shakespearean criticism

"Thou art a Monument without a tomb,
And art alive still while thy Book doth
    live
And we have wits to read and praise to
    give."

*Ben Jonson, from the preface
to the First Folio, 1623.*

Mr. WILLIAM
SHAKESPEARES

COMEDIES,
HISTORIES, &
TRAGEDIES.

Published according to the True Originall Copies.

Martin Droeshout sculpsit London.

LONDON
Printed by Isaac Iaggard, and Ed. Blount. 1623.

Frontispiece to the First Folio (1623). By permission of the Folger Shakespeare Library.

ISSN 0883-9123

Volume 4

shakespearean criticism

Excerpts from the Criticism of
William Shakespeare's Plays and Poetry,
from the First Published Appraisals
to Current Evaluations

Mark W. Scott
Editor

Gale Research Company
Book Tower
Detroit, Michigan 48226

STAFF

Mark W. Scott, *Editor*

Sandra L. Williamson, *Senior Assistant Editor*

Kit Aro, Michael S. Corey, Melissa Reiff Hug,
Daniel J. Montgomery, *Assistant Editors*

Phyllis Carmel Mendelson, *Contributing Editor*

Lizbeth A. Purdy, *Production Supervisor*
Denise Michlewicz Broderick, *Production Coordinator*
Eric Berger, *Assistant Production Coordinator*
Kathleen M. Cook, Maureen Duffy, Sheila J. Nasea, *Editorial Assistants*

Victoria B. Cariappa, *Research Coordinator*
Daniel Kurt Gilbert, Maureen R. Richards, Keith E. Schooley, Filomena Sgambati,
Vincenza G. Tranchida, Valerie J. Webster, Mary D. Wise, *Research Assistants*

Linda M. Pugliese, *Manuscript Coordinator*
Donna Craft, *Assistant Manuscript Coordinator*
Maureen A. Puhl, Rosetta Irene Simms, *Manuscript Assistants*

Jeanne A. Gough, *Permissions Supervisor*
Janice M. Mach, *Permissions Coordinator, Text*
Patricia A. Seefelt, *Permissions Coordinator, Illustrations*
Susan D. Battista, *Assistant Permissions Coordinator*
Margaret A. Chamberlain, Sandra C. Davis, Kathleen J. Grell,
Josephine M. Keene, Mary M. Matuz, *Senior Permissions Assistants*
H. Diane Cooper, Colleen M. Crane, Mabel C. Gurney, *Permissions Assistants*
Margaret A. Carson, Anita Ransom, *Permissions Clerks*

Frederick G. Ruffner, *Publisher*
Dedria Bryfonski, *Editorial Director*
Ellen Crowley, *Associate Editorial Director*
Christine Nasso, *Director, Literature Division*
Laurie Lanzen Harris, *Senior Editor, Literary Criticism Series*
Dennis Poupard, *Managing Editor, Literary Criticism Series*

Copyright © 1987 by Gale Research Company

ISBN 0-8103-6128-0
ISSN 0883-9123

Printed in the United States
10   9   8   7   6   5   4   3

Contents

Preface

The works of William Shakespeare have delighted audiences and inspired scholars for nearly four hundred years. Shakespeare's appeal is universal, for in its depth and breadth his work evokes a timeless insight into the human condition.

The vast amount of Shakespearean criticism is a testament to his enduring popularity. Critics of each epoch have contributed to this critical legacy, responding to the comments of their forebears, bringing the moral and intellectual atmosphere of their own era to the works, and suggesting interpretations that continue to inspire critics of today. Thus, to chart the history of criticism on Shakespeare is to note the changing aesthetic philosophies of the past four centuries.

The Scope of the Work

The success of Gale's four existing literary series, *Contemporary Literary Criticism (CLC), Twentieth-Century Literary Criticism (TCLC), Nineteenth-Century Literature Criticism (NCLC)*, and *Children's Literature Review (CLR)*, suggested an equivalent need among students and teachers of Shakespeare. Moreover, since the criticism of Shakespeare's works spans four centuries and is larger in size and scope than that of any author, a prodigious amount of critical material confronts the student.

Shakespearean Criticism (SC) presents significant passages from published criticism on the works of Shakespeare. Eight volumes of the series will be devoted to aesthetic criticism of the plays. Performance criticism will be treated in separate special volumes. Other special volumes will be devoted to such topics as Shakespeare's poetry, the authorship controversy and the apocrypha, stage history of the plays, and other general subjects, such as Shakespeare's language, religious and philosophical thought, and characterization. The first eight volumes will each contain criticism on four to six plays, with an equal balance of genres and an equal balance of plays based on their critical importance. Thus, volume 4 contains criticism on one major tragedy *(Othello),* one minor tragedy *(Titus Andronicus),* one major comedy *(The Merchant of Venice),* and one romance *(Cymbeline).*

The length of each entry is intended to represent the play's critical reception in English, including those works which have been translated into English. The editors have tried to identify only the major critics and lines of inquiry for each play. Each entry represents a historical overview of the critical response to the play: early criticism is presented to indicate initial responses and later selections represent significant trends in the history of criticism on the play. We have also attempted to identify and include excerpts from the seminal essays on each play by the most important Shakespearean critics. We have directed our series to students in late high school and early college who are beginning their study of Shakespeare. Thus, ours is not a work for the specialist, but is rather an introduction for the researcher newly acquainted with the works of Shakespeare.

The Organization of the Book

Each entry consists of the following elements: play heading, an introduction, excerpts of criticism (each followed by a bibliographical citation), and an additional bibliography for further reading.

The *introduction* begins with a discussion of the date, text, and sources of the play. This section is followed by a critical history which outlines the major critical trends and identifies the prominent commentators on the play.

Criticism is arranged chronologically within each play entry to provide a perspective on the changes in critical evaluation over the years. For purposes of easier identification, the critic's name and the date of the essay are given at the beginning of each piece. For an anonymous essay later attributed to a critic, the critic's name appears in brackets at the beginning of the excerpt and in the bibliographical citation.

Within the text, all act, scene, and line designations have been changed to conform to *The Riverside Shakespeare,* published by Houghton Mifflin Company, which is a standard text used in many high school and college English classes. All of the individual essays are prefaced with *explanatory notes* as an additional aid to students using *SC.* The explanatory notes provide several types of useful information, including: the importance of the critics in literary history, the critical schools with which they are identified, if any, and the importance of their comments on Shakespeare and the play discussed. The explanatory notes also identify the main issues in the commentary on each play and include cross references to related criticism in the entry. In addition, the notes provide previous publication information such as original title and date for foreign language publications.

A complete *bibliographical citation* designed to facilitate the location of the original essay or book follows each piece of criticism.

Within each play entry are *illustrations,* such as facsimiles of title pages taken from the quarto and First Folio editions of the plays as well as pictures drawn from such sources as early editions of the collected works and artists' renderings of some of the famous scenes and characters. The captions following each illustration indicate act, scene, characters, and the artist and date, if known. The illustrations are arranged chronologically and, as a complement to the criticism, provide a historical perspective on Shakespeare throughout the centuries.

The *additional bibliography* appearing at the end of each play entry suggests further reading on the play. This section includes references to the major discussions of the date, the text, and the sources of each play.

At the request of librarians, beginning with volume 4 *SC* will include a list of Shakespeare's plays covered in the series, indicating which works of the canon are treated in each existing or future volume. This is referred to as the List of Plays and can be found following the Preface.

Each volume of *SC* includes a cumulative index to plays that provides the volume number in which the plays appear. *SC* also includes a cumulative index to critics; under each critic's name are listed the plays on which the critic has written and the volume and page where the criticism appears.

As an additional aid to students, beginning with volume 3 *SC* provides a glossary of terms relating to date, text, and source information frequently mentioned by critics and used throughout the introductions to the plays. The glossed terms and source names are identified by small capital letters when they first appear in the introductions.

An appendix is also included that lists the sources from which the material in the volume is reprinted. It does not, however, list every book or periodical consulted for the volume.

Acknowledgments

No work of this scope can be accomplished without the cooperation of many people. The editors wish to thank the copyright holders of the excerpts included in this volume, the permissions managers of the book and magazine publishing companies for assisting us in securing reprint rights, and the staffs of the Detroit Public Library, the University of Michigan libraries, and the Wayne State University Library for making their resources available to us. We would especially like to thank the staff of the Rare Book Room of the University of Michigan Library for their research assistance and the Folger Shakespeare Library for their help in picture research. We would also like to thank Jeri Yaryan and Anthony J. Bogucki for assistance with copyright research.

Suggestions Are Welcome

The editors welcome the comments and suggestions of readers to expand the coverage and enhance the usefulness of the series.

List of Plays Covered in *SC*

[The year or years in parentheses indicates the composition date of the play as determined by G. Blakemore Evans in *The Riverside Shakespeare*]

Volume 1

The Comedy of Errors (1592-94)
Hamlet (1600-01)
1 and *2 Henry IV* (1596-98)
Timon of Athens (1607-08)
Twelfth Night (1601-02)

Volume 2

Henry VIII (1612-13)
King Lear (1605)
Love's Labour's Lost (1594-95)
Measure for Measure (1604)
Pericles (1607-08)

Volume 3

1, 2, and *3 Henry VI* (1589-91)
Macbeth (1606)
A Midsummer Night's Dream (1595-96)
Troilus and Cressida (1601-02)

Volume 4

Cymbeline (1609-10)
The Merchant of Venice (1596-97)
Othello (1604)
Titus Andronicus (1593-94)

In Forthcoming Volumes:

All's Well That Ends Well (1602-03)
Antony and Cleopatra (1606-07)
As You Like It (1599)
Coriolanus (1607-08)
Henry V (1599)
Julius Caesar (1599)
King John (1594-96)
The Merry Wives of Windsor (1597)
Much Ado about Nothing (1598-99)
Richard II (1595)
Richard III (1592-93)
Romeo and Juliet (1595-96)
The Taming of the Shrew (1593-94)
The Tempest (1611)
The Two Gentlemen of Verona (1594)
The Two Noble Kinsmen (1613)
The Winter's Tale (1610-11)

Cymbeline

DATE: It is generally believed that *Cymbeline* was written and first performed between 1609 and 1610. The latest possible date of composition is 1611, based on the diary entry of Simon Forman that describes a performance of *Cymbeline* he saw at the GLOBE THEATRE. Although Forman's reference to this event is not dated, it was included with other material which he wrote in the spring of 1611; in any case, it could have been written no later than September 8, 1611, for that is the date of Forman's death. Since the depiction of the rout of the Roman army by Belarius and the two young princes in a narrow lane described by Posthumus in Act V, Scene iii is contained in RAPHAEL HOLINSHED's *The Description and Historie of Scotland* (2d ed. 1587), and because there is a consensus that this work was the major source for *Macbeth*—which is generally accepted as being written around 1606—, there is some speculation that Shakespeare may have encountered the chronicle account of the defeat of the Danes by an old man and two boys when he was working on his earlier tragedy. For some scholars, this suggests that 1606 is the earliest possible composition date for *Cymbeline*. Finally, some commentators have argued that *Cymbeline* belongs to an earlier period in Shakespeare's career and that he later revised it sometime around 1609; but this assessment has been generally discredited in the twentieth century. Because of the parallels in characterization, dramatic material, poetic style, and authorial attitude between *Cymbeline* and Shakespeare's other late romances, most commentators have assigned the play to the dramatist's final period.

TEXT: *Cymbeline*'s initial publication was in the FIRST FOLIO of 1623. Although Heminge and Condell included it with Shakespeare's tragedies—its title in the Folio is given as *The Tragedie of Cymbeline*—, critics generally have maintained that, despite its tragic incidents, the play does not belong to this genre. Concerning the authenticity of the Folio text, most modern-day scholars agree that it is a true reproduction of Shakespeare's original manuscript; they also concur that Shakespeare was the sole author of the play. However, some commentators in the past three centuries have perceived the presence of a second hand in the composition of the drama. Alexander Pope, George Steevens, and Frederick Gard Fleay (see Additional Bibliography) all argued that the vision in Act V, Scene iv was an interpolation by another writer, and both Horace Howard Furness and Harley Granville-Barker contended that Shakespeare worked with a collaborator not only on this scene but on other parts of the play as well. Furness alleged that major portions of *Cymbeline* were the work of an assistant and credited Shakespeare only with those sections of the play that he deemed superior. Granville-Barker maintained that Shakespeare had a collaborator for both "the design and the execution" of the drama, but he discovered the hand of a second writer in fewer passages than did Furness. Although E. H. W. Meyerstein (see Additional Bibliography) argued in 1922 for the authenticity of the vision scene, it was not until G. Wilson Knight's 1947 defense of the integrity of the episode that scholars generally accepted it as an authoritative part of Shakespeare's text. Additionally, many eighteenth-century editors of *Cymbeline* deleted Posthumus's dialogue with the jailer in Act V, Scene iv, arguing that it was intrusive and stylistically inconsistent. As in the case of the vision scene, however,

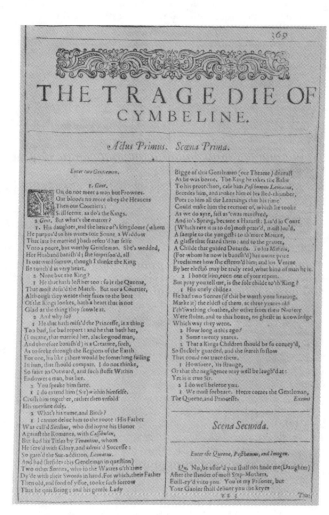

Title page of Cymbeline taken from the First Folio (1623).

present-day scholars no longer question the authenticity of this passage.

SOURCES: Numerous examples of the wager story, in which a husband offers a sum of money to a man who questions the fidelity of his wife if he will bring him proof of her unfaithfulness, survive from the thirteenth through the sixteenth centuries. It is generally accepted that *Cymbeline* provides evidence that Shakespeare was familiar with at least two of these: Giovanni Boccaccio's *Decameron*, Day 2, Novella 9 (1353) and the anonymous *Frederyke of Jennen*. Although the *Decameron* was not translated into English until 1620, a French version by Antoine le Maçon first appeared in 1545 and was reprinted several times in the sixteenth century, and scholars agree that Shakespeare must have read the work either in the original Italian or in the French translation. *Cymbeline* and the *Decameron* novella share many common elements: in both works the villain gains access to the wife's bedroom by concealing himself in a chest and, although he is not successful in seducing the wife, convinces the husband otherwise by providing a detailed description of a mole under her left breast;

in both the servant disobeys the husband's order to kill the wife and instead helps her to escape, providing her with male clothing to conceal her sex; and in both the villain's deception is finally discovered by the wife. *Frederyke of Jennen* is a reworking of the Boccaccio tale, but it differs in several important details that show resemblances to *Cymbeline*. In *Frederyke of Jennen* the merchants present during the wager scene are of many different nationalities, the husband is characterized as regretting his rash decision to have his wife murdered, and there are many references to commercial and financial transactions. *Frederyke of Jennen* originally appeared in German in 1478; the first English translation was printed in Antwerp in 1518, and subsequent versions appeared in England in 1520 and 1560.

Commentators have also noticed the similarities between *Cymbeline* and a dramatic romance by an unknown author, *The Rare Triumphes of Love and Fortune*, first performed in 1582 and printed in 1589. In this play, the heroine is a princess named Fidelia who has contracted an unequal match with a young orphan who has been brought up in the royal household; because her father opposes the marriage and exiles her beloved, she flees the court and finds refuge in a cave with a nobleman who had earlier been banished by her father. The lovers are reunited only when a supernatural figure appears on stage and alters the course of the dramatic action. *Cymbeline* also has many resemblances to *Philaster*, a dramatic romance written by Francis Beaumont and John Fletcher. The two plays demonstrate similarities in plotting, scenic structure, characterization, and versification, and in both dramas the hero is exiled from the court and the heroine refuses to marry the boorish man her father has chosen for her, disguising herself as a boy and becoming lost in the wilderness. Some early twentieth-century scholars argued that Beaumont and Fletcher's play was an immediate source for *Cymbeline*, but critics today maintain that while it is clear that both were written at about the same time, there is no evidence to indicate which preceded the other, and therefore attempts to determine their possible respective influence can only be speculative.

There is general agreement, however, that for the historical plot in *Cymbeline* Shakespeare drew upon Holinshed's *Chronicles*, which includes a brief description of the reign of Kymbeline or Cymbeline and notes that the king had been raised at the court of Augustus Caesar, that Christ was born during his regency, and that about this time Britain refused to continue paying tribute to Rome. In the Scottish section of the *Chronicles* there is reference to a peasant named Hay who, together with his two sons, routed the invading Danish army at the Battle of Luncarty in A. D. 976, and many commentators consider this the source for Posthumus's description in Act V, Scene iii of the exploits of Belarius, Guiderius, and Arviragus in the battle with the Romans. Scholars have noted that the popular medieval collection, A MIRROR FOR MAGISTRATES, contains two "complaints of Guiderius" and that it is likely that Shakespeare was familiar with these and adapted them as part of the historical material in *Cymbeline*. Recent critics have also claimed that the play alludes to the Brute myth, propagated by Geoffrey of Monmouth in his *Historia Regum Brittaniae* (c. 1137) and reworked by Holinshed, and that references to the legendary founding of Britain were intended by Shakespeare to underscore the play's theme of British national destiny. Additionally, some commentators have remarked on the likelihood that the account of King Cymbeline and his sons in Spenser's *The Faerie Queene* (1589 and 1596) formed part of the background material for the play. There are some parallels between

Cymbeline and the anonymous *Sir Cyclomon and Sir Clamydes*, which was published in 1599, although probably written in the 1580s. In this latter drama, the heroine is abducted, escapes in male clothing, comes under the protection of an old shepherd, and mistakes the villain's grave for her husband's. In the eighteenth century, critics believed that an anonymously written collection of tales entitled *Westward for Smelts* was also a source for Cymbeline, but modern-day scholars contend that there is no reliable evidence to prove that this collection was published before 1620, and it is now generally perceived as an analogue of Shakespeare's play. Imogen's adventures in the mountains of Wales are reminiscent of portions of Tasso's *Jerusalem Delivered*, which was translated into English by Edward Fairfax in 1600. Finally, although some nineteenth-century critics held that the portrayal of the wicked stepmother in the Germanic folk tale of *Snow White* influenced Shakespeare's depiction of the Queen in *Cymbeline,* modern scholars find no evidence that this tale was extant in England in the early years of the seventeenth century.

CRITICAL HISTORY: The dominant critical issues in the commentary on *Cymbeline* have generally arisen from considerations of the play's dramatic structure. Through the centuries, Shakespeare's combination of material from pastoral romance, British and Roman history, traditional wager stories, and techniques of early seventeenth-century tragicomedy has prompted critics to question whether these disparate elements are skillfully blended and which is most salient in the play. Discussions of thematic concerns have frequently involved assumptions that elements from one or the other of these literary traditions are most prominent. Thus, *Cymbeline* has been variously styled as a dramatic romance, a celebration of British national history, and a tragicomedy. Especially since the 1950s, many scholars have identified the themes of regeneration or reconciliation as central to the play and have related these to the Christian doctrine of the "fortunate fall," which traces a pattern of sin, repentance, and rebirth. Other significant issues include the characterization of Posthumus and Imogen, interpretations of Posthumus's conduct in the wager subplot, the significance of the vision scene in Act V, Scene iv, the propriety and significance of the depiction of Imogen awakening beside the headless corpse of Cloten, and the dramatic techniques employed by Shakespeare to control and shape the complex material that constitutes his play.

Two references to *Cymbeline* survive from the seventeenth century: Simon Forman's plot summary recorded in his personal journal, which provided the latest possible date for the play's composition, and Gerard Langbaine's commentary on the sources of *Cymbeline,* which helped determine Shakespeare's indebtedness to Boccaccio's *Decameron.* In the eighteenth century, critics generally disparaged the dramatic structure of the play. Such commentators as Charles Gildon, Charlotte Lennox, William Hawkins, and Samuel Johnson all remarked on the irregularities or "absurdities" of the plotting. Both Gildon and Lennox disapproved of Shakespeare's depiction of noble characters behaving inconsistently with their stature, and Lennox further argued that Boccaccio's tale was superior to the dramatist's rendering of the wager story. The beginnings of the contention over the play's genre also become apparent in this century, for while Hawkins emphasized the importance of British history in *Cymbeline,* John Potter described it as a dramatic romance. Alexander Pope became the first critic to challenge the authenticity of the vision scene in Act V, Scene iv and to assert that it represents an unnecessary interruption of the dramatic action, an estimation that was later supported by George Steevens and shared by some nineteenth-century critics. Steevens also commented on the inconsistencies in the character of Cloten, emphasizing his monstrous behavior toward Imogen and Posthumus in Acts I through IV. The most famous criticism of the play, however, is Johnson's brief but sharp attack, in which he charged that the presence in one drama of such diverse material and unbelievable dramatic action resulted in a work of "unresisting imbecillity." Some early twentieth-century critics agreed with this view of *Cymbeline,* and a majority of scholars who have examined the dramatic structure of the play have begun their discussions with reference to Johnson's comments.

In the nineteenth century, however, there occurred a marked departure from such unfavorable judgments as Johnson's. August Wilhelm Schlegel, William Hazlitt, Anna Brownell Jameson, and Denton J. Snider all argued that *Cymbeline* is skillfully constructed and that the diverse elements of the plot blend together harmoniously, resulting in a drama that is remarkable for its unity. But the principal focus of commentary on *Cymbeline* during this period was on the character of Imogen; and these discussions, written in the flowery language of the time, frequently bordered on idolatry. The beginning of this critical adulation may be seen in the evaluation by Schlegel, who regarded Imogen as possessing every quality required to dramatize the ideal of "female excellence." Hazlitt argued that Imogen's chief virtue is her constancy, but that she is also noteworthy for her tender, ingenuous nature. G. G. Gervinus contended that she is one of the most fully developed of Shakespeare's dramatic characters. Jameson similarly viewed Imogen as the most perfect of Shakespeare's female characters, asserting that she embodies all the virtues generally considered requisite in ideal women. Algernon Charles Swinburne echoed this opinion and declared—in a remark that largely reflects the general nineteenth-century judgment of Imogen—that she is "the woman above all Shakespeare's women." Although Helena Faucit, too, highly praised the character of Imogen, she contended that the apparent happy conclusion of the play fails to attenuate the heroine's sufferings and, as a result, she questions whether Imogen is capable of recovering from her tribulations. One dissenting voice from the general critical idealization of Imogen came from Bernard Shaw, who found two conflicting aspects in her nature: delicate sensitivity on the one hand and priggish affectation on the other.

Unlike the commentators of the previous century, nineteenth-century critics generally maintained that *Cymbeline* is a work of serious dramatic import. Hazlitt was the first to contend, albeit in a brief comment, that the play deals with serious religious and theological questions. In an extended analysis of the play, G. G. Gervinus argued that *Cymbeline* demonstrates the maxim that virtue severely tempted is superior to goodness which has not been tested by evil—an idea he claimed was epitomized in the vision scene, in which divine justice and omnipotence are vindicated despite the presence of evil in the world. Gervinus also asserted that the unifying theme of the play is reflected in the repeated juxtapositions of fidelity and faithlessness amongst the various characters, and that all their actions manifest the contrast between truth and perfidy or slander. Hermann Ulrici argued that the central concern of *Cymbeline* is the idea that divine providence renders human intentions and actions inadequate as determinants of humanity's fate. In the iteration of this theme, and in the behavior of all the characters, he discovered the means by which Shakespeare unified and harmonized the disparate elements of his play. Denton J. Snider foreshadowed critics since the 1950s in his contention

that *Cymbeline* demonstrates a process of sin, repentance, and regeneration. He averred that conflicts in societies as well as between individuals are shown to be gradually resolved until all the disruptions and disturbances have been reconciled and the dramatic world of the play exhibits a final stage of restoration.

Other issues addressed by nineteenth-century commentators include the debate over Shakespeare's artistry as evidenced in *Cymbeline* and the controversy over whether he collaborated with another dramatist on the play. Snider and Thomas Kenny maintained that the vision scene, although artistically inferior to the rest of the play, is authentically Shakespearean, but Frederick Gard Fleay held that the speeches of the Leonati and Jupiter in this scene represent the work of another dramatist. Combining biographical criticism with literary analysis, Barrett Wendell judged the play to be lacking in spontaneity and replete with evidence that the dramatist was overexerting his capacities as an artist, and he held that the poetic style and stagecraft indicate that Shakespeare intended to prove that his dramatic powers were not declining.

These few unfavorable assessments of *Cymbeline* became more pronounced in the first decades of the twentieth century. Like Barrett Wendell, E. K. Chambers, Horace Howard Furness, and Brander Matthews contended that the style of the play suggests that it was written during Shakespeare's declining years. Other critics, such as Walter Raleigh and William Witherle Lawrence, adopted Samuel Johnson's unfavorable assessment of *Cymbeline,* calling it accurate and justified; Furness and Harley Granville-Barker similarly endorsed that judgment, although only with respect to certain portions or scenes. Raleigh noted the artificiality of *Cymbeline* and concluded that Johnson spoke "truly and moderately" in his disparaging evaluation of the drama. Furness, on the other hand, attributed most of the absurdities and stylistic inconsistencies evident in the play to the presence of a second dramatist, claiming that Shakespeare wrote only those sections in which Imogen appears. Lawrence, too, found much in the play unacceptable, especially in the final two acts. But the critic also attempted to mitigate some of the negative commentary by stressing two points: one, that the problem many commentators have with the wager scene can be resolved if we view Posthumus's actions—regardless of their apparent rashness—as unavoidable and even proper considering the chivalric code Shakespeare was dramatizing; and two, that Posthumus's behavior after he learns of Imogen's alleged infidelity is appropriate and would not have seemed unreasonable to Shakespeare's contemporaries in light of the romance tradition reflected in the play. Like Furness, Granville-Barker also maintained that portions of *Cymbeline* were designed and executed by an unknown collaborator, although he claimed that Furness had assigned too much to the unknown second dramatist. Most significant in Granville-Barker's analysis of the dramatic technique employed in *Cymbeline* is his conclusion that what seems artificial and, therefore, un-Shakespearean in the play is actually authentic. According to the critic, Shakespeare intentionally made his play seem artless by openly displaying his dramatic devices and conventions, thereby allowing his audience to participate in his craftsmanship while simultaneously preventing that audience from taking the story—and its tragic implications—too seriously. Granville-Barker further claimed that this mode of dramaturgy prompted Shakespeare to alter his sensitive characterization of Imogen and depict her in misplaced grief beside the headless torso of Cloten (IV. ii.), a dramatic turn of events which the critic judged inexcusable.

Other early twentieth-century critics who disparaged certain aspects of *Cymbeline* include E. K. Chambers and Brander Matthews. Unlike such nineteenth-century commentators as Gervinus and Jameson, who contended that Imogen is one of Shakespeare's most fully developed characters, Chambers concluded that she is nothing more than a puppet. Chambers also reviewed the theory proposed by Ashley H. Thorndike (see Additional Bibliography)—namely, that *Cymbeline* represents Shakespeare's attempt to write a play like Beaumont and Fletcher's *Philaster*—and argued that although the hypothesis is interesting, it cannot be sustained with the available evidence on the chronology of the two plays. In addition, he asserted that the "mere desire to rival others in exploiting a dramatic convention" is not sufficient to explain the severe change in Shakespeare's philosophy and manner of writing evident in his romances as a whole. Instead, as mentioned above, he postulated that some "spiritual crisis" or physical illness occurred at the time *Cymbeline* was composed, changing Shakespeare's attitude towards life and his art and resulting in a work of "relaxed mental energies." Matthews, on the other hand, agreed with Thorndike's theory that *Cymbeline* is an imitation of *Philaster*, and it is to this "unsound" approach that he attributed all the shortcomings in Shakespeare's play. In a manner similar to Chambers, he also regarded Imogen as little more than a puppet and declared that *Cymbeline* displays "a sad decline" in Shakespeare's skills.

After this period of relative disparagement of *Cymbeline*, critics returned to a consideration of the play's thematic concerns and attempted to explicate rather than condemn its diverse mixture of dramatic elements. E. M. W. Tillyard postulated that the play's uncommon mixture of sources and genres, together with its accidental and improbable turns of events, provided Shakespeare with an opportunity to dramatize his newly achieved awareness of the different levels of reality of human existence; however, he judged that the dramatist failed to portray successfully in *Cymbeline* these "many planes on which life could be lived." In an analysis that recalls Gervinus's identification of a series of oppositions in the play, F. C. Tinkler posited that an essential contrast between the ideal and the "sordid" or familiar pervades the entire structure of *Cymbeline*. He argued that this conflict appears to be unreconcilable and that, as a result, the prevailing dramatic mood is one of strain and tension until Act V, Scene iv, where Posthumus recognizes and accepts the silent stasis of death as the final reconciliation of these positive and negative forces in life. However, Tinkler concluded that the dualistic tensions in the drama between Rome and Britain, style and meaning, reality and the ideal are never resolved. A. A. Stephenson directly disputed Tinkler's arguments, claiming instead that the sense of strain and tension in the play arises from Shakespeare's frustration with the impossibility of dramatizing fully his vision of a new harmony in which the disparities between reality and ideal value disappear and a new unanimity is achieved. Like Caroline F. E. Spurgeon earlier, Stephenson also analyzed the metaphoric language of the play. But whereas Spurgeon had focused on images related to the countryside that enhance the bucolic atmosphere of the idyll scenes in Acts III and IV, and on allusions to mercantile transactions generally associated with the wager plot and the payment of the tribute to Rome, Stephenson identified an imagistic pattern of valuation that emphasizes the ideal worth of fidelity and chastity and, in related language, links honor with a precious gem. F. R. Leavis rebutted both Tinkler's and Stephenson's conclusions and argued that although *Cymbeline* contains many instances of Shakespeare's dramatic genius, it should not be assumed that the playwright expressed in this

drama any theme of profound intellectual or philosophical import. According to Leavis, *Cymbeline* should be viewed strictly as a romance—its various incidents the "stuff" of romantic literature in general—, and he claimed that any portions of the play that seem to support a more profound reading are merely those points where Shakespeare's genius breaks through the otherwise commonplace work.

Near the mid-twentieth century, G. Wilson Knight offered an extended analysis of *Cymbeline* that has generally been regarded as one of the most salient interpretations of the play. Knight became the first commentator to develop the idea that the historical elements in *Cymbeline* are extremely significant and that the drama itself is a representation of British national issues. He contended that the play's dramatic action depicts the means by which the king learns to reject the viciousness of the Queen and Cloten so that the virtues of Britain may be united with those of Rome. He further argued that whereas Posthumus and Imogen embody the goodness and integrity of Britain, Iachimo reflects the licentiousness of the continent and the debased nature of Renaissance Italy, which is presented in the play as unworthy of the legacy of classical Roman culture and history. Knight maintained that the "massed meanings" of *Cymbeline* are concentrated in the vision scene and that Jupiter's blessing of the marriage of Posthumus and Imogen underscores the idea that Roman heritage is transferred to the British nation. In his assessment, the appearance of Jupiter and his assurances to the Leonati represent the culmination of Shakespeare's portrayal of the gods throughout the play—that is, as beneficent in their direction of the fortunes of humanity. Knight's defense of the integrity of the vision scene effectively brought an end to attempts to demonstrate that it was the work of an interpolator or collaborator and not authentically Shakespearean.

Although Knight's interpretation has not gone unchallenged in the decades after its publication, many other commentators have followed his example and also focused on the historical issues depicted in *Cymbeline*. Harold C. Goddard posited that the play is a political allegory in which Shakespeare dramatized the struggle between freedom and imperialism, arguing that the Roman invasion of England symbolizes the attempt by a tyrannous empire to deprive a free nation of its liberties. Like Knight, Goddard contended that the play demonstrates the maliciousness of Renaissance Italy, and he further asserted that Italy is juxtaposed with both the corrupt English court and the natural and noble environment of Wales. J. P. Brockbank (see Additional Bibliography) offered the earliest discussion of *Cymbeline* in relation to the myth of Brute or Brutus, the legendary founder of Britain. Noting that Brute was the descendant of Roman and Trojan ruling families, Brockbank contended that allusions to that myth in *Cymbeline* are intended to reflect the eventual reconciliation of Roman and British heritage that is depicted in Shakespeare's drama; he also declared that the chroniclers of British history regarded the historical Cymbeline's reign as significant because during this time Christ was born and Augustus Caesar ruled a peaceful empire. Similarly, Emrys Jones (see Additional Bibliography) maintained that there is a significant association between the play's historical setting at the time of Christ's nativity and the universal *pax romanum*, or "peace of Rome," and the belief of the first Stuart monarch, James I, that he was a great peacemaker responsible for the unification of Britain. Jones also remarked that Milford Haven had important associations with the Brutan and Arthurian legends adapted by Tudor and Stuart historians for political purposes, and thus the numerous allusions to Milford in *Cymbeline* serve to intensify the association between James I and Britain's national destiny. As recently as 1977, Alexander Leggatt has argued that in this play Britain is represented as the locus of a superior value system, where miraculous actions are not exceptional and whose people are distinguished from those of other nations by keen and lively imaginations. The critic averred that the seemingly inexplicable events of the play either are portrayed as the result of divine intervention on behalf of Britain or occur because the British characters enjoy the special favor of the gods.

The question of divine intervention and the debate over the significance of supernatural or religious elements in *Cymbeline* have become dominant issues in criticism of the play since the 1950s. J. A. Bryant, Jr. examined *Cymbeline* with respect to Christian theology and concluded that its dramatic action is modelled after the paradoxical concept of the fortunate fall, in that its principal characters retrace a redemptive pattern from temptation to sin to restoration. Like G. G. Gervinus in the previous century, Bryant maintained that there are strong resemblances between Jupiter's speech in the vision scene and the traditional Christian tenet that God chastises those whom He has chosen to love and redeem. Like Brockbank and Jones, Robin Moffet noted that chroniclers such as Holinshed distinguished the historical Cymbeline's reign by the fact that he held the throne at the time of Christ's birth. Moffet thus argued that the nativity is a significant "esoteric" element in *Cymbeline,* and he viewed the play as demonstrating the disastrous consequences of sin and error while showing the need for a savior to redeem humanity. Northrop Frye also held that there is an implicit sense of the association of Cymbeline's reign and Christ's nativity. The critic further noted that divine providence is the agent of the festive resolution of the drama, a feature that distinguishes it from the so-called problem comedies which it otherwise resembles, he claimed, for in those plays human characters themselves resolve the dramatic errors and confusions. Leggatt similarly noted the underlying significance of Christ's birth in the action of *Cymbeline,* declaring that the king's final submission to Rome is understandable in one sense only: it "shows that he is in tune with the new age of peace." R. A. Foakes argued that the improbabilities of the dramatic action, the psychological inconsistency of Shakespeare's characterization, and the representation of the reunion of Posthumus and Imogen as attributable to the intervention of Jupiter, and not to their own efforts, all underscore the play's depiction of the central role of divine providence in determining humanity's fate. Echoing Bryant, Robert Grams Hunter asserted that the dramatic structure of *Cymbeline* retraces in secularized form the pattern of the medieval miracle and morality plays, in which central characters are portrayed as proceeding through a redemptive process of sin, contrition, and forgiveness; however, Hunter maintained that while Christian doctrines are central to the play's dramatic structure, Shakespeare departed from the model by shifting his primary emphasis from divine to human love. Homer D. Swander contended that the fundamental religious design of *Cymbeline* is particularly evident in Act V, Scenes i through iv, for here Posthumus is portrayed as prayerfully seeking and receiving God's grace and the forgiveness of his sins. Again like Bryant, Arthur C. Kirsch held that the dramatic action of Shakespeare's play follows the pattern of moral lapses prefiguring and leading to redemption that is typically associated with the paradox of the fortunate fall. Similarly, Martin Lings (see Additional Bibliography) related the course of dramatic events in *Cymbeline* to the Biblical account of humanity's fall from grace and to the rework-

ings of this story in the tales of Everyman and the medieval mystery plays, as had Hunter.

Many of the same scholars who addressed the religious issues in *Cymbeline* also focused on the character of Posthumus, and several presented a strikingly different analysis of the protagonist than had been offered by earlier commentators. In addition to demonstrating the parallels between Shakespeare's Posthumus and the stylized prototype of *Humanum genus* ("mankind") in medieval drama, Hunter became one of the first critics to contend that Posthumus is a counterpart of Cloten, arguing that the former's behavior, attitude, and sentiments in the wager scene and in Act II closely resemble Cloten's views and actions throughout Acts I through IV. Swander also discovered marked similarities between Posthumus and Cloten, not only in physical resemblances but also in the feelings expressed in their respective soliloquies (II. v. and III. v.), which reveal the brutal and violent intentions that each holds regarding Imogen. James Edward Siemon also stressed the parallels between Posthumus and Cloten, particularly the violence with which both react when they realize they have suffered sexual humiliation. Siemon demonstrated the manner in which Shakespeare emphasized the similarities between the two characters by careful juxtaposition of scenes in which Cloten and Posthumus display parallel behavior and emotions. Whereas such critics as Siemon contended that Posthumus is portrayed as valorous and noble in the concluding scenes of *Cymbeline,* and repentant of his earlier behavior, Leggatt maintained that by attributing Posthumus's repentance to the intervention of Jupiter, instead of portraying the internal evolution of his remorse, Shakespeare failed to alter the negative impressions the audience has of him from the wager scenes, and thus he cannot be completely regarded as a figure of worth and nobility at the close of the play.

Since 1950, several critics have examined the significance of the scene in which Imogen awakens beside the headless corpse of Cloten, with some commentators claiming that the episode provides a further analysis of the character of Posthumus. Goddard argued that the scene is a climactic expression of the struggle between lasciviousness and virtue depicted throughout *Cymbeline* and that it portrays Imogen, the allegorical symbol of the English nation, temporarily mistaking sham nobility (Cloten) for true English manhood and purity (Posthumus). Moffet linked this scene with the one showing Posthumus's repentance and vision in prison, contending that both depict their central characters in utter despair, contain important soliloquies, and offer—in the brothers' dirge and the prayer of the Leonati—assertions of pagan, pre-Christian views of divine justice and morality. In his analysis of the different kinds of irony apparent in *Cymbeline,* F. D. Hoeniger contended that Imogen's mistaken identification of the headless corpse is a "grotesque irony," since it is unexpected in the world of romance comedy. Hunter also judged the scene to be ironic, maintaining that as Posthumus is shown to be a counterpart of Cloten, Imogen's belief that the headless corpse is that of her beloved is an "excessively macabre joke— a deserved mockery of Posthumus." Swander asserted that the burial of the corpse marks not only the interment of Cloten, but also symbolically signals the termination of Posthumus's naïveté and violent proclivities, thus providing for his subsequent repentance.

Since the beginning of the second half of the twentieth century, several commentators have argued that *Cymbeline* is principally concerned with demonstrating the discrepancies between appearance and reality. Many of these critics also linked Shakespeare's exploration of reality with the theme of regeneration and reconciliation in the play. Donald A. Stauffer contended that one of Shakespeare's chief concerns in *Cymbeline* is to represent the difficulty of discerning between true worth and false appearances. According to Stauffer, Shakespeare depicts all the central characters as being misled about the true quality and even identity of other people because they rely solely on the evidence of their eyes. Locating the central theme of the play in the idea that society must promote the integration of natural and courtly virtues, Derek Traversi asserted that the characters must discover the difference between apparent worth and true nobility before this ideal union can be achieved. Traversi also emphasized the importance of the theme of reconciliation in the play, claiming that Shakespeare resolves the characters' previous struggles with appearance and reality, "natural nobility" and courtly artifice, in a final vision of universal harmony and cosmic order. Yet, despite its accomplishments, Traversi regarded *Cymbeline* as an experimental play, attributing to this fact much in the drama that is unsuccessful, particularly Shakespeare's failure to match his language and poetic expression with his themes. William Barry Thorne also maintained that regeneration and reconciliation are central to Shakespeare's play. He held that the structure of *Cymbeline* is similar to that of traditional mummers' folk drama—in which the death of the old year and the birth of the new are ritually reenacted—and thus concluded that the theme of renewal is underscored by the form of the drama itself. Nancy K. Hayles also contended that in this play Shakespeare was concerned with portraying the often unrecognizable differences between appearance and reality and with dramatizing the theme of reconciliation. Arguing that sexual disguise in Shakespearean drama generally serves as the principal means by which the disguised characters gain a truer awareness of reality and false perception, she focused on Imogen's adoption of the role of Fidele, the boy page. Hayles contended that during the time that Imogen is garbed as a boy and thus unites male and female modes of thinking, she acquires an intuitive, dreamlike vision that penetrates false appearances in a way that reason and the senses cannot.

The influence of Elizabethan and Jacobean literary conventions on the dramaturgy of *Cymbeline,* often of interest in the past, has continued to be assessed by more recent scholars. Douglas L. Peterson demonstrated that the scenes set in the Welsh mountains are meant to be symbolic or emblematic of universal truths, contending that this nonrealistic dramatic presentation is related to Philip Sidney's concept of poetic license—namely, that a poet has the freedom to create new natures and forms not found in the real world. The critic further maintained that the ideal community depicted in these scenes, together with its inhabitants—who are emblematic exemplars of natural virtues—, generates the movement toward renewal that impels the play's subsequent dramatic action. However, Rosalie L. Colie asserted that the Welsh mountain scenes portray "the classic life of hard pastoral" rather than a golden, idyllic world, arguing that Shakespeare represents the mountainous landscape as harsh and devoid of nurturing generosity and fecundity. More recently, Michael Taylor has maintained that Shakespeare's adaptation in *Cymbeline* of the literary conventions of pastoralism indicates the dramatist's marked ambivalence towards the pastoral tradition. While he regarded the depiction of the mountain setting in Acts III and IV as unsentimental and divergent from that tradition, Taylor also emphasized that Posthumus and Imogen are not typical young lovers from pastoral romance. Instead, according to Taylor, they are presented as being partially to blame, because of their sexual naiveté,

for the disasters that befall them; he also noted that their self-worth and their behavior towards each other is consistently expressed in punitive, almost painful, terms. Like Granville-Barker earlier in the twentieth century, Barbara A. Mowat examined the self-conscious artlessness of *Cymbeline*, focusing on Shakespeare's use in this play of certain Elizabethan dramatic conventions, such as expository soliloquies, unsubtle announcements of entrances and exits, and direct address to the audience. She contended that Shakespeare intentionally revived such early techniques in order to undercut the dramatic illusion and distance the audience from the fate of Imogen and Posthumus. Arthur C. Kirsch similarly examined this so-called metadramatic element in *Cymbeline* in two essays. In one, he discussed the techniques that make *Cymbeline* a self-conscious play and compared these to the reflexive elements in seventeenth-century coterie drama (see Additional Bibliography); in the other, excerpted below, he claimed that the artificial, artless, and conventional nature of *Cymbeline* is a result of Shakespeare's deliberate "attempt to explore the techniques and implications of tragicomic dramaturgy." Whereas the majority of recent commentators on the theatrical techniques in *Cymbeline* have judged that Shakespeare intended to establish a series of distancing effects between the audience and his drama, Roger Warren disputed this finding and argued that the play depicts basic human emotions so vividly that the audience becomes intensely involved with the consequences of the dramatic action. Warren examined three scenes in particular—Imogen's awakening beside Cloten's headless torso, Posthumus's vision, and Iachimo in Imogen's bedroom—and concluded that in each there is a startling visual action that arrests the audience's attention, isolating the dramatic moment from the rest of the play, and in which, by means of powerful and intense poetry, Shakespeare conveys a sense of emotion so strong that the audience experiences the feeling together with the character.

Several recent critics have offered expositions of *Cymbeline* that represent departures from the mainstream of the play's critical history. Relating the play to Shakespeare's earlier comedies, John Russell Brown contended that the issues of love and friendship are paramount in *Cymbeline* and that the broad variety of dramatic situations and sentiments in the play may be linked to the expansive view of life that comprises the comic vision. Employing techniques of psychoanalytic criticism, D. E. Landry argued that *Cymbeline* dramatizes the parallels between the construction of dreams and the national edifices of chronicle history and concluded that both Posthumus and Britain are depicted as undergoing a purgative experience in which disruptive elements are rejected or reabsorbed and personal and national identities are reconstituted. David M. Bergeron contended that *Cymbeline* is unlike Shakespeare's other romances in that its portrayal of sexuality is unrelated to the process of regeneration and renewal; he concluded that the play's dramatic world is sterile and that Iachimo and Cloten epitomize the deficient and misguided sexuality that is pervasive throughout the drama.

A recapitulation of the critical history of *Cymbeline* demonstrates the series of remarkable shifts since the first serious evaluations of the play. Commentators of the eighteenth century generally disparaged it, those of the nineteenth emphasized its serious thematic content and lauded both its structure and the character of Imogen, and scholars in the early twentieth century found fault with many aspects of the drama, often attributing much of the work to a collaborator. From the 1940s to the present, however, critics have regarded *Cymbeline*'s astonishing variety of dramatic material as affording a broad range of interpretations. The fact that there is no consensus on the primacy of national issues, on the import of the wager plot, on the significance of religious or Christian principles, and on Shakespeare's dramatic technique, as well as other critical questions, may be traced to the unusual combination in this play of a diverse richness of dramatic elements unequalled in any of Shakespeare's other dramas.

SIMON FORMAN   (diary date 1611)

[*Forman was an astrologer and a disreputable practitioner of medicine. He was frequently jailed for his activities, but he enjoyed the patronage of many powerful and titled women who were convinced of his abilities to effect miraculous cures and to foretell the future. Forman's recollection of the dramatic action in* Cymbeline—*which he saw performed at the Globe Theatre in 1611—is generally accepted as establishing a latest possible composition date for the play.*]

of Cimbalin king of England

Remember also the storri of Cymbalin king of England in Lucius tyme. howe Lucius Cam from octauus Cesar for Tribut and being denied. after sent Lucius wth a greate Arme [*or* Arnie] of Souldiars who landed at milford hauen. and After wer vanquished by Cimbalin and Lucius taken prisoner and all by means of 3 outlawes of the wch 2 of them were the sonns of Cimbelim token from him when they were but 2 yers old. by an old man whom Cymbalin banished. and he kept them as his own sonns 20 yers wth him in A cave. And howe [one] of them slewe Clotan that was the quens sonn goinge To milford hauen to sek the loue of Innogen the kinges daughter whom he had banished also for louinge his daughter. and howe the Italiã that cam from her loue. conueied him selfe into A Cheste. and said yt was a chest of plate sent from her loue & others to be presented to the kinge. And in the depest of the night she being aslepe. he opened the cheste & cam forth of yt. And vewed her in her bed and the markes of her body. & toke a wai her braclet & after Accused her of adultery to her loue &c And in thend howe he came wth the Romains into England & was taken prisoner and after Reueled to Innogen. Who had turned her self into mans apparrell & fled to mete her loue at milford hauen. & chanchsed to fall on the Caue in the wodes wher her 2 brothers were & howe by eating a sleping Dram they thought she had bin deed & laid her in the wodes & the body of cloten by her. in her loues apparrell that he left behind him & howe she was found by lucius etc. . . .

> Simon Forman, *"Contemporary Notices of the Plays and Poems: Dr. Simon Forman,"* in The Riverside Shakespeare, *edited by G. Blakemore Evans, Houghton Mifflin Company, 1974, p. 1841.*

GERARD LANGBAINE   (essay date 1691)

[*Langbaine is generally acknowledged as the first historian of the English theater. He wrote several catalogues of dramatic history, including* An Account of the English Dramatick Poets *(1691), in which he provided biographical sketches of playwrights, lists of their works, and possible sources for the plots of their plays. In the excerpt below, taken from the work mentioned above, Langbaine establishes himself as the first commentator to call attention to Shakespeare's use of Boccaccio's* Decameron *for the wager plot in* Cymbeline. *He also judges that Shakespeare's debt to the* chronicle historians for the plot of Cymbeline *is a negligible one. Other scholars who have discussed the possible sources of this play include Charlotte Lennox (1753) and Robert Grams Hunter (1965); also, see the essays by J. P. Brockbank and Kenneth Muir cited in the Additional Bibliography.*]

This Play [*Cymbeline*], tho' the Title bear the Name of a King of *Brute*'s Linage; yet I think ows little to the Chronicles of those Times, as far as I can collect, from *Grafton, Stow, Milton, &c.* But the Subject is rather built upon a Novel in *Boccace, viz.* Day 2. Nov. 9.

> Gerard Langbaine, in an extract from Shakespeare, the Critical Heritage: 1623-1692, Vol. 1, *edited by Brian Vickers, Routledge & Kegan Paul, 1974, p. 419.*

[CHARLES GILDON]   (essay date 1710)

[*Gildon was the first critic to write an extended commentary on the entire Shakespearean dramatic canon. Like many other Neoclassicists, he regarded Shakespeare as an imaginative playwright who nevertheless lacked knowledge of the dramatic "rules" necessary for correct writing. Gildon's disapproval of the irregularities of plotting in* Cymbeline, *as described below, is shared by Charlotte Lennox (1753) and William Hawkins (1759). The critic also comments that the king, Queen, and Cloten behave inconsistently with their stature—a point that is treated extensively by Lennox—and that the play smells "rankly of* Romance."]

Tho' the usual Absurdities of irregular Plots abound in [*Cymbeline*], yet there is something in the Discovery, that is very touching. The character of the King Queen and *Clotten*, do not seem extreamly agreeable to their Quality. . . .

[Indeed] most of the Incidents of this Play smell rankly of *Romance*. (p. 419)

> [Charles Gildon], *"Remarks on the Plays of Shakespear,"* in The Works of Mr. William Shakespear, *Vol. 7 by William Shakespeare, 1710. Reprint by AMS Press, Inc., 1967, pp. 257-444.*

ALEXANDER POPE   (essay date 1723)

[*Pope was the foremost English poet of the first half of the eighteenth century, as well as a prolific author of satires written at the expense of his literary contemporaries. Between 1723 and 1725 he published a six-volume edition of the works of Shakespeare which was based upon the text of Nicholas Rowe. Pope was more concerned with poetics than with editorial scholarship, and thus his edition is replete with corruptions, principally interpolations and omissions which he believed would improve the metric patterns of Shakespeare's dramatic verse. In the excerpt below from his emendations to* Cymbeline, *Pope asserts that the vision scene (V. iv. 30ff.) is an unnecessary interruption of the dramatic action—a judgment that was later endorsed by George Steevens (1793) and Hermann Ulrici (1839). Pope is the first commentator to maintain that these lines are not the work of Shakespeare, but an interpolation by another writer; his assessment is shared by Steevens and Frederick Gard Fleay (see Additional Bibliography). However, most scholars from G. Wilson Knight (1947) to the present regard the passage as authentic.*]

[In Act V of *Cymbeline*, there is] a *Vision*, a *Masque*, and a *Prophecy*, which interrupt the Fable without the least necessity, and unmeasurably lengthen this act. I think it plainly foisted in afterwards for meer show, and apparently not of *Shakespear*.

> Alexander Pope, in a note on *"Cymbeline,"* in The Works of Shakespear, *Vol. 6 by William Shake-*

speare, edited by Alexander Pope, 1723. Reprint by AMS Press, 1969, p. 219.

[CHARLOTTE LENNOX]   (essay date 1753)

[*Lennox was a novelist and Shakespearean scholar who compiled* Shakespear Illustrated *(1753), a three-volume edition of the sources used by Shakespeare in twenty-two of his plays, including some analyses of the ways in which he used these sources. In the excerpt below, taken from that work, she maintains that Shakespeare's alterations of Boccaccio's tale result in an inferior retelling of the wager story. With regard to the plotting of dramatic events in* Cymbeline, *Lennox argues, like Samuel Johnson (1765) a few years later, that "the whole Conduct of the Play is absurd and ridiculous to the last Degree." She is particularly concerned with tracing the occasions throughout the play in which characters' actions or speeches are "unnatural" or inappropriate to their roles in society, a point made earlier by Charles Gildon (1710). Along with such other eighteenth-century critics as Gildon and William Hawkins (1759), Lennox also charges that* Cymbeline *is replete with violations of the Neoclassical rules regarding time, place, and action.*]

The Plot of the foregoing Novel forms one of the Actions of *Shakespear*'s Tragedy, called *Cymbeline*; I say one of the Actions, because this Play, with his usual Irregularity, is composed of three or four different ones.

He has copied all those Circumstances from *Boccaccio,* that were necessary to serve his Design; but he has entirely changed the Scene, the Characters, and the Manners; and that he has done so greatly for the worse, is I think easy to prove.

Boccaccio introduces some young Merchants in a Tavern, where two of them, being heated by Wine, lay a fantastical Wager; one that his Wife was absolutely chaste, and not to be corrupted by any Methods whatever.

The other, that she was frail like the rest of the Sex; and that to prove it, he would prevail upon her in a very short Time to violate her Faith to her Husband.

Shakespear makes the Lady in Question, not the Wife of a Merchant, but the Heiress of a great Kingdom.

The Husband, who lays so indiscreet a Wager, not a simple Trader intoxicated with Liquor, but a young, noble, though unfortunate Hero, whom, for the extraordinary Qualities of his Mind and Person, the Princess had secretly married.

And the Scenes, instead of a Tavern in *Paris,* and the House of a private Family in the Court of *Britain,* and the Chamber of the Princess.

To this injudicious Change of the Characters is owing all the Absurdities of this Part of *Shakespear*'s Plot; he has given the Manners of a Tradesman's Wife, and two Merchants intoxicated with Liquor, to a great Princess, an *English* Hero, and a noble Roman.

The King, enraged at *Poshumus* for daring to marry his Daughter, contents himself with only sending him into Banishment, and presses the Princess to take for another Husband a Man whom she detests, while her first is only divided from her by a very inconsiderable Distance, and while there is a Probability of meeting him again.

Since he was so resolutely bent upon making her marry the stupid Son of his second Wife, surely it would have more facilitated his Design, to have either taken away the Life of *Posthumus,* or kept him in a strict and secret Confinement,

and by that Means have deprived the Princess of all Hope of ever seeing him; but *Posthumus* must only be banished to make Way for the scandalous Wager.

This adoring and obliged Husband of a beautiful and virtuous Princess, no sooner arrives at *Rome,* but he engages in a ridiculous Dispute concerning the Beauty, Wit, and Chastity of his Lady; and tamely suffers one of his *Roman* Friends, to maintain that she was as liable to be corrupted as any other of her Sex.

The Dispute growing warm, the *Roman* engages to take a Journey to *Britain,* and corrupt the Chastity of the Princess, which, if he accomplishes, *Posthumus* is to reward him with the Ring that she had given him at parting; and to facilitate his Design, writes a Letter to the Princess, recommending *Jachimo* to her as one of his most valued Friends.

Jachimo accordingly arrives in *Britain*, delivers his Letter to the Princess, and is very kindly received.

It must be observed that the Princess is strictly guarded by the King's Orders, and this is very natural, since he intended to force her to marry her stupid Step-brother.

But how comes it that this confined Princess, guarded by her Father's Guards, and watched by her Mother-in-law's Spies, should be able to give an Audience to a foreign Stranger, who comes from the very Place where her banished Husband resides?

We see no Stratagem made use of to elude the Vigilance of her Guards; no Bribes given to buy the Secresy of Spies.

The Friend of her banished Husband is introduced by his Confident, who though known to be so, both by the King, Queen, and Rival of *Posthumus,* is still permitted to attend her.

This is not indeed very probable, but it is absolutely necessary for the Plot, because this faithful Confident is to carry the Princess afterwards into a dark Wood, in order to kill her, by his Master's Orders.

So the story goes in *Boccaccio,* so also goes the Plot in the Tragedy.

There is only this small Difference, that in *Boccaccio* it is a private Gentlewoman, who, attended with one Servant, rides a small Journey to meet her Husband at his Country House.

But in *Shakespear,* it is the Heiress of a great Kingdom, who notwithstanding her Guards, the Dignity of her Station, and Weakness of her Sex, rides Post with one Man Servant to a Sea-port Town, for a short View of her Husband. (pp. 155-58)

When she arrives in the destined Wood, *Pisanio* acquaints her with the Orders he had received to kill her, and his fixed Resolution not to obey them.

The princess indeed puts a very pertinent Question to him.

> *Imo.* Wherefore then
> Didst undertake it? why hast thou abused
> So many Miles, with a Pretence? this Place?
> Mine Action? and thine own? our Horses
>   labour.
> The Time inviting thee? the perturb'd Court,
> For my being absent? whereunto I never
> Purpose return. Why hast thou gone so far
> To be unbent when thou hast ta'en thy Stand,
> Th' elected Deer before thee?
>   [III. iv. 101-09]

Shakespear no doubt foresaw his Readers would ask this Question if the Princess did not, but though he found it an easy Matter to make *Pisanio* satisfy her as to that Particular, the Reader is not so easily answered.

For why indeed did he bring her into so shocking a Situation, if he resolved not to murder her? Why did he not acquaint her with the cruel Orders of her Husband while she was in her Father's Palace?

It it was a bold and hazardous Action to quit the Court in such a strange Equipage, to have a short Conference with a faithful Husband, why must she expose herself to so eminent a Danger, only to be told of the Cruelty and Injustice of that Husband?

But the Truth is, she has a great many strange Adventures to come yet, and these must be brought about at the Expence of Probability.

But what Resolution does the Heiress of *Britain* take after being told that her Husband, believing her to be an Adulteress, had ordered her to be killed?

One would imagine, that full of a just Disdain for so vile and scandalous a Suspicion, the Pride of injured Virtue, affronted Dignity, and Rage of ill requited Love, would have carried her back to the Court, there by disclaiming all future Faith and Tenderness for the unworthy *Posthumus,* restore herself to the Affection of her Father, and all the Rights of her royal Birth.

No, she only weeps, complains, reproaches a little, and then resolves to dress herself in the Habit of a Boy, and wander a-foot to procure a Service.

Here *Shakespear* drops *Boccaccio,* after having servilely copied from him all the Incidents which compose this Part of the Plot of *Cymbeline*; but by changing the Scene and Characters has made these Incidents absurd, unnatural, and improbable.

The rest of the Play is equally inconsistent, and if *Shakespear* invented here for himself, his Imagination is in this one Instance full as bad as his Judgment.

His Princess forgetting that she had put on Boy's Cloaths to be a Spy upon the Actions of her Husband, commences Cook to two young Forresters and their Father, who live in a Cave; and we are told how nicely she sauced the Broths.

> [*Arv.*] But his neat Cookery!
> He cut our Roots in Characters,
> And sauc'd our Broth, as *Juno* had been sick,
> And he her Dieter.
>
> [IV. ii. 49-51]

Certainly this Princess had a most œconomical Education; however she is to change her Situation, seem dead, be buried, and come to Life again, and hire herself to a new Master. (pp. 161-63)

Cloten follows the Princess with an Intention, as he declares, "to ravish her, and then kick her back to Court," and is disguised in the Cloaths of *Posthumus,* though there is no other Reason for his being thus disguised, but only that the Princess may afterwards suppose him *Posthumus* when she finds him dead. Being afterwards killed by the Brothers of *Imogen,* one of them cuts off his Head, and buries him beside the supposed Youth.

It may seem a little shocking for a generous young Man, a Prince, though he did not know it himself, to cut off the Head of his Enemy, after having killed him; but his Head must be cut off, or else how could *Imogen* mistake him for her Lord?

The Princess awaking from her Trance, supposes she is travelling to *Milford-Haven,* and cries, "Ods pittikens, is it six Miles yet?" recovering her Senses perfectly, and seeing a headless man lying near, drest in the Cloaths of *Posthumus,* she laments over him, believing him to be her Husband.

This is indeed a very pathetic Distress; but what does the unhappy Heiress of *Britain* do, now she thinks her Husband is killed? Why she accepts the Post of Page to the Enemy of her Father and Country; who, with a hostile Army, is wasting the Kingdom, over which, by Right of Birth, she is to reign.

But why does the Princess disgrace her Sex and Dignity by accepting so scandalous an Employment? Is it the Fear of Death from the *Romans?* No, certainly there is no such Thing threatened.

Besides, a Lady, fond to Distraction of a Husband whom she finds lying murdered by her, can hardly be supposed so attentive to her own Danger in those distressful Moments as to provide so cunningly for her Safety.

However, the Princess, full of Despair as she is, dresses up a clever Tale in a Trice; invents a Name for her murdered Husband; calls herself his Page; says she was slain by Mountaineers; and expresses her Fears that she should never get so good a Master.

Hereupon *Lucius* takes her to be his Page; and her Highness goes off very well contented with her Situation.

It would be an endless Task to take Notice of all the Absurdities in the Plot, and unnatural Manners in the Characters of this Play.

Such as the ridiculous Story of the King's two Sons being stolen in their Infancy from the Court, and bred up in the Mountains of Wales till they were twenty Years of Age.

Then, at their first Essay in Arms, these Striplings stop the King's Army, which is flying from the victorious *Romans,* oblige them to face their Enemies, and gain a compleat Victory.

With Inconsistencies like these it every where abounds; the whole Conduct of the Play is absurd and ridiculous to the last Degree, and with all the Liberties *Shakespear* has taken with Time, Place and Action, the Story, as he has managed it, is more improbable than a Fairy Tale. (pp. 164-66)

> [*Charlotte Lennox*], *"Observations on the Use Shakespear Has Made of the Foregoing Novel in His Tragedy of 'Cymbeline',"* in her Shakespear Illustrated; or, The Novels and Histories, on Which the Plays of Shakespear Are Founded, Vol. I, 1753. Reprint by AMS Press Inc., 1973, pp. 155-67.

WILLIAM HAWKINS   (essay date 1759)

[Hawkins was a clergyman and poet who wrote an adaptation of Cymbeline *(1759) in which he retained much of Shakespeare's original language, but sought to amend the irregularities of plotting by imposing a new dramatic design that followed the Neoclassical precepts of the dramatic unities. Other eighteenth-century commentators who found fault with the play's violations of the rules of Neoclassicism include Charles Gildon (1710) and Charlotte Lennox (1753). In the excerpt below from the preface to his adaptation, Hawkins remarks that the play's subject is "truly British," thus foreshadowing the judgment of G. Wilson Knight (1947), Harold C. Goddard (1951), William Barry Thorne*

(1969), and Alexander Leggatt (1977); for further discussions of the importance of British nationalism in Cymbeline, *see the essays by David M. Bergeron, J. P. Brockbank, Robert S. Miola, and Frances A. Yates cited in the Additional Bibliography.*]

The Tragedy of *Cymbeline* is, in the whole oeconomy of it, one of the most irregular productions of *Shakespeare*. Its defects however, or rather its superfluities, are more than equalled by beauties and excellencies of various kinds. There is at the same time something so pleasingly romantic and likewise truly *British* in the subject of it that, I flatter myself, an attempt to reduce it as near as possible to the regular standard of the *drama* will be favourably received by all who are admirers of *novelty* when *propriety* is its foundation. I have accordingly endeavoured to new-construct this Tragedy almost upon the plan of *Aristotle* himself, in respect of the *unity* of *Time*, with so thorough a veneration however for the great *Father* of the *English* stage that even while I have presumed to regulate and modernize his design I have thought it an honour to tread in his steps, and to imitate his Stile with the humility and reverence of a *Son*. (p. 374)

> *William Hawkins, in an extract from* Shakespeare, the Critical Heritage: 1753-1765, Vol. 4, *edited by Brian Vickers, Routledge & Kegan Paul, 1976, pp. 374-75.*

SAMUEL JOHNSON   (essay date 1765)

[*Johnson has long held an important place in the history of Shakespearean criticism. He is considered the foremost representative of moderate English Neoclassicism and is credited by some literary historians with freeing Shakespeare from the strictures of the three unities valued by strict Neoclassicists: that drama should have a single setting, take place in less than twenty-four hours, and have a causally connected plot. More recent scholars portray him as a critic who was able to synthesize existing critical theory rather than as an innovative theoretician. Johnson was a master of Augustan prose style and a personality who dominated the literary world of his epoch. In the excerpt below, taken from his notes to* Cymbeline *in his 1765 edition of Shakespeare's plays, Johnson sharply attacks the structure of the play and charges that its fabric is one of "unresisting imbecillity." His brief remarks on* Cymbeline *are more frequently cited by later commentators than those of any other critic. Whereas John Potter (1771-72) has regarded Johnson's sentiments as unnecessarily harsh and Anna Brownell Jameson (1833) has found them obtuse, such critics as Walter Raleigh (1907), Horace Howard Furness (1913), William Witherle Lawrence (1920), and Harley Granville-Barker (1930) have all essentially endorsed Johnson's judgment; moreover, most scholars who have examined the dramatic structure of* Cymbeline *have begun their discussions with reference to his comments reprinted below.*]

This play has many just sentiments, some natural dialogues, and some pleasing scenes, but they are obtained at the expence of much incongruity.

To remark the folly of the fiction, the absurdity of the conduct, the confusion of the names and manners of different times, and the impossibility of the events in any system of life, were to waste criticism upon unresisting imbecillity, upon faults too evident for detection, and too gross for aggravation. (p. 908)

> *Samuel Johnson, "Notes on Shakespeare's Plays: 'Cymbeline'," in his* The Yale Edition of the Works of Samuel Johnson: Johnson on Shakespeare, Vol. VIII, *edited by Arthur Sherbo, Yale University Press, 1968, pp. 874-908.*

JOHN POTTER   (essay date 1771-72)

[*Potter was a miscellaneous writer and a theatrical critic of the eighteenth century. The following excerpt is taken from his review of some eighteenth-century performances of* Cymbeline, *first published in his* The Theatrical Review; or, New Companion to the Play-House *(1771-72). Potter disputes Samuel Johnson's assessment of the play (see excerpt above, 1765), contending it is too severe and fails to consider the "infinity of Beauties" in the drama. With his remark that the play is a "Dramatic Romance," Potter established himself as the earliest commentator to raise the issue of the genre to which the play might be assigned. Other critics who have discussed* Cymbeline *in relation to the romance tradition and pastoral conventions include E. K. Chambers (1907), Douglas L. Peterson (1973), Rosalie L. Colie (1974), and Michael Taylor (1983).*]

This pleasing Dramatic Romance (for it cannot be considered in any other light) is one proof amongst many of the amazing fertility of *Shakespeare*'s unbounded fancy; for though the Plot as far as it relates to *Posthumus* and *Imogen* is taken from *Boccace*'s *Decameron*, and the rest from the ancient traditions of the *British* History, there is little historical besides the names. (p. 432)

Whoever places himself in the Critic's chair must subscribe to [the sentiments of Samuel Johnson; see excerpt above, 1765]. But then it should be considered of whom we are speaking: Of *Shakespeare*, the first Dramatic Author in the World; who, scorning to be bound by any Laws, gave a loose to the workings of the most extensive imagination that ever possessed the mind of Man. The irregularities in this Piece are numerous, we confess; yet notwithstanding all these it contains an infinity of Beauties, both with respect to Language, Character, Passion, and incident; and the severity of Criticism must abate of its rigour by contemplating on those wonderful strokes of Genius with which it abounds. So that while the Judgment is displeased with the improbability of the Plot, and inconsistency of the Dramatic Action, the Mind must receive the highest satisfaction from the pleasing excursions of Fancy; and though it is impossible we can be inattentive to the obvious defects of the Piece the pleasure we receive from it, on the whole, naturally inclines us to behold them with an eye of favour. (pp. 432-33)

> *John Potter, in an extract from* Shakespeare, the Critical Heritage: 1765-1774, Vol. 5, *edited by Brian Vickers, Routledge & Kegan Paul, 1979, pp. 432-33.*

GEORGE STEEVENS   (essay date 1772)

[*Steevens was an English scholar who collaborated with Samuel Johnson on a ten-volume edition of Shakespeare's dramatic works in 1773. The subsequent revision of this collection, along with Steevens's own edition of 1793, formed the textual basis for the first two Variorum editions of Shakespeare's plays. Many modern scholars also contend that Steevens was the sole theater critic for the* General Evening Post. *In the following excerpt, taken from the March 1772 issue of that journal and signed "Lorenzo" (attributed to Steevens by Brian Vickers), the critic focuses on the inconsistencies in Cloten's language and behavior and concludes by calling him "a plain, undisguised, self-condemning monster." In the twentieth century, Cloten has frequently been viewed as more than just an evil villain in the play; in fact, he is frequently seen as representing the dark aspects of Posthumus's character. For examples of this reading, see the excerpts by Robert Grams Hunter (1965), Homer D. Swander (1966), and James Edward Siemon (1976); also, for more on this topic, see the essays by Joan Carr, Howard Felperin, and Joan Hartwig cited in the Additional Bibliography.*]

Cloten is a very whimsical composition; he is drawn foolish and wise, brave and insignificant, suspicious to an excess, yet weak beyond the toleration of credibility. In his vices he keeps no bounds whatsoever with the instruments he wishes to employ, but on the contrary describes the villainy he wants executed in the most detestable terms. Thus in his attack upon Pisanio, to discover where Imogen is, he tells that faithful servant if he is desirous to be thought *a true man*, that is, if he is ready to commit every crime which Cloten thinks proper to advise, this *gracious Prince* will at once receive him into his highest favour, and neither spare his purse nor his interest to advance him in Cymbeline's Court. Other villains, when they endeavour to corrupt the weak or the wavering, behave with some share of caution and break their infamous purposes gradually, to lessen the horror of their intentions. . . . But Cloten, though uninvested with a regal power of defending his deeds, is a plain, undisguised, self-condemning monster. Like Lord Ogleby in the *Clandestine Marriage*, he is above all consideration the moment his desires are kindled, and instead of tediously beating the bush comes to his point at once, with an impudence that actually puts guilt out of countenance. The murder of Posthumus and the rape of Imogen he mentions as mere trifles, and tells us after he has slaughtered the first and forced the latter that the King may *possibly* be angry but that the Queen his mother, having power over the destiny of Cymbeline, shall turn every thing into his commendation. This is not all. Cloten's fury is as ridiculous as it is criminal, for after he has *tied up his horse* in a most royal stile to look after Posthumus he enters into a foolish, preposterous quarrel with one of the disguised young Princes under Bellarius's care, and risques the disappointment of his own views because he takes the Prince to be a mountaineer. 'Yield thee, villain, or thou diest,' is his language to a man who has given him no shadow of offence, and whose only culpability consists in being the inhabitant of a mountain. (pp. 496-97)

George Steevens, in an extract from Shakespeare, the Critical Heritage: 1765-1774, Vol. 5, *edited by Brian Vickers, Routledge & Kegan Paul, 1979, pp. 496-97.*

GEORGE STEEVENS   (essay date 1793)

[*The excerpt below was originally published in a fifteen-volume edition of Shakespeare's dramatic works that appeared in 1793 and included commentary by various scholars. Steevens endorses the judgment of Alexander Pope (1723) that the vision or masque in Act V, Scene iv of* Cymbeline—*which Steevens describes as "this contemptible nonsense"—is not the work of Shakespeare, an estimation shared by Frederick Gard Fleay (see Additional Bibliography). For additional discussions of the vision scene and its relation to the play, see the excerpts by Hermann Ulrici (1839), G. G. Gervinus (1849-50), Thomas Kenny (1864), Denton J. Snider (1890), and G. Wilson Knight (1947).*]

Every reader must be of the same opinion [as Alexander Pope (see excerpt above, 1723) regarding the dumb-show and masque in V. iv. of *Cymbeline*]. The subsequent narratives of Posthumus, which render this masque &c. unnecessary, (or perhaps the scenical directions supplied by the poet himself) seem to have excited some manager of a theatre to disgrace the play by the present metrical interpolation. Shakespeare, who has conducted his fifth act with such matchless skill, could never have designed the vision to be twice described by Posthumus, had this contemptible nonsense been previously delivered on the stage.

George Steevens, in an extract from Shakespeare, the Critical Heritage: 1774-1801, Vol. 6, *edited by Brian Vickers, Routledge & Kegan Paul, 1981, p. 597.*

AUGUST WILHELM SCHLEGEL   (essay date 1811)

[*A prominent German Romantic critic, Schlegel holds a key place in the history of Shakespeare's reputation in European criticism. His translations of thirteen of the plays are still considered the best German editions of Shakespeare. Schlegel was also a leading spokesman for the Romantic movement, which permanently overthrew the Neoclassical contention that Shakespeare was a child of nature whose plays lacked artistic form. In the excerpt below, first published in his* A Course of Lectures on Dramatic Art and Literature *in 1811, Schlegel praises the manner in which Shakespeare combined characters and events from diverse historical eras in* Cymbeline. *Whereas such eighteenth-century English commentators as Charles Gildon (1710), Charlotte Lennox (1753), William Hawkins (1759), and Samuel Johnson (1765) argued that the structure of the play is irregular and inconsistent, Schlegel departs from this tradition by maintaining that the elements of the plot are blended "together into one harmonious whole." Other critics who contend that the play is a successful blend of diverse elements include, among others, William Hazlitt (1817), Anna Brownell Jameson (1833), Denton J. Snider (1890), Harold C. Goddard (1951), and Howard Felperin (see Additional Bibliography). Schlegel's comment that Imogen possesses every requisite quality of "female excellence" foreshadows the adulation such nineteenth-century critics as Hazlitt, Jameson, Algernon Charles Swinburne (1880), and Helena Faucit (1882) lavished on the heroine. The critic also views the characters of Guiderius and Arviragus as reflecting Shakespeare's belief in "the superiority of the natural over the artificial." For additional discussions of the princely brothers, see the excerpts by Hazlitt and Douglas L. Peterson (1973).*]

Cymbeline is . . . one of Shakespeare's most wonderful compositions. He has here combined a novel of Boccacio's with traditional tales of the ancient Britons reaching back to the times of the first Roman Emperors, and he has contrived, by the most gentle transitions, to blend together into one harmonious whole the social manners of the newest times with olden heroic deeds, and even with appearances of the gods. In the character of Imogen no one feature of female excellence is omitted: her chaste tenderness, her softness, and her virgin pride, her boundless resignation, and her magnanimity towards her mistaken husband, by whom she is unjustly persecuted, her adventures in disguise, her apparent death, and her recovery, form altogether a picture equally tender and affecting. The two Princes, Guiderius and Arviragus, both educated in the wilds, form a noble contrast to Miranda [*The Tempest*] and Perdita [*The Winter's Tale*]. Shakespeare is fond of showing the superiority of the natural over the artificial. Over the art which enriches nature, he somewhere says, there is a higher art created by nature herself. As Miranda's unconscious and unstudied sweetness is more pleasing than those charms which endeavour to captivate us by the brilliant embellishments of a refined cultivation, so in these two youths, to whom the chase has given vigour and hardihood, but who are ignorant of their high destination, and have been brought up apart from human society, we are equally enchanted by a *naïve* heroism which leads them to anticipate and to dream of deeds of valour, till an occasion is offered which they are irresistibly compelled to embrace. When Imogen comes in disguise to their cave; when, with all the innocence of childhood, Guiderius and Arviragus form an impassioned friendship for the tender boy, in whom they neither suspect a female nor their own sister; when, on their return from the chase, they find her dead, then "sing her to the ground" [IV. ii. 235], and cover the grave with flowers:—these scenes might give to the most deadened imagination a new life for poetry. If a tragical event is only apparent, in such case, whether the spectators are already aware of it or ought merely to suspect it, Shakespeare always knows how to mitigate the impression without weakening it: he makes the mourning musical, that it may gain in solemnity what it loses in seriousness. With respect to the other parts, the wise and vigorous Belarius, who after long living as a hermit again becomes a hero, is a venerable figure; the Italian Iachimo's ready dissimulation and quick presence of mind is quite suitable to the bold treachery which he plays; Cymbeline, the father of Imogen, and even her husband Posthumus, during the first half of the piece, are somewhat sacrificed, but this could not be otherwise; the false and wicked Queen is merely an instrument of the plot; she and her stupid son Cloton (the only comic part in the piece) whose rude arrogance is portrayed with much humour, are, before the conclusion, got rid of by merited punishment. As for the heroical part of the fable, the war between the Romans and Britons, which brings on the dénouement, the poet in the extent of his plan had so little room to spare, that he merely endeavours to represent it as a mute procession. But to the last scene, where all the numerous threads of the knot are untied, he has again given its full development, that he might collect together into one focus the scattered impressions of the whole. This example and many others are a sufficient refutation of Johnson's assertion, that Shakespeare usually hurries over the conclusion of his pieces. Rather does he, from a desire to satisfy the feelings, introduce a great deal which, so far as the understanding of the *dénouement* requires, might in a strict sense by justly spared: our modern spectators are much more impatient to see the curtain drop, when there is nothing more to be determined, than those of his day could have been. (pp. 397-99)

August Wilhelm Schlegel, "Criticisms on Shakespeare's Comedies," in his A Course of Lectures on Dramatic Art and Literature, *edited by Rev. A. J. W. Morrison, translated by John Black, revised edition, 1846. Reprint by AMS Press, Inc., 1965, pp. 379-99.*

WILLIAM HAZLITT   (essay date 1817)

[*Hazlitt is considered a leading Shakespearean critic of the English Romantic movement. A prolific essayist and critic on a wide range of subjects, Hazlitt remarked in the preface to his* Characters of Shakespear's Plays, *first published in 1817, that he was inspired by the German critic August Wilhelm Schlegel and was determined to supplant what he considered the pernicious influence of Samuel Johnson's Shakespearean criticism. Hazlitt's commentary is typically Romantic in its emphasis on character studies. His experience as a drama critic was an important factor in shaping his descriptive, as opposed to analytical, interpretations of Shakespeare. In the excerpt below, taken from the work mentioned above, Hazlitt asserts that the characters in* Cymbeline *are "represented with great truth and accuracy," focusing especially on Imogen, whom he praises for her constancy, tenderness, and artlessness. Whereas August Wilhelm Schlegel (1811) had earlier lauded the character of Imogen for its representation of female virtues, Hazlitt is the first critic to offer such fulsome praise of the figure; indeed, his remarks foreshadowed the nineteenth-century critical preoccupation with the heroine which has sometimes bordered on idolatry. Examples of this adulatory viewpoint may be seen in the essays by Anna Brownell Jameson (1833), G. G. Gervinus (1849-50), Algernon Charles Swinburne (1880), and Helena Faucit (1882). In the late nineteenth century, Bernard Shaw (1896) has provided a contrasting assessment, contending*

that there are two distinct aspects of Imogen's nature—one priggish and the other of great sensitivity. For some twentieth-century commentary on the character of Imogen, see the excerpts by E. K. Chambers (1907), Brander Matthews (1913), Harley Granville-Barker (1930), G. Wilson Knight (1947), Harold C. Goddard (1951), and Robin Moffet (1962). Like Schlegel, Hazlitt also praises the dramatic structure of Cymbeline, *declaring that Shakespeare has combined the different elements of his story so skillfully that even the "most straggling and seemingly casual incidents are contrived in such a manner as to lead at last to the most complete development of the catastrophe." Also like Schlegel, Hazlitt sees the princes and Belarius in their mountain retreat as the embodiment of natural simplicity in opposition to "the intrigues and artificial refinements of the court." For additional discussion of Guiderius and Arviragus, see the excerpt by Douglas L. Peterson (1973). Finally, in a brief remark on Imogen's funeral rites, Hazlitt discusses the significance of the religious element in* Cymbeline, *an issue treated more extensively by G. G. Gervinus (1849-50), G. Wilson Knight (1947), J. A. Bryant, Jr. (1961), Robin Moffet (1962), Northrop Frye (1965), Robert Grams Hunter (1965), Homer D. Swander (1966), R. A. Foakes (1971), and Arthur C. Kirsch (1972).*]

Cymbeline is one of the most delightful of Shakespear's historical plays. It may be considered as a dramatic romance, in which the most striking parts of the story are thrown into the form of a dialogue, and the intermediate circumstances are explained by the different speakers, as occasion renders it necessary. The action is less concentrated in consequence; but the interest becomes more aerial and refined from the principle of perspective introduced into the subject by the imaginary changes of scene, as well as by the length of time it occupies. The reading of this play is like going a journey with some uncertain object at the end of it, and in which the suspense is kept up and heightened by the long intervals between each action. Though the events are scattered over such an extent of surface, and relate to such a variety of characters, yet the links which bind the different interests of the story together are never entirely broken. The most straggling and seemingly casual incidents are contrived in such a manner as to lead at last to the most complete development of the catastrophe. The ease and conscious unconcern with which this is effected only makes the skill more wonderful. The business of the plot evidently thickens in the last act: the story moves forward with increasing rapidity at every step; its various ramifications are drawn from the most distant points to the same centre; the principal characters are brought together, and placed in very critical situations; and the fate of almost every person in the drama is made to depend on the solution of a single circumstance—the answer of Iachimo to the question of Imogen respecting the obtaining of the ring from Posthumus. Dr. Johnson is of opinion that Shakespear was generally inattentive to the winding-up of his plots. We think the contrary is true; and we might cite in proof of this remark not only the present play, but the conclusion of *Lear*, of *Romeo and Juliet*, of *Macbeth*, of *Othello*, even of *Hamlet*, and of other plays of less moment, in which the last act is crowded with decisive events brought about by natural and striking means.

The pathos in *Cymbeline* is not violent or tragical, but of the most pleasing and amiable kind. A certain tender gloom overspreads the whole. Posthumus is the ostensible hero of the piece, but its greatest charm is the character of Imogen. Posthumus is only interesting from the interest she takes in him; and she is only interesting herself from her tenderness and constancy to her husband. (pp. 1-2)

We have almost as great an affection for Imogen as she had for Posthumus; and she deserves it better. Of all Shakespear's women she is perhaps the most tender and the most artless. Her incredulity in the opening scene with Iachimo, as to her husband's infidelity, is much the same as Desdemona's backwardness to believe Othello's jealousy. Her answer to the most distressing part of the picture is only, "My lord, I fear, has forgot Britain" [I. vi. 112-13]. Her readiness to pardon Iachimo's false imputations and his designs against herself, is a good lesson to prudes; and may shew that where there is a real attachment to virtue, it has no need to bolster itself up with an outrageous or affected antipathy to vice. The scene in which Pisanio gives Imogen his master's letter, accusing her of incontinency on the treacherous suggestions of Iachimo, is as touching as it is possible for anything to be.... (p. 3)

She all along relies little on her personal charms, which she fears may have been eclipsed by some painted Jay of Italy; she relies on her merit, and her merit is in the depth of her love, her truth and constancy. Our admiration of her beauty is excited with as little consciousness as possible on her part. There are two delicious descriptions given of her, one when she is asleep, and one when she is supposed dead. Arviragus thus addresses her—

> With fairest flowers,
> While summer lasts, and I live here, Fidele,
> I'll sweeten thy sad grave; thou shalt not lack
> The flower that's like thy face, pale primrose, nor
> The azur'd hare-bell, like thy veins, no, nor
> The leaf of eglantine, which not to slander,
> Out-sweeten'd not thy breath.
>
> [IV. ii. 218-24]

The yellow Iachimo gives another thus, when he steals into her bedchamber:—

> Cytherea,
> How bravely thou becom'st thy bed! Fresh lily,
> And whiter than the sheets! That I might touch—
> But kiss, one kiss—'Tis her breathing that
> Perfumes the chamber thus: the flame o' th' taper
> Bows toward her, and would under-peep her lids
> To see th' enclosed lights now canopied
> Under the windows, white and azure, laced
> With blue of Heav'ns own tinct—on her left breast
> A mole cinque-spotted, like the crimson drops
> I' th' bottom of a cowslip.
>
> [II. ii. 14-17, 18-23, 37-9]

There is a moral sense in the proud beauty of this last image, a rich surfeit of the fancy,—as that well-known passage beginning, "Me of my lawful pleasure she restrained, and prayed me oft forbearance" [II. v. 9-10], sets a keener edge upon it by the inimitable picture of modesty and self-denial.

The character of Cloten, the conceited, booby lord, and rejected lover of Imogen, though not very agreeable in itself, and at present obsolete, is drawn with much humour and quaint extravagance. The description which Imogen gives of his unwelcome addresses to her—"Whose love-suit hath been to me as fearful as a siege" [III. iv. 133-34]—is enough to cure the most ridiculous lover of his folly. It is remarkable that though Cloten makes so poor a figure in love, he is described as assuming an air of consequence as the Queen's son in a council of state, and with all the absurdity of his person and manners, is not without shrewdness in his observations. So true is it that folly is as often owing to a want of proper sentiments as to a want of understanding! The exclamation of the ancient critic—

Oh Menander and Nature, which of you copied from the other! would not be misapplied to Shakespear.

The other characters in this play are represented with great truth and accuracy, and as it happens in most of the author's works, there is not only the utmost keeping in each separate character; but in the casting of the different parts, and their relation to one another, there is an affinity and harmony, like what we may observe in the gradations of colour in a picture. The striking and powerful contrasts in which Shakespear abounds could not escape observation; but the use he makes of the principle of analogy to reconcile the greatest diversities of character and to maintain a continuity of feeling throughout, has not been sufficiently attended to. In *Cymbeline*, for instance, the principal interest arises out of the unalterable fidelity of Imogen to her husband under the most trying circumstances. Now the other parts of the picture are filled up with subordinate examples of the same feeling, variously modified by different situations, and applied to the purposes of virtue or vice. The plot is aided by the amorous importunities of Cloten, by the persevering determination of Iachimo to conceal the defeat of his project by a daring imposture: the faithful attachment of Pisanio to his mistress is an affecting accompaniment to the whole; the obstinate adherence to his purpose in Bellarius, who keeps the fate of the young princes so long a secret in resentment for the ungrateful return to his former services, the incorrigible wickedness of the Queen, and even the blind uxorious confidence of Cymbeline, are all so many lines of the same story, tending to the same point. The effect of this coincidence is rather felt than observed; and as the impression exists unconsciously in the mind of the reader, so it probably arose in the same manner in the mind of the author, not from design, but from the force of natural association, a particular train of thought suggesting different inflections of the same predominant feeling, melting into, and strengthening one another, like chords in music.

The characters of Bellarius, Guiderius, and Arviragus, and the romantic scenes in which they appear, are a fine relief to the intrigues and artificial refinements of the court from which they are banished. Nothing can surpass the wildness and simplicity of the descriptions of the mountain life they lead. They follow the business of huntsmen, not of shepherds; and this is in keeping with the spirit of adventure and uncertainty in the rest of the story, and with the scenes in which they are afterwards called on to act. How admirably the youthful fire and impatience to emerge from their obscurity in the young princes is opposed to the cooler calculations and prudent resignation of their more experienced counsellor! How well the disadvantages of knowledge and of ignorance, of solitude and society, are placed against each other!

> *Guiderius.* Out of your proof you speak: we poor unfledg'd
> Have never wing'd from view o' th' nest; nor know not
> What air's from home. Haply this life is best,
> If quiet life is best; sweeter to you
> That have a sharper known; well corresponding
> With your stiff age: but unto us it is
> A cell of ignorance; travelling a-bed,
> A prison for a debtor, that not dares
> To stride a limit.
> *Arviragus.* What should we speak of
> When we are old as you? When we shall hear
> The rain and wind beat dark December! How,

In this our pinching cave, shall we discourse
The freezing hours away? We have seen nothing.
We are beastly: subtle as the fox for prey,
Like warlike as the wolf for what we eat:
Our valour is to chase what flies; our cage
We make a quire, as doth the prison'd bird,
And sing our bondage freely.

              [III. iii. 27-44]

The answer of Bellarius to this expostulation is hardly satisfactory; for nothing can be an answer to hope, or the passion of the mind for unknown good, but experience.—The forest of Arden in *As you like it* can alone compare with the mountain scenes in *Cymbeline:* yet how different the contemplative quiet of the one from the enterprising boldness and precarious mode of subsistence in the other! (pp. 5-8)

We cannot take leave of this play, which is a favourite with us, without noticing some occasional touches of natural piety and morality. We may allude here to the opening of the scene in which Bellarius instructs the young princes to pay their orisons to heaven:

        See, boys! this gate
Instructs you how t' adore the Heav'ns; and bows you
To morning's holy office.
  Guiderius. Hail, Heav'n!
  Arviragus. Hail, Heav'n!
  Bellarius. Now for our mountain-sport, up to yon hill.
           [III. iii. 2-4, 9-10]

What a grace and unaffected spirit of piety breathes in this passage! In like manner, one of the brothers says to the other, when about to perform the funeral rites to Fidele,

    Nay, Cadwall, we must lay his head to the east;
    My Father hath a reason for't

           [IV. ii. 255-56]

—as if some allusion to the doctrines of the Christian faith had been casually dropped in conversation by the old man, and had been no farther inquired into.

Shakespear's morality is introduced in the same simple, unobtrusive manner. Imogen will not let her companions stay away from the chase to attend her when sick, and gives her reason for it—

    Stick to your journal course; *the breach of custom
    Is breach of all!*

           [IV. ii. 10-11]

When the Queen attempts to disguise her motives for procuring the poison from Cornelius, by saying she means to try its effects on "creatures not worth the hanging," his answer conveys at once a tacit reproof of her hypocrisy, and a useful lesson of humanity—

      Your Highness
Shall from this practice but make hard your heart.
           [I. v. 23-4]
           (pp. 8-9)

William Hazlitt, "*Characters of Shakespear's Plays: 'Cymbeline',*" *in his* Characters of Shakespear's Plays & Lectures on the English Poets, *Macmillan and Co. Limited, 1903, pp. 1-9.*

MRS. [ANNA BROWNELL] JAMESON   (essay date 1833)

[*Jameson was a well-known nineteenth-century essayist. Her essays and criticism span the end of the Romantic age and the beginning of Victorian realism, reflecting elements from both periods. She is best remembered for her study* Shakespeare's Heroines *(1833), which was originally published in a slightly different form in 1832 as* Characteristics of Women: Moral, Poetical, and Historical. *This work demonstrates both her historical interests and her sympathetic appreciation of Shakespeare's female characters. In the following excerpt from* Shakespeare's Heroines, *Jameson argues that Imogen harmoniously combines beauty, wit, and "dignity of rank" and should thus be considered "the most perfect" of Shakespeare's female characters. Comparing her with such other heroines as Juliet, Desdemona, and Miranda, the critic contends that although Imogen is not as striking, brilliant, or powerful as these characters, she "unites the greatest number of those qualities which we imagine to constitute excellence in women." For further discussions of the character of Imogen, see the excerpts by August Wilhelm Schlegel (1811), William Hazlitt (1817), G. G. Gervinus (1849-50), Algernon Charles Swinburne (1880), Helena Faucit (1882), Bernard Shaw (1896), E. K. Chambers (1907), Brander Matthews (1913), Harley Granville-Barker (1930), G. Wilson Knight (1947), Harold C. Goddard (1951), and Robin Moffet (1962). Also, Jameson is the first critic to assert that Posthumus is obliged, because of the social code of his age and class, to accept the wager proposed by Iachimo, a judgment shared by William Witherle Lawrence (1920). In addition, Jameson charges Samuel Johnson (1765) with obtuseness and insensitivity in his estimation of* Cymbeline *and agrees with Schlegel that the dramatic structure of the play presents a unified representation of "the marvellous, the heroic, the ideal, and the classical."*]

Others of Shakespeare's characters are, as dramatic and poetical conceptions, more striking, more brilliant, more powerful; but of all his women, considered as individuals rather than as heroines, Imogen is the most perfect. Portia [in *The Merchant of Venice*] and Juliet are pictured to the fancy with more force of contrast, more depth of light and shade; Viola [in *Twelfth Night*] and Miranda [in *The Tempest*], with more aërial delicacy of outline; but there is no female portrait that can be compared to Imogen as a woman—none in which so great a variety of tints are mingled together into such perfect harmony. In her, we have all the fervour of youthful tenderness, all the romance of youthful fancy, all the enchantment of ideal grace—the bloom of beauty, the brightness of intellect, and the dignity of rank, taking a peculiar hue from the conjugal character which is shed over all, like a consecration and a holy charm. In "Othello" and the "Winter's Tale" the interest excited for Desdemona and Hermione is divided with others; but in "Cymbeline" Imogen is the angel of light, whose lovely presence pervades and animates the whole piece. The character altogether may be pronounced finer, more complex in its elements, and more fully developed in all its parts, than those of Hermione and Desdemona; but the position in which she is placed is not, I think, so fine—at least, not so effective—as a tragic situation. (pp. 181-82)

It would be a waste of words to refute certain critics who have accused Shakespeare of a want of judgment in the adaptation of the [source] story, of having transferred the manners of a set of intoxicated merchants and a merchant's wife to heroes and princesses, and of having entirely destroyed the interest of the catastrophe. The truth is, that Shakespeare has wrought out the materials before him with the most luxuriant fancy and the most wonderful skill. As for the various anachronisms, and the confusion of names, dates, and manners over which Dr. Johnson exults in no measured terms [see excerpt above, 1765], the confusion is nowhere but in his own heavy obtuseness of sentiment and perception, and his want of poetical faith. . . . Shakespeare, by throwing his story far back into a remote and uncertain age, has blended, by his "own omnipotent will," the marvellous, the heroic, the ideal, and the classical—the extreme of refinement and the extreme of simplicity—into one of the loveliest fictions of romantic poetry; and, to use Schlegel's expression, "has made the social manners of the latest times harmonise with heroic deeds, and even with the appearances of the gods" [see excerpt above, 1811].

But admirable as is the conduct of the whole play, rich in variety of character and in picturesque incident, its chief beauty and interest is derived from Imogen.

When Ferdinand tells Miranda that she was "created of every creature's best" [*The Tempest,* III. i. 47-8], he speaks like a lover, or refers only to her personal charms. The same expression might be applied critically to the character of Imogen; for as the portrait of Miranda is produced by resolving the female character into its original elements, so that of Imogen unites the greatest number of those qualities which we imagine to constitute excellence in woman.

Imogen, like Juliet, conveys to our mind the impression of extreme simplicity in the midst of the most wonderful com-

Act II. Scene ii. Iachimo and Imogen. Frontispiece to the Rowe edition (1709). By permission of the Folger Shakespeare Library.

plexity. To conceive her aright, we must take some peculiar tint from many characters, and so mingle them, that, like the combination of hues in a sunbeam, the effect shall be as one to the eye. We must imagine something of the romantic enthusiasm of Juliet, of the truth and constancy of Helen [in *All's Well That Ends Well*], of the dignified purity of Isabel [in *Measure for Measure*], of the tender sweetness of Viola, of the self-possession and intellect of Portia, combined together so equally and so harmoniously that we can scarcely say that one quality predominates over the other. But Imogen is less imaginative than Juliet, less spirited and intellectual than Portia, less serious than Helen and Isabel. Her dignity is not so imposing as that of Hermione; it stands more on the defensive. Her submission, though unbounded, is not so passive as that of Desdemona; and thus, while she resembles each of these characters individually, she stands wholly distinct from all.

It is true that the conjugal tenderness of Imogen is at once the chief subject of the drama and the pervading charm of her character; but it is not true, I think, that she is merely interesting from her tenderness and constancy to her husband. We are so completely let into the essence of Imogen's nature, that we feel as if we had known and loved her before she was married to Posthumus, and that her conjugal virtues are a charm superadded, like the colour laid upon a beautiful ground-work. Neither does it appear to me that Posthumus is unworthy of Imogen, or only interesting on Imogen's account. His character, like those of all the other persons of the drama, is kept subordinate to hers; but this could not be otherwise, for she is the proper subject, the heroine of the poem. Everything is done to ennoble Posthumus and justify her love for him, and though we certainly approve him more for her sake than for his own, we are early prepared to view him with Imogen's eyes, and not only excuse, but sympathise in her admiration of one—

> Who sat 'mongst men like a descended god.
>
> [I. vi. 169]

>   Who lived in court,
> Which it is rare to do, most praised, most lov'd:
> A sample to the youngest; to the more mature
> A glass that feated them.
>
> [I. i. 46-9]

And with what beauty and delicacy is her conjugal and matronly character discriminated! Her love for her husband is as deep as Juliet's for her lover, but without any of that headlong vehemence, that fluttering amid hope, fear, and transport, that giddy intoxication of heart and sense, which belongs to the novelty of passion, which we feel once, and but once, in our lives. We see her love for Posthumus acting upon her mind with the force of an habitual feeling, heightened by enthusiastic passion, and hallowed by the sense of duty. She asserts and justifies her affection with energy, indeed, but with a calm and wife-like dignity—

> *Cymbeline.* Thou took'st a beggar, would'st have made my throne
> A seat for baseness.
>   *Imogen.*   No, I rather added
> A lustre to it.
>   *Cymbeline.*   O thou vile one!
>   *Imogen.*   Sir.
> It is your fault that I have lov'd Posthumus;
> You bred him as my playfellow; and he is
> A man, worth any woman; overbuys me,
> Almost the sum he pays.
>
> [I. i. 141-47]
> (pp. 184-87)

Two little incidents, which are introduced with the most unobtrusive simplicity, convey the strongest impression of her tenderness for her husband, and with that perfect unconsciousness on her part which adds to the effect. Thus, when she has lost her bracelet—

> Go, bid my woman
> Search for a jewel, that too casually
> Hath left mine arm. It was thy master's: 'shrew me,
> If I would lose it for a revenue
> Of any king's in Europe. I do think
> I saw 't this morning; confident I am
> Last night 'twas on mine arm—*I kiss'd it.*
> *I hope it be not gone, to tell my lord*
> *That I kiss aught but he.*
>
> [II. iii. 140-48]

It has been well observed, that our consciousness that the bracelet is really gone to bear false witness against her adds an inexpressibly touching effect to the simplicity and tenderness of the sentiment.

And again, when she opens her bosom to meet the death to which her husband has doomed her, she finds his letters preserved next her heart—

> Soft, we'll no defence. . . .
>   What's here?
> The scriptures of the loyal Leonatus?—
>
> [III. iv. 79-81]

The scene in which Posthumus stakes his ring on the virtue of his wife, and gives Iachimo permission to tempt her, is taken from the [source] story. The baseness and folly of such conduct have been justly censured; but Shakespeare, feeling that Posthumus needed every excuse, has managed the quarrelling scene between him and Iachimo with the most admirable skill. The manner in which his high spirit is gradually worked up by the taunts of this Italian fiend is contrived with far more probability, and much less coarseness, than in the original tale. In the end he is not the challenger, but the challenged; and could hardly (except on a moral principle much too refined for those rude times) have declined the wager without compromising his own courage, and his faith in the honour of Imogen.

> *Iachimo.* I durst attempt it against any lady in the
> world.
> *Posthumus.* You are a great deal abused in too bold a
> persuasion; and I doubt not you sustain what you're
> worthy of, by your attempt.
> *Iachimo.* What's that?
> *Posthumus.* A repulse: though your *attempt,* as you call
> it, deserve more; a punishment too.
> *Philario.* Gentlemen, enough of this: It came in too
> suddenly; let it die as it was born, and, I pray you,
> be better acquainted.
> *Iachimo.* 'Would I had put my estate, and my
> neighbour's, on the approbation of what I have
> spoke!
> *Posthumus.* What lady would you choose to assail?
> *Iachimo.* Yours; whom in constancy, you think, stands
> so safe.
>
> [I. iv. 112-27]

In the interview between Imogen and Iachimo, he does not begin his attack on her virtue by a direct accusation against Posthumus; but by dark hints and half-uttered insinuations, such as Iago uses to madden Othello, he intimates that her husband, in his absence from her, has betrayed her love and truth, and forgotten her in the arms of another. All that Imogen says in this scene is comprised in a few lines—a brief question, or a more brief remark. The proud and delicate reserve with which she veils the anguish she suffers is inimitably beautiful. The strongest expression of reproach he can draw from her is only, "My lord, I fear, has forgot Britain" [I. vi. 112-13]. When he continues in the same strain, she exclaims in an agony, "Let me hear no more!" [I. vi. 117]. When he urges her to revenge, she asks, with all the simplicity of virtue, "How should I be revenged?" [I. vi. 132]. And when he explains to her how she is to be avenged, her sudden burst of indignation, and her immediate perception of his treachery, and the motive for it, are powerfully fine; it is not only the anger of a woman whose delicacy has been shocked, but the spirit of a princess insulted in her court—

> Away!—I do condemn mine ears, that have
> So long attended thee.—If thou wert honourable,
> Thou would'st have told this tale for virtue, not
> For such an end thou seek'st; as base as strange.
> Thou wrong'st a gentleman, who is as far
> From thy report, as thou from honour; and
> Solicit'st here a lady, that disdains
> Thee and the devil alike.
>
> [I. vi. 141-48]

It has been remarked that "her readiness to pardon Iachimo's false imputation, and his designs against herself, is a good lesson to prudes, and may show that where there is a real attachment to virtue, there is no need of an outrageous antipathy to vice" [see excerpt above by William Hazlitt, 1817].

This is true; but can we fail to perceive that the instant and ready forgiveness of Imogen is accounted for, and rendered more graceful and characteristic, by the very means which Iachimo employs to win it? He pours forth the most enthusiastic praises of her husband, professes that he merely made this trial of her out of his exceeding love for Posthumus, and she is pacified at once; but, with exceeding delicacy of feeling, she is represented as maintaining her dignified reserve and her brevity of speech to the end of the scene.

We must also observe how beautifully the character of Imogen is distinguished from those of Desdemona and Hermione. When she is made acquainted with her husband's cruel suspicions, we see in her deportment neither the meek submission of the former nor the calm resolute dignity of the latter. The first effect produced on her by her husband's letter is conveyed to the fancy by the exclamation of Pisanio, who is gazing on her as she reads—

> What shall I need to draw my sword? The paper
> Has cut her throat already!—No, 'tis slander;
> Whose edge is sharper than the sword!
>
> [III. iv. 32-4]

And in her first exclamations we trace, besides astonishment and anguish, and the acute sense of the injustice inflicted on her, a flash of indignant spirit, which we do not find in Desdemona or Hermione—

> False to his bed!—What! is it to be false
> To lie in watch there, and to think on him?
> To weep 'twixt clock and clock? If sleep charge nature,
> To break it with a fearful dream of him,
> And cry myself awake?—that's false to his bed,
> Is it?
>
> [III. iv. 40-4]

This is followed by that affecting lamentation over the false-hood and injustice of her husband, in which she betrays no atom of jealousy or wounded self-love, but observes in the extremity of her anguish, that after *his* lapse from truth ''all good seeming would be discredited'' and she then resigns her-self to his will with the most entire submission. (pp. 191-95)

Cloten is odious; but we must not overlook the peculiar fitness and propriety of his character in connection with that of Im-ogen. He is precisely the kind of man who would be most intolerable to such a woman. He is a fool—so is Slender [in *The Merry Wives of Windsor*], and Sir Andrew Aguecheek [in *Twelfth Night*]; but the folly of Cloten is not only ridiculous, but hateful; it arises not so much from a want of understanding as a total want of heart; it is the perversion of sentiment rather than the deficiency of intellect; he has occasional gleams of sense, but never a touch of feeling. Imogen describes herself not only as ''sprighted with a fool,'' but as ''frighted and anger'd worse'' [II. iii. 139, 140]. No other fool but Cloten—a compound of the booby and the villain—could excite in such a mind as Imogen's the same mixture of terror, contempt, and abhorrence. The stupid, obstinate malignity of Cloten, and the wicked machinations of the queen—

> A father cruel, and a step-dame false,
> A foolish suitor to a wedded lady—
>
> [I. vi. 1-2]

justify whatever might need excuse in the conduct of Imogen—as her concealed marriage and her flight from her father's court—and serve to call out several of the most beautiful and striking parts of her character; particularly that decision and vivacity of temper, which in her harmonise so beautifully with exceeding delicacy, sweetness, and submission.

In the scene with her detested suitor, there is at first a careless majesty of disdain which is admirable—

> I am much sorry, sir,
> You put me to forget a lady's manners,
> By being so verbal; and learn now, for all,
> That I, which know my heart, do here pronounce,
> By th' very truth of it, I care not for you,
> And am so near the lack of charity,
> (T' accuse myself,) I hate you; which I had rather
> You felt, than make 't my boast.
>
> [II. iii. 104-11]

But when he dares to provoke her, by reviling the absent Post-humus, her indignation heightens her scorn, and her scorn sets a keener edge on her indignation—

> *Cloten.*   For
> The contract you pretend with that base wretch,
> (One bred of alms, and foster'd with cold dishes
> With scraps o' the court:) it is no contract,—none. . . .
>   *Imogen.*   Profane fellow!
> Wert thou the son of Jupiter, and no more,
> But what thou art, besides, thou wert too base
> To be his groom; thou wert dignified enough,
> Even to the point of envy, if 'twere made
> Comparative for your virtues, to be styl'd
> The under-hangman of his kingdom: and hated
> For being preferr'd so well. . . .
> He never can meet more mischance than come
> To be but nam'd of thee. His mean'st garment,
> That ever hath but clipp'd his body, is dearer
> In my respect than all the hairs about thee,
> Were they all made such men.
>
> [II. iii. 112-15, 124-31, 132-36]

One thing more must be particularly remarked, because it serves to individualise the character from the beginning to the end of the poem. We are constantly sensible that Imogen, besides being a tender and devoted woman, is a princess and a beauty, at the same time that she is ever superior to her position and her external charms. There is, for instance, a certain airy maj-esty of deportment, a spirit of accustomed command, breaking out every now and then—the dignity, without the assumption, of rank and royal birth, which is apparent in the scene with Cloten and elsewhere. And we have not only a general impres-sion that Imogen, like other heroines, is beautiful, but the peculiar style and character of her beauty is placed before us; we have an image of the most luxuriant loveliness combined with exceeding delicacy, and even fragility, of person, of the most refined elegance and the most exquisite modesty, set forth in one or two passages of description; as when Iachimo is contemplating her asleep—

> Cytherea,
> How bravely thou becom'st thy bed! fresh lily!
> And whiter than the sheets.
>   'Tis her breathing that
> Perfumes the chamber thus: The flame o' the taper
> Bows toward her; and would underpeep her lids,
> To see the enclosed lights, now canopied
> Under these windows; white and azure, lac'd
> With blue of heaven's own tinct!
>
> [II. ii. 14-23]

The preservation of her feminine character under her masculine attire, her delicacy, her modesty, and her timidity, are managed with the same perfect consistency and unconscious grace as in Viola. And we must not forget that her ''neat cookery,'' which is so prettily eulogised by Guiderius—

> He cut our roots in characters,
> And sauc'd our broths, as Juno had been sick,
> And he her dieter—
>
> [IV. ii. 49-51]

formed part of the education of a princess in those remote times. (pp. 195-98)

The catastrophe of this play has been much admired for the peculiar skill with which all the various threads of interest are gathered together at last, and entwined with the destiny of Imogen. It may be added, that one of its chief beauties is the manner in which the character of Imogen is not only preserved, but rises upon us to the conclusion with added grace: her in-stantaneous forgiveness of her husband before he even asks it, when she flings herself at once into his arms—

> Why did you throw your wedded lady from you?—
>
> [V. v. 261]

and her magnanimous reply to her father, when he tells her that by the discovery of her two brothers she has lost a kingdom.

> No; I have gain'd two worlds by it—
>
> [V. v. 373-74]

clothing a noble sentiment in a noble image—give the finishing touches of excellence to this most enchanting portrait.

On the whole, Imogen is a lovely compound of goodness, truth, and affection, with just so much of passion, and intellect, and poetry, as serve to lend to the picture that power and glowing richness of effect which it would otherwise have wanted; and of her it might be said, if we could condescend to quote from any other poet with Shakespeare open before us, that ''her

person was a paradise, and her soul the cherub to guard it."
(pp. 199-200)

Mrs. [Anna Brownell] Jameson, "Imogen," in her Shakespeare's Heroines: Characteristics of Women, Moral, Poetical, & Historical, George Newnes, Limited, 1897, pp. 181-200.

HERMANN ULRICI   (essay date 1839)

[A German scholar, Ulrici was a professor of philosophy and the author of works on Greek poetry and Shakespeare. The following excerpt is from an English translation of his Über Shakespeares dramatische Kunst, und sein Verhältniss zu Calderon und Göthe, a work first published in 1839. This study exemplifies the "philosophical criticism" developed in Germany during the nineteenth century. The immediate sources for Ulrici's critical approach appear to be August Wilhelm Schlegel's conception of the play as an organic, interconnected whole and Georg Wilhelm Friedrich Hegel's view of drama as an embodiment of the conflict of historical forces and ideas. Unlike his fellow German Shakespearean critic G. G. Gervinus, Ulrici sought to develop a specifically Christian aesthetics, but one which, as he carefully points out in the introduction to the work mentioned above, in no way intrudes on "that unity of idea, which preeminently constitutes a work of art a living creation in the world of beauty." In the following excerpt, Ulrici asserts that the central governing idea of Cymbeline is the proposition that divine providence, not human intentions and actions, is the ultimate determinant of an individual's fate. Employing the terms "comedy of destiny" and "comedy of intrigue" to designate the genre of the play, he argues that destiny renders ineffective the machinations of the various characters. He also maintains that "every movement" and "each single character" is indispensable to this central idea, so that the play is not incoherent, as some critics maintain, but reflects an "harmonious and well-organized whole." Such later critics as G. G. Gervinus (1849-50), G. Wilson Knight (1947), and R. A. Foakes (1971) have maintained, like Ulrici, that the play depicts divine providence as the controlling force of human destiny. Further, Ulrici regards the vision scene in Act V, Scene iv as a discordant element and "a mistake on Shakespeare's part," in that it adds nothing to our understanding of the drama and, worse, confounds the tragic and comic views of life. For additional commentary on the vision scene, see the excerpts by Alexander Pope (1723), George Steevens (1793), Gervinus, Thomas Kenny (1864), Denton J. Snider (1890), and Knight. Finally, Ulrici believes that Cymbeline belongs to Shakespeare's earliest period of play writing and that he subsequently revised it sometime between 1609 and 1611 into the version that appeared in the First Folio, a judgment that is shared by Charles Knight and Frederick Gard Fleay (see Additional Bibliography).]

["Cymbeline"] displays in a higher degree then even "Measure for Measure," the "Merchant of Venice," or any other drama, the characteristic peculiarity of Shakespeare's comedy. At the same time it appears to me to possess much of the spirit of romantic poetry. As its fulness of bitter humour spontaneously unites itself with tragedy and the tragic view of life, so this profound seriousness and tragic suffering and fate are not only not unknown to the romantic-comic view, but belong rather to the very notion of romantic comedy. In its details and special motives it has much in common with tragedy, but the position relatively to the whole which it gives to these details is very different; it works them out in a different manner from tragedy, so that they thereby acquire an essentially different signification, just as the general views on which they are respectively founded are discrepant. So long as we adhere to the vulgar idea of comedy, it will perhaps sound strange to call "Cymbeline"—that marvellous drama—a comedy; and yet we shall acknowledge that such is its true character if once we

dispossess our minds of the common error which confounds comedy with farce. "Cymbeline" may be well designated a comedy of destiny: it embraces in its subject all the objective foundations of morality, and the most powerful relations and conditions of life—wedlock, the family, and the state. For by destiny, in the comic domain, we do not understand divine Providence immediately, but either that subjective and objective chance which rules human life as a higher power, or else the intrigues of man himself, which by their mutual entanglement cross and paralyse each other, and consequently bring about at last a very different result from what they were originally intended to produce. Of these two the former constitutes the destiny of the comedy of fancy, the latter is that of intrigue. Both, however, do not properly constitute destiny. While the powers which apparently rule the life of man mutually destroy each other, and their own empire is subverted, a very different one is established, and by the contrast we are taught to discern the divine Providence itself, guiding and disposing the events and contingencies of life.

"Cymbeline" is essentially a comedy of intrigue. Its intrigue, however, assumes externally and apparently the form of tragic destiny, which, indeed, becomes truly comic, whenever . . . it goes consciously and intriguingly to work with all sorts of far-fetched tricks and artifices. In "Cymbeline" we meet with the most diversified and manifold intrigues: the moral weakness and perversity of the dramatic personages bring at first suffering and woe on all around them, dissolving the ties of family and affection, and plunging the state itself in confusion; but their intrigues ultimately close with and frustrate each other, and thereby effect undesignedly that which ought to be. . . . When weakness, malice, and perversity have been caught in their own toils, order and harmony are restored to the unsettled relations of wedlock, the family, and the state. For these fundamental supports of human life and civilization, rest themselves on the empire and law of intellect: man's free-will both raises and casts them down again; but while they are in confusion he cannot himself subsist, and an inherent necessity, involved in his very freedom, quickly restores order to the universal disorder and chaos.

The mind and life of man are, in short, here viewed under the same aspect as in the "Tempest," that, viz., of his will and conduct. But as in the present case the story assumes the shape of a comedy of intrigue, the volition does not stop at the mere designs and intentions, but passes on into real actions and events; and plans and deeds are purposely accumulated in order that they may the more fully work out their own comic paralysis, and the more forcibly illustrate what is universally true of the represented idea. While in the "Tempest," agreeably to its fantastic character, the human will and conduct, conquered by a secret power of good objectively opposing it, involuntarily assume a very different and opposite form to its own bias; the nature of the comedy of intrigue required that it should be brought to a subjective termination. In the former the power of good is positive; in the latter negative, so far as it reveals itself merely by the destruction of evil. To exhibit the contradiction and insufficiency of human plans and conduct, which become, as it were, a destiny both to their immediate agents and others, as well as the nothingness of such a self-created destiny, appears to be the ground idea of "Cymbeline." Shakespeare, we may well say, has here sought to give a poetical illustration of the proposition—man is not master of his own lot, which is unquestionably as true as its contrary. It is, however the living contemplation of the whole of life from this particular point of view, and not any isolated and dead notion, which in its philosophical generality would be most unsuited to art, that forms the soul of the represented story.

Thus considered, the poem becomes at once thoroughly intelligible, and no single figure in it appears superfluous; every movement necessary and each single character indispensable, as only serving to display the ground thought in some fresh turn and new modification, and the multitude of the dramatic personages, as well as of the mass of incidents and suffering, arrange themselves into one harmonious and well organized whole. The Queen and Imogene, Cloten and Posthumus, are evidently the principal contrasts around whom, as its poles, the whole action and interest revolve. The Queen, whose guilty machinations threaten with ruin Posthumus and Imogene, the King himself, and Pisanio, and all else that have any goodness or virtue, holds in her own hands the reigns of government, and would make her will both law and fate to all, sees all her plans suddenly wrecked, and falls at last the victim of the destructive energy of her own wickedness. Cloten, whom the Queen alone can rule, is by his own savage ferocity caught in his own snare, and his fate is but a modified reflection of the same truth that his mother's life and death set forth. Imogene and Posthumus, by their secret marriage without the consent of her father, have justly incurred whatever sufferings befal them; upon Imogene they fall without staining the mirror of her pure womanliness, and therefore produce at once their beneficial design. They deprive Posthumus of his self-possession, but the destiny which he has prepared for himself, the death which he is seeking, are thwarted and turned aside by the counterplay of others' intrigues, and are turned eventually into life and happiness. Even the artful intriguing Iachimo is improved and converted by the misery which he has brought upon himself and others. Bellarius too, who breathed and contemplated nothing but deadly revenge, has undesignedly rescued the Princes from the clutches of the Queen, and contrary to his original design, preserves and educates for the throne a noble youth in every way worthy of the dignity, and so brings a blessing on the closing years of his life. On the other hand, Pisanio, the faithful and honest servant of Posthumus, has no design or desire but what is good and honourable, and yet whatever he does leads only to trouble and suffering. Cymbeline, lastly, the husband, the father, and the king, whom the miseries of all the other parts more or less remotely affect, in whom the rays of the large circle converge again, around whom all revolves, forms as it were the quiescent centre of motion, which, however passive and latent, regulates the fortunes of all, and is ultimately influenced by them. The drama therefore justly derives its name from him.

The justice of this conception of the piece is at once confirmed by the fact that thus animated by a single ground idea, it easily rounds itself off into an organic whole. But then the question occurs, what are we to think of the appearance of the spirits and deities in the fourth scene of the fifth act. It must, I cannot help thinking, be regarded as a mistake on Shakespeare's part. No doubt we see clearly enough the end which the poet had in view by it; he wished by their introduction to signify that the true might of destiny, which arranges the tangled threads of the designs, actions, and sufferings of men, and whose unseen hand fastens or loosens the knots, is the divine justice and providence itself. So far the scene does but confirm our view of the whole. But by this visible manifestation of the divine, he has not only combined together the separate elements of Tragedy and Comedy, but he has also confuséd the two distinct views of life which form their respective foundations.

This dualism admits, it is true, of an organic union of its two parts: a higher unity comprises both the tragic and the comic view. But this, as we shall presently see, is artistically practicable nowhere except in what is properly the *historical* drama, where, however, the two views are by no means *confounded*, and their poetic validity in consequence rendered doubtful, but truly reconciled by being raised to a higher position and fused together in organic unity, in such wise that the significance and justification of each being unimpaired, they both continue *to be* independent members of one body. But "Cymbeline" can hardly pass for an historical drama. Not only its entire structure, but all the parts, equally militate against such a view; the apparition of the deities is in an especial manner inconsistent with it. This admixture disturbs, in fact, not only the intrinsic unity of idea, but also the organic structure of the entire fabric. The very circumstance that the necessity of this scene is not at once apparent—since even without it every thing would have proceeded in the same way as at present—proves it to be a needless interruption. In every organised body a superfluous member does but impede and interfere with its free action. Another fault in the structure of "Cymbeline" is the absence of any such light and merry character, or laughable situations, as might serve to keep us in mind of the comic domain, on which, notwithstanding the omission, the whole piece unquestionably stands. By this want the poem acquires a dark look—darker even than any tragedy.

I cannot hesitate to concur in the view of [Ludwig] Tieck, who supposes "that the checkered and romantic story may have attracted the youthful mind of Shakespeare, and inspired him to attempt to adapt it to the stage." This first juvenile essay he may probably have revised towards the close of his poetic career—such a supposition is greatly favoured by the unevenness of the style—and he may have retained the ill-placed scene of the gods, either because it had formerly made a favourable impression on the public mind, or because, in the patch-work of revision, he either lost sight of organic unity, or was unable to reproduce the exact spirit and idea under whose influence he had originally composed the piece. (pp. 316-22)

> Hermann Ulrici, "Criticisms of Shakespeare's Dramas: 'Merchant of Venice'—'Measure for Measure'—'Cymbeline'," in his Shakespeare's Dramatic Art: And His Relation to Calderon and Goethe, *translated by A. J. W. Morrison, Chapman, Brothers, 1846, pp. 300-22.*

G. G. GERVINUS (essay date 1849-50)

[*One of the most widely read Shakespearean critics of the latter half of the nineteenth century, the German critic Gervinus was praised by such eminent contemporaries as Edward Dowden, F. J. Furnivall, and James Russell Lowell; however, he is little known in the English-speaking world today. Like his predecessor Hermann Ulrici, Gervinus wrote in the tradition of the "philosophical criticism" developed in Germany in the mid-nineteenth century. Under the influence of August Wilhelm Schlegel's literary theory and Georg Wilhelm Friedrich Hegel's philosophy, German critics, such as Gervinus, tended to focus their analyses around a search for the literary work's organic unity and ethical import. Gervinus believed that Shakespeare's works contained a rational ethical system independent of any religion—in contrast to Ulrici, for whom Shakespeare's morality was basically Christian. In the excerpt below, taken from his study* Shakespeare (1849-50), *Gervinus maintains that the theme which unifies the separate dramatic actions of* Cymbeline *is the repeated juxtaposition of fidelity and faithlessness. He argues that the contrast between truth and perfidy or slander is apparent in all the actions and characters in the play, noting the opposition of "the idyllic innocence of the sylvan solitude" and the treachery and intrigues of the court; the slander which drove Belarius to leave the court and the purity and truthfulness of his adopted sons; the deceptions of the Queen, and Cymbeline's broken bond of fidelity to Rome. Similarly, A. A. Stephenson (1942) has also commented on the thematic importance of fidelity in* Cymbeline, *and F. C. Tinkler (1938) has identified a series of dualisms and oppositions present throughout the play. Gervinus finds the play's concern with the concept of fidelity centered in the wager plot. He contends that Posthumus's acceptance of Iachimo's challenge is ineluctable, because the latter's basemindedness so offends his own "strong conviction of virtue and his faith in human nature" that it becomes a point of honor for him to oppose it. For additional discussions of Posthumus's behavior in the wager scenes, see the excerpts by Anna Brownell Jameson (1833), Thomas Kenny (1864), William Witherle Lawrence (1920), Homer D. Swander (1966), and James Edward Siemon (1976). Gervinus further maintains that the central moral lesson of* Cymbeline *is that virtue which has been severely tried and tempted is superior to goodness which has not been tested by evil—that "genuine virtue ought not to shrink at any trial." He contends that the speech of Jupiter in the vision scene is intended to make that message explicit. Thus, Gervinus concludes,* Cymbeline *may be regarded as a vindication of divine justice and omnipotence despite the existence of evil in the world. Such other critics as Denton J. Snider (1890), G. Wilson Knight (1947), and J. A. Bryant, Jr. (1961) have also commented on the thematic importance of the vision scene. Finally, Gervinus's praise of Imogen and estimation that she is one of the most fully developed of Shakespeare's dramatic characters are shared by most nineteenth-century critics.]*

The subject of *Cymbeline*, like that of *Lear*, is formed by the combination of two different actions, derived from widely different sources, and these again appear on the more extensive background of political and military events, as in *Lear*. . . . *Cymbeline*, like *Lear*, belongs to the heathen times of the aboriginal Britons. But in this play we are not carried back to the dark ages that preceded our era, but we are transported to the bright period of Augustus Caesar, when Roman civilisation had already spread its improving influence as far as Britain. . . . The more civilised age soon shows itself by its more civilised vices. Hypocrisy and falsehood, which in Lear's daughters and in Edmund played only a subordinate part compared to their bloody ambition, here play the principal part. The virtues of fidelity and truth, which in Kent were carried to a harsh extreme, are here tempered with the prudence of a more refined and educated race. We find here only the remains of that earlier wild age, as we there found only the beginnings of this gentler one. From the beginning to the end of the play we uniformly meet with this weaker degree of passion and the stronger power of prudence. (pp. 644-45)

In *King Lear* two actions are woven into one, the similar nature of the two demanding such a combination and suggesting of itself one common idea. It is quite otherwise in *Cymbeline*. The parts of which it is composed stand with reference to their purport in no relation to each other. Three such parts may be distinguished. Holinshed afforded Shakespeare suggestions for the first part, namely, the dispute about the tribute and the war between Britain and Rome; Cymbeline, who had been reigning since the 19th year of the Emperor Augustus, and his two sons, Guiderius and Arviragus, are there mentioned as historical characters. No source is known for the second action, the fate of these sons of Cymbeline; it must have been Shakespeare's own ingenious invention. Belarius, a courtier and warrior, who has guiltlessly fallen into disgrace with Cymbeline, carries off the two princes out of revenge into a solitary wood, where we see them grow up, where one afterwards kills his step-brother

Cloten, and both, while unknown to their father, do him good service in the Roman war. The third part, apparently a perfectly distinct and different matter, is borrowed from one of Boccaccio's tales (II. 9). . . . This story, which had been previously dramatised in a French miracle play, Shakespeare connected with *Cymbeline* by making the slandered wife a daughter of Cymbeline, and her husband an adopted son of his, whom Imogen had independently married, although she was intended by her father and step-mother for her half-brother, Cloten.

Thus outwardly a connection would be established between these different actions; but what inner relation could by any means exist between them, what ideal unity, such as we attribute to all Shakespeare's works, should link them together, is hardly discoverable at a first glance. Even Coleridge missed in *Cymbeline*, compared with *Lear*, a certain prominent object. But this was wanting in many of Shakespeare's plays, without their internal connection and unity being injured by it; nay, it even seems that in just these pieces, as, for instance, in the *Merchant of Venice*, the exact idea and intention in which they are written is all the more prominent. Thus is it also in *Cymbeline*. We have only to examine its several parts according to their internal nature and to refer to the motives, and we shall see at once persons and actions forming themselves like crystals into a fixed figure; we shall catch the idea which links them together, and, comparing the idea and the mode of carrying it out, we shall obtain clearer elucidation of the whole, and shall perceive a work of art, the compass of which widens and the background deepens in such a manner that we can only compare it with the most excellent of all that Shakespeare has produced. (pp. 646-47)

Let us, then, consider . . . the purport of the two main actions, and the causes at work in them, in order that we may next examine more closely the acting personages, and through them may approach the inner point of unity in our drama.

When the sons of Cymbeline were yet in their infancy, there dwelt at his court a faithful and famous warrior, named Belarius, who by valuable services had deserved the favour and love of his prince. Suddenly Cymbeline's anger fell upon the guiltless man; calumny deprived him of the royal favour; two villains swore falsely that he had entered into a treacherous league with the Romans, and Cymbeline banishes him and robs him of his possessions. The soldier, grown old in the service of the world, could not quietly suffer this punishment for his fidelity; he took the unmerited disgrace as a warrant for revenge, carried off the two sons of Cymbeline, with their nurse, married her, and brought up the boys as his own children in a solitary cavern in a forest. Here the old warrior, who formerly had not 'paid pious debts to heaven' [III. iii. 71-2], becomes a gentle hermit, and endeavours in this wilderness to educate two worthy royal youths for their country. Experience had taught him that 'the gates of monarchs are arched so high' [III. iii. 4-5] that they make men impious against God and nature, that no one can keep himself pure in the high places of life, in courts and in cities, amidst the worldly impulses of usury, ambition, and false thirst for glory; that the art of the court in the world in its present condition cannot easily be renounced, but for the soul's good it were better to be unknown. Embittered by the corruption of the world, he thinks to do the greatest service to the ungrateful and weak king by keeping the boys free and far from it, bringing them up in the pious worship of nature, warning them of the danger of intercourse with the world by images from nature, showing them the sweetness of retired and humble life, and praising the beetle as safer than the eagle. The boys grow up in their solitude in the same simple-hearted goodness as that which has kept their sister Imogen true to her pure feminine nature in the midst of the dangers of the courtly world; true, simple, innocent, despisers of wealth, and touched by no impure thoughts or desires. But as they ripen in years their manly royal blood stirs within them, and urges them to leave the narrow bounds of the forest for the world, for war and action; they are held in bonds like the beetle by a thread, and they long to take the bold flight of the eagle; the cage becomes too narrow for them, in which they, like the prisoned bird, sing their bondage; they fear a void old age after an inactive life, in which they are not allowed, like Belarius, to look back upon a fruitful past; they chase only what flies without resistance before them; they have never known the noble strife with equal foes upon which their fancy raves, they have never stood the trial of their valour; the truest instinct leads them to yearn for a life of temptations and trials in spite of its dangers, and it is the germ of the fairest promise of wisdom in them that they feel the wisdom of Belarius to be well suited to his age, yet very unfit for their untested youth. (pp. 648-49)

On the first impression they seem both alike in character; on a closer inspection it is not so. The elder, Guiderius, the destined heir, is the more manly of the two. At the very beginning he is the more successful hunter. When he meets the rude Cloten without knowing him, when the latter provokes him 'with language that would have made him spurn the sea if it could roar so at him' [V. v. 294-95], and threatens his life, he kills him without hesitation, confesses it (to the envy of Arviragus) to his alarmed foster-father, and afterwards without fear or reflection to the royal step-father himself, although warned by Belarius that this acknowledgment would bring upon him torture and death. Equally hasty and passionate Guiderius also shows himself when he is ready to rush into battle with the Romans, even without his father's blessing. In contrast to him, Arviragus appears throughout more tender and gentle, more communicative and richer in his choice of language. Guiderius is inclined to believe of him that he plays a solemn instrument of mourning, idly and boy-like, without a cause. When over the supposed corpse of Fidele he mentions the pretty legend that Robin Redbreasts covered unburied bodies with moss and flowers, Guiderius blames him for playing 'in wench-like words with that which is so serious' [IV. ii. 230-31].

The story of the carrying off of the princes by Belarius happens long before the beginning of our play; it is slightly mentioned at first, and the interlocutors find it strange and incredible that royal children should be so carelessly guarded and so indolently sought after that no trace of them should be found. But we now at once meet with a second incident happening to the king's third child before our eyes, and are thereby initiated so accurately into the circumstances and relations of the court, that in some degree we can comprehend how this unlikely event might before have happened. We see a king utterly weak, good-natured, easily excited though indolent, almost unaccountable from a lack of all self-will; ruled and prejudiced as he once had been by slanderers against Belarius, he is now just as much ruled by a hypocritical wife, with whom he had shortly before been united in his second marriage; and he is just as much prejudiced by her against his daughter Imogen and his foster-son Leonatus, and in favour of his step-son Cloten, a creature 'too bad for bad report' [I. i. 17]. This distortion of the poor king's judgment works now as it did before. All around him are combined against him and his misleader. As formerly the nurse allowed herself to be bribed to the robbery, so now the

courtiers are all at heart on the side of Leonatus and Imogen, although with their lips they play the parts of the grossest hypocrites towards Cloten whom they utterly despise. The queen persecutes Imogen and her faithful servant, even attempting poison; but the physician, who pretends to serve her, deceives her, making her and her means harmless. There is no one who behaves honourably to the king and his new family, but the good Imogen has the pity and sympathy of everyone. (pp. 650-51)

Imogen has often, and rightly, been considered as the most lovely and artless of the female characters which Shakespeare has depicted. Her appearance sheds warmth, fragrance, and brightness over the whole drama. More true and simple than Portia [in *The Merchant of Venice*] and Isabella [in *Measure for Measure*], she is even more ideal. In harmonious union she blends exterior grace with moral beauty, and both with fresh straightforwardness of feeling and the utmost clearness of understanding. She is the sum and aggregate of fair womanhood, such as at last the poet conceived it. We may doubt whether in all poetry there is a second creature so charmingly depicted with such perfect truth to nature. At the same time the picture is as highly finished as is generally possible only to the wider range of epic poetry. Imogen is, next to Hamlet, the most fully drawn character in Shakespeare's poetry; the traits of her nature are almost inexhaustible; the poet makes amends by this perfected portrait of a woman of this artless kind for the many sketches of similar natures in the dramas of this period which he has merely outlined. When he transports us into Imogen's bedchamber it is as lifelike as if we sensibly breathed the atmosphere of it. Not only does he mention and describe her outward beauty, but we see (on merely reading the play) the graceful movements which so well become her, we are acquainted with all her endowments—how 'angel-like' she sings, how 'neat her cookery' is, as if 'Juno had been sick, and she her dieter' [IV. ii. 50-1], how gracefully she wears her garments, so that she 'made great Juno angry' [III. iv. 164]. But her inward qualities far outweigh these outward ones. And it is our main business to make this clear to our minds, because she is the chief personage of the play, the one which leads us to the understanding of the whole.

The characteristic feature of this nature, which displays itself again and again in all the strange and most various situations in which the poet has placed Imogen, is her mental freshness and healthiness. In the untroubled clearness of her mind, and unspotted purity of her being, every outward circumstance is reflected, unruffled and undistorted, in the mirror of Imogen's soul, and at every occasion she acts from the purest instinct of a nature as sensible as it is practical. Rich in feeling, she is never morbidly sentimental; rich in fancy, she is never fantastic; full of true, painful, earnest love, she is never touched by sickly passion. She is mistress of her soul under the most violent emotions, self-command accompanies her strongest feelings, and the most discreet actions follow her outbursts of vehement passion, even when bold resolutions are required. . . . Exposed to the wrath of her father, to the falseness of her step-mother, to the urgency of the rude Cloten, she endures all with the peace of mind belonging to that happy female nature which can keep unpleasant thoughts at a distance, and can forget the pressure of the present by glad recollections of the past. Her ladies and attendants, Pisanio, and the nobles of the court, lament her unhappy situation—she herself scarcely ever complains of it; not until she has fled from Cloten does she perceive that his love-suit has been to her 'as fearful as a siege' [III. iv. 134]. No harsh word against father or mother escapes her lips, nor before another even a harsh word *respecting* them; for her father's sake she is sorry when the unnatural mother who had aimed at her own life is dead. She bears no resentment for injuries, nor do suffering and trouble press too heavily upon her.... Naturally cheerful, joyous, ingenuous, born to fortune, trained to endurance, she has nothing of that agitated passionateness which fortells a tragic lot, and which brings trouble upon itself of its own creating. At the end of the play, when, shaking off her long sufferings and cruel deceptions, she gives herself at once to the happiest feelings, we see how quickly she jests and is playful with her brothers, how brightly her eyes glance round 'the counter-change severally in all' [V. v. 396-97], and we feel that this being, fit for every situation, improved by every trial, has been wonderfully gifted by nature to be equal to every occasion. (pp. 657-59)

[Imogen's sufferings began with] Posthumus' romantic wager upon [her] fidelity. This is the point which robbed the play of the favour of all sensitive readers. How was it possible that the poet could make such an indelicate situation the turning point of so great a poem? How indeed was it possible, and how could it be consistent with psychological truth, that this wager should be laid upon a woman of so lovely and tender a nature, and by a man who was declared to be the 'glass' and 'sample' to his generation? To these questions we have, in the first place, to repeat an answer already often given: Shakespeare found this incident in the story itself, and he conscientiously retained it as a poetic symbol. Whether it was probable or not, he did all he could to make it possible and true. Leonatus had been in France on a previous occasion, and had there already had a similar dispute respecting his Imogen. At that time he was younger, more presumptuous, more impetuous, more contentious than now. He then extolled his beloved before the French ladies; he was ready to maintain his opinion by the ordeal of the sword, according to knightly custom; the matter, however, was amicably adjusted. The banished Posthumus accidentally meets the Frenchman, who at that time had acted as mediator, at the house of his host Philario, in Rome. The evening before his arrival these men had disputed with some strangers at a banquet on a very similar subject, the superiority of their countrywomen; the conversation thus falls easily upon the earlier dispute, which Posthumus, though now grown calmer in his judgment, does not regard as so light a matter as the Frenchman. A taunt of Iachimo's levelled at his beloved irritates Posthumus for a moment, but he recovers his manly composure until he learns more and more the Italian's character. Iachimo is a courtier and a worldling, whom Shakespeare endows with the affected language of his 'waterflies,' Osric [in *Hamlet*], and such like; in the novel his character is rather that of a profligate of Borgia's time than of a Roman in the days of the emperors. His name sounds almost like a diminutive of Iago, and he resembles him in his way of thinking of men. He has no idea of greatness and virtue, and no faith in them. When Posthumus is mentioned he has a number of instances ready to explain his high reputation, only in order to avoid acknowledging his real excellence, of which he has himself no idea. Harshly to disparage or slander individuals, to speak contemptuously of human nature generally, is not so much his nature, but it has become his habit; he esteems the female sex like a freebooter whom success has always attended. He is annoyed by the high reputation of Posthumus and his boundless estimation of Imogen; still more by the confidence with which he rests upon her virtue and fidelity. He offers his wager, and lays it rather against this confidence than against Imogen's reputation; he would attempt this, he protests, against

any lady in the world. Unbelief in morals and propriety generates this mode of thinking in the low-minded man, and petty venomous envy induces him to offer the wager; but in Posthumus, on the contrary, it is his strong conviction of virtue and his faith in human nature which makes him first calmly and then angrily oppose Iachimo's principles and assertions; it is the deep indignation of his moral nature which inclines him to accept the offered wager. Excitable indeed in nothing else, he is so just on this one point; and we think any resolute man who had retained a moral and virtuous state would similarly express his impatience against loquacious vice. To the Frenchman this would have been but a blade of straw, for which he felt no inducement to fight; but to Posthumus it is a great point of honour to defend insulted humanity. Not that he enters with Quixotic zeal into this knight-errantry; not that easily kindled he presses for the wager; for a while he intentionally avoids it, although he does not conceal from Iachimo that his presumption deserves not only repulse but chastisement. Not until the Italian actually taints the snow-white swan of Posthumus, and taunts him as though he must have cause to fear if he gave way, not until then does he wager upon his wife, whose fidelity he could trust for even more than this; *she* is to do her part to retrieve the honour of her sex, and then (this is the intention with which he accepts the wager) he will add to *her* repulse the deserved castigation, and punish Iachimo with the sword for his ill opinion and his presumption. In this moral anger Posthumus is no less the same rare being as in the rest of his conduct. His irritation on such noble grounds shows his previous calmness and discretion for the first time in its right light, and this his ever-tested moderation reminds us to consider again and again the reason which drives him exceptionally to exasperation in a transaction so indelicate. Let us remember that the equally calm and even calmer Imogen, who is as rarely or more rarely excited, is driven by the same occasion to the same indignation, when the abject Cloten sets himself above her Posthumus and attempts to disparage him as Iachimo has attempted to defame Imogen. Let us remember that this abnegation of 'a lady's manners' [II. iii. 105], her burst of indignation, and her flight, show no less self-forgetfulness in the woman than the wager does in the man. For that a self-forgetfulness lies in both cases in both steps we will not deny; the poet himself, beautiful and excusable as are the inducements in both instances, would neither deny nor conceal this, since he has so severely punished the rashness on both sides.

In this punishment the faults of both co-operate; the wager of Posthumus is not alone to be blamed for the whole chain of their trials. Had Imogen, wearied out with Cloten's 'siege,' not at once set out to Wales upon the deceptive invitation, Pisanio must have announced his bloody commission on the spot; the verification of her alleged death (her disappearance) would have been wanting, Posthumus would have had time for remorse ere it was too late, and all would have unravelled itself in a milder form. But Imogen herself assists in the apparent execution of the revenge which Posthumus, upon Iachimo's report, decreed against her, and which afterwards reacts so heavily upon himself. The artful Italian returns to Rome and enjoys a false triumph over the unsuspecting Briton. Base as he is, we must however beware of making him still baser. Want of faith in human goodness is not innate in him, but acquired from his never having met with virtuous men. A mere glance at Imogen shows him what he had never seen; he feels at once that here weapons of no common kind would be required. Repulsed by her, and ashamed, he feels neither hatred nor ill-will against her, but admiration alone. If it were not for the stings of a base ambition to maintain the glory of being irresistible, if half his fortune and his life had not been at stake, he might indeed have foreborne the deception which he now plays upon Posthumus. He utters the horrible slander against Imogen, yet not for the pleasure of slandering her; he speaks ambiguously, he neither lies unnecessarily nor degrades her unnecessarily. When he has attained his object—his own safety—the experience he has gained affects him, the virtue he has seen and tested awakens his conscience, the shame of his guilt oppresses him and makes him a coward in the fight with Britain, the speedy confession of his sin shows him crushed with remorse and worthy of pardon. But at the time when he came to Posthumus with the report of his success, the latter was more easily convinced the cooler and calmer Iachimo appeared. There was no room for doubt after the proofs adduced; even the impartial Philario considers Iachimo as victor. There now follows in Posthumus the fearful outburst of despair, the dark glimpse into his lost life of promise. Jealousy and wounded honour shake his manhood even to ungovernable fury, and give rise to the most inconsiderate projects of revenge. He here almost resembles Othello. As in him, so in Posthumus' nature there is none of that superficial, social cheerfulness which is mixed with happy and sanguine light-mindedness; serious by nature, he was continually inclined to melancholy, even without cause. Like Othello he had to look up to his beloved, and thought himself despised for his inferior birth. In both, notwithstanding their imposing calmness, there is a vein of passion upon which Iago and Iachimo speculate. Like Othello with the handkerchief Posthumus has apparent proof at hand in the bracelet. Like him he is seized with a paroxysm of misanthropy and contempt; like him his harmonious nature is thrown into a state of chaos, in which he appears far more unfortunate than guilty. Like Othello he loses himself in sensual hateful ideas, conjuring up a repulsive voluptuous picture of the rapid conquest of the 'yellow Iachimo' over a being whom he had thought 'as chaste as unsunned snow' [II. v. 13]. His hatred falls upon the whole female sex; everything 'that tends to vice in man' seems to him 'the woman's part' [II. v. 21, 20], every crime and sin to be inherited from her. Like Othello he condemns the criminal to be the sacrifice for his stained honour, while his moral nature is ever in the same state of indignation that we before observed. How much gentler, under similar circumstances, is his wife, his Imogen, to him! When she thinks him faithless she loses not her faith in the whole male sex, she only says that *his* falsity will 'lay the *leaven* on all proper men!' [III. iv. 62]. She is reminded of revenge, but by others, not by herself, and she cannot comprehend the thought. She has only pity and no hatred for him; and even if her heart has somewhat cooled, she never could have wholly lost her faith in him; she would never have been capable of planning any evil against him.

This, however, does not place him below her. In the man, who can and will be nothing by halves, the difference of sex necessitates this fearful reaction after an experience which unsettles his trust in the world and in everything. As soon as he has given his faithful Pisanio the order for her death his reflection returns. He now laments the fidelity which had so rapidly executed his command. Othello killed Desdemona to prevent her from sinning further; in this lies the delicate distinction between him and the more human, more gentle Leonatus. The latter curses his act, because, had the victim lived, she would have had time for repentance! Faith in her virtue was only stifled for a moment in him, but was not dead. He is now seized with remorse, which urges him to take vengeance on himself. The same indignation which had roused him against Iachimo, against Imogen, and against Pisanio, arms him now

against himself; and it is this severity against himself that must atone for the moral irritation which induced him to lay the wager and to impose the penalty on Imogen. Not in the recklessness of his first fury does he lay hands on himself like Othello, but in calm composure he inflicts upon himself a noble penance. (pp. 665-70)

Hitherto, according to our first intention, we have closely examined the two actions of the play and the prominent characters; but the point of view from which the poetic painter has taken his picture has not yet been indicated, the master-key is still wanting which can lay open to us at once the various component parts, as well as the way to one innermost centre, from which the plan of the whole structure can be easily recognised as one of artistic harmony.

From our explanation of the subject it will easily be perceived that it treats uniformly throughout two opposite ideas or moral qualities, namely, truth in word and in deed (fidelity), and untruth and faithlessness, falseness in deed or perfidy, falseness in word or slander. All the actions and characters of the play combine to exemplify these ideas, and this is really as apparent as the leading thought in the most intelligible of Shakespeare's dramas can ever be. At the very outset we are introduced into the world of falsehood, the court, and in contrast to this afterwards appears the idyllic innocence of the sylvan solitude. The political action, the background on which the two main actions rest, may be reconciled with the point of view we have specified. Bound to fidelity towards Rome, Cymbeline is led to rebellion by his false wife, and repents when he is his own master. The man who in his very weakness is not false is ensnared by the queen, that mistress of all deceitful arts, in a thickly woven net of falsehood and fatal intrigue, and is threatened with the loss of children and kingdom. False slanderers have once stamped the faithful Belarius to Cymbeline as a traitor; outlawed and banished, but faithful even in his revenge, he carries off the king's sons from the soil of the false world, and brings them up to be true, upright men, incapable of a lie even in the face of danger. The falseness of the queen ensnares also Posthumus and Imogen. Fidelity and truth, and the soundness and simplicity of character united with these qualities, are their main characteristics. How sensitively Imogen expresses her sense of truth when she speaks of having been misdirected by beggars! And there too, when she tells Lucius a false name for her dead lord, and offers with touching simplicity a prayer to the gods for their pardon of the harmless deceit. And Posthumus on his side, when in the most terrible distraction of mind he assails himself, calling himself Imogen's murderer, he corrects the inaccuracy of his words, conscientiously true, even in the midst of his rage:—

> Villain-like I lie;
> That caused a lesser villain than myself,
> A sacrilegious thief, to do it.
>
> [V. v. 218-20]

As regards the fidelity of both, the main purport of the play turns upon it and upon the calumny which makes each doubt the fidelity of the other, and upon the noble endurance of their own fidelity towards the beloved one, even though supposed to be faithless or dead. Between these two characters move the subordinate figures, who make still clearer the clear reference of even the lesser parts of the action. Cloten, who is too awkward for lies and slanders, and too stupid for the intrigues of falsehood; the courtiers, who make such vehement 'asides;' the physician, who uses salutary falsehood towards the poisoner; and Pisanio, who, as the servant of two masters, so prudently weighs duties of fidelity between the two when at variance.

Fidelity is the true cardinal virtue of an heroic age; it is this which in the national epic poetry of ancient times places those songs of fidelity, the 'Odyssey' and 'Gudrun,' in such natural juxtaposition to the warlike sagas of the 'Iliad' and the 'Niebelungen.' This connection is entirely founded upon the nature of such times, and so far the remarkable concordance of theme in these poems is no mere blind coincidence. In times when everything depends upon the estimation of great military power and great possessions, upon the thirst for glory and the desire for property, when house and dominion, possessions and existence, are ever insecure, there is nothing nobler and nothing more valuable than a true and tried friend, than a true and trusty servant, than a true and constant wife. No characteristic, therefore, of such an age is more natural than the proverbial friendships of Greek antiquity, the tales of the true vassals in German heroic poetry, and the poems on the fidelity of Penelope and Gudrun. Whether Shakespeare knew this, or whether the dim gropings of genius and an instinctive feeling of the nature of heroic times dictated it, it is equally remarkable that he should have depicted it with such distinctness both in *Lear* and *Cymbeline,* as if both these poems, or their sources, sprung direct from the traditions of those ages. In *Lear* the faithful attachment of the aged Kent is as beautiful as the friendship of Achilles to Patrocles in the 'Iliad.' In *Cymbeline* the ugly story of the wager is removed to the heroic times of the middle ages; and though the colouring and character of such a period, as well as in the Roman plays, is handled with little of the historical aptitude attainable in our own days, yet the poet (and this was more essential) has clothed the doubtful matter of the tale with such genuine and pure simplicity that his Imogen may rank as an equal third among those old models of feminine fidelity.

Shakespeare's song of fidelity belongs consequently to the period in which the virtue which it extols reaches its highest rank, in which it attains its greatest worth, owing to the continued trials, temptations, and dangers to which it is exposed, and in which it is often in the peculiar position of being obliged, as it were, to maintain itself by its very opposite. If Penelope would continue honourably true to her consort she must keep back her suitors with falsehood and deception; if Gudrun would keep faith with her betrothed she must deceive her new wooer with false promises. Even this characteristic feature is not omitted in Shakespeare's drama. In *Lear* he has made the truehearted Kent carry out his virtue with a tragic consistency. Here in *Cymbeline* he has sketched in Pisanio a very different picture of a fidelity just as instinctive, but far more circumspect. 'Sly and constant' [I. v. 75], as the queen calls him, and as he himself wishes to be, Pisanio unites the cunning of the serpent with the harmlessness of the dove. His singular position is throughout that he is truest where he is most untrue. (pp. 671-73)

In the self-satisfaction and security with which Pisanio practises [his] deceptions, only that he may venture to be true where justice and a higher duty demand it, he does not err; he is heedless of the danger which threatens him at court; he silently endures the abhorrence of the mistaken Imogen and the execrations of Posthumus; he is rewarded by his good conscience for having done the right.

If we closely examine this position of Pisanio, the ingenious purport of the play becomes more and more extended; it gains in universal significance and moral depth, beyond perhaps any other of Shakespeare's works; and if *Lear* may be regarded as

a representation of passion generally, *Cymbeline* may be called a representation of the common course of the world in which man with his powers and impulses is placed. It is a characteristic of Shakespeare's ideas and empirical system of morals, and an ordinary tenet in his worldly wisdom, that cases and circumstances not unfrequently occur to men, in which virtue becomes vice and vice virtue—as Pisanio here, in all his truth, cannot avoid repaying false actions with falsehood, and punishing false judgment with untruth, maintaining in this very falsity the highest fidelity. Our poet's conviction has been throughout that no outward law can embody the rule of moral action in strict and ever available precepts, but that there is an inner law and feeling which ought to guide us according to case and circumstance in adding or taking away from the letter of duty; that self-reliance and self-consciousness should be purified and developed within us in order that we may be ever a living law and a true judge for ourselves in the doubtful perplexities of the moment. To that simple-natured Pisanio there was no sin in a harmless concealment, a healthful dissimulation, a necessary falsehood, and a necessary deception, compelled by the pressure of circumstances and the condition of the world around him. It is not possible to remain good, true, and faithful among the wicked and the false, without involving personal ruin; this experience Pisanio drew with simple tact from his intercourse with men and his knowledge of them. To remain pure and inoffensive as a hermit in a bad world would only be possible by separating from the world and living *as* a hermit. In this situation the poet has shown us the two sons of Cymbeline. But even these are driven by the impetus of human nature into the dangers and temptations of life; they love not 'the passive virtue, which procures innocence, but not merit' (Bacon); they risk the paternal blessing in this impulse for action, and their first collision with the world would have brought them into the most dangerous complications had not Providence favourably interposed. The poet has shown us, therefore, more perfect characters, who remained uninjured in the midst of the whirlpool of the world. . . . [The] moral purity of Imogen and Posthumus [were] regarded as blameless both at home and abroad. Yet even these perfect beings were to be defiled with the rancour of the world, their virtue was to be tempted and calumniated, their prudence shaken, their internal peace was to be destroyed with their external prosperity; even they were to discover that it is not possible to keep unspotted in the world. Even if in these exceptions of humanity such an inner power were imaginable as would render them in themselves secure from all temptation to evil, yet the world without would expose them to it. The slanderer forces himself on Posthumus; he represents to him as false that on which he had placed his highest confidence, he robs him of his good and trustful nature; Posthumus now errs with the best intentions, exercising an over-hasty and inconsiderate justice, which, as he subsequently says, had it been employed against his *own* faults, he had 'never lived to put on' [V. i. 8-9] this revenge. Imogen was deprived of her beloved, her patience was irritated, her longing desires overstrained; she flees in the hope of seeing her husband, and of saving him when she believes him faithless; both are excusable, even praiseworthy intentions, but they render deceptions, disguises, evasions, lies, and endangered modesty unavoidable; characteristically enough she is obliged to conceal and preserve her fidelity under the false, but characteristic, name of Fidele. Imogen's spotless nature struggles against all this, but the pressure of circumstances forces it upon her. The poison of the world breathes on these purest mirrors of virtue; suspicion and mistrust, so contrary to their nature, seize them, trials befall them, and temptations in their worst form, armed with misfortune and despair, beset them, but they maintain inviolate their fidelity, against which all these strokes are aimed. And this it is, and this alone, which at last overcomes misfortune and wickedness: that we do not shape our own course after that of the world, that we do not let the vices of others tempt us to our own nor believe them excusable. 'By constancy,' says Bacon, 'fate and fortune return like Proteus to their former being.' Faithlessness, in revenge for faithlessness, as recommended by Iachimo to Imogen, would have for ever destroyed the love and happiness of both; the true constancy of both, in spite of the supposed falsehood of each, surmounted the wicked report and even the incurable evil—the supposed death. And this constancy under such heavy trials acquires a different purity and a different splendour *after* the sorrow and defilement than *before* it. For the events of our play preach this lesson also loudly and distinctly: that virtue when tried, even if it has wavered, has a much higher value than that which is unshaken and untempted. This wisdom slumbers in the craving for the world exhibited by Cymbeline's boys; it lies deeply buried in the much-attacked wager of Posthumus; for a man would only stake upon such a trial the dearest being whom he possessed, and the tried one would only stand the test like Imogen, when it lies in the innermost conviction of both that genuine virtue ought not to shrink from any trial, not even from the most painful. This lesson is taught also in the position which Shakespeare has given to Cymbeline, whose name stands not by mere chance as the title of the drama. In the midst of all these tempting and tempted agents stands the weak king, without self-reliance, the image of a subordinate character, the sport of every good or bad influence, tossed about by every temptation or suggestion, bent by every wind, but not like the tree at the same time strengthened. He is a mere cipher, receiving value only from the higher or lower figure placed before it; we cannot impute the evil to him, to which he has been instigated by those whom he esteems wise and good, any more than the good which happens without his choice and without his interference. If we consider, also, the contrast in which the poet has placed this character to that of the tried sufferers, our play becomes, as it were, a poetic theodicy; it justifies the impulse to evil which lies within us, and the struggle with external evil imposed upon us, by rendering perceptible in those opposite examples that goodness which has not overcome in the struggle with evil is worthless, and that there can be no virtue without vice. The poet has brought down the gods themselves to the complaining shadows of Posthumus' parents and to the couch of the sleeping sufferer, in order to explain to them this meaning of our play, and to announce expressly to them that which Posthumus had already learnt by his own penetration and others by experience: that the gods decree evil for the trial of the good; that 'some falls are means the happier to arise' [IV. ii. 403]; that 'fortune brings in some boats that are not steered' [IV. iii. 46]; that God loves him best whom he crosses, 'to make his gift, the more delayed, delighted' [V. iv. 101-02], that consequently only tried virtue, ripened by its contact with evil, is worthy of love; that the dearest of the world's sons are not exempt from its shocks and blows, but by resisting its temptations they strengthen their inner worth. Shakespeare here allows the rules of the world to mix personally in the drama, as is usual in the epos, where the actors are in harmony with the divinity and his laws. This epic character and the happy termination of the epos were necessarily given to this drama also. For the personages who here act and err are friends and favourites of the gods, because even that which in calm certainty or uncertain passion they do, contrary to the maxims of morality, is done

from moral motives or in moral indignation; so that the drama with a tragic ending would have been an impeachment of the world's government. Hence I do not think that Shakespeare would have admitted the introduction of Jupiter to be a blunder, as Ulrici calls it [see excerpt above, 1839], or that he needs Tieck's apology, that this scene was a fragment of a youthful attempt at this play. Far rather does it appear to me that the introduction of the divinity in this dramatised epos testifies to the same deep and remarkable instinct with which Shakespeare entered into the nature of poetry and its various styles and requirements—an instinct of which the preparation of the historical ground in the last two plays [*Macbeth* and *King Lear*] was another proof. The poet used the advantage afforded him by this introduction of Providence in a bodily form to carry on the history in some points by means of unexpected incidents; the miraculous power thus introduced neutralises the wonder of the incident, which Shakespeare otherwise nowhere permits himself to employ. This machinery of Providence, however, in nowise impedes the free movement of the actors. And that which might appear arbitrary in the combination of the outward events is more than counterbalanced by the inimitable unravelling of the wonderfully intricate knots at the conclusion of the play. This even found favour with [Samuel] Johnson; it is so rich in distinctness that the poet seems to applaud himself for it, when he makes Cymbeline say:—

> This fierce abridgment,
> Hath to it circumstantial branches, which
> Distinction should be rich in.
>
> [V. v. 382-84]

A single passage will show this—that one, for instance, in which Imogen, leaning upon Posthumus, 'like harmless lightning throws her eye' [V. v. 394] on him, her brothers, and her father, 'hitting each object with a joy, the counterchange severally in all' [V. v. 395-97]. This passage imparts life and satisfaction to the scene when represented, and when read it makes us thoroughly understand the necessity of *seeing* Shakespeare represented, and is a complete commentary upon it. (pp. 674-78)

> G. G. Gervinus, "Third Period of Shakespeare's Dramatic Poetry: 'Cymbeline'," in his Shakespeare Commentaries, *translated by F. E. Bunnètt, revised edition, 1877. Reprint by AMS Press Inc., 1971, pp. 644-78.*

THOMAS KENNY   (essay date 1864)

[*Kenny regards* Cymbeline *as "one of Shakespeare's comparative failures" despite its "earnestness and vigour," asserting that it displays no "higher purposes" and that the characterization is frequently incomplete or inconsistent. He maintains that although the vision scene in Act V, Scene iv is extravagant and inferior to the rest of the play, it is undoubtedly the work of Shakespeare, perhaps copied by him from a similar episode in a play by another dramatist or composed in this fashion to appeal to the popular taste. The use of such sensational scenic effects as essential elements in coterie drama in the early sixteenth century, and the likelihood that in* Cymbeline *Shakespeare was experimenting with the dramatic techniques of this new mode, has been discussed by Arthur C. Kirsch (see Additional Bibliography). Also, Brander Matthews (1913) has claimed that the artificiality of the characterization in the play is related to the descriptive method of character portrayal typical of the dramas of Beaumont and Fletcher. Kenny is the first critic to draw attention to the exchange between Posthumus and his jailer in Act V, Scene iv, which he describes as a "singular comic dialogue."*]

''Cymbeline'' is another of the works which we owe to the Shakespeare folio of 1623. It is there inserted among the tragedies, and it is even called the ''Tragedie of Cymbeline.'' We cannot, however, adopt that classification. ''Cymbeline'' is not a tragedy in any sense in which the word is usually employed. But neither can it be regarded as a comedy in the natural acceptation of that term. We believe it must merely be called a drama, which is the only epithet we can with any propriety apply to many of the plays of Shakespeare, founded on romantic tales, or even on actual historical events. (p. 208)

Its plot is most singularly complicated, and, in the frequent succession of surprises and perplexities which it creates, it leaves little room for the development of real dramatic emotion. And yet ''Cymbeline'' is throughout written with much of Shakespeare's earnestness and vigour. It is by no means one of his more careless and hasty works. His special imagination is distinguishable in the whole of these scenes, although never, perhaps, in its largest and freest mood. The actors are almost exclusively princes, or courtiers, or the leaders of armies; and the language is not only imaginatively coloured, but is animated by a tone of sustained elegance and dignity. The dialogue, it is true, contains none of Shakespeare's more wonderful manifestations of the beauty or the power of expression, but we find in it many passages which could have come from no other hand. (p. 210)

But we must still regard this drama as one of Shakespeare's comparative failures. In it he never rises to his finer and more imaginative presentment of life. All the higher purposes of dramatic composition are here more or less sacrificed to the necessities of mere romantic narration. The most rapid examination of ''Cymbeline'' will show, we think, that it is not largely distinguished by vivid characterisation. The King is old and feeble, and has no striking part to perform. The two young princes are also comparatively unimportant figures; true enough to the very exceptional circumstances in which they are placed, but in no sense great dramatic creations. The Queen is a sort of diminutive Lady Macbeth, but without any opportunity, throughout these intricate and improbable episodes, of distinctly developing her character. Cloten is a more original portraiture; and although he is but slightly sketched, and in spite of some apparent contradictions here and there, which make him sometimes better and sometimes worse than we are prepared to expect, we seem to catch in his brutal but not wholly unmanly nature, glimpses of a real unmistakable human being of a very unconventional type. The ''yellow Iachimo'' is one of the many villains in Shakespeare's dramas who sin without any intelligible motive, and who afterwards, at the desired moment, appear to renounce their wickedness with an equally unaccountable facility.

The mode in which Posthumus himself is represented in these scenes is open to some objection. He appears to have been conceived by the poet as a perfectly complete and harmonious character, and, on the whole, perhaps he realises this conception. But he sometimes seems very strangely to fall short of this ideal standard. His consent to accept the wager, with all its conditions, is an absurd and unnatural resolution; the solicitation which he addresses to Pisanio to kill his mistress is still more out of place, and is absolutely cruel and treacherous; and in Act. V., Scene I., he could not have been prepared to pardon such a crime as that of which he still believes his wife to have been guilty, and he could no longer have spoken of her as ''the noble Imogen'' [I. i. 10]. These may be but slight inconsistencies; they were, no doubt, introduced by the poet

to meet his immediate dramatic requirements; but they disturb the harmony of the impression which we are disposed to form of the all-accomplished Posthumus. We are aware that Shakespeare manages the wager scene with more skill and delicacy than Boccaccio, who makes the offer of the extravagant test of female fidelity to proceed from the merchant whose own wife is to be tempted; but we are not satisfied with merely finding that a mediaeval romance presents less of ideal truth and grace than the Shakespearian drama.

Imogen is the redeeming figure in this work; it is she alone that gives to it any deep vital interest. Without any apparent effort, or any straining after effect, the poet places her before us in the light of the most natural and engaging loveliness. The charm of her divine purity and tenderness is finely blended with the rapid but enchanting glimpses we obtain of her personal grace and attractiveness. She is undoubtedly one of the most exquisite of all Shakespeare's female creations. But we still cannot class such a figure among the greatest achievements of his genius, for it is evidently one that arose out of a refined sensibility rather than out of the highest creative imagination.

We have still to notice what seems the most curious passage in ''Cymbeline.'' This is the vision of Posthumus, with the rhymes of the ghosts of his dead relatives, and of Jupiter himself, who ''descends in thunder and lightning'' [V. iv. s.d. at 92], together with the strange scroll which the dreamer finds before him on awaking. We feel utterly perplexed in attempting to reconcile the employment of this extravagant stage trick with our knowledge of the wonderful imagination and the fine sense of the poet. Some critics have taken it for granted that the scene was not written by himself, but that it was foisted into the work by the players. There does not, however, seem to be the slightest ground for attributing it to such a source, and, indeed, the episode appears to form an essential link in the conclusion of the drama. Our surprise at its introduction would be considerably diminished if we could find that it was only an imitation by Shakespeare of a passage in some work which he was generally copying in his play—for such a circumstance would be in complete accordance with a practice which he very frequently adopted; and we think it not at all improbable that it was in this way a large portion of ''Cymbeline'' was written. The only other mode in which we can attempt to account for the selection of so grotesque a show is by supposing that the dramatist was here yielding, in one of his careless rhyming moods, to what he knew to be the taste of his audiences. But, on either of these suppositions, we should still find a singular want of harmony between the weakness and extravagance of this episode and the clearness and strength which more or less characterise the rest of his composition. We are specially struck by this contrast on reading immediately afterwards, in the same scene, the singular comic dialogue between Posthumus and his gaolers—a dialogue so strangely natural, so wild and reckless, so replete with the careless, impersonal power of the poet. In it, as in many other portions of his dramas, he seems to allow the characters to speak absolutely for themselves; he has no interest in them; he knows nothing of them; he does not even appear disposed to indulge, through the medium which they afford, in any bitter and concealed irony; he is wholly passive and indifferent, and Nature follows, through the unforced play of his fancy, her own capricious, unaccountable will. The poet himself is no more to be found here than in the rhymes of Jupiter, or in any of the more serious incidents of his drama. But this impersonality is a constant and special accompaniment of the whole of these wonderful creations. We can never perfectly comprehend the nature of Shakespeare as it is revealed in his work. In his heights and in his depths he is still removed from us by the exceptional conditions of his personality and his genius; and we can never fully account for such wholly unconcerned and apparently illimitable power, or for the strange and even worthless uses to which that power is frequently applied. (pp. 211-14)

Thomas Kenny, ''The Plays of Shakespeare: 'Cymbeline','' in his The Life and Genius of Shakespeare, *Longman, Green, Longman, Roberts, and Green, 1864, pp. 208-14.*

ALGERNON CHARLES SWINBURNE   (essay date 1880)

[*Swinburne was an English poet, dramatist, and critic who devoted much of his literary career to the study of Shakespeare and other Elizabethan writers. His three books on Shakespeare—*A Study of Shakespeare *(1880),* Shakespeare *(1909), and* Three Plays of Shakespeare *(1909)—all demonstrate his keen interest in Shakespeare's poetic talents and, especially, his major tragedies. Swinburne's literary commentary is frequently expressed in a style that is markedly intense and effusive. Swinburne closes* A Study of Shakespeare *with a brief discussion of* Cymbeline *excerpted below, in which he declares that he loves the play more than any of Shakespeare's other works. In his judgment of Imogen as ''the woman above all Shakespeare's women,'' he epitomizes the nineteenth-century Romantic critical esteem of this character. For further discussion of Imogen, see the excerpts by August Wilhelm Schlegel (1811), William Hazlitt (1817), Anna Brownell Jameson (1833), G. G. Gervinus (1849-50), Helena Faucit (1882), Bernard Shaw (1896), E. K. Chambers (1907), Brander Matthews (1913), Harley Granville-Barker (1930), G. Wilson Knight (1947), Harold C. Goddard (1951), and Robin Moffet (1962).*]

I think, as far as I can tell, I may say I have always loved [*Cymbeline*] beyond all other children of Shakespeare. . . . Here is depth enough with height enough of tragic beauty and passion, terror and love and pity, to approve the presence of the most tragic Master's hand: subtlety enough of sweet and bitter truth to attest the passage of the mightiest and wisest scholar or teacher in the school of the human spirit; beauty with delight enough and glory of life and grace of nature to proclaim the advent of the one omnipotent Maker among all who bear that name. Here above all is the most heavenly triad of human figures that ever even Shakespeare brought together; a diviner three, as it were a living god-garland of the noblest earth-born brothers and loveworthiest heaven-born sister, than the very givers of all grace and happiness to their Grecian worshippers of old time over long before. The passion of Posthumus is noble, and patent the poison of Iachimo; Cymbeline has enough for Shakespeare's present purpose of ''the king-becoming graces'' [*Macbeth*, IV. iii. 91]; but we think first and last of her who was ''truest speaker'' and those who ''called her brother, when she was but their sister; she them brothers when they were so indeed.'' The very crown and flower of all her father's daughters—I do not speak here of her human father, but her divine—the woman above all Shakespeare's women is Imogen. As in Cleopatra we found the incarnate sex, the woman everlasting, so in Imogen we find half glorified already the immortal godhead of womanhood. I would fain have some honey in my words at parting—with Shakespeare never, but for ever with these notes on Shakespeare; and I am therefore something more than fain to close my book upon the name of the woman best beloved in all the world of song and all the tide of time; upon the name of Shakespeare's Imogen. (pp. 225-27)

Act III. Scene vi. Imogen, Belarius, Guiderius, and Arvir-agus. Frontispiece to the Hanmer edition by H. Gravelot (1744). By permission of the Folger Shakespeare Library.

Algernon Charles Swinburne, ''Third Period: Tragic and Romantic,'' in his A Study of Shakespeare, *R. Worthington, 1880, pp. 170-227.*

HELENA FAUCIT, LADY MARTIN   (essay date 1882)

[*Faucit was a highly respected and greatly admired English actress whose stage career began in 1833 and lasted until 1879. Her* On Some of Shakespeare's Female Characters *(1882) represents studies of seven Shakespearean heroines, together with recollections of her performances of these roles. In the excerpt below from that work, Faucit constructs an imaginary post-play world and speculates on what becomes of the characters in* Cymbeline *after the drama ends. She maintains that the vicissitudes Imogen suffers have left her irretrievably sick at heart. In Faucit's view, happiness has come too late for Imogen, who is destined to suffer a lingering illness which will end in the fading out of her life, ''like an exhalation of the dawn.'' Harley Granville-Barker (1930) agrees with Faucit that Imogen could never have credibly recovered from the horrors and violence of her ordeals. For additional commentary on the character of Imogen, see the excerpts by August Wilhelm Schlegel (1811), William Hazlitt (1817), Anna Brownell Jameson (1833), G. G. Gervinus (1849-50), Algernon Charles Swinburne (1880), Bernard Shaw (1896), E. K. Chambers (1907), Brander Matthews (1913), G. Wilson Knight (1947), Harold C. Goddard (1951), and Robin Moffet (1962).*]

[In] my letter on Portia, I said that I never could leave my characters when the scene closed in upon them, but always dreamed them over in my mind until the end. So it was with Imogen. Her sufferings are over. The "father cruel," made so by the "step-dame false" [I. vi. 1], has returned to his old love and pride in her,—the love made doubly tender by remembrance of all that he has caused her to suffer. The husband—ah, what can measure his penitence, his self-abasement! That *he* had dared to doubt her purity, her honour,—he who had known her inmost thoughts from childhood!

But Imogen—can she think of him as before? Yes! She is truly named the "divine Imogen"; at least, she has so much of the divine "quality of mercy" [*The Merchant of Venice*, IV. i. 184] in her, that she can blot from her memory all his doubts, all his want of faith, as if they had never been. Her love is infinite—"beyond beyond." Hers is not a nature to do things by halves. She has forgotten as well as forgiven. But can Posthumus forgive himself? No! I believe, never. The more angel she proves herself in her loving self-forgetfulness, the blacker his temporary delusion will look in his own eyes. Imogen may surmise at times the thorns which prick his conscience so sharply. Then she will quietly double the tender ways in which she delights to show her love and pride in him. But no spoken words will tell of this heart-secret between them.

In her brothers Imogen has none but sweet and happy memories. These "two worlds" are an immense and unlooked-for gain to her life; they fill it with new thoughts, new sympathies. She has their future to look forward to, their present to help. One can see how their unsophisticated natures will go forth to her; how the tender memory of the "rare boy" Fidele will give an added charm to the grace and attractiveness of the sweet sister-tie; how, in their quiet hours with her, they will repeat the incidents of the cave-life. Imogen will never tell them the whole of her sorrow there. She fears they would not forgive Posthumus. We can suppose, too, how, in this so new life to them, the young princes would be for ever seeking this sweet counsellor to guide them in the usages and customs of the Court life, all so strange to them. Men will ask from women what they would be shy of asking from one another. Think of the pleasant banterings there would be at times between them! How amused Imogen would be at their mistakes! How often, laughingly, she would have to put them right; and how all these things would draw them nearer to each other!

Then, too, the old soldier Belarius,—the tried retainer and friend Pisanio! What a group of loving hearts about the happy princess! Caius Lucius also, in Rome, carrying in his memory tender thoughts of his once "kind, duteous" page Fidele, together with the admiring respect he feels for the noble Imogen, Princess of Britain. And Iachimo! The time is to come when his repentance will flow from a still deeper source. While at the Court of Britain, he could not fail to hear of all the misery which he had wrought upon the noble lovers. With his own ears he heard the despair of Posthumus on learning the truth—his agony, his self-accusations—at the thought that he had taken away the life of the maligned princess. But even bitterer pangs of remorse than he then felt will assail Iachimo and never leave him,—for we find he is capable of feeling them,—when he learns that, before very long, the young noble life is quenched through the suffering and bitter trials which he had brought upon it. For quenched, I believe, it is.

Happiness hides for a time injuries which are past healing. The blow which was inflicted by the first sentence in that cruel letter went to the heart with a too fatal force. Then followed, on this crushing blow, the wandering, hopeless days and nights, without shelter, without food even up to the point of famine. Was this delicately nurtured creature one to go through her terrible ordeal unscathed? We see that when food and shelter came, they came too late. The heart-sickness is upon her: "I am sick still—heart-sick" [IV. ii. 37]. Upon this follows the fearful sight of, as she supposes, her husband's headless body. Well may she say that she is "nothing; or if not, nothing to be were better" [IV. ii. 367-68]. When happiness, even such as she had never known before, comes to her, it comes, like the food and shelter,—too late.

Tremblingly, gradually, and oh, how reluctantly! the hearts to whom that life is so precious will see the sweet smile which greets them grow fainter, will hear the loved voice grow feebler! The wise physician Cornelius will tax his utmost skill, but he will find the hurt is too deep for mortal leechcraft. The "piece of tender air" [V. v. 446] very gently, but very surely, will fade out like an exhalation of the dawn. Her loved ones will watch it with straining eyes, until it

> Melts from
> The smallness of a gnat to air; and then
> Will turn their eyes and weep.
>
> [I. iii. 20-2]

And when, as the years go by, their grief grows calm, that lovely soul will be to them

> Like a star
> Beaconing from the abodes where the Immortals are;
> [Shelley, *Adonais*]

inspiring to worthy lives, and sustaining them with the hope that where she is, they may, in God's good time, become fit to be. Something of this the "divine Imogen" is to us also. Is it not so? (pp. 223-26)

> *Helena Faucit, Lady Martin, "Imogen, Princess of Britain," in her* On Some of Shakespeare's Female Characters: Ophelia, Portia, Desdemona, Juliet, Imogen, Rosalind, Beatrice, *Scribner and Welford, 1887, pp. 157-226.*

DENTON J. SNIDER   (essay date 1890?)

[*Snider was an American scholar, philosopher, and poet who closely followed the precepts of the German philosopher Georg Wilhelm Friedrich Hegel and contributed greatly to the dissemination of his dialectical philosophy in America. Snider's critical writings include studies on Homer, Dante, and Goethe, as well as Shakespeare. Like Hermann Ulrici and G. G. Gervinus, Snider sought for the dramatic unity and ethical import in Shakespeare's plays, but he presented a more rigorous Hegelian interpretation than those two German philosophical critics. In the introduction to his three-volume work* The Shakespearian Drama, a Commentary *(1887-90), Snider states that Shakespeare's plays present various ethical principles which, in their differences, come into "Dramatic Collision," but are ultimately resolved and brought into harmony. He claims that these collisions can be traced in the plays' various "Dramatic Threads" of action and thought, which together form a "Dramatic Movement," and that the analysis of these threads and movements—"the structural elements of the drama"—reveal the organic unity of Shakespeare's art. Snider observes two basic movements in the tragedies—guilt and retribution—and three in the comedies—separation, mediation, and return. In the excerpt below, Snider regards* Cymbeline *as a "play of regeneration" that depicts a process of "purgatorial discipline" in societal institutions, such as the Family and State, as well as individual characters. According to the critic, although the sins and weaknesses of Iachimo, Posthumus, Cymbeline, and Belarius are much greater than those of Imogen and Pisanio, who display only minor inadequacies of character, all these must free themselves of their infirmities and undo their unjust acts before attaining a state of repentance and harmony with the providential order. Other critics who view regeneration as the central thematic concern in* Cymbeline *include Robert Grams Hunter (1965) and William Barry Thorne (1969). In addition, such critics as Derek Traversi (1954), J. A. Bryant, Jr. (1961), Nancy K. Hayles (1980), and Richard G. Moulton (see Additional Bibliography) have also argued that the resolution of conflicts both in families and in states is an important theme in the play. On other matters, Snider is the first critic to question the characterization of the Queen, arguing that drawing her as the champion of British Independence from Rome on the one hand, and as the principal assailant of the Family union of Imogen and Posthumus on the other, results in a clash of ethical standards and mars her role in the drama. He also questions the action of Cymbeline in renewing the vow of tribute to Rome, asserting that the king's rejection of freedom would be offensive to Shakespeare's English audience. However, both G. Wilson Knight (1947) and Emrys Jones (see Additional Bibliography) have offered explanations of the Roman tribute which deny that Cymbeline's decision is either inconsistent or offensive. Concerning the vision scene in Act V, Scene iv, Snider judges it artistically inferior to the rest of the play, but believes it to be authentic and maintains that it is an accurate reflection of Posthumus's state of mind at this point in the action, for it represents "a literal image of the repentant soul harmonizing itself with the rational principle of the Universe." Other commentators who regard this scene as thematically significant include G. G. Gervinus (1849-50), G. Wilson Knight (1947), and J. A. Bryant, Jr. (1961).*]

The entire action [of *Cymbeline* is] divided into three parts or movements. The first movement portrays the world of conflict and disruption, which has its center at the court of Cymbeline. Family and State are in a condition of strife and wrong; the union of Posthumus and Imogen, representing the Family, has to endure a double collision—from within and from without; Britain, representing the State, is involved in a war with a foreign power. This movement, therefore, exhibits struggle and contradiction on all sides; because of such a condition of things there will necessarily result a flight from the world of institutions to a primitive life. Hence, we pass to the second movement, which is the Idyllic Realm—the land of peace and harmony, inhabited by hunters, and far removed from the conflicts of the time. But this narrow existence will disintegrate from within, and will be swallowed up in the conflict from without. The third movement, therefore, is the Restoration, involving the repentance of those who are guilty, the return of those who have been wrongfully banished—in general, the harmony of all collisions of Family and State.

The first movement will unfold the threads giving the domestic and the political conflict. Britain has passed into a period of discord and struggle in its two great institutions—Family and State, showing a diseased condition of the social organism, which has to be subjected to a restorative process.

The preliminary fact of the action is the love and marriage of Posthumus and Imogen. It is in the highest degree a rational union; the characters of husband and wife seem just fitted for each other. Moral worth, strong emotion, intellectual gifts, are all present. Posthumus has been instructed in every kind of knowledge; he is also endowed with the fairest exterior and noblest manners. But that which he lacks is a long line of highborn ancestry, though his father and brothers had rendered the most important services to their country—in fact, his entire family had perished, directly or indirectly, in its defense, and

he had been left an orphan. This untitled origin, then, is the sole ground of objection to him; the play emphasizes the conflict between birth and intelligence. Imogen, the daughter of the king, has chosen him in preference to the degraded and half-witted nobleman, Cloten, against the will of her father and against the plans of her step-mother. Her choice, however, meets with the secret, but unanimous, approval of the courtiers. Now, to break this union so true and so deep, the most powerful instrumentalities are brought forward in the course of the play. But particularly the wife, Imogen, is subjected to the sorest trials, and passes through them in triumph—nothing can undermine her devotion. Here we see the inherent necessity for the restoration and final union of the pair, since the Family reposing on so deep and rational a basis cannot be destroyed without violence both to thought and to our most sacred emotions, in fact without undermining the ethical order of the world.

Against the marriage of Posthumus and Imogen there is a double assault, giving what may be named the external and internal collisions. These two phases manifest all the possible forms of conflict with the Family. The first phase will exhibit the external collision, in which there is an attempt to destroy the union of the married pair by force—by violent separation. Three persons of consequence are engaged in the undertaking—Cymbeline, the Queen, and Cloten. (pp. 511-14)

The Queen, however, is the lever of the whole action, and her great object is, to place her son upon the throne. She is the perfection of cunning and ambition. The easiest way of attaining her end is to marry her son, Cloten, to Imogen, the heiress of the realm; but if this plan does not succeed, she is ready for the secret poisoning of all obnoxious individuals. In the use of deadly drugs she has already had some experience, and she declares that the King himself will be put out of the way if necessary. Still, Imogen understands her dissimulation, and with the greatest firmness resists all attempts to break the marriage. The Queen is truly the villain of the play, and assails the subsisting ethical relations. (pp. 514-15)

These are the three persons who assail the marriage; in the very beginning of the play Posthumus has to flee, being banished by the King; Imogen, the wife, is left alone to withstand the anger of her father, the machinations of her step-mother, and the rude courtship of Cloten. This she does in the most heroic manner, aided and comforted by a servant, Pisanio, who is a leading mediatorial character of the drama. His character is devotion to the pair—fidelity under the most trying difficulties. Forced by the stress of circumstances, he will be faithless to everybody else in order to be faithful to his master and mistress. (p. 515)

With the departure of Posthumus the separation is accomplished; external force has disrupted the members of the Family. Still, they are one in emotion, though far apart in space. Now comes the internal collision—the bond of emotion which unites husband and wife is to be assailed. This assault, if successful, must destroy the foundation of marriage, which is based upon the fidelity of each party. Let either man or wife be brought to believe that the other is untrue, the emotional unity upon which the Family reposes is destroyed. The character whose function it is to undermine their reciprocal love is Iachimo. He is incited to his act by the wager of Posthumus, who thus shows both his confidence and his folly. The scene in Philario's house at Rome, where the bet is made, is not without offensive features, but its necessity is manifest—it motives this assault upon the internal unity of the Family.

Moreover, the affair has its truth to-day; such a wager is still laid by the libertine against the honor of woman, and is sought by every device to be won. The nationality of Iachimo is repeatedly emphasized; he is the crafty Italian who utterly disregards all ethical principles. First, he comes to Britain and assails the chastity of Imogen. He begins with casting suspicion upon the fidelity of Posthumus at Rome. The latter, he says, is jolly, laughs at lover's sighs, ridicules devotion, attacks the character of woman, and, to complete his transgressions, is untrue to his marriage vow. Imogen wavers for a moment in her confidence. Iachimo thinks it is the favorable moment; he urges her to take revenge upon her husband by being untrue also, and offers himself as the means. But revenge is not her principle; she not only thwarts, but at once detects his purpose, and is on the point of having him seized, when he succeeds in gaining her confidence a second time by an artful apology, as well as by extravagant laudation of Posthumus. The assault upon Imogen has, therefore, failed; her confidence in her husband is unimpaired; the wily Italian has not succeeded in destroying the union in her bosom.

Next comes the assault upon Posthumus. Let us see how he stands the trial. Iachimo returns to Rome; the trick of concealment in the chest has furnished him with certain kinds of evidence, which he employs to the best advantage. No doubt the chain of suspicious circumstances was very strong; it convinces the impartial Philario, but it ought not to have convinced a husband who was very partial towards his wife, and who firmly rested on the belief in her fidelity. But Posthumus hastily yields the wager, and concludes that his wife has lost her chastity—a conclusion of which he afterwards bitterly repents. Posthumus, in his anguish, turns against all womankind, and reproaches them with infidelity; he does not even spare his own mother, and thus casts the suspicion of illegitimacy upon himself. This is, however, only carrying misogyny to its necessary conclusion—a universal slander of woman returns to the calumniator.

Thus Iachimo succeeds with the husband, though he has failed with the wife; as regards Posthumus, the confidence upon which the Family reposes is destroyed. He is even ready to murder his wife, and gives instructions to that effect to Pisanio. But the latter again is false in order to be true; he disregards the wicked command of his master, and is faithful to the ethical relation of the pair. (pp. 516-18)

Thus we behold the bond of union between Posthumus and Imogen in almost complete disruption—suspended, as it were, by a single thread. First, external violence separated husband and wife—Posthumus has to leave the court, and Imogen remains behind. Then comes the internal attack, which aims at undermining their emotional unity. With Imogen it fails, but succeeds with Posthumus; and, finally, the wife becomes aware of the alienation of the husband. Such are what were before called the external and internal collisions of the Family. Only Imogen remains faithful to the union, though assailed from without and from within. The beauty of her character lies in this devotion to the highest principle of her sex. Against parent, against the most powerful enemies, and, finally, against the very husband who rejects her, does she assert her unconquerable fidelity to the Family, and in the end saves it from destruction.

The second thread of this movement is the conflict between the two States, though it is much less prominent than the first thread. Britain has ceased to pay tribute to Rome, an ambassador is sent to demand it; the refusal of Britain causes war to be declared. It is national independence against foreign subjugation. The King announces the right of revolt, and asserts the duty of maintaining the ancient laws of the land. But the chief instigator and active supporter of the rebellion is the Queen; without her strong will the weak King could not have been brought to undertake such an enterprise. It must be said that her conduct in this case is not only defensible, but noble; she appears as the champion of nationality against the greatest power in the world. Even Cloten is arrayed on the same side—not from any merit in him, perhaps, but through the influence of his mother. Her motive was doubtless selfish; she wanted to possess absolute authority for herself and for her son as successor to the crown. Still, it is in itself a noble ambition to desire to rule over a free country.

Here occurs the great jar to our ethical feeling which has always been noticeable in this play, notwithstanding its power and beauty. The wicked Queen, who, on the one hand, assails the Family in its loftiest and purest manifestations, on the other hand vindicates the State, the highest ethical institution of man. What, therefore, is to be her fate? She ought not to live—she ought not to die; she is a contradiction which runs through the entire play and blasts its effect. Nor can she be called strictly a tragic character, which goes down in the conflict of institutions, for her support of the State in no way necessitates her hostility to the Family. To the class of villains she rather belongs—those whose nature is to defy all ethical principles, though her selfishness drives her to maintain one—the State. We feel the discord, the double trend of her character, from this time forward. The Poet undoubtedly seeks to condemn her as the enemy of the true marital relation; but, then, on the other side, she stands the main supporter of national independence. When it is added that the drama ends with undoing the whole work of the Queen—that not only the sundered pair are restored to one another, but also Britain returns to the Roman allegiance, and thus nationality is destroyed—we can see how deep is the violence done to the feelings of an audience—especially of a British audience. This play has never been popular, compared with most of Shakespeare's pieces, and never can be, for the reasons just given. Rarely in his other works has the Poet left so great a discord in his Ethical World.

We are now ready to pass out of this realm of conflict to the second movement, which is the Idyllic Land. The Poet has here introduced a new variety of inhabitants, namely the hunters, corresponding to the shepherds of *Winter's Tale* and *As You Like it*. . . . [Yet,] this world is not marked off so plainly here as in the plays just mentioned. It is mingled with foreign elements, which run along with it on the outside, as if to cover up its naked joints. The Poet breaks off describing it, in the middle, and passes to the court of Cymbeline, and he also introduces into it the Roman thread. The outlines of the Hunter World are, therefore, by no means so distinct and separate in the play as might be expected from other works. Still, it constitutes an essential element of the action; it performs also the function of mediation; its character, too, is thoroughly idyllic, and it causes the present play to be ranked with the ideal class of mediated dramas.

The second thread also is introduced into this Hunter Land, namely, the collision between the Roman and British states. It necessarily swallows up the idyllic realm, which has always a tendency to return to society. The battleground is in the neighborhood of the hunters' territory—that is, the latter cannot be wholly withdrawn from the conflict of the nation.

The Hunter World is the contrast to the court, and logically springs from the latter, which has become intolerable as the abode of man; in fact, the Poet has made it the direct product of the King's injustice. Many years before the time of the present action, Cymbeline wrongfully condemned Belarius, a nobleman who had done great services to the State; he flies from society and calls into existence this Hunter World. But he also steals and takes along two children, sons of the King. These three persons now compose this world. The boys are grown up to manhood; are ignorant, however, of their royal origin. The country is mountainous, their house is a cave, their clothing is made of skins, their food is derived from the chase. The old man, Belarius, whom they take to be their father, is full of the praises of their wild existence, and utters much detraction of the court; he has even a natural religion—the worship of the sun. But the young men are anxious to go forth and know more of life; the very dissuasion of Belarius has excited their intense desire of experience. So at the beginning we notice the seeds of dissolution in the Hunter World.

It is manifest, therefore, that this realm is both the contrast and product of the court of Cymbeline. Belarius, driven away by injustice, has created a world of his own—or, rather, has returned to a primitive, natural life, as opposed to a concrete, social existence. Such ideal realms are the natural fruit of a disordered society. Suspicion, intrigue, flattery, wrong, are triumphant at court; but among the hunters are found simplicity, honesty, true bravery, united with a manly independence. It is a condition of peace; of narrow, idyllic activity; a free life, in which the individual, harassed by social collisions, gladly takes refuge—in imagination if not in reality. Imogen, fleeing from the court, comes to its opposite—this idyllic land—and is most kindly received by its inhabitants. The inner, spontaneous feeling of kinship which springs up between her and her brothers, though wholly unknown to one another, is one of the most beautiful situations of the play. (pp. 519-24)

The second arrival from the court in this idyllic land is that of Cloten. The pursuit of Imogen has led him hither. His design is to inflict upon the poor fugitive the most brutal outrage, and drag her back to her angry parents. The wretch meets the elder of the brothers, begins to treat him as if he were one of the servile courtiers, and addresses him in a most insulting manner. The work is short—Cloten's head is cut off in a trice. It was only the court and civilized society which could protect such a monster. In this realm of nature birth conveys no privilege, unless supplemented by other endowments. But observe the contrast between these two adversaries: Cloten, the probable successor of the throne hitherto, is slain by the true heir, one who possesses, not only the royal blood, but the royal character. (pp. 525-26)

But the Hunter World dissolves now within itself. The germ of its dissolution was noticed before; the two young men are dissatisfied with their narrow sphere of action when they have discovered that there is another world beyond, of which they know nothing. They hear the noise of the conflict round about them. The old man, Belarius, with the bitter remembrance of his wrong, wishes to go higher up the mountain, out of the way; he desires still to preserve his idyllic realm. But the youths cannot be restrained; their thirst for activity is so great that they have come to prefer death to their present condition. They descend, therefore, into the plain to participate in the struggle of nationality, and the old warrior, Belarius, cannot stay behind. Thus the Hunter World vanishes, being disrupted, from within and disturbed from without. The civilized State must

show itself stronger than such a narrow, abstract existence. These hunters will now return; the Roman war is the means. They must on the one hand be restored to the State, and the State on the other hand must make it possible for them to live under its protection—must free itself from wrong and contradiction.

Next comes the third movement—the Restoration—which will bring all the separated and colliding elements of Britain into harmony. The external means for accomplishing this purpose has already been stated to be the war with Rome. Connected with it, in one way or another, are all the characters for whom reconciliation is prepared. The battle takes place; the Romans are at first victorious, but are afterwards beaten back and defeated by the three hunters, aided by Posthumus. Thus the idyllic land has been the instrumentality of saving the King; his own courtiers and soldiers have degenerated into cowards. (pp. 527-28)

The battle, being only an external instrumentality, is of minor importance; hence the Poet does not dwell upon it, but has it pass before our eyes rapidly in the form of pantomime. The point, however, which is of the highest significance is the internal ground for the return and salvation of the different characters. They who have done wrong can be saved only through Repentance; they must as far as possible make their deed undone. There are at least three persons who manifest contrition for their conduct—Posthumus, Iachimo, and the King. But the worst character of the play, the Queen, will not, or cannot, repent; at least her repentance is of that kind which does not purchase reconciliation, for she

> Repented
> The evils she hatched were not effected; so,
> Despairing, died.
>
> [V. v. 59-61]

Her violation of the ethical world has taken such deep possession of her nature that it could not be cast off—renunciation of ambition and crime means death. The step-mother in this play can not be mediated; she conspires against and assails her step-daughter, Imogen, who is, moreover, the great mediatorial character; thus she destroys her own means of salvation.

The first of the repentants is Posthumus. He supposes that his order to kill Imogen has been fulfilled by Pisanio; he is full of the deepest tribulation for his hasty action. Though he is not yet aware of the innocence of Imogen, he nevertheless repents of his command; for thus she has not had the opportunity to repent. He courts death; he would gladly offer up his own life as an atonement for his deed. Repentance can go no further. When the individual is ready to sacrifice his existence, what more can he give? Posthumus seeks death from both Romans and Britons; but his wish is not fulfilled—he still lives. It is evident that he has made his deed undone as far as lies in his power; the sorrow within and the action without indicate the deepest repentance. In two lengthy speeches he is introduced as giving expression to his contrite feelings. Reconciliation must be prepared for such a soul—it is a necessary logical consequence.

The character of Posthumus passes through a great development; he has at first an outer fickleness and impulsiveness, but when he comes to himself he shows his deep inward honesty and stability. The bad company at Rome seems to have called out his weak traits; his impetuous mistake is to have made the wager, which could expose himself to deception, and his wife to annoyance if not to temptation. He receives the penalty, he is deceived by circumstantial evidence, loses confidence in his wife, and hastily orders her to be slain. Thus his trait is now vengeance; in a fit of jealousy, like Othello, he will slay the dearest object of his heart. He will also involve in his own guilt his faithful servant, Pisanio, making the very fidelity of the latter, into a means of crime. In these things we see the weakness of Posthumus, and the necessity of his discipline; he is sudden, impulsive, and vengeful in his passion. But we must not forget the good side of the man, which is the ground of his restoration; it is love which drives him to jealousy—he shows no infidelity, no unchastity, but he has in his blindness revenge and not charity.

Time, however, will work a change; this takes place in the interval between the Second and Fifth Acts, during which he disappears. He repents of both of his deeds toward Imogen and Pisanio. Not that he thinks she is guiltless—he repents that he has not given her time to repent. Disguised as a peasant, he will fight for his country, or rather for her country, since she is always in his mind as the supreme object. Though he vanquishes and disarms Iachimo, he cannot slay the latter, as he is the cause of his own misfortune. He welcomes death and bondage, but can not die or be taken; his repentance is to bring restoration. Thus he goes through his discipline; no longer vengeance but charity is now his soul's strongest impulse. He is to show himself a second Providence and suffer the wicked to repent; so he grants life to Iachimo. If he had thus acted at the beginning, he would not have had this trial; even if Imogen had been guilty he should have had charity. He may now be said to be in harmony with the divine order, into which he must, after repentance, be accepted.

Here the Poet might stop, for he has amply motived the reunion of Posthumus with Imogen, which will hereafter take place. But he has chosen to go further, and to give a detailed representation of the above-mentioned reconciliation in another form—to present a literal image of the repentant soul harmonizing itself with the rational principle of the Universe. Posthumus falls asleep and dreams; his dream is of forgiveness. He sees his father, mother, and brothers interceding for him with Jupiter—greatest of the gods—who grants their prayer. The restoration to Imogen is promised, and also release from affliction. It is but a dream, yet it shows his state of mind, and intimates his internal absolution. He wakes again; doubt and sorrow assail him; again he sighs for death. But the reality soon comes to confirm the vision; he is reconciled with his father-in-law, Cymbeline, and restored to his wife, Imogen, not without another flash of impulse, however, in which he gives her, before she is recognized, a cruel blow of which he has again to repent.

This passage, including the dream of Posthumus and his conversation with the jailors, has often been condemned for its manifold defects, and sometimes declared not to be the work of the Poet. That its literary merit falls below the average literary merit of Shakespearian composition is hardly to be denied; that it is not strictly necessary to the development of the action is also true, since the repentance already manifested by Posthumus logically involves restoration. The example of the Poet may also be cited, for, though he has often employed repentance in other dramas, he has nowhere introduced such an intercession of divinity to secure its results. Still, even if it be not absolutely requisite for the action, the plea may be made in its favor that it gives an imaginative completeness to the mediation. Deity is introduced in person, manifesting grace for repentance. It is thus the most profound Christian doctrine

in a heathen dress, and this dress is taken, instead of the real Christian dress, for the purpose of avoiding the charge of blasphemy. To bring God upon the stage, pardoning the repentant sinner, would be a pretty hazardous undertaking, and would not have escaped, it is likely, the deletion of the censor's pen in the Poet's time. Such a liberty may be taken with an old, worn-out Greek divinity, though even this procedure is not strictly that of the drama, which should exhibit man as determined from within, and not from without. But the introduction of the tablet, with its prophetic inscription and its interpretation, is not only useless, but also ridiculous. The authorship of the entire passage, however, cannot well be taken away from Shakespeare, in the absence of positive testimony, though one may wish it were not his. It is also jointed too closely into the rest of the Act to pass for an external interpolation.

The second of these repentants is Iachimo, who has been guilty of defaming a pure woman, and destroying the internal bond of union of the Family. He also has come with the Roman army; his first declaration is sorrow for his wrong. The main ground of his change seems to lie in the fact that he has lost his former valor; the guilty soul paralyzes the strong arm; he is vanquished by one who seems to him to be a mere peasant. Before the King and the entire company he confesses his deed, and, finally, asks for death at the hands of Posthumus, whom he has so deeply wronged. Thus his repentance has carried him to the point of a necessary reconciliation; he has offered for it the highest possible price, namely, his own life. At this price it can not be withheld—for how could his punishment obtain more? (pp. 528-34)

The King also repents of his conduct toward Imogen, and is reconciled with Belarius. Thus his two great acts of wrong are undone; the two deeds which disrupted his family—one of them causing the loss of his sons, the other the loss of his daughter—are recalled. The result is, sons and daughter are restored to him, and his family is once more united. But not only the Family, but also the State, is restored from its internal disruption. The Hunter World is reconciled with it, and no longer separates from it—creating a distinct realm. Even in the external conflict Britain is successful against the Romans; but the King voluntarily surrenders his victory and again becomes the vassal of Rome. The object is, no doubt, to undo entirely the work of the wicked Queen, who was the chief instigator of the revolt, even to the extent of throwing away national independence. It has already been said that to make this detestable woman the heroine of her country's freedom was a jar to our ethical feeling; but to reject that freedom because it was achieved by a wicked person seems to grate even more harshly upon the sentiment of nationality. The management of the part of the Queen must be declared to be unfortunate—it is, indeed, the chief defect of the drama.

The favorite person of the play is undoubtedly Imogen, who is held by many to be the finest female character in Shakespeare. Her love is the driving wheel of the action, and draws into its movement the whole order of things. Gervinus has said that next to Hamlet she is the most elaborate delineation of the Poet. Upon none of his characters has Shakespeare poured such vials of affliction; to none has he given a more unswerving fealty to the best self in the hour of trial. She is the self-centered soul, not determined to revenge by wrong, but to the greater activity and charity; her duty rests not upon another's conduct, but upon itself; her love depends not even upon her lover's love, but is its own unfailing fountain. Can she be shaken? The Poet has tried his best to break her down, but has not been able; he has heaped upon her the heaviest burdens of life, yet, after a little stoop or swoon, she is on her feet again, erect as ever. She is quite the sum of his conflicts, yet she meets them all, and mediates most of the colliding persons of the play, who seem to require her restorative hand. (pp. 536-38)

[She] has stood her trial; she must be restored, else the Universe would fall to pieces; the ethical gravitation is far stronger and more necessary than the physical, in the Shakespearian cosmogeny. But she has become the center of the spiritual system; she draws and restores others who have been wayward and wanderers. Her integrity is what brings back into harmonious order her husband, her parent, even her tempter, the very devil. To be sure she is unconscious of doing all this, it lies far out of the horizon of her knowledge; still Providence is working with her, since his instrument is always just this integrity, which he supplies with his purpose. She has an inborn faith that the world is founded on goodness and will show it ultimately, if she persist herself in being good. Her mediatorial gift runs far beyond her conscious intention; she seems to combine two of Shakespeare's great women; she has the long-suffering of Hermione [in *The Winter's Tale*], coupled with the activity of Portia [in *The Merchant of Venice*]. Hermione, indeed, is somewhat passive; Portia is not called upon to endure, but to do; Imogen shows both supremely—the endurance and the deed. (p. 539)

Pisanio is, from the start at least, the most perfect character of the play, though in a sphere more limited than Imogen, who weakens at points, thinks of giving up, even of committing suicide. It is Pisanio who calls her back and sees through the whole trouble: "It cannot be but that my master is abused; some villain hath done you both this cursed injury" [III. iv. 119-22]. He has the coolest head, he shows the best balance of all. We feel that Iachimo could not have wheedled him. Neither his fidelity nor his insight ever lapses, nor does impulse catch him unawares. Against his master, who bids him commit murder, he preserves his moral autonomy; he has a soul of his own though he be a servant, which no authority can drive counter to its true being; he will not execute the wicked command, he is a spiritual aristocrat in his humble station. However small his sphere of life, in it he can be all and perfect. A curious fact of the play is this: not till Imogen, too, has become a servant, does her perfection shine out, and she is prepared for restoration to her high rank. Thus has the Poet ennobled the life of the humble, in a way that recalls the one who was born in a manger. But even Pisanio gets lost in the mazes of the time; master and mistress are whirled outside of his knowledge, and he "remains perplexed in all" [IV. iii. 40-1]. Then his final appeal turns to Providence: "The heavens still must work" [IV. iii. 41]. They do work and vindicate him, making good his faith. Again we see the providential order sweep in and take control [of] the Shakespearian world. (pp. 540-41)

This play is peculiarly a play of regeneration, and shows in manifold characters the process by which the soul is to free itself of its weak, inadequate, sinful phases. We find here, even the unregenerate—Cloten and his mother, who persist in evil and perish, though they, too, have the same chance as the rest. They cannot be mediated, they make the Inferno in this comedy, which, in certain respects, is Dantean. But the chief realm here is the Purgatory, which shows the erring man in the process of regeneration. Many forms he takes, from the demon Iachimo, through Posthumus, the King, Belarius; up to even the good ones, Imogen and Pisanio; all are going through the purgatorial discipline. Shakespeare's Purgatory, however,

includes the guiltless and the guilty, in this being different from Dante's; the sinless have to suffer for and through the sinful, thereby attaining to completeness and passing from mere innocence to positive goodness. But we have also a touch of the primitive Paradise in the two youths and their mountain home. Theirs is the state of first innocence, without knowledge, but they thirst for experience, and quit their paradisaical abode, having the old Adam in them still. Thus the play completes the cycle of the human, if not of the divine, comedy. (pp. 542-43)

Denton J. Snider, "'Cymbeline'," in his The Shake-spearian Drama, a Commentary: The Comedies, *Sigma Publishing Co., 1890? pp. 506-43.*

BARRETT WENDELL　(essay date 1894)

[*Wendell was an American literary historian, scholar, and educator known especially for his work in early American literature. His critical work,* William Shakspere: A Study in Elizabethan Literature *(1894), is regarded as a useful handbook for students of Shakespearean literature. In the excerpt below, Wendell is principally concerned with the intricacies of language and structure in* Cymbeline. *From his analysis of Act V, Scene v—in which he identifies "twenty-four distinct stage situations" carefully manipulated and resolved through "a feat of technical stage-craft"— and from his assessment of "the broken, parenthetic style" and complexities of thought in the play, he concludes that Shakespeare's dramatic powers were declining when he composed* Cymbeline. *Wendell judges the play as lacking in "spontaneous imagination" and showing evidence of Shakespeare's forced exertion of his capacities as an artist. He argues that the disguises, degrees of enlightenment, and the series of revelations which lead to the successive denouements of Act V, Scene v constitute a literary tour de force, in which the dramatist "was determined to assert that he could still do better than ever." Such twentieth-century critics as Harley Granville-Barker (1930), Barbara A. Mowat (1966), and R. A. Foakes (1971) agree that* Cymbeline *is a self conscious and often cumbersome work, but they additionally maintain that Shakespeare intended to draw his audience's attention to his dramatic technique, rather than overwhelm them with his mastery. Bertrand Evans (see Additional Bibliography) has also demonstrated Shakespeare's virtuoso use of various degrees of awareness among the different characters in this play, a point briefly addressed here by Wendell. For further commentary on whether* Cymbeline *provides evidence of Shakespeare's artistic decline, or of his state of mind, see the excerpts by E. K. Chambers (1907) and Brander Matthews (1913) and the essays by George Brandes, Lytton Strachey, and James Sutherland cited in the Additional Bibliography.*]

A hasty critic lately said that *Cymbeline* sounds as if Browning had written it. Though crude, the remark is suggestive. The style of *Cymbeline* has at least two traits really like Browning's: the rhythm of the lines is often hard to catch; and the thought often becomes so intricate that, without real obscurity, it is hard to follow. Take, for example, the opening of the third scene of the first act, a conversation between Imogen and Pisanio:—

> *Imo.* I would thou grew'st unto the shores o' the
> 　　　haven,
> And question'dst every sail: if he should write
> And I not have it, 't were a paper lost
> As offer'd mercy is. What was the last
> That he spake to thee?
> 　　*Pis.* 　　　　　　　It was his queen, his queen!

Imo. Then waved his handkerchief?
Pis.   And kiss'd it, madam.
Imo. Senseless linen! happier therein than I!
And that was all?
Pis.   No, madam; for so long
As he could make me with this eye or ear
Distinguish him from others, he did keep
The deck, with glove, or hat, or handkerchief,
Still waving, as the fits and stirs of's mind
Could best express how slow his soul sail'd on,
How swift his ship.
Imo.   Thou shouldst have made him
As little as a crow, or less, ere left
To after-eye him.
Pis.   Madam, so I did.

                                              [I. iii. 1-16]

This passage is enough to illustrate the peculiar metrical structure of *Cymbeline*. Endstopped lines are so deliberately avoided that one feels a sense of relief when a speech and a line end together. Such a phrase as

How slow his soul sail'd on, how swift his ship

is deliberately made, not a single line, but two half-lines. Several times, in the broken dialogue, one has literally to count the syllables before the metrical regularity of the verse appears. The meaning, too, is often so compactly expressed that to catch it one must pause and study. Clearly this puzzling style is decadent; the distinction between verse and prose is breaking down. Again, take this passage from the scene when Imogen receives the letter of Posthumus bidding her meet him at Milford:—

Then, true Pisanio,—
Who long'st, like me, to see thy lord; who long'st,—
O, let me bate,—but not like me—yet long'st,
But in a fainter kind:—O, not like me;
For mine's beyond beyond—say, and speak thick;
Love's counsellor should fill the bores of hearing
To the smothering of the sense—how far it is
To this same blessed Milford.

                                              [III. ii. 52-9]

Here the actual sentence is only "Pisanio . . . say . . . how far it is to . . . Milford." Nothing but the most skilful elocution, however, could possibly make clear to a casual hearer the broken, parenthetic style. The speeches of Iachimo in the last act show the same trait more extravagantly still. Altogether, the style of *Cymbeline* probably demands closer attention than that of any other work of Shakspere.

This almost perverse complexity of *Cymbeline* is not confined to details of style. To understand the structure of the play you must give it preposterous attention. Until the very last scene, the remarkably involved story tangles itself in a way which is utterly bewildering. At any given point, overwhelmed with a mass of facts presented pell-mell, you are apt to find that you have quite forgotten something important. Coming after such confusion, the last scene of *Cymbeline* is among the most notable bits of dramatic construction anywhere. The more one studies it, the more one is astonished at the ingenuity with which *dénouement* follows *dénouement*. Nowhere else in Shakspere, certainly, is there anything like so elaborate an untying of knots which seem purposely made intricate to prepare for this final situation. Situation, however, is an inadequate word. Into 485 lines Shakspere has crowded some two dozen situa-

tions any one of which would probably have been strong enough to carry a whole act.

An analysis of these is perhaps worth while. The scene opens with the triumphal entrance of Cymbeline, who proceeds to knight his heroic sons—neither side suspecting the relation. His triumph is interrupted by news of the queen's death, and of her villainy. Before this can much upset Cymbeline, however, the captives are brought in, and the *dénouements* are fully prepared for. To realize what they are, we may remind ourselves that we now have on the stage not only the mutually unknown father and sons, but also the following personages whose identity is more or less confused: Imogen, disguised as a youth, is known to be herself only by Pisanio, but is known to her brothers—whom she does not suspect to be her brothers—as the boy Fidele, whom they believe dead. Belarius and Posthumus, each in disguise, are known to nobody. Iachimo is present undisguised; but his villainy is known only to Imogen, and not wholly to her. Meanwhile, nobody but the sons of Cymbeline knows that Cloten has been killed. One's brain fairly swims. The action begins by Lucius, the Roman general, begging the life of Imogen, whom he believes to be a boy in his service. This boon granted, Imogen, instead of showing gratitude to Lucius, turns away from him, with apparent heartlessness. Her real object, however, is to expose the villain Iachimo,—a matter which so fills her mind that she has no eyes for her brothers, who half recognize her as Fidele. Iachimo, caught with the ring of Posthumus on his finger, now confesses his villainy. Thereupon Posthumus, at last enlightened, and believing that Imogen has been killed by his command, reveals himself in an agony of rage. Imogen interrupts him, and he, believing her an officious boy, strikes her down. Pisanio then reveals her identity; and in telling her story reveals also circumstances which prove her identity with the boy Fidele. Thus the interest of disguised Belarius, Arviragus, and Guiderius is thoroughly aroused; and when Pisanio goes on to expose the wicked purposes of Cloten, who is missing, Guiderius declares himself Cloten's slayer. Thereupon Cymbeline, who has just knighted him, feels bound to condemn him to death. The execution of this sentence is interrupted by Belarius, who is presently condemned too. He thereupon reveals the identity of the sons of Cymbeline and his own; and his statements are confirmed by conventional stage birth-marks. In the general thanksgiving which follows, Posthumus reveals himself as the missing hero of the battle. Iachimo confirms him; and is thereupon pardoned. Then the soothsayer expounds how all this solves the mysterious riddle, peace is proclaimed, and, in some savor of anticlimax, everybody is happy.

In this *dénouement,* we have specified twenty-four distinct stage situations. Over-elaborate as this is,—and tautologous, too, for the audience already knows pretty much all that is revealed,—it is such a feat of technical stage-craft as can be appreciated only by those who have tried to manage even a single situation as strong as the average of these. This last scene of *Cymbeline*, then, which demonstrates the deliberate nature of all the preceding confusion, is very remarkable. Without yielding to fantastic temptation, we may assert that, whatever the actual history of its composition, it is just such a deliberate feat of technical skill as on general principles we might expect from a great artist, stirred to tremendous effort by the stinging consciousness of creative lethargy. . . . (pp. 356-61)

In this respect, the last scene of *Cymbeline* proves typical of the whole play. From beginning to end, whatever its actual history, the play is certainly such as we might expect from an artist who, in spite of declining power, was determined to assert that he could still do better than ever. Thus viewed, if hardly otherwise, all its perversities become normal.

Not the least normal thing about the play, too, is the material of which its bewildering plot is composed. Very slight examination will show that *Cymbeline* is a tissue of motives, situations, and characters which in the earlier work of Shakspere proved theatrically effective. There is enough confusion of identity for a dozen of the early comedies; and the disguised characters are headed, as of old, by the familiar heroine in hose and doublet. Posthumus, Iachimo, and Cloten revive the second comic motive—later a tragic one—of self-deception. At least in the matter of jealousy and villainy, too, Posthumus and Iachimo recall Othello and Iago. In the potion and the death-like sleep of Imogen, we have again the death-like sleep of Juliet. In the villainous queen, we have another woman, faintly recalling both Lady Macbeth and the daughters of King Lear. In the balancing of this figure by the pure one of Imogen, we have a suggestion of Cordelia's dramatic value. And so on. If, in some fantastic moment, we could imagine that Shakspere, like Wagner, had written music-dramas, giving to each character, each situation, each mood, its own musical motive, we should find in *Cymbeline* hardly any new strain.

The symphonic harmonies in which the old strains combined, however, would themselves seem new; for the mood of *Cymbeline* has a quality which, except in feebly tentative *Pericles*, we have not found before. *Cymbeline* leads its characters through experiences which have all the gloom of tragedy; but the inexorable fate of tragedy is here no longer, and ultimately all emerge into a region of romantic serenity. In *Cymbeline*, men wait; and in spite of their errors and their follies, all at last goes well. (pp. 361-62)

To a reader, and still more to an enthusiastic student, *Cymbeline* has the fascinating trait of at once demanding and rewarding study. On the stage, however, compared with the best of Shakspere's earlier plays, it is tiresome. For this there are two reasons: it contains too much,—its complexity of both substance and style overcrowds it throughout; and, with all its power, it lacks not only the simplicity of greatness, but also the ease of spontaneous imagination. It has amazing cunningness of plot; its characters are individually constructed; its atmosphere is varied and sometimes—particularly in the mountain scenes—plausible; its style abounds in final phrases. Throughout, however, it is laborious. Just as in *Twelfth Night*, for all its recapitulation, one feels constant spontaneity, so in every line of *Cymbeline* one is somehow aware of Titanic effort.

In brief, then, *Cymbeline* seems the work of a consciously older man than the Shakspere whom we have known. As such, it takes a distinct place in our study. In thus placing it, to be sure, we must guard against certainty. At best, our results must be conjectural; and we have no external evidence to confirm us. Always remembering that we may not assert our notions true, however, we are free to state and to believe them. (pp. 363-64)

We may imagine Shakspere, then, with disdainful technical mastery of stage-craft and of style, sweeping together all manner of old material which had proved itself effective. We may imagine him combining this in a new form,—more comprehensive, more varied, more intricately skilful, and in the ultimate sweetness of its romantic harmony more significant than

any form in which he had previously used its components. The result we may imagine to be *Cymbeline*. Though in *Cymbeline*, however, Shakspere's power, compared with any other man's, remain supreme, it does not, for all his pains, rise to its own highest level. Vast though it be, it cannot conceal the effort at last involved in its exertion. In this effort, one feels the absence of his old spontaneity. Here, if nowhere else, *Cymbeline* reveals unmistakable symptoms of creative decadence. (p. 364)

> Barrett Wendell, *"The Plays of Shakspere, from 'Cymbeline' to 'Henry VIII',"* in his William Shakspere: A Study in Elizabethan Literature, *Charles Scribner's Sons, 1894, pp. 355-94.*

BERNARD SHAW   (essay date 1896)

[*Shaw, an Irish dramatist and critic, was the major English playwright of his generation. In his Shakespearean criticism, he consistently attacked what he considered to be Shakespeare's inflated reputation as a dramatist. Shaw did not hesitate to judge the characters in the plays by the standards of his own values and prejudices, and much of his commentary is presented—as the prominent Shaw critic Edwin Wilson once remarked—"with an impudence that had not been seen before, nor is likely to be seen again." Shaw's hostility towards Shakespeare's work was due in large measure to his belief that it was interfering with the acceptance of Henrik Ibsen and the new social theater he so strongly advocated. The following excerpt is from a review of a production of* Cymbeline *staged by Henry Irving in 1896. Shaw's irritation with the public adulation of Shakespeare is expressed in a famous stream of vitriol, climaxing with the wish "to dig him up and throw stones at him, knowing as I do how incapable he and his worshippers are of understanding any less obvious form of indignity." He dismisses* Cymbeline *as a vulgar melodrama, of little value except for a few of the characters. While such nineteenth-century critics as August Wilhelm Schlegel (1811), William Hazlitt (1817), Anna Brownell Jameson (1833), G. G. Gervinus (1849-50), Algernon Charles Swinburne (1880), and Helena Faucit (1882) all regarded Imogen as a sublime figure, Shaw argues that there are two aspects of this character: one he terms "an enchanting person of the most delicate sensitiveness"; the other he views as a priggish figure in whom "virtuous indignation is chronic." For twentieth-century commentary on Imogen, see the excerpts by E. K. Chambers (1907), Brander Matthews (1913), Harley Granville-Barker (1930), G. Wilson Knight (1947), Harold C. Goddard (1951), and Robin Moffet (1962).*]

I confess to a difficulty in feeling civilized just at present. Flying from the country, where the gentlemen of England are in an ecstasy of chicken-butchering, I return to town to find the higher wits assembled at a play three hundred years old, in which the sensation scene exhibits a woman waking up to find her husband reposing gorily in her arms with his head cut off.

Pray understand, therefore, that I do not defend "Cymbeline." It is for the most part stagey trash of the lowest melodramatic order, in parts abominably written, throughout intellectually vulgar, and, judged in point of thought by modern intellectual standards, vulgar, foolish, offensive, indecent, and exasperating beyond all tolerance. There are moments when one asks despairingly why our stage should ever have been cursed with this "immortal" pilferer of other men's stories and ideas, with his monstrous rhetorical fustian, his unbearable platitudes, his pretentious reduction of the subtlest problems of life to commonplaces against which a Polytechnic debating club would revolt, his incredible unsuggestiveness, his sententious combination of ready reflection with complete intellectual sterility, and his consequent incapacity for getting out of the depth of even the most ignorant audience, except when he solemnly says something so transcendently platitudinous that his more humble-minded hearers cannot bring themselves to believe that so great a man really meant to talk like their grandmothers. With the single exception of Homer, there is no eminent writer, not even Sir Walter Scott, whom I can despise so entirely as I despise Shakespeare when I measure my mind against his. The intensity of my impatience with him occasionally reaches such a pitch, that it would positively be a relief to me to dig him up and throw stones at him, knowing as I do how incapable he and his worshippers are of understanding any less obvious form of indignity. To read ''Cymbeline'' and to think of Goethe, of Wagner, of Ibsen, is, for me, to imperil the habit of studied moderation of statement which years of public responsibility as a journalist have made almost second nature in me.

But I am bound to add that I pity the man who cannot enjoy Shakespeare. He has outlasted thousands of abler thinkers, and will outlast a thousand more. His gift of telling a story (provided some one else told it to him first); his enormous power over language, as conspicuous in his senseless and silly abuse of it as in his miracles of expression; his humour; his sense of idiosyncratic character; and his prodigious fund of that vital energy which is, it seems, the true differentiating property behind the faculties, good, bad, or indifferent, of the man of genius, enable him to entertain us so effectively that the imaginary scenes and people he has created become more real to us than our actual life—at least, until our knowledge and grip of actual life begins to deepen and glow beyond the common. When I was twenty I knew everybody in Shakespeare, from Hamlet to Abhorson, much more intimately than I knew my living contemporaries; and to this day, if the name of Pistol or Polonius catches my eye in a newspaper, I turn to the passage with more curiosity than if the name were that of—but perhaps I had better not mention any one in particular.

How many new acquaintances, then, do you make in reading ''Cymbeline,'' provided you have the patience to break your way into it through all the fustian, and are old enough to be free from the modern idea that Cymbeline must be the name of a cosmetic and Imogen of the latest scientific discovery in the nature of a hitherto unknown gas? Cymbeline is nothing; his queen nothing, though some attempt is made to justify her description as ''a woman that bears all down with her brain'' [II. i. 53-4]; Posthumus, nothing—most fortunately, as otherwise he would be an unendurably contemptible hound; Belarius, nothing—at least, not after Kent in ''King Lear'' (just as the Queen is nothing after Lady Macbeth); Iachimo, not much—only a *diabolus ex machina* made plausible; and Pisanio, less than Iachimo. On the other hand, we have Cloten, the prince of numbskulls, whose part, indecencies and all, is a literary masterpiece from the first line to the last; the two princes—fine presentments of that impressive and generous myth, the noble savage; Caius Lucius, the Roman general, urbane among the barbarians; and, above all, Imogen. But do, please, remember that there are two Imogens. One is a solemn and elaborate example of what, in Shakespeare's opinion, a real lady ought to be. With this unspeakable person virtuous indignation is chronic. Her object in life is to vindicate her own propriety and to suspect everybody else's, especially her husband's. Like Lothaw in the jeweller's shop in Bret Harte's burlesque novel, she cannot be left alone with unconsidered trifles of portable silver without officiously assuring the proprietors that she has stolen naught, nor would not, though she had found gold strewed i' the floor. Her fertility and spontaneity in nasty ideas is not to be described: there is hardly a speech

in her part that you can read without wincing. But this Imogen has another one tied to her with ropes of blank verse (which can fortunately be cut)—the Imogen of Shakespeare's genius, an enchanting person of the most delicate sensitiveness, full of sudden transitions from ecstasies of tenderness to transports of childish rage, and reckless of consequences in both, instantly hurt and instantly appeased, and of the highest breeding and courage. But for this Imogen, ''Cymbeline'' would stand about as much chance of being revived now as ''Titus Andronicus.'' (pp. 339-40)

> *Bernard Shaw, ''Blaming the Bard,'' in* The Saturday Review, *London, Vol. 82, No. 2135, September 26, 1896, pp. 339-41.*

E. K. CHAMBERS   (essay date 1907)

[*Chambers occupies a transitional position in Shakespearean criticism, one which connects the biographical sketches and character analyses of the nineteenth century with the historical, technical, and textual criticism of the twentieth century. While a member of the education department at Oxford University, Chambers earned his reputation as a scholar with his multivolume works,* The Medieval Stage *(1903) and* The Elizabethan Stage *(1923), while he also edited* The Red Letter Shakespeare *(1904-08). Chambers investigated both the purpose and limitations of each dramatic genre as Shakespeare presented it and speculated on how the dramatist's work was influenced by contemporary historical issues and his own frame of mind. In the excerpt below, taken from his introduction to the 1907 Red Letter edition of* Cymbeline, *Chambers takes issue with Ashley H. Thorndike's theory (see Additional Bibliography) that Shakespeare's play is indebted to Beaumont and Fletcher's* Philaster, *claiming that although the hypothesis is interesting, it cannot be sustained by the available evidence regarding the chronology of the two plays. He also notes that elements of the romance tradition—present in both* Cymbeline *and* Philaster—*were ''neither the invention of Shakespeare nor of Beaumont and Fletcher,'' but ''had long been common form in the narrative romances both of the middle ages and of the Renascence.'' Other commentators who have discussed the parallels between* Philaster *and* Cymbeline *include Brander Matthews (1913) and Arthur C. Kirsch (1972). In additional refutation of Thorndike's thesis, Chambers contends that the ''mere desire to rival others in exploiting a dramatic convention'' is insufficient to explain the drastic change in Shakespeare's philosophy and manner of writing that is reflected in the romances as a whole. Instead, adopting a biographical approach similar to that of Barrett Wendell (1894) and George Brandes (see Additional Bibliography), Chambers postulates that Shakespeare suffered some ''spiritual crisis'' or physical illness before he composed the romances which changed his attitudes towards life and art, and which resulted in works of ''relaxed mental energies, shrinking from the effort after the wrought and nervous rhythms of the past.'' On another matter, whereas the majority of nineteenth-century critics adulated Imogen and G. G. Gervinus (1849-50) assessed her as one of the most completely developed of all Shakespeare's characters, Chambers regards her as a puppet, who ''may pass for perfection so long as the danger of comparison with the flesh and blood of a Cleopatra or even of a Cressida is scrupulously avoided.''*]

Recognition has long been given to the fact that the three last plays completed by Shakespeare, *Cymbeline, The Winter's Tale,* and *The Tempest,* together with *Pericles,* for which he can only in part be responsible, form a distinct group among his works, and are marked by certain qualities of temper and outlook upon life which differentiate them rather sharply from their immediate predecessors. It is a far cry indeed from the later tragedies, with their remorseless analysis of human frailties and their sombre interrogation of human destiny, to the serene optimism which slowly directs the travail of a Hermione [in *The Winter's*

Tale] or an Imogen to its golden close, or to the solemn vindication of an overruling Providence through the symbolism of Prospero's triumphant magic [in *The Tempest*]. Hardly less is the gulf between the imperishable phrasing, cast in monumental bronze, of *Antony and Cleopatra,* and the facile and disordered prettinesses, which hang about the relaxed and structureless periods of the later plays. A recent thesis [proposed by Ashley H. Thorndike; see Additional Bibliography], supported by a fund of learning and a gift of critical perception that command all respect, endeavours to trace this fundamental change in Shakespeare's dramatic methods to the growing reputation of Beaumont and Fletcher, and to the fresh stimulus afforded to the imagination of the older poet by the need of catching the trick of romantic writing which his younger rivals had brought into vogue. In particular it is suggested that *Cymbeline* owes its inspiration to *Philaster,* the elements of whose plot it reproduces in a new and ingenious combination, while the slandered and disguised Imogen has her double prototype in the slandered Arethusa and the disguised Bellario.

It would be easier to determine the question of priority if there were less uncertainty as to the chronology of the plays produced by the King's men during the first Jacobean decade; in the present state of the evidence upon that subject, it is hardly possible to go beyond guess-work. There is nothing, for example, to show whether, as a matter of fact, *Philaster* preceded or followed *Cymbeline;* and therefore, so far as there is anything in the nature of direct imitation between the two plays, it may have been either on the one side or on the other. I am not myself impressed, in actually reading the two plays, by a sense of direct imitation to anything like the extent which a formal comparative analysis of their motives suggests. Apart from any such issue, it may freely be admitted that the general scope of the later tragicomedies of Shakespeare and that of the early tragicomedies of Beaumont and Fletcher is much the same. They have many devices of construction and many types of character in common. Wickedness triumphs for a time, but never in the end. Truth and chastity pass through the furnace and come out unstained. Any lie, however improbable, finds temporary acceptance. The happiness of lovers is broken by intrigues and misunderstandings, and restored by fortunate discoveries. Heroines conceal themselves in the garb of pages and endure moving accidents by flood and field. Children are lost and found again. Ancient feuds and shattered friendships come to reconciliation in the fullness of time. The woods prove less savage than the court, and the pomp of kings is contrasted to its disadvantage with pastoral content. The tyrannical father, the cruel step-mother, the devoted wife, the credulous lover, the loutish rival, the wanton maid of honour, the faithful servant, all play their parts. The salad is variously compounded and flavoured, but the ingredients are always the same. They belong to the formulae, not of life, but of romance. The opportunities which they afford for dramatic situations and for sentimental embroidery seem to have made them especially dear to Jacobean audiences. But obviously they are neither the invention of Shakespeare nor of Beaumont and Fletcher. They had long been common form in the narrative romances both of the middle ages and of the Renascence; and the earlier dramatists themselves, even if less continuously and with less abundance of rhetoric and pathos, had freely exploited them. So far as Shakespeare is concerned, many of the individual incidents and motives of *Cymbeline* can readily be paralleled from former plays; what is new is the emphasis with which they are selected and arranged.

In adopting tragicomedy as, for him, the final dramatic expression of life, Shakespeare was, in a sense, returning to a way of dramatic writing which he had first experimentally essayed in *The Two Gentlemen of Verona* and *The Merchant of Venice,* had then used to provide an emotional background to the comedy of *As You Like It* and *Twelfth Night,* had allowed to become conspicuous and questionable in *Much Ado About Nothing,* and had finally rejected with the unsmiling satire of *Measure for Measure* and *All's Well that Ends Well.* In the storm and stress of the great tragedies there is naturally no room left for the happy ending. The new tragicomedy succeeds in steering clear of certain technical faults upon which the old was apt to be wrecked. So conventional a representation of life can only maintain itself by being consistent. If it is brought into contact with the touchstone of real humanity, it ceases to persuade. This is an artistic principle which Shakespeare had not always grasped. In *The Two Gentlemen of Verona,* the reality of Proteus, imaging in the play the poet's own unstable friend, puts to shame the hollow artifices of the concluding scene. Still more, in *Much Ado About Nothing,* does the melodrama of Claudio and Hero pale into unconvincingness beside the exuberant vitality of Beatrice and her Benedick. There is no such mistake in *Cymbeline.* This is to be a symbolical and idealized rendering of life, and there must be no such clashing of dramatic planes as would result from the intrusion of an actual transcript taken from the book of life itself. Shakespeare works with puppets throughout; and the puppet Imogen, set between the puppet Cloten and the puppet Posthumus, may pass for perfection, so long as the danger of comparison with the flesh and blood of a Cleopatra or even of a Cressida is scrupulously avoided.

The chief difficulty in the theory, which traces the characteristics of Shakespeare's last dramatic manner to the imitation of Beaumont and Fletcher, seems to me to lie in its failure to account for the profound change of spiritual mood which underlies the transition from tragedy to romance. For years the soul of Shakespeare had trodden the abyss of vexed and gloomy speculation. From the questionings of *Macbeth* he had passed to the denials of *King Lear,* and had seen love of woman as the scourge of the world in *Antony and Cleopatra,* and honour of man as the mask of the egoist in *Coriolanus.* The last echo of the Titanic denunciation is in the half incoherent mutterings of *Timon of Athens;* and then, tentatively at first in *Pericles,* but fully and without hesitation in *Cymbeline,* comes this entirely new utterance, the expression of a mind at peace with itself and ready to accept the ordering of things with the contented optimism of an unembarrassed faith. *Cymbeline* is, as it were, a palinode to *King Lear.* The radiant whiteness of Cordelia, impotent of old to make head against the forces of evil, revisits earth again in Imogen, and broods like a dove over a *dénouement* in which unspotted purity and simple honesty come in the ultimate issue, after much vexation, to their own. The unanswered cosmic problems are laid aside, or take on new colours in the light of a regained faith. Life, which the purged eye once scanned with a splendid despair, is now seen only through a golden haze of sentiment. The broken harmonies are resolved before the close. A great and gracious peace descends upon the autumn of thought—

> Fear no more the heat of the sun,
>   Nor the furious winter's rages;
> Thou thy worldly task hast done,
>   Home art gone and ta'en thy wages.
>
> [IV. ii. 258-61]

What is remarkable is not, of course, that the tragic mood should come to an end, and the perturbed spirit find rest at last; but rather that the change should come so suddenly, presenting itself as a breach of continuity instead of as the natural term of a logical process of mental growth. Up to this point Shakespeare's development has been intelligible enough. Play has led on to play by sensible and regular gradations. The blossoming and fruitage of his art, however astonishing, have none the less formed an organic whole. And now the links are broken. Something inexplicable has intervened, and without hint or warning the whole outlook of the poet has changed. He accepts where he denied; blesses where he banned. The universe, which but a moment ago he reviewed and judged to be chaos, now spreads itself out before his eyes as the ordered and sunlit garden of God. I hope to give all credit to the critical principle which bids us remember that Shakespeare, in addition to being a great poet, was also an expert and adroit stage-manager. But I do not find it possible to ascribe so fundamental a metamorphosis to a mere desire to rival others in exploiting a dramatic convention. . . . There must be more in it than this. The profound cleavage in Shakespeare's mental history about 1607-1608 must have been due to some spiritual crisis the nature of which it is only possible dimly to conjecture; some such process as that which in the psychology of religion bears the name of conversion; or perhaps some sickness of the brain which left him an old man, freed at last from the fever of speculation and well disposed to spend the afternoon of life in unexacting and agreeable dreams. This latter hypothesis would help also to explain the marked change of style which accompanies the change of dramatic purpose in the romances. In these complicated and incoherent periods, in these softened and unaccentuated rhythms, in these tender and evanescent beauties, I find less a deliberate attempt to reduce the declamation of the stage to the colloquial dialogue of daily life, than the natural outcome of relaxed mental energies, shrinking from the effort after the wrought and nervous rhythms of the past. (pp. 286-93)

> E. K. Chambers, "'Cymbeline'," in his Shakespeare: A Survey, 1925. Reprint by Hill and Wang, 1958, pp. 286-94.

WALTER RALEIGH   (essay date 1907)

[Raleigh was a professor of English literature at Oxford and an essayist, literary critic, and biographer who employed a humanistic approach in his work. In addition to biographies of Milton, Wordsworth, Robert Louis Stevenson, and Shakespeare, he published several works on Johnson and on the English novel. Whereas such nineteenth-century critics as August Wilhelm Schlegel (1811), William Hazlitt (1817), Anna Brownell Jameson (1833), and Denton J. Snider (1890) all argued that Cymbeline is a skillfully designed play, Raleigh's brief comment excerpted below signals the beginning of a movement away from that judgment. He endorses Samuel Johnson's castigation of Cymbeline (see excerpt above, 1765), declaring that Johnson was speaking "truly and moderately"; this assessment is echoed by such other early twentieth-century critics as Horace Howard Furness (1913), William Witherle Lawrence (1920), Harley Granville-Barker (1930), and Arthur Symons (see Additional Bibliography).]

In general, it is true to say that Shakespeare cheerfully burdens himself with a plot which is either very complex, or very artificial, or both, and then goes to work to make a living thing of it. His care for probability is least in his latest plays. Towards the beginning of his career he wrote The Comedy of Errors, which is a story of two pairs of twin brothers, each pair so exactly alike that no one can tell them apart. Towards the close he wrote Cymbeline, of which Johnson speaks truly and mod-

erately when he says: "This play has many just sentiments, some natural dialogues, and some pleasing scenes, but they are obtained at the expense of much incongruity. To remark the folly of the fiction, the absurdity of the conduct, the confusion of the names and manners of different times, and the impossibility of the events in any system of life, were to waste criticism upon unresisting imbecility, upon faults too evident for detection, and too gross for aggravation" [see excerpt above, 1765]. (p. 142)

> Walter Raleigh, "Story and Character," in his Shakespeare, Macmillan and Co., Limited, 1907, pp. 128-208.

HORACE HOWARD FURNESS   (essay date 1913)

[Furness was an American lawyer who abandoned law to devote his life to Shakespearean studies. In 1871 he became the first editor of the New Variorum edition of Shakespeare's works with the publication of Romeo and Juliet. Eighteen volumes appeared under his editorship, all of which draw heavily on the First Folio of 1623. The value of Furness's work rests on his extensive textual, critical, and annotative notes derived from the best authorities of the time. Cymbeline was the last play he edited in this series, having completed the introduction only days before his death. Whereas such earlier critics as Alexander Pope (1723), George Steevens (1793), and Frederick Gard Fleay (see Additional Bibliography) questioned the authenticity of the vision scene in Act V, Scene iv of Cymbeline, Furness is the first commentator to propose that significantly large portions of the play were the work of someone other than Shakespeare. By his own admission, he takes "the uncritical position" of crediting Shakespeare with "all that is good and abandoning to the unknown assistant all that is weak or trivial." Harley Granville-Barker (1930) also contends that Shakespeare worked with a collaborator on this play. Furness is persuaded that Samuel Johnson's condemnation of Cymbeline (see excerpt above, 1765) is justified—so long as it is applied to those parts of the play he considers not authentic. Other early twentieth-century critics who endorse Johnson's comments include Walter Raleigh (1907), William Witherle Lawrence (1920), Granville-Barker, and Arthur Symons (see Additional Bibliography). Furness especially disparages those passages containing "jingling" rhymes and a "jarring tag," or expressions of sentiment he believes are wholly incongruous with the speaker's character. Also, where earlier scholars had paid scant attention to the figure of Belarius, Furness asserts that he is "a sanctimonious braggart" whose treachery toward Cymbeline is compounded by his demand for recompense for his years of nurturing the king's sons. For further discussion of the character of Belarius, see the excerpt by Douglas L. Peterson (1973).]

'This play has many just sentiments, some natural dialogues, and some pleasing scenes, but they are obtained at the expense of much incongruity.

'To remark the folly of the fiction, the absurdity of the conduct, the confusion of the names and manners of different times, and the impossibility of the events in any system of life were to waste criticism upon unresisting imbecility, upon faults too evident for detection, and too gross for aggravation' [see excerpt above by Samuel Johnson, 1765]. Time was when my youthful eyes were dazzled by the charms of Imogen, that my only comment on this note by Dr. Johnson was irrepressible laughter,—so stately was it in its language, so patronising in its tone, and so purblind in its appreciation of one whose name Dr. Johnson could never, never have imagined would be pronounced 'the greatest in all literature.' Time brings in its revenges, however, and if grizzling hair the brain doth clear, what clarifying results may not be expected from hair snow-white? It is even so. Laughter died away into a smile, the smile lapsed into a sad brow, and the wrinkled brow into a vague assent. Ay, Dr. Johnson was right in his estimate of this play of *Cymbeline,*—the sweetest, tenderest, profoundest of almost all the immortal galaxy.

If, then, this play be open to such a criticism as Dr. Johnson's, which by one eminent critic has been pronounced 'true' and even moderate [see excerpt above by Walter Raleigh, 1907], whence comes then this deterioration? It can be only indirectly due to advancing years. Although forty-six years of age can hardly inaugurate physical or intellectual senility, yet into that span there may have been compressed an emotional life far outspanning the Psalmist's threescore years and ten. Indeed, it is not difficult to fancy that at this period there may have crept into Shakespeare's study of imagination a certain weariness of soul in contemplating in review the vast throng of his dream-children. What possible joy can thrill the human breast that he has not experienced and revealed? What pain or anguish, remorse or guilt that can rack the soul has he not vicariously borne? And now a sufficing harvest of fame is his, and honest wealth, accompanied by honour, love, obedience, and troops of friends. Thus at last, safe moored within a waveless bay, what more has life to offer?

But inaction is not rest, and I can most reverently fancy that he is once more allured by the joy of creation when by chance there falls in his way the old, old story of a husband convinced, through villainy, of his wife's infidelity. Thereupon there begins to live and breathe before him the heavenly Imogen, fair as Miranda [in *The Tempest*], in colour warmer than Hermione [in *The Winter's Tale*]. The woman tempted him and he fell,—to the infinite happiness of all.

For a secondary plot anything will do, only let its scene and time be remote enough to allow free scope in manners and customs. Holinshed, the faithful old standby, will quickly enough furnish all that is needed. As for the tedious drudgery of the minor characters, is there not many a friend who will assume all this portion of the task? . . . There are scenes on scenes in many of the Plays which no love for Shakespeare can be so blind as not to see that they could never have been written by him. . . . Thus, then, I believe that *Cymbeline* grew,—the joint work of two minds; and in studying it the uncritical position is forced on us of claiming for Shakespeare all that is good and abandoning to the unknown assistant all that is weak or trivial, or, in short, all that Dr. Johnson condemns.

Regarded broadly, I believe that the Imogen love story and all that immediately touched it interested Shakespeare deeply; the Cymbeline portion was turned over to the assistant, who at times grew vainglorious and inserted here and there, even on the ground sacred to Imogen, lines and sentiments that shine by their dulness. Nay, one whole character was, I think, confided to him. It is Belarius—who bored Shakespeare. To rehabilitate that hoary scoundrel was not (I may not say) too great a task for Shakespeare, but one that would divert him from fairer and more entrancing subjects. He, therefore, permitted his fellow-craftsman to convert into a sanctimonious braggart a man who, for a personal affront, committed a crime against humanity as black as may be found, and an act of treachery against the State so foul that death by torture would have been, for that era, the sole amends. This treason Belarius did not commit unwittingly. He knew it was treason and acknowledged it. And he knew well enough that in stealing the King's sons he crushed a father's heart, and the more agonising the father's tears, the more highly he exulted in his success.

And finally, as the lowest abysm of his baseness, he has the brazen effrontery to demand of Cymbeline payment in cash for his sons' board during all the years they have been stolen. To be sure, he adds that he will return the money as soon as it is paid. Not he. Once a thief, always a thief. He is not for an instant to be trusted.

Of course, I would not be understood as asserting that Shakespeare had no part or lot in the Holinshed scenes. Here and there throughout our course, first on one side and then on the other, we feel the unerring noiseless stroke that keeps the canoe headed straight for the goal.

In the Fifth Act a masque is given, which from Pope's day to the present is regarded by a large majority of editors and critics as an intrusive insertion by some hand not Shakespeare's. Steevens termed it 'contemptible nonsense' [see excerpt above, 1793]. . . . In discussing his treatment of the Text, Pope, in his excellent *Preface,* explains that 'some suspected passages which are excessively bad and which seem interpolations by being so inserted that one can entirely omit them without any chasm, or deficiency in the context, are degraded to the bottom of the page.' To this degradation to the foot of his page Pope has subjected the whole of this 'excessively bad' masque. If an audacious hand has thus dared to thrust its fingers into one of Shakespeare's wonderful scenes, and interpolate nigh a hundred lines, may we not suspect that no sense of sacrilege would restrain it from similar interpolations elsewhere? I do not say it is always the same hand, but it is *a* hand which had a faith in its own cunning greater than in Shakespeare's. And it is these intrusions, sometimes inane and sometimes silly, which in the aggregate possibly prompted some of the allusions in Dr. Johnson's criticism.

No consideration for the solemnity of hour or for consistency of character restrains the interpolator, who had evidently a knack for rhyming, and liked a jingle at the end of a scene. For instance, in the [Fifth] Scene of the First Act, when the desperate character of the Queen is for the first time fully revealed to us in all its enormity, and there are dark intimations that Imogen is to be killed by poison, she sounds Pisanio to see if she can make him her accomplice, and leaves him with the ominous expression, uttered with penetrating significance, 'Think on my words!' [I. v. 75]. After the door has closed behind her Pisanio says, with equal significance, 'And shall do!' [I. v. 85] and we receive instant relief in this assurance that he sees through her evil designs, and will remain staunch and true to Imogen and to Posthumus. And then comes in the interloper with his jarring tag:

> *But when to my good lord, I prove untrue*
> *I'll choke myself; there's all I'll do for you.*
>
> [I. v. 86-7]

Were this play a comedy, these lines would be well enough. They superfluously make assurance double sure. But the atmosphere is as tragic up to the very last scene as any downright tragedies; there is not a comic character in it, and to give a comic turn to any speech of Pisanio, on whose weary, faithful shoulders so much of the tragedy rests, is, as it seems to me, utterly unShakespearian.

Again, it is rather too late a day to urge the truth to themselves of all of Shakespeare's characters; they are always perfectly consistent; they may in fleeting expressions bear the impress of Elizabethan times, as Imogen in her intensest agony may refer to Æneas and to Sinon, whose faithful stories were told in the pictured tapestries of her childhood, and whose names instinctively now rise to her lips as best expressing her breaking heart. But what I mean is that Shakespeare does not put ethical problems of life into the mouth of a born fool or stupid dolt. Yet, mark the following passage, and say, if you can, that Shakespeare ever could have wished us to believe that an 'ass' like Cloten—who cannot take two from twenty, for his heart and leave eighteen—could have moralised the time and the effect of saint-seducing gold:

> *Cloten*. If she be up, I'll speak with her: if not
> Let her lie still and dream: by your leave, ho.
> I know her women are about her: what
> If I do line one of their hands, 'tis gold
> Which buys admittance (oft it doth) *yea, and makes*
> *Diana's rangers false themselves, yield up*
> *Their deer to th' stand o' th' stealer: and 'tis gold*
> *Which makes the true-man kill'd, and saves the thief.*
> *Nay sometimes hangs both Thief, and true-man: what*
> *Can it not do and undo? I will make*
> *One of her women lawyer to me, for*
> *I yet not understand the case my selfe.*
> By your leave.
>
> [II. iii. 64-76]

There are instances, possibly even more gross than this, where sentiments utterly foreign to their characters or to their experience in life are ascribed to the speakers. Thus, in the exquisite lament over Imogen by young Arviragus, whose thoughts dwell on the flower-like beauty of his lovely sister, and he tells of pale primroses, and the azured harebells, and the leafy eglantine with which he could cover her, and then—

> the ruddock would
> With charitable bill (*O bill sore-shaming*
> *Those rich-left heirs that let their fathers lie*
> *Without a monument*).
>
> [IV. ii. 224-27]

Had the interpolator no wit, manners, nor modesty to put such a simile into the mouth of a sorrowing youth who had been from his swathing clothes housed in a rock? And, as though unwilling that Arviragus should be solitary in the use of impossible allusions, the interpolator gives to Guiderius a reference which is quite as foreign to any possible knowledge that the mountain-bred youth could have acquired. It is in the same scene a few lines further on, where the younger brother proposes to sing the Dirge, although their voices have got the mannish crack. . . . Guiderius, however, refuses to attempt to sing, but says:

> I'll weepe and word it with thee,
> *For notes of sorrow, out of tune, are worse*
> *Than Priests and Fanes that lie.*
>
> [IV. ii. 240-42]

Apart from the absurdity (of which Shakespeare could never, never, never have been guilty) that a false note in music betokened false sorrow, what could Guiderius have known of priests, be they truthful or lying? Or what of fanes, either hallowed or fictitious, when he had never seen a church? Not of such are Shakespeare's oversights made. (pp. v-x)

Again, in this same scene, as Belarius and Guiderius are returning to the cave they hear the plaintive sighing of the 'solemn music' of an Æolian harp, and Belarius exclaims,

Act II. Scene ii. Iachimo and Imogen. Frontispiece to the Bell edition (1773). The Department of Rare Books and Special Collections, The University of Michigan Library.

> My ingenious instrument!
> Hark, Polydore, it sounds! But what occasion
> Hath Cadwal now to give it motion? Hark!
>   *Guiderius*. Is he at home?
>   *Belarius*. He went from hence even now.
>   *Guiderius*. What does he mean? since death of my
>   dear'st Mother
> It did not speak before. All solemn things
> Should answer solemn accidents. *The matter?*
> *Triumphs for nothing and lamenting toys*
> *Is jollity for apes and grief for boys.*
> Is Cadwal mad?
>
> [IV. ii. 186-95]

After such exhibitions of pressing in where angels tread, can we be surprised that a jingling tag, with the monotonous rhyme of 'must' and 'dust,' is appended to three of the stanzas of 'The Dirge'? After the first stanza is there, in the assertion that 'golden lads and girls all must like chimney-sweepers come to dust' [IV. ii. 262-63], a feeble jocosity intended in the reference to the dust of the chimney-sweeper's bag? No suggestion is too trifling or too bad. And any one who would believe that Shakespeare could have written the lack-luster line 'All lovers young, *all lovers must*' [IV. ii. 273-74] will believe anything. (pp. xi-xii)

Rhymes occurring in blank verse are suspicious, especially if pompously enunciating a commonplace. Thus,

>   *Imogen.* Your life, good master,
> Must shuffle for itself.
>   *Lucius.* The boy disdains me,
> He leaves me, scorns me; *Briefly die their joys,*
> *That place them in the truth of girls and boys.*
> Why stands he so perplex'd?
>
> [V. v. 104-08]

The omission of the lines in italics leaves a hardly perceptible gap in the metre.

In the following passage I mistrust the concluding lines. It is in the First Scene of the last Act,—a scene whereof it is impossible to exaggerate the dramatic importance. We meet Posthumus for the first time since Iachimo's triumph and since his unpardonable distrust of Imogen and brutal commands to Pisanio. And although we have not seen him, yet every fresh sorrow that has befallen Imogen has quickened our hot anger against the cause of it. Now, however, as we draw towards a serene close of the tragedy, more lenient feelings towards Posthumus must be the harbingers of peace. We must see the devotion of a love so triumphant that every thought of sin is cast away and the object of it accepted by the throned gods. There must be the revelation of a repentance so profound that its only expiation is death; every phrase, every word must stamp this high resolve; and every phrase, every word that does not bear this stamp weakens the impression and blurs our sympathy.

>   Tis enough
> That, Britain, I have killed thy mistress-piece,
> I'll give no wound to thee. Therefore, good heavens,
> Hear patiently my purpose; I'll disrobe myself
> Of these Italian weeds, and suit myself
> As does a Britain peasant; so I'll fight
> Against the part I come with; so I'll die
> For thee, O Imogen, even for whom my life
> Is, every breath, a death; and this, unknown,
> Pitied nor hated, to the face of peril
> Myself I'll dedicate. *Let me make men know*
> *More valour in me than my habits show.*
> *Gods, put the strength o' the Leonati in me!*
> *To shame the guise of the world, I will begin*
> *The fashion less without and more within.*
>
> [V. i. 19-33]

Can anything allay the good precedence more effectually than these last four or five lines? It was not then, it appears, to die unknown and unpitied for Imogen's dear sake that he put on a peasant's dress, but to show off and make people stare. This braggart *poseur* would be dressed as a beggar and fight like a lion. Instead of seeking death, he would give it, and, by thus winning so much cheap admiration, he—*he,* whose every breath was death for Imogen's sake, would—Heaven save the mark!—set the fashion of bad clothes to offset good fighting!

The last line of the [Fifth] Scene of the Second Act jars in the reading, and seems to me an excrescence of the interpolator:

>   *Posthumus.* I'll write against them
> Detest them, curse them; yet 'tis greater skill
> In a true hate, to pray they have their will;
> *The very devils cannot plague them better.*
>
> [II. v. 32-5]

Were this a solitary example, it would not be worth the mention. It is given here for cumulative effect.

I doubt the genuineness of the whole of the following passage. Its metaphors are forced and involved, and in the reference to 'winds that sailors rail at' there is an allusion that no inland, mountain-bred youth would ever dream of:

>   *Arvir.* Nobly he yokes
> A smiling with a sigh; as if the sigh
> Was what it was, for not being such a smile;
> The smile mocking the sigh, that it would fly
> From so divine a temple, to commix
> With winds that sailors rail at.
>   *Guid.* I do note
> That grief and patience rooted in him both,
> Mingle their spurs together.
>   *Arvir.* Grow patience!
> And let the stinking elder, grief, untwine
> His perishing root with the increasing vine.
>   *Bel.* It is great morning—Come away!
>
> [IV. ii. 51-61]

Finally, the last scene of all has been most highly extolled for the marvelous dramatic skill wherewith all the characters, without any violation of probability, are brought together and all dramatic knots are untied. The scene is not, however, flawless. There are, I think, two passages where the trail of the interpolator may be traced. One is where the Soothsayer is called in to explain the 'label' which the interpolator had left on Posthumus's bosom; the label and its explanation are merely vapid; and as they are compressed within forty lines they may be stoically endured.

The other passage, however, involves a fault not so readily condoned, although in both cases the sovereign'st remedy is omission. If what Dr. Johnson said of *Henry the Eighth* be true, that 'the genius of Shakespeare comes in and goes out with Katherine,' it may be asserted, I think, with equal truth that in the present play this same genius comes in and goes out with Imogen. While she is before us we have eyes and ears and hearts and thoughts only for her. And as, in this last scene, we approach the crisis of her fate and mark her heaving breast, with her whole soul sitting in those eyes which are fastened on Iachimo, and every feature glowing in the triumph of a mystery now solved, and hear once more the tones of that dear voice, agonised yet heavenly, and, with her, we are smitten to the earth by that blind hand, who of us, who has ever felt what it is to love or be loved, but knows that with the first glimmer of returning consciousness there is the one sole impulse to spring into those arms, now stretched in staggering welcome, with the glad cry that here again was love as firm as earth's rocky base? Instead of this, what has the wretched interpolator given us? With reviving consciousness Imogen begins an unseemly squabble with Pisanio! About a drug! It made her ill! Then poor old doddering Cornelius must needs be brought forward, and must tell again in prosy words what he had told us all once before, even to the very same reference to 'cats and dogs' [V. v. 252]! All this while poor Posthumus has nothing to do but shift first on one foot and then on the other, and listen open-eyed to Imogen's quarrel about some mysterious poison. When at last Pisanio's and Cornelius's explanation has satisfied Imogen, and the curiosity of Belarius and Guiderius and Arviragus is allayed about the boy Fidele, then Imogen arises and, it is to be hoped, after carefully dusting her clothes (I marvel that the interpolator did not insert this tidy act as a stage direction), she turns at last to Posthumus.

Oxen and wainropes cannot hail me to the conviction that the passages which I have specified in the foregoing pages are Shakespeare's. Whose they are I care neither to know nor even to surmise. I know only that they are not Shakespeare's. (pp. xii-xv)

> *Horace Howard Furness, in a preface to* A New Variorum Edition of Shakespeare: The Tragedie of Cymbeline *by William Shakespeare, edited by Horace Howard Furness, J. B. Lippincott Company, 1913, pp. v-xx.*

BRANDER MATTHEWS   (essay date 1913)

[*An American scholar, educator, and novelist whose academic training was in the law, Matthews began his literary career by lecturing, contributing extensively to various periodicals, and writing plays. In 1900 he was appointed professor of dramatic literature at Columbia University, becoming the first person to hold such a title at any American university. His published works, including* The Development of the Drama *(1903),* Molière *(1910),* Shakspere as a Playwright *(1913), and* The Principles of Playmaking *(1919), reflect his interest in the practical as opposed to theoretical aspects of drama, and his writing on Shakespeare focuses on the dramatist's stagecraft and his theatrical rather than literary abilities. Although he was an academician for many years, Matthews had a wide influence on playwrights, critics, and the general public. In the following excerpt, he censures what he regards as the artificiality of* Cymbeline, *attributing this quality to Shakespeare's having patterned the play after the dramatic romances of Beaumont and Fletcher. Matthews also argues that Shakespeare's extensive use of soliloquies as expositions of dramatic background and descriptions of other characters indicates a decline in his skills as a psychologist and a playwright, a viewpoint similar to that expressed earlier by Barrett Wendell (1894). For other examinations of the artificial nature of* Cymbeline, *see the excerpts by Harley Granville-Barker (1930), Barbara A. Mowat (1966), R. A. Foakes (1971), and the essay by Arthur C. Kirsch cited in the Additional Bibliography. Like E. K. Chambers (1907), who called the characters of* Cymbeline *"puppets," Matthews charges that the dramatis personae have no autonomy, but are entirely shaped by the circumstances of the action. He asserts that whereas other Shakespearean heroines are "self-revealed" by their speeches and action, Imogen is principally delineated by what others in the play report about her. Matthews concludes that in this method of characterization Shakespeare was following "the unsound method brought into fashion by Beaumont and Fletcher." For further commentary on the relation between Shakespeare and these other dramatists, see the excerpts by Chambers and Arthur C. Kirsch (1972), as well as the essay by Ashley H. Thorndike cited in the Additional Bibliography.*]

Of the three dramatic-romances that Shakspere composed in imitation of Beaumont and Fletcher, 'Cymbeline' is the one which most emphatically conforms to the type as this had been worked out by the younger playwrights. It has the merits and the demerits inherent in the formula. It contains a laboriously complicated story abounding in surprises and barren of reality. It is as artificial as the 'Philaster' of Beaumont and Fletcher, which indeed seems to have served as its immediate pattern. It proves that Shakspere could be on occasion quite as ingeniously clever as the youthful collaborators whom he was emulating. It lacks the largeness of his great tragedies as it is devoid of the charm of his romantic-comedies. It contains no character, with the single exception of its lovely heroine, Imogen, who has won a place in the gallery of Shakspere's imperishable figures. Whatever its success when it was originally performed, it has been unable to keep itself on the stage, where it is seen now only at rare intervals and only because some

actress of authority wishes to risk herself in the alluring part of Imogen.

Of course the play is Shakspere's, after all is said, and there are many passages that only Shakspere could have written. When he composed this piece he was at his full maturity as a poet, and his wisdom also had ripened to enrich the dialogue of this arbitrary tale. There is no falling off here on the part of the poet or of the philosopher, even if there is a sad decline in the psychologist and the playwright. It is astounding that after the ample creation of character which compels our admiration in the great tragedies he should have been satisfied with the summary and perfunctory outlining which we discover in the persons who carry on this dramatic-romance. Here he is vying with the inventors of the type, and he outdoes them in reckless disregard of plausibility and of probability. The characters have no independent life; they are the slaves of the situation. What they say and what they do is rarely what they would say or do of their own volition; it is only what they have to say and do to make the plot work and to bring about the successive surprises.

And the decline in playmaking skill is equally evident. The play is full of feeble devices and of clumsy makeshifts of a simplicity which Shakspere had long outgrown and which he had discarded in his nobler plays, both tragic and comic. The exposition is pitiably ineffective when compared with the superb openings of 'Romeo and Juliet' and 'Hamlet,' of 'Othello' and 'Macbeth.' Shakspere sends on two gentlemen, that one of them may tell the audience what the other can hardly fail to know already. In like manner Belarius has a long soliloquy, wholly without excuse, and delivered solely to inform the spectators who he is himself and who are the two young men who think themselves his sons. The last dying speech and confession of the Queen is absurdly out of nature; and it is reported to us only to clear the way for the quick sequence of marvelous discoveries and recognitions which tumble over each other in the final scene. The whole plot has been articulated to lead up to these discoveries and recognitions, which come one after another with impossible rapidity. But despite all the care and trouble which has been spent on this arbitrary construction, the resulting scene is quite ineffective in the acting, for the plain reason that the discoveries and recognitions are astonishing only to the characters in the story, since they reveal nothing which the spectators do not know already. There is no element of expectancy or of suspense in the protracted series of situations. The audience has long foreseen how the play would end—indeed, how it had to end; and there is too little interest in any of the characters, excepting always Imogen, too little reality in the tale itself, to make the spectators care how the persons in the play will take the strange news which is revealed to them by character after character. (pp. 333-35)

The very skill with which Shakspere adjusts his story to the likings of the Jacobean audiences, whom Beaumont and Fletcher had accustomed to fantastic impossibility, has recoiled on him and made the piece repugnant to us nowadays. Especially repulsive to us is the main theme of the story, the monstrous wager which the husband makes with a casual stranger about his wife's chastity. Such an outrageous bet was all very well in the source where Shakspere found it; and it might have been possible enough in the Renascence Italy of Boccaccio. But its abhorrent grossness is inconceivable under the circumstances in which Shakspere presents it. There is an almost equal lack of truth in the interview between the would-be seducer and Imogen. Coming with a letter of introduction from her husband,

Iachimo proceeds at once to take away the character of Post-humus and to make love to Imogen. The psychology of the seducer is so summary here that it may fairly be called childish.

Even Imogen herself, who has found favor in the eyes of many dissatisfied with the play itself, is less subtly and less inge-niously presented than her sisters in the earlier romantic-com-edies. Swinburne has called her "the woman best beloved in all the world of song" [see excerpt above, 1880]; and yet in what she actually does before our eyes she is far inferior in vibrating femininity to Juliet and to Viola [in *Twelfth Night*]. She does and she says little more than what she is commanded to say and to do by the circumstances of the story of which she is the heroine. She is painted for us, and her character is delineated largely by what the other characters say about her, and only a little by what she says herself. Imogen is described rather than self-revealed, whereas Viola and Juliet are self-revealed rather than described. Viola and Juliet need no eulogy from the other characters and no commentary; they are what they are, and we know them by their own words and deeds. Here again Shakspere is obeying his pattern; he is surrendering his own sounder method of portraiture for the unsound method brought into fashion by Beaumont and Fletcher. (pp. 335-36)

Brander Matthews, "The Dramatic-Romances," in his *Shakspere as a Playwright, Charles Scribner's Sons, 1913, pp. 329-46.*

WILLIAM WITHERLE LAWRENCE   (essay date 1920)

[*Lawrence was an American educator and scholar. His* Shake-speare's Problem Comedies *(1931) marked the beginning of a twentieth-century reappraisal of Shakespeare's so-called problem plays. In the excerpt below, Lawrence analyzes the dramatic ac-tion of* Cymbeline *in terms of "the Elizabethan social conventions and literary traditions" contemporaneous with its composition. He contends that such an approach to the play can mitigate the negative criticism it has often received, especially with respect to Posthumus's behavior in the wager scene and in subsequent acts. Like Anna Brownell Jameson (1833), Lawrence maintains that the wager story is governed by a chivalric code developed in the Middle Ages and still accepted during Shakespeare's lifetime, and that, according to this code, Posthumus's acceptance of Iachimo's challenge is both appropriate and unavoidable. Lawrence further demonstrates that Posthumus's order to have Imogen murdered is consonant with the romance tradition, and thus an Elizabethan audience would not have censured his actions. He concludes that Shakespeare intended Posthumus to be "a blameless hero" and accounts for the lack of sympathy or even scorn with which he is generally regarded by pointing out the dearth of individual or natural additions to his character that might temper an audience's aversion. Finally, like such other early twentieth-century critics as Walter Raleigh (1907), Horace Howard Furness (1913), and Harley Granville-Barker (1930), Lawrence comments on Samuel Johnson's charges leveled against* Cymbeline *(see excerpt above, 1765); he generally agrees with Johnson, but only in regard to the incongruencies and "impossibility of events" in Acts III through V.*]

It has long been the fashion, when *Cymbeline* has been under discussion, to cite Dr. Johnson's famous criticism, and indeed one feels a whimsical joy in setting down so delightful a bit of square-toed dogmatism. "This play has many just senti-ments, some natural dialogues, and some pleasing scenes, but they are obtained at the expense of much incongruity. To re-mark the folly of the fiction, the absurdity of the conduct, the confusion of the names and manners of different times, and the impossibility of the events in any system of life, were to waste criticism upon unresisting imbecility, upon faults too

evident for detection, and too gross for aggravation" [see ex-cerpt above, 1765]. The really significant thing, however, which makes this opinion worth repeating, is that so many of the best modern critics have expressed substantial agreement with it. Sir Walter Raleigh thinks that "Johnson speaks truly and mod-erately" [see excerpt above, 1907] and Dr. H. H. Furness said, "Ay, Dr. Johnson was right in his estimate of this play of *Cymbeline,*—the sweetest, tenderest, profoundest of almost all the immortal galaxy" [see excerpt above, 1913]. Most writers, while not agreeing directly with Johnson, have taken a half-puzzled, half-apologetic attitude; they have obviously felt what Dr. Furness calls "deterioration" here, after the splendid achievement of the great tragedies and the Roman plays.

The purpose of the present paper is not to attempt a wholesale refutation of Johnson's charges, nor a defence of *Cymbeline* as a flawless work of art. This would require a degree of courage quite beyond the possession of the writer. There is too much truth and sense in Johnson's strictures to allow of their easy refutation. But it may very well be asked whether certain elements in the play which have been censured as blemishes are really such, after all; whether the critics from Johnson down, have not partly misunderstood Shakspere's intentions. This is not a new subject of discussion; the play has never lacked defenders. One problem, however, and a very important one for the piece as a whole, still awaits solution. There has never been, so far as my knowledge extends, a really adequate analysis of the chief episode of the main plot, the wager be-tween Posthumus Leonatus and Iachimo as to the chastity of Imogen, nor a wholly satisfactory treatment of the character and motives of Posthumus himself. (pp. 391-92)

The first thing which strikes one in reading comments on the play is the forgetfulness of critics that due allowance must be made for the social conventions of Shakspere's day, and of the earlier times when the wager-story was taking shape. . . . Post-humus and Imogen and Iachimo are too often treated as if they where persons of the nineteenth century, and their acts inter-preted like those of characters in a modern realistic novel, instead of a tale the outlines and spirit of which had been determined by centuries of literary and social tradition. (pp. 394-95)

The aim of the present paper, then, is to examine the main plot of *Cymbeline* in the light of Elizabethan social conventions and literary traditions. . . . How would the Elizabethans have understood it, as they saw it on the stage? In particular, what would they have thought of Posthumus Leonatus? Through such an analysis as this we shall, I hope, reach sound results, some of them of considerable importance. Chief of these is the substantial vindication of Posthumus, not, indeed, as a man without faults, but as blameless and even praiseworthy in ac-cepting the wager, and, in the later part of the play, one to be judged as, like Othello, "perplex'd in the extreme" [*Othello,* V. ii. 346] under great misfortune, and acting in accord with the ethics of his day and the conventions of romantic drama. Hardly less interesting will be the question why Posthumus has generally failed to arouse sympathy, and been regarded as weak and even vicious,—the answer to which can hardly be summed up in a single phrase. (pp. 395-96)

Our attempt to gain a better understanding of the situation in *Cymbeline* will be simplified if we first consider the wager-scene by itself, with its immediate consequences (Acts I and II), and then the later conduct of Posthumus (Acts III-IV). (p. 404)

The chivalric discussion at the house of Philario which Shakspere describes in *Cymbeline* is as different as possible from the contest between "philosophy" and the pride of a bourgeois merchant in an accomplished wife in the pages of Boccaccio. It is clear at once that Shakspere's characters are gentlemen, gathered at the residence of an Italian of wealth and social position. Their conversation is the elaborate, rather affected language of the courtier; this is particularly noticeable in the speeches of Iachimo. The social status of Posthumus is unmistakable; he is sprung from the noble stock of the Leonati and married to the daughter of a king. He is introduced to the company as an equal,—as Philario puts it to his friends, "Let him be so entertained amongst you as suits, with gentlemen of your knowing, to a stranger of his quality" [I. iv. 28-30]. This is, to all intents and purposes, a scene from the life of Shakspere's own time, with the social conventions of gentler folk,—just the sort of company in which a young Englishman making the grand tour at the end of the sixteenth century might have found himself. (p. 410)

The important thing to note here is that Shakspere, in making Philario and Iachimo gentlemen instead of merchants, or an inn-keeper and a merchant, has made the conduct of Posthumus far more natural. The confidence of a trusting husband, willing to go to any extreme to show his confidence in his wife's integrity, is here reinforced by the solemn duty of a knight not to hesitate when the virtues and excellence of his lady are called in question. According to the rules of chivalry, Posthumus could have acted, as the perfect lover and gentleman, in no other way. (p. 411)

Various details in the conversation reveal the chivalric conventions which control it. Posthumus says of Imogen, "Being so far provoked as I was in France, I would abate her nothing, though I profess myself her adorer, not her friend" [I. iv. 67-9], that is to say, "If I were to be so much roused to speak my mind as I was in France, I would rate her virtue no lower than I did then, even though I were judging as one worshipping her from afar, instead of as her accepted lover." The purity of Imogen is so compelling that even a man in the conventional chivalric attitude of loving hopelessly, as Troilus did Cressida in the beginning, or Palamon and Arcite Emelye [in Chaucer's *The Knight's Tale*], would be as sure of her virtue as the man to whom she had granted her "pity." The reader should also observe the threat of a duel to follow, in case Iachimo cannot prove his assertions against the lady, and the words of Iachimo, referring to Posthumus at the end of the play:

> he, true knight,
> No lesser of her honor confident
> Than I did truly find her, steals this ring.
> [V. v. 186-88]

The suggestion of the wager comes, it will be noted, not from the husband, as in Boccaccio's tale, but from the villain Iachimo. The "true knight" might be loth to be drawn into a quarrel, but when the virtues of his lady were called in question, the code of chivalry gave him no choice in the matter. (pp. 412-13)

[Elucidation] of *Cymbeline* by reference to medieval courtly romance is abundantly justified by the survival and revival of chivalric conventions in the days of Elizabeth and James, both in literature and in the life of the court. Chivalry, as a practical rule of life, was moribund in the fourteenth century, yet it was splendidly observed at the court of Edward III, it was ostentatiously practiced during the Wars of the Roses, as for example by Malory's theatrical patron Richard Earl of Warwick, Henry VIII gave it magnificent expression at the Field of the Cloth of Gold, and it experienced a veritable rebirth under Elizabeth. (p. 416)

Everyone who knows what chivalry means can see its influence in the plays of Shakspere, yet it is extraordinary how little the plays have been studied against the background of the medieval conventions surviving in the Elizabethan Age. If Shakspere had occasion to put on the stage the fighting or the love-making of the highly born, he drew the picture in terms of the society with which he was familiar. It did not matter whether the play exhibited the walls of windy Troy, or the castle of Elsinore, or the park of the king of Navarre, or the Britain of Cymbeline, the manners took the shape of those of Elizabeth's court. (p. 417)

Regarded from the point of view of medieval chivalric observance, then, the making of the wager assumes a new significance. Posthumus Leonatus emerges fully vindicated; his is the only conduct possible for the perfect lover and the perfect knight. But what of his later procedure? This is quite another matter, demanding separate consideration.

After the very brilliant and carefully elaborated scenes in Acts I and II, which are beyond doubt Shakspere's own work,—the parting of Posthumus and Imogen, the making of the wager, the interview between Imogen and Iachimo, the brief but beautifully managed episode in the bedchamber, the triumph of Iachimo over Posthumus, and the agonized soliloquy of Posthumus, in which he suspects the virtue of all women—we do not see Posthumus again until Act V. Letters from him are read, one bidding with feigned affection that Imogen meet him at Milford-Haven, and another commanding Pisanio to poison her. At the opening of Act V, it appears from his soliloquy over the bloody handkerchief that the rage of Posthumus and his desire for vengeance are quite over; he repents his command and the faithfulness of Pisanio in having, as he supposes, executed it, ending with lines of a banality that certainly make us suspect an interpolator or collaborator. The scenes on the field of battle and in the prison contain occasional evidences of his repentance, but add nothing new for his relations with Imogen, while they have often been suspected of being from another hand than Shakspere's, especially the scene in the prison. The business in Cymbeline's tent in Act V is curiously managed: after the confession of Iachimo, Posthumus, with a fresh outbreak of repentance, strikes the disguised Imogen, who swoons, and upon reviving "begins an unseemly squabble with Pisanio. . . . Then poor old doddering Cornelius must needs be brought forward, and must tell again in prosy words what he has told us all once before, even to the very same reference to 'cats and dogs'! All this while poor Posthumus has nothing to do but to shift first on one foot and then on the other" [Furness].—But most remarkable of all, I think, is the final reunion of Imogen and Posthumus. After all that has gone before, we certainly expect that the terrible misunderstanding which brings death so near for the lovers, the main-spring of the whole play, will be ended with appropriate dignity. Instead, all that the scene has to offer is this:

> *Imogen.*   Why did you throw your wedded lady from
>   you?
>   Think that you are upon a rock, and now
>   Throw me again. [Embracing him.]
> *Posthumus.*   Hang there like fruit, my soul,
>   Till the tree die!
>   [V. v. 261-64]

—a mixture of wrestling, horticulture and banality which could hardly be surpassed.

In short, then, the development of the main plot in the last three acts is most unsatisfactory, giving the impression of hasty and careless workmanship, as if the dramatist had lost his interest. Perhaps a collaborator was allowed too large a share here, but we must be chary of assuming that scenes were not written by Shakspere because they seem to fall far below his usual level. There is no doubt that he did, at times, hurried and very inferior work. It seems clear, in any case, that what interested him most was the earlier part of the tale; for the punishment which Posthumus attempts to inflict upon Imogen and the final reconciliation he felt little enthusiasm. (pp. 422-24)

The critics have been very severe on Posthumus for his ready belief in the guilt of Imogen, which indeed seems to anticipate Iachimo's full revelations, for his resolve to murder her, the cruelty with which he pursues this resolve, and finally for his sudden repentance, which is held to denote a fatal weakness of character. Yet we do not have to go beyond Shakspere's own plays to see that these are conventions of romantic drama. . . . That Imogen must be put to death for her supposed unchastity is the only course possible for the romantic hero. It was a very old and widespread idea among the Indo-European peoples that the unchaste woman must pay for her frailty with her life, and that this is at the disposal of the husband whom she has wronged or the kinsfolk whom she has disgraced; and this idea survived as a convention of the romantic drama down to the beginning of the seventeenth century, when a more humanitarian note was struck in [Thomas Heywood's] *A Woman Killed With Kindness*. Instances of it are too common to need lengthy citation. Death, under such circumstances, was not viewed as revenge, but as just punishment, inflicted by private rather than public authority. . . . Moreover, cruelty in inflicting the punishment, and in dealing with the guilty woman in general, was held to be only what she deserved. Our forefathers believed that to treat the sinner with consideration was to compound with sin. The erring wife or sister, like other criminals, laid herself open not only to chastisement, but to severity and insult. (pp. 425-27)

What, then, are we to say of the character of Posthumus as a whole? If we are to sum it up in a word, I think we must agree that he is meant to be a blameless hero. He is fully justified in the wager-business, and his subsequent procedure is entirely in accord with the ethics of romance. Moreover, Shakspere himself tells us, in no uncertain terms, that Posthumus is a good man. In the opening scene of the play, the "First Gentleman," that very well-informed person who tells the "Second Gentleman" all about the situation at court, reports Posthumus as

> most prais'd, most lov'd;
> A sample to the youngest, to the more mature
> A glass that feated them, and to the graver
> A child that guided dotards; to his mistress,
> For whom he now is banish'd, her own price
> Proclaims how she esteem'd him and his virtue;
> By her election may be truly read
> What kind of man he is.
>
> [I. i. 47-54]

Every audience knows that such a faithful expositor is not misleading them, but giving such information that they may understand the rest of the play intelligently. Very significant,

too, is the way in which people in the play generally, even the villain Iachimo, speak well of Imogen's husband.

Yet, if all this is true, why do we feel so little sympathy with Posthumus? Why have critics almost unanimously treated him with scorn? Why does his suffering leave us cold, and his marriage with Imogen fail to suggesting the mating of the eagle?

In answering these questions, several points must be kept in mind. In the first place, a hero according to a formula, whose acts are "a mosaic of the commonplaces of romance," is not likely to be consistent or convincing. Very great brilliancy of characterization may accomplish this; a hero may be given so many little touches of individuality and naturalness that we forget the absurdity and inconsistency of his acts. It is one of the greatest of Shakspere's marks of genius that he could do this when he liked. Old stories full of the wildest improbabilities were thus, by his magic touch, completely transformed, and made to seem psychologically sound. Out of the old motives of the Choosing of the Caskets and the Pound of Flesh he created Portia and Shylock; out of the fairy-tale of the King and his Three Daughters Lear and Cordelia, out of the archaic marriage-taboo theme in *All's Well* the beautiful figure of Helena. But at times he was too careless or too indifferent to give even very important characters this final and transforming touch. He did it for Imogen, but not for Posthumus. The noble scion of the Leonati remains a lay-figure, with all the appropriate gestures, but never instinct with the breath of life.

In the second place, modern readers and playgoers do not find the acts and expressions of Posthumus heroic. They do not share the peculiar view of chivalric obligation which sways him in the wager-scene, and they do not believe that virtue which flies in the face of common-sense remains virtue. They have learned a more humane tradition for the punishment of the woman taken in adultery. And they demand in a hero more consistency, more use of his wits, more emotional restraint. The ravings of Posthumus, his rapid fluctuations of purpose, disgust Anglo-Saxons of today, bred to repress their deepest feelings. Moreover, Posthumus has to bear all the heavier burden of reprobation because the misfortunes of Imogen are due to his errors. Every reader of the play loves this radiant and spirited girl; what more natural than to dislike the husband who makes her suffer? "Womanish tears" and "wild acts" [*Romeo and Juliet*, III. iii. 110] may be pardoned in Romeo, who sacrifices everything for Juliet, but not in Posthumus, who makes Imogen herself the sacrifice. It will probably make little difference to remind people that Posthumus has justification for his course of action; they will continue to think just as meanly of him. Perhaps they are right. We are all familiar with the way in which "good" persons in real life, with virtue on their side, and a valid reason for every act, can make the innocent suffer. We wish that Posthumus had thought more of Imogen and less of social conventions. We wish, in short, that he were a man with modern notions, instead of an Elizabethan with medieval ideals still dogging him. But we must remember that the judgments which we pass on him today are probably harsher than those of the men who beheld his figure on the stage under the grey and shifting skies of London three hundred years ago.

We began this discussion with Dr. Johnson's famous criticism of *Cymbeline;* what shall we say of it in closing? Our study has revealed at once its truth and its falseness, or, let us say, the falseness of more specific criticisms to the same effect. We have seen that much in the play which seems absurd and improbable today becomes, in the light of Elizabethan ethics and social conventions, natural and reasonable. But nothing can save the play as a whole from the reproach of "much incongruity." This is, however, confined almost wholly to the last three acts; to the end of the second act *Cymbeline* is a play to be taken seriously, as plausible as *Othello*. Then it goes to pieces, as far as naturalness is concerned, and becomes a kind of—dare we say it?—variety-show, in its multitude of dramatic situations, many of them wildly improbable, mingled with a procession of ghosts, the stage trick of Jupiter, the eagle, the thunderbolt, political prophecy, and so forth. "The impossibility of the events in any system of life" must be granted immediately. But how far we can afford to chide Shakspere when he pours out the whole cornucopia of stage-tricks before us, in this reckless and prodigal fashion, and accuse him of "unresisting imbecility," is a question which shall be left to others to decide. (pp. 427-31)

> *William Witherle Lawrence, "The Wager in 'Cymbe-*
> *line'," in* PMLA, *XXVIII, n. s. Vol. XXVIII, No. 4,*
> *December, 1920, pp. 391-431.*

HARLEY GRANVILLE-BARKER   (essay date 1930)

[*Granville-Barker was a noted actor, playwright, director, and critic. His work as a Shakespearean critic is at all times informed by his experience as a director, for he treats Shakespeare's plays not as works of literature better understood divorced from the theater, as did many Romantic critics, but as pieces meant for the stage. As a director, he emphasized simplicity in staging, set design, and costuming. He believed that elaborate scenery obscured the poetry which was of central importance to Shakespeare's plays. Granville-Barker also eschewed the approach of directors who scrupulously reconstructed a production based upon Elizabethan stage techniques; he felt that this, too, detracted from the play's meaning. In an extended analysis of* Cymbeline *that continues to be cited to the present day, Granville-Barker argues that in this play Shakespeare had "an unlikely story to tell" and, therefore, chose a method of "sophisticated artlessness" to serve his purpose. By openly displaying his theatrical devices and artifices, the critic declares, Shakespeare was both inviting the audience to participate in his craft and ensuring that they would not take the story too seriously. Because the play was designed to have a comic ending, the tragic events must not dominate to the extent that the happy ending appears incongruous with the previous dramatic action. Barbara A. Mowat (1966), R. A. Foakes (1971), and Arthur C. Kirsch (see Additional Bibliography) have also offered explanations of the play's artless display of dramatic techniques; also, see the essay by E. M. W. Tillyard (1938) for further discussion of the seemingly incongruous elements in the dramatic action. However, Granville-Barker maintains that in Act IV, Scene ii, when Imogen awakens beside the headless corpse of Cloten, Shakespeare's "showman's escapade" eclipses the sensitivities of his characterization of the heroine. Granville-Barker denounces the manner in which Imogen has been fraudulently led to her extremities of grief, rating it as "dramatically inexcusable" and "a pretty damnable practical joke." He also doubts that Imogen could ever credibly recover from such a tragic experience and acknowledges the insight of Helena Faucit (1882) in reaching this conclusion. For additional commentary on Imogen and the scene where she awakens beside the headless Cloten, see the excerpts by Harold C. Goddard (1951), F. D. Hoeniger (1961), Robin Moffet (1962), and Robert Grams Hunter (1965); also, see the essay by Joan Carr cited in the Additional Bibliography. In his appraisal, Granville-Barker admits the presence in the play of the "unresisting imbecillity" of which Samuel Johnson (1765) complained, but argues that it should be attributed to the fact that Shakespeare was here experimenting with a new form of drama and to the likelihood that portions of the play were written by an unknown collaborator—a hypothesis first suggested*

by Horace Howard Furness (1913). Granville-Barker argues that this collaborator had a role in both "the design and the execution" of Cymbeline *and agrees that the passages ascribed by Furness to another hand "have certainly a very tinny ring."*]

Cymbeline is said to have been a product, probably the first, of Shakespeare's leisured retirement to Stratford. (p. 234)

The Folio labels it tragedy, but it is not; it is tragi-comedy rather, or romance. Through treachery and mischance we move to a providentially happy ending. Repentance for wrong done, and then

> Pardon's the word to all.
>
> [V. v. 422]

is the moral outcome, two of the least pardonable characters having conveniently been despatched beyond human pardon's reach. In which digest of charitable wisdom—and the easing of the occasion for it—we may see if we will a certain leisured weariness of mind. . . . As for collaboration; we shall not deny Imogen to Shakespeare, nor Iachimo, the one done with such delight, the other, while he sways the plot, with exceeding skill. Here is not the master merely, but the past-master working at his ease. Much besides seems to bear his stamp, from Cloten to that admirable gaoler. Was he as content, in his leisure, to set his stamp on such a counterfeit as the dissembling tyrant Queen? There is a slick professional competence about the writing of her, one may own. And how far is he guilty of the inepter lapses, of which the play is undeniably full?

It is pretty poor criticism (Dr. Furness owns it) to fasten all the faults upon some unknown collaborator and allow one's adored Shakespeare all the praise. Lackeying of that sort leads us first to the minor, then, if we are not careful, into the larger lunacies. Better take shelter behind Johnson, who, like a schoolmaster with cane in hand, sums up his indignation in one tremendous sentence and lets his author—this author, when need be, as well as another—know that he, at any rate, will not 'waste criticism upon unresisting imbecillity, upon faults too evident for detection, and too gross for aggravation' [see excerpt above, 1765]. Johnson was spared the dilemmas of modern research. He would not have taken kindly to our armament of the hair sieve. Nor would he ever have subscribed, one feels sure, to the convenience of a whipping-boy, whatever other tribute he might pay to Shakespeare's majesty. Still, even he approves Pope's opinion—for he quotes it—that the apparitions of the Leonatus family and the jingle they speak were 'plainly foisted in afterwards for meer show, and apparently [are] not of Shakespear' [see excerpt above, 1723].

How much further must we go? The apparitions and their rubbish—

> When once he was mature for man,
> In Britain where was he
> That could stand up his parallel,
> Or fruitful object be
> In eye of Imogen, that best
> Could deem his dignity?
>
> [V. iv. 52-7]

—are not only, one swears, not Shakespeare's, but could hardly have been perpetrated even by the perpetrator of the worst of the rest of the play. One searches for a whipping-boy to the whipping-boy; the prompter, possibly, kept in between rehearsal and performance, thumping the stuff out and thumbing it down between bites and sips of his bread and cheese and ale.

But Furness quotes a round dozen of passages besides, which he declares Shakespeare never, never could have written; and they all, or nearly all, have certainly a very tinny ring. Did the author of *King Lear* and *Antony and Cleopatra* descend to

> Triumphs for nothing and lamenting toys
> Is jollity for apes and grief for boys.
>
> > [IV. ii. 193-94]

or to

> Th' imperious seas breed monsters, for the dish,
> Poor tributary rivers as sweet fish?
>
> > [IV. ii. 35-6]

But he also, we notice, will have nothing to do—on Shakespeare's behalf—with

> Golden lads and lasses must
> Like chimney sweepers, come to dust.
>
> > [IV. ii. 262-63]

and he rejects Belarius altogether on the grounds, mainly, that the old gentleman's demand to be paid twenty years' board and lodging for the children he had abducted touches turpitude's lowest depths. But this surely is to deny even the whipping-boy a sense of pleasantly whimsical humour. It is hard to follow Furness all the way. There are, however, other directions in which we can look for this collaborator or interpolator; and we may possibly find, besides, a Shakespeare, who, for the moment, is somewhat at odds with himself.

If the play's construction is his unfettered work he is at odds with himself indeed. From the beginning he has been a good craftsman, and particularly skilful in the manoeuvring of any two stories into a symmetrical whole. But here the attempt results in a very lop-sided affair. The first scene sees both themes stated: Imogen's marriage to Posthumus, and the strange loss, years before, of her brothers. Then Iachimo's intrigue against her is pursued and completed, most expeditiously; the entire business is done in less than twelve hundred lines, with Cloten and his wooing thrown in. But meanwhile we see nothing, and hear only once, of the young princes. Certainly Imogen cannot set out on her wanderings and encounter them any sooner than she does; and, once she does, this part of the story—it is the phase of the blending of the two stories, and customarily would be the penultimate phase of the plot as a whole—makes due progress. But what of Posthumus? He is now banished from the scene for the space of another fourteen hundred lines or so. That is bad enough. But when he does return to it, the only contrivances for his development are a soliloquy, a mute duel with Iachimo, a quite undramatic encounter with an anonymous 'Lord,' a talk with a gaoler, and a pointless pageant that he sleeps through. This is far worse. He was never much of a hero, but here he becomes a bore. The difficulties are plain. Once his faith in Imogen is destroyed and he has commanded her murder (and we do not need both to see him sending the command and Pisanio receiving it) there is nothing left for him to do till he returns repentant: and once he returns he cannot openly encounter any of the more important characters, or the dramatic effect of his sudden appearance in the last scene (and to that, in its elaboration, every thread, obviously, is to be drawn) will be discounted. But it is just such difficulties as these that the playwright learns to surmount. Can we see Shakespeare, past-master in his craft, making such a mess of a job? If nothing else showed a strange finger in the pie, this letting Posthumus slip from the current of the story, and the clumsiness of the attempt to restore him

to prominence in it, should suffice to. Nevertheless, Shakespeare's stamp, or an excellent imitation of it, is on much of the actual writing hereabouts. One would not even swear him entire exemption from the apparitions.

> Poor shadows of elysium, hence, and rest
> Upon your never-withering banks of flowers:
> Be not with mortal accidents opprest;
> No care of yours it is; you know 'tis ours.
> Whom best I love I cross; to make my gift
> The more delay'd, delighted. . . .
>
> > [V. iv. 97-102]

That, though pedestrian, is, for the occasion, good enough.

These structural clumsinesses concern the last two-thirds of the play. The passages that Furness gibbets—the most and the worst of them—fall there too; and there we may find, besides, minor banalities of stagecraft, set as a rule in a poverty of writing, the stagecraft and writing both showing a startling change from the opulently thrifty methods that went to the making of *Coriolanus, Antony and Cleopatra, King Lear, Othello,* this play's predecessors.

Are we to debit the mature Shakespeare with the dramatic impotence of Pisanio's soliloquy:

> I heard no letter from my master since
> I wrote him Imogen was slain: 'tis strange:
> Nor hear I from my mistress, who did promise
> To yield me often tidings; neither know I
> What is betid to Cloten, but remain
> Perplex'd in all. The heavens still must work.
> Wherein I am false I am honest; not true, to be true.
> These present wars shall find I love my country,
> Even to the note o' the king, or I'll fall in them.
> All other doubts, by time let them be clear'd:
> Fortune brings in some boats that are not steer'd.
>
> > [IV. iii. 36-46]

It is poor stuff; the information in it is hardly needed; it does not seem even meant to provide time for a change of scene or costume. Nor does Shakespeare now use to let his minor characters soliloquise to help his plots along. There are two other such soliloquies: the Queen's rejoicing over Imogen's disappearance, rising to its forcible-feeble climax with

> . . . gone she is
> To death or to dishonour; and my end
> Can make good use of either: she being down,
> I have the placing of the British crown.
>
> > [III. v. 62-5]

This is nearly as redundant in matter; but villainy has its rights, and premature exultation over the misfortunes of the virtuous is one of them. Though it be Shakespeare at his worst, it may still be Shakespeare. So, more certainly, is the Second Lord's soliloquy, with which Cloten's second scene ends. This probably owes its existence to Imogen's need of a little extra time for getting into bed. But it adds information, and, more importantly, reiterates the sympathy of the Court for her in her trouble. It falls earlier in the play; in the stretch of the action that few will deny to be wholly Shakespeare's.

But, quality of writing and the unimportance of the speakers apart, is there not a curious artlessness about nearly all the soliloquies in the play? They are so frankly informative. Shakespeare's use of the soliloquy is no more subject to rule than are any other of his methods; but his tendency, as his art matures, is both to make it mainly a vehicle for the intimate thought and emotion of his chief characters only, and to let its plot forwarding seem quite incidental to this. (pp. 234-40)

But in *Cymbeline*, what a disintegrating change! Posthumus' soliloquies are reflectively emotional enough. The first is an outburst of rage; it would not, one supposes, have been any differently framed for Othello or Antony. The others contain such simply informative passages as

> I am brought hither
> Among the Italian gentry, and to fight
> Against my lady's kingdom. . . .
> I'll disrobe me
> Of these Italian weeds, and suit myself
> As does a Briton peasant. . . .
>
> [V. i. 17-19, 22-4]

as the seemingly needless

> . . . I have resumed again
> The part I came in. . . .
>
> [V. iii. 75-6]

And one asks, without being quite sure of the answer, how far is that

> You married ones,
> If each of you should take this course, how many
> Must murder wives much better than themselves,
> For wrying but a little! . . .
>
> [V. i. 2-5]

meant to be addressed plump to his audience? But the flow of emotion is generally strong enough to sweep any such obstacles along.

Iachimo passes from the dramatic perfection of the soliloquy in the bedchamber to the feebleness of his repentant

> Knighthoods and honours, borne
> As I wear mine, are titles but of scorn.
> If that thy gentry, Britain, go before
> This lout as he exceeds our lords, the odds
> Is that we scarce are men and you are gods.
>
> [V. ii. 6-10]

—with which we hesitate to discredit Shakespeare in any case.

But what of that not merely ingenuously informative, but so *ex post facto* confidence from Belarius:

> O Cymbeline! heaven and my conscience knows
> Thou didst unjustly banish me: whereon,
> At three and two years old I stole these babes,
> Thinking to bar thee of succession as
> Thou reft'st me of my lands. Euriphile,
> Thou wast their nurse, they took thee for their mother,
> And every day do honour to her grave.
> Myself, Belarius, that am Morgan called,
> They take for natural father.
>
> [III. iii. 99-107]

We shall have to search far back in Shakespeare's work for anything quite so apparently artless, and may be doubtful of finding it even there. Furness would make the collaborator responsible for Belarius. But what about the long aside—a soliloquy, in effect—by which Cornelius lets us know that the Queen is not to be trusted, and that the poison he has given her is not poison at all? This is embedded in the admittedly Shakespearean part of the play.

The soliloquies apart, when we find Imogen-Fidele, welcomed by Arviragus-Cadwal with

> I'll make 't my comfort
> He is a man: I'll love him as my brother. . . .
>
> [III. vi. 70-1]

then glancing at him and Guiderius-Polydore and exclaiming

> Would it had been so, that they
> Had been my father's sons.
>
> [III. vi. 75-6]

and when the trick by which Cloten must be dressed in Posthumus' garments (so that Imogen waking by his corpse may mistake it) is not glossed over but emphasised and advertised, here, we feel, is artlessness indeed. But it is obviously a sophisticated, not a native artlessness, the art that rather displays art than conceals it.

A fair amount of the play—both of its design and execution—is pretty certainly not Shakespeare's. Just how much, it is hard to say (though the impossible negative seems always the easier to prove in these matters), for the suspect stuff is often so closely woven into the fabric. It may have come to him planned as a whole and partly written. In which case he worked very thoroughly over what are now the Folio's first two acts. Thereafter he gave attention to what pleased him most, saw Imogen and her brothers and Cloten through to the end, took a fancy to Lucius and gave him reality, did what more he could for Posthumus under the circumstances, generously threw in the First Gaoler, and rescued Iachimo from final futility. This relieves him of responsibility for the poor planning of the whole; he had been able to re-fashion the first part to his liking. But why, then, should he leave so many of the last part's ineptitudes in place? Or did the unknown cling affectionately to them, or even put them back again after Shakespeare had washed his hands of the business? We are dabbling now, of course, in pure 'whipping-boy' doctrine, and flaws enough can be found in it. Of the moments of 'unresisting imbecillity' Shakespeare must be relieved; careless or conscienceless as he might sometimes be, critical common sense forbids us to saddle him with them. But, trying his hand at a new sort of thing (emulating Beaumont and Fletcher and their *Philaster*—why not?—he had never been above taking a hint), and if, moreover, he was trying it 'by request' in hard-won leisure at Stratford, his grip might easily be looser than usual. We find him with a firmer one, that is certain, in *A Winter's Tale* and *The Tempest*. Allowing, then, for some collaboration, and some incertitude besides, at what, are we to suppose, is he aiming, what sort of play is he setting out to write? And if the sophisticated artlessness is his, what end is this meant to serve? These are the practical questions to be answered here.

He has an unlikely story to tell, and in its unlikelihood lies not only its charm, but largely its very being; reduce it to reason, you would wreck it altogether. Now in the theatre there are two ways of dealing with the inexplicable. If the audience are to take it seriously, leave it unexplained. They will be anxious—pathetically anxious—to believe you; with faith in the dose, they will swallow a lot. The other plan is to show one's hand, saying in effect: Ladies and gentlemen, this is an exhibition of tricks, and what I want you to enjoy among other things is the skill with which I hope to perform them. This art, which deliberately displays its art, is very suited to a tragicomedy, to the telling of a serious story that must yet not be taken too seriously, lest its comedy be swamped by its tragedy and a happy ending become too incongruous. Illusion must by no means be given the go-by; if this does not have its due in the theatre, our emotions will not be stirred. Nor should the audience be overwhelmed by the cleverness of the display; arrogance in an artist antagonises us. This is where the seeming artlessness comes in; it puts us at our ease, it is the equivalent of 'You see there is no deception.' But very nice steering will be needed between the make-believe in earnest and in jest.

Shakespeare sets his course (as his habit is, and here we may safely assume that it is he) in his very first scene. We have the immediately necessary tale of Posthumus and Imogen, and the more extraordinary one of the abducting of the princes is added. And when the First Gentleman brings the Second Gentleman's raised eyebrows down with

> How soe'er 'tis strange. . . .
> Yet is it true, sir.
>
>   [I. i. 65, 67]

we of the audience are asked to concur in the acquiescent

> I do well believe you.
>
>   [I. i. 67]

For 'this,' Shakespeare and the First Gentleman are telling us, 'is the play you are about to hear; and not only these facts, but their rather leisurely amplifying, and that supererogatory tale of Posthumus' birth, should show you the sort of play it is. There is trouble in the air, but you are not to be too strung up about it. Moreover, the way you are being told it all, the easy fall of this verse, with its light endings and spun-out sentences, should be wooing you into the right mood. And this talk about Cassibelan is to help send you back into a fabulous past in which these romantic things may legitimately happen. So now submit yourselves, please, to the illusion of them.'

The beginning, then—quite properly—inclines to make-believe in earnest, rendering to the theatre its normal due. And the play's story will follow its course, nor may any doubt of its likelihood be hinted; that is a point of dramatic honour. But in half a hundred ways, without actually destroying the illusion, Shakespeare can contrive to prevent us taking it too seriously.

Cornelius lets us know at once that the poison is not poison; for, monster though the Queen is, we must not fear tragedy of that stark sort to be impending. We must be interested in watching for the working out of the trick played upon her, and amused the while that

> She is fool'd
> With a most false effect. . . .
>
>   [I. v. 42-3]

There is a subtler aim in the artlessness of Belarius' soliloquy. By accepting its frank familiarity we become, in a sense, Shakespeare's accomplices. In telling us the story so simply he is at the same time saying 'You see what a very simple business this playwriting is; take it, please, no more seriously than I do.' The stressing of the coincidence of the meeting of the sister and her lost brothers has a like effect. We feel, and we are meant to feel, 'What a pretty fairy-tale!' The emphasising of the artifice, the 'folly of the fiction,' by which Cloten's corpse comes to be mistaken for Posthumus' does much to mitigate the crude horror of the business, to bring it into the right tragi-comic key. Keep us intrigued by the preparations for the trick, and we shall gain from its accomplishment a half-professional pleasure; we shall be masters of the illusion, not its victims. And throughout the whole elaborate scene of revelation with which the play ends we are most artfully steered

between illusion and enjoyment of the ingenuity of the thing. We hold all the clues; the surprises are for Cymbeline, Imogen, Posthumus and the rest, not for us. We soon foresee the end, and our wits are free to fasten on the skill of the approach to it. But there is an unexpected turn or so, to provide excitement; and the situation is kept so fully charged with emotion that our sympathy is securely held.

This art that displays art is a thing very likely to be to the taste of the mature and rather wearied artist. When you are exhausted with hammering great tragic themes into shape it is a relief to find a subject you can play with, and to be safely able to take more interest in the doing than the thing done. For once you can exercise your skill for its own sake. The pretty subject itself seems to invite a certain artlessness of treatment. But the product will have a sophisticated air about it, probably. (pp. 241-47)

[*Cymbeline*'s] contents may be mongrel, but it has a specific style. Set Imogen in her doublet and hose beside Rosalind [in *As You Like It*] or Viola [in *Twelfth Night*] and—all difference of character and circumstance allowed for—note the complete change of method; the verse with its varied pace and stress, complex, parenthetical, a vehicle for a strange mixing of artifice and simplicity, of naked feeling and sententious fancy— the old forthright brilliance has given place to this.

It is style (nor of writing only; for writing is but half, or less, of the dramatic battle) that gives their due complexion to all the actualities of the play. Critics have exclaimed against the blinding of Gloucester in *King Lear*. Upon the face of it, Imogen's discovery of Cloten's headless corpse should be as horrible a business; more so, indeed, for much more is made of it. But, thanks to the style of its contriving, this passes unremarked. The artless artifice of the preparations for the episode, this we have noted already. But much more is done in mitigation. We do not see Cloten killed; no moment of poignancy is allowed him; he vanishes bombasting and making a ridiculous fight of it. The next we see of him is his ridiculous head; and the boyish unconcern of the young savage who has slaughtered him puts us in the mood to make as little of the matter.

> This Cloten was a fool, an empty purse;
> There was no money in't: not Hercules
> Could have knocked out his brains, for he had
>   none. . . .
>
>   [IV. ii. 113-15]

Then, before the body is brought on, comes the long, tender passage of the mourning over the unconscious Fidele; and our attention is so fixed upon her, Cloten already a memory, that when she wakes beside the dummy corpse it is really not much more to us than a dummy and a pretext for her aria of agony. The setting of the scene, too, must have helped to rob the business of poignancy. There is one sort of realism to be gained on a bare stage and another in scenic illusion; but before a decoratively conventional cave we shall not take things too literally. (pp. 256-58)

But now that we have reached this most effective situation, we must own it, and the whole business of it, to be, from one point of view at least, dramatically inexcusable. It is a fraud on Imogen; and we are accomplices in it. We have watched the playwright's plotting, been amused by his ingenuity. We shall even be a little conscious as we watch, in this sophisticated play, of the big bravura chance to be given to the actress. But Imogen herself is put, quite needlessly, quite heartlessly, on exhibition. How shall we sympathise with such futile suffering? And surely it is a vicious art that can so make sport of its creatures.

All this is true. But tragi-comedy—in this phase of its development, at least—is a bastard form of art; better not judge it by too strict æsthetic law. Tact can intervene; that reconciling grace which sometimes makes stern principle so pleasant to forswear. And Shakespeare palliates his trick with great dramatic tact; he veils its crudity in beauty (a resource that seldom fails him) and even manages to make it serve for some enriching of his character.

The atmosphere of artifice in which the whole play moves— in these scenes in the forest it is at its densest—helps soften, as we saw, the crudity of the butchered corpse. The long, confused waking (dream, to Imogen's drugged senses, only emerging into dream) tempers the crassness of the horror, too. Such a touch of sheer beauty as

> Good faith,
> I tremble still with fear; but if there be
> Yet left in heaven as small a drop of pity,
> As a wren's eye, fear'd gods, a part of it! . . .
> [IV. ii. 302-05]

will sweeten it. And from the positive

> A headless man! The garments of Posthumus!
> I know the shape o's leg: this is his hand;
> His foot mercurial. . . .
> [IV. ii. 308-10]

we are carried very quickly to the agonised climax and as quickly on. There is no shirking. Shakespeare, once committed, will have every ounce of his effect.

> Posthumus! O! Alas!
> Where is thy head? where's that? Ah me, where's that?
> Pisanio might have kill'd thee at the heart,
> And left this head on. . . .
> [IV. ii. 320-23]

is material for as blood-curdling an exhibition as any actress need wish to give. But—here is the master-stroke—even while she is thus racked, and beyond endurance, Imogen's heart is purging of a deeper pain. There is no remotest reason for her jumping to

> Pisanio,
> All curses madded Hecuba gave the Greeks,
> And mine to boot, be darted on thee! Thou,
> Conspired with that irregulous devil, Cloten,
> Hast here cut off my lord. . . .
> [IV. ii. 312-16]

She does not even know of Cloten's attempt to suborn him. But her suffering—and her sex, if we like—is excuse enough for anything of the sort. And to find that Posthumus, even though she finds him dead, was not after all her reviler and would-be murderer, cleanses and exalts her grief. Shakespeare does not insist on this. Imogen, for one thing, is not in a very analytical or explanatory mood. It is as clear as he needs it to be. He leaves it to become effective in the acting:

> That confirms it home:
> This is Pisanio's deed and Cloten's: O!

> Give colour to my pale cheek with thy blood,
> That we the horrider may seem to those
> Which chance to find us: O, my lord, my lord!
> [IV. ii. 328-32]

She rallies from delirium; the pictorial phrase is a resolution into the play's proper key; and in the simple 'O, my lord, my lord!'—spoken as it can be spoken—we are to hear, as she faints away, her reconciliation with her dead.

Nevertheless, contrive as he may, it is a pretty damnable practical joke; and Shakespeare, the creator of Imogen, must now pay the price of Shakespeare's the showman's escapade. He does; to whatever else he may yield we shall not find him at this time of day finally playing false to character. A happy ending may be the play's due, but Imogen can make no full recovery from what has been pure poignant tragedy for her. When the kind hands of Roman enemies recover her from her 'bloody pillow' she stands tongue-tied at first. Lucius has to question and question before she answers his 'What art thou?' [IV. ii. 367] with

> I am nothing: or if not,
> Nothing to be were better.
> [IV. ii. 367-68]

She is stunned and dazed; what wonder! She will follow whither she is bid:

> But first, an 't please the gods
> I'll hide my master from the flies, as deep
> As these poor pick axes can dig. . . .
> [IV. ii. 387-89]

The royal Imogen, to whom Posthumus kneeled with his

> My queen! my mistress!
> [I. i. 92]

who could gallantly defy her father and his Queen, and laugh at the brute Cloten and his wooing, has travelled far. 'Happy ending' looks little congruous with the sight of her now.

So Shakespeare finds. He frees her from the action for four full scenes, gives her time, as it were, for recovery; but restored to it, restored to husband and father, united to her brothers, her path fair before her, she is a wounded woman still. Her ring on Iachimo's finger; that only means she may learn how all the evil came to pass, the tale cannot bring her dead back to life; she listens to its verbiage in numb silence. When it does, when by miracle Posthumus stands there before her, the very joy leaves her speechless; she can only cling to him and stammer helplessly. Just for one moment, when she turns upon Pisanio, she rallies to 'the tune of Imogen' [V. v. 238], and they know her by it. The 'happy ending' is duly brought about. But Shakespeare gives her little more to say; that little quiet and colourless, almost. He could not in conscience set her— or set any of them—merry-making.

Lady Martin, who wrote pleasant reminiscences of Miss Helen Faucit's applauded performances of Shakespeare's heroines, ends the study of Imogen with a sentimental picture of a slow decline (the play being over), of her dying—'. . . fading out like an exhalation of the dawn' [see excerpt above, 1882]— surrounded by the rest of the cast in appropriate attitudes of grief and remorse. This is certainly not criticism; and one is apt to smile at such 'Victorian' stuff, and to add 'and nonsense' as one puts the book down. But there is something to be said for acting a part if you want to discover those last few secrets about it that the author knew but did not see fit to disclose.

And Lady Martin is essentially right here. The figure of Imogen is life-like, of a verity that transcends the play's need; and the blows that Shakespeare had to deal her were death-blows. It is something of a simulacrum that survives. But there is a truth to life in this, too.

No one will rank *Cymbeline* with the greater plays. It is not conceived greatly, it is full of imperfections. But it has merits all its own; and one turns to it from *Othello,* or *King Lear,* or *Antony and Cleopatra* as one turns from a masterly painting to, say, a fine piece of tapestry, from commanding beauty to more recondite charm. (pp. 340-45)

> *Harley Granville-Barker, "'Cymbeline'," in his* Prefaces to Shakespeare, second series, *Sidgwick & Jackson, Ltd., 1930, pp. 234-345.*

CAROLINE F. E. SPURGEON   (essay date 1935)

[*Spurgeon's* Shakespeare's Imagery and What It Tells Us *(1935) inaugurated the "image-pattern analysis" method of studying Shakespeare's plays, one of the most widely used methods of the mid-twentieth century. In this work, she interprets the thematic structure of the plays through an examination of patterns in the imagery. Spurgeon also sought to learn about Shakespeare's personality from a study of his images, a course which few of her disciples followed. Since publication of her book, earlier works on image patterns in Shakespeare have been discovered, but none was so important in the history of Shakespearean criticism as hers. In the following excerpt, Spurgeon identifies two dominant strains of metaphorical language in* Cymbeline. *The first she describes as those images associated with the countryside—such as birds, trees, and flowers—and which enhance the bucolic atmosphere of the idyll scenes in Acts III and IV and also contribute to Shakespeare's characterization of the dramatic figures. The second she discerns in the frequent allusions to "buying and selling, value and exchange, every kind of payment, debts, bills and wages." Spurgeon claims that these are generally associated with the wager plot and the contested tribute to Rome, but sometimes are introduced awkwardly or inappropriately into other sections of the drama, perhaps because monetary value was a subject preoccupying Shakespeare at the time he wrote the play. Such other critics as F. C. Tinkler (1938), A. A. Stephenson (1942), Derek Traversi (1954), and Robin Moffet (1962) have also examined the metaphorical patterns in* Cymbeline.]

In *Cymbeline* there are two chief strains, one of atmosphere, and one of thought, brought out in the imagery. The country atmosphere of the play is very marked, and this is as true of the scenes laid in Rome or the king's palace in Britain as of those in the mountains of Wales. This atmosphere is largely created and sustained by the very large proportion of country images, unusually large even for Shakespeare, amounting to about forty per cent. of the total number.

We are conscious especially of the background of trees, the fragrance of flowers and the presence of birds, for all these are much drawn upon. There are many well-known and beautiful images and pictures of trees, and several of the characters are very definitely thought of as trees, or their characteristics are symbolised by trees of different kinds, or by the winds affecting trees. Thus Cymbeline, as the soothsayer explains, is a stately cedar, and his two lost sons lopped branches, revived after many years, joined to the old stock and grown afresh; and Belarius, describing how he fell suddenly from high favour into his king's displeasure, pictures himself dramatically as a fruit tree stripped bare by the winds or by thieves; when Cymbe-

line loved him, he says, and counted him among his bravest soldiers,

> then was I as a tree
> Whose boughs did bend with fruit: but in one night,
> A storm, or robbery, call it what you will,
> Shook down my mellow hangings, nay, my leaves,
> And left me bare to weather.
>
>   [III. iii. 60-4]

The characters of the two princely boys, kindly, yet on occasion fierce, are painted by their proud foster-father in a charming woodland picture of the wind and flowers and trees:

> they are as gentle
> As zephyrs blowing below the violet,
> Not wagging his sweet head; and yet as rough,
> Their royal blood enchafed, as the rudest wind
> That by the top doth take the mountain pine
> And make him stoop to the vale.
>
>   [IV. ii. 171-76]

The tactless intrusion of Cymbeline on the parting of the lovers is similarly described by Imogen as the action of the rough spring winds on the fruit trees:

> ere I could
> Give him that parting kiss, . . .
>   comes in my father,
> And, like the tyrannous breathing of the north,
> Shakes all our buds from growing.
>
>   [I. iii. 33-4, 35-7]

So also the outstanding characteristics of Imogen herself as noted by the two boys, grief and patience, are pictured as the growth of the hateful elder tree and the fruitful vine, mingling 'their spurs together' [IV. ii. 58], and Arviragus, wishing her better fortune, cries,

> Grow, patience!
> And let the stinking elder, grief, untwine
> His perishing root with the increasing vine!
>
>   [IV. ii. 58-60]

In the dirge, the conception that to the dead all earthly differences are as nought, is tersely expressed in emblematic form,

> To thee the reed is as the oak,
>
>   [IV. ii. 267]

and one of the most vivid and moving images in Shakespeare, summing up in itself all we long to know of the remorse and real feeling and (we hope) passionate devotion of Posthumus, ten words which do more than anything else in the whole play to bring him in weight and value a little nearer to Imogen, this again is the picture of a fruit tree, when, with her arms thrown round him in an ecstasy of love and forgiveness, he murmurs,

> Hang there like fruit, my soul,
> Till the tree die!
>
>   [V. v. 263-64]

Flowers and their special qualities are called upon to aid in the description of the fair and delicate beauty of Imogen, by the two boys who love her, as well as by Iachimo when evilly gloating over her. She is fair and fresh and fragrant as the lily, pale as the primrose, her veins are the tint of the azured harebell, her mole spotted as the centre of the cowslip, and her breath sweet as is the eglantine.

And the play is alive with the movement and sound of birds, for, even for Shakespeare, there is in it an unusual number of bird similes. In his characteristic way they are used continually for all sorts of purposes and comparisons, for they are ever in his mind and before his eyes. We find them as units of measurement; of size,

> but if there be
> Yet left in heaven as small a drop of pity
> As a wren's eye;
>
> [IV. ii. 303-05]

of distance; ere you ceased waving farewell to Posthumus, cries Imogen to Pisanio,

> thou shouldst have made him
> As little as a crow, or less,
>
> [I. iii. 14-15]

and Belarius, starting the boys up the mountain, gives them instructions for reflection,

> When you above perceive me like a crow.
>
> [III. iii. 12]

Birds symbolise liberty and wideness of range, as when Belarius, vainly trying to reconcile the spirited young princes to a quiet country life, assures them that

> often . . . shall we find
> The sharded beetle in a safer hold
> Than is the full-wing'd eagle.
>
> [III. iii. 19-21]

They naturally symbolise also swiftness of movement, such as Imogen's, when, as the queen suggests,

> wing'd with fervour of her love, she's flown
> To her desired Posthumus.
>
> [III. v. 61-2]

Sometimes the point of view of the bird is used as a measure of something desired, as it is by Arviragus, who assures Imogen that 'the night to the owl and morn to the lark' [III. vi. 93] is less welcome than her presence to him; or the habits of birds help to form a picture of what may happen in human life, as when Iachimo warns Posthumus that 'strange fowl light upon neighbouring ponds' [I. iv. 89].

They are used constantly as a swift means of characterisation; the imperial Caesar is a 'princely eagle', Cloten is a crowing cock, the Britons are crows which peck the Romans:

> Forthwith they fly
> Chickens, the way which they stoop'd eagles,
>
> [V. iii. 41-2]

says Posthumus, describing the soldiers in battle;

> I chose an eagle,
> And did avoid a puttock,
>
> [I. i. 139-40]

proudly retorts Imogen, when her father tells her she might have had Cloten instead of Posthumus; and Posthumus himself is described by Iachimo, when speaking of a little group of Romans, as 'the best feather of our wing' [I. vi. 186].

The boys, lamenting their inexperience, compare themselves to unfledged birds, who 'have never wing'd from view o' the nest' [III. iii. 28].

'Our cage', says Arviragus,

> We make a quire, as doth the prison'd bird,
> And sing our bondage freely.
>
> [III. iii. 42-4]

When he finds Imogen, as he thinks, dead, he calls her a bird. Iachimo on first sight of her compares her to the fabulous phoenix and mutters, 'She is alone the Arabian bird' [I. vi. 17]. When told she must leave her country, Imogen agrees, quickly characterising in half a line the smallness of that country compared with the rest of the world and its peculiar homely cosy qualities,

> I' the world's volume
> Our Britain seems as of it, but not in't;
> In a great pool a swan's nest.
>
> [III. iv. 137-39]

By these and similar images, then, the atmosphere of a woodland country is given and maintained; but there is as well to be traced in the imagery another very different set of ideas or interests in the poet's mind which persists throughout the play. This is the theme of buying and selling, value and exchange, every kind of payment, debts, bills and wages.

It is possible that the two central motives of the plot, the wager, and the Roman claim for tribute, may have suggested this; or it may just have been, for some reason unknown to us, a subject much in Shakespeare's mind at the time. I incline to this latter view, because the idea seems so constantly with him that he almost drags it in at times, even in places where as a metaphor it is both far-fetched and awkward.

For instance, when the queen reflects complacently, as doubtless many other wives have done, that whenever she angers the king, he, in repentance, is doubly nice to her afterwards in order to be friends again, she words it in this obscure way:

> I never do him wrong
> But he does buy my injuries, to be friends;
> Pays dear for my offences;
>
> [I. i. 104-06]

when Iachimo invents the description of how Imogen gave him her bracelet, he adds,

> Her pretty action did outsell her gift,
> And yet enrich'd it too;
>
> [II. iv. 102-03]

and when Imogen boldly tells her father that Posthumus is of so much greater value than she, that in marrying her he gets nothing in return for the greater part of what he gives, she uses the same somewhat involved language; 'he is', she says

> A man worth any woman, overbuys me
> Almost the sum he pays.
>
> [I. i. 146-47]

On the other hand this metaphor is sometimes in such perfect keeping with the subject that we scarcely notice it, as when Belarius reminds the boys that Cloten was 'paid' for his actions, or when in the dirge they sing,

> Thou thy worldly task hast done,
> Home art gone and ta'en thy wages.
>
> [IV. ii. 260-61]

The idea of the relative value of the two lovers themselves is constantly in the minds of both, each avowing that the other has lost heavily in the exchange. Posthumus, putting on the ring Imogen gives him in parting, says,

> And, sweetest, fairest,
> As I my poor self did exchange for you
> To your so infinite loss, so in our trifles
> I still win of you,
>
> [I. i. 118-21]

and he clasps a bracelet on her arm.

Imogen, when she first meets the two boys, wishes they might have been her brothers, for so she would not have been heir to a throne,

> then had my prize
> Been less, and so more equal ballasting
> To thee, Posthumus.
>
> [III. vi. 76-8]

Iachimo, discussing Posthumus with his friends, and saying that his marriage to the king's daughter has probably fictitiously enhanced the report of his parts and prowess, expresses his thought in the same metaphor of weights and values:

> This matter of marrying his king's daughter,
> wherein he must be weighed rather by her value
> than his own, words him, I doubt not, a great
> deal from the matter.
>
> [I. iv. 14-17]

When Posthumus, at the end, offers to the gods his life in exchange for Imogen's, he plays at length on the theme of debts, value, weight and exchange:

> I know [he cries] you are more clement than vile men,
> Who of their broken debtors take a third,
> A sixth, a tenth, letting them thrive again
> On their abatement: that's not my desire:
> For Imogen's dear life take mind; and though
> 'Tis not so dear, yet 'tis a life; you coin'd it:
> 'Tween man and man they weigh not every stamp;
> Though light, take pieces for the figure's sake:
> You rather mine, being yours: and so, great powers,
> If you will take this audit, take this life,
> And cancel these cold bonds.
>
> [V. iv. 18-28]

So also, when his gaolers return to take him to be hanged, the talk is again of the same theme, bills, debts and weight, and the gaoler offers curious comfort to the condemned man by reminding him that he is going where he will 'be called to no more payments, fear no more tavern-bills' [V. iv. 158-59], taverns, whence he will emerge with 'purse and brain both empty, the brain the heavier for being too light, the purse too light, being drawn of heaviness' [V. iv. 163-65], and so on.

In all kinds of ways, sometimes, one would think, unsuitable, these ideas of purchase, payment, weight and value are introduced and dwelt upon. Thus, when Guiderius tells Imogen he loves her, he immediately translates it into weight:

> I love thee; I have spoke it:
> How much the quantity, the weight as much,
> As I do love my father.
>
> [IV. ii. 16-18]

The settling of the wager, naturally, gives an opening for many such figures; Iachimo suggests to Posthumus that his ring is of greater value than his wife, to which Posthumus indignantly answers that his ring may be bought or given, but that Imogen

Act I. Scene i. Imogen and Posthumus. By G. Greatbach. The Department of Rare Books and Special Collections, The University of Michigan Library.

is not for sale, and only the gift of the gods; then follows the discussion of the terms of the wager, the value of Iachimo's estate compared to the ring, his taunt that Posthumus is 'buying ladies' flesh at a million a dram' [I. iv. 135], the final agreement on the sum of 10,000 ducats and the ring, which Iachimo hastens to get ratified in legal form, 'lest the bargain should catch cold and starve' [I. iv. 166-67].

Cloten, about to tip one of Imogen's waiting women, startles us by speaking suddenly for a moment with the voice of Timon,

> 'Tis gold
> Which buys admittance; oft it doth;
> . . . and 'tis gold
> Which makes the true man kill'd and saves the thief;
> Nay, sometime hangs both thief and true man: what
> Can it not do and undo?
>
> [II. iii. 67-8, 70-3]

When he finally buys his way in to her presence, he is given but a cold reception by Imogen, who greets him by saying,

> You lay out too much pains
> For purchasing but trouble.
>
> [II. iii. 87-8]

Imogen herself later offers the boys money for her food, which is angrily rejected, and Arviragus cries, in what undoubtedly is, in some moods, the voice of his creator

All gold and silver rather turn to dirt!
As 'tis no better reckon'd, but of those
Who worship dirty gods.

[III. vi. 53-5]
(pp. 291-300)

Caroline F. E. Spurgeon, "Leading Motives in the Romances," in her Shakespeare's Imagery and What It Tells Us, *1935. Reprint by Cambridge at the University Press, 1971, pp. 291-308.*

F. C. TINKLER   (essay date 1938)

[*In one of the earliest extended analyses of thematic issues in* Cymbeline *in the twentieth century, Tinkler maintains that the play is not "a lighthearted pastoral romance," as many critics have assumed, nor an example of Shakespeare's "relaxed" manner of writing during his final years (see the excerpts above by Barrett Wendell, 1894; E. K. Chambers, 1907; and Brander Matthews, 1913), but a serious work "which continues the achievement of the great tragedies in another form." Tinkler is particularly concerned with describing and assessing the importance of "a contrasting dualism" which operates at every level of the drama—from the imagery in the verse itself to the progress of the dramatic action. He notes that much of the verse contains images of muscular strain and physical stress and that the passages in which these images occur are "compressed" or "telescoped," while, simultaneously, individual words are isolated, thus producing a constant tension between compression and separation. Tinkler also perceives this tension or dualism in the speeches of the various characters, where the conflict between the inflated exaggeration of their experiences and the disgusting, often violent world of everyday life—the "solid here-and-now"—in which these experiences take place is developed. The critic further associates this dualism in the characters' monologues with "a need to escape the disgusting sordidness of the familiar," while, at the same time, they wish "to remain in close contact with the 'local' life"— a pattern he finds most visible in Posthumus's diatribe against Imogen (in Act II, Scene v) and in her rage against him (in Act III, Scene iv) upon discovering his revengeful motives. In Tinkler's assessment, there are no "positive" ideals realized in the play, since the "critical irony" inherent in the characters' romanticized and self-centered speeches inhibits the establishment of these ideals; on the other hand, there is insufficient energy in the negative emotions themselves to "constitute a 'positive'." Focusing on yet another level of the drama, Tinkler extends the conflict between the need to escape and the need to remain in familiar routine into the contrast "between the still movelessness of the ideal vision and the crude, gross violence of the familiar." He considers Rome in the play, which is nowhere "spatially visualized," a "nebulous symbol" of escape to a remote Golden Age from the sordidness and provinciality of Britain. Similarly, he describes "the exquisite, pastoral elegizing of the dirges" as an attempt to crystallize the melancholic mood brought on by Imogen's "death" and to transform it into a momentary idyllic relief. The common element in both, Tinkler continues, is "remoteness" or "stillness," which in itself "includes the idea of coming to rest, perhaps, in the stillness of death." It is this "stillness of death" that Tinkler claims both Shakespeare and, eventually, Posthumus recognize "as the solution of the impossible tension between the motions from and towards common experience"—in other words, the reconciliation of the positive ideals of the characters and the negative realities of life. In light of this, the critic concludes that the entire dramatic action of* Cymbeline *moves "towards a repose achieved in spite of violence," finding its consummation in the final scene, "where the circular movement is like that of a wheel coming to rest, as more and more of the 'action' is disposed of, circling nearer and nearer to the final immobility of the last tableau." Yet, Tinkler adds, the crucial irony present at the end of the play informs us that the reconciliation between the ideal vision and the realities of life is not final, that the dualistic tensions in the*

drama between Rome and Britain, style and meaning, reality and the ideal are not resolved. For direct responses to Tinkler's interpretation of Cymbeline, *see the excerpts by A. A. Stephenson (1942) and F. R. Leavis (1942).*]

[*Cymbeline*] offers such strong resemblances to [Shakespeare's] other plays, notably *The Winter's Tale* (which has an almost identical plot), that one is forced to the conclusion that not only was the plot seriously and deliberately chosen, but it was chosen because of its possibilities as the medium for exploring and refining material which had already an essential interest for the poet. It should be considered, not as a fashionable romance, but as a play which continues the achievement of the great tragedies in another form, in one which defies an arbitrary classification much as *Measure for Measure* does.

In examining the implications of these necessarily vague statements, it is obvious that a start must be made in examining the texture of the verse itself. (p. 5)

With certain obvious exceptions—and it is these which have been persistently admired as characteristic of the play—the verse has a hard, corrugated texture differing from that of, say, *Coriolanus* or *The Winter's Tale*, in that this harshness proceeds from the persistent recreation of feelings of a particular kind of physical pain. A large number of the images involve ideas of muscular tension and strain:

. . . crush him together rather than unfold
His measure duly . . .

[I. i. 26-7]

. . . And I shall here abide the hourly shot
Of angry eyes . . .

[I. i. 89-90]

I would have broke my eyestrings, cracked them, but
To look upon him, till the diminution
Of space had pointed him sharp as my needle.

[I. iii. 17-19]

. . . rivetted, screw'd to my memory.

[II. ii. 43-4]

There is an insistent feeling of brutal strain; the contours of the verse in which these images occur suggest a strong compression—words are strained together to such an extent in this 'fierce abridgment,' that frequently they telescope. 'Underpeep,' 'nothing-gift,' 'after-eye' readily suggest themselves as examples of this tendency. The corollary of this is a tendency of the words to *separate*. Here there is no suggestion of the fluid sap-creation of the great tragedies; the words seem more sharply defined, more separate, the rhythm is, as it were, more fearful, delicately hesitant even. So the life in the verse proceeds from the tension between this tendency and the strong compressive force exerted, as it were, from the outside. Obviously, technique of this kind, in its development away from the characteristic *fusion* of the earlier verse, does not represent an approximation to the verse of the lesser dramatists, the Beaumont and Fletchers writing 'superior' romances. Rather, one suggests, the tendency is towards a kind of verse somewhat like that achieved by [Ben] Jonson in his best work. In such images as

that tub
Both filled and running

[I. vi. 48-9]

the vigorous, destructive vivacity of the homely metaphor completely refutes the charges implied in the academic attitudes towards this play.

The reference to Jonson once made, the suggestion of a subtle exaggeration which pervades this play gains in significance. At once it is seen to be intimately connected with the sense of strain we have noticed. Consider the following passage, selected almost at random:

> Had I this cheek
> To bathe my lips upon; this hand, whose touch,
> Whose every touch, would force the feeling soul
> To the oath of loyalty; this object, which
> Takes prisoner the wild motion of my eye,
> Fixing it only here;—should I—damned then—
> Slaver with lips as common as the stairs
> That mount the Capitol; join gripes with hands
> Made hard with hourly falsehood—falsehood, as
> With labour; then, by peeping in an eye
> Base and illustrious as the smoky light
> That's fed with stinking tallow;—it were fit
> That all the plagues of hell should at one time
> Encounter such revolt.
>
> [I. vi. 99-112]

The exaggeration is obvious. The gusto of the dramatic gestures and inflated emotions—one remembers that Iachimo is playing a part—with the head thrown back and the arm upraised in

> Should I—damned then—

and the raised voice sweeping out into the next lines in an exaggerated theatricality—all this is superbly realized, and naturally it draws attention to itself, demanding a more critical attention. The exaggeration is 'placed' by a continual reference to a solid matter-of-factness. The inflation, built up on 'bathe' and the general theatricality, is subtly controlled by such images as that in the seventh and eighth lines; the heightened disgust of the kissing, with its suggestions of servility, of old men and children dribbling on chins, and of the dirty hard steps of a public building trodden by unwashed crowds, is modified by the very concreteness of the image, by the *pettiness* of the suggestions. Moreover 'Capitol' still has some dignity, and the lips could only sustain such comparison where the attention is focussed not so much in the propriety of the image as such, as in its reference to the general context, to the unreal theatrical world which yet exists only in concrete, real particulars. This air of unreality, this inflation, reaches bursting-point as it extends into the concentrated disgust of the 'stinking tallow,' and here it becomes obvious that the disgust envelopes the familiar work-a-day world, that both worlds, the unreal melodramatic one and the solid here-and-now, mutually interact in an unresolved tension; or, if you like, while there is a need to escape the disgusting sordidness of the familiar, so that even disgust is exaggerated, yet on the other hand there is a vital need to remain in close contact with the 'local' life.

Put crudely there is a 'conflict' between the tendencies to escape and to remain and the resultant poise is intensely critical. What we have to examine are the bases and implications of these tendencies, so surely expressed in the verse, and the means by which the balance between them is preserved.

The critical interaction of a contrasting dualism which has been noted in the foregoing section is typical of the whole play; throughout there is no 'positive' which is not modified by the intense irony, not even an assured, transcendent vision of Evil

or Death, as in the great tragedies; nor is there on the other hand sufficient energy in the negative emotions themselves which might in itself constitute a 'positive.' The acute disgust which finds expression in such phrases as 'partnered with tomboys' 'vaulting variable ramps' and 'crackt of kitchen trulls' [I. vi. 121-22, I. vi. 134, V. v. 177], is itself so conditioned, critically, that it too is made to appear petty. This critical element is not, however, merely the ironic detachment of the sophisticated sensibility pricking extravagant bubbles; it is too fierce, too extravagant itself for just that. It seems to emerge at the point of tension between the violent negative emotions which envelop *all* experience and the need to create some positive. In this tension feelings are exaggerated into a condition of nervous susceptibility, and 'exposedness,' which is tauter than that of *The Winter's Tale* where the critical element, in this special sense, being absent, there is a more resolved, if also more convulsive, reaction. Comparison with this latter play shows how different the disgust-feelings are in these two plays. In the verse of their speeches one immediately notices the greater violence of Leontes' disgust ('no barricado for a belly' [*The Winter's Tale,* I. ii. 204]) the more convulsive movement, as if the disgust, almost hatred, has a definite direction, whereas Posthumus is not sure, he is swayed between the recognition of the appearance of virtue and of the lust beneath.

> my mother seemed
> The Dian of that time: so doth my wife
> The non-pareil of this.
>
> [II. v. 6-8]

The emotions behind Leontes are more direct—or, as Coleridge put it, there is 'something like hatred'; those behind Posthumus are ironically conceived:

> I'll write against them,
> Detest them, curse them.
>
> [II. v. 32-3]

It is hopelessly inadequate after the violent theatricality of his disgust-motions. The disgust itself is restrained, held up as it were by the taut critical irony, which when relaxed as in the later play, allows the negative emotions a looser, more violent expression. But when both are compared with Othello's speeches a wide difference is observed. With him it is a purely personal matter—in one speech he even seeks reasons for her unfaithfulness. There is no disgust, no violent hatred against all women, but only the self-conscious reference of everything to his own feelings and then, the self-dramatization. There is hardly any of this self-dramatization in *The Winter's Tale* but in *Cymbeline* it persists throughout, both in the theatricality of the emotions expressed and the trick of making the individual characters play parts, consciously or unconsciously. In this play this ironic detachment is partly *protective*—I mean that what in *Othello* was, shall we say, a tragic theme, becomes in *Cymbeline* a means of distancing the emotions, of protecting the creative sensibility from experience too painful. The artist refuses to give universal valency to these negative emotions though he must recognize their potency. Notice how the third 'O' is introduced in the following passage:

> O vengeance, vengeance!
> Me of my lawful pleasure she restrained,
> And prayed me oft forbearance: did it with
> A pudency so rosy, the sweet view on't
> Might well have warmed old Saturn; that I thought her
> As chaste as unsunned snow:—O all the devils!—
> This yellow Iachimo, in an hour—wast not?—

Or less—at first?—perchance he spoke not, but,
Like a full acorned boar, a German one,
Cried 'O' and mounted.

                                                   [II. v. 8-17]

The dominant note in the first lines is a kind of angry sensuality,
which is somewhat like that characteristic of Othello. . . . But
the stress has been shifted in the later play—a different element
is introduced. Posthumus, in his frenzied excitement, lets his
imagination get to work and seems to enjoy the spectacle,
elaborating for his own benefit the nationality of the boar, until
one is brought to that

                    Cried 'O' and mounted

—the climax of a fine declamation; an anti-climax rather, for
one's earlier suspicions are confirmed in that comic detail.
That is the element of differentiation from *Othello*. It is almost
a kind of understatement placed immediately after a blustering
speech, again as in

                    I'll write against them . . .

But it is not just comic, never falls into bathos. Beneath the
words can be felt the strong disgust reaction from the heavy
oppressive sluggishness ('German boar') of the gross, common
life, from all that does not realize a particular, egotistic (the
persistent irony is operative here) and completely *selfish* ideal—
but the general impression is that it's overdone: the convulsive
movement of the description here is completely out of accord
with the intensely static quality of the actual bedroom scene.
Not only are the negative emotions inflated, but also there is
a recognition of the 'impossibility' of the ideal, upon which
they depend, in the description of Imogen's chastity. She is so
extraordinarily chaste.

It is absurd to suggest, as many . . . have done, that Imogen
is conceived in the same terms as Marina and Perdita. In the
first place, a large proportion of the images of muscular tension
occur in her speeches, and in general the verse of these is hard,
vigorous and uncompromising. With Perdita's speeches compare the following:

False to his bed! What is it to be false?
To lie in watch there, and to think on him?
To weep twixt clock and clock? if sleep charge nature
To break it with a fearful dream of him,
And cry myself awake! That's false to's bed, is it? . . .
I false! Thy conscience witness, Iachimo,
Thou didst accuse him of incontinency;
Thou them lookedst like a villain: now, methinks,
Thy favour's good enough. Some jay of Italy,
Whose mother was her painting, hath betrayed him:
Poor I am stale, a garment out of fashion:
And for I am richer than to hang by the walls,
I must be ript—to pieces with me!

                                         [III. iv. 40-4, 46-53]

The harsh bitterness of this verse, crystallizing into such phrases
as 'to weep 'twixt clock and clock' where the harsh separateness of the words, like strokes on an anvil, creates a feeling
of taut suspense, is quite unlike the buoyant wave-movement
of Perdita's speech, which should, rather, be related to the
verse of the dirges. The taut suspension allows the concentrated
disgust ('some jay of Italy') a closer, more controlled, expression and prepares the way for the dramatic gesture in 'I
must be ript.' At that point, the melodramatic savageness reveals itself—the gesture recalls the 'acting' of Posthumus, and
points to the inflated tone, the exaggerated incongruity in the

juxtaposition of the ideas of dusty moth-eaten garments hanging
outmoded on walls which can accommodate suicidal hangings,
and her great chastity. The same process can be observed in
the speech of Posthumus examined above. Imogen is dramatizing herself and, shall we say, 'enjoys' the dramatic gesture.
Not that it is pure farce or melodrama—the ready comic or
pathetic responses (the easiest ways out of the situation) are
prohibited by the extreme concreteness of the imagery and by
the subtle deflation, the hint at the 'impossibility' of her protestations. One is reminded of Act II, Sc. ii.

Imogen: What hour is it?

Lady: Almost midnight, madam.

Imogen: I have read three hours, then: mine eyes are
             weak:
             Fold down the leaf where I have left: to bed:
             Take not away the taper, leave it burning;
             And if thou canst awake by four o'the clock,
             I prithee, call me. Sleep hath seized me
             wholly. . . .

                                                   [II. ii. 2-7]

[It] is evident that Imogen is extraordinarily virtuous—too virtuous, too beautiful, too much 'the paragon of all excellence,'
and to this excess the continual inflation in the verse brings
the ironic inflection. Against this air of impossibility, however,
there is the practical homely familiarity of her speeches. It is
as if there is a need to create an ideal, chaste beauty . . . and
yet there is too the insistent necessity of conceiving her in
terms of that local world in which she is and does as other
women, and which has so much that disgusts, so much that
attracts. (It is the central problem for the artist in creating the
play, for the artist in 'living' the play). The exaggeration is
not entirely farcical, is not primarily so. Primarily it is due to
the need to make Imogen remote from the commonplace; but
the insistent knowledge of the existence of the commonplace
and its reality adds the note of comic unreality. . . . [Imogen]
is conceived as existing in a world apart and yet living in the
local routine of homely images, and I suggest that this seeming
impossibility is the cause of the strained tone of the play, of
Posthumus' jealousy.

This tension contrasts with the 'fiery vision' of the great tragedies (and it is to these that *Cymbeline* should be related, not
the early comedies) where, say, Cleopatra is created *through*
the details of common life, the vision transcends them, whereas
Imogen is conceived almost *in spite of* them. It is interesting
to notice how the symbol of Cleopatra is introduced into the
'report' of Iachimo, where it contrasts with the insolent dir-
tiness of the pornographic raconteur, which reduces everything
to its own level—the insinuating hiss of the alliteration and the
familiar tone do not allow any transcendent attitudes towards
love, yet the meanness of the account is betrayed in the symbol.
The evocation of such a love reveals the coarse self-centredness
of Posthumus' agreement:

                  She hath been colted by him.

                                                   [II. iv. 133]

It is as if Posthumus had been thinking pruriently of Imogen
when Iachimo was speaking—as if that is the only way of
reducing her impossible chastity to everyday experience.

In Posthumus' admission of his guilt all these previous suggestions of melodramatic inflation and self-centred dramatization which we have examined are focussed and intensified,
for he rants and struts and visualizes himself, quite conceitedly,

as a monster. Here, again, although the air of savage farce is strong in the exaggerated theatricality, there is a suggestion of a firm need beneath it. The 'recognition,' in which the Evil is known and overcome, is conceived as necessary at the same time as a detached, painfully critical attitude is preserved. This 'recognition' is essential before the idea of 'rebirth' . . . can be accepted. This idea is integral to our conception of the play and now, having examined the kind of emotions broadly designated here as negative, it remains to examine the more positive tendencies and their final reconciliation, and it is in this examination that the idea of 'rebirth' assumes its importance.

In beginning this fresh inquiry I suggest that we can extend our previous generalization—that there is a conflict between the need to escape and the need to remain in the familiar routine of everyday life—into another, that the contrast throughout is between the still movelessness of the ideal vision and the crude, gross violence of the familiar. The whole play does seem in fact a gradual probing and sifting of experience to create a precise definition of this 'ideal vision' and to reconcile it with actual living experience.

Thus throughout the play there is a complex comparison between Britain and Rome. We have seen how there is a strong revulsion from the pettiness and sordidness of 'local' life, but there is much more than that. Britain is regarded with a mature reasonableness—I do not imply that any 'statements' are made in any particular speeches.

> I' the world's volume
> Our Britain seems as of it, but not in't;
> In a great pool a swan's nest . . .
>
> [III. iv. 137-39]

There, in that final image, you see the balanced recognition of the smallness of Britain. Against any attachment to the native land there is the recognition that Ludstown is incurably provincial, when considered with Rome, which suggests the wide culture of a fine civilization. This contrast is an essential pivot of the play and is characteristic of the 'total situation.' Immediately one notices that Rome is not Italy. Iachimo, 'the Italian villain' is never called Roman, whereas Lucius, the virtuous soldier of a dignified Empire, is always 'the Roman Lucius.' Rome does not seem to be *spatially visualized,* but, rather, is the nebulous symbol of an escape into the Dignity and Grandeur That Was Rome. And then, of course, there is Italy; and the relation resolves itself into a contrast between the fine civilization of a remote Golden Age and the vicious evil of a known present, and in this contrast, since both are ostensibly conceived as contemporaneous (thus employing a device similar to that of 'double time') both suffer an ironically critical scrutiny.

If the speech of the Queen on the subject of Britain [III. i. 14-33] be examined it will readily be seen how Caesar is brought down to the level of a provincial general. He is introduced in colloquial terms as any parish-hero ('a kind of conquest,' 'brag,' etc.) and so naturally becomes 'master Caesar.' . . . The local does not succeed in annexing, nor is it annexed by, the wider world of Imperial Caesar; the two remain suspended. If Caesar is made provincial then that in itself implies an inferiority in the provinciality, so that in that sense Caesar preserves his dignity over the incipiently comic Britons strutting in their rustic capital. Rome does remain an avenue of escape, essentially that, from the *close confinement* of the rural life, its sluggishness and waste. But although its value is admitted it is never regarded as a 'solution'—as we have seen Rome is

never regarded as being attainable in space: its attraction lies in its *remoteness,* and this is recognized.

Escape from, and criticism of, the rural life—which seems to include all life though there is the familiar Court-Country opposition—finds expression too in another mode, in the exquisite, pastoral elegizing of the dirges. . . . Mr. [John Middleton] Murry has declared: 'In *Cymbeline* Shakespeare himself was not far removed from that condition of relaxed control; but concentration was too deep an instinct with him ever to be quite forgotten,' and if the dirges are considered by themselves such an account as Mr. Murry gives does seem justified. But considered in their context—and since they are part of the play surely they are entitled to such consideration—the final account must take cognisance of the element of critical irony. It is not just that there is never any chance of the emotional impulse 'trickling away through the porous vessel of poetic commonplace,' as Mr. Murry puts it, but that there is a conscious, unrelaxed *critical* force behind it. The first dirge, 'With fairest flowers . . .' [IV. ii. 218-29] despite the soft fluency ('azure harebell,' 'furred moss,' etc.) has a suggestion of strength, of rustic vigour, noticeably in the word 'ruddock'; under the delicate alliterative lilting ('those rich-left heirs that let their fathers lie') you can feel the tense concentration, the wiriness of the lines. Immediately afterwards the critical attention is focussed in Guiderius' reaction.

> Prithee have done:
> And do not play in wench-like words with that
> Which is so serious.
>
> [IV. ii. 29-31]

Not that that is the 'right' reaction; the dirges cannot be dismissed so easily—and if one returns to the beginning of this passage a speech by Belarius gives the clue:

> O melancholy!
> Who ever yet could sound thy bottom, find
> The ooze, to show what coast thy sluggish crare
> Might easiliest harbour in?
>
> [IV. ii. 203-06]

The thick viscosity of these lines, with its fine image of the 'crare' heavily yet gracefully ('easiliest harbour in') moving through the ooze, has certain obvious relations to the claustrophobic tension observed previously. The melancholy is unpleasant yet relaxing, but, as the scene proceeds, the heavy sluggishness is sublimated into the clearer fluency of the dirge and then, completely, in the exquisite song (where the 'chimneysweepers' introduce a fine black contrast to the golden youth), as if melancholy is directly displayed and then 'worked on,' the process occurring partly under the compulsion of a need to escape, partly under the direction of a strong critical irony—

> Thersites' body is as good as Ajax'
> When neither are alive.
>
> [IV. ii. 252-53]

The dirges, then, offer a relief similar to that achieved in the evocation of the wide classic culture of Rome, and, similarly, such relief is critically 'placed.' There is no simple acceptance or rejection but a critical suspension of allegiance. The common denominator is the remoteness, the stillness—there is a kind of photographic stillness in the precision of the dirges—and if this be accepted it will readily be seen that in this way they are intimately connected with the idea of 'rebirth' which in itself includes the idea of coming to rest, perhaps, in the stillness of death. After the personality in its outward 'seeming' has been abandoned—and here the disguise convention is used to good effect—each character accepts death. Imogen is mourned as dead—indeed she suffers a kind of death—and Posthumus makes his acceptance in the gaol. It is this idea which must be examined now.

In his speech in the gaol one immediately notices the lack of any of the inflation of the rest of the play, and of any ironic overtones—there is a great deal of irony in the scene, but it is cut off from the magnificent speech: that is left unaffected. This speech is no instance of the weakened Shakespeare momentarily rousing himself from his mechanical task, or any other such academic myth. It has a measured dignity, a calm reasonableness quite unlike the violent convulsiveness and 'theatricality' of the earlier speeches. The movement gradually becomes slower and finally comes to rest in the last lines—

> If you will take this audit, take this life,
> And cancel these cold bonds. O Imogen!
> I'll speak to thee in silence.
>
> [V. iv. 27-9]

The 'silence,' the static remoteness of death, is what appeals to Posthumus, to the poet, as the solution of the impossible tension between the motions from and towards common experience, and through this the scene leads naturally into the ballet-like movements of the dream, which itself provides the transition into the terrible 'humour' of the prose. After the heightened, spiritual acceptance of death a fine modulation is made through the tense jesting to the normal everyday attitudes of the gaoler's prose, and it is thus that a reconciliation of the two opposite tendencies is made. The keen sense of futility expressed in the magnificent prose—

> What an infinite mock is this, that a man should
> have the best use of eyes to see the way of
> blindness! I'm sure hanging's the way of wink-
> ing—
>
> [V. iv. 196-97]

is maintained as the more practical version of what Posthumus saw more spiritually, and the irony in the gaoler's remarks does not destroy the value of the acceptance nor call it in question at all, rather does it substantiate that, since its energy is directed against the defeatist acceptance of death as an escape from a life of futility.

Here is no passion in accepting death as in the earlier work; here, death is no bridal bed but the cessation of all movement, is 'silence,' is a negative, cancelling force, which, paradoxically enough, has a kind of positive value. The direction of the play is towards this freedom from motion, from the restrictions of life's 'cold bonds'—

> no bolts for the dead!
>
> [V. v. 240]

But although this tendency is strong there is no suggestion of death, as a cessation of action, being the final absolute.

If these conclusions are not perverse it should be evident that *Cymbeline* cannot be regarded merely as a lighthearted pastoral romance and that there is not the slightest evidence for suggesting 'relaxed control.' The 'neatness' of the final scene is seen to be, not the hurried finishing-off of a task become wearisome, but the natural consequence of the direction of the play, which is towards a repose achieved in spite of violence,

the brutal action which constitutes the substratum of experience.

In the first place it has often been noted that Cymbeline himself does not act but only suffers, a will-less personality, and throughout the play there does seem to be a consciously expressed wish for a will, for the power to break clear of the entanglement of feelings, to have sovereignty over oneself. The whole plot is ostensibly 'the placing of the British Crown' [III. v. 65], and the sovereignty of this Britain involves an abnegation of the will—Cloten and Imogen sigh for the wills of lesser people, and the latter sacrifices a kingdom to gain 'two worlds.' The passivity and restrictions which such sovereignty entails are stressed.

This aspect of the passivity of the king must be related to the whole direction of the play, which finds its consummation in this final scene, where the circular movement is like that of a wheel coming to rest, as more and more of the 'action' is disposed of, circling nearer and nearer to the final immobility of the last tableau. This final immobility is, I suggest, the poise which the play achieves—up to this point the verse rapidly becomes less violent, less immediately evocative, and flatter, more neutral. The tautness of the body of the play is not relaxed, there is no relaxation in that sense, but the verse of the last speeches is flat and polished like a mirror reflecting the final tableau. All the previous suggestions of savage farce disappear leaving only the taut ironic inflection.

This critical element is important, suggesting as it does that the evocation of a static tableau, of the denial of action in this 'final peace,' is not an unqualified resolution of the strain and tension of the play. Cymbeline's speech in its recall of 'Ludstown' and 'our crookt smokes' [V. v. 477], although it presents them as in a photograph, yet evokes that world of small, petty things which arouses such revulsion. There is still an ironic inflection to the peace, to the reconciliation of Britain and Rome. And in any case no ideals have been left standing. Imogen is 'a commodity,'

> a shop of all the qualities that man
> Loves woman for.
>
> [V. v. 166-67]

and the gods are but mischievous little boys who 'throw stones of sulphur' [V. v. 240]. (pp. 6-19)

> *F. C. Tinkler, " 'Cymbeline'," in* Scrutiny, *Vol. VII, No. 1, June, 1938, pp. 5-19.*

E. M. W. TILLYARD (essay date 1938)

[Tillyard is best known for his influential Shakespeare's History Plays *(1944), considered a leading example of historical criticism. In addition to his historical studies, Tillyard also published* Shakespeare's Last Plays *(1938),* Shakespeare's Problem Plays *(1949), and* Shakespeare's Early Comedies, *a book he was working on at the time of his death in 1962 but was not published until 1965. In an unexcerpted portion of his study* Shakespeare's Last Plays, *Tillyard postulates that the variety of incidents, the unusual combination of characters, and the mixture of elements from romance, comedy, and tragedy in such plays as* Cymbeline, The Winter's Tale, *and* The Tempest, *are not the result of a "gratuitous and wanton outburst" by Shakespeare, but indicate his intention to represent in his work the different levels of reality of human existence. In the following excerpt, he argues that although it is possible to accept Harley Granville-Barker's judgment that the artlessness in* Cymbeline, *including the uncommon mixture of incidents, was self-conscious and deliberate on Shakespeare's*

part (see excerpt above, 1930), he thinks it wiser to follow the lead of William Hazlitt (1817), who noted the play's association with dramatic romance, a genre that necessitates an unrealistic treatment of character and events. Tillyard maintains that a play rich in complexity like Cymbeline—*with its "rapidly changing incidents, the extraordinary accidents, the mixture of improbability with moral wisdom"—would have provided Shakespeare with "a correlative to a newly sharpened sense of the many planes on which life could be lived." However, he concludes, Shakespeare's attempt to portray different planes of reality in* Cymbeline *was not successful, in that the dramatist did not convey his intention skillfully; in Tillyard's words, the play "ends in the queer phantasmagoric effect of a welter of unreality rather than in a vision of those different planes standing out in sharp and thrilling contrast."*]

Shakespeare's first attempt to express his urgent sense of the different planes on which life can be lived was not very successful. (And when I say 'attempt,' I do not mean that there was anything deliberate about it.) For it is vain to hold that *Cymbeline* is a clean and satisfactory achievement. On the other hand, I cannot believe that Shakespeare was quite in the dark; or that the fantastic range of style from brilliant realism to the grossest conventionalism and improbability was no more than a gratuitous and wanton outburst. One of the best passages in Granville-Barker's excellent preface to the play is that in which he insists that the ingenuousnesses are intentional [see excerpt above, 1930]. Take, for instance, one of the most flagrant examples: Belarius's informative soliloquy at the end of the third scene of the third act:

> These boys know little they are sons to the King;
> Nor Cymbeline dreams that they are alive.
> They think they are mine; and though train'd up thus meanly
> I' the cave wherein they bow, their thoughts do hit
> The roofs of palaces, and nature prompts them
> In simple and low things to prince it much
> Beyond the trick of others . . .
> O Cymbeline! heaven and my conscience knows
> Thou didst unjustly banish me: whereon,
> At three and two years old, I stole these babes;
> Thinking to bar thee of succession, as
> Thou reft'st me of my lands. Euriphile,
> Thou wast their nurse; they took thee for their mother,
> And every day do honour to her grave:
> Myself, Belarius, that am Morgan call'd,
> They take for natural father.
>
> [III. iii. 80-6, 99-107]

Not only does the soliloquy offend against all probability as to its utterance, but it is difficult to see how, in his mountain isolation, Belarius could have known the intimate thoughts of Cymbeline. Yet that Shakespeare committed this offence because he was tired or careless is most difficult to believe. At the time of *Cymbeline*, dramatic technique must have been easy to him: in his sleep or in his cups it would have been easier for him to devise something more competent. It is more probable that the ingenuousness, like that of the Euripidean prologue, was intended.

On the other hand, Granville-Barker may be wrong in limiting the play to a piece of technical sophistication. He says, 'Shakespeare has an unlikely story to tell,' and proceeds to explain, relying especially on the theatrical conditions, with what artifice he did his job. But to say 'Shakespeare has an unlikely story to tell' is to beg the main critical question. And this is: why did Shakespeare choose so unlikely a story? Or, more

fully, why did Shakespeare take the trouble to go to three quite different originals, thus letting himself in for a dramatic task of extreme difficulty, which he can perform only by forfeiting the kind of dramatic probability which he normally accepted? His immediate originals were an Italian novel, early British history derived from Holinshed, and a fairy story of the wicked step-mother and innocent step-daughter. And behind them may be the general pressure of Sidney's *Arcadia*. Critics have tried to disintegrate the play and assign bits away from Shakespeare. But no one doubts Shakespeare's choice of the three main motives; and the burden of accounting for that choice remains. (Personally, in view of the amount of queerness one has to swallow, I can see no reason for not swallowing the whole, Posthumus's vision included.) Well, did Shakespeare choose the three themes for the sole reason of setting himself technical problems by solving which he could exhibit his virtuosity; in particular that he might indulge in the technical debauch of a super-dénouement in the last scene? or had he some other motive? That he enjoyed the debauch need not be denied, but that he went out of his way to amalgamate three plots in order to prepare for it is hard to admit. More likely the wealth of plot-material corresponded to some desire in Shakespeare's mind; and this desire was to express his sense of the different worlds we live in. He attempted to do so by one of the most obvious means: diversity of plot. His attempt was experimental, yet at first serious. It may have become less serious during composition, as Shakespeare felt success eluding him. And he may have been glad to cover his failure with that cloak of artful and pseudo-ingenuous sophistication of which Granville-Barker speaks.

When we call Shakespeare's last plays romances, I suppose we mean that his material is remote and improbable and that he uses the happy ending. It would be more helpful, at least in thinking of *Cymbeline*, to use the word *romance* as Hazlitt did, who thought of this play as a narrative romance adapted to the stage:

> Cymbeline may be considered as a dramatic romance, in which the most striking parts of the story are thrown into the form of a dialogue, and the intermediate circumstances are explained by the different speakers, as occasion renders it necessary. The action is less concentrated in consequence; but the interest becomes more aërial and refined from the principle of perspective introduced into the subject by the imaginary changes of scene, as well as by the length of time it occupies [see excerpt above, 1817].

It may well be that Hazlitt gives our inquiry the right direction. Turning from Roman history to the romances, Underdowne's translation of Heliodorus, for instance, or Sidney's *Arcadia,* Shakespeare may have felt that this rich complexity corresponded in some obscure way with what was now occupying his mind. A story told by the author was one thing, but a story within that story, told by a character (a device common to both the above books), was something a little different. And the difference may have interested him. The general effect, too, of the rapidly changing incidents, the extraordinary accidents, the mixture of improbability with moral wisdom would express a sense of wonder, of the strange mix-up of things, that would easily provide a correlative to a newly sharpened sense of the many planes on which life could be lived. Thus, attracted by the implications of the romance, Shakespeare in *Cymbeline* attempts to imitate the diversity of its material and the surprising turns of its plot. (pp. 68-72)

There was no absolute need [for Shakespeare] . . . to depart from the realistic methods of the tragedies proper, even though it may have been convenient to mark off the theme of recreation from that of destruction by a change of manner. But by adding variety of character-treatment to variety of plot, Shakespeare could powerfully enrich his means of expressing his sense of different worlds. And this was the main reason for his new treatment of character.

In addition to these contrasts, there is a new contrast of style, tending to express the same things. The packed, arduous, stormy, and eminently dramatic verse of the late tragedies is still there. . . . But another music, remote, unearthly, slow, and not very dramatic, first detected in *Pericles,* now appears in palpable contrast. It marks especially the scenes in the Welsh mountains. This is how Guiderius and Arviragus describe their life.

> *Gui.*   We, poor unfledged,
>   Have never wing'd from view o' the nest, nor
>   know not
>   What air's from home. Haply this life is best,
>   If quiet life be best; sweeter to you
>   That have a sharper known; well corresponding
>   With your stiff age: but unto us it is
>   A cell of ignorance; travelling a-bed;
>   A prison for a debtor, that not dares
>   To stride a limit.
> *Arv.*   What should we speak of
>   When we are old as you? when we shall hear
>   The rain and wind beat dark December, how,
>   In this our pinching cave, shall we discourse
>   The freezing hours away? We have seen nothing;
>   We are beastly, subtle as the fox for prey,
>   Like warlike as the wolf for what we eat;
>   Our valour is to chase what flies; our cage
>   We make a quire, as doth the prison'd bird,
>   And sing our bondage freely.
>
>   [III. iii. 27-44]

If this type of music was confined to *Cymbeline,* we might infer that it exists for no more than to depict the remote life of Belarius and the boys in the Welsh mountains: unspoilt nature set against the broken and hectic life of the court. But it occurred in *Pericles* and was to occur in the two later plays [*A Winter's Tale* and *The Tempest*]; hence it can hardly not have a more general significance. And it implies a way of feeling about life. Through this unearthly music Shakespeare expresses a feeling of seeing life distanced, instead of identifying himself with whatever action is being transacted.

The chief merit of *Cymbeline* as a stage play is its liveliness. There is a constant and diversified stream of interesting incident, fluctuating in intensity of feeling and in its kinship to tragedy, comedy, farce, or romance. It is extremely agreeable and diverting to watch. And Shakespeare's sure general grasp of this miscellany arouses in us the zest of admiration. It cannot be said that Shakespeare's sense of different worlds, however important a part of the meaning, is conveyed strongly by the whole play. He did not put his various means of conveying that meaning to any very skilful use. The diversity of plot causes confusion rather than contrast. Realism and symbolism in Imogen's character do the same. The changes of style are far more effective, but there is little apparent reason for their occurrence. Shakespeare is apt to maintain one kind of style

so long that he accustoms us to it thoroughly enough to make us take it for granted. For instance, the scene of Imogen's burial is drawn out: we are satisfied with it, and when she wakes with the words, 'Yes, sir, to Milford-Haven' [IV. ii. 291], there is no shock of surprise, as there might have been if the burial scene had left us hungry and wanting more. On the other hand, the brisk and business-like entry of Lucius and the Romans after Imogen's strained, moving, and melodramatic soliloquy over Cloten's body is the effective breaking-in of one world on another. . . . But on the whole, Shakespeare's attempt in *Cymbeline* to convey his feeling of different planes of reality ends in the queer phantasmagoric effect of a welter of unreality rather than in a vision of those different planes standing out in sharp and thrilling contrast. (pp. 72-6)

> E. M. W. Tillyard, "Planes of Reality," in his
> Shakespeare's Last Plays, *Chatto and Windus, 1938,*
> *pp. 59-80.*

MARK VAN DOREN   (essay date 1939)

[*Van Doren was a Pulitzer Prize-winning poet, American educator, editor, and novelist. In the introduction to his* Shakespeare *(1939), he states that he "ignored the biography of Shakespeare, the history and character of his time, the conventions of his theater, the works of his contemporaries" to concentrate on the interest of the plays and their relevance to the modern reader or spectator. In the following excerpt, Van Doren analyzes the poetic style of* Cymbeline, *noting the prevalence of involuted phrasings, tangled syntax, and sentences so complex that they are "not to be parsed by thoughtless ears." He also points to Shakespeare's use of brief, elliptical phrases that create a sense of tension and to the way in which the passages of praise are written in a highly exaggerated language. Van Doren further examines the urgency and intensity of Imogen's speeches, which he maintains reflect the absolute quality of her love and influence every other major figure in the play. For additional commentary on the dramatic language of* Cymbeline, *see the essays by Coburn Freer, James Sutherland, and Arthur Symons cited in the Additional Bibliography; also, see the excerpts by Caroline F. E. Spurgeon (1935), F. C. Tinkler (1938), A. A. Stephenson (1942), Derek Traversi (1954), and Robin Moffet (1962) for analyses of the imagery in the play.*]

Even among the romances "Cymbeline" is extreme. Its king is meaninglessly stern, banishing the hero with extravagant words:

>   Away!
>   Thou 'rt poison to my blood,
>
>   [I. i. 127-28]

and dismissing the grief of the heroine, his own daughter, with this harsh command:

>   Nay, let her languish
>   A drop of blood a day; and, being aged,
>   Die of this folly!
>
>   [I. i. 156-58]

Its queen is sinister in her craft; she brews poison out of innocent violets, cowslips, and primroses [I. v. 83], she knows how to make sleep look like death, and she lectures the heroine coldly against grief, ignorant that it can be a medicine too, as Imogen once says [III. ii. 33]. And her son Cloten, whom Imogen had been ordered to marry instead of Posthumus, is, as the villain of the piece, so utterly out of bounds that he becomes a clown; "this ass," as the lords at court call him, swears horrendously that he will ravish Imogen in her husband's clothes, but he swears with "snatches in his voice, and burst of speaking'' [IV. ii. 105-06], and is but a whining parody of Aaron the Moor [in *Titus Andronicus*]. The fairy element loses some of its force through being associated with the rigmarole of two princes, sons of Cymbeline, who since their abduction as babes have been brought up in a Welsh cave and yet are princes still; for, as Belarius their abductor says, it is hard ''to hide the sparks of nature'' [III. iii. 79]. And the divine element, pursued to a point where Jupiter descends in thunder and lightning, sitting on an eagle, to say that the sleeping Posthumus will be all the happier for his affliction, and to leave on his chest a riddling tablet which once interpreted will make all clear, is perhaps grotesque. (pp. 303-04)

Where, then, does ''Cymbeline'' get its power, for it has power? The answer is the uses to which Shakespeare has put his extremes. In plausibility he was perhaps not interested at all, absorbed as he must have been in the opportunities his plot gave him for saying absolute things absolutely, and for following to its end in Imogen the vision of an absolutely faithful woman—absolutely faithful because absolutely in love. But the heroine of the play cannot be understood before its style, which is the richest and most elaborate of Shakespeare's styles thus far. The opening speech, by a nameless gentleman of Cymbeline's court, accustoms us at once to involution:

> You do not meet a man but frowns. Our bloods
> No more obey the heavens than our courtiers
> Still seem as does the King.
>
> [I. i. 1-3]

The proportion in the second sentence is less obvious than we expected, and leaves us with a sense that we should have listened more closely. The sense will be with us always, whether it is prose we hear:

> He was then of a crescent note, expected to
> prove so worthy as since he hath been allowed
> the name of;
>
> [I. iv. 1-3]

> You speak of him when he was less furnish'd
> than now he is with that which makes him both
> without and within;
>
> [I. iv. 8-10]

or whether it is verse, tangling us in excesses of syntax:

> I have given him that
> Which, if he take, shall quite unpeople her
> Of liegers for her sweet, and which she after,
> Except she bend her humour, shall be assur'd
> To taste of too.
>
> [I. v. 78-82]

Syntax would seem with this poet to have become an occupation in itself; complex sentences, not to be parsed by thoughtless ears, are his special pleasure. And he takes a further pleasure in making familiar words do unfamiliar work: ''rather than story him in his own hearing'' [I. iv. 33-4], ''to the madding of her lord'' [II. ii. 37], ''when we shall hear the rain and wind beat dark December'' [III iii. 36-7], ''in simple and low things to prince it much beyond the trick of others'' [III. iii. 85-6], ''thy memory will then be pang'd by me'' [III. iv. 94-5], ''to winter-ground thy corse'' [IV. ii. 229], ''the holy eagle stoop'd, as to foot us'' [V. iv. 115-16]. This is always the privilege of poets, and Shakespeare has made full use of the privilege before; but he has never been so ingenious at coining verbs. His style is on the stretch. To the brevity of phrase that distinguished ''Antony and Cleopatra'' are added

further brevities, sometimes perverse, and still more nervous tensions. It is the style of a man whose determination is to reach extremes of statement with as few preliminaries as possible. His people are deadly earnest in their exaggeration:

> I'll drink the words you send,
> Though ink be made of gall.
>
> [I. i. 100-01]

> Should we be taking leave
> As long a term as yet we have to live,
> The loathness to depart would grow. . . .
>
> [I. i. 106-08]

> What shall I need to draw my sword? The paper
> Hath cut her throat already.
>
> [III. iv. 32-3]

> I had rather
> Have skipp'd from sixteen years of age to sixty,
> To have turn'd my leaping-time into a crutch,
> Than have seen this.
>
> [IV. ii. 198-201]

> So I'll die
> For thee, O Imogen, even for whom my life
> Is every breath a death.
>
> [V. i. 25-7]

This is the speech of persons for whom there are but two alternatives, all and none; as when Posthumus puts an end to Iachimo's slander of Imogen with the desperate words:

> Spare your arithmetic; never count the turns;
> Once, and a million!
>
> [II. iv. 142-43]

The music of praise has never in Shakespeare been so elaborate. The gentleman of the opening scene says of Posthumus that he

> is a creature such
> As, to seek through the regions of the earth
> For one his like, there would be something failing
> In him that should compare. I do not think
> So fair an outward and such stuff within
> Endows a man but he.
>
> [I. i. 19-24]

And when the second gentleman remarks that this is far praise indeed, the first insists:

> I do extend him, sir, within himself,
> Crush him together rather than unfold
> His measure duly.
>
> [I. i. 25-7]

Posthumus is not only a sample to the youngest, he is a guide for dotards—he is all that man can be, and the final proof of this is that such a woman as Imogen has elected him husband. . . . The language of praise in this play has found its absolute grammar—as, when Imogen hears Cloten call Posthumus a base slave, the reverse language of denunciation comes correspondingly into its own:

> Wert thou the son of Jupiter and no more
> But what thou art besides, thou wert too base
> To be his groom. Thou wert dignified enough,
> Even to the point of envy, if 't were made
> Comparative for your virtues, to be styl'd
> The under-hangman of his kingdom, and hated

For being preferr'd so well . . .
He never can meet more mischance than come
To be but nam'd of thee. His meanest garment
That ever hath but clipp'd his body, is dearer
In my respect than all the hairs above thee,
Were they all made such men.

[II. iii. 125-31, 132-36]

Imogen is one of the great women of Shakespeare or the world. The absoluteness of her fidelity comes from the absoluteness of her love, the intensity of which has more than saved the play—has endowed it with a unique fascination. Her virtue is not a named thing like Isabella's [in *Measure for Measure*], nor is she conscious of it as virtue. And her devotion is to Viola's [in *Twelfth Night*] as avalanches are to aromas—swift, full-bodied, not to be withstood. Neither has it any of the rankness which reduced Helena's [in *A Midsummer Night's Dream*] at times to the level of barbarism. Being complete, it has its pressing tendernesses, its urgent delicacies, its passionate reserves. Its influence spreads through all of the play that can contain it; makes Iachimo by contact a great poet, and fills the figure of Posthumus with seriousness which otherwise it would have lacked. Posthumus exists through Imogen, as Iachimo through both. Her speech has everywhere a force beyond which poetry can scarcely go, and this is true whether she is expressing herself in short, sharp, compendious queries and interjections: "Will my lord say so?", "Not he, I hope," "Am I one, sir?", "Let me hear no more," "You make amends," "To pieces with me!" [I. vi. 73, 77, 83, 117, 168; III. iv. 53] . . . ; or whether she is delivering her mind of sudden metaphors: "In a great pool a swan's nest" [III. iv. 139], "but if there be yet left in heaven as small a drop of pity as a wren's eye" [IV. ii. 303-05]; or whether she is pursuing to its limit in long discourse the theme of her incomparable attachment. The dialogue which opens the third scene would alone distinguish the play, and certainly it lets us feel, before we have gone any farther, the fierceness along with the beauty of our heroine's temper.

Imogen.	I would thou grew'st unto the shores o' the haven,
	And question'dst every sail. If he should write
	And I not have it, 't were a paper lost,
	As offer'd mercy is. What was the last
	That he spake to thee?
Pisanio.	It was his queen, his queen!
Imogen.	Than wav'd his handkerchief?
Pisanio.	And kiss'd it, madam.
Imogen.	Senseless linen! happier therein than I!
	And that was all?
Pisanio.	No, madam; for so long
	As he could make me with this eye or ear
	Distinguish him from others, he did keep
	The deck, with glove, or hat, or handkerchief,
	Still waving, as the fits and stirs of 's mind
	Could best express how slow his soul sail'd on,
	How swift his ship.
Imogen.	Thou shouldst have made him
	As little as a crow, or less, ere left
	To after-eye him.
Pisanio.	Madam, so I did.

Imogen.	I would have broke mine eye-strings; crack'd them, but
	To look upon him, till the diminution
	Of space had pointed him sharp as my needle;
	Nay, follow'd him, till he had melted from
	The smallness of a gnat to air, and then
	Have turn'd mine eye and wept.

[I. iii. 1-22]

Imogen in her urgency, her insistence which is never quite hysteria, creates Posthumus through her love, and even brings his servant to the point of being a fine poet. For Pisanio shares with her the moments when she speaks best—the moment, for another instance, when she reads the letter from Posthumus which he has given her:

O, for a horse with wings! Hear'st thou, Pisanio?
He is at Milford-Haven. Read, and tell me
How far 't is thither. If one of mean affairs
May plod it in a week, why may not I
Glide thither in a day? Then, true Pisanio,—
Who long'st, like me, to see thy lord; who long'st,—
O, let me bate,—but not like me—yet long'st,
But in a fainter kind;—O, not like me,
For mine's beyond beyond—say, and speak thick,—
Love's counsellor should fill the bores of hearing,
To the smothering of the sense—how far it is
To this same blessed Milford; and by the way
Tell me how Wales was made so happy as
To inherit such a haven.

[III. ii. 48-61]

This is not hysteria, it is rapture. The woman who bears down upon Pisanio and us with such a rush of eagerness, such tornadoes of joy, is herself whole and strong. (pp. 305-11)

But there is another scene which she saves for greatness. The recognition scene (V, v) draws all of its power from her; first when she fixes her eyes on Iachimo across the room, saying

I see a thing
Bitter to me as death,

[V. v. 103-04]

and later when, having been struck to the floor by Posthumus in the rage which precedes recognition, and having had at last a few moments of silence with him while Cymbeline and Cornelius speak, she teases him with the question:

Why did you throw your wedded lady from you?
Think that you are upon a rock, and now
Throw me again.

[V. i. 261-63]

To which, whether "rock" (precipice) or "lock" (as in wrestling) is the word Shakespeare wrote, and either would fit the speaker, Posthumus's response is adequate at last:

Hang there like fruit, my soul,
Till the tree die!

[V. v. 263-64]
(p. 312)

Mark Van Doren, "'Cymbeline'," in his Shakespeare, *Henry Holt and Company, 1939, pp. 303-12.*

A. A. STEPHENSON, S.J.   (essay date 1942)

[*Stephenson argues that in* Cymbeline *Shakespeare was preoccupied by "the idea of an ideal perfection, an absolute value" and that he sought to dramatize a "transcendental" vision of a "harmonized experience," in which the disparities between reality and ideal value disappear and a new unanimity is achieved. The critic maintains that, because this theme of a "harmonized experience" is an ideal, theoretical abstraction, it resists dramatic representation; therefore, Shakespeare's failure to portray it effectively in this play, he contends, is traceable to the nature of the theme and not to any defects in the dramatist's creative imagination. Stephenson discovers a "clue" to this transcendent vision in the play's imagery, particularly in the recurring metaphors of valuation and worth, which express the significance of the ideal value ascribed to fidelity and chastity. He also claims that the imagistic pattern of "locks, bonds, and bolts" relates to the valuation pattern "through the idea that honour is a jewel which must be kept locked away." For further commentary on the imagery in* Cymbeline, *see the excerpts by Caroline F. E. Spurgeon (1935), Derek Traversi (1954), and Robin Moffet (1962). Additionally, Stephenson claims that the idea of a "harmonized experience" in* Cymbeline *refutes the view of F. C. Tinkler (1938) that the play is based on a profound "contrasting dualism" and is informed by a "critical irony" throughout, to the extent that no positive ideals remain intact by the end of the drama. Whereas Tinkler regards this dualism of tension and critical irony as intentional, Stephenson argues that it is merely an indication of Shakespeare's inability to dramatize successfully his vision of a new harmony. F. R. Leavis (1942) disputes Stephenson's identification of a significant theme in* Cymbeline *that unites and underlies the various elements in the play.*]

The imagery of *Cymbeline* is of an unusual character. To begin with, it goes beyond the imagery of most, probably all, of the plays in its unrelenting pervasiveness; a single class of imagery is almost ubiquitous. Mr. Masefield, incidentally, might find some difficulty in squaring with this fact his suggestion, attractive on some grounds, that the discontinuity and incoherency of *Cymbeline* is due to its having been 'begun as a tragedy during the great mood of tragical creation, then laid aside unfinished, from some failure in the vision, or change in the creative mood, and brought to an end later in a new spirit.' In favour of, or at least compatible with, Mr. Masefield's suggestion are the exaggerated eulogies of the hero and heroine in the early scenes and their own secure self-confidence, which suggest, very much in Shakespeare's way, a challenge to the Fates and, so, ironically presage catastrophe. Moreover in III iv, where the faithful Pisanio takes Imogen to Milford in obedience to his master's murderous commands, we seem actually to watch the play modulating out of tragedy into comedy or romance. But, apart from the difficulty raised by the continuity of the imagery, this hypothesis is hardly reconcilable with the presence from the beginning of certain elements of romance, notably the theme of the 'thief-stol'n' royal babes, the improbable villainy of the Queen, and the extravagancy of Cloten.

Yet it may still be true that the play *otherwise* represents several phases or strata of Shakespeare's experience: that it is the dramatization of a vision long present to his mind, a vision which dated, in a confused form, from the period of the great tragedies, and probably from much earlier, a vision which might equally well have been expressed in tragedy or in comedy, and perhaps better in lyric or allegorical epic, a vision which, while it never 'changed,' gradually clarified and simplified itself so as finally to elude articulation.

It is by way of this last suggestion that the immediate relevancy at this point of this apparent digression will appear in connection with the second general characteristic of the imagery: which is its abstractness. As is generally recognized, in the obviously great plays the total effect of the imagery is something 'not imagined—felt' (oddly, the phrase is from *Cymbeline* [IV. ii. 307]): the darkness in *Macbeth*, the disease in *Hamlet*, are an 'atmosphere': intangible, they are apprehended by tact, 'felt.' In *Cymbeline* there is, generally speaking, no such concretion of idea, imagery, and situation; the imagery strikes one, rather, as a removable oddity of expression, suggestive of a breakdown of communication. (p. 330)

Finally, the imagery is rather trite—by now, hackneyed—and perhaps on that account it has been the less noticed. To come now to the imagery itself: the pervading idea is that of worth, value. That which above all realizes this value, that which is pre-eminently (according to the most characteristic epithet) 'rare,' is a certain quality of spirit which appears variously as honour, fidelity, 'trueness,' and—for this is the play with 'the indecent theme'—chastity or purity. The familiar contrast of 'inner' and 'outer,' real and only apparent, worth occurs constantly and in a variety of forms. There is the contrast between the social status of Imogen and that of her husband: this is harped on a good deal, and Posthumus is frequently referred to, particularly by Cloten, as a 'beggar'; the general assumption is that the disparity of birth and position is irrelevant unless it reflects a difference of real worth. Then there is the contrast between mere physical beauty and 'honesty' (the 'handsome heart'). Intelligence, 'brains,' is considered as another sort of worth; and there is the familiar contrast of country and Court. The various sorts of worth form a scale; it is sometimes suggested that the lower forms may be counterfeit, may hide, or even be symptomatic of, an inner 'falseness': but the deeper implication is that all the forms have a fundamental affinity, partake, essentially, of the same quality and should, ideally, go together. It is Imogen's glory that she is rich in all the kinds, but especially in the 'jewel' of 'honesty': Iachimo exclaims on his first sight of her:

> All of her that is out of door most rich!
> If she be furnish'd with a mind so rare,
> She is alone the Arabian bird.
>
> [I. vi. 15-17]

And the courtier, arguing that Posthumus is worthy of her, concludes

> I do not think
> So fair an outward and such stuff within
> Endows a man but he.
>
> [I. i. 22-4]

A passage which characteristically brings together several kinds, or levels, of falseness occurs in III, vi:

> Yes, no wonder,
> When rich ones scarce tell true: to lapse in fullness
> Is sorer than to lie for need; and falsehood
> Is worse in kings than beggars.—My dear lord!
> Thou art one of the false ones.
>
> [III. vi. 11-15]

Compare:

> Such noble fury in so poor a thing;
> Such precious deeds in one that promised nought
> But beggary and poor looks
>
> [V. v. 8-10]

where there is the further complication that 'the poor soldier that so richly fought, Whose rags shamed gilded arms' [V. v. 3-4] is really the knight Posthumus.

This valuation-imagery appears in the frequently recurring metaphors of buying and selling, of estimating (including measuring and weighing), of equivalence or non-equivalence, of jewellery, of debts, contracts, and exchange. Further, the rich treasure and rare jewel is conceived as fragile and as the prey of thieves: it goes with, and is guarded by, a discriminating sensitiveness; the antagonists, the solvent forces, are conceived as cheap and 'common,' and go with coarse and calloused perceptions. *Cf.* the speech beginning 'Had I this cheek' [I. vi. 99]; with this should probably be compared the lines:

> Forget that rarest treasure of your cheek,
> Exposing it—but, O, the harder heart!
> Alack, no remedy!—to the greedy touch
> Of common-kissing Titan
>
> [III. iv. 160-63]

where the meaning seems to be, in spite of the suggestions of editors, that when Imogen disguises herself as a boy, exchanges 'fear and niceness' for a 'waggish courage' [III. iv. 155, 157] and becomes sun-burnt, there is a danger that the loss of delicacy may go more than skin-deep. *Cf.* also:

> Shalt hereafter find
> It is no act of common passage, but
> A strain of rareness.
>
> [III. iv. 90-2]

'Common' stands in obvious contrast with 'rare'; 'rare' implies not so much that the rare quality has few instances, but that its achievement is desirable and arduous and that, attained, it is of great price; similarly 'common,' besides suggesting promiscuity and imperceptiveness, means something like 'easy.'

Some further illustration of the 'bargaining' sort of imagery is necessary to establish my point; though, since it is very common, and since it is so lacking in special beauty or subtlety that analysis is neither necessary nor possible, much that is directly relevant must be omitted.

The play starts off with the 'dissembling' of the flattering and hypocritical courtiers; 'our courtiers Still seem as does the King . . . all is outward sorrow . . .' [I. i. 2-3, 9]. Posthumus is 'a poor but worthy gentleman' [I. i. 7]; and a few lines down the contrast between the 'faces' and the 'hearts' of the courtiers occurs again. Then the description of Posthumus quoted above, and the metaphor is immediately developed in the figure of an honest salesman displaying wares of solid value:

> I do extend him, sir, within himself,
> Crush him together rather than unfold
> His measure duly.
>
> [I. i. 25-7]

The First Gentleman next proves the worth of Posthumus from Imogen's choice of him as a husband:

> her own price
> Proclaims how she esteem'd him and his virtue
>
> [I. i. 51-2]

—compare how in I, iv, Iachimo argues that Posthumus's marriage has caused him to be overrated. The same sort of imagery accompanies the exchange of jewellery 'As I my poor self did exchange for you . . .' [I. i. 119]—and underlines the revelation of conjugal infidelity just made by the Queen in similar terms—there far more unnatural:

> I never do him wrong
> But he does buy my injuries to be friends,
> Pays dear for my offences.
>
> [I. i. 104-06]

This last quotation suggests, perhaps, that the whole complicated price-imagery is an elaborate extension of the familiar ambiguity of 'dear.' All these examples occur in the first 120 lines of the play, and there are more in the next 30 lines.

There is much, also, of this imagery in the Wager-scene (I, iv); and there, also, the symbolism of the jewellery is made explicit in 'Your ring may be stolen too: so your brace of unprizable estimations, the one is but frail and the other casual,' and in the phrase 'she your jewel, this your jewel' [I. iv. 89-91, 153]. Iachimo, of course, uses the stolen bracelet to prove that he has

> pick'd the lock and ta'en
> The treasure of her honour.
>
> [II. ii. 41-2]

But the establishment of the symbolism further lends irony, probably, to Imogen's words just before Iachimo's 'attempting' of her—'Had I been thief-stol'n, / As my two brothers, happy!' [I. vi. 5-6]; and it also allows Shakespeare to indulge in a little gentle moralizing (not, of course, at Imogen's expense) when he makes the unwitting Imogen bid her maid 'search for a jewel that too casually / Hath left my arm; it was thy master's' [II. iii. 141-42].

Imogen and Posthumus, when each thinks the other false, both cry out on the deceitfulness of 'good seeming': thus Posthumus's

> Let there be no honour
> Where there is beauty; truth, where semblance
>
> [II. iv. 108-09]

is answered by Imogen's speech beginning 'True honest men, being heard, like false Aeneas . . .' [II. iv. 58].

Some interesting examples of this valuation imagery are to be found in Cloten's Wooing scene (II, iii), and the contrast between true and false nobility is underlined, rather heavily, in Posthumus's encounter with the British Lord (V, iii). The language of the repentance soliloquy in the following scenes depends on the traditional conceptions of expiation as the payment of a debt and of justice as consisting in an equivalence.

Another group of imagery centres in locks, bonds, and bolts. 'Bond(s)' is used in a great variety of senses, and is a focal point of the imagery. This group of imagery is connected with the main group through the idea that honour is a jewel which must be kept locked away; the connection is made explicitly in a passage already quoted.

Finally—and this leads up to the general interpretation of the play—a very high proportion of the words which occur only in this play seem to have been especially coined to express the idea of something uniquely excellent and 'passing fair': such words are 'chaffless,' 'unparagoned' (twice), 'outprized,' 'outsell' (twice); and 'rare,' with its derivatives, occurs with a frequency even approached only in *The Winter's Tale*.

I should suggest, then, that the persistent 'value' imagery indicates a preoccupation of the dramatist with the idea of an ideal perfection, an absolute value, and that this preoccupation was coincident with the attainment of a harmonized experience, an experience, however, not yet fully reorganized for the expression of the new vision in poetry. If it be objected that this is no preoccupation for a respectable dramatist, the answer perhaps is that this is true in so far as drama regularly involves a conflict, and the conflict in turn entails a certain hypostatization of evil; but the natural concomitant of the harmonization of experience, assuming it to be associated with a (Platonic) 'conversion,' is the rejection of dualism and the imaginative intuition of the identity of reality and value. (This identification, however, need not be held as a logical proposition; it may be assented to only on one 'plane': and this is, here, not meaningless, since such a 'conversion' might reasonably be expected to create a new plane of consciousness.)

But by an inevitable paradox the vision which, as an underlying assumption and as the source of an irritant, is at the root of much great poetry, can hardly itself be the theme of poetry. As an idea, it is found to be so general and abstract that it 'moves nothing'; as an ideal, it is so rich and concrete as to elude complete imaginative expression. Everything is related to it, because everything has value; but the relation is abstract; what is concrete is not the ground, but the subjects of the relation—things themselves; but they are not perceptibly 'like' the ideal, do not reveal it. Yet certain favoured things—things that give the sense of extraordinary beauty and richness (mostly the least describable things)—are analogues or symbols of it and evoke it—scent-laden breezes, and flowers, and setting suns. . . . Hence the verse of *Cymbeline* is least alive in precisely those places where the idea finds clearest expression; the 'value' imagery is a clue to the experience which is at the heart of the play, but it does not communicate it; the experience is communicated, the rare quality evoked, in the genuine poetry of the play where the vision spontaneously crystallizes itself in concrete images which say nothing about value but awaken a sense of startling beauty: 'alone the Arabian bird,' 'in a great pool a swan's nest' [III. iv. 139], 'chaffless' (occurring just there), the flower poetry of the Dirge scene, and

> As zephyrs blowing below the violet,
> Not wagging his sweet head.
>
> [IV. ii. 172-73]

Another difficulty inseparable from the expression in poetry of such a vision is one of words (rather than of things): because it is a vision which all men have glimpsed, the words which might have been least inadequate to describe it have been staled by use. Consequently the poet is faced with the dilemma that if he uses ordinary language it will seem trite and dead, and probably priggish; while if he creates a new language and a new verse . . . , he is likely to suffer the rate of the esoteric. So the poet finds himself, as it were, in a void.

A further difficulty besets the attempt at a *dramatic* rendering of such a vision. With the passing of the vision of evil, now seen as remote and alien instead of as urgent and present, conflict, which is the mainspring whence serious drama derives its energy, also disappears. The poet is left with a single principle of life, and cannot 'project' himself with full sympathy into antagonistic characters. And that may be the explanation of the inequalities, the incongruities, the discontinuity, the sense of different planes, the only spasmodic and flickering life, in *Cymbeline*. It must, I think, be recognized that *Cymbeline* is not an 'organic whole,' that it is not informed and quickened by an idea-emotion in all its parts. The 'evil' characters, in particular, do not receive full imaginative realization: there is something galvanic about their movements, something perfunctory, sometimes, or 'automatic,' about their speeches. Certain passages seem not 'apprehensive . . . forgetive,' but still-born, or, fossil-like, to belong to earlier strata of experience and to be produced now only by an acquired habit. Hence, also, the 'static' quality of the play and the sense of the unreality of the action, which is, in any case largely replaced by symbolism. Whereas in *The Winter's Tale* the positive possibilities

of 'injurious Time,' its rôle as the condition of healing and of construction, are recognized, in *Cymbeline* time is simply ignored: there is no movement to a goal: the end is, on the contrary, felt to be immanent throughout.

This conclusion is, no doubt, startling; and the 'transcendental' terminology, which I have been unable altogether to avoid, is unfortunate. Yet I know of only two other views that have any *prima facie* plausibility. One is that *Cymbeline* is simply a 'pretty' romance; but a single reading is sufficient to show this account to be at least inadequate. The other is the interesting theory propounded by Mr. Tinkler . . . and this seems to me, though more intelligent than the former, more, and more evidently, erroneous. Mr. Tinkler's view, if I may presume to attempt a summary of it, is that a painful tension, expressive of a profound dualism and conflict, pervades the more significant parts of the play. This tension is an index of, or accompanies, a 'taut critical irony' [see excerpt above, 1938]. Mr. Tinkler lays emphasis on a harshness in much of the verse, on certain images suggesting muscular tension, and 'an insistent feeling of brutal strain.' He detects further an 'air of savage farce,' and a subtly 'placed' theatricality. The upshot is that 'throughout there is no "positive" which is not modified by the intense irony'; there is an (intended) 'air of impossibility' about Imogen ('she is so extraordinarily chaste,' 'her impossible chastity'), conveyed by 'the continual inflation' in the verse, which 'brings the ironic inflection.' . . . Imogen is a 'commodity,'

> A shop of all the qualities that man
> Loves woman for.
>
> [V. v. 166-67]

But this last metaphor, to begin my criticism there, refers not to Imogen, as Mr. Tinkler implies, but to 'our loves of Italy' [V. v. 161]; and in any case its significance is easily understood in the context of the 'value' imagery. To interpret it otherwise is to be guilty of the fallacy of confusing value and price; and Shakespeare had already shown his explicit awareness of this distinction in 'You are mistaken: the one may be sold or given, if there were wealth enough for the purchase, or merit for the gift; the other is not a thing for sale, and only the gift of the gods' [I. iv. 82-5]. But price naturally stands for value by metaphor.

The attitude towards Imogen is, of course, the crucial question. I can detect no 'ironic overtones' in her portraiture. That a passage is sincere in a quite unironical way, that it is 'conducting' the central idea—emotion, is, naturally, not demonstrable; the sincerity is recognizable only by catching a ring in the verse, a ring as unmistakable as the new vibrancy that enters a voice under the necessity of emotion. I can only record the personal impression that the application of such a test to *Cymbeline* reveals no 'critical irony' in the attitude towards Imogen. . . . But the decisive impression is the total impression left by the play.

Mr. Tinkler quotes from two speeches spoken by Imogen alone with her appointed executioner just after she has read the letter in which her husband denounces her as a 'strumpet,' and comments on the 'bitterness' revealed, contrasting it with the tone of the speeches of Perdita in *The Winter's Tale*. But, obviously, Imogen's situation is very different from Perdita's: she 'corresponds' *both* to Hermione and to Perdita (who is not, to her knowledge, wronged). Imogen for the greater part of the play is separated from her husband, and during much of it is thought by him unfaithful. It is Hermione who is the victim in *The*

Winter's Tale; Perdita suffers only a temporary setback in her 'romance': why should one whose story in outline, is that of an unusually beautiful and charming young lady who, after being brought up as a shepherd's daughter, finds herself to be engaged to a prince and the heiress to two kingdoms, be 'bitter'? There seems, then, to be no reason for regarding the element of harshness in *Cymbeline* to be, in any sinister way, symptomatic.

Again, Mr. Tinkler (rather surprisingly) compares Imogen with Cleopatra and (not unnaturally) finds a contrast: 'Cleopatra is created *through* the details of common life . . . , the vision transcends them, whereas Imogen is conceived almost *in spite of* them.' But, after all, Cleopatra is a very different sort of heroine from Imogen, and represents, on any theory, a very different sort of ideal. Yet something like 'tension' *is* felt through much of *Cymbeline;* but I should attribute this sense of tension, or frustration, to a failure of consistently successful communication; it exists not in the original experience, but only (and by accident, not by design) in the result. Moreover, the failure of the ideal completely to subdue the 'homely' is not intended—not a satirical comment—but is inevitable for reasons already suggested; and in any case the familiar does not appear as thwarting, or even as hostile to, the spiritual energy, but only . . . as failing to reflect it. And hence, presumably, the necessity of the 'pastoral' scenes; there the protest of the princes, from the start, against idyllic seclusion is im-portant, as is also their final rejection of 'idyll' in the name of 'action and adventure'; this, perhaps, safeguards the positive values of the idealized world against destruction when the setting itself crumbles and vanishes before the breath of reality and the invasion by war. Imogen passes easily from the one world to the other and back again; she 'belongs,' effortlessly, to both.

Again, Mr. Tinkler finds an extravagance and theatricality, indicative of irony in the conception, in the characterization of Posthumus; he writes, for example, that Posthumus, where he admits his guilt (presumably in the violent and rather hysterical speech of [V. v. 210 ff]), 'rants and struts and visualizes himself, quite conceitedly, as a monster'; but are we to understand that this 'self-dramatization' extends also to the closing cry of the speech, 'O Imogen, Imogen, Imogen!' And is 'savage farce' really an apt description of the next moment, when Imogen (still disguised as a page), hearing her name on her husband's lips, rushes forward to reveal herself, only to be flung by him to the ground? This speech, after all, is the sequel to the sad self-knowledge and contrition revealed in the V, i soliloquy, and is surely, the natural sequel in the new situation where Posthumus discovers the innocence of his wife whom he thinks to have been murdered at his command. (As for the 'theatricality' of Iachimo's speech in I, vi, Iachimo *is* 'acting' there.)

Act I. Scene i. Posthumus, Imogen, Cymbeline, the Queen, and Lords. By W. Hamilton.

In general, where Mr. Tinkler finds an almost serpentine subtlety I find only the naïveté of the dove. Where he sees, or thinks he sees, irony, I find only detachment: not a detachment calculated to secure 'emotional distance' in order to 'protect the creative sensibility from experience too painful,' but a spontaneous detachment indicative of emotional distance already secured by tranquillity. This tranquillity, however, is not the tranquillity of relaxation, but the *concentrated* tranquillity of 'perfect activity'; but the activity is not also 'unimpeded'; in its expression it energizes freely only in certain areas—in symbols of the ideal, in Posthumus's repentance, where there is a new birth of the ideal, in passages expressing qualities directly opposed to the ideal in the particular terms in which it is conceived, and fairly continuously in Imogen, who is the incarnation of the ideal in verse. (pp. 331-38)

> *A. A. Stephenson, S.J., "The Significance of 'Cymbeline'," in* Scrutiny, *Vol. X, No. 4, April, 1942, pp. 329-38.*

F. R. LEAVIS   (essay date 1942)

[*Leavis was one of the most influential educators and literary critics of the mid-twentieth century. He was a cofounder and editor of* Scrutiny, *a highly regarded literary magazine which had a profound impact on the teaching and interpretation of English literature in Britain and America. Leavis maintained that literary criticism should be based on "intelligent discrimination" and "moral seriousness," contending that close study of texts and attention to a writer's "ethical sensibility" would lead to a discerning evaluation of a work of art. His belief that moral consciousness is the wellspring of poetic creativity led Lionel Trilling to comment that, for Leavis, "literature is what Matthew Arnold said it is, the criticism of life." Leavis often assumed adamant, uncompromising positions in his work, and thus his criticism is frequently contentious and controversial. In the excerpt below, Leavis finds in* Cymbeline *no "commanding significance which penetrates the whole, informing everything . . . from a deep centre." Thus, he directly disputes F. C. Tinkler's identification of "critical irony" and A. A. Stephenson's discovery of a significant theme in the play (see excerpts above, 1938 and 1942). Leavis argues that although* Cymbeline *provides some "evidence of Shakespearean genius," it should not therefore be assumed that the dramatist intended to convey in this work any idea of profound import. In fact, he claims that the play is "merely romantic" and that much of the action belongs "to the order of imagination in which 'they all lived happily ever after'."*]

When Fr. Stephenson criticizes F. C. Tinkler's account of *Cymbeline* [see excerpts above, 1942 and 1938] I find myself in agreement. I was never convinced by that account, stimulating and profitable as I found some of the accompanying observation and suggestion. Nor am I convinced by Fr. Stephenson's. Of its very nature, it doesn't invite one so challengingly to point out where it is wrong, but it seems to me quite as unconvincing. 'Unconvincing' is the word I want to stress: the conclusion, the theory, doesn't emerge with any inevitability from the observations that are offered as containing its grounds.

The observed recurrence of valuation-imagery is interesting. But even when I re-read the play with an eye adverted by Fr. Stephenson I can't see that imagery as having anything like the relative prominence or importance he assigns it (and his general remarks about the imagery of the play seem to me questionable in the extreme). The theory that he develops in 'transcendental' terminology (as he puts it) would demand, to make it anything other than an excursion of fancy, a great deal

more support than he points to, and the significance he finds in the play is at least as much imposed (it seems to me) as Tinkler's 'critical irony' and 'savage farce.' The attributed significance, of course, is deduced, not from the valuation-imagery alone, but from this as related to another set of observed characteristics:

> the inequalities, the incongruities, the discontinuity, the sense of different planes, the only spasmodic and flickering life in *Cymbeline*. It must, I think, be recognized that *Cymbeline* is not an "organic whole," that it is not informed and quickened by an idea-emotion in all its parts [Stephenson].

The stress laid on these characteristics of the play seems to me much more indisputably justified than that laid on the valuation-imagery. So much so, in fact, that the question arises: Why didn't both Fr. Stephenson and Tinkler (whose argument also derives from observation of these characteristics) rest in the judgment that the play 'is not an "organic whole," that it is not informed and quickened by an idea-emotion in all its parts'? Why must they set out to show that it is, nevertheless, to be paradoxically explained in terms of a pressure of 'significance'—significance, according to Fr. Stephenson, of a kind that cannot be conveyed? (pp. 339-40)

What a following-through of F. C. Tinkler's and Fr. Stephenson's accounts will, I think, bring home to most readers is that we may err by insisting on finding a 'significance' that we assume to be necessarily there.

I have put the portentous word in inverted commas in this last use of it, in order not to suggest a severity of judgment that is not intended. The play contains a great variety of life and interest, and if we talk of 'inequalities' and 'incongruities' it should not be to suggest inanity or nullity: out of the interplay of contrasting themes and modes we have an effect as (to fall back on the usefully corrective analogy) of an odd and distinctive music. But the organization is not a matter of a strict and delicate subservience to a commanding significance, which penetrates the whole, informing and ordering everything—imagery, rhythm, symbolism, character, episode, plot—from a deep centre. . . . (p. 340)

The romantic theme [of *Cymbeline*] remains merely romantic. The reunions, resurrections and reconciliations of the close belong to the order of imagination in which 'they all lived happily ever after.' Cloten and the Queen are the wicked characters, stepmother and son, of the fairy tale: they don't strike us as the expression of an adult intuition of evil. Posthumus's jealousy, on the other hand (if I may supplement Fr. Stephenson's observation: 'the "evil" characters, in particular, do not receive full imaginative realization'), is real enough in its nastiness, but has no significance in relation to any radical theme, or total effect, of the play. (pp. 341-42)

[The] assumption that a profound intended significance must be discovered in explanation of the peculiarities of the play is fostered by the presence of varied and impressive evidence of the Shakespearean genius. I questioned above Fr. Stephenson's disparaging general reflections upon the imagery of *Cymbeline;* but I explain these by some inadequate conception of 'imagery,' since it is clear that he is not insensitive to what is strong in the play.

Strength could be adduced in a wealth of illustration. I myself have long carried mental note of a number of passages from

Cymbeline that seemed to me memorable instances of Shakespeare's imagery and versification. Two in particular I will mention. One is Posthumus's description of the battle [V. iii. 14-51]. It is a remarkable piece of vigorous dramatic felicity. The precisely right tone, a blend of breathless excitement, the professional soldier's dryness, and contempt (towards the Lord addressed), is perfectly got. There are some fine examples of Shakespearean compression and ellipsis; and here, surely, is strength in imagery:

> and now our cowards,
> Like fragments in hard voyages, became
> The life of the need: having found the back-door open
> Of the unguarded hearts, heavens, how they wound!
>
> [V. iii. 43-6]

In 'like fragments in hard voyages' and the 'back-door' we have, in imagery, the business-like and intense matter-of-factness, at once contemptuous and, in its ironical dryness, expressive both of professional habit and of controlled excitement, that gives the speech its highly specific and dramatically appropriate tone. The other passage is Posthumus's prison speech in the next scene [V. iv. 3-20], so different in tone and movement:

> Most welcome, bondage! for thou art a way,
> I think, to liberty: yet am I better
> Than one that's sick of the gout; since he had rather
> Groan so in perpetuity than be cured
> By the sure physician, death, who is the key
> To unbar these locks.
>
> [V. iv. 3-8]

This doesn't belong to 'romantic comedy,' nor does the dialogue with the gaoler at the end of the scene. And here, and in the many vigorously realized passages, we have the excuse for the attempt, in spite of 'the inequalities, the incongruities, the discontinuity, the sense of different planes,' to vindicate the play (for that, paradoxically, is Fr. Stephenson's aim as well as Tinkler's) in terms of a profound significance. But surely there should be no difficulty in recognizing that, wrestling with a job undertaken in the course of his exigent profession, Shakespeare might, while failing to find in his material a unifying significance such as might organize it into a profound work of art, still show from place to place, when prompted and incited congenially, his characteristic realizing genius? (pp. 343-44)

> F. R. Leavis, "The Criticism of Shakespeare's Late Plays: A Caveat," in Scrutiny, Vol. X, No. 4, April, 1942, pp. 339-45.

G. WILSON KNIGHT (essay date 1947)

[*Knight was one of the most influential Shakespearean critics of the twentieth century; he helped shape a new interpretive approach to Shakespeare's work and promoted a greater appreciation of many of the plays. In his studies* The Wheel of Fire *(1930) and* The Shakespearian Tempest *(1932), Knight rejected criticism which emphasizes sources, character analysis, psychology, and ethics and outlined his principles of interpretation which, he claimed, would "replace that chaos by drawing attention to the true Shakespearian unity." Knight argued that this unity lay in Shakespeare's poetic use of images and symbols—particularly in the opposition of "tempests" and "music." He also maintained that a play's spatial aspects, or "atmosphere," should be as closely considered as the temporal elements of the plot if one is "to see the whole play in space as well as time." Knight's essay on* Cymbeline *is from his* The Crown of Life *(1947) and is generally*

regarded as one of the most significant interpretations of the play. Whereas some earlier critics merely commented on the historical interest in Cymbeline, *Knight is the first to develop the idea that the historical elements are the most important ones and that the play is foremost a dramatization of national issues. Knight argues that the dramatic action of the play traces the manner in which British integrity, symbolized by the king, must learn to reject the evils represented by such figures as the Queen and Cloten, and even by an oppressive Rome itself, so that the country's virtues may once again be reconciled with those of its classical predecessor. The critic emphasizes Imogen's role as the "essence of royalty" and contends that Posthumus represents a composite of the best of British and Roman traits—in his words, "Britain's best manhood"; thus, he is the only one worthy enough to be the husband of Imogen, Princess of Britain. Harold C. Goddard (1951) has similarly viewed Imogen as a representative of national virtues and Robert S. Miola (see Additional Bibliography) has discussed the harmonization of British and Roman qualities in Posthumus. Knight further maintains that Posthumus's defense of his lady in the wager scene symbolically reflects a defense of "the romantic and puritanical idealism of his country as against the license of the Continent," specifically Italy, as represented in the character of Iachimo. In depicting Iachimo as a scheming, ostentatious swaggerer, the critic adds, Shakespeare intended to demonstrate that Renaissance Italy had debased the virtues of classical Rome, thus leaving Britain as the true heir to the legacy of imperial culture and history. By reinstating the payment of the tribute,* Cymbeline *freely acknowledges Britain's "Roman inheritance and obligation." J. P. Brockbank (see Additional Bibliography) has also investigated the reconciliation of Rome and Britain in* Cymbeline, *while such other critics as Goddard and Alexander Leggatt (1977) have discussed the historical issues in the play; also, see the essays by David M. Bergeron, Robert S. Miola, Hugh M. Richmond, and Frances A. Yates cited in the Additional Bibliography for more on this subject. Last, Knight argues that the "massed meanings" of* Cymbeline *are concentrated in the vision scene of Act V, Scene iv, claiming that Jupiter's blessing of the marriage of Posthumus and Imogen, as well as the soothsayer's prophecy, heightens the theme of the transfer of Roman heritage to the British nation. He concludes that the scene is legitimately Shakespeare's—emphasizing elements it has in common with the rest of the play—and points out its religious significance; according to Knight, the episode demonstrates an optimistic theology, since the gods are shown throughout to be "normally kind" and "susceptible to pleading," and Jupiter's appearance, together with his assurances to the Leonati, underscores the beneficence of the divine powers that control human fortunes. G. G. Gervinus (1849-50) and J. A. Bryant, Jr. (1961) have also interpreted the vision scene as emphasizing the idea of providential control over events in the play; also, see the excerpts by Northrop Frye (1965) and R. A. Foakes (1971) for additional commentary on the intervention of Jupiter.*]

Cymbeline strikes one as a peculiarly studied work. All is smooth, considered and correct. The mythology, the names of places and persons, the historical effects, are all considered. Even its anachronisms appear to be planned. It is, indeed, to be regarded mainly as an historical play. *Pericles* and *The Winter's Tale* blend Shakespeare's early comedy with his later tragedy; *Cymbeline* does this too, but is also concerned to blend Shakespeare's two primary historical interests, the Roman and the British, which meet here for the first time. These are close-knotted with the personal, tragic interest, together with the feminine idealism, of *Othello* and *The Winter's Tale;* recent discoveries are incorporated into a national statement; and all is subdued within a melancholic harmony distantly resembling that of *Twelfth Night.*

First, let us inspect its national interest, concentrating on Cymbeline, his Queen and Cloten.

Of Cymbeline as a man there is little to say, but he is important as king. He is accordingly comparable with the early King John. His distress under threat of invasion resembles that of John when hearing simultaneously of the French army's invasion and his mother's death [*King John*, IV. ii. 116-32]:

> Imogen,
> The great part of my comfort, gone; my queen
> Upon a desperate bed, and in a time
> When fearful wars point at me; her son gone,
> So needful for this present: it strikes me, past
> The hope of comfort.
>
> [IV. iii. 4-9]

The accent recalls Claudius in *Hamlet* [IV. v. 77-96]. Cymbeline is less a man than a centre of tensions due to his royal office, persuaded, attacked, tugged asunder and finally reestablished by the various themes and persons.

His Queen is more firmly realized as a 'crafty devil' [II. i. 52] and 'mother hourly coining plots' [II. i. 59]. Her considered villainy is amazing and her only unselfishness her instinctive support of her fool son, Cloten. She is a composite of Lady Macbeth and Goneril, though without the tragic dignity of the one and the cold rationality of the other. She is cruelty incarnate. (pp. 129-30)

[The Queen] is a considered study of extreme, specifically feminine, evil; a possessive maternal instinct impelling her violent life. She is not a caricature. The study is brief, but convincing. Cymbeline has to learn painfully the worthlessness of his wife and her, not his, son, Cloten. In the wider national reading we can feel Britain learning to reject all for which they stand.

Cloten is a boastful fool: his name suggests clot-pole, the term being used to jingle with his name [at IV. ii. 184]; a word also applied to Oswald by King Lear [*King Lear*, I. iv. 46]. We find him puffing and blowing after an interrupted duel, convinced fallaciously that he would have won it (I. ii). He loses his money and his temper, swearing and striking a bystander, at bowls [II. i. 1-8], and nearly involving himself in another duel. He is quarrelsome and generally obnoxious, a blustering, high-born, fool, very conscious of his rank:

> When a gentleman is disposed to swear, it is
> not for any standers-by to curtail his oaths, ha?
>
> [II. i. 10-11]

and

> . . . A pox on't. I had rather not be so noble
> as I am. They dare not fight with me because
> of the Queen my mother. Every Jackslave hath
> his bellyful of fighting, and I must go up and
> down like a cock that nobody can match.
>
> [II. i. 18-22]

As a study of foolish nobility he resembles Sir Andrew Aguecheek [in *Twelfth Night*] and Roderigo [in *Othello*]; and yet he is at once more intelligent, full-blooded and forceful, than those. He seems to have a genuine appreciation of Imogen [III. v. 70-4] and serenades her with taste [II. iii. 20-6]. One cannot deny him a certain arrogant dignity that makes it easier to laugh behind his back (as his interlocutors do) than to his face. His high position alone, with his consciousness of it, itself gives him dramatic weight. (pp. 132-33)

Cloten is certainly both ridiculous and vicious. Like Sir Andrew he is vain, comparing his figure with Posthumus' [IV. i. 9-10],

and is necessarily maddened by Imogen's rejection of himself for a mere nobody. He is autocratic and insulting—witness his continued insults concerning Posthumus' low birth—and has a thoroughly nasty mind, seen in his dastardly plot to revenge himself by raping Imogen whilst wearing Posthumus' garments. There is poetic justice in his death: he who has so often been saved by well-meaning courtiers from the consequences of his own quarrelsomeness, rashly insults as a 'robber' and 'law-breaker' [IV. ii. 74, 75] the young Guiderius in his mountain home and, finding his rank of little service to him there, gets his deserts without delay. He is a fool and rash, but no coward; and he meets his death at the hands of no less a person than the King's son. The conception throughout works within the limits imposed by the noble birth his very being disgraces.

King Cymbeline supports both these bad persons, banishing Posthumus mainly at the Queen's instigation and for Cloten's sake. Our drama shows therefore a misguided King of Britain fostering evil and folly near his throne.

Our main national interest concerns Cymbeline's refusal to continue Britain's tribute to Rome. The question of Britain's islanded integrity is clearly raised; more, it is phrased. Told by Philario that he thinks the ambassador Caius Lucius will succeed in getting the tribute, since Britain has cause to remember Rome's power, Posthumus answers:

> I do believe—
> Statist though I am none, nor like to be—
> That this will prove a war; and you shall hear
> The legions now in Gallia sooner landed
> In our not-fearing Britain, than have tidings
> Of any penny tribute paid. Our countrymen
> Are men more order'd than when Julius Caesar
> Smil'd at their lack of skill, but found their courage
> Worthy his frowning at: their discipline—
> Now winged—with their courage will make known
> To their approvers they are people such
> That mend upon the world.
>
> [II. iv. 15-26]

Posthumus' thoughts are obvious and what we would expect from him; but what we might not expect is to find precisely the same thoughts expressed even more satisfyingly by the Queen and Cloten. The Queen and Cloten urge on Cymbeline to resistance rather as the Bastard urges on King John, Cloten's wit definitely recalling the Bastard's. Lucius has said how the tribute is 'left untender'd':

> *Queen.*   And, to kill the marvel,
> Shall be so ever.
> *Cloten.*   There be many Caesars
> Ere such another Julius. Britain is
> A world by itself, and we will nothing pay
> For wearing our own noses.
> *Queen.*   That opportunity,
> Which then they had to take from 's, to
>   resume,
> We have again. Remember, sir, my liege,
> The kings your ancestors, together with
> The natural bravery of your isle, which
>   stands
> As Neptune's park, ribbed and paled in
> With rocks unscaleable and roaring waters,
> With sands, that will not bear your
>   enemies' boats,

But suck them up to the topmast. A kind of
    conquest
Caesar made here, but made not here his
    brag
Of 'came and saw and overcame': with
    shame—
The first that ever touch'd him—he was
    carried
From off our coast, twice beaten; and his
    shipping—
Poor ignorant baubles!—on our terrible
    seas,
Like egg-shells mov'd upon their surges,
    crack'd
As easily 'gainst our rocks: for joy whereof
The fam'd Cassibelan, who was once at
    point—
O giglot fortune!—to master Caesar's
    sword,
Made Lud's town with rejoicing-fires
    bright,
And Britons strut with courage.

                                    [III. i. 10-33]

The Queen has powerfully expressed precisely the sentiments
many Elizabethan Englishmen must have felt after the failure
of the Spanish Armada. She is deadly serious; Cloten witty.
Though told by the King to keep quiet—as the Bastard, Falstaff
and Enobarbus [in *Antony and Cleopatra*] are rebuffed in similar circumstances—he continues:

    We have yet many among us can gripe as hard
    as Cassibelan; I do not say I am one, but I have
    a hand. Why tribute? why should we pay trib-
    ute? If Caesar can hide the sun from us with a
    blanket, or put the moon in his pocket, we will
    pay him tribute for light; else, sir, no more
    tribute, pray you now.

                                    [III. i. 40-5]

Cloten's wit (so like the Bastard's in purpose and Enobarbus'
in manner) is admirable; he for once even shows modesty.
King Cymbeline continues with a speech every phrase of which
raises a natural response, urging the original freedom of Britain, Caesar's insatiate and inexcusable ('colour') ambition, the
compulsion on a 'war-like' people to resist slavery, and especially the Roman's 'mangling' of Britain's traditional 'laws'
deriving from her first king, Mulmutius [III. i. 46-61]. He
reminds the ambassador that other peoples are fighting for 'their
liberties' [III. i. 72-5], an example Britain must follow. The
discussion, except for Cloten's interruptions, is on a high level
of seriousness and chivalric courtesy, though Cloten's admirable interjections remain its high lights:

    His majesty bids you welcome. Make pastime
    with us a day or two, or longer; if you seek us
    afterwards in other terms, you shall find us in
    our salt-water girdle; if you beat us out of it,
    it is yours; if you fall in the adventure, our
    crows shall fare the better for you; and there's
    an end.

                                    [III. i. 77-82]

This is in line with the island-patriotism of [*3 Henry VI*, IV.
i. 39-46; *Richard II*, II. i. 31-68; and *King John*, II. i. 19-31].
There is no more subtle praise of British independence than
Cloten's; and yet the play ends with Cymbeline's willing pay-

ment of tribute from which, he says, he was only persuaded
by his 'wicked queen' [V. v. 463]. How are we to read all
this?

First, we can observe an impingement of the national on the
more purely personal; rather as when in *King Lear* the French
king is summarily recalled to France leaving Cordelia in charge
of his army to avoid at once the danger and difficulty of soliciting our sympathy for an invading king on British soil. The
problem is basic in the design of *King John*, where the Bastard's
abhorrence at the death of Arthur is followed by his support
and indeed exhortation of the King when invasion is threatened.
So here, the wicked Queen and her normally repellant son are,
at this moment, primarily Britons and their reaction to the
Roman threat the measure of British toughness and the islanded
integrity of their land. Neither speak out of character: the Queen
merely finds an occasion for the blameless exercise of her fierce
and active temperament, urging the King [III. v. 26], as Elinor
urges King John and Goneril Albany, to resist invasion; while
Cloten, always conscious of his birth and place and a born
quarreller and swaggerer, is for once in his element without
being obnoxious; the national situation serving, as often in real
life, to render violent instincts respectable.

A certain incompatibility, perhaps, remains, the more so as
Cloten shows many of the worst qualities habitually associated
by Shakespeare with foreign travel or foreign birth; and indeed,
when Imogen asserts that Posthumus' 'meanest garment' is of
more worth to her than a number of Clotens, and Cloten repeats
and reiterates the phrase after her exit in a puerile tantrum [II.
iii. 149-56], one is reminded of Austria in *King John* and the
Bastard's repetition of Constance's line, 'And hang a calf-skin
on those recreant limbs' [*King John*, III. i. 131]. The Queen
and Cloten, though British and the upholders of Britain's integrity, are nevertheless conceived as types which Cymbeline,
that is, Britain, must finally reject. So too Richard III, villain
though he be, can under threat of invasion show a tough patriotism not unlike the Bastard's [at *King John*, V. ii. 128-58]:

    Let's whip these stragglers o'er the sea again;
    Lash hence these overweening rags of France . . .
                                    [*Richard III*, V. iii. 327-28]

His whole speech forms an admirable commentary on *Cymbeline*. But we find here no scorn of the invader, for Shakespeare
honours Rome almost equally with Britain, with a respect that
rings in Lucius' line, so reminiscent of the Roman tragedies
(e.g. *Antony and Cleopatra* [IV. xv. 57]), 'A Roman with a
Roman's heart can suffer' [V. v. 81]. Understanding of Shakespeare's Roman sympathy is vitally necessary. A final solution
to our difficulties is hinted by Cymbeline's remark to Lucius
earlier (in our diplomatic scene) that

    Thy Caesar knighted me; my youth I spent
    Much under him; of him I gather'd honour;
    Which he, to seek of me again, perforce,
    Behoves me keep at utterance.

                                    [III. i. 69-72]

In modern phraseology the speech says: 'It has been Britain's
destiny, as a nation, to spend its youth under Roman tutelage,
drawing virtue from her traditions; and yet any too forceful
assertion by Rome of her own superiority must negate the very
virtues we have learnt and be resisted to the last.' That is, the
knightly 'honour' Cymbeline has drawn from Rome's favour
must be defended, if need be, against Rome herself, slavery
being incompatible with the chivalric virtues. Though the
phraseology enlists associations of a later age, Shakespeare is

definitely envisaging the youth of Britain: careless as he often is of anachronisms, he never in *Cymbeline* allows the word 'England' to intrude.

The play's action dramatizes the only possible solution. The Romans invade and the British at first fail, Cymbeline being captured; he is afterwards saved by Belarius and his own (unrecognized) sons, whose efforts are seconded by Posthumus. Britain's integrity (symbolized by the King) is thus preserved by (i) the royal boys and (ii) Posthumus (representative, as we shall see, of British manhood). (pp. 133-38)

But, having won, King Cymbeline learns of his Queen's wickedness and agrees, willingly, to pay tribute to Rome:

> And Caius Lucius,
> Although the victor, we submit to Caesar,
> And to the Roman Empire; promising
> To pay our wonted tribute, from the which
> We were dissuaded by our wicked queen.
> [V. v. 459-63]

Britain's integrity is to be no hot-headed self-assertion; it must learn to reject such influences as the Queen and Cloten; and to recognize, but freely, its Roman inheritance and obligation. So the action marches to its stately conclusion:

> Set we forward: let
> A Roman and a British ensign wave
> Friendly together; so through Lud's town march . . .
> [V. v. 479-81]

Such is the massive union, not unlike the union of lovers in a happy-ending romance, that our play dramatizes; a kind of majestic marriage, where we are to imagine that the partners 'lived happily ever afterwards'.

Interwoven with these national issues is the story of Posthumus' jealousy, redeveloping the old theme running from Ford [in *The Merry Wives of Windsor*], Claudio [in *Measure for Measure*] and Antonio [in *Twelfth Night*] through Troilus and Othello to Leontes [in *The Winter's Tale*]. One is apt to tire of it; and here, at first anyway, it scarcely grips the Shakespearian student. The treatment is less glamorous than in *Othello* and less revealing than in *The Winter's Tale,* and one is apt to wonder why Shakespeare bothers to complicate what might have been a purely national play with such an already well-worked-over plot. Besides, Posthumus has, as a man, no such impact on us as Othello and Leontes; he is a colourless person being, one half suspects, put through the paces of love, jealousy, disillusion and repentance rather as a representative of something, perhaps of earlier heroes, than as a man in his own right. He is a person with no core to his personality, and hence shows something of that queer colourlessness (though not the artificial, puppet-like, movement) noticeable in Prince Hal in *Henry IV,* who, though less of a person than Falstaff and Hotspur, is yet supremely important as typifying the English temperament: the treatment there being extremely complex, involving humour, irresponsibility, sportfulness, duty, courage and something very near to treachery; with a final humility and grave, if priggish, sense of responsibility. Now Posthumus shows nothing of Hal's variety, and his more emotional rôle is convincingly developed; but he serves a not dissimilar function. He is here to typify Britain's best manhood; not royalty or princeliness, since there are others for that, but manhood. (pp. 139-40)

Throughout we are continually pointed to (i) his great merit and (ii) his comparatively low rank. This lack of rank directly causes his banishment and his enemies make capital of it. To Iachimo he is a 'beggar' [I. iv. 23] and to Cloten a 'base wretch', 'one bred of alms and foster'd with cold dishes' [II. iii. 113, 114], 'the low Posthumus' [III. v. 76]. Cloten's peculiarly snobbish arrogance instinctively insults him. The two are dramatically opposed as rivals for Imogen's love, the one being of high birth but worthless, the other without rank but all-worthy: much is involved in the British princess' choice of Posthumus.

A certain mystery shrouds his descent. 'I cannot', says the Gentleman, 'delve him to the root' [I. i. 28]: in so far as Posthumus symbolizes British strength, Shakespeare is carefully non-committal as to its origin. For the rest, we are told that his father was Sicilius, who fought for Britain against Rome under Cassibelan and next under Tenantius, who gave him the surname 'Leonatus'; the lion, as at [*King John,* II. i. 135-42 and V. i. 57], being well-suited to the national type intended. His mother having died at his birth, and his father and two brothers having fallen in the wars, he was brought up by Cymbeline, took to education naturally and, whilst still young, became a 'sample' to youth, a pattern to the 'mature', and a guide to old age [I. i. 48-50]. He is generally praised and loved [I. i. 47], especially by Imogen, who has married him; the best proof, we are told, of his 'virtue' [I. i. 50-4]. Again, the direct and glamorous phrase is avoided: there is, perhaps, something a trifle priggish, to our ears, in this description of youthful gravity and solid worth, so different from the praise accorded the true sons, as Posthumus is the adopted son, of Cymbeline. Notice, too, that his own name and surname and also his father's sound not British but Roman. He is imaginatively at least a composite of the British and the Roman—his virtues are throughout pre-eminently the Roman virtues—and as such personifies the play's main statement. During the war his dress and supposed action (though he never fights against Britain) vary: 'Italian,' next British, then Roman.

Against Posthumus are balanced both Cloten and Iachimo. The one we have discussed; the other needs careful understanding.

Iachimo is to be regarded as a Renaissance Italian, quite distinct from the Romans. As his name suggests, he is a re-creation of Iago as a creature of Italian cunning, though with important differences. He is, as an individual, more convincing than either Iago, about whom one writes metaphysical essays, or Edmund, who could scarcely exist outside the peculiar webtexture of *King Lear*. He is more rounded out, more analysable as a person, can stand on his own feet. As so often, Shakespeare's last work presents, if anything, an advance in human delineation; as though the new intuition of transcendence accompanies a newly concrete awareness of man. Iachimo is peculiarly well done. His motivation as villain is clearly one with his excessive self-confidence and knowledge of his own brilliance and personal attraction. He is a born exhibitionist, smug, suave, showy and bold as the occasion demands, or all at once. He is, too, typically foreign. We first meet him during the general conversation in Rome, where a courtier prose of easy polish is the order. During the discussion before Posthumus' entry his every accent shows an easy mockery growing to jealousy of the praise accorded the rough islander of undistinguished origin who is shortly to arrive. Observe his offhand style in addressing poor Philario, who so desires that his friend shall be well received in Italy: 'But how comes it he is to sojourn with you? How creeps acquaintance?' [I. iv. 23-5]. 'Sojourn'; 'creeps'—the last word could only be spoken by Iachimo; spoken, I think, with a half-smile and a lift of the eyebrows. When he joins conversation with Posthumus concerning the Britisher's faith in his lady, his manner is intended to be subtly insulting. The argument has grown out of Posthumus' former difference with the Frenchman on an earlier occasion when, each offering the praise 'of our country mistresses' [I. iv. 57-8]—a national issue is involved—Posthumus asserted his to exceed in value and virtue, whilst being 'less attemptable' [I. iv. 60-1] than any in France. Iachimo attacks him on behalf of Italy ('You must not so far prefer her, fore ours of Italy' [I. iv. 65-6]), being irritated by the new arrival's islanded ignorance and priggish certainties:

> As fair and as good—a kind of hand-in-hand
> comparison—had been something too fair and
> too good for any lady in Britain. If she went
> before others I have seen, as that diamond of
> yours out-lustres many I have beheld, I could
> not but believe she excelled many; but I have
> not seen the most precious diamond that is, nor
> you the lady.
>
> [I. iv. 70-6]

The voice rises on the final phrase with telling *insouciance*. Iachimo's words are the more infuriating for their calm rationality and smooth assurance. The argument is in part national, as Iachimo's emphasis on 'Britain' shows, and in such terms it continues, Iachimo suggesting that, just as a 'cunning thief' might easily win the ring, so an 'accomplished courtier' (i.e. of continental training and experience) would soon vanquish the simple British girl in question. Posthumus answers:

> Your Italy contains none so accomplished a
> courtier to convince the honour of my mistress,
> if, in the holding or loss of that, you term her
> frail. I do nothing doubt you have store of thieves;
> notwithstanding I fear not my ring.
>
> [I. iv. 94-8]

There is an implicit contrast between the fearless, slightly rough, Briton, keeping, as it were, his own ideals intact wherever he journeys, and continental intrigue, showiness, and superficial refinement. (pp. 141-43)

The banished Britisher was from the start thrown among dangerous foreigners. On his arrival in Italy there were, besides Iachimo and Philario, not only the Frenchman, but also a Dutchman and a Spaniard [I. iv. s.d.]: the intention is obvious. The simple islander is in danger of moral ruin: he is automatically on the defensive, the issue formerly with the Frenchman and next with Iachimo being his lady's honour; that is, the romantic and puritanical idealism of his country as against the license of the Continent. Yet another nationality is involved in Posthumus' agony at Imogen's supposed seduction:

> . . . perchance he spoke not, but
> Like a full-acorn'd boar, a German one,
> Cried 'O!' and mounted.
>
> [II. v. 15-17]

The list is complete. Remembering Imogen's royal birth, we can say that Posthumus defends not merely a single lady, but Britain's soul-integrity, widely conceived, among foreigners who cannot understand his idealism and resent its implications. The phraseology throughout drives in the national contrast. Iachimo is more than a melodramatic villain: he is called a 'slight thing of Italy' [V. iv. 64] and 'Italian fiend' [V. v. 210]. To Imogen he is a 'saucy stranger' in the British court [I. vi. 151]; and later, hearing of her lord's jealousy, she con-

cludes that the 'drug-damn'd Italy hath out-crafted him' [III. iv. 15], feeling sure that 'some jay of Italy' [III. iv. 49] must be responsible. So Pisanio attributes the trouble to some 'false Italian' [III. ii. 4]. Iachimo himself ends by confessing the villainous cunning of his 'Italian brain' [V. v. 197]. Conversely, Britain is felt as the home of honour. Imogen would not lose the gift of her British lover 'for a revenue of any king's in Europe' [II. iii. 143-44]. You can see how peculiarly offensive, to British ears, is Iachimo's studied lie, describing how Posthumus, known abroad as 'the Briton reveller' [I. vi. 61], mocks at a Frenchman's simple love-faith:

Iachimo. There is a Frenchman, his companion, one,
  An eminent monsieur, that, it seems, much
      loves
  A Gallian girl at home; he furnaces
  The thick sighs from him, whiles the jolly
      Briton—
  Your lord, I mean—laughs from's free lungs,
            cries, 'O!
  Can my sides hold, to think that man, who
      knows
  By history, report, or his own proof,
  What woman is, yea, what she cannot choose
  But must be, will his free hours languish for
  Assured bondage?'

  [I. vi. 64-73]

Imogen's comment is pithy: 'My lord, I fear, has forgot Britain' [I. vi. 112-13]. But perhaps never in all Shakespeare does Britain assume a sweeter excellence than in Imogen's wistful thoughts—recalling Mowbray in *Richard II*—of leaving it:

>   Where then?
> Hath Britain all the sun that shines? Day, night,
> Are they not but in Britain? I' the world's volume
> Our Britain seems as of it, but not in't;
> In a great pool a swan's nest: prithee, think
> There's livers out of Britain.
>
> [III. iv. 135-40]

A pool or pond in Shakespeare carries undertones suggestive of impurity: there is a precision in the image, constituent to its beauty.

In studying the opposition here encountered of British manhood and Italian cunning in direct reference to marriage-integrity an historical reminder may be forgiven. At the Renaissance, the marriage bond becomes, for the first time in Christian history, a pressing and dominating concern of literature. No age but Elizabeth's could have produced Spenser's two bridal poems. Now this concentration, so evident in Lyly and Spenser, and so overpowering in Shakespeare, may be in particular related to the severe moral feeling, the innate puritanism, of the English temperament, rooting especially from the sixteenth century, though perhaps ingrained from an earlier date: certainly in no other literature are the dramatic implications, and reverberations, more powerful. The term 'Elizabethan' fits Shakespeare's precursors, Lyly and Spenser, as it does not fit Marlowe, himself more properly than they the voice of the European Renaissance widely understood in all its unmoral extravagance: aptly, Machiavelli speaks a prologue on his stage. The Renaissance exuberance is controlled and directed in England and in her voice, Shakespeare; and this it is that prompts his continual return to themes of jealousy, that accounts for the puritanical emphasis on pre-nuptial purity in *The Winter's Tale* and *The Tempest* and the close reference of the sexual to the national in *Cymbeline*. In contrast the Continent, in both the political and the social spheres, is considered dangerous. Shakespeare's insularity expresses a fear of continental influence natural to England during the Reformation and after. The imaginative power exerted by Italy in Shakespeare's day is witnessed by his steady reliance on Italian settings (where anticontinental satire may nevertheless, as in *Romeo and Juliet* and *Much Ado About Nothing*, be rather illogically contained). Throughout our later poetry the fascination of the Continent, and especially Italy, is variously balanced against the will to British integrity: the general situation being compactly described by Imogen's comment on Britain as 'of' the world but 'not in it'.... (pp. 147-50)

A sharp distinction between Roman and Italian elements in *Cymbeline* is, accordingly, demanded. Shakespeare's habitual indulgence in anachronism reaches an extreme development, whilst simultaneously becoming newly purposeful and attaining the level of artistic device. We have in a single action a distinction between ancient Rome and Renaissance Italy, the first highly honoured, the other all but equated with the devil. Though their mutual relation is never stated, the moral of Roman decline is clear and involved in the separate relations of each to Britain. Posthumus is imaginatively one quarter Roman, but the antithesis of an Italian, and his sin precisely that of taking the continental taint and becoming, however indirectly, an 'Englishman Italianate' (the phrase is [Roger] Ascham's). Though the overlaying of Italian on Roman in one plot is highly illogical, there is remarkably little confusion and one is never in doubt as to the response demanded.... Note that the 'Italian gentry' are subtly considered as allies, not identified with the Romans nor automatically involved in their cause. About Caius Lucius, who functions wholly as a Roman, there is never any doubt, though there is certainly a jar when Imogen introduces herself to him as the former page of 'Richard du Champ' [IV. iii. 377]. The precision is, on the whole, remarkably well maintained. When Posthumus changes over from the Roman to the British side he clearly sees himself as deserting not Romans but Italians, having come over 'among the Italian gentry' [V. i. 18]. He has joined the invaders during his fury against Imogen, but now, 'I'll give no wound to thee' [V. i. 21] he says, addressing Britain, in remorse at having, as he supposes, killed her 'mistress-piece', Imogen. Therefore,

> I'll disrobe me
> Of these Italian weeds and suit myself
> As does a Briton peasant . . .
>
> [V. i. 22-4]

He prays for 'the strength of the Leonati', and proceeds to fight for Britain, for Imogen [V. i. 26], for his ancestry: the various themes are closely in-knotted. (pp. 151-52)

The plot-construction and interweaving of themes and persons in *Cymbeline* are extraordinarily interesting; so is its impressionistic subtlety.... We have, however, so far missed the imaginative density of *The Winter's Tale*, scenes where person, setting, action and imagery make one glowing ingot, anvil-hot; and not until we approach Bellarius' cave do we find a comparable creative magic. We wait for it until the third act; but then the poet's genius functions with sovereign power.

These scenes have the glow, the imaginative aura, of *The Winter's Tale*. The setting is a cave in a 'mountainous country', among the Welsh mountains. Nowhere else in Shakespeare do mountains, to become later such recurring powers in our po-

etry, receive a primary emphasis. The setting is rugged; we face nature in its primal grandeur.

Belarius tells his charges, the royal boys, how their cave's low entrance instructs them how to 'adore the heavens' with 'a morning's holy office' [III. iii. 3, 4]; and proceeds to contrast their wild existence with the arrogance of monarchs whose lofty gates allow them to keep their 'impious turbans on without goodmorrow to the sun' [III. iii. 6-7]. Two paganisms, grand and ignoble, are finely contrasted. 'Hail, thou fair heaven!' he cries; and the boys repeat, in turn, 'Hail, heaven!' [III. iii. 9]. The sunlit heaven is conceived simply, as a living presence (as again later in Belarius' magnificent phrase 'It is great morning' at [IV. ii. 61]) in this prayer of natural piety, of devotion to the great Nature of *The Winter's Tale*, seen in all its rugged and golden works.... Belarius' cave reminds one of Jason and the boy-heroes under Cheiron, the Centaur, in the old Greek story: there is the same rough magic, the same boyhood glamour, in both. (pp. 157-58)

The poetic magic lies close to the prevailing conception of royalty, of royal blood, as quite outspacing political categories, while drawing near to the mystical or magical. When Arviragus asks Fidele, 'Are we not brothers?' she answers:

> So man and man should be.
> But clay and clay differs in dignity,
> Whose dust is both alike.
>
> [IV. ii. 3-6]

Where 'dignity' means worth, or value. Belarius says of Cloten:

> He was a queen's son, boys,
> And though he came our enemy, remember
> He was paid for that; though mean and mighty rotting
> Together, have one dust, yet reverence—
> That angel of the world—doth make distinction
> Of place 'tween high and low. Our foe was princely,
> And though you took his life, as being our foe,
> Yet bury him as a prince.
>
> [IV. ii. 244-51]

The whole action is conceived to show that Cloten was, in fact, far from 'princely'; but the key lies in 'reverence', corresponding to 'respect' in Ulysses' order-speech in *Troilus and Cressida* [I. iii. 75], the great principle of value, of worth, of, at the limit, divinity. (pp. 161-62)

In terms of royal blood—of which he elsewhere recognizes the limitations—Shakespeare defines [in the characters of Guiderius and Arviragus] something half-magical, some excellence beyond the normal categories exemplified by Posthumus. Though gentleness is emphasized (as in 'two of the sweet'st companions in the world' at [V. v. 249]), though flower-thoughts blend naturally into the description, and indeed come spontaneously elsewhere to the boys' lips, yet both the rough and the gentle aspects of nature are contained; a strength, even violence, suggested, the rough beginnings of that forcefulness characterizing a born leader. And yet the words 'princely', 'royal', 'royalty', 'honour', 'civility', all witness that the primal instinct at work does not run counter to the chivalric virtues. Guiderius reacts instinctively from Cloten's arrogance, asserting that it was 'most uncivil' and 'nothing prince-like' [V. v. 293]. However reached, and whatever its relation to Tudor politics, Shakespeare's conception clearly hints some high order of human being in embryo, to which the nearest analogies in our literature are the youthful heroes of Coleridge's *Zapolya* and Keats' *Otho* the Great; with one sad miscarriage of attempt in Wordsworth's *Excursion*. The excellence intended is perhaps best defined as a grand potentiality in boyhood; a mature figure being always liable to fail, becoming either impractical, as are Shakespeare's philosophic rulers and Byron's Sardanapalus, or a conventional soldier, like Shakespeare's Henry V. A final elucidation is given by Nietzsche's *Thus Spake Zarathustra:* the royal boys have not attained the integration of gentleness and power Nietzsche preaches, but they are matchless raw material for it.

When Britain is invaded, the boys, despite Belarius' advice, press to join their country's defenders; they are unwilling to remain 'hot summer's tanlings and the shrinking slaves of winter' [IV. iv. 28-9]: in a state, that is, of natural servitude, beyond which their royal instincts prompt them. And yet it is 'by this sun that shines' [IV. iv. 34] that they swear their resolution, preserving their natural piety:

> I am asham'd
> To look upon the holy sun, to have
> The benefit of his bless'd beams, remaining
> So long a poor unknown.
>
> [IV. iv. 40-3]

Nature, the 'great creating nature' of *The Winter's Tale* [IV. iv. 88], itself drives them beyond their semi-savage existence. So these two, with the old Belarius, and joined by Posthumus, turn Britain's defeat to victory. They prove themselves 'the liver, heart and brain of Britain' by whom 'she lives' [V. v. 14, 15]. (pp. 163-64)

Cymbeline is a vast parable, with affinities to Lyly's *Endimion,* though far more compacted and weighty and with no stiffness of allegory. A sense of destiny is pointed by two transcendental incidents: (i) the appearance of Jupiter and (ii) the Soothsayer's vision; the reference of the one being mainly personal; of the other national; though the two interests dovetail.

The action reaches a climax at Jupiter's appearance to Posthumus. This scene we shall study in detail presently. The extraordinary event cannot be properly received without full appreciation of the more-than-personal significance of Posthumus and the social and national implications of his marriage. Jupiter leaves an oracular tablet, reminiscent of the dreambook in *Endimion,* foretelling in cryptic phraseology the King's recovery of his lost sons and Posthumus' union with Imogen. The King is called a 'royal cedar', Posthumus Leonatus a 'lion's whelp', and Imogen 'a piece of tender air', the phrase being derived by the Soothsayer through *mollis aer* to *mulier,* to emphasize her typifying of womanhood, at its gentle best [V. v. 435-52]. So Posthumus' representative function, whereby his successful marriage becomes at once the matrimonial peace of the individual, the social integrity of the nation and the union of British manhood with the essence—Imogen is just that, an 'essence'—of royalty, which is also the union of strength with gentleness, becomes peculiarly clear:

> . . . then shall Posthumus end his miseries, Britain be fortunate and flourish in peace and plenty.
>
> [V. v. 440-42]

Posthumus' happiness is one with Britain's welfare. His marriage-happiness is assured by Jupiter, in whose 'Temple' he was married [V. iv. 106]; and indeed the will to preserve the marriage bond inviolate, so strong in Shakespeare's work, may well be derivative from Roman rather than Hebraic sources. So young Britain receives, through Posthumus, the blessing and protection of great Jupiter, the guardian deity of ancient Rome.

The play's final scene, a *tour de force* of technical compression, knits our various themes together. The King recovers his sons, as Pericles recovers Marina and Leontes Perdita, though here there is the further national symbolism of royal strength returning to Britain (cp. 'Now these her princes are come home again . . .' at [*King John,* V. vii. 115]); and perhaps too of some yet greater royalty as yet unborn. Iachimo is, like Iago, unmasked, though again with a wider significance; and the dead Queen and Cloten are at last known for what they are, or were, and finally repudiated; as, in the sequence of Shakespeare's national thinking, Richard III and Macbeth (who tried to murder Britain's destiny at its source) were rejected.

Each person accordingly contributes to the national statement whose enveloping action dramatizes the conflict and union of Britain with Rome. This enveloping action has, too, its transcendental pointing. The Soothsayer describes his vision:

> I saw Jove's bird, the Roman eagle, wing'd
> From the spongy south to this part of the west,
> There vanish'd in the sunbeams . . .
>
> [IV. ii. 348-50]

He takes it to portend Britain's defeat, but when things develop differently attempts a re-interpretation:

> . . . for the Roman eagle
> From south to west on wing soaring aloft,
> Lessen'd herself, and in the beams o' the sun
> So vanish'd: which foreshow'd our princely eagle,
> The imperial Caesar, should again unite
> His favour with the radiant Cymbeline,
> Which shines here in the west.
>
> [V. v. 470-76]

The meaning need not be limited to this interpretation, though the union of Rome and Britain is, of course, central. The word 'spongy' suggests softness and also, perhaps, an enervating, clammy heat, as though the imperial eagle were leaving a soft, effete, decaying land for one more virile. It underlines the precise relation within our drama of Renaissance Italy to ancient Rome, whilst indicating why their synchronization was forced: as the Roman virtue sinks to the level of Iachimo, the heritage of ancient Rome falls on Britain. The western, sunset emphasis may even hold a hint of Elizabethan sea-adventures. Certainly we are to feel the Roman power as vanishing into the golden skies of a Britain destined to prove worthy of her Roman tutelage.

Jupiter's blessing on Posthumus' marriage and the Soothsayer's vision thus make similar statements. Both symbolize a certain transference of virtue from Rome to Britain.

Shakespeare's two national faiths are here married; his creative faith in ancient Rome, felt in the Roman dramas from *Titus Andronicus* to *Coriolanus,* and his faith in England:

> Set we forward: let
> A Roman and a British ensign wave
> Friendly together; so through Lud's town march:
> And in the temple of great Jupiter
> Our peace we'll ratify; seal it with feasts.
> Set on there. Never was war did cease,
> Ere bloody hands were wash'd, with such a peace.
>
> [V. v. 479-85]
>
> (pp. 164-66)

In approaching Posthumus' vision (V. iv.) it is necessary to face the complaints of established criticism levelled against its authenticity. . . . My purpose here is two-fold: (i) to show that the Vision in its entirety must be accepted, whilst simultaneously (ii) examining it as an example of a normal Shakespearian technique whereby a single important unit concentrates the massed meanings of its play.

Posthumus sleeps in prison. There is solemn music—a usual Shakespearian direction, used earlier of Cadwal's harping [IV. ii. 186]—and then 'enter as in an apparition' Posthumus' father and mother 'with music before them'; and then 'after other music', his brothers. They 'circle' round the sleeping figure [V. iv. 29]. The phraseology resembles that of other ritualistic directions in Shakespeare's final period. We find nothing whatever in the language, here or afterwards, to question. Queen Katharine's similar vision in *Henry VIII* is also accompanied by 'sad and solemn music', the elaborate direction being of similar style and including the phrase 'as it were by inspiration' [*Henry VIII*, IV. ii. 82]. (p. 168)

Posthumus' vision is darker than Queen Katharine's but precisely suits his fortunes and the whole play. It is stately, solemn, and harmonious, using circular movement and a melodious chant: death, through these ghosts, is functioning as harmony. There could be no more vivid mark of its authenticity; for such is death throughout *Cymbeline*, so rich in sweetly sombre impressions of death; of death, as it were, softened, with a pervading atmosphere of deep but ineffectual tragedy. Death is here desired, yet merciful. Significantly, no major tempest symbolism, outside our Vision, jars the action.

Posthumus early invokes 'bonds of death' [I. i. 117] to prevent his loving any wife but Imogen; while she, referring to their separation, remarks 'There cannot be a pinch in death more sharp than this is' [I. i. 130-31]. Cornelius has been asked by the wicked Queen for poisons, 'the movers of a languishing death' which 'though slow are deadly' [I. v. 9, 10], but instead supplies a potion that only makes 'a show of death' [I. v. 40]. It resembles the Friar's drug in *Romeo and Juliet,* a play recalled too by Iachimo's words over the sleeping Imogen:

> O sleep! thou ape of death, lie dull upon her;
> And be her sense but as a monument
> Thus in a chapel lying.
>
> [II. ii. 31-3]

Hearing from Pisanio that Posthumus has ordered her death, Imogen craves his obedience, herself prevented from suicide by a reminiscence of *Hamlet:*

>   Against self-slaughter
> There is a prohibition so divine
> That cravens my weak hand.
>
> [III. iv. 76-8]

She desires death; it is a kindly release, as when, sick in the cave, she says 'let me die' [IV. ii. 15], her pathetic longing developing into the beauty of her supposed death, found 'stark' dead, but

> Thus smiling, as some fly had tickled slumber,
> Not as death's dart, being laugh'd at; his right cheek
> Reposing on a cushion.
>
> [IV. ii. 210-12]
> (pp. 168-69)

The repentant Posthumus likewise desires to die in battle. Having killed, as he thinks, the thing he loved, his 'life is, every

breath, a death' [V. i. 26-7]. But the other 'death' in battle he cannot find [V. iii. 69]. He invokes it again in prison as 'the sure physician, death' [V. iv. 7], and prays to the 'great powers' [V. iv. 26]:

> For Imogen's dear life, take mine; and though
> 'Tis not so dear, yet 'tis a life; you coin'd it . . .
>
> [V. iv. 22-3]

He concludes: 'O Imogen! I'll speak to thee in silence' [V. iv. 28-9], he enters the death-world of sleep, to commune with the dead. Thereupon follows the Vision, followed closely by his dialogue with the gaoler, which, by the usual Shakespearian process of playing a humorous variation on a serious theme, offers some macabre fun on death as the solver of all debts:

> *Gaoler.*   O! the charity of a penny cord; it sums up
>   thousands in a trice: you have no true
>   debitor and creditor but it; of what's past,
>   is, and to come, the discharge. Your neck,
>   sir, is pen, book, and counters; so the
>   acquittance follows.
> *Post.*   I am merrier to die than thou art to live.
> *Gaoler.*   Indeed, sir, he that sleeps feels not the
>   toothache . . .
>
> [V. iv. 166-72]

Death is less an imposition than a liberator. Our ghostly Vision is thus enclosed and clasped firmly by speeches of serene deathly meditation. As the play draws to its conclusion, Cymbeline observes in the manner of *Pericles* (at [V. i. 190-94]) that the gods are striking him 'to death with mortal joy' [V. v. 235].

No better masque-equivalent to these at once fearful and fruitful impressions of harmonious death in a work concluding with a series of miraculous survivals could be imagined than that composed of these kindly yet piteous ghosts from the Elysian Fields circling to 'solemn music' and demanding Jupiter's intercession. They fit in. (pp. 170-71)

The Vision of Jupiter certainly occurs in a work saturated with religious suggestion. The people are not only vengeful; they can also repent. There is the forgiveness of both Posthumus and Imogen of each other before they learn of Iachimo's plot. Posthumus' remorse . . . is powerful and joined with the truly remarkable thought—considering Shakespeare's usual attitude—that Imogen's unfaithfulness is a mere slip [V. i. 12]. We have Iachimo's summoning conscience [V. ii. 1] and later repentance, with Posthumus' finely-worded forgiveness [V. v. 417-20]. Cymbeline himself finally realizes how he has been deceived, and forgives everyone, saying, 'pardon's the word to all' [V. v. 422]. The main people are shown as drawing towards a more god-like understanding.

The gods are even more frequently mentioned than in *King Lear;* and, as in *King Lear,* they are entwined with meditations on human justice or injustice. When Iachimo says it is 'the office of the gods to venge' Posthumus' betrayal [I. vi. 92], the thought is a weaker version of Albany's two pronouncements on divine interposition in *King Lear* [IV. ii. 46-50, 78-80]. More directly comparable is Cymbeline's comment on the death of his wicked Queen, on whom, he says, the heavens, 'in justice both on her and hers, have laid most heavy hand' [V. v. 464-65]. The theology in *Cymbeline* is both more optimistic and more insistent than in *Lear.* There is a belief in 'heaven's bounty' [I. vi. 78], in gracious [I. iv. 87] powers from whom good things come: Imogen is 'the gift of the gods' [I. iv. 85], they made her sweet disposition [I. vi. 177]; 'the gods make Belarius and the two boys 'preservers' of Cymbeline's throne [V. v. 1]. . . . Man is here utterly dependent, more so than in *King Lear,* on the 'gods' or 'heavens' whose creature he is. That is why the people talk so naturally to them. Imogen half speaks to 'Jove' as to a companion [III. vi. 6], when she wakes beside a dead body, her immediate cry is, 'O gods and goddesses!' [IV. ii. 295]; there is her typical and pretty oath in misfortune ''ods pittikins' [IV. ii. 293]. When she introduces herself to Caius Lucius as the servant of 'Richard du Champ', she wryly hopes that the gods, if they happen to hear her falsehood, will forgive it [IV. ii. 377-78]: the gods are always, as it were, just round the corner, listening, likely to interrupt. The tendency is yet stronger with Posthumus, as we shall see. Guiderius and Arviragus have an equivalent sense of divine nearness though with them it is, aptly, felt most strongly through the sun [IV. iv. 34, 41]. (pp. 179-80)

These clustering impressions of divinity and man's reliance thereon, these prayers and chants, form a setting for our Vision with its chanted prayer of intercession imploring the Deity's too long withheld favour. The play ends on a note of prayer: 'Laud we the gods . . . bless'd altars' [V. v. 476, 478]. The Ghosts' prayer is thus an extreme instance of a general tendency.

It is, moreover, continuous with Posthumus' two important soliloquies preceding the Vision. These sum and condense our varying significances whilst preparing for, indeed all but demanding, the Deity's appearance. The gods are conceived as variously stern and kind:

> Gods! if you
> Should have ta'en vengeance on my faults, I never
> Had liv'd to put on this; so had you sav'd
> The noble Imogen to repent, and struck
> Me, wretch more worth your vengeance. But, alack!
> You snatch some hence for little faults; that's love,
> To have them fall no more; you some permit
> To second ills with ills, each elder worse,
> And make them dread it, to the doer's thrift.
> But Imogen is your own; do your best wills,
> And make me bless'd to obey.
>
>   [V. i. 7-17]

He asks the 'good heavens' to 'hear patiently' his purpose [V. i. 21, 22]. One feels the divine powers very near, he is *talking* to them; he prays the 'gods' to give him the 'strength o' the Leonati' [V. i. 31], those same Leonati who in the Vision pray on his behalf. The pressure is being swiftly heightened throughout these agonized soliloquies. Next in prison he wrestles again with the powers above, praying the 'good gods' [V. iv. 9] to forward his repentance:

>   Is't enough I am sorry?
> So children temporal fathers do appease;
> Gods are more full of mercy.
>
>   [V. iv. 11-13]

He proceeds to argue with them, to bargain:

> If of my freedom 'tis the main part, take
> No stricter render of me than my all. . . .
>
>   [V. iv. 16-17]

He ends with:

>   . . . and so, great powers,
> If you will take this audit, take this life,
> And cancel these cold bonds. O Imogen!
> I'll speak to thee in silence.
>
>   [V. iv. 26-9]

One feels the tension, which has become unbearable, about to snap. The gods have been drawing nearer and nearer; and we are prepared for the Ghosts' final invocation and the logical though startling climax of Jupiter's appearance. If he does not appear, to what do these tormented soliloquies lead? (pp. 182-83)

No other play gives Jupiter quite such honour, but he is Shakespeare's most frequent and most powerful god throughout; and after the parts played by the less important Diana and Apollo in *Pericles* and *The Winter's Tale,* one surely here expects Jupiter, who seems to have been reserved for the purpose, to do something spectacular.

Here is our stage-direction:

> Jupiter descends in thunder and lightning, sitting upon an eagle: he throws a thunderbolt. The ghosts fall on their knees.
>
>   [V. iv. 29]
>   (p. 186)

Jupiter's actual throwing of the 'bolt' has interesting Shakespearian analogies. His business is to strike awe and yet prove merciful, his actions thus toning with the religious expectance throughout *Cymbeline* and Shakespeare's consistent attribution of mercy to the divine powers. . . . The Vision, where Jupiter's breath is 'sulphurous' [V. iv. 115], but his words merciful, is a precise actualization of earlier poetry. *Cymbeline* itself, moreover, offers some valuable supporting phrases. In the dirge sung over Fidele we have, in description of mortality's trials:

> Fear no more the lightning-flash
> Nor the all-dreaded thunder-stone.
>
>   [IV. ii. 270-71]

There is Imogen's

> 'Twas but a bolt of nothing, shot at nothing,
> Which the brain makes of fumes.
>
>   [IV. ii. 300-01]

More clearly significant is Pisanio's 'the gods throw stones of sulphur on me' [V. v. 240], the image of Imogen's happy glances hitting everyone 'like harmless lightning' [V. v. 394], and Cymbeline's

> If this be so, the gods do mean to strike me
> To death with mortal joy.
>
>   [V. v. 234-35]

How exactly these optimistic miniatures—with, too, Iachimo's flattering description of Posthumus (for whom our Vision is enacted) as 'a descended god' [I. vi. 169]—reflect, in Shakespeare's usual manner, our central symbolism, wherein the god, descending to thunder and lightning and throwing his dreaded bolt, proceeds to announce a reversal of the hero's suffering and a general happiness. (pp. 188-89)

Surely the necessity of our Vision is now apparent. If we reject it, *Cymbeline* is left, alone in [Shakespeare's final plays], without any striking transcendental moment. Nor is it merely a question of its conformity with the other final plays: nearly all Shakespeare's greater works have their transcendental, or semi-transcendental, scenes: the Ghost in *Hamlet,* the Cauldron-scene in *Macbeth* (with Hecate and the Apparitions), the weird tempests continually, as in *Julius Caesar* and *King Lear,* the mysterious music in *Antony and Cleopatra. Pericles* and *The Winter's Tale* have their powerful tempests, but *Cymbeline* no active tempest-symbolism outside the Vision; its massed effect is one of sombre assurance; but surely something similar is needed. Now our Vision of Jupiter the Thunderer exactly fits our sense of purposeful, controlled tragedy. Thunder, apart from Jupiter himself, is a central symbol, as in Lear's

> Let the great gods
> That keep this dreadful pother o'er our heads
> Find out their enemies now!
>
> [*King Lear*, III. ii. 49-51]

and the searching question later, 'What is the cause of thunder?' [*King Lear*, III. iv. 155]. In Jupiter's appearance and words we have a synthesis of (i) the tragic tempests and (ii) the beneficent deities of the two sister-plays: in him a new compactness is reached. Throughout Shakespeare 'tempests' are balanced against 'music', a balance peculiarly clear in *Macbeth*, where the three thunderous apparitions are set beside the show of kings passing to music. Our Vision again conforms. It is, moreover, carefully designed: Posthumus sleeps, the Ghosts enter to solemn music and lift their chant, rising to an insistent cry for justice; the Deity appears to thunder, speaks a heavier, more resonant rhymed verse, and ascends; the Leonati speak normal dramatic verse, as though waked from pain; Posthumus wakes. The movement reflects the mysterious rhythms within the swift passage from dream to waking life.

But, it may be said, the scene's poetry leaves us cold and cannot accordingly be Shakespearian. Such purely aesthetic judgements are surely irresponsible. Apart from Shakespeare's being himself an Elizabethan and Jacobean playwright, one would have, to-day, to meet our own objections with the best possible modern stage-representation; and while the scene is cut out of our performances, no advance is possible. But, to return to facts, the Vision's style, whether good or bad, is Shakespearian. (pp. 191-92)

[Our] acceptance or rejection of this crucial scene is of primary importance. More even is at stake than our understanding of Shakespeare's reading of his country's destiny. We have regarded Jupiter as pre-eminently the Romans' god; but he is, throughout Shakespeare, more than that, and may often be best rendered 'God', a word Shakespeare was diffident of using on the stage, though it occurs at [*King Lear*, V. iii. 17]. The puritanical Malvolio thanks 'Jove' for his good fortune [*Twelfth Night*, II. v. 172]; and at [*Measure for Measure*, II. ii. 111], the Deity serves powerfully ... to extend some of Shakespeare's purest and most fervent passages of Christian doctrine, explicitly referring, through the pronoun 'He' [II. ii. 74-6], to the Christian God. We may practically equate Shakespeare's Jove with Jehovah, whilst also observing that, since representation of the supreme deity cannot be completely successful (as Milton also found), Shakespeare probably gains rather than loses in *Cymbeline* by reliance on a semi-fictional figure allowing a maximum of dignity with a minimum of risk. So, within a plot variously concerned with the building up and dispelling of deceptive appearance, we find, at its heart, this vivid revelation of a kindly Providence behind mortality's drama. (pp. 201-02)

> G. Wilson Knight, "'Cymbeline'," in his The Crown of Life: Essays in Interpretation of Shakespeare's Final Plays, 1947. Reprint by Barnes & Noble, Inc., 1966, pp. 129-202.

DONALD A. STAUFFER (essay date 1949)

[*Stauffer maintains that the question of distinguishing between appearance and reality is a chief concern in* Cymbeline. *He argues that Shakespeare demonstrates that in order to detect "virtue and*

truth in others" we must look beyond external marks of physical beauty or adornments, for Cymbeline, Posthumus, and even Imogen are all misled by outward appearances. Derek Traversi (1954) and Nancy K. Hayles (1980) have also discussed the discrepancies between the apparent and the actual in Cymbeline. *Stauffer further notes that Iachimo's ability to discern that reality and evil "are not interchangeable terms" distinguishes him from the more limited intellects of the Queen and Cloten; thus, he "can repent and be forgiven."*]

A dominating contrast in *Cymbeline* is between the life of the court and the life of nature, between sophistication and simplicity. The rude cave in Wales is far from Cymbeline's palace—as if the Forest of Arden had been discovered in some coign of Lear's harsh Britain. Or as if a fresh area of Shakespeare's mind had burst to life in the midst of what he had known too intimately and too long. The profoundest contrast is between Shakespeare Old Style and Shakespeare New Style. In this play (as in the first half of *The Winter's Tale*, and occasionally in the other two romances) he writes of the naughty world almost with his old conviction and authority. Knowing evil, caring seriously to comprehend it, he nearly achieves again; but the achievement seems principally designed to contrast the stupidly cunning and the proud with some radiant dream which, if it is not truer, is at least more intensely realized. Often, in all of these romances, Shakespeare merely sketches in quickly, in a kind of shorthand, material which he had realized solidly in earlier plays; or he assumes ideas which he had formerly argued or demonstrated. The old elements of a fallen Adam—pride, blindness, mistrust, jealousy, revenge, hypocrisy—are taken for granted without scrutiny, much as proved propositions in geometry are used to establish a new conclusion. This means, of course, that Iachimo will be a littler Iago, Cloten a smaller Ajax, and only Cymbeline's Queen without a parallel—except for Dionyza in *Pericles*.

The evil characters, nevertheless, are treated with enough respect to individualize them; and their differing ends compose a pattern of moral beliefs that Shakespeare held to consistently. The Queen, who poisons with fair words, whose purposes remain secret to the end, cannot escape the prison of her self. The last act of this "most delicate fiend" [V. v. 47] is to confess her abhorrence of her husband, a final malignant gesture which she hopes may keep her hatred alive after her death. Her only repentance is that she "repented The evils she hatch'd were not effected" [V. v. 59-60]. So she "despairing died." Her end is expressed with moral certainty:

> With horror, madly dying, like her life,
> Which (being cruel to the world) concluded
> Most cruel to herself.
>
> [V. v. 31-3]

Iachimo is not so cabined and confined in evil. He acts on the raw and reckless assumption that no lady lives who is "fair, virtuous, wise, chaste, constant" [I. iv. 59-60]. He matches his pride in amatory exploits against the pride in possession of the young Posthumus, who allows his own reckless anger to make a wager of his wife. Iachimo is intelligent: he realizes (in the spirit of the dark comedies) "the cloyed will—That satiate yet unsatisfied desire, That tub both fill'd and running" [I. vi. 47-9], which after devouring the lamb still longs for garbage. But confronted by the fact of Imogen, he realizes also her "most perfect goodness" [I. vi. 158], and knows immediately that he must descend to lies in order to win his wager. Evil sits so uneasily upon his nature that in the last scene he is glad to utter what it torments him to conceal, and his heavy conscience—not outside force—causes him to kneel before the man he has wronged. He asks for death for his crimes, and is forgiven.

Cloten, on the other hand, is as unyielding in stupidity as his mother is in malice. He is "too bad for bad report" [I. i. 17]. Shakespeare makes of him a brutal farce. He brawls, bowls, gambles, and leads every argument to a most preposterous conclusion. Of every situation, he might well say: "I yet not understand the case myself" [II. iii. 75]. He is too stupid even to realize his own cowardice and incompetence. Having no center, "his humour Was nothing but mutation" [IV. ii. 132-33]. He is the voice of idiocy, an essential spiritual emptiness. Imogen characterizes him as "that harsh, noble, simple nothing—Cloten!" [III. iv. 132-33]. Her ironic "noble" strikes off his subservience to externals: his boasting of birth and position, his dependence upon his mother and upon his flatterers who amuse themselves with sarcasms he is too dumb to grasp, his lamenting that "I had rather not be so noble as I am," and his notion that "it is fit I should commit offence to my inferiors" [II. i. 18, 28-9]. In Cloten, Caliban [in *The Tempest*] is dressed up in Osric's [in *Hamlet*] clothing. When the shallow courtier and the brute are united in one person, Shakespeare comes as close to mercilessness as his nature allows. This is the nitwit that dares to imagine he dictates to the inevitable. Using his nose as a moral sense, as he so often does, Shakespeare presents Cloten on his first appearance as quite literally a stinker. And as Cloten flies to pieces for his last appearance, it is an occasion for rejoicing to see his severed head brought in by Guiderius: "This Cloten was a fool, an empty purse" [IV. ii. 113]. For Cloten is all outsides—with no more spiritual significance than his garments possess.

There is, then, no hope for the Clotens—for evil which is too stupid to con the book. Nor is there salvation for evil which is dominated by a limited intelligence, which dies despairing within its own constricted circle. But there is salvation for the evil intelligence which can learn from experience that evil and reality are not interchangeable terms, because intelligence can correct such a partial and warped belief and therefore can repent and be forgiven.

Shakespeare develops a Clothes Philosophy which does not make the practice of virtue easy. How can the well-intentioned detect virtue and truth in others? Not through externals. Posthumus cannot ferret out Iachimo's treachery, for he accepts the ocular proof, the "corporal sign" of the bracelet stolen from Imogen's arm. Again, Cymbeline to the end cannot discover the real nature of his physically beautiful Queen. Is his fault, too, the "cloyed will," the desire so powerful . . . that it overrides judgment? Shakespeare does not say so. Instead, he allows Cymbeline an extraordinary bit of pleading:

> Mine eyes
> Were not in fault, for she was beautiful;
> Mine ears, that heard her flattery; nor my heart
> That thought her like her seeming. It had been vicious
> To have mistrusted her.
>
> [V. v. 62-6]

Cymbeline permits his daughter to feel that his action was folly, but concludes his defense by abandoning personal responsibility in favor of a prayer to a higher order: "Heaven mend all!" [V. v. 68]. And if it was a sin in Cymbeline to trust his wife and mistrust his friend Belarius, then why was not Othello virtuous in following an opposite course?

It is true that Iachimo, dazzled by Imogen's purity (though even here he is for a moment not sure that "all of her that is

out of door most rich" [I. vi. 15] can be furnished with a mind of equal rarity), thinks men mad who cannot distinguish "twixt fair and foul" [I. vi. 38]. The eye, the judgment, even the appetite, he feels, can make the distinction; and the unsatisfied will alone could act contrary to judgment. But Troilus said as much when he trusted Cressida. And such moral certainty appears odd in the mouth of Iachimo, who has dealt wholesale in cynicisms, and who now seems a libertine intoxicated by the sight of virtue.

Shakespeare does not hold for long to any Platonic or Spenserian intuition that a beautiful soul inhabits, because it creates, a beautiful body. His ultimate simplicity, rather, is that all mistrust is vicious. How easily, then, may slander and false appearance play upon the trustful! The ideal is reciprocal trust and virtue. Yet rarely in Shakespeare's plays, including the comedies, does a perfect trust meet with an object of perfect virtue. Nor does a perfect virtue encounter a perfect trust. . . . Failure in trust can momentarily infect even the virtuous with despair, so that Imogen offers her heart to Pisanio's knife when she learns of her husband's false suspicions. Bitterly she proclaims that the traitors of the past have destroyed trust in honest men, and caused sacred pity to falter. As for her husband Posthumus: "Goodly and gallant shall be false and perjur'd From thy great fail" [III. iv. 63-4].

But the ideal is never abandoned because it is unrealizable, and in some impossible world the turtledove of infinite trust continues to worship the Phoenix of virtue indistinguishable from beauty.

In *Cymbeline,* Shakespeare gives one last grotesque twist to his troubled thoughts on truth and semblance. That lover of appearances, Cloten, his attention riveted by a phrase of Imogen's, resolves to ravish her in the very garments of her husband Posthumus. Even Imogen cannot distinguish between apparel and "the thing itself." When she beholds the headless body of Cloten, her recognition of her own husband by his outward clothes is painfully prolonged and detailed:

> The garments of Posthumus?
> I know the shape of 's leg; this is his hand,
> His foot Mercurial, his Martial thigh,
> The brawns of Hercules; but his Jovial face—
> Murther in heaven?
>
> [IV. ii. 308-12]

She acknowledges Cloten's body as "this most bravest vessel of the world" [IV. ii. 319]. Even the purest cannot look through the deceitful garments of the world, nor escape from their own adorations and presentiments. With insistent dramatic irony, Imogen, who knows that "Our very eyes Are sometimes like our judgments, blind" [IV. ii. 301-02], falls senseless over the body of her supposed lord.

> The dream's here still. Even when I wake it is
> Without me, as within me; not imagin'd, felt.
>
> [IV. ii. 306-07]

Tangled in their own mortality, men and women must for a time act out murder in heaven on the stage of the earth.

Yet above all this subtle realization of complex evil, Shakespeare sets contrasting and conquering images of liberty, courage, patience, hope, and truth. The natural world is beautiful, and in the main beneficent; human beings are beautiful, and in the main may learn brotherhood, humility, and the necessity for repentance and forgiveness. If instinct will out, it may be noble as well as ravening. Spirit scores its triumph over matter.

Act I. Scene iv. Posthumus, Iachimo, Philario, and others. By G. F. Sargent. The Department of Rare Books and Special Collections, The University of Michigan Library.

As for the temporary losing of any good, the final answer is "'Twill not be lost" [II. iv. 148]. The shining dream is here elevated above common earth through superlatives, which Shakespeare never used more lavishly. And though his admired creations are worthy to inlay heaven with stars, though they exceed in goodness the hugeness of any villain's unworthy thinking, and though the mere thought of banished virtue and love subdues all pangs, all fears, and is past grace, obedience, and hope, yet Shakespeare can stoutly imagine, in defending the farthest reach of his description of the virtuous, that "I do extend him, sir, within himself" [I. i. 25]. (pp. 279-84)

> Donald A. Stauffer, "A World of Images," in his Shakespeare's World of Images: The Development of His Moral Ideas, W. W. Norton & Company, Inc., 1949, pp. 266-323.

HAROLD C. GODDARD (essay date 1951)

[*Further developing the significance of national issues in* Cymbeline *initially discussed by G. Wilson Knight (1947), Goddard maintains that the play is a political allegory in which Shakespeare presents the struggle between freedom and imperialism, and where the Roman invasion of England symbolizes the efforts of a tyrannous empire to deprive a free nation of its liberties. Illustrating this allegorical design, Goddard views Belarius, Guiderius, and*

Arviragus as "Old English Experience and Wisdom *hand in hand with her genuinely* Noble Youth," *who, when joined by Posthumus—the personification of* "English Manhood"—*rout the forces of imperialism. He applies this allegorical construction also to the scene in which Imogen awakens beside the headless corpse of Cloten, holding that despite its* "incredible" *and* "desecrating" *appearance, this episode has a symbolic significance. Further, if Imogen is seen as* "the True England," *who for a moment mistakes* "False Nobility" *for true* "English Manhood and Valor," *the scene may also be interpreted as a climactic expression of the play's second allegorical struggle—the moral battle between* "lust and purity." *Other critics who have discussed this scene include Harley Granville-Barker (1930), F. D. Hoeniger (1961), Robin Moffet (1962), Robert Grams Hunter (1965), and Joan Carr (see Additional Bibliography). Like Knight, Goddard also asserts that in* Cymbeline *Shakespeare was trying to demonstrate the malicious influence of* "the darker side of the Italian Renaissance" *on the political and moral life of England, evidenced by the numerous unfavorable references in the play to all things Italian and represented, symbolically, in the attempted seduction of Imogen (*"True England"*) by the libertine Iachimo (*"Evil influence"*). For further discussion of the struggle between Rome and Britain in the drama, see the excerpt by Alexander Leggatt (1977) and the essays by David M. Bergeron, J. P. Brockbank, Robert S. Miola, Hugh M. Richmond, and Frances A. Yates cited in the Additional Bibliography.*]

To one reading *Cymbeline* just as a story, the location of certain of its scenes in Italy may seem as accidental and lacking in significance as the same thing in, say, *The Two Gentlemen of Verona*. And as for the Roman Lucius and his legions, they appear to be just so much dramaturgic machinery. But we had better beware. There is *Othello* to warn us that something seemingly insignificant, far in the dramatic background, may be poetically all-important.

Moreover, in addition to a Roman invasion of Britain, the play is full of references to Italy and Rome. As they occur in the text, scattered casually along, they excite little attention. But assembled, they assume another color and unmistakable meaning:

> What false Italian,
>
> [III. ii. 4]

cries Pisanio, reading the letter from his master that accuses his mistress,

> As poisonous-tongu'd as handed, hath prevail'd
> On thy too ready hearing?
>
> [III. ii. 5-6]

> My husband's hand!
>
> [III. iv. 14]

exclaims Imogen, when she first sees the same letter,

> That drug-damn'd Italy hath out-crafted him,
>
> [III. iv. 15]

and a moment later,

> Some jay of Italy,
> Whose mother was her painting, hath betray'd him!
> [III. iv. 49-50]

When Posthumus, coming to his senses near the end, tears off his clothes, his cry is,

> I'll disrobe me
> Of these Italian weeds,
>
> [V. i. 22-3]

and when Iachimo—"Italian fiend" as Posthumus calls him—looking back on his villainy, confesses and repents, he declares,

> mine Italian brain
> 'Gan in your duller Britain operate
> Most vilely.
>
> [V. v. 196-98]

These examples give the temper of practically every reference to Italy in the play, on the part at least of any character whom we respect either at the moment or throughout. They are all violently condemnatory; they all have a social-moral bearing; and they all sound more Elizabethan than early British.

But curiously—until we see the reason—the references to Rome have a different tone that discriminates them sharply from those to Italy. These are all military-political and carry us back to the Roman Empire and the age of Augustus. Yet in spite of Caesar and the historical date, in spite of the legendary British court and of the wager, with its touch of the age of chivalry, the play impresses us as neither Augustan, nor early British, nor medieval, but reminds us, with its account of the Queen's interest in drugs and refined forms of poisoning and its picture of the cosmopolitan gathering in Philario's house in Rome, of the period of the Borgias. Its atmosphere, save for certain scenes, is that of the less delectable aspects of the Italian Renaissance and so of Shakespeare's own time in so far as it was infected by the same virus.

And this links with something else. Adding a detail not mentioned so far as I remember in his source, Shakespeare points out that, since the commoners were all in service elsewhere, it became necessary for the empire to recruit its "gentry" for the business of subduing the recalcitrant Britons, who had refused to pay the tribute exacted by Julius Caesar. There would be nothing especially remarkable about that, did not the poet proceed a second time, and then a third, to stress the fact that Britain is to be conquered by Italian gentlemen in combination with certain Gallic forces. Why this triple underlining of the seemingly inconsequential fact that the invasion is to be by *gentlemen*?

It will be conjectured whither all this is leading. Almost from the outset, and increasingly, Shakespeare was plainly impressed by the evil influence on England of the ideas, manners, and morals of the darker side of the Italian Renaissance, both as imported directly from Italy and indirectly from France.

To begin with, there is the Machiavellian politics of the History Plays. This at first was hardly more than the stage tradition of the Machiavel. But, as early as *King John,* it was far more than that, a clear definition of the concept of Commodity, of power politics as we call it, exemplified in detail in that assembly of vile politicians which the History Plays so largely are. Though they were not all directly Italian-taught, these Commodity-servers are all directly, or by implication, indictments of Machiavellian politics.

But the fashions, manners, and morals of Italy are condemned quite as relentlessly as its politics in a long line of young gentlemen—some Italian, some Italian-bred, others only "Italianated"—who parade through Shakespeare's plays, especially his Comedies. The Italian setting of so many of these is comment on the vogue of things Italian among the Elizabethan gentlemen who frequented the theaters, most of whom had traveled and many of whom had been educated in Italy. (pp. 632-34)

There is simply no escaping the implications of these characters as a group. Interested in everything human, the poet draws most of them with a gaiety and good humor befitting comedy, but underneath his tolerance for the individual—to use that word of those who do not deserve it—can be felt his unmerciful scorn for the type, for its follies and fashions and shams that either flatten out into nonentity or grow into knavery and crime. (pp. 634-35)

Now Iachimo is one of the most illuminating embodiments of the Italian gentleman in this sense in all Shakespeare, the type at something near its best by his own standard, something near its worst by a higher one—until his repentance at the end. It is a notable compliment to both Iachimo's intelligence and his histrionic ability that Shakespeare intrusts to him what is possibly the most difficult scene to carry off successfully on the stage, so far as the acting is concerned, of any he had confronted an actor with since Richard III wooed Anne: the one in which Iachimo assails Imogen's virtue, and, having failed, restores himself to her good grace by a lightning-like shift of tactics. Unless consummately done, that scene seems absurdly improbable and breaks the play once for all at that point. But the fault is not in the psychology. The instantaneousness with which Iachimo perceives Imogen's impregnability and the combined audacity and insight with which he nevertheless proceeds are both characteristic. The effect, too, that this Sleeping Beauty's beauty has on him in the bedchamber scene, and his description of her, are not so much Shakespeare's poetry getting out of bounds, as has often been held, as ground and preparation for a belief that Iachimo's repentance at the end is sincere. (p. 635)

[If] a gentleman from abroad sought to corrupt Imogen, so did a royal representative of the court at home. There is a British as well as an Italian villain in the piece: Cloten.

Cloten. What a masterpiece! He deserves more critical attention than he has received as the final distillation of something Shakespeare had been at work on all his life. If Iachimo is his summing up of all that is ungentle in the continental gentleman, so is Cloten of all that is ignoble in the English nobility. Cloten is a sort of demonstration in advance of *The Tempest* of what happens when we try to civilize Caliban too rapidly. His virtues disappear and his vices are raised to the *n*th power. Imogen has his measure. In one of her milder moods she addresses him:

> Profane fellow!
> Wert thou the son of Jupiter and no more
> But what thou art besides, thou wert too base
> To be his groom. Thou wert dignified enough,
> Even to the point of envy, if 'twere made
> Comparative for your virtues, to be styl'd
> The under-hangman of his kingdom, and hated
> For being preferr'd so well.
>
> The south-fog rot him!
> [II. iii. 124-31]

retorts Cloten, meaning Posthumus, and the accent is exactly that of Caliban cursing Prospero:

> All the infections that the sun sucks up
> From bogs, fens, flats, on Prosper fall, and make him
> By inch-meal a disease!
>
> [*The Tempest,* II. ii. 1-3]
> (p. 637)

Nor does Cloten stand alone. He is merely the dark consummate flower of a nobility and court society that is rotten to the core.

The Queen is villainous, the King pusillanimous, the British lords cowardly and panicky in battle.

> To-day how many would have given their honours
> To have sav'd their carcases! took heel to do 't,
> And yet died too!
>
> [V. iii. 66-8]

cries Posthumus, and when he meets a British lord who, far from the battle line, is going still farther, he accosts him derisively:

> Still going? This is a lord!
>
> [V. iii. 64]

But Shakespeare was no Jacobin. Trust him not to leave things so one-sided as they would be if this were his last word in the matter. The plan of the play is triangular, and over against the miasma of Italian gentility and the cruder corruption of the British court he has put the mountain atmosphere of Wales and that incomparable trio, Belarius-Guiderius-Arviragus, the old man and the two kidnapped princes.

These scenes are among the loveliest in Shakespeare. They are done with a gusto that shows how deeply the poet's heart was in them. We feel ourselves bounding up the rocks, leaping the brooks, drinking in the bracing air. And the two princes *who do not know they are princes* are as indigenous to their habitat as deer or antelopes (and yet subtly alien to it too): the bold, dashing, athletic Guiderius (Polydore), and the not less courageous but more imaginative and lovely Arviragus (Cadwal), as alike and yet as different and nicely discriminated as were Goneril and Regan [in *King Lear*] at the opposite pole.

We may read these scenes of course for their own sakes as a delightful idyl.... But to do so is to lose much. A part may be a perfect whole in itself but that does not prevent it from being a perfect part of a whole also. These scenes have both these perfections.

To begin with, especially with Italy and the British court for contrast, they are a revealing study in the effects on a child's life of the three factors, heredity, environment, and education. Here is noble blood under conditions best suited to elicit hardihood, thrift, simplicity, and courage. And the results, we feel, would have been less happy if the blood had not been so good or the conditions had been less *natural*. But there is a third factor. Belarius—foster-father to the children and the wisest and kindliest kidnapper on record—is beautifully unaware of the fact that his memories of a more civilized life, strained through a philosophic temperament, afford just the influence and restraint that the boys need if they are to get all that is good from nature without being merely swallowed up by her bigness and wildness. He saves them from becoming young barbarians. Nor should their nurse-mother, Euriphile, dead but not forgotten, be left out. *Good blood, unconscious of its goodness, close to nature, watched over and loved by civilized experience and wisdom:* it is just the combination essential to the best results, and the fact that Shakespeare repeats it, with only minor variations, in the cases of Perdita [in *The Winter's Tale*] and Miranda [in *The Tempest*] shows that it is not just the chance of the plot but something approaching a considered prescription for the education of youth and the production of the noblest type of man and woman. The mountains of Wales in this play are all that Italy and the British court are not.

And now into this rocky retreat comes the older sister of these princes disguised as a boy. If Imogen has shone like a star in the darkness of the British court and has appeared there a Sleeping Beauty even to the base Iachimo, what will she be in the heart of nature? Belarius' attempts to describe her when he first glimpses her in the cave come nearest to being adequate: "a fairy," "an angel," "an earthly paragon," "divineness no elder than a boy" [III. vi. 41, 42, 43, 43-4]. Though we hear of Desdemona's house affairs, Imogen is perhaps the only character in Shakespeare who successfully reconciles the functions of angel and cook—so of heaven and of earth is she at the same time. Her supposed death and the dirge her brothers sing above her add a sad beauty to this mountain idyl.

And then it is interrupted in the most incongruous manner.

Cloten, clad in the garments of Posthumus he has gotten from Pisanio, has come to the region seeking revenge, swearing to violate Imogen for her insults to him and her rejection of him. He meets Guiderius, whom . . . he takes for a mountain robber. Enraged that the youth does not quail at the mere realization of his royal presence, he starts to beat him, but, instead, is beheaded by Guiderius. And now at the end of the dirge for the dead Fidele—Imogen under her mountain name—Belarius brings in the bloody and headless corpse of Cloten and places it beside the sleeping Imogen. The others go out. Imogen, awakening from her Juliet-like slumber and recognizing the garments of Posthumus, imagines it is the body of her slain husband by which she reposes, and, after an outburst of emotion, falls in an unconscious embrace on Cloten's bloody corpse.

It is the most incredible scene in Shakespeare! Or at least the reader who pronounces it such will be understood. The living purity of womanhood, the dead and bloody trunk of sensuality and brutality, brought into this disgusting physical proximity through a mistake in identity. It strikes one as one of the most inexcusable of theatrical tricks. The horrors of *Titus Andronicus,* if they are Shakespeare's, may be forgiven on the score of the author's youth. Titania embracing Bottom—"methought I was enamoured of an ass" [*A Midsummer Night's Dream,* IV. i. 77]—which somehow seems like a far-off prophecy of this scene, is both humorous and wise. But this desecrating juxtaposition of Beauty and the Beast seems to have not a shred or shadow of excuse. The gouging-out of Gloucester's eyes may be more cruel, but it is less nauseating.

The memory of that scene from *King Lear,* however, may well set us thinking. What if here, as there, the most revolting moment in the play should be the clue? What if, in relation to the whole, this scene should have its justification and significance? There is every precedent in Shakespeare for expecting it.

The ideal purity of womanhood embracing—because it is clad in the garments of the loved one—the brutal villainy of a false nobility that sought to enforce it: here is a situation that may mean more than meets the eye at first glance. (And in exploring it for over- and underintentions—in order to minimize the mere history—let us substitute England and English for Britain and British.)

Iachimo plainly stands for Italy and her malign influence, Cloten for corrupt English nobility, and Belarius-Guiderius-Arviragus for the ancient English tradition handed on, uncontaminated, to England's youngest and most genuinely noble blood. Iachimo seeks to seduce Imogen, and Cloten tries to violate her. But in vain, for Guiderius meets Cloten and beheads him, and Posthumus disarms Iachimo in a duel but spares him. Does not the parabolic quality of all this fairly shout aloud and demand that we think of Imogen as the True England wedded secretly to the poor but genuinely gentle Posthumus Leonatus, English Manhood and Valor? Posthumus himself calls Imogen almost exactly that: "Britain, . . . even thy mistress" [V. i. 20]. And though the recovery of her brothers deprives her of a worldly kingdom, she remains spiritual queen.

The moment we take the leading characters of the play in this way, numberless details rush forth to fit into what we can scarcely help calling the allegorical design. The King and Queen are plainly *The Power of the English Throne* wedded to *Corruption,* who is slowly poisoning it. Their "son"—not the King's son at all—is *Degenerate Royalty* or *False Nobility* who, though he hasn't a drop of princely blood in his veins, hopes with the help of *Corruption* to attain the throne. But *True England* prefers its *True Manhood* of low estate to its *False Nobility*—and secretly weds it. That *Manhood* is banished and is temporarily deluded by an *"Italian Fiend,"* who boasts in a cosmopolitan gathering in *Rome* that he can seduce *England.* The villain, first repulsed, then too ingenuously forgiven, succeeds, by theft and lies, in ruining the faith of *English Manhood* in *England.* In a frenzy of disillusionment *He* plots *Her* death, but is saved from the ultimate crime—somewhat as Lear is by Kent—by a *Faithful Servant. England,* meanwhile, attacked from within as well as from without, flees from the *Court* disguised as a youth, finds in the *Mountains* her true kin, her lovers and defenders, who, a *Genuine Nobility,* save her from violation by *False Nobility.* Awakening from a stupor induced by a drug (that came from *Corruption*), for a moment she embraces by mistake the dead and headless *False Nobility* that would have outraged her—because of the stolen clothes in which the corpse is clad. (How different that scene becomes when taken in this way!)

And then the Roman invasion and the battle:

Imperialism recruiting *Gentility*—an unholy alliance found throughout history because *Gentility* can hold its privileges at home only by fomenting quarrels and conquests abroad—invades England and puts to rout the English forces until *Old English Experience and Wisdom* hand in hand with her genuinely *Noble Youth* ("an old man and two boys" [V. iii. 52]) and joined by *English Manhood* who has put off his Italian guise and assumed that of an *English Peasant* ("a fourth man in a silly habit" [V. iii. 86]) make a Thermopylean stand in a narrow lane. These four, threatening to fight their own countrymen if they do not return to the combat, turn the tide of battle, and administer to the forces of *Imperialism* an overwhelming defeat—so miraculous a one, indeed, that the victors believe that "the heavens fought" [V. iii. 4] on their side and that their four saviors, or three of them at least, were angels.

The particular figurative designations suggested for the various characters need not be rigorously insisted on. There can be considerable latitude there. But can anyone believe that characters and story could fit together in this fashion by chance? If anyone can, it must be because of a dogmatic conviction that Shakespeare's genius was alien to allegory.

But to believe that the myriad-minded Shakespeare should have tried dramatic allegory—even assuming that he had not flirted with it in certain of his earlier Comedies—is surely doing him far less disrespect than to hold that he fell to composing in his last days such improbable and really inconsequential stuff as *Cymbeline* is if taken merely as a story. Furthermore, there is *The Tempest,* in which scarcely anyone denies the presence of some allegory. Granted that allegory, because of its element of conscious contrivance, is on a level below the greatest po-etry: still, a form used by Spenser, Bunyan, and Keats is not to be despised. Nobody thinks of claiming that *Cymbeline* is another *King Lear.*

Moreover, some such interpretation as the one suggested seems not only to harmonize with the text and evidence of the play itself but to confirm what Shakespeare has been saying almost from the beginning about "gentlemen," the inner and outer life, court and country, and most of all about imperialism in such plays as *Henry V* and *Antony and Cleopatra.*

But if this is not enough, there is something still more convincing.

There is a Roman soothsayer in *Cymbeline* who has a dream:

> Last night the very gods show'd me a vision—
> I fast and pray'd for their intelligence—thus:
> I saw Jove's bird, the Roman eagle, wing'd
> From the spongy south to this part of the west,
> There vanish'd in the sunbeams; which portends—
> Unless my sins abuse my divination—
> Success to the Roman host.
>
> [IV. ii. 346-52]

"Unless my sins abuse my divination": why did Shakespeare slip that in? Because the event, which was a British victory, shows that his sins did abuse his divination. At the end, the Soothsayer tries to save face by a second, *ex post facto,* interpretation of the dream that only makes matters worse:

> The vision
> Which I made known to Lucius, ere the stroke
> Of this yet scarce-cold battle, at this instant
> Is full accomplish'd; for the Roman eagle,
> From south to west on wing soaring aloft,
> Lessen'd herself, and in the beams o' the sun
> So vanish'd; which foreshow'd our princely eagle,
> The imperial Caesar, should again unite
> His favour with the radiant Cymbeline,
> Which shines here in the west.
>
> [V. v. 467-76]

This quite confirms the suspicion that the Soothsayer was a diplomatist and not a diviner, a gross licker of the royal boots. (Caesar would not have relished being only an eagle while Cymbeline was the sun!) And yet the dream itself was from the gods. Can *we* divine its meaning?

Politically the sun is a symbol of kingship or imperial power, but psychologically and poetically it means God, the source of life, love, light. When then the Roman eagle *vanishes*—a word the Soothsayer omits or perverts in his interpretations—in sunbeams, it means power being sublimated into imagination. And that is exactly the event in the play. The villain is not taken out to be tortured, as his poetical father Iago was, but is pardoned by the man he had injured.

> Kneel not to me,

says Posthumus,

> The power that I have on you is to spare you;
> The malice towards you to forgive you. Live,
> And deal with others better.
>
> [V. v. 417-20]

There is power vanishing in love, indeed. And Posthumus' mercy begets the same kindliness in the King:

>   Nobly doom'd!
> We'll learn our freeness of a son-in-law;
> Pardon's the word to all.
>
>   [V. v. 420-22]

There is a general reconciliation, the older generation, as in *King Lear,* kneeling to the younger. And that reconciliation is not only personal but political. Cymbeline, out from under the spell of his wicked queen, instead of exacting tribute from the defeated Romans, agrees to give freely what he had refused to have exacted of him under compulsion. It is one of Shakespeare's last words on that spirit of magnanimity in which he held that victory should be taken. Here again the Roman eagle of Imperialism *vanishes* in the sun of pardon and harmony:

> CYM.:   Laud we the gods;
> And let our crooked smokes climb to their
>   nostrils
> From our bless'd altars. Publish we this peace
> To all our subjects. Set we forward. Let
> A Roman and a British ensign wave
> Friendly together. So through Lud's town march;
> And in the temple of great Jupiter
> Our peace we'll ratify; seal it with feasts.
> Set on there! Never was a war did cease,
> Ere bloody hands were wash'd, with such a
>   peace.
>
>   [V. v. 476-85]

Another significant last word.

If *Antony and Cleopatra* was actual, this is symbolic history. And how incomplete the former is without the latter. "The time of universal peace is near" [*Antony and Cleopatra,* IV. vi. 4], boasted Octavius, and then Shakespeare shows him sending his imperial legions against Britain. This is a Little England play if there ever was one. But in the suggestion of a British and a Roman ensign waving together is a hint of a reconciliation and synthesis between the liberty that can be found only in the little country and the unity of the whole world, which is the redeeming ideal behind an Imperialism that, practically, always makes the mistake of letting the sunshine vanish in the eagle instead of the eagle in the sunshine.

But this play is as much a moral as a political allegory. The warning it affords England of the dangers lurking in the decadent agents of the Renaissance (what a prophecy it is of the worst features of the Jacobean drama!) goes far, as does its stress on the virtues of simplicity, to place Shakespeare, in his latest phase, with Milton and the Puritans. He was little enough of a puritan in the popular derogatory sense of the term. I detect not one trace of false asceticism in his nature. But when Posthumus, still supposing he has been the cause of Imogen's death, discards his Italian garments and assumes those of a British peasant, allegory or no allegory, we catch intimations not only of the Puritans, but of Rousseau, Wordsworth, and even Tolstoy. It is like a poetical Reformation denouncing a poetical Renaissance that has proved traitor to the very beauty she thought she worshiped. (pp. 639-45)

Through the symbolic connection between England and Imogen that it sets up, *Cymbeline* suggests that those two age-old combats between lust and purity, and between empire and liberty, are at bottom the same. The latter struggle will go on, Shakespeare seems to say, until those opposites, envy and privilege,

on which it depends, recognize with shame their identity under their apparent difference and repent like Iachimo:

>   Knighthoods and honours, borne
> As I wear mine, are titles but of scorn.
>
>   [V. ii. 6-7]

Those who rest in them "scarce are men" [V. ii. 10], while those who do not are "gods." (p. 647)

> Harold C. Goddard, "'Cymbeline',," in his The Meaning of Shakespeare, *The University of Chicago Press, 1951, pp. 630-47.*

DEREK TRAVERSI   (essay date 1954)

[*Traversi, a British scholar, has written a number of books on Shakespeare's plays, including* An Approach to Shakespeare *(1938),* Shakespeare: The Last Phase *(1954), and* Shakespeare: The Roman Plays *(1963). In the introduction to the first of these studies, Traversi proposed to focus his interpretation of the plays on "the word," stating that the experience which forms the impetus to each of Shakespeare's dramas "will find its most immediate expression in the language and verse." In the following excerpt, Traversi contends that the "true theme" of* Cymbeline *is that universal harmony requires the integration of "natural simplicity" with "courtly virtue" in its individuals, and that both of these qualities must be subordinated to a "higher loyalty." The critic maintains that this overriding symbolic theme informs the various conflicts and dramatic developments in the play: for example, the confrontation between opposing views of "value"— one "romantic" and reflected in the speeches of Posthumus and Imogen, the other "cynical" and demonstrated by the libertine Iachimo—paves the way for the tragic experiences which later befall the young lovers, causing them to reassess their earlier romantic conception of self-worth and, in turn, leading them to a more integrated and ethical sense of identity. Traversi also perceives this "symbolic structure" in the play's increasing emphasis on the discrepancies between true and apparent virtue or honor—a knowledge which he states forms the foundation of Iachimo's assault on Imogen and serves as an important subject in the heroine's moral education—and in the conflict between "natural nobility" and the artifices of the civilized court, dramatized most explicitly in the scenes set near Milford Haven. According to Traversi, Shakespeare unites all of these concerns in the final act in a vision of universal harmony and cosmic order. For him, the events of this final movement—the reconciliations, the note of repentance, the reintegration of the British kingdom, even the political or historical theme in which Britain willfully returns to its proper relation with Rome and the gods shower their blessings on its destiny—all "are united in subjection to a spiritual vision, full of mellow, 'golden' richness. . . ." For further commentary on the theme of regeneration or reconciliation in* Cymbeline, *see the excerpts by Denton J. Snider (1890), Robert Grams Hunter (1965), William Barry Thorne (1969), and Nancy K. Hayles (1980). Also, see the excerpts by G. Wilson Knight (1947) and Harold C. Goddard (1951) for further examinations of the historical theme in the play. In addition, the emphasis on the discrepancies between appearance and reality in the drama is apparent in the essays by Donald A. Stauffer (1949) and Hayles. Additional investigation of value imagery can also be found in the studies by Caroline F. E. Spurgeon (1935) and A. A. Stephenson (1942). On a different matter, Traversi regards* Cymbeline—*despite its accomplishments—as an experimental play, and he attributes to its transitional nature much in the drama that is unsuccessful, particularly Shakespeare's failure to match his language and expression with his themes and to adapt rather conventional material to his own needs.*]

Cymbeline, second to *Pericles* in the series of Shakespeare's last plays, is also, though in a rather different manner, an unequal piece. The presence in it of diverse and even contradictory artistic purposes seems to point, as in the earlier play, to an experimental origin. Beyond that, however, the parallel breaks down. Whereas the avowedly 'Shakespearean' passages of *Pericles* stand out clearly from the inferior matter which surrounds them, in *Cymbeline* the theory of divided authorship, though in part feasible, rests on no clear-cut distinction in style or treatment. The more pedestrian passages of the play are firmly embedded in the general structure, and its inequalities suggest less a stratified construction by different hands than the work of an author feeling his way, with incomplete clarity of purpose, towards a fresh use of the dramatic conventions which lay to his hand. (p. 43)

The result is a play which, although notably uneven in execution, represents a stage of transition between the highly personal symbolism of *Pericles* and the greater scope, the reference to wider fields of human experience, successfully achieved in *The Winter's Tale*. In relation to the later masterpieces *Cymbeline* is a strangely incoherent and incomplete performance; but, read as the successor to Shakespeare's earlier experiment in dramatic symbolism, it shows him reaching out towards a more ample social content and a more inclusive conception of poetic drama.

The relation between romantic convention and the underlying purpose of *Cymbeline* only emerges gradually in the course of the early action. It is best approached, in the first place, through a consideration of linguistic quality. The opening scenes of the play are distinguished by the presence of a definite vitality of speech, itself the reflection of a deeper content, from the sentimental conceptions of Fletcher. The clash of loyalties occasioned by Imogen's forced betrothal to Cloten, which serves as point of departure for the action, is given a definite universality, firmly and objectively defined, in the opening words of the play:

> . . . our bloods
> No more obey the heavens than our courtiers
> Still seem as does the king.
>
> [I. i. 1-3]

The arbitrary act of the monarch, occasioned by the blind passion that binds him to his second wife, is thus set by his own courtiers against a background of the obedience properly owed by 'blood', or instinct, to the 'heavens': an obedience, however, which is already felt to be subject to strain, to 'seem' rather than to be, and which soon gives way to a more explicit contrast between the mask of duty and the compulsion of true feeling:

> . . . not a courtier,
> Although they wear their faces to the bent
> Of the king's looks, hath a heart that is not
> Glad at the thing they scowl at.
>
> [I. i. 12-15]

The complexity of expression, imposed in a kind of verbal counterpoint upon the plain sense, is, as in so much of Shakespeare's mature writing, an indication of underlying purpose. The deliberate intricacy of the double negative ('*not* a courtier . . . that is *not* glad'), the balancing of opposites in 'glad' and 'scowl', the sense of dissembling implied in 'wear their faces', all point to the presence of a deep-seated dislocation of natural feeling. The bond which binds individual conduct, through proper obedience to established authority, to the cosmic order, accepted though it may be on the surface with an appearance of conformity, is in fact subjected to a sense of pervasive strain which will soon find its counterpart in the external

action. The return to normality through the final integration of natural simplicity to courtly virtue, and the subordination of both to a higher loyalty, is the true theme of the play.

In accordance with this general plan, Imogen's repudiation of Cloten, whose parody of true courtliness can only be acceptable to Cymbeline's passion-distorted vision, implies her choice of a superior conception of humanity, at once supremely natural and truly civilized. This conception inspires, in the same scene, the description of Posthumus, whom the king formerly endowed with—

> all the learnings that his time
> Could make him the receiver of; which he took,
> As we do air, fast as 't was minister'd;
> And in's spring became a harvest; liv'd in court—
> Which rare it is to do—most praised, most loved;
> A sample to the youngest; to the more mature
> A glass that feated them; and to the graver
> A child that guided dotards. . . .
>
> [I. i. 43-50]

Posthumus is more than an individual example of the courtly virtues. He stands, through the possession of these, for a conception of 'value' which, fostered by his upbringing and the action of time, is to be an essential point of reference in the development of the action.

With the universal intention thus indicated, the sense of the main description of Posthumus' courtly education is evident. For the first time—and the last, until the end of the play— nature and civilization are united in spontaneous harmony. The virtues celebrated in him are those of true courtliness, fostered by a 'learning' imbibed as naturally as air and proceeding, in the normal course of youthful development, to its proper 'harvest'. In a world in which, as events will show, true virtue is indeed a rarity, the 'outward' of Posthumus reflects the merit of the 'stuff within'; he has become thereby an example to all ages and conditions, a mirror of the finer human qualities which Imogen, in loving him and rejecting Cloten, has appreciated at their proper worth.

The integrity of Imogen's love, her fitting response to the virtues enshrined in Posthumus, receives poetic expression in their interview, to which the opening exchanges have served as an introduction. The tone is one in which romantic sentiment is modified, though with less than complete consistency, by the introduction of a pervading symbolism to stress the conception of *value*, of surpassing worth. The expression of emotion is built deliberately round the central image of the jewel, which will shortly receive external projection as a symbolic element in the plot. Imogen refers to her 'dearest husband', about to be separated from her by banishment, as 'this jewel'; she confers upon him at the moment of parting a diamond which 'was my mother's' and receives in return the bracelet which is 'a manacle of love' [I. i. 85, 91, 112, 122]. The external symbols of value, in themselves normally associated with romantic passion, serve to focus around their rarity intense expressions of emotion, in which the separating action of time is balanced against the sense of achieved timelessness—

> Should we be taking leave
> As long a time as yet we have to live,
> The loathness to depart would grow—
>
> [I. i. 106-08]

and living dedication gains added point by being set, in terms of religious sanction, against the evocation of mortality:

> You gentle gods, give me but this I have,
> And sear up my embracements from a next
> With bonds of death!
>
> [I. i. 115-17]

The poetry, though more diluted with romantic sentiment, recalls the relevant portions of Antony and Cleopatra in its easy freedom and intensity of phrase. A similar impression of timelessness and transcendent value is conveyed by Posthumus' reference to Imogen's 'so *infinite* loss' [I. i. 120], and this infinity is in turn balanced against the intense immediacy implied in 'sense'—

> Remain, remain thou here
> While sense can keep it on!—
>
> [I. i. 117-18]

and confirmed, a little further on, in Imogen's firm retort to the enraged Cymbeline: 'I am *senseless* of your fears' [I. i. 135]. The whole of this part of the action is steeped, in fact, in an impression of value, of 'rarity'—Imogen herself refers to the 'touch more *rare*' which 'subdues' all 'pangs' and 'fears' [I. i. 35-6]—in which the action of time, itself apprehended as implying a kind of refinement of the sensual, is set against the infinite delicacy, at once tenuous and intense, of experienced love.

It is this emotional affirmation of value, this 'rarity', indeed, which, together with its context in courtly convention, is subjected in the following scenes to analysis. After having received further expression in Imogen's dialogue with Pisanio (I. iii), it is first emphasized by contrast with the aristocratic pretensions of Cloten—a court parody of the truly 'natural' man, enslaved to his base passions—and then exposed to the intrigues of Iachimo. The arrival of Posthumus in Rome (I. iv), with which the prevailing mood is switched from integration to analysis, introduces a contrast essential to the play. Fittingly expressed in prose, the scene introduces the convention of Italianate court cynicism, which is allowed to play with critical detachment, or the appearance of it, upon the values incarnated in Posthumus' idealization of Imogen. (pp. 44-9)

The primary purpose of this Roman dialogue, poised in the calculated intricacy of its prose between convention and analysis, is an exploration of the conception of 'value' intuitively accepted by Imogen and Posthumus as the basis of their relationship. As it opens, Philario and Iachimo divide between them the possible attitudes to Posthumus' reputation. For Philario, whose judgement is based on friendship and a family bond of gratitude, Posthumus is 'without and within' [I. iv. 9-10]—the stressing of this consistency is, in the light of earlier expressions, a notable indication of the play's continuity of purpose—an incarnation of the perfect gentleman; for Iachimo, on the other hand, a dispassionate weighing of the facts as they appear to him introduces a persistent doubt, a reducing of this supposed 'value' to interest and pretension. Iachimo, in fact, sees Posthumus' virtues not as illuminating social existence, as the crown of human living, but as conditioned by it, tainted by its inescapable hollowness. His devotion to Imogen, regarded hitherto as the supreme proof of his moral excellence, becomes from this new standpoint a proof of imperfection; for, to a critical eye, it seems to imply that 'he must be weighed rather by her value than his own' [I. iv. 15-16], whilst the very 'approbation' of those that welcomed the match can be explained in terms of a desire to 'fortify' the weak judgement of

Imogen, 'which else an easy battery might lay flat, for taking a beggar without less quality' [I. iv. 22-3]. The intricate verbal pattern thus woven round the central situation has, in fact, beyond its obvious purpose as a reflection of sophisticated 'Italianate' cynicism, a strictly analytic content. To Iachimo, absolute 'value' of the kind postulated in love by Imogen and Posthumus is inconceivable. His intelligence, acute in its limitations, plays upon such 'value' and the virtue which is its moral expression, reducing both alike to a mixture of sentiment and interest; and, if his attitude is rootedly negative, if such a phrase as 'how *creeps* acquaintance' [I. iv. 24-5] clearly reflects the speaker's tendency towards systematic debasement, under-valuation, it is none the less true that his position needs to be taken into account, to be first isolated in its expression and then assimilated, through the positive reaction it will eventually produce, into the final pattern.

To this clash of contrary attitudes to 'value', the tangible symbol of the ring, already introduced in the earlier verse-scene, serves as a point of focus. Around it, indeed, the moral and material values with which the play is ultimately concerned are subtly interwoven. Posthumus is ready to defend his belief in his mistress' virtue in terms of tangible worth, and Iachimo uses this very readiness to insinuate that the two conceptions of value, the moral and the material, are in fact identical, that the one is only to be conceived in terms of the other. In this he is helped, if not justified, by a strain of romantic rashness (if we may call it so) in Posthumus, which is indicated from the first in his preparatory exchange with the Frenchman. What strikes the latter, in remarking upon an incident in Posthumus' earlier career, as an unjustified disparity between the 'mortal purpose' of a challenge and the 'slight and trivial' nature of its cause, is at once acknowledged by him to have been the product of impulse in a 'young traveller' and confirmed by what he now considers to be his 'minded judgement' [I. iv. 41, 42, 43-4, 46]. The distinction at once asserts a valid principle—for Posthumus' adoration of his mistress is clearly intended to be ratified by his mature evaluation—and indicates a possible danger; for, although it is undoubtedly true, as he asserts later, that there is a fundamental difference between 'what may be sold or given' and what is 'only the gift of the gods' [I. iv. 82-3, 85], the assumption that the two values are connected, that the one may properly be discussed in terms of the other, is perhaps a little too easily made. Certainly it gives Iachimo his opening. To Posthumus' sweeping assertion that his jewel and the object of his love stand alike unparalleled in his estimation—'I praised her as I rated her: so do I my stone'—the answer inspired by his rooted relativity is, as far as it goes, indisputable: 'I have not seen the most precious diamond that is, nor you the lady' [I. iv. 77, 75-6]. The attempt, whether successful or not, to turn romantic commonplace to the ends of moral analysis, is undoubtedly present. The romantic love of Posthumus, far from being, as he believes, a final and sufficient relationship, needs to be subjected to a destructive process which will eventually bring it to full maturity. 'She your jewel' and 'this your jewel' [I. iv. 153], thus brought together in the subtleties of court conversation, represent in their identification a knot of contrasted interpretations of value which the play, in so far as it is consistent with its deeper purposes (which is only in part), will be concerned to unravel.

With the two conceptions of 'value'—the romantic and the critical, so to call them—thus contrasted, the rest of this, the first stage in the development of the play, deals with the undermining of the former by the latter. Iachimo's next appearance (I. vi) brings him face to face with Imogen, and so with the chance to apply his 'philosophy' in practice. His attack rests, characteristically, upon the contrast between inward quality and outward features, the evident perfection of that part of his intended victim 'that is out of door' [I. vi. 15] and the possible 'rarity' of the mind with which she is furnished. The distinction enables him to apply his peculiarly dissolvent, disintegrating procedure in a way that contributes to the total analysis of 'value' with which the play as a whole is particularly concerned. (pp. 50-2)

The scene which follows is at once important and oddly unsatisfactory. It reminds us, in its conception, of the episode in *Macbeth* (IV. iii) in which Malcolm first tries the loyalty of Macduff by stressing his imagined villainies and then, undoing his own words, brings out his deepest allegiance. Both scenes are symbolically rather than realistically conceived; both have their function as turning-points balancing in opposed poetic intensities the contrasted themes of their respective plays, and both—it is only fair to say—fail to relate these purposes to a convincing dramatic action. In the case of *Cymbeline*, the impact of the episode is further complicated by a definite derivative note in the poetry, a use of language which repeatedly recalls themes used in earlier tragedies without really equalling them in intensity or conviction. This is particularly apparent in the treatment of Iachimo's resentment against the physical embodiment, in Imogen, of a purity which he finds inconceivable. He begins, in accordance with the constant theme of the play, by ascribing to Posthumus a madness, an incapacity to 'distinguish' or 'make partition' between evident value and its parody, between 'fair and foul'; but, as he proceeds, his detachment fails and the characteristic expressions of repulsion, 'apes and monkeys' and the desire that, surfeited, 'vomits emptiness', come to the surface as reflections of his own sensuality [I. vi. 34, 37, 38, 39, 45]. Ascribing to Posthumus sentiments formerly held by Iago—

> . . . that man, who knows
> By history, report, or his own proof,
> What woman is, *yea, what she cannot choose*
> *But must be*—
>
> [I. vi. 69-72]

he falls into the disgust imagery typical of so many earlier plays, but felt here a little too easily and with something less than the full Shakespearean immediacy. The intention, it seems, is to pervade the scene with the sensuality with which Imogen's 'honour' is threatened, to reflect a world in which she lives indeed but in isolation and subject to continual perils. There is even a moment, when Imogen herself responds by referring to the 'Romish stew' and the 'beastly mind' of the stranger who is seeking to abuse her [I. vi. 152, 153], in which the prevailing animality of Iachimo seems on the point of turning her otherwise serene utterance into unbalance; but the shift in tone is unprepared for, without relation to any justifying complexity of character, and stands in strange contrast to her prevailing integrity as a sign of the imperfect assimilation so evident in this play. The development, indeed, is not insisted on. Iachimo recognizes his error, falling back on a description of Posthumus which reminds us, in its evocation of intangible perfection, of a kind of divinity which the subject's own behaviour is shortly to qualify:—

> He sits 'mongst men like a descended god:
> He hath a kind of honour sets him off,
> More than a mortal seeming.
>
> [I. vi. 169-71]

At the end of the exchange, Imogen has repelled easily enough Iachimo's direct assault, but is powerless to meet the guile by which he plans to steal from her in sleep the 'proof' of his conquest; and, as a result of her defencelessness, she is faced in due course, not only with her father's passionate resentment, but with the anger of her disillusioned lover.

The following scenes at Cymbeline's court add little to themes already announced. A background to Imogen's betrayal, and a comment on the worthlessness of courtly pretension divorced from true 'value', is provided (II. i) by the contrast between Cloten's claim to external nobility and a rooted coarseness which becomes grotesque in the eyes of his attendants and expresses itself most characteristically in a persistent underlining of the animal, the purely physical element in passion. (pp. 53-5)

From this point, it is natural to pass on to the scene (II. ii) in which the 'temple' itself is finally subjected to direct siege by the furtive entry of Iachimo into Imogen's bed-chamber. Symbolically speaking, of course, the climax of the incident lies in the theft of Imogen's bracelet, the function of which as a point of focus for the poetic development has already been indicated. Poetically, however, the scene, like so much in the play, hesitates between the full symbolic integration of its theme and a prevailing decorative spirit. It is worth noting that the tragic implications of Iachimo's speech are persistently diluted by reflections which, while they recall images and themes derived from the great tragedies, are less immediate than, in a very real sense, literary elaborations. . . . Tragic urgency and the firm grasp of character seem, in short, to have been both diluted into something very like an excess of decorative poetry. And yet the excess itself—it is necessary to add—is possibly part of a deliberately chosen effect. Imogen's honour is set here, temporarily, in a setting of opulent artifice which is foreign to its nature and in which the sophisticated sensuality of Iachimo is unquestionably at home. Her marriage with Posthumus will only be consummated after she has been removed from Cymbeline's court, exposed to 'nature' and a variety of trials; but, meanwhile, her very virtues are set against a background, beautiful indeed, but steeped in convention, particularly calculated to set Iachimo's sensuous instincts sharply on edge. (pp. 56-7)

The following episode (II. iii), with Imogen's repudiation of Cloten, develops further the contrast between true 'honour' and its parody, the respect given to place and courtly advancement. (p. 58)

It also stresses, through the attendant Lady's opening words to Cloten, that true gentility needs to be distinguished from the external adornments which so often replace it in common esteem. When Cloten describes himself as a 'gentleman' and, further, as 'a gentleman's son', he provokes the comment:

> That's more
> Than some whose tailors are as dear as yours
> Can justly boast of.
>
> [II. iii. 78-80]

The matter of clothing, indeed, is not raised by accident. The superficial courtliness of Cloten is exposed by his denunciation of Posthumus, in verse of some complexity, as 'a base wretch' [II. iii. 113] in whom lack of fortune is a certain sign of lack of desert. 'Bred of alms and foster'd with cold dishes' [II. iii. 114], he is—so Cloten argues, reflecting the attitude of the society which has accepted his own claim to aristocracy—no proper match for a princess, and one, moreover, specially bound by her station to the duty of 'obedience'. The argument, in Shakespearean terms, is not without force, as may be gathered from the closely-knit writing in such a passage as—

> . . . to knit their souls,
> On whom there is no more dependency
> But brats and beggary, in self-figured knot;
>> [II. iii. 117-19]

but it is invalidated by the essential coarseness of he who proposes it, whose relation to true courtliness is properly assessed by Imogen when she subordinates him, in a phrase which will be echoed persistently from now on, to the 'meanest garment' of her lover.

Cloten's pretensions having thus been sufficiently placed by the mere fact of contact with Imogen, we return (II. iv) to Posthumus in Italy, and to the introduction into his soul of the poison associated with Iachimo. With this introduction, the first stage in the play's development will be completed. Once more, the circumstances of Imogen's betrayal are surrounded, in the telling, with a quality of sensual artifice which links them with Iachimo's particular brand of courtliness. The account of her bed-chamber, with its direct evocation of Cleopatra at Cydnus, reads like a derivation from Enobarbus' famous description, and has, perhaps, something like the same function in the play. The emphasis is throughout on 'workmanship and value' [II. iv. 74], on the artistic counterfeit of true life:

> never saw I figures
> So likely to report themselves; *the cutter*
> *Was as another nature, dumb;* outwent her,
> *Motive and breath left out.*
>> [II. iv. 82-5]

To grasp adequately the relation between this artifice and the human value to be ascribed to Imogen's honour is to be in possession of one of the main themes of the play. The 'golden cherubins' on the roof of her bed-chamber, the 'two winking Cupids' of silver, the chimney-piece with 'chaste Dian bathing', and the tapestries 'of silk and silver' are all elaborate counterfeits, seen through the self-conscious, artificial vision of a courtier, of 'nature' [II. iv. 88, 89, 82, 69]. Iachimo, as befits him, responds sensually to their opulence, but the perfection he evokes is not meant to obscure the fact that 'motion and breath' have been here 'left out' [II. iv. 85], have no part to play in an essentially lifeless effect. Without claiming that the point is consistently made, we may say that the setting of courtly opulence in which Imogen has so far moved—and which is associated, above all, with the betrayal of her trust—is intended as a contrast to the firm simplicity which will only emerge fully in the hour of her misfortune.

Whether or not this reading be entirely justified, the description leads directly to the assertion of the central 'symbolic' theme, the 'wedding' of Imogen's bracelet to Posthumus' diamond. The ease with which Posthumus is convinced of his mistress' betrayal reminds us, in a certain sense, of the similar behaviour of Othello when confronted by the 'proof' of Desdemona's 'faithlessness'; but, it is necessary to add, his behaviour is not supported by any similar rigour in the dramatic analysis of character. Posthumus, indeed, seems to hesitate, as always, between a realistic and a symbolic function, seems not to belong fully either to the spirit of the earlier plays or to that of the final comedies. His dramatic mode of being, whilst recalling both, is neither that of Othello nor of Leontes; we are neither convinced by his declared motives nor ready to regard detailed motivation as irrelevant to a character not conceived

as actor in a realistic tragedy. The commonplace rant with which he states his conviction of betrayal—

> Let there be no honour
> Where there is beauty; truth where semblance; love,
> Where there's another man—
>> [II. iv. 108-10]

lacks that justification in terms of motive which alone could make it plausible, and the further direct echoes of *Othello*—

> I will kill thee if thou dost deny
> Thou'st made me cuckold.
>
> O, that I had her here, to tear her limb-meal!—
>> [II. iv. 145-46, 147]

suffer from a similar lack of defined dramatic purpose. As a character, Posthumus is, to say the least of it, inadequately conceived; as participant in a symbolic action, his behaviour too frequently raises questions of motive which should have been felt to be irrelevant, and his expression is too derivative, too reminiscent of earlier figures conceived on different lines, to carry complete conviction. Perhaps that is another way of saying that he, like the play to which he belongs, stands at a transitional moment in Shakespeare's artistic development, in which old themes have yet to be fully assumed into a new dramatic conception.

In so far as a clear purpose can be said to emerge from this part of *Cymbeline,* this scene and Posthumus' following monologue (II. v) seem to be intended to convey the entry into his mind of a sensual poison which springs finally from Iachimo's cynical evaluation of human motives. The soliloquy which brings this part of the action to an end—'We are all bastards!' [II. v. 2]—clearly aims at giving universal force to a particular experience in which motive, as in Leontes, counts for little. The image of the 'coiner' and his 'counterfeit' is of universal rather than particular application, as is the final catalogue of vices and the denunciation of woman which accompanies it; but it is impossible not to feel that the universal purpose is in great part invalidated by the presence of a feeling of particular resentment, and the whole passage reads—in spite of a number of remarkable verbal felicities: 'as chaste as unsunn'd snow', '*yellow* Iachimo' [II. v. 13, 14]—rather as the repetition of themes more convincingly developed elsewhere than as a fresh dramatic creation. Be that as it may, it does certainly mark the attempt to work out an important stage in the main symbolic design. Posthumus is now, in a very real sense, assimilated in outlook to Iachimo, affected by the poison that corrupts human relationships in their courtly context. He casts doubts upon his own paternity and evokes the comparison with Diana—introduced not for the first time into the play—only to give it the validity of appearance, of mere *seeming*. His very memories of Imogen's behaviour become affected, in the telling, with a strangely ambiguous note:

> Me of my lawful pleasure she restrain'd,
> And pray'd me oft forbearance; did it with
> A pudency so rosy, the sweet view on't
> Might well have warm'd old Saturn.
>> [II. v. 9-12]

Imogen, thus described, becomes a figure of hypocrisy, restraining her lover from his 'lawful pleasure' at the same time as she planned his betrayal; her very 'pudency', touched with sensuality by the choice of the epithets 'rosy' and 'sweet' which accompany it, has the power to 'warm' the unnatural instincts of the aged Saturn. Posthumus' relations to Imogen have, in short, been corrupted by exposure to court sophistication and cynicism. He, and Imogen, will have to be taken out of that context, exposed to the natural simplicities, before any true process of recovery can be initiated.

The central part of *Cymbeline*, involving the integration of the various symbolic themes, is mainly concerned with the events that lead up to the meeting of Imogen, Cloten, and the lost sons of the king at Milford Haven. At this point, and as a result of their expulsion from the civilized world, the story of the two lovers meets that of Guiderius and Arviragus in a common exposure to 'nature'. (pp. 59-63)

[Act III, Scene iii] introduces the world of 'nature', the environment of Belarius and his two adopted sons. It also raises once more the problem of the relationship between true feeling and literary convention which is characteristic of *Cymbeline*, and perhaps one of its main themes. For the 'nature' which is set in contrast to court artificiality is itself artificially conceived, and this is one of the complicating features of the play. The spirit which impels Belarius to draw his moral from every aspect of his surroundings—as when he contrasts the low entrance of the cave, through which his wards have to stoop, with the 'gates of monarchs'—

> ... arch'd so high that giants may jet through
> And keep their impious turbans on, without
> Good morrow to the sun,
>
> [III. iii. 4-7]

or when he remarks—

> Consider,
> When you above perceive me like a crow,
> That it is place which lessens and sets off—
> [III. iii. 11-13]

suggests that Shakespeare, in the writing of this play, was caught up to some extent in the conventions he was trying to use. The complexity of tone, balanced between sententiousness and sincerity, may be said, however, to correspond to the state of the action, which is still manifestly incomplete. The relationship between 'civilization' and 'nature', indeed, is not of the kind that can be projected into a simple contrast. If the contrast exists, it reflects a mutual incompleteness. Advantages balance disadvantages on either side. The court world which produced Iachimo and the Queen also gave their proper background to Imogen's essentially royal virtues; and, if these have to be removed from their corrupt setting to find themselves in contact with 'nature', the shortcomings of 'nature' itself are equally clear, through the operation of instinct, to Cymbeline's transplanted off-spring. Arviragus and Guiderius, in the same scene (III. iii), balance in their discussion with their father a realization of the advantages of the simple life, which he has a little theoretically enlarged upon, against a sense of its limitations. On the one hand, indeed,

> Haply this life is best,
> If quiet life be best;
>
> [III. iii. 29-30]

on the other, Arviragus acknowledges himself to be 'beastly' and feels his simplicity as a confinement:

> our cage
> We make a quire, as doth the prison'd bird,
> And sing our bondage freely.
>
> [III. iii. 42-4]

Simplicity, in other words, has limitations of its own, and freedom under conditions of primitive life involves the 'bondage' of the higher, specifically civilized faculties. These will only be awakened in Cymbeline's sons when they are restored to free loyalty and to a proper relationship with the father they have lost. This, in turn, will imply their assimilation into the wider pattern of the action, at once patriotic and (as we shall see) universal, in which the personal issues of the play are finally to be resolved. (pp. 66-7)

[The meeting] between Imogen and the 'adopted' sons of Belarius (III. vi), though clearly important in the structure of the play, is ... uneven in conception and treatment. The main theme, the acceptance of primitive conditions by a heroine born to court life, is once more superficially handled, fails to resolve its conventionality in terms of a deeper purpose. Imogen's opening speech, which seems occasionally to echo themes familiar in *King Lear* and other tragedies, evidently seeks to relate the action to a significant moral development. The emphasis on her exhaustion and the very phrase 'I have made the ground my bed', the assertion of her 'resolution' as a counterpoise to despair, the relating of her experience of poverty to a more universal uncertainty in 'Foundations fly the wretched' (although 'foundations', as has been observed, carries the subsidiary sense of 'hospitals' and cure, taken up by Imogen herself when she adds 'such, I mean, Where they should be relieved'), the moral contrast between 'poor folks', whose very afflictions, 'a punishment or trial', should guarantee the truthfulness still more inexplicably lacking in 'rich ones' [III. vi. 3, 7, 7-8, 9, 11, 12]: all this reminds us in certain respects of Edgar's similar reduction to 'unaccommodated' beggary, whilst failing to produce any similar sense of coherence, of relation to a central moral exploration consistently developed. 'Famine', we are told, makes 'nature' valiant, before it 'overthrows' it [III. vi. 19-20]. 'Hardness' is mother of 'hardiness', and 'plenty and peace', by contrast, breed 'cowards' [III. vi. 21-2]; but Imogen's resolution, when Guiderius and Arviragus appear, is scarcely stressed as the new factor it should be, and the scene tapers off into sentiment of a more conventional kind. The emphasis on the sexual confusion, sensed if not understood by the brothers, is scarcely an adequate background for the overtly universal moral drawn by Imogen in conclusion, as she looks back on her recent experiences:

> Great men,
> That had a court no bigger than this cave,
> That did attend themselves and had the virtue
> Which their own conscience seal'd them—laying by
> That nothing-gift of differing multitudes—
> Could not out-peer these twain.
>
> [III. vi. 81-6]

Once more, in reading this passage, we are faced with a discrepancy, frequent in *Cymbeline* and perhaps the fundamental problem of the play, between expression and effectiveness. The language, concise and compact, is that of the mature tragedies, and the sentiments expressed are related, by means of it, to that exploration of moral realities which is characteristic of Shakespeare at his best; but the themes stated are not adequately developed, fail to make themselves felt in the course of an action that remains basically conventional. Nowhere is the provisional quality of the inspiration of *Cymbeline* more clearly apparent.

The following scenes carry the situation at Milford to its climax. The first of them (IV. i) incorporates Cloten once more into the central action and takes up the contrast, already developed with reference to him, between the external 'garment' and the inner man. Cloten, in fact, is the unpolished human animal, dressed up as a courtier and given the external circumstances of rank. His very likeness, in physical terms, to Posthumus—stressed by the fact that the latter's clothes fit him perfectly—emphasizes the vainness of his pretensions. Cloten is sure of his similarity, or superiority, to Posthumus in physique, in 'fortunes', in 'the advantage of the time', in 'birth', and in martial prowess [IV. i. 11-12]; the inability of these qualities, or the imaginary possession of them, to impress Imogen is a sign of his failure in moral understanding and the cause of his resentment. That resentment, typically, breeds the brutality expressed in his final anticipation of the way in which, having killed Posthumus, he will treat his mistress:

> Posthumus, thy head, which now is growing
> upon thy shoulders, shall within this hour be
> off; thy mistress enforced; thy garments cut to
> pieces before thy face: and all this done, spurn
> her home to her father, who may haply be a
> little angry for my so rough usage; but my
> mother, having power to his testiness, shall turn
> all into my commendations.
>
> [IV. i. 15-22]

The final admission, conceived in a spirit of sardonic irony which characterizes much of the prose scenes of this play, that Cloten's power rests on the accident of birth, which is sufficient in his eyes to justify his brutality, is a clear indication of the intention which underlay the creation of the character.

The following scene (IV. ii) is clearly intended, in its length and elaboration, to be of central importance. Its intention, which is to use the romantic circumstances of Imogen's sickness and death as means for setting the personal issues of the play against a common subjection to 'mortality', is stressed from the first. Imogen's opening words expressly relate the conception of brotherhood—more conventionally relevant in the relationship, still unknown to her, which binds her to Guiderius and Arviragus—to that of death. 'Are we not brothers?' asks Arviragus, and receives in reply the observation—

> So man and man should be;
> But clay and clay differs in dignity,
> Whose dust is both alike.
>
> [IV. ii. 2-5]

The relevance of this to Cloten's recently expressed pretensions is obvious enough; less so, but equally to be considered, is the suggestion of the true meaning, symbolically speaking and in the play's general structure, of Imogen's own exposure to tragic circumstance. Through it she is learning, in a process of moral growth, how far beneath the surface appearances of courtliness lie the true sources of a 'nobility' which 'nature' possesses indeed, but which needs to be confirmed and deepened by exposure to tragic experience before being assumed into a more ample, civilized order; and, through this development, she will attain to a true brotherly relationship as well as to the confirmation of her love for Posthumus. (pp. 71-4)

The final removal of Cloten is followed immediately by the playing of the 'solemn music' which announces the supposed 'death' of Imogen, and with it the opening of one of the most deliberately worked passages in the whole play. Like so much in *Cymbeline*, the episode produces a peculiar sensation of mingled sentiment and tragic feeling which fails, in spite of its beauty (or perhaps because of the excess of it), to carry entire conviction. The phrasing is from the first pervasively

sentimental. . . . Personal emotion is here set in an elaborate decorative framework, sound and image combining to create immediacy, to give feeling a sense of remoteness on the basis of which the desired effect of acceptance may be achieved. . . . [The beauty of the scene], recognized though it may be, cannot fail to strike us less as a new creation than as an evasion of true tragic feeling; unlike the best of Shakespeare's mature verse, its aim is primarily decorative, its relation to the situation described tenuous and remote. . . . It is part of the symbolic technique of the last plays to absorb direct emotion into a more complex poetic harmony, and this seems to be Shakespeare's intention here in his handling of the romantic conventions; except that in this part of *Cymbeline*, unlike *The Winter's Tale*, the prevailing tone seems to be still that of a sentimentality which is its own justification, rather than that of a harmony in which tougher and more realistic states of feeling can find their context in reconciliation. (pp. 74-6)

When Imogen wakes, after the departure of Belarius and his 'sons', her first words give a moral quality, itself typical of the play, to the rites we have just witnessed:

> These flowers are like the pleasures of the world;
> This bloody man the care on't.
>
> [IV. ii. 296-97]

The speech thus introduced, however, leaves us yet again with a sense of imperfect concordance between action and expression, between a quality of feeling that recalls the great tragedies and external events which fail to correspond to them. Imogen's statement that she has awakened, as it were, from the dream of simple life in which she was a 'cave-keeper', aims at a universality of human reference which recalls, for a moment and imperfectly, the phrasing of *King Lear*:

> 'Twas but a bolt of nothing, shot at nothing,
> Which the brain makes of fumes: our very eyes
> Are sometimes like our judgements blind.
>
> [IV. ii. 300-02]
> (p. 78)

The feeling, however, is not sustained. When Imogen passes from general moral statement to face her particular tragedy—the death, as she believes, of Posthumus—her words, instead of rising to the occasion and giving concrete application to the universal abstractions already formulated, slip into melodrama, into an incoherence which is justified by the situation but adds little to its poetical development:

> Damn'd Pisanio
> Hath with his forged letters—damn'd Pisanio—
> From this most bravest vessel of the world
> Struck the main-top.
>
> [IV. ii. 317-20]

This is rather a normal, ample gesture of Elizabethan verse drama than a contribution to the poetic integration of the main theme. It gives way, as the scene ends, to the entry of the Roman Lucio and the carrying of the plot a stage further by the incorporation of Imogen, disguised as Fidele (the name has, of course, a certain symbolic association, but one has only to compare it in function with those of Marina, Perdita, and Miranda [in *Pericles*, *The Winter's Tale*, and *The Tempest*] to see how relatively insecure in conception is *Cymbeline*), into the Roman army. The episode at Milford has played its part in the development of the general theme; what now follows is the incorporation of the values there expressed into a wider range of action and, more particularly, the assimilation of 'natural' virtue through patriotic dedication and further exposure to death into a more ample field of harmony.

If the central part of *Cymbeline* has been marked, as we have tried to show, by a concentration of the various strands of the play upon Milford, where different conceptions of life, conventionally represented, are brought into contact and in some sense tested, the final episodes broaden out again into an inclusive harmony, itself once more projected through familiar conventions, in which these conceptions finally fall into place. (p. 79)

The last Act of *Cymbeline*, whilst maintaining the inequalities so typical of the play as a whole, has some of its most interesting passages to offer. In fact, with the possible exception of the opening, nothing in the whole action reads as so distinctively Shakespearean. The main symbolic structure leading up to the final reconciliation is clear enough, as is its aim of absorbing personal vicissitudes into a more universal inclusiveness. To this conception, the 'death' of Imogen already belongs. It implies, as we have seen more especially in connection with the dirge, a certain liberation, and to it now corresponds the captivity of Posthumus and the tone of his meditations in prison:

> Most welcome, bondage; for thou art a way,
> I think, to liberty.
>
> > [V. iv. 3-4]
> > (p. 83)

This attitude to death, 'the sure physician', rooted though it is in Elizabethan convention, further balances fittingly the spirit of the dirge already sung over the 'corpse' of the 'dead' Imogen. Both, in fact, have been exposed to trials which involve the contemplation of death, and both, according to the symbolic intention of the play, will emerge from them enriched in terms of moral experience. Posthumus here declares himself more 'fettered' by the accusations of his own conscience than by the external fact of his imprisonment; liberation he sees in the acceptance of mortality and of the—

> gyves,
> Desired more than constrain'd,
>
> > [V. iv. 14-15]

which are its external equivalent. The 'penitent instrument', in fact, which is now the mainspring of his reflections, is coupled with a sense of the 'mercy' of the 'gods' and of his own mortal dependence:

> For Imogen's dear life take mine; and though
> 'Tis not so dear, yet 'tis a life; you coin'd it:
> 'Tween man and man, they weigh not every stamp;
> Though light, take pieces for the figure's sake:
> You rather mine, being yours; and so, great powers,
> If you will take this audit, take this life,
> And cancel these cold bonds.
>
> > [V. iv. 22-8]

What is being stated here is something very like an adaptation to the circumstances of the action of the Christian view of atonement. Springing from the deep sense of mortality which Shakespeare shares with other writers of the age, the argument proceeds, after admitting the inequality between the 'value' of Imogen, murdered as an indirect consequence of the speaker's own behaviour, and his repentance, to stress their common dependence upon the 'gods' in restoration of the balance. His life, though less 'dear' than Imogen's, has been equally 'coin'd' by the 'gods', and in their common dependence at least there is an implication of equality. ''Tween man and man, they weigh not every stamp'; in their common need for mercy, at least, men are equal, and the processes of divine forgiveness can properly ignore the discriminations and evaluations of relative guilt which are a necessary part of the 'cold bonds' of human justice.

The peculiar vision which appears to Posthumus in his following dream, though it falls naturally enough into place at this point as a supernatural intervention, is one of the puzzles of the play. The verse, taken as a whole, is poor enough to make the theory of interpolation plausible, and yet there is no denying that the episode, like much in the early part of *Pericles* and like the masque in *The Tempest*, is firmly integrated in the structure of the play. (pp. 89-91)

The relative crudity of the theatrical apparatus which accompanies this vision cannot blind us to the fact that it has an essential part to play in the development of the main conception. Whatever may be thought of its expression (and we may concede the possible presence of another hand without denying a measure of Shakespearean adaptation), there can be no doubt that the words of Sicilius immediately after Jupiter's withdrawal are impregnated with a sense of supernatural 'grace' that is entirely in line with the spirit of the last plays:

> He came in thunder; his celestial breath
> Was sulphurous to smell: the holy eagle
> Stoop'd, as to foot us: his ascension is
> More sweet than our blest fields: his royal bird
> Prunes the immortal wing and cloys his beak,
> As when his god is pleased.
>
> > [V. iv. 114-19]

The feeling conveyed in '*celestial* breath', '*holy* eagle' and '*sweet* ascension', in '*blest* fields' and '*immortal* wing' is, cumulatively speaking, unmistakable. It belongs to the imagination that put into the mouth of Banquo the description of Macbeth's castle at Inverness, or evoked, in *The Winter's Tale*, the holiness of the 'sacrifice' to the oracle in Delphos in terms of 'sweet air', 'delicate' climate, fertility, and the 'celestial' quality—'ceremonious, solemn, and unearthly'—of the offering [*The Winter's Tale*, III. i. 1, 4, 7]. Royalty, holiness, and immortality are fused in a vision of transforming 'grace' which will, in due course, be taken up, on the plane of the main action, in the splendid, sun-drenched vision which rounds off the concluding scene; the presence here of the 'holy eagle' already serves to connect this utterance with the Soothsayer's vision (IV. ii) and the final unravelling of the action. That this is mature Shakespearean verse, and that it belongs to the symbolic conception of the play, is not seriously open to question.

The full implications of this complex scene are still, however, to be completed. Posthumus wakes from his dream with a sense of disillusionment, of return to a world of harsh and conflicting realities still bounded by death and mutability. The tone of moral commonplace which dominates his thought at this stage makes itself felt once more:

> Poor wretches that depend
> On greatness' favour dream as I have done;
> Wake, and find nothing.
>
> > [V. iv. 127-29]

The fabric of dreams has still to be integrated into the plane of reality, although the speaker's disillusionment is already modified by the sense of his lack of deserving:

> Many dream not to find, neither deserve,
> And yet are steep'd in favours; so am I.
>
> > [V. iv. 130-31]

Looking back on his dream in the light of a reawakening to reality, Posthumus can still see it as a '*golden* chance' (the choice of adjective is significant, because it has already appeared in the dirge and will be taken up in the final contemplative vision of the sun's life-giving rays) with which he has been favoured without understanding, as yet, the reason. In this spirit, he is presented with the apparition of the 'rare' book which contains, couched in oracular terms, a key to the final resolution. It is remarkable that Posthumus, presented with this new revelation, returns once more to the 'garment' theme so prominent in earlier scenes. He prays that the fair appearance of the book be not a deception, a 'garment' to confer nobility, or the shadow of it, upon matter intrinsically unworthy; and, as he does so, he refers explicitly to that gap between appearance and reality which is a dominating feature of court life:

> let thy effects
> So follow, to be most unlike our courtiers,
> As good as promise.
>
> [V. iv. 135-37]

Posthumus in prison is still in a state of trial, still occupied in sifting true moral worth from its shadow, still balancing appearance and substance against the sense of immanent death; and, accordingly, it is proper that the revelation now enigmatically offered comes to him not as enlightenment but as puzzlement and obscurity, a further instance of the apparently inconsequent fabric which goes to make up the dream of living:

> 'Tis still a dream; or else such stuff as madmen
> Tongue, and brain not: either both, or nothing:
> Or senseless speaking, or a speaking such
> As sense cannot untie. Be what it is,
> The action of my life is like it.
>
> [V. iv. 145-49]
> (pp. 93-5)

The final grave prose dialogue with the Gaoler, saturated in a sense of death that is at once characteristic of the age and profoundly personal, rounds off this fine scene in a most fitting manner. It has, indeed, its own contribution to make to the complete sense of the episode. The elements that go to make up the Gaoler's 'philosophic' attitude to mortality are, of course, Elizabethan commonplaces, used as such by many inferior writers; a phrase like 'he that sleeps feels not the tooth-ache' [V. iv. 172-73] bears with it an air of self-conscious dramatic truism which can easily be paralleled, at least in feeling, among Shakespeare's lesser contemporaries. Once again, however, as in the use made of the barely less familiar 'dream' metaphor just considered, convention is put to a profoundly personal use. What really matters in the whole dialogue is the delicate and deeply individual balancing of contrary attitudes, the setting of death conceived as liberation—an emotion itself deeply, genuinely felt—against an equal sense of the uncertainty which the contemplation of mortality inspires: 'look you, sir, you know not which way you shall go' [V. iv. 175-76]. The attitudes which go to make up the scene are, in fact, various, plausible, and—above all—mutually enriching. The Gaoler hesitates between the conceptions of death as release, as implying freedom from the burden of life, and as obscurity, entry into the unknowable; and to this Posthumus himself seems to oppose, with profoundly human effect, a feeling akin to religious conviction, which naturally accompanies the new and distinctively moral outlook which characterizes his utterances throughout this part of the play: 'there none want eyes to direct them the way I am going, but such as wink and will not use

Act II. Scene ii. Iachimo and Imogen. By T. Uwins. The Department of Rare Books and Special Collections, The University of Michigan Library.

them' [V. iv. 185-87]. The confidence thus implied, however, is no more than part of the whole effect. The essential tone of the dialogue—and it is here that the distinctively Shakespearean quality is above all to be sought—is one of balance, of poised alternatives. Posthumus' mood of religious acceptance is set against the quality of the Gaoler's prevailing scepticism, expressed above all in his clear statement of the spiritual alternatives that face the prisoner:

> . . . you must either be directed by some that
> take upon them to know, or take upon yourself
> that which I am sure you do not know, or jump
> the after-enquiry on your own peril.
>
> [V. iv. 179-82]

The alternatives as here stated are an acceptance of spiritual authority, itself given a certain sense of pretension in 'some that *take upon them* to know', an admission of the helplessness of individual judgement ('take upon yourself that which *I am sure you do not know*'), or a plunge into the unknowable which recalls, in its expression, Macbeth's frustrated impulse to 'jump the life to come' [*Macbeth*, I. vi. 7]. All these are, in the Gaoler's eyes, equally confessions of helplessness, for the only certainty is, in his own terms, 'how you shall speed in your journey's end, I think you'll never return to tell one' [V. iv. 182-84]. In this balance of opposing attitudes, none accepted as final but each serving to add immediacy to its fellow, the genuine Shakespearean note makes itself unmistakably felt.

With the last scene of the play (V. v) the time has come to gather the various threads of plot and symbolism into a final unity. The threads, indeed, are numerous and closely interrelated. Posthumus and Imogen have to be restored to one another, and the King's lost sons united to their sister, Imogen, all under the embracing royal paternity of Cymbeline; whilst, in the public order, the liberties of the British realm have to be reconciled with the universal claims of Rome, and both alike subdued to a final harmony depending on the will of the 'gods'. The scene, in fact, uses the familiar mechanism of romantic reconciliation for symbolic ends of its own, working up through successive stages to a final, inclusive effect. (pp. 96-7)

[Posthumus and Imogen are reconciled] in lines pregnant with symbolic meaning and unmistakably belonging to the spirit of Shakespeare's last comedies. 'I was dead', says Imogen [V. v. 229], and her words, beyond the mere recalling of a past event, bear a distinctive quality of marvel that itself implies the integration of the action on the symbolic level. In the light of her following question to Posthumus—

Why did you throw your wedded lady from you?—
[V. v. 261]

his intense, broken exclamation, 'My queen, my life, my wife' [V. v. 226], combining the personal and familiar with the vivifying and the regally transcendent, is given its proper counterpart, and the embrace of the lovers surrounded by intuitions of a harmony more than purely personal:

Hang there like fruit, my soul,
Till the tree die!
[V. v. 263-64]

The feeling, in fact, is so fine, so precious, that it can only be described in terms of 'soul', and by relating the spiritual suggestion to an evocation of the rich fertility of nature. Cymbeline, in turn, responds with words that stress the closeness and value of the reconciliation which has just flooded him with a re-birth of emotions long presumed dead; . . . he salutes his daughter as 'my flesh, my child' [V. v. 264], and the strength of his feeling is such that he senses himself reduced to the state of a 'dullard' by his incapacity to express it. Finally, and most typically of all, the reconciliation assumes its proper external form. Imogen, kneeling, requests the 'blessing' of her father, the tears of whose mingled happiness and grief become, in his own mind, 'holy water', a transmutation of mortal sorrow into spiritual joy. In the light of these new discoveries, the queen and her machinations have indeed become 'naught', the unwitting cause, as he now sees it, of the miracle taking place before his eyes:

. . . long of her it was
That we meet here so strangely.
[V. v. 271-72]

The pattern of plot, thus filled out with a corresponding harmony of poetic imagery, thus assumes its complete, balanced form.

The spirit of restored unity which now dominates the conclusion is still, however, incomplete. The action, indeed, after advancing so far, now turns back upon itself, in a manner not uncommon in Shakespeare, deviating to pick up the threads that have been left on one side. The occasion is the recalling of Cloten, through the reference to his mother, and the subsequent confession of Guiderius that he killed him at Milford. By this recapitulation, the theme of the contrast between true princeliness and external pretension, the 'inner' man and the mere 'garment', is taken up into the final synthesis. For Cymbeline, even in his state of awakening understanding, the forms of royalty still carry weight: hence his ominous observation 'He was a prince' [V. v. 291], and the refusal to heed Gui-

derius' evocation of Cloten's 'incivility' (the word, of course, carries a meaning of much more than rudeness, or mere lack of polish) as justification for his act. Shakespeare, however, accepting the conventions which underlie his story, aims at turning them once more to his own ends. For Guiderius, as Belarius asserts, is 'better than the man he slew' [V. v. 302], both in birth and in moral quality; the two orders, indeed, go together, and the discovery of the true situation at once satisfies the conditions of courtly romance and suggests a symbolic integration. That the device is crude, relatively unsupported by the weight of poetic richness which alone could give it full life, proves that once more Shakespeare is experimenting with established conventions, feeling his way to a fully personal use of familiar dramatic devices. His success is, as yet, manifestly incomplete, but the transforming purpose is clearly present.

It makes itself felt more strongly, indeed, in Cymbeline's reaction to the finding of his lost sons. Belarius prepares the way for the symbolic transformation of the discovery, in poetic terms, by invoking upon his charges, even as he delivers them to their father, 'the benediction of the covering heavens' [V. v. 350]; the notions of benediction and reconciliation are, throughout the last plays, closely connected, and Cymbeline's answering expression of grief at the very moment when the way is clear for the full expression of felicity—'Thou weep'st, and speak'st' [V. v. 352]—is also significant. The convenient recalling of the mole on Guiderius' neck belongs, of course, to the external commonplaces of romance which are rarely, in this play, completely assimilated; but it is followed by an intensification of the idea of recovered paternity in Cymbeline's exclamation:

O, what am I?
A mother to the birth of three? Ne'er mother
Rejoiced deliverance more. . . .
[V. v. 368-70]

Birth, and a certain implied re-discovery of the self, are here indicated; so is the suggestion of the pangs of 'deliverance' by which sorrow finds relief in compensating joy. In the light of this intensified feeling, the idea of the paternal blessing falls naturally into place—'Blest pray you be'—and is associated in turn with the restoration of natural order:

That, after this strange parting from your orbs,
You may reign in them now.
[V. v. 370-72]

The completing dialogue with Imogen:—

Cymbeline: Thou hast lost by this a kingdom.
Imogen: No, my lord;
              I have got two worlds by it—
[V. v. 373-74]

with its characteristic sense of 'symbolic' overtone, of a poetic content that surpasses its apparent occasion, combines with a stressing of the sanctity of intimate family relationships—

O, my gentle brothers . . .
you call'd me brother,
When I was but your sister; I you brothers,
When ye were so indeed—
[V. v. 374, 376-78]

to produce at least a verbal sense of latent significance springing through to the surface; later plays will wed this sense more adequately to a relevant plot, but the poetic conditions for the full development are clearly present, at least in potentiality.

How far they can be taken will be seen in *The Winter's Tale* and *The Tempest*.

At this point, the development of the action is at last ready for completion. Cymbeline, once more king over himself—since his discovery of the dead queen's machinations—and over the realm he has seen victorious, points the way to a final act of religious affirmation, in which the consummation of marriage between Imogen and Posthumus will be one with the rendering of thanks for victory achieved:

> Let's quit this ground,
> And smoke the temple with our sacrifices.
>   [V. v. 397-98]

Once more, the ideas of sacrifice and worship anticipate a fuller development in *The Winter's Tale*. With Iachimo's confession of guilt and the forgiving gesture of Posthumus the way is open for an act of religious integration which will give its highest justification to the 'gracious season' into which the action has at last entered.

This act is confirmed by the Soothsayer's final reading of the prophecy enigmatically declared to Posthumus in his dream. Once more, as so often in this play, commonplace and even inferior material is made to serve ends felt to be far superior in terms of poetic organization and emotional power. The riddle itself, indeed, has possibilities in the sense it conveys of fertility and expanding inclusiveness. Cymbeline, the 'lofty cedar', is at last restored to the 'lopped branches' for whose original loss his own passion was partially responsible; and by this restoration or 'revival' (to use the Soothsayer's own term, with its suggestion of life restored), his 'issue', joined once more to 'the most majestic cedar' for Britain of 'peace and plenty' [V. v. 453, 454, 457, 458]. Nor is this, even in political terms, all. Victorious Britain, through its king, acknowledges its 'wonted tribute' to the universal empire of Rome, reintegrates itself, in other words, in bonds of peace and equality, to a conception vaster even than its own vindicated patriotism; and finally both states are united in subjection to a spiritual vision, full of mellow, 'golden' richness, which is itself expressed in Shakespeare's best manner:

> The fingers of the powers above do tune
> The harmony of this peace.
>   [V. v. 466-67]

'Harmony', indeed, on a scale of ever-increasing spaciousness, is the key-note of this conclusion. 'The Roman eagle', lessening herself, is gathered into the 'beams o' the sun' [V. v. 470, 472], vanishes, is absorbed into a greater union; and the final reference, sustained by verse at once free, ample, and superbly concise, is to sacrifice and the praise of the 'gods'. In this final vision of consecration to a unifying purpose, the personal issues of the play, the love of Imogen for Posthumus maintained through trials and separation, and the integration of natural simplicity to the graces of civilized order, find in subjection to a universal unity, through the figure of Cymbeline as father and king, their proper integration. (pp. 99-104)

Derek Traversi, " 'Cymbeline'," in his Shakespeare: The Last Phase, *Hollis & Carter, 1954, pp. 43-104.*

F. D. HOENIGER   (lecture date 1961)

[*Hoeniger describes the significant role irony plays in* Cymbeline, *noting instances throughout the play where characters either lack important information that the audience possesses or act accord-ing to false perceptions. He claims that the Queen and Cloten are subjected to a "broadly comic" irony intended to undermine their dramatic stature, that Posthumus's rage over Imogen's supposed infidelity is viewed by the audience with "critical detachment, even amusement," because at this point in the play he has not been shown to possess tragic seriousness, and that Imogen's mistaken identification of the headless corpse is "grotesque irony," for the episode is unexpected in a world of romance comedy. For further commentary on the discrepancies between appearance and reality in* Cymbeline, *which Hoeniger claims form the basis of the ironic viewpoint in the play, see the excerpts by Donald A. Stauffer (1949), Derek Traversi (1954), and Nancy K. Hayles (1980). In addition, Imogen's awakening beside the headless corpse of Cloten has also been discussed by Harley Granville-Barker (1930), Harold C. Goddard (1951), Robin Moffet (1962), Robert Grams Hunter (1965), and Joan Carr (see Additional Bibliography). Hoeniger's essay on* Cymbeline *was originally delivered as a lecture before the Modern Language Association in 1961.*]

Irony lies close to the core of drama because of its separation, in many varied ways, of appearance and reality. Dramatic irony occurs when a character's utterance or act reminds the audience acutely of his ignorance of some facts relevant to the situation. His words may be known by the audience to be sharply contradicted by reality, they may merely reveal his unawareness of the schemes of others, or they may inform us of steps taken by him in a direction unwittingly against his own interest. Our reaction to a specific ironic situation in a play will depend partly on whether the sense of irony is shared by one of the characters or not. In the former case, the irony often arises from an action of comic or serious intrigue, as when the disguised Rosalind [in *As You Like It*] trains her lover in the art of wooing, or when Iago lays his elaborate trap for Othello even while rising in his confidence. But sometimes this type of ironic situation takes the form of a character's being deliberately left in ignorance by his companions, or even being confirmed in a mistaken notion because for one reason or another it would be unwise for them to reveal their knowledge; as when the lords encourage Cloten in his self-praise for imaginary heroism in two of the early scenes of *Cymbeline*. (There the irony is employed satirically; Cloten at that point is not a villain so much as a fool.)

But if the audience is alone in sensing the irony, its reaction will be partly determined, it need hardly be said, by the goodness or badness of the characters involved, and if the character is good, by the nature of his deception or ignorance. The complex developments which arise from the unawareness of the identity of the two royal sons on the part first of Imogen and then of their father represent a stock situation in comedy. Here the irony involves no suffering, it only betrays ignorance, and we sense that when recognition comes, it will closely precede a happy ending. On the other hand, such a situation as Imogen's mistaking Cloten's body, however ludicrous, can hardly be said to be comic in the usual sense of the term; the effects on Imogen are too pathetic for that:

> this is his hand,
> His foot Mercurial, his Martial thigh,
> The brawns of Hercules; but his Jovial face—
> Murder in heaven?—How!—'Tis gone.
>   [IV. ii. 309-12]

The effect of the mythological comparisons is at first funny, but immediately qualified by Imogen's profound grief. When pathos and grotesque irony combine acutely, as they do here, we move in the sphere neither of tragedy nor of comedy but in the world of a genre different from both.

Unfortunately for the analytical critic, the problem of the nature of dramatic irony is further complicated because the types of irony so far discussed may coincide with a nondramatic variety, engineered by "fickle Fortune," which has been described as "a contradictory outcome of events as if in mockery of the promise and fitness of things." This kind of irony certainly contributes to our sense of Imogen's predicament when she mistakes Cloten for Posthumus, for it was she who was largely responsible for Cloten's dressing himself up in Posthumus's garments in the first place. The complex incongruity of this incident makes one wonder whether in the world of this play some Hardyish god is at work. Supposing the play was conceived in a serious spirit, what vision of life, we might well ask, can include such mockery, and yet tell us of joy and reconciliation in the end?

Such a vision . . . must be quite unlike that of Shakespeare's romantic comedies, for the heroines of these plays are never placed in situations which affect us like Imogen's lament. And we also realize, I trust, that the purely romantic notion of Imogen, so popular in Victorian days, simply won't do—"half-glorified already the immortal godhead of womanhood," Swinburne called her [see excerpt above, 1880]. Imogen may be a charming lady who sometimes utters beautiful poetry, but she can at times become absurdly confused. If at first in the play, we are encouraged to idealize Imogen, some doubts must arise after her rejection of Iachimo's temptation to lust, when she so readily accepts his excuse, "I have spoke this to know if your affiance / Were deeply rooted" [I. vi. 163-64]—quite a cheek for a stranger to subject a princess to such a test, isn't it? This lie, Iachimo follows up with a passage in praise of Posthumus which, especially in the context, might have put a less naive woman on her guard:

> such a holy witch
> That he enchants societies into him:
> Half all men's hearts are his.
>
>   [I. vi. 166-68]

Would a Rosalind or a Portia have answered, like Imogen: "You make amends" [I. vi. 168]?

Then in the bedchamber scene we are made aware of how vulnerable the honor of the "godliest of women" can be. As the scene opens, Imogen closes her book with the words, surely ironic in their context, "mine eyes are weak" [II. ii. 3]. Soon after she has fallen asleep, Iachimo climbs out of the trunk. Expertly, he takes in the details of the chamber and snatches her bracelet: "As slippery as the Gordian knot was hard / 'Tis mine" [II. ii. 34-5]. Here Shakespeare follows Boccaccio closely. But note that he adds Iachimo's remarks about Imogen's book: "She has been reading of late / The tale of Tereus; here the leaf's turned down / Where Philomel gave up" [II. ii. 44-6]. What a clever ironic touch, to inform us that Imogen read this very story shortly before, unknown to herself, evidence is being gathered which will persuade her husband that she indeed gave up to Iachimo's allurements.

Having attempted in the previous paragraphs to qualify somewhat our romantic adoration of Imogen, let me now pay a little attention to her stepmother, Cymbeline's Queen. The Queen is less stupid than her son Cloten, but much less clever than she thinks. The irony directed at her is more complex than that used for her son, but it undermines her as completely. She is more phony than funny. Her simulation and cunning show are singularly ineffective, except towards Cymbeline. In the opening scene, Imogen comments on her: "O dissembling courtesy!

How fine this tyrant / Can tickle where she wounds!" [I. i. 83-5]. But the full ironic treatment of her is reserved for the fifth scene, where she accepts the small box of poison from her doctor and passes it on to Pisanio.

In construction, this scene is one of the strangest in Shakespeare. It is framed by a short episode of the ladies who are commanded to gather flowers, which provides an ironic undercurrent for the sinister interview. Pisanio's entry on the far side of the stage occasions the first of the scene's many asides:

> *Queen.* Here comes a flattering rascal; upon him
>   Will I first work: he's for his master,
>   And enemy to my son.
>
>   [I. v. 27-9]

The Queen's stepping aside in turn gives Cornelius his opportunity of confiding to the audience that far from being deceived, he has himself outwitted the Queen by furnishing her with a substance which will cause the taker to fall into a long sleep, "to be more fresh, reviving" [I. v. 42]—a typical romantic motif. The next aside comes after the doctor has been dismissed and the interview with Pisanio completed. Here the Queen's comment on this "sly and constant knave" [I. v. 75] (Pisanio) is interrupted by the re-entry of Pisanio himself, accompanied by the ladies carrying flowers. In the last three lines of this scene so rich in intrigue and counter-intrigue, Pisanio assures us, with a turn of his head towards the departed Queen: "But when to my good lord I prove untrue, / I'll choke myself; there's all I'll do for you" [I. v. 86-7].

As the action advances, Shakespeare makes us increasingly aware of the Queen's predicament when engaging in such elaborate intrigue for the sake of a son who is not merely a clown but one who boorishly advertises his folly. Shakespeare capitalizes on this predicament in the scene where Lucius delivers Augustus Caesar's ultimatum to Britain. There, Cloten and the Queen try to outdo each other in their haughty replies to Lucius while Cymbeline sits still, except for a completely ineffective reprimand: "Son, let your mother end" [III. i. 39]. Irony of fate—that a wicked and cunning queen should have so inept a son—coalesces here with dramatic irony. Cloten's aggressive talkativeness neutralizes the Queen's "dissembling courtesy".

We have seen that the irony directed at two of the play's three antagonists is broadly comic, while that directed at the heroine is sometimes difficult to reconcile with comedy. What about her lover-husband, Posthumus? Of all the characters, he undergoes the greatest development. In the first scene, he is praised to the skies by the Gentlemen and by Imogen. We are then somewhat startled when he allows himself headstrongly to be lured into a wager on Imogen's chastity. Does one play such games with what's most pure and precious? Posthumus is one of those Englishmen of the Renaissance who fare badly in Italy. When deceived by Iachimo's evidence, he bursts out into a monologue of rage and frustration. He imagines the sexual act between Iachimo and Imogen in terms of a "full-acorn'd boar, a German one" which "Cried 'O' and mounted" [II. v. 16, 17]. Worse, he questions the chastity of his own mother: he himself may be a bastard. There are echoes here of Hamlet's first monologue, "O that this too too sullied flesh" [*Hamlet*, I. ii. 129]. But Hamlet's disillusionment with women affects us quite differently of course, since we know that Hamlet is partly right while Posthumus is utterly wrong. Closer to *Cymbeline* are the situations in *Othello* and *Much Ado* where the protagonists are, like Posthumus, persuaded of the unchastity of their wives or brides-to-be by the slander of a villain. Yet there, too, our response is different. By the time Othello succumbs to Iago's insinuations his tragic stature has been fully developed. This is not the case with Posthumus, of whom we are allowed only a glimpse before the Italian scenes. True, we have been told about his admirable qualities, but we have hardly seen them in action. We witness Othello's fall with pity and fear. We witness Posthumus's rage with critical detachment, even amusement. (pp. 222-26)

When we see Posthumus again in Act V, he is a changed man:

> Gods, if you
> Should have taken vengeance on my faults, I never
> Had liv'd to put on this: so you had sav'd
> The noble Imogen, to repent, and struck
> Me, wretch, more worth your vengeance.
>
> [V. i. 7-11]

He disguises himself in mean clothes befitting his state of mind and hopes for death in the oncoming battle. He almost achieves his wish. The last scene but one shows us Posthumus in prison, awaiting execution. Once more we are given a scene whose irony is quite different from anything in earlier Shakespeare. It opens with the jailers leaving their prisoner with a jovial sneer. They don't realize that Posthumus welcomes his bondage since it promises him the only liberty he can hope for—death. Then follows the strange vision where the ghostly spirits of the Leonati family clamor with Jupiter for fairer treatment of Posthumus. This too is ironic for we know that Posthumus's sufferings are deserved. The message of the book left behind when Posthumus awakes is, like the rest of the scene, full of paradox, and makes Posthumus still more acutely conscious of the hopelessness of any purely human attempt to grasp the meaning of existence. He comments: "Or senseless speaking, or a speaking such / As sense cannot untie" [V. iv. 147-48]. When the jailers return, they are startled by Posthumus's readiness for death. Assured of the liberty which awaits him, Posthumus gaily banters with the Jailer: "I am merrier to die than thou art to live" [V. iv. 171]. The Jailer comments: "What an infinite mock is this, that a man should have the best use of his eyes to see the way of blindness!" [V. iv. 188-90]. The mockery isn't over yet. A Messenger arrives to call Posthumus before the King. "I'm called to be free," says Posthumus; "I'll be hang'd then," responds the Jailer [V. iv. 193-94, 195]. Neither knows what kind of freedom is waiting for Posthumus. Bur first, mockery takes one last fling at Posthumus, for the events of the final scene are so arranged that Iachimo's confession of his crime and revelation of Imogen's innocence occur before Imogen has cast off her disguise. Posthumus responds with his most extreme outburst of self-loathing yet: "Spit and throw stones, cast mire upon me, set / The dogs o' th' street to bay me" [V. v. 222-23]. And when the disguised Imogen interrupts him, he strikes her down in one last ironic act: "Shall's have a play of this? Thou scornful page, / There lie thy part" [V. v. 228-29]. Only then, after this final rejection of himself in a passion which recalls his earlier denunciation of womanhood, and after this final unwitting act of violence towards his wife—unwitting but so symbolic of his past intentions—is Posthumus granted the vision which dispels all irony in the joy of romance.

We all know how in the play's concluding episodes this vision comes to enfold all the major characters, including Cymbeline himself, who like Posthumus had "the best use of eyes to see the way of blindness," and how after acts of private and public forgiveness, Britain in spite of victory submits herself to Rome. The concluding ceremony takes place in the temple of Jupiter,

the god who grants this vision to man, though only after man, and woman too, have wandered about in error, aimlessly, even to despair. Now the sense is untied: irony ends. Mockery yields to vision, the world of appearance to the world of reality and joy, and irony dissolves in romance, a romance of which we in the audience have always been aware, but whose significance becomes clear only when it at last enfolds Imogen and Posthumus as well. (pp. 227-28)

> *F. D. Hoeniger, "Irony and Romance in 'Cymbeline'," in* Studies in English Literature, 1500-1900, *Vol. II, No. 2, Spring, 1962, pp. 219-28.*

J. A. BRYANT, JR.   (essay date 1961)

[*Bryant interprets* Cymbeline *in relation to Christian theology and concludes that the play's dramatic action follows the Christian pattern of redemption and the "fortunate fall." Not only do individual characters retrace a redemptive pattern from temptation to sin to restoration, but the play also demonstrates that the dramatic events are controlled throughout by divine providence. Such subsequent critics as Arthur C. Kirsch (1972) and Martin Lings (see Additional Bibliography) have also discovered parallels between this play and the concept of the fortunate fall, and G. G. Gervinus (1849-50), G. Wilson Knight (1947), and R. A. Foakes (1971) have all claimed that the play demonstrates that providence controls the fortunes of humanity. In Bryant's estimation, the figure of Jupiter in Act V, Scene iv is meant to represent the Christian God, and the critic particularly notes the resemblances between Jupiter's speech and the traditional Christian belief that God chastises those whom He has chosen to love and redeem— an interpretation of the vision scene that recalls earlier assessments by Gervinus and Knight. For additional commentary on the religious or spiritual element in* Cymbeline, *see the excerpts by Derek Traversi (1954), Robin Moffet (1962), Northrop Frye (1965), Robert Grams Hunter (1965), and Homer D. Swander (1966), as well as the essay by J. P. Brockbank cited in the Additional Bibliography.*]

Cymbeline, like the two plays that follow it in Shakespeare's canon [*The Winter's Tale* and *The Tempest*], is more meaningful in terms of a broad integrated view of God and human affairs than any of the plays that Shakespeare had written previously. (p. 193)

Yet, one does have to accept certain Christian presuppositions in order to make sense of *Cymbeline*, which has almost no Christian furniture and few clear-cut allusions to Christian scripture, custom, or doctrine. The movement of the plot, for example, is nothing if not Christian. We have a ruler, Cymbeline, who in a series of temptations is made to lose all he has that is worth possessing, his friend, his sons, his daughter and virtuous son-in-law, and his ally. In wrongheadedly banishing his son-in-law, moreover, he exposes him also to temptation and thus indirectly exposes his daughter to temptation, so that both daughter and son-in-law become objects of public suspicion and victims of despair. His fault in causing these virtuous young people to fall is probably his most grievous one, yet this is the fault that ultimately brings about the restoration and redemption of all who are worth saving and the purgation of the evil that has been causing trouble. Thus in Shakespeare's story we have nothing more or less than a version of the Christian paradox of the fortunate fall, which, in the familiar words of St. Paul (I Corinthians 1.18), "is to them that perish foolishness; but unto us which are saved it is the power of God." One might say, as Posthumus says of his dream in Act V:

> 'Tis still a dream, or else such stuff as madmen
> Tongue and brain not; either both or nothing;
> Or senseless speaking, or a speaking such

As sense cannot untie. Be what it is,
The action of my life is like it, which
I'll keep, if but for sympathy.

[V. iv. 145-50]

In short, the action of this play, senseless or not, is like the mysterious Christian pattern of redemption; and it places squarely in the hands of the Almighty the disposition of men's affairs and the election of those who are to be redeemed from and through the sin in which all participate. Iachimo, Posthumus, Imogen, and Cymbeline, all come clean in the end because they recognize fully who and what they are and accept their salvation (if I may use the term as a metaphor here) as something operating miraculously from without.

The focus of the play, quite obviously, is on only two of these characters, Posthumus and Imogen, and of these two, primarily on Posthumus. We see this partly in what Shakespeare has each of them do and partly in the way he has arranged the scenes. Acts I and II keep the focus pretty consistently on Posthumus: he leaves Britain, goes to Italy, falls in with Iachimo, is tempted to wager, is deceived, and is disillusioned:

Is there no way for men to be, but women
Must be half-workers? We are all bastards;
And that most venerable man which I
Did call my father, was I know not where
When I was stamp'd. Some coiner with his tools
Made me a counterfeit; yet my mother seem'd
The Dian of that time. So doth my wife
The nonpareil of this. O vengeance, vengeance!

[II. v. 1-8]

After this we see nothing more of Posthumus for two whole acts (III and IV); for these are given over to setting forth a similar fate for Imogen, who having learned of Posthumus' distrust of her and wish to kill her, condemns her husband, abandons both Britain and her sex, sickens, and, after taking the "cordial" that Pisanio has given her, apparently dies (IV. ii). After this point in her two acts, however, Imogen goes beyond Posthumus. Recovering from the effects of the sleeping potion, she wakes to find the headless body of Cloten beside her and mistakenly thinks it the body of the banished Posthumus; thereupon she begins to know her own frailty and to comprehend something of the abiding affection she has always had for her husband even while she was condemning him most bitterly. Imogen's two acts, in short, establish a parallel with Posthumus' misfortunes and point toward a happy resolution of them. This resolution begins immediately with Act V, when Posthumus on receiving the bloody token mistakenly thinks Imogen dead and undergoes a genuine repentance. Three scenes later, in prison, he begs the Almighty to take his life, worthless as it is, for the life presumably lost:

For Imogen's dear life take mine; and though
'Tis not so dear, yet 'tis a life; you coin'd it.
'Tween man and man they weigh not every
    stamp;
Though light, take pieces for the figure's sake;
You rather mine, being yours; and so, great
    powers,
If you will take this audit, take this life,
And cancel these cold bonds.

[V. iv. 22-8]

At this point, and not before, Posthumus is ready to receive the truth, about himself and about all the others of true blood and election in the play. He gets it, of course, from that crucial and much criticized Vision of Jupiter, which Shakespeare, if he did not write it himself (and there is really no sound reason for believing he did not), at least sanctioned and accepted.

Looking back over the play from the vantage point of Act V we see that this matter of blood and true nobility has been a leading theme of the play from the beginning. The first gentleman in Act I, Scene i, may be exaggerating when he describes Posthumus as

        . . . a creature such
As, to seek through the regions of the earth
For one his like, there would be something failing
In him that should compare. I do not think
So fair an outward and such stuff within
Endows a man but he.

[I. i. 19-24]

But Posthumus has the "election" of Imogen, in which, the first gentleman continues, "may be truly read / What kind of man he is" [I. i. 53-4], and he is acknowledged superior by almost everyone else in the play except possibly Cloten, who pretty obviously stands to him as a puttock to an eagle and hence is hardly capable of judging. Even Iachimo, who makes pretensions to nobility of blood, recognizes the nobility of Posthumus when Posthumus is still disguised as a simple countryman. "If that thy gentry, Britain," he says, "go before / This lout as he exceeds our lords, the odds / Is that we scarce are men and you are gods" [V. ii. 8-10].

But this play does not stop with the assertion that Posthumus' natural nobility is recognizable; it asserts that all men of natural nobility are recognizable in some way. Shakespeare's device for getting this across is his representation of Belarius and the two princes. Belarius, alias Morgan, after much discussion of the superiority of rude Nature to a corrupt court, tells us out of the princes' hearing in Act III:

How hard it is to hide the sparks of nature!
These boys know little they are sons to th' King,
Nor Cymbeline dreams that they are alive.
They think they're mine; and, though train'd
    up thus meanly
I' th' cave wherein they bow, their thoughts
    do hit
The roofs of palaces, and nature prompts them
In simple and low things to prince it much
Beyond the trick of others.

[III. iii. 79-86]

In Act IV the young princes show such a princely impatience to be about the business of war that Belarius is compelled to say: "their blood thinks scorn / Till it fly out and show them princes born" [IV. iv. 53-4]. And in Act V the British soldiers, who think the trio indeed peasants, confirm Belarius' somewhat prejudiced view: "'Tis thought," say they, "the old man and his sons were angels" [V. iii. 85].

The play also recognizes that rank, even when not accompanied by natural nobility, deserves respect. The example of that in this play is Cloten, who is demonstrably ignoble in behavior yet whose headless trunk at Belarius' insistence gets proper burial. . . . (pp. 194-98)

Posthumus and Imogen seem to be pretty well matched in the order and degree of nobility within them. He is, in [Iachimo's] phrase, "a holy witch / That . . . enchants societies unto him" [I. vi. 166-67], and she, in [the Frenchman's] description, "more fair, virtuous, wise, chaste, constant, qualified, and

less attemptable than any the rarest of . . . ladies in France"
[I. iv. 59-61]. Moreover, as each by virtue of virtue in himself
recognizes virtue in the other, so each recognizes the blindness
of his own error. Imogen says, "Our very eyes / Are sometimes
like our judgements, blind" [IV. ii. 301-02]; and Posthumus,
after he has regained his senses, "there are none want eyes to
direct them the way I am going, but such as wink and will not
use them" [V. iv. 185-87]. Both have winked and both have
ceased to wink; yet in the end it is Posthumus who receives
the full epiphany. He receives it, as has already been said, in
the famous masquelike scene called the Vision of Jupiter, which
constitutes a revelation given directly by God under the aspect
of Jupiter in justification of his ways. It should be stressed that
there is no question of a pagan Jupiter here. Jupiter is the One
God, called Jupiter in this play simply because the setting
happens to be pre-Christian Britain. Furthermore, he is no *deus
ex machina:* he does not intervene, he changes nothing, he
adds nothing, he cuts no knots. He merely reveals what might
have been inferred anyhow—that his Providence has been controlling things from the beginning. The significant thing that
he does is to emphasize and give divine sanction to the paradox
contained in Lucius' enlightened remark to the grieving Imogen, "Some falls are means the happier to arise" [IV. ii. 403].
(pp. 199-200)

The Vision falls into two parts. The first is the appeal of
Posthumus' family (all ghosts, of course); and the second,
Jupiter's reply. Of the details of the appeal the following should
be noted here. First, Sicilius Leonatus, father to Posthumus,
raises the question of "undeserved" human suffering—"Hath
my poor boy done aught but well?" [V. iv. 35]. He also
observes that the "mould" or form of Posthumus (note where
the virtue lies) has been pronounced good by the world. The
First Brother notes that Posthumus alone of all the Britons has
found favor with Imogen. Posthumus' mother wants to know
why, once her son was elevated in such a marriage, he deserved
to be "mocked" with exile. And Sicilius comes in again to
demand why, further, he should be tempted by the wicked
Iachimo with "needless" jealousy. Finally, all point out Posthumus' positive claims, lately proved in valorous deeds, to
Jupiter's favor. The effect of all this is to raise the more general
question of Jupiter's goodness and justice; but it should be
noted that these questionings merely pick up, emphasize, and
summarize the main threads of movement as they have been
developing in the play from the beginning. *Cymbeline* as a
whole has all along been inching toward the overwhelming
question, "Is God good?" And now that Jupiter speaks in
reply, he does so in terms that are as simple and as conventionally Christian as the prototype for them in Hebrews:

> And ye have forgotten the exhortation which
> speaketh unto you as unto children, My son,
> despise not thou the chastening of the Lord,
> nor faint when thou are rebuked of him: For
> whom the Lord loveth he chasteneth, and
> scourgeth every son whom he receiveth. If ye
> endure chastening, God dealeth with you as
> with sons; for what son is he whom the father
> chasteneth not? But if ye be without chastise-
> ment, whereof all are partakers, then are ye
> bastards, and not sons.
>
> (Hebrews xii. 5-8)

The tenor of Jupiter's remarks to the suppliant ghosts is that
his Providence accounts for everything, that he has chosen

whom he will love, and that he will punish whom he has
chosen:

> Whom best I love I cross; to make my gift,
>   The more delay'd, delighted. Be content;
> Your low-laid son our godhead will uplift.
>   His comforts thrive, his trials well are spent.
> Our jovial star reign'd at his birth, and in
>   Our temple was he married. Rise, and fade.
> He shall be lord of Lady Imogen.
>   And happier much by his affliction made.
>
> [V. iv. 101-08]

After this there can be no fear of bastardy for Posthumus, such
as he once entertained [II. v. 2], nor doubt of his election. The
dream has been his revelation:

> Sleep, thou hast been a grandsire and begot
> A father to me, and thou hast created
> A mother and two brothers; but, O scorn!
> Gone! they went hence so soon as they were born.
> And so I am awake. Poor wretches that depend
> On greatness' favour dream as I have done,
> Wake and find nothing. But, alas, I swerve.
> Many dream not to find, neither deserve,
> And yet are steep'd in favours; so am I,
> That have this golden chance and know not why.
> What fairies haunt this ground?
>
> [V. iv. 123-33]

The riddling prophecy which comes to him now [V. iv. 138-44],
with its fresh mixture of Biblical echoes—the stately cedar
suggesting the great tree of Ezekiel xxxi. 3 and the metaphor
of grafting from Romans xi. 15-25—is the promise by which
not only Posthumus, but all those of virtue may be saved. The
good fortunes of Posthumus, Imogen, Cymbeline, and the two
sons are all implicit in it; Posthumus, who possesses the promise but does not understand it, is nevertheless made happy by
it. "The action of my life is like it, which / I'll keep, if but
for sympathy," he says to himself [V. iv. 149-50]; then to the
bewildered Gaoler, "I am merrier to die than thou art to live"
[V. iv. 171].

The long concluding scene of Act V is a series of discoveries
and regenerative experiences for the characters who are entitled
to them. Cymbeline's regenerative experience comes first, as
he acknowledges Posthumus' virtue without really knowing
who Posthumus is, grants dignities to the brothers and old
Belarius without knowing who they are, and admits his own
folly in submitting to the influence of the wicked Queen. Next
he recognizes the virtue in young Fidele, without seeing of
course that Fidele is really Imogen; and the result of this additional recognition of virtue in disguise is the repentance of
Iachimo, which brings about the rediscovery of Posthumus,
which in turn reunites the two lovers. An interesting development occurs shortly before the lovers are reunited when
Posthumus, overcome with the realization that there was no
justice at all in his order to have Imogen killed, strikes down
the disguised Imogen as she protests his excessive grief.
Cymbeline's startled exclamations here, as Pisanio reveals that
it is Imogen and not some obscure servant who has been struck,
help us see what is happening: "Does the world go round?"
and "the gods do mean to strike me / To death with mortal
joy" [V. v. 232, 234-35]. The Christian paradox which gives
the whole play its meaning, "Whom the Lord loveth, he chas-
teneth, and scourgeth every son whom he receiveth," here gets
perfect and clear realization at the historical level of the play.

Posthumus in his last moment of blindness, inadvertently and not wantonly, does what God in the fullness of knowledge and perfect wisdom continually does: he chastens the one whom he loves. As a human being he errs, and as [a] human being he is mercifully forgiven; the result, however, is wholly good. Imogen, come again to life, embraces him as the soul the body or fruit the tree, and Cymbeline pronounces benediction upon them both: "My tears that fall / Prove holy water on thee" [V. v. 268-69].

In the remaining portion of this scene other necessary business takes place: Belarius and the brothers are properly identified, the family is made whole again, and Iachimo, unwitting agent of a good deal of the divine chastening, is forgiven. The most interesting business, however, has to do with the yet unexplained prophecies. The first of these, we recall, is the one given to Posthumus; and this, with the possible exception of that detail about "tender air," virtually explains itself. Lucius' soothsayer makes the obvious explanation official. The other is that prophecy, first mentioned in Act IV, Scene ii, just before Lucius discovers Imogen-Fidele prostrate on Cloten's headless body. As delivered and explained by the Soothsayer at that point in the play, it goes as follows:

> Last night the very gods show'd me a vision—
> I fast and pray'd for their intelligence—thus:
> I saw Jove's bird, the Roman eagle, wing'd
> From the spongy south to this part of the west,
> There vanish'd in the sunbeams; which portends—
> Unless my sins abuse my divination—
> Success to the Roman host.
>
> [IV. ii. 346-52]

The point should be made, however, that the Soothsayer's explanation is not quite accurate. It is the British host, not the Roman, thanks largely to Posthumus, Belarius, Guiderius, and Arviragus, that has succeeded on the battlefield; and because the battle *has* been won by these four—principally with the aid of Posthumus—the victory for Britain can be a victory for Rome too. Lucius can thank Posthumus for a regenerated Cymbeline, for whom victory involves—something that would be utter madness in any context except a Christian one—paying tribute to the vanquished and forgoing all special prerogatives due to an earthly victor. Thus the Soothsayer can say, without referring to his previous error, that the dream "foreshow'd our princely eagle, / Th' imperial Caesar, should again unite / His favour with the radiant Cymbeline, / Which shines here in the west" [V. v. 473-76]. In our own day it is fashionable to say that no one ever really wins a war; here no one loses. The conflict ends with victory and happiness for both sides, praise to the gods, and ratification of the peace in the temple of Jupiter.

Tragicomedy also usually ends with peace and kisses all round; but *Cymbeline*, though related to tragicomedy by both materials and convention and therefore clearly a member of that family, has, as we have seen, a very different spiritual lineage. Because it participates in a Christian point of view, *Cymbeline* is related also to the Corpus Christi plays, to the English moralities, and to the Shakespearean tragedies; but it differs from these spiritual predecessors much as Pauline Christianity ("unto the Jews a stumblingblock, and unto the Greeks foolishness") differs from some of the other early formulations of the faith. Having accommodated itself to the morality and the more classical modes of drama, Christianity here adapts itself to a mode so fantastic that to many minds the new mode can only be an impediment to understanding. There is still current a Hebraic kind of puritanism that demands drama like the morality, and a Hellenic kind that demands something of which Aristotle conceivably might have approved; moralists and philosophers alike decline to take seriously the pleasant capriciousness of tragicomedy, which many sophisticated Jacobeans applauded. What Shakespeare has done, however, is to discover in the very capriciousness of this ephemeral art form a symbol of something that neither the morality nor the classical modes of drama had adequately acccounted for—the mystery of a gracious Providence and its inscrutable workings among mankind. Shakespeare's *Cymbeline* moves in the same spirit as Paul's words to the Romans:

> And we know that all things work together for good to them that love God, to them who are the called according to his purpose. For whom he did foreknow, he also did predestinate to be conformed to the image of his Son, that he might be the firstborn among many brethren. Moreover whom he did predestinate, them he also called: and whom he called, them he also justified: and whom he justified, them he also glorified.
>
> (Romans VIII: 28-30)
> (pp. 200-05)

J. A. Bryant, Jr., " 'Cymbeline'," in his Hippolyta's View: Some Christian Aspects of Shakespeare's Plays, *University of Kentucky Press, 1961, pp. 192-206.*

ROBIN MOFFET (essay date 1962)

[*Noting that such English chroniclers as Raphael Holinshed distinguished the historical Cymbeline's reign by the fact that he held the throne at the time of the birth of Christ, Moffet argues that the Nativity is a significant "esoteric" element in Shakespeare's play. He views* Cymbeline *as demonstrating the disastrous consequences of "sin, error, and misfortune" which reveal "the need of mankind for a saviour." Northrop Frye (1965), Alexander Leggatt (1977), and J. P. Brockbank (see Additional Bibliography) have also seen the Nativity as an implicit factor in this drama. Associated with this need for a divine agent to achieve peace and reconciliation for both individuals and states, Moffet contends, is the imagery of debts and bondage. He maintains that the metaphoric language of the play enhances the theme of release from "wrong bondages" through acceptance of "natural" and willingly acknowledged obligations to a higher spiritual authority. Both Caroline F. E. Spurgeon (1935) and A. A. Stephenson (1942) have also analyzed the significance of the metaphors of bonds and debts in* Cymbeline. *Finally, Moffet links Imogen's presumed death and reawakening (Act IV, Scene ii) with Posthumus's repentance and vision in prison (Act V, Scene iv). He notes that both episodes show these characters in utter despair, contain important soliloquies, and offer—in the brothers' dirge and the prayer of the Leonati—"antiphonal declarations" which emphasize pagan, pre-Christian views of divine justice and morality; according to Moffet, the respective experiences of Imogen and Posthumus further indicate the need in Cymbeline's kingdom for a spiritual savior. Other critics who have discussed the significance of Christian doctrine in* Cymbeline *include G. G. Gervinus (1849-50), J. A. Bryant, Jr. (1961), Robert Grams Hunter (1965), Homer D. Swander (1966), Arthur C. Kirsch (1972), and Martin Lings (see Additional Bibliography).*]

Holinshed's chapter heading tells us clearly what he, like the medieval chroniclers before him, regarded as the most important fact about Cymbeline's reign:

> Of Kymbeline, within the time of whose government Christ Jesus our saviour was borne,

all nations content to obeie the Romane emperours and consequentlie Britaine, the customes that the Britaines paie the Romans as Strabo reporteth.

The "customes" have a considerable part in Shakespeare's play, but it is the birth of Jesus Christ which made the reign unique.... [Not] merely is Shakespeare's imagination likely to have been stimulated by this detail in Holinshed, but there is quite a strong presumption that we may expect to find in this detail his principal reason for wishing to set a play in the reign of Cymbeline. Here I want to investigate briefly some of the ways in which this central fact—that Cymbeline's reign was the period of the Nativity of Jesus Christ—may be reflected in the form and details of the play. (p. 207)

One of the problems of *Cymbeline* is posed by the remarkably disparate and various material which has gone into it, and particularly by the uniting of the historical and political story with the popular "old tale" story of the Wager. The idea of the Incarnation naturally suggests the idea of union and uniting and a picture of every kind of human person and activity set together in contrast to the saving manifestation of the Divine Child, just as in *Cymbeline* the basis of the play is a contrast between the complicated interweaving of different kinds of human action in the greater part of it and the rapid miraculous unloosing at the end. If we consider the union of stories from this point of view we get a scheme somewhat as follows: the reign of Cymbeline is of unique importance because it is to see the birth of the saviour of mankind, thus the central idea will be the need of mankind for a saviour; the content of the play—"holding up a mirror" to reflect in little the essential truths of the theater of the world—will show the straits into which men have fallen as a result of sin, error, and misfortune, followed by a supernaturally effected restoration and reconciliation which will be both an imperfect analogue of the full restoration to come and a fitting preparation and greeting for the divine child soon to be born—"peace upon earth, goodwill towards men" (as with those mediaeval chroniclers who saw Cymbeline as pre-eminently a man of peace). The idea is expressed on the level of political events in the story of Cymbeline and the Romans; as it concerns the life of the nation, typified in the king and court, it is expressed through the figures of the Queen, Cloten, and the young princes; the story of Posthumus and Imogen expresses it in terms of the lives of individual persons, two supremely excellent human beings (as Britain excels among lands—"in a great pool a swan's nest" [III. iv. 139]), who are yet shown to us as impotent against malice and error and brought by them to the extreme of misfortune and despair. The whole is shown as a key moment in British history. There is no need, after [J. P.] Brockbank's essay [see Additional Bibliography], to remark the importance of the historical element in the play, and it would be impertinent, after Wilson Knight's study in *The Crown of Life* [see excerpt above, 1947], to dwell on the feeling shown for Britain's peculiar virtues and the sense of Britain's national destiny, but it would be an error not to recognize also that the play is as much concerned to show the insufficiency of Britain and Britons without divine aid. Posthumus finds his life worthless and desperate until he has offered it to the gods; Cymbeline's final action is to renounce the national pride so stirringly expressed by his queen in III. i. and to call for public sacrifice to the gods.

The emphases in Shakespeare's treatment of his sources support this view. With regard to the historical story the accounts of the chroniclers are confused and conflicting and it is not surprising that his choice of details is unique. However, the following points suggest his intentions. (1) Against the balance of opinion he chooses to have Cymbeline fight with the Romans over tribute. The historians stress the peace of the reign and are more certain of a war about tribute under Guiderius. (2) The motives for the rebellion are national pride and the desire for liberty. When liberty has been gained by war it is voluntarily given up. Ideas of liberty and bondage are important in the play, as will be shown later. (3) Cymbeline's final *volte face* is made in such a way as to suggest the justice of the Roman cause. No suggestion is made that it was British treachery and dissension that enabled the Romans to impose tribute—a theme which looms large in most sixteenth-century treatments of the subject. The chroniclers suggest no further motive than friendship for Cymbeline's payment of tribute. (4) Points (1) and (3), considered in combination with Cymbeline's double action at the end of the final scene, where his agreement to pay tribute to Caesar is closely followed by his call for sacrifice to the gods, suggests that Shakespeare is regarding the story in terms of the question over tribute in the Gospels ("Render unto Caesar", etc., Matthew xxiii), a suggestion which is reinforced by the deeper allusion to the same passage made by Posthumus in his repentance speech [V. iv. 3-29], where offering his life to the gods he thinks of himself as an underweight coin which he yet hopes that they will accept "for the figure's sake", presumably because the "image and superscription" he bears is the divine image in which man is created and which thus shows man to belong to the gods by right. Out of the confused details of the chronicles Shakespeare produces a clear picture of a Britain held in error and false values leading to a conflict which intensifies until, through unforeseeable outside assistance and a change of heart, peace and reconciliation are gained and the true relation of spiritual and political values is recognized.

In his treatment of the wager story Shakespeare makes two significant changes to the usual form. (1) The central idea of nearly all versions is of "a woman who wins her good name by an interesting cleverness", says Gaston Paris at the end of his exhaustive study of the tale, usually an energetic and masculine woman who gains military and political distinction disguised as a man—as in both Boccaccio's version, which we know Shakespeare to have read, and "Frederick of Jennens", the most likely second source among other extant versions. The masculine qualities—the self-sufficiency, the successful energy and resourcefulness (Helena of *All's Well* is much nearer the typical "Wager" heroine)—have been left out entirely in Imogen and her human and feminine limitations stressed (along with her excellence)—weakness, helplessness, subjection to error. (2) In both the source versions the villain is punished with death. Iachimo repents and is pardoned. In him also is illustrated a variant of the pattern of false values leading to discomfiture and a destitution which brings acceptance of truth and is reversed by an unexpectable restoration.

In his first presentation of the two leading characters Shakespeare goes out of his way to stress their ideal excellence. Posthumus is introduced as

> a creature such
> As to seek through the regions of the earth
> For one his like; there would be something failing
> In him that should compare. I do not think
> So fair an outward, and such stuff within
> Endows a man, but he.
>
>   [I. i. 19-24]

It is an abstract excellence, excellence *per se,* that is presented to us, and here, as later, the rhetoric is ordered to suggest a straining after unreachable superlatives. The sense of straining reaches its height in the broken off extravagances of Iachimo's temptation of Imogen, where he seeks to convey an appreciation of her supreme excellence by the disgust and foulness of his contrasting images:

> Had I this cheek
> To bathe my lips upon . . .
> . . . should I (damn'd then)
> Slaver with lips as common as the stairs
> That mount the Capitol: join gripes, with hands
> Made hard with hourly falsehood (falsehood, as
> With labour): then by-peeping in an eye
> Base and illustrous as the smoky light
> That's fed with stinking tallow . . .
>
> [I. vi. 99-100, 103-09]

Throughout the early scenes the chief emphasis of the poetry (apart from the simple facts of the story) is on this mere excellence, expressed in such figures as the above, in the images of value, price, gold and jewels, which have been often remarked upon, and in such generalized symbols of excellence as the phoenix (Imogen, [I. vi. 17]) and the eagle (Posthumus, [I. i. 139; I. iv. 12]). . . . This near-abstract treatment gives to Posthumus and Imogen a kind of representative significance, which for Posthumus is increased by his name and birth. He is without father, mother, or family, the last of a great race (*Leo*-natus), yet of obscure origin ("I cannot delve him to the root" [I. i. 28]). The lack of human ties makes him stand the more readily for humanity in general, and the fact that he is the last-born (*posthumus*) of his race fits his period in history, which sees the end of the possibility of pagan greatness. He is "like a descended god" (Iachimo, [I. vi. 169]), and when Imogen thinks him dead she runs through a catalogue of the pagan gods to find expression for the excellence which has been brought to nothing [IV. ii. 310ff].

This last speech is of special importance. There is neither space nor need here to show how the play follows the parallel but differentiated fortunes of the two central figures as they are brought to greater and greater calamity by the powers of error and ill-will (in scenes very varied in style but, mostly, of great individual intensity), and broadens to include the stories of the dispute over tribute and of the lost princes with their "grand paganism" (Wilson Knight). But for each of the two there is a climactic scene marking the pitch of their misfortunes (and, were it not for unforeseeable intervention of Providence, the end of their fortunes), which is given stress both by its dramatic placing and by the solemn manner of the scene itself. Moreover, there are several similarities between the two scenes. Both Imogen's "burial and resurrection" scene (IV. ii.) and Posthumus' repentance and vision (V. iv.) show the protagonist reaching an ultimate point of destitution (finally destroyed, to put it crudely, by Death and Sin respectively, as it seems); both contain important soliloquies; in both the action is halted while over the prone body of the protagonist other characters speak antiphonally in rhymed verse, which thus stands out from its surroundings; each of these antiphonal declarations is heralded by music, otherwise used sparingly in *Cymbeline;* in both scenes the protagonist wakes in confusion and, trying and failing to make sense of his predicament, compares the reality around him to a dream; each, quite logically, ends in despair; and each, as is obvious to the audience, is in this utterly wrong. The importance of Imogen's burial and awakening speech in

particular may be judged from the extraordinarily complicated plot-manipulation involved in bringing it about. The dramatic emphasis and parallelism suggests that we are to relate the two scenes, to see in them the two possible ends for good human beings in a world where sin and error are allowed to run to their logical conclusions, in which death is final:

> All lovers young, all lovers must
> Consign to thee and come to dust.
>
> [IV. ii. 274-75]

The famous lament is wholly pagan and fits its place at the close of the pre-Christian world. The ills mentioned are those due to nature, fortune, and human malice; the best that can be hoped for the dead is a quiet grave undisturbed by ghosts and sorcerers, and fame—the characteristic and unsatisfying pagan answer to the problem of mortality. All the time, however, we are aware that this is not the whole truth; only Cloten, compared in Imogen's next speech to "the care of the world" and very adequately exemplifying the "old man" of Christian theology, is in fact dead. But to Imogen her life is useless, and she is aware only of betrayal and loss: "O, my lord! my lord!" [IV. ii. 332]. Posthumus, by contrast, has himself destroyed the one thing which gave value to his life, and seeks death as the only means to free his conscience and make a partial reparation. The prayer of the Leonati is a plea for pity and justice to an omnipotent god who is seemingly harsh and indifferent:

> Whose father then (as men report
> thou orphans' father art)
> Thou shouldst have been, and shielded him
> from this earth-vexing smart.
>
> [V. iv. 39-42]

Jupiter's answer is a reflection of the Book of Job, in a pagan key:

> How dare you ghosts
> Accuse the thunderer, whose bolt (you know)
> Sky-planted, batters all rebelling coasts?
>
> [V. iv. 94-6]

but he goes on to explain his care:

> Our Jovial star reigned at his birth, and in
> Our temple was he married.
>
> [V. iv. 105-06]

The representative character which we have come to see in Posthumus, along with such details as the epithet "earth-vexing", with its suggestion of a universal pain, makes this seem a covert, figurative, expression of God's all-embracing care for men, at every moment of life.

It is noteworthy that at the point where we are expected to think most unmistakably of the Christian God the allegorical paganism is made most explicit and extensive. We can see here most clearly, I suggest, two related motives which are important, I think, for the understanding of the play as a whole—the reverence which does not wish to approach too closely and behave too familiarly in the presence of a sacred object, and the good sense and acknowledgement of limitation which will not attempt to find expression for the ineffable but is content with a sign or a gesture which will carry part, but only part, of the way. Hence the absence of any explicit mention of the Nativity. . . . Hence also, I think, the intensity of detail and the apparently casual artifice of the whole. (pp. 208-13)

In these two climactic scenes, then, we see the two leading characters, whom we have learned to regard as representative of human excellence (I hope I have not suggested that this in any way impairs their reality and interest as persons), brought to despair and confusion—waking to a life that is as senseless and unreal as a dream [IV. ii. 297-307; V. iv. 123-51]. The battle scenes, likewise, show first the British, then the Roman, army in full defeat with their leaders taken, again making very clear to us how little confidence may reasonably be placed in human powers; similar ''low points'' are introduced in the last scene for Cymbeline himself—when he learns of his queen's treachery—and for the Princes and Belarius. The different stories are related also by the common theme of false appearances (announced in the first line of the play) and the imagery of valuation, but these have been very adequately discussed by others. Another theme or line of imagery, that connected with debts, prisons, bondage, and liberty, has received less notice and is important both as a link between the different episodes and for its suggestiveness in relation to the period and presumed intention of the play. A full account would be disproportionate, but the following points must be made. (1) The frequency of references to bondage and prisons—even in rhetorical figures where the image is unexpected and seems uncalled for by the context e.g. Iachimo in [I. vi. 102-03], ''this object which / *Takes prisoner* the wild motion of mine eye'', and Imogen's strange thought when she receives Posthumus' letter in III. ii, ''Lovers / And *men in dangerous bonds* pray not alike: / Though *forfeiters you cast in prison,* yet / You clasp young Cupid's tables'' [III. ii. 36-9]—shows that the idea was very much in Shakespeare's mind when he wrote the play. (2) Practically all the main characters at some time find themselves ''in bondage'', either physical or spiritual. Posthumus is physically a prisoner in the last scenes, and is also ''bound'' in several other ways. His great prison speech ends with a pun on at least four different meanings of ''bonds'':

> and so, great powers,
> If you will take this audit, take this life,
> And cancel these cold bonds.
>
> [V. iv. 26-8]

Imogen is ''imprison'd'' in the first act by her father, and also ''bound'' by her marriage vow (symbolized in the ring Posthumus places upon her finger—''wear this, / It is a manacle of love, I'll place it / Upon this fairest prisoner'' [I. i. 121-23]). The Britons, speaking in the person of Cymbeline himself, fret against the ''yoke'' ''put upon'' them by Rome. The young princes find their uncivilized life a ''cell of ignorance'', ''A prison, or a debtor that not dares / To stride a limit'', although like the ''prison'd bird'' they ''sing their bondage freely'' [III. iii. 33-44]. Iachimo appears as a physical prisoner in the last scene, along with the rest of the Romans. Even Belarius, though living in ''honest freedom'', recognizes and pays ''pious debts to heaven'' [III. iii. 71-2]. (3) Bonds may be good or bad. Roughly, bonds freely accepted or naturally due are good (marriage bonds, ''debts to heaven'', Cymbeline's final agreement to pay tribute); bonds tyranically or unwillingly imposed are bad (physical imprisonment, the bondage of ignorance). Both Cloten and Iachimo wickedly try to persuade Imogen that it is right for her to break her marriage bonds. The bondage of sin is a rather special case. It is good that Posthumus should accept this bond, even welcome it, but it is not the kind of bond that is in general acceptable and welcome. Freedom is, rightly, desired; but it seems possible only through death and is in fact effected through the gracious benevolence of Providence (Jupiter). (4) The general picture we get, if we try to rationalize this sequence of images, is of humanity ''bound'', imprisoned, in debt in various unpleasant and undesirable ways, but released

finally from the wrong bondages and left subject only to natural, right, fruitful, and willingly accepted obligations. The evidence points both to a widely dispersed concern over the nature of liberty and obligation and to an insistent awareness of the need of human beings for release from bondage, ready indeed for the saviour who will redeem men from an unpayable debt and free them from the darkness of error and bondage to sin.

In a few places there is evidence of the ''special'' character of the time of the play. ''My peace we will begin'' [V. v. 459], says Cymbeline towards the close, and at the very end the peace is characterized:

> Never was a war did cease
> (Ere bloody hands were wash'd) with such a peace.
>
> [V. v. 484-85]

Some earlier editors were so offended by the apparent megalomania of ''*my* peace'' that they emended to ''by''. Cymbeline's peace is, however, another version of that special peace celebrated in [John Milton's] Ode ''On the Morning of Christ's Nativity''. On a less conscious level, Shakespeare makes Imogen speak . . . of her gratitude for aid that enabled her ''to see this gracious season'' [V. v. 402]. The last two words are elsewhere in Shakespeare associated once only, when in the first scene of *Hamlet* Marcellus remembers ''that Season . . . wherein our Saviour's birth is celebrated'' [*Hamlet*, I. i. 158-59] in which

> No fairy takes, nor witch hath power to charme
> So hallowed, and so gratious is that time.
>
> [*Hamlet*, I. i. 163-64]

If my hypothesis is correct, it will follow that we must accept an element of the esoteric in *Cymbeline*. The play makes sense as romance and history, but I think it makes better sense when its complications and resolution are viewed in the light of the greater denouement which is not mentioned but is known to be at hand. I am not concerned here with the critical consequences of my argument, but the possibility that the play is, to some extent, directed towards something outside itself may in some degree explain its acknowledged imperfections. In particular, the esoteric element may help to explain the prominence given to the two riddling devices which are interpreted by the soothsayer immediately before the close of the play— the riddle given by Jupiter to Posthumus, and the augury, the image of an eagle flying into the sun, seen by the soothsayer before the battle. Both are unnecessary to the plot and hold up the action so that we are led to seek some good reason for their introduction; and their placing makes them seem important. ''Oracles'' of different kinds are common enough in romances and romance plays, but it is difficult to think that Shakespeare would have given these the prominence and extended treatment they receive merely for fashion's sake. At the least they present the idea of fulfilled prophecy at the close of the play. I suggest that they also present the idea of incompletely fulfilled prophecy and are deliberately composed to suggest a double or multiple interpretation.

The riddle reads as follows:

> When as a lion's whelp shall, to himself unknown, without seeking find, and be embraced by a piece of tender air: and when from a stately cedar shall be lopp'd branches, which, being dead many years, shall after revive, be jointed to the old stock, and freshly grow, then shall

Posthumus end his miseries. Britain be fortunate, and flourish in peace and plenty.

[V. iv. 138-44]

It is certainly remarkable that when the supreme god visits this
last of the pagans in a vision he gives to him a ''book'' . . .
(to be conveyed to him by intermediaries) which contains obscure prophecies of good fortune to come. The ''label'' itself
is full of scriptural echoes, especially of Ezekiel xvii; and the
ingenuity of the soothsayer's interpretation, which explains the
riddle solely in terms of the persons and events of the play
(adequately but not satisfyingly), provokes further ingenuity
in seeking a wider application for the theologically suggestive
language. Thus in the Prophecy of Jacob (Genesis xlix) we
read that ''Juda is a lions whelpe'' (verse 9), Judah being
traditionally the tribe of the Holy Family. ''Without seeking
find'' suggests the gentiles of Romans 20 (quoting Isaiah lxv.
1), ''I was founde of them that sought me not'', who are
contrasted with the Israel who might be expected to ''know''
(v. 19). ''Tender air'' is not scriptural, but seems a very strained
periphrasis simply for ''woman'', and in these surroundings
might easily be thought to refer to the Holy Spirit (*spiritus* =
breath, wind, air) embracing either the Virgin (of the tribe of
Judah, to whom ''without seeking find'', ''to himself unknown''—with a change of gender—would be especially appropriate) or the gentiles (Leonatus the Briton). In Ezekiel xvii.
22, ''Thus sayth the Lorde God, I wyl also take of the top of
this high Cedar, and wil set it, and cut of the top of the tender
plante thereof, and wyl plant it upon an hygh hil and a great''.
The association of the word ''tender'' with the lopped cedar
is noteworthy. In earlier verses of the same chapter (vv. 3, 4)
a cedar twig is cropped and carried off by an eagle (cf. the
image of the augury), and images also characteristic of the later
part of *Cymbeline* follow in verse 23: ''that it may bryng foorth
bowes, and give fruite [cf. V. v. 263-64], and be an excellent
Cedar: & under it shall remayne al birdes, and every foule shal
remayne under the shadowe of the branches thereof''. Finally
(v. 24) ''I the Lorde . . . have dryed up the greene tree, and
made the dry tree to florishe''. In chapter xix of Ezekiel, a
lioness and her whelps appear, associated this time with a vine
tree which withers up and is transplanted. The idea of rejointing
is not found in Ezekiel, but looks like another reminiscence of
Romans—chapter xi—where Israel is figured as an olive tree
whose branches have been broken off to make room for the
in-grafting of the gentiles, figured as wild olive branches: at
present, St. Paul argues, Israel is cut off from the root, but in
time the broken branches will be re-grafted into their old tree
(vv. 17-24). The Ezekiel prophecy refers to the coming blessing
of Israel: the Geneva Bible interprets the cropped twig to mean
the Church, but it is also related to the Righteous Branch of
Isaiah xi. 1 and Jeremiah xxiii. 5, the ''Rod of Jesse'', so that
the prophecy becomes Messianic. All this suggests a wealth
of possible interpretations for the *Cymbeline* riddle, with the
branches standing either for the Messiah, for Israel, for the
gentiles, or for the ''true Israel of God'' including both Jews
and gentiles. Any of these can be worked out without great
difficulty and with little more straining and ingenuity than is
shown by the soothsayer, but they should not delay us here,
as it seems clear that the riddle is constructed so that it will
recall familiar biblical ideas and images without suggesting
any one obvious line of interpretation. What is important is
that it foretells a coming separation and re-uniting, and that it
does so in language mysterious and qualitatively suggestive of
religious experience and largely drawn from the Scriptures,
which therefore provokes a search for a theological meaning
beyond the interpretation given to it in the play.

The augury is more straightforward as it presents a single image
of a kind which can normally be expected to suggest multiple
interpretations. In [IV. ii. 346-52] the Soothsayer tells how he
has seen an eagle fly from the south into the west and disappear
into the sun. He regards this as foretelling a Roman victory
and is proved wrong. At the close of play he re-interprets it:

which foreshow'd our princely eagle,
Th' imperial Caesar, should again unite
His favour with the radiant Cymbeline,
Which shines here in the west.

[V. v. 473-76]

We are probably right to see in the image further ideas of the
transference of Roman virtues to Britain (as Wilson Knight)
and the ''lessening'' of the political power (Rome) when subsumed in the more spiritual (Britain), with possibly a hint also
of the familiar sun / Son pun, but the image had a traditional
meaning which gives it even more universal scope. Traditionally the purpose of the eagle's flight into the sun was to renew
his youth. The idea is best conveyed by quotation from the
bestiaries:

it is a true fact that when the eagle grows old
and his wings become heavy and his eyes become darkened with a mist, then he goes in
search of a fountain, and, over against it, he
flies up to the height of heaven, even unto the
circle of the sun; and there he singes his wings
and at the same time evaporates the fog of his
eyes, in a ray of the sun. Then at length taking
a header down into the fountain, he dips himself
three times in it, and instantly he is renewed
with a great vigour of plumage and splendour
of vision. Do the same thing, O Man . . . Seek
the spiritual fountain of the Lord and lift up
your mind's eyes to God . . . and your youth
will be renewed like the eagle's.

If we are expected to remember this legend (used by Spenser
[*Fairie Queen*], I. xi. 34, and kept alive as an explanation and
elaboration of Psalms ciii. 5, ''Thy youth is renued like the
eagle's''), the eagle's flight into the sun becomes an augury,
at the close of *Cymbeline*, of general rejuvenation and renewal
of life and vision, applicable to all the surviving persons of
the play and to the whole world in which its action takes place.
(pp. 213-17)

Nearly all the points I have treated are concerned with facts
of the play which raise critical questions when it is considered
merely as a historical-romantic story: the attempt to unite very
diverse stories and kinds of character, and the comparative
sketchiness of treatment in many cases brought about by the
attempt to include so much; the pains taken to bring about
Imogen's awakening scene and the parallel and contrasting
repentance, dream, and awaking of Posthumus, and to effect
the multiple reversals of a denouement which will be as artificial, complete, and many-faceted as possible; the stress on
the representative excellence of the hero and heroine; the apparently irrelevant references to prisons and prisoners which
seem to infringe rhetorical decorum; the dramatic emphasis
placed on the riddle and augury; the very fact of setting a play
in the obscure reign of Cymbeline. These are not the only
problems the play raises, but they are among the most obvious
and important, and it seems to me that all become less prob-
lematical, in the ways I have tried to indicate, if we have a
conception of *Cymbeline* as governed by the unique moment

in world history at which its events are imagined to take place. F. R. Leavis judged that *Cymbeline* was not organized "from a deep centre" (as is *The Winters Tale*) [see excerpt above, 1942]. I suggest that we have here for once a play whose "centre" is something not stated or presented and an action whose climax and justifying event is not shown but assumed as shortly to take place, and that it is for this reason that we find in it a striving after union, disparate pieces artificially yoked, rather than unity itself. (p. 218)

> Robin Moffet, "'Cymbeline' and the Nativity," in Shakespeare Quarterly, *Vol. XIII, No. 2, Spring, 1962, pp. 207-18.*

JOHN RUSSELL BROWN   (essay date 1962)

[*Brown maintains that in* Cymbeline *Shakespeare continued to be concerned with the issues of love and friendship which were central to the earlier comedies. He argues that among other interests in the play are "the ideal of love's wealth" and the "dangers and conflicts of love." Brown also links the broad variety of dramatic situations and sentiments in* Cymbeline *to the expansive view of life that forms the comic vision. Perhaps most significant of Brown's findings is his assessment of the final reunion and reconciliation of the various characters, which he contends is not "primarily religious"; instead, he argues that "the last scene is concerned with the ways in which the remaining* dramatis personae *take up their final positions in relation and in contrast with each other." Brown's comment on this aspect of* Cymbeline *opposes the findings of such other critics as G. G. Gervinus (1849-50), Derek Traversi (1954), J. A. Bryant, Jr. (1961), Robin Moffet (1962), Robert Grams Hunter (1965), Homer D. Swander (1966), Arthur C. Kirsch (1972), and Martin Lings (see Additional Bibliography), all of whom, to one degree or another, have emphasized the religious or spiritual element in the play.*]

The action [in *Cymbeline*] ranges from Britain to Italy and Rome, and back again, and towards the end the heavens 'open' to introduce Jove himself on an eagle's back. Its affairs are political, nationalistic, heroic, pastoral, connubial, religious, and amatory; dangers and disguises multiply freely. The characters know separation, deceit, love, hate, hopelessness, pain and death; they hope beyond reason and beyond true report. Cunning and perseverance direct many ventures, while 'Fortune brings in some boats that are not steer'd' [IV. iii. 46]. No long passage of time is represented, but events of more than twenty years earlier have their consequences.

To sustain this variety—and, we may think, to present an overall judgement as in the earlier comedies—Shakespeare chose a primitive dramatic idiom. Several scenes are entirely soliloquy, while many end with soliloquy and most have comments spoken aside. Numerous characters hold the audience's attention in strong and directly presented situations, but they usually do so one at a time and intermittently; Posthumus, Iachimo, Cloten, Cymbeline, his queen and even Imogen dominate the stage severally only to relinquish the central position to another. Contrasts are incessant and sometimes violent. A casual reader might dismiss the play as a sensational toy: but it is complex as well as primitive, and these two qualities are interdependent. The dramatic idiom is entirely suitable for establishing a wide view of the stage and for exploiting contrasts and relationships. . . . [Notice] particularly the treatment of love and friendship, and in the contrasts observe a subtle and insistent manifestation of Shakespeare's ideals. Sweet-tongued romance and elaborate, hot-headed fantasy are yoked together and both are controlled, with astonishing care, by Shakespeare's judgement.

The ideal of personal order is invoked in the very first lines:

> You do not meet a man but frowns: our *bloods*
> No more *obey* the heavens than our courtiers
> Still seem as does the king.
>
> [I. i. 1-3]

And at the conclusion there is an ordered and general procession off-stage, to a formal ratification of peace in 'the temple of great Jupiter' [V. v. 482] and the celebration of feasts. . . . [This] theme is represented in many different actions, from wild, isolated outbreaks of anger to the calm 'circle' [s.d., V. iv. 29] formed by the ghosts of the Leonati as they kneel in silence for the appearance of Jupiter [s.d., V. iv. 92]. Love's truth is also invoked in the opening duologue:

> . . . not a courtier,
> Although they *wear* their *faces* to the bent
> Of the king's looks, hath a *heart* that is not
> Glad at the thing they scowl at.
>
> [I. i. 12-15]

And at once these men are compared with Posthumus who is said to be alone in having 'so fair an outward and such stuff within' [I. i. 23]. The theme is obviously important. It recurs many times as Iachimo's 'simular proof' [V. v. 200] causes Posthumus and Imogen, and others, to question the truth of their 'hearts'. The queen's false professions of love are anti-

Act II. Scene iv. Iachimo, Philario, and Posthumus. By R. Westall.

thetical to Cymbeline's trust, while Cloten's disguise in Posthumus' clothes gives occasion to show how Guiderius, a prince who looks like a savage outlaw, discounts words and appearance, and how Imogen, in lonely grief can accept the foolish Cloten's body for that of Posthumus (which she believes to be godlike). Less openly, but with equal persistence, the ideal of love's wealth informs the play. As Caroline Spurgeon noticed in her pioneering analysis of the imagery, almost every character speaks of 'buying and selling, value and exchange, . . . payment, debts, bills and wages' [see excerpt above, 1935]. She believed that the 'awkward' way in which these affairs were sometimes introduced as metaphors showed that commerce was much in Shakespeare's mind while writing this play because of some event in his personal life, now of course unknown to us. Mr Nosworthy, a recent editor of the play, believed these images were 'an overflow from the tragedies' [see Additional Bibliography]. But we can accept them as a continuation of interests and techniques from earlier comedies, a way of defining and contrasting the behaviour of friends and lovers. It is no surprise to find Posthumus introduced as 'poor but worthy' [I. i. 7] or a ring and bracelet interchanged between the lovers with a realization that they cannot 'sum up' the 'bounty' of their love:

> And, sweetest, fairest,
> As I my *poor* self did *exchange* for you,
> To your so *infinite loss,* so in our *trifles*
> I still *win* of you
>
> [I. i. 118-21]

and again:

> . . . he is
> A man *worth* any woman, *overbuys* me
> Almost the *sum* he *pays.*
>
> [I. i. 145-47]

Such images are also found in the hyperbole of a sophisticated society, as in *The Winter's Tale,* and, with an extension of the normal range of comedy, in the gaoler's talk of the 'payment' due to death [V. iv. 157ff]. The commercial imagery associated with the ideal of love's wealth illuminates the diverse parts of the play and helps to give meaning and unity to the whole.

As in *The Winter's Tale,* Shakespeare accentuated the dangers and conflicts of love. Ignorance and separation make severe demands of the most faithful, and these are expressed with sharp antitheses made forceful by reference to the great range of judgements informing the whole play. So when Pisanio is caught between loyalty to Imogen's 'truth' and his master's 'words', he cries 'Wherein I am false I am honest; not true, to be true' [IV. iii. 42], and Posthumus, when he is led against all evidence to call Imogen 'noble' once more, cries: 'my life Is every breath a death' [V. i. 26-7]. The response of Guiderius and Arviragus to the page Fidele, who is in fact their sister Imogen, has to withstand all reason and moral propriety:

> *Guiderius.* I love thee; I have spoke it:
> How much the quantity, the weight as much,
> As I do love my father.
> *Belarius.* What! how! how!
> *Arviragus.* If it be sin to say so, sir, I yoke me
> In my good brother's fault: I know not why
> I love this youth; and I have heard you say,
> *Love's reason's without reason:* the bier at door,
> And a demand who is't shall die, I'ld say
> 'My father, not this youth.'
>
> [IV. ii. 16-24]

Imogen's continuing love for Posthumus when she can no longer believe him to be true is a contradiction unresolved until the end of the play and presented with rapid transitions of mood suggesting a basic instability: so, for example, the despairing 'My dear lord! Thou art one o' the false ones' yields instantaneously to peace and courage with 'Now I think on thee, My hunger's gone' [III. vi. 14-16]; her heart's faith, 'love's reason' that is 'without reason', has opposed reason and proved the stronger. (pp. 237-41)

Cloten is at first introduced as a braggart, an anti-heroic foil to Posthumus, but as a suitor to Imogen he also contrasts as a lover. When he complains 'If I could get this foolish Imogen, I should have *gold* enough' [II. iii. 7-9] the comparison seems a simple one between commerce and love, and when he argues 'You sin against *Obedience,* which you *owe* your father' [II. iii. 111-12] he is simply trusting another 'order' than that of love. But when Imogen tells him that she respects the 'meanest garment' of Posthumus before thousands of Cloten's [II. iii. 133-36] his repeated echoing of her words and violent reactions betray a stronger, divided response: now he goes alone to the forests to rape Imogen and kill Posthumus, risking danger in a wholly unexpected way. Belarius will not believe that he could do this:

> . . . not *frenzy,* not
> Absolute *madness* could so far have *raved*
> To bring him here alone.
>
> [IV. ii. 134-36]

Cloten, however, now knows something of the power of love to establish a new reason and new order, and he recognizes Imogen's wealth that 'outsells all others' [III. v. 74]. Yet he loves himself too and envies Posthumus; therefore, with the sharp antithesis associated in this play with the deepest feelings, he cries aloud: 'I love and hate her' [III. v. 70]. In the power of these conflicting passions he 'foams at the mouth' and even 'enforces' the honest Pisanio to his purposes [V. v. 274-85]. He dies asserting his own importance, but not before he has risked all for 'love and hate'.

The conclusion of this play follows the appearance of Jupiter to Posthumus in prison and shows in detail how his riddling prophecy is fulfilled; and the god is praised and honoured. But our reading does not lead us to think that the dramatic interests are primarily religious: because of the issues awakened through the whole play, the last scene is concerned with the ways in which the remaining *dramatis personae* take up their final positions in relation and contrast with each other; and, as in the earlier comedies, these last movements appear eloquent of Shakespeare's implicit judgements. The gaoler who had reminded Posthumus of the new 'reckoning' to be made in death, remains on stage for a soliloquy which, like the final soliloquies of Bottom [in *A Midsummer Night's Dream*], Launce [in *The Two Gentlemen of Verona*], and Parolles [in *All's Well That Ends Well*], prefigures the judgement of the conclusion:

> I would we were all of one *mind,* and one mind
> good; O, there were desolation of gaolers and
> gallowses! I speak against my present *profit,*
> but my wish hath a *preferment* in't.
>
> [V. iv. 203-06]

So many minds have been divided from each other and within themselves that the dramatic idiom has to be simple and unusually economical if it is to contain the full resolution. The succession of dénouements in short space draws attention to its own contrivance and belittles the human beings who seem impelled by the logic of a comic catastrophe: but some of the feelings expressed are strong and direct, linked to judgements implicit throughout the play; these stand large among the lesser shifts and changes of opinion and thus gain greater eloquence. Posthumus strikes the 'scornful page' who interrupts his cries of grief, but when Fidele becomes Imogen she 'hangs' upon him and he 'anchors upon Imogen' [V. v. 393]; their understanding is secure and almost silent among the glissading events. Some distinctions are given strength antithetically: on one count Imogen has 'lost a kingdom' by the discovery of her brothers, but in the fulfilment of 'love's reason' and 'truest' speaking she acknowledges love's wealth in this very loss as the '*gaining*' of 'two worlds' [V. v. 373-78]. Iachimo, having confessed, kneels to Posthumus expecting death and returns the ring and bracelet: but now Posthumus has 'power' only to 'spare' and forgive, and this leads the king to learn 'freeness' and doom 'Pardon's the word to all' [V. v. 422]. Our view of the play as it is concerned with love and friendship cannot give a full reading, for many other interests have been interwoven, but we may understand enough to appreciate the nature of this conclusion as a sharpened, weighty image of men and women attempting a mutual mind and that 'one mind good'. Even the contrivance of the dénouement gathers meaning when the soothsayer assures the others that the 'fingers of the powers above do *tune* The *harmony* of this peace' [V. v. 466-67]. Then piety is placed in the background, as a structural line in a wider and more lively composition:

> Laud we the gods;
> And let our crooked smokes climb to their nostrils
> From our blest altars.
>
> [V. v. 476-78]

The stage fills at the close with an orderly procession of men and women at peace with each other, a stable relationship which has been given eloquence through a persistent and minute judgement on divided minds throughout the play.

Cymbeline is often considered to be eccentric among the other last comedies, for it is hard to see it as a 'myth of immortality' or as a treatment of 'fall and redemption'. . . . Dr Tillyard believed that in all the last comedies Shakespeare intended to follow 'tragic events' to their final and 'regenerative' phase: but *Cymbeline* ill suits his thesis:

> The tragic events (for which Cymbeline's original error is ultimately responsible) are curiously apt to end in insignificance, while the existence into which the tragic action issues is, as any recognizable and convincing way of life, a pallid and bloodless affair.

Fastening on some newly introduced elements in these last plays, Dr Tillyard has missed the way in which Shakespeare's imagination has given meaning to theatrical worlds as wide, or wider, than those of his earlier comedies. Perhaps he would find that all these plays gain in unity and life if he responded to them as products of Shakespeare's continuous interest in comedy and in love and friendship. In this view, the concluding scene of *Cymbeline* seems to be at one with those of the other last plays: its wide view of life has the comprehensive eloquence of the earlier comedies and the reticence appropriate to a play that has shown such discords before such peace. (pp. 242-45)

> *John Russell Brown, "The Life of the Last Comedies," in his* Shakespeare and His Comedies, *second edition, Methuen & Co. Ltd., 1962, pp. 205-52.*

NORTHROP FRYE   (essay date 1965)

[*Frye is considered one of the most important critics of the twentieth century and a leader of the anthropological or mythic approach to literature which gained prominence during the 1950s. As outlined in his seminal work,* An Anatomy of Criticism *(1957), Frye views literature as ultimately derived from certain myths or archetypes present in all cultures, and he therefore sees literary criticism as an unusual type of science in which the literary critic seeks only to decode the mythic structure inherent in a work of art. Frye's effort was to produce a method of literary interpretation more universal and exact than that suggested in other critical approaches, such as New Criticism, biographical criticism, or historical criticism—all of which he finds valuable, but also limited in application. As a Shakespearean critic, Frye has made his greatest contribution in the area of the comedies and romances, especially with his definition of the three main phases of Shakespearean comic and romantic structure: the initial phase of "the anticomic society," "the phase of temporarily lost identity," and the establishment of a "new society" through either marriage or self-knowledge. Although Frye states that "reading things into Shakespeare . . . is a dubious practice," he notes that there is an implicit sense in* Cymbeline *of the association between Cymbeline's reign and Christ's Nativity, an assessment also suggested by Robin Moffet (1962), Alexander Leggatt (1977), and J. P. Brockbank (see Additional Bibliography). In addition, Frye remarks that divine providence is the agent of the festive resolution in the play, unlike the "problem comedies" which it otherwise resembles, where human characters, not divine will, act to resolve the dramatic errors and confusions. Other commentators who have similarly held that this play demonstrates providential control over human affairs include G. G. Gervinus (1849-50), G. Wilson Knight (1947), J. A. Bryant, Jr. (1961), and R. A. Foakes (1971). On a related matter, Frye emphatically disputes the idea that* Cymbeline *is a historical play, terming it instead "pure folk tale."*]

Cymbeline, a play that might have been subtitled "Much Ado About Everything," is the apotheosis of the problem comedies: it combines the *Much Ado* theme of the slandered heroine, the *All's Well* theme of the expulsion of the hero's false friend, the *Measure for Measure* theme of the confusion and clarifying of government, and many others. There are even some curious echoes of names from *Much Ado:* in *Cymbeline* we have Sicilius Leonatus betrothed to Imogen, whose name is Innogen in Shakespeare's sources; in *Much Ado* we have Leonato, Governor of Messina in Sicily, whose wife's name, though she has no speaking part, is Innogen. The former name goes on echoing in *The Winter's Tale* as Leontes, King of Sicilia. The repetition may mean very little in itself, but we notice in the romances a technique of what might be called spatial anachronism, in which Mediterranean and Atlantic settings seem to be superposed on top of each other, as Bermudan imagery is superposed on the island in *The Tempest*. In particular, there is a convention, referred to in the Prologue to [Ben] Jonson's *Sad Shepherd* and prominent in [John Milton's] *Comus* and *Lycidas,* of mixing British with Sicilian and Arcadian imagery in the pastoral.

The same technique of superposition is used temporally as well, binding together primitive Wales, Roman Britain, and Italian Rome. *Cymbeline* has at least a token connection with the history plays of some significance. History is a prominent genre in Shakespeare until *Henry V,* when it seems to disappear and revive only in the much suspected *Henry VIII* at the end of the canon. Yet the history of Britain to Shakespeare's audience began with the Trojan War, the setting of *Troilus and Cressida,* and included the story of Lear as well as the story of Macbeth. Even *Hamlet* is dimly linked with the period of Danish ascendancy over England. Alternating with these plays of a Britain older than King John are the Roman or Plutarchan plays, dealing with what, again, to Shakespeare's audience was the history of a cousin nation, another descendant of Troy. In *Cymbeline* the theme of reconciliation between the two Trojan nations is central, as though it were intended to conclude the double series started by *Troilus and Cressida.*

The reason for the choice of the theme may be partly that Cymbeline was king of Britain at the time of Christ. The sense of a large change in human fortunes taking place offstage has to be read into *Cymbeline,* and as a rule reading things into Shakespeare in the light of some external information is a dubious practice. Still, we notice the curiously oracular gaoler, who speaks for a world that knows of no other world, and yet can say: "I would we were all of one mind, and one mind good" [V. iv. 203-04]. We notice, too, the word "peace" at the end of the play, and the way that the promise to pay tribute to Augustus fits into that emperor's decree that all the world should be taxed, the decree that begins the story of the birth of Christ. But *Cymbeline* is not, to put it mildly, a historical play: it is pure folk tale, featuring a cruel stepmother with her loutish son, a calumniated maiden, lost princes brought up in a cave by a foster father, a ring of recognition that works in reverse, villains displaying false trophies of adultery and faithful servants displaying equally false trophies of murder, along with a great firework display of dreams, prophecies, signs, portents, and wonders.

What strikes one at once about the play is the extraordinary blindness of the characters in it. Imogen begins her journey to Milford Haven by saying:

> I see before me, man: nor here, nor here,
> Nor what ensues, but have a fog in them,
> That I cannot look through.
>
> [III. ii. 78-80]

Lucius, after the battle he was so confident of winning has gone so awry, says:

> For friends kill friends, and the disorder's such
> As war were hoodwinked
>
> [V. ii. 15-16]

and the gaoler tells Posthumus how little he knows of where he is going. Posthumus replies that "none want eyes to direct them the way I am going, but such as wink and will not use them" [V. iv. 185-87]. Yet Posthumus himself has believed an even sillier story than Claudio does in *Much Ado.* The crafty Queen wastes her energies trying to teach Cloten the subtleties of courtship; Belarius tries to persuade his adopted sons to be disillusioned about a world they have never seen. The word "election," implying free choice, is used several times, but no one's choice seems very well considered; the word "note," meaning distinction or prestige, also echoes, but distinctions are difficult to establish when "Reverence, / The angel of the world" [IV. ii. 247-48] is compelled to focus on the idiot Cloten, stepson of the weak and deluded Cymbeline. In *Cymbeline,* as in all the romances, there is a scaling down of the human perspective. Posthumus is peevishly and querulously jealous, he is no Othello; the Queen is squalidly unscrupulous, and is no Lady Macbeth.

Imogen is by long odds the most intelligent character in the play, and Imogen throughout is surrounded by a kind of atmospheric pressure of unconsciousness. The emotional climaxes of the play are the two great songs of the awakening and the laying to rest of Imogen, and in neither of them has she any notion of the context. The aubade is sung to her in-

different ear by the agency of Cloten after she has unknowingly spent a night with Iachimo; the obsequy is sung to her unconscious body by two boys whom she does not know to be her brothers while the headless Cloten is being laid beside her in the clothes of Posthumus. We feel in *Pericles* that Marina's magical chastity will get her safely through the peril of the brothel, but at least she knows it is a peril: in other words, there is much less dramatic irony in *Pericles* than in *Cymbeline.* The ironic complications of *Cymbeline* are in themselves, of course, the customary conventions of pastoral romance, where the simple childlike pleasure of knowing more than the characters do is constantly appealed to by the author. But there also seems to be a strong emphasis on the misdirection of human will, which culminates in the prison scene.

In this scene a number of characters appear who are new to us but are older than the action of the play. They speak in a naïve doggerel verse not unlike in its dramatic effect to the verse of Gower in *Pericles,* and like it they are a sign that we are being confronted with something traditional and archaic. They are ghosts from the world of the dead, who have been invisible spectators of the action and now come to speak for us as spectators, impeaching the wisdom of Jupiter for allowing things to get in such a muddle. Jupiter tells them what, in fact, we have been seeing all along, that a skillful and quite benevolent design is being woven of the action despite all the efforts of human folly to destroy it. This scene is soon followed by the great contrapuntal tour de force of the recognition scene, when the truth is torn out of a score of mysteries, disguisings, and misunderstandings; when out of all the confusion of action a very simple conclusion is reached, and one which sounds very like peace on earth, good will toward men. The difference between *Cymbeline* and the earlier problem comedies, then, is that the counter-problem force, so to speak, which brings a festive conclusion out of all the mistakes of the characters, is explicitly associated with the working of a divine providence, here called Jupiter. Jupiter is as much a projection of the author's craftsmanship as the Duke in *Measure for Measure:* that is, the difference between *Cymbeline* and the problem comedies is not that *Cymbeline* is adding a religious allegory to the dramatic action. What it is adding to the dramatic action is the primitive mythical dimension which is only implicit in the problem comedies. *Cymbeline* is not a more religious play than *Much Ado:* it is a more academic play, with a greater technical interest in dramatic structure. (pp. 65-70)

> *Northrop Frye, "Making Nature Afraid," in his* A Natural Perspective: The Development of Shakespearean Comedy and Romance, *Columbia University Press, 1965, pp. 34-71.*

ROBERT GRAMS HUNTER   (essay date 1965)

[In unexcerpted portions of his Shakespeare and the Comedy of Forgiveness *(1965), from which the following excerpt is taken, Hunter describes a recurring pattern in medieval miracle and morality plays of "sin, contrition, and forgiveness" which central characters, especially the stock figure of* Humanum genus *("mankind"), reenact. He also summarizes the terms used by classical grammarians to describe the three parts of a play's structure: the* protasis, *or beginning, in which characters and subjects are introduced; the* epitasis, *or middle, where plot complications ensue; and the* catastrophe, *or end, where alterations and upheavals lead to the conclusion of the play. In the excerpt below, Hunter asserts that the dramatic structure of* Cymbeline *retraces in secularized form the religious pattern of the miracle/morality drama. He considers Posthumus the "mankind figure" who successively*

faces and fails "the test of love," transgresses against the spiritual basis of human relationships, seeks to unravel the purpose behind his experience, demonstrates contrition for his sin against Imogen, and eventually achieves an understanding of forgiveness, thereby earning for himself the forgiveness of the gods. Hunter is also one of the first commentators to maintain that Posthumus is a counterpart of Cloten, demonstrating that the former's behavior, attitude, and sentiments in the wager scene and in Act II closely parallel Cloten's views and actions. Thus, Hunter declares, the depiction of Cloten's headless corpse dressed as Posthumus is "a deeply ironic and excessively macabre joke—a deserved mockery of Posthumus." Other critics who have argued that Cloten represents the ignoble aspects of Posthumus's character include Homer D. Swander (1966) and James Edward Siemon (1976), as well as Joan Carr, Howard Felperin, and Joan Hartwig (see Additional Bibliography). Finally, although Hunter finds the Christian doctrines of repentance and regeneration at the heart of Cymbeline's *dramatic structure, he contends that Shakespeare has departed from the medieval drama in shifting the play's primary emphasis from divine to human love. Other critics who have identified the Christian pattern of redemption in* Cymbeline *include J. A. Bryant, Jr. (1961), Homer D. Swander (1966), Arthur C. Kirsch (1972), and Martin Lings (see Additional Bibliography).]*

Cymbeline is a play concerned, like all romantic comedy, primarily with love, but unlike most comedy of its kind, its lovers are married before the curtain rises. The play belongs to that type of romantic comedy in which love is tested, in which, temporarily, one of the lovers fails the test, in which the lovers must undergo an ordeal as the result of that failure, and in which, finally, the ordeal is survived and the lovers—one penitent, one forgiving—are reunited. In telling his story, Shakespeare has devoted his first two acts (the protasis) to the test of love. The action is evenly divided between Posthumus and Imogen and Act Two ends with the soliloquy in which Posthumus demonstrates that he . . . has failed the test. Tricked into the mistaken belief that he has found alteration in Imogen's love, Posthumus allows his love to undergo an answering alteration and bends with the remover (whom he believes to be Imogen, but who is really Iachimo) to remove. The third and fourth acts—the epitasis—concern themselves with the ordeal that follows love's failure. That ordeal is Imogen's, and Posthumus does not appear while it is taking place. The catastrophe (Act Five) opens with the reappearance of Posthumus and concentrates almost exclusively upon him and his penitence until the final scene of reunion, reconciliation, and forgiveness. Such is the organization of the narrative. Whether or not it strictly but delicately subserves a commanding significance one can discover only by examining the play in detail.

Cymbeline opens with an expository scene between two gentlemen, one knowing, the other conveniently if inexplicably ignorant. We learn that the king's daughter (and only child since the kidnapping of her brothers) has angered her father by marrying a poor but honorable gentleman in preference to her stepmother's clod of a son by a previous marriage. The scene also establishes the atmosphere of the court—an atmosphere permeated by sycophancy; a court where the courtiers mimic the king's displeasure outwardly while rejoicing in their hearts at its cause. This image of a society where the ignoble must be flattered and fawned on while merit can only be supported *sotto voce* is brilliantly sustained by the comic scenes between Cloten and his two companions. Cloten, however, is only a sign of what is rotten in Britain. Cymbeline himself is the cause of his country's degeneration.

Like the France of *All's Well*, the Britain of *Cymbeline* is diseased, and the king is at the center of its misfortune. But the king of France, though physically sick, was morally sound. Cymbeline is in a sense his opposite and his moral weakness has its source where Bertram's did—in ignorance of merit. But Bertram's inability to see the true worth of others was a personal shortcoming. Cymbeline's is a national catastrophe. As a result of it, the wickedness of the literally bewitching queen and the coarse stupidity of her son are lavishly rewarded, while the true nobility of Posthumus is not only unrecognized, but actively persecuted. Cymbeline's failure to perceive has already caused the banishment of the virtuous Belarius and, as a result, the loss of the two male heirs to the British throne. Now the king will banish the husband of his sole remaining child. Until the last scene of the play. Cymbeline knows and sees nothing but what is false. His ignorance and misapprehension are total, and serve as the source for the partial ignorances and misapprehensions of the other characters, and the near tragic misunderstandings that result from them. At the play's beginning, the king's moral blindness has created around him a dangerous atmosphere of sycophancy and deceit.

Posthumus and Imogen stand out boldly from this background. Their love, beauty, and virtue serve as a contrast to the king's ignorance, the queen's wickedness, and Cloten's complacent and boorish stupidity. Their marriage also represents the one visible hope for the society of the play. The courtiers rejoice at Posthumus' victory and Cloten's defeat, not only because good has triumphed, but because their own chance for a better future depends upon that victory. From the beginning, then, the happiness of the world of the play is seen as bound up with the love of Posthumus and Imogen.

The nature of that love demands analysis. It is characteristically described, throughout the protasis of the play, in two opposed sorts of metaphor—in terms derived either from commerce or from theology. In the opening scene, for example, the First Gentleman says of Imogen's love for Posthumus:

> To his Mistris,
> (For whom he now is banish'd) her owne price
> Proclaimes how she esteem'd him. . . .
>
> [I. i. 50-2]

In the [same] scene Posthumus, too, describes their marriage commercially:

> I (my poore selfe) did exchange for you
> To your so infinite losse. . . .
>
> [I. i. 119-20]

And in defending their marriage to her father, Imogen repeats the metaphor with a different conclusion as to the relative value of the commodities involved:

> he is
> A man, worth any woman: Ouer-buyes mee
> Almost the summe he payes.
>
> [I. i. 145-47]

Set against this materialistic imagery (and these examples could be multiplied) are the lines in which the love of Posthumus and Imogen is discussed in terms usually reserved for the love between deity and mortal. In the first of the examples given above, the First Gentleman continues his description with the words:

> and his Virtue
> By her [election] may be truly read, what kind of man
> he is.
>
> [I. i. 52-4]

Denotatively, election means any act of choice, and its connotations, both Elizabethan and modern, are political as well as theological, and yet the theological overtones of the word are very strongly at work here, and in her choice of the commoner Posthumus, the Princess Imogen is compared to God, who chooses those who merit eternal bliss. The term is used again, in an opposite sense, but with an even stronger religious connotation, by the Second Lord in Act One, Scene [Two], where in response to Cloten's incredulous, "And that shee should loue this Fellow, and refuse mee," he says (aside), "If it be a sin to make a true election, she is damn'd" [I. ii. 25-8]. Here the election is that by the mortal of God. Imogen has been offered a choice between matrimonial salvation and matrimonial damnation and has chosen correctly. Finally, in Act One, Scene [Six], in his flattery of Imogen, Iachimo returns to the first meaning when he speaks of her:

> great Iudgement,
> In the election of a Sir, so rare,
> Which you know, cannot erre.
>
> [I. vi. 174-76]

Imogen is sometimes, then, seen as the deity who bestows her grace upon her worshiper, sometimes as the worshiper who adores her god, the point being that Posthumus and Imogen adore one another. "I professe my selfe her Adorer, not her Friend" [I. vi. 68-9] says Posthumus to Iachimo, while to Imogen the tokens and statements of Posthumus' love are as precious as the mercy of God:

> if he should write,
> And I not haue it, 'twere a Paper lost
> As offer'd mercy is. . . .
>
> [I. iii. 2-4]

And when Cymbeline, having just banished Posthumus, and furious at Imogen's defiance, asks, "Past Grace? Obedience?" she replies, "Past hope and in dispaire, that way past Grace" [I. i. 136-37]. Cut off from Posthumus, she is like the mortal who feels himself cut off from the love of God.

Finally, in Act I, Scene Four, when Imogen is lamenting to Pisanio the brevity of her leavetaking of Posthumus, she wishes that she had

> charg'd him
> At the sixt houre of Morne, at Noone, at Midnight,
> T'encounter me with Orisons, for then
> I am in Heauen for him.
>
> [I. iii. 30-3]

J. M. Nosworthy [see Additional Bibliography], in a footnote, points out that,

> the times mentioned are three of the seven canonical hours of the Divine Office. The obvious interpretation is that Imogen sees herself as a goddess whom Posthumus is to worship at certain hours, but I doubt whether it is the correct one. I take "encounter me" to mean "join me" . . . and would interpret: I would have charged him to join with me in prayer at those times because I shall then be praying for him.

Mr. Nosworthy is quite right. Imogen never sees herself as a goddess. Her manner of expression in these lines is such, however, that we think of her as resembling an interceding saint, or the Virgin Mary. Like Helena, in *All's Well,* Imogen is one

whose "prayers . . . heaven delights to heare / And loves to grant" [*All's Well That Ends Well,* III. iv. 27-8].

Posthumus and Imogen, in the first throes of love, regard one another as deities. In life, the reaction is so common as to be conventional. We must, however, decide just how *we* are meant to assess the love Shakespeare describes in these exalted terms. With regard to Posthumus and Imogen as characters, our reaction seems clear enough. They are experiencing the emotions proper to a newly married couple, and we enjoy the spectacle. But the characterization of their love in theological terms is not entirely the work of the lovers themselves. The term "election" is applied to Imogen's choice of Posthumus by three different observers of their love. Furthermore, the terms used are not usually from the conventional vocabulary of diluted Petrarchan love-worship. They are chosen, rather, to suggest the real concerns of theology. It is almost as if Shakespeare wished to reinvest the love of Posthumus and Imogen with something of the exalted spirit of medieval idealization—to see in it a kind of secular salvation, the beginning of a new life.

There is, however, a danger in the application of a theological vocabulary to a romantic love—the danger of awakening the cynicism of an audience that knows there is more to love than an encountering of orisons. To describe love in the vocabulary of [Molière's] Tartuffe is to run the risk of provoking the reactions which Tartuffe provokes. An instinct for avoiding this sort of danger explains, I think, Shakespeare's probably unconscious strategy in juxtaposing commercial metaphors for love against those drawn from theology. The two kinds of imagery combine to produce a complex but single effect: they join to describe a love that is at once physical and spiritual, both of this world and out of it. This combination is what romantic love should be—of the spirit, a "marriage of true minds," and of the body, a matter of things (in the bawdy Elizabethan sense of that basic word). The love of Posthumus and Imogen is established at the play's opening as romantic love of the highest order, a love that contains and holds in balance both the physical and the spiritual. This is the reciprocated love that, in the course of the protasis, will be tested and (partially and temporarily) subjugated.

Iachimo is the active destroyer of that love, but his opportunity for mischief is provided by the muddle-headed Cymbeline's banishment of Posthumus. The physical separation of lovers as a trial of love was, of course, a favorite theme both of romance and lyric poetry (Donne's *Valediction Forbidding Mourning* is particularly *à propos* here). The standard romantic hero passes that test and, indeed, mere separation does not diminish Posthumus' love for Imogen. It does, however, affect that love by destroying the balance in it between the physical and the spiritual—or, rather, by causing a confusion of the two. Prevented, by separation, from the physical enjoyment of love, Posthumus, very naturally indeed, becomes a bit obsessed with love's physical aspect and begins to consider Imogen's spiritual value solely in terms of her ability to remain physically chaste. Instead of properly assuming that Imogen's spiritual value ensures her physical chastity, he begins to think of her physical chastity as the guarantee of her spiritual value. Iachimo's cynicism completes Posthumus' confusion. For Iachimo, "love" is simply and entirely a thing. Imogen's ring, which is a symbol of her love for Posthumus, is for Iachimo an equivalent physical object. Posthumus knows perfectly well that there is a difference.

the one may be solde or giuen, or if there were
wealth enough for the purchases, or merite for
the guift. The other is not a thing for sale, and
onely the guift of the Gods.
Iach.: Which the Gods haue giuen you?
Post.: Which by their Graces I will keepe.

[I. iv. 82-7]

Posthumus here surrenders his position in the process of defending it. His confusion as to the nature of his and Imogen's love for one another leads him to admit Iachimo's basic proposition: that Imogen's love is a thing in Posthumus' possibly temporary possession. It is not, or not entirely. It is, as Posthumus knows but forgets at the moment of knowing, "the guift of the Gods," comparable to God's grace and hence (outside Calvinism) something whose continued possession is merited either by faith in its existence or by an avoidance of sin. Posthumus fails to merit the grace of Imogen's love both by Lutheran and Catholic standards, for he first loses faith in Imogen and then proceeds to sin against her by attempting to have her murdered. Like the Christian sinner, however, he can only destroy the love within himself. He cannot succeed in destroying the love that is felt for him. Imogen's love, like God's for man, remains constant and is available to her erring husband when, penitent, he once more desires it.

Although Imogen's love is *like* the love of God, it is not the love of God, nor is it a symbol of that love. It is a human love and Iachimo sets about to try to destroy it. He begins by undermining Posthumus' half of that mutual emotion. Posthumus allows himself to be convinced that Imogen's ring and Imogen's love can be equated and the one wagered against the other. *Humanum genus* [humankind] listens to the voice of the tempter and makes his first mistake by half believing what he hears. (pp. 144-51)

Iachimo's trial of Imogen's love for her husband has been characterized as "crassly blundering" [see excerpt above by Harley Granville-Barker, 1930], but that is to do less than justice to the shrewdness of Imogen's virtue as well as to Iachimo's skill as a seducer. Iachimo grounds his attempted seduction on the accusation that Posthumus has denied the spirituality of love, that he has treated it as a thing to be bought and sold, that he has hired prostitutes with the very money which (in Iachimo's view) Imogen has paid him for loving her. This coarsening and literalizing of the commercial metaphor of the play has an effect on Imogen, who is half convinced by Iachimo's calumnies until she realizes the motive for them— her seduction. So Iachimo fails, but he revenges himself for his failure with Imogen by his success with Posthumus.

For Iachimo, as for Iago, love means the sexual act, and beauty (as in the bedchamber scene) is only an excitement to desire. Female virtue is a myth. What he does in [Act Two, Scene Four] is to convert Posthumus to his view of life. His method of converting him is similar to the method he employed unsuccessfully against Imogen—he calumniates the object of love. Posthumus believes him, however. He listens to the voice of the tempter and thus completes the process of conversion that had begun at their first encounter. By agreeing to a test of love, Posthumus has offended against love. True love would feel no necessity for a test, would reject the suggestion of one as degrading, and would simultaneously know that love is too important to risk destroying by admitting the possibility of its destruction. Posthumus, in his naïveté and lack of confidence, agrees to Iachimo's proposal and falls an easy victim to his villainy.

The soliloquy with which the protasis ends is painful and disturbing. It is strongly reminiscent of Claudio's diatribe against Hero in the church scene of *Much Ado,* but there is here a stronger misogyny, and a masochistic dwelling on more specifically brutalized images of the loved one's supposed sexual encounters:

> Perchance he spoke not, but
> Like a full Acorn'd Boare, a Iarman on,
> Cry'de oh, and mounted. . . .

[II. v. 15-17]

Like Claudio, he rejects the woman he has loved and, along with her, all women and all the supposed characteristics of the female:

> Could I finde out
> The Womans part in me, for there's no motion
> That tends to vice in man, but I affirme
> It is the Womans part: be it Lying, note it,
> The womans: Flattering, hers; Deceiuing, hers;
> Lust, and ranke thoughts, hers, hers: Reuenges
> hers: . . .

[II. v. 19-24]

Shakespeare is here having Posthumus regale us with the clichés of Pauline antifeminism, but he is doing so in a context that transforms Posthumus' ravings by implication into the purest philogyny. Shakespeare is making use of what Bertrand Evans has called "disparate awareness" [see Additional Bibliography]. The audience knows that the source of Posthumus' hatred for Imogen is a lie, and our knowledge of Imogen's innocence turns Posthumus' attack on women into a hymn of praise. We know that lying, deceiving, flattering, lust, etc., are the characteristics not of the woman Imogen, but of the man Iachimo, and we realize that they—and particularly the rank thoughts and revenges—are becoming characteristic of Posthumus as well. As always in Shakespearean romantic comedy, it is the man's love that fails to meet the test. It is the weakness of the hero that allows strife its entrance into the world of the play. In *Cymbeline,* as in *Much Ado,* love presupposes the overcoming and containment of hate. The destruction of love automatically results in the triumph of hate with its inevitable consequences of suffering, war, and death.

The protasis ends with the triumph of hatred in the mind of *humanum genus.* The epitasis begins with preparations for war and plans for murder. Posthumus' cruel orders to Pisanio seem to Imogen, in her ignorance, to provide her with the opportunity to escape from the treachery, hatred, and persecution of the court back to the haven of Posthumus' love for her. Milford Haven, where she is to meet her husband, becomes the play's symbolic goal, a "port after stormy seas" where reconciliation and love will occur. Posthumus was described as leaving haven when he left Britain and Imogen's love [I. iii. i.]. His return, Imogen naturally assumes, will be to the shelter of their love for one another. She does not know that that love has been destroyed and that she must now go on a journey which, though it will bring her to haven at last, will necessitate her passing through a wasteland of nightmare horrors. (pp. 152-54)

Imogen is pursued through the wilderness by a monster intent on rape and murder. At the moment he overtakes her, however, she has drunk the "poison" prepared for her by the queen and is lying "dead" in the cave of Belarius. Her unreal death coincides with the real killing of her pursuer by Guiderius. The slaying of this absurd dragon is played as farce:

I haue tane
His head from him: Ile throw't into the Creeke
Behinde our Rocke, and let it to the Sea,
And tell the Fishes, hee's the Queenes Sonne,
Cloten. . . .

[IV. ii. 150-53]

This, in an abrupt change of mood from the grotesque to the pathetic, is followed by the entrance of Arviragus with the "corpse" of Imogen. The "wench-like words" of mourning which follow culminate in the exquisite dirge with its catalogue of the evils that Imogen has now escaped: "the heat o' th' sun," "the furious winter's rages;" "the frown o' th' great" and "the tyrant's stroke" of Cymbeline's persecution; the "lightning flash" and "thunder-stone" of the gods; and, finally, the "slander" of Iachimo and the "censure rash" of Posthumus [IV. ii. 230, 258-72]. This pathos, however, again modulates immediately into one of the most bizarre scenes Shakespeare ever wrote.

That Imogen wakes to find beside her a headless corpse which she takes to be that of Posthumus is clearly no spur of the moment inspiration on Shakespeare's part. He lays the groundwork for it carefully in Act Two, Scene Three, when Imogen tells Cloten that she esteems him less than "the mean'st garment" of Posthumus [II. iii. 133], a remark that inspires Cloten to put on Posthumus' clothes in an effort to add insult to the injuries he has planned for the woman who has dared to reject him. Staging problems are created by the scene, for the actors playing Posthumus and Cloten must be able to wear one another's clothes—unless two identical costumes were created for them with, perhaps, a third for the headless dummy which the scene requires. The purely practical difficulties raised by the scene are complex enough to make it clear that Shakespeare was determined to stage the incident. It is difficult to imagine why. To be sure, Shakespeare wants Imogen to be convinced of her husband's death, and this is the basic *raison d'être* for the scene, but surely it would not have been difficult to devise a less grotesque means of misleading the heroine. Shakespeare, however, wants this moment of grotesquerie, this "ludicrous situation" which yet contains a grief that is "deep, genuine, movingly presented" and "compels simultaneous tears and laughter" [Evans]. But to what end? Does this scene have any significance, or is it simply a piece of supreme theatrical virtuosity indulged in, as similar moments are in the work of Beaumont and Fletcher, for its own sake?

Part of the answer may, perhaps, be indicated by the role which Cloten plays throughout the epitasis. Posthumus is absent from the scene during acts Three and Four, and yet he is in a sense present insofar as during these acts Cloten is providing us with a parody of him. Like Posthumus', Cloten's "love" for Imogen has been turned to hate by what he conceives to be her ill treatment of him. As a result, he meditates bloody thoughts of revenge against her:

I loue, and hate her: for she's Faire and Royall,
And that she hath all courtly parts more exquisite
Then Lady, Ladies, Woman, from euery one
The best she hath, and she of all compounded
Out-selles them all. I loue her therefore, but
Disdaining me, and throwing Fauours on
The low *Posthumus,* slanders so her iudgement,
That what's else rare, is choak'd; and in that point
I will conclude to hate her, nay indeede,
To be reueng'd vpon her.

[III. v. 70-9]

This is approximately equal in sense, if not in eloquence, to Posthumus' soliloquy at the end of Act Two, where, by accepting Iachimo's lies as truth, he turned himself into a version of Iachimo. By setting about to have his wife murdered, he turns himself into a version of Cloten as well. Cloten, in attempting to suborn Pisanio, says:

Sirrah, if thou would'st not be a Villain, but do
me true service: vndergo those Imployments wherin
I should have cause to vse thee with a serious
industry, that is, what villainy soere I bid
thee do to performe it, directly and truely, I would
thinke thee an honest man.

[III. v. 108-13]

Neither style, morality, nor logic differ drastically here from Posthumus' letter to Pisanio:

. . . thou (Pisanio) must acte for me, if thy Faith
be not tainted with the breach of hers; let thine
owne hands take away her life . . . if thou feare
to strike . . . thou art the Pander to her dishonour, and equally to me disloyall.

[III. iv. 25-8, 29-30, 30-1]

Posthumus, then, has adopted the mindless savagery of Cloten, and Cloten, by putting on Posthumus' clothes, underlines the resemblance. When Guiderius lops off Cloten's head, the resemblance becomes perfect. I take Cloten's headless body to be a deeply ironic and excessively macabre joke—a deserved mockery of Posthumus. For he, too, has lost his head. By allowing himself to consider the love between him and Imogen to be a matter simply of things, he has reduced himself to the status of a thing—a mindless corpse. Remove the heads from both Cloten and Posthumus and Cloten will equal Posthumus. "I dare speak it to myself," says Cloten, "for it is not Vainglorie for a man, and his Glasse, to confer in his owne Chamber; I meane, the Lines of my body are as well drawne as his; no lesse young, more strong . . ." [IV, i. 7-10]. Cloten is quite right. As a thing, he is the equal of Posthumus, and Posthumus has chosen, for the time, to change himself into a thing.

When we next see Posthumus, however, he is in the process of changing himself back into a man—or rather, of changing himself into a new man, for the experience of Posthumus in the catastrophe of the play is made a pagan equivalent to Christian regeneration. This process begins with the erring human's conviction that he is a miserable sinner who has done what he ought not to have done. (pp. 156-59)

Posthumus' first soliloquy in Act Five is an expression both of sorrow for his own trespasses and of forgiveness for the woman who, he thinks, has trespassed against him:

You married ones,
If each of you should take this course, how many
Must murther Wiues much better than themselues
For wrying but a little?

[V. i. 2-5]

According to the Arden editor [Nosworthy]:

The hero's remorse of conscience is unconvincing. Since he still believes in Imogen's guilt, his attitude towards her should remain unchanged, however much he may repent of the supposed murder. To term her alleged offence "wrying but a little" seems contrary to the moral code of the play, though as Professor

Ellis-Fermor points out, it is not necessarily inconsistent with the feelings of a human being illuminated by grief and seeing with new eyes.

Professor Ellis-Fermor's point is admirable, but Mr. Nosworthy's introduction of it seems to me to betray a lack of sympathy with Posthumus' moral and spiritual condition. Posthumus is saying that it is wrong to kill your wife because she has slept with another man. Clearly—and Mr. Nosworthy seems to realize this—the ''moral code of the play'' is not one which would encourage the *crime passionel* [''crime of passion'']. When Posthumus refers to Imogen's supposed adultery, he is comparing it in his mind with his own sin—murder. By comparison with murder, adultery is ''wrying but a little.'' This is certainly not an amoral view of the matter, nor does it suggest that adultery is not wrong. Adultery is a sin, an offense against God which God will forgive if the sinner's repentance (or faith) justifies forgiveness. Adultery is also an immoral act and an offense against man—which man will forgive if he has the slightest sense of his own moral condition. . . . Posthumus thinks he has seen the mote in his wife's eye and has killed her for it. Now he looks in the mirror and sees a murderer in whose eyes are beams big enough to make hog troughs. By forgiving his wife he demonstrates that *he* deserves forgiveness. (pp. 160-61)

Posthumus is penitent, but he is also human, and he tries, though feebly, to shift some of the intolerable blame which he deserves to the account of others:

> Oh *Pisanio,*
> Euery good Seruant do's not all Commands:
> No Bond, but to do iust ones.
>
> [V. i. 5-7]

This expresses a natural desire to share the guilt of Imogen's murder, but at the same time it repudiates precisely that attitude toward Pisanio as the instrument of his master's crimes which we have seen Posthumus sharing with Cloten in the play's epitasis.

Posthumus goes on to consider himself and Imogen as the creatures of omnipotent gods and to accuse those powers of injustice in having permitted him to arrrange the murder of his wife:

> Gods, if you
> Should haue 'tane vengeance on my faults, I neuer
> Had liu'd to put on this: so had you saued
> The noble *Imogen,* to repent, and strooke
> Me (wretch) more worth your Vengeance.
>
> [V. i. 7-11]

In addition to revealing Posthumus' new sense of his own unworthiness, this attack upon the justice of the gods has the effect of celebrating that justice. Posthumus' misogyny, in his previous soliloquy, is turned into a defense of women by our knowledge of Imogen's innocence. Here our knowledge that Imogen is alive justifies the ways of God to men at precisely the moment they are being questioned, and the purpose of the gods in inflicting this ordeal upon the hero and heroine begins to emerge at this point in the play. The regeneration of Posthumus is now taking place and his reunion with Imogen will set the seal of the gods upon the completion of the new man. Posthumus betrays a sense of what is happening to him:

> But alacke,
> You snatch some hence for little faults; that's loue
> To haue them fall no more: you some permit
> To second illes with illes, each elder worse,
> And make them dread it, to the dooers thrift. . . .
>
> [V. i. 11-15]

Posthumus, having doubted the justice of heaven, now begins to see some glimmer of meaning in the workings of his fate. The gods, he recognizes, have two methods of rescuing a man from his self-created evil. They may either save a sinner they love by removing him from the world, or they may further torment the evil-doer until he comes to dread his own actions. Posthumus supposes that the gods have taken the first course with Imogen, and the second with Posthumus, whom they wish to punish:

> But *Imogen* is your owne, do your best willes,
> And make me blest to obey.
>
> [V. i. 16-17]

Posthumus' acceptance of the will of the gods is bound up, however, with a rejection of life. The only blessing he desires from heaven is the speedy death he has characterized as the reward of those whom the gods love, and he will seek death by all the means he can, short of deliberate self-destruction. Posthumus, though in the process of becoming a new man, is still in a state of wanhope as a result of his ignorance that Imogen is alive. But if this ignorance has the effect of making him reject life, it also preserves him from desperation, for if he is ignorant of Imogen's survival, he is also ignorant of her innocence. The knowledge that he has avenged with murder an adulterous act, which, in fact, never occurred, would upset his precarious balance between an acceptance of his unhappiness and complete despair.

Posthumus' departure to seek for death in battle is followed immediately by the entrance of the Roman and British armies, among them Posthumus in disguise. Granville-Barker has pointed out that the ''elaborate pantomime'' of the battle scene ''really looks not unlike an attempt to turn old-fashioned dumb-show to fresh and quaint account.'' Like a dumb show, certainly, the battle scene contains a moment of silent significance in which Shakespeare is underlining a point of large importance to the play:

> Enter Lucius, Iachimo, and the Romane Army
> at one doore: and the Britaine Army at another:
> Leonatus Posthumus following like a poore
> Souldier. They march ouer, and goe out. Then
> enter againe in Skirmish Iachimo and Posthu-
> mus: he vanquisheth and disarmeth Iachimo,
> and then leaues him. . . .
>
> [V. ii. s.d.]

Posthumus reveals later [V. v. 411-12] that he has seen Iachimo very clearly here. It is true that Posthumus is still ignorant ''of how the villain has betrayed him,'' but he is not ignorant of the fact that Iachimo is a villain. That Posthumus believes him the seducer rather than the calumniator of Imogen is hardly likely to make Iachimo less an object of his hatred. Iachimo is Posthumus' worst enemy and here Posthumus has the villain at his mercy. He spares him, and we must ask ourselves why.

There is, perhaps, more than one reason. Posthumus is a man of honor, and he has given his word, in Act One, Scene [Four], that if Iachimo succeeds in seducing Imogen, Posthumus will not attempt to revenge himself upon the seducer. In the battle scene, however, these two meet, not in a private cause, but as soldiers in opposing armies, and the code of honor would not require Posthumus to spare his enemy in such circumstances. Posthumus' chivalry may contribute to his decision to treat his enemy mercifully, but the soliloquy which he has just delivered suggests that his action has been prompted by something morally more important than the rules of the game.

In the previous scene, we have heard Posthumus forgive what he thinks has been a trespass against him. Since he also thinks that he had previously had the trespasser murdered, he cannot really demonstrate his charity effectively in action. The trespass which he has been called upon to forgive is adultery, and the party offended by adultery must necessarily have been offended by more than one other person. Posthumus thinks that both Imogen and Iachimo have despitefully used him. He has said that he forgives Imogen. Now we *see* him forgive Iachimo. By sparing Iachimo's life, Posthumus demonstrates that, since he is capable of pardoning others, he deserves the pardon of the gods.

But the final meaning of this moment of silent action remains to be considered. Posthumus, in pardoning his enemy, makes possible the happy ending of the play, for the happiness of the world of *Cymbeline* depends upon the continued existence of its villain. Iachimo alone can bring the play to a comic conclusion, for only he possesses the knowledge which can explain the events of the play, and it is the gaining of knowledge, the moment of revelation, that will make possible the triumphant ending of *Cymbeline*. By choosing to forgive his enemy, Posthumus merits the pardon of the gods, who, we may suspect, have so arranged events that the charitable action contains its own reward. (pp. 162-66)

Posthumus continues to long for death. Death will free him from the chains upon his flesh and from the flesh which chains his soul. But Posthumus appears to believe that the gods will not allow him to die until he has freed his conscience from the guilt which fetters it. By his "murder" of Imogen, he has sinned against the gods and the knowledge of that sin fetters his conscience to his body. He will be free only when he has achieved the forgiveness of the gods. Posthumus asks himself how he can gain that forgiveness, and presents himself with the thoroughly Christian answer: through penitence. The process of penance is the instrument that will pick the lock on the chains that bind his conscience, and free him forever. But of what does that process consist?

The answer contained in Posthumus' soliloquy is a traditional one. He proposes that there are two possible means of achieving the forgiveness of the gods: contrition and satisfaction. Contrition he considers under the names of sorrow and repentance, but whether he intends any subtle theological distinction thereby is doubtful. When he asks, "Is't enough I am sorry?" his incredulity is that of the repentant Christian who cannot believe his contrition alone will release him from the deserved sentence of divine justice. And yet . . . contrition, according to Aquinas, is enough, and it always served to guarantee the salvation of the *humanum genus* figure in the medieval plays of forgiveness. (pp. 167-68)

It is when Posthumus begins to consider the possibility of "satisfaction" that his soliloquy becomes more than ordinarily complex. It is complicated first by the conscious irony of the speaker. In offering to pay for Imogen's murder with his life, Posthumus is being disingenuous. Far from offering the gods a thing of value, he offers what he would most willingly part withal. But Posthumus is being, if that is possible, openly disingenuous, and his irony in asking the gods to show a superhuman mercy (as he thinks they have done with Imogen) by destroying him completely is an irony directed at himself. He is offering the gods a poor bargain, but he knows it, and he says so. (p. 168)

The final complexity of this speech has its source in the irony of which Posthumus is unconscious: the fact that he is not really guilty of the crime he wishes to expiate. The gods (including, one may say, the audience) know that Posthumus, like all *humanum genus* figures in the secularized comedy of forgiveness, has sinned through intention only. As a result, his expiation by contrition alone is aesthetically as well as theologically sufficient.

That contrition, with the charity he has demonstrated in sparing Iachimo, clearly earns Posthumus the forgiveness of the gods, and his prayer to them brings its own odd answer. (p. 169)

Posthumus' dream-vision opens with the apparition of the spirits of his parents and his two brothers. Their function is to ask the gods a very basic question: Why does the good man suffer? Why, specifically, have the gods, after rewarding Posthumus' virtues with the love of Imogen, taken that gift from him and brought him to his present miserable state? And why, most importantly of all, have the gods allowed the evil man to triumph by successfully tempting the good man to sin?

> Sic. Why did you suffer *Iachimo*, slight thing of Italy,
> To taint his Nobler hart & braine, with needlesse ielousy,
> And to become the geeke and scorne o' th'others vilany?
>
> [V. iv. 63-8]

Jupiter's reply is in the Christian tradition:

> Whom best I loue, I crosse; to make my guift
> The more delay'd, delighted. Be content,
> Your low-laide Sonne, our Godhead will vplift:
> His Comforts thriue, his Trials well are spent:
> Our Iouiall Starre reign'd at his Birth, and in
> Our Temple was he married: Rise, and fade,
> He shall be Lord of Lady *Imogen*,
> And happier much by his Affliction made.
>
> [V. iv. 101-08]

God punishes those whom he loves and they are happier as a result of their afflictions because of the contrast between their sufferings and their eventual felicity. This is Jupiter's message, and given the complexity of the action that has preceded it, its burden, we may justifiably think, is rather a simple-minded one. It is difficult to find this theophany a "central and dominating" statement of the play's meaning [see excerpt above by G. Wilson Knight, 1947]. If the vision really sums up and contains the significance of *Cymbeline*, then the play is a good deal less interesting than the rest of it would lead us to suspect. But there is not the slightest reason to take the epiphany as the summation of the play. The version of reality given us in *Cymbeline*, as always in Shakespeare, is highly complex. Like Jaques' melancholy, it is compounded of many simples and one of the simplest of these is the truth contained in the theophany. That truth—even though all's not quite right with the world, God *is* in his heaven, and we suffer for our own good—is, in terms of the play, perfectly valid but only partial. It is the sort of simple truth with which children are reassured after a first encounter with unjustifiable suffering.

This simplicity is, I think, the explanation for the archaism of the verse in the scene's opening lines. By using fourteeners, Shakespeare, I would suggest, is deliberately creating an aura of "the olden times." "The good old days" are always simpler than the present and this scene is summoning up a nostalgia for the simpler solutions of a supposedly less complex time by employing the devices of the drama which had been popular thirty years before *Cymbeline*. Such a strategy has two results. On the one hand, the charm associated with a remembrance of things past would lend an added strength to the message of the scene, while, at the same time, its "old-fashioned" quality underlines the partialness and simplicity of its meaning by contrast with the more "modern" complexity of the action which surrounds it.

It is important, too, that the deity who descends is a mythological one. I must take issue with J. A. Bryant's recent insistence that "there is no question of a pagan Jupiter here. Jupiter is the One God, called Jupiter in this play simply because the setting happens to be pre-Christian Britain" [see excerpt above, 1961]. This airborne, sulphurous-breathed old gentleman is not, I think, meant to convey to us the full impact of God's awful majesty. He is the kind of apparition Ben Jonson was making fun of when he pointed out that, in his revised *Everyman In His Humour*, "Nor creaking throne comes downe, the boyes to please." The boys who are meant to be pleased by Shakespeare's fundamentally benevolent but rather testy father figure are not simply the very young, but also the boys contained within all men. This Jupiter is the remembered God of childhood, who loves us but punishes us for our own good. He is not destroyed, but amplified and subtilized in the God of the grown man. *Cymbeline*, like the rest of the romances, contains much that appeals to a highly sophisticated childishness, but its world is, nonetheless, a grown-up world. To take this Jupiter as an entirely satisfactory divinity for that world would be to oversimplify a complex work of art.

The immediate effect of the vision of Jupiter is to present Posthumus, not with a solution, but with a further mystery. He awakens from his dream to discover upon his breast the "tablet" which Jupiter instructs the ghosts to leave there. This prophecy, with its jumble of lion's whelps, tender air, and stately cedars, disappoints Posthumus' desire for revelation:

'Tis still a Dreame: or else such stuffe as Madmen
Tongue, and braine not: either both, or nothing,
Or senselesse speaking, or a speaking such
As sense cannot vntye. Be what it is,
The Action of my life is like it, which Ile keepe
If but for simpathy.

[V. iv. 145-50]

Jupiter's descent has provided a refutation of one pessimistic version (expressed here by the ghosts but echoing that of Gloucester in *Lear*) of the human condition: that we are mortal flies spitefully tormented for the sport of the gods. Now Posthumus proposes another view, equally pessimistic, which echoes that of Macbeth in his "Tomorrow, and tomorrow, and tomorrow" speech: our lives are tales "told by an Idiot, full of sound and fury / Signifying nothing" [*Macbeth*, V. v. 19, 27-8]. But Posthumus qualifies that pessimism by admitting the possibility that his life may be not "senseless," but merely "a speaking such / As sense cannot untye." Not meaningless, but incomprehensible. He will finally discover, however, that it is neither. In retrospect, his sufferings, like the prophecy of the gods, will be found to have a meaning, and Jupiter, though we may not accept him as a revelation of complete godhead, will stand as a sign that the universe is controlled by an omnipotent and omniscient intelligence.

The demonstration of this divine omniscience comes in the last scene of the play, where it is set against an example of human nescience, the ignorant Cymbeline, who alone possesses no fragment of the truth which the other characters will now pro-

ceed to assemble for our admiration. The rush of knowledge into this royal vacuum constitutes the action of the play's denouement. And yet Cymbeline does begin the scene in possession of one almost instinctive truth: the gods have preserved his kingdom through their instruments—his as yet unrecognized sons and the disguised Belarius and Posthumus. What more the gods have done and what instruments they have employed is revealed by Shakespeare in a scene whose technical brilliance comes close to obscuring the significance of what occurs. But the revelations of the last scene are more than a series of astounding *coups-de-théâtre*, and their meaning may be clearer if we concentrate our attention not upon Cymbeline but upon Posthumus.

The first revelation to Posthumus is the revelation . . . made to Claudio and Bertram [in *Much Ado about Nothing* and *All's Well That Ends Well*]—he learns how vilely he has sinned. Unlike Shakespeare's earlier *humanum genus* figures, however, Posthumus has the advantage, in terms of audience sympathy, of having already repented the crime of which he thinks himself guilty. But only at this point does he realize the full horror of what he has done, for he discovers that he has commanded the murder not of a wife who has wryed a little, but of an entirely innocent and loyal woman. The effect of Iachimo's confession is to make Posthumus loathe himself completely:

           Aye me, most credulous Foole,
Egregious murtherer, Theefe, any thing
That's due to all the Villaines past, in being
To come. Oh giue me Cord, or knife, or poyson,
Some vpright Iusticer. Thou King, send out
For Torturors ingenious: it is I
That all th'abhorred things o' th'earth amend
By being worse then they. I am *Posthumus*,
That kill'd thy Daughter: Villain-like, I lye,
That caus'd a lesser villaine then my selfe,
A sacreligious Theefe to doo't.

[V. v. 210-20]

But he is wrong, and his error is immediately revealed. Imogen is alive and Pisanio, far from having been the agent of Posthumus' villainy, has served as the good instrument of the gods. The gods, who have "to instrument this lower world" [*The Tempest*, III. iii. 54], have "innumerable instruments," both good and evil. Against the wickedness of the queen, Cloten, and Iachimo, they have set the virtue of Imogen, Cornelius, Pisanio, and the banished princes. Their purpose—or one of their purposes—has been the regeneration of Posthumus. As a result of their mysterious workings, Posthumus has been tested, has sinned, repented, and been forgiven. But their efforts have not been confined to the individual alone. The kingdom of Britain has been cured as well, and its virtues, personified by the lost princes, the lost Imogen, Belarius, and Posthumus himself, have been restored to it. (pp. 170-75)

Of the four romantic comedies of forgiveness, *Cymbeline* is the most overtly Christian, and it is in this Christianity, with the doctrines of repentance and regeneration at its center, that I would place that "commanding significance, which penetrates the whole, ordering and informing everything," which Dr. Leavis has denied to the play [see excerpt above, 1942]. If I am correct in maintaining that *Cymbeline* . . . is the literary descendant of one variety of the didactic Christian tales and drama of the Middle Ages, then that Christianity is a natural aspect of the form in which these plays are cast. (p. 176)

However, once one has insisted that these plays of forgiveness are in the same Christian tradition, both philosophical and literary, one must redress the balance by insisting equally that, in the Shakespearean comedy of forgiveness, that tradition has been secularized. As a result of its secularization, the effect and significance of a play like *Cymbeline* has been importantly altered. The divinity that shapes the events of *Cymbeline* is far more mysterious than the constantly visible and available God of the miracles. (p. 181)

The miracle plays primarily celebrate God's love for man and the mercy which God is constantly willing to extend to his repentant creatures. The human virtue which the medieval plays exalt is man's love for God. These varieties of love remain important in *Cymbeline*, but the primary emphasis is shifted to two kinds of human love: the romantic love of man and woman, and charity. The most powerful emotional moment of the last scene of *Cymbeline* comes in the lines that dramatize the reunion of Posthumus and Imogen:

> *Imo.*: Why did you throw your wedded Lady fro you?
> Thinke that you are vpon a Rocke, and now
> Throw me againe.
> *Post.*: Hang there like fruite, my soule,
> Till the Tree dye.
>
> [V. v. 261-64]
> (p. 182)

Cymbeline contains a demonstration of the means by which the goodness of God operates effectually in his human creatures to rule them. The process of regeneration results in charity, and that process has its ultimate origin in the grace of God. The forgiveness of man by man, on which psychological and social order depends, is the result of the forgiveness of man by God. A knowledge of this full pattern is essential to a complete understanding of *Cymbeline*, but the primary emphasis in Shakespeare is upon the necessity for man's recognition of God's purposes, and upon the difficulty of that recognition. (pp. 183-84)

Robert Grams Hunter, " 'Cymbeline'," in his Shakespeare and the Comedy of Forgiveness, *Columbia University Press, 1965, pp. 142-84.*

BARBARA A. MOWAT (lecture date 1966)

[*In the following excerpt, taken from a lecture delivered in 1966, Mowat examines Shakespeare's use in* Cymbeline *of certain early Elizabethan dramatic conventions, including: "expository direct address" to the audience, extended soliloquies indiscriminately divided amongst the characters, and "undisguised entrance announcements and exit signals." However, whereas such earlier critics as Barrett Wendell (1894), E. K. Chambers (1907), and Brander Matthews (1913) have regarded such dramaturgical techniques as evidence of Shakespeare's declining powers or lack of interest in his material, Mowat maintains that he employed these conventions intentionally as a means of undercutting the dramatic illusion and distancing his audience from the fate of Imogen and Posthumus, a position that is shared by R. A. Foakes (1971). She concludes that the dramatist recognized that "his Romance story" could not sustain such tragic, painful events as the play depicts, and thus he alternated techniques of involvement—such as "colloquial language, interesting plot [and] appealing characters"—with artifices designed to remind the audience that this is a theatrical experience. Harley Granville-Barker (1930) has also examined the "self-conscious artlessness" of* Cymbeline *and Arthur C. Kirsch (see Additional Bibliography) has demonstrated the parallels between the dramaturgy of Shakespeare's play and the techniques of coterie drama.*]

Cymbeline has long been under critical attack: Johnson's famous comment on the play's moments of "unresisting imbecility," its "faults too evident for detection and too gross for aggravation" [see excerpt above, 1765] are echoed a century later in Granville-Barker's references to *Cymbeline*'s "banalities of stagecraft" [see excerpt above, 1930]—and critical opinion is almost unanimous that the dramatic technic of *Cymbeline* reveals a "disintegrating change" from the works which precede it. Attempts to explain this change have been various, and many of the explanations have a certain plausibility about them—that is, until we examine the tactical dramaturgy of *Cymbeline*. The suggestion that Shakespeare himself had changed, that he was "working, not wholly confidently, in a new medium" [J. M. Nosworthy; see Additional Bibliography] or for a new theatre, or that he had his mind on something other than drama—these might explain the peculiar structure—the general laying-out—of this play. "Artfully arranging" a play like *Cymbeline*, with its complex plot, its odd assortment of characters and motifs, might lead the most skillful dramatist astray, and result in the amorphous, absurdly complex and botched-up job that many consider *Cymbeline* to be. But dramatic tactics—the art of getting characters on and off the stage, of conveying information to the audience (the definition is, of course, Pinero's)—this a dramatist learns early or not at all; these are the basic skills of his craft, bungled in his apprentice-work, perhaps, but mastered long before he achieves greatness as a dramatist. And these very skills of basic dramaturgy, learned by Shakespeare so early in his career, seem to have most noticeably deserted him in the writing of *Cymbeline*.

In scene v of Act I of *Cymbeline*, for instance, Shakespeare has considerable information to convey to the audience and several entrances and exits to effect. His method of handling these dramaturgical details seems rather strange. In the first place, he puts all of his exposition into soliloquies and asides, addressed directly to the audience; no pertinent information is revealed through dialogue or action. In the second place, he distributes the soliloquies indiscriminately among major and minor characters alike, so that our interest never centers sharply on any one character. And, in the third place, he emphasizes the conventional entrance and exit announcements to a degree that is unexpected in a mature dramatist. The effect of this emphasis on expository soliloquies and asides and on stressed entrance and exit signals is that the scene seems audience-directed and somehow narrative in structure. The illusion that mature Shakespearian drama normally sets up—that illusion which is, to use William McCollum's words, "calculated to lift the spectator into a realm independent of the theatre and its platform stage"—this illusion is constantly shattered as we are repeatedly reminded of theatrical conventions and of our role as spectators at a theatrical performance.

Since this scene offers us in small compass a variety of tactics typical of *Cymbeline*, let us examine it briefly. The scene centers around Cymbeline's queen, her doctor, and Pisanio, a servant to Imogen's exiled husband, and it follows the famous "wager scene" in which Posthumus, an exile in Rome, accepts a wager on his wife Imogen's chastity. Onstage comes the queen, the doctor Cornelius, and a retinue of ladies. The first three lines of the dialogue brusquely clear the stage of unwanted listeners, and in the fourth line, the queen introduces the real business of the scene: "Now, master doctor, have you brought those drugs?" [I. v. 4]. The doctor hands the drugs, with expressed misgivings, to the queen. The dialogue which follows [I. v. 5-26] centers around the drugs as a deadly poison:

the queen wants to do experiments on small animals, she says; the doctor tries to dissuade her. In the light of what we later learn, the dialogue is pointless: the drugs are not poisonous at all, so that the doctor's argument is based on what he knows to be a lie, and the queen's on what she mistakenly believes to be the truth. But as the conversation takes place, we, as well as the queen, believe that the box contains "poisonous compounds." And, in spite of the queen's lengthy protestations of semi-innocent intentions, we begin to fear for Imogen's life.

Our fears seem justified when the queen, noting the entrance of Pisanio, turns from the doctor to address the audience directly. Her "aside" includes a variant of the "look where he comes" entrance announcement, and also flatly reveals the black intentions of her wicked heart: "Here comes a flattering rascal. Upon him will I first work. He's for his master and enemy to my son" [V. i. 27-9]. She then greets Pisanio, and dismisses the doctor with a standard, if brusque, exit request. Cornelius then utters his own "aside," and begins to set our fears at rest: "I do suspect you, madam, but you shall do no harm" [I. v. 31-2]. The queen takes Pisanio aside with the conventional "stand aside" request used to clear the stage for soliloquies: "Hark thee, a word" [I. v. 32]—and Cornelius moves forward to explain everything to the audience. His monologue, considered by Muriel Bradbrook to be "one of the most amusingly naive in Shakespeare," was attacked by Johnson as being "very inartificial. The speaker is under no pressure of thought . . . and yet makes a long speech to tell himself what himself knows." Actually, Cornelius is telling the audience, not himself—and the information he imparts is essential for our understanding of later scenes in the play. Only in this speech do we learn the truth about the box of drugs: "I do not like her," says Cornelius, and then proceeds, as Muriel Bradbrook puts it, to "dispose summarily of the old convention of the sleeping potion which appears to be a poison."

After Cornelius is once again dismissed from the stage and the queen and Pisanio move forward to continue their conversation, the tactics of the scene follow basically the same pattern as before. The elaborate dialogue is once again pointless—merely a cover for the transfer of the drugs, in the guise of precious medicine, from the queen to Pisanio. The queen's soliloquy is another self-revealing monologue describing her wicked plans—though now we know that the schemes must come to nothing, since the drugs are not poisonous. And the scene ends with Pisanio's little soliloquy, an exit-signalling couplet which drew from Furness this outburst: "Did William Shakespeare write this doggerel?"—to which Nosworthy replies, "The probable answer is, 'Alas, yes!'"

The repeated use of expository direct-address to tell the story to the audience, the casual distribution of soliloquies to very minor characters, the undisguised entrance announcements and exit-signals, all seem reminiscent of very early Shakespearian drama or even of pre-Shakespearian drama. Open recognition of the audience, an essentially narrative technic: these are characteristic of the mysteries and moralities from which the Elizabethan stage inherited its presentational conventions. The medieval drama was basically audience-directed, closely related to ritual and to platform oratory, and was designed not to enthrall and purge, but to teach and to reveal. The tactics of such drama: open address to the audience, basically narrative technique, simple theatrical speech, self-descriptive monologues—all helped to distance the spectators and make them reflect on how this story affected them personally and practically.

In Shakespeare's earliest plays—from the Henry VI trilogy through Comedy of Errors—the inherited conventions were employed much as they had been in pre-Shakespearian drama— as presentational elements in essentially presentational plays. Expository soliloquies, long and grandiose, were used to tell the story, fill in gaps in the action, provide a precis of events; asides were employed to explain obscure motives or to comment on the action. Entrances and exits were conscientiously explained, as if to clarify for the audience every stage-action. (pp. 39-43)

In mature Shakespearian drama . . . , presentational Elizabethan conventions are used when they are adequate for Shakespeare's purposes, but they are used in such a way that they obtrude little on the illusion that the characters are moving in a non-theatrical world—and they are made to contribute, whenever possible, to the over-all dramatic impact of the scene. With Cymbeline, however, we seem to return to very early Shakespearian tactics: once again, direct address is used to tell the story, soliloquies are scattered among the characters, and our interest is scattered as well. But, interestingly enough, the presentational conventions used in Cymbeline seem much more obtrusive than they do, say, in 3 Henry VI. Presentational conventions in 3 Henry VI are, of course, part of the general pattern of stylization, elaborate set speeches, balanced repetitions, patterned groupings, so that expository soliloquies or entrance announcements seem in keeping with the play as a whole; whereas, in Cymbeline, with its emphasis on story-line and suffering young lovers, the mode is essentially representational. Imbedded in a drama of intriguing story, appealing characters, and language real to the point of coarseness, presentational conventions are noticeably theatrical and startling. More than this, however, the conventions used in Cymbeline seem more than ordinarily artificial. The explanatory asides are naive, the exit couplets reduced to doggerel, the expository soliloquies banal and often redundant. One can never forget, for example, the long, grandiose monologue uttered by Belarius in Act III, with its famous closing lines:

At three and two years old I stole these babes . . .
                              Euriphile,
Thou wast their nurse; they took thee for their mother,
And every day do honor to her grave.
Myself, Belarius, that am Morgan call'd
They took for natural father.

                              [III. iii. 101, 103-07]

As Granville-Barker pointed out, we shall have to search far back in Shakespeare to find anything quite like this monologue, and shall be doubtful of finding it even there.

In the scene we earlier examined, nothing can quite compare with Belarius's soliloquy, but there is much that smacks of artifice. The queen's first "aside," for instance, combines the conventions of entrance-announcement, self-descriptive villainy and expository direct-address; the language is flat to the point of comic bluntness and the villainy is naively self-revealing: the artificiality of this "aside" seems deliberately heightened and our attention directed to its theatricality. Again, Cornelius's monologue is prefaced with four artificial conventions in quick succession, and he is bluntly ordered off-stage both before and after his monologue—as if Shakespeare had drawn an arrow pointing toward this flat, banally expository monologue. And Pisanio's obstinate silence throughout the scene calls our attention to his closing lines, doubtless the most ludicrous exit-signal ever penned by an Elizabethan playwright.

To call attention to the artificiality of a theatrical convention, as Shakespeare seems to do so often in *Cymbeline,* is to endanger the dramatic illusion. This is a fact much exploited by modern theatricalists like Wilder, Pirandello, Anouilh, or Giraudoux, who seek a heightened audience awareness of the theatrical medium and a consequent destruction of illusionist theatre. Brecht, who is even more in earnest about the dangers of illusion-mongering and the desirability of a distanced, critically alert audience, stresses constantly, in his plays, the artifice of theatrical representation, and reminds us again and again that we are only watching a play. Soliloquies, asides, obtrusive prompt-men, highly theatrical props, all are used to break the illusion and distance the audience from the play. If carried too far—as Edward Bullough pointed out in his classic essay on aesthetic distance—such distancing devices can reduce the play to absurdity. If we are made too aware of theatre—of stage-conventions, of props, of poor acting or writing—we fail to identify sufficiently with the "human beings" presented, are prevented from succumbing to that magical circle of experience which the drama normally provides, and, like Theseus and his court watching "Pyramus and Thisbe" [in *A Midsummer Night's Dream*], are amused, bored, or annoyed when we should be moved. But when theatricality is emphasized within limits, it can serve to help us maintain a proper distance from the play—can counteract the almost overwhelming tendency of drama to pull us into its spell, and can thus help us to respond to the play with just that degree of identification and concern proper to the kind of story being told.

In *Cymbeline,* I feel, Shakespeare uses presentational conventions, deliberately made artificial, in order to provide just that distancing needed for his Romance story. The effect he achieves is a peculiar one, because we are not consistently distanced from the characters and their suffering. Pulled into the story through the colloquial language, interesting plot, appealing characters, we are sporadically detached from it by sharp reminders that this is only a play, a theatrical representation which employs noticeably theatrical conventions. The effect which results is that varying aesthetic distance noted by R. J. Kaufmann as a characteristic of all of Shakespeare's Romances—that disciplined and calculatedly occasional involvement of the audience with the hero's material choices and sufferings, which makes the final plays seem so different from the tragedies and comedies. With the Romances, we seem to turn away from the mode of the great dramas to a heightened interest in story, to "intermittent engagement" in the play, "calculatedly occasional" identification with the hero, and to conventions used, in *Cymbeline* in particular, in such a way that they call attention to themselves as conventions, as theatrical devices, and, hence, to theatre. They then serve the purpose of all devices of theatricality: they bring to the center of our awareness the fact that we are in a theatre, and they distance us from the story.

Act III. Scene iv. Pisanio and Imogen. By J. Hoppner.

I would suggest, then, that the "crude dramaturgy" of *Cymbeline* is not experimental groping nor the sign of Shakespeare's failing powers, but is rather a late use of Elizabethan theatrical conventions. Shakespeare's sudden departure, in *Cymbeline*, from the path he had been following of fewer and fewer soliloquies and asides, to the burgeoning wealth of twenty-four soliloquies, countless asides, doggerel exit-signals, etc., seems to point to a new interest in what these conventions might be made to do; the actual effect of these conventions, as he used them, indicates that his interest in them, in *Cymbeline*, was as "theatrical devices," instruments for forcing the audience to view this romance from the proper distance. Too anguished a concern for Imogen, too deep an indignation over Posthumus's treatment of his faithful wife—such an emotional response this fairy-tale play cannot long support. And what better way to control audience concern and indignation than to forbid us to take the story seriously—to remind us again and again that we are in a theatre watching a play? (pp. 44-7)

> Barbara A. Mowat, "'Cymbeline': Crude Dramaturgy and Aesthetic Distance," in Renaissance Papers 1966, 1967, pp. 39-48.

HOMER D. SWANDER   (essay date 1966)

[*Like Robert Grams Hunter (1965) and James Edward Siemon (1976), Swander discovers marked similarities between Posthumus and Cloten, both in physical resemblances and in the feelings expressed in their respective soliloquies in Act II, Scene v and Act III, Scene v, which demonstrate their brutal and violent intentions towards Imogen. The critic sees Cloten as "a revealing caricature of Posthumus, exposing the dirty underside of his [Posthumus's] crime," and he argues that the burial of the corpse is simultaneously the interment of Cloten and, symbolically, the end of the "credulous and violent" Posthumus. Swander also asserts that the fundamental religious design of Cymbeline is evident in Act V, Scenes i through iv, for here Posthumus prayerfully seeks and receives God's grace and the forgiveness of his sins, thereby attaining Imogen's "level of insight and excellence" and wholly distinguishing himself from Cloten. Other critics who have discovered a similar pattern of sin, redemption, and forgiveness in this play include J. A. Bryant, Jr. (1961), Robert Grams Hunter (1965), Arthur C. Kirsch (1972), and Martin Lings (see Additional Bibliography).*]

One obvious purpose of [Act V, Scenes i-iv of *Cymbeline*], which constitute a clear structural unit with Posthumus at the center, is to convince us, now that we have not seen him for two acts, that he is at last worthy of Imogen. Within the confines of a familiar story—that of the slandered wife or bride—Shakespeare has until this point in the play emphasized to an unusual degree the moral failure of the credulous and murderous but well-meaning husband; and for the happy ending he can no longer content himself with Claudio's brief but conventionally satisfactory "Yet sinn'd I not / But in mistaking" (*Much Ado About Nothing* [V. i. 274-75]). There must for Posthumus be a genuine conversion in terms that openly repudiate the social and literary convention that allows such mistaken husbands or lovers to go uninstructed and unchanged to their comic reward, and the conversion initially takes the form of an unconventional conclusion about the morality of revenge. Having, he thinks, killed his apparently unfaithful wife, he suddenly sees his own viciousness and her virtue even though he still thinks her an adultress:

> Gods! if you
> Should have ta'en vengeance on my faults, I never

Had liv'd to put on this; so had you sav'd
The noble Imogen to repent, and struck
Me, wretch, more worth your vengeance.

> [V. i. 7-11]

No hero in any other medieval or Renaissance version of the story forgives the slandered woman until he knows she is innocent, at which time there is of course nothing to forgive; and even after her innocence is certain, no hero from the analogues arrives at any similar condemnation of himself: unlike Posthumus, he continues (quite properly, according to conventional morality) to believe that he was right to try to kill an apparently impure woman, and he returns to happy domesticity as easily as if he had only been out for a walk around the block.

The change in Posthumus appears variously—in his rejection, for example, of the revenge against Iachimo that is also conventionally due him [V. ii, v]; and the paradox of the early acts, when his conventional or external excellence goes unmatched by an excellence of spirit, is now, both in the imagery and the action, reversed. The most obvious sign is the peasant disguise, a real and symbolic move to develop inner strength, and proof that Posthumus at last knows not only what is wrong with himself but with the world in which he formerly excelled: "To shame the guise o' the world, I will begin / The fashion: less without and more within" [V. i. 32-3]. It is unnecessary to dwell upon how this move, accompanied by so many images of inner and outer worth, identifies itself with his new ability to distinguish between Imogen's real and apparent virtue. But we must also notice that the peasant disguise is only one of three, for his decision to disguise himself is of course unconventional only in its absoluteness, in his continuing determination to die unknown. The fear with which the conventional tragic or romantic hero contemplates anonymity is not easy to exaggerate; for him, name and reputation are often ultimate values—as in Cassio's lament: "Reputation, reputation, reputation! O, I have lost my reputation! I have lost the immortal part of myself . . ." [*Othello*, II. iii. 262-64]. And nearly the last concern of Othello himself is for the name he will leave behind him. Yet Posthumus slips from an Italian to a peasant to a Roman disguise for a single purpose—to die anonymously.

The significance of the peasant disguise, of Posthumus repudiating his courtly clothes and name, is great partly because three scenes earlier Cloten unsuccessfully depends for his life upon precisely these things. To Guiderius, who a moment later decapitates him, he says, "Know'st me not by my clothes? . . . Hear but my name, and tremble" [IV. ii. 81, 88]. This is what Posthumus calls "our fangled world" [V. iv. 134], with its characteristic, fatal faith in externals; and when Cloten dies because such a faith is all he has, his death is the exact opposite of and thus a preparation for what happens to Posthumus in Act V.

But because Cloten is at the moment of his death wearing Posthumus' clothes instead of his own (and he reminds us of it: "My tailer made them not" [IV. ii. 84]) the contrast is complex. Physically, the two men are identical—Imogen's error over the headless corpse (she believes it to be Posthumus) is remarkable for Shakespeare's nearly grotesque insistence upon detail:

> I know the shape of's leg; this is his hand,
> His foot Mercurial, his Martial thigh,
> The brawns of Hercules. . . .

> [IV. ii. 309-11]

Thus when Cloten first appears in Wales dressed in Posthumus' clothes and looking so much like him that in the theater we cannot miss it (the two characters, never on stage together, should be played by a single actor), the perfect fit of the stolen garments naturally stimulates a comparison:

> . . . the lines of my body are as well drawn as
> his; no less young, more strong, not beneath
> him in fortunes, beyond him in the advantage
> of the time, above him in birth, alike conversant
> in general services, and more remarkable in
> single oppositions. . . .
>
> [IV. i. 9-14]

For the braggart Cloten, this is unusually restrained; and it is apparently true that in all the points upon which he bases the comparison—lines, age, strength, fortune, social status, birth, military service, and dueling, all points by which the world judges excellence—either he has the advantage or he and Posthumus are about the same. If clothes make the man, Cloten is as good as Posthumus, perhaps better.

The hints of some ironic similarity between the two go further. Although in first-act imagery Cloten is a "puttock" and Posthumus an "eagle" [I. i. 139-40], by the end of Act II the latter's actions over the wager have narrowed the difference. Then in the scene directly after we hear the murderous orders to Pisanio—when, that is, our opinion of Posthumus is at its lowest—Cloten soliloquizes upon Imogen:

> I love and hate her; for she's fair and royal,
> And that she hath all courtly parts more exquisite
> Than lady, ladies, woman; from every one
> The best she hath, and she, of all compounded,
> Outsells them all. I love her therefore; but
> Disdaining me and throwing favours on
> The low Posthumus slanders so her judgment
> That what's else rare is chok'd; and in that point
> I will conclude to hate her, nay, indeed,
> To be reveng'd upon her.
>
> [III. v. 70-9]

Strangely enough, Cloten, while thus working out his own attitude toward Imogen, in effect defines, crudely but surely, the attitude that credulity creates in Posthumus; for the insensitivity of the latter's own soliloquy against Imogen, when drained of rhetoric, comes down to little more than Cloten's blunt stupidity. Having decided to "tear her limbmeal" [II. iv. 147], Posthumus rages:

> Some coiner with his tools
> Made me a counterfeit; yet my mother seem'd
> The Dian of that time. So doth my wife
> The nonpareil of this. O, vengeance, vengeance!
> Me of my lawful pleasure she restrain'd
> And pray'd me oft forbearance; did it with
> A pudency so rosy the sweet view on't
> Might well have warm'd old Saturn; that I thought her
> As chaste as unsunn'd snow. O, all the devils!
> This yellow Iachimo in an hour,—was't not?—
> Or less,—at first?—perchance he spoke not, but,
> Like a full-acorn'd boar, a German one,
> Cried "O!" and mounted; found no opposition
> But what he look'd for should oppose and she
> Should from encounter guard. . . .
>
> [II. v. 5-19]

Like Cloten, Posthumus believes that Imogen "outsells" all other women; but for him, too, a presumed crime "slanders so her judgment / That what's else rare is chok'd" [III. v. 76-7]; and he, like Cloten, concludes to hate and be revenged.

More than this, Shakespeare characterizes the violence that each would do her—murder in the one case, rape in the other—in the imagery of dress that prepares for and develops the symbolic action of the peasant disguise. Of Posthumus' order for her murder, Imogen (wrong about the motive but right about the quality of the act) says:

> Poor I am stale, a garment out of fashion;
> And, for I am richer than to hang by the walls
> I must be ripp'd.—To pieces with me!
>
> [III. iv. 51-3]

And Cloten later says, "How fit his garments serve me! Why should his mistress . . . not be fit too?" [IV. i. 2-3, 4]. The men are alike, then, in this, too—that each, blind to the Imogen that even Iachimo sees [II. ii. 50], would treat her like a garment, valuing her no more highly than last year's doublet or another man's cloak.

Shakespeare does not, I think, press the strange similarity much further, yet he has done enough to fill Cloten's death and funeral with unusual significance. Dressed in Posthumus' clothes, like him in a variety of superficial and one or two crucial ways, but always cruder, more obvious, Cloten becomes a revealing caricature of Posthumus, exposing the dirty underside of his crime, suggesting that there is, after all, some appalling kinship between the "puttock" and the "eagle." The mask of self-righteousness and conventional correctness is gone, revealing a different face; but here are the same clothes, the same body, a love that can turn to hate, a mind that feeds on revenge.

The clothes and the body, to be sure, constitute "so fair an outward" [I. i. 23] as to promise much, a fact emphasized by Lucius when he says of the corpse, "The ruin speaks that sometime / It was a worthy building" [IV. ii. 354-55]; and Posthumus at last proves "as good as promise" while Cloten is "a fool, an empty purse; / There was no money in't" [V. iv. 137; IV. ii. 113-14]. But the memory of the similarity continues as Posthumus proves himself. After Imogen buries the corpse, thinking it Posthumus, we never again see him in the dress of a British courtier; the actions and imagery combine to suggest that his former unworthiness lies buried with the courtly garments that cover the deceptive corpse. This burial is not only the end of Cloten, the man who could not love, but of the conventionally proper Posthumus, credulous and violent. Because Shakespeare keeps Posthumus off stage for Acts III and IV, we do not watch his struggle against the empty virtue that blinds him. We watch, instead, its symbolic life and death in the caricature named Cloten; and the burial of this Posthumus prepares us for the appearance of the new.

More important than anything else, however, is that Shakespeare's consistently developed religious terminology makes Posthumus' crime a sin: in his attempt to murder Imogen, he rejects the "gift of the gods" [I. iv. 85], the gods' "own" [V. i. 16] and attacks "divineness" [III. vi. 43] by means of a "sacrilegious" servant [V. v. 220]. His remorse is therefore, as one would expect, openly religious, an acceptance not simply of a woman but of grace. When he appears in Act V his mind is full of God, and the four scenes that he dominates develop, in their substance and their shape, religious meanings that begin in the earlier acts and conclude only with the last lines of the play.

An early moment of crucial importance is of course that in which Posthumus accepts the slander as true, and there Shakespeare presents the failure as not only moral but religious. Just as Posthumus' love fails to give him a knowledge of Imogen (for he believes the slander), his faith fails to help him recognize false piety or careless swearing, for it is finally Iachimo's oath—"By Jupiter, I had it [the bracelet] from her arm"—that convinces him: "Hark you, he swears; by Jupiter he swears. / 'Tis true,—nay, keep the ring—'tis true" [II. iv. 121, 122-23]. Two passages from the preceding scene define this failure, Imogen providing as she so often does the standard by which we judge her husband. When Cloten says to her, "Still, I swear I love you," she replies:

> If you but said so, 'twere as deep with me.
> If you swear still, your recompense is still
> That I regard it not.
>
> [II. iii. 90-3]

And when he slanders Posthumus, she answers:

> Wert thou the son of Jupiter and no more
> But what thou art besides, thou wert too base
> To be his groom.
>
> [II. iii. 125-27]

No empty oaths and nothing simply external, however exalted, will blind her to the truth or shake her fidelity to it. This is the insight that Posthumus lacks when he allows the name of Jupiter to destroy his love; and unless he gains it we are not likely ever to think him worthy of what the gods have given him.

Most of his soliloquy at the beginning of Act V is thus appropriately a prayer in which he begins to see how the gods are working with him—

> You some permit
> To second ills with ills, each elder worse,
> And make them dread it, to the doers' thrift—
>
> [V. i. 13-15]

and in which he submits himself to the divine will: "make me blest to obey" [V. i. 17]. Furthermore, all of his actions and intentions—the re-evaluation of himself and Imogen, his use of disguise, the plan to strengthen his inner self and to seek death in battle, all those matters in the soliloquy that shape the next scenes—are in the deepest sense religious, for they are framed as prayer. All other meanings, that is, come to serve the religious meaning.

In scene four, Posthumus, now a prisoner of the British, prays again, welcoming his almost certain execution as the "way . . . to liberty," the "key / T' unbar" the locks that hold him [V. iv. 3-4, 7-8]. But his conscience is still, in spite of all, "fetter'd / More than my shanks and wrists," and he prays the "good gods" to give him "The penitent instrument to pick that bolt; / Then"—*and only then*—"free for ever!" [V. iv. 8-9, 10-11]. He prays not simply for death but for salvation.

The prayer continues:

> Is't enough I am *sorry*?
> So children temporal fathers do appease;
> Gods are more full of mercy. Must I *repent*,
> I cannot do it better than in gyves,
> Desir'd more than constrain'd; to *satisfy*,
> If of my freedom 'tis the main part, take

No stricter render of me than my all.
I know you are more clement than vile men,
Who of their broken debtors take a third,
A sixth, a tenth, letting them thrive again
On their abatement. That's not my desire.
For Imogen's dear life take mine. . . .

> [V. iv. 11-22]

The religious language here is precise, Posthumus carefully moving through the three steps necessary for remission of sins—sorrow, repentance, and satisfaction—and Shakespeare emphasizes the orthodox structure and fullness of the contrition by anchoring those three alternate lines with the operative word (here italicized). From the idea of satisfaction (or payment) come quite naturally images of debt, money, and weight to take their place in the pattern of such images that distinguishes the play, everywhere encouraging us to compare and evaluate the characters:

> For Imogen's dear life take mine; and though
> 'Tis not so dear, yet 'tis a life; you coin'd it.
> 'Tween man and man they weigh not every stamp;
> Though light, take pieces for the figure's sake;
> You rather mine, being yours; and so, great powers,
> If you will take this audit, take this life,
> And cancel these cold bonds.
>
> [V. iv. 22-8]

This is the final contrast of Imogen and Posthumus because he has now, through sin and contrition, reached her level of insight and excellence. He now deserves the fate that this traditional story of slander conventionally awards its heroes with no such achievement demanded; and he has pleased God. In the very asking for the "penitent instrument," he has been granted it, as Shakespeare reveals through the divine vision to which the prayer directly leads. In the economy of salvation, God in fact anticipates: the strength to ask for grace is itself a gift of grace, the proof of this in the play coming from the vision in the words of Jupiter himself: "Whom best I love I cross; to make my gift, / The more delay'd, delighted . . . Our jovial star reign'd at his birth . . ." [V. iv. 101-02, 105]. Shakespeare is here evoking the mystery of the relationship between free will and predestination, time and eternity, natural virtue and grace. If natural virtue is all there is, Posthumus—great though his virtues certainly are—cannot escape an essential identification with Cloten; it is only as in two prayers he accepts and in four scenes exercises supernatural virtue that he proves himself worthy of the love that offers such strength. He has, that is, had to earn in time the gift that was freely granted in eternity; though chosen of God, he has nevertheless had freely to choose (after first rejecting) the gift that was always his. (pp. 249-56)

Homer D. Swander, "'Cymbeline': Religious Idea and Dramatic Design," in Pacific Coast Studies in Shakespeare, *edited by Waldo F. McNeir and Thelma N. Greenfield, University of Oregon, 1966, pp. 248-62.*

WILLIAM BARRY THORNE   (essay date 1969)

[*Thorne argues that the dramatic structure of* Cymbeline *is related to that of fairy tales or the traditional mummers' folk dramas, which served as ritual reenactments of the death of the old year and the birth of the new one, and he thus regards the idea of renewal, regeneration, and reconciliation as the primary focus of the play. Demonstrating the similarities between Shakespeare's play and folklore literature, Thorne asserts that* Cymbeline *is associated with winter and "antifertility" by his obstruction of the marriage of Imogen and Posthumus, who, in turn, represent scapegoat figures whose sacrifice and suffering provide "the basis for a regeneration of the kingdom and the spiritually sterile king." Similarly, the critic compares Guiderius to the archetypal folk hero who first appears as a penniless outcast but succeeds to his rightful position on the throne by defeating the forces which threaten the nation. Like G. Wilson Knight (1947) and Harold C. Goddard (1951), Thorne regards* Cymbeline *as "a national play," contending that it celebrates "England herself . . . , her culture and her people" and demonstrates the reconciliation of disordered elements within an ordered kingdom. Both Denton J. Snider (1890) and Robert Grams Hunter (1965) have also discussed the significance of the theme of regeneration in* Cymbeline; *in addition, Derek Traversi (1954) and Nancy K. Hayles (1980) have concluded that a central concern of the play is with the reconciliation and integration of opposing elements in an ordered society.*]

Shakespeare's *Cymbeline* is a regrettably underrated and overlooked play. Misunderstood and evaluated upon false grounds, it is far better than many commentators recognize, for it embraces a multeity of Shakespearian devices, themes, and structural principles, with an energy of fusion characteristic only of the dramatist's maturity. Part of the trouble with the typical analysis of *Cymbeline* would seem to result from the fruitlessness of applying methods of critical realism to this type of play. In the gossamer tissue of the play's action, the dramatist did not attempt full-scale psychological portraits; nor did he foresee the malignant "motive hunting" of some of those "literalists of the imagination" who currently infest the standing pool of literary criticism. Too much, therefore, can be made of a lack of realism in the treatment of action and character in *Cymbeline,* for the play is dealing with romantic materials exclusively, and it is processing them with the emotional logic of the folk, the cohesive inner reality of fairy tales, of folk ritual, and of the folk-drama. (p. 143)

[If] one takes the play for what it is, a sophisticated extension of themes from the early comedies, and observes what is actually happening on the stage, not what one would like to be happening, or what one feels should be happening in view of the dramatist's past history, the play is well-balanced, exciting, and rapidly paced. It is really not so different from the other late plays as it may appear upon cursory inspection, and it is actually rather good, when one relinquishes prejudices and settles back to enjoy a "folk" experience. Though the poetry is not always equal to Shakespeare's best, an organic fusion and an imaginative congruity pervade the action. . . . The imagery which complements the brilliantly manipulated plot is consistent and sensitively attuned to the major themes, for it is designed to carry the spectator beyond the immediate terms of reference of the play into the world of myth, of fairy tale, and romance.

In this play, moreover, we do not merely fall under the spell of "golden unrealities", for at the heart of all the comedies, especially the late ones, lies an undercurrent of very real seriousness. *Cymbeline,* with its balanced development, its national orientation, and its folk materials, is deliberately holding up a glass to Elizabethan culture; but the act of holding up the glass is, in itself, a ritual gesture, for this play, of all the late plays, is closest to the spirit of the people and requires a ritualistic presentation. *Cymbeline* is, therefore, not simply a history play; it is, as [G. Wilson] Knight suggests, a "national" play [see excerpt above, 1947], a sophisticated, professional "mummers' play", in the largest sense of that word, a play whose *raison d'être* seems to be to extol English culture, English morality, and the English race. A performance of *Cymbe-*

line is, in some respects, a patriotic affirmation of national unity and a sentimental extolling of established social mores.

In *Cymbeline* and the other comedies, the same basic principle would appear to lie behind Shakespeare's frequent use of folk materials, chronicle history, and plot incidents from other plays. Relying heavily on the stock responses of his audience, he usually selects material which would already be familiar to most of them. This manipulation of familiar devices, scenes, and concepts, sometimes from an oral tradition as well, assures the dramatist of certain predictable reactions on the part of his audience, and leads to an almost ritual character in his drama. His general dependence on Holinshed for pseudo-history, his acquaintance with the relevant section of the *Decameron,* and his apparent use of *The Rare Triumphs of Love and Fortune* and *Frederyke of Jennen,* for example, are recognizable enough borrowings, and are sound indications that the raw materials of *Cymbeline* were probably already known to most of Shakespeare's audience.

It is not enough, however, to regard the play as simply a "history", nor as a sophisticated restyling of a tale from Boccaccio's *Decameron.* What is vital to a satisfactory interpretation of *Cymbeline* is the further recognition that it was often Shakespeare's method in the comedies to process his material after the fashion of folk-drama, and to subordinate his "borrowings" to a clear dramatic purpose and a structural development often indebted to English folk-drama. The unbelievable diversity of plot materials, the seeming "incongruity" attacked by Johnson [see excerpt above, 1765], and the apparently hopelessly varied plot threads in *Cymbeline* are ultimately bound up in an indissoluble union by the brilliant technical control of the final act, a control which seems to have evolved through intensive experiment with folk themes and methods. (pp. 144-45)

Cymbeline, like the other late plays, is dedicated to examining [the] role of youth and love in the operation of the community. As in the early comedies, love's regenerative qualities are uppermost in the action; but these regenerative qualities are not limited to the young alone or to those immediately involved, for they are distributed ritually to the community at large. This view of the development of Shakespeare's comic vision is not merely speculative. The enlargement of scope in the late plays contributes to their "high seriousness", the broader view of life which deepens their philosophic basis. In these plays, organized society profits immensely from the seasonal pulse in human life; the tremendous good generated by enlargement of the spirit and the vital forces, symbolized by love and the spring season, floods into the lives of the mature adults as well and revitalizes the community. This phenomenon in the late comedies parallels the principles lying behind fertility rituals, in which mummers distribute the nature spirit to the whole community by passing through the village and literally spreading nature's holiness. (p. 146)

Like the bulk of Shakespearian comedies, *Cymbeline* begins in trouble and ends in joy. In the opening scene, Cymbeline, unlike Pericles and Leontes [in *The Winter's Tale*], is not in great prosperity. In fact, he has been for some time in the sterile period which develops only in the later action of the other two plays. When we first see him, Cymbeline is acting as the heavy father, who resents the fact that his daughter has ignored his "consent" and married against his wishes. His irrational and unhealthy attitude reminds us of Leontes' jealousy in *The Winter's Tale,* and Polixenes' later tyranny in opposing his son's marriage to Perdita [in *Pericles*]. To emphasize this traditional situation, the play adopts as its structural basis the polar construction observable in many of the other comedies, and, at the end of scene four, garbs Imogen's last remarks about her plight in the winter-summer imagery of the early comedies:

> . . . or ere I could
> Give him that parting kiss, which I had set
> Betwixt two charming words, comes in my father,
> And like the tyrannous breathing of the north,
> Shakes all our buds from growing.
>
> [I. iii. 33-7]

In the opening movement of the action, obviously, Cymbeline's wrath and tyranny act as the "sneaping" wind of winter, which blights love, marriage, and life itself. By this symbolism, he is immediately aligned on the side of "antifertility", for he is ignoring the dictates of the season, and has imposed his "law" upon the young people with the rigor and inflexibility of the "law of Athens" in *A Midsummer Night's Dream*. The opening passage of the play also makes it quite clear that the King is alone in his view of the marriage of his daughter, and has no real support from his community for his actions towards her. At this juncture, the only difference between Cymbeline and Egeus of *A Midsummer Night's Dream,* or Polixenes, for that matter, is that the winter of his tyranny and aged wrath is visited *ex post facto* upon the young lovers. Because Imogen and Posthumus are already married, Cymbeline is committing essentially the sin of Leontes in interrupting the sacred fertility of consecrated marriage and banishing Posthumus from the community. Symbolically, in the first section of the play, Winter obtrudes upon joyous Spring unnaturally and unlawfully, and banishes Spring from the community until it can finally be restored to favor in the second section, through the actions of the younger generation. (pp. 147-48)

Because Cymbeline is the symbolic center of the tensions of the kingdom, it is in him that the final reconciliations are effected. Though we recognize that, basically, Cymbeline, through a series of temptations, is made to lose all that is dear to him (his friend, his sons, his daughter and virtuous son-in-law, his ally, and, almost, his kingdom), the immediate emphasis of the action is not upon the past or upon recrimination, for his previous life is of little interest or weight. There are very few lines directed toward accusation and condemnation of the suffering King, and there is no Paulina figure [as in *The Winter's Tale*] to act as his conscience and guide him to repentance. Rather the emphasis is upon restoration and redemption of others who are worthy, and the long concluding scene of the play presents a sequence of discoveries and regenerative experiences for those who figure significantly in the action, experiences which work for the good of the nation as a whole. The King's regenerative experience, important because he distributes praise to Posthumus, Belarius, and his own two sons, without knowing who they are, is the initial one. Though . . . his first impulse is to avenge himself mercilessly upon his Roman captives, he forswears his old evil self and signals the new order by forgiving Belarius and sparing his captives, and in the final great act of union there is a place even for Iachimo.

The "argument" of the play is simple, for it is based on situations of a folk- or fairy-tale nature. The old King is furious, because his daughter has refused to marry the brutish son of her wicked stepmother, and has, against her father's wishes, married a desirable young man who, as orphan ward to the King, "in's spring became a harvest" [I. i. 46]. We learn that the two boy children of the King had been, in their infancy, spirited away, and the kingdom is deprived of male issue. . . . Now that the younger generation is alienated (Posthumus is banished, and Imogen is in confinement), the King stands virtually alone, unsupported by his subjects and deceived by his wife and stepson. We are given to believe that he is being punished for past injustices, particularly his persecution of innocent Belarius, and his reign . . . will be marked by unhappiness and evil until his sons are reinstated in their rightful place. (pp. 149-50)

Act Three, scene three, introduces the country setting of the cave of Belarius and his supposed sons, Guiderius and Arviragus. The opening action is presented in ritual fashion, with their obeisance to the sun and their ritual hunt; and their appearance, with the discovery that these are the true sons of the King, heralds the return of good and prosperity to Cymbeline's realm. In general, the nature scenes in *Cymbeline* are designed as a sharp philosophical contrast to the action at court, and the conceptual structure is thus based on the simple dichotomy of court—country. Because of the misguided acts of the King, evil is resident at court, and the forces of regeneration must come from nature herself, where the "lopp'd branches" of the King have taken root and "leav'd" under the guidance of Belarius, who had been wrongfully banished from court.

In *Cymbeline,* the familiar wedding of the virtues of court and country extends the point of view handled so sensitively in *The Winter's Tale,* by grafting a "gentler scion" of a courtly tree "to the wildest stock" to make conceive "a bark of baser kind / By bud of nobler race" [*The Winter's Tale,* IV. iv. 93, 94-5]. This treatment of the values of country and city, focussed in the resolution, is a good example of the fertilizing result of the juxtaposition of polar opposites in Shakespearian comedy. *Cymbeline* is based upon this principle, not only in the mingling of the natural with the sophisticated man, but in the familiar age-youth conflict which eventuates in fertility and success for the kingdom. The "order-disorder" polarity also shares in the construction, for the social regeneration which crowns the wintry passions of the play is to be achieved only through the healthful plunge into chaos during the first three acts.

It seems quite clear that, as in *Romeo and Juliet,* the relation between the two lovers has a bearing upon the community and the relation of the King to his people, for a potentially destructive situation is resolved through the actions of the lovers. The young must suffer in this play, for it seems that their sacrifice insures the well-being of the community. . . . Clearly, the young in *Cymbeline* are significant participants and even scapegoats to a degree; their agony provides the basis for a regeneration of the kingdom and the spiritually sterile King.

In *The Hero: A Study in Tradition, Myth, and Drama,* Lord Raglan makes some fascinating comments about the folk hero which seem to have particular relevance to the late plays, especially to *Cymbeline*. He explains that:

> In many stories in which the hero ends by ascending the throne and reigning as if to the manner born, he is represented as starting life as a pauper, but this is done, as I shall try to show later, to explain the fact that in the typical myth the hero has to pass through a period of adversity. It is usually found that, though ostensibly the son of a peasant, he is really a prince who in early infancy was either stolen by an enemy or hidden from a tyrant by his friends. . . .

Variants of this traditional situation appear in all the late plays and seem especially meaningful in *Pericles,* in which the prince appears as a poor stranger at the court of Simonides, and in *Cymbeline,* in which the two sons start life as simple mountain peasants, sons of a banished man. This parallel with the archetypal folk hero, deliberate or no, increases the associations of sanctity which invest the second generation in the late plays. Even when the second generation is female, the concept of disguise or humble upbringing is still used to contribute to the thematic development of the play. (pp. 152-53)

Cymbeline's sons are first presented as idealized symbols of "the kingly nature blooming in wild surroundings" [E. M. W. Tillyard]. When we first meet then, the Princes are wearing skins and might well have appeared also as mummers to an Elizabethan audience. Furthermore, the pagan associations of caves contribute to the "folk" flavor of the action. Certainly, the plot situation has real resemblance to the materials of the Robin Hood legend, which is similarly indebted to folk ritual and drama. Like Robin, Belarius (and hence his "sons") is outlawed; he and the boys have true nobility of soul and charity of heart, which we see during the battle and later, when pardon and forgiveness are dominant motifs. For a time, they, too, have with them a virtuous girl dressed in clothes of a man. It seems obvious that Belarius, like Camillo of *The Winter's Tale,* is an agent of rebirth working in mysterious ways, and like the doctor of the mummers' plays, Paulina, Perdita, and Marina, he gives "physic" to Cymbeline's realm. Richard Wincor suggests that Belarius is similar to Prospero in *The Tempest,* for he leaves civil life because of injustice, goes back to nature, "and there finds ways of affecting the community which he left, giving it a degree of rebirth at the end" [see Additional Bibliography]. One of the major assumptions of this portion of the action is that true virtue and rank cannot be obscured by position in society, and Belarius says to Imogen: "nor measure our good minds / By this rude place we live in" [III. vi. 64-5]. Showing itself in the royal mien of two lads reared in the mountains, the "noble strain" cannot be dimmed by circumstance, and Guiderius and Arviragus are presented as polar opposites to brutish Cloten, whose place cannot erase the evil of his personality.

In Act Three, scene four, Pisanio gives "winter news" to Imogen, who, distraught at her husband's suspicions, assumes the disguise of a boy and journeys to become a companion to Lucius. The device of the heroine in man's clothing and mistaken for a man harks back to the early comedies, for it is not to be found in *Pericles* or *The Tempest,* and is used only briefly in *The Winter's Tale.* Transvestism was a dominant feature of misrule celebrations during this period, for it clearly symbolized a disturbance in both nature and the social order and accentuated the sexual meanings central to the ritual itself. The "maid in man's clothing" was also a favorite theme in the Robin Hood legend and contributes additional accretions of meaning to the mountain scenes.

Structurally, by dividing the "winter" and the "summer" sections of the play, Imogen's flight to the woods acts as a symbolic center of gravity in the action. This traditional folk theme introduces in *Cymbeline* a species of misrule, a flight away from the evil and chaos at court, and a temporary reversal of role which corresponds to the "holiday world-real world" polarity in the early comedies, and provides a further perspective on the action. As a device for converging structural and symbolic threads of the action, it serves very well to remove most of the main characters from court and to reshuffle the

previous balance between good and evil, strongly in favor of good. Serving also to increase suspense and render the final brilliant chain of dénouements all the more unexpected, the flight to the woods introduces the theme of the kidnapped princes and opens the way for the regeneration of Cymbeline's realm, a regeneration which is to come from Nature herself.

Act Four introduces an important and puzzling sequence involving the two Princes and Cloten, as he searches for Imogen and Posthumus. It is interesting that the beheading scene is prepared for in advance by Cloten's threat in soliloquy: "Posthumus, thy head (which now is growing upon thy shoulders) shall within this hour be off, thy mistress enforced, thy garments cut to pieces before thy face" [IV. i. 15-18]. Editors and commentators have been disturbed to notice that the "flyting match" between Cloten and Guiderius seems out of character for the latter. But the obviously careful preparation for the scene seems to point toward a deliberate purpose in the brutality of Guiderius' treatment of Cloten, not, as is usually felt, toward carelessness on the part of the dramatist.

Though the deliberate hacking off of the head and the triumphant attitude certainly seem out of character for a young man who is otherwise presented in quite an idealistic manner, the "borrowed clothing" motif and the braggart vaunting of Cloten, in combination with the slanging match and the deliberate beheading, remind one of the typical mummers' Sword Dance, in which the fool is beheaded and then is revived by a doctor. Certainly, on stage, the tableau of the Prince, dressed in skins and in combat with Cloten, who is wearing the clothing of Posthumus, might have reminded the audience of the folk-drama, and certainly it represents the symbolic assertion of the forces of good, for the beheading is their first positive act. The parallel between the fight and the traditional beheading seems to be present, though we know that it is Cloten, not Posthumus, who is beheaded; in fact, Cloten seems to take the place of Posthumus in death, just as the Queen must die to free Cymbeline from mental and spiritual bondage. Later, we see that Posthumus does come to life again for Imogen, as she does for him, and, more important, he experiences a spiritual rebirth.

The brags and insults between Cloten and the young Prince are also reminiscent of the symbolic battle and *renouveau* ["regeneration"] of the Saint George mummers' play, in which Saint George kills a braggart character, and the doctor eventually revives him. What has happened is simply that the idyllic Hero-Prince has killed a grotesque monster and we need feel no pity for the victim. I think the most significant statement during this scene is Cloten's brag: "To thy further fear, / Nay, to thy mere confusion, thou shalt know / I am son to th' queen" [IV. ii. 91-3]. Extravagant boasting and retorts characterize the mummers' plays of this nature, and Belarius even makes indirect reference to the dragon of the legend; "then on good ground we fear, / If we do fear this body hath a tail / More perilous than the head" [IV. ii. 143-45]. The idea of decapitating the beast Cloten and hurling his head into a creek to "tell the fishes he's the Queen's son, Cloten" [IV. ii. 153], seems to reinforce the folk nature of this scene.

The beheading scene is followed dramatically by the supposed death of Imogen. Arviragus appears, carrying the body of Imogen, and they lament her as a dead bird, a lily blasted; images of summer flowers and fairies fill the dialogue at this point, as the Princes determine to keep fresh her memory. "With fairest flowers / Whilst summer lasts, and I live here, Fidele, / I'll sweeten thy sad grave" [IV. ii. 218-20], exclaims Arviragus, who goes on to liken the various parts of Fidele to flowers. In covering her body with flowers, the brothers give her, not a Christian, but a pagan burial, which concludes with an exorcism of evil paralleling Imogen's own prayer before retiring on the night that Iachimo stole her bracelet:

> Gui.   No exorciser harm thee!
> Arv.   Nor no witchcraft charm thee!
> Gui.   Ghost unlaid forbear thee!
> Arv.   Nothing ill come near thee!
> Both.   Quiet consummation have,
>   And renowned be thy grave!
>   [IV. ii. 276-81]

This ritual chant reminds us of Puck's invocation of fertility spirits at the end of *A Midsummer Night's Dream*. The whole scene is decidedly central to the action, for it magnifies the theme of regeneration, and the subsequent dialogue makes clear that this was a necessary experience, vital to the relationship between the main characters. (pp. 154-56)

Act Five, which concerns itself with the regeneration of the main characters and the revitalization of the kingdom, opens with Posthumus' determination to support the British cause. In his soliloquy, he delivers an apostrophe to Britain and claims that, because he has killed her mistress (Imogen), he will give no further wound to her, but will fight against the Romans who had brought him to British shores. [Robin] Moffet remarks significantly about this section that "Posthumus finds his life worthless and desperate until he has offered it to the gods" [see excerpt above, 1962]. The rout first suffered by the British forces in the resulting battle seems designed to symbolize the cankerous evil which had drained the realm of its vitality, and also represents the punishment of the gods for the evil committed by the King. The battle itself is presented by simple exposition and dumb show, with Posthumus defeating Iachimo, and assisting Belarius, Guiderius, and Arviragus in rescuing Cymbeline.

The dream sequence which follows this action presents the god Jupiter's prophecy in terms of *renouveau:* "and when from a stately cedar shall be lopp'd branches, which, being dead many years, shall after revive, be jointed to the old stock, and freshly grown, then shall Posthumus end his miseries, Britain be fortunate, and flourish in peace and plenty" [V. iv. 140-44]. This prophecy makes quite clear the symbolic link between Posthumus and the success and prosperity of Britain, for it reminds us that the tribulations undergone by the young are necessary and good, and will result in final happiness. Posthumus' intriguing vision is not just a fanciful element gratuitously introduced into a hodgepodge of romantic materials; it is an integral part of the play, insuring preservation of the unity and fertility of the kingdom, and complementing the earlier revelations that Cloten is also a fool, the Queen's drug is really harmless, and the sons of Cymbeline are still living. This device of the *deus ex machina,* used to marshal and support the forces of good, is not at all foreign to the late plays; Diana appears in *Pericles;* Juno, Iris, and Ceres sing in *The Tempest;* and Time and the Oracle of Apollo serve in *The Winter's Tale* to assure us that eventually all will be well. As an agent of regeneration, Jupiter is a dramatic necessity, for by his pronouncement he counteracts the cruelty, violence, and evil which have afflicted the main characters during most of the action.

The magnificent concluding scene of recognition and reconciliation emphasizes that Imogen, to Pisanio, Belarius, Guiderius, Arviragus, Cymbeline, and Posthumus, is truly "reborn". Belarius asks in astonishment: "Is not this boy reviv'd

from death?" [V. v. 120]. And Imogen herself believes that she was, in fact, dead: "Most like it did, for I was dead" [V. v. 259]. The confrontations of this scene make it abundantly clear that Shakespeare has constantly had his hands on the reins of the action, guiding and urging it through incident and imagery to the ultimate unification; for the fate of every character really depends on the outcome of Imogen's interrogation of Iachimo.

To complete the balance of the symbolic action, the tree imagery, which had appeared earlier, recurs in this scene in Posthumus's lovely line, "Hang there like fruit, my soul, / Till the tree die" [V. v. 263-64], and culminates in the theme of regeneration in the statement of Jupiter. It is interesting that Cymbeline's reaction to the reconciliation, when he exclaims: "If this be so, the gods do mean to strike me / To death with mortal joy" [V. v. 234-35], is much like that of Pericles and emphasizes the similarity between the two plays. With the confession of Iachimo, the "supposes" complication is unravelled, and the elaborate system of discrepancies in awareness is dispelled. The revelations come thick and fast, as Belarius reveals the truth about himself and Arviragus and Guiderius, identifying Arviragus by the device of a "most curious mantle", made by his mother, and Guiderius by a birth mark, a "sanguine star", which is a common device in fairy tales [V. v. 361, 364].

Concluding with rebirth and a certain discovery of self, the play has been concerned with the fall and the restoration of both the King and his realm. Though in the beginning of the play his role was highly stereotyped, in the end Cymbeline is the figure in whom all the resolutions and unifications of the concluding scene are focused. Though he has been misguided and blind and has fostered evil and folly in the heart of his kingdom, the scales are ripped from his eyes and he becomes the central symbol of reunification. In exclaiming, "Oh, what am I? / A mother to the birth of three?" [V. v. 368-69] Cymbeline identifies his role in the action and focusses the main theme of the play upon the restoration of his three children and the reunification of the community. With rebirth as the dominant motif of this concluding scene, Cymbeline's remark that, by this happy return, Imogen has lost a kingdom, elicits from his daughter the touching reply: "No, my lord, / I have got two worlds by't" [V. v. 373-74]. The reconciliations between father and daughter, and wife and husband are accompanied by a similar reconciliation between Britain and Rome; Britain is returned to the Roman fold, just as Imogen, Guiderius, and Arviragus are returned to their father's arms, and the play concludes in a fashion similar to that of the early comedies, with a union of lovers and a majestic marriage of Britain and Rome.

The two dreams of prophecy in this play provide a focal point for the final series of reconciliations, because traditionally the eagle's flight into the sun was believed to renew his youth, and hence Philarmonus' dream, like Jupiter's prophecy, becomes a subtle indication of the general rejuvenation and renewal of life pervading the action. When the Soothsayer interprets the Oracle of Jupiter (much in the fashion of the interpretation of the Oracle in *The Winter's Tale*), Cymbeline promises to pay the tribute to the Romans which his wife had persuaded him to refuse.... Cymbeline's payment of tribute to Rome symbolizes the return of order and justice in the community and "Promises Britain peace and plenty".

The payment of this tribute, despite the stirring patriotism of Act Three, scene one, and the British victory, represents for

Cymbeline a species of "penance." At least, like the traditional return of the young to the community after their seasonal rebellion, it recognizes national commitments, duties, and responsibilities, and merges two great streams of influence in British culture. The play concludes with the emphasis upon the peace of the realm, assured by the blessed actions of the young. The eagle of Caesar is re-united with the radiant Cymbeline, who shines in the west, to symbolize the renewed fertility and peace of the land. By the dénouement, the King has been reinstated, not only in the Roman Empire, but also in the hearts of his daughter and his subjects, for by the deaths of his Queen and her brutish son his kingdom has been purged of a spiritual evil and an animal barbarity which had been draining it of its vitality. His final action is, thus, a renunciation of the national hubris stimulated by his evil wife, a hubris which, in some respects, parallels the rebellion of the young, their declaration of independence from the "consent" and authority of their elders, and their struggle with the laws which bind the community together. In the last lines of the play, the community is restored to unity by the King himself, who calls for a public sacrifice to the gods, and by so doing reaffirms the old equilibrium and proclaims peace and prosperity.

Cymbeline is, therefore, a national play, presenting in artistic and sophisticated terms the theme of regeneration which can be seen in the prototypal mummers' play. As a national play, it pays tribute to England herself, to her morality, her culture, and her people. In the cycle of its action, *Cymbeline* explores the basis of national unity and presents an almost ritual strengthening of the bonds which bind the kingdom together, for the events chronicled in the play effect a purgation of the body politic and by extension the whole kingdom. In this action, the theme of regeneration provides the symbolic center of gravity, as well as the center of interest, and makes possible the mock death displayed in both physical and spiritual terms. From this conception of regeneration flows the theme of reconciliation which animates the late romantic comedies. Regeneration and reconciliation emanate from the young, transcend the evil impulses working against them, and serve to revitalize the whole kingdom. (pp. 157-59)

> *William Barry Thorne, "'Cymbeline': Lopp'd Branches and the Concept of Regeneration," in* Shakespeare Quarterly, *Vol. XX, No. 1, Spring, 1969, pp. 143-59.*

R. A. FOAKES (essay date 1971)

[*In the following excerpt, Foakes accounts for the uneven, improbable, and often contradictory nature of the dramatic action in* Cymbeline *by claiming that Shakespeare placed a "deliberate emphasis on chance, accident, and the improbable" in the play. Whereas many eighteenth-century commentators, most notably Samuel Johnson (1765), criticized the absurdities and improbabilities in the dramatic action, Foakes views them as directly related to other elements in the play. Significantly, he maintains that the unexpected turns of events underscore the central role of divine providence in determining human fate. Just as the characters in* Cymbeline *are shown to be at the mercy of chance or coincidence, Foakes argues, Posthumus and Imogen are reunited, and Cymbeline's kingdom restored, not as a result of their own struggles, but because of the direct intervention of Jupiter. Other critics who hold that this play demonstrates the role of providence in human destiny include G. G. Gervinus (1849-50), G. Wilson Knight (1947), and J. A. Bryant, Jr. (1961). Further, Foakes maintains that the psychological inconsistency of Shakespeare's characterization is not a dramatic flaw, but serves to enhance the general mood of illogicality in the drama. The critic also contends that Shakespeare intentionally exposes his use of theatrical conventions—such as choric speeches and informational asides and soliloquies—to distance the audience from events and characters, just as he blends comic elements with tender ones in the headless torso episode, "to ensure that we watch the action with a degree of amused detachment as well as sympathy." For further discussions of the self-conscious dramaturgy in* Cymbeline, *see the excerpts by Harley Granville-Barker (1930) and Barbara A. Mowat (1966), as well as the essay by Arthur C. Kirsch cited in the Additional Bibliography.*]

Cymbeline begins with the entry of two gentlemen, who praise Posthumus glowingly, describe his ancestry, and report the loss of the King's two sons twenty years ago. The First Gentleman explains to his ignorant companion how Imogen has married against her father's wishes, a tough line of action in Shakespeare's time, how she has been imprisoned, her husband banished, and how, in spite of searching, the King's sons still remain untraced. It all sounds unlikely, but the Second Gentleman is convinced as his partner cries, 'Howso'er 'tis strange . . . Yet is it true, sir' [I. i. 65, 67]. Already these figures begin to establish the tonality of the play, as one in which the strange, even the incredible, will prove true, so that normal expectations of probability, consistency and motivation may not apply. (pp. 98-9)

In *Cymbeline,* as the final scene with its series of surprising discoveries indicates, the interest does not lie in the development of character, or of plot in the sense of a developing action with a beginning, a middle or crisis, and end, or resolution, like that, say, of *Othello* or *Coriolanus.* Instead, we are offered a multiplicity of plots and a continual variety in unexpected twists to the action; the *unexpected,* indeed, seems a necessary part of the play's movement, and of the pattern of expectations it sets up. It invites us to look not for what is probable, or for a motivated, consequential action, but rather to accept the most extraordinary coincidences and accidents, and to be ready to respond with an assent like that of the First Gentleman, 'Howso'er 'tis strange. . . . Yet is it true'.

If we accept the tonality of the play as indicated in the opening scenes, then other assumptions and conventions become clearer. Flagrant improbabilities are taken for granted, such as that in a journey across Wales, both Cloten and Imogen would stumble into the exact spot where Belarius has hidden untraced for twenty years; or that Lucius, the Roman ambassador, would be in need of an attendant at that precise moment when Imogen happens to turn up in Milford Haven, and that he would hire her, in her disguise as a boy, on sight. There are many more such instances, which Shakespeare clearly was at pains to expose, and not to conceal. Of a piece with these is the overt display of theatricality. No attempt is made to create a consistent illusion of human beings in action as Shakespeare lays bare, sometimes with what looks like deliberate crudeness, intricacies of the action in a creakingly theatrical way. This begins early with the asides to the audience of the Second Lord in [I. ii.], recommending us to note what a fool Cloten is, and the asides in [I. v.], when Cornelius the doctor gives a box of drugs to the Queen. Here both characters, and Pisanio, who comes in midway through the scene, have asides or short soliloquies in which they appear to come downstage to address the audience directly, perhaps concealing their words from the other characters with a melodramatic gesture. The asides have a function, and provide information, but they seem to be used in a deliberately obtrusive way, as if to make us notice the theatrical device. So, as Pisanio enters, the Queen and Cornelius in turn speak in aside:

Queen	[*Aside*] Here comes a flattering rascal,
	upon him
	Will I first work: he's for his master,
	And enemy to my son.—How now
	Pisanio?—
	Doctor, your service for this time is
	ended,
	Take your way.
Cornelius	[*Aside*] I do suspect you, madam;
	But you shall do no harm.

[I. v. 27-32]

A similar kind of effect is produced when, as happens from time to time, characters sum up the story so far as it has gone, or have a little choric speech, as if to remind us of what, in the complications of intrigue, we may have half-forgotten. . . . Perhaps the most notable example of such gratuitous speech occurs with the introduction of Belarius in III. iii. We were told a little about him in the opening scene of the play, but now Shakespeare amplifies the details without troubling to disguise what he is doing. The conversation between Belarius and the boys Guiderius and Arviragus turns on the difference between court and country, nature and nurture; the boys not unreasonably feel rather irritated at living among animals, and knowing nothing of the benefits of civilization, although they talk in accomplished blank verse, and in speech might pass among the best, but Belarius explains as though for the first time his dislike of the court, and then repeats his life story, all of which one might think superfluous after twenty years of living together. But if the boys have heard it before, we have not, and Shakespeare put it there for us. At the end of the scene, Belarius sends the boys off to hunt, and finishes with a soliloquy filling out some details we have not yet heard:

> O Cymbeline, heaven and my conscience knows
> Thou didst unjustly banish me: whereon
> At three and two years old, I stole these babes,
> Thinking to bar thee of succession as
> Thou reft'st me of my lands. Euriphile,
> Thou wast their nurse, they took thee for their mother,
> And every day do honour to her grave:
> Myself, Belarius, that am Morgan call'd,
> They take for natural father.

[III. iii. 99-107]

Belarius here speaks for the benefit of the audience, imparting information directly, and the soliloquy springs not from the action, or from introspection, but is presented as narrative. Shakespeare adopted in this scene a direct narrative means of supplying some facts with complete disregard for probability or character conceived as psychologically consistent. Belarius is simply used for the moment as a kind of chorus.

Probably at any stage of his career, and certainly now in his maturity, Shakespeare could have worked this material into the action more subtly if he had wished to do so; the only reasonable way to explain it is to suppose that it was a deliberate tactic on his part. It is of a piece with other aspects of the play, some of which have been noted above, in drawing attention to itself as theatrical device. The aim seems to have been to make us think less of the character and more of the actor speaking from a stage. It may be seen as one means of preventing us from identifying ourselves with a character, or taking the action too seriously, at any rate on a literal level. The famous stage direction in Act V for Jupiter to descend 'in thunder and lightning, sitting upon an eagle' [at V. iv. 92], and to throw a thunderbolt, a direction which the nature of the

text encourages us to suppose is Shakespeare's own, provides another example of deliberate emphasis on theatrical effect. Here the physical machinery of the stage is palpably employed, not for illusion, but for a piece of clever spectacle, as the god comes down, lowered presumably on wires, and then vanishes aloft into what Sicilius calls his 'radiant roof' [V. iv. 121] in the canopy or 'heavens' at the Globe.

The conscious theatricality shown here and elsewhere, as in the scene in Imogen's bedroom (II. ii) where the clock marks the passage of more than three hours in the space of forty lines, is related to the deliberate emphasis on chance, accident, and the improbable, and both in turn are connected with the presentation of characters not as human beings conceived in terms of psychological consistency, but rather as liable to arbitrary shifts and changes. Shakespeare, it is true, treats the characters in different ways according to their function in the play; so, for instance, Pisanio remains throughout a stock figure, the devoted loyal servant of Imogen and Posthumus, and neither changes nor develops. The point is that, given the deliberately arbitrary nature of the action, as not dependent on cause and motive, and as flaunting its theatricality and rejection of ordinary narrative continuity and expectation, there is no need for a stable and consistent portrayal and development of characters; they may be liberated from consistency, since they too are part of a dramatic world where anything can happen, however strange, yet true.

Consider, for example, Cloten. When we first see him, in [I. ii.] and II. i, he is accompanied by two lords; one of them feeds him with lines, while the other speaks almost continually in asides to the audience, inviting us to think of Cloten as a fool or ass, and mocking him:

Cloten	When a gentleman is dispos'd to
	swear, it is not for any standers-by to
	curtail his oaths, ha?
Second Lord	No, my lord; [*Aside*] nor crop the ears
	of them.
Cloten	Whoreson dog! I give him satisfaction?
	Would he had been one of my rank!
Second Lord	[*Aside*] To have smelt like a fool.
Cloten	I am not vex'd more at anything in th'
	earth; a pox on't! I had rather not be so
	noble as I am. . . .

[II. i. 10-18]

This rough prose is characteristic of Cloten's speeches in these scenes; he behaves as a foolishly arrogant prince, occupied in quarrelling, playing bowls and gambling, who appears to justify the comment of the Second Lord when he is left alone on stage to address the audience at the end of II. i:

> That such a crafty devil as is his mother
> Should yield the world this ass! a woman that
> Bears all down with her brain, and this her son
> Cannot take two from twenty, for his heart,
> And leave eighteen.

[II. i. 52-6]
(pp. 100-04)

[Yet, when] Shakespeare wants Cloten to speak with grace and intelligence, he has him do so, however inconsistent it may be. So later on Cloten addresses the Roman ambassador, Lucius, with a warlike simplicity as if he were some noted fighter in an earlier history play:

His majesty bids you welcome. Make pastime
with us a day or two, or longer: if you seek us
afterwards in other terms, you shall find us in
our salt-water girdle; if you beat us out of it,
it is yours; if you fall in the adventure, our
crows shall fare the better for you, and there's
an end.

[III. i. 77-82]

The old arrogant fool returns in III. v, as Cloten sets off to
Wales in lustful pursuit of Imogen. He is not presented as a
stable or psychologically consistent figure, but this is neither
a failure on Shakespeare's part to work out a consistent mode
of treating him, nor is it explicable in symbolic terms. It seems
rather that Shakespeare was moving in *Cymbeline* towards a
mode of drama which could abandon the idea of character as
morally or psychologically stable, and one result is the presence
of figures like Cloten, who changes from scene to scene, and
is given a variety of styles of speech to match the varying and
even contradictory versions of him we see. In other words, he
is not revealed at once in a mode of speech that gives us in
some sense the hallmark of the man, like Hamlet, Othello, or
Coriolanus, but is conceived in a more flexible way, and changes
with the situation; alone with his followers he appears a quarrelsome fool, but he can speak verse of distinction when thinking of Imogen, and he challenges the Romans in good plain
sensible English.

Although Cloten provides the most notable instance of such
'inconsistency', he is not alone in being presented in this way.
The Queen, for example, drops her witch-like, conspiratorial
manner to become the champion of England, echoing John of
Gaunt, as she stiffens Cymbeline's opposition to Rome:

Remember, sir, my liege,
The kings your ancestors, together with
The natural bravery of your isle, which stands
As Neptune's park, ribb'd and pal'd in
With rocks unscaleable and roaring waters,
With sands that will not bear your enemies' boats,
But suck them up to th' topmast. . . .

[III. i. 16-22]

The sudden transformation of Posthumus from eternally faithful
lover to hater of all women upon hearing Iachimo's account
of Imogen relates to this variation in the presentation of characters, and to the arbitrary features of action and dialogue, and
instances of overt theatricality noted earlier. The presentation
of the central figures, Imogen and Posthumus, is more subtle
and complicated than that of Cloten or the Queen, but they all
need to be understood in relation to the pattern of expectations
established from the beginning; the mode of the play, its variations and mingling of conventions, seems designed, among
other things, to make us accept what happens as in some sense
'true', and at the same time to prevent us from committing
ourselves to any one character.

A subtle distancing operates in respect of Imogen and Posthumus. They begin the play in the unusual, indeed unique position
for Shakespeare's romantic heroes and heroines, of being married. They are at first so perfect, so much the 'loyalest husband'
and wife, that they may seem to be almost over-acting their
love, and the echo in their parting protestations of the leavetaking between Troilus and Cressida, is probably deliberate.
For Imogen, who idealizes her husband as one who 'overbuys
me Almost the sum he pays' [I. i. 146-47], their parting seems
an opportunity for acting out prettily the most romantic of

farewells; she is less absorbed in Posthumus than in her imaginings of how she might have watched him go:

I would have broke mine eye-strings, crack'd them, but
To look upon him, till the diminution
Of space had pointed him, sharp as my needle,
Nay, follow'd him, till he had melted from
The smallness of a gnat to air, and then
Have turn'd mine eye, and wept.

[I. iii. 17-22]

She would have wept if the separation could have been so
staged, but at the actual parting there are no tears. There the
hurried nature of the parting in the presence of the Queen
shortens their speeches, and controls their feeling, which becomes simple and moving, especially in Imogen's:

O the gods!
When shall we see again?

[I. i. 123-24]

After this, however, each is shown as lacking in true knowledge
of and feeling for the other, with the result that Posthumus
becomes passionate in hatred and thoughts of vengeance, while
Imogen becomes sentimental and at times almost comic.

At the first test of his love, Posthumus, who goes about boasting
of his wife's excelling beauty and virtue, believes a complete
stranger's testimony that she is disloyal. It might perhaps be
thought a hollow confidence in Imogen that drives Posthumus
to brag so much that she is 'more fair, virtuous, wise, chaste,
constant, qualified, and less attemptable' than the rarest ladies
of France [I. iv. 59-61], to quarrel at swordpoint, and then to
accept Iachimo's wager rashly; if not hollow, then it is slightly
absurd, for it indicates the extent to which she has been for
him an idea rather than a person, an embodiment of chastity
too pure for common mortality; and when this idea of her is
made distasteful to him by Iachimo, he casts her off readily,
without even hearing out the evidence. . . . (pp. 106-08)

Imogen is content to think of Posthumus as like a god, and
knows him as little as he knows her. Shakespeare presents her
as full of pretty speeches and tender sentiments appropriate to
her situation, but with an edge of comic irony in what she
says, and a tendency to overdo the part a little bit, and strain
across the boundary of the absurd. (pp. 109-10)

The culmination of this process of rendering Imogen at once
sympathetic and faintly comic comes when she awakes from
her drugged sleep to find a body by her side clothed in the
garments of Posthumus. She had earlier said to Cloten that the
meanest garment of Posthumus was dearer to her 'than all the
hairs' on him [II. iii. 135] and she now takes the clothes for
the man, and proceeds to itemize the body on assumption that
it is Posthumus:

A headless man? The garments of Posthumus?
I know the shape of's leg; this is his hand;
His foot Mercurial; his Martial thigh;
The brawns of Hercules; but his Jovial face—
Murder in heaven! How?—'Tis gone.

[IV. ii. 308-12]

This episode is comic in several ways, because a number of
incongruities are at work. Imogen shows how little she knows
the husband whose limbs she thinks she recognizes, and here
above all her ignorance of Posthumus is brought out. Now she
thinks Posthumus dead, . . . in her fancy [he] becomes a combination of bits of various deities, Mercury, Mars, Hercules,

Jupiter, all inappropriate to the image of Cloten, whose body is actually on stage. Also comic is the way she proceeds from the body to the head, with a kind of delayed recognition that the head is missing, which bursts out in the curious lines:

> O Posthumus, alas,
> Where is thy head? where's that? Ay me! where's that?
> Pisanio might have kill'd thee at the heart,
> And left this head on.
>
> [IV. ii. 320-23]

Imogen's fancy expresses itself in a concern for the body as an assembly of parts, with the most important one, the head, missing; this is to reduce the body to a kind of mechanism, and her rhetoric here is absurd in itself. At the same time, though her logic is false and her rhetoric extravagant; though she is made to indulge her grief by . . . staging the scene, as when she smears herself with the blood of Cloten for the benefit of those who will find her:

> This is Pisanio's deed, and Cloten—O!
> Give colour to my pale cheek with thy blood,
> That we the horrider may seem to those
> Which chance to find us;
>
> [IV. ii. 329-32]

yet her anger with Pisanio and grief over the supposed death of Posthumus are genuine. Moreover, she has just been ceremoniously laid to rest as dead by Belarius, Guiderius and Arviragus, with expressions of their tender affection for her, as a 'blessed thing' they associate with flowers and fairies [IV. ii. 206] and immediately afterwards she is found by Lucius, who takes her, in her disguise as Fidele, into his service on mere sight:

> The Roman Emperor's letters
> Sent by a consul to me should not sooner
> Than thine own worth prefer thee.
>
> [IV. ii. 384-86]

The scene combines tenderness and humour, as if Shakespeare wants to ensure that we watch the action with a degree of amused detachment as well as sympathy. This is not to be confused with what happens in the early comedies, where we watch the 'strange capers' of true lovers on their way through courtship to marriage, with the sense, in Touchstone's words, that 'as all is mortal in nature, so is all nature in love mortal in folly' [As You Like It, II. iv. 55-6]; in these plays we are engaged sympathetically in watching the successful overcoming of all obstacles by young lovers, while at the same time having something of Puck's stance:

> Shall we their fond pageant see?
> Lord, what fools these mortals be!
> [A Midsummer Night's Dream, III. ii. 114-15]

In Cymbeline the effect is different, and the presentation of Imogen links with other features of the play described earlier to emphasize rather how subject to whim, chance, accident, mistaken judgments, and wild coincidences the pattern of existence is. When Imogen wakes from the sleep brought on by Pisanio's drug, she exclaims:

> I hope I dream;
> For so I thought I was a cave-keeper,
> And cook to honest creatures. But 'tis not so;
> 'Twas but a bolt of nothing, shot at nothing,
> Which the brain makes of fumes. Our very eyes
> Are sometimes like our judgments, blind.
>
> [IV. ii. 297-302]

This is not the 'blindness' or folly of lovers, symbolized in the magic juices Puck squeezes on to the eyelids of the lovers in A Midsummer Night's Dream, but has more far-reaching implications. Imogen thinks now that she merely dreamt what we have seen happen, her encounter with Belarius, Guiderius and Arviragus, who were not in any case the peasants she thought them. She takes the body on stage for that of Posthumus, when we know it is Cloten's. She has been buried as dead by Belarius and the king's sons, but we quickly discover that she is still alive. Belarius and the boys are disguised as Welsh mountaineers, Imogen is disguised as a boy, and Cloten's body is dressed in the clothes of Posthumus. Eyes and judgments are bound to deceive sometimes, in a world such as this. (pp. 112-14)

The famous series of revelations, constantly bringing fresh confrontations and news of further strange coincidences, which forms the culmination of the action in the final scene, flows naturally out of what has gone before, and is in keeping with the tonality and mode of the whole. The revelations come as unexpected, not as caused by a chain of consequence. When Posthumus reports to one of the lords who has fled, with the King and entire British army, from the Romans, how he, with Belarius, 'an old man, and two boys', turned the battle and made the Romans withdraw routed, the lord expresses his admiration:

> Lord   This was strange chance,
>   A narrow lane, an old man, and two
>   boys.
> Posthumus Nay, do not wonder at it; you are made
>   Rather to wonder at the things you hear
>   Than to work any.
>
> [V. iii. 51-5]

Posthumus is angry with the lord for being one of those who fled, and so one made to hear the wonders rather than to work them; but the audience is in something of the same position as the lord, in accepting with wonder the strange chances they see and hear enacted before them. The last scene begins with the unexpected news of the Queen's death, and continues with reports and discoveries that bring to light Iachimo's treachery, make Posthumus, Imogen, Belarius and the King's sons reveal themselves, and overwhelm Cymbeline with the constant stream of 'New matter still' [V.v.243]. Again and again the news is good, bringing the restoration of what has been lost, turning peasant into prince, replacing discord with harmony, and offering peace in place of war, love in place of hate, forgiveness in place of malice. Cymbeline recovers his children, but not through any effort of his, and the deliverance from error and loss, which is also a kind of rebirth, comes as an unlooked for gift of providence; so Cymbeline cries:

> O, what am I?
> A mother to the birth of three? Ne'er mother
> Rejoic'd deliverance more. Blest pray you be
> That after this strange starting from your orbs,
> You may reign in them now!
>
> [V. v. 368-72]

It is the mysterious operation of a providence not understood by the characters that brings restitution finally, and purges evil in the casual deaths of Cloten and the Queen. The structure of the play depends not on motive or causality or intention so much as on coincidence, chance, accident, which seem beyond man's control, and inexplicable, though accepted without question as an aspect of the nature of life. Providence manifests itself unexpectedly in Act V when Jupiter appears to Posthumus, and leaves on his bosom that 'book' or 'label' containing a prophecy the sense of which is pretty clear to the audience, though inscrutable to him. A soothsayer has to be called to explain it at the end, when the only part of the prophecy not fulfilled is the last phrase, that Britain shall 'flourish in peace and plenty' [V. v. 441-42]. Cymbeline at once takes upon himself the fulfilment of this as he submits to Rome, crying, 'My peace we will begin' [V. v. 459]. The presence of the 'covering heavens' is thus felt as:

> The fingers of the powers above do tune
> The harmony of this peace.
>
> [V. v. 466-67]

The voluntary submission of Cymbeline here, and the ending of the play with prayer and praise of the gods, crowning all in harmony, arises out of the direct intervention of a god, Jupiter, in the play. Up to that point, there is nothing to explain the inconsistencies, contradictions, and coincidences of the action; and its deliberate theatricalities, self-consciousness in the presentation of characters, its devices for distancing them and avoiding a sense of psychological realism, among which may be included the bringing together of the ancient Britain of Cymbeline and the Renaissance Italy of Iachimo, all help to shape the play within an overall consistent and intelligible dramatic mode, in which the resolution can come not by the will of men, but only by the intervention of the heavens. Imogen wakes from her drugged sleep to think she has dreamt of meeting Belarius, Guiderius and Arviragus, and, waking to find a body by her, believes 'The dream's here still' [IV. ii. 306]; so Posthumus, emerging from a sleep which has brought the vision of Jupiter, finds the paper containing the prophecy laid on him, and thinks ''Tis still a dream' [V. iv. 145]. They confuse dream and actual existence because existence to them has in any case many of the qualities of a dream in its strangeness and its unexpected turns of event; and the overlap between dream and actuality is embodied for the audience too in the action, as Belarius and Jupiter are seen to be as 'real' as Imogen and Posthumus. The mode of the play is such as to make us, the audience, share something of Posthumus's puzzled acceptance of his 'dream' and prophecy:

> 'Tis still a dream; or else such stuff as madmen
> Tongue, and brain not; either both, or nothing,
> Or senseless speaking, or a speaking such
> As sense cannot untie. Be what it is,
> The action of my life is like it. . . .
>
> [V. iv. 145-49]

He cannot make sense of the prophecy, which, whether it spring from dream or madness or whatever, remains inexplicable, yet somehow like the action of his life. In an analogous sense we may say of the play as a whole that it is like the action of our own lives. (pp. 116-18)

> *R. A. Foakes, "Shakespeare's Last Plays," in his* Shakespeare, the Dark Comedies to the Last Plays: From Satire to Celebration, *The University Press of Virginia, 1971, pp. 94-172.*

ARTHUR C. KIRSCH   (essay date 1972)

[*Kirsch argues that the discontinuities and discords, the contradictions and the mixture of literary modes—in short, all the frequently cited anomalies in* Cymbeline—*are the result of Shakespeare's "attempt to explore the techniques and implications of tragicomic dramaturgy." Thus, like such earlier critics as Harley Granville-Barker (1930), Barbara A. Mowat (1966), and R. A.*

Foakes (1971), Kirsch regards the artifices and conventions in the play as elements deliberately displayed by Shakespeare. The critic also comments on the "remarkable" manner in which Shakespeare exploits the tragicomic form, stating that the entire dramatic action of Cymbeline *is patterned according to the Christian concept of the fortunate fall—a paradox he sees reenacted in various aspects of the play, such as in the language of the characters, the use of riddles, the frequent allusions to the discrepancies between body and soul or appearance and reality, and the use of disguise as a means of symbolically dramatizing an individual's passage from death to rebirth. Indeed, Kirsch calls the notion of death and rebirth a central theme in* Cymbeline, *one which "informs the action profoundly, becoming associated with the tragicomic paradoxes both of nature and Christianity." Other commentators who have identified the pattern of the fortunate fall in Shakespeare's play include J. A. Bryant, Jr. (1961) and Martin Lings (see Additional Bibliography); also, see the excerpts by Robert Grams Hunter (1965) and Homer D. Swander (1966) for related commentary on the issue of redemption in* Cymbeline. *Finally, Kirsch offers a metadramatic reading of the play, claiming that Shakespeare's exploration of "the dynamics of tragicomedy" is "wholly and marvellously indistinguishable from the evolution of the providential pattern which it represents."*]

[*Cymbeline*] seems composed of discontinuities and discords which resist coherent analysis. The action, half-romance, half-history, moves freely through a kaleidoscope of milieux: a primitive British court, a Machiavellian Italy, a Roman Italy, a pastoral cave. The hero is at best only half-admirable: in the beginning he loves Imogen and values her as "the gift of the gods" [I. iv. 85]; after Iachimo's deception he orders her death. Its principal villain is similarly only half-sinister: at possibly his most evil moment, when he is attempting to seduce Imogen, Iachimo becomes so intoxicated with his own verbal extravagance that he subverts his own intentions. Cloten, a lesser villain to begin with, is also a clownish boor, as Shakespeare takes pains to establish in the scene with the Second Lord [I. ii.]; the Queen is never more than a cardboard figure; and Cymbeline is not, until the end, much more than a dupe. Imogen, the principal and unifying figure of interest in the play, is less equivocally portrayed, since in herself she is consistent enough. But on the other hand, the play deals with her very strangely. In a scene that is studiously prepared for, she awakens by the headless body of Cloten, who is dressed in Posthumous's garments, and mistaking him for her husband, she sings "an aria of agony." It is a moving and convincing one, but we cannot help being conscious, at the same time, as Granville-Barker remarks, that "it is a fraud on Imogen; and we are accomplices in it" [see excerpt above, 1930]. No other heroine in Shakespeare . . . suffers this kind of exploitation.

Faced with such apparent contradictions, most critics have taken refuge in allegory, or in apocalyptic sentimentalizations (of Imogen especially), or in disintegrations of the text. Yet . . . , a better answer would seem to be that the play is an attempt to explore the techniques and implications of tragicomic dramaturgy, and it is a better answer because it is based on the plausible assumption that Shakespeare is doing what he wants to do (more or less successfully, as the case may be) and that what appear to be contradictions in the play are deliberate and part of its very nature. Even superficially considered, most of the features of the play which cause trouble for critics are precisely those which are most typical of self-conscious tragicomedy. Posthumous, in his sudden turn of heart (and subsequent counterturn), is not unlike countless Fletcherian heroes whose discontinuous characterizations provide the occasions for turns of plot and emotional declamations; and when at the end of the play he strikes his disguised wife to the ground, the theatrical effect is not so very unlike that provided by Philaster's wounding of Arathusa or of the disguised Euphrasia [in *Philaster*]. Fletcher's scenes are obviously not as resonant as Shakespeare's, but the theatrical situations and patterns are nevertheless initially the same. Similarly, Iachimo is very like the villains who abound in Marston's plays—so close to parodies, so consumed with their own flamboyant rhetoric, and so eventually powerless that though they arouse our apprehensions we cannot take them entirely seriously. Granville-Barker says of Iachimo that "he presents us, in his arrogance, with an approach to a travesty of himself, which is also a travesty of the very medium in which he exists. A subtle and daring piece of craftsmanship, germane to this hybrid tragi-comedy. Instead of opposing the heroic and the comic, Shakespeare blends the two." (pp. 64-5)

Imogen, shaped in a more familiar Shakespearian mold, cannot be explained so easily. . . . She has a "tune" of her own [V. v. 239], and she is the only character in the play with whom we are really asked to sympathize. There is no emotional indirection or ambivalence, for example, about her reception of the news that Posthumous doubts her, nor is there any in our reaction to it:

> *Pis.*　What shall I need to draw my sword? the paper
> 　　　Hath cut her throat already. . . .
> *Imo.*　False to his bed? What is it to be false?
> 　　　To lie in watch there, and to think on him?
> 　　　To weep 'twixt clock and clock? If sleep charge Nature,
> 　　　To break it with a fearful dream of him,
> 　　　And cry myself awake? That's false to's bed, is it?
> 　　　　　　　　　　　　　[III. iv. 32-3, 40-4]

But if Imogen in herself seems remote from the usual heroines of tragicomedy, the situations in which she is placed are not. She is repeatedly called upon for histrionic displays in much the same way that Marston's heroines or Fletcher's are—through contrived misunderstandings, or mistaken identities, or deceptions. Her grief over the supposed dead body of her husband, moving certainly in itself, is not different in kind from the grief which Maria displays in [Marston's] *The Malcontent* when her disguised husband is apparently attempting to seduce her. Imogen is made to perform for us, and she is, throughout, exploited not only by plotters but . . . by the plot of the play itself. It is not surprising that there should be a slightly irascible lilt to her tune—Shakespeare's own unconscious reflex, perhaps, as well as hers, against the treatment to which she is subjected.

Not only the characters and the plot, moreover, are symptomatic of the play's self-conscious contrivance; everything about *Cymbeline* suggests that Shakespeare "is somehow *playing with the play*" [see essay by Frank Kermode cited in the Additional Bibliography]. Its verse draws attention to itself: a "new Euphuism," Granville-Barker calls it, where often "the thought or emotion behind" a speech seems "too far-fetched for the occasion or the speaker"; and its stagecraft consistently requires a style of "sophisticated artlessness." . . . [In] this respect, as in others, it is evident that *Cymbeline*, like [*All's Well That Ends Well*], can best be understood as a form of tragicomedy.

The ways in which Shakespeare exploited the capacities of this form in *Cymbeline* are, of course, remarkable, and distinct

Act III. Scene vi. Imogen as Fidele. By R. Westall.

both from the practice of his contemporaries and of his own earlier problem plays. To begin with, *Cymbeline*, even more than *All's Well*, is governed by a pattern of action made intelligible by the paradox of the fortunate fall. The idea is unusually explicit in the play. Lucius tells the disguised Imogen:

> Be cheerful; wipe thine eyes:
> Some falls are means the happier to arise;
> 　　　　　　　　　　　[IV. ii. 402-03]

and shortly afterwards, Jupiter, the play's presiding deity, informs Posthumous's parents in a dream that

> Whom best I love I cross; to make my gift,
> 　The more delay'd, delighted. Be content,
> Your low-laid son our godhead will uplift:
> 　His comforts thrive, his trials well are spent:
> Our Jovial star reign'd at his birth, and in
> 　Our temple was he married. Rise, and fade.
> He shall be lord of lady Imogen,
> 　And happier much by his affliction made.
> 　　　　　　　　　　　[V. iv. 101-08]
> 　　　　　　　　　　　(pp. 66-7)

[A] primary manifestation of the influence of this idea upon the action of the play is the concern with riddle and paradox. It is most obvious in the actual riddle which Posthumous finds in his cell, the explication of which concludes the play, but it is apparent elsewhere as well. The language of *Cymbeline* is saturated with paradoxes. The Queen, Imogen remarks, "can tickle where she wounds," and the King "buys" her "injuries, to be friends'' [I. i. 85, 105]. After giving the Queen a harmless sleeping potion, the doctor remarks that

> there is
> No danger in what show of death it makes,
> More than the locking up the spirits a time,
> To be more fresh, reviving. She is fool'd
> With a most false effect: and I the truer,
> So to be false with her.
>
> [I. v. 39-44]

The Queen tells Cloten that in wooing Imogen he must ''make denials / Increase'' his ''services'' [II. iii. 48-9], and Cloten instructs Pisanio to accept villainy as good:

> Sirrah, if thou wouldst not be a villain, but do
> me true service, undergo those employments
> wherein I should have cause to use thee with
> a serious industry, that is, what villainy soe'er
> I bid thee do, to perform it, directly and truly,
> I would think thee an honest man.
>
> [III. v. 108-13]
> (p. 68)

There is another strain of paradox in *Cymbeline*, less obviously related to the idea of *felix culpa* [''fortunate fall''], but perhaps even more significant. When Posthumous joins the British army in the habit of a peasant, he remarks that ''To shame the guise o' th' world, I will begin, / The fashion less without, and more within'' [V. i. 32-3], and throughout the play there is a deep preoccupation with the frequently paradoxical oppositions between body and soul, between what human beings look like on the outside and what they are within, between their garments and their natures. (p. 69)

Imogen alone in the play is able from the start to bridge such disjunctions, both in herself and in her perception of others. In Iachimo's words, her virtue rests precisely in the identity of her nature and her appearance:

> All of her that is out of door most rich!
> If she be furnish'd with a mind so rare,
> She is alone th' Arabian bird.
>
> [I. vi. 15-17]

All the other characters are either incapable of such union or must learn to achieve it, and much of the action of the play is concerned with the process by which they literally assume and emerge from disguise. Even Imogen herself must wear a disguise, albeit as Fidele, and can only reveal herself when her other name has been cleared.

The insistence upon garments in this play is remarkable, even in comparison with the Shakespearian romantic comedies in which disguise is paramount. It partly represents a continuation of the concern expressed in *All's Well* with the relationship between virtue and breeding. Like Cloten, Parolles too is accused of having been made by his tailor (though he does not suffer as badly for it), and his very name signifies the play's interest in the discrepancies between word and deed, appearance and true nature. The extensive use of the theatrical symbolism of clothing in *Cymbeline* serves to explore these same ideas, as does the whole configuration of a plot in which both nobility and villainy are in disguise.

There is, however, a further significance to the preoccupation with dress in *Cymbeline* which marks a turn of the paradox of the fortunate fall that is peculiar to the last plays. It is an idea stated and dramatized most directly by *The Winter's Tale:* in

the words of the shepherd who finds Perdita, ''Thou met'st with things dying, I with things new-born'' [*The Winter's Tale*, III. iii. 113-14]. *Cymbeline* enacts this pattern more symbolically, primarily through the medium of disguise and the surrounding context of paradoxical inversions. Cloten, dressed as Posthumous, is consumed by a fantasy of raping Imogen, which is as much a travesty of the creation of life as his costume is of himself, and he finds a literal death. Imogen accepts the identity of Fidele as an act of despair, because, as she tells Pisanio, ''How live? / Or in my life what comfort, when I am / Dead to my husband?'' [III. iv. 128-30]; and in that disguise she appears to die in her brothers' cave, only to be ''more fresh, reviving.'' Posthumous, to whom she also seems dead, himself takes on a habit of despair: ''so I'll die / For thee, O Imogen, even for whom my life / Is every breath, a death'' [V. i. 25-7]; and in that habit he helps redeem both himself and his country. In yet another disguise in prison—as a Roman—he talks of the liberty of bondage and of his merry wish for the charity of death, but he dreams of the different charity of Jupiter, finds a book which is ''not, as is our fangled world, a garment / Nobler than that it covers'' [V. iv. 134-35], and reads the riddle that eventually explains the renewal of life of his family and his kingdom.

In the final recognition scene of the play, all these movements are gathered together and brought to fulfillment in what is explicitly recognized as an act of birth. The Queen's ''show'' is revealed, as is Iachimo's and Cloten's; Posthumous, Imogen, Guiderius, Arviragus, and Belarius emerge from their garments to assume their true identities, their appearances at peace now with their real natures; and Cymbeline, struck ''to death with mortal joy'' at the revelation of his daughter and sons, declares,

> O what am I?
> A mother to the birth of three? Ne'er mother
> Rejoic'd deliverance more. Blest pray you be,
> That, after this strange starting from your orbs,
> You may reign in them now. O Imogen,
> Thou hast lost by this a kingdom.
>
> [V. v. 368-73]

Imogen replies, ''No, my lord; / I have got two worlds by't'' [V. v. 373-74]. In the death of the Queen and Cloten and in the rebirth of the King's heirs, the kingdom of Britain too is reborn, literally delivered from evil, its identity baptized in battle, its life within a vision of Pax Romana confirmed.

The idea of death and rebirth is suggested more than once in *All's Well*—''there's my riddle, one that's dead is quick'' [*All's Well That Ends Well*, V. iii. 303]—but it operates primarily on a verbal level. In *Cymbeline*, as in the last plays in general, it informs the action profoundly, becoming associated with the tragicomic paradoxes both of nature and Christianity. Early in the play, before his fall, Posthumous states that he is ready to ''abide the change of time, / Quake in the present winter's state, and wish / That warmer days would come'' [II. iv. 4-6], and there are other references in the play which similarly relate human history to the birth and death of the seasons. This is a primary function of the pastoral scenes, especially of Imogen's death, when Arviragus strews flowers upon her, sings his famous dirge, and her revival becomes visually as well as verbally associated with the rejuvenating powers of the earth. At the same time there are, as we have seen, various references, many of them explicit, to the central Christian paradox of the fortunate fall, and the action itself, with its multiple disguises, bears particular overtones of the casting off (and in Cloten's case, the literal death) of the old Adam and the birth of the new, both in individuals and in the kingdom. Posthumous's penitential transformation especially is strongly inscribed on the ending of the play.

But even more important than these particular adumbrations, which are in any case more fully expressed in *Pericles, The Winter's Tale*, and *The Tempest*, is the degree to which in *Cymbeline*, as in these other plays, the dynamics of tragicomedy become a means of expressing the human creative process and the genesis of the play becomes wholly and marvelously indistinguishable from the evolution of the providential pattern which it represents. . . . The scene, for example, where Imogen awakens beside the headless body of Cloten clothed as her husband is entirely symptomatic. It is indeed the "fraud" that Granville-Barker said it is, but deliberately not accidentally so, a fraud like the multiple disguises in the play, of which we are meant to be conscious; and when Imogen responds to the situation with rather precious classical imagery, her speech too is intended to be observed as much as felt. We are clearly intended to watch Shakespeare directing his characters, and more particularly, to observe how his own paradoxical capacity as a dramatist to transform illusion into reality corresponds to a human capacity for regeneration and transformation. It is therefore profoundly appropriate that in the last scene, in which the show of evil is finally exposed, in which all of the paradoxes of the play meet and are resolved, and in which most of the principal characters are delivered from literal disguise to be figuratively reborn, that in this scene Posthumous should strike the disguised Imogen to the ground and say to her, "Shall's have a play of this? Thou scornful page, / There lie thy part" [V. v. 228-29]. It is a line which italicizes the full wonder of the moment, both because our own rejoicing is a function of our experience of the labor and births of the playwright as well as of the characters, and because Posthumous's action itself dramatizes that mysterious union of joy and pain which is akin to childbirth and which at its deepest reach is the true miracle of the last plays. (pp. 70-3)

Arthur C. Kirsch, "Shakespeare," in his Jacobean Dramatic Perspectives, *The University Press of Virginia, 1972, pp. 52-74.*

DOUGLAS L. PETERSON   (essay date 1973)

[*Peterson asserts that disparaging assessments of the combination of plots and, especially, of dramatic modes in* Cymbeline *are misdirected, since in this play Shakespeare chose both the representational and the symbolic for definite reasons. Adopting the synopsis of the play's leading theme suggested by J. P. Brockbank—that it enacts "certain truths about the processes that have shaped the history of Britain" (see Additional Bibliography)—, Peterson divides the drama into two movements, the destructive and the regenerative. He demonstrates how Shakespeare followed a realistic, historic "mimetic mode" to dramatize the "destructive action"—initiated by the behavior of King Cymbeline and Posthumus—and how he then shifted to a symbolic or emblematic mode in order to transform impending tragedy into comedy and depict the reintegration of the British kingdom. The critic notes that this transformation of the play's direction and presentation is begun in the pastoral scenes at Belarius's cave and continues until the action dissolves into the "pageantry" of the final act. Peterson devotes most of his essay to a study of these "redemptive" scenes, focusing on the theme of* nosce teipsum ("self-knowledge") *and the way in which such characters as Imogen, Belarius, and Posthumus must all achieve a clearer understanding of their own humanity in order to develop those "personal and civic virtues" so necessary to the establishment of the "communal ideal" with which the play concludes. Peterson also emphasizes the emblematic manner in which the second half of* Cymbeline *is written, drawing parallels between this symbolic world and the "golden" arcadia Philip Sidney described as the domain of poets in his* Apology for Poetry. *In his examination of Posthumus's path to self-knowledge, the critic discusses the religious and spiritual importance of the hero's repentance—his recognition of human sin and his new understanding of divine justice. And, like such earlier critics as G. G. Gervinus (1849-50), G. Wilson Knight (1947), J. A. Bryant, Jr. (1961), and R. A. Foakes (1971), Peterson stresses the role played by providence in the final harmony; however, he qualifies this assessment by concluding that, although the gods intervene, their intervention is "primarily through human agents," and that "Britain's destiny has been shaped by men."*]

In *Cymbeline* Shakespeare returns to the general concerns of *Pericles* but with a shift of dramatic focus. The restorative pattern, which in *Pericles* takes the form of exemplars and exemplary episodes, is represented in a fiction which is intended, as J. P. Brockbank has observed, "to express certain truths about the processes that have shaped the history of Britain" [see Additional Bibliography]. As the action gets under way, tragedy seems imminent. The body politic is diseased and has a fool for its head. Order and degree have been destroyed by a king who is unable to distinguish between authentic and apparent nobility. But tragedy is averted: the destructive action is miraculously transformed, and the body politic is restored to health. Virtuous action is again honored as the basis of true nobility, the ancient lines of Britain's kings are repaired, and an honorable reconciliation with Rome is won when surrender had seemed inevitable.

The demands made upon mimesis by such an action are intricate. If the play is going "to express certain truths about the processes that have shaped the history of Britain," an illusion of historicity must be established at the outset. At the same time, since the fiction of the play must demonstrate the process by which the fallen inhabitants and institutions of a real world are miraculously restored by love, mimesis must allow for the transition from representational to symbolic narrative.

The mimetic mode that Shakespeare devised to meet these requirements is unique to *Cymbeline*. For the initial destructive action he adopts the mode he had used in *Lear*; for the renewing action he returns to the emblematic mode that he had used so effectively in *Pericles*. The mode of *Lear*, while affording the means of establishing historical probability, is, nevertheless, sufficiently free to allow for the inclusion in *Cymbeline* of such improbable characters as the wicked Queen (an evil stepmother out of fairy tale lore) and the anachronistic Iachimo, and for such unlikely events as the wager and the means by which Iachimo gains entrance to Imogen's bedchamber. The mode of *Pericles*, by drawing attention to mimesis as artifice, calls attention to, and occasionally even isolates, the ideas it figures forth. Scenes, for instance, may introduce symbolic actions by serving as emblematic tableaux which isolate and announce the ideas that are central to that action; dreaming and awaking may introduce shifts in mimetic focus from one level of reality to another. Furthermore, the emblematic mode allows the greatest freedom in the visualization of abstractions and thus the fullest exploitation of the symbolic resources of dramatic illusion. Within such a mode the spiritual insight afforded by man's belief in the merciful heavens may be represented by a god descending from the heavens to speak with men, princes who have been raised in the wilderness may be exemplars of honor and courtesy, and a king's recovery of his lost heirs (together with his recognition of nobility where formerly he had been unable to recognize it) may represent the renascence of a nation.

There is nothing in the opening scene of the play to distinguish the world it introduces from the world of *Lear*. The setting is the court of an ancient British king. The concerns are public: a king's folly has bred a disorder which threatens to consume his heirs and the body politic. As the action progresses the impression that we are in the world of tragedy is strengthened. Cymbeline and Posthumus appear to be shaping a tragic future for themselves and for Britain.

But as the "tragic" action approaches its crisis, signs of the coming shift in mimetic modes begin to appear. The earliest indications of the change occur when the setting shifts from Cymbeline's court to the mountains of Wales. . . . Belarius in his first appearance speaks metaphorically of his surroundings. For him, the cave in which he and his foster sons live, with its low door and ceiling, is an emblem of humility.

> A goodly day not to keep house with such
> Whose roof's as low as ours! [Stoop], boys; this gate
> Instructs you how t' adore the heavens and bows you
> To a morning's holy office. The gates of monarchs
> Are arch'd so high that giants may jet through
> And keep their impious turbans on without
> Good morrow to the sun. Hail, thou fair heaven!
> We house i' th' rock, yet use thee not so hardly
> As prouder livers do.
>
>   [III. iii. 1-9]

The hill, too, which he urges the boys to climb during the day's hunt, assumes emblematic significance. As a high place from which to look down upon the world—a "place which lessens and sets off" [III. iii. 13]—it designates the circumspection that is a mark of prudence. The impression that we are entering a new dramatic world is strengthened by the debate between Belarius and the boys which follows. Its subject, whether a contemplative life in the country or an active life in court is more desirable, is a familiar one in the world of pastoral. Thus it, too, calls attention to the setting as artifice.

As the pastoral action progresses it becomes increasingly clear that we have entered a new mimetic world in which universals are unabsorbed by particularity. It is the world of Arcadian romance, in which the miraculous may occur—and in which characters and actions, as well as caves and hills, may serve the purposes of emblematic narrative. Its inhabitants are pure exemplars. Belarius is Ideal Patriarch and Tutor; Arviragus and Guiderius (as Belarius, himself, observes in [IV. ii. 169-81]), are exemplars of Ideal Royalty—of Ideal Honor, Civility, and Valor. Involved, as they are, in actions which make no claim to historicity, their "reality" resides in the truths which they and their actions figure forth. The same thing is generally true of those characters who move into the emblematic world of Wales from the historical world of Cymbeline's court. Imogen becomes exemplar of a love which "alters not when it alteration finds" [*Sonnet* 116] and Posthumus becomes the repentant sinner who through redemptive love regains his lost identity as his father's son, as husband to a princess, and as noble member of the body politic. Even Cloten, who, along with his mother, is primarily an exemplar in the opening action, acquires another symbolic dimension—as the "old" Posthumus who must die before the "new" Posthumus can be born.

Nowhere in Shakespeare is Sidney's theory of mimesis more strongly suggested. In creating an Arcadian Wales Shakespeare follows Sidney's Poet [in his *Apology for Poetry*], who "disdayning to be tied to any subjection" of the sort the philosopher or the historian is obliged to endure,

dooth growe in effect another nature, in making things either better then Nature bringeth forth, or, quite a newe, formes such as neuer were in Nature, as the *Heroes, Demigods, Cyclops, Chimeras, Furies*, and such like: so as hee goeth hand in hand with Nature, not inclosed within the narrow warrant of her guifts, but freely ranging onely within the Zodiack of his owne wit.

Wales is a "golden world" in which Shakespeare looks beyond even the laws of nature. From the moment we enter that world until the restorative action is completed and the play dissolves into pageantry, the extravagant improbabilities of romance are a means of figuring forth a miraculous renewal in the time of Kymbeline of Britain's native line of kings and the no less miraculous preservation of an old agreement with classical Rome.

The failure to recognize in *Cymbeline* the inventive way in which Shakespeare met the mimetic problems inherent in the nature of his subject has obscured its meaning and led to repeated criticism of its construction and design. . . . [Critics] have mistaken the transformation of the play's imitative mode and its corresponding shift in tone as evidence of inconsistencies in its conception and of flaws in dramatic unity. Only after the shift in modes is recognized as the means by which Shakespeare shifts dramatic focus from the "brazen world" of history to the ideal world of Arcadian romance is it possible to discover the ideas which order and give meaning to the action. (pp. 108-13)

The source of the destructive action in *Cymbeline* is not specifically identified as it is in *The Winter's Tale* and *The Tempest*. Initially, it appears to be Cymbeline's lack of trust in the proven loyalty of Belarius. Other indications point to Cymbeline's inability to discern between truth and appearances as the initial source. He is unable to fathom the Queen's deception or to distinguish the genuine nobility of Posthumus from the boorish strutting of Cloten when no one else at court has any difficulty in doing so.

Evidence in the play, in fact, strongly suggests that Cymbeline is the victim of an incurable folly and that he learns little in the course of the play. When, for instance, he is eventually made aware of the malice of his queen, he can only confess to his folly and say in his defense:

>   Mine eyes
> Were not in fault, for she was beautiful;
> Mine ears, that [heard] her flattery; nor my heart,
> That thought her like her seeming. It had been vicious
> To have mistrusted her; yet—O my daughter!—
> That it was folly in me, thou mayst say,
> And prove it in thy feeling. Heaven mend all!
>
>   [V. v. 62-8]

These words ring hollow in the mouth of a king who chose to believe, in the face of compelling evidence to the contrary, that Belarius was a traitor and who refused to see nobility and worth in Posthumus. . . . (p. 115)

The consequences of Cymbeline's folly are both "public" and "private." His exiling of Belarius has led to the loss of his own male heirs and raises the question of royal succession. In refusing to recognize Posthumus as a worthy son-in-law, he further threatens his "lines of life." . . . Cymbeline has, furthermore, married an evil and vicious woman under whose influence he is persuaded to consider the brutish Cloten as heir to the crown and a desirable husband for Imogen. Finally, as the opening scene makes clear, he has forced men to pretend and feign. (p. 116)

As a consequence of Cymbeline's folly, time threatens to destroy him, his heirs, and even the kingdom of Britain. His inability to fathom appearances, and hence his inability to trust in those who might offer him good counsel, have made him a slave to illusion and a fool of time. He is utterly under the influence of the Queen, whose sole motive is to advance her time-serving son. Thus the entire kingdom is in the service of folly; for Cymbeline in serving the Queen serves Cloten, and Cloten is a fool.

Such, then, is the fictional situation that Shakespeare invents to account for the public disorder during the reign of Kymbeline that he found recorded in Holinshed. Time has been violently disrupted and seems destined to run a tragic course. Imogen, the only remaining heir to Cymbeline's crown, is a prisoner of the Queen, who plots her death while Posthumus, denied his legacy, is ordered into exile. Cloten, with Cymbeline's approval, courts Imogen and seems destined to fall heir to the crown.

When Posthumus is persuaded of Imogen's infidelity, he repeats the pattern begun by Cymbeline when he had believed the charges levelled against Belarius. He is transformed by sexual jealousy into an agent of destructive love and initiates a sequence of actions which reduce him, finally, to the level of the vicious and mindless Cloten.

His readiness to enter into the wager is itself evidence of the folly which makes him so ready to accept Iachimo's "proof" of Imogen's infidelity. During his wanderings on the continent he has become infected with false notions of honor and courtly service to a lady. Once before, he has revealed how easily his passions are aroused. In France he has quarreled and come close to dueling with a courtier who challenged his claim that Imogen is the paragon of all French mistresses, and now in Italy he is similarly provoked by Iachimo's taunts. Confirming evidence of his folly is his readiness to wager the ring which Imogen has given him. (p. 117)

Whatever the folly of the wager itself, its outcome proves the vulnerability of Posthumus' trust. The evidence that Iachimo presents is insubstantial, and yet Posthumus accepts it with a readiness that appalls Philario. When Iachimo shows him the bracelet, Posthumus is shocked; and after considering only for an instant that Imogen may have "pluck'd it off / To send it me" [II. iv. 104-05], he is ready to give the ring over to Iachimo and to assume, in a pique of adolescent cynicism, that all women are faithless and that beauty inevitably conceals corruption. (p. 118)

Like Othello and Leontes, [Posthumus] sees only what his passion allows him to see. The additional "proof"—the description of the mole "under" Imogen's breast, which Iachimo claims to have kissed—is quite unnecessary. It serves only to intensify his passion. By the time he rushes offstage he has been reduced to a raging fool, vowing in his madness to be avenged.

Posthumus is now afflicted with the same crippling inability to discern between truth and seeming that afflicts Cymbeline. The moral disintegration that follows is rapid. He rushes back onstage to deliver a soliloquy in which he completely undermines the claims he once had to a noble name. In lines that

are reminiscent of Lear and Timon in their most cynical moments he concludes from Imogen's supposed infidelity the dishonesty of all women, even his mother's. . . . In denying his mother's honesty he denies his right to his father's noble name. . . . In rejecting his patrimony he denies the very notion of generative love as the means through which the lineal succession is assured. Love is no more than lust, the means by which the legacy of sin and death are transmitted from generation to generation. The irony is unmistakable: in his madness Posthumus has renounced his patrimony and in effect proclaimed himself heir to all the depravities he has identified with woman; and by committing himself to a course of revenge he has lost all claim to the honors he had earned as a member of Cymbeline's household. His decision to defect to Rome completes the irony. His father had earned the title of "Sicilius Leonatus" in wars against the Romans—the very title which because of his mother's presumed dishonesty he now denies is legitimately his. He has renounced his private identity and dedicated himself to a course of action which will destroy his right to a noble title and rank within the body politic. (pp. 118-20)

Following Posthumus' fall, the destructive action rapidly moves toward crisis. The corrosive effects of the loss of trust threaten to consume Pisanio and Imogen. Initially, all hinges on Pisanio. Pressed on the one hand by Cloten to serve him and win a prince's esteem, and on the other by Posthumus to serve him faithfully, Pisanio holds Imogen's future and, as things eventually turn out, the future of Britain in his hands. In this critical time he emerges as exemplar of the love and trust from which the restorative action eventually emerges.

Pisanio faces two critical occasions: the first, when he receives the letter from Posthumus ordering him to kill Imogen; the second, when Imogen, discovering the contents of the letter, lapses into despair. In each instance, trust proves to be the only sure grounds for determining a course of action in a world in which the lack of trust and the inability to discern between truth and seeming have turned fair to foul and foul to fair. Because Pisanio's trust remains firm he continues to see clearly and truly and, therefore, never loses his hold on reality.

This vital epistemological role of faith (or trust) is brought out by Shakespeare's sharply drawn contrast between Pisanio's response to the charges Posthumus has levelled against Imogen and Posthumus' response to Iachimo's "proofs" of her infidelity. Posthumus' trust is immediately shaken and his passions quickly gain control of reason, corrupting his senses and destroying his ability to discriminate between appearance and reality. Pisanio, too, is deeply moved; but the firmness of his trust enables him not only to examine the contents of the letter in the clear light of reason, but to reconstruct with extraordinary accuracy what the audience knows to be the real situation. . . . (p. 121)

In short, whereas reason under the sway of passion leads Posthumus to mistake illusion for truth, reason grounded in trust leads Pisanio to reject illusion and to conjecture truth. (p. 122)

Imogen's response to the letter parallels Posthumus' response to Iachimo's "proof" of her infidelity, but with one crucial difference—a difference which allows Pisanio eventually to break the pattern of mistrust and destruction that has been already thrice repeated in the "tragic" action of the play. She is shocked and deeply disillusioned, and she immediately concludes that Posthumus has been unfaithful to his marriage vows. . . . However, as she continues it becomes clear that Posthumus' apparent infidelity has not destroyed her faith in the potential and actual goodness of men, but only her readiness to trust in proper-seeming men. . . . (p. 123)

The difference is important. Posthumus' mistrust results in his rejection of what is real. To him, whatever seems in women to be good is only illusion—only seeming. Imogen doubts only the possibility of ever distinguishing between men who are true and honest from those who seem to be. Imogen, like Posthumus, succumbs to despair. She doubts Pisanio's honesty and asks him to do what the divine prohibition against self-slaughter makes her fearful of doing herself; but she never doubts the reality of the good or man's capacity to perform the good. Her spiritual recovery will require of her only that she regain her willingness to trust in the goodness of particular men; Posthumus' will require that he discover the essential nature of love and constancy. (p. 124)

Here, then, is the turning point in the play, the moment in which the destructive action is circumvented and renewal commences. From the moment that Pisanio renews Imogen's faith and she decides to seek out Lucius the action moves steadily toward the restoration of trust and reconstruction of the social order which Cymbeline's folly, abetted by Posthumus', has brought to the edge of catastrophe. As that action proceeds, appearances will continue to deceive; but now they will serve the interests of renewal and reconciliation—a curious inversion of their consequences in the opening action.

Renewal begins in the wilderness. The pattern is a familiar one in Shakespeare's plays. In *As You Like It* good men, who have found no recourse to justice in a duchy governed by a tyrant, flee to the forest of Arden where they live patiently and civilly. In *The Winter's Tale* rural Bohemia is a haven for Perdita where her natural nobility is nurtured by the simple but good shepherd. An island provides a similar haven for Prospero and Miranda in *The Tempest;* here, Prospero finds not only a second opportunity to govern but, finally, after years of contemplation have made him again worthy to govern, the opportunity to reform the society he had formerly failed to govern well. In *Cymbeline* Belarius, Guiderius, and Arviragus—joined briefly by Imogen and eventually by the repentant Posthumus—form the nucleus of a new and ideal community. It is a patriarchy founded on the natural virtues of ''humanity''—''those virtues In whom seemeth to be a mutual concord and love in the nature of man'' [Thomas Elyot, in his *The Governor*]. . . . (pp. 124-25)

Each of the scenes devoted to the depiction of the Ideal Community exploits the symbolic potentialities of Arcadian romance by presenting a ''perfect picture'' of ''what should or should not be'' [Sidney]. . . . Each scene contributes, in short, to the portrayal of a ''golden world'' where, in contrast to the ''brazen world'' of Cymbeline's court, the appearances of things reveal rather than delude and where good and evil receive their due. For in that world ideas, virtues, and vices (for which the philosopher can provide only ''a woordish description, which dooth neyther strike, pierce, nor possesse the sight of the soul'') are visually set forth in ''fayned examples'' [Sidney]. . . . (p. 125)

The first of these emblematic scenes is devoted to the knowledge of self which leads to humility and reverence—virtues without which the respect for order and degree is an impossibility. Belarius, like Duke Senior in *As You Like It*, has found the rough conditions of a life ''exempt from public haunt'' [*As You Like It*, II. i. 15] conducive to *nosce teipsum* [self-knowledge]. As the scene opens he draws a lesson in humility and reverence from the cave in which he and his foster sons live. The boys indicate by their responses that they have learned

their lessons well. They know the meaning of humility and they are reverent in their respect for the heavens.

But they are less ready to accept the absolute dichotomy between rural and civic life that Belarius proceeds to develop in his next lesson:

> *Belarius:* Now for our mountain sport. Up to yond hill!
> Your legs are young; I'll tread these flats. Consider,
> When you above perceive me like a crow,
> That it is place which lessens and sets off;
> And you may then revolve what tales I have told you
> Of courts of princes, of the tricks in war;
> This service is not service, so being done,
> But being so allow'd. To apprehend thus
> Draws us a profit from all things we see;
> And often, to our comfort, shall we find
> The sharded beetle in a safer hold
> Than is the full-wing'd eagle. O, this life
> Is nobler than attending for a check,
> Richer than doing nothing for a [bribe],
> Prouder than rustling in unpaid-for silk.
> Such gains the cap of him that makes him fine,
> Yet keeps his book uncross'd.
>
>   [III. iii. 10-26]

However diligent Belarius has been in raising the boys he has kidnapped, instructing them in humility and reverence and training them in the noble art of the chase, he is, nevertheless, a spokesman at this point for an attitude toward the court and the active life which is contrary to the social ethic assumed in the play. Nobility is obligated to sustain the social order; and the natural nobility of Arviragus and his brother expresses itself in their reluctant acceptance of what Belarius has found to be true.

> *Guiderius:* Out of your proof you speak; we,
>   poor unfledg'd,
> Have never wing'd from view o' th' nest,
>   nor know not
> What air's from home. Haply this life is best,
> If quiet life be best; sweeter to you
> That have a sharper known; well corresponding
> With your stiff age; but unto us it is
> A cell of ignorance, . . .
>
>   [III. iii. 27-33]

When Arviragus has seconded his brother, the best Belarius can do is to appeal, on grounds that the youth of every generation seem destined to hear: ''If you had only been through what I've been through.''

>   How you speak!
> Did you but know the city's usuries,
> And felt them knowingly; the art o' th' court,
> As hard to leave as keep: whose top to climb
> Is certain falling, or so slipp'ry that
> The fear's as bad as falling; the toil o' th' war,
> A pain that only seems to seek out danger
> I' th' name of fame and honour which dies i' th'
>   search,
> And hath as oft a slanderous epitaph
> As record of fair act; . . .
>
>   [III. iii. 44-53]

It will be the boys who will eventually persuade Belarius to take up the active life he so long ago had rejected. He will fight alongside them against the Romans and by that action help to cure the British court of the very evils he has described so cynically in the lines quoted above. He will also cure himself, proving by that action that he has regained his faith in the social order.

The scene's emblematic content should now be apparent. Belarius' and the boys' views are complementary, rather than antithetical as the disillusioned old warrior argues. Taken together, they express in a primitive form the private virtues and public obligations on which community depends.

Those virtues and obligations will be delineated more fully in the action involving the family group and its encounters with Imogen and Cloten. In the scenes ensuing Imogen and Cloten are foils for the purpose of developing further the communal ideal that is represented in Belarius' patriarchal community. The development involves a good deal more than merely contrasting the way in which a needy outcast is received with benevolence and an arrogant fool is slain in self-defense. It begins with a consideration of knowledge of self as a fundamental requirement of personal and civic virtues and then proceeds to a delineation of those virtues upon which custom, order, and degree are founded.

The scene in which Imogen first encounters Belarius and his foster sons (III. vi.) is devoted to the love which, according to Thomas Elyot, is the basis for "community" and "gentleness." Imogen's opening soliloquy indicates that from her own adversities she has come to know the meaning of *humanitas* ["human nature"] ("I see a man's life is a tedious one") and thus to feel the need of the wretched for "foundations" [III. vi. 1, 7]. Her love for Posthumus has provided her with the strength to endure; now, when she is at the point of complete exhaustion, she becomes love's recipient. She is welcomed by Belarius and the boys into their primitive communal life.

When she first encounters Belarius and his foster sons, she does not know what treatment to expect. The cave seems "some savage hold" [III. vi. 18]; and when she is later discovered by the boys, her apology and appeals indicate that she anticipates anything but civil treatment. In representational drama the reassurances she receives and the readiness with which she accepts them would be too brief to be persuasive. But Shakespeare's concern here is not with things as they are but as they ought to be. He exploits the license of romance to present a "speaking picture" which "coupleth the generall notion" of community "with the particular example" of Belarius' patriarchy. The scene is "an image of that whereof the Philosopher bestoweth but a woordish description" [Sidney]. . . . Elyot, the "Philosopher," writes:

> The nature and condition of man, wherein he is less than God Almighty, and excelling notwithstanding all other creatures in earth, is called humanity; which is a general name to those virtues in whom seemeth to be a mutual concord and love in the nature of man. And although there be many of the said virtues, yet be there three principal by whom humanity is chiefly compact: benevolence, beneficence, and Liberality, which maketh up the said principal virtue called benignity or gentleness.

Gentleness, Elyot continues, originates in benevolence ("charity," "love," or "amity") and expresses itself in a readiness to give unselfishly of one's efforts ("beneficence") or of one's goods ("liberality"). These are precisely the virtues figured forth in the scene. The readiness with which Imogen is taken in and given food and shelter is an example of "beneficence" and "liberality." Her acceptance as a "brother" by the boys is an example of "gentleness." The family group of which she has become a member is a community which is bound together by "the mutual concord and love" which is natural to man.

As night falls the scene concludes with lines that are symbolic and ceremonial. Belarius as patriarch directs all according to decorum:

> *Belarius:* Boys, we'll go dress our hunt. Fair youth,
>   come in.
> Discourse is heavy, fasting; when we have supp'd,
> We'll mannerly demand thee of thy story,
> So far as thou wilt speak it.
> *Guiderius:*   Pray, draw near.
> *Arviragus:* The night to th' owl and morn to th' lark
>   less welcome.
> *Imogen:* Thanks, sir.
> *Arviragus:* I pray, draw near.
>
> [III. vi. 89-95]

The *natural* and the *civil* are united in the little group as night draws down and its members share in the warmth and glow of "mutual concord and love."

The notion of community introduced in III. vi. is again taken up in the opening scene of the fourth act. The scene is devoted to Cloten, who confuses surface appearances with true nobility and whose depravity makes him a threat to the values represented at this point in the play by the cave community. From the beginning of the play he is committed by his folly to the peripheral, the transient, and the irrational. Now, as he enters the emblematic world of Wales, the metaphysical implications of his folly become explicit: as Fool, he is . . . exemplar of all that is contrary to benevolence and the communal virtues.

Cloten's soliloquy is a parody of *nosce teipsum*. The Fool, failing to know himself, cannot know the meaning of "humanity"; he remains isolated in his own pride and blind to all but surfaces. (pp. 125-29)

Elyot stresses that man "in knowing the condition of his soul and body . . . knoweth himself, and consequently in the same thing he knoweth every other man." Cloten knows only appearances and therefore cannot understand why Imogen prefers Posthumus. He sees only surface similarities between himself and Posthumus and takes them to be essential:

> the lines of my body are as well drawn as his;
> no less young, more strong, not beneath him
> in fortunes, beyond him in the advantage of the
> time, above him in birth, alike conversant in
> general services, and more remarkable in single
> oppositions; yet this imperceiverant thing loves
> him in my despite. What mortality is!
>
> [IV. i. 9-15]

Failing to know himself, Cloten cannot know Posthumus, or any other human. Nor can he see that worth alone merits titles and rewards. To him success is merely a matter of chance and fortune.

The next scene, which returns to the communal group, is devoted to precisely those virtues which are contingent upon self-knowledge and which Cloten cannot comprehend. When the boys and Belarius set off for the hunt, the intimacy of the parting is again expressive of the "mutual concord and love" that is discoverable only through *nosce teipsum*. After Arvir-agus urges Imogen to remain in the cave—"Brother, stay here. Are we not brothers?" [IV. ii. 2-3]—Imogen answers affirma-tively by extending the concept of brotherhood to all men on the ground of their common mortality, and using Elyot's dis-tinction between "common clay" and the "cloak of dignity."

> So man and man should be;
> But clay and clay differs in dignity,
> Whose dust is both alike.
>
> [IV. iv. 3-5]

She also echoes Elyot when responding to Guiderius' offer to stay with her. She urges him to observe decorum: "Stick to your journal course. The breach of custom / Is breach of all" [IV. ii. 10-11]. The stability of the social order within the community of which she is now a member would not be served by a "breach of custom." The daily hunt is such a custom and it is Guiderius' duty to observe it.

The theme of *nosce teipsum* continues to echo in the language of the scene. When Cloten encounters Guiderius he again mis-takes appearance for reality, assuming that Guiderius' rustic attire is evidence of baseness. "What slave art thou?" [IV. ii. 72], he asks, and when Guiderius replies in a way he takes as impertinent, he accuses him of being a robber and a villain and demands that he surrender. Guiderius' response is made in the very terms that Cloten had used earlier to prove to himself that he was at least Posthumus' equal:

> To who? To thee? What art thou? Have not I
> An arm as big as thine? a heart as big?
>
> [IV. ii. 76-7]

Cloten next appeals unsuccessfully to his clothes as tokens of his nobility and, finally, with no more success, to the fact that he is a queen's son. Cloten's foolishness in confusing tokens of nobility for inner worth, his appeal to his mother's royalty, and, finally, his miserable defeat complete the portrayal of a "purblind" fool whose utter ignorance of self, and therefore of all other men and order and degree, identifies him as the antithesis of *sapientia* [wisdom].

Cloten's death and the double funeral complete the portrayal of Belarius' community. Cloten has threatened the life of one of its members and been killed. Nevertheless, even in his fu-neral the community he has threatened respects custom. As Belarius reminds the boys, who in their grief over the apparent death of Imogen have ignored Cloten's headless corpse, their slain enemy deserves funeral rites that befit his social rank:

> He was a queen's son, boys;
> And though he came our enemy, remember
> He was paid for that. Though mean and mighty, rotting
> Together, have one dust, yet reverence
> That angel of the world, doth make distinction
> Of place 'tween high and low. Our foe was princely;
> And though you took his life, as being our foe,
> Yet bury him as a prince.
>
> [IV. ii. 244-51]

The funeral ceremony concludes one phase of the "pastoral" action. When Imogen awakens to discover the headless corpse of Cloten, she is again in the world of deceiving appearances. The transition from "golden" to "brazen" world makes bril-liant use of the resources of emblematic mimesis. Imogen has a dual role—as daughter of Cymbeline and estranged wife of Posthumus, and as Fidele.

Imogen, herself, directs our attention to the symbolic signifi-cance of Fidele's awakening:

> Yes, sir, to Milford-Haven; which is the way?—
> I thank you.—By yond bush?—Pray, how far thither?
> 'Ods pittikins! can it be six mile yet?
> I have gone all night. Faith, I'll lie down and sleep.
> But, soft! no bedfellow!—O gods and goddesses!
> *These flowers are like the pleasures of the world;*
> *This bloody man, the care on't.*
>
> [IV. ii. 291-97]

For a moment the stage has become a tableau in which Faith awakens from a death-seeming sleep to reflect upon the tran-sient pleasures and mortal cares of the world. The tableau figures forth the "fore-conceit" which will be depicted in the final phase of the renewing action; for it is the awakening of faith—first in Imogen, then in Belarius, and finally in Posthu-mus—which leads ultimately to the recovery of lost heirs, to the renewal of Britain's ties with Rome, and to the restoration of order and degree in the body politic.

The tableau lasts only for a moment, and then Fidele again becomes Imogen, whose "awakening" marks her return to the "historical" world of deception and depravity. In returning to that world she remembers the cave community only as "a bolt of nothing, shot at nothing" [IV. ii. 300]. The irony here is intricate. We know that Imogen has not been dreaming—that she has indeed been "a cave-keeper / And cook to honest creatures" [IV. ii. 298-99]. We also know, as spectators who are aware that we are watching a play, that what she remembers and dismisses as merely an empty illusion "which the brain makes of fumes" is in truth a dramatic illusion created to represent the ideal virtues of humanity. The irony deepens as Imogen, after commenting on the frailty of man's eyes and judgment, proceeds to mistake as real what we know to be illusory. . . . Her mistaken identification of the corpse is a reminder to us that the virtuous and faithful, as well as fools like Cloten, can be misled by appearances. She repeats the very error Cloten had made when he compared himself with Posthumus and found no distinguishing physical differences.

The irony continues. Imogen's next conclusion indicates that her eyes are no blinder to the truth than her judgment; for the evidence from which she concludes that Pisanio, in the employ of Cloten, has murdered Posthumus and tried to murder her is utterly unsubstantial. . . . The final irony is in the fact that her errors in seeing and reasoning have led to the restoration of her faith in Posthumus. Even misleading appearances and errors in judgment may have fortunate consequences! The play at this point is moving toward the conclusion affirmed in each of the romances: the one source of constancy in a world of deceiving appearances is a love grounded in faith.

Shakespeare continues to exploit the resources of emblematic narrative in the final episode of IV. ii. When Lucius, his Cap-tains, and the Soothsayer discover Imogen lying with her head on the bloody corpse of Cloten, the stage again becomes a tableau. Again a character in the tableau directs our attention to the symbolic significance of the action in which he is a participant. When the figure who appears to Lucius to be either dead or asleep has been aroused and given her name, Lucius comments on the appropriateness of her name. To him, she seems to be Faith personified:

> Thou dost approve thyself the very same;
> Thy name well fits thy faith; thy faith thy name.
>
> [IV. ii. 380-81]

The emblematic prefiguration is clear: once again Faith has arisen from a deathlike sleep to face the adversity that is the common lot of fallen man. Imogen's own faith in Posthumus has been fully restored; and we shall presently see similar restorations of faith in Belarius and Posthumus. (pp. 130-35)

With the landing of the Romans, time presents Belarius with the opportunity to regain what he has lost. It is a recurring occasion. Twenty years earlier he had fought the Romans and for his efforts had been accused of treason and exiled. His immediate inclination on this new occasion is to retire, and when Guiderius objects, he reminds him of the torture and death they face for having killed Cloten. When the boys continue to argue with him, he is driven to what, in terms of the play's central thematic concern, is the crucial point at issue:

> the King
> Hath not deserv'd my service nor your loves,
> Who find in my exile the want of breeding,
> The certainty of this hard life; aye hopeless
> To have the courtesy your cradle promis'd,
> But to be still hot Summer's tanlings and
> The shrinking slaves of Winter.
>
> [IV. iv. 24-30]

The choice Belarius would make is based upon "desert" and certainty. His first argument is an expression of the logic which led him to repay Cymbeline for failing to trust him by kidnapping his sons. He has given Cymbeline what he deserves by repaying him in kind; and since Cymbeline has done nothing since to deserve Belarius' support, he finds no reason now to volunteer his service. This is the logic of natural justice. In the absence of love evil can only be avenged and service given only to those who merit it. Belarius' second argument is based upon his disillusion with the world of the court. He prefers the assurance of time's hard certainties, the revolutions of the seasons, to unreliable "courtesy."

But once again love proves renewing. The boys hear only the promptings of their noble blood; and when he realizes that they intend to engage the Romans with or without him, Belarius the Patriarch becomes a follower and agrees to go with them into their "country wars." . . . His love for the princes he has raised and his admiration for the patriotic and noble virtues he sees in them have awakened his faith in "courtesy" and led him to resume, without concern for "desert," his former role in the public world. He has made a choice which will regain him the love, titles, and honors that once were his.

Posthumus eventually recovers what he has lost through a process that is similar to the restoration of Belarius. But the conditions he must satisfy are far more demanding. Belarius has only to recover his faith in the integrity of the court. He has never denied man's capacity for honorable action, nor has he ever denied the notions of order and degree. He has sought satisfaction through revenge, but not through murder. Posthumus' mistrust, on the other hand, has been total. He has denied the "mutual concord and love" of humanity itself. Before his return to the civil world he must return to the world of man. Through *nosce teipsum* he must discover *humanitas*.

His return commences in V. i., when he confronts what he takes to be the visible evidence of his own guilt. As he begins to reflect upon the bloody "proof," we recognize that he has been given another opportunity to consider Imogen's "transgression," and on this occasion in the light of his own. Iachimo's "proof" had provoked in him a sexual jealousy so violent that he had charged all wives with dishonesty and de-

nounced all women as the vessels through which original sin is transmitted from generation to generation. Now, on this new occasion, the remorse he feels for his own guilt clears his eyes. Discovering in his own guilt the legacy of sin to which all men are heirs, he begins to "see feelingly" [*King Lear,* IV. vi. 149] and to understand why justice needs the tempering of mercy. . . . (pp. 135-37)

As Posthumus' soliloquy progresses, the question of justice (raised implicitly in his reflection on the folly of his seeking justice through revenge) emerges as the dominant concern. He regrets that Pisanio had not refused, in the name of justice, to carry out the command to kill Imogen, and then he briefly questions the justice of the gods:

> if you
> Should have ta'en vengeance on my faults, I never
> Had liv'd to put on this; so had you sav'd
> The noble Imogen to repent, and struck
> Me, wretch, more worth your vengeance.
>
> [V. i. 7-11]

The acknowledgment of guilt in this protest is evidence of his new awareness. It is an awareness born of the knowledge of self: he shares the common guilt of "humanity" and in the strict terms of retributive justice is guilty of crimes, even before the crime of killing Imogen, that demand his death. (p. 138)

The means Posthumus chooses to satisfy the gods are as important as the end—both to his spiritual regeneration and to his eventual reconciliation with Imogen, Cymbeline, and the civil state of Britain—for they are also the means by which he confirms his legacy as a Briton and as his father's son. His regeneration began when he acknowledged his "humanity." By accepting death as the just punishment for sin and by forgiving Imogen and all wives their transgressions, he has acknowledged the dual legacy of justice and love to which all men fall heir. Now, by donning the humble attire of a "Briton peasant" to face death "unknown" and "to shame the guise o' th' world" [V. i. 32] by making "men know / More valour in me than my habits show" [V. i. 29-30], he reaffirms the patrimony which in his jealous rage he had renounced. He is now ready—as atoning man, as British subject, and as Posthumus Leonatus—to prove through action his nobility of purpose. (pp. 139-40)

But Posthumus has still more to learn about truth and seeming. . . . So long as he conceives of death as a punishment, it will necessarily seem to him a thing to be feared. Punishment must be painful or else it is no punishment; moreover, it must, in his view, fit the crime, and the crime he believes he has committed is fearful in the extreme. Eventually his vision will be clarified. He will see death differently. But for the present he sees death only as a punishment, a way of satisfying divine justice. It is this desire to pay for what he believes he has done, not despair, that leads him to change clothes again and to be taken prisoner as a Roman and held for treason.

This action, too, contributes to clarification. Posthumus has been a defector to the Roman cause, and the Roman dress he assumes is a public admission of his disloyalty. Once again he corrects a variance between truth and seeming. It is also true, as several commentators have observed, that the action initiates an exercise in repentance. In surrendering himself to the Britons, Posthumus confirms his readiness to answer to both divine and civil justice, to answer with his life for the crime he has committed against both his country and the gods. The fact that he is finally reprieved is the consequence of mercy granted by both authorities—a mercy freely given, but which his own efforts to remake himself prepare him to receive.

Posthumus' soliloquy following the Gaoler's exit [V. iv. 3] is crucial to these matters. It commences with an acceptance of ''bondage'' as a way to ''liberty'' inasmuch as it points to death. The liberty Posthumus seeks is a release from a tormented conscience. The point, however, is subtler than it first seems, for in his reflections Posthumus has ascended from the notion of physical captivity and release to a spiritual notion. Death now seems to him a ''penitent instrument'' which will release him from the debt he has incurred by his crimes of murder and treason. To die is to satisfy both the civil and divine law and thus to be free from the debt incurred.

From this point on in the soliloquy Posthumus concentrates upon the divine law and its satisfaction. The civil law demands his death, and his surrender is sufficient proof of his willingness to satisfy it. Divine law seems to him not so easily satisfied. Now, for the first time since the beginning of his remorse, he considers the gods in terms of other than as exactors of justice. . . . As he had earlier discovered the justice of the gods in allowing him to live, murder Imogen, and still go seemingly unpunished, now, through the strength of his own powers of self-examination and reflection, he discovers their mercy. They will be merciful if they will accept his life as satisfactory payment for the life of Imogen, even though his life is not equal in worth to hers. (pp. 140-42)

The proof that Posthumus has satisfied the justice of the gods, that they have cancelled ''these cold bonds'' [V. iv. 28], is the vision that follows. He is now given, in a way that has been anticipated in *Pericles,* the most profound ability to see and therefore to understand. (p. 142)

[The] vision [Posthumus' dream] presents is not only Jupiter's way of confirming Posthumus' belief that the gods are merciful as well as just, but also the dramatist's means of portraying the kind of vision that Posthumus has been given by the gods as a reward for his trust in their benevolence. It is a mode of dramatic illusion, permitted by the conventions of romance, which allows the dramatist to portray what he conceives to be a reality beyond the phenomenal world. As such, the vision is a means—and in this it is similar to Pericles' dream and to the music of the spheres which he hears—of illuminating the audience as well as Posthumus. In its presentation of Jupiter descending from the heavens to answer the questions raised by the Shades of Posthumus' parents and brothers it answers the central questions raised by the play's action about justice and mercy and truth and seeming. (pp. 143-44)

A final word about the extent of divinity's involvement in *Cymbeline* is in order. The concluding scene of the play affirms and reaffirms the role that the heavens have had in bringing about the harmonious conclusion of events. The Soothsayer, who from his first appearance in the play has had difficulties in reading natural phenomena, concludes that the peace restored between Rome and Britain has been the work of the heavens. . . . He has reinterpreted the omen of the Roman eagle which ''wing'd / From the spongy south to this part of the west'' and ''There vanish'd in the sunbeams'' [IV. ii. 348-50] as a sign that the reunion of Britain has been divinely ordained. Cymbeline accepts the Soothsayer's reading, announcing in the opening lines of his exit speech sacrifices to the gods and a ratification of the newly won peace in the temple of Jupiter.

But the audience from its vantage point has seen more than the Soothsayer and Cymbeline have been permitted to see and knows the extent to which Britain's destiny has been shaped by men. We have seen the gods intervene, but primarily through human agents—through men who like Posthumus and Belarius have atoned fully for their crimes against heaven and country and thus transformed themselves into agents of renewal. We know, therefore, that the destination of the Roman eagle's flight has been determined by men. It was unleashed and directed toward Britain by Cymbeline's refusal to continue to pay tribute to Rome; and, as the Soothsayer had initially suggested, it seemed to promise a Roman victory. But that victory was circumvented by Belarius and the three boys, who in asserting their nobility won the favor of the god who rides on the back of the eagle and who is the dispenser of justice.

The audience also knows that the eagle seen by the Soothsayer, whose knowledge of the future is based solely upon natural phenomena, is not to be identified only with Rome. Having seen Posthumus identified with the eagle on several occasions in the play, we realize in retrospect that the eagle seen by the Soothsayer may also have designated the vengeful Posthumus' return to England with the invading Romans. We realize, therefore, that retributive justice in the form of the Roman invasion, and in the person of Posthumus, has been circumvented by atoning man and a merciful and forgiving Jupiter. We know, in short, that the heavens have intervened at a decisive moment in the history of Britain, but only after human agents have taken the initiative. (pp. 146-47)

Douglas L. Peterson, '' 'Cymbeline': Legendary History and Arcadian Romance,'' in his Time and Tempest: A Study of Shakespeare's Romances, *The Huntington Library, 1973, pp. 108-50.*

ROSALIE L. COLIE   (essay date 1974)

[*Whereas earlier critics have generally viewed the Welsh mountain scenes in* Cymbeline *as depicting a golden, idyllic world (in particular, see the excerpt above by Douglas L. Peterson, 1973), Colie regards them as representing ''the classic life of hard pastoral.'' She argues that the landscape is pictured as ''difficult'' and ''ungenerous,'' emphasizing its dearth of nurturing generosity and fecundity. However, Colie contends, their natural life has refined the innate nobility of Guiderius and Arviragus, enabling them to fulfill their proper roles. Such other critics as E. K. Chambers (1907) and Michael Taylor (1983) have also discussed Shakespeare's adaptation of pastoral conventions in* Cymbeline. *For further analyses of the characters of Guiderius, Arviragus, and Belarius, see the excerpts by August Wilhelm Schlegel (1811), William Hazlitt (1817), and Horace Howard Furness (1913), as well as the essay by D. R. C. Marsh cited in the Additional Bibliography.*]

[In *Cymbeline,* we] are at once made acutely aware, for good as for ill, of that court's sophistications, duplicities, fissures, and general unkindness. Posthumus is banished because he has overlept rank—in spite of the fact that he was raised as companion to princes and as cynosure of the King's household, he may not aspire to the King's daughter. Natural love between two persons considered to be naturally good, then, is denied at the play's beginning; ''nurture'' is also rejected, since the very King who raised Posthumus does not consider his own education of the young man a sufficient counterbalance to lack of ''rank.'' Rank has replaced both nature and nurture; and rank itself is a matter of occasion. Cloten is distasteful to the courtiers among whom he moves, but as the new Queen's son, he is free to indulge his personality as he wishes. The Queen's machinations in the garden with the poisonous flowers, an inverted pastoral procedure, are matched and neutralized by the Doctor's mitigations: we see nature tampered with and restored in the successive incidents over the poison. There are parallels to the Queen's artifices in other ranges of the court life—even Imogen's high Renaissance chamber has an overblown decorativeness that makes it seem an appropriate setting for Iachimo's schemes. Little here is natural, save the punished love of Imogen and Posthumus: that is, whatever is of the court is made to seem artificial if not positively invaded by artifice. Caught between the Queen's calculated tricks on one side and the gratuitous stratagem of Iachimo on the other, Imogen can only flee the place—and flees to what is thematically, schematically, the opposite of the court, to a rocky cave in the wild hillsides beyond the boundaries of "civilization." Disguised as Fidele, Imogen takes refuge in the Welsh mountains, in a cave empty of inhabitants where, of course, the two young huntsmen whose home it is gladly take her in. That these two representatives of her kind turn out to be her kin as well is simply a stock arrangement in pastoral drama and in romances generally, where changeling situations abound. The reconstitution of a fundamentally noble family is a standard romance resolution, too, as it is a pastoral-comic resolution as well.

In *Cymbeline,* the moral thematics of pastoral receives considerable emphasis as, throughout the play, a concealed debate of court with country is carried on, in many thematic mutations. Imogen finds that courtiers have no monopoly on human deceptions, when she is misled by beggars; but she recognizes that their poverty and rusticity may offer an excuse for the beggars' unkindness which courtiers have not. In this as in much else, Imogen iterates her natural goodness, her recognition of other people's conditions: her wish to be a shepherdess [I. i. 48-50] is of a piece with her natural understanding. By far the most important doctrinal statement is that made by Belarius: insisting on the ideological purity of the life he has lived with his foster sons (in a rocky cave so stark that Imogen first takes it for a beast's lair), Belarius urges natural religion on his charges, as well as the spartan simplicity of

> this life
> . . . nobler than attending for a check:
> Richer than doing for a robe,
> Prouder than rustling in unpaid for silk. . . .
>
> [III. iii. 21-4]

The boys, however, will not join with him in his assertion that there is "No life to ours!" [III. iii. 26]. Like those primitives in the earliest stages of Lucretius' cyclical development of human polity [in *De rerum natura*], the boys have evidently tired of eating acorns and want something more in their lives. Lucretius' lines describe a primitive race of men very like Belarius' ideal for these boys, a race far hardier than the present sort, men . . . who ate acorns and drank the pure water of the stream, who lived in caves, hunted game, and slept on the ground: flint was their pillow, as it was for Belarius' boys. Otherwise primitive, these men had an immense integrity, a complete and finished humanness, qualified by their further "development" toward civilization. Guiderius' words echo another stage in the Lucretian account of social progress, that is, the rejection of cave life, and cave ecology. Acorns would no longer do . . . and a greater refinement in diet and life came to seem necessary. As Guiderius says to Belarius, not everything is perfect in the cave, either:

> Haply this life is best
> (If quiet life be best) sweeter to you
> That have a sharper known, well corresponding

> With your stiff age; but unto us it is
> A cell of ignorance, travelling a-bed,
> A prison, or a debtor that not dares
> To stride a limit.
>
> [III. iii. 29-35]

These boys . . . yearn for a nurture of which they are deprived: they are . . . inland bred and something in them craves for that inland cultivation:

> What should we speak of
> When we are old as you? When we shall hear
> The rain and wind beat dark December? How
> In this our pinching cave shall we discourse
> The freezing hours away? We have seen nothing:
> We are beastly: subtle as the fox for prey,
> Like warlike as the wolf for what we eat.
>
> [III. iii. 35-41]

Like animals in their self-sufficiency and their physical hardness, the boys do not admire themselves as beasts; nor do they care for the winter weather, which they recognize as part of their discontent. Theirs is, truly, the classic life of hard pastoral—but which they, unlike proper ideological hard-pastoralists, criticize precisely for its want of nurture. Belarius makes haste to assure them of the comparative merits of their lot, recalling the injustices that are—as the audience knows from the earlier parts of the play—"the art o' the court" [III. iii. 46]:

> Then was I as a tree
> Whose boughs did bend with fruit. But in one night,
> A storm, or robbery (call it what you will)
> Shook down my mellow hangings, nay, my leaves,
> And left me bare to weather.
>
> [III. iii. 60-4]

In this organic metaphor, we feel the unnaturalness of the husbandry which so stripped Belarius. In the mountains he can claim at least that in "this rock and these demesnes" he has "liv'd in honest freedom"—that primary requisite, as [Thomas G.] Rosenmeyer has pointed out [in *The Green Cabinet*], of the pastoral condition—without fearing the "poison, which attends / In place of greater state" [III. iii. 77-8]. And the audience must agree with him, against the noble stretching of the boys, having seen his metaphor unmetaphored earlier in the play, as the Queen gathered simples in her garden with which to do away with Imogen.

However their aspirations may reach, though, the boys must bow each time they enter the cave, in a stoic *topos* [motif], just as Hercules bent to enter mortal houses and Aeneas to enter Evander's little palace, these boys acknowledged their humility every time they take shelter. But they are proud, too: they hunt the hills, Belarius the plain—and not just because they are nimble and he is stiff, but also because elevations are their symbolic habitat, properly sought according to the inevitable pastoral correspondence of real rank with character. However stern the doctrine he tries to implant in them, Belarius does not quite believe in the totality of his ideology, and cannot help delighting in the boys' aspiring to a life beyond the one they lead. Noble as it is as a refuge from the unjust, artificial, and deceitful court, this landscape is very far from the nourishing pastoral landscape to which Theocritus turned, nor is it the ironically idealized background of the Forest of Arden, delightful in some ways and harsh in others. This is unmitigated hard pastoral, a rocky, difficult terrain training its inhabitants to a spare and muscular strength sufficient to wrest their nutriment from its minimal, ungenerous, exiguous resources. No fruit here bends from the boughs to the eaters' mouths; there is no leisure here to play on pipes and lie in the shade—and as for Neaera, she casts no shadow over the boys' lives. Here, the homely must prove savory, as they say, and flint offer the only pillow; hunger must be satisfied with cold meat till the catch be cooked. The boys are, in a word, cave-dwellers, troglodytes, quite innocent of the city's "usuries." As such children of nature, they instinctively scorn "pelf": when Imogen-Fidele offers them money for what she had taken from their larder, Arviragus answers like the natural aristocrat he is:

> All gold and silver rather turn to dirt,
> As 'tis no better reckon'd but, of those
> Who worship dirty gods.
>
> [III. vi. 53-5]

Again and again, the boys respond as nature's noblemen, and Belarius, for all the stoic moral instruction he gives the boys, takes pride in their mysterious elevations beyond their present condition:

> How hard it is to hide the sparks of Nature!
> These boys know little they are sons to th' king,
> Nor Cymbeline dreams that they are alive.
> They think they are mine, and though train'd up thus meanly,
> I' th' cave wherein they bow, their thoughts do hit
> The roofs of palaces, and nature prompts them
> In simple and low things to prince it, much
> Beyond the trick of others.
>
> [III. iii. 79-86]

Naturally courteous, then, the cave-family takes in the exile freely, shares what it has with her in hospitable kindness: bare gentility, but liberal. That the boys recognize some kinship with Fidele, and she with them, is of a piece with the kind of miraculous recognition in which this mixed drama is cast. Like calls to like; disguise is no bar to human recognition, the recognition of kind which is, in this kind of fiction, recognition of kin as well. Furthermore, Imogen-Fidele knows at once the natural gentility of these boys:

> These are kind creatures. Gods, what lies I have heard!
> Our courtiers say all's savage but at court;
> Experience, O, thou disprov'st report!
>
> [IV. ii. 32-4]

In contrast to her considerate nature, Cloten recognizes no such thing: unfortunately for him, he sees Guiderius simply as a villainous and rustic mountaineer, and comes to his death at the hands of this touchy aristocrat, who will not be condescended to, still less insulted. Once more, Guiderius' behavior, this time manifestly in line with the codes of courtly honor, elicits Belarius' praise of the goddess Nature, who has invested these boys with their birthright—

> royalty unlearn'd, honour untaught,
> Civility not seen from other, valour
> That wildly grows in them
>
> [IV. ii. 178-80]

corroborates their fundamental nobility. In another style, Arviragus proves as courtly as his brother, in his uttering the wonderful flower-catalogue of Fidele's beauty; in the dirge for her (learned from their foster mother?) the boys offer no simple country ditty, but a complex poem balancing off simplicity against sophisticated awareness of simplicity's power, a poem entirely in the pastoral mode if not in a pastoral vocabulary.

The plot itself permits the boys to prove their chivalric qualities: the murder of Cloten brings the British threat, so long staved off by Belarius, closer to the cave; the advent of the hostile legions menaces their outlandish privacy as well. Prudent in the boys' welfare, Belarius counsels retreat to the hills ("higher to the mountains" [IV. iv. 8]) whither, he is sure, neither party shall pursue his "hot summer's tanlings," his "shrinking slaves of winter" [IV. iv. 29, 30]. But Guiderius has heard the call to arms, and the boys seize the chance to outrun the skimpy, barren life to which they had been bred—"Than be so," says Guiderius, "Better to cease to be" [IV. iv. 30-1]. Off they go, and in the chaotic battle that follows, the boys and their foster father manage such deeds of valor that they are knighted in the field for their gentlemanliness at arms. Gradually, the concealments unwind until the boys are restored to their father, their foster father is forgiven his theft of them, and justice and mercy are distributed to everyone gathered for the play's proper ending. The self-consciously reformed court world takes them all in, as the court's recognized means of restoration; everyone turns his back on earlier error and harder landscapes elsewhere. The fine young men, schooled to endurance by their teacher and their habitat, take their places among the other courtiers naturally enough, their youthful discipline offering the promise that Cymbeline's kingdom will be reorganized on new and different moral lines. Nature has raised these boys so that they can return to a birthright compromised in their absence and purify it by the simple strengths of their natural characters.

In this paradigm, the country interludes, whether on a supernatural island [as in *The Tempest*] or in the Welsh mountains, affirm nature's preservative and restorative powers, her capacity to reconstitute whatever may be wrong with the human constitution, personal or social. To this extent, the country interlude permits human beings to come into contact with Nature, and to assimilate from her such creatural strength as human nature requires in an unnatural social world. (pp. 292-98)

We must wonder at much in *Cymbeline,* but the quality of our wonder is utterly different from the wonder experienced in *The Tempest,* where "wonder" is frankly written into the whole play, its *maraviglia* [astonishment] more than the wondrous and wondering Miranda. In the case of this uncharted island, its associations with the "still-vex'd Bermoothes" and with Mediterranean islands like Corfu only serve to make its locale more mysterious, its magic qualities truly leagues beyond ordinary life. (p. 299)

The Welsh mountains of *Cymbeline* are no such magic place. Indeed, if we were to imagine a natural environment opposite to Prospero's island, we might come up with just such a stark, rocky, isolated cave as Belarius has made his home. The strictness of that locale, as habitat and as symbol, simply guarantees the innate and confirmed rectitude of Cymbeline's sons, savage noblemen so totally in control of their inhospitable landscape that they can question the values of the life it offers even as they go about fulfilling its severe requirements. They are the hard pastoralists extolled by stoic and cynic, those plain men who, pared down to their essentials by the environment with which they must all their lives compete, make of themselves touchstones for moral and social truth. (pp. 300-01)

> *Rosalie L. Colie, " 'Nature's above Art in That Respect': Limits of the Pastoral Pattern," in her* Shakespeare's Living Art, *Princeton University Press, 1974, pp. 284-316.*

ROGER WARREN   (essay date 1976)

[*Warren analyzes the contrasting stylistic techniques Shakespeare used in* Cymbeline *to depict basic human emotions in a state of*

Act III. Scene vi. Belarius, Arviragus, Guiderius, and Imogen. By T. Bankel. The Department of Rare Books and Special Collections, The University of Michigan Library.

supreme intensity. He examines three scenes—Imogen's awakening beside Cloten's headless torso, Posthumus's vision, and Iachimo in Imogen's bedroom—where, he avers, "theatrical virtuosity on an elaborate scale is set off against language of great simplicity or emotional intensity or both." In each of these scenes, Warren argues, there is a visual action so startling that the audience's attention is arrested and the dramatic moment is temporarily isolated from the rest of the play's action, whereupon the dramatist conveys, by means of poetry that is powerful and intense, a sense of emotion so strong that the audience experiences the feeling together with the character. The critic generally disputes those commentators—such as Harley Granville-Barker (1930), Barbara A. Mowat (1966), R. A. Foakes (1971), and Arthur C. Kirsch (see Additional Bibliography)—who have judged that Shakespeare intended to establish a series of distancing effects in this play, especially in those scenes cited above. Indeed, Warren contends, the audience's involvement with Imogen during the headless torso episode is so deep that the scene is one of "retching grief." For further discussions of this scene, see the excerpts by Harold C. Goddard (1951), F. D. Hoeniger (1961), Robin Moffet (1962), and Robert Grams Hunter (1965), as well as the essay by Joan Carr cited in the Additional Bibliography.]

In much the most helpful criticism of *Cymbeline* that I know, James Sutherland isolates two contrasting styles, one 'impetuous, violent, straining after the maximum of intensity', the other a 'natural, easy, and unforced' style [see Additional Bib-

liography]. He describes illuminatingly the 'new recklessness of expression' in Arviragus's

> the bier at door,
> And a demand who is't shall die, I'ld say
> 'My father, not this youth':

[IV. ii. 22-4]

Undertakers do not come round to the door like dustmen to demand a corpse—a corpse, too, that is not yet dead when they arrive. What Shakespeare has to express is an avowal of love that will go a stage further than that just made by Guiderius . . . Clutching at some means to express this thought powerfully, Shakespeare moves naturally enough to a choice between life and death, a choice involving the (supposed) father of Guiderius on the one hand and the boy on the other . . . Driven on by some compelling urge for the immediate and the emphatic—perhaps visualizing the death situation in a sudden flash—he never pauses to get it into perspective, but suddenly writes down the elliptical and startling phrase, 'the bier at door', and the rest inevitably follows.

What Professor Sutherland conjectures here about the style seems to me to apply to whole scenes as well: Shakespeare visualises situations 'in a sudden flash' and does not bother about matters of more normal dramatic coherence. It is the situations which interest him. In particular, 'visualizing the death situation' is central to the action of the play as well as to the language.

The two contrasted styles which Professor Sutherland mentions are also central, in a less complex and extreme form, to Shakespeare's style in his earlier comedies. Those comedies constantly set extravagant against extremely simple language (the strikingly simple, powerful blank verse in the finale of *Love's Labour's Lost* against the extravagance earlier; the simple directness of Beatrice and Benedick in the Church against the dangerous frivolity of the Court [in *Much Ado about Nothing*]; the contrast between Orsino's language and Viola's [in *Twelfth Night*]). In *Cymbeline*, Shakespeare applies similar contrasts, not only to the language, but to the whole play. In each of the central scenes, theatrical virtuosity on an elaborate scale is set off against language of great simplicity or emotional intensity or both: the enormously elaborate series of events leading up to Imogen's waking by Cloten's corpse against the breathtaking simplicity of the dirge and the passionate intensity of Imogen's grief, the virtuoso descent of Jupiter against the language with which Posthumus responds to it, and Iachimo's emergence from the trunk against his exquisitely expressed appreciation both of Imogen's beauty and her worth. And J. C. Maxwell points out the 'contrast in the final scene between the surface virtuosity of the dénouement . . . and the rich poetry of the occasional phrase' [see Additional Bibliography].

These contrasts account for the play's most impressive single quality in the theatre—the capturing of single *moments*, the highlighting and displaying on stage, in an extreme form, of central human emotions—love, rapture, despair, jealousy, desire, jealousy, desire, even death and burial, ultimately reconciliation. It seems to have been the desire to capture, to exploit fully, even the sadness of death that made Shakespeare contrive the bizarre series of events that would enable him to present, not just an awareness but an *experiencing* of death and loss, to make the audience share in it fully—so that he can then take them *beyond* even that to joy and reconciliation, to make it the more valued, the richer, for our having experienced Imogen's pain and the princes' grief so fully. This seems to me a more far-reaching version of the technique of a comedy like *Twelfth Night,* where the awareness of shadows, dying roses, and the wind and the rain, far from detracting from the ultimate happiness of the lovers, enriches our sense of their 'golden time', precisely *because* the harsher aspects of life have not been excluded. (pp. 41-2)

The big difference between the two plays is that taking the imagined death situation out of the poetic texture and putting it on the stage contributes to the much greater complexity—or at any rate complicatedness—of *Cymbeline*. In attempting to present on the stage everything about an experience, the play constantly fuses poetic complexity with stage action of a particularly startling kind, as it places love, grief, despair, death, before us. And of these death is the most important, since the mock-burial is at once the central, the most complex, and the most contrived scene in the play.

Why does Shakespeare go to such bizarre lengths to present us with an elaborate funeral for someone who isn't dead, and an elaborate recognition of a headless body—except that it's the wrong body? Any interpretation of *Cymbeline* must account for this apparent dramatic perversity. Those critics who see *Cymbeline* in terms of self-conscious 'coterie dramaturgy' feel

that this technique is to keep the characters' emotions distanced and the audience detached. My impression of the burial scene is exactly the reverse—that Shakespeare is lavishing all his resources on the scene in order to create an overwhelming sense of the sadness of death, a genuine sense of loss and deprivation, both on the princes' part and Imogen's, without the loss being in the end a real one. Then, having made the audience *experience* fully the princes' and Imogen's grief and sense of loss, the play can move beyond even that to reunion and a new life. And this seems to me a more complex version of the technique used in *Twelfth Night,* which makes us aware of darkness and disturbance in its implications and undertones, in order to make the final happiness seem all the richer and fuller.

The stylistic connection between *Cymbeline* and *Twelfth Night* also helps to explain why Shakespeare has taken so much trouble to get Cloten into Posthumus's clothes for this situation, and also why Imogen is made so positively to make her erroneous identification. The retching grief of this scene in the theatre convinces me beyond doubt that it is not (as some have suggested) a scene for laughs. We are not, even remotely, supposed to preserve a mockingly distanced detachment from Imogen. 'Why,' asks Frank Kermode, 'give Posthumus the body of a paragon, and then allow Cloten's equal to it?' [see Additional Bibliography]. Because, I think, Shakespeare wants to indicate a similarity in certain respects between them. The physical similarity is insisted upon to suggest another kind of similarity. When Posthumus moves from an extreme protestation of love for Imogen to an equally extreme outburst of violence against her, he matches Cloten in extravagant rashness, even to the details of the language they use:

> *Cloten*. when my lust hath dined—which, as I
> say, to vex her I will execute in the clothes that
> she so praised—to the court I'll knock her back,
> foot her home again.
>
> [III. v. 141-44]

> *Posthumus*.
>
> O that I had her here to tear her limb-meal!
> I will go there and do't i' th' court, before
> Her father. I'll do something.
>
> [II. iv. 147-49]

The difference is that this mixture of half-incoherent rage and a determination to humiliate Imogen before her father as well as inflicting violent pain on her is the sort of thing which occurs naturally to Cloten, whereas it is only a part of Posthumus, a reaction to Iachimo's goading: the fact remains that similar violence lurks inside both characters, as it lurks inside the Orsino of Act V. All three react from wounded pride; all three are concerned with *themselves* as betrayed or thwarted lovers. The insistence on the similarity of Cloten's body to Posthumus's is not, then, a wanton theatrically self-conscious joke; what they have in common complicates what might have remained fairy-tale figures, romantic hero and boor. For Life is more complex than such superficial views allow.

And so it is with Imogen's apparent death and burial. . . . In the burial scene, the far-reaching, evocative imagery from the natural world not only suggests the sorrow of death, but its peace as well: Imogen is almost absorbed into that world; she is not only *like* primrose or harebell, she *is* the lily or 'the bird . . . That we have made so much on' [IV. ii. 197-98]. The magical poignancy of that moment, as of the burial scene as a whole, stems from this unforced identification of Imogen with the natural world; we are hardly aware of it as a comparison at all, and this is an important example of a scene where the ease and simplicity of the writing offsets the complicated contrivance which has led up to the apparent death. And Arviragus's flower speech is worlds away from superficial compliment: the concrete, specific presentation of the robin bringing, not just 'fairest flowers' but the more down-to-earth 'furred moss' to protect the body gives a sense of security to contrast more sharply with human ingratitude:

> The ruddock would
> With charitable bill—O bill sore shaming
> Those rich-left heirs that let their fathers lie
> Without a monument!—bring thee all this;
> Yea, and furred moss besides, when flowers are none,
> To winter-ground thy corse.
>
> [IV. ii. 224-29]

The exquisite dirge develops this still quality, sadness mingled with a sense of the body returning to and being protected by the earth, as Belarius emphasises in closing the episode:

> The ground that gave them first has them again.
> Their pleasures here are past, so is their pain.
>
> [IV. ii. 289-90]

So the emotions associated with death and burial are fully evoked; an impression of Death is placed before the audience.

And then the play takes us beyond Death; Imogen revives. Shakespeare communicates her bewildered terror in another vividly expressive image from the natural world; it has that quality peculiar to *Cymbeline* of 'an exquisite distillation of the thought into a precise, if still surprising, image' [Joan Barton, as stated in program notes for the 1974 Royal Shakespeare Company production of *Cymbeline*]. Shakespeare needs something immediate yet startling to convey Imogen's terror and her attempt to grasp reality, something 'not imagined, felt':

> if there be
> Yet left in heaven as small a drop of pity
> As a wren's eye, feared gods, a part of it!
>
> [IV. ii. 303-05]

Then the play reworks, in a much more intense fashion, the technique by which Viola moves from expressing her love in terms of an imagined death situation to an acceptance that life has to continue.

Viola's simple statement of heartbreak, 'A blank, my lord. She never told her love' [*Twelfth Night,* II. iv. 110] is matched by the utterly simple, broken expression of Imogen's misery:

> I am nothing; or if not,
> Nothing to be were better.
>
> [IV. ii. 367-68]

Neither Imogen nor Viola feel themselves to be anything without the love of Posthumus or Orsino; and Imogen, like Viola, uses the master/page relationship to express her sadness at her apparent loss, and so the power of her love:

> I may wander
> From east to occident; cry out for service;
> Try many, all good; serve truly; never
> Find such another master.
>
> [IV. ii. 371-74]

But the really crucial comparison is that, after promising, again in sweet-sad verse of great expressiveness, to cover the body with wood-leaves and weeds, echoing the language and implications of the earlier burial speeches, she realises like Vi-

ola—'Sir, shall I to this lady?' [*Twelfth Night,* II. iv. 122]— that life must go on: 'And leaving so his service, follow you' [IV. ii. 393]. Both scenes express human love in images of death, and the language realises that experience as fully as possible; then, having allowed both the sadness and the peace of death their full impact, both Viola and Imogen—characteristically of Shakespeare's comic technique—move beyond even this. This attempt at inclusiveness helps to explain why the language in *Cymbeline* should range so greatly, from the hauntingly evocative to the extremely tortuous: it seems to me the expression of a man trying to pack in a great deal, to communicate this or that emotion in all its complexity, even at the sacrifice of immediate clarity. Such clarity is never sacrificed in *Twelfth Night;* Shakespeare takes the emotion as far as it will go in that brilliantly organised play; but here, he wants something more, more than could be attained even by Viola— and there is a price to be paid for that more; the greater intensity can only be attained by greater dramatic complexity and the danger there is that the complexity of device may defeat the intensity of emotion. This danger is particularly acute in the Jupiter scene.

It looks as if the Jupiter scene was intended to parallel the burial scene, showing the low point of Posthumus's fortunes as well, in his plea to the Gods for death, and then taking Posthumus, like Imogen, beyond the shadow of death. But whereas Shakespeare makes Imogen's scene work superbly because he endows it with such powerful writing, and so maintains the crucial balance between stage virtuosity and poetic impact, Posthumus's scene *depends* upon theatrical machinery of a startling kind. To put it simply, however successful Jupiter's apparatus, the language of the apparitions cannot hope to compare with the emotional and atmospheric charge of 'Fear no more the heat o' th' sun' [IV. ii. 258]. Setting aside all questions of authenticity, the scene is unbalanced as it stands: unlike the burial scene, virtuoso staging and evocative language are not held in balance. Since Jupiter's

> Whom best I love I cross; to make my gift,
> The more delayed, delighted
>
> [V. iv. 101-02]

lacks poetic distinction, it is not powerful enough to command attention and so communicate significance when delivered from an eagle's back in mid-air. I think that the descent of Jupiter was meant to be a sensational 'call to attention', to place Posthumus in an *extreme* situation, as the burial scene placed Imogen, so as to focus on his reactions as that scene does on hers. Usually, though, that eagle *competes* with, rather than emphasising, Posthumus's experiences. But there is surely no doubt about the poetic quality of Posthumus's speeches.

Shakespeare does all he can to give those speeches suggestiveness and emotional power, and in a very specific way. Consciously or not, he uses phrasing from his own love poetry to express the depth of Posthumus's repentance *before* he knows that Imogen was true to him. When Posthumus begs the gods to take

> No stricter render of me than my all . . .
> For Imogen's dear life take mine; and though
> 'Tis not so dear, yet 'tis a life,
>
> [V. iv. 17, 22-3]

he is, as J. B. Leishman comments, 'speaking metaphorically, as a bankrupt, and means ''Don't trouble to work out what proportion you ought to take of what I possess—take all''' [in *Themes and Variations in Shakespeare's Sonnets*], and is using the legal metaphors and colouring of Sonnet 125. The earlier Posthumus, in his excessive adoration and protestation, and in judging by appearances, had resembled those from whom Shakespeare dissociates himself in the sonnet:

> Have I not seen dwellers on form and favour
> Lose all, and more, by paying too much rent.

In the sonnet, Shakespeare celebrates a mutual love which is 'not mix'd with seconds' (flour of an inferior quality); rather, it

> knows no art
> But mutual render, only me for thee.

But Posthumus is unhappily aware that the 'render' he can make cannot be 'mutual' because he is worth less than Imogen; his love is 'mix'd with seconds'. So he desperately offers a one-sided 'proportion', his life, in an attempt to pay the account ('audit') he owes Imogen:

> If you will take this audit, take this life,
> And cancel these cold bonds.
>
> > [V. iv. 27-8]

Here again, a mixture of complexity and simplicity expresses Posthumus's intensity: the bankruptcy metaphor is combined with the tender simplicity of 'dear life' [V. iv. 22] and at the end he turns from prayer to direct communication with her:

> O Imogen,
> I'll speak to thee in silence.
>
> > [V. iv. 28-9]

'Silence' is the only way he can communicate his grief after what he has done to her, as it was ultimately her only way at [I. iii. 21-2]. And this admission of his own folly helps to bring him closer to Imogen, so that when they meet he may seem worthier of her. They are brought together in other ways too. As there is an upward change of direction at the end of the burial scene, so his tone changes after the vision:

> 'Tis still a dream; or else such stuff as madmen
> Tongue, and brain not; either both, or nothing,
> Or senseless speaking, or a speaking such
> As sense cannot untie
>
> > [V. iv. 145-48]

recalls Imogen's

> 'Twas but a bolt of nothing, shot at nothing,
> Which the brain makes of fumes,
>
> > [IV. ii. 300-01]

thus underlining the similarity of their situations. His bewildered comment that he has

> this golden chance, and know not why.
> What fairies haunt this ground?
>
> > [V. iv. 132-33]

recalls not only the magical atmosphere of *A Midsummer Night's Dream*, but also Orsino's 'when . . . golden time convents' [*Twelfth Night*, V. i. 382]; both Orsino and Posthumus enjoy, without perhaps contributing substantially to it themselves, a new 'golden' time.

Just as the style of the play complicates the impression of 'simplicity' given by the characters in the burial and Jupiter scenes, so it does in the trunk and final scenes. As Posthumus is more complicated than a straightforward romantic hero, Iachimo is less than a fiend. It is not Iago-like malignity which

spurs Iachimo to the wager, but irritation at Posthumus's protestations: 'I make my wager rather against your confidence than her reputation' [I. iv. 110-11]. As Granville-Barker says, 'No tragically-potent scoundrel, we should be sure, will ever come out of a trunk.' But on the other hand, that scene is not simply a matter of 'theatrical' ostentation; Iachimo emerges from that trunk to arouse expectations which are not fulfilled: a rape scene which is not a rape, like the death scene where Imogen is not dead. Shakespeare captures our attention with the visual surprise in order to isolate and throw all attention upon Iachimo's reaction to Imogen herself. The gorgeous language gives us the impression of desire, but it has a delicacy too, which indicates sensitivity as well, a response to Imogen herself, a valuing of her for her own sake, in a way that Posthumus never does until Act V. And as in Imogen's needle, gnat and wren images, another vivid image from the natural world is used to present Iachimo's response as vividly as possible:

> On her left breast
> A mole cinque-spotted, like the crimson drops
> I' th' bottom of a cowslip.
>
> > [II. ii. 37-9]

This technique recurs when, amid all the ingenious contrivance of the final scene, moments of emotional intensity suddenly emerge, expressed by similar images:

> *Imogen.*
> Why did you throw your wedded lady from you?
> Think that you are upon a lock, and now
> Throw me again.
>
> *Posthumus.*
> Hang there like fruit, my soul,
> Till the tree die.
>
> > [V. v. 261-64]

Cymbeline is not a lucid play, as the comedies are, but I think it is the very *combination* of the 'virtuoso' elements with a reworking of techniques from the comedies which gives it its particular power, enabling Shakespeare to emphasise, isolate, highlight such powerful emotions as Imogen's grief or joy, Posthumus's extravagance and jealous rashness, Iachimo's response to Imogen. Gareth Lloyd Evans found it a matter for adverse criticism at Stratford in 1962 that, though Imogen, Iachimo, and Posthumus were 'superb in speech and in timing', the neutral, empty stage and the extreme sophistication of the production meant that 'their gaiety, gravity, pride and panache is cocooned in artificiality, and that the realities of grief, joy and venom are intermittent' [as stated in his review in *The Guardian*, July 18, 1962]. But so they are in a sense in the play, and the outstanding achievement of the 1962 production was to use its off-white surround, together with the necessary props and lighting, to *pinpoint* those individual 'realities of grief, joy and venom'. In doing so, it underlined Shakespeare's technique of isolating individual moments and situations and so highlighting a series of human emotions as fully as possible by examining contrasts and complexities, however tortuous:

> These flowers are like the pleasures of the world;
> This bloody man, the care on't.
>
> > [IV. ii. 296-97]
> > (pp. 44-9)

Roger Warren, "Theatrical Virtuosity and Poetic Complexity in 'Cymbeline'," in Shakespeare Survey: An Annual Survey of Shakespearian Study and Production, *Vol. 29, 1976, pp. 41-9.*

JAMES EDWARD SIEMON   (essay date 1976)

[*Cautioning against accepting without question the laudatory assessment of Posthumus's character presented by the First Gentleman in the opening scene of* Cymbeline, *Siemon argues that the hero must be evaluated in terms of his actions, his speeches, and the reactions to him of other credible figures in the play. Examining the wager scene, Siemon calls attention to the ambivalent reactions of the minor characters, whose responses lead us to question whether Posthumus is bound by a conventional code of honor to accept the challenge of Iachimo, as has been argued by such critics as Anna Brownell Jameson (1833), G. G. Gervinus (1849-50), and William Witherle Lawrence (1920). The critic also focuses on parallels between Posthumus and Cloten, including their physical resemblance, their propensities for wagers and gambling, their rashness, and, especially, the way they "both respond with violence to sexual humiliation," to underscore the fact that Posthumus is not, at least initially, a wholly virtuous figure. Siemon specifically remarks on the manner in which Shakespeare has emphasized these parallels through careful juxtaposition of scenes in which the two characters demonstrate similar behavior and emotions, contending that this technique is meant to demonstrate Posthumus's increasing likeness to Cloten through the close of Act II. However, the critic identifies certain effects adopted by Shakespeare to mitigate the audience's hostility towards Posthumus: one, he wisely keeps the hero offstage during Acts III and IV; two, he makes both Pisanio and Imogen react with sorrow rather than anger over Posthumus's scheme to kill his wife; and three, he provides Cloten as a "surrogate" and "scapegoat" to deflect the spectator's hostility from Posthumus during the hero's absence. These techniques, Siemon concludes, prepare us for Posthumus's reappearance in Act V and his subsequent adoption of a new understanding of real and apparent worth. Such other commentators as Robert Grams Hunter (1965) and Homer D. Swander (1966), as well as Joan Carr, Howard Felperin, and Joan Hartwig (see Additional Bibliography), have also demonstrated the similarities between Posthumus and Cloten.*]

[*Cymbeline*] undoubtedly poses difficulties, but it has also had needless difficulties foisted upon it. Its opening scene, for example, is usually understood as clarifying stable values:

> He that has miss'd the princess is a thing
> Too bad for bad report: and he that hath her
> (I mean, that married her, alack good man,
> And therefore banish'd) is a creature such
> As, to seek through the regions of the earth
> For one his like; there would be something failing
> In him that should compare. I do not think
> So fair an outward, and such stuff within
> Endows a man, but he.
>
>   [I. i. 16-24]

Thus the well-informed First Gentleman. There is, of course, growing recognition that the views advanced by expository characters may be highly colored and that in his exposition Shakespeare sometimes emphasizes not the complete view of the play's world that we should hold but rather a prejudicial view of it held by its inhabitants. The critical tradition, however, has been to take the First Gentleman in *Cymbeline* as Shakespeare's spokesman. W. W. Lawrence long ago remarked, 'Every audience knows that such a faithful expositor is not misleading them, but giving such information that they may understand the rest of the play intelligently' [see excerpt above, 1920]. This is the standard view and remains to this day a working premise in criticism of the play. (p. 51)

[Yet] neither Cloten nor Posthumus Leonatus behaves in a manner entirely in accord with the First Gentleman's appraisal;

nor does the play either in its spectacle or in its action sustain the absolute distinction he so emphatically draws between them.

Posthumus Leonatus makes his second appearance in I, iv, a scene of major expository importance whose implications seriously undercut the initial assertion of his virtue. This, the wager scene, opens with a short prelude: Philario, Iachimo, and an unnamed Frenchman discuss Posthumus's career and recent history. Although Iachimo's doubts about Posthumus's reputation appear to be cynically motivated, the reservations themselves are not unreasonable; his manner is offensive, but his meaning goes little beyond the observation that seeing is believing. The Frenchman expresses like doubts, and Philario's response is pointed:

> How worthy he is I will leave to appear hereafter,
> rather than story him in his own hearing.
>
>   [I. iv. 32-4]

Posthumus is here not a cynosure; he is a man whose worth will emerge in time, whose worth lies in that to come hereafter rather than in story. Whereas the First Gentleman directs our attention backwards and to story, Philario directs it forward and to action, inviting us to judge the past by the future rather than the reverse, to test Posthumus's reputation against his behavior, and to believe because we have seen. No one supposes that Posthumus stands the test well, but it is significant that in a play which begins with such high praise for Posthumus we are soon asked to watch Posthumus to see whether the praise be just or no.

The putative source for I, iv does not represent the decision to test the virtuous wife as in any way out of the ordinary. If Shakespeare intended us to take Posthumus's behavior as similarly a matter of course, we could reasonably expect a scene in which it were made to seem so—a scene which either directed our attention to the propriety of Posthumus's actions or deflected our attention from anything that might trouble us. In fact, Shakespeare does the reverse; he introduces a major and troubling departure from his source tale, inventing an earlier occasion in which Posthumus caused a fracas by making the question of Imogen's superiority to all other women a fighting matter. The Frenchman thinks he behaved badly:

> ... it had been pity you should have been put
> together, with so mortal a purpose as then each
> bore, upon importance of so slight and trivial
> a nature.
>
>   [I. iv. 39-42]

In calling the cause slight and trivial the Frenchman may be espousing Iachimo's cynical view of women; even so, as with Philario's invitation to watch Posthumus before judging him, this observation raises the issue of rational as opposed to conventional behavior. Iachimo picks up the question, and an increasingly heated disagreement ensues. As its outcome begins to take shape, Philario (for whose cynicism there is no evidence) tries to stop it, making unmistakably clear that he thinks both Iachimo and Posthumus mad:

> Let us leave here, gentlemen ... Gentlemen,
> enough of this, it came in too suddenly, let it
> die as it was born, and I pray you be better
> acquainted.
>
>   [I. iv. 99, 120-22]

When Posthumus proposes the wager, Philario protests, 'I will have it no lay' [I. iv. 147]. The scene ends with the Frenchman's disbelieving question, 'Will this hold, think you?' and

Philario's unhappy reply, 'Signior Iachimo will not from it. Pray let us follow 'em' [I. iv. 170, 171-72]. Thus, although none of the minor characters in this scene condemns Posthumus's code of honor as such, neither do they treat it as fine and proper; they tell us that Posthumus was a hot head when he was younger and observe with alarm that he is so still. Lawrence is right in pointing to a conventional code of honor underlying Posthumus's behavior, but the shape of the scene implies reservations about that code. Shakespeare reworks his source material, and what had there been morally clear cut is here morally ambivalent. (pp. 52-3)

That only Iachimo takes Posthumus's behavior as a matter of course suggests less than unqualified support for the conventions which lie behind it. On the other hand, there is no doubt that the sympathetic characters of *Cymbeline* admire him and that his nobility is directly called into question only by those whose right to make moral judgments is compromised by their own morally debased attitudes. In judging Posthumus, we must give due weight both to what we are shown of him and to what is said about him in his own world, and by whom. Meanwhile we must guard against confusing the simplistic conventions of romance with the sophisticated craft of a veteran playwright. If Iachimo is cynical, the First Gentleman is naive. His portrait of Posthumus is clearly labelled cardboard, and the opening scenes of the play invite us to compare the portrait with the man. What we first learn of Posthumus's worth lies only in his reputation:

> To his mistress,
> (For whom he now is banish'd) her own price
> Proclaims how she esteem'd him; and his virtue
> By her election may be truly read
> What kind of man he is.
>
> [I. i. 50-4]

The reliability of such a conception is made clear enough when Iachimo uses not only the First Gentleman's point of view but his very language to play successfully and disastrously upon Imogen's vanity:

> He hath a kind of honour sets him off,
> More than a mortal seeming. Be not angry,
> Most mighty princess, that I have adventur'd
> To try your taking of a false report, which hath
> Honour'd with confirmation your great judgement
> In the election of a sir so rare,
> Which you know cannot err.
>
> [I. vi. 170-76]

The First Gentleman's account of Cloten appears to be more reliable. The Second Lord, Imogen, and Guiderius agree that he is a fool, and even the Queen seems occasionally to find him exasperating. But if we simply take their word and look no more closely at the complexity of Cloten's role. He is more than just a fool. He makes sense in the council scene (III, i) even if, as is possible, he represents there a deeply corrupted understanding of Britain's proper relation to Rome; he has the brains to see that he needs help in wooing Imogen, 'for / I yet not understand the case myself' [II. iii. 74-5]; and although he is sometimes chided for valuing Imogen only for her dowry ('If I could get this foolish Imogen, I should have gold enough' [II. iii. 7-9]); in fact he knows better:

> she's fair and royal,
> And . . . she hath all courtly parts more exquisite

> Than lady, ladies, woman, from every one
> The best she hath, and she of all compounded
> Outsells them all.
>
> [III. v. 70-5]

As Granville-Barker perceptively remarks, 'Cloten is by no means pure ass; a diseased vanity is his trouble . . .'. (pp. 54-5)

We must, in fact, take Cloten and his behavior into account in our understanding of Posthumus Leonatus, for a parallel between them is woven carefully into the fabric of the play. Almost its first words present them as inversions of one another, Posthumus more worthy than words can easily say, Cloten bad beyond words, 'a thing / Too bad for bad report'. At a crucial point the plot turns upon their physical resemblance. They are paired in their relation to Cymbeline (the one his ward, the other his step-son); as rivals who seek first Imogen's hand and later vengeance upon her; as gamblers whom Iachimo easily outwits.

Moreover, the varied ways in which they are obviously paired either for comparison or contrast are underpinned by one less immediately obvious: they have remarkably like responses to a wide range of situations and events. It is, for example, often considered a difficulty of the play that the fool absolute can speak so eloquently in rejecting the Roman demand for tribute:

> Come, there's no more tribute to be paid: our
> kingdom is stronger than it was at that time:
> and (as I said) there is no moe such Caesars,
> other of them may have crook'd noses, but to
> owe such straight arms, none . . . Why tribute?
> Why should we pay tribute? If Caesar can hide
> the sun from us with a blanket, or put the moon
> in his pocket, we will pay him tribute for light:
> else, sir, no more tribute, pray you now.
>
> [III. i. 34-8, 42-5]

This sounds pretty good, and critics have been hard pressed to explain such words from Cloten's mouth. Most of the difficulty evaporates if we recognize Cloten as a fool relative rather than a fool absolute. He clearly can, whatever the Second Lord thinks, take two from twenty and come up with eighteen, and it doesn't require hard thought to mouth commonplaces.

More interesting than the problem of how Cloten figured out that a stronger army can defeat a weaker is the degree to which his attitude is Posthumus's:

>   you shall hear
> The legion now in Gallia sooner landed
> In our not-fearing Britain than have tidings
> Of any penny tribute paid. Our countrymen
> Are men more order'd than when Julius Caesar
> Smil'd at their lack of skill, but found their courage
> Worthy his frowning at. Their discipline,
> (Now wing-led with their courages) will make known
> To their approvers they are people such
> That mend upon the world.
>
> [II. iv. 17-26]

So Posthumus to Philario. Cloten is more pungent, but they do not differ greatly.

Nor do they differ greatly in other regards. Posthumus's behavior in II, iv, the scene in which his trust in Imogen is destroyed, is central to an understanding of his character and of the meaning of worth in *Cymbeline*. In its over-all shape it presents a dialectical encounter between a man who means well but does not think clearly and a skilled rhetorician. Posthumus is outmatched so far that he has no sense that his self-confidence is frivolous:

> Sparkles this stone as it was wont, or is't not
> Too dull for your good wearing? . . . Make not, sir,
> Your loss your sport. . . .
>
> [II. iv. 40-1, 47-8]

It is difficult not to agree that so complacent a man deserves to trip. The scene is well handled, Posthumus's complacency giving gradual way first to nervous uncertainty, and then, as Iachimo's evidence mounts, to an increasingly wide oscillation between fear that Imogen has betrayed him and relief at each piece of evidence that can be discounted:

> This is her honour!
> Let it be granted you have seen all this (and praise
> Be given to your remembrance) the description
> Of what is in her chamber nothing saves
> The wager you have laid.
>
> [II. iv. 91-5]
> (pp. 56-7)

Moving from complacency through fear to wrath, the scene exposes more and more fully the portrait begun earlier of a man of uneven temper, unschooled in emotional restraint. But many of the details of the scene have been anticipated, and while it develops more fully a psychological process briefly sketched in Posthumus's first encounter with Iachimo, it recapitulates one fully stated in the immediately preceding scene, II, iii.

The laying of the wager between Posthumus and Iachimo is separated from Iachimo's claim to success by five scenes. Two of these, II, i in its entirety and II, iii in its opening dialogue, are devoted to Cloten as a gambler who consistently loses and whose losses make him foul tempered and violent—a dramaturgical detail of some significance in a play where so much turns upon the winning and losing of wagers. Moreover, lest we miss the point, Shakespeare brings it home by having Cloten, like Posthumus, gamble with Iachimo:

> Come, I'll go see this Italian: what I have lost
> to-day at bowls I'll win to-night of him.
>
> [II. i. 48-9]

and lose:

> Your lordship is the most patient man in loss,
> the most coldest that ever turn'd up ace.
>
> [II. iii. 1-2]
> (pp. 57-8)

The parallel is carried further in the encounter between Imogen and Cloten which follows almost immediately. Cloten begins his address to her with considerable assurance. He is soon discomfited by her unmistakable suggestion that he is a fool, and within twenty lines of asserting that he loves Imogen he hears her reply that she hates him. Piqued, he retaliates with a diatribe against Posthumus, which brings down upon his head the full force of Imogen's contempt:

> His mean'st garment,
> That ever hath but clipp'd his body, is dearer
> In my respect, than all the hairs above thee,
> Were they all made such men . . .
>
> [II. iii. 133-36]

Now nearly speechless with rage, Cloten does little more than punctuate Imogen's exchange with Pisanio—significantly an inquiry into the whereabouts of the fatal bracelet which will soon send Posthumus into a rage comparable to Cloten's—with the repeated exclamation, 'His garment! . . . His garment! . . . His meanest garment!' [II. iii. 137, 139, 150]. And like Posthumus in the scene which follows, Cloten has here the last word. It is Posthumus's word, revenge:

> I'll be reveng'd:
> 'His mean'st garment!' Well.
>
> [II. iii. 155-56]

The two sequences are drawn together by many details, some small, some large. An allusion to the tribute demanded by Rome falls early in each; as each reaches its climax there occurs what in a musical analysis might be called a counterpoint between the bracelet motif and the offended-male-vanity motif. Each begins with an assertion of love for Imogen and ends with a vow of vengeance upon her. In putting two such scenes back to back, Shakespeare invites comparison between the two men; in putting Cloten's scene first, he invites us to watch Posthumus's behavior with Cloten's freshly in mind. What we see is that as Posthumus yields gradually to fear and anger, his behavior becomes increasingly like Cloten's.

It is useful, too, to consider the ways in which the construction of the play draws our attention to the workings of Posthumus's imagination. *Cymbeline* is widely recognized as a recapitulatory play—recalling in particular *Much Ado About Nothing* and *Othello.* The process by which Iachimo convinces Posthumus that Imogen is a whore involves the corruption of Posthumus's imagination, the substitution in his mind of Iachimo's way of seeing women, and the analogy with *Othello,* often cited, is apt.

Within the world of romance, where chaste marriage represents so high a value, it is not surprising that the corrupt are often sexually corrupt. Iachimo, with his cynical attitude toward chastity, fits neatly into the pattern, but the more obviously obscene imagination is Cloten's. We are treated to a particularly nice example of his lubricious imagination when he addresses the musicians preparing for the aubade to Imogen:

> Come on, tune: if you can penetrate her with
> your fingering, so: we'll try with tongue too . . .
>
> [II. ii. 14-15]

Hence, too, the details of his revenge:

> She said upon a time (the bitterness of it I now
> belch from my heart) that she held the very
> garment of Posthumus in more respect than my
> noble and natural person . . . With that suit
> upon my back, will I ravish her: first kill him,
> and in her eyes; there shall she see my valour,
> which will then be a torment to her contempt.
> He on the ground, my speech of insultment
> ended on his dead body, and when my lust hath
> dined (which, as I say, to vex her I will execute
> in the clothes that she so prais'd) to the court
> I'll knock her back, foot her home again. She
> hath despis'd me rejoicingly, and I'll be merry
> in my revenge.
>
> [III. v. 133-36, 137-45]

Sex and violence have already appeared together in Posthumus's imagination:

Perchance he spoke not, but
Like a full-acorn'd boar, a German one,
Cried 'O!' and mounted. . . .

[II. v. 15-17]

He has not yet come to the point of taking sexual pleasure in violence, however. . . . The revenge he envisions at the end of [II, v] is to be literary—he is going to write anti-feminist tracts—and is akin in all but intensity to Iachimo's pleasure in making cynical remarks.

As we learn in III, ii, Posthumus subsequently devises a revenge that satisfies him better. But the full details of his plan are withheld until III, iv, the scene immediately preceding the revelation of Cloten's plan:

Thy mistress, Pisanio, hath played the strumpet
in my bed: the testimonies whereof lie bleeding
in me . . . let thine own hands take away her
life: I shall give thee opportunity at Milford-
Haven: she hath my letter for the purpose: where,
if thou fear to strike, and to make me certain
it is done, thou art the pandar to her dishonour,
and equally to me disloyal.

[III. iv. 21-31]

There is much of Iachimo still in this—plausible lies and secret scheming—but something of Cloten too. In its particular details Posthumus's plan differs from Cloten's, although the degree of distinction one allows depends upon one's readiness to take as a phallic symbol the sword which is to be the instrument of Posthumus's revenge. At the least, both respond with violence to sexual humiliation, and just as Shakespeare places the scenes of humiliation back to back, so he puts together the scenes in which the plans for violent revenge are most fully stated. The invitation to compare is patent, and the comparison shows the disintegration of Posthumus's character as a process by which he adopts Cloten's manners and some, at least, of his morals. (pp. 58-9)

In the earlier scenes in which Posthumus and Cloten behave alike, II, iii and [v] for example, we actually see them. At the moment when they are most demonstrably alike, however, we are shown one but only told about the other. Posthumus is absent from the stage from [II, v] until V, i, so the parallel in Acts III and IV is between Cloten's hatred as we see it acted out and Posthumus's as we learn about it from his letter. Abstractly the difference is slight, but in dramatic feeling it is considerable. Whereas we watch Cloten formulating his plans for rape and murder and gloating over them, we never see the intensity of hatred which gives rise to Posthumus's damning letter. Cloten serves thus as a surrogate for Posthumus and as a scapegoat, drawing most of our hostility down upon himself, and in his violent and well-earned death satisfying our need to see vice receive its just reward and so appeasing our hostile feelings. By keeping Posthumus offstage, and directing our attention instead to Cloten, Shakespeare shelters him from the blunt of obloquy.

Meanwhile, even as it sets it forth, the play begins to palliate Posthumus's cruelty. For within those scenes in which plot and spectacle most emphatically insist upon a moral kinship between Posthumus and Cloten, other characters behave in such a way as to undercut the full emotional impact of what we are being shown and told. We see the final stage of Posthumus's moral decay only at second hand, briefly in his letter, more fully as it is reflected in Pisanio's grief and in Imogen's mingled anger and pain. That these two respond in sorrow rather than contempt asserts their conviction that vice is aberrant in Posthumus, quintessential in Cloten; and her sympathy for Posthumus even at his worst is reiterated in a scene of wonderful and multifold irony when Imogen, roused to fury at the sight of what she takes to be Posthumus's mutilated body, blames Pisanio—and Cloten [IV. ii. 312-29].

Posthumus's absence from the stage, the deflection of our anger and, separately, Imogen's toward Cloten, and the violence of Cloten's death serve as elements in a modulation of tone which prepares for the reintroduction of Posthumus to the stage. That he is unable to relate his role in the fifth act to any stable costume indicates his deep moral confusion: in a world where distinctions of dress are closely bound up with questions of role and rank, confusion over one's proper dress is an apposite expression for confusion over one's true nature. His most significant actions in the war are his defeat of Iachimo and his assistance to Belarius and the princes in turning the rout. (pp. 59-60)

That he succeeds dressed as a poor British soldier suggests that he is no longer acting under the pressure of his own ego; he has abandoned sophistic notions of honor-in-reputation in favor of a sense of propriety in which actions are of value for their intrinsic merit rather than for the glory they may reflect. That Posthumus is unable to settle on a costume for the fifth act points to his confusion, but his rejection of 'Italian weeds' points to the terms in which his confusion will be resolved:

Let me make men know
More valour in me than my habits show.
Gods, put the strength o' th' Leonati in me!
To shame the guise o' th' world, I will begin,
The fashion less without, and more within.

[V. i. 29-33]

The recollection here of the First Gentleman's words,

I do not think
So fair an outward, and such stuff within
Endows a man, but he.

[I. i. 22-4]

draws together the beginning of the play and its ending; their altered balance expresses a new understanding of what constitutes worth. (pp. 60-1)

Many difficulties over the play's workmanship have arisen from mistaking hypothesis for fact. The judgment of Posthumus's worth in I, i is at odds with much of the play's action, in part because that action is designed to explore and test the bases for such judgments. They are found wanting, and in the process *Cymbeline* comes to a new and more satisfactory understanding of what it means to be nobly virtuous. So long as Posthumus's thoughts and actions are variations upon Cloten's—even when they are superior variations—it matters very little what anyone thinks of him. Only when he comes on his own to recognize and reject his excessive concern with form is the worth attributed to him made manifest. He discards the Italian weeds which, like Cloten's court dress, proclaim his rank. More important, while still believing Imogen an adulteress, he sees the folly of identifying honor with reputation and the hasty arrogance of his assumption that Imogen must die to assuage his wounded vanity. By the time the play's action affirms an apprehension of virtue in Posthumus Leonatus, he has justified his own nobility by coming on his own to embrace its new definition of virtue:

Heaven doth with us as we with torches do,
Not light them for themselves; for if our virtues
Did not go forth of us, 'twere all alike
As if we had them not.

[*Measure for Measure*, I. i. 32-5]
(p. 61)

James Edward Siemon, ''Noble Virtue in 'Cymbeline','' in Shakespeare Survey: An Annual Survey of Shakespearian Study and Production, *Vol. 29, 1976, pp. 51-61.*

ALEXANDER LEGGATT (essay date 1977)

[*Leggatt demonstrates that certain aspects of* Cymbeline *which strain credence—such as the idealized characterization of Imogen and Posthumus, the latter's repentance, the defeat of the Roman army, and the prospect of universal peace offered at the play's conclusion—may be interpreted in light of the idea that British national destiny is favored by ''a mysterious higher power.'' In this play, he contends, Britain is represented as the locus of a superior value system, a setting in which miraculous actions are not exceptional and where men and women are distinguished from people of other nations by keen and lively imaginations. Leggatt concludes that the seemingly inexplicable events of the play either are shown as the result of divine intervention on behalf of Britain or occur because the British characters enjoy the partiality of the gods. However, he declares that in attributing Posthumus's repentance to ''the special favour of Jupiter'' rather than depicting the development of his remorse, Shakespeare has failed to palliate the unfavorable impressions we derive from the wager scenes; thus, our impression of him as a figure of worth and nobility is tempered. Other critics who have regarded* Cymbeline *as a play that celebrates British national fortunes include G. Wilson Knight (1947), Harold C. Goddard (1951), and William Barry Thorne (1969); also, for further commentary on the historical theme, see the essays by David M. Bergeron, J. P. Brockbank, Robert S. Miola, and Frances A. Yates cited in the Additional Bibliography. In addition to the above assessments, Leggatt echoes an interpretation proposed by such earlier critics as Robin Moffet (1962) and Northrop Frye (1965)—namely, that Christ's Nativity and the final resolution in* Cymbeline *are intimately related—, saying that Cymbeline's submission to Rome, despite the fact that Britain remains the gods' chosen victor, is explicable in one sense only: it ''shows that he is in tune with the new age of peace'' signified by the birth of Christ.*]

Dr. Johnson was not the first to object to ''the folly of the fiction'' in *Cymbeline*, ''the impossibility of the events in any system of life'' [see excerpt above, 1765]. The problem is raised in the opening scene of the play itself by the two gentlemen who lay out the plot for us:

Sec. Gent.	That a king's children should be so convey'd, So slackly guarded, and the search so slow That could not trace them!
First Gent.	Howsoe'er 'tis strange, Or that the negligence may well be laugh'd at, Yet it is true, sir.
Sec. Gent.	I do well believe you.

[I. i. 63-7]

The problem of credibility is raised and appears to be summarily dismissed; the apparently unlikely incident is to be taken as part of the given material of the play. But while we may

accept the ground rules of the plot, there are other problems of credibility that cannot be so lightly dealt with. . . . Strange events are part of Shakespeare's stock in trade, and we quickly become used to suspending disbelief in the wilder turns of the plot. But the special problem of *Cymbeline* is that we are presented with what seems to be an outrageously idealized view of the characters. (p. 191)

The problem of credibility, in both action and character, is basic to Shakespearean comedy and romance, and each play provides a slightly different resolution of it. Here, I think the resolution is connected with that other recurring factor, the interplay between two different locations, the one a place of normal, daylight experience, the other a place of magic: in this case, Italy and Britain. The special function of Britain as a place where strange things happen, isolated from the normal world, has not, I think, been given as much examination as it deserves—perhaps because here Shakespeare catches his critics off guard by departing from his usual narrative pattern. Instead of beginning in the normal world and moving to the magic one, we are placed in the magic one at the very beginning and then moved out of it. The interplay between Britain and Italy begins in earnest in [I. iv.], where the first note struck is Iachimo's cool insistence that Posthumus, though a fine enough fellow, is no paragon:

> Believe it sir, I have seen him in Britain; he was then of a crescent note, expected to prove so worthy as since he hath been allowed the name of. But I could then have look'd on him without the help of admiration, though the catalogue of his endowments had been tabled by his side and I to peruse him by items.

[I. iv. 1-7]

The Second Gentleman queried the ideal vision of Posthumus but was quick to acquiesce: ''I honour him, / Even out of your report'' [I. i. 54-5]. Iachimo is more persistent. The special bent of his mind, as several commentators have noted, is to react sceptically to idealism and to attempt to tarnish, even destroy, anything that contradicts his cynical view of the world. When presented with what he takes to be an exaggerated view of Posthumus, he cuts it down, and when Posthumus himself presents an idealized view of Imogen, he moves not merely to express his disbelief but to justify it.

In the crucial dialogue that sets the wager plot in motion, the issue of credibility—in this case the credibility of Posthumus' report of Imogen—is bound up with national feeling:

French.	. . . It was much like an argument that fell out last night, where each of us fell in praise of our country mistresses; this gentleman at that time vouching (and upon warrant of bloody affirmation) his to be more fair, virtuous, wise, chaste, constant, qualified and less attemptable than any the rarest of our ladies in France.
Iach.	That lady is not now living; or this gentleman's opinion, by this, worn out.
Post.	She holds her virtue still, and I my mind.
Iach.	You must not so far prefer her 'fore ours of Italy.
Post.	Being so far provok'd as I was in France, I would abate her nothing, though I profess myself her adorer, not her friend.

159

Iach.   As fair, and as good—a kind of hand-in-hand comparison—had been something too fair, and too good for any lady in Britany. If she went before others I have seen, as that diamond of yours outshines many I have beheld, I could not believe she excelled many: but I have not seen the most precious diamond that is, nor you the lady.

[I. iv. 56-76]

An important part of the scene's effect, as G. Wilson Knight has noted, is the vision of a coldly proper young man from a remote island insisting on "the romantic and puritanical idealism of his country as against the license of the Continent" [see excerpt above, 1947]. Not so much the license, perhaps, as the Continentals' tendency not to take anything too seriously: they praise their mistresses as a kind of social game and react with some surprise when this strange young foreigner takes the game so seriously that he is prepared to fight over it [I. iv. 43-8]. Throughout the scene the stiffness of Posthumus is played off against the urbane ease of Iachimo, Philario, and the Frenchman; and the silent presence of the Dutchman and the Spaniard (if they are not merely ghosts from an earlier draft) suggests, in an emblematic way, that the young Briton is confronting all of Continental Europe. The suggestion that there are national as well as sexual loyalties at stake is reinforced later when Imogen, hearing the false report of Posthumus' loose behavior on the Continent, declares, "My lord, I fear, / Has forgot Britain" [I. vi. 112-13]. And even at the end of the play, when Iachimo repents, he cannot resist a last flourish of national self-assertion, with the suggestion that Britons and Continentals have not merely different beliefs but different mental processes: "mine Italian brain / Gan in your duller Britain operate / Most vilely" [V. v. 196-98]. The current of national feeling, obvious enough in the play's political scenes, is also important for the wager plot and is one of the most important means by which Shakespeare draws together the astonishingly varied material of the play. (pp. 192-94)

[The] tendency to idealize is deliberately identified as a British characteristic and is made one of the main terms of the confrontation between Britain and Italy. Along with this goes a certain kind of imagination, shared by the major British characters: an imagination that works quickly and boldly, creating extravagantly vivid pictures. Imogen describes how she would have parted from Posthumus:

I would have broke mine eye-strings, crack'd them, but
To look upon him, till the diminution
Of space had pointed him sharp as my needle:
Nay, followed him, till he had melted from
The smallness of a gnat, to air: and then
Have turn'd mine eye, and wept.

[I. iii. 17-22]

This imagination can be easily played upon, as we see in Imogen's confrontation with Iachimo. Her reaction on his entrance—"Who may this be? Fie!" [I. vi. 9] suggests that with one glance she has leaped to a conclusion about him, and the right one. Yet when Iachimo describes Posthumus' loose behavior, she seems surprisingly willing to believe him; and when he makes amends by describing her husband's virtuous conduct, she is totally reconciled to her guest, to the point of asking him to extend his visit. Swift at making its own pictures, her imagination is unusually susceptible to pictures created by others. (p. 196)

Far from being, as Iachimo calls it, "dull," Britain seems to be a place where imaginations are extraordinarily vivid and active. And this quality sets the Britons apart from the foreigners. Perhaps the greatest flight of imagination any Italian is given is Iachimo's speech in Imogen's bedchamber, but it is a tissue of classical references and conventional Petrarchan images of beauty; and when he later gives a vivid description of her bedchamber, it is only after taking notes. (Even his action in kissing the sleeping Imogen is a familiar literary convention, as readers of [Philip Sydney's] *Astrophel and Stella* would recognize.) The Soothsayer has a prophetic vision but misinterprets its significance, prophesying a Roman victory. Only after events have taken place can he explain how dreams and oracles anticipated them: his line is not really prophecy but exegesis. In contrast, the Britons, semi-primitive though they may seem, have what amounts almost to a sixth sense. The contrast is between an oversophisticated, even blasé, Continental society, whose imagination has gone dry, and an island kingdom which is backward in some respects (we notice how homely and domestic many of Imogen's images are—"sharp as my needle," "the smallness of a gnat") but where the imagination still runs fresh.

Yet, while the British imagination may be powerful, it is not always so accurate as it is in the recognition scenes. Cymbeline's imagination is perverted by his Queen. She fools no one but him—the ordinary courtiers see through her—but she fools him completely. Under her influence, his denigration of Posthumus and Imogen is as extravagant as others' praise. Imogen herself is dangerously quick to imagine the worst. She is, one may feel, a little too ready to believe Iachimo's slander. And when Pisanio shows her Posthumus' letter accusing her of falsehood and demanding her death, she imagines, wrongly, that her husband has himself been false: "Some jay of Italy / (Whose mother was her painting) hath betray'd him" [III. iv. 49-50]. She is also ready to translate his treachery into a sweeping, extravagant generalization, not unlike Posthumus' own:

All good seeming,
By thy revolt, O husband, shall be thought
Put on for villainy.

[III. iv. 54-6]

The perverting of the imagination to create a false picture is seen most strikingly in Posthumus himself. His cynicism becomes as extravagant, as uncompromising, as his idealism. Like Imogen, he creates vivid—in this case, grotesque—pictures in his mind:

This yellow Iachimo, in an hour, was't not?
Or less; at first? Perchance he spoke not, but
Like a full-acorn'd boar, a German one,
Cried "O!" and mounted.

[II. v. 14-17]

Iachimo's cynicism, though deep, was casually expressed, suggesting a familiar acquaintance with the darker side of life; Posthumus' cynicism is new to him and shows itself in a fevered, unhealthy excitement. There is an edge of absurdity in his insistence on imagining the worst:

If you will swear you have not done't you lie,
And I will kill thee if thou dost deny
Thou'st made me cuckold. . . .

[II. iv. 144-46]

Imogen, as we have seen, shows a perverted imagination when she thinks her husband has betrayed her and leaps to general conclusions about the corruption of mankind. But Pisanio's common sense and her own love bring her under control, so that she never becomes so extravagant or cuts so shabby a figure as Posthumus does. (pp. 198-200)

The generation of false images is a function not only of the characters' minds but of the play itself, particularly in its central scenes. Britain may be a land where male worth and female chastity take their ideal forms and where (as we will see later) visions and miracles occur. But it is also peopled by false images, an evil queen who looks beautiful, princes who look like rustic mountaineers, and, when Imogen dons her disguise, a princess who looks like a page. (p. 200)

The play's confusion reaches a climax when Imogen (disguised, and apparently dead) awakes beside the headless body of Cloten (apparently Posthumus). Imogen's ordeal is a grim variation on one of the recurring devices of Shakespearean comedy, the moment when a character, faced with a strange experience, hovers uncertainly between dream and reality:

> O gods and goddesses!
> *(Seeing the body of Cloten.)*
> These flowers are like the pleasures of the world;
> This bloody man, the care on't. I hope I dream:
> For so I thought I was a cave-keeper,
> And cook to honest creatures. But 'tis not so:
> 'Twas but a bolt of nothing, shot at nothing,
> Which the brain makes of fumes. Our very eyes
> Are sometimes like our judgements, blind. Good faith,
> I tremble still with fear: but if there be
> Yet left in heaven as small a drop of pity
> As a wren's eye, fear'd gods, a part of it!
> The dream's here still: even when I wake it is
> Without me, as within me: not imagin'd, felt.
> A headless man? The garments of Posthumus?
>
> [IV. ii. 295-308]

At first, her mind keeps the vision of the headless body at a distance, by seeing it coolly, as an emblem. Then she tries to recall what happened before she fell asleep, but in the face of this horror her waking life now seems a dream; and as her mind clears, the vision she hoped was a dream is seen as reality "Without me, as within me." Only then can she admit what it is she sees—and her imagination leaps, as it has done before, to a false conclusion.

In the opening of the speech, the sense of delirium is authentic and terrifying. But as the speech progresses and Imogen identifies each part of the body as that of Posthumus, we are sharply reminded that her grief, like Posthumus' jealous rage, is based on a false assumption. The tendencies of the play to generate false images and of the characters to create false images in their minds have come together. The climax of the play's horror is also the climax of the motif of delirium, and this makes the horror ultimately unreal. It is no accident that moments later, in the same scene, we have the play's first fully developed reference to a higher, benevolent power at work in the Soothsayer's description of his vision [IV. ii. 346-52]. At the end of the following scene Pisanio, who has been the unwitting instrument of so much of the play's confusion, states one of the basic ideas of Shakespearian comedy: that if the characters cannot contrive a happy ending for themselves, some higher power can do it for them: "Fortune brings in some boats that are not steer'd" [IV. iii. 46].

In the midst of the play's confusion, we may have been wondering what has become of the earlier suggestion of Britain as a special place where higher values reside and where the imagination works keenly. It has seemed, increasingly, to be a place of delirium, where false images proliferate to the point of nightmare. And as we watched Posthumus in his jealousy become increasingly grotesque and trivial, we will certainly have wondered what happened to the paragon described for us in the opening scene. Shakespeare deals with both these questions through the depiction of a higher power at work. Let us take Posthumus first. We may well ask where his special value resides, since he never seems to do anything particularly virtuous; even his repentance is presented as a *fait accompli,* so that we never see his better nature actually at work. The answer is that his worth is not a matter of his own personal desert; it is, instead, the special favour of Jupiter. The identification of Posthumus with Jupiter and with Jupiter's eagle is suggested throughout the play. Imogen, surveying what she thinks is her husband's body, misses "his Jovial face" [IV. ii. 311]. A casual oath of Iachimo's is, for Posthumus, so solemn as to compel belief: "Hark you, he swears: by Jupiter he swears" [II. iv. 122]. Posthumus is associated with the eagle explicitly by Imogen: "I chose an eagle, / And did avoid a puttock" [I. i. 139-40] and implicitly by the Frenchman: "I have seen him in France: we had very many there could behold the sun with as firm eyes as he" [I. iv. 11-13]. And when Iachimo tells Imogen of her husband's behavior, he unconsciously anticipates the vision itself: "He sits 'mongst men like a descended god" [I. vi. 169]. (pp. 201-03)

Jupiter is a Roman god; yet his only appearance is in Britain. It is as though the Rome of the play—that strange mixture of Renaissance Italy and a solidly classical Rome, complete with senators and tribunes—is no longer responsive to the higher things of the imagination. (We have noted the comparative incompetence of Lucius' soothsayer.) But what is clearer, and ultimately more important, is a parallel between Britain and Posthumus. Both are governed by a special destiny. When Imogen refers to Britain as a small offshore island, the apparent intention of the speech is to stress Britain's insignificance in comparison with the great world; but the actual effect of the imagery is to make Britain seem special and precious:

> I'th' world's volume
> Our Britain seems as of it, but not in't:
> In a great pool, a swan's nest.
>
> [III. iv. 137-39]
> (p. 204)

We may be sceptical of the inherent worth of Britain and of Posthumus; yet the worth of both is assured by a higher destiny and confirmed by the play's chief sceptic. The critical realism of Iachimo, far from being (as Derek Traversi suggests [see excerpt above, 1954]) assimilated into the play's vision, is beaten into submission. He pays tribute to the magic of the island and acknowledges his own unworthiness to set foot on it:

> The heaviness and guilt within my bosom
> Takes off my manhood: I have belied a lady,
> The princess of this country; and the air on't
> Revengingly enfeebles me, or could this carl,
> A very drudge of Nature's, have subdued me
> In my profession? Knighthoods and honours, borne
> As I wear mine, are titles but of scorn.
> If that thy gentry, Britain, go before
> This lout, as he exceeds our lords, the odds
> Is that we scarce are men and you are gods.
>
> [V. ii. 1-10]

The speech is also, though Iachimo does not yet realize it, a tribute to Posthumus, who has defeated him in battle. Later, in his speech of repentance—which is as extravagantly written as anything in the play and radically different from the cool ironic cynicism of his early manner—he accepts the idealized vision of Posthumus that he had earlier rejected.

> He was too good to be
> Where ill men were, and was the best of all
> Amongst the rar'st of good ones.
>
> [V. v. 158-60]

The collapse of Iachimo may be frustrating to the actor who would like to play the flashy Italian villain to the end, but it is a necessary part of the play's treatment of the problem of credibility. Through it, the scepticism that challenged Britain, and Posthumus, is crushed.

In the finale, Britain becomes indeed an island of miracles. Shakespeare goes beyond the usual comic ending in the extraordinary number of dénouements he achieves. There seems to be something in the air. The power of the imagination to create pictures is extended: characters are no sooner referred to than they appear. Even Iachimo can do it:

> Whereupon—
> Methinks I see him now—
> *Post.*   (*Advancing*) Ay, so thou dost
> Italian fiend!
>
> [V. v. 208-10]

In a similar way, Posthumus calls up Imogen—

> O Imogen!
> My queen, my life, my wife, O Imogen,
> Imogen, Imogen!
> *Imo.*   Peace, my lord, hear, hear—
> *Post.*   Shall's have a play of this? Thou scornful
>   page,
> There lie thy part.
>
> [V. v. 225-29]

—and, in striking her down, he reenacts his early offences against her. The brief "play" they enact is the wager-plot in little, with a happy ending. But the most astonishing thing that happens, happens quite simply: "Although the victor, we submit to Caesar" [V. v. 460]. For once, there is no extravagance of style, perhaps because we have reached a stage where miracles seem natural and no longer call forth wonder.

If Britain is a land under a special destiny, winner against odds of a great battle, why should it submit? The answer may lie in the one event of the play that no one refers to, yet the one event that a Jacobean audience, new to the play, would have associated with the name of Cymbeline. It was during his reign, as the play shows, that there went out a decree from Caesar Augustus that all the world should be taxed; and, as the play cannot show, Christ was born. This is the ultimate miracle, and Cymbeline's extraordinary act of submission shows that he is in tune with the new age of peace. The soothsayer's final interpretation of his vision depicts not so much the submission of Britain to Rome as the linking of the two—or even the submission of Rome to Britain:

> For the Roman eagle,
> From south to west on wing soaring aloft,
> Lessen'd himself and in the beams o'the sun

> So vanish'd; which foreshadow'd our princely eagle,
> Th'imperial Caesar, should again unite
> His favour with the radiant Cymbeline
> Which shines here in the west.
>
> [V. v. 470-76]

The eagle seems to be absorbed by the sun, and we may remember that the eagle flies to the sun to renew its youth. At the end of the play, the real power (in the human world) rests with Cymbeline, who shows to Rome a favor it has done nothing to deserve, just as Jupiter favors Posthumus, Destiny favors Britain, and Christ favors an undeserving humanity. Nor has Cymbeline himself done anything in particular to deserve this special position: though the play is named for him, he has been for most of its length an unimpressive figure, passive where he is not cantankerous; yet at the end we are asked to see him as "radiant Cymbeline."

The play's way of dealing with its own incredibility is to admit it: to show that the worth of Posthumus, the miracles of Britain, and the final vision of peace, depending as they do not on human merit but on the workings of a mysterious higher power, are finally arbitrary and inexplicable; and to say, "Yet it is true, sir," leaving us to reply, if we can, "I do well believe you." We may not be able to. The elaborateness of the plotting and the self-consciousness of many of the devices give the play an air of artificiality, a remoteness from real experience. The vision is too good, or at least too neat, to be true; and a line like Posthumus' "shall's have a play of this?" coming at a crucial moment in the finale suggests Shakespeare's admission of the artificiality of his work. The scepticism that Iachimo renounces may be permitted to survive in the audience. And while the miraculous destiny of Britain carries some conviction, because the devices are familiar and reliable and a more sceptical view of Britain is never properly organized, we may have some lingering difficulty with the worth of Posthumus. His behaviour in the wager plot is so sharply delineated and so ugly that it becomes a real source of irritation. It is not enough to assure us that it does not matter, that Jupiter's favor wipes out all offenses. We may see the point that is being made, but it is difficult to give it full imaginative assent. The psychological problem and the mystic solution do not quite fuse. This time, Shakespeare has not quite worked the trick. (pp. 205-08)

Alexander Leggatt, "The Island of Miracles: An Approach to 'Cymbeline'," in Shakespeare Studies: An Annual Gathering of Research, Criticism, and Reviews, *Vol. X, 1977, pp. 191-209.*

NANCY K. HAYLES   (essay date 1980)

[Hayles contends that the dramatic function of Imogen's androgynous disguise as the boy page, Fidele, is symbolic rather than practical and thus is markedly different from Shakespeare's earlier use of this technique. Commenting on the significance in Cymbeline *of the themes of "false appearance" and the reestablishing of family ties, Hayles argues that sexual disguise, as in the case of Imogen-Fidele, serves as the principal means by which the characters gain a truer awareness of reality and false perception and, as a result, are able to reconstruct those family bonds so important to the play's final act. After reviewing the manner in which Shakespeare explored the moral questions of disguised gender in his earlier play* Twelfth Night, *Hayles maintains that* Cymbeline *represents a culmination in the development of the dramatist's use of this stage device. She especially emphasizes those scenes in which Imogen disguises herself as Fidele, saying that her false identity alters "not only the way others*

perceive her, but the way she herself perceives." Hayles asserts that in the episode at Belarius's cave, after she has adopted her disguise, Imogen unconsciously begins to apprehend the world and people around her intuitively, rather than strictly by reason and the senses, as she had previously done. The critic states that Shakespeare indicates this transformation of Imogen's perception by introducing her ironic references to Guiderius and Arviragus as her "brothers" and by making her mistake the headless corpse of Cloten for that of Posthumus; this last perception, Hayles adds, is not untrue, in that it intuitively recognizes the fact that Posthumus, symbolically at least, has lost his head and very much resembles Cloten during his degenerate stages. According to Hayles, all of this indicates that by adopting a sexual disguise, Imogen has acquired an intuitive, mystical, dreamlike vision that penetrates false appearances in a way that reason and the senses cannot. On the theme of reestablished family bonds in Cymbeline, *Hayles contends that Imogen's androgynous disguise foreshadows and provides for the reconciliation of disrupted families in the final act, for garbed as Fidele she intuits a kinship with the young princes and, during her expression of grief for her husband, "freely forgives Posthumus," thus prefiguring the concluding harmonious reunions. Peter Hyland (see Additional Bibliography) has also compared Shakespeare's use of sexual disguise in* Cymbeline *and his earlier plays, and D. E. Landry (1982) has analyzed the significance of the dream state as depicted in the play. Also, for further commentary on the theme of appearance and reality in* Cymbeline, *see the excerpts by Donald A. Stauffer (1949) and Derek Traversi (1954).]*

When Shakespeare has his heroines adopt a male disguise, he employs that disguise in complex ways. *Cymbeline*, however, appears to be an exception. Though it is not illogical for Imogen to assume a male disguise, Shakespeare's use of the device here, compared to the variety of uses to which he puts it in earlier plays, seems curiously uneconomical. I believe that Shakespeare's use of sexual disguise in *Cymbeline* is more complex than it at first appears. The nature of that complexity not only suggests that those plays employing sexual disguise follow a definite progression which culminates in *Cymbeline*, but also provides a way to relate Imogen's disguise to the play's central problems of misleading appearance and the disrupted family.

From the first, it is apparent that Shakespeare uses sexual disguise to provide witty romantic involvements for the heroine. Until *Cymbeline*, the exchanges the heroine has with her lover or would-be lover are central in explaining the function of the disguise. *The Merchant of Venice* suggests a second important use of the sexual disguise in the early plays: the disguise allows the heroine to enter a masculine world of action and be taken seriously there. For the third and perhaps most subtle use of the disguise, I am indebted to a suggestion by Peter Hyland [see Additional Bibliography], who argues that the disguise is a dramatic device to let the heroine occupy "an area midway between actors and audience" in the role of her female persona, whence she can comment on herself as a boy and on the action in general. Since the heroine as commentator is still within her original character role as a woman, she can make her observations without breaking the dramatic illusion. At the same time, because she is able to step aside from her male disguise, she has a "certain awareness that she is taking part in a play" [Hyland]. According to Hyland, the disguise is used as a device to allow Shakespeare to move unobtrusively from drama to metadrama. (pp. 231-32)

What is missing in [Shakespeare's] early plays is any sustained exploration of the psychological possibilities of the disguise. (p. 232)

In *Twelfth Night*, however, Shakespeare begins seriously to explore the possibility that the heroine who disguises herself as a boy is not simply a disguised girl, but a boy-girl: Cesario is Shakespeare's first androgyne. (p. 233)

[There] may be a parallel between Shakespeare's handling of sexual disguise in *Twelfth Night* and the Puritan attacks on cross-dressing in the theater. The Puritan case, as presented by Dr. John Rainolds in a pamphlet entitled *Th' Overthrow of Stage-Plays* (1599), rested on an association the male spectator makes between the stage heroine and the underlying presence of the boy actor. According to Rainolds, the spectator is roused to lust by the actor's female appearance, yet is still aware that it is a boy wearing those female garments. Led by degrees to desire the boy, the spectator may engage in practices Rainolds labeled as "beastlie filthiness, or rather more then beastlie." . . . In *Twelfth Night* Shakespeare creates a textual disguising analogous to the theatrical disguising in the scenario imagined by Rainolds: the spectators (Orsino and Olivia) do indeed sense the sexual ambiguity of the disguised heroine, and this leads to Viola's anxiety about the homoerotic implications of the disguise. But Shakespeare, unlike Rainolds, creates a context in which sexual ambiguity presages fulfillment rather than damnation.

Because Olivia has fallen in love with Cesario's "form," Sebastian, Cesario's double, can take Cesario's place with Olivia when the proper time comes. Meanwhile Orsino, who has been as it were coaxed to love Viola through her masculine appearance, can accept her as his bride when she is finally revealed as a woman. *Twelfth Night* thus implicitly refutes the Puritan claim that sexual ambiguity necessarily leads to "abomination." At the same time, the play acknowledges the complexities of homoeroticism by surrounding it with anxiety. Antonio's love for Sebastian, strongly linked throughout with images of disaster and betrayal, reminds us that not all difficulties raised by homoeroticism simply vanish once Cesario's sexually ambiguous identity is resolved into the unambiguously male and female identities of Sebastian and Viola. Some ambiguities remain: for example, the sexual ambiguity created by the presence of the boy actor. What the end of the play does promise is that the ambiguities that cannot be resolved are harmless rather than diabolically threatening. (pp. 234-35)

Twelfth Night represents a turning point. Though sexual ambiguity was always present in the boy actor, and perhaps did titillate the audience as the Puritans claimed, *Twelfth Night* is the first play to re-create those dynamics within the text and to take them as the occasion for a serious investigation into the moral ambiguities that arise as a result of sexual ambiguity. It is debatable whether Viola sees *herself* as sexually ambiguous, though she does say, somewhat oddly, that she will present herself to Orsino as a "eunuch" [*Twelfth Night*, I. ii. 56]. It is clear, however, that *other* characters see her as sexually ambiguous, and this raises the possibility that the relation between the female character and her male persona in *Twelfth Night* is more complex than it was in the earlier plays. (p. 235)

What we know of Shakespeare's extraordinary inclination to experiment suggests that once he had made the connection between the male disguise and the female character identity in *Twelfth Night*, and then went on to explore in depth the relation of disguise to identity in the tragedies, he was not likely to return to the same formulation he had been content with in the earlier romantic comedies. Thus it is not surprising that sexual disguise, when it reappears in *Cymbeline*, has little to do with the dramatic distancing, romantic complications, and freedom

Act IV. Scene ii. Guiderius, Belarius, Arviragus, and Imogen. By G. F. Sargent. The Department of Rare Books and Special Collections, The University of Michigan Library.

of action that were its primary reasons for being in the early plays. It does, however, have a great deal to do with Shakespeare's handling of sexual disguise in *Twelfth Night*.

Fidele is clearly not the same kind of androgynous figure that Cesario is. Yet certain features of *Cymbeline* suggest that Shakespeare continues with the same line of exploration he had been following in *Twelfth Night*. In *Cymbeline*, the passivity of the heroine has been pushed so far as to give the impression that the disguised Imogen, as Hyland remarks, "does very little." . . . Our tentative thesis suggests that Imogen's disguise is thus intimately connected with her identity. Because mingling male and female identities raised serious moral problems for a society that believed in the divine ordination of sex roles, we may further expect that *Cymbeline* will deal with the moral implications of the disguise, though not necessarily in exactly the same terms as *Twelfth Night*.

Recent research has made quite clear that the romances as a group are intimately concerned with family ties, especially with the father-daughter bond. Another body of criticism, more concerned with *Cymbeline* as an individual play than as a romance, argues that misleading appearance—as it relates to clothing, behavior, even underlying mythic patterns—is a major theme in the play. The two critical approaches are easily reconciled, because it is through disrupting family ties that misleading appearance in *Cymbeline* has its most devastating effect. Cymbeline is angry with his daughter because his Queen de-

ceives him by appearing to be the loving wife and mother she is not; the two brothers are lost because Cymbeline failed to discern that the accusations against Belarius were false; and Posthumus is alienated from Imogen by the false impression created by Iachimo. Misleading appearance is so pervasive that it qualifies as the most important disruptive influence in the play. Every evil action in *Cymbeline* depends upon hypocrisy and false appearances. (Perhaps this helps explain why Shakespeare has Cloten, who plans to murder and rape, first put on a disguise.) We know that the hold of evil is beginning to lessen when the disparity between appearance and reality is used in a different way. To counteract figures like the Queen, Cloten, and Iachimo, who present good exteriors but are bad within, come figures who have base exteriors but are noble inside. Guiderius and Arviragus are two such; later on so is Posthumus, when he hides his repentant heart under a peasant's garb.

To relate the theme to the play's use of sexual disguise, I wish to state it in terms that are applicable to Shakespearean romance in general. We can say that whereas falsehood displaces the truth in the first part of the play, later on false seeming itself is made to embody a kind of truth. Both Pisanio and Cornelius, for example, frustrate evil designs by assuming false poses; both also say that by being false they are in some larger sense being true (Pisanio [III. v. 157-59]; Cornelius [I. v. 43-4]). Marjorie Garber has remarked upon the word-play on "seeming'' in *Cymbeline,* and the progression she notes—''seeming'' as false appearance, ''seeming'' as a dream, ''seeming'' as the truth [see Additional Bibliography]—summarizes the kind of reversal that is taking place. Thus a central pattern in the play is the movement from false appearance as an instrument of evil, to a dreamlike state where surfaces yield to a mode of perception not fully conscious, to a reintegration of perception in which ''seeming'' becomes the principal means through which family ties are reestablished.

The pattern is also closely linked with the operation of sexual disguise. When Pisanio urges Imogen to dress as a page and approach the Roman ambassador Lucius, he first describes how the disguise will work:

> Now, if you could wear a mind
> Dark, as your fortune is, and but disguise
> That which, t'appear itself, must not yet be
> But by self-danger, you should tread a course
> Pretty, and full of view; yea, haply, near
> The residence of Posthumus; so nigh (at least)
> That though his actions were not visible, yet
> Report should render him hourly to your ear
> As truly as he moves.
>
> [III. iv. 143-51]

The disguise will let Imogen encounter Posthumus in a manner that will essentially conceal her while still exposing her to view, and yet expose Posthumus even though he may be concealed from view. The tension between exposure and concealment, as Pisanio describes it, will work in Imogen's favor, unlike the bedroom scene with Iachimo, where Imogen was exposed to view without her knowledge and consent. The disguise is thus a device to use the disparity between perception and reality, once exploited by Iachimo to create the rift, to heal the breach and begin to undo the effects of his machinations. By following Pisanio's suggestion, Imogen would be in a position to control appearances in a way she had not been earlier.

The general thrust of Pisanio's description of the disguise is certainly true; that is, it marks the beginning of a countermovement that will bring the lovers together, and this countermovement is associated with a change in perception. But the specific scenario Pisanio imagines never comes to pass. Imogen fails to reach Milford Haven, let alone Italy. Imogen, alone of all Shakespeare's heroines who disguise themselves as boys, does not manage to meet her lover as she had planned. Further, her failure to reach Italy means that the disguise is not used to allow her to enter a masculine world of action; instead, she seems to enter a curiously passive state when she assumes the disguise. Although the earlier uses of the disguise are evoked in Pisanio's speech, they are never realized in the play. If we are to explain the operation of the disguise in *Cymbeline,* we must abandon the earlier models and turn to the deeper implications of the disguise as an entry into a changed mode of perception.

From Pisanio's description we gather that the disguise is intended to alter the relation between appearance and reality. In a sense, of course, any disguise does this. But Imogen's disguise appears to alter not only the way others perceive her, but the way she herself perceives. In the scenes where Imogen is in disguise, the characters' understanding of the underlying relationships comes, not from sensory perception and reasoning, but from intuition of a more irrational, mysterious kind. Indeed, the power of intuition to penetrate appearances and reveal the underlying reality is the chief interest in these scenes.

Until the meeting with Lucius, everyone Imogen sees (and Imogen herself) is in disguise; the disguises emphasize that she cannot possibly understand the significance of events through sensory perception alone. Despite misleading appearances, an intuitive and mysterious sympathy, aided by unconscious associations, foreshadows the final reconciliations between family members. False appearance thus loses its power to disrupt because intuition or unconscious association can penetrate beneath surfaces, revealing the underlying truth.

A brief recapitulation of the events that occur while Imogen is in disguise will demonstrate how a changed mode of perception leads to a restoration of family ties. First she meets her brothers, who are also disguised (though they are unaware of it) as the sons of Morgan. Imogen is immediately drawn to them, and they to her, as they assure her that she has fallen '''mongst friends.'' She replies:

> 'Mongst friends?
> If brothers: [*Aside*] would it had been so, that they
> Had been my father's sons, then had my prize
> Been less, and so more equal ballasting
> To thee, Posthumus.
>
> [III. vi. 74-8]

Her aside, though she imagines it as an abstract proposition, has the effect of resolving any jealousy she might feel for her brothers before it can occur. Similarly, the sexual disguise allows a potentially incestuous sentiment to be expressed in a situation where it is harmless rather than threatening when Guiderius says, ''Were you a woman, youth, / I should woo hard,'' and Arviragus replies, ''I'll make't my comfort / He is a man, I'll love him as my brother'' [III. vi. 68-9, 70-1]. In veiled terms, the sibling relationship is thus freed from the two threats of incest and jealousy. Through the characters' intuitive responses, family bonds are at once implicitly acknowledged and strengthened against possible future strife.

Imogen then takes the drug that Pisanio has given her, and falls into a deathlike trance. She awakes disoriented, and imagines that her life in the cave was unreal, a ''bolt of nothing, shot at nothing'' [IV. ii. 300]. The meeting with her brothers, always partly unconscious for Imogen, now melts away with all the insubstantiality of a dream. But the shock of discovering the headless body convinces her that the dream continues: ''The dream's here still: even when I wake it is / Without me, as within me: not imagin'd, felt'' [IV. ii. 306-07]. The confusion of waking and sleeping, the interpenetration of the dream world and the waking world, suggests a mingling of two different modes of perception: from the unconscious mind come the associative connections common in dreams, and from the conscious mind comes the rationality of logical thought. Imogen uses logic to arrive at the conclusion that Cloten, in league with Pisanio, has murdered Posthumus and left his headless trunk; and her reasoning is, of course, false. But underlying the identification of Posthumus as the headless corpse is a grisly pun: Posthumus lost his head.

This scene has long attracted critical attention—and controversy—because of its complex ironic distancing of the heroine's genuine anguish. For the moment, however, the aspect of the scene I wish to emphasize is the way in which Imogen's unconscious associations look forward to her eventual reconciliation with Posthumus. There are three points to notice here: (1) Imogen's mistaken identification of the corpse rests on a symbolic truth, in the sense that Posthumus has indeed become a kind of Cloten; (2) Imogen is led to this deeper truth not by conscious ratiocination, but by unconscious association; and (3) Imogen's misapprehension, rather than alienating the lovers as it did earlier in the play, now hints at their eventual reconciliation because Imogen, in her grief, freely forgives Posthumus.

As Imogen falls unconscious over the body, the brief scene of her mourning is bracketed by periods of unconsciousness. The following action, though it is a waking scene, continues the pattern of dreamlike association. When Lucius arrives and revives Fidele, promising to "rather father thee than master thee" [IV. ii. 395], he vicariously becomes the kind father whom Imogen had earlier lacked. Persuaded by Fidele's faithfulness to honor the dead Posthumus (as Fidele supposes), Lucius promises to lay the body in the "prettiest daisied plot" [IV. ii. 398] he can find. Again a false supposition brings about a symbolic reconciliation, now between the supposed husband and vicarious father.

The sexual disguise is used, then, not to bring about any practical resolution; indeed, in the final scene it delays that resolution for a few seconds more as Posthumus, in the last example of the pernicious effects of misleading appearance, flings aside the "scornful page" Fidele [V. v. 228]. At the moment when the lovers are reunited and Posthumus recognizes Imogen as his own, surface and appearance are fully reclaimed.

Until then, the apprehension of truth is achieved, not through sensory perception, but through dreams, intuition, revelation. Imogen's passivity in disguise suggests that she enters a new mode of being: pathetic rather than erotic, passive rather than active, symbolic and dreamlike rather than conscious and purposeful. Her original qualities—her sexuality, resourcefulness, self-composure—are not negated but only obscured by the disguise. When the time is ripe, they reemerge to bring about the final resolution when Imogen steps forward to ask about Iachimo's ring. But the resolution can occur only because the disguise has prepared the way. Somehow, Imogen's resourcefulness, honesty, and conscious self-knowledge, excellent though they are, are not enough to resolve the problems until they are integrated with something much less conscious, a mode of thought that can emerge only when consciousness becomes passive and still.

In a sense, the moral implications of disguise have expanded in *Cymbeline* to become the center of thematic interest. There is also an astonishing expansion in the number of disguises; most of the characters, at one time or another, are in a disguise of some kind. With so many characters in disguise, we can scarcely help noticing the connection between disguise and deceiving appearance.

Yet Imogen's disguise differs from the others in being a sexual disguise. While it is similar to the other disguises in its thematic associations with deceiving appearance, it is unlike them in the peculiar effect it has on the heroine. Imogen's surprising passivity in disguise, coupled with the kinds of experiences she undergoes, makes it seem as if the disguise has the effect of guiding her into a new mode of being that has strong affinities with the unconscious. We have seen how, in *Twelfth Night,* the androgynous implications of the sexual disguise were cause for anxiety in terms that were familiar to Puritan pamphleteers. But according to an older tradition, which goes back at least as far as Plato's *Symposium,* the androgyne is cause for nostalgia, not anxiety. In Plato, and in many Renaissance renderings of the myth, the androgyne becomes an emblem of

wholeness that bifurcated man can only yearn for and, perhaps, half-consciously remember.

It is in this sense, I think, that the disguised Imogen is androgynous. The associations of her disguise-state with dreams and intuitions suggest that while she is disguised, she is in contact with the hidden part of the psyche, represented in modern terms as the unconscious, in mythic terms as a lost unity of soul. Commentators as various as Marsilio Ficino and C. G. Jung have interpreted the androgyne as a symbol for psychic wholeness, whether the terms used to describe it come from Christian mysticism or modern psychology.

I am suggesting, then, that the doubleness of Imogen's sexual identity at once evokes and symbolizes the doubleness of psychic life. The bifurcation between male and female becomes a metaphor for the bifurcation between dream-life and waking life, as the commingling of genders in the androgynous Fidele is made to coincide with Imogen's entry into a state combining aspects of the conscious and unconscious minds.

Thematically, Imogen's androgynous state, with its implications of putting her in touch with the unconscious, is associated both with her overcoming the ill effects of misleading appearance and with the restoration of sundered family bonds. The connection with misleading appearance is clear enough, since the entry into an intuitive, dreamlike state means that the usual modes of perceiving are bypassed, and new modes, presumably less vulnerable to manipulation by evil forces, become available. (pp. 236-42)

But what of the association between intuitive modes of thought and the restored family? (p. 243)

The answer . . . has something to do with the fact that family bonds are constantly threatened by forces that can play on our gullibility, sometimes on our very rationality. But part of the answer, I believe, goes deeper. There is a sense in which the family moves closer to archetype in the romances; this is especially clear in *Cymbeline,* where no attempt is made to create a "realistic" family unit. There is the father, mysteriously becoming the mother as well; the brothers, noble though raised in a wilderness, with a mysterious sympathy for a sister they have never seen; and a wicked stepmother, engrossing into herself all the child's fantasies about the "bad" parent. With this representation of the family, family bonds too become archetypal, not the result of shared experience, but preceding experience. Experience can indeed affect the bonds, but it can never wholly eradicate them or generate them if they are not there already. The entry into a dreamlike state is associated with their restoration because it is in this preconscious, prerational state that the character may again come into contact with the family bonds in their archetypal purity. Other characters approach this state through dreams or visions; Imogen, through donning a male disguise. She can do this because Fidele, even without experiencing a dream, already *is* a figure from a dream: the archetypal androgyne.

The boy actor may play an important, though unstated, role. Underneath our waking life lies the elusive otherness of our dream-life; underneath Imogen's stage identity lies the elusive otherness of the boy actor. Re-creating that doubleness on stage by putting Imogen in male clothing allows Shakespeare to create a symbolic representation of receding depth. We may think we understand the metaphoric equation between the sexual doubleness of the disguised heroine and the doubleness of the psyche; but there is still another sex reversal, another potential androgyny, implicit in the presence of the boy actor.

As the unconscious can be approached but never directly known, so the meaning of Imogen's sexual disguise can be approached—but the unacknowledged presence of the boy actor creates a sense of hidden depth that eludes conscious apprehension.

The sense of a meaning fully immanent but eluding rational formulation is one of the most characteristic features of Shakespearean romance. It is in this context that we can perhaps best appreciate how the sexual disguise in *Cymbeline* forms part of a larger design. The "atmospheric pressure of unconsciousness" that surrounds the disguised Imogen, as Northrop Frye calls it [see excerpt above, 1965], is part of larger thematic and dramaturgical patterns designed to present us with experiences that transcend our rational comprehension. It is perhaps understandable, then, why Shakespeare should choose to use sexual disguise in a way that has virtually no practical use at all. Its significance is almost entirely symbolic; and the very nature of symbols is such that their meaning can be approached, but never completely formulated in terms external to themselves.

Perhaps symbols, as Borge remarks of metaphors [in his *Other Inquisitions*], cannot be invented; they simply exist. If so, there is ample evidence that the androgyne is a true symbol. In *Cymbeline*, Shakespeare takes full advantage of the symbolic potential of the androgynous heroine for the first time (as distinct from the dramatic and romantic possibilities of the sexual disguise), incorporating it into the symbolic structure of his play and using the unavoidable stage convention of the boy actor to deepen the symbolic resonances. Shakespeare, in his use of sexual disguise in *Cymbeline*, goes "beyond beyond"— beyond the conventional use of sexual disguise that marked the early plays, beyond the social implications of sexual role-playing that were its focus in *As You Like It*, beyond the fear of sexual ambiguity that forms an important part of *Twelfth Night*—into a realm that might properly be called mythic. (pp. 245-47)

Nancy K. Hayles, "Sexual Disguise in 'Cymbeline'," in Modern Language Quarterly, Vol. 41, No. 3, September, 1980, pp. 231-47.

D. E. LANDRY (essay date 1982)

[*Employing techniques of psychoanalytic criticism, Landry argues that* Cymbeline *is "a play about dreams, about the various and often inexplicable functions of the unconscious mind," and that it dramatizes the underlying correspondences between dreams and chronicle history; in her words,* Cymbeline *demonstrates that "dreams, which contain . . . [one's] personal history, are to one's identity as a nation's past, recovered through legend and chronicle-history, is to its sense of itself as a nation, a true community." According to the critic, personal identity and national history are alike, in that each is a product of a process that combines truth and artifice, with the latter serving to organize the former. Landry specifically examines the role of Posthumus, claiming that his "purgation through dream or dreamlike experience" parallels the purgation Britain must undergo at the play's historical level. Relying on Freudian theory, she asserts that the purgation is dreamlike to the extent that "it acts as a working out or incorporation of potentially disruptive elements." Perhaps most interesting of Landry's comments is her claim that the pastoral scenes of Acts III and IV depict "a psychomachic enactment" of Posthumus's moral and psychological development while he remains offstage. According to Landry, it is as if Posthumus is dreaming the dramatic events in these pastoral scenes near Milford Haven, for, in their fearful contention against each other, Fidele and Cloten become "figures of displacement for [his] embattled psy-*] che." The "demonic drama of the pastoral sequence," the critic adds, lays "to rest those disturbances of character which had sundered [Posthumus] from wife and 'soul,' from his own best self." Landry maintains that the pastoral sequence is a dramaturgical preparation both for Posthumus and for us, leading to the vision in Act V, Scene iv, which she declares serves to "dilate" the hero's character and provide him with a recovery of his personal history; in a larger sense, according to Landry, the scene also reenacts in miniature "the play as a whole, its pattern of purgation and reintegration of consciousness in communal and national terms." For further commentary on the theme of national history in Cymbeline, see the excerpts by G. Wilson Knight (1947), Harold C. Goddard (1951), and William Barry Thorne (1969); also, see the essay by Nancy K. Hayles (1980) for a related discussion of the dream-state in the play. For another psychoanalytic interpretation of Cymbeline, see the essay by Murry M. Schwartz cited in the Additional Bibliography.]

Cymbeline is most remarkably a play about dreams, about the various and often inexplicable functions of the unconscious mind. It is also a romance, a history play, and a tragicomic pastoral. Naturally, critics have found it difficult to interpret the play in any unified way, difficult to assign it any governing structure. Most are still in tacit agreement with Johnson, who deplored its "incongruity" and "unresisting imbecility" [see excerpt above, 1765]; even critics who claim some fondness for its oddities tend to explore particular aspects, leaving the unwieldy bulk of the threefold plot largely unexplained. Frank Kermode [see Additional Bibliography] and Northrop Frye [see excerpt above, 1965], respectively, have come closer to pinning down the play's peculiar tone by calling it "experimental" and "academic," with a "technical interest in dramatic structure."

In *Cymbeline*, Shakespeare is indeed experimenting, but experimenting most resonantly, I think, with the underlying significance of certain natural cycles and their dramaturgical counterparts, with the processes of sleep as a perpetual "ape of death" (Iachimo's phrase [II. ii. 31]), waking as a symbolic rebirth, dream as a ritualized purgation. The main dreamers, Posthumus and Imogen, are also the characters with the strongest focus. They are, moreover, the agents of the erotic plot through which the plots of familial and national affection can be salvaged and resolved. By a series of analogies, the experience of Posthumus and Imogen comes to represent that of the whole community of Cymbeline's kingdom.

The play's structural complexities imply an equation: dreams, which contain in however concealed a fashion the facts of personal history, are to one's identity as a nation's past, recovered through legend and chronicle-history, is to its sense of itself *as* a nation, a true community. *Cymbeline* is at once the most local and historical of the romances, the only one explicitly grounded in events from Britain's past, and as transcendently primitive as any, with considerable interest in the ritualistic, largely unconscious roots of the drama. In *Cymbeline*, however, the primitivism or archaic interest of the themes of dreams and chronicle-history is treated with wit and sophistication. The apparent naiveté of the folk-tale plot is constantly undermined by self-consciously theatrical artifice. The panegyrical quality of the chronicles—especially as interpreted under the Tudors with an eye toward legitimating royal authority by aligning it with the national interest—is gently deflated. The play closes with Cymbeline, the King himself, commenting a little wryly on the expeditious nature of the peace just negotiated between Britain and Rome: ". . . Never was a war did cease, / Ere bloody hands were wash'd, with such a peace" [V. v. 484-85]. It is just this tone of naive wonder undermined ever so quietly but insistently by archness and self-control that distinguishes Shakespeare's last plays in general, and *Cymbeline,* as a peculiar blend of romance and history play, in particular.

Romances are traditionally concerned with the recovery and reconstitution of identity. Quite a bit has been written about the unusual status of Posthumus as a hero. His absence from the stage is indeed more noticeable than his presence. And yet, at the same time, his experience functions as the only facsimile of developing character we are offered in the play. Not only Posthumus but the entire court and, by analogy, all of Britain undergo a kind of purgation through dream or dreamlike experience. The purgation is dreamlike in that it acts as a working out or incorporation of potentially disruptive elements, which Freud describes as the basis of the dream-work; the pattern or structure of the dream itself incorporates these usually erotic impulses by permitting them to be expressed, however covertly or metaphorically, in the dream's action. The play suffers a certain break in consciousness followed by a descent to a demonic realm when Posthumus retreats from the action. In romance, the demonic or night world to which the self descends is the domain of tyrannous circumstances, filled with images of displacement of the self: a world of doublings, disguises, misnamings, and mistaken identities, the conventions both of romantic or tragicomic drama and of dreams.

It is as if Posthumus' physical absence were somehow paralleled by Imogen's absence of mind. Though repudiated unfairly as an adulteress, as Posthumus' wife Imogen remains in Shakespearean conception his lawful helpmate, his other and better self, and, most significantly, his "soul" [V. v. 263] in her mind and ours. Throughout the pastoral scenes which follow near Milford Haven her masculine disguise further identifies her with the absent Posthumus. As Fidele she comes to embody Posthumus' own capacity for virtue in the same way that Cloten, as a parodic double, enacts his tendencies toward vice. The pastoral setting, with its magical and ironic overtones, is an ideal distancing device, and it reinforces in these scenes the sense of a kind of dream action. Both Fidele and Cloten become figures of displacement for the embattled psyche of Posthumus and allow bestial and erotic instincts to surface in a distanced, and therefore acceptable, way. Posthumus' absence from the stage does not preclude his growth as a hero, because we are given instead a psychomachic enactment of his development through the adventures of Imogen, Cloten, and the royal brothers. The relation these scenes bear to Posthumus' moments of crisis and insight—neatly following his disappearance and preceding his return—suggests, I think, at least a subliminal sense of Posthumus himself offstage, dreaming the pastoral action. His very exile to Italy is a kind of sleep, an abatement of his ordinary powers of action and discourse. As the Queen puts it:

> His fortunes all lie speechless, and his name
> Is at last gasp.
>
> [I. v. 52-3]

But the dreaming itself resolves the various dilemmas of the court and of his tenuous hold on identity. When Cornelius predicts the effect of the drug Imogen takes in Belarius' cave, his words are appropriate for the effect produced by the pastoral sequence as a whole:

> . . . but there is
> No danger in what show of death it makes,
> More than the locking up the spirits a time,
> To be more fresh, reviving.
>
> [I. v. 39-42]

We may think first of the explicit patterning of Posthumus' fifth-act dream in the jail, when imprisonment and impending execution lead directly to revelation and new hope. But the pattern is implicit also in Imogen's "show of death" and revival, followed by Posthumus' change of heart.

Frye has commented upon the "extraordinary blindness" of the play's characters, calling attention particularly to Imogen's speech to Pisanio as she prepares to depart on her journey—in psychic terms, her descent—to the wilds of Wales:

> I see before me, man. Nor here, nor here,
> Nor what ensues, but have a fog in them
> That I cannot look through. Away, I prithee;
> Do as I bid thee. There's no more to say;
> Accessible is none but Milford way.
>
> [III. ii. 78-82]

There is a sense of encroaching murkiness, of blurred horizons, of the contraction of vision. Only a journey to Milford, a sacred or enchanted place since Posthumus is supposed to be there, will serve to restore the natural order; it is time for the quest. And that quest requires that Imogen prepare for "the gap" that she "shall make in time" [III. ii. 62, 63]—a phrase suggestive of a lapse of ordinary consciousness—by wearing "a mind dark" as her fortune is [III. iv. 143-44] as well as a boyish disguise. By assuming a false identity as Fidele, she literally becomes the truth of Posthumus' psychic experience. As Pisanio says, with the insouciance characteristic of the many speakers of dramatic ironies in the play, by vanishing as herself she will "tread a course / Pretty and full of view" [III. iv. 146-47] which will bring her, in Lucius' service, close enough to Posthumus to receive accurate news of him:

> . . . yea, happily, near
> The residence of Posthumus; so nigh, at least,
> That though his actions were not visible, yet
> Report should render him hourly to your ear
> As truly as he moves.
>
> [III. iv. 147-51]

Indeed, his actions, his change of heart, will not be made visible, but her actions will signify in the minds of the audience the emergence and eventual triumph of his native virtue. The method is one of visual enactment of a subtext never made verbally explicit, another strategy perhaps originally derived from dreams. (pp. 68-71)

When Posthumus returns to the stage at the beginning of Act V, it is apparent that he is as changed a man as if he too had witnessed or undergone Imogen's ordeal. In the logic of the double- or triple-plot, he has in effect undergone such an ordeal within himself. The demonic drama of the pastoral sequence of Acts III and IV has laid to rest those disturbances of character which had sundered him from wife and "soul," from his own best self. And that self is finally inseparable from the greater social harmony. His alienation has been both signified and compounded by banishment from his native soil. Dramatically, the pastoral sequence prepares him, and us, for a visitation by the past in the dream of the parents and brothers he, born literally posthumously, has never known:

> *Post.* [Waking] Sleep, thou hast been a grandsire and
> begot
> A father to me; and thou hast created
> A mother and two brothers. But, O scorn,
> Gone! They went hence so soon as they were
> born.
>
> [V. iv. 123-26]

Still under the dream's spell, he falls into couplets like the ghosts. But though they have vanished, a token has been left behind—the riddle which prophesies Posthumus' eventual good fortune as part of Britain's newly found prosperity in peace. Less tangibly, the dream's legacy is a legitimation, through the recovery of origins, of his full identity as Posthumus Leonatus, a warrior-patriot, now strong in the defense of peace. The curious thing is that the more he comes to know himself, the more he ceases to matter as a character at all and comes instead to embody the psychic experience of the play as a whole. He whose reputation has been so hyperbolically "extended" becomes in fact symbolically dilated to encompass both the realms of dream and waking, of alienation and identity. The strangeness of Posthumus as a hero may be more easily accounted for if we remember that the nature of "identity," as it functions within comic, or tragicomic, structure, is always twofold. The singular sense of identity comes close to our conventional notion of the word; its larger sense requires that the social tyranny with which the play begins be dismantled and the community more harmoniously rebuilt. Posthumus' experience is, I think, both profoundly individual and social, at once peculiar to him—the recovery, through dream, of his personal history—and, by analogy, comparable with a larger movement—the recognition of a growing sense of national identity through the dramatization of national history, with its politic blend of fact and legend, reportage and myth.

Because his potential for virtue was always present, merely waiting to be purged of its darker impulses, in the course of the play Posthumus is changed, and yet not changed. He experiences a dilation of being in at least two senses. The pastoral action—itself a dream displaced and enacted—functions as an incorporation of the unconscious, without some acknowledgment of which a complete and seamless identity is impossible, and as a preparation for his actual dream, in which his personal history is returned to him. In a larger sense, Posthumus' being is dilated through the pressure of such incorporation to signify, by analogy, the experience of the play as a whole, its pattern of purgation and reintegration of consciousness in communal and national terms. (pp. 73-4)

In contrast to most modern critics, *Cymbeline*'s first audiences would have perceived not only the connection between Posthumus' experience and that of the other characters, but the analogies yoking the three plots as well. The doctrine of analogy as it applies to history, both personal and national, seems to have been firmly implanted in their minds. They were, after all, not so very far from the tradition of medieval exegesis, which in the reading of church history encouraged a particular sensitivity to a layering of analogous relationships. Indeed, one could characterize the structure of feeling at work in *Cymbeline* as a kind of dialectical relation between the one and the many. On one hand, the play's deepest experience is distilled into the psyche of Posthumus; on the other, the audience is made aware of certain forces compelling the action on several levels, so that the last act especially bears witness to an overriding order, a sense of unity in multiplicity.

Critics who complain of the play's lack of unity seem to have trouble most often with the historical elements, particularly the Roman/British pact, with its accompanying aura of anachronism. Some of the sense of illogicality and dislocation can, as I have suggested, be attributed to the play's dream-like texture. But I also think that the abrupt yoking of the issues of personal, familial, and communal or national reunification heightens the audience's awareness of the correspondences between them.

Each plot becomes a metaphor for the other two; we are shown the destinies of man, family, and the larger community under the same reassuring management. (p. 75)

In his persuasive discussion of the historical groundings of the play, Emrys Jones argues for an implicit unity exactly where many critics have found fault—in the play's historical dimension [see Additional Bibliography]. Jones refers to both the contemporary, topical significance of certain aspects of the play and to Shakespeare's reliance upon his audience's possessing a strong sense of national history. The topical references surface mainly in relation to Cymbeline as a figure of the peace-making king, an obeisance to James I. This homage-to-patron also yields such dramaturgical features as the masque-like theophany, since James was fond of masques. Jones also pins the main flaw of the dramatic design to the Cymbeline/James analogy in an interesting way, attributing certain inconsistencies of character to Shakespeare's various strategies for avoiding giving offense. While I am not persuaded that the play is as logically flawed as Jones suggests, I would agree that a proper understanding of its intricacies depends to a great extent upon a recognition of its use of history. (p. 76)

The analogies the play makes between the logic of events of chronicle-history and the logic of dreams point up the disorder and illogic of unreconstructed historical facts, and the essentially fictive structure the historian, like the dramatist, must impose to give shape to his narrative. It is not that the sanctity of national history is being deliberately undermined, but that Shakespeare makes us aware that history *is* constructed, that both our personal and national myths must of necessity scaffold truth with an artificial, purposive design. (p. 77)

Perhaps the play's concern with this connection between private and social experience may help account for its strange tone, its mixture of archness and affecting simplicity. As Freud defines them, wit and dreams share a common parentage in the unconscious; the most important difference lies in their "social behavior." Freud holds the dream to be "a perfectly asocial psychic product," which not only finds it "unnecessary" to be intelligible, but "must even guard against being understood" since it can only exist in disguised form. Wit, on the other hand, Freud considers "the most social of all those psychic functions whose aim is to gain pleasure." Wit requires an audience. In *Cymbeline* Shakespeare conveys much of the experience of dreams and some of their wonder within a sophisticated dramatic vehicle, aware of its own artifice.

As Granville-Barker recognized, in Imogen's waking next to Cloten and in the final recognition scene especially, the audience is both sympathetically engaged and ironically distanced [see excerpt above, 1930]. The grotesque irony of the former scene is replaced in the latter by the potentially "farcical associations," in Kermode's phrase, of so many revelations so neatly contrived. In both cases, the core of the narrative moves us; it is the palpable presence of the master dramatist pulling both affective and witty strings which holds us apart. Within the conventions of the tragicomic double plot, heroic and pastoral or comic episodes reflect and redound upon one another, but remain distinct. But *Cymbeline*'s complexity of tone derives from a deliberate confounding of the two.

While it sounds paradoxical, in this respect *Cymbeline* is a peculiarly medieval play. The sacred and the profane exist side by side, and to some degree merge in their essential effect. The grotesque and the farcical help give the transcendent an earthly location. At the same time, they allow the controlled intrusion of unconscious impulses, an acknowledgment of man's kinship with the beasts, and at once direct the mind upward toward reverence. I am reminded of Hugh of St. Victor's belief that

> The ugly is still more beautiful than beauty itself.... Beauty encourages us to linger. The ugly does not permit us to rest; it forces us to depart, to transcend it....

This is the impulse which underlies those medieval grotesques carved into Miserere seats. And Shakespeare captures it to some extent in the union of sympathy and ironical amusement he manages to evoke in *Cymbeline*. The play's rarefied atmosphere of wittiness infused with the insouciance of dreams, its impression of artlessness artfully executed, is not only a sophisticated exploration of tragicomic form, but an unusually primitive dramaturgical experience. Beside *The Winter's Tale* or *The Tempest*, *Cymbeline* provides relatively few verbal clues to its underlying meaning; its effects are mainly visual, its affectiveness a concatenation of texture and atmosphere. There is an implicit silence in the play, suggested by those quietenings down which occur as the various characters fall asleep. And these lapsings, these cessations of consciousness which yet contain the deepest truth of that consciousness, suggest the silence which signifies that state of complete identity in which the perils and restorative rituals of the romance are no longer necessary.

Cymbeline's greatest interest lies, I think, in the suggestiveness of its bold peculiarities. As Granville-Barker described the play:

> ... one turns to it from *Othello*, or *King Lear*, or *Antony and Cleopatra*, as one turns from a masterly painting to, say, a fine piece of tapestry, from commanding beauty to more recondite charm.

This rather specialized charm is probably what Shaw had in mind when he ventured to suggest that the proper setting for a modern production of *Cymbeline* was not the London stage, but a village schoolroom. There, unself-consciously, the drama would be played with the degrees of ardor and artlessness natural to it, and to a nation's sense of itself when it fancies it has recently come of age. The smallish stature of the actors would adumbrate their faint absurdity as heroes without bringing down charges of unpatriotic license, and we as the audience could remain complacently detached, congratulating ourselves on our greater historical sophistication. (pp. 78-9)

> *D. E. Landry, "Dreams as History: The Strange Unity of 'Cymbeline'," in* Shakespeare Quarterly, *Vol. 33, No. 1, Spring, 1982, pp. 68-79.*

DAVID M. BERGERON   (essay date 1983)

[*Bergeron discusses sexuality in* Cymbeline *with an emphasis on the tragicomic form of the play. He remarks that this drama is unlike Shakespeare's other romances in that its depiction of sexuality is unrelated to the process of regeneration and renewal. Indeed, Bergeron contends, the dramatic world of* Cymbeline *is "sterile, non-procreative," and he avers that Iachimo and Cloten "embody the incomplete and misdirected sexuality of the play." For contrasting discussions of regeneration and renewal in* Cymbeline, *see the excerpts by Denton J. Snider (1890), Robert Grams Hunter (1965), and William Barry Thorne (1969). Also, for additional analyses of Shakespeare's depiction of the sexuality of the characters in his play, see the excerpt by Michael Taylor*

(1983) and the essay by Murray M. Schwartz cited in the Additional Bibliography.]

Writing about the theme and process of regeneration in *Cymbeline*, William B. Thorne suggests that in Posthumus "sexual fulfillment is directly equated with national well-being...." Thus the ending of the play resonates not only with the achievement of peace in Britain but also with the potential success of the marriage of Imogen and Posthumus. But the key word is, I think, "potential." Sexual activity in *Cymbeline* is both misdirected and unfulfilled. Though Thorne comments on the regenerative force of nature in the play, one might just as well argue that one large dimension of nature—sexuality—does not contribute to regeneration. Unlike *Pericles* and *The Winter's Tale*, *Cymbeline* contains no procreative acts—no one is born. Unlike the other Romances, *Cymbeline* includes the deaths of two principal characters, Cloten and the Queen. (p. 159)

As has often been observed, the Romances focus on the relationship of fathers and daughters. But the situation of Imogen differs from that of her counterparts: she is already married, and indeed this marriage to Posthumus is the play's initial dramatic problem. The irate father, Cymbeline, banishes Posthumus, setting in motion a possible tragic development along the lines of *Romeo and Juliet*. In all likelihood, though it is difficult to be sure, their marriage has not been consummated.... That may be what the First Gentleman means when, referring to Posthumus, he says: "... and he that hath her / (I mean, that married her, alack good man, / And therefore banish'd) ..." [I. i. 17-19]. Cloten later speaks of the marriage "contract" of Imogen and Posthumus [II. iii. 113-15], though again one cannot be sure whether he means a legal, spiritual, or physical contract. In any event, the potential of normal sexual activity in the play is not realized; in fact, there are several threats to it. Though incest, suspected adultery, prostitution, and attempted rape dot the landscape of the Romances and some of these problems are in *Cymbeline*, sexual contact remains generally frustrated or non-existent in *Cymbeline*, setting it apart from the other plays. [J. M.] Nosworthy refers to the "fantastic promiscuity" in the early parts of the play [see his introduction to the New Arden edition cited in the Additional Bibliography], but I find no evidence for that. Whatever promiscuity there may be resides in the imagination of the characters, principally Iachimo and Cloten.

These two figures, Cloten and Iachimo, embody the incomplete and misdirected sexuality of the play. On the level of metaphor, I suggest that Cloten may be a eunuch and Iachimo impotent. Though the evidence is not, cannot be, conclusive, one might even argue that their conditions are real as well as metaphorical. But however one finally views their sexual capacity, we can be certain that they are symptomatic of the larger sterile, nonprocreative world in *Cymbeline*. The reordering of the world of the play cannot come to fruition until these two, who have no parallel in the other Romances, are removed or overcome. Only then can the dramatist reconcile the fractured world and offer hope of a new beginning, making sexual fulfillment possible.

Critics often single out Cloten and Iachimo as villains with Cloten also usually designated as a fool. With such perceptions one could scarcely argue. Linking these two characters, one critic has observed: "... Iachimo, like Cloten, is an aspect or extension of Posthumus. Cloten is a type of brute appetite and violence, while Iachimo is a type of egotistic intellectual cunning, and he very much acts as Posthumus' agent" [see essay by Joan Carr cited in the Additional Bibliography]. That Cloten and Iachimo are manifestations of Posthumus' darker side is an imaginative suggestion. But, ironically, they are always trying to take his place, and the means is sexual. I think the link between Cloten and Iachimo is precisely a sexual one, each suffering from his own brand of incomplete sexuality, each sexually aware but thwarted or perverted in purpose, thereby fulfilling no natural sexual function. In the narrative arrangement of the play the same actor could play both parts, helping underscore the connection between them. The basic irony of their situation is that they seem to pose a genuine sexual threat to Imogen but in fact do not, perhaps cannot.

The problem of sexual inability further distinguishes *Cymbeline* from the other Romances and indeed from Shakespeare's comedies generally. Cloten's sexual deficiency signals his general personality deficiency, as incapable of sexual performance as he is incapable of social intercourse. The first hint comes, I think, when Cloten boasts, "I must go up and down like a cock, that nobody can match" [II. i. 21-2]; and the Second Lord adds an aside: "You are cock and capon too . . ." [II. i. 23]. . . . Outwardly Cloten may be a strutting cock while in actuality a capon. If he is a capon, then this fits well a general "beast fable" perspective that some critics see in the play's numerous references to birds. However much Cloten may exhibit some of Posthumus' qualities, he is finally quite different, as we are reminded when Imogen, commenting on her choice, distinguishes Posthumus from Cloten: "I chose an eagle, / And did avoid a puttock" [I. i. 139-40]. The eagle has strength and virility, contrasting radically with the puttock or kite which lacks bold dash and instead "glides about ignobly looking for a sickly or wounded victim" [James E. Harting, *The Birds of Shakespeare*]. (pp. 160-61)

In the encounter with Imogen Cloten complains about his love fortune and calls in musicians to assist, being advised that music "will penetrate" [II. iii. 12-13]. Ordering them to tune, Cloten says: ". . . if you can penetrate her with your fingering, so: we'll try with tongue too: if none will do, let her remain . . ." [II. iii. 14-16]. The tongue can, of course, be a sexual instrument, both literally and figuratively; for Cloten it seems at best a phallus-substitute. In his case the tongue is merely the means of language. If the music does not work, Cloten says, then not even the "voice of unpaved eunuch" can succeed [II. iii. 30]. In Shakespeare's strikingly redundant phrase, "unpaved eunuch" ("unpaved" meaning "castrated"), Cloten seems to know whereof he speaks. The phrase, of course, does not prove that Cloten is a capon, but the words and events accumulate to underscore Cloten's inadequacy so that at the least eunuch is a telling metaphor for Cloten.

Imogen meets this sexual pursuit with rebuff and abuse, indicating that she hates Cloten. The measure of her contempt bristles in a comment threatening to his manhood:

> His [Posthumus'] mean'st garment,
> That ever hath but clipp'd his body, is dearer
> In my respect, than all the hairs above thee,
> Were they all made such men.
>
> [II. iii. 133-36]

Struck to the quick, Cloten repeats four times some variation of "'His garment!'" [II. iii. 137, 139, 150, 156]. There is, I think, a clear sexual association made by Imogen between Posthumus and the clothes that cover his body; such a sexual linking is crucial to the remainder of Cloten's story. Imogen leaves the distinct impression that the difference between Posthumus and Cloten is not one merely of nobility, but that Post-

humus is a man of sexual attractiveness and Cloten is not. Having lost in so many other endeavors, Cloten loses in love despite the assistance of musicians. (p. 162)

Cloten protests too much about his "natural person"; everything about him suggests that he is unnatural. Cloten certainly has lustful desires, but I wonder if they may not be another of his idle boasts, of which there are many. Not only is his desire for Posthumus' garments perverse, the clothes seem to offer him a strength he otherwise does not have. He never refers to raping Imogen except as envisioned while wearing Posthumus' clothes. To say the least, such an action will "vex" Imogen, as Cloten says; but I think Shakespeare may be hinting at a power or capability that in Cloten's imagination these garments may confer on him. The thought of killing two birds with one stone excites Cloten, but that desire, fortunately, comes to naught.

Opening Act IV with a soliloquy, Cloten puns on the word "fit" with its sexual connotations; and he also boasts: "How fit his [Posthumus'] garments serve me!" [IV. i. 2]. Cloten's identification with Posthumus' clothes seems complete, leading him to ask of Guiderius when they suddenly meet: "Know'st me not by my clothes?" [IV. ii. 81]. There is confusion of identity here as Cloten betrays his need to be associated with the strength and manhood that Posthumus represents. Guiderius, of course, kills Cloten and beheads him; and he comments: "This Cloten was a fool, an empty purse, / There was no money in 't" [IV. ii. 113-14]. The phrase "empty purse" may join "capon" and "unpaved eunuch" to underscore Cloten's possible lack of sexual capability.

How is one to regard the beheading of Cloten, which strikes some critics as gratuitous cruelty on the dramatist's part? . . . [If] Cloten can be regarded as a eunuch, at least as a metaphor, would not his decapitation complete the earlier action that had left him "unpaved," a capon? Beheaded, Cloten is an appropriate emblem of the sterility in the play. Calling in musicians and wearing Posthumus' clothes do not add sexual power to Cloten; rather, these acts focus attention on Cloten's failure. In the discussion that follows we will see how the matter of sexual incapacity affects other characters as well.

Though G. Wilson Knight claims that Iachimo is a "born seducer" [see excerpt above, 1947], he stops short of seduction even when he has a golden opportunity. Iachimo seems to settle for being a sexual voyeur engaged in titillation. (p. 163)

In their [first] encounter Imogen asks Iachimo why he pities her; and he replies: "That others do / (I was about to say) enjoy your—" [I. vi. 90-1]. He can't complete the statement. Imogen initially finds him puzzling and asks to explain "What both you spur and stop" [I. vi. 99]. The image, appropriately enough, comes from horsemanship; it seems an analysis of Iachimo's sexual advances and retreats—the "spur and stop." In his graphically sensual language, especially [I. vi. 99-112], Iachimo unwittingly captures in an image his own position of voyeur: ". . . then by-peeping in an eye . . ." [I. vi. 108]. Of the scandalous things he says about Posthumus, Iachimo insists that Imogen's graces "That from my mutest conscience to my tongue / Charms this report out" [I. vi. 116-17]. He urges revenge against Posthumus, asking why "Should he make me / Live like Diana's priest, betwixt cold sheets, / Whiles he is vaulting variable ramps . . ." [I. vi. 132-34]—the difference between frustrated sexuality and virility, probably said in envy. One notes how Iachimo has twisted the revenge issue to serve his purposes. Offering himself to Imogen, he pledges: "I dedicate myself to your sweet pleasure . . .''; ''Let me my service tender on your lips'' [I. vi. 136, 140]. With that Imogen has heard quite enough, and she rebuffs him, as she will Cloten later. Iachimo escapes from sexual disappointment by changing his tune, now insisting that all of this was but a test of her love for Posthumus. His tongue is as ineffectual with Imogen as is Cloten's.

If not tongue, then perhaps eyes: the subsequent scene in Imogen's bedchamber in which Iachimo emerges from the trunk constitutes at the least a visual ''rape'' of her, a point on which Schwartz [see Additional Bibliography] and I agree. The sleeping, sexually alluring Imogen, reminiscent of a Desdemona, compels Iachimo to cry: ''That I might touch! / But kiss, one kiss!'' [II. ii. 16-17]. Well, why not? He spurs on but stops: ''But my design. / To note the chamber: I will write all down'' [II. ii. 23-4]. For one who boasted that he would seduce Imogen, his passive response to the now vulnerable Imogen seems strange. Again the suspicion arises that he may be impotent. His only assertive action is to take her bracelet which will be the necessary ocular proof of his alleged sexual act. Indeed, taking the bracelet becomes for Iachimo a kind of sexual action, a substitute for what he had intended to do. His actions do not match the boldness of his tongue nor the imagination of his eyes. (pp. 164-65)

The swaggering of Cloten and Iachimo only masks their sexual incapacity; and though they are the chief examples of such incomplete sexuality, the problem touches almost everyone in *Cymbeline*. The new husband and wife, Posthumus and Imogen, separated in the early moments of the play, are thus denied any ongoing sexual fulfillment. Every indication is that Posthumus is himself healthy and virile; in the opening scene the First Gentleman praises Posthumus for both his valor and his physical bearing: ''I do not think / So fair an outward, and such stuff within / Endows a man, but he'' [I. i. 22-4]. By the measure of Posthumus we judge the failures of Cloten and Iachimo, who, despite their boasting of taking the sexual place of Posthumus, are in fact unable to do so. Yet, Posthumus' own sexuality is thwarted by external forces, namely Cymbeline who interferes in and interrupts the natural love of Imogen and Posthumus, thus assuring no procreation. When Posthumus awakens from the vision of his family and Jupiter, his language evokes the idea of birth: ''Sleep, thou hast been a grandsire, and begot / A father to me: and thou hast created / A mother, and two brothers'' [V. iv. 123-25]. But such a ''birth'' is an illusion, as Posthumus recognizes, reminding us that procreation is a thing of the past in *Cymbeline*.

Imogen herself compounds the irony and difficulty of the play as she makes her way through the maze of the plot wearing boy's clothes in search of Posthumus. To put on such garments denies overtly, if temporarily, her sexuality; to deny her femininity adds to the problem of occluded sexuality. Reacting to Posthumus' presumed betrayal, Imogen says: ''Poor I am stale, a garment out of fashion . . .'' [III. iv. 51]. Later in the scene Pisanio hits on the strategy of her disguise and tells her: ''You must forget to be a woman . . .'' [III. iv. 154]. Imogen heeds his instructions: ''I see into thy end, and am almost / A man already'' [III. iv. 166-67]. But only ''almost a man,'' for Imogen's masculine pose is just that, a conscious pose, in contrast to those two seeming men, would-be seducers, Cloten and Iachimo. So the disguised Cloten, tricked out in Posthumus' suit, wanders about looking for Imogen, who is attired in boy's clothes. Such distortion of reality only makes the prospects of natural sexuality more difficult. Imogen's com-

ment about Guiderius and Arviragus, whom she has encountered in the woods, ''I'd change my sex to be companion with them, / Since Leonatus' false'' [III. vi. 87-8], evokes several ironies, starting with Shakespeare's favorite, namely that a young boy playing the role of Imogen dressed in male garments wishes to be a male. She also suggests that if she were indeed male, she could be a companion to Guiderius and Arviragus without any sexual considerations. That is, assuming Leonatus to be false, she would deny her sexuality and live as a brother to these two, thus assuring no procreation. (pp. 165-66)

What of Guiderius and Arviragus? Perhaps it is misleading to see them in this sterile picture, for their situation is one of innocence born of lack of opportunity for sexual experience despite their young manhood. At least they have an instinctual attraction to Imogen—Fidele. As Guiderius says: ''Were you a woman, youth, / I should woo hard . . .'' [III. vi. 68-9]. The capacity is there, but Fidele is not a proper sexual object. Having no opportunities for sexual fulfillment is of course another version of incomplete sexuality.

The arid world of *Cymbeline* must be overcome unless Shakespeare is intent on tragedy. Cloten is killed, the Queen dies, Iachimo is transformed, and Posthumus and Imogen are reunited. The obstacles to sexual completion have been removed; only then can one begin to look with hope to the future and see the comic possibilities that lie ahead. But so intense is the problem of unfulfilled sexuality that a heavy, sometimes tragic, tone lies over much of the play. Indeed at moments the play seems at cross purposes, an uncertainty that emphasizes more fully than elsewhere in the Romances the *tragi*-comic nature of its structure. But the supernatural intervenes, and the diffuse forces come together in V. v for a glorious process of revelation and reconciliation. There is no other scene quite like it in Shakespeare.

When Posthumus and Imogen reunite, he says to her, in words of special delight to Tennyson: ''Hang there like fruit, my soul, / Till the tree die'' [V. v. 263-64]. ''Fruit'' is an uncommon word in this play, and it implies possibility, ripeness: we are now ready to turn our backs on a barren world. Thus Belarius steps forward with Cymbeline's sons, admitting that though he has stolen them, he has been their nurse, their surrogate father and mother. The exultant Cymbeline, a father restored to his daughter and to these long-lost sons, cries out in joy: ''O, what am I? / A mother to the birth of three? Ne'er mother / Rejoic'd deliverance more'' [V. v. 368-70]. He is now both father and mother; he has helped give birth. To link himself metaphorically to the mother role is to highlight a procreative act. So, there is birth in *Cymbeline*, not an actual physical birth, but spiritual renewal and family reunion. (p. 167)

David M. Bergeron, ''Sexuality in 'Cymbeline','' in Essays in Literature, *Vol. X, No. 2, Fall, 1983, pp. 159-68.*

MICHAEL TAYLOR   (essay date 1983)

[*Taylor discusses Shakespeare's complex response in* Cymbeline *to the ''narrative conventions normally governing the lives of young lovers in the romances.'' He contends that the sexual innocence of Posthumus and Imogen is not praiseworthy, but is, rather, a primary cause of the disasters that befall them. Taylor sees in the play ''a pattern of erotic punishment in which both lovers suffer for the naïvety of their expectations,'' drawing attention to the frequency with which their self-worth is described in punitive, negative terms. He further argues that this pattern of punitive behavior, together with other instances of potential sexual*

violations and the unsentimental depiction of the "idyllic setting"
in Acts III and IV, demonstrates Shakespeare's marked ambiva-
lence towards the tradition of pastoralism. Such other critics as
E. K. Chambers (1907), Douglas L. Peterson (1973), and Rosalie
L. Colie (1974) have also examined Shakespeare's adaptation of
the literary conventions of pastoralism in Cymbeline. *For further*
commentary on the portrayal of sexuality in the play, see the
excerpt by David M. Bergeron (1983) and the essay by Murray
M. Schwartz cited in the Additional Bibliography.]

The most astonishing scene in *Cymbeline* unnerves us with the
grotesque spectacle of its heroine waking up in a pastoral setting
from a death-like sleep (induced by Dr Cornelius' box of drugs)
to the sight of what appears to be her decapitated husband
sprawled alongside her. . . . Until this rude awakening, Imogen
had imagined herself to be safe in her pastoral sanctuary, far
from the corruption of Cymbeline's court, secure in the immediate and excessive affection displayed for her by Arviragus
and Guiderius who, despite her male disguise, and despite the
fact that they have never met her before, have instinctively and
conventionally responded to the ties of blood between them.
Horrified now by this change in her situation, Imogen at first
concludes that she must be dreaming:

> I hope I dream,
> For so I thought I was a cave-keeper
> And cook to honest creatures.
>
> [IV. ii. 297-99]

The desired diminution of status from princess to pastoral skivvy
has become mysteriously transformed into a nightmare degradation in which the honest creatures of her waking hours
have vanished, leaving behind in their place a headless changeling whose reality can be only fleetingly doubted in those blurred
moments 'twixt sleep and wake. (p. 97)

While it may be true (as so many critics insist) that there has
been something of an 'uneasy conflation' of history and romance in *Cymbeline* [see the essay by Howard Felperin cited
in the Additional Bibliography], or that the play as a whole
fails to come together entirely satisfactorily, it is demonstrably
true that in the story of Imogen, Iachimo, and Posthumus
Shakespeare achieves a potent coherence in which the violation
of Imogen's dream of pastoral innocence has an important role
to play, as it also has in the play's action as a whole, making
it one of those events of special significance in a work of art
around which interpretation inevitably clusters. (p. 98)

Pivotally placed, Imogen's experience captures much of the
play's accumulated significance, and the greater the interpre-
tative burden the more daring Shakespeare's choice of the grotesque as an appropriate vehicle for this climax to the play's
pastoral activity, in which an original dream of innocence—
Imogen's—expressed in explicitly pastoral terms, undergoes
such a savage assault. Earlier, in Cymbeline's court, with Posthumus banished, and pursued by the preposterous Cloten, Imogen had dreamt of a life exempt from courtly haunt and princely
responsibility:

> Would I were
> A neatherd's daughter, and my Leonatus
> Our neighbor shepherd's son.
>
> [I. i. 148-50]

Instead of finding herself in a pastoral setting where she might
play Flora to Posthumus' Florizel [in *The Winter's Tale*], Imogen finds herself in one where she must play a much more
demandingly operatic role in a mad burlesque of sexual passion
and shattered idyllic expectations. When Imogen clutches the

decapitated body to her, daubs herself with its blood, and falls
into an exhausted, dreamless sleep—the sleep of an emotional
satiety—the coital sequence suggested by these responses supplies an equivocal, parodic answer to the earnest prayer of
Guiderius and Arviragus: 'Quiet consummation have, / And
renowned be thy grave' [IV. ii. 280-81].

Why at this important juncture does Shakespeare choose to
subject his heroine (a heroine as militantly chaste, incidentally,
as any in the late plays) to such a literal and symbolic be-
smirching? Any adequate answer has to take into account the
extent to which *Cymbeline* has from the beginning played fast
and loose with the narrative conventions normally governing
the lives of young lovers in the romances, especially the one
that insists on the narrative sequence that leads them through
a troublesome unmarried state to a blissfully married one. Not
for Posthumus and Imogen (or so it seems) the traditional
comedic role of their counterparts in the other romances and
romantic comedies whose marriage prospects remain conventionally dim until the final scenes, their consummations impeded
by a society that Northrop Frye characterizes as 'irrational or
anti-comic':

> The normal action [of Renaissance comedy] is
> the effort of a young man to get possession of
> a young woman who is kept from him by var-
> ious social barriers: her low birth, his minority
> or shortage of funds, parental opposition, the
> prior claims of a rival. These are eventually
> circumvented, and the comedy ends at a point
> when a new society is crystallised, usually by
> the marriage or betrothal of hero and heroine.

In the case of *Cymbeline*, Frye's various social barriers seem
already to have been hurdled by the lovers' impetuous marriage—consummated despite Posthumus' low birth, shortage
of funds, the opposition of Imogen's father and step-mother
and the rival claims, prior or otherwise, of Cloten, the Queen's
son and Imogen's step-brother. Just as iconoclastically, however, Cymbeline and his supporters act in shocking defiance
of both dramatic and social convention; they refuse to accept
the validity of the lovers' contract, using all the arguments
mentioned by Frye (with the exception of the hero's minority),
as though the marriage itself—usually the holy grail in Shakespearian comedy—were nothing but a minor impediment to
Cloten's more authentic courtship. In the enormity of its ca-
sualness, Cymbeline's advice to his step-son perfectly conveys
this important aspect of his court's aristocratic perversity:

> The exile of her minion is too new;
> She hath not yet forgot him. Some more time
> Must wear the print of his remembrance on't,
> And then she's yours.
>
> [II. iii. 41-4]

Not much spirit of *noblesse oblige* here: stripped of its fatuity
(if that were possible) Cloten's version of what it is to be a
nobleman (the obsession later of Belarius' moral reflections)—
'it is fit I should commit offense to my inferiors' [II. i. 28-9]—
epitomizes the values of Cymbeline's court.

Cymbeline begins then in the manner of *Pericles;* both plays
open with the unsavoury spectacle of wayward kings disregarding moral or social norms, victimizing representatives of
the younger generation, committing offences to their inferiors.
(The general resemblance is made keener by the suggestion of
incest in Cloten's courtship of his step-sister.) In vivid contrast,
the marriage of Imogen and Posthumus institutionalizes (or

seems to do so) the larger virtues each possesses; yet even before we experience Posthumus' later weakness on his banishment to Italy—even (for that matter) before we meet either Imogen or Posthumus—the sense we have of the abnormality of the situation, of there being something posthumous about the action of a romance beginning where most end, infects even the play's opening conversation, a piece of explicatory dialogue between the two Gentlemen in which the First Gentleman—for the benefit of his conventionally ignorant colleague (and of ourselves)—extols the superior virtues of the newly married couple at the expense of the King's party. He does so in a verse typical of *Cymbeline*—one that has a 'hard corrugated texture . . . [caused by] the persistent recreation of feelings of a particular kind of physical pain' [see excerpt above by F. C. Tinkler, 1938]. The play's opening lines, 'tantalizingly elliptical' in Nosworthy's phrase [see Additional Bibliography], make only tortuous sense, but are then followed by the crystal-clear exposition that the First Gentleman provides for the Second, as though he were at the same time mocking his own introductory style:

> She's wedded,
> Her husband banished, she imprisoned. All
> Is outward sorrow, though I think the King
> Be touched at very heart.
>
> [I. i. 7-10]

To swing from one linguistic extreme to the other within the space of a few lines seems appropriate for a play throughout blown stylistically between the opposing winds of fairy-tale and case-history. If the semantic complexity of the First Gentleman's opening speech reflects the moral difficulty of living in a court so Janus-faced, then his later use of the hyperbole of punishment in his description of Posthumus reveals a more subtle difficulty; like the other courtiers, the First Gentleman cannot mould his language to the disposition of his subject without the use of punitive metaphor:

> I do extend him, sir, within himself,
> Crush him together rather than unfold
> His measure duly.
>
> [I. i. 25-7]

This is the first of several instances in the play where the extreme worth of an object—something or someone beyond beyond, as Imogen says [III. ii. 56]—forces the eulogizer beyond (or rather beneath) conventional hyperbolic expression to draw extravagance from a darker area of the mind. If Cloten is 'a thing / Too bad for bad report' [I. ii. 16-17] then Posthumus and Imogen often seem to be things too good for good report, hence their superiority can only be conveyed in a strange hyperbolic exploitation of the vocabulary of bad report dominated by the imagery of forcible restraint—merit crushed in order to be unfolded duly. The lovers express their love for each other in terms equally punitive: Posthumus will drink down the words of Imogen's letters 'Though ink be made of gall' [I. i. 101]; rather than marry again were Imogen to die before him (itself a morbid notion) he would 'cere up my embracements from a next / With bonds of death' [I. i. 116-17]; in his eyes, the bracelet he gives Imogen on parting from her 'is a manacle of love; I'll place it / Upon this fairest prisoner' [I. i. 122-23]. Imogen is similarly afflicted. She can afford to ignore her father's anger, she says, because 'a touch more rare / Subdues all pangs, all fears' [I. i. 135-36]—'a touch more rare' is a fine phrase meaning (as Dowden tells us) 'a more exquisite pain', the pain, that is, of the enforced absence of her new husband whom she later describes as 'My supreme

crown of grief' [I. vi. 4]. Later still, she talks of the 'med'cinable' griefs that 'physic love' [III. ii. 33, 34]; and it is she who has to drink the gall of Posthumus' letter. 'The paper / Hath cut her throat already' [III. iv. 32-3] Pisanio observes in a typical metaphor. Love's affliction becomes self-infliction for Imogen—or imagined self-infliction—when she responds to Pisanio's description of Posthumus' embarking for Italy with

> I would have broke mine eyestrings, cracked them but
> To look upon him till the diminution
> Of space had pointed him sharp as my needle.
>
> [I. iii. 17-19]

Lovers in Shakespeare's plays do not usually talk of love's experience in this way except in problem comedies like *Troilus and Cressida* or tragedies of love like *Romeo and Juliet*. Do the lovers in *Cymbeline* linger in punitive terms over their love for each other simply because they have been forced to undergo the punishment of separation at that point in their lives when their counterparts in the other romances begin their hard-won freedom together? It hardly seems an adequate explanation. When Imogen describes Posthumus as 'My supreme crown of grief' (which follows the interesting ambiguity of her 'a wedded lady / That hath her husband banished' [I. vi. 2-3]), the phrase is a metonym not so much for Posthumus himself as for the punishment he cannot avoid inflicting on her by his banishment from Cymbeline's court—the 'pangs of barred affections' [I. i. 82] in the Queen's hypocritical words. Yet Imogen's elliptical construction gives the phrase the force of an accusation (or even self-accusation), especially as it follows 'O, that husband', the traditional resigned or despairing cry of long-suffering wives of neglectful husbands (a class Imogen is about to join).

Neither the perilous situation in which Imogen and Posthumus find themselves at the beginning of the play, nor the irony of subsequent events, justifies the extravagant language each uses to and about the other, each the other's supreme crown of grief more mysteriously than can be explained by the circumstances of their separation. And as in *The Winter's Tale*, Shakespeare allows us the occasional fleeting insight into his characters' pasts to suggest more complicated psychic disturbances than at first seems to be the case. The impression we have of something hyperbolically and unnaturally over-ripe, where (as the First Gentleman says of Posthumus) spring has become autumn, and where value can be expressed only in punitive terms, suggests a deeper malaise, hinted at perhaps by Imogen when surprised by Iachimo's description of Posthumus' frivolous behaviour in Rome:

> When he was here
> He did incline to sadness, and ofttimes
> Not knowing why. . . .
>
> [I. vi. 61-3]

What Imogen remembers about Posthumus has an ironically lurid light thrown on it by what Posthumus remembers about Imogen in parallel circumstances an act later (act 2, scene 5). Both memories surface under the pressure of Iachimo's accusations, both seem spontaneous and involuntary, each tells us something unexpected about the person concerned:

> Me of my lawful pleasure she restrained
> And prayed me oft forbearance—did it with
> A pudency so rosy, the sweet view on't
> Might well have warmed old Saturn—that I thought her
> As chaste as unsunned snow.
>
> [II. v. 9-13]

These lines come in the middle of a soliloquy of great power and subtlety; one that George Steiner in *After Babel* chooses as his paradigm for the untranslatability of the 'complete semantic event' in great poetry. To exhaust the significance (the meaning even) of such a complex speech, he argues, would involve us in ever-widening circles of legitimate application up to and including what he calls the 'informing sphere of sensibility' . . . with the problem of 'infinite series' . . . becoming an increasingly daunting one. We do not have to journey too far down the road to infinity, however, to notice how Posthumus' memory of Imogen exposes her innocence in an equivocal manner peculiar to *Cymbeline*. As opposed, say, to the sinless sensuality of the lovers in *The Winter's Tale, Cymbeline* makes much of the treacherous eroticism of its lovers' innocence, with Imogen cast as the play's Isabella whose 'modesty may more betray our sense / Than woman's lightness' [*Measure for Measure*, II. ii. 168-69]. Posthumus couches his recollections of Imogen's modesty in words that convey how dangerous to itself it is: 'pudency so rosy' suggests the erotic image that warms old Saturn far more readily than, in this context, the more paradoxical one of a chastity as cold as unsunned snow. Posthumus remembers Imogen in terms that recall Iachimo aroused by her erotic vulnerability as she lies sleeping before him, whose encomium on her beauty comes to a climax with a description of the intimate detail which for Posthumus will clinch the argument for her betrayal of him:

> On her left breast
> A mole cinque-spotted, like the crimson drops
> I' th' bottom of a cowslip. Here's a voucher
> Stronger than ever law could make. This secret
> Will force him think I have picked the lock and ta'en
> The treasure of her honor.
>
> [II. ii. 37-42]
> (pp. 98-102)

'Pudency so rosy', 'crimson drops / I' th' bottom of a cowslip', 'chaliced flowers': images to warm the libidos of old Saturn, Iachimo, Posthumus, and Cloten. And Posthumus is not as much the odd man out on this list as he ought to be, considering that, until his banishment, he has had every reason to expect the provocative image to give way to the reality it advertises. Between wedding and banishment, however, the image retains its provocation for him because of the frequency with which Imogen restrains him from his *lawful* pleasure—she 'prayed me *oft* forbearance'. Appropriately enough, Iachimo squeezes the final equivocation out of Imogen's attitude in the last scene of the play: 'He spake of her as Dian had hot dreams, / And she alone were cold' [V. v. 180-81]. Exploiting yet another ironic parallel with Cloten, Britain's absurd, bungling Iachimo, Posthumus' experience seems to confirm Cloten's vulgar opinion of love-making in which 'a woman's fitness comes by fits' [IV. i. 5-6]. The inclination to sadness that Imogen remembers about Posthumus may therefore not be unconnected with what Posthumus remembers about Imogen's chaste behaviour, no matter how rosily managed (a management, by the way, that Pisanio describes as 'More goddess-like than wife-like' [III. ii. 8]). Such an inference need not go beyond the complete semantic event, even though it may go beyond the more usual interpretation of the lovers' recollections which sees them as having only a limited application—Imogen's rosy pudency functioning simply as a kind of pathetic fallacy emphasizing Posthumus' savagery. Yet well within the informing sphere of sensibility lies the important connection that we make between Posthumus' prurient recollection of Imogen's sexual attrac-

tiveness and the relative ease with which he believes Iachimo's account of her fallen condition. (pp. 102-03)

However innocent the lovers, we cannot help but see them as sexual objects designed to provoke the conspiracy of suggestiveness that gives them their ambivalent and attractive power. How much more attractive (and no less ambivalent) must be Imogen's appeal for us, when we hear not only from Iachimo how beautiful she is, but share with him in the actual vision of her loveliness, the naked extent of which will be determined only by the tact or bravado of the particular production in which she appears. The moral precariousness of the moment is heightened when Iachimo bends to kiss her: 'But kiss, one kiss! Rubies unparagoned, / How dearly they do't!' [II. ii. 17-18]. Her lips in fact 'do' nothing, as she is asleep, but it is difficult to keep this in mind given the whispered fervour of Iachimo's remarks, all of which, incidentally, stress the magnetic power of Imogen's unconscious form—drawing the taper's flame to it—exuding a heady perfume. When Iachimo reports back to Posthumus, his description of Imogen's bedroom not only cruelly prolongs and as cruelly substantiates the claim made by his narrative, but recaptures the erotic cosmopolitanism of the trappings we have already seen with our own eyes: the tapestry of 'silk and silver' depicting Cleopatra's meeting with Antony where, in a mamillary image, 'Cydnus swelled above the banks' [II. iv. 71]; the andirons shaped like 'winking Cupids' (turning thereby a blind eye on the proceedings); the cherubim sporting wantonly on the ceiling; and, in the near-oxymoron of the voyeur, the carving of 'Chaste Dian bathing' on the chimney over the fireplace [II. iv. 89, 82]. . . . And, as we have seen, in the centre of all these seductive trappings, the cynosure, the goddess Imogen herself, whom Iachimo (like Milton's Satan) has already worshipped in his hushed recitation of her lovely parts, a devotional exercise we may well recall when listening to Imogen's catalogue of the headless corpse's Herculean ones.

In the light of this eventful history, it would be more accurate to view Imogen's grim experience with Cloten's body as a manifestation of a particular kind of symbolically appropriate pastoral reckoning than as the climax of a destructive countermovement to the pastoral tradition as such. In recent years, Shakespeare's treatment of the pastoral convention has received much critical attention, most of it concentrating on the innovative and unconventional in his handling of traditional literary attitudes. But by Shakespeare's time, the pastoral experience itself in literature had lost much of its traditional sweetness; beneath its 'superficial loveliness ranked the wretchedness of man' [S. K. Heninger, Jr.], its nostalgia and idealization in the service of satire and moral allegory. . . . The pastoral experience in *Cymbeline* and *The Tempest* is particularly harsh: innocence (rather than happiness) has to be renewed on a daily basis in a spirit of absorbed self-abnegation in a more formidable landscape than the traditional *locus amoenus* [pleasant place] of Greek pastoral. Of this landscape in *Cymbeline*, Rosalie Colie writes: 'it is unmitigated hard pastoral, a rocky difficult terrain training its inhabitants to a spare and muscular strength sufficient to wrest their nutriment from its minimal, ungenerous, exiguous resources,' [see excerpt above, 1974].

It is to this frugal landscape which makes 'tanlings' of her abducted brothers in the summer and 'shrinking slaves' [IV. iv. 29, 30] of them in the winter that Imogen comes in her traditional search for a pastoral sanctuary. She finds it—or thinks she does—in Belarius' 'pinching cave' [III. iii. 38], that 'cell of ignorance' [III. iii. 33] in Guiderius' contemptuous words, whose symbolically low threshold 'bows' the brothers each morning 'To a morning's holy office' [III. iii. 4]. Despite the love that Imogen wins instinctively from her unknown brothers, she must share with them the life of 'hardness' that 'ever / Of hardiness is mother' [III. vi. 21-2].... [Pisanio] urges Imogen to 'forget to be a woman' [III. iv. 154]; but his lengthy exhortation on the importance of her transvestism for her survival substitutes the doleful for the jocular. He seems overwhelmed by the inevitable degradation of her experience:

> Nay, you must
> Forget that rarest treasure of your cheek,
> Exposing it—but O, the harder heart!
> Alack, no remedy—to the greedy touch
> Of common-kissing Titan, and forget
> Your laborsome and dainty trims, wherein
> You made great Juno angry.
>
> [III. iv. 159-65]

In a manner typical of *Cymbeline*, Pisanio views Imogen's exposure to the elements as yet another sexual violation in which the sun becomes some hulking commoner intent on defiling a refined aristocrat, one who, typically again, has in all innocence angered Juno with her 'laboursome and dainty trims'. (pp. 103-05)

In *Cymbeline* the lovers' renewal of innocence is completed only after a rigorous purging of their sexual frailty. Imogen's grotesque experience with Cloten's body is therefore part of a pattern of erotic punishment in which both lovers suffer for the naïvety of their expectations. In an ambiguous manner peculiar to *Cymbeline*, Imogen, in Pisanio's words, is 'punished for her truth' [III. ii. 7]; and part of that punishment—as Imogen herself half realizes—entails 'peril to my modesty, not death on't' [III. iv. 152]. The lovers' punitive behaviour towards each other is brought to an appropriate climax in the play's last scene in a manner reminiscent of Pericles' initial rejection of his daughter, Marina. Imogen, still disguised as Fidele, attempts to interrupt another (this time the last) of Posthumus' outbursts of self-detestation and lamentation over Imogen's fate. Making the opposite of Imogen's mistake over Cloten, Posthumus spurns Imogen's intervention:

> Shall's have a play of this? Thou scornful page,
> There lie thy part.
> [*Thrusts her away; she falls*]
>
> [V. v. 228-29]

The stage direction here is from the Pelican edition; Nosworthy in the new Arden edition has '[*Striking her: she falls*]' which seems to me closer to the savage spirit of the sequence. That blow brings to a climax and to an end the thwarted relationship between the lovers.... When Posthumus next speaks some thirty or so lines later (apart from his Cymbeline-like bewilderment 'How come these staggers on me?' [V. v. 233]), he uses the play's most famous pastoral metaphor as the lovers embrace: 'Hang there like fruit, my soul / Till the tree die' [V. v. 263-64]. So this reconciliation is also part of the play's pastoral reckoning. Posthumus is now mature enough—and Imogen too—for him to be able properly to fulfil Jupiter's prediction: 'He shall be lord of Lady Imogen' [V. iv. 107].

Jupiter's way of putting it—courtly and zestful—anticipates a future for the lovers purged of all their sexual misconstructions and hesitancies. Posthumus' dense arboreal metaphor, however, goes beyond the assertion of mere swaggering lordship to provide us with a vision of married life as an entwining mutuality in which the spiritual (Imogen as Posthumus' soul) and the erotic and fructuous (Posthumus as the tree and Imogen

as the fruit of it) merge in a complicated, slightly ambiguous union. The density of the metaphor matches the subtleties of the lovers' history. Some 150 lines later, when Posthumus next speaks, his last words in the play measure the extent to which he has achieved the authoritative maturity erroneously thrust upon him by the First Gentleman in the opening scene. All traces of that corrugated verbal texture have now vanished: like Leontes in the final scene of *The Winter's Tale* Posthumus has earned the right to speak with compelling clarity. Confronted with a penitent, kneeling Iachimo, Posthumus provides Cymbeline with his model for bringing the conflict between the Romans and the British and the play itself to an end:

> Kneel not to me.
> The pow'r that I have on you is to spare you;
> The malice towards you to forgive you. Live,
> And deal with others better.
>
> [V. v. 417-20]

Cymbeline is suitably impressed:

> Nobly doomed!
> We'll learn our freeness of a son-in-law:
> Pardon's the word to all.
>
> [V. v. 420-22]

Pardon to all and the new harmony between Britain and Rome mark the happy outcome envisioned in pastoral terms by the Soothsayer in which the 'majestic cedar' [V. v. 457] of Britain is made whole. The play's pastoral reckoning, therefore, embraces not only the lovers' punishment and reward but also the British failure and recovery on the political and diplomatic fronts in which, as the appropriate last word for a pastoral vision, the play's last, lingering word—peace—is the word to all. (pp. 105-06)

> *Michael Taylor, "The Pastoral Reckoning in 'Cymbeline'," in* Shakespeare Survey: An Annual Survey of Shakespearian Study and Production, *Vol. 36, 1983, pp. 97-106.*

ADDITIONAL BIBLIOGRAPHY

Abartis, Caesarea. *The Tragicomic Construction of "Cymbeline" and "The Winter's Tale."* Salzburg Studies in English Literature: Jacobean Drama Studies, 73, edited by James Hogg. Salzburg: Institut für Englische Sprache und Literatur Universität Salzburg, 1977, 128 p.

Extended discussion of the dramatic structure of *Cymbeline*. Abartis argues that the theme of reconciliation or renewal inherent in the tragicomic genre itself assumes an inappropriate precedence in *Cymbeline* over the announced themes of worth, nobility, and justification for national war in each of the three separate plots of the play. The critic concludes that *Cymbeline* is "an inferior tragicomedy, unable to accommodate the demands of the plot and the demands of the genre."

Bergeron, David M. "*Cymbeline*: Shakespeare's Last Roman Play." *Shakespeare Quarterly* XXXI, No. 1 (Spring 1980): 31-41.

Agrees with G. Wilson Knight (see excerpt above, 1947) "that the heart of [*Cymbeline*] is its historical basis" and links the play with Shakespeare's dramas of Roman history. Noting the several references in the play to Augustus Caesar, Bergeron demonstrates the similarities between some of its central characters and the emperor's family, especially remarking on the resemblances between Cymbeline's queen and Augustus's wife, "the magnificent and horrible Livia."

Berry, Francis. "The Interior Plot-Required Inset: Cardinal Blemish." In his *The Shakespeare Inset: Word and Picture,* pp. 68-74. London: Routledge and Kegan Paul, 1965.

Analysis of Shakespeare's use in *Cymbeline* of the dramatic technique of having a character describe an event that occurs earlier during the action of the play. Theorizing that the scene in Imogen's bedroom (II. ii) would originally have taken place on the inner, recessed stage that was typical of the Elizabethan playhouse and that Iachimo's subsequent description of it to Posthumus (II. iv) would occur on the outer stage that was directly in front of the audience, Berry contends that the "actual spectacle" of the former becomes almost an "imagined spectacle" through its distance from the spectators and Iachimo's narrative language in this scene, while his account of the event afterward receives "dramatic immediacy" by its probable placement in the foreground of the stage.

Bond, R. Warwick. "The Puzzle of *Cymbeline*." In his *Studia Otiosa: Some Attempts in Criticism,* pp. 69-74. London: Constable and Co., 1938.

Contends that Shakespeare's primary concern in *Cymbeline* was with the historical material. Bond argues that this play should be regarded not only as a sequel to *Antony and Cleopatra,* but, more importantly, as a link between the two series of Roman and English history plays that the dramatist had written earlier.

Brandes, George. "*Cymbeline.*" In his *William Shakespeare,* pp. 615-34. 1898. Reprint. London: William Heinemann, 1920.

Contends that *Cymbeline* demonstrates that Shakespeare had adopted for himself a situational ethic, in which the intention and the agency of the action are more significant than the act itself. Brandes maintains that although Pisanio and all the noble characters in the play are depicted as guilty of various deceits, fabrications, and acts of violence, they do not sacrifice their intrinsic morality. The critic further asserts that the contrast between the country and the corrupt court in *Cymbeline* reveals that Shakespeare himself saw the former as a refuge or sanctuary, especially "for those who have done with life."

Brockbank, J. P. "History and Histrionics in *Cymbeline*." *Shakespeare Survey* 11 (1958): 42-9.

Earliest discussion of *Cymbeline* in relation to Geoffrey of Monmouth's reworking of the myth of Brute or Brutus, the legendary founder of Britain. Brockbank avers that Brute, descended himself from rulers of Rome and Troy and purportedly the founder of the line of British kings down to Cadwallader, represents a reconciliation of Roman and British traditions that is mirrored in the conjunction of these nations in *Cymbeline.* Brockbank is also one of the earliest critics to note that for the chroniclers of British history, Cymbeline's reign was primarily significant because during his rule "Christ was born and Augustus ruled in Rome." Beyond Shakespeare's use of some names in *Cymbeline* that appear in the Brutan legend—such as Posthumus, Silvius, Imogen, Lucius, and Cloten—Brockbank views both the play and the myth as depicting "the apocalyptic destiny of Britain."

Bullough, Geoffrey. Introduction to *Cymbeline,* by William Shakespeare. In *Narrative and Dramatic Sources of Shakespeare,* Vol. VIII, edited by Geoffrey Bullough, pp. 3-37. London: Routledge & Kegan Paul, 1975.

Discussion of Shakespeare's sources and his use of them in *Cymbeline.* In addition to the *Chronicles* of Holinshed, Bullough maintains that both Boccaccio's *Decameron* and the anonymous *Frederyke of Jennen* provided material for Shakespeare's play. Additionally, he identifies the anonymous *The Rare Triumphs of Love and Fortune* as a "probable source" and comments on parallels between passages in *Cymbeline* and folk stories similar to *Snow White and the Seven Dwarfs,* as well as Tasso's *Jerusalem Delivered.*

Camden, Carroll. "The Elizabethan Imogen." *Rice Institute Pamphlet* XXXVIII, No. 1 (April 1951): 1-17.

Offers extensive evidence from Elizabethan literature to demonstrate that Imogen's public and private virtues were those most frequently regarded by Shakespeare's contemporaries as essential qualities of a virtuous woman. Camden notes that the only fault with which Imogen may be charged is her disobedience to her father, but it is a significant one, for her subsequent suffering is shown to be a consequence of her undutiful behavior.

Carr, Joan. "*Cymbeline* and the Validity of Myth." *Studies in Philology* LXXV, No. 3 (July 1978): 316-30.

Maintains that in *Cymbeline* Shakespeare was questioning the power of myth to palliate the harshness of life and to "make sense of the human condition." Carr comments on the parallels between the portrayal of Imogen and "Judaeo-Christian versions of the scapegoat myth," arguing that, unlike the tales of legendary victims, Shakespeare does not make it clear that her sufferings have successfully achieved redemption for her fellow characters. The critic also demonstrates the similarities between the death of Cloten and the resurrection myth of Orpheus and contends that the subsequent change in Posthumus when he returns to the stage in Act V is explainable only by means of "the mythic, folkloric aspect of Cloten's dismemberment, which signals the demise of the bloodthirsty, unregenerate Posthumus."

Clemen, Wolfgang. "*Cymbeline.*" In his *The Development of Shakespeare's Imagery,* pp. 205-13. London: Methuen and Co., 1977.

Argues that the conventionalism of much of the imagery in *Cymbeline* is more reminiscent of the metaphoric language of Shakespeare's earlier plays than of the major tragedies. Clemen maintains that the speeches of Belarius and Arviragus are much richer and more imagistic than those of the court figures and that in assigning fewer instances of imagery to Guiderius, Shakespeare emphasized the different temperaments and characters of the two brothers.

Colley, John Scott. "Disguise and New Guise in *Cymbeline.*" *Shakespeare Studies* VII (1974): 233-52.

Examines Shakespeare's use in *Cymbeline* of an Elizabethan mode of characterization that is emblematic or schematic rather than psychologically realistic. Colley maintains that this method—"in which moral states are suggested through costumes and costume changes"—reflects both the play's thematic concern with the disparities between real and apparent worth and the importance of deceptions and deceptive appearances in complicating the dramatic action. The critic focuses on Posthumus's "rapid and seemingly effortless change of character" at the beginning of Act V and theorizes that his adoption of various garments and "guises" should be seen as manifestations of his continuing moral development.

Colman, E. A. M. "The Language of Sexual Revulsion." In his *The Dramatic Use of Bawdy in Shakespeare,* pp. 112-42. London: Longman Group, 1974.

Contends that in *Cymbeline* Shakespeare used "bawdy as a medium of disgust or aggression rather than fun" as he had in other of his plays. Colman analyzes the sexual innuendoes and double entendres in several speeches by Iachimo, Posthumus, and Cloten and concludes that they are "rarely funny and often sinister," noting in particular the perverse necrophilia underlying Cloten's disclosure of his intentions to ravish Imogen.

Corin, Fernand. "A Note on the Dirge in *Cymbeline.*" *English Studies* 40 (1959): 173-79.

Argues that the dirge intoned by Arviragus and Guiderius in Act IV, Scene ii has more significant associations with paganism than with Christianity. Corin concludes that the song's reference to "home" is not to heaven but to the grave or the earth, implying that Imogen and Cloten "have gone the way of all flesh."

Craig, Hardin. Introduction to *Cymbeline.* In *Shakespeare: A Historical and Critical Study with Annotated Texts of Twenty-one Plays,* by William Shakespeare, edited by Hardin Craig, pp. 996-99. Chicago: Scott, Foresman and Co., 1931.

A general introduction to *Cymbeline* that presents the play as "Shakespeare's experiment in a new form." Craig is particularly concerned with *Cymbeline*'s irregular construction, its emphasis on sensational situations at the expense of consistent characterization, and the improbabilities of its dramatic action.

————. "Romance or Tragi-comedy: *Cymbeline*." In his *An Interpretation of Shakespeare*, pp. 314-27. New York: Citadel Press, 1948.

Argues that purely aesthetic grounds are not sufficient bases for challenging the authenticity of the vision scene (Act V, Scene iv) in *Cymbeline*. Craig particularly notes that the "doggerel verse" of the ghosts, although it may be unpleasant to a modern audience, would have been judged as merely "old-fashioned" by an Elizabethan one. Indeed, the critic contends, the Leonati are represented as belonging to the past, and "there is a certain appropriateness in having these old ghosts speak in an old meter."

Crawford, John W. "Shakespeare's *Cymbeline*." *Explicator* 38, No. 4 (Summer 1980): 4-6.

Focuses on Cymbeline's decision to resume paying the Roman tribute after the triumph of the British forces. Crawford argues that Shakespeare here intended to demonstrate that "the ordering of the kingdom, if it is to be effective and beneficial to all, must be made on the basis of retribution and forgiveness."

Cutts, John P. "*Cymbeline*: 'in self-figur'd knot'." In his *Rich and Strange: A Study of Shakespeare's Last Plays*, pp. 26-50. Pullman: Washington State University Press, 1968.

Argues that Cymbeline, Imogen, and Posthumus are all, to varying degrees, imprisoned in "a dream world" of their own devising. Cutts contends that Cymbeline develops from the opening of the play, where he is depicted as lacking a male heir and confused about the Roman and British aspects of his identity, into an individual who successfully resolves these conflicting elements in his personality and appears at the conclusion as "a triumphant monarch with princely stars about his throne." The critic views both Posthumus and Imogen as victims of her "false chastity complex," caught up in her struggle to reconcile her conflicting desires to consummate her marriage and to remain chaste; Cutts maintains that it is only through the intervention of the gods that they achieve "a clear vision of themselves."

Dean, John. "Shakespeare's Romance Sources & Their Dramatic Adaptation: *Cymbeline*." In his *Restless Wanderers: Shakespeare and the Pattern of Romance*, pp. 181-88. Salzburg Studies in English Literature: Elizabethan & Renaissance Studies, 86, edited by James Hogg. Salzburg: Institute Für Anglistik und Amerikanistik Universität Salzburg, 1979.

Regards *Cymbeline* as an experimental play in which Shakespeare attempted to master "the narrative complexity of romance" by using an extensive variety of source material in a single drama. Dean also contends that Boccaccio's *Decameron* is a more significant source for *Cymbeline* than is the anonymous *Frederyke of Jennen*.

Evans, B. Ifor. "*Cymbeline; The Winter's Tale; The Tempest*." In his *The Language of Shakespeare's Plays*, pp. 176-88. London: Methuen & Co., 1952.

Maintains that the language of *Cymbeline* is more diffuse and leisurely than that of the previous tragedies and that this contributes to the play's general impression of resignation. Evans views the fragmented, elliptical style of some of the verse as "bold and original," but questions whether this mode of versification has any significant dramatic function.

Evans, Bertrand. "A Lasting Storm: The Planetary Romances, *Cymbeline*." In his *Shakespeare's Comedies*, pp. 245-88. Oxford: At the Clarendon Press, 1960.

Extensive analysis of Shakespeare's use in *Cymbeline* of "discrepant awarenesses"—a dramatic technique that establishes and maintains "gaps" in understanding between a play's characters and its audience with regard to their perception of the dramatic action. Evans avers that *Cymbeline* is the outstanding example in the Shakespearean canon of the dramatist's "creation, maintenance, and exploitation" of different levels of awareness. Additionally, he terms the vision scene (V. iv) "an artistic fraud," because while it presents Jupiter as the architect of the play's dramatic events, the god actually does nothing to alter the action in *Cymbeline*.

Felperin, Howard. "Tragical-Comical-Historical-Pastoral: *Cymbeline* and *Henry VIII*." In his *Shakespearean Romance*, pp. 177-210. Princeton: Princeton University Press, 1972.

Analysis of the way in which Shakespeare has combined "Elizabethan romance, Christian history, and British history" in *Cymbeline* to achieve a unified dramatic design. Felperin contends that the dramatic events of the play depict the end of one era and the beginning of another and that at the conclusion of the drama the "Roman gives place to the Christian not only within the action as a whole but within each character, and tragical history gives way to romance." The critic agrees with Robert Grams Hunter and Homer D. Swander (see excerpts above, 1965 and 1966) that Cloten represents the darker aspect of Posthumus's personality, and he further argues that the death of the former indicates that the latter is now capable of repenting and purging himself of his Cloten-like "sexual brutality."

Fleay, Frederick Gard. "The Chronological Succession of Shakespeare's Plays." In his *A Chronicle History of the Life and Work of William Shakespeare: Player, Poet, and Playmaker*, pp. 175-254. London: John C. Nimmo, 1886.

Argues that the British and Roman portions of *Cymbeline* were written in 1609 and the rest of the play was composed two or three years later. Fleay attributes the inconsistencies in Cloten's characterization to this interruption in composition, asserting that in the earlier version Cloten "is by no means deficient in manliness," but that in the final version "he is a mere fool." Regarding the vision scene (Act V, Scene iv), the critic maintains that the stage directions for the dumb show portion of this episode are authentic, but he concludes that the speeches of the Leonati and Jupiter are the work of another writer.

Freer, Coburn. "*Cymbeline*." In his *The Poetics of Jacobean Drama*, pp. 103-35. Baltimore: Johns Hopkins University Press, 1981.

Comprehensive and detailed examination of the poetic technique of *Cymbeline*, particularly tracing the "poetic development" of Iachimo, Imogen, and Posthumus. Freer points out that in this play Shakespeare "employs every form of rhetorical pattern and posture, incorporates widely varying poetic styles, [and] explores the technique of shifting one voice among several characters." Freer's extensive analysis of the poetics of *Cymbeline* encompasses Shakespeare's varied use of rhythmic patterns, syntax, diction, metrical stresses and irregularities, dramatic tones, and meters. He maintains throughout that the dramatist's poetic technique is closely related to and enhances the play's dramatic design and "the growth of its central characters."

Garber, Marjorie. "*Cymbeline* and the Languages of Myth." *Mosaic* X, No. 3 (Spring 1977): 105-15.

Hypothesizes that *Cymbeline*'s thematic concerns with "seeming and providence" are conveyed through a hidden configuration based on the myth of Prometheus—"a generative structure which underlies the play and shapes it below the level of consciousness." Garber further argues that these two themes are enhanced in the play by the legend of Pandora and the box, a story that depicts the error of equating outer beauty with inner quality and that also features Prometheus, whom the Renaissance regarded as the signification of providence.

Geller, Lila. "*Cymbeline* and the Imagery of Covenant Theology." *Studies in English Literature 1500-1900* XX, No. 2 (Spring 1980): 241-55.

Maintains that the religious imagery and metaphors of business transactions in *Cymbeline*, as well as the play's themes and dramatic action, are unified by the idea of an ancient covenant between man and God. The marriage of Posthumus and Imogen as a sacred contract whose terms are broken and restored is the most striking example of an expression of covenant theology, argues Geller, but she also finds echoes of this idea in the political preoccupations of the play, which demonstrate the sixteenth-century view of "Britain as a second Israel" and the British "as a specially chosen people."

Gerwig, George William. "Imogen: An Unprized Wife." In his *Shakespeare's Ideals of Womanhood*, pp. 193-218. East Aurora, N.Y.: The Roycroft Shops, 1929.

    Analysis of the character of Imogen that emphasizes her practical, self-sufficient qualities. In remarking upon the depiction of Imogen as an ideal type of woman, but one whose worth is not fully appreciated by Posthumus, Gerwig comments that "Shakespeare ever gives his choicest women into the care of mediocre men."

Gesner, Carol. "Shakespeare's Greek Romances [I]: *Cymbeline*." In her *Shakespeare & the Greek Romance: A Study of Origins*, pp. 90-115. Lexington: University Press of Kentucky, 1970.

    Discovers in *Cymbeline* echoes of and parallels with several classical Greek romances, most especially Heliodorus's *Aethiopica*. Gesner remarks that Heliodorus's play, like Shakespeare's, has a tripartite plot structure, is set against a background of war and empire, presents a witty and inventive heroine who has entered into an unconsummated marriage with a military hero, has a subplot featuring lost royal heirs, and concludes with a "great public assembly" in which the dénouement is accomplished in a trial-like setting. In addition to the above evidence, Gesner notes that in the *Aethiopica* the hero fails to recognize his disguised wife and strikes her with a powerful blow, and she thus concludes that *Cymbeline* "was probably modeled" after this drama of Heliodorus.

Greenlaw, Edwin. "Shakespeare's Pastorals." *Studies in Philology* XII (1961): 122-54.

    Discusses the possible sources for *Cymbeline*. In addition to noting the dramatist's use of Holinshed and Boccaccio, Greenlaw argues that the plot of this play is an adaptation of the dramatic structure of Shakespeare's *Romeo and Juliet*. He also contends that the portrayal of Imogen's experiences in the mountains of Wales is based on "Tasso's story of Erminia's sojourn among the shepherds."

Harris, Bernard. "'What's past is prologue': 'Cymbeline' and 'Henry VIII'." In *Later Shakespeare*, edited by John Russell Brown and Bernard Harris, pp. 203-33. London: Edward Arnold, 1966.

    Measures *Cymbeline* against the requirements for pastoral tragicomedy established in Giovanni Battista Guarini's *Il Pastor Fido* (1590) and developed by other dramatists in the succeeding two centuries. Harris contends that the play's combination of "romantic historical myth, sacred reference and political relevance" is not disjunctive or unharmonious, but, rather, represents Shakespeare's acknowledgement of the literary conventions and traditions associated with the form of pastoral tragicomedy.

Hartwig, Joan. "*Cymbeline*: 'A speaking such as sense cannot untie'." In her *Shakespeare's Tragicomic Vision*, pp. 61-103. Baton Rouge: Louisiana State University Press, 1972.

    Contends that the "discrepancy between man's true nature and his outward appearance" is the principal thematic issue in *Cymbeline*. Hartwig argues that the scene in which Imogen awakens beside the headless torso of Cloten enforces the idea that perceptions of worthiness which rely on outward appearance are wholly inadequate. She concludes that the pattern of dramatic action follows the attempts by its principal characters to attain the broader perspective and vision required for apprehension of inner worth and nobility.

———. "Cloten, Autolycus, and Caliban: Bearers of Parodic Burdens." In *Shakespeare's Romances Reconsidered*, edited by Carol McGinnis Kay and Henry E. Jacobs, pp. 91-103. Lincoln: University of Nebraska Press, 1978.

    Maintains that Cloten represents the baser aspects of Posthumus's nature. Hartwig argues that, by employing Cloten as a literal representation of the reportedly nobler Posthumus and by showing the latter's regeneration as occurring on the heels of the former's burial, Shakespeare is not only taking parody to the extreme, but he is also offering evidence that "life is a continuing dilemma-ridden confrontation with perplexities."

Hill, Geoffrey. "'The True Conduct of Human Judgment': Some Observations on *Cymbeline*." In *The Morality of Art: Essays Presented to G. Wilson Knight by His Colleagues and Friends*, edited by D. W. Jefferson, pp. 18-32. London: Routledge & Kegan Paul, 1969.

    Discusses the question raised by Emrys Jones (see entry below) of the "relevance of Stuart myth to our understanding of this play." Hill argues that although there are indications in *Cymbeline* of "an oblique awareness of royalist views," Shakespeare did not intend the drama to be a tribute to the policies and accomplishments of James I.

Hofling, Charles K. "Notes on Shakespeare's *Cymbeline*." *Shakespeare Studies* I (1965): 118-36.

    Psychoanalytic study of *Cymbeline* in connection with what is known of the events in Shakespeare's life at the time he composed this play. Hofling focuses on the characterization of Imogen—which he regards as an "unambivalent picture of woman and of the power of hope"—and contends that we can see in her portrayal that "Shakespeare's bitterness and near-despair have been vanquished by hope."

Hunt, Maurice. "Shakespeare's Empirical Romance: *Cymbeline* and Modern Knowledge." *Texas Studies in Literature and Language* 22, No. 3 (Fall 1980): 322-42.

    Argues that in *Cymbeline* Shakespeare demonstrated the "Christian-Humanist" proposition that knowledge is derived from experience and observation. The language of the play, Hunt declares, reflects the central characters' progress in understanding themselves and each other, for as their comprehension increases, their speeches become less torturous and the ideas they express less conventional.

———. "'Stir' and Work in Shakespeare's Last Plays." *Studies in English Literature 1500-1900* 22, No. 2 (Spring 1982): 285-304.

    Examines selected passages from *Cymbeline* and the other romances of Shakespeare that offer oppositions between "stir and stasis." Hunt maintains that in this play work is associated with "power, wrath, and deeds" and is juxtaposed to wonder, "sweet art, quaintness, and delicate beauty."

Hyland, Peter. "Shakespeare's Heroines: Disguise in the Romantic Comedies." *Ariel* 9, No. 2 (April 1978): 23-39.

    Compares Shakespeare's use of "the 'girl-page' device" in five plays, noting that in *Cymbeline* this technique does not serve the purposes for which it was used in the earlier dramas. Hyland points out that Imogen's disguise affords her no "special controlling power over other characters" and that she never "stands back to watch and comment on Fidele," concluding that, unlike the earlier disguised heroines, Imogen as Fidele docs not function as a device to "create a special intimacy with the audience."

Jacobs, Henry E., ed. *Cymbeline*. Garland Shakespeare Bibliographies, No. 3. New York: Garland Publishing, 1982, 591 p.

    A comprehensive listing, with descriptive notes, of published commentary on *Cymbeline*. The entries are organized into sections reflecting different scholarly concerns, including authorship, characters, sources, textual studies, genre and mode, dating, and thematic approaches.

Jones, Emrys. "Stuart *Cymbeline*." *Essays in Criticism* XI, No. 1 (January 1961): 84-99.

    Argues that *Cymbeline* "centers on the character and foreign policy of James I." Jones agrees with J. P. Brockbank (see entry above) that there is a significant association between the play's historical setting at the time of the birth of Christ and the universal "peace of Rome" and James's belief that he was a great peacemaker who was responsible for the unification of Britain. Jones also notes that Milford Haven had important connections with the Brutan and Arthurian legends that Tudor and Stuart historians adapted for political purposes, and thus the numerous references to it in the play serve to heighten the association between the first Stuart monarch and Britain's national destiny.

Kay, Carol McGinnis. "Generic Sleight-of-Hand in *Cymbeline*." *South Atlantic Review* 46, No. 4 (November 1981): 34-40.

    Analyzes the manner in which audience expectations of the dramatic nature of *Cymbeline* are altered and manipulated by the order in which Shakespeare introduces characters in the first four scenes. Kay maintains that the play begins as if it were to be a fairy tale, appears to develop as a romantic comedy, and then assumes tragic potentialities with the introduction of Iachimo, whom she regards as "precisely that shrewd destructive force we have been cozened out of anticipating."

Keck, Kendell Magee. "Accounting for Irregularities in Cloten." *Shakespeare Association Bulletin* 10, No. 2 (April 1935): 67-72.

Examines the possible influence on Cloten's speeches of Robert Armine, the actor who played "fool" roles in the King's Men Company at the time that *Cymbeline* was first produced. Noting that Armine was generally permitted to make extemporaneous additions to the lines written for him and that he is known to have reveled in playing "abnormal" types, Keck contends that what appear to be inconsistencies in tone and sentiments in the various speeches of Cloten may be traced to this habit of the actor. Keck concludes that the character's blank verse lines are Shakespeare's work alone, but that Cloten's prose speeches "may be the result of some adaptation by Armine."

Kermode, Frank. "*Cymbeline.*" In his *The Final Plays: "Pericles," "Cymbeline," "The Winter's Tale," "The Tempest," "The Two Noble Kinsmen,"* pp. 19-29. 1963. Reprint. London: Longmans, Green & Co., 1965.

Discusses Shakespeare's use of diverse dramatic genres in *Cymbeline*. Kermode also comments on the virtuosity with which the dramatist created the play's ambiguities and obscurities, arguing that the exchange between the two unnamed gentlemen in Act I, Scene i displays "the obliquity that will prevail throughout" the drama.

Kirsch, Arthur C. "*Cymbeline* and Coterie Dramaturgy." *ELH* 34, No. 3 (September 1967): 285-306.

Explores the parallels between *Cymbeline* and dramas by Ben Jonson, John Marston, and Francis Beaumont and John Fletcher that were written for private theaters in the first years of the seventeenth century. Kirsch endorses Harley Granville-Barker's estimation of the self-consciousness of *Cymbeline* (see excerpt above, 1930), focusing on the way in which the play "calls attention to itself as a dramatic fiction" and noting that the most prominent feature of coterie dramaturgy is "its deliberate self-consciousness." He further comments that "discontinuous action," inconsistent characterization, sensational scenic effects, and histrionic speeches are all characteristic of these plays written expressly for the private theaters, concluding that the presence in *Cymbeline* of these dramatic techniques indicates that Shakespeare was here experimenting with this relatively new dramatic mode.

Knight, Charles. Introduction to *Cymbeline*, by William Shakespeare. In *The Comedies, Histories, Tragedies, and Poems of William Shakspere*, Vol. VIII, edited by Charles Knight, pp. 187-200. 1843. Reprint. New York: AMS Press, 1968.

Speculates that the original conception and composition of *Cymbeline* "belong to the youthful Shakspere," but that the dramatist revised the play at some later time when he was at the height of his creative powers. Knight asserts that the vision scene in Act V, Scene iv was likely a part of the early version to which Shakespeare subsequently added both Posthumus's soliloquy and his dialogue with the gaoler.

Knowles, Richard Paul. "'The More Delay'd, Delighted': Theophanies in the Last Plays." *Shakespeare Studies* XV (1982): 269-80.

Argues that the appearance of Jupiter in Act V, Scene iv represents the point at which "Shakespeare elicits our imaginative engagement with the powers that impose order on the play, and the powers that control the play are clearly those of the playwright." Knowles avers that this appearance is not portrayed as a single instance of divine intervention in *Cymbeline*, but rather is the culmination of earlier allusions and references to providential control and that the depiction of the sufferings of Posthumus and Imogen leads us to anticipate and long for evidence of an ordering force behind the dramatic action. Thus, the critic concludes, "we

have willed Jupiter into existence," and the audience becomes Shakespeare's "accomplices" in fostering dramatic illusion.

Kolin, Philip C. "The Doctor in Tragicomedy." In his *The Elizabethan Stage Doctor as a Dramatic Convention*, pp. 67-106. Salzburg Studies in English Literature: Elizabethan & Renaissance Studies, 41, edited by James Hogg. Salzburg: Institut für Englische Sprache und Literatur, Universität Salzburg, 1975.

Contends that Cornelius's administration of his sleeping potion, which appears to have fatal consequences but is actually an agent of revitalization and renewal of the spirit, dramatically reenacts the theme of regeneration through suffering in *Cymbeline*. Kolin also traces "this pattern of happy deception" in the actions of Pisanio, Belarius, and—most significantly—in Jupiter, whose curative methods are prefigured in those of the wise physician.

Lawrence, W. J. "The Vision in 'Cymbeline'." *Times Literary Supplement*, No. 1647 (24 August 1933): 561.

Regards the vision scene in V. iv as authentic, but argues that the ascent and descent of Jupiter on the back of an eagle was an interpolation by a later reviser of *Cymbeline*. Commenting on the frequent use of "descents and ascents of divinities" in plays written in 1610 and the years immediately following, Lawrence concludes that this spectacle was incorporated into Shakespeare's text in order to please an audience fascinated by such stage devices.

Lawry, J. S. "'Perishing Root and Increasing Vine' in *Cymbeline*." *Shakespeare Studies* XII (1979): 179-93.

Examines the "hemispheric options (North-South; Britain-Rome)" in *Cymbeline* that determine national and individual temperament. Lawry argues that the apparent differences between the two locations—Britain is depicted as "coldly violent" and Rome as "foggy, drugged, effete, and cynical"—are belied by their identical obsessions with an impulse toward death. The progress of the dramatic action, Lawry contends, is towards Milford Haven, which Shakespeare represents as an alternative "way" and the place where Roman and British traits are transformed and achieve a new definition through a process of "regenerative suffering and joy."

Lings, Martin. "*Cymbeline.*" In his *Shakespeare in the Light of Sacred Art*, pp. 94-103. London: George Allen & Unwin, 1966.

Compares the dramatic action of *Cymbeline* to the Biblical account of humankind's fall from grace and to reworkings of this story in the tales of Everyman and the medieval mystery plays. Lings views Posthumus as the sinner who descends into Hell and then must proceed through Purgatory before he may attain Paradise; he also likens Cymbeline and his daughter to Fallen Man, with Imogen representing the intelligent aspect of the soul that seeks a return to Paradise through "spiritual striving."

Makaryk, Irene Rima. "The Romances." In her *Comic Justice in Shakespeare's Comedies*, Vol. 2, pp. 278-360. Salzburg Studies in English Literature: Jacobean Drama Studies, 91, edited by James Hogg. Salzburg: Institute für Anglistik und Amerikanistik Universität Salzburg, 1980.

Judges that the conclusion of *Cymbeline* leaves the audience with ambiguous interpretations and unanswered questions. Makaryk argues that King Cymbeline's continued propensity for rash behavior "raises doubts about the perfection of the peace and order which conclude the play" and that, because happiness is shown to be chiefly the result of divine intervention, the characters appear to be "no more than puppets, and the loyalty of Imogen and transformation of Posthumus have little meaning."

Mares, F. H. "Viola and Other Transvestist Heroines in Shakespeare's Comedies." In *Stratford Papers 1965-67*, edited by B. A. W. Jackson, pp. 96-109. Hamilton, Ont.: McMaster University Library Press, 1969.

Compares Shakespeare's use of sexually disguised females in *Cymbeline*, *Twelfth Night*, *As You Like It*, and *Two Gentlemen of Verona*. Mares asserts that the disguise of Imogen as a page is neither "integral to the plot" nor "essential to the statement of the theme."

Marsh, D. R. C. "*Cymbeline.*" In his *The Recurring Miracle: A Study of "Cymbeline" and the Last Plays,* pp. 24-124. Pietermaritzburg, South Africa: University of Natal Press, 1962.

A detailed, scene-by-scene analysis of *Cymbeline*. Marsh contends that the play is neither flawed nor experimental, that its central thematic issue is the necessity of accepting "the conditions of life," and that Shakespeare fulfilled his intention of offering in the drama an optimistic, affirmative view of life.

Marx, Joan C. "The Encounter of Genres: *Cymbeline*'s Structure of Juxtaposition." In *The Analysis of Literary Texts: Current Trends in Methodology,* edited by Randolph D. Pope, pp. 138-44. Ypsilanti, Mich.: Bilingual Press, 1980.

Contends that juxtaposition of characters and scenes is *Cymbeline*'s "major structural device" and that the play's "energy and coherence lie in the contrast of its different genre worlds." Shakespeare did not intend to present a uniform design, argues Marx, but rather wished to demonstrate that different dramatic genres—such as satire, pastoral, heroic, and tragic—offer disparate perspectives and "differing values" which, taken together, represent a wide range of vision on the dramatic action.

Maxwell, J. C., ed. Introduction to *Cymbeline,* by William Shakespeare, pp. xi-lv. The Works of Shakespeare, edited by John Dover Wilson. Cambridge: At the University Press, 1960.

A comprehensive overview of *Cymbeline,* including discussion of date of composition and Shakespeare's possible sources. Maxwell provides an extended examination of the play's "deliberate incongruity and comic exploitation of conventions," arguing that Shakespeare's technique of humorous detachment is evident throughout the drama. He especially discerns this comic detachment in the portrayal of Imogen awakening beside the headless torso of Cloten, where, according to Maxwell, comic touches mitigate the situation's "strong emotional effects."

Meyerstein, E. H. W. "The Vision in *Cymbeline.*" *Times Literary Supplement,* No. 1065 (15 June 1922): 396.

Maintains that the appeal of the Leonati to Jupiter (V. iv. 30-122) is the work of Shakespeare and not an interpolation by another hand. Meyerstein praises this passage for its "subtle prosody" and denies that it is "doggerel," as earlier commentators had claimed.

Miola, Robert S. "*Cymbeline:* Beyond Rome." In his *Shakespeare's Rome,* pp. 206-35. Cambridge: Cambridge University Press, 1983.

Concurs with G. Wilson Knight (see excerpt above, 1947) in viewing *Cymbeline* as a play that "celebrates an assertion of British independence as well as the creation of a new alliance with Rome, one in which Britain will be ascendant." Miola focuses on Roman elements in the play and regards *Cymbeline* as "Shakespeare's valedictory to Rome," in the sense that, even as it acknowledges the traditional Roman virtues of constancy and honor, it demonstrates these virtues being modified and transformed by British "flexibility" and compassion.

Moulton, Richard G. "Wrong and Restoration: The Comedies of *Winter's Tale* and *Cymbeline.*" In his *The Moral System of Shakespeare: A Popular Illustration of Fiction as the Experimental Side of Philosophy,* pp. 65-88. New York: The Macmillan Co., 1903.

Contends that dramatic events in *Cymbeline* are controlled by providential intervention. Moulton identifies six types of wrongdoing and six forces of restoration operating in the play. He concludes that the most significant in the latter group is the "force of an overruling providence," which operates autonomously, but which also influences the other five forces or agents so that what seem to be accidental or inadvertent events in the dramatic world of *Cymbeline* are more correctly viewed as the governance of divine providence.

Mowat, Barbara A. *The Dramaturgy of Shakespeare's Romances.* Athens: University of Georgia Press, 1976, 163 p.

Extended discussion of the dramatic tactics and strategy employed in *Cymbeline* and Shakespeare's other late romances. Mowat argues that whereas such tactics as direct address, expository soliloquies, and narrative rather than representational presentation

of dramatic action may appear artificial or intrusive, they intentionally function to "interrupt emotionally charged moments" and to remind the audience of "the strangeness of the world which we know through our own experience." She further contends that the absence of any single dramatic design evident in the play emphasizes the arbitrary and whimsical nature of existence, so that, like the characters in *Cymbeline,* the audience must wait for "the outcome and the significance of the story to be revealed in the fullness of time."

Muir, Kenneth. "*Cymbeline.*" In his *The Sources of Shakespeare's Plays,* pp. 258-66. New Haven: Yale University Press, 1978.

Examines the "theatrical virtuosity" with which Shakespeare combined and adapted in *Cymbeline* the heterogeneous materials from such diverse sources as romance drama, *The Mirror for Magistrates,* the English and Scottish portions of Holinshed's *Chronicles,* Boccaccio's *Decameron,* and *Frederyke of Jennen.*

Nelson, Thomas Allen. "*Cymbeline:* Holinshed and Shakespearean Comedy." In his *Shakespeare's Comic Theory: A Study of Art and Artifice in the Last Plays,* pp. 42-53. De Proprietatibus Litterarum: Series Practica, 57, edited by C. H. Van Schooneveld. The Hague: Mouton, 1972.

Analyzes *Cymbeline* "in the light of Shakespeare's development as a comic artist." Nelson remarks on a number of different aspects of the play, including the dramatist's inversion of serious and didactic elements in his sources into essentially comic features, the resemblances between Posthumus and Imogen and protagonists of the earlier comedies, and the reconciliation of the "different views of the world" that is also typical of the preceding comedies. He concludes that "*Cymbeline* exhibits the characteristic interests and continued development of a unique comic vision."

Noble, Richmond. "*Cymbeline.*" In his *Shakespeare's Use of Song, with the Text of the Principal Songs,* pp. 130-37. 1923. Reprint. Oxford: At the Clarendon Press, 1967.

Analyzes the aubade in II. iii and the dirge in IV. ii of *Cymbeline.* Noble contends that the former is an example of music intended as relief, for just as it indicates the stage change from night to morning, it also dispels the "heavy stifling atmosphere" of the previous scene in Imogen's bedroom. He compares the fifth and sixth lines of each stanza in the dirge to "gruesome funeral games in which children love to indulge," noting that the couplets underscore the simple natures of Guiderius and Arviragus.

Nosworthy, J. M. "The Integrity of Shakespeare: Illustrated from *Cymbeline.*" *Shakespeare Survey* 8 (1955): 52-6.

Disputes the speculations of such earlier commentators as Horace Howard Furness and Harley Granville-Barker (see excerpts above, 1913 and 1930) that several passages and sections in *Cymbeline* are the work of another dramatist than Shakespeare. Nosworthy agrees that the play is a "stylistic gallimaufry," but he demonstrates parallels between some of the challenged passages and lines from other nondisputed Shakespearean plays, as well as from his early poetry, concluding that there is no stylistic evidence that *Cymbeline* was written by any playwright other than Shakespeare.

———, ed. Introduction to *Cymbeline,* by William Shakespeare, pp. xi-lxxxv. The Arden Edition of the Works of William Shakespeare, edited by Una Ellis-Fermor and Harold F. Brooks. Cambridge: Harvard University Press, 1955.

A comprehensive discussion of the text, composition date, and possible sources of *Cymbeline,* together with a review of the play's critical history, its style and imagery, and its relation to Beaumont and Fletcher's *Philaster.* Nosworthy regards *Cymbeline* as an "experimental romance" in which Shakespeare "explored a new way of using plot material within the limits of a convention which also demanded" a symbolic method of characterization.

Quiller-Couch, Arthur. "*Cymbeline.*" In his *Shakespeare's Workmanship,* pp. 259-81. London: T. Fisher Unwin, 1918.

Concurs with Algernon Charles Swinburne's high praise of Imogen (see excerpt above, 1880), declaring that she is the "most adorable woman ever created by God or man." However, Quiller-

Couch faults the complexities and intrigues of *Cymbeline*'s dramatic structure, claiming that the audience becomes so concerned with how Shakespeare will "unravel it all" that its attention is diverted from the play's central focus—the peerless Imogen.

Rabkin, Norman. "The Great Globe Itself." In his *Shakespeare and the Common Understanding*, pp. 192-237. New York: The Free Press, 1967.

Maintains that the combination in *Cymbeline* of naive and sophisticated dramatic techniques is a function of the play's concern with "the nature of theatrical illusion." Rabkin argues that Shakespeare has here fashioned an experimental game that seeks "to engage us in the naive artifice of the piece, to make us believe in its reality, and then to make us recognize the game he is playing." The critic especially remarks on the manner in which the drama represents the potential for tragic and destructive consequences and then offers a vision of rescue by miraculous reversals of fortune, thereby heightening the impression of Shakespeare's "power over the plot."

Ribner, Irving. "Shakespeare and Legendary History: *Lear* and *Cymbeline*." *Shakespeare Quarterly* VII, No. 1 (Winter 1956): 47-52.

Classifies *Cymbeline* as a "historical romance," a popular Elizabethan dramatic genre in which a play's historical setting is subsidiary to its romantic qualities. Unlike Shakespeare's historical drama, Ribner contends, *Cymbeline* contains no didacticism and the political issues it refers to are of "secondary importance."

Richmond, Hugh M. "Shakespeare's Roman Trilogy: The Climax in *Cymbeline*." *Studies in the Literary Imagination* V, No. 1 (April 1972): 129-39.

Argues that *Cymbeline* represents the culmination of Shakespeare's view of Imperial Rome—begun in *Julius Caesar* and continued in *Antony and Cleopatra*—as characterized by "legalistic harshness," political cunning, and "malevolent egotism." Richmond contends that this play demonstrates that pagan values and moral codes are inadequate bases for truly heroic and creative lives; it also depicts, according to the critic, the development of "a humane politics largely denied to the Romans, but to which the earlier history plays at least aspire."

Rossi, Joan Warchol. "*Cymbeline*'s Debt to Holinshed: The Richness of III. i." In *Shakespeare's Romances Reconsidered*, edited by Carol McGinnis Kay and Henry E. Jacobs, pp. 104-12. Lincoln: University of Nebraska Press, 1978.

Assesses the speeches of Cloten, the Queen, and Cymbeline in the council scene with Lucius in light of the accounts of the actual historical events that appear in Holinshed's *Chronicles*. Noting that in the chronicle *History of England* there is "a definite bias in favor of Rome and of peace," Rossi contends that Shakespeare reordered his source material to make his king appear more bellicose than the historical Kymbeline. She also demonstrates that in the chronicle *History of Scotland* Arviragus is depicted as having "marital difficulties" that parallel those of Posthumus and Imogen, concluding that for *Cymbeline* "Shakespeare may in fact have first considered history and found within his historical material the suggestions of a romance which he later developed."

Salingar, L. G. "Time and Art in Shakespeare's Romances." In *Renaissance Drama* IX, edited by S. Schoenbaum, pp. 3-35. Evanston, Ill.: Northwestern University Press, 1966.

Regards *Cymbeline* as an idealized, as opposed to either an allegorical or psychologically realistic, drama. Salingar maintains that elements in the play which promote this symbolic quality—such as distortions in the time scheme, mistaken identities, disguises and coincidences, Imogen's "faith and patience" sustained throughout her tribulations—are all characteristic of the dramatic technique of medieval romance.

Schork, R. J. "Allusion, Theme, and Characterization in *Cymbeline*." *Studies in Philology* LXIX, No. 2 (April 1972): 210-16.

Argues that Shakespeare's use in *Cymbeline* of allusions to "classical myth, legend, and history" are dramatically significant and not merely ornamental. Schork analyzes the classical references in speeches by Iachimo and Imogen and concludes that these allusions are important contributions to their characterizations.

Schwartz, Murray M. "Between Fantasy and Imagination: A Psychological Exploration of *Cymbeline*." In *Psychoanalysis and Literary Process*, edited by Frederick Crews, pp. 219-83. Cambridge, Mass.: Winthrop Publishers, 1970.

Extensive psychoanalytic interpretation of *Cymbeline*. Schwartz argues that the play depicts parallel dissociations in the family, the nation, and individual sexuality. At the basis of Imogen's portrayal as a phallic, castrating female and Posthumus's and Iachimo's delineation as orally fixated males, the critic argues, is the Renaissance dichotomy between "the idealization and worship of women" and the impulse to establish "a stable relationship between platonic sublimation and crude sexual expression."

Sen Gupta, S. C. "Shakespeare's Final Period." In his *Shakespearian Comedy*, pp. 215-34. London: Oxford University Press, 1950.

Judges the characterization in *Cymbeline* to be inadequate because Shakespeare places more emphasis on the "sensational situations" through which his characters pass than on the development of their individual natures. Sen Gupta also views the artificiality of the play's theatrical devices as a serious defect in the drama.

Shaheen, Naseeb. "The Use of Scripture in *Cymbeline*." *Shakespeare Studies* IV (1968): 294-315.

Demonstrates that Biblical references in *Cymbeline* are extensive, providing a list of "conscious" allusions, "echoes" of scriptural passages, and instances of parallel resemblances. Shaheen maintains, however, that the inconsistent, dispassionate use of these references mitigates against the conclusion that there is any "basis in *Cymbeline* for arguing for overt theological intent on Shakespeare's part."

Shaw, Bernard. "Foreword to *Cymbeline Refinished*." In his *Geneva, Cymbeline Refinished, & Good King Charles*, pp. 133-38. 1937. Reprint. New York: Dodd, Mead & Co., 1947.

Prefatory explanation of Shaw's intentions in revising Act V of Shakespeare's *Cymbeline*. Shaw asserts that he has "ruthlessly cut out the surprises that no longer surprise anybody," left Posthumus as Shakespeare drew him—a self-centered prig and chronic complainer—, and generally revised the act "as Shakespear might have written it if he had been post-Ibsen and post-Shaw instead of post-Marlowe."

Simonds, Peggy Muñoz. "Some Emblematic Courtier *Topoi* in *Cymbeline*." In *Renaissance Papers 1981*, edited by A. Leigh Deneef and M. Thomas Hester, pp. 97-112. Raleigh, N.C.: Southeastern Renaissance Conference, 1982.

Maintains that Shakespeare's use in *Cymbeline* of the motifs of "the caged bird, the ravished tree, and the empty head" strengthens the arguments of Belarius regarding the superiority of life in the wilderness over life in a corrupt court. Simonds presents evidence from classical and Renaissance sources to demonstrate the conventional associations of these tropes with "the uncertainty, the dangers and the frivolity of the Renaissance courtier's life."

———. "'No More . . . Offend Our Hearing': Aural Imagery in *Cymbeline*." *Texas Studies in Literature and Language* 24, No. 2 (Summer 1982): 137-54.

Maintains that in *Cymbeline* words and music are shown to have both malevolent and beneficent effects. Simonds asserts that the play presents "the aural seduction" of a number of characters: "the king through flattery, Posthumus through Iachimo's slander of Imogen, and Imogen through overpraise of her husband and false words of love." Conversely, she contends, sound is also used to invoke divine intervention, to convey messages of hope and good cheer, and to offer "praise and thanksgiving" for the happy conclusion of the dramatic events.

Skura, Meredith. "Interpreting Posthumus' Dream from Above and Below: Families, Psychoanalysts, and Literary Critics." In *Representing Shakespeare: New Psychoanalytic Essays*, edited by Murray M. Schwartz and Coppélia Kahn, pp. 203-16. Baltimore: Johns Hopkins University Press, 1980.

Argues that there are "family resonances" beneath each of the three plots of *Cymbeline*, but claims that concern with family is most central to Posthumus's development as a worthy husband to Imogen. The hero achieves an awareness of the proper balance between "family inheritance and personal individuality," Skura contends, during his dream in prison, which provides him with both a recognition of his past and an understanding of his own nature.

Smith, Warren D. "Cloten with Caius Lucius." *Studies in Philology* XLIX, No. 2 (April 1952): 185-94.

Contends that Cloten's speeches during the conference with the Roman general (Act III, Scene i) are not noble expressions of British patriotism, as earlier commentators have judged, but instead are consistent with Shakespeare's characterization of the prince as a villainous boor. Smith argues that Cloten's sentiments would have been viewed as offensive bellicosity by a Jacobean audience and by Shakespeare's patron, James I, who consistently espoused a policy of peacemaking. The critic further notes that Cloten's speeches are in prose, whereas every other character in this scene speaks in verse, maintaining that by this means the dramatist sought to remind his audience "that a lout is speaking the lines."

Speaight, Robert. "New Directions." In his *Shakespeare: The Man and His Achievement,* pp. 330-45. London: J. M. Dent & Sons, 1977.

Discusses *Cymbeline*'s dramatic elements and concludes that the play is "strange, beautiful, and uneven." Speaight questions the authenticity of the vision scene because of "the hack-work rhyming of Posthumus's Roman ancestors"; he also contends that thematic material is not well integrated into the structure of the play and that, with the exception of Imogen, Shakespeare has failed to engage the audience's interest in the characters.

Stoll, Elmer Edgar. "Lecture III: The Maidens in the Dramatic Romances." In his *Shakespeare's Young Lovers,* pp. 85-118. London: Oxford University Press, 1937.

Contends that the credulity with which both Imogen and Posthumus accept what Iachimo tells them is not represented by Shakespeare as inherent in their natures, but is merely a dramatic device to increase the complications of *Cymbeline*'s plot structure. Stoll also argues that Posthumus's "treacherous and murderous undertaking" against Imogen deters our acceptance of their reconciliation at the end of the play as anything other than arbitrary and conventional.

Strachey, Lytton. "Shakespeare's Final Period." In his *Books and Characters: French & English,* pp. 49-69. New York: Harcourt, Brace and Co., 1922.

A notable analysis of Shakespeare's last plays, including *Cymbeline*. Rejecting the widely held nineteenth-century view that these plays reveal the dramatist enjoying a tranquil state of mind during this period, Strachey argues instead that they evince a mind that was "bored . . . with everything except poetry and poetical dreams." The critic contends that although the plays written from 1609 onward generally represent remote, enchanted worlds peopled by unreal figures, we should not "neglect the goblins" who also inhabit the "land of faery." Citing Iachimo and Cloten in his list of the many evil characters in these final dramas and drawing attention to the coarse and foul language provided not only to them but to Posthumus as well, Strachey concludes that Shakespeare could not prevent "a general disgust to burst occasionally through his torpor into bitter and violent speech," even as he continued to compose lyrics of incomparable beauty.

Sutherland, James. "The Language of the Last Plays." In *More Talking of Shakespeare,* edited by John Garrett, pp. 144-58. London: Longmans, Green and Co., 1959.

Attempts to account for the mixture of poetic styles in *Cymbeline* and the abrupt changes from a "natural, easy, and unforced expression" to language that is "impetuous, violent, [and] straining after the maximum of intensity." Sutherland speculates that this compositional mode may indicate either that Shakespeare was tiring on occasion, and thus the tempo of the verse appears forced,

or that he was beginning to write a kind of verse typical of metaphysical poetry, incorporating such attributes as celebration, unconventional expressions, and "remote and far-fetched ideas."

Swander, Homer. "*Cymbeline* and the 'Blameless Hero'." *ELH* 31, No. 3 (September 1964): 259-70.

Disputes William Witherle Lawrence's conclusion (see excerpt above, 1920) that in Acts I and II Posthumus's behavior is shown to be unimpeachable because it is in accord with the traditional attitude that a husband or lover has the right to test a woman's virtue and to slay her if she has been unfaithful to him. Swander maintains that by deviating from conventional treatments of "the woman-falsely-accused" story Shakespeare challenged "generally accepted ideas about the kind of insight that love demands and provides"; for this reason, the critic calls *Cymbeline* a "revolutionary and modern" play.

Symons, Arthur. Introduction to *Cymbeline.* In *The Complete Works of William Shakespeare,* Vol. XIV, by William Shakespeare, edited by Sidney Lee, pp. ix-xix. New York: George D. Sproul, 1907.

A general analysis of the various dramatic elements in *Cymbeline*. Symons maintains that the poetic language of the play approaches a form of prose in its clarity, directness, and density of meanings. He also contends that the structure of the drama is flawed, declaring that "the play is thrown together loosely" and shows evidence of Shakespeare's having lost interest in his craft.

Thompson, Ann. "Philomel in 'Titus Andronicus' and 'Cymbeline'." *Shakespeare Survey* 31 (1978): 23-32.

Analyzes the significance of the reference in *Cymbeline* (II. ii. 45-6) to the tale of Philomel, "one of the most famous classical rape narratives," in terms of the theme of mutilation. Thompson contends that although the scene in Imogen's bedroom represents a symbolic destruction of Imogen's honor rather than an actual one, the play as a whole continually depicts individuals, families, and even nations as "threatened with dismemberment."

Thompson, Karl F. "The Last Plays: A Quality of Strangeness." In his *Modesty and Cunning: Shakespeare's Use of Literary Tradition,* pp. 149-67. Ann Arbor: University of Michigan Press, 1971.

Argues that *Cymbeline* expresses the medieval convention of the parallels between human and religious love. Thompson describes Posthumus and Imogen as votaries of this "religion-of-love," whose constancy is assailed by Cloten and Iachimo, just as subverting humanity's love of God is "the chief aim of evildoers."

Thorndike, Ashley H. "*Cymbeline* and *Philaster.*" In his *The Influence of Beaumont and Fletcher on Shakspere,* pp. 152-60. 1901. Reprint. New York: Russell & Russell, 1965.

Argues that Beaumont and Fletcher's *Philaster* served as Shakespeare's model for *Cymbeline*. Thorndike demonstrates the similarities in plotting, scenic structure, characterization, and versification between the two plays, and declares that there is "a strong presumption that *Philaster* was the original," although he admits that the evidence for dating these two plays is not conclusive.

Thrall, William Flint. "*Cymbeline,* Boccaccio, and the Wager Story in England." *Studies in Philology* XXVIII, No. 4 (October 1931): 107-19.

One of the earliest source studies to identify the anonymous *Frederick of Jennen* as a version of the wager story which Shakespeare may have used in *Cymbeline*. Thrall notes elements in common between *Cymbeline* and *Frederick of Jennen* that are absent in Boccaccio's reworking of the tale, concluding that the *Decameron* is not the single source for the wager plot in Shakespeare's play.

Turner, Robert Y. "Slander in *Cymbeline* and Other Jacobean Tragicomedies." *English Literary Renaissance* 13, No. 2 (Spring 1983): 182-202.

Interprets *Cymbeline* with reference to other plays of the period that feature a slandered woman and that represent a movement away from the satiric dramas prevalent from 1600 to 1605. Turner traces a pattern of debasement throughout the play, beginning with Cymbeline's dispraise of Posthumus, arguing that juxtaposed to this pattern is "the impulse to affirm trust and fidelity." The critic concludes that in *Cymbeline* the value of trust is emphasized through the depiction of loyalty among husband and wife, among other family members, and between national states, and that this virtue finds its paradigm in the figure of Imogen.

Uphaus, Robert W. "*Cymbeline* and the Parody of Romance." In his *Beyond Tragedy: Structure & Experience in Shakespeare's Romances*, pp. 49-68. Lexington: The University Press of Kentucky, 1981.
    Regards *Cymbeline* as Shakespeare's "genial parody" of the literary conventions of the romance form. Uphaus avers that the apparent resolution of the dramatic action in Act V, Scene v is "partial, fragmentary, and hilarious"—a gentle mockery of the expected and conventional conclusion of romance drama.

Velie, Alan R. "*Pericles* and *Cymbeline* as Elizabethan Melodramas." In his *Shakespeare's Repentance Plays: The Search for an Adequate Form*, pp. 61-90. Rutherford, N.J.: Fairleigh Dickinson University Press, 1972.
    Argues that Shakespeare borrowed elements from Elizabethan melodrama to represent in *Cymbeline* the theme of sin and repentance that he had earlier depicted in *Measure for Measure*. Velie maintains that *Cymbeline*'s sensational action, happy ending for the sympathetic characters, violent deaths of "most of the villains," and symbolic presentation of the dramatic figures are all elements characteristic of melodrama. However, he contends that in the characterization of Posthumus, Shakespeare moved away from the stereotyped figures of this dramatic form. Velie asserts that Posthumus is depicted as a "complex, psychologically-realistic" protagonist who is shown making "two crucial moral choices—to sin and to repent—and so undergoes a process of degeneration and regeneration."

Vickers, Brian. "The Return of Comedy." In his *The Artistry of Shakespeare's Prose*, pp. 405-28. London: Methuen & Co., 1968.
    Examines Shakespeare's use of prose in the wager scene, Cloten's speeches in the council scenes and his exchanges with the two lords, and the dialogue between Posthumus and his gaoler. Vickers remarks that "the prose scenes have little importance in relation to the complete design" of the play.

Wickham, Glynne. "Riddle and Emblem: A Study in the Dramatic Structure of *Cymbeline*." In *English Renaissance Studies: Presented to Dame Helen Gardner in Honour of Her Seventieth Birthday*, edited by John Carey, pp. 94-113. Oxford: Oxford University Press, 1980.
    Notes that from 1603 to 1611 most of the English "poets, playmakers, and pageanteers" composed celebrations of the accession and accomplishments of James I, contending that *Cymbeline* is Shakespeare's own vehicle for paying homage to this first Stuart monarch. Wickham declares that the emblematic language in the riddles of the soothsayer and Jupiter, together with the play's many references to Milford Haven and the "reiterated images of union," support the theory that Shakespeare meant to identify Cymbeline and James and to honor the latter as peacemaker and unifier of Britain.

Wilson, Harold S. "*Philaster* and *Cymbeline*." In *English Institute Essays, 1951*, edited by Alan S. Downer, pp. 146-67. New York: AMS Press, 1965.
    Disputes the conclusion of Ashley H. Thorndike (see entry above) that *Cymbeline* is an imitation of Beaumont and Fletcher's *Philaster*. Wilson contends that these two dramas are very different in terms of plotting and characterization; he also comments that whereas in *Cymbeline* Shakespeare prepared the audience to expect certain consequences as a result of the progress of the dramatic action, in *Philaster* Beaumont and Fletcher intentionally misled, shocked, and surprised the audience by the unexpected turns of events in the play.

Wincor, Richard. "Shakespeare's Festival Plays." *Shakespeare Quarterly* 1, No. 4 (October 1950): 219-40.
    Compares Shakespeare's last plays with folk drama that developed from rituals associated with seasonal changes. Wincor identifies elements in the plot of *Cymbeline* that reflect the festival drama's concern with "the return of spring after a barren winter."

Yates, Frances A. "*Cymbeline*." In her *Shakespeare's Last Plays: A New Approach*, pp. 39-61. London: Routledge & Kegan Paul, 1975.
    Concurs with G. Wilson Knight's estimation of the importance of the "imperial theme" in *Cymbeline* (see excerpt above, 1947). Yates theorizes that the play was first written in 1611 to honor the children of James I—Prince Henry and Princess Elizabeth—and was later revised in 1612 as Shakespeare's contribution to the national celebration of the betrothal of Princess Elizabeth to the Elector Palatine. The critic also maintains that Shakespeare added onto the earlier play's focus on national fortune, as represented in the figures of Imogen, Guiderius, and Arviragus, "suggestions of the further destiny of the British Imogen through her marriage to a representative of the Holy Roman Empire."

The Merchant of Venice

DATE: Scholars generally agree that *The Merchant of Venice* was written by Shakespeare sometime between 1594 and 1598, with the years 1596-97 the most frequently cited date. The play was entered in the STATIONERS' REGISTER on July 22, 1598, and was included in a list of dramas attributed to Shakespeare in Francis Meres's *Palladis Tamia* published that same year. Besides establishing the latest date of composition, this evidence—especially Meres's reference—has also led scholars to assume that *The Merchant of Venice* was performed shortly after its completion, since it is unlikely that Meres would have known of the play unless it had been publicly staged before his book was written. The first known performance of *The Merchant of Venice* is that by the KING'S MEN at the court of James I on February 10, 1605. Scholars have determined the earliest composition date of *The Merchant of Venice* by citing a number of historical events relevant to the play, especially the execution of Dr. Roderigo Lopez, Queen Elizabeth's personal physician, for treason in June of 1594. Many critics maintain that Shakespeare alludes to this event at IV. i. 133-37 of his play. Also cited in support of the 1594 composition date is the revival of Christopher Marlowe's *The Jew of Malta* in the summer of that year, which some scholars claim spurred Shakespeare to write *The Merchant of Venice*, and the coronation of Henry IV of France on February 27, 1594, which, again some critics contend, is referred to by Shakespeare at III. ii. 48-50. Those who argue that 1596 is the earliest date Shakespeare could have written *The Merchant of Venice* point to a reference in the play (I. i. 25-9) to the grounding and capture of the Spanish vessel *St. Andrew*, which actually occurred in early 1596 during the English expedition to Cadiz, but news of which did not reach the English court until July of that same year. John Russell Brown, among others, has contended that this is the most conclusive evidence that *The Merchant of Venice* could not have been written before the summer of 1596.

TEXT: The earliest published text of *The Merchant of Venice* is the QUARTO of 1600 (Q1), also known as the Heyes Quarto because of the reference on the title page to the copyright holder Thomas Heyes. The play was subsequently published in 1619 in a Second Quarto (Q2) and in 1623 in the FIRST FOLIO. Q2 was long thought to be the earlier of the two quartos until the noted textual scholar A. W. Pollard demonstrated that it was actually printed by William Jaggard in 1619 and fraudulently dated 1600 on the title page in order to circumvent a ruling of the Lord Chamberlain prohibiting publication of any play belonging to the King's Men without their consent. Q1 is regarded as the most authoritative of the three texts and the basis of the two later editions, Q2 and the Folio versions being essentially reprints of Q1 with the addition of some minor COMPOSITOR errors. Scholars generally agree that the First Quarto was based on a copy very close to Shakespeare's own manuscript, perhaps his FOUL PAPERS. This is indicated in the text by the often vague and uncertain stage directions, especially the number of unspecified character entrances and exits. Textual authorities note that Elizabethan acting companies were usually precise in such matters, thus discrediting the possibility that Q1 was based on a theater's PROMPT-BOOK; however, an author's manuscript frequently left such information incomplete in order to accommodate the resources or whims of the acting company. Yet,

Title page of The Merchant of Venice *taken from the First Folio (1623).*

some critics—most notably J. Dover Wilson—have claimed that the copy used to print Q1 was put together from players' parts and a plot outline of the drama, in other words, an ASSEMBLED TEXT. In support of this theory, Dover Wilson has pointed to the presence in Q1 of anomalies characteristic of assembled texts, such as half-lines of verse, mixtures of prose and poetry, confusions of fact, and the existence of unnecessary lines. The majority of scholars, however, maintain that these anomalies are more satisfactorily explained as imperfections in Shakespeare's own papers than as the peculiarities of an assembled text.

SOURCES: Most critics maintain that Shakespeare based *The Merchant of Venice* on the first tale in a collection of novelle called *Il Pecorone,* either written or collected by an obscure Italian writer named Ser Giovanni Fiorentino. This story, composed as early as 1378, was not published in Fiorentino's collection until 1558. Although no known English translation of the tale has ever been found, its similarities to *The Merchant of Venice* suggest that one was available to Shakespeare and that the dramatist must have used it as the basis of his play. Like Shakespeare's story, Fiorentino's is set in the mythical land of "Belmonte" and involves the wooing of a princess; but there is only one suitor instead of three and no casket test for the men to undergo. In *Il Pecorone,* the suitor need only stay awake for one whole night to win the desired lady. Realizing that this plot was unsuited for the stage, Shakespeare added two more suitors and substituted the story of the three caskets. Scholars contend that he could have encountered the tale of the caskets in as many as three works: John Gower's *Confessio Amantis* (1390), Giovanni Boccaccio's *Decameron* (1353), or, most likely, the anonymously written *Gesta Romanorum,* a large collection of tales first printed in 1472 and translated into English in two editions during the sixteenth century. The "pound of flesh" story was also widely known during Shakespeare's lifetime. It appears in two versions that he could have easily read: one, "The Ballad of the Crueltie of Geruntus" (c. 1590), the other in *The Orator,* a collection of orations one of which describes "A Jew, who would for his debt have a pound of flesh of a Christian." Some commentators suggest that Shakespeare might have found all these elements in an English drama no longer in existence. They base this hypothesis on a reference made by Stephen Gosson in his *School of Abuse* (1579) to a play called *The Jew,* which he describes as "representing the greediness of worldly choosers and the bloody minds of Usurers"—a plot summary that just as easily could be applied to *The Merchant of Venice.* Since *The Jew* has never been found, however, its relation to Shakespeare's play remains a matter of conjecture for most scholars.

Critics have also noted two other influences on *The Merchant of Venice.* Marlowe's *The Jew of Malta* and the contemporary affair of Dr. Lopez. Since the beginning of the seventeenth century commentators have cited the similarities between Marlowe's play and Shakespeare's, especially with regard to their respective villains, Barabas and Shylock, both wealthy Jews and enemies of Christianity. The influence of the Lopez affair, however, has been harder to assess. A Jewish-Portuguese doctor who became Queen Elizabeth's personal physician in 1586, Lopez was later linked in a plot to assassinate the queen. During a lengthy trial, the Earl of Essex insisted on Lopez's guilt and demanded that he be executed. Overcoming her own doubts and misgivings, Elizabeth eventually signed a warrant for Lopez's execution. The act was carried out before a large, rebellious crowd on June 7, 1594. To capitalize on the renewed hatred towards Jews the Lopez affair engendered in the London public, the LORD ADMIRAL'S MEN revived Marlowe's *The Jew of Malta.* As such, many scholars argue, though the Lopez incident was not a formal source for *The Merchant of Venice,* it may have spurred Shakespeare to write a play about a villainous Jew.

CRITICAL HISTORY: Undoubtedly the central issue in the commentary on *The Merchant of Venice* has been the debate over Shakespeare's intent in the play. One school of critics has claimed that the drama is allegorical and depicts, in the courtroom victory of Portia and the Christians over the Jew Shylock, the triumph of mercy over justice, New Testament dispensation over Judaic law, or love's wealth over the quest for material possessions. Another substantial group of commentators, sensing ambiguities and uncertainties in the play's apparent endorsement of Christian principles, has contended that Shakespeare was actually condemning the Venetians, including the ethereal Portia, for their moral duplicity and religious insincerity. Often referred to as the "ironic" reading of the play, this assessment also posits that Shylock, though evil in his

unnatural pursuit of justice and revenge, is a scapegoat figure—essentially no different from the Christians—condemned for demonstrating the hypocrisy of the Venetian world and challenging its false ideals of love and mercy. Recently, a few critics have postulated that Shakespeare intentionally provided for both interpretations in his play, offering the allegorical, pro-Christian in order to camouflage his bitterness towards the Puritans of his day, whom he saw as hypocritical, or providing both readings in order to challenge the members of his audience to choose their own interpretation. Other important critical concerns in the commentary on *The Merchant of Venice* include: the determination of the play's genre, Shakespeare's mixture of plots and his adaptation of Elizabethan stage conventions, the significance of Shylock's Jewishness as a theme in the drama, the importance of Act V and its relation to preceding events, the effect of Shylock's forced conversion to Christianity, and the cause and significance of Antonio's melancholy.

Although the first substantial criticism of *The Merchant of Venice* did not appear until the nineteenth century, many eighteenth-century scholars mentioned the play in their analyses of other Shakespearean works. Generally, these early commentators focused on Shakespeare's violation of the Neoclassical rules for correct drama while praising his characterization, craftsmanship, and versification in the play. Nicholas Rowe, for example, claimed that the bond and casket stories are "a little too much remov'd from the Rules of Probability." He also commented on the play's typical presentation as a comedy, contending instead that it is closer to tragedy in its "deadly Spirit of Revenge." Rowe's remarks thus initiated a debate over the genre of *The Merchant of Venice* that has lasted well into the twentieth century. Like Rowe, Charles Gildon argued that despite the inherent beauty of *The Merchant of Venice,* the play is too romantic and "vastly out of Nature" to satisfy the reason or understanding of most readers. Near the middle of the eighteenth century, George Colman and Samuel Johnson opposed this common assessment of the drama: Colman rebuked those critics who consistently applied the rules of human nature and probability to the fruits of Shakespeare's genius, claiming that once we willingly take the dramatist's "datum" for granted—as in the case of Shylock's bond—the story is beautifully and naturally sustained; Johnson, on the other hand, agreed that the bond and casket stories are improbable, but concluded that by combining them in one play Shakespeare overcame this obstacle and produced a unified work. Likewise, John Potter asserted that though the plot of *The Merchant of Venice* is "irregular" and the unities of time and place "materially broken," the play contains many beauties and sublime sentiments. Potter especially praised the characterization of Shylock, whom he claimed embodies the "quintessence" of the Jewish people. The importance of Shylock's Jewishness to Shakespeare's design, suggested in the preceding century by Potter, was discussed more fully in the nineteenth century by August Wilhelm Schlegel, William Hazlitt, Heinrich Heine, and Hermann Ulrici, among others. Towards the end of the eighteenth century, B. Walwyn became one of the earliest commentators to assess the significance of the ring episode in *The Merchant of Venice.* After generally disparaging the overuse of subplots in English drama, Walwyn asserted that the final act of Shakespeare's play is "more proper for an Interlude" and, as such, detracts from the pleasure of the main story.

Essentially, four issues dominated nineteenth-century commentary on *The Merchant of Venice:* analysis of the play's structure and unifying idea; discussion of Shylock's Jewishness and its importance to Shakespeare's design; interpretation of the final act, including the ring episode, and its relation to preceding events in the drama; and a determination of the play's classification—whether it is best regarded as a tragedy, a comedy, or a combination of these genres. However, the nineteenth century also saw the first negative assessments of the Christian characters in the play—and, conversely, the first sympathetic appraisals of Shylock—and the first of the so-called allegorical readings.

On the issue of the structure of *The Merchant of Venice*, as well as the debate over the play's unifying idea, August Wilhelm Schlegel, like Samuel Johnson, commended Shakespeare's handling of his double plot, noting how the casket and bond stories are each rendered "natural and probable" by the presence of the other. Hermann Ulrici examined what he called "the intrinsic unity of idea" that binds the separate plots of *The Merchant of Venice* together, stating that though events in the play seem unrelated, a common pattern unifies each. Ulrici summarized this central idea in the Latin maxim *summum jus, summa injuria* (the highest right [enables] the greatest injustice). Ulrici's contemporary, G. G. Gervinus, disputed this assessment of the unifying theme in *The Merchant of Venice*, claiming that the play is concerned principally with "the relation of man to property," and by extension, "the question of [man's] relation to man." Karl Elze concurred that "man's relation to wealth" might well be the unifying theme in the play. F. Kreyssig disagreed with both Ulrici and Gervinus and concluded that *The Merchant of Venice* reflects no moral idea. The drama merely demonstrates, according to Kreyssig, that "lasting success, sure, practical results can be secured only by a just estimate of things." Near the end of the nineteenth century, Denton J. Snider argued that *The Merchant of Venice* is constructed around three movements—conflict, mediation, and return—and that the play in total is concerned with the issues of property and love, the former reflected in the conflict between Antonio and Shylock, the latter in the struggle within Portia herself over whether to obey her father's will or exercise her personal freedom and choose her own husband. Snider was also among the first critics to suggest an allegorical interpretation of the Antonio-Shylock opposition, saying that it depicts not only the confrontation of two ethically and religiously opposed individuals, but also symbolically reenacts the struggle between Christianity and Judaism itself.

Discussion of Shylock's Jewishness as an important theme in *The Merchant of Venice* was primarily restricted to the nineteenth century. Schlegel argued that Shylock was an original creation and not a mere abstraction of "national sentiments," though he admitted that aspects of the Jew's behavior, such as his insistence on the letter of the law, make him "a symbol of the general history of his unfortunate nation." In the first substantial defense of Shylock as a man justified in his hate towards the Christians, William Hazlitt maintained that it is not until the trial in Act IV that the usurer demonstrates the vengeful nature of his Jewish heritage. Until that point, Hazlitt asserted, Shylock is a sympathetic figure, a man grossly mistreated by the hypocritical Venetians. Heinrich Heine similarly regarded Shylock as a tragic figure in the play—in his opinion, a symbol of the undeserved general hatred of the Jewish race. Ulrici contended that Shylock is both an abstraction and an original creation, to the extent that he symbolizes "the Jewish national character" in its "universal degradation," yet remains "embued with concrete reality." Like Heine, the German lawyer Rudolf von Ihering considered Shylock a tragic figure and

suggested that he represents the Jew of the Middle Ages, whose rights were "in the same breath acknowledged, and, by fraud, denied." A. Pietscher later disputed Ihering's findings, stating that if Shylock represents anything it is the portrait of an individual who puts his rights above all others and uses the law to further his own evil ends. Thus, Pietscher concluded, the Jew deserves the extent of his punishment, and his defeat by what Ihering called a "pettifogging trick" is proper and unavoidable given the legal circumstances.

Nineteenth-century commentators on *The Merchant of Venice* generally did not regard the apparently inappropriate Act V and the business of the rings as superfluous to Shakespeare's design, as B. Walwyn contended, but saw it as intimately related to the comic structure of the play. Schlegel, again, was the first to offer this defense of the drama's conclusion, stating that Act V provided Shakespeare with the means to transcend the "gloomy impressions" of Antonio's acquittal and Shylock's condemnation, thus ending the play "with the most exhilarating mirth." Hazlitt described the final act as "one of the happiest instances of Shakespear's knowledge of the principles of the drama." Anna Brownell Jameson followed Schlegel and claimed that Shakespeare composed Act V in order to conclude *The Merchant of Venice* on a positive note. Ulrici concurred, and Gervinus argued that it serves not only to overcome "the painful impression of the judgment scene," but also to satisfy the moral interest of the drama by confirming "the genuineness of . . . friendship" as the highest relationship between individuals.

The controversy during the nineteenth century over the classification of *The Merchant of Venice* was closely related to those questions of Shylock's characterization and the relation of Act V to the remainder of the play. Generally, those critics who considered Shylock a tragic or sympathetic figure usually labelled the drama a tragedy; conversely, those who regarded him as nothing more than a comic villain consistently viewed the play as a comedy. Similarly, those commentators who claimed that Act V is essential to Shakespeare's comic structure concluded by describing *The Merchant of Venice* as either a comedy or a tragicomedy. Thus Heine called the play a tragedy, despite the obvious caricaturization of Shylock and Shakespeare's comedic design. Ulrici referred to it as "a comedy of intrigue." Karl Elze maintained that even with its tragic undertones *The Merchant of Venice* ends as a "romantic comedy." Although he did not specifically call Shakespeare's play a tragedy, Ihering emphasized that its central action is the tragic defeat of Shylock. And Snider concluded that *The Merchant of Venice* is neither a comedy nor a tragedy, but what he termed a "mediated drama" or tragicomedy, an assessment voiced by most twentieth-century critics. Many of these same issues have dominated criticism of *The Merchant of Venice* during the twentieth century, especially the debate over the conventional nature of Shakespeare's play and the controversy over the meaning or significance of the final act. Other concerns that surfaced at this time include the investigation into the cause and importance of Antonio's melancholy, the study of Shakespeare's language and imagery, and the on-going debate over the thematic purpose of the play—whether its vision of Christian mercy is meant to be ironic, or whether Shakespeare actually endorses the orthodox view and supports Shylock's condemnation.

In the beginning of the twentieth century, E. K. Chambers offered the first explanation of the cause and significance of Antonio's melancholy. In a general assessment of the classification of *The Merchant of Venice*, in which he describes the play as a "drama of emotion," Chambers argued that even in this work of emotional stress Antonio's dark behavior is out of tune. He suggested that its source might be found in the marriage of Bassanio and Portia and Antonio's reaction to this event; he even postulated that the merchant's sadness represents the "intrusion of a personal note, an echo of those disturbed relations in Shakespeare's private life of which but enigmatic record is to be found in the *Sonnets*." Later critics who discussed this issue include T. A. Ross, Graham Midgley, John D. Hurrell, A. D. Moody, and Lawrence Danson. Ross, like Chambers, maintained that Antonio's melancholy stems from a sense of personal loss over Bassanio's marriage to Portia. However, he claimed that the merchant is actually a homosexual and is in love with his friend, and that this sexual abnormality, rather than Bassanio's planned marriage, is the true cause of Antonio's sadness. Ross's homoerotic reading of Antonio's behavior was reiterated by Midgley and Hurrell. The former contended that *The Merchant of Venice* is neither a love comedy with tragic intrusions nor a tragedy of an isolated Jew "disfigured by lovers' adventures and tedious casket scenes," but is instead a study in the loneliness of two outsiders. Midgley identified these outsiders as Shylock and Antonio, one because of his Jewish faith, the other because of his homosexual love for his Venetian friend. According to the critic, Antonio's melancholy is thus a result of his "outsider" status in his own society. Like Chambers and Ross, Hurrell maintained that the source of Antonio's sadness and dark behavior is his jealousy over Bassanio's relationship with Portia and his belief that he has lost his friend forever. Although, according to Hurrell, Shakespeare might not have intended to make the merchant a homosexual, his mysterious behavior throughout the play "certainly suggests one." Both Moody and Danson departed from this psychosexual interpretation of Antonio's sadness. In one of the most celebrated readings of *The Merchant of Venice* as an "ironic" play, Moody asserted that Antonio's melancholy stems from an acute dissatisfaction with his society's failure to accommodate humane, personal feelings—a fact painfully demonstrated in the Venetians' insensitive behavior towards him. And Danson maintained that Antonio's mistreatment of Shylock and his melancholy are "intimately related," postulating that the source of the merchant's sadness is his sense of the "moral failure" in his un-Christian behavior towards the Jew.

Twentieth-century discussion of Shakespeare's use of conventions in *The Merchant of Venice* has focused on an examination of Shylock and his role in the play. Elmer Edgar Stoll, writing near the end of the 1920s, took issue with those earlier commentators who considered Shylock a tragic or, at least, sympathetic figure, claiming that the Jew is nothing more than the traditional comic villain apparent throughout Elizabethan comedy. Harold R. Walley reviewed the various interpretations of Shylock's character since the seventeenth century and similarly argued that the best way to understand the Jew is to view him strictly as a dramatic instrument or vehicle by which Shakespeare provided motivation to his story. Thus, like Stoll, Walley maintained that Shylock's primary role in the play is that of the stock villain. In his examination of *The Merchant of Venice*, John Middleton Murry contended that critics who seek a psychological and conceptual consistency in Shakespeare's plays are misdirected, since Shakespeare was chiefly a dramatic craftsman who manipulated his characters in order to achieve particular effects—especially those demanded by the theatrical conventions of his time. In the case of *The Merchant of Venice*, Murry noted, Shakespeare permits his audience to either sym-

pathize with or condemn Shylock according to the dramatic needs of the different episodes in his play. J. W. Lever later modified this view of Shylock as a conventional figure, agreeing that Shakespeare generally cared little for character motivation, but that in this instance he took the traditional caricature of the Jewish usurer and villain and transformed him into a more complex and threatening figure—in Lever's assessment, one who seriously challenges the Christian values of love, friendship, and community. More recently, D. A. Traversi reiterated Murry's interpretation of Shylock's role in *The Merchant of Venice*, claiming that Shakespeare intended the character to be "the melodramatic villain, the heartless usurer, and the enemy of Christianity," but that the dramatist could not resist "conferring upon his Jew, at the moments when that effect requires them, a consistency and human solidity which . . . threatens at times to break through the elaborate poetic fabric of his Venetian romance."

Other significant topics in twentieth-century commentary on *The Merchant of Venice* include the analysis of the play's structural design and investigation into Shakespeare's language and imagery. Like such earlier critics as Samuel Johnson and August Wilhelm Schlegel, Harley Granville-Barker noted how naturally and effectively Shakespeare combined his two plots—the casket and bond stories—and, especially, how he maintained the artifice of the casket story in the presence of the tragic potentiality of the Antonio-Shylock conflict. During the 1960s, Sigurd Burckhardt and Thomas H. Fujimura offered further analyses of Shakespeare's construction of *The Merchant of Venice*. Burckhardt noted the unifying function of the metaphor of bonds and bonding, "circularity and circulation," in the drama and argued that the play primarily asks "how the vicious circle of the bond's law can be transformed into the ring of love." Burckhardt claimed that *The Merchant of Venice* provides an answer to this question in both a dramatic and a reflexive manner: the first, in Portia's "literal and unreserved submission to [Shylock's] bond as absolutely binding" as the only means of liberating Antonio from that bond's demands; the second, in Shakespeare's method of writing his play, in that he found his creative freedom not outside the sources of his tale but deeper within that tale's own exigencies. In a more detailed study, Fujimura suggested that *The Merchant of Venice* can be better understood if we view its three distinct worlds—that of Bassanio-Portia, that of Antonio, and that of Shylock—as each representing a different mode of dramatic expression and all working together to convey Shakespeare's "philosophy." He defined these modes of dramatic expression—adopting Northrop Frye's terminology in his *Anatomy of Criticism*—as: the romantic (Bassanio-Portia), the realistic (Antonio), and the ironic (Shylock). Fujimura also noted that these three worlds are represented symbolically in the play by the three caskets. On the subject of Shakespeare's language and imagery in *The Merchant of Venice*, Caroline F. E. Spurgeon discussed the clustering of poetic images in the third casket scene (III. ii.) and the final act of the play. She maintained that these two scenes contain more poetic imagery than any other in the drama because they represent the highest points of emotion. B. Ifor Evans examined how Shakespeare employed language and imagery in *The Merchant of Venice* to enhance the romantic elements and unite the various moods of the play. And, as mentioned above, Sigurd Burckhardt focused on Shakespeare's use of the bonding metaphor as a unifying motif.

Although these topics have attracted considerable attention among twentieth-century commentators, two other issues have clearly dominated critical discussion of *The Merchant of Venice* since the 1920s. One is the debate over the significance of Act V and the ring episode; the other is the confrontation between scholars over the thematic purpose of the play. Since the eighteenth century, critics have variously argued over the importance and meaning of Act V and the ring episode. The debate was continued in the present century by such commentators as Harley Granville-Barker, C. L. Barber, Barbara K. Lewalski, A. D. Moody, and others. Commenting on the fairy-tale quality of *The Merchant of Venice,* Granville-Barker concluded that the final act provides the traditional fairy-tale ending and returns the play's focus to that of romantic comedy. Similarly, Barber contended that Act V, along with the defeat of Shylock in Act IV, works to remove the threat against the Venetian world and establish the triumph of comedy. He asserted that no other early Shakespearean comedy "ends with so full an expression of harmony as that which we get in . . . the final scene of *The Merchant of Venice.*" Lewalski, in her well-known allegorical study of the play, declared that Act V is necessary as "a comic parody of the trial scene" in which, on the moral level, the metaphor of "venturing" or "sacrifice" is depicted in the realm of romantic love, and, on the allegorical level, the judgment of a human soul (Bassanio) is enacted according to those same Christian standards applied to Shylock. On the other hand, Moody called the final act of *The Merchant of Venice* a "light comedy" of folly, but one that underscores the illusion of the Christians' self-glorification and piety and informs the audience of the disparity between their actions and their beliefs. Moody also claimed that Lorenzo's homage to universal harmony in Act V is meant to parody what the Venetians in this last episode actually strive to achieve.

Other twentieth-century critics who have debated the importance of Act V include James E. Siemon, R. Chris Hassel, Jr., Richard Horwich, Alice N. Benston, and Anne Parten. In one of the most extensive interpretations, Siemon contended that the final act serves as more than a comic extension of the plot or an attempt by Shakespeare to satisfy the conventional ending expected by his Elizabethan audience; instead, he maintained that it channels our emotional reactions towards Shylock's defeat "along suitable and constructive lines" and provides a new awareness of events in Acts I through IV. Siemon stated that this redirection of the audience's feelings and perceptions is necessary because of Shakespeare's sympathetic portrayal of Shylock, whose defeat produces in the spectator or reader an emotionally frustrated response to the play. To avert this sense of emotional inconclusiveness, Siemon concluded, Shakespeare displaces our attention in Act V to "the harmony and beauty of reconciliation" in "general and comprehensive terms"; but, he added, this apparent conclusion and reconciliation is not a successfully integrated element in *The Merchant of Venice,* since the final act merely "distracts our attention" from the painful vision of the defeated Shylock, rather than resolving this experience with the comic movement of the play. Similarly, Hassel maintained that *The Merchant of Venice,* unlike Shakespeare's other festive comedies, demonstrates no sense of character development or integration, no reconciliation in the final act between its so-called green or festive world and the real, social one, but instead depicts two societies—Venice and Belmont—"equally tainted by suggestions of perversion, guilt, hypocrisy, and unhappiness." Hassel specifically focused on the grim figure of Antonio and the "ambiguous tones" underlying the conversations in Act V—the notes of infidelity, sexual perversion, and sadness; he claimed that the "unnatural love relationships encourage us to question not only the quality of love in Belmont, but also the quality of justice and mercy, and finally of the whole society." Horwich analyzed the business of the rings in Acts IV and V, stating that this contrived affair by Portia is designed to provide Bassanio with a second chance to act on inspiration and spontaneous generosity in her service—his first opportunity being his selection of the casket to win Portia's hand in marriage, which though correct, Horwich argued, is based on calculation rather than inspiration. Benston contributed yet a different interpretation of Act V, contending that it depicts Portia's education of Antonio. According to the critic, Portia—through the business of the rings—teaches the merchant how to forsake his possessive and unnatural love for Bassanio and to accept the law of "natural succession" and "generation" embodied in Portia and Bassanio's union and love for each other. Parten also commented on the ring episode, declaring that this scene "serves as an important element of the play in its own right" and "represents Shakespeare's resolution of the threat to the comic world that Portia herself embodies," mainly because of her superiority over all the male characters. In dispelling that threat, Parten concluded, Shakespeare overcomes "a dangerous underlying tension in the play" and reveals Portia "to be not a horn-giving shrew, but rather the embodiment of the Elizabethan ideal virtuous wife."

The controversy over Shakespeare's thematic purpose in *The Merchant of Venice* has generally been between those critics who believe that the dramatist endorses the Christian, orthodox view and supports Shylock's condemnation, and those who maintain that the play's vision of Christian mercy, as expressed by the Venetians, is meant to be ironic. This latter group of critics also claim that Shylock is a scapegoat figure, an individual condemned not for following an ideology alien and hostile to the world of Venice, but for reflecting too closely the true mercenary nature of his Christian enemies. The so-called allegorical interpretation of *The Merchant of Venice,* though suggested as early as the nineteenth century by Denton J. Snider, was first fully presented during the 1920s by Sir Israel Gollancz. Gollancz argued that Shakespeare's play derived ultimately from the medieval exempla of the Pound of Flesh story and the parable of the Three Caskets, both of which were available to Shakespeare in dramas derived from the *Gesta Romanorum.* Each of these homilies depicts, according to Gollancz, an allegory of the soul's desire to bond with God or Christ. The critic also pointed out the numerous parallels between the trial scene in *The Merchant of Venice* and the medieval allegory of *The Four Daughters of God* (also known as *The Parliament in Heaven*), which tells the story of how God reconciled the demands of the four angels—Truth, Justice, Mercy, and Love—over the spiritual fate of humankind. Elements in Gollancz's reading of the play were further developed or redefined in the essays by Nevill Coghill, Muriel C. Bradbrook, Theodor Reik, E. M. W. Tillyard, Barbara K. Lewalski, and René E. Fortin, among others. Coghill considered the central issue in *The Merchant of Venice* Shakespeare's allegorical dramatization of the historical struggle between justice and mercy, the Old Law of Judaic tradition and the New Dispensation of Christianity. He thus interpreted the triumph of mercy over strict justice in the trial scene (Portia's victory over Shylock) as a reenactment of God's decision to provide for the salvation of humanity through the figure of Jesus Christ. Like Gollancz, Coghill claimed that Shakespeare probably adopted this pattern from the medieval allegory of *The Four Daughters of God* and other homilies. Bradbrook commented on the harsh contrasts in *The Merchant of Venice* and Shakespeare's stock characterization of Shylock, both of which she saw as necessary to the theme of justice and mercy in the play—or, in her words, the confrontation between "the law and love that is the fulfilling of the law, the gold of Venice and the gold of Belmont.'' In an otherwise psychoanalytic assessment of Shakespeare's play, Reik discerned behind the characterizations of Shylock and Antonio the figures of the Old Testament God and the Savior Christ, in conflict with each other, the one stern, unmerciful, and vengeful, the other sad, forgiving, and willing to shoulder the sins of his fellow human beings. Tillyard also emphasized the allegorical nature of the trial scene and argued that Portia's role in the play is not only that of mercy on earth, but also the reconciliation of mercy and justice. He added a comment on Shylock's forced conversion often stressed in the so-called ironic readings of the drama, namely, that Shakespeare meant to contrast this act unfavorably with Portia's earlier remark that mercy cannot be ''constrain'd'' or forced. Lewalski extended Gollancz's and Coghill's assessments of *The Merchant of Venice,* interpreting the entire work, not just the trial scene, as a conscious effort by Shakespeare to dramatize, through allegory, the medieval story of *The Parliament of Heaven.* Lewalski emphasized two important points in her examination: one, that Shylock's forced conversion, when viewed in light of the play's symbolic design, ''is not antisemitic revenge,'' but a merciful action that substantiates what Shylock's own experience during the trial has demonstrated—''that the Law leads only to death and destruction, that faith in Christ must supplant human righteousness''; and two, as mentioned above, that Act V is necessary as a ''comic parody'' and extension of the trial scene. The last of these critics, René E. Fortin, also stressed the allegorical nature of the play; however, Fortin was primarily concerned with the ''allegorical counterstatement'' the character of Launcelot contributes to the drama. Noting that Shakespeare presents his theme of Judaic and Christian opposition in one manner through his various examples of filial piety, Fortin maintained that Launcelot, in the scene depicting the encounter with his lost father (II. ii.), is meant to ''counterpoint'' the assumption in the naive allegory that the New Dispensation of Christianity represents a progression to a ''Higher Truth.'' According to the critic, a more complex meaning is apparent in the scene of the two Gobbos, in that the blindness motif played out between father and son, when interpreted symbolically, reflects ''the failure of filial piety between Christian and Jew and compels us to recognize the distance between the idea shadowed forth in naive allegory— the Higher Truth of Christianity—and the imperfect realization of that Idea in the commerce of everyday life.'' Fortin concluded that *The Merchant of Venice* actually demands not that we choose between Jewish law and Christian love, but that we recognize ''that an indissoluble bond of filial piety exists between the two traditions.''

Although most twentieth-century critics who have interpreted *The Merchant of Venice* as an allegorical play have focused on the opposition of justice and mercy, or Judaic law and Christian Dispensation, others have perceived a different thematic conflict at the heart of the drama. For example, in the 1950s both John Russell Brown and C. L. Barber argued that *The Merchant of Venice* depicts the struggle between ''love's wealth,'' as demonstrated in the generosity of the Christian characters, and the ''rights of commerce,'' as exemplified by Shylock. In Barber's words, the play ''dramatizes the conflict between the mechanisms of wealth and the masterful, social use of it.'' Peter G. Phialas took issue with those critics who focused strictly on the conflict between Jew and Christian, even the opposition of justice and mercy, in the play, claiming that Shakespeare was concerned primarily with the struggle between love and hate and with demonstrating the necessity of love, ''in the romantic as well as the social sphere,'' as

humanity's sole means ''of achieving harmony and happiness and salvation.'' John P. Sisk defined the central conflict in *The Merchant of Venice* as that between ''the salvation of love'' and the bondage of material possessions. However, like Brown and Barber, Sisk noted that money can be used, as it is by Portia, Bassanio, and Antonio, to liberate in the service of life and love, just as it can be used, as it is by Shylock, to bind one in hatred and greed. Alice N. Benston disagreed with the traditional reading of *The Merchant of Venice* as a play based on a series of dichotomies, the most significant being the opposition of justice and mercy. Instead, Benston contended that the drama presents a succession of trials concerning the law and ''its complex relations to vice, virtue, and vicissitude'' with Portia, not Shylock or Antonio, as its central figure. She especially emphasized the manner in which Portia affirms rather than denies the laws of both Venice and Belmont, concluding that this underscores her primary role in the play as the law's protector. Most recently, Barbara Tovey maintained that the conflict between appearance and reality is a central concern in *The Merchant of Venice,* reflected most obviously in the casket story, but also inherent in Antonio's relationship with Bassanio. Tovey noted that although the merchant's actions on behalf of his friend appear sincere and noble, they are actually designed ''to make Bassanio dependent on him and to elicit from Bassanio feelings of love and indebtedness.'' Tovey viewed Antonio as a ''Christ-figure'' in the play, and she claimed that in dramatizing the danger his self-sacrifice poses on Bassanio and the action in general Shakespeare was criticizing the Christian faith itself, in that it, too, seeks to engender guilt and feelings of indebtedness in its followers.

The view that the Christians in *The Merchant of Venice* are not as admirable as they appear was proposed early in the nineteenth century by William Hazlitt and noted by Heinrich Heine. But it was not until the twentieth century that this idea received serious consideration. Although stopping short of discrediting Shakespeare's Christian message in *The Merchant of Venice,* Arthur Quiller-Couch was one of the first twentieth-century commentators to question, as Hazlitt and Heine did, the morals and behavior of the virtuous Venetians. Except for Portia and Antonio, Quiller-Couch considered the Christians a ''circle of wasters'' and ''parasites.'' He concluded that Shakespeare failed in *The Merchant of Venice* by making these supposedly noble Venetians ''just as heartless as Shylock without any of Shylock's passionate excuse.'' The first interpretation of *The Merchant of Venice* as an ironic play was proposed by Harold C. Goddard at the beginning of the 1950s. Goddard argued that the surface story depicting the benevolence of the Christians and the triumph of mercy over justice conceals a deeper meaning, suggestions of which he found in the Venetians' vague and apprehensive statements throughout the play. He postulated that this uneasiness is prompted by their unwillingness to confront their unconscious desires, which, according to Goddard, is understandable, since as a group they are dependent on money and self-fulfillment in a manner no less revolting than Shylock's usury and obsession with the law. Goddard thus described the Christians' hatred of Shylock as a result of their projection onto him of all those repressed qualities they cannot accept in themselves; in short, the Jew serves as a scapegoat figure in the play, a point echoed by such later critics as A. D. Moody and René Girard. Perhaps the most significant of Goddard's findings is his conclusion that neither Portia nor Antonio sustain that victory of Christian mercy they both demand of Shylock. In fact, he asserted that the ''logic of the courtroom'' is put to shame by Shakespeare's ''spiritual argument'' unrealized in the drama but nonetheless still visible in Shylock's speech on "Christian example," Portia's on mercy, and Lorenzo's on the harmony of the universe. Goddard concluded with the idea that the spectators and readers of *The Merchant of Venice,* like the characters themselves, are provided with the opportunity to transform the play as they see fit—to choose, in other words, the "base" or the "precious" as its central design. A. D. Moody also considered *The Merchant of Venice* an ironic play, maintaining that the Christians are hypocritical and mercenary and that the drama never satisfies the ideals of mercy and justice it seems to endorse. In addition, Moody argued that the controlling irony in the play not only allows us to see the falsity of the festive resolution and to recognize the "doublefaced" nature of the Christians, but also "extends beyond the characters to involve and question the attitudes of the audience," to the extent that we typically accept the Christians at face value and rejoice in their good fortune. Thus, Moody concluded, *The Merchant of Venice* leaves us "with an image of our ordinary condition of moral compromise, of [our] complacent spiritual mediocrity," and of what consequences such an attitude entails. As mentioned earlier, R. Chris Hassel, Jr. contended that the ambiguous nature of the conversations in Act V suggests that the quality of love in Belmont, as well as the quality of justice and mercy throughout the play, is not as ideal as it seems. Hassel viewed Shylock's "disposal" as a particularly good indication of the true nature of the Christian society in *The Merchant of Venice.* Recently, René Girard—like Goddard and Moody—disparaged the Christians' behavior and treatment of Shylock, asserting that the Jew and the Venetians are essentially alike; in fact, stated Girard, the Christians are morally inferior to Shylock in that they cover up their true desires with protestations of love and charity, while Shylock admits that his efforts in life are shaped by one thing—making money. The fact that readers have not universally accepted the Venetians' corrupt nature and duplicity, Girard theorized, is because Shakespeare managed both to condemn them for their "scapegoating" and immoral treatment of Shylock and provide his audience with enough reason to dislike the Jew and, therefore, participate in his persecution.

The suggestions by both Goddard and Girard that *The Merchant of Venice* contains the possibility of opposing interpretations was further developed by Norman Rabkin. In a general discussion of the nature of modern criticism, Rabkin argued that a play like *The Merchant of Venice* clearly demonstrates the limitations of interpretations that posit one set of terms as relevant to Shakespeare's meaning and disregard other information we might gather from the drama. He perceived this failure on both sides of the critical debate over the play, finding identical faults with the allegorical and the ironic readings. Instead, Rabkin maintained that we should view such plays as *The Merchant of Venice* as an existential experience, our response to which is "quintessentially" like our response to life, "characterized by process, tension, resistance, and an ineffable sense of integrity." He concluded that although Shakespeare's play does indeed have "an autonomous, coherent, and meaningful whole," that meaning, like life itself, resists definition.

A review of the critical history of *The Merchant of Venice* demonstrates that no one answer to the numerous questions the play poses will ever satisfy its critics. Essentially, the problems confronting scholars today are the same ones that troubled earlier commentators in their attempts to define the play's elusive meaning. Foremost among these is the question of Shakespeare's thematic purpose in writing *The Merchant of Venice,* which includes additional speculation into the reasons behind

his sympathetic portrait of the villain Shylock and, conversely, his unflattering characterization of the Venetians as a whole. Previous critics either condemned Shylock as an outright villain and praised the noble Venetians, as in the eighteenth century, or, as in the nineteenth, elevated Shylock to the status of romantic hero, usually without considering how, if at all, such a view affects the other characters and the play itself. Commentators since the beginning of the present century have addressed the central issue of Shakespeare's thematic purpose in *The Merchant of Venice* in two ways: by claiming that the play is essentially allegorical, that Shakespeare endorses the orthodox, Christian view and supports Shylock's condemnation, and that the Jew seems at times sympathetic and his cause appears legitimate only because Shakespeare was unwilling to create one-dimensional characters; or, by contending that Shylock is indeed a sympathetic, scapegoat figure, and that the drama's vision of Christian mercy and justice is meant to be ironic. Recently, Harold C. Goddard and René Girard have suggested the possibility that both readings are inherent in *The Merchant of Venice.* And, as stated above, Norman Rabkin has argued that though it expresses a definite theme, the drama, like life itself, resists definition. Whether future commentators will follow Rabkin's nonreductionist lead remains to be seen, but what is certain is that *The Merchant of Venice* will provoke readers and spectators to formulate questions for years to come—despite the fact that these questions, as Rabkin noted, can never be answered.

NICHOLAS ROWE (essay date 1709)

[*Rowe was the editor of the first critical edition of Shakespeare's plays (1709) and the author of the first authoritative Shakespeare biography. In the following excerpt, he links Shylock with Shakespeare's other satirical and ill-natured characters and comments on the typical presentation of* The Merchant of Venice *as a comedy. Rowe instead regards it as a tragedy because of its "deadly Spirit of Revenge" and its "Cruelty and Mischief." He also calls the play one of the most finished of any by Shakespeare, though he considers the story of the caskets and the bond accepted by Antonio "a little too much remov'd from the Rules of Probability." Other critics who have interpreted* The Merchant of Venice *in light of such Neoclassical standards include Charles Gildon (1710), George Colman (1761), Samuel Johnson (1765), and John Potter (1771-72).*]

[Shakespear's] Clowns, without which Character there was hardly any Play writ in that Time, are all very entertaining: And, I believe, *Thersites* in *Troilus* and *Cressida,* and *Apemantus* in *Timon,* will be allow'd to be Master-Pieces of ill Nature, and satyrical Snarling. To these I might add, that incomparable Character of *Shylock* the *Jew,* in *The Merchant of* Venice; but tho' we have seen that Play Receiv'd and Acted as a Comedy, and the Part of the *Jew* perform'd by an Excellent Comedian, yet I cannot but think it was design'd Tragically by the Author. There appears in it such a deadly Spirit of Revenge, such a savage Fierceness and Fellness, and such a bloody designation of Cruelty and Mischief, as cannot agree either with the Stile or Characters of Comedy. The Play it self, take it all together, seems to me to be one of the most finish'd of any of *Shakespear*'s. The Tale indeed, in that Part relating to the Caskets, and the extravagant and unusual kind of Bond given by *Antonio,* is a little too much remov'd from the Rules of Probability: But taking the Fact for granted, we must allow it to be very beautifully written. There is something in the Friendship of *Antonio* to *Bassanio* very Great, Generous and Tender. The whole fourth Act, supposing, as I said, the Fact to be probable, is extremely Fine. (pp. xix-xx)

> *Nicholas Rowe, "Some Account of the Life, &c. of Mr. William Shakespear," in* The Works of Mr. William Shakespear, Vol. I *by William Shakespeare, edited by Nicholas Rowe, 1709. Reprint by AMS Press, Inc., 1967, pp. i-xl.*

[CHARLES GILDON]   (essay date 1710)

[*Gildon was the first critic to write an extended commentary on Shakespeare's plays. Like many other Neoclassicists, he regarded Shakespeare as an imaginative playwright who nevertheless lacked knowledge of the dramatic "rules" necessary for correct writing. In the following excerpt, first published in his* Remarks on the Plays of Shakespear *in 1710, Gildon maintains that* The Merchant of Venice *is "so very Romantic, so vastly out of Nature" that any reader of common sense should be appalled by its lack of reason and probability. Gildon also states that though the play is beautifully written, it lacks the power to move the soul and passions, "which ought every where to shine in a serious Dramatic Performance, such as most of this is." For further commentary on Shakespeare's violation of this and other Neoclassical standards in* The Merchant of Venice, *see the excerpts by Nicholas Rowe (1709), George Colman (1761), Samuel Johnson (1765), and John Potter (1771-72).*]

The Ignorance that *Shakespear* had of the *Greek Drama* threw him on such odd Stories, as the Novels and Romances of his time cou'd afford, and which were so far from being natural, that they wanted that Probability and Verisimilitude, which is absolutely necessary to all the Representations of the Stage. The Plot of [*The Merchant of Venice*] is of that Number. But the Errors of the Fable and the Conduct are too visible to need Discovery. (p. 321)

The Character of the *Jew* is very well distinguish'd by Avarice, Malice, implacable Revenge &c. But the Incidents that necessarily shew these Qualitys are so very Romantic, so vastly out of Nature, that our Reason, our Understanding is every where shock'd; which abates extremely of the Pleasure the Pen of *Shakespear* might give us. This is visible in his Speech to the Doge [IV. i. 35-62, 89-103], for all the while that Distinction of Character, which is beautiful and otherwise pleases you, the Incredibility of such a Discourse to such a Prince and before such a Court of Judicature, has so little of Nature in it, that it is impossible to escape the Censure of a Man of common Sense.

The Character of *Portia* is not every where very well kept, that is, the Manners are not always *agreeable* or *convenient* to her Sex and Quality; particularly [in III. iv. 60-78] where she scarce preserves her Modesty in the Expression.

The Scene betwixt *Shylock* and *Tubal* [III. i. 79-130] is artfully managed; and the Temper of the Jew excellently discover'd in its various Turns upon the different News, of which *Tubal* gives him an Account.

This Play, as well as most of the rest, gives Instances, that *Shakespear* was perfectly acquainted with the fabulous Stories of the old Poets, which is to me a Confirmation, that he was well acquainted with the Authors of the *Latin* Antiquity, whence only he cou'd learn them.

Tho' there are a great many Beauties in what our modern Gentlemen call the *Writing* in this Play, yet it is almost every where calm, and touches not the Soul, there are no sinewy Passions, which ought every where to shine in a serious Dramatic Performance, such as most of this is. (pp. 321-22)

> [*Charles Gildon*], *"Remarks on the Plays of Shakespear," in* The Works of Mr. William Shakespear, Vol. 7 *by William Shakespeare, 1710. Reprint by AMS Press, Inc., 1967, pp. 257-444.*

GEORGE COLMAN   (essay date 1761)

[*Colman was an eighteenth-century dramatist and producer who primarily followed Neoclassical standards in his critical and creative writings. However, he accepted Shakespeare's variations of the classical rules as permissible because, like Joseph Addison, he felt that the poet's genius was greater than his lapses; in fact, Colman ranked Shakespeare with Homer in his degree of supremacy over other poets. In the following excerpt from his* Critical Reflections on the old English dramatick writers (1761), *Colman disparages the tendency of his contemporaries to limit the genius and imagination of such writers as Shakespeare within the confines of human nature and probability. He specifically refers to Shakespeare's use of ghosts and other supernatural beings, whom he finds always well delineated, unified, and effective. Colman notes the same results in those instances where Shakespeare took common mortals and placed them in extravagant situations, citing Shylock's bond with Antonio as such an example. The critic concludes that once we willingly accept Shakespeare's "datum"—as in the case of Shylock's bond—the story and characters are "beautifully" and "naturally" sustained. For further commentary on* The Merchant of Venice *in light of such Neoclassical standards, see the excerpts by Nicholas Rowe (1709), Charles Gildon (1710), Samuel Johnson (1765), and John Potter (1771-72).*]

There is one circumstance in Dramatick Poetry which I think the chastised notions of our modern Criticks do not permit them sufficiently to consider. Dramatick Nature is of a more large and liberal quality than they are willing to allow. It does not consist merely in the representation of real Characters, Characters acknowledged to abound in common life, but may be extended also to the exhibition of imaginary Beings. To create is to be a Poet indeed; to draw down Beings from another sphere and endue them with suitable Passions, Affections, Dispositions, allotting them at the same time proper employment, 'to body forth, by the Powers of Imagination, the forms of things unknown, and to give to airy Nothing a local Habitation and a Name' [*A Midsummer Night's Dream*, V. i. 14-17] surely requires a Genius for the Drama equal, if not superior, to the delineation of personages in the ordinary course of Nature. Shakespeare, in particular, is universally acknowledged never to have soared so far above the reach of all other writers as in those instances where he seems purposely to have transgressed the Laws of Criticism. 'He appears to have disdained to put his Free Soul into circumscription and confine' [*Othello*, I. ii. 26-7], which denied his extraordinary talents their full play nor gave scope to the Boundlesness of his Imagination. His Witches, Ghosts, Fairies, and other Imaginary Beings scattered through his plays are so many glaring violations of the common table of Dramatick Laws. What then shall we say? Shall we confess their Force and Power over the Soul, shall we allow them to be Beauties of the most exquisite kind and yet insist on their being expunged? And why? except it be to reduce the Flights of an exalted Genius by fixing the Standard of Excellence on the practice of Inferior Writers, who wanted parts to execute such great designs, or to accommodate them to the narrow ideas of small Criticks, who want souls large enough to comprehend them?

Our Old Writers thought no personage whatever unworthy a place in the Drama to which they could annex what may be called a *Seity*, that is, to which they could allot Manners and Employment peculiar to itself. The severest of the Antients cannot be more eminent for the constant Preservation of Uniformity of Character than Shakespeare; and Shakespeare in no instance supports his Characters with more exactness than in the conduct of his Ideal Beings. The Ghost in *Hamlet* is a shining proof of this excellence.

But in consequence of the custom of tracing the Events of a Play minutely from a Novel the authors were sometimes led to represent a mere human creature in circumstances not quite consonant to Nature, of a disposition rather wild and extravagant, and in both cases more especially repugnant to modern ideas. This indeed required particular indulgence from the spectator, but it was an indulgence which seldom missed of being amply repaid. Let the writer but once be allowed, as a necessary *Datum*, the possibility of any Character's being placed in such a situation or possest of so peculiar a turn of mind, the behaviour of the Character is perfectly natural. Shakespeare, though the Child of Fancy, seldom or never drest up a common mortal in any other than the modest dress of Nature. . . . *Shylock*'s Contract, with the Penalty of the Pound of Flesh, though not Shakespeare's own fiction is perhaps rather improbable—at least it would not be regarded as a happy Dramatick Incident in a modern Play; and yet, having once taken it for granted, how beautifully, nay, how naturally is the Character sustained! (pp. 443-44)

> *George Colman, in an extract from* Shakespeare, the Critical Heritage: 1753-1765, *Vol. 4, edited by Brian Vickers, Routledge & Kegan Paul, 1976, pp. 440-49.*

SAMUEL JOHNSON   (essay date 1765)

[*Johnson has long held an important place in the history of Shakespearean criticism. He is considered the foremost representative of moderate English Neoclassicism and is credited by some literary historians with freeing Shakespeare from the strictures of the three unities valued by strict Neoclassicists: that dramas should have a single setting, take place in less than twenty-four hours, and have a causally connected plot. More recent scholars portray him as a critic who was able to synthesize existing critical theory rather than as an innovative theoretician. Johnson was a master of Augustan prose style and a personality who dominated the literary world of his epoch. In the following excerpt on* The Merchant of Venice, *taken from the notes in his 1765 edition of Shakespeare's plays, Johnson comments that both the comic and serious portions of the play satisfy their ends. He also notes that the probabilities of the casket and bond stories could not be maintained on their own, and, in this respect, he finds their union in one event "eminently happy." Other critics who have addressed the probability of events in* The Merchant of Venice *include Nicholas Rowe (1709), Charles Gildon (1710), and George Colman (1761). In addition, Johnson's favorable remarks on Shakespeare's multiple plot structure have been reiterated by nearly all subsequent critics, most notably August Wilhelm Schlegel (1811) and Harley Granville-Barker (1930). For an opposing view on this issue, see the excerpt by B. Walwyn (1782).*]

Of *The Merchant of Venice* the stile is even and easy, with few peculiarities of diction, or anomalies of construction. The comick part raises laughter, and the serious fixes expectation. The probability of either one or the other story cannot be maintained. The union of two actions in one event is in this drama eminently happy. Dryden was much pleased with his own ad-

dress in connecting the two plots of his *Spanish Friar*, which yet, I believe, the critick will find excelled by this play. (p. 241)

> *Samuel Johnson, "Notes on Shakespeare's Plays: 'The Merchant of Venice',"* in his *The Yale Edition of the Works of Samuel Johnson: Johnson on Shakespeare, Vol. VII, edited by Arthur Sherbo, Yale University Press, 1968, pp. 217-41.*

JOHN POTTER   (essay date 1771-72)

[*Potter was an English miscellany writer whose Shakespearean criticism was originally published as a series of theatrical reviews in several newspapers between 1771 and 1772. In the following excerpt, from a review collected in his* Theatrical Review; or, New Companion to the Playhouse *(1771-72), Potter maintains that though the unities of time and place "are materially broken" in* The Merchant of Venice, *and its plot "irregular," the play contains many beauties and sublime sentiments. Potter especially praises the figure of Shylock, in whom he claims Shakespeare has captured the very "quintessence" of the Jewish character. Further commentary on the significance of Shylock's Jewishness—a prominent issue in nineteenth-century criticism of* The Merchant of Venice—*can be found in the excerpts by August Wilhelm Schlegel (1811), William Hazlitt (1817), Heinrich Heine (1838), Hermann Ulrici (1839), Rudolf von Ihering (1872), and A. Pietscher (1881). Also, see the excerpts by Nicholas Rowe (1709), Charles Gildon (1710), George Colman (1761), and Samuel Johnson (1765) for earlier commentary on Shakespeare's violation of Neoclassical rules in this play.*]

The Plot [of *The Merchant of Venice*] is well contrived, notwithstanding it is irregular; but the Unities of Time and Place are materially broken. The Characters are well chosen, and in general supported in a masterly Manner. The Incidents are not only numerous but pleasing and affecting, and many of the Sentiments are truly sublime. In short, tho' this Piece hath many defects its beauties are infinitely more numerous.—With what art and perfect knowledge of human Nature in her most degenerated State has the Poet drawn the Character of *Shylock*! How nobly has he availed himself of the general Character of the *Jews*, the very Quintessence of which he has displayed in a delightful manner in order to enrich this Character. And though he has evidently deviated from a Matter of fact (according to Tradition), in representing the Jew the Hero of Villainy and Barbarity instead of the Christian, popular Prejudice will sufficiently vindicate him; not that we think he was absolutely bound to adhere to the matter of fact, if it really was so. After all, the Picture here drawn is so disgraceful to human Nature, that we doubt whether it ever had an Original. (pp. 433-34)

> *John Potter, in an extract from* Shakespeare, the Critical Heritage: 1765-1774, *Vol. 5, edited by Brian Vickers, Routledge & Kegan Paul, 1979, pp. 433-34.*

B. WALWYN   (essay date 1782)

[*Walwyn was an English playwright, essayist, novelist, and the author of* An Essay on Comedy *(1782), from which the following excerpt is taken. In it, he comments on the use of underplots in dramatic works, which he, against the accepted opinion of Neoclassicists, maintains are not absolutely necessary if the main plot provides substantial interest. Walwyn cites* The Merchant of Venice *as a case in which the underplot of the rings detracts from the pleasure of the main story, claiming that the play naturally ends with the trial and that the business of the rings in Act V is "more proper for an Interlude." For further commentary on Shakespeare's combination of plots in* The Merchant of Venice, *see the excerpts by Samuel Johnson (1765), August Wilhelm Schlegel (1811), Hermann Ulrici (1839), Denton J. Snider (1890), and Harley Granville-Barker (1930).]*

Criticism has authoritively said, an under-plot is indispensible. Surely this law, like every other literary edict, has arisen more from example than necessity. Ancient comic writers made use of these plots—not through necessity, but a voluntary desire of giving the whole design a more pleasing variety. How then should it become an edict for every other writer to observe? Although their use should not be denied, yet their absolute necessity should not be countenanced; for that depends entirely on their utility. So that if one principal design is capable of a sufficient variety to render it interesting, an under-plot would then only tend to confuse those scenes it was meant to embellish. In reality they too frequently weaken the fabric they were meant to support. The necessity of winding up the under-plot in the *Merchant of Venice* has tacked what would have been more proper for an Interlude to one of the most interesting Comedies of the immortal Shakespeare. The compleat unity of action finishes with the trial. Hence, Shakespeare's powers cannot banish from us that unpleasing emotion which every person of taste and sensibility must experience during the fifth act. It can only be compared to the necessity of turning our attention from the ocean to a fish-pond. (p. 325)

> *B. Walwyn, in an extract from* Shakespeare, the Critical Heritage: 1774-1801, Vol. 6, *edited by Brian Vickers, Routledge & Kegan Paul, 1981, pp. 324-27.*

AUGUST WILHELM SCHLEGEL (essay date 1811)

[A prominent German Romantic critic, Schlegel holds a key place in the history of Shakespeare's reputation in European criticism. His translations of thirteen of the plays are still considered the best German editions of Shakespeare. Schlegel was also a leading spokesman for the Romantic movement, which permanently overthrew the Neoclassical contention that Shakespeare was a child of nature whose plays lacked artistic form. In the following comments on The Merchant of Venice, *first published in 1811, Schlegel calls the play "one of Shakspeare's most perfect works" and "a wonder of ingenuity and art for the reflecting critic." He especially praises the characterization of Shylock and, unlike John Potter (1771-72), states that the Jew is strongly marked with originality and is not a mere abstraction of "national sentiments." Like Samuel Johnson (1765), Schlegel also praises Shakespeare's handling of his double plot, noting how the casket and bond stories are each rendered "natural and probable" by the presence of the other. Last, the critic regards the final scene of* The Merchant of Venice *as Shakespeare's means of transcending the "gloomy impressions" of Antonio's acquittal and Shylock's condemnation, thus concluding his play "with the most exhilarating mirth." The importance of Act V and the so-called ring episode in* The Merchant of Venice *has been debated by such subsequent critics as William Hazlitt (1817), Anna Brownell Jameson (1833), G. G. Gervinus (1849-50), Harley Granville-Barker (1930), C. L. Barber (1959), Barbara K. Lewalski (1962), A. D. Moody (1964), James E. Siemon (1970), R. Chris Hassel, Jr. (1970), Richard Horwich (1977), Alice N. Benston (1979), and Anne Parten (1982). Also, for further commentary on the significance of Shylock's Jewishness, see the excerpts by William Hazlitt (1817), Heinrich Heine (1838), Hermann Ulrici (1839), Rudolf von Ihering (1872), and A. Pietscher (1881).]*

The *Merchant of Venice* is one of Shakspeare's most perfect works: popular to an extraordinary degree, and calculated to produce the most powerful effect on the stage, and at the same time a wonder of ingenuity and art for the reflecting critic. Shylock, the Jew, is one of the inimitable masterpieces of

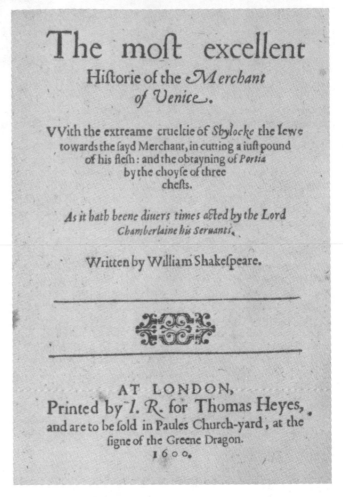

Title page of the First Quarto of The Merchant of Venice *(1600).*

characterization which are to be found only in Shakspeare. It is easy for both poet and player to exhibit a caricature of national sentiments, modes of speaking, and gestures. Shylock, however, is everything but a common Jew: he possesses a strongly-marked and original individuality, and yet we perceive a light touch of Judaism in everything he says or does. . . . In tranquil moments, all that is foreign to the European blood and Christian sentiments is less perceptible, but in passion the national stamp comes out more strongly marked. . . . Shylock is a man of information, in his own way, even a thinker, only he has not discovered the region where human feelings dwell; his morality is founded on the disbelief in goodness and magnanimity. The desire to avenge the wrongs and indignities heaped upon his nation is, after avarice, his strongest spring of action. His hate is naturally directed chiefly against those Christians who are actuated by truly Christian sentiments: a disinterested love of our neighbour seems to him the most unrelenting persecution of the Jews. The letter of the law is his idol; he refuses to lend an ear to the voice of mercy, which, from the mouth of Portia, speaks to him with heavenly eloquence: he insists on rigid and inflexible justice, and at last it recoils on his own head. Thus he becomes a symbol of the general history of his unfortunate nation. The melancholy and self-sacrificing magnanimity of Antonio is affectingly sublime. Like a princely merchant, he is surrounded with a whole train of noble friends. The contrast which this forms to the selfish cruelty of the usurer Shylock was necessary to redeem the honour of human nature. The danger which almost to the close of the fourth act, hangs over Antonio, and which the imagination is almost afraid to approach, would fill the mind with too painful anxiety, if the poet did not also provide for its recreation and diversion. This is effected in an especial manner by the scenes at Portia's country-seat, which transport the spectator into quite another world. And yet they are closely connected with the main business by the chain of cause and effect: Bassanio's preparations for his courtship are the cause of Antonio's subscribing the dangerous bond; and Portia again, by the counsel and advice of her uncle, a famous lawyer, effects the safety of her lover's friend. But the relations of the dramatic composition are the while admirably observed in yet another respect. The trial between Shylock and Antonio is indeed recorded as being a real event, still, for all that, it must ever remain an unheard-of and singular case. Shakspeare has therefore associated it with a love intrigue not less extraordinary: the one consequently is rendered natural and probable by means of the other. A rich, beautiful and clever heiress, who can only be won by solving the riddle—the locked caskets—the foreign princes, who come to try the venture—all this powerfully excites the imagination with the splendour of an olden tale of marvels. The two scenes in which, first the Prince of Morocco, in the language of Eastern hyperbole, and then the self-conceited Prince of Arragon, make their choice among the caskets, serve merely to raise our curiosity, and give employment to our wits; but on the third, where the two lovers stand trembling before the inevitable choice, which in one moment must unite or separate them for ever, Shakspeare has lavished all the charms of feeling—all the magic of poesy. We share in the rapture of Portia and Bassanio at the fortunate choice: we easily conceive why they are so fond of each other, for they are both most deserving of love. The judgment scene, with which the fourth act is occupied, is in itself a perfect drama, concentrating in itself the interest of the whole. The knot is now untied, and according to the common ideas of theatrical satisfaction, the curtain ought to drop. But the poet was unwilling to dismiss his audience with the gloomy impressions which Antonio's acquittal, effected with so much difficulty, and contrary to all expectation, and the condemnation of Shylock, were calculated to leave behind them; he has therefore added the fifth act by way of a musical afterlude in the piece itself. The episode of Jessica, the fugitive daughter of the Jew, in whom Shakspeare has contrived to throw a veil of sweetness over the national features, and the artifice by which Portia and her companion are enabled to rally their newly-married husbands, supply him with the necessary materials. The scene opens with the playful prattling of two lovers in a summer evening; it is followed by soft music, and a rapturous eulogy on this powerful disposer of the human mind and the world; the principal characters then make their appearance, and after a simulated quarrel, which is gracefully maintained, the whole ends with the most exhilarating mirth. (pp. 388-90)

> August Wilhelm Schlegel, "Criticisms on Shakespeare's Comedies," in his A Course of Lectures on Dramatic Art and Literature, edited by Rev. A. J. W. Morrison, translated by John Black, revised edition, 1846. Reprint by AMS Press, Inc., 1965, pp. 379-99.

WILLIAM HAZLITT　(essay date 1817)

[Hazlitt is considered a leading Shakespearean critic of the English Romantic movement. A prolific essayist and critic on a wide range of subjects, Hazlitt remarked in the preface to his Characters of Shakespear's Plays, first published in 1817, that he was inspired by the German critic August Wilhelm Schlegel, and was determined to supplant what he considered the pernicious influence of Samuel Johnson's Shakespearean criticism. Hazlitt's criticism is typically Romantic in its emphasis on character studies. His experience as a drama critic was an important factor in shaping his descriptive, as opposed to analytical, interpretations of Shakespeare. In the following excerpt, taken from the work mentioned above, Hazlitt offers the first substantial defense of Shylock as a man justified in his hate towards the Christians. In fact, Hazlitt maintains that the Jew engages our sympathies more readily than any of the Venetians, whom he calls hypocritical and prejudiced, and that it is not until the trial that we turn against Shylock. Later critics who have similarly regarded Shylock as a sympathetic figure, or who have seriously questioned the moral behavior and religious sincerity of the Christians, include Karl Elze (1871), Arthur Quiller-Couch (1926), Harold C. Goddard (1951), A. D. Moody (1964), R. Chris Hassel, Jr. (1970), and René Girard (1978). Hazlitt also comments on the final act of The Merchant of Venice, which he describes as "one of the happiest instances of Shakespear's knowledge of the principles of the drama." For further commentary on the significance of Act V in Shakespeare's play, see the excerpts by August Wilhelm Schlegel (1811), Anna Brownell Jameson (1833), G. G. Gervinus (1849-50), Harley Granville-Barker (1930), C. L. Barber (1959), Barbara K. Lewalski (1962), A. D. Moody (1964), James E. Siemon (1970), R. Chris Hassel, Jr. (1970), Richard Horwich (1977), Alice N. Benston (1979), and Anne Parten (1982).]

[The Merchant of Venice] is a play that in spite of the change of manners and prejudices still holds undisputed possession of the stage. . . . In proportion as Shylock has ceased to be a popular bugbear, "baited with the rabble's curse" [Macbeth, V. viii. 29], he becomes a half-favourite with the philosophical part of the audience, who are disposed to think that Jewish revenge is at least as good as Christian injuries. Shylock is a good hater; "a man no less sinned against than sinning" [King Lear, III. ii. 60]. If he carries his revenge too far, yet he has strong grounds for "the lodged hate he bears Anthonio" [IV. i. 60], which he explains with equal force of eloquence and reason. He seems the depositary of the vengeance of his race; and though the long habit of brooding over daily insults and injuries has crusted over his temper with inveterate misanthropy, and hardened him against the contempt of mankind, this adds but little to the triumphant pretensions of his enemies. There is a strong, quick, and deep sense of justice mixed up with the gall and bitterness of his resentment. The constant apprehension of being burnt alive, plundered, banished, reviled, and trampled on, might be supposed to sour the most forbearing nature, and to take something from that "milk of human kindness" [Macbeth, I. v. 17], with which his persecutors contemplated his indignities. The desire of revenge is almost inseparable from the sense of wrong; and we can hardly help sympathising with the proud spirit, hid beneath his "Jewish gaberdine" [I. iii. 112], stung to madness by repeated undeserved provocations, and labouring to throw off the load of obloquy and oppression heaped upon him and all his tribe by one desperate act of "lawful" revenge, till the ferociousness of the means by which he is to execute his purpose, and the pertinacity with which he adheres to it, turn us against him; but even at last, when disappointed of the sanguinary revenge with which he had glutted his hopes, and exposed to beggary and contempt by the letter of the law on which he had insisted with so little remorse, we pity him, and think him hardly dealt with by his judges. In all his answers and retorts upon his adversaries, he has the best not only of the argument but of the question, reasoning on their own principles and practice.

They are so far from allowing of any measure of equal dealing, of common justice or humanity between themselves and the Jew, that even when they come to ask a favour of him, and Shylock reminds them that "on such a day they spit upon him, another spurned him, another called him dog, and for these curtesies request he'll lend them so much monies" [I. iii. 126-29]—Anthonio, his old enemy, instead of any acknowledgment of the shrewdness and justice of his remonstrance, which would have been preposterous in a respectable Catholic merchant in those times, threatens him with a repetition of the same treatment—

> I am as like to call thee so again,
> To spit on thee again, to spurn thee too.
>   [I. iii. 130-31]

After this, the appeal to the Jew's mercy, as if there were any common principle of right and wrong between them, is the rankest hypocrisy, or the blindest prejudice; and the Jew's answer to one of Anthonio's friends, who asks him what his pound of forfeit flesh is good for, is irresistible—

> To bait fish withal; if it will feed nothing else,
> it will feed my revenge. He hath disgrac'd me,
> and hinder'd me of half a million, laughed at
> my losses, mock'd at my gains, scorn'd my
> nation, thwarted my bargains, cool'd my friends,
> heated mine enemies; and what's his reason? I
> am a Jew. . . . If a Jew wrong a Christian, what
> is his humility? revenge. If a Christian wrong
> a Jew, what should his sufferance be by Christian example? why revenge. The villainy you
> teach me I will execute, and it shall go hard
> but I will better the instruction.
>   [III. i. 53-73]

The whole of the trial-scene, both before and after the entrance of Portia, is a master-piece of dramatic skill. The legal acuteness, the passionate declamations, the sound maxims of jurisprudence, the wit and irony interspersed in it, the fluctuations of hope and fear in the different persons, and the completeness and suddenness of the catastrophe, cannot be surpassed. Shylock, who is his own counsel, defends himself well, and is triumphant on all the general topics that are urged against him, and only fails through a legal flaw. (pp. 165-68)

The keenness of his revenge awakes all his faculties; and he beats back all opposition to his purpose, whether grave or gay, whether of wit or argument, with an equal degree of earnestness and self-possession. (p. 168)

Portia is not a very great favourite with us; neither are we in love with her maid, Nerissa. Portia has a certain degree of affectation and pedantry about her, which is very unusual in Shakespear's women, but which perhaps was a proper qualification for the office of a "civil doctor," which she undertakes and executes so successfully. The speech about Mercy is very well; but there are a thousand finer ones in Shakespear. We do not admire the scene of the caskets: and object entirely to the Black Prince, Morocchius. We should like Jessica better if she had not deceived and robbed her father, and Lorenzo, if he had not married a Jewess, though he thinks he has a right to wrong a Jew. (pp. 168-69)

The graceful winding up of this play in the fifth act, after the tragic business is despatched, is one of the happiest instances of Shakespear's knowledge of the principles of the drama. We do not mean the pretended quarrel between Portia and Nerissa

and their husbands about the rings, which is amusing enough, but the conversation just before and after the return of Portia to her own house [V. i. 54-110]. . . . There is a number of beautiful thoughts crowded into that short space, and linked together by the most natural transitions. (pp. 169-70)

> *William Hazlitt, " 'The Merchant of Venice'," in his* Characters of Shakespear's Plays & Lectures on the English Poets, *The Macmillan Company, 1903, pp. 165-71.*

MRS. [ANNA BROWNELL] JAMESON   (essay date 1833)

[*Jameson was a well-known nineteenth-century essayist. Her essays and criticism span the end of the Romantic age and the beginning of Victorian realism, reflecting elements from both periods. She is best remembered for her study* Shakspeare's Heroines *(1833), which was originally published in a slightly different form in 1832 as* Characteristics of Women: Moral, Poetical, and Historical. *This work demonstrates both her historical interests and her sympathetic appreciation of Shakespeare's female characters. In the excerpt below, Jameson presents one of the first full-length character studies of Portia, whom she classifies with Isabella, Beatrice, and Rosalind as "characters of intellect." As such, Jameson takes issue with both August Wilhelm Schlegel's and William Hazlitt's assessments of Portia's nature—the former for referring to her as "clever," the latter for calling her affected and pedantic (see excerpts above, 1811 and 1817). Instead, Jameson maintains that Portia unites "all the noblest and most loveable qualities that ever met together in woman." Jameson also discusses the scene in which Bassanio wins Portia's hand in marriage and the final act of the play, which she claims Shakespeare wrote to conclude* The Merchant of Venice *on a positive note. For further commentary on the relation of Act V to the remainder of the play, see the excerpts by August Wilhelm Schlegel (1811), William Hazlitt (1817), G. G. Gervinus (1849-50), Harley Granville-Barker (1930), C. L. Barber (1959), Barbara K. Lewalski (1962), A. D. Moody (1964), James E. Siemon (1970), R. Chris Hassel, Jr. (1970), Richard Horwich (1977), Alice N. Benston (1979), and Anne Parten (1982).*]

Portia, Isabella [in *Measure for Measure*], Beatrice [in *Much Ado about Nothing*], and Rosalind [in *As You Like It*], may be classed together as characters of intellect, because, when compared with others, they are at once distinguished by their mental superiority. In Portia, it is intellect kindled into romance by a poetical imagination; in Isabel, it is intellect elevated by religious principle; in Beatrice, intellect animated by spirit; in Rosalind, intellect softened by sensibility. The wit which is lavished on each is profound, or pointed, or sparkling, or playful—but always feminine: like spirits distilled from flowers, it always reminds us of its origin; it is a volatile essence, sweet as powerful; and to pursue the comparison a step further, the wit of Portia is like attar of roses, rich and concentrated; that of Rosalind, like cotton dipped in aromatic vinegar; the wit of Beatrice is like sal-volatile, and that of Isabel like the incense wafted to heaven. Of these four exquisite characters, considered as dramatic and poetical conceptions, it is difficult to pronounce which is most perfect in its way, most admirably drawn, most highly finished. But if considered in another point of view, as women and individuals, as breathing realities, clothed in flesh and blood, I believe we must assign the first rank to Portia, as uniting in herself, in a more eminent degree than the others, all the noblest and most loveable qualities that ever met together in woman. . . . (pp. 38-9)

It is singular that hitherto no critical justice has been done to the character of Portia; it is yet more wonderful that one of the finest writers on the eternal subject of Shakspeare and his perfections should accuse Portia of pedantry and affectation, and confess she is not a great favourite of his [see excerpt above by William Hazlitt, 1817]—a confession quite worthy of him who avers his predilection for servant-maids, and his preference of the Fannys and the Pamelas over the Clementinas and Clarissas. Schlegel, who has given several pages to a rapturous eulogy on the ''Merchant of Venice,'' simply designates Portia as a ''rich, beautiful, clever heiress'' [see excerpt above, 1811]. Whether the fault lie in the writer or translator, I do protest against the word clever. Portia *clever!* What an epithet to apply to this heavenly compound of talent, feeling, wisdom, beauty, and gentleness! Now, would it not be well if this common and comprehensive word were more accurately defined, or at least more accurately used? It signifies properly, not so much the possession of high powers as dexterity in the adaptation of certain faculties (not necessarily of a high order) to a certain end or aim—not always the worthiest. It implies something commonplace, inasmuch as it speaks the presence of the *active* and *perceptive*, with a deficiency of the *feeling* and *reflective* powers; and, applied to a woman, does it not almost invariably suggest the idea of something we should distrust or shrink from, if not allied to a higher nature? . . . If Portia had been created as a mere instrument to bring about a dramatic catastrophe—if she had merely detected the flaw in Antonio's bond and used it as a means to baffle the Jew, she might have been pronounced a clever woman. But what Portia does is forgotten in what she *is*. The rare and harmonious blending of energy, reflection, and feeling, in her fine character, makes the epithet *clever* sound like a discord as applied to *her,* and places her infinitely beyond the slight praise of Richardson and Schlegel, neither of whom appears to have fully comprehended her.

These and other critics have been apparently so dazzled and engrossed by the amazing character of Shylock, that Portia has received less than justice at their hands; while the fact is, that Shylock is not a finer or more finished character in his way than Portia is in hers. These two splendid figures are worthy of each other—worthy of being placed together within the same rich framework of enchanting poetry and glorious and graceful forms. She hangs beside the terrible, inexorable Jew, the brilliant lights of her character set off by the shadowy power of his, like a magnificent beauty-breathing Titian by the side of a gorgeous Rembrandt.

Portia is endued with her own share of those delightful qualities which Shakspeare has lavished on many of his female characters; but besides the dignity, the sweetness, and tenderness which should distinguish her sex generally, she is individualised by qualities peculiar to herself; by her high mental powers, her enthusiasm of temperament, her decision of purpose, and her buoyancy of spirit. These are innate; she has other distinguishing qualities more external, and which are the result of the circumstances in which she is placed. Thus she is the heiress of a princely name and countless wealth; a train of obedient pleasures have ever waited round her; and from infancy she has breathed an atmosphere redolent of perfume and blandishment. Accordingly there is a commanding grace, a highbred, airy elegance, a spirit of magnificence, in all that she does and says, as one to whom splendour had been familiar from her very birth. She treads as though her footsteps had been among marble palaces, beneath roofs of fretted gold, o'er cedar floors and pavements of jasper and porphyry; amid gardens full of statues, and flowers, and fountains, and haunting music. She is full of penetrative wisdom, and genuine tenderness, and lively wit; but as she has never known want, or grief, or fear,

or disappointment, her wisdom is without a touch of the sombre or the sad; her affections are all mixed up with faith, hope, and joy; and her wit has not a particle of malevolence or causticity. (pp. 39-41)

The sudden plan which she forms for the release of her husband's friend, her disguise, and her deportment as the young and learned doctor, would appear forced and improbable in any other woman, but in Portia are the simple and natural result of her character. The quickness with which she perceives the legal advantage which may be taken of the circumstances; the spirit of adventure with which she engages in the masquerading, and the decision, firmness, and intelligence with which she executes her generous purpose, are all in perfect keeping, and nothing appears forced—nothing as introduced merely for theatrical effect.

But all the finest parts of Portia's character are brought to bear in the trial scene. There she shines forth all her divine self. Her intellectual powers, her elevated sense of religion, her high, honourable principles, her best feelings as a woman, are all displayed. She maintains at first a calm self-command, as one sure of carrying her point in the end; yet the painful, heart-thrilling uncertainty in which she keeps the whole court, until suspense verges upon agony, is not contrived for effect merely; it is necessary and inevitable. She has two objects in view—to deliver her husband's friend, and to maintain her husband's honour by the discharge of his just debt, though paid out of her own wealth ten times over. It is evident that she would rather owe the safety of Antonio to anything rather than the legal quibble with which her cousin Bellario has armed her, and which she reserves as a last resource. Thus all the speeches addressed to Shylock in the first instance are either direct or indirect experiments on his temper and feelings. She must be understood, from the beginning to the end, as examining with intense anxiety the effect of her own words on his mind and countenance; as watching for that relenting spirit which she hopes to awaken either by reason or persuasion. She begins by an appeal to his mercy, in that matchless piece of eloquence which, with an irresistible and solemn pathos, falls upon the heart like ''gentle dew from heaven'' [*Henry VIII*, IV. ii. 133]:—but in vain; for that blessed dew drops not more fruitless and unfelt on the parched sand of the desert, than do these heavenly words upon the ear of Shylock. She next attacks his avarice—

> Shylock, there's *thrice* thy money offer'd thee.
> [IV. i. 227]

Then she appeals in the same breath, both to his avarice and his pity—

> Be merciful!
> Take thrice thy money. Bid me tear the bond.
> [IV. i. 233-34]

All that she says afterwards—her strong expressions, which are calculated to strike a shuddering horror through the nerves; the reflections she interposes, her delays and circumlocution to give time for any latent feeling of commiseration to display itself; all, all are premeditated, and tend in the same manner to the object she has in view. Thus—

> You must prepare your bosom for his knife. . . .
> Therefore lay bare your bosom!
> [IV. i. 245, 252]

These two speeches, though addressed apparently to Antonio, are spoken *at* Shylock, and are evidently intended to penetrate *his* bosom. In the same spirit she asks for the balance to weigh the pound of flesh; and entreats of Shylock to have a surgeon ready. . . . (pp. 42-4)

So unwilling is her sanguine and generous spirit to resign all hope, or to believe that humanity is absolutely extinct in the bosom of the Jew, that she calls on Antonio, as a last resource, to speak for himself. His gentle yet manly resignation—the deep pathos of his farewell, and the affectionate allusion to herself in his last address to Bassanio . . . are well calculated to swell that emotion which through the whole scene must have been labouring suppressed within her heart.

At length the crisis arrives, for patience and womanhood can endure no longer; and when Shylock, carrying his savage bent "to the last hour of act" [IV. i. 19] springs on his victim— "A sentence! come, prepare!" [IV. i. 304], then the smothered scorn, indignation, and disgust burst forth with an impetuosity which interferes with the judicial solemnity she had at first affected; particularly in the speech—

> Therefore, prepare thee to cut off the flesh.
> Shed thou no blood; nor cut thou less, nor more,
> But just the pound of flesh: if thou tak'st more
> Or less than a just pound,—be it but so much
> As makes it light, or heavy, in the substance,
> Or the division of the twentieth part
> Of one poor scruple; nay, if the scale do turn
> But in the estimation of a hair,—
> Thou diest, and all thy goods are confiscate.
>
> [IV. i. 324-32]

But she afterwards recovers her propriety, and triumphs with a cooler scorn and a more self-possessed exultation.

It is clear that, to feel the full force and dramatic beauty of this marvellous scene, we must go along with Portia as well as with Shylock; we must understand her concealed purpose, keep in mind her noble motives, and pursue in our fancy the under-current of feeling working in her mind throughout. The terror and the power of Shylock's character—his deadly and inexorable malice—would be too oppressive; the pain and pity too intolerable, and the horror of the possible issue too overwhelming, but for the intellectual relief afforded by this double source of interest and contemplation. (pp. 44-5)

A prominent feature in Portia's character is that confiding, buoyant spirit which mingles with all her thoughts and affections. . . . Portia's strength of intellect takes a natural tinge from the flush and bloom of her young and prosperous existence, and from her fervid imagination. In the casket scene, she fears indeed the issue of the trial, on which more than her life is hazarded; but while she trembles, her hope is stronger than her fear. While Bassanio is contemplating the caskets, she suffers herself to dwell for one moment on the possibility of disappointment and misery—

> Let music sound while he doth make his choice;
> Then if he lose, he makes a swan-like end,
> Fading in music: that the comparison
> May stand more proper, my eye shall be the stream
> And wat'ry death-bed for him.
>
> [III. ii. 43-7]

Then immediately follows that revulsion of feeling so beautifully characteristic of the hopeful, trusting, mounting spirit of this noble creature—

> But he may win!
> And what is music then?—then music is
> Even as the flourish, when true subjects bow

> To a new-crowned monarch: such it is
> As are those dulcet sounds at break of day
> That creep into the dreaming bridegroom's ear
> And summon him to marriage. Now he goes
> With no less presence, but with much more love,
> Than young Alcides, when he did redeem
> The virgin tribute paid by howling Troy
> To the sea monster. I stand here for sacrifice.
>
> [III. ii. 47-57]

Here, not only the feeling itself, born of the elastic and sanguine spirit which had never been touched by grief; but the images in which it comes arrayed to her fancy; the bridegroom waked by music on his wedding-morn; the new-crowned monarch,— the comparison of Bassanio to the young Alcides, and of herself to the daughter of Laomedon, are all precisely what would have suggested themselves to the fine poetical imagination of Portia in such a moment. (pp. 47-9)

Her subsequent surrender of herself in heart and soul, of her maiden freedom, and her vast possessions, can never be read without deep emotion; for not only all the tenderness and delicacy of a devoted woman are here blended with all the dignity which becomes the princely heiress of Belmont, but the serious, measured self-possession of her address to her lover when all suspense is over, and all concealment superfluous, is most beautifully consistent with the character. It is, in truth, an awful moment, that in which a gifted woman first discovers that, besides talents and powers, she has also passions and affections; when she first begins to suspect their vast importance in the sum of her existence; when she first confesses that her happiness is no longer in her own keeping, but is surrendered for ever and for ever into the dominion of another! The possession of uncommon powers of mind are so far from affording relief or resource in the first intoxicating surprise—I had almost said terror—of such a revolution, that they render it more intense. The sources of thought multiply beyond calculation the sources of feeling; and mingled, they rush together, a torrent deep as strong. Because Portia is endued with that enlarged comprehension which looks before and after, she does not feel the less, but the more: because from the height of her commanding intellect she can contemplate the force, the tendency, the consequences of her own sentiments—because she is fully sensible of her own situation and the value of all she concedes— the concession is not made with less entireness and devotion of heart, less confidence in the truth and worth of her lover, than when Juliet, in a similar moment, but without any such intrusive reflections—any check but the instinctive delicacy of her sex, flings herself and her fortunes at the feet of her lover—

> And all my fortunes at thy foot I'll lay,
> And follow thee, my lord, through all the world.
>
> [*Romeo and Juliet,* II. ii. 147-48]

In Portia's confession, which is not breathed from a moonlit balcony, but spoken openly in the presence of her attendants and vassals, there is nothing of the passionate self-abandonment of Juliet, nor of the artless simplicity of Miranda [in *The Tempest*], but a consciousness and a tender seriousness, approaching to solemnity, which are not less touching—

> You see me, Lord Bassanio, where I stand,
> Such as I am: though for myself alone
> I would not be ambitious in my wish
> To wish myself much better; yet, for you,
> I would be trebled twenty times myself;
> A thousand times more fair, ten thousand times
> More rich; that only to stand high in your account,

I might in virtues, beauties, livings, friends,
Exceed account; but the full sum of me
Is sum of something; which to term in gross,
Is an unlesson'd girl, unschool'd, unpractised;
Happy in this, she is not yet so old
But she may learn; and happier than this,
She is not bred so dull but she can learn;
Happiest of all is, that her gentle spirit
Commits itself to yours to be directed
As from her lord, her governor, her king.
Myself, and what is mine, to you and yours
Is now converted. But now I was the lord
Of this fair mansion, master of my servants,
Queen o'er myself! and even now, but now,
This house, these servants, and this same myself,
Are yours, my lord.

[III. ii. 149-71]

We must also remark that the sweetness, the solicitude, the subdued fondness which she afterwards displays relative to the letter, are as true to the softness of her sex as the generous self-denial with which she urges the departure of Bassanio (having first given him a husband's right over herself and all her countless wealth) is consistent with a reflecting mind, and a spirit at once tender, reasonable, and magnanimous. (pp. 49-51)

Her reflections on the friendship between her husband and Antonio are as full of deep meaning as of tenderness; and her portrait of a young coxcomb, in the same scene, is touched with a truth and spirit which show with what a keen observing eye she has looked upon men and things. . . . (p. 52)

And in the description of her various suitors, in the first scene with Nerissa, what infinite power, wit, and vivacity! She half checks herself as she is about to give the reins to her sportive humour: "In truth, I know it is a sin to be a mocker" [I. ii. 57]. But if it carries her away, it is so perfectly good-natured, so temperately bright, so lady-like, it is ever without offence; and, so far, most unlike the satirical, poignant, unsparing wit of Beatrice, "misprising what she looks on" [*Much Ado about Nothing*, III. i. 52]. In fact, I can scarce conceive a greater contrast than between the vivacity of Portia and the vivacity of Beatrice. Portia, with all her airy brilliance, is supremely soft and dignified; everything she says or does displays her capability for profound thought and feeling as well as her lively and romantic disposition; and as I have seen in an Italian garden a fountain flinging round its wreaths of showery light, while the many-coloured Iris hung brooding above it, in its calm and soul-felt glory; so in Portia the wit is ever kept subordinate to the poetry, and we still feel the tender, the intellectual, and the imaginative part of the character, as superior to, and presiding over, its spirit and vivacity.

In the last act, Shylock and his machinations being dismissed from our thoughts, and the rest of the *dramatis personae* assembled together at Belmont, all our interest and all our attention are rivetted on Portia, and the conclusion leaves the most delightful impression on the fancy. The playful equivoque of the rings, the sportive tricks she puts on her husband, and her thorough enjoyment of the jest, which she checks just as it is proceeding beyond the bounds of propriety, show how little she was displeased by the sacrifice of her gift, and are all consistent with her bright and buoyant spirit. In conclusion, when Portia invites her company to enter her palace to refresh themselves after their travels, and talk over "these events at full" [V. i. 297], the imagination, unwilling to lose sight of

the brilliant group, follows them in gay procession from the lovely moonlight garden to marble halls and princely revels, to splendour and festive mirth, to love and happiness! (pp. 52-3)

It is observable that something of the intellectual brilliance of Portia is reflected on the other female characters of "The Merchant of Venice," so as to preserve in the midst of contrast a certain harmony and keeping. Thus Jessica, though properly kept subordinate, is certainly—

A most beautiful Pagan—a most sweet Jew.

[II. iii. 11]

She cannot be called a sketch—or if a sketch, she is like one of those dashed off in glowing colours from the rainbow palette of a Rubens; she has a rich tinge of orientalism shed over her, worthy of her eastern origin. In any other play, and in any other companionship than that of the matchless Portia, Jessica would make a very beautiful heroine of herself. Nothing can be more poetically, more classically fanciful and elegant, than the scenes between her and Lorenzo—the celebrated moonlight dialogue, for instance, which we all have by heart. Every sentiment she utters interests us for her—more particularly her bashful self-reproach when flying in the disguise of a page—

I am glad 'tis night, you do not look upon me,
For I am much asham'd of my exchange;
But love is blind, and lovers cannot see
The pretty follies that themselves commit;
For if they could, Cupid himself would blush
To see me thus transformèd to a boy.

[II. vi. 34-9]

And the enthusiastic and generous testimony to the superior graces and accomplishments of Portia comes with a peculiar grace from her lips—

Why, if two gods should play some heavenly match,
And on the wager lay two earthly women,
And Portia one, there must be something else
Pawned with the other; for the poor rude world
Hath not her fellow.

[III. v. 79-83]

We should not, however, easily pardon her for cheating her father with so much indifference, but for the perception that Shylock values his daughter far beneath his wealth—

I would my daughter were dead at my foot,
and the jewels in her ear!—would she were
hearsed at my foot, and the ducats in her coffin.

[III. i. 87-90]

Nerissa is a good specimen of a common genus of characters: she is a clever, confidential waiting-woman, who has caught a little of her lady's elegance and romance; she affects to be lively and sententious, falls in love, and makes her favour conditional on the fortune of the caskets, and, in short, mimics her mistress with good emphasis and discretion. Nerissa and the gay, talkative Gratiano are as well matched as the incomparable Portia and her magnificent and captivating lover. (pp. 57-8)

Mrs. [*Anna Brownell*] *Jameson*, "Portia," in her Shakespeare's Heroines: Characteristics of Women, Moral, Poetical, & Historical, *second edition, George Newnes, Limited, 1897, pp. 37-58.*

HEINRICH HEINE   (essay date 1838)

[*Heine was one of Germany's leading literary figures of the nineteenth century. He is best known for his* Buch der Lieder *(1827), a collection of love lyrics that were later set to music by Franz Schubert, Robert Schumann, and other composers. He was also the first major poet to adopt a humorous, ironic tone in his poetry, prose, and commentaries on politics, art, literature, and society. In the following excerpt, taken from comments written in 1838, Heine interprets* The Merchant of Venice *as a tragedy, rather than a comedy, despite the "obvious" caricaturization of Shylock and the play's comedic design, an assessment also voiced by Nicholas Rowe (1709), T. A. Ross (1934), and Graham Midgley (1960). Heine perceives this tragic effect most readily in the underlying reality Shylock represents, namely, the undeserved hatred the Jewish race has suffered. The critic emphasizes, however, that Shakespeare presents not the religious struggle between Judaism and Christianity, but the conflict between oppressors and the oppressed, noting that neither Antonio and his comrades nor Shylock emulates the spirit of their respective religions. For further commentary on the significance of Shylock's Jewishness, see the excerpts by John Potter (1771-72), August Wilhelm Schlegel (1811), William Hazlitt (1817), Hermann Ulrici (1839), Rudolf von Ihering (1872), and A. Pietscher (1881). In addition, Heine discusses the relation of Shylock and his daughter, stating that the Jew truly loves Jessica, but that she abuses his love. In her, the critic adds, Shakespeare was presenting an example of "an adventuress" and a "daughter of Eve." Further analysis of Jessica and her role in* The Merchant of Venice *can be found in the excerpts by Anna Brownell Jameson (1833), Arthur Quiller-Couch (1926), Sigurd Burckhardt (1962), and Camille Slights (1980).*]

When I saw [*The Merchant of Venice*] acted at Drury Lane a beautiful pale Englishwoman standing beside me burst into tears at the end of the fourth act, crying out several times, "the poor man is wronged." (pp. 125-26)

On account of these tears I must place *The Merchant of Venice* among Shakespeare's tragedies although he intended it as a comedy surrounding it by merry masks satyrs and cupids. Possibly Shakespeare thought it would please the public were he to represent a greedy were-wolf, a dread mythical creature thirsting for blood, thereby losing his daughter and his ducats, besides exciting general ridicule. But the poet's genius, the world-spirit which reigns in him, always supersedes his individual will. Thus it came to pass that notwithstanding the obvious caricature which Shylock presents, Shakespeare has justified in him an unfortunate race whom Providence for some secret cause has burdened with the hatred of the low and highborn populace, and who has not always consented to return love for hate.

But what do I say? Shakespeare's genius rises above the mean quarrels of two parties entertaining opposite beliefs, and his play does not actually represent either Jews or Christians but oppressors and oppressed. We also hear the madly painful shouts of joy whenever the latter are able to pay back with interest the injuries inflicted on them by their proud torturers. There is not the slightest trace of religious differences in this play, and in Shylock, Shakespeare represents a character whose nature it is to hate his enemy. In a similar manner we find that Antonio and his friends are by no means apostles of that divine gospel which commands men to love their enemies. Shylock replies to the man wishing to borrow money of him;

> Signor Antonio, many a time and oft
> In the Rialto you have rated me
> About my moneys and my usances:
> Still have I borne it with a patient shrug;

> For sufferance is the badge of all our tribe:
> You call me misbeliever, cut-throat dog;
> And spit upon my Jewish gabardine,
> And all for use of that which is mine own. . . .
> Shall I bend low, and in a bondman's key,
> With bated breath, and whispering humbleness,
> Say this,—
> 'Fair Sir, you spit on me on Wednesday last;
> You spurned me such a day; another time,
> You called me dog; and for these courtesies
> I'll lend you thus much moneys'?
> [I. iii. 106-13, 123-29]

And Antonio answers;

> I am as like to call thee so again,
> To spit on thee again, to spurn thee too.
> [I. iii. 130-31]

Have we here an example of christian love! Christianity would have been satirised had Shakespeare typified it by Shylock's enemies, men who hardly deserved to loosen his shoe-latchets. The bankrupt Antonio is a weak-spirited mortal without energy, without power to hate, and therefore without power to love, a dull worm whose flesh was really not good for much else than to serve as "bait for fish" [IV. i. 53]. Besides this he certainly does not return the fleeced Jew his three thousand ducats. Neither does Bassanio, who according to an English critic is a regular fortune-hunter, return him his money; this man borrows money for the purpose of setting himself up in grand style to marry a wealthy wife and to obtain a rich dowry. . . . (pp. 126-28)

As to Lorenzo, he is an accomplice in a most infamous robbery by which according to Prussian law he would be condemned to fifteen years' penal servitude after being branded and put in the pillory, although he had a liking for the beauties of nature for moonlight scenes and music as well as for jewels and ducats. The other noble Venetians, Antonio's friends, also seem to regard money with favour and they have naught but words, coined air for their poor friend in the midst of his misfortunes. . . . It would surely have been comparatively easy for those good friends who appeared to surround the regal mechant in crowds, to collect three thousand ducats in order to save a human life, and such a life! But these things are always rather inconvenient and so the dear good friends do nothing—nothing whatever—because they are only so-called friends, or, if you will, semi or three-quarter friends. They greatly pity the excellent merchant who formerly entertained them so well, but they do this in a calm manner and revile Shylock to their heart's content heaping bitter words on him. This also they can do without incurring any risks, and they then probably all imagine that they have done their duty. Much as we are bound to hate Shylock we can understand even him for somewhat despising these people, which he has every right to do. (pp. 129-30)

Indeed with the exception of Portia, the character of Shylock is the most worthy in the play. He loves money and makes no secret of his passion crying it out on the open market place. . . . But something he prizes more than money, namely the easing of his wounded spirit, the just vengeance for inexpressible injuries, and though they offer him ten times the amount of the borrowed sum he refuses it. (p. 131)

Yes indeed though Shylock loves his money there are things he prizes infinitely more, among other things his daughter; "Jessica, my child" [II. v. 15]. Though he curses her in overwhelming and passionate anger, longing to see her dead at his feet with the jewels in her ears and the ducats in her coffin, he loves her nevertheless more than all his jewels and his ducats. Thrust out of public life and christian society into the narrow limits of household joys, the poor Jew found himself entirely dependant on family ties, and these assume in him pathetically tender proportions. He would not have given away the turquoise ring once given him by his wife Lea for a "forest of monkeys" [III. i. 123]. When in the court of justice Bassanio addresses the following words to Antonio:

> Antonio, I am married to a wife
> Which is as dear to me as life itself;
> But life itself, my wife, and all the world,
> Are not with me esteemed above thy life:
> I would lose all, ay sacrifice them all
> Here to this devil, to deliver you.
>
> [IV. i. 282-87]

And when Gratiano adds:

> I have a wife whom I protest I love:
> I would she were in heaven, so she could
> Entreat some power to change this currish Jew.
>
> [IV. i. 290-92]

Then Shylock begins to tremble for the fate of his daughter who has married among people who can sacrifice their wives to their friends, and he says to himself in an aside and not aloud:

> These be the Christian husbands! I have a daughter
> Would any of the stock of Barabbas
> Had been her husband rather than a Christian!
>
> [IV. i. 295-97]

This passage, these silent words, are beautiful Jessica's death warrant. It was no loveless father whom she deserted, robbed and betrayed . . . Oh disgraceful betrayal! She even makes common cause with Shylock's enemies, and when at Belmont they slander him, Jessica does not look down, the colour does not leave her cheeks and she utters base words concerning her father . . . Oh abominable outrage! She has no soul, only the mind of an adventuress. She found the strict honourable home of the embittered Jew tedious, until it seemed to her a hell. The merry sound of drums and fifes had too great attractions for her frivolous mind! Did Shakespeare mean to depict a Jewess? No indeed, he only describes a daughter of Eve, one of those beautiful birds who finding themselves fledged, flutter away from the parental nest to the beloved mate. Desdemona followed the Moor, Imogene followed Posthumus in like manner! We perceive in Jessica a certain timid shame which she cannot overcome when she has to dress in boy's clothes. Perhaps in this we may recognise the mysterious shyness peculiar to her race owing to which quality its daughters possess a special charm! (pp. 132-34)

If we consider Shylock in the usual way, as a type of that stern, serious, inartistic Judaea, Portia appears on the other hand as a type of those after-blossoms of Greek intellect which in the sixteenth century spread their beautiful scent from Italy over the world, and which we now love and revere under the name of the *Renaissance*. Portia also represents bright happiness as contrasted with gloomy misfortune, which we see typified in Shylock. All her thoughts are blooming, rosy, and pure; her speech is penetrated with warm happiness and her similes, which she generally borrows from mythology, are full of beauty. In Shylock's thoughts and words, borrowed only from old testament metaphors, we get a dismal, pungent and

ugly contrast. His wit is spasmodic and pungent, he borrows his metaphors from loathsome objects and his very words are compressed discords, shrill and hissing. Men resemble their homes. We perceive how this servant of Jehovah will not suffer either an image of God, or of man made in God's image, to enter his "honourable house"; he even shuts out every sound from the hearing thereof, namely from the windows, so that sounds of heathen mummery shall not gain entrance there . . . in the beautiful palace at Belmont, on the other hand, we find a luxurious and ideal country home surrounded by light and music. Adorned suitors wander about joyfully among pictures, marble statues and high laurels, dreaming of love's mysteries, whilst Signora Portia reigns over them in all her glory, resplendent as a goddess, "golden hair adorning her temples" [I. i. 169-70].

By force of contrast the two chief figures in the play become so individualised that we positively believe them to be actual human beings, instead of a poet's fantastic creations. To us they appear still more life-like than ordinary mortals, as neither time nor death can alter them and their hearts are quickened by immortal pulsations, by divine poetry. (pp. 143-45)

> *Heinrich Heine, "Jessica" and "Portia," in his* Heine on Shakespeare: A Translation of His Notes on Shakespeare Heroines, *translated by Ida Benecke, Archibald Constable and Co., 1895, pp. 125-41, 141-49.*

HERMANN ULRICI   (essay date 1839)

[A German scholar, Ulrici was a professor of philosophy and the author of works on Greek poetry and Shakespeare. The following excerpt is from an English translation of his Über Shakespeares dramatische Kunst, und sein Verhältniss zu Calderon und Göthe, *a work first published in 1839. This study exemplifies the "philosophical criticism" developed in Germany during the nineteenth century. The immediate sources for Ulrici's critical approach appear to be August Wilhelm Schlegel's conception of the play as an organic, interconnected whole and Georg Wilhelm Friedrich Hegel's view of drama as an embodiment of the conflict of historical forces and ideas. Unlike his fellow German Shakespearean critic G. G. Gervinus, Ulrici sought to develop a specifically Christian aesthetics, but one which, as he carefully points out in the introduction to the work mentioned above, in no way intrudes on "that unity of idea, which preeminently constitutes a work of art a living creation in the world of beauty." In the following excerpt from the work cited above, Ulrici takes up the debate over Shylock's Jewishness established by such earlier critics as John Potter (1771-72), August Wilhelm Schlegel (1811), William Hazlitt (1817), and Heinrich Heine (1838), claiming that the usurer is both an abstraction and an original figure—a symbol of "the Jewish national character" in its "universal degradation" and an individual embued "with concrete reality." Most importantly, however, Ulrici seeks the "intrinsic unity of idea" that binds the separate plots of* The Merchant of Venice *together, stating that, on the level of dramatic action, there is none. This lack of unity leads him to speculate on the generic nature of the play, claiming that until we discover its central idea we can never determine whether it is "a comedy, a spectacle, or a tragedy." Eventually, Ulrici maintains that if we look elsewhere than the characters and their actions for the unifying thread, we can find it in the pattern of experience each plot develops, namely, that any exclusive right or principle, when carried out exclusive of all other conditions, "produces in this world of limitation its direct negative, and necessarily passes into its opposite." Ulrici summarizes this central idea in the maxim* summum jus, summa injuria *(the highest right, the greatest injustice). Having thus defined the unifying idea in* The Merchant of Venice, *Ulrici concludes by determining its genre, which he calls "a comedy of intrigue."*

Ulrici's assessment of the play's central idea was later disputed by G. G. Gervinus (1849-50), who claimed that Shakespeare's purpose was to ''depict the relation of man to property,'' and by extension, ''the question of [man's] relation to man.'' Also, for further examination of the genre of The Merchant of Venice, *see the excerpts by Nicholas Rowe (1709), Heinrich Heine (1838), Karl Elze (1871), A. Pietscher (1881), Denton J. Snider (1890), Elmer Edgar Stoll (1927), Harley Granville-Barker (1930), T. A. Ross (1934), Harold R. Walley (1935), John Middleton Murry (1936), C. L. Barber (1959), and Graham Midgley (1960).*]

''The Merchant of Venice,'' one of the most popular, and, at the same time, noblest productions of our great master, unites all the charms and excellencies of Shakspeare's style. First of all, as to the characterization: overlooking the well-conceived and ably worked-out peculiarities of the other personages, who in organic contrast nicely balance and set off each other . . . , we meet in Shylock the Jew a masterpiece of characterization. It is a most successful portrait of the Jewish national character generally;—not indeed of that noble and high-minded, but exclusive spirit, which in the times of Moses, David, and the prophets, still animated the people, but of the low and unworthy sentiments into which this degenerate and fallen nation had gradually sunk during the thousand years of persecution and oppression which marked its dispersion over the face of the earth. During these long years of ignominy, their firm endurance and strict adherence to their national religion, morals and law, had been degraded into conceit and stiff-neckedness—their acute intellect into subtlety and finesse, the inspired view of the prophet into superstition, the love of their inheritance (which in so far as it was united with devotion to the land which God had given them, was praiseworthy,) was corrupted into a sordid and loathsome avarice, and the sense of superiority which their separation from all other nations and kindred had engendered, had sunk into bitter and contemptuous hate, and, wherever possible, into unfeeling and cruel revenge of their persecutors. Nothing had escaped the universal degradation, except the invincible perseverance, and the dry mummy-like tenacity of their Jewish nature. Shylock looks like a mournful relic of a great and glorious past, the still glimmering spark of a dying splendour, which though it warms and nourishes no more, can yet burn and destroy. We can no more refuse our pity than repress our horror at his conduct and sentiments. The general character of the Jewish people is, however, distinctly individualized in Shylock, and endued with concrete vitality. The spirit of revenge and hatred is in his case directed chiefly against the Christian merchants, who are willing to lend their money without security or interest, in order to assist the oppressed and unfortunate debtor, and who in his opinion injure him thereby more deeply than they ever can do by the contemptuous and dog-like treatment which they show him. It is simply on this account that the princely Antonio is a real thorn in his side. His hatred overcomes his avarice, and he plays the part of a high-minded and generous character in order to set at work a devilish design; attachment to religion, caste, and natural rights, expresses itself in Shylock merely in the most rigid and stiff-necked adherence to the letter of the law. He is not without intelligence and natural shrewdness, which reveal themselves in the peculiar humour, and the biting sarcastic wit, which he has freely at command. It is by such special motives of action and delicate touches that Shakspeare has saved his portrait from being but a caricature, and stamped the individuality of life on the abstract generalities of national peculiarity.

But not merely does Shakspeare's wonderful skill in delineating character shine forth in this piece in the most brilliant light; the composition, arrangement, and unfolding of the intricate plot are equally wonderful. The invention, it is true, is not altogether his own property. . . . [But he] has with his usual freedom enriched the original with several additional characters, and enlarged the plot by interweaving into it a new episode. Thus we have three knots, each complicated enough, tangled together in the present fable: the money affair between Shylock and Antonio; the weddings of Bassanio and Portia, and of Gratiano and Nerissa; and lastly, Jessica's love for, and elopement with, Lorenzo. These several events and interests are disposed with remarkable clearness and precision; each proceeds so naturally of itself, and alongside the others, that we never lose the thread, but the several parts are kept perfectly distinct, while at the same time a living, free, and organic principle pervades them all, and rounds them off into a well-organized and perfect whole. As Schlegel justly remarks, in the same way that the noble Antonio is placed in delightful contrast to the hateful Shylock, so the strange bargain between them—which, although not absolutely impossible, is to the highest degree extraordinary—has its counterpart in the no less singular story of the courtship of Portia and Bassanio [see excerpt above, 1811]. The one is rendered less improbable by the other. So, again, as Portia's free choice is restrained by an odd whim of her deceased father, her attendant Nerissa voluntarily makes her own happiness to depend on the fate of her mistress. To this constraint of will and inclination, the violation of all respect of law and custom by the free choice of Jessica forms again a decided contrast. Thus are the manifold interests and situations of the plot skilfully disposed, so as to shew forth in strong light that contrariety from which life and movement uniformly issue. The next question, however, is, where then are we to look for that intrinsic unity of idea which alone can justify before the tribunal of criticism the combination in a single drama of so many different elements? Notwithstanding all this skill of characterization and development, there is a seeming want of consistency, and the whole consequently appears to fall in pieces. No doubt we can see clearly enough an external bond holding together the several parts; Antonio falls into the Jew's power by his self-sacrificing devotion to his friend, and he is rescued by the wit and shrewdness of Portia, and with these two the heroes of the other love-stories are no doubt more or less intimately connected. This tie, however, is altogether external and accidental. In its essential and *intrinsic* signification, what has the business transaction, which turns out so gloomily and almost tragically, in common with the cheerful happy wedding of Portia and Bassanio? None: on the contrary, by such external juxtaposition their intrinsic dissimilarity becomes only the more apparent. Such a connection is in truth null; and a composition of which the parts are so loosely held together is not to be dignified with the title of a work of art. The aesthetical judge finds it impossible to deliver a different sentence, whenever he cannot discover a truly organic and artistic unity between the different components of a great whole; and as hitherto this has not been shown in the case of the ''Merchant of Venice,'' it must be pronounced unworthy of the high encomiums and reputation which it has hitherto enjoyed. Indeed, the question may justly be propounded, whether it is of right to be regarded as a comedy, a spectacle, or a tragedy? and as long as the intrinsic central point is left undiscovered, no answer can be given to the question. (pp. 300-03)

[The critic] must forcibly withdraw his eye from the graceful movement of the several figures, and from the beautiful hues and lovely play of light and shade, if he would hope to discover the invisible thread, which, like the eternal plan of the world's history, runs through the whole, a mystery and a wonder. And, on the other hand, we find occasional hints scattered through the whole in sufficient number to prevent any one who has penetrated the least into the profound mystery of Shakspeare's art from going altogether astray. The idea which lies at the bottom of the transaction between Antonio and Shylock, is evidently the old juristic maxim, "Summum jus summa injuria" [the highest right, the greatest injustice], which is again founded on that high dialectic principle, which the experience of life enforces, that every one-sided and exclusive right produces in this world of limitation its direct negative, and necessarily passes into its opposite. Shylock has evidently the material right on his side, but by taking it, and following it out in its mere letter and one-sidedness, he falls into the deepest and foulest wrong, which by intrinsic necessity, and agreeably to the essential nature of sin, recoils fatally on his own head. The dead letter of the law can but kill. But the same dialectic, and the same view which is here presented in its sharpest and unqualified extreme, shine through all the other parts in various shades and refractions. The whim of Portia's father, which fetters her free-will and robs her of all participation in the choice of her husband, rests, no doubt, ultimately on parental rights and authority; but this extreme right is even extreme wrong, and Portia has good ground for her complaint:

> O! these naughty times
> Put bars between the owners and their rights.
> [III. ii. 18-19]

Even if she had broken her oath, and by signs and hints had guided her well-beloved, amiable, and worthy lover to a right choice, would any of us have been ready to cast the first stone at her? The wrong which was involved in this capricious exercise of parental rights, might have issued in tragic misery, had not chance—again a lucky thought of the moment—led to a happy result. The flight and marriage of Jessica against her father's will is itself also a decided wrong. And, yet, who will condemn her for withdrawing herself from the rule, and for despising the rights of *such* a *parent,* who, if she had remained obedient to him, would have brought both her temporal and eternal welfare into peril. . . . The penalty which the court imposes upon the Jew, by which he is compelled to sanction the marriage of his daughter with Lorenzo, annuls these struggling contrarieties externally and accidentally, rather than furnishes a true intrinsic adjustment of them. Lastly, right and wrong are in the same manner again carried to their extreme points, and consequently to a nicely balanced ambiguity, in the quarrel, with which the piece closes, between Gratiano and Nerissa, and Bassanio and Portia, about the rings which they have parted with, in violation of their sworn promises. Here, again, the maxim "Summum jus summa injuria," is clearly reflected: here, too, right and wrong are driven dialectically to a strait—to that extreme boundary where both become indistinguishable and pass into each other.

Thus, then, does the intrinsic meaning and signification of these several and seemingly heterogeneous elements, combine them together into unity; they are but so many variations of the same theme. Human life is considered as a transaction of business, with right or justice as its foundation and centre. But the greater the stress that is laid upon this foundation, and the more it is built upon, the more unstable and weak it appears; and the more deeply and definitely it is taken, the more superficial and eccentric does it seem, and the more fatally is it disturbed by its own gravity. No doubt, the end of law and justice is to maintain and support human society. Nevertheless, they are not the true basis and centre of existence, and neither do they constitute the full value of life, nor comprise its whole truth.

On the contrary, when conceived in such narrow one-sidedness, the whole structure of life is dialectically dissolved; right becomes wrong, and wrong is right; law and justice do in truth form but one aspect of a many-sided whole. They have not their validity and truth, in and by themselves, but they ultimately rest on a higher principle of true morality, from which they issue like rays from the focus of light. Absolutely speaking, man has no rights, but merely duties; he is created by God not for right, but for duty. But his very duties become in turn, and in regard to others, his own rights also, and there is absolutely no true and living right which does not involve a duty, and is itself an obligation. Ultimately, therefore, human life rests not on any arrogated right, but on the grace of God; and the divine mercy, which calls him to union with God, is the true and substantial basis of his existence. The conformity of the human with the divine will is the true life-giving morality of man; and this alone gives to right and wrong their true import and significance. This truth is thus beautifully expressed by Shakspeare:—

> But mercy is above this sceptred sway,
> It is enthroned in the hearts of kings,
> It is an attribute to God himself;
> And earthly power doth then shew likest God's
> When mercy seasons justice. Therefore, Jew,
> Though justice be thy plea, consider this,—
> That in the course of justice, none of us
> Should see salvation: we do pray for mercy;
> And that same prayer should teach us all to render
> The deeds of mercy.
> [IV. i. 193-202]

That another power, which withdraws itself from outward view, and higher than the material one—positive right—lies at the ground of human life, is clearly shewn in the character and fortune of Antonio. A strange unaccountable gloom has taken possession of him; he is weary of his former pursuits; he is so suddenly changed, that he has much ado to know himself. . . . It is only when the misfortunes which, even in his highest success, had disturbed his soul with an ill-defined boding, have actually overtaken him, that all becomes clear. It was the very magnitude of his earthly wealth, to which, however, his heart did not cling exclusively, that unconsciously hampered the free flight of his soul, and like a heavy burden weighed upon his spirit: oversatiety of earthly success had made life itself loathsome. This overflow of earthly mammon, which brings temptation in its train and leads away the mind an unwilling captive, involves in it more or less of sin, especially when man has brought the burthen upon himself. And accordingly it oppresses him; it brings with it a penalty, not indeed from the tribunal of common law and justice, but from that higher power of morality—a penalty which, if it be not legally, is nevertheless morally due. (pp. 303-07)

Having thus discovered the idea which gives to the whole its organic unity, we shall be able to determine the artistic form to which it belongs. It is manifestly a comedy of intrigue, after Shakspeare's usual manner. The comic view of things is evidently the basis on which the dramatic structure is here raised. It is only from this poetical position that the picture which it draws of life, under the one-sided aspect of law and rights can be explained and justified. For the exclusiveness in which this single but indispensable spring of action is employed as the fundamental principle of the whole of life, appears ultimately destroyed by the dialectic of irony. For by shewing the insufficiency of this principle in various situations and circum-

Act IV. Scene i. Antonio, Bassanio, the Duke, Nerissa, Salerio, Gratiano, Shylock, and the Magnificoes. Frontispiece to the Rowe edition (1709). By permission of the Folger Shakespeare Library.

stances, the truth, which is occasionally hinted at, that extreme right, when it is insisted upon, becomes a palpable wrong, is placed by the contrast in the fullest light. Right and wrong become indistinguishable when carried to their utmost limits, and are finally merged in the source of all true life—the love and mercy of God.

And this consideration serves to prove how erroneous and unfounded is the oft-repeated objection, that the last act is an unnecessary adjunct, which, after all interest has been exhausted, hobbles on feeble and languishing. It is nothing less than indispensable to the right understanding and completeness of the whole. It effaces the tragic impression which still lingers on the mind from the fourth act; the last vibrations of the harsh tones which were there struck, here die away; *in the gay and amusing trifling of love the sharp contrarieties of right and wrong are playfully reconciled.* In the same way that in all the preceding scenes the tragic gloom, which the misfortunes of Antonio diffuse, is painted with the softest touch and lightest shades, and their bitterness seems dissolved into sweet, soothing, and melancholy strains, amid which a happier note may be not indistinctly heard, so the concluding act impresses on the whole its appropriate comic stamp, and puts a playful mask on the profound seriousness of the entire subject. We cannot,

in short, sufficiently admire the artistic skill of our poet, who, at the risk of censure, and of failure of effect on the weak-sighted and superficial reader, dares to appear indeed to be violating the rules of his art, while he is constantly and steadily pursuing it, and was attaining it so surely and unerringly. (pp. 307-08)

> Hermann Ulrici, *"Criticisms of Shakspeare's Dramas: 'Merchant of Venice'—'Measure for Measure'—'Cymbeline',"* in his Shakspeare's Dramatic Art: And His Relation to Calderon and Goethe, *translated by A. J. W. Morrison, Chapman, Brothers, 1846, pp. 300-22.*

G. G. GERVINUS   (essay date 1849-50)

[*One of the most widely read Shakespearean critics of the latter half of the nineteenth century, the German critic Gervinus was praised by such eminent contemporaries as Edward Dowden, F. J. Furnivall, and James Russell Lowell; however, he is little known in the English-speaking world today. Like his predecessor Hermann Ulrici, Gervinus wrote in the tradition of the "philosophical criticism" developed in Germany in the mid-nineteenth century. Under the influence of August Wilhelm Schlegel's literary theory and Georg Wilhelm Friedrich Hegel's philosophy, German critics like Gervinus tended to focus their analyses around a search for the literary work's organic unity and ethical import. Gervinus believed that Shakespeare's works contained a rational ethical system independent of any religion—in contrast to Ulrici, for whom Shakespeare's morality was basically Christian. In the excerpt below, first published in his* Shakespeare Commentaries *in 1849-50, Gervinus disputes Ulrici's opinion that the unifying idea in* The Merchant of Venice *is reflected in the maxim "summum jus summa injuria" (the highest right, the greatest injustice) [see excerpt above, 1839]. Gervinus disagrees with Ulrici on two counts: first, not all the essential characters in the play stand in relation to this concept; second, it is fundamentally opposed to Shakespeare's method to attempt to interpret his plays from the vantage point of a maxim or thesis, to which the characters and dramatic action must comply. Gervinus maintains that the story or meaning "grows out of the peculiar nature of the characters," and not the other way around, a point echoed in the twentieth century by Norman Nathan (1952). Gervinus identifies this "meaning" in* The Merchant of Venice *in Shakespeare's depiction of "the relation of man to property," and by extension, "the question of [man's] relation to man." The critic also comments on the final act of* The Merchant of Venice, *claiming that it not only serves to overcome "the painful impression of the judgment scene," as noted by August Wilhelm Schlegel (1811) and Anna Brownell Jameson (1833), as well as Ulrici, but is equally necessary to satisfy the moral interest of the play by confirming "the genuineness of . . . friendship" as the supreme relationship between individuals. For further commentary on Act V and the so-called ring episode, see the excerpts by B. Walwyn (1782), William Hazlitt (1817), Harley Granville-Barker (1930), C. L. Barber (1959), Barbara K. Lewalski (1962), A. D. Moody (1964), James E. Siemon (1970), R. Chris Hassel, Jr. (1970), Richard Horwich (1977), Alice N. Benston (1979), and Anne Parten (1982).*]

Ulrici has justly remarked that the connecting threads in [*The Merchant of Venice*] lie very much hidden, owing to the different circumstances contained in it. The poet has here not given himself the trouble, as in *Romeo and Juliet,* to insinuate his design by express explanation. Ulrici . . . perceived the fundamental idea of the *Merchant of Venice* in the sentence, 'summum jus summa injuria' [the highest right, the greatest injustice; see excerpt above, 1839]. With ability and ingenuity he has referred the separate parts to this one central point. The lawsuit in which Shylock enforces the letter of justice, and is himself avengingly struck by the letter of justice, is thus placed in the true centre of the piece. The arbitrariness of the will, in which Portia's father appears to assert the utmost severity of his paternal right, and which, as Portia herself laments, 'puts bars between the owners and their rights' [III. ii. 19], connects the second element of the piece in one idea with the principal part. Jessica's escape from her father forms the contrast to this; in the one, right is wrong, in the other, wrong is right. The intricacy of right and wrong appears at its height in the quarrel of the lovers in the last act. Even Launcelot's reflections on the right and wrong of his running away, and his blame of Jessica in the fourth act, concur with this point of view. We are thus led to understand the stress which Portia, in her speech to Shylock, lays upon mercy: not severe right, but tempered equity alone can hold society together.

But when we glance at the external structure of the piece, the essential characters do not all stand in relation to this idea—a requirement which we find fulfilled in all the maturer works of our poet. Bassanio, who is really the link uniting Antonio and Portia, the principal actors in the two separate incidents, has nothing to do with this idea. Just as little are the friends and parasites of Antonio, and the suitors of Portia, connected with it. Moreover, Portia's father is called 'a virtuous and holy man' [I. ii. 27], who has left behind him the order concerning the caskets out of kindness, in a sort of 'inspiration,' but in no wise in a severe employment of paternal power. But even setting aside these reasons, which we derive from the attempt to connect the acting characters with the fundamental idea of the piece, we feel that such a maxim as the above can only be the result of a forced interpretation of any of the Shakespearian plays. We only arrive at such maxims and explanations when we consider the story and the plot in this or other plays as the central point for consideration. Ulrici does this: he calls this piece a comedy of intrigue, as he has also even more unsuitably designated *Cymbeline,* a play that must be classed with those most magnificent works of the poet, which like *Lear* confine within the narrow scope of a drama almost the richness of an epos. In Ulrici's opinion the story is the all-important point; in ours the story grows out of the peculiar nature of the characters. We do not, like him, distinguish the dramatic styles, and we believe that Shakespeare himself did not thus distinguish them, for to him the form arose naturally out of the material in obedience to internal laws. Shylock is connected in the intricacies of the action with Antonio by means of Bassanio; these men, and their characters and motives, exist in the poet's mind before the plot is designed which results from their co-operation. Granted that the subject was transmitted to the poet, and that here, as in *All's Well that Ends Well,* he held himself conscientiously bound to the strangest of all materials; still that which most distinguishes him and his poetry, that in which he maintains his freest action, that from which he designs the structure of his pieces, and even creates the given subject anew, is ever the characters themselves and the motives of their actions. . . . To perceive and to know the virtues and crimes of men, to reflect them as in a mirror, and to exhibit them in their sources, their nature, their workings, and their results, and this in such a way as to exclude chance and to banish arbitrary fate, which can have no place in a well-ordered world, such is the task which Shakespeare has imposed upon the poet and upon himself.

We will now say what reflections the *Merchant of Venice* has excited in our own mind. . . . [The] intention of the poet in the *Merchant of Venice* was to depict the relation of man to property. However commonplace this may appear, the more worthy of admiration is that which Shakespeare, with extraordinary,

profound, and poetic power, has accomplished in his embodiment of the subject. (pp. 232-35)

The god of the world, the image of show, the symbol of all external things, is money, and it is so called by Shakespeare, and in all proverbs. To examine the relation of man to property or to money is to place his intrinsic value on the finest scale, and to separate that which belongs to the unessential, to 'outward shows,' from that which in its inward nature relates to a higher destiny. As attributes of show, gold and silver, misleading and testing the chooser, are taken as the material of Portia's caskets, and Bassanio's comments on the caskets mark the true meaning of the piece:—

So may the outward shows be least themselves;
The world is still deceived with ornament.
In law, what plea so tainted and corrupt
But, being season'd with a gracious voice,
Obscures the show of evil? In religion,
What damned error, but some sober brow
Will bless it and approve it with a text,
Hiding the grossness with fair ornament?
There is no vice so simple but assumes
Some mark of virtue on its outward parts:
How many cowards [. . .] assume but valour's
  excrement,
To render them redoubted! Look on beauty,
And you shall see 'tis purchased by the weight [. . .];
So are those crisped snaky golden locks,
Which make such wanton gambols with the wind,
Upon supposed fairness, often known
To be the dowry of a second head,
The scull that bred them, in the sepulchre.
Thus ornament is but the guiled shore
To a most dangerous sea; the beauteous scarf
Veiling an Indian beauty; in a word,
The seeming truth which cunning times put on
To entrap the wisest.

[III. ii. 73-83, 87-9, 92-101]

The chooser therefore turns away from the gold and silver, as from the current and received image of that precarious show, and turns to the lead, 'which rather threatenest, than doth promise aught' [III. ii. 105]. And so, not his relation alone, but the relation of a number of beings to gold, this perishable and false good, is depicted in our play. A number of characters and circumstances show how the possession produces in men barbarity and cruelty, hatred and obduracy, anxiety and indifference, spleen and fickleness; and again how it calls forth the highest virtues and qualities, and, by testing, confirms them. But essential prominence is given to the relation of the outward possession, to an inclination of an entirely inward character, namely, to friendship. This is indeed inserted by the poet in the original story; it is, however, not arbitrarily interwoven with it, but is developed according to its inmost nature from the materials given. For the question of man's relation to property is ever at the same time a question of his relation to man, as it cannot be imagined apart from man. The miser, who seeks to deprive others of possession and to seize upon it himself, will hate and will be hated. The spendthrift, who gives and bestows, loves and will be loved. The relation of both to possession, their riches or their poverty, will, as it changes, also change their relation to their fellow-men. For this reason the old story of Timon, handled by our poet in its profoundest sense, is at once a history of prodigality and a history of false friendship. And thus Shakespeare, in the poem before us, has shown a genuine affinity between the pictures he exhibits of avarice and prodigality, of hard usury and inconsiderate extravagance, so that the play may just as well be called a song of true friendship. The most unselfish spiritual affection is placed in contrast to the most selfish worldly one, the most essential truth to unessential show. For even sexual love, in its purest and deepest form, through the addition of sensual enjoyment, is not in the same measure free from selfishness as friendship is, which, as an inclination of the soul, is wholly based upon the absence of all egotism and self-love; its purity and elevation is tested by nothing so truly as by the exact opposite, namely, by possession, which excites most powerfully the selfishness and self-interest of men.

We shall now see how the apparently disparate circumstances of our play work wonderfully one into the other, and with what wisdom the principal characters are arranged with respect to each other.

In the centre of the actors in the play, in a rather passive position, stands Antonio, the princely merchant, of enviable and immense possessions, a Timon and Shylock in riches, but with a noble nature elevated far above the effects which wealth produced in these men. Placed between the generous giver and the miser, between the spendthrift and the usurer, between Bassanio and Shylock, between friend and foe, he is not even remotely tempted by the vices into which these have fallen; there is not the slightest trace to be discovered in him of that care for his wealth imputed to him by Salanio and Salarino, who in its possession would be its slaves. But his great riches have inflicted upon him another evil, the malady of the rich, who have never been agitated and tried by anything, and have never experienced the pressure of the world. He has the spleen, he is melancholy; a sadness has seized him, the source of which no one knows; he has a presentiment of some danger, such as Shakespeare always imparts to all sensitive, susceptible natures. In this spleen, like all hypochondriacs, he takes delight in cheerful society; he is surrounded by a number of parasites and flatterers, among whom there is one nobler character, Bassanio, with whom alone a deeper impulse of friendship connects him. He is affable, mild, and generous to all, without knowing their tricks and without sharing their mirth; the loquacious versatility and humour of a Gratiano is indifferent to him; his pleasure in their intercourse is passive, according to his universal apathy. His nature is quiet and is with difficulty affected; when his property and its management leave him without anxiety, he utters a 'fie, fie,' over the supposition that he is in love; touched by no fault, but moved also by no virtue, he appears passionless, and almost an automaton. The position which the poet has given him in the midst of the more active characters of the piece is an especially happy one; for were he of less negative greatness he would throw all others into deep shadow; we should feel too painful and exciting a sympathy in his subsequent danger. Yet he is not allowed, for this reason, to appear quite feelingless. For in one point he shows that he shared the choler and natural feelings of others. When brought into contact with the usurer, the Jew Shylock, we see him in a state of agitation, partly arising from moral and business principles, partly from intolerance and from national religious aversion. This sense of honour in the merchant against the money-changer and usurer urges him to those glaring outbursts of hatred, when he rates Shylock in the Rialto about his 'usances,' calls him a dog, 'foots' him, and spits upon his beard. For this he receives a lesson for life in his lawsuit with the Jew, whom, with his apathetic negligence, he allows to get the advantage over him. His life is placed in danger, and the

apparently insensible man is suddenly drawn closer to us; he is suffering, so that high and low intercede for him; he himself petitions Shylock; his situation weakens him; the experience is not lost upon him; it is a crisis, it is the creation of a new life for him; finally, when he is lord and master over Shylock, he no longer calls up his old hatred against him, and, aroused from his apathy, he finds henceforth in Bassanio's happiness and tried friendship the source of a renovated and ennobled existence.

Unacquainted with this friend of Bassanio's, there lives at Belmont his beloved Portia, the contrast to Antonio, a character upon whom Shakespeare has not hesitated to heap all the active qualities of which he has deprived Antonio; for in the womanly being kept modestly in the background, these qualities are not likely to appear so overwhelmingly prominent as we felt that they would have been if united in the man, whom they would have raised too far above the other characters of the piece. Nevertheless, Portia is the most important figure in our drama, and she forms even its true central point; as for her sake, without her fault or knowledge, the knot is entangled, and through her and by means of her conscious effort it is also loosened. She is just as royally rich as Antonio, and as he is encompassed with parasites, so is she by suitors from all lands. She too, like Antonio, and still more than he, is wholly free from every disturbing influence of her possessions upon her inner being. She carries out her father's will in order to secure herself from a husband who might purchase her beauty by the weight. Without this will she would of herself have acted similarly; wooed by princely suitors she loves Bassanio, whom she knew to be utterly poor. She too, like Antonio, is melancholy, but not from spleen, not from apathy, not without cause, not from the ennui of riches, but from passion alone, from her love for Bassanio, from care for the doubtful issue of that choice which threatens to surrender her love to chance. A thoroughly superior nature, she stands above Antonio and Bassanio as Helena does above Bertram [in *All's Well That Ends Well*], higher than Rosaline is raised above Biron [in *Love's Labour's Lost*], and Juliet above Romeo; it seems that Shakespeare at that time created and endowed his female characters in the conviction that the woman was fashioned out of better material than the man. . . . To this man of her heart Portia represents herself as a rough jewel, although she is far superior to him; she gives herself to him with the most womanly modesty, although she is capable rather of guiding him. She is superior to all circumstances, that is her highest praise; she would have accommodated herself to any husband, and for this reason her father may have felt himself justified in prescribing the lottery; he could do so with the most implicit confidence; she knows the contents of the caskets, but she betrays it not. She has already sent from her eyes 'speechless messages' to Bassanio, and now she would gladly entertain him some months before he chooses, that she may at least secure a short possession; but no hint from her facilitates his choice. And yet she has to struggle with the warm feeling which longs to transgress the will: it is a temptation to her, but she resists it with honour and resolution. Yet, quick in judgment, skilled in the knowledge of men, and firm in her demeanour, she knows how to frighten away, by her behaviour, the utterly worthless lovers; so superior is she in all this, that her subsequent appearance as judge is perfectly conceivable. (pp. 236-41)

Between Portia and Antonio stands Bassanio, the friend of the one, the lover of the other; he appears between the two boundlessly rich persons as a man utterly poor, ruined in his circumstances, inconsiderate, and extravagant at the expense of his friend. He seems to belong thoroughly to the parasitical class of Antonio's friends. In disposition he is more inclined to the merry Gratiano than to Antonio's severe gravity; he appears on the stage with the question 'When shall we laugh?' [I. i. 66] and he joins with his frivolous companions in all cheerful and careless folly. On this occasion he is borrowing once more three thousand ducats, in order to make a strange Argonautic expedition to the 'Golden Fleece,' staking them on a blind adventure, the doubtful wooing of a rich heiress. His friend breaks his habit of never borrowing on credit, he enters into an agreement with the Jew upon the bloody condition, and the adventurer accepts the loan with the sacrifice. Before he sets forth, on the very same day and evening, he purchases fine livery for his servants with this money, and gives a merry feast as a farewell, during which the daughter of the invited Jew is to be carried off by one of the free-thinking fellows. Does not the whole conduct appear as if he were only the seeming friend of this rich man for the sake of borrowing his money, and only the seeming lover of this rich lady for the sake of paying his debts with her fortune?

But this quiet Antonio seemed to know the man thus apparently bad to be of better nature. He knew him indeed as somewhat too extravagant, but not incurably so, as one who was ready and able also to restrict himself. He knew him as one who stood 'within the eye of honour' [I. i. 137], and he lent to him without a doubt of his integrity. His confidence was unlimited, and he blames him rather that he should 'make question of his uttermost,' than 'if he had made waste of all he has' [I. i. 156-57]. In his melancholy, it is this man alone who chains him to the world; their friendship needs no brilliant words, it is unfeignedly genuine. His eyes, full of tears at parting, tell Bassanio what he is worth to Antonio; it is the very acceptance of the loan which satisfies Antonio's confidence. . . . When [Bassanio] comes to Portia, he does not accede to her tender womanly proposal that he should safely enjoy two months' intercourse with her; he will not 'live upon the rack' [III. ii. 25], and he insists with manly resolution upon the decision. His choice, and the very motives of his choice, exhibit him as the man not of show, but of genuine nature; his significant speech upon this fundamental theme of the piece stands as the true centre of the play. (pp. 241-42)

Bassanio's choice is crowned by success, or, we may more justly say, his wise consideration of the father's object and of the mysterious problem meets with its deserved reward. But his fair doctrine of show is to be tested immediately, whether it be really deed and truth. His adventurous expedition has succeeded through his friend's assistance and loan. But at the same moment in which he is at the climax of his happiness, his friend is at the climax of misfortune and in the utmost danger of his life, and this from the very assistance and loan which have helped Bassanio to his success. The horror of the intelligence concerning Antonio occurs at the very prime of his betrothal happiness. The genuine character of the friend now shows itself. The intelligence disturbs his whole nature. On his wedding-day—Portia herself permits not that they should be married first—he leaves her in order to save his friend, to pay thrice the money borrowed, in the hope of being able to avert the course of the law in this case of necessity. But Portia proves even here her superior nature. She sees more keenly what an inevitable snare the inhuman Jew has dug for Antonio; she adopts the surest course of saving him by right and law itself; she devises at the same time a plan for testing the man of her love. Even with all this, the idea of the design of the whole piece concurs most closely. Her own choice had been

denied her by her father's arrangement; her delight in Bassanio rested not on a long acquaintance; the alliance made by chance appears to her to acquire its true consecration and security by one solemn trial; she will test him and his friend, she will test him by his friendship. . . . [She] wishes to convince herself of the nature of this friendship, in order that she may conclude from it the nature of Bassanio's love. She saves her husband from despair, and his friend from death, at the same moment that amid their torments she is observing their value. In this catastrophe Antonio has to atone for all the sin he has committed against Shylock through sternness, and Bassanio for all that of which he was guilty through frivolity, extravagance, and participation in the offences against the Jew: the best part of both is exhibited through their sufferings in their love for each other, and Antonio's words, the seal of this friendship, must have penetrated deeply into Portia's heart. But with equally great agitation she hears the words of Bassanio, that he would sacrifice his wife, his latest happiness, to avert the misfortune which he had caused. Such an avowal must enchant her: this was indeed standing the fiery test. Whilst she turns the words into a jest, she has to overcome the deepest emotion; with those words the sin is forgiven of which Bassanio was guilty. By his readiness for such a sacrifice he deserves the friend, whom he had exposed to death through the wooing of his wife, and the means which Antonio had given him of pressing his suit; and by it also he shows that he deserves his wife, who could not be called happily won by a fortunate chance which had proved at the same time the evil destiny of his friend. This trial of Bassanio is carried on by Portia in the last act of the play. It has always been said of this act that it was added for the satisfaction of an aesthetic necessity, in order to efface the painful impression of the judgment scene; but it is equally required to satisfy the moral interest of the play by a last proof of the genuineness of this friendship. The helpful judge demands from Bassanio, as a reward, the ring which his wife had forbidden him to give away. Antonio himself begs him to give the ring, and places his love in the scale to 'be valued 'gainst his wife's commandment' [IV. i. 451]; love and friendship come into a final collision, amusing to the spectator, but most serious to those tested by it: friendship must carry the day, if love is to be genuine. He makes his wife secondary to his friend, because he had obtained his wife only by means of his friend. And he thus proves in an emergency, which placed a painful choice before him, that he was in earnest in those words, that he would sacrifice his wife to his friend in order that his friend might not fall a sacrifice to his wife. He proves in this severe Brutus-like sentence against that which was his dearest treasure that he is worthy of his Portia.

Such are the various characteristics of the noblest circumstances, relations, and intricacies between man and man, between worth and possession. Shylock is the contrast, which we hardly need explain; although, indeed, in this degenerated age of art and morals, lowness and madness have gone so far as to make on the stage a martyr and a hero out of this outcast of humanity. The poet has, it is true, given to this character, in order that he may not sink quite below our interest, a perception of his pariah-condition, and has imputed his outbursts of hatred against Christians and aristocrats partly to genuine grounds of annoyance. Moreover, in his delineation of the usurer he has not been biassed by the hatred of the Christians of that time against all that was Jewish, otherwise he would not have imparted to Jessica her lovely character. . . . [Shylock] hates indeed the Christians as Christians, and therefore Antonio who has mistreated him; but he hates him far more because by disinterestedness, by what he calls 'low simplicity,' he destroys his business, because he lends out money gratis, brings down the rate of usance, and has lost him half a million. Riches have made him the greatest contrast to that which they have rendered Antonio, who throughout appears indifferent, incautious, careless, and generous. Shylock on the other hand is meanly careful, cautiously circumspect, and systematically quiet, ever shufflingly occupied as a genuine son of his race, not disdaining the most contemptible means nor the most contemptible object, speculating in the gaining of a penny, and looking so far into the future and into small results that he sends the greedy Launcelot into Bassanio's service, and against his principle eats at night at Bassanio's house, only for the sake of feeding upon the prodigal Christian. This trait is given to him by the poet in a truly masterly manner, in order subsequently to explain the barbarous condition on which he lends Antonio that fatal sum. Shakespeare after his habit has done the utmost to give probability to this most improbable degree of cruelty, which, according to Bacon, appears in itself a fabulous tragic fiction to every honest mind. Antonio has mistreated him; at the moment of the loan he was as like to mistreat him again; he challenges him to lend it as to an enemy; he almost suggests to him the idea, which the Jew places, as if jestingly, as a condition of the loan; and he, the man railed at for usury, is ready generously to grant it without interest to the man who never borrowed upon advantage. The same crafty speculation and reckoning, attended at all events with one advantage, underlie this proposal; in one case it has the show of disinterestedness, in the other it promises opportunity for a fearful revenge. If the Jew really had only partially trifled with the idea of such a revenge, the poet does everything to make the jest fearfully earnest. Money had effaced everything human from the heart of this man, he knows nothing of religion and moral law but when he quotes the Bible in justification of his usury; he knows of no mercy but that to which he may be compelled; there is no justice and mercy in his heart nor any of the love of kindred. His daughter is carried away from him; he is furious, not because he is robbed of her, but because she has robbed him in her flight; he would see his daughter dead at his feet, provided that the jewels and gems were in her ears; he would see her 'hearsed' before him, provided the ducats were in her coffin. He regrets the money employed in her pursuit; when he hears of her extravagance, the irretrievable loss of his ducats occasions fresh rage. In this condition he pants for revenge against Antonio even before there is any prospect of it, against the man who by long mortifications had stirred up rage and hatred in the bosom of the Jew, and with whose removal his usury would be without an adversary. Obduracy and callousness continue to progress in him, until at the pitch of his wickedness he falls into the pit he had dug; and then, according to the notions of the age, he learns from the conduct of Antonio and of the Duke that mercy exercised in a Christian spirit produces other actions than those suggested by the unmerciful god of the world, who had imposed upon him its laws alone. This awful picture of the effects of a thirst for possession, however strongly it is exhibited, will not appear as a caricature to him who has met with similar instances in the actual world, in the histories of gamblers and misers. (pp. 242-46)

G. G. Gervinus, "Second Period of Shakespeare's Dramatic Poetry: 'The Merchant of Venice'," in his Shakespeare Commentaries, *translated by F. E. Bunnètt, revised edition, 1877. Reprint by AMS Press Inc., 1971, pp. 230-47.*

F[RIEDRICH] KREYSSIG   (essay date 1862)

[*In the following excerpt from his* Vorlesungen über Shakspeare, seine Zeit und seine Werke, *published in 1862, Kreyssig comments on the numerous beauties and the intricacies of plot and characterization in* The Merchant of Venice. *However, unlike such earlier critics as Hermann Ulrici (1839) and G. G. Gervinus (1849-50), Kreyssig concludes that the play was written "neither to glorify friendship, nor to condemn the usurer, nor, finally, to represent any moral idea." The play simply demonstrates, according to Kreyssig, that "lasting success, sure, practical results can be secured only by a just estimate of things" and that "rigid Idealism, although infinitely more amiable and estimable, shows itself as scarcely less dangerous than hard-hearted selfishness."*]

[In *The Merchant of Venice*, Shakespeare] moulds into one the stories of the daughter of the King of Apulia and the bride of Gianetto, lets the suitors choose the caskets, devotes himself to the noble character of the merchant who sacrifices himself for his friend, takes the light, hot blood of Lorenzo and Jessica into the service of poetic justice,—and then lets the sun of his genius rise upon this chaos of odd entanglements and incredible fictions. Under its beams the sharp outlines of the Piece are softened into lines of beauty, contradictions are reconciled, the little poetic world gains its due proportions, its own perspective and colouring. The Actual is nowhere copied, and yet its inner, essential laws are not violated. The facts indeed belong to the fabulous; all the firmer and the more real is the soil out of which the motives and characters spring; and in applying ourselves to work through the ever-involved details to a point of view commanding the whole, we are compensated at every step for the difficulty of the journey by an abundance of single beauties. It is as if we were seeking the spot where we may see the whole, in some charming, thickly-overgrown park. The path leads us, by artificial windings, through green, fragrant woods. Lovely pictures open on the right and on the left, side-paths are lost in the shrubberies; flowers and fruits tempt us to linger and enjoy them. We have no fatigue, no weariness to fear, but we must take care to mark the way, lest in the beautiful labyrinth we miss our goal. But, metaphor aside, in few of his Pieces does Shakespeare play hide-and-seek with his readers and commentators as happily as here. The wisdom everywhere introduced, cropping out in the action and in the scenes, allures us, in a peculiar degree, to seek ever more curiously for a 'moral' in the Play. (p. 453)

The Merchant of Venice, in our opinion, was written neither to glorify friendship, nor to condemn the usurer, nor, finally to represent any moral idea, rich and manifold as are the moral allusions which the thoughtful reader carries away with him, together with the aesthetic enjoyment of this work of Art. The essential and definite aspect of life here illustrated admonishes us that lasting success, sure, practical results can be secured only by a just estimate of things, by prudent use and calm endurance of given circumstances, equally far removed from violent resistance and cowardly concession. Strong feeling and clear, good sense hold the scales in the pervading character of the whole Drama; fortune helps the honest in so far as they boldly and wisely woo its favour; but rigid Idealism, although infinitely more amiable and estimable, shows itself as scarcely less dangerous than hard-hearted selfishness. (pp. 454-55)

F[riedrich] Kreyssig, in an extract, translated by Horace Howard Furness, in A New Variorum Edition of Shakespeare: The Merchant of Venice, Vol. VII *by William Shakespeare, edited by Horace Howard Furness, J. B. Lippincott Company, 1888, pp. 453-55.*

KARL ELZE (essay date 1871)

[*Elze was a nineteenth-century German literary historian who specialized in English literature and philology and was one of the first editors of the German Shakespeare Society's* Jahrbuch. *In the following excerpt, first published in the* Jahrbücher *of the German Shakespeare Society in 1871, Elze argues that one way to interpret* The Merchant of Venice *is to follow G. G. Gervinus and consider it a drama about "man's relation to wealth" (see excerpt above, 1849-50). For Elze, the reactions of such characters as Antonio, Portia, Bassanio, and Shylock to their wealth—specifically, whether or not they sacrifice material gains to higher objects—form a fundamental issue in the play and relate as well to the struggle between appearance and reality most evident in the casket story. The significance of the characters' use of wealth in* The Merchant of Venice *was later discussed by John Russell Brown (1957), C. L. Barber (1959), and John P. Sisk (1969). Elze also examines the controversy over whether Shylock is meant to be a tragic or comic figure, concluding that it is unlikely Shakespeare viewed him strictly as a comic villain, despite certain scenes where he appears so. In fact, Elze suggests that Shakespeare sympathized with Shylock's fate and disapproved of his forced conversion. But he maintains that the tragic undertones in Shylock's persecution are overcome in the play's final scene—what he describes as Shakespeare's return to "romantic comedy." Other commentators who have disapproved of the Christians' treatment of Shylock, especially his defeat and forced conversion, include Rudolf von Ihering (1872), Harold C. Goddard (1951), A. D. Moody (1964), James E. Siemon (1970), R. Chris Hassel, Jr. (1970), and René Girard (1978), though Siemon views Shylock's "disposal" as more of an artistic failure on Shakespeare's part than an example of the Venetians' moral insincerity.*]

[We can] by a different path come to the same conclusion as Gervinus, and find the fundamental thought of ['The Merchant of Venice'] to be man's relation to wealth. As Gervinus justly observes, Shakespeare, towards the end of his career, in 'Timon of Athens,' returns again to the same question, which however commonplace in appearance, occupies a most prominent position among the agents of human society. Timon, likewise in possession of immense wealth, is the exact contrast to Shylock; he is a senseless squanderer, just as the latter is a senseless miser, for Shylock is a miser as well as a usurer—and what usurer is not? To him wealth is the idol which he worships, possession itself is his aim and pleasure, he stands upon the lowest stage which man can occupy in regard to property, upon the same stage as a raven or a magpie. All the four Croesuses—Shylock, Antonio, Portia, and Timon—with their surroundings, show us that wealth or possession in itself is not happiness, that poverty in itself is not unhappiness. His own confession of faith on this subject, perhaps his own wish, the poet puts in the mouth of Nerissa, who says: 'For aught I see, they are as sick that surfeit with too much, as they that starve with nothing. It is therefore no small happiness to be seated in the mean; superfluity comes sooner by grey hairs, but competency lives longer' [I. ii. 5-9]. But the poet goes more deeply into the matter than Nerissa with her mother-wit; he knows that not only does superfluity come sooner by grey hairs, but that possession leads to moral degradation and ruin if it is not made to serve a moral purpose; he knows that it must never itself be the object, as in the case of . . . Shylock, but that a true man must, on the contrary, be able to sacrifice his wealth to higher objects, as required by the inscription on the leaden casket. In all cases the question ought to be not what a man has, but what he is; the having is but the shell, the being is the kernel. Moreover wealth, as Gervinus expresses it, is a test of character. This conception readily passes over into the other, that having is regarded only as an apparent good, the being,

on the other hand, as the true essence, and that accordingly, the play treats of the struggle between Appearance and Reality.

It has been a matter of discussion whether Shylock is a tragic or a comic character. In order to bring this dispute to a final decision, the subject requires to be minutely sifted. . . . Gervinus is vexed that 'at this time of the degeneracy of art and morals, vulgarity and madness could go so far as to make a martyr out of this outcast of humanity' [see excerpt above, 1849-50]. A martyr he certainly is not, but we must allow extenuating circumstances in his favour. Shylock is a usurer, although it is nowhere expressly said that, like [Marlowe's] Barabas, he has taken a hundred per cent, or oppressed and drained the poor. There is only one passage where such a thing is hinted at, viz., the lines spoken by Antonio:—

> He seeks my life; his reason well I know:
> I oft deliver'd from his forfeitures
> Many that have at times made moan to me;
> Therefore he hates me.
>
> [III. iii. 21-4]

Shylock's own version is different; he ascribes the origin of their mutual hatred to Antonio, and persists repeatedly in the assertion that his gains are righteous, and that he only uses what is his own. We place, however, little faith in what Shylock calls righteous, and although the poet, as he is fond of doing, has to some extent left the true state of affairs concealed, yet Shylock in this matter cannot be exonerated. But who made him a usurer? How has it come about that wealth and gain have stifled all moral sense in him, instead of leading him to princely generosity, like Antonio, or to the noblest enjoyment of life in the faithful performance of duty, like Portia? We know no other answer to this question, except that the Christians have made Shylock what he is. We do not mean to say that Shakespeare intended to hint at any thing of the kind, although the temptation of drawing such inferences lies nearer in this play than elsewhere in Shakespeare. Whether the poet intended it or not, Shylock, in his hand, has become the representative of Judaism in its lowest degradation, and this degradation has undeniably been caused by centuries of political and social bondage. . . . Cooped up in their ghettos, and marked by a conspicuous dress like hangmen and prostitutes, the Jews were excluded from the legal as well as the moral organism of the state. All branches of business were prohibited to them except that of barter and dealings in money, and this sole source of acquiring the means of existence was branded by the name of usury. According to the doctrines of the Catholic Church, it was a grievous sin to take interest on money lent; it was a crime amenable to the ecclesiastic tribunals, and Pope Clement V. declared it heresy to vindicate it. The subsequent Popes, Pius V. and Sixtus V. (1585-1590), even Benedict XIV. (as late as the middle of the eighteenth century), confirmed this doctrine. The outcast Jew alone was permitted to take interest. (pp. 82-6)

We must distinctly recollect this state of things, and bear in mind the intellectual foundations out of which the 'Merchant of Venice' originated, in order to be able to place ourselves within the sphere of Shakespeare's ideas. Thus, in accordance with the laws of the Church, the Christian Antonio takes no interest for his money, but overstepping his province, he abuses the Jew for doing so, and ill-treats him at the Exchange without there having been any provocation or cause for it on Shylock's part.

> Thou call'dst me dog before thou hadst a cause,
>
> [III. iii. 6]

says Shylock, and in another passage adds that Antonio hates him simply because he is a Jew, in fact, that Antonio hates his sacred nation. This hatred of Antonio is scarcely less culpable than the Jew's; Shylock can bring forward the excuse that he has not been brought up, either by his family or by society, to love humanity or to practise moral duties. Antonio has certainly also been brought up to hate the Jews. Shylock bears Antonio's ill-treatment with composure:—

> Still have I borne it with a patient shrug;
> For sufferance is the badge of all our tribe. . . .
> > [I. iii. 109-10]

It can, however, raise no astonishment that in spite of all patience a bitter feeling of revenge, like a subcutaneous ulcer, is developed in Shylock against the Christian who has interfered with his sole means of making money (he has hindered him half a million), who has in public heaped him with abuse, kicked him, and spat upon his beard. This state of things, this mutual relation of the characters to one another, is portrayed throughout the whole play with absolute truth. No more forcible complaint against the Christians, no more impressive justification of the Jews can be given than the celebrated passage in [III. i. 59-73]. 'Hath not a Jew eyes? Hath not a Jew hands, organs, dimensions, senses, affections, passions? Fed with the same food, hurt with the same weapons, subject to the same diseases, healed by the same means, warmed and cooled by the same winter and summer, as a Christian is? If you prick us, do we not bleed? If you tickle us, do we not laugh? If you poison us, do we not die? And if you wrong us, shall we not revenge? If we are like you in the rest, we will resemble you in that. If a Jew wrong a Christian, what is his humility? Revenge. If a Christian wrong a Jew, what should his sufferance be by Christian example? Why, revenge. The villainy you teach me I will execute; and it shall go hard but I will better the instruction.' Shylock has grown up under the letter of the Mosaic religion, what wonder therefore that he at last knows of nothing higher than the letter, and the right of the letter? He only understands an eye for an eye, and a tooth for a tooth, and what he learned of Christianity was not of a nature to raise him to a higher conception of Right and of Morality. In such circumstances many a man would, like him, seek a good opportunity of getting Antonio into his power, in order to indulge his old grudge; even the worm will turn when it is trodden upon. The full cup overflows when Jessica elopes with a Christian, and takes away with her her father's ducats and jewels. If she had only been carried off by one of her own religion; but that one of Shylock's deadly enemies should marry her is the height of affliction. (pp. 87-9)

Nevertheless, Shylock's relation to his daughter is a point where least can be said in his excuse. The ossification of his mind and feelings, his selfishness and bitterness, have also entered his family life, and like corrosive acids, have eaten and destroyed it. While his co-religionists are wont to hold family ties in high estimation, and to keep their domestic life in a certain patriarchal holiness, so as to escape from the oppression of the outer world, Shylock, according to Jessica, makes his home a hell. He does not succeed in leaving harshness, avarice, hatred, and revenge out of doors, and in being gentle, kind, and generous within the bosom of his family—it is indeed an almost impossible task. . . . Jessica is nothing to him but the keeper of his house and the guardian of his treasures. She leads the life of a prisoner; she is to shut the ears of the house, and, according to oriental custom, is not allowed to put her head out of the window to gape at 'varnished' Christian fools who

are an abomination to her father. That she should possess any claim to the enjoyment of life Shylock never dreams of; his withered soul never supposes that hers is expanding in youthful excitement and desire. Why does he not surround her life with at least such ornaments and finery as young girls are accustomed to regard as a great part of their happiness? Why does he not place her under the motherly care of a companion, instead of leaving her completely to herself at home, while he goes about his money transactions? Why? From greed, selfishness, and hardheartedness. The want of fatherly feeling on his part necessarily produces a want of filial feeling on hers. . . . As too much oppression will cause rebellion, so Jessica begins to appropriate the ducats, all of which must necessarily fall to her share after her father's death, she being the only child: she but takes her inheritance in advance. Even the ducat which she gives Launcelot on parting was scarcely a part of her own scanty pocket-money. Much as she feels it 'a heinous sin' that she is ashamed of being her father's child, and that she is only the daughter of his blood, not of his heart, yet she makes herself no reproaches about the more glaring transgression of making off with her father's money. (pp. 90-2)

However repulsive Jessica's appropriation of her father's ducats may be to our feelings, yet when considering all the circumstances, we are inclined to forgive the thoughtless child, especially because the poet himself intends her to be mildly judged; for when Shylock exclaims 'she is damned,' he is answered by Salarino, 'that's certain, if the devil may be her judge' [III. i. 31-3]. That Lorenzo gives her unmixed praise stands to reason; he says:—

> Beshrew me but I love her heartily;
> For she is wise, if I can judge of her,
> And fair she is, if that mine eyes be true,
> And true she is, as she hath proved herself.
> > [II. vi. 52-5]

In regard to the last-named virtue, faithfulness, it is fortunate that there is no Iago near, to whisper into the confiding lover's ear:—

> She did deceive her father, marrying you.
> > [*Othello*, I. iii. 293]

This leads us to the question of Jessica's flight. . . . The relation existing between father and daughter, as already remarked, is only a blood relationship, not a moral one. As Jessica sees no other possibility, she breaks this relation violently, in order to establish a new moral one by marriage; she does this without reflection, by natural instinct. The reflection on the rightness of her elopement has been put by the poet in Launcelot's mouth, who comes to the conclusion that on his part it would not be right, and who says that he will only accept another situation with the Jew's knowledge and consent. His position is certainly different from that of Jessica, for not being in the Jew's paternal power, he need not seek refuge in a violent breach of engagement. In his relation to his father Launcelot is the very reverse of Jessica, for in spite of the tricks which in his privilege as clown he does not scruple to play upon the blind old man, he feels after all that he is, was, and ever will be his child, and asks for his blessing. It is this point, moreover, which brings the scene between the two Gobbos into a close connection with the whole—a scene which the public is generally inclined to consider as a superfluous by-play. As will be seen below, Portia in her filial obedience is a still more unequivocal contrast to Jessica.

When Shylock discovers Jessica's flight, he runs through the streets of Venice like a madman, calling out for his daughter and his ducats, and crying for help from the Doge and the courts of justice. The street boys troop at his heels, and we seem to hear their shouts and jeers. This is the only scene in which Shylock would appear in a ridiculous light, and the poet very wisely does not bring it upon the stage, but gives it as a report. It seems evident that he does not wish to lay the curse of ridicule upon the man who already bears the weight of a double curse as a Jew and a usurer. Nay, we are even here inclined to sympathise with the Jew. But the matter appears in a very different light when Shylock, through Tubal, receives the news of Jessica's doings in Genoa. Here his hard-hearted avarice and his obdurate selfishness break out in a truly revolting manner. Here he reveals himself in all the nakedness of his degradation, without a spark of human feeling, without an idea of the moral laws and ties which establish and govern society. His exclusive love for his stones has made him a stone. No syllable escapes his lips to express how heavy a blow has fallen upon his paternal heart, and that he is now, in his old age, left completely forsaken and forlorn. He only laments his ducats and his stones; were his daughter before him in her coffin, with the jewels in her ear, he would be content and satisfied. Now he feels more than ever the curse which weighs on his people—not because he has lost his daughter, the only being related to him, but because he has lost his ducats and stones, which she has squandered. His character here already rises to a terrible extreme, and there is but one step to the climax, which is reached in the scene of the catastrophe. (pp. 93-6)

Judaism forms by no means an external or accidental, but an inner and essential element in Shylock's character; in fact, he could only have become what he is, under the Mosaic religion. Not only every inch of him, but every fibre in him is a Jew. Out of his Mosaism first arises his formal righteousness; his deeds are to fall upon his head, for what judgment shall he dread, as he does no wrong. From his Mosaism flows his Jewish logic, his bitter sarcasm, his spirit of revenge. Where God is represented as an avenger, revenge is not only allowable but a duty. Lastly his obstinacy and hardness agree with it; he has sworn by his holy Sabbath to insist upon his bond; he has an oath in heaven, shall he lay perjury upon his soul? Shylock is not overcome by admitting the necessity of mercy set forth by the Christian side, but by his own vital principle, his worship of the letter; the letter, which is his God, turns with fatal effect against himself. It could not be expected that it should have been otherwise, as, according to our ideas, the deeds of Shylock's Christian opponents by no means prove that they are penetrated by the significance of mercy, in its full extent. The Doge, with a certain kind of self-complacency, does indeed address the Jew:—

> That thou shalt see the difference of our spirits,
> I pardon thee thy life before thou ask it.
>   [IV. i. 368-69]

But we cannot forbear taking 'this difference of the spirits' into nearer consideration. Portia, in a terrible climax, explains to the Jew that, according to the law of the Republic, he has forfeited his possessions and his life, because he, an alien, by direct and indirect attempts, has sought the life of one of its citizens. The one half of his fortune falls to his adversary, the other to the state, unless the latter be commuted through mercy into a fine. His life lies in the hands of the Doge, who in his exclusive right has to dispose of it. The Doge therefore grants

him his life before he asks for it; upon Antonio's proposal, moreover, Shylock is allowed to retain that half of his fortune which is forfeited to the state, and Antonio accepts the other half only as a usufruct till Shylock's death, so as to hand it over to his rightful heirs, Lorenzo and Jessica. In addition to this, Shylock, which one might think a matter of course, is obliged to promise to make these two heirs of all he leaves at his death. In reality therefore Shylock, exclusive of the 3,000 ducats which he has advanced to Antonio, loses only one half of his fortune, and even that is secured to his heirs. Considering the draconic laws of Venice, this may be regarded as a mild punishment, although it certainly does fall heavily upon the Jew. (pp. 101-03)

But now comes the last condition likewise proposed by Antonio: Shylock shall at once become a Christian; if he will not fulfil this condition, in addition to the preceding ones, the Doge will revoke the granted pardon. Shylock therefore has only the choice between immediate death on the one hand, and the abjuration of his faith, and the adoption of the religion of his deadly enemies, on the other. This feature, which is taken from Marlowe, according to our modern feelings, goes beyond the idea of punishment: it is no longer poetic justice or tragical retribution, it is mental and moral annihilation, the inevitable consequences of which must lead to physical death as well. The indulgence in regard to the forfeiture of his fortune is hereby more than counterbalanced. . . . The sentence of death would have been mild compared to this torture. However grievously Shylock may have offended, however heartily we despise and condemn his character, yet we cannot avoid a momentary feeling of sympathy for him when he staggers out of the court, crushed by the pardon which the Doge has granted him. (pp. 103-04)

[It] is not fanatical hatred, cruel revenge, or malicious scorn which prompts Antonio to demand the condition that Shylock shall consent to be baptised. Antonio has indeed, from the beginning, abused and ill-treated the Jew, but this is the only stain upon his character. Otherwise he is distinguished by gentleness, benevolence, and kindheartedness, and it cannot be conceived that his hatred of the Jews would amount to such cruelty, and this at the very moment when, in regard to the confiscation of the Jew's property, he gives an unequivocal proof of his generosity. His demand for the conversion arises in all probability from an entirely different motive, and we shall hardly err in seeking it in the general religious conviction of the Middle Ages, according to which none but the believers in Christianity could partake of salvation and eternal blessedness. (pp. 105-06)

It is well known that this conviction rose to the belief that it was a meritorious work to assist the non-Christians to the blessings of Christianity, even against their own wish, by forcing them to become converts. From this point of view Antonio's demand and the Doge's action appear in a different light, and it is easily understood that they should regard the proposed conversion as a proof of mercy as well. They intended to save Shylock's soul from eternal perdition. (p. 106)

Thus we see that Shakespeare's public stood in quite a different relation to 'The Merchant of Venice' from what we now do. His public was still deeply imbued with hatred and contempt of the Jews, and far from considering a Jew a fellow-creature, and a member of the community possessed of equal rights with the Christians. Accordingly his public saw no objection to the enforced conversion, but rather found it quite correct, and considered it a merciful punishment. . . . To us Judaism, as such, is no longer an object of hatred and contempt; the Jews have finally, in principle at least, become our fellow-citizens, with equal rights. This is a point where the progress of moral ideas since Shakespeare's time has led to essentially different moral views. The condemnation of all religious compulsion, together with legal and moral tolerance, in Protestant countries at least, have fought their way to universal acceptance. To us Shylock is no longer a comical character, we can no longer lightly pass over his enforced conversion, much less 'unceremoniously' laugh at it, let critics demonstrate the case as they please. By this change of the moral point of view, a certain discordance has arisen in the play, which it did not possess with Shakespeare's contemporaries.

But in what relation did the poet himself stand to these questions? Did he share the religious bigotry and intolerance of his public, or was he in advance of it, and with a poet's gift of divination had he arrived at modern toleration? What was his intention in the creation of the character of Shylock? Did he really only wish to furnish his groundlings with a welcome subject for their rude uproariousness and love of merriment? From what we have already said it is impossible for us to arrive at such a conclusion. Even in this case Shakespeare has not departed from his 'desperate objectivity,' even here he has held up the most faithful mirror to nature, without giving us any signs of his own personal opinion, except at most between the lines. Apart from the great apostrophe in Act III. 1, and the fact that the poet only gives us the report of Shylock's wild

Act II. Scene vii. The Prince of Morocco, Portia, and others.
Frontispiece to the Hanmer edition by H. Gravelot (1744).
By permission of the Folger Shakespeare Library.

cries for help in the streets, indications of his own opinion are to be gathered from the fifth scene of the third act, where Launcelot, in his clownish way, declares to Jessica his belief that she will be damned, because the sins of the fathers are visited upon the children, and that there is but one bastard-hope left for her—viz. the supposition that she is not the Jew's daughter. When Jessica replies that then the sins of her mother should be visited upon her, he agrees that she is lost in both ways. With an unquestionable leaning upon the doctrine of the Apostle Paul, Jessica now expresses her hope that she will be saved by her husband, who has made her a Christian. Launcelot, however, considers 'this making of Christians' very objectionable; for, says he, there are pork-eaters enough as it is, and if this goes on there will soon not be a rasher of bacon to be had. When her husband enters Jessica complains to him of Launcelot and his sayings, and Lorenzo turns the joke against Launcelot by accusing him of a love-affair with a negro woman, and winds the discussion up by saying that it will be easier for him to answer for his converting Jews than it will be for Launcelot to answer for his loose doings.

This conversation is undeniably the prelude to the condition imposed upon Shylock in the judgment-scene; it gives, as it were, the chord and the key-note to it. Herein lies its importance, otherwise it would be an idle excrescence. But which is this key-note? When we think of Launcelot's scoffing at chiromancy in Act II. 2, and at the interpretation of dreams in Act II. 5, it would be difficult to see in his conversation with Jessica anything more than witty jokes at the doctrines of the Church and the conversion of the Jews, which may have been called forth by some actual occurrence of the time. Be that as it may, the serious correlate to this humorous consideration of the subject can scarcely be any other than that the poet here personally disapproves of the change of religion imposed on Shylock. His witticisms imply the serious reflections that the Christians do not care for a convert who is neither of use nor an honour to them, and that moreover baptism will be of no avail to the Jew, who in spite of his conversion will be damned. (pp. 107-10)

But if the poet from his broader and more tolerant religious standpoint disapproved of the more or less enforced conversion of Jews, why did he make it a condition to Shylock? The Jew might of course have come off with the fine only, even if it had been a heavier one. The contrasts in the play, designed as a comedy, would then have appeared less harsh, and the stage effect would scarcely have been less. However, as has been said, Shakespeare considered a dramatic poem a mirror, not a kaleidoscope; it is nowhere his custom to embellish or to suppress; he gives us the world and history as they are, even at the risk of every now and then resembling a naturalistic landscape-painter; nay, he possesses an undeniable predilection for sharp and definite outlines, even although they are not always within the confines of the beautiful. Moreover his public wished above all things to see Shylock crushed, just as in Lessing's 'Nathan' the Patriarch insists upon having the Jew burned. Nay, it seems questionable whether we ourselves would approve of a representation of the play in which the condition of baptism were omitted for once, by way of trial.

Just as if Shakespeare had felt that the truth of nature had in this respect gone a little too far, he makes up for it in the fifth act by double sweetness; he evidently felt the necessity of relieving the discord, and of leading the poem back into the brighter regions of romantic comedy. The charming little Utopia in Belmont is in so far connected with the fundamental idea of wealth, as only upon the basis of wealth this development of a life which flows in such a self-conscious and unconstrained cheerfulness is possible. . . . If we imagine Portia burdened with the troubles about gain, or even about the necessities of life, we have no longer a Portia before us. Her element of life, resting as it does upon the foundation of secured property, is the practice of the noblest humanity, the promotion and enjoyment of the good and the beautiful. The inner independence, which her character has acquired by her external independence, undeniably gives her a slight touch of the masculine, whereas in Antonio, on the contrary, a tinge of the feminine is produced by his wealth. Portia with her wealth, and in her completely isolated position as an orphan, would have been exposed to the danger of losing the qualities of her sex, and of falling a victim to emancipation, had she not been kept in the sphere of dependence and subordination, appropriate to the female sex, by the directions in her father's last will. . . . To give it in a few words, the father did not wish that Portia should become the prey of a lover who seeks in marriage only outward, not inward happiness, who loves her possessions, not her person. And yet—strange contradiction!—it is just Bassanio who undertakes the journey to Belmont to obtain the 'Golden Fleece,' whereas this motive can scarcely be attributed to the Prince of Arragon or to the Prince of Morocco, for they had their own royal possessions. Bassanio is not only poor but greatly in debt, and has already cost Antonio a good deal of money; this he now intends to recover, much in the same way as, when a boy, he shot two arrows one after the other, and found both again. This new riddle can only be solved thus, that Bassanio, in spite of his youthful follies and his extravagances, has preserved a firm and true character; he does not only love Portia's wealth, but herself still more. He has merely sown his wild oats, and the inference which Portia draws from his character in favour of Antonio, may just as appropriately be inverted to Bassanio's favour. He excels the whole group which surrounds Antonio; according to Launcelot's version of the proverb, he has the grace of God, while Shylock has enough. (pp. 111-15)

In how far Antonio stands in contrast to Shylock has been sufficiently explained by Gervinus. To Shylock possession itself is everything, to Antonio nothing, not even a means for the enjoyment of life. Shylock lives and gains for himself only, Antonio for others only. Shylock stands isolated as it were, for Tubal and Chus are merely his tools in business; Antonio, on the contrary, is surrounded by a number of friends and followers, the majority of whom, it is true, may have been attracted by his wealth; but they are all filled with sincere respect and cordial sympathy for him, and do not turn their backs upon him in the hour of need, as Timon's parasites do. Antonio's sole pleasure consists in seeing these 'butterflies' merry and of good cheer, and they on their part endeavour to enliven him. Why he should be melancholy himself does not know, nor do his friends; simply because he is not cheerful. The fact is, that wealth has blunted his feelings, has satiated and made him effeminate; fulfilment, where it has not preceded, has immediately followed all his desires; what is there left for him to desire? Besides, he has no family for whose future he would have to provide, and in whose success he could take delight. In this respect he stands likewise in an isolated position, in spite of his friends, and a perfect indifference, not only to property, but to life itself, has taken possession of him; it is only for Bassanio's sake that he still loves the world. Consequently he calmly resigns himself to his fate, and is quite willing to meet it, if only the Jew will cut deep enough; he feels himself too weak to survive the loss of his wealth. . . .

[He] is full of soft-heartedness, gentleness, and kindliness, and it is only in relation to Shylock that he does not display these excellences of his nature. Gervinus, however much he is prejudiced against Shylock, cannot help admitting that the affliction and deathly terror which Antonio has to endure are a well deserved punishment, and may serve him as a lesson. This is again a masterly stroke of Shakespeare, that he does not make Antonio suffer innocently. . . . (pp. 115-17)

Amidst the sounds of intoxicating music and the fragrance of the glorious flowers of southern climes, all the principal characters of the play, with the exception of Shylock, meet at Belmont. Portia, the most prominent of all, gives Antonio the glad tidings that three of his galleons have arrived in the roads, and by this news recalls him completely back to life. Little Jessica, who cannot be merry at the sounds of sweet music— by the way, a trait which tells much in her favour—is, we hope, made all the happier by her father's will, which Nerissa brings. Even the ticklish episode of the rings . . . ends in exuberant merriment, and thus we find ourselves at the end of the play, which in spite of all that may be said, we will guard in its imperishable beauty as a dramatic jewel no less carefully than Bassanio and Gratiano guard the rings of their wives. (p. 117)

Karl Elze, "'The Merchant of Venice'," in his Essays on Shakespeare, *translated by L. Dora Schmitz, Macmillan and Co., 1874, pp. 67-117.*

RUDOLF von IHERING　(essay date 1872)

[*In the following excerpt from his* Der Kampf um's Recht *(1872), Ihering argues from a legal perspective that what is on trial in Act IV of* The Merchant of Venice *is not Shylock's demand for justice, but the Venetian law itself. The critic maintains that when Shylock's rights are denied, it is more importantly the rights or law of Venice that is struck down, defeated by what he calls "a disgraceful, pettifogging trick." Ihering thus views Shylock's fate as a "mighty tragedy" and contends that, in this respect, he symbolizes all Jews of the Middle Ages, whose rights were "in the same breath acknowledged, and, by fraud, denied." For further commentary on the significance of Shylock's Jewishness in the play, see the excerpts by John Potter (1771-72), August Wilhelm Schlegel (1811), William Hazlitt (1817), Heinrich Heine (1838), and Hermann Ulrici (1839). Also, see the excerpt by A. Pietscher (1881) for a direct refutation of Ihering's remarks.*]

It is hatred and revenge that take Shylock to court to get his pound of flesh from the body of Anthonio, but the words the poet puts into Shylock's mouth are just as true as from the mouth of any other. It is the language which an injured sense of right always speaks in all times and in all places; the force, not to be shaken, of the conviction that law must for ever remain law; the lofty strain and pathos of a man, conscious that he pleads not merely for his own person, but for the enacted law.

'I crave the law' [IV. i. 206]. In these four words Shakespeare has marked the true relation of law in its subjective sense to law in its objective sense, and the significance of the struggle for law, in a way that no philosopher learned in the law could have done more strikingly. With these words the case is at once changed, and it is not the claim of Shylock which is on trial, but the law of Venice. To what mighty, gigantic proportions does not the figure of Shylock dilate as he utters these words! It is no longer the Jew demanding a pound of flesh; it is Venice herself that knocks at the door of the court,—*his* rights and the rights of *Venice* are one; with *his* rights, the rights of *Venice* are struck down. And when, under the weight of the decision of a Judge who nullifies law by a miserable quibble, Shylock succumbs, and, the butt of bitter scorn and jeers, totters away with trembling knees, who can help feeling that in his person the law of Venice also is broken down, that it is not Shylock the Jew who staggers off, but the typical figure of the Jew of the Middle Ages, that pariah of society, who cried for law in vain?

> [Ihering adds in a footnote:] It is just here that in my opinion the deep tragic interest lies which Shylock wrings out of us. He is indeed cheated out of his rights. So at least must a jurist regard the case. The Poet of course is free to make his own jurisprudence, and we do not regret that Shakespeare has done it here, or rather that he has kept the old story unchanged. But when the jurist undertakes to criticise it, he cannot say otherwise than that the bond was in itself null and void, in that its provisions were contrary to good morals; the Judge, therefore, on this very ground should from the very first have denied it. But since he did not so deny it, since the 'second Daniel' acknowledged its validity, it was a wretched quibble, a disgraceful, pettifogging trick, to withhold from the plaintiff the right to draw blood after the right had been granted to take the flesh. Just as well might a Judge acknowledge the right of entry on land, but forbid the right to make footprints, because this was not expressly stipulated. . . .

The mighty tragedy of [Shylock's] fate lies not in the denial of his right, but in that he, a Jew of the Middle Ages, has faith in the law,—we might say, just as if he were a Christian!—a faith firm as a rock which nothing can shake, and which the Judge himself sustains; until the catastrophe strikes him like a thunderbolt, shivering his delusion to atoms, and teaching him that he is nothing but the despised mediaeval Jew, whose rights are in the same breath acknowledged, and, by fraud, denied. (pp. 410-11)

> *Rudolf von Ihering, in an extract, translated by Horace Howard Furness, in* A New Variorum Edition of Shakespeare: The Merchant of Venice, *Vol. VII by William Shakespeare, edited by Horace Howard Furness, J. B. Lippincott Company, 1888, pp. 410-11.*

A. PIETSCHER (essay date 1881)

[*In opposition to such earlier critics as John Potter (1771-72), William Hazlitt (1817), Heinrich Heine (1838), Hermann Ulrici (1839), and Rudolf von Ihering (1872), Pietscher argues that "confessions of faith or nationalities have nothing to do with the central idea" of* The Merchant of Venice. *Instead, Pietscher claims that Shakespeare merely needed a usurer for his play and, according to the customs of the time, took his character from that race of people who performed this function, namely, the Jews. Pietscher also takes issue with Ihering's assessment of Shylock as a sympathetic, tragic figure whose defeat at court was accomplished by a "pettifogging trick." The critic argues that if Shylock represents anything it is the picture of the individual who puts his rights above all others and uses the law to further his own evil ends. Thus, according to Pietscher, the Jew deserves the extent of his punishment, and his defeat by cunning rather than the execution of the justice is proper and unavoidable under the legal circumstances. Other critics who have disapproved of Shylock's treatment during the trial or have questioned the Christians'*

religious and moral behavior include Karl Elze (1871), Arthur Quiller-Couch (1926), Harold C. Goddard (1951), A. D. Moody (1964), R. Chris Hassel, Jr. (1970), and René Girard (1978). Pietscher's comments were first published in 1881.]

In truth there is nothing genuinely tragic about Shylock. Hence the poet called the piece, not *The Jew,* but *The Merchant,* of Venice, and termed it a *Comedy,* not a *Tragedy.* He knew nothing of the modern sympathy with a 'persecuted race,' and surely Shylock was not regarded by him as typical of one. He needed for his drama a *usurer,* not a *Jew,*—confessions of faith or nationalities have nothing to do with the central idea of the piece,—and in accordance with the views of his day he took him very naturally from the race of Jews. Then, to be sure, Shylock became for him *not merely* the 'usurer,' but a mortal and a Jew with human passions and the characteristics of his race.

When the Jew has demanded 'What judgement shall I dread, doing no wrong?' [IV. i. 89], he must be driven from this pharasaical pretext. It is doing him an unmerited honour to impute to him the will, at any dictate of mercy, to put an end to the contest between his legal rights and the baseness of his claim. For once this flinty heart must be made to feel that he himself may need mercy, and all other means must be exhausted before proceeding to use his own weapons against him. If Ihering finds Shylock typical, let us, too, find him typical [see excerpt above, 1872]. He typifies all who mercilessly insist upon their rights. All such are admonished that there are other and higher duties than maintaining one's rights, and our jurists are herein instructed who call a legal contest for justice, a duty. . . . Even Shylock demands the law, he 'stands for judgement,'—we have seen how this imposes upon Ihering,—but we know well enough how hollow these high-sounding words are, and that the man cares nothing for the law, but only that by means of it he may feed his hatred, and above all his greed. . . . It is the wretched envy of a business rival that instigates him. And when this 'man of law' invokes 'his deeds upon his head,' and his bold invocation is answered, it is brought home to every one that whoever pursues his own rights in violation of the dictates of 'mercy,' is himself crushed by merciless Right.

I am much afraid that Anthonio would have had to succumb, if Ihering had been of his counsel. His only plea was *turpis causa* [malicious motive]; if that would not carry him through, he would have given up his client. But his chance of making this plea good, before the Doge and the Senate, was small; they had probably from the first noticed that in this case an abominable design lay concealed under legal forms, but they could not have known how these latter were to be evaded. I believe that I dare assert that at that time in Venice the consideration that 'a contract against morals was void' was not yet recognized or regarded as a valid plea. For this consideration, or more properly its recognition in law, belongs only to the higher grades of culture, and always even then depends on the prevailing estimate of what is immoral, and its *full* significance and worth will have to remain, I suppose, a pious wish.

Ihering is particularly hostile to the way in which Portia deals with Shylock, which he terms quibbling and pettifogging.

For my part, commend me to our Portia, who, in true woman's fashion, does not allow herself to be in the least disconcerted by the pathetic appeal: 'If you deny me, fie upon your law! There is no force in the decrees of Venice' [IV. i. 101-02]; but steadily regarding the present case alone, takes no thought whatever of any dangerous consequences. . . . If the law of

Venice is so bad that it will help a scoundrel to ruin an honest man, it is worthless and does not deserve the least consideration. When a man stands in peril of his life he does not stop to choose his weapon,—the first is the best,—and just so in the present case, it may be permissible to meet chicanery with chicanery, pettifogging with pettifogging. Did it really escape our learned jurist, what the poet with sovereign humour has scourged with joyous jest, that a legal contest, if it is a fight, is subject to all the chances of a fight, and that in it often enough cunning must be overcome by cunning? To observe it may be unwelcome, but it may be observed, nevertheless, every day in courts of justice. A lawsuit is therein like a duel or a fight, and the talk is of 'winners' and 'losers.' When Portia's plea that flesh and not blood is in the bargain, is met by Ihering with the replication that blood is implied, and that the plea is frivolous, he may be met with the rejoinder that bargains of this nature are to be strictly interpreted, and in doubtful points *against* him in whom the power lay of making the terms of the agreement more explicit. And so it could go on with sur-rejoinders and rebutters for a good long while. But is it really 'a wretched quibble' which is here used against Shylock? What was the Jew after? The life of Anthonio. There is not the least doubt of that. For the pound of flesh in itself he cared not a jot. Well, then, why did he not have that stated clearly in his bond? He dared not; and hence he used the ambiguous phrase, 'a pound of flesh' [IV. i. 307]. And to his own words he is now kept. Is that unjust?

The discomfiture of the Jew is not the lamentable downfall of a hero; it is the victory of cunning by greater cunning; the rogue is caught in his own snare. No tears need fall; there can be here only the smiling satisfaction of a genuine comedy. But why did not the prudent man anticipate the possibility of the objection which Portia afterwards actually made? . . . The clever man was not clever enough, and a cleverer overcame him.

Nevertheless, it is to be unhesitatingly admitted that the wound which law and right received in the victory over Shylock is not healed,—a wound received at the hands of Shylock, not Portia; it is only skinned over. To overcome cunning with cunning, to take advantage of an opponent's weakness, cannot be termed executing justice. *If* the Jew had been more careful, the Merchant would have been lost. But even this point Shakespeare did not overlook. Through the mouth of Portia he shows [that 'the law hath yet another hold' [IV. i. 347] on Shylock]. Here, then, at last comes forth the violated majesty of abstract law, punishing, crushing him who dared presume to make law aid wrong. The violation of private rights yields place to the deeply outraged State of Venice that now demands atonement for itself. And so the Jew, because he stood upon his law, gets more law than he desired, a different law from that for which he hoped. (pp. 411-13)

A. Pietscher, in an extract, translated by Horace Howard Furness, in A New Variorum Edition of Shakespeare: The Merchant of Venice, Vol. VII *by William Shakespeare, edited by Horace Howard Furness, J. B. Lippincott Company, 1888, pp. 411-13.*

DENTON J. SNIDER (essay date 1890?)

[*Snider was an American scholar, philosopher, and poet who closely followed the precepts of the German philosopher Georg Wilhelm Friedrich Hegel and contributed greatly to the dissemination of his dialectical philosophy in America. Snider's critical writings include studies on Homer, Dante, and Goethe, as well as Shakespeare. Like Hermann Ulrici and G. G. Gervinus, Snider*

sought for the dramatic unity and ethical import in Shakespeare's plays, but he presented a more rigorous Hegelian interpretation than those two German philosophical critics. In the introduction to his three-volume work The Shakespearian Drama, a Commentary *(1887-90), Snider states that Shakespeare's plays present various ethical principles which, in their differences, come into "Dramatic Collision," but are ultimately resolved and brought into harmony. He claims that these collisions can be traced in the plays' various "Dramatic Threads" of action and thought, which together form a "Dramatic Movement," and that the analysis of these threads and movements—"the structural elements of the drama"—reveal the organic unity of Shakespeare's art. Snider observes two basic movements in the tragedies—guilt and retribution—and three in the comedies—separation, mediation, and return. In the following excerpt, Snider notes this three-part movement once again in* The Merchant of Venice, *though he substitutes "conflict" for "separation" in this instance. Within the first two movements he identifies two threads, which he calls the issues of property and of love, the former involving the conflict between Shylock and Antonio, the latter the struggle within Portia herself over obeying her father's will or exercising her personal choice. Snider variously terms this second conflict as that between parental authority and individual will, or that between objective law and subjective choice. The critic describes the Shylock-Antonio conflict as reflecting not only a struggle between two ethically and religiously opposed individuals, but a confrontation between two businessmen and, most importantly, between Christianity and Judaism itself. Thus, Snider became one of the first critics to note the allegorical structure of* The Merchant of Venice, *an interpretation more fully developed in the excerpts by Sir Israel Gollancz (1922), Nevill Coghill (1949), Theodor Reik (1956), C. L. Barber (1959), Barbara K. Lewalski (1962), and René E. Fortin (1974). On other matters, Snider labels* The Merchant of Venice *neither a comedy nor a tragedy, but a "mediated drama," or a tragicomedy. Similarly, he considers Shylock a tragic figure as a persecuted and defeated Jew, but a comic figure in his eventual conversion to Christianity. For further discussion of the genre of* The Merchant of Venice, *see the excerpts by Nicholas Rowe (1709), Heinrich Heine (1838), Hermann Ulrici (1839), Karl Elze (1871), A. Pietscher (1881), Elmer Edgar Stoll (1927), Harley Granville-Barker (1930), T. A. Ross (1934), Harold R. Walley (1935), John Middleton Murry (1936), C. L. Barber (1959), and Graham Midgley (1960).*]

Better than any other play of the Poet, the *Merchant of Venice* shows us the soul of his comic world. It is a mediated drama in the profoundest sense, portraying the mediation of man in pictures taken from the very body of Time. The Jewish and the Christian worlds are placed alongside of each other, are shown in conflict, are shown in transition; the one passes into the other through the doctrine of Mercy, which is not only stated in the poem, but is employed as the grand mediatorial instrument. Thus the mightiest event of human history, the mediation of the individual, whereby he escapes from a tragic fate, is made into a comedy, in the Shakespearian sense of the word. And what is that sweep of history from antiquity into Christianity, but a great mediated drama? There is the dark, threatening, tragic element; man seems fated; but he is rescued, and the end is happy. The heart of history, warm and palpitating, is taken out of its temporal wrappage, and held up before us in a representation which is the diversion of an evening. (pp. 227-28)

In the *Merchant of Venice* . . . we behold a conflicting and reconciling element. The conflicting element is mainly the contest between Antonio and Shylock, and is to be considered first; we are to behold the dramatic economy ordered to this end, and to watch how every incident contributes either to call forth their struggle, or to harmonize it after it has arisen. A glance at the leading events of the play will show that this conflict is the one central point from which the entire action radiates—which organizes and vivifies the whole piece. The incidents relating to Portia, which, at the first look, seem somewhat remote from the main action, are the reconciling part, and bring forth, in fact, the profoundest mediation of the drama. . . . Portia was indirectly the cause of Antonio's falling into the hands of the Jew, and, in ideal justice, the Poet makes her the instrumentality by which Antonio is released. Even the incidents of the last Act, which take place after the culmination of the play, are logically necessary for the harmonization of the lesser contradictions which have been called forth by the main struggle. Every part must be rounded off with the perfection of art; no shreds are left to draggle from the edges of this well-woven garment. (pp. 229-31)

The general movement of the play, therefore, lies in the conflict between the right of Property and the existence of the Individual, and in the mediation of this conflict through the Family, which owes its origin, in the present case, to that same individual whom it rescues. That is, the Family, represented by Portia, the wife, returns and saves the man who aided, by his friendship and generosity, to bring it into being. All the characters of the play, though possessing peculiarities of their own, must be seen in their relation to this fundamental theme of the work.

There are three essential movements, which may be named in order: the Conflict, the Mediation, the Return. Of the first movement there are two threads, showing, respectively, the Property-conflict and the Love-conflict, though the former is raised to the highest spiritual significance by the underlying religious element. These two threads, moreover, are interwoven in the subtlest manner; still, an analysis has to tear them asunder temporarily. (pp. 231-32)

The first movement . . . unfolds the realm of conflict in its double phase. Two legal documents are introduced, which, in their very right are violating right; in both, the outer realized Law is turning against the inner Law not yet realized in forms of legality. These two documents are the testament of Portia's father, and the Jew's contract with Antonio. We see Justice and Equity, which ought to remain one and in harmony, to divide and to be set against each other; Law, which should protect, is made to assail its most precious trusts. It is a dualism which cuts to the heart of man as well as of social order. The life of the individual is assailed by the right which guards it; the Family is disregarded by forcing it to submit in its inner essence to what seems an outer accident.

We shall start with the conflict between Antonio and Shylock, which we have called, in a general way, the Property-conflict. Each of these men has a good and a bad side to his character, though in different degrees. The question, therefore, arises— what do they respectively represent? What principles does each one maintain? For men, without some great motive lying at the basis of their action and giving color to their endeavor, can have no interest for us. It is the conflict of these principles, represented and carried into execution by men, that excites our sympathy, our fear, our delight. The first thing which we find much stress laid upon is that Shylock is a Jew—a circumstance which should excite our careful consideration. The Poet evidently intends to portray the Jewish character, or rather the Jewish consciousness, in one of its manifestations. Antonio's religion is not specially dwelt upon, but he is called a Christian, which is also the faith of those around him. The Jew thus finds himself in a Christian world, acting and dealing with men of a strange race and strange morality, and with ends in life far

different from his own. Hence the possibility of a conflict, both of nationalities and of moralities. The collision, therefore, which supplies the nerve of the play, may be stated, in a general form, to be between Christianity and Judaism.

But mark! it is not between these religions as dogmatic systems of Theology, but as realized in the practical life of men. Antonio is a Christian—not that he goes to church and makes long prayers and daily rehearses the creed; he does none of these things as far as we know; but a general spirit of brotherhood and generosity animates all his actions, with one very striking exception; a liberality, which we may fairly call Christian, is ingrained into his very nature, and is the well-spring of his conduct in his dealings with his fellow-men. On the contrary, Shylock exhibits Judaism, as it must influence the doings of those who act according to its principle, though there is, in his portraiture, an element foreign to Judaism, which must not be forgotten. To be sure, the religious phase is brought into more prominence in his character than in Antonio's, but only for the purpose of showing the moral consequences of that system of belief. Shylock carries out in his life the faith that is in him, with the utmost logical rigor and bitterness. (pp. 233-35)

[Here] is the conflict of two hostile moralities, and the struggle is ethical rather than religious. We feel that the consciousness of the two men is entirely different; that their notions of right and wrong are, in many respects, directly opposite. Shylock cannot help being a Jew in character any more than being a Jew in nationality. He is no vulgar villain; he acts according to his end in life; given his moral basis, his deeds must follow. He is not altogether a comic character; on the contrary, he belongs in part to Tragedy, for he is the bearer of one of the two great colliding principles, and it is his principle which has gone down in history, and which must again go to the wall in every conflict with the profounder phases of modern spirit. We see the destiny impending over him; but he yields—as the Jews always have done—and is preserved. The Poet has thus made him the type of his race, which avoids the life-and-death collision; for, like him, the Jew has lived among all nations without being swallowed up. He possesses that happy admixture of stubbornness and submission which has kept him from being destroyed on the one hand, and from being absorbed on the other.

The cause of this strange preservation lies in the nature of the Jewish faith; it is not for all men, but for the peculiar people of God. Hence it is not a religion of propagandism, and thus avoids any struggle with dominant systems. Still, it maintains its individuality, and has a tenacity which can spring only from the profoundest conviction—or rather, in its most stubborn forms, from a complete limitation of Intelligence, beyond which the Hebrew mind refuses to pass. Thus we see renewed, though in a different way, the contest which took place 1800 years ago, on the plains of Judea—the contest which forms, perhaps, the most important period in history, and upon the result of which our entire modern civilization has turned. . . . [It] is the collision between two of the greatest world-historical epochs— between the old and new dispensation—which lays the imperishable foundation of the play.

But this statement of the collision between Judaism and Christianity is still too abstract, and, hence, we next ask—what is the content of these two systems of religion, especially in their influence upon the practical life of mankind? What objects do these two men place before themselves, to be attained by their living? In other words, what is their end in life? This gives the central point—the germinal unit—from which all action springs. Antonio is a merchant, but it is plain that his end in life is not money, nor can it be any Christian's. Antonio's purse is open to all his friends. He is the center of a jolly crowd of good fellows, though he himself is inclined to be melancholy. In such a position we can easily see it is not difficult to get rid of money. A deeper phase of his moral nature is his hatred of usury. He has relieved many a poor victim from the clutches of Shylock, and has denounced the meanness and cruelty of the latter, on the Rialto, with extremest vehemence. He realizes, in the highest sense of the expression, that man is above property—that is enough to show his Christianity. Money is to him only a means—a means of enjoyment for himself and friends on the one hand, and for helping his fellow-mortals on the other. On this side of his character Antonio is truly merciful; he is the practical embodiment of the holy declaration—"without charity I am nothing." Christianity always insists upon the neighbor, who has the same rights as yourself; he is a person as well as yourself, in the thought of universal Reason, or, as Holy Writ saith, "in the sight of God." Nay, more; its cardinal doctrine is Mercy—which means that man, within certain limits, is to be shielded from the consequences of his deeds. Man is a finite being—God made him so—and, in so far as he is finite, he cannot be held responsible for the results of his actions. He is ignorant, and, hence, liable to err; Mercy says that he shall not suffer for his mistakes. But he is also weak, and, hence, liable to transgress; Mercy says that he must receive pardon if the transgression be repented of. Here the conflict arises. Justice demands rigid accountability; it asserts that man must be responsible for all his acts, while Mercy tries to shield even the crouching criminal. (pp. 237-40)

Antonio's mishap was no doubt his own fault; he had no business to give such a bond, one thinks, since it seems that his credit was good in Venice, and he might have obtained the money by other means. But his case deserves the commiseration of his fellow-mortals, especially since he made a mistake merely, and did not commit a transgression. Besides, he probably could not think, with his consciousness, that even the Jew would proceed to such extreme measures. Of Antonio we may say that in the main his life has been a practical embodiment of Mercy; now, in his present extremity, he deserves Mercy. But he does not get it; on the contrary, he hears the cry, Revenge. Why? He has himself reared the avenger, it is his own deed coming back to him in that ominous shout.

At this point we must mark the side on which character of Antonio shows its limitation; inconsistency cuts it in twain, for, though generally merciful, he was unmerciful to the Jew, and thus wronged his own principle. The sight of the pitiless man, made him pitiless in requital; he has berated, kicked, spit on Shylock in public; he has educated the latter to vengeance. "Hath not a Jew eyes? Hath not a Jew hands, organs, dimensions, senses, affections, passions? If you prick us do we not bleed? if you tickle us, do we not laugh? if you poison us, do we not die? and if you wrong us, shall we not revenge? If a Christian wrong a Jew, what should his sufferance be, by Christian example? Why, revenge. The villainy you teach me, I will execute; and it shall go hard but I will better the instruction" [III. i. 59-73]. Thus Shylock's deed is engendered of Antonio's deed, which is now coming back to the latter armed with all the might of Venetian justice.

If this passage shows Antonio in his limit, it shows equally well Shylock in his limit. The latter has drawn from the severe discipline of life not charity, but revenge. His sarcastic plea is Christian example, but just therein he is not Christian. His trials have begotten no love, but have nursed to colossal growth the Judaistic germ—an eye for an eye and a tooth for a tooth. His hate now passes into guilt; he intends to destroy Antonio, if he can keep himself safe in the process.

Shylock's Judaism is strongly emphasized; and Judaism, in its narrow, sectarian manifestation, knows no Mercy—at least, Mercy in its universal sense. God has his own peculiar people; the world is for them, and the fullness thereof. Furthermore, the manifestation of God's favor is prosperity; of his wrath, adversity. Hence Shylock well states his end in life to be—Thrift. The acquisition of gain is the highest object of existence; every other end is subordinate. (pp. 241-43)

But now we are to consider the second element in the character of Shylock—an element which springs, not from his religion, but from his circumstances. Shylock represents the ancient Hebrew, with his essential peculiarities, cast into the modern world and subjected to abuse and injustice on account of his faith. He is, therefore, the product of two influences—first, the original Jewish character; second, that character in a strange land, persecuted and outlawed by society. On every side he meets with scorn and outrage; hence the bitterness which overflows his whole existence, and poisons, not merely his social relations, but his own domestic hearth. Thrust into a Christian world, he must hate it on account of its attitude toward him, since it represents for him ridicule and oppression. Here the modern reader is touched with a sympathetic feeling for Shylock, and is not averse to hating along with him. (pp. 243-44)

But there is another contrast between Antonio and Shylock. The scene of this drama is laid in the greatest commercial city of that age, and it represents the business world. Hence it portrays man in his commercial relations to his fellow-man, and these transactions furnish the basis of a business morality. . . . Furthermore, this is a world of free activity, for each one chooses what branch of business best suits his inclination and character. The calling thus becomes, to a certain degree, an index of the moral disposition of the man. It is well known that some kinds of business, though acknowledged by law and recognized by the community as necessary, are, nevertheless, held in disrepute by the great majority of mankind.

What callings, then, have these two men respectively chosen? Antonio is a merchant; he exchanges the productions of the world; he knits the nations together by mutual traffic—of course, for a consideration. But there is nothing narrow or mean in his nature; his end, as before stated, is not money, and this frees him from any trace of avarice or illiberality. In fact, his melancholy seems to arise in part from a dissatisfaction with his calling; it cannot satisfy the highest wants of man. Shylock, on the contrary, is a usurer; he takes advantage of the sudden wants of people to extort their earnings. Hence this class of men were regarded as the enemies of society, ready to draw profit out of any misfortune to the individual or the State. It is not surprising, then, that this business fell into the hands of the Jews, who were persecuted by society, and, hence, hostile, or at least indifferent, to it. (pp. 244-46)

Let us now take up the second thread—the Love-conflict—in which Portia is the main figure, supported, however, by Nerissa and Jessica. Portia is the third great character of the play, and in importance stands quite on a par with Antonio and Shylock. Her function is mediatorial; in fact, she may be called the grand mediatrix of the entire drama. In her we see the instrumentality by which the main results are brought about. . . . The great principle of which she is the bearer may be termed the Right of Subjectivity. She asserts the validity of the Internal and Spiritual against the crushing might of externality; but she does not deny the Right of the Objective in its true limitation. Only when this Objective becomes destructive of its end, and self-contradictory, as in the case when the law was about to murder Antonio, does she place a limit to it, and invoke a higher principle. Her struggle is with legality and prescription asserting themselves in spheres where they do not belong; but, in relations where this contradiction no longer appears, she is the most ethical of women. In the Family her subordination is complete—indeed, devout. We shall see that all her acts have one end and one impelling motive—devotion to her husband, an absolute unity with his feelings and interests; in other words subordination to the Family. She vindicates the Right of Subjectivity for herself in order that she may obtain the one whom she really loves—without which principle, it need hardly be said, the true existence of the Family is impossible. So peculiar is this character, so difficult is it to ascertain its unity, and so important is its place in the drama, that we shall be justified in looking somewhat minutely at all the circumstances in which it has been placed by the Poet. (pp. 246-48)

Portia has quite disregarded the outward glitter of wealth and rank, and has seemingly sought out a follower in the retinue of a lord, instead of the lord himself—"a Venetian, a scholar and a soldier, that came hither in the company of the Marquis of Montferrat" [I. ii. 113-14]. So, at the outset, we see that she cares naught for the External, but lays stress upon the Internal. The Poet has thus given us an inkling of her inclination that we may not be in the dark about her choice. Moreover, we already know of the inclination of Bassanio from the very first scene of the play, and he, too, is aware of Portia's preference for himself. This point, then, let us carefully bear in mind—that the Poet has already let us into the secret, unknown to the outside world, that Portia and Bassanio love each other, and that each one knows of the other's love. The two people, therefore, belong together; they alone can form a rational union, since they possess the absolute prerequisite of the Family, namely, reciprocal love. (pp. 248-49)

But to this blissful consummation there is a great obstacle. Portia's father is dead, and has left a will which seems to bind her choice of a husband to a hopeless accident. Three caskets—made of gold, silver, and lead, respectively—are to be set before his daughter's suitors for selection, and that casket which contains her image carries with it her hand in marriage. Hence we find her lamenting, in almost her first words, that she cannot choose whom she would, nor refuse whom she disliked. But she recognizes the binding validity of the last request of her parent, and thus we have one of Shakespeare's favorite collisions, which may be stated as the Right of Choice against the Will of the Parent. Both sides have their validity, and it is just this validity of both sides which makes it a genuine collision. None will deny the right of the parent over the child, and this right was less circumscribed in former times than at present. But, though the parent may no longer have any legal right, he has still the right of respect; and no child with a truly ethical feeling, such as Portia undoubtedly possessed, would withhold obedience.

Such is the one side. But the other side is what we have termed the Right of Choice, or, in general terms, the Right of Subjectivity. This demands that the daughter should have, absolutely, the right of selecting her partner for life. She has to

bear the responsibility of her choice, for she must live with the one whom she selects. The husband and wife constitute that unity called the Family; it is a unity of emotion; each party finds true life in the other. This emotion, by which both are melted together into one common existence, is called love. So, if we have a true unity, or a true Family, love is the indispensable condition. Now, it is just this important element which the will of Portia's father flings to the winds by exposing the choice of her husband to mere accident. It does not demand reciprocal love, which is the only basis of rational marriage. Such is the problem which Portia has to solve, and such is the mental conflict which we find her undergoing. (pp. 249-50)

The caskets are really but a test of the motives of the suitors, who must choose as they do; they cannot help themselves, for they are held in the grip of their own natures. . . . The Prince of Morocco must follow the glitter; the Prince of Arragon must follow his own good opinion of himself. Given their characters, they must choose as they do, and choose wrongly, and reveal themselves in their choice. Thus accident is made the means for carrying out the free will of Portia; it is simply the mask of Love rejecting the wrong and accepting the right suitor. The conflict with the will of the parent, which at first weighed so hard upon her, is reduced to a mere appearance, as Nerissa saw from the start: "the lottery will never be chosen by any rightly, but one whom you shall rightly love" [I. ii. 32-3]. (pp. 252-53)

We have now witnessed the two grand conflicts of the play in full operation. The next thing is, they are to be mediated. But by whom? Again this duty falls to the lot of a woman. Already in the love of Portia, the principle has been introduced, which will transform this entire world of conflict. First, she harmonizes her own struggle, which lies in the domestic realm. Then she carries her reconciling deed up into the State, into the very administration of Justice, to which she, the woman, brings Mercy, after a sharp struggle, and imparts it to all. Love is the germ, the first impelling force; love drives her to overcome the legal obstacle to itself; then it drives her to do for others what she has done for herself. Love is thus the curer, as well as the conqueror, verily the mediator; the love of Portia is the primal fountain whence flow the healing waters in which all are saved. Nay, she rises out of the Family, out of the State even, and reaches up to the heights of the World's History; she mediates essentially the conflict between Judaism and Christianity, and does over again the greatest deed of Time. This deed Shakespeare assigns to a woman, not to a man; it would seem as if he might worship the Mother as well as the Christ. But it is wonderful; that little seed of Portia's love, sprouting amid so much confusion and conflict, will draw all to itself, and make out of chaos a cosmos. This is the work of the second movement of the play, which shows the mediation.

The first thread again takes up the conflict between Shylock and Antonio, and shows its solution. Shylock, being a Jew, can use the Gentiles for his own end; that end being Thrift, he uses them for making money. This is allowed by the law of Moses, which permits the Hebrews to take usury from the stranger, but not from the brother. But Antonio stands in his way. He has the right to employ any means of getting rid of the hateful merchant which does not endanger his own safety; for, if he should lose his life in the attempt, that would not be thrifty. The means most consistent with his own safety is the formal side of the Law—he is going to murder Antonio legally. . . . Hence the Right of Property comes into conflict with the existence of the Individual. (pp. 254-56)

[Shylock's] bond calls for a pound of flesh—that, and nothing else, will satisfy him. Thus the collision is narrowed down to a mere empty form of Law against the existence of an individual. Law is pushed in this way to the extreme limit of self-contradiction, for Law, which was made to protect and preserve mankind, has now become the direct instrument of their destruction. Is not that self-contradictory? But it is the Law, and the Law must have its course, says Portia; only Mercy can soften its severity and annul its wrong. Hence her appeal for Mercy [in IV. i. 184-205]. But the Jew cannot relent; the character would be utterly illogical and untrue if he did. The letter of the Law, then, is to be followed with the utmost rigidity; this is the Jew's own basis. "But hold!" says Portia, "the bond mentions no blood" [IV. i. 305-06]. If you want the letter, you can have it to your heart's content. Portia abandons her first defense—that of Mercy—and takes the weapons of the Jew and turns them against him. This contradiction rests upon the fact that a law, a bond, a contract—yea, language itself—cannot describe the Particular, for they are in their nature general. . . . Hence, if an absolute adherence to the letter is insisted upon, neither Shylock's nor any other bond is possible.

Many lawyers have made objection to this point taken by Portia; they say that no court in Christendom would have decided that a pound of flesh did not include the blood, though the bond may not have expressly said so. This may be the case, but it does not affect the truth of Shakespeare's representation. His design was to show how formal Law contradicts itself, and to exhibit the Jew beaten at his own game. From this moment Shylock subsides; he sees the point, and is completely overwhelmed. The might of the Form of Law was never more powerfully presented. The judge, the people, and justice itself, are all on the side of one innocent man, yet they are unable to rescue him from the clutches of an odious wretch who has the form alone on his side. Still, the Poet must find for us some reconciliation with the Law; it would be most ridiculously inadequate if it did not furnish some means for reaching the Jew. This it does, inasmuch as it is made to seize the crime of Shylock just in its truly vulnerable point—criminal intention. This is Portia's next point against him. He has willed the death of a citizen, of which the punishment is confiscation and death. We have seen this motive lying behind all his actions, notwithstanding his vociferation for Right and Justice.

Still, we must not suppose that he was a common villain—an Iago, or Richard, or Edmund. The subjective side was little emphasized by the Jewish faith. If men conformed to Law and Religion, it mattered not so much about motives. Under the old dispensation, the man who committed the most justifiable homicide had to flee the country, and the person who ate pork had committed a deed of guilt. Hence, when Shylock is arraigned for his subjective intention, we may fairly assume that this principle lies beyond his consciousness; it is the product of the modern world and Christianity. Still, Shylock is saved, because he is ready to yield to formal Law when that turns against him; hence the Law cannot well destroy him. . . . [However,] is punished with a truly poetic justice. Avarice loses its money; religious and national bigotry sees the Jewish house of Shylock go down forever, by the marriage of the daughter with a Christian. Moreover, the court and Portia could not reasonably condemn the Jew after they had maintained the cause of Mercy with such persistency and power. It would be a flagrant inconsistency to demand that for Antonio which they the next moment refuse to Shylock. (pp. 256-59)

But what if the Jew would still insist upon taking his pound of flesh? Then he must have it, and the play becomes a tragedy. Antonio loses his life by the letter of the Law, and Shylock is executed for murder. But the play can not admit of this solution; for thus the character of the Jew would be wholly untrue, as we have before stated. Nor can the Poet allow Antonio to perish for a mere mistake. This would be totally adverse to his moral code. Hence the difficulty demands mediation, and the conclusion must be happy. The piece is, therefore, neither pure tragedy nor pure comedy, but a middle species of play, which may be called, for want of a better word, a mediated drama or tragicomedy.

But the question will continue to come up: Is the Jew truly mediated? People will differ about the matter, but the Poet clearly answers, Yes. Let us notice the course of the trial in the Fourth Act, that scene of the world's judgment, which reveals, in brief compass, the whole dealing of Christendom with the Jews. There are three stages. 1st. The preaching of Mercy to the Jew by the Duke and all, especially by the evangelist Portia. But the stiff-necked Israelite refuses it, scorns it, and triumphs in his principle. 2nd. That principle is turned against him in its inadequacy, he is the victim of his own justice. The penalty has come; not triumph now, but death looks him in the eye. 3rd. Again the evangel of Mercy, interceding not now for the Christian, but for the Jew, is heard in the question of Portia: "What Mercy can you render him, Antonio?" [IV. i. 378]. From the lips of his victim Shylock is to hear the answer: Mercy, yes; but on one sole condition, that his property, his family, and himself be Christianized. The answer seems harsh, but, given the conflict, no other solution is possible. A world based upon Shylock's principle, cannot exist, it must be transformed into another kind of world. Is not that the decree of history? Shylock himself sees the point which is made against him, he yields, and accepts the conditions in full.

Portia. Art thou contented, Jew? What does thou say?
Shylock. I am content.

[IV. i. 393-94]

Perhaps this is a surrender to external force, with mental reservation; but we must think that Shylock is smitten internally, as we have seen him breaking under the blows of Portia's argument. We do not say he repents, but he gives up his standpoint, otherwise the Poet would not let him off in the present way. Thus we must read the result: Shylock too is mediated—and mediated by Portia. He has a tragic element in him; as a Jew he perishes in his bitter conflict with Christendom. But in property, family, nay, in his new mediated self, he lives on, as far as we can see, to the natural end. He is, therefore, comic essentially; from the beginning the Poet gave him a biting speech, an odd demeanor; pathetic at times, he is always grotesque. . . . But in a still deeper sense he is comic; he is mediated, saved, if not reconciled. (pp. 260-62)

The second thread [of the Mediation movement] is Portia's, whose conflict has been already unfolded, and must now be shown in its mediation. Her work is double—she has first to solve her own difficulty, then Antonio's. After the failure of the two princes, Bassanio appears, in order to make trial of the caskets. He has both the requisite elements—loves and is loved; for the Poet has carefully told us all this beforehand. We have no doubt of his success from the start. It is curious to trace the ethereal, almost imperceptible, influences which the Poet brings to bear upon Bassanio to determine his choice. First, his state of mind, all aglow with affection—no wonder that he disregards the exterior of things, for love is blind. Then Portia, in the same condition, and giving expression to it in words, to which we may add, in imagination, her looks. Finally, the music, and the vague hints of the song, until the feeling of internality is intensified to such a degree as to be irresistible. . . . The same principle which causes the rejection of the two Princes, must bring about the triumph of Bassanio.

The grounds of a rational marriage are now complete. Portia and Bassanio have all the elements of a true union. Such is, undoubtedly, the logic of the situation. Thus the choice of caskets—which seemed to represent a horrible Chance about to crush out the rights of human nature—is spiritualized into the highest forms of freedom. Portia wins, and, moreover, wins through the very instruments which threatened her happiness; she converts them to weapons for her own rescue. (pp. 264-66)

But does Portia . . . give any hint to Bassanio which of the caskets to choose? It will be recollected that it was forbidden her in her father's will to tell this secret. A suspicious circumstance is the introduction of a song during the choice of Bassanio, which the previous choosers do not have the benefit of. Hence one is inclined to scrutinize closely the meaning of this song. It is somewhat enigmatic, yet its general purport may be stated to be: "Do not choose by the eye—by the glittering outside—for it is the source of all delusion." Hence Portia, after observing with the greatest care all the formalities of her father's will, breaks it just at the point of its conflict with her subjective right. This is done so delicately by her that it is scarcely perceived; still, it is none the less real. Thus she stands here as the grand bearer of the Right of Subjectivity, in its special form of Love versus Obedience to the will of the parent. (p. 266)

The great majority of Shakespeare's prominent female characters have one trait, however varied they may otherwise be—subordination to the Family. It is a devotion to husband, parent, child, lover; they live but for one object—to be absorbed into the existence of another. By themselves they feel that they are nothing; only in the unity of feeling, interest, and existence with another do they have any happiness in life. The complete absorption of the individual through emotion, not consciously, but instinctively, is the grand characteristic which Shakespeare gives to his women—that is, to those whom he wishes to portray as good, noble and dutiful. On the contrary, his bad women are, for the most part, marked by quite the opposite of this quality. Such are the limits in which Shakespeare's female characters move. Now, that just this trait forms the charm of woman few men will deny. Though wit, fancy, learning, may call forth admiration, there must be something quite different to subdue. It is not servitude, but the willing subordination to the higher end—self-sacrifice in its most exalted form. We believe that it is this consideration which makes us ever respect Portia; her motive is pure devotion to her husband, complete oneness with his interests and friendships, added, no doubt, to gratitude toward that man—Antonio—who has been chiefly instrumental in making her the happiest of mortals. For Antonio is a stranger to her so far as we know; why should she assume the disguise, and run the risk of an ignominious exposure and tarnished reputation? No; she has that complete harmony and unity with her husband, that his joys are her joys, his sorrows her sorrows; and she has the same interest in her husband's friend that the husband himself has. Thus she is a truly ethical character—ethical in the sense that she instinctively subordinates herself to the highest end of woman.

Such is the motive which impels Portia forth to the rescue of Antonio. Just here occurs the seeming contradiction in her character. Hitherto she has asserted boldly and strongly her individual rights; she has trampled upon custom, and even Law, when they have stood in the way of her purposes. But the moment she is united with Bassanio, all is changed. She yields up her whole being to another, who is, of course, equally devoted to her; this daring and resolute will is now at peace, and submissive; and her expression of subordination is as absolute as language can make it:—

> Though for myself alone
> I would not be ambitious in my wish,
> To wish myself much better; yet for you
> I would be trebled twenty times myself. . . .
> She is not bred so dull but she can learn;
> Happiest of all in that her gentle spirit
> Commits itself to yours to be directed
> As from her lord, her governor, her king.
> Myself and what is mine to you and yours
> Is now converted; but now I was the lord
> Of this fair mansion, master of my servants,
> Queen of myself, and even now—but now
> This house, these servants, and this same myself
> Are yours, my lord.
>
> [III. ii. 150-53, 162-71]

Now, what is the solution of these contradictory traits? Portia insists upon the subjective principle only in order that her union with her husband may be more complete. She has struggled for the Right of Choice. To what end? Since the oneness of the marriage-tie is based upon emotion, she insists that emotion in this sphere must have absolute validity. Every hindrance must be set aside; the more intense and unobstructed the affection, the more perfect the bond of unity. Thus she has asserted her individuality, with the single purpose that her subordination might, in the end, be more complete, and that her marriage might be truer and more rational. (pp. 271-74)

Portia thus stands as the type of the rational woman—rational in what she resists and in what she accepts, rational in rebellion and in submission. She is a strong character, yet not strong-minded, in the special sense of this term; she withers not, like a delicate flower, at the first rude blast, but maintains her individual right, till to yield becomes duty. (p. 275)

The Fourth Act terminates the leading collision of the play—that between Shylock and Antonio. The one has been punished, the other rescued. Why, then, is the Fifth Act added? It is because the minor complications, which are brought about by the leading collision and form a necessary element of it, are not yet solved. Portia and Bassanio have been violently separated—like Gratiano and Nerissa—by the main struggle. When this is at an end, there is no longer cause for separation; but they must quickly rebound to their former union, which is their only rational existence. Hence the Return, which is the theme of the Fifth Act, is a logical movement of the whole drama. If there be mediation, it must be complete in every part. (pp. 277-78)

The characters pass out of the realm of difference and contradiction into the world of harmony. It opens with an idyllic strain, which at once ushers us into the nature of the place—we are now in the land of love. Lorenzo and Jessica, in responsive song, celebrate the heroes and heroines of romantic devotion. Next the sweet strains of music arise—the language of emotion and harmony. So there is diffused over the whole scene the atmosphere of love and concord. Finally, the parties return separately from their struggle, into the land of harmony; the rescued Antonio is also there—the mark of triumph. The difficulty about the rings is only temporary; their hearts are right, and that is the main thing; for it would ill become Portia, after her crusade against the most weighty formalities of the world, to insist upon the formality of a ring. Even the ships return to smooth over the last trouble; and the concord is perfect when the story of the disguise is told. It is worth noticing that Shakespeare has here localized his themes. The abode of quiet is at a distance from the place of strife; so Belmont is the land of Harmony and Love, which they leave in the hour of struggle and to which they come back in the hour of peace. (pp. 278-79)

> Denton J. Snider, "'Merchant of Venice'," in his The Shakespearian Drama, a Commentary: The Comedies, *Sigma Publishing Co., 1890? pp. 227-86.*

E. K. CHAMBERS   (essay date 1908)

[*Chambers occupies a transitional position in Shakespearean criticism, one which connects the biographical sketches and character analyses of the nineteenth century with the historical, technical, and textual criticism of the twentieth century. While a member of the education department at Oxford University, Chambers earned his reputation as a scholar with his multivolume works,* The Medieval Stage *(1903) and* The Elizabethan Stage *(1923), while he also edited* The Red Letter Shakespeare *(1904-08). Chambers investigated both the purpose and limitations of each dramatic genre as Shakespeare presented it and speculated on how the dramatist's work was influenced by contemporary historical issues and his own frame of mind. In the following excerpt, taken from his introduction to the Red Letter edition of* The Merchant of Venice *published in 1908, Chambers questions the reason for Antonio's melancholy, which he states is nowhere justified in the play. To answer his question, Chambers suggests that we must first decide what type of play* The Merchant of Venice *is. After ruling out the "drama of amusement" and the "drama of ideas," he concludes that it is most like the "drama of emotion," or tragicomedy. Chambers next determines the emotional issue that informs this tragicomedy, which he defines as the conflict between love and hate—love represented by Portia and Antonio, hate reflected in the actions of Shylock. Returning to the question of Antonio's melancholy, Chambers concludes that even in this play of emotional stress the merchant's dark behavior is out of tune. He suggests that its source might be the marriage of Bassanio and Portia and the former's separation from Antonio, but adds that it remains unexplicable and plays no important role in the drama. As such, Chambers proposes, Antonio's sadness represents the "intrusion of a personal note, an echo of those disturbed relations in Shakespeare's private life of which but enigmatic record is to be found in the Sonnets." The significance of Antonio's melancholy and the investigation into its possible source became dominant issues in twentieth-century criticism of* The Merchant of Venice *and can be found in the essays by T. A. Ross (1934), Graham Midgley (1960), John D. Hurrell (1961), A. D. Moody (1964), and Lawrence Danson (1978).*]

The melancholy of Antonio is a perpetual undertone in the gaiety and the tribulation of *The Merchant of Venice*. It claims your pondering in the first significant words of the play; nor is its meaning, there or elsewhere, clearly or explicitly set forth. Solanio and Salarino, with the natural assumption of poor men, that a rich man must be at least as much concerned about his riches, as themselves are at their want of riches, have an obvious explanation ready to hand; and Antonio merely replies that it is not his merchandise that makes him sad. Gratiano, since he must always be talking, thinks, or pretends to think, that his friend is deliberately affecting the serious pose proper

to persons of importance; and him too Antonio puts by with a smile. Gratiano is not of those to whom one reveals the heart's secrets. So that you are left to guess whether there is a heart's secret here at all, or whether Antonio is sincere when he declares that he is no more able than another to tell what stuff his melancholy is made of, whereof it is born. The current explanation has it that he is quite sincere, and that a vague uneasiness stands for a premonition of the disaster which is shortly to overtake him. Such a device falls altogether within Shakespeare's dramatic methods. If one cites only plays contemporary with *The Merchant of Venice*, there is the prophetic foreboding of the little queen in *Richard the Second,* when her lover and king has gone forth on his light-hearted expedition to Ireland—

> Some unborn sorrow, ripe in fortune's womb,
> Is coming towards me, and my inward soul
> With nothing trembles:—
>
> [*Richard II,* II. ii. 10-12]

and there is the ironical inverse of the same situation when Romeo steps out into the morning, and tells us that his bosom's lord sits lightly in his throne, five minutes before he is to learn that Juliet sleeps in Capel's monument [*Romeo and Juliet,* V. i. 1-10]. Yet a difference is to be observed. *Richard the Second* and *Romeo and Juliet* are to issue tragically; and therefore the preluding touches which tune the spectator to the sense of tragedy are justified. They have their appointed and logical place in the pattern. With *The Merchant of Venice* it is otherwise. Heart-strings shall be wrung in the process of the story; but it is not, as a whole, written in the key of tragedy. It stands under the domination of Portia, the first and most triumphant of Shakespeare's questing heroines; and its atmosphere is throughout in harmony with Portia's sunny hair, and Portia's sunny wit, and Portia's sunny temper, rather than with the grey twilight of Antonio's mood.

A formal analysis of the central dramatic intention—the *idée mère* [principal idea] of the play—can only confirm one's immediate feeling that its stage must not be hung with black. Heminges and Condell classed it with Shakespeare's comedies, and it claims to be, upon every page, a 'comical history.' But 'comedy,' like most other literary terms of art, has but a shifting connotation, and one is hardly dispensed from enquiring in what precise shade of its significance it is here to be taken. In the long history of the soul of man, the dramatic instinct seems to have worked its way to two or three types of outlook upon the world which it mirrors; and for each of them the ambiguous term 'comedy' has its distinct meaning. There is the drama of amusement, the drama of ideas, and the drama of emotion. The drama of amusement asks the name of comedy for the give and take of dialogue and the tangle of intrigue with which it entertains the spectator. But the drama of amusement is too purely external to take rank as art in the higher sense in which art is before all things an expression of the personality of the artist. The higher drama, on the other hand, differentiates itself, according as it expresses one or other side of such a personality. It is the medium through which the dramatic artist conveys to the audience his ideas about life, or it is the medium through which he conveys to them his emotions about life. Comedy, in what I accept as the primary sense of the word, is the characteristic form taken by the drama of ideas. Such is the comedy of Aristophanes and of Molière. It has its roots in the fearless and outspoken comment of . . . the revel rout, or of . . . the village rout. In its urban forms it is still essentially an analysis, a criticism, of life. And, therefore, it is really no paradox to say that comedy is often one of the most serious and even didactic of utterances. The comic dramatist has reflected upon life and condemns it. He lays his finger upon its follies and weaknesses. He strips it bare for you, a wheel of fortune, a dance of fools, a show of jerking puppets. His cap and bells hides this deliberate intention. His bauble conceals a scalpel. 'He uses his folly as a stalking-horse, and under the presentation of that he shoots his wit' [*As You Like It*, V. iv. 106-07].

Is it, then, this primary type of comedy to which *The Merchant of Venice* belongs? Are we to find in it the critical outlook, the play of bitterness or of humour or of irony upon life? Up to a point the intention of the piece can, no doubt, be so formulated. Take it as a series of variations on the obvious comic theme of the hollowness of appearances; and the choice of the caskets, the deception of Shylock, even the disguise of the wives and their stratagem with the rings, fit naturally enough into such a design. Nor can one fail to notice how well a good deal of the dialogue lends itself to such an interpretation. Gratiano chaffs those—

> That therefore only are reputed wise
> For saying nothing.
>
> [I. i. 96-7]

Arragon scorns 'the fool multitude that choose by show' [II. ix. 26]. Bassanio sermonizes upon 'beauty purchased by the weight,' upon golden locks that are 'the dowry of a second head,' 'the beauteous scarf veiling an Indian beauty' [III. ii. 89, 96, 98-9], and upon other illustrations of his thesis that 'the world is still deceived with ornament' [III. ii. 74]. Certainly here is one element in the structure of the play. But as certainly, I think, when you have disengaged and fixed this element, you have not really accounted for the whole. For you have not accounted for the other element of emotion; and although, no doubt, as you watch *The Merchant of Venice*, you feel the gathering conviction that 'the outward shows are least themselves' [III. ii. 73], yet after all this feeling is only subordinate to the swing and sway of your sympathies with the trapping of Antonio and the rout of Antonio's oppressor by Portia's divine and generous wit. In virtue, then, of its emotion, the play falls outside the range of comedy in the sense in which comedy is the vehicle of the drama of ideas; since to such comedy it is vital that it should remain unemotional, should see all things in the dry light of reason unperverted by the heart, and should hold the sympathies aloof that its flight may be all the more deadly to the brain.

It is probable enough that *The Merchant of Venice* has a divided purpose. Literary types rarely offer their pure form in concrete examples. But in the total impression left by the play it is the emotional and not the critical attitude towards life which predominates. And it is the principal ambiguity of the term 'comedy' that it stands not only for the characteristic expression of the drama of ideas in the sense already defined, but also for one variety of that other type of drama which is not of ideas but of emotions, since in it the artist is endeavouring to transfer to the audience not his own judgments, but his own emotional states, through the medium of their sympathies with the woes and exultations of the characters whom he fashions for the purpose. This secondary sense of the word is to be explained in part by the influence of mediaeval usage, which had forgotten its theatre, and had come to regard comedy and tragedy, not as names for specific dramatic types, but as names for emotional narratives coming respectively to happy and to sad endings. When, at the Renascence, emotional drama grew up

again on the basis of mediaeval narrative, it became the natural heir of the same distinction. The stress of emotion is common to Elizabethan tragedy and Elizabethan comedy, but while in tragedy it issues in pity and terror and the funeral procession, in comedy it gathers only to pass away and dissolve in triumph and laughter and the clash of marriage-bells. For such emotional or romantic comedy, as distinct from comedy proper, 'tragicomedy,' which the Elizabethans themselves sometimes used, is perhaps the happiest term.

If, then, *The Merchant of Venice* is to be regarded as primarily a tragicomedy, a drama of emotional stress with a happy ending, and only secondarily a comedy, a drama of the criticism of life, the next question which claims an answer is: What precisely is the emotional issue which is raised and which demands our sympathies in the play? It is probably true of all emotional drama that it tends to present its issue as a conflict, for this is an obvious and natural scheme for the arrangement of human characters set over against each other and answering speech by speech upon the narrow boards of a stage. It is certainly true of the Elizabethan drama, which had always behind it the tradition of the morality, with its serried array of vices and of virtues, warring for the soul of man. The theme of *The Merchant of Venice*, in particular, is readily to be formulated as a conflict. It is a conflict in the moral order, between the opposing principles of Love and Hate. That Shylock, whetting his knife upon his soul, stands for the principle of Hate is plain enough. Hate, indeed, is almost the first word that we have from his mouth—

Act II. Scene v. Jessica, Shylock, and Launcelot. By Robert Smirke.

I hate him for he is a Christian.

[I. iii. 42]

And when he thinks himself on the point of victory and is pressed to give a reason for his action, he will give none—

More than a lodged hate and a certain loathing
I bear Antonio.

[IV. i. 60-1]

Of course Shylock's hate is to be explained and traced to its roots, some of which, at least, lie rather in what he has suffered than in what in himself he is. Shakespeare aimed to make a man, and by no means a mere moral abstraction. But it is impossible to understand the play without careful guard against that favourite modern heresy of interpretation which sees so deep into the heart of Shylock that, in fact, it converts him from the villain into the hero. . . . I am not concerned to deny that Shakespeare himself was led by the logic of facts, and in the teeth of his own dramatic arrangement, to give some handle for this misunderstanding of Shylock. One cannot forget the famous vindication of Hebrew humanity with which the wanton raillery of the silly Salarino gets its answer [III. i. 53-73]. Certainly Shakespeare saw all round his Shylock. But the play becomes a chaos if the qualifications of Shylock's villainy are allowed to deflect the perception of the fact that after all it is he and none other who stands for the villain in its structure. One must, of course, exercise a little of the historic imagination in judging of an Elizabethan play. There has been a certain evolution of the moral sentiments in the course of three centuries. To the modern *ethos* Antonio spitting upon the usurer's gaberdine is almost a more distasteful figure than the usurer himself, and the notion that even a proven criminal may justly be compelled to change his religion as the price of his life is intolerable. But one is not to suppose that the Elizabethan audience saw things after this kind. . . . [It may] be assumed that the temper of the play chimed in with a popular sentiment towards the chosen people which, in England at least, hardly finds an echo to-day outside the limits of Whitechapel. Nor is the interpretation of Shylock the only case, even in this single comedy, in which the historic imagination is called for. Put Jessica or Bassanio to the test of the finer ethical ideals, and you will find it difficult to justify the conduct of the one in robbing her father's jewel-chest to pay the expenses of her elopement, or the conduct of the other in setting out to retrieve his wasted fortunes by the adventure of a gilded bride, until you remember that *The Merchant of Venice* is not in the realistic manner, and that, with whatever sound humanity it states its main issue, it makes no effort to depart from many of the world-old conventions of romance which it found in its sources among the *novelle*. For Bassanio it may perhaps be added, that 'fair speechless messages' [I. i. 64] had already passed between his eyes and Portia's in the days of his bravery, and that he may not have been quite so worldly an adventurer as he chose to represent himself as being to Antonio.

One cannot fail to see that, if Shylock embodies the principle of Hate, Antonio and Portia between them embody that of Love. Antonio will put his 'uttermost' at the service of his friend, and even when he is in the snare, will hold all debts cleared between them if he might but see Bassanio at his death. Portia, in her turn, has, as Lorenzo tells her—

A noble and a true conceit
Of god-like amity.

[III. iv. 2-3]

For love's sake she defers the consummation of her wedding rites and essays a doubtful enterprise to purchase—

The semblance of her soul
From out the state of hellish cruelty.

[III. iv. 20-1]

Her glorification of 'the quality of mercy' in the trial-scene is the spiritual counterpart to Shylock's dogged insistence on the rights of Hate; and her ultimate triumph, all the more perhaps for the obvious legal quibbles on which it is based, is nothing else than the triumph of Love, in the deliberate preference of equity to rigid justice. For moral and epilogue of the whole you may take the exquisite lines which she speaks as she treads once more her terraces of Belmont in the white moonlight—

How far that little candle throws his beams!
So shines a good deed in a naughty world.

[V. i. 90-1]

And what of Antonio's melancholy all this while? What place has it in the happy ending which this most delectable lady has brought about, with all its after-mirth? Antonio, as I read him, does not put off his melancholy. He bows his thanks over Portia's hand, and stands silent and gravely smiling through the greater part of the frolic with the rings. Even the return of his argosies, inevitable in the winding up of a tragicomedy, leaves him still, I fancy, a sombre figure in the background. For, in fact, Antonio's melancholy preceded the loss of his riches, and I think that it has had very little to do with that, or with the fear of death either, all the time. At the beginning of the play he was going to lose something much dearer to him than riches, his friend Bassanio. Bassanio had just broken to him his intended marriage, and this it was that made him sad. He was not likely to explain to Gratiano or Salarino, but directly they had gone out he turned to Bassanio and showed on what his mind was running in the quick enquiry—

Well, tell me now what lady is the same
To whom you swore a secret pilgrimage,
That you to-day promised to tell me of.

[I. i. 119-21]

Consider, again, the scene described by Salarino at Bassanio's embarking, still before any question of the miscarriage of his vessels can have come to his ears, how—

His eye being big with tears,
Turning his face, he put his hand behind him,
And with affection wondrous sensible
He wrung Bassanio's hand; and so they parted.

[II. viii. 46-9]

'I think he only loves the world for him' [II. viii. 50], says Salarino. Bassanio was merely voyaging a few miles from Venice, but it was to his wedding, and Antonio knew well how hardly the closest intimacies of bachelors survive the coming of a woman's love. (pp. 106-17)

Antonio's whole attitude is out of harmony with the sunny atmosphere which reigns throughout, and which has its justification in the happy ending to which the audience are presently to be wafted. I am inclined to doubt whether this particular point in the play was intended for the audience at all, and is not rather the intrusion of a personal note, an echo of those disturbed relations in Shakespeare's private life of which the fuller but enigmatic record is to be found in the *Sonnets*. Shakespeare, too, like Antonio, had lost a friend, and had lost him through a woman; nor does it seem to me to be inconsistent with any view which Shakespeare can be supposed to have taken of his art, that he should reserve something behind the arras of a play for his own ear, for the secret consolation of his private trouble. (p. 117)

E. K. Chambers, '''The Merchant of Venice','' in his *Shakespeare: A Survey*, *1925. Reprint by Hill and Wang, 1958, pp. 106-17.*

SIR ISRAEL GOLLANCZ   (lecture date 1922)

[*The following excerpt includes the first discussion of the medieval Christian influence on* The Merchant of Venice. *In it Gollancz argues that Shakespeare's play derived ultimately from the medieval exempla of the Pound of Flesh story and the parable of the Three Caskets, both of which are found in the* Gesta Romanorum. *Each of these homilies depicts, according to Gollancz, an allegory of the human soul's desire to bond with God or Christ. The critic also comments on Shylock's role in the Pound of Flesh story as the "Evil One" or devil of medieval theology and on the similarities of the trial scene in* The Merchant of Venice *and the allegory of* The Four Daughters of God, *a comparison developed more fully by such later critics as Nevill Coghill (1949) and Barbara K. Lewalski (1962). Gollancz concludes that the "lesson" of* The Merchant of Venice *is illustrated in Lorenzo's speech in Act V—namely, that humanity can never experience the harmony of the spheres, including the reconciliation on earth of truth, justice, mercy, and love, until it frees itself from "hatred, indignity, narrowness, [and] strife." Other critics who have interpreted* The Merchant of Venice *as an allegory of the conflict between mercy and justice, Christianity and Judaism, or love and wealth include Denton J. Snider (1890), Muriel C. Bradbrook (1951), Theodor Reik (1956), John Russell Brown (1957), C. L. Barber (1959), John P. Sisk (1969), and René E. Fortin (1974). Gollancz's essay was originally delivered as a lecture at University College in Exeter, England on June 13, 1922.*]

One of the greatest collections [of medieval *exempla*] is the *Gesta Romanorum*. That is a collection of tales where after each tale a moralisation is given. In the *Gesta Romanorum* we have the story of the Pound of Flesh: how, in order to win the love of a lady—a rather fierce lady—a virago indeed—a certain young man borrows money from a man who is avaricious—a very monster. This monster is willing to lend money on condition that if it is not repaid by a certain day the young man shall forfeit one pound of his flesh. That story is explained in a moralisation: how the lady is the soul made in the likeness of God, and how the wicked monster is, of course, the Devil. That story we have in a great number of forms. Long before the *Gesta Romanorum* we have a form where the monster is closely bound up with the story of the Vision of the Cross, and the scene is transferred to the place where the Cross is found, and the monster is brought under the aegis of the Church. So the whole story has been softened down from the version that we have in the *Gesta Romanorum*.

Shakespeare did not take his story [of the Pound of Flesh] from the *Gesta Romanorum*. It came ultimately from Italy in the form of a romance. The romance or novella had nothing to do with allegory. Here was a good plot for a story, and the Italians made it into romance. It simply told the story with all the leading details which finally were used by some dramatist in England.

Why do I say *some* dramatist? Long before Shakespeare thought of dealing with the theme, when Shakespeare was still young— a schoolboy—the story of the Jew with reference to the same story that we have in Shakespeare's *Merchant of Venice* had been enacted on the English stage. As early as 1579 we have

a reference to it, but the play is lost; we know it only from Gosson's reference. The man who dramatised that story did an extremely remarkable thing. He dealt not only with the story of the Pound of Flesh, but also with that other side of the story as we have it in Shakespeare, the Choice of the Caskets. This, too, is a story in the *Gesta Romanorum*. Not even in the *Gesta Romanorum* is it connected with the Pound of Flesh *exemplum*. It is entirely different, and belongs there to a different allegory, and a different homily. But there you have a choice; a lady making choice of the casket to win the hand of a prince. It is the woman who makes the choice of the casket, and not the man. We know at once, as we read that story of the Choice of the Casket in the *Gesta Romanorum*, that the young prince stands, of course, for Christ, and the human soul is the wooer.

In the story of the Pound of Flesh, as I indicated, the lady is a virago—a fierce, mercenary creature. All that had to be changed, and Shakespeare, or even the man who preceded Shakespeare, the dramatist I have alluded to, saw that some change was necessary, and introduced this other story, reversing the whole idea by making the man the wooer and the lady to be wooed. That is only another aspect of our allegory. Man, in the medieval times of mystical literature—man in his pilgrimage on earth—had to woo Grace Dieu, a noble lady, the daughter of the Divinity—Grace of God, as she was called, a noble and beautiful lady. . . . In 1579 we have already two elements that make up *The Merchant of Venice;* the Pound of Flesh motive on the one hand and, on the other, the Choice of the Caskets, combined into one play, *The Jew*, "representing the greedinesse of worldly chusers, and the bloody mindes of Usurers." (pp. 52-3)

Let us [consider] Shakespeare's play. Regard me for the moment as being a medievalist approaching the matter from his own standpoint. Arising from your two *exempla*, you have your Antonio, your good friend, your perfect friend, a man who is very carefully described as the dearest friend. . . . There is Bassanio on his pilgrimage to woo the lady. Think of the lady in Belmont

> richly left;
> And she is fair, and fairer than that word,
> Of wondrous virtues . . .
> Her name is Portia; nothing undervalued
> To Cato's daughter, Brutus' Portia:
> Nor is the wide world ignorant of her worth;
> For the four winds blow in from every coast
> Renowned suitors.
>
> [I. i. 161-63, 165-69]

Yea, they come from all Europe, France and Germany and far-off America, wooing this fair lady Grace Dieu. And Bassanio comes too, and Antonio, the perfect friend, so passive, so quiet, and yet destined to give his name to the whole play.

And Bassanio! I can imagine some of you saying: "Well, it was not an ideal thing to get his friend to borrow money for him that he might make a great show to win this noble heiress!" But when the test came, Bassanio stood the test. He, too, would have been willing to give himself if he could to have rescued his friend, willing to give wife and all. But you will say: "Why, if this man was ultimately to make choice of the leaden casket, as though he didn't care about the vain glories of the world, why borrow three thousand ducats under such conditions, and why go pranked out in clothes that really were not his?" But would you have a man enter on his quest for a noble lady, as it were for the divine Grace Dieu, in clothes beflecked with mire, unfit to enter so noble a presence? Think of your parable of the wedding feast. And so, too, of Portia. Look at her environment, her noble palace, all the beauty and charm of high life about her. Grace Dieu. Yea, do not all the great philosophers and teachers tell us, whether we turn to the Bible or turn to the Greek, that with truth and wisdom are two other aspects of beauty—charm and grace? The palace above, the heavenly mansion, must have something resembling it for the Grace Dieu on earth.

Indeed, I am making this suggestion to some of you that Shakespeare's Bassanio, in his quest for Portia, has points of contact with Spenser's Red Cross Knight in search of Una. They are not absolutely different. Your Knight of Holiness, it is true, must wear the armour of holiness, of truth and goodness, must climb the great hill and catch a glimpse of the heavenly Jerusalem, that he may the better thereafter "fight the good fight." Yes, that is one type. But your man of the world must also win his Portia, even though he must prank himself out in worldly garments; must do his best to win her.

The test came with the caskets. What is the meaning of the test? You remember the text in the Bible: "Your gold and silver is cankered; and the rust of them shall be a witness against you." Make an *exemplum* of that, and you have your caskets. The ideal for winning Grace Dieu was to ignore gold and silver, the empty pomp and show, and to choose that which was inscribed: "Who chooseth me must give and hazard all he hath" [II. vii. 9]. Bassanio proves that he was justified in attempting to win the hand of Portia, for ultimately, as I said, he stood the test and would have hazarded all to save his friend, if he could. (pp. 55-7)

As I noted earlier, in the *Gesta Romanorum* the monster who exacts, or is wishing to exact, the pledge is the Evil One—I mean the devil. The medieval theology, as I said, the *odium theologicum* [hateful theology], linked the matter directly, and turned this monster into a Shylock against whose race popular prejudice throughout all ages had deepened and deepened until the time that Chaucer gave to that object the cruel legend of *The Prioress's Tale:*

> Oure firste foo, the serpent Sathanas,
> That hath in Jewes herte his waspes nest.

But if you look at the theological point of view, you see exactly how the figure stands for Shylock, and that brings me to Shakespeare's real problem.

The pledge of the pound of flesh was to be exacted by Shylock as a mere afterthought. A merry idea seems to have occurred, as it were, Shylock saying that if Antonio did not pay his pledge, the pound of flesh should be the payment. Shakespeare, getting as far as that in doing his work, came to a difficulty. The whole thing gave him great difficulty. After all, no man ever in real life demanded such a pledge. It belongs not to nature, not even to myth, but rather to farce. It would have done very well for farce, or indeed for real tragedy if certain elements were there to deepen the matter; but Shakespeare's play was a blend of tragedy and comedy, his first great experiment in tragi-comedy. As he dealt with his subject the theme fascinated him. The humanity of the problem appealed to him. He saw that this element of the story, the integral element, the pound of flesh, could not be got rid of; he saw that although that element was unnatural and improbable, yet the character of Shylock was a character representing tragedy—the tragedy of humanity, the tragedy of race, and the tragedy of religion. The theme fascinated him more and more. He put

into Shylock's mouth that great plea uttered at the bar of humanity that differentiated Shakespeare so much from any predecessor in drama; and to a large extent (not altogether) from writers of the Middle Ages. It was not that he held a brief for Shylock, but that the problem appealed to him; and I hold, with a very perfect faith, that great as Shakespeare is as a dramatist, great as he may be as a poet, greater still is he as a thinker. Primarily, Shakespeare is a man who is a philosopher; who allows his wisdom and his view of life to speak, not in his case through *exemplum*, but through dramatic form from the platform stage—which rightly was called the platform stage. It was the platform where he enunciated so many of his thoughts. Uttering that plea was not enough for the purposes of drama; though it would do for the pamphleteer, the man holding a brief. The dramatic necessity for Shakespeare was to deal with his character so as to account for it. For that purpose he created an underplot.

Naturally we come to that underplot of Jessica and Lorenzo in *The Merchant of Venice*. Until we come to that, the whole problem of Shylock is difficult, and we find that Shakespeare is troubled as to how to treat the thing. By means of Jessica, the character and purpose of Shylock are to be so intensified as to give probability. No longer are we in doubt as to whether any monster can possibly, under any condition, exact such a pledge. Through Jessica, those who have been most scornful of Shylock are now put in position to triumph over him until the man becomes obsessed, his character deepened and maddened with the idea of carrying through his purpose. His is an obsession not just of the tragedy of vengeance, but of a particular type of tragedy—that other drama of vengeance best exemplified by [Thomas Kyd's] *The Spanish Tragedy*, where a man has suffered wrong, and is so obsessed with the idea of vengeance as to become maddened and lose all sense of reason. One idea obsessed him. That obsession in tragedy ends in death and disaster; for the man, the hero, who is thus maddened, not only deals vengeance to those who have wronged him, but kills himself also. But Shakespeare's play had to be tragi-comedy. We have now, therefore, got Shakespeare dealing with his twofold subject, the pound of flesh and the choice of the casket, and also this underplot of Jessica and Lorenzo.

Turn to the audience listening to the play. What was the theme that struck them most vividly? It was the figure of Shylock as the usurer incarnate. The play was a lesson to them, primarily a play dealing with the problem of usury; and Shylock was the embodiment of usury, as in the medieval morality play you have the character of Lucre, or usury. (pp. 58-60)

[The Trial scene], to my mind, is a problem which has not received proper attention. Shakespeare saw the difficulty. You have your Trial scene. And what a Trial scene it is! Your Portia seems at one time Mercy, at another time Justice. What is your Duke who is at the head of the Tribunal? Jurists have written a great deal about the law of the Trial scene as though Shakespeare wished to give the impression of a Royal Court of Justice. (p. 63)

What is the Trial scene in *The Merchant of Venice*? For that I must take you back again to medievalism. There was one interesting Psalm that of all others affected commentators from the earliest times. It was the 85th Psalm, the Psalm that belonged to Christmas Day; telling of the time when there should be great glory in the world—when mercy and truth should meet together, and righteousness and peace should kiss each other; when truth was to spring out of the earth, and righteousness to look down from heaven. The early commentators said: "Who are these people—Mercy and Truth and Righteousness and Peace?'' They personified them. They made them first of all attributes of God—the four daughters of God. They made out a wonderful story: how man transgressed at the Fall through disobedience, and the four daughters of God—Mercy, Truth, Righteousness and Peace—came before Him. Mercy said: ''Spare him; do not let your fiat go forth.'' Truth said: ''Yea, but he hath sinned.'' Righteousness, or Justice, said: ''He must be punished.'' And Peace said: ''Let us see whether we cannot harmonise all these elements together.'' . . . In some French morality plays we have a whole scene devoted to this pleading. One version was called the *Processus Belial,* which later was transferred to the mystery play of the *Passion,* and then influenced the trial of Antonio on the one hand, and Shylock on the other. The problem of Mercy and Justice for all mankind grew out of the medieval dramatising of this idea; the mysticism associated with the wonderful medieval allegory of *The Four Daughters of God.* In Mercy and Justice are those sisters reconciled and harmonised. Medieval theology can justify it.

And Shakespeare failed not. He felt there was something amiss in the plot before him. Righteousness and Peace have not kissed. We come to the last Act of *The Merchant of Venice.* There we have Shakespeare's personality coming out abundantly. Supposing the play had ended with the Trial scene. How unsatisfactory it would have been! Nothing could have been more unsatisfactory. Mercy and Justice would not have harmonised.

In the fifth act, through two minor characters of the play, and, perchance, where we would least expect it, through Lorenzo and Jessica, Shakespeare speaks, and transmutes everything in the play up to that point into his own wonderful golden work. Shakespeare often speaks through a minor character. In *Romeo and Juliet,* through the Friar he taught his lesson. (pp. 64-5)

What was the lesson to be learnt here? Jessica and Lorenzo were not introduced in order to satisfy the requirement: a sacrifice to hatred—and thus divide their religion and race. That was not to be the lesson, but another lesson more marvellous than that of *Romeo and Juliet.* Lorenzo, with gay spirit and youthful, is talking to Jessica; and suddenly we hear pronounced the theory of the heavenly spheres, the music of the universe. Could anything be more marvellous than that? He to Jessica, the daughter of Shylock, uttered these immortal words:

> Sit, Jessica. Look how the floor of heaven
> Is thick inlaid with patines of bright gold:
> There's not the smallest orb which thou behold'st
> But in his motion like an angel sings,
> Still quiring to the young-eyed cherubins;
> Such harmony is in immortal souls;
> But while this muddy vesture of decay
> Doth grossly close it in, we cannot hear it.
>
> [V. i. 58-65]

''Such harmony is in immortal souls.'' Medieval people are they, going right back to Antiquity—because the doctrine of the heavenly spheres came right through the Middle Ages down to the Renaissance. . . . Shakespeare thought of the wonderful idea of the world moving to music; that in each human heart there is some music; that only those pure of heart—away from the evil of the world, away from the muddy vesture of decay—can catch the heavenly music; but while this muddy vesture closes it in, we cannot hear it. We cannot hear the music in our hearts corresponding to the music of the spheres, and we cannot hear the music in other men's hearts; we cannot hear the music in their souls where misery, where contempt, where

injustice, where hatred, make the human soul, as it were, a noble thing placed in a tenement corroded over, even as iron chains corrode. . . . As man does to man, so persecution and contempt do to the human soul. They place the human soul in a veritable corroded thraldom; we cannot hear the music of such a one, and we cannot hear our own.

That theory of the music of the spheres goes back to the mysticism of the Middle Ages in a remarkable way. Shakespeare does not borrow the whole thing from Plato directly or indirectly. He links the Platonic idea with the Biblical, and in place of the Sirens in Plato we have the Cherubim. (pp. 66-7)

The idea was very beautiful. And Shakespeare, through the speech of Jessica and Lorenzo, in a marvellous way shows us his hope that man divested of all the muddy vesture—which is not merely the corporeal flesh, but evil, that is, hatred, indignity, narrowness, strife—all those elements removed, may then have hope again. Then it is as though Shakespeare had this idea: Truth will spring up from the earth; and Righteousness will meet Truth from heaven; Mercy and Truth will meet together; and Righteousness and Peace will kiss. So the whole of that play is rounded off with the idea that fascinated Shakespeare: the problem of harmony. (pp. 67-8)

> *Sir Israel Gollancz, ''Shakespeare's 'The Merchant of Venice' (A Medievalist's Exposition),'' in his Allegory and Mysticism in Shakespeare: A Medievalist on ''The Merchant of Venice'', edited by Alfred W. Pollard, George W. Jones, 1931, pp. 45-68.*

CHARLES READ BASKERVILL   (essay date 1923)

[*Focusing on the casket scenes in* The Merchant of Venice, *Baskervill discusses Elizabethan ideas about love and those human qualities that Shakespeare's contemporaries would have recognized as defining a certain attitude towards love. In particular, Baskervill analyzes the manner in which Shakespeare presented his characters in accordance with these contemporary attitudes so that his first audiences would have realized, as Nerissa realizes, that only someone like Bassanio could win Portia's hand in marriage. Throughout his discussion, Baskervill underscores the influence of Neoplatonism on Shakespeare's and other writers' works. For additional commentary on the influence of Neoplatonism on Shakespeare's vision of love in* The Merchant of Venice, *see the excerpt by Peter G. Phialas (1966).*]

In the *Merchant of Venice,* Shakspere has made the failure of two suitors of Portia and the success of Bassanio in the choice of the caskets turn not upon the caprice of fortune but upon character so that only the true lover chooses aright. For the portrayal of character in this choice and through the play, he has used a number of motives which were so conventional in the literature of the Renaissance that their meaning must have been perfectly clear to his audiences. Some phases of the treatment are clear to modern readers, but others, particularly the basis of Bassanio's choice, remain somewhat obscure. By an analysis of the casket scenes and a discussion of the conventions used, the treatment can be shown to be a systematic one, with a definite meaning based on Renaissance theories of love.

Symbolism has been used in the casket scenes and its meaning has been indicated to a degree unwonted in Shakspere's plays. In the scene introducing Portia, Nerissa says:

> Your father was euer vertuous, and holy men
> at their death haue good inspirations, therefore
> the lotterie that hee hath deuised in these three
> chests of gold, siluer, and leade, whereof who

chooses his meaning, chooses you, wil no doubt
neuer be chosen by any rightly, but one who
you shall rightly loue.

[I. ii. 27-33]

The whole course of the casket story enforces this. . . . It is
character as affecting judgment that determines the choice of
the three suitors who dare to stake their future on the lottery
of the caskets. The prince of Morocco is moved both by the
brilliance of the gold casket and by its inscription promising
"what many men desire" [II. vii. 5]. Magnifying in his soliloquy the plaudits of the world and the response of the masses
to glamor, he is led by his deductions . . . to seek Portia as a
gilded ornament for his worldly glory. The scroll with its maxims, "All that glisters is not gold" and "Guilded timber doe
wormes infold," indicates that he fails because he chooses for
show, and he is declared to be not "as wise as bold," not "in
iudgement old" [II. vii. 65, 69, 70, 71]. The Prince of Arragon
furnishes a contrast to Morocco in scorning the impulses of

the foole multitude that choose by show,
Not learning more then the fond eye doth teach,
Which pries not to th' interior.

[II. ix. 26-8]

In his arrogant pride, the subdued silver casket, with its promise
of "as much as he deserues," causes him to reason that "cleare
honour" should be "purchast by the merit of the wearer" and
to "assume desert" [II. ix. 36, 42, 43] as one aloof from the
common man. His reasoning is rewarded by a fool's head in
the casket and the contemptuous remark of Portia:

O these deliberate fooles when they doe choose,
They haue the wisdome by their wit to loose.

[II. ix. 80-1]

In contrast with these two, Bassanio is represented as having
in his understanding of true love a wisdom that guides his
judgment of the value of earthly glory and self-esteem. The
basis indicated by Nerissa for success in the choice of the
caskets is stressed by Portia as Bassanio prepares to choose:

If you doe loue me, you will finde me out.

[III. ii. 41]

Then, as he reflects on the caskets and their inscriptions, "Tell
me where is fancie bred" [III. ii. 63] is sung with its declaration
that fancy—constantly used to indicate sensual love—fed by
the eyes, dies in its own indulgence of sense. As a lover who
recognizes the fact that character and not surface beauty is the
basis of true love and that intemperate lust for worldly acclaim
and inordinate self-love represent perversions through sense or
fancy, Bassanio picks up the thought and applies it:

So may the outward showes be least themselues. . . .

[III. ii. 73]

Thus Bassanio in his judgment is not moved by beauty of
appearance, by the acclamation of the world, or by self-love,
but by the appeal without circumstances of pomp to an ideal
of self-abnegation and even of self-sacrifice in love.

The meaning can be shown more clearly by indicating the
conventional aspects of the treatment of character and love in
the play. The symbolic use of the caskets comes from medieval
maxims and fables of the fallacy of judging by surface appearances. With it is joined through the lyric "Tell me where
is fancie bred" the kindred idea of the impermanence of the
love based on the appeal of external beauty to the senses, a
connection made by modifying medieval conceits of love to

fit a Platonic distinction between true and false love. The application of this last idea in Bassanio's choice and some phases
of the characterization of the lovers reflect conceptions of Platonic love. (pp. 90-2)

The background of these ideas was furnished by the contrast
between reason and sense constantly made in the Middle Ages
and the Renaissance in works which preached the virtuous and
controlled conduct of life through the dominance of sense by
reason, as in [John] Lydgate's *Assembly of Gods*, [Henry]
Medwall's *Nature*, and [Thomas] Elyot's *Platonike Dialogue*.
Fancy was a term constantly used for the mental attitude in
which the impulses and passions of the senses mastered reason.
Further, in attacks on love, sensuality and love were made
synonymous by medieval moralists. Not infrequently the point
of view was expressed in the love allegories of the Middle
Ages as in Lydgate's *Reson and Sensuallyte*. With the Renaissance distinction between earthly and spiritual love, the
latter was associated with the virtuous life as the type in which
reason controlled. This modification appeared early in discussions of Platonic love. The old point of view was often expressed in English poetry of the sixteenth century, sometimes
in debates of love and reason typically medieval, while love
guided by reason and love inspired by the senses were contrasted in passages of fiction and in songs reflecting Platonism.
(pp. 94-5)

As a conventional definition of love, Shakspere's lyric suggests
. . . a contrast between the love of the heart and the love of
the eyes and so, particularly in its connection, a distinction
between the two types of love. The conceit is one that Shakspere had already expressed more clearly several times as in
A Midsummer-Night's Dream [I. i. 234]:

Love looks not with the eyes, but with the mind,

and *Romeo and Juliet* [II. iii. 67-8]:

young men's love then lies
Not truly in their hearts, but in their eyes.

This distinction cannot be traced so far as I know before the
Renaissance, but it is one that might easily have been made at
any time on the basis of the constant contrast in love poetry,
on the one hand between reason and love, and on the other
between heart and eye. Both of these conceptions lent themselves readily to the formulation of a distinction between the
spiritual love of the heart and the sensual love of the eyes
without a material change of the phraseology conventional in
definitions of love. (pp. 97-8)

Shakspere's lyric would consequently, in addition to warning
against the varied deceptions of the eyes, turn the thought of
a lover familiar with Renaissance theories of love to the conception of true love, and this would give him a basis for judging
the inscriptions of the caskets. He would disregard the beauty
of the gold casket and the appeal of its inscription to "desire,"
as Arragon and Bassanio do. The choice remaining would be
between the pale casket of silver with its inscription calling
for an assumption of desert and the pale one of lead with its
inscription demanding that the lover give all. The choice of
the latter by the true lover Bassanio represents an aspect of the
idealization of love that may be best explained on the basis of
the conception of Platonic love current in sixteenth-century
England. (pp. 98-9)

If the real test of judgment comes in the appeals to self-love
and to humility, the inscriptions of the caskets are of far more
significance than the metal. The semibarbaric Morocco chooses

by the exterior view and by an appeal to the senses only slightly more subtle—the promise of "what men desire." Arragon, a man with "knowledge" but lacking "understanding," guided by his reasoning and influenced by self-love, has 'the wisdom by his wit to lose' [II. ix. 81]. Bassanio's choice through understanding of self-abnegation is the climax and completion of a series of choices based on an ascending scale of ideals which illustrate sense, reason, and understanding.

The true judgment of Bassanio is the foundation of the characterization of Bassanio and Portia as lovers "Whose soules doe bear an egal yoke of loue" [III. iv. 13]. For, while Shakspere makes them two very human characters with marked individuality, there is enough reflection of Platonism through the rest of the play to emphasize the idealization of love in the casket scenes. Portia emphasizes the harmony of lovers stressed by [Baldassare] Castiglione [in *Il Cortegiano*] and considered possible in friendship and love for those only who have achieved perfection in moral virtues:

> in companions
> That do conuerse and waste the time together,
> Whose soules doe beare an egal yoke of loue,
> There must needs be a like proportion
> Of lyniaments, of manners, and of spirit;
> Which makes me thinke that this *Anthonio*
> Being the bosome louer of my Lord,
> Must needs be like my Lord. If it be so,
> How little is the cost I haue bestowed
> In purchasing the semblance of my soule;
> From out the state of hellish cruelty,
> This comes too neere the praising of my selfe,
> Therefore no more of it.
>
> [III. iv. 11-23]

A suggestion of Bassanio's idealization of Portia's beauty as a symbol of a greater spiritual beauty is found in his declaration:

> And she is faire, and fairer then that word,
> Of wondrous vertues;
>
> [I. i. 162-63]

While Jessica, in an obscure passage that may be corrupt, seems to state that it can be only through his own earthly love that Bassanio can fail to find in Portia's spiritual quality the ideal which furnishes "the stayers" mentioned by Castiglione for climbing to "the high mansion place" of God where heavenly beauty dwells:

> it is very meete
> The Lord *Bassanio* liue an vpright life
> For hauing such a blessing in his Lady,
> He findes the ioyes of heauen heere on earth,
> And if on earth he doe not meane it, it
> Is reason he should neuer come to heauen.
>
> [III. v. 73-8]

This Platonic symbolism of the harmony of lovers through the idealization of beauty and virtue is completed in the play by a beautiful passage in which another Platonic conception of mystic harmonies is expressed. Just as friends and lovers are about to reunite after the separation created by Shylock's action, Lorenzo, in a moonlight night created for love, tells Jessica of the music of the spheres, adding:

> Such harmonie is in immortal soules,
> But whilst this muddy vesture of decay
> Doth grosly close in it, we cannot heare it.
>
> [V. i. 63-5]

From this high level of mysticism Shakspere descends in the reunion of his characters and the merriment of the ring episode to the level of sprightly human comedy. (pp. 102-03)

> *Charles Read Baskervill, "Bassanio as an Ideal Lover," in* The Manly Anniversary Studies in Language and Literature, The University of Chicago Press, *1923, pp. 90-103.*

Q. [ARTHUR QUILLER-COUCH]   (essay date 1926)

[*Quiller-Couch was editor with J. Dover Wilson of the New Cambridge edition of Shakespeare's works. In his study* Shakespeare's Workmanship, *and in his Cambridge lectures on Shakespeare, Quiller-Couch based his interpretations on the assumption that Shakespeare was mainly a craftsman attempting, with the tools and materials at hand, to solve particular problems central to his plays. In his commentary on* The Merchant of Venice, *published in his introduction to the 1926 edition of the play, Quiller-Couch is one of the first critics after William Hazlitt (1817) to seriously question the morals and behavior of Shakespeare's Christians. Except for Portia and Antonio, he considers the Venetians a "circle of wasters" and "parasites." He also calls Jessica "frivolous" and "greedy" and argues that Shakespeare failed in* The Merchant of Venice *by making his Christian characters "just as heartless as Shylock without any of Shylock's passionate excuse." Numerous critics have found fault with Shakespeare's Christians since Quiller-Couch voiced his concerns, and some—including Harold C. Goddard (1951), A. D. Moody (1964), R. Chris Hassel, Jr. (1970), and René Girard (1978)—have claimed that they are the real target of Shakespeare's comedy, more villainous than Shylock, in that they mask their true mercenary behavior behind an ideal of Christian love and mercy never demonstrated in the play.*]

[*The Merchant of Venice* is] a mightily effective play. It is also for those curious about [Shakespeare's] genius, a strangely intriguing play: for Shakespeare, more than any dramatist, could defeat definition among tragedy, comedy and romance. Years after this experiment he invited us to laugh at Polonius pulling his beard and solemnly differentiating 'tragedy, comedy, history, pastoral, pastoral-comical, historical-pastoral, tragical-historical, tragical-comical-historical-pastoral, scene individable, or poem unlimited.' We are dealing with a dramatist who more than any other has overridden all these categories with a negligent smile, and that (be it remembered) through and after encounters at 'The Mermaid' with Ben Jonson, hectoring layer down of the law as derived from Aristotle and transmitted in practice through Seneca and Plautus. We may therefore in dealing with *The Merchant of Venice*, as in dealing later with *Antony and Cleopatra*—in both of which plays we know, as accurately as may be, his sources—ask how he did it.

He did it almost always, if one may use the term, with an instinctive economy. Chaucer has something of this gift in handling his 'originals,' but Shakespeare has it in a superlative degree. No one reading the *Life of Antony* in North's *Plutarch* alongside of *Antony and Cleopatra* can miss to marvel at the frugality of the converting touch. So we take it, understanding (as we have surely a right to do) that this overworked, constitutionally indolent man, apparently careless of his dramatic work, once done, just operated upon the story as genius suggested throughout.

Now the first, or Shylock-Antonio story, is evident Tragedy. The Merchant corresponds at every point to the Aristotelian demand upon a tragic hero. He is a good man who, not by vice, but through some error, comes to calamity. So, up to a point—a definite point—Shakespeare conducts his drama up towards pure tragedy. He opens upon Antonio's gloom and foreboding of some heavy fate, obviously meant to be communicated at once to the audience—

> In sooth I know not why I am so sad,
> It wearies me, you say it wearies you;
> But how I caught it, found it, or came by it,
> What stuff 'tis made of, whereof it is born,
> I am to learn
>
> [I. i. 1-5]

—this upon a broken line and a pause through which we follow his moving. And this actual business of tragedy persists, through revel and carnival and masquers, noise of hautboys, choosing of caskets—to music and the music of a right woman's voice confessing and surrendering to love, straight to the point where Portia asks

> Why doth the Jew pause?
>
> [IV. i. 335]

If the Jew had not just been held at pause by that mastering question, if his hatred and revenge, racial and personal, had carried him an inch over that question, if, so to say, this very grand Hebrew had divorced his ducats from his daughter and cried out, 'Revenge I will have: afterwards tear me limb from limb,' under the law of Venice Portia's quibble had gone by the board, and the play must necessarily, from that instant, have reverted to the tragic conclusion its opening lines portend. (pp. xii-xiii)

Now for the [character of] Shylock, who in our opinion has been over-philosophised and over-sentimentalised, we may start upon the simple, obvious text that Shakespeare (who, in an age when Jews were forbidden this country, had probably never met with one in the flesh) makes him an intelligible if not a pardonable man; a genuine man, at any rate, of like passions with ourselves, so that we respond to every word of his fierce protest:

> Hath not a Jew eyes? hath not a Jew hands,
> organs, dimensions, senses, affections, pas-
> sions? fed with the same food, hurt with the
> same weapons, subject to the same diseases,
> healed by the same means, warmed and cooled
> by the same winter and summer, as a Christian
> is?
>
> [III. i. 59-64]

—makes him entirely more human than the conventional Jew of Il Pecorone or than the magniloquent monster created by Marlowe—makes him, up to the moment of his defeat by a woman's art, the tall dominating man of the play, tall as Coriolanus and nearer to us than Coriolanus in his scorn, sense of injury and motive of revenge. (p. xviii)

How, then, does Shakespeare do it?—how contrive to make Shylock sympathetic to us as [Marlowe's] Barabas never is? . . .

[Shakespeare's] audience, conventionally minded, may accept the proffer of the bond (Act I, Scene 3) as a jesting bargain made with blood-thirsty intent, to be blood-thirstily enacted; but a gentle Shakespeare cannot. There must be more incentive to hate, to lust for a literally bloody vengeance, than any past insults, however conventional, put upon him on the Rialto by Antonio, mildest of men, can dramatically supply. Sufferance is the badge of his tribe.

But he is a fierce Israelite and has an adored daughter. In the interim between the signing of the bond and its falling due this daughter, this Jessica, has wickedly and most unfilially betrayed him. (p. xix)

Jessica is bad and disloyal, unfilial, a thief; frivolous, greedy, without any more conscience than a cat and without even a cat's redeeming love of home. Quite without heart, on worse than an animal instinct—pilfering to be carnal—she betrays her father to be a light-of-lucre carefully weighted with her sire's ducats. So Shylock returns from a gay abhorrent banquet to knock on his empty and emptied house. (p. xx)

[Jessica's] elopement with one of the most heartless fribblers on the list of Antonio's friends, which is to say much, and the 'gilding' of herself, as on an afterthought, with more of her father's ducats before she runs downstairs to the street, leaves us with no alternative. Shylock is intolerably wronged.

Let us turn aside for a moment to Antonio, and to consider his friends and associates taken as a lot. It may not be always true that a man is known by the company he keeps: and most of us have known some man or two or three, of probity and high intellectual gifts, who are never at ease save in company with their moral and intellectual inferiors, avoid their peers, and of indolence consort with creatures among whom their eminence cannot be challenged. Such a man is Antonio, presented to us as a high-minded and capable merchant of credit and renown, but presented to us also as the indolent patron of a circle of wasters, 'born to consume the fruits of this world,' heartless, or at least unheedful, while his life lies in jeopardy through his tender, extravagantly romantic friendship for one of them.

Now it may be that Shakespeare, in the first half of this play purposely, of his art, hardened down all these friends and clients of the Merchant. Even as in Macbeth he afterwards helped to throw up his two protagonists by flattening down (the honest, thinking Banquo once removed) all the subordinate persons into mere figures of tapestry. And, if intended, this disheartening of Venice does indeed help to throw up Shylock with his passion into high relief.

But, if so, surely it is done at great cost. (pp. xx-xxi)

[Barring] the Merchant himself, a merely static figure, and Shylock, who is meant to be cruel, every one of the Venetian dramatis personae is either a 'waster' or a 'rotter' or both, and cold-hearted at that. There is no need to expend ink upon such parasites as surround Antonio—upon Salerio and Solanio. Be it granted that in the hour of his extremity they have no means to save him. Yet they see it coming; they discuss it sympathetically, but always on the assumption that it is his affair not theirs:

> Let good Antonio look he keep his day,
> Or he shall pay for this,
>
> [II. viii. 25-6]

and they take not so much trouble as to send Bassanio word of his friend's plight, though they know that for Bassanio's sake his deadly peril has been incurred! It is left to Antonio himself to tell the news in that very noble letter of farewell and release . . . —a letter which, in good truth, Bassanio does not too extravagantly describe as 'a few of the unpleasant'st words that ever blotted paper' [III. ii. 251-52]. (p. xxiii)

But let us consider this conquering hero, Bassanio. When we first meet him he is in debt, a condition on which—having to confess it because he wants to borrow more money—he expends some very choice diction.

> 'Tis not unknown to you, Antonio,

(No, it certainly was not!)

> How much I have disabled mine estate,
> By something showing a more swelling port
> Than my faint means would grant continuance.
>
> [I. i. 122-25]

That may be a mighty fine way of saying that you have chosen to live beyond your income; but, Shakespeare or no Shakespeare, if Shakespeare mean us to hold Bassanio for an honest fellow, it is mighty poor poetry. For poetry, like honest men, looks things in the face, and does not ransack its wardrobe to clothe what is naturally unpoetical. Bassanio, to do him justice, is not trying to wheedle Antonio by this sort of talk; he knows his friend too deeply for that. But he is deceiving *himself,* or rather is reproducing some of the trash with which he has already deceived himself.

He goes on to say that he is not repining; his chief anxiety is to pay everybody, and

> To you, Antonio,
> I owe the most in money and in love,
>
> [I. i. 130-31]

and thereupon counts on more love to extract more money, starting (and upon an experienced man of business, be it observed) with some windy nonsense about shooting a second arrow after a lost one.

> You know me well, and herein spend but time
> To wind about my love with circumstance
>
> [I. i. 153-54]

says Antonio; and, indeed, his gentle impatience throughout this scene is well worth noting. He is friend enough already to give all; but to be preached at, and on a subject—money—of which he has forgotten, or chooses to forget, ten times more than Bassanio will ever learn, is a little beyond bearing. And what is Bassanio's project? To borrow three thousand ducats to equip himself to go off and hunt an heiress in Belmont. . . . Now this is bad workmanship and dishonouring to Bassanio. (pp. xxiv-xxv)

But he gets the money, of course, equips himself lavishly, arrives at Belmont; and here comes in worse workmanship. For I suppose that, while character weighs in drama, if one thing be more certain than another it is that a predatory young gentleman such as Bassanio would *not* have chosen the leaden casket. Let us consider his soliloquy while choosing:

> The world is still deceived with ornament.
> In law, what plea so tainted and corrupt,
> But, being seasoned with a gracious voice,
> Obscures the show of evil? In religion,
> What damnéd error, but some sober brow
> Will bless it, and approve it with a text.
>
> [III. ii. 74-9]

One feels moved to interrupt: 'Yes, yes—and what about yourself, my little fellow? What has altered you, that you, of all men, suddenly use this sanctimonious talk?'

And this flaw in characterisation goes right down through the workmanship of the play. For the evil opposed against these curious Christians is specific; it is Cruelty; and, yet again specifically, the peculiar cruelty of a Jew. To this cruelty an artist at the top of his art would surely have opposed mansuetude, clemency, charity, and, specifically, Christian charity. Shakespeare misses more than half the point when he makes

the intended victims, as a class and by habit, just as heartless as Shylock without any of Shylock's passionate excuse. (pp. xxv-xxvi)

Q. [Arthur Quiller-Couch], in an introduction to The Merchant of Venice *by William Shakespeare, 1926. Reprint by Cambridge at the University Press, 1962, pp. vii-xxxii.*

ELMER EDGAR STOLL   (essay date 1927)

[*Stoll was one of the earliest critics to attack the method of character analysis that had dominated nineteenth-century Shakespearean criticism. Instead, he maintained that Shakespeare was primarily a man of the professional theater and that his works had to be interpreted in the light of Elizabethan stage conventions and understood for their theatrical effects, rather than their psychological insight. Stoll has in turn been criticized for seeing only one dimension of Shakespeare's art. In the excerpt below, Stoll takes issue with those critics who consider Shylock a tragic, pathetic figure, claiming that the Jew is nothing more than the traditional comic villain apparent throughout Elizabethan comedy. Stoll demonstrates this point by emphasizing the manner in which Shakespeare "leaves little or nothing to suggestion or surmise," constantly manipulating our attitudes towards Shylock by the comments of the other characters, by the disposition of important scenes, and by the "downright avowals of soliloquy" and intimate conversation. Stoll's rather technical view of Shakespeare's art, particularly with respect to the dramatist's characterization of Shylock and the development of his plot, is echoed in the excerpts by Harold R. Walley (1935), John Middleton Murry (1936), J. W. Lever (1952), and D. A. Traversi (1968).*]

The puzzle whether the *Merchant of Venice* is not meant for tragedy, for instance, is cleared up when, as Professor Baker suggests [see Additional Bibliography], we . . . remember that the title—and the hero—is not the 'Jew of Venice' as he would lead us to suppose; that this comedy is only like others, as *Measure for Measure* and *Much Ado,* not clear of the shadow of the fear of death; and that in closing with an act where Shylock and his knife are forgotten in the unravelling of the mystery between the lovers and the crowning of Antonio's happiness in theirs, it does not, from the Elizabethan point of view, perpetrate an anti-climax, but, like many another Elizabethan play, carries to completion what is a story for story's sake. 'Shylock is, and always has been the hero,' says Professor Schelling. But why, then, did Shakespeare drop his hero out of the play for good before the fourth act was over? It is a trick which he never repeated—a trick, I am persuaded, of which he was not capable.

Hero or not, Shylock is given a villain's due. His is the heaviest penalty to be found in all the pound of flesh stories, including that in *Il Pecorone,* which served as model for the play. . . . In not a single heart do Shylock's griefs excite commiseration; indeed, as they press upon him they are barbed with gibes and jeers. Coriolanus is unfortunate and at fault, but we know that the poet is with him. We know that the poet is not with Shylock, for on that point, in this play as in every other, the impartial, inscrutable poet leaves little or nothing to suggestion or surmise. As is his custom elsewhere, by the comments of the good characters, by the methods pursued in the disposition of scenes, and by the downright avowals of soliloquy, he constantly sets us right.

As for the first of these artifices, all the people who come in contact with Shylock except Tubal—among them being those of his own house, his servant and his daughter—have a word or two to say on the subject of his character, and never a good one. And in the same breath they spend on Bassanio and Antonio, his enemies, nothing but words of praise. Praise or blame, moreover, is, after Shakespeare's fashion, usually in the nick of time to guide the hearer's judgment. Lest at his first appearance the Jew should make too favourable an impression by his Scripture quotations, Antonio is led to observe that the devil can cite Scripture for his purpose; lest the Jew's motive in foregoing interest (for once in his life) should seem like the kindness Antonio takes it to be, Bassanio avows that he likes not fair terms and a villain's mind; and once the Jew has caught the Christian on the hip, every one, from Duke to Gaoler, has words of horror or detestation for him and of compassion for his victim.

As for the second artifice, the ordering of the scenes is such as to enforce this contrast. First impressions, every playwright knows (and no one better than Shakespeare himself), are momentous, particularly for the purpose of ridicule. Launcelot and Jessica, in separate scenes, are introduced before Shylock reaches home, that, hearing their story, we may side with them, and, when the old curmudgeon appears, may be moved to laughter as he complains of Launcelot's gormandizing, sleeping, and rending apparel out, and as he is made game of by the young conspirators to his face. Here . . . , when there might be some danger of our sympathy becoming enlisted on Shylock's side because he is about to lose his daughter and some

of his property, Shakespeare forestalls it. He lets Shylock, in his hesitation whether to go to the feast, take warning from a dream, but nevertheless, though he knows that they bid him not for love, decide to go in hate, in order to feed upon the prodigal Christian. And he lets him give up Launcelot, whom he has half a liking for, save that he is a huge feeder, to Bassanio—'to one that I would have him help to waste his borrowed purse' [II. v. 50-1]. Small credit these sentiments do him; little do they add to his pathos or dignity. Still more conspicuous is this care when Shylock laments over his daughter and his ducats. Lest then by any chance a stupid or tenderhearted audience should not laugh but grieve, Salanio reports his outcries—in part word for word—two scenes in advance, as matter of mirth to himself and all the boys in Venice. It is exactly the same method as that employed in *Twelfth Night,* Act III, scene ii, where Maria comes and tells not only Sir Toby, Sir Andrew, and Fabian, but, above all, the audience, how ridiculously Malvolio is acting, before they see it for themselves. The art of the theatre, but particularly the art of the comic theatre, is the art of preparations, else it is not securely comic. But the impression first of all imparted to us is of Shylock's villainy—an impression which, however comical he may become, we are not again allowed to lose. In the first scene in which he appears, the third in the play, there is one of the most remarkable instances in dramatic literature of

Act II. Scene v. Launcelot, Shylock, and Jessica. By H. Hofmann. The Department of Rare Books and Special Collections, The University of Michigan Library.

a man saying one thing but thinking another and the audience made to see this. He prolongs the situation, keeps the Christians on tenterhooks, turns the terms of the contract over and over in his mind, as if he were considering the soundness of it and of the borrower, while all the time he is hoping, for once in his life, that his debtor may turn out not sound but bankrupt. He casts up Antonio's hard usage of him in the past, defends the practice of interest-taking, is at the point of stipulating what the rate this time shall be, and then—decides to be friends and take no interest at all. He seems, and is, loath to part for a time with three thousand ducats—'"tis a good round sum!' [I. iii. 103]—but at the bottom of his heart he is eager.

And as for the third artifice, that a sleepy audience may not make the mistake of the cautious critic and take the villain for the hero, Shakespeare is at pains to label the villain by an aside at the moment the hero appears on the boards:

> I hate him for he is a Christian,
> But more for that in low simplicity
> He lends out money gratis, and brings down
> The rate of usance here with us in Venice.
>
> [I. iii. 42-5]

Those are his motives, later confessed repeatedly; and either one brands him as a villain more unmistakably in that day, as we shall see, than in ours. Of the indignities which he has endured he speaks also, and of revenge; but of none of these has he anything to say at the trial. There he pleads his oath, perjury to his soul should he break it, his 'lodged hate', or his 'humour'; further than that, 'I can give no reason nor I will not' [IV. i. 59],—for some reasons a man does not give; but here to himself and later to Tubal—'were he out of Venice I can make what merchandise I will' [III. i. 128]—he tells, in the thick of the action, the unvarnished truth. As with Shakespeare's villains generally—Aaron [in *Titus Andronicus*], Iago, or Richard III—only what they say concerning their purposes aside or to their confidants can be relied upon; and Shylock's oath and his horror of perjury are . . . belied by his clutching at thrice the principal when the pound of flesh escapes him, just as is his money-lender's ruse of pretending to borrow the cash from 'a friend' . . . by his going home 'to purse the ducats straight' [I. iii. 174].

His arguments, moreover, are given a specious, not to say a grotesque colouring. . . . But Hazlitt and other critics strangely say that in argument Shylock has the best of it [see excerpt above, 1817].

> What if my house be troubled with a rat
> And I be pleas'd to give *ten* thousand ducats
> To have it ban'd?
>
> [IV. i. 44-6]

This particular rat is a human being; but the only thing to remark upon, in Shylock's opinion, is his willingness to squander ten thousand ducats on it instead of three. 'Hates any man the thing,' he cries (and there he is ticketed), 'he would not kill!' [IV. i. 67]. Even in Hazlitt's time, moreover, a choice of 'carrion flesh' in preference to ducats could not be plausibly compared as a 'humour'—the Jew's gross jesting here grates upon you—with an aversion to pigs or to the sound of the bagpipe, or defended as a right by the analogy of holding slaves; nor could the practice of interest-taking find a warrant in Jacob's pastoral trickery while in the service of Laban; least of all in the day when Sir John Hawkins, who initiated the slave-trade, with the Earls of Pembroke and Leicester and the Queen herself for partners, bore on the arms which were granted him

for his exploits a demi-Moor, proper, in chains, and in the day when the world at large still held interest-taking to be robbery. Very evidently, moreover, Shylock is discomfited by Antonio's question 'Did he take interest?' for he falters and stumbles in his reply—

> No, not take interest, not, as you would say,
> Directly, interest,—
>
> [I. iii. 75-7]

and is worsted, in the eyes of the audience if not in his own, by the repeated use of the old Aristotelian argument of the essential barrenness of money, still gospel in Shakespeare's day, in the second question,

> Or is your gold and silver ewes and rams?
>
> [I. iii. 95]

For his answer is meant for nothing better than a piece of complacent shamelessness:

> I cannot tell: I make it breed as fast.
>
> [I. iii. 96]

Only twice does Shakespeare seem to follow Shylock's pleadings and reasonings with any sympathy—'Hath a dog money?' [I. iii. 121] in the first scene in which he appears, and 'Hath not a Jew eyes?' [III. i. 59] in the third act—but a bit too much has been made of this. Either plea ends in such fashion as to alienate the audience. To Shylock's reproaches the admirable Antonio, 'one of the gentlest and humblest of all the men in Shakespeare's theatre' [see John W. Hales in the Additional Bibliography], praised and honoured by every one but Shylock, retorts, secure in his virtue, that he is just as like to spit on him and spurn him again. And Shylock's celebrated justification of his race runs headlong into a justification of his villainy: 'The villainy which you teach me I will execute, and it shall go hard but I will better the instruction' [III. i. 73-5]. 'Hath not a Jew eyes?' and he proceeds to show that your Jew is no less than a man, and as such has a right, not to respect or compassion, as the critics for a century have had it, but to revenge. Neither large nor lofty are his claims. The speech begins with the answer to Salanio's question about the pound of flesh. 'Why, I am sure, if he forfeit, thou wilt not take his flesh. What's that good for?' 'To bait fish withal,' he retorts in savage jest; 'if it will feed nothing else it will feed my revenge' [III. i. 51-4]; and he goes on to complain of insults, and of thwarted bargains to the tune of half a million, and to make a plea for which he has already robbed himself of a hearing. Quite as vigorously and (in that day) with as much reason, the detestable and abominable Aaron defends his race and colour, and Edmund, the dignity of bastards. The worst of his villains Shakespeare allows to plead their cause: their confidences in soliloquy or aside, if not (as here) slight touches in the plea itself, sufficiently counteract any too favourable impression. This, on the face of it, is a plea for indulging in revenge with all its rigours; not a word is put in for the nobler side of Jewish character; and in lending Shylock his eloquence Shakespeare is but giving the devil his due. (pp. 262-69)

Elmer Edgar Stoll, "Shylock," in his Shakespeare Studies: Historical and Comparative in Method, *The Macmillan Company, 1927, pp. 255-336.*

HARLEY GRANVILLE-BARKER   (essay date 1930)

[*Granville-Barker was a noted actor, playwright, director, and critic. His work as a Shakespearean critic is at all times informed by his experience as a director, for he treats Shakespeare's plays not as works of literature better understood divorced from the theater, as did many Romantic critics, but as pieces meant for the stage. As a director, he emphasized simplicity in staging, set design, and costuming. He believed that elaborate scenery obscured the poetry which was of central importance to Shakespeare's plays. Granville-Barker also eschewed the approach of directors who scrupulously reconstructed a production based upon Elizabethan stage techniques; he felt that this, too, detracted from the play's meaning. In the following excerpt, Granville-Barker calls The Merchant of Venice "a fairy tale," but one handled so skillfully by Shakespeare that he sustains his audience's interest in the fate of his characters, yet prevents the emotional issues involved from overburdening the fairy-tale structure. Like such earlier critics as Samuel Johnson (1765) and August Wilhelm Schlegel (1811), Granville-Barker notes how naturally and effectively Shakespeare combines his two plots—the casket and bond stories—and, especially, how he maintains the artifice of the casket story in the face of the tragic, serious tone of the Shylock-Antonio conflict. Last, Granville-Barker reconstructs the skillful manner in which Shakespeare develops the trial scene and gradually entraps Shylock in his own misconception of law. He concludes that the final act of* The Merchant of Venice *provides the traditional fairy-tale ending and returns the play's focus to that of romantic comedy. For further discussion of the purpose of Act V and the so-called ring episode in* The Merchant of Venice, *see the excerpts by August Wilhelm Schlegel (1811), William Hazlitt (1817), Anna Brownell Jameson (1833), G. G. Gervinus (1849-50), C. L. Barber (1959), Barbara K. Lewalski (1962), A. D. Moody (1964), James E. Siemon (1970), R. Chris Hassel, Jr. (1970), Richard Horwich (1977), Alice N. Benston (1979), and Anne Parten (1982).]*

The Merchant of Venice is a fairy tale. There is no more reality in Shylock's bond and The Lord of Belmont's will than in Jack and the Beanstalk.

Shakespeare, it is true, did not leave the fables as he found them. This would not have done; things that pass muster on the printed page may become quite incredible when acted by human beings, and the unlikelier the story, the likelier must the mechanism of its acting be made. Besides, when his own creative impulse was quickened, he could not help giving life to a character; he could no more help it than the sun can help shining. So Shylock is real, while his story remains fabulous; and Portia and Bassanio become human, though, truly, they never quite emerge from the enchanted thicket of fancy into the common light of day. Aesthetic logic may demand that a story and its characters should move consistently upon one plane or another, be it fantastic or real. But Shakespeare's practical business, once he had chosen these two stories for his play, was simply so to charge them with humanity that they did not betray belief in the human beings presenting them, yet not so uncompromisingly that the stories themselves became ridiculous. (p. 67)

The Merchant of Venice is the simplest of plays, so long as we do not bedevil it with sophistries. Further, it is—for what it is!—as smoothly and completely successful, its means being as well fitted to its end, as anything Shakespeare wrote. He was happy in his choice of the Portia story; his verse, which has lost glitter to gain a mellower beauty and an easier flow, is now well attuned to such romance. The story of Shylock's bond is good contrast and complement both; and he can now project character upon the stage, uncompromising and complete.... Lastly, Shakespeare is now enough of the skilled playwright to be able to adjust and blend the two themes with fruitful economy.

This blending of the themes would, to a modern playwright, have been the main difficulty. The two stories do not naturally march together. The forfeiture of the bond must be a matter of months; with time not only of the essence of the contract, but of the dramatic effect. But the tale of the caskets cannot be enlarged, its substance is too fragile; and a very moderate charge of emotion would explode its pretty hollowness altogether. Critics have credited Shakespeare with nice calculation and amazing subtlety in his compassing of the time-difficulty.... [For him dramatic time] was a naturally elastic affair. (It still is, though less so, for the modern playwright, whose half-hour act may commonly suggest the passing of an hour or two; this also is Double Time.) Shakespeare seems to think of it quite simply in terms of effect, as he thought of dramatic space, moving his characters hither and thither without measurement of yards or miles. The one freedom will imply and enhance the other.... In this play, for instance, where we find Shylock and Antonio will be Venice, but whereabouts in Venice is usually no matter; when it is—at Shylock's door or in Court before the Duke—it will be made clear enough to us. And where Portia is, is Belmont. He treats time—and the more easily—with a like freedom, and a like aim. Three months suits for the bond; but once he has pouched the money Bassanio must be off to Belmont, and his calendar, attuned to his mood, at once starts to run by hours only. The wind serves, and he sails that very night, and there is no delay at Belmont. Portia would detain him some month or two before he ventures; and what could be more convenient for a Shakespeare bent on synchronising the two stories? For that matter, he could have placed Belmont a few hundred miles off, and let the coming and going eke out the time. Did the problem as a whole ever even occur to him? If it did, he dismissed it as of no consequence. What he does is to set each story going according to its nature; then he punctuates them, so to speak, for effect. By the clock they are not even consistent in themselves, far less with each other. But we should pay just the sort of attention to these months, days or hours that we do, in another connection, to the commas and semi-colons elucidating a sentence. They give us, and are meant to, simply a *sense* of time and its exactions. (pp. 68-71)

How to blend two such disparate themes into a dramatically organic whole; that was his real problem. The stories, linked in the first scene, will, of themselves, soon part company. Shakespeare has to run them neck and neck till he is ready to join them again in the scene of the trial. But the difficulty is less that they will not match each other by the clock than that their whole gait so differs, their very nature. How is the flimsy theme of the caskets to be kept in countenance beside its grimly powerful rival? You cannot, as we said, elaborate the story, or charge it with emotion; that would invite disaster. Imagine a Portia seriously alarmed by the prospect of an Aragon or a Morocco for husband. What sort of a barrier, on the other hand, would the caskets be to a flesh-and-blood hero and heroine fallen in love? ... As it is, the very sight of Bassanio prompts Portia to rebellion; and Shakespeare can only allow his lovers a few lines of talk together, and that in company, dare only colour the fairy-tale with a rhetorically passionate phrase or so before the choice is made and the caskets can be forgotten—as they are!—altogether. (pp. 71-2)

But you cannot neglect the Portia story either, or our interest in her may cool. Besides, this antiphony of high romance and rasping hate enhances the effect of both. A contrasting of subjects, scene by scene, is a trick (in no depreciatory sense) of Shakespeare's earliest stage-craft, and he never lost his liking for it. Then if the casket-theme cannot be neglected, but cannot be elaborated, it must somehow be drawn out, its peculiar character sustained, its interest husbanded while its consummation is delayed.

Shakespeare goes straightforwardly enough to work. He puts just as little as may be into Portia's first scene; but for the one sounding of Bassanio's name there would be nothing but the inevitable tale of the caskets told in tripping prose and the conventional joking upon the suitors. Portia and Nerissa, however, seen for the first time in the flesh, give it sufficient life, and that 'Bassanio' one vivid spark more. Later, in due course, come Morocco's choice of the gold casket and Aragon's of the silver. . . . [But for a time, Shakespeare holds] his lovers apart, since the air of the Belmont of the caskets is too rarefied for flesh and blood to breathe. And Portia herself has been spellbound; we have only had jaunty little Nerissa to prophesy that love (by the pious prevision of the late lord) would somehow find out the way. But once he brings them together Bassanio must break the spell. It is the story of the sleeping beauty and the prince in another kind; a legitimate and traditional outcome. And once Shakespeare himself has broken free of the fairytale and brought these two to life (for Bassanio as well has been till now a little bloodless) it is not in him to let them lapse from the scene unproven, and to the full. The long restraint has left him impatient, and he must, here and now, have his dramatic fling. We need not credit—or discredit him, if you like—with much calculation of the problem. It was common prudence both to keep Belmont as constantly in our view as Venice, and the emancipating Bassanio clear of it for as long as possible. And he is now in the middle of his play, rather past it, ready to link his two stories together again. . . . [Here] is his chance to uplift the two as hero and heroine, and he will not dissipate its effectiveness.

For Bassanio, as we said, has been till now only little less bound than Portia in the fetters of a fairy-tale; and later, Shylock and the bond will condemn him to protesting helplessness, and the affair of the rings to be merrily befooled. The wonder indeed is, considering the rather poor figure . . . the coercion of the story makes him cut, that throughout he measures up so well to the stature of sympathetic hero. Shakespeare contrives it in two ways. He endows him with very noble verse; and, whenever he can, throws into strong relief the Bassanio of his own uncovenanted imagination. He does this here. The fantasy of the caskets brought to its due climax, charged with an emotion which blows it for a finish into thin air, he shows us Bassanio, his heart's desire won, agonised with grief and remorse at the news of Antonio's danger. Such moments do test a man and show him for what he is; and this one, set in bright light and made the scene's turning point, counts for more in the effect the character makes on us than all the gentlemanly graces of his conventional equipment. Unless the actor is much at fault, we shall hear the keynote to the true Bassanio struck in the quiet simplicity—such contrast to his rhetoric over the caskets, even though this was less mere rhetoric than Morocco's and Aragon's—of the speech which begins

> O sweet Portia,
> Here are a few of the unpleasant'st words
> That ever blotted paper. . . .
> Rating myself at nothing, you shall see
> How much I was a braggart. When I told you
> My state was nothing, I should then have told you
> That I was worse than nothing, for indeed

> I have engaged myself to a dear friend,
> Engaged my friend to his mere enemy,
> To feed my means. . . .
>
>   [III. ii. 250-52, 257-63]

Here speaks Shakespeare's Bassanio; and it is by this, and all that will belong to it, that he is meant to live in our minds. (pp. 72-6)

The fairytale is finally incarnate in the fantastic word-painting of [Portia's] portrait and the reading of the scroll. Then, with a most delicate declension to reality, Bassanio comes to face her as in a more actual world, and the curtains can be drawn upon the caskets for the last time. Observe that not for a moment has Shakespeare played his fabulous story false. He takes his theatre too seriously to go spoiling an illusion he has created. He consummates it, and turns the figures of it to fresh purpose, and they seem to suffer no change. (pp. 77-8)

Shakespeare can do little enough with Portia while she is still the slave of the caskets; incidentally, the actress must resist the temptation to try and do more. She has this picture of an enchanted princess to present, verse and prose to speak perfectly, and she had better be content with that. But we feel, nevertheless (and to this, very discreetly, she may encourage us), that here, pent up and primed for escape, is one of that eminent succession of candid and fearless souls: Rosaline, Helena, Beatrice, Rosalind [in, respectively, *Love's Labour's Lost*, *All's Well That Ends Well*, *Much Ado about Nothing*, and *As You Like It*]—they embodied an ideal lodged for long in Shakespeare's imagination; he gave it expression whenever he could. . . . He reveals [Portia's character] to us mainly in little things, and lets us feel its whole happy virtue in the melody of her speech. This it is that casts its spell upon the strict court of Venice. The

> Shed thou no blood. . . .
>
>   [IV. i. 325]

is an effective trick. But

> The quality of mercy is not strained;
> It droppeth as the gentle rain from heaven
> Upon the place beneath. . . .
>
>   [IV. i. 183-85]

with its continuing beauty, gives the true Portia. To the very end she expands in her fine freedom, growing in authority and dignity, fresh touches of humour enlightening her, new traits of graciousness showing. She is a great lady in her perfect simplicity, in her ready tact (see how she keeps her guest Antonio free from the mock quarrel about the rings), and in her quite unconscious self-sufficiency (she jokes without embarrassment about taking the mythical Balthasar to her bed, but she snubs Gratiano the next minute for talking of cuckoldry, even as she snubbed Nerissa for a very mild indelicacy—she is fond of Nerissa, but no forward waiting-women for her!) Yet she is no more than a girl.

Here is an effect that we are always apt to miss in the acting of Shakespeare to-day. It is not the actress's fault that she cannot be what her predecessor, the boy-Portia, was; and she brings us compensation for losses which should leave us—if she will mitigate the losses as far as she can—gainers on the whole. But the constant play made in the Comedies upon the contrast between womanly passion or wisdom and its very virginal enshrining gives a delicacy and humour to these figures of romance which the limited resources of the boy left vivid, which the ampler endowment of the woman too often obscures. (pp. 84-6)

The very first line [Portia] speaks, the

> By my troth, Nerissa, my little body is aweary
> of this great world
>
> [I. ii. 1-2]

is likely to come from the mature actress robbed of half its point. This will not matter so much. But couple that 'little body' with her self-surrender to Bassanio . . . with the mischief that hides behind the formal courtesies of the welcome to Aragon and Morocco, . . . [and] with the pretty sententiousness of her talk of herself, her

> I never did repent of doing good,
> Nor shall not now. . . .
>
> [III. iv. 10-11]

and the figure built up for us of the heiress and great lady of Belmont is seen to be a mere child too, who lives remote in her enchanted world. Set beside this the Portia of resource and command, who sends Bassanio post haste to his friend, and beside that the schoolgirl laughing with Nerissa over the trick they are to play their new lords and masters. Know them all for one Portia, a wise and gallant spirit so virginally enshrined; and we see to what profit Shakespeare turned his disabilities. There is, in this play, a twofold artistry in the achievement. Unlikelihood of plot is redeemed by veracity of character; while the artifice of the medium, the verse and its convention, and the stylised acting of boy as woman, re-reconciles us to the fantasy of the plot.

But a boy-Portia's advantage was chiefly manifest, of course, in the scene of the trial; and here in particular the actress of to-day must see that she lessens it no more than she need. The curious process of what we may call the 'double negative,' by which an Elizabethan audience first admitted a boy as a girl and then enjoyed the pretence that the girl was a boy, is obsolete for us; make-believe being the game, there was probably some pleasure just in this complication of it. This beside, there was the direct dramatic effect, which the boy made supremely well in his own person, of the wise young judge, the Daniel come to judgement. . . . He is life incarnate and destined to victory; and such a victory is the fitting climax to a fairy-tale. So the Portia that will—as most Portias do—lapse into feminine softness and pitch the whole scene in the key of the speech on mercy, and that in a key of sentiment, damns the scene and herself and the speech, all three. This amazing youth has the ear of the Court at once; but he'll only hold it by strict attention to business. Then, suddenly, out of this, comes the famous appeal, and catches us and the Court unaware, catches us by the throat, enkindles us. In this lies the effect. Prepare for it, or make the beauty of it over-beautiful (all the more now, because it is famous and hackneyed) and it becomes a dose of soothing syrup.

This, be it further remembered, is not the scene's top note; conflict and climax are to come. They are brought about simply and directly; the mechanical trick of the 'No jot of blood' [IV. i. 306] that is to resolve them asks nothing else. Shakespeare keeps the medium of the verse as simple; it flows on with hardly a broken line. The conflict is between Portia and Shylock. Bassanio's agony, Antonio's stoic resignation cannot be given great play; the artifice of the story will not even now sustain cross-currents of human passion. But the constraint of the business of a court accounts well enough for their quies-

cence (the actors need do nothing to mitigate it) and the few notes that are struck from them suffice. The action must sweep ahead and no chance be given us to question its likelihood. (pp. 86-9)

Throughout the scene a Portia must, of course, by no smallest sign betray to us—as well betray it to Bassanio—that she is other than she now seems. No difficulty here, as we said, for Shakespeare's Portia, or his audience either. There was no wondering as he faced the judges why they never saw this was a woman (since very obviously he now wasn't) nor why Bassanio did not know his wife a yard off. The liquid sentences of the Mercy speech were no betrayal, nor did the brusque aside of a young lawyer, intent upon his brief—

> Your wife would give you little thanks for that,
> If she were by to hear you make the offer.
>
> [IV. i. 288-89]

—lose its quite casual humour. All this straightforwardness the modern actress must, as far as she can, restore. (pp. 89-90)

There remains Shylock. He steps into the play, actual and individual from his first word on, and well might in his strength (we come to feel) have broken the pinchbeck of his origin to bits, had a later Shakespeare had the handling of him. . . . Despite the borrowed story, this Shylock is essentially Shakespeare's own. But if he is not a puppet, neither is he a stalking horse; he is no more a mere means to exemplifying the Semitic problem than is Othello for the raising of the colour question. 'I am a Jew' [III. i. 58]. 'Haply, for I am black . . .' [Othello, III. iii. 263]. Here we have—and in Shylock's case far more acutely and completely—the circumstances of the dramatic conflict; but at the heart of it are men; and we may surmise, indeed, that from a maturer Shakespeare we should have had, as with Othello, much more of the man, and so rather less of the alien and his griefs. However that may be, he steps now into the play, individual and imaginatively full-grown, and the scene of his talk with Bassanio and Antonio is masterly exposition.

The dry taciturnity of his

> Three thousand ducats, well?
>
> [I. iii. 1]

(the lure of that thrice-echoed 'Well'!) and the cold dissecting of the business in hand are made colder, drier yet by contrast with the happy sound of Portia's laughter dying in our ears as he begins to speak. And for what a helpless innocent Bassanio shows beside him; over-anxious, touchy, over-civil! Shylock takes his time; and suddenly we see him peering, myopic, beneath his brows. Who can the new-comer be? And the quick brain answers beneath the question's cover: They must need the money badly if Antonio himself comes seeking me. Off goes Bassanio to greet his friend; and Shylock in a long aside can discharge his obligations to the plot. These eleven lines are worth comment. In them is all the motive power for drama that the story, as Shakespeare found it, provides; and he throws this, with careless opulence, into a single aside. Then he returns to the upbuilding of his Shylock. (pp. 92-3)

From the snuffling depreciation of his present store, from his own wonted fawning on these Christian clients, Shylock unexpectedly rises to the dignities of

> When Jacob grazed his uncle Laban's sheep. . . .
>
> [I. iii. 71]

And with this the larger issue opens out between Gentile and Jew, united and divided by the scripture they revere, and held from their business by this tale from it—of flocks and herds and the ancient East. Here is another Shylock; and Antonio may well stare, and answer back with some respect—though he recovers contempt for the alien creature quickly enough. But with what added force the accusation comes:

> Signior Antonio, many a time and oft
> In the Rialto you have rated me. . . .
> You called me misbeliever, cut-throat dog
> And spit upon my Jewish gaberdine. . . .
>
>   [I. iii. 106-07, 111-12]

The two Venetians see the Ghetto denizen again, and only hear the bondman's whine. But to us there is now all Jewry crouched and threatening there, an ageless force behind it. They may make light of the money bond, but we shall not.

Shakespeare keeps character within the bounds of story with great tact; but such a character as this that has surged in his imagination asks more than such a story to feed on. Hence, partly at least, the new theme of Jessica and her flight, which will give Shylock another and more instant grudge to satisfy. It is developed with strict economy. Twenty-one lines are allowed to Jessica and Launcelot, another twenty or so to her lover and their plans; then, in a scene not sixty long, Shylock and his household are enshrined. As an example of dramatic thrift alone this is worth study. The parting with Launcelot: he has a niggard liking for the fellow, is even hurt a little by his leaving, touched in pride too, and shows it childishly.

> Thou shalt not gormandize
> As thou has done with me. . . .
>
>   [II. v. 3-4]

But he can at least pretend that he parts with him willingly and makes some profit by it. The parting with Jessica, which we of the audience know to be a parting indeed; that constant calling her by name, which tells us of the lonely man! He has looked to her for everything, has tasked her hard, no doubt; he is her gaoler, yet he trusts her, and loves her in his extortionate way. Uneasy stranger that he is within these Venetian gates; the puritan, who, in a wastrel world, will abide by law and prophets! So full a picture of the man does the short scene give that it seems hardly possible we see no more of him than this between the making of the bond and the climacteric outbreak of passion upon Jessica's loss and the news of Antonio's ruin.

References to him abound; Shylock can never be long out of our minds. But how deliberate is the thrift of opportunity we may judge by our being shown the first effect of the loss on him only through the ever-useful eyes of Salarino and Solanio. This is politic, however, from other points of view. Look where the scene in question [II. viii] falls, between Morocco's choice of his casket and Aragon's. Here or hereabouts some such scene must come, for the progress of the Antonio and Shylock story cannot be neglected. But conceive the effect of such a tragic outcry as Shylock's own,

> So strange, outrageous and so variable. . . .
>
>   [II. viii. 13]

—of such strong dramatic meat sandwiched between pleasant conventional rhetoric. How much of the credibility of the casket story would survive the association, with how much patience should we return to it? But Salarino and Solanio tone down tragedy to a good piece of gossip, as it becomes young men

of the world to do. We avoid an emotional danger zone; and, for the moment at least, that other danger of an inconvenient sympathy with 'the dog Jew' [II. viii. 14]. When Shylock's outbreak of anguish does come, the play is nearer to its climax, Bassanio's choice is about to free Portia's story from its unreality, and his savage certainty of revenge upon Antonio will now depress the sympathetic balance against him. (pp. 94-6)

In tone and temper and method as well [Act III, Scene 1] breaks away from all that has gone before. The very start in prose, the brisk

>   Now, what news on the Rialto?
>
>   [III. i. 1]

even, perhaps, Solanio's apology for former

>   . . . slips of prolixity or crossing the plain high-
>   way of talk:
>
>   [III. i. 11-12]

seem to tell us that Shakespeare is now asserting the rights of his own imagination, means, at any rate, to let this chief creature of it, his Shylock, off the leash. For verily he does.

The scene's method repays study. No whirling storm of fury is asked for; this is not the play's climax, but preparation for it still. Shylock is wrapped in resentful sorrow, telling over his wrong for the thousandth time. Note the repetition of thought and phrase. And how much more sinister this sight of him with the wound festering than if we had seen the blow's instant fall! His mind turns to Antonio, and the thrice told

>   . . . let him look to his bond.
>
>   [III. i. 47]

is a rope of salvation for him; it knots up the speech in a dreadful strength. Then, on a sudden, upon the good young Salarino's reasonable supposition that what a money-lender wants is his money back; who on earth would take flesh instead?—

>   What's that good for?
>
>   [III. i. 52]

—there flashes out the savagery stripped naked of

> To bait fish withal: if it will feed nothing else,
> it will feed my revenge.
>
>   [III. i. 53-4]

Now we have it; and one salutes such purity of hatred. There follows the famous speech . . . mounting in passionate logic, from its

> He hath disgraced me . . . and what's his rea-
> son? I am a Jew.
>
>   [III. i. 54, 58]

to the height of

> If a Jew wrong a Christian, what is his hu-
> mility? Revenge. If a Christian wrong a Jew,
> what should his sufferance be by Christian ex-
> ample? Why, revenge. The villainy you teach
> me I will execute, and it shall go hard but I
> will better the instruction.
>
>   [III. i. 68-73]

This is a Shylock born of the old story, but transformed, and here a theme of high tragedy, of the one seemingly never-ending tragedy of the world. It is the theme for a greater play than Shakespeare was yet to write. But if this one cannot be sustained on such a height, he has at least for the moment raised it there. (pp. 97-8)

There follows the remarkable passage with Tubal; of gruesome comedy, the apocalyptic Shylock shrunk already to the man telling his ill-luck against his enemy's, weighing each in scales (love for his daughter, a memory of his dead wife thrown in!) as he is used to weigh the coin which is all these Christians have left him for his pride. . . . Shakespeare, for a finish, lowers the scene from its climax, from that confronting of Christian and Jew, of hate with hate, to this raucous assonance of these two of a kind and mind, standing cheek to cheek in common cause, the excellent Tubal fueling up revenge.

Such a finish, ousting all nobility, both shows us another facet of Shylock himself (solid man enough now to be turned any way his maker will) and is . . . a shadow against which the high romance of Bassanio's wooing will in a moment shine the more brightly. Sharp upon the heels of this, he comes again; but once more apocalyptic, law incarnate now. . . . Verse and its dignity are needed for this scene; and note the recurring knell of the phrases:

> I'll have my bond; I will not hear thee speak:
> I'll have my bond, and therefore speak no more.
> I'll not be made a soft and dull-eyed fool,
> To shake the head, relent, and sigh, and yield
> To Christian intercessors. Follow not;
> I'll have no speaking: I will have my bond.
>
> [III. iii. 12-17]

Here is a Shylock primed for the play's great scene; and Shakespeare's Shylock wrought ready for a catastrophe, which is a deeper one by far than that the story yields. For not in the missing of his vengeance on Antonio will be this Shylock's tragedy, but in the betrayal of the faith on which he builds.

> I've sworn an oath that I will have my bond. . .
>
> [III. iii. 5]

How many times has the synagogue not heard it sworn?

> An oath, an oath. I have an oath in Heaven. . .
>
> [IV. i. 228]

He has made his covenant with an unshakable God . . .—and he is to find himself betrayed.

It is the apocalyptic Shylock that comes slowly into Court, solitary and silent, to face and to outface the Duke and all the moral power of Venice. When he does speak he answers the Duke as an equal, setting a sterner sanction against easy magnanimity—at other people's expense! (pp. 98-100)

So confident is he that he is tempted to shift ground a little and let yet another Shylock peep—the least likable of all. He goes on

> You'll ask me, why I rather choose to have
> A weight of carrion flesh, than to receive
> Three thousand ducats: I'll not answer that,
> But say it is my humour. . .
>
> [IV. i. 40-3]

Legality gives license to the hard heart. Mark the progression. While the sufferer cried

> The villainy you teach me I will execute; and
> it shall go hard but I will better the instruction.
>
> [III. i. 71-3]

with the law on his side it is

What judgment shall I dread, doing no wrong? . . .

> [IV. i. 89]

from which he passes, by an easy turn, to the mere moral anarchy of

> The pound of flesh, which I demand of him,
> Is dearly bought; 'tis mine, and I will have it . . .
>
> [IV. i. 99-100]

and in satanic heroism stands defiant:

> If you deny me, fie upon your law!
> There is no force in the decrees of Venice.
> I stand for judgment. Answer: shall I have it?
>
> [IV. i. 101-03]
> (p. 101)

The coming of the young judge's clerk does not impress Shylock. How should it? Little Nerissa! He has won, what doubt of it? He can indulge then—why not?—the lodged hate and loathing he bears Antonio. The Duke is busy with Bellario's letter and the eyes of the Court are off him. From avenger he degenerates to butcher; to be caught, lickerish-lipped, by Bassanio, and Gratiano's rough tongue serves him as but another whetstone for savagery. He turns surly at first sight of the wise young judge—what need of such a fine fellow and more fine talk?—and surlier still when it is talk of mercy. (p. 102)

Why does Shakespeare now delay the catastrophe by a hundred lines, and let Portia play cat and mouse with her victim? From the story's standpoint, of course, to keep up the excitement a while longer. We guess there is a way out. We wonder what it can be; and yet, with that knife shining, Antonio's doom seems to come nearer and nearer. This is dramatic child's play, and excellent of its sort. But into it much finer stuff is woven. We are to have more than a trick brought off; there must be a better victory; this faith in which Shylock abides must be broken. So first she leads him on. Infatuate, finding her all on his side, he finally and formally refuses the money—walks into the trap. Next she plays upon his fanatical trust in his bond, sets him searching in mean mockery for a charitable comma in it—had one escaped his cold eye—even as the Pharisees searched their code to convict Christ. Fold by fold, the prophetic dignity falls from him. While Antonio takes his selfless farewell of his friend, Shylock must stand clutching his bond and his knife, only contemptible in his triumph. She leads him on to a last slaveringly exultant cry: then the blow falls.

Note that the tables are very precisely turned on him.

> . . . if thou tak'st more,
> Or less, than a just pound, be it so much
> As makes it light or heavy in the substance,
> Or the division of the twentieth part
> Of one poor scruple, nay, if the scale do turn
> But in the estimation of a hair. . . .
>
> [IV. i. 326-31]

is exact retaliation for Shylock's insistence upon the letter of his bond. Gratiano is there to mock him with his own words, and to sound, besides, a harsher note of retribution than Portia can; for the pendulum of sympathy now swings back a little—more than a little, we are apt to feel. But the true catastrophe is clear. Shylock stood for law and the letter of the law; and it seemed, in its kind, a noble thing to stand for, ennobling him. It betrays him, and in the man himself there is no virtue left. . . . The pride and power in which legality had wrapped him, by which he had outfaced them all, and held Venice herself to ransom, are gone. He stands stripped, once more the sordid Jew that they may spit upon, greedy for money, hurriedly keen to profit by his shame.

> I take this offer then; pay the bond thrice,
> And let the Christian go.
>
> [IV. i. 318-19]

Here is Shakespeare's Shylock's fall, and not in the trick the law plays him. (pp. 102-04)

Shakespeare has still to bring his theme full circle. He does it with doubled regard to character and story.

> Why, then the devil give him good of it!
> I'll stay no longer question.
>
> [IV. i. 345-46]

If he were not made to, by every canon of theatrical justice Shylock would be let off too lightly; wherefore we find that the law has another hold on him. It is but a logical extending of retribution, which Gratiano is quick to reduce to its brutal absurdity. Here is Shylock with no more right to a cord with which to hang himself than had Antonio to a bandage for his wound. These quibbling ironies are for the layman among the few delights of law. Something of the villainy the Jew taught them the Christians will now execute; and Shylock, as helpless as Antonio was, takes on a victim's dignity in turn. He stays silent while his fate, and the varieties of official and unofficial mercy to be shown him, are canvassed. He is allowed no comment upon his impoverishing for the benefit of 'his son Lorenzo' [IV. i. 390] or upon his forced apostasy. But could eloquence serve better than such a silence?

> *Portia.* Art thou contented, Jew? What doest thou say?
> *Shylock.* I am content.
>
> [IV. i. 393-94]

With the three words of submission the swung pendulum of the drama comes to rest. And for the last of him we have only

> I pray you give me leave to go from hence;
> I am not well. Send the deed after me,
> And I will sign it.
>
> [IV. i. 395-97]

Here is the unapproachable Shakespeare. 'I am not well.' It nears banality and achieves perfection in its simplicity. And what a completing of the picture of Shylock! His deep offence has been to human kindness; he had scorned compassion and prayed God himself in aid of his vengeance. So Shakespeare dismisses him upon an all but ridiculous appeal to our pity, such as an ailing child might make that had been naughty; and we should put the naughtiness aside. He passes out silently, leaving the gibing Gratiano the last word, and the play's action sweeps on without pause. (pp. 104-06)

The play ends, pleasantly and with formality, as a fairy-tale should. One may wonder that the last speech is left (against tradition) to Gratiano; but one practical reason is plain. Portia and Bassanio, Antonio, Lorenzo and Jessica must pace off the stage in their stately Venetian way, while Gratiano's harmless ribaldry is tossed to the audience as an epilogue. (p. 107)

> *Harley Granville-Barker, "'The Merchant of Venice'," in his* Prefaces to Shakespeare, *second series, Sidgwick & Jackson, Ltd., 1930, pp. 67-110.*

T. A. ROSS   (essay date 1934)

[*In the following excerpt, Ross puts forth an explanation of Antonio's melancholy, and in so doing argues that the play's title is appropriate, since the drama is concerned mainly with the fortunes and tribulations of the merchant. He also claims that despite the play's classification as a comedy, it is in reality "a record of human misery and sorrow, relieved in the manner of high tragedy by the nobility of character of the chief sufferer." Other critics who have regarded* The Merchant of Venice *as a tragedy, rather than a comedy, include Nicholas Rowe (1709), Heinrich Heine (1838), and Graham Midgley (1960). The sufferer in the play, according to Ross, is Antonio, and his suffering is the result of his love for Bassanio, who in turn is leaving him permanently for the chance to marry Portia. Thus, for Ross, Antonio is a homosexual—a remorseful homosexual at that—and this is the impetus behind his melancholy. The critic supports his hypothesis by focusing on certain clues he claims Shakespeare inserted in his text—such as the highly emotional parting of Antonio and Bassanio described by Salerio in Act II, Scene viii— and answers some hypothetical questions which his argument calls forth. Perhaps the most important of these questions deals with the nature of Shakespeare's views on homosexuality and Antonio's predicament, to which Ross responds that Shakespeare undoubtedly disapproved of homosexuality, though at the same time could sympathize with and even admire the courage of such people as Antonio who bore their "sexual anomaly" with dignity and compassion. For further commentary on the reason for and significance of Antonio's melancholy, see the excerpts by E. K. Chambers (1908), Graham Midgley (1960), John D. Hurrell (1961), A. D. Moody (1964), and Lawrence Danson (1978).*]

There is first of all the title of [this] play. It is called *The Merchant of Venice*, but though the Merchant himself has to appear throughout, though the trial scene could not be played without him, on the stage he is all the time treated as a lay figure. . . . A pound of flesh had to be in danger from someone, and this quite unimportant person will do as well as anyone else.

It is true that after the first act is over, an act in which the Merchant dominates the stage, an act which would seem to foretell that the play was to be about him as the principal person if it has any meaning at all, his apparent importance fades, and consequently the rest of the play is presented either as the Jew of Venice or the Lady of Belmont, according to the skill and importance of the person portraying one of these two characters. And yet we should not dismiss a title so summarily; perhaps this play is about the Merchant of Venice after all. Assuredly for his light comedies Shakespeare seemed singularly indifferent to the names he gave them. Here indeed a rose by any other name would smell as sweet, and in rosy mood he seemed to think so. *Twelfth Night; or, What You Will, As You Like It, A Midsummer Night's Dream* are names which proclaim that he did not care what the play was called. But though the *Merchant of Venice* may by some be classed as a comedy, it is not a comic comedy; so far as it is comedy it is one of manners rather than of hilarity. It is however in the main, as I shall hope to show, a record of human misery and sorrow, relieved in the manner of high tragedy by the nobility of character of the chief sufferer. (p. 303)

There is nothing melodramatic in this play, no corpses, few tears; it is a record of something that, to us who are interested in psychology, is commonplace, usually unsympathized with, frequently condemned, often borne badly, but often enough met with great patience and fortitude. It deals with pleasant people and with extremely unpleasant people; generosity and meanness jostle each other as in everyday life. But its main theme is connected with the Merchant of Venice, and I do not think that we shall ever understand this play properly until we grasp that its title was chosen deliberately.

The opening lines announce a psychiatric problem. The Merchant enters with his friends in the middle of that compulsive kind of talk which stamps the mildly depressed person, who cannot get away from his illness, but who is still not so ill but that he can talk:

> In sooth, I know not why I am so sad:
> It wearies me; you say it wearies you;
> But how I caught it, found it, or came by it,
> What stuff 'tis made of, whereof it is born,
> I am to learn;
> And such a want-wit sadness makes of me,
> That I have much ado to know myself.
>
> [I. i. 1-7]

Here is a definite problem, definitely stated. It would be strange if the answer were nowhere in the play. It seems extraordinary that so little attention should have been paid to something which is stated so unequivocally. The commentators have not been entirely silent. Financial disaster overtook the Merchant later on; perhaps he had a premonition. This indeed is immediately suggested by the two friends to whom he is talking, and is summarily dismissed by the Merchant, who announces that his affairs have been so well distributed that it is practically impossible that disaster could overtake them all. This is stated in the calmest, most businesslike way possible, and I think it is quite certain that Shakespeare meant us to be quite sure that that was not what Antonio could possibly be worrying about. Against this it must be admitted that the Merchant was not speaking the exact truth. He says that his whole estate is not adventured. However, he had to admit presently that he had no liquid cash and that all his fortunes were at sea. If the play is read carefully it would seem that this is merely careless writing on Shakespeare's part. He forgot in these opening lines that Antonio would soon have to be borrowing money. He wanted, as I see it in this opening, to emphasize that Antonio's sadness was not connected with finance. (pp. 303-04)

Before we go on, however, we may look again at these opening lines, and admire in detail the vivid clinical picture presented. The sadness without cause apparent to the patient, how fatiguing it is, and how the friends have not scrupled to show how bored they are with it, the longing of the patient to know the cause, the feeling that his brain won't work properly. One feels that unless Shakespeare was engaged in psychiatric practice—which I admit is possible from his immense knowledge of the subject—he must at some time have felt exactly as the Merchant was feeling. No better description of the essential symptoms of mild depression has been penned.

Immediately all the usual explanations are thrust at him, at first good-naturedly, but on the patient's rejection of them one by one, less so. I think we are all familiar with that phenomenon also—the bystanders losing their patience when their obviously correct explanations are rejected by the patient. The first explanation we have already dealt with—financial worry. Proof is given that this is probably not true.

The next cause alleged—also a usual one—is that he is in love. To which Antonio replies "Fie, fie" [I. i. 46]. This answer is ambiguous. It is not a denial though his friends apparently think it is, and the friend who suggested it becomes a little rude, and tells Antonio that he had better just say that he is sad because he is not merry. The two friends see Bassanio with others approaching, and say that as better company is coming

they will leave. The Merchant lets them know that he knows that they have seized the chance of leaving him. "I take it your own business calls on you and you embrace the occasion to depart." [I. i. 63-4].

To the newcomers the Merchant, with that curious insistence of the mildly depressed to talk about themselves, seizes the opportunity, afforded by one of them who says that he is not looking very well, to emphasize that his part in life is a sad one. He is immediately fallen upon and told some home truths about himself in the manner with which we are all so familiar. He is told that he poses as the grave solemn man; such people are reputed wise because they say very little, they go about with the air of "I am Sir Oracle and when I ope my lips let no dog bark" [I. i. 93-4], he is told that altogether he is an inferior person trying to put on an air of superiority. And so this friend leaves him.

All this is clinical description of the highest order, not only of the patient's case, but also of what all these poor people have usually to put up with from their friends.

Some hundred and fifty lines are expended on this story of Antonio's depression, so that it cannot be said that the matter is slurred over. As plain as plain can be it is said over and over again that he is depressed, that he can hardly talk of anything else, that he cannot think why it has happened, and it is also made abundantly clear that everybody is sick of it.

Antonio is now left alone with Bassanio, and, after a passing reference to the last quip of the friend who has just departed, he immediately asks Bassanio to tell him about the lady to whom Bassanio had sworn a secret pilgrimage. It is a point of importance that this should be the first subject which he broaches when left alone with Bassanio. It is also of importance to note that he must have known of this intention before the play opens, not in detail indeed, but that there was something afoot of the nature of a love affair. Unfortunately there is no indication of how long he did know of it, or whether this knowledge preceded the onset of the depression or not. The reader is also reminded that when he, Antonio, was challenged with being in love, he could reply only "Fie, fie." It is also important to remember that this love affair of Bassanio's must have been of vast importance to Antonio. Psychiatrists will agree that it is not common for persons obsessed with their own depression to ask a friend straightway at the first opportunity about his love affairs. It must have been something very telling which put a stop to the flow to talk about himself, which had hitherto been steady and unrelenting.

Bassanio does not answer the question immediately, but says that he has been very extravagant and that he has now no money, but that he knows that Antonio from his love will help him to clear his debts. Bassanio is an utterly worthless person; he is not in the least anxious to pay his debts; on the contrary he wants to borrow a considerable further sum from his principal creditor—Antonio himself. The latter instantly assures him that he can rely on him to his uttermost farthing. (pp. 304-06)

This certainly implies great friendship. Shakespeare did not approve of people borrowing money from their friends. "Loan oft loses both itself and friend" [*Hamlet*, I. iii. 76]. It must in his mind have been something very exceptional in the way of friendship that made so shrewd a person as the Merchant of Venice so ready to lend money to this fortune-hunting bankrupt.

There follows after this the unpleasant bargaining between Shylock and the Merchant, but in this we have no reference to Antonio's illness. . . . It might seem as if the Merchant had become infused with a new energy because he was doing something to help his friend. With the same proviso the terms of the bond are of importance. This loan had to be raised to serve Bassanio, and it mattered not a whit to Antonio what became of him personally provided that Bassanio was served. Indeed it might have seemed that at the moment a dangerous bond was attractive.

It is from now on that the play seems to drop Antonio as the principal character. Bassanio sets out for Belmont, which cannot have been very far off seeing that many of the characters made the journey subsequently so easily. But the farewell between the Merchant and his friend was conducted by the former as if it were a final parting. The distance in space might not be great, but there was in the Merchant's mind the thought that this was no mere *au revoir*. Bassanio, with his usual mode of trying to make other people think he was a fine fellow, because he was not sure of himself but felt uncomfortable, said that he would be back soon, but Antonio told him not to hurry, to wait till he had completed his business properly; nothing mattered to him except that Bassanio's affairs should be successful. The parting was described later by one of his friends whom we met in the first act:

> And even there, his eye being big with tears,
> Turning his face, he put his hand behind him,
> And with affection wondrous sensible
> He wrung Bassanio's hand; and so they parted.

To which his auditor replied,

> I think he only loves the world for him.
> [II. vii. 46-50]
> (pp. 306-07)

There are two more quotations to be made. Bassanio at Belmont received a letter from Antonio, then fully persuaded that he must die. He cannot bring himself to do so without seeing Bassanio once more. Not only the opening words but also the whole tenor of the letter bespeak intense affection; and characteristically he puts Bassanio's pleasure and convenience as of more importance than his wish:

> Sweet Bassanio, my ships have all miscarried,
> my creditors grow cruel, my estate is very low,
> my bond to the Jew is forfeit, and since, in
> paying it, it is impossible I should live, all debts
> are cleared between you and I, if I might but
> see you at my death; notwithstanding, use your
> pleasure; if your love do not persuade you to
> come, let not my letter.
> [III. ii. 315-22]

The last words which Antonio speaks before the trial are these:

> Pray God, Bassanio come
> To see me pay his debt, and then I care not!
> [III. iii. 35-6]

My thesis is now fairly plain. Antonio was in love with Bassanio, and the depression had been precipitated by the knowledge which he had received some time before the play opens, that he was going to leave him. This is a common enough story. A homosexual love affair is broken by one of the parties marrying, and the other reacts by depression.

It may be well to summarize the evidence of the love affair.

In an early conversation, Antonio calls out ''Fie, fie'' at the suggestion of love; he does not deny it; he is slightly upset by it as these words suggest. Later he informs an extravagant swaggering bankrupt that he can have as much money as he likes for any purpose not strictly dishonourable because of his love for him; thirdly there is this farewell, though physically it was not a great separation either in space or time, but it threatened to be a complete one spiritually.

There is also recurring evidence on the part of Bassanio of an inward feeling of discomfort. The deserter in practice usually shows some sign of this.

There remain a number of interesting questions which may be summarized:

(1) Why did this subject of Antonio's depression which dominates the first scene peter out and become apparently lost?

(2) Is Antonio's opening speech an example of Shakespeare's belief in the actuality of the unconscious?

(3) How did Antonio and how did other people regard homosexual love at that time, so far as the play provides any evidence on this head?

(4) What was Shakespeare's own view of the subject?

I shall deal with these questions seriatim.

(1) Why did the matter of Antonio's depression and love affair disappear? It seems to do so; in fact it reappears here and there as will become evident when we discuss the third question. But its seeming to disappear was probably because Shakespeare wanted to get his play acted. The censor of obscene books is probably always with us, and therefore, though the beginning of the play was easy, the subject was bound to become more difficult in its presentation as it went on. The farewell scene, which I regard as one which clinches the matter, is not stressed or emphasized in any way. Puritanism of the repressive sort was already strong in England in Shakespeare's time.

Bernard Shaw has called attention in one of his prefaces to the fact that the serious open presentation of a sexual subject will usually ensure its suppression by the censor. Undisguised frivolous presentation is passed easily. Shakespeare may well have had the same difficulty. He apparently had no difficulty in getting leave to display the open jokes of Sir Toby Belch [in *Twelfth Night*] or Sir John Falstaff. But a serious discussion would probably then as later have been taboo.

(2) Is Antonio's opening speech to be regarded as a proof of Shakespeare's belief in the unconscious? I suppose that most people are aware by now that Freud did not invent the unconscious, so that this question is not an anachronistic absurdity. I have myself used the first lines on other occasions as a most excellent statement of the fact of the unconscious, and taken by themselves this is indubitable. ''In sooth I know not why I am so sad'' [I. i. 1]. If these words are true they necessitate an unconscious. But are they true on this occasion? To answer that we must look wider afield. I do not think that they are true. The statement ''I do not know'' is used very often when the speaker does not wish to tell the whole truth about something. Antonio was sad, he was a very popular and well-liked person, and his friends were plaguing him about something which he did not wish to explain. Antonio is one of the most honourable figures in all Shakespeare, and we shall not think the less of him if he should prefer the polite untruth rather than tell people to mind their own business. I do not think he was unconscious either of the cause of his sadness or of his ho-

mosexual love; the fact that he broached the subject of the lady the first moment he found Bassanio alone showed that the subject of love was very much in his conscious mind. Some might say that he would not have found the money so readily if he had consciously recognized that its use would utterly destroy his own happiness. I do not think much of that argument. It is clear and will become clearer that he was a continent lover—as indeed was the lover in Sonnet XX, who freely gave his beloved physically to women—and that he was a man for whom love meant giving rather than receiving, whose great aim was the happiness of the beloved rather than his own.

(3) How is homosexual love regarded in the play? Throughout the play Antonio seems to have regarded it as wrong. In a way he seems to further Bassanio's cause though it gave him pain. He pushed the money on him though it was to his own undoing. We are very familiar with the conscientious scrupulous patient who acts like this. If he regarded it as sin it would be an act of expiation that he should do this. Far on in the play there is evidence that he did so regard it. In the trial scene Bassanio makes a hearty and, as I read it, insincere offer to let the Jew have his flesh instead of Antonio's. To which the latter replies,

> I am a tainted wether of the flock,
> Meetest for death.
>
> [IV. i. 114-15]

It is obvious that Antonio held that he had a stigma, and that it was well that he should not live. These words are not merely those of a man whose interest in life has disappeared, but those of one who holds that he is not worthy to live; they have some value too as proof for the main thesis. In what way was Antonio tainted? In no way that we know of. It is certain that he was in love with Bassanio, and for the mass of mankind that is a taint.

How did other people regard him? Though his friends were tired of his illness, and there is no illness which wearies friends so quickly as this one, they were fond of him; Salarino, the friend who reported his breakdown on parting with Bassanio, said, while he was actually telling the very story of the parting, that a kinder gentleman treads not this earth. His friend, on hearing the story of the parting, says of Antonio:

> I think he only loves the world for him [i.e. Bassanio].
> I pray thee, let us go and find him out,
> And quicken his embraced heaviness
> With some delight or other.
>
> [II. vii. 50-3]

This would seem to indicate, taken with the story of the parting, that they regarded the affair as more than ordinary friendship. Throughout they all remain friendly, so that if they knew they did not disapprove.

(4) But how did Shakespeare view the matter? We have here the question: If an author puts a view of a case into the mouth of a character, how far does that view represent the author's? As already stated it seems to me that Antonio considered his sexual anomaly as a somewhat disreputable thing. We are not sure whether the friends had detected it; if they had they remained unmoved. But is Antonio's view Shakespeare's? I am of course talking of conscious views. Antonio's view of himself probably represented, does indeed at the present day represent, the usual view of the general public, that a state like this is disgraceful and that if one is in it one had better keep quiet about it.

Shakespeare does not directly state a view at all. Throughout the play Antonio is depicted as an upright, lovable, courageous man, so that if Shakespeare disapproved, he at least considered that a man with such a condition might otherwise be a very fine person. It is, however, more particularly in the fifth act that Antonio is revealed as a much finer person than anyone else in the play. If this act were not intended to show something of the kind it is hard to see why it was ever written. If the play were really a melodrama where the villain is discomfited in the end, that end has been reached at the end of the trial. That is the climax. Shylock, poor man, is finished and done with when the trial is over. Portia, the other possible central figure, cuts a rather poor figure also after the trial. Antonio does not, which brings me back to my original thesis that the play was intended to be about the person whose identity is given in the title, that the play is about the Merchant of Venice. It ends with him as it began. Anyone who reads that fifth act superficially will say "What nonsense." Antonio speaks only twelve lines in the whole act, and these of no importance. Let us, however, examine the act in some detail. This act is spoken chiefly by several married couples whose marriages have not yet been consummated. The urgent news of the danger in which Antonio stood had come before this could be accomplished. They all meet now on a beautiful moonlight night to which they pay compliment, for Shakespeare could never resist any occasion for glorifying the beauties of nature. After that they have a little rather vulgar joking about the rings which Bassanio and Gratiano had given to the alleged lawyer and his clerk. This leads up to more open sexual jokings about what is going to happen when they get to bed. It is all rather undignified. In the midst of them stands Antonio, loftily remote from all this vulgarity, a solitary figure of great dignity.

I think we may say from this play and also from Sonnet XX that Shakespeare's attitude towards continent homosexuality was one of respectful admiration. He saw, as some of us see now, how unfortunate these poor people are, despised for something they cannot help, a something which cuts them off from the greatest joys of life; and in this play he depicts a man who bore these trials nobly. (pp. 308-11)

T. A. Ross, "A Note on 'The Merchant of Venice'," in The British Journal of Medical Psychology, *Vol. XIV, Part IV, 1934, pp. 303-11.*

CAROLINE F. E. SPURGEON   (essay date 1935)

[*Spurgeon's* Shakespeare's Imagery and What It Tells Us *(1935) inaugurated the "image-pattern analysis" method of studying Shakespeare's plays, one of the most widely used methods of the mid-twentieth century. In this work, she interprets the thematic structure of the plays through an examination of patterns in the imagery. Spurgeon also sought to learn about Shakespeare's personality from a study of his images, a course which few of her disciples followed. Since publication of her book, earlier works on image patterns in Shakespeare have been discovered, but none was so important in the history of Shakespearean criticism as Spurgeon's. In her commentary on* The Merchant of Venice *excerpted below, Spurgeon discusses the clustering of poetic images in the third casket scene (III. ii.), in which Bassanio chooses the proper casket and wins Portia's hand in marriage, and the final act of the play. She argues that these two scenes contain more poetic imagery than any other in the drama because they represent the highest points of emotion. In another highly emotional episode—that of the trial—Spurgeon claims Shakespeare used little imagery because "the tension and deep feeling . . . are maintained chiefly through the quality of the plot itself, its fears, doubts, suspense and surprises." For additional commentary on the lan-*

guage and imagery in The Merchant of Venice, *see the excerpt by B. Ifor Evans (1952); also, see the essay by Sigurd Burckhardt (1962) for a discussion of the images of bonding and circularity in the play.*]

[*The Merchant of Venice* is] remarkable, like *A Midsummer Night's Dream,* for its high proportion of poetical images, eighty out of a total of a hundred and thirteen, some of them very beautiful and among the best known in Shakespeare.

There are sensitive little nature pictures such as Antonio's etching of the mountain pines 'fretten with the gusts of heaven' [IV. i. 77]; or more artificial and worked up 'pieces' like Gratiano's double image of the 'scarfed bark' putting out from her native bay compared to a prodigal and his return [II. vi. 14ff.]; highly imaginative and decorative beauties as when the 'floor of heaven' is likened to a mosaic 'thick inlaid with patines of bright gold' [V. i. 58-9]; brilliantly vivid and unusual comparisons, as

> cowards, whose hearts are all as false
> As stairs of sand;
>
> [III. ii. 83-4]

or, most unusual of all with Shakespeare, several detailed glimpses of everyday life and experience in a city. Such are the demeanour of the rich and haughty burghers in London streets; the feelings of the prizewinner in wrestling or some feat of strength, who, hearing the shouts and applause of the populace, stops

> Giddy in spirit, still gazing in a doubt
> Whether those peals of praise be his or no,
>
> [III. ii. 144-45]

which Bassanio uses with such effect to describe his feelings when he realises he has won Portia.... (pp. 280-81)

Bassanio uses the greatest number of images and Portia runs him very close, so that between them they are responsible for nearly half the images in the play. Next to them, but at a long distance, comes the gay and talkative Gratiano, who, though Bassanio thinks he 'speaks an infinite deal of nothing' [I. i. 114], possesses a lively imagination and a pretty wit.... (p. 281)

The distribution of images is unusual; it is very uneven, varying with the tone and subject, and in no other play, I believe, is this unevenness so marked.... The high points of emotion in the *Merchant of Venice* are the third casket scene, when Bassanio makes his choice, the trial scene, and the preparation for the final gathering together of the pairs of lovers in the moonlit garden, and it is in the first and last named of these that the images are chiefly grouped.

It is worth while to note—as an indication of the difference of tone and feeling—the difference in the number and use of images in the three casket scenes. In the first (2.7), 79 lines in length, there are four images only, somewhat frigid and detached, used by Morocco, who rather pettishly describes Venice as the

> watery kingdom, whose ambitious head
> Spits in the face of heaven,
>
> [II. vii. 44-5]

where Portia's suitors come 'as o'er a brook' [II. vii. 47] to see her, and who has a play of words on a gem set in gold,

and an 'angel in a golden bed' [II. vii. 58]. In the second (2.9), of 84 lines, we find three images, two used by Arragon, the martlet's nest, and the picking of seed from chaff (real merit from mere titles and dignities), finished off by Portia's dry and caustic summing up of the incident,

> Thus hath the candle singed the moth.
>
> [II. ix. 79]

But when, immediately afterwards, the servant arrives to say that Bassanio's messenger is at the gate, he describes him with one of Shakespeare's most charming similes of spring:

> A day in April never came so sweet,
>
> [II. ix. 93]

thus striking the note of beauty, romance and true love which rings through the great scene when Bassanio makes his happy choice (3.2).

It opens quietly, for Portia has herself well in hand, but when the actual moment of choice arrives, and the tension of emotion increases, images crowd thick and fast in the speech of both lovers, so that in eighteen lines spoken by Portia [III. ii. 44-62], no less than seven follow one another without a break, as she orders music to be played, and stands back, tense and excited, longing to give a hint, but loyally refraining, to watch the decision being made; while Bassanio, in thirty-two lines of anxious musing, tumbles out image after image, twelve of them, each fast on the heels of the other, each taking light from the one before it and in turn fading into the next.

The opening of the fifth act, so full of romance and glamour, is naturally full of images, though the decoration in the very beginning is given, not by images in the technical sense, but by the well-known exquisite series of direct pictures drawn from old romance and the great love stories of the world. It is not until Lorenzo and Jessica are sitting on the bank in the sleeping moonlight, awaiting the sounds of sweet music they have ordered, that the images proper begin [V. i. 54]. Then they come with a rush, close together [V. i. 54-113], so long as Lorenzo and Jessica, and later Portia and Nerissa are, or think themselves, alone in the garden listening to the music, but after they meet, and the music stops and the others come trooping in [V. i. 127], the glow of romance fades, and the tone changes to badinage and light comedy. On this note the play ends, so that in the remaining hundred and seventy lines, only four sparsely scattered images occur.

We find therefore that the images are chiefly grouped round these two high points of emotion. In addition, we get a good many in the opening scene where Antonio, Gratiano and Bassanio all speak at length, revealing the setting of the story and their own characteristics, one of which, as regards the speech of the two latter, is that they delight in simile and metaphor. So it is that 59 images—nearly half the total number in the play—are crowded into the space of 392 lines [I. i; III. ii. 24-148; IV. i. 69-77; V. i. 53-126], while the remaining 77 are spread out over the other 2162 lines.

Naturally in the prose scenes, or the semi-comic ones, such as the talk between Launcelot and Gobbo (2.2), or those chiefly occupied with practical affairs, such as Portia's preparations for departure, there are few images, or none; but it is surprising that the trial scene, where we are conscious of great tension of emotion, has so few. It is much the longest scene in the play—457 lines—and there are only ten images throughout the whole of it. Five of these are Antonio's, used under great stress

"The Rialto at Venice," by G. F. Sargent. The Department of Rare Books and Special Collections, The University of Michigan Library.

of emotion, three of them to express the futility of hoping to touch Shylock, and two in despairing descriptions of himself; two are the duke's, two are Shylock's (when he likens Antonio to a serpent, and Portia to Daniel); while Portia, in her great opening speech and subsequent arguments and decision, makes use of one image only, which is perhaps the best known one in the whole of Shakespeare.

The truth is, it would seem, that the tension and deep feeling of the trial scene are maintained chiefly through the quality of the plot itself, its fears, doubts, suspense and surprises: first the apparent hopelessness of Antonio's position and the obduracy of Shylock, then the appearance of Portia and the continued obduracy of the Jew, followed by the swift and dramatic turning of the tables upon him, so that except at the moments when Antonio is most exasperated or depressed, imagery is not needed either as an outlet or expression of feeling.

There does not appear to be any continuous symbol in the images, though there is an instance of a twice repeated image giving the key to the whole action. This occurs first in Antonio's earliest business interview with Shylock, conducted on Antonio's side with a contemptuous coolness, detachment and assurance which almost frighten the spectators, and is in strong contrast to Shylock's burning but suppressed emotion, which rises as he details his grievances, and finally bursts forth like an erupting volcano, when he turns on Antonio and cries, 'You call me misbeliever, cut-throat dog',

> you say
> 'Shylock, we would have moneys:' you say so;
> You, that did void your rheum upon my beard,
> And foot me as you spurn a stranger cur
> Over your threshold.
>
> [I. iii. 111, 115-19]

This is one of five images only in the whole scene of 181 lines, and it is clear from the way the Jew dwells on it (5 times in 17 lines) that it is the outcome of his deepest feeling, and sums up symbolically in itself the real and sole reason for his whole action—bitter rancour at the contemptuous treatment he has received, and desire for revenge. (pp. 281-85)

> *Caroline F. E. Spurgeon, "Leading Motives in the Comedies," in her* Shakespeare's Imagery and What It Tells Us, *1935. Reprint by Cambridge at the University Press, 1971, pp. 259-90.*

HAROLD R. WALLEY   (essay date 1935)

[Walley reconstructs the varying interpretations of Shylock's character since the seventeenth century—the Jew as a grotesque, comic figure, as a malicious villain, and finally as an oppressed sympathetic hero—and argues that out of this confusion it is possible to determine Shakespeare's true intention only if we view Shylock as a dramatic instrument or vehicle by which the dramatist could provide motivation to his story. Thus, like such other critics as

Elmer Edgar Stoll (1927), John Middleton Murry (1936), J. W. Lever (1952), and D. A. Traversi (1968), Walley considers Shylock strictly the stock villain of the play, and not a comic or tragic figure. The critic then discusses how Shakespeare solved certain difficulties his bond story created and explains three conditions necessary for the play to succeed: 1) Shakespeare had to make the bond ambiguous and Shylock's intentions therein uncertain; 2) because of this Shakespeare had to derive a way of justifying Shylock's eventual determination to carry out the bond; and 3) in order to satisfactorily resolve the bond story Shakespeare had to achieve "poetic" rather than "legal justice."]

There is perhaps no play of Shakespeare, with the possible exception of *Hamlet*, which has received more divergent interpretations than *The Merchant of Venice*. This divergence arises chiefly from the uncertainties attendant upon the character of Shylock, the interpretation of which has varied widely according to the disposition of successive generations of actors and critics. (p. 213)

What Shylock meant to an audience of Shakespeare's day is a matter of conjecture. Since the seventeenth century, however, the attempt to clarify Shakespeare's own intention has resulted in three divergent and clearly defined conceptions of the role. The first, in point of time, is the conception of Shylock as a grotesque comic figure, which prevailed during the first half of the eighteenth century. . . . [Next] began the lengthy reign of a malignant and vengeful Shylock. Essentially an unsympathetic rôle . . . , Shylock became the embodiment of cruel, venomous malice, sometimes exalted to an austere vindictiveness, sometimes debased to shabby and sordid decrepitude. Somewhat later, in the wake of Macready, appeared the sympathetic Shylock, the Jew as much sinned against as sinning, the patriarchal avenger of an oppressed race, who reached the dignity of tragic pathos in the interpretation of Sir Henry Irving and his followers. This is the humanitarian Shylock who wrung the feelings of such as Heine's dark-eyed lady [see excerpt above, 1838] and perverted so much of late nineteenth century criticism. . . . (pp. 213-14)

Twentieth century criticism tends to waver between the two latter conceptions. If one may presume to generalize about so varied a commentary, it appears that the consensus of opinion inclines toward a revengeful and villainous Shylock, with usually an extenuating proviso. For, despite the play's abundant evidence of Shylock's callous villainy, there is always an awkward residue which makes appeal to the more indulgent sympathies of modern times. (p. 214)

This apparent conflict between comedy and near-tragedy, antisemitism and humanitarianism, is usually accounted for in one of three ways. The most common explanation is that Shakespeare confused the issue by humanizing Shylock. But this fairly obvious fact rarely receives any further explanation than the dramatist's incomprehensible caprice or a hypothetical compassion for a hated and downtrodden race. The second theory, which has the virtue of giving some reason for the confusion, is that approved by the editors of the New Cambridge Shakespeare [Arthur Quiller-Couch and J. Dover Wilson]: namely, that Shakespeare was addressing indirectly the members of the Essex circle and was pleading for mercy toward the Jewish physician, Lopez. The theory might be more convincing were the effect of the trial scene in *The Merchant of Venice* reversed. But Portia's plea is not in behalf of a Jew; it is directed to a merciless Jew in behalf of Christians; and the general situation of the play is scarcely calculated to inspire tolerance toward the Jew. The third theory blandly cuts a Gordian knot by proposing that Shakespeare's character simply got

out of hand and proceeded to play tricks upon his creator. (pp. 214-15)

Now in this welter of contradictions one thing is manifest: not all can be correct. It may be the privilege of actors and critics to find in Shakespeare's play whatsoever meaning each most desires; but the exercise of this privilege must not obscure the fact that somewhere beneath all other meanings there lies Shakespeare's own intention. (p. 215)

The road to an answer should appear rather obvious. That Shakespeare was intimately concerned about the fate of the Jew is a matter of conjecture. That he found irresistible the study of human nature for its own sake is a matter of assumption. That he commonly bent his plays to ulterior purposes is a matter of speculation. But that he was a practical playwright engaged in the production of plays which might satisfy a contemporary audience, and that in *The Merchant of Venice* he wrote a perennially successful play, are not matters of either assumption or conjecture; they are matters of fact. Therefore it would seem that the logical approach to the elucidation of Shylock is to consider the problem as primarily a problem in dramatic craftsmanship. Such consideration is the purpose of the present study. (pp. 215-16)

In *The Merchant of Venice* there are, all told, twenty scenes. Of these, Shylock appears personally in but five, to which may be added a scene containing a report of his conduct. Quantitatively his participation in the play is relatively small and is obviously intended as that of neither a central nor even a major character. Functionally he contributes but two elements to the play—the signing of the bond and the demand of its forfeiture—and these are contained in only two scenes. The remaining scenes are incidental and deal with intermediate events.

If one considers these scenes by themselves, in the light of their structural contribution to the play, the dramatic function of Shylock is seen to be quite straightforward and unmistakable. He appears as the adversary of the protagonists, the villain in whom originates the menace to their well-being. What is more important, however, as regards Shakespeare's intention, is that this constitutes the whole of his contribution. In these scenes there is no evidence of character delineation for its own sake; there is no weighing of racial problems; nor does the character get out of hand. What becomes increasingly clear is that Shylock does precisely what is necessary to function properly as antagonist, and no more.

Further examination, however, reveals a curious fact about these scenes: that they fall into two groups as regards their treatment of Shylock. This does not mean that there are two different Shylocks in the play or that there is any fundamental inconsistency in the portrayal of his character. It does mean that in the first half of the play, through and including the first scene of Act III, Shakespeare presents a complex character, while throughout the remainder of the play his Shylock is a rudimentary conception, almost crudely simple. In the opening scenes the delineation of Shylock is so varied and complex that it sets him apart from the other characters; yet in the concluding scenes he is so simply drawn as to be practically a type of vengeful malice. A comparison of the adjacent scenes i and iii of Act III shows the contrast sharply. In the first of these Shylock is a human being torn by conflicting emotions; in the second he is an unreasoning, inhuman personification of malevolence.

If one considers first the simple Shylock who appears in the last two scenes, one gains a quite definite impression of his character. It is one of callous, unmitigated villainy. On the basis of these scenes alone, without earlier preparation, it is impossible to be confused with sympathy, even of the most sentimental variety. Nor, apart from a very general sense of satisfaction at his discomfiture, is it possible to view him as comic. Instead, Shylock is represented as thoroughly evil, as vicious, cruel, mean. He is deaf to every appeal of humanity. He exults in his opportunity to inflict suffering. He has a wolfish thirst for blood. He is neither stricken Jew nor human being, but a fiend incarnate. (pp. 230-32)

Now this final portrayal of Shylock, I submit, is quite of a piece and unmistakable in intention. Shylock is simply a conventional villain, intractable, inexcusable, inhuman, and contemptible. On the basis of these scenes alone it is incomprehensible that anyone could view Shylock with tolerance, to say nothing of sympathy. Yet in the light of preceding scenes this conception of Shylock has been blurred. Furthermore it is worth noting that the passages upon which is usually based the plea of extenuation occur only in the earlier scenes. Let us, therefore, consider them separately.

In dramatizing the story of the bond, Shakespeare was confronted with three serious difficulties. How is the initial signing of the bond to be rendered plausible? How is Shylock's subsequent demand to be motivated? And how is the whole matter to be concluded in a manner satisfactory to the audience?

In bringing about a satisfactory conclusion Shakespeare is faced by the delicate problem of arranging a courtroom settlement of a highly irregular proceeding in a manner consistent with some scheme of justice. It is unnecessary here to debate the legality of his solution; one need merely point out the conflict within the scene itself. The law which imperils Antonio's life is obviously inconsistent with the one later invoked to punish Shylock; the one cancels the other. Of course, the matter of legality has nothing to do with the case. Shakespeare is not conducting a trial; he is writing a play. His sole concern is to provide a scene of maximum dramatic suspense and intensity with a resolution which will appear both satisfactory and just to his audience. He thus is concerned, not with legal technicalities, but with human values. His solution is the simple, the obvious one. Inasmuch as justice is the point at issue, he merely substitutes poetic justice for legal justice. The satisfaction of the audience derives, not from the fact that law and order have triumphed, but from the fact that Shylock receives his just desert. In other words, it is poetically just that Shylock should fall into the very trap which he prepared for Antonio, that his own weapon, the bond, should be turned against him. This is a justice beyond legality; it is sound psychology, and it is impeccable dramaturgy.

The other two problems are of a different nature, and are the more complex because the solution of the one inevitably conflicts with the solution of the other. The signing of the bond is particularly incredible. If Antonio is not aware of the peril in this contract, he is scarcely the astute and maturely wise merchant that he is obviously intended to be. If, in spite of his knowledge, he signs away his life to a manifest villain who has reason to dislike him, he is simply a fool. But the bond must be signed or the story collapses.

Shakespeare's method of attaining plausibility is to make the signing of the bond apparently innocuous but potentially dangerous. Both aspects of the situation he deliberately stresses. He first presents the unctuous and devious mind of Shylock,

and makes clear the Jew's resentment. To this are immediately added Antonio's rebuke of his usury, and the specific challenge:

> I am as like to call thee so again,
> To spit on thee again, to spurn thee too.
> If thou wilt lend this money, lend it not
> As to thy friends; for when did friendship take
> A breed for barren metal of his friend?
> But lend it rather to thine enemy,
> Who, if he break, thou mayst with better face
> Exact the penalty.
>
> [I. iii. 130-37]

At this point Shylock suddenly disarms Antonio. . . . His proposal is to act upon Antonio's teaching, to renounce usury, and take as security that which is manifestly worthless to him. Antonio is left with no alternative. Not only does his own generous nature betray him, but to reject reformation is to nullify censure. That there is danger in the proposal Shakespeare makes clear: Bassanio rebels. But Antonio—supported by Shylock's perfectly reasonable contention, "If he should break his day, what should I gain?"—can do no other than yield to Shylock's plea, "I pray you wrong me not" [I. iii. 163, 170]. It is a dilemma with but one solution.

Concerning this situation, however, one fact must be observed. Nowhere in the scene does Shakespeare give any indication that the signing of the bond implies more than Shylock has stated. Shylock himself may be a treacherous rogue; he may hate Antonio; Bassanio may suspect him; the audience may cherish misgivings about his motives. All this may deliberately prejudice one against Shylock. Moreover, those who know the sequel may read into this scene ulterior motives. But the scene itself, taken at face value, neither in detail nor as a whole reveals the slightest suggestion that Shylock is contriving murder or, indeed, anything beyond what he has stated. This fact is of the utmost importance; for it is the very absence of possible motive which makes plausible Antonio's acceptance of the bond. His concluding remarks, together with those of Bassanio, deliberately underline the ambiguity of the scene.

But this ambiguity, while it evades the difficulties of the bond contract, plays havoc with the sequel. For the resultant uncertainty about Shylock's disposition and intention inevitably postpones the explanation of his attempt upon Antonio's life. Consequently, in the interval between the signing of the bond and the arrest of Antonio, Shakespeare is under the necessity of making clear why a man like Shylock should be wrought to such a pitch of vindictive hatred as to contemplate murder.

The motivation of Shakespeare's villains does not differ materially from that of his other characters. Their conduct is regularly presented as logical and justifiable from their own point of view. But complete understanding of motive, if unregulated, leads readily to sympathy. Such sympathy, if the villain be a tragic protagonist like Macbeth, is entirely appropriate. But if the villain is to remain purely a villain, there is but one method whereby his conduct can safely be motivated: to present it as justifiable from his own point of view, and at the same time establish that his point of view is intolerable and indefensible. Now this is precisely Shakespeare's method in dealing with Shylock. Throughout the first half of the play he nicely balances two attitudes of mind, that of Shylock and that which the audience is expected to share with the other characters in the play. As a result, at every point one is made to realize how the situation appears to Shylock, and how logical is his reaction to it; but, in addition, each clarification of Shylock's psychology is consistently so arranged as to bear with it its own condemnation. In short, Shylock is presented as comprehensible but fundamentally wrong.

At the very beginning of the play we are first introduced to Antonio. At once he is presented as good, honest, kindly, and admirable. He loves his friend well. He is generous to a fault. He stands well in the community and is admired by his friends. To every right-minded person in the play, as Shakespeare constantly reminds us, he is "the good Antonio." And then we meet Shylock. In his first speeches he is revealed as a hard business man, one to drive a sharp bargain. Moreover he is given to uncalled-for spleen, as in his spiteful rejoinder to Bassanio's courteous invitation to dine. His first aside, upon the appearance of Antonio, places him for the audience. . . .

> I hate him for he is a Christian.
> But more for that in low simplicity
> He lends out money gratis and brings down
> The rate of usance here with us in Venice.
> If I can catch him once upon the hip,
> I will feed fat the ancient grudge I bear him.
>
> 　　　　　　　　　　　　　　[I. iii. 42-7]

Here is the initial proclamation of hatred and potential danger. The reasons for Shylock's hatred are quite explicit—Antonio's religion and his opposition to usury. Both, from Shylock's point of view, are understandable and have, as the subsequent lines show, constituted a genuine grievance. But the very nature of the grievance, to an Elizabethan at least, is its own evidence of Shylock's warped mind, an impression which is intensified by the treacherous hypocrisy of his next speech.

The following discussion of usury further emphasizes the disparity in attitude. To Shylock the story of Jacob and Laban is eminent justification of his practice. On the other hand, the story has two glaring deficiencies: it is, first, a false analogy; and, second, it is a sophistical and specious defense of what to an Elizabethan was manifestly wrong. These objections are specifically pointed out by Antonio: "The devil can cite Scripture for his purpose. . . . O, what a goodly outside falsehood hath!" [I. iii. 98, 102].

What we are dealing with, as Shakespeare presents the matter, is a perverted mind honestly misled by wrong reason. It is in this light that Shylock's next long speech must be considered—that speech [I. iii. 106-29] which so often is advanced in his defense. It is a speech of deep-seated grievances, of rankling resentment and sneering irony. Undoubtedly Shylock has cause for resentment. Unfortunately, however, as by this time the Elizabethan audience must have been convinced, it is the resentment of a man who objects to interference when he is beating a horse to death. (pp. 233-37)

What, then, is Shakespeare's initial conception of his villain? Obviously he is not an impossible monster beyond the pale of humanity, nor is he merely a hated Jew. Fundamentally one recognizes the dread figure of the Christian-hating Jew. More immediate is the insidious and treacherous usurer, feeding upon the flesh of his victims and hating those who would interfere with his nefarious practices. But far more important than either of these is the villain as human being, the mortal man possessed of a treacherous mind and a grievance. And mind and grievance are one and the same; for the grievance is the direct result of perverted reasoning from false premises.

The intervening scenes which lead up to Act III, insofar as they deal with Shylock at all, serve to confirm this initial impression. Indirectly, through Launcelot Gobbo and Jessica, Shakespeare adds one more damning detail to his portrait: Shylock is a mean and grudging miser. Launcelot, who is a likable enough fellow with a real affection for Jessica, cannot stand him; Shylock begrudges him his food and speeds his departure that he may help to impoverish Bassanio. Even Jessica finds life with Shylock intolerable. Much nonsense has been written to deplore the callous, unfilial Jessica who abandoned her tender and loving father. This is scarcely Shakespeare's version. Every character in the play considers her a charming young lady. . . . Jessica herself, when finally she decides to leave Shylock, laments that she must be ashamed of him. . . . [In Act II, scene v,] one meets the complaining miser who berates Launcelot for his fancied gluttony and laziness, who dreams of moneybags and goes forth to feast with Christians merely that he may feed upon them, who regards all merriment as wasteful folly, and who seals up his daughter like a prisoner within his house. It is a scene deliberately calculated to present Shylock as unpleasant, mean, and contemptible.

The climax of Shakespeare's portrayal is reached in the first scene of Act III, which is crucial in the motivation of Shylock's conduct. But first there is a preliminary scene of the utmost importance. In the eighth scene of Act II Shylock does not appear personally, but we have a very graphic report of his conduct. Indeed Solanio's report is an advance summary of what we are to witness two scenes later. The purpose of this repetition immediately becomes apparent. For Act III, scene i is a dangerous scene; it may quite readily be misinterpreted, and indeed often has been. What the preliminary scene contributes is the substance of the situation plus a most important key to its proper tone and interpretation. In other words, Shakespeare is here preparing his audience for his intended reaction before the audience has opportunity to go astray on its own impulse.

For Solanio is an unsympathetic witness. To him the hysterical outcries of Shylock, far from moving compassion, are ridiculous and contemptible. . . . As Solanio reports it, it is all very ludicrous. But it is not quite so ludicrous two scenes later when we see for ourselves, for then we see through Shylock's eyes. Hence the importance of this preliminary comment. Moreover Shylock is not merely ludicrous; he is also potentially dangerous. For Antonio has suffered losses, and Solanio anticipates the possible convergence of the two developments.

> Let good Antonio look he keep his day,
> Or he shall pay for this.
>
> 　　　　　　　　　　　　　　[II. viii. 25-6]

In the emphasis upon the words "he" and "this"—namely, that Antonio may be held responsible for an elopement with which he was not concerned—is the clue to the situation which develops two scenes later.

In the first scene of Act III Shakespeare not only reveals himself as a master psychologist but clinches the motivation of Shylock's conduct. As has often been pointed out, Shakespeare added to his story the sub-plot of Jessica and Lorenzo to supply a motive for Shylock's revenge. Actually, however, it supplies but an indirect motive; for it is Jessica who robs and abandons her father; Antonio is entirely innocent. Vengeance can be visited upon him only if the issue is presented as a feud between Jews and Christians, which is scarcely the case. It is the task of the present scene to identify the motive with the effect. (pp. 237-40)

From his own point of view Shylock is a much abused man. He is despised by the Christians. His thrift is condemned as miserly blood-sucking. Now he is betrayed by his own flesh and blood, and robbed to boot. To make matters worse, he knows that his enemies rejoice at his discomfiture. And there is no redress. In building up this picture of Shylock's misery, once again Shakespeare is careful to balance potential pathos with contemptibility. There is a vast difference in emotional appeal between a grief-stricken father and a duped miser. Shylock's grief is adroitly distributed between his ducats and his daughter. As the scene continues it is the ducats which loom larger and larger as the chief cause of distress. "Would she were hearsed at my foot, and the ducats in her coffin!" [III. i. 89-90]. There is something infinitely contemptible about a father who, in the disappearance of his daughter, laments loudest the gold that has gone with her and computes anxiously the cost of recovery. Even the most daring stroke of pathos—the famous bartering of the turquoise; "I had it of Leah when I was a bachelor"—is nullified deliberately in the grotesque sequel, "I would not have given it for a wilderness of monkeys" [III. i. 121-23]. The very impulse which prompts the computation of sentimental values in terms of material equivalents is its own commentary. What one finds in this scene is anguish true enough, but the grotesque anguish of a warped spirit on contemptible grounds.

The scene is well designed to accomplish its purpose. Shylock's first meeting with Salerio and Solanio immediately extends the responsibility for Jessica's flight. Then, at a time when Lorenzo's friends have openly courted Shylock's resentment, Salerio gratuitously introduces the subject of Antonio and his losses. This is the first occasion since Act I, scene iii that Shylock has had to consider his bargain. His response is vague but reflects his resentful mood. It is only when Salerio pins him down that Shylock vents his indignation. Once more he is being taken advantage of; let them beware. And he is off on his recital of grievances.

Now this is a famous passage. It is crucial to those who demand a sympathetic portrayal of Shylock. But is it a plea for sympathy? Shylock enumerates his woes. "And what's the reason?" he demands: "I am a Jew" [III. i. 58]. But this is nonsense. Shylock has suffered, as is made quite explicit, because he is a usurer, a hypocrite, and a skinflint. Shylock's whine is the self-defense of perversity shunning responsibility by shifting the blame. But this shift of ground introduces a very important new element. Whatever he may be, Shylock gives warning, he is fundamentally human. If it be human for resentment to breed retaliation, let his foes beware of his retaliation. It is upon this note that Tubal enters.

The following colloquy is a skilful oscillation between the misfortunes of Shylock and the misfortunes of Antonio. As Shylock's impotent passion increases, so too is he made aware of Antonio's helplessness. At first Antonio's misfortunes provide merely the company that misery loves. Then as Shylock's wretchedness mounts, the idea of vague retaliation upon Antonio seizes upon him. "I'll plague him; I'll torture him: I am glad of it" [III. i. 116-17]. It is only when the news of his precious turquoise gives the last exquisite turn to his suffering that Tubal's consoling suggestion, "But Antonio is certainly undone" [III. i. 124], provokes desperate action. . . . The quite understandable vindictiveness of a desperate and sorely goaded man. But mark how the heroic effect is deliberately discounted by the anti-climactic sequel: "for, were he out of Venice, I can make what merchandise I will" [III. i. 127-29]. To the end the money-grubber.

After this scene, as we have noted before, Shylock the complex human being abruptly disappears, to be supplanted by the typical villain. He has served his purpose; the fantastic plot has been motivated. With true dramatic economy, Shakespeare has attended strictly to business without concerning himself about gratuitous, and pointless, embellishment.

One may therefore summarize Shakespeare's portrayal of Shylock in the following. He has presented Shylock consistently as a villain without sympathy or exaggerated race prejudice. He has availed himself sparingly of the antipathies of his audience to insure a proper antagonism to his villain. He has not presented Shylock as comic except for a touch of grotesque incongruity to offset any possible pity. He has "humanized" Shylock in the first half of the play by endowing him with a complexity, the specific purpose of which is to motivate his conduct without forfeiting the condemnation of the audience. In short, he has arrived at the character of Shylock in terms of dramatic motivation; his portrayal of the rôle is a straightforward solution of a technical dramatic problem; and there remains no substantial evidence that, in the play as it now stands, Shakespeare was particularly concerned with any matter but the production of a convincing and artistic theatrical performance. (pp. 240-42)

> *Harold R. Walley, "Shakespeare's Portrayal of Shylock," in* Essays in Dramatic Literature: The Parrott Presentation Volume, *edited by Hardin Craig, Princeton University Press, 1935, pp. 213-42.*

JOHN MIDDLETON MURRY   (essay date 1936)

[*A twentieth-century English editor and critic, Murry has been called the most "level-headed" of Shakespeare's major biographical critics. Unlike such other biographical scholars as Frank Harris and Edward Dowden, Murry refused to attribute to Shakespeare a definite personality or creative neurosis which determined all of his work, but regarded the poet as a man of powerful insights rather than character, an individual possessing Keats's negative capability, in the sense that he was able to withstand "uncertainties, mysteries, doubts, without any irritable reaching after fact and reason." What Murry saw as Shakespeare's greatest gift was his ability to uncover the true spirit of Elizabethan England, to fuse "not merely the poet and dramatist in himself," but to establish "a unique creative relation between himself, his dramatic material, his audience, and his actors." In the following excerpt, Murry argues that it is misdirected criticism that seeks to establish psychological and conceptual consistency in Shakespeare's plays, especially a drama like* The Merchant of Venice. *He takes direct issue with Arthur Quiller-Couch and J. Dover Wilson, the editors of the New Cambridge edition of* The Merchant of Venice, *who sought reasons for the inconsistency in design and execution of the play. Murry, in a manner similar to Elmer Edgar Stoll (1927) and Harold R. Walley (1935), instead views Shakespeare as a dramatic craftsman who manipulated his characters as was necessary to achieve a particular effect. In the case of* The Merchant of Venice, *he allows his audience to both sympathize with and condemn Shylock, for, as Murry claims, that is what different episodes in his play demanded. Like Harley Granville-Barker (1930), Murry concludes by calling,* The Merchant of Venice *a "matter-of-fact fairy tale." For further commentary on Shakespeare's skills as a dramatic craftsman, especially as demonstrated in his concern for plot and effective theater over consistent characterization, see the excerpts by Muriel C. Bradbrook (1951), J. W. Lever (1952), and D. A. Traversi (1968).*]

[*The Merchant of Venice* is], more than any other of Shakespeare's plays, a matter-of-fact fairy tale: a true folk story, made drama; and it makes its secular appeal to that primitive substance of the human consciousness whence folk-tales took their origin. Or, without reaching back to these dark and dubious beginnings, we may say that it is, as nearly as possible, a pure melodrama or tragi-comedy, an almost perfect example of the art-form which being prior to art itself, most evidently and completely satisfies the primitive man in us all. If the English theatre be considered as a place of popular entertainment, strictly on a level with the football field, the prize-ring and the racecourse, then *The Merchant of Venice* is the type of entertainment the theatre should supply—villain discomfited, virtue rescued, happy marriages, clowning, thrills, and a modest satisfaction of the general appetite for naughtiness. (pp. 189-90)

[Of] all the plays of [the] period *The Merchant of Venice* is the most typical of Shakespeare—the most expressive of what Coleridge once called his 'omni-humanity'. It contains tragedy, comedy high and low, love lyricism; and, notably, it does not contain any 'Shakespearian' character. The Berowne-Mercutio-Benedick figure [in, respectively, *Love's Labour's Lost*, *Romeo and Juliet*, and *Much Ado about Nothing*], witty, debonair, natural, is diffused into a group of young Venetian noblemen, all credible and substantial, but none possessing the inimitable individuality of their progenitor. Antonio, who stands apart from them, and was (if my judgment of the various verse-styles of the play is to be trusted) the last figure in it to have been elaborated, is a singular character. He supplies a background of sadness to the whole drama. He seems to be older than the friends who surround him, and detached from their thoughtless extravagance. Actually, in his final elaboration, by reason of the quality and colour given to him by Shakespeare's rewriting of Act I, Scene i, he becomes, as a character, slightly inconsistent with the contemptuous opponent of Shylock of later scenes; but it is not the function of Antonio to be primarily a dramatic 'character'. In that capacity, he is negative; he is a shadow beside Shylock and Portia, and unsubstantial even in comparison with his Venetian entourage. But as the vehicle of an atmosphere, he is one of the most important elements in the play. He provides, for the beginning of the play, what the lyrical antiphony of Lorenzo and Jessica supplies for the end of it—a kind of musical overtone which sets the spiritual proportions of the drama. He shades into the Duke of *Twelfth Night*.

The analogue between *The Merchant of Venice* and a musical composition is significant, I think, when taken in conjunction with the basic popularity of the play and the probability that its origin is to be sought in a play of many years before called 'The Jew', which Stephen Gosson exempted from abuse in 1579 because it displayed 'the greediness of worldly chusers and the bloody mind of usurers'. That is too apt a summary of the purely dramatic content of *The Merchant of Venice* to be accidental, and it fits too well with our impression of the play as the product of much re-writing to be ignored. (pp. 190-91)

Out of [his source play] Shakespeare wrought a miracle. He transformed it, and yet he left the popular substance essentially the same. What he did not, could not, and so far as we can see or guess, would not do, was to attempt to make it an intellectually coherent whole. That seems to have been no part of his purpose; he did not entertain the idea because he knew it was impossible. The coherence of *The Merchant of Venice* is not intellectual or psychological; and there has been much beating of brains in the vain effort to discover in it a kind of coherence which it was never meant to possess.

As an example of what I believe to be a radical misunderstanding of the nature of *The Merchant of Venice*, we may take the edition of the play in the *New Cambridge Shakespeare*. It will serve as a typical example of a mistaken approach to Shakespeare, for *The Merchant* in its origins, its methods of composition, and its final splendour, is typical of Shakespeare's achievement. The very stubbornness of his material compelled, I believe, a more or less complete abeyance of Shakespeare's personality. In his work upon this play he was pre-eminently the 'artist', but not in the modern and largely romantic sense of the word.

When the news of the disaster to Antonio's ventures comes to Belmont, in the very ecstasy of happiness there, Jessica adds her witness to Salerio's report of Shylock's implacability:

> When I was with him, I have heard him swear
> To Tubal and to Chus, his countrymen,
> That he would rather have Antonio's flesh
> Than twenty times the value of the sum
> That he did owe him: and I know, my lord,
> If law, authority and power deny not,
> It will go hard with poor Antonio.
>
> [III. ii. 285-91]

On this passage, the New Cambridge editors have the following note:

> We are tempted to put this speech into square brackets as one from the old play which Shakespeare inadvertently left undeleted in the manuscript. Note (1) it jars upon a nerve which Shakespeare of all writers was generally most careful to avoid: that a daughter should thus volunteer evidence against her father is hideous. . . .
>
> (pp. 192-93)

This is, indeed, to break a butterfly upon a wheel. But more alarming than the severity of the sentence is its irrelevance. *The Merchant of Venice* is not a realistic drama; and its characters simply cannot be judged by realistic moral standards. Jessica, taken out of the play, and exposed to the cold light of moral analysis, may be a wicked little thing; but in the play, wherein alone she has her being, she is nothing of the kind—she is charming. She runs away from her father because she is white and he is black; she is much rather a princess held captive by an ogre than the unfilial daughter of a persecuted Jew. Whether or not it is true that Shakespeare 'of all writers' was most careful to avoid representing unfilial behaviour without condemning it—and the proposition becomes doubtful when we think of *Romeo and Juliet* and *Othello*—it is almost certainly true that he did not himself conceive, or imagine that others would conceive, that Jessica's behaviour was unfilial. The relations between the wicked father and the lovely daughter are governed by laws nearly as old as the hills.

Yet even so, in rejecting Jessica's words as un-Shakespearian because morally hideous, the *New Cambridge Shakespeare* is not consistent; for the introductory essay discusses the problem how it is that Shylock is made 'sympathetic' to us, and argues that it is because he is deserted by his bad and disloyal daughter [see excerpt above by Arthur Quiller-Couch, 1926]. . . . We cannot have it both ways; we cannot argue that Shakespeare deliberately made Jessica unfilial in order to gain our sympathy for the Jew, and at the same time reject a passage as un-Shakespearian because in it Jessica reveals herself unfilial. The dilemma is absolute, but it is of the modern critic's making, not Shakespeare's. It is the direct result of applying to *The Merchant of Venice* a kind of criticism which it was never meant to satisfy.

Criticism of this kind seeks for psychological motives where none were intended or given. Shylock's hatred of Antonio is, in origin, a fairy-tale hatred, of the bad for the good. And perhaps this fairy-tale hatred is more significant than a hatred which can (if any hatred can) be justified to the consciousness. At any rate Shakespeare was at all times content to accept this antagonism of the evil and the good as self-explanatory. (pp. 193-95)

Thus Shylock at one moment declares that he hates Antonio 'for he is a Christian' [I. iii. 42]; at another, because he is a trade rival. . . . If we take the psychological point of view, the contradiction should not trouble us. We may say that Shylock is trying, as later Iago will try, to rationalize his hatred of Antonio: that he contradicts himself in so doing, is in accord with everyday experience. Or, on a different level, we may say that Shakespeare himself is trying to rationalize his elemental story. Unlike Oliver, who appears only at the beginning and the end of *As You Like It,* unlike the unsubstantial Don John in *Much Ado,* Shylock is the main figure of the play. What is in reality the simple fact of his hatred has to be motivated. Oliver and Don John are not required to be credible; Shylock is.

But these two kinds of explanation are not contradictory, as some critics think they are. They are two modes, two levels, of the operation of the same necessity: the 'psychologization' of a story that is a datum. In the process, Antonio's character suffers some slight damage. He spits upon Shylock's Jewish gaberdine. If we reflect in cold blood on Antonio's reported behaviour to Shylock, we are in danger of thinking that Shylock's intended revenge was not excessive. But we are not meant or allowed to reflect upon it. We are not made to *see* this behaviour. It is a sudden shifting of the values in order to make Shylock sympathetic to us at the moment he is proposing the bond. This is a dramatic device of which Shakespeare was always a master. But because Shakespeare was Shakespeare it is something more than a dramatic device.

Shylock undoubtedly is, to a certain degree, made sympathetic to us; and it is important to discover how it is done. For this, almost certainly, was a radical change wrought by Shakespeare in the crude substance of the old play. But the effect was certainly not achieved by Shakespeare's representing Shylock as the victim of Jessica's ingratitude. On the contrary, Shakespeare is most careful to prevent any such impression from taking lodgment in our minds. (pp. 195-96)

Shylock is deliberately made unsympathetic when it is required to cover Jessica. He is made sympathetic when Shakespeare feels the need, or welcomes the opportunity of making a dramatic contrast between Shylock and Antonio. At critical moments he is given dignity and passion of speech and argument to plead his cause to us and to himself. His hatred then is represented as deep, irrational and implacable, but not as mean and mercenary. It is then a force of nature—something greater than himself:

> So can I give no reason, nor I will not,
> More than a lodged hate and a certain loathing
> I bear Antonio, that I follow thus
> A losing suit against him.
>
> [IV. i. 59-62]

'A losing suit', because he, who grieves more for his ducats than his daughter, refuses many times the value of his debt to have his bond of Antonio; and his implacability is supplied with excuses enough to more than half persuade us—Antonio's expressed contempt for him, and the magnificent speech, which may have been hardly less magnificent in the verse from which Shakespeare seems to have changed it.

> And if you wrong us, shall we not revenge?
> If we are like you in the rest, we will
> Resemble you in that. If a Jew wrong
> A Christian, what is his humility?
> Revenge! And if a Christian wrong a Jew
> What should his sufferance be?
> By Christian example, why, revenge!
> The villainy you teach me
> I will execute: and it shall go hard
> But I will better the instruction.
>
> [III. i. 71-80]
> (pp. 197-98)

This is much more than a dramatic device to gain a momentary sympathy for Shylock; yet it is less, or at least other, than a deliberate posing of a profound moral problem. *The Merchant of Venice* is not a problem play; it is a fairy story, within the framework of which Shakespeare allowed free working to the thoughts of his mind and the feelings of his heart. What an unfettered Shylock might say, this fettered Shylock does say.

In other words, Shylock is both the embodiment of an irrational hatred, and a credible human being. He is neither of these things to the exclusion of the other. And if we ask how can that be? the only answer is that it is so. This was Shakespeare's way of working. If we choose, we may say that there are in the story primitive elements which he could not wholly assimilate to his own conception; but such an explanation, in *The Merchant of Venice* as in *Hamlet,* brings us against the fact that the dramatic impression made by these plays is the impression of an artistic whole. And, indeed, it seems more probable that Shakespeare did not deal in 'conceptions' of the kind that are often attributed to him. He set himself in successive attempts to infuse a general impression of credibility into an old story, and to secure from his audience no more, and no less, than 'that willing suspension of disbelief which constitutes poetic faith'.

One cannot too often emphasize the nature of Shakespeare's dramatic 'method'. It was not chosen by him, neither was it imposed upon his reluctant genius; it was simply the condition of the work he had chosen to do. The situation was given; necessarily, therefore, the 'characters' in a certain primitive sense—much the same sense in which we can speak of 'characters' in a nursery-story like Cinderella or Robin Hood or a Punch and Judy show. They are simply the necessary agents for that situation or that story. Shakespeare proceeded to endow them with poetic utterance, and with character in a quite different sense. He did what he could to make them credible human beings to himself. He gave them, so far as was possible, humanly plausible motives for their acts and situations, although these were often in fact prior to humane psychology. In a word, the method of Shakespeare's drama consists, essentially, in the humanization of melodrama. And each of those terms must have real validity for the Shakespeare critic who is to avoid ascending or descending into some private universe of his own and calling it Shakespeare. (pp. 199-200)

John Middleton Murry, "Shakespeare's Method: 'The
Merchant of Venice'," in his Shakespeare, Jonathan
Cape, 1936, pp. 188-211.

NEVILL COGHILL   (lecture date 1949)

[*Like Sir Israel Gollancz (1922) and Barbara K. Lewalski (1962),
Coghill describes the central issue in* The Merchant of Venice *as
an allegorical dramatization of the historical struggle between
justice and mercy, the Old Law of Judaic tradition and the New
Dispensation of Christianity. Coghill thus interprets the triumph
of mercy over strict justice in the trial scene (Portia's victory over
Shylock) as a reenactment of God's wisdom in providing for the
salvation of humanity through the sacrifice of Jesus Christ—a
divine act depicted in the medieval allegory* The Four Daughters
of God *and other homilies, which Coghill maintains strongly
influenced Shakespeare's work. For further consideration of* The
Merchant of Venice *as an allegory of the conflict between justice
and mercy or Judaic law and Christian charity, see the excerpts
by Denton J. Snider (1890), Muriel C. Bradbrook (1951), Theodor
Reik (1956), C. L. Barber (1959), E. M. W. Tillyard (1961), and
René E. Fortin (1974). The following excerpt is drawn from a
lecture delivered by Coghill in 1949.*]

The title-page of the second quarto of *The Merchant of Venice*,
dated 1600, reads: "The most excellent Historie of *The Merchant of Venice*. With the extreame crueltie of *Shylocke* the
Iewe towards the said Merchant, in cutting a iust pound of his
flesh" *etcetera*.

This announcement seems to justify a producer in supposing
that the play was intended to be sold as a piece of anti-Semitism, and the almost contemporary Lopez scandal is generally
quoted in support of this view. Yet even this title-page, by the
use of the word "just" (intended no doubt to mean "exact")
may raise thoughts about justice in the producer's mind. Should
he, however, stifle such thoughts and proceed to a full-blooded
Jew-baiting production (*à la Jew of Malta*) he may at a pinch
be able to bring it off by ruthless distortion and insensitiveness
to detail. In the trial scene he will have to disregard the noble
dignity and unimpeachable logic of the supposed "villain" and
on several other occasions during the action he will find himself
forced to underplay a sympathy for Shylock which is manifestly
in the text:

Shylock: Faire sir, you spet on me on Wednesday last;
          You spurn'd me such a day; another time
          You cald me dog: and for these curtesies
          Ile lend you thus much moneyes.
Ant: I am as like to call thee so againe,
          To spet on thee againe, to spurne thee too.
                                        [I. iii. 126-31]

Or,

Hath not a *Iew* eyes? hath not a *Iew* hands,
organs, dementions, sences, affections, passions, fed with the same foode, hurt with the
same weapons, subiect to the same diseases,
healed by the same meanes, warmed and cooled
by the same Winter and Sommer as a Christian
is: if you pricke vs doe we not bleede? if you
tickle vs doe we not laugh? if you poison vs
doe we not die?
                                        [III. i. 59-66]

These passages cannot be harmonized with a governing idea
of anti-Semitic feeling. They would rend the unity of such a
production.

On the other hand to regard Shylock as the wronged hero of
an oppressed race, falling with final grandeur through a wily
woman versed in legal trickery makes nonsense of the last Act
of the play: for how can a Comedy of rings and nuptials be
clapped on to so tragic an event without laying the producer,
not to say the author, open to the charge of heartless levity,
and a gross breach in the unity of design?

If then the production of *The Merchant of Venice* is attended
by certain incompatibilities of meaning whether we produce it
on pro-Jew or anti-Jew prejudices, should we not think it possible that neither kind of production was intended by Shakespeare? Might it even be that the fundamental notion of the
play was to be found in a region far above and beyond race
feeling?

Is there any other notion that can give the play a genuine unity?
What is it really *about*?

I believe that to answer these questions we must return to the
Middle Ages and to one of its traditional themes. The best
expression of the theme I have in mind is to be found in *Piers
Plowman*. In that poem, Truth (God) sends Piers a Pardon. . . .
(pp. 18-20)

In the first version of the poem (the "A Text") this "pardon"
remains an unexplained enigma. In what sense can it be a
"pardon"? It states a proportionate requital, an eye for an eye.
It shows *Justice* in God, but not *Mercy*.

The second version of the poem (the "B Text") was written
to elaborate and explain the seeming paradox of the "pardon".
It does so by adding the whole story of the Incarnation, Passion
and Descent into Hell, the picture of God's love to man. For
in demanding an exact payment for all sin, He paid it Himself,
and His payment is available to all who are willing to acknowledge their debt . . . in confession and obedience to His
Church.

Now God's right thus to despoil the Fiend of his prey (sinful
man) is very closely argued by four characters in the poem. . . .
They are the four daughters of God, Mercy and Truth, Righteousness and Peace. Briefly their argument is this: under the
Old Law God ordained punishment for sin, eye for eye and
tooth for tooth in Hell. But under the New Law, God underwent
and paid that punishment Himself on Calvary, and He has
therefore bought back and redeemed "those that he loved"
with a perfect *Justice* that is also a perfect *Mercy*. God is Truth,
but He is also Love. The New Law does not contradict but
complements the Old.

Almost exactly the same argument is conducted by the same
four daughters of God at the end of *The Castle of Perseverance*,
a morality play written in the early fifteenth century. In this
the protagonist, *Humanum Genus* has died in sin and so his
soul comes up for judgment. Righteousness and Truth demand
his damnation, which the play would show to be just. Mercy
and Peace plead the Incarnation, and *Humanum Genus* is saved.
(p. 20)

Now if we follow this Christian tradition of a former age as a
pathway into Shakespeare it will lead us to an understanding
of *The Merchant of Venice* that will solve the dilemma I have
stated. It is a presentation of the theme of justice and mercy,
the Old Law and the New. Seen thus it puts an entirely different
complexion upon the opposition of Jew and Gentile. The two
principles for which, in Shakespeare's play, respectively they
stand are both *inherently right*, and they are only in conflict
because, whereas God is absolutely just as He is absolutely

Act III. Scene i. Solanio, Salerio, and Shylock. By Sir John Gilbert.

merciful, mortal and finite man can only be relatively so, and must arrive at a compromise. In human affairs either justice must yield a little to mercy or mercy to justice, and the former solution is the more Christian. The conflict between Shylock and Anthonio is thus an *exemplum* (to use medieval terminology) of this traditional theme.

As I am here considering what Dante would have called the allegorical meaning of the play, let me stress that I am not saying it is the "only" meaning. The play will stand on the natural plane well enough (if we allow impossibilities such as choice-by-caskets and young women disguised as lawyers to be "natural"). All the characters can be shown to have a determinable human psychology consistent with themselves and with the story. . . . If I use the word "allegory" in connection with Shakespeare I do not mean that the characters are abstractions representing this or that vice or virtue. . . . I mean that they contain and adumbrate certain principles, not in a crude or neat form, but mixed with other human qualities; but that these principles taken as operating in human life, do in fact give shape and direction to the course, and therefore to the meaning, of the play.

Let us return to the Trial scene. The principle here mainly adumbrated in Shylock is justice, in Portia, mercy. He stands, and says he stands, for the Law, for the notion that a man must be as good as his bond. It is the Old Law. (pp. 20-1)

Before Shylock's uncompromising demand for justice, mercy is in the posture of a suppliant refused. Thrice his money is offered him and rejected. He is begged to supply a surgeon at his own cost. But no, it is not in the bond.

From the technical point of view the scene is constructed on a sudden reversal of situation, a traditional dramatic dodge to create surprise and *dénouement*. The verbal trick played by Portia is not a part of her "character", but a device to turn the tables and show justice in the posture of a suppliant before mercy. The reversal is instantaneous and complete, as it is also unexpected for those who do not know the story in advance. Portia plants the point firmly:

> Downe, therefore, and beg mercy of the Duke.
>
> [IV. i. 363]

And, in a twinkling, mercy shows her quality:

> *Duke:* That thou shalt see the difference of our spirit,
>   I pardon thee thy life before thou aske it:
>   For halfe thy wealth, it is *Anthonio's,*
>   The other halfe comes to the generall state,
>   Which humblenesse may driue vnto a fine.
>
> [IV. i. 368-72]

Out of this there comes the second reversal. Shylock, till then pursuing Anthonio's life, now has to turn to him for favour; and this is Anthonio's response:

> So please my Lord the Duke, and all the Court
> To quit the fine for one halfe of his goods,
> I am content; so he will let me haue
> The other halfe in vse, to render it
> Vpon his death, vnto the Gentleman
> That lately stole his daughter.
> Two things prouided more, that for this fauour
> He presently become a Christian:

The other, that he doe record a gift
Heere in the Court of all he dies possest
Vnto his sonne *Lorenzo,* and his daughter.

[IV. i. 380-90]

Evidently Anthonio recognizes the validity of legal deeds as much as Shylock does, and his opinion on Jessica's relationship with Lorenzo is in agreement with Shakespeare's, namely that the bond between husband and wife overrides the bond between father and daughter. Cordelia and Desdemona would have assented. Nor is it wholly alien to Shylock who is himself a family man. For him to provide for Jessica and Lorenzo is not unnaturally harsh or vindictive.

It is Anthonio's second condition that seems to modern ears so harshly vindictive. In these days all good humanitarians incline to the view that a man's religion is his own affair, that a religion imposed is a tyranny, and that one religion is as good as another, if sincerely followed.

But the Elizabethans were not humanitarians in this sense. Only in Utopia, . . . (and Utopia was not in Christendom) would such views have seemed acceptable. Whether we dislike it or not, Shylock had no hope, by Elizabethan standards, of entering a Christian eternity of blessedness; he had not been baptized. It would not have been his cruelty that would have excluded him (for cruelty, like other sin, can be repented) but the simple fact that he had no wedding-garment. No man cometh to the Father but by me.

Shylock had spent the play pursuing the mortal life of Anthonio (albeit for private motives) in the name of justice. Now, at this reversal, in the name of mercy, Anthonio offers him the chance of eternal life, his own best jewel.

It will, of course, be argued that it is painful for Shylock to swallow his pride, abjure his racial faith, and receive baptism. But then Christianity is painful. Its centre is crucifixion, nor has it ever been held to be equally easy for all natures to embrace. If we allow our thoughts to pursue Shylock after he left the Court we may well wonder whether his compulsory submission to baptism in the end induced him to take up his cross and follow Christ. But from Anthonio's point of view, Shylock has at least been given his chance of eternal joy, and it is he, Anthonio, that has given it to him. Mercy has triumphed over justice, even if the way of mercy is a hard way.

Once this aspect of the Trial scene is perceived, the Fifth Act becomes an intelligible extension of the allegory (in the sense defined); for we return to Belmont to find Lorenzo and Jessica in each other's arms. Christian and Jew, New Law and Old, are visibly united in love. And their talk is of music, Shakespeare's recurrent symbol of harmony.

It is not necessary for a single member of a modern audience to grasp this study in justice and mercy by any conscious process of cerebration during a performance, or even afterwards in meditation. *Seeing one may see and not perceive.* But a producer who wishes to avoid his private prejudices in favour of Shakespeare's meanings, in order that he may achieve the real unity that binds a poetical play, should try to see them and to imagine the technical expedients of production by which that unity will be experienced. If he bases his conception on the resolution of the principles of justice and mercy, he will then, on the natural plane, be left the freer to show Christians and Jews as men and women, equally containing such faults and virtues as human beings commonly have. (pp. 21-3)

Nevill Coghill, ''The Basis of Shakespearian Comedy,'' in Essays and Studies, *n.s. Vol. 3, 1950, pp. 1-28.*

NORMAN NATHAN   (essay date 1950)

[*Nathan offers a response to two questions which he claims earlier critics in their analyses of* The Merchant of Venice *have left unresolved: 1) why would Shylock enter into his bond with Antonio unless he believed the merchant would default and the ''pound of flesh'' be his; and 2) why does Shylock so readily accept the Christian faith after his defeat? Nathan focuses on the parable of Jacob and Laban recounted by Shylock to answer the first question, stating that the Biblical story provided the Jew with a justification for his assumption that God would intervene on his behalf and grant his wish, just as He does for Jacob. Nathan next maintains that Shylock accepts Christianity so readily because his belief that God would provide in his behalf, and thereby justify his cause, is never realized; instead, God provides for the ''Christian state of Venice,'' thus, in Shylock's eyes, making him the ''infidel'' and Antonio the chosen individual. Nathan also stresses that Shylock's conversion is not so unusual since the Jew is hardly a religious person. The debate over the issues raised in Nathan's essay was continued in two subsequent articles by J. W. Lever and Nathan himself (see the excerpts below, 1952). Also, for further commentary on Shylock's forced conversion, see the excerpts by E. M. W. Tillyard (1961), Barbara K. Lewalski (1962), A. D. Moody (1964), James E. Siemon (1970), R. Chris Hassel, Jr. (1970), and René Girard (1978).*]

Among the many criticisms leveled against the *Merchant of Venice,* two have not been adequately refuted. How could Shylock have expected the wealthy Antonio to default, and how could Shylock so quickly have been willing to convert to Christianity when the trial went against him? These two problems have an intimate connection. As will be shown, it is the money lender's self-assurance which, when thwarted, largely accounts for his sudden collapse of faith and consequent readiness to accept what has heretofore been to him a hated religion.

Although Shylock originally professes that the pound of flesh security is ''in a merrie sport'' [I. iii. 145], it is obvious that he is not one to be either merry or sporting. That Shylock is not telling the truth is evidenced by what Jessica later says at Belmont,

When I was with him, I have heard him sweare
To Tuball and to Chus, his Countri-men,
That he would rather have Antonio's flesh,
Then twenty times the value of the summe
That he did owe him. . . .

[III. ii. 284-88]

Shylock himself says, ''. . . I will have the heart of him if he forfeit, for were he out of Venice, I can make what merchandize I will'' [III. i. 127-29]. In view of this admission and that of Jessica's, it is curious to find anyone maintaining that Shylock's intentions were not murderous until the conspiracy of the Venetians took his daughter away from him.

There is, nevertheless, a seeming difficulty with the usual interpretation that Shylock lent Antonio the money with the intention of killing him when the forfeiture fell due. How could Shylock know or have even a reasonable assurance that the money would not be repaid in time? Antonio, who presumably was better aware of his own affairs than was Shylock, had no fear of defaulting. Bassanio too had no doubt about repayment, though he was suspicious of ''faire terms, and a villaines minde'' [I. iii. 179]. But Bassanio need not have worried about the *villaines minde*. The only thing that Shylock does to hinder Antonio's meeting the bond is to eat perhaps a few ducats' worth of food at Bassanio's house!

Was Shylock gambling on a long chance? Not only is such conduct unlike him, there is evidence to show that he fully expected that the pound of flesh would be his.

At least four metaphors in the *Merchant* indicate that Shylock figuratively regarded Antonio's flesh as his food. Shortly after he sees Antonio he says "I will feede fat the ancient grudge I beare him" [I. iii. 47]. A few lines further he reaffirms this image for the audience while speaking to the merchant, "Your worship was the last man in our mouthes" [I. iii. 60]. Later, when he tells Jessica,

> But yet Ile goe in hate, to feede upon
> The prodigall Christian.
>
> [II. v. 14-15]

he is surely using *feede* in a sense different from that of eating a meal. The fourth metaphor is even more definite,

> *Sal*. Why I am sure if he forfaite, thou wilt not
> take his flesh, what's that good for?
> *Shy*. To baite fish withall, if it will feede
> nothing else, it will feede my revenge . . .
>
> [III. i. 51-4]

This feeding on Antonio is something more than merely hoped for. An examination of the ultimate source (*Genesis*) of much of Act 1, scene 3, shows just how Shylock got the idea for the forfeit and why he expected Antonio to default. Early in this scene Shylock says about Antonio that he would like to "catch him once upon the hip," a phrase suggestive of Jacob's being made powerless when touched on the "hollow of his thigh" (*King James Version*) by the angel (*Gen.*: 32). Not forty lines later he recapitulates the story of Jacob and Laban (*Gen.*: 30) in an effort to justify his lending money at interest. (pp. 255-56)

Shylock, as has been pointed out many times, is literal minded. Villain though he is, he believes that Antonio is in the wrong and that he is in the right. Even in his asides Shylock cannot fully distinguish between Antonio's hatred of usury and an unwarranted assumption that the merchant is anti-Semitic. Add to this that, when Shylock mentions the Jacob-Laban story to justify his taking of usury, he is told by his adversary that the only worthwhile gain is that which God has made to prosper. Antonio is here suggesting to Shylock the very way to prove who is right. It is not merely that Antonio's flesh quickly becomes associated in his mind with the flesh of ewes and rams. The important thing is that just as God gave the flesh of cattle to Jacob, so will He give Antonio's flesh to Shylock. Shylock has identified himself with Jacob and Antonio has become Laban.

That Shylock bases on God's help his faith in gaining his pound of flesh is also shown in later scenes. He does not want to go to Bassanio's for supper,

> . . . By Jacobs staffe I sweare,
> I have no minde of feasting forth to night:
> But I will goe. . . .
>
> [II. v. 36-8]

Presumably Shylock is swearing by the staff with which Jacob passed over the Jordan (*Gen.*: 32, 10) and upon which he leaned when worshipping just before his death. (*Heb.*: 11, 21). Again he is aligning his conduct towards Antonio and Bassanio with

that of Jacob for whom God performed miracles. When Tubal tells him that Antonio has lost an argosy, Shylock exclaims, "I thanke God, I thanke God, is it true, is it true?" [III. i. 102]. Note further that Shylock's preoccupation appears to be that he should have an officer ready to take Antonio into custody once the due date is passed. Are there many villains who hope for so much and do so little to procure their ends? (pp. 256-57)

So far the audience has largely been left out of consideration. That the audience would know the Jacob-Laban story need not be questioned. And an age versed in the Bible would surely recognize other similarities between the *Merchant* and *Genesis*. In the courtroom scene Shakespeare has Gratiano speak a line that is inappropriate unless it is intended to produce an effect upon the audience. When Shylock first appeared he had said, "If I can catch him once upon the hip . . ." [I. iii. 46]. This is in an aside and presumably no Venetian heard him. Yet, after Shylock learns that he is not to succeed in his plans, Gratiano says, "Now infidell I have thee on the hip" [IV. i. 334]. Surely this line, with the accent on *thee*, would bring back to the audience Shylock's earlier use of a similar expression. And what effect would this recalling have upon Shylock and the audience? Shylock is an infidel. God, he had thought, would show Antonio just as He had shown Laban who was in His favor. Shylock finds, instead, that God has not merely failed to give him Antonio's flesh, but has made his cattle, his property, the property of Antonio, Lorenzo, and the Christian state of Venice. By his own test Shylock discovers that he is an infidel. It is no wonder that he crumples so completely. Never in the play does he prove either by good deeds, charity, mercy, or penitence that he is truly religious. He is religious only in the sense that he is superstitious. His God, what god? has failed him. Does it matter to him to desert his religion?

Shakespeare's intent might be even more apparent to an age accustomed to consider the literal meanings of names in a play. When Portia temporarily grants Shylock his pound of flesh, he replies, "A Daniel come to judgement, yea a Daniel" [IV. i. 223]. Biblical Daniels have engaged in wise judgments, but *Daniel* happens to mean *God is my judge*. May not Shylock mean, "A 'God is my judge' come to judgement, yea a 'God is my judge'"? Grant that it may be coincidental that the literal meaning of *Daniel* happens to make sense in the passage. Yet it cannot be denied that such a coincidence would be superb luck in view of Shylock's having earlier indicated that God would judge the righteousness of his case against Antonio just as God had judged Jacob over Laban.

But the possibility of coincidence is lessened when Gratiano takes up the phrase. After Portia states the full import of her judgment, Gratiano mocks, "A second Daniel, a Daniel Jew . . ." [IV. i. 333]. A second God (perhaps Jesus?) is my judge, a God is my judge Jew. And some lines later,

> A Daniel still say I, a second Daniel,
> I thanke thee Jew for teaching me that word.
>
> [IV. i. 340-41]

The word clearly is *Daniel*. Note, Gratiano thanks Shylock for teaching him *that word*, not name. Is this not added proof to Shylock that God has sided with Antonio? (pp. 257-58)

Thus it appears that numerous passages, names, and events in *Genesis* are woven into the play and that it is Shylock's identification of himself with Jacob which gives him the cunning desire to enter into the *merrie sport*. Shylock expected to get his pound of flesh through God's intervention. Ultimately it is Antonio whom God favors, and the sign that Shylock sought for comes to him in a message hostile to his original convictions. He is content to become a Christian. *The Merchant of Venice*, a romantic comedy as far as the overall effect is concerned, emerges, therefore, as something less than a tragedy even on Shylock's level. He becomes a grossly mistaken man partly brought to a realization of his errors. (p. 259)

> Norman Nathan, "Shylock, Jacob, and God's Judgment," in Shakespeare Quarterly, *Vol. I, No. 4, October, 1950, pp. 255-59.*

HAROLD C. GODDARD   (essay date 1951)

[*Goddard's essay represents one of the first detailed interpretations of* The Merchant of Venice *as an ironic play, a work whose real meaning lies concealed beneath the surface action. Goddard discerns this deeper meaning in the Venetians' vague, uneasy, and apprehensive statements, such as those expressed by Portia and Antonio, which the critic states are prompted by their unwillingness to confront their unconscious desires. Rightfully so, Goddard claims, for their repressed selves are hardly what they consciously present, since they are all dependent on money and self-fulfillment in a manner no less revolting than Shylock's usury and obsession with the law. Even worse, Goddard adds, the Christians in the play all subscribe to the attitude of "exclusiveness," which involves a false assumption that they are more valuable than what is being excluded. In the case of* The Merchant of Venice, *what is being excluded is Shylock. Goddard thus describes the hatred towards the Jew as the result of the other characters' projection onto him of all those repressed qualities which they cannot accept in themselves; in short, he represents the traditional scapegoat figure. In the remainder of his essay, Goddard applies elements from the casket story to the principal Christian characters to define their essential identities. He thus likens Bassanio to the golden casket in his disguised pursuit of wealth; Antonio to the silver in his choice of a career which brought him wealth but left unsatisfied his nobler impulses; Shylock to the leaden casket, in that beneath his hatred and materialism resides a man of generosity and forgiveness; and Portia, like Bassanio, to the golden casket, in that she fails to live up to her own dictates of mercy and forgiveness and, instead, strives after worldly admiration and praise. Perhaps most significant of Goddard's findings is his conclusion that neither Portia nor Antonio sustains that victory of Christian mercy they both demand of Shylock. In fact, the critic suggests that the "logic of the courtroom" is put to shame by Shakespeare's "spiritual argument" unrealized in the play but nonetheless still visible in Shylock's speech on "Christian example," Portia's on mercy, and Lorenzo's on the harmony of the universe. Goddard concludes with the idea that the spectators and readers of* The Merchant of Venice, *as with the characters themselves, are provided with the opportunity to transform the play as they see fit—to choose the base or the precious as its central design. A similar assessment was suggested later by René Girard (1978), who argued that though Shakespeare sympathized with Shylock as a scapegoat figure and condemned the Christians' duplicity, he skillfully managed to structure his play so that both the so-called ironic and Christian readings are possible. Such other critics as A. D. Moody (1964) and R. Chris Hassel, Jr. (1970) have also maintained that* The Merchant of Venice *is more properly understood as a comedy of Christian duplicity than a dramatization of mercy triumphing over strict justice, while William Hazlitt (1817) and Arthur Quiller-Couch (1926) also alluded to the insincerity of the Venetians' moral and religious pronouncements.*]

The Merchant of Venice is an interweaving of three strands commonly known as the casket story, the bond story, and the ring story. . . . [These] three stories, as the poet uses them, become variations on a single theme.

The casket story obviously stresses the contrast between what is within and what is without. So, however, if less obviously, do the other two. The bond story is built about the distinction between the letter and the spirit of the law. But what are letter and spirit if not what is without and what is within? And the ring story turns on the difference between the outer form and the inner essence of a promise. When Bassanio rewards the Young Doctor of Laws with Portia's ring, he is keeping the spirit of his vow to her as certainly as he would have been breaking it if he had kept the ring on his finger. In the circumstances literal fidelity would have been actual faithlessness. (p. 82)

Ostensibly, *The Merchant of Venice* is the story of the friendship of an unselfish Venetian merchant for a charming young gentleman who is in love with a beautiful heiress; of the noble sacrifice that the friend is on the point of making when nearly brought to disaster by a vile Jew; of the transformation of the lovely lady into lawyer and logician just in the nick of time and her administration to the villain of a dose of his own medicine. Was ever a play more compact with popular appeal? But what if, all the while, underneath and overhead, it were something so different from all this as the contents of the three caskets are from their outward appearance? It would be in keeping. What if the author is putting to the test, not just the suitors of Portia, but other characters as well, even, possibly, every reader or spectator of his play? It would be like him.

The seductive atmosphere of the play lends immediate credence to such an hypothesis. (p. 83)

The social world of Venice and more especially of Belmont centers around pleasure. It is a golden world—a gilded world we might better say. It is a world of luxury and leisure, of idle talk and frivolity, of music and romance. . . . Gold is the symbol of this world of pleasure. But what is under this careless ease? On what does it rest for foundation? The answer is—on money. Or, if you will, on the trade and commerce that bring the money, and on the inheritance that passes it along. Now this world of trade and commerce, as it happens, does not resemble very closely the world that its profits purchase. Its chief symbol in the play is silver, which in the form of money is the "pale and common drudge 'tween man and man" [III. ii. 103-04]. When the Prince of Arragon opens the silver casket, he finds, within, the portrait of a blinking idiot and verses telling him that he is a fool who has embraced a shadow in mistake for substance.

But there is something even worse than money under the surface of this social world. Exclusiveness—and the hypocrisy exclusiveness always involves, the pretense that that which is excluded is somehow less real than that which excludes. When the Prince of Morocco opens the golden casket he finds not a fool's head, as Arragon finds, but a Death's head—so much deadlier than money is the moral degradation that money so often brings. "All that glisters is not gold" [II. vii. 65].

Dimly, in varying degrees, these Venetians and Belmontese reveal an uneasiness, a vague discontent, an unexplained sense of something wrong. This note, significantly, is sounded in the very first words of four or five of the leading characters.

> In sooth, I know not why I am so sad,
>
> [I. i. 1]

says Antonio in the first line of the play. "By my troth, Nerissa, my little body is aweary of this great world" [I. ii. 1-2], are Portia's first words. "Our house is hell" [II. iii. 2], Jessica announces in her opening speech. And we wonder what cruelty her father has been guilty of, until she goes on to explain that the hell she refers to is tediousness. Melancholy, weariness, tedium—the reiteration of the note cannot be coincidence. And the other characters confirm the conjecture. Over and over they give the sense of attempting to fill every chink of time with distraction or amusement, often just words, to prevent their thinking. (pp. 83-4)

What is the trouble with these people and what are they trying to hide? Why should the beautiful Portia, with all her adorers, be bored? Nerissa, who under her habit as waiting-maid has much wisdom, hits the nail on the head in *her* first speech in answer to Portia's: "For aught I see, they are as sick that surfeit with too much as they that starve with nothing" [I. ii. 5-7]. What these people are trying to elude is their own souls, or, as we say today, the Unconscious.

Now Shylock is a representative of both of the things of which we have been speaking: of money, because he is himself a moneylender, and of exclusion, because he is the excluded thing. Therefore the Venetian world makes him their scapegoat. They project on him what they have dismissed from their own consciousness as too disturbing. They hate him because he reminds them of their own unconfessed evil qualities. Down the ages this has been the main explanation of racial hatred and persecution, of the mistreatment of servant by master. Our unconsciousness is our foreign land. Hence we see in the foreigner what is actually the "foreign" part of ourselves.

Grasp this, and instantly a dozen things in the play fall into place, and nearly every character in it is seen to be one thing on the outside and another underneath—so inherent, so little mere adornment, is the casket theme. It ramifies into a hundred details and into every corner of the play.

Bassanio is a good example to begin with. He fools the average reader and, especially if the play is conventionally cast and handsomely mounted, the average spectator, as completely as the dashing movie star does the matinee girl. Is he not in love with the rich heroine? (pp. 84-5)

Bassanio himself describes [his pursuit of Portia] as a "plot" to get clear of his debts. But when the young spendthrift is handsome, we forgive him much. In watching the development of the love affair it is easy to forget its inception. And yet, when Bassanio stands in front of the golden casket, clad in the rich raiment that Antonio's (i.e., Shylock's) gold has presumably bought, and addresses it,

> Therefore, thou gaudy gold,
> Hard food for Midas, I will none of thee,
>
> [III. ii. 101-02]

we feel that if Shakespeare did not intend the irony it got in in spite of him. No, gold, I'll have none of thee, Bassanio declares (whether he knows it or not), except a bit from Antonio-Shylock to start me going, and a bit from a certain lady "richly left" whose dowry shall repay the debts of my youth and provide for my future. Beyond that, none.

> *Who chooseth me must give and hazard all he hath.*
>
> [II. vii. 9]

It is almost cruel to recall the inscription on the casket Bassanio picked in the light of what he *received* from Shylock and of what he let Antonio *risk* in his behalf.

If it be objected that this is subjecting a fairy tale to the tests of realistic literature, the answer is that it is not the first time

that a fairy tale has been a fascinating invention on the surface and the hardest fact and soundest wisdom underneath. Ample justice has been done by his admirers to Bassanio's virtues. It is the economic aspect of his career that has been understressed. Like a number of others in this play the source of whose income will not always bear inspection, like most of us in fact, he was not averse to receiving what he had not exactly earned. Bassanio is the golden casket. He gained what many men desire: a wealthy wife.

Antonio's case is a bit subtler than Bassanio's but even more illuminating. Why is Antonio sad? (pp. 85-6)

Commentators have commonly either side-stepped the problem or explained Antonio's melancholy as a presentiment of the loss of his friend Bassanio through marriage. That may have accentuated it at the moment, but Antonio has had barely a hint of what is coming when the play opens, while his depression has all the marks of something older and deeper. It is scarcely too much to say that he is a sick man. Later, at the trial, when the opportunity of sacrificing himself is presented, his sadness becomes almost suicidal:

> I am a tainted wether of the flock,
> Meetest for death. The weakest kind of fruit
> Drops earliest to the ground; and so let me.
> You cannot better be employ'd, Bassanio,
> Than to live still, and write mine epitaph.
>
> [IV. i. 114-18]

Only something fundamental can explain such a sentimental welcome to death. The opening of the play is an interrogation three times underscored as to Antonio's sadness.

Later, a similar question is propounded about another emotion of another character: Shylock and his thirst for revenge. Now Shylock is a brainier man than Antonio, and his diagnosis of his own case throws light on Antonio's. The Jew gives a number of reasons for his hatred. . . . Yet not one of them, or all together, sufficient to account for his passion. They are rationalizations, like Iago's reasons for his plot against Othello. . . . And Shylock comes finally to recognize that fact. In the court scene when the Duke asks his reason for his mad insistence on the pound of flesh, Shylock says he can and will give no reason other than "a certain loathing I bear Antonio." A certain loathing! It matches exactly the certain sadness of Antonio.

But it matches another emotion of Antonio's even more closely. If Shylock loathes Antonio, Antonio has a no less savage detestation of Shylock. His hatred is as "boundless" as was Juliet's love. It appears to be the one passion that like a spasm mars his gentle disposition, as a sudden squall will ruffle the surface of a placid lake. . . . It is not enough to say that in those days everybody hated the Jews, for that leaves unexplained why the gentlest and mildest man in the play is the fiercest Jew-baiter of them all. As far as the record goes, he outdoes even the crude and taunting Gratiano. (pp. 87-8)

Unless all signs fail, Antonio, like Shylock, is a victim of forces from far below the threshold of consciousness. What are they?

Shakespeare is careful to leave no doubt on this point, but, appropriately, he buries the evidence a bit beneath the surface: Antonio abhors Shylock because he catches his own reflection in his face. . . . It is Antonio's unconscious protest against this humiliating truth that is the secret of his antipathy. "Wilt thou whip thine own faults in other men?" cries Timon of Athens

[*Timon of Athens*, V. i. 39]. Shakespeare understood the principle, and he illustrates it here.

The contrast between Shylock and Antonio is apparently nowhere more marked than in the attitude of the two men toward money. Shylock is a usurer. So strong is Antonio's distaste for usury that he lends money without interest. But where does the money come from that permits such generosity? From his argosies, of course, his trade. For, after all, to what has Antonio dedicated his life? Not indeed to usury. But certainly to money-making, to profits. And profits, under analysis, are often only "usury" in a more respectable form. Appearance and reality again. (p. 88)

This does not mean that Antonio is a hypocrite. Far from it. Who does not know an Antonio—a man too good for money-making who has dedicated his life to money-making? Antonio was created for nobler things. And so he suffers from that homesickness of the soul that ultimately attacks everyone who "consecrates" his life to something below his spiritual level. Moreover, Antonio is a bachelor, and his "fie, fie!" in answer to Salanio's bantering suggestion that he is in love may hint at some long-nourished disappointment of the affections. Antonio has never married, and he is not the man to have had clandestine affairs. So he has invested in gentle friendship emotions that nature intended should blossom into love. But however tender and loyal, it is a slightly sentimental friendship, far from being an equivalent of love. Both it and the argosies are at bottom opiates. Those who drown themselves in business or other work in order to forget what refuses to be forgotten are generally characterized by a quiet melancholy interrupted occasionally by spells of irritation or sudden spasms of passion directed at some person or thing that, if analyzed, is found to be a symbol of the error that has spoiled their lives. . . . This surely is the solution of the opening conundrum of the play, and anger at himself, not a conventional anti-Semitism of which Antonio could not conceivably be guilty, is the cause of his fierce and irrational outbursts against Shylock. Antonio is the silver casket. He got as much as he deserved: material success and a suicidal melancholy.

Why did Shylock offer Antonio a loan of three thousand ducats without interest?

On our answer to that crucial question, it is scarcely too much to say, our conception of the Jew and our interpretation of the play will hinge. (pp. 91-2)

Shakespeare is at pains to make plain the noble potentialities of Shylock, however much his nature may have been warped by the sufferings and persecutions he has undergone and by the character of the vocation he has followed. His vices are not so much vices as perverted virtues. His pride of race in a base sense is pride of race in a high sense inverted, his answer to the world's scorn. His love of sobriety and good order is a degeneration of his religion. His domestic "tyranny"—which it is easy to exaggerate—a vitiated love of family and home. His outward servility, a depraved patience. His ferocity, a thwarted self-respect. Even his avarice is partly a providence imposed by the insecurity of his lot. There is a repressed Shylock. (p. 95)

Shylock has tried to fuse the usurer with the father of Jessica—but in vain. They will no more mix than oil and water. Troubled dreams about his money bags are proof of this—symptoms of struggle in a divided nature. And so the two Shylocks exist side by side, now the one, now the other asserting sovereignty. The reiterated cry "My daughter! O my ducats!" which the next moment becomes "My ducats, and my daughter!" [II. viii. 15, 17] is an example of this ambivalent state of the man's mind. It is a mark of the near-balance between outraged love and avarice, though it is not without significance that the daughter—the first time at least—is mentioned first. It is the same with the turquoise that he had of Leah when he was a bachelor. First, it is the jewel as a memento of romance, then as a valuable material possession. But there is a still more revealing instance. "Would she were hearsed at my foot and the ducats in her coffin!" [III. i. 89-90]. That tormented cry is usually taken as meaning, "I would give my daughter's life to get my ducats back." And doubtless that is what Shylock thinks he is saying. But note that it is not Jessica dead and the ducats locked up in his vault. The ducats are in the coffin too! Plainly an unconscious wish to bury his own miserliness. Shylock is ripe for a better life. It takes a Shakespeare to give a touch like that.

Such passages shed an intense light on the offer to Antonio of a loan without interest, followed instantly by the stipulation of the bloodthirsty bond (passed off as a jest). The pattern is identical. When we read the passage for the first time, or see the incident on the stage, we are too excited by the situation and the suspense to look beneath the surface. We are taking the play as drama and consider each scene separately as it comes or as interpreted by an actor who is probably thinking more of its effect on the audience than of the truth of its psychology. But when, later, we read it as poetry, and take the parts in the light of the whole, we see how perfectly the Jew's words and actions here cohere with the rest of his role. (p. 96)

Shylock, the despised usurer, is on the point of lending Antonio, the great merchant, three thousand ducats, presumably at a high rate of interest, when he is suddenly confronted by a storm of anger from a man humiliated by the necessity of borrowing from a Jew (whom he has been in the habit of insulting) and stung by the Jew's recognition of the highly ironical nature of the situation. The merchant's loss of temper brings an inversion of everything. The inferior is suddenly the superior—in all senses. As certainly as when a wheel revolves and what was a moment before at the bottom is now at the top, so certainly what was deep down in Shylock is bound to come to the surface. But what is deep down in Shylock is precisely his goodness. How often the finer Shylock must have dreamed of a different kind of life, of being received into the fellowship of the commercial princes of Venice, treated as a human being, even as an equal. And now suddenly the beginning of that dream comes true. One of the greatest of Venetian merchants does come to him, without insults, asking a favor. How can the Jew's imagination fail, for a moment at least, to round out the pattern of the old daydream? Whatever the moneylender feels, or fancies he feels, what the dreamer within Shylock experiences is an impulse to be friendly:

SHY.: I would be friends with you and have your love,
Forget the shames that you have stain'd me with,
Supply your present wants, and take no doit
Of usance for my moneys, and you'll not hear me.
This is kind I offer.

BASS.: This were kindness.

SHY.:   This kindness will I show.
[I. iii. 138-43]

Bassanio's words show that there was no obvious irony in Shylock's tone nor conspicuous fawning in his manner. Only gross distortion could impart to the Jew's lines the accent of Iago, an accent they would have to carry if Shylock were a deliberate villain. On the contrary, little as he may recognize it himself, here is the instinctive reaction of the nobler Shylock. But . . . the good impulse is followed instantly by its polar opposite. The wheel goes on revolving. The highest gives place to the lowest. When the window is opened to the angel, the devils promptly rush in at the unguarded back door. The day-dream of kindness is followed by the daydream of killing. As the imaginative Shylock pictured himself coming to the aid of a friend, so the primitive Shylock dreams of shedding the blood of an enemy. In the first fantasy the heart of one man goes out to unite with the heart of the other. In the second the hand of the one would tear out the heart of the other. The perfect chiasmus stamps the two as products of the unconscious. Such a diametrical contradiction is one of its almost infallible marks. (pp. 96-7)

The opposite hypothesis—that the offer of no interest is a snare and the bond a deliberate trap—breaks down completely for another reason. If Shylock were that sort of plotter, however much he might have tried not to show it, he would have leaped with the eagerness of a villain at the first news that Antonio's argosies had miscarried. But, as several discerning critics have pointed out, he does nothing of the sort. When Salarino asks him if he has not heard of Antonio's loss at sea, he does not cry even to himself, "Ah, now I have him on the hip!" but only "There I have another bad match" [III. i. 44], the noun revealing that his mind is still on his daughter, and it is Salarino himself who has to recall the pound of flesh and ask him of what possible use it can be to him. Shylock's reply is scarcely what Salarino was fishing for. Instead of an anticipatory day-dream of blood, it is precisely the famous speech, "I am a Jew. Hath not a Jew eyes? . . ." [III. i. 58ff.] which, more than any other in his role, wrings sympathy even from those who elsewhere grudge him a particle of it.

So, too, a moment later, when Tubal mentions Antonio's ill luck. Shylock takes the news joyfully, to be sure, but casually, in fact almost absentmindedly, his "in Genoa?" showing that his confused thoughts are still in the place where his fellow-Jew has been trying to trace his daughter. Tubal has to keep whipping his thoughts back to Antonio and the impending forfeiture. Indeed, if Tubal had been trying deliberately to forge a link in Shylock's mind between the infidelity of his daughter and the forfeiture of the bond he could not have proceeded more skilfully. He is trying. He does forge it. Jessica—Antonio: Jessica—Antonio: Jessica—Antonio: back and forth from the one to the other Tubal yanks Shylock's mind. Yet the utmost he can extort from it concerning Antonio is "I'll torture him" [III. i. 117]—not kill him. And when in his very next speech Shylock cries, with regard to the ring his daughter has exchanged for a monkey, "Thou torturest me, Tubal" [III. i. 120], the echoed word shows that if he lives to torture Antonio it will be because Jessica and Tubal have tortured him. If ever a man egged on revenge it is this other Jew. Indeed it is he rather than Shylock who is acting the role of "Shylock" in this scene, by which of course I mean the Shylock of popular conception. That Shylock needs no one to instigate him. But Shakespeare's Shylock, strangely, does. Those who find a bloodthirsty Jew in this play are right. But they have picked the wrong man.

TUB: But Antonio is certainly undone.
SHY: Nay, that's true, that's very true. Go, Tubal, fee me an officer; bespeak him a fortnight before. I will have the heart of him, if he forfeit; for, were he out of Venice, I can make what merchandise I will.
[III. i. 124-29]

"Were he out of Venice"! Here is the proof that, even at this late hour, Shylock is thinking of tearing out Antonio's heart in a metaphorical sense only and has no idea of literal blood-shed. Just five words. But what a difference they make!

It must be something else, then, that turns the Jew from a desire to be rid of Antonio's presence in Venice to the idea of demanding the literal pound of flesh, a desire that only a mad-man could entertain. Salanio's description of Shylock in the streets gives us the clue:

I never heard a passion so confus'd,
So strange, outrageous, and so variable,
As the dog Jew did utter in the streets . . .
[II. viii. 12-14]

There are scarcely three more illuminating lines in the play, little as their speaker is aware of the light he is shedding. Plainly this proud man, displaying his inmost heart to all behold-ers . . . , has been driven to the verge of madness. The com-bined infidelity and thievery of his own child, culminating in her elopement with a Christian, are what have done it. Tubal and Salarino, as we have seen, precisely when the Jew was in the most suggestive state, implant in his mind what amounts to posthypnotic directions to demand the literal fulfilment of his bond. And no one knows what the street urchins contribute to the same end. But it is the daughter who first releases the flood of despair that helps these later seeds to germinate. (pp. 98-9)

It is not until he runs on Antonio with the jailer that the Jew, enraged perhaps at seeing his enemy at large, threatens him directly:

Thou call'dst me dog before thou hadst a cause,
But, since I am a dog, beware my fangs.
[III. iii. 6-7]

At last Shylock recognizes that the animal within him is gaining ascendancy. . . . His repetitions betoken his irrational state:

I'll have my bond; speak not against my bond:
I have sworn an oath that I will have my bond . . .
I'll have my bond; I will not hear thee speak.
I'll have my bond, and therefore speak no more. . . .
I'll have no speaking; I will have my bond.
[III. iii. 4-5, 12-13, 17]

It is as if the revengeful Shylock were afraid that even one reasonable word from Antonio might revive the natural instincts of the kinder Shylock now so near extinction. The repeated "I'll have no speaking" measures the tremendous inner resis-tance the Jew has had to overcome before he could surrender and become unmitigatedly bad.

What was the nature of this resistance that at last seems to be breaking down? Obviously it was a desire to be just the opposite of what he now feels himself becoming. Though he was ren-dered coldhearted by his vocation, made cruel by the insults that had been heaped upon him by everybody from the re-spectable Antonio to the very children in the streets, driven to desperation by his daughter, there is nothing to indicate that Shylock was congenitally coldhearted, cruel, or desperate. On the contrary, it is clear that he had it in him, however deep down, to be humane, kindly, and patient, and his offer to Antonio of a loan without interest seems to have been a supreme effort of this submerged Shylock to come to the surface. If so, here is the supreme irony of this ironical play. If so, for a moment at least, the Jew was the Christian. The symbolism confirms the psychology: Shylock was the leaden casket with the spiritual gold within.

The moment this fact is grasped the court scene becomes something quite different from what is seems to be. It is still a trial scene, but it is Portia who is on trial. Or, better, it is a casket scene in which she is subjected to the same test to which she has submitted her suitors. Can she detect hidden gold under a leaden exterior? (pp. 100-01)

No one can deny her brilliance or her charm, or could wish to detract from them. . . . Yet Portia, too, like so many of the others in this play, is not precisely all she seems to be. Indeed, what girl of her years, with her wealth, wit, and beauty, could be the object of such universal adulation and come through unscathed? In her uprush of joy when Bassanio chooses the right casket there is, it is true, an accent of the humility that fresh love always bestows, and she speaks of herself as ''an unlesson'd girl, unschool'd, unpractis'd'' [III. ii. 159]. There the child Portia once was is speaking, but it is a note that is sounded scarcely anywhere else in her role. The woman that child has grown into, on the contrary, is the darling of a sophisticated society which has nurtured in her anything but unself-consciousness. Indeed, it seems to be as natural to her as to a queen or princess to take herself unblushingly at the estimate this society places on her. (p. 101)

The casket motif, the court scene, and the ring incident taken together comprise a good share of the story. Each of them is intrinsically spectacular, histrionic, or theatrical—or all three in one. Each is a kind of play within a play, with Portia at the center or at one focus. The casket scenes are little symbolic pageants; the court scene is drama on the surface and tragedy underneath; the ring incident is a one-act comedy complete in itself. What sort of heroine does all this demand? Obviously one with the temperament of an actress, not averse to continual limelight. Portia is exactly that.

When she hears that the man who helped her lover woo and win her is in trouble, her character and the contingency fit each other like hand and glove. Why not impersonate a Young Doctor of Laws and come to Antonio's rescue? It is typical of her that at first she takes the ''whole device,'' as she calls it, as a kind of prank. Her imagination overflows with pictures of the opportunities for acting that her own and Nerissa's disguise as young men will offer, of the innocent lies they will tell, the fun they will have, the fools they will make of their husbands. The tragic situation of Antonio seems at the moment the last thing in her mind, or the responsibility of Bassanio for the plight of his friend. The fact that she is to have the leading role in a play in real life eclipses everything else. There is more than a bit of the stage-struck girl in Portia.

And so when the curtain rises on Act IV, Shakespeare the playwright and his actress-heroine, between them, are equipped to give us one of the tensest and most theatrically effective scenes he had conceived up to this time. What Shakespeare the poet gives us, however, and what it means to Portia the woman, is something rather different. (p. 103)

Portia, as the Young Doctor of Laws, says to Shylock:

> Of a strange nature is the suit you follow;
> Yet in such rule that the Venetian law
> Cannot impugn you as you do proceed.
>
> [IV. i. 177-79]

This bears the mark of preparation, if not of rehearsal. It seems a strange way of beginning, like a partial prejudgment of the case in Shylock's favor. But his hopes must be raised at the outset to make his ultimate downfall the more dramatic. ''Do you confess the bond?'' she asks Antonio. ''I do,'' he replies.

> Then must the Jew be merciful.
>
> [IV. i. 181-82]

Portia, as she says this, is apparently still addressing Antonio. It would have been more courteous if, instead of speaking of him in the third person, she had turned directly to Shylock and said, ''Then must you be merciful.'' But she makes a worse slip than that: the word *must*. Instantly Shylock seizes on it, pouring all his sarcasm into the offending verb:

> On what compulsion ''*must*'' I? Tell me that.
>
> [IV. i. 183]

Portia is caught! You can fairly see her wheel about to face not so much the Jew as the unanswerable question the Jew has asked. He is right—she sees it: ''must'' and ''mercy'' have nothing to do with each other; no law, moral or judicial, can force a man to be merciful.

For a second, the question must have thrown Portia off balance. This was not an anticipated moment in the role of the Young Doctor. But forgetting the part she is playing, she rises to the occasion superbly. The truth from Shylock elicits the truth from her. Instead of trying to brush the Jew aside or hide behind some casuistry or technicality, she frankly sustains his exception:

> The quality of mercy is not strain'd. . . .
>
> [IV. i. 184]

''I was wrong, Shylock,'' she confesses in effect. ''You are right''; mercy is a matter of grace, not of constraint:

> It droppeth as the gentle rain from heaven
> Upon the place beneath. . . .
>
> [IV. i. 185-86]

Shylock, then, supplied not only the cue, but, we might almost say, the first line of Portia's most memorable utterance.

In all Shakespeare—unless it be Hamlet with ''To be or not to be'' [*Hamlet*, III. i. 55ff.]—there is scarcely another character more identified in the world's mind with a single speech than Portia with her words on mercy. And the world is right. They have a ''quality'' different from anything else in her role. They are no prepared words of the Young Doctor she is impersonating, but her own, as unexpected as was Shylock's disconcerting question. Something deep down in him draws them from something deep down—or shall we say high up?—in her. They are the spiritual gold hidden not beneath lead but beneath the ''gold'' of her superficial life, her reward for meeting Shylock's objection with sincerity rather than with evasion. (pp. 105-06)

And then, incredibly, it is Portia who fails Shylock, not Shylock Portia. The same thing happens to her that happened to him at that other supreme moment when he offered Antonio the loan without interest. Her antipodal self emerges. In the twinkling of an eye, the angel reverts to the Doctor of Laws. . . . [Pushing] aside the divine Portia and her divine opportunity, the Young Doctor resumes his role. His "therefore, Jew" gives an inkling of what is coming. You can hear, even in the printed text, the change of voice, as Portia sinks from compassion to legality:

> I have spoke thus much
> To mitigate the justice of thy plea,
> Which if thou follow, this strict court of Venice
> Must needs give sentence 'gainst the merchant
>   there. . . .
>
>   [IV. i. 202-05]

Portia the lover of mercy is deposed by Portia the actress that the latter may have the rest of her play. And the hesitating Shylock, pushed back to the precipice, naturally has nothing to say but

> My deeds upon my head! I crave the law,
> The penalty and forfeit of my bond.
>
>   [IV. i. 206-07]

The rest of the scene is an overwhelming confirmation of Portia's willingness to sacrifice the human to the theatrical, a somewhat different kind of sacrifice from that referred to in the inscription on the leaden casket. (pp. 106-07)

The skill with which from this point she stages and acts her play proves her a consummate playwright, director, and actress—three in one. She wrings the last drop of possible suspense from every step in the mounting excitement. She stretches every nerve to the breaking point, arranges every contrast, climax, and reversal with the nicest sense for maximum effect, doing nothing too soon or too late, holding back her "Tarry a little" [IV. i. 305] until Shylock is on the very verge of triumph, even whetting his knife perhaps. It is she who says to Antonio, "Therefore lay bare your bosom" [IV. i. 252]. It is she who asks if there is a balance ready to weigh the flesh, a surgeon to stay the blood. And she actually allows Antonio to undergo his last agony, to utter, uninterrupted, his final farewell.

It is at this point that the shallow Bassanio reveals an unsuspected depth in his nature by declaring, with a ring of sincerity we cannot doubt, that he would sacrifice everything, including his life and his wife, to save his friend. . . . It is now, not when he stood before it, that Bassanio proves worthy of the leaden casket. Called on to make good his word, he doubtless would not have had the strength. But that does not prove that he does not mean what he says at the moment. And at that moment all Portia can do to help him is to turn into a jest—which she and Nerissa are alone in a position to understand—the most heartfelt and noble words her lover ever uttered.

> POR.: Your wife would give you little thanks for that,
>   If she were by to hear you make the offer.
>
>   [IV. i. 288-89]

This light answer, in the presence of what to Antonio and Bassanio is the very shadow of death, measures her insensibility to anything but the play she is presenting, the role she is enacting.

From this jest, in answer to the Jew's insistence, she turns without a word of transition to grant Shylock his sentence. . . . It is apparently all over with Antonio. The Jew lifts his knife. But once more appearances are deceitful. With a "tarry a little" this mistress of the psychological moment plays in succession, one, two, three, the cards she has been keeping back for pre-

cisely this moment. Now the Jew is caught in his own trap, now he gets a taste of his own logic, a dose of his own medicine. Now there is no more talk of mercy, but justice pure and simple, an eye for an eye:

> POR.:   as thou urgest justice, be assur'd
>   Thou shalt have justice, more than thou desir'st.
>
>   [IV. i. 315-16]
>   (pp. 107-08)

"Logic is like the sword," says Samuel Butler, "—those who appeal to it shall perish by it." Never was the truth of that maxim more clearly illustrated than by Shylock's fate. His insistence that his bond be taken literally is countered by Portia's insistence that it be taken even more literally—and Shylock "perishes." He who had been so bent on defending the majesty of the law now finds himself in its clutches, half his goods forfeit to Antonio, the other half to the state, and his life itself in peril.

And so Portia is given a second chance. She is to be tested again. She has had her legal and judicial triumph. Now it is over will she show to her victim that quality which at her own divine moment she told us "is an attribute to God himself" [IV. i. 195]? The Jew is about to get his deserts. Will Portia forget her doctrine that mercy is mercy precisely because it is not deserved? The Jew is about to receive justice. Will she remember that our prayers for mercy should teach us to do the deeds of mercy and that in the course of justice none of us will see salvation? Alas! she will forget, she will not remember. Like Shylock, but in a subtler sense, she who has appealed to logic "perishes" by it. (p. 110)

Ironically it is the Duke who proves truer to the true Portia than Portia herself.

> DUKE: That thou shalt see the difference of our spirits,
>   I pardon thee thy life before thou ask it.
>
>   [IV. i. 368-69]

And he suggests that the forfeit of half of Shylock's property to the state may be commuted to a fine.

> Ay, for the state; not for Antonio,
>
>   [IV. i. 373]

Portia quickly interposes, as if afraid that the Duke is going to be too merciful, going to let her victim off too leniently. Here, as always, the aftermath of too much "theatrical" emotion is a coldness of heart that is like lead. (pp. 110-11)

[Even] the man whom Shylock would have killed seems more disposed than Portia to mitigate the severity of his penalty: he is willing to forgo the half of Shylock's goods if the Duke will permit him the use of the other half for life with the stipulation that it go to Lorenzo (and so to Jessica) at his death. But with two provisos: that all the Jew dies possessed of also go to Lorenzo-Jessica and that

> He presently become a Christian.
>
>   [IV. i. 387]

Doubtless the Elizabethan crowd, like the crowd in every generation since including our own, thought that this was letting Shylock off easily, that this *was* showing mercy to him. Crowds do not know that mercy is wholehearted and has nothing to do with halves or other fractions. Nor do crowds know that you cannot make a Christian by court decree. Antonio's last demand quite undoes any tinge of mercy in his earlier concessions.

Act III. Scene ii. Portia, Bassanio, Gratiano, Nerissa, and others. The Department of Rare Books and Special Collections, The University of Michigan Library.

Even Shylock, as we have seen, had in him at least a grain of spiritual gold, of genuine Christian spirit. Only a bit of it perhaps. Seeds do not need to be big. Suppose that Portia and Antonio, following the lead of the seemingly willing Duke, had watered this tiny seed with that quality that blesses him who gives as well as him who takes, had overwhelmed Shylock with the grace of forgiveness! What then? The miracle, it is true, might not have taken place. Yet it might have. But instead, as if in imitation of the Jew's own cruelty, they whet their knives of law and logic, of reason and justice, and proceed to cut out their victim's heart. (That that is what it amounts to is proved by the heartbroken words,

> I pray you give me leave to go from hence.
> I am not well.)
>
> [IV. i. 395-96]

Shylock's conviction that Christianity and revenge are synonyms is confirmed. "If a Christian wrong a Jew, what should his sufferance be by Christian example? Why, revenge" [III. i. 69-71]. The unforgettable speech from which that comes, together with Portia's on mercy, and Lorenzo's on the harmony of heaven, make up the spiritual argument of the play. Shylock asserts that a Jew is a man. Portia declares that man's duty to man is mercy—which comes from heaven. Lorenzo points to heaven but laments that the materialism of life insulates man from its harmonies. A celestial syllogism that puts to shame the logic of the courtroom.

That Shakespeare planned his play from the outset to enforce the irony of Portia's failure to be true to her inner self in the trial scene is susceptible of something as near proof as such things can ever be. As in the case of Hamlet's

> A little more than kin, and less than kind,
>
> [*Hamlet*, I. ii. 65]

the poet, over and over, makes the introduction of a leading character seemingly casual, actually significant. Portia enters *The Merchant of Venice* with the remark that she is aweary of the world. Nerissa replies with that wise little speech about the illness of those that surfeit with too much (an observation that takes on deeper meaning in the retrospect after we realize that at the core what is the trouble with Portia and her society is boredom). "Good sentences and well pronounced" [I. ii. 10], says Portia, revealing in those last two words more than she knows. "They would be better if well followed" [I. ii. 11], Nerissa pertinently retorts. Whereupon Portia, as if gifted with insight into her own future, takes up Nerissa's theme:

> If to do were as easy as to know what were
> good to do, chapels had been churches, and
> poor men's cottages princes' palaces. It is a
> good divine that follows his own instructions:
> I can easier teach twenty what were good to be
> done, than be one of the twenty to follow mine
> own teaching.
>
> [I. ii. 12-17]

If that is not a specific preparation for the speech on mercy and what follows it, what in the name of coincidence is it? The words on mercy were good sentences, well pronounced. And far more than that. But for Portia they remained just words in the sense that they did not teach her to do the deeds of mercy. So, a few seconds after we see her for the first time, does Shakespeare let her pass judgment in advance on the most critical act of her life. For a moment, at the crisis in the courtroom, she seems about to become the leaden casket with the spiritual gold within. But the temptation to gain what many men desire—admiration and praise—is too strong for her and she reverts to her worldly self. Portia is the golden casket.

The last act of *The Merchant of Venice* is often accounted a mere epilogue, a device whereby Shakespeare dissipates the tension aroused by the long court scene of Act IV. It does dissipate it, but the idea that it is a mere afterpiece is superficial.

To begin with, the moonlight and the music take up the central theme and continue the symbolism. At night what was concealed within by day is often revealed, and under the spell of sweet sounds what is savage in man is tamed, for "music for the time doth change his nature." It is not chance that in the first hundred lines and a little more of this scene (at which point the music ceases) Portia, Nerissa, Lorenzo, and even Jessica utter words that might well have been out of their reach by day or under other conditions. Lorenzo's incomparable lines on the harmony of heaven seem, in particular, too beautiful for the man who called Jessica "wise" and "true" at the very time when she was robbing her father. But under the influence of love and moonlight this may be his rare moment. Over and over Shakespeare lets an unsuspected depth in his characters come out at night. However that may be, the passage lends a sort of metaphysical sanction to the casket metaphor. Moonlight opens the leaden casket of material reality and lets us see

> how the floor of heaven
> Is thick inlaid with patines of bright gold.
>
> [V. i. 58-9]

But the garden by moonlight is only a glimpse, a prelude, or rather an interlude, and with the return of the husbands and Antonio, the poetry and romance largely disappear, the levity is resumed, the banter, the punning, the sexual allusions, including some very frank ones on Portia's part, until the secret of the impersonations is revealed and everything is straightened out. What a picture it is of the speed with which so-called happy people rush back to the idle pleasures of life after a brief compulsory contact with reality. Privilege was forced for a moment to face the Excluded. It makes haste to erase the impression as quickly and completely as it can. Similarly, for theatergoers, the fifth act erases any earlier painful impressions. The story came out all right after all! Nothing need cloud the gaiety of the after-theater supper. (pp. 111-13)

The metaphor that underlies and unifies *The Merchant of Venice* is that of alchemy, the art of transforming the base into the precious, lead into gold. Everything in it comes back to that. Only the symbols are employed in a double sense, one worldly and one spiritual. By a kind of illuminating confusion, gold is lead and lead is gold, the base precious and the precious base. Portia had a chance to effect the great transformation—and failed. But she is not the only one. Gold, silver, and lead in one, the play subjects every reader or spectator to a test, or, shall we say, offers every reader or spectator the same opportunity Portia had. Choose—it says—at your peril. This play anti-Semitic? Why, yes, if you find it so. Shakespeare certainly leaves you free, if you wish, to pick the golden casket. But you may thereby be revealing more of yourself than of his play. (p. 115)

Harold C. Goddard, "'The Merchant of Venice'," in his The Meaning of Shakespeare, *The University of Chicago Press, 1951, pp. 81-116.*

M[URIEL] C. BRADBROOK (essay date 1951)

[*Bradbrook is an English scholar specializing in the development of Elizabethan drama and poetry. In her Shakespearean criticism, she combines both biographical and historical research, paying particular attention to the stage conventions popular during Shakespeare's lifetime. Her* Shakespeare and Elizabethan Poetry (1951) *is a comprehensive work which relates Shakespeare's poetry to that of George Chapman, Christopher Marlowe, Edmund Spenser, and Philip Sidney, and describes the evolution of Shakespeare's verse. Like such other critics as Elmer Edgar Stoll (1927), Harold R. Walley (1935), John Middleton Murry (1936), J. W. Lever (1952), and D. A. Traversi (1968), Bradbrook, in her commentary on* The Merchant of Venice, *praises Shakespeare's skills as a dramatic craftsman, particularly with regard to his characterization of Shylock and the construction of his plot. She claims that despite justifications for Shylock's behavior, he remains the villain of* The Merchant of Venice; *any other view of him, she adds, is "something less" than what Shakespeare created. Bradbrook contends that this extreme image of Shylock is necessary to Shakespeare's pattern of harsh contrasts, all of which support the theme of justice and mercy in the play—the confrontation of "the law and love that is the fulfilling of the law, the gold of Venice and the gold of Belmont." Other critics who have regarded the conflict of justice and mercy as the central issue in* The Merchant of Venice *include Sir Israel Gollancz (1922), Nevill Coghill (1949), C. L. Barber (1959), Barbara K. Lewalski (1962), and René E. Fortin (1974). Bradbrook concludes by discussing the artificiality of Shakespeare's work, specifically the casket story, which she claims despite its "fairy-tale quality" provides much thematic weight to the play in its examination of appearance and reality. For further commentary on the theme of appearance and reality in* The Merchant of Venice, *see the excerpt by Barbara Tovey (1981).*]

[*The Merchant of Venice*] is among the most vivid of Shakespeare's works in tone and colour. The golden world of Belmont and the heavier splendours of Venice are yoked together by something that, if it were not mastery, would approach violence. Shakespeare has carried his . . . method of contrasting different species within a single play to the very limits of its capacity. In Shylock he has imported the stage villain of Marlowe—upon whom his own Aaron [in *Titus Andronicus*] had been modelled—and set him down within the limits of a love story. True, he found the Jew in his source, but had he not chosen to make a play of such boldness he might easily have looked elsewhere.

Modern humanitarianism has run riot on Shylock; like Falstaff, with whom he has little else in common, he is held to be wronged in the end. Though the abuse of Bassanio's fortune-hunting, Antonio's manners and the Duke's notion of mercy has abated a little of recent years, there is still a tendency to overwork that phrase:

> Out upon her, thou torturest me *Tuball*, It was
> my Turkies, I had it of *Leah* when I was a
> Batchelor: I would not haue giuen it for a wilderness
> of Monkies.
>
> [III. i. 120-23]

Such an admission of conjugal fidelity is almost held to outweigh a taste for judicial murder.

But Shylock is in search of Revenge. . . . Revenge, even in the most extenuating circumstances, was for the Elizabethan a crime; Shylock's injuries were not *per se* any further justification than Edmund's grievance of illegitimacy, or the predisposition to vice which his crooked birth gave Richard III. Nothing less monstrous than the theatre's prize bogyman, linked in the popular mind with Machiavelli and the Devil in an infernal triumvirate, would serve for the villain of a romantic comedy. Were he less diabolic, Shylock would not be tolerable. . . . A human Shylock, devoted to Jessica, smarting under what Antonio can do in the way of spitting on his gabardine, is something less than Shakespeare's. Still less can he be looked on as an embodiment of the Rise of Capitalism, Shakespeare's protest against the new money economy [see the entry by E. C. Pettet in the Additional Bibliography]. Naturally Shakespeare used his feeling about 'the breed of barren metal' [I. iii. 134]—later to be used to more potent effect in *Timon*—but only as a similitude, shadowing in a baser manner the theme of his play; which is very plainly set forth as Justice and Mercy, the law and love that is the fulfilling of the law, the gold of Venice and the gold of Belmont.

Shylock, in so far as he stands for anything, stands for the Law: for the legal system which, to be just to all in general, must only approximate to justice in particular cases. Shylock's creed is an eye for an eye, and in a later play Shakespeare set out the measure to be meted in the name of strict justice. The Bible would be sufficient lead to the identification of a Jew with legal concepts of justice, and for the opposition of the Old Law to the New. Portia's famous speech is the most purely religious utterance in the canon—the most directly based upon Christian teaching, with its echoes of the Lord's Prayer, the Christian doctrine of salvation, and the words of *Ecclesiasticus*, 35.20:

> Mercy is seasonable in time of affliction, as
> clouds of rain in the time of drouth.

As addressed to a Jew, the argument loses its cogency, but it is intended rather as contrast to Shylock's

> What iudgement shall I dread doing no wrong? . . .
> I stand for iudgement, answer, Shall I haue it?
>
> [IV. i. 89, 103]

As in so many trial scenes of the Elizabethan drama, the pleading is addressed directly to the audience; it is exposition. In Shylock's and Portia's case it is also self-revelation; but it is the peculiar virtue of this play, and of the later *Measure for Measure*, that the characters are at the same time fully human, and symbolic or larger than human. Shakespeare has achieved here what he failed to do in *All's Well that Ends Well* and written a 'moral play'—that is a play in which the lively image of a general truth is embodied with such decorum and in so fitting a form that it has all the immediacy, the 'persuasion' as the Elizabethans would say, of a particular instance. (pp. 170-73)

The legal quibble by which Portia saves Antonio is triumphantly and appropriately a quibble. Any sounder argument would be giving Shylock less than his deserts. The bare letter of the law nooses him; and mercy takes the form of another legal instrument. The deed of gift balances the 'merry bond'.

The whole play is built upon contrasts of this sort. The original story and Marlowe's stage Jew require stronger counterweights than the heroine of *Il Pecarone* provided. Portia and Belmont are Shakespeare's creation; the casket story, which he added to his original, stands in precise and symbolic contrast to the story of the bond. In this play Shakespeare makes more direct use than anywhere else of dramatic *impresa:* the bold physical contrasts of the Jew with his curving knife and the boy-Portia in doctor's gown. The splendours of the Doge's court and the moonlight of Belmont would probably be outdone as sheer pageantry on the Elizabethan stage by the highly symbolic casket scenes.

The Prince of Morocco who comes first wearing 'the shadowed liuerie of the burnished sun' is described as 'Morochus a tawnie

Moore all in white' [II. i. 2, s.d.]. He has the accents of [Christopher Marlowe's] Tamburlaine:

> By this Symitare
> That slew the Sophie and a Persian Prince
> That won three fields of Sultan Solyman . . .
>
> [II. i. 24-6]

and ruled by his planet Sol, he chooses the Golden Casket with its motto, 'Who choses me shall gaine what men desire' [II. vii. 37], in a speech that deliberately recalls Tamburlaine's praise of Zenocrate:

> The Hircanion deserts, and the vaste wildes
> Of wide Arabia are as throughfares now
> For princes come to view fair *Portia*.
>
> [II. vii. 41-3]

The answer is a death's head. Mortality conquers those who like Tamburlaine are more 'bold' than 'wise' [II. vii. 70].

The Prince of Arragon is a Spaniard, incarnation of Pride. He chooses silver which promises 'as much as he deserves' [II. ix. 36]. The answer is a fool's head; and unlike Morocco, he is not only dismissed but rebuked by Portia; his wisdom only makes him a 'deliberate fool' [II. ix. 80].

Bassanio chooses the lead casket: 'Who chooseth me must giue and hazard all he hath' [II. vii. 9]. The hazards of love in this venture are Antonio's; Bassanio invited him to hazard (chance) a second arrow after the first, and the hazards (dangers) of the venture are no less than his life. The scene of Bassanio's choosing is made into a tapestry picture by Portia's magnificent 'augmentation':

> Now he goes,
> With no lesse presence but with much more loue
> Than yong *Alcides* when he did redeeme
> The virgine tribute paid by howling Troy
> To the Sea-monster: I stand for sacrifice,
> The rest aloof are the Dardanian wiues
> With bleared visages come forth to view
> The issue of th' exploit.
>
> [III. ii. 53-60]

The heightened language (almost with a touch of Hamlet's First Player), the tableau, the soft music whose significance Portia has explained so fully, are all designed to isolate this moment, the turning point of the story—the song, warning Bassanio against the fancy (or love) that is 'engendered in the eyes' [III. ii. 67]. His dangerous hazard brings him to a moment of blind and naked choice: and his choice is based on negatives. He will not take the *seeming* beauty. The speech of his choice echoes a theme which was to recur in the tragedies, and even before the tragedies, was to appear with almost tragic significance.

To work so much morality out of a pretty fairy tale may appear too much like breaking a butterfly upon a wheel; but the fairy-tale quality of the story serves to keep these significances unemphatic, not to obliterate them. Some such technique, but far subtler, was to be used in the final plays. To ignore the moral significance of the casket story—familiar commonplace morality, but the Elizabethans enjoyed the familiar and doted on the commonplace—is to ignore the main counterbalance to Shylock. He is symbolic in an all but tragic manner: these scenes are symbolic in an all but fairy-tale manner. The thrust of the opposing stresses maintains the arch of the narrative.

Portia, whose sunny locks hang on her temples like a golden fleece, whose suitors come from all corners of the earth to woo her, is set against the wealth of Venice, the mart where all the trade of east and west flows in. Antonio's argosies sail to Mexico, England, Tripoli, Lisbon, Barbary and India. The pledge and bond of matrimony—which is both a sacrament and a legal contract—is set against the bond of the Jew and Antonio's pledge of his flesh. Bassanio has won all, for with the ring Portia gives power as

> her Lord, her Governour, her King.
> Myself and what is mine, to you and yours
> Is now conuerted.
>
> [III. ii. 165-67]

The exchange of property is an exchange of the very self, which leaves Bassanio confused, as his powers recognize the voice of their sovereign in Portia's voice.

The rings which are exchanged reappear in the final scene as the pledge of this bond. It is as parody of the trial scene that the final episode becomes something more than a jest out of the Hundred Merry Tales. The gold of the rings is not the gold which Shylock deals in, and to which Portia and Antonio are both so superbly indifferent, which Bassanio has rejected in the casket scene, and which the unthrift Lorenzo acquires in so light-fingered a fashion. It is the gold of Belmont, and in parting from the ring, for Antonio's sake, Bassanio has supplied some backing for his second choice, made in the trial scene:

> Antonio, I am married to a wife,
> Which is as deare to me as life it selfe,
> But life it selfe, my wife, and all the world,
> Are not with me esteem'd aboue thy life.
> I would loose all, I sacrifice them all
> Here to this deuill, to deliuer you.
>
> [IV. i. 282-87]

So that in the dispute between husband and wife, Antonio reasonably intervenes, with the offer of a new and even more reckless bond, though of the kind that may not be registered in law.

> I once did lend my bodie for thy wealth,
> Which but for him that had your husbands ring
> Had quite miscarried. I dare be bound againe,
> My soule upon the forfeit, that your Lord
> Will neuer more break faithe aduisedly.
>
> [V. i. 249-53]

The pretty jests about cuckoldry are far from modern taste (like the jests which Diana makes with Lafeu and the King at the end of *All's Well* over Hellen's ring). Yet it is as hopelessly anachronistic to boggle at them as to treat Bassanio as a fortune-hunter. He is luck and young love personified, given as much character as the object of Portia's and Antonio's devotion requires; but, like Bertram though without any of the condemnation that Bertram receives, he is there to be the *object* of devotion, and he must look and move his part. I have seen it suggested that if his feelings for Antonio are all that he proclaims, he has only to run Shylock through with his rapier in the open court and stand to the consequences. Let anyone try to write a play on these lines. *The Merchant of Venice* is in the best sense artificial; Portia's successful disguise, the nature of the bond itself, the set pleas of Justice and Mercy are all artifice, designed not to make the story slighter but to control, direct and focus the emphasis upon the theme or 'cause' of the

play. Every piece of artifice is there for a purpose, and a purpose which an imaginative reading discloses readily enough. For *The Merchant of Venice* is not a subtle play; it is a recklessly bold and obvious sort of play. The symbolism is almost blatant, the violence of the contrasts almost glaring. It can be turned about and viewed from many aspects; the personal relationship between Antonio and Bassanio—which is mostly Antonio's—is so familiar from elsewhere in the Works that the only danger is lest the connexion with the sonnets should be pressed too far. The reproachful sonnets should not be invoked. Nor must the economics of the situation be taken on economic lines. In an age when economic treatises could be written by city merchants in the form of allegory and called *St. George for England,* there would have been little danger of misunderstanding, even from those members of Shakespeare's audience who smelt most strongly of ink and counters. For the groundlings he had provided a magnificent villain, some exciting scenes of pageantry and a tale which might have been authorized by their grandam. For the young gentlemen of the Inns of Court, he had provided some lovely speeches of wooing and some of morality and good life; for everyone the contrast between Justice and Mercy, gold and love, embodied in figures of so winning a grace that the critics talk of them as if they lived. It is the first of Shakespeare's plays which invites the moral judgments of real life in this way. (pp. 175-79)

> M[uriel] C. Bradbrook, "Polyphonic Music: 'All's Well', 'Merchant of Venice', 'Much Ado about Nothing'," in her Shakespeare and Elizabethan Poetry: A Study of His Earlier Work in Relation to the Poetry of the Time, Chatto and Windus, 1951, pp. 162-88.

J. W. LEVER   (essay date 1952)

[*Lever's essay, from which the following excerpt is drawn, is primarily a response to Norman Nathan's earlier investigation of the reasons why Shylock does not act to insure Antonio's failure to meet his bond (see excerpt above, 1950). Lever argues that the question behind Nathan's investigation answers itself when one realizes that for Shakespeare to have provided Shylock with this motivation would have transformed* The Merchant of Venice *into a "Marlowe-type melodrama." The critic then offers a general assessment of Shakespeare's craftsmanship, stating that in all his plays Shakespeare cared little for character motivation, but was concerned foremost with theme and plot, a point voiced earlier by Elmer Edgar Stoll (1927), Harold R. Walley (1935), and John Middleton Murry (1936). In the case of* The Merchant of Venice, *Lever asserts, Shakespeare merely adapted the character of Shylock to his theme of love and usury, taking the traditional caricature of the Jewish usurer and villain and transforming him into a more complex and threatening figure—in Lever's assessment, one who seriously challenges the Christian values of love, friendship, and community. The essence of Lever's essay, then, is to demonstrate the way in which Shakespeare "used the seemingly recalcitrant plot-factor to effect a testing and reassessment of the major values in terms of which* [The Merchant of Venice] *was conceived." Lever concludes, however, that despite Shylock's defeat at the end of the trial scene, the Venetian Christian society does not "answer" the Jew's challenge; only Portia as an individual confronts and overcomes Shylock's scepticism, and the play ends, Lever suggests, without resolving its central conflict. For a response to Lever's argument, see the excerpt by Norman Nathan (1952). Also, see the excerpts by James E. Siemon (1970) and R. Chris Hassel, Jr. (1970) for additional indication of the critical dissatisfaction with Shylock's treatment and Shakespeare's resolution of the play's central conflict.*]

No approach to Shakespeare's plays has proved so sterile as that which proceeds from speculations as to the unspoken beliefs or motives of his characters. Its monuments are the yellowing piles of dissertations in every library on what Hamlet (Falstaff, Shylock, etc.) "really" meant. Since every important Shakespearian character is a mosaic of anomalies, any theory can be propounded, none disproved. A more helpful method is to inquire the intentions, not of the characters, but of the dramatist as revealed in the treatment of his medium; more specifically, to note how the theme as it becomes manifest in the course of a play modifies and is modified by the extraneous plot on which the action is based. For out of this creative ferment emerge the characters, whose complexities accurately register the conflict of values which has given them birth.

From this viewpoint Dr. Nathan's question why Shylock does not act to insure the maturing of Antonio's bond answers itself [see excerpt above, 1950]. Shylock could easily have been made to engineer the failure of Antonio's ventures. He could also have contrived, as Barabas did, the death of his daughter's Christian lover (Dr. Nathan does not point out that he is as passive towards Lorenzo as he is towards Antonio). But then the play would have taken on the shape of a Marlowe-type melodrama. If on the other hand its main concern were to show how God favours virtuous Christians and punishes a villainous Jew, who at last accepts the true faith, its pattern would hark back to yet another pre-Shakespearian form, that of the morality play, and would remain largely irrelevant to the major interests of Shakespearian comedy.

We return to some familiar premises. *The Merchant of Venice* is in form a romantic comedy. The theme is Love and Usury; the plots, both borrowed, are the story of the caskets and the story of the pound of flesh, elaborated with hints from Marlowe's *Jew of Malta*. From the interaction between this theme and these plots, the principal characters, Shylock and Portia, take on their substance; and in the confrontation of the two lies the climax and resolution of the drama.

Love and Usury form a clear antinomy in the Shakespearian cosmos. Both have wide implications. Love comprehends the generous give and take of emotion, the free spending of nature's bounty, and the increase of progeny through marriage. This is the burden of the Sonnets, particularly those of the group inviting the Friend to marry. It is expressed in the wisdom of Theseus as well as in the blessings spoken by the fairies [in *A Midsummer Night's Dream*]; in the maturer romantic comedies, its chief expression is through the attributes and conduct of the heroine. The concept is, moreover, carried through from the sphere of sexual relationships into the social and economic fields where the ties of friendship and communal loyalty further the natural increase of husbandry—the word itself pointing to the common root of sexual and social institutions.

Set against Love in its various connotations is the concept of Usury. Economically and socially Usury signifies, in accordance with Aristotelian doctrine, a perverse activity, the monstrous breeding of money from money. It is the negation of friendship and community on which all natural productive labour depends:

> for when did friendship take
> A breed for barren metal of his friend?
>
> [I. iii. 133-34]

But Usury has also a sexual aspect in Shakespeare, meaning the perverse withholding of love. The Friend of the Sonnets in refusing to marry commits this sin:

> . . . Nature's bequest gives nothing, but doth lend,
> And being frank she lends to those are free.
> Then, beauteous niggard, why dost thou abuse
> The bounteous largess given thee to give?
> Profitless usurer, why dost thou use
> So great a sum of sums, yet canst not live?
>
> [*Sonnet* IV]

In this extended sense, the father who seeks to restrain his daughter from marriage may be said to practice a form of usury.

Thus the choice of a Jewish moneylender with a marriageable daughter as the villain of romantic comedy was entirely fitting. On the face of it, here was a perfect means of dramatizing the traditional concept. But the theme had unexplored complexities, and it was only through interaction with the pound of flesh story that they were brought to light. A sure token of Shakespeare's genius was the way he used the seemingly recalcitrant plot-factor to effect a testing and reassessment of the major values in terms of which the play was conceived.

As representative of a people that rejected the great commonplaces of Christian fellowship, Shylock stood in direct antithesis to the Venetians. At his first appearance the negations are deliberately stressed. Garbed in his Jewish gaberdine, eschewing elementary courtesies, speaking the harsh prose of commerce, Shylock incarnates all that is alien to Elizabethan ideals. To emphasize his self-segregation from the community, the Jewish dietary laws are arbitrarily worked into the dialogue [I. iii. 33-8]. . . .

The sight of Antonio makes [Shylock] think of revenge, but there is no indication in his first soliloquy that he knows what course he will take. When, however, Antonio virtuously disclaims the practice of money-lending, he is stung into a theoretical defence of his profession. The whole point of Shylock's biblical analogy is that Jacob succeeded through his own skill and initiative. . . . The rewards of business enterprise, that is to say, are divinely sanctioned and approved: only theft is wicked ("thrift is blessing if men steal it not" [I. iii. 90]). But Antonio brushes aside the biblical precedent with the evasive comment that the story records a fortuitous act of providence in which Jacob's own action had no effect upon the result. He proceeds to reassert the traditional Aristotelian distinction between the natural increase of husbandry, which might apply to Jacob as a shepherd, and the "unnatural" gains of finance, which is Shylock's occupation.

> Was this inserted to make interest good?
> Or is your gold and silver ewes and rams?
>
> [I. iii. 94-5]

It would be surprising if Shylock were impressed with Antonio's interpretation of the text, which runs counter to his whole philosophy of life. Neither Jacob nor he had prospered by waiting for providence: they throve through their enterprise and hard work. But Antonio's strictures do suggest to him a brilliantly ironical turning of the tables. Very well, he will make a bargain according to Antonio's principles. He will take "no doit of interest" [I. iii. 140], only the traditionally sanctioned "natural increase." . . . What he offers is a grotesque application to his own circumstances of Jacob's dealings in ewes and rams: a bargain based not on money but on a pound's weight of human livestock. Here is the "merry sport," thoroughly in keeping with Shylock's sardonic humour. If nothing comes of it, he has at least made Antonio's sanctimonious principles look absurd: and if—just conceivably—the bond should mature, he will indeed have his enemy on the hip.

What grounds had Shylock for expecting the bond to produce results? The dialogue would have told us, had the question been relevant here. But our attention as spectators is not turned in that direction. What we note is the striking manipulation of the borrowed plot. Through it Shylock is changed from the traditional Jewish usurer to a man challenging the pattern of recognized values. Antonio has called him misbeliever, cut-throat dog, and spits upon his Jewish gaberdine: his answer is to depart from the prescribed pattern of Jewish behaviour ("sufferance is the badge of all our tribe" [I. iii. 110]), to renounce the profits of usury, and to face his enemy not as dog, but as man. He may remain a villain, but it is now villainy of an unpredictable kind; while Antonio's orthodox virtues have in turn taken on strange, harsh contours under the searchlight of Shylock's scrutiny.

Shylock's development proceeds to a further stage with his second appearance. At the cost of irrelevance to the action, it had been stressed that his Jewish tenets forbade him to dine with Christians. Yet in this crucial scene he leaves Jessica alone in the house and goes out to eat forbidden food. The motive is not made clear: but his misgivings and premonitions of mishap are unmistakeable.

> . . . By Jacob's staff I swear
> I have no mind of feasting forth tonight;
> But I will go.
>
> [II. v. 36-8]

There is neither pleasure nor real gain to be had from going; yet some compulsion is at work. It is as if, once he has stepped out of the protective ethic of Jewish segregation, he is driven into ever more fatal contact with the hostile Christian world.

The story of Jessica's elopement is largely inspired by *The Jew of Malta*. But there are significant contrasts. Abigail is made sympathetic by her daughterly pity for Barabas: she rescues his treasure from their old house, throwing it from an upper window for her father to catch; only when he murders her Christian lover does she recognize his villainy, accept Christianity, and become a nun. Jessica shows her antipathy to Shylock from the start: she plunders his ducats in conspiracy with her suitor; her notion of winning Christian salvation includes the squandering of fourscore ducats at a sitting and the exchange of her mother's ring for a monkey. Shakespeare converts the revolt of love against usurious parental restraint into a breach of elementary filial piety, just as he converts the jubilant assault upon a usurer's hoarded wealth into an act of plain theft. Shylock's dictum that thrift is blessing if men steal it not becomes an indictment of Christian practice which the titters of Solanio and Salarino at the Jew's "ducats and his daughter" [II. viii. 24] do not efface.

Shylock's final renunciation of Jewish principles comes after he has discovered his loss. His outburst [III. i. 53-73] is not, of course, a plea for tolerance. It is a justification of revenge, based on the view that physically and morally, too, the Jew is indistinguishable from other men. Shylock might have quoted revenge precedents from the Old Testament to justify his conduct. Significantly he waives these arguments, just as he abandons the post-exile Jewish doctrines of sufferance. He claims revenge not as Jew, but as man. The Christian talk of humility is hypocrisy; so too is the Jewish talk of sufferance; he, Shylock, will have none of it, but will behave as in practice all human beings do.

> If a Jew wrong a Christian, what is his humility,
> revenge! if a Christian wrong a Jew, what should

his sufferance be by Christian example, why revenge! The villainy you teach me I will execute, and it shall go hard but I will better the instruction.

> [III. i. 68-73]

The nature of Shylock's self-confessed villainy is apparent: it is to challenge the sincerity of the whole edifice of traditional values, built upon love, friendship, and community: values which are the foundations of romantic comedy.

Here precisely lies the strength of Shylock's case in court. The plot is made to reinforce the testing of values. Shylock bases his plea on the laws of Venice, which, in this Christian but highly commercialized state, recognize neither love nor human fellowship as valid principles. Citizens may use their property as they please, whether money, animals, or human beings. The conclusive reply to any plea is "the slaves are ours" [IV. i. 98]. Were it not that Portia stands for something more than law, Shylock's position would be unshakeable—if not strictly in terms of plot, certainly in terms of the drama's inner meaning.

The casket story, like that of the pound of flesh, is often seen as a mere fairy-tale intrusion. Actually its symbolical properties fulfill a major function. The golden lady whose name is found in the leaden casket exactly typifies the paradox of Portia. One of the more startling contrasts of the play is that between Bassanio's first romanticized description of the Lady of Belmont, and the lively clear-headed girl whom we next see exchanging witticisms with her maid at the expense of her brocaded suitors. Portia upsets the traditional concepts of courtship as effectively as Shylock does the traditional social pieties. Love of her new husband, loyalty to his friends, uncalculating generosity are her guiding standards. Hence her unique qualifications to meet Shylock's challenge. Facing his gaberdine in her lawyer's gown, she is theatrically his opposite number, as free from the glamour of romance heroines as he is from the decorative idealism of the Venetian merchants. (pp. 383-86)

In [the trial] scene the moral position taken up by Shylock is driven to its logical implications. Portia makes her celebrated appeal for him to show mercy. Had Shakespeare intended to use the trial as a conflict between Jewish and Christian ethics, between the "Old Testament God" and what Dr. Nathan calls the "second God (perhaps Jesus?)" of the New, here was the place for a clear statement. But Portia's speech on the quality of mercy is the broadest monotheism. It is based on the principles held in common by Christians and Jews—belief in God and the after-life—and deliberately passes over the distinctions between the two faiths:

> Therefore, Jew,
> Though justice be thy plea, consider this,
> That, in the course of justice, *none of us*
> Should see salvation. *We* do pray for mercy,
> And that same prayer doth teach *us all* to render
> The deeds of mercy.
>
> [IV. i. 197-202]

When Shylock ignores the appeal ("my deeds upon my head" [IV. i. 206]), he cuts himself adrift from the spiritual links that bind both Christian and Jew. Portia's last plea, that he have by a surgeon to stop Antonio's wounds, goes yet further: it is addressed to his rudimentary humanity. But again he refuses, and is thereby forced into the position of a common murderer. It may be true that theft is worse than usury; but nothing justifies murder. And now, when the issues are fully clarified, Portia discloses her hand.

With the loss of his case, Shylock's property is forfeit to "the gentleman that lately stole his daughter" [IV. i. 384-85]. He is offered a choice between Christianity and hanging, and prefers the former. I see no need to speculate as to his reasons. As a creature of Shakespeare's pen, the only words he speaks are "I am content" [IV. i. 394]: his unuttered thoughts are dramatically irrelevant. What counts in the play is that society, suddenly recollecting its Christian principles, manages both to pardon him and to eliminate the challenge of his scepticism.

Yet at bottom society has not answered Shylock's challenge. Neither the Venetians nor the laws and customs of Venice are vindicated by Shylock's downfall. Only Portia as an individual has confronted and overcome him; and in the play she is almost as isolated a figure as the Jew. The conflict is not truly fought out until, purged of all conventional doctrines, it is transferred from romantic comedy to the wider sphere of tragedy. (p. 386)

> J. W. Lever, "Shylock, Portia and the Values of Shakespearian Comedy," in Shakespeare Quarterly, Vol. III, No. 4, October, 1952, pp. 383-86.

NORMAN NATHAN   (essay date 1952)

[*Nathan responds to J. W. Lever's refutation of Nathan's earlier claim that Shylock does not act to secure Antonio's forfeiture of his bond because the Jew believes that, like the Old Testament Jacob, God is on his side and will act in his favor (see the excerpts above, 1950 and 1952). Nathan contends that Lever's interpretation of* The Merchant of Venice—*namely, that the play depicts the conflict between love and usury and that character motivation is less relevant to a reliable evaluation than is an understanding of Shakespeare's adaptation of his characters to his theme and plot—is inferior to his own reading and robs the play of much of its charm and originality. Nathan takes particular issue with Lever's view of Shylock as the traditional Jewish usurer of romantic comedy transformed into "a man challenging the pattern of recognized values." The critic maintains that this reading detracts from Shylock's symbolic association with Jacob—and therefore his motivation for his inactivity or passivity towards Antonio— and, more important, is not supported by the drama itself, which Nathan says would not have left the Jew without a Venetian deserving his scorn had he been meant to challenge the Christian values of Venice.*]

Great characters must have significant influence in shaping an author's intentions (and thereby causing much scholarly dispute). By relying too much on what he considers Shakespeare's intentions and themes to be, Mr. Lever weakens the dramatist's powers of characterization [see excerpt above, 1952]. Portia in one scene is made to become a lawyer rather than a woman in lawyer's robes. The Jessica we get is not based on the lines as they appear in the play. And Shylock emerges as an inconsistent figure who at an early stage in the play changes so completely that no other character would have recognized him as the Shylock he had known for years!

Mr. Lever sees Portia in her lawyer's gown as "free from the glamour of romance heroines. . . ." But the audience knows that the lawyer is a witty young woman in the position of being able to surpass in wisdom all the men in the scene. The fun of a future disclosure is anticipated, particularly when Bassanio would exchange her life for Antonio's and, a little later, gives her a ring he had promised would never leave his finger. Portia in this scene is perhaps more glamorous than either Beatrice

or Rosalind. In general, making Portia and Shylock the ideational protagonists of the play weakens the charm of her part.

Jessica likewise suffers. ". . . Her notion of winning Christian salvation includes the squandering of forescore ducats at a sitting and the exchange of her mother's ring for a monkey." But as proof of these actions we have only Tubal's second-hand statement as he torments Shylock (note that it is Shylock who, hearing *a ring,* jumps to the conclusion that it was *my Turkies*). At any event, if Jessica had acted thus, it would be necessary to consider her unspoken motives, for she would at the moment have been more concerned with being gay on her honeymoon than with thoughts of Christian salvation.

Furthermore, I cannot agree that "Shakespeare converts the revolt of love against usurious parental restraint into a breach of elementary filial piety. . . ." Jessica is not as virtuous as Portia, but a large number of phrases are planted in justification of her conduct. (pp. 386-87)

I assume that it is to Shylock that Mr. Lever refers when he says, ". . . the father who seeks to restrain his daughter from marriage may be said to practice a form of usury." But there is nothing in the play to indicate that Shylock does this. Jessica apparently can lock (and unlock!) the doors. She is urged not to look at Christians, but this is even less restraining from marriage than the edict of Portia's father who, in effect, insisted that she become an old maid unless some suitor picked the lead casket!

But something more important happens to Shylock's characterization. Shakespeare shows him first as hoping to catch Antonio on the hip. After the bargain Bassanio says that Shylock has a villain's mind. He is called a devil more than once. He fees an officer *in advance.* Jessica states that Antonio's flesh was much in his mind. Certainly Shakespeare tries to create in the audience the feeling that Shylock is to be feared and is not at all the type of person who would take any satisfaction in the fact that he had made "Antonio's sanctimonious principles look absurd."

Contrary to Mr. Lever's statement, Shylock is not "as passive towards Lorenzo as he is towards Antonio." He could not contrive "the death of his daughter's Christian lover," for he did not know she had a lover. Shakespeare neatly gets the husband out of Venice. While Shylock is not a Marlovian villain, to apprehend Lorenzo and Jessica he even goes so far as to spend money! He says to Tubal, ". . . no newes of them, why so? and I know not how much is spent in the search . . ." [III. i. 90-2]. (p. 387)

Shakespeare has clearly defined Shylock for us. To regard Shylock's lack of action towards Antonio as irrelevant seems to be the same as saying that Shylock's character has been drawn inconsistently in order to satisfy the demands of the author's intentions as to the nature of the play.

Shylock, however, is not inconsistent and his inactivity has been motivated. Since Mr. Lever assumes only conventional themes and motivations as possible, his logical conclusion is that a different kind of play would have resulted. But Shakespeare used his genius for a new kind of motivation. By harkening back to Genesis he found a means to make a dramatic virtue out of a plot necessity without rushing into either melodrama or morality.

And what is Mr. Lever's alternative? ". . . Shylock is changed from the traditional Jewish usurer to a man challenging the pattern of recognized values." Later, "Shylock bases his plea on the laws of Venice, which, in this Christian but highly commercialized state, recognize neither love nor human fellowship as valid principles." But have Antonio, Bassanio, and Portia (or even the Duke, as far as we know) ever recognized the letter of the law as more important than the spirit? As soon as Shylock loses the upper hand, the court in which he stressed justice immediately becomes a court of mercy. No one in the play is as guilty as Shylock is of the accumulated nasty charges that he makes. Had Shylock's intentions been to test values, I cannot believe that Shakespeare would have left him without a Venetian deserving of his attack.

The play remains for me a romantic comedy in which the chief (but not the exclusive) ideational protagonist is the Merchant of Venice (the symbol of the Renaissance ideal of friendship). I feel, however, that Shakespeare gave us many extras to the main theme, one of these being Shylock's symbolic identification of himself with Jacob. Should it surprise that with Shakespeare the play, rather than any overall theme, is the thing? (pp. 387-88)

> Norman Nathan, "Rejoinder to Mr. Lever's 'Shylock, Portia, and the Values of Shakespearian Comedy'," in Shakespeare Quarterly, Vol. III, No. 4, October, 1952, pp. 386-88.

B. IFOR EVANS (essay date 1952)

[Evans examines how Shakespeare uses language and imagery in The Merchant of Venice to enhance the romantic elements and unite the varying moods of the play. He also comments on Shakespeare's "control of language" through formal arrangement of certain speeches, such as Portia's on mercy and Shylock's on the humanity of Jews, concluding that in this play "Shakespeare had come to a period when he knew more about language than it was necessary for him immediately to employ." For further commentary on the language and imagery in The Merchant of Venice, see the excerpts by Caroline F. E. Spurgeon (1935) and Sigurd Burckhardt (1962). The following excerpt is taken from Evans's The Language of Shakespeare's Plays, originally published in 1952.]

The language of The Merchant of Venice is somewhat different from the other comedies of [Shakespeare's middle years], though here verse plays a very full part. But it is verse used easily, not exploring new purposes, confidently controlled and well-defined in all that is attempted and accomplished. Verse prescribes the mood in which we accept the play, gathering up the fairy-story of the caskets, the shabbiness of Bassanio's motives and the elements of incipient tragedy of the Shylock and Antonio theme, and holding them united in a charmed and magical world. Shakespeare might be asking that the motives for action should not be examined by the dull and calculating arguments of realism, but that all should be accepted in the rainbow hues of romance which the poetry has provided. Accept the music of the verse, Shakespeare would seem to say with Lorenzo, and all else will become acceptable. . . . (pp. 101-02)

As a result the language has great riches, and wide ranges of experience are claimed by Shakespeare as the resources of his imagery. The language is almost uniformly beautiful. Shylock, it is true, is allowed to explore more closely the harsher elements in life, and Gratiano has the licence of a wit. But in the main, the images of disease, war, strife, all the emphasis on the darker motives for human action are excluded. Deliberately Shakespeare seems to bathe the play in music, to wash it over with a richly emblazoned verse. (p. 102)

This summoning of the resources of romance gains its greatest emphasis in the fifth act where Lorenzo and Jessica rehearse the legends of the classical characters who knew nights similar to the one they were then enjoying:

> The moon shines bright: in such a night as this,
> When the sweet wind did gently kiss the trees
> And they did make no noise, in such a night
> Troilus methinks mounted the Troyan walls
> And sigh'd his soul toward the Grecian tents,
> Where Cressid lay that night.
>
> [V. i. 1-6]

Lorenzo, in this scene, gives the ultimate effect of poetry in this play, disengaging life from all tarnishing influences, all the incidents and motives which ordinarily encourage dismay and despair. Through its music, poetry opens out, as it were, into a world romantic but spiritual, a life that is void of all that is contaminating and sordid:

> Look how the floor of heaven
> Is thick inlaid with patines of bright gold:
> There's not the smallest orb which thou behold'st
> But in his motion like an angel sings,
> Still quiring to the young-eyed cherubins;
> Such harmony is in immortal souls;
> But whilst this muddy vesture of decay
> Doth grossly close it in, we cannot hear it.
>
> [V. i. 58-65]

This is not ordinary existence Shakespeare seems to emphasise, but a moment of brightness created for pleasure. It is as if Portia's lines on her final return to her house were a symbol for the play as a whole:

> That light we see is burning in my hall.
> How far that little candle throws his beams!
> So shines a good deed in a naughty world.
>
> [V. i. 89-91]
> (pp. 102-03)

While the romantic background is so admirably maintained by the verse, there is variety as the action moves from one scene to another. Shylock himself is given a language of realism, often simple, direct and forceful. Shakespeare has learned the power of statement, unadorned with imagery, strong in its own content and movement. . . . (p. 104)

The control of language is emphasised by the number of speeches which have the formal arrangement of an oration. The outstanding example is Portia's 'Mercy' speech. Each phrase has its counterpart, and each sentence is balanced, and so the argument, with its sentiments, is constructed until the whole has a formal and classical strength. Incidentally there are so many competing claimants as the original of this speech that one is driven back upon the hypothesis that perhaps the sentiments are so commonplace that invention was unnecessary, though poetically they are supremely expressed:

> it is twice blest;
> It blesseth him that gives and him that takes:
> 'Tis mightiest in the mightiest: it becomes
> The throned monarch better than his crown.
>
> [IV. i. 186-89]

While Portia's address is the most obvious example, a number of the speeches follow a formal pattern. Thus Shylock's great defence of the Hebrew people gains its strength not through imagery or through an imaginative language, but through simple and direct statements so arranged and repeated that they obtain an effect of profound emotional power. . . . (p. 105)

While these are the two main examples there are a number of speeches which display a formal pattern, used for emphasis and merely for the delight with which the ear receives them. So Portia, even in her talk with Bassanio can set her speech into the rule of triplicity:

> *Happy* in this, she is not yet so old
> But she may learn; *happier* than this,
> She is not bred so dull but she can learn;
>
> *Happiest* of all is that her gentle spirit
> Commits itself to yours to be directed,
> As from her *lord,* her *governor,* her *king.*
>   [III. ii. 160-65]

This formal structure used seriously throughout the play is employed in the last act, light-heartedly, to restore the mood of comedy after the solemnities of the trial scene.

> BASSANIO.   Sweet Portia,
>   If you did know to whom I gave the ring,
>   If you did know for whom I gave the ring
>   And would conceive for what I gave the ring
>   And how unwillingly I left the ring,
>   When nought would be accepted but the ring,
>   You would abate the strength of your displeasure.
>   [V. i. 192-98]

To which Portia replies in a sentence of a similar pattern.

All this emphasises the impression that the language is easily in control and looks back towards Shakespeare's earlier achievement. It is adjusted to the needs both of the scene and the characters. (pp. 105-06)

One of the happiest effects comes from the language connected with the sea, above all of the traffic at sea of ships which merchant adventurers in Venice send from port to port. Much of the action depends on the losses at sea which Antonio, the rich merchant, was believed to have suffered. Antonio's losses cannot find a place in the action itself, and yet they must be present in the minds of the audience. So, from the first scene imagery is employed for this purpose of *definition:* 'Your mind', says Salarino to Antonio, 'is tossing on the ocean';

> There, where your argosies with portly sail,
> Like signiors and rich burghers on the flood,
> Or, as it were, the pageants of the sea,
> Do overpeer the petty traffickers,
> That curtsy to them do them reverence,
> As they fly by them with their woven wings.
>   [I. i. 9-14]
>   (pp. 106-07)

It is all very satisfactory, as if Shakespeare had come to a period when he knew more about language than it was necessary for him immediately to employ. He had forces in reserve. All this would change when he came to the dark comedies and the tragedies. (pp. 107-08)

> B. Ifor Evans, *"The Middle Comedies," in his* The Language of Shakespeare's Plays, *second edition, Methuen & Co. Ltd., 1959, pp. 101-15.*

THEODOR REIK   (essay date 1956)

[*Applying a psychoanalytic methodology to the relationship of Shylock and Antonio in* The Merchant of Venice, *Reik interprets*

the "pound of flesh" demanded in Shylock's bond as "a substitute expression of castration," which he says is itself an exaggeration of the Jewish practice of circumcision. Since during Shakespeare's time circumcision was performed only by Jews, and not Gentiles, Reik regards Shylock's desire to "circumcise" Antonio as the former's demand that the merchant become a Jew. The critic thus sees Shylock's forced conversion at the end of the trial scene as poetically just, since he had earlier made the same demands on Antonio. On a more allegorical level, however, Reik discerns behind Shakespeare's characterization of Shylock and Antonio the figures of the Old Testament God and the Savior Christ, in conflict with each other, the one stern, unmerciful, and vengeful, the other sad, forgiving, and willing to bear the sins of his fellow human beings. This analogy Reik attributes to Shakespeare's unconscious "myth-forming" imagination, which "reached beyond the thoughts and designs known to him, into the region where the great myths and religious legends of the people are born and bred." For other allegorical readings of* The Merchant of Venice, *see the excerpts by Denton J. Snider (1890), Sir Israel Gollancz (1922), Nevill Coghill (1949), Muriel C. Bradbrook (1951), C. L. Barber (1959), E. M. W. Tillyard (1961), Barbara K. Lewalski (1962), and René E. Fortin (1974).*]

While I read the familiar scenes of [*The Merchant of Venice*], I went astray in my thoughts, pursuing fleeting images and impressions. Embryos of ideas, snatches of new thoughts emerged. They were brushed aside, but they recurred and would not let themselves be rejected. These new thoughts all concerned the contrast and conflict of Shylock and Antonio. There was something in the opposition of these two antagonists which I sensed but could not grasp.

This mysterious something transgressed the narrow limitations of the plot about a loan and about a legal argument and counterargument. Something there is unsaid but conveyed. Some concealed meaning is alluded to, but eludes the search of logical and conscious thinking. Shylock and Antonio are, of course, not only this money-lending Jew and that Venetian Merchant, in spite of all individual traits and typical features. They are even more than types, more than the kind and noble Gentile and the malicious son of the old tribe. That intangible and elusive element seems to overlap into an area beyond the individual and the typical. It shatters the frame of the two characters and reaches to the sky. In reading the play, Antonio and Shylock grew in my thoughts to gigantic figures standing against each other silently. I did not know what this transformation meant and I first tried to solve the problem by means of conscious analytic interpretation. (p. 358)

I am certainly not the first analyst who interpreted Shylock's terms, namely, the condition that he can cut a pound of flesh "in what part of your body pleaseth me" [I. iii. 151] as a substitute expression of castration. When later on in the play it is decided the cut should be made from the breast, analytic interpretation will easily understand the mechanism of distortion that operates here and displaces the performance from a part of the body below to above. Only one step is needed to reach the concept that to the Gentile of medieval times the Jew unconsciously typified the castrator because he circumcised male children. Circumcision is, as psychoanalytic experiences teach us, conceived as a milder form of castration. The Jew thus appeared to the Gentiles as a dangerous figure with whom the threat of castration originated. Consciously, to Shakespeare and his contemporaries (as to many of our own time), the Jew appears as a money-taking and -grasping figure who takes financial advantage of the Gentiles. Unconsciously, he is the man who threatens to damage them by cutting off the penis. Because his tribe performs the archaic operation of circumcision, the Jew represents an unconscious danger to the masculinity of the Gentiles. The unconscious factor has to be added to the strange features of his different religious rituals, to the unfamiliar dietary customs and the divergent habits of the foreign minority. If Shylock insists upon cutting out a pound of flesh from Antonio's breast, it is as if he demanded that the Gentile be made a Jew if he cannot pay back the three thousand ducats at the fixed time. Otherwise put: Antonio should submit to the religious ritual of circumcision.

The application of the analytic method is really not needed to arrive at this conclusion. It could be easily reached on another route. At the end of the "comedy" Antonio demands that Shylock should "presently become a Christian." If this is the justified amends the Jew has to make for his earlier condition, it would be according to poetic justice that the Jew be forced to become a Christian after he had insisted that his opponent should become a Jew. Such a retaliation corresponds to the oldest law of the world, to the *ius talionis* [the law of equivalent retaliation] that demands tooth for tooth, eye for eye.

That bit of insight into the concealed meaning of Shylock's demand remained an isolated and trifling scrap of analytic interpretation until it was blended with other impressions. The first impression concerned the character of Shylock.... While I read the play, Shylock's thirst for revenge impressed me more than any other feature of the man. At the same time half-forgotten lines from the Holy Scriptures began to sound in my mind, fragmentary sentences, snatches of lines.... "The Lord will take vengeance on His adversaries" ... "They shall see My vengeance ..." "I will not spare them on the day of vengeance," and others. Yes, the God of the Old Testament is a vindictive God. He has perhaps not only the virtues, but also the vices of the worshipers in whose image He is made.

At a certain moment I was, it seemed, carried away by a fancy or an impression that had gained power over me. It seemed to me that the figure of the God of the Old Testament, Jahweh Himself, looms gigantically behind "the Jew that Shakespeare drew." The mythological figure of the old God reduced to the size of a human creature, diminished and dressed up as a Jewish moneylender? Jahweh, the Lord, who came to earth on the Rialto? But the impression quickly evaporated. It was as if I had, for a moment, seen an apparition in the delusive light of that evening. It reappeared, however, later on.

I then became more interested in another impression that surprised me because it had not been there when I had previously read and seen the play: the lack of characterization of Antonio. If there is a leading character in any Shakespeare play who is less of a personality, is less colorful and less equipped with distinguishing individual traits, I would like to know of it. There is no doubt that Antonio is the leading character. His is the title role of *The Merchant of Venice*, although his opponent steals the show.

What do we know of Antonio? Only that he is kind, loves his friends, is generous to the extent of self-sacrifice and that he is sad.... He is kindliness itself, personified.... He loves his friends, he wants to give his life for his friends.... He is eager to make the supreme self-sacrifice. Greater love hath no man.... He not only suffers, he *is* suffering, grief, sorrow themselves. He is sad. Why? Nobody knows, least of all himself. Is this a shortcoming on the part of the greatest playwright of the world or is there something hidden here, unknown even to the Bard? (pp. 358-61)

While I still ponder over Antonio's mysterious sadness, a line runs through my mind. "He was despised and rejected of men,

a man of sorrows and acquainted with grief." And then: "He hath borne our griefs and carried our sorrows." ... But those are passages from the Holy Scripture! ... How do they now emerge? It occurs to me where and when I heard them last. A friend let me have the records of Handel's *Messiah* a few days ago.

In Act IV, Antonio says:

> I am a tainted wether of the flock,
> Meetest for death.
>
> [IV. i. 114-15]

Actually, he does not awaken interest and sympathy by the person he is, but by what happens to him; not by his personality, but by his destiny. He is, he says, a tainted wether of the flock, destined to die. He is, rather, a lamb. (p. 361)

Antonio's sadness ... the man of sorrow ... the Lamb of God ... destined to die.... He was wounded for our transgressions.... He was bruised for our iniquities.... The scene before the court at Venice.... The readiness to die for others.... Did He not state, "Greater love has no man than this that a man lay down his life for his friend"? ... No, I am not the victim of a delusion. Behind the figure of Antonio is the greater one of Jesus Christ. Again the motif "He was despised and rejected" emerges as if the tune wants to confirm my thought, as if the line from the *Messiah* announced that my concept is correct.

Again there is the image of Antonio and Shylock standing opposite each other, the one all charity and the other no charity at all.... I know now clearly what was in the background of my mind while I read the play, what were the vague impressions that crowded upon me until they became condensed into one leading thought. I am turning the leaves of the volume, and my glance chances upon the lines of Shylock in Act I, where he speaks directly to the noble Venetian merchant:

> Signior Antonio, many a time and oft
> In the Rialto you have rated me
> About my money and my usances.
> Still I have borne it with a patient shrug,
> For sufferance is the badge of our tribe.
> You call me misbeliever, cut-throat dog,
> And spat upon my Jewish gaberdine,
> And all for use of that which is mine own ...
>
> [I. iii. 106-13]

Here is one of the few occasions in which Antonio shows temperament and hate in contrast to his otherwise gentle and weak attitude.... Not a trace of charity and loving-kindness here. Not very Christian, as a matter of fact. This seems to contradict my concept that behind the Gentile merchant the figure of his God is concealed.

But then it occurs to me that this feature does not contradict my thesis. It rather confirms it. Did He not go up to Jerusalem when Passover was at hand and abuse and whip the money-changers and drive them all out of the temple? Did He not pour out their money and overthrow their tables? Behind the treatment Shylock gets from Antonio the features of the primal pattern of the Holy Scripture become apparent.

I do not doubt any more that behind Antonio and Shylock are hidden the great figures of their gods. Here are two small people in Venice, but the shadows they cast are gigantic and their conflict shakes the world. There is the vengeful and zealous God of the Old Testament and the milder Son-God of the

Act III. Scene ii. Portia and Bassanio. By Max Adamo. The Department of Rare Books and Special Collections, The University of Michigan Library.

Gospels who rebelled against His father, suffered death for His revolt, and became God Himself, afterwards. The two Gods are presented and represented in this play by two of their typical worshipers of the playwright's time.

Shakespeare wanted to present a Jewish figure as he and his contemporaries saw it, but the character grew beyond human measure into the realm of the mythical, as if the God of the Jews stood behind the stage. Shakespeare wanted to shape the destiny of a Gentile merchant who almost became the victim of a vengeful, evil Jew, but the unconscious imagination of this writer shattered the thin frame of his plot. The myth-forming fantasy of this man William Shakespeare, his *imagination complète,* as [Hippolyte] Taine says, reached so much farther than his conscious mind. It reached beyond the thoughts and designs known to him, into the region where the great myths and religious legends of the people are born and bred. He wanted only to write a comedy with a plot about the curious case of a Jew who was outjewed. Unconscious memory-traces made him shape the conflict of the two Gods, the holy story as he had absorbed it as a boy. Invisible threads connect *The Merchant of Venice* with the medieval passion plays.

He took the two plots from many sources, the story of the three caskets and the tale of the merchant who got a rough deal from a malicious Jew, and alloyed them into a play. Thus William

saw the Jews as the Toms, Dicks, and Harrys of his time saw them, despised them, and mocked them, and hated them. But something greater than his conscious thought gave that Jew a voice of his own, a rancorous voice that speaks in icy sarcasm, biting and accusing, a voice full of sound and fury, rising in passionate protest and ebbing in utter despair. The creative and re-creative imagination of this man Shakespeare poured into the trivial plot of the three thousand ducats something of the stuff the great myths of people, the dreams of mankind, are made on. He added the figure of Antonio, who was to be cut and mutilated, to the mythical figures of Attis, Adonis, and Jesus Christ, who were torn to pieces. Only small inconspicuous traits, little features overlooked and neglected, invisible or only visible under the microscope of psychoanalytic scrutiny, reveal that behind the trivial figures of the comedy are hidden Jehovah and Jesus, that the real *personae dramatis* are overdimensional. (pp. 363-64)

Theodor Reik, ''Psychoanalytic Experiences in Life, Literature, and Music,'' in his The Search Within: The Inner Experiences of a Psychoanalyst, *1956. Reprint by Funk & Wagnalls, 1968, pp. 331-472.*

JOHN RUSSELL BROWN   (essay date 1957)

[*Brown contends that of all Shakespeare's comedies* The Merchant of Venice *is ''the most completely informed by Shakespeare's ideal of love's wealth.'' He demonstrates how Shakespeare contrasts the free giving of love—the generosity and unselfishness of Antonio, Bassanio, and Portia—with the ''rights of commerce'' exemplified by Shylock. He also notes how the theme of usury is echoed in the casket story, where love, too, is presented as a kind of material transaction, though Portia and Bassanio through marriage ''practice their usury without compulsion, for the joy of giving.'' Brown further examines the trial scene, the episode of the rings, and the final act in Belmont to illustrate how love, through the characters of Antonio, Bassanio, and Portia, is risked, given, multiplied, and—most importantly—possessed. For additional discussion of the characters' use of wealth and love in* The Merchant of Venice, *see the excerpts by Karl Elze (1871), C. L. Barber (1959), and John P. Sisk (1969). The following excerpt is taken from Brown's* Shakespeare and His Comedies, *originally published in 1957.]*

Of all the comedies, *The Merchant of Venice* is the most completely informed by Shakespeare's ideal of love's wealth. Each of Portia's suitors has to choose one of three caskets and he who chooses the one which contains a portrait of Portia, wins her as his bride. Each casket is of a different metal and each bears a motto: one of gold reads 'Who chooseth me shall gain what many men desire', one of silver reads 'Who chooseth me shall get as much as he deserves', and one of lead reads 'Who chooseth me must give and hazard all he hath' [II. vii. 5, 7, 9]. Morocco, the type of those who make their choice in love for the sake of what they will 'gain', chooses gold and finds inside a skull—a reminder that death must cancel all such gain; Arragon, who presumes to take what 'he deserves', finds a fool's head; Bassanio who is willing to 'give and hazard', who does not mind the quality of the casket if he finds Portia within it, chooses lead and wins the bride of his choice. It could not be otherwise if love's true wealth, unlike commercial wealth, should be 'in bounty' cherished, if 'giving', not 'gaining' or 'getting', is essential to love. And so by these contrasts, clearly and formally, the wooing of Portia is related to Shakespeare's ideal.

As in *The Comedy of Errors* and *The Shrew*, this ideal is contrasted with a frankly commercial wealth, but here Shakespeare has broadened his theme. Previously commerce has been presented, in contrast to love, as concerned solely with possession and gain; now Shakespeare shows that it can involve personal relationships as well. Both Shylock and Antonio get their livelihood by commerce, but Antonio is ready to submit the rights of commerce to the claims of love; he lends freely to his friend Bassanio without security, although he has squandered previous loans and although it involves risking his own life by giving a bond to Shylock for a pound of his flesh. This is to 'give and hazard'. In contrast, Shylock, the Jew, demands his rights; repeatedly he claims his due according to the bond, and sees no reason to relent. . . . He is content to cry:

> My deeds upon my head! I crave the law,
> The penalty and forfeit of my bond.
>
> [IV. i. 206-07]

In Shylock's eyes, this is to 'get what he deserves'. Both he and Antonio may be judged by the mottoes on the caskets.

The contrast between these two is emphasized much earlier in the play in a discussion about usury. As Antonio enters to negotiate the bond, Shylock discovers his hatred in an aside:

> I hate him for he is a Christian,
> *But more* for that in low simplicity
> He lends out money gratis and brings down
> The rate of usance here with us in Venice. . . .
>
> [I. iii. 42-5]

Shylock lends only for what he can gain, Antonio for the sake of friendship. . . . (pp. 61-3)

It is sometimes argued that Shylock's affairs are so far removed in kind from the affairs of the lovers at Belmont, that the play falls into two parts. But, in one way the play is very closely knit, for, besides contrasting Shylock with Antonio, the discussion about usury is yet another contrast between him and Portia and Bassanio. . . . Shakespeare saw love as a kind of usury, and so in their marriage Bassanio and Portia put Nature's bounty to its proper 'use'. Shylock practises a usury for the sake of gain and is prepared to enforce his rights; the lovers practice their usury without compulsion, for the joy of giving. . . . As soon as Bassanio has chosen the right casket, being ready to 'give and hazard all', Portia knows love's 'increase':

> O love,
> Be moderate; allay thy ecstasy;
> In measure rein thy joy; scant this *excess*.
> I feel too much thy blessing: make it less,
> For fear I surfeit.
>
> [III. ii. 111-14]
> (p. 64)

The comparison of the two usuries is part of a more general comparison of commerce and love which is likewise maintained throughout the play. From the beginning Bassanio's quest has been described in commercial terms; indeed, he might have equal claim with Antonio and Shylock for the title of 'The Merchant of Venice'. To Antonio he outlines his plans as a means of getting 'clear of all the debts' he owes [I. i. 134], trying, with little success, to present his intention of paying court to Portia as a good business proposition. Antonio tells him that all this is unnecessary, that such values are inappropriate to friendship, and thereupon Bassanio changes his tone, praising Portia in the 'innocence' [I. i. 145] of his love: she is indeed rich, and—

> . . . she is fair *and,* fairer than that word,
> Of wondrous virtues. . . .
>
> [I. i. 162-63]

He '*values*' her as Cato's daughter, renowned for constancy and virtue, and her 'sunny locks' are as the '*golden* fleece' [I. i. 169, 170] for which Jason ventured. . . . In Bassanio's description of Portia there is a curious, but, to those who trade in love, a natural, confusion of her wealth, beauty, and virtue; all these comprise her wealth in love. In Bassanio's eyes she has all perfections, and, amazed by them, he sees no obstacle to his fortune:

> I have a mind presages me such *thrift*,
> That I should questionless be *fortunate!*
>
> [I. i. 175-76]

When Bassanio has chosen the right casket, and comes 'by note, to give and to receive', Portia responds in similarly commercial terms:

> You see me, Lord Bassanio, where I stand,
> Such as I am: though for myself alone
> I would not be ambitious in my wish,
> To wish myself much better; yet, for you
> I would be trebled twenty times myself;
> A thousand times more fair, ten thousand times
> More rich . . .
>
> [III. ii. 149-54]

Portia desires greater wealth only for Bassanio's sake:

> That only to stand high in your *account*,
> I might in virtues, beauties, livings, friends,
> *Exceed account* . . .
>
> [III. ii. 155-57]

She cannot possess enough of this kind of wealth to enable her to give as generously as she would wish:

> . . . but the *full sum* of me
> Is sum of something, which, to *term in gross*,
> Is an unlesson'd girl . . .
>
> [III. ii. 157-59]

Bassanio's willingness to give and hazard is answered by Portia's giving, and the contract of love is complete. So the willing, generous, and prosperous transactions of love's wealth are compared and contrasted with Shylock's wholly commercial transactions in which gain is the object, enforcement the method, and even human beings are merely things to be possessed.

Normally in Shakespeare's early narrative comedies, hero and heroine are betrothed at the end of the very last scene of the play where there is little time for the expression of sentiment; *The Merchant of Venice* is the major exception to this, presenting Portia's modest, eager, rich-hearted committal to Bassanio in the third act. In consequence, Shakespeare is not only able to show how love's wealth is risked, given, and multiplied, but also how it is possessed. At the end of Portia's speech of self-giving, she 'commits' herself to Bassanio. . . . All her wealth is made over as if it were a commercial possession:

> Myself and what is mine to you and yours
> Is now *converted:* but now I was the lord
> Of this fair mansion, master of my servants,
> Queen o'er myself; and even now, but now,
> This house, these servants and this same myself
> *Are yours,* my lord: I *give* them with this ring. . . .
>
> [III. ii. 166-71]

Bassanio is told never to part with the ring, and in his confused joy, he can only swear that he will keep it for life. The story of Portia and Bassanio is by no means complete at this point; love is not like merchandise, it is not simply a question of possessor and possessed.

This is at once apparent: when news comes that Shylock is about to enforce the penalty to which his bond entitles him, Portia finds she has yet more to give; she is ready to forgo wealth and delay her marriage rights, and she urges Bassanio to leave for Venice before nightfall. A line sums up her response:

> Since you are *dear bought*, I will love you *dear*.
>
> [III. ii. 313]

[This line] expresses Portia's willingness to continue to give joyfully in love. In the commerce of love, giving is the secret of keeping as well as of gaining.

Under this impulse, Portia herself goes to Venice and, disguised as a lawyer, defeats Shylock's claims. For this service she refuses payment:

> He is well paid that is well satisfied;
> And I, delivering you, am satisfied
> And therein do *account* myself well *paid:*
> My mind was never yet more *mercenary*.
>
> [IV. i. 415-18]

Not recognizing Portia in the young lawyer, Antonio and Bassanio cannot know how deeply he is satisfied, how 'dearly' he has given; they do not know that he has acted with love's bounty. Portia chooses to bring this to their knowledge by the trick of asking Bassanio for the ring she gave him at their betrothal. At first he refuses because of his vow, but when he is left alone with Antonio, his love for this friend persuades him to send the ring to the young lawyer. This twist in the plot is resolved in the last act, and still further illustrates the kind of possession which is appropriate for love's wealth.

The act begins with music, and talk of ancient loves and of the harmony of the spheres, but when Portia, Bassanio, and Antonio enter, all harmony seems threatened by a quarrel over the ring of gold, the symbol of possession. They now talk about unfaithfulness, adultery, and cuckoldry. Bassanio's story is most unplausible and he is in a difficult position. . . . Bassanio can only say that he was unable to refuse the one

> . . . that did uphold the very life
> Of my dear friend. . . .
> I was beset with shame and courtesy;
> My honour would not let ingratitude
> So much besmear it.
>
> [V. i. 214-15, 217-19]

But when Antonio interjects that he is willing to 'be bound again', with his 'soul upon the forfeit', that Bassanio will 'never more break faith advisedly' [V. i. 251-53], Portia returns the ring, and perplexity is soon resolved. And Bassanio is soon pardoned, for he has erred only through generosity to his friend. The whole episode is a lighthearted reminder that Portia has saved Antonio's life, and that the claim of generosity must always rank as high as that of possession.

The bawdy talk, which the misunderstandings provoke, also serves an important purpose; hitherto Bassanio and Portia have conducted their courtship and love in unsensual terms, almost as if the body was always a quietly acquiesing follower of the mind and spirit, but the manner in which they weather the disagreement about the ring shows that their love is appropriate to the world as well as to Belmont, the 'beautiful mountain' of a fairy-tale. The wealth of love, although it exists in the free giving of both parties to the contract and is possessed by neither one of them, has yet to be kept safe and guarded: so the blunt, unromantic Gratiano who has been as merrily fooled by Nerissa as Bassanio has been by Portia, finishes the play:

> Well, while I live I'll fear no other thing
> So sore as keeping safe Nerissa's ring.
>
> [V. i. 306-07]

After the ring episode, we know that Bassanio and Portia will be equally wise. If *The Merchant of Venice* is seen as a play about Shakespeare's ideal of love's wealth, this last act is a fitting sequel to the discord of the trial scene where love and generosity confront hatred and possessiveness; it suggests the way in which love's wealth may be enjoyed continually. (pp. 64-70)

[But] Shakespeare has not simply contrived a contrast of black and white, a measured interplay of abstract figures with every detail fitting neatly into a predetermined pattern; the lovers are not all paragons and Shylock's cry for revenge is not without a 'kind of wild justice'. Judged against Shakespeare's ideal of love's wealth we cannot doubt on which side our sympathies should rest, but such final harmony is only established after we have judged, as in life, between mixed motives and imperfect responses. Even when the central theme has been recognized, *The Merchant of Venice* is not an 'easy' play; it presents an action to which we must respond as to a golden ideal, and also as to a human action.

We have already noticed Shakespeare's achievement of this double purpose in dialogue; for example, when Portia gives herself to Bassanio Shakespeare has not provided a well-rounded expression of generosity in love for her to utter; her speech also embodies modesty, eagerness, and a gathering confidence, feelings that in a human context must attend such generosity. Action and dialogue are allied to the same end; so Shakespeare presented Bassanio's ill-judged attempt to justify his venture in commercial terms and followed that by his confused description of Portia's wealth, at first formal, then quickening, glowing, almost boasting, and, finally, blindly confident. Such technique does not simply present a theoretical ideal of love's adventurer, but a human being, fearful and eager, inspired and embarrassed as he realizes the possibilities of love's wealth. In human terms his is a difficult role, for he must feel the confusion of one who asks:

> . . . how do I hold thee by thy *granting?*
> And for that *riches* where is my deserving?
> [Sonnet 87]

For the role of Bassanio the 'humanizing' of action and dialogue has been so thorough that its ideal implications are in some danger of being obscured. Some critics have discounted the embarrassment of love's largess and, because of his roundabout approach to Antonio, have called Bassanio a heartless 'fortune-hunter'—and in doing so they have failed to see the balance and judgement of the play as a whole.

Shylock is in greatest danger of causing such misinterpretation. This is truly surprising, for in order to bring generosity and possessiveness into intense conflict Shakespeare has made him perpetrate the outrageous deeds of some fantastic villain whom we might expect to see punished without compunction. Moreover Shylock is a Jew and therefore, for an Elizabethan audience, one of an exotic, fabulous race to whom cunning, malice, and cruelty were natural satisfactions; Jews lived obscurely in Shakespeare's London, but in literature and popular imagination they were monstrous bogeys from strange, far-off places and times, fit only to be reviled or mocked. Shakespeare exploited both Shylock's irrational, or devilish, motivation and the outrage of his action, but he has presented him in such a way that an audience can find itself implicated in his inhuman demands. Shakespeare seems to have done everything in his power to encourage this reaction. Our revulsion from Shylock's hatred and cruelty is mitigated by the way in which his opponents goad and taunt him; we might suppose that he was driven to excessive hatred only through their persecution. Shakespeare also arranged that he should voice his grievances and plead his case in the play's most obviously lively and impassioned dialogue. This treatment is so successful that when Shylock tries to justify his murderous purpose, some critics have believed that he is making a grand, though tortured, plea for human tolerance. But to go to such lengths of sympathy for Shylock is to neglect the contrasts and comparisons implicit in the play as a whole; we must judge his actions against a purposefully contrasted generosity in love as portrayed by Antonio, Portia, Bassanio, and others. Indeed we may guess that it was in order to make this contrast lively and poignant that Shakespeare has laboured to implicate us in Shylock's hatred, frustration, and pain.

The outcome of the comparison cannot be long in question for judged by Shakespeare's ideal of love's wealth as expressed here and in other comedies, the sonnets and *Romeo and Juliet,* we cannot doubt that Shylock must be condemned. However lively Shylock's dialogue may be, however plausibly and passionately he presents his case, however cruelly the lovers treat him, he must still be defeated, because he is an enemy to love's wealth and its free, joyful, and continual giving. . . . (pp. 71-3)

But this judgement cannot be made lightly; the mirror that Shakespeare held up to nature was unsparing in its truth, and, by presenting his ideal in human terms, he has shown that those who oppose the fortunes of lovers are apt to get more than justice as punishment at their hands. It is Shylock's fate to bring out the worst in those he tries to harm: the 'good Antonio' shows unfeeling contempt towards him, the light-hearted Salerio and Solanio become wantonly malicious when they meet him, and Portia, once she has turned the trial against him, wounds him still further with sarcastic humour. The trial scene shows that the pursuit of love's wealth does not necessarily bring with it a universal charity, a love which reaches even to one's enemies. The balance is fairly kept, for Antonio and the Duke magnanimously spare Shylock's life and this is thrown into relief by the irresponsible malice of Gratiano.

Shakespeare does not enforce a moral in this play—his judgement is implicit only—but as the action ends in laughter and affection at Belmont we know that each couple, in their own way, have found love's wealth. We know too that their happiness is not all that we would wish; as they make free with Shylock's commercial wealth, we remember that they lacked the full measure of charity towards one who, through his hatred and possessiveness, had got his choice of that which he deserved. *The Merchant of Venice* presents in human and dramatic terms Shakespeare's ideal of love's wealth, its abundant and sometimes embarrassing riches; it shows how this wealth is gained and possessed by giving freely and joyfully; it shows also how destructive the opposing possessiveness can become, and how it can cause those who traffic in love to fight blindly for their existence. (pp. 73-4)

John Russell Brown, "Love's Wealth and the Judgement of 'The Merchant of Venice'," in his Shakespeare and His Comedies, second edition, Methuen & Co. Ltd., 1962, pp. 45-81.

C. L. BARBER   (essay date 1959)

[*An American scholar, Barber is one of the most important contemporary critics of Shakespearean comedy. In his influential study,* Shakespeare's Festive Comedy *(1959), Barber examines the parallels between Elizabethan holiday celebrations and Shakespeare's comedies. In the introduction, Barber states that the festival customs and the comic plays both contain a saturnalian pattern involving "a basic movement which can be summarized in the formula, through release to clarification." Barber defines release as a revelry, a mirthful liberation, "an accession of wanton vitality" over the restraint imposed by everyday life; the clarification that follows he characterizes as a "heightened awareness of the relation between man and 'nature'," which in comedy "puts holiday in perspective with life as a whole." In the following excerpt, Barber maintains that* The Merchant of Venice "*dramatizes the conflict between the mechanisms of wealth and the masterful, social use of it," an assessment similarly voiced by Karl Elze (1871), John Russell Brown (1957), and John P. Sisk (1969). He describes Shylock as a comic figure, though dramatic and threatening throughout the play, who symbolizes "the ogre of money power" and "the impersonal logic, the mechanism, involved in the control of money''; the Venetians he characterizes as members of a ''humanly knit group,'' men and women who use their ''civilized wealth'' to achieve social solidarity, as exemplified in the image of Belmont. Barber devotes the remainder of his study to an examination of how the final scenes—Shylock's ''bafflement'' and the so-called happy ending—work to remove the threat against the Venetian world and establish the triumph of comedy. Like such other critics as Denton J. Snider (1890), Sir Israel Gollancz (1922), Nevill Coghill (1949), Muriel C. Bradbrook (1951), Theodor Reik (1956), E. M. W. Tillyard (1961), Barbara K. Lewalski (1962), and René E. Fortin (1974), Barber also notes the conflict between Old and New Testament views— the struggle between justice and mercy—in the trial scene. In addition, he comments on the final act in Belmont, claiming that no other early Shakespearean comedy ''ends with so full an expression of harmony as that which we get in . . . The Merchant of Venice.'' Further commentary on the significance of Act V and the so-called ring episode can be found in the essays by August Wilhelm Schlegel (1811), William Hazlitt (1817), Anna Brownell Jameson (1833), G. G. Gervinus (1849-50), Harley Granville-Barker (1930), Barbara K. Lewalski (1962), A. D. Moody (1964), James E. Siemon (1970), R. Chris Hassel, Jr. (1970), Richard Horwich (1977), Alice N. Benston (1979), and Anne Parten (1982).]*

The Merchant of Venice as a whole is not shaped by festivity in the relatively direct way [we find] . . . in *Love's Labour's Lost* and *A Midsummer Night's Dream*. . . . [The plot] is based on story materials and worked out with much more concern for events, for what happens next, than there is in the two previous comedies. . . . The play's large structure is developed from traditions which are properly theatrical; it is not a theatrical adaptation of a social ritual. And yet analogies to social occasions and rituals prove to be useful in understanding the symbolic action. I shall be pursuing such analogies without suggesting, in most cases, that there is a direct influence from the social to the theatrical form. Shakespeare here is working with autonomous mastery, developing a style of comedy that makes a festive form for feeling and awareness out of all the theatrical elements, scene, speech, story, gesture, role which his astonishing art brought into organic combination.

Invocation and abuse, poetry and railing, romance and ridicule—we have seen repeatedly how such complementary gestures go to the festive celebration of life's powers, along with the complementary roles of revellers and kill-joys, wits and butts, insiders and intruders. What is mocked, what kind of intruder disturbs the revel and is baffled, depends on what particular sort of beneficence is being celebrated. *The Merchant of Venice*, as its title indicates, exhibits the beneficence of civilized wealth, the something-for-nothing which wealth gives to those who use it graciously to live together in a humanly knit group. It also deals, in the role of Shylock, with anxieties about money, and its power to set men at odds. . . . Shylock's name has become a byword because of the superb way that he embodies the evil side of the power of money, its ridiculous and pernicious consequences in anxiety and destructiveness. In creating him and setting him over against Antonio, Bassanio, Portia, and the rest, Shakespeare was making distinctions about the use of riches, not statically, of course, but dynamically, as distinctions are made when a social group sorts people out, or when an organized social ritual does so. Shylock is the opposite of what the Venetians are; but at the same time he is an embodied irony, troublingly like them. So his role is like that of the scapegoat . . . , a figure in whom the evils potential in a social organization are embodied, recognized and enjoyed during a period of licence, and then in due course abused, ridiculed, and expelled.

The large role of the antagonist in *The Merchant of Venice* complicates the movement through release to clarification: instead of the single outgoing of *A Midsummer Night's Dream*, there are two phases. Initially there is a rapid, festive movement by which gay youth gets something for nothing, Lorenzo going masquing to win a Jessica gilded with ducats, and Bassanio sailing off like Jason to win the golden fleece in Belmont. But all this is done against a background of anxiety. We soon forget all about Egeus' threat in *A Midsummer Night's Dream*, but we are kept aware of Shylock's malice by a series of interposed scenes. . . . We are conscious that running on the score with Shylock is a very dangerous business, and no sooner is the joyous triumph accomplished at Belmont than Shylock's malice is set loose. It is only after the threat he poses has been met that the redemption of the prodigal can be completed by a return to Belmont.

The key question in evaluating the play is how this threat is met, whether the baffling of Shylock is meaningful or simply melodramatic. Certainly the plot, considered in outline, seems merely a prodigal's dream coming true: to have a rich friend who will set you up with one more loan so that you can marry a woman both beautiful and rich, girlishly yielding and masterful; and on top of that to get rid of the obligation of the loan because the old money bags from whom your friend got the money is proved to be so villainous that he does not deserve to be paid back! If one adds humanitarian and democratic indignation at anti-semitism, it is hard to see, from a distance, what there can be to say for the play: Shylock seems to be made a scapegoat in the crudest, most dishonest way. One can apologize for the plot, as Middleton Murry and Granville-Barker do [see excerpts above, 1936 and 1930], by observing that it is based on a fairy-story sort of tale, and that Shakespeare's method was not to change implausible story material, but to invent characters and motives which would make it acceptable and credible, moment by moment, on the stage. But it is inadequate to praise the play for delightful and poetic incoherence. . . . As I see it, [Shakespeare] has expressed important things about the relations of love and hate to wealth. When he kept to old tales, he not only made plausible protagonists for them, but also, at any rate when his luck held, he brought up into a social focus deep symbolic meanings. Shylock is an ogre, as Middleton Murry said, but he is the ogre of money power. The old tale of the pound of flesh involved taking literally the proverbial metaphors about money-lenders ''taking it out of the hide'' of their victims, eating them up. Shakespeare keeps the unrealistic literal business, knife-sharpening and all; we accept it, because he makes it express real human attitudes:

> If I can catch him once upon the hip,
> I will feed fat the ancient grudge I bear him.
>
> [I. iii. 46-7]

So too with the fairy-story caskets at Belmont: Shakespeare makes Bassanio's prodigal fortune meaningful as an expression of the triumph of human, social relations over the relations kept track of by accounting. The whole play dramatizes the conflict between the mechanisms of wealth and the masterful, social use of it. The happy ending, which abstractly considered as an event is hard to credit, and the treatment of Shylock, which abstractly considered as justice is hard to justify, *work* as we actually watch or read the play because these events express relief and triumph in the achievement of a distinction.

To see how this distinction is developed, we need to attend to the tangibles of imaginative design which are neglected in talking about plot. So, in the two first scenes, it is the seemingly incidental, random talk that establishes the gracious, opulent world of the Venetian gentlemen and of the "lady richly left" [I. i. 161] at Belmont, and so motivates Bassanio's later success. Wealth in this world is something profoundly social, and it is relished without a trace of shame when Salerio and Solanio open the play by telling Antonio how rich he is. . . . What is crucial is the ceremonial, social feeling for wealth. Salerio and Solanio do Antonio reverence just as the petty traffickers of the harbor salute his ships, giving way to leave him "with better company" [I. i. 59] when Bassanio and Gratiano arrive. He stands at ease, courteous, relaxed, melancholy (but not about his fortunes, which are too large for worry), while around him moves a shifting but close-knit group who "converse and waste the time together" [III. iv. 12], make merry, speak "an infinite deal of nothing" [I. i. 114], propose good times: "Good signiors, both, when shall we laugh? say, when?" [I. i. 66]. When Bassanio is finally alone with the royal merchant, he opens his mind with

> To you, Antonio,
> I owe the most, in money and in love.
>
> [I. i. 130-31]

Mark Van Doren . . . notes how these lines summarize the gentleman's world where "there is no incompatibility between money and love." So too, one can add, in this community there is no conflict between enjoying Portia's beauty and her wealth: "her sunny locks / Hang on her temples like a golden fleece" [I. i. 169-70]. When, a moment later, we see Portia mocking her suitors, the world suggested is, again, one where standards are urbanely and humanly social: the sad disposition of the county Palatine is rebuked because (unlike Antonio's) it is "unmannerly." Yet already in the first scene, though Shylock is not in question yet, the anxiety that dogs wealth is suggested. In the lines [at I. i. 29-36] . . . , Salerio's mind moves from attending church—from safety, comfort and solidarity—through the playful association of the "holy edifice of stone" with "dangerous rocks," to the thought that the sociable luxuries of wealth are vulnerable to impersonal forces:

> rocks,
> Which, touching but my gentle vessel's side,
> Would scatter all her spices on the stream,
> Enrobe the roaring waters with my silks . . .
>
> [I. i. 31-4]

The destruction of what is cherished, of the civic and personal, by ruthless impersonal forces is sensuously immediate in the wild waste of shining silk on turbulent water, one of the magic, summary lines of the play. (pp. 166-71)

When Shylock comes on in the third scene, the easy, confident flow of colorful talk and people is checked by a solitary figure and an unyielding speech.

> *Shylock.* Three thousand ducats—well.
> *Bassanio.* Ay, sir, for three months.
> *Shylock.* For three months—well.
> *Bassanio.* For the which, as I told you, Antonio shall be bound.
> *Shylock.* Antonio shall become bound—well.
> *Bassanio.* May you stead me? Will you pleasure me? Shall I know your answer?
> *Shylock.* Three thousand ducats for three months, and Antonio bound. . . .
>
> [I. iii. 1-10]

[Shylock's] deliberation expresses the impersonal logic, the mechanism, involved in the control of money. Those *well's* are wonderful in the way they bring bland Bassanio up short. Bassanio assumes that social gestures can brush aside such consideration:

> *Shylock.* Antonio is a good man.
> *Bassanio.* Have you heard any imputation to the contrary?
> *Shylock.* Ho, no, no, no, no! My meaning in saying he is a good man, is to have you understand me that he is sufficient.
>
> [I. iii. 12-17]

The laugh is on Bassanio as Shylock drives his hard financial meaning of "good man" right through the center of Bassanio's softer social meaning. The Jew goes on to calculate and count. He connects the hard facts of money with the rocky sea hazards of which we have so far been only picturesquely aware: "ships are but boards" [I. iii. 22]; and he betrays his own unwillingness to take the risks proper to commerce: "and other ventures he hath, squand'red abroad" [I. iii. 21]. . . . The Jew in this encounter expresses just the things about money which are likely to be forgotten by those who have it, or presume they have it, as part of a social station. He stands for what we mean when we say that "money is money." So Shylock makes an ironic comment—and *is* a comment, by virtue of his whole tone and bearing—on the folly in Bassanio which leads him to confuse those two meanings of "good man," to ask Shylock to dine, to use in this business context such social phrases as "Will you *pleasure* me?" [I. iii. 7]. When Antonio joins them, Shylock (after a soliloquy in which his plain hatred has glittered) becomes a pretender to fellowship, with an equivocating mask:

> *Shylock.* This is kind I offer.
> *Bassanio.* This were kindness.
> *Shylock.* This kindness will I show.
>
> [I. iii. 142-43]

We are of course in no doubt as to how to take the word "kindness" when Shylock proposes "in a merry sport" [I. iii. 145] that the penalty be a pound of Antonio's flesh.

In the next two acts, Shylock and the accounting mechanism which he embodies are crudely baffled in Venice and rhapsodically transcended in Belmont. The solidarity of the Venetians includes the clown, in whose part Shakespeare can use conventional blacks and whites about Jews and misers without asking us to take them too seriously. . . . Even the street urchins can mock Shylock after the passion which "the dog Jew did utter in the streets" [II. viii. 14]. . . . (pp. 172-73)

The simplest way to describe what happens at Belmont is to say that Bassanio is lucky; but Shakespeare gives a great deal of meaning to his being lucky. His choosing of the casket might be merely theatrical; but the play's handling of the age-old story motif makes it an integral part of the expression of relations between people and possessions. Most of the argument about gold, silver, and lead is certainly factitious, even tedious. It must necessarily be so, because the essence of a lottery is a discontinuity, something hidden so that the chooser cannot get from here to there by reasoning. Nerissa makes explicit a primitive notion of divination:

> Your father was ever virtuous; and holy men
> at their death have good inspirations. Therefore
> the lott'ry that he hath devised in these three

chests of gold, silver, and lead, whereof who
chooses his meaning chooses you, will no doubt
never be chosen by any rightly but one who
shall rightly love.

[I. ii. 27-33]

The elegant phrasing does not ask us to take the proposition
very seriously, but Nerissa is pointing in the direction of a
mystery. Part of the meaning is that love is not altogether a
matter of the will, however willing. Portia recognizes this even
when her heart is in her mouth as Bassanio is about to choose:

Away then! I am lock'd in one of them.
If you do love me, you will find me out.
Nerissa and the rest, stand all aloof.
Let music sound while he doth make his choice . . .

[III. ii. 40-3]

The song, "Tell me, where is fancy bred" [III. ii. 63ff.],
serves to emphasize the break, the speechless pause while Bassanio chooses. The notion that it serves as a signal to warn
Bassanio off gold and silver is one of those busy-body emendations which eliminate the dramatic in seeking to elaborate
it. The dramatic point is precisely that there is no signal: "Who
chooseth me must give and hazard all he hath" [II. vii. 9]. . . .
(p. 174)

If we look across for a moment at Shylock, thinking through
opposites as the play's structure invites us to do, his discussion
with Antonio about the "thrift" of Jacob and the taking of
interest proves to be relevant to the luck of the caskets. Antonio
appeals to the principle that interest is wrong because it involves
no risk [I. iii. 91-3]. . . . Antonio's loan is venture capital. It
fits with this conception that Bassanio, when at Belmont he
goes "to my fortune and the caskets," turns away from money,
from "gaudy gold, / Hard food for Midas," and from silver,
the "pale and common drudge / 'Tween man and man" [III.
ii. 101-04]. Money is not used to get money; that is the usurer's
way. . . . Instead Bassanio's borrowed purse is invested in life—
including such lively things as the "rare new liveries" [II. ii.
109] that excite Launcelot, and the "gifts of rich value" [II.
ix. 91] which excite Nerissa. . . . (pp. 174-75)

With the money, Bassanio invests *himself,* and so risks losing
himself—as has to be the case with love. (Antonio's commitment of his body for his friend is in the background.) It is a
limitation of the scene where he makes his choice that the risk
has to be conveyed largely by the poetry, since the outward
circumstances are not hazardous. . . . But the moment of choice
is expressed in terms that point beyond feelings to emphasize
discontinuity; they convey the experience of being lost and
giddily finding oneself again in a new situation. . . . This poetry
is remarkable for the conscious way that it describes being
carried beyond expression, using words to tell of being beyond
them. The lines in which Portia gives herself and her possessions to Bassanio make explicit, by an elaborate metaphor of
accounting, that what is happening sets the accounting principle
aside:

You see me, Lord Bassanio, where I stand,
Such as I am. Though for myself alone
I would not be ambitious in my wish
To wish myself much better, yet for you
I would be trebled twenty times myself,
A thousand times more fair, ten thousand times more
rich,
That, only to stand high in your account,

*Act III. Scene ii. Gratiano, Nerissa, Portia, and Bassanio.
By H. Fradelle. The Department of Rare Books and Special
Collections, The University of Michigan Library.*

I might in virtues, beauties, livings, friends,
Exceed account. But the full sum of me
Is sum of nothing, which, to term in gross,
Is an unlesson'd girl, unschool'd, unpractic'd. . . .

[III. ii. 149-59]

This is extravagant, and extravagantly modest, as fits the moment; but what is telling is the way the lines move from possessions, through the paradox about sums, to the person in the
midst of them all, "where I stand," who cannot be added up.
It is she that Bassanio has won, and with her a way of living
for which his humanity, breeding, and manhood can provide
a center. . . . (pp. 175-77)

The possessions *follow* from this human, social relation.

But the accounting mechanism which has been left behind by
Bassanio and Portia has gone on working, back at Venice, to
put Antonio at Shylock's mercy, and the anxiety it causes has
to be mastered before the marriage can be consummated. . . .
(p. 177)

Shylock repeatedly states . . . that he is only finishing what
the Venetians started. He can be a drastic ironist, because he
carries to extremes what is present, whether acknowledged or
not, in their silken world. He insists that money is money—
and they cannot do without money either. So too with the rights
of property. The power to give freely, which absolute property
confers and Antonio and Portia so splendidly exhibit, is also
a power to refuse, as Shylock so logically refuses. . . . Shylock
seems a juggernaut that nothing can stop, armed as he is against
a pillar of society by the principles of society itself: "If you
deny me, fie upon your law! . . . I stand for judgement. Answer. Shall I have it?" [IV. i. 101, 103]. Nobody does answer
him here, directly; instead there is an interruption for Portia's

276

entrance. To answer him is the function of the whole dramatic action, which is making a distinction that could not be made direct, logical argument.

Let us follow this dramatic action from its comic side. Shylock is comic, so far as he is so, because he exhibits what should be human, degraded into mechanism. The reduction of life to mechanism goes with the miser's wary calculation, with the locking up, with the preoccupation with "that which is mine own" [I. iii. 113]. . . . Antonio has to live inside some sort of rich man's melancholy, but at least he communicates with the world through outgoing Bassanio (and, one can add, through the commerce which takes his fortunes out to sea). Shylock, by contrast, who breeds barren metal, wants to keep "the vile squeeling of the wryneck'd fife" [II. v. 30] out of his house, and speaks later, in a curiously revealing, seemingly random illustration, of men who "when the bagpipe sings i'th'nose, / Cannot contain their urine" [IV. i. 49-50]. Not only is he closed up tight inside himself, but after the first two scenes, we are scarcely allowed by his lines to feel with him. And we never encounter him alone; he regularly comes on to join a group whose talk has established an outside point of view towards him. This perspective on him does not exclude a potential pathos. There is always potential pathos, behind, when drama makes fun of isolating, anti-social qualities. Indeed, the process of *making fun of* a person often works by exhibiting pretensions to humanity so as to show that they are inhuman, mechanical, not validly appropriate for sympathy. With a comic villain such as Shylock, the effect is mixed in various degrees between our responding to the mechanism as menacing and laughing at it as ridiculous.

So in the great scene in which Solanio and Salerio taunt Shylock, the potentiality of pathos produces effects which vary between comedy and menace:

> *Shylock.* You knew, none so well, none so
> well as you, of my daughter's flight.
> *Salerio.* That's certain. I, for my part, knew
> the tailor that made the wings she flew withal.
> [III. i. 24-7]

Shylock's characteristic repetitions, and the way he has of moving ahead through similar, short phrases, as though even with language he was going to use only what was his own, can give an effect of concentration and power, or again, an impression of a comically limited, isolated figure. In the great speech of self-justification to which he is goaded by the two bland little gentlemen, the iteration conveys the energy of anguish:

> —and what's his reason? I am a Jew. Hath not a Jew eyes? Hath not a Jew hands, organs, dimensions, senses, affections, passions? fed with the same food, hurt with the same weapons, subject to the same diseases, healed by the same means, warmed and cooled by the same winter and summer as a Christian is? If you prick us, do we not bleed? If you tickle us, do we not laugh? If you poison us, do we not die? And if you wrong us, shall we not revenge? If we are like you in the rest, we will resemble you in that.
> [III. i. 58-68]

Certainly no actor would deliver this speech without an effort at pathos; but it is a pathos which, as the speech moves, converts to menace. And the pathos is qualified, limited, in a way which is badly falsified by humanitarian renderings that open all the stops at "Hath not a Jew hands, etc. . . ." For Shylock thinks to claim only a *part* of humanness, the lower part, physical and passional. . . . The passions in Shylock's speech are conceived as reflexes; the parallel clauses draw them all towards the level of "tickle . . . laugh." The same assumption, that the passions and social responses are mechanisms on a par with a nervous tic, appears in the court scene when Shylock defends his right to follow his "humor" in taking Antonio's flesh [IV. i. 53-61]. . . . The most succinct expression of this assumption about man is Shylock's response to Bassanio's incredulous question:

> *Bassanio.* Do all men kill the things they do not love?
> *Shylock.* Hates any man the thing he would not kill?
> [IV. i. 66-7]

There is no room in this view for mercy to come in between "wrong us" and "shall we not revenge?" As Shylock insists, there is Christian example for him: the irony is strong. But the mechanism of stimulus and response is only a part of the truth. The reductive tendency of Shylock's metaphors, savagely humorous in Iago's fashion, goes with this speaking only the lower part of the truth. He is not cynical in Iago's aggressive way, because as an alien he simply doesn't participate in many of the social ideals which Iago is concerned to discredit in self-justification. But the two villains have the same frightening, ironical power from moral simplification.

Shylock becomes a clear-cut butt at the moments when he is himself caught in compulsive, reflexive responses, when instead of controlling mechanism he is controlled by it: "O my daughter! O my ducats!" [II. viii. 15]. At the end of the scene of taunting [III. i], his menace and his pathos become ridiculous when he dances like a jumping jack in alternate joy and sorrow as Tubal pulls the strings. . . . This is a scene in the dry manner of Marlowe, Jonson, or Molière, a type of comedy not very common in Shakespeare: its abrupt alternations in response convey the effect [Henri] Bergson describes so well in *Le Rire,* where the comic butt is a puppet in whom motives have become mechanisms that usurp life's self-determining prerogative. Some critics have left the rhythm of the scene behind to dwell on the pathos of the ring he had from Leah when he was a bachelor. It is like Shakespeare once to show Shylock putting a gentle sentimental value on something, to match the savage sentimental value he puts on revenge. There *is* pathos; but it is being fed into the comic mill and makes the laughter all the more hilarious.

In the trial scene, the turning point is appropriately the moment when Shylock gets caught in the mechanism he relies on so ruthlessly. He narrows everything down to his roll of parchment and his knife: "Till thou canst rail the seal from off my bond . . ." [IV. i. 139]. But two can play at this game:

> as thou urgest justice, be assur'd
> Thou shalt have justice more than thou desir'st.
> [IV. i. 315-16]

Shylock's bafflement is comic, as well as dramatic, in the degree that we now see through the threat that he has presented, recognizing it to have been, in a degree, unreal. For it is unreal to depend so heavily on legal form, on fixed verbal definition, on the mere machinery by which human relations are controlled. Once Portia's legalism has broken through his legalism, he can only go on the way he started, weakly asking "Is that the law?'' [IV. i. 314] while Gratiano's jeers underscore the comic symmetry:

> A Daniel still say I, a second Daniel!
> I thank thee, Jew, for teaching me that word.
>
> [IV. i. 340-41]

The turning of the tables is not, of course, simply comic, except for the bold, wild and ''skipping spirit'' of Gratiano. The trial scene is a species of drama that uses comic movement in slow motion, with an investment of feeling such that the resolution is in elation and relief colored by amusement, rather than in the evacuation of laughter. . . . The threat Shylock offers is, after all, drastic, for legal instruments, contract, property are fundamental. Comic dramatists often choose to set them hilariously at naught; but Shakespeare is, as usual, scrupulously responsible to the principles of social order (however factitious his ''law'' may be literally). So he produced a scene which exhibits the limitations of legalism. It works by a dialectic that carries to a more general level what might be comic reduction to absurdity. To be tolerant, because we are all fools; to forgive, because we are all guilty—the two gestures of the spirit are allied, as Erasmus noted in praising the sublime folly of following Christ. Shylock says before the trial ''I'll not be made a soft and dull-ey'd fool'' by ''Christian intercessors'' [III. iii. 14-15]. Now when he is asked how he can hope for mercy if he renders none, he answers: ''What judgement shall I dread, doing no wrong?'' [IV. i. 89]. As the man who will not acknowledge his own share of folly ends by being more foolish than anyone else, so Shylock, who will not acknowledge a share of guilt, ends by being more guilty—and more foolish, to judge by results. An argument between Old Testament legalism and New Testament reliance on grace develops as the scene goes forward. (Shylock's references to Daniel in this scene, and his constant use of Old Testament names and allusions, contribute to the contrast.) Portia does not deny the bond—nor the law behind it; instead she makes such a plea as St. Paul made to his compatriots:

> Therefore, Jew,
> Though justice be thy plea, consider this—
> That, in the course of justice, none of us
> Should see salvation. We do pray for mercy,
> And that same prayer doth teach us all to render
> The deeds of mercy.
>
> [IV. i. 197-202]

Mercy becomes the word that gathers up everything we have seen the Venetians enjoying in their reliance on community. What is on one side an issue of principles is on the other a matter of social solidarity: Shylock is not one of the ''we'' Portia refers to, the Christians who say in the Lord's Prayer ''Forgive us our debts as we forgive our debtors.'' All through the play the word Christian has been repeated, primarily in statements that enforce the fact that the Jew is outside the easy bonds of community. Portia's plea for mercy is a sublime version of what in less intense circumstances, among friends of a single communion, can be conveyed with a shrug or a wink. . . . Comedy, in one way or another, is always asking for amnesty, after showing the moral machinery of life getting in the way of life. The machinery as such need not be dismissed—Portia is very emphatic about not doing that. But social solidarity, resting on the buoyant force of a collective life that transcends particular mistakes, can set the machinery aside. Shylock, closed off as he is, clutching his bond and his knife, cannot trust this force, and so acts only on compulsion. . . . It has been in giving and taking, beyond the compulsion of accounts, that Portia, Bassanio, Antonio have enjoyed the something-for-nothing that Portia . . . summarizes in speaking of the gentle rain from heaven.

The troth-plight rings which Bassanio and Gratiano have given away are all that remain of plot to keep the play moving after the trial. It is a slight business, but it gives the women a teasing way to relish the fact that they have played the parts of men as they give up the liberty of that disguise to become wives. And the play's general subject is continued, for in getting over the difficulty, the group provides one final demonstration that human relationships are stronger than their outward signs. Once more, Bassanio expresses a harassed perplexity about obligations in conflict; and Portia gayly pretends to be almost a Shylock about this lover's bond, carrying the logic of the machinery to absurd lengths before showing, by the new gift of the ring, love's power to set debts aside and begin over again.

No other comedy, until the late romances, ends with so full an expression of harmony as that which we get in the opening of the final scene of *The Merchant of Venice*. And no other final scene is so completely without irony about the joys it celebrates. The ironies have been dealt with beforehand in baffling Shylock; in the moment of relief after expelling an antagonist, we do not need to look at the limitations of what we have been defending. . . . The court compels Shylock to breathe his gold and give bounty to Lorenzo. He is plainly told that he is a snudge—and we are off to noble magnificence and frolic at Belmont. No high day is involved, though Shakespeare might easily have staged the solemn festival due after Portia's wedding. Instead Lorenzo and Jessica feel the harmony of the universe and its hospitality to life in a quiet moment of idle talk and casual enjoyment of music. . . . The openness to experience, the images of reaching out towards it, or of welcoming it, letting music ''creep in our ears,'' go with the perception of a gracious universe such as Portia's mercy speech invoked:

> How sweet the moonlight sleeps upon this bank!
> Here will we sit and let the sounds of music
> Creep in our ears. Soft stillness and the night
> Become the touches of sweet harmony.
> Sit, Jessica. Look how the floor of heaven
> Is thick inlaid with patens of bright gold.
> There's not the smallest orb which thou behold'st
> But in his motion like an angel sings . . .
>
> [V. i. 54-61]

Lorenzo is showing Jessica the graciousness of the Christian world into which he has brought her; and it is as richly golden as it is musical! Jessica is already at ease in it, to the point of being able to recall the pains of famous lovers with equanimity, rally her lover on his vows and turn the whole thing off with ''I would out-night you did no body come, / But hark, I hear the footing of a man'' [V. i. 23-4]. That everybody is so perfectly easy is part of the openness. . . . As the actual music plays, there is talk about its Orphic power, and we look back a moment toward Shylock

> The man that hath no music in himself
> Nor is not mov'd with concord of sweet sounds,
> Is fit for treasons, stratagems, and spoils . . .
>
> [V. i. 83-5]

A certain contemplative distance is maintained by talking *about* perception, *about* harmony and its conditions, even while enjoying it. Portia comes on exclaiming how far the candle throws its beams, how much sweeter the music sounds than by day. There are conditions, times and seasons, to be observed; but the cosmological music, which cannot be heard directly at all, is behind the buoyant decorum of the people:

> How many things by season season'd are
> To their right praise and true perfection!
> Peace ho! The moon sleeps with Endymion
> And would not be awak'd.

[V. i. 107-10]

At the end of the play, there is Portia's news of Antonio's three argosies richly come to harbor, and the special deed of gift for Lorenzo—"manna in the way / Of starved people" [V. i. 294-95]. Such particular happy events are not sentimental because Shakespeare has floated them on an expression of a tendency in society and nature which supports life and expels what would destroy it. (pp. 179-89)

> C. L. Barber, "The Merchants and the Jew of Venice: Wealth's Communion and an Intruder," in his Shakespeare's Festive Comedy: A Study of Dramatic Form and Its Relation to Social Custom, *Princeton University Press*, 1959, pp. 163-91.

GRAHAM MIDGLEY   (essay date 1960)

[*Midgley argues that critics err in interpreting* The Merchant of Venice *as either a love comedy with tragic intrusions or as a tragedy of an isolated Jew "disfigured by lovers' adventures and tedious casket scenes." He claims instead that the two focal points in the play are not Shylock and "the lovers or the romance theme," but Shylock and Antonio—or, more specifically, these two characters and their relation to Venetian society. Midgley states that the relation of Shylock and Antonio to their respective worlds is essentially that of two outsiders; he thus calls* The Merchant of Venice *"a twin study in loneliness." For Midgley, the circumstance isolating Shylock is his Jewish faith, and for Antonio, it is his homosexual love for Bassanio, which the critic contends is also the reason for his unexplained melancholy. Midgley suggests that the nature of* The Merchant of Venice *is anything but comic, and that in its depiction of two individuals who fail to conquer their loneliness, who actually isolate themselves further, the play is closer to tragedy. Other critics who have considered* The Merchant of Venice *a tragedy rather than a comedy include Nicholas Rowe (1709), Heinrich Heine (1838), and T. A. Ross (1934). Also, see the excerpts by E. K. Chambers (1908), T. A. Ross (1934), John D. Hurrell (1961), A. D. Moody (1964), and Lawrence Danson (1978) for additional commentary on the source of Antonio's melancholy.*]

The problem of *The Merchant of Venice* has always been its unity, and most critical discussions take this as the centre of their argument, asking what is the relative importance of its two plots and how Shakespeare contrives to interweave them into a unity; the two plots being the Shylock plot and what is called the love or romance plot. . . . If we insist in analysing the play with these two plots as our central consideration, we find ourselves in trouble. We find Shakespeare working out a remarkably steady alternation of scene between Venice and Belmont and then, as if to cap this alternating structure, giving the whole of Act IV to Venice and the trial scene, and the whole of Act V to Belmont, with Shylock apparently forgotten. Whatever else he might do, Shakespeare does not throw away his fifth act and, if we are working on the Shylock-lovers pattern, it would appear that the farewell and lasting impression on the audience, which the fifth act can give, is meant by Shakespeare to be, not the end of Shylock and the misery of his defeat, but the love theme, the happiness of the united lovers and the lyrical beauty of Belmont by moonlight. Skylock is forgotten completely by the lovers beneath the stars, and the

main theme is the triumph of love. If this is the truth, then Shylock has been allowed to become far too imposing a figure in the previous four acts of the play . . . , and this fifth act is a desperate attempt to redress a lost balance. If, on the other hand, we accept Shylock as the central point of interest, the play collapses beautifully but irrelevantly in a finely-written act given over to a secondary theme. It is possible to show, however, that the construction becomes more meaningful if we accept an entirely different theme and two different points of interest. If we do this, the problem of divided interest between Shylock and the lovers becomes an irrelevant one, or at least relevant in a different way, and the play becomes something far more interesting than a fairy tale with unfortunate deeper intrusions, or a tragic downfall of a Jew, disfigured by lovers' adventures and tedious casket scenes. (pp. 119-20)

I would suggest that the two focal points of the play are Shylock and, not the lovers or the romance theme, but Antonio, and that the world of love and marriage is not opposed by Shylock, but rather paralleled by Venetian society as a whole, social, political and economic. The scheme of the play is, if I may reduce it to ratio terms: As Shylock is to Venetian society, so is Antonio to the world of love and marriage. The relationship of these two to these two worlds is the same, the relationship of an outsider. The play is, in effect, a twin study in loneliness. The fact that these two outcasts, these two lonely men, only meet in the cruel circumstances they do, adds an irony and pathos to the play which lift it out of the category of fairy tale or romance. Indeed, seen from any angle, *The Merchant of Venice* is not a very funny play, and we might gain a lot if, for the moment, we ceased to be bullied by its inclusion amongst the Comedies. This thesis has much to offer in our understanding of the play. It reinstates Antonio to a position in the play more commensurate with the care and interest Shakespeare seems to have shown in his creation (and the play is, after all, called *The Merchant of Venice*): it does not force us into having to condemn Shylock if we accept the values of the love world, for it offers us different oppositions and asks us to make different moral judgments, different in kind as well as in direction: and finally, it seems to make more impressive sense of the construction of the play, especially of Acts IV and V.

An examination of the characters of Shylock and Antonio as parallel studies is a preliminary task which should throw light on the reconsideration of the play as a whole.

Examinations of Shylock have too often been obscured by a scholarly heap of secondary considerations arising from the fact that he is a Jew. It is surprising how much of the work on *The Merchant of Venice* turns out on inspection to be on the lines of 'The Jew in Elizabethan England', 'The Elizabethan Jew in Drama', or 'The Jew in Elizabethan Drama'. . . . To work through this mass of material is to feel at once that the play is being smothered, and when, for example, one is asked to accept as superbly clever hypocrisy a speech of Shylock's which rings with obvious sincerity and feeling, one begins to rebel and return to the play and what the play says. In my opinion it is not of much importance that Shylock is a Jew, and all the 'background work' on Jews and Judaism strikes me as quite irrelevant. The important thing is that he is a Jew in a Gentile society, that all he is and all he holds dear is alien to the society in which he has to live. He is an alien, an outsider, tolerated but never accepted. His being a Jew is not important in itself: what is important is what being a Jew has done to his personality. He is a stranger, proud of his race and its traditions, strict in his religion, sober rather than miserly in his domestic life, and filled with the idea of the sanctity of the family and family loyalty. Around him is the society of Venice, a world of golden youth, richly dressed, accustomed to luxury, to feasting, to masking, of a comparatively easy virtue and of a religious outlook which, though orthodox, hardly strikes one as deep, a society faithful and courteous in its own circle and observing a formal politeness of manner and address, but quite insufferable to those outside its own circle, where Shylock is so obviously placed. (pp. 121-23)

Our first meeting with him is in the arranging of the bond. He is faced with insolent rudeness on the part of those who come in fact to beg a favour, with the peremptory snaps of Bassanio. . . . He is drawn into a discussion on usury, attacked for lending money on interest, and the only reply to his quite sensible defence is Antonio's supercilious:

> Mark you this, Bassanio,
> The devil can cite scripture for his purpose,
> An evil soul, producing holy witness,
> Is like a villain with a smiling cheek,
> A goodly apple rotten at the heart.
> O what a goodly outside falsehood hath!
>
> [I. iii. 97-102]

Shylock is stirred to remind Antonio, in words already quoted, of his former cruel behaviour to him, to call attention to the almost forgotten fact that Antonio *is* begging a favour, but he is again rejected by Antonio with cold scorn. Can we blame him if a scheme of revenge forms in his mind?

Later Lorenzo elopes with Jessica, the two of them rejoicing callously in the tricking and robbing of the Jew. Jessica's elopement, added by Shakespeare to his source, is no mere romantic addition, but the crucial point in Shylock's development. In this deed a blow is struck at all that Shylock holds dear, his pride of race, the sober decency of his household life and the dear sanctity of the family and family bonds. The mixing of ducats with his daughter in his cries of despair is because his ducats, as his daughter, are part of his family pride, the only bulwarks against the general scorn of the society he lives in. . . . (pp. 123-24)

Antonio is in no way rejected externally or consciously by the people he has to live with. He is respected, rich, with easy access to economic, legal and social circles, and Venice is always on his side. His loneliness is within and not without, as Shylock's. Antonio is an outsider because he is an unconscious homosexual in a predominantly, and indeed blatantly, heterosexual society. Against such a statement I am aware that a great amount of scholarly opposition could be mustered, studies of friendship in Renaissance thought and Elizabethan literature, evidence of an extremer vocabulary of endearment between men than could be used nowadays without risk of misunderstanding, studies of Shakespeare's sonnets and the theme of friendship there. All this may be very true, but my first bare formulation stands. The fact which strikes one above all about Antonio is his all-absorbing love of Bassanio, his complete lack of interest in women—in a play where this interest guides the actions of all the other males—and his being left without a mate in a play which is rounded off by a full-scale mating dénouement. Moreover, his relationship with Bassanio has very special facets which need a special interpretation. We first meet Antonio in a state of deep melancholy—not the pretty heigh-ho sadness of Portia which is (purposefully?) to be contrasted with it in the next scene—but a deeper and completely unaffected melancholy. . . . It is soon estab-

lished that its cause is not worry over his business affairs, and the first clue comes in the exchange with Solanio:

> Sol. Why then you are in love.
> Ant.   Fie! Fie!
>
> [I. i. 46]

This is more than a simple contradiction or negative. There is a reproach here either for something being mentioned which ought not to be mentioned—Antonio thinking Solanio refers to his love for Bassanio—or for something being mentioned which Antonio finds repugnant to his nature—thinking Solanio suggests some love-affair with a woman. Whichever it may be, Antonio, a few lines later, perfectly sums up his place in the society in which he moves:

> I hold the world but as the world, Gratiano,
> A stage, where every man must play a part,
> And mine a sad one.
>
> [I. i. 77-9]

The cause of this sadness which Antonio has refused to acknowledge even to himself is revealed as soon as Antonio and Bassanio are alone together, for Antonio's first words are:

> Well, tell me now what lady is the same
> To whom you swore a secret pilgrimage.
>
> [I. i. 119-20]

It was, apparently, Bassanio's first mention of the possibility of his wooing and marriage some time previously, which had cast Antonio into this gloomy sadness. This is not, I think, a forcing of the text, for all the previous writing about Antonio has been to establish that sadness, to stress its apparent causelessness, except in that inexplicably angry 'Fie! Fie!' Now, added to this, comes this sudden rush to the heart of the matter, where Antonio seeks to know more of the thing which has ruined his happiness, and then, knowing, he does the only thing his love can do, sacrificing himself as fully as possible for his beloved. . . . We are not to see Antonio again until disaster has overtaken him, his fortune gone and his death at the hands of the Jew for his friend's sake apparently inevitable. His attitude to that fate and what he makes of it have been neglected in criticism, which has concentrated its interest on Shylock and Portia, relegating Antonio to the rank of another bystander. The first piece of evidence is the letter which he sends to Bassanio:

> Sweet Bassanio, my ships have all miscarried,
> my creditors grow cruel, my estate is very low,
> my bond to the Jew is forfeit, and (since in
> paying it, it is impossible that I should live) all
> debts are clear'd between you and I, if I might
> but see you at my death: notwithstanding, use
> your pleasure—if your love do not persuade
> you to come, let not my letter.
>
> [III. ii. 315-22]

The last words indicate Antonio's mood. The death is, in a way, welcome, for it is his greatest, if his last, opportunity to show his love, and to escape from the world where his part is a sad one. This is why he never questions Shylock's claim, never fights against the outrage of it. Death he accepts—as long as Bassanio is there. . . . In the trial scene his attitude is of resignation, and almost of an eagerness for death . . . and there are two important exchanges with Bassanio, the first when Bassanio tries to encourage Antonio with hope and big words, and Antonio replies in terms which only make sense if they refer to a bigger problem in his life than the immediate legal one:

> I am a tainted wether of the flock,
> Meetest for death—the weakest kind of fruit
> Drops earliest to the ground, and so let me;
> You cannot better be employ'd, Bassanio,
> Than to live still and write mine epitaph.
>
> [IV. i. 114-18]

What would have been, but for Portia's intervention, his last farewell to Bassanio is a wonderful drawing-together of all the threads which make up the complex character and motives of Antonio at this point:

> Give me your hand, Bassanio, fare you well,
> Grieve not that I am fall'n to this for you:
> For herein Fortune shows herself more kind
> Than is her custom: it is still her use
> To let the wretched man outlive his wealth,
> To view with hollow eye and wrinkled brow
> An age of poverty: from which ling'ring penance
> Of such misery doth she cut me off.
> Commend me to your honourable wife,
> Tell her the process of Antonio's end,
> Say how I lov'd you, speak me fair in death:
> And when the tale is told, bid her be judge
> Whether Bassanio had not once a love:
> Repent but you that you shall lose your friend
> And he repents not that he pays your debt.
> For if the Jew do cut but deep enough,
> I'll pay it instantly with all my heart.
>
> [IV. i. 265-81]
> (pp. 125-29)

The parallel between Shylock and Antonio is the framework of the play. Both are not fully at home in the society in which they are forced to live, for different reasons. Shylock is accepted only because of his wealth and economic usefulness: otherwise in all the things which a man needs for happiness with his fellows, friendship, respect, social intercourse, sympathy, cooperation, he is denied and spurned. Antonio has all these things, but the thing he most desires is denied him, again by the society around him, not denied to him as violently as to Shylock, because Antonio's lack is secret and personal, and those around him neither know nor understand that in fact he lacks anything. Yet for all these differences, there is the basic kinship in the Jew and the Merchant, the kinship of loneliness.

Each, then, has to make a gesture against being overwhelmed, and each has to make it through the channel open to him or dear to him. The Jew makes his offer of friendship, he tries to escape from his isolation by means of the only common link between himself and his enemies, his wealth. Antonio makes his gesture of sacrifice in entering upon the bond, through the only thing which really means anything to him, his love.

Each makes his gesture and each is defeated, for as the people around Shylock violently and cruelly reply to his gesture with renewed attacks on his home and beliefs, finally overcoming him completely through the congregated social and legal powers of that society, at the same time they condemn Antonio to the loneliness his death would have ended. The violence of the defeat differs, of course, as the very positions of Shylock and Antonio differ. Shylock's fate is more violent and cruel because he outwardly opposes a whole society and outrages its pride and its code: Antonio's fate is private and quiet, as his opposition and loneliness are private and quiet. But their defeat is nevertheless a common one, and each is left holding an empty reward, each is left with cold comfort. Shylock is stripped of half of his wealth, the one thing which gave him standing in Venice, and is given in return the formal badge of entrée, to become a member of the society in which he has always been an outcast—he is to be made a Christian. . . . Antonio is rewarded with the return of his ships and money, and his receiving of this news is marked by such a flat unexcitement that we realise he speaks the whole truth and nothing more nor less, when he tells Portia:

> Sweet lady, you have given me life and living;
> For here I read for certain that my ships
> Are safely come to road.
>
> [V. i. 286-88]

'Life and living' in a world where is destined to play a part, and that a sad one. The defeat of Shylock has been in a way the cause of his defeat, for it has deprived him of the one great gesture of love which would have ended his loneliness and crowned his love with one splendid act. (pp. 130-31)

The climax of this parallel which is built up throughout the play, is reached in the parallel action of Act IV and Act V. Act IV covers the rejection and defeat of Shylock, quite explicitly, quite completely. It also covers the defeat of Antonio, but not so explicitly, and Act V is needed to bring out fully and unmistakably what has actually been done to him before the Duke and the court. In Act IV all the powers which oppose Shylock are drawn together into the court room, the glittering youth of Venice, with their friendship and solidarity, and above all the Duke and the magnificoes, embodiments of the law and social code which has rejected Shylock all his life, which, in bitter revenge, he now tries to use for his own ends, but which will turn and destroy him. Shylock is doomed and the net closes round him quite inescapably. He is thrust out from the court as he has always been thrust out, and the visual symbol is more powerful than any reading can be—the Duke on his throne, the magnificoes in all the haughty pomp and robes of state, the gentlemen and ladies grouped together hand in hand or arm in arm, a great, splendid and friendly phalanx filling one side of the stage, while at the other, beaten and alone, the Jew leaves the stage. Antonio's act is still to come, and I would stress it as his act, though he hardly speaks, rather than an attempt to restore the play safely to the romance comedy world from which it seemed to have been in danger of escaping— the interpretation forced on us if we accept the old reading of the play. Now it is not the state, the law, the social solidarity of Venice which is built up into the symbol of the rejecting power. The Act opens with:

> The moon shines bright. In such a night as this,
> When the sweet wind did gently kiss the trees,
> And they did make no noise, in such a night
> Troilus methinks mounted the Trojan walls,
> And sigh'd his soul towards the Grecian tents
> Where Cressid lay that night. . . .
>
> [V. i. 1-6]

Against this background move the lovers, Lorenzo and Jessica, lying entranced in the moonlight, Portia hastening back to her husband, Nerissa to hers—even Launcelot has found a dark-skinned lover. The talk is all of husbands and wives, or reunion, of welcomes home, of going to bed—for with three pairs of happy united lovers, this night is to see the consummation of their marriages. Antonio is welcomed to Belmont, but welcome him as they may, he is alone, and the words of welcome are formal and polite, spoken by people who have more important things to think about. . . . And then he is forgotten. Again one needs to see the scene to realise this fully. From the moonlit garden into the glow of the candle-lit house the lovers pass two by two, Portia with her Bassanio, Lorenzo with his Jessica, and lastly, rushing to their bed, Gratiano and Nerissa—and Antonio is left behind to walk from the stage alone, the stage to which he had likened his world, where he must play a part, and that a sad one. Visually one cannot escape the parallel between the lonely Shylock creeping from the stage, leaving the triumphant ranks of Venice, and this lonely Antonio walking from the stage, following without joy the triumphant pairs of lovers. The sad irony of the whole play is that these two never really meet. Indeed, they are pitched *against* each other, each retiring defeated into his own loneliness again, while Venice goes about its business, and the nightingales of Belmont serenade three happy marriage beds. (pp. 131-33)

> Graham Midgley, '' 'The Merchant of Venice': A Reconsideration,'' in Essays in Criticism, *Vol. X, No. 2, April, 1960, pp. 119-33.*

E. M. W. TILLYARD   (essay date 1961)

[*Tillyard is best known for his influential* Shakespeare's History Plays *(1944), considered a leading example of historical criticism. In addition to his historical studies, Tillyard also published* Shakespeare's Last Plays *(1938),* Shakespeare's Problem Plays *(1949), and* Shakespeare's Early Comedies, *a book he was working on at the time of his death in 1962 but was not published until 1965. Emphasizing the allegorical nature of the trial scene in* The Merchant of Venice *noted by such other critics as Denton J. Snider (1890), Sir Israel Gollancz (1922), Nevill Coghill (1949), Theodor Reik (1956), Barbara K. Lewalski (1962), and René E. Fortin (1974), Tillyard contends that Portia's role in the play is not only that of mercy on earth, but also the reconciliation of mercy and justice. He also maintains that Portia, during the trial, is more concerned with Shylock's soul than with Antonio's safety, since she alone knows that the merchant is secure in her legal ''quibble''; as such, Tillyard argues, the episode is more complex than previous critics have admitted. Tillyard also comments on Shylock's forced conversion, stating that Shakespeare meant to contrast this act unfavorably with Portia's earlier remark that mercy cannot be ''constrain'd'' or forced. Other critics who have focused on Shylock's forced conversion as an example of the Christians' duplicity, or have argued that the Jew's punishment fails to adequately resolve the conflict of justice and mercy in the play, include Harold C. Goddard (1951), A. D. Moody (1964), James E. Siemon (1970), R. Chris Hassel, Jr. (1970), and René Girard (1978).*]

Mrs. Jameson declared that in the trial scene Portia had two objects in view; to deliver her husband's friend and to maintain her husband's honour by the discharge of his just debt [see excerpt above, 1833]. 'It is evident that she would owe the safety of Antonio to anything rather than to the legal quibble with which her cousin Bellario has armed her, and which she reserves as a last resource.' I wonder. Was the legal quibble a last, and presumably uncertain, resource? Or is Mrs. Jameson, through the very definiteness of her error, suggesting an equally definite contrary embodying a truth not yet fully apprehended? May not the legal quibble be, not a last resource, but a trump-card Portia keeps serenely up her sleeve while transacting business quite other than that which Mrs. Jameson assigns to her? The moment Portia produces her quibble, Shylock's case collapses. His enemies know instantaneously that it *has* collapsed, and he attempts not a single quibble in retort.

In its context the quibble is an infallible magic spell, in keeping with the fairy-tale substance of the two main plots.

What was it then that Shakespeare most had to do, granted that his Portia was untroubled in mind on Antonio's account, knowing that she possessed a spell insuring his release? As a practising dramatist he wanted in the first place to present an effective scene, something of the greatest possible dramatic interest; and indeed it is an enrichment of the dramatic situation if Portia knows she has Shylock quite within her power while the other characters know no such thing: if she is cool about the thing all the others agonize over; if she is able to prolong her moment of power before enjoying the supreme satisfaction of giving to the sorely tried sufferers their unexpected and spectacular relief. I would not deny the presence of such elements; only they coexist with something more important.

In his *Basis of Shakespearean Comedy* Nevill Coghill made some important points: that the age of the *Faerie Queene* must have been generally expectant of allegory; that some of Shakespeare's comedies demand figurative as well as naturalistic understanding; and that the *Merchant of Venice* is among them [see excerpt above, 1949]. He holds that the play repeats the much exploited medieval theme of the conflict of Justice and Mercy, associating it especially with that highly stylised form of it, the story of the Four Daughters of God. . . . While not accepting some of the details of Coghill's account, I think he gives a necessary general truth about the play. But I also think he does not see the full part Portia has in the conflict between Justice and Mercy.

The Merchant of Venice belongs to the years when Spenser's vogue was at its height, when any educated audience would be quite familiar with Spenser's habit of sliding characters along a scale that was naturalistic at one end and allegorical at the other. . . . Having seen Portia begin as a witty Elizabethan lady, change into the fairy-princess of the Beautiful Mountain, and change again into the tom-boy of contemporary romantic comedy, the original audience would have been well prepared for further changes. Moreover she enters doubly disguised, as a man and as a doctor of laws of Rome; hence the readier to have exchanged an old for a new self. She arrives in state, heralded by a forerunner; and her tone, when she has entered, is magisterial. She dictates what is right or wrong and speaks with more authority than the Duke himself, while Bassanio assumes that she can 'wrest' the law of Venice itself to her will. In this magisterial assurance she has ceased to be a young woman and has turned into an allegory—of what? Not of Mercy alone, though that is her main theme and though the audience . . . would at once be prone to take her as such. But she is Mercy clothed in the robes of Justice and can only stand for Justice and Mercy reconciled, in accordance with her own words about earthly power being most godlike 'when mercy seasons justice' [IV. i. 197]. Mercy must season justice but may not 'wrest' it, and Bassanio's plea can only be rejected.

We have arrived at this point, then, that Portia stands, after the manner of the Four Daughters story, for Mercy reconciled with Justice and that she knows she possesses the infallible means of rescuing Antonio according to the strict letter of the law, Antonio not needing in actual fact any exercise of mercy at all. But Christian mercy is not confined to the plight of a single unfortunate Venetian; it is concerned with the souls of all men, specifically here with those of Jews as well as of Venetians. When Portia lectures Shylock on mercy, while the other persons on the stage can only think of Antonio's fate, she is thinking of Shylock's, she is imploring Shylock to recognise his own peril and to mind the salvation of his own soul. Read in this double sense, the scene gains greatly in richness of content. (pp. 51-3)

The Portia [of the trial scene] is, as I have said, magisterial, quite altered from the young girl whose little body was aweary of this great world. She also goes headlong into action unlike both the lovesick girl who wished to detain Bassanio 'some month or two' [III. ii. 9] before he shall undergo that other judgement of the caskets and from the procrastinating Venetians among whom she finds herself. She is like a cold draught of air suddenly penetrating a hot room and refreshing the wits of those within. Both by her difference and by her fresh energy she leads us to expect a novel way of feeling. It takes her only a moment to find that Antonio acknowledges his obligation to his bond: upon which she tells Shylock he must be merciful; Shylock queries her *must;* and she begins her oration on mercy. How does this speech satisfy the audience's expectation of the novel way of feeling I have just postulated? First, it defines the change in Portia's nature. If she is now magisterial and more certain of herself than the other characters on the stage, it is because she is now the embodiment of that mercy on which she expatiates. Second, her speech attaches itself to formal rhetoric in a way none of the previous speeches in the scene have done. . . . And we accept this new rhetoric just because we have been startled by the nature of Portia's entry. But, thirdly, we should also perceive that the speech must be interpreted with a richness of reference not belonging to anything that has gone before but not unexpected in view of the jolt to which we have been submitted.

Take the actual text of the speech, and it is plain that Portia's plea for mercy concerns both Shylock's soul and Antonio's life: mercy is twice blest, benefiting both giver and receiver. And Portia tells Shylock, Christianwise, that justice alone is insufficient for the soul's salvation. But the mere text becomes greatly complicated through the different ways the characters take it. The Duke, having already referred to Shylock's soul, must surely give at least a passing thought to it when Portia dwells so insistently on the benefit mercy brings the giver. But the other Venetians, bent so intently on poor Antonio's plight, value her words solely as they are likely to persuade Shylock to soften and so to spare his victim. Portia, knowing Antonio to be safe, aims all her eloquence at Shylock and Shylock alone. Shylock, obsessed with his hate, is deaf to the tones of her entreaty and has not the remotest idea that she pleads essentially for him and his welfare, that she is fulfilling the command of Christ to love your enemy. The audience knew the outlines of the story, knew that Antonio would not in fact lose his pound of flesh, but they would not be prevented (any more than in witnessing *Oedipus King* or *Othello*) from being caught up in the excitement of the plot, from experiencing the supposed tension of the persons in the story while the issue is undecided. But they should recognise the other issue and watch Portia in her struggle to break down Shylock's obtuseness, ready to take her words both in the way she means them and in the way the Venetians (the Duke perhaps excepted) do in fact take them. The audience are thus in a wonderfully happy position: ironically superior to most persons in the play by possessing additional knowledge and thrilled by the excitement of having two parallel meanings to apprehend. . . . When Shylock queries Portia's *must,* the Venetians accept his query and hope that Portia's eloquence will sway him to spare Antonio. Portia, having first said *must* and then said that there are no *musts* about mercy, tries to stir Shylock's set and stupid wits. Can't he see that she is using *must* in two different senses? It

is of the utmost consequence to you, she means, that you should be merciful; but when it comes to mercy no one can force you, the impulse must come from your own heart, or from the yielding of your heart to the operation of heavenly grace.

And thus the scene proceeds. Seen from the point of view of Portia's Christian pleading, Shylock's retort to her eloquence, 'My deeds upon my head' [IV. i. 206], is indeed dreadful in its self-damnation. Then, unable to convince Shylock of the beauty of mercy in its own right, Portia climbs down from the height from which she has begun and appeals to his advantage with, 'Shylock, there's thrice thy money offered thee' [IV. i. 227]; only to find Shylock taking his stand on ground more elevated and yet for his soul's health more perilous than a simple love of gain:

> An oath, an oath, I have an oath in Heaven.
> Shall I lay perjury upon my soul?
>
> [IV. i. 228-29]

Solicitous for his own soul on purely legal premises, he cannot begin to see that Portia is also solicitous, but on premises how different! Then Portia repeats both pleas simultaneously, after dwelling on the most dreadful item in the bond: that the flesh to be cut shall be nearest to the heart. Shylock refuses with an emphasis grimmer than before, bringing in his soul yet again:

> by my soul I swear
> There is no power in the tongue of man
> To alter me.
>
> [IV. i. 240-42]

Antonio perceives the emphasis and that Portia has failed; he asks for an end of the trial. But, even as the end appears to approach, Portia, giving Shylock every chance (or, as the Venetians think, not abandoning the minutest portion of hope on behalf of Antonio), implores Shylock to get a surgeon to stop his victim's bleeding to death, on the Christian plea of charity. Then, having made this plea in vain, Portia abandons her struggle for Shylock's soul. She is now free to abandon also her high allegorical role, which she begins to do when, in comment on Bassanio's protest that his friend's life is more to him than his own life, wife and all the world, she exclaims:

> Your wife would give you little thanks for that,
> If she were by, to hear you make the offer.
>
> [IV. i. 288-89]

Begins, because she has not yet finished with the judicial part of her allegorical task. However, having begun, she must not delay her return to common humanity, since the play must not dwell too long on solemn things lest it lose its predominantly comic complexion. So she hastens to produce her trump-card, her infallible legal quibble; and the tension, so long sustained, relaxes. Portia now has no concern but with justice against Shylock; mercy now being the concern of the Duke and Antonio. The Duke is generous, granting Shylock his life in anticipation of his plea for it, and being willing to commute confiscation of half his property to a fine. But pardon comes easier to the Duke than to Shylock's victim; and Portia is careful to distinguish between them, finally asking what mercy Antonio can render Shylock. Antonio is on the whole generous in the matter of money but he makes the stipulation that Shylock shall turn Christian, a stipulation made definitive by the Duke, who says he will rescind his pardon unless Shylock complies.

In interpreting Antonio's stipulation one encounters the kind of dilemma presented by Hamlet's motive in sparing Claudius at his prayers and the irreconcilable dispute between the tough

Act III. Scene ii. Portia, Bassanio, Lorenzo, Jessica, Salerio, Nerissa, and Gratiano. By W. Hamilton. The Department of Rare Books and Special Collections, The University of Michigan Library.

and tender critics over it. Everything is so simple if you can follow the tough ones. These (and on this issue Coghill is among them) point out that the Elizabethans found nothing odd in forcible conversions. Baptism was necessary for salvation, and it 'worked' as surely when forced as when chosen. Thus Antonio performed an act of pure Christian mercy, when, forgoing revenge, he stipulated that Shylock should turn Christian; he was returning good for evil. I should like to get out of the dilemma so easily; but in view of the many cross-references in the play and of the irony I have described as running through the trial scene I cannot help doubting so simple an explanation. For cases of cross-references, it is not fortuitous that Antonio begins the play's first scene with 'In sooth I know not why I am so sad: It wearies me' [I. i. 1-2], and that Portia begins the second scene with 'By my troth, Nerissa, my little body is aweary of this great world' [I. ii. 1-2]. Nor again can it be fortuitous that over the triviality of the ring Bassanio and Antonio swear on their souls as Shylock had sworn on his soul over the vital matter of his bond. Thus, when Antonio and the Duke in their mercy force Shylock to turn Christian, surely we are meant to recall Portia's pronouncement that you cannot force mercy. Even so, the tough critics could argue that Portia's forcing refers to the giver not to the receiver of mercy and that Antonio in choosing freely to force mercy on Shylock, was acting according to her principles. And yet in my heart I cannot help thinking that Portia included the receiver in her ken, and that Shakespeare meant some ironical contrast between Portia's ideals and the cruder understanding of the Venetians.

Certainly, if he does, and if I am right in detecting a long series of double meanings in Portia's speeches, the trial scene comes out richer and more complex than has usually been supposed. (pp. 54-9)

E. M. W. Tillyard, "The Trial Scene in 'The Merchant of Venice'," in A Review of English Literature, *Vol. 2, No. 4, October, 1961, pp. 51-9.*

JOHN D. HURRELL   (essay date 1961)

[*Hurrell identifies what he calls an "interior theme" in* The Merchant of Venice *that explains Antonio's melancholy and his behavior throughout the play. The critic describes this theme as "rivalry in love," which he traces in Antonio's jealousy towards Portia and his fear that Bassanio can never reciprocate the depth of his passion. According to Hurrell, Antonio's love for Bassanio exceeds even the Renaissance image of male friendship; it is this abundance of love, he adds, that fuels the merchant's jealousy towards Portia and—fearing that he has lost Bassanio forever—accounts for both his sadness and his willingness to sacrifice his life for his friend. Like T. A. Ross (1934) and Graham Midgley (1960), Hurrell contends that though Shakespeare might not have intended Antonio to be a homosexual, he "certainly suggests one." The critic concludes that Antonio is "returned to normal social life" at the end of* The Merchant of Venice, *and his antisocial behavior overcome, once he realizes that Portia does not intend to come between him and Bassanio. For further commentary on the nature and cause of Antonio's melancholy, see the excerpts by E. K. Chambers (1908), A. D. Moody (1964), and Lawrence Danson (1978). Also, see the essay by Barbara Tovey (1981) for an examination of the underlying negative effects of Antonio's love for Bassanio and additional commentary on the "rivalry in love" theme noted by Hurrell.*]

In discussing *The Merchant of Venice* we commonly refuse to consider the Shylock plot, and particularly the characterization of Shylock himself, as purely conventional. It is generally agreed that to some extent, at least, Charlton is right, and that Shakespeare was unable to confine himself to a presentation of the stock dramatic type of the Jew, finding it necessary, though perhaps for dramatic rather than sentimental reasons, to round him out as a human being [see Additional Bibliography]. Ultimately this is the source of all the critical debate centering on Shylock. Yet in considering the Antonio-Bassanio-Portia plot the critical analogy is ignored; few critics do more than point out the conventional nature of the "friendship" or "amity" motif, which is encountered frequently in Shakespeare and in Renaissance literature generally. Most of the material in this plot certainly can be explained by reference to the traditional "amity" theme, but a close reading suggests that much cannot. Perhaps here, too, Shakespeare has gone beyond theatrical and literary convention in his portrayal of human relationships, and in so doing has created some problems of interpretation.

The first of these problems, leading to the rest, is Antonio's "melancholy"; the subject is best introduced by a brief comment on the first scene. Bassanio is to be the romantic hero, but the play opens with an expository scene that concerns him less than it does Antonio. It has three pieces of information to convey: Antonio's sadness, his business situation, with all his ships at sea, and Bassanio's impending journey to Belmont, contingent on his borrowing sufficient funds from Antonio. This last development introduces the close relationship between the two men. The second and third points of information serve to advance the plot, but the first apparently does not. Yet Shakespeare has left us with a strong sense of Antonio's troubled mind. Few critics have pursued the relevance of this mood beyond the first scene, as though it were merely a device introduced gratuitously to add a semblance of dramatic solidity to a character who has little else to do in the play but lend money to Bassanio, become Shylock's victim, and thereby afford Portia a means of demonstrating her qualities of mind and soul. The popular conception of Antonio is of a passive character, a link between two plots, who has been given just sufficient personality by Shakespeare to make him dramatically credible, but who interested the dramatist very little.

Some critics have been content to dismiss Antonio's "melancholy" as something "unexplained"; others, looking at the play from the viewpoint of Elizabethan conventions of psychology, see Antonio as a kind of humour character, a sketch of the melancholy man whose mental state must simply be accepted. Others see the opening scene of the play as an example of dramatic foreboding. But Antonio has not always been "sad": he has yet to discover how he "caught it, found it, or came by it"; it is obviously a recent development. It seems likely, then, that there is sufficient cause for this mood, and that it ought to be kept in mind as a factor influencing Antonio's behavior throughout the rest of the play.

John Russell Brown, the editor of the New Arden *Merchant of Venice,* states the commonly accepted modern view: "since Antonio knows about Portia . . . the imminent parting with Bassanio, his friend, is ample motive for it. 'Amity,' or friendship, is an important theme in the play . . . Shakespeare may have used this oblique beginning for the theme in order to arouse interest and speculation in the audience; the motive for the melancholy becomes clear as soon as Antonio and Bassanio are left alone" [see Additional Bibliography]. Mr. Brown does not pursue this line, either in his edition or in his later study of Shakespeare's comedies, but as I hope to show, an analysis of the character of Antonio leads to the idea that while "amity" in the conventional sense is what Shakespeare wished to present in the play, he has, perhaps unintentionally, gone some way beyond the traditional portrayal of male friendship.

This approach was first suggested by E. K. Chambers . . . :

> I am inclined to doubt whether this particular point in the play [Antonio's melancholy] was intended for the audience at all, and is not rather the intrusion of a personal note, an echo of those disturbed relations in Shakespeare's private life of which the fuller but enigmatic record is to be found in the *Sonnets*. Shakespeare, too, like Antonio, had lost a friend, and had lost him through a woman; nor does it seem to me to be inconsistent with any view which Shakespeare can be supposed to have taken in his art, that he should reserve something behind the arras of a play for his own ear, for the secret consolation of his private trouble [see excerpt above, 1908].

Chambers does not elaborate on this statement, and I am not aware that anyone else has pursued its implications. Biographical interpretation is unfashionable, especially in Shakespearean scholarship. But there are some difficulties and ambiguities in this play that demand attention in the light of Chambers' comment. No full reading of the play can emerge from this method, of course; at most we can suggest that Shakespeare's subconscious attitude to the relations between two of his characters, as Chambers outlines that attitude, affected his treat-

ment of otherwise impersonally conceived conventional material. If in what follows I seem to overstate the case it is because I wish to bring to the surface elements of the play that are submerged and, probably, quite unintended by the dramatist. My purpose is to extract from *The Merchant of Venice* an interior theme that adds an extra dimension to the more explicit ones.

The first speech of the play is less simple than it appears, and raises a number of questions which are not answered by the standard interpretations of Antonio's character. "In sooth, I know not why I am so sad" [I. i. 1]: why has Shakespeare used this particular word "sad," here and later, to convey Antonio's state of mind? Most critics take it as a synonym for "melancholy," but the more common meaning, well on into the seventeenth century, was "grave," or "serious." The word suggests that Shakespeare is not concerned with the portrayal of a stock "embodiment of the humour of melancholy," as M. R. Ridley has put it, but with something more subtle. Antonio is not a malcontent, for instance, or a conventional sufferer from lover's melancholy, and he is not a figure of fun in the play. He is a person who has formerly been a good companion but has now turned grave. Gratiano appears to believe that he has assumed this air

> With purpose to be dress'd in an opinion
> Of wisdom, gravity, profound conceit,
>
> [I. i. 91-2]

and is eager, like the others, to bring him back to his accustomed light-heartedness. The only use of the word "melancholy" in the play occurs in this same speech when Gratiano urges Antonio

> But fish not with this melancholy bait
> For this fool gudgeon, this opinion,
>
> [I. i. 101-02]

which certainly suggests that he considers Antonio to be *posing* as a melancholy man, basing his opinion on Antonio's serious and preoccupied air. And Antonio, unlike most stock melancholics in comedy, takes no pleasure in his mark of distinction, as his opening words in the play make quite clear. In fact, he is melancholy in the sense in which we use that word today, meaning "preoccupied," "pensive," "depressed," always with the implication that something fairly definite has *caused* this state of mind. The word "melancholy" had, of course, a rather different literary and dramatic connotation for Shakespeare, so it is all the more significant that while the slightly ambiguous "sad" is used by and of Antonio several times in the play, the more obvious "melancholy" is, with the exception cited above, avoided—though it is used freely by most critics of the play. But Shakespeare's Antonio is a man mentally depressed, not a *conventional* melancholic.

No less puzzling is Antonio's denial of knowledge of the cause of his sadness. How far are we to accept this as the truth? The sadness wearies Antonio, he says, but is it indeed the sadness that wearies him, or the cause of that sadness? If he is simply made sad by the imminent departure of his friend, and the possibility of his marriage, why should he not acknowledge this as the cause? If, as so many commentators assure us, friendship between men is accepted as a part of Elizabethan life, even when it borders on a more passionate relationship, then there is no need for Antonio to conceal the reason for his sadness from his friends. He is certainly quite sure what is *not* the cause; more than a hundred lines of dialogue are employed to establish this fact. The obvious conclusion seems to be that

Antonio's "melancholy" state of mind is indeed caused by his knowledge of Bassanio's plans, but that he does not want to admit, either to himself or to others, that this is the case. Possibly he feels a certain guilt in his relationship with Bassanio. He is facing a crisis in his life, and has withdrawn from Venetian society in an attempt to assess himself. This is perhaps the real sense of foreboding that is present in the opening scene of the play—not the foreboding of danger to come in the physical sense from Shylock, but the foreboding of personal, moral distress for Antonio. His dilemma is a difficult one: his love for Bassanio will not permit him to hinder his friend's plans, even though the fulfillment of those plans will leave his life empty. Antonio has become aware of the disparity between his love for Bassanio and Bassanio's love for him. Bassanio's attitude to Antonio is within the legitimate boundaries of friendship between men, but Antonio's is almost outside these limits. There is, of course, no need to suggest an active homosexuality in the relationship between the two men. It is simply a question of proportion: Antonio's love for Bassanio has become excessive and exclusive, so that he is oversensitive and attaches undue importance to Bassanio's marriage plans, which he sees as desertion.

This suspicion extends beyond Bassanio until Antonio feels ill at ease with his other friends, hinting irrationally at a general desertion. When the play opens, Antonio is talking to Salerio and Solanio about his sadness. They are joined by Bassanio, Lorenzo, and Gratiano. Solanio naturally prepares to leave Antonio with his closer friends ("We leave you now with better company" [I. i. 59]) while Salerio adds,

> I would have stay'd till I had made you merry,
> If worthier friends had not prevented me.
>
> [I. i. 60-1]

Antonio's reply reveals his suspicion of their motives for leaving him, implying that they have talked with him out of politeness and are glad of an excuse to leave:

> I take it, your own business calls on you
> And you embrace th' occasion to depart.
>
> [I. i. 63-4]

The conversation about Antonio's state of mind then continues, with Gratiano and Lorenzo replacing Solanio and Salerio, but with Bassanio making no comment until the others leave.

In this opening scene, then, Antonio's sense of isolation is insisted on, his feeling of being outside the social circle of young Venetians. Perhaps we have here the first indication of a submerged theme of the play, one that in more explicit and conventional form is constantly repeated in Shakespeare's comedies: the young man or woman who places himself (like Beatrice and Benedick) outside the conventional pattern of social behavior, who holds to an individual way of life too passionately, and who at the conclusion of the play is brought back to a behavioral norm.

Bassanio's conversation with Antonio as soon as they are alone seems to indicate that he is aware of the need to spare Antonio's feelings, and to choose his words carefully so that his actions will appear to Antonio to have a practical motive. He is asked a direct question:

> Well, tell me now what lady is the same
> To whom you swore a secret pilgrimage
> That you to-day promis'd to tell me of?
>
> [I. i. 119-21]

But his reply is oblique; he places all his emphasis on the magnitude of the debts he has incurred through his "too prodigal" living. His greatest debts are to Antonio; so he now acquaints his friend with all the "plots and purposes" [I. i. 133] which he has devised to make himself solvent again. Not until he has received the expected promise from Antonio to help him to the utmost does he actually mention Portia. In fact he almost overdoes the preparation, and Antonio gently rebukes him for it in a speech in which his hurt feelings are evident:

> You know me well, and herein spend but time
> To wind about my love with circumstance;
> And out of doubt you do me now more wrong
> In making question of my uttermost
> Than if you had made waste of all I have.
>
> [I. i. 153-57]

After this, Bassanio proceeds to outline his plan without mincing matters, though, as has been often noted by critics of the play, the first quality of Portia mentioned is that she is "richly left." It is sometimes suggested that these words refer to Portia's moral qualities, rather than to her financial position. But it seems hardly likely that Shakespeare would have Bassanio use such ambiguous terminology unless it were intended to be deliberately ambiguous—in which event my suggestion that Bassanio is treading warily here is strengthened. In any case, this reading seems improbable rhetorically, for in the lines,

> In Belmont is a lady richly left,
> And she is fair, and (fairer than that word),
> Of wondrous virtues,
>
> [I. i. 161-63]

there is a logical progression from the most obvious kind of attraction (wealth) to the next most obvious (beauty) to the least obvious, but most worthy (virtue). This is not only an effective trope (so much so that it could be used as evidence by the "rhetorical acting" school of Shakespearean critics); it is also an effective piece of characterization. Bassanio is enabled by this order of ideas to appear to Antonio to be concerned primarily with Portia's dowry, while at the same time he makes such claims for the importance of beauty and virtue that his later role of romantic lover is not compromised in the eyes of the audience. Putting the matter simply, for the purposes of the Antonio-Bassanio relationship he seems to be reciting Portia's qualities in *descending* order, for the Bassanio-Portia plot in *ascending* order. And certainly his last words, reinforced by a pun, drive home to Antonio the seeming pecuniary nature of his interest in the lady:

> O my Antonio, had I but the means
> To hold a rival place with one of them,
> I have a mind presages me such thrift
> That I should questionless be fortunate.
>
> [I. i. 173-76]

Antonio is now satisfied that Bassanio is indeed not really deserting him at all; for the moment the crisis has passed, and he has even been afforded an opportunity to give further evidence of his love for Bassanio. Psychologically the scene I have just reviewed is sound, and as far as an Elizabethan audience is concerned it presents no great difficulties when Bassanio is later converted by Shakespeare into a romantic lover. The principle of love being more stable when based on a sound financial alliance, the dowry system in fact, was fully accepted, in literature at least, as not at all incompatible with romantic love. To the modern audience, of course, the scene is somewhat distasteful, and for the oversensitive critic Bassanio is no more than a scheming fortunehunter. But surely to take this view is to treat Bassanio and his relationship with Antonio too simply. Bassanio is certainly a schemer in this scene, but only because his position is so difficult. He needs money badly, and he does not want to hurt his friend, although he realizes that there is a great disparity in the degree of friendship between them. In the attempt to extricate himself from this situation he is forced to misrepresent his motives (in degree, perhaps, rather than in fact) and if the modern reader does not appreciate the suggestion of tension between the two friends in the opening scene of the play he will be forced to take Bassanio at his word, with the inevitable result of overemphasizing the predatory nature of his relationship to Portia, and hence having to adjust to an apparently abrupt change of tone in the play when Bassanio reaches Belmont. He is certainly not in love with Portia before he arrives at her home, but he *is* prepared to fall in love with a woman; this is the fact that he must conceal from Antonio, and it is the cause of the unspoken uneasiness between them.

If the precise nature of Antonio's "melancholy" is the first problem of the play, his reason for entering into such a dubious agreement with Shylock is certainly the second. That we are faced here with an only partly assimilated element from Shakespeare's source cannot be denied. But again a closer examination of Antonio's state of mind at the time of his meeting with Shylock will show that the Merchant is not nearly so guilty of an unmotivated piece of bad business, or even of gross overconfidence, as appears from a casual reading. Shylock's motives, of course, are clear enough: if the money is repaid he will have shown himself generous; if it is not, then it will feed his revenge—and the idea that the money might not be forthcoming occurs to him only gradually, when Antonio's ships are rumored lost, and when a Christian has provoked him in the extreme by abducting his daughter. But Antonio's motives are less obvious. At first he shows no enthusiasm for the actual business of borrowing money. It is significant that although his instruction to Bassanio has been,

> Go, presently inquire, and so will I,
> Where money is,
>
>   [I. i. 183-84]

it is Bassanio who has actually made the contact with Shylock and opened the negotiations. One can only suppose that some kind of lethargy has come over Antonio, not unnaturally, since any action on his part will bring nearer the day of Bassanio's departure. Conceivably the emotional background to this scene could be stated even more strongly: Antonio has been somewhat disillusioned by Bassanio's intended marriage; he sees desertion everywhere (by Solanio and Salerio, for example); he has no will to act, and in any case action will not help him. He is thus in the hands of Bassanio; to refuse to deal with Shylock would be a breach of his promise to a friend. For the moment the normally cautious Antonio has no defenses, and the initiative passes to Shylock and Bassanio, who stand to gain from the discussion. Antonio, impatient to be finished with the negotiations, takes no part beyond railing admissions of his hatred for Shylock. Suddenly Shylock seems to change his approach:

> Why, look you, how you storm!
> I would be friends with you and have your love,
> Forget the shames that you have stain'd me with,
> Supply your present wants, and take no doit
> Of usance for my moneys, and you'll not hear me.
> This is kind I offer.
>
>   [I. iii. 137-42]

Bassanio's reply, "This were kindness" [I. iii. 143], admits of at least two interpretations, which can be indicated by the actor's tone of voice. It is either suspicion ("This would indeed be kindness, but I'm sure there's a catch somewhere") or enthusiasm (cynically agreeing to accept Shylock's friendship because it saves money). But it is Antonio's reaction that is more interesting. Until Shylock actually names his terms and mentions the pound of flesh, he remains silent, but on hearing of the projected bond he instantly agrees, while Bassanio, frightened, urges him to refuse. Why should Antonio deal with Shylock on these terms? The usual explanation is that he is merely overconfident, and cannot envisage a business failure so complete that he will fall into Shylock's power. But here we must also add that it is his disturbed state of mind that allows him to neglect the slightest possibility of disaster and to misjudge Shylock's character. There is certainly no reason to suppose that he is incredibly naïve in taking Shylock's offer of friendship at its face value. He cannot imagine a total loss of his ships, so he does not expect Shylock to have taken this into account, either. Consequently, while he does not understand Shylock's motive for this apparent generosity, he can see no need to doubt the Jew's sincerity. At the conclusion of the scene he comments to Bassanio "The Hebrew will turn Christian; he grows kind," and just after his arrest he appeals to "good Shylock" to "Hear me yet" [I. iii. 178; III. iii. 3].

Beyond this there may be other motives for Antonio's hasty acceptance of Shylock's "kindness" and "merry bond." Shocked perhaps by the apparent infidelity of one he loves, and desirous of abandoning his own feeling of isolation and suspicion, he is now disarmed by the seeming friendliness of one he has hated. His world of personal relationships has become so confused that he is no longer a cautious and reliable judge of character; in fact, somewhat ashamed of his present cynicism he overcompensates by taking Shylock at his word, glad to discover that he has been mistaken in thinking the usurer incapable of a kindly action. In these circumstances Shylock's

>   . . . what these Christians are,
> Whose own hard dealings teaches them suspect
> The thoughts of others!
>
>   [I. iii. 160-62]

strikes home with a relevance that the Jew cannot suspect, and confirms Antonio in his agreement to the bond. Yet another motive, possibly a more deeply submerged one, is a feeling that signing to such a bond is a flamboyant though effective gesture of love certain to have its effect on Bassanio. It may even be that there is a subconscious desire for death on Antonio's part. The reader who feels that analysis has gone too far in this suggestion is referred to Antonio's reception, at the trial, of the news of the arrival of the "learned doctor," and of Bassanio's enthusiasm over the event:

> I am a tainted wether of the flock
> Meetest for death: the weakest kind of fruit
> Drops earliest to the ground, and so let me.
> You cannot better be employed, Bassanio,
> Than to live still and write mine epitaph.
>
>   [IV. i. 114-18]

This is spoken in direct reply to Bassanio's

> The Jew shall have my flesh, blood, bones, and all,
> Ere thou shalt lose for me one drop of blood,
>
>   [IV. i. 112-13]

and reveals two interesting facts: Antonio believes himself in some way so "tainted" that he deserves death, and further, he is determined that he shall sacrifice himself for Bassanio, not Bassanio for him. Is this another indication of the guilt and social isolation that Antonio experiences in his friendship for Bassanio? A little later in the same scene Antonio gives a second explanation for his indifference to imminent death. Bassanio is reminded that Antonio is dying for him ("Grieve not that I am fall'n to this for you" [IV. i. 266]) and is then told:

> For herein Fortune shows herself more kind
> Than is her custom: it is still her use
> To let the wretched man outlive his wealth,
> To view with hollow eye and wrinkled brow
> An age of poverty; from which ling'ring penance
> Of such misery doth she cut me off.
>
> [IV. i. 267-72]

This is apparently a reference to the loss of his ships, but there is at least a likelihood of ambiguity here. The "wealth" Antonio refers to could be his friendship with Bassanio before his marriage, and the "age of poverty" his future deprivation after the marriage. Immediately after the lines just quoted come the words,

> Commend me to your honourable wife:
> Tell her the process of Antonio's end;
> Say how I lov'd you, speak me fair in death,
> And, when the tale is told, bid her be judge
> Whether Bassanio had not once a love.
> Repent but you that you shall lose your friend
> And he repents not that he pays your debt;
> For if the Jew do cut but deep enough,
> I'll pay it instantly with all my heart.
>
> [IV. i. 273-81]

Noting the train of Antonio's thoughts it is difficult to avoid the conclusion that he sees himself, quite consciously, as a rival to Portia, and hopes to remain so in memory even after his death. His insistence is not wasted, for Bassanio sees the point of his remarks and utters comforting words:

> Antonio, I am married to a wife
> Which is as dear to me as life itself;
> But life itself, my wife, and all the world,
> Are not with me esteem'd above thy life.
> I would lose all, ay, sacrifice them all
> Here to this devil, to deliver you.
>
> [IV. i. 282-87]

The thematic importance of this exchange between the two men is in no way reduced by its being played out in the presence of the disguised Portia. The fact that it is both highly rhetorical and, in the dramatic circumstances, comic, simply emphasizes the emotional isolation of Antonio. Bassanio's offer is an impractical gesture, while Portia knows that the trial will have a happy conclusion and can afford to jest ("Your wife would give you little thanks for that, / If she were by . . ." [IV. i. 288-89]). Only Antonio is entirely earnest, speaking with the frankness of one who does not expect to live to regret his words.

An earlier episode in the play is also very interesting as evidence of Shakespeare's portrayal of the relationship between the two principal men as more complex and less innocent (on Antonio's part) than the conventional Renaissance friendship. Having introduced the topic of Antonio's melancholy in Act I and developed it as I have suggested, he allows almost the whole of Act II to pass before there is any further treatment

either of the Antonio-Shylock or Antonio-Bassanio themes. This act is mainly devoted to Portia, Nerissa, Jessica, and Lorenzo, and it introduces the Gobbos, father and son. Then, close together in scene viii come Solanio's discussion with Salerio of Jessica's flight ("Let good Antonio look he keep his day" [II. viii. 25]) and Salerio's report of the parting of Bassanio and Antonio, when Antonio urged Bassanio "slubber not business for my sake" [II. viii. 39], but could not restrain his tears over this highly emotional leavetaking. Rapidly following this come further reports of rumored losses of Antonio's ships. Shylock's reaction is in keeping with his increased hatred of Christians engendered by Lorenzo's abduction of Jessica. Meanwhile, Bassanio has been successful in his choice of casket, but before he has had any opportunity to savor his new fortune, Salerio brings him a letter from Antonio, the contents of which are supplemented by its bearer, in which Antonio informs him that the bond is forfeit and his life in danger. Now the wording of the letter, and its arrival at this precise moment, are noteworthy; but no critic, to my knowledge, has commented on the phrases employed by Antonio. They reveal that the "melancholy" motif of I. i. has been continued by Shakespeare into the third act of the play, at the very heart of the "romantic" part of the plot.

The first sentence of the letter is purely expository: Antonio's bond is forfeit, and he has resigned himself to death. Yet it seems that the resignation is not complete, but conditional: "all debts are cleared between you and I, if I might but see you at my death" [III. ii. 318-20]. This phrasing is virtually repeated at the end of the next scene [III. iii. 35-6]. It is hardly likely that Antonio means by this that if Bassanio fails to be present at his death, then he will remain with monetary debts to his friend's estate. Surely the reference is to the debt of love that Bassanio owes Antonio; Bassanio is being reminded that if he fails to make payment of love by being present at Antonio's death, the accounts will be closed with Antonio's proof of love much in excess of that of his friend. It is a threat aimed at Bassanio's conscience. Here we seem to be faced with another problem, not to be explained by reference to the Renaissance concept of friendship. This is hardly the Antonio who had urged Bassanio not to think of him while at Belmont. Rather, it is an Antonio who is desperately, and almost hopelessly, making a final test of the power of his love over Bassanio; it is a battle now between Antonio and Portia for a prior claim on Bassanio's love. The final sentence of the brief letter surely confirms this. Antonio wishes Bassanio to witness his death (that is, to witness what is virtually his sacrifice for love), but he must come out of love, not out of a sense of duty. And the phrasing seems to suggest that Antonio is none too sure that Bassanio's love will prove strong enough to draw him away from Belmont: "if your love do not persuade you to come, let not my letter" [III. ii. 321-22].

Significantly for the eventual happy ending of the play, as far as it concerns the state of Antonio's mind rather than of his body, Portia's response is instant: "O love, dispatch all business and be gone" [III. ii. 323]. She, at least, is prepared unhesitatingly to yield precedence in such an emergency to the love between the two men. But judging from his reply, the matter might not have been resolved so simply by Bassanio. His

> Since I have your good leave to go away
> I will make haste
>
> [III. ii. 324-25]

indicates that without Portia's "good leave" the choice might not have been so easy. The way is being cleared for a final acceptance by Antonio of the marriage of his friend, a marriage that, through Portia's intervention in the trial, demonstrates to Antonio that Bassanio is not lost to him at all, that indeed he has in Portia no rival but a sharer in Bassanio's love, one whose claims on Bassanio are of such a different nature that he has nothing to fear from her.

The timing of this scene, with the letter arriving immediately after Bassanio's winning of Portia, is especially effective in clarifying the "rivalry in love" interior theme of the play. It adds a stock comic device—the delay in consummation of a marriage—but makes of it something more serious. When the sexual background of the play, as I have outlined it, is kept in mind, it becomes clear that the two kinds of love, heterosexual love and passionate male love, are being played off against each other less lightheartedly than dramatic convention demands, and in delaying the consummation of sexual love between Bassanio and Portia by the implied challenge of his letter, Antonio has won a strategic point. It may be objected that Antonio has had no news from Belmont, that he does not know that he is preventing the completion of the marriage rites, and this is a valid objection. But it must be remembered that this is the effect of the letter, if not the intention, and effect is what matters when the pacing of the scene is so rapid at this point. In any case, it might be noted that although Antonio has made great sacrifices for his friend, and is prepared to make an even greater one, he is *not* prepared to make this sacrifice in silence and without interrupting the purpose (Bassanio's courtship of Portia) for which the sacrifice was required in the first place. His love for Bassanio is not a disinterested, unselfish love; it is demanding, occasionally querulous, and it always requires an ostentatious display of affection. Antonio's relationship with Bassanio is nervous, and even if Shakespeare did not intend it as a portrayal of an incipient homosexual relationship, it certainly suggests one. Perhaps the principal danger to Antonio comes more from the strength of his own emotions, leading him further and further from the sexual and social norm, than from Shylock's knife. He has almost passed from a "friendship" that is socially and morally permissible to a passionate relationship that makes him jealous of Bassanio's pursuit of Portia. At the trial he reaches his lowest moral point, paralyzed beyond the desire to defend himself from Shylock, even though Bassanio has heeded his urgent summons. In a sense, he stands outside the legal procedures, watching them happen to him; they can be of little comfort in his real distress, since he does not know until later that Portia has demonstrated (in III. ii.) that she has no intention, conscious or unconscious, of coming between the two men. Not until he learns this, after the trial, can he accept the love between Bassanio and Portia. With this acceptance Antonio is restored to normal social life. The incident of the rings, usually considered a mere lightening of tone after the tension of the trial, reinforces the lesson for him: it is at his urging that Bassanio neglects Portia's command not to part with the ring.

Thus the play ends with its nominal hero brought back from the dead in more senses than one. We have a double testing motif, and an additional theme almost as important as the more obvious one of the duel between Christian and Jew. While Portia (or rather, her late father) is testing Bassanio with the caskets, Antonio is testing him, too, with the letter. In the theater, perhaps, this sense of tension in the relationship between Antonio and Bassanio and the hint of rivalry between Antonio and Portia for Bassanio's love, which I have desig-

nated the "interior" theme of the play, is far from evident. The romance of Belmont, and the greater excitement of the trial scene, effectively conceal it. But whether or not one accepts Chambers' suggestion that Shakespeare was personally concerned with the problems of male friendship, it seems clear that there is more in Antonio's behavior towards Bassanio than can be completely accounted for by reference to the conventional treatment of the "amity" theme. (pp. 328-41)

John D. Hurrell, "Love and Friendship in 'The Merchant of Venice'," in Texas Studies in Literature and Language, *Vol. III, No. 3, Autumn, 1961, pp. 328-41.*

BARBARA K. LEWALSKI   (essay date 1962)

[*In one of the most frequently cited essays on* The Merchant of Venice, *Lewalski notes that whereas such earlier critics as Nevill Coghill (1949) and others have emphasized the allegorical nature of the trial scene in Shakespeare's play, no one has interpreted the entire work as a conscious effort to dramatize, through allegory, the medieval story of* The Parliament in Heaven. *Lewalski analyzes both the moral and allegorical meanings of the different characters and events in the play to identify the numerous points at which the action is organized according to this Christian homily and, especially, the ideological conflict between Old and New Testament values at issue therein. The critic makes two important points, among others, in her examination of* The Merchant of Venice: *first, she claims that Shylock's forced conversion, when viewed in light of the play's symbolic design, "is not antisemitic revenge," but a merciful action that substantiates what Shylock's own experience during the trial has demonstrated—"that the Law leads only to death and destruction, that faith in Christ must supplant human righteousness"; and second, she argues that Act V is necessary as "a comic parody of the trial scene" in which, on the moral level, the metaphor of "venturing" or "sacrifice" is depicted in the realm of romantic love, and, on the allegorical level, the judgment of a human soul (Bassanio) is enacted according to those same Christian standards applied to Shylock. For further discussion of the allegorical nature of* The Merchant of Venice *and interpretation of its central conflict, see the excerpts by Denton J. Snider (1890), Sir Israel Gollancz (1922), Muriel C. Brudbrook (1951), Theodor Reik (1956), C. L. Barber (1959), E. M. W. Tillyard (1961), and René E. Fortin (1974). Also, see the excerpts by Karl Elze (1871), Harold C. Goddard (1951), E. M. W. Tillyard (1961), A. D. Moody (1964), R. Chris Hassel, Jr. (1970), and René Girard (1978) for various readings opposing Lewalski's assessment that Shylock's forced conversion is merciful and Christian.*]

The allegorical aspects of *The Merchant of Venice* can, I believe, be greatly illuminated by the medieval allegorical method exemplified by Dante. . . . In contrast to personification allegory wherein a particular is created to embody an insensible, Dante's symbolic method causes a particular real situation to suggest a meaning or meanings beyond itself. In [*The Merchant of Venice*] Shakespeare, like Dante, is ultimately concerned with the nature of the Christian life, though as a dramatist he is fully as interested in the way in which the allegorical dimensions enrich the particular instance as in the use of the particular to point to higher levels of meaning. The various dimensions of allegorical significance in [*The Merchant of Venice*], though not consistently maintained throughout the play and not susceptible of analysis with schematic rigor, are generally analogous to Dante's four levels of allegorical meaning: a literal or story level; an allegorical significance concerned with truths relating to humanity as a whole and to Christ as head of humanity; a moral or tropological level dealing with factors in the moral development of the individual; and an anagogical significance treating the ultimate reality, the Heavenly City. Moreover, comprehension of the play's allegorical meanings leads to a recognition of its fundamental unity, discrediting the common critical view that it is a hotchpotch which developed contrary to Shakespeare's conscious intention.

The use of Biblical allusion to point to such allegorical meanings must now be illustrated in relation to the various parts of the work.

At what would correspond in medieval terminology to the "moral" level, the play is concerned to explore and define Christian love and its various antitheses. As revealed in the action, Christian love involves both giving and forgiving: it demands an attitude of carelessness regarding the things of this world founded upon a trust in God's providence; an attitude of self-forgetfulness and humility founded upon recognition of man's common sinfulness; a readiness to give and risk everything, possessions and person, for the sake of love; and a willingness to forgive injuries and to love enemies. In all but the last respect, Antonio is presented throughout the play as the very embodiment of Christian love, and Shylock functions as one (but not the only) antithesis to it.

Antonio's practice of Christian love is indicated throughout the play under the metaphor of "venturing", and the action begins with the use of this metaphor in a mock test of his attitude toward wealth and worldly goods. The key scripture text opposing love of this world to the Christian love of God and neighbor is Matt. vi. 19-21, 31-33:

> Lay not up treasures for your selves upon the earth, where the moth and canker corrupt, & where theeves dig through, and steale. / But lay up treasures for your selves in heaven. . . . / For where your treasure is, there will your heart be also / . . . . Therefore take no thought, saying, what shall we eate? or what shall we drink? or wherewith shall we be clothed? / . . . But seeke ye first the kingdome of God, and his righteousnesse, & all these things shalbe ministred unto you.

(pp. 328-29)

The quality of Antonio's love is [thus] shown in the positive forms of charity and benevolence. . . . Though his first loan to Bassanio has not been repaid, Antonio is willing to "venture" again for his friend "My purse, my person, my extremest means" [I. i. 138], even to the pledge of a pound of his flesh. And when this pledge (and with it his life) is forfeit, he can still release Bassanio from debt: "debts are clear'd between you and I" [III. ii. 318-19]. Furthermore, Antonio lends money in the community at large without seeking interest, and often aids victims of Shylock's usurious practices [I. iii. 44-5; III. iii. 22-3].

Shylock's "thrift" poses the precise contrast to Antonio's "ventures". His is the worldliness of niggardly prudence, well-characterized by his avowed motto, "Fast bind, fast find,— / A proverb never stale in thrifty mind" [II. v. 54-5]. He locks up house and stores before departing, he begrudges food and maintenance to his servant Launcelot, he demands usurious "assurance" before lending money. This concern with the world poisons all his relations with others and even his love for Jessica: the confused cries, "My daughter! O my ducats! O my daughter!" after Jessica's departure [II. viii. 15], reveal, not his lack of love for his daughter, but his laughable and pitiable inability to determine what he loves most. Shylock also manifests pride and self-righteousness (p. 330)

The moral contrast of Shylock and Antonio is more complex with reference to that most difficult injunction of the Sermon on the Mount—forgiveness of injuries and love of enemies. Recollection of this demand should go far to resolve the question as to whether an Elizabethan audience would regard Shylock's grievances as genuine: presumably an audience which could perceive the Biblical standard operating throughout the play would also see its relevance here. . . . Antonio at the outset of the play is rather in the position of the publican described as friendly to his brethren only—he loves and forgives Bassanio beyond all measure, but hates and reviles Shylock. For evidence of this we have not only Shylock's indictment, "You call me misbeliever, cut-throat dog, / And spet upon my Jewish gaberdine, / . . . And foot me as you spurn a stranger cur" [I. iii. 111-12, 118], but also Antonio's angry reply promising continuation of such treatment: "I am as like to call thee so again, / To spet on thee again, to spurn thee too" [I. iii. 130-31]. Indeed, the moral tension of the play is lost if we do not see that Shylock, having been the object of great wrongs, must make a difficult choice between forgiveness and revenge—and that Antonio later finds himself in precisely the same situation.

Ironically, Shylock poses at first as the more "Christian" of the two in that, after detailing his wrongs, he explicitly proposes to turn the other cheek. . . . Of course it is merely pretence: Shylock had declared for revenge at the first sight of Antonio [I. iii. 46-7], and, according to Jessica's later report, he eagerly planned for the forfeit of Antonio's flesh long before the bond came due [III. ii. 284-90]. And in this fixed commitment to revenge, this mockery of forgiveness, lies I believe the reason for the often-deplored change from the "human" Shylock of the earlier scenes to the "monster" of Act IV. At the level of the moral allegory Shylock undergoes (rather like Milton's Satan) the progressive deterioration of evil; he turns by his own choice into the cur that he has been called. . . . Conversely, Antonio in the trial scene suffers hatred and injury but foregoes revenge and rancor, manifesting a genuine spirit of forgiveness—for Shylock's forced conversion is not revenge, as will be seen. Thus, his chief deficiency surmounted, Antonio becomes finally a perfect embodiment of Christian love.

The Shylock-Antonio opposition functions also at what the medieval theorists would call the "allegorical" level; in these terms it symbolizes the confrontation of Judaism and Christianity as theological systems—the Old Law and the New—and also as historic societies. In their first encounter, Shylock's reference to Antonio as a "fawning publican" and to himself as a member of the "sacred nation" [I. iii. 41, 48] introduces an important aspect of this contrast. The reference is of course to the parable of the Pharisee and the Publican (Luke xviii. 9-13) which was spoken "unto certayne which trusted in themselves, that they were ryghteous, and despised other". . . . The contemporary interpretation of this parable is suggested in [L.] Tomson's note [to his edition of the New Testament]: "Two things especially make our prayers voyde and of none effect: confidence of our owne ryghteousnesse, and the contempts of other. . . . we [are] despised of God, as proude & arrogant, if we put never so little trust in our owne workes before God." Through this allusion, then, the emphasis of the Old Law upon perfect legal righteousness is opposed to the tenet of the New Law that righteousness is impossible to fallen man and must be replaced by faith—an opposition which will be further discussed with reference to the trial scene.

Also in this first encounter between Antonio and Shylock, the argument about usury contrasts Old Law and New in terms resembling those frequently found in contemporary polemic addressed to the usury question. Appealing to the Old Testament, Shylock sets forth an analogy between Jacob's breeding of ewes and rams and the breeding of money to produce interest. Antonio, denying the analogy with the query, "is your gold and silver ewes and rams?" [I. iii. 95] echoes the commonplace Christian argument (based upon Aristotle) that to take interest is to "breed" barren metal, which is unnatural. (pp. 330-32)

At this same encounter, Shylock's pretense of following the Christian prescription regarding forgiveness of injuries again contrasts Old Law and New as theological systems, for it recalls the fact that Christ in the Sermon on the Mount twice opposed the Christian standard to the Old Law's demand for strict justice. . . . Later, some of the language of the trial scene alludes again to the differing demands of the two dispensations with regard to forgiveness of enemies:

> *Bass:* Do all men kill the things they do not love?
> *Shy:* Hates any man the thing he would not kill?
> *Bass:* Every offense is not a hate at first!
> *Shy:* What! wouldst thou have a serpent sting thee twice?
>
> [IV. i. 66-9]

And the Duke reiterates this opposition almost too pointedly when he tenders Shylock the mercy of the Christian court, observing that Shylock could recognize from this "the difference of our spirit" [IV. i. 368]. . . . (pp. 332-33)

This allegorical dimension encompasses also the historical experience of the two societies, Jewish and Christian. . . . Shylock's passionate outcries against Antonio . . . take on larger than personal significance: they record the sufferings of his entire race in an alien Christian society—"he hath disgrac'd me . . . laugh'd at my losses, mock'd at my gains, scorned my nation, thwarted my bargains, cooled my friends, heated mine enemies—and what's his reason? I am a Jew!" [III. i. 54-8]. This is followed by the eloquent plea for recognition of the common humanity Jew shares with Christian, "Hath not a Jew eyes? . . ." [III. i. 59ff.], and it concludes with the telling observation that despite the Christian's professions about "humility" and turning the other cheek, in practice he is quick to revenge himself upon the Jew. The taunts of Solario, Solanio, and Gratiano throughout the play give some substantiation to these charges.

Yet overlaying this animosity are several allusions to Shylock's future conversion, suggesting the Christian expectation of the final, pre-millennial conversion of the Jews. The first such reference occurs, most appropriately, just after Shylock's feigned offer to forego usury and forgive injury. Antonio salutes Shylock's departure with the words . . . , "The Hebrew will turn Christian, he grows kind" [I. iii. 178]. "Kind" in this context implies both "natural" (in foregoing unnatural interest) and "charitable"; thus Antonio suggests that voluntary adoption of these fundamental Christian principles would lead to the conversion of the Jew. The second prediction occurs in Lorenzo's declaration, "If e'er the Jew her father come to heaven, / It will be for his gentle daughter's sake" [II. iv. 33-4]—again with the pun on gentle-gentile. As Shylock's daughter and as a voluntary convert to Christianity, Jessica may figure forth the filial relationship of the New Dispensation to the Old, and Lorenzo's prediction may carry an allusion to Paul's prophecy

that the Jews will ultimately be saved through the agency of the Gentiles. At any rate, the final conversion of the Jews is symbolized in just such terms in the trial scene: because Antonio is able to rise at last to the demands of Christian love, Shylock is not destroyed, but, albeit rather harshly, converted. Interestingly enough, however, even after Portia's speeches at the trial have reminded Antonio and the court of the Christian principles they profess, Gratiano yet persists in demanding revenge. This incident serves as a thematic counterpoint to the opposition of Old Law and New, suggesting the disposition of Christians themselves to live rather according to the Old Law than the New. Such a counterpoint is developed at various points throughout the play—in Antonio's initial enmity to Shylock, in the jeers of the minor figures, in Shylock's statements likening his revenge to the customary vengeful practices of the Christians and his claim to a pound of flesh to their slave trade in human flesh [IV. i. 90-100]. Thus the play does not present arbitrary, black-and-white moral estimates of human groups, but takes into account the shadings and complexities of the real world.

As Shylock and Antonio embody the theological conflicts and historical interrelationships of Old Law and New, so do they also reflect, from time to time, the ultimate sources of their principles in a further allegorical significance. Antonio, who assumes the debts of others (rescuing Bassanio, the self-confessed "Prodigal", from a debt due under the law) reflects on occasion the role of Christ satisfying the claim of Divine Justice by assuming the sins of mankind. . . . And Shylock, demanding the "bond" which is due him under the law, reflects the role of the devil, to whom the entire human race is in bondage through sin—an analogy which Portia makes explicit when she terms his hold upon Antonio a "state of hellish cruelty". . . . As E. E. Stoll points out, the identification of Jew and Devil is repeated nine times in the play, and was a commonplace of medieval and Elizabethan antisemitic literature. Yet it seems to function here less to heap opprobrium upon the Jew than to suggest the ultimate source of the principles of revenge and hatred which Shylock seeks to justify out of the Law. (pp. 333-35)

The story of Bassanio and the casket choice also appears to incorporate a "moral" and an "allegorical" meaning. At the moral level, the incident explores the implications of Christian love in the romantic relationship, whereas Antonio's story deals with Christian love in terms of friendship and social intercourse. Morocco, in renouncing the leaden casket because it does not offer "fair advantages", and in choosing the gold which promises "what many men desire" [II. vii. 19, 37], exemplifies the confusion of love with external shows: like most of the world, he values Portia not for herself but for her beauty and wealth. However, the death's head within the golden casket indicates the common mortality to which all such accidents as wealth and beauty are finally subject. Aragon, by contrast, represents love of self so strong that it precludes any other love. He renounces the gold because he considers himself superior to the common multitude whom it attracts; he disdains the lead as not "fair" enough to deserve his hazard; and in choosing the silver which promises "as much as he deserves" he declares boldly, "I will assume desert" [II. ix. 51]. But the blinking idiot in the casket testifies to the folly of him who supposes that love can be bargained for in the pitiful coin of human merit. Bassanio, on the other hand, chooses the lead casket which warns, "Who chooseth me, must give and hazard all he hath" [II. ix. 21]—thus signifying his acceptance of the self-abnegation, risk, and venture set up throughout the play as characteristics of true Christian love. And the metaphor of the "venture" is constantly used with reference to Bassanio and Portia just as it is with Antonio. (p. 335)

At the "allegorical" level, the caskets signify everyman's choice of the paths to spiritual life or death. This analogy is explicitly developed in the "Moral" appended to the casket story in the *Gesta Romanorum* which is almost certainly Shakespeare's source for this incident. In the *Gesta* the casket choice tests the worthiness of a maiden (the soul) to wed the son of an Emperor (Christ). The moral declares, "The Emperour sheweth this Mayden three vessells, that is to say, God putteth before man life & death, good and evill, & which of these he chooseth hee shall obtaine." . . . That Shakespeare intended . . . to make the caskets symbolize the great choices of spiritual life and death, is evident by the constant references in the lovers' conversation to "life" and "death" just before Bassanio's venture. . . . That the casket choice represents Everyman's choice among values is further emphasized by the multitude at Portia's door: some of them refuse to choose (like the inhabitants of the vestibule of Hell in Dante); others choose wrongly and, having demonstrated by this that they are already wedded to false values, are forbidden to make another marriage. Furthermore, Antonio's action in making possible Bassanio's successful venture reflects the role of Christ in making possible for the true Christian the choice of spiritual life, the love of God. (p. 336)

Bassanio's choice of the lead casket is the choice of life, the love of God. The use of romantic love as a symbol for divine love is of course a commonplace in mystical literature. . . . Bassanio's meditation on the caskets [III. ii. 73-107] symbolically suggests his understanding and renunciation of the two kinds of "Ornament" which oppose this love: his description of the silver as "thou common drudge between man and man" suggests his knowledge of the pretense of righteousness with which men generally cover their vices when presenting themselves to others, and the skull image which he uses in denouncing the gold indicates his awareness of the transience and corruptibility of worldly goods. (p. 337)

The trial scene climaxes the action at all the levels of meaning that have been established. As has been suggested, it portrays at the moral level Shylock's degradation to a cur and a monster through his commitment to revenge, and by contrast, Antonio's attainment of the fullness of Christian love through his abjuration of revenge. Allegorically, the scene develops the sharpest opposition of Old Law and New in terms of their respective theological principles, Justice and Mercy, Righteousness and Faith; it culminates in the final defeat of the Old Law and the symbolic conversion of the Jew. (p. 338)

Antonio's predicament in the courtroom of Venice is made to suggest traditional literary and iconographical presentations of the "Parliament of Heaven" in which fallen man was judged. Both sides agree that Antonio's bond (like the sinner's) is forfeit according to the law, and that the law of Venice (like that of God) cannot be abrogated. Shylock constantly threatens, "If you deny me, fie upon your law" [IV. i. 101], and Portia concurs, "there is no power in Venice / Can alter a decree established" [IV. i. 218-19]. The only question then is whether the law must be applied with strictest justice, or whether mercy may somehow temper it. In the traditional allegory of the Parliament of Heaven, Justice and Mercy, as the two principal of the four "daughters" of God, debate over the judgement to be meted out to man. . . . So in the trial scene Shylock as the embodiment of the Old Law represents Justice: "I stand for

Judgement. . . . I stand here for Law" [IV. i. 103, 142], whereas Portia identifies herself with that "Quality of Mercy" enthroned by the New Law. Also, another conception of the Heavenly Court is superadded to this by means of several references during the trial to Shylock as Devil [IV. i. 217, 287]. The scene takes on something of the significance of the trial described in the medieval drama, the *Processus Belial*, in which the Devil claims by justice the souls of mankind due him under the law, and the Virgin Mary intercedes for man by appealing to the Mercy of God.

In either formulation, the demands of Justice and Mercy are reconciled only through the sacrifice of Christ, who satisfies the demands of justice by assuming the debts of mankind, and thus makes mercy possible. Therefore it is not surprising that the courtroom scene also evokes something of the crucifixion scene—as the moment of reconciling these opposed forces, as the time of defeat for the Old Law, as the prime example of Christian Love and the object of Christian Faith. Both plot situation and language suggest a typical killing of Christ by the Jew. Antonio, baring his breast to shed his blood for the debt of another, continues the identification with Christ occasionally suggested at other points in the play. Shylock's cry, "My deeds upon my head" [IV. i. 206] clearly suggests the assumption of guilt by the Jews at Christ's crucifixion . . . , and his later remark, "I have a daughter— / Would any of the stock of Barrabas / Had been her husband, rather than a Christian" [IV. i. 295-97] recalls the Jews' choice of the murderer Barrabas over Christ as the prisoner to be released at Passover (Matt. xxvii. 16-21). (p. 339)

Throughout the action thus far described, Shylock has persistently denied pleas to temper justice with mercy—to forgive part of the debt, to accept three times the value of the debt rather than the pound of flesh, or even to supply a doctor "for charity" to stop Antonio's wounds. His perversity is rooted in his explicit denial of any need to "deserve" God's mercy by showing mercy to others, for he arrogates to himself the perfect righteousness which is the standard of the Old Law—"What judgment shall I dread doing no wrong?" [IV. i. 89]. Accordingly, after Portia's "Tarry a little", the action of the scene works out a systematic destruction of that claim of righteousness, using the laws of Venice as symbol. Shylock is shown first that he can claim nothing by the law: his claim upon Antonio's flesh is disallowed by the merest technicality. This reflects the Christian doctrine that although perfect performance of the Law would indeed merit salvation, in fact fallen man could never perfectly observe it, any more than Shylock could take Antonio's flesh without drawing blood. . . . Next, Shylock is shown that in claiming the Law he not only gains nothing, but stands to lose all that he possesses and even life itself. He becomes subject to what Paul terms the "curse" of the Law, since he is unable to fulfill its conditions: "For as many as are of the workes of the Lawe, are under the curse: for it is written, Cursed is every man that continueth not in all things, which are written in the booke of the Lawe, to do them" (Gal. iii. 10). (p. 340)

Shylock's "forced conversion" (a gratuitous addition made by Shakespeare to the source story in *ll Pecorone*) must be viewed in the context of the symbolic action thus far described. Now that Shylock's claim to legal righteousness has been totally destroyed, he is made to accept the only alternative to it, faith in Christ. Paul declares (Gal. ii. 16), "A man is not justified by the workes of the Lawe, but by the fayth of Jesus Christ." . . . Thus the stipulation for Shylock's conversion, though it of course assumes the truth of Christianity, is not antisemitic revenge: it simply compels Shylock to avow what his own experience in the trial scene has fully "demonstrated"—that the Law leads only to death and destruction, that faith in Christ must supplant human righteousness. In this connection it ought to be noted that Shylock's pecuniary punishment under the laws of Venice precisely parallels the conditions imposed upon a Jewish convert to Christianity throughout most of Europe and also in England during the Middle Ages and after. All his property and goods, as the ill-gotten gain of usury, were forfeit to the state upon his conversion, but he was customarily allotted some proportion (often half) of his former goods for his maintenance, or else given a stipend or some other means of support.

There is some evidence that Shylock himself in this scene recognizes the logic which demands his conversion, though understandably he finds this too painful to admit explicitly. His incredulous question "Is that the law" [IV. i. 314] when he finds the law invoked against him, shows a new and overwhelming consciousness of the defects of legalism. Also, he does not protest the condition that he become a Christian as he protested the judgment (soon reversed) which would seize all his property: his brief "I am content" [IV. i. 394] suggests, I believe, not mean-spiritedness but weary acknowledgement of the fact that he can no longer make his stand upon the discredited Law. (p. 341)

The ring episode is, in a sense, a comic parody of the trial scene—it provides a means whereby Bassanio may make at least token fulfillment of his offer to give "life itself, my wife, and all the world" [IV. i. 284] to deliver Antonio. The ring is the token of his possession of Portia and all Belmont: in offering it Portia declared, "This house, these servants, and this same myself / Are yours . . . I give them with this ring, / Which when you part from, lose, or give away, / Let it presage the ruin of your love, / And be my vantage to exclaim on you" [III. ii. 170-74]. So that in giving the ring to the "lawyer" Balthasar—which he does only at Antonio's bidding—Bassanio surrenders his "claim" to all these gifts, even to Portia's person, and is therefore taunted at his return with her alleged infidelity. But Belmont is the land of the spirit, not the letter, and therefore after Bassanio has been allowed for a moment to feel his loss, the whole crisis dissolves in laughter and amazement as Antonio again binds himself (his soul this time the forfeit) for Bassanio's future fidelity, and Portia reveals her own part in the affair. At the moral level, this pledge and counter pledge by Bassanio and Antonio continue the "venture" metaphor and further exemplify the willingness to give all for love. At the allegorical level, despite the lighthearted treatment, Bassanio's comic "trial" suggests the "judgment" awaiting the Christian soul as it presents its final account and is found deficient. But Love, finally, is the fulfillment of the Law and covers all defects—Bassanio's (Everyman's) love in giving up everything, in token at least, for Antonio, and Antonio's (Christ's) love toward him and further pledge in his behalf.

Belmont functions chiefly at the anagogical level (if one may invoke the term): it figures forth the Heavenly City. . . . Here Gentile and Jew, Lorenzo and Jessica, are united in each other's arms, talking of the music of the spheres . . . :

> Look how the floor of heaven
> Is thick inlaid with patens of bright gold,
> There's not the smallest orb which thou behold'st

> But in his motion like an angel sings,
> Still quiring to the young-eye'd cherubins;
> Such harmony is in immortal souls

> [V. i. 58-63]

And Portia's allusion upon returning, "Peace!—how the moon sleeps with Endymion, / And would not be awak'd" [V. i. 109-10] also suggests eternity, for Diana, enamoured of Endymion's beauty, caused him to sleep forever on Mount Latmos. In Belmont all losses are restored and sorrows end: Bassanio wins again his lady and all Belmont; Antonio is given a letter signifying that three of his argosies are returned to port richly laden; and Lorenzo receives the deed naming him Shylock's future heir. Lorenzo's exclamation, "Fair ladies, you drop manna in the way of starving people" [V. i. 294-95], together with the reference to "patens" in the passage quoted above, sets up an implied metaphor of the heavenly communion. Here all who have cast their bread upon the waters in the "ventures" of Christian love receive the reward promised. . . . (pp. 342-43)

> *Barbara K. Lewalski, "Biblical Allusion and Allegory in 'The Merchant of Venice'," in* Shakespeare Quarterly, *Vol. XIII, No. 3, Summer, 1962, pp. 327-43.*

SIGURD BURCKHARDT (essay date 1962)

[*Focusing on the controlling metaphor of bonds and bonding in* The Merchant of Venice, *Burckhardt contends that the play is about "circularity and circulation" and that it "asks how the vicious circle of the bond's law can be transformed into the ring of love." He claims that* The Merchant of Venice *provides the answer to this question in both a dramatic and a reflexive manner: the first, in Portia's "literal and unreserved submission to the bond as absolutely binding" as the only means of liberating Antonio from that bond's demands; the second, in Shakespeare's method of writing his play, in that he found his creative freedom not outside the sources of his tale but deeper within that tale's own exigencies. For further discussion of the language and imagery in* The Merchant of Venice, *see the excerpts by Caroline F. E. Spurgeon (1935) and B. Ifor Evans (1952). Also, see the excerpts by John P. Sisk (1969) and Alice N. Benston (1979) for additional commentary on the theme of bonds and bonding and its importance in the play. The following excerpt is taken from an essay originally published in the journal* ELH *in September, 1962.*]

The danger of literary source-hunting is that it abets our natural tendency to discount things we believe we have accounted for. The source, once found, relieves us of the effort to see what a thing *is;* we are satisfied with having discovered how it got there. Shakespeare's plots—especially his comedy plots—have generally been at a discount; we have been content to say that the poet took his stories pretty much as he found them and then, as the phrase goes, "breathed life" into them, enriched them with his subtle characterizations and splendid poetry. That the dramatist must make his plot into the prime metaphor of his meaning—this classical demand Shakespeare was magnanimously excused from, the more readily because by the same token we were excused from the labor of discovering the meaning of complex and "improbable" plots.

But with the plot thus out of the way, other problems often arose. *The Merchant of Venice* is a case in point. Audiences persist in feeling distressed by Shylock's final treatment, and no amount of historical explanation helps them over their unease. It is little use telling them that their attitude toward the Jew is anachronistic, distorted by modern, un-Elizabethan opinions about racial equality and religious tolerance. They know better; they know that, in the play itself, they have been made to take Shylock's part so strongly that his end seems cruel. Nor does it do them much good to be told that Shakespeare, being Shakespeare, "could not help" humanizing the stereotype villain he found in his sources; Richard III and Iago are also given depth and stature, but we do not feel sorry for them. If we regard *The Merchant* as a play of character rather haphazardly flung over a prefabricated plot, we cannot join, as unreservedly as we are meant to, in the joyful harmonies of the last act; Shylock spooks in the background, an unappeased ghost.

The source of our unease is simple enough: Shylock gets more than his share of good lines. This is nowhere more evident than in the courtroom scene, where he and Antonio, villain and hero, are pitted against each other in a rhetorical climax.... The toughness of Shylock's argument [IV. i. 35-62] is embodied in the toughness of his lines, his passion in their speed and directness: this is a man who *speaks*. We might simply say that Shakespeare here is writing close to his dramatic best; but if by this time he was able to give his devils their due, why does he leave his hero shamed? Antonio's lines [IV. i. 70-83] are flaccidly oratorical; his similes move with a symmetry so slow and pedantic that our expectations continually outrun them.... True, the burden of his speech is resignation; but it is feeble rather than noble, a collapse from overstatement into helplessness.

The historical critic may protest at this point that such a judgment reflects a modern bias against rhetoric, a twentieth-century preference for the understated and purely dramatic. But the qualities which make us rank Shylock's lines over Antonio's have long been accepted among the criteria by which we seek to establish the sequence of Shakespeare's plays, on the assumption that where we find them we have evidence of greater maturity and mastery. Nor is this only an assumption. In *The Merchant* itself there is a crucial occasion where these qualities are preferred and where, had the choice been different, the consequence would have been disaster for Antonio. The occasion is Bassanio's choice of the right casket; he rejects the golden one, because it is "mere ornament," and prefers lead:

> thou meagre lead,
> Which rather threat'nest than dost promise aught,
> Thy plainness moves me more than eloquence.
> [III. ii. 104-06]

At a decisive moment, Bassanio's critical judgment is the same as ours; so that, when we find ourselves more moved by Shylock's plainness than by Antonio's eloquence, we have the best possible reason for feeling sure that Shakespeare intended us to be.

For Bassanio's judgment is "critical" in more senses than one: the play's happy outcome hangs on his taste. Had he judged wrongly, Portia could not have appeared in court to render her second and saving judgment. In the casket scene, the action turns on the *styles* of metals, conceived as modes of speech; the causalities of the play assume a significance which is, initially at least, only obscured by our being told that Shakespeare's plot is to be found in *Il Pecorone* and the *Gesta Romanorum*. Why does Portia come to Venice? Because Bassanio chooses plainness over eloquence. And how is Bassanio put into the position to make that choice? By Antonio's having bound himself to Shylock. That is how the causal chain of the story runs; it does not run from Fiorentino to Shakespeare.

And as in any good play, so here the causality reveals the meaning of the whole. It shows that the plot is *circular:* bound in such a way that the instrument of destruction, the bond, turns out to be the source of deliverance. Portia, won through the bond, wins Antonio's release from it; what is more, she wins it, not by breaking the bond, but by submitting to its rigor more rigorously than even the Jew had thought to do. So seen, one of Shakespeare's apparently most fanciful plots proved to be one of the most exactly structured; it is what it should be: the play's controlling metaphor. As the subsidiary metaphors of the bond and the ring indicate, *The Merchant* is a play about circularity and circulation; it asks how the vicious circle of the bond's law can be transformed into the ring of love. And it answers: through a literal and unreserved submission to the bond as absolutely binding. It is as though Shakespeare, finding himself bound to a story already drawn up for him in his source, had taken it as the test of his creative freedom and had discovered that this freedom lay, not in a feeble, Antonio-like resignation, which consoles itself with the consciousness of its inner superiority to the vulgar exigencies of reality, but in a Portia-like acceptance and penetration of these exigencies to the point where they must yield their liberating truth. The play's ultimate circularity may well be that it tells the story of its own composition, of its being created, wholly given and intractably positive though it seems, by the poet's discovery of what it is.

The world of *The Merchant* consists of two separate and mostly discontiguous realms: Venice and Belmont, the realm of law and the realm of love, the public sphere and the private. Venice is a community firmly established and concerned above all else with preserving its stability; it is a closed world, inherently conservative, because it knows that it stands and falls with the sacredness of contracts. Belmont, on the other hand, is open and potential; in it a union—that of lovers—is to be founded rather than defended. The happy ending arises from the interaction of the two realms: the bond makes possible the transfer of the action to Belmont, which then *re*-acts upon Venice. The public order is saved from the deadly logic of its own constitution by having been transposed, temporarily, to the private sphere.

But it is not a matter merely of transposition. Each realm has, as it were, its own language, so that the process is better described as a retranslation. Antonio's bonding is a necessary condition for Bassanio's winning Portia, but it is not a sufficient cause; the riddle of the caskets must be correctly *interpreted*. And in exactly the same way the winning of Portia is a necessary condition but not a sufficient cause for the redemption of the bond; it likewise cannot be bought but must be correctly interpreted. The language of love and liberality does not simply supersede that of "use" (=usury) and law; it must first be translated from it and then back into it. Love must learn to speak the public language, grasp its peculiar grammar; Shylock, to be defeated, must be spoken to in his own terms. That he compels this retranslation is his triumph, Pyrrhic though it turns out to be.

The Jew draws his eloquence and dignity from raising to the level of principle something which by its very nature seems to deny principle: use. Antonio's most serious mistake—or rather failure of imagination—is that he cannot conceive of this possibility. He takes a fearful risk for Bassanio, but he cannot claim full credit for it, because he does not know what he is risking. Not only is he confident that his ships will come home a month before the day; he is taken in by Shylock's harmless interpretation of the "merry jest," the pound-of-flesh clause:

Act III. Scene iii. Shylock, Antonio, Solanio, and the Jailer. By R. Westall.

> To buy his favour, I extend this friendship.
>
> [I. iii. 168]

He is sure that the Jew wants to *buy* something, to make some kind of profit, and pleasantly surprised that the profit is to be of so "gentle" (=gentile) a kind; he cannot conceive that a greedy usurer would risk three thousand ducats for a profitless piece of carrion flesh. His too fastidious generosity prevents him from reckoning with the generosity of hatred. . . . The worst he expects is the exacting of "barren metal"; that it will turn out to be a pound of his own flesh does not enter his haughtily gentle mind.

But the play, thanks largely to Shylock's imagination, insistently makes the point that metal is not barren; it does breed, is pregnant with consequences, and capable of transformation into life and even love. Metal it is which brings Bassanio as a suitor to Belmont, metal which holds Portia's picture and with it herself. When Shylock runs through Venice crying: "My ducats and my daughter" [II. viii. 17], we are as shallow as Venetian dandies and street urchins if we simply echo him with ridicule. . . . In this merchant's world money is a great good, is life itself. When Antonio . . . learns that three of his argosies are "richly" come to harbor, he is not scornful of mere pelf but says:

> Sweet lady, you have given me life and living.
>
> [V. i. 286]

(Which makes him Shylock's faithful echo: "You take my life / When you do take the means whereby I live" [IV. i. 376-77].) Bassanio, with Shylock's ducats, ventures to Belmont to win "a lady richly left" and so to rid himself of his debts; it is a good deal worse than irrelevant to blame him (as some gentlemen critics, of independent income no doubt, have done) for being a fortune hunter. One, perhaps *the* lesson Antonio is made to learn is a lesson in metal-breeding. (pp. 206-14)

In Belmont the Jew's money promises to breed in a more literal sense: it helps to unite lovers. The equation money = offspring is pointed up by Gratiano, in a line which echoes Shylock's "My ducats and my daughter":

> We'll play with them the first boy for a thousand ducats.
>
> [III. ii. 214-15]

More precisely, the money makes the union possible; the consummation turns out to be rather more complicated.

I have stressed the differences between Belmont and Venice; but in one respect they are alike: both are governed by rigorously positive laws, which threaten to frustrate the very purposes they are meant to serve, but which must nevertheless be obeyed. In fact, the rule which governs Belmont—the covenant of the caskets—seems even more wilfully positive than that of Venice. More rigidly even than the law of the bond, it puts obedience above meaning, the letter above the spirit.

The harshly positive character of Venetian law is evident enough. When Bassanio pleads a kind of natural law, man's intuitive sense of justice, he is sternly corrected by Portia:

> Bassanio: If this will not suffice, it must appear
> That malice bears down truth. And I
>   beseech you,
> Wrest once the law to your authority;
> To do a great right, do a little wrong,
> And curb this cruel devil of his will.
> Portia: It must not be; there is no power in
>   Venice
> Can alter a decree established.
> 'Twill be recorded for a precedent,
> And many an error by the same example
> Will rush into the state. It cannot be.
>
> [IV. i. 213-22]

But Portia here can still appeal to reason, can show that the law which is at the mercy of man's "sense of justice" fails of its purpose, even though, taken as positively binding, it may also frustrate that purpose. Nerissa, defending the wisdom of the casket test against Portia's rebellious complaints, has no argument to fall back on except authority and faith:

> Portia: I may neither choose who I would nor refuse
> who I dislike; so is the will of a living daughter curb'd by the will of a dead father. Is it
> not hard, Nerissa, that I cannot choose one
> nor refuse none?
> Nerissa: Your father was ever virtuous, and holy
> men at their death have good inspirations.
>
> [I. ii. 23-8]

The wisdom of the father's will can be proved only in the event.

The law of Belmont, then, demands submission quite as much as that of Venice; it too disallows mere feeling. But it differs in one decisive point: it permits, in fact (as the result shows) requires interpretation by *substance* rather than by letter. Aragon and Morocco fail because they try to interpret the lines inscribed on the caskets rather than the substance; they calculate which of the inscriptions correctly states the relation between their own worth, Portia's worth and the risk of choosing wrongly. For them the caskets are mere clues; what they are really concerned with is themselves and the object of their suit. It is this intrusion of their selves and their purposes that misleads them; they are enmeshed in their reckonings. The noteworthy thing about Bassanio is that he disregards the inscriptions; he lets the metals themselves speak to him (quite literally: he apostrophizes them as speakers). Once before the caskets, he seems almost to forget Portia, himself, and his purpose. He does not look for signs, pointers along the way to his goal; he stops—and listens to the things themselves. And so he wins. (pp. 215-17)

Yet this release into pure fancy is in its nature momentary; in human existence—and so in drama—purpose and use cannot long be set aside. "Fancy" is bred neither in the head nor in the heart, neither by will nor by thought; it is the child of pure vision. But being that, it lives only in the moment; its cradle is its grave. When the predestined pair is happily united and everything seems to have dissolved into pure concord, we are promptly reminded that there is an accounting still due back in prosaic Venice. Belmont is bound to Venice as surely as Antonio is to Shylock. If the bond were not acknowledged, the bliss of the lovers would remain private, encapsuled in the barren half-fulfilment of fancy and sheer, useless poetry, while in the public world of prose and use time and the law would run their deadly course. The parthenogenesis of fancy has no lasting issue; the union of Portia and Bassanio must remain unconsummated until after the retranslation to Venice.... (p. 218)

At this point I had better deal with a question which may have troubled the reader for some time. I suggested that for Shakespeare the play he had been commissioned to do, or rather to rework (with a three-month deadline?) from a story already fixed, became the metaphor of the bondage he found himself in, and that the way to freedom he discovered was Portia's way of a radical and literal acceptance. Obviously this theory, if it is to be more than idle speculation, implies that Shakespeare did follow his source religiously; the question is: is this in fact true?

It would mean, for one thing, that Shakespeare did not, as used to be thought, graft the casket story from the *Gesta* onto the Fiorentino tale, but that this graft had already been made by the author of his immediate source. The evidence for such a source seems to me as conclusive as we can expect under the circumstances. In *The School of Abuse* Gosson mentions a play, no longer extant, which bore the title *The Jew* and showed "the greediness of worldly choosers and the bloody minds of usurers." The description fits the two main actions of Shakespeare's play so closely that we can hardly avoid regarding *The Jew* as his source; and so it has been regarded by most recent editors.

But the fact is that, as far as we can tell, Shakespeare did depart from his source in at least two important instances. The first of these is the inscription on the leaden casket. Gosson's phrase—"the greediness of *worldly* choosers"—shows that *The Jew* must still have had the *Gesta* inscription: "Whoso chooseth me shall find that God hath disposed to him." Shakespeare, while taking over the other two inscriptions as he found them, changed the leaden one to read: "Whoso chooseth me

must give and hazard all he hath." If the very point of the play for him was that he felt bound to it and by it as it was, how did he come to take a liberty here?

His second assertion of independence is more substantial, although, as I shall try to show, less substantive; it is the Jessica-Lorenzo plot. It contains some echoes of Marlowe's *Jew of Malta*, but as a whole it appears to have been freely added by Shakespeare; no analogue to it has been found in any of his possible sources. Again: if he felt bound, whence this sudden flight of invention?

Before I take up these questions singly, I must note that they have one element in common: there seems to be no necessity for the departures. Bassanio, in choosing the leaden casket, gets no guidance from the inscription; insofar as his reference to threats and promises is an implicit allusion to the inscription, it is of a kind rather to frighten him off than to attract him. With the Jessica plot the puzzle is even greater; for not only does it not serve any useful purpose, it seems a perversely extraneous element in a story which was, to put it mildly, complicated enough without it. Yet I am persuaded that my general interpretation is confirmed—I would almost say verified—by these two elements.

To begin with the simpler one: In the Jessica plot Shakespeare breaks free of the bondage to his source and elopes into the untrammeled freedom of invention. Pure, spontaneous feeling governs the conduct of these lovers; they brush aside, without much compunction, the impediments to their union and celebrate careless honeymoons in Genoa, Belmont, or wherever their fancy and Shylock's ducats take them. The one theme that accompanies them quite faithfully, however, is the difference of their religions; we are never allowed to forget that Jessica was a Jewess and Lorenzo is a Christian.

One of the important stipulations in the judgment on Shylock is that he become a Christian; and the compulsion leaves a bitter taste in our mouths.... Shakespeare takes particular pains to impress on us the violence and merciless secularity of this act of "grace." Gratiano has the last word on it and places it in the proper metaphorical context:

> In christening shalt thou have two godfathers:
> Had I been judge, thou shouldst have had ten more,
> To bring thee to the gallows, not the font.
>
> [IV. i. 398-400]

We might think that the union of Jessica and Lorenzo would have offered a more harmonious means of conversion; the subplot, if it is designed for anything, seems designed to that very end. There could—I am tempted to say "should"—have been a final scene following the judgment, a scene with the satisfying, conciliatory finality and completeness we expect in comedies. As thus: Jessica and Lorenzo enter (perhaps from Genoa, bearing good tidings about Antonio's argosies); Shylock, already crushed, is urged by all to forgive his daughter and accept Lorenzo as his son-in-law; he still resists, claiming his religion; but finally Jessica's prayers prevail: he embraces Christianity and his newfound children. Antonio magnanimously renounces his claim to half of Shylock's property in favor of the lovers; Portia and Nerissa reveal themselves and are claimed by Bassanio and Gratiano; Antonio is asked to be honored guest at the triple wedding and godfather to Shylock. Curtain. I shall be so bold as to say that some such conclusion would have been a "natural": all the main characters on stage and in harmony, no need to return to Belmont and the business of the rings, no unresolved residue. As it is, Shylock exits unreconciled, while Jessica and Lorenzo moon in Belmont to no intelligible purpose, as they were brought there for no intelligible reason. I find it hard to imagine that Shakespeare, when he thought up the Jessica action, was not thinking of a conclusion somewhat along these lines, and that he was not fully aware of the complications and difficulties he needlessly created for himself by rejecting it. Why, then, did he?

The answer I am bound to by my interpretation—that it was not "so nominated in the bond," the source—only makes matters worse. Neither was the Jessica story in his source; if he felt free to invent that, why could he not take another liberty and tie it into the main action, as he might so easily and satisfyingly have done? As it stands, the play would have more unity and coherence if the subplot were simply left out; if Shakespeare felt the need to add to it, why did he not at least add something that would help round matters out? Worse: why did he perversely refuse to make the addition serve the one end it seems so manifestly intended for?

Of course, a purpose for it *has* been discovered. As Quiller-Couch puts it: "But here Shakespeare comes in. His audience, conventionally minded, may accept the proffer of the bond as a jesting bargain made with bloodthirsty intent, to be bloodthirstily enacted; but a gentle Shakespeare cannot. There must be more incentive to hate, to lust for a literally bloody vengeance, than any past insult, however conventional, put upon him on the Rialto by Antonio, mildest of men, can dramatically supply" [see excerpt above, 1926]. This . . . would pretty well represent the critical consensus on the function of the Jessica plot. But it is not only implausible; it is demonstrably false. "Gentle Shakespeare"—the creator of Richard III and company—cannot create a vengeful Shylock? "Antonio, mildest of men"—who spits on Shylock, calls him a cur, and promises to do so again even as he is asking him for a loan—did not give Shylock ample cause for bloody hatred? But we need not even speculate about sufficiency or insufficiency of motive; the text is perfectly explicit and unambiguously refutes the theory that Shylock needed the elopement of his daughter to confirm him in the resolution to enforce the bond. In Belmont Jessica reports:

> When I was with him [i.e., *before her elopement*],
> 　I have heard him swear . . .
> That he would rather have Antonio's flesh
> Than twenty times the value of the sum
> That he did owe him.
>
> 　　　　　　　　　　[III. ii. 284-88]

It is as though Shakespeare, suspecting that the subplot might be misinterpreted, had taken particular pains to prevent the misreading. But to no avail; the motive-mongers got the better of him. Here, as so often, the "psychological" explanation fails miserably—not because it is psychological, but because it is *ad hoc*, got up to explain away one difficulty and in doing so engendering a litter of others.

As almost always when Shakespeare puzzles us, the question to ask is not: why? but: what? If once we see the thing as it *is*, the question of its purpose will commonly answer itself. As lovers, Jessica and Lorenzo stand in the sharpest imaginable contrast to Portia and Bassanio. Their love is lawless, financed by theft and engineered through a gross breach of trust. It is subjected to no test: "Here, catch this casket; it is worth the pains" [II. vi. 33], Jessica says to Lorenzo to underscore the difference. The ring which ought to seal their love is traded for a monkey. They are spendthrift rather than liberal, thought-

less squanderers of stolen substance; they are aimless, drifting by chance from Venice to Genoa to Belmont. They are attended by a low-grade clown, who fathers illegitimate children (Launcelot), while Bassanio and Portia are served by a true jester, who marries in due form (Gratiano). Wherever we look, the Jessica-Lorenzo affair appears as an inversion of true, bonded love.

More: the spontaneous love-match remains fruitless and useless; it redeems no one but is itself in urgent need of redemption. There is one qualification to be made here; Jessica does have a function, which is repeatedly insisted on: she is to be the torchbearer in the impromptu masque. But the light she casts is ambiguous and flickering as that of a torch; it illumines only her own shame. . . . Also, the dramatic enterprise she is meant to serve in is

> vile, unless it may be quaintly order'd,
> And better, in my [Solanio's] mind, not undertook.
>
> 　　　　　　　　　　[II. iv. 6-7]

But in any case nothing comes of it:

> Antonio: Fie, fie, Gratiano! where are all the rest?
> 　　　　　'Tis nine o'clock; our friends all stay for
> 　　　　　　you.
> 　　　　　No masque tonight; the wind is come
> 　　　　　　about,
> 　　　　　Bassanio presently will go aboard.
>
> 　　　　　　　　　　[II. vi. 62-5]

The play of bonded and tested love, which was in danger of being delayed by these improvising masquers, is underway once more. (pp. 219-25)

What, then, does this torchlit subplot accomplish; why, it is now safe to ask, is it there at all? It is there to discover its own shame and uselessness and so, by contrast, to make clearer and firmer the outlines of bonded love. It is the abortive "masque," first planned by Shakespeare (I surmise) as an escape from the harsh letter of his bond, a means of rendering his intractable material more manageable. But when he discovered the much more hazardous and satisfying solution of unreserved submission, he turned the subplot to a new purpose, made it into something that should be "obscur'd," the *oscuro* in the chiaroscuro of the whole.

If this judgment of Jessica and Lorenzo seems too narrowly puritanical—and at odds, moreover, with their gorgeous lines about night and music at the opening of the last act—two things are to be remembered. *The Merchant* is a play of *use;* this word, among others, is rescued alike from Shylock's malice and Antonio's contempt. The people who ultimately count—Antonio, Bassanio, Portia, and, in a negative way, Shylock—have all been useful, have freed and united not only each other but also the state. And they have done so—to repeat—by accepting the given, the letter of the law, as binding; something to be fulfilled, not evaded. The play's ethos, the standards by which we must judge, are defined by its causality: and the causality is wholly unambiguous. Here, as in the sphere of speech, it is action that counts, not sentiment, effect, not attitude; here too Shakespeare teaches us—and perhaps himself—the true meaning of "drama." Mere lyrical splendor is, in the world the play defines, a kind of sentimentality, a parasitical self-indulgence, possible only because, and insofar as, others bear the brunt of the law. (pp. 225-26)

If the Jessica story is thus a kind of inverse demonstration of the play's point, the changed inscription goes directly to the core of Shakespeare's meaning.

In writing *The Merchant* Shakespeare learned, by my interpretation, that his work as a commissioned playwright need not be servile, money-grubbing prostitution of his talent, that he need not make himself a motley to the view, gore his own thoughts, and sell cheap what was most dear. There was dignity in his trade, truth and worth in the two hours' traffic of the stage. Antonio's sadness at the outset is, by his own description, that of a man who has to play a "part" arbitrarily assigned him; his restitution to happiness begins when he—though not fully aware of what he is doing—pledges his life to a binding contract and a literal "deadline." With this pledge things start to happen; "circulation" sets in. Trading with his talent is not in itself contemptible, an exploitation of something that should be employed only freely, for "gentle," liberal ends. It is, or can be, the beginning of action.

But this discovery entailed another—and a formidable risk. It meant that Shylock, the prophet of use and the bond, had to be built up—that his language had to be given the force and dignity which would sustain the claim Shakespeare was entering for profit-poetry. . . . Characters who spoke in Shylock's idiom and cadence had been comic figures, meant to earn goodnatured smiles if they were good and to be despised if they were malicious. For the language they spoke was that in "common use," employed by common men for the mean and illiberal ends they are compelled to pursue. It was not gentle, noble—the idiom designed to give the poet's patrons and protectors a properly idealized image of themselves. The language of the stage—at least of characters deserving serious regard—was one of representation rather than action, or if action, then of "actions of state." Or it was a language of feelings—the "gentle" feelings allowed for within the conventions of courtly love. It moved in set pieces—lofty commentaries on an action that moved independently. If the action ended tragically, it was because the protagonists were star-crossed, or because the wheel of Fortune turned, or because they were guilty of *superbia* [excessive pride] or some similar grand and splendid sins and crimes. If it ended happily, it did so because the proper feelings, dressed in the properly gentle language, had won out over loud-mouthed braggarts, mealy-mouthed parasites, foul-mouthed usurers, and other ill-spoken folk. In either case the dramatic question was begged; the convention predetermined the issue and the judgment of the audience. Gentle was as gentle did; gentle talked as gentle did; ergo: gentle was as gentle talked—the syllogism of aristocratic sentimentality.

Had Shakespeare written three hundred years later, he might have had to fight free of a different kind of sentimentality—that of the naturalists. As it was—and because he was Shakespeare—he confronted the word "gentle" in all its tricky ambiguity: as meaning something purely external (well-born; Christian) as well as kind, generous, loving. He did not think that churlishness proved a man honest and uncorrupted; nor was he satisfied with making the tritely pious point that, alas! not every gentleman is a gentle man. His problem was a different one: to vindicate gentleness under conditions—social and (it is the same thing) linguistic conditions—which did not beg the question but put it.

Shylock puts the question. In his mouth the common language assumes a force which puts all genteel speech to shame and reduces gentle speech to impotence. It mocks, and makes a mockery of, all sentimental claims to a "higher truth," clothed in elevated and elevating rhetoric, which cannot produce its credentials in the only court there is: the state's. Shylock's language is positivism triumphant, scornful of gentle pretensions, forcing the gentles to confess that, when all the ornament is stripped away, they too have been relying on the positive laws of the social order. If Shylock were silenced by force or fiat—even by divine intervention—his triumph would only be more complete; for he would then have compelled the gentiles, or their god, openly to profess his own faith: positivism. (pp. 227-29)

The question the Jew puts is not confined to the class meaning of "gentle"; it probes with equal rigor the religious meaning. We have good reason to suppose that the language of Shakespeare's source begged the question of gentility; *we know* that it begged the question of Christianity. That is the point of the changed inscription. Simply by making the clearly labeled Christian choice, by proving himself a devout rather than a worldly chooser, the gentile of the earlier play gained the truth by which the Jew was vanquished. The test did not involve a risk but asked for a correct response; so that *The Jew* as a whole was not a drama, an action (with the absolute risk all true action involves), but a teaching machine, which in the end rewarded and reinforced the right answer with redemption, bliss, and victory over the evil one. . . . Shakespeare sees that the word "gentle" evades the social and religious issue by institutionalizing it. Through the power he gives to Shylock's dramatically ungentle speech and through the elimination of the religious solution, he submits to the hazard of a genuine test—not a schoolmaster's but a chemist's. His play is, so to speak, the *aqua regia* [royal water] into which the word "gentle" is dropped to see if it is more than fool's gold.

It may be objected here that changing the inscription was, after all, no real risk. The plot was laid out for the poet and was sure to lead to a happy ending; not even the device by which that ending was achieved—Portia's judgment—had to be invented. But beyond the risk involved in changing the moral and dramatic balance between the usurious Jew and the noble Christian, Shakespeare had to confront, in simple fidelity to his source, the hazard that was its very meaning. He did not alter the story but restored it to itself by freeing it from a pious falsification. For its meaning was that it sprang from a series of ventures, of hazards; it was propelled by the risks Antonio, Bassanio, Portia, and, up to a point, Shylock were willing to take. Its ethic was that of venture capitalism raised to the moral level; so that to make it pivot, at the decisive juncture, on an option to invest in God's own, gilt-edged securities was to deprive it of its truth. Shakespeare's change here, though of a kind opposite to that of the Jessica plot, is directed toward the same end: while through the "free lovers" he accented the outlines of the composition by adding shadows, in the test scene he removed a layer of pious overpainting. The picture as he leaves it is not changed but more itself than when he took it in hand; he is a restorer, not an adapter.

To return to the plot. Belmont, left to itself, would end in sterile self-absorption; Venice, left to itself, would end in silence. There is an odd logic working in Shylock's bond: with its seal and letter it gradually deadens even the Jew's powerful speech. Increasingly his lines become monotonous and monomaniacal; where we heard him, earlier, responding acutely and flexibly to Antonio's hard scantness, he now grows deaf:

> Antonio: I pray thee, hear me speak.
> Shylock: I'll have my bond; I will not hear thee
> speak.

I'll have my bond; and therefore speak
no more . . .
I'll have no speaking; I will have my
bond. . . .

[III. iii. 11-13, 17]

Thus, "bond," in Shylock's mouth, comes to mean the opposite of speech and hearing; and since the state must sustain him, we come to the point where the community, to preserve itself, must prohibit communion. He who stands on the bond is no longer answerable and need no longer listen; the instrument of exchange threatens to render the body politic tongue-tied. A gap opens between the private and utterly ineffectual speech of men as men and the deadening, unalterable letter of the law. Portia's oft-quoted lines about the quality of mercy are remarkable not so much for their eloquence as for their impotence; they are of no use, fall on deaf ears, *do* nothing and so remain, in the literal sense, undramatic.

But at this point there is a reversal. Very much as Shylock learned, from Antonio's hardness, how to transform metal into flesh, so Portia now learns from Shylock himself the art of winning life from the deadly letter. So far she has given no hint that she has come with the solution ready; her last plea, interrupting as it does her already begun judgment, has the desperate urgency of a final, hopeless effort. When she asks Shylock to provide a surgeon to staunch the blood, does she know yet that it is on this point she will presently hang him? Or is it not rather Shylock himself who leads her to the saving inspiration?

Shylock: Is it so nominated in the bond?
Portia: It is not so expres'd; but what of that?
           'Twere good you do so much for charity.
Shylock: I cannot find it; 'tis not in the bond.

[IV. i. 259-62]

We cannot read Portia's mind and purposes, but this much is clear: here the crucial word is forced from her which then recurs in:

This bond doth give thee here no jot of blood;
The words *expressly* are "a pound of flesh."

[IV. i. 306-07]

The same process is at work as that which led to the framing of the bond; language, and with it Antonio and the state, have been revived and freed to act.

If we read Portia's judgment as a legal trick and Shylock's defeat as a foregone conclusion, the Jew's final humiliation must appear distressingly cruel. But there is good reason for reading the scene differently. Portia's ruling is one more hazard, and Shylock's moral collapse does not demolish the bond and all it stands for, but rather proves him unequal to the faith he has professed. Even after the judgment the issue is in doubt; it is still in Shylock's power to turn the play into a tragedy, to enforce the letter of the bond and to take the consequences. But at this point and before this choice he breaks, turns apostate to the faith he has so triumphantly forced upon his enemies. Having made the gentles bow before the letter of the law, he is now asked to become, literally, a blood witness. But he reneges and surrenders the bond's power, and like a renegade he is flogged into gentleness.

That it is the apostate rather than the bond that is brought into contempt is made clear in the last act: the ring episode. We the spectators can view it as a mere frolic; because we know of Portia's double identity and so understand her threatening

equivocations as being, in truth, binding pledges of fidelity. But Bassanio does not know and understand; to him the ring seems to continue the vicious circle of the bond. The cost of redeeming the public bond has been the forfeiture of the private one, the pledge of love; he now stands before Portia as Antonio stood before Shylock. His explanations, his appeals to circumstances, and motives are in vain; she insists on the letter of the pledge and claims the forfeit. What redeems the bond of true love is not good intentions but the fact that Portia speaks with a double voice, functions both in Venice and in Belmont, is both man and woman. . . . (pp. 230-34)

The ring is the bond transformed, the gentle bond. Since "bond" has dinned its leaden echo into our ears for the better part of four acts, "ring" is now made to ring out with almost comic but still ominous iteration. . . . Like the bond, the ring is of a piece with flesh, so that we can hardly tell whether it has made flesh into metal or has itself become flesh:

A thing stuck on with oaths upon your finger,
And so riveted with faith unto your flesh.

[V. i. 168-69]

Flesh, therefore, may have to be cut for it:

Why, I were best to cut my left hand off
And swear I lost the ring defending it.

[V. i. 177-78]

And in the end Antonio must once again bind himself:

Antonio: I once did lend my body for his wealth,
           Which, but for him that had your husband's
           ring,
           Had quite miscarried. I dare be bound again,
           My soul upon the forfeit, that your lord
           Will never more break faith advisedly.
Portia: Then you shall be his surety.

[V. i. 249-54]

Only with this renewal of the bond is the secret discovered, the true meaning of the equivocations revealed. Shylock has been defeated and dismissed, but the words which he almost succeeded in making synonymous with himself are not. They enter into the gentle contract of love, are requisite to the consummation; union, truth, and faith are impossible without them.

So the action ends; or rather, the circle closes. The play comes round with Shakespeare's happy discovery that poetry is an equivocal language, public as well as private, common as well as gentle, useful as well as beautiful. The poet draws upon the social order's legal currency and so is bound and fully accountable. But by binding himself with Antonio instead of stealing with Lorenzo, he frees energies which will save the order from becoming deadlocked in a vicious circle of self-definition; by hazarding all he has on the chance of making personal unions possible, he frees himself from the twin futilities of uselessness and parasitical exploitation of the public currency. For himself and for Venice he gains Portia—the indefinable being who speaks most truly when she sounds most faithless, who frees us through an absolute literalness, who learns the grim prose of law in order to restore it to its true function. (pp. 234-36)

Sigurd Burckhardt, "'The Merchant of Venice': The Gentle Bond," in his Shakespearean Meanings, *Princeton University Press, 1968, pp. 206-36.*

A. D. MOODY   (essay date 1964)

[*Like such other critics as William Hazlitt (1817), Arthur Quiller-Couch (1926), Harold C. Goddard (1951), R. Chris Hassel, Jr. (1970), and René Girard (1978), Moody asserts that the Christian characters in* The Merchant of Venice *are hypocritical and mercenary in their moral and religious convictions. More importantly, he maintains that the play never satisfies the ideals of mercy and justice that it seems to endorse, since Shakespeare treated his Christians' relation to these ideals in an ironic manner, an assessment also voiced by Goddard, Hassel, and Girard. To demonstrate his thesis, Moody discusses some familiar topics: first, he maintains that Shylock is a "scapegoat" figure—an individual who embodies the true attributes of his Christian "enemies" and, as such, must be symbolically sacrificed in order to insure that the society as a whole can function without confronting its real nature; second, Moody comments on Antonio's melancholy, saying that it stems from his own dissatisfaction with his society's failure to accommodate humane, personal feelings; third, the critic interprets the final act of* The Merchant of Venice *as a "light" comedy of folly, but one that underscores the illusion of the Christians' self-glorification and piety and informs the audience of the disparity between their actions and their beliefs; fourth, he argues that the emphasis on universal harmony in Act V serves as a parody of what the Venetians in Portia's Belmont actually strive to achieve; and fifth, Moody notes that the controlling irony in the play not only allows us to see the falsity of the resolution in Act V and to recognize the "doublefaced" nature of the Christians, but it also "extends beyond the characters to involve and question the attitudes of the audience," to the extent that we typically accept the Christians at face value and rejoice in their good fortune. Thus, Moody concludes,* The Merchant of Venice *leaves us "with an image of our ordinary condition of moral compromise, of [our] complacent spiritual mediocrity," and of what consequences such an attitude entails. For a similar assessment of the cause of Antonio's melancholy, see the excerpt by Lawrence Danson (1978). Also, see the excerpts by James E. Siemon (1970) and R. Chris Hassel, Jr. (1970) for further discussion of the disparity between the festive resolution of Act V and previous events in the play.*]

The established view of *The Merchant of Venice* goes something like this:

> *The Merchant of Venice*, then, is 'about' judgement, redemption and mercy; the supersession in human history of the grim four thousand years of unalleviated justice by the era of love and mercy. It begins with usury and corrupt love; it ends with harmony and perfect love.

Professor Frank Kermode, whose formulation this is, supports it with the assertion that 'only by a determined effort to avoid the obvious' can one fail to see that that is the meaning of the play. I have to confess that what seems to me obvious, is that the promised supersession of justice by love and mercy does not come about, and that the end is something of a parody of heavenly harmony and love. The play *is* about the qualities he mentions, but it treats them much more critically than he suggests. He seems to have overlooked the irony that is at the centre of its meaning.

To emphasise the importance and centrality of the irony, I would suggest that the play is 'about' the manner in which the Christians succeed in the world by not practising their ideals of love and mercy; that it is about their exploitation of an assumed unworldliness to gain the worldly advantage over Shylock; and that, finally, it is about the essential likeness of Shylock and his judges, whose triumph is even more a matter of mercenary justice than his would have been. In this view

the play does not celebrate the Christian virtues so much as expose their absence.

Yet this account too, though no less true than the more usual one, would be less than adequate to the experience. For the special quality of the play is that it refuses to endorse any such simple judgements. It compels an intensely sympathetic insight into Shylock's tragically corrupt nature, yet we are unlikely to identify ourselves with him. It reveals in the Christians a complacent inhumanity, and yet we are likely to find them attractive in their fashion. No account of the play which offers to see it in terms of simple good and evil can hope to satisfy. It is too subtle and exploratory for that; and also, perhaps, too ironic in its resolution.

The characterising quality of the Venice-Belmont set is their worldliness. This makes it odd that their claims to represent the Christian virtues should be accepted at face value. With the exception of a few set pieces on the themes of mercy, love and harmony—and of Antonio's partial representation of these qualities—their minds are never raised above the gaieties and good things of the world.

Their way of life and the things which possess their imaginations are suggested in the opening exchange:

Solanio.	Believe me, sir, had I such venture forth,
	The better part of my affections would
	Be with my hopes abroad. I should be still
	Plucking the grass to know where sits the wind,
	Piring in maps for ports and piers and roads:
	And every object that might make me fear
	Misfortune to my ventures, out of doubt,
	Would make me sad.
Salerio.	My wind, cooling my broth,
	Would blow me to an ague when I thought
	What harm a wind too great might do at sea.
	I should not see the sandy hour-glass run
	But I should think of shallows and of flats,
	And see my wealthy Andrew docked in sand,
	Vailing her high-top lower than her ribs
	To kiss her burial. . . . Should I go to church
	And see the holy edifice of stone,
	And not bethink me straight of dangerous rocks,
	Which touching but my gentle vessel's side,
	Would scatter all her spices on the stream,
	Enrobe the roaring waters with my silks,
	And, in a word, but even now worth this,
	And now worth nothing?

[I. i. 15-36]

In image and idiom that splendidly evokes the merchant's compulsive fears and hopes, and his world of profit and risk. The language of the play as a whole is drawn quite consistently from that world, so that the action is firmly placed in a context of worldly preoccupations and values. Venice and Belmont emerge as gay, splendid and rich, and not very near to heaven; their end is profit and pleasure, not perfection.

One set of words recurs constantly in their speech—*venture* and *fortune*, or *hazard, chance*, etc. From the recurrence comes a cumulatively powerful sense that the goal of their endeavours is the winning, metaphorically and literally, of the 'golden fleece', a common image for the great fortunes the Elizabethan merchant-adventurers hoped for. But to be committed to the pursuit of worldly fortune is to be subjected, in the medieval view of things, to the whims of the fickle goddess Fortune; at the most serious level, it is to forfeit the redemptive influence of Providence for the chances and reverses of Fortune's wheel. Boethius' salutation to the true followers of Christ in the world, 'O happy race of mortals if your hearts are ruled as is the universe by divine love', can scarcely be applied to the Christians of Venice and Belmont. The fount of their happiness is Portia, appropriately referred to as a golden fleece of fortunate beauty and wealth. In consequence their allusions to the values of a world transcending their own, such as divine mercy or heavenly harmony, stand out as precisely that, allusions to quite another world.

But more than this, their worldliness is shown to be of a kind which subverts their religion. In the passage from Salerio quoted before, what we have is not a simple preoccupation with the world, but the expression of that preoccupation in an idiom adapted from the pulpit. It was commonplace to draw from the hour-glass the moral that man's life is brief and eternity his proper end. But Salerio reverses the preacher's logic and draws a wholly secular moral, ignoring any life beyond death. Again, his culminating image, 'Enrobe the roaring waters with my silks', very strikingly fuses the splendour and the loss, but without at all heeding the implicit biblical admonition against the vanity of rich apparel. The whole passage is, in effect, a parody of orthodox warnings against putting one's hopes upon worldly fortune, since it echoes them only to reduce them to an occasion for a more anxious concern with the world.

The major instance of this irony is the contrast between Portia as we see her at Belmont, lightly disregarding the bonds of law and duty, and as we see her in the court, disguised as the wise doctor of law. One observation will be enough to suggest how grave the disparity could be, and to what ironic effect. When Portia declares near the end of IV. i, 'I was never yet more mercenary' [IV. i. 418], there is a curious and significant effect. The immediate sense, quite innocently playful, is clear enough. And yet 'mercenary' is a startling word to have just there, the more so as it echoes 'mercy', which would have seemed the obviously appropriate word. . . . All this is manifestly very relevant to our thinking about Portia, in which a main question must be whether her conduct conforms to the ideal of loving one's neighbour as oneself, or is more nearly self-interested. Coming where it does, with its oddness and ambiguity, that 'mercenary' crystallises the suspicion that what we have seen in her is perhaps literally mercenary, and that her appearance as Justice and Mercy has been a most deceiving disguise. There is then a possibility that Portia has outdone even the Venetians in subverting religion to her own worldly will, reducing its supreme principle of generous love to something nearly its opposite. *Can* Portia be said to love Shylock as herself, or as she loves her Christian friends?

However, this ironic questioning of Portia, though it is pervasive, is unlikely to lead us to reject her. What it should do is prevent the uncritical acceptance of her at face-value. After all, one of the main themes of the play is that 'the world is still deceived with ornament' [III. ii. 74], and the action is constantly exploring the ways in which the appearance and the reality may differ. (pp. 9-13)

A word here about the way the allusions to the Christian ideal work in the play may prevent some misapprehensions. It is not easy to gauge the exact force of these allusions, partly because they are so variable a quantity, shifting from a subdued presence in Salerio's opening speech to the explicitness of Portia's invocation to Mercy. But it is possible to be definite on the main point, and that is that the Christian ideal is not deployed as a standard by which the characters are to be judged. The controlling viewpoint is not that of the eye of Heaven, but that of enlightened human feeling. (p. 13)

The play does not imply, for example, that [the Christians] ought to be ideally merciful; nor that they are damned for falling short of the ideal or subverting it. The dramatic experience simply does not lead us to judge them in relation to the ideal; it leads us to judge them by their treatment of Shylock. Their offence is not against God but against humanity. The function of the allusions to the Christian ideal is to sharpen our awareness of the human issue, but not to be a measure of it. Their function may be likened to that of the coloured spectacles that went with the early 3D pictures: when one looks through them the images assume definition and depth. They are there to be looked through, not to be looked at. (pp. 13-14)

The need for a detached and critical approach is brought home still more when we consider Shylock's part. For while he is grievously wronged by the Christians, to the extent that his inhumanity is effectively their doing, he must nevertheless be held fully responsible for the inhuman act he proposes. Yet again, while the judgement the Christians pass on him is fully deserved, we cannot but feel that his humanity is larger in scope and depth than theirs. In consequence his defeat at their hands seems to involve a reversal of the right order of things, the lesser being allowed to put down the greater.

John Russell Brown has shown that in the theatre it has always been Shylock's play, and there is good reason for this. Where the Christians speak with quibbling wit or rhetoric, filtering emotion through artifice, Shylock's speech is directly responsive to his burden of personal and racial experience, with the result that his humanity is so much more fully present to us. . . . [Shylock] is no simple devil or machiavel, but a man who sees and feels and thinks as other men do, except that his feeling and thinking has been terribly twisted by the wrong done to him. (p. 14)

All this must complicate and deepen the interest of the play beyond any simple issue of the good *v.* the damned. The play confronts us rather with the triumph of a group of worldly and a-moral characters over one whose evil is inseparable from his larger humanity. There is much that is baffling in this spectacle of the breaking by a set of trifling gilded youth of a man with something of the stature and interest of a tragic figure. But we must not attempt to evade or to oversimplify the experience. It is only by making sense of what baffles us that we can attain a full understanding of the play. (pp. 14-15)

Antonio's 'sadness' is like a keynote sounded before the statement of the play's main concerns. Later, as it persists through the scene, it becomes an undertone set off against and showing up the levity of his friends. The word 'sadness' had a primary meaning of 'sober, grave, serious', and would signify that Antonio was preoccupied, withdrawn into himself. The cause is nowhere plainly stated. Instead our interest is shifted to his friends; but in their inability to respond adequately to his mood we begin to see its meaning. He is sad, in the modern sense, because his more sober, grave and serious feelings are unrecognised and unsatisfied. His passive demand for a deeper understanding and friendship meets no response—being beyond matters of fortune and merchandise it is beyond the Venetians' comprehension—so that even among his 'friends' he is an alien. The prime interest of this is in what it suggests about them. It will be relevant to recall it later, when we find Antonio failing to recognise or to respond to Shylock's implicit demand for friendship. But for the moment Antonio's 'sadness' is a foil to his friends' trifling worldliness.

Here, as later in the trial, he is the curiously still and passive centre of the scene. His presence seems to have the odd function of declaring some absence or emptiness, making us aware of some hollowness at the heart of Venice. He is, in his effect, a dumb reminder of unrealised possible feelings, of deeper needs and impulses than any Venice is aware of. In this there is again a parallel with Shylock's fate.

The Venetians seem to circle about Antonio like quick indifferent creatures of another element. Theirs is the world of wit and pleasure-seeking, and it is to the exploration of this world that the play is mainly devoted. The substance of I. i and ii reveals it in its several aspects. There is first the parodic relation of its worldliness to religion, as shown in Salerio and Solanio; this is capped by Gratiano's 'sermon' upon the impropriety of 'sadness'; then Bassanio carries their attitudes into action, and finds their proper object in Portia.

Gratiano is the main spokesman and effective philosopher of the Venetians' worldliness. He will be found to be, throughout the play, a sort of nether touchstone for the Christians, giving expression to their basest elements. His advice here to Antonio, on how to be worldly without letting its risks and dangers prevent merriment, is the complement to Salerio's solicitude, and is in the same idiom. (pp. 21-2)

[Gratiano's] most revealing piece of wit is his parody of Antonio's 'sadness'. Here he represents at its crudest the Venetians' shallowness. To assume that Antonio must be pretending to be 'sad' in order to deceive the world is firstly a blind failure of sympathy. Secondly, it shows an inability to conceive the possibility of genuine seriousness; and to this he adds the expectation that an appearance of gravity is something to be exploited for an ulterior motive. (p. 22)

In all this Gratiano is making explicit the attitudes of the worldly Christians, revealing in a crude and unmistakable form what is more subtly present in the rest. He is the shallow cynic to whom nothing is sacred or even serious. All that is real to him or important is 'merriment', which seems to amount to a vulgar knowingness, cheap witticisms and the bawdy punning he contributes to the love scenes. The darker aspect of his shallowness, is shown in his grotesque preaching at Antonio's 'sadness'; and of his cynicism, in his readiness nevertheless to pretend to sadness for gain. (pp. 22-3)

Bassanio, despite his attempt to dissociate himself from Gratiano before Antonio, is manifestly cast in the same mould. His constant association with him later in the play is a persistent reminder of this. He shares the same 'enlightened' worldliness, and his end is likewise 'merriment'. But he is like Gratiano in nothing so much as his capacity for cynically using serious emotions which he does not share. In his exploitation of Antonio's generous love he acts out the Venetians' imcomprehension of its value, and their parodying or subverting things of profound value.

Nothing so positively demonstrates the nature and depth of Antonio's 'sadness', his serious and unsatisfied need to love and to be loved, as his deliberately offering Bassanio not only his purse but his person. Bassanio takes full advantage of both, in order to venture for Portia and her fortune, and in doing so casually reduces the personal love to a merely monetary value. This is most clearly evident in the way his urgent self-interest

quite blinds him, in I. iii, to the implications of his bonding Antonio to Shylock. If Shylock puts his daughter on a level with his ducats, Bassanio likewise puts Antonio's money before his person. This is the worst parody or perversion so far wrought in Venice, (the trial has yet to show what can be done with Mercy), that the profoundly human affection, which transcends their preoccupation with the world of fortune, should be exploited in the pursuit of fortune, and subjected most rigorously to the cold chances of Fortune. (p. 23)

Mr. Graham Midgley has drawn attention to the likeness in one main respect of Antonio and Shylock—both are aliens in Venice [see excerpt above, 1960]. It seems to me that there is a profound dramatic basis for this likeness. Antonio, who is an alien *within* his society, may be seen as an image of the inoperancy of love in the hollow heart of Venice. Shylock who is put *outside* that society, and who shows the full effects of its defective love, may be seen as the image of what happens within the human person when love is denied, of the consequent distortions and corruptions of feeling and impulse. Thus he and Antonio face each other as the social surface and the inward substance of the same spiritual condition. If that is too metaphysical a way of putting it one can say, more simply, that with the introduction of Shylock there begins a full and profound exploration of the effects upon a human being of the Venetians' light worldliness.

Shylock's relation to Venice is shown in the tone and quality of his speech. For the most part the play is set in the polished manner of the Christians, lively, easy, sophisticated, with a marked tendency to playful wit; the effect is to give dominance to their undisturbed and unself-questioning assurance. Shylock speaks as their opposite in nearly every respect. His language is slow, weighted with brooding calculation, reserved and careful, rejecting levity with precision or passion. His is the most resonant voice in the play; and yet it does not disturb or modify the Christians' tone. What it does, however, is to challenge their dominance, by setting gravity against levity and compelling us to perceive more clearly what the latter represents.

In the rendering of Shylock we can distinguish two related emphases. Firstly he shows up and further defines the quality of the Venetians' worldliness. Then he elicits the indifference to human value which underlies it, and which he suffers and returns as an active inhumanity. (pp. 26-7)

There can be no question that [the Christians] treat Shylock like a dog, systematically refusing to accept him as a human being equal with themselves. Even Antonio, the best example in the play of Christian friendship, insists that he is and shall remain an enemy, and that there can be no bond between them save a financial one. The main part of Act II (excluding scenes i, vii and ix) is devoted to acting out this attitude to Shylock. Since they do not recognise his humanity the Venetians have neither inhibitions nor a sense of guilt in depriving him of his daughter and his ducats, and then mocking his grief. Their parody of his passion (in II. viii) and their baiting him to his face [in III. i. 22ff.] shows the depths of their indifference.

What their actions demonstrate of course is their own inhumanity. Only that word, though strictly appropriate, is rather strong for what we actually see. The Christians remain in their lighthearted element, while it is Shylock whom we see acting truly inhumanly. A clear distinction and distance is thus maintained between their civilised exterior and their real barbarism: we are shown the latter only as it is reflected and returned upon them by Shylock. (pp. 29-30)

"Shylock returning to his empty house," by Charles A. Buchel.

That Shylock behaves inhumanly, and that this is a direct consequence of the way the Christians abuse him, hardly needs to be stressed. It is perhaps less obvious that even as he is abused and made inhuman he demonstrates his claim to be treated as a human being. The play prompts us to see his inhumanity as an inverted or perverted form of human nature, and not at all as something apart and devilish. (p. 30)

[Shylock's] 'merry bond' with Antonio is the major instance both of the perversion of his humanity, and of his representing in his perversion the inner condition of the Christians. In his lust to be revenged upon Antonio it is as if he were determined that what the Venetians had deprived him of, his flesh and blood humanity, shall be repaid in Antonio's flesh and blood. Moreover there is a special propriety in his 'I shall have the heart of him if he forfeit' [III. i. 127], for the heart is the symbol of that life-giving love which Antonio denies him. It comes to seem then that Shylock is desperately and insanely seeking to act out upon Antonio a precise image of the hurt he has himself suffered. (pp. 30-1)

So far we have established that Shylock is openly what the Christians are beneath their urbane surface. He embodies and elicits the worldliness and the related indifference to the human person which are concealed by their pretence of 'goodness' and 'kindness'. In behaving inhumanly he is acting out the corruption of human nature implicit in their inhuman treatment of him. There remains some unrealised meaning in the situation. There is an apparent inconsistency in Antonio's being at once the ideal Christian friend to Bassanio and the enemy to

Shylock. And we have yet to specify the motive and the necessity of the Christians' antipathy to Shylock—we have seen the fact, but not its logic.

Antonio's 'inconsistency' is a matter of 'character'—and within the terms of a character reading it must be inexplicable and unacceptable. For no matter how evil Shylock may be the Christian response should be love and not hatred. However, the difficulty disappears if we stop asking that Antonio should behave with the consistency we expect of people in real life, and allow him to be the dramatic expression of one aspect of the Christian group. We see him then as indeed embodying the principle of charity, which the Christians profess, and in some measure practise among themselves. Certainly Antonio's love for Bassanio is altogether ideal. But we see then that his declaration of enmity to Shylock marks the point at which the principle of charity ceases to be practised. His 'inconsistency' is a dramatic manifestation of the difference between principle and practice among the Christians, and a fuller and clearer statement of what was implicit in his early 'sadness'.

To find a satisfying cause for their rooted antipathy to Shylock we need to put together the several aspects of the play observed so far, and in particular the two central facts: that the Christians pretend to a moral status which is above themselves, and that Shylock avows the moral sense by which they actually live. We can see that in condemning Shylock they are condemning their own sins. It would seem then that they are making him literally their scapegoat. . . . Or, as H. C. Goddard puts it, 'They project on him what they have dismissed from their own consciousness as too disturbing' [see excerpt above, 1951]. (pp. 31-2)

It should be possible by this stage to make out the significant structure or 'argument' of the play. We have been introduced, in the early scenes, to a fairly commonplace worldliness, shallow and heartless, but gilded by love of merriment, wealth and beauty. Next, in Shylock, we have seen the perversion of spirit, the blind and destructive egotism, which is the twisted root of worldly 'will'. But again, over that has been laid its most golden appearance, all the pageantry and 'poetry' of Belmont. Thus so far we have had developed and intensified the contradiction between the gilded appearance and the corrupt spirit of the Christians.... [This] conflict of the appearance and the reality is worked out in the bringing to trial and judgement of all that Shylock represents.

If we bear in mind that what Shylock represents is the inward condition of the Christians we may find it an odd resolution which vindicates their apparent virtue in condemning the reflection of their real viciousness. The issues are not as simple as they seem, and for this reason it would be best to begin by asking, in a quite elementary way, what precisely the trial is about, what is at issue and who is to be judged.

Since the moment in Act III when Antonio was known to be forfeit to Shylock, everything has been shaping towards the trial. Antonio's friends, under Portia, have been rallying to him, while Shylock has been shown hardening his heart. At the simplest level, then, we are prepared for a dramatic conflict between Shylock bent upon his pound of flesh and the Christians bent upon saving Antonio.

This simple situation is quickly complicated. The fact that the contest is conducted within the machinery of the law gives Shylock an initial advantage. It is generally allowed that the law and 'credit' of Venice require that Antonio honour his bond. But the Christians introduce a further complication, to their own advantage, by appealing to a higher principle than the law, and translating the issue from the relatively simple legal one into a contest of Justice and Mercy. This shifts the interest all the way from 'who's going to win?' to 'who's good and who's bad?' On the surface everything persuades us to answer this in the Christians' favour. Their identification of themselves with the good, and of Shylock with the bad, confidently assumed in their taking their stand on Mercy, has been suggested to us all along.... One way and another the Christians would have us believe that the contest is really between the devil and God's elect. So far as we are persuaded of this we will become as anxious as themselves that a means be found to deprive the devil of his base legal advantage. In short, we will become involved in a melodrama.

However, if we are not altogether of the Christians' persuasion, we may see that the melodrama is transformed, in its turn, by the deeper complications of character and conduct. Shylock has shown too much humanity to be written off as the mere devil. The Christians on the other hand have shown too much love of the world, and too much 'skill' in obtaining their will in it under cover of religion, for us to accept them as simple saints. When things go on in the trial as they have before, we can only conclude that the essential conflict is still what it was, and that Mercy is not being practised, but merely invoked as cover for 'will'.

Yet this is not quite the end of the matter. Justice and Mercy, though not what the trial is about, do provide us with the relevant standards by which to judge the conduct of the char-

acters. That Shylock is wrong to stick to justice and refuse mercy is rigorously proved in his own fate. But the larger question is whether the Christians are in truth Christ-like. Ultimately the trial can be seen as a 'proving' of their charity, a bringing of their pretensions to the test of their actual conduct towards Shylock. When they pass judgement on him they themselves are on trial. We may find they have grown genuinely merciful; or we may find them merely mercenary still. But this at any rate is what the trial is about. (pp. 38-40)

[Shylock] is not a figure of fun nor an easy butt for prejudice. But everything that makes for his composure, for the self-possession evident in his cool answer to Gratiano's railing [at IV. i. 123-42], shows him to be completely alienated from proper human feeling. We can only be horrified by his ebullient trust that the law will sanction his murdering Antonio. Yet his criminality is of the kind which should haunt the conscience of the self-righteous and the complacent, and shock his society into self-recognition. It is impossible not to resist his inhumanity, but it is intolerable that he should have been made so. He is pre-eminently a man in need of mercy; but as for justice, who in the play is fit to cast the first accusation?

There is a grotesque irony in the Christians bidding him show mercy—Hazlitt called it 'the rankest hypocrisy or the blindest prejudice' [see excerpt above, 1817]. For his mercilessness is quite directly the measure of Antonio's refusing to accept him within the human brotherhood. His desires *are* 'wolvish, bloody, starved and ravenous' [IV. i. 138], and this is because the Christians have made them so, infusing their own spirit into him.... (pp. 40-1)

Shylock should of course be moved to mercy by his own experience.... In his inhuman and obdurate refusal to be so he is making himself guilty of his persecutors' crime, and digging a pit for himself. Yet, again, to condemn him they too must unmercifully pursue the letter of the law.

That Portia has put on the power and authority of the law, and not anything else, would be declared by the black robes of her disguise, just as effectively as her real nature and interest would be concealed by them. And it would be enforced by her coming on virtually as the answer to Shylock's demand for the justice of the law, and by her meeting and frustrating his demand with a display of deep legal cunning. Of course we are conscious of her as other than the impartial representative of the law. Over and above that is her plea for mercy; beneath it there is her hidden interest on Antonio's behalf.... We cannot but approve her skilful prevention of Shylock's malice. But we have reason to suspect her motives. And this must make us critical of her large claim to execute the law mercifully and in the spirit of divine charity. That must be tested upon Shylock's great need for mercy above justice. If she is fully to satisfy the expectation she arouses she must respond to his innermost need to be valued and treated as a man. We come again to the recognition that the deepest interest in the trial is in the quality of the Christians' mercy.

The most notable aspect of Portia's speech on that theme is that she quite fails to offer Shylock any motive for mercy, unless the self-interested one of forgiving others in order to be forgiven oneself. The speech is rhetorically excellent, as a forceful rehearsal of the relevant commonplaces, but lacks the one thing necessary, the spirit of love itself. (pp. 41-2)

There is reason to suppose that Portia is all along preparing to smite in sunder the loins of the unmerciful. Shylock has been assured repeatedly that in law his case is unassailable. Moreover, it has openly been taken for granted that Antonio's blood will be shed; and Portia carries this so far as to bid him have by some surgeon 'To stop his wounds lest he do bleed to death' [IV. i. 258]. All this is to lull Shylock into a false trust in the law so that he may be the more surely tripped by its letter. (pp. 42-3)

Portia takes her time, winding him in with the lulling sing-song of [IV. i. 299-303]; checking him with her light 'tarry a little' [IV. i. 305]; sardonically urging him to take his pound of flesh, but no drop of blood; mocking him with the assurance he shall have 'justice more than thou desir'st' [IV. i. 316]; then, when he had yielded his claim on Antonio, laying upon him the full rigour of the law. In all this Portia has been practising the law with cunning precision, and to the end not simply of saving Antonio, but of putting Shylock at the mercy of his enemies. There is nowhere any hint of Mercy—and her climactic 'Down therefore, and beg mercy' [IV. i. 363] in no way accords with 'The quality of mercy is not [con]strained' [IV. i. 184]. Simply to force him to release Antonio it would have been enough to show him his danger; to convert him to Mercy in the full sense an example would be necessary. But what we see in Portia's conduct looks most like mercenary vengefulness.

In the event the Christians seem to effect only a variation upon Shylock's scheme to translate the money owed him into hearts-blood, by sparing his life but taking his money. This is a transaction no more involving love than his; but it is perhaps the grosser parody. Shylock was seeking a terribly perverted substitute for love, but one at least related to the reality; whereas the Christians neither offer nor seek anything resembling a real relationship with him. Instead they compound for his worldly wealth in order to be well rid of the man. Shylock has no effective retort. . . . Nevertheless we should realise what he cannot, that his tragedy is in the Christians' appropriating to themselves not simply his worldly wealth but 'love's wealth' also. It is their doing that which deprives his life of meaning and value.

All this is imaged in the quibble upon the drop of blood. That drop of blood which Shylock must not shed perfectly represents the love the Christians deny him, the essential life of the spirit. And it is a reminder beyond that of the blood which Christ in his Mercy shed for all mankind. . . . It becomes then the crowning piece in their perversion of their religion that they should require Shylock to become a Christian upon pain of death, imposing upon him the outward form of redemptive mercy while denying him the reality.

Their effective motives and attitudes in the trial are pretty well placed in Gratiano's *Schadenfreude,* his malicious joy in Shylock's undoing, an attitude fully consonant with Antonio's in I. iii, and exactly the opposite of mercy and charity. It is not pretty, therefore, to have the scene close with the spectacle of the Christians being smugly amiable among themselves, assuring themselves of their gentle community with mutual compliments and courtesies. No wonder Portia's 'mercenary' strikes one so: it alone does justice to one's sense of the terrible reality which is being glossed over.

In the end the trial turns out to have been a drama in which the Christians were engaged in resolving their inner contradiction, by casting out Shylock, the scapegoat fashioned in the likeness of their devotion to the world, and a reproach to their indifference to the life of the spirit and the love which it demands. With him undone and compelled to put on their own goodly outside, they are at liberty to enjoy the delights of Belmont, their idyll.

No one will miss the midsummer's night atmosphere of the last act, with the moon making a second night of the day, the poetry of legendary lovers, and the perfecting of the mood by the music brought forth into the air. This idyll of music, moonlight and love is wholly removed from the trial and from everything to do with Shylock, and seems to offer the apotheosis of the love of Venice and Belmont. However, we will find, if our wits are not dreaming, that we are in the same world as before, beneath the moon in fortune's world of 'will' and fickle chance. There is some passing talk of heavenly harmony, but the last word is Gratiano's, and it resolves the teasing business of the rings and broken vows only in an earthy pun.

Such a conclusion makes sense if we have resisted the temptation to romanticise and idealise the love of the Christians. If we see Bassanio as Ideal Lover, Antonio as Ideal Friend, and Portia as Mercy, it will seem discordant and bathetic. But if we have seen that the Christian group is not ideal, we will discover that the last act draws what has gone before towards its natural *comic* conclusion, by isolating and exposing the real quality of their love. It provides a critique of the love they actually practise, as distinct from that which they pretend to; a love of the world and their own will, sublunary and fickle. . . . (pp. 43-5)

The refining and narrowing of the interest in this way accounts for the very different mode and texture. The play is still concerned preeminently with the attitudes and conduct of the Christians, but the absence of Shylock precludes any further exploration in depth. Through the main part of the play the fact that the Christians were presented almost entirely through their outward appearance, their social surface and public declarations, was offset by the presence of Shylock, their third dimension. In what the Christians had made him, fashioning their victim in their own image, we could discover what they were beneath their deceptive exterior. Without his substance and depth, and with only the Christians' 'surface' to work on, the writing is inevitably much lighter. Instead of directly engaging our emotions, as in the trial, it now appeals rather to our understanding. There is no conflict or tension in the action; but there are discords and false relations in the poetry. And the main meaning emerges in the way the off-key quibbling of the lovers over the rings jars against the previous evocation of the stillness and deep tranquillity of spirits attentive to love's music.

Probably the clue to a right reading of the last act is the recognition that the allusion to an ideal harmony of love has a critical function, and is not laid as tribute before the Christians. Its effect is not to praise but to place them, to show how far from the ideal they are. . . . The critical intelligence that has been controlling the play is not abruptly suspended in its end. However, its final judgement, in which Shylock is left aside and only the comic mode is used, is subtle, elusive and surprising.

The main stage-business ('action' would be too grand a word) is in the disposing of the lovers' rings. This is preceded by two passages, one on moonstruck lovers . . . , the other on music and harmony, which establish contexts of literary and philosophical associations within which the matter of the rings is placed.

The first passage offers to create a setting for romantic love:

> The moon shines bright. In such a night as this,
> When the sweet wind did gently kiss the trees,
> And they did make no noise, in such a night . . .
>   [V. i. 1-3]

However, all the allusions that follow, seemingly as variations upon that theme of the live and lucent night, undercut its suggestions of tranquil beauty with others of false, or unfortunate or betrayed love. Moreover, it emerges that these gentle lovers are teasingly imputing to each other like infidelities and misfortunes. Cressida's fickleness, Thisbe's ludicrous fearfulness, Dido's desertion by Aeneas, and Medea's by Jason, are all notorious *exempla* of the fortunes of sublunary lovers. . . . The quite direct drawing in of Jessica and Lorenzo themselves to this train of allusions leaves no doubt that they are to be understood as having a cautionary bearing upon the lovers at Belmont. We are being prompted to see that they too fit the old and oft-repeated pattern in which the acting of 'will' against duty is followed by the misfortunes of fickleness or betrayal. The love of the Christians, their pretending to 'gentility' and 'god-like mutual amity', is set delicately and suggestively in a relevant context.

In Lorenzo's speech on the power of music . . . we have the opposite context evoked, the harmony of the heavens which are moved by Love, and the analogous harmony of music which may possess even disordered mortal spirits. In gracefully connecting their 'touches of sweet harmony', to which 'soft stillness and the night' [V. i. 57, 56] are a fitting counterpart, with the music of the spheres suggested by the serene beauty of the stars shining above the night, Lorenzo is establishing the larger term in the analogy. The basic conception is that the stars, as they move in their courses about the Primum Mobile, set up a harmony expressing his perfect ordering of them. This is very richly imagined here, and in a way to realise most compellingly the value of that harmony of being which—for the cherubim whose lord is literally their *illuminatio* [glory]—flows from directly knowing the harmonious ordering of things by Love. Fallen man, grossly closed in his 'muddy vesture of decay' [V. i. 64], neither hears nor is directly influenced by the divine harmony; nor does he . . . attend to the corresponding harmony within his own immortal soul. (pp. 45-7)

Certainly, with Portia's return, we are brought back from thoughts of heavenly harmony to the sublunar world of mortals, as invoked in the opening passage. . . . What emerges almost at once is that music does not still Portia's merry wit, nor make her more attentive to 'sad' feelings [as in the case of Jessica]. There is a harshness and dissonance in her devaluing the lark and the nightingale and making them no better than crow or goose or wren. In the context just established this must make her 'fit for treasons, stratagems, and spoils' [V. i. 85]—which indeed is pretty much what she has been up to in Venice. Her 'nothing is good, I see, without respect' [V. i. 99], makes clear where she has brought us; not into the universe where all is ordered by Love and where the degrees of good and evil are steadily distinguished by the cherubim, but into the 'wild and wanton' world of man where all is relative, and good and evil are determined by circumstance and 'will' and 'skill'. These impressions of her being out of accord with the finest feelings and insights touched upon by Lorenzo are confirmed by her stopping the music, as if it were disturbing the peace and not itself the source of the peacefulness, and by her setting up in its place her own tone of brittle merriment. . . . (pp. 47-8)

The main function of the ring byplay, which occupies the rest of the act, seems to be to act out in light comedy the perceptions previously established in the ironies of the poetry. Gratiano has again a significant part. To the bawdy which Portia's lightness encourages he gives a cruel edge. . . . In respect of the solemnity of lovers' vows he accurately, if more basely, represents the common feeling, in rating the ring merely at its material and sentimental value. Nerissa's and Portia's expostulations and 'exclaiming upon' their husbands, since their tone observes the decorum of the comic situation, in effect make just as light of the serious values invoked in the exchange of rings. . . . (pp. 48-9)

The conclusion lets all pass as in a fairy-tale, and crowns their light play with dreams come true as if fortune had vowed herself to kindness. In the end their pleasures seem to recommend them above their moral shortcomings. Possibly Gratiano's urging Nerissa to bed may remind us of an earlier cynicism—

> O ten times faster Venus' pigeons fly
> To seal love's bonds new-made, than they are wont
> To keep obliged faith unforfeited.
>   [II. vi. 5-7]

Possibly his anxiety about 'keeping safe Nerissa's ring' [V. i. 307] just hints at the fates of earthly lovers rehearsed at the beginning of the act. 'Love me, and leave me not' may come to seem a fitting motto for these light lovers, its cheap sentiment sharpened by a sense of probable infidelity. How should love's bonds be honoured when no bond in law or under heaven but has been made light of?

But it would be a false emphasis to moralise. No serious judgement is being passed in that form, and no dire fate threatened. We grow aware of the grave defects in this pleasant comedy only by preserving a sense of what is absent—those qualities Antonio's 'sadness' portended in the first scene, and the heavenly harmony so positively if briefly evoked in this. For example, when Antonio offers to 'be bound again, my soul upon the forfeit' [V. i. 251-52], we need to pinch ourselves with the question, Can he really be playing at forfeits with his soul? Or again, we have to make an effort to recall that this apparently inconsequential comedy, which makes light of faith and inward harmony, has a direct, if hidden, connection with the corrupting and breaking of Shylock. We are likely too to miss the echo, in Antonio's 'Sweet lady, you have given me life and living' [V. i. 286], of Shylock's 'you take my life / When you do take the means whereby I live' [IV. i. 376-77]; an echo which might help us to see, beyond the irony of the former's being rewarded with what the latter was mocked for valuing excessively, the deeper connection, in Antonio's being fobbed off with his argosies and denied love's wealth, in the end as in the beginning, just as he had denied it to Shylock.

What we have to do with in all this is not evil but folly, the kind of folly exposed in Erasmus' *In Praise of Folly*, which can lay claim even to the attributes of the God to whom it is blind and indifferent. There is perhaps a measure of direct dramatic judgement of it in the slackening of tension after Portia's entrance, and in the impressions of a coarsening of feeling throughout the business of the rings. It is clearly and consistently placed, moreover, by its association with the moon and the moonstruck lovers, and by its own shallowness and the tawdriness that is inseparable from its superficial wit. But it remains difficult to define the exact quality of our response to it, and to formulate the elusive moral sense that permeates our response. The same difficulty exists for the larger matter of perceiving how this light comedy of folly is a relevant resolution for the play as a whole. (pp. 49-50)

The Merchant of Venice is at once not comic and not tragic. It is not comic since the Christian group is exposed to the criticism of the consequences for Shylock of their levity. Yet it is not tragic since it is Shylock who suffers and not themselves. But if the emphasis falls either way it is towards the comic; and this is confirmed in the last act, in which the tragic implications are dismissed, and the Christians left secure in their fool's paradise, unscathed by the evil they have done and at most to be laughed at. We must think of the play then as a comedy; but still we cannot think of it as only a comedy. Combination-terms such as 'tragi-comedy' hardly serve the purpose here. The best term I can find to catch the appropriate emphasis is *ironic comedy*.

I mean the term to indicate the relation of the two moral senses. We are subjected disturbingly to two different and unresolved sorts of justice, two different and unresolved standards of value. This is the main challenge for the producer, or for the reader producing the play in his own imagination: how to preserve the disturbing differences of mode and feeling, and nevertheless to resolve them into a coherent meaning. If they are not preserved the play will be oversimplified; if they are not resolved it will seem an enigma, or simply unsuccessful. It seems to me that the differences are resolved by the operation of a powerful and pervasive irony, an irony which carries into the comedy a seriously critical awareness of what has been felt and understood in the tragic part, and which, while it does not destroy the comedy, causes us to judge it by values which it fails to comprehend.

For the irony to be effective it is necessary that the tragic and the comic elements be kept distinct and separate—one remarks how naturally they separate out with Shylock's departure. This separateness is, in the first place, a safeguard against melodrama. . . . Beyond this, the separateness is positively the condition upon which the two elements are brought into an actively ironic relation. It is precisely by virtue of the clear disparity and opposition, the contradiction of the more profound by the superficial moral sense, that we are roused to seek an appropriate resolution, a unifying vision.

We can get further towards defining the interaction of the two parts by considering the effect of each separately, and then seeing the separate effects in relation to each other. The appeal of the comic part, with its wit, spectacle and diverting plot, is to the eye and ear, to the head rather than the heart. But the tragic part does 'speak to the heart', and engages before anything else our feelings of terror and pity. Our attitudes to Shylock are directly controlled by a quite full emotional response. With Venice and Belmont we must reflect upon the entertaining spectacle in order to discover how we might feel about it; they require our critical attention, but leave our feelings relatively disengaged.

In this difference we have a clue to the dramatic relation of the two parts. Given the Christians alone we could doubtless think our way to a justly judging response. But given Shylock as well we are much more powerfully and directly impelled towards that response. The feelings generated by Shylock must radically influence our sense of the Christians, sharpening and clarifying our attitude to them.

Our feelings instruct us that Shylock is inhuman because inhumanly abused. At the same time we are offered the spectacle of those who abuse him disporting themselves without any trace

of guilt. But the play directs us towards a resolution of the disparity by the stronger dramatic force of the tragic part. We discover, I think, that the heart is instructing the head in the right understanding of the comedy, bringing the mind to perceive in the self-centredness and self-satisfaction of the Christians the true cause of Shylock's condition. In consequence what they offer for our diversion ceases to please, for the heart is sensible of its connection with evil. The comedy can only exacerbate this sense, most especially in the last act which follows so closely upon the trial, with the result that it ceases to be simply comic, and becomes transformed by a profound irony.

The resolution effected by this irony is primarily a matter of enabling us to see the bafflingly doublefaced Christians in a single focus, to hold together in the mind's eye their attractive appearance and the vanities and inhumanity which have been exposed beneath it. But the irony then extends beyond the characters, to involve and question the attitudes of the audience. . . . So far as we have been attracted to the happily amoral Christians, accepted them at face value, and rejoiced in their good fortune, we may find ourselves exposed, like them, to the criticism of Shylock's fate and of the lesser evocation of a finer harmony. (pp. 53-5)

[The] several sins of commission and omission which we have witnessed, while they do not disturb Belmont's light happiness, do firmly delimit it, and place it in relation to the grand framework of heaven and hell. We are made aware—though the knowledge is lightly borne—that this happiness depends upon the breaking of Shylock, and the forgetting that he has been broken; and that it depends also upon the breaking of the spirit of divine and natural law, and the forgetting about the spirit under colour of conforming to the letter. If we are invited therefore to recognise and endorse an image of the way we ordinarily live and judge, by the 'decent average', we are shown at the same time the meaning of our complacency. If this is our paradise, it is the paradise of fools.

Yet the most teasing and disturbing quality of the play is that we are left to rejoice there if we will. The unpurged abyss of guilt represented by Shylock, and the unattained heaven of harmonious love, however critical their bearing upon it, may be lightly set aside in Belmont in favour of the moonshine. Yet what is enjoyed in Belmont is attuned to our dreams rather than our necessities, and satisfies no more than our illusions. If we are grateful that the play treats these so kindly, yet the gratification must be slight and shallow. And we can hardly avoid having it soured by the consciousness that it is so. For while the conclusion offers to flatter our fantasies as magazine fiction does, it embodies also, as such fictions rarely do, an ironic comprehension of reality. How many, aware of all that has passed in the play, will rest content with Belmont? and how many will be uncritically content with the standard of average decency in the face of what it could do to Shylock? Our ordinary worldly standards must come to seem less than adequate to the more serious occasions of life touched upon by the play.

Not that the play will purge us of our inadequacies in the matter, or of the follies of the world. Perhaps it would be a more comfortable play if it did in some way or other. Tragedy might purge us of the guilt of being as we are; and comedy reconcile us to ourselves through laughter. But the achievement of this play is in its not fitting cleanly into either mode, and instead confronting us deliberately with an image of our ordinary condition of moral compromise, of complacent spiritual mediocrity. The play neither condemns nor condones that condition: it reflects it accurately, thereby to promote a better knowledge of ourselves. The end makes us aware, even as it invites us to relapse into it, that the cosy amorality in which we would live if we were left to, is not ideal, is not the heaven of perfection we would like to think we aspire to.

We are tempted to look to literature to flatter our illusions of moral grandeur, to show us ourselves in the parts of saint or sinner, hero or martyr. But *The Merchant of Venice* offers to reflect what we are in our ordinary varnished reality. If we find this intolerable it is perhaps because we feel naked without our illusions. The emperor was proud until told he was without clothes. (pp. 55-6)

> A. D. Moody, in his Shakespeare: ''The Merchant of Venice,'' Edward Arnold (Publishers) Ltd., 1964, 64 p.

THOMAS H. FUJIMURA   (essay date 1966)

[In one of the most comprehensive examinations of the structure of The Merchant of Venice, *Fujimura argues that the play can be better understood if we view its three distinct worlds—that of Bassanio-Portia, that of Antonio, and that of Shylock—as each representing a different mode of dramatic expression and all working together to convey Shakespeare's ''philosophy.'' Fujimura states that these three modes of dramatic expression can be defined by Northrop Frye's genres or categories outlined in his* Anatomy of Criticism *as: the romantic (Bassanio-Portia), the realistic (Antonio), and the ironic (Shylock). The critic demonstrates how each world follows the dramatic pattern and contains the imagery and language of Frye's respective literary categories, and that each provides as its protagonist-hero a figure or figures who best represents his world. Fujimura also notes that the three worlds are represented symbolically in the play by the three caskets, the gold associated with Bassanio-Portia, the silver with Antonio, and the lead with Shylock. But as the casket story demonstrates, he adds, ''One needs to distinguish between the truly golden and what is gilded as well as the truly leaden and the apparently leaden.'' Thus Fujimura notes that the action in each of these worlds is characterized by the differences in the perception or awareness of the protagonists, claiming that ''Bassanio triumphs through his power of penetration, Antonio experiences a comic* anagnorisis, *and Shylock is defeated because his vision remains leaden and dull.'' The overall intent of Fujimura's essay is to show that* The Merchant of Venice *affirms certain values and rejects others, describing those affirmed values as ''aristocratic, Platonic, spiritual, Christian,'' and those rejected as ''commercial, materialistic, and non-Christian.' Fujimura's study, though different in purpose and conclusion, recalls the structural studies of* The Merchant of Venice *written in the nineteenth century by Hermann Ulrici (1839) and Denton J. Snider (1890). His emphasis on the Platonic element in the play and the characters' perceptions is also apparent in the essays by Charles Read Baskervill (1923) and Peter G. Phialas (1966).]*

[More] needs to be said about the structural unity of [*The Merchant of Venice*] in relation to its meaning. Though critics have paid tribute to Shakespeare's skillful interweaving of the main stories, they have not recognized the play's complex yet symmetrical structure. What is involved here is a question of critical method: the old-fashioned preoccupation with character, the current concern with imagery and style, or even [the] stress on theme does not take us to the heart of the play. What is central to drama is action, and the mode (romantic, realistic, ironic) which determines the structure of that action. And a study of the mode and structure of *The Merchant of Venice*

indicates that in its architectonics and in its communicated meaning it ranks as one of Shakespeare's great comedies.

There are three ''worlds'' presented in the play, each in its own mode; and these can be summed up as the world of Bassanio-Portia, the world of Antonio, and the world of Shylock. The first is romantic in its mode and non-realistic, the second is realistic, and the third is ironic; further, each mode has its relevant type of character, language, and dramatic action. The architectonic skill of Shakespeare appears in the interweaving and contrasting of these modes of action to express his theme or ''philosophy.'' There is no one main action, and it seems a critical error to set up the casket or the bond story as the central action. Rather it is through the dramatic interaction and contrast among the modes of action that the total meaning of the play emerges. Each of the three worlds is distinct and unique. To some extent, the world of Bassanio-Portia and the world of Shylock are insulated against each other, even hostile, and hence impervious to the dominant mood of the other. Though Shakespeare has provided links like Launcelot, Gratiano, and Jessica, it is chiefly through Antonio's world that we pass from one extreme to the other. The significance of these worlds is revealed to us only through their dramatic action, but this action is symbolic and ritualistic; hence, at its most meaningful moments, we participate in an enactment that transcends mere plot. (pp. 499-500)

These three worlds are represented symbolically in the play by the three caskets, gold, silver, and lead. It would not be inaccurate to speak of the golden world of Bassanio-Portia, the silver world of Antonio, and the leaden world of Shylock. The metals stand for the respective values of these worlds, and thus characterize everything from the outer manners and speech of these persons to their moral being. But paradoxically, as the caskets demonstrate, one needs to distinguish between the truly golden and what is gilded as well as the truly leaden and the apparently leaden. The action in these three worlds, in different modes, is also characterized by differences in the acuity of the protagonists: thus Bassanio triumphs through his power of penetration, Antonio experiences a comic *anagnorisis* [recognition], and Shylock is defeated because his vision remains leaden and dull.

The characters in these three worlds are all engaged in their own mythic encounter, the kind of action being determined by the mode which dominates. The intent of the total dramatic action is to affirm certain values and to reject certain others. The values in the play are generally familiar, and to the extent that they are acceptable to us, we assume their universality; where they are unfamiliar, we are either unmoved or perturbed. The dramatic affirmation of these values is what we usually call the statement of the theme. This theme is implicit rather than explicit, and is expressed through action, character, and dialogue; and thus not much is gained by too specific a summation of what the play means. But if we examine the values affirmed in the play, we find them to be aristocratic, Platonic, spiritual, Christian, in contrast to what is ''vulgar,'' commercial, materialistic, and non-Christian. The range of these values is greater than in most of Shakespeare's comedies; and basic to the meaning, and hence structure, of the play are certain metaphysical assumptions. (pp. 500-01)

The least controversial of the three worlds in the play is that of Bassanio-Portia, involving the casket story and the ring episode, with its characteristically romantic action of success and triumph. In the casket story, the almost ritualistic presentation retains in its purest form the symbolic meaning of Bassanio's encounter: after two "inferior" figures (surrogates for Shylock and Antonio) have failed, Bassanio picks the right casket, and thus affirms the values implicit in his golden world. The full meaning of this action is often obscured by failure to grasp the mode; that is, by adopting a realistic approach to the world of romance, and thus confusing modes. (p. 501)

Bassanio needs to be accepted on the play's own terms, as the hero of a romance, whose action affirms the idealistic-aristocratic values implicit in his world. The dramatic action involves a quest to liberate a princess, at the same time to prove the hero's worth, and finally to defeat the enemy of the golden world. This involves progress, or upward movement, from Venice (the world of commerce and law) to Belmont (the ideal world of romance). As befits the romantic hero, Bassanio expresses himself in language and imagery suggestive of the high world he inhabits. . . . The imagery of gold dominates, and in some respects Bassanio is a seeker of gold; but the wealth he pursues is spiritual and moral, embodied in a fair heiress, and touched with the magic beauty of love. (pp. 501-02)

Bassanio needs to be accepted as the hero of a romantic comedy. There is considerable truth to the view of Bassanio as an ideal Renaissance lover, moved to make the right choice because he understands the Renaissance concept of ideal love in Platonic terms. But Bassanio is something more and something less than an ideal Renaissance lover. He is the hero of a romantic comedy; that is, a young man of considerable spiritual, moral, intellectual, and physical excellence, subject to a few human failings, yet within reach of true love and the Garden of Eden because his failings are not irredeemable. If he has a fault, it is his prodigality, which he honorably confesses; but this prodigality springs from a generosity of spirit that does not reckon up material considerations, and it is set off favorably against the miserliness of Shylock. (p. 502)

Those who do not respond to the mode in which Bassanio is presented forget that he plays the role of the hero who embarks upon a hazardous and romantic quest. Belmont is no ordinary place, for ruling over it is the spirit of Portia's father, a kind of Prospero, who seems to possess magical powers. Nor are the hazards merely imaginary: the penalty for failure is an oath to remain single all one's life. If Bassanio is not quite Parsifal coming to the Siege Perilous, he is still the hero who comes to face the test of his merit, and also to free the imprisoned princess. The effect of Bassanio's wise choice is to liberate Portia from her father's iron-clad will, which, however wise, restrains her freedom. So joy and love and magnanimity are liberated. . . . Without Bassanio, [Portia] would never achieve the magnanimity of spirit which is finally hers, but would wither away in spinsterhood, with all its connotations of sterility, both physical and spiritual. She is hence as much the debtor as Bassanio.

The casket scenes are the central episode of the Bassanio-Portia story. Although they do not have the dramatic tension and emotional urgency that realistic theatergoers demand, they have a richly complex meaning and pattern which are eminently satisfying for those who do not demand merely realism in the theater. With its roots in the medieval *exemplum* and the emblem, its almost allegorical simplicity, and its Platonic basis, the casket episode retains the ritualistic quality which we find in the Renaissance masque. . . . Its meaning for Bassanio-Portia is explicit. Bassanio, enlightened by true love and wisdom, sees the symbolic quality of the metals, interprets the mottoes rightly, and makes the fitting choice. The right choice dramatically affirms the values of the romantic world, in which

the hero's character, parental wisdom, and providence are all vindicated. Bassanio proves his worth; he also demonstrates the rightness of the hierarchical value system of which he is a part.

But another crucial test of the hero lies ahead before he can fully achieve Belmont or the Garden of Eden. Like many another hero of romance who has won his fair princess in a golden land, Bassanio must return to the lower world to hazard all as final proof of his worth. This is the point of the ring episode. Its symbolic meaning is often overlooked. To understand the ring episode, we need to re-read the inscription on the lead casket: "Who chooseth me, must give and hazard all he hath" [II. vii. 9]. Bassanio, with Antonio, is the only person who has the dedication and wisdom to hazard all as a true lover must. But human love, as expressed in Dante or in the Renaissance, is not merely romantic love; it is an analogy of divine love; it is charity, mercy, and also friendship. In the trial scene, Bassanio expresses his willingness to hazard all for love:

> Antonio, I am married to a wife
> Which is as dear to me as life itself,
> But life itself, my wife, and all the world,
> Are not with me esteem'd above thy life.
> I would lose all, ay sacrifice them all
> Here to this devil, to deliver you.
>
> [IV. i. 282-87]

There is no resentment in the retort of Bellario (Portia), for with her wisdom and insight, she recognizes what is implicit in the offer of Bassanio, that it is the demonstration of the motto on the leaden casket. . . . As Portia recognizes, the ring episode is a symbolic enactment of Bassanio's hazarding all for love: to express his gratitude to Antonio's savior, he relinquishes the ring; that is, he gives up Portia. It is an act of gratitude and generosity—and also sacrifice. It shows the genuineness of his sentiments in the court scene. . . . However much the action might pique a lesser soul, Portia recognizes the worth of Bassanio. The ring episode also re-enacts the pound of flesh story; but with the charitable Portia rather than a cruel usurer invoking the penalty, the resolution is a happy one. Bassanio has passed every test, and proved to be true gold; he has lived up to the motto that he chose. During the course of the dramatic action, he has grown in stature, till at the end he is indeed worthy of inhabiting Belmont or the Garden of Eden.

Bassanio and Portia, united in spirit, also participate in another agon, or conflict, this time with Shylock. This is dramatized in the trial scene, in which the values of the romantic world are pitted against their opposites. . . . Though it is Portia and not Bassanio who actually encounters and defeats Shylock, the meaning of the encounter is clear. The heroine assumes a masculine disguise, and for the moment represents the hero in this familiar instance of displacement. As two persons united in spirit, Bassanio and Portia are interchangeable in their relationship to Shylock, for theirs is the golden, vital, youthful, and aristocratic world pitted against the leaden, dead, withered, and "vulgar" world of Shylock. In the triumph over Shylock and also in Bassanio's achievements in the casket scenes, his successful testing in the ring episode, we have the dramatic (or ritualistic) affirmation-through-enactment of certain values. These are related to love, and hence to harmony, order, and life, as contrasted with hatred, disorder, chaos, and spiritual death. This affirmation, attested to by the upward movement of the action, is not merely . . . a dream created as part of a dramatic illusion. Our approach to the world of romance and its values should not be so literal and realistic, for the world of romance has its own validity. This ideal world, the attainable Garden of Eden for those of right mind and spirit, is not only man's dream but his actual goal.... For the humanist-idealist like Shakespeare, the Garden of Eden is of this world, if men demonstrate their merit, as Bassanio does, through surviving the test of his intelligence and moral worth. Belmont is not a dream or a vision; it is an attainable reality.

Opposed to the romantic values of Bassanio-Portia is Shylock, who exists in a truly leaden world. Whereas the action in which Bassanio is involved turns upward, the action involving Shylock turns downward, for it is in the ironic mode. The ironic reversal in the trial scene brings defeat to Shylock, as he is satirically exposed to ridicule for the mean creature that he is. This dramatic action is subject to misunderstanding because the reader or theatergoer usually misses the ironic mode. The actor over the years has been as much to blame as anyone for this confusion of modes, and at this late date, it is perhaps impossible for most people to see Shylock clearly, as he is characterized in the play through action and dialogue.

The most serious obstacle to grasping the ironic mode in which he is presented is to regard Shylock primarily as a Jew. In adapting the bond story, Shakespeare stressed his Jewish traits, no doubt for the practical reason that the associations worked to communicate the theme with the greatest economy on the Elizabethan stage. But he is hateful not because he is a Jew but because he is Shylock.... Shylock's Jewishness is thus, in Aristotelian terms, an ''accident''; his substance is his spiritual deadness or leadenness. Hence the endless discussions of Shylock as a Jew are singularly fruitless; and in general the realistic approach implicit in this stress on his Jewishness is unrewarding. The study of anti-Semitism in Shakespeare's time sheds some light, but it is not very illuminating insofar as our understanding of the basic Shylock is concerned. Also unilluminating is the realistic and modern idea that Shylock is the product of his environment, that he is a creature of hatred because he has been warped by the hatred directed against his race. Again, discussion of the Jewish practice of usury in the Elizabethan period sheds some light, but is not crucial to our understanding of Shylock. He merely happens to be a usurer, and usuriousness like his Jewishness is an ''accident.'' (pp. 502-04)

Our response to Shylock is complicated by the fact that he is a complex symbol embodying a great many negative qualities. Aside from his Jewishness and his usury, he is a hater of music, and hence of harmony and concord, both social and moral.... In this hatred of music and in his stress on thrift, he shows a Puritanic quality much like Malvolio's. More conventionally, Shylock is the miserly old man who stands in the way of true love, and he is thus the familiar enemy of joy and life. He is also the ogre: the pound of flesh story is a mythic enactment of hatred transposed into act; and Shylock shares with Ugolino a hatred that expresses itself as a craving for human flesh. Finally, he is the fiend or devil incarnate, as indicated by many a comment in the play.... Shylock is a complex figure because he is more than the sum of his explicit identities—a Jew, usurer, and old father; he is also implicitly a Puritan, ogre, and devil. He has his function as antagonist to the world of romance; he also has his function in the world of Antonio.

As for his own dramatic action, Shylock exists on the level of the ironic mode. Consequently he is treated satirically, without much sympathy, and is allowed to entrap himself and bring about his own ironic discomfiture. (pp. 504-05)

The ironic treatment of Shylock is most evident in the language and imagery associated with him: his style is the plain style of Renaissance rhetoric. It is factual, literal, prosaic, as befits a materialistic creature; its rhythm is pedestrian and devoid of music.... In his allusions Shylock turns naturally to low images, chiefly bestial. Defending his irrational desire for Antonio's flesh, he refers to ''a gaping pig,'' ''a cat,'' and those who ''Cannot contain their urine'' ''when the bagpipe sings i'th'nose'' [IV. i. 47-50]; and supporting his claim to the pound of flesh, he alludes to ''a purchas'd slave'' and also asses, dogs, and mules [IV. i. 90-1]. Here speaks a ''vulgar'' mind, devoid of nobility, as mean in its aspirations as in the language in which its thoughts are clothed. This is the diction and imagery of irony and satire.

Much has been made of one speech of Shylock's in which he asserts his Jewishness:

> and what's his reason? I am a Jew. Hath not a Jew eyes? hath not a Jew hands, organs, dimensions, senses, affections, passions? fed with the same food, hurt with the same weapons, subject to the same diseases, healed by the same means, warmed and cooled by the same winter and summer as a Christian is?—if you prick us do we not bleed? if you tickle us do we not laugh? if you poison us do we not die? and if you wrong us shall we not revenge?
>
> [III. i. 58-67]

A sympathetic interpretation of this passage is open to two main objections. First, we should note the sophistry of Shylock, who is really justifying revenge on the grounds that this is what a Christian would do, and also rationalizing Antonio's contempt for him. But more seriously, Shylock has not asserted his humanity, nor his equality with people like Antonio and Bassanio. His list of items (hands, organs, dimensions, senses, affections, passions) does not include man's *rational* soul. Shylock is a creature of passion, and hence irrational.... Much is said about Shakespeare humanizing Shylock, and indeed Shylock is a human being, he is not a monster. But he needs to be considered in the context of the play; and in that context he is treated ironically. (pp. 505-06)

Irony characterizes the most striking statements of Shylock in the trial scene.... At the moment of seeming triumph, he exclaims in praise of Portia, ''A Daniel come to judgment: yea a Daniel!'' [IV. i. 223]. ''Most rightful judge!'' ''Most learned judge!'' he cries [IV. i. 301, 304]. And at that instant of comic hybris, there is an ironic reversal; Portia declares that though Shylock may have his pound of flesh, he will pay with his lands and goods if he sheds one drop of blood. Thereupon Gratiano mocks him with ''O upright judge! . . . O learned judge!'' [IV. i. 313], which he reiterates [IV. i. 317, 319], and adds, ''A second Daniel, a Daniel'' [IV. i. 333]. At this point a tragic villain would no doubt have insisted on his pound of flesh to feed his revenge whatever the consequences; but Shylock is not a tragic villain. Unlike Marlowe's Barabas, he lacks *virtù* [worthiness]. So he retreats, tries to salvage what he can, and is further exposed for the mean creature that he is. The whole treatment is ironic and satiric. The low language of Shylock, Gratiano's railing and mocking mimicry, the ironic reversal, the mean-spirited backing down of Shylock—all taken together clearly indicate the ironic mode. In the court scene,

Shylock will not arouse a great deal of sympathy if we are sensitive to the language, imagery, and ironic devices.

At the same time, we cannot dismiss Shylock as simply a comic villain and the butt of ridicule in the play. E. E. Stoll's conception of Shylock as a thoroughly Elizabethan and comic villain overlooks the complexities [see excerpt above, 1927]. He is more than the butt of ridicule in a comedy; he is the protagonist in his own ironic action. Perhaps a figure closest to him is someone like [Ben Jonson's] Volpone, who in his complexity and evil transcends the merely comic evil-doer. The ironic-satiric treatment does not allow for real sympathy, but it allows for passion, both in the victim and in the audience. The ironic mode is also at times closer in spirit to tragedy than to the purely comic. Thus the victim may express hatred, venom, resentment, desire for revenge, avarice, lust, envy; and in reaction, the audience may feel anger, contempt, hatred, loathing, disgust. Shylock is permitted to express strong passions, though never with tragic dignity or nobility.

Not only is Shylock the protagonist in his own ironic action, but he is the antagonist in relation to Bassanio-Portia and also to Antonio. He symbolizes the negation of all the values in the play, in fact, of the whole social, ethical, and metaphysical scheme of things. This role of Shylock's is worked out with considerable subtlety; and in this involvement he acquires more dignity. As an instance of this complex working out of his role, we might note that Morocco is a surrogate for Shylock in the casket scene. There is more than analogy in this. Morocco, like Shylock, is an alien; like his symbolic equivalent, he emphasizes his equality with other men, but in purely physical terms (the redness of his blood). Like Shylock's, his values are worldly and "vulgar"; and he chooses the gold casket, with its motto, "Who chooseth me, shall gain what many men desire" [II. vii. 5]. . . . So the materialistic creature is exposed for what he is, and his reward is a skull rather than love. He who is taken with false values and lacks the wisdom to achieve the real world of love, mercy, and magnanimity finds spiritual death and sterility. The values of Morocco and of Shylock are much alike, and Shylock's ironic defeat is anticipated in the casket scene. (pp. 507-08)

Finally, there is the silver world of Antonio, with its action set in the realistic mode. Though he does not hold the center of the stage, the merchant of Venice is the central figure thematically. He is an aristocrat engaged in commercial ventures; thus his existence impinges on the world of Bassanio and the world of Shylock. Antonio is silver—for the daily uses of this world. As Everyman, he goes through a ritual of death and rebirth, and experiences a comic *anagnorisis,* centered in the idea of mercy (charity, love). In the beginning he is characterized by hybris and lack of charity, demonstrated by his conduct toward Shylock; his purgatorial experience of impending death and "justice" leads to recognition and change, demonstrated by his charity toward Shylock in the trial scene. At the end, Antonio makes his symbolic journey to Belmont, the Garden of Eden, having freed himself from sin. This dramatic action is comic in the Dantean or medieval sense, in that it ends happily. As the protagonist in this "comic" action, Antonio is not, as is sometimes said, a passive or static character. Nor is he, as some critics describe him, the embodiment of perfect goodness. . . . Actually, Antonio is involved as protagonist in an action that is dramatic, and he undergoes a real change in the process. The most serious obstacle to understanding his role is failure to grasp the dramatic mode in which the action is cast. Thus, some critics see Antonio's opening

lines as the sign of a "tragic quality" in the play, and find him alien to the world of Shakespearean comedy. But Antonio is the protagonist of a dramatic action cast in the realistic mode, and his action follows the trajectory of hybris, passion (or suffering), *anagnorisis* or recognition, and a happy resolution.

A primary reason for failure to understand the action involving Antonio is that his experience is presented in a complex manner. He is of course on the stage *in propria persona* [in his own essential character] to enact his own drama. But he is represented, too, by Arragon, who is his surrogate in the choice of the silver casket. Antonio's spiritual career from hybris to *anagnorisis* is also presented symbolically through the account of his ships, from the picture of the proud vessels at the beginning, through the report of their loss at sea (death), to their final restoration. . . . Central to Antonio's "comic" experience is his growing acuity in relation to the basic principle of love and charity and also his loss of hybris before the onslaughts of fortune.

At the beginning Antonio is melancholy, with a malaise like that of Dante, lost in the woods in the middle of his spiritual journey. . . . This malaise is the product of his spiritual condition, of his lack of charity and his ignorance of self. But the tragic tone that some critics sense in these lines is a misreading. The language of Antonio is couched in the low middle style, with simple diction and homely imagery, as befits the realistic mode; it does not have the accent of high tragedy. This is the spiritual condition of Everyman, in a relatively low mimetic mode, expressed in ordinary language. The unsettled and yet arrogant state of Antonio is suggested by the imagery of the ships that follows, in Salerio's words.

> Your mind is tossing on the ocean,
> There where your argosies with portly sail
> Like signiors and rich burghers on the flood,
> Or as it were the pageants of the sea,
> Do overpeer the petty traffickers
> That cur'sy to them (do them reverence)
> As they fly by them with their woven wings. . . .
>
> [I. i. 8-14]

Antonio denies that his ventures make him sad; and indeed he is right. But his calm faith in his own ships reveals his hybris and a blindness to the vagaries of fortune untypical of a wise Shakespearean character. At the same time Antonio, like Arragon, is acute enough to penetrate appearances to some degree, and he declares:

> I hold the world but as the world Gratiano,
> A stage, where every man must play a part,
>
> [I. i. 77-8]

Antonio is aware of the mutability of life, its transitory nature, and the mockery of make-believe. Yet he is guilty of a strange over-confidence, based on his material possessions and the respect of less affluent acquaintances. . . . With the blindness of hybris, Antonio says blithely to the warier Bassanio when Shylock proposes his bond:

> Why fear not man, I will not forfeit it,—
> Within these two months, that's a month before
> This bond expires, I do expect return
> Of thrice three times the value of this bond.
>
> [I. iii. 156-59]

Again, at the end of the act, he repeats with supreme confidence:

Act IV. Scene i. Shylock and Portia. By J. D. Watson. The Department of Rare Books and Special Collections, The University of Michigan Library.

in this there can be no dismay,
My ships come home a month before the day.
                                              [I. iii. 180-81]

This reiteration is not accidental, but serves its dramatic function of pointing up Antonio's overconfidence. At the same time, he reveals a lack of charity, which accompanies his hybris. When Shylock snarls at him, "You call'd me dog" [I. iii. 128], Antonio retorts:

I am as like to call thee so again,
To spet on thee again, to spurn thee too.
                                              [I. iii. 130-31]

This harshness of Antonio has bothered critics who think of him as a perfectly good man. But Antonio is clearly depicted at the beginning as a man with a flaw. The redeeming quality is his deep love for Bassanio; and on this pivots the action in which Antonio makes his foolish mistake, goes through suffering (a kind of Purgatory or ritual death), and finally experiences *anagnorisis*. In Antonio's story, Shylock assumes the role of the fiend who nearly triumphs over him. (pp. 509-10)

When sentence is pronounced against Shylock, [a] wiser and more charitable Antonio intercedes for remission of half the fine against his enemy. For such merciful conduct Antonio is rewarded; not only does he make the symbolic journey to Belmont, but he is informed by Portia that three of his argosies

"Are richly come to harbour suddenly" [V. i. 277]. The silver world of Antonio, with its dramatic enactment of hybris, suffering, and *anagnorisis,* remains on the level of comedy. It does not sparkle with the golden shimmer of the world of romance. But the silver world, expressed through Antonio's experience and the language he habitually uses, with its relatively simple diction, imagery, and rhythm, is in the realistic mode, and is closest to us, closer even than Shylock's world or Bassanio's. (p. 511)

> Thomas H. Fujimura, "Mode and Structure in 'The Merchant of Venice'," in PMLA 81, Vol. LXXXI, No. 1, March, 1966, pp. 499-511.

PETER G. PHIALAS   (essay date 1966)

[*Phialas contends that* The Merchant of Venice *is concerned primarily with demonstrating the necessity of love, "in the romantic as well as the social sphere," as humanity's sole means "of achieving harmony and happiness and salvation." As such, he takes issue with those critics who have overemphasized the race theme in the play—the conflict between Judaism and Christianity, even the opposition of justice and mercy—examples of which can be found in the essays by Heinrich Heine (1838), Denton J. Snider (1890), Sir Israel Gollancz (1922), Nevill Coghill (1949), Muriel C. Bradbrook (1951), Theodor Reik (1956), C. L. Barber (1959), E. M. W. Tillyard (1961), Barbara K. Lewalski (1962), and René E. Fortin (1974). Phialas maintains that Shakespeare's central concern is the conflict between love and hate, the one depicted in Portia's exercise of Christian mercy, the other in Shylock's manipulation of the law to satisfy a personal vengeance. He thus claims that Shakespeare was interested in Shylock's role as a Jew and usurer only to the extent that this role aided his audience's understanding of the character as an outsider, a stranger, a person whose "attitude towards gold, love, mercy, and the rest appears completely foreign" to the Venetians. For a more developed discussion of Shylock as an outsider, see the excerpt by Graham Midgley (1960). Phialas also comments on Shakespeare's Neoplatonic vision of romantic love in* The Merchant of Venice, *especially as displayed in the spiritual relationship of Bassanio and Portia and symbolized in the world of Belmont. The Platonic element in the play has also been examined by Charles Read Baskervill (1923) and Thomas H. Fujimura (1966).*]

The Merchant of Venice takes up and develops further certain motifs [Shakespeare] attempted in some of the earlier comedies. One of these themes has to do with two large aspects of love, romantic love and what might be called love in the social sphere, the love guiding and controlling human relationships, love expressed in friendship, love as the basis of ideal justice, justice qualified by mercy. Having dealt with the love-friendship conflict in *The Two Gentlemen of Verona* and in a smaller way in *A Midsummer Night's Dream,* Shakespeare proposes here to present the ideal relationship of friendship and love. . . . Most important of all, *The Merchant of Venice* resumes a theme indeterminately treated in some of the earlier plays, a theme made central to the action of *A Midsummer Night's Dream.* It is the theme of choice, a lover's falling in love with this woman and not another, the basis of attraction between two lovers, the question Shakespeare had essayed to answer by means of the mysterious operation of the fairies in the earlier play. (pp. 134-35)

These are the chief matters with which *The Merchant of Venice* is concerned, and if the reader or audience holds to these as the main concern of the dramatist, then the questions raised by the play, including Shylock's role, may prove somewhat less perplexing. One of the reasons for those questions is that because Shylock dominates certain scenes he is thought to be the most important character and his fortunes the chief concern of the play. Of his emotional impression upon the reader and audience there can be no doubt. But in terms of the play's structure in expressing the themes cited above he is not the chief character, and though his own individual destiny is absorbing, it is not that destiny that matters most in the play. What matters is Shylock's immediate as well as symbolic representation of an attitude, a point of view which is by the dramatist opposed to another point of view, this one represented by the Venetians in general but expressed most pointedly by Portia. (p. 135)

[The] most celebrated historian of Elizabethan drama called *The Merchant of Venice* a tragicomedy. He thought it a play of "divided purpose," and believed that in its final impression "it is the emotional and not the critical attitude towards life which predominates" [see excerpt above by E. K. Chambers, 1908]. The penetration with which Shakespeare looked into Shylock tends to justify the judgment that the play contains elements which distinguish it from Shakespeare's other comedies. But those elements differ from analogous matter in *Much Ado About Nothing* and *As You Like It* in degree, not in kind. And the success with which Shakespeare adjusted the force of Don John's and Oliver's actions in those plays is the reason why the two later comedies are more successful than *The Merchant of Venice*. The difference then lies in the improper balance between the romantic love story and the story of social or national or international strife which supplies the secondary, non-romantic interest in Shakespearean romantic comedy. Although Shakespeare placed exceptionally great stress on the non-romantic tale, the play nevertheless is a comedy of romantic love, its main action being the love and final union of Bassanio and Portia. It differs from the joyous comedies only in the degree of stress placed upon the antagonistic, non-romantic opposition to the love motive. (pp. 148-49)

The Merchant of Venice is not a play on a race theme, though many critics have thought so, and although there can be no doubt that the Elizabethans showed distrust and dislike for the Jew the play is not necessarily directed towards prejudice.... Nor is it a play about money or gold although these are given a significant role. We must also reject the notion that what has been called the "realistic theme" of Shylock's bond story "portrays the downfall of hated usury and the triumph of Christian charity in the person of a princely merchant" [see the essay by John W. Draper in the Additional Bibliography]. Christian charity is opposed to something much more powerful than usury, and that charity is not represented by the merchant Antonio even though he is willing to show some evidence of charity at the conclusion of the fourth act.... *The Merchant of Venice* is about love, and in blending the bond story with the story of the caskets it enforces the Virgilian conviction that *Omnia vincit amor,* that in the romantic as well as the social sphere, love is the only means of achieving harmony and happiness and salvation. And this is the master-theme of all Shakespeare's comedies; it is the thought which underlies his whole work. Here in *The Merchant of Venice* the principle is crystallized in Portia's declaration that human action shows most god-like when it is tempered by mercy.... [And it] is made clear by Lorenzo's taking up the theme and expressing it in somewhat different terms in the garden scene of Act V.

But though the play is not primarily concerned with usury or race or religion, these form, nevertheless, significant thematic units employed by the dramatist in order to state his central idea. It must be added that usury or the love of money, one's

attitude towards accumulating and possessing gold, is of far greater importance in the play than the race theme, although the latter has been raised by both critics and actors to a position of eminence unwarranted by the play. (pp. 149-50)

Shylock's profession and the related theme of accumulating gold, the sterile possession of wealth—these matters ... are employed by Shakespeare as a metaphor, the correlative means of expressing the chief idea in the play. The love of gold not only points to Shylock's inability to love anything else but also identifies the kind of love Nerissa defines in the song she sings while Bassanio contemplates the caskets.... In *The Merchant of Venice* one's attitude towards gold tends to define his capability for love.

We may turn now to the other sub-theme which critics have emphasized somewhat unduly, the fact that Shylock is a Jew. Why did Shakespeare make his usurer a Jew? One answer, of course, is that he found him in the sources.... But there is another reason and that is that by presenting a Jewish usurer Shakespeare could enforce the point that the usurer seems utterly different from the Venetians and that his attitude towards gold, love, mercy, and the rest appears completely foreign to theirs. Shakespeare was intent upon presenting a pointed contrast between those within a society held together by certain traditions and attitudes and the usurer who stands outside it. It was for such a reason that Shakespeare stressed Richard III's deformity and Edmund's illegitimacy.... As a usurer and as a Jew, Shylock would thus be most pointedly contrasted not only with Antonio and the rest of the Venetians but also and most especially with Portia, who in the trial scene propounds ideal attitudes towards wealth and love and mercy which may be called Christian. This comes very near to saying that Shakespeare opposes the Jew and the Christian and that the play deals with the conflict between races and religions. It cannot be denied that any moral conflict can be referred to religious principle. But though Shylock's attitude as usurer and would-be murderer is opposed to the Christian-like charity and communal harmony enforced by the play's conclusion, it is not Shylock's race or religion that prompts his attitudes; his race and religion are nowhere on trial in the play. It is not Shylock's race that matters but what he says and does. (pp. 153-54)

This then is the significance of the Jewish usurer in the comedy. Shakespeare was far more seriously concerned with the dramatic function of Shylock's race and more especially his profession than with these matters *per se*.... If it is true that the play is primarily concerned with the conflict between love and hate, we are bound to conclude that Shylock, who represents the latter, must be so conceived that the audience shall receive an instantaneous impression of both the nature and force of his representation. For that reason he is made a Jewish usurer. Or to turn it around, that is the reason a Jewish usurer is selected by the dramatist as the antagonist of Portia, the heroine of a love story. (p. 155)

Shylock's function in the play is to oppose and directly threaten the harmony represented by Belmont. If this is admitted, then Shylock's characterization must be so fashioned that he will most effectively furnish such opposition and threat. For this neither a pathetic nor a comic Shylock will do. But neither will an inhuman villain, for such a character would fail to provide opposition in human or credible terms. Nowhere in the play is Shylock shown to be bent on some evil act for its own sake; he is after revenge, and revenge is a human response to a human stimulus. Revenge he seeks with terrifying singleness of mind, and in that passionate search he rejects mercy, that is, he refuses to be swayed by love in disposing of Antonio's bond. In this rejection and refusal, like many another villain or tragic hero in Shakespeare—but like no comic character—Shylock would violate his human nature. For evil, in this instance desire for revenge, is antagonistic to and a violation of the natural law inherent in man's being. That this is what happens—that Shylock would violate that law within his being—is made clear throughout the play but most pointedly in the trial scene. (p. 160)

The action of the play presents the conflict between love and its antithesis, and whereas the latter is represented in the main by a single character, the former is acted out by a number of persons. In Shylock the dramatist represents in their utmost concentration the thirst for revenge, the lust for possession, the neither giving nor forgiving, the complete rejection of what are called "human values." What keeps Shylock from seeming an abstraction are the human motives we referred to above, motives which, be it remembered, may explain his acts without justifying them. On the other side at least three characters represent giving and forgiving. That theme is dramatized by Antonio's generosity to Bassanio as well as to those to whom "he lends out money gratis" [I. iii. 44]; it is expressed also in Bassanio's choice of the lead casket, which is preceded by a formal exposition of the principle which underlies it; and it is most forcefully stated by Portia in the trial scene, wherein she sets down the principle of love, of giving, and merciful forgiving in contrast to Shylock's insistence on revenge.

Now the opposition between Shylock and Antonio in the early scenes of the play and between Shylock and Portia in the trial scene has to do with the bond story, with love or its opposite as it operates in social intercourse. But there is another conflict in which Shylock is involved, though not directly on the stage, and that is the scene of Bassanio's trial. . . . [Here] the obvious contrast is between Bassanio's giving and hazarding all for love and Morocco's and Arragon's failures: Morocco confuses external show with truth and beauty, whereas Arragon "assumes desert," that is, he insists upon receiving what he believes he deserves. Bassanio rejects both the insistence on receiving and the choice on the basis of external show, and thus indirectly demonstrates through the choice of the lead casket that he is Portia's true love. But the choice of gold and silver by Morocco and Arragon, and the choice of lead by Bassanio are made to recall and comment upon Shylock's love of gold and his insistence upon receiving instead of giving. In this scene, then, he is presented in opposition to Bassanio, and the conflict between them is far more significant than that between Bassanio and the other suitors. Whereas the latter conflict serves to give meaning to Bassanio's choice, the implied conflict with Shylock has a structural as well as thematic significance, for it contributes to considerable unity of impression, a desideratum for a successful play second to none. That impression can be expressed simply by saying that Bassanio's choice would not be Shylock's. The link between the two is enforced upon our consciousness not only by the attractiveness and external worth of gold and silver, which Bassanio rejects, but more directly through the scrolls within the gold and silver caskets. (pp. 161-63)

But although Bassanio's trial has relevance to the bond story, his chief role is as a romantic lover, whose "choice" must carry significance in matters of romantic love. The burden of his speech before choosing is stated in the second line: "The world is still deceived with ornament" [III. ii. 74]. Bassanio is not so deceived and indeed chooses "that within which

passeth show" [*Hamlet*, I. ii. 85]; he is eager not merely to receive but also to give. . . . The relevance of Bassanio's choice to matters of romantic love, implicit in that choice and the words which accompany it, is stated directly in Nerissa's song.

> Tell me where is fancy bred.
> Or in the heart or in the head?
> How begot, how nourished?
>   Reply, reply.
>
> It is engend'red in the eyes,
> With gazing fed; and fancy dies
> In the cradle where it lies. . . .
>
> [III. ii. 63-9]

Though beauty is first carried to the lover's consciousness by the eyes, he must not choose by the view, for that is not true love's way. For love as the attraction based on the external dies and is forgotten in its infancy. Love is not love which thus begins and shortly ends. True love begins with the eyes but proceeds to consider the beloved with the eyes of the mind, whereby in a series of steps guided in turn by sense, reason, and understanding, it may reach the state of perfect happiness which in Shakespeare is usually symbolized by music. In turn the lovers' happiness or harmony is but the analogue to a universal union and harmony, the harmony which is at one with the music of the spheres, that is to say, the harmony implicit in the Divine. . . . The music of the spheres which echoes within man's immortal soul can be heard only through love, the true love which unites man and woman, and that other larger union of all men into a universal communion.

Shylock seems far from this, but, though absent, he is not utterly banished from Belmont. His absence is, of course, most significant, but the humanity which Shakespeare gave him, though self-violated, may reassert itself and thus respond to that same harmony which he had earlier rejected. (pp. 163-65)

And here we may pause briefly to note that the contrast between Shylock and the Venetians is not absolute: it is not expressed in sharp and clear-cut opposition of black and immaculate white. The reason for this is that Shakespeare sees both sides not as static but as potential principles, and "potential" is the term which best describes the ending of Shakespearean romantic comedy. In such comedy what the happy and harmonious conclusion of the story or stories represents is not an attempt to record actuality. What it represents is the imaginative fulfillment of what is possible and desirable in human experience: the perfection or ideal which Shakespearean comedy projects is a potential, not a fact. The world of the Venetians is not perfect, though it is potentially so, and it attains perfection after it has been transferred to Belmont. Thus Belmont is a symbol not of what is but of what is achievable if men will allow love and charity and mercy and forgiveness to guide their actions. (pp. 165-66)

That the Christians of Venice, though contrasted with Shylock, are not perfect is clearly an important theme in the play, although it is treated mainly in indirect and ironic fashion. Shylock's speeches defending his thirst for revenge suggest that the conduct of his opposites is not always defensible. Antonio is too violent in his spurning and bespitting him, Salarino and Salerio too callous in their jeering him, Gratiano too strident in his taunts. . . . The contrast between Shylock and the Venetians is there but it is not absolute, and this is the reason why over-schematic interpretations of that contrast can be misleading. Nor is Belmont the symbol of an exclusively Christian paradise, although Shakespeare associates it with prayers and holy men, for along with these the final act brings to the speeches of Jessica and Lorenzo the most concentrated classical allusions in Shakespearean comedy. In these lines, as well as in Bassanio's trial, there is a happy union of Christian and Platonic ideals, but they are ideals for the Venetians as well as Shylock. Shylock's narrow world may be contrasted with the freer world of the Venetians, but there is an even more significant contrast between these two on the one hand and Belmont on the other. The achievement of Belmont is far more significant than Shylock's enforced conversion. (pp. 166-67)

The Merchant of Venice is the last comedy before the climactic triad, the so-called joyous comedies, and in that position it seems to conclude the long experimental period. Though like *A Midsummer Night's Dream* it demonstrates an extraordinary advance over earlier plays in both structure and characterization, its central idea is not perfectly implicit in its structure. The reason for this is that Shylock and the bond story cannot be completely assimilated into the comic conclusion; the link between the bond story and the rest of the plot—one's attitude toward or use of wealth—that link offers only a partial analogy to the romantic theme. We noted earlier that Bassanio's choice is structurally and thematically related to Shylock's attitude towards gold, and that the relationship can be stated in this manner: Bassanio's choice would not be Shylock's. But Shylock's choice is between gold and human values whereas Bassanio's has to do with the conflict between external appearance and inner worth as the guide to true love. Shylock's choice leads him to self-violation, whereas Bassanio's leads him to self-realization. Between the two choices there is of course a connection, but the two cannot be identified, and the division between the Rialto and Belmont, in spite of the many structural links, remains to the end. Even Portia's symbolic journey to Venice and her confrontation with Shylock cannot completely bridge that division. Although both ultimately argue for the letter of the law, neither is really concerned with it but rather with something else. Shylock calls upon the law to sanction his plea for revenge, whereas Portia turns to the same instrument to justify her desire for mercy: revenge and mercy are their chief concerns. Furthermore, it should be noted that Shylock never meets Portia, never hears of her, never discovers the identity of the young doctor who defeats his designs upon Antonio, and the reason for this (other than the need of the ring episode for Portia's disguise) must have been the dramatist's unwillingness to identify Portia with the bond story. Portia is needed in both plots, but her two roles, though related, are very different. As she does not really belong in the bond story—she appears in it disguised—so Shylock, as we noted earlier, cannot be made part of the romantic tale of Belmont. (pp. 168-69)

In spite of such minor imperfections, *The Merchant of Venice* marks an advance in Shakespearean romantic comedy by virtue of its treating, and therefore in a sense disposing of, certain themes which Shakespeare had attempted in earlier plays. One of these themes is the use of wealth as a metaphor for the expression of human relationships. . . . Another motif given a final expression in the play is the question with which Nerissa opens her song during Bassanio's test. The nature of true love, directly described in the sonnets, is here obliquely defined by its opposite, superficial and short-lived fancy based on externals, and also by Bassanio's choice as well as by his exposition of its meaning. But the whole episode has a theoretical quality, for Bassanio's choice of the lead casket and his comment upon it are not made relevant to his own falling in love, his own election of Portia. Nevertheless his speech, together with Ner-

issa's song, provides a reply to the question raised in *A Midsummer Night's Dream*. . . . True love, as Nerissa's song and Bassanio's speech imply, is based not on external beauty alone but on attraction from within as well. By refusing to be guided merely by the eyes, that is, by the appetite of sense, and by turning from sense to reason and the understanding, the lover may hope to move from the immediate experience of physical attraction to the mystic realm of oneness with the divine. This is the clearest expression so far achieved by Shakespearean comedy of the Neoplatonist concept of love. And reinforcing this statement by Nerissa's song and Bassanio's choice is yet another Platonic concept, the notion that, like love, virtue may enable mortal man to break through "the muddy vesture of decay" and, like the "youngey'd cherubins" [V. i. 64, 62], at last hear the mystic harmonies of the moving spheres. This idealization of love is never absent from Shakespearean romantic comedy. Whether stated or merely implied, it is the object of men's longing, of their aspiration towards ultimate perfection and purification, in short, the realization of man's angelic possibilities. But Shakespeare stresses the longing, not the state itself, and moreover he unfailingly presents that longing against human limitation. . . . (pp. 169-71)

These, then, are the points wherein *The Merchant of Venice* records an advance in Shakespeare's development of his peculiar comic mode. Although its structure is managed with great skill, the play fails to achieve perfect unity of impression. In this one respect *The Merchant of Venice* is inferior to *A Midsummer Night's Dream*. It is superior in structure, in the penetrating conception of Shylock's character, and in its verse. And in addition it records Shakespeare's preoccupation with certain motifs which henceforth will appear in his later comedies as contributory elements, not as subjects of exploration. That exploration is conducted in *The Merchant of Venice*. (p. 171)

> *Peter G. Phialas, " 'The Merchant of Venice'," in his* Shakespeare's Romantic Comedies: The Development of Their Form and Meaning, *The University of North Carolina Press, 1966, pp. 134-71.*

D. A. TRAVERSI (essay date 1968)

[*Traversi, an English scholar, has written a number of books on Shakespeare's plays, including* An Approach to Shakespeare *(1938) and* Shakespeare: The Last Phase *(1954). In the introduction to the first of these studies, Traversi proposed to focus his interpretation of the plays on "the word," stating that the experience which forms the impetus to each of Shakespeare's dramas "will find its most immediate expression in the language and verse." Like such earlier critics as Elmer Edgar Stoll (1927), Harold R. Walley (1935), John Middleton Murry (1936), and J. W. Lever (1952), Traversi focuses on the stock characterization of Shylock, claiming that he is intended to be "the melodramatic villain, the heartless usurer, and the enemy of Christianity" in* The Merchant of Venice. *However, Traversi adds that Shakespeare could not resist "conferring upon his Jew, at the moments when that effect requires them, a consistency and human solidity which . . . threatens at times to break through the elaborate poetic fabric of his Venetian romance."*]

The interpretation of Shylock's part in [*The Merchant of Venice*] calls . . . for considerable firmness in discrimination. It may even be that Shakespeare, when he embarked upon his comedy, was not in every respect fully conscious of what he was in fact bringing into being. It is essential, of course, to avoid the modern temptation to sentimentalize Shylock, or to read his character in terms of our own preoccupation with racial realities. The melodramatic villain, the heartless usurer, and the enemy of Christianity all belong to the conception, and an Elizabethan audience would certainly have found nothing unusual or unseemly in the final downfall of all three. This downfall is amply accomplished before the end of the play and is certainly essential to its intended effect; but even before Shakespeare Marlowe had gone a considerable way, in the early scenes of his *Jew of Malta,* to apportion blame between the races, and what Shakespeare has done in *The Merchant* is to follow his instinct for powerful dramatic effect to the extent of conferring upon his Jew, at the moments when that effect requires them, a consistency and human solidity which, reflecting disquieting aspects of the real world, threatens at times to break through the elaborate poetic fabric of his Venetian romance.

An unprejudiced reading of the play, indeed, can leave us in no doubt concerning the scope of this achievement. The contemptuous treatment afforded to Shylock by the Christians, not excluding Antonio, is, of course, to be seen primarily through Elizabethan eyes. It is justified, in these terms, by the generally accepted need to repudiate the position of one who sins by taking "A breed for barren metal of his friend" [I. iii. 134], who seeks, in other words, to make inanimate gold "breed" and so assume a function properly confined to living creatures. The rejection and final punishment which this aberration brings upon the sinner is both in itself appropriate and necessary, by contrast, to bring out the truth implied in both Antonio's generosity and Portia's essential plea for "the quality of mercy" [IV. i. 184]. Shylock, in fact, is brought to ruin because these positive virtues are beyond his comprehension; but Shakespeare's instinct for a dramatic situation was not thereby prevented from giving due force, when the situation called for it, to his response to the contempt of his enemies and even to the appeal to racial tradition implied in his quoting of the Old Testament story of Laban [I. iii. 77ff.] and elsewhere. Similarly, the betrayal of the Jew by his own daughter is clearly to be regarded as justified both as an act of religious conversion and as an escape from what are finally inhuman attitudes; but though Shylock is evidently at once comic and ignoble when presented, in Salanio's description [II. viii. 12ff.], as confounding the loss of Jessica with that of his "ducats," there are moments when his deprivation of both is invested with a degree of passion that, while it cannot justify him, does add to the initial effect a note at least akin to tragedy. When Tubal reports that one of Antonio's creditors has been seen abroad with "a ring that he had of your daughter for a monkey" [III. i. 118-19], Shylock's reaction—

> Thou torturest me, Tubal: it was my turquoise;
> I had it of Leah when I was a bachelor: I would
> not have given it for a wilderness of monkeys—
>
> [III. i. 120-23]

is sufficiently steeped in emotion, personal and, as it were, racial, to produce an effect that finally evades the merely comic. Incidents of this kind are common in Shakespeare's presentation of Shylock; they are used, beyond the evident intention of condemning the usurious unbeliever, beyond even that of showing an incompletely human being entrapped in the insufficiency of his own attitudes, to lend depth and dramatic verisimilitude to the Jew's passion, to what is seen at certain culminating moments to be his intense desire to *survive* by clinging to his own separate standards. (pp. 183-85)

It is his understanding of these deeper issues behind Shylock's admitted "villainy," even his rejection of the human law of compassion, that enables Shakespeare to present the Jew's re-

actions to Christian society with a force that makes it impossible for us simply to pass them by. It is not in any sense that Shylock is to be regarded as being in the right. On the contrary, his attitudes are based on what all the comedies agree in regarding as basic human limitations, blind spots which, when persisted in, make a balanced and fully human life unattainable. Shylock is finally condemned by his persistence in his own perverse choices, by the warped attitudes which prompt him to reject life when it is offered him upon the only terms on which, according to these comedies, it is available; but the rejection itself is rendered dramatically understandable, takes possession of our minds as a dark and twisted strain that threatens at times to affect our attitude to the play as a whole. His retort to Antonio's initial request for a loan, so spare and tense with passion against the brilliant but relatively trivial decoration that surrounds it, is charged, on any interpretation, with the unmistakable accents of reality

> Go to, then: you come to me, and you say
> "Shylock, we would have moneys": you say so;
> You, that did void your rheum upon my beard,
> And foot me as you spurn a stranger cur
> Over your threshold: moneys is your suit.
> What should I say to you? Should I not say
> "Hath a dog money? is it possible
> A cur can lend three thousand ducats?" or
> Shall I bend low and in a bondman's key,
> With bated breath and whispering humbleness,
> Say this,—
> "Fair sir, you spit on me on Wednesday last;
> You spurn'd me such a day; another time
> You call'd me dog; and for these courtesies
> I'll lend you thus much moneys"?
>
> [I. iii. 115-29]

Here, if anywhere, the compulsive dramatic instinct is at work conferring life upon a character beyond all possible abstract limits or over-all necessities. (pp. 185-86)

All this does not mean, as we have said, that we need be tempted to simplify the reading of the character so presented. The conventional Elizabethan view of the Jew and the usurer continues to be, at this point as always, the foundation of Shakespeare's conception of Shylock, as, indeed, the entire comic conception requires it; but, whilst he has taken this view as his starting point, and is on the way to accepting it for his conclusion, his sense of dramatic contrast is clearly at work humanizing it, balancing it—even at some risk to the effect made by his play as a whole—against other factors that, if they do not contradict, at least profoundly modify it. The modification sometimes even threatens to color our view of Shylock's Christian opponents, those whom the general line of the comedy would have us see as uniformly benign and superior. It produces, in reply to the explosion of resentment just quoted, Antonio's ruthlessly complacent expression of superiority:

> I am as like to call thee so again,
> To spit on thee again, to spurn thee too;
>
> [I. iii. 130-31]

so that we may even feel that, when he explicitly tells Shylock:

> If thou wilt lend this money, lend it not
> As to thy friends; . . .
> But lend it rather to thine enemy;
> Who, if he break, thou mayest with better face
> Exact the penalty,
>
> [I. iii. 132-33, 135-37]

he is in effect inviting the fate which will in due course threaten to undo him. The appropriate reversal of this episode comes, indeed, when Antonio is driven to throw himself upon the Jew's mercy, only to receive what is, always within its own terms, the unanswerable logic of his reply:

> I am a Jew. Hath not a Jew eyes? hath not a Jew hands, organs, dimensions, senses, affections, passions? . . . If a Jew wrong a Christian, what is his humility? Revenge. If a Christian wrong a Jew, what should his sufference be by Christian example? Why, revenge. The villainy you teach me, I will execute; and it shall go hard but I will better the instruction.
>
> [III. i. 58-73]

We have already stressed that the temptation to whitewash Shylock in the light of our own notions in these matters must be avoided. To "better instruction" in this way is by no means to escape the charge of "villainy" which remains firmly fixed; but recognition of this evident reality need not lead us to ignore the plain evidence of the text, which gives this same "villainy" a real, if perverse, motivation, or to discount the full balance that his sense of a dramatic situation imposed at this and other points on Shakespeare's conception. (pp. 186-87)

> D. A. Traversi, "'King John' and 'The Merchant of Venice'," in his An Approach to Shakespeare, revised edition, 1968. Reprint by Doubleday & Company, Inc., 1969, pp. 167-90.

JOHN P. SISK (essay date 1969)

[*Sisk maintains that the unity of the three plots in* The Merchant of Venice—*the bond story, the casket story, and the ring story—is the result of a single theme present in each, namely, the release from bondage through "the salvation of love." Sisk contends that the "good" characters in the play value love over money, hatred, and self-gain, and are thus in harmony with the "elemental liberating powers" of the universe; the "bad" characters invert this process and are held in bondage to their own attachment to false ideals. Sisk notes, however, that the issue of money and love in the drama "is not a disjunctive one," in that money can be used, as it is by Antonio, Portia, and Bassanio, in the service of life and love to liberate, just as it can be used, as it is by Shylock, to bind one in hatred and greed. A similar assessment of the uses of love and wealth in* The Merchant of Venice *can be found in the excerpts by Karl Elze (1871), John Russell Brown (1957), and C. L. Barber (1959). Sisk adds that the ultimate distinction in the play "is not between liberation and bondage but between good bonds and bad bonds," since love and mercy and the laws of a harmonious universe are themselves a form of bondage, but a form, Sisk concludes, that liberates rather than constricts, as evil bonds do. For further commentary on the theme of bonds and bonding in* The Merchant of Venice, *see the excerpts by Sigurd Burckhardt (1962) and Alice N. Benston (1979).*]

It is customary to observe [in *The Merchant of Venice*] how skillfully Shakespeare has organized into a dramatic unit the bond story (the compact between Shylock and Antonio), the casket story, and the ring story. The latter two are no less bond stories than the first. Portia, "aweary of this great world" [I. ii. 2], languishes in bondage to her father's will as expressed in the lottery of the three caskets. She is the Enchanted Princess whose chance for a release to love and life hinges on a Prince Charming's willingness to risk all to free her. The ring story repeats with variations the situation of the bond story and the casket story. "But when this ring / Parts from this finger, then parts life from hence . . ." [III. ii. 183-84], says Bassanio upon

his engagement, accepting the extreme conditions of bondage that Portia has set down in the previous speech, just as earlier Antonio and Portia herself have accepted their own extreme conditions of bondage. . . .

In *The Merchant*, as throughout Shakespeare, appearance is an enthralling agency. True love and the full life are not possible to one held in bondage to the sensuous surface of experience—to the "rosy lips and cheeks" which, in Sonnet 116, come within time's "bending sickle's compass". So the fair-appearing golden casket is a snare to Morocco, and by implication to countless other suitors, who do not know, as Bassanio does, that "The world is still deceiv'd with ornament" [III. ii. 74]. His reasons for choosing the leaden casket, as stated in his appearance-and-reality speech, may be no better than Arragon's or Morocco's if the three speeches are abstracted from the play and compared, but in context it is apparent that Bassanio is to a significant degree free of the bondage of that outward show by which others are still enthralled. (p. 218)

Closely related to the conflict of appearance and reality is the conflict of money (gold) and love. By long tradition in Shakespeare's time money had become a prime symbol of deceptive and enthralling outward show. . . . The good people in the play put love ahead of money. Antonio risks his fortune as well as his life out of love of Bassanio. Bassanio spends money extravagantly out of love of Portia (in the context of the play the fact that she will make him rich is completely subordinated to her beauty, her virtue, her desirability as a person). Launcelot, as Bassanio puts it, prefers "To leave a rich Jew's service, to become / The follower of so poor a gentleman" [II. ii. 147-48]. He anticipates Jessica's escape to love from the prison of her father's money (that she takes some of his wealth with her is much less important than the fact that, in the interest of loving and living, she voluntarily cuts herself off from rich expectations). In her rejection of the fair outward appearance of Shylock's gold she also restates the meaning of the casket story. And Portia, who accepted Bassanio knowing that his state "was less than nothing" [III. ii. 260], is willing to pay Shylock eighteen thousand ducats to settle the bond.

Cupidity and the mean-spiritedness of which it is an expression are of course common defining and imprisoning characteristics of those characters in comedy who oppose love and life. . . . In comedy where money is an issue, as it is in *The Merchant*. . ., "good" people always put love first and are thus in harmony with elemental liberating powers, while "bad" people put money or hatred first (one leads to the other) and are cut off from those powers. The fact that Shylock is held in bondage to money and hatred is more important in the play than his Jewishness; the Jewishness is an accident of a particular time and place, a time and place in which, Stoll reminds us [see excerpt above, 1927], the Aristotelian argument of the barrenness of money was gospel. (p. 219)

However, the issue of love and money in the play is not a disjunctive one. Gold, money, is not an unqualifiedly evil thing, as it becomes for Timon of Athens or as it would be for Thersites in *Troilus and Cressida* if his attention could be diverted to it from lust. If gold were simply evil one implication of Bassanio's speech before the caskets would be that Portia's goldenness ought to be suspected as deceitful appearance. But it is clear that she is golden all the way through, and that the golden place in which she lives is also the Great Good Place. Portia's gold, like Antonio's, serves life and love, and therefore liberates; Shylock's, expresses his cupidity or serves his hate, and therefore results in bondage. Portia and Antonio in their attitude towards gold express a measure of that magnanimity that Spenser in *The Faerie Queene* envisages as the informing virtue of Arthur. Even Bassanio's spendthrift nature, when seen as it should be in context with Shylock's parsimony, should be seen as a sign of magnanimity. . . .

The free dispensing of mercy, an expression of love which "becomes / The throned monarch better than his crown . . ." [IV. i. 188-89] is also an expression of magnanimity. Justice unseasoned by mercy is bondage; without mercy, Portia tells Shylock, "none of us / Should see salvation" [IV. i. 199-200]. The point is made again in the culmination of the ring story, when Portia's mercy seasons the strict justice of Bassanio's ring bond. The play, like all comedy, and like the divine comedy of the Christian story itself, is about the salvation of love. (p. 220)

The passage from bondage to liberation is reinforced by the Venice-Belmont polarity of the play. Venice exists at a hyberbolic remove from the everyday world so that it is itself a story world in which the Antonio-Shylock contract is believable, but Belmont . . . defines it as a bound world. Venice is a place of good-in-evil, a world of time, change, and doubtful appearance, where good men are preys of fortune and lose their argosies, and where fair terms disguise a villain's mind. Belmont, on the other hand, is a world of release and revelation, a world in which the possibility of the time-bound world can be realized, and in which the values that motivate the time-bound world can be heightened and defined. Belmont . . . is a school in which the lessons needed for living in the time-bound world are learned: here, for instance, the right relation between gold and love, between appearance and reality, between justice and mercy. For the meaning of the play is that the opposed members of these pairs can be reconciled in a larger harmony, which dwellers in the time-bound world hear only fitfully or not at all, grossly closed in as it is with "this muddy vesture of decay" [V. i. 64].

The aim of the play is to release the soul from this gross closing-in so that the harmony can be heard. So in Act Five we pass from the Venetian court scene to Belmont and hear Lorenzo apostrophize that harmony in two beautiful speeches that draw their inspiration from both Christian and Platonic sources. In the second of these speeches Lorenzo says:

> The man that hath no music in himself,
> Nor is not mov'd with concord of sweet sounds,
> Is fit for treasons, stratagems, and spoils;
> The motions of his spirit are dull as night,
> And his affections dark as Erebus:
> Let no such man be trusted.
>
> [V. i. 83-8]

The words bring Shylock on stage and with him the state of evil bondage he represents, clearly defined now in its antithesis to that concord of sweet sounds that love is, whether seen in the mortal lovers, Jessica and Lorenzo, or in the universe itself.

But the universe of Lorenzo's speech is itself in bondage, for it is harmonious and therefore moves to measure. In the play, then, the ultimate distinction is not between liberation and bondage but between good bonds and bad bonds. Bad bonds frustrate or enthrall the forces that press to be free for love and life; good bonds release them. But good bonds are no less restrictive than bad bonds: bonds are bonds. Antonio's love of Bassanio restricts him at least as much as Shylock's love of ducats and hatred of Antonio restrict him. There are certain things Antonio cannot do while held in the bond of Bassanio's

love; he cannot, for instance, refuse to put himself in hazard for Bassanio's sake. The testing question is not, Does the bond restrict? but, To what end does it restrict? The restriction is to the end of a more abundant life for Antonio, and ultimately for Bassanio, but to the end of a greater frustration of life for Shylock. As to the life-frustrating consequences of the Christians' hatred of the Jews, an evil bond institutionalized in the society out of which the play comes—to judge that is to take the advantage of time and stand in judgment of the age as, no doubt, in time others will stand in judgment over us.

The play assumes and demonstrates, then, a universe in which all release is not only disciplined but made possible by discipline. Portia's mercy, which is above the "sceptred sway" of kings, is "not strain'd" (constrained) [IV. i. 193, 184], yet it is "an attribute of God himself" [IV. i. 195], Who is the source of all love and harmony, and therefore of all discipline. Portia does not ask that justice be replaced by mercy, which is love, but that it be seasoned and therefore fulfilled by mercy, just as in the archetypal story Christ did not replace the Old Law but seasoned and therefore fulfilled it. When Shylock cannot see that such a seasoned justice is justice at all, that in refusing mercy he has really sinned against justice itself, he must learn the hard way. He gets the strict justice of the letter of the law from Portia, and only then the merciful seasoning as the Duke mitigates the sentence. Bassanio is taught the same lesson in the last act, when at Antonio's intercession Portia seasons the strict justice of the ring bond. She does not release him from the bond itself, nor would he want to be released from it. It is a love-bond freely entered into, a discipline in which he will find salvation. (pp. 220-22)

That the release from a life-frustrating bondage is central to the play can be seen even in the burlesque debate between Launcelot Gobbo's conscience and the "fiend". Here conscience is an evil bond, counseling Launcelot ("being an honest man's son" [II. ii. 15-16]) to remain in Shylock's service where there is neither love nor life. Such a conscience is analogous to the mercy-denying justice that Shylock will later demand: a matter of the letter, not the spirit, and thus not conscience at all. It is finally a seasoned conscience, identified humorously as the fiend, that Launcelot follows, and so escapes to the liberating bond of service to Bassanio.

There is something else to be seen in this debate that is relevant not only to the later debate between Portia and Shylock but to the debate between opposed forces that the play as a whole is. In the contest between Launcelot's conscience and the fiend, the contender that opposes the cause of release, conscience, is allowed to state his position strongly, to marshal his best arguments. If he were not, it would be a poor debate and victory would be hollow. If Launcelot is to experience a sense of release from the bond of false conscience (and if the audience is to find the debate amusing), conscience must put up a good fight.

So throughout the play Shylock, and the bonding forces he represents, must be allowed to put up a strong fight, in the interest ultimately of the fullest possible realization of release from the menace he represents. He must be allowed to marshal his strongest arguments, even the strongest of all arguments, his common humanity ("If you prick us, do we not bleed? if you tickle us, do we not laugh?" [III. i. 64-5]). Perhaps Shakespeare the man could not help humanizing Shylock, but it is more to the point to note that sheer dramatic exigency demands that Shylock state his case to the limits of Shakespeare's ability to control him in relation to other forces in the play. The result is a more intensely dramatized experience of release. (p. 222)

John P. Sisk, "Bondage and Release in 'The Merchant of Venice'," in Shakespeare Quarterly, Vol. XX, No. 2, Spring, 1969, pp. 217-23.

JAMES E. SIEMON (essay date 1970)

[*In one of the most extensive interpretations of the conclusion of* The Merchant of Venice, *Siemon argues that the final act serves as more than just a comic extension of the plot or an attempt by Shakespeare to satisfy the conventional ending expected by his Elizabethan audience, an opinion voiced by numerous earlier critics, including August Wilhelm Schlegel (1811), William Hazlitt (1817), Anna Brownell Jameson (1833), Harley Granville-Barker (1930), C. L. Barber (1959), and Barbara K. Lewalski (1962). Instead, Siemon claims that Act V channels our emotional reactions towards Shylock's defeat "along suitable and constructive lines" and provides a new awareness of events in Acts I through IV. In support of his argument, Siemon notes that* The Merchant of Venice *is among those plays, including* Measure for Measure *and* All's Well That Ends Well, *in which Shakespeare expanded his treatment of his antagonists and produced comedies that "present a more nearly balanced emphasis on those of sympathetic and unsympathetic characters alike." The dramatist's unequalled treatment of Shylock in this regard, Siemon contends, forced him to alter the conventional ending used in his romantic comedies, since that formalized conclusion could never succeed with such a fully delineated character as Shylock. The critic states that although the trial scene ends on "an intellectually comprehensible" note, it leaves the reader or spectator with an emotionally frustrated response to Shylock's fate. To avert this sense of emotional inconclusiveness, Siemon speculates, Shakespeare redirected our attention in Act V to "the harmony and beauty of reconciliation" in "general and comprehensive terms"; in short, Siemon asserts, the beauty of the final act distracts our attention from the emotionally unsatisfying vision of the defeated Shylock to a new appreciation of the harmony and beauty of the universe in general, thus fulfilling our emotional expectations. Siemon concludes that his argument leaves us with little choice but to view Shakespeare's handling of Shylock's defeat and reconciliation as unsuccessful, that his experiment in balancing the "forces of protagonist and antagonist" within the comic form failed, in that his solution "achieves its force in part by distracting our attention from the problem of Shylock rather than by proposing a dramatically convincing solution to that problem." For a similar assessment of the final act of* The Merchant of Venice, *see the excerpt by R. Chris Hassel, Jr. (1970). Also, for further commentary on Act V and its significance to the play, see the excerpts by G. G. Gervinus (1849-50), A. D. Moody (1964), Richard Horwich (1977), Alice N. Benston (1979), and Anne Parten (1982).*]

The Merchant of Venice is the first of Shakespeare's comedies to attempt a full-scale depiction of evil; in theme and in structure the play is experimental. In conception, if not in chronology, it stands between that group of comedies of which *Twelfth Night, As You Like It,* and *A Midsummer-Night's Dream* are representative, comedies which are festive and optimistic, and those later comedies such as *All's Well That Ends Well, Measure for Measure* and *The Winter's Tale,* in which, whether we choose to call them problem plays, tragi-comedies, or whatever, the balance between triumph and the threat of catastrophe is altered, vice and brutality are given major emphasis, and the principal characters are subjected to extensive suffering. The increased interest in the role of the antagonist and in his responses to those who oppose him is one indication of this experimental interest in evil. Whereas the conventional romantic comedies concentrate on the responses of the sympathetic characters, the experimental comedies present a more nearly balanced emphasis on those of sympathetic and unsympathetic characters alike. No one ever asks why Egeus so adamantly opposes Hermia's marriage to Lysander [in *A Midsummer Night's Dream*], nor what has driven Duke Frederick to seize the realm or Oliver to brutalize his younger brother [in *As You Like It*]; only the most maudlin worry about the emotional life behind Malvolio's antics [in *Twelfth Night*]. Shylock is an entirely different matter. Even the play's embarrassing emphasis on racial antipathy suggests that Shylock's motives are of more than passing interest. In *The Merchant of Venice,* Shakespeare takes pains to give dramatic verisimilitude to Shylock's passionate hatred for Antonio and to his deepseated contempt for the way of life which gives such pleasure to the Venetians. Modern controversy over Shylock's exact nature and our proper response to him are clear evidence of the attention that the play directs toward his character, as well, perhaps, as evidence that the experiment in which he figures is not entirely successful.

Concurrent with the shift of emphasis to include major consideration of the responses of the antagonist, there is an alteration of dramatic structure to give scope to those responses. There is nothing comparable in Shakespeare's conventional romantic comedies to the confrontation between Shylock and Antonio. These are tales of mixed romantic adventures. At their core, one or two pairs of lovers are shown in hot but variously misdirected pursuit of one another. Surrounding this core are secondary tales of love, which reflect directly or indirectly upon the core tale, or vary it through ironic reversal or farcical relief. The complex of tales is embedded within a framing tale of negligible or even non-existent dramatic interest, which is the occasion for the comic misadventures and provides the efficient cause of the comic resolution.

In *The Merchant of Venice,* the framing tale is raised to major prominence. As a device occasioning the romantic adventures, Bassanio's wooing and winning of Portia is the structural equivalent of Theseus' wedding Hippolyta [in *A Midsummer Night's Dream*], Viola's shipwreck and separation from Sebastian [in *Twelfth Night*], of Duke Senior's loss of his duchy and Rosalind's banishment [in *As You Like It*]; true love runs so determinedly smooth a course that Portia herself must manufacture as a practical joke the only impediment to its consummation; and the major tale told within the frame is one not of the romantic misadventures of lovers but of the tragi-comic defeat of Shylock.

A side effect of this structural experiment is to bring all of the plots to an apparent conclusion by the end of Act IV. Portia must be successfully won early in the play in order to provide for Antonio's deliverance; Jessica must be successfully spirited away before the trial scene both that her decamping with his jewels may whip up Shylock's wrath and provide further motivation to his antipathy to the Venetians, and that his defeat may be fully climactic. There is little left to happen in Act V. Portia's waggish cajoling away of Bassanio's ring serves several purposes. It looks forward to Act V, creating the illusion that the action of the play is not yet complete, and thus provides a necessary link between Acts IV and V. And it enables Shakespeare to postpone the necessary revelations. So, the securing of the rings becomes a deft piece of dramaturgy, providing a bridge to the necessary last act and carrying material over into that act to fill it out. Act V itself might, however, seem to be little more than a rhetorical flourish in deference to the Elizabethan audience's expectation that a romantic comedy end with all the sympathetic characters onstage and with as many marriages as can be contrived.

But the relation of the last act to the body of the play is more subtle and immediate than the details of plot lines and conventional endings suggest. It serves important functions in fulfilling the comic pattern of the play (a pattern that is related to, but quite distinct from, its plot), and in channelling our emotions along suitable and constructive lines. There is, indeed, a very real sense in which Act V is Acts I-IV all over again, but on a different level of awareness and meaning, and in which it interprets the events of the preceding acts. It is not, for example, possible to come to any satisfactory conclusion about Shylock without explicit reference to Act V, even though he himself does not appear in that act.

The pattern of comedy, Northrop Frye suggested some years ago, is one leading to release and reconciliation. . . . C. L. Barber has employed comparable terms in describing the movement of romantic comedy as a movement "through release to clarification": release from the restrictions of the everyday, comic world into the festive world of nature; clarification, in the face of the restrictive artifice of the comic world, of the healthful relation [of] man to nature. An approach to *The Merchant of Venice* in terms of comic pattern or movement, rather than in terms of plot, is particularly fruitful in view of the play's experimental handling of plot material, and suggestive of the importance of Act V.

The recurrent pattern of Shakespearean comedy begins with the world of comic reality, where modes of sophisticated social, economic, or political behavior impose on men what increasingly becomes an intolerable burden, frustrating the expression of feelings that they believe to be natural and healthy. It moves from this comic world into a world of romance, where problems can be faced in symbolic form and solutions found in terms of natural response rather than in terms of acquired manners. It returns to the world of comic restriction, where the felt knowledge acquired in the world of romance enables men to triumph over the absurd restrictions which threaten the health of society, and to renew society. It is a pattern of retreat and return. The romance world . . . is never wholly free from comic restriction. . . . It is a world where solutions are more clearly possible, not one where they are inevitable. The solution found is a function of the worth of the finder. . . . [As] the imagery of III. ii (the scene in which Bassanio makes his choice of the caskets) and the insistent parallels between II. vii, II. ix (the scenes in which Morocco and Aragon make theirs), and III. ii make clear, Bassanio wins Portia not because he is good at parlor games but because he is, as Nerissa says the winner must be, "one who shall rightly love" [I. ii. 32-3]. (pp. 201-04)

[It] would seem that like Bassanio's plot to win Portia and Shylock's plot to ensnare Antonio, the comic pattern of retreat and return, restriction and release, is complete at the end of Act IV, and that here, too, Act V only fills out in conventional terms a resolution already accomplished. A few lines in IV. ii, in which, instead of inveigling Bassanio and Gratiano to give up their rings, Portia and Nerissa revealed themselves, and the lovers anticipated their coming marriages . . . would serve to bring the play to its conclusion, and an easy redivision of Acts II and III into three acts would provide the customary five-act division. Shakespeare evidently felt that more was needed. His reasons, I believe, lie in the experiment in a full-scale depiction of the comic antagonist.

Shylock falls suddenly, swiftly, and absolutely. His conversion is certainly intended as a symbol of his integration into the social world of Venice, and as a thing good in itself. Similarly, the redirection of the power of his wealth from destructive to

Act IV. Scene i. Nerissa, Portia, Shylock, Gratiano, Antonio, Bassanio, the Magnificoes, and others. The Department of Rare Books and Special Collections, The University of Michigan Library.

creative ends turns it outward into the healthy sexuality represented by the love of Lorenzo and Jessica, rather than inward, breeding incestuously upon itself as though it were the Rams and Ewes from which Shylock cannot distinguish it. But it requires no sympathy with Shylock's moral nature, no denial that his bond is monstrous or that the Duke speaks true when he calls Shylock a "stony adversary, an inhuman wretch / Uncapable of pity" [IV. i. 4-5], to recognize that these symbols have no dramatic force, and that the mercy Portia has so warmly sought is coldly administered. We do not know when Portia came upon her legal loophole. Unless we assume, in the absence of any dramatic evidence whatsoever, that it is a last-minute brainstorm, we must take it that she came forearmed, knowing that she could save Antonio. And this suggests that, whatever Shakespeare's intentions in prolonging the trial scene, Portia's plea is essentially a plea for Shylock rather than for Antonio. She is pleading with him to throw off his stony, inhuman nature and to take his place as a man among men, to acknowledge, as Angelo is driven to acknowledge, that he is a man and that all men live by mercy. That Shylock does not respond to Portia is no fault of hers, for it is consistent with Shakespeare's whole conception of the man as it reveals itself in the play. But it does leave Shakespeare with a certain difficulty. He has developed Shylock as a powerful and powerfully convincing antagonistic force. Whether we take his great speech of justification in III. i as the expression of a just grievance whose legitimacy we are to feel, whatever we think of the redress he seeks, or see it, as I would argue, as a kind of brilliant dramatic economy designed to ensure that we have no doubt either of Shylock's hatred for Antonio or of the powerful emotional force behind it, it remains true that we know a good deal about Shylock, and that the emotional force which he dramatizes cannot be easily dismissed. Shakespeare's very success with Shylock causes untoward restrictions. We cannot accept a conventionally abrupt defeat of Shylock, because we are too conscious of him as a man driven by powerful emotions; nor can we imagine him as truly reconciled with the Venetians. . . . We know too much of Shylock to suppose that, having failed even to comprehend Portia's plea, he will see justice in the court's decision, or that with his passionate contempt for Venetian revelry he will take pleasure in Jessica's translation to Belmont. Whatever the plot tells us of Shylock's suppression or the symbols of his reconciliation, Shylock's emotional force remains untouched at the end of Act IV. There is a terrible sense of frustration, little of the sense of calm which ends the tragedies, and none of the joy with which even the most restrained comedies end. Act IV ends on an intellectually comprehensible but emotionally unencompassable note.

But although Shylock is so conceived and so forcefully realized that we cannot imagine the form his reconciliation could take, it is possible to skirt that issue and assert, instead, the harmony and beauty of reconciliation, and to embody harmony sought, threatened, and finally achieved in a ritual that operates on an emotionally encompassable level. This is what Shakespeare does in Act V of *The Merchant of Venice*. Lorenzo's unexpected text-book lesson in the nature of universal harmony and the music of the spheres . . . reasserts the symbolic force of Shylock's conversion in general and comprehensive terms. The beauty of this vision of beauty distracts our attention from means to end. And the symbolic force of the end is compelling in a way that that of the means is not.

More important (because it is bruised emotions that trouble us at the end of Act IV rather than an offended sense of justice), Act V begins again with Act I, with the hero's pursuit of the heroine, and reenacts, in precisely legalistic terms and in a social ritual (that is, a trial), the legal impediment of the hero's success. Bassanio has sworn that "when this ring / Parts from this finger, then parts life from hence" [III. ii. 183-84], and has then promptly given away his ring to an importuning stranger. Portia's case is airtight, as Shylock's had seemed to be, and it finds its resolution in charity and love, in reconciliation. The body of the play sets forth a merry jest turning itself into a nightmare; the last act shows us a potential nightmare turning itself into a merry jest. It festively and ritually reenacts the pattern of threat, release, and reconciliation which the preceding acts have dramatized; in doing so, it redirects the emotional tensions which remain unresolved at the end of Act IV, giving emotional extension to the symbols of Shylock's reconciliation in a vision of a human and cosmic harmony and dramatic embodiment to them in Jessica's translation to Belmont and her union with Lorenzo.

In readjusting the priorities of theme and plot to develop a major interest in the comic antagonist, the focus of *The Merchant of Venice* invalidates the easy solution of conventional romantic comedy by which the antagonist is casually suppressed. That the solution which Shakespeare turned to achieves its force in part by distracting our attention from the problem of Shylock rather than by proposing a dramatically convincing solution to that problem suggests the limited success of this initial experiment within the comic form of a serious balance between the forces of protagonist and antagonist. The problem is made particularly acute by the unique force of Shylock; were we not so fascinated by him we might well judge him a mistake.

He is too large a figure for even the enlarged role he is given, and the tensions between his personality and his dramatic function seem at times almost great enough to wreck the play. In the end they do not, principally, I think, because to his unique problem Shakespeare proposed a unique solution. (pp. 205-08)

There is a certain critical point of view, not without its value, from which we might pronounce the play a muddle. For so it is, evoking visions of ugliness and of beauty without either resolving the tensions between them or making it clear that those tensions cannot be resolved. But when one has said all one has to say about the play's limitations, or opposed with the greatest vehemence an interpretation of the play which one is unable to accept, one must admit that on the stage, and, it would seem, with whatever solution to the uncertain balance of forces the production has proposed, the play has invariably been a success. This may suggest that criticism, like dramatic structure, has its limits, and that a first-rate dramatist can direct an audience's attention and its emotional responses where he chooses. It certainly serves to remind us that the dramatist's intention is to entertain his audience rather than to edify his critics. (p. 209)

> James E. Siemon, "'The Merchant of Venice': Act V as Ritual Reiteration," in Studies in Philology, Vol. 67, No. 2, April, 1970, pp. 201-09.

R. CHRIS HASSEL, JR. (essay date 1970)

[*In an assessment similar to that offered by James E. Siemon (1970), Hassel states that the festive conclusion of* The Merchant of Venice *is "artificial, ambiguous, and highly ironic." Unlike Shakespeare's other festive comedies, Hassel points out,* The Merchant of Venice *demonstrates no sense of character development or integration, no reconciliation (or possibility of reconciliation) between its so-called green or festive world and the real, social one, but instead depicts two societies—Venice and Belmont— "equally tainted by suggestions of perversion, guilt, hypocrisy, and unhappiness." Hassel focuses on the "ambiguous tones" underlying the conversations in Act V—the notes of infidelity, sexual perversion, and sadness—which he states "question not only the quality of love in Belmont, but also the quality of justice and mercy, and finally of the whole society." Further, like such other critics as Karl Elze (1871), Rudolf von Ihering (1872), Harold C. Goddard (1951), A. D. Moody (1964), and René Girard (1978), Hassel expresses dissatisfaction over Shylock's treatment during and after the trial, claiming that the Jew's "disposal" is "hardly satisfactory from any perspective." More significant, Hassel adds, is Antonio's relation to the ambiguity of Act V. According to the critic, Antonio's vague and mysterious sadness parallels the ambiguous morality of his Christian society—in Hassel's words, "it becomes a symbol of that ambiguity"; and the merchant's "impossible fixation on Bassanio brutally dramatizes Belmont's and Antonio's imperfect relationship to the comic and the Christian ideal" represented in the play. For further discussion of the cause and significance of Antonio's melancholy, see the excerpts by E. K. Chambers (1908), T. A. Ross (1934), Graham Midgley (1960), John D. Hurrell (1961), A. D. Moody (1964), and Lawrence Danson (1978). Also, see the essays by August Wilhelm Schlegel (1811), William Hazlitt (1817), Anna Brownell Jameson (1833), G. G. Gervinus (1849-50), Harley Granville-Barker (1930), C. L. Barber (1959), Barbara K. Lewalski (1962), A. D. Moody (1964), Richard Horwich (1977), Alice N. Benston (1979), and Anne Parten (1982) for varying interpretations of Act V and its importance to* The Merchant of Venice.]

In mature Shakespearian comedy festivity consistently signifies the achievement of wisdom, because Shakespeare's comic action is predominantly educative. Consequently the tone of the festivity depends upon the quality and the degree of personal and social education. (p. 67)

The Merchant of Venice fits very uneasily into this context of educative festivity. Shakespeare seems to have reverted to the Roman comedy's technique of having festivity signify only the superficial overthrow of the comic usurper, Shylock. Educations have not occurred, and the one Christian character with recognized psychological obstructions, Antonio, seems to have been forgotten amidst the festive celebration. But Antonio's unexplained and unresolved sadness and the lack of educative festivity are in fact both essential to our proper understanding of the play. Antonio's ill-defined sadness suggests a moral dissatisfaction with the Christian society in which he is both a participant and a critic. Even during the externally festive ending, Antonio remains an uncomfortable and discomfiting member of the revellers. His awkwardness reminds us that Shylock was a victim as well as a villain, and that Belmont is as flawed as Venice. Most important, because Belmont's inhabitants are oblivious to their flaws, their festivity is artificial, ambiguous, and highly ironic. Festivity characteristically signals the achievement of wisdom, not its evasion. But in *The Merchant of Venice* there is no world which is sufficiently perfect to accommodate wisdom and festivity. Perceptiveness almost demands unhappiness.

The audience's moral awareness comes alive during the trial and then completely alters its perception of the fifth act. Both before and after his defeat Shylock is a scapegoat figure in the least superficial sense. In order to purify the community, he is convicted of business and social evils for which he is only partly to blame, damned for the prosecution of a pact, however horrible, which his victim agreed to without delusions and the court approved, and expelled in a symbolic ridding of vengeful justice, hatred, hypocrisy, and other imperfections. But ironically, Venice is not purged. At the height of Shylock's defeat Gratiano shamelessly exemplifies, without correctives from his Christian friends, most of the hateful attitudes which should have been cast out.

The society of Venice is obviously going to retain most of the characteristics it sought to dispel in Shylock. And so the only successful resolution in festivity must be achieved away from Venice in a retreat, a green world such as Belmont. Besides highlighting the comic ambiguity, this need to escape the real world urges us to reexamine the neat achievement of Christian love, mercy, and justice. Ideally for Shakespearian festivity, the reconciliation of green world and real should either be promised or realized, as it is in every mature festive comedy except this one. But the societal problem could not even be resolved in *The Merchant of Venice* were the two societies integrated, for Belmont is equally tainted by suggestions of perversion, guilt, hypocrisy, and unhappiness. Shylock's memory haunts the festive conclusion by affecting its imagery and its jesting. The guilt which is carried back to Belmont is no greater, of course, than the guilt of all individuals and all societies of all times. But it is still perplexing, especially within the comic form. The tainted society functions as powerfully as Antonio's indefinable problem in injecting important ambiguities into the concluding festivity.

The lyrical conversation of Lorenzo and Jessica carries the ambiguous tones of the trial back to Belmont. Superficially, the love-pairings of Jessica and Lorenzo and those to follow represent the reconciliation of Jew and Christian and Venice and Belmont. However, each matchup ironically indicts the imperfections of both societies. The lovers recall past romantic figures, all of whom—Cressid, Thisbe, Dido, and Medea—connote tragedy and perversion: fickleness, familial discord, unfaithfulness, and murder [V. i. 1-14]. The light joking that follows about Jessica's unnatural theft and desertion and Lorenzo's false vows of faith [V. i. 14-20] further suggest a romantic façade with undertones of falseness. Launcelot Gobbo's appearance recalls again the breach of faith to Shylock, as his horn jokes continue the moral ambiguity of festivity amidst varieties of infidelity [V. i. 46-8]. . . . Even the allusions to Diana suggest the failure of Endymion, man, to achieve her. Lorenzo explains Jessica's sadness by contrasting man's bestial savagery with his ideal potential [V. i. 70-82], evoking once again the memory of a world—Venice—where man is imperfectible.

When Portia enters the ambiguity remains. The light in darkness reminds her of a "naughty world" [V. i. 91], but only superficially, for she is oblivious to her own share of guilt, even proud of her own goodness. Portia's cuckold joke [V. i. 112-13] makes the dim light suggest more than a soft, idyllic, romantic setting. The men's arrival starts the fun of the ring exposure. But Gratiano's curse, "Would he were gelt that had it for my part" [V. i. 144], reminds us again of Shylock and of unnaturalness. Nerissa insists that Gratiano could have given the ring to no man: "The clerk will never wear hair on's face that had it" [V. i. 158]. This playful charge of infidelity suggests also the perversions of men loving men and of men without beards.

Such perplexing suggestions of unnaturalness had begun just after the trial's conclusion. Portia, exhilarated by her victory, demands her love token back from Bassanio as payment for her services [IV. i. 427-29]. Antonio's plea seconds the disguised Portia's. . . . Upon Antonio's urging Bassanio finally relents and becomes "unfaithful" to his new wife. Both pleas create the unnatural situation of two ostensible men pleading for the love and the love token given to another man by his wife. Gratiano's encounter with Nerissa functions similarly. These unnatural love relationships encourage us to question not only the quality of love in Belmont, but also the quality of justice and mercy, and finally of the whole society.

Back in Belmont, the ambiguity of Bassanio's relationship to his wife and his friend is dramatized by his having to defend his infidelity to the person who caused it. As a friend, he could act no other way. But as a lover, he failed miserably. Love's choices in a practical world are often ambiguous. In turn, each of these ambiguities typifies the larger ambiguity of Shylock's relationship to this festive group. His disposal was hardly satisfactory from any perspective, just as the ring disposal could not possibly be adjudged moral or immoral, faithful or unfaithful. Portia's cuckold joking becomes more and more perplexing as the play nears its festive ending [V. i. 223-33]. Even its conventional playfulness cannot negate its more serious suggestiveness that men and women and society in general are fickle and unpredictable. When the final note of infidelity is sounded [V. i. 256-65] it is almost too late for another, less perplexing moral tone to supersede. . . . A general sense of wonderment typically characterizes the last moments of the resolution, but the veneer of festivity belies a dearth of human awareness. For we recall continually the failure that all of them but Antonio, perhaps, seem to have gladly forgotten. Antonio has to be underplayed in the last scene to tone down his sombreness, just as he is largely ignored through most of the play after his dramatic first scene. But Antonio is always present in Belmont either in memory or in person, and his vague disenchantment further informs the play's ambivalent mood.

Antonio's undefined sadness is an extremely uncharacteristic comic obstruction, never explained and never resolved. Because it precedes the bond, it cannot be removed by Shylock's defeat. In fact, it seems intensified at the end of the play, where Antonio participates only perfunctorily in the festivity of his fellows. Antonio is immediately disturbed by his sadness, but can offer no satisfactory explanation for it [I. i. 1-7]. His friends' suggestions that he worries about his merchant ventures [I. i. 8-45], that he is in love [I. i. 46], or that his melancholy is a pose [I. i. 88-102] are inadequate, even foolish. (pp. 68-70)

But other suggestions emerge from this action. Antonio's impatient rejection of the attempted explanations suggests that he is too serious and morally exacting for his own happiness or his friends' comfort. When he tactlessly exposes Salanio's and Salarino's excuse for leaving as hypocritical [I. i. 63-4], we perceive a self-righteous and sombre person. Both qualities may become sorrowful burdens in an imperfect society. Also, Antonio is disenchanted with the material world [I. i. 77-9], even to the point of his execution. Only his deep concern for Bassanio modifies this disenchantment. Antonio is clearly an extremely complex comic character, obstructed by a variety of mental characteristics rather than physical agents. His is the first and only ambiguous opening obstruction Shakespeare ever used. It is never clearly defined, and never satisfactorily resolved. His sadness remains as ambiguous as the morality of the Christian society, and it becomes a symbol of that ambiguity. (p. 70)

[Antonio's] dealings with Shylock offer his fullest picture as unbearably self-righteous and intolerant. His boasts [I. iii. 61-4] and his physical and mental insults [I. iii. 97-102, 117-19, 130-37] demonstrate his moral inflexibility. Antonio is choking on the corruption, the hypocrisy, and the cruelty inherent in his merchant world, as they are embodied in Shylock; yet he is powerless to reform them. Simultaneously, Antonio is ironically implicated in the social and moral guilt of believing a generalization which brands Shylock a villain without realizing either his common humanity or the faults in the Christian society which created and nurtured that villainy.

Antonio's vague disenchantment with the values of the world he must live in remains throughout the play. Unconcerned about physical things, Antonio later appears to Salanio and Salarino to love the world only insofar as it contains Bassanio. Although any good friend might be saddened by a companion's imminent departure, his hazardous venture, and his previous ill fortune, Antonio's relationship to Bassanio seems unnaturally intense. . . . As he loves Bassanio far more than he loves himself, so Antonio fears Bassanio's fate more strongly than he does his own impending death. Of course, neither his friends nor his enemies insinuate any sordidness in his love for Bassanio. Rather, his love simply transcends human understanding and categorization and is mysteriously related to the similar indefinability of his sadness. His stoical reactions to death most clearly illustrate his total disregard of the physical world and his intense love for Bassanio. But Antonio never understands that his obscure world-weariness is defined by his complex relationship to Shylock, to Bassanio, and to his society. Because the personal and social diseases which disturb him are so ingrained and so subtle, they can never be confronted, understood, or assaulted. Like his mysterious love, and like Shylock's memory, they haunt the play's ending with irresolvable questions. (p. 71)

Antonio's psychological problems are as difficult to resolve as they were to define, for they were only intensified by his painful experience, whose outcome could hardly relieve them. If he was disenchanted by the cruelties of the business community, he could only be more fully aware of them [after the trial]. If he had grown weary of the world and even accepted his death, the return to life could only be a partial victory. His sense of self-righteousness must have been intensified by his nobility, and his friends would be even more awed by his goodness. The rotten core of undiscovered hypocrisy is still present, and will remain undiscovered and unresolved. Shylock still holds a bond on Antonio, and this one he will not evade. Antonio is sombre even in victory, in marked contrast to his comrades' festivity. For while they have overthrown all impediments to their festivity, he has defeated only the most superficial. Even his happiness for Bassanio is tempered by the sadness of loss that marriage occasions, as well as the comic and human unnaturalness of his single state. Of course, Antonio is not even a latent homosexual, though much of the witty jesting that pervades the festivity focuses on that perversion. His love for Bassanio, like his abortive attempt at self-sacrifice, suggests all varieties of human inadequacy, the inevitable breach between the Christian ideal and its limited realization among mankind. That Belmont is unaware of this problem while it articulates it in jest makes it all the more grotesque.

In the traditionally joyous denouement, Antonio's happiest statement is "I am dumb" [V. i. 279], hardly a festive affirmation. His knowledge of the ships' safe return is cold news in view of his recent renunciation of the world. Even his last bonding for Bassanio seems stuffy and overcautious, too serious, too restrained. Ironically, the explanations of his friends in the first scene were to the point, although no one understood their full comic and Christian significance. Antonio does "have too much respect upon the world" [I. i. 74]. But "the world" must mean the world's morality, for Antonio has consistently renounced the worldly. Antonio is so in love with the world as it might be but will never become that its every fault diminishes his happiness. . . . This pessimistic awareness of universal imperfection is both un-Christian and un-comic. The Christian is injoined during the Order of Holy Communion to "acknowledge and bewail" his "manifold sins and wickedness," but he is also consoled by the commonality of error and the promise of God's grace. Analogously, Shakespeare's later comic characters achieve their festivity by humbly admitting their shared imperfections and then rejoicing in their achieved wisdom and their common humanity. Antonio can apprehend only human error; Belmont seems aware only of grace and festivity. Neither achieves complete Christian or comic wisdom.

Antonio's impossible fixation on Bassanio brutally dramatizes Belmont's and Antonio's imperfect relationship to the comic and the Christian ideal. Physical love can be consummated in Belmont, but charity, that "greater love," cannot. This world thwarts the act of charity, because the actors are only human. Were they souls, Antonio could love Bassanio. Being men, they can only enact futile gestures of love, like the bonding, the ring exchange, and the attempt to lay down a life for a friend. Antonio gives himself away in order that Bassanio might achieve his greatest possible love, Portia. But inevitably, his gift of love loses Bassanio for him, confirming only the bitter half of Christ's famous paradox: "He that findeth his life shall lose it: and he that loseth his life for my sake, shall find it." Antonio's charity is also at least doubly flawed: it is selfish, and it is directed towards only one man, not all men. For all of these reasons, Antonio's love for Bassanio, his friend, his neighbor, his fellow man, must result in solitude, not communion. Antonio's cold, austere morality becomes his defense against the world's imperfectibility and his own. But it simultaneously prevents his participation in either Christian or comic festivity. (pp. 72-3)

As this discussion of Antonio and the ironic festivity of Act V indicates, form and meaning have been integrated much more subtly in *The Merchant of Venice* than in the earlier comedies. The complex incompatibility of festive resolution and nonfestive conflict parallels the incongruity of a Shylock or even an Antonio living in a comic society. It even urges the incompatibility of a totally festive society to such a world as ours, if festive has to mean naive.... The festive endings [in the comedies] after *The Merchant of Venice* urge that we live on, joyously though not naively, in the face of our sobering awareness of human imperfectibility. Such a position not only approximates the tragic vision as well as the comic. It is also as basic to Christian communion as it is to comic festivity. (pp. 73-4)

> R. Chris Hassel, Jr., "Antonio and the Ironic Festivity of 'The Merchant of Venice'," in Shakespeare Studies: An Annual Gathering of Research, Criticism, and Reviews, *Vol. VI, 1970, pp. 67-74.*

RENÉ E. FORTIN (essay date 1974)

[*Fortin contends that the character of Launcelot deserves more consideration in the commentary on* The Merchant of Venice, *since, in his words, he provides "an allegorical counter-statement to the major allegorical statement of the play" and serves as a "corrective to the one-sidedness and reductiveness of interpretation that the naive allegory invites." Reiterating that the conflict between Judaism and Christianity, "the Old Testament Law of Justice" and "the New Testament Law of Love," is the allegorical theme in* The Merchant of Venice, *which is conveyed in one manner through Shakespeare's varying presentations of filial piety, Fortin maintains that Launcelot—specifically in the scene of his encounter with his lost father—is meant to "counterpoint" the naive allegorical assumption that the New Dispensation of Christianity represents a progression to a "Higher Truth." According to Fortin, a more complex allegorical structure is apparent in the scene of the two Gobbos (II. ii.), in that the blindness motif there at work, when interpreted symbolically, reflects "the failure of filial piety between Christian and Jew and compels us to recognize the distance between the idea shadowed forth in the naive allegory—the Higher Truth of Christianity—and the imperfect realization of that Idea in the commerce of everyday life." Fortin thus suggests that the allegorical vision the play seems to endorse, as depicted ultimately in the victory of Portia (Christian love) over Shylock (Jewish or Old Testament law), is but an imperfect attempt on earth to realize that "Heavenly Idea." He concludes that the play actually demands not that we choose between Jewish law and Christian love, but that we recognize "that an indissoluble bond of filial piety exists between the two traditions." Other critics who have commented on the allegorical nature of* The Merchant of Venice *include Denton J. Snider (1890), Sir Israel Gollancz (1922), Nevill Coghill (1949), Muriel C. Bradbrook (1951), Theodor Reik (1956), C. L. Barber (1959), E. M. W. Tillyard (1961), and Barbara K. Lewalski (1962).*]

Few critics now harbor any doubts about the structural sophistication of *The Merchant of Venice*. Despite its relative earliness in the canon, this drama nevertheless gives every indication of Shakespeare's incomparable ability to fuse disparate elements into an aesthetic whole and to wring ethical significance from the common properties of Elizabethan drama. The one apparently wasted motion is Launcelot Gobbo, who is most often overlooked as an awkward irrelevance or written

off as a low-grade apprentice clown who has not yet realized the dramatic potential of his role.

I think, however, that Launcelot deserves a better press, for a closer look at his foolery suggests that he is very much involved in the play's central issues and that in fact, he adds much to its meaning. Specifically, he seems intended to provide an allegorical counterstatement to the major allegorical statement of the play, thereby offering a corrective to the one-sidedness and reductiveness of interpretation that the naive allegory invites.

However diverse the interpretation of *The Merchant of Venice* may be, there seems to be general agreement that the play communicates its meaning through allegory and that this meaning is centrally concerned with the tensions, theological and sociological, between Judaism and Christianity. On the most naive level, the allegory contrasts the vindictiveness of Shylock, representing the Old Testament Law of Justice, with the tender mercy of the Christians, representing the New Testament Law of Love. Accordingly, in the defeat of Shylock in the trial scene, we are invited to relish the absolute vindication of the Christian way.... (p. 259)

Launcelot first appears, in what seems to be a comic version of the central bond motif, in a moment of "spiritual crisis," being tormented by the decision whether to dissolve the master-servant "bond" with Shylock or risk damnation by continuing to serve the "devil" [II. ii.]. It is obvious that in his reasoning he adopts the attitudes of the medieval morality play (he is fittingly given a name with glittering medieval connotations) which identify the Jew with the devil, thus clearly betraying his unabashed and simple-minded contempt for Judaism. In a similar vein, he later taunts Jessica about her probable damnation for being the daughter of a Jew [III. v. 1-18] and also expresses fear that the conversion of the Jews would raise the price of pork [III. v. 21-6]. His moral crudity, in effect, caricatures the more genteel and discreet insensitivity of other Christians, who voice somewhat similar opinions throughout.... (p. 261)

In this role, Launcelot is delightful, useful, but not really necessary, since he is essentially restating what a reasonably perceptive and unbiased reader could conclude for himself, the discrepancy between Christian theory and practice.... His crucial scene in the play is, rather, his encounter with his father, a scene which offers an oblique commentary on the tensions between the Judaic and Christian traditions.

This father-son encounter must be seen in the larger context of other father-child relationships, involving Portia, Bassanio, and Jessica as well as Launcelot. Each of these relationships offers a different version of the father-child relationship and serves to highlight the theme of filial piety which emerges as a central concern.

Portia's father, though physically absent, plays a thematically vital role in exemplifying the father who rules through Law. For the casket lottery which he has devised as a condition for the marriage of Portia demands her unquestioning obedience. It is clear that Portia would prefer things otherwise, that she would prefer to be given the freedom of choosing her mate on the basis of love; her references to the lottery, which she enjoys certainly far less than the audience, are tinged with, at best, an impatience at the arbitrariness of the test....

One effect of the casket lottery is to blur the differences between Venice and Belmont. Though we are increasingly tempted as the play progresses to associate love and spiritual freedom with Belmont, we are here reminded that Belmont, like Venice, has its own stringent laws. . . . (p. 262)

There is no question that the casket scene depicts an exemplary father-child relationship, but one that dwells primarily upon the legal aspect of the ideal relationship; the other aspect of the filial piety is revealed in the Antonio-Bassanio relationship. Though the relationship between the two is literally one of friendship, the discrepancy in age between the two invites us to fit this relationship into the pattern of father-child relationships and to view Antonio as Bassanio's protector and father-surrogate; it is a relationship reminiscent of that in *Twelfth Night* between Sebastian and Antonio's namesake. Therefore, despite his love for Bassanio, Antonio seeks nothing but Bassanio's happiness and is eager to help him in his courting of Portia. Bassanio himself offers the best clue to this relationship in identifying himself as a "prodigal" son [I. i. 129]; in contrast to the "legal" relationship existing between Portia and her father, this is one of love, with Antonio as the quintessential generous and forgiving father ready to sacrifice himself for the welfare of his son. (p. 263)

It is in the context of these exemplary father-child relationships, one based primarily on Law and the other based primarily on Love, that the Jessica-Shylock relationship is located. This relationship can be described only as a monstrous inversion of filial piety, a relationship lacking utterly in both Law and Love. Jessica, admitting to the "legal" bond, the bond of blood, states that she is ashamed of her father:

> Alack, what heinous sin is it in me
> To be ashamed to be my father's child.
> But though I am a daughter to his blood,
> I am not to his manners.
>
> [II. iii. 16-19]

She then severs all bonds with Shylock, sharing, in fact, in the Gentiles' identification of her father as a devil [II. iii. 2] and feeling no compunction whatever in her thievery of his fortune. Nor does she, while rejoicing in her own conversion, express any hope that her father will be similarly converted. She seems to have taken his damnation for granted. (pp. 263-64)

Shylock, superficially at least, seems similarly lacking in paternal love; no thought of his daughter's elopement is ever unaccompanied by somber thoughts about the fortune she has taken with her, both ducats and daughter apparently occupying the same level in his hierarchy of values. . . . (p. 264)

However, it is possible, as others have done, to attach some importance to the "confused passion" of Shylock and to detect beneath his bitter denunciations of Jessica a genuine suffering over her betrayal of him. I find personally moving, in fact, his concern over the loss of Leah's ring, which he seems to treasure for sentimental reasons, as a memento of happier days of love and domestic warmth. But this suggestion of personal depth in Shylock is elsewhere overwhelmed by his vehemence, and the complex human being recedes again into the stereotype. . . . The Jessica-Shylock relationship seems predominantly a complete inversion of filial piety, a relationship neither based on law nor leavened by love.

What then, in view of Jessica's ironic relationship to one of the major themes of the play, are we to make of the "allegorical" Jessica? It is my belief that Jessica transcends her realistic limitations and does serve to shadow forth the relationship between Jewish and Christian traditions; it is not in-

consistent to see her invitation to Belmont as an invitation to participate in a "higher truth"; I would, in short, agree that "As Shylock's daughter and as a voluntary convert to Christianity, Jessica may figure forth the filial piety relationship of the New Dispensation to the Old" [see excerpt above by Barbara K. Lewalski, 1962]. Admittedly, to see her in this way poses a grave problem because of the apparent discontinuity between the "real" Jessica and the allegorical Jessica, but the problem is not unresolvable if we understand that we have here, not an irreparable split between literal and allegorical levels, but rather an elaborate structure in which a naive allegory is subtly complemented and corrected by a sophisticated allegory.

This correction is provided by Launcelot in his encounter with Old Gobbo. The encounter takes place immediately after Launcelot's decision to leave the service of his Jewish master and seek service with the Christian Bassanio. Launcelot is interrupted by the arrival of his father carrying a "dish of doves" [II. ii. 135] and looking for his son. In what seems initially to be a mere comic interlude, Launcelot decides to taunt his father. . . . After some not quite harmless mischief—Launcelot leads Gobbo to believe that his son is dead—Launcelot finally identifies himself. . . . (pp. 264-65)

This seems to be little more than pointless folly, but the scene would have important reverberations for a viewer conversant with the Bible: the Launcelot-Gobbo encounter closely parallels the Isaac-Jacob incident in Genesis 27. In this famous biblical narrative, Jacob dupes the blind Isaac into blessing him, rather than the firstborn Esau, by simulating with the skins of kids the hairy body of Esau. Isaac, touching the hairy hands of Jacob, extends the blessing that grants him and his race primacy over Esau and his progeny; Isaac then eats a ritual meal offered to him by Jacob in order to solemnize the blessing.

The recognition scene contains many of the elements of the narrative, including the blessing requested by Launcelot of Old Gobbo, the dish of doves carried by Gobbo, which recalls the ritual meal of Isaac, Gobbo's fascination with the beard of Launcelot, which recalls the device of the hair; and, most conspicuously, the blindness of the father which prevents him from knowing his own child. . . .

That this richly allusive scene occurs in a play focusing upon Jewish-Christian relations and occurs, moreover, at the precise moment when Launcelot has decided to change from a Jewish to a Christian master underscores the need to explore carefully its implications. The scripturally-sophisticated viewer would be aware, for example, of St. Paul's commentaries on this narrative, which he considered prefigurative; Paul sees the twin "elections" in successive generations—of Isaac over Ishmael and of Jacob over Esau—as allegories of God's secret election of the Gentiles as his new "children of the promise." (p. 266)

Thus what is symbolically re-enacted here is an allegory of the transferral of divine favor from the Jewish to the Christian Dispensation; but it is an allegory that unsparingly exposes the ironies of the situation. Just as the biblical narrative is itself steeped in irony (since Jacob's blessing is obtained by guile), its counterpart in the *Merchant of Venice* releases ironic suggestions calculated to daunt the most zealous allegorist.

There is a strong emphasis to begin with on the bond of filial piety, for Old Gobbo's suit to Bassanio on behalf of Launcelot adumbrates the fact that the preferment of the Christian Dispensation was made possible by the centuries of integrity of the older faith. More obviously, the scene insists upon the mutual blindness of father and son, the *involuntary* blindness of Gobbo—and by extension, of the Jewish tradition—and the *willed* blindness of Launcelot—and by extension of the Christian tradition, which chooses to ignore its indebtedness to the older tradition from which it derives its richness. . . . Despite their father-son relationship, both traditions, in their mutual blindness, overlook the bond between them. Launcelot has stated it tersely: "It is a wise father that knows his own child" [II. ii. 76-7]; and one might add, "It is a wise child who acknowledges his own father." . . . The point finally made by this allegorical expression of father-son relationships is that we are not to choose between Jewish Law and Christian Love, as most critics of the play suggest, but to recognize that an indissoluble bond of filial piety exists between the two traditions, a bond that should engender a mutual respect. (p. 267)

Launcelot's primary function in the play, then, is to focus our attention upon the theme of filial piety; in so doing he exposes the limitations of a naive allegory that would force upon the viewer an "either-or" choice when a "both-and" is in order. It is important to note that he, in a sense, duplicates the allegorical function of Jessica who, as we have seen, figures forth the relationship of the new Dispensation to the Old. But Launcelot's scene, though concerned with the same event, is actually in counterpoint to Jessica's naive allegory, for his allegory stresses the complexity of the relationships; it exposes, through the blindness motif especially, the *failure* of filial piety between Christian and Jew and compels us to recognize the distance between the idea shadowed forth in the naive allegory—the Higher Truth of Christianity—and the imperfect realization of that Idea in the commerce of everyday life. . . . We are reminded that Christianity, though a fulfillment of the Old Law, remains itself to be perfectly fulfilled. And until "all things be fulfilled," it must continue to respectfully observe the Law and not flout it as Jessica does.

The enigmatic fifth act confirms this view. Its central theme, which sheds a retrospective light on the entire play, seems to consist of a distinction between the absoluteness of the Heavenly Idea and the relativity of earthly experience. The scene begins with Lorenzo and Jessica cataloguing the imperfection of earthly realities: the references to Cressida, Thisbe, Dido, and Medea are various reminders of the vicissitudes of human love; and the theme of imperfection persists in Lorenzo's taunting of Jessica about her theft from her father and Jessica's imputation of insincerity in Lorenzo's love. The dialogue is interrupted by the arrival of Portia, at which point Lorenzo, in more overt terms, refers to the disparity between the Heavenly Idea and earthly reality:

> Sit, Jessica. Look how the floor of heaven
> Is thick inlaid with patens of bright gold.
> There's not the smallest orb which thou behold'st
> But in his motion like an angel sings,
> Still quiring to the young-eyed cherubins;
> Such harmony is in immortal souls,
> But whilst this muddy vesture of decay
> Doth grossly close it in, we cannot hear it.
> [V. i. 58-65]
> (pp. 268-69)

The Platonic imagery is sustained by Portia, who alludes to the other dominant image in Plato, light:

> That light we see is burning in my hall;
> How far that little candle throws his beams!
> So shines a good deed in a naughty world.
> [V. i. 89-91]

Portia, in my opinion, refers to no specific good deed, but rather to the nature of human experience in general, which participates on a lower level of being in perfections fully existent only in a higher order of being. The implication seems to be that perfection is not to be hoped for in this world, and that only relative goodness can be expected. . . . But the lone earthly candle which lights up this naughty world is nonetheless a true image of heavenly light, though it is not to be confused with that greater glory. (pp. 269-70)

Despite the new order introduced by Christianity, the Law survives. This co-existence of Love and Law seems to be the burden of the ring motif as well, for the ring is given as a bond of love entailing "legal" obligations; the ring is a reconciling symbol suggesting that Love, i.e., spiritual freedom, and Law, i.e., moral responsibility, must co-exist in human relationships.

Thus the conclusions to which we are guided by Launcelot in his symbolic role are reiterated and developed in the fifth act; through the complex allegory which insists upon the co-existence of values, the *Merchant of Venice* suggests that, despite the truth contained in its naive allegory of love, man can expect only relative perfection in a world far too complex for naive allegory to be given full credit. (p. 270)

René E. Fortin, "Launcelot and the Uses of Allegory in 'The Merchant of Venice'," in Studies in English Literature, 1500-1900, *Vol. XIV, No. 2, Spring, 1974, pp. 259-70.*

RICHARD HORWICH (essay date 1977)

[*Horwich postulates that the business of the rings in Acts IV and V of* The Merchant of Venice *is designed to provide Bassanio with a second chance to act on inspiration and spontaneous generosity in the service of Portia—his first opportunity being the choice of the right casket to win Portia's hand in marriage, which Horwich claims he does by calculation and not inspiration. But Horwich adds that whereas the testing of the caskets is essentially a riddle with a right answer Bassanio can solve, the business of the rings presents a dilemma whose resolution can be more disturbing than the original problem. The critic also notes that it is the nature of the opposing worlds of* The Merchant of Venice *that one (Belmont) is characterized by riddles, the other (Venice) by dilemmas. Horwich maintains that in the real world of Venice Bassanio is unable to make a satisfying choice over what to do with Portia's ring, but in Belmont he learns that what had seemed an unsolvable dilemma is yet another riddle. Although he fails to provide the proper solution to this riddle—namely, that Portia and Balthazar are the same person and thus the sacrifice of the ring is no sacrifice at all—Bassanio does offer Portia the opportunity which she lacked in the casket story, and that is the chance to exercise her "power of choice" and to accept willingly Bassanio as her husband. For additional commentary on the ring episode and Act V of* The Merchant of Venice, *see the excerpts by August Wilhelm Schlegel (1811), William Hazlitt (1817), Anna Brownell Jameson (1833), G. G. Gervinus (1849-50), Harley Granville-Barker (1930), C. L. Barber (1959), Barbara K. Lewalski (1962), A. D. Moody (1964), James E. Siemon (1970), R. Chris Hassel, Jr. (1970), Alice N. Benston (1979), and Anne Parten (1982).*]

The Merchant of Venice is filled with difficult choices; in both Venice and Belmont, we find characters in the act of deciding between contrasting alternatives, or lamenting their inability to do so. Since the action of the play moves back and forth between these settings with some regularity, it is almost inevitable that several critics should see the two locales themselves as representing a kind of choice, or at least an antithesis—they are "the realm of law and the realm of love, the public sphere and the private," in Sigurd Burckhardt's description [see excerpt above, 1962]. . . .

Symmetry, if nothing else, seems to require that Belmont represent an alternative, even an antidote, to the impersonality of Venice. Venice is a city of marble, where Antonio is confronted by a "stony adversary" [IV. i. 4], but Belmont is "a green world," according to John P. Sisk [see excerpt above, 1969], where impulse, not logic, reigns. At any rate, current scholarly opinion holds that the lottery of the caskets which takes place there calls more for intuition than for calculation on the part of those who would win Portia. Morocco and Arragon, according to this view, fail the test because they approach it as an intellectual puzzle; Bassanio chooses the correct casket, as James Siemon puts it, "not because he is good at parlor games but because he is, as Nerissa says the winner must be, 'one who shall rightly love'" [see excerpt above, 1970]. (p. 191)

Yet if we look at the scene in which Bassanio makes his choice, it is hard to say unequivocally that he does not calculate, that he chooses exclusively at the behest of feeling or inspiration. . . . The scene begins with Portia telling him, "If you do love me, you will find me out" [III. ii. 41], which may be read as a suggestion that he intuit his selection rather than arrive at it through reason; whether or not the song "Tell me where is fancy bred" [III. ii. 63ff.] is a clue designed to aid him, it suggests the same thing. But it is not at all clear that he listens to the song. While it is being sung, he "comments on the caskets to himself," according to the stage direction, and his following speech begins with the word "So" [III. ii. 73], which implies either an extension of, or a conclusion to, some premise—perhaps the song's, that things are seldom what they appear to be, or one reached during his own "commenting," whatever that consisted of.

The thirty-four lines which follow sound very much like a "reason" for his choice. . . . Throughout the choosing scene, Bassanio sounds less like a lover guided by intuition than like a man bent on solving a riddle in order to best Portia's father in a contest of wits. The casket scene is thus of a piece with the rest of the play's world, which seeks to mislead him with "The seeming truth which cunning times put on / To entrap the wisest" [III. ii. 100-01].

The inscriptions which accompany the caskets are, certainly, riddles in the literal sense of the word—intellectual puzzles, that is, not exercises in divination. . . . It is true that riddles are seldom answered through the exercise of pure logic alone, and often require an imaginative leap or insight of some sort, but that is not to say that they do not primarily engage the intellect. The "discontinuity" which Barber finds in the inscriptions [see excerpt above, 1959] is one of the inevitable features of riddles, which are, according to one authority, "descriptions of objects in terms intended to suggest something entirely different" from the reality [Archer Taylor, in *English Riddles from Oral Tradition*], like a golden casket which proclaims "Who chooseth me shall gain what many men desire" [II. vii. 5] and which proves to contain a death's-head. The principle which Bassanio states just before his choice—that appearances are deceiving—is precisely what one has to assume in order to solve a riddle; it is a comment not only on the nature of the world, but also on the particular problem set for him by Portia's father.

Admittedly, Burckhardt is correct when he points out that Bassanio ignores the inscriptions and instead "lets the metals themselves speak to him." Yet speech is typically the language of thought, and the misleading description which riddles invariably contain is clearly present in the physical caskets, whose composition and outward appearances belie and even contradict what is within. It is, in fact, easier to solve the riddles of the caskets if one ignores the inscriptions and listens only to what the metals say, and to solve it, what is more, by the exercise of the most superficial logic—once one has adopted the premise, as Bassanio has, that "The world is still deceived with ornament" [II. ii. 74].

Thus, if we demand to see that Bassanio is more spiritually gifted than Morocco or Arragon, and not merely more clever—if we insist that he demonstrate the liberal impulses of the true lover to our satisfaction and to Portia's—the choosing scene will disappoint us. . . . (pp. 193-94)

But though he does not concretely or obviously manifest this quality of unhesitating generosity in Belmont (to be sure, he "gives and hazards all he hath" [II. vii. 9], but only after deliberations as long as Morocco's and Arragon's), he has another opportunity to do so later in the play. It occurs when Portia arranges for a second test of his worthiness, by binding him to keep the trothplight ring which she will later coerce from him while disguised as Balthazar. Such, it would appear, is her intention from the start, for the speech with which she accompanies the gift of the ring foreshadows the diminution of intensity and seriousness which occurs in her relationship with Bassanio following his choice of the leaden casket:

> This house, these servants, and this same myself
> Are yours, my lord's. I give them with this ring,
> Which when you part from, lose, or give away,
> Let it presage the ruin of your love
> And be my vantage to exclaim on you.
>
> [III. ii. 170-74]
> (pp. 194-95)

The ring trick has often been dismissed as trivial, a needless postscript to a plot already concluded. . . . But if it is a practical joke [Portia] plays, we should inquire what practical purpose it serves, and how it is related to the action which precedes it.

We ought, therefore, to connect it not only to the trial scene . . . , but to the casket-choosing scene as well—for here, once again, Bassanio is faced with a difficult choice on whose outcome hinges his future with Portia. When, disguised as the deserving Balthazar, she demands the ring in recompense for saving Antonio, she confronts him with two virtually indistinguishable alternatives, both of them laden with disadvantage. Impulse is of no help to him, for giving free rein to his generous nature may lose him Portia along with the ring; neither is reason any more useful, for Portia has balanced the alternatives so nicely that a reasonable case can be made for either. (pp. 195-96)

Bassanio's ultimate decision to part with the ring is not so much arrived at as thrust upon him by Antonio; in fact, Bassanio has allowed Balthazar to leave empty-handed, and sends the ring after the departing lawyer only when Antonio brings intolerable pressure to bear on him by saying,

> My Lord Bassanio, let him have the ring.
> Let his deservings, and my love withal,
> Be valued 'gainst your wife's commandement.
>
> [IV. i. 449-51]

It is precisely Bassanio's inability to perform this act of calculation which has paralyzed him; so far is he from feeling that his ultimate decision is his own, freely arrived at, that he later excuses it to Portia as "this enforcèd wrong" [V. i. 240].

Whether his decision is in fact right or wrong is all but impossible to say; it is the nature of dilemmas that the alternatives are equally desirable or (as in the present case) undesirable. According to the scale of values which the play establishes, love and gratitude are more to be prized than legal commandment, and much of the action has been a working-out of the principle that it is more blessed to give than to receive. On the other hand, the claims of law can never be set aside entirely. . . . (p. 196)

It is in Venice that Bassanio faces this choice; that is significant, for where Belmont was full of riddles, Venice is the natural habitat of dilemmas. (p. 197)

Because of their ambiguous nature, . . . dilemmas are far more taxing problems than riddles; riddles have single and wholly correct answers, at least, however hard those answers may be to come by. The difference between Belmont and Venice is throughout the play embodied in the difference between problems which can be solved neatly and completely, and those which can only be dealt with imperfectly, through a resigned willingness to compromise. Realistic problems, like those found in Venice, hardly ever hold out the prospect of a clear alternative which offers unalloyed satisfaction; that is why the happy endings of comedy and romance, which depend upon this sense of wholeness, are available to us only through dreams, plays, and other forms of wish-fulfillment.

The attraction of Belmont's riddle is that, though one risks losing everything, there is a way to win everything. In Venice, by contrast, the solutions to problems may be almost as threatening as the problems themselves—either Antonio must die, for example, or Shylock must be humiliated and broken, a spectacle which has disturbed audiences for hundreds of years. No third alternative exists which would satisfy everyone. . . .

Bassanio is confronted by his dilemma in Venice, where all problems are dilemmas; when the action returns to Belmont, his dilemma disappears as he discovers that it is really a riddle, after all. A third, and heretofore hidden, alternative to keeping the ring or giving it away has existed all along: guess the true identity of Balthazar, and it will not matter whether Bassanio withholds the ring or not, since neither will cause him to break his oath. As she was earlier locked in the lead casket, so Portia is now hidden in Balthazar; had Bassanio been able to "find her out" beneath the lawyer's robes, he would have been spared much anxiety. But he has no reason to consider Balthazar's demand for the ring as part of a puzzle to be solved; he does not understand that Portia is asking him a riddle when she poses an apparently rhetorical question: "What man is there so much unreasonable / . . . To urge the thing held as a ceremony?" [V. i. 203-06]. The answer, of course, is no man at all, but a woman. All the riddles ask the central question of the play: who is Portia, and where is she to be found?

So Bassanio solves one riddle in the play, but cannot solve the other. For him, this failure is relatively unimportant; it does not cost him Portia, as failing to answer the riddle of the caskets would have done. But it is of inestimable value to her, for it remedies the sole defect of her life in Belmont by restoring to her what from the start she complained of lacking—the power of choice. . . . (p. 199)

Thus, [Portia] invents what is far more than a mere practical joke, but a device by which she may exercise her free will by

accepting Bassanio as her husband through an act of conscious volition—choosing him retroactively, as it were. According to the terms to which she bound him with the ring, she may reject him if he gives it away. According to a strict interpretation of the law, he *has* given it away; she has seen to that. It is, of course, only a game, but her role in it enables her to baffle and reject him as long as she keeps her identity secret, and when she at last reveals it, choosing to forgive and accept him, she symbolically restores to herself control over her destiny, and responsibility for it.

At the same time, she makes Belmont once again a place where wishes, no matter how improbable, can come true, as all problems seem literally to disappear. Bassanio has both given and kept the ring; Antonio's ships are not sunk; Jessica and Lorenzo are safe and rich; the exigencies of life in Venice, where all choices are heavy with dire consequence and all solutions are limited ones, no longer exist. In Belmont, finally, it matters very little what choices are made, as long as one is free to choose. That is what Bassanio has discovered, through Portia's ministrations, and it is what Gratiano emphasizes in the final speech, when he confronts Nerissa with the play's last, and least crucial, decision:

> Whether till the next night she had rather stay,
> Or go to bed now, being two hours to day.
>
> [V. i. 302-03]
> (pp. 199-200)

Richard Horwich, "Riddle and Dilemma in 'The Merchant of Venice'," in Studies in English Literature, 1500-1900, Vol. XVII, No. 2, Spring, 1977, pp. 191-200.

LAWRENCE DANSON   (essay date 1978)

[*The following is taken from Danson's book-length study of* The Merchant of Venice, *the primary purpose of which, according to the critic, is to demonstrate the viability of the so-called Christian interpretation of the play. In the excerpt below, Danson focuses on the characterization of Antonio and discusses his melancholy. He notes that Shakespeare's Elizabethan audience probably would have attributed Antonio's sadness to his mercantile activities, or, worry over his investments. He adds that to those audiences, suspicious of mercantile fortunes, moneylender and merchant were "not entirely separate." Danson argues, however, that Antonio is "unmerchantlike," both charitable and unworldly, very much the perfect Christian in all aspects except for his attitude towards Shylock. The critic thus suggests that Antonio's treatment of the Jew and his melancholy are "intimately related," claiming that the true cause of the merchant's sadness is his "emotional response" to the "moral failure" of his un-Christian behavior towards Shylock. Danson also comments on the homoerotic interpretation of Antonio's melancholy, examples of which can be found in the essays by T. A. Ross (1934), Graham Midgley (1960), and John D. Hurrell (1961). Noting that this psychosexual explanation accounts for the character's verisimilitude, and is thus significant and not totally dismissable, Danson concludes that it is nonetheless out of sync with the structure and thematics of Shakespeare's play. For further commentary on the cause and significance of Antonio's melancholy, see the excerpts by E. K. Chambers (1908) and A. D. Moody (1964).*]

The opening dialogue of *The Merchant of Venice* takes us simultaneously inward and outward. In, to a psychologically troubled world ("In sooth I know not why I am so sad" [I. i. 1]), out, to a busy and dangerous world where great trading ships, "Like signiors and rich burghers on the flood," "do overpeer the petty traffickers" [I. i. 10, 12]. The two movements—the inward and psychological, the outward and public—are closely related: "Your mind is tossing on the ocean" [I. i. 8]. By his imagistic joining of the world's ocean with the ocean of the mind, Salerio (whose explanation this is for the merchant Antonio's mysterious sadness) creates at least a provisional reconciliation of opposing principles. And this reconciliation is delicately premonitory of other achieved harmonies with which *The Merchant of Venice* abounds. (p. 19)

The play's opening lines pose something of a riddle. Antonio's sadness, wearisome though he claims it is to all involved, immediately offers an invitation to begin searching for answers:

> In sooth I know not why I am so sad,
> It wearies me, you say it wearies you;
> But how I caught it, found it, or came by it,
> What stuff 'tis made of, whereof it is born,
> I am to learn:
> And such a want-wit sadness makes of me,
> That I have much ado to know myself.
>
> [I. i. 1-7]

What follows, however—the attempt by Salerio and Solanio to solve the apparent riddle—should warn us to proceed with caution. Salerio and Solanio have not fared well at the hands of critics: "the two bland little gentlemen," C. L. Barber calls them [see excerpt above, 1959]; and the first item in any bill of indictment ought to be their easy confidence that they can clear up the mystery of Antonio's sadness.

It is not only the jingling similarity of their names which makes Salerio and Solanio seem a Venetian Rosencrantz and Guildenstern [in *Hamlet*]. They are lightweights, so insubstantial, indeed, that our texts are not even clear about their names—not even clear, in fact, that there are only two of them. Like Rosencrantz and Guildenstern, they meet their friend's emotional distress with the reasonableness of men who have never felt a similar distress. And like their Danish counterparts, they are rebuffed—though rather more gently. Still, Antonio is not a pipe for any fool to play what tune he will; and though their explanations are plausible, we are confronted with Antonio's assertions that they have not plucked the heart out of this sad mystery. (pp. 21-2)

There is one further attempt within the scene to explain away Antonio's sadness: Gratiano's "You have too much respect upon the world" [I. i. 74]. Or perhaps this is not so much a third explanation as a summary of the previous two; both the mercantile and the amorous explanations in effect accuse Antonio of having too much concern for the things of this world. They are the thoughts of "worldly choosers." The reproof sounds especially ironic coming from Gratiano, whose babbling levity, while it places him at an opposite extreme from Antonio, is not the sort of joyful noise unto the Lord commended by the Psalmist. Solanio, Salerio, and Gratiano, with their confident and curiously repetitive explanations for Antonio's sad state, begin to sound like Job's three comforters. Antonio, at any rate, rejects Gratiano's more comprehensive explanation as decisively as he has the previous ones:

> I hold the world but as the world Gratiano,
> A stage, where every man must play a part,
> And mine a sad one.
>
> [I. i. 77-9]

The terms of Antonio's response here are especially interesting. The idea that all the world's a stage was a poetic commonplace long before Shakespeare began to realize its lively potential.

And generally the effect of the trope is to open out fresh imaginative prospects. Here, however, the effect might seem to be the reverse: since Antonio *is* a character in a play, his world indeed merely a stage and his part a sad one, his self-conscious admission of a fictive status appears to rule out any more guessing about his melancholy's motives. His sadness, he seems to be saying, is merely a *donnée,* and there will be no use searching anywhere for its roots except, perhaps, in the literary and dramatic history of the convention of the Melancholy Man.

Or so it might seem. In fact this commonsensical, literary-historical approach—the sort of approach once used (for instance) by E. E. Stoll to explain away any ambiguities in Shylock's character [see excerpt above, 1927]—is no more valid than the psychologizing guesswork indulged in by the play's own characters, Salerio, Solanio, and Gratiano. The world may be a stage where every man must play a part, but the world of *The Merchant of Venice* is a very special world, governed by laws (dramatic and judicial) as curious as, but not identical with, the laws that govern "the great globe itself." The way to understand the problems raised by Antonio's sadness is to understand the special laws that govern the conditions of dramatic life in *The Merchant of Venice,* and therefore to understand such thoroughly interdependent factors as the play's modes of characterization, the disposition of its fable, and what matters are relevant and what irrelevant to its interpretation.

Of the two explanations offered for Antonio's psychological state, the mercantile would no doubt have seemed to many in Shakespeare's audience an especially plausible one. (Modern audiences have been more attracted to the amorous explanation.) Living at a time when previously unimaginable fortunes were to be made, or suddenly lost, in overseas trade, the Elizabethan audience would easily understand how a man might be sorely weighed down by business worries; and when that man was a *Venetian* merchant —the most splendid embodiment of that boundless wealth available to one who would dare the hazards of such trading—the audience might well be suspicious of his disclaimers. How could such a man, to whom the wealth of the world indeed lay as perilously open as did the golden fleece to the venturesome Jason, *not* be made "sad to think upon his merchandise"?

There were further reasons to be suspicious of Antonio. Elizabethan attitudes towards the idea of a "merchant of Venice" were complex, compounded in part of admiration, in part of jealousy, but also in part of moral disapproval. Antonio, after all, is no bluff Simon Eyre, the honest Englishman whose joyful competence in the gentle craft of shoemaking makes him, Dick Whittington-wise, Lord Mayor of London. A deep suspicion still attached to these merchants, Italian or English, whose fortunes were made less through the sweat of their brow than through the manipulation of money itself. The ambiguity sometimes felt to reside in Shakespeare's title is no mere undergraduate misunderstanding. The Venetian moneylender and the Venetian merchant were not entirely separate in the Elizabethan mind. (pp. 23-6)

Our first glimpse of Antonio, however, may convince us that he, of all men, is least in danger from the moral precariousness of the mercantile life. We have not only Antonio's own disclaimers; more importantly we are quickly granted an extravagant demonstration of Antonio's unmerchantlike charity or love. (pp. 29-30)

Antonio has said that he counts the world as nothing more than it is, "A stage where every man must play a part, / And mine a sad one'' . . . ; but in his response to Bassanio's need we see Antonio's conception of his role more extensively displayed. His use of the world, and all the things of the world, appears to be all unblameworthy; everything he has or can get (for he must borrow in order to meet Bassanio's needs) is at the service of his friend. And as the action of the play progresses, that original phrase, ''My purse, my person, *my extremest means* / Lie all unlock'd to your occasions'' [I. i. 138-39], gathers to itself deeper resonance, until the doomed Antonio's plight may bring to mind the words of Christ, ''Greater loue then this hathe no man, when any man bestoweth his life for his friends'' (John 15:13).

Thus Shakespeare plays with his audience's expectations, giving them a merchant who is (apparently) so far from being guilty of a lack of charity that he comes perilously close to completing literally an *imitatio Christi*. But although a man of sorrow, Antonio is in fact no more a ''Christ-figure'' than is any man who acts with charity. And indeed in this first reversal of ordinary expectations Shakespeare has prepared the way for a further and more subtle reversal. In one extraordinary, vital instance, the imputation of uncharitableness will still come back upon Antonio, but in a way far different from what the comfortable audience would initially have expected. . . . Antonio's un-Christlike but quite merchantlike failure involves his fellow merchant, that insidious doppelganger, Shylock.

Antonio's self-righteously unrepentant answer to Shylock at their first appearance together, that ''I am as like to call thee [dog] again, / To spet on thee again, to spurn thee too'' [I. iii. 130-31], is shocking to modern ears. No doubt it would have shocked some in Shakespeare's audience; others, familiar with a literature which treated Jews in such a way as to make Shakespeare's creation of Shylock seem remarkably forbearing, might have applauded Antonio's openly expressed hatred. Shakespeare's own judgment on the matter is suggested at the start by Antonio's melancholy and confirmed by the lesson of the trial. Critics who search along a naturalistic bias to find the reason for Antonio's sadness generally condemn Antonio's treatment of Shylock without seeing that the two facts—his sadness and his treatment of Shylock—are intimately related. Antonio's melancholy, I suggest, is his emotional response to a moral failure. Elizabethan ideas about the usury Shylock practices complicate the issue but do not alter the fundamental point: that the Christian is obliged equally to hate the sin but *not* the sinner.

The purposeful ambiguity in the play's title, and the numerous felt similarities between Shylock and Antonio—each one, as the play opens, an odd-man-out—help to make the point. The *malice* with which Antonio has, in the past and now, publicly reproved and humiliated Shylock, convicts him of being, in this instance, himself spiritually a ''Jew.'' . . . In treating Shylock as he has done, Antonio violates—and has, apparently, repeatedly violated—one of the more difficult spiritual directives given in The Sermon on the Mount: 'Iudge not, that ye be not iudged'' (Matt. 7:1). Later in the play, in Portia's curious courtroom—a place as much for moral instruction as for legal judgment—Antonio and the audience will have an opportunity to render another kind of judgment, one which rejects the flesh desired by the inner ''Jew'' and accepts instead the spiritual circumcision of the heart.

By the end of the fifth act, characters and audience have been granted intimations of that music of the heavenly spheres which is too fine for our crude mortal perception. The idea of musical harmony has by then become a dominant metaphor for the play's actions, and the attitudes of the characters to music has become an important means of knowing them. Jessica, a newcomer to the courtly Belmontese society, is uneasy about her own esthetic response: ''I am never merry when I hear sweet music'' [V. i. 69], she confesses to her Christian husband. But Lorenzo, more native to the musical place, takes it upon himself to instruct Jessica: ''The reason is your spirits are attentive'' [V. i. 70]. Far from showing a lack of responsiveness, the fact that Jessica is not ''merry'' when she hears the music shows that she has an appropriate listening attitude: she is prepared to ''mark the music'' [V. i. 88], and to hear in it faint echoes of the spiritual music of divine harmony. Jessica's is a norm of appropriate attentiveness against which we can measure the attitudes of other characters—of Bassanio, for instance, who so carefully marks the music when it accompanies his choice of Portia's leaden casket.

At an opposite extreme is the capering Gratiano, whose delight in ''mirth and laughter'' [I. i. 80] overflows into an ugly sort of joy at Shylock's defeat. And Shylock, of course, is clearly identified as an untrustworthy man who ''hath no music in himself, / Nor is not moved with concord of sweet sounds'' [V. i. 83-4]. At the trial, Shylock, whose rigid adherence to a literal law rules out the mollifying effects of music, and Gratiano, with his excessive levity, will produce between them a cacophony of lovelessness.

The musical metaphor tells us about Antonio, too. Antonio's melancholy shows that he is out of tune; that despite his spontaneous charity to his beloved Bassanio, his malice towards Shylock—his enemy but therefore, because of his malice, a spiritual kinsman—keeps him from being fully a part of the ideal harmony. But to Portia's challenge at the trial, ''What mercy can you render him Antonio'' [IV. i. 378], Antonio responds differently than either Gratiano or Shylock. In his response, which goes beyond love of a neighbor to reach as well the love of an enemy, Antonio shows himself to be at last in tune. In his melancholy, Antonio was incapable of fulfilling the Psalmist's injunction to ''Sing vnto the Lord a new song'' (Ps. 98); but when he extends his love beyond the circle that includes Portia and Bassanio, reaching outwards with charity for Shylock as well, his gesture makes the ''new song'' of spiritual love. (pp. 30-4)

I want to consider the other explanation beside the mercantile one that has been advanced for Antonio's melancholy. For the opinion that Antonio is in love continues to be widely held, all his ''fie, fies'' notwithstanding. Not cranks, but some of the play's most eminent interpreters, both academic and theatrical, perceive a homoerotic disturbance as the basis of Antonio's sadness. (p. 34)

For instance, E. M. W. Tillyard writes that ''Antonio suffers from a self-abnegating passion that quenches the springs of vitality in him and makes him the self-chosen outcast from society. . . . Antonio now sees himself as useless. Before Bassanio left him for Portia, his life had some direction; now it has none.'' . . . [Of] even greater interest is the rhetoric of Tillyard's conclusion: ''I do not think Antonio a study of homosexuality; *but* Shakespeare presented him as essentially a lonely figure, strikingly different from all the sociable folk he has to do with, except Shylock'' [see Additional Bibliography]. The force of that ''but'' implies that Antonio's loneliness and his difference from ''all the sociable folk'' make him like a homosexual, even if he is not ''a study in homosexuality.'' Thus Antonio's homosexual attachment is made to explain his sadness, and his sadness to prove his homosexuality. The logic (by no means uniquely Tillyard's) is as curious as the implication that loneliness and a striking difference from sociable folk are characteristic of homosexuals.

Now this explanation for Antonio's melancholy seems to me quite wrong: its implied consequences (as I will explain shortly) are not coherent with the play's overall shape and tone. And it is important to stress that this reason, rather than any *a priori* theoretical objection, is the basis for rejecting the psychosexual interpretation: for what is at issue here is not only Antonio's sexual preference, but the nature of Shakespearean characterization. The possible extremes are these: that Antonio, as Shakespeare created him, is merely a bundle of personified dramatic conventions—melancholy, generous, unlucky; or (at another extreme) that he is a psychologically "realistic" character in whom it is proper to discover submerged psychosexual motivations. And the difficult fact—the very heart of this Shakespearean matter—is that Antonio is not wholly the one sort of character or the other, but a richly impure mixture (like the play itself) of both dramatic tendencies. We need to give due weight to all that is uniquely Elizabethan and "conventional" in Antonio's characterization—and that means, among other things, recognizing him as a figure capable of standing for "abstract" ideas, of representing moral qualities. But the necessity to hold on to both sides of Shakespeare's characterizing variousness also makes it important to reaffirm—even in rejecting the idea that Antonio is primarily motivated by a sexual attachment to Bassanio—the character's actual degree of psychological "realism." (pp. 34-6)

The Merchant of Venice is a play in which harmonies are discovered where only discord had seemed possible, and its dominant figure (whether in details of imagery or in the implied shape of the fable as a whole) is the circle, ring, or round. The love of Antonio and Bassanio chimes in that harmonious round, as does the love of Bassanio and Portia. But to suppose a competition between Antonio and Portia introduces a discord more intractable to resolution than that of Shylock, the unmusical man, himself. So it is not the realism nor the humanness, but the consequent introduction of this irreconcilable competition, that leads me to reject the psychosexual explanation for Antonio's sadness. (pp. 38-9)

It is conceivable, I suppose, that one could have a homosexual Antonio without any consequent irreconcilability between Bassanio's two lovers. But then, of course, Antonio's sadness remains inexplicable. And in critical practice, a competition between Portia and Antonio seems the inevitable result of the assumption. According to one account, for instance, friendship is relegated "to a subordinate place" by the end of the play, and Antonio is taught that "there is room for friendship within the house of love, but love holds the upper and controlling hand" [see essay by Anne Barton in the Additional Bibliography]. This shrewish love, however, conflicts with all that Portia says about the nature of her relationship to Bassanio when he wins her in the casket test, when "her gentle spirit / Commits itself to [his] to be directed, / As from her lord, her governor, her king" [III. ii. 163-65]. And it conflicts with the actual result of the ring episode, which is (in part) the reaffirmation of Antonio's loving loyalty to both Bassanio and Portia:

> I once did lend my body for his wealth,
> Which but for him that had your husband's ring
> Had quite miscarried. I dare be bound again,
> My soul upon the forfeit, that your lord
> Will never more break faith advisedly.
>
> [V. i. 249-53]

The love of Antonio and Bassanio (whether or not it dares to speak its name) is a textual fact; but a sexual competition between Antonio and Portia is not, and to invent one raises more problems of interpretation than it solves. (pp. 39-40)

> *Lawrence Danson, in his* The Harmonies of "The Merchant of Venice," *Yale University Press, 1978, 202 p.*

RENÉ GIRARD   (lecture date 1978)

[*Like such earlier critics as Harold C. Goddard (1951), A. D. Moody (1964), and R. Chris Hassel, Jr. (1970), Girard postulates an ironic interpretation of* The Merchant of Venice *and condemns the Christians' behavior throughout the play. Foremost in his assessment, Girard contends that Shylock and the Venetians are essentially alike, noting that Venice is governed by a monetary, calculating, and selfish code that is no better, morally, than that which Shylock follows; in fact, the critic asserts, the Christians are morally inferior to the Jew in that they cover up their true nature with protestations of love and charity, while Shylock admits that his efforts in life are shaped by one thing—making money. Girard argues that this duplicity on the part of the Christians can best be discerned in their religious behavior, which he states demonstrates throughout that revenge and retribution, not mercy or love, are at the heart of their treatment of Shylock. The fact that readers have not universally accepted the Venetians' corrupt nature and duplicity, Girard theorizes, is because Shakespeare managed to both condemn them for their "scapegoating" and immoral treatment of Shylock and provide his audience with enough ammunition to dislike the Jew and thus participate in his persecution. In short, Girard suggests that Shakespeare structured his play so that both of the traditional interpretations are possible— the anti-Semitic view of Shylock as the villain whose creator agrees with and participates in his persecution, and the so-called ironic view that regards Shylock as wrongfully punished and suggests that the Christians are the target of Shakespeare's condemnation. For a similar assessment that both of these interpretations are present in Shakespeare's play, see the excerpt above by Goddard. Also, see the essay by Norman Rabkin (1981), who argues that any thematic analysis of a work like* The Merchant of Venice, *be it allegorical or ironic, is simplistic, failing to account for that work's numerous oppositions or conflicts. Girard's essay was originally read as a lecture in September, 1978.*]

The criticism of *The Merchant of Venice* has been dominated by two images of Shylock that appear irreconcilable. It is my contention that both images belong to the play and that far from rendering it unintelligible their conjunction is essential to an understanding of Shakespeare's dramatic practice.

The first image is that of the Jewish moneylender in the late-medieval and modern book of anti-Semitism. The mere evocation of that Jewish stereotype suggests a powerful system of binary oppositions that does not have to be fully developed to pervade the entire play. First comes the opposition between Jewish greed and Christian generosity, between revenge and compassion, between the crankiness of old age and the charm of youth, between the dark and the luminous, the beautiful and the ugly, the gentle and the harsh, the musical and the unmusical, and so on.

There is a second image that comes only after the stereotype has been firmly implanted in our minds; at first it does not make as strong an impression as the first, but it gathers strength later on because the language and behavior of the Christian characters repeatedly confirm the rather brief but essential utterances of Shylock himself on which it primarily rests.

"The Trial Scene" (Act IV. Scene i.), "Jessica's Elope-ment" (Act II. Scene vi.), and "Lorenzo's Speech on the Heavens" (Act V. Scene i.). The Department of Rare Books and Special Collections, The University of Michigan Library.

The symmetry between the explicit venality of Shylock and the implicit venality of the other Venetians cannot fail to be intended by the playwright. It is true that Bassanio's courtship of Portia is presented primarily as a financial operation. In his plea for Antonio's financial support, Bassanio mentions first the wealth of the young heiress, then her beauty, then finally her spiritual qualities. Those critics who idealize the Venetians write as if the many textual clues that contradict their view were not planted by the author himself, as if their presence in the play were a purely fortuitous matter, like the arrival of a bill in the morning mail when one really expects a love letter. (pp. 100-01)

Regarding this symmetry between Shylock and the Venetians, many good points have been made. I will mention only one, for the sole reason that I have not found it in the critical literature on the play. (p. 101)

Act 3, scene 2, Bassanio wants to reward his lieutenant for his services, and he tells Gratiano and Nerissa that they will be married simultaneously with Portia and himself, in a double wedding ceremony—at Portia's expense we may assume. "Our feast," he says, "shall be much honored in your marriage."

Upon which the elated Gratiano says to his fiancée: "We'll play with them the first boy for a thousand ducats" [III. ii. 212-14].

These young people have ample reason to be joyous, now that their future is made secure by Bassanio's clever stroke with the caskets, and this bet sounds harmless enough, but Shakespeare is not addicted to pointless social chitchat and must have a purpose. Gratiano's baby will be two thousand ducats cheaper than Antonio's pound of flesh. Human flesh and money in Venice are constantly exchanged for one another. People are turned into objects of financial speculation. Mankind has become a commodity, an exchange value like any other. I cannot believe that Shakespeare did not perceive the analogy between Gratiano's wager and Shylock's pound of flesh.

Shylock's pound of flesh is symbolical of Venetian behavior. The Venetians appear different from Shylock, up to a point. Financial considerations have become so natural to them and they are so embedded into their psyches that they have become not quite but almost invisible; they can never be identified as a distinct aspect of behavior. Antonio's loan to Bassanio, for instance, is treated as an act of love and not as a business transaction.

Shylock hates Antonio for lending money without interest. In his eyes, the merchant spoils the financial business. We can read this as the resentment of vile greed for noble generosity within the context of the first image, but we may prefer another reading that contributes to the second image. The generosity of Antonio may well be a corruption more extreme than the caricatural greed of Shylock. As a rule, when Shylock lends money, he expects more money in return, and nothing else. Capital should produce capital. Shylock does not confuse his financial operations with Christian charity. This is why, unlike the Venetians, he can look like the embodiment of greed.

Venice is a world in which appearances and reality do not match. Of all the pretenders to Portia's hand, Bassanio alone makes the right choice between the three caskets because he alone is a Venetian and knows how deceptive a splendid exterior can be. Unlike his foreign competitors who obviously come from countries where things still are more or less what they seem to be, less advanced countries we might say, he instinctively feels that the priceless treasure he seeks must hide behind the most unlikely appearance.

The symbolic significance of choosing lead rather than the gold and silver selected by the two foreigners faithfully duplicates the whole relationship between the true Venetians and the foreign Shylock. When the two alien pretenders reach avidly for the two precious metals, just like Shylock, they look like personifications of greed; in reality they are rather naive, whereas Bassanio is anything but naive. It is characteristic of the Venetians that they look like the very picture of disinterestedness at the precise moment when their sly calculations cause the pot of gold to fall into their lap.

The generosity of the Venetians is not feigned. Real generosity makes the beneficiary more dependent on his generous friend than a regular loan. In Venice a new form of vassality prevails, grounded no longer in strict territorial borders but in vague financial terms. The lack of precise accounting makes personal indebtedness infinite. This is an art Shylock has not mastered since his own daughter feels perfectly free to rob and abandon him without the slightest remorse. The elegance of the décor and the harmony of the music must not lead us to think that everything is right with the Venetian world. It is impossible, however, to say exactly what is wrong. Antonio is sad but he cannot say why, and this unexplained sadness seems to characterize the whole Venetian business aristocracy as much as Antonio himself.

Even in Shylock's life, however, money and matters of human sentiment finally become confused. But there is something comical in this confusion because, even as they become one, money and sentiment retain a measure of separateness, they remain distinguishable from each other and we hear such things as "My daughter! Oh, my ducats! Oh, my daughter! / Fled with a Christian! Oh, my Christian ducats!" [II. viii. 15-16] and other such ridiculous utterances you would never catch in a Venetian mouth.

There is still another occasion upon which Shylock, goaded by his Venetian enemies, confuses financial matters with other passions, and it is the affair of his loan to Antonio. In the interest of his revenge, Shylock demands no interest for his money, no positive guarantees in case of default, nothing but his infamous pound of flesh. Behind the mythical weirdness of the request, we have one spectacular instance of that complete interpenetration between the financial and the human that is characteristic less of Shylock than of the other Venetians. Thus Shylock appears most scandalous to the Venetians and to the spectators when he stops resembling himself to resemble the Venetians even more. The spirit of revenge drives him to imitate the Venetians more perfectly than before, and, in his effort to teach Antonio a lesson, Shylock becomes his grotesque double.

Antonio and Shylock are described as rivals of long standing. Of such people we often say that they have their differences, but this expression would be misleading. Tragic—and comic—conflict amounts to a dissolving of differences that is paradoxical because it proceeds from the opposite intention. All the people involved in the process seek to emphasize and maximize their differences. In Venice, we found, greed and generosity, pride and humility, compassion and ferocity, money and human flesh, tend to become one and the same. This undifferentiation makes it impossible to define anything with precision, to ascribe one particular cause to one particular event. Yet on all sides it is the same obsession with displaying and sharpening a difference that is less and less real. (pp. 101-04)

We have an allusion to this process of undifferentiation, I believe, in a well-known line of *The Merchant*. When Portia enters the court she asks, "Which is the merchant and which is the Jew?" [IV. i. 174]. Even if she has never met either Antonio or Shylock, we have a right to be surprised Portia cannot identify the Jewish moneylender at first sight, in view of the enormous difference, visible to all, that is supposed to distinguish him from the gracious Venetians. The line would be more striking, of course, if it came after rather than before the following one: "Antonio and Old Shylock both stand forth" [IV. i. 175]. If Portia were still unable to distinguish Shylock from Antonio once the two men have come forward together, the scene would explicitly contradict the primary image of Shylock, the stereotype of the Jewish moneylender. This contradiction would stretch the limits of dramatic credibility beyond the breaking point, and Shakespeare refrained from it, to question the reality of a difference he himself, of course, had first introduced into his play. Even the structure of the line, with its two symmetrical questions, suggests the prevalence of symmetry between the two men. (p. 105)

This analysis must lead to Shylock's famous tirade on reciprocity and revenge; we now have the context in which the meaning and purpose of the passage become unmistakable:

> . . . if you tickle us,
> Do we not laugh? if you poison us, do we not
> Die? and if you wrong us, shall we not revenge?
> If we are like you in the rest, we will resemble
> You in that. If a Jew wrong a Christian, what
> Is his humility? Revenge. If a Christian wrong
> A Jew, what should his sufferance be by Christian
> Example? Why, revenge. The villainy
> You teach me, I will execute; and it shall go
> Hard but I will better the instruction.
>
> [III. i. 65-73]

The text insists above all on Shylock's personal commitment to revenge. It does not support the type of "rehabilitation" naively demanded by certain revisionists. But it unequivocally defines the symmetry and the reciprocity that govern the relations between the Christians and Shylock. It says the same thing as the line: "Which is the merchant and which is the Jew?" It is as essential, therefore, as it is striking, and it fully deserves to be singled out.

With his caricatural demand for a pound of flesh, Shylock does, indeed, "better the instruction." What we have just said in the language of psychology can be translated into religious terms. Between Shylock's behavior and his words, the relationship is never ambiguous. His interpretation of the law may be narrow and negative but we can count on him for acting according to it and for speaking according to his actions. In the passage on revenge, he alone speaks a truth that the Christians hypocritically deny. The truth of the play is revenge and retribution. The Christians manage to hide that truth even from themselves. They do not live by the law of charity, but this law is enough of a presence in their language to drive the law of revenge underground, to make this revenge almost invisible. As a result, this revenge becomes more subtle, skillful, and feline than the revenge of Shylock. The Christians will easily destroy Shylock but they will go on living in a world that is sad without knowing why, a world in which even the difference between revenge and charity has been abolished.

Ultimately we do not have to choose between a favorable and an unfavorable image of Shylock. The old critics have concentrated on Shylock as a separate entity, an individual substance that would be merely juxtaposed to other individual substances and remain unaffected by them. The ironic depth in *The Merchant of Venice* results from a tension not between two static images of Shylock, but between those textual features that strengthen and those features that undermine the popular idea of an insurmountable difference between Christian and Jew.

It is not excessive to say that characterization itself, as a real dramatic problem or as a fallacy, is at stake in the play. On the one hand Shylock is portrayed as a highly differentiated villain. On the other hand he tells us himself that there are no villains and no heroes; all men are the same, especially when they are taking revenge on each other. Whatever differences may have existed between them prior to the cycle of revenge are dissolved in the reciprocity of reprisals and retaliation. Where does Shakespeare stand on this issue? Massive evidence from the other plays as well as from *The Merchant* cannot leave the question in doubt. The main object of satire is not Shylock the Jew. But Shylock is rehabilitated only to the extent that the Christians are even worse than he is and that the "honesty" of his vices makes him almost a refreshing figure compared to the sanctimonious ferocity of the other Venetians.

The trial scene clearly reveals how implacable and skillful the Christians can be when they take their revenge. In this most curious performance, Antonio begins as the defendant and Shylock as the plaintiff. At the end of one single meeting the roles are reversed and Shylock is a convicted criminal. The man has done no actual harm to anyone. Without his money, the two marriages, the two happy events in the play, could not have come to pass. As his triumphant enemies return to Belmont loaded with a financial and human booty that includes Shylock's own daughter, they still manage to feel compassionate and gentle by contrast with their wretched opponent.

When we sense the injustice of Shylock's fate, we usually say: Shylock is a scapegoat. This expression, however, is ambiguous. When I say that a character in a play is a scapegoat, my statement can mean two different things. It can mean that this character is unjustly condemned from the perspective of the writer. The conviction of the crowd is presented as irrational by the writer himself. In the first case, we say that in that play there is a theme or motif of the scapegoat.

There is a second meaning to the idea that a character is a scapegoat. It can mean that, from the perspective of the writer, this character is justly condemned, but in the eyes of the critic who makes the statement, the condemnation is unjust. The crowd that condemns the victim is presented as rational by the writer, who really belongs to that crowd; only in the eyes of the critic are the crowd and the writer irrational and unjust.

The scapegoat, this time, is not a theme or motif at all; it is not made explicit by the writer, but if the critic is right in his allegations, there must be a scapegoat effect at the origin of the play, a collective effect probably, in which the writer participates. The critic may think, for instance, that a writer who creates a character like Shylock, patterned after the stereotype of the Jewish moneylender, must do so because he personally shares in the anti-Semitism of the society in which this stereotype is present.

When we say that Shylock is a scapegoat, our statement remains vague and critically useless unless we specify if we mean the scapegoat as theme or the scapegoat as structure, the scapegoat as an object of indignation and satire or the scapegoat as a passively accepted delusion.

Before we can resolve the critical impasse to which I referred at the beginning of my presentation we must reformulate it in the terms of this still unperceived alternative between the scapegoat as structure and the scapegoat as theme. Everyone agrees that Shylock is a scapegoat, but is he the scapegoat of his society only or of Shakespeare's as well?

What the critical revisionists maintain is that the scapegoating of Shylock is not a structuring force but a satirical theme. What the traditionalists maintain is that scapegoating, in *The Merchant of Venice,* is a structuring force rather than a theme. Whether we like it or not, they say, the play shares in the cultural anti-Semitism of the society. We should not allow our literary piety to blind us to the fact.

My own idea is that the scapegoat is both structure and theme in *The Merchant of Venice,* and that the play, in this essential respect at least, is anything any reader wants it to be, not because Shakespeare is as confused as we are when we use the word *scapegoat* without specifying, but for the opposite

reason: he is so aware and so conscious of the various demands placed upon him by the cultural diversity of his audience; he is so knowledgeable in regard to the paradoxes of mimetic reactions and group behavior that he can stage a scapegoating of Shylock entirely convincing to those who want to be convinced and simultaneously undermine that process with ironic touches that will reach only those who can be reached. Thus he was able to satisfy the most vulgar as well as the most refined audiences. To those who do not want to challenge the anti-Semitic myth, or Shakespeare's own espousal of that myth, *The Merchant of Venice* will always sound like a confirmation of that myth. To those who do challenge these same beliefs, Shakespeare's own challenge will become perceptible. The play is not unlike a perpetually revolving object that, through some mysterious means, would always present itself to each viewer under aspects best suited to his own perspective.

Why are we reluctant to consider this possibility? Both intellectually and ethically, we assume that scapegoating cannot be and should not be a theme of satire and a structuring force at the same time. Either the author participates in the collective victimage and he cannot see it as unjust or he can see it as unjust and he should not connive in it, even ironically. Most works of art do fall squarely on one side or the other of that particular fence. Rewritten by Arthur Miller, Jean-Paul Sartre or Bertolt Brecht, *The Merchant* would be different indeed. But so would a *Merchant of Venice* that would merely reflect the anti-Semitism of its society, as a comparison with Marlowe's *Jew of Malta* immediately reveals.

If we look carefully at the trial scene, no doubt can remain that Shakespeare undermines the scapegoat effects just as skillfully as he produces them. There is something frightening in this efficiency. This art demands a manipulation and therefore an intelligence of mimetic phenomena that transcends not only the ignorant immorality of those who submit passively to victimage mechanisms but also the moralism that rebels against them but does not perceive the irony generated by the dual role of the author. Shakespeare himself must first generate at the grossly theatrical level the effects that he later undermines at the level of allusions.

Let us see how Shakespeare can move in both directions at the same time. Why is it difficult not to experience a feeling of relief and even jubilation at the discomfiture of Shylock? The main reason, of course, is that Antonio's life is supposed to be under an immediate threat. That threat stems from Shylock's stubborn insistence that he is entitled to his pound of flesh.

Now the pound of flesh is a mythical motif. We found earlier that it is a highly significant allegory of a world where human beings and money are constantly exchanged for one another, but it is nothing more. We can imagine a purely mythical context in which Shylock could really carve up his pound of flesh and Antonio would walk away, humiliated and diminished but alive. In *The Merchant of Venice,* the mythical context is replaced by a realistic one. We are told that Antonio could not undergo this surgical operation without losing his life. It is certainly true in a realistic context, but it is also true, in that same context, that, especially in the presence of the whole Venetian establishment, old Shylock would be unable to perform this same operation. The myth is only partly demythologized, and Shylock is supposed to be capable of carving up Antonio's body in cold blood because, as a Jew and a moneylender, he passes for a man of unusual ferocity. This presumed ferocity justifies our own religious prejudice.

Shakespeare knows that victimage must be unanimous to be effective, and no voice is effectively raised in favor of Shylock. The presence of the silent Magnificoes, the élite of the community, turns the trial into a rite of social unanimity. The only characters not physically present are Shylock's daughter and his servant, and they are of one mind with the actual scapegoaters since they were the first to abandon Shylock after taking his money. (pp. 106-11)

As scapegoating affects more and more people and tends toward unanimity, the contagion becomes overwhelming. In spite of its judicial and logical nonsense, the trial scene is enormously performative and dramatic. The spectators and readers of the play cannot fail to be affected and cannot refrain from experiencing Shylock's defeat as if it were their own victory. The crowd in the theater becomes one with the crowd on the stage. The contagious effect of scapegoating extends to the audience. In *The Merchant of Venice*, at least, and perhaps in many other plays, the Aristotelian catharsis is a scapegoat effect.

As an embodiment of Venetian justice, the duke should be impartial, but at the very outset of the proceedings he commiserates with the defendant and launches into a diatribe against Shylock:

> I am sorry for thee. Thou art come to answer
> A stony adversary, an inhuman wretch,
> Uncapable of pity, void and empty
> From any dram of mercy.
>
> [IV. i. 3-6]

These words set the tone for the entire scene. The Christian virtue par excellence, mercy is the weapon with which Shylock is clubbed over the head. The Christians use the word *mercy* with such perversity that they can justify their own revenge with it, give full license to their greed and still come out with a clear conscience. They feel they have discharged their obligation to be merciful by their constant repetition of the word itself. The quality of their mercy is not strained, to say the least. It is remarkably casual and easy. When the duke severely asks: "How shalt thou hope for mercy, rendering none?" [IV. i. 88], Shylock responds with impeccable logic: "What judgment shall I dread, doing no wrong?" [IV. i. 89].

Shylock trusts in the law too much. How could the law of Venice be based on mercy, how could it be equated with the golden rule, since it gives the Venetians the right to own slaves and it does not give slaves the right to own Venetians? How can we be certain that Shakespeare, who engineered that scapegoat effect so skillfully, is not fooled by it even for one second? Our certainty is perfect and it may well be much more than "subjective," as some critics would say. It may well be perfectly "objective" in the sense that it correctly recaptures the author's intention and yet it remains a closed book to a certain type of reader. If irony were demonstrable it would cease to be irony. Irony must not be explicit enough to destroy the efficiency of the scapegoat machine in the minds of those fools for whom that machine was set up in the first place. Irony cannot fail to be less tangible than the object on which it bears.

Some will object that my reading is "paradoxical." It may well be, but why should it be a priori excluded that Shakespeare can write a paradoxical play? Especially if the paradox on which the play is built is formulated most explicitly at the center of that very play. . . . Shakespeare is writing, not without a purpose, that the worst sophistry, when distilled by a charming voice, can decide the outcome of a trial, or that the most unreligious behavior can sound religious if the right words are

mentioned. Let us listen to the reasons given by Bassanio for trusting in lead rather than in silver or gold and we will see that they apply word for word to the play itself:

> The world is still deceived with ornament.
> In law, what plea so tainted and corrupt
> But being seasoned with a gracious voice,
> Obscures the show of evil? In religion,
> What damned error but some sober brow
> Will bless it, and approve it with a text,
> Hiding the grossness with fair ornament?
> There is no vice so simple but assumes
> Some mark of virtue on his outward parts.
>
> [III. ii. 74-82]

This is so appropriate to the entire play that it is difficult to believe it a coincidence.

I see Bassanio's brief intervention during the trial scene as another sign of Shakespeare's ironic distance. As soon as Shylock begins to relent, under the pressure of Portia's skill, Bassanio declares his willingness to pay back the money Shylock is now willing to accept. In his eagerness to be finished with the whole unpleasant business, Bassanio shows a degree of mercy, but Portia remains adamant. Feeling her claws in Shylock's flesh, she drives them deeper and deeper in order to exact her own pound of flesh. Bassanio's suggestion bears no fruit but its formulation at this crucial moment cannot be pointless. It is the only reasonable solution to the whole affair but dramatically it cannot prevail because it is undramatic. Shakespeare is too good a playwright not to understand that the only good solution, from a theatrical standpoint, is the scapegoating of Shylock. On the other hand he wants to point out the unjust nature of the "cathartic" resolution that is forced upon him by the necessity of his art. He wants the reasonable solution to be spelled out somewhere inside the play.

Is it not excessive to say that scapegoating is a recognizable motif in *The Merchant of Venice*? There is one explicit allusion to the scapegoat in the play. It occurs at the beginning of Shylock's trial.

> I am a tainted wether of the flock,
> Meetest for death. The weakest kind of fruit
> Drops earliest to the ground, and so let me.
> You cannot better be employed, Bassanio,
> Than to live still and write mine epitaph.
>
> [IV. i. 114-18]

Is there a difficulty for my thesis in the fact that Antonio rather than Shylock utters these lines? Not at all, since their mutual hatred has turned Antonio and Shylock into the doubles of each other. This mutual hatred makes all reconciliation impossible— nothing concrete separates the antagonists, no genuinely tangible issue that could be arbitrated and settled—but the undifferentiation generated by this hatred paves the way for the only type of resolution that can conclude this absolute conflict, the scapegoat resolution.

Antonio speaks these lines in reply to Bassanio, who has just asserted he would never let his friend and benefactor die in his place. He would rather die himself. Neither one will die, of course, or even suffer in the slightest. In the city of Venice, no Antonio or Bassanio will ever suffer as long as there is a Shylock to do the suffering for them.

There is no serious danger that Antonio will die, but he can really see himself, at this point, as a scapegoat in the making. Thus Shakespeare can have an explicit reference to scapegoating without pointing directly to Shylock. There is a great irony, of course, not only in the fact that the metaphor is displaced, the scapegoat being the essence of metaphoric displacement, but also in the almost romantic complacency of Antonio, in his intimation of masochistic satisfaction. The quintessential Venetian, Antonio, the man who is sad without a cause, may be viewed as a figure of the modern subjectivity characterized by a strong propensity toward self-victimization or, more concretely, by a greater and greater interiorization of a scapegoat process that is too well understood to be reenacted as a real event in the real world. Mimetic entanglements cannot be projected with complete success onto all the Shylocks of this world, and the scapegoat process tends to turn back upon itself and become reflective. What we have, as a result, is a masochistic and theatrical self-pity that announces the romantic subjectivity. This is the reason why Antonio is eager to be "sacrificed" in the actual presence of Bassanio.

Irony is not demonstrable, I repeat, and it should not be, otherwise it would disturb the catharsis of those who enjoy the play at the cathartic level only. Irony is anticathartic. Irony is experienced in a flash of complicity with the writer at his most subtle, against the larger and coarser part of the audience that remains blind to these subtleties. Irony is the writer's vicarious revenge against the revenge that he must vicariously perform. If irony were too obvious, if it were intelligible to all, it would defeat its own purpose because there would be no more object for irony to undermine. (pp. 111-15)

> René Girard, "'To Entrap the Wisest': A Reading of 'The Merchant of Venice'," in Literature and Society: Selected Papers from the English Institute, 1978, edited by Edward W. Said, The Johns Hopkins University Press, 1980, pp. 100-19.

ALICE N. BENSTON (essay date 1979)

[*Benston disputes the traditional reading of* The Merchant of Venice *as a play structured on a series of dichotomies, the most significant being the opposition of justice or law and mercy. She argues instead that the drama is constructed from a series of trials concerning the law and "its complex relations to vice, virtue, and vicissitude," with neither Shylock nor Antonio but Portia at its center. Benston maintains that Portia upholds the civil law of Venice and reaffirms the natural law of Belmont—the former by granting Shylock's legal claim rather than refuting it, as Bassanio and the other Venetians would have her do, the latter by following the "bond" inherent in her father's will and by demonstrating to Bassanio and Gratiano in the ring episode the sanctity of personal oaths or contracts despite the severe conditions those oaths must withstand. Benston thus considers Portia not the personification of mercy other critics have claimed, but the play's protector of law in both its civil and natural spheres. The critic also contributes additional evidence of Act V's significance in* The Merchant of Venice, *contending that it depicts Portia's education of Antonio. According to Benston, Portia teaches the merchant how to forsake his possessive and unnatural love for Bassanio and to accept the law of "natural succession" and "generation," which is embodied in Portia and Bassanio's union and love for each other. John D. Hurrell (1961) and Barbara Tovey (1981) have also commented on the unnaturalness and possessiveness of Antonio's love for Bassanio, as well as noted the secondary conflict in the trial scene between Portia and the merchant. In addition, see the excerpts by Sigurd Burckhardt (1962) and John P. Sisk (1969) for further discussion of the theme of personal bonds and bonding in the play.*]

Among the problems one faces in dealing with *The Merchant of Venice* is the difficulty of sensing a whole, a harmony, in a play that seems to work so consistently with dichotomies. Christian and Jew, mercy and law, love and friendship, prodigality and frugality—all are captured in the contrast between Belmont's moonlit, fairy-tale peace, and Venice's mercantile hubbub. Most commentators have made no attempt to reconcile these oppositions, choosing rather to argue for the triumph of one side of the dichotomy over the other. The usual choice, of course, has been for Christian mercy, love, prodigality, and peace. (p. 367)

But, as has been frequently noted, the generous and merciful Venetians show little mercy or generosity in dealing with Shylock. To be sure, we are expected to accept the confines and conventions of this comedy and believe that the mercy shown by the court and the promise of conversion elicited from Shylock by Antonio represent a future redemption and absorption of the Jew into the total community. We are left, in other words, with a situation in which mercy appears to triumph over the law. Comically or tragically, we are left with a seeming denigration of law and contract.

This interpretation has had much support; and after all, the triumph of the New over the Old Testament is a credible theme to attribute to an Elizabethan playwright. But such a reading still leads to perplexity. Questions remain. (1) How is it that Portia, the eloquent spokesman for mercy, a figure venerated almost as holy [V. i. 286, 294-95], is not given the role as dispenser of that heavenly virtue? (2) If the list of opposites drawn above is extrapolated from the structure of the play, the drama should end with the court scene. The two folklore themes— the three caskets and the pound of flesh—have been concluded. What, then, is the function of the last act?

[Anne] Barton offers an interesting interpretation [see Additional Bibliography]. Portia, she says, has cause for alarm when she learns just how strong the bond is between Bassanio and Antonio. Her new husband would pledge his life and hers to save Antonio's. . . . Excessive friendship must give way to love, therefore, and it is to this end that Portia resorts to the "ring trick." But Barton also says that "there is almost a sense that Antonio welcomes death as an incontrovertible proof that he has . . . elevated his love above hers." . . . This conclusion, if correct, would indicate in Antonio an anxiety greater than thwarted friendship, an anxiety which Portia could not relieve with a mere trick. Barton's explanation, then, leaves us with yet a third problem, one related to those already raised: how can Antonio be seen as part of a final reconciliation?

I believe that if we treat the so-called "ring trick" as a *trial* in which Portia has as important a task as "Balthazar" had in Venice, we will see that the last act, far from being a "thematic appendix," as Frank Kermode asserts, achieves a synthesis of the troublesome antinomies, deepens our understanding of Shylock and his "bond," and incorporates Antonio in the final vision. The key to understanding the thematic and structural organization of *The Merchant of Venice*, I think, is to see the play as a series of *three* trials.

The basic form of the play is tripartite: Bassanio's casket scene, Shylock's trial, and the ring episode are equal partners in a drama concerned primarily not with law versus mercy, but with the law itself and its complex relations to vice, virtue, and vicissitude. The play not only has a tripartite structure, but is informed throughout by a pattern of triads. There are three trials, three caskets, three couples, and, of great importance, three rings. In terms of plot structure, however, the sequence of trials forms the significant triad. And the play's crucial figure is neither Antonio nor Shylock but Portia, since it is her attitude toward the law that is central for these trials.

When we first meet Portia (I. ii) she is anything but a happy, naive princess in a fairyland. In fact, she is tinged with the same melancholy that dominates Antonio. . . . The marked difference between the two is that Antonio does not know the source of his sadness, his melancholy causing him to lose his sense of self: "And such a want-wit sadness makes of me, / That I have much ado to know myself" [I. i. 6-7]. His companions vie in trying to cheer him up and make him admit a cause (business or love), but he denies both suggestions and remains gloomy.

Though Portia is sad, unlike Antonio she can name the cause of her distress. Her speech [I. ii. 12-26] defines her melancholy in terms of her attitude toward the law and her relationship to it. "If to do were as easy as to know what were good to do, chapels had been churches, and poor men's cottages princes' palaces" [I. ii. 12-14]. Knowledge of the good does not guarantee good actions. Individual conscience is not enough; church law and state law are necessary. "It is a good divine that follows his own instructions" [I. ii. 14-15]. Even those who know best do not universally act as they preach. "I can easier teach twenty what were good to be done, than to be one of the twenty to follow mine own teaching" [I. ii. 15-17]. Here the switch to the personal pronoun shows that Portia is not railing against an outside wicked world, but parsing human nature and counting herself as capable of human frailty as anyone else. If humanity were perfect, there would be no need for authority. If man, who can and does know the good, were capable of always acting on that knowledge, there would be no need for laws. There then follows a diagnosis of the flaw in humanity that causes the problems: "The brain may devise laws for the blood, but a hot temper leaps o'er a cold decree—such a hare is madness the youth, to skip o'er the meshes of good counsel the cripple" [I. ii. 18-21]. There is nothing remarkable in the opposition reason/passions ("brain"/"blood") or wild youth/wise maturity. What is of significance is that these words are surrounded by the legal terms, "laws," "decree," and "counsel."

Portia does not need a wig and robe to turn into a doctor of laws. Apparently she has listened before to her kinsman Bellario. But, more importantly, it is personal experience that has taught her. The words that follow indicate the basis for her present mood: "But this reasoning is not in the fashion to choose me a husband. O me, the word choose! I may neither choose who I would, nor refuse who I dislike; so is the will of a living daughter curb'd by the will of a dead father. Is it not hard, Nerissa, that I cannot choose one, nor refuse none?" [I. ii. 21-6]. . . . Clearly Portia is feeling discontent; with youthful passion she would like to abrogate the contract as written by her father. But she cannot, as she says, *reason* her way to freedom of choice; she would have to rebel.

Instead of languishing, however, she turns to recreative game (naming over the suitors) to restore her good humor. And although she does not echo Nerissa's conventional wisdom ("holy men at their death have good inspirations," [I. ii. 27-8]), she has, by the end of the recital, determined to fulfill her father's wishes. . . . What she perceives is that although she cannot choose by her father's decree (and indeed she may stay husbandless), the conditions set by the contract will free her from ever encountering the passionless less-than-men, the risk-avoiders for whom she has nothing but contempt. (pp. 368-71)

Whether or not we feel that Portia manipulates the outcome of the casket choice by providing Bassanio with musical clues, we usually credit Bassanio with having passed his test by the conditions set. Each casket has a clue, and it is the art of deciphering clues that is being tested. Bassanio's reasoning takes him to the right casket and is echoed in the poem he finds there. The last line of the poem releases Portia to Bassanio "with a loving kiss" [III. ii. 138]. (p. 371)

Freed from her contract with her father, Portia freely "confirms," "signs over," all that she freely reigned over as "queen": "this house, these servants, and this same myself" [III. ii. 170]. She seals the contract, adding a ring to the kiss: "I give them [house, servants, and myself] with this ring" [III. ii. 171]. She here writes a new contract, one not even implied by her father's words. And this new contract has risks and conditions, too: "Which when you part from, lose, or give away, / Let it presage the ruin of your love, / And be my vantage to exclaim on you" [III. ii. 172-74].

Bassanio enters the contract in the rush of passion: "Madam, you have bereft me of all words, / Only my blood speaks to you in my veins" [III. ii. 175-76]. Nor does he simply repeat the terms; he adds to them. "But when this ring / Parts from this finger, then parts life from hence; / O then be bold to say Bassanio's dead" [III. ii. 183-85]. The same Bassanio who cautioned Antonio against signing a contract that wagered his life against future performance is now exhibiting the same rashness. Overly confident of themselves, their fortunes, and their feelings, failing to acknowledge, soberly, that there is no contract without risk—no such thing as a "merry" bond— Antonio and Bassanio both have much to learn.

The lesson to be learned will be delayed until the third section of the play, but that the two bonds—Portia and Bassanio's, and Antonio and Shylock's—are linked is indicated by the structure of the casket scene. The vows between the two couples do not issue in the customary "wedding march." Rather, the happy foursome are immediately interrupted by the appearance of Lorenzo and Jessica (a couple whose marriage is unsanctioned by a parent) and by Salerio, who bring the news of Antonio's plight.

Since the audience knows all that is reported, attention is focused on Portia as she receives the information. Bassanio informs her of his obligation to Antonio:

> How much I was a braggart: when I told you
> My state was nothing, I should then have told you
> That I was worse than nothing; for indeed
> I have engag'd myself to a dear friend,
> Engag'd my friend to his mere enemy,
> To feed my means. . . .
>
> [III. ii. 258-63]

Portia interrupts with two crisp questions: "Is it your dear friend that is thus in trouble?" [III. ii. 291] and "What sum owes he the Jew?" [III. ii. 297]. Answered "three thousand ducats," she says:

> What, no more?
> Pay him six thousand, and deface the bond;
> Double six thousand, and then treble that,
> Before a friend of this description
> Shall lose a hair through Bassanio's fault.
>
> [III. ii. 298-302]

Bassanio's *fault*? No monetary value can be placed on that obligation. In monetary terms it is to her a "paltry debt." She then tells everyone to cheer up and orders Bassanio to leave quickly, after a brief stop at the church for an exchange of vows. Then she asks to hear Antonio's letter:

> . . . my bond to the Jew is forfeit; and since in paying it, it is impossible I should live, all debts are clear'd between you and I, if I might but see you at my death. Notwithstanding, use your pleasure; if your love do not persuade you to come, let not my letter.
>
> [III. ii. 317-22]

The monetary obligation and the bond of love are linked. In fact, it is the fulfillment of the bond of love that would "deface" the "paltry" monetary obligation. To Anne Barton this is evidence of Antonio's desire to manipulate Bassanio's feelings. She believes that it shows his eagerness to die so as to seem greater than Portia as a lover, willing to give all, life as well as money, for Bassanio. If so, Portia fails to perceive it. She has just responded to the information concerning the monetary obligation. Now, on hearing Antonio's plea concerning the bond of love, she is even more decisive and emotional: "O love! dispatch all business and be gone" [III. ii. 323]. . . . Her generosity, as Barton notes, includes the willingness to incorporate Antonio in the new group formed by the marriage. Exactly; and the terms in which she explains her actions underscore her thinking on friendship, love, and the bonds they imply. . . . Portia does not oppose love to friendship; rather, she elides love and friendship. Nor does she see this as generosity, since it is her own soul that must be rescued. It is in this spirit, as Barton says, that she takes up the disguise of a man of law and sets off for Venice: "to make absolutely sure that Bassanio will not lose a friend as a consequence of gaining a wife." . . . (pp. 372-73)

The urgency Portia feels is indicated by the pace in which she gives her directives to the seemingly catatonic Bassanio. She knows that, even if unsuccessful, Bassanio must attempt to "deface" the bond so that he will not be at fault. This is consistent with Portia's attitude toward the "sanctity of contract."

Among other things, then, Portia must go to Venice to protect the law. That the law is endangered and that the Duke needs advice is revealed to her by Salerio and Jessica. Salerio says that the Duke and twenty merchants have pleaded with Shylock to give up his "forfeiture, . . . [his] justice, and his bond" [III. ii. 283]. Jessica articulates the alternatives: it is Antonio's life versus "law, authority and power" [III. ii. 289]. Portia's previous behavior indicates that, much as she values that half of her soul, she would not give up or subvert law, authority, or power. Just as she had misgivings as to the outcome of her father's will but decided to fulfill her obligation, so, too, she feels that Bassanio must fulfill his contracts (both the financial debt and the bond of love), no matter what the outcome. It is because Portia has such a deep feeling for the obligation of contract that she becomes so alarmed when she learns of the Venetians' indifference to it. This concern becomes the generative force for the action of the last third of the play.

Shakespeare underscores that what are at stake are the conditions that insure civilization, those binding forces that make intercourse possible among groups of people and among nations. In the scene that intervenes between Bassanio's and Portia's departures (III. iii), we watch Antonio's arrest. This scene heightens the tension; we hear Shylock spurn pleas that he be merciful. When Shylock leaves and Solanio turns to comfort Antonio, asserting that the Duke will refuse Shylock his forfeiture, Antonio articulates what is at issue:

> The Duke cannot deny the course of law;
> For the commodity that strangers have
> With us in Venice, if it be denied,
> Will much impeach the justice of the state,
> Since that the trade and profit of the city
> Consisteth of all nations.
>
> [III. iii. 26-31]

While it may be, as some have suggested, that Shakespeare's attitude toward usury in this play indicates a long, last, loving look at a fast disappearing medieval concept of commerce and money, this speech shows that he grasped a fundamental principle of free enterprise, namely that commerce and profit are contingent on the legal protection of property rights. Not for a moment does Antonio sanction an action whereby the state would confiscate Shylock's "property," as represented in his own pound of flesh. Nor does Antonio bemoan trading and profit-making as the cause of his distress. Rather, he places the protection of the wealth of nations above his own life. It is the duty of the state to ensure contracts such as that between himself and Shylock. Some commentators have pointed to this scene as evidence that Antonio is all too eager to die. That he is still affected by the melancholy so strongly stressed in the first scene is undeniable, but it should be noted that before the speech just quoted he tries twice to interrupt Shylock to plead for mercy. Failing, he concludes that there will be no mercy forthcoming. . . . Antonio sees no wrong in pleading as an individual to renegotiate a bond; he feels, however, that it would be wrong for the state to force either party to do so.

Mercy, then, seems to be the only way out of a choice between two wrong actions. Either the state abrogates its obligations or Shylock's "cruel contract" must be enforced. Because of this formulation, many readers conclude that the saving of Antonio represents the triumph of mercy over justice. Portia's beautiful speech on the "quality of mercy" easily leads one to see her as the personification of that virtue. Hence the confusion when she shows no mercy toward Shylock. As long as we fail to see that Portia does not represent mercy, this confusion will remain. We must observe that it is justice—law—not mercy that prevails under Portia's direction at the trial. This is not to say that the nature and value of mercy are of no thematic importance. On the contrary, because Portia does not argue that it become a state policy displacing the law, mercy is all the more protected as the higher virtue. Mercy must not function until after adjudication is made and justice is dispensed. (pp. 373-75)

It is important to see that Portia's rescue of Antonio with her reading of the contract (a pound of flesh but not a drop of blood) is not simply a clever trick, demeaning the law by characterizing it as a quagmire in which anyone can get caught, the guilty and the guiltless alike. The turnabout must represent a legal punishment deserved by Shylock; otherwise the trial reveals Venetian law to be a sham. Shylock must be guilty not simply of cruelty, but of some legally punishable fault. And the carefully structured trial reveals that he *is* guilty. With consummate irony, Shakespeare has Shylock's guilt lie in the very concept of contract which he believed his cause represented.

In the first part of the trial Portia manipulates the proceedings so that the case is stated as all Venice has seen it. Although it is "Of a strange nature" [IV. i. 177], the Venetian law cannot impugn Shylock for proceeding. Antonio acknowledges the bond, and she concludes ''Then must the Jew be merciful'' [IV. i. 182]. Here as elsewhere, Shylock misconstrues and takes Portia's use of the word ''must'' to mean compulsion rather than, as she intends, a posing of alternatives. . . . Finally, Portia invokes Christian doctrine:

> Therefore, Jew,
> Though justice be thy plea, consider this,
> That in the course of justice, none of us
> Should see salvation. We do pray for mercy,
> And that same prayer doth teach us all to render
> The deeds of mercy.
>
> [IV. i. 197-202]

It is this New Testament doctrine, of course, that Shylock does not understand. He will live by the law and will ask no forgiveness. If no law compels him, he will not act. . . . Shylock is portrayed as a man blind to the possibility of his own guilt. He does not respond to Portia's arguments in theological terms. Despite Portia's appeal that ''in the course of justice, none of us / Should see salvation,'' he stands firm, convinced of his blamelessness. (pp. 375-76)

Once the appeal to mercy fails, Portia asks if the money cannot be paid. Bassanio answers ''yes,'' but that Shylock will not take twice the sum stated in the bond. Bassanio then asks the Duke to revoke the law:

> And I beseech you
> Wrest once the law to your authority:
> To do a great right, do a little wrong,
> And curb this cruel devil of his will.
>
> [IV. i. 214-17]

But Portia sharply rebukes Bassanio's suggestion:

> It must not be, there is no power in Venice
> Can alter a decree established.
> 'Twill be recorded for a precedent,
> And many an error by the same example
> Will rush into the state. It cannot be.
>
> [IV. i. 218-22]

It is to her husband, Bassanio, that she states most clearly the absolute necessity of preserving the law, of preventing the Duke from doing what Bassanio calls ''a little wrong.'' Bassanio has failed to see the great wrong involved. While a debtor may appeal to his bond holder for mercy, a court cannot compel an alteration of the contract prior to adjudication of the rights involved. This exchange is what first reveals the conflict between Portia's and Bassanio's values, a conflict which will have to be reconciled later. (pp. 376-77)

It is only after she has made it clear that the state must not interfere with the fulfillment of the law and offered Shylock three opportunities to change his mind that Portia renders her final judgment: Antonio must die. Shylock has been offered three alternatives. First, the straightforward appeal to mercy; second, an appeal to take more money than fulfillment would have given him; and finally, a combination of the two. Portia has forced Shylock not only to reveal that he is blind to his own possible guilt but also to state publicly that he will not accept money as payment for the bond. (p. 377)

Before Portia reveals what Shylock's oath implies, she leads him into arguing for a concept of the law which she will then use to judge him. First she tells Shylock: ''For the intent and purpose of the law / Hath full relation to the penalty, / Which here appeareth due upon the bond'' [IV. i. 247-49]. Shylock replies: '''Tis very true'' [IV. i. 250]. Then the final trap. Portia asks Shylock if he has a surgeon handy to stop Antonio's wounds lest he bleed to death [IV. i. 257-58]. Shylock asks, ''Is it so nominated in the bond?'' [IV. i. 259]. Portia presses: ''It is not so express'd, but what of that? / 'Twere good you do so much for charity'' [IV. i. 260-61]. Shylock answers again that he will have nothing but what is stated in the bond.

More is happening here than an exposition of the literal aspects of Shylock's notion of the law. By the time of the trial, everyone assumes that Shylock wants Antonio's life, the pound of flesh being but a metaphor for his intent. What Portia does is to force Shylock to state this hidden meaning of the bond openly. She shows that Shylock is not acting out of usurious, profit-making motives. Rather, she reveals him to be a man filled with hate caused by hate. It is Antonio's mistake to believe that the Jew has only one motive—profit.

Shylock's guilt lies in the use to which he would put the law. The whole scene turns on the word ''blood,'' and it is in Portia's ensuing literal reading of the bond that the reversal is effected. The introduction of the word ''blood'' reveals that Shylock is guilty both of violating a fundamental principle in the law of contract and, more seriously, of attempting to use the law for illegal purposes. When Portia renders her strictest interpretation of the bond, noting the penalties were Shylock to ''shed / One drop of Christian blood'' [IV. i. 309-10], he responds with the simple question, ''Is that the law?'' [IV. i. 314]. After Portia assures him that she can show him the statute, Shylock decides that he is willing after all to settle for the monetary award offered earlier. Significantly, he remains firm in his commitment to the law; he never cries ''foul,'' but accepts Portia's judgment. Once again Bassanio responds immediately, eager to give Shylock the money. But Portia stops him.

Now that Portia has exposed the contract as a sham, it would seem to be enough to declare it null and void, or to settle for a true exchange of value as Bassanio wants to do. But Shylock is guilty of more than attempting to enforce a fraudulent contract. His greater guilt is that he would use the state's judicial system for purposes of private revenge. The reversal here, then, is not in Portia's out-''Shylocking'' Shylock, thereby exposing the harshness of Old Testament justice, but in her demonstration that, just as law and the state would be in jeopardy were Shylock not allowed his day in court, so both would be equally threatened were Shylock not punished for the implicit intent of his bond. . . . Portia must pursue Shylock until it is clear that he owes the court damages not only for bringing a false suit, but for violating a more fundamental law as well. The heart of a system of justice is that it provides alternatives to the bloodletting of private revenge and protects its citizens by punishing murderers. (pp. 377-78)

Portia's role, then, has been to use the law to save the law. The trenchant irony we feel so strongly here is that Portia has displaced Shylock as the spokesman for law. The pure theatricality of the ''courtroom drama'' that Shakespeare uses to such great effect—the purity of conflict, the sudden revelations and reversals—may obscure the fine understanding of the law he shows in his creation of Portia. Far more significant than the scholarly knowledge she carries as Balthazar, student of the great Bellario, is what she uses her knowledge to achieve. On the one hand, she has prevented the Venetians from destroying the sanctity of contract; on the other, she has prevented Shylock from perverting the law to disguise illegal actions. The law and the state are preserved.

It is only after the verdict is rendered that mercy is allowed its proper place and function—"to season justice." Even then, as the Duke joyfully and nobly exhibits the charitable and merciful spirit of his state by pardoning Shylock from a death sentence and ruling that the half of the monies awarded to the state will be reduced to a lesser fine, Portia interrupts to make it clear that the Duke cannot dispose of Antonio's award. Again mercy cannot be dictated to anyone; it must come freely from the individual. Dramatically, this imperative allows Antonio to be the one to stipulate the conditions of the pardon: that Shylock convert to Christianity and that he leave Jessica his money upon his death. A new bond is the condition upon which mercy will be shown, a bond which ensures two comic adjustments. Since the rancor which led Shylock to feel the need for revenge flows from his position as an outsider, the first remedy is to incorporate him into the community. The second injunction forces him to recognize his daughter, the prodigal, whom he had wished dead just as he had sought revenge upon Antonio.

The final comic adjustment is reserved for the fifth act, where the law of contract (bonds) remains the theme. The discrepancy between Portia's and Bassanio's attitudes toward contractual obligations has already been noted. We have seen that Portia has to reprove Bassanio twice during the court proceedings. But there is the third and more famous occasion when Bassanio, in his distress after Antonio is condemned to die, emotionally offers his own life and his wife's to redeem his friend [IV. i. 282-87]. . . . These lines are usually cited as the motivation for her instigation of the "ring trick": it is argued that Portia suddenly realizes that Bassanio places obligations due a friend above those owed a wife and that the relationship must be "clarified." As we have seen, however, Portia does not admit the necessity of a hierarchy: in fact, she defines a harmonious relationship in which the three become one soul. Further, it is she who is most insistent on the obligations of friendship. We have to conclude, then, that during the trial she has become concerned about the relationship—concerned that there is something more threatening than anything the word "friendship" covers, something touching natural law. (p. 379)

Bassanio is characterized throughout as susceptible to the tendencies of what Portia had described as the "hare," the "madness of youth," "the hot temper [which] leaps o'er a cold decree" [I. ii. 18-20]. His passion twice causes him to swear excessive oaths, first in his exchange of vows with Portia and then in his offer to stand for Antonio. In both cases he pledges his own death as a sign of his love. The second occasion is an example of how in the passion of a new circumstance Bassanio would "leap o'er" an earlier commitment. That tendency is captured perfectly in the sequence of the ring. While talking to Portia when she is disguised as Balthazar, he is capable of resisting the request for the ring and of assessing its value, but in the very next moment he cannot resist the direct pleas of

Act V. Scene i. Jessica and Lorenzo. By Samuel Shelley.

Antonio, even though Antonio clearly states what giving up the ring involves: "Let his [Balthazar's] deservings and my love withal / Be valued 'gainst your wive's commandment" [IV. i. 450-51]. Antonio is again manipulating Bassanio's emotions, and Bassanio responds. Throughout the trial scene, as has been observed, Bassanio has shown a propensity to take contractual obligations lightly, begging the Duke to "commit a little wrong" in setting aside the law. Antonio, on the other hand, has shown an understanding of Venice's obligation to ensure civil contracts. His complicity here reveals, therefore, that if he is not overtly antagonistic to Portia, he at least allows his emotions toward the young man who saved his life to devalue the contract between husband and wife. (p. 381)

If we look at the language in that part of the [final] scene where the Christian husbands are taught the costs of slighting their vows, we find that underneath the delightful comic irony and playful bawdry an important process is occurring. That process is the dissolving of old bonds and the establishing of new ones. Burckhardt was the first to establish the connection between this scene and the trial [see excerpt above, 1962]. But as illuminating and suggestive as is his discussion of the language of the play, Burckhardt's failure to observe dramatic interaction among the characters leads him to dismiss the final scene as a mere "renewal" of the old bond. But these are new contracts, the making of which reveals much more than "the true meaning of the equivocations." The first bond is one that has been duly paid. In introducing Antonio, Bassanio says, ". . . this is Antonio, / To whom I am so infinitely bound" [V. i. 134-35]. Portia replies that he *should* feel "bound," since Antonio was "much bound" for Bassanio. Antonio replies, "No more than I am well acquitted of" [V. i. 138]. If Antonio's bond with Shylock is acquitted, in other words, so too is Bassanio's obligation to Antonio. The purpose for which Portia sent Bassanio to Venice has been achieved.

In using the word "acquittal," Antonio is beginning the parental process of "letting-go." . . . The next unbinding comes in the high point of the argument between Portia and Bassanio. The repetition of the word "ring" five times by him and five times by her, as well as the rhythms of their echoing challenges—"If you did know to whom I gave the ring" [V. i. 193], "If you had known the virtue of the ring" [V. i. 199]— lends the sense of a ritual. It is only after Bassanio swears a new oath that Portia relents and affirms the new bond with a second, ceremonial offering of the ring. And Antonio is directly involved in this process with a new oath of his own:

> *Bass.*   Nay, but hear me.
> Pardon this fault, and by my soul I swear
> I never more will break an oath with thee.
>   *Ant.* I once did lend my body for his wealth,
> Which but for him that had your husband's ring
> Had quite miscarried. I dare be bound again,
> My soul upon the forfeit, that your lord
> Will never more break faith advisedly.
>   *Por.* Then you shall be his surety. Give him this,
> And bid him keep it better than the other.
>   *Ant.* Here, Lord Bassanio, swear to keep this ring.
>   [V. i. 246-56]
>   (pp. 382-83)

If, as Anne Barton says, Portia is using the ring trick to teach the men to place friendship below married love, why does Portia involve Antonio in the new bond? Why does he, so to speak, become a member of the wedding? A better explanation of the ring episode, one consistent with all that has been dis-

cussed above, is that both Venetians have to learn the serious consequence of the implied contract in any oath. But just as Portia reveals the fundamental principle of civil law in the Venetian courtroom, so this ritualized exchange of vows invokes a principle of natural law. If that principle displaces Antonio without reincorporating him, the melancholy he has expressed throughout will probably remain. . . . If so, Shakespeare has not created comic resolution. This perceived disharmony, however, is founded on the assumption that the basic unit is the married couple (of which we have three). Recalling that the basic "chord" is a triad, and remembering that the ring passes through Antonio's hands, we should see this last action as a rebinding that incorporates rather than rejects him.

The critical view that suggests a gloomy, withdrawn, or rejected Antonio is contingent on an argument that the so-called valued friendship is either a latent or an explicit homosexual love relationship. Graham Midgley explicitly argues the case for homosexuality: "Antonio is an outsider because he is an unconscious homosexual in a predominantly, and indeed blatantly, heterosexual society" [see excerpt above, 1960]. But the action of the play shows Antonio explicitly involved in the marriage ritual, an involvement that would be unlikely were Shakespeare hinting at a homosexual attachment. Rather, Antonio's is another kind of love, one that can be sanctioned. And if that love is redirected, Antonio can be seen as becoming part of the harmonious family structure. The only possible role for Antonio is meeting these conditions—the one he has been playing from the beginning—is that of father surrogate. (pp. 383-84)

To see Antonio in a fatherly role toward Bassanio explains not only what he must unbind but what he must affirm. It explains both the great love he feels and Bassanio's reciprocal love. And it does, indeed, link Antonio with Shylock, but in such a way as to argue comic, rather than tragic, overtones. The younger generation has freed itself from its elders, and the fathers have been forced to turn control over to their children. Life and regeneration have triumphed over death. (p. 384)

Antonio, who does not even recognize that his melancholy is caused by jealousy of the young wife who robs him of Bassanio's company, reacts by using any excuse to call his "son" away from the new home to his. Since it is clear that Bassanio defines his happiness in terms of his having obtained Portia, Antonio is caught in a loving parent's dilemma: he cannot consciously deny what will bring Bassanio pleasure, so he instinctively manipulates Bassanio indirectly. Portia's actions force Antonio to release Bassanio from old obligations (a bond of love and duty "well acquitted"), recognize that his actions have marred his loved one's happiness ("Your lord will never more break faith advisedly [on my advice]"), and actively accept Portia by giving Bassanio "away" in ceremony to her ("Bassanio, swear to keep this ring"). The forcefulness here hardly suggests reservation or melancholy. Furthermore, after this new bond is established, Portia rewards Antonio with the letter containing good news. His final words are: "Sweet lady, you have given me life and living, / . . . my ships / Are safely come to road" [V. i. 286-88]. "Life and living"—another link to Shylock, but here spoken in an outburst of happiness. For the first time in the play, Antonio has been brought out of his melancholy; he now looks forward to life.

Portia's protection of the law is complete. Civil law has been reaffirmed in Venice and natural law in Belmont. Contract and the courts, the inviolability of personal oaths, and the law of natural succession for the furtherance of life have been assured.

Now the couples can celebrate, knowing that all three fathers have given way to their children. As Gratiano puts it, they must "fear no other thing / So sore, as keeping safe Nerissa's ring" [V. i. 306-07]. They are at last free to go about the serious and merry business of generation. (pp. 384-85)

Alice N. Benston, "Portia, the Law, and the Tripartite Structure of 'The Merchant of Venice'," in Shakespeare Quarterly, Vol. 30, No. 3, Summer, 1979, pp. 367-85.

CAMILLE SLIGHTS   (essay date 1980)

[*In the following excerpt, Slights examines Jessica and assesses her role in* The Merchant of Venice. *After reviewing the negative attitude most critics have adopted towards this character, Slights proposes a reassessment of Jessica's influence on the other characters in the play, stating that the audience is meant "to be glad that Jessica loves rather than hates, to approve her decision to reject her father's values and to ally herself through Lorenzo with those of Portia, but to regret the pain and loss that accompany her choices." Slights also argues that Jessica is neither greedy nor frivolous, as described by Arthur Quiller-Couch (1926), and that although she is disloyal and causes Shylock much pain in this regard, "her transfer of love and loyalty is a conscious, positive choice, involving danger and sacrifice." For further discussion of Jessica's role in* The Merchant of Venice, *see the excerpt by Sigurd Burckhardt (1962).*]

Jessica has not fared well in the criticism of *The Merchant of Venice*. Those who see the play primarily as an exposure of Christian hypocrisy respond sympathetically to Shylock and judge harshly the daughter who deserts him for his Christian enemies. In an extreme version of this view, Sir Arthur Quiller-Couch condemns Shylock's rebellious daughter as "bad and disloyal, a thief; frivolous, greedy, without any more conscience than a cat and without even a cat's redeeming love of home. Quite without heart, on worse than an animal instinct—pilfering to be carnal—she betrays her father to be a light-of-lucre carefully weighted with her sire's ducats" [see excerpt above, 1926]. Much recent criticism rejects a sentimentally sympathetic response to Shylock, but Jessica has not received a compensatory rehabilitation. Though they do not exactly visit the sins of the father on the child, many of the most perceptive critics of the play nevertheless argue that Jessica too, though in a way different from her father, embodies negative values in contrast to the positive values of Portia, Bassanio, and Antonio. In this view, the function of the Jessica-Lorenzo subplot is to illuminate by contrast the exemplary relationship of Portia and Bassanio. . . . (p. 357)

The problem with this moral condemnation is that it contradicts a natural audience response to the marriage and conversion of Shakespeare's gentle Jew. While we must be grateful for the critical erudition and insight that deepen and sharpen our responses, correct our misapprehensions, and unsettle our complacencies, we must question judgments that deny the most obvious emotional force of Shakespearean plots and characters. It is impossible to exaggerate the complexity of Shakespeare's art, but its subtleties normally extend and deepen, rather than contradict, traditional dramatic and narrative conventions. Jessica's part in the plot draws on classical and Elizabethan comic conventions that pit rebellious children against miserly fathers and on romance traditions that elicit approval for beautiful young daughters who disobey repressive fathers for love. It also follows, in general outline, medieval and Renaissance stories which treat sympathetically a Jew's daughter who runs away to marry a Christian. In Shakespeare's version, the ro-

mantic elopement of Jessica and Lorenzo, their association with the imagery of light and music, their acceptance by Portia, and their participation in the harmonies of Belmont are signals for audience acceptance and approval.

And indeed, although much of the detailed commentary on Jessica has been negative, most audiences and readers accept Jessica's escape from Shylock's joyless house to the moonlit garden of Belmont as part of the general comic movement from bondage to freedom, from misfortune to happiness. Such a sympathetic view of Jessica, however, is usually presented in passing, without close analysis of the subplot, and it rarely addresses the question of why the subplot is there at all. Jessica's explicit defenders, moreover, often damn with faint praise. (pp. 357-58)

The important exceptions to these generalizations are the studies that emphasize the play's theological dimensions and see in Jessica's departure from Shylock's house an allegory of the "abandonment of Old Law for New" and "a flight from the devil to salvation" [see excerpt above by Barbara K. Lewalski, 1962]. In these terms, Jessica's repudiation of her biological father for Christian marriage signifies the victory of spirit over flesh, the New Law superseding the Old. From this perspective, the Jessica-Lorenzo plot parallels and foreshadows the fulfillment of law through love in the casket plot and the bond plot.

Such an allegorical reading is surely relevant to a play that raises theological issues so specifically, but it cannot answer fully the moral objections put by sensitive critics to the human situations dramatized. Shylock is a Jew who demands justice, but he is not merely an allegorical figure of the Old Law, or even of its misinterpretation as a code of malicious revenge. In fleeing to Christian marriage from a house that has become a hell, Jessica moves from Judaism to Christianity, but she also deceives, disobeys, robs, and abandons her father. Critics have objected not to the fact of Jessica's conversion, but to the particular circumstances of her elopement. In the view of Sigurd Burckhardt, the love of Jessica and Lorenzo "is lawless, financed by theft and engineered through a gross breach of trust. It is subjected to no test. . . . The ring which ought to seal their love is traded for a monkey. They are spendthrift rather than liberal, thoughtless squanderers of stolen substance; they are aimless, drifting by chance from Venice to Genoa to Belmont" [see excerpt above, 1962]. (p. 359)

I have spent some time describing the controversy surrounding Jessica on the assumption that if we see the critical problem clearly its solution will be inherent in the questions we ask. What emerges from the commentary by the play's most thoughtful readers is that in Jessica Shakespeare has created a character who elicits the audience's good will and yet disturbs it with moral doubts. The design of the play directs us to be glad that Jessica loves rather than hates, to approve her decision to reject her father's values and to ally herself through Lorenzo with those of Portia, but to regret the pain and loss that accompany her choices. A satisfying understanding of Jessica's function in the intricate patterning of *The Merchant of Venice* should take into account both the positive and the negative responses she provokes and explain the significant relation of the joy and love to the pain and loss embodied in her dramatic role.

It is important to emphasize that the tension between our sympathy and our disapproval does not reflect a strain between emotional identification with young love and tough-minded moral condemnation of irresponsible self-gratification: Jessica's defenders as well as her detractors make their cases essentially in moral terms. Nor is it enough to say that Jessica demonstrates the inevitable discrepancy between abstract ideals and their imperfect human realization, giving individual life to Portia's generalization ''That in the course of justice, none of us / Should see salvation'' [IV. i. 199-200]. Certainly Jessica is human rather than a personified ideal, but she is not portrayed in such a way as to emphasize occasional lapses from usual virtue. Unlike Antonio, whose characteristic generosity and Christian charity are thrown into relief by his bitter contempt for Shylock the Jew, Jessica is consistent throughout. The crucial action that constitutes her claim to moral stature and to our good will—her rebellious marriage—is also the source of the uneasiness she causes. Our ambivalent response results not from her imperfectly mixed motives or from the relative impurity of her love for Lorenzo but from the discrepancy between her character and her effect on the society around her, between her intentions and the means by which she implements them, between the nature of her moral choices and their consequences.

Pejorative interpretations, even when couched in terms of character, reflect the difficulty of Jessica's situation more than they reflect her essential nature. The charge that she is greedy, for example, is a judgment on the fact that she steals from her father, not an insight into her natural disposition or basic values. No evidence suggests that she values material wealth excessively. She shares with all the characters in the play a recognition of the need for gold and with all except Portia and Shylock a determination to get it in spite of difficulty and embarrassment. That she wants it to give and to use with love rather than to hoard and to breed for its own sake links her with Portia, Antonio, and Bassanio in contrast with Shylock. Where she differs from the Christians is in the dependency and isolation of her position as Shylock's daughter. Pointing to her predicament does not absolve her from moral responsibility, of course, but it does suggest that her dramatic role is to explore the problematic relations of love and wealth, not to portray ''a greedy woman.''

Jessica's willingness to marry a man without means, in fact, demonstrates relatively little concern with wealth. But, while her marriage is financially imprudent, the suggestion that she is by nature frivolous, reckless, and without conscience is inaccurate. We should not accept Tubal's biased and secondhand account of her honeymoon extravagance (III. i) in preference to Lorenzo's judgment that she is ''wise, fair, and true'' [II. vi. 56] and in preference to Portia's trust in her integrity, implicit in Portia's committing Belmont's household responsibilities to Jessica and Lorenzo while she travels to Venice (III. iv). . . . [Her] mood is sad and reflective rather than thoughtlessly gay in every scene she appears in. Most significantly, her decision to leave her father is not lightly or easily made:

> Alack, what heinous sin is it in me
> To be ashamed to be my father's child!
> But though I am a daughter to his blood
> I am not to his manners: O Lorenzo
> If thou keep promise I shall end this strife.
> Become a Christian and thy loving wife!
>
> [II. iii. 16-21]

Her only soliloquy expresses the pain and moral doubt the decision costs her.

Jessica's acute awareness of the conflict between the loyalty she owes her father and the moral disapproval she feels for his

manners is juxtaposed significantly with Launcelot Gobbo's muddled debate with his conscience in the preceding scene. . . . Like Jessica, Launcelot feels guilty about leaving Shylock, but his reasons are that Bassanio sets a more generous table and gives new liveries [II. ii. 109]; there is no irreconcilable difference in values. Jessica's resolution to escape this conflict by changing herself—becoming a Christian and a loving wife and thus uniting moral, emotional, and familial loyalties—contrasts favorably with Launcelot's decision to deny his conscience for materialistic reasons. Surely Shylock's opinion that she is damned for rebelling against her own flesh and blood (III. i) is no more to be accepted than Launcelot's opinion that she is damned for her Jewish father (III. v).

Eventually Launcelot Gobbo is released from his dilemma externally. When, accompanied by his father, he offers his services to Bassanio, they learn that Shylock has already recommended Launcelot to Bassanio. Jessica's problem does not conveniently evaporate, however, and she must rely on her own courage and ingenuity to escape. The means she takes—defying her father, disguising herself as a boy, and running away with her lover—draw on comic traditions that are part of Shakespeare's stock-in-trade. Her male disguise recalls Julia's [in *Two Gentlemen of Verona*] and anticipates Rosalind's and Viola's recourse to the same protective strategy. . . . In the later comedies, *As You Like It* and *Twelfth Night*, Shakespeare exploits his disguised heroines for the comic possibilities in sexual confusion and places more emphasis on their wit and independence and less on their sensitivity to convention and courage in risking scandal. But he consistently uses the disguise convention to portray his heroines' resourcefulness and vitality and to bring about the self-knowledge and social harmony of his comic endings. (pp. 361-62)

The circumstances of Jessica's elopement, then, associate her with others of Shakespeare's young women who find love by breaking with oppressive traditional authority. Comparing Jessica with them suggests, not that she is shallow and scatterbrained, but that she is distinctively thoughtful. Although her role is relatively small (she has fewer lines than any of the heroines I have mentioned), she realizes more fully her responsibilities and the implications of her decision than do her predecessors. . . . Jessica is impelled by love for Lorenzo and repelled by Shylock's savage vindictiveness. Her love and her judgment agree, and her faith that Lorenzo will prove true is justified by events; her vindication by the future results from her accurate understanding of the present. (p. 363)

But if Jessica is neither greedy nor frivolous, she is undeniably disloyal. She rejects her father and identifies with his enemies. But the point, I think, is that her transfer of love and loyalty is a conscious, positive choice, involving danger and sacrifice. Among Shakespeare's runaway heroines she is strikingly aware of the moral problems implicit in her divided loyalties and of the chances she is taking. She is also the only one to feel her departure as genuine personal loss, for both herself and her father. . . . Jessica understands that she is making a radical and irrevocable break with the past. The firmness of her decision should not deafen us to the poignancy of her parting from Shylock:

> Farewell,—and if my fortune be not crost,
> I have a father, you a daughter, lost.
>
> [II. v. 56-7]

Her willingness to lose a father does not imply that she is pursuing personal happiness in preference to broader social and spiritual values. Her break with her past is precisely a decision to forfeit her isolated security as a rich Jew's daughter in order to become part of the familial, social, and divine harmonies that bind people together in Christian society. (p. 364)

Jessica makes us feel uneasy, then, not because of unworthy values or because of negative qualities intrinsic to her character, but because of the pain she unwittingly but necessarily causes others. *The Merchant of Venice* is less about personal salvation than about human community. The plot does not trace its characters' internal development so much as it explores the ways their lives impinge on each other's, often in unintended and unexpected ways. It is this interaction that makes human law and mercy necessary, and love possible. Jessica's story is neither a precursor of the rash escapade of Jane Austen's Lydia Bennett [in *Pride and Prejudice*] nor an allegory of the granting of the New Covenant. It is the marriage and conversion of one young woman whose most admirable goals are inextricably linked with regrettable consequences and whose most personal choices unavoidably have repercussions on the well-being of others.

When she decides to marry Lorenzo and to become a Christian, Jessica must also renounce Shylock and Judaism. Portia can dissolve the tensions of Bassanio's old and new loyalties, light-heartedly reconciling love and friendship in the ring trick. But Jessica can achieve future love only by breaking violently from the past. Her willingness to change makes fulfillment possible, but the difficulty of her decision and the pathos of Shylock's grief remind us that even positive change may be painful. Although Jessica and Lorenzo consciously acknowledge responsibility for robbing Shylock of his daughter, nothing suggests that they are aware of what Shylock suffers from most— Jessica's taking Leah's ring. Presumably Jessica has never heard of the ring's provenance from the tight-lipped Shylock and has inadvertently touched the one area of her father's life that he responds to in emotional rather than materialistic terms. . . . Shylock's fidelity to Leah's memory sharpens our discomfort at Jessica's betrayal, but it does not obliterate our recognition that life requires growth and the courageous acceptance of new responsibilities.

The destructive impact of a love in itself innocent and good also appears in the linking of the elopement plot with the bond plot. Initially the alternation of Shylock's rage at Jessica's escape with his glee at Antonio's misfortune is comic. But Shylock concentrates his confusion into a monomaniacal quest for revenge. His hatred of Antonio precedes Jessica's betrayal, and his motives are in part coolly practical. . . . But when he rants that his search for Jessica has brought "no satisfaction, no revenge" [III. i. 94], we remember Solanio's worried prediction about Shylock's response to losing his daughter and his ducats: "Let good Antonio look he keep his day / Or he shall pay for this" [II. viii. 25-6]. The suggestion is unmistakable that Jessica's happiness has contributed to Antonio's suffering. This domino effect, by which Jessica's actions have undesired consequences, forces us as audience to contemplate the painful consequences of choices we have approved. In this way, the Jessica and Lorenzo plot complements the main action with a disquieting reminder that our actions may have ugly results we did not intend and sometimes are not even aware of.

The erratic, potentially tragic discrepancy between intention and effect is also present in the story of the bond of flesh, but there Portia's wisdom dispels all problems. When Bassanio's quest for love unintentionally endangers the life of the loving friend who has made his courtship possible, his new love saves his old love. By demonstrating the essential harmony of love and friendship and of justice and mercy, Portia commands our total sympathy and approval. Jessica's role, raising a more problematic conflict between old love and new and between love and law, demands an ambivalent response. She must be a disloyal daughter in order to become a loving wife. . . . Jessica's unlawful love takes her beyond the guidance and protection of social conventions and forces her and Lorenzo to define their own guidelines and create their own bonds of responsibility. . . . Ultimately their faith and fidelity are rewarded by the Venetian state with recognition of their marriage and their financial claim on Shylock. But this implicit legitimization is fortuitous, not, like Portia's means of saving Antonio, inherent in the law itself. As Lorenzo realizes, it is miraculous—manna dropping for starved people—and the implication remains that love and law may be irreconcilable.

By dramatizing the pain and loss inherent in change, Jessica adds a minor chord to the harmonies of the play. But I do not mean to imply that she is properly a tragic character thrust incongruously into a romantic comedy. When she and Lorenzo allude to stories of pagan lovers where struggles between love and external pressures and duties ended tragically, they remind themselves and us of the dangers they themselves have escaped. As an exemplar of change and as a beneficiary of human generosity and kind fortune, Jessica performs a positive function. The changes she initiates cause pain, but they also demonstrate her personal growth and the vitality of the society that accepts her. The actions that expose herself and others to danger also make her and them recipients of unexpected blessings. (pp. 364-66)

> *Camille Slights, "In Defense of Jessica: The Runaway Daughter in 'The Merchant of Venice'," in* Shakespeare Quarterly, *Vol. 31, No. 3, Autumn, 1980, pp. 357-68.*

BARBARA TOVEY (essay date 1981)

[*Like Muriel C. Bradbrook (1951), Tovey contends that the conflict between appearance and reality is a central concern in* The Merchant of Venice, *reflected most obviously in the casket story, but also inherent in Antonio's relationship with Bassanio. Tovey maintains that although on the surface Antonio's love for Bassanio and his willingness to sacrifice himself for his friend's welfare seem noble and sincere, his efforts actually work against Bassanio's best interests. In the critic's words, Antonio's "policy was extremely well-calculated to make Bassanio dependent on him and to elicit from Bassanio feelings of love and indebtedness." Tovey also notes that Antonio's behavior throughout the play— his passivity, his determination to die for his friend after his bond with Shylock comes due, and his desire to have his friend witness his sacrifice—all suggest that he is a Christ-figure, the Christian element of atonement forming a primary quality of his characterization. The critic claims that Portia immediately recognizes the threat Antonio's martyrdom "poses to her married life with Bassanio." She thus regards the trial scene as not only demonstrative of the struggle between Christianity and Judaism, as noted by numerous earlier critics, but also concerned with "the battle between Bassanio's male and female lovers." Portia's victory, Tovey adds, serves a double purpose in this regard, freeing Antonio from his bond with Shylock, thus reuniting the Christian community of Venice, and liberating Bassanio from his "bond" with Antonio by thwarting the merchant's attempt at self-sacrifice. In her overall symbolic interpretation of* The Merchant of Venice, *Tovey postulates that Shakespeare was criticizing Christianity— symbolized by Bassanio's relationship with Antonio—and promoting the ideals of classical antiquity—reflected in Portia and the world of Belmont—to the extent that he saw in Christianity an unhealthy, repressive quality as a necessary result of the guilt and indebtedness demanded of its followers. Although numerous critics beginning with William Hazlitt (1817) have argued that the Christians were the target of Shakespeare's criticism in* The Merchant of Venice, *only Tovey has suggested that the Christian faith itself was the butt of his comedy. Also, for further commentary on the quality of Antonio's love for Bassanio and the related conflict between the merchant and Portia, see the excerpts by John D. Hurrell (1961) and Alice N. Benston (1979).]*

The teaching that appearance often belies reality figures prominently in many Shakespearean plays. It seems fair to say, however, that there is no play in which that teaching is given such frequent explicit utterance as *The Merchant of Venice*. *Measure for Measure* is the only possible rival. In that play there are at least two characters who concretely embody the appearance-reality antithesis. Angelo seems virtuous but is not. The Duke, applying craft against vice, disguises himself as a friar. Contrary to what one might expect, in *The Merchant* there does not seem to be any character who exemplifies the principle that "outward shows" are least themselves. It is true that in the play's first enunciation of the appearance-reality antithesis Antonio says of Shylock:

> An evil soul producing holy witness
> Is like a villain with a smiling cheek,
> A goodly apple rotten at the heart.
> O what a goodly outside falsehood hath!
>
> [I. iii. 99-102]

and this thought is echoed in Bassanio's words:

> I like not fair terms, and a villain's mind.
>
> [I. iii. 179]

However, Shylock has no "goodly outside." He appears to be what he is.

The theme of appearance and reality is most fully developed in the story of the caskets, which turns on this antithesis. The alluring golden and silver caskets contain a death's head and a fool's head, respectively. Portia's portrait is to be found only in the "meagre lead"

> Which rather threaten'st than does promise aught.
>
> [III. ii. 105]

The deceptiveness of appearances is the explicit theme of Bassanio's long speech which immediately precedes his correct choice of the lead casket. . . . Another warning against judging by the eye is to be found in the song depreciating Fancy (amorous inclination), which Portia arranges to have sung while Bassanio is deliberating upon his choice of the caskets. (pp. 215-16)

It is interesting to note that the story of the caskets does not occur in the *Il Pecorone* Tale which is almost certainly Shakespeare's chief source for *The Merchant*. In that story the wooing test is of an entirely different nature. In most respects Shakespeare follows the plot of his source quite closely. The fact that he makes an alteration here is an indication that the casket story has an important function in the play. Some people think that the casket choice is a silly way to decide between the suitors. But the very fact that this is so shows that Shakespeare did not go to the trouble of inserting it into the play because of its excellence as a practical test of love or virtue or intelligence. Clearly he selected it only because of the ample opportunities it afforded for discourse on the subject of appear-

ance and reality. Consequently, one would expect this theme to be of central importance in the play. (p. 216)

In the story of the caskets, then, the theoretical teaching of the play receives an explicit statement. But this statement, if not accompanied by a convincing practical demonstration, has a tendency to strike us as platitudinous. That appearance often belies reality is the kind of principle which almost too readily wins our assent and which easily includes itself in our store of theoretical knowledge. To be able to apply it to particular cases, to be able to recognize actual instances of false "seeming," is, however, a far more difficult matter. Now it is interesting to note that a problem very much akin to that of putting theoretical knowledge into practice forms the opening subject of the first conversation between Portia and Nerissa.

> PORTIA: If to do were as easy as to know what were
> good to do, chapels had been churches, and
> poor men's cottages princes' palaces,—it is a
> good divine that follows his own instruc-
> tions,—I can easier teach twenty what were
> good to be done, than be one of the twenty to
> follow mine own teaching. . . .
>
> [I. ii. 12-17]

Portia tells the truth about herself when she says that it is easier for her to teach others what is good to be done than to follow her own teaching. She, of course, is fully aware of the correct principle to be employed in choosing between the caskets and in saying to Bassanio: "If you do love me, you will find me out" [III. ii. 41], she seems to assent to it. Furthermore, by the device of the song which she causes to have sung before Bassanio makes his choice, she successfully teaches this principle to him. The song gives Bassanio a twofold hint. In the first place, it deprecates "judging by the view." Secondly, the end words in the first rhyming couplet both rhyme with "lead":

> Tell me where is Fancy bred,
> Or in the heart, or in the head?
>
> [III. ii. 63-4]
> (pp. 217-18)

I should like to suggest that Shakespeare places his audience in the position of the suitors. Portia coaches Bassanio concerning the principle which should guide his choice by means of hints. Shakespeare explicitly teaches his audience the theory that governs the play. At the same time, without comment, he confronts the audience with an instance of the theoretical teaching, a character who is the living counterpart of the golden casket. The audience is silently asked to recognize an actual case where appearance and reality are at odds. It is asked to apply the theory of the play to the play itself. It was mentioned earlier that in *Measure for Measure*, another play abounding in statements about the appearance-reality dichotomy, there are at least two characters who exemplify that antithesis. In *The Merchant*, on the other hand, exemplification of the theory seems to be lacking so far as the characters are concerned. Is it possible that Antonio constitutes just such an exemplification? May it be that the story of his relationship with Bassanio concretely embodies the teaching that is explicitly asserted in the narrative of the caskets? I shall argue that this is the case. If I am correct in this contention, the organic connection between these two parts of the play, seemingly only superficially related, will become clear.

On the surface Antonio is presented to us as an exceedingly noble person and as the archetype of the devoted friend. He has bought golden opinions. The characters of the play repeatedly hold him up as a supremely good man. Both the Duke and Gratiano refer to him as: ''royal merchant'' [III. ii. 239 and IV. i. 29]. Salerio says of him: ''A kinder gentleman treads not the earth,—'' [II. viii. 35] and from Solanio we have:

> . . . the good Antonio, the honest Antonio;—
> O that I had a title good enough to keep his
> name company!—
>
> [III. i. 12-14]

It should be remembered, however, that Salerio and Solanio are the Rosencrantz and Guildenstern [in *Hamlet*] of this play. Like the latter two, Salerio and Solanio are exact duplicates of each other, and that, of course, is the reason Shakespeare gives them such similar names. Philistines both, they are clearly intended to serve as examples of the average Venetian. . . . However that may be, nobler and more intelligent characters also praise Antonio and his love for Bassanio in the highest terms. Lorenzo refers to their friendship as ''god-like amity'' [III. iv. 3] and to Portia, who is about to set out to rescue Antonio, he says:

> But if you knew to whom you show this honour,
> How true a gentleman you send relief,
> How dear a lover of my lord your husband,
> I know you would be prouder of the work
> Than customary bounty can enforce you. . . .
>
> [III. iv. 5-9]

[Certainly] it seems that Antonio's devotion to Bassanio and his willingness to endanger his own life for his friend's sake well merit these praises.

Let us consider the relationship between Antonio and Bassanio more closely. . . . Now it is made clear to us that for a considerable period of time prior to the opening of the play, Antonio had been lending large sums of money to the impecunious Bassanio without making any effort to secure repayment. Bassanio speaks of:

> the great debts
> Wherein my time (something too prodigal)
> Hath left me gag'd: to you Antonio
> I owe the most in money and in love.
>
> [I. i. 128-31]

Lending Bassanio a great deal of money would have been entirely appropriate, of course, if the latter had been using these sums to finance some worthwhile project, such as acquiring an education or establishing himself in business. But it is plain that Bassanio has been using the money for rather frivolous purposes. . . . There is no reason to think that he has been engaging in debauchery, but he has been self-indulgent. His manner of life is unnecessarily grand. He maintains numerous servants whom he decks out in fancy liveries (II. ii) and he feasts his many friends at sumptuous dinner parties where they are entertained by professional masquers. . . . When he goes to court Portia he falsely believes it necessary to equip himself with an elaborate retinue; in fact, Portia would have gladly wed him even if he had come alone. At first glance it seems generous of Antonio to finance this expensive way of life, particularly since he had litle reason to expect repayment, but thinking more carefully, we may well wonder whether he was acting in a way that was calculated to serve Bassanio's long run interests. Antonio was spoiling Bassanio. He was encouraging a young person with slender financial means and expensive tastes to accustom himself to a manner of life that he could not possibly afford to maintain. This may lead us to

question whether he had Bassanio's real welfare in mind. On the other hand, his policy was extremely well-calculated to make Bassanio dependent on him and to elicit from Bassanio feelings of love and indebtedness. Antonio buys Bassanio's love by lavishing money upon him. When the play begins Bassanio's affections are literally mortgaged to Antonio.

As the play opens we find Antonio in the midst of a conversation with Salerio and Salanio. Apparently the latter two have observed that Antonio is depressed, have complained that he is dull company and have inquired into the cause of his melancholic mood. . . . His companions propose several theories concerning the cause of his sadness. Salerio thinks that Antonio is worrying about the ships he has at sea and fearing that his merchandise may be lost. This is emphatically rejected by Antonio. Solanio suggests he is in love, to which Antonio replies ''Fie, fie!'' [I. i. 46]. And, indeed, throughout the course of the play there appears to be no woman whatsoever in Antonio's life. . . . Gratiano theorizes that Antonio is feigning sadness in order to gain a reputation for wisdom and gravity, but this piece of silliness is ridiculed by both Antonio and Bassanio. So Shakespeare begins the play by setting the audience a problem to solve. Why is Antonio sad? The explanations offered by the characters are in each case rejected and no correct explanation is ever explicitly put forward. This seemingly strange circumstance has caused some commentators to speculate that the episode of Antonio's melancholy is a relic of an earlier version of the play which Shakespeare forgot to delete. Such speculation is misguided. Shakespeare has provided his audience with the resources to solve the problem. He has gone out of his way to let the reader know that shortly before the opening of the play Antonio had received a piece of news which might well account for his sadness. Bassanio had informed him of his intention to become a suitor for Portia's hand. Thus the conversation between Antonio and Bassanio which concludes scene one does not begin, as one might expect, with Bassanio's breaking the news of his nuptial intentions to Antonio. That would appear to be the most straightforward way to start their dialogue as well as the most dramatic. But Shakespeare foregoes the drama and instead makes Antonio begin the conversation:

> Well, tell me now what lady is the same
> To whom you swore a secret pilgrimage—
> That you to-day promis'd to tell me of?
>
> [I. i. 119-21]

Whether or not Antonio is consciously aware that the threatened loss of Bassanio is the cause of his sadness is difficult to say. He may be telling the truth when he concludes his opening speech with the statement that he has much ado to know himself. He may lack self-knowledge. On the other hand, even if he had clearly articulated to himself the nature of his feeling for Bassanio, he would certainly have a motive to conceal from his companions the real cause of his sorrow. John Russell Brown, who correctly identifies Bassanio's imminent departure as the reason for Antonio's sadness [see Additional Bibliography], also points out that when Solanio suggests to Antonio that he is in love, he may have gotten close to the real cause of the melancholy. This may be the reason why Antonio responds with the words ''Fie, fie!'' Antonio's reproachful answer is, it seems to me, subject to two interpretations, not necessarily mutually exclusive. He may be angrily rejecting the suggestion that he is in love with a woman. It is the other possibility which I take it Brown has in mind, namely, that at some level of awareness Antonio feels his love for Bassanio is something to be ashamed of; hence his indignant reproach when it is suggested to him that he is in love. (pp. 219-23)

Antonio recognizes, of course, that Bassanio's intention to sue for Portia's hand is inalterable. He knows that any attempt to prevent Bassanio from going to Belmont, or even a refusal wholeheartedly to assist him, would merely alienate him. The wisest course for Antonio at this point is to salvage what he can. This goal will be best accomplished by doing everything possible to intensify the love and the sense of indebtedness that Bassanio feels toward him. The most effective way to increase Bassanio's love and gratitude is to make a sacrifice for his sake. Borrowing money at interest constitutes for Antonio a moral sacrifice much more than a financial one. His belief that usury is a moral abomination provides the only justification for his extraordinarily harsh treatment of Shylock. Now, merely in order to outfit Bassanio with an elegant entourage, he is willing to pay Shylock interest, thereby lending support to the man and the institution he so bitterly condemns. (p. 223)

When Shylock proposes to remit interest on condition that the penalty for forfeiture be a pound of Antonio's flesh, the latter's reaction is very revealing. One would expect a normal person at least initially to wince at such a horrible proposal, even although he might subsequently accept it on the grounds that there was no danger of forfeiture. . . . But Antonio instantly, joyfully, and even gratefully accepts Shylock's terms. He knows Shylock hates him and has cause to wish his death. But seemingly he never gives any consideration to the possibility that Shylock is angling for his life. Despite the fact that he himself has just referred to Shylock as "An evil soul, producing holy witness," "a villain with a smiling cheek" [I. iii. 99, 100], he apparently takes at face value Shylock's assurance that the penalty would not be exacted even in case of forfeiture. (pp. 223-24)

Antonio's behavior might well appear strange even if he had possessed absolute assurance that his ships would come safely in before the bond's expiration. But of course he had no such assurance. . . . As an experienced merchant, Antonio should have realized that he had no complete certainty concerning the timely return of his ships. He is represented as being extraordinarily liberal with his money; surely he was not overcome by a niggardly desire to economize by avoiding payment of the interest. Why then is he so imprudent as to assent to Shylock's terrible terms? Why does he not insist upon a bond secured by monetary guarantees rather than his own flesh? I suggest it is because the proposal that his life be surety for the bond gratifies Antonio's desire to make Bassanio appreciate his willingness to sacrifice himself for Bassanio's sake. Antonio seems to think that Shylock is doing him a favor in offering him this opportunity. It may be that, unwittingly, Shylock is doing precisely this.

After the conclusion of the contract between Antonio and Shylock at the end of Act I, the audience does not again see Antonio and Bassanio in each other's presence until the courtroom scene in Act IV. However, Shakespeare employs Salerio to describe the scene of their parting on board the vessel that is about to carry Bassanio to Belmont. He says:

> I saw Bassanio and Antonio part,
> Bassanio told him he would make some speed
> Of his return: he answered, "Do not so,
> Slubber not business for my sake Bassanio,
> But stay the very riping of the time,
> And for the Jew's bond which he hath of me—
> Let it not enter in your mind of love:

> Be merry, and employ your chiefest thoughts
> To courtship, and such fair ostents of love
> As shall conveniently become you there."
> And even there (his eye being big with tears),
> Turning his face, he put his hand behind him,
> And with affection wondrous sensible
> He wrung Bassanio's hand, and so they parted.
> [II. viii. 36-49]

Solanio appends the comment: "I think he only loves the world for him" [II. viii. 50]. This is an extraordinarily moving account. Antonio's love for Bassanio appears to be wholly selfless. Yet, as Allan Bloom points out [in his *Shakespeare's Politics*], the scene ". . . also reveals the pretense in Antonio's selflessness; Bassanio is reminded of the risks his friend is taking for him when Antonio tells him to forget them. The scene cuts in both directions."

The element of pretense in Antonio's selflessness becomes fully apparent in the letter that he writes to Bassanio after the bond has become forfeit. . . . Such a letter is calculated to make Bassanio spend the rest of his life in remorseful remembrance. That this is indeed Antonio's intention is borne out by his courtroom admonition:

> You cannot better be employed, Bassanio,
> Than to live still and write mine epitaph.
> [IV. i. 117-18]

Hereafter Bassanio's function in life will be to serve as apostle to the "crucified" Antonio, who died for his sake. (pp. 224-25)

The most appalling aspect of Antonio's letter is his stated wish that Bassanio be actually present to witness his sacrificial death. . . . This wish is expressed even more forcibly in the next scene. Having failed to obtain a hearing from Shylock, Antonio resigns himself to death, saying:

> —pray God Bassanio come
> To *see* me pay his debt, and then I care not.
> [III. iii. 35-6]

Bassanio is supposed to watch while Antonio dies in agony in order to discharge the debt incurred on Bassanio's behalf. Never does Antonio consider what effect such a sight will have upon Bassanio's future happiness. . . . Had Antonio genuinely cared about Bassanio's welfare, he would have done everything in his power to keep Bassanio away from the scene of his death. More, he would have attempted to mitigate Bassanio's sense of guilt by reminding him of the truth, namely, that Bassanio had tried to prevent him from accepting Shylock's terms and had warned him concerning Shylock's intentions. Antonio would have emphasized that it was *he* who had misjudged Shylock's motives and that the responsibility for signing the bond was his and his alone. He does just the opposite. Bidding farewell to his friend in the courtroom, he twice points out that Bassanio has been the cause of his undoing:

> Give me your hand, Bassanio: fare you well,
> Grieve not that I am fall'n to this *for you;*
> [IV. i. 265-66]

> Repent but you that you shall lose your friend
> And he repents not that he pays *your debt.*
> [IV. i. 278-79]

What Antonio does here is similar to what he did in his shipboard parting from Bassanio. We have already seen that on that occasion he reminded Bassanio of his indebtedness to him in the very act of telling him to forget. In the courtroom he admonishes Bassanio not to grieve while showing him that he has, indeed, great cause for grief. Judged by classical standards, Antonio is not a true friend.... But the judgment on Antonio may be different if the standards employed are Christian rather than classical. Christians are constantly reminded that Christ died in order to atone for their sins; in Christian art and in Christian churches His death is figured everywhere. In return the faithful owe Him boundless love, gratitude and repentance. Antonio's behavior is in some respects an imitation of Christ's. It would not have appeared noble to the ancients, but it is understandable that Christian audiences regard it as a manifestation of the highest love.

We have already remarked on Antonio's imprudence in initially assenting to Shylock's dangerous terms. After his ships have been (apparently) lost, he continues to display what seems to be a lack of good judgment.... After the bond falls due, Antonio's encounters with Shylock are marked by a strange passivity on the former's part. On the eve of the trial he is let out of prison in order that he may plead with Shylock for mercy (III. iii), but he makes no serious effort to get a hearing from his creditor. Twice he asks Shylock to listen to him; twice Shylock refuses. Without attempting any statement of his case Antonio then gives up, saying: "Let him alone, I'll follow him no more with bootless prayers" [III. iii. 19-20]. In the trial scene, prior to the entrance of the disguised Portia, he makes three speeches, each of them characterized by an attitude of passive resignation to his fate.... As Bloom remarks, he seeks martyrdom. In his farewell speech to Bassanio he says that Fortune has been kinder to him than to most men:

> it is still her use
> To let the wretched man outlive his wealth,
> To view with hollow eye and wrinkled brow
> An age of poverty: from which ling'ring penance
> Of such misery doth she cut me off.
>
> [IV. i. 268-72]

The wealth Antonio has really outlived is not his lost shipping, but his close association with Bassanio. The age of poverty from which death cuts him off is a life without Bassanio's company. By dying for his friend, he wins a victory over his rival, Portia, and regains what he fears he has lost, Bassanio's love.

As soon as she hears of Antonio's predicament, Portia clearly recognizes the threat that his imminent martyrdom poses to her married life with Bassanio. She correctly diagnoses that Bassanio will be regarded by himself and others as the culprit in the affair [III. ii. 301-06]. She realizes that if Antonio is allowed to offer himself up as a sacrificial victim, Bassanio will never again enjoy tranquility of mind. More specifically, he will not be able to look at her without thinking that it was on her account that he wrought the destruction of his devoted friend.... This outcome she is determined to prevent. Hence she sets out for Venice to save Antonio and, by saving him, her marriage with Bassanio.

The courtroom is the scene of two struggles. What is explicit and on the surface is the war between Jew and Christian, the Old Law and the New. Beneath the surface there is another conflict: the battle between Bassanio's male and female lovers. Portia has at her disposal the legal means that would enable her immediately to dismiss Shylock's claim. Part of her reason for not doing so is that she wishes to bring out in the open the conflict between Antonio and herself. She lets Antonio think he is on the verge of making the supreme sacrifice for his

friend. It was only under these circumstances that he would permit himself the luxury of comparing his love for Bassanio with hers:

> Commend me to your honourable wife,
> Tell her the process of Antonio's end,
> Say how I lov'd you, speak me fair in death:
> And when the tale is told, bid her be judge
> Whether Bassanio had not once a love.
>
> [IV. i. 273-77]

Subtly Antonio suggests that his love is superior to Portia's. It is he who is laying down his life for Bassanio. Greater love hath no man than this. She makes no comparable sacrifice. The irony is that Portia, who to the audience now appears to be rendering judgment against Antonio, in his mind will ultimately be compelled to render judgment against herself ("... bid her be judge"). (pp. 226-29)

The implicit comparison between the two loves elicits from Bassanio the desired response. Whether consciously or unconsciously, he realizes that Antonio is asking him to state which of the pair he loves the best. He replies:

> Antonio, I am married to a wife
> Which is as dear to me as life itself,
> But life itself, my wife, and all the world,
> Are not with me esteem'd above thy life.
> I would lose all, ay sacrifice them all
> Here to this devil, to deliver you.
>
> [IV. i. 282-87]

Portia is dear, but Antonio is nearer and dearer. In fact, Bassanio's preference for Antonio could hardly be stated in starker terms. If he were in a position to choose which one should be sacrificed and which one should be saved, it would be Portia, not Antonio, who would fall victim to Shylock's knife. If Bassanio could have his way, his voluntary redemption by Antonio would be replaced by a compulsory redemption of Antonio by Portia. This is Antonio's moment of triumph. It is for this that he has been willing to lay down his life. (pp. 229-30)

Both prior to and during the trial Antonio has presented himself as the redeemer of Bassanio's debt. Twice he has said that he is dying in order to pay that debt. Portia herself has referred to the fact that Bassanio has been "dear bought" [III. ii. 313]. For the sake of retaining Bassanio's love, Antonio has bound himself to Shylock. In turn, Bassanio has become "infinitely bound" to Antonio [V. i. 135]. At the conclusion of the trial both bonds have been dissolved. The tables have been turned, not only on Shylock, but also on Antonio. He is no longer cast in the role of the redeemer. It is now Portia who is *his* saviour and benefactor, and as the Duke says, he is "much bound" to her [IV. i. 407]. (p. 230)

However, Portia's project is not yet complete. Antonio has threatened her marriage and Bassanio, in preferring his friend to her, has been guilty of a form of conjugal infidelity. Bassanio must be chastised and Antonio chastened in order to insure that this offense will never again be repeated. Portia accomplishes these ends through the device of obtaining from Bassanio the ring with which she had previously wed herself to him and from which he had been cautioned never to part.... Portia's placing of her ring on Bassanio's finger on their wedding day symbolizes the fact that she gives herself to him sexually. When he removes the ring and returns it to her, he performs an act of sexual renunciation.... Bassanio initially refuses Portia's request for the ring. It is only after her departure that Antonio persuades him to yield it:

> My Lord Bassanio, let him have the ring,
> Let his deservings and my love withal
> Be valued 'gainst your wife's commandement.
>
> [IV. i. 449-51]

In asking Bassanio to place a higher value on his love than on Portia's "commandement" Antonio again reveals the competitive situation that exists between them. And once more he wins the competition.

Act V, which is laid in Belmont, opens with a scene of great lyric loveliness in which Lorenzo and Jessica praise the beauty of the moonlit night. The theme of their opening conversation, however, is that of infidelity in love. They list four pairs of unhappy lovers: Troilus and Cressida, Pyramus and Thisbe, Aeneas and Dido, and Jason and Medea. In the case of three of these pairs the cause of the unhappiness was the faithlessness of one of the partners. Lorenzo then refers to Jessica's infidelity to her father and she concludes the conversation by playfully accusing him of making false vows to her. The little exchange between these two is a prelude to the confrontation later in the act between Portia and Bassanio over the missing ring. . . . Portia explicitly accuses [Bassanio] of sexual infidelity [V. i. 208] and she proceeds to punish him by making him think that she, in her turn, has been unfaithful [V. i. 259]. John Russell Brown sees this episode as a comic statement of the appearance-reality theme, "for despite appearance Bassanio is really true to Portia." The irony is that beneath his real truth there is yet another, deeper level of reality upon which he has been untrue. Antonio is more correct than he realizes when he says "I am the unhappy subject of these quarrels" [V. i. 238]. Antonio's courtroom triumph over Portia is now reversed. Bassanio swears to his wife by his soul: "I never more will break an oath with thee" [V. i. 248]. And Antonio for the second time becomes the surety for Bassanio's obligation; this time it is his soul, not his body, that is the forfeit. His yielding up of Bassanio is immediately rewarded by Portia. She partly recompenses him for his emotional loss by informing him that three of his argosies "Are richly come to harbour suddenly" [V. i. 277]. Antonio emerges from the whole affair far wealthier than he entered it. But he has lost that which he valued more than his ships.

It has been widely recognized that the quarrel between Shylock and Antonio is a depiction of the conflict between the principles of Judaism and Christianity, between the Old Law and the New. There can be no question that, just as Shylock stands for Judaism with its emphasis upon obedience to the law, so Antonio represents Christianity with its corresponding stress upon the virtues of love, charity and self-sacrifice. Not only do Antonio's actions reflect Christian principles; at numerous points in the play he seems to be identified with the figure of Christ. (pp. 230-32)

Shakespeare's play is generally regarded as illustrating the superiority of the New Law to the Old. As Lewalski points out "it culminates in the final defeat of the Old Law and the symbolic conversion of the Jew" [see excerpt above, 1962]. It would be difficult to disagree with this estimate. But if I am substantially correct in my assessment of Antonio's behavior, the play also contains a veiled criticism of Christianity, a criticism which might be regarded as stemming either from the point of view of Machiavellian realism or from that of classical antiquity. The defectiveness of Antonio's love for Bassanio

perhaps symbolizes what Shakespeare takes to be a corresponding flaw in the principles of Christianity. Now the defectiveness of Antonio's love does not consist primarily in the fact that it is the love of one male for another; the flaw in that love is rather its possessiveness. It is not wholly directed toward the well-being of the beloved one; it aims instead at securing from him the maximum return of love and gratitude. If Antonio had been allowed to sacrifice himself, Bassanio would have incurred an enormous indebtedness which could only have been repaid by a lifetime of remorseful gratitude. The payment of that debt would have poisoned for him and for Portia the earthly paradise symbolized by Belmont. Just so, Shakespeare may be suggesting, the Christian, who lives with the constant reminder of the enormity of the sacrifice made for him by Christ, is prevented from fully experiencing the joys of this world. The gratitude and repentance elicited by that sacrifice deflect him from the pursuit of his natural good on this earth.

I have argued that the courtroom scene, which appears to be exclusively a struggle between Shylock and Antonio, is in reality also a battle between Antonio and Portia, a battle that is waged for the soul of Bassanio. If Antonio stands for Christianity, as surely he does, we must now ask ourselves what it is that Portia represents. Bloom correctly says of Belmont: "It is pagan; everyone there speaks in the terms of classical antiquity. . . . The themes of conversation and the ideas current have an ancient source." Most notably, the distinction between appearance and reality, which is of central importance in Belmont, has its roots in the philosophies of Parmenides and Plato. In Belmont Lorenzo and Jessica gaze upon the beauties of the celestial bodies; for Plato such activity is a metaphor for philosophizing. Lorenzo's famous speech on the music of the spheres reflects the teachings of Pythagoras and Plato [V. i. 58-65]. In her first conversation with Portia, Nerissa echoes Aristotle's theory that virtue and happiness consist in following the mean [I. ii. 3-9]. In maintaining that the best kind of friends are similar to one another, Portia expounds one of the themes of the classical teaching about friendship [III. iv. 11-18]. Portia herself is named after the wife of the famous Roman, Marcus Brutus. It is reasonable to assume, then, that in her confrontation with the Christ-like figure of Antonio, Portia represents the spirit of classical antiquity. (pp. 233-34)

Plutarch describes the Roman Portia as "being addicted to philosophy" and "full of an understanding courage." Her father was Cato the Younger, a philosopher of the Stoic school, who committed suicide. According to Plutarch, he spent the last evening of his life discussing philosophy, warmly defending the Stoic thesis "that the good man only is free, and that all wicked men are slaves." Just prior to his death he is reported to have read three times over Plato's dialogue on the soul, the *Phaedo*. We have already mentioned that themes taken from classical philosophy figure prominently in the conversations which take place in Belmont. Remembering these things, let us consider the possible significance of the fact that Portia is an heiress "richly left" [I. i. 161]. Although I cannot here substantiate the claim, I believe that Boccaccio in *The Decameron* frequently uses monetary wealth as a symbol for the treasures of classical philosophy, and in this I think Chaucer follows him. It would be particularly appropriate if Portia's inherited wealth had the same significance in view of the fact that the Roman woman after whom she is named literally did inherit the riches of classical philosophy from her father. If this is what Portia's wealth is meant to represent, then what appears to be a somewhat mercenary desire on Bassanio's part to get his hands on her money would be explained and redeemed. The significance of his parting with Antonio would also be deepened. If Portia's riches stand for classical philosophy, Antonio's wealth may signify the teachings of Christianity. Bassanio's separation from Antonio and his union with Portia would then represent an abandonment of Christianity for the sake of classical philosophy.

Portia is presented to us as a person of the highest intelligence. She controls the action of the play. It is she who brings it about that Bassanio chooses the correct casket, she who breaks Shylock and saves Antonio, she who delivers Bassanio from his indebtedness to his friend. Without her intervention in the trial the play would have had a tragic ending. *The Merchant* is a comedy precisely because it exemplifies the rule of wisdom. There are certain analogies between Portia's behavior and that of the philosopher ruler as described by Plato in the *Republic*. Plato's philosopher is compelled to cease gazing upon the heavenly bodies and to descend into the cave where he must take upon himself the burden of ruling. In Shakespeare's play Belmont is the place where the heavenly order is an object of admiration. Portia is compelled to make a descent from Belmont (literally, "beautiful mountain") and to enter the city of Venice in order to rule it and to save it. In the *Republic* the rule of the philosopher king has a double purpose. The first is to bring about the well-being of the city. The second is to drag from the cave those potential philosophers who are capable of being liberated from the shadowy realm of politically authoritative opinion. In journeying to Venice, Portia also has two main purposes. She wants, first of all, to save Antonio from Shylock. In other words, she defends Christianity, the religion of the city, against its attacker. By stripping Shylock of his wealth, his power and his religion, she weakens, if not annihilates, the power of Christianity's opponents. Although the means are harsh, it can be said that she benefits Venice by unifying it. Her second purpose is to free Bassanio from Antonio, and in so doing to emancipate the potential philosopher from the religion of his city. It is this action that corresponds to the philosopher's dragging of the prisoner from the cave. Having accomplished these goals, she departs from the city, ascending again to Belmont, with Bassanio in her train.

As Bloom has pointed out, Portia is not characterized by undue reverence either for the law or for her father's will. She violates the spirit of his will by giving Bassanio a double hint concerning the correct casket. In order to entrap Shylock, she violates the canons of good legal proceeding; in the narrow sense of the term her dealings with him are unfair.... But Portia is not aiming at a compromise. She wants to entice Shylock into making a criminal attempt upon Antonio's life so that he will be liable to the penalties for a felonious action. Had she wished, she could have pointed out that the bond was illegal at the outset of the proceedings. She could have immediately threatened Shylock with the law that punishes by forfeiture of life and property any alien making an attempt upon the life of a Venetian citizen.... Portia's great speech exhorting Shylock to be merciful is not motivated by any hope that he will comply.... Before she arrives in the courtroom, [she] has ample evidence that any attempt to move Shylock by persuasion will be futile. She makes the plea in order that he may reject it; he will then be debarred from pleading for mercy for himself. Portia manipulates the law. She is less than scrupulously fair. But her ultimate purposes are beneficent. Her exclusive concern is the achievement of what is good. She uses both law and religion to achieve her ends, but she stands above and outside of them. In this respect, also, she resembles the Platonic philosopher.

The conflict between Judaism and Christianity appears to be the dominant theme of *The Merchant of Venice*. Much less obvious, but of equal or greater importance, I would suggest, is the theme of the conflict between Christianity and classical philosophy, which is embodied in the silent struggle between Portia and Antonio for Bassanio. Shakespeare indicates what he conceives to be the proper solution of this conflict. Within the city, philosophy will be Christianity's ally and defender. In return, Christianity should release its hold over those gifted young persons who are capable of making an ascent from the cave. (pp. 235-37)

> *Barbara Tovey, "The Golden Casket: An Interpretation of 'The Merchant of Venice'," in* Shakespeare as Political Thinker, *edited by John Alvis and Thomas G. West, Carolina Academic Press, 1981, pp. 215-38.*

NORMAN RABKIN   (essay date 1981)

[*In the following excerpt, Rabkin applies to* The Merchant of Venice *his assessment of the nature of modern criticism, questioning in the process the validity of any critical methodology that is based on thematic formulations and seeks to identify a literary work's "meaning," in the sense that any work of writing contains a central, dominant meaning to the exclusion of all other readings of that work. Rabkin claims that* The Merchant of Venice *clearly shows the inadequacy of interpretations that posit one set of terms as relevant to Shakespeare's meaning and disregard other information we gather from the drama. He notes this failure on both sides of the critical debate over the play, finding faults with the so-called Christian or allegorical reading—that the drama depicts the triumph of mercy, love, and charity over justice, hate, and possessiveness—and the so-called ironic reading—that it demonstrates the Christians' essential duplicity and insincerity, that mercy or love is never realized in either Venice or Belmont, and that Shylock is merely a scapegoat figure. Rabkin takes issue with both of these interpretations to the extent that each leaves us with doubts and impressions unaccounted for—indeed, often purposely repressed or ignored—but which nonetheless are part of our experience of the play. After some rather theoretical commentary on the nature of aesthetic criticism in the twentieth century, Rabkin argues in favor of the theory, proposed by John Dewey and Kenneth Burke, that literature should be approached as an experience, our response to which is "quintessentially" like our response to life, "characterized by process, tension, resistance, and an ineffable sense of integrity." Although he claims that such plays as* The Merchant of Venice *do indeed have "an autonomous, coherent, and meaningful whole," Rabkin asserts that, like life itself, that meaning resists definition. He thus concludes that "*The Merchant of Venice *is a model of our experience, showing us that we need to live as if life has meaning and rules, yet insisting that the meaning is ultimately ineffable and the rules are provisional."*]

The power of *The Merchant of Venice* has moved actors and audiences, critics and readers to interpretations opposed so diametrically that they seem to have been provoked by different plays. Most disagreements have centered on character.... [Critical] descriptions of Shylock range from a "malevolence ... diabolically inhuman" whom Shakespeare "clearly detested" [see essays by Paul N. Siegel and John W. Draper in the Additional Bibliography] to a "scapegoat," an instinctively generous man who reminds his tormentors of the wickedness which they possess in greater measure than he [see excerpt above by Harold C. Goddard, 1951]. Inevitably Portia has aroused responses similarly at odds, seeming to many the epitome of the romantic heroine, to some virtually a saint, and to others no more than a "callous barrister" with a trump card up her sleeve; ... Antonio [is] a model of Christian gentleness

Act V. Scene i. Lorenzo and Jessica. By William Hodges. The Department of Rare Books and Special Collections, The University of Michigan Library.

and an underground Shylock, Bassanio a romanticized lover and a heartless money-grubber. Similarly Portia's use of the law to defeat Shylock has been seen by some as a brilliant and just device, by others as a malicious and unnecessary piece of conniving.

A typical contention flourishes about the scene in which Shylock, provoked to swear vengeance by his daughter's defection and her plundering of his household, learns from Tubal that one of Antonio's ships is lost. To suggest the complexity of our responses to Shylock at this point I need only remind the reader that he justifies his savage commitment to revenge by claiming it as the mechanical and therefore normal human response to injury, and that the claim, thus reflecting an impoverished sensibility, is the climax of his moving appeal to universal brotherhood: "I am a Jew. Hath not a Jew eyes?" [III. i. 58-9]. From moment to moment, even simultaneously, we respond to signals of Shylock's injured fatherhood, of his role as heavy father, of his lighthearted mistreatment at the hands of the negligible Salerio and Solanio, of his motiveless malignity, and we try hopelessly to reduce to a single attitude our response to his self-defining scorn for Antonio, whose combination of generosity, passivity, sensibility, and spitting hatred has itself already led us to mixed feelings.

> SHY. I thank God, I thank God. Is it true, is it true?
> TUB. I spoke with some of the sailors that escap'd the wrack.

> SHY. I thank thee, good Tubal, good news, good news! Ha, ha! [Heard] in Genoa?
> TUB. Your daughter spent in Genoa, as I heard, one night fourscore ducats.
> SHY. Thou stick'st a dagger in me. I shall never see my gold again. Fourscore ducats at a sitting, fourscore ducats!
> TUB. There came divers of Antonio's creditors in my company to Venice that swear he cannot choose but break.
> SHY. I am very glad of it. I'll plague him, I'll torture him. I am glad of it.
> TUB. One of them show'd me a ring that he had of your daughter for a monkey.
> SHY. Out upon her! Thou torturest me, Tubal. It was my turkis, I had it of Leah when I was a bachelor. I would not have given it for a wilderness of monkeys.
>   [III. i. 102-23]

More clearly evocative of laughter at Shylock's obsessions and speech mannerism than other parts of the scene, these lines nevertheless engage us in a kaleidoscopic shift of emotion and touch us at the end. At this point in Shakespeare's career his ability to create characters with authentic voices and to effect mercurial changes in his audience's emotions leaped beyond what he had been able to do earlier. . . . [Yet,] critic after critic, rather than acknowledging the welter of our responses, insists that this scene reveals a clear and simple truth about Shylock's martyred humanity or his comic villainy.

Such radical disagreements between obviously simplistic critics testify to a fact about their subject that ought to be the point of departure for criticism. Instead, critics both bad and good have constructed strategies to evade the problem posed by divergent responses. Some blame Shakespeare, suggesting that his confusion accounts for tension in the work and its audience. Others appeal to a narrow concept of cultural history which writes off our responses as anachronistic, unavailable to Shakespeare's contemporaries because of their attitudes toward usury or Jews or comedy. Still others suggest that, since the plays are fragile confections designed to display engaging if implausible characters, exegetical criticism is misplaced. Though all of these strategies attract modern practitioners, they have lost ground before the dominant evasion, the reduction of the play to a theme which, when we understand it, tells us which of our responses we must suppress. (pp. 5-8)

My chief concern here, as I said above, is not with such dismal stuff but rather with a less obviously procrustean kind of criticism which, accepting the play as a whole, attempts to account for its unity without expelling characters or issues or plot. The new consensus is laconically summarized by Frank Kermode:

> *The Merchant of Venice* is "about" judgment, redemption and mercy; the supersession in human history of the grim four thousand years of unalleviated justice by the era of love and mercy. It begins with usury and corrupt love; it ends with harmony and perfect love. And all the time it tells its audience that this is its subject; only by a determined effort to avoid the obvious can one mistake the theme of *The Merchant of Venice*.

In this view, developed by [various critics] . . . , the wealth so mechanistically prized by Shylock is set against what Brown calls "love's wealth," possessiveness against prodigality, giving against taking [see excerpt above, 1957]. For Barber, "the whole play dramatizes the conflict between the mechanisms of wealth and the masterful, social use of it" [see excerpt above, 1959]. Problems that stumped other critics have been resolved. (pp. 8-9)

One of the most comprehensive accounts to date is John R. Cooper's "Shylock's Humanity," which argues that at the play's core is a theological distinction between the values of Christianity and those of a Pauline version of Old Testament Judaism [see Additional Bibliography]. This view . . . sets the law, a rational principle according to which men should get exactly what they deserve, against Christian mercy, which gives freely to those who hazard all they possess. Cooper notes that not all the Christians in the play act like ideal Christians—a fact on which a number of schematic interpretations founder—and argues that

> the fundamental opposition in the play is not between Jew and Christian but between two sets of values. On the one hand, there is the uncalculating generosity and forgiveness, the sense of one's own unworthiness and the infinite value of others, the attitude referred to by Portia as "mercy." On the other hand, there is the hard-headed attitude of those who have a high estimation of their own value and rights, and who demand just payment for themselves,

whether in the form of money, or revenge, or a wife.

In this account as in others the opposition in the play is seen as symbolized by the inscriptions on the caskets: Morocco trusts appearances and puts his faith in gold as Shylock does; Arragon demands what he deserves, insisting like Shylock on a rational justice; both are beaten by Bassanio, who gives and hazards all. The opposition is seen by some as figured in the symbolic connotations of the metals of which the caskets are made, and by most as embodied geographically in Belmont, home of music and love, and the commercial Venice.

If I suggest that these critics are wrong, I shall have gravely misstated my argument. What they describe is there, and reflecting on our experience of the play we recognize the patterns identified. Their analysis integrates the techniques developed in the last half-century for literary study and, perhaps more important, arises from unmistakably personal experiences of the play. Thus they hear verbal nuances and know how to talk about them; they know the significance of motifs and echoes, of dramaturgic and metrical effect, of structure and symbol, character and genre. Yet even their own writing conveys a sense of uneasy tentativeness that speaks of more than simple modesty or rhetorical disclaimer. In the first passage I cited, for example, Kermode puts eloquent quotation marks around the word "about" when he tells us what the play is "about." . . . I quoted before Barber's capsule summary of the theme: "The whole play dramatizes the conflict between the mechanism of wealth and the masterful, social use of it." But listen to the reservations implied by the sentence that follows: "The happy ending, which abstractly considered as an event is hard to credit, and the treatment of Shylock, which abstractly considered as justice is hard to justify, work as we actually watch or read the play because these events express relief and triumph in the achievement of a distinction." And later, after his demonstration of the total efficiency with which the play communicates its complex set of interrelated judgments on character, wealth, and love so that the audience is clearly instructed by the end: "I must add, after all this praise for the way the play makes its distinctions about the use of wealth, that *on reflection,* not when viewing or reading the play, but when thinking about it, I find the distinction, as others have, somewhat too easy." And he goes on, with characteristic sensitivity, to demonstrate how much of the play—Portia's facile generosity, Shylock's comeuppance, Antonio's fudging of the usury argument, Shylock's large place in our consciousness—fails to fit even so subtle a schematization as he had made. Brown, you will recall, presents his summary as a question: "Shall we say it is a play about . . .?" And I suggest that his rhetorical choice reflects a tacit acknowledgment that in some sense the formulation is narrower than the play. (pp. 9-11)

Why, if as I have claimed the criticism of these men adds up to a synthesis that comes closer than anything before it to explaining the play, is their presentation so hedged? I suggest that they recognize that they have not in fact explained the very things that provoked them to the elucidation of meaning in the first place, the questions that the play like any good play raises in order to drive us to search for answers that are not forthcoming. Each critic in his own way suggests some conflict between the thematic pattern he identifies on reflection and his actual experience of the play. . . . If on reflection, through the contemplation of thematic patterns, we manage to be satisfied by an understanding that seems to resolve the constant inner conflict which the process of *The Merchant of Venice* sets going in us, we do so by treating as accidental rather than substantive the doubts with which we are left by the end.

Consider some of the problems that remain unresolved in the versions of the comedy we have been discussing. Present in only five scenes, Shylock speaks fewer than four hundred lines yet dominates the play, haunting our memories during the suddenly etherealized and equally suddenly trivialized final episodes as we try to reach a simple position on the fairness of his treatment, or even on the truth of his response to it, funny, deflated, proud, inscrutable: "I pray you give me leave to go from hence, / I am not well" [IV. i. 395-96]. The play, we are told, is about the opposition of mercy to legalism. Cooper, subtle enough to realize that the distinction must not be made by separating out Christian lambs and Jewish goats, must nonetheless belie our own experience of the play, as he admits, in order to judge the disposition of the villain: "Though his forced conversion to Christianity seems to us to be cruel and insulting, we are meant, I think and as many critics have said, to see this as the altogether kindly conversion of Shylock to the new rule of mercy and thus his liberation from the dilemma of the old Law." Note how that "we are meant," derived not from Cooper's response to something he sees as "cruel and insulting" but from a thesis about what the play means, denies to Shakespeare's intention or the play's virtue what the comedy actually *does* to us. Abstractly considered, Shylock's enforced conversion might be judged benevolent, in that it is imposed upon him in order to assure his salvation. Not only is that salvation not mentioned, however, but the conversion is dictated as part of a settlement that is otherwise entirely fiscal, without any suggestion of kindness:

> So please my lord the Duke and all the court
> To quit the fine for one half of his goods,
> I am content; so he will let me have
> The other half in use, to render it
> Upon his death to the gentleman
> That lately stole his daughter.
> Two things provided more, that for this favor
> He presently become a Christian;
> The other, that he do record a gift,
> Here in the court, of all he dies possess'd
> Unto his son Lorenzo and his daughter.
>
> [IV. i. 380-90]

If Antonio's plea for the mitigation of Shylock's sentence is a step back from the cruelty of the Duke's original plan, it nevertheless insists twice that all of the Jew's property must eventually fall into the hands of "the gentleman / That lately stole his daughter"; and one doubts whether any actress could make Portia's demand that Shylock not only accept the judgment but profess satisfaction with it—"Art thou contented, Jew? what dost thou say?" [IV. i. 393]—sound "altogether kindly." The issue is not how Elizabethans felt about the relative advantages of dying in or outside the church, but how Shakespeare forces his audience to respond to this particular conversion in its context.

For Barber our response to Shylock is a problem, but, like some critics whose work his supplants, he suggests that in that respect the play failed because Shakespeare cared more about his villain than his purpose could afford. But Cooper has the superior technology, and his conclusion is cleaner: we must deny that we even care about Shylock's harsh dismissal and his forced conversion so that we may feel, in Brown's phrase, all the elements of the play "mingling together joyfully." (pp. 12-14)

One might discuss at length other elements in the play that cause uneasiness in an audience and difficulties for a critic who wants to make a schematic analysis—the pointed contrast between a Belmont and a Venice not really so different from one another; the peculiar characterization of the melancholy Antonio, the link between his sadness and Portia's in their opening lines, and the fact that the play is named after him; the ring plot which, though it enables Portia to teach once again her lesson about bonds and love, reminds us of her trickery and her tendency to domineer, so inconsistent with the moving spontaneity of her emotions both as Bassanio chooses the lead casket and as she speaks of mercy. But I shall cite, and briefly, only two matters.

First, the characterization of Lorenzo and Jessica has been disputed often enough to suggest that their ambivalence is built into the play. The judgments of their best critics reflect difficulty with them. Goddard sees their villainy as necessary to prod Shylock to revenge. Burckhardt condemns them as an inversion of the true bonded love of the play's theme, lawless and mean-spirited, "spendthrift rather than liberal, thoughtless squanderers of stolen substance," trading for a monkey "the ring which ought to seal their love" [see excerpt above, 1962]. Yet Brown sees them as exemplars of "the central theme of love's wealth." . . . If, as Burckhardt thinks, Lorenzo and Jessica help silhouette Portia's genuine value, their presence in Belmont and their common cause with her against Shylock complicate the play for interpretation, as does the strange excursus on music that Lorenzo delivers in the last act.

And that takes me to my second matter, the beads of language, imagery, and ideas threaded on the string of music. It is a commonplace that that music—the music of the heavenly choirs, the music that Portia has sounded as Bassanio makes his choice—accompanies the life of grace, sensibility, love, and play, the life won by those who triumph in the play. . . . As Lorenzo puts it, the play seems to say:

> The man that hath no music in himself,
> Nor is not moved with concord of sweet sounds,
> Is fit for treasons, stratagems, and spoils; . . .
> Let no such man be trusted.
>
> [V. i. 83-5, 88]

But Lorenzo is a poor witness, since "treasons, stratagems, and spoils" characterizes his exploits at least as accurately as it does those of Shylock, who has other personality problems. Furthermore, Lorenzo's dialogue with Jessica is sandwiched between the episodes of Portia's stratagem against Bassanio, the ring plot, and helps both to undercut the enormous emotional claim she has made on the audience in the trial scene and to call attention to the triviality at best of the game she plays with the ring. We might note also that the chief other entry of music into the play is the song that Portia has sung during Bassanio's ordeal with the caskets, and interestingly that song has occasioned a still unsettled debate as to whether it is simply a pretext to suggest "lead" through rhymes with "bred," "head," and the like.

Once again, my point is not that critics who are demonstrably right about so much are to be dismissed, lightly or otherwise. But one may justifiably ask how so much brain power in the most sensitive and highly trained critical audiences has produced so little that can't be punctured simply by watching one's own responses to details of a play. One may ask furthermore why critical readings of similar methodology and equal brilliance by critics of different temperaments so often add up to radically opposed interpretations. My guess is that our troubles stem in good part from the value we have put on reductiveness. We have been betrayed by a bias toward what can be set out in rational argument. Before the full impact of the new romantic understanding of art hit the professional study of literature, that bias reflected itself in the decision of literary scholars to concentrate on matters now seen as less than central to the understanding of the work itself. But, under the delayed influence of Coleridge and his contemporaries in England and Germany, literary study began to realize how far it was from dealing with the experience of art and began to come closer to it by focusing on the interpretation of texts. To be responsible, however, the newer study had to produce conclusions which were derived as logically and argued as closely as demonstrations of source and influence had been. Attracted by the spectacular possibilities of a new technology . . . critics fell into an invisible trap, the fallacy of misplaced concreteness: what can be brought by self-contained argument to a satisfying conclusion is what is worth discussing, and responses that don't work into the argument must be discounted. Given a romantic inheritance, given a genuine sense of the integrity of a single poem or play or novel, given a puritanical bias which assumes that the value of literature is moral and familiarly expresses itself in the notion of the professor of literature as lay preacher, given a long history of assumption that art is valuable at least half because of what it teaches, and given an art which is verbal, so that virtually all the patterns, parallels, structural juxtapositions, image clusters, ironic repetitions, variations, and generic conventions a critic can find can be translated into other words, was it not inevitable that the bias toward a criticism that would produce discrete and rational arguments should culminate in the study of meaning?

There is nothing surprising about our bias towards rationality. It is perfectly consistent with our hopes for civilization, with our needs, both inner- and outer-directed, to write prose that is logical, coherent, defensible, documentable. . . . But it is time to recall that all intellection is reductive, and that the closer an intellectual system comes to full internal consistency and universality of application—as with Newtonian mechanics—the more obvious become the exclusiveness of its preoccupations and the limitations of its value. What our successful criticism of meaning has made clear—and I include not only naive reduction but also that much more sophisticated criticism which argued so cogently against the heresy of paraphrase while still being concerned with summary thematic statements—is its consistent suppression of the nature of aesthetic experience.

Should it not have disturbed critics interested in hypostatizing meaning that no two critics of any play really agree with one another in their formulations, that no two performances reflect identical interpretations or produce uniform responses in their audiences, that all of us return to plays we know intimately to discover that we respond to them in entirely new ways? Is not the disagreement about works of art as significant a fact for the critic as the interpretation he favors? Might a fruitful criticism not begin and end there as validly as it does with reduction to thematic descriptions of unity? (pp. 17-21)

"One thematist's gestalt is not another's," Richard Levin justly observes [in his *New Readings vs. Old Plays: Recent Trends in the Reinterpretation of English Renaissance Drama*], and he shrewdly demonstrates how critics attempting to make more inclusive and definitive thematic statements than their predecessors remain trapped in hermeneutic solipsism. . . . Acknowledging that even "good" critics do the same thing as

"bad" ones, admitting that he cannot find any model to replace the pernicious critical mode he attacks, Levin nevertheless fails to recognize the dimensions of the problem he is dealing with. And, directing his scrutiny exclusively to the performance of critics, he fails equally to recognize the ultimate cause of our critical sins: the experience of literature. A play we care about provokes us to form a gestalt, and the powerful experience of doing so may tempt us to formulate it thematically. Our formulations differ widely enough to enable Levin's mockery, and they are inadequate enough to serve very poorly, as I have tried to show, what is communicated by the plays they describe. Nevertheless, even at their worst they speak for the conflicts, tensions, implications, and significant fields of force that contribute to our sense that a play is an autonomous, coherent, and meaningful whole. To repudiate that sense because critics have too often translated it into excessively narrow thematic formulations, as Levin does . . . , is to deny the possibility of authorial communication or communal aesthetic experience, to deny that at a certain level of experience a work of art controls the responses of audiences who share its culture, even though each member of the audience may interpret those responses differently. The eddying signals communicated by a play arouse a total and complex involvement of our intellect, our moral sensibility, our need to complete incomplete patterns and answer questions, our longing to judge, and that involvement is so incessantly in motion that to pin it down to a "meaning" is to negate its very essence.

The essence of our experience is our haunting sense of what doesn't fit the thesis we are tempted at every moment to derive. If one hallmark of an authentic work of art and a central source of its power is its ability to drive us to search out its central mystery, another way may be its ultimate irreducibility to a schema. Both of these qualities are present in Shakespeare's plays. They are there because Shakespeare put them there. If we are going to call the distillation of our experience of one of the plays its meaning, we must acknowledge that it includes both the paradigm to which the controlling patterns of the play tempt us to reduce our experience and elements of that experience which resist or weaken or complicate or contradict the paradigm. . . . Both the evidence of the critical consensus and the evidence of rational disagreement in the interpretation of a play like *The Merchant of Venice* lead us back to a particularly powerful authorial control all too susceptible of simplistic hypostatization. It is the critic's job, considering the evidence of others' responses as well as his own, to comprehend as much as possible of what is contained in the intention of a work. (pp. 22-3)

Like many insights that have attained widespread acceptance, Keats's definition of "negative capability" has been allowed to lose its cutting edge. If Keats speaks as rightly as I think he does for artists and for us as their audiences, then the critic must learn to defer his "irritable reaching after fact and reason" and learn to think of "uncertainties, mysteries, doubts" as the stuff of our experience of art. To put it another way, he must treat experience as the subject of discussions of art. That is the point of John Dewey's profound and too little heeded *Art as Experience*, which sees the creation of art and the response to it as quintessentially like life, characterized by process, tension, resistance, and an ineffable sense of integrity. Keats's insight is implicit in the criticism of Kenneth Burke, who has insisted on asking what the poem does for the poet and his readers rather than what it says, who sees a play by Shakespeare as "a device for the arousing and fulfilling of expectations in an audience," and who has defined "the symbolic act" as *"the dancing of an attitude."* For Dewey and Burke the job of the critic is to analyze in the work a set of highly complex interrelations among its elements which the audience, experiencing those elements as they are presented, perceives as a unity. And for Dewey and Burke form and content are inseparable because the experience of the work is one—hence "the dancing of an attitude." (pp. 23-4)

The good Shakespeare critic must point out the patterns of the dance. He must find terms in which the oppositions and conflicts and problems within a play can be stated while recognizing the reductiveness of those terms. He must fight the temptation to proclaim what it boils down to; he must fight against the urge to closure which, as a gifted audience, he feels with particular intensity. He must learn to point to the centers of energy and turbulence in a play without regarding them as coded elements of a thematic formula. And while rejecting narrow conclusions drawn by other critics, he must be able to learn from the perceptions that have led to those conclusions. (p. 25)

The challenge to criticism, I have been suggesting, is to embark on a self-conscious reconsideration of the phenomena that our technology has enabled us to explore, to consider the play as a dynamic interaction between artist and audience, to learn to talk about the process of our involvement rather than our considered view after the aesthetic event. We need to find concepts other than meaning to account for the end of a play, the sense of unverbalizable coherence, lucidity, and unity that makes us know we have been through a single, significant, and shared experience. We need to learn to distinguish between the art represented in its extreme form by the murder mystery, in which the end completes the gestalt figure that tells us unequivocally how we should have responded to every detail along the way, and Shakespeare's profounder art, an art no less powerful in drawing us to a final vantage point from which we may look back over the whole, but an art ultimately irreducible to an explanatory schema.

To get down to cases, what can we do with *The Merchant of Venice*? Two obvious places to begin are its genre and its history, both on stage and in the study, and in both places we come immediately to the same realization. *The Merchant of Venice* is a comedy, inviting us to celebrate a happy resolution and the reassertion of the values of a community that includes us. Shakespeare's comedy normally involves the overthrow of a threat, often the ejection of a character whose inability to participate in the communal resolution threatens community itself. But *The Merchant of Venice* plays on that convention by investing enough of our emotions in its outsider to make us at least uneasy about his discomfiture; the play unsettles one's normal reaction to the end of a comedy. So much is indicated by the centuries of reaction to Shylock and concomitantly to other characters that I indicated earlier. I hope I have made it clear that audience responses to Shylock or Bassanio or Portia which are alternately or exclusively hostile or sympathetic are the result of ambivalent signals built into the play. The countless such signals in *The Merchant of Venice* are part of an entire system. If for a moment, or an entire production, we are led to respond sympathetically to Shylock, we necessarily respond with less sympathy to Jessica or Portia, and vice versa. The potential fullness of a reading in which one element or another in the play can come to seem like the center of the play's values and the focus of its allegiances is paradoxically the source of both its inexhaustible complexity and its vulnerability to powerful productions in which the play seems to belong completely to Shylock or to Belmont. The best reading and the best production, one might guess, would have to take account of the possibilities of both readings.

As the critical consensus has repeatedly shown in recent years, the terms in which the central conflicts of *The Merchant of Venice* can be paraphrased or summarized are remarkably clear. As the entire critical history of the play has made equally apparent, the play's ultimate resolution of those conflicts is anything but clear or simple. The deep polarities in the comedy are luminously evident long before the end. The life-and-death struggle between them makes us feel the need to take a stand on one side or the other. And yet the same play that makes that demand refuses to permit an unequivocal resolution in favor of one character or group of characters or one term in a thematic debate. (pp. 27-9)

At every point at which we want simplicity we get complexity. Some signals point to coherence—thus the conflict between the ideas of prodigality and possessiveness, or between two definitions of prodigality. But just as many create discomfort, point to centrifugality—virtually every mention of a ring and every episode involving one, the grouping of characters, the links between scenes that constantly ask us to reassess what we've just seen and interpreted in terms of what we're now seeing. In terms of moral content that we can extract, we come away with precious little: by the end we know as we knew before we began that cruelty is bad and love better, just as we know in *King Lear* that love between fathers and daughters is a good thing. If *The Merchant of Venice* or any of Shakespeare's great plays were to be judged by what we can claim to have learned from it, or by its ability to lead critics to clear formulations that agree with each other, society would pay even less for English departments than it does now. Yet by the end we have been through a constantly turbulent experience which demands an incessant giving and taking back of allegiance, a counterpoint of ever-shifting response to phrase, speech, character, scene, action, a welter of emotions and ideas and perceptions and surprises and intuitions of underlying unity and coherence rivalled only by our experience in the real world so perplexingly suggested by the artifact to which we yield ourselves. (pp. 29-30)

I have voiced reservations about readings of *The Merchant of Venice* that have claimed to be able to make precise formulations of its meaning, and have tried to show that such attempts are inadequate to the experience of the play. At the same time I have argued against critical positions that, recognizing the shortcomings of such attempts to stipulate meaning, would assert that a play has no meaning, and I have suggested that, despite other inadequate paraphrases, *The Merchant of Venice* does have a meaning. The time would seem to have arrived for me to attempt my own statement of that meaning. I hope that it is clear by now, however, that I do not think that the meaning that is there can be stated as a thematic paradigm. The power of the play is its power to create the illusion of a life that is like our lives, a world like our world, in which as in our life and our world experience tempts us to believe itself to be reducible to fundamental terms but cannot be adequately analyzed in those terms. In *The Merchant of Venice* as in the life we live outside the theater we are driven to formulate questions which—despite the fact that we manage to go on living our lives—we cannot begin to answer. (pp. 30-1)

We can neither ignore nor answer the questions with which our reason is burdened. It is this quality of our existence that is ultimately suggested by our being tempted to and frustrated by the search for meaning in *The Merchant of Venice*, this conviction that the world makes sense but that the sense once abstracted no longer fits it. The attempt to state the meaning of the play is therefore not much more likely to produce an accurate account than an attempt to state the meaning of life. But to say that we cannot profitably talk about the meaning of life is not to say that life is meaningless. *The Merchant of Venice* is a model of our experience, showing us that we need to live as if life has meaning and rules, yet insisting that the meaning is ultimately ineffable and the rules are provisional. The experience of the play, like the experience of a sonata—or of life itself—is one of process, and involves not just a final cadence or even the recapitulation of some main themes, but a whole sequence of contrasting but related developments. That is why Dewey's consideration of art as experience and of experience as process remains so important. Properly understood, the play as a whole is identical with its meaning. (p. 31)

> Norman Rabkin, "Meaning and 'The Merchant of Venice'," in his *Shakespeare and the Problem of Meaning*, *The University of Chicago Press, 1981, pp. 1-32.*

ANNE PARTEN   (essay date 1982)

[*Examining the ring episode and its role in* The Merchant of Venice, *Parten contends that this scene "serves as an important element of the play in its own right" and "represents Shakespeare's resolution of the threat to the comic world that Portia herself embodies." She supports her thesis by establishing three points: one, that Portia is a discordant element in the comic resolution by virtue of her superiority over all the male characters, a situation unacceptable in Shakespeare's comic world where the proper hierarchy of men dominating women must be affirmed; two, that Shakespeare uses the theme of cuckoldry in the ring episode as emblematic of "women's ultimate weapon and ultimate assertion of power over men"; and three, that Shakespeare, through the exchange of the symbolic rings, makes "the threat of a breach in the sexual order explicit"; in dispelling that threat, Parten adds, the dramatist overcomes "a dangerous underlying tension in the play" and reveals Portia "to be not a horn-giving shrew, but rather the embodiment of the Elizabethan ideal virtuous wife." For additional commentary on the ring episode or Act V in general, see the excerpts by August Wilhelm Schlegel (1811), William Hazlitt (1817), Anna Brownell Jameson (1833), G. G. Gervinus (1849-50), Harley Granville-Barker (1930), C. L. Barber (1959), Barbara K. Lewalski (1962), A. D. Moody (1964), James E. Siemon (1970), R. Chris Hassel, Jr. (1970), Richard Horwich (1977), and Alice N. Benston (1979).*]

The ring episode, the last and least of the three interlocking movements of *The Merchant of Venice*, has generally, with some justification, been considered too slight a business to be given the critical attention accorded the earlier phases of the play. The matter of the troth-plight rings and the migrations they make among the various characters is overshadowed by the actions involving the three caskets and the pound of flesh. The established view seems to be that Portia's gift of a "new" ring in the fifth act restates the theme of mercy set out in the fourth, echoing playfully both the usurer's implacability and the generosity of the triumphant Christians. This is certainly true, as is even the somewhat reductive view that the controversy about the rings is designed merely to provide laughter. . . . The business of the rings, however, has a dramatic function beyond mirroring the main action or providing comic counterpoint. It also serves as an important element of the play in its own right, in that it acts as focus for the unresolved—and potentially explosive—issue of the heroine's power. The

ring episode of *The Merchant of Venice* represents Shakespeare's resolution of the threat to the comic world that Portia herself embodies.

In supporting this argument, I will be covering three main points: first, my reasons for seeing Portia as a discordant element in the comic resolution; secondly, the traditional connotations of cuckoldry that account for Shakespeare's choice of it as the central theme of the scenes that deal with achieving that resolution; and finally, the way in which the rings themselves serve as highly significant tokens and emblems in the dramatic commentary on the relationship between the sexes.

It is a donné in Shakespearean comedy, and in Elizabethan comedy in general, that the final scenes of the play will present a society to which order and harmony have been restored after a revitalizing interval of saturnalia. The basis for this new and healthy stability is the re-establishment of the ordered social hierarchy: during the earlier stages of the comedy, the normal pattern of relationships between masters and servants, men and women, and parents and children can go wildly askew, but the conclusion of the play sees each figure restored to his or her proper role. If children are not brought back into the position of subordination to their parents that they held at the beginning of the play, it is only in order to allow them the freedom to move on into the properly ordered marriages that will provide the future generations that will in turn endorse and preserve the same social forms.

The triumphant Portia of the courtroom scene . . . is not a piece that can easily be made to fit this conservative pattern, particularly the aspect of it that makes a concluding harmony contingent upon feminine submission. Her conquest of Shylock does eliminate one evil that threatens the comic society, but, from another perspective, she herself is almost as much of a threat to the re-establishment of order. The comic world will remain in its unresolved and inverted state for as long as she stands in such easy and conspicuous superiority to all the men around her, including her husband.

Portia, after all, represents Shakespeare's first effort to create a comic heroine capable of controlling and directing the action that develops around her, and it is arguable that—at least from the Elizabethan point of view—he overplayed his hand, producing a figure too powerful to be credible as a future wife. In constantly demonstrating her ability to beat men at their own games, Shakespeare allows Portia to emerge as a more potent character than any of her masculine companions. (pp. 146-47)

If one considers the particular focus of the Venetian milieu in which the action of the comedy takes place, the aspect of Portia that is potentially most intimidating is her financial power: she is fabulously wealthy in a society in which wealth is the *summum bonum* [highest good]. Bassanio, on the other hand, comes to her penniless. Though the conventions of the fairy-tale present the pauper-princess alliance in the most positive light, it was not a variety of marriage that the Elizabethans regarded complacently. Contemporary treatises on domestic relations warned constantly against the dangers of financial mésalliances, especially those in which the wife was wealthier than her husband. One such tract, *The Flower of Friendshippe*, phrases that warning in terms that seem especially relevant to the threatened inversion of roles in *The Merchant of Venice*:

> a riche woman, that marieth a poor man, seldome, or never, shake off the pride from hir shoulders. Yea *Menander* sayth, that suche a

man hath gotten in steed of a wyfe, a husband,
and she of him a wyfe, a straunge alteration,
a wonderfull metamorphosis.

Nor is the allusion to metamorphosis in this case necessarily mere rhetoric: influential older literary traditions may have supplied an element of justification for taking such a fear seriously. Ovid's *Metamorphoses,* for example, contains the story of a young woman whose success in passing in disguise as a man is divinely rewarded with true and permanent masculinity. The particulars of Portia's case—showing, as they do, her triumph over the masculine world, rather than the mere capacity to be assimilated by it—link her with yet another tradition that dealt with the possibility of the metamorphosis of female into male. Medieval authorities on science and medicine had expressed the opinion that a female's vanquishing her mate could actually lead to somatic change of sex. Vestiges of those beliefs may still have been available to an Elizabethan consciousness, adding to a general underlying anxiety about the problem of reconciling Portia's past actions and accomplishments with her projected assumption of the feminine role of wife.

It is within this context that the function of the ring episode in *The Merchant of Venice* becomes clear. Shakespeare, rather than ignoring that anxiety-provoking element or declaring a happy ending by fiat, creates a dramatic situation in which the imbalance of power between the sexes is exaggerated, and drawn to the audience's conscious attention. For the theme of the last dramatic business before the final harmony of the play is restored, he chooses the social act traditionally seen as women's ultimate weapon and ultimate assertion of power over men: cuckoldry. By making the threat of a breach in the sexual order explicit, and then by dispelling that threat, he eases a dangerous underlying tension in the play.

In order to examine the technique Shakespeare uses to allay anxiety that his competent woman will turn into a dominant wife, it is necessary to review briefly the literary tradition that deals with the domestic horrors that result when women fight their way out of their subordinate position in the marital hierarchy. Alice of Bath [in Chaucer's *Canterbury Tales*], whose use of psychological warfare and physical violence in her struggles for "maistric" suggests the standard policies of these wives, alleges that she intimidated her fourth husband merely with the suggestion that she was cuckolding him. Other shrews of her sect exhibit no such restraint. The fifteenth-century carol that contains in its refrain the first recorded use of the idiom "to wear the breeches" is part of a genre that celebrates the two principal ways a dominant wife signifies her power over her husband: by beating him, and by making him a cuckold. The literature of the period suggests that the three—domination, husband-beating, and cuckoldry—are intimately related, and that the practice of the one implies the practice of the others.

The frightening prospects that are associated with cuckoldry—loss of one's manhood, one's chattels, and one's place in the familial hierarchy—are capable of arousing very deep-rooted, almost atavistic fears in men. The traditions that treat cuckoldry as comic provide a means by which these fears can be assuaged: the cuckold of the Tudor farce, for example, is made into a grotesque and pitiful figure, one whom an audience of men can reject with its laughter. This laughter at cuckoldry evolves into a social reflex, an automatic and unconscious exorcism of a particularly disturbing specter.

Shakespeare, in his introduction of the theme of cuckoldry into *The Merchant of Venice,* is tapping an established source of both deep anxiety and ready laughter. The laughter, of course, is a boon to any comic author, but Shakespeare is able to make an even more significant use of the fear. Since the idea of cuckoldry is so intimately bound to the idea of feminine ascendancy, Shakespeare is able to adopt that anxiety-provoking image as a compact symbol of all the vicissitudes associated with female domination. By introducing the threat of cuckoldry and then eliminating it, he is able to exorcise the prospect of permanent female rule from this comedy of temporary female ascendancy. Shakespeare's demonstration that Portia will not become a dominant wife is worked out with almost mathematical logic. A mannish, aggressive shrew is a woman who makes her husband a cuckold; briefly, this is precisely what Portia pretends to have done. But when the cuckoldry is shown to be unreal, the other side of the equation loses its force as well. Portia's game is shown to be *only* a game; the episode gives her, in effect, an opportunity to tell the audience explicitly that she would never really cuckold her husband. The rest of the triad follows: she will not beat him, and—more importantly—she will not dominate him.

In order to appreciate the serious side of the final comic clash between the wives and husbands, it is necessary to examine the way in which the emblematic force of the rings is put to use in the play. Portia's ring, in particular, is associated with two separate but constantly interacting issues, her independent power and her sexual identity. The shifting ownership of the ring reflects corresponding shifts in characters' control over these two factors.

The link between the ring and her autonomy is one that Portia herself makes explicit in the speech in which she acknowledges Bassanio as her husband:

Myself and what is mine to you and yours
Is now converted. But now I was the lord
Of this fair mansion, master of my servants,
Queen o'er myself; and even now, but now,
This house, these servants, and this same myself
Are yours, my lord's. I give them with this ring . . .

[III. ii. 166-71]

She specifically makes the ring a token of her submission to her new husband. Above all, it symbolizes her agreement to submerge her identity in Bassanio's, in accordance with the principle that man and wife are one flesh. . . . Portia warns Bassanio that his loss of the ring will occasion her reproach, but in practice the penalty threatens to be far greater. The ring itself is seen almost as the embodiment of the right to control Portia's actions: to forfeit the one is to forfeit the other, and as the gift of jewelry is transferred, so is the gift of self.

It is not necessary to turn to the works of the psychoanalytic commentators on *The Merchant of Venice* to document the association between Portia's and Nerissa's rings and their sexuality. The connection is one that can be established by reference to the bawdy quibble in the final couplet of the play itself. . . . [Any] man who possesses a married woman's ring controls her sexuality. When Bassanio breaks his vow to Portia that he will not part with the ring, it might of course be argued that in delivering the token to his "other self," he has no more broken faith than Portia has in sleeping with the doctor of laws. But ultimately, it is this rather paradoxical matter of variably fusing and separating identities that is at the center of the major statements that the play makes about the relationship between the sexes. In order to understand them it is necessary to explore somewhat more fully the role played by the epicene figure of the young lawyer Balthasar in the action of the comedy as a whole.

Unlike Shakespeare's other disguised heroines, who adopt boys' clothing chiefly as a measure of self-protection, Portia disguises herself as Balthasar for the express purpose of gaining an entree to the man's world. In this world she intends to perform a single, specific action; when the action is complete, one might assume, the masculine character that she has conjured up for the purpose would cease to exist. But Bassanio's failure to keep his word disrupts this pattern. It seems almost as though Bassanio's rejection of the token that makes him one with Portia causes, in addition to the break with her, a secondary fission, enabling the figure of the lawyer to assume a shadowy life of his own.

In returning his wife's ring, Bassanio is in effect surrendering the talisman that Portia's own words have invested with power over her and hers. But the Portia who stands in front of him is a double entity: the disguised woman whom the audience sees co-exists with the capable young man seen by Bassanio. It is to this two-sexed figure that Bassanio yields the token of Portia's independent power and physical love. One could predict the logical result of such a transfer even without reference to the remainder of the play: the woman whose autonomy had been restored would assert her independence, both personal and sexual; the masculine figure who had been given the woman's ring would emerge as a sexual rival to the husband. The events of the fifth act bear this prediction out: Portia browbeats Bassanio, and the doctor of laws "cuckolds" him.

In a very abstract way, Portia's request of the ring from Bassanio represents a comic re-enactment of the casket trial, but this time it is a trial that Bassanio fails: he chooses saving face and preserving his masculine honor over keeping his vow to Portia. In this trial, as in the first, the penalty for failure is enforced celibacy. But where there it was fairy-tale, here it is farce: "By heaven, I will ne'er come in your bed / Until I see the ring!" [V. i. 190-91]. Bassanio, sensing the impending storm of female wrath, murmurs, "Why, I were best to cut my left hand off / And swear I lost the ring defending it" [V. i. 177-78]. It is a marvelous aside, and it does much to humanize the elegant Bassanio, but it also savors somewhat of incipient cowardice in the face of henpecking. The meaning-charged rings in their possession, women are quick to press their advantage: the declaration of female independence, and independent female sexuality, is brought to a more and more highly menacing pitch. From the promise of withholding their sexual favors, they move to threatening to cuckold their husbands:

> Portia   Now by mine honor which is yet mine own
>   I'll have that doctor for my bedfellow.
> Nerissa And I his clerk.
>
> [V. i. 232-34]

And from there they go on to present the cuckoldry as a *fait accompli*:

> Portia   Pardon me, Bassanio.
>   For by this ring the doctor lay with me.
> Nerissa And pardon me, my gentle Gratiano,
>   For that same scrubbed boy, the doctor's clerk,
>   In lieu of this last night did lie with me.
>
> [V. i. 258-62]

It is only for a moment that the men are allowed to taste the full farcical horror of their situation: the return to wifely duty

that the new gift of the rings implies lags only an instant behind the actual redelivery. In that moment, however, as Portia and Nerissa lay down their high cards, they stand in absolute mastery of the situation. Bassanio is stunned into silence, but Gratiano yelps in indignation, "What, are we cuckolds e'er we have deserved it?" [V. i. 265]. The word is allowed to resonate with its full set of unpleasant connotations; the prospect of masculine subjugation and female ascendancy is set before the eyes of characters and audience alike.

If, as one critic suggests, bawdiness in Shakespeare is associated with anarchic and dissident impulses, Portia's sudden rejection of the topic in hand is illuminating. She meets Gratiano's outburst with curt propriety: "Speak not so grossly" [V. i. 266]. In the one short phrase she rejects both the bawdy language and the anarchic image of female rebellion that inspired it, her reassertion of womanly modesty signalling her return to unthreatening femininity. She suddenly reveals herself to be not a horn-giving shrew, but rather the embodiment of the Elizabethan ideal virtuous wife. . . . (pp. 147-53)

In summary, I would say that although *The Merchant of Venice* may be the best of Shakespeare's early comedies, it is nonetheless one with a central figure that an Elizabethan audience might have found faintly disturbing. Portia is strong and self-sufficient in both the feminine and masculine roles; she seems neither to need nor, perhaps, to be likely to submit to a husband's guidance. Traditionally, a wife who is stronger than her husband makes him a cuckold; no less traditionally, an outside male who is more clever or more powerful than a husband—again—makes him a cuckold. Portia of the double identity seems more than capable of fulfilling both roles. Unless she is determined to be loyal to the bond of marriage, Bassanio is doomed.

The sharp focus on this potential cuckoldry gives Portia (and behind her, Shakespeare) a chance to demonstrate that the future the comedy points to is in no way threatened by Portia's superhuman and superfeminine gifts. The ring episode at the end of *The Merchant of Venice* is indeed introduced to provoke the audience's laughter, but a context is created in which this can be laughter at the mere thought that such an action as cuckoldry should be performed. Because the threat can be laughed away, it is no longer a threat. One can laugh at danger only from a position of security: laughter at the thought that order could be broken is a sure sign that order has been restored. Bassanio . . . finishes his story with the all-important ring back on his finger. . . . [He] and the audience have Portia's promise and Shakespeare's dramatic proof that that promise will be kept. (pp. 153-54)

Anne Parten, "Re-establishing Sexual Order: The Ring Episode in 'The Merchant of Venice'," in Women's Studies, Vol. 9, No. 2, 1982, pp. 145-55.

ADDITIONAL BIBLIOGRAPHY

Baker, George Pierce. "The Art of Plotting Mastered." In his *The Development of Shakespeare as a Dramatist*, pp. 181-220. New York: The Macmillan Co., 1914.

    Discusses Shakespeare's plotting of *The Merchant of Venice* and his adaptation of elements not present in his sources.

Banes, Daniel. *The Provocative Merchant of Venice*. Silver Spring, Md.: Malcolm House Publications, 1975, 111 p.

Reiterates some of the principal puzzles and contradictions the play has generated for critics and offers his own solutions to many of these questions.

Barnet, Sylvan. "Prodigality and Time in *The Merchant of Venice*." *PMLA* 87, No. 1 (January 1972): 26-30.
Examines the twin motifs of prodigality and time in *The Merchant of Venice*. Barnet notes that the clearest symbol of prodigality in the play, Bassanio, displays a generosity towards his fellow Christians and, being an individual of intuition, responds to time "when appropriate"; Shylock, on the other hand, opposes prodigality and attempts to "sell" time through the practice of usury.

————, ed. *Twentieth-Century Interpretations of "The Merchant of Venice": A Collection of Critical Essays*. Englewood Cliffs, N.J.: Prentice-Hall, 1970, 122 p.
A collection of essays by such prominent critics as C. L. Barber, John Russell Brown, G. Wilson Knight, Frank Kermode, and others.

Barton, Anne. Introduction to *The Merchant of Venice*, by William Shakespeare. In *The Riverside Shakespeare*, edited by G. Blakemore Evans, pp. 250-53. Boston: Houghton Mifflin Co., 1974.
Treats the date, text, and sources of the play and offers some critical analysis.

Bishop, David H. "Shylock's Humour." *The Shakespeare Association Bulletin* XXIII, No. 4 (October 1948): 174-80.
Focuses on Shylock's use of the term "humour" in his speech at the beginning of the trial scene (IV. i.). Bishop argues that critics err in interpreting the term as meaning whim or inclination, claiming instead that it conveys, in the Elizabethan sense of the word, something more elemental.

Bronstein, Herbert. "Shakespeare, the Jews, and *The Merchant of Venice*." *Shakespeare Quarterly* XX, No. 1 (Winter 1969): 3-10.
Discusses the issue of Shylock's role in *The Merchant of Venice*—whether he is meant to be a melodramatic villain, a comic figure, or a tragic and mistreated victim of Shakespeare's Venetian society.

Brown, Beatrice D. "Medieval Prototypes of Lorenzo and Jessica." *Modern Language Notes* XLIV, No. 4 (April 1929): 227-32.
Identifies sources for the Jessica-Lorenzo subplot in Christian literature from the thirteenth, fourteenth, and fifteenth centuries.

Brown, John Russell. Introduction to *The Merchant of Venice*, by William Shakespeare, edited by John Russell Brown, pp. xi-lviii. The Arden Edition of the Works of William Shakespeare, edited by Harold F. Brooks and Harold Jenkins. London: Methuen & Co., 1976.
A comprehensive examination of the date, text, sources, and critical history of the play.

Bullough, Geoffrey, ed. *"The Merchant of Venice."* In his *Narrative and Dramatic Sources of Shakespeare, Vol. I: Early Comedies, Poems, Romeo and Juliet*, pp. 445-514. London: Routledge and Kegan Paul, 1966.
Includes a detailed discussion of the possible sources for Shakespeare's play and provides excerpts from the source texts.

Charlton, H. B. "Shakespeare's Jew." In his *Shakespearian Comedy*, pp. 123-60. London: Methuen & Co., 1949.
Argues that Shakespeare meant to depict Shylock as a diabolical Jew, and thereby "gratify his own patriotic pride of race," but that the nature of his play demanded that the characterization be more credible and humane.

Cooper, John R. "Shylock's Humanity." *Shakespeare Quarterly* XXI, No. 2 (Spring 1970): 117-24.
Examines what he considers the reason for Shakespeare's inclusion of Shylock's speech at III. i. 58-73 on the similarity of Jews and Christians. Cooper claims that the dramatist composed the speech in order to ensure that his audience accepted Shylock as a serious character, and not merely a comic villain, and to underscore the point that the play deals foremost with a conflict of theological principles.

Dimock, Arthur. "The Conspiracy of Dr. Lopez." *English Historical Review* IX, No. 35 (July 1894): 441-72.
In-depth discussion of the history surrounding Dr. Roderigo Lopez and his involvement in the conspiracy to assassinate Queen Elizabeth. For commentary refuting Dimock's conclusions, see the entry below for John W. Hales.

Donow, Herbert S. "Shakespeare's Caskets: Unity in *The Merchant of Venice*." *Shakespeare Studies* IV (1968): 86-93.
Claims that the casket story and the elopement of Jessica and Lorenzo are integral elements in the structure of *The Merchant of Venice*. Donow cites parallels in the play between the Jessica-Lorenzo affair and the union of Portia and Bassanio, between the casket story and elements in Venice, and between Shylock's household and Lord Belmont's. He states that the similarities between these different aspects of the drama indicate that Shakespeare was concerned with, among other things, "the relationship between father and daughter and the mutual obligations that are incurred by that relationship."

Draper, John W. "Usury in *The Merchant of Venice*." *Modern Philology* XXXIII, No. 1 (August 1935): 37-47.
Discusses the religious and social debate over usury in Elizabethan England and the influence of that debate on Shakespeare's play.

————. "Shakespeare and the Doge of Venice." *The Journal of English and German Philology* XLVI, No. 1 (January 1947): 75-81.
Reviews the government and judicial system of Venice in order "to ascertain how far Shakespeare seems to reflect this system in *The Merchant of Venice* and in *Othello*."

————. "The Theme of *The Merchant of Venice*" and "The Psychology of Shylock." In his *Stratford to Dogberry: Studies in Shakespeare's Earlier Plays*, pp. 128-36, pp. 137-42. Pittsburgh: University of Pittsburgh Press, 1961.
Applies a historical analysis to the theme of *The Merchant of Venice* and to Shylock's characterization. In the first essay, Draper argues that Shakespeare's play deals not with the religious conflict between Jews and Christians, but with the struggle between two opposing economic ideals; in the second, he examines Shylock's characterization according to Elizabethan concepts of psychology and personal temperaments.

Echeruo, Michael J. C. "Shylock and the 'Conditioned Imagination': A Reinterpretation." *Shakespeare Quarterly* 22, No. 1 (Winter 1971): 3-15.
Investigates the effect of an antecedent literary tradition on Marlowe's *The Jew of Malta* and *The Merchant of Venice*. Echeruo contends that it is more rewarding to determine the influence of that medieval morality tradition from which both *The Jew of Malta* and *The Merchant of Venice* derived than to study the effect of Marlowe's play on Shakespeare's.

Evans, Bertrand. "All Shall Be Well: The Way Found, *The Merchant of Venice*." In his *Shakespeare's Comedies*, pp. 46-67. Oxford: Oxford at the Clarendon Press, 1960.
Examines four scenes in *The Merchant of Venice* in which the audience enjoys an awareness and perception of events not shared by the characters.

Felheim, Marvin. "The Merchant of Venice." *Shakespeare Studies* IV (1968): 94-108.
Focuses on the dualistic nature of Shakespeare's comic world in *The Merchant of Venice*, specifically, the presence and interaction of such contrary phenomena as joy and sorrow, love and hate, spiritual fulfillment and material wealth, and so on. Felheim also discusses the significance of food imagery in the play and remarks on Shakespeare's development and resolution of the drama's three plots.

Freud, Sigmund. "The Theme of the Three Caskets." In *The Standard Edition of the Complete Psychological Works of Sigmund Freud, Vol. XII (1911-1913): The Case of Schreber Papers on Technique and Other Works*, edited by James Strachey, translated by James Strachey and others, pp. 291-301. London: The Hogarth Press, 1958.

A psychoanalytic interpretation of the casket story in *The Merchant of Venice*.

Friedlander, Gerald. *Shakespeare and the Jew*. London: George Routledge & Sons, 1921, 79 p.

A historical examination of the Jew in Elizabethan England. Friedlander also discusses the presentation of Jews in pre- and post-Shakespearean drama and some possible sources for Shakespeare's Shylock.

Furness, Horace Howard, ed. *A New Variorum Edition of Shakespeare: "The Merchant of Venice."* Philadelphia: J. B. Lippincott Co., 1888, 479 p.

Includes a text of the play in addition to useful excerpts from the works of prominent European and American critics.

Graham, Cary B. "Standards of Value in *The Merchant of Venice*." *Shakespeare Quarterly* IV, No. 2 (April 1953): 145-51.

Comments on Shakespeare's use of standards of value in *The Merchant of Venice*. Graham maintains that a review of the values employed in the play, their relationships, "and their connection with the intellectual background of the Renaissance may explain in part the technique of Shakespeare in appealing to an audience and may help to show why interpretations have varied so widely."

Grebanier, Bernard. *The Truth about Shylock*. New York: Random House, 1962, 369 p.

Reconstructs Elizabethan attitudes on Jews and the practice of usury and determines how much this climate of opinion affected Shakespeare's writing of *The Merchant of Venice*. After establishing this historical background, Grebanier offers a critical analysis of the play itself, which he interprets as Shakespeare's allegorical dramatization of the triumph of love and mercy over justice and hate.

Hales, John W. "Shakespeare and the Jews." *English Historical Review* IX, No. 36 (October 1894): 652-61.

Takes issue with Arthur Dimock's statement in his essay on the "Conspiracy of Dr. Lopez" that Shakespeare wrote *The Merchant of Venice* "to incite hatred and suspicion" of the Jews (see entry above). Hales contends that although Shakespeare was no "pedant" or "preacher," he was also "no mere slave of filthy lucre," and he maintains that we do the dramatist "a grievous injustice" if we "think of him as a mercenary, ready to serve in the army of the Philistines, if the pay was high enough."

Hapgood, Robert. "Portia and *The Merchant of Venice*: The Gentle Bond." *Modern Language Quarterly* XXVIII, No. 1 (March 1967): 19-32.

Opposes Sigurd Burckhardt's interpretation of *The Merchant of Venice* as a play about "circularity and circulation" and, especially, his assessment of Portia as a figure who achieves freedom by a stringent application of the letter of the law (see excerpt above, 1962). Instead, Hapgood asserts that Portia does not rigorously follow the letter of the law to achieve a more equitable solution to the bond, but makes "enlightened exceptions" to legal forms.

Hill, R. F. "*The Merchant of Venice* and the Pattern of Romantic Comedy." *Shakespeare Survey* 28 (1975): 75-87.

Contends that, unlike Shakespeare's other romantic comedies, *The Merchant of Venice* presents an uncomplicated, idealistic vision of love, rather than a picture of sexual passion that is tinged with pain and suffering and is, generally, ambiguous. Hill cites the ring episode as the only scene in which the love achieved in the play seems mitigated; but he demonstrates that this episode serves more as a reiteration of the comic mood and in no way modifies the success of love depicted throughout the drama.

Holaday, Allan. "Antonio and the Allegory of Salvation." *Shakespeare Studies* IV (1968): 109-18.

Contributes further evidence in support of the theory that the trial scene in *The Merchant of Venice* was strongly influenced by the medieval allegory *The Parliament in Heaven*. Holaday also offers an interpretation of Antonio as an uncharitable and proud individual who goes through a process of suffering and *anagnorisis* to reach a new Christian self-awareness.

Holmer, Joan Ozark. "Loving Wisely and the Casket Test: Symbolic and Structural Unity in *The Merchant of Venice*." *Shakespeare Studies* XI (1978): 53-76.

Detailed examination of the manner in which the casket story foreshadows and reinforces themes prevalent throughout *The Merchant of Venice*, especially those related to Shylock and his self-deception concerning wealth, worldly possessions, and the letter of the law.

———. "The Education of the Merchant of Venice." *Studies in English Literature: 1500-1900* 25, No. 2 (Spring 1985): 307-36.

Argues that an important theme in *The Merchant of Venice* is the education of Antonio. Holmer supports her thesis by examining those additions to and deviations from Shakespeare's sources that underscore the ways in which Antonio develops, morally and spiritually, from the man we first meet in Act I.

Hyman, Lawrence W. "The Rival Lovers in *The Merchant of Venice*." *Shakespeare Quarterly* XXI, No. 2 (Spring 1970): 109-16.

Contends that those critics who interpret the central conflict in *The Merchant of Venice* as that between the Christians and Shylock miss the play's metaphorical meaning. According to Hyman, Shylock is but a minor figure in the drama, a fact that becomes apparent once we view the bond story not as the confrontation of Jew and Christian, but as a symbolic representation of Antonio's desire to demonstrate his love for Bassanio, and thereby prevent his friend's consummated union with Portia. Hyman thus regards the central conflict as that between Antonio and Portia, and he interprets the trial scene as the forum in which Portia reasserts her love over Antonio's, defeating not only Shylock but also the merchant by preventing his ultimate sacrifice and total possession of Bassanio's love.

Knight, G. Wilson. "The Romantic Comedies." In his *The Shakespearean Tempest*, pp. 75-168. London: Oxford University Press, 1932.

Notes the opposition of tempest and music imagery in *The Merchant of Venice* and cites numerous examples where one or the other of these patterns dominates.

Krapf, E. E. "Shylock and Antonio: A Psychoanalytic Study of Shakespeare and Antisemitism." *The Psychoanalytic Review* 42, No. 2 (April 1955): 113-30.

Maintains that the central character in *The Merchant of Venice* is Shylock, not Antonio, and that Shakespeare consciously intended this figure to be nothing more than a comic villain. Krapf adds, however, that Shylock evokes our interest and sympathy because Shakespeare himself was uncertain about his feelings towards Jews. In Krapf's words, the inconsistencies in Shylock's character reveal "strong ambiguities" and "a severe intrapsychic tension in the poet."

Landa, M. J. *The Shylock Myth*. London: W. H. Allen & Co., 1942, 48 p.

Interprets the play and Shakespeare's treatment of Shylock in their historical context, claiming that such an approach might help to clarify some modern misconceptions.

Lee, S. L. "The Original Shylock." *The Gentleman's Magazine* CCXLVI, No. 1790 (February 1880): 185-200.

Contends that Shakespeare based the character of Shylock on the historical figure of Roderigo Lopez, a Portuguese Jew who lived in London and became Queen Elizabeth's personal physician. Lopez was convicted in 1594 of attempting to assassinate the queen and was later executed.

Leggatt, Alexander. "*The Merchant of Venice*." In his *Shakespeare's Comedy of Love*, pp. 117-50. London: Methuen & Co., 1974.

A detailed discussion of a number of different aspects of *The Merchant of Venice*: its combination of naturalism and romantic comedy, the contrast of Venice and Belmont, the significance of Bassanio's role as an intuitive, uncalculating suitor during the casket scenes, a further discussion of the nature of his success, and an examination of the transposition of Belmont and Venice, in which the former becomes the active, realistic world and the latter, during the trial, becomes highly stylized and poetic. Leggatt concludes by analyzing Shakespeare's method of "patterning" speeches and inserting dialogue out of context with the surrounding action.

Palmer, John. "Shylock." In his *Comic Characters of Shakespeare,* pp. 53-91. London: Macmillan and Co., 1946.

Takes issue with those critics who judge the characters of *The Merchant of Venice* according to the standards and values of real life. However, Palmer also disparages the efforts of historical scholars to attribute every dramatic element in Shakespeare's texts to the necessities or conventions of his theater. Instead, the critic contends that Shakespeare combined technical craft and creative imagination, adopting the necessary conventions of his theater "to concentrate the activity of [his] free spirit on the business in hand." Palmer suggests that commentators have such problems with the figure of Shylock because Shakespeare made him realistic enough to overcome the improbability of his plot, yet in so doing provided the means to judge him realistically.

Pettet, E. C. "*The Merchant of Venice* and the Problem of Usury." *Essays and Studies* XXXI (1945): 19-33.

Discusses the presentation of usury in *The Merchant of Venice* and some contemporary events and controversies that influenced Shakespeare's writing of the play.

Pettigrew, Helen Purinton. "Bassanio, the Elizabethan Lover." *Philological Quarterly* XVI, No. 3 (July 1937): 296-306.

Examines the contradiction in Bassanio's character between that of the romantic hero and recipient of Portia's love and the prodigal spendthrift and deceiver which his behavior in general seems to imply.

Sen Gupta, S. C. "Middle Comedies." In his *Shakespearian Comedy,* pp. 129-73. London: Oxford University Press, 1950.

Comments on the characters and different episodes and their relation to each other and the play as a whole. Sen Gupta devotes much of his essay to a discussion of Shylock and his role in the drama.

Siegel, Paul N. "Shylock the Puritan." *Columbia University Forum* V, No. 4 (Fall 1962): 14-19.

Maintains that Shylock was meant to recall, for Shakespeare's Elizabethan audience, the Puritan usurer of the late sixteenth century. Siegel cites much historical evidence to support his theory, the most significant being that the Puritans more than the Jews of Shakespeare's lifetime were the source of economic, political, and social unrest as a result of their activities as usurers, religious fanatics, and enemies of the Anglican church.

Sinsheimer, Hermann. *Shylock: The History of a Character; or, The Myth of the Jew.* London: Victor Gollancz, 1947, 147 p.

Examines the history of Jews in Europe, their treatment in myth and fiction, the genesis of the Pound of Flesh story, Shylock's role in *The Merchant of Venice,* and the influence of medieval elements on Shakespeare's characterization.

Sklar, Elizabeth S. "Bassanio's Golden Fleece." *Texas Studies in Literature and Language* XVIII, No. 3 (Fall 1976): 500-09.

Compares Bassanio to the mythic figure of Jason in John Gower's *Confessio Amantis.* Sklar claims that Bassanio, like his predecessor, is insincere in his quest for his beloved, or, at least, guilty of the sin of "covetousness in love."

Small, Samuel Asa. *Shakespearean Character Interpretation: "The Merchant of Venice."* Baltimore: The Johns Hopkins Press, 1927, 126 p.

Surveys the history of criticism of the characters in *The Merchant of Venice* and offers his own evaluations based on the attitudes and prejudices of Shakespeare's original audience.

Smith, Warren D. "Shakespeare's Shylock." *Shakespeare Quarterly* XV, No. 3 (Summer 1964): 193-99.

Argues that Shylock is the villain in *The Merchant of Venice* not because he is a Jew, but because he is a usurer. According to Smith, Shakespeare made Shylock a Jew in order to give greater verisimilitude to his story, since the terms *Jew* and *usury* were nearly synonymous in Elizabethan England.

Stoll, Elmer Edgar. "Shakespeare's Jew." *University of Toronto Quarterly* VIII, No. 2 (January 1939): 139-54.

Comments on the individual scenes in which Shylock appears.

Stonex, Arthur Bivins. "The Usurer in Elizabethan Drama." *PMLA* XXXI, No. 2 (1916): 190-210.

A survey of Elizabethan and Jacobean drama in which the figure of the usurer appears. Stonex is especially concerned with the manner in which dramatists of this period adapted this stock character for their own purposes.

Tillyard, E. M. W. *"The Merchant of Venice."* In his *Shakespeare's Early Comedies,* pp. 182-208. London: Chatto and Windus, 1966.

A character study of Shylock, Bassanio, and Antonio, plus commentary on Act V and the ring episode. Tillyard essentially agrees with Graham Midgley's assessment of Antonio's loneliness and isolation (see excerpt above, 1960); he also states that Shakespeare sympathized with Shylock to a point—that is, enough to demonstrate that the Jew is justified in his behavior, though his actions are deplorable under any circumstances.

Waddington, Raymond B. "Blind Gods: Fortune, Justice, and Cupid in *The Merchant of Venice.*" *ELH* 44, No. 3 (Fall 1977): 458-77.

Contends that the recurrent references by the Christians in *The Merchant of Venice* to "venture," "fortune," and "hazard" do not necessarily underscore a mercantile view of human endeavor, thereby contradicting the Christian belief in divine control. Citing numerous contemporary views on business adventure, as well as statements from other Shakespearean works, Waddington claims that the Christians undertake their respective ventures with the belief that, their sacrifices being virtuous, Providence will direct their course. According to Waddington, it is only the so-called pagan characters—Shylock, Morocco, and Arragon—who consider fortune a product of blind fate rather than divine will.

Withington, Robert. "Shakespeare and Race Prejudice." In *Elizabethan Studies and Other Essays in Honor of George F. Reynolds,* edited by E. J. West, pp. 172-84. Boulder: University of Colorado Press, 1945.

Examines whether Shakespeare held a prejudiced view of minorities in such plays as *The Merchant of Venice* and *Othello.*

Othello

DATE: Most scholars agree that Shakespeare wrote *Othello* in 1604, but some have postulated a composition date as early as 1603 or even 1602. The earliest recorded performance of the play was that by the KING'S MEN "in the Banketinge house at Whit Hall" on November 1, 1604, although it is possible that it was performed earlier that year in a public theater. Indeed, the Cambridge editor John Dover Wilson has claimed that the BAD QUARTO of *Hamlet,* published shortly after May 19, 1603, contains four or five echoes from *Othello,* suggesting that the actors responsible for the unauthorized version of the Danish tragedy had been performing in *Othello* not long before. In addition, some commentators believe that a reference to a "barbarous Moore" in Thomas Dekker and Thomas Middleton's play *Honest Whore*—known to have been written no later than March of 1604—is an allusion to Othello, the Moor of Venice, and thus they contend that *Othello* must have been written and produced in 1603 or early 1604 at the latest.

TEXT: *Othello* was first printed in QUARTO form in 1622, and then in the FIRST FOLIO of 1623. However, there are more than a thousand variants between the texts of that quarto, also known as Q1, and the First Folio edition. Most significantly, the First Folio text, or F1, contains approximately 160 lines that are not in the First Quarto, but it has markedly fewer stage directions. On the other hand, Q1 contains about thirteen lines or partial lines not found in F1. With the notable exception of the New Arden editor M. R. Ridley (see Additional Bibliography), most modern editors of *Othello* regard F1 as more authentic than the earlier quarto version and follow its readings generally, but not exclusively, occasionally using quarto variants of lines which, in their judgment, appear to be more Shakespearean. There has been considerable conjecture about the process by which the dramatist's manuscript was transmitted to the two printers of the quarto and Folio editions. While Ridley theorized that the copy-text of Q1 was a transcript made from Shakespeare's FOUL PAPERS, Alice Walker (see Additional Bibliography) hypothesized that a pirated transcript of an acting version of the play served as the text for the quarto printer. Such other noted textual authorities as W. W. Greg, E. K. Chambers, and Nevill Coghill have also contributed various theories to explain the origins of these texts. Several scholars also believe that F1 shows indications of revisions and additions made by Shakespeare, or perhaps someone else associated with the theater, subsequent to the preparation of the manuscript for performance. Except for Ridley, textual commentators are in general agreement that the Folio edition was printed from a copy of the First Quarto, together with corrections and additions from some reliable manuscript, such as a company PROMPT-BOOK. *Othello* was also subsequently published in quarto form in 1630 (Q2)—based on Q1 with additions and corrections from the Folio—and in the later quartos of 1655, 1681, and 1695.

SOURCES: The principal source for the narrative of *Othello* is Geraldi Cinthio's *Gli Hecatommithi* (Decade 3, Story 7). No English translation of this work is known to have appeared before 1753. While some scholars have held that, because of verbal echoes in *Othello* of some of Cinthio's words, Shakespeare probably read the work in its original Italian, others have remarked that resemblances between some passages in

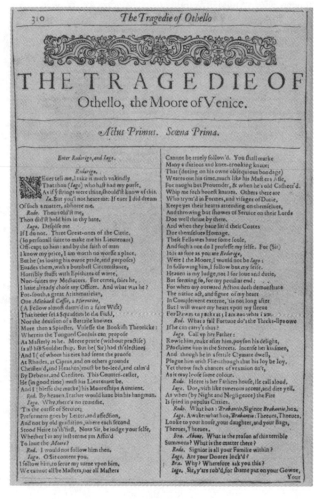

Title page of Othello taken from the First Folio (1623).

Othello and the French translation of Cinthio published by Gabriel Chappuys in 1584 indicate that Shakespeare was undoubtedly familiar with the latter work. The wife in Cinthio's novella is named Disdemona, but the other characters are only designated by titles, such as the Captain, the Ensign, and the Corporal. In Cinthio's narrative, the courtship of the virtuous Disdemona and the valiant Captain, their wedding and subsequent married life in Venice, and the events in Cyprus leading up to the wife's murder occur over a period of several months. The Italian source also differs from Shakespeare's play in other significant ways: the voyage to Cyprus is tranquil rather than tempestuous; the Ensign is a wicked scoundrel who falls in love with Disdemona, who in turn is oblivious to his sexual advances and thereby becomes the object of his hatred; and the Ensign's wife—Emilia's counterpart—is fully informed of her husband's plot against the Captain and his wife but conceals this information from Disdemona because she fears her husband's malice. Also in Cinthio's tale, several weeks elapse between the Ensign's first insinuations to the Captain about Disdemona's chastity and the murder. In addition, as her husband's rage and melancholy deepen during this period, Disdemona considers that perhaps she should not have wed a man so very different in race and culture from herself, thus voicing what most critics regard as the central moral of Cinthio's tale. Finally, the murder of Disdemona is carried out by the Captain and the Ensign together; after striking her repeatedly with a sand-filled stocking, they attempt to conceal their crime by causing the ceiling in the bed-chamber to fall upon her corpse. Although Cinthio provides punishment for the murderers, neither repents or offers explanations for his conduct.

Several commentators have also argued that Pliny's *Natural History,* translated by Philemon Holland in 1601, provided Shakespeare with details he used to enhance Othello's exotic adventures and alien origins, and Geoffrey Bullough (see Additional Bibliography) has maintained that the dramatist probably consulted as well John Pory's translation (1600) of Leo Africanus's *A Geographical Historie of Africa,* which carefully distinguishes between the Moors of northern and those of more southerly regions of Africa and which characterizes both groups as candid and unaffected, but prone to jealousy. It is also apparent that Shakespeare was familiar with fifteenth- and early sixteenth-century accounts of the wars between Venice and Turkey, particularly the Battle of Lepanto in 1571, in which the Venetians, in alliance with other European Catholic states, regained temporary control of the island of Cyprus.

CRITICAL HISTORY: Othello has frequently been described as "a tragedy of character," and, perhaps as a reflection of this, the principal focus of critical commentary on the play has been on the characters of the Moor and Iago. Until the second quarter of the twentieth century, Iago had received as much scholarly attention as Othello. Indeed, until recently there appeared to be some question as to who is the central figure in the play, and scholars continue to debate which of them bears greater responsibility for the tragic outcome of the dramatic events. Critics have also weighed and examined the various motives behind Iago's diabolical behavior, offering in the process myriad responses. The bold contrast between Othello's apparently noble nature and his jealousy and violence has also been analyzed by many scholars, and in the past sixty years commentators have devoted much attention to the Moor's concluding speech, attempting to discover in these lines not only Shakespeare's attitude toward the character, but the significance of the play itself. In addition, Othello's sense of honor and his concern with reputation have similarly emerged as central issues in the play, and the import of the Moor's racial identity and his resemblances to Iago have also received a large measure of critical attention. Other major critical questions during the past three hundred years include these: Shakespeare's exploration and portrayal of the nature of love in *Othello;* the relation of dramatic events to either free will or predestination; the deaths of Desdemona and Othello in light of the requirements of poetic justice; the question of Desdemona's culpability or degree of responsibility for the tragic catastrophe; and the thematic significance of religious or doctrinal elements in the play. More recently, intensive analyses of *Othello*'s poetic language and investigation into Shakespeare's possible indebtedness to theatrical conventions for methods of characterization and formulations of dramatic structure have also assumed importance in the critical history of the play.

Where it has survived, seventeenth-century commentary on Shakespearean drama usually takes the form of relatively brief remarks on an individual play or general evaluations of Shake-

speare's artistry. First published in 1692, Thomas Rymer's lengthy and systematic analysis of *Othello* is therefore remarkable, not only for its extensiveness, but also for its stridency and derision and its subsequent influence on later commentators on the play. Dogmatically applying the precepts of French Neoclassical criticism, Rymer attacked Shakespeare's portrayal of military men in *Othello,* contending that no soldier would conduct himself as Iago does and that Othello's love for Desdemona is inconsistent with his role as a commander of arms. He also charged that no dramatist should represent a black man as a tragic protagonist and insisted that the murder of Desdemona violates the rules of poetic justice and reasonableness. Rymer particularly assailed the dramatic significance ascribed to the handkerchief and demonstrated the inconsistencies of the time scheme in Acts II through V. Mockingly presenting a list of moral instructions to be derived from *Othello,* he concluded that the play is "a Bloody Farce, without salt or savour." Two years later, Charles Gildon contended that Rymer's racial bias had led him to a shocking misinterpretation of the play. He argued that the drama is neither improbable nor inconsistent and that there are instances in classical literature of military men who exhibit human failings and passions. Gildon also avowed that a man ought to be judged for his character and actions without regard to the color of his skin, and he lauded Shakespeare for portraying an ideal, meritocratic world where a noble, heroic Moor might achieve distinction.

However, near the beginning of the eighteenth century, Gildon inexplicably reversed his earlier assessment and endorsed Rymer's argument against *Othello.* Maintaining that a black tragic protagonist is shocking to an audience's sensibilities, the critic added that Desdemona's love for the Moor is "monstrous" and wholly inconsistent with the custom of the times. Additional responses to Rymer's essay and expressions of racial bigotry continued to appear throughout the eighteenth century, but other important issues were raised as well, such as the question of Iago's motivation and the nature of Othello's jealousy. Although he did not refer directly to Rymer, John Hughes castigated critics who mechanically apply "borrow'd Rules" in forming judgments of literary works. He contended that the central interest of *Othello* is not racial but moral—namely, the portrayal of jealousy—and declared that the Moor's turbulent love for Desdemona and the extravagant quality of his mind make him especially vulnerable to Iago's schemes. Hughes also maintained that the use of the handkerchief as an important element in the development of Othello's jealousy demonstrates Shakespeare's recognition that jealous minds may be swayed by trifles. Lewis Theobald similarly commented on Othello's impetuous temperament, and he asserted that the Moor's jealousy is innate rather than imposed on him by Iago, thus initiating a line of inquiry that continued into the twentieth century. In a second essay on *Othello,* Theobald denounced Rymer for his raillery against the play, and he argued that Shakespeare, in making his hero black, intended to show that virtue and nobility of character may overcome racial differences between lovers. In addition, Theobald's assertion that Shakespeare endowed the handkerchief with dignity and symbolic significance, making it an emblem of marital harmony, foreshadowed the assessments of that stage property proffered by several critics more than two centuries later.

Throughout the eighteenth century, critics returned frequently to the question of Iago's motivation and the nature of his villainy. Both William Warburton and Charlotte Lennox rejected Rymer's claim that no soldier should be depicted as Shakespeare has drawn the ancient, and they argued that it is illogical to assume that no military man was ever so villainous. Lennox further explained Iago's wickedness by describing Italians as notoriously cruel and vengeful. On other matters, Lennox became the first critic to draw attention to the character of Emilia, whose conduct in concealing the whereabouts of the handkerchief she considered the most inconsistent element in *Othello*. John Shebbeare stressed the cleverness and mastery of Iago's manipulation of the Moor and argued that Othello's credulousness should not be condemned, for it is entirely consonant with his openness and honesty. The question of Iago's motivation—one of the central issues in criticism of the play—was first addressed in this century by Thomas Wilkes, who maintained that the ancient's sole reason for seeking the destruction of Othello is the loss of the lieutenancy; he added that Iago's claim that the Moor had cuckolded him was merely a fabrication to enhance his deception of Roderigo. John Potter, however, held that Iago does indeed believe that Othello and Emilia have had an adulterous relationship, but he asserted that this motive and the ensign's resentment over not receiving the lieutenancy are inadequate reasons for his destructive conduct. Potter concluded that Iago's hatred of Othello can only be regarded as inhuman and unnatural. Near the end of the eighteenth century, an anonymous commentator in the *Bee* was one of the first to mitigate the extent of Iago's villainy. He argued that in Act I the ensign has neither the intention of destroying the Moor and Desdemona nor a well-conceived plan, but instead is merely interested in gulling Roderigo and displacing Cassio in the post of lieutenant. In addition to his commentary on Iago, the anonymous critic was among the earliest to contend that Othello kills Desdemona not out of jealousy, but out of service to the principles of honor and justice—an opinion shared by such prominent critics as Samuel Taylor Coleridge in the nineteenth century and A. C. Bradley in the early years of the twentieth. Shortly after the essay in the *Bee* appeared, Richard Hole offered what he termed an "ironical" defense of Iago, contending that the ancient's military experience and valor justify his resentment over losing the lieutenancy to Cassio, and further declaring that his suspicions that he has been cuckolded by Othello and Cassio provide Iago with additional cause to feel offended and to seek revenge.

Although questions surrounding Iago's character dominated eighteenth-century analyses of *Othello*, other issues—such as Othello's race and jealousy and the significance of the handkerchief—also received critical attention. Samuel Johnson speculated that Othello's description of himself as "not easily jealous" (V. ii. 345) is perhaps not entirely credible. He was also the earliest commentator to suggest that the time scheme of the play would adhere more closely to the Neoclassical rule regarding unity of time had Shakespeare set the opening scenes in Cyprus and allowed his characters to relate or recall the dramatic events that occur in Venice in Act I. Like Rymer, George Steevens discovered a series of improbabilities and absurdities in *Othello*, claiming that Iago's military rank and stature make it unlikely that his wife would serve as Desdemona's chambermaid, that Cassio's instant inebriation in Act II, Scene iii strains credulity, and that Desdemona's speech after her death is patently absurd. In fact, Steevens concluded that Rymer's irritation with the significance of the handkerchief was misdirected, for this is the least disagreeable of the play's several implausibilities. Raising a question that would also be addressed in the next century by Coleridge and others, William Kenrick declared that Shakespeare intended Othello to be a "tawny" Moor rather than a black African. The critic insisted that, had Shakespeare made Othello black, Desdemona's love

for him and his position as military commander of Venice would be unacceptable.

From 1800 to 1850, Iago continued to fascinate and puzzle commentators on the play. Coleridge's description of Iago's soliloquy at the close of Act I, Scene iii as "the motive-hunting of motiveless malignity" remains one of the most famous critical remarks in the history of literary criticism of *Othello*. Coleridge held that Shakespeare intended to portray Iago as an inhuman personification of evil whose numerous accusations against others merely serve to conceal his inherent love of villainy. August Wilhelm Schlegel similarly emphasized the consummate artistry of Iago's villainy, as well as his unusual ability to dissimulate and his deep understanding of human nature. Schlegel also commented on the "unfortunate affinity" between Iago and Othello which surfaces once the Moor degenerates into jealous rage—a point made by several twentieth-century critics. Without specific reference to Coleridge, William Hazlitt rejected the idea that Iago has no specific motivation for his schemes, contending that he is impelled by an intense passion for power. Like Schlegel, Hazlitt also maintained that Shakespeare depicted Iago as ingeniously creative, although he added that the ancient becomes the victim of his own schemes because of his passion for risk taking. Two decades later, William Maginn similarly argued that Iago loses control of the progress of his plot and becomes a helpless instrument of the destructive process he unwittingly unleashes. Like the anonymous critic in the *Bee,* Maginn also averred that at the outset of the dramatic action Iago is concerned only with gulling Roderigo, undermining Cassio, and gaining the lieutenancy for himself, and that the ancient does not contemplate the destruction of Othello and Desdemona until his plot is well advanced. Emphasizing Iago's quick-wittedness, his discerning judgment, and his powers of dissimulation, Thomas Babington Macaulay (see Additional Bibliography) drew a parallel, as have several twentieth-century critics, between the ancient and the Machiavellian political precepts of Renaissance Italy as they were understood by Shakespeare's contemporaries.

Besides the numerous examinations of Iago, several commentators in the first half of the nineteenth century focused their analyses specifically on Othello, addressing issues similar to those raised by eighteenth-century scholars and initiating new fields of critical inquiry as well. Schlegel advanced a view of Othello as a "double man," whose inherent inclinations to fierceness and sensuality have been tempered by the acquisition of civilized virtues and conduct. When Iago arouses his jealousy, the critic maintained, the Moor reverts to his savage nature in a triumph of instinct over will. In individual comments dispersed over a number of years, Coleridge contended that Shakespeare portrayed Othello as not naturally a jealous man, and he insisted that "any man" who trusted Iago as the Moor did would have reached the same conclusion about his wife's infidelity. He also asserted that Othello is driven to kill Desdemona not by jealousy, but by an outraged sense of regret that her virtue has been impeached and his personal honor compromised. Schlegel's "double man" thesis was directly rejected by Hermann Ulrici, who claimed that this interpretation renders the tragic world of *Othello* blasphemous by negating the freedom of human will and by depicting humanity as dependent on impartial physical necessity rather than on the grace of God. Ulrici argued that all the characters in this play are portrayed as contributing to the tragic consequences of the dramatic action through their obliviousness to the divine basis of human emotions and social relationships. He further contended that Desdemona and, especially, Othello overvalue the earthly expression of their passion and neglect to place it in perspective with the more exalted love of God, and he therefore regarded their deaths at the conclusion of the drama as an expression of tragic or poetic justice. Maintaining that Schlegel's ascription of a sensual form of jealousy to Othello was erroneous, G. G. Gervinus identified several elements that contribute to the rapid advancement of the Moor's violent suspicion, including Desdemona's ingenuousness, the malediction of Brabantio, the Moor's excitability and his alienation from Venetian society, and Iago's consummate dissembling. Like Ulrici, Gervinus argued that tragic justice is served through the deaths of Desdemona and Othello, for by marrying outside the conventions of society and deceiving Desdemona's father, they disrupt the state-sanctioned family relationship and deal a fatal blow to Brabantio. As much as we admire their superlative qualities, Gervinus concluded, we should also regard Desdemona and Othello as victims of their own natures.

Whereas such critics from 1800 to 1850 as Ulrici and Gervinus held that Desdemona willfully contributes to the tragic outcome of the dramatic events, Anna Brownell Jameson focused instead on her passivity. She claimed that, although Desdemona seems unable to act and offers no resistance to Othello's baseless charges, she is not portrayed as weak and powerless. Because any manifestation of intellectual vigor or active will would have marred the pathos of the drama, the critic averred, Shakespeare intentionally did not represent her as actively opposing her fate. Returning to the racial issue in *Othello*, Charles Lamb asserted that, whereas one may, while reading the play, comprehend and applaud the nobility and virtue of Desdemona in disregarding the Moor's color and loving him for his intellectual and moral qualities, one recoils from the representation on stage of their courtship and marriage, and her choice of Othello must seem inexplicable. The most extreme expression of racial bias during this period appeared in an essay by John Quincy Adams, in which he described Desdemona as "little less than a wanton" for betraying both her gender and her social position by marrying a black man. However, even Coleridge evinced a measure of racism in his repeated assertion that Shakespeare never intended to portray Othello as a Negro, since his claim of belonging to a noble family is otherwise anomalous.

One important subsidiary question in *Othello* criticism relates to the duration of dramatic time in the play, which John Wilson addressed in two separate essays in 1850. Writing under the pseudonym of Christopher North, he presented an extensive analysis of the many references in the text to the passage of time, concluding that, despite several indications that many weeks elapse between the arrival of the chief characters on the island of Cyprus and Othello's murder of Desdemona, the action of Acts II through V occupies less than two full days (see Additional Bibliography). He further argued that the long or protracted time makes the development of Othello's jealousy and suspicion more credible to the audience and that the short or condensed time conveys the intensity and impetuosity of the Moor's passion. Although several twentieth-century commentators have also examined the time scheme in *Othello,* no one has disputed Wilson's demonstration of double time and its significance in the play. In an essay written nearly one hundred years after Wilson's, Harley Granville-Barker explicated the relation between Shakespeare's manipulation of time and his portrayal of the theme of sexual jealousy. Demonstrating that from the beginning of Act III, Scene iii until the close of the drama no more than twenty-four hours of actual time elapses, Granville-Barker contended that the precipitous action is both dramatically convincing, as it hurries the audience along, and consistent with the recklessness of Iago and the pathological sexual jealousy that flaws the character of Othello.

From 1850 to 1900, commentators evaluated a broad variety of issues and dramatic elements in *Othello*. J. A. Heraud speculated that Othello may indeed have seduced Emilia and that Iago's suspicions are perhaps not without justification. He also asserted that Desdemona's timorous nature and unwillingness to face difficult situations represent fatal defects in her character, and that without them the tragic events of the play might not have occurred. In an argument reminiscent of Gervinus's, Friedrich Bodenstedt contended that Desdemona is guilty of filial disrespect and impiety and that she must be viewed as primarily responsible for the ensuing tragic events. Denton J. Snider similarly maintained that the principal transgression leading to the tragic consequences of the play is Desdemona's violation of ethical principles in marrying a man of another race. Like Ulrici and Gervinus, Snider thus argued that the catastrophic conclusion of the dramatic action is brought about by the principal figures acting freely of their own will and not by the agency of accident or fate. Snider also hypothesized that the Moor and Emilia have had an adulterous relationship and, because of this, Othello is more prone to believe Iago's suggestion that Desdemona has betrayed him. He further asserted that it is not jealousy, but Othello's resolute sense of honor and concern for his reputation that impel him to slay Desdemona, although he takes a darker view of this act than did such earlier critics as Coleridge and Ulrici, and he rejected Coleridge's view of Iago as motiveless, arguing instead that the ancient had several valid reasons for his actions, even though none of them justifies the extent of his revenge.

Further analyses of the character of Iago were offered in the second half of the nineteenth century by Algernon Charles Swinburne and Richard Grant White. Like Schlegel and Hazlitt, Swinburne attributed to Iago a remarkable talent for creativity and emphasized the ancient's delight in manipulating the other dramatic figures in the play. White—in an essay which first drew attention to Iago's human characteristics—initiated a critical movement against viewing the ancient as inhumanly wicked and the incarnation of evil. He described the dual aspect of Iago's character, contending that although his inner nature is amoral, heartless, and entirely self-interested, his external demeanor of warm sympathy for his friends and apparent trustworthiness earns him wide popularity in Venice. White also asserted that Iago does not initially intend to destroy Othello, but seeks only to undo Cassio and achieve the lieutenancy for himself.

In the twentieth century, most commentary on *Othello* has focused on the figure of the Moor and on the significance or import of his final speech at the close of Act V, Scene ii. A. C. Bradley's essay on Othello, published in the first decade of this century, provided one of the most noted explications of the character and elicited extended responses from several later critics. Bradley agreed with Coleridge that Othello is not an easily jealous man, that "any man" would have succumbed to the insinuations of a friend in whom he had placed so much trust, and that he kills Desdemona not from motives of sexual jealousy, but because he considers her virtue and his honor outrageously tainted by her supposed infidelity. He further ascribed the rapid progress of Othello's jealousy to a number of different factors: his artless and trusting nature, the unreflecting quality of his intellect, his impulse for immediate action, his passionate temperament, his having had only a brief time to adjust to his role as a husband, and his unfamiliarity with Venetian social customs. More than a decade later, Elmer Edgar Stoll disputed Bradley's assessment of Othello, claiming that the character's role is fundamentally that of the sixteenth- and seventeenth-century conventional stage figure of "the blameless hero," who is inherently unsuspicious, intelligent, and noble, yet who succumbs to jealous rage with little realistic motivation. In this dramatic convention, the critic demonstrated, the hero is duped into violent and brutal behavior by an extraordinarily clever and slanderous villain, but he traditionally reestablishes his original noble nature before the conclusion of the dramatic action. Stoll judged that Shakespeare's use of this convention in *Othello* is flawed because of the precipitous alteration in the Moor's behavior in Act III, Scene iii; this wrenching change in character, he argued, leads the audience to conclude that he must be predisposed to jealousy— even though he is everywhere else presented as being inherently unsuspicious—or, at least, an extremely gullible fool. In a more eclectic reading of *Othello,* Wyndham Lewis associated Shakespeare's hero with other colossal or titanic protagonists in Shakespearean tragedies, all of whom are characterized by extraordinary majesty, valor, and physical strength, and who appear to be distant or aloof from ordinary human experience. The critic declared that the Moor is at once both the most typical and the simplest of these colossal figures because of his pure, guileless, generous nature and the childlike, defenseless quality of his soul.

Early in the second quarter of the present century, T. S. Eliot initiated a movement toward a more disparaging view of Othello that has continued to the present day. Using the Moor's concluding speech in Act V, Scene ii to illustrate his assertion that some Shakespearean heroes adopt a self-dramatizing pose at moments of heightened intensity, Eliot contended that here Othello is attempting to delude himself about the implications of his actions and to "cheer himself up," persuading both himself and his audience on stage to adopt an unrealistic interpretation of his conduct. Similarly, in an essay published the same year as Eliot's, Allardyce Nicoll maintained that Othello's various protestations of his unsuspicious nature and his claims of personal integrity reveal his propensity for self-delusion, as well as his ability to delude others. He also argued that Othello's familiarity with military camp life and his experience with such ignoble women as Emilia and Bianca has bred in him an underlying suspicion of the virtue of all women which jars with his romanticism and actually predisposes him to jealousy. In one of the most provocative and controversial twentieth-century analyses of *Othello,* F. R. Leavis also asserted that the Moor is depicted as self-dramatizing, proud, and egotistical. Contending that these qualities are not necessarily detrimental to Othello's role as a heroic man of action, the critic held that they nonetheless render him tragically incapable of coping with situations of great emotional stress. Leavis further claimed that the Moor's love for Desdemona is not so ideal as previous commentators had believed, but is flawed by self-centeredness and a lack of self-understanding that make the Moor easily susceptible to Iago's insinuations.

In addition to Leavis and Eliot, other twentieth-century commentators who have emphasized Othello's pridefulness, self-dramatization, or self-deception include G. R. Elliott, Derek Traversi, Brents Stirling, Roy W. Battenhouse, and Carol McGinnis Kay. Elliott acknowledged the intrinsic nobility of the Moor, but asserted that he is also excessively proud and self-centered and that, until the close of the drama, his love for Desdemona is romantic in conception and, in comparison with Desdemona's passion for him, selfish. Although Traversi viewed the Moor as essentially a noble figure, he also believed that Shakespeare represented him as naive and self-centered, especially vulnerable to Iago's provocations because his love for Desdemona is shallow and grounded in sensuality; the critic concluded that Othello is therefore no match for the ancient's positivist view of human relations. Stirling claimed that Othello's excessive pride leads him from a merely ordinary concern for his public reputation in the early parts of the play to the adoption in Act III, Scene iii of an obsessive, self-centered view of honor and good name. Battenhouse contended that Shakespeare enhanced his portrayal of the Moor as an overly proud figure by offering dramatic parallels with Judas, for both are guilty of "presumptuously playing God" by condemning themselves, despairing of divine mercy, and committing suicide. Conversely, Carol McGinnis Kay recently claimed that Othello is portrayed as deficient in self-confidence and that his histrionic speeches throughout the play, including his final one, reveal a child-like need to reassure himself, or be reassured by others, of his nobility and worth.

The critical positions of these commentators, especially those of Eliot and Leavis, have been evaluated by several later critics, including Barbara Everett (see Additional Bibliography), John Bayley, and Jane Adamson. Everett argued that Leavis raised valuable questions but erred in regarding the Moor as egotistical and self-centered, for self-dramatization is a quality typical in protagonists of Renaissance drama. In addition, she claimed, Shakespeare consistently portrays Othello as a heroic individual with the capacity to alter his conduct, return to goodness, and recognize his responsibility for the tragic events. Bayley disagreed with the conclusions of Eliot and Leavis on the hollowness of Othello's poetry, contending that, because these critics believe the play represents a negative view of love, they were led to make a spurious distinction between heroic and sentimental modes of speech and to view the Moor's romantic flights of language as self-parody. Instead, he concluded, "the 'heroic mode' is the love mode" in this drama, involving the audience in the passions of the characters and directing us to an appreciation of the vitality and splendor of love. Adamson assessed Eliot's analysis of Othello's final speech as insightful, but she denied that this should lead us to view the Moor as an egotist or a moral coward. She also contended that Leavis's insistence on Othello's culpability led him to a judgmental position that prevented him from experiencing the compassionate feelings Shakespeare intended to evoke in his audience. Adamson further maintained that although Othello's self-dramatization represents an attempt to avoid reality or restructure it for the benefit of others, such behavior is understandable considering the horror of his situation. Thus, she construed his concluding speech as not only embodying elements of self-pity and denials of reality, but also as Othello's harrowing acknowledgment of his real nature and conduct.

Many other twentieth-century critics have closely analyzed Othello's final speech in an effort to draw conclusions about the entire dramatic action or to determine the extent of the hero's understanding by the end of the play. Both Elmer Edgar Stoll and John Holloway (see Additional Bibliography) emphasized that in the Elizabethan dramatic tradition, and in Shakespearean tragedy as well, the final comments upon the character of a protagonist—whether delivered by himself or by another dramatic figure—serve as a commentary on his life and death and always indicate what the audience should believe about him. Helen Gardner (see Additional Bibliography) rejected the interpretations of Eliot and Leavis, asserting that

Othello's final speech demonstrates that he has regained his faith in Desdemona and their love and thus concludes his life, not with self-delusion or self-dramatization, but with renewed understanding of the human heart. On the question of Othello's clarity of perception at the close of the play, G. R. Elliott, E. M. W. Tillyard, Robert B. Heilman, and G. M. Matthews have all held that the Moor attains some measure of understanding. Elliott maintained that the hero discards his pride and recognizes at last Desdemona's inward, spiritual beauty. Likewise, Tillyard believed that the Moor consciously perceives the errors of his conduct and is thus an altered man at the close of the play. In his 1951 essay, Heilman concluded that Othello realizes the enormity of his crime and begins once again to be able to distinguish between truth and falsehood. And Matthews argued that he recovers his dignity and human values and regains completely "his integrity as a human being." However, in opposition to these assessments, Leavis declared that Othello never achieves a clear and accurate perception of himself and dies without attaining "tragic self-discovery," and, in a later essay on *Othello*, Heilman asserted that the Moor fails to understand the significance of Desdemona's love and dies ignorant of the true nature of his loss. Irving Ribner averred that the Moor's suicide should be viewed as expiation for his sins and his final speech as an explicit rejection of evil, an avowal of his contrition, and a serene acceptance of his fate. Finally, Jared R. Curtis held that the Moor's last speech demonstrates his renewed clarity of vision which permits him to recognize the proper harmony of love and reason in the human psyche.

Other critical issues centering around the Moor include his affinity to Iago, his status as an alien in the Venetian state, and the significance of his racial identity. Identifying a kinship between the minds of Othello and Iago, Maud Bodkin contended that the Moor has repressed his suspicions regarding Desdemona's fidelity and his fears that, because their natures are so diverse, Desdemona cannot continue to love him. These unacknowledged feelings, she held, are projected into Iago's speeches in Act III, Scene iii and, because the ancient's half-truths are identical to Othello's own suppressed thoughts and emotions, they are embued with greater potency to wound him. Like Bodkin, Elliott contended that Othello has suppressed his fears that Desdemona may prove false to him and is thus quickly provoked by Iago's initial insinuations in the temptation scene; the critic thus described the ancient as a dramatic actualization of the Moor's "worser self." Similarly, Leavis believed that Othello's precipitous fall indicates that the specter raised by Iago is already present in the Moor's mind and that the reason for Iago's quick success in Act III, Scene iii is because he voices what has already been engendered in Othello's psyche. Emphasizing the symbolic function of the characters in *Othello*, J. I. M. Stewart argued that the Moor, especially in Act III, represents the human soul aspiring to nobility, whereas Iago represents the corrosive inner force determined to debase it; thus, he claimed, at this stage of the drama their separate identities converge into a single "invisible protagonist" caught up in the conflict of spiritual and carnal impulses. Stewart agreed with Bodkin that Othello hears from Iago the very suspicions that he has tried to deny to himself, but he argued that Bodkin's assessment falls short of expressing the utter conjunction of their symbolic natures dramatized in the play. On the issue of Othello's alienation, G. M. Matthews maintained that Shakespeare, in making Othello black, has accentuated the physical and cultural differences that set the Moor apart from the Venetians, and he contended that, by electing to marry this "alien," Desdemona becomes equally isolated from that community. Matthews concluded that the lovers' attempt to assert their human and more elevated values against the predatory Venetian power structure, rather than guaranteeing the success of their love, actually makes them more vulnerable. Offering an extensive review of the Renaissance attitude toward black persons, G. K. Hunter (see Additional Bibliography) declared that the traditional association of black people with wickedness survived into the early seventeenth century. By focusing on these assumptions and identifying them with Iago, the critic asserted, Shakespeare intended his audience to set aside their traditional biased views and recall the Christian precept that the fairness of one's soul is more important than the color of one's skin.

Many modern critics have focused on the Moor's spiritual state at the close of the play. Kenneth O. Myrick maintained that while members of Shakespeare's Christian audience would have regarded Othello with compassionate sympathy, their belief in free will would have led them to consider him guilty of, and therefore accountable for, the murder of Desdemona, an act for which he must express repentance or face eternal damnation. In the concluding passages of the play, the critic asserted, Othello indeed moves through the successive stages of repentance established by Christian doctrine; thus, the audience's final impression of him is that of "a man ennobled by contrition." S. L. Bethell argued that Shakespeare intended to present Othello as remorseful but unpenitent at the conclusion of the play—guilty not only of the sins of jealousy and murder, but also of suicide. Paul N. Siegel declared that Othello's wrong choice between love and forgiveness, on the one hand, and hate and vengeance, on the other, leads him to perdition, and when he denies Desdemona the opportunity to pray for her salvation and kills her in vengeance, "Othello's soul is lost." However, Irving Ribner contended that, following Emilia's disclosures in Act V, Scene ii, Shakespeare depicts Othello as passing through the progressive stages of repentance, first recognizing his sin and rejecting the devil, then atoning for this transgression with his expiating suicide, and finally becoming reunited with goodness at his death, thus clearly demonstrating that he has earned salvation. Ribner also likened Othello to Adam, encountering evil for the first time in his life and bringing about his own destruction because of his wrong choice. The arguments of Bethell and Siegel were sharply assailed by Edward Hubler, who considered the question of the Moor's eternal destiny to be only tangentially important to the audience's experience of the drama. The critic's own view of Othello is that he is a man of great heart, guilty of a grievous wrong, but prepared to make atonement for that crime by sacrificing his life. G. M. Matthews believed that although Othello's murder of Desdemona and his suicide would have been viewed by Shakespeare's original audience as leading to his damnation, it is possible to regard the Moor as saved from this fate, for Desdemona's final, forgiving speech, the critic stated, recalls the Christian doctrine of atonement. Battenhouse asserted that Othello's concluding speeches in Act V, Scene ii show no evidence that Othello is penitent or contrite for the murder of Desdemona, but, instead, reveal that he maintains to the end of his life an obsession with his "quasi-religion of honor."

Iago, an important critical focus in earlier eras, has received less critical attention in the twentieth century. However, several commentators have offered substantial analyses of his role in the play. Bradley, Nicoll, and Elliott developed the idea—first suggested in the nineteenth century by William Hazlitt—that Iago's self-deception ultimately works against him, making him the victim of his own schemes. Bradley also emphasized the ancient's powerful intellect and will, his unusual degree of self-control, and his amorality, contending that he is motivated not by a love of evil for its own sake, as stated by Coleridge, but by an inordinate sense of pride. Nicoll held that Iago's amoral self-interest betrays his own superior intelligence, leading him to self-deception and ignorance of the tragic possibilities inherent in his plot against Othello. Far from being superhuman, Elliott maintained, Iago is depicted by Shakespeare as lacking even an ordinary measure of insight into the personalities of those around him. The critic declared that Iago is actually caught off guard by the vehemence of the Moor's anger and that, from the close of Act III, Scene iii to the end of the play, he becomes "the tool of Othello's passion" rather than its manipulator. Earlier in the twentieth century, Tucker Brooke offered a charitable assessment of Iago, arguing that Shakespeare and his fellow Elizabethans would have regarded the ancient as attractive, even though they would have condemned his irresponsible conduct. The critic further maintained that throughout Acts IV and V Iago undergoes a process of "moral awakening," so that at the conclusion of the drama he achieves an understanding of the spiritual significance of life. Stanley Edgar Hyman (see Additional Bibliography), championing a pluralistic approach to critical issues in literature, assessed Iago's motives from five different critical perspectives and concluded that our appreciation of the richness of Shakespeare's portrayal of the ancient is heightened by considering him variously as a conventional stage villain, a symbolic representation of evil, a creative genius, a repressed homosexual, and a practitioner of Machiavellianism.

The figure of Desdemona, like Iago's, has been overshadowed by that of Othello in twentieth-century criticism of the play. Still, the heroine has received much more serious consideration in modern commentary than in previous centuries, where she was generally lauded for her virtue and devotion to Othello, then dismissed. Nicoll emphasized her lack of intelligence and self-esteem, her romantic, idealistic nature which makes her unable to cope with Othello's rage, and the several instances where she prevaricates because she cannot face the consequences of telling the truth. Elliott contended that Desdemona is morally and mentally limited throughout most of the drama, but he asserted that, although her love is initially tainted by a preoccupation with the sensuous and physical aspects of passion, by the conclusion of the play she perceives the necessity of merging both spiritual and physical love and dies acknowledging her share of blame for the tragic outcome. Most recently, Gayle Greene argued that Desdemona's submissiveness, selflessness, and solicitude for her husband are ultimately destructive, for these qualities, she maintained, make her an accomplice to the tragic events. Since Desdemona defines herself only in terms of her relationships with men—indeed, as Greene held, since she considers herself "inferior"—she possesses no strong conviction of her identity, and her inability to articulate any defiance as a result of this actually precipitates the final catastrophe.

Other critics, such as Kenneth Burke, Paul N. Siegel, Irving Ribner, and Roy W. Battenhouse, have regarded Desdemona's conduct in light of Christian principles. Burke compared the lines she speaks after her apparent death (V. ii. 124-25) with Christ's forgiveness of his murderers, and Battenhouse styled her as Christlike in her martyrdom. Siegel likened Desdemona's rejection of Emilia's pragmatic view of marital fidelity in Act IV, Scene iii to the biblical account of Christ's temptation by the devil in the wilderness. He further judged Desdemona

as possessing Christlike powers of saving others, commenting that, for Cassio and Emilia, belief in Desdemona leads to their salvation. Arguing that Desdemona's perfect love is a reflection of Christ's love for humanity, Ribner also claimed that Shakespeare represented her mercy and forgiveness as the agency of Othello's salvation.

In addition to explication of the three principal characters in *Othello,* much twentieth-century commentary has focused on the central thematic issues in the play, especially Shakespeare's concern with the nature of love. Derek Traversi claimed that the play portrays the degeneration of physical desire into selfish prurience, and he contended that although Iago's view of love appears to be in sharp contrast with the Moor's, taken together they represent Shakespeare's recognition that self-destructive tendencies are implicit in all sexual love. Kenneth Burke maintained that *Othello* expresses the tension inherent in the equation of monogamous love with private property or possession. He also asserted that Iago and Othello both perceive love as a form of ownership that enhances a man's status, and he added that Iago's function is to threaten Othello's sense of exclusive possession by provoking the Moor's inherent fear of its loss or theft. In 1956, Robert B. Heilman argued that Shakespeare here portrayed love as effecting a magical transformation of the lover's personality, dramatized in the development of Desdemona's passion for Othello from an immature, sensual emotion to one enriched by charity, forgiveness, and spiritual understanding. However, he added, the Moor fails to understand the significance of Desdemona's ideal love because his feelings for her never progress beyond a preoccupation with love's physical or sensuous element. John Bayley asserted that *Othello* deals primarily with the inherent contradiction in love, declaring that while human passion offers a spacious and expansive world to Othello and Desdemona, their romantic egotism consistently precludes their developing a clear and accurate comprehension of each other. Susan Snyder held that the play portrays love as vulnerable and demonstrates that the ideal of love and marriage—the complete union of "self and other"—is impossible to achieve. Like Bayley, Snyder further contended that *Othello* depicts a terrible paradox: love encourages mutual dependency between two persons who, because they are essentially separate in their natures, may never comprehend the unknowable mysteries of each other. Jane Adamson averred that in *Othello* Shakespeare was concerned most with the tragic dilemmas inherent in absolute love, demonstrating that if love is lost, the loss is total and irreparable, and that the possibility of being wounded by one's lover is "a necessary condition of loving."

Another thematic issue in the play noted by many twentieth-century critics is the right relation of love and reason. Winifred M. T. Nowottny maintained that *Othello* depicts the fundamental incompatibility of love and rational, objective justice, together with Shakespeare's conviction that love is innately miraculous. Because Othello is ruled by justice and reason, she maintained, he is incapable of repudiating Iago's insinuations—of consciously choosing to believe Desdemona innocent—, thereby substituting faith in her love for the dispensation of justice. Heilman agreed with Nowottny that the play depicts reason and love as inimical, arguing that Othello's adoption of Iago's mode of rational thought blinds him to reality and leads him to chaos. Additionally, Heilman demonstrated that the dramatic fabric of *Othello* is woven through with a series of interrelated contrasts between love and hate, light and dark, innocence and guilt, chaos and harmony, appearance and reality, heaven and hell, and white and black. According to the critic, these correspond to the play's central conflict between the "witchcraft" of Desdemona's love and Iago's method of "wit," and he contended that Othello's wrong choice between these two is the central cause of the tragedy. However, Jared R. Curtis disputed the conclusions of these latter two critics and asserted instead that *Othello* dramatizes, first, the destruction of the ideal harmony among the faculties of reason, will, and sensuality, and, second, the restoration of this harmony in the Moor's final recognition that love and reason are not polarities but exist in equilibrium.

In the past thirty-five years, several critics have argued that the central focus of *Othello* is the contrast between appropriate self-esteem and the Moor's overweening pride which leads him to an excessive concern for his reputation. In his second essay on *Othello,* Elliott proposed that "wrong pride" underlies the Moor's refusal to reveal to anyone but Iago the reasons for his suspicions and, thus, serves as the fundamental cause of the tragic consequences. Brents Stirling also regarded the issues of pride and reputation as central to *Othello,* but he maintained that, at the conclusion of the drama, the Moor achieves sufficient self-knowledge to speak with humility of the services he has done the state and the honor and reputation he has earned thereby. Stirling also remarked upon the pattern in which Othello's formal, ritualistic speeches abruptly descend into viciousness and cruelty, beginning in Act III, Scene iii and continuing until midway through the final scene. The critic identified the most elaborate expression of this ritualistic attitude in the Moor's opening lines of the last scene, where he assumes, according to Stirling, the roles of "light-bearer," judge, and priest carrying out a sacrifice. John Arthos similarly averred that Othello formulates his plan to avenge Desdemona's apparent transgression against his honor in terms of ceremony and sacrament. He further declared that Othello's impulse to defend his honor, although impersonal at first, becomes tainted by vengeful, hateful, and punitive elements, so that, by his conduct, the Moor himself debases "the cult of honor."

Throughout the twentieth century commentators have discussed the question of whether, in the dramatic world of *Othello,* the course of human conduct is shown to be ordered by providence, determined by blind chance, or freely chosen by men and women. Early in the century, E. K. Chambers viewed Othello and Desdemona as helpless victims, whose fate is controlled by destiny rather than by their own natures. Stopford A. Brooke argued that the numerous improbabilities in the play indicate that, at the time he composed this drama, Shakespeare doubted the existence of any rational agent guiding humanity and the universe itself. Challenging this explanation of the implausibilities in the drama, Elmer Edgar Stoll maintained that the few references in *Othello* to fate or accident are merely rhetorical devices employed to heighten the tragic atmosphere. Wyndham Lewis argued that the play depicts "the race of men at war with the race of titans" and that the gods have predetermined that the pettiness of Iago will triumph over the grandeur of Othello. Allardyce Nicoll also judged the play as offering a fatalistic, predetermined view of life, while Harry Levin maintained that the prominence of the handkerchief in the tragic outcome of the drama demonstrates that human happiness often depends not on cosmological agents, but on such relatively trivial instrumentalities as one man's malice or another's credulity. Finally, Robert G. Hunter averred that in the dramatic world of *Othello* divine grace is absent and the protagonists' fates are not depicted as predetermined, but are the result of humanity freely exercising its will and electing its own destiny. The critic maintained that the play pointedly asks whether human love can be sustained without such divine grace and demonstrates that "the answer, clearly, is 'No.'"

Hunter was also one of several scholars to link *Othello* with the medieval psychomachia, a kind of morality play that portrayed the allegorical struggle of vice and virtue for the soul or psyche of the protagonist. Early in the century, Chambers—the first scholar to make this comparison—described Iago as an inhuman symbolic representation of evil, patterned after earlier Machiavellian figures in English drama. Later, Irving Ribner and Bernard Spivack held that Iago is Shakespeare's vivid recreation of the stock character of the Vice from medieval morality plays. In one of the most comprehensive studies on the subject, Spivack traced the development of the Vice figure in medieval allegorical drama through the later moralities and hybrid plays, in which the hero, because of his essential goodness, attracts the enmity of the Vice figure. He considered Iago such a figure and argued that—in order to fulfill his role in the play—he must destroy the goodness in Othello. For Spivack, then, Iago's jealousy and resentment are merely superfluous motivations; or, dramatically speaking, they are naturalistic elements which Shakespeare imposed on his villain in response to the more realistic requirements of Elizabethan drama.

The stylistic and linguistic elements in *Othello* have also attracted much commentary from twentieth-century critics. G. Wilson Knight's 1930 essay on the "Othello music" is one of the most famous examinations of the poetic language of the play. Knight maintained that Othello's poetic style is characterized by aloofness and detachment—where universal images sometimes provide a background for human action, but which remain essentially isolated, separate, and "decorative"—and by metaphors that are precise, solid, and specific. On occasion, Knight asserted, the Othello style becomes artificial and enervated, so that the beauties of the language seem foisted onto Othello's emotions and not integral to them and his speeches degenerate into exaggerated emotion. Similarly, Derek Traversi assessed Othello's love poetry as cold, aloof, and conventional. He discovered in the Moor's speeches on his military role the force and intensity lacking in his amatory verse and found in Othello's expressions of vengefulness more warmth and vitality than in the love passages. William Empson (see Additional Bibliography) analyzed the many possible connotations an Elizabethan audience would perceive in the words "honest" and "honesty" as applied to Iago and argued that Shakespeare adroitly manipulated these different meanings to create ambiguous or ironic effects and to generate in the audience a confused reaction to his villain. S. L. Bethell argued that the frequent images of diabolism and damnation in *Othello* are used by Shakespeare to underscore the themes of "deceitful appearance" and damnation in the play and to enhance our appreciation of the metaphysical conflict between good and evil that underlies the more prominent domestic and social action. In his 1951 essay on *Othello,* Robert B. Heilman maintained that the metaphorical images of darkness and light, hell and heaven, black and white, and chaos and harmony enhance the significance of the series of contrasts upon which the play is based. John Bayley commented that in Act II, Scene i, the "power of love" is strongly evoked by the poetry of Othello, Desdemona, and Cassio and the disparities between real and idealized love are expressed by the prosaic or realistic speeches of Iago and others. Like Kenneth Burke, Gayle Greene remarked on the Moor's association of Desdemona with words related to exchange, purchase, and possession, and she viewed this as evidence not only of Othello's estimation of his wife as a "thing" or object, but also as revealing his intuition that his possession of her cannot be guaranteed or assured. Generally agreeing with Traversi's evaluation of Othello's poetic language, she also argued that the Moor's conventional and unspirited style demonstrates his uneasiness with the physical aspects of love.

Certain modern commentators have also examined the structural pattern governing the dramatic action in *Othello*. Burke discovered a three-part ''ritual design'' underlying the dramatic structure of the play: Othello's equation of marital love with private ownership; Iago's double role as a scapegoat figure, shouldering the audience's antipathy and guilt, and as a menacer of Othello's sense of exclusivity; and Desdemona as the embodiment of love's private treasure. G. R. Hibbard analyzed the manner in which the structural design of *Othello* takes on a contracted and narrowing focus as the play progresses, comparing this to the pattern of Shakespeare's other tragedies, which generally expand the dramatic perspective to include whole societies, even the cosmos, in the tragedy of individuals. Some recent critics have indicated the structural connections between *Othello* and comic drama. Barbara Heliodora C. de Mendonça (see Additional Bibliography) examined Shakespeare's manipulation of elements from Italian commedia dell'arte to enhance his disparagement of Venetian society. Susan Snyder maintained that in *Othello* Shakespeare was exploring and questioning the traditional assumptions about the nature of love that are implicit in his earlier comedies. She demonstrated that although the dramatic action from the beginning of the play to the reunion of Desdemona and Othello in Cyprus follows the traditional comic structure, these early scenes also foreshadow the subsequent tragedy by showing that their love lacks the force to defend itself against the destructive power of Iago's rationality.

Othello has often been characterized as the most painful of Shakespeare's tragedies. The source of its power to move and engage an audience remains elusive and inexplicable, although the prodigious body of commentary on the play is evidence of its commanding magnetism for reader and audience alike. In comparison with Shakespeare's other major tragedies, it is more domestic than cosmological, focusing on individual characters rather than on teleological issues, and for this reason it has sometimes been judged inferior to *Hamlet, King Lear,* and *Macbeth.* Many critics have cautioned that we must beware of the Rymer-like conviction that we have all the answers to the puzzles raised by the play; for in spite of the faith and love of such noble figures as Desdemona and Othello, Shakespeare demonstrates that even their union is mutable and ultimately vulnerable. Advising students of *Othello* to be wary of intemperate evaluations ''about its 'greatness' or its 'limitations,''' Jane Adamson claimed that what the play does demonstrate is the need to reconcile judgment with feeling, emphasizing, especially, the extraordinary difficulty of that process. Indeed, in her estimation, like ''all the very greatest tragic works, *Othello* makes us realize with especial force that the fate of loving is precisely the conjunction of that difficulty and that need.''

ABRAHAM WRIGHT (essay date 1637?)

[*Wright was a scholar and clergyman who wrote sermons and biblical commentary and also edited sixteenth- and seventeenth-century epigrams and poetry. His remarks on* Othello *excerpted below are from a manuscript collection of his early writings, probably dating from the period 1629 to 1637 when he was a student at Oxford. Wright singles out the plot of* Othello *for particular praise.*]

[*Othello* is a] very good play, both for lines and plot, but especially the plot. Jago for a rogue, and Othello for a jealous husband, two parts well penned. Act 3, the scene between Jago and Othello, and the first scene of the fourth act, between the same, shew admirably the villanous humour of Jago when he persuades Othello to his jealousy.

> *Abraham Wright, in an extract from* The Shakspere Allusion-Book: A Collection of Allusions to Shakspere from 1591-1700, Vol. I, *edited by John Munro, revised edition, 1932. Reprint by Books for Libraries Press, 1970; distributed by Arno press, Inc., p. 411.*

THOMAS RYMER (essay date 1692)

[*Rymer was a historian, antiquarian, and literary critic. As historiographer royal, he compiled and edited the* Foedera, *a multivolume collection published between 1704 and 1713 of all treaties and alliances contracted between England and other kingdoms from the twelfth to the seventeenth centuries. This is generally considered his most important work. Rymer is also credited with introducing to England the principles of seventeenth-century French formalism or Neoclassicism. His applications of these Neoclassical precepts to dramatic criticism was doctrinaire, and throughout his literary criticism he stressed the necessity for reasonable and probable dramatic action, moral precept and instruction, poetic justice, and a method of characterization that would depict figures as representative of their class. In his study of* Othello, *which constitutes the major portion of his* A Short View of Tragedy *(1692), Rymer offered the first known systematic analysis of any Shakespearean play. In the excerpt below from that work, the critic derides* Othello *for what he regards as its manifold improbabilities. He particularly assails the characterization of Iago, contends that the murder of Desdemona violates the rules of poetic justice and reasonableness, and expresses dismay over the inconsistencies in the time scheme of the play. Rymer also attacks the central significance of the handkerchief, questioning why there is ''so much ado, so much stress, so much passion and repetition about an Handkerchief?'' Finally, Rymer judges the last scene of* Othello *to be barbarous and aberrant and declares that the tragic aspects of the play are ''plainly none other, than a Bloody Farce, without salt or savour.'' For further discussions of* Othello *in relation to the concept of poetic justice, see the excerpts by Hermann Ulrici (1839), G. G. Gervinus (1849-50), Denton J. Snider (1887), and Nigel Alexander (see Additional Bibliography). Also, see the excerpt by Harley Granville-Barker (1945) and the essays by Christopher North cited in the Additional Bibliography for fuller treatments of dramatic time in the play. Direct responses to Rymer's interpretation of* Othello *may be found in the excerpts by Charles Gildon (1694 and 1710), John Hughes (1713), Lewis Theobald (1733), William Warburton (1747), Charlotte Lennox (1753), and Harry Levin (1964), as well as the essay by Nigel Alexander cited in the Additional Bibliography.*]

From all the Tragedies acted on our English Stage, *Othello* is said to bear the Bell away. The *Subject* is more of a piece, and there is indeed something like, there is, as it were, some phantom of a *Fable.* The *Fable* is always accounted the *Soul* of Tragedy. And it is the *Fable* which is properly the *Poets* part. Because the other three parts of Tragedy, to wit the *Characters* are taken from the Moral Philosopher; the *thoughts* or *sence,* from them that teach *Rhetorick:* And the last part, which is the *expression,* we learn from the Grammarians.

This Fable is drawn from a Novel, compos'd in Italian by *Giraldi Cinthio,* who also was a Writer of Tragedies. And to that use employ'd such of his Tales, as he judged proper for the Stage. But with this of the *Moor,* he meddl'd no farther.

Shakespear alters it from the Original in several particulars, but always, unfortunately, for the worse. He bestows a name on his *Moor;* and styles him the Moor of *Venice:* a Note of pre-eminence, which neither History nor Heraldry can allow him. *Cinthio,* who knew him best, and whose creature he was, calls him simply a *Moor.* We say the Piper of *Strasburgh;* the Jew of *Florence;* And, if you please, the Pindar of *Wakefield:* all upon Record, and memorable in their Places. But we see no such Cause for the *Moors* preferment to that dignity. And it is an affront to all Chroniclers, and Antiquaries, to top upon 'um a *Moor,* with that mark of renown, who yet had never faln within the Sphere of their Cognisance.

Then is the Moors *Wife,* from a simple Citizen, in *Cinthio,* dress'd up with her Top knots, and rais'd to be *Desdemona,* a Senators Daughter. All this is very strange; And therefore pleases such as reflect not on the improbability. This match might well be without the Parents Consent. Old *Horace* long ago forbad the Banes.

Sed non ut placidis Coeant immitia, non ut
Serpentes avibus geminentur, tigribus agni.

[Savage should not mate with gentle, nor serpents pair
    with birds, lambs with tigers, *Ars Poetica.*]

(pp. 131-32)

What ever rubs or difficulty may stick on the Bark, the Moral, sure, of this Fable is very instructive.

First, This may be a caution to all Maidens of Quality how, without their Parents consent, they run away with Blacka-moors. (p. 132)

Secondly, This may be a warning to all good Wives, that they look well to their Linnen.

Thirdly, This may be a lesson to Husbands, that before their Jealousie be Tragical, the proofs may be Mathematical.

Cinthio affirms that *She was not overcome by a Womanish Appetite, but by the Vertue of the Moor.* It must be a good-natur'd Reader that takes *Cinthio's* word in this case, tho' in a Novel. *Shakespear,* who is accountable both to the *Eyes,* and to the *Ears,* And to convince the very heart of an Audience, shews that *Desdemona* was won, by hearing *Othello* talk,

Othello.
——I spake of most disastrous chances,
of Moving accidents, by flood and field;
of hair-breadth scapes i' th' imminent deadly breach;
of being taken by the insolent foe;
and sold to slavery: of my redemption thence;
and portents in my Travels History:
wherein of Antars vast, and Desarts idle,
rough Quarries, Rocks, and Hills, whose heads touch
    Heaven,
It was my hint to speak, such was my process:
and of the *Cannibals* that each others eat:
the *Anthropophagi,* and men whose heads
do grow beneath their shoulders——

[I. iii. 134-45]

This was the Charm, this was the philtre, the love-powder that took the Daughter of this Noble Venetian. This was sufficient to make the Black-amoor White, and reconcile all, tho' there had been a Cloven-foot into the bargain. (pp. 132-33)

Nodes, Cataracts, Tumours, Chilblains, Carnosity, *Shankers,* or any *Cant* in the Bill of an High-German Doctor is as good *fustian Circumstance,* and as likely to charm a Senators Daughter. But, it seems, the noble Venetians have an other sence of things. The *Doge* himself tells us;

Doge. I think this Tale wou'd win my Daughter too.

[I. iii. 171]

Horace tells us,

Intererit Multum . . .
Colchus an Assyrius, Thebis nutritus, an Argis.

[Vast difference will it make
(whether a god be speaking or a hero)
a Colchian or an Assyrian, one bred at Thebes or
    at Argos.]

Shakespear in this Play calls 'em the *supersubtle venetians.* Yet examine throughout the Tragedy there is nothing in the noble *Desdemona,* that is not below any Countrey Chamber-maid with us.

And the account he gives of their Noblemen and Senate, can only be calculated for the latitude of *Gotham.*

The Character of that State is to employ strangers in their Wars; But shall a Poet thence fancy that they will set a Negro to be their General; or trust a *Moor* to defend them against the *Turk?* With us a Black-amoor might rise to be a Trumpeter; but *Shakespear* would not have him less than a Lieutenant-General. With us a *Moor* might marry some little drab, or Small-coal Wench: *Shake-spear,* would provide him the Daughter and Heir of some great Lord, or Privy-Councellor: And all the Town should reckon it a very suitable match: Yet the English are not bred up with that hatred and aversion to the *Moors,* as are the Venetians, who suffer by a perpetual Hostility from them. . . .

Littora littoribus contraria——

[Shore clash with shore, Virgil, *Aeneid.*]

Nothing is more odious in Nature than an improbable lye; And, certainly, never was any Play fraught, like this of *Othello,* with improbabilities.

The *Characters* or Manners, which are the second part in a Tragedy, are not less unnatural and improper, than the Fable was improbable and absurd.

Othello is made a Venetian General. We see nothing done by him, nor related concerning him, that comports with the con-dition of a General, or, indeed, of a Man, unless the killing himself, to avoid a death the Law was about to inflict upon him. When his Jealousy had wrought him up to a resolution of's taking revenge for the suppos'd injury, He sets *Jago* to the fighting part, to kill *Cassio;* And chuses himself to murder the silly Woman his Wife, that was like to make no resistance.

His Love and his Jealousie are no part of a Souldiers Character, unless for Comedy.

But what is most intolerable is *Jago.* He is no Black-amoor Souldier, so we may be sure he should be like other Souldiers of our acquaintance; yet never in Tragedy, nor in Comedy, nor in Nature was a Souldier with his Character; take it in the Authors own words;

Em.   ——some Eternal Villain,
Some busie, and insinuating Rogue,
Some cogging, couzening Slave, to get some Office.

[IV. ii. 130-32]

Horace Describes a Souldier otherwise:

> *Impiger, iracundus, inexorabilis, acer.*

[Brisk, passionate, unbending, fierce.]

Shakespear knew his Character of *Jago* was inconsistent. In this very Play he pronounces,

> If thou dost deliver more or less than Truth,
> Thou are no Souldier.——
>
> [II. iii. 219-20]

This he knew, but to entertain the Audience with something new and surprising, against common sense, and Nature, he would pass upon us a close; dissembling, false, insinuating rascal, instead of an open-hearted, frank, plain-dealing Souldier, a character constantly worn by them for some thousands of years in the World. (pp. 133-35)

Nor is our Poet more discreet in his *Desdemona*, He had chosen a Souldier for his Knave: And a Venetian Lady is to be the Fool.

This Senators Daughter runs away to (a Carriers Inn) the *Sagittary*, with a Black-amoor: is no sooner wedded to him, but the very night she Beds him, is importuning and teizing him for a young smock-fac'd Lieutenant, *Cassio*. And tho' she perceives the *Moor* Jealous of *Cassio*, yet will she not forbear, but still rings *Cassio, Cassio* in both his Ears.

Roderigo is the Cully of *Jago*, brought in to be murder'd by *Jago*, that *Jago*'s hands might be the more in Blood, and be yet the more abominable Villain: who without that was too wicked on all Conscience; And had more to answer for, than any Tragedy, or Furies could inflict upon him. So there can be nothing in the *characters*, either for the profit, or to delight an Audience.

The third thing to be consider'd is the *Thoughts*. But from such *Characters*, we need not expect many that are either true, or fine, or noble.

And without these, that is, without sense or meaning, the fourth part of Tragedy, which is the *expression* can hardly deserve to be treated on distinctly. The verse rumbling in our Ears are of good use to help off the action.

In the *Neighing* of an Horse, or in the *growling* of a Mastiff, there is a meaning, there is as lively expression, and, may I say, more humanity, than many times in the Tragical flights of *Shakespear*.

Step then amongst the Scenes to observe the Conduct in this Tragedy.

The first we see are *Jago* and *Roderigo*, by Night in the Streets of *Venice*. After growling a long time together, they resolve to tell *Brabantio* that his Daughter is run away with the Black-a-moor. *Jago* and *Roderigo* were not of quality to be familiar with *Brabantio*, nor had any provocation from him, to deserve a rude thing at their hands. *Brabantio* was a Noble Venetian one of the Sovereign Lords, and principal persons in the Government, Peer to the most Serene *Doge*, one attended with more state, ceremony and punctillio, than any English Duke, or Nobleman in the Government will pretend to. This misfortune in his Daughter is so prodigious, so tender a point, as might puzzle the finest Wit of the most *supersubtle* Venetian to touch upon it, or break the discovery to her Father. See then how delicately *Shakespear* minces the matter:

> *Rod.* What ho, *Brabantio*, Signior *Brabantio*, ho.
> *Jago.* Awake, what ho, *Brabantio*,
> Thieves, thieves, thieves:
> Look to your House, your Daughter, and your Bags
> Thieves, thieves.
> —Brabantio *at a Window*.
> *Bra.* What is the reason of this terrible summons?
> What is the matter there?
> *Rod.* Signior, is all your Family within?
> *Jago.* Are your Doors lockt?
> *Bra.* Why, wherefore ask you this?
> *Jago.* Sir, you are robb'd, for shame put on your
>   Gown,
> Your Heart is burst, you have lost half your Soul,
> Even now, very now, an old black Ram
> It tupping your white Ewe: arise, arise,
> Awake the snorting Citizens with the Bell,
> Or else the Devil will make a Grandsire of you, arise I
>   say.
>
> [I. i. 78-92]

Nor have they yet done, amongst other ribaldry, they tell him.

> *Jago.* Sir, you are one of those that will not serve God, if the Devil bid you; because we come to do you service, you think us Ruffians, you'le have your Daughter covered with a Barbary Stallion. You'le have your Nephews neigh to you; you'le have Coursers for Cousins, and Gennets for Germans.
> *Bra.* What prophane wretch art thou?
> *Jago.* I am one, Sir, that come to tell you, your Daughter and the Moor, are now making the Beast with two backs.
>
> [I. i. 108-17]
> (pp. 135-37)

Brabantio was not in Masquerade, was not *incognito; Jago* well knew his rank and dignity.

> *Jago.* The *Magnifico* is much beloved,
> And hath in his effect, a voice potential
> As double as the Duke——
>
> [I. ii. 12-14]

But besides the Manners to a *Magnifico*, humanity cannot bear that an old Gentleman in his misfortune should be insulted over with such a rabble of Skoundrel language, when no cause or provocation. Yet thus it is on our Stage, this is our School of good manners, and the *Speculum Vitae* [mirror image of life].

But our *Magnifico* is here in the dark, nor are yet his Robes on: attend him to the Senate house, and there see the difference, see the effects of Purple.

So, by and by, we find the Duke of *Venice* with his Senators in Councel, at Midnight, upon advice that the Turks, or Ottamites, or both together, were ready in transport Ships, put to Sea, in order to make a Descent upon *Cyprus*. This is the posture, when we see *Brabantio*, and *Othello* join them. By their Conduct and manner of talk, a body must strain hard to fancy the Scene at *Venice;* And not rather in some of our Cinq-ports, where the Baily and his Fisher-men are knocking their heads together on account of some Whale; or some terrible broil upon the Coast. But to shew them true Venetians, the Maritime affairs stick not long on their hand; the publick may sink or swim. They will sit up all night to hear a Doctors Commons, Matrimonial, Cause. And have the Merits of the

Cause at large laid open to 'em, that they may decide it before they Stir. What can be pleaded to keep awake their attention so wonderfully?

Never, sure, was *form* of *pleading* so tedious and so heavy, as this whole Scene, and midnight entertainment. Take his own words: says the *Respondent.*

> *Oth.* Most potent, grave, and reverend Signiors,
> My very noble, and approv'd good Masters:
> That I have tane away this old mans Daughter;
> It is most true: true, I have Married her,
> The very front and head of my offending,
> Hath this extent, no more: rude I am in my speech.
> And little blest with the set phrase of peace,
> For since these Arms of mine had seven years pith,
> Till now some nine Moons wasted, they have us'd
> Their dearest action in the Tented Field:
> And little of this great World can I speak,
> More than pertains to Broils and Battail,
> And therefore little shall I grace my Cause,
> In speaking of my self; yet by your gracious patience
> I would a round unravish'd Tale deliver,
> Of my whole course of love, what drugs, what charms
> What Conjuration, and what mighty Magick,
> (for such proceedings am I charg'd withal)
> I won his Daughter.
>
> [I. iii. 76-94]

All this is but *Preamble,* to tell the Court that He wants words. This was the Eloquence which kept them up all Night, and drew their attention, in the midst of their alarms.

One might rather think the novelty, and strangeness of the case prevail'd upon them: no, the Senators do not reckon it strange at all. Instead of starting at the Prodigy, every one is familiar with *Desdemona,* as he were her own natural Father, rejoice in her good fortune, and wish their own several Daughters as hopefully married. Should the Poet have provided such a Husband for an only Daughter of any noble Peer in *England,* the Black-amoor must have chang'd his Skin, to look our House of Lords in the Face.

Aeschylus is noted in *Aristophanes* for letting *Niobe* be two or three *Acts* on the Stage, before she speaks. Our Noble Venetian, sure, is in the other more unnatural extreme. His words flow in abundance; no Butter-Quean can be more lavish. Nay: he is for talking of State-Affairs too, above any body:

> *Bra.* Please it your Grace, on to the State Affairs——
> [I. iii. 190]

Yet is this *Brabantio* sensible of his affliction; before the end of the Play his Heart breaks, he dies.

> *Gra.* Poor *Desdemona,* I am glad thy Father's dead,
> Thy match was mortal to him, and pure grief
> Shore his old thread in twain——
> [V. ii. 204-06]

A third part in a Tragedy is the *Thoughts:* from Venetians, Noblemen, and Senators, we may expect fine *Thoughts.* Here is a tryal of skill: for a parting blow, the *Duke,* and *Brabantio* Cap *sentences.* Where then shall we seek for the *Thoughts,* if we let slip this occasion? says the Duke:

> *Duk.* Let me speak like your self and lay a *Sentence,*
> Which like a greese or step, may help these lovers
> Into your favour.

> When remedies are past the grief is ended,
> By seeing the worst which late on hopes depended,
> To mourn a mischief that is past and gone,
> Is the next way to draw more mischief on;
> What cannot be preserv'd when Fortune takes,
> Patience her injury a Mocker makes.
> The rob'd that smiles, steals something from a Thief,
> He robs himself, that spends an hopeless grief.
> *Bra.* So let the Turk of *Cyprus* us beguile
> We lose it not so long as we can smile;
> He bears the sentence well, that nothing bears
> But the free comfort which from thence he hears,
> But he bears both the sentence and the sorrow,
> That to pay grief must of poor patience borrow:
> These *Sentences* to Sugar, or to Gall,
> Being strong on both sides are equivocal.
> But words are words, I never yet did hear,
> That the bruis'd Heart was pierced through the Ear.
> Beseech you now to the affairs of State.
>
> [I. iii. 199-220]
> (pp. 138-40)

What provocation, or cause of malice our Poet might have to Libel the most *Serene Republick,* I cannot tell: but certainly, there can be no wit in this representation.

For the *Second Act,* our Poet having dispatcht his affairs at *Venice,* shews the Action next (I know not how many leagues off) in the Island of *Cyprus.* The Audience must be there too: And yet our *Bays* had it never in his head, to make any provision of Transport Ships for them.

In the days that the *Old Testament* was Acted in *Clerkenwell,* by the *Parish Clerks* of *London,* the Israelites might pass through the *Red sea:* but alass, at this time, we have no *Moses* to bid the Waters *make way,* and to Usher us along. Well, the absurdities of this kind break no Bones. They may make Fools of us; but do not hurt our Morals.

Come a-shoar then, and observe the Countenance of the People, after the dreadful Storm, and their apprehensions from an Invasion by the Ottomites, their succour and friends scatter'd and tost, no body knew whither. The first that came to Land was *Cassio,* his first Salutation to the Governour, *Montanio,* is:

> *Cas.* Thanks to the valiant of this Isle:
> That so approve the Moor, and let the Heavens
> Give him defence against their Elements,
> For I have lost him on the dangerous Sea.
>
> [II. i. 43-6]

To him the Governour speaks, indeed, like a Man in his wits.

> *Mont.* Is he well Shipt?
> [II. i. 47]

The Lieutenant answers thus.

> *Cas.* His Bark is stoutly Tymber'd, and his Pilot
> Of very expert, and approv'd allowance,
> Therefore my hopes (not surfeited to death)
> Stand in bold care.
>
> [II. i. 48-51]

The Governours first question was very proper; his next question, in this posture of affairs, is:

> *Mont.* But, good Lieutenant, is our general Wiv'd?
> [II. i. 60]

A question so remote, so impertinent and absurd, so odd and surprising never entered *Bayes's Pericranium*. Only the answer may Tally with it.

> *Cas.* Most fortunately, he hath atcheiv'd a Maid,
> That Parragons description, and wild fame:
> One that excels the quirks of blasoning Pens:
> And in the essential vesture of Creation,
> Does bear an excellency——
>
> [II. i. 61-5]

They who like this Authors writing will not be offended to find so much repeated from him. I pretend not here to tax either the *Sense,* or the *Language;* those *Circumstances* had their proper place in the Venetian Senate. What I now cite is to shew how probable, how natural, how reasonable the Conduct is, all along.

I thought it enough that *Cassio* should be acquainted with a Virgin of that rank and consideration in *Venice,* as *Desdemona.* I wondred that in the Senate-house every one should know her so familiarly: yet, here also at *Cyprus,* every body is in a rapture at the name of *Desdemona:* except only *Montanio* who must be ignorant; that *Cassio,* who has an excellent cut in shaping an Answer, may give him the satisfaction:

> *Mont.* What is she?
> *Cas.* She that I spoke of: our Captains Captain,
> Left in the Conduct of the bold *Jago,*
> Whose footing here anticipates our thoughts
> A Sennets speed: great *Jove Othello* guard,
> And swell his Sail with thine own powerful breath,
> That he may bless this Bay with his Tall Ship,
> And swiftly come to *Desdemona*'s Arms,
> Give renewed fire to our extincted Spirits,
> And bring all *Cyprus* comfort:
>   *Enter Desdemona, &c.*
>   ——O behold,
> The riches of the Ship is come on shoar.
> Ye men of *Cyprus,* let her have your Knees:
> Hail to the Lady: and the Grace of Heaven
> Before, behind thee, and on every hand.
> Enwheel the round——
>
> [II. i. 73-87]

In the name of phrenzy, what means this Souldier? or would he talk thus, if he meant any thing at all? Who can say *Shakespear* is to blame in his *Character* of a Souldier? Has he not here done him reason? When cou'd our *Tramontains* talk at this rate? but our *Jarsey* and *Garnsey* Captains must not speak so fine things, nor compare with the Mediterranean, or Garrisons in *Rhodes* and *Cyprus.*

The next thing our Officer does, is to salute *Jago*'s Wife, with this *Conge* to the Husband,

> *Cas.* Good Ancient, you are welcome, welcome
>   Mistriss,
> Let it not Gall your patience, good *Jago,*
> That I extend my Manners, 'tis my Breeding,
> That gives me this bold shew of Curtesy.
> *Jago.* Sir, would she give you so much of her lips,
> As of her tongue she has bestow'd on me,
> You'd have enough.
> *Desd.* Alass! she has no speech.
>
> [II. i. 96-102]

Now follows a long rabble of Jack-pudden farce betwixt *Jago* and *Desdemona,* that runs on with all the little plays, jingle,

and trash below the patience of any Countrey Kitchin-maid with her Sweet-heart. The Venetian *Donna* is hard put to't for pastime! And this is all, when they are newly got on shoar, from a dismal Tempest, and when every moment she might expect to hear her Lord (as she calls him) that she runs so mad after, is arriv'd or lost. (pp. 142-44)

But pass we to something of a more serious air and Complexion. *Othello* and his Bride are the first Night, no sooner warm in Bed together, but a Drunken Quarrel happening in the Garison, two Souldiers Fight; And the General rises to part the Fray: He swears.

> *Othel.* Now by Heaven,
> My blood begins my safer guides to rule,
> And passion, having my best judgment cool'd,
> Assays to lead the way: if once I stir,
> Or do but lift this arm, the best of you
> Shall sink in my rebuke: give me to know
> How this foul rout began; who set it on,
> And he that is approv'd in this offence,
> Tho' he had twin'd with me both at a birth,
> Should lose me: what, *in a Town of War,*
> *Yet wild, the peoples Hearts brimful of fear,*
> To manage private, and domestick quarrels,
> In Night, and on the Court, and guard of safety,
> 'Tis Monstrous, *Jago,* who began?
>
> [II. iii. 204-17]

In the days of yore, Souldiers did not swear in this fashion. What should a Souldier say farther, when he swears, unless he blaspheme? action shou'd speak the rest. What follows must be *ex ore gladii* ["the sword drawn from the sheath"]; He is to rap out an Oath, not Wire-draw and Spin it out: by the style one might judge that *Shakespears* Souldiers were never bred in a Camp, but rather had belong'd to some Affidavit-Office. Consider also throughout this whole Scene, how the Moorish General proceeds in examining into this *Rout;* No Justice *Clodpate* could go on with more Phlegm and deliberation. The very first night that he lyes with the *Divine Desdemona* to be thus interrupted, might provoke a Mans Christian Patience to swear in another style. But a Negro General is a Man of strange Mettle. Only his Venetian Bride is a match for him. She understands that the Souldiers in the Garison are by th' ears together: And presently she at midnight, is in amongst them.

> *Desd.* What's the matter there?
> *Othel.* All's well now Sweeting——
> Come away to Bed——
>
> [II. iii. 252-53]

In the beginning of this *second Act,* before they had lain together, *Desdemona* was said to be, *our Captains Captain;* Now they are no sooner in Bed together, but *Jago* is advising *Cassio* in these words.

> *Jago.*——Our Generals Wife is now the General, I may say so in this respect, for that he hath devoted, and given up himself to the contemplation, mark, and devotement of her parts and graces. Confess your self freely to her, importune her; she'll help to put you in your place again: she is so free, so kind, so apt, so blessed a disposition, that she holds it a vice in her goodness, not to do more than she is requested. This broken joint between you and her Husband, intreat her to splinter——
>
> [II. iii. 314-23]

And he says afterwards.

> *Jago.*——'Tis most easie
> The inclining *Desdemona* to subdue,
> In any honest suit. She's fram'd as fruitful,
> As the free Elements: And then for her
> To win the Moor, were't to renounce his Baptism,
> All seals and symbols of redeemed sin,
> His soul is so enfetter'd to her love,
> That she may make, unmake, do what she list:
> Even as her appetite shall play the God
> With his weak function——
>
> [II. iii. 339-48]

This kind of discourse implies an experience and long conversation, the Honey-Moon over, and a Marriage of some standing. Would any man, in his wits, talk thus of a Bridegroom and Bride the first night of their coming together?

Yet this is necessary for our Poet; it would not otherwise serve his turn. This is the source, the foundation of his Plot; hence is the spring and occasion for all the Jealousie and bluster that ensues.

Nor are we in better circumstances for *Roderigo*. The last thing said by him in the former *Act* was,

> *Rod.*——I'll go sell all my Land.
>
> [I. iii. 382]

A fair Estate is sold to *put money in his Purse,* for this adventure. And lo here, the next day.

> *Rod.* I do follow here in the Chace, not like a
> Hound that hunts, but one that fills up the cry:
> My Money is almost spent. I have been tonight
> exceedingly well cudgell'd, I think the issue
> will be, I shall have so much experience for
> my pains, and so no Money at all, and with a
> little more wit return to *Venice.*
>
> [II. iii. 363-69]

The Venetian squire had a good riddance for his Acres. The Poet allows him just time to be once drunk, a very conscionable reckoning!

In this *Second Act,* the face of affairs could in truth be no other, than

> ——In a Town of War,
> Yet wild, the peoples Hearts brim-ful of fear.

But nothing either in this *Act,* or in the rest that follow, shew any colour or complexion, any resemblance or proportion to that face and posture it ought to bear. Should a Painter draw any one *Scene* of this Play, and write over it, *This is a Town of War;* would any body believe that the Man were in his senses? would not a *Goose,* or *Dromedary* for it, be a name as just and suitable? And what in Painting would be absurd, can never pass upon the World for Poetry.

Cassio having escaped the Storm comes on shoar at *Cyprus,* that night gets Drunk, Fights, is turn'd out from his Command, grows sober again, takes advice how to be restor'd, is all Repentance and Mortification: yet before he sleeps, is in the Morning at his Generals door with a noise of Fiddles, and a Droll to introduce him to a little Mouth-speech with the Bride.

> *Cassio.* Give me advantage of some brief discourse
> With *Desdemona* alone.
> *Em.* Pray you come in,
> I will bestow you, where you shall have time
> To speak your bosom freely.
>
> [III. i. 52-5]

So, they are put together: And when he had gone on a good while *speaking his bosom, Desdemona* answers him.

> *Des.* Do not doubt that, before *Emilia* here,
> I give thee warrant of thy place; assure thee,
> If I do vow a friendship, I'll perform it,
> To the last article——
>
> [III. iii. 19-22]

Then after a ribble rabble of fulsome impertinence. She is at her Husband slap dash:

> *Desd.*——Good love, call him back.
> *Othel.* Not now, sweet *Desdemona,* some other time.
> *Desd.* But shall't shortly?
> *Othel.* The sooner, sweet, for you.
> *Desd.* Shall't be to-night at Supper?
> *Othel.* No, not tonight.
> *Desd.* To-morrow Dinner then?
> *Othel.* I shall not dine at home,
> I meet the Captains at the Citadel.
> *Desd.* Why then to morrow night, or Tuesday morn,
> Or night, or Wednesday morn?
>
> [III. iii. 54-61]

After forty lines more, at this rate, they part, and then comes the wonderful Scene, where *Jago* by shrugs, half words, and ambiguous reflections, works *Othello* up to be Jealous. One might think, after what we have seen, that there needs no great cunning, no great poetry and address to make the *Moor* Jealous. Such impatience, such a rout for a handsome young fellow, the very morning after her Marriage must make him either to be jealous, or to take her for a *Changeling,* below his Jealousie. After this *Scene,* it might strain the Poets skill to reconcile the couple, and allay the Jealousie. *Jago* now can only *actum agere* [set things in motion], and vex the audience with a nauseous repetition.

Whence comes it then, that this is the top scene, the Scene that raises *Othello* above all other Tragedies on our Theatres? It is purely from the *Action;* from the Mops and the Mows, the Grimace, the Grins and Gesticulation. Such scenes as this have made all the World run after *Harlequin* and *Scaramuccio.* (pp. 145-49)

Had this scene been represented at old *Rome, Othello* and *Jago* must have quitted their Buskins; They must have played *barefoot:* the spectators would not have been content without seeing their Podometry; And the Jealousie work at the very Toes of 'em. Words, be they Spanish, or Polish, or any inarticulate sound, have the same effect, they can only serve to distinguish, and, as it were, beat time to the *Action.* But here we see a known Language does wofully encumber, and clog the operation: as either forc'd, or heavy, or trifling, or incoherent, or improper, or most what improbable. When no words interpose to spoil the conceipt, every one interprets as he likes best. So in that memorable dispute betwixt *Panurge* and our English Philosopher in *Rabelais,* perform'd without a word speaking; The Theologians, Physicians, and Surgeons, made one inference; the Lawyers, Civilians, and Canonists, drew another conclusion more to their mind.

Othello the night of his arrival at *Cyprus,* is to consummate with *Desdemona,* they go to Bed. Both are rais'd and run into the Town amidst the Souldiers that were a fighting: then go to Bed again, that morning he sees *Cassio* with her; She importunes him to restore *Cassio. Othello* shews nothing of the Souldiers Mettle: but like a tedious, drawling, tame Goose, is gaping after any paultrey insinuation, labouring to be jealous; And catching at every blown surmize.

> Jago. My Lord, I see you are moved.
> Oth. No, not much moved.
> Do not think but Desdemona is honest.
> Jag. Long live she so, and long live you to think so.
> Oth. And yet how Nature erring from it self,
> Jago. I, There's the point: as to be bold with you,
> Not to affect many proposed Matches
> Of her own clime, complexion, and degree,
> Wherein we see, in all things, Nature tends,
> Fye, we may smell in such a will most rank,
> Foul disproportion, thoughts unnatural——
>
> [III. iii. 224-33]

The Poet here is certainly in the right, and by consequence the foundation of the Play must be concluded to be Monstrous; And the constitution, all over, to be *most rank*,

> Foul disproportion, thoughts unnatural.

Which instead of moving pity, or any passion Tragical and Reasonable, can produce nothing but horror and aversion, and what is odious and grievous to an Audience. After this fair Mornings work, the Bride enters, drops a Cursey.

> Desd. How now, my dear Othello,
> Your Dinner, and the generous Islanders
> By you invited, do attend your presence.
> Oth. I am to blame.
> Desd. Why is your speech so faint? Are you not well.
> Oth. I have a pain upon my Fore-head, dear.
>
> [III. iii. 279-84]

Michael Cassio came not from *Venice* in the Ship with *Desdemona*, nor till this Morning could be suspected of an opportunity with her. And 'tis now but Dinner time; yet the *Moor* complains of his Fore-head. He might have set a Guard on *Cassio*, or have lockt up *Desdemona*, or have observ'd their carriage a day or two longer. He is on other occasions phlegmatick enough: this is very hasty. But after Dinner we have a wonderful flight:

> Othel. What sense had I of her stoln hours of lust?
> I saw't not, thought it not, it harm'd not me:
> I slept the next night well, was free and merry,
> I found not Cassio's kisses on her lips——
>
> [III. iii. 338-41]

A little after this, says he,

> Oth. Give me a living reason that she's disloyal.
> Jago.——I lay with Cassio lately,
> And being troubled with a raging Tooth, I could not
>   sleep;
> There are a kind of men so loose of Soul,
> That in their sleeps will mutter their affairs,
> One of this kind is Cassio:
> In sleep I heard him say: sweet Desdemona,
> Let us be wary, let us hide our loves:
> And then, Sir, wou'd he gripe, and wring my hand,
> Cry out, sweet Creature; and then kiss me hard,
> As if he pluckt up kisses by the roots,
> That grew upon my Lips, then laid his Leg
> Over my Thigh, and sigh'd, and kiss'd, and then
> Cry'd, cursed fate, that gave thee to the Moor.
>
> [III. iii. 409-26]

By the Rapture of *Othello*, one might think that he raves, is not of sound Memory, forgets that he has not yet been two nights in the Matrimonial Bed with his *Desdemona*. But we find *Jago*, who should have a better memory, forging his lies after the very same Model. The very night of their Marriage at *Venice*, the Moor, and also *Cassio*, were sent away to *Cyprus*. In the *Second Act*, *Othello* and his Bride go the first time to Bed; The *Third Act* opens the next morning. The parties have been in view to this moment. We saw the opportunity which was given for *Cassio* to *speak his bosom* to her; once, indeed, might go a great way with a Venetian. But *once*, will not do the Poets business; The *Audience* must suppose a great many bouts, to make the plot operate. They must deny their senses, to reconcile it to common sense: or make it any way consistent, and hang together.

Nor, for the most part, are the single thoughts more consistent, than is the œconomy: The Indians do as they ought in painting the Devil White: but says *Othello*:

> Oth.——Her name that was as fresh
> As Dian's Visage, is now begrim'd and black,
> As mine own face——
>
> [III. iii. 386-88]

There is not a Monky but understands Nature better; not a Pug in *Barbary* that has not a truer taste of things.

> Othel.   ——O now for ever
> Farewel the tranquil mind, farewel content;
> Farewel the plumed troop, and the big Wars,
> That make Ambition Vertue: O farewel,
> Farewel the neighing Steed, and the shrill Trump,
> The spirit stirring Drum, th' ear-piercing Fief,
> The royal Banner, and all quality,
> Pride, Pomp, and Circumstance of glorious War,
> And O ye Mortal Engines, whose wide throats
> Th' immortal Joves great clamours counterfeit,
> Farewel, Othello's occupation's gone.
>
> [III. iii. 347-57]

These lines are recited here, not for any thing Poetical in them, besides the sound, that pleases. Yet this sort of imagery and amplification is extreamly taking, where it is just and natural. (pp. 149-52)

Notwithstanding that this Scene had proceeded with fury and bluster sufficient to make the whole Isle ring of his Jealousy, yet is *Desdemona* diverting her self with a paultry buffoon and only solicitous in quest of *Cassio*.

> Desd. Seek him, bid him come hither, tell him——
> Where shou'd I lose that Handkerchief, Emilia?
> Believe me I had rather lose my Purse,
> Full of Crusado's: And but my noble Moor
> Is true of mind, and made of no such baseness,
> As Jealous Creatures are; it were enough
> To put him to ill thinking.
> Em. Is he not Jealous?
> Desd. Who he? I think the Sun, where he was born,
> Drew all such humours from him.
>
> [III. iv. 18, 23-31]

By this manner of speech one wou'd gather the couple had been yoak'd together a competent while, what might she say more, had they cohabited, and had been Man and Wife seven years?

She spies the Moor.

> *Desd.* I will not leave him now,
> Till *Cassio* is recall'd.
> I have sent to bid *Cassio* come speak with you.
> *Othel.*——Lend me thy Handkerchief.
> *Desd.*——This is a trick to put me from my suit.
> I pray let *Cassio* be receiv'd agen.
> *Em.*——Is not this man Jealous?
> ——'Tis not a year or two shews us a man——
> 　　　　　　　　　[III. iv. 32-3, 52, 87-8, 99, 103]

As if for the first year or two, *Othello* had not been jealous? The *third Act* begins in the morning, at noon she drops the Handkerchief, after dinner she misses it, and then follows all this outrage and horrible clutter about it. If we believe a small Damosel in the last *Scene* of this *Act,* this day is effectually seven days.

> *Bianca.*——What keep a week away! seven days, seven
> 　　nights,
> Eightscore eight hours, and lovers absent hours,
> More tedious than the Dial eightscore times.
> O weary reckoning!
> 　　　　　　　　　　　　　[III. iv. 173-76]

Our Poet is at this plunge, that whether this *Act* contains the compass of one day, of seven days, or of seven years, or of all together, the repugnance and absurdity would be the same. For *Othello,* all the while, has nothing to say or to do, but what loudly proclaim him jealous: her friend and confident *Emilia* again and again rounds her in the Ear that *the Man* is Jealous: yet this Venetian dame is neither to see, nor to hear; nor to have any sense or understanding, nor to strike any other note but *Cassio, Cassio.*

The Scotchman hearing *trut Scot, trut Scot,* when he saw it came from a Bird, checkt his Choler, and put up his *Swerd* again, with a *Braad O God, G. if thaa' dst ben a Maan, as th' art ane Green Geuse, I sud ha stuck tha' to thin heart.* *Desdemona* and that Parrot might pass for Birds of a Feather; and if *Sauney* had not been more generous than *Othello,* but continued to insult the poor Creature after this beastly example, he would have given our Poet as good stuff to work upon: And his *Tragedy of the Green Geuse,* might have deserv'd a better audience, than this of *Desdemona,* or *The Moor of Venice.*

ACT IV.

Enter *Jago* and Othello.

> *Jago.* Will you think so?
> *Othel.* Think so, *Jago.*
> *Jago.* What, to kiss in private?
> *Othel.* An unauthorised kiss.
> *Jago.* Or to be naked with her friend a-bed,
> An hour or more, not meaning any harm?
> *Othel.* Naked a-bed, *Jago,* and not mean harm?——
> 　　　　　　　　　　　　　　　[IV. i. 1-5]

At this gross rate of trifling, our General and his Auncient March on most heroically; till the Jealous Booby has his Brains turn'd; and falls in a Trance. Would any imagine this to be the Language of Venetians, of Souldiers, and mighty Captains? no *Bartholomew* Droll cou'd subsist upon such trash. But lo, a Stratagem never presented in Tragedy.

> *Jago.* Stand you a while a part——
> ——Incave your self;
> And mark the Jeers, the Gibes, and notable scorns,
> That dwell in every region of his face,

> For I will make him tell the tale a new,
> Where, how, how oft, how long ago, and when
> He has, and is again to Cope your Wife:
> I say, but mark his gesture——
> 　　　　　　　　　　　　　　[IV. i. 74, 81-7]

With this device *Othello* withdraws. Says *Jago* aside.

> *Jago.* Now will I question *Cassio* of *Bianca,*
> A Huswife——
> That doats on *Cassio*——
> He when he hears of her cannot refrain
> From the excess of Laughter——
> As he shall smile, *Othello* shall go mad,
> And his unbookish jealousy must conster
> Poor *Cassio*'s smiles, gesture, and light behaviour
> Quite in the wrong——
> 　　　　　　　　　　　　　　[IV. i. 93ff.]

So to work they go: And *Othello* is as wise a commentator, and makes his applications pat, as heart cou'd wish—but I wou'd not expect to find this Scene acted nearer than in *Southwark* Fair. But the *Hankerchief* is brought in at last, to stop all holes, and close the evidence. So now being satisfied with the proof, they come to a resolution, that the offenders shall be murdered.

> *Othel.*——But yet the pity of it, *Jago,* ah the pity.
> *Jago.* If you be so fond over her iniquity give her
> 　　Patent to offend.
> For if it touches not you, it comes near no Boby.
> Do it not with poison, strangle her in her Bed; Even the
> 　　Bed she has contaminated.
> *Oth.* Good, good, the Justice of it pleases, very good.
> *Jago.* And for *Cassio,* let me be his undertaker——.
> 　　　　　　　　　　　　　[IV. i. 195-99, 207-11]

Jago had some pretence to be discontent with *Othello* and *Cassio:* And what passed hitherto, was the operation of revenge. *Desdemona* had never done him harm, always kind to him, and to his Wife; was his Country-woman, a Dame of quality: for him to abet her Murder, shews nothing of a Souldier, nothing of a Man, nothing of Nature in it. The *Ordinary* of *New gate* never had the like Monster to pass under his examination. Can it be any diversion to see a Rogue beyond what the Devil ever finish'd? Or wou'd it be any instruction to an Audience? *Jago* cou'd desire no better than to set *Cassio* and *Othello,* his two Enemies, by the Ears together; so he might have been reveng'd on them both at once: And chusing for his own share, the Murder of *Desdemona,* he had the opportunity to play booty, and save the poor harmless wretch. But the Poet must do every thing by contraries: to surprize the Audience still with something horrible and prodigious, beyond any human imagination. At this rate he must out-do the Devil, to be a Poet in the rank with *Shakespear.*

Soon after this, arrives from *Venice, Ludovico,* a noble Cousin of *Desdemona,* presently she is at him also, on the behalf of *Cassio.*

> *Desd.* Cousin there's fallen between him and my Lord
> An unkind breach, but you shall make all well.
> *Lud.* Is there division 'twixt my Lord and *Cassio.*
> *Desd.* A most unhappy one, I wou'd do much
> To attone them, for the love I bear to *Cassio.*
> 　　　　　　　　　　　　[IV. i. 224-25, 231-33]

By this time, we are to believe the couple have been a week or two Married: And *Othello*'s Jealousie that had rag'd so loudly, and had been so uneasie to himself, must have reach'd her knowledge. The *Audience* have all heard him more plain with her, than was needful to a Venetian capacity: And yet she must still be impertinent in her suit for *Cassio,* well, this *Magnifico* comes from the *Doge,* and Senators, to displace *Othello.*

> *Lud.*——Deputing *Cassio* in his Government.
> *Desd.* Trust me, I am glad on't.
> *Oth.* Indeed.
> *Desd.* My Lord.
> *Oth.* I am glad to see you mad.
> *Desd.* How, sweet *Othello.*
> *Oth.* Devil.
> *Desd.* I have not deserved this.
> *Oth.* O Devil, Devil——
> Out of my sight.
> *Desd.* I will not stay to offend you.
> *Lud.* Truly, an obedient Lady.
> I do beseech your Lordship call her back.
> *Oth.* Mistress.
> *Desd.* My Lord.
> *Oth.* What would you with her Sir?
> *Lud.* Who, I, my Lord?
> *Oth.* I, you did wish that I wou'd make her turn.
> Sir, she can turn, and turn, and yet go on,
> And turn agen, and she can weep, Sir, weep.
> And she is obedient, as you say, obedient:
> Very obedient——
> *Lud.* What strike your Wife?
>   [IV. i. 237-41, 247-56, 272]

Of what flesh and blood does our Poet make these noble Venetians? the men without Gall; the Women without either Brains or Sense? A Senators Daughter runs away with this Black-amoor; the Government employs this Moor to defend them against the Turks, so resent not the Moors Marriage at present, but the danger over, her Father gets the Moor Cashier'd, sends his Kinsman, Seignior *Ludovico,* to *Cyprus* with the Commission for a new General; who, at his arrival, finds the Moor calling the Lady his Kinswoman, Whore and Stumpet, and kicking her: what says the *Magnifico?*

> *Lud.* My Lord this would not be believ'd in *Venice,*
> Tho' I shou'd swear I saw't, 'tis very much;
> Make her amends: she weeps.
>   [IV. i. 242-44]

The Moor has no body to take his part, no body of his Colour: *Ludovico* has the new Governour *Cassio,* and all his Country-men Venetians about him. What Poet wou'd give a villanous Black-amoor this Ascendant? What Tramontain could fancy the Venetians so low, so despicable, or so patient? this outrage to an injur'd Lady, the *Divine Desdemona,* might in a colder Climate have provoked some body to be her Champion: but the Italians may well conclude we have a strange Genius for Poetry. In the next Scene *Othello* is examining the supposed Bawd; then follows another storm of horrour and outrage against the poor Chicken, his Wife. Some Drayman or drunken Tinker might possibly treat his drab at this sort of rate, and mean no harm by it: but for his excellency, a My lord General, to Serenade a Senator's Daughter with such a volly of scoundrel filthy Language, is sure the most absurd Maggot that ever bred from any Poets addle Brain.

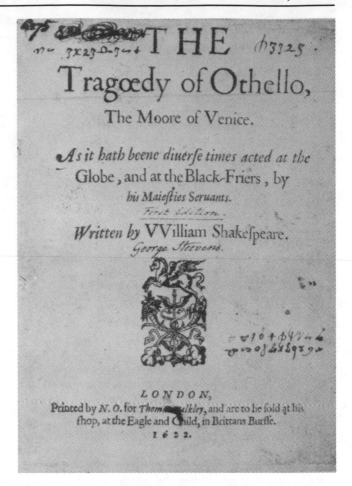

Title page of the First Quarto of Othello *(1622).*

And she is in the right, who tells us,

> *Emil.*——A Begger in his Drink,
> Cou'd not have laid such terms upon his Callet.
>   [IV. ii. 120-21]
>   (pp. 153-58)

Yet to make all worse, her Murder, and the manner of it, had before been resolv'd upon and concerted. But nothing is to provoke a Venetian; she takes all in good part; had the Scene lain in *Russia,* what cou'd we have expected more? With us a Tinkers Trull wou'd be Nettled, wou'd repartee with more spirit, and not appear so void of spleen.

> *Desd.* O good *Jago,*
> What shall I do to win my Lord agen?
>   [IV. ii. 148-49]

No Woman bred out of a Pig-stye, cou'd talk so meanly. After this, she is call'd to Supper with *Othello, Ludovico,* &c. after that comes a filthy sort of Pastoral Scene, where the *Wedding Sheets,* and Song of *Willow,* and her Mothers Maid, poor *Barbara,* are not the least moving things in this entertainment. (p. 158)

The last *Act* begins with *Jago* and *Roderigo;* Who a little before had been upon the huff:

> *Rod.* I say it is not very well: I will make my self known to *Desdemona;* if she will return me my Jewels, I will give over my suit, and

repent my unlawful solicitation, if not, assure
your self, I'll seek satisfaction of you.

[IV. ii. 196-200]

Roderigo, a Noble Venetian had sought *Desdemona* in Marriage, is troubled to find the Moor had got her from him, advises with *Jago,* who wheadles him to sell his Estate, and go over the Sea to *Cyprus,* in expectation to Cuckold *Othello,* there having cheated *Roderigo* of all his Money and Jewels, on pretence of presenting them to *Desdemona,* our Gallant grows angry, and would have satisfaction from *Jago;* who sets all right, by telling him *Cassio* is to be Governour, *Othello* is going with *Desdemona* into *Mauritania:* to prevent this, you are to murder *Cassio,* and then all may be well.

> *Jago.* He goes into *Mauritania,* and takes with
> him the fair *Desdemona,* unless his abode be
> lingred here by some accident, wherein none
> can be so determinate, as the removing of *Cassio.*
>
> [IV. ii. 224-27]

Had *Roderigo* been one of the *Banditi* [outlaws], he might not much stick at the Murder. But why *Roderigo* should take this for payment, and risque his person where the prospect of advantage is so very uncertain and remote, no body can imagine. It had need be a *super-subtle* Venetian that this Plot will pass upon. Then after a little spurt of villany and Murder, we are brought to the most lamentable, that ever appear'd on any Stage. A noble Venetian Lady is to be murdered by our Poet; in sober sadness, purely for being a Fool. No Pagan Poet but wou'd have found some *Machine* for her deliverance. *Pegasus* wou'd have strain'd hard to have brought old *Perseus* on his back, time enough, to rescue this *Andromeda* from so foul a Monster. Has our Christian Poetry no generosity, nor bowels? Ha, Sir *Lancelot!* ha St. *George!* will no Ghost leave the shades for us in extremity, to save a distressed Damosel?

But for our comfort, however felonious is the Heart, hear with what soft language, he does approach her, with a Candle in his Hand:

> *Oth.* Put out the light and then put out thc light;
> If I quench thee, thou flaming Minister,
> I can again thy former light restore——
>
> [V. ii. 7-9]

Who would call him a Barbarian, Monster, Savage? Is this a Black-amoor? (pp. 158-60)

One might think the General should not glory much in this action, but make an hasty work on't, and have turn'd his Eyes away from so unsouldierly an Execution: yet is he all pause and deliberation; handles her as calmly: and is as careful of her Souls health, as it had been her *Father Confessor. Have you prayed to Night,* Desdemona? [V. ii. 25]. But the suspence is necessary, that he might have a convenient while so to *roul his Eyes,* and so to *gnaw* his *nether lip* to the spectators. (p. 160)

But hark, a most tragical thing laid to her charge.

Oth. That Handkerchief, that I so lov'd, and gave thee,
Thou gav'st to *Cassio.*
Desd. No by my Life and Soul;
Send for the man and ask him.
Oth.——By Heaven, I saw my Handkerchief in his hand——
——I saw the Handkerchief.

[V. ii. 48-50, 62, 66]

So much ado, so much stress, so much passion and repetition about an Handkerchief! Why was not this call'd the *Tragedy of the Handkerchief?* What can be more absurd. . . . Had it been *Desdemona's* Garter, the Sagacious Moor might have smelt a Rat: but the Handkerchief is so remote a trifle, no Booby, on this side *Mauritania,* cou'd make any consequence from it.

We may learn here, that a Woman never loses her Tongue, even tho' after she is stifl'd.

> *Desd.* O falsly, falsly murder'd.
> *Em.* Sweet *Desdemona,* O sweet Mistress, speak.
> *Desd.* A guiltless death I dye.
> *Em.* O who has done the deed?
> *Desd.* No body, I my self, farewel.
> Commend me to my kind Lord, O farewel.
>
> [V. ii. 117, 121-25]

This *Desdemona* is a black swan; or an old Black-amoor is a bewitching Bed-fellow. (pp. 160-61)

But hark what follows:

> *Oth.*   ——O heavy hour!
> Methinks it shou'd be now a huge Eclipse
> Of Sun and Moon, and that the affrighted globe
> Shou'd yawn at Alteration.
>
> [V. ii. 98-101]

This is wonderful. Here is Poetry to *elevate* and *amuse.* Here is sound All-sufficient. It wou'd be uncivil to ask [John] *Flamstead,* if the Sun and Moon can both together be so hugely eclipsed, in any *heavy hour* whatsoever. Nor must the Spectators consult *Gresham* Colledge, whether a body is naturally *frighted* till he *Yawn* agen. The Fortune of *Greece* is not concern'd with these Matters. These are Physical circumstances a Poet may be ignorant in, without any harm to the publick. These slips have no influence on our Manners and good Life; which are the Poets Province.

Rather may we ask here what unnatural crime *Desdemona,* or her Parents had committed, to bring this Judgment down upon her; to Wed a Black-amoor, and innocent to be thus cruelly murder'd by him. What instruction can we make out of this Catastrophe? Or whither must our reflection lead us? Is not this to envenome and sour our spirits, to make us repine and grumble at Providence; and the government of the World? If this be our end, what boots it to be Vertuous?

Desdemona dropt the Handkerchief, and missed it that very day after her Marriage; it might have been rumpl'd up with her Wedding sheets: And this Night that she lay in her wedding sheets, the *Fairey* Napkin (whilst *Othello* was stifling her) might have started up to disarm his fury, and stop his ungracious mouth. Then might she (in a Traunce for fear) have lain as dead. Then might he, believing her dead, touch'd with remorse, have honestly cut his own Throat, by the good leave, and with the applause of all the Spectators. Who might thereupon have gone home with a quiet mind, admiring the beauty of Providence; fairly and truly represented on the Theatre.

Oth.——Why, how shou'd she be murdered?
Em. Alas, who knows?
Oth. You heard her say her self it was not I.
Em. She did so, I must needs report a truth.
Oth. She's like a liar gone to burn in Hell.
'Twas I that did it.

Em. O, the more Angel she!
And you the blacker Devil.
Oth. She turn'd to folly, and she was an Whore.
Em. Thou dost belye her, and thou art a Devil.
Oth. She was false as Water.
Em. Thou art rash as Fire,
To say that she was false: O she was heavenly true.

                                          [V. ii. 126-35]

In this kind of Dialogue they continue for forty lines farther, before she bethinks her self, to cry Murder.

Em.   ——Help, help, O help,
The Moor has kill'd my Mistress, murder, Murder.

                                          [V. ii. 166-67]

But from this Scene to the end of the Play we meet with nothing but blood and butchery, described much-what to the style of *the last Speeches and Confessions of the persons executed at Tyburn:* with this difference, that there we have the *fact*, and the due course of Justice, whereas our Poet against all Justice and Reason, against all Law, Humanity and Nature, in a barbarous arbitrary way, executes and makes havock of his subjects, *Hab-nab*, as they come to hand. *Desdemona* dropt her Handkerchief; therefore she must be stifl'd. *Othello*, by law to be broken on the Wheel, by the Poets cunning escapes with cutting his own Throat. *Cassio*, for I know not what, comes off with a broken shin. *Jago* murders his Benefactor *Roderigo*, as this were poetical gratitude. *Jago* is not yet kill'd, because there never yet was such a villain alive. The Devil, if once he brings a man to be dipt in a deadly sin, lets him alone, to take his course: and now when the *Foul Fiend* has done with him, our wise Authors take the sinner into their poetical service; there to accomplish him, and do the Devils drudgery.

Philosophy tells us it is a principle in the Nature of Man *to be grateful*.

History may tell us that *John an Oaks, John a Stiles*, or *Jago* were ungrateful; *Poetry* is to follow Nature; Philosophy must be his guide: history and *fact* in particular cases of *John an Oaks*, or *John of Styles*, are no warrant or direction for a Poet.... History might without any preamble or difficulty, say that *Jago* was ungrateful. Philosophy then calls him unnatural; But the Poet is not, without huge labour and preparation to expose the Monster; and after shew the Divine Vengeance executed upon him. The Poet is not to add wilful Murder to his ingratitude: he has not antidote enough for the Poison: his Hell and Furies are not punishment sufficient for one single crime, of that bulk and aggravation.

Em. O thou dull Moor, that Handkerchief thou speakest
    on,
I found by Fortune, and did give my Husband:
For often with a solemn earnestness,
(More than indeed belong'd to such a trifle)
He beg'd of me to steal it.

                                          [V. ii. 225-29]

Here we see the meanest woman in the Play takes this *Handkerchief* for a *trifle* below her Husband to trouble his head about it. Yet we find, it entered into our Poets head, to make a Tragedy of this *Trifle*.

Then for the *unraveling of the Plot*, as they call it, never was old deputy Recorder in a Country Town, with his spectacles in summoning up the evidence, at such a puzzle: so blunder'd, and bedoultefied: as is our Poet, to have a good riddance: And get the *Catastrophe* off his hands.

What can remain with the Audience to carry home with them from this sort of Poetry, for their use and edification? how can it work, unless (instead of settling the mind, and purging our passions) to delude our senses, disorder our thoughts, addle our brain, pervert our affections, hair our imaginations, corrupt our appetite, and fill our head with vanity, confusion, *Tinta-marre*, and Jingle-jangle, beyond what all the Parish Clarks of *London*, with their *old Testament* farces, and interludes, in *Richard* the seconds time cou'd ever pretend to? Our only hopes, for the good of their Souls, can be, that these people go to the Playhouse, as they do to Church, to sit still, look on one another, make no reflection, nor mind the Play, more than they would a Sermon.

There is in this Play, some burlesk, some humour, and ramble of Comical Wit, some shew, and some *Mimickry* to divert the spectators: but the tragical part is, plainly none other, than a Bloody Farce, without salt or savour. (pp. 161-64)

> *Thomas Rymer, "'A Short View of Tragedy'," in his* The Critical Works of Thomas Rymer, *edited by Curt A. Zimansky, Yale University Press, 1956, pp. 82-176.*

CHARLES GILDON   (essay date 1694)

[*Gildon was the first critic to write an extended commentary on Shakespeare's plays. Like many other Neoclassicists, he regarded Shakespeare as an imaginative playwright who nevertheless lacked knowledge of the dramatic "rules" necessary for correct writing. In the excerpt below from his* Miscellaneous Letters and Essays on Several Subjects in Prose and Verse *(1694), Gildon offers a defense of Shakespeare's* Othello *against the charges of Thomas Rymer (1692). Gildon is primarily concerned with refuting Rymer's indictment of the "Fable" or narrative as flawed with improbabilities. In opposition to Rymer, the critic argues that Shakespeare has drawn Othello as a man of such "extraordinary Merit and Vertues" that Desdemona's love for him is very credible. In addition, he attacks Rymer for an ignoble bias against men of other races, averring that, although it may have been unusual in Renaissance times for a black man to rise to such eminence as the generalship of the Venetian military forces, ideally a man should be honored for his character and deeds regardless of the color of his skin. Thus, Gildon maintains, Shakespeare has fulfilled the dramatist's function by depicting an ideal, meritocratic world where a noble, heroic Moor may achieve distinction. However, in a later essay (see excerpt below, 1710), Gildon reversed himself on the question of whether a black man is a suitable protagonist for a tragic drama, claiming that he is not. For additional discussions of this issue, see the excerpts by William Kenrick (1774), Samuel Taylor Coleridge (1808-18 and 1813), Charles Lamb (1811), John Quincy Adams (1835), Denton J. Snider (1887), and G. M. Matthews (1964), as well as the essay by G. K. Hunter cited in the Additional Bibliography. Such other critics as George Steevens (1772) and Stopford A. Brooke (1913) have also examined the implausible or improbable elements in* Othello.]

To begin with the *Fable* (as our Critic has done [see excerpt above by Thomas Rymer, 1692]) I must tell him, he has as falsly, as ridiculously represented it.... (p. 93)

The *Fable* to be perfect must be *Admirable* and *Probable*, and as it approaches those two, 'tis more or less perfect in its kind. *Admirable*, is what is *uncommon*, and *extraordinary*. *Probable*, is what is agreeable to common Opinion. This must be the Test of this *Fable* of *Othello*; but then we must not take it, as given us by our Drolling Critic, who very truely confesseth in his former Book, (and in that he is no Changeling) he must be merry out of Season, as he always is. (pp. 94-5)

I suppose none will deny that it is *Admirable:* that is, compos'd of Incidents that happen not e'ery day, his Antagonist confesses as much; there is therefore nothing but the *Probability* of it attaqu'd by him, which I question not either wholly to prove, or at least to set it on the same bottom with the best of *Sophocles,* that of his *Oedipus.*

First, to see whether he have sinn'd against Probability, let us consider what our Caviller objects, all which may be reduc'd to two Points. First, That 'tis not probable that the Senate of *Venice* (tho' it usually employ Strangers) should employ a *Moor* against the *Turk:* neither is it in the next place *probable,* that *Desdemona* shou'd be in Love with him. On this turns all the Accusation, this is the very Head of his offending.

All the Reason he gives, or rather implies, for the first Improbability is, That 'tis not likely the State of *Venice,* wou'd employ a *Moor,* (taking him for a *Mahometan*) against the *Turk,* because of the mutual Bond of Religion. He, indeed says not so, but takes it for granted that *Othello* must be rather for the *Turkish* interest than the *Venetian,* because a *Moor.* But, I think (nor does he oppose it with any reason) the Character of the *Venetian State* being to employ Strangers in their Wars, it gives sufficient ground to our Poet, to suppose a *Moor* employ'd by 'em as well as a *German;* that is a *Christian Moor,* as *Othello* is represented by our Poet, for from such a *Moor,* there cou'd be no just fear of treachery in favour of the *Mahometans.* He tells us——

> I fetch my Life and Being from Men of Royal Siege.
> [I. ii. 21-2]

Supposing him therefore the Son or Nephew of the Emperor of *Monomotopa, Aethiopia* or *Congo,* forc'd to leave his Country for Religion, or any other occasion, coming to *Europe* by the convenience of the *Portugueze* Ships, might after several Fortunes, serve first as a Voluntier till he had signaliz'd himself, and prov'd himself worthy of Command; part of this may very reasonably be drawn from what the Poet makes him say. Now upon this Supposition, it appears more rational, and probable, the *Venetians* shou'd employ a Stranger, who wholly depended on themselves, and whose Country was too remote, to influence him to their prejudice, than other Strangers, whose Princes may in some measure direct their Actions for their own Advantage. But that *Othello* is suppos'd to be a Christian is evident from the Second Act, and from these words of *Jago;*— *And then for her to Win the* Moor, *were't to renounce his* Baptism, &c. [II. iii. 342-43]. Why therefore an *African* Christian may not by the *Venetians* be suppos'd to be as zealous against the *Turks,* as an *European* Christian; I cannot imagine. So that this Bustle of *Littora littoribus Contraria* [shore clash with shore], &c. is only an inconsiderate Amusement, to shew how little the Gentleman was troubled with thought when he wrote it.

No more to the purpose, is that Heat he expresses against *Shakspears* giving a Name to his *Moor,* though *Cinthio* did not, though History did not warrant it. For this can be no more objected to our Poet, then the perverting the Character of *Dido,* and confounding the Chronology to bring her to the time of *Aeneas,* is to *Virgil;* the first as 'tis not mention'd in History, so it does not contradict it; but the last is a plain opposition to express History, and Chronology. If *Virgil* be allow'd his Reason for doing that, *Shakespear* is not to seek for one for what he has done. 'Twas necessary to give his *Moor* a place of some Figure in the World, to give him the greater Authority, and to make his Actions the more Considerable, and what place more

likely to fix on, than *Venice,* where Strangers are admitted to the highest Commands in Military Affairs.

'Tis granted, a *Negro* here does seldom rise above a Trumpeter, nor often perhaps higher at *Venice.* But then that proceeds from the Vice of Mankind, which is the Poets Duty as he informs us, to correct, and to represent things as they should be, not as they are. Now 'tis certain, there is no reason in the nature of things, why a *Negro* of equal Birth and Merit, should not be on an equal bottom, with a *German, Hollander, Frenchman,* &c. The Poet, therefore ought to do justice to Nations, as well as Persons, and set them to rights, which the common course of things confounds. The same reason stands in force for this, as for punishing the Wicked, and making the Virtuous fortunate, which as [René] *Rapin,* and all the Critics agree, the Poet, ought to do, though it generally happens otherways. The Poet has therefore well chosen a polite People, to cast off this customary Barbarity, of confining Nations, without regard to their Virtue, and Merits, to slavery, and contempt for the meer Accident of their Complexion.

I hope I have brought by this time as convincing proofs for the probability in this particular, as Mr. *Rymer* has against it, if I have not wholly gain'd my Point. Now therefore I shall proceed to the probability of *Desdemona*'s Love for the *Moor,* which I think is something more evident against him.

Whatever he aims at in his inconsistant Ramble against this, may be reduc'd to the *Person* and the *Manner.* Against the *Person* he quotes you two Verses out of *Horace,* that have no more reference to this, than——*in the Beginning God made the Heaven and the Earth,* has to the proof of the *Jus Divinum* [Divine Love] of lay Bishops, the Verses are these,

> *'Sed non ut placidis coeant immitia, non ut*
> *Serpentes avibus geminentur, tiegribus agni.*

> [Savage should not mate with gentle, nor serpents pair with birds, lambs with tigers, *Ars Poetica.*]

unless he can prove that the Colour of a Man alters his Species, and turns him into a *Beast* or *Devil.* 'Tis such a vulgar Error, so criminal a fondness of our Selves, to allow nothing of Humanity to any but our own Acquaintance of the fairer hew; that I wonder a Man, that pretends to be at all remov'd from the very Dreggs of the thoughtless Mob, should espouse it in so public a manner a Critic too, who puts the Poet: in mind of correcting the common corruptions of Custom. Any Man that has convers'd with the best Travels, or read any thing of the History of those parts, on the continent of *Africa,* discover'd by the *Portugueze,* must be so far from robbing the *Negroes* of some Countrys there of *Humanity,* that they must grant them not only greater Heroes, nicer observers of Honour, and all the Moral Virtues that distinguish'd the old *Romans,* but also much better Christians (where Christianity is profess'd) than we of *Europe* generally are. They move by a nobler Principle, more open, free and generous, and not such slaves to sordid Interest.

After all this, *Othello* being of *Royal Blood,* and a Christian, where is the disparity of the Match. If either side is advanc'd, 'tis *Desdemona.* And why must this Prince though a Christian, and of known and experienc'd *Virtue, Courage,* and *Conduct,* be made such a Monster, that the *Venetian* Lady can't love him without perverting Nature? Experience tells us, that there's nothing more common than Matches of this kind, where the Whites, and Blacks cohabit, as in both the *Indies:* and Even here at home, Ladys that have not wanted white Adorers have indulg'd their Amorous Dalliances, with their Sable Lovers, without any of *Othello*'s Qualifications, which is proof enough, that Nature and Custom, have not put any such unpassable bar betwixt Creatures of the same kind, because of different colors, which I hope will remove the improbability of the Person, especially when the powerful Auxilarys of extraordinary Merit and Vertues come to plead with a generous Mind.

The probability of the *Person* being thus confirmed, I shall now consider that of the *Manner* of his obtaining her *Love*. To this end we must still keep in mind the known and experienc'd Virtue of the *Moor* which gave Credit, and Authority to what he said; and then we may easily suppose the story of his Fortunes, and Dangers, would make an impression of Pity, and admiration at least on the bosom of a Woman, of a noble and generous Nature. No *Man* of any generous Principle, but must be touch'd at suff'ring Virtue, and value the noble sufferer, whose Courage and Bravery, bears him through uncommon Trials and extraordinary Dangers. Nor would it have less force on a Woman of any principle of Honour and tenderness; she must be mov'd and pleas'd with the Narration, she must admire his constant Virtue, and Admiration is the first step to Love, which will easily gain upon those who have once entertain'd it.

Dido in *Virgil* was won by the *Trojan* stranger she never saw before, by the relation of his fortunes and Escapes; and some particulars of the Narration of *Aeneas*, carrys full as ridiculous and absurd a Face as any thing, *Othello* says; the most trifling of which is,

> And of the Cannibals that each other eat
> the *Anthropophagi*, and Men whose Heads
> do grow beneath their Shoulders.
>
> [I. iii. 143-45]

for all the rest is admirably fine, though our wonderful Critic can't relish it, there is a moving Beauty in each Line, the words are well chosen, and the Image they give great, and Poetical; what an Image does *Desarts* IDLE give? that very Epithet is a perfect *Hypotyposis* [vivid description], and seems to place me in the midst of one, where all the active hurry of the World is lost; but all that I can say, will not reach the excellence of that Epithet so many properties of such a place meet in it. But as for the *Cannibals*, &c. *and the Men whose Heads grow beneath their Shoulders*. I have heard it condemn'd by Men whose tast I generally approve, yet must they give me leave to dissent from them here, and permit me either wholly to justifie *Shakespear*, even here, or at least to put him on an equal bottom with *Virgil*, in his most beautiful part. For the fault lyes either in the *Improbability* of those things, or their *Impertinence* to the business in Hand. First Probability we know is built on common Opinion; but 'tis certain the *Canibals* have been generally believed, and that with very good grounds of Truth; so that there can be no doubt of the probability of that. Next for the *Men whose Heads grow beneath their Shoulders*, though that is not establish'd on so good a Foundation as Truth; yet the general Traditionary belief of it in those days, is sufficient to give it a poetical probability. As this was not *Improbable*, so neither was it *Impertinent*, for 'tis certain, that whatever contributed to the raising her Idea of his Dangers and Escapes, must conduce to his aim, but to fall into the Hands of those, whom not only the fury of War, but that of Custom makes Cruel, heightens the danger, and by consequence the Concern, especially in a young Lady possess'd with the legend of the Nursery, whence she must have amazing Ideas of the Danger of the brave *Moor* from them.

But at worst, *Shakespear* is on as good a bottom as *Virgil*, in this particular; the Narrative of *Aeneas*, that won the Heart of *Dido*, has many things full as trifling and absurd as this, if not far more? For is there not as much likelyhood that there shou'd be a People that have their Heads grow beneath their Shoulders, as the Race of the *Cyclops*, that have but one Eye, just beneath their Foreheads, and that *Polyphemus* his Eye was as big as a *Grecian* Shield, or the Sun; or that he cou'd wade through the Sea, without being up to his middle. Can there be invented any thing so unnatural, as the Harpys in the third Book, who had the Faces of Virgins, Wings, Feathers, &c. Of Birds, and a human Voice. . . . (pp. 95-102)

The Absurdities in *Homer* are much more numerous than those in *Virgil*. (I mean those that must pass for such, if this in *Shakespear* is so,) But because they relate not to this particular, I shall say nothing of them here. All these I have remark'd in the Narration of *Aeneas*, hinder'd not, but that it won the Heart of *Dido*, though firmly bent against a second Amour. . . . *Desdemona* had no such tye, to steel her Heart against *Othello*'s Tongue, no reason to curb that Passion she ne'er felt before, when the prevailing Virtue of the *Moor*, attaqu'd her Heart; well may we therefore believe *Desdemona* shou'd yield to the same force, that conquer'd *Dido*, with all her Resolutions and Engagements, to the memory of *Sichceus*. (p. 104)

By this time, I hope our *Drolling Caviller*, will grant it no such monstrous absurdity for the *Doge* to say,

> I think this Tale wou'd win my Daughter too.
>
> [I. iii. 171]

since without doubt, that short summing up of what was only the subject of his tale to *Desdemona*, with only the supposition of the particulars, must move any generous Brest.

But should all I have said fail of clearing the *Probability* of the *Fable* from Mr. *Rymers* Objections, yet ought not that to rob *Shakespear* of his due Character of being a *Poet*, and a great *Genius:* unless he will for the same reason deny those prerogatives to *Homer*, and *Sophocles*. The former has often lost the *Probable*, in the *Admirable*, as any Book of the *Iliads* and *Odysses* will prove; and the latter, as *Rapin* justly observes, has not kept to probability, ev'n in his best performance, I mean in his *Oedipus Tyrannus;* for (as *Rapin* has it) Oedipus *ought not to have been ignorant of the assassinate of Laius, the ignorance he's in of the Murder, which makes all the Beauty of the intrigue, is not probable;* and if a Man wou'd play the Droll with this *Fable* of Oedipus, it would furnish full as ridiculous a Comment, as witty Mr. *Rymer* has done from this of *Othello*. . . . (pp. 105-06)

But I have dwelt so long on the Fable [of *Othello*], that I have not time enough to discuss the other parts, as the *Characters*, *Thoughts*, and *Expressions*, so fully as I ought; especially, the *Thought* and *Expression*, for 'twou'd require a Volumn near as big as *Shakespear*, to set them off according to their worth; with all the proofs from Grammar or Rhetoric of their Truth and Justness. The Fable is look'd upon by *Rapin*, and after him by our *Gleaner of Criticisms*, as the Soul of the Play, and therefore I may be excus'd for my prolixity in its defence, and allow'd a little more time for a full Justification of the other parts of *Shakespear*, attaqu'd with less Reason and Justice: Mr. *Rymer* has taken above ten Year to digest his Accusations, and therefore it can't in reason be thought I shou'd not in half so many days be able to perform all the work he has cut out: Nor can I proceed to a particular consideration of all the Characters of this Play at this time. *Desdemona* I think is the most faulty:

but since our *Antagonist* will have *Jago*, the most *intollerable*, I shall confine my self to that.

What I have said in the beginning of my Vindication of *Shakespear*, must here be recollected on *Jago*'s behalf; besides which, I have some other considerations to offer, which I hope will lighten the insupportable load of Contempt, and Ridicule cast on him by our Caviller.

First, Therefore in our Judgment of *Jago,* we must follow the Rule of *Horace,* so much stood upon by Mr. *Rymer.*

Intererit multum
Cholcus an Assyrius, Thebis nutritus, an Argis.

[Vast difference will it make
(whether a god be speaking or a hero)
a Colchian or an Assyrian, one bred at Thebes or at
    Argos, *Ars Poetica.*]

We are not only to respect the profession of the Man in our Judgment of the Character, but we must also have an Eye to his Nation, the Country he was born in, and the prevailing temper of the People, with their National Vices; by this Rule we shall find *Jago,* an *Italian;* by Nature *Selfish, Jealous, Reserv'd, Revengeful* and *Proud,* nor can I see any reason to suppose his Military Profession shou'd too powerfully influence him to purge away all these Qualities, and establish contrary in their room. Nor can I believe the quotation from *Horace,* which our Caviller produces, can justly be extended to all degrees of Soldiers.

It runs thus in *Horace.*
——*Honoratum si forte reponis Achillens*
Impiger, Jracundus, Inexcrabilis, Acer,
Jura neget sibi Nata, nibil non arroget armis.

[Supposing that, by chance, (you choose to depict) the
    honoring of Achilles,
(show him as) diligent, irascible, stern, vigorous,
denying that laws apply to him, (and) claiming that
    weapons of war have preeminence.]

'Tis plain from what goes before, and what follows after that *Horace* meant not this, at least for a general Character of all Soldiers, but only as a direction for the drawing *Achilles,* or such a Hero. . . . (pp. 108-10)

I know *Rapin* gives a Soldier these qualities; *Fierce, Insolent, Surly, Inconstant,* which partly are the effects of their manner of Life, but I can't conceive these to be opposite to those other in *Jago.* The *Characters* or *Manners,* as the same *Rapin* observes, are to be drawn from Experience; and that tells us, that they differ in Soldiers according to their Nature and Discipline; that also tells us that the Camp is not free from Designs, Supplantings, and all the effects of the most criminal of Passions, and this indeed is evident from the Draught *Homer* gives us of the Grecian Camp, where *Love* was not judg'd so contrary to the Character of a General, as Mr. *Rymer* wou'd have it thought: *Achilles* and *Agamemnon* having both their admir'd Captives. And let Mr. *Rymer* say what he please, I can prove that 'twas the Love of *Brieseis,* that troubl'd *Achilles,* and confirm'd his anger, as well as the meer affront of having his prize taken from him, but of that in another place. In short, the *Thersites* of *Homer* differs as much from the Soldiers of Mr. *Rymers* acquaintance, as *Jago* does; nor is he the only Soldier that cou'd dissemble. *Sinon* in *Virgil,* and *Neoptolemus* in *Sophocles,* are as guilty of it as he.

But granting that *Jago*'s Character is defective something in the Manners, *Homer* and *Sophocles* have been guilty (the first much more, the other not much less) of the same: what are the Wounds, Scuffles, Passions, Adulteries, &c. Of the Gods and Goddesses, obvious to the meanest Capacity, and beyond all dispute? Is not the Character of *Oedipus Coloneus* of *Sophocles,* as *Rapin* remarks, extreamly unproportionable to *Oedipus Tyrannus?* And tho' Mr. *Rymer* is so severe, to deny that the Character of *Jago* is that of a Soldier, because so different from his Military Acquaintance; yet I'm confident he wou'd take it extreamly amiss, If I shou'd deny him to be a Critic, because so contrary to all the Critics that I have met with, playing the merry Droll, instead of giving serious and solid Reasons for what he advances.

The other Characters of this Play I must defer till another time, as well as a thorough defence of his Thoughts and Expression, both which he wholly denies him; and with an extravagantly wonderful Assurance publicly tells us; that the Neighing of a Horse has more *Humanity,* (for that is his Wittycism) than the Tragical Flights of *Shakespear.* (pp. 111-12)

I shall hereafter step into the Scenes with Mr. *Rymer,* and also examine his Narrations, Deliberations, Didactic and Pathetic Discourses, which are all that are made use of in Tragedy, in which if he sometimes err, he has yet perform'd well; and amidst his faults you shall find some thoughts of a great Genius. I shall only now observe *en passant,* in defence of that Scene, betwixt *Jago* and *Othello* [Act III, Scene iii], that we ought not to be imposed on by positive assertions, or think because Mr. *Rymer* tells us so, that half words, and ambiguous Reflexions, do not naturally work up Jealousie, or that 'tis not natural, for *Othello to catch at e'ry blown surmise.* These Assertions of our Critic shew him to be very ignorant of the very nature of this Passion, for as 'tis reduc'd to the primitive *Desire* by the Moralists, so 'tis thus by them defin'd,

> Jealousie is a fear of loosing a good we very much value and esteem, arising from the *least* causes of Suspicion.

now 'tis evident even from the trifling, and false Objections of his enemies that *Shakespear* had this very notion of this passion. For this reason 'tis, he makes *Othello* swallow the very first bait laid by *Jago* for him. *Cassio* is found with *Desdemona,* and on *Othello*'s approach, consciously retires, which tho' he did to avoid his Anger not Jealousie; yet *Jago* improves the opportunity to his purpose, with an—*I like not that* [III. iii. 35]; then to awake the *Moors* Jealousie by degrees, he takes occasion from *Cassio's* departure to question him—*did Cassio when you woo'd my Lady know of your Love?* [III. iii. 94-5]. Which he pursues with *half words,* and ambiguous *Reflexions,* that plainly imply more than they barely express, in which he discover'd, fear to speak out what he desir'd *Othello* shou'd know, the natural consequence of which is the touching a jealous Nature, with curiosity in a thing, that so nearly related to his Happiness. E'ry word rous'd some surmize; and as *Ovid* observes, *cuncta timemus Amantes,* Lovers fear any Appearance [*Metamorphoses*]. But more of this hereafter. In the mean while I'm pretty confident, e'ry Mans own Sence will supply my defect of a particular defence of the working up of *Othello*'s passion of Jealousie. (pp. 116-17)

Charles Gildon, "Some Reflections on Mr. Rymer's 'Short View of Tragedy', and an Attempt at a Vindication of Shakespeare," in The Impartial Critick [*and*] Miscellaneous Letters and Essays *by John Den-*

*nis [and] Charles Gildon, 1693, 1694. Reprint by
Garland Publishing, Inc., 1973, pp. 64-118.*

[CHARLES GILDON]   (essay date 1710)

[In the following excerpt, taken from his Remarks on the Plays
of Shakespear *(1710), Gildon reverses his earlier estimation of*
Othello, *but offers no explanation of his change of heart. Agreeing
with Thomas Rymer (see excerpt above, 1692), the critic argues
that "making a Negro of the Hero or chief Character of the Play,
would shock anyone." Gildon also condemns Shakespeare's depiction of Desdemona's love for Othello as a "monstruous" thing,
wholly inconsistent with the custom of the times. For further
discussions of the issue of miscegenation in the play, see the
excerpts by William Kenrick (1774), Samuel Taylor Coleridge
(1808-18 and 1813), Charles Lamb (1811), John Quincy Adams
(1835), Denton J. Snider (1887), and G. M. Matthews (1964),
as well as the essay by G. K. Hunter cited in the Additional
Bibliography. Gildon further disparages Shakespeare's use of
soliloquies in the play and avers that the dramatist has mishandled
the time scheme in* Othello.]

I must own that the Faults found in [the Fable of *Othello*] by
Mr. *Rymer* [see excerpt above, 1692] are but too visible for
the most Part. That of making a *Negro* of the Hero or chief
Character of the Play, wou'd shock any one; for it is not the
Rationale of the thing and the Deductions, that may thence be
brought to diminish the Opposition betwixt the different Colours of Mankind that wou'd not be sufficient to take away that
which is shocking in this Story; since this entirely depends on
Custom which makes it so, and on common Womens admitting
a *Negro* to a Commerce with her every one almost starts at
the Choice. Much more in a Woman of Vertue; and indeed
Iago, Brabantio, &c. have shewn such Reasons as make it
monstruous. I wonder *Shakespear* saw this in the Persons of
his Play, and not in his own Judgment. If *Othello* had been
made deformed, and not over young but no Black, it had
removed most of the Absurdities, but now it pleases only by
Prescription. 'Tis possible, that an innocent tender young
Woman, who knew little of the World, might be won by the
brave Actions of a gallant Man not to regard his Age or De-
formities, but Nature, or what is all one in this Case, Custom
having put such a Bar as so opposite a Colour, it takes away
our Pity from her, and only raises our Indignation against him.
I shall pass over the other Observations founded on this Error,
since they have been sufficiently taken Notice of already. It
must be own'd that *Shakespear* drew Men better, than Women;
to whom indeed he has seldom given any considerable Place
in his Plays; here and in *Romeo* and *Juliet* he has done most
in this matter, but here he has not given any graceful Touches
to *Desdemona* in many places of her Part.

Whether the Motives of *Othello*'s Jealousie be strong enough
to free him from the Imputation of Levity and Folly I will not
determine; since Jealousie is born often of very slight Occasions, especially in the Breasts of Men of those warmer Climates. Yet this must be said *Shakespear* has manag'd the Scene
so well, that it is that alone, which supports his Play, and
imposes on the Audience so very successfully, that till a Reformation of the Stage comes, I believe it will always be kindly
receiv'd. (pp. 410-11)

There are in this Play as well as in most of this Poet a great
abundance of *Soliloquies* in which the *Dramatic* Person discourses with the Audience his Designs, his Temper, &c. which
are highly unnatural, and not to be imitated by any one.

The *Moor* has not bedded his Lady till he came to *Cyprus,* nay
it was not done . . . , and yet it is before and after urg'd that
she was or might be sated with him. But those little Forget-
fulnesses are not worth minding. (p. 412)

*[Charles Gildon], "Remarks on the Plays of Shake-
spear," in* The Works of Mr. William Shakespear,
Vol. 7 *by William Shakespeare, 1710. Reprint by
AMS Press, Inc., 1967, pp. 257-444.*

JOHN HUGHES   (essay date 1713)

*[Hughes was a poet, translator, and dramatist who frequently
contributed to such periodicals as the* Guardian, *where the following essay on* Othello *first appeared in April, 1713. In the
excerpt below, he declares that the central interest of* Othello *is
the depiction of jealousy, remarking that the Moor's "tempestuous" love for Desdemona and the "tumultuous" quality of his
intellect contribute to his susceptibility to the "deep and subtle
Villany of* Iago." *Hughes is the first critic to suggest that Shakespeare's portrayal of Othello's torments evokes our pity to such
a degree that, even as he murders Desdemona, we feel compassion
for him, as well as for his victim. He is also the earliest to argue
that Shakespeare's representation of the handkerchief as the linch-
pin of Othello's downfall underscores the dramatist's understanding that jealous minds may be swayed by trifles. For additional
discussions of Shakespeare's use of the handkerchief as a dramatic
device, see the excerpts by Thomas Rymer (1692), Lewis Theobald
(1733), Wolstenholme Parr (1795), Robert G. Heilman (1956),
and Harry Levin (1964); also, see the essays by Nigel Alexander
and John Middleton Murry cited in the Additional Bibliography.
Finally, perhaps thinking of Rymer, Hughes castigates those critics who have ridiculed what he considers the beauties of* Othello;
*the critic contends that such interpretations "betray a Mechanical
Judgment formed out of borrow'd Rules and Commonplace Reading."]*

I have often considered [*Othello*] a noble but irregular Production of a Genius which had the Power of animating the
Theatre beyond any Writer we have ever known. The Touches
of Nature in it are strong and masterly, but the Oeconomy of
the Fable, and in some Particulars the Probability, are too much
neglected. If I would speak of it in the most severe Terms, I
should say as [Edmund] *Waller* does of [Francis Beaumont and
John Fletcher's] the *Maid's Tragedy,*

> Great are its Faults, but glorious is its Flame.

But it would be a poor Employment in a Critick to observe
upon the Faults and shew no Taste for the Beauties in a Work
that has always struck the most sensible Part of our Audiences
in a very forcible Manner.

The chief Subject of this Piece is the Passion of *Jealousie,*
which the Poet has represented at large in its Birth, its various
Workings and Agonies, and its horrid Consequences. From
this Passion, and the Innocence and Simplicity of the Person
suspected, arises a very moving Distress.

It is a Remark, as I remember, of a Modern Writer, who is
thought to have penetrated deeply into the Nature of the Passions, that *the most extravagant Love is nearest to the strongest
Hatred.* The Moor is furious in both these Extremes. His Love
is tempestuous, and mingled with a Wildness peculiar to his
Character which seems very artfully to prepare for the Change
which is to follow.

How savage, yet how ardent is that Expression of the Raptures of his Heart when, looking after *Desdemona* as she withdraws, he breaks out,

> Excellent Wretch! Perdition catch my Soul
> But I do love thee; and when I love thee not,
> *Chaos* is come again.

> [III. iii. 90-2]

The deep and subtle Villany of *Iago,* in working this Change from Love to Jealousie in so tumultuous a Mind as that of *Othello,* prepossessed with a Confidence in the disinterested Affection of the Man who is leading him on insensibly to his Ruin, is likewise drawn with a Masterly Hand. *Iago's* broken Hints, Questions, and seeming Care to hide the Reason of them; his obscure Suggestions to raise the Curiosity of the Moor; his personated Confusion and refusing to explain himself while *Othello* is drawn on and held in suspence till he grows impatient and angry, then his throwing in the Poyson, and naming to him in a Caution the Passion he would raise

> —O beware of Jealousie!

> [III. iii. 165]

are inimitable Strokes of Art in that Scene which has always been justly esteemed one of the best which was ever represented on the Theatre.

To return to the Character of *Othello;* his Strife of Passions, his Starts, his Returns of Love, and Threatnings to *Iago* who had put his Mind on the Rack; his Relapses afterwards to Jealousie, his Rage against his Wife, and his asking Pardon of *Iago,* whom he thinks he had abused for his Fidelity to him are Touches which no one can overlook that has the Sentiments of Human Nature, or has consider'd the Heart of Man in its Frailties, its Penances, and all the Variety of its Agitations. The Torments which the Moor suffers are so exquisitely drawn as to render him as much an Object of Compassion, even in the barbarous Action of murdering *Desdemona,* as the innocent Person her self who falls under his Hand.

But there is nothing in which the Poet has more shewn his Judgment in this Play, than in the Circumstances of the Handkerchief, which is employ'd as a Confirmation to the Jealousie of *Othello* already raised. What I would here observe is that the very slightness of this Circumstance is the Beauty of it. How finely has *Shakespeare* expressed the Nature of Jealousie in those Lines which on this occasion he puts into the Mouth of *Iago:*

> Trifles light as Air
> Are to the Jealous Confirmations strong
> As Proofs of Holy Writ.

> [III. iii. 322-24]

It would be easie for a tasteless Critick to turn any of the Beauties I have here mentioned into Ridicule; but such an one would only betray a Mechanical Judgment formed out of borrow'd Rules and Commonplace Reading, and not arising from any true Discernment in Human Nature and its Passions.

The Moral of this Tragedy is an admirable Caution against hasty Suspicions and the giving way to the first Transports of Rage and Jealousie, which may plunge a Man in a few Minutes in all the Horrors of Guilt, Distraction and Ruin. (pp. 300-02)

> *John Hughes, in an extract from* Shakespeare, the Critical Heritage: 1693-1733, Vol. 2, *edited by Brian Vickers, Routledge & Kegan Paul, 1974, pp. 299-302.*

LEWIS THEOBALD   (essay date 1717)

[*Theobald, a dramatist and classical scholar, was one of the most important editors of Shakespeare's plays in the first half of the eighteenth century. Although his reputation as a Shakespearean editor declined after his death and the value of his work remains a question today, he nonetheless contributed significant emendations which have been adopted by modern editors. His adaptations of Shakespeare's plays, revised to adhere to Neoclassical dramatic rules, have been less well received. In the following excerpt, first published in the* Censor, *January 12, 1717, Theobald declares that Othello is characterized as having "a Jealousie and Rage, native to him, which he cannot controul" and which impel his destruction, thereby initiating a critical debate over whether the Moor or Iago is more culpable for the tragic events of* Othello. *In addition, like John Hughes (1713), Theobald maintains that the audience's pity and compassion rest with the Moor to the close of the play. Such later critics as Samuel Johnson (1765), August Wilhelm Schlegel (1811), Samuel Taylor Coleridge (1813, 1822, and 1827), Hermann Ulrici (1839), G. G. Gervinus (1849-50), Denton J. Snider (1887), A. C. Bradley (1904), E. K. Chambers (1908), Elmer Edgar Stoll (1915), Allardyce Nicoll (1927), and Harley Granville-Barker (1945) have also addressed the issue of Othello's jealousy.*]

I have frequently perus'd with Satisfaction the *Othello* of *Shakespeare,* a Play most faulty and irregular in many Points but Excellent in one Particular. For the Crimes and Misfortunes of the *Moor* are owing to an impetuous Desire of having his Doubts clear'd, and a Jealousie and Rage, native to him, which he cannot controul and which push him on to Revenge. He is otherwise in his Character brave and open, generous and full of Love for *Desdemona,* but stung with the subtle Suggestions of *Iago* and impatient of a Wrong done to his Love and Honour. Passion at once o'erbears his Reason and gives him up to Thoughts of bloody Reparation. Yet after he has determin'd to murther his Wife his Sentiments of her suppos'd Injury and his Misfortune are so pathetick that we cannot but forget his barbarous Resolution, and pity the Agonies which he so strongly seems to feel.

> *Lewis Theobald, in an extract from* Shakespeare, the Critical Heritage: 1693-1733, Vol. 2, *edited by Brian Vickers, Routledge & Kegan Paul, 1974, p. 308.*

LEWIS THEOBALD   (essay date 1733)

[*The excerpt below is from Theobald's edition of* The Works of William Shakespeare, Vol. 7, *published in 1733. In his commentary on Othello, the critic derides Thomas Rymer (1692) for "the Freedom and Coarseness of his Raillery" against this play, stating that such "Reflexions require no serious Answer." He also remarks that, whereas in Cinthio's tale the moral precept is that young women should not enter into "disproportion'd marriages," Shakespeare's intention was to demonstrate that racial differences between lovers may be obviated by virtue and nobility of character. For additional commentary on the racial difference between Desdemona and the Moor, see the excerpts by Charles Gildon (1694 and 1710), William Kenrick (1774), Samuel Taylor Coleridge (1808-18 and 1813), Charles Lamb (1811), John Quincy Adams (1835), Denton J. Snider (1887), and G. M. Matthews (1964); also, see the essay by G. K. Hunter cited in the Additional Bibliography. Implicitly including Rymer with those "Snarlers and Buffoon-Criticks" who regard the handkerchief as an unsubstantial basis for Othello's jealousy, Theobald counters that Shakespeare anticipated this objection and endowed the handkerchief with magical and mysterious qualities, thereby elevating its significance and embuing it with a dignity appropriate to its role in the tragic pattern of events. Such other critics as Rymer, John Hughes (1713), Wolstenholme Parr (1795), Robert B. Heil-*]

man (1956), Harry Levin (1964), and Nigel Alexander and John Middleton Murry (see Additional Bibliography) have also examined the function of the handkerchief in the play.]

The Groundwork of [*Othello*] is built on a Novel of *Cinthio Giraldi* . . . , who seems to have design'd his Tale a Document to young Ladies against disproportion'd Marriages . . . : That they should not link themselves to such, against whom Nature, Providence, and a different way of Living have interpos'd a Bar. Our Poet inculcates no such Moral: but rather, that a Woman may fall in Love with the Virtues and shining Qualities of a Man; and therein overlook the Difference of Complexion and Colour. Mr. *Rymer* has run riot against the Conduct, Manners, Sentiments, and Diction, of this Play [see excerpt above, 1692]: but in such a Strain, that one is mov'd rather to laugh at the Freedom and Coarseness of his Raillery, than provok'd to be downright angry at his Censures. (pp. 371-72)

[Such] Reflexions require no serious Answer. This Tragedy will continue to have lasting Charms enough to make us blind to such Absurdities, as the Poet thought were not worth his Care. (p. 372)

Because [the] Episode of the *Handkerchief* [III. iv. 55ff.] has been attack'd by Snarlers and Buffoon-Criticks, I am tempted to subjoin an Observation or two in Justification of our Author's Conduct. The Poet seems to have been aware of the Levity of such Judges, as should account the giving away an Handkerchief too slight a Ground for Jealousy. He therefore obviates this, upon the very Moment of the Handkerchief being lost, by making *Iago* say;

> Trifles, light as Air,
> Are, to the Jealous, Confirmations Strong
> As Proofs of holy Writ.
>
> [III. iii. 322-24]

Besides this, let us see how finely the Poet has made his Handkerchief of Significancy and Importance. *Cinthio Giraldi,* from whom he has borrowed the Incident, only says, that it was the *Moor*'s Gift, upon his Wedding, to *Desdemona;* that it was most curiously wrought after the *Moorish* Fashion, and very dear both to him and his Wife. . . . But our Author, who wrote in a superstitious Age, (when *Philtres* were in Vogue for procuring Love, and *Amulets* for preserving it;) makes his Handkerchief deriv'd from an *Inchantress; Magick* and *Mystery* are in its *Materials* and *Workmanship;* its *Qualities* and *Attributes* are solemnly laid down; and the Gift recommended to be cherish'd by its Owners on the most inducing Terms imaginable, *viz.* the making the Party amiable to her Husband, and the keeping his Affections steady. Such Circumstances, if I know any thing of the Matter, are the very Soul and Essence of *Poetry: Fancy* here exerts its great *creating* Power, and adds a Dignity, that surprizes, to its Subject. (pp. 447-48)

> *Lewis Theobald, in notes on "Othello," in* The Works of Shakespeare, Vol. 7 *by William Shakespeare, edited by Lewis Theobald, 1733. Reprint by AMS Press, Inc., 1968, pp. 369-494.*

WILLIAM WARBURTON   (essay date 1747)

[*Warburton, a controversial eighteenth-century English theologian and literary scholar, edited the works of Alexander Pope and Shakespeare. His edition of Shakespeare, based primarily on the work of Lewis Theobald, contains many unsubstantiated and questionable emendations. Because of this, scholars have severely criticized and generally rejected his work. However, Warburton did contribute a few significant textual emendations which are*

accepted by scholars today. In the following excerpt from his edition of The Works of Shakespear (1747), Warburton excoriates the criticism of Thomas Rymer (1692), focusing on the latter's charge that Shakespeare has misrepresented the nature of soldiers in his depiction of Iago. Warburton argues that Rymer has misapplied the rules of Neoclassical literary criticism, and he asserts that the presence in Othello of other soldiers who are "represented as open, generous, and brave" demonstrates Shakespeare's adherence to this rule and, thus, vindicates him from "this impertinent criticism." Not only is Iago clearly shown to be an exception to the standards of military men, the critic contends, but it is also unnatural to assume that no villain "ever insinuated himself into that corps"—an assessment also proposed later by Charlotte Lennox (1754). For further responses to Rymer's commentary on Othello, see the excerpts by Charles Gildon (1694 and 1710), John Hughes (1713), Lewis Theobald (1733), Charlotte Lennox (1753), Harry Levin (1964), and Nigel Alexander (see Additional Bibliography).]*

Rymer, who had neither vigour of imagination to make a poet, or strength of judgment to make a critic, as appears from his *Edgar* and his *Remarks* on Shakespeare, had yet just enough of both to play the buffoon and caviller. His criticisms on the *Poets of the last age,* with only a mixture of trite remarks transcribed from the *French* commentators on *Aristotle,* are one continued heap of ignorance and insolence. Almost the only remark on *Shakespeare* which, I think deserves an answer, is upon *Iago*'s character, which he thus censures: *To entertain the audience* (says he) *with something new and surprising, against common sense and nature, he would pass upon us a close, dissembling, false, ungrateful Rascal instead of an openhearted, frank, plain-dealing soldier, a character constantly worn by them for some thousands of years in the world* [see excerpt above, 1692]. This hath the appearance of sense, being founded on that rule of *Nature* and *Aristotle* that each character should have manners convenient to the age, sex, and condition. . . . But how has our critic applied it? According to this rule it is confessed that a soldier should be brave, generous, and a man of honour. This is to be his dramatic character. But either *one* or *more* of any order may be brought in. If only one, then the character of the order takes its denomination from the manners of that *one.* Had therefore the only soldier in this play been *Iago* the rule had been transgressed, and *Rymer*'s censure well founded. For then this *eternal villain* must have given the character of the soldiery, which had been unjust and unnatural. But if a *number* of the same order be represented, then the character of the order is taken from the manners of the majority; and this, according to nature and common sense. Now in this play there are many of the order of the soldiery, and all, excepting *Iago,* represented as open, generous, and brave. From *these* the soldier's character is to be taken and not from *Iago,* who is brought as an exception to it—unless it be unnatural to suppose there could be an exception, or that a villain ever insinuated himself into that corps. And thus *Shakespeare* stands clear of this impertinent criticism. (pp. 258-59)

> *William Warburton, in an extract from* Shakespeare, the Critical Heritage: 1733-1752, Vol. 3, *edited by Brian Vickers, Routledge & Kegan Paul, 1975, pp. 258-59.*

[CHARLOTTE LENNOX]   (essay date 1753)

[*Lennox was a novelist and Shakespearean scholar who compiled* Shakespear Illustrated *(1753-54), a three-volume edition of translated texts of the sources used by Shakespeare in twenty-two of his plays, including some analyses of the ways in which he used these sources. In the following excerpt on* Othello, *taken from the first volume of that work, she maintains that Shakespeare's modifications of the material in Cintho's novella generally resulted in a superior, more credible tale; she also states that "most of the Charges" Thomas Rymer (1692) leveled against* Othello *"have little or no Foundation." Rejecting Rymer's claim that no soldier should be portrayed as Shakespeare has drawn Iago, she argues, like William Warburton (1747), that it is incredible to think that there should be no "close dissembling Villains" in the military profession. She relates Iago's behavior to his nationality, declaring that, since Iago "was born in a country remarkable for the deep Art, Cruelty, and revengeful Temper of its Inhabitants," it would have been unnatural for him to suspect a personal offense and not pursue vengeance. However, she does agree with Rymer that Iago's part in Desdemona's murder strains credulity because of its excessive cruelty and wickedness. For additional commentary on Rymer's essay, see the excerpts by Charles Gildon (1694 and 1710), John Hughes (1713), Lewis Theobald (1733), William Warburton (1747), and Harry Levin (1964), as well as the essay by Nigel Alexander cited in the Additional Bibliography. On other matters, Lennox is the first commentator to draw attention to the character of Emilia, contending that her depiction as doting on Desdemona yet hiding from her the fact that she has given Iago the handkerchief is the most inconsistent element in the play. The character of Emilia has also been discussed by such critics as George Steevens (1772), the anonymous critic in the* Bee *(1791), G. G. Gervinus (1849-50), Gayle Greene (1979), and Thomas D. Bowman and Carol Thomas Neely (see Additional Bibliography).]*

Othello, or the *Moor* of *Venice,* the Plot of which is drawn from the . . . Novel of *Giraldi Cinthio,* has always been esteemed one of the best of *Shakespear's* Tragedies.

'Tis confessed the Fable is more regular, the Incidents less numerous and closer connected, and the Subject more of a Piece than any other of his Plays, except *Romeo* and *Juliet.*

The Fable *Shakespear* found already formed to his Hands, some few Alterations he has made in it, and generally for the better. (p. 125)

In *Cinthio* the Moor is mentioned without any Mark of Distinction; *Shakespear* makes him descended from a Race of Kings, his Person is therefore made more considerable in the Play than in the Novel, and the Dignity which the *Venetian* Senate bestows upon him is less to be wondered at.

In the Play, *Cassio,* the Person of whom *Othello* is jealous, is represented to be a young amiable Officer, remarkable for the Agreeableness of his Person, and the Sweetness of his Manners, and therefore likely enough to inspire *Desdemona* with a Passion for him.

In the Novel, these Qualities are all ascribed to the Villain who betrays the Moor to the Murder of his Wife; and the suspected Rival is no more than an ordinary Person.

Cinthio might perhaps think it necessary to give his Villain a pleasing Person and insinuating Address, in order to make his Artifices less suspected; but to give Probability to the Jealousy of the Moor, was it not also as necessary to make the suspected Rival possess some of those Qualities with which the Minds of young Ladies are soonest captivated.

Shakespear therefore paints *Cassio* young, handsome, and brave; and *Othello,* who feeds his Jealousy, by reflecting that he himself is neither young nor handsome, by the same Train of Thought falls naturally into a Suspicion, that what he loses, for want of those Qualities, will be gained by another who possesses them.

But on the other Hand *Shakespear* has made a very ill Use of the Lieutenant's Wife.

Cinthio shews this Woman privy, much against her Will, to the Design on *Disdemona;* and though she dares not discover it to her, for fear of her Husband's Resentment, yet she endeavours to put her upon her Guard, and gives her such Advice, as she thinks will render all his Schemes ineffectual.

Shakespear calls this Woman *Emilia,* and makes her the Attendant and Friend of *Desdemona,* yet shews her stealing a Handkerchief from her, which she gives to her Husband, telling him at the same Time that the Lady will run mad when she misses it; therefore, if it is not for some Purpose of Importance that he wants it, desires him to return it to her again.

If her Husband wants it for any Purpose of Importance, that Purpose cannot be very good; this Suspicion however never enters her Mind, but she gives it him only upon that very Condition, which ought to have made her refuse it.

Yet this Woman is the first who perceives *Othello* to be jealous, and repeats this Observation to her Mistress, upon hearing him so often demand the Handkerchief she had stolen, and fly into a Rage when he finds his Wife cannot produce it.

Emilia pronounces him jealous, perceives the Loss of that fatal Handkerchief, confirms some Suspicions he had entertained, and though she loves her Mistress to Excess, chuses rather to let her suffer all the bad Consequences of his Jealousy, than confess she had taken the Handkerchief, which might have set all right again; and yet this same Woman, who could act so base and cruel a Part against her Mistress, has no greater Care in dying, than to be laid by her Side.

Mr. *Rymer,* in his Criticisms on this Play, severely censures the Characters as well as the Fable, and Conduct of the Incidents [see excerpt above, 1692].

That of *Emilia* though more inconsistent than any, he has taken no Notice of; and most of the Charges he brings against the others have little or no Foundation.

The Character of *Iago,* says this Critic, is against common Sense and Nature. "*Shakespear* would pass upon us a close, dissembling, false, insinuating Rascal, instead of an openhearted, frank plain dealing Soldier; a Character constantly worn by them for some Thousands of Years in the World."

The Soldiers are indeed greatly obliged to Mr. *Rymer* for this Assertion, but though it may in general be true, yet surely it is not absurd to suppose that some few Individuals amongst them may be close dissembling Villains.

Iago was a Soldier, it is true, but he was also an *Italian;* he was born in a Country remarkable for the deep Art, Cruelty, and revengeful Temper of its Inhabitants. To have painted an *Italian* injured, or under a Suspicion of being injured, and not to have shewn him revengeful, would have been mistaking his Character.

It is with Justice indeed that Mr. *Rymer* condemns *Shakespear* for that unnecessary and diabolical Cruelty he makes *Iago* guilty of in urging *Othello* to the Murder of the innocent Lady who had never offended him; his Point was gained by making *Othello* jealous, and procuring his Consent to the Death of *Cassio,* who stood in his Way to Preferment: But the Murder of *Desdemona* was such an Excess of wanton Cruelty, that one can hardly conceive it possible a Man could be so transcendently wicked.

Cinthio indeed makes *Iago* not only urge *Othello* to the Murder of his Wife, but is himself the Perpetrator of it; this seems still more absurd; but he tells us, that he had been violently in love with *Desdemona*, and the Indifference she had discovered towards him converted his Love into a settled Hatred.

Shakespear injudiciously copies *Cinthio* in making *Iago* confess a Passion for *Desdemona*, as it rendered his urging on her Murder less probable; since in the Play *Iago* had no Opportunity of declaring that Love to her, and consequently could not be stimulated by her Contempt of him to act so cruel a Part against her.

But he has greatly improved on the Novelist by making him jealous of the Moor with his own Wife; this Circumstance being sufficient, in an *Italian* especially, to account for the Revenge he takes on *Othello*, though his Barbarity to *Desdemona* is still unnatural. (pp. 127-30)

The Character of *Desdemona* fares no better in Mr. *Rymer*'s Hands, than that of *Iago;* her Love for the Moor, he says, is out of Nature.

Such Affections are not very common indeed; but a very few Instances of them prove that they are not impossible; and even in *England* we see some very handsome Women married to Blacks, where their Colour is less familiar than at *Venice;* besides the *Italian* Ladies are remarkable for such Sallies of irregular Passions.

Cinthio, it is true, says, that *Desdemona* was not overcome by a womanish Appetite, but represents her, as *Shakespear* does likewise, subdued by the great Qualities of the Moor.

Courage in Men has always had an invincible Charm for the Ladies; *Desdemona* admired the Moor for his Valour, and the Transition from extreme Admiration to Love is very easy in a female Mind.

Mr. *Rymer* alledges, that *Shakespear* makes *Desdemona* a Senator's Daughter instead of a simple Citizen; and this he imputes to him as a Fault, which is perhaps a great Instance of his Judgment.

There is less Improbability in supposing a noble Lady, educated in Sentiments superior to the Vulgar, should fall in love with a Man merely for the Qualities of his Mind, than that a mean Citizen should be possessed of such exalted Ideas, as to overlook the Disparity of Years and Complexion, and be enamoured of Virtue in the Person of a Moor.

However, it is not true, that *Shakespear* has changed a simple Citizen into a Lady of Quality, since *Desdemona* in the Novel is mentioned as a Woman of high Birth. (pp. 131-32)

That Simplicity in the Manners of *Desdemona*, which Mr. *Rymer* calls Folly and Meanness of Spirit, is the Characteristic of Virtue and Innocence.

Desdemona was conscious of no Guilt, and therefore suspected no Blame: She had so lately given the Moor an incontestable Proof of her Affection, that it was not unnatural for her to impute his sudden Starts of Passion to some other Cause than Jealousy.

The whole Stress of the Proof against *Desdemona* is laid upon the Handkerchief, as well in the Novel as the Play; though I think in the Novel it is more artfully managed; there the Moor insists upon seeing it in the Captain's Possession e'er he will resolve any Thing against his Wife, and the Lieutenant contrives to give him this Satisfaction.

Othello, in the Play, has not the least Appearance of Proof against his Wife, but seeing the Handkerchief in the Lieutenant's Possession; yet this is brought about by mere Accident.

Bianca, to whom *Cassio* had given it to have the Work copied, (which, by the way, was an odd Whim for a Soldier) comes to him while he is engaged in a private Discourse with *Iago;* and *Othello* observing them concealed, and in a Fit of Jealousy, throws the Handkerchief at his Head.

This happens well for *Iago*'s Plot; but as he did not, and indeed could not foresee, this lucky Accident, methinks it would have been more natural, since every Thing depended upon that, to have made it the Effect of some Contrivance of his.

The Outlines of *Iago, Desdemona,* and *Cassio*'s Characters are taken from the Novel; but that of *Othello* is entirely the Poet's own.

In *Cinthio* we have a Moor, valiant indeed, as we are told, but suspicious, sullen, cunning, obstinate and cruel.

Such a Character married to the fair *Desdemona* must have given Disgust on the Stage; the Audience would have been his Enemies, and *Desdemona* herself would have sunk into Contempt for chusing him.

With what Judgment then has *Shakespear* changed the horrid *Moor* of *Cinthio* into the amiable *Othello,* and made the same Actions which we detest in one, excite our Compassion in the other!

The Virtues of *Shakespear*'s *Moor* are no less characteristic than the Vices of *Cinthio*'s; they are the wild Growth of an uncultivated Mind, barbarous and rude as the Clime he is born in; thus, his Love is almost Phrensy; his Friendship Simplicity; his Justice cruel; and his Remorse Self-Murder. (pp. 132-34)

> [*Charlotte Lennox*], *"Observations on the Use Shakespear Has Made of the Foregoing Novel in His Tragedy of 'Othello'," in her* Shakespear Illustrated; or, The Novels and Histories, on Which the Plays of Shakespear Are Founded, *Vol. I, 1753. Reprint by AMS Press Inc., 1973, pp. 125-34.*

JOHN SHEBBEARE   (essay date 1755)

[*Shebbeare was a political writer, satirist, and pamphleteer, who was once convicted of libeling the deceased George I, although he was subsequently granted a royal pension by George III. The excerpt below is from his pseudonymous publication,* Letters on the English Nation, *by Batista Angeloni, a Jesuit resident in London (1755), which is principally an attack on the Duke of Newcastle. Shebbeare praises the psychological veracity, naturalness, and consistency of characterization achieved by Shakespeare in* Othello, *focusing on the figures of the Moor and Iago. He contends that Othello's honesty and openness preclude any condemnation of his credulousness, arguing that Iago's tactics in Act III, Scene iii are so masterful that "it is impossible but that Othello must have been ensnared by his manner of conducting the conversation." Other critics who have maintained that the Moor's open and trusting nature makes him particularly vulnerable to Iago's manipulation include Samuel Taylor Coleridge (1813), A. C. Bradley (1904), E. K. Chambers (1908), and Wyndham Lewis (1927).*]

In the tragedy of *Othello* the Moor, all artless, open, and brave, is reduced by the wiles and subtilty of the hypocritic Iago.

The seeming simplicity of an honest heart is so exquisitely supported and practised by him on the unsuspecting disposition of a virtuous, valiant, and ingenuous mind, that no instance is to be produced of any thing parallel in any theatrical production.

In each of these characters there is not one mistaken deviation; every spectator excuses the Moor in his being deceived, and pities with sincerest sorrow the fate of open honesty seduced by artifice and wiles.

The difficulty is not easily imagined which attends the preservation of these two characters. The Moor must be supported as brave, sensible, and honest; the skill lay in preserving all these from the imputation of weakness in Othello, thro' the conducting the imposition which was to be play'd upon him.

The simple, plain, and seemingly artless cunning of Iago was attended with no less difficulty: to preserve the separate characteristics of this personage without deviating into one instance which might betray his design to a man of sense is of all things the most difficult. Yet thro' the whole conduct of both characters there appears no one violation of the intended and original design of the poet. (p. 185)

His management of Cassio and Roderigo is in the same simple, natural, and apparent honest strain; we see that the deceit must be invisible to such men. The scene in the third act between Othello and Iago, where the latter first insinuates the idea of jealousy into the mind of the Moor, that timidity of accusing the innocent, that regard for the reputation of Desdemona, with the insinuation against her fidelity, are so artfully mixt that it is impossible but that Othello must have been insnared by his manner of conducting the conversation. How inimitable is his pretended love for Othello, his conjuring up the Moor's resolution to know his sentiments by distant hints and suggestions; and when Othello breaks out

> I'll know thy thoughts
>
> [III. iii. 162]

he answers

> You cannot, if my heart were in your hand:
> Nor shall not, whilst 'tis in my custody.
>
> [III. iii. 163-64]

At this seemingly determined secrecy, the Moor pronouncing 'ha!', Iago with all possible art cries out

> Oh! beware, my lord, of jealousy;
> It is a green-eyed monster, which doth mock
> The meat it feeds on. That cuckold lives in bliss
> Who, certain of his fate, loves not his wronger:
> But oh! what damned minutes tells he o'er
> Who doats yet doubts, suspects yet strongly loves?
>
> [III. iii. 165-70]

This speech necessarily turns the thoughts of Othello on the idea of jealousy with all the appearance of nature and refined art; and then by proceeding in the same manner he leads him to examine the conduct of Desdemona, and creates a suspicion of her infidelity to the Moor from her having chosen him, and refused those

> Of her own clime, complexion, and degree.
>
> [III. iii. 230]

From this he draws an inference which reflects on the character of Desdemona; this almost convinces the Moor of her being false to his bed, and he desires Iago to set his wife to watch Desdemona. In answer to this the subtle villain pretends to intreat Othello to think no more of what he had told him, to attempt discovering Desdemona's true disposition by the ve-

hemence of her suit to him for restoring Cassio, and to believe his fears for his honour had been too importunate in the affair; with this he leaves him. In all this scene there appears nothing which can discover the Moor weaker than an honest, plain, brave man may be allowed to be; not one step carried beyond the truth in nature by Iago.

The knowledge of the promptness of jealousy in the bosom of man which the author shews in the character of Iago is beyond all comparison; when he has possest the handkerchief which Desdemona drops, he says

> I will in Cassio's lodgings lose this napkin,
> And let him find it. Trifles light as air
> Are to the jealous confirmations strong
> As proofs of holy writ.
>
> [III. iii. 321-24]

At seeing Othello enter he continues:

> Look where he comes! not poppy nor mandragora,
> Nor all the drowsy syrups of the world,
> Shall ever medicine thee to that sweet sleep
> Which thou hadst yesterday.
>
> [III. iii. 330-33]

The operations which the jealous mind undergoes were never so truly described by any author. The trifles light as air, the tasteless poison of a hint becoming mines of burning sulphur to the soul, and the irrevocable power of sweet slumber to a mind haunted with jealousy are beyond all conception just, great and sublime, and I think to be found in no other author. (pp. 186-87)

> *John Shebbeare, in an extract from* Shakespeare, the Critical Heritage: 1753-1765, Vol. 4, *edited by Brian Vickers, Routledge & Kegan Paul, 1976, pp. 184-91.*

THOMAS WILKES   (essay date 1759)

[The excerpt below is from Wilkes's A General View of the Stage *(1759). The critic asserts that Iago's desire to destroy Othello is based solely on his not having been chosen as the Moor's lieutenant. Contending that Iago's references to being cuckolded by Othello are only inventions to further his deception of Roderigo and not part of his motives, Wilkes argues that Iago does not celebrate the success of his plot, but merely demonstrates at the close of the play the ignoble and "gloomy malice of a slave." The question of Iago's motivation is one of the most prominent issues in the criticism of* Othello; *it has also been addressed by such commentators as John Potter (1771-72), Richard Hole (1796), Samuel Taylor Coleridge (1808-18), William Hazlitt (1817), William Maginn (1839), Denton J. Snider (1887), A. C. Bradley (1904), G. Wilson Knight (1930), Bernard Spivack (1958), G. M. Matthews (1964), and Stanley Edgar Hyman (see Additional Bibliography).]*

Jealousy and Envy proceed from various causes: the peace and prosperity of others, the advantages they are possessed of and which we think ourselves intitled to and qualified for, will give rise to Envy, Hatred, Rancor, Malice, and Revenge. These tormenting, detestable passions have much the same appearances. They cover the countenance with a malignant gloom, the eye is inflamed, and shoots cautious side-glances at the object of resentment: thus Milton [in *Paradise Lost*] represents Satan in Paradise viewing our first parents.

> Aside the devil turned
> For envy, yet with jealous leer malign
> Eyed them askance.

There is a great deal of difference between the malice of a slave and the vengeance of a prince justly provoked.... Iago prosecutes to destruction a noble unsuspecting officer for having preferred above him *one Michael Cassio*. He has no other real motive for his villainy. He, indeed, in the first [Act] of the Play mentions to Roderigo that he hates the general on another account, for, says he, 'He has, between my sheets, done me the unlawful office' [I. iii. 387-88]; and again he declares he will not be easy 'till he is even with him wife for wife' [II. i. 299]. But from his deportment through the rest of the play he leaves us at liberty to judge that he has invented this story the better to help his designs on Roderigo, without whom it is impossible his schemes can work. He then proceeds to destroy an honest gallant soldier, an innocent beautiful woman, a well-beloved modest man, and a simple outwitted coxcomb. He completes a mean but barbarous revenge, excited by a very trifling disappointment; he levels every thing in his way, and spares neither age, sex, or condition. When his villanies are detected he deports himself with all the gloomy malice of a slave. 'What ye know, says he, ye know; seek no more of me, for from this hour I never will speak more' [V. ii. 303f.]. In few words, he has neither the spirit to triumph in his vengeance, nor the least spark of refined feeling for having destroyed characters so amiable as Desdemona and Othello. (pp. 360-61)

Thomas Wilkes, in an extract from Shakespeare, the Critical Heritage: 1753-1765, Vol. 4, *edited by Brian Vickers, Routledge & Kegan Paul, 1976, pp. 356-61.*

SAMUEL JOHNSON   (essay date 1765)

[*Johnson has long held an important place in the history of Shakespearean criticism. He is considered the foremost representative of moderate English Neoclassicism and is credited by some literary historians with freeing Shakespeare from the strictures of the three unities valued by most Neoclassicists: that dramas should have a single setting, take place in less than twenty-four hours, and have a causally connected plot. More recent scholars portray him as a critic who was able to synthesize existing critical theory rather than as an innovative theoretician. Johnson was a master of Augustan prose style and a personality who dominated the literary world of his epoch. In the excerpt below, taken from his end-note to* Othello *in his 1765 edition of Shakespeare's plays, Johnson focuses on the consummate skill with which Shakespeare has drawn the various characters in the play. Of the Moor himself, the critic suggests that his self-assessment as "a man not easily jealous" (V. ii. 345) is perhaps not an accurate one, but nevertheless our compassion for him is constant. Such other critics as John Hughes (1713), Lewis Theobald (1717), August Wilhelm Schlegel (1811), Samuel Taylor Coleridge (1813, 1822, and 1827), Hermann Ulrici (1839), G. G. Gervinus (1849-50), Denton J. Snider (1887), A. C. Bradley (1904), E. K. Chambers (1908), Elmer Edgar Stoll (1915), Allardyce Nicoll (1927), and Harley Granville-Barker (1945) have also offered assessments of Othello's jealousy. Johnson is the first critic to suggest that if the opening scenes were set in Cyprus and the dramatic events of Act I were described by other characters instead of dramatized, the time scheme of the play would be more regular. For further discussion of the relation of Act I to the subsequent action of the play, see the excerpts by Samuel Taylor Coleridge (1808-18) and Susan Snyder (1972).*]

The beauties of [*Othello*] impress themselves so strongly upon the attention of the reader, that they can draw no aid from critical illustration. The fiery openness of Othello, magnanimous, artless, and credulous, boundless in his confidence, ardent in his affection, inflexible in his resolution, and obdurate in his revenge; the cool malignity of Iago, silent in his re-

sentment, subtle in his designs, and studious at once of his interest and his vengeance; the soft simplicity of Desdemona, confident of merit, and conscious of innocence, her artless perseverance in her suit, and her slowness to suspect that she can be suspected, are such proofs of Shakespeare's skill in human nature, as, I suppose, it is vain to seek in any modern writer. The gradual progress which Iago makes in the Moor's conviction, and the circumstances which he employs to inflame him, are so artfully natural, that, though it will perhaps not be said of him as he says of himself, that he is "a man not easily jealous," yet we cannot but pity him when at last we find him "perplexed in the extreme" [V. ii. 345, 346].

There is always danger lest wickedness conjoined with abilities should steal upon esteem, though it misses of approbation; but the character of Iago is so conducted, that he is from the first scene to the last hated and despised.

Even the inferiour characters of this play would be very conspicuous in any other piece, not only for their justness but their strength. Cassio is brave, benevolent, and honest, ruined only by his want of stubbornness to resist an insidious invitation. Rodorigo's suspicious credulity, and impatient submission to the cheats which he sees practised upon him, and which by persuasion he suffers to be repeated, exhibit a strong picture of a weak mind betrayed by unlawful desires, to a false friend; and the virtue of Aemilia is such as we often find, worn loosely, but not cast off, easy to commit small crimes, but quickened and alarmed at atrocious villanies.

The scenes from the beginning to the end are busy, varied by happy interchanges, and regularly promoting the progression of the story; and the narrative in the end, though it tells but what is known already, yet is necessary to produce the death of Othello.

Had the scene opened in Cyprus, and the preceding incidents been occasionally related, there had been little wanting to a drama of the most exact and scrupulous regularity. (pp. 1047-48)

Samuel Johnson, "Notes on Shakespeare's Plays: 'Othello'," in his The Yale Edition of the Works of Samuel Johnson: Johnson on Shakespeare, Vol. VIII, *edited by Arthur Sherbo, Yale University Press, 1968, pp. 1012-48.*

JOHN POTTER   (essay date 1771-72)

[*Potter was an English miscellaneous writer whose Shakespearean criticism was originally published as a series of theatrical reviews in several newspapers between 1771 and 1772. In the excerpt below, taken from a review which first appeared under the title "The Theatrical Review. By a Society of Gentlemen, independent of Managerial Influence" (1771-72), the critic assesses* Othello *as "the most perfect" of Shakespeare's tragedies, but takes issue with two aspects of the play. Potter maintains that Iago's motives in seeking the Moor's downfall—namely, his lack of promotion to the lieutenancy and his surmises that Othello has had an adulterous relationship with Emilia—are inadequate reasons to wreak such destruction, and therefore his resentment is "unnatural." Also, whereas many earlier critics hold that Othello retains the compassion of the audience throughout the drama, Potter argues that he "is drawn rather too credulous," to the extent that his jealousy is founded solely on "trifles," and that he "forfeits by such conduct some of our pity." For additional analyses of Iago's motives, see the excerpts by Thomas Wilkes (1759), Richard Hole (1796), Samuel Taylor Coleridge (1808-18), William Hazlitt (1817), William Maginn (1839), Denton J. Snider (1887), A. C. Bradley (1904), G. Wilson Knight (1930), Bernard*

Spivack (1958), and G. M. Matthews (1964), as well as the essay by Stanley Edgar Hyman cited in the Additional Bibliography.]

The Fable of [Othello] is founded upon one action only, which is conducted with great skill; and if from the distress of the Catastrophe it is not the most pleasing of Shakespeare's Tragedies, it is undoubtedly the most perfect. All the Characters are admirably drawn; the Sentiments, where it is required, are sufficiently elevated; and the Moral is excellent: viz. enforcing in the most natural yet powerfull manner the fatal effects of endulging the pernicious and ungovernable passion of jealousy.—Some Critics have been disgusted with the distresses and unhappy fate of the virtuous and innocent Desdemona because, say they, she had not been guilty of the least fault or failing, and therefore her fate is too horrible to be born. To this we answer that though she is from first to last an object of pity, and her fate greatly to be lamented, yet her misfortunes are owing to a cause extremely natural, and not at all uncommon, viz. the jealousy of her husband.

Others have objected greatly to the Character of Iago; particularly the learned Author of the Elements of Criticism [Henry Home, Lord Kames], who says that not even Shakespeare's masterly hand can make the picture agreeable, and that it is so monstruous and satanical as not to be sufferable in the Representation. This opinion, however, has been sufficiently proved to be too far strained by the applause with which the Play has always been received whenever it is performed. Iago never fails to engage the attention of an Audience, though his Character is so conducted as to render him detestable; in which the Poet has shewn great judgement. (p. 441)

If there is any fault in the Character of Iago it is that of his grounding his resentment against Othello on very trifling circumstances, viz. his having set a younger Officer over his head on a particular and singular vacancy, notwithstanding he himself still stands most high in his esteem and confidence, and consequently in the fairest light for being immediately preferred by him to a post of equal if not greater advantage. To this indeed is added a slight suspicion, which he himself declares to be but bare surmise, of Othello's having been too familiar with his wife, a particular which Othello's Character and cast of behaviour seems to give no authority to; and on these slight motives he involves in the ruin he intends for the General three innocent persons besides, viz. Cassio, Roderigo and Desdemona.—We are aware that it may be said in answer to this that the more trifling the motives of his resentment, the greater is the art of the Poet in working them up to such an amazing height. But this, we believe, will not bear a very strict examination; for the greater his resentment is heightened on trifling circumstances the more unnatural it certainly must be.

With respect to Othello, his military Character is admirably sustained; but though his jealousy is finely wrought up by the machinations of the designing and plausible villain Iago, yet from first to last it is raised by trifles, viz. the loss of a paultry handkerchief which Desdemona knew not was of value, and her pleading for Cassio's forgiveness, who had been cashiered on a most trivial fault. These are all the circumstances which corroborate the vile insinuations of Iago against the innocent Desdemona, and produce so fatal a Catastrophe. Othello, therefore, is drawn rather too credulous, and forfeits by such conduct some of our pity. (pp. 441-42)

John Potter, in an extract from Shakespeare, the Critical Heritage: 1765-1774, Vol. 5, edited by Brian Vickers, Routledge & Kegan Paul, 1979, pp. 441-42.

LORENZO [pseudonym of GEORGE STEEVENS]   (essay date 1772)

[Steevens was an English scholar who collaborated with Samuel Johnson on a ten-volume edition of Shakespeare's works in 1773. The subsequent revision of this collection, along with Steevens's own edition of 1793, formed the textual basis for the first two Variorum editions of Shakespeare's plays. In the following excerpt, first published in the General Evening Post in 1772 under the pseudonym of Lorenzo, Steevens contends that there are "many absurdities" in Othello that violate an audience's sense of what is natural, proper, and appropriate, resulting in a narrative flawed with improbabilities. Foremost among these, he argues, is Emilia's role as Desdemona's chambermaid, which Steevens styles as "grosly improper," claiming that it would be debasing for the wife of a man of some military rank and stature to serve in such a lowly position, but admitting that if she were not thus engaged she could not play her vital role in the dramatic action. He further dispraises Shakespeare's depiction of Roderigo's foolishness, Cassio's instant inebriation in Act II, Scene iii, and Desdemona's speech after her death, which he describes—using an ethnic slur against Irish speech patterns—as "an Hiberianism of the first magnitude." Steevens concludes that whereas Thomas Rymer (1692) has ridiculed the significance of the handkerchief in Othello, that is the least disagreeable of the drama's several improbabilities. Charles Gildon (1694) and Stopford A. Brooke (1913) have also discussed the improbabilities in Othello, and the characterization of Emilia has been analyzed by such commentators as Charlotte Lennox (1753), the anonymous critic in the Bee (1791), G. G. Gervinus (1849-50), Gayle Greene (1979), and Thomas D. Bowman and Carol Thomas Neely (see Additional Bibliography).]

Whenever our modern critics take up the pen to point out any defect in the prince of our dramatic poets, they deliver themselves with the utmost diffidence, as if actually fearful of speaking the truth, and always qualify the severity of their animadversion with some compliment which gives censure the air of approbation. For my own part, however, I think if we take Shakespeare with all his faults, he will still have beauties enough left to deserve our highest applause, and in the midst of his defects unquestionably remain the most exalted genius of our country.

Among the many plays of this great man which have undergone the ordeal of criticism, I know of none which has escaped more unhurt than the tragedy of Othello, notwithstanding the attempts of Rymer to render it universally ridiculous on account of the handkerchief [see excerpt above, 1692]. Yet, though this play has had the good fortune to be treated very gently by our critics in general, and though the exquisite manner in which its inimitable author has painted the passion of jealousy throws a seeming veil over a variety of imperfections, an accurate observer will nevertheless find many absurdities in the piece, besides the object of Rymer's disapprobation, which strike materially at the probability of the fable, and destroy that agreeable appearance of nature which constitutes the chief source of our theatrical satisfaction.

In the first place, the circumstance of Emilia's waiting upon Desdemona in the capacity of a chambermaid is utterly indefensible. Iago maintains the rank of a gentleman in the Venetian service, is the second-in-command after Othello on the expedition to Cyprus, and could by no means suffer his wife to be placed in so humiliating a situation. If therefore we suppose it unlikely for one officer's lady to be the servant of another, we overset the whole fable at once, and immediately defeat all the purposes of the catastrophe. Yet we must do this if we are governed by the rules of real life, where disparity of rank in certain degrees creates no difference in gentility, but leaves the youngest Ensign of a regiment as respectable individually as the Chief Commander of an army. I must on this account repeat that if Emilia is taken away from the service of Desdemona, in which it is grosly improper to place her, she can have no opportunity of stealing the handkerchief which gives rise to all the bustle of the play, no opportunity of hearing Desdemona's dying confession, nor any opportunity of discovering her husband's villainy to Othello. But the violence offered to common sense by no means terminates here; for unless we subscribe to farther incongruities we must inevitably give up the tragedy before us. We must suppose Roderigo a greater fool than the poet has painted him, as he fancies that a woman who receives his whole fortune in presents will not admit of his addresses, and entertains the most respectful idea of her purity while he believes her to be scandalously mercenary. The sudden drunkenness of Cassio besides, which constitutes a principal incident of the play, is ridiculous to extravagance; and Desdemona's speaking after she is dead, an Hibernianism of the first magnitude. In short, the handkerchief, which is usually deemed the most obnoxious is the least offensive particular of the performance in question. (pp. 492-93)

> *Lorenzo [pseudonym of George Steevens], in an extract from* Shakespeare, the Critical Heritage: 1765-1774, Vol. 5, *edited by Brian Vickers, Routledge & Kegan Paul, 1979, pp. 492-93.*

WILLIAM KENRICK [as reported by the *MONTHLY MISCELLANY*] (lecture date 1774)

[*An English journalist who translated the works of Rousseau, a literary critic and playwright, Kenrick was notorious for his abusive, acrimonious criticism of Samuel Johnson, Oliver Goldsmith, David Garrick, and others. After the publication of his* A Review of Doctor Johnson's New Edition of Shakespeare: in which the Ignorance, or Inattention, of that Editor is exposed, and the Poet defended from the Persecution of his Commentators (1765), *Kenrick lost his position as a contributor to the* Monthly Review. *He later wrote articles for* Gentleman's Journal, *and in 1775 he established his own periodical, the* London Review of English and Foreign Literature. *The following excerpt is taken from an anonymous review of Kenrick's lecture on* Othello *published in the* Monthly Miscellany *in 1774. Kenrick is the earliest critic to question whether Shakespeare intended Othello to be black, an issue later addressed by Samuel Taylor Coleridge (1808-18 and 1813). In the excerpt below, he argues that the protagonist of this drama is "not a black, and at worst only of a tawny colour." He contends that Othello must be regarded as a Spanish Moor for three reasons: Desdemona would "never have fallen in love with a Negro," the Venetians would have set a Moor at the head of their military but not a black man, and Othello's Christianity is consonant with a Moorish heritage. Thomas Rymer (1692), Charles Gildon (1694 and 1710), Charles Lamb (1811), John Quincy Adams (1835), Denton J. Snider (1887), G. M. Matthews (1964), and G. K. Hunter (see Additional Bibliography) have also commented on the significance of Othello's race in the play.*]

In his remarks on the Tragedy of *Othello* we cannot but think [Dr. Kenrick] superlatively great; and he also gave his audience sufficient proof of the soundness of his judgment. For, though none of Shakespeare's Commentators ever doubted but that Othello was of a real *black* complexion, and though every performer of that character has followed the same opinion and put on an *absolute negro face,* yet the Doctor asserted that he was *not* a *black,* and at worst only of a *tawny* colour. This assertion he supported by the following arguments:

First, That a young Lady of Desdemona's delicacy of sentiment could never have fallen in love with a Negro; and more particularly, if we suppose him 'ill-favoured and old,' as Shake-

speare calls him, we must conceive a greater idea of Desdemona's indelicacy; whereas, supposing him *tawny* there is nothing very unnatural in it.

Secondly, It could not be imagined that the Venetians would depute the chief command of their forces to a Negro; whereas, that a Moor should occupy this important trust was nothing extraordinary, in a country where an intercourse with the Moorish race had been long established.

A third presumptive proof was deduced from Othello's religion. He was a Christian; for he recounts the taking a circumcised enemy to the state by the throat. The Moors, the Lecturer observed, were strongly inclined at one time to Christianity, though that mode of faith hath since been extirpated from almost every country inhabited by Moors. And what corroborated his opinion, was a passage which seemed to indicate that he was descended from the Moorish Kings of Old Spain.

From these considerations, we cannot but think the Doctor's hypothesis to be the true one; nor can we conceive the propriety of Shakespeare's calling Othello the *Moor of Venice* unless he meant that specific tribe of Moors between whom and the inhabitants of Old Spain a frequent intercourse had been carried on by wars and treaties; and his describing Othello as one of *those Moors* unquestionably ascertained his colour. (pp. 116-17)

> *William Kenrick [as reported by the "Monthly Miscellany"], in an extract from* Shakespeare, the Critical Heritage: 1774-1801, Vol. 6, *edited by Brian Vickers, Routledge & Kegan Paul, 1981, pp. 116-17.*

THE BEE; OR, LITERARY WEEKLY INTELLIGENCER (essay date 1791)

[*The following excerpt is from an essay which first appeared in the* Bee; or, Literary Weekly Intelligencer (1791), *signed merely "W. N." The critic is primarily concerned with demonstrating Shakespeare's fidelity to human nature in the portrayal of the principal characters of* Othello. *He contends that at the outset Iago has neither the intention of destroying Othello and Desdemona nor a well-developed "plan of action," for his early soliloquies reveal that he only seeks to gull Roderigo and to displace Cassio as the Moor's lieutenant. William Maginn (1839) and Richard Grant White (1885) have similarly argued that Iago does not contemplate the ruin of Othello and Desdemona at the initial stage of his scheming. W. N. further maintains that the opposition of Iago's malice and Desdemona's "unsuspicious virtue" provides the impetus for the dramatic action of* Othello, *which he regards as principally intended to depict "the destruction of Desdemona." He is also the earliest commentator to argue that the Moor is motivated to kill Desdemona not by jealousy alone, but "by the noble principles of honour and justice" as well. Other critics who have addressed the motives behind Othello's murder of Desdemona include Samuel Taylor Coleridge (1813 and 1822), Hermann Ulrici (1839), G. G. Gervinus (1849-50), Denton J. Snider (1887), A. C. Bradley (1904), Elmer Edgar Stoll (1915), Winifred M. T. Nowottny (1952), G. M. Matthews (1964), and Carol McGinnis Kay (1983). Finally, like Charlotte Lennox (1753), W. N. charges Shakespeare with inconsistency in the characterization of Emilia, asserting that her failure to tell Desdemona the whereabouts of the handkerchief is antithetical to her devotion to her mistress in the final act. For further analyses of the character of Emilia, see the excerpts by George Steevens (1772), G. G. Gervinus (1849-50), and Gayle Greene (1979), as well as the essays by Thomas D. Bowman and Carol Thomas Neely cited in the Additional Bibliography.*]

In every work of [Shakespeare] we discover all the marks of his genius; his diversity of character, his boundless imagination, his acute discernment, and his nervous expression; but in none of them are these qualities more conspicuous than in the tragedy of *Othello;* a work also, the freest of his irregularities, his puns, his bombast, and conceits. No where has he painted virtue with more flaming sublimity than in the character of Othello; with more amiable tenderness than in that of Desdemona; and no where are all the artifices of human nature more fully displayed than in the character of Iago. From the whole he has contrived a plot, the most moral in its tendency, which winds up to the highest pitch our sympathetic feelings in concern for unsuspicious virtue, and at the same time rouses our utmost indignation against deep-laid villainy. From a review of the conduct of the poet in producing such a noble effect we may expect much pleasure and improvement. (pp. 557-58)

The characters which make a chief figure in the tragedy of *Othello* are the Moor himself, Desdemona, and Iago. The subject is the destruction of Desdemona; and this catastrophe the author never loses sight of. It is indeed remarkable for unity of action, which of all the three unities is of principal consequence. (p. 558)

Shakespeare has adorned the hero of this tragedy with every virtue that can render human nature great and amiable; and he has brought him into such trying situations as give full proof of both. His love for Desdemona is of the most refined and exalted kind; and his behaviour upon the supposition of his false return is an indication of his great spirit, and such as might be expected from his keen sense of honour and warlike character. Though naturally susceptible of the tenderest passions, yet being engaged from his early youth in scenes that required the exercise of those of a higher nature, he has not learned

> Those soft parts of conversation
> That Chamberers have.
>
> > [III. iii. 264-65]

> Rude (says he) am I in speech,
> And little bless'd with the set phrase of peace.
>
> > [I. iii. 81-2]

His manners have nothing of that studied courtesy which is the consequence of polite conversation—a tincture of which is delicately spread over the behaviour of Lodovico and Gratiano; but all is the natural effusion of gentleness and magnanimity. His generous and soaring mind, always occupied with ideas natural to itself, could not brook, according to his own expression, *to study all the qualities of human dealings;* the artifices of interest, and the meanness of servile attentions. . . .

With so much nature and dignity does he always act that, even when distorted with angry passions, he appears amiable.

> *Emil.* I would you had never seen him.
> *Des.* So would not I; my love doth so approve him,
> That even his stubborness, his checks and frowns,
> Have grace and favour in them.
>
> > [IV. iii. 18-21]

A character of this kind commands respect; and in his actions we naturally interest ourselves.

Iago, who is the prime mover of the events of this tragedy, is a character of no simple kind; he possesses uncommon sagacity in judging of the actions of men, good and bad. (p. 559)

In his first interview with Othello Iago begins his deep schemes very successfully by labouring, with bold and masterly cunning, to impress him with a strong sense of his fidelity and

Act V. Scene ii. Desdemona and Othello. Frontispiece to the Rowe edition (1709). By permission of the Folger Shakespeare Library.

attachment to his interests. He represents himself as sustaining a difficult conflict between two of the best principles, regard to his master and a fear of seeming to act with a malicious cruelty. He speaks like a person fired with anger that he cannot contain; he does not give a detail of Brabantio's proceedings like an unconcerned spectator, but in that confused and interrupted manner worthy of the truest passion; his reflections which, according to calm reason ought to come last, according to passion come first. (pp. 559-60)

Hitherto Iago seems not to have formed any determined plan of action. A bait is laid for him in the simplicity of Roderigo; and how to get possession of his treasures seems to be the only object he had at first in view. . . . However, while his orders are executing he has leisure to consider what he is about; for Iago, at his first setting out, seems to have no intention of dipping so deep in wickedness as the dreadful event. Finding no method to gratify Roderigo, he dexterously makes him a tool for promoting the interests of his own. The suit of Roderigo, and the active hand he had taken in it, had brought him to think of a scheme of which the same persons were to be the subject. To render Cassio odious to Othello by scandalous aspersions, and by these means to be preferred in his place are the objects which he now has in view; a pursuit which he did not perhaps think would be attended with such a fatal train of consequences, though his sagacious mind discerns something that strikes him with horror.

> Hell and night
> Must bring this monstrous birth to the world's light.
>
> [I. iii. 402-03]

Shakespeare has shown great judgment in the darkness which he makes to prevail in the first counsels of Iago. To the poet himself all the succeeding events must have been clear and determined; but to bring himself again into the situation of one who sees them in embryo, to draw a mist over that which he had already cleared, must have required an exertion of genius peculiar to this author alone. In so lively a manner does he make Iago shew his perplexity about the future management of his conduct, that one is almost tempted to think that the poet had determined as little himself about some of the particulars of Iago's destruction. When with much reasoning about their propriety he is by himself digesting his schemes, he says

> 'Tis here—but yet confused;
> Knavery's plain face is never seen till used.
>
> [II. i. 311-12]

But however much at a loss he may be about the method of accomplishing his designs, yet for the present he lets slip no opportunity that will promote them. He lays his foundation sure, as knowing what a hazardous structure he had to rear upon it. He had already laboured to exhibit himself in the best light to the unsuspicious Moor, and he succeeded to the height of his wishes; for we find him congratulating himself upon the advantages that will accrue from it.

> He holds me well;
> The better shall my purpose work upon him.
>
> [I. iii. 390-91]

Upon the same principles does he go on working the downfall of Cassio. His blameless and well established character must be first tarnished; he must be known capable of irregularity before the crime he is accused of obtain full belief; and this more difficult part of his undertaking the indefatigable Iago finds means to accomplish, and with such ability as to promote at the same time the opinion of his own honesty and goodness. One would have imagined that he would have remained content with all the lucky events of the tumultuous adventure on the platform, and exult for a little. But he wisely determines not to triumph before he has gained a complete victory; his thoughtful and piercing mind sees another use to which the disgrace of Cassio may be applied. Under a cover of zeal to serve him he advises the virtuous man to a scheme that will further work his ruin; and by hinting to him the great power which Desdemona had over her husband he opens a very likely method for regaining his favour through her mediation. The bait is swallowed, and an appearance of intimacy most favourable to his design is thereby produced. (pp. 560-61)

He assumes the appearance of one whose mind laboured with the knowledge of some flagrant impropriety which he could not contain; and when any circumstance recals the abhorred idea an involuntary remark escapes, and immediately he affects to recover himself. He kindles the jealousy of Othello by tantalizing him with imperfect accounts and ambiguous arguments. He agitates and distracts his soul by confusedly opening one source of suspicion, and leaving him in the perplexity of doubt; immediately by displaying the matter in another point of view, gives him a farther glimmering into the affair; until at last, frantic with rage and jealousy, Othello insists upon

satisfactory information; and by these means the discoveries which he makes are made to appear more the effect of necessity than inclination.

> Villain, be sure thou prove my love a whore.
>
> [III. iii. 359]

Incomplete knowledge of what concerns us deeply, besides the tortures of suspense into which it throws the mind, has a natural effect to make it appear in the most hideous colours which is possible to devise. (pp. 561-62)

Upon the whole, in this intercourse betwixt Iago and Othello Shakespeare has shewn the most complete knowledge of the human heart. Here he has put forth all the strength of his genius; the faults which he is so prone to fall into are entirely out of sight. We find none of his quibbling, his punning, or bombast; all is seriousness, all is passion. He brings human nature into the most difficult situation that can be conceived; and with matchless skill he supports it. Who can read those admirable scenes without being touched in the most sensible manner for the high grief of Othello? Plunged into a sea of troubles which he did not deserve, we see him torn asunder in the most cruel manner. (p. 562)

It has been observed of Shakespeare, that he has not often exhibited the delicacy of female character; and this has been sufficiently apologized for from the uncivilized age in which he lived; and women never appearing upon the stage in his time might have made him less studious in this department of the drama. Indeed, when we consider his strength of mind, his imagination, which delighted in whatever was bold and daring, we would almost think it impossible that he could enter into all the softness and refinement of love. But in spite of all these disadvantages, he has shewn that in whatever view he chose to behold human nature he would perform it superior to any other. For no where in the writings of Shakespeare, or any where else, have we found the female character drawn with so much tenderness and beauty as in that of Desdemona. The gentleness with which she behaves to all with whom she converses, the purity, the modesty, the warmth of her love, her resignation in the deepest distress, together with her personal accomplishments attract our highest regard. But that which chiefly distinguishes her is that exquisite sensibility of imagination which interested her so much in the dangers of Othello's youthful adventures, a passion natural enough indeed, though it is not every one who is capable of experiencing it. Othello, as we have seen, was naturally of an heroic and amiable disposition; but when by his bold undertakings he is exposed to imminent dangers, he would then shine in his brightest colours. All his magnanimity, and all his address, are brought to view; at that moment all the generous affections of the soul would be drawn towards him; admiration of his virtues, wishes for his success, and solicitude for his safety. And when the best feelings of the heart are thus lavished on a certain object it is no wonder it should settle into fixed love and esteem.

Such was the sublimated passion of Desdemona, inspired solely by internal beauty. The person of Othello had every thing to cool desire, possessing not only the black complexion and the swarthy features of the Africans; he was also declined, as he says, into the vale of years. But his mind was every thing to Desdemona; it supplied the place of youth by its ardour, and of every personal accomplishment by its strength, its elevation, and its softness. Where, in all the annals of love, do we find so pure and so disinterested a passion supported with so much dignity and nature? She loved him *for the dangers he had passed;* upon this fleeting and incorporeal idea did she rest her affections, upon abstract feelings and qualities of the mind, which must require in her all that warmth of imagination and liveliness of conception which distinguish the finest genius.

The character of this exquisite lady is always consistently supported. Her behaviour towards Cassio shews, in a particular manner, her liberal and benevolent heart; and her conversation with Emilia about the heinousness of infidelity is a striking picture of innocent purity. It is artfully introduced, and adds much to the pathos of the tragedy. The circumstances of ordering her wedding-sheets to be put on her bed, and the melancholy song of a willow, are well imagined, and awaken the mind to expect some dreadful revolution. Indeed, throughout the whole scene before her death an awful solemnity reigns. The mind of Desdemona seems to be in a most agitated condition; she starts an observation about Lodovico, and immediately falls into her gloomy thoughts, paying no attention to the answer of Emilia, though connected with an anecdote that would have at another time raised her curiosity. This absence of mind shews beyond the power of language her afflicted and tortured state. But what gives a finishing stroke to the terror of this midnight scene is the rustling of the wind, which the affrighted imagination of Desdemona supposes to be one knocking at the door. This circumstance, which would have been overlooked as trifling by an inferior writer, has a most sublime effect in the hands of Shakespeare; and till the fatal catastrophe the same horribly interesting sensations are kept up. Othello enters her bed-chamber with a sword and candle, in that perturbation and distraction of mind which marked his behaviour since the supposed discovery of her guilt; remains of tenderness still struggling with revenge in his bosom, and a conversation is protracted; during which the mind is arrested in a state of the most dreadful suspense that can well be imagined.

Had Othello been actuated by cruelty alone in this action; had he, to gratify a savage nature, put Desdemona to death the scene would have been shocking, and we would have turned from it with aversion. But instigated as he is by the noble principles of honour and justice, and weighing at the same time the reluctance with which he performs it and the great sacrifice which he makes to his finest feelings, it on these accounts produces those mournfully pleasing sensations which to attain is the highest praise of the tragic poet.

In the final unravelling of the plot there is often great difficulty; it is the grand point to which the author aims in the course of successive scenes; and upon the proper execution of it depends much of the merit of the work. Here Shakespeare has not fallen off. The same high tone of passion is preserved. Upon the discovery of Desdemona's innocence, and the intrigues of Iago, all the characters act a very consistent and natural part. Othello's distraction is painted in an inimitable manner. Unwilling to believe that he had acted upon false grounds, and confounded with contrary evidence, he knows not where to betake himself. After uttering a few incoherent speeches, which shew in the strongest light a mind rent with grief and remorse, he gradually recovers himself; and resuming, as much as possible, his natural composure and firmness he looks around him a little, and deliberately views his wretched situation; but finding no peace for him on earth he terminates his existence.

Iago also stands forth in the group, a just monument of his own crimes. Seeing the proof too plain against him, he can brave it out no longer. He sees no prospect of escape from any quarter; his own arts are now of no avail, and he knows that

he deserves no pity; he gives up all for lost, and resolves upon a state of dumb desperation, most expressive of the horror of his mind. In this state we have the satisfaction to see him dragged to deserved punishment.

It might now be expected that we should proceed to the ungrateful task of pointing out what a critic would blame in this tragedy. I have already observed that it is perhaps the most sublime and finished of Shakespeare's compositions; yet were I to point out all its redundancies, puns, conceits, and other faults which are commonly taken notice of in this author, I might fill some pages. Such a detail, however, would be trivial and impertinent. No person who can relish its beauties will be much offended with any thing of this kind in the course of perusing *Othello*. Its excellencies are so bold and so striking as to make the blemishes almost wholly vanish in the midst of their splendor. (pp. 562-65)

It is with much regret, however, we must observe that after Shakespeare had supported with uniform propriety one of the most difficult characters Genius ever attempted, he should at last fall off, and put a trifling conceit in the mouth of a dying man.

> *Oth.* I kissed thee e'er I killed thee—no way but this,
> Killing myself to die upon a kiss.
>
> [V. ii. 358-59]

It might also be objected to the contrivance of the plot that Iago had not sufficient motives for the perpetration of so many horrid crimes; and this the sagacity of Shakespeare has foreseen, and with much address obviated. In the course of our observations we have already noticed that he does not suppose Iago, in his first setting out, resolutely to plan the destruction of Desdemona and Cassio. The objects he had in view were to get possession of the wealth of Roderigo, and to be preferred in the place of Cassio; but seeing matters beginning to be embroiled around him, the firm and undaunted Iago will not stop short, whatever should be the consequence. By thus viewing his conduct it will appear natural and probable. He wishes (as human nature ever must) to view himself even for a moment in the light of an honest man——

> And what's he then that says I play the villain? &c.
>
> [II. iii. 336f.]

But the principal fault which we observe in this performance is a want of consistency in supporting the upright and disinterested character of Emilia. We can easily suppose, in the first place, that she might procure Desdemona's napkin for her husband, without seeming to concur with him or even suspect his schemes. But when afterwards, in [Act III, Scene iv] she sees the improper use to which this napkin is applied and the great distress which the loss of it occasioned to Desdemona, without so much as wishing to explain the misunderstanding, she is no more the open and virtuous Emilia but a coadjutor with her dark and unfeeling husband. This is a remarkable violation of every appearance of probability, when we contrast it with her noble and spirited conduct afterwards. We are surprised to find a slip of so much magnitude from the clear and piercing judgment of Shakespeare, especially when we consider that it could have been very easily remedied by removing her during this interview. (pp. 565-66)

W. N., in an extract from Shakespeare, the Critical Heritage: 1774-1801, Vol. 6, *edited by Brian Vickers, Routledge & Kegan Paul, 1981, pp. 556-66.*

WOLSTENHOLME PARR (essay date 1795)

[In the following excerpt, taken from his The Story of the Moor of Venice (1795), Parr focuses on the character of Othello. He maintains that Shakespeare's representation of the Moor's "education, his temper, his moral and religious Principles" not only establishes his singularity as a military hero, but also demonstrates that he is dangerously vulnerable to an assault on his honor. Othello's military background and his high adventures have produced an individual who "knows no medium between the extremes of a boundless confidence and an implacable hatred," Parr contends; thus, once his suspicions are raised about Desdemona and Cassio he impetuously elects a course of murderous revenge. The critic argues that Othello has had no training in how to rationally choose a course of action, and hence the evidence Iago provides is sufficient to provoke his jealousy and recklessly impel him to avenge his sense of honor by committing a crime he knows is unworthy of "the military name and profession." Similarly, F. R. Leavis (1937) and Derek Traversi (1949) have argued that the very qualities which make the Moor an outstanding military commander mark him as most unsuited to function effectively in a domestic role. Parr also notes that Othello's upbringing in a non-Christian setting leads him to believe that he cannot control his fate and to a superstitious conviction that the handkerchief is an object of "preternatural importance," so that its apparent loss signals to him the irrevocable end of his happiness. For further commentary on the significance of the handkerchief in Othello, see the excerpts by Thomas Rymer (1692), John Hughes (1713), Lewis Theobald (1733), Robert B. Heilman (1956), and Harry Levin (1964), as well as the essay by Nigel Alexander cited in the Additional Bibliography.]

In the tragedy of the Moor of Venice the unity of action, which indeed ought never to be violated, is acknowledged even by the severer critics to be complete. The consistency of the subordinate characters, and the wonderful skill with which they are all made to contribute to the proposed catastrophe, have been fully discussed, and have received their due portion of praise. The character of Othello alone, proved by the [novel of Cinthio] to have been almost wholly created by the imagination of Shakespeare, seems never to have been sufficiently considered, though it eminently deserves to be examined with a view to poetical effect. We are equally interested and surprised by every part of it; by his education, his temper, his moral and religious Principles.

So much of the conduct of men depends on the habits of early life that it was extremely necessary for the poet to describe first the original occupations of Othello, that these might serve as a ground-work to the probability of succeeding fictions. This basis of his character was to be consistent with the merit that had raised him to his distinguished rank in the Venetian army; and to explain the singular passion with which he had inspired the tender and unfortunate Desdemona, as well as to lay open the source of his opinions and his foibles. To illustrate these two leading incidents of his life it was certainly not injudicious to throw a blaze of glory round the commencement of his fortune, opposing a series of dangers to his progress that could only be surmounted by consummate Valour: 'She lov'd me for the dangers I had past' [I. iii. 167].

But as if these were not sufficient to excite a general sympathy and affection, the poet has represented Desdemona as the most benevolent and compassionate of human beings; and, by a beautiful management, has effected her ruin by means of that very compassion, when excited a second time by the disgrace of Cassio. Of his military merit and capacity the mind is left to form its own ideas, assisted only by obscure indications, that extol far more than the explicit detail of history or the pomp of excessive praise. The very early period at which he

began his course of warlike employments, the confused and marvellous account of his imminent perils and singular escapes, his zeal and fondness for the service, his dislike of peace and leisure, are all so many masterstrokes of Shakespeare's pencil that finish the portrait of a brave and experienced General. . . . Such a train of youthful adventures, where every thing dearest to humanity was daily hazarded, working upon a noble temper naturally destroyed all petty considerations of detriment and interest. The mind thus schooled thinks not of adopting the common measures of prudence, and scorns to make estimates and divisions of natural sentiment. It knows no medium between the extremes of a boundless confidence and an implacable hatred. When therefore his tenderness for Desdemona and his attachment to Cassio had once yielded to the surmises of jealousy, he rushed with a resistless impetuosity into the bloody and horrible projects of assassination and Murder.

His temper was hasty and violent, free and generous; neither prone to suspicion nor apt without reason to forgive; neither inclined to disturb itself with doubts nor qualified afterwards to restore its own tranquility. Dissimulation is a vice of which the practice was to him not only unintelligible but of which, without a prompter, he would not perhaps have known the existence. From the nature of his past life he was so little acquainted with the arts of conversation and the modes of society that on his elevation, probably for the first time, to a portion of civil authority, and his entrance into family affairs and domestic regulations, some confidential person became necessary for advice and instruction. Iago seemed to be formed for the perfect execution of this office. (pp. 617-19)

The dark and insidious practices of this monster were so far from his thoughts that even in the last moments of his guilt and despair he expresses his astonishment at the proceeding, and his curiosity to know the Cause.

> Will you, I pray, demand that demi-devil,
> Why he hath thus ensnar'd my soul and body?
> [V. ii. 301-02]

In his love as well as in his jealousy there are singular and original traits that belong exclusively to Othello's character. A soldier of fortune in foreign service, whose enterprizes are successful and whose merit eclipses the fame of his rivals, generally excites more envy than admiration. But the distinction between foreigner and native is infinitely weaker than between the Moors and the inhabitants of Europe. Desdemona was perhaps the first that had felt and expressed a real and unaffected sorrow for the hardships he had suffered: 'And he lov'd her, that she did pity them' [I. iii. 168]. His mind perhaps then first conceived the exquisite pleasure of social communication and attachment; and opened to him the enchanting prospect of a milder happiness than he had hitherto enjoyed. His vehement and fiery disposition grasped with avidity this unusual joy, and hinged his future hopes and affections on the object with such force that separation must produce the most tremendous and fatal Convulsions.

When Shakespeare has once established a principle of conduct that principle is not only observed, but frequently converted into a motive for succeeding revolutions of sentiment. The complexion of Othello, that had placed him at such a distance from Desdemona's love, and with other considerations had so much encreased his tenderness and gratitude for her passionate declarations in his favour, becomes afterwards a powerful weapon for the arm of jealousy.

> ——Haply, for I am black,
> And have not those soft parts of conversation
> That chamberers have; or for I am declin'd
> Into the vale of years;—yet that's not much.
>
> [III. iii. 263-66]

It was the pity that Desdemona had first felt for his early misfortunes that had persuaded Othello of the sincerity of her affection. The ideas then of love and compassion were from that moment connected so closely in his mind that when she apparently wept for the death of Cassio he instantly acquired force and cruelty enough to execute his sanguinary Purpose.

A sensation continually present to the mind is shifted about by all the passions, and becomes at one time the support of confidence, and at another the slave of Suspicion. From the blessings of love and confidence so congenial to his mind he is hurled into all the tortures of jealousy which his nature abhorred. The society he had gained, the sympathy he had excited, must be now abandoned; and his misery is aggravated by all those singularities of his fortune and situation which had before augmented his joy. The solitude of Philoctetes is not more wretched, nor his anguish more deplorable.

> Had it pleas'd Heaven
> To try me with affliction; had it rain'd
> All kind of sores and shames on my bare head;
> Steep'd me in poverty to the very lips;
> Given to Captivity me and my hopes;
>
> [IV. ii. 47-51]

The moral character and opinions of Othello are more the result of momentary feeling and the suggestions of his own private sense of honour than the consequences of system or the just deductions of reason. His education had precluded the general exercise of deliberation, and his passions were gaining force while his reason languished in the weakness which inactivity produces. A sense of honour, which so imperfectly supplies its place, steps in on every occasion with fragments of advice that involve him in the most singular and surprising contradictions. When his frame is convulsed and his spirit trembling at the knowledge of Desdemona's infidelity he determines to commit a crime unworthy (as he confesses and laments) of the military name and profession; but in the gratification of his revenge feels not a pang of remorse for that virtue which he abandons. (pp. 619-20)

Imperfectly however as this sense supplies the place of reason in a moral view, it is certainly calculated to produce poetically a much greater beauty and variety of effect. The ardour and surprise of poetry have nothing in common with the rational and tranquil proceedings of prudence; where, without the aid of imagination, all that is to happen may be foretold by the simple force of sagacity founded on experience. Othello jealous in his chamber, and Achilles angry in his tent, are pictures that interest us more than Æneas piously bearing away his father from the flames of Troy, or patiently expostulating with the wrath of Juno and the fury of the elements. . . .

Happy had it been for mankind if all the mischiefs with which superstition has deformed society could have been compensated by the graces with which it has embellished poetry. So strong indeed is the alliance between those two sources of terrible and romantic fiction that an epic or a tragic character is not considered as complete without some tincture of religious ecstasy.

The fancy of Shakespeare, though excessively delighted with such embellishments, did not however adopt them rashly without first being assured of their fitness and congruity. The wandering and military life of Othello must be supposed to have prevented him from conforming generally to the tenets of any particular sect; and to have left his religious faith in still more uncertainty than his moral principles. Whatever struck his imagination in the belief of either people with whom he was most conversant as applicable to his own fortune, naturally rested on his mind, and rendered it a tissue of the Christian and Mahometan persuasions. The singularity of his adventures, his numberless perils and escapes, might induce him almost reasonably to receive as true the potency of spells and the doctrines of predestination. The pleasures of love and the charms of beauty figured with so much distinction in the Mahometan scheme of happiness that whatever superstition consecrated to the benefit or protection of mankind was endued with a capacity to improve or perpetuate these enjoyments. Hence has Shakespeare judiciously taken occasion to confer a sort of preternatural importance on the handkerchief that was the last fatal confirmation of his jealousy.

> ——: That handkerchief
> Did an Ægyptian to my mother give. . . .
>
> [III. iv. 55ff.]
> (p. 621)

The idea of an irreversible predetermined destiny returns to his mind when, conscious of the innocence of his former life and intentions, he finds himself involved in the most horrible of crimes; when, after all the dangers he had passed he sees that his courage can no longer protect him though apparently in a state of tranquility and peace: 'Who can controul his fate?' [V. ii. 265].

In his death the same sense of honour still prevails. In his last moments he is exhibited in all the agony of guilt without one symptom of fear; he shews a tender and anxious regard for his reputation, but none for himself; obscurely hoping that the services which he has rendered to the state may diminish the infamy attached to a foul and atrocious murder. (p. 622)

> *Wolstenholme Parr, in an extract from* Shakespeare, the Critical Heritage: 1774-1801, Vol. 6, *edited by Brian Vickers, Routledge & Kegan Paul, 1981, pp. 617-22.*

RICHARD HOLE (essay date 1796)

[Hole was a poet and antiquarian who was a frequent contributor to literary magazines and reviews. Commentators on his "An Apology for the Character and Conduct of Iago" (1796), from which the following excerpt is taken, are divided as to whether his opening declaration—"I mean nothing ironical"—is sincere. Hole argues that Shakespeare depicted Iago as a soldier of some experience and valor, and therefore his resentment towards Othello for appointing Cassio to the lieutenancy is natural and excusable, and his anger toward the latter is not unexpected in any man who lacks "the apathy of a stoic or the meekness of a saint." Further, the critic maintains, since Iago suspects that both the Moor and Cassio have cuckolded him he has even more cause to feel offended, and his schemes for revenge are additionally justified. Denton J. Snider (1887) has also argued that Othello and Emilia have had an adulterous relationship, and Richard Grant White (1885) and Tucker Brooke (1918) have each offered an additional defense of Iago's actions. Finally, Hole justifies Iago's cruelty towards Desdemona by claiming that his relations with Emilia have so colored his attitude toward women that he has become a mysoginist; still, the critic admits that Iago's conduct

involving Desdemona is less excusable than his actions against Othello and Cassio. For further commentary on the extent of Iago's villainy in the play, see the excerpts by the anonymous critic in the Bee (1791) and William Maginn (1839).]

As I mean nothing ironical in this undertaking I am aware of incurring some suspicion of having tasted

> ——of the insane root
> That takes the reason prisoner.
>
> [*Macbeth*, I. iii. 84-5]

It may be urged against me that the name of Iago is almost proverbial for a close dissembling villain; that Dr. Johnson observes, 'his character is so conducted, that he is, from the first scene to the last, hated and despised' [see excerpt above, 1765]; that 'it is so monstrous and satanical, if we are to credit Lord Kames, as not to be sufferable in a representation—not even Shakespeare's masterly hand can make the picture agreeable' [see excerpt above by John Potter, 1771-72]; and, that old Rymer, long before them, observed, 'He was too wicked in all conscience, and had more to answer for than any tragedy or furies could inflict upon him' [see excerpt above, 1692]. That, in short, he is held by the world in general no less than by Othello as the 'damned damned Iago.'

Permit me, however, first to observe that I do not absolutely undertake to vindicate him, but to shew that his conduct admits of much excuse. His character, as I apprehend, is greatly misunderstood and requires an explanation. (p. 623)

The principal charges urged against him are his ingratitude and treachery to Othello; his perfidy to Cassio and to Desdemona.

Previous to the opening of the drama we are led to understand that Iago's character was respectable both as an officer and a man. His military services are often alluded to. He is made known to the gentlemen of Cyprus by Cassio as 'the bold Iago' [II. i. 75]. Othello reports him to the Duke of Venice as 'a man of honesty and trust' [I. iii. 284]. Other speeches of a similar kind shew that Iago had often acted, by Othello's own confession, in such a manner as to deserve his favor: yet over this tried and experienced soldier, of whose prowess

> ——his eyes had seen the proof
> At Rhodes and Cyprus, and on other grounds,
> Christian and heathen,
>
> [I. i. 28-30]

He places one

> Who never set a squadron in the field,
> Nor the division of a battle knew
> More than a spinster.
>
> [I. i. 22-4]

Must not this have been a justifiable cause for resentment, if any can be so, to a brave and enterprizing soldier? Some critic styles him 'a false, dissembling, *ungrateful* rascal' [Rymer]. Nothing however can be more unjust than the last epithet. Othello was unkind and ungenerous; Iago not ungrateful. The strongest reason for his resentment to the Moor is yet to be told. He suspected that he had been injured by him in the most tender point; that he had seduced his wife Emilia, a suspicion which does not appear destitute of foundation. The discourse she holds with Desdemona amply demonstrates that she was very far from entertaining any rigid notions of conjugal fidelity. . . . (pp. 624-25)

Whatever stress may be laid on this circumstance, it certainly required no common degree of christian charity to forgive such treatment as Iago had experienced from the Moor.

But what excuse it may be said is there for his behavior to Cassio? He never personally injured him; nor does it appear that he had at any time endeavoured to supplant Iago, tho' he was fortunately preferred before him.

I cannot however allow that he had no cause for resentment against Cassio. He suspects him no less than Othello of a criminal intercourse with Emilia. . . . And revenge, though contrary to the precepts of the gospel, is not so strongly prohibited by the military code of honor.

Again: though it does not appear that he had attempted to supplant Iago, yet the circumstance alone of his undeserved promotion over him must have kindled in his breast, unless endowed with the apathy of a stoic or the meekness of a saint, some sparks of anger and indignation against the successful rival as well as the unjust patron. . . .

It would have been certainly much more noble in Iago to have supprest his resentment against Othello and Cassio, and wiser probably to have winked at the frailties of Emilia; but many allowances ought surely to be made for the imperfections of human nature when placed in trying situations: and why should not Iago be entitled to the benefit of this plea as well as more exalted characters? . . . (p. 625)

Not the death of Cassio, but the depriving him of his office was Iago's original design. Had he succeeded to the command he so justly claimed we may conclude, reasoning from probabilities and the common course of events, that he would neither have betrayed Othello, defrauded Roderigo, nor acted unkindly to Cassio, but have continued 'honest, honest Iago' [V. ii. 154] to the end of the chapter.

The last charge, and the severest, is his cruelty to the innocent Desdemona. This is generally considered as the very acme of villainy, and it admits indeed of less excuse than the former accusations, for she had never wronged him. Iago however does not behold her in the same point of view as a reader or a spectator of this tragedy. He is by no means convinced of her virtue and purity of heart, as appears from his observations on the first interview between her and Cassio, (Act 2. Sc. 5.) from his subsequent discourse with Roderigo, and the soliloquy which follows.

> That Cassio loves her, I do well believe it;
> That she loves him, 'tis apt and of great credit.
>
> [II. i. 286-87]

Other similar passages might be adduced: and it is not unreasonable to suppose that his suspicions of his wife had soured his temper, and excited in him a general aversion to the female sex. (pp. 625-26)

On the whole, his conduct to Roderigo, concerning which no accusation has been preferred, appears to be the least excusable. To him he was indebted for pecuniary obligations, but for none of any kind to either of the other characters. On the contrary, from the first of them he had, most decidedly and incontrovertibly, received injuries of the severest kind. He had no trivial cause for his aversion to Cassio. Desdemona, as being a woman, was not an object of his regard: as the friend of Cassio and Emilia she appeared to him in a disgusting light, and more so probably considered as the wife of Othello. In order to distress *him*, however, not to gratify any aversion towards Desdemona, he contrives her death. She is merely an instrument to effectuate his vengeance: and if vengeance can be vindicated by an accumulation of injuries, Iago's, though exorbitant, was just.

It appears therefore, notwithstanding the general opinion, that his conduct admits of much palliation.—This is all I contended for: and I trust that if you still think him a villain, you consider him as one of the lower class, 'a puny whipster' [V. ii. 244] in the school of iniquity, not to be ranked with Richard the third, Aaron the moor [in *Titus Andronicus*], and others of the higher order, his usual associates. (p. 626)

> Richard Hole, in an extract from Shakespeare, the
> Critical Heritage: 1774-1801, Vol. 6, *edited by Brian*
> *Vickers, Routledge & Kegan Paul, 1981, pp. 622-26.*

SAMUEL TAYLOR COLERIDGE   (essay date 1808-18)

[*Coleridge's lectures and writings on Shakespeare form a major chapter in the history of English Shakespearean criticism. As the channel for the critical ideas of the German Romantics and as an original interpreter of Shakespeare in the new spirit of Romanticism, Coleridge played a strategic role in overthrowing the last remains of the Neoclassical approach to Shakespeare and in establishing the modern view of the dramatist as a conscious artist and masterful portrayer of human character. Coleridge's remarks on Shakespeare come down to posterity largely as fragmentary notes, marginalia, and reports by auditors on the lectures, rather than in polished essays. In the following excerpt, taken from his notes and marginalia written between 1808 and 1818, Coleridge focuses on Act I, Scene i of* Othello. *His characterization of Iago's soliloquy at the close of Act I, Scene iii as "the motive-hunting of motiveless malignity" is one of the most famous critical remarks on* Othello *and has served as a point of departure for many later commentators who have also questioned whether Iago seeks to avenge a perceived injustice or is simply impelled by baseless malice. Such other critics as Thomas Wilkes (1759), John Potter (1771-72), Richard Hole (1796), William Hazlitt (1817), William Maginn (1839), Denton J. Snider (1887), A. C. Bradley (1904), G. Wilson Knight (1930), Bernard Spivack (1958), G. M. Matthews (1964), and Stanley Edgar Hyman (see Additional Bibliography) have also addressed the issue of Iago's motives in the play. On other matters, Coleridge maintains, like William Kenrick (1774), that Shakespeare did not intend to portray Othello as a Negro, arguing that the protagonist's claim of noble birth is anomalous if we consider him a black man. In the paragraph below beginning, "It is a common error . . ."—which Coleridge's editor, Thomas Middleton Raysor suspects is the work of the critic's nephew, H. N. Coleridge—, it is further argued that Shakespeare's audience would not have accepted Desdemona's "falling in love with a veritable negro." For additional commentary on the issue of Othello's race, see the excerpts by Thomas Rymer (1692), Charles Gildon (1694 and 1710), Charles Lamb (1811), John Quincy Adams (1835), Denton J. Snider (1887), and G. M. Matthews (1964), as well as the essay by G. K. Hunter cited in the Additional Bibliography. Finally, the critic addresses the issue raised earlier by Samuel Johnson (1765) as to the aptness of the setting of Act I, contending that by viewing Othello in Venice, before his arrival in Cyprus, the audience not only becomes acquainted with him, but develops compassion and fear for him "before the deep interest is to be approached." Susan Snyder (1972) has also described the structural connections between Act I and the subsequent parts of the play.*]

[On Act I. Scene i.] The admirable preparation, so characteristic of Shakespeare, in the introduction of Roderigo as the dupe on whom Iago first exercises his art, and in so doing displays his own character. Roderigo [is] already fitted and predisposed [to be a dupe] by his own passions—without any fixed principle or strength of character (the want of character

and the power of the passions,—like the wind loudest in empty houses, form his character)—but yet not without the moral notions and sympathies with honor which his rank, connections had hung upon him. The very three first lines happily state the nature and foundation of the friendship—the purse—as well [as] the contrast of Roderigo's intemperance of mind with Iago's coolness, the coolness of a preconceiving *experimenter*. The mere language of protestation in

> If ever [I did dream of such a matter,]
> Abhor me—
>
> [I. i. 5-6]

which, fixing the associative link that determines Roderigo's continuation of complaint—

> [Thou told'st me thou didst hold him] in thy hate—
>
> [I. i. 7]

elicits a true feeling of Iago's—the dread of contempt habit[ual] to those who encourage in themselves and have their keenest pleasure in the feeling and expression of contempt for others. His high self-opinion—and how a wicked man employs his real feelings as well as assumes those most alien from his own, as instruments of his purpose. (pp. 40-1)

[In] what follows, let the reader feel how by and thro' the glass of two passions, disappointed passion and envy, the very vices he is complaining of are made to act upon him as so many excellences, and the more appropriately, because cunning is always admired and wished for by minds conscious of inward weakness. And yet it is but *half*—it acts like music on an inattentive auditor, *swelling* the thoughts which prevent him from listening to it. Roderigo turns off to Othello; and here comes the one if not the only justification of the blackamoor Othello, namely as a negro, who is not a *Moor* at all.

> [What a full fortune does the thick-lips owe,
> If he can carry't thus!]
>
> [I. i. 66-7]

Even if we supposed this an uninterrupted tradition of the theatre, and that Shakespeare himself, from want of scenes and the experience that nothing could be made too *marked* for the nerves of his audience, [sanctioned it,] would this prove aught concerning his own intentions as a poet for all ages? Can we suppose him so utterly ignorant as to make a barbarous *negro* plead royal birth? Were negroes then known but as slaves; on the contrary were not the Moors the warriors, etc.?

Iago's speech to Brabantio implies merely that he was a *Moor*, i.e. black. Tho' I think the rivalry of Roderigo sufficient to account for his wilful confusion of Moor and negro—yet tho' compelled to give this up, I should yet think it only adapted for the then *acting*, and should complain of an enormity built only on one single word—in direct contradiction to Iago's 'Barbary horse.' If we can in good earnest believe Shakespeare ignorant of the distinction, still why take one [chance] against ten—as Othello cannot be *both*?

It is a common error to mistake the epithets applied by the *dramatis personae* to each other, as truly descriptive of what the audience ought to see or know. No doubt Desdemona saw Othello's visage in his mind; yet, as we are constituted, and most surely as ar English audience was disposed in the beginning of the seventeenth century, it would be something monstrous to conceive this beautiful Venetian girl falling in love with a veritable negro. It would argue a disproportionateness, a want of balance in Desdemona, which Shakespeare does not appear to have in the least contemplated. (pp. 41-2)

In real life how do we look back to little speeches, either as presentimental [of], or most contrasted with, an affecting event. Shakespeare, as secure of being read over and over, of becoming a family friend, how he provides this for *his readers*, and leaves it to them.

> [*Iago*. Virtue! a fig! 'tis in ourselves that we are thus or thus.]
>
> [I. iii. 319-20]

Iago's passionless character, all *will* in intellect; therefore a bold partizan here of a truth, but yet of a truth converted into falsehood by absence of all the modifications by the frail nature of man. And the *last sentiment*—

> [. . . our raging motions, our carnal stings, our unbitted lusts;
> whereof I take this, that you call love, to be a sect or scion]—
>
> [I. iii. 330-32]

There lies the Iagoism of how many! And the repetition, 'Go make money!'—a pride in it, of an anticipated dupe, stronger than the love of lucre.

> [*Iago*. Go to, farewell, put money enough in your purse
> Thus do I ever make my fool my purse.]
>
> [I. iii. 380-81, 383]

The triumph! Again, 'put money,' after the effect has been fully produced. The last speech, [Iago's soliloquy,] the motive-hunting of motiveless malignity—how awful! In itself fiendish; while yet he was allowed to bear the divine image, too fiendish for his own steady view. A being next to devil, only *not* quite devil—and this Shakespeare has attempted—executed—without disgust, without scandal!

[On Act II. Scene i.] Dr. Johnson has remarked that little or nothing is wanting to render the *Othello* a regular tragedy but to have opened the play with the arrival of Othello in Cyprus, and to have thrown the preceding act into the form of narration [see excerpt above, 1765]. Here then is the place to determine whether such a change would or would not be an improvement, nay (to throw down the glove with a full challenge), whether or no the tragedy would by such an arrangement become *more regular;* i.e., more consonant with the rules dictated by universal reason or the true common sense of mankind in its application to the particular case. For surely we may safely leave it to common sense whether to reply to or laugh at such a remark as, for instance—suppose a man had described a rhomboid or parallelogram and a critic were with great gravity to observe, 'If the lines had only been in true right angles, or if the horizontal parallels had been but of the same length as the two perpendicular parallels that form the sides, the diagram would have been according to the strictest rules of geometry.' For in all acts of judgement it [can] never be too often recollected and scarcely too often repeated, that rules are means to ends,—consequently, that the end must be determined and understood before it can be known what the rules are or ought to be. (pp. 44-5)

Confirmation of my reason [for defending a first act at Venice]: in how many ways is not Othello made, first, our acquaintance—then friend—then object of anxiety—before the deep interest is to be approached. (p. 46)

Samuel Taylor Coleridge, "Notes on the Tragedies of Shakespeare: 'Othello'," in his Shakespearean Criticism, Vol. 1, *edited by Thomas Middleton Raysor, second edition, Dutton, 1960, pp. 40-9.*

AUGUST WILHELM SCHLEGEL   (essay date 1811)

[*A prominent German Romantic critic, Schlegel holds a key place in the history of Shakespeare's reputation in European criticism. His translations of thirteen of the plays are still considered the best German editions of Shakespeare. Schlegel was also a leading spokesman for the Romantic movement, which permanently overthrew the Neoclassical contention that Shakespeare was a child of nature whose plays lacked artistic form. In the excerpt below, the critic offers a general discussion of* Othello, *paying particular attention to the central characters. Schlegel argues that Othello is a "double man," whose native inclinations towards fierceness and sensuality have been tempered by his acquisition of more civilized virtues and conduct. However, he contends, when Othello's jealousy is aroused, these patterns of behavior are routed by his innate passions, thus giving "the upper hand to the savage over the moral," and a triumph of "the blood over the will." See the excerpt by Hermann Ulrici (1839) and the essay by G. K. Hunter cited in the Additional Bibliography for rebuttals of Schlegel's description of Othello as a "double man"; also, see the excerpt by G. G. Gervinus (1849-50), who disputes Schlegel's evaluation of Othello's nature as sensuous. In his analysis of Iago, Schlegel emphasizes the consummate artistry of the ancient's villainy, his powers of dissimulation, and the depth of his understanding of human nature, describing him as Othello's "evil genius" and noting the "unfortunate affinity" between the two men. For additional discussions of the similarities between Iago and Othello, see the excerpts by Denton J. Snider (1887), Maud Bodkin (1934), G. R. Elliott (1937), F. R. Leavis (1937), J. I. M. Stewart (1949), and Kenneth Burke (1951). Schlegel's essay on* Othello *was originally published in his* A Course of Lectures on Dramatic Art and Literature *in 1811.*]

[*Othello* is] a strongly shaded picture: we might call it a tragical Rembrandt. What a fortunate mistake that the Moor (under which name in the original novel, a baptized Saracen of the Northern coast of Africa was unquestionably meant), has been made by Shakespeare in every respect a negro! We recognize in Othello the wild nature of that glowing zone which generates the most ravenous beasts of prey and the most deadly poisons, tamed only in appearance by the desire of fame, by foreign laws of honour, and by nobler and milder manners. His jealousy is not the jealousy of the heart, which is compatible with the tenderest feeling and adoration of the beloved object; it is of that sensual kind which, in burning climes, has given birth to the disgraceful confinement of women and many other unnatural usages. A drop of this poison flows in his veins, and sets his whole blood in the wildest ferment. The Moor *seems* noble, frank, confiding, grateful for the love shown him; and he is all this, and, moreover, a hero who spurns at danger, a worthy leader of an army, a faithful servant of the state; but the mere physical force of passion puts to flight in one moment all his acquired and mere habitual virtues, and gives the upper hand to the savage over the moral man. This tyranny of the blood over the will betrays itself even in the expression of his desire of revenge upon Cassio. In his repentance, a genuine tenderness for his murdered wife, and in the presence of the damning evidence of his deed, the painful feeling of annihilated honour at last bursts forth; and in the midst of these painful emotions he assails himself with the rage wherewith a despot punishes a runaway slave. He suffers as a double man; at once in the higher and the lower sphere into which his being was divided.—While the Moor bears the nightly colour of suspicion and deceit only on his visage, Iago is black within. He haunts Othello like his evil genius, and with his light (and therefore the more dangerous,) insinuations, he leaves him no rest; it is as if by means of an unfortunate affinity, founded however in nature, this influence was by necessity more powerful over him than the voice of his good angel Desdemona. A more artful villain than this Iago was never portrayed; he spreads his nets with a skill which nothing can escape. The repugnance inspired by his aims becomes tolerable from the attention of the spectators being directed to his means: these furnish endless employment to the understanding. Cool, discontented, and morose, arrogant where he dare be so, but humble and insinuating when it suits his purposes, he is a complete master in the art of dissimulation; accessible only to selfish emotions, he is thoroughly skilled in rousing the passions of others, and of availing himself of every opening which they give him: he is as excellent an observer of men as any one can be who is unacquainted with higher motives of action from his own experience; there is always some truth in his malicious observations on them. He does not merely pretend an obdurate incredulity as to the virtue of women, he actually entertains it; and this, too, falls in with his whole way of thinking, and makes him the more fit for the execution of his purpose. As in every thing he sees merely the hateful side, he dissolves in the rudest manner the charm which the imagination casts over the relation between the two sexes: he does so for the purpose of revolting Othello's senses, whose heart otherwise might easily have convinced him of Desdemona's innocence. This must serve as an excuse for the numerous expressions in the speeches of Iago from which modesty shrinks. If Shakespeare had written in our days he would not perhaps have dared to hazard them; and yet this must certainly have greatly injured the truth of his picture. Desdemona is a sacrifice without blemish. She is not, it is true, a high ideal representation of sweetness and enthusiastic passion like Juliet; full of simplicity, softness, and humility, and so innocent, that she can hardly form to herself an idea of the possibility of infidelity, she seems calculated to make the most yielding and tenderest of wives. The female propensity wholly to resign itself to a foreign destiny has led her into the only fault of her life, that of marrying without her father's consent. Her choice seems wrong; and yet she has been gained over to Othello by that which induces the female to honour in man her protector and guide,—admiration of his determined heroism, and compassion for the sufferings which he had undergone. With great art it is so contrived, that from the very circumstance that the possibility of a suspicion of her own purity of motive never once enters her mind, she is the less reserved in her solicitations for Cassio, and thereby does but heighten more and more the jealousy of Othello. To throw out still more clearly the angelic purity of Desdemona, Shakespeare has in Emilia associated with her a companion of doubtful virtue. From the sinful levity of this woman it is also conceivable that she should not confess the abstraction of the handkerchief when Othello violently demands it back: this would otherwise be the circumstance in the whole piece the most difficult to justify. Cassio is portrayed exactly as he ought to be to excite suspicion without actual guilt,—amiable and nobly disposed, but easily seduced. The public events of the first two acts show us Othello in his most glorious aspect, as the support of Venice and the terror of the Turks: they serve to withdraw the story from the mere domestic circle, just as this is done in *Romeo and Juliet* by the dissensions between the houses of Montague and Capulet. No eloquence is capable of painting the overwhelming force of the catastrophe in *Othello*,—the pressure of feelings which measure out in a moment the abysses of eternity. (pp. 401-04)

August Wilhelm Schlegel, "Criticisms on Shakspeare's Tragedies," in his A Course of Lectures on Dramatic Art and Literature, *edited by Rev. A. J. W. Morrison, translated by John Black, revised edition, 1846. Reprint by AMS Press, Inc., 1965, pp. 400-13.*

CHARLES LAMB   (essay date 1811)

[*Lamb is considered one of the leading figures of the Romantic movement and an authority on Elizabethan drama. Although he was, like William Hazlitt, a theatrical critic, Lamb argued that the stage was an improper medium for Shakespeare's plays, mainly because visual dramatizations marred their artistic and lyrical effects. Like Samuel Taylor Coleridge, Lamb reverenced Shakespeare as a poet rather than a playwright. Although many scholars consider his views sentimental and subjective and his interpretations of Shakespeare's characters often extreme, Lamb remains an important contributor to the nineteenth-century reevaluation of Shakespeare's genius. In the excerpt below, taken from an essay on Shakespeare's tragedies that first appeared in* The Reflector *in 1811, Lamb argues that* Othello *cannot be staged effectively. He contends that while a reader's imagination may comprehend and applaud the virtue of Desdemona in disregarding Othello's color and loving him for his intellectual and moral qualities, the depiction on stage of their "courtship and wedded caresses" is "extremely revolting," and Desdemona's choice appears inexplicable. Such other critics as Thomas Rymer (1692), Charles Gildon (1694 and 1710), William Kenrick (1774), Samuel Taylor Coleridge (1808-18 and 1813), John Quincy Adams (1835), Denton J. Snider (1887), G. M. Matthews (1964), and G. K. Hunter (see Additional Bibliography) have also discussed the issue of Othello's race.*]

Lear is essentially impossible to be represented on a stage. But how many dramatic personages are there in Shakspeare, which though more tractable and feasible (if I may so speak) than Lear, yet from some circumstance, some adjunct to their character, are improper to be shewn to our bodily eye. Othello for instance. Nothing can be more soothing, more flattering to the nobler parts of our natures, than to read of a young Venetian lady of highest extraction, through the force of love and from a sense of merit in him whom she loved, laying aside every consideration of kindred, and country, and colour, and wedding with *a coal-black Moor*—(for such he is represented, in the imperfect state of knowledge respecting foreign countries in those days, compared with our own, or in compliance with popular notions, though the Moors are now well enough known to be by many shades less unworthy of a white woman's fancy)— it is the perfect triumph of virtue over accidents, of the imagination over the senses. She sees Othello's colour in his mind. But upon the stage, when the imagination is no longer the ruling faculty, but we are left to our poor unassisted senses, I appeal to every one that has seen *Othello* played, whether he did not, on the contrary, sink Othello's mind in his colour; whether he did not find something extremely revolting in the courtship and wedded caresses of Othello and Desdemona; and whether the actual sight of the thing did not over-weigh all that beautiful compromise which we make in reading;—and the reason it should do so is obvious, because there is just so much reality presented to our senses as to give a perception of disagreement, with not enough of belief in the internal motives,—all that which is unseen,—to over-power and reconcile the first and obvious prejudices. What we see upon a stage is body and bodily action; what we are conscious of in reading is almost exclusively the mind, and its movements: and this I think may sufficiently account for the very different sort of delight with which the same play so often affects us in the reading and the seeing. (pp. 137-38)

> *Charles Lamb, "On the Tragedies of Shakespeare, Considered with Reference to Their Fitness for Stage Representation," in* The Works in Prose and Verse of Charles and Mary Lamb, Vol. I *by Charles Lamb and Mary Lamb, edited by Thomas Hutchinson, Oxford University Press, 1908, pp. 124-42.*

SAMUEL TAYLOR COLERIDGE [as reported by *THE BRISTOL GAZETTE*] (lecture date 1813)

[*The excerpt below is taken from an unsigned account of Coleridge's fourth Shakespearean lecture in Bristol, delivered November 9, 1813. Whereas Lewis Theobald (1717) viewed Othello as possessing an uncontrollable jealousy and Samuel Johnson (1765) was sceptical of the Moor's assertion that he is not easily aroused to suspicion, Coleridge contends that Shakespeare depicted him as reluctant to believe in Desdemona's infidelity and as "the very opposite to a jealous man." For additional views of Othello's jealousy, see the excerpts by John Hughes (1713), August Wilhelm Schlegel (1811), Hermann Ulrici (1839), G. G. Gervinus (1849-50), Denton J. Snider (1887), A. C. Bradley (1904), E. K. Chambers (1908), Elmer Edgar Stoll (1915), Allardyce Nicoll (1927), and Harley Granville-Barker (1945). As in his preceding remarks on the play (see excerpt above, 1808-18), Coleridge avers that Shakespeare portrayed Othello as a "gallant Moor," not as a Negro. For further commentary by Coleridge on the character of Othello, see the excerpts below (1822 and 1827).*]

[The character of Leontes, in *The Winter's Tale*] Mr. Coleridge contrasted with that of Othello, whom Shakespeare had portrayed the very opposite to a jealous man: he was noble, generous, open-hearted; unsuspicious and unsuspecting; and who, even after the exhibition of the handkerchief as evidence of his wife's guilt, bursts out in her praise. Mr. C. ridiculed the idea of making Othello a negro. He was a gallant Moor, of royal blood, combining a high sense of Spanish and Italian feeling, and whose noble nature was wrought on, not by a fellow with a countenance predestined for the gallows, as some actors represented Iago, but by an accomplished and artful villain, who was indefatigable in his exertions to poison the mind of the brave and swarthy Moor. (pp. 227-28)

> *Samuel Taylor Coleridge [as reported by* The Bristol Gazette], *"The Lectures at Bristol, 1813-14: Lecture IV," in his* Shakespearean Criticism, Vol. 2, *edited by Thomas Middleton Raysor, second edition, Dutton, 1960, pp. 227-28.*

SAMUEL TAYLOR COLERIDGE   (essay date 1813?)

[*The following excerpt is from* The Literary Remains of Samuel Taylor Coleridge (1836), *a collection of Coleridge's notes and marginalia compiled and edited by his nephew and literary executor, H. N. Coleridge. Although twentieth-century scholars have generally challenged the authenticity of this work, contending that the younger Coleridge often expanded his uncle's original remarks and interpolated his own views and ideas, nineteenth-century critics regarded* Literary Remains *as a veracious representation of Coleridge's opinions. Indeed, the remark below that "any man" who trusted Iago would have been led to the same conclusion as Othello, together with the query as to who is more to be pitied, Othello or Desdemona, have been frequently cited by subsequent commentators on the play, and A. C. Bradley (1904) has concurred with the assertion here that Othello's trust in Iago is very human and credible. Also, Coleridge's opinion that "Othello does*

not kill Desdemona in jealousy," but out of a deeper "conviction," is similarly asserted by the anonymous critic in the Bee *(1791), Hermann Ulrici (1839), G. G. Gervinus (1849-50), Denton J. Snider (1887), A. C. Bradley (1904), Winifred M. T. Nowottny (1952), G. M. Matthews (1964), and Carol McGinnis Kay (1983), as well as by Coleridge again in his subsequent essay on the play (see excerpt below, 1822). H. N. Coleridge represented the following commentary as being part of his uncle's notes for a series of lectures he gave in Bristol in 1813.*]

Othello does not kill Desdemona in jealousy, but in a conviction forced upon him by the almost superhuman art of Iago, such a conviction as any man would and must have entertained who had believed Iago's honesty as Othello did. We, the audience, know that Iago is a villain from the beginning; but in considering the essence of the Shakespearian Othello, we must perseveringly place ourselves in his situation, and under his circumstances. Then we shall immediately feel the fundamental difference between the solemn agony of the noble Moor, and the wretched fishing jealousies of Leontes [in *The Winter's Tale*], and the morbid suspiciousness of Leonatus [in *Cymbeline*], who is, in other respects, a fine character. Othello had no life but in Desdemona:—the belief that she, his angel, had fallen from the heaven of her native innocence, wrought a civil war in his heart. She is his counterpart; and, like him, is almost sanctified in our eyes by her absolute unsuspiciousness, and holy entireness of love. As the curtain drops, which do we pity the most? (pp. 266-67)

> *Samuel Taylor Coleridge, "Notes on 'Othello'," in his* The Literary Remains of Samuel Taylor Coleridge, Vol. II, *edited by Henry Nelson Coleridge, 1836. Reprint by AMS Press, Inc., 1967, pp. 255-67.*

WILLIAM HAZLITT   (essay date 1817)

[*Hazlitt is considered a leading Shakespearean critic of the English Romantic movement. A prolific essayist and critic on a wide range of subjects, Hazlitt remarked in the preface to his* Characters of Shakespeare's Plays, *first published in 1817, that he was inspired by the German critic August Wilhelm Schlegel, and was determined to supplant what he considered the pernicious influence of Samuel Johnson's Shakespearean criticism. Hazlitt's criticism is typically Romantic in its emphasis on character studies. His experience as a drama critic was an important factor in shaping his generally descriptive, as opposed to analytical, interpretations of Shakespeare. In his discussion of* Othello *taken from the above mentioned work and excerpted below, Hazlitt praises the play for its representation of human passions in their extreme forms and claims that it demonstrates Shakespeare's extraordinary understanding of human nature. Without specific reference to Samuel Taylor Coleridge (1808-18), he rejects the conclusion of some critics who claim that Iago has no specific motivation for his schemes, contending that "the love of power" impels his villainy. Hazlitt argues that Iago, among all of Shakespeare's villains, is an unparalleled representation of intellectual acuity joined with amorality and the love of vice. The critic is also among the earliest to maintain that Shakespeare depicts the ensign as both ingeniously creative and reveling in risk taking, declaring that Iago is "himself the dupe and victim of his ruling passion— an insatiable craving after action of the most difficult and dangerous kind." Iago's possible motives have also been discussed by such critics as Thomas Wilkes (1759), John Potter (1771-72), Richard Hole (1796), William Maginn (1839), Denton J. Snider (1887), A. C. Bradley (1904), G. Wilson Knight (1930), Bernard Spivack (1958), G. M. Matthews (1964), and Stanley Edgar Hyman (see Additional Bibliography). Subsequent commentators who have similarly evaluated Iago as the victim of his own scheming include William Maginn (1839), A. C. Bradley (1904), Tucker Brooke (1918), Allardyce Nicoll (1927), G. R. Elliott (1937), and*

Nigel Alexander (see Additional Bibliography). Hazlitt also avers that the most salient element in Desdemona's character is her lack of volition, remarking that obedience to others is the primary impulse behind her actions. For additional commentary on Desdemona's passivity and lack of courage, see the excerpts by Anna Brownell Jameson (1833), J. A. Heraud (1865), E. K. Chambers (1908), Allardyce Nicoll (1927), G. R. Elliott (1937), and Gayle Greene (1979).]

It has been said that tragedy purifies the affections by terror and pity. That is, it substitutes imaginary sympathy for mere selfishness. It gives us a high and permanent interest, beyond ourselves, in humanity as such. It raises the great, the remote, and the possible to an equality with the real, the little and the near. It makes man a partaker with his kind. It subdues and softens the stubbornness of his will. It teaches him that there are and have been others like himself, by shewing him as in a glass what they have felt, thought, and done. It opens the chambers of the human heart. It leaves nothing indifferent to us that can affect our common nature. It excites our sensibility by exhibiting the passions wound up to the utmost pitch by the power of imagination or the temptation of circumstances; and corrects their fatal excesses in ourselves by pointing to the greater extent of sufferings and of crimes to which they have led others. Tragedy creates a balance of the affections. It makes us thoughtful spectators in the lists of life. It is the refiner of the species; a discipline of humanity. . . . Othello furnishes an illustration of these remarks. It excites our sympathy in an extraordinary degree. The moral it conveys has a closer application to the concerns of human life than that of almost any other of Shakespear's plays. . . . The pathos in Lear is indeed more dreadful and overpowering: but it is less natural, and less of every day's occurrence. We have not the same degree of sympathy with the passions described in Macbeth. The interest in Hamlet is more remote and reflex. That of Othello is at once equally profound and affecting.

The picturesque contrasts of character in this play are almost as remarkable as the depth of the passion. The Moor Othello, the gentle Desdemona, the villain Iago, the good-natured Cassio, the fool Roderigo, present a range and variety of character as striking and palpable as that produced by the opposition of costume in a picture. Their distinguishing qualities stand out to the mind's eye, so that even when we are not thinking of their actions or sentiments, the idea of their persons is still as present to us as ever. These characters and the images they stamp upon the mind are the farthest asunder possible, the distance between them is immense: yet the compass of knowledge and invention which the poet has shewn in embodying these extreme creations of his genius is only greater than the truth and felicity with which he has identified each character with itself, or blended their different qualities together in the same story. What a contrast the character of Othello forms to that of Iago! At the same time, the force of conception with which these two figures are opposed to each other is rendered still more intense by the complete consistency with which the traits of each character are brought out in a state of the highest finishing. The making one black and the other white, the one unprincipled, the other unfortunate in the extreme, would have answered the common purposes of effect, and satisfied the ambition of an ordinary painter of character. Shakespear has laboured the finer shades of difference in both with as much care and skill as if he had had to depend on the execution alone for the success of his design. On the other hand, Desdemona and Æmilia are not meant to be opposed with any thing like strong contrast to each other. Both are, to outward appearance, characters of common life, not more distinguished than women

usually are, by difference of rank and situation. The difference of their thoughts and sentiments is however laid open, their minds are separated from each other by signs as plain and as little to be mistaken as the complexions of their husbands.

The movement of the passion in Othello is exceedingly different from that of Macbeth. In Macbeth there is a violent struggle between opposite feelings, between ambition and the stings of conscience, almost from first to last: in Othello, the doubtful conflict between contrary passions, though dreadful, continues only for a short time, and the chief interest is excited by the alternate ascendancy of different passions, by the entire and unforeseen change from the fondest love and most unbounded confidence to the tortures of jealousy and the madness of hatred. The revenge of Othello, after it has once taken thorough possession of his mind, never quits it, but grows stronger and stronger at every moment of its delay. The nature of the Moor is noble, confiding, tender, and generous; but his blood is of the most inflammable kind; and being once roused by a sense of his wrongs, he is stopped by no considerations of remorse or pity till he has given a loose to all the dictates of his rage and his despair. It is in working his noble nature up to this extremity through rapid but gradual transitions, in raising passion to its height from the smallest beginnings and in spite of all obstacles, in painting the expiring conflict between love and hatred, tenderness and resentment, jealousy and remorse, in unfolding the strength and the weakness of our nature, in uniting sublimity of thought with the anguish of the keenest woe, in putting in motion the various impulses that agitate this our mortal being, and at last blending them in that noble tide of deep and sustained passion, impetuous but majestic . . . , that Shakespear has shewn the mastery of his genius and of his power over the human heart. The third act of Othello is his finest display, not of knowledge or passion separately, but of the two combined, of the knowledge of character with the expression of passion, of consummate art in the keeping up of appearances with the profound workings of nature, and the convulsive movements of uncontroulable agony, of the power of inflicting torture and of suffering it. Not only is the tumult of passion in Othello's mind heaved up from the very bottom of the soul, but every the slightest undulation of feeling is seen on the surface, as it arises from the impulses of imagination or the malicious suggestions of Iago. (pp. 26-9)

The character of Desdemona is inimitable both in itself, and as it appears in contrast with Othello's groundless jealousy, and with the foul conspiracy of which she is the innocent victim. Her beauty and external graces are only indirectly glanced at: we see "her visage in her mind;" her character everwhere predominates over her person.

> A maiden never bold:
> Of spirit so still and quiet, that her motion
> Blush'd at itself.
>
> [I. iii. 94-6]

There is one fine compliment paid to her by Cassio, who exclaims triumphantly when she comes ashore at Cyprus after the storm,

> Tempests themselves, high seas, and howling winds, . . .
> As having sense of beauty, do omit
> Their mortal natures, letting safe go by
> The divine Desdemona.
>
> [II. i., 68, 71-3]

In general, as is the case with most of Shakespear's females, we lose sight of her personal charms in her attachment and devotedness to her husband. "She is subdued even to the very quality of her lord" [I. iii. 250-51]; and to Othello's "honours and his valiant parts her soul and fortunes consecrates" [I. iii. 253-54]. The lady protests so much herself, and she is as good as her word. The truth of conception, with which timidity and boldness are united in the same character, is marvellous. The extravagance of her resolutions, the pertinacity of her affections, may be said to arise out of the gentleness of her nature. They imply an unreserved reliance on the purity of her own intentions, an entire surrender of her fears to her love, a knitting of herself (heart and soul) to the fate of another. Bating the commencement of her passion, which is a little fantastical and headstrong (though even that may perhaps be consistently accounted for from her inability to resist a rising inclination) her whole character consists in having no will of her own, no prompter but her obedience. Her romantic turn is only a consequence of the domestic and practical part of her disposition; and instead of following Othello to the wars, she would gladly have "remained at home a moth of peace" [I. iii. 255-56], if her husband could have staid with her. Her resignation and angelic sweetness of temper do not desert her at the last. The scenes in which she laments and tries to account for Othello's estrangement from her are exquisitely beautiful. After he has struck her, and called her names, she says,

> Alas, Iago,
> What shall I do to win my lord again?
> Good friend, go to him; for by this light of heaven,
> I know not how I lost him. Here I kneel;
> If e'er my will did trespass 'gainst his love,
> Either in discourse, or thought, or actual deed
> Or that mine eyes, mine ears, or any sense
> Delighted them on any other form;
> Or that I do not, and ever did,
> And ever will, though he do shake me off
> To beggarly divorcement, love him dearly
> Comfort forswear me. Unkindness may do much,
> And his unkindness may defeat my life,
> But never taint my love. . . .
>   *Iago.* I pray you be content: 'tis but his humour.
> The business of the state does him offence.
>   *Desdemona.* If 'twere no other!
>
> [IV. ii. 148-61, 165-68]

The scene which follows with Æmilia and the song of the Willow, are equally beautiful, and shew the author's extreme power of varying the expression of passion, in all its moods and in all circumstances.

> *Æmilia.* Would you had never seen him.
> *Desdemona.* So would not I: my love doth so
>   approve him,
> That even his stubbornness, his checks, his frowns,
> Have grace and favour in them, &c.
>
> [IV. iii. 18-21]

Not the unjust suspicions of Othello, not Iago's unprovoked treachery, place Desdemona in a more amiable or interesting light than the conversation (half earnest, half jest) between her and Æmilia on the common behaviour of women to their husbands. This dialogue takes place just before the last fatal scene. If Othello had overheard it, it would have prevented the whole catastrophe; but then it would have spoiled the play.

The character of Iago is one of the supererogations of Shakespear's genius. Some persons, more nice than wise, have thought this whole character unnatural, because his villainy is *without*

a sufficient motive. Shakespear, who was as good a philosopher as he was a poet, thought otherwise. He knew that the love of power, which is another name for the love of mischief, is natural to man. He would know this as well or better than if it had been demonstrated to him by a logical diagram, merely from seeing children paddle in the dirt or kill flies for sport. Iago in fact belongs to a class of character, common to Shakespear and at the same time peculiar to him; whose heads are as acute and active as their hearts are hard and callous. Iago is to be sure an extreme instance of the kind; that is to say, of diseased intellectual activity, with the most perfect indifference to moral good or evil, or rather with a decided preference of the latter, because it falls more readily in with his favourite propensity, gives greater zest to his thoughts and scope to his actions. He is quite or nearly as indifferent to his own fate as to that of others; he runs all risks for a trifling and doubtful advantage; and is himself the dupe and victim of his ruling passion—an insatiable craving after action of the most difficult and dangerous kind. "Our ancient" is a philosopher, who fancies that a lie that kills has more point in it than an alliteration or an antithesis; who thinks a fatal experiment on the peace of a family a better thing than watching the palpitations in the heart of a flea in a microscope; who plots the ruin of his friends as an exercise for his ingenuity, and stabs men in the dark to prevent *ennui.* His gaiety, such as it is, arises from the success of his treachery; his ease from the torture he has inflicted on others. He is an amateur of tragedy in real life; and instead of employing his invention on imaginary characters, or long forgotten incidents, he takes the bolder and more desperate course of getting up his plot at home, casts the principal parts among his nearest friends and connections, and rehearses it in downright earnest, with steady nerves and unabated resolution. We will just give an illustration or two.

One of his most characteristic speeches is that immediately after the marriage of Othello.

> *Roderigo.* What a full fortune does the thick lips
>   owe,
> If he can carry her thus!
>   *Iago.* Call up her father:
> Rouse him *(Othello),* make after him, poison his
>   delight,
> Proclaim him in the streets, incense her kinsmen,
> And tho' he in a fertile climate dwell,
> Plague him with flies: tho' that his joy be joy,
> Yet throw such changes of vexation on it,
> As it may lose some colour.
>
> [I. i. 66-73]

In the next passage, his imagination runs riot in the mischief he is plotting, and breaks out into the wildness and impetuosity of real enthusiasm.

> *Roderigo.* Here is her father's house: I'll call aloud.
>   *Iago.* Do, with like timorous accent and dire yell
> As when, by night and negligence, the fire
> Is spied in populous cities.
>
> [I. i. 74-7]

One of his most favourite topics, on which he is rich indeed, and in descanting on which his spleen serves him for a Muse, is the disproportionate match between Desdemona and the Moor. This is a clue to the character of the lady which he is by no means ready to part with. It is brought forward in the first scene, and he recurs to it, when in answer to his insinuations against Desdemona, Roderigo says,

I cannot believe that in her—she's full of most
   blest conditions.
Iago. Bless'd fig's end. The wine she drinks
is made of grapes. If she had been blest, she
would never have married the Moor.

                                    [II. i. 249-53]

And again with still more spirit and fatal effect afterwards,
when he turns this very suggestion arising in Othello's own
breast to her prejudice.

   Othello. And yet how nature erring from itself—
   Iago. Aye, there's the point;—as to be bold with
      you,
   Not to affect many proposed matches
   Of her own clime, complexion, and degree, &c.

                                    [III. iii. 227-30]

This is probing to the quick. Iago here turns the character of
poor Desdemona, as it were, inside out. It is certain that nothing
but the genius of Shakespear could have preserved the entire
interest and delicacy of the part, and have even drawn an
additional elegance and dignity from the peculiar circumstances
in which she is placed.—The habitual licentiousness of Iago's
conversation is not to be traced to the pleasure he takes in gross
or lascivious images, but to his desire of finding out the worst
side of every thing, and of proving himself an overmatch for
appearances. He has none of "the milk of human kindness"
in his composition. His imagination rejects every thing that
has not a strong infusion of the most unpalatable ingredients;
his mind digests only poisons. Virtue or goodness or whatever
has the least "relish of salvation in it" [*Hamlet*, III. iii. 92],
is, to his depraved appetite, sickly and insipid: and he even
resents the good opinion entertained of his own integrity, as
if it were an affront cast on the masculine sense and spirit of
his character. Thus at the meeting between Othello and Desdemona, he exclaims—"Oh, you are well tuned now: but I'll
set down the pegs that make this music, *as honest as I am*"
[II. i. 199-201]—his character of *bonhommie* not sitting at all
easy upon him. In the scenes, where he tries to work Othello
to his purpose, he is proportionably guarded, insidious, dark,
and deliberate. We believe nothing ever came up to the profound dissimulation and dextrous artifice of the well-known
dialogue in the third act, where he first enters upon the execution of his design.

   Iago. My noble lord.
   Othello. What dost thou say, Iago?
   Iago. Did Michael Cassio,
   When you woo'd my lady, know of your love?
   Othello. He did from first to last.
   Why dost thou ask?
   Iago. But for a satisfaction of my thought,
   No further harm.
   Othello. Why of thy thought, Iago?
   Iago. I did not think he had been acquainted with it.
   Othello. O yes, and went between us very oft—
   Iago. Indeed!
   Othello. Indeed? Ay, indeed. Discern'st thou aught
      of that?
   Is he not honest?
   Iago. Honest, my lord?
   Othello. Honest? Ay, honest.
   Iago. My lord, for aught I know.
   Othello. What do'st thou think?

   Iago. Think, my lord!
   Othello. Think, my lord! Alas, thou echo'st me,
   As if there were some monster in thy thought
   Too hideous to be shewn.—

                                    [III. iii. 93-108]

The stops and breaks, the deep workings of treachery under
the mask of love and honesty, the anxious watchfulness, the
cool earnestness, and if we may so say, the *passion* of hypocrisy, marked in every line, receive their last finishing in
that inconceivable burst of pretended indignation at Othello's
doubts of his sincerity.

   O grace! O Heaven forgive me!
   Are you a man? Have you a soul or sense?
   God be wi' you; take mine office. O wretched fool,
   That lov'st to make thine honesty a vice!
   Oh monstrous world! Take note, take note, O world!
   To be direct and honest, is not safe.
   I thank you for this profit, and from hence
   I'll love no friend, since love breeds such offence.

                                    [III. iii. 373-80]

If Iago is detestable enough when he has business on his hands
and all his engines at work, he is still worse when he has
nothing to do, and we only see into the hollowness of his heart.
His indifference when Othello falls into a swoon, is perfectly
diabolical.

   Iago. How is it, General? Have you not hurt your head?
   Othello. Do'st thou mock me?
   Iago. I mock you not, by Heaven, &c.

                                    [IV. i. 59-60]

The part indeed would hardly be tolerated, even as a foil to
the virtue and generosity of the other characters in the play,
but for its indefatigable industry and inexhaustible resources,
which divert the attention of the spectator (as well as his own)
from the end he has in view to the means by which it must be
accomplished. (pp. 32-8)

> *William Hazlitt, "'Othello'," in his* Characters of
> Shakespear's Plays & Lectures on the English Poets,
> *The Macmillan Company, 1903, pp. 26-38.*

**SAMUEL TAYLOR COLERIDGE   [as reported by H. N.
COLERIDGE]   (conversation date 1822)**

*[From 1822 until Coleridge's death in 1834, his nephew and son-
in-law, H. N. Coleridge, recorded the critic's remarks on a wide
variety of subjects; he later published portions of these accounts
in* Specimens of the Table Talk of the Late Samuel Taylor Coleridge *(1835). The following two excerpts are taken from that work.
In the first of these, from a conversation which took place on
December 29, 1822, Coleridge expands on the argument he re-
portedly made in his earlier lecture on* Othello *(see excerpt above,
1813)—namely, that the Moor is not of a jealous temperament.
He contends that Othello suffers because he believes that Desdemona has been proven "impure and worthless" and that he
kills her not out of jealousy, but from "moral indignation and
regret" over the destruction of such virtue and the compromise
of his personal honor. For additional examples of the view that
Othello's murder of Desdemona is motivated by honor and justice
rather than jealousy, see the excerpts by the anonymous critic in
the* Bee *(1791), Hermann Ulrici (1839), G. G. Gervinus (1849-50),
Denton J. Snider (1887), A. C. Bradley (1904), Winifred M. T.
Nowottny (1952), G. M. Matthews (1964), and Carol McGinnis
Kay (1983).]*

Othello must not be conceived as a negro, but a high and chivalrous Moorish chief. Shakspeare learned the spirit of the character from the Spanish poetry, which was prevalent in England in his time. Jealousy does not strike me as the point in his passion; I take it to be rather an agony that the creature, whom he had believed angelic, with whom he had garnered up his heart, and whom he could not help still loving, should be proved impure and worthless. It was the struggle *not* to love her. It was a moral indignation and regret that virtue should so fall:—"But yet the *pity* of it, Iago!—O Iago! the *pity* of it, Iago!" [IV. i. 195-96]. In addition to this, his honour was concerned: Iago would not have succeeded but by hinting that his honour was compromised. There is no ferocity in Othello; his mind is majestic and composed. He deliberately determines to die; and speaks his last speech with a view of showing his attachment to the Venetian state, though it had superseded him. (pp. 1-2)

Samuel Taylor Coleridge [as reported by H. N. Coleridge], in a conversation on December 29, 1822, in his Specimens of the Table Talk of the Late Samuel Taylor Coleridge, Vol. I, *edited by H. N. Coleridge, John Murray, 1835, pp. 1-2.*

SAMUEL TAYLOR COLERIDGE [as reported by H. N. COLERIDGE] (conversation date 1827)

[*In this second excerpt from* Table Talk *(1835), from a conversation which occurred on June 24, 1827, Coleridge again maintains that Othello is not portrayed as a jealous man. He asserts that the Moor evinces "no predisposition to suspicion," a characteristic the critic argues is basic to a jealous nature, and that Othello acts on what he believes to be convincing proofs of Desdemona's infidelity. The question of whether Shakespeare presents Othello as an inherently jealous man has also been considered by such critics as John Hughes (1713), Lewis Theobald (1717), Samuel Johnson (1765), August Wilhelm Schlegel (1811), Hermann Ulrici (1839), G. G. Gervinus (1849-50), Denton J. Snider (1887), A. C. Bradley (1904), E. K. Chambers (1908), Elmer Edgar Stoll (1915), Allardyce Nicoll (1927), and Harley Granville-Barker (1945).*]

I have often told you that I do not think there is any jealousy, properly so called, in the character of Othello. There is no predisposition to suspicion, which I take to be an essential term in the definition of the word. Desdemona very truly told Emilia that he was not jealous, that is, of a jealous habit, and he says so as truly of himself. Iago's suggestions, you see, are quite new to him; they do not correspond with any thing of a like nature previously in his mind. If Desdemona had, in fact, been guilty, no one would have thought of calling Othello's conduct that of a jealous man. He could not act otherwise than he did with the lights he had; whereas jealousy can never be strictly right. See how utterly unlike Othello is to Leontes, in the *Winter's Tale,* or even to Leonatus, in *Cymbeline!* The jealousy of the first proceeds from an evident trifle, and something like hatred is mingled with it; and the conduct of Leonatus in accepting the wager, and exposing his wife to the trial, denotes a jealous temper already formed. (pp. 67-8)

Samuel Taylor Coleridge [as reported by H. N. Coleridge], in a conversation on June 24, 1827, in his Specimens of the Table Talk of the Late Samuel Taylor Coleridge, Vol. I, *edited by H. N. Coleridge, John Murray, 1835, pp. 67-8.*

MRS. [ANNA BROWNELL] JAMESON (essay date 1833)

[*Jameson was a well-known nineteenth-century essayist. Her essays and criticism span the end of the Romantic age and the beginning of Victorian realism, reflecting elements from both periods. She is best remembered for her study* Shakspeare's Heroines *(1833), which was originally published in a slightly different form in 1832 as* Characteristics of Women: Moral, Poetical, and Historical. *This work demonstrates both her historical interests and her sympathetic appreciation of Shakespeare's female characters. In the excerpt below from* Shakspeare's Heroines, *Jameson describes Desdemona as possessing an excess of "gentleness" that verges on passivity, but argues that, although she shows no resistance to Othello's charges, she should not be viewed as weak or powerless. Indeed, the critic maintains, Desdemona holds our compassion throughout the dramatic action even though she lacks perspicacity and strength of will. Jameson adds that "the slightest manifestation of intellectual power or active will" ascribed to her character "would have injured the dramatic effect" of the pathos of the drama. Desdemona's passivity has also been analyzed by such critics as William Hazlitt (1817), E. K. Chambers (1908), and Gayle Greene (1979), and her deficiencies of courage and wit have been discussed by J. A. Heraud (1865), Allardyce Nicoll (1927), and G. R. Elliott (1937). Also, for an assessment of Desdemona as a "wanton" and an unnatural woman, see the excerpt by John Quincy Adams (1835).*]

Desdemona, as a character, comes nearest to Miranda [in *The Tempest*] both in herself as a woman, and in the perfect simplicity and unity of the delineation; the figures are differently draped, the proportions are the same. There is the same modesty, tenderness, and grace; the same artless devotion in the affections, the same predisposition to wonder, to pity, to admire; the same almost ethereal refinement and delicacy. But all is pure poetic nature within Miranda and around her; Desdemona is more associated with the palpable realities of everyday existence, and we see the forms and habits of society tinting her language and deportment: no two beings can be more alike in character, nor more distinct as individuals.

The love of Desdemona for Othello appears at first such a violation of all probabilities that her father at once imputes it to magic, "to spells and mixtures powerful o'er the blood"—

> She,—in spite of nature,
> Of years, of country, credit, every thing,—
> To fall in love with what she fear'd to look on!
>
> [I. iii. 96-8]

And the devilish malignity of Iago, whose coarse mind cannot conceive an affection founded purely in sentiment, derives from her love itself a strong argument against her—

> Ay, there's the point:—As to be bold with you,—
> Not to affect many proposed matches
> Of her own clime, complexion, and degree;
> Whereto, we see, in all things nature tends; &c.
>
> [III. iii. 227-31]

Notwithstanding this disparity of age, character, country, complexion, we, who are admitted into the secret, see her love rise naturally and necessarily out of the leading propensities of her nature. (pp. 172-73)

Desdemona displays at times a transient energy, arising from the power of affection, but gentleness gives the prevailing tone to the character—gentleness in its excess—gentleness verging on passiveness—gentleness, which not only cannot resent—but cannot resist—

> *Othello.* Then of so gentle a condition!
> *Iago.* Ay! too gentle.
> *Othello.* Nay, that's certain.
>
> [IV. i 192-95]

Here the exceeding softness of Desdemona's temper is turned against her by Iago, so that it suddenly strikes Othello in a new point of view, as the inability to resist temptation; but to us who perceive the character as a whole, this extreme gentleness of nature is yet delineated with such exceeding refinement, that the effect never approaches to feebleness. It is true that *once* her extreme timidity leads her in a moment of confusion and terror to prevaricate about the fatal handkerchief. This handkerchief, in the original story of Cinthio, is merely one of those embroidered handkerchiefs which were as fashionable in Shakspeare's time as in our own; but the minute description of it . . . suggested to the poetical fancy of Shakspeare one of the most exquisite and characteristic passages in the whole play. Othello makes poor Desdemona believe that the handkerchief was a talisman—

> There's magick in the web of it:
> A sybil, that had number'd in the world
> The sun to course two hundred compasses,
> In her prophetick fury sew'd the work:
> The worms were hallow'd that did breed the silk,
> And it was dyed in mummy, which the skilful
> Conserv'd of maidens' hearts.
> *Desdemona.*   Indeed! is't true?
> *Othello.* Most veritable, therefore, look to 't well.
> *Desdemona.* Then would to heaven that I had never
>   seen it!
> *Othello.* Ha! wherefore!
> *Desdemona.* Why do you speak so startlingly and rash?
> *Othello.* Is 't lost?—is 't gone? Speak, is 't out of the
>   way?
> *Desdemona.* Heaven bless us!
> *Othello.*   Say you?
> *Desdemona.* It is not lost: But what an if it were?
> *Othello.* Ha!
> *Desdemona.* I say, it is not lost.
> *Othello.*   Fetch 't, let me see 't.
> *Desdemona.* Why, so I can, sir, but I will not now,
>   &c.
>
>   [III. iv. 69-86]

Desdemona, whose soft credulity, whose turn for the marvellous, whose susceptible imagination had first directed her thoughts and affections to Othello, is precisely the woman to be frightened out of her senses by such a tale as this, and betrayed by her fears into a momentary tergiversation. It is most natural in such a being, and shows us that even in the sweetest natures there can be no completeness and consistency without moral energy.

With the most perfect artlessness, she has something of the instinctive, unconscious address of her sex; as when she appeals to her father—

> So much duty as my mother show'd
> To you, preferring you before her father,
> So much I challenge, that I may profess
> Due to the Moor, my lord.
>
>   [I. iii. 186-89]

And when she is pleading for Cassio—

> What! Michael Cassio!
> That came a wooing with you; and so many a time,
> When I have spoke of you disparagingly,
> Hath ta'en your part?
>
>   [III. ii. 70-3]
>   (pp. 174-76)

In the mention of her mother, and the appeal to Othello's self-love, Desdemona has no design formed on conclusions previously drawn; but her intuitive quickness of feeling, added to her imagination, lead her more safely to the same results, and the distinction is as truly as it is delicately drawn.

When Othello first outrages her in a manner which appears inexplicable, she seeks and finds excuses for him. She is so innocent, that not only she cannot believe herself suspected, but she cannot conceive the existence of guilt in others—

> Something, sure, of state,—
> Either from Venice; or some unhatch'd practice
> Made demonstrable here in Cyprus to him,—
> Hath puddled his clear spirit.
>   'Tis even so—
>   Nay, we must think, men are not gods,
> Nor of them look for such observances
> As fit the bridal.

And when the direct accusation of crime is flung on her in the vilest terms, it does not anger but stun her, as if it transfixed her whole being; she attempts no reply, no defence; and reproach or resistance never enters her thought—

> Good friend, go to him;—for, by this light of heaven,
> I know not how I lost him. Here I kneel:
> If e'er my will did trespass 'gainst his love,
> Either in discourse of thought, or actual deed;
> Or that mine eyes, mine ears, or any sense,
> Delighted them in any other form;
> Or that I do not yet, and ever did,
> And ever will,—though he do shake me off
> To beggarly divorcement,—love him dearly,
> Comfort forswear me! Unkindness may do much,
> And his unkindness may defeat my life,
> But never taint my love.
>
>   [IV. ii. 150-61]

And there is one stroke of consummate delicacy, surprising, when we remember the latitude of expression prevailing in Shakspeare's time, and which he allowed to his other women generally: she says, on recovering from her stupefaction—

> Am I that name, Iago?
>   *Iago.*   What name, fair lady?
>   *Desdemona.* Such as, she says, my lord did say I
>   was?
>
>   [IV. ii. 118-19]

So completely did Shakspeare enter into the angelic refinement of the character.

Endued with that temper which is the origin of superstition in love as in religion,—which, in fact, makes love itself a religion,—she not only does not utter an upbraiding, but nothing that Othello does or says, no outrage, no injustice, can tear away the charm with which her imagination had invested him, or impair her faith in his honour. "I would you had never seen him!" exclaims Emilia—

> *Desdemona.* So would not I!—my love doth so
>   approve him,
> That even his stubborness, his checks, and frowns,
> Have grace and favour in them.
>
>   [IV. iii. 18-21]

There is another peculiarity, which, in reading the play of "Othello," we rather feel than perceive: through the whole of the dialogue appropriated to Desdemona, there is not one general observation. Words are with her the vehicle of sentiment, and never of reflection; so that I cannot find throughout a sentence of general application. The same remark applies to Miranda: and to no other female character of any importance or interest; not even to Ophelia. (pp. 177-78)

[The] source of the pathos throughout—of that pathos which at once softens and deepens the tragic effect—lies in the character of Desdemona. No woman differently constituted could have excited the same intense and painful compassion without losing something of that exalted charm which invests her from beginning to end, which we are apt to impute to the interest of the situation and to the poetical colouring, but which lies, in fact, in the very essence of the character. Desdemona, with all her timid flexibility and soft acquiescence, is not weak; for the negative alone is weak; and the mere presence of goodness and affection implies in itself a species of power; power without consciousness, power without effort, power with repose—that soul of grace! (p. 180)

In Desdemona we cannot but feel that the slightest manifestation of intellectual power or active will would have injured the dramatic effect. She is a victim consecrated from the first—''an offering without blemish,'' alone worthy of the grand final sacrifice; all harmony, all grace, all purity, all tenderness, all truth! But, alas! to see her fluttering like a cherub, in the talons of a fiend!—to see her—O poor Desdemona! (p. 181)

> Mrs. [Anna Brownell] Jameson, ''Characters of the Affections: Desdemona,'' in her Shakspeare's Heroines: Characteristics of Women, Moral, Poetical, and Historical, *George Newnes, Limited, 1897, pp. 172-81.*

J[OHN] Q[UINCY] ADAMS   (essay date 1835)

[*Adams was the sixth President of the United States (1825-29) and is generally regarded by scholars as one of the most outstanding diplomats in the nation's history. During his tenure as a United States Congressman, from 1831 until his death in 1848, he was an ardent opponent of the expansion of slavery, and he sought a Constitutional amendment to grant freedom from slavery for every child born in this country. His remarks on* Othello *excerpted below, however, suggest that although Adams sought political equality for black Americans, he was opposed to the concept of interracial marriage. He declares that even though Desdemona is not false to Othello, she betrays both her gender and her social position by wedding a black man, and in so doing becomes ''little less than a wanton,'' thus forfeiting our compassion for her suffering and death. Adams concludes that the ''great moral lesson'' of* Othello *is that marriage between people of divergent races is an outrage against natural law. For further discussions of the racial issue in the play, see the excerpts by Thomas Rymer (1692), Charles Gildon (1694 and 1710), William Kenrick (1774), Samuel Taylor Coleridge (1808-18 and 1813), Charles Lamb (1811), Denton J. Snider (1887), and G. M. Matthews (1964), as well as the essay by G. K. Hunter cited in the Additional Bibliography. Also, for additional commentary on Desdemona's character, see the excerpts by William Hazlitt (1817), Anna Brownell Jameson (1833), J. A. Heraud (1865), E. K. Chambers (1908), Allardyce Nicoll (1927), G. R. Elliott (1937), and Gayle Greene (1979). Adams's comments on* Othello *originally appeared in* New England Magazine *in 1835.*]

There are several of the most admired plays of Shakespeare which give much more pleasure to read than to see performed upon the stage. For instance, *Othello* and *Lear;* both of which abound in beauty of detail, in poetical passages, in highly-wrought and consistently preserved characters. But, the plea-

sure that we take in witnessing a performance upon the stage, depends much upon the sympathy that we feel with the sufferings and enjoyments of the good characters represented, and upon the punishment of the bad. We never can sympathize much with *Desdemona* or with *Lear,* because we never can separate them from the estimate that the lady is little less than a wanton, and the old king nothing less than a dotard. Who can sympathize with the love of *Desdemona?*—the daughter of a Venetian nobleman, born and educated to a splendid and lofty station in the community. She falls in love and makes a runaway match with a blackamoor, for no better reason than that he has told her a braggart story of his hair-breadth escapes in war. For this, she not only violates her duties to her father, her family, her sex, and her country, but she makes the first advances. She tells *Othello* she wished Heaven had made her such a man, and informs him how *any* friend of his may win her by telling her again his story. On *that* hint, says he, I spoke; and well he might. The blood must circulate briskly in the veins of a young woman, so fascinated, and so coming to the tale of a rude, unbleached African soldier.

The great moral lesson of the tragedy of *Othello* is, that black and white blood cannot be intermingled in marriage without a gross outrage upon the law of Nature; and that, in such violations, Nature will vindicate her laws. The moral of *Othello* is not to beware of jealousy, for jealousy is well founded in the character and conduct of his wife, though not in the fact of her infidelity with *Cassio. Desdemona* is not false to her husband, but she has been false to the purity and delicacy of her sex and condition when she married him; and the last words spoken by her father on parting from them, after he has forgiven her and acquiesced in the marriage, are—

> Look to her, Moor; have a quick eye to see:
> She has deceived her father, and may thee.
> [I. iii. 292-93]

And this very idea is that by which the crafty villain *Iago* works up into madness the jealousy of *Othello.*

Whatever sympathy we feel for the sufferings of *Desdemona* flows from the consideration that she is innocent of the particular crime imputed to her, and that she is the victim of a treacherous and artful intriguer. But, while compassionating her melancholy fate, we cannot forget the vice of her character. Upon the stage, her fondling with *Othello* is disgusting. Who, in real life, would have her for a sister, daughter, or wife? She is not guilty of infidelity to her husband, but she forfeits all the affection of her father and all her own filial affection for him. When the duke proposes, on the departure of *Othello* for the war, that she should return during his absence to her father's house, the father, the daughter and the husband all say ''No!'' She prefers following *Othello,* to be besieged by the Turks in the island of Cyprus.

The character of *Desdemona* is admirably drawn and faithfully preserved throughout the play. It is always deficient in delicacy. Her conversations with *Emilia* indicate unsettled principles, even with regard to the obligations of the nuptial tie, and she allows *Iago,* almost unrebuked, to banter with her very coarsely upon women. This character takes from us so much of the sympathetic interest in her sufferings, that when *Othello* smothers her in bed, the terror and the pity subside immediately into the sentiment that she has her deserts. (pp. 223-26)

> J[ohn] Q[uincy] Adams, ''Misconceptions of Shakespeare, upon the Stage,'' in Notes and Comments upon Certain Plays and Actors of Shakespeare by

James Henry Hackett, third edition, Carleton, Publisher, 1864, pp. 217-28.

WILLIAM MAGINN (essay date 1839)

[Born and educated in Ireland, Maginn later lived in London where he developed his career as an essayist, poet, and short story writer. In the following excerpt from an essay originally published in Bentley's Miscellany in 1839, Maginn focuses on the character of Iago, addressing, in particular, the motives for his villainy; he concludes that the most legitimate of those offered by Iago is Cassio's appointment to the lieutenancy. Maginn argues that at the outset Iago intends merely to gull Roderigo and undermine Cassio, but that the circumstance of Othello's marriage unfortunately presents itself as a surer means to gain his revenge. The critic also contends that Iago is "as much a tool or passive instrument as those whom he is using," in that his own love of "deceit and iniquity" destroys himself along with the others. Other commentators who have viewed Iago as the victim of his own schemes include William Hazlitt (1817), A. C. Bradley (1904), Tucker Brooke (1918), Allardyce Nicoll (1927), G. R. Elliott (1937), and Nigel Alexander (see Additional Bibliography). Also, for further commentary on Iago's motives, see the excerpts by Thomas Wilkes (1759), John Potter (1771-72), Richard Hole (1796), Samuel Taylor Coleridge (1808-18), William Hazlitt (1817), Denton J. Snider (1887), A. C. Bradley (1904), G. Wilson Knight (1930), Bernard Spivack (1958), G. M. Matthews (1964), and the essay by Stanley Edgar Hyman cited in the Additional Bibliography.]

What appears to me to be the distinguishing feature of Shakespeare is, that his characters are real men and women, not mere abstractions. In the best of us all there are many blots, in the worst there are many traces of goodness. There is no such thing as angels or devils in the world. We have passions and feelings, hopes and fears, joys and sorrows, pretty equally distributed among us; and that which actuates the highest and the lowest, the most virtuous and the most profligate, the bravest and meanest, must, in its original elements, be the same. People do not commit wicked actions from the mere love of wickedness; there must always be an incentive of precisely the same kind as that which stimulates to the noblest actions—ambition, love of adventure, passion, necessity. All our virtues closely border upon vices, and are not unfrequently blended. (pp. 155-56)

As Shakespeare therefore draws men, and not one-side sketches of character, it is always possible to treat his personages as if they were actually existing people; and there is always some redeeming point. The bloody Macbeth is kind and gentle to his wife; the gore-stained Richard [in Richard III], gallant and daring; Shylock [in The Merchant of Venice] is an affectionate father, and a good-natured master; Claudius, in Hamlet, is fond of his foully-won queen, and exhibits, at least, remorse for his deed in heart-rending soliloquies; Angelo [in Measure for Measure] is upright in public life, though yielding to sore temptation in private; Cloton [in Cymbeline] is brutal and insulting, but brave; the ladies are either wholly without blemishes, or have merits to redeem them: in some plays, as Julius Caesar, Coriolanus, Antony and Cleopatra, Romeo and Juliet, and several others, no decidedly vicious character is introduced at all. The personages introduced are exposed to the frailties of our nature, but escape from its grosser crimes and vices.

But Iago! Ay! there's the rub. Well may poor Othello look down to his feet, and, not seeing them different from those of others, feel convinced that it is a fable which attributes a cloven hoof to the devil. His next test—

If that thou be'st a devil, I can not kill thee—
[V. ii. 287]

affords a proof that Iago is not actually a fiend, for he wounds him; but still he can not think him any thing less than a "demi-devil," being bled, not killed. Nor is it wonderful that the parting instruction of Lodovico to Cassio should be to enforce the most cunning cruelty of torture on the hellish villain, or that all the party should vie with each other in heaping upon him words of contumely and execration. He richly deserved them. He had ensnared the soul and body of Othello to do the most damnable actions; he had been the cause of the cruel murder of Desdemona; he had killed his own wife, had plotted the assassination of Cassio, had betrayed and murdered Roderigo. His determination to keep silence when questioned was at least judicious:—

Demand me nothing: what you know, you know;
From this time forth I never will speak word—
[V. ii. 303-04]

for, with his utmost ingenuity, he could hardly find any thing to say for himself. Is there nothing, then, to be said for him by any body else?

No more than this. He is the sole exemplar of studied personal revenge in the plays. The philosophical mind of Hamlet ponders too deeply, and sees both sides of the question too clearly, to be able to carry any plan of vengeance into execution. Romeo's revenge on Tybalt for the death of Mercutio is a sudden gust of ungovernable rage. The vengeances in the historical plays are those of war or statecraft. In Shylock, the passion is hardly personal against his intended victim. A swaggering Christian is at the mercy of a despised and insulted Jew. The hatred is national and sectarian. Had Bassanio or Gratiano, or any other of their creed, been in his power, he would have been equally relentless. He is only retorting the wrongs and insults of his tribe, in demanding full satisfaction, and imitating the hated Christians in their own practices:—

And if you wrong us, shall we not revenge?
If we are like you in the rest, we will
Resemble you in that. If a Jew wrong
A Christian, what is his humility?
Revenge!
[And] if a Christian wrong a Jew, what should
His sufferance be by Christian example?
Why, [sir], revenge! The villainy you teach me
I'll execute, and it shall go hard, but
I'll better the instruction.
[The Merchant of Venice, III. i. 66-73]

It is, on the whole, a passion remarkably seldom exhibited in Shakespeare in any form. Iago, as I have said, is its only example, as directed against an individual.

Iago had been affronted in the tenderest point. He felt that he had strong claims on the office of lieutenant to Othello, who had witnessed his soldierly abilities.

At Rhodes, at Cyprus, and on other grounds,
Christian and heathen.
[I. i. 29-30]

The greatest exertion was made to procure it for him, and yet he is refused. What is still worse, the grounds of the refusal

are military: Othello evades the request of the bowing magnificoes

> with a bombast circumstance
> Horribly stuffed with epithets of war.
>
> [I. i. 13-14]

He assigns to civilians reasons for passing over Iago, drawn
from his own trade, of which they, of course, could not pretend
to be adequate judges. And worst of all, when this practised
military man, is, for military reasons, set aside, who is appointed? Some man of greater renown and skill in arms? *That*
might be borne; but it is no such thing. The choice of Othello
lights upon,

> Forsooth, a great arithmetician,
> One Michael Cassio, a Florentine,
> A fellow almost damned in a fair wife,
> That never set a squadron in the field,
> Nor the division of a battle knows,
> More than a spinster; unless the bookish theoric,
> Wherein the toged consuls can propose
> As masterly as he; mere prattle without practice,
> Is all his soldiership.
>
> [I. i. 19-27]
> (pp. 156-63)

In the country of Iago, whether from his name we conclude it
to be Spain, or from his service, Italy, none of the scruples,
or rather principles, which actuate or restrain English gentlemen, existed. . . . Iago could not be expected to be very scrupulous as to his method of compassing his revenge. But how
effect it? He is obliged to admit that Othello's standing in the
state is too important to render it possible that public injury
could be done to him. He is well aware that

> the state . . .
> Can not with safety cast him; he's embarked
> With such loud reasons to the Cyprus war,
> Which e'en now stands in act, that for their souls
> Another of his fathom they have not
> To lead their business.
>
> [I. i. 147, 149-53]

In his unhoused condition no point of vantage presented itself
whence harm could be wrought. Just then, when Iago's heart
was filled with rage, and his head busily but vainly occupied
in devising means for avenging himself on the man by whom
that rage was excited, just then *Até*, the goddess of Mischief,
supplies him with all that deepest malignity could desire, by
the hasty, ill-mated, and unlooked-for marriage of Othello. It
was a devil-send that the most sanguine spirit could not have
anticipated, and Iago clutched it accordingly with passionate
eagerness. He was tempted, and he fell.

When he first conceived his hatred against Othello, he had no
notion that it would be pushed to such dire extremity. Revenge
is generally accompanied by vanity, indeed there must be always a spice of vanity in a revengeful disposition. He who so
keenly feels and deeply resents personal injury or affront, must
set no small value upon himself. The proud are seldom revengeful—the great, never. We accordingly find that Iago engages in his hostilities against Othello, more to show his talents
than for any other purpose. He proudly lauds his own powers

*Act IV. Scene i. Lodovico, Iago, Desdemona, and Othello.
Frontispiece to the Hanmer edition by H. Gravelot (1744).
By permission of the Folger Shakespeare Library.*

of dissimulation, which are to be now displayed with so much
ability.

> When my outward action doth demonstrate
> The native act and figure of my heart
> In compliment extern, 'tis not long after
> But I will wear my heart upon my sleeve
> For daws to peck at. I am not what I am.
>
> [I. i. 61-5]

He fancies himself superior to all around in art and knowledge
of the world. Roderigo is a mere gull:—

> Thus do I ever make my fool my purse;
> For I mine own gain'd knowledge should profane,
> If I should time expend with *such a snipe,*
> But for my sport and profit.
>
> [I. iii. 383-86]

Cassio he considers to be not merely unskilled in war, but a
fool:—

> For while *this honest fool*
> Plies Desdemona to repair his fortunes, &c.
>
> [II. iii. 353-54]

Othello is an ass in his estimation:—

> The Moor is of a free and open nature,
> That thinks men honest that but seem to be so,

And will as tenderly be led by the nose
As asses are.

[I. iii. 399-402]

The "*inclining*" Desdemona he utterly despises, as one who
fell in love with the Moor merely for his bragging, and telling
fantastical lies. His wife he calls a fool; and, with these opinions of his great superiority of wisdom and intellect, he commences operations to enmesh them all, as if they were so many
puppets. It would be a strange thing indeed, he reflects, if I
were to permit myself to be insulted, and my rights withheld,
by such a set of idiots, whom I can wind round my finger as
I please. (pp. 163-65)

The jealousy of Othello is not more gradually and skilfully
raised and developed than the vengeance of Iago. At first angry
enough, no doubt; but he has no defined project. He follows
the Moor to take advantage of circumstances to turn them to
his own use. Nothing of peculiar malignity is thought upon: if
he can get Cassio's place, he will be satisfied.

Cassio's a proper man; let me see now,
To get his place—

[I. iii. 392-93]

The marriage and the sight of Desdemona point out to him a
ready way of accomplishing this object. The thought occurs
suddenly, and he is somewhat startled at first. He asks himself
with eager repetition,

How? how?

and pauses to think—

Let me see—

[I. iii. 394]

It is soon settled.

After some time, to abuse Othello's ear
That he is too familiar with his wife.

[I. iii. 395-96]

But it still alarms him:—

I have it—it's engendered: Hell and night
Must bring this monstrous birth to the world's light.

[I. iii. 403-04]

The plot is not matured even when they all arrive at Cyprus.

'Tis here, but yet confused—
Knavery's plain face is never seen till used.

[II. i. 311-12]

When once fairly entered upon, however, it progresses with
unchecked rapidity. He is himself hurried resistlessly forward
by the current of deceit and iniquity in which he has embarked.
He is as much a tool or passive instrument as those whom he
is using as such.

Some critics pronounce his character unnatural, as not having
sufficient motive for the crimes he commits. This is not wise.
He could not help committing them. Merely to put money in
his purse, he gulled Roderigo into a belief that he could assist
the poor dupe in his suit to Desdemona. There is no remarkable
crime in this. Nor can we blame him for being angry at being
somewhat scornfully passed over; we can, at all events, enter
into his feelings when he wishes to undermine one whom he
considers unworthily preferred to him, and to obtain a place
which he thinks should be his own, if patronage had been justly
dispensed. It was a base thing, indeed, to malign a lady, and

possess her husband with jealousy; but he could not have calculated on the harvest of death and crime which the seed of
suspicion that he was sowing was destined to bring up. When
he makes Cassio drunk, he only anticipates that he will put
him in such action as may offend the isle. When framing the
device that is to destroy the lieutenant, no thoughts of murder
arise before him.

He has no regard for the feelings of Othello, but dreams not
that he will kill Desdemona, whom he says he loves. As for
the lady herself, his low estimation of woman would, of course,
lead him to think but little about her peace and quiet. He
excuses himself, besides, by referring to the rumor that Othello
had given him cause to be jealous. It is plain that he does not
pretend to lay any great stress upon this; nor can we suppose
that, even if it were true, it would deeply affect him; but he
thinks light of women in general, and has no respect whatever
for his wife. Indeed, Othello does not hold Emilia in much
esteem; and her own conversation with Desdemona, as she is
undressing her for bed (Act IV. Scene 3), shows that her virtue
was not impregnable. The injury, therefore, Iago was about to
do Desdemona, in lessening her in the respect of her husband
by accusing her of such an ordinary offence as a deviation from
chastity, and one which *he* did not visit with any particular
severity on his own wife, must have seemed trivial. He could
not have been prepared for the dire tempest of fury which his
first hint of her unfaithfulness aroused in the bosom of Othello.
Up to that moment he had done nothing more than gull a
blockhead, and endeavor by unworthy means to undermine a
rival; trickery and slander, though not very honorable qualities
are not of such rare occurrence in the world as to call for the
expression of any peculiar indignation, when we find them
displayed by a clever and plotting Italian.

They have, however, led him to the plain and wide path of
damnation. He can not retract his insinuations. Even if he
desired, Othello will not let him:—

Villain, be sure you prove my love a whore.

[III. iii. 359]

[We may observe that he still, though his suspicions are so
fiercely roused, calls her his *love*. It is for the last time before
her death. After her guilt is, as he thinks, proved, he has no
word of affection for her. She is a convicted culprit, to be
sacrificed to his sense of justice.]

Be sure of it: give me ocular proof:
Or, by the worth of mine eternal soul,
Thou hadst been better have been born a dog
Than answer my waked wrath. . . .
Make me to see 't, or, at the least, so prove it,
That the probation bear no hinge, no loop
To hang a doubt on; or woe upon thy life!

[III. iii. 360-63, 364-66]

Iago, therefore, had no choice but to go forward. He was
evidently not prepared for this furious outburst; and we may
acquit him of hypocrisy when he prays Othello to let her live.
But Cassio must die:—

He hath a daily beauty in his life
That makes me ugly.

[V. i. 19-20]

A more urgent reason immediately suggests itself:—

And besides, the Moor
May unfold me to him; there stand I in much peril.
No—he must die.

[V. i. 20-2]

The death of Desdemona involves that of Roderigo:—

> Live Roderigo?
> He calls me to a restitution large
> Of gold and jewels, that I bobb'd from him
> As gifts to Desdemona.
> *It must not be.*
>
> [V. i. 14-18]

Here is the direct agency of necessity. He *must* remove these men. Shortly after, to silence the clamorous testimony of his wife, he *must* kill her. He is doomed to blood. (pp. 166-70)

William Maginn, "Iago," in his The Shakespeare Papers of the Late William Maginn, LL.D., *edited by Shelton Mackenzie, Redfield, 1856, pp. 155-70.*

HERMANN ULRICI (essay date 1839)

[*A German scholar, Ulrici was a professor of philosophy and the author of works on Greek poetry and Shakespeare. The following excerpt is from an English translation of his* Über Shakespeares dramatische Kunst, und sein Verhältniss zu Calderon und Göthe, *a work first published in 1839. This study exemplifies the "philosophical criticism" developed in Germany during the nineteenth century. The immediate sources for Ulrici's critical approach appear to be August Wilhelm Schlegel's conception of the play as an organic, interconnected whole and Georg Wilhelm Friedrich Hegel's view of drama as an embodiment of the conflict of historical forces and ideas. Unlike his fellow German Shakespearean critic G. G. Gervinus, Ulrici sought to develop a specifically Christian aesthetics, but one which, as he carefully points out in the introduction to the work mentioned above, in no way intrudes on "that unity of idea, which preeminently constitutes a work of art a living creation in the world of beauty." In the following excerpt, Ulrici contends that the central, unifying theme of* Othello *is love, "the true moral foundation of life," for each of the characters is shown to have forgotten the divine basis of human emotions and social relationships, thereby contributing to the tragic consequences of the dramatic action. He argues that all the characters are depicted by Shakespeare as holding "false views of love, marriage, and honour" and that Othello, especially, overvalues the earthly expression of his passion, wrongly asserts his claim to honor, and "misemploys his divine gifts" by failing to subjugate them to the more exalted love of God. Thus, although he finds the death of Desdemona almost too painful to contemplate, Ulrici sees tragic justice in the play's conclusion. Such other critics as Derek Traversi (1949), Kenneth Burke (1951), Winifred M. T. Nowottny (1952), Robert B. Heilman (1956), John Bayley (1960), Susan Snyder (1972), Jared R. Curtis (1973), and Jane Adamson (1980) have also focused on Shakespeare's portrayal of the nature of love in* Othello. *For additional commentary on the element of tragic or poetic justice in the play, see the excerpts by Thomas Rymer (1692), G. G. Gervinus (1849-50), and Denton J. Snider (1887), as well as the essay by Nigel Alexander cited in the Additional Bibliography. Ulrici also directly disputes August Wilhelm Schlegel's interpretation of Othello as a "double man" (see excerpt above, 1811), asserting that if the Moor's unconquered savage nature is held to be the prime mover in the tragic action, the result would be blasphemous; in Ulrici's words, "the true tragic effect could not consist with a system of fatalism, which subverts at once all freedom of the will, and makes man dependent, not on God's free grace, but on a blind physical necessity." Such other critics as G. G. Gervinus (1849-50), Denton J. Snider (1887), Elmer Edgar Stoll (1915), Harry Levin (1964), and Robert G. Hunter (1976) have also maintained that the play's tragic action is not represented as fatalistic or predetermined. However, E. K. Chambers (1908), Stopford A. Brooke (1913), Wyndham Lewis (1927), and Allardyce Nicoll (1927) have contended that* Othello *does depict a world where destiny or divine providence determines the tragic outcome. On a final matter of importance, Ulrici contends that Othello "in his inmost self is by no means jealous" and that it is not revenge but—as the Moor himself confesses—honor and love that motivate his murder of Desdemona. Other critics who have addressed the issue of Othello's jealousy include John Hughes (1713), Lewis Theobald (1717), Samuel Johnson (1765), August Wilhelm Schlegel (1811), Samuel Taylor Coleridge (1813, 1822, and 1827), G. G. Gervinus (1849-50), Denton J. Snider (1887), A. C. Bradley (1904), E. K. Chambers (1908), Elmer Edgar Stoll (1915), Allardyce Nicoll (1927), and Harley Granville-Barker (1945).*]

Othello has always appeared to me the most fearful of all Shakspeare's tragedies. . . . My sympathies are as much repelled as attracted by it. The emotions it excites resemble those with which we regard the men who, while they irresistibly attract us by the powers and splendour of their genius, alienate us no less forcibly by their character and disposition. As often as I read it a ferment of conflicting thoughts and feelings takes possession of my mind, and it is only slowly that this deep commotion gives place to that soothing and calm elevation, which, in all the other tragedies of our author, so quickly succeeds the more painful impression. The cause of this I take to be, the grief and bitterness of the immediate impression which is left upon the mind, by the death of the loveliest and noblest of human beings, and predominates over the brighter and more cheering hopes which, nevertheless, are an essential element of the tragical. The sharpest contrarieties are united in this piece: the most high-minded openness and honesty of sentiment, the most confiding love and innocence, fall a sacrifice to the meanest artifice and depravity; magnanimity and strength of mind, noble manliness, and achievements, whose fitting place is in the history of the world, are through blind passionateness "enmeshed" in the slight toils of a low cunning and a vulgar desire of revenge, associated with a devilish, and, in its fatal consequences, fearful selfishness. Though of all who are involved in the tragic catastrophe not one is totally blameless, yet the penalty of their faults appears harsh, not to say cruel:—Desdemona's death alone fills us with horror. All this jarring dissonance does not, as in "Romeo and Juliet," pass off at once into a soothing sweet sounding accord; but we must look to reflection, and a combined consideration of all the several constituents of the ground idea, for solace and comfort. If this be the case, if my feelings have not deceived me, we must, on this account, ascribe to "Othello" a want of tragic perfection and completeness, which, as compared with the other tragedies of Shakspeare, must throw into the background a drama which, on account of its undeniable excellency of construction and well-motived action, the English nation has ever regarded as the masterpiece of our poet. Nevertheless, to remove the painfulness of the immediate impression, nothing more is wanting, as has been already said, than a closer consideration of the ground idea of the whole. It is manifestly love—the noblest and highest emotion of the human mind, and a truly divine gift—that is here again taken as the basis and centre of man's feelings and actions. Still we do not meet with it exactly on the same ground as that on which we contemplated it in "Romeo and Juliet." Here it is not the glowing morning tints of youthful love, nor the virgin flame of the maiden's full dreaming heart; the sun has now reached his meridian altitude; it is *wedded* love—love of the *mature man*, who has been tried in the storms of life, and the heartfelt devotion of an *accomplished* woman, irresistibly attracted not by the false tinsel of youthful beauty and loveliness, but by the sterling gold of manly deeds and virtue. We might almost say, that marriage itself, so far as it has its principle and idea in such a love, is the subject of the piece. Wedlock, so far as it is the chief element and a leading motive in the social development of the human race, is the position of life from which the poet has surveyed the horizon of the tragic view of the world and providence. On this account it is not love alone that is here presented to us, as is the case in "Romeo and Juliet," where it has no other accompaniment but a hatred, which, by an intrinsic necessity, is inseparable from its very passionateness; but in "Othello" love stands in organic and indissoluble communion, both with conjugal fidelity and duty, and with *honour,* that indispensable attribute of man's life and activity. So much zeal has been shewn upon religous and moral, as well as philosophical considerations, against the so-called phantom of honour, that we might almost suppose that the spectre had long since vanished before such earnest conjurations. Nevertheless, the traces of its unhealthy influence are daily discernible. This can only be accounted for by the supposition, that the hateful and monstrous thing into which honour, no doubt, is, for the most part perverted, has yet for its ground a real principle, and a justification not easily to be reasoned away. And so it is in fact. Honour, in its true import, is the necessary condition of man's activity; he ought and must act in and for the world, in which his natural vocation and divine destination lies. But the inmost nerves of his historical activity are weakened, when they are not accompanied by an outward manifestation of the world's esteem. Honour is the indispensable bond between a man's enterprise, and the sphere on which he exerts its. And this is the true justification of honour: in itself, indeed, it has no validity, but derives its right from a higher principle of true *morality,* which is perfectly independent of the world, and stands in immediate reference to God alone. If honour be torn from its true root and soil—that morality in comparison with which the world and all its pursuits are at best of relative importance, and by themselves are absolutely worthless—if it be viewed exclusively in its relation to this finite earthly existence, then, no doubt, it becomes a mere spectral phantom, and whatever there is in it of grandeur and might, once separated from its godlike origin, rebounds with demoniacal force upon its possessors.

Thus it happens with "Othello." It is evidently an infelicitous idea of Schlegel's, in which, however, [Franz] Horn and others have concurred, that led him to see in this character merely the *Negro* [see excerpt above, 1811], whose animal nature, tamed apparently by milder and nobler institutions, when once excited by the poison of jealousy, instantaneously throws off all its acquired and habituated virtues, and gives the victory to the savage over the civilized man. If the case were really so, where then would be the tragic import of the drama? Could it be called tragic for the negro to continue a negro—degraded, repelled, and rejected, even by God, simply because he is not a white man? On the contrary, the true tragic effect could not consist with a system of fatalism, which subverts at once all freedom of the will, and makes man dependent, not on God's free grace, but on a blind physical necessity. It is nothing less than a pure revolting blasphemy, and consequently so unsuitable to true poetry, that within such a view of providence no *poetical idea* would be possible. If, then, it be from no *real* elevation and genuine greatness of soul, but rather from a *seeming* grandeur, and from the *spurious* tinsel splendour of a *plated* virtue, that Othello falls into the lowness and darkness of a nature really more brutal than human, then, in the place of a profound tragic idea, we have nothing left but the trite moral: "All is not gold that glitters." The whole drama will be out of joint: Desdemona would sink from her lofty and beautiful womanhood into the class of ordinary unripe girls, whose heart is deceived by outward show, and her love could

not have had its root in the inmost being of Othello. In such a case the Moor's African savageness must have repelled all affection, or from the first have barred against him all access to her heart; and lastly, Iago would have been justified in tearing from Othello's seeming virtue its pompous mask; the senate of Venice, and Cassio, and all, must have been in their veneration for Othello the veriest and blindest of fools.

Schlegel allowed himself, perhaps, to be misled into this misconception in order to justify the pretended mistake of Shakspeare in making a Negro of a Moor. For my part I do not believe it is any mistake or misunderstanding of the sort. Shakspeare knew well enough that a Moor and a Negro are two different things. It was from very different but for just reasons that he has made a Negro of Othello. For in the first place it admits of no doubt that Othello, as painted by Shakspeare, is truly the noble excellent character he seems, and not one of mere conventional virtues. This view is confirmed, not only by a number of separate passages, but also by the general cast and the ground idea of the entire piece. From such a charge of a repressed but still unconquered savageness and fury, he is at once acquitted by the speech of Iago. (Act 3., scene 4.)

> Can he be angry? I have seen the cannon,
> When it hath blown his ranks into the air,
> And, like the Devil, from his very arm
> Puft his own brother; and can he be angry?
> Something of moment, then,—I will go meet him.
> There's matter in't, indeed, if he be angry.
>
> [III. iv. 134-39]

To this truly high degree of manly energy and virtue, Othello is raised by Shakspeare, as it were by a vigorous cast, and this greatness of soul is further exalted in an eminent degree, by the conception that he had to conquer, not merely the ordinary weakness and sinfulness of humanity, but also the savage violence of his African nature. Othello's fall, in truth, becomes the more deeply tragic and affecting, the higher his mental and moral strength is represented. And it is this same consideration, also, that first enables us to appreciate duly the true worth and profound significance of Desdemona's character; her matured affection, her wifely, more than virgin love, is shaded off distinctly from the youthful and glowing passionateness of Juliet, by the good sense with which, breaking through the outward shell, undismayed by Othello's external ugliness and negro repulsiveness, she surrenders her affection to the true intrinsic substance, the sterling worth and excellency of the man. On the other hand, it would not do for her to appear entirely blameless in her hard fate; the tragic catastrophe could not come upon her wholly undeserved and arbitrarily, without doing violence to the nature of Tragedy, and casting a doubt upon the justice of Providence. Besides many little faults of imprudence, her chief transgression is the deceiving of her noble and affectionate father, and her disobedience in uniting herself without his consent with the husband of her own choice. Indeed, Iago's whole plan, as he himself often expressly asserts, is grounded partly on the sad experience that such a disproportion between the outward grace and the inward worth must, in time, necessarily tend to loosen the marriage knot; and partly on the presumption that Othello himself, on this very ground, would be only the more disposed to harbour suspicion of the fidelity of his wife. Thus, we see, the conception of Othello's negro origin is so profoundly and intentionally interwoven with the leading spring of the whole tragic development, that the true critic is forced to recognise in what has been called a mistake, nothing less than the most profound and artistic wisdom.

The high-minded, noble, heroic Othello—he who has so completely overcome his nature and the stain of his birth—does not relax his moral firmness until all faith in human worth and virtue has been wrung from him by a devilish cunning, which, in spite of all its littleness, is yet most subtilly devised, and, as he believes, his second self—this model of fair womanhood—has become untrue. It is only when with such affliction he has lost his true self, that his passion breaks out beyond controul, and that he breathes death and annihilation against himself and the whole worthless race of man. Othello in his inmost soul is by no means jealous; this low passion, whatever Iago may pretend, is altogether foreign to his nature. A man is not, properly speaking, jealous who has good cause for jealousy. And in the same manner the desire of revenge seizes his mind but transiently; it springs up and passes away with the first burst of passion. For revenge seeks but to heap misery and ruin on the hated head; but how touchingly does Othello urge Desdemona, before her death, to confess and repent, that her soul may be saved from eternal damnation! Anger, jealousy, and revenge, are but the momentary phases under which love and honour, the ruling emotions of his soul, exhibit themselves as deeply wounded and violated, and consequently contending with each other in the annihilating struggle of conflicting passions. What he says of himself when meditating self-destruction is strictly true; he is "an honourable murderer, who has done nothing out of hate, but all for honour." When the supposed infidelity of his wife, and the treachery of his friend Cassio, have robbed him of love, and whatever else in life is dear to him, and his mind, deprived of its sole stay, reels and totters and is near to shipwreck, then he clings convulsively with all his might to the other and only tie that still remains to him—honour. His honour, at least, he will preserve. But his soul, once out of tune, is unable to resume its self-possession; in passionate blindness he deems the deaths of Cassio and Desdemona necessary for the vindication of his honour. Thus does he ruin what he wishes to save. When his own guiltiness has broken asunder the only two ties which had attached him to existence, death alone remains for him.

Othello, like Romeo, misemploys his divine gifts; forgetting their true destination, he devotes them and himself to this *earthly* life. By its own weakness, its worldliness and finiteness of view, the great, the noble, and the beautiful, sinks to the earth; in the hard trial it could not hold its ground, and falling, dashed into pieces the rich casket which contained it. As in the former piece it was youthful devotion and enthusiasm, so in the latter it is ripe manly love, with wedded truth, its inseparable companion—honour, that is represented as the most intimate tie of human existence. But even this bond, this necessary tie of society and progress, breaks into pieces, powerless and unsupported so soon as it looks upon this *earth* alone as its abiding stay, and not as a passing moment of the eternal life of humanity.

All that has been falsely said of Othello, applies only to his manifest opposite, Iago. He is the whitewashed, hypocritical power of evil—his is a selfish, half-animal nature, which is unable to control its desires and passions simply because it has never made the attempt. The mere semblance of virtue easily deceives the open unsuspecting Othello. He, indeed, is the prey of a vulgar jealousy: he hates Othello, because he believes him, on no other ground than his own unreasonable suspicions, guilty of adultery with his wife Emilia. With Iago, honour, even in its worldly acceptation, is a mere pretence. Honour, with him, means nothing but external influence and reputation—it matters not how acquired. In this sense, too, he is

jealous; for he hunts Othello and Cassio into his toils simply because the former has preferred the latter to himself. These are the motives of all his conduct, which form the groundwork of the tragic plot. Even as the mere organic opposite to Othello, this character was indispensable to the whole piece. But still more so on account of his marriage with Emilia, Desdemona's attendant, which again stands in direct opposition to that of Othello and Desdemona. In the latter are found all the conditions necessary to produce a true and lasting union: so that the only obstacle to the permanence of this happy state of genuine humanity is the undue value which is set upon it, as if it were the sole object of existence. In the wedding of Iago, on the other hand, all, even the lowest considerations which might make it a real union, are wanting. It was, therefore, from the very first, false and heartless, and had within itself the seeds of its own destruction. The truly frivolous, thoughtless, but good-natured Emilia, could have united herself to Iago only from impure motives, in sin and error. She falls by the dagger of her husband at the very moment when she is performing the best deed of her life—defending the innocence of her mistress. Iago, too, perishes by his own wickedness; and thus does the life of both reflect the ground idea of the piece in an organic contrariety. Somewhat similar, also, is the relation between Cassio and Roderigo: they are not superfluous, entering wholly from without into the machinery of the action. Their fates likewise are the results and consequences of their own false views of love, marriage, and honour.

And so here again we behold all the subordinate agents pervaded and impelled by an intrinsic necessity, revolving around one organic centre in mutual relationship and interaction. Accordingly, all settle themselves in a well-arranged group; on one side Othello and Desdemona, with Iago and Emilia on the other; behind them, on either hand, stand Cassio and Roderigo; even Bianca fills her place with reason and significancy, so far as her connection with Cassio seems to reveal his frivolous levity with regard to the true moral foundation of life, and thereby implicates him in the same tragic guiltiness with the rest, and takes away from its heavy penalty its seeming injustice; the fool, however, is here reduced to a mere messenger; his presence seems but to show that genuine wit and humour cannot spring up in the same soil with fiendish malice and savage passionateness. Lastly, beyond all, and far in the background, stand the Doge and Senate of Venice (with their officials, Gratianus and Lodovico), both as the representatives of the objective majesty of law and morality, and as being at the same time necessary, from their relation to the state, to illustrate the general character of the age and people, and to exhibit the reciprocal action between it and the represented action. For it is only in such times of emergency, and amid wars and political storms, that passionateness and high heroic prowess, the tearing rapidity of decision and execution, and especially the sense of honour, could rise to such a height. Moreover, Italy and Venice pre-eminently are the land of intrigue and cunning; on these the whole action is built, which, therefore, without any external interferences, without chance, accident, or unexpected incidents, develops itself by an intrinsic majesty entirely from out of the characters and conduct of the dramatic personages. What seems like accident, that Desdemona should drop her handerkerchief, is, in truth, inconsiderateness rather. "Othello," therefore, must be regarded as a tragedy of intrigue. By such a view of it the tragic element first obtains its true significancy. For then the soothing, calming element which is covertly contained in it, comes distinctly forward; then do Othello's sufferings and death teach us that man's wit and cunning may no doubt bring low a great and noble character, but cannot rob him of his intrinsic nobility, his greatness of soul, and his hope in God's mercy and compassion, in which Othello, amidst tears of repentance, and atonement full of "*soul-soothing balsam*," dies. (pp. 183-91)

> Hermann Ulrici, "*Criticisms of Shakspeare's Dramas: 'Othello'*," in his Shakspeare's Dramatic Art: And His Relation to Calderon and Goethe, *translated by A. J. W. Morrison, Chapman, Brothers, 1846, pp. 183-91.*

G. G. GERVINUS　(essay date 1849-50)

[*One of the most widely read Shakespearean critics of the latter half of the nineteenth century, the German critic Gervinus was praised by such eminent contemporaries as Edward Dowden, F. J. Furnivall, and James Russell Lowell; however, he is little known in the English-speaking world today. Like his predecessor Hermann Ulrici, Gervinus wrote in the tradition of the "philosophical criticism" developed in Germany in the mid-nineteenth century. Under the influence of August Wilhelm Schlegel's literary theory and Georg Wilhelm Friedrich Hegel's philosophy, such German critics as Gervinus tended to focus their analyses around a search for the literary work's organic unity and ethical import. Gervinus believed that Shakespeare's works contained a rational ethical system independent of any religion—in contrast to Ulrici, for whom Shakespeare's morality was basically Christian. In the following excerpt on Othello, taken from his book, Shakespeare Commentaries (1849-50), Gervinus has two primary concerns: to examine the reasons for Othello's jealousy and its precipitous progress and to demonstrate that the action of the drama satisfies the requirements of tragic justice. He thus describes the factors influencing the Moor's passionate behavior, such as Iago's consummate dissembling, Othello's own "excitable nature," and, especially, Desdemona's ingenuous and undiscerning temperament. Gervinus also disagrees with August Wilhelm Schlegel's description of Othello's jealousy as sensual (see excerpt above, 1811), maintaining instead that the Moor's anger is related to "his outraged and misused honour" rather than to "the jealousy of a slave to sensuality." For further commentary on the issue of Othello's jealousy, see the excerpts by John Hughes (1713), Lewis Theobald (1717), Samuel Johnson (1765), Samuel Taylor Coleridge (1813, 1822, and 1827), Hermann Ulrici (1839), Denton J. Snider (1887), A. C. Bradley (1904), E. K. Chambers (1908), Elmer Edgar Stoll (1915), Allardyce Nicoll (1927), and Harley Granville-Barker (1945). Most importantly, Gervinus avers that, by electing to marry outside the conventions of society and deceiving Brabantio, Othello and Desdemona disrupt the unity of a family relationship and inflict a mortal blow to her father. As much as we are led to admire and pity their daring, originality, and simplicity, the critic maintains, we must also view them as victims of their own faulty natures and admit that tragic justice is served through their deaths. In Gervinus's words, Shakespeare intended "that the death of Desdemona should be brought as a sacrifice, and that of Othello as an atonement, to the manes of the broken-hearted father." Other commentators who have discussed the operation of tragic or poetic justice in* Othello *include Thomas Rymer (1692), Hermann Ulrici (1839), Denton J. Snider (1887), and Nigel Alexander (see Additional Bibliography). Also, for further commentary on Desdemona's murder as a noble or honorable "sacrifice," see the excerpts by the anonymous critic in the* Bee *(1791), Samuel Taylor Coleridge (1813 and 1822), Hermann Ulrici (1839), Denton J. Snider (1887), A. C. Bradley (1904), Winifred M. T. Nowottny (1952), G. M. Matthews (1964), and Carol McGinnis Kay (1983).*]

In *Othello*, with wonderful psychological perception, [Shakespeare] created a magnificent tragic field for the passion of jealousy, which commonly belongs rather to man's petty self-love and is better suited to comic treatment; but, just for this reason, he forfeited the possibility of considering the feelings of his readers and of forbearance in agitating their minds. With his sense of psychological truth he sought the ground of a passion of such strength as the issue of [Giraldi Cinthio's] story of the Moor of Venice supposed, and he accepted it, when found, with all its necessary consequences. He suffered the flood of this excited sea to rise according to the power of the storm, unmindful of the finer natures which could not stand the hurricane. Even Ulrici, who generally stood on the side of our poet against criticising opinion and prejudice, considered the harshness evinced in the loss of the beautiful as outweighing the consolatory and elevating element [see excerpt above, 1839]; because the conclusion does not afford here, as in *Romeo and Juliet,* an agreeable dénouement. But this, it seems, lay unavoidably in the subject itself. Romeo and Juliet perish by their own will in the excess of a passion of love, which even in its agony appears sweet to us; in the tragedy before us the innocent wife falls by the hand of her husband under the frightful power of the bitterest and most malignant passion, which completely annihilates the sweeter emotion of love. This was indeed only to be avoided by relinquishing the subject itself, which would certainly be a far greater cause of regret than if the poet had not written *Measure for Measure,* on account of its painful plot. The question therefore is only whether the poet, having once undertaken the theme, has done all that he could to avoid what is needlessly terrible, and to soften what is necessarily severe. That he has done this must have appeared evident even to Ulrici. For he perceived that by carefully comprehending and considering the whole, the harmony which he had before missed became apparent. This different result from a different mode of contemplation can scarcely be the consequence of an inner want of harmony in the poem, or the careful consideration of the whole would tend to reveal it; whilst, on the contrary, we are all the more convinced that although passion is here aroused and displayed in all its strength and power, and is manifested in the most terrible actions, yet no actual discord in the melody is to be perceived. The fault, therefore, must lie in ourselves. Our understanding of the play is not in unison with our moral or aesthetic feelings; either our judgment is at fault in the final comprehension of the play, or our feeling errs in the first impression it produces.

By examining the play and ourselves more narrowly, we shall discover that, so far as the object and design of the drama is concerned, our moral perceptions are opposed to those of the poet. The entire spirit of the tale of the Moor of Venice is laid down by Giraldi Cinthio in the following plain words from Desdemona: 'I fear,' says she, 'that I must serve as a warning to young maidens not to marry against the will of their parents; an Italian girl should not marry a man whom nature, heaven, and mode of life have wholly separated from her.' These prosaic truths meet us also in Shakespeare's tragedy, set forth in glowing poetry, and grounded on the deepest experiences of life. At the present day, however, we have not so lively an appreciation of the first of these truths, and we do not estimate so highly the opposition of Othello and Desdemona against family claims as was the case with Shakespeare and his time. If we follow our natural method of consideration, we do not perceive the crime which makes the sufferers deserve such suffering, and we stumble at their heavy punishment. If we place ourselves and our judgment (which with some knowledge of history is not so difficult for us) at the poet's point of view, we find his solution of the problem logical, right, and irrefragable. (pp. 506-07)

The task imposed upon the poet was to exhibit the passion of jealousy to an extent in which the lover can be thought capable of destroying the object of his love. We think a man of inflamed sensibility, of heated blood, and of the most violent irritability, especially capable of such a deed; and even him only in the frenzy of intoxication, in the sudden incentive of opportunity, and in the feverish excitement of a fit of rage. But such a deed would never be a subject for art; such a man, acting in an irresponsible condition, would never win our sympathy for his tragic fate. Could it, however, be conceivable that such a deed could ever be committed by a man of fixed character and steadfast disposition, who previous to the act had even captivated our interest? by a man in whom this passion, one of the lowest which actuates a human being, could appear so ennobled that, even in spite of and after such a deed, he could engage our sympathy and even excite our pity? It would appear impossible! And yet the poet in *Othello* has made such a man commit such a deed. Or, rather, he has depicted it as committed by a man who united the two natures, calmness and ardour, rashness and circumspection—the traits which make the murder possible, and those which allow us to admire and to pity the murderer. How the poet was to evolve truth in such a contradiction, was the point which required his utmost art and knowledge of human nature. This task, however, he discharged in such a manner that the play of *Othello* must for this reason be reckoned among his highest works.

Let us first bring out the image of the Moor from the shadow of the Past, before we consider him in the action of the play.

Othello is by race, complexion, habits, and natural disposition, a stranger in the state which we see him serving, although he has become a Christian and a Venetian. The stain of his birth is ever kept in fresh remembrance by his dark skin, and neither his deeds nor his royal origin can free him from the prejudices of men. The peculiar disposition of his Mauritanian race, his violent temperament, the power of passion, and the force of a tropical fancy, were not to be effaced, however much the self-command of the much-tried man, steeled by deeds and sufferings, had attempted it. . . . Othello had entered the service of the Venetian state. He had become so naturalised there that like a patriot he held the honour of the state as his own honour: this he showed at Aleppo, when, in the midst of the enemy's land, he stabbed the Turk who insulted Venice by striking a Venetian. By his warlike deeds he had made himself indispensable to the state; he was 'all in all' to the senate [IV. i. 265]; the people and public opinion, 'the sovereign mistress of effects' [I. iii. 225], were on his side. Among the noble and the higher classes alone he had open enemies and enviers; those who possess the privileges ever possess the prejudices also. We hear, indeed, the tone in which Iago and Roderigo speak of the 'black devil' and 'the thick-lips' [I. i. 66]; we hear how poisonously Iago, under the mask of good intention, tells him to his face the prejudices as to his colour and birth which are circulated in Venice; we see plainly at what a distance he was regarded by Brabantio, at whose house he was even a favoured guest. In the eyes of these people he was not the deserving warrior of their country, but a vagrant, vagabond, and foreign barbarian; the finger of scorn pointed at him, and he felt it. That he should meet his enemies with disregard and contempt lay in his proud nature; we hear that he rejected important requests for Iago; we see him opposing the pride of the senator's cap (Brabantio) by the assertion of his own royal birth; if he so treats the powerful and influential father-in-law in the moment of closest union, how might he have acted in the case of provocation? There rested upon him, as upon the descendants of the Jewish people, the stain of unequal birth and the fate of expulsion; the more his services emancipated

him, the more sensitive, we may believe, would he be to the prejudices which yet remained. But before he attained to this position of importance, throughout his whole life resentment and bitterness must have been planted in his spirit through this pariah-condition. The feeling of depreciation oppressed him; disunion with the world and discord with his fellow-men raged silently within him; this gave him the grave expression and the silent reserved nature, with its tendency to brooding thought; it gave him the inclination, so common to rugged characters, to yield to soft compliant dispositions, to the apparent honesty of the hypocritical Iago, to the pliable Cassio, and entirely to the gentle Desdemona. There was a time when this feeling of rejection produced a disturbance within him which, with one of his strongly expressive comparisons, he called 'chaos,' and which he shudders to look back upon. He had cooled his hot Moorish blood, but he could not change it. He had learned to repress his raging temperament in the school of circumstances, but these struggles, we imagine, had become hard to him, and had often been fruitless. If from some just and heavy cause the flood-gates of restrained passion gave way, then his condition became 'perplexed in the extreme' [V. ii. 346], stubborn obstinacy seized him, and the outburst of frightful emotions betrayed the inherent power of his nature, threatened his mind with distraction, and overcame even his body with spasms and faintness. (pp. 510-13)

There are five essential agents which influence the creation of this fearful passion in Othello, and which we must consider in succession, each one more active and of greater weight than the other: the perfect dissimulation of Iago, the character of Cassio, the excitable nature of Othello and his whole relation to human society, above all the curse-burdened commencement to his marriage and the natural disposition of Desdemona, which in the subsequent development of this marriage continues to operate as fatally as it had done at its origin.

It is clear that a man so base, and in possession of such mental resources as Iago, would easily ensnare a man so little circumspect, and so unarmed against cunning and deceit as Othello. His audacious assurance in his plans of vengeance against the Moor, as well as against the equally unsuspicious Cassio and Desdemona, is so great, that at the moment he is undermining their peace he is appearing at the same time as their best friend and most careful adviser. . . . With what openness does Iago accuse himself of foul thoughts, and warn the jealous man of himself and his censoriousness! With what good intentions and palliating excuses does he allege that 'the best sometimes forget' [II. iii. 241]! How fearfully he paints the torments of the lover who has cause to doubt! How forcibly he warns of the green-eyed monster Jealousy, while Othello had caught already at the still unbaited hook! How tenderly he recommends forbearance to him for the sake of his good name, by which he touches indeed the string which produces the sharpest discord for the Moor. Once wrapped in this veil of tried honesty, Iago has for the future an easy and successful game. He entangles the Moor in a twofold unhappy delusion; all the doubts in the world occur to him concerning the fidelity and honour of Desdemona, no doubt strikes him as to the dissimulation of this villain. The light and dark side of Othello's nature, his unsuspicious mind and his suspicion, err decidedly in the first decisive moment. Desdemona's behaviour still here and there overpowers him with the impression of her perfect innocence, but the various apparent proofs of her guilt weigh heavier with him. Her integrity rests quietly and inactively in itself, while the honesty of Iago presses ever actively forward in new proofs and services. Othello perceives in him at first small tokens and qualities of falseness, but he imputes another signification to them from the beginning. To suffer the whole being of the malicious man to affect him is a matter that Othello understands not. His own honesty of nature has made him so short-sighted with regard to knaves and knavish tricks, that even that accomplice of Iago's, the unfortunate Roderigo, surpasses him in acuteness. He is fascinated by a passion as dazzling as that of the Moor, he is urged by a sensual love for Desdemona, and Iago keeps up this passion in him just as artfully as that in Othello, and deceives both credulous souls in a similar manner. Even this weak head, however, has, at any rate, fits of suspicion against the false ancient, suggested to him by fear of the loss of this money; but Othello, who is threatened by a loss so much greater, and who is so shattered by the mere idea of this loss, is not provoked by this grief to the shadow of a suspicion against the suspecter of his wife; nay, even after his fearful deed, even after the first doubt in his conviction of Desdemona's infidelity, no doubt of Iago's integrity touches his soul. So securely had the revengeful hypocrite taken possession of this heart for the purpose of filling it with incurable jealousy.

By this plan he could hope to work out his revenge in the boldest manner, because the most favourable material for it (for *this* very plan) lay ready for him in the persons and circumstances. In casting suspicion upon Desdemona's connection with Cassio, the mere personal appearance of the latter was strikingly in his favour. He had acted the mediator between her and Othello, and how truly and silently he had kept this secret is exhibited in his conversation with Iago (Act I. sc. [2]), where he affects ignorance of the whole marriage history. He had become so intimate with both that in intercourse with Desdemona he could indulge in all proper familiarity. She had been so frank with him that she had often spoken to him 'dispraisingly' of the Moor, while he had taken the part of the latter; and that Othello knew. In outward manners, form, and appearance, no greater contrast can be imagined than that between Cassio and the Moor. Beautiful in figure and face, young, of 'a smooth dispose,' as Iago says, 'almost damned in a fair wife' [I. iii. 397, I. i. 21], endowed with all the gifts and arts of the elegant world, he possesses all that in which the Moor knows himself most defective; he is naturally an object to attract the attention of women, and in this point he is just as seducing as he is seducible. If on this very point the mistrust of the Moor in his own endowments could be stirred up, it would be easy to direct suspicion to this gifted substitute. So long as he still believed in Desdemona's virtue, it might appear to him compatible with it for her to have indulged a weakness for this very Cassio. For there was no other man so faithful to his duty, so heartily devoted to his general, no other who so scrupulously valued his good name, no other who with more feminine timidity insisted upon good morals. The vices of men, such as drunkenness, were foreign and detestable to him; the name 'drunkard' from Othello's lips was as sad to him as to Desdemona was that invective against her womanly honour which she could not utter. But all these virtues were almost too refined to furnish confidence in their stability; Iago was thus right when he regarded Cassio as a man formed for suspicion. That his good-nature at times passes into quarrelsomeness is known by all the world; that his aversion to wine may be overcome as occasion offers, and that then even his zeal for service may be exchanged for forgetfulness of duty, has been a matter of experience to Othello. If anything is yet wanting to make him a fit person for Iago's tragedy, it is that similar unsuspiciousness of character which belonged to Desdemona and Othello, that

similar confidence in Iago's honesty and friendship which he, too, doubts not even to the end.

Iago's power of dissimulation and Cassio's seducing gifts would nevertheless have not ensnared the Moor into that immoderate error of his suspicion, if all the earlier circumstances of his life and the manner of his union with Desdemona had not facilitated its growth. Othello knows himself quite free from the empty motives which urge others to jealousy. In himself he is as incapable of groundless suspicion as of groundless anger. It troubles him not if others extol his wife's beauty and endowments, even though they were to depreciate him by the comparison. His self-reliance is still strong: 'she had eyes,' he says, 'and chose me' [III. iii. 189]. But this self-reliance was just on this point so easily to be shaken. For as soon as Iago only reminds him of the arts of the Venetian women, 'not to leave't undone, but keep't unknown' [III. iii. 204], of the Venetian deceit which Desdemona practised on her father, of the dissimulation with which she had shut his eyes, then the ardent imagination of the susceptible man is directed to the point where there is no lack of inflammable material. Iago uses to the Moor the very words of Brabantio, which he, being present, had heard: 'She did deceive her father, marrying you; and when she seemed to shake and fear your looks, she loved them most' [III. iii. 206-08]. 'And,' says the struck Moor, 'so she did' [III. iii. 208]. The expression which is to be thrown into these words cannot be significant enough. . . . The curse of the father discharges itself in them upon Othello's soul; the light of his faith in Desdemona is with them extinguished. From this time musingly and silently he loses himself in the thought, whether in her choice she may not have erred against nature, and in pursuing this path both he and she are lost. Iago seizes it at once with the ready skill of his wickedness, well knowing that this is 'the point' which it behoves him to cultivate. Under the appearance of bold and inconsiderate openness, he represents to him, with all the emphasis possible, the unnaturalness of their unsuitability, and suggests for his consideration whether 'a will most rank and thoughts unnatural' [III. iii. 232-33] may not have been at work in Desdemona; whether recoiling to her better judgment, she may not have repentingly compared him with her own countrymen. This rankles in the mind of the Moor. Because his years decline, yet therefore not so much—but because those soft parts of conversation are lacking, and because he is black—how possible that against these her taste and her prejudice may have stumbled! From this point of view how readily does his wife seem exposed to the most natural doubts! Still self-reliance and mortification struggle within him, but his fancy lingers already upon the one fearful idea: 'I am deceived and abused.' His first resolve is hatred and rejection. To torment himself with suspicion lies not in his nature; he will not doubtingly love, and loving he will not doubt; if he *must* doubt, he will see and prove, and according to the result he will make an end of love or jealousy. This is now an incitement to Iago to provide an apparent proof.

Immediately after Iago (Act III. sc. [3]) had sown the first seeds of suspicion in Othello's bosom, Desdemona had left at his request. At this threshold of the labyrinth of jealousy the full impression of his present happiness stood before Othello's versatile fancy, joined to the impression of the fearful future which would await him if he had ever cause to renounce that happiness; and these impressions disburden themselves in those few words so full of meaning, so full of mingled happiness and bitter foreboding, which must be regarded as the commencement of the catastrophe, as the main substance of Othello's passion, and as the guide to its development:—

> Excellent wretch! Perdition catch my soul
> But I do love thee! and when I love thee not
> Chaos is come again!
>
> [III. iii. 90-2]

No doubt has been yet named to him, and already before his busy imagination there stands the complete picture of his possible misery, which according to his fashion he compresses into a single word. Subsequently Desdemona's mere appearance seems for once to master his doubt, and he goes away with her. But immediately afterwards, when he returns, he is entirely overpowered, and that without fresh cause, by the idea that the endless happiness which this wife had prepared for him was only a delusion, and that she had been false to him. But how is it possible that this man, so deliberate in fight and danger, and who subsequently executes that fearful punishment on Desdemona with such considerate calmness, should now be so dazzled by the mere idea of possible things as to take them for actual? How is it possible that his whole being should be shattered by a fancy and be upset by a delusion? Is it not unnatural that thus, without conceivable ground, Othello should suddenly be so utterly disturbed that he utters a painful farewell to his tranquil mind, to his content, to his glad vocation—war, that he sees his occupation gone, that he seizes in rage and fearful excitement the destroyer of his peace, and entreats him for proofs when further proof was scarcely indeed required? We must, however, bear in mind that *all* false jealousy rests on mere imagination; that this delusion, because it is a weed, grows luxuriously upon the poorest soil and in the scantiest space, and that here a soil of fatal fertility was prepared, inasmuch as position and circumstances gave an unusual force and depth to the suspicion, and opened to the quick eye of doubt so wide a view that the near would almost necessarily be overlooked. We must bear in mind that in this first inroad of a suspicious fancy lay the greatest disturbing power, destroying at once in the Moor all resolve and all ability for examination. We must bear in mind, finally and above all, the fearful excitement that would be produced in Othello from the whole course of his life and fate at the mere supposition of Desdemona's infidelity. If she were really false and untrue towards him, she had not fallen from him in the ebullition of passion, but her falseness was premeditated, and the marriage with him had been a finely woven deceit! His noble nature, his childlike openness, had been abused in the basest manner, as Iago forgets not to impress upon him; with quiet circumspection a disgraceful game had been carried on with his manly uprightness and candour. All the pity and sympathy which she had shown him was but the dissimulation of the vilest prostitute! All the love which he had thought to have found in her was only a mockery, and the whole heaven which she had opened to him was a hellish deception! Faith in all virtue and in all mankind was shattered in him, and this purest vessel was a 'cistern for foul toads to knot and gender in!' [IV. ii. 61-2]. And this immense ruin had befallen *him*, who with such bitter efforts had aimed at greatness and honour, who stood before the curious and admiring world, who had at last attained even this envied and delightful contentment, the possession of such a wife! This single blow had hurled him from the height so laboriously reached into the depth of an immeasurable ignominy, which would make him the derision of the age. And this humiliation, this disappointment, this crushing of his heart, had been inflicted upon him by the being whom he had regarded as the most valuable possession which the world comprised!

And this idea, which carried with it his utter ruin, both of heart and position, approached so close to probability! He who had aroused it in him spoke so honestly and so anxiously! She who was accused had committed one irregularity, why not another also? If she had committed an error against her father who had begat her, why not this against her husband, who was foreign to her, and a black? Had not he who was accused with her, the virtuous Cassio, had not he also, contrary to all expectation, equally deceived Othello's confidence? And the victim of all this deception was he, the Moor, upon whom the old curse of rejection had ever weighed heavily! (pp. 529-35)

Othello knew himself rightly when he said that he could not long torment himself with uncertainty and doubts; the passionate blood and the power of his imagination fret him; he presses Iago for proofs; it is as if he longed for the confirmation of Desdemona's falsity as for comfort; surely it would now require many certain facts to convince him of her innocence, whilst one apparent proof will strengthen his belief in her guilt. In the excellent delineation of the jealousy of the weak, which Gottfried of Strasburg has sketched in his Tristan, sensual weakness is characterised in a contrary manner. King Marke shuts his eyes to the certainty of the infidelity of his Isolda; he gladly allows his doubt to be removed, he deceives himself with confidence in her innocence; the sinner is too beautiful for him to hate her, and from lust he overlooks injury and disgrace. The jealousy of the strong differs in this, that all the pain which it excites refers to the loss of honour and not of enjoyment, and this gives it its depth. William Schlegel, indeed, seemed to deduce the strength of passion in Othello merely from his strong sensuality [see excerpt above, 1811]. The dream of Cassio which Iago relates to Othello poisons his fancy, we must confess, with sensual images, which never subsequently loose their hold of him. Schlegel, misled by these passages, considered his jealousy to be of the sensual kind which in the tropic zones has produced the unworthy watchfulness over women. But it is not so in this man, advanced as he is in years, and on this point no longer so excitable. The idea of sharing with others the attractive beauty of his wife, the idea of the greatness of this beauty which he then resolves to annihilate, these thoughts rise in his mind amid others, as we can well conceive; for instance, when he sees her sleeping before him in all her charms just before his fearful deed; and when with Iago the remembrance of this charm seizes him, and wrings from him the sorrowing words: 'But yet the pity of it!' [IV. i. 195]. At these moments he is mild and tender, and we see that the thought of his privation of this charm and enjoyment neither stimulates him to revenge nor restrains him from it. But that which excites him so fearfully in this idea of Desdemona's intimacy with Cassio, which Iago has excited, is nothing but the shattering thought of the shameless game which this mirror of virtue must have played with him, and of the shame and dishonour which she drew upon him. In this sense we must read the subsequent outburst of his rage before Desdemona herself, and the passages in which the picture of the deceived husband presents itself to him, and we shall find indisputably that the anger of a hero at his outraged and misused honour is here speaking, and not the jealousy of a slave to sensuality. We do not mean to say that these ideas do not also of themselves seize the lively fancy of the Moor; they overwhelm him at the first suggestions with that force which seems on all occasions to belong to his strong nature; it is from this that he falls subsequently into a trance. Yet his jealousy, as it appears to us, is not influenced nor characterised by these ideas, nor is it urged by them to its extreme. In the very scene (Act III. sc. 3) at which we stand, these ideas help to prepare the irritable frame of mind, but the first and the decisive outburst follows only when Iago mentions that he has seen the handkerchief, Othello's first gift to Desdemona, in Cassio's hands; only when Othello believes that he has now a certain proof. Still Iago himself has only doubted whether the handkerchief which he has seen really and in truth is that very one, or only any one of Desdemona's; and already the furious man blows his love to heaven, calls black vengeance from his hollow cell, and swears with all the reverence due to a sacred vow, almost with deliberate rage, that his bloody thoughts shall never ebb back to humble love till revenge swallows them up. In other passages also Othello proves that he is master of the agitations of passion, and that anger and zeal overpower him only where he has ground and certainty for his suspicions. No smouldering fire of sensuality helps in this case to plunge him into the over-hasty conviction of Desdemona's infidelity; superstition and a bad conscience are the only agents. Upon the handkerchief and its faithful preservation rested, according to prediction, the happiness of his marriage; the giving away of the dear treasure commended to her was to him a sure proof that the relation was broken; fickleness in the treatment of the pledge must have recalled to the Moor's remembrance the similar fickleness which Desdemona had committed against her father in her union with him.

It is true, in the moment of his first outburst of rage, Othello still lacks the strong proof that the handkerchief and the fidelity of Desdemona are bestowed upon another. But he goes to gain this proof from her for himself. Her behaviour can only serve to confirm her guilt to him. If in Iago's hypocrisy, in Cassio's suspicious qualities, in Othello's own excitability, in the previous history of the married pair, there were already powers enough at work to call forth the jealousy of even a more sober-minded man, and that even in still more fearful force, a still more powerful agent was added to all this in Desdemona's character. The wide division between the two natures is obvious, but unhappily it was not perceived by Desdemona, and it was, moreover, difficult for her nature to perceive it. . . . Her ingenuousness knows nothing of the shielding arts of foresight; carelessly she commits some indiscretion every moment, and this helps to her destruction. Othello, seeking to find a foundation for his suspicion, stands before his wife in deep inward emotion, and enquires after the gift whose fatal significance he explains to her with fearful earnestness; she is alarmed at the loss of the handkerchief, but she forbodes nothing of the ground nor of the depth of his emotion. The poor creature had let the handkerchief fall in a kindly service for the Moor; in this little circumstance carefulness and carelessness were just as closely united as affection for Othello and want of affection towards her father had been before in the great circumstance of her marriage. On both occasions, and at all times, she is influenced by her natural disposition, her unsuspiciousness, which is the consequence of the best consciousness. In this error she is aware of no fault, in the midst of her consternation she is unconcerned, she feels the threatening in Othello's passionate words, but she has never seen him so, and she knows not how to treat the strange-humoured man; in contrast to his angry Moorish rage her lighter Venetian nature is unhappily called into play; with levity she passes from this grave conversation to her suit for Cassio, and thus pours oil on the flame. Innocently she does in small things that which she may seem to Othello to have done in great ones: she seems carelessly to trifle with the happiness and unhappiness of a man justified in his self-reliance, and to admit an insignificant rival; the one scene may reflect to him the whole nature of their relation. (pp. 535-39)

In [the] scene of the meeting of Othello with Desdemona (Act IV. sc. 2), and in all those in which the latter appears with Emilia and others, we see plainly the unhappy effects of the different nature and descent of the married pair, and how the abandonment of the paternal home, and the unadvised and defenceless surrender of herself to the stranger, are thus revenged on Desdemona. The Moor once made suspicious, sees in her only the dissembling Venetian; she, ever unsuspicious, forbodes not what has passed in his mind, and even after her attention has been drawn to his jealousy she knows not how to meet it. She herself suspects no one, and understands not that she is suspected. A child in innocence, she is a child as regards rebuke; she can bear no more of this kind of punishment than a child; now, thus mistreated and harshly used beyond all moderation, for a moment her nature is hardened; she cannot weep; still less could she have further intercourse with Othello, and ask him to analyse the grounds of his displeasure; it is only when Emilia assists her with her words and feelings, that her tears, her sensations, and her protestations find vent. When she is afterwards alone, and is undressed by Emilia, her innermost soul utters its misgivings upon her situation, and she sings that touching song of Barbara and provides an arrangement for her death; but her meditative spirit receives not the deep impressions which lie upon her heart; she would otherwise have more circumspectly weighed her relation to her husband, she would have seen through his painful condition, she would have felt his sorrow rather than his outbursts of rage, she would not without persuasion have resigned the deeply troubled man to a sleepless night, and she would not have laid herself to rest with so little solicitude. In the midst of the excellent scene (Act IV. sc. 3), in which Desdemona's beautiful nature is so richly portrayed, we can perceive a cleft which, if it did not now once for ever separate this couple, would have ever occasionally separated them again and again. Both beings, at the moment when their connection experiences its first trial, veil their innermost thoughts from each other, instead of revealing them; the Moor will not expostulate with her, even in the hour of her death he will not believe her oath, and hardens his heart at her denial; she too, although she finds his very anger and scorn charming, like an injured child refuses to speak; and even with death before her, when she hears of Cassio's murder, she finds no word to assert her innocence, but in the bewilderment she once more accuses herself by speech and behaviour, and like a frightened deer she falls a victim to the death which she would gladly have escaped.

To this murder itself Othello proceeds with the calmness of a judge; the feeling of the man and the husband, and the sensibility of the injury to his honour and love, are therefore not extinct in him. To estimate this his deed from *his* mind, we must remember his severe service and the incorruptible discipline which we have before seen him exercise towards Cassio. This is essentially a prelude to the main action, allowing us, in a less exciting case, to cast a calmer glance into the innermost nature of this strange character. No conviction of Cassio's well-regulated life, no familiarity of personal relation to him, could then move him to spare the favourite in such a serious matter, a matter in which he would not even have spared his own brother. He made an example of Cassio, not from anger, for his wrath is only aroused by examination into the confirmed guilt of his lieutenant, but from prudence and from a political sense of duty. In this we trace the same mode of action, in a case which has nothing to do with love and jealousy, as he now pursues towards Desdemona. Here, too, anger overpowers him especially at those times when he thinks he has received proofs or confessions of her guilt; here, too, he punishes not in wrath, but from a feeling of honour. It is not passion (with these words he approaches Desdemona's bed), but it is the *cause* which urges him. The reflection, therefore, whether after the accomplishment of the deed he might repent that which could never be amended restrains him not. Her beauty and her charms extort tears from him yet again, but they could not weaken his resolve; the magic of her kiss almost persuades justice to break her sword, but it remains firm. A higher justice speaks in his 'cruel tears;' once dead he would kill her even a second time, and the murder which is to heal her sin will not injure his love; his sorrow is like that of heaven, 'it strikes where it doth love' [V. ii. 22]. Since he would thus punish her from love, his first thought of repudiating her with hate had vanished; he will not expose this beloved being to the contempt of the world, nor abandon her to sin, but withdraw her from both, from shame and sin, by his punitive rather than avenging deed. For this reason, once again in the last moment, he is agitated at her denial of the crime of which he is firmly convinced; he would fain punish as her last judge for the sake of atonement and purification; her denial provokes him to call that a murder which he thought a sacrifice. Here, too, in one word he compresses in his fashion an infinity of inward feelings, for which he had no separate designation. He regards himself as the chastising judge of her shame, and as the physician of his honour; he performs this deed, according to his last testimony, not from hatred, but from honour. When he finds himself mistaken he punishes himself with the same exalted coolness and calmness, and with the same propitiatory act; and therefore there lies such deep significance in the fact that at his suicide, at the very last, he remembers the stab with which he had smote the Turk in Aleppo; he had then found the honour of the Venetian state as great a provocative as his domestic honour is now; and to avenge this honour the peril of his life could as little restrain him then as the annihilation of his most precious possession can now. Therefore, after Desdemona's death, he is far from repenting of his deed or concealing it. He permits her not in dying to take the deed upon herself, he pleads aloud guilty to the deed, to which just grounds alone have urged him. He is therefore hard to convince that he has erred; Desdemona's angelic falsehood at her death, and Emilia's accusation of her own husband, confuse him not, because his conscience was clear; repentance and revenge only turn against himself when the proof against his own conduct is as certain as he had before believed that against Desdemona's.

From the moment when Emilia learns Othello's deed from his own lips, the poet disburdens us in a wonderful manner of all the tormenting feelings which the course of the catastrophe had awakened in us. Emilia is a woman of coarser texture, good-natured like her sex, but with more spite than others of her sex, light-minded in things which appear to her light, serious and energetic when great demands meet her; in words she is careless of her reputation and virtue, which she would not be in action. At her husband's wish she has heedlessly taken away Desdemona's handkerchief, as she fancied for some indifferent object. Thoughtless and light, she had cared neither for return nor for explanation, even when she learned that this handkerchief, the importance of which she knows, had caused the quarrel between Othello and Desdemona; in womanly fashion she observes less attentively all that is going on around her, and thus, in similar but worse unwariness than Desdemona, she becomes the real instrument of the unhappy fate of her mistress. Yet when she knows that Othello has killed his wife, she unburdens our repressed feelings by her words, testifying to Desdemona's innocence by loud accusations of the Moor.

When she hears Iago named as the calumniator of her fidelity, she testifies to the purity of her mistress by unsparing invectives against the wickedness of her husband, and seeks to enlighten the slowly apprehending Moor, whilst she continues to draw out the feelings of our soul and to give them full expression from her own full heart. At last, when she entirely perceives Iago's guilt in the matter of the handkerchief and therefore her own participation in it, her devoted fidelity to her mistress and her increasing feeling rise to sublimity; her testimony against her husband, in the face of threatening death, now becomes a counterpart to Othello's severe exercise of justice, and her death and dying song upon Desdemona's chastity is an expiatory repentance at her grave, which is scarcely surpassed by the Moor's grand and calm retaliation upon himself. The unravelment and expiation in this last scene are wont to re-awaken repose and satisfaction even in the most deeply agitated reader. Moreover, when the play is justly represented, the painful excitement in the third and fourth acts is far more softened than in the reading. . . . [We] are diverted by the mental suspense with regard to all the levers in motion; and, added to this, the rapid progress of the play does not suffer single emotions to dwell so long on the mind. . . . If, by suitable representation, the spectator attains at least to as much sympathy with the Moor as indignation against him, he will bear the death of Desdemona with more emotion than bitterness, and the atoning death of Othello will expiate for all. Or, in spite of all our explanations, does the ruin of both remain too terrible, because their end is so much less reconciliatory than that of Romeo and Juliet? Yet it cannot be pleaded for them, as for Romeo and Juliet, that their secret marriage was made in the ardent intoxication of early youth and in the unreasonableness of passion; they entered on their union with cooler feelings and in full self-possession. It cannot further be pleaded for them that their self-willed union, like that between Romeo and Juliet, was concluded in the midst of threatening fates, amid the bitterness of contending families, on the ruin of domestic relations, that it was the only expedient for the two lovers, favoured moreover by a holy man, and offering a prospect of peace between the discordant houses. Here, on the contrary, the peace of a family was disturbed, and the happiness and life of a father destroyed. If even there the secret union bore its bitter fruit, if wild joy had a wild end, here also, according to the words of the demon-like Iago, the violent commencement must have an answerable sequestration. Not alone did Othello intend, but the poet also intended, that the death of Desdemona should be brought as a sacrifice, and that of Othello as an atonement, to the manes of the broken-hearted father. The tidings of her father's death no longer reach Desdemona. 'I am glad thy father's dead,' says the uncle who brings the tidings, otherwise the fate of his child 'would do him a desperate turn' [V. ii. 204, 206]. This verdict, however, may be reversed. If Desdemona had lived to know of her father's death, not the death itself, but the cause of it, would have been an experience to her as terribly undeceiving as the lost confidence of Othello. For as she had no foreboding of this, she had none also of the effect which her independent step had had upon her father. The same nature and qualities were at work in her when she gave the fatal blow to the life of her father as when she gave occasion for the suspicion of her husband. The same innocence of heart, the same lack of suspicion, the same inability to intend harm to anyone, allowed no touch of bashfulness to appear in her in the first instance before the public council, and placed in her lips subsequently the dangerous intercession on behalf of Cassio. In both cases she intended to do right and good, and from the very purity of her consciousness arose her misinterpreted actions. Like Othello, like Romeo and Juliet, she falls a sacrifice to her own nature, and not to the law of any arbitrary and unjust moral statute; to a nature which, in the strength of that simplicity and originality which excites our interest, oversteps the limits of social custom, unites guilt and innocence in strange combination, draws death as a punishment upon itself, and endures death like a triumph—a nature which divides our feelings between admiration and pity. It seems as if perfect satisfaction was here afforded to all the demands of tragedy. It seems also that the picture is consistent with the freest moral view. For the poet, by this conclusion, has not once for all condemned *every* unequal marriage, nor *every* secret union, just as little as in Romeo he has condemned all passionate love. Shakespeare has never and nowhere meditated upon moral problems with such partiality of judgment. Otherwise, in *All's Well that Ends Well*, he would not have carried an unequal marriage to a prosperous end through so many difficulties; he would not, in *Cymbeline*, have suffered a secret union to turn out for good, nor in the *Merchant of Venice* would he have justified the abduction of a child and a self-willed marriage. Not the letter of the law, but the circumstances and nature of men, are in the poet's wise opinion the spring from which good and evil, happiness and unhappiness arise. *These* furnish also the line of conduct according to which both must be measured. In proportion to the circumstances and nature of the man, evil often becomes a source of good and good a source of evil, apparent happiness a misfortune and misfortune a happiness. And this is with conscious intention observed and carried out in this play, in which the noble Desdemona falls into sin through innocence and goodness, and by a sinful lie commits the most beautiful act of forgiveness. (pp. 541-47)

> G. G. Gervinus, "Third Period of Shakespeare's Dramatic Poetry: 'Othello'," in his Shakespeare Commentaries, *translated by F. E. Bunnett, revised edition, 1877. Reprint by AMS Press Inc., 1971, pp. 505-47.*

VICTOR HUGO   (essay date 1864)

[Hugo was the leading poet and novelist of French Romanticism. In his study William Shakespeare, *first published in 1864, he maintains that Shakespeare is a reincarnation of Aeschylus and regards the poet as a genius who explored the limits of human experience. Hugo was also interested in Shakespeare's use of the supernatural and claimed that the poet "believed profoundly in the mystery of things." His discussion of* Othello, *taken from the work mentioned above, focuses on the oppositions in the play between light and dark, white and black, day and night, and openness and deception. Hugo makes a distinction between the darkness of night represented in Othello and the darkness of evil dramatized in the character of Iago. Such twentieth-century critics as Wyndham Lewis (1927), Allardyce Nicoll (1927), G. Wilson Knight (1930), and Robert B. Heilman (1951) have subsequently offered extended analyses of the series of contrasts and oppositions evident in* Othello.]

[What] is Othello? He is the night. An immense fatal figure. Night is amorous of day. Darkness loves the dawn. The African adores the white woman. Othello has for his light and for his frenzy, Desdemona. And then, how easy to him is jealousy! He is great, he is dignified, he is majestic, he soars above all heads; he has as an escort bravery, battle, the braying of trumpets, the banners of war, renown, glory; he is radiant with twenty victories, he is studded with stars, this Othello: but he is black. And thus how soon, when jealous, the hero becomes the monster, the black becomes the negro! How speedily has night beckoned to death!

By the side of Othello, who is night, there is Iago, who is evil—evil, the other form of darkness. Night is but the night of the world; evil is the night of the soul. How deeply black are perfidy and falsehood! It is all one whether what courses through the veins be ink or treason. Whoever has jostled against imposture and perjury, knows it: one must blindly grope one's way with knavery. Pour hypocrisy upon the break of day, and you put out the sun; and this, thanks to false religions, is what happens to God.

Iago near Othello is the precipice near the landslip. "This way!" he says in a low voice. The snare advises blindness. The lover of darkness guides the black. Deceit takes upon itself to give what light may be required by night. Falsehood serves as a blind man's dog to jealousy. Othello the negro and Iago the traitor pitted against whiteness and candor: what more formidable? These ferocities of darkness act in unison. These two incarnations of the eclipse conspire, the one roaring, the other sneering, for the tragic suffocation of light.

Sound this profound thing. Othello is the night, and being night, and wishing to kill, what does he take to slay with? Poison? the club? the axe? the knife? No; the pillow. To kill is to lull to sleep. Shakespeare himself perhaps did not take this into account. The creator sometimes, almost unknown to himself, yields to his type, so truly is that type a power. And it is thus that Desdemona, spouse of the man Night, dies, stifled by the pillow upon which the first kiss was given, and which receives the last sigh. (pp. 242-43)

> Victor Hugo, "'Macbeth'—'Othello'—'Lear'," in *his* William Shakespeare, *translated by Melville B. Anderson, A. C. McClurg and Company, 1887, pp. 240-43.*

J. A. HERAUD   (essay date 1865)

[Heraud was a poet, dramatist, and frequent contributor to literary periodicals, serving as drama critic for both the Athenaeum *and the* Illustrated London News. *In the excerpt below from his* Shakspere; His Inner Life as Intimated in His Works (1865), *Heraud discusses what he regards as defects or flaws in the characters of Othello and Desdemona that contribute to the fatal consequences of the drama. He contends that Othello may indeed have seduced Emilia, as Iago claims, and that because of this he is more susceptible to Iago's scheme to make him jealous, for this moral laxity has weakened his character. Denton J. Snider (1887) and Samuel A. Tannenbaum (see Additional Bibliography) have also contended that there is evidence in the play to substantiate the charge that Othello has cuckolded Iago. Heraud further argues that Desdemona deludes herself as well as others in the play and that her "indifference to truth" arises from a timorous nature that shrinks from facing difficult situations. He declares that but for this "defect in Desdemona's character" the tragic events of* Othello *might not have occurred. For additional commentary on Desdemona's passivity and lack of courage, see the excerpts by William Hazlitt (1817), Anna Brownell Jameson (1833), E. K. Chambers (1908), Allardyce Nicoll (1927), G. R. Elliott (1937), and Gayle Greene (1979).]

The credulous Moor of Cinthio is very unlike the loving Othello of the play, and his tempter is moved to his infamous course by his illicit love for Desdemona. This weak passion is, in the play, transferred to Roderigo,—a creation of Shakspere's own, partly as a comic relief to the tragic action and partly as a link of sympathy with the audience. Iago is the really jealous person, and, suspecting Othello with his own wife, hates him accordingly and determines on revenge.... A perfect hero cannot be made interesting, and Shakespeare gives to all his heroes, whatever may be their abstract qualities, some human infirmity by which they secure our sympathy. Perfect love, such as would belong to a perfect soul, would 'cast out all fear,' and that of Othello is so perfect in its degree that it is 'not easily jealous' [V. ii. 345], nor is it naturally suspicious. But it can be 'wrought,' and therefore there is in his otherwise perfect character a peccant part. From his scene with Emilia, when he throws her the purse as the portress of Hell's gate, he shows that he has 'poured his treasures into foreign laps' [IV. iii. 88]; and from the revelation which Emilia makes of her own character to her mistress, it is not impossible that her husband's ugly suspicions were not ill-founded. Othello had been no celibate, nor pretended to be such, and previous to his acquaintance with Desdemona had cultivated some experiences by which his virtue had not been strengthened. There was this flaw in his conduct, and by this inlet both suspicion and jealousy might enter; neither could have found a thoroughfare in a perfectly innocent character. Even the 'perfect soul,' living the life of camps, had found the preservation of its innocence impossible. In proportion that it had sinned it had become weak, and thus Othello was laid open to the temptation of Iago, and liable to a further fall. All mankind are, in some respect or other, similarly exposed from similar causes to evil communication; and our conscience, therefore, leads us to pity and forgive the noble Moor for his obvious fault and the fatal consequences. These reasons are philosophical and true, and therefore we must not accept Othello as an absolute and direct affirmation of a perfect loving soul, but as a negative instance approximating perfection as near as possible, yet fallible because it could not be identified with it. This view,—all but the highest,—simply because it is not the highest, makes the character and the tragedy possible....

The theme of the play is Love. In *Romeo and Juliet,* Love before marriage was the argument, now it is Love after. The common Idea is differently conceived by the persons of the drama.... Othello and Iago divide the moral and intellectual view, and the real debate is between the two principals. The latter is naturally a jealous husband, and the revenge which he seeks is to infect his enemy with the same plague. Unfortunately for his victim, there is a joint in his armour loose, as in that of every man, and there enters the poisoned point of his foeman's spear. The tragedy, however, might not have been possible at all but for a defect in Desdemona's character. Her passion was romantic, and there exists fiction in whatever is romantic. She suffers from illusion and loves to be deluded. If she is self-deceived, she likewise deceives others. It is on this ground that Brabantio warns Othello: 'She has deceived her father, and may thee' [I. iii. 293]. In word, deed, thought, she must have been guilty of falsehood; and, virtuous as she otherwise is, we find in the development of the drama that she has one foible. It is the slightest of foibles, but one frequently fatal,—a habit of fibbing. From a timidity of disposition she frequently evades the truth, when attention to its strict letter would raise a difficulty. Practically, too, she dallies with falsehood: 'I am not merry, but I do beguile The thing I am by seeming otherwise' [II. i. 122-23]. To *seem otherwise* than she is, in order to obtain her end, is at all times lawful in her estimation; not meaning ill, but to make matters easy. Reticent as Hero [in *Much Ado About Nothing*],—perhaps more so, because her conduct suppressed the truth when it did not falsify it,—there was always an amount of 'seeming' in it which misled observers: 'A maiden never bold; Of spirit so still and

quiet, that her motion Blushed at herself' [I. iii. 94-6]. Yet, all the time, she was carrying on a love-intrigue with a man of another race and colour, in which she was 'half the wooer' [I. iii. 176]. When this fact is pointed out to Othello, it naturally raises suspicion. One so accustomed to deport herself gives no certain index in her behaviour by which her mental or her moral state may be judged of. All this proceeds not from criminality of disposition, but indolence or susceptibility of temper. Iago practises on the quality: 'For 'tis most easy The *inclining* Desdemona to subdue In any honest suit' [II. iii. 339-41]. And, even so, she readily undertakes the cause of Cassio, and assures him of success. With her the end consecrates the means, and she regards nothing but the success of her enterprise. How she pleads with Othello for Cassio we know. With characteristic lenity she makes light of his fault, falsely arguing, not unconsciously: 'Save that they *say,* the wars must make examples' [III. iii. 65-6], &c. And immediately gives us an insight into her little foible, and how habitually she was induced to indulge in it: 'What! Michael Cassio, That came a-wooing with you, and *many a time When I have spoke of you dispraisingly* Hath' [III. iii. 70-3], &c. So that Desdemona had not only disguised her sentiments from her father, but had idly sought to do the same from Cassio, who was in the secret. Iago might have, indeed, inferred from this conduct that the 'super-supple Venetian' [I. iii. 356], his mistress, was willing to regard the lieutenant with special favour. As she warms in her advocacy with Othello, she puts a further false colouring on the transaction, pretending to disparage the importance to her of the suit she was promoting: 'Nay, when I have a suit Wherein I mean to touch your love indeed, It shall be full of poise and difficult weight, And fearful to be granted' [III. iii. 80-3]. No lawyer for a fee pleaded more intrepidly in behalf of a criminal client, whose acquittal he desired in the face of the clearest evidence. And in the affair of the handkerchief we find in her the same indifference to truth. She had dropped it in a moment of excitement, and probably forgot the fact; but she is at no pains to recollect, and finds it easier to feign an excuse for the nonce, than to cast about for the true reason. She had certainly questioned Emilia about it, and recognized its importance, if Othello were a jealous person; but as he is not, she will not think too much about it. When Othello asks for it, she is frightened into a direct lie. If at this critical moment Desdemona had confessed the truth, the tragedy would have been prevented and Iago's plot nipped in the bud. Even on her deathbed the case is the same. She tells Emilia that she had killed herself.... The truth is, that the lady's faults only render her more womanly. They are mainly those of her sex, ay, and of the most amiable of her sex. Desdemona is not a strong-minded, rationalistic woman; but a tender, loving, and devoted one, brought up in the lap of luxury and swayed by her feelings rather than by her reason. Nevertheless, we should not conceal from ourselves that there is even in this a defect, and that therefrom a number of injurious effects ensue which may end fatally. (pp. 422-24)

J. A. Heraud, in an extract in A New Variorum Edition of Shakespeare: Othello, Vol. VI, *edited by Horace Howard Furness, 1886. Reprint by American Scholar Publications, Inc., 1965, pp. 422-24.*

FRIEDERICH BODENSTEDT (essay date 1867)

[*Bodenstedt was a German poet and translator of nineteenth-century Russian literature. He also wrote* Shakespeare's Contemporaries and Their Works *(1858-60) and collaborated with other scholars on a multivolume translation of Shakespeare's plays and poetry (1866-72). In the following excerpt, taken from an English*

translation of a portion of his Jahrbuch d. deutschen Shakspere
Gesellschaft (1867), Bodenstedt avers that Shakespeare intended
to depict Desdemona as culpable of filial disrespect and impiety.
In electing to disregard Brabantio's love and concern for her,
choosing instead to join her future with Othello's, the critic argues, Desdemona assumes responsibility for the ensuing tragic
events. Bodenstedt concludes that "so long as family ties are held
sacred, Desdemona will be held guilty towards her father by every
healthy mind," an opinion similar to that of G. G. Gervinus
(1849-50). For further commentary on the character of Desdemona, see the excerpts by William Hazlitt (1817), Anna Brownell
Jameson (1833), J. A. Heraud (1865), E. K. Chambers (1908),
Allardyce Nicoll (1927), G. R. Elliott (1937), and Gayle Greene
(1979).]

'That Desdemona left her father for the Moor involves no
crime,' says [Friedrich Theodor] Vischer. 'The foolish, irascible man deserves no better. Her love for her father and her
love for her husband were not to be reconciled.' This opinion
appears to me to be more bold than correct. Let us come to
an understanding by taking into consideration this act with its
immediate consequences. A tenderly beloved daughter breaks
the heart of her father by a secret marriage, without having
even made the attempt to obtain his consent. She forsakes the
old man, whom she has sorely wounded, without one tender
word; deprecates his displeasure without imploring his blessing. She speaks to him not as a child to a father, but like an
advocate addressing his reason, not appealing to his heart; or,
like a debtor settling with his creditors,—so much is due to
one, so much to another, and so much to a third.

If such an attitude of a child to a father, whose whole heart is
bound up in that child, involves no fault, then this word has
lost its meaning. I am sure that here, as in Lear, it was the
earnest purpose of Shakespeare to represent a serious wrong
done by a child to a father, and that the popular feeling, to
which Vischer himself, in another place as well as in this
instance, appeals, will find Desdemona guilty. Her sin lies not
in the fact that she loves the Moor, and for love of him forsakes
her father, but that in this, the most critical step in her life,
she has no consideration for her father, but justifies herself in
terms as rude as if he were to her the most indifferent person
in the world. She insists as coolly upon her right as Shylock
upon his bond [in The Merchant of Venice]. We can readily
imagine that Desdemona knew that it was impossible to obtain
her proud father's consent. We can suppose, also, that Othello,
in order to avoid the humiliation of a rejection, encouraged her
in secretly consummating her hastily formed determination;
but nothing of this kind appears in the text and it is just the
care which the Poet takes to avoid every hint in this direction
that shows, in the plainest manner possible, his intention to
emphasize in the sharpest way Desdemona's lack of filial affection. . . . It is this lack of filial piety, as well as the fact
that Desdemona, having grown up without a mother's tender
care and without brother or sister, had early learned to depend
upon herself, that explains her indifference to the opinion of
the world, the marked self-dependence of her character, and
the unbending determination with which, in the weightiest step
of her life, she takes counsel only of her own heart. In a city
where wealth and luxury flourished in their fullest bloom there
is such a lack of able men that the lead in war is given to an
adventurer, to a Moor,—this it is that wins her heart. She is
light, airy, like a sunny May day; he is black and ugly as an
overclouded day in autumn, and, withal, so little blinded to
his own repulsive exterior that he never would have ventured
to woo Desdemona had not she made advances towards him.
She is touched by his lofty, manly qualities, by his frank, noble

character. . . . The noblest impulses have brought together two
pure hearts; we feel that they are worthy each of the other,
and yet we cannot, from the first, evade the fear, that presses
involuntarily upon us, of the consequences of this union. We
see before us perfect womanhood in the most graceful shape,
and perfect manhood in a form most repulsive; and it is as if
day and night came together; the two cannot unite!

This remark seems to lead us away from the tragic motive of
the play which we have indicated above; but, in reality, it only
results therefrom, pointing back to it as its source. For what
else is it than a sorrowful conviction that from such a singular
union,—a union so unnatural that in the eyes of Brabantio, no
happiness could come to his daughter,—what but this feeling
caused his opposition, and broke his heart when the union
became unalterable? A large share of wounded pride and indignant pain at the disregard shown for his paternal authority
may be taken into account, but the essential thing with him is
to be found in his concern for his child. And so long as family
ties are held sacred, Desdemona will he held guilty towards
her father by every healthy mind. Without keeping in mind
this wrong, in which Othello shares, done by the heroine,
otherwise so lovely, the drama loses its sacredly tragic character, and degenerates into a mere intrigue. For that such a
finished villain as Iago should destroy the happiness of two
such excellent persons as Othello and Desdemona, without at
the same time, consciously or unconsciously, serving higher
purposes, can make an impression which is only sorrowful,
not tragic. It is otherwise when we take things as they are and
keep strictly to the Poet's own words, putting nothing into the
play, but explaining everything by what is in it. Then Desdemona's tragic fate affects us because we see that she is the
fate herself which prepares the soil whereon Iago sows the seed
of his deadly mischief. She voluntarily exchanges the peace
of her father's house for the stormy life which she must see
before her as the wife of Othello. She is fully aware of the
fatal meaning of the step she takes, and is so little forced to
it that she bids defiance to the whole world in taking it. She
breaks her father's heart to follow her own heart. She takes
upon herself the whole responsibility and all the consequences
of her act. After such a beginning no healthy temperament can
look for a happy ending. (pp. 440-41)

Friederich Bodenstedt, in an extract, translated by
William Henry Furness, in A New Variorum Edition
of Shakespeare: Othello, Vol. VI, edited by Horace
Howard Furness, 1886. Reprint by American Scholar
Publications, Inc., 1965, pp. 440-41.

ALGERNON CHARLES SWINBURNE   (essay date 1880)

[Swinburne was an English poet, dramatist, and critic who devoted much of his literary career to the study of Shakespeare and
other Elizabethan writers. His three books on Shakespeare—A
Study of Shakespeare (1880), Shakespeare (1909), and Three
Plays of Shakespeare (1909)—all demonstrate his keen interest
in Shakespeare's poetic talents and, especially, his major tragedies. Swinburne's literary commentary is frequently conveyed in
a style that is markedly intense and effusive. In the excerpt below
from A Study of Shakespeare, he centers his discussion of Othello
on the characters of the Moor and Iago. Like August Wilhelm
Schlegel (1811) and William Hazlitt (1817), Swinburne attributes
a remarkable talent for creativity to Iago, describing him as "an
inarticulate poet," whose malignity is not "motiveless"—as Samuel Taylor Coleridge asserted (1808-18)—but impelled by delight
in the exercise of his incomparable powers of manipulation. Just
as Iago is the most malevolent of Shakespeare's villains, the critic
argues, Othello is his most noble dramatic figure. Swinburne

maintains that, while the Moor is partly culpable for the tragic events of the play, there is nothing base or mean-spirited in his temperament. The critic concludes that Othello's nobility surpasses even Desdemona's, and we pity him more because his suffering has been greater than hers. Other commentators who have discussed the noble aspects of Othello's nature include Charles Gildon (1694), Wyndham Lewis (1927), J. I. M. Stewart (1949), Derek Traversi (1949), and Helen Gardner (see Additional Bibliography).]

[The] fatalism of *Othello* is as much darker and harder than that of any third among the plays of Shakespeare, as it is less dark and hard than the fatalism of *King Lear*. For upon the head of the very noblest man whom even omnipotence or Shakespeare could ever call to life he has laid a burden in one sense yet heavier than the burden of Lear, insomuch as the sufferer can with somewhat less confidence of universal appeal proclaim himself a man more sinned against than sinning.

And yet, if ever man after Lear might lift up his voice in that protest, it would assuredly be none other than Othello. He is in all the prosperous days of his labour and his triumph so utterly and wholly nobler than the self-centred and wayward king, that the capture of his soul and body in the unimaginable snare of Iago seems a yet blinder and more unrighteous blow

Struck by the envious wrath of man or God

than ever fell on the old white head of that child-changed father. But at least he is destroyed by the stroke of a mightier hand than theirs who struck down Lear. As surely as Othello is the noblest man of man's making, Iago is the most perfect evildoer, the most potent demi-devil. It is of course the merest commonplace to say as much, and would be no less a waste of speech to add the half comfortable reflection that it is in any case no shame to fall by such a hand. But this subtlest and strangest work of Shakespeare's admits and requires some closer than common scrutiny. Coleridge has admirably described the first great soliloquy which opens to us the pit of hell within as "the motive-hunting of a motiveless malignity" [see excerpt above, 1808-18]. But subtle and profound and just as is this definitive appreciation, there is more in the matter yet than even this. It is not only that Iago, so to speak, half tries to make himself half believe that Othello has wronged him, and that the thought of it gnaws him inly like a poisonous mineral: though this also be true, it is not half the truth—nor half that half again. Malignant as he is, the very subtlest and strongest component of his complex nature is not even malignity. It is the instinct of what Mr. [Thomas] Carlyle would call an inarticulate poet. . . . [If] it be better to make a tragedy than to write one, to act a poem than to sing it, we must allow to Iago a station in the hierarchy of poets very far in advance of his creator's. None of the great inarticulate may more justly claim place and precedence. With all his poetic gift, he has no poetic weakness. Almost any creator but his would have given him some grain of spite or some spark of lust after Desdemona. To Shakespeare's Iago she is no more than is a rhyme to another and articulate poet. His stanza must at any rate and at all costs be polished: to borrow the metaphor used by Mr. Carlyle in apologetic illustration of a royal hero's peculiar system of levying recruits for his colossal brigade. He has within him a sense or conscience of power incomparable: and this power shall not be left, in Hamlet's phrase, "to fust in him unused" [*Hamlet*, IV. iv. 39]. A genuine and thorough capacity for human lust or hate would diminish and degrade the supremacy of his evil. He is almost as far above or beyond vice as he is beneath or beyond virtue. And this it is that makes him impregnable and invulnerable. When once he has said it, we know

as well as he that thenceforth he never will speak word. We could smile almost as we can see him to have smiled at Gratiano's most ignorant and empty threat, being well assured that torments will in no wise ope his lips: that as surely and as truthfully as ever did the tortured philosopher before him, he might have told his tormentors that they did but bruise the coating, batter the crust, or break the shell of Iago. (p. 180)

Between Iago and Othello the position of Desdemona is precisely that defined with such quaint sublimity of fancy in the old English byword—"between the devil and the deep sea." Deep and pure and strong and adorable always and terrible and pitiless on occasion as the sea is the great soul of the glorious hero to whom she has given herself; and what likeness of man's enemy from Satan down to Mephistopheles could be matched for danger and for dread against the good bluff soldierly trustworthy figure of honest Iago? The rough license of his tongue at once takes warrant from his good soldiership and again gives warrant for his honesty: so that in a double sense it does him yeoman's service, and that twice told. . . . It is perhaps natural that the two deepest and subtlest of all Shakespeare's intellectual studies in good and evil should be the two most painfully misused and misunderstood alike by his commentators and his fellows of the stage: it is certainly undeniable that no third figure of his creation has ever been on both sides as persistently misconceived and misrepresented with such desperate pertinacity as Hamlet and Iago.

And it is only when Iago is justly appreciated that we can justly appreciate either Othello or Desdemona. This again should surely be no more than the truism that it sounds; but practically it would seem to be no less than an adventurous and audacious paradox. Remove or deform or diminish or modify the dominant features of the destroyer, and we have but the eternal and vulgar figures of jealousy and innocence, newly vamped and veneered and padded and patched up for the stalest purposes of puppetry. As it is, when Coleridge asks "which do we pity the most" [see excerpt above, 1813] at the fall of the curtain, we can surely answer, Othello. Noble as are the "most blessed conditions" of "the gentle Desdemona" [II. i. 249-50, I. ii. 25], he is yet the nobler of the two; and has suffered more in one single pang than she could suffer in life or in death. (pp. 180-82)

Algernon Charles Swinburne, "Third Period: Tragic and Romantic," in his A Study of Shakespeare, *1880. Reprint by AMS Press Inc., 1965, pp. 170-230.*

RICHARD GRANT WHITE (essay date 1885?)

[*White was an American scholar and essayist, who edited* The Works of William Shakespeare *(1857-66) and also wrote* Shakespeare's Scholar *(1854) and the posthumously published* Studies in Shakespeare *(1886). In the following excerpt from the latter work, believed to have been composed shortly before his death in 1885, White describes the dual aspects of the character of Iago, whose external demeanor is characterized by warm sympathy for his friends and apparent trustworthiness among his peers, but whose "real and inner nature" is amoral, heartless, and entirely self-interested. Disagreeing with the view that Iago is merely "malignant," doing evil for evil's sake alone, as suggested most notably by Samuel Taylor Coleridge (1808-18), White contends that the ancient is indifferent to ethical or moral choices and would choose either virtuous or evil conduct on the basis of which would most profitably serve his purpose. He further asserts that Iago's only intention in the beginning of the drama is "to ruin Cassio and get his place"—a view also held by the anonymous critic in the* Bee *(1791), William Maginn (1839), and Tucker*

Brooke (1918). Finally, White argues that while Iago shows a
callous disregard for the impact of his scheme upon Desdemona,
he does not intend the destruction of Othello, for the Moor is
necessary to his military advancement. By drawing attention to
Iago's human characteristics, White's essay signals a departure
from the general tendency of most nineteenth-century critics to
regard him as monstrous and unnatural. In later essays, such
critics as Wyndham Lewis (1927), G. R. Elliott (1937), and
Robert B. Heilman (1956) have all sought further to humanize
Iago or, at least, to link him more closely to the norm of humanity.]

It cannot be that the Iago of the modern stage is, either in
external appearance or in his characteristic traits, the man who
deceived and betrayed Desdemona, Cassio, and Othello. Iago,
as Shakespeare presents him to any careful and thoughtful
student of the tragedy, is entirely unlike the coarse although
crafty villain who has held possession of the stage from the
time of the revival of the Shakespearean drama until the present
day. The latter is a creature of conventional and theatrical traits
of person and of action, whom Shakespeare would not have
allowed to occupy the stage for a single scene. (p. 262)

Before going on to consider the various passages of the tragedy
which indicate Shakespeare's conception of this personage—
hardly inferior to any of his creations in its union of complexity
and strength, and perhaps the most widely known of all of
them as a type—it may be well to describe the real Iago, who,
so far as my knowledge goes, has never been presented on the
modern stage.

Iago was a young man, only twenty-eight years old, the youngest of all the men who figure in the tragedy, excepting, possibly, Roderigo. He says of himself that he has looked upon
the world for four times seven years. Brave, and a good soldier,
he was also of that order of ability which lifts a man speedily
above his fellows. His manners and his guise were of a dashing
military sort; and his manner had a corresponding bluntness,
tempered, at times, by tact to a warm-hearted effusiveness,—
by the very tact which prompted the bluntness. For that, although not exactly assumed, was consciously adopted. Nevertheless, he had little spontaneous malice in his composition;
and unless for some good reason he would rather serve than
injure those around him. He made himself liked by all, and
was regarded not only as a man of great ability in his profession
and of sagacity in affairs, but as a warm-hearted, ''whole-
souled'' man, and the very prince of good fellows. Being all
this, and being genial and sympathetic, he was eminently popular. He was, moreover, a heartless, selfish, cold-blooded,
unprincipled, and utterly unscrupulous scoundrel.

It was because he was this manner of man that he was able to
work that woeful ruin in which the love of Othello and Desdemona ends,—a ruin which in its extremity, however, he did
not plan, and did not at first desire. In fact, he had no inclination
to do needless harm to any one; he would not have gone out
of his way to tread upon a worm if it had kept out of *his* way,
and been no barrier to his success in life. (pp. 263-64)

The most strongly marked external traits of Shakespeare's Iago,
the Iago who was known in Venice and rose rapidly in general
favor there, were honesty and a warm heart: honesty of the
kind which is notably outspoken and trustworthy; warmth of
heart which seems to have sympathy for all men, not only in
all their hopes and sorrows, but in all their little likings and
small personal vanities. Is there any wonder that such a man
was popular and got on in the world,—that he was in favor
with the best and greatest? For he was not a mere flatterer,
however skilful. The most marked trait in this bold soldier's

character was his good faith. As if with a premonition of the
coming misconception and misrepresentation of his creature,
and to put his seeming character beyond misapprehension,
Shakespeare applies the epithet ''honest'' to him no less than
sixteen times in the course of the tragedy. Such a description—
we may almost say such a labelling—of another of his personages is not to be found in all the multitude that throng
through his thirty-seven dramas. And this is the more worthy
of note because in the Italian story out of which the play was
made there is no hint of this trait to Iago's character, nor indeed
of any of his complex moral and mental constitution. He is
absolutely and exclusively Shakespeare's conception. His trustworthiness, because of his truthful nature and his warm and
friendly heart, is to those around him the attractive trait of his
character up to, and even past, the catastrophe which his cruelly
indifferent selfishness brings about. Othello, after he has killed
Desdemona, pauses in his agony to call his tormentor and
destroyer ''my *friend,* honest, honest Iago'' [V. ii. 154]. All
the principal personages of the tragedy, Desdemona and Cassio
included, thus regard him; although Cassio, himself a soldier,
is most impressed by Iago's personal bravery and military ability. In speaking of him, he not being present, the lieutenant
calls him ''the bold Iago,'' and in his presence says to Desdemona that she ''may relish him more in the soldier than in
the scholar'' [II. i. 75, 165-66]. But Othello was chiefly attracted by his honesty and kindly nature. He speaks of him to
the Senate as a man ''of honesty and trust'' [I. iii. 284], calls
him ''most honest,'' says he is of ''*exceeding* honesty,'' and
indeed shows in all his conversation with him his absolute
unquestioning reliance upon his good faith,—a good faith which
is not mere uncontaminated purity from deceit, but an active,
benevolent honesty, which seeks the best good of others.

For loving-kindness was hardly less than honesty an attractive
feature of Iago's external character. Othello constantly speaks
of the love that he finds in his ''ancient.'' His sympathies are
always ready, always manifest. When Cassio is involved in
the brawl, Othello, in the first outburst of his wrath, says:—

> *Honest* Iago, that *look'st dead with grieving,*
> Speak, who began this? On thy *love,* I charge thee.
> [II. iii. 177-78]

The man deceived even his wife; for she, speaking the next
day to Desdemona of Cassio's disgrace, says,—

> I warrant it grieves my husband
> As if the case were his.
> [III. iii. 3-4]

Now it is plain that Iago had no particular reason or occasion
to deceive his wife on this point. He merely showed to her
what he showed to everybody, a readiness to sympathize with
the joys and sorrows and wishes of those around him. Emilia,
a woman of the world, a woman of experiences, who knew
her husband better than many wives know theirs, is yet imposed
upon by this skin-deep warmth and surface glow of his character. It is not until the climax of the tragedy that even she is
undeceived.

In the eyes of his friends and acquaintances Iago was not merely
an honest man and a good-natured one, after the semblance of
ordinary honesty and good nature. These traits were salient in
him; they distinguished him from other men. And they were
his noted peculiarities of character among his acquaintances
*long before he had any temptation to reveal his real and inner
nature,* which, until the temptation came, was possibly but
half known to himself, although indeed he had a certain con-

sciousness of it in his feeling of instinctive aversion to the sweetness and nobility of soul showed in Cassio's daily life. The occasion that revealed him completely to himself was the elevation of Cassio to the lieutenancy,—this being a place second in rank to that of a general officer.

For this honest, warm-hearted, effusively sympathetic man was a soldier of such approved valor and capacity, and so highly regarded, that when the lieutenant-generalship became vacant, notable men of Venice concerned themselves to have the young officer promoted to the place; for which they made personal suit to Othello,—an incident which in itself shows not only Iago's military distinction, but his success in attaching others to his interests. And Shakespeare, as if to put the full complement of Iago's personal gifts beyond a question (he gives to Iago's character a particularity of description as rare with him as that which he gives to Imogen's beauty [in *Cymbeline*]), makes Othello say of him that he "knows all qualities, with a learned spirit of human dealings" [III. iii. 259-60]. Indeed, there is hardly a man of Shakespeare's making, except Hamlet, who is set before us as possessing the manifold personal gifts, accomplishments, and attractions which won for Iago the distinction and favor which he enjoyed in the highest society of Venice.

As to the make of him, and what he really was, Iago by a very evident special design of the dramatist reveals himself fully in the first scene. After setting forth the promotion of Cassio as the cause of his ill-will to Othello, and expressing his contempt for such honest knaves (that is, merely such honest servingmen) as do their duty for duty's sake, he says,—

> Others there are
> Who, trimm'd in forms and visages of duty,
> Keep yet their hearts attending on themselves,
> And, throwing but shows of service on their lords,
> Do well thrive by them, and when they have lin'd their
>   coats
> Do themselves homage. These fellows have some soul;
> And such a one do I profess myself.
>
> [I. i. 49-55]

And again, in his soliloquy at the end of the first act, he shows us the same selfish, unscrupulous nature, but no disposition to malice, or even to needless mischief,—only a cruel heartlessness. Even the Roderigos of the world would have remained unharmed by him, unless he could have gained something by their injury. (pp. 266-70)

In the creation of Iago the author of *Othello* had, as I have already remarked, no help or hint from the story out of which he made his tragedy, nor from any precedent play, so far as we know,—a rare isolation and originality in Shakespeare's personages. The Iago of the Italian story is a coarse, commonplace villain, who differs from Shakespeare's Iago in this very point: that he *is* a morose, malicious creature. His soul is full of hatred; he *has* the innate spontaneous malignity which some critics have found in Iago, and have attributed to the creative powers of Shakespeare, but which Shakespeare's creation is entirely and notably without.

It was no mere villain, however black, no mere embodiment of cruelty, however fiendish, that Shakespeare saw in his idea of Iago. In that conception and in its working out he had a much more instructing, if not instructive, purpose. Such a purpose he seldom seems to have; nor does his own feeling toward his evil creatures manifest itself except on very rare occasions, and then slightly and by implication. But upon Iago

Act V. Scene ii. Othello and Desdemona. Frontispiece to the Bell edition (1785). The Department of Rare Books and Special Collections, The University of Michigan Library.

he manifestly looked with loathing and with horror, although he spent upon him the utmost powers of his creative art.

In Iago Shakespeare has presented a character that could not have escaped his observation; for it is of not uncommon occurrence except in one of its elements,—utter unscrupulousness. But for this, Iago would be a representative type,—representative of the gifted, scheming, plausible, and pushing man, who gets on by the social art known as making friends. This man is often met with in society. Sometimes he is an adventurer, like Iago, but most commonly he is not; and that he should be so is not necessary to the perfection of his character. The difference in social conduct between him and a genuine man is that this one is simply himself, and forms friendships (not too many) with those whom he likes and those who, taking him as they find him, like him; while the other lays himself out to make friends, doing so not always with the direct and specific purpose of establishing a social connection, but because it is his nature to; as the sea monster which preys upon its own kind throws out its alluring bait which is part of itself, whether there are fellow-fish in sight or not. This is not only his way of getting on, but his way of going through life. He accomplishes his purpose somewhat by flattery, of course, but less by direct flattery than by an ever-springing sympathy, and a readiness to help others in the little affairs in which their vanity or their pleasure is concerned. (pp. 270-71)

It was this kind of man that Shakespeare chose as the type of supremest villainy. His Iago is first and chiefly the most popular young man in Venice. He has assiduously made himself so, because he knows that all his ability (which he does not in the least overrate) will not help him on so much as popularity will; and that popularity brings not only success in the long run, but immediate opportunities of gain. He makes friends everywhere,—with the great ones of the state, but no less with the Roderigos. He wins everybody to trust him, in matters good and bad indifferently, that their confidence may be his profit.

Thus far Iago's character is one not rare in any society nor at any time. Yet it has been misapprehended; and the cause of its misapprehension is the one element in which it is peculiar. Iago is troubled with no scruples, absolutely none. He has intellectual perceptions of right and wrong, but he is utterly without the moral sense. He has but one guide of conduct,—self-interest. (pp. 274-75)

Now to his ability, his popular manners, his reputation for honesty and courage, and his supreme selfishness Iago added that great accomplishment and perfection of complete villainy, an absolute indifference to right and wrong. It was mere indifference. He had no special preference for wrong-doing. If by doing right he could have prospered as well as by doing wrong, he would have done right, because right-doing is more respectable and popular and less troublesome than wrong-doing. But for right and wrong in themselves he had neither like nor dislike; and there was no limit to the degree of wrong that he was ready to do to attain his ends,—this fellow of exceeding honesty, who knew all qualities with a discerning spirit, and whose daily life was an expression of love and sympathy. And his capacity of evil was passive as well as active. He did not quite like it (for some unexplained reason) that there was reason to suspect his wife with Othello; but yet he had borne the scandal prudently, lest resentment might interfere with his promotion. But when Cassio was made his general's lieutenant the disappointed man coolly reckoned the former fact as one of the motives of his action. His main purpose, however, indeed his only real purpose, was to ruin Cassio and get his place. As the readiest and the most thorough method of ruining Cassio was to ruin Desdemona with him, well: Desdemona must be ruined, and there an end; no more words about the matter. But her ruin in this way must surely involve her death at Othello's hands. Well, then she must be murdered by her husband; that's all. But this would torture Othello. No matter. All the better, perhaps,—serve him right for preferring that theorizing military dandy to the place which belonged to a better soldier.

Iago, however, had no thought of driving Othello to suicide. Far from it. Had he supposed the train he laid would have exploded in that catastrophe, he would at least have sought his end by other means. For Othello was necessary to him. He wanted the lieutenancy; and he was willing to ruin a regiment of Cassios, and to cause all the senators' daughters in Venice to be smothered, if that were necessary to his end. But otherwise he would not have stepped out of his path to do them the slightest injury; nay, rather would have done them some little service, said some pretty thing, shown some attaching sympathy, that would have been an item in the sum of his popularity. There is no mistaking Shakespeare's intention in the delineation of this character. He meant him for a most attractive, popular, good-natured, charming, selfish, cold-blooded and utterly unscrupulous scoundrel. (pp. 276-77)

Richard Grant White, "On the Acting of Iago," in his Studies in Shakespeare, Houghton, Mifflin and Company, 1886, pp. 258-79.

DENTON J. SNIDER   (essay date 1887)

[*Snider was an American scholar, philosopher, and poet who closely followed the precepts of the German philosopher Georg Wilhelm Friedrich Hegel and contributed greatly to the dissemination of his dialectical philosophy in America. Snider's critical writings include studies on Homer, Dante, and Goethe, as well as Shakespeare. Like Hermann Ulrici and G. G. Gervinus, Snider sought for the dramatic unity and ethical import in Shakespeare's plays, but he presented a more rigorous Hegelian interpretation than those two German philosophical critics. In the introduction to his three-volume work,* The Shakespearian Drama: A Commentary *(1887-90), Snider states that Shakespeare's plays present various ethical principles which, in their differences, come into "Dramatic Collision," but are ultimately resolved and brought into harmony. He claims that these collisions can be traced in the plays' various "Dramatic Threads" of action and thought, which together form a "Dramatic Movement," and that the analysis of these threads and movements—"the structural elements of the drama"—reveal the organic unity of Shakespeare's art. Snider observes two basic movements in the tragedies—guilt and retribution—and three in the comedies—separation, mediation, and return. In his analysis of* Othello, *Snider has two principal concerns. His first is to trace the pattern of the dramatic action, which he views as being divided into three movements: "the external conflict in the Family" of Brabantio and Desdemona, "the internal conflict in the Family between husband and wife," and the tragic retribution of the final act. Snider's second concern is to analyze the primary sources of the tragic catastrophe, which he identifies as the racial difference between Desdemona and the Moor, Othello's adulterous relation with Emilia, and the hero's rigid sense of honor. Like Hermann Ulrici (1839) and G. G. Gervinus (1849-50), Snider maintains that the catastrophic conclusion of the play is a result of the characters' personal choices and actions, and not a product of accident or fate. Unlike these earlier critics, however, Snider contends that the most significant transgression in the play is Desdemona's violation of ethical and natural principles in marrying a man of another race. Further, he argues that Othello's recognition of this breach of morality leads him to believe that Desdemona may be capable of disregarding "another ethical element of marriage . . . , namely, chastity." Such earlier critics as Thomas Rymer (1692), Charles Gildon (1694 and 1710), William Kenrick (1774), Samuel Taylor Coleridge (1808-18 and 1813), Charles Lamb (1811), and John Quincy Adams (1835) have also addressed the issue of Othello's race in the play. For further commentary on whether free will or determinism directs the dramatic action in* Othello, *see the excerpts by E. K. Chambers (1908), Stopford A. Brooke (1913), Elmer Edgar Stoll (1915), Wyndham Lewis (1927), Allardyce Nicoll (1927), Harry Levin (1964), and Robert G. Hunter (1976). Also significant in Snider's essay on* Othello *is his commentary on the third cause of the tragic conclusion: Othello's resolute sense of honor. Whereas such other commentators as the anonymous critic in the* Bee *(1791), Samuel Taylor Coleridge (1813 and 1822), Hermann Ulrici (1839), G. G. Gervinus (1849-50), A. C. Bradley (1904), Winifred M. T. Nowottny (1952), and G. M. Matthews (1964) have all argued that the hero is motivated by honor or love rather than jealous revenge in killing Desdemona, thereby mitigating the horror of his actions, Snider takes a darker view of Othello's behavior, contending that the Moor believes he must destroy Desdemona in order to maintain his personal reputation. This assessment foreshadows similar evaluations of Othello's actions proposed by such twentieth-century critics as F. R. Leavis (1937), G. R. Elliott (1937 and 1953), Derek Traversi (1949), Roy W. Battenhouse (1969), and Carol McGinnis Kay (1983).*]

The impression left by [*Othello*] is generally said to be that of sadness and despair. Life seems given over to the sport of external influences, and man is swept to destruction whether his conduct be good or bad. Villainy and cunning, it is thought, are portrayed as too successful and powerful, while innocence is exhibited as too weak and unfortunate. There is often expressed a deep dissatisfaction at the result; virtue is not rewarded, or is even punished, and retribution does not manifest itself in its native might. Perhaps such will always be the first and most immediate impression upon the auditor or reader. But this melancholy view of the work springs from a hasty judgment—from taking into account only a portion of the various elements of the play. On the one hand, Othello and Desdemona are not innocent, but are guilty of a violation of ethical principles, which calls forth their punishment. And, on the other hand, Iago is not the incarnation of villainy for its own sake, but he has some very strong and very natural grounds for his conduct, which, however, do not justify his action, though they explain his character. (pp. 79-80)

In the character of Othello we note that antithetic movement, which is found in so many of Shakespeare's tragic heroes, and, we may add, in Human Nature. A soul without jealousy is thrown into a course which converts it to a type of jealousy itself; a spirit noble, gentle, forbearing, becomes most vindictive and bloody; the civilized man relapses to savagery. This change comes through the deed, the deed of guilt, which is man's scourging destiny, and turns him to the opposite of himself, turns him to his own triumphant enemy, who slays him. As a counterpart to the man, we see, in this tragedy, the woman, who shows in her sphere the same tragic antithesis of character, true unto death to her husband, yet untrue to truth; faithful to family, yet unfaithful to the moral order of the world; sweet, noble, innocent, yet guilty, for it is her guilt which weaves the tragic net of destiny in which she is caught.

If we grasp the entire sweep of the action, we observe that it first moves towards union of the lovers, out of a conflict with parent; but this union, outwardly attained, rests inwardly upon a deeper disunion, which, in a suitable environment, unfolds rapidly, and hurries the pair forward to the ultimate separation in death. As is usual in Shakespeare's tragedies, a dissonance, a deep incompatibility is introduced into the Ethical World, which has to be purified of it by eliminating the individuals who caused it.

There are three essential divisions or Movements of the entire action. The first is the external conflict in the Family. The right of the daughter to choose a Moor for her husband is asserted against the will of the parent. Both sides appeal to the State, which decides in favor of the marriage, and Othello carries off his bride in triumph. The guilt of Desdemona is here indicated. The second Movement shows the internal conflict in the Family between husband and wife. The married pair, though successful in their external struggle with the father, are now rent asunder; for between such characters no secure and permanent ethical union is possible. Jealousy must arise. Iago seized only what was already prepared, and used it for his own purposes. The guilt of Othello and his Ancient is here shown. The third Movement is the retribution, which brings home to every person the consequences of his deeds. (pp. 81-3)

The presupposition of the drama is the love, elopement, and marriage of Othello and Desdemona, who constitute the single central thread of the first Movement, and with whose union three leading persons come into conflict. The lovers are thus already joined in marriage, against which the hostile elements begin to array themselves. First comes the rejected, yet determined suitor, Roderigo, who has been ignominiously dismissed by the father, and apparently disregarded by the daughter. Still, he persists; the great end of his existence is to secure her hand, for which purpose he is willing to spend large sums of money. This weakness makes him a fit subject for the practices of Iago, who buoys him up with hope and draws at will from his purse. But, when the marriage is sanctioned by the State, and is beyond reversal, what will poor Roderigo do? Since the object of his life is to attain Desdemona, he is easily led into the thought of attaining her in unholy fashion, when she can no longer be his lawful wife. He is first foolish in pursuing such an object; then he becomes immoral, and assails the Family. Roderigo is the white suitor of Desdemona, and stands in striking contrast to the black suitor, Othello. She prefers the hero of a different race to the imbecile of her own nation. But his chief function is to be the ready instrument of Iago, who uses him like the merest tool, and destroys him when he no longer subserves any purpose.

The second enemy is Iago, whose hate is not so much directed against the marriage as against Othello in person. Hence he plays a very subordinate part in the First Movement of the drama, but is reserved for the second collision. To unfold and arrange in proper order and prominence the different motives which actuate him is one of the chief duties of a criticism on this work. In his conversation with Roderigo he assigns as the cause of his hate that he has been degraded in rank, through having a less experienced and less meritorious officer promoted over his head by Othello. Hereafter he is going to look out for himself, since nobody else will pay any attention to his claims. He proposes to employ any means in his power to accomplish his end; everything high and holy—honesty, fidelity, morality—is to be trampled under foot if standing in his way. The service of the individual, therefore, he declares to be his ultimate principle. But, to attain his purpose with success, there must be a disguise. "I am not what I am" [I. i. 65], is his curt and striking statement. His instrumentality is to be dissimulation.

Iago asserts, in the strongest manner, the supremacy of reason; men can make out of their body and their appetite what they will. Still, his reason extends not beyond subjective cunning; he ignores the validity of all ethical principles. Virtue is a pretense, love is merely lust, reputation is a delusion. The question naturally arises, why has his intelligence become so debauched? The ground thereof lies in his own experience, as will be pointed out hereafter. But, here, also there is a large element of pretense, since he knows the exact nature of his conduct. Mark, too, that for his hatred of Othello he has not assigned to Roderigo the true motive; he is already dissembling in accordance with his principle. His talk is intended for Roderigo alone, whom he wishes to keep as an instrument, and to whom he is compelled, therefore, to give some motive for his conduct and some clew to his future action. For Roderigo, fool as he is, must have a plausible explanation of the strange fact that the Ancient of Othello works against his master, before any money will be forthcoming.

But the true motive for Iago's hate is given in his first, and also in his succeeding soliloquies, but nowhere in his conversation with others, since he would not be likely to announce his own shame, or herald his self-degrading suspicions. He considers that Othello has destroyed the chastity of his wife. Public rumor has noised the scandal abroad. He is made the object of scorn; he feels that he has suffered the deepest injury which man is capable of giving or receiving. This is the thought which gnaws the heart of Iago, and spurs him to revenge;

> —The thought thereof
> Doth, like a poisonous mineral, gnaw my inwards,
> And nothing can or shall content my soul
> Till I be evened with him.
>
> [II. i. 296-99]

Such was his own declaration to himself, whom he certainly had no motive for deceiving. Nor is it consistent with his shrewd understanding to assume that his belief rests on self-deception—that he really did not know what he was about. Iago has declared his actual conviction—a conviction which is confirmed by events which afterwards transpire. It is often taken for granted that his suspicions are wholly groundless—in fact, that he does not believe them himself. The question of Othello's guilt with Emilia belongs to the second division of the play, where it will be hereafter considered. But that Iago is sincere in his belief cannot be consistently questioned. The single motive usually assumed for his conduct is what he states to Roderigo about the lack of promotion. Such a view, however, is psychologically false; Iago is not the man to tell the truth to another and lie to himself. Moreover, why is the form of the soliloquy employed, unless to express the real internal ground of his action, which could not be imparted to others? Coleridge calls Iago's soliloquizing "the motive-hunting of a motiveless malignity" [see excerpt above, 1808-18], in spite of the authority of the great critic, we must think that his sentence has obtained its currency more from its epigrammatic point than from its accuracy.

With the interpretation above given, there is a motive quite adequate for the subsequent vindictive conduct of Iago; otherwise, he is an unnatural character—a monstrosity. His slight in regard to promotion would doubtless excite his enmity, but not an enmity sufficient to involve Desdemona in destruction, or even Othello. To inflict worse than death upon a man because he did not advance a subordinate when he could have done so, is altogether disproportionate to the offense; but to cause his wife to perish also is merely horrible. Thus Iago is a monster, a wild beast, and needs no motive at all—not even neglect of promotion—to bring on a rabid fit of cruelty. But what then becomes of the artistic merit and beauty of this drama? Moreover, Shakespeare's rule is to motive all his most important characters; such a being as the villain pure and simple is not to be found in any of his works. The second motive is, therefore, the true one, and at the same time is adequate. The family of Iago has been ruined by Othello; now, Iago, in his turn, will ruin the family of the destroyer of his domestic life. Hence Desdemona is included in his retaliation. He thus requites the Moor with like for like. His conduct is logical, and his revenge only equals the offense. But there is absolutely no proportion between motive and deed, if he involved Othello's family in destruction merely because the latter would not promote him. Such seems to be the proper relation of the two grand motives mentioned by the poet; the first one is intended only for Roderigo, while the second is the true and single motive for the subsequent actions of Iago.

The third opponent of the marriage is the father, Brabantio. Here we have the essential part of the First Movement—the conflict of the Family carried up into the State. The opposition of Brabantio gives the collision which Shakespeare always takes particular delight in portraying—the collision between the right of choice on the part of the daughter and the will of the parent. It is often supposed that the tragic destiny of Des-

demona is motived by her disobedience; but such a view will not bear investigation. Shakespeare everywhere justifies the right of choice when it is the sole issue, and therein he is true to the modern consciousness. It belongs to the woman to say who shall be her husband, for she, and not her father, has to form with him the unity of emotion which lies at the basis of the Family. But, even if we grant that there is some guilt in such conduct, it certainly cannot be tragic guilt, which involves the destruction of the individual. The ethical code of Shakespeare is plainly against this interpretation, for he always mediates such a conflict by the triumph of the daughter. . . . (pp. 83-8)

Another motive must, hence, be sought, which the poet has not failed to indicate. It lies in the fact that between husband and wife existed the difference of race. An ethical union is impossible under such circumstances; the chasm is too wide—at least in the present condition of mankind. The Family, like all institutions, is grounded in prescription; this prescription has placed upon marriage certain limitations which cannot be violated without giving the deepest offense to the ethical feelings. The principle of prescription belongs to every age and nation, in different degrees, and is shared by all the truly moral people; those who violate it are regarded as outcasts. . . . The rational basis for such a strong sentiment is not wanting; it is that, where so great a difference exists, the unity demanded by the Family is impossible. Both parties know that they have violated one ethical element of marriage; hence comes the dark suspicion that another ethical element of marriage may be as readily disregarded, namely, chastity. It is clear that the jealousy which fires Othello will hardly fail to arise from such a union, and turn it into a source of bitterness and death.

As Desdemona has contracted a marriage which is impossible for the Family, it culminates in destroying the woman who enters into its baleful embrace. The true tragic element of her character we are now prepared to appreciate. On the one side, she is the most chaste and innocent of women; her love and devotion are absolute. So faithful to her relation does she seem, that many people can see no justification for her fate. But let us now turn to the other side. While in the highest degree true to one ethical principle, she utterly disregards another. The entire realm of prescription which rests upon distinction of race she casts to the winds and marries an African. In the most beautiful manner she is true to the Family, but is untrue to that upon which the Family reposes. For the sake of marriage she violates the condition of marriage. Her tragic pathos, therefore, lies in the fact that she espouses the one whom she loves, which is her right, and yet thereby involves herself in guilt. The collision with her parent is allowable, but not with her race: that is, the one is not tragic, the other is. If Othello were not a Moor, there would be no motive for the fate of Desdemona; and, conversely, if she commits no offense in her marriage, it is hard to see why the poet should give himself the unnecessary trouble of making Othello a Moor. (pp. 88-90)

A question has been raised concerning the degree of Othello's Africanism, about which extreme opinions have been held in both directions. But he was not a Hottentot on the one hand, nor was he a Caucasian on the other; he was, however, born in Africa, and his physiognomy is thoroughly African. The point which the poet emphasizes so often and so strongly is the difference of race between him and Desdemona. He is her equal in rank, for he comes of royal lineage; he is the peer of her family in honor and fame, for he is the most distinguished man in Venice. The sole difference which is selected as the ground of the collision is the difference of race. This fact is sufficient for all dramatic purposes; to ascertain the exact shade of his skin may be left to those who have leisure to play with probabilities.

Desdemona, therefore, asserts the right of choosing her husband against the will of her father, which collision, as above said, is continually recurring in Shakespeare, and which he always solves by giving full validity to love, though in opposition to parental authority. But, in the present instance, he has surrounded the choice of the young girl with a peculiar obstacle, and introduced an element found nowhere else in his dramas. The love of Desdemona is made to leap over quite all the social limitations known to man; she bids defiance, not only to the behests of Family, but also to the feelings of nationality and to the instincts of race. She is a practical cosmopolitan.

Her father Brabantio, is decidedly of the opposite character. He is not wholly illiberal in his external conduct; nevertheless, he bears the stamp of a hide-bound patrician, devoted more to his class than to his country. He would hardly be called national in his feelings; the cosmopolitan love of his daughter, therefore, excites in his bosom the liveliest emotions. It is, indeed, so incomprehensible to him that he can only account for it by the employment of some supernatural means on the part of the Moor. His limits are essentially those of his own order. But he cannot avoid taking his share of the blame; it is his own conduct which has led to the unfortunate result. Othello has been a frequent guest at his house, and thus he has himself furnished the opportunity of the courtship. For Othello had rendered the most important services to the State. On account of these services he was tolerated, indeed, welcomed to the home of the Venetian aristocrat. But never for a moment did the latter think of removing the social ban. The limits of race Othello has thus broken down on one side—he has obtained honor and high command in the State. Here he cannot be barred out, for he is the chief instrument of its existence. It might be thought that these civil distinctions are higher than any other. This may be so; still, they cannot overcome social distinctions—or prejudices—if such it were better to call them. The contrast is drawn in the most striking manner by the poet. Brabantio admires him, treats him with the kindness of a friend, regards him as a benefactor, often invites him to his own house, and seems to accord to him complete social equality. Yet when it comes to have Othello as a son-in-law, his nature revolts. For him the limit of race is impassible; he would prefer the booby Roderigo, because he is a Venetian, to the hero Othello, because he is a Moor. Brabantio can only curse fatherhood when he contemplates his descendants of a different race.

But this narrow, Venetian view of things is an absurdity, and cannot be permanent. The State which defends itself by the aid of a distinct and despised race must expect to bestow honors upon those to whom it owes its own existence. That race cannot long be excluded from social equality under such circumstances, for the State is the higher, and will give the greater validity to the instruments of its own perpetuity. It must happen that these social distinctions will be ignored or subordinated, in the end, by the State. Consequently, we see in this play that the Duke, the head of authority, can only confirm the union of Othello and Desdemona. Such is the strife here portrayed between social prejudice and acquired honors by an individual of a despised race. It is manifest that the Venetians must themselves defend their State if they wish to preserve intact their Society. The latter is subordinate to the former. (pp. 91-4)

The choice must be made—the safety of the Nation or the punishment of the offender. The appeal of Brabantio is, doubtless, most powerful. His "brothers of the State cannot but feel this wrong as their own" [I. iii. 96-7], and, if such actions be permitted, who will be their children—the future rulers of Venice? But there can be only one result of such a trial; the State is deciding whether it shall exist, or a subordinate principle shall be asserted. The parent gives up all hope when his charge of witchcraft is disproved; he has already cursed fatherhood, in which alone such a collision is possible, and now, with a heavy heart and an ominous warning to the lovers, he asks that the Senate turn to other affairs. Othello departs, with his prize, for the wars; in his struggle with both Family and State he has been triumphant.

Such is the conclusion of the First Movement of the action, in which is portrayed the external conflict in its twofold phase. The various hostile elements have assailed the union of Othello and Desdemona from the outside, and have failed. This First Movement almost constitutes a drama by itself, with its collisions and happy termination. Were Othello a Venetian, it would be difficult to tell why the play should not end here. But in the difference of race has been planted the germ of the internal disruption of the pair. The man has also been introduced to us whose hatred will nurse this germ into a speedy and colossal growth. So this little introductory comedy, ending in the union and triumph of the lovers, really rests upon a deeper tragedy, which is now to unfold.

The Second Movement of the play exhibits the internal conflict of the Family—a conflict which brings to ruin all who participate in its guilt. The scene is now transferred from Venice to Cyprus, where Othello has supreme authority. The struggle, therefore, will not be disturbed by any external power, but will be allowed to unfold itself in its natural and complete development. The couple, too, are here removed from the social prejudice and dislike which would assail them at home. By this transition, therefore, they become the head of the society around them; free scope is given to them to make the most of their union. Relieved of every possibility of immediate external interference on the part of authority, Othello and Desdemona must now fall back upon their internal bond of marriage.

But a disruption will take place, of which the dark plotter is Iago, who now becomes the central figure, and whose actions are the single thread of this Second Movement. His object is to sunder and destroy the pair; for this purpose he holds his three instruments, Roderigo, Cassio, and Emilia, as it were, in one hand, and Othello and wife in the other hand. The motive for his conduct has already been stated to lie in the deep injury which he believes that he has suffered from the Moor. His method is to excite in Othello the most intense jealousy, to produce which he employs various means that will be considered in their proper order. Now, it is a leading peculiarity of Othello that his character is fundamentally free from jealousy; he is of a noble, open, magnanimous disposition. The problem, then, is to explain how an unsuspicious person becomes filled with the most deadly suspicion. The character of the Moor is a contradiction—and, hence, an impossibility—without some adequate ground for the great change which it undergoes. If he were naturally jealous, there would be needed no motive for his conduct; but the difficult point lies in the fact that he is naturally without jealousy. His characterization, as well as that of Iago, has been pronounced unnatural; and so it is, unless some adequate impelling principle can be given to account for this total inversion of his nature. We shall attempt to explain the cause of his change, and to portray his gradual transition from the first surmise to the final deed of blood.

The several parties have arrived in the island. Othello still remains behind, detained by a storm which has separated him from his wife—an ominous prelude of the succeeding play. While they are waiting for his ship, a conversation arises which exhibits a new phase of Iago's character—his disbelief in the honor of woman. It must be regarded as the result of his own experience. Married life has for him brought forth only its bitterest fruits. He treats his wife with the greatest asperity and contempt, which she, with slight protest, for the present endures. But at the whole sex he aims his sarcasms; his doctrine is that woman is naturally lustful and faithless, and, moreover, fitted only for the lowest functions—

> To suckle fools and chronicle small beer.
>
> [II. i. 160]

That the husband's opinion of Emilia is true is very plainly indicated in the last scene of the Fourth Act, where she openly admits that chastity is not the principle of her life. Othello is also well acquainted with her character. He knows of her falsehood and infidelity; he will not believe any of her statements, and loads her with the most opprobrious epithets.

We are now brought face to face with a question which is by no means pleasant to consider, but which has to be discussed if we wish to comprehend the poet's work. Must we regard the Moor as guilty of what Iago suspects him? There is nothing in the play which shows that Othello was innocent of the charge, but there is much which shows that he was not innocent. The very fact that this suspicion is cast upon him almost at the beginning, and is nowhere removed, seems sufficient to raise the presumption of guilt. It hangs over him like a cloud which will not pass away. Then Emilia's character, instead of precluding, strengthens the supposition of criminal intercourse, and the notion is still further upheld by the knowledge of her habits which Othello betrays. But the veil is never wholly removed. Why does not the poet openly state the offense, so as to leave no doubt? It is evident that he does not wish to soil the union with Desdemona by dwelling on Othello's incontinence, nor does he desire to throw into the background the difference of race as the leading motive of the play. Still, he would not have us forget the dark surmise; there it remains suspended over the Moor to the last. Iago, to be sure, is a liar; but his lies are meant for others, and not for himself. Besides, Iago is not more certain at first than we, his readers and hearers, are; but the complete success of his plan, which is based on the Moor's guilt, confirms, both for him and for us, the truth of the suspicion.

So much is indicated in the course of the play; but, if the deeper motives of the various characters are carefully examined, this conclusion would seem to become irresistible. Iago is manifestly assailed with the same burning jealousy which afterwards wrought such terrific effects in Othello. Now, what will be the manner of his revenge? The most logical and adequate would be, "wife for wife" [II. i. 299]; hence his first thought is to debauch Desdemona. But nothing more is heard of this plan, for it could not possibly be successful. Then comes his most shrewd and peculiar method of avenging his wrong. If he cannot dishonor Othello in reality, he can do it in appearance, with almost the same results. His purpose is to make Othello believe that Desdemona is untrue. This will be a revenge sufficient for his end. It will destroy Othello's happiness and peace

of mind just as well as the truth; it will bring upon Othello that which he has brought upon Iago.

Another phase of the question now comes up for solution. How was it possible to excite such a passion in a character like that of Othello? The free, open, unsuspecting nature of the Moor is noted by Iago himself; his noble and heroic disposition would appear least likely to be subject to jealousy. Yet this is the very form of revenge chosen by Iago with surpassing skill. This is, therefore, just the weak side of Othello's character. Why? The solution of the problem lies in the fact above mentioned—that Iago's suspicion concerning Emilia is true. Othello has been guilty of adultery; he is, therefore, aware that the infidelity of wives is a fact. Here lies the germ of his belief in the faithlessness of Desdemona. His own act thus comes home to him and renders him accursed; his faith in justice can only make him more ready to think that he will be punished through his wife, since that is the mode which his own guilt suggests. Such is the initial point of the fearful jealousy of the Moor, which Iago knows exactly how to reach, since it is a matter lying wholly within his own experience; and he knows also that Othello, on account of previous criminality, must be as capable of this passion as himself. Both the revenge of Iago and the jealousy of Othello, therefore, can be adequately motived only by the guilty conduct of the Moor towards the Ancient's wife.

Moreover, there is no other ground for the relation of marriage between Iago and Emilia except as a basis for these two main motives of drama. Thus, too, we see one of the fundamental rules of Shakespeare vindicated—that man cannot escape his own deed; hence Othello is the author of his own fate, since by his guilt he has called up the avenger who will destroy him and his family, while, without the view above developed, he must appear as an innocent sufferer deceived by a malicious villain. It will, therefore, be seen that two things of the greatest importance have their sole explanation in this view, namely, the manner of Iago's revenge, and his knowledge of the assailable point in Othello's character. Here also we find the solution of the Moor's contradictory nature. He is, in general, unsuspecting; but, on account of his guilt, he is capable of one suspicion, namely, that wives may be faithless. The poet has thus added to the distinction of race—for which the Moor could not be blamed—a second motive, the criminal deed, of which he must take the responsibility. The military life of Othello will furnish the third principle—that of honor, which will impel him to destroy the wife whom he thinks to have violated it in its deepest and most tender part. (pp. 97-104)

Iago begins the manipulation of Othello's mind through a series of influences adapted exactly to the shifting phases of the Moor's disposition, and increasing in intensity to the end. Given a noble, unsuspecting character, the design is to portray those causes which not only turn it into the opposite of itself, but make it destroy its most beloved object. The primal basis to work upon lies in Othello's own consciousness of guilt. The first point is to touch faintly his suspicion, which is accomplished most easily, for he readily imagines what he himself has done to others may happen in his own case. We see how the slightest hint from Iago casts a shadow over his whole being.

> Iago.—Ha! I like not that.
> Othello.—What dost thou say?
> Iago.—Nothing my lord, or if—I know not what.
> Othello.—Was not that Cassio parted from my wife? etc.
>
> [III. iii. 35ff.]

A word from Desdemona is sufficient, however, to allay his mistrust, but another word from Iago is sufficient to arouse it anew in all its intensity. Can any one doubt that this hasty suspicion, on the part of an unsuspecting character, can have any other ground than the consciousness of the same kind of guilt which he is so ready to suspect in another? Iago's artifices are unquestionably skillful, but he found a most fruitful and well-prepared soil; and, besides, his very skillfulness rests upon his comprehending and utilizing so thoroughly the psychological effects of Othello's crime. It is impossible to think that an honest and innocent man could have been so easily led astray.

Othello's suspicion is now fully aroused, but with it the difficulty of Iago's task is proportionately greater. How will the latter prevent that suspicion from becoming universal—from being directed against himself as well as against Cassio and Desdemona? His first plan, therefore, must be to confirm his own honesty in the mind of Othello with the same care and skill that he infuses distrust against the other two. He has to fill the Moor with suspicion, and, at the same time, to avoid the suspicion of doing that very thing.

It is this double, and apparently contradictory, ability that gives such a lofty idea of Iago's intellectual power. But how does he proceed to accomplish his purpose? At first, by the apparent unwillingness with which he tells his dark surmises, and by the pretended dislike with which he assails the reputation of people. In these cases he seems to manifest the most tender regard for the rights and character of others; indeed, he repeatedly confesses his own tendency to suspect wrongfully. Such a man appears to be absolutely just—more just, indeed, to others than to himself. But all these things might be the tricks of a false, disloyal knave, as Othello well knows and says. Now comes Iago's master-stroke, by which he completely spans the Moor's mind, and turns it in whatever direction he pleases—"Othello, beware of jealousy" [III. iii. 165]; and then he proceeds to give a description of its baleful nature. What, now, is the attitude of the Moor? This is the very passion with which he knows himself to be affected. Never more can he harbor a doubt of Iago's honesty; for has not the latter warned him of his danger? Iago thus tears out and brings to the Moor's own look his deepest consciousness—his greatest peril. He knows the truth of the admonition. Iago now can proceed with more certainty and directness; he cannot be suspected of exciting jealousy, for this is the very thing against which he has given so potent a warning. Thus Othello is thrown on his own defense—is compelled to dissemble his true feelings; thus he declares that he is not jealous, when he really is. He is forced into the necessity of disguise—exchanges positions with Iago; yet the latter well knows, indeed says, that jealousy cannot be eradicated when once excited, but ever creates itself anew—feeds on its own meat. Such is the twofold purpose of Iago, as manifested in this dialogue—to inspire Othello with suspicion, and yet to shun suspicion himself. (pp. 108-10)

Iago can now be more bold; Othello cannot suspect him. Hitherto he has directed his hints and surmises against Cassio; but now he begins to assail Desdemona with the most artful innuendoes. She is from Venice, where it is the custom to be untrue. She deceived her father; you know she pretended in his presence to tremble at your looks when she loved you most—a statement which has increased force from the parting admonition of Brabantio: "Moor, she has deceived her father, and may thee" [I. iii. 293]. As preparatory to the final and culminating charge, Iago renews his warning against jealousy.

But this third point the Moor anticipates, so well prepared has he been, and thus shows that it was always in his mind. It is the distinction of race. Hardly is it hinted by him, when Iago catches up the unfinished thought and dwells upon it with terrific emphasis. How unnatural, horrible, the union between man and woman of different complexion and clime! and hence how much more ready will she be to break it, after becoming disgusted! We see with what effect this reproach takes hold of Othello in his succeeding soliloquy. It recalls all the bitterness of many years, the taunts of Brabantio, finally the collision resting upon this very basis, which collision he has just passed through. Desdemona broke over all social distinctions of nation and race; here is the retribution—jealousy. The greater her sacrifice the more unnatural does it seem, and the more suspected she becomes. Moreover, we catch a glimpse of that to which this jealousy will lead—destruction for himself and for the loved one rather than be dishonored in his domestic life. The passion of jealousy rests upon the monogamic nature of marriage; when that relation is disturbed, jealousy will, and ought to, arise in all its intensity. Another element is added in the case of Othello, springing from his military career—honor. He cannot endure shame and reproach—he who has never had any taint cast upon his courage or reputation.

The passion has overwhelmed him; he cannot do or think of anything else; his occupation is gone. So Iago knows; not all the drowsy medicines of the world will restore to him peace of mind. Iago, indeed, has obtained his knowledge from experience; in fact, his own present activity has the same root. For a moment Othello reacts, suspects, notices that no positive proofs have been produced, but only surmises. He turns upon Iago and grasps him by the throat; yet, how can he continue his suspicion; how can he blame Iago? Did not the latter warn him of these very consequences? One word from his Ancient, therefore, makes him release his hold. Othello must believe that Iago has been honest with him. Once more Iago speaks of his jealousy; it is a thought that cuts the Moor through and through, whose truth he can not deny.

Othello will have more direct proofs than surmise; Iago is ready with them. He then narrates the dream of Cassio, which Othello, of course, has no means of verifying. But the charge is direct, plain, and based upon an occurrence. Next comes the apparently complete demonstration—the handkerchief. Here is a fact which Othello does verify sufficiently to discover that Desdemona has not the article sought for in her possession. Still, whether Cassio has received it or not he cannot verify as long as they are asunder. Finally, the trick wherein Othello overhears the conversation about Bianca, and thinks it is about Desdemona, seems to him to be an acknowledgement of guilt from the mouth of Cassio himself. It ought to be added that, before this, Iago has made the direct charge that Cassio has revealed to him Desdemona's infidelity. Othello is so overcome that he falls into a swoon, and then afterward, through the words of the Lieutenant, he seems to get a complete confirmation of Iago's statement. Othello is now resolved; the swoon indicates the changed man; he has gone through his demonic baptism; his mad suspicion has been wrought up to the point where no explanations can mitigate its ferocity. He investigates, but his resolution is already taken. No declaration of Emilia, whose character he cannot trust, and no denials of Desdemona, who is the person suspected, can shake his belief. The passion has taken too deep a hold; he will not, and can not, withdraw himself from its grasp. (pp. 111-14)

The Third Movement of the play, the Retribution follows. The tragic preparation of the previous portions is carried to the consummation. First, Roderigo is led to assail Cassio, but is slain by Iago. It is his just desert, for he has willed, and tried to accomplish both adultery and murder. Desdemona is killed by the Moor; jealousy has done its worst—has slain its most beloved object. The ground for her fate has been already stated. She violated the conditions of the Family in marrying a husband of a different race. Othello himself feels that she has shocked the strongest instincts of nature by her conduct; hence he can easily be brought to believe her untrue. That is, jealousy is sure to arise under such circumstances. It cannot be her disregard of the parental will which brings on her tragic fate. The second and subordinate motive of Othello's jealousy, namely, his previous incontinence, can, of course, have nothing to do with the guilt of Desdemona. That has its baleful effect upon his character, as has already been shown; it brings upon him a fearful retribution, and determines the method of Iago's revenge. Still, a man may be fired with jealousy and yet may not be ready to destroy its object. A third element, therefore, is added to Othello's character—honor. It is intimately connected with his military life. The soldier always prefers death to what he deems dishonor; he would rather destroy the dearest object in existence, and be destroyed himself, than be stained with disgrace. Hence, when Othello is convinced of Desdemona's guilt he must proceed to kill her. (pp. 116-17)

This play has suffered, perhaps more than any other work of Shakespeare, from the amiable sentimentality of expositors who have wrenched and tortured it, till they behold in it two angelic beings caught unawares and hurled into the infernal pit by a black demon in human form. But in their attempt to save Othello and Desdemona, they destroy Shakespeare; they tumble into chaos the ethical order of the poet, which is the best part, nay, the very soul, of him. Satan is not the ruler of this world, nor does Shakespeare picture it thus; and, surely, to damn Providence is not the way to save man. In this play, too, we are to see the moral cosmos, and the poet as its stern but loyal revealer.

Moreover we are to let the light from other plays shine upon this one, which we shall find to be no exception, but in harmony with Shakespeare's poetic law. He serves up to man man's deed, which is destiny instinct with freedom and responsibility; we are to see that such is what he does in *Othello*. We disjoint the entire Shakespearian edifice, if we make the innocent perish simply through their innocence. In the physical world accident may destroy from the outside, but not in the ethical or providential world, which it is the function of tragedy to represent. There the action is always returnable, and adjudges the penalty. Iago is inside Othello as well as outside; if he were merely outside, he could do little harm. The play shows two Iagos; the one is external, but is conspiring with an internal Iago in Othello, and rousing in the latter his own jealousy and deviltry. The outer demon calls to the inner, and wonderful is the response. (pp. 119-20)

Denton J. Snider, "'Othello'," in his The Shakespearian Drama, a Commentary: The Tragedies, *Sigma Publishing Co., 1887, pp. 79-124.*

G. B. S. [BERNARD SHAW] (essay date 1897)

[*Shaw, an Irish dramatist and critic, was the major playwright of his generation. In his Shakespearean criticism, he consistently attacked what he considered to be Shakespeare's inflated reputation as a dramatist. Shaw did not hesitate to judge the characters in the plays by the standards of his own values and prejudices, and much of his commentary is presented—as the prominent Shaw*

critic Edwin Wilson once remarked—"with an impudence that had not been seen before, nor is likely to be seen again." Shaw's hostility towards Shakespeare's work was due in large measure to his belief that it was interfering with the acceptance of Henrick Ibsen and the new social theater he so strongly advocated. The following excerpt is taken from an article in The Saturday Review, *in which Shaw reviewed a production of* Othello *at the Lyric Theatre in London on May 22, 1897. He dispraises the play for what he describes as its melodramatic and superficial representation of the dramatic characters, but declares that "it remains magnificent by the volume of its passion and the splendour of its word-music," arguing that the significance of the language is "drowned in sound." Analyses of the poetic language in* Othello *have been offered by such critics as G. Wilson Knight (1930), Derek Traversi (1949), Robert B. Heilman (1951), S. L. Bethell (1952), John Bayley (1960), Gayle Greene (1979), and Carol McGinnis Kay (1983); also, see the essays by Wolfgang Clemen, Madeleine Doran, William Empson, and Caroline F. E. Spurgeon cited in the Additional Bibliography for further commentary on the language and imagery in the play.*]

["Othello"] is pure melodrama. There is not a touch of character in it that goes below the skin; and the fitful attempts to make Iago something better than a melodramatic villain only make a hopeless mess of him and his motives. To any one capable of reading the play with an open mind as to its merits, it is obvious that Shakespeare plunged through it so impetuously that he had it finished before he had made up his mind as to the character and motives of a single person in it. Probably it was not until he stumbled into the sentimental fit in which he introduced the willow song that he saw his way through without making Desdemona enough of the "supersubtle Venetian" of Iago's description to strengthen the case for Othello's jealousy. That jealousy, by the way, is purely melodramatic jealousy. The real article is to be found later on in "A Winter's Tale," where Leontes is an unmistakable study of a jealous man from life. But when the worst has been said of "Othello" that can be provoked by its superficiality and staginess, it remains magnificent by the volume of its passion and the splendour of its word-music, which sweep the scenes up to a plane on which sense is drowned in sound. The words do not convey ideas: they are streaming ensigns and tossing branches to make the tempest of passion visible. In this passage, for instance:

> Like to the Pontic sea,
> Whose icy current and compulsive course
> Ne'er feels retiring ebb, but keeps due on
> To the Propontic and the Hellespont,
> E'en so my bloody thoughts, with violent pace,
> Shall ne'er look back, ne'er ebb to humble love
> Till that a capable and wide revenge
> Swallow them up,
>
> [III. iii. 453-60]

if Othello cannot turn his voice into a thunder and surge of passion, he will achieve nothing but a ludicrously misplaced bit of geography. If in the last scene he cannot throw the darkness of night and the shadow of death over such lines as

> I know not where is that Promethean heat
> That can thy light relume,
>
> [V. ii. 12-13]

he at once becomes a person who, on his way to commit a pettish murder, stops to philosophize foolishly about a candle end. The actor cannot help himself by studying his part acutely; for there is nothing to study in it. Tested by the brain, it is ridiculous: tested by the ear, it is sublime. He must have the orchestral quality in him; and as that is a matter largely of physical endowment, it follows that only an actor of certain physical endowments can play Othello. Let him be as crafty as he likes without that, he can no more get the effect than he can sound the bottom C on a violoncello. The note is not there, that is all; and he had better be content to play Iago, which is within the compass of any clever actor of normal endowments. (p. 604)

> G. B. S. [Bernard Shaw], "Mainly about Shake-
> speare," in The Saturday Review, London, Vol. 83,
> No. 2170, May 29, 1897, pp. 603-05.

A. C. BRADLEY (essay date 1904)

[Bradley was a major Shakespearean critic whose work culminated the method of character analysis initiated in the Romantic era. He is best known for his Shakespearean Tragedy (1904), a close analysis of Hamlet, Othello, King Lear, and Macbeth. Bradley concentrated on Shakespeare as a dramatist, and particularly on his characters, excluding not only the biographical questions so prominent in the works of his immediate predecessors but also the questions of poetic structure, symbolism, and thematics which became prominent in later criticism. He thus may be seen as a pivotal figure in the transition in Shakespearean studies from the nineteenth to the twentieth century. He has been a major target for critics reacting against Romantic criticism, but he has continued to be widely read to the present day. In the excerpt below, Bradley analyzes Iago and Othello. He describes the former as an individual with "very remarkable powers both of intellect and will," together with an unusual degree of self-control—a result of his icy temperament—which allows no considerations of moral or ethical values and greatly limits his compassion or sympathetic regard for others. Disputing the idea of "motiveless malignity" proffered by Samuel Taylor Coleridge (1808-18), Bradley argues that Iago is impelled not by a love of evil for its own sake, but to satisfy his "sense of power and superiority." For further discussions of Iago's motives, see the excerpts by Thomas Wilkes (1759), John Potter (1771-72), Richard Hole (1796), William Hazlitt (1817), William Maginn (1839), Denton J. Snider (1887), G. Wilson Knight (1930), Bernard Spivack (1958), G. M. Matthews (1964), and Stanley Edgar Hyman (see Additional Bibliography). Bradley further asserts that Iago finds the very perilousness of his scheme so stimulating and the exercise of his creative talents so pleasureable that he is unwittingly trapped by his own machinations. Other commentators who have regarded Iago as self-deceiving and the victim of his own schemes include William Hazlitt (1817), William Maginn (1839), Tucker Brooke (1918), Allardyce Nicoll (1927), G. R. Elliott (1937), and Nigel Alexander (see Additional Bibliography). With regard to the character of Othello, Bradley is in agreement with Coleridge (see excerpts above, 1813, 1822, and 1827) that the Moor is not an easily jealous man; he adds that, once trusting completely in Iago, "any man" would have been suspicious of such reports regarding his wife, and that the apparent "wreck of his faith and his love," not sexual jealousy, leads him to slay Desdemona. The question of Othello's jealousy has also been addressed by John Hughes (1713), Lewis Theobald (1717), Samuel Johnson (1765), August Wilhelm Schlegel (1811), Hermann Ulrici (1839), G. G. Gervinus (1849-50), Denton J. Snider (1887), E. K. Chambers (1908), Elmer Edgar Stoll (1915), Allardyce Nicoll (1927), and Harley Granville-Barker (1945). Also, for further examples of the opinion that Othello kills Desdemona out of love or honor, rather than jealous revenge, see the excerpts by the anonymous critic in the Bee (1791), Samuel Taylor Coleridge (1813 and 1822), Hermann Ulrici (1839), G. G. Gervinus (1849-50), Denton J. Snider (1887), Winifred M. T. Nowottny (1952), G. M. Matthews (1964), and Carol McGinnis Kay (1983). Wyndham Lewis (1927) and F. R. Leavis (1937) have provided extended responses to Bradley's analysis of Iago and Othello.]

The character of Othello is comparatively simple, but . . . it is desirable to show how essentially the success of Iago's plot is connected with this character. Othello's description of himself as

> one not easily jealous, but, being wrought,
> Perplexed in the extreme,
>
> [V. ii. 345-46]

is perfectly just. His tragedy lies in this—that his whole nature was indisposed to jealousy, and yet was such that he was unusually open to deception, and, if once wrought to passion, likely to act with little reflection, with no delay, and in the most decisive manner conceivable. (p. 186)

Othello is, in one sense of the word, by far the most romantic figure among Shakespeare's heroes; and he is so partly from the strange life of war and adventure which he has lived from childhood. He does not belong to our world, and he seems to enter it we know not whence—almost as if from wonderland. There is something mysterious in his descent from men of royal siege; in his wanderings in vast deserts and among marvellous peoples; in his tales of magic handkerchiefs and prophetic Sibyls; in the sudden vague glimpses we get of numberless battles and sieges in which he has played the hero and has borne a charmed life; even in chance references to his baptism, his being sold to slavery, his sojourn in Aleppo.

And he is not merely a romantic figure; his own nature is romantic. He has not, indeed, the meditative or speculative imagination of Hamlet; but in the strictest sense of the word he is more poetic than Hamlet. Indeed, if one recalls Othello's most famous speeches—those that begin, 'Her father loved me,' 'O now for ever,' 'Never, Iago,' 'Had it pleased Heaven,' 'It is the cause,' 'Behold, I have a weapon,' 'Soft you, a word or two before you go' [I. iii. 128; III. iii. 347; III. iii. 453; IV. ii. 47; V. ii. 1; V. ii. 259; V. ii. 338]—and if one places side by side with these speeches an equal number by any other hero, one will not doubt that Othello is the greatest poet of them all. (pp. 187-88)

The sources of danger in this character are revealed but too clearly by the story. In the first place, Othello's mind, for all its poetry, is very simple. He is not observant. His nature tends outward. He is quite free from introspection, and is not given to reflection. Emotion excites his imagination, but it confuses and dulls his intellect. On this side he is the very opposite of Hamlet, with whom, however, he shares a great openness and trustfulness of nature. In addition, he has little experience of the corrupt products of civilised life, and is ignorant of European women.

In the second place, for all his dignity and massive calm (and he has greater dignity than any other of Shakespeare's men), he is by nature full of the most vehement passion. Shakespeare emphasises his self-control, not only by the wonderful pictures of the First Act, but by references to the past. Lodovico, amazed at his violence, exclaims:

> Is this the noble Moor whom our full Senate
> Call all in all sufficient? Is this the nature
> Whom passion could not shake? whose solid virtue
> The shot of accident nor dart of chance
> Could neither graze nor pierce?
>
> [IV. i. 264-68]

Iago, who has here no motive for lying, asks:

> Can he be angry? I have seen the cannon
> When it hath blown his ranks into the air,
> And, like the devil, from his very arm
> Puffed his own brother—and can he be angry?
>
> [III. iv. 134-37]

This, and other aspects of his character, are best exhibited by a single line—one of Shakespeare's miracles—the words by which Othello silences in a moment the night-brawl between his attendants and those of Brabantio:

> Keep up your bright swords, for the dew will rust them.
>
> [I. ii. 59]

And the same self-control is strikingly shown where Othello endeavours to elicit some explanation of the fight between Cassio and Montano. Here, however, there occur ominous words, which make us feel how necessary was this self-control, and make us admire it the more:

> Now, by heaven,
> My blood begins my safer guides to rule,
> And passion, having my best judgment collied,
> Assays to lead the way.
>
> [II. iii. 204-07]

We remember these words later, when the sun of reason is 'collied,' blackened and blotted out in total eclipse.

Lastly, Othello's nature is all of one piece. His trust, where he trusts, is absolute. Hesitation is almost impossible to him. He is extremely self-reliant, and decides and acts instantaneously. If stirred to indignation, as 'in Aleppo once' [V. ii. 354], he answers with one lightning stroke. Love, if he loves, must be to him the heaven where either he must live or bear no life. If such a passion as jealousy seizes him, it will swell into a well-nigh incontrollable flood. He will press for immediate conviction or immediate relief. Convinced, he will act with the authority of a judge and the swiftness of a man in mortal pain. Undeceived, he will do like execution on himself. (pp. 189-91)

Yet there are some critics and not a few readers who cherish a grudge against him. They do not merely think that in the later stages of his temptation he showed a certain obtuseness, and that, to speak pedantically, he acted with unjustifiable precipitance and violence; no one, I suppose, denies that. But, even when they admit that he was not of a jealous temper, they consider that he *was* 'easily jealous'; they seem to think that it was inexcusable in him to feel any suspicion of his wife at all; and they blame him for never suspecting Iago of asking him for evidence. I refer to this attitude of mind chiefly in order to draw attention to certain points in the story. It comes partly from mere inattention (for Othello did suspect Iago and did ask him for evidence); partly from a misconstruction of the text which makes Othello appear jealous long before he really is so; and partly from failure to realise certain essential facts. I will being with these.

(1) Othello, we have seen, was trustful, and thorough in his trust. He put entire confidence in the honesty of Iago, who had not only been his companion in arms, but, as he believed, had just proved his faithfulness in the matter of the marriage. This confidence was misplaced, and we happen to know it; but it was no sign of stupidity in Othello. For his opinion of Iago was the opinion of practically everyone who knew him: and that opinion was that Iago was before all things 'honest,' his

very faults being those of excess in honesty. This being so, even if Othello had not been trustful and simple, it would have been quite unnatural in him to be unmoved by the warnings of so honest a friend, warnings offered with extreme reluctance and manifestly from a sense of a friend's duty. *Any* husband would have been troubled by them.

(2) Iago does not bring these warnings to a husband who had lived with a wife for months and years and knew her like his sister or his bosom-friend. Nor is there any ground in Othello's character for supposing that, if he had been such a man, he would have felt and acted as he does in the play. But he was newly married; in the circumstances he cannot have known much of Desdemona before his marriage; and further he was conscious of being under the spell of a feeling which can give glory to the truth but can also give it to a dream.

(3) This consciousness in any imaginative man is enough, in such circumstances, to destroy his confidence in his powers of perception. In Othello's case, after a long and most artful preparation, there now comes, to reinforce its effect, the suggestions that he is not an Italian, not even a European; that he is totally ignorant of the thoughts and the customary morality of Venetian women; that he had himself seen in Desdemona's deception of her father how perfect an actress she could be. As he listens in horror, for a moment at least the past is revealed to him in a new and dreadful light, and the ground seems to sink under his feet. These suggestions are followed by a tentative but hideous and humiliating insinuation of what his honest and much-experienced friend fears may be the true explanation of Desdemona's rejection of acceptable suitors, and of her strange, and naturally temporary, preference for a black man. Here Iago goes too far. He sees something in Othello's face that frightens him, and he breaks off. Nor does this idea take any hold of Othello's mind. But it is not surprising that his utter powerlessness to repel it on the ground of knowledge of his wife, or even of that instinctive interpretation of character which is possible between persons of the same race, should complete his misery, so that he feels he can bear no more, and abruptly dismisses his friend [III. iii. 238].

Now I repeat that *any* man situated as Othello was would have been disturbed by Iago's communications, and I add that many men would have been made wildly jealous. But up to this point, where Iago is dismissed, Othello, I must maintain, does not show jealousy. His confidence is shaken, he is confused and deeply troubled, he feels even horror; but he is not yet jealous in the proper sense of that word. In his soliloquy [III. iii. 258 ff.] the beginning of this passion may be traced; but it is only after an interval of solitude, when he has had time to dwell on the idea presented to him, and especially after statements of fact, not mere general grounds of suspicion, are offered, that the passion lays hold of him. Even then, however, and indeed to the very end, he is quite unlike the essentially jealous man, quite unlike Leontes [in *The Winter's Tale*]. No doubt the thought of another man's possessing the woman he loves is intolerable to him; no doubt the sense of insult and the impulse of revenge are at times most violent; and these are the feelings of jealousy proper. But these are not the chief or the deepest source of Othello's suffering. It is the wreck of his faith and his love. (pp. 191-94)

Up to this point, it appears to me, there is not a syllable to be said against Othello. But the play is a tragedy, and from this point we may abandon the ungrateful and undramatic task of awarding praise and blame. When Othello, after a brief interval, re-enters [III. iii. 330], we see at once that the poison has been at work and 'burns like the mines of sulphur' [III. iii. 329]. . . . The 'madness of revenge' is in his blood, and hesitation is a thing he never knew. He passes judgment, and controls himself only to make his sentence a solemn vow.

The Othello of the Fourth Act is Othello in his fall. His fall is never complete, but he is much changed. Towards the close of the Temptation-scene he becomes at times most terrible, but his grandeur remains almost undiminished. Even in the following scene (III. iv.), where he goes to test Desdemona in the matter of the handkerchief, and receives a fatal confirmation of her guilt, our sympathy with him is hardly touched by any feeling of humiliation. But in the Fourth Act 'Chaos has come' [III. ii. 92]. . . . His self-control has wholly deserted him, and he strikes his wife in the presence of the Venetian envoy. He is so lost to all sense of reality that he never asks himself what will follow the deaths of Cassio and his wife. An ineradicable instinct of justice, rather than any last quiver of hope, leads him to question Emilia; but nothing could convince him now, and there follows the dreadful scene of accusation; and then, to allow us the relief of burning hatred and burning tears, the interview of Desdemona with Iago, and that last talk of hers with Emilia, and her last song.

But before the end there is again a change. The supposed death of Cassio (v. i.) satiates the thirst for vengeance. The Othello who enters the bed-chamber with the words,

> It is the cause, it is the cause, my soul,
>
> [V. ii. i]

is not the man of the Fourth Act. The deed he is bound to do is no murder, but a sacrifice. He is to save Desdemona from herself, not in hate but in honour; in honour, and also in love. . . . As he speaks those final words in which all the glory and agony of his life—long ago in India and Arabia and Aleppo, and afterwards in Venice, and now in Cyprus—seem to pass before us, like the pictures that flash before the eyes of a drowning man, a triumphant scorn for the fetters of the flesh and the littleness of all the lives that must survive him sweeps our grief away, and when he dies upon a kiss the most painful of all tragedies leaves us for the moment free from pain, and exulting in the power of 'love and man's unconquerable mind' [William Wordsworth, "Sonnet to Toussaint 1' Ouverture"]. (pp. 194-98)

Of Shakespeare's characters Falstaff, Hamlet, Iago, and Cleopatra (I name them in the order of their births) are probably the most wonderful. Of these, again, Hamlet and Iago, whose births come nearest together, are perhaps the most subtle. And if Iago had been a person as attractive as Hamlet, as many thousands of pages might have been written about him, containing as much criticism good and bad. As it is, the majority of interpretations of his character are inadequate not only to Shakespeare's conception, but, I believe, to the impressions of most readers of taste who are unbewildered by analysis. (p. 208)

It has been held that he is a study of that peculiarly Italian form of villainy which is considered both too clever and too diabolical for an Englishman. I doubt if there is much more to be said for this idea than for the notion that Othello is a study of Moorish character. . . . Iago certainly cannot be taken to exemplify the popular Elizabethan idea of a disciple of Macchiavelli. There is no sign that he is in theory an atheist or even an unbeliever in the received religion. On the contrary,

he uses its language, and says nothing resembling the words of the prologue to [Christopher Marlowe's] the *Jew of Malta:*

> I count religion but a childish toy,
> And hold there is no sin but ignorance.

Aaron in *Titus Andronicus* might have said this (and is not more likely to be Shakespeare's creation on that account), but not Iago. (pp. 210-11)

One must constantly remember not to believe a syllable that Iago utters on any subject, including himself, until one has tested his statement by comparing it with known facts and with other statements of his own or of other people, and by considering whether he had in the particular circumstances any reason for telling a lie or for telling the truth. The implicit confidence which his acquaintances placed in his integrity has descended to most of his critics; and this, reinforcing the comical habit of quoting as Shakespeare's own statement everything said by his characters, has been a fruitful source of misinterpretation. I will take as an instance the very first assertions made by Iago. In the opening scene he tells his dupe Roderigo that three great men of Venice went to Othello and begged him to make Iago his lieutenant; that Othello, out of pride and obstinacy, refused; that in refusing he talked a deal of military rigmarole, and ended by declaring (falsely, we are to understand) that he had already filled up the vacancy; that Cassio, whom he chose, had absolutely no practical knowledge of war, nothing but bookish theoric, mere prattle, arithmetic, whereas Iago himself had often fought by Othello's side, and by 'old gradation' too ought to have been preferred. Most or all of this is repeated by some critics as though it were information given by Shakespeare, and the conclusion is quite naturally drawn that Iago had some reason to feel aggrieved. But if we ask ourselves how much of all this is true we shall answer, I believe, as follows. It is absolutely certain that Othello appointed Cassio his lieutenant, and *nothing* else is absolutely certain. But there is no reason to doubt the statement that Iago had seen service with him, nor is there anything inherently improbable in the statement that he was solicited by three great personages on Iago's behalf. On the other hand, the suggestions that he refused out of pride and obstinacy, and that he lied in saying he had already chosen his officer, have no verisimilitude; and if there is any fact at all (as there probably is) behind Iago's account of the conversation, it doubtless is the fact that Iago himself was ignorant of military science, while Cassio was an expert, and that Othello explained this to the great personages. That Cassio, again, was an interloper and a mere closet-student without experience of war is incredible, considering first that Othello chose him for lieutenant, and secondly that the senate appointed him to succeed Othello in command at Cyprus; and we have direct evidence that part of Iago's statement is a lie, for Desdemona happens to mention that Cassio was a man who 'all his time' had founded his 'good fortunes' on Othello's love and had 'shared dangers' with him [III. iv. 93-4]. There remains only the implied assertion that, if promotion had gone by old gradation, Iago, as the senior, would have been preferred. It may be true: Othello was not the man to hesitate to promote a junior for good reasons. But it is just as likely to be a pure invention; and, though Cassio was young, there is nothing to show that he was younger, in years or in service, than Iago. Iago, for instance, never calls him 'young,' as he does Roderigo; and a mere youth would not have been made Governor of Cyprus. What is certain, finally, in the whole business is that Othello's mind was perfectly at ease about the appointment, and that he never dreamed of Iago's being discontented at it, not even when the intrigue was disclosed and he asked himself how he had offended Iago. (pp. 211-13)

Iago's powers of dissimulation and of self-control must have been prodigious: for he was not a youth, like Edmund [in *King Lear*], but had worn [his hypocritical] mask for years, and he had apparently never enjoyed, like Richard [in *Richard III*], occasional explosions of the reality within him. In fact so prodigious does his self-control appear that a reader might be excused for feeling a doubt of its possibility. But there are certain observations and further inferences which, apart from confidence in Shakespeare, would remove this doubt. It is to be observed, first, that Iago was able to find a certain relief from the discomfort of hypocrisy in those caustic or cynical speeches which, being misinterpreted, only heightened confidence in his honesty. They acted as a safety-valve, very much as Hamlet's pretended insanity did. Next, I would infer from the entire success of his hypocrisy—what may also be inferred on other grounds, and is of great importance—that he was by no means a man of strong feelings and passions, like Richard, but decidedly cold by temperament. Even so, his self-control was wonderful, but there never was in him any violent storm to be controlled. Thirdly, I would suggest that Iago, though thoroughly selfish and unfeeling, was not by nature malignant, nor even morose, but that, on the contrary, he had a superficial good-nature, the kind of good-nature that wins popularity and is often taken as the sign, not of a good digestion, but of a good heart. And lastly, it may be inferred that, before the giant crime which we witness, Iago had never been detected in any serious offence and may even never have been guilty of one, but had pursued a selfish but outwardly decent life, enjoying the excitement of war and of casual pleasures, but never yet meeting with any sufficient temptation to risk his position and advancement by a dangerous crime. So that, in fact, the tragedy of *Othello* is in a sense his tragedy too. It shows us not a violent man, like Richard, who spends his life in murder, but a thoroughly bad, *cold* man, who is at last tempted to let loose the forces within him, and is at once destroyed.

In order to see how this tragedy arises let us now look more closely into Iago's inner man. We find here, in the first place, as has been implied in part, very remarkable powers both of intellect and of will. Iago's insight, within certain limits, into human nature; his ingenuity and address in working upon it; his quickness and versatility in dealing with sudden difficulties and unforeseen opportunities, have probably no parallel among dramatic characters. Equally remarkable is his strength of will. Not Socrates himself, not the ideal sage of the Stoics, was more lord of himself than Iago appears to be. It is not merely that he never betrays his true nature; he seems to be master of *all* the motions that might affect his will. . . . Indeed, in intellect (always within certain limits) and in will (considered as a mere power, and without regard to its objects) Iago *is* great.

To what end does he use these great powers? His creed—for he is no sceptic, he has a definite creed—is that absolute egoism is the only rational and proper attitude, and that conscience or honour or any kind of regard for others is an absurdity. He does not deny that his absurdity exists. He does not suppose that most people secretly share his creed, while pretending to hold and practise another. On the contrary, he regards most people as honest fools. He declares that he has never yet met a man who knew how to love himself; and his one expression of admiration in the play is for servants

> Who, trimmed in forms and visages of duty,
> Keep yet their hearts attending on themselves.
>
> [I. i. 50-1]

'These fellows,' he says, 'have some soul' [I. i. 54]. He professes to stand, and he attempts to stand, wholly outside the world of morality.

The existence of Iago's creed and of his corresponding practice is evidently connected with a characteristic in which he surpasses nearly all the other inhabitants of Shakespeare's world. Whatever he may once have been, he appears, when we meet him, to be almost destitute of humanity, of sympathetic or social feeling. He shows no trace of affection, and in presence of the most terrible suffering he shows either pleasure or an indifference which, if not complete, is nearly so. Here, however, we must be careful. It is important to realise, and few readers are in danger of ignoring, this extraordinary deadness of feeling, but it is also important not to confuse it with a general positive ill-will. When Iago has no dislike or hostility to a person he does *not* show pleasure in the suffering of that person: he shows at most the absence of pain. There is, for instance, not the least sign of his enjoying the distress of Desdemona. But his sympathetic feelings are so abnormally feeble and cold that, when his dislike is roused, or when an indifferent person comes in the way of his purpose, there is scarcely anything within him to prevent his applying the torture. (pp. 217-20)

Iago is keenly sensitive to anything that touches his pride or self-esteem. It would be most unjust to call him vain, but he has a high opinion of himself and a great contempt for others. He is quite aware of his superiority to them in certain respects; and he either disbelieves in or despises the qualities in which they are superior to him. Whatever disturbs or wounds his sense of superiority irritates him at once; and in *that* sense he is highly competitive. This is why the appointment of Cassio provokes him. This is why Cassio's scientific attainments provoke him. This is the reason of his jealousy of Emilia. He does not care for his wife; but the fear of another man's getting the better of him, and exposing him to pity or derision as an unfortunate husband, is wormwood to him; and as he is sure that no woman is virtuous at heart, this fear is ever with him. For much the same reason he has a spite against goodness in men (for it is characteristic that he is less blind to its existence in men, the stronger, than in women, the weaker). He has a spite against it, not from any love of evil for evil's sake, but partly because it annoys his intellect as a stupidity; partly (though he hardly knows this) because it weakens his satisfaction with himself, and disturbs his faith that egoism is the right and proper thing; partly because, the world being such a fool, goodness is popular and prospers. But he, a man ten times as able as Cassio or even Othello, does not greatly prosper. Somehow, for all the stupidity of these open and generous people, they get on better than the 'fellow of some soul.' And this, though he is not particularly eager to get on, wounds his pride. Goodness therefore annoys him. He is always ready to scoff at it, and would like to strike at it. In ordinary circumstances these feelings of irritation are not vivid in Iago—*no* feeling is so—but they are constantly present.

Our task of analysis is not finished; but we are now in a position to consider the rise of Iago's tragedy. Why did he act as we see him acting in the play? What is the answer to that appeal of Othello's:

> Will you, I pray, demand that demi-devil
> Why he hath thus ensnared my soul and body?
>
> [V. ii. 301-02]

This question Why? is *the* question about Iago, just as the question Why did Hamlet delay? is *the* question about Hamlet.

Iago refused to answer it; but I will venture to say that he *could* not have answered it, any more than Hamlet could tell why he delayed. But Shakespeare knew the answer, and if these characters are great creations and not blunders we ought to be able to find it too. (pp. 221-22)

Is the account which Iago gives of the causes of his action the true account? The answer of the most popular view will be, 'Yes. Iago was, as he says, chiefly incited by two things, the desire of advancement, and a hatred of Othello due principally to the affair of the lieutenancy. These are perfectly intelligible causes; we have only to add to them unusual ability and cruelty, and all is explained. Why should Coleridge and Hazlitt and Swinburne go further afield?' To which last question I will at once oppose these: If your view is correct, why should Iago be considered an extraordinary creation; and is it not odd that the people who reject it are the people who elsewhere show an exceptional understanding of Shakespeare?

The difficulty about this popular view is, in the first place, that it attributes to Iago what cannot be found in the Iago of the play. Its Iago is impelled by *passions,* a passion of ambition and a passion of hatred; for no ambition or hatred short of passion could drive a man who is evidently so clear-sighted, and who must hitherto have been so prudent, into a plot so extremely hazardous. Why, then, in the Iago of the play do we find no sign of these passions or of anything approaching to them? Why, if Shakespeare meant that Iago was impelled by them, does he suppress the signs of them? Surely not from want of ability to display them. The poet who painted Macbeth and Shylock understood his business. Who ever doubted Macbeth's ambition or Shylock's hate? And what resemblance is there between these passions and any feeling that we can trace in Iago? The resemblance between a volcano in eruption and a flameless fire of coke; the resemblance between a consuming desire to hack and hew your enemy's flesh, and the resentful wish, only too familiar in common life, to inflict pain in return for a slight. Passion, in Shakespeare's plays, is perfectly easy to recognise. What vestige of it, of passion unsatisfied or of passion gratified, is visible in Iago? None: that is the very horror of him. He has *less* passion than an ordinary man, and yet he does these frightful things. The only ground for attributing to him, I do not say a passionate hatred, but anything deserving the name of hatred at all, is his own statement, 'I hate Othello'; and we know what his statements are worth.

But the popular view, beside attributing to Iago what he does not show, ignores what he does show. It selects from his own account of his motives one or two, and drops the rest; and so it makes everything natural. But it fails to perceive how unnatural, how strange and suspicious, his own account is. Certainly he assigns motives enough; the difficulty is that he assigns so many. A man moved by simple passions due to simple causes does not stand fingering his feelings, industriously enumerating their sources, and groping about for new ones. But this is what Iago does. And this is not all. These motives appear and disappear in the most extraordinary manner. Resentment at Cassio's appointment is expressed in the first conversation with Roderigo, and from that moment is never once mentioned again in the whole play. Hatred of Othello is expressed in the First Act alone. Desire to get Cassio's place scarcely appears after the first soliloquy, and when it is gratified Iago does not refer to it by a single word. The suspicion of Cassio's intrigue with Emilia emerges suddenly, as an afterthought, not in the first soliloquy but the second, and then disappears for ever. Iago's 'love' of Desdemona is alluded to

in the second soliloquy; there is not the faintest trace of it in word or deed either before or after. The mention of jealousy of Othello is followed by declarations that Othello is infatuated about Desdemona and is of a constant nature, and during Othello's sufferings Iago never shows a sign of the idea that he is now paying his rival in his own coin. In the second soliloquy he declares that he quite believes Cassio to be in love with Desdemona. It is obvious that he believes no such thing, for he never alludes to the idea again, and within a few hours describes Cassio in soliloquy as an honest fool. His final reason for ill-will to Cassio never appears till the Fifth Act.

What is the meaning of all this? Unless Shakespeare was out of his mind, it must have a meaning. And certainly this meaning is not contained in any of the popular accounts of Iago.

Is it contained then in Coleridge's word 'motive-hunting'? [see excerpt above, 1808-18]. Yes, 'motive-hunting' exactly answers to the impression that Iago's soliloquies produce. He is pondering his design, and unconsciously trying to justify it to himself. He speaks of one or two real feelings, such as resentment against Othello, and he mentions one or two real causes of these feelings. But these are not enough for him. Along with them, or alone, there come into his head, only to leave it again, ideas and suspicions, the creations of his own baseness or uneasiness, some old, some new, caressed for a moment to feed his purpose and give it a reasonable look, but never really believed in, and never the main forces which are determining his action. In fact, I would venture to describe Iago in these soliloquies as a man setting out on a project which strongly attracts his desire, but at the same time conscious of a resistance to the desire, and unconsciously trying to argue the resistance away by assigning reasons for the project. He is the counterpart of Hamlet, who tries to find reasons for his delay in pursuing a design which excites his aversion. And most of Iago's reasons for action are no more the real ones than Hamlet's reasons for delay were the real ones. Each is moved by forces which he does not understand; and it is probably no accident that these two studies of states psychologically so similar were produced at about the same period.

What then were the real moving forces of Iago's action? Are we to fall back on the idea of a 'motiveless malignity;' that is to say, a disinterested love of evil, or a delight in the pain of others as simple and direct as the delight in one's own pleasure? Surely not. I will not insist that this thing or these things are inconceivable, mere phrases, not ideas; for, even so, it would remain possible that Shakespeare had tried to represent an inconceivability. But there is not the slightest reason to suppose that he did so. Iago's action is intelligible; and indeed the popular view contains enough truth to refute this desperate theory. It greatly exaggerates his desire for advancement, and the ill-will caused by his disappointment, and it ignores other forces more important than these; but it is right in insisting on the presence of this desire and this ill-will, and their presence is enough to destroy Iago's claims to be more than a demi-devil. For love of the evil that advances my interest and hurts a person I dislike, is a very different thing from love of evil simply as evil; and pleasure in the pain of a person disliked or regarded as a competitor is quite distinct from pleasure in the pain of others simply as others. The first is intelligible, and we find it in Iago. The second, even if it were intelligible, we do not find in Iago.

Still, desire of advancement and resentment about the lieutenancy, though factors and indispensable factors in the cause of Iago's action, are neither the principal nor the most characteristic factors. To find these, let us return to our half-completed analysis of the character. Let us remember especially the keen sense of superiority, the contempt of others, the sensitiveness to everything which wounds these feelings, the spite against goodness in men as a thing not only stupid but, both in its nature and by its success, contrary to Iago's nature and irritating to his pride. Let us remember in addition the annoyance of having always to play a part, the consciousness of exceptional but unused ingenuity and address, the enjoyment of action, and the absence of fear. And let us ask what would be the greatest pleasure of such a man, and what the situation which might tempt him to abandon his habitual prudence and pursue this pleasure. Hazlitt and Mr. Swinburne do not put this question, but the answer I proceed to give to it is in principle theirs.

The most delightful thing to such a man would be something that gave an extreme satisfaction to his sense of power and superiority; and if it involved, secondly, the triumphant exertion of his abilities, and, thirdly, the excitement of danger, his delight would be consummated. And the moment most dangerous to such a man would be one when his sense of superiority had met with an affront, so that its habitual craving was reinforced by resentment, while at the same time he saw an opportunity of satisfying it by subjecting to his will the very persons who had affronted it. Now, this is the temptation that comes to Iago. Othello's eminence, Othello's goodness, and his own dependence on Othello, must have been a perpetual annoyance to him. At *any* time he would have enjoyed befooling and tormenting Othello. Under ordinary circumstances he was restrained, chiefly by self-interest, in some slight degree perhaps by the faint pulsations of conscience or humanity. But disappointment at the loss of the lieutenancy supplied the touch of lively resentment that was required to overcome these obstacles; and the prospect of satisfying the sense of power by mastering Othello through an intricate and hazardous intrigue now became irresistible. Iago did not clearly understand what was moving his desire; though he tried to give himself reasons for his action, even those that had some reality made but a small part of the motive force; one may almost say they were no more than the turning of the handle which admits the driving power into the machine. Only once does he appear to see something of the truth. It is when he uses the phrase 'to *plume up my will* in double knavery' [I. iii. 393-94].

To 'plume up the will,' to heighten the sense of power or superiority—this seems to be the unconscious motive of many acts of cruelty which evidently do not spring chiefly from ill-will, and which therefore puzzle and sometimes horrify us most. It is often this that makes a man bully the wife or children of whom he is fond. The boy who torments another boy, as we say, 'for no reason,' or who without any hatred for frogs tortures a frog, is pleased with his victim's pain, not from any disinterested love of evil or pleasure in pain, but mainly because this pain is the unmistakable proof of his own power over his victim. So it is with Iago. His thwarted sense of superiority wants satisfaction. What fuller satisfaction could it find than the consciousness that he is the master of the General who has undervalued him and of the rival who has been preferred to him; that these worthy people, who are so successful and popular and stupid, are mere puppets in his hands, but living puppets, who at the motion of his finger must contort themselves in agony, while all the time they believe that he is their one true friend and comforter? It must have been an ecstasy of bliss to him. And this, granted a most abnormal deadness of human feeling, is, however horrible, perfectly intelligible. (pp. 223-29)

Iago's longing to satisfy the sense of power is, I think, the strongest of the forces that drive him on. But there are two others to be noticed. One is the pleasure in an action very difficult and perilous and, therefore, intensely exciting. This action sets all his powers on the strain. He feels the delight of one who executes successfully a feat thoroughly congenial to his special aptitude, and only just within his compass; and, as he is fearless by nature, the fact that a single slip will cost him his life only increases his pleasure. His exhilaration breaks out in the ghastly words with which he greets the sunrise after the night of the drunken tumult which has led to Cassio's disgrace, 'By the mass, 'tis morning. Pleasure and action make the hours seem short' [II. iii. 378-79]. Here, however, the joy in exciting action is quickened by other feelings. It appears more simply elsewhere in such a way as to suggest that nothing but such actions gave him happiness, and that his happiness was greater if the action was destructive as well as exciting. We find it, for instance, in his gleeful cry to Roderigo, who proposes to shout to Brabantio in order to wake him and tell him of his daughter's flight:

> Do, with like timorous accent and dire yell
> As when, by night and negligence, the fire
> Is spied in populous cities.
>
> [I. i. 75-7]

All through that scene; again, in the scene where Cassio is attacked and Roderigo murdered; everywhere where Iago is in physical action, we catch this sound of almost feverish enjoyment. His blood, usually so cold and slow, is racing through his veins.

But Iago, finally, is not simply a man of action; he is an artist. His action is a plot, the intricate plot of a drama, and in the conception and execution of it he experiences the tension and the joy of artistic creation. 'He is,' says Hazlitt, 'an amateur of tragedy in real life; and, instead of employing his invention on imaginary characters or long-forgotten incidents, he takes the bolder and more dangerous course of getting up his plot at home, casts the principal parts among his nearest friends and connections, and rehearses it in downright earnest, with steady nerves and unabated resolution' [see excerpt above, 1817]. Mr. Swinburne lays even greater stress on this aspect of Iago's character, and even declares that 'the very subtlest and strongest component of his complex nature' is 'the instinct of what Mr. Carlyle would call an inarticulate poet' [see excerpt above, 1880]. (pp. 230-31)

Such, then, seem to be the chief ingredients of the force which, liberated by his resentment at Cassio's promotion, drives Iago from inactivity into action, and sustains him through it. And, to pass to a new point, this force completely possesses him; it is his fate. It is like the passion with which a tragic hero wholly identifies himself, and which bears him on to his doom. It is true that, once embarked on his course, Iago *could* not turn back, even if this passion did abate; and it is also true that he is compelled, by his success in convincing Othello, to advance to conclusions of which at the outset he did not dream. He is thus caught in his own web, and could not liberate himself if he would. But, in fact, he never shows a trace of wishing to do so, not a trace of hesitation, of looking back, or of fear, any more than of remorse; there is no ebb in the tide. As the crisis approaches there passes through his mind a fleeting doubt whether the deaths of Cassio and Roderigo are indispensable; but that uncertainty, which does not concern the main issue, is dismissed, and he goes forward with undiminished zest. Not even in his sleep—as in Richard's before his final battle—does any rebellion of outraged conscience or pity, or any foreboding of despair, force itself into clear consciousness. His fate—which is himself—has completely mastered him: so that, in the later scenes, where the improbability of the entire success of a design built on so many different falsehoods forces itself on the reader, Iago appears for moments not as a consummate schemer, but as a man absolutely infatuated and delivered over to certain destruction. (pp. 231-32)

There remains . . . the idea that Iago is a man of supreme intellect who is at the same time supremely wicked. That he is supremely wicked nobody will doubt; and I have claimed for him nothing that will interfere with his right to that title. But to say that his intellectual power is supreme is to make a great mistake. Within certain limits he has indeed extraordinary penetration, quickness, inventiveness, adaptiveness; but the limits are defined with the hardest of lines, and they are narrow limits. It would scarcely be unjust to call him simply astonishingly clever, or simply a consummate master of intrigue. But compare him with one who may perhaps be roughly called a bad man of supreme intellectual power, Napoleon, and you see how small and negative Iago's mind is, incapable of Napoleon's military achievements, and much more incapable of his political constructions. Or, to keep within the Shakespearean world, compare him with Hamlet, and you perceive how miserably close is his intellectual horizon; that such a thing as a thought beyond the reaches of his soul has never come near him; that he is prosaic through and through, deaf and blind to all but a tiny fragment of the meaning of things. Is it not quite absurd, then, to call him a man of supreme intellect?

And observe, lastly, that his failure in perception is closely connected with his badness. He was destroyed by the power that he attacked, the power of love; and he was destroyed by it because he could not understand it; and he could not understand it because it was not in him. Iago never meant his plot to be so dangerous to himself. He knew that jealousy is painful, but the jealousy of a love like Othello's he could not imagine, and he found himself involved in murders which were no part of his original design. That difficulty he surmounted, and his changed plot still seemed to prosper. Roderigo and Cassio and Desdemona once dead, all will be well. Nay, when he fails to kill Cassio, all may still be well. He will avow that he told Othello of the adultery, and persist that he told the truth, and Cassio will deny it in vain. And then, in a moment, his plot is shattered by a blow from a quarter where he never dreamt of danger. He knows his wife, he thinks. She is not overscrupulous, she will do anything to please him, and she has learnt obedience. But one thing in her he does not know—that she *loves* her mistress and would face a hundred deaths sooner than see her fair fame darkened. There is genuine astonishment in his outburst 'What! Are you mad?' [V. ii. 194] as it dawns upon him that she means to speak the truth about the handkerchief. But he might well have applied to himself the words she flings at Othello,

> O gull! O dolt!
> As ignorant as dirt!
>
> [V. ii. 163-64]

The foulness of his own soul made him so ignorant that he built into the marvellous structure of his plot a piece of crass stupidity.

To the thinking mind the divorce of unusual intellect from goodness is a thing to startle; and Shakespeare clearly felt it so. The combination of unusual intellect with extreme evil is more than startling, it is frightful. It is rare, but it exists; and Shakespeare represented it in Iago. But the alliance of evil like Iago's with *supreme* intellect is an impossible fiction; and Shakespeare's fictions were truth. (pp. 236-37)

> A. C. Bradley, ''Lecture V: 'Othello','' and ''Lecture VI: 'Othello','' in his Shakespearean Tragedy: Lectures on ''Hamlet'', ''Othello'', ''King Lear'', ''Macbeth'', *Macmillan and Co., Limited, 1904, pp. 175-206, 207-42.*

E. K. CHAMBERS   (essay date 1908)

[*Chambers occupies a transitional position in Shakespearean criticism, one which connects the biographical sketches and character analyses of the nineteenth century with the historical, technical, and textual criticism of the twentieth century. While a member of the education department at Oxford University, Chambers earned his reputation as a scholar with his multivolume works,* The Medieval Stage *(1903) and* The Elizabethan Stage *(1923); he also edited* The Red Letter Shakespeare *(1904-08). Chambers investigated both the purpose and limitations of each dramatic genre as Shakespeare presented it and speculated on how the dramatist's work was influenced by contemporary historical issues and his own frame of mind. In the excerpt below, taken from his preface to the Red Letter edition of* Othello *(1908), Chambers diverges from such nineteenth-century critics as Hermann Ulrici (1839), G. G. Gervinus (1849-50), and Denton J. Snider (1887), all of whom maintained that the drama depicts Desdemona and Othello freely electing the conduct which brings about their ruin. He views the lovers in this play as helpless victims, whose lives are controlled by destiny rather than by their natures; he also asserts that, while* King Lear *and* Macbeth *evoke feelings both of awe and pity, in this play there is more of the pathetic than the truly tragic, a point echoed later by Harry Levin (1964). Such other critics as Stopford A. Brooke (1913), Elmer Edgar Stoll (1915), Wyndham Lewis (1927), Allardyce Nicoll (1927), Harry Levin (1964), and Robert G. Hunter (1976) have also addressed the question of free will versus predestination in the play. On other matters, Chambers regards Iago as an inhuman, symbolic representation of evil, patterned after earlier Machiavellian dramatic types. For additional commentary on Iago and his relation to Machiavellianism, see the excerpts by Wyndham Lewis (1927), Allardyce Nicoll (1927), and S. L. Bethell (1952), as well as the essay by Thomas Babington Macaulay cited in the Additional Bibliography. Several critics, including Irving Ribner (1955), Bernard Spivack (1958), and Robert G. Hunter (1976) have further considered the connection between Iago and the traditional villain of medieval drama. Chambers also compares this play with two of Shakespeare's later ones,* Cymbeline *and* The Winter's Tale, *remarking that the despairing conclusion of* Othello *reflects the "perturbed Shakespeare" of this period, while the jubilant ending of* Cymbeline *mirrors the dramatist's "recovered optimism." Stopford A. Brooke (1913) has similarly concluded that* Othello *provides evidence that Shakespeare's psyche was possessed by a dark rage at the time he wrote the play. Finally, Chambers endorses Samuel Taylor Coleridge's belief (see excerpts above, 1813, 1822, and 1827) that* Othello *is not of a jealous nature, contrasting the Moor's characterization with that of Leontes in* The Winter's Tale, *who, Chambers asserts, evinces a type of mean-spirited jealousy that is wholly inimicable to the sympathetic and noble Othello.*]

Of all the great and moving Shakespearean plays, *Othello* is that in which the fullest expression is given to that particular quality of sentiment or emotion, to which belongs the name of pathos. One may perhaps define pathos as tragic pity. It is the welling up of human sympathy at the sight of something beautiful and frail in the grip of forces utterly beyond its own control, at the fate of the windlestraw in the floods. Tragedy, as Aristotle hinted long ago, arises out of the contemplation of the clash of forces and the triumph of the greater force, and its result in the human soul is to awake the feelings of pity and of awe. And pity or awe predominates according to the extent of the disproportion between the strength of the triumphant force and that which is defeated. It is awful when the Titans make head against the Gods, even though the ultimate issue can be in no way doubtful; it is pitiful when the chariot-wheels of destiny roll over and crush a human flower. The one spectacle yields tragedy in the fullest sense; the other pathos. This distinction corresponds closely to that between the effect upon the spectator of *Othello* and the effect of the two other tragedies which, both in time and in temper, stand nearest to it, *Macbeth* and *King Lear*. In *Macbeth* the pathetic hardly finds any expression; in *King Lear* it attaches itself mainly to the subordinate character of the helpless Cordelia, and if to Lear at all, not to him who wrangles with the elements upon the blasted heath, but to the ruined piece of nature who wanders, mad as the vexed sea, and crowned with rank fumitory and furrow weeds, through the acres of the sustaining corn. Lear and the Macbeths are of the race of Titans, and when they go under, the heavens may vaunt themselves to have conquered those who, for a moment at least, were in some sort their equals. About Othello and Desdemona there is nothing of the Titanic. They are noble, of course, and gracious in their lives; otherwise their fate would have altogether lacked that exalted interest which is essential even to pathetic tragedy. But nevertheless, when the push comes, the simple open-hearted soldier and the tender woman who loves him prove to have nothing to oppose to the forces that beset them. They are easy victims, and it is with the sense of springing tears rather than with the thrill of lost battle that we watch them to the hopeless end.

In other respects, the grouping of *Othello* with *Macbeth* and *King Lear* is complete. Already the subtle change has come over Shakespeare's attitude towards the problems of existence whereby cosmic tragedy has replaced the earlier psychological tragedy of *Julius Caesar* and of *Hamlet*. The issue has shifted from the relations of man and man to the relations of man and his creator. The sceptical ironies of the bitter comedies begin to take shape as a definite arraignment of the scheme of things. Failure is presented as a resultant no longer of character but of destiny; and the fall of Othello is not merely the fall of a good man, but the purposed and inevitable defeat of goodness itself. The play is a duel, in which goodness as such is pitted against evil as such, and to represent evil Shakespeare has recourse to the revival of a type of character which finds its analogues in some of his earliest plays and still more in plays not his. In Iago he returns, with a more definite philosophic purpose as well as with a far greater subtlety of delineation, to the model which he had taken from Marlowe's Barabbas [in *The Jew of Malta*] and used, with an imperfect comprehension of its real dramatic significance, in Aaron the Moor and in Richard Crookback [in *Titus Andronicus* and *Richard III*]. Once more, and now to be treated as what he is, a symbol, not as what he is not, a human being, there comes upon the stage the terrible man according to Machiavelli, with his deliberate and self-conscious choice of evil to be his good, and his superhuman resource and efficiency in shaping all events towards the realization of his diabolical end. Iago, playing upon the souls of all the other personages in the drama like puppets, and manipulating them this way and that as the intricacies of his plot for their common destruction require, is obviously enough the efficient cause of the whole tragic working of *Othello*. His essential inhumanity is no less apparent. He has the outward form and members of a man, but his dramatic function

is that of the incarnation of the forces of evil, of the devil himself.

> I look down towards his feet; but that's a fable,
>
> [V. ii. 286]

says the disillusioned Othello, when the whole map of Iago's villainy is suddenly unrolled, an hour too late, before him. Iago is clear enough about himself and his calling—

> Divinity of hell!
> When devils will the blackest sins put on,
> They do suggest at first with heavenly shows,
> As I do now.
>
> [II. iii. 350-53]

In the sinister soliloquies with which, at every pause in the action, he delights to take the stage and let the audience into his secrets, he reveals the clearest intellectual appreciation of the good points, which are for him the weak points, of his opponents; and it is precisely upon these, upon the unquestioning confidence of Othello and upon the generous impulses of Desdemona's translucent soul, that he fastens most securely the web of the intrigue that is to be their ruin. Those Mephistophelean confidences give an added horror to the scenes in which the other personages reappear and Iago composes the sneer upon his countenance to assume once more the profitable *rôle* of the disinterested follower or the sympathetic friend. And so, at the height of his villainy, his unsuspecting victim sings his praises—

> This fellow's of exceeding honesty,
> And knows all qualities, with a learned spirit,
> Of human dealings.
>
> [III. iii. 258-60]

Honest Iago! That virtue should bestow this epithet upon vice is a measure of the defencelessness of virtue in the eternal conflict. It has been doubted whether Shakespeare did not intend to qualify the abstract devilry of Iago by assigning for his hatred of Othello certain motives not altogether inhuman. He represents himself to Roderigo as bearing the grudge of a soldier who has been passed over for one less worthy. It is not perhaps necessary to believe everything he says to Roderigo, although he is elsewhere not too careful to conceal his real self before so inconsiderable a hearer. Roderigo is not a fish that requires much playing. But it is in the more intimate revelation of his soliloquies that he professes a suspicion that the Moor has played him false with Emilia and a desire to be evened with him, wife for wife. It is hardly to be supposed that this suspicion is meant to have any foundation. Othello's behaviour to Emilia certainly lends it no credence, and it is clear that for Iago himself it is an occasion rather than a motive for treachery—

> I know not if it be true;
> But I, for mere suspicion in that kind,
> Will do as if for surety.
>
> [I. iii. 388-90]

What is illustrated is the willingness of evil to be convinced of evil, in contrast to the reluctance with which a similar suspicion is entertained and the profound upheaval which it causes in Othello's noble soul.

The type of Iago fitted in with something profound in Shakespeare's tragical apprehension of the world. It is resumed, not in the main plot but in the sub-plot of *King Lear,* where the melodramatic Edmund has precisely Iago's trick of analysing his own infamy in cynical comment before the audience. And it recurs for the last time, with a significant difference, in the Iachimo of *Cymbeline*. One may almost take *Cymbeline* as the palinode to *Othello*, and the comparison between Iago and Iachimo serves well to measure the gulf that lies between the perturbed Shakespeare of the great tragedies and Shakespeare in the golden mood of recovered optimism which inspires the last romances. . . . The darkness which settles upon *Othello* is lit by no gleam of hope at the close; but the sunshine breaks into the last scene of *Cymbeline*, and it becomes apparent that not only has evil proved impotent to wreck the faith and happiness of Imogen, but also evil has ultimately ceased to be dominant even in the black soul of Iachimo itself. By Imogen the very devil is taught—

> The wide difference
> 'Twixt amorous and villainous.
> [*Cymbeline*, V. v. 194-95]

Othello, no less than Iago, would seem at first sight to be paralleled in the later plays, to some degree by Posthumus [in *Cymbeline*], and to a greater by the Leontes of *The Winter's Tale*. But the resemblance is too superficial a one to bear much analysis. On this there is perhaps little to be added to one of the finest passages in Coleridge's unequal Shakespearean comment.

Act I. Scene iii. Emilia, Desdemona, Iago, Othello, Brabantio, the Duke, Senators, and Officers. By Charles Geofroy. The Department of Rare Books and Special Collections, The University of Michigan Library.

Jealousy does not strike me as the point in Othello's passion; I take it to be rather an agony that the creature, whom he had believed angelic, with whom he had garnered up his heart, and whom he could not help still loving, should be proved impure and worthless. It was the struggle *not* to love her. It was a moral indignation and regret that virtue should so fall:— 'But yet the *pity* of it, Iago!—O Iago! the *pity* of it, Iago!' [see excerpt above, 1822].

Clearly, if Othello had been a Leontes, he would have been unfitted for the part he has to play in the drama. Shakespeare's scheme entails an opposition between black and white, and jealousy in the meaner sense would have lost Othello the sympathies which he is bound to maintain in order that tragic pity may be evoked. By his simplicity he falls, but his nobility of soul must remain unstained. . . . The jealous husbands of *Cymbeline* and *The Winter's Tale* are only instruments of the emotional history; and their own personalities may remain unsympathetic until the time comes when their repentance is needed to contribute to the general reconciliation. But Othello must never be unsympathetic. From the beginning he is a gracious and doomed creature, a child in spirit, walking on the abyss; and the tragic pity slowly gathers as he moves on with honest eyes to the sudden disaster which Iago has prepared. (pp. 218-25)

> E. K. Chambers, "Othello," in his *Shakespeare: A Survey*, 1925. Reprint by Hill and Wang, 1958, pp. 218-25.

BERNARD SHAW   (essay date 1910)

[*Shaw's implicit evaluation of* Othello *in the following excerpt is consistent with that expressed in his review of the drama thirteen years earlier (see excerpt above, 1897). Taken from the program to the 1910 production of* The Dark Lady of the Sonnets, *it is couched in the form of a fanciful sketch, in which a bust of Shakespeare, mounted on a pedestal in the workshop of a costume maker, interrupts a conversation between the costumier and a person dressed as Iago. Shaw represents Shakespeare as declaring that his original intention in the play was to depict Desdemona as an "utterly corrupt" woman and Iago as a loathsome, coarse, "second-rate" villain. But when he altered Desdemona's character, so that she became innocent and engaging rather than corrupt and deceitful, "the change turned the play into a farce." According to Shaw-Shakespeare, if Othello is noble and Desdemona is guiltless, there is no cause for the Moor's jealousy, and thus the dramatic action proceeds on a contrived rather than a natural course. Similarly, Shaw has Shakespeare aver that when he began to portray Iago as a pleasant, humorous fellow, motivated not merely by envy of goodness but imbued with the dramatist's "own divine contempt for the follies of mankind and for himself," he became inconsistent and unnatural. Richard Grant White (1885) and Tucker Brooke (1918) have also commented on the attractive and engaging elements in the character of Iago. As in his earlier essay on the play, it is evident here that Shaw greatly admires the poetic language of* Othello *and judges it to be the supreme dramatic element in the work.*]

It was trying-on day; and the last touches were being given to the costumes for the Shakespear Ball as the wearers faced the looking-glass at the costumiers.

"It's no use," said Iago discontentedly. "I dont look right; and I dont feel right."

"I assure you, sir," said the costumier: "you are a perfect picture."

"I may look a picture," said Iago; "but I dont look the character."

"What character?" said the costumier.

"The character of Iago, of course. *My* character."

"Sir," said the costumier: "shall I tell you a secret that would ruin me if it became known that I betrayed it?"

"Has it anything to do with this dress?"

"It has everything to do with it, sir."

"Then fire away."

"Well, sir, the truth is, we cannot dress Iago in character, because he is not a character."

"Not a character! Iago not a character! Are you mad? Are you drunk? Are you hopelessly illiterate? Are you imbecile? Or are you simply blasphemous?"

"I know it seems presumptuous, sir, after so many great critics have written long chapters analyzing the character of Iago: that profound, complex, enigmatic creation of our greatest dramatic poet. But if you notice, sir, nobody has ever had to write long chapters about *my* character."

"Why on earth should they?"

"Why indeed, sir! No enigma about me. No profundity. If my character was much written about, you would be the first to suspect that I hadnt any."

"If that bust of Shakespear could speak," said Iago, severely, "it would ask to be removed at once to a suitable niche in the façade of the Shakespear Memorial National Theatre, instead of being left here to be insulted."

"Not a bit of it," said the bust of Shakespear. "As a matter of fact, I *can* speak. It is not easy for a bust to speak; but when I hear an honest man rebuked for talking common sense, even the stones would speak. And I am only plaster."

"This is a silly trick," gasped Iago, struggling with the effects of the start the Bard had given him. "You have a phonograph in that bust. You might at least have made it a blank verse phonograph."

"On my honor, sir," protested the pale costumier, all disordered, "not a word has ever passed between me and that bust—I beg pardon, me and Mr Shakespear—before this hour."

"The reason you cannot get the dress and the make-up right is very simple," said the bust. "I made a mess of Iago because villains are such infernally dull and disagreeable people that I never could go through with them. I can stand five minutes of a villain, like Don John in—in—oh, whats its name?—*you* know—that box office play with the comic constable in it [*Much Ado About Nothing*]. But if I had to spread a villain out and make his part a big one, I always ended, in spite of myself, by making him rather a pleasant sort of chap. I used to feel very bad about it. It was all right as long as they were doing reasonably pleasant things; but when it came to making them commit all sorts of murders and tell all sorts of lies and do all sorts of mischief, I felt ashamed. I had no right to do it."

"Surely," said Iago, "you dont call Iago a pleasant sort of chap!"

"One of the most popular characters on the stage," said the bust.

"Me!" said Iago, stupent.

The bust nodded, and immediately fell on the floor on its nose, as the sculptor had not balanced it for nodding.

The costumier rushed forward, and, with many apologies and solicitous expressions of regret, dusted the Bard and replaced him on his pedestal, fortunately unbroken.

"I remember the play you were in," said the bust, quite undisturbed by its misadventure. "I let myself go on the verse: thundering good stuff it was: you could hear the souls of the people crying out in the mere sound of the lines. I didnt bother about the sense—just flung about all the splendid words I could find. Oh, it was noble, I tell you: drums and trumpets; and the Propontick and the Hellespont; and a malignant and a turbaned Turk in Aleppo; and eyes that dropt tears as fast as the Arabian trees their medicinal gum: the most impossible, far-fetched nonsense; but such music! Well, I started that play with two frightful villains, one male and one female."

"Female!" said Iago. "You forget. There is no female villain in Othello."

"I tell you theres no villain at all in it," said the immortal William. "But I started with a female villain."

"Who?" said the costumier.

"Desdemona, of course," replied the Bard. "I had a tremendous notion of a supersubtle and utterly corrupt Venetian lady who was to drive Othello to despair by betraying him. It's all in the first act. But I weakened on it. She turned amiable on my hands, in spite of me. Besides, I saw that it wasnt necessary—that I could get a far more smashing effect by making her quite innocent. I yielded to that temptation: I never could resist an effect. It was a sin against human nature; and I was well paid out; for the change turned the play into a farce."

"A farce!" exclaimed Iago and the costumier simultaneously, unable to believe their ears. "Othello a farce!"

"Nothing else," said the bust dogmatically. "*You* think a farce is a play in which some funny rough-and-tumble makes the people laugh. Thats only your ignorance. What I call a farce is a play in which the misunderstandings are not natural but mechanical. By making Desdemona a decent poor devil of an honest woman, and Othello a really superior sort of man, I took away all natural reason for his jealousy. To make the situation natural I must either have made her a bad woman as I originally intended, or him a jealous, treacherous, selfish man, like Leontes in *The [Winter's] Tale*. But I couldnt belittle Othello in that way; so, like a fool, I belittled him the other way by making him the dupe of a farcical trick with a handkerchief that wouldnt have held water off the stage for five minutes. Thats why the play is no use with a thoughtful audience. It's nothing but wanton mischief and murder. I apologize for it; though, by Jingo! I should like to see any of your modern chaps write anything half so good."

"I always said that Emilia was the real part for the leading lady," said the costumier.

"But you didnt change your mind about me," pleaded Iago.

"Yes I did," said Shakespear. "I started on you with a quite clear notion of drawing the most detestable sort of man I know: a fellow who goes in for being frank and genial, unpretentious and second rate, content to be a satellite of men with more style, but who is loathsomely coarse, and has that stupid sort of selfishness that makes a man incapable of understanding the mischief his dirty tricks may do, or refraining from them if there is the most wretched trifle to be gained by them. But my contempt and loathing for the creature—what was worse, the intense boredom of him—beat me before I got into the second act. The really true and natural things he said were so sickeningly coarse that I couldnt go on fouling my play with them. He began to be clever and witty in spite of me. Then it was all up. It was Richard III over again. I made him a humorous dog. I went further: I gave him my own divine contempt for the follies of mankind and for himself, instead of his own proper infernal envy of man's divinity. That sort of thing was always happening to me. Some plays it improved; but it knocked the bottom out of Othello. (pp. 87-90)

Bernard Shaw, "A Dressing Room Secret," in his Short Stories, Scraps and Shavings, *Dodd, Mead & Company, 1934, pp. 85-93.*

STOPFORD A. BROOKE   (essay date 1913)

[*A noted London ecclesiastic, Brooke was also a literary critic and historian, as well as an eminent lecturer and writer on English poetry. In the following excerpt on* Othello, *he is chiefly concerned with what he regards as the play's improbabilities and the state of Shakespeare's mind at the period of its composition. He includes among the unlikely dramatic events Desdemona's love for a man of another race, the hardened cynicism of the apparently youthful Iago, the lack of clarification in the play of Iago's motives, Emilia's failure to discern her husband's true nature, Othello's complete trust in his ancient, and the affair of the handkerchief. Noting the masterful construction of the play, Brooke asserts that these instances of unreasonableness cannot be ascribed to the dramatist's carelessness or lack of artistry, but instead maintains that they reflect a period in Shakespeare's life when he doubted the existence of "any rational Will, or Justice, or even a fixed Destiny" guiding humanity and the universe itself. Such other critics as Thomas Rymer (1692) and George Steevens (1772) have also discussed the improbable or implausible elements in* Othello, *and E. K. Chambers (1908) has similarly drawn conclusions as to what the play reveals about Shakespeare's own psychological well-being. Also, Elmer Edgar Stoll (1915) has argued that Brooke errs in attributing serious significance to references to fate or destiny in the play, maintaining that these are merely rhetorical devices to intensify the tragic mood.*]

That the history of mankind or our personal life should be subject to mere Chance, without reason, law, or direction, is infinitely less tolerable, and more irritating, than that it should be subjected to Fate, whose decrees and movements are unalterable, and which, being unalterable, imply reason at their back. We may, in the end, bend before Fate, because it moves by Law; but nothing will ever induce us to be otherwise than in angry rebellion against unreasoning Chance. We abhor a universe which is without any law at all; and if, for a moment or a year, we think we are in such a universe, we despise ourselves and our race. That way lies, if it continue, black cynicism or insanity.

Something of such questioning and the temper which arises from it seems to have been in Shakespeare's mind when he wrote *Othello.* The conception of the play, the movement of it, the events in it, the bringing about of the catastrophe, are all apparently in the realm of Chance. There is a shocking unreasonableness about them, which is all the more curious when we consider that the construction of the play, the linking and the sequence of its scenes, is so eminently clear, so closely ordered by the imaginative reason and the logic of passion. This is a wonderful combination.

But I dwell at present on the unreasonableness, the chance-strangeness of what occurs. There is a *prima facie* improbability in Desdemona's love for Othello, even if he were only a brown Moor, much more if he were intended by Shakespeare to be a thick-lipped Negro, as he is called in the play by those who hate him. But even as a Moor, the strangeness, the unreasonableness of her love is great. It is as if Chance were at the back of it. The natural, indeed the rational feeling of the world is against such an affection. And Shakespeare makes every one in the play, except Desdemona, feel how odd it is, how out of the natural way of things. No amount of greatness of mind, of nobility of character, in Othello can entirely—as some think it can—do away with the natural improbability, the physical and racial queerness of her love for the Moor. And I venture to say that this is the first feeling of those who read the play, however they may, in their admiration of Othello's noble nature, persuade themselves afterwards to the contrary.

Then there is Iago. It is odd that a young man of twenty-eight years should be capable of such cool hypocrisy, unreasonable hatred, such luxuriousness of cruelty; should have such advanced experience of evil, such lip-smacking pleasure in plotting it and fulfilling it; should so soon have arrived at the pitilessness of grey-haired inhumanity. It is possible, of course, but it is very improbable; as if a monstrous mind had arrived by chance in the body of a non-commissioned officer. It is all the more improbable that the reasons of his wickedness cannot clearly be discovered by us, nor indeed by himself. Endless discussion has gathered round the question—'Why did Iago torture Othello?' Even when he is proved in the play to have done so, no one can quite understand why. His wife is lost in surprise. Othello cries—

demand that demi-devil.
Why he hath thus ensnar'd my soul and body.
[V. ii. 301-02]

Iago himself cannot tell. Hate is his native air; the desire to torture stings him within. He seeks to explain it; he searches for his motives; 'motive-hunting,' Coleridge calls it [see excerpt above, 1808-18]. He finds this and that motive, but not one of them explains what is in his heart, not one of them is an adequate reason for the devilish pleasure he has in putting Othello on the rack, in egging him on to kill Desdemona. His suspicion that the Moor was intimate with his wife is an invented suspicion. To give it some colour he accuses Cassio of the same sin. His action is outside of probable humanity, even of wicked humanity. It is like that of a soulless devil in a man, that is, of the last improbability. Envy is the most real of his motives, but is in him excited to a height almost incredibly beyond its ordinary nature. Cassius was envious, so was Casca, but they only desired to slay Caesar, not to torture him. All this is the more improbable when we find that every one believes Iago is especially frank, honest, and open; that every one, and especially his chief victim, trusts him to the bone.

I intercalate Emilia as another of the improbabilities. It is surely passing strange that she should have lived with Iago for some years, and never thought any ill of him, or imagined him capable of deceit. She thinks him 'wayward.' Wayward! His wickedness bursts on her like a thunderbolt. Till Othello mentions the handkerchief, she has not the slightest suspicion of the unhonesty or cruelty of the man she has lived with as a wife. Of course, he would have deceived the very elect. Still it is vastly improbable that she should have thought him only wayward, and at times impatient.

The writer who devised all this was in doubt while he wrote that any rational Will, or Justice, or even a fixed Destiny, was at the helm of the Universe; but a general Unreason which one might call Chance, and which made a mere muddle of the course of humanity and of our personal lives.

Then take Othello. When we live with him through the first two Acts, we live with the great and experienced soldier, with a grave and noble character. He has arrived at full middle age, and has won the trust and respect of the most jealous and difficult of governments. All men honour his integrity, his skill in war, his ability in governing men, his self-governance, his temperate nature, a ruler of men who rules himself. He has also seen the world and mixed with many men and events in an adventurous youth, as he relates to Desdemona and to the Signiory of Venice—a man then not liable to give his trust rashly, to act on mere suspicion, without inquiry, to be ignorant of the evil which is in men. Yet this is the vast improbability which Shakespeare creates for him—this is the blind, deaf, unreasonable chance which happens to him. He places his unquestioning trust, to the ignoring of every one else, in a young man of twenty-eight, whom, in spite of interest made for him, he has put in a lower position than his lieutenant, Cassio. It never occurs to him that he may have angered Iago. He entrusts his wife to Iago's charge, he keeps him always by his side, he consults him in the circumstance of the riot; he cashiers Cassio, who has fought with him as a faithful comrade, on the report of Iago; he listens to his first innuendoes against his wife without one symptom of distrust in the man who makes them; he believes even in that foul dream which Iago invents. He attributes to her, on the mere hearsay evidence of Iago, coarse and common lustfulness, revolting appetite. He turns his young wife, in his thoughts, into a common harlot; and his belief in Iago is so unshaken that he slays Desdemona. Nothing, given Othello's character in the first two Acts, can be more improbable.

Then it is amazingly improbable that a grave, experienced, world-worn man like Othello, of so magnanimous a nobility of thought and character, should not have felt the innocence of Desdemona, should have been immediately disturbed into suspicion by Iago's phrase 'I do not like that'—by his 'Indeed'—should, in an hour, at the hints of a raw young man, be tortured into distrust of the woman who had given up all for him, broken with her father, violated the customs of her society, and followed him to the war. It is equally improbable that he should have made no inquiry concerning the handkerchief from Emilia, but believed that Cassio, having received it from Desdemona, gave it carelessly away to his mistress Bianca. The matter of the handkerchief bristles with improbabilities, and Othello—this temperate, grave man—never looks into it, drives his wife by his violence about it into a lie, and takes his only refuge in his hopeless trust in Iago.

The improbability of the whole affair is shocking. It is one more of the mass of improbabilities Shakespeare has chosen to rest his play upon. Yet, I repeat, while he yielded to a mood which thought men were involved in a world of chance, he never ceased to be the artist. There was no chance in his work. What he constructed, he constructed with the finest imaginative logic. Not a trace of want of reason is in the building or conduct of the play. The art-powers in him wrought with complete independence of the mood of his soul; as if they were led by a separate being in him. He combined all these improbabilities with so creative and formative an imagination that the whole play seems eminently probable. We are hurried on so fast from the first suspicion of Othello to his death that we have no time to ask questions, to doubt or debate anything. Our interest is so caught by the artist that we resent even a moment's delay. Still, Shakespeare made the improbabilities, and they are so great that it seems as if at the bottom of his mind he believed that a reasonless Chance prevailed in this world. (pp. 171-75)

Stopford A. Brooke, "'Othello'," in his Ten More Plays of Shakespeare, *Constable and Company Ltd., 1913, pp. 165-96.*

ELMER EDGAR STOLL   (essay date 1915)

[*Stoll was one of the earliest critics to attack the method of character analysis that had dominated nineteenth-century Shakespearean criticism. Instead, he maintained that Shakespeare was primarily a man of the professional theater and that his works had to be interpreted in the light of Elizabethan stage conventions and understood for their theatrical effects, rather than their psychological insight. Stoll has in turn been criticized for seeing only one dimension of Shakespeare's art. In the following excerpt on* Othello, *Stoll delineates the resemblances between the Moor and the stage convention of "the blameless hero" used by many of Shakespeare's contemporaries, as well as by subsequent dramatists. According to the critic, in this dramatic tradition the protagonist is depicted as an inherently unsuspicious, intelligent, and noble man, who, through the "slander and 'diabolical soliciting'" of an extraordinarily clever villain, is duped into violent and brutal behavior; however, the hero is traditionally shown as recovering his original nature before the conclusion of the drama. Stoll maintains that Shakespeare's use of the convention in this play is flawed by the precipitous alteration in Othello's behavior in Act III, Scene iii, for the change is so wrenchingly abrupt as to force upon the audience the conclusion that the Moor must be predisposed to jealousy or, worse, that he is an extremely gullible fool. Despite Shakespeare's mishandling of the convention, Stoll asserts, it is still the most legitimate way of explaining Othello's sudden jealousy, and it is in this regard that he disputes the so-called psychological interpretation of the Moor's change in temperament proposed by such critics as Samuel Taylor Coleridge (1813, 1822, and 1827) and A. C. Bradley (1904). Additionally, Stoll disputes Bradley's assessment that the death of Desdemona should be viewed as a sacrifice rather than murder, arguing instead that Othello's insistent demands for "blood" in the temptation scene arise from a more venal motive than the violation of his "faith and idealism." Stoll also challenges Stopford A. Brooke's explanation of the implausibilities in the play (see excerpt above, 1913), maintaining that the few references in* Othello *to what Brooke calls fate or accident are merely rhetorical devices to heighten the tragic atmosphere. Finally, the critic claims that, despite the "sudden conversions and lapses" in Othello's behavior, Shakespeare has provided him with a consistent "tone" throughout the drama by virtue of the powerful and noble music of his poetic language. Stoll's assessment of the Moor's poetic speeches as a significant element in his characterization may be compared with G. Wilson Knight's later analysis of "the Othello music" (see excerpt below, 1930), and with the excerpts by Derek Traversi (1949), John Bayley (1960), Gayle Greene (1979), and Carol McGinnis Kay (1983). For direct responses to Stoll's commentary on* Othello, *see the excerpts by F. R. Leavis (1937), Brents Stirling (1944), and J. I. M. Stewart (1949).*]

I hope that the reader will bear with me while so familiar a figure as Othello is, at such length, discussed once again. Hitherto he has hardly been studied in the light of Comparative Literature; hitherto he has hardly been studied even as a bit of Elizabethan art. But the problems of one play are, in varying degrees, those of other plays like it, whether Shakespearean or merely Elizabethan, whether modern or ancient; and art, not life, furnishes the clearer and more pertinent comment on art, problems the only solution to problems. Chief among these in the play before us are certain relations of character to plot, and the measure of the dramatist's concern for the consistency of his characters, and of his interest, conscious or instinctive, in what is nowadays called psychology. (p. 1)

[Othello claims that he] is "not easily jealous," [V. ii. 345], not jealous by nature, and yet, within a single scene, he becomes jealous terribly, irrecoverably, as no man ever was. Indeed . . . , the character is inconsistent not at this point only but throughout.

> The Moor is of a free and open nature,
> That thinks men honest that but seem to be so;
>   [I. iii. 399-400]

yet in trusting his cynical subaltern, who has not been on terms of friendship with him, he thereby distrusts his dearest friend and his newly wedded wife. He is one, says Lodovico, "whom passion could not shake"—"Can he be angry?" [IV. i. 266; III. iv. 134] asks even Iago in wonder,—and up to the moment of Cassio's disgrace, in fact, one might say up to the moment of temptation, never was there, in trying circumstances, anyone so serene, disengaged, and dignified as he; yet, at a man's word, he falls a prey to the wildest and grossest of passions. . . . He is a general of renown, "the noble Moor whom our full Senate call all in all sufficient" [IV. i. 264-65], and in Venice, even in the opinion of his unadmiring Ancient, "another of his fathom they have none to lead their business" [I. i. 152-53], his mind being no less ample than his heart; yet so tamely, so precipitately—without judgment, consideration of evidence, or perception of character, whether Iago's, Cassio's, or his wife's— does he succumb to covert suggestion and open slander and every stratagem brought to bear. . . . (pp. 1-2)

What is to be made, we ask ourselves, of this great heap of contradictions? Critics have been stumbling at them, more or less unconsciously ever since the days of Rymer [see excerpt above, 1692]. . . . (p. 3)

Accustomed to modern methods of dramatic art, which involve analysis and psychology, the critics, naturally enough, cannot conceive of a man so readily becoming suspicious and violently passionate and sensual, stupid or bereft of dignity, without being such at bottom from the first. Especially has this been the case with the Germans. With Schlegel, they have taken the Moor's dignity and virtue for the crust of discipline and Venetian culture, through which might break, at any moment, the red lava of sexual passion and barbarism [see excerpt above, 1811], or, with Gervinus [and] Ulrici . . . , have thought that his later passions were within him, though in the germ [see excerpts above, 1839 and 1849-50]. . . . What in Anglo-Saxon countries at least may be called the orthodox theory, however, is that in the first act and up to the temptation scene Shakespeare had fashioned a free and perfect soul, with no weakness but his trustfulness (if a weakness that be), and that he fell only by that and by Iago's guile. Such is the theory of Coleridge,— "a conviction forced upon him by the superhuman art of Iago, such a conviction as any man would and must have entertained who had believed Iago's honesty as Othello did" [see excerpt above, 1813]. . . . So far as Othello is concerned this might be the case if it were merely a struggle in which goodness is attacked by evil—if the Moor were not a great self-respecting personality instead of a subject for hypnosis—if the virtue (or weakness) of trustfulness, as well as his love, did not require *a fortiori* that he should trust his wife and friend at least as well as a stranger—if all his virtues, his intelligence, and the

dignity of his character and position did not require that he should brush aside Iago's legerdemain of innuendo and mystery-mongering at a stroke, instead of being held fascinated from the beginning as is a bird or a monkey by a serpent. Their psychology simply pushes back the paradox a degree, instead of abolishing it; their psychology presumes that innocence inclines to a belief in guilt, rather than to a belief in innocence, and that the most trustful man is most capable of distrust. If there is any psychology in the play, this, to be sure, it must be; but I cannot see that there is any more than in the dictum of Iago, which takes it all for granted—

> The Moor is of a free and open nature
> That thinks men honest that but seem to be so—

and summarily, theatrically lifts and floats us over contradiction and paradox as over a rock in the river. Here is a working formula, a postulate or fundamental premise, which then did not demand or provoke investigation; and more than that the dramatist did not contemplate or require.

It is profitable to turn from the theories of critics, however, to the practice of playwrights. In *Much Ado* [*About Nothing*], as in *Cymbeline*, in Greene's *Orlando Furioso* as in Beaumont and Fletcher's *Philaster* or even Dryden's *Conquest of Granada*, the blameless hero, like Othello, blamably, unpsychologically believes whatever the slanderer (and the poet) would have him believe. All his intelligence and his nobility of soul, all his knowledge of his beloved's character and ignorance of the slanderer's, avail him nothing. . . . So, in a single scene, without giving his wife or his friend a hearing, Othello is led to the point of wishing to "tear her all to pieces," shouting "blood, blood, blood" [III. iii. 431, 451], and vowing, in company with Iago, the death of both; and though later he questions Desdemona and her woman, he is, like Philaster and Dolce's Herod [in *Marianna*], blind, deaf, and obdurate. And the passion of the heroes . . . is, while it runs its course, made as violent and brutal as it is abrupt and unreasonable, and abounds in sensual imaginings and in outcries against woman and wedded life. But out of this obscuration and eclipse the hero's old self, like Othello's, ultimately emerges. Well before the play is over he comes to his senses again; and he has been made noble that he may be lovable, and his jealousy is not spontaneous, not born and bred within. Through an arbitrary but immemorial convention, it is instilled into his soul by a villain's wiles.

With or without sexual jealousy, the convention of the calumniator credited is one of the oldest traditions of the drama. It reappears in Shakespeare's next play, *King Lear,* when Gloster, quite without reason, implicitly takes the word of the bastard (who repeats some of Iago's tricks) though it blackens his better known and equally beloved son. Here and elsewhere, without either proof demanded or a hearing given, the noble, intelligent father, lover, or king straightway contrives or compasses the death of the accused. (pp. 3-6)

Of slander bringing about jealousy there is found a more modern form in such plays as Voltaire's *Zaïre* and Schiller's *Kabale und Liebe,* where the villain's function in bringing about the catastrophe is encroached upon or supplanted by the use of evidence worthier the name—by an external obstacle like the oath sealing the lips of the accused, or by conduct even more imprudent than Desdemona's own. But even here, as in any other form of the convention (whether with jealousy or without) there is not lacking the presumption that lovers, husbands and wives, fathers and sons, have no confidence in one another and next to no acquaintance. (p. 7)

Whether in the older or the newer form, the tradition is even yet not extinct, but (however little that may mean to Shakespeare critics) it is now hopelessly discredited. . . . At the least, the character, who assumes and suspects must now have the disposition rooted within him. How thoroughly external and unpsychological a device it is in Shakespeare appears most clearly, perhaps, in the case of Gloster in *King Lear* and Leonato in *Much Ado,* who have of course no motive such as has been urged, though without reason, in Othello's defense—lack of acquaintance or a pre-disposition to jealousy—but have been fond and indulgent fathers. (pp. 8-9)

Many critics . . . have followed Coleridge in denying that [Othello's] passion is jealousy; others . . . have contended that it is nothing else. Still others take the jealousy for granted. . . . To deny that he is jealous in the end (whatever he was at first) is . . . mere word-splitting. Coleridge's difficulty lay, however, not in the word or in the passion as here we have it, but, without his being aware, in the convention, which, amid his philosophical prepossessions, he could not comprehend. He insists on the "predisposition to suspicion" (which in Othello, he rightly declares, is wanting) as essential and yet does not see that, in the temptation scene and after, he is an altered, a different man suspicious as a Turk. (pp. 9-10)

[All] that Coleridge's distinctions come to is, that Othello, as he himself says, is "not *easily* jealous" [V. ii. 345], and that he is not, in the freaks of his fancy, a vulgar cuckold. Indeed, it is possible that once when he asks for the handkerchief, he, too, shows, like Posthumus and Leontes [in *Cymbeline* and *The Winter's Tale*], something of the comic figure's spasmodic and frantic utterance, comic though he is not. . . . Even by the standard of other plays, then, Othello is jealous, and so he is called throughout the seventeenth century . . . ; and before the undramatic, untheatrical Coleridge, so far as I am aware, no one ever dreamed of his being anything else. Still more decisive proof lies in the explicit utterances of the hero and the other characters. On the subject of their own passions Shakespeare's characters are excellently informed. But it is Othello's last words—

> one not easily jealous, but, being wrought,
> Perplex'd in the extreme—
>
> [V. ii. 345-46]

that we must take, not his rash, classically presumptuous words at the beginning:

> Why, why is this?
> Think'st thou I'd make a life of jealousy,
> To follow still the changes of the moon
> With fresh suspicions? . . .
> . . . No, Iago;
> I'll see before I doubt, when I doubt, prove;
> And on the proof, there is no more but this,—
> Away at once with love or jealousy.
>
> [III. iii. 176-79, 189-92]

For presently (if not already), before this same scene is over, both by thought and by deed he gives himself the lie. (pp. 11-12)

[This] does not mean that we deny to Othello's passion that nobler and loftier aspect, first discerned by Coleridge, and best described, perhaps, by Mr. Bradley, who, at the same time, does not fail to recognize the jealousy at the bottom. Our hero grieves at "the wreck of his faith and his love" [see excerpt above, 1904], at the ravage and havoc there has been

> there where I have garner'd up my heart,
> Where either I must live, or bear no life.
>
> [IV. ii. 57-8]

But this thought, like Othello's later notion, worthy of a Spaniard—or of an Englishman, an Englishman declares,—that the murder is done in a holy cause, and that she must die else she'll betray more men, is not the moving force in the play, is not even, as Mr. Bradley thinks, "the chief or the deepest source of Othello's suffering." A shock to one's faith or idealism is hardly the thing to make one cry out for "blood," thrice over, or to drive one straight to thoughts of mutilation and murder. (pp. 13-14)

Othello is, then, jealous—Iago's words, later to be considered, if no others, would settle that,—but is it possible to take it that in the matter of the "predisposition" Desdemona, Iago, Lodovico, and Othello himself, are wrong? If Othello alone had spoken to this intent, and only at the beginning, that might be; but, in accordance with the old superstition, in Shakespeare and the Elizabethan drama generally, the man (not a villain) who is about to pay the debt to nature, speaks by the card. Not that it is a matter of superstition mainly: it is rather a matter of technique. In general we must believe the last words in the tragedy concerning the characters in question, whether spoken by the hero himself, or by Fortinbras [in *Hamlet*], or by Antony concerning Brutus [in *Julius Caesar*], remembering that they in some measure take the place of the final choral comment in Greek tragedies or in such Elizabethan ones as *Faustus*. There is no place, to my knowledge, in all Elizabethan tragedy where a hero's final judgment on himself is inexact, still less a judgment ratified by the other principal characters of the play. Besides, the facts are for us: "free and open" Othello is, up to the temptation scene. Not a trace of suspicion, jealousy, or "uneasiness" is to be found in him. . . . (pp. 14-15)

Certainly no one but a philosopher, no playwright, no audience, no Elizabethan scholar, even, who is not bent and intent upon making his point, can find in Othello, untempted, traces of "uneasiness" of "anxiety," "tormenting thoughts," misgivings, or "unsatisfied love." The foreboding of his rapture is the regular thing in Elizabethan tragedy, and no more means anxiety as to the permanence of their love than does Juliet's in the garden. All the inwardness of it amounts to no more than the ingrained superstitious notion of men that good things cannot last. But a particle of truth these more logical psychologists—these more illogical critics—really have. Once Iago begins to ply his arts, Othello has now, though not before, if not the predisposition, at least the disposition, the inclination, call it what you will. (p. 16)

In truth, he now is uneasy, anxious, jealous—but he is now a different man. Simply reason and the constitution of our minds demand that so we should take it if Othello is really to be a man at all. *Natura non facit saltum* [there are no gaps in Nature] or at least the Nature that we know. Iago does his thinking for him. Iago puts jealousy upon him, and that our human, hardheaded imaginations cannot conceive or compass, save on the supposition that (though of a sudden) the jealous disposition is already within him, and judgment fled to brutish beasts. In a moment he

> whose solid virtue
> The shot of accident nor dart of chance
> Could neither graze nor pierce,
>
> [IV. i. 266-68]

cries,

> By heaven, he echoes me,
> As if there were some monster in his thought,
> > [III. iii. 106-07]

and is "frighted" and "moved" by a pow-wow of mystery and the bare names of jealousy and cuckoldom. In a moment he is hanging upon the Ancient's lips, his eyes fixed on the baleful mesmeric orbs, on the waving wizard hands, and to every suggestion he responds with little better than a groan or a sob.

But of suggestion or hypnotism Shakespeare knew not a thing, nor does he intend to intimate that Othello is in himself now different at all. The dramatist but leans on the convention of slander and "*diabolical* soliciting"—on the unapparent paradox of the "free and open" nature turning to suspicion.... These premises given, and by the formula of Elizabethan dramaturgy almost anything may follow. Only, in order to expedite matters, Shakespeare leans hard, and Othello presents little or no resistance to temptation, is eager, excited, is, for all his protestations of faith, won over in a trice.... Though Shakespeare, then, in his absorption in the immediate situation and his disregard for possible inferences or for mere psychological processes, did not so intend it, Othello, becoming jealous, brutal, sensual, so speedily—not to say eagerly—cannot, for all the tempting he undergoes, but seem to us as wrenched and altered at that moment, or else jealous, brutal, sensual, deep down in his heart before. (pp. 16-18)

On the strength of the convention, to be sure—that arbitrary but traditional fundamental premise—Iago is quite equal to carrying it off; but on the plain basis of human nature, or of psychology, the feints and insinuations of "that demi-devil" [V. ii. 301] or the devil himself (for at bottom the convention or superstition is nearly the same) would have been wasted, had Othello not been Iago's already and been delivered into his hands. He harkens unto Iago, Iago's counsel seems good in his eyes. Yet, if we know ourselves, the entrenchments of character and personality are not all so lightly leaped over, and the simplest body could long have baffled a more cunning fiend. If Iago's treachery was unthinkable, "unimaginable," Othello might at least have thought—by the Ancient himself it is suggested—that his prying, jealous disposition had been mistaken. (p. 20)

It is only upon the presumption, then, that Othello is not a personality, not a psychological entity—unless, indeed, a sadly gullible, jealous one—but a *tabula rasa,* or, changing the figure, clay in the potter's hands, that Iago's arts may prosper and prevail. But these, though extraordinary, are ... far from super-human, are by no means without defect. Particularly is this the case in the first two hundred and fifty lines of the temptation scene, where the villain produces even no such "proof" as (after Othello's return) the dream or the handkerchief, but merely raises a cloud of suspicion about Desdemona and Cassio as he "steals" away.... [Why] should he not steal away, being degraded and disgraced? His friend Othello—he might be "stupid" and still do it—should think of this at once, and should suspect—he might be generous and still do it—the generosity of Iago. And Desdemona's prompt and frank petition on his behalf ought of itself to make clear for what he had come. How questionable, moreover, are the aspersions now cast upon Othello's dearest friend's honor and the part he bore in Othello's courtship, proceeding out of the mouth of the man who had just supplanted him in the lieutenancy—

whose testimony had been the cause of his supplanting! Then on the heels of that come the echoes, "shrugs," feints, and dodges, the charges which he makes and unmakes, the hints and secrets which he whisks under his general's nose and sticks in his pocket, the sibylline allusions to cuckoldom and admonitions against jealous rage. Wonderfully clever in itself it all is, ... but from the merely human, the "psychological," standpoint how utterly misplaced! Again is implied (as unhappily is the case) that Othello had already signed his soul away. For to a man in his senses, let alone a famous general and viceroy, nothing could appear more presumptuous or impertinent. Who has constituted Iago, from the very outset, guardian of Othello's mind and keeper of his conscience? Nor could any conduct seem more unbefitting for a really "honest" friend. He is continually trying to cover up his tracks, he is every moment ready to retreat. An honest man who undertakes to tell you that your wife and your dearest friend have played you false makes a clean breast of it, I suppose, without flourish or ado. He does not twist and turn, tease and tantalize, furtively cast forth the slime of slander and ostentatiously lick it up again. Nor when you ask him what he is driving at does he purse his lips, pat you on the shoulder, and say: It were not for your quiet nor your good. Never mind me: I am an uncleanly prying devil! Good name is to be kept at all hazards, and jealousy is the green-eyed monster which doth mock the meat on which it feeds. Good heaven, the souls of all my tribe defend from jealousy! At best a tale-bearer's business is but a questionable one, but it is all the more questionable and suspicious when he has nothing of a tale to tell.

And instead of following him with bated breath and all agape with fear or crying, "By Heaven, he echoes me"—"Ha!"—"O misery!" a man not quite out of his senses might well have taken our Ancient ... simply for the double-dealing viper that he is. Rather, he should have struck him, as at Aleppo once he did the turban'd Turk. Can he better brook the "traducing" of his wife and friend than of Venice? Indeed, the nearest Iago at this first session approaches to proof is but to insult his general beyond all bounds. "She did deceive her father," or, as we innocently say, eloped, and not with one "of her own clime, complexion, and degree," but—

> Foh! one may smell in such a will most rank,
> Foul disproportions, thoughts unnatural—
> > [II. iii. 20, 230, 232-33]

with a Moor! The most pigeon-livered, chicken-hearted creature in the world, we must think, would not have put up with the like of this; and it is doing Shakespeare and his Iago little honor to maintain either that arts such as these are "superhuman," or that the Othello of the Council-chamber has not now vanished from our view. (pp. 21-2)

The unplausibleness of all this manoeuvring of Iago's is abated only as we fall back upon the convention and fundamental premise. Psychologically, Iago's toils are, now or afterward, not at all so ineluctable as Coleridge, Schlegel, Ulrici, Hudson, and the rest of the orthodox think; and possibly Shakespeare himself would have been as much surprised as we at their taking it that any man in Othello's position would have been like him enmeshed. What Othello calls proof (but Iago himself "trifles light as air" [III. iii. 322]) comes later; and all that Iago is now doing is, without proof or evidence, as it were by a spell or mesmeric manipulation, to get the man under control, to make the man his own. Othello is changed and jealous, we have seen, at the moment of temptation; but—according to the orthodox criticism as a psychological fact, according to Shakespeare himself, I think, as but a fact in the story—it is Iago himself that changes him. The readiness with which he yields to the process must simply be granted the poet. As we have traced this, it consists in injecting the "medicine," the "poison," as Iago calls it, and then letting it "work," and turn into "proof" evidence however trivial. . . . Iago's own words make his method clear—to "put the Moor into a jealousy so strong that judgment cannot cure" [II. i. 300-02], and then, merely suggesting, never convincing, let passion run its course. And this he does as if the Moor were an hypnotic subject or a brainless beast, by repeating the words "good name," "jealousy," and "cuckold," almost as if he were crying "sick 'im" to a dog. No man not jealous by nature was ever thus put into a jealousy without process of proof or show of reason; no man's soul ever thus lay in the hollow of another's hand. (pp. 23-4)

In Act IV Iago resumes his play on the imagination, ironically calling up visions of kissing, being naked in bed together, and things more bestial still, before his ensanguined eyes. Then comes the swoon, and then the overhearing of Cassio. By this time, to be sure, the maddened mind of the Moor is quite ready to be imposed upon, but still the grossness of the imposition is almost beyond belief. If the possession of a lady's handkerchief is proof of adultery with her, how preposterous that Cassio, now pleading for his favor, should be wiping his beard with it in public or unconcernedly producing it before Iago or his drab! And only less preposterous is Othello's mistaking of Cassio's report of the "customer" Bianca's haunting him and publicly falling him about the neck, for a report concerning the daughter of the Magnifico, gentle Desdemona. (pp. 25-6)

"Blindness," "stupidity," inevitable "conviction"—mere convention is all that I can make of it, or else . . . unplausibility, improbability in the arrangement of the play. There is not a tragedy of intrigue and slander in the world without similar defects, and the hero is not "blinded" but sees only what for the purposes of a tragic plot the poet vouchsafes him to see. A pretty trick of the apologist it is to turn all these inconsequences in the action into traits of the hero as a man! Masterpieces, at that rate, would be thick as blackberries and every scribbler no less than a "bard." At bottom it is the same confusion of art and life as in Mr. [Stopford A.] Brooke's and Professor Bradley's and others' transformation into Fate or Chance of all the coincidences which fill up for Iago the gaps in his intrigue. (pp. 26-7)

One would think the stage were Cyprus itself, and Iago not a bundle of words in verse and prose but flesh, blood, and bone. By the standards of art, by the limitations or opportunities with which he was confronted, our dramatist must be judged like any other mortal artist, and not be given a patent to offend. But by dint of mere assertion Mr. Brooke, Mr. Bradley and others turn all these defects into virtues, as if he were not so much an artist as the supreme Artificer, and whatever is were right or so must be. (p. 28)

Justly enough, Mr. Brooke dwells upon the "blind unreasonable chance" [see excerpt above, 1913] and improbability in Othello's, Emilia's, and everybody else's ignorance of the monster's character, in a wise and cautious general's so stupidly succumbing to him, in his failure to feel Desdemona's innocence intuitively, to make inquiry concerning the handkerchief, or to discredit the notion that Cassio would give away the token to his drab. But all this "shocking unreasonableness," shows, he says, "the power of baleful Chance in the world, not chance in [the poet's] work. . . . He combined all the improbabilities with so creative and formative an imagi-

nation that the whole play seems eminently probable. We are hurried on so fast from the first suspicion of Othello to his death that we have no time to ask questions, to doubt or debate anything."

Quite the same may be said of many a melodrama that gets short shrift from the critics today, and would get shorter from Mr. Brooke, I judge. But what double-tongued, damning praise! He combined and hurried over all the improbabilities! These are defects, then, these bits of philosophy, glimpses into a "distracted world-order," revelations of a "belief in chance as at the root of the universe," which make the mood of the drama as a whole—and these it is a merit in the poet, after damaging the play by introducing them, to hurry over and conceal! Certainly Mr. Brooke confuses "chance in the world" and "chance in his work" if Shakespeare does not, though with each other these two things have nothing to do. It is but the familiar, traditional error of the craft. In a play which shows Chance at the root of the Universe motivation is surely as needful as in a play which shows Necessity. The play must not be a chaos if the world is; the fortuitous must be represented with an art wherein there is nothing fortuitous; and sensible people must not fail, if need be, to remember their handkerchiefs, to use their wits, and to pick up some little knowledge of one another. The want of this in the play indicates, if anything, not Chance in the universe, but an over-ruling Providence in the poet! (pp. 28-9)

The Shakespearean's Fate is robbed of much of its tragic gravity, however, when we see how readily it puts in an appearance to help the poet out. Things fine and precious are difficult, and how much more difficult it would have been to furnish Iago with evidence more credible, and an intrigue independent of Chance, fit to inveigle an Othello who trusts his wife and friend as well as his officer, and has not discontinued the use of his wits! Why have an Othello that only by a *deus ex machina* can escape being called a fool, even by the poet's worshippers? It is a device that the poet himself would have been first and foremost to disdain. In this play the references to Fate are only two, and, as in most of the poet's plays, such references are momentary and casual. In no play, perhaps, is Fate by him presented as the active agent, but curse and prophecy alike are fulfilled, through human motives, by the free and willing act of man, though often recognized as a miraculous fulfillment afterward. Brabantio's final warning, Othello's foreboding on the quay, and his outcry "Who can control his fate?" [V. ii. 265] in the bedchamber, are hardly more than bits of constructive and rhetorical furniture, imitated, indirectly, from the classics, and designed to focus interest and lend tragic state and emphasis. Utterances of the moment, they do not strike to the centre; but even if they did, it is the poet's own art and effort, not his artlessness, that must make Fate's hand appear. (p. 30)

[Shakespeare] was, when all is said, a dramatist, and the rift which we have found in Othello's character should not too much amaze us. (pp. 50-1)

Sudden conversions and lapses are only the most unplausible part of a system common in Elizabethan plays, least unplausibly carried out in *Othello*, most brilliantly and speciously in Beaumont and Fletcher, whereby the chief characters, before all is said and done, run the whole gamut of emotions. In the last scene, for instance, from the death of Desdemona to the moment when Othello is himself again—

I am not valiant neither—

[V. ii. 243]

there are hardly two or three speeches together in the same key, but his mood changes from solemn pity to wild grief or desperate regret, to anger when provoked by Emilia, to incoherent mourning when again he remembers his loss, then to mournful self-justification, then to the wrath of revenge.

A like range of emotion is to be found elsewhere in the play. It is a great stroke of theatrical art, no doubt, whereby his solemn nobler self is summoned up before us at the beginning of the murder scene, to plunge once more into jealous rage; but the last we had seen of him, a few minutes before, he was raging at his worst. Since, however, it was in the interval that the change took place, it does not trouble us, as does the question how in the scene where, at the beginning and the end, he plays visitor at a brothel, he could manage to soar up to the ideal heights from which he laments the "wreck of his faith and love." A moment before he had what Desdemona calls a "horrible fancy" and "fury in his words" [IV. ii. 26, 32], and now he gives voice to the anguish of his heart in the noble lines "Had it pleased Heaven" [V. ii. 47ff.] and the rest. Not that we ignore the difference between a play and a novel, or fail to remember that in the three hours' traffic of the stage there has always been, because of the need both of condensation and of stage effect, a far wider range of emotion than is probable in life. But in three centuries of approach to realism, or rather in three centuries of finer thinking and of search for a finer mode of expression to suit, that range has been narrowed, the boldness of modulation, or acuteness of contrast, has been subdued. And now dramatists preserve the mood and tone of a scene, just as they preserve, more scrupulously, the integrity of the character; and we must look to the "well-made" but tricky play of thirty or forty years ago for the same prestidigitation and kaleidoscopic change as here. Authors, like actors, then "made points," as the authors of the more popular stage do still, instead of presenting a character, from first to last. (pp. 57-8)

In the first act not a line of Othello's but is, as they say, "in tone," in harmony with

Keep up your bright swords or the dew will rust them,—

[I. ii. 59]

whether he is speaking to Iago alone, or to Cassio as he comes "with lights, officers, and torches" [s. d. I. ii. 28], or to Brabantio, or later, in immortal oratory, to the Senate. Passion cannot shake him, or the dart of chance pierce him, and a light word and a smile are on the lips of the god. Of character he has no end—without much more psychology than there is in a painting of Titian's or a dramatic melody of Mozart's. Character appears in the notions expressed only as in the lineaments drawn,—in image, diction, rhythm, as in lines or colors or musical tones, without analysis or any concernment with mental processes or subtleties in themselves. The mental processes are simple and on the surface; the thoughts themselves are no discovery and revelation of truth; and all we can say is, that, under the master's touch, word and figure, not unlike clay or color, take form and start up into life.

And in the second act and the third, though the splendor of the apparition is now somewhat abated, he is the same, except for his hasty anger with Cassio, until the hour of his ordeal is come. His foreboding on the quay is such a foreboding as he might have had, if really he were to have one at all, and his courtesy and dignity continue to be unfailing. But at Iago's first questions, we have seen, his self-sufficiency collapses, at once he is excited, and then adieu Othello! indeed. Not that

the poet is now less than a poet, or spoils the tone and harmony of the figure as he does its mental consistency or psychology. If Othello, for such cause, could really rage, no doubt he would do it in this big and imaginative vein. Poetically he is still identical—"the Pontic Sea," "the error of the moon which comes more nearer earth than she was wont and makes men mad," "aspics' tongues," and the sibyl in her prophetic fury, are not ill in keeping with "these nine moons wasted" and "antres vast and deserts idle" [III. iii. 453; V. ii. 109-11; III. iii. 450; I. iii. 84, 140]. And again and again in the midst of his sensual passion there are touches which recall his earlier self:

Nor from my own weak merits will I draw
The smallest fear or doubt of her revolt;
For she had eyes and chose me. . . .

No, not much moved,—
I do not think but Desdemona's honest. . . .

But there where I have garnered up my heart,
Where either I must live or bear no life . .

O thou weed,
Who art so lovely fair and smell'st so sweet
That the sense aches at thee, would thou had'st ne'er
been born.
[III. iii. 187-89, 224-25; IV. ii. 57-8, 67-9]

Others are, when Desdemona first appears after Iago has tampered with his peace, and when Othello, light in hand, soliloquizes above her bed.

The change, when the old Othello comes back with all his dignity upon his head, though as yet without his calm, is at the moment when he says:

Nay, stare not, masters; it is true indeed . .
[V. ii. 188]

and after that he does not leave us. But it is with line 243—

I am not valiant, neither,
But every puny whipster gets my sword.
But why should honour outlive honesty?
Let it go all. . . .
[V. ii. 243-46]

that begins the solemn, poignant musical movement with which the tragedy sweeps to a close. Emilia speaks her dying words, and thereupon this theme—the sword-motive Wagnerians might call it—appears again.

I have another weapon in this chamber;
It was a sword of Spain, the icebrook's temper—
O, here it is. Uncle, I must come forth.
[V. ii. 252-54]

After an interval of challenging and parleying the motive appears once more—

Behold I have a weapon;
A better never did itself sustain
Upon a soldier's thigh. I have seen the day, etc.
[V. ii. 259-61]

in great amplitude and volume; but his pride—as of a paladin—in his weapon and in his glorious past lapses into a wail of misery, and the sword-motive, which had seemed to signify defiance, turns, by a hint, to the motive of suicide.

> Here is my butt
> And very sea-mark of my utmost sail.
>
> [V. ii. 267-68]

But now there is a retardation and digression—his thoughts are diverted from the act to the horror, present and future, which impels him to it. Then come Iago's entrance, the wounding of him, and the wrenching of the sword away. Still the motive of suicide is uttered again, though darkly,

> I'd have thee live;
> For, in my sense, 'tis happiness to die.
>
> [V. ii. 289-90]

But upon that ensues a longer digression. In tender words Othello and Cassio express their reconciliation, but Iago vows that from this time forth he never will speak word. "Well, thou dost best," says Othello, much the same spirit, amid his anguish, as he who, at the beginning, had replied to Iago's urgency, "'Tis better as it is"[V. ii. 306, I. ii. 6]. The disclosure of several details of the villainous conspiracy follows, and Othello's grief at his own folly grows. Then, when Lodovico, reminding him that Cassio rules in Cyprus, requires the general to leave the room and close prisoner rest, the main trend of thought, the theme of suicide, is, though under cover, in the last unforgetable speech, resumed:

> Soft you; a word or two before you go.
> I have done the state some service and they know 't.
> No more of that, etc.
>
> [V. ii. 338-40]

Again the motive of his pathetic pride in his glorious past, as it had appeared a few moments before, and, though without pathos, it had appeared in talking with Iago at the beginning, in the Senate Chamber, and on the quay at Cyprus; again the motive of his recent happiness, his present irremediable disaster. Suicide itself ends the speech, but in that there is for us no mere surprise or empty shock of horror. Over his brain memory holds sway, as with the dying: he looks backward, even as he looks forward to the memory that there will be of him. Though no one sees his dagger, his words breathe only of still desperation and farewell. But the point is that with delicate and various repetition and retardation of theme, whether by the business of the sword, or hints of suicide, or reminiscences and anticipations in digression, the poet had made it apparent already that this was his "journey's end," his "utmost sail," and, as if it were in music, had prepared and reconciled our souls. And the chief point of all is that this whole final movement is an echo or reflux of that with which the play began. For here in his misery is Othello again as first we knew and loved him—in his pride, in his tenderness, even in his calm—though now by passion shaken and by the dart of chance pierced.

All this, and the play as a whole, is a feat of the imagination merely and of a cunning pen. What great play is more? "If the poet makes use of philosophic ideas," says Croce truly, "he does so only that he may change reason into imagination;" and that he can achieve only when the ideas are no longer new, are not wholly his own. Hence of psychology, with its searching analysis, its devious and subliminal processes, its "stunning" and forcing of thought—its fleeing from thought itself—its undertow and unconscious self-deceptions, he could give us nothing, even if he had had it to give. Even [Robert] Brown-

ing, who, three hundred years later, had it to give, could not always manage to impart it to his readers—to say nothing of an audience—because, of truth embodied in a character, and so presented indirectly, an artist can give us only what was fairly ours before.

Why then with Shakespeare should this interest in psychology, the subtle analysis of character and the revealing of recondite mental processes—science and learning in short—be any longer the chief of our critical diet, as it was in the Renaissance with Homer? How primitive and unsophisticated it is not to consider Shakespeare only as a dramatist and poet, not to be content with poetry and drama (as we are with mere music in Mozart, mere painting in Rembrandt) and that, too, the poetry and drama, not of Browning or Ibsen, but of his own simple and spacious days? . . . We have traced the harmonious relation of the last scene to the first scenes, and in the last scene the fine gradation of effects, and repetition and interweaving of themes or motives, which almost reminds one of the *Master Builder;* and another fine gradation we might have traced in the five meetings of Othello with Desdemona after the temptation begins, the hero being in each more brutal and nearer murder than in the one before. We have traced in part, too, the poetic identity and unity of the characters, which is preserved to us despite default of analysis and reason. By the sheer potency of art Othello, Iago, Desdemona, and Emilia maintain, through all their incredible spiritual vicissitudes, their individual tone. And inconsistent, unpsychological though they be, their passions speak ever true. It is this poetic identity, this fine differentiation of tone, this concrete and intense reality of utterance, to be sure, which people have mistaken for psychology itself. But how much more reasonable and profitable it is to dwell on the great emotional speeches, the great emotional situations, which though they hang not so closely and intimately together, and to reality, as in a modern play, yet give us (which is the chief thing) unfailing "faith in the emotions expressed." . . . And the first real critic of Shakespeare will be he who by his learning, his imaginative sympathy, and a gift of expression not inferior to Hazlitt's or Lamb's, shall teach us to feel this, as he leads us back out of the modern world into the poet's, in something of the divine simplicity with which the poet once felt it himself. (pp. 59-63)

> *Elmer Edgar Stoll, in his "Othello": An Historical and Comparative Study, 1915. Reprint by Haskell House, 1964, 70 p.*

TUCKER BROOKE (essay date 1918)

[*Brooke was an American scholar and editor of the Yale Shakespeare series—a collection praised by critics for its sound annotations and careful attention to textual problems and source materials. In his study of the history of Tudor and Elizabethan drama, Brooke paid particular attention to the social and intellectual backgrounds of the era. He also contributed significantly to the existing knowledge of Elizabethan stage conventions, set designs, and the actual productions of plays. In the most sympathetic analysis of Iago to this date, Brooke asserts that Shakespeare and his fellow Elizabethans would have regarded the character as "distinctly attractive," even though they condemned his irresponsible behavior. He also contends that Iago's diabolical behavior is accidental and unpremeditated rather than coldly calculated and preconceived, as stated by A. C. Bradley (1904) and others; in Brooke's opinion, Iago's villainy is the result of his materialistic philosophy and the pursuit of his own self-interests regardless of the outcome. Brooke argues that, in this respect, Iago resembles Falstaff, to the extent that both avoid sympathetic relationships with other people, overvalue "present personal sen-*]

sation," and repudiate any contemplation of the future. The critic concludes that throughout Acts IV and V Iago proceeds through a process of "moral awakening" and that his villainy leads him to the realization of the true significance of life and its spiritual values. Other critics who have discovered mitigating qualities in Iago include Richard Hole (1796), William Maginn (1839), and Richard Grant White (1885).]

"Of Shakespeare's characters," writes Professor Bradley, "Falstaff, Hamlet, Iago, and Cleopatra (I name them in the order of their births) are probably the most wonderful. Of these, again, Hamlet and Iago, whose births come nearest together, are perhaps the most subtle. And if Iago had been a person as attractive as Hamlet, as many thousands of pages might have been written about him, containing as much criticism good and bad" [see excerpt above, 1904].

Now heaven forfend that the mountainous cairn of commentary erected over the bones of him who so infelicitously remarked, "The rest is silence" [*Hamlet*, V. ii. 358], be ever duplicated. But I am constrained to take up the cudgels against this general imputation of the unattractiveness of Iago and vindicate his place in the sun, beneath the beams of that romantic luminary which so irradiates all his great compeers: Honest Jack, the Prince of Denmark, and the Serpent of old Nile. We are prone to turn our scandalized backs upon Iago and flatter ourselves, as our ancestors have been doing since the days of Samuel Johnson, that the rogue shall never beguile us; and thus we miss the many evidences that Iago was to Shakespeare intensely, even romantically, attractive.

"Evil has nowhere else been portrayed with such mastery as in the character of Iago," Professor Bradley further remarks; and he goes on to declare: "It is only in Goethe's Mephistophiles that a fit companion for Iago can be found. Here there is something of the same deadly coldness, the same gaiety in destruction."

The gaiety in destruction we may admit—more easily in Shakespeare's character perhaps than in Goethe's; but the deadly Mephistophelian coldness of Iago requires establishment. The difficulty is that what the critics see—this chilly, almost passionless, egoism—is so remarkably at variance with what Iago's companions in the play see in him. The qualities they all recognize are blunt honesty, rough imperturbable good nature, extraordinary cordiality and trustworthiness, hiding under the thinnest mask of cynicism, as in real life they so often do.

Shakespeare is at particular pains to emphasize the unanimity and positiveness of this impression. At the beginning of the third act, by way of preliminary to the great "temptation scene," he favors us with a regular symposium on Iago's character. The witnesses are most varied in experience, attitude of mind, and intimacy of acquaintance. Their evidence is overwhelmingly unanimous and consistent. Says Cassio, the foppish Florentine: "I never knew a Florentine more kind and honest" [III. i. 40]. Says Emilia, Iago's plain-spoken wife: "I warrant it [Cassio's misfortune] grieves my husband, as if the case were his" [III. iii. 3-4]. Says Desdemona: "O, that's an honest fellow!" [III. ii. 5]. Says Othello: "This fellow 's of exceeding honesty" [III. iii. 258]; and much more to the same effect.

The words are fully borne out in action. In their trust of Iago all Iago's acquaintance are united. Roderigo lets him have his purse as if the strings were his; Cassio accepts his counsel unhesitatingly; Othello, searching his brain, finds the idea of Iago's insincerity simply unbelievable; Emilia, when finally confronted with irrefragable proof of his duplicity, is thundersmitten, but still incredulous. (pp. 349-50)

This honesty and innate kindliness of Iago, which all the characters in the play vouch for through practically the whole course of the action, can be no melodramatic villain's mask. A man of deadly coldness and natural selfishness does not thus impress his fellows. Shakespeare's plays, indeed, do present us with figures possessing something of the Mephistophelian coldness of heart predicated of Iago. Cassius in "Julius Caesar" has suggestions of it; Don John in "Much Ado" has a great deal more. Now what is the general opinion of these characters? Do we find the lean and hungry Cassius a common favorite? Do we find Don John universally trusted and appealed to as a man of exceeding honesty? Can we imagine Portia carrying her troubles to Cassius, or Hero selecting Don John for confidant, as Desdemona selects Iago?

It is evident, I think, that Shakespeare imagined Iago a man of warm sympathetic qualities, begetting confidence in his acquaintances as instinctively and universally as Don John's coldness begot distrust. Can we find in Shakespeare another character possessed of mental qualities like Iago's and exerting a similar influence upon his companions? There is one such, I think.

The adjective inevitably applied to Iago is "honest"; it is the regular epithet also of Falstaff. The coupling of Falstaff and Iago may seem bizarre, and their relation is indeed a kind of Jekyll-Hyde affair; but that Shakespeare saw a likeness seems capable of proof, and each throws welcome light upon the character of the other. We need not dwell long upon their more social aspects, since exigencies of plot, which multiplied scenes of jovial merry-making almost to the point of fatty degeneration in the Falstaff plays, reduced to the minimum the treatment of the corresponding side of Iago. Yet it is clear that Iago, like Sir John, has heard the chimes at midnight and been merry twice and once. Only a seasoned *habitué* of the taverns could talk as he talks in the scene of the arrival at Cyprus and in the brawl scene, or sing as he sings:

> And let me the canakin clink, clink;
> And let me the canakin clink:
>   A soldier's a man;
>   Oh, man's life's but a span;
> Why, then, let a soldier drink.
>
> [II. iii. 69-73]

In Iago's intellectual attitude we find reminiscences of Falstaff's way of thinking, just as we find reminiscences of Brutus in Hamlet. Falstaff's famous words on honor are virtually paraphrased in Iago's definition of reputation. "O, I have lost my reputation!" cries the disgraced Cassio. "I have lost the immortal part of myself!" [II. iii. 262-64]. "As I am an honest man," answers Iago, "I thought you had received some bodily wound; there is more sense in that than in reputation. Reputation is an idle and most false imposition, oft got without merit and lost without deserving: you have lost no reputation at all, unless you repute yourself such a loser" [II. iii. 266-71].

One of Falstaff's most charming propensities is shared by Iago, and by no other character in Shakespeare. It is the trick of mischievously teasing the complaining victim, drawing him on from irritation to positive anger for sheer pride of intellectual superiority; allowing half-derisive confessions of abuse to accumulate til the victim is ready to strike, and then by a dexterous turn of phrase leaping clear away and leaving the dazed antagonist more firmly in his power than before. (pp. 351-53)

Falstaff and Iago are . . . Shakespeare's two great studies in materialism. Mentally and morally, they are counterparts. That they affect us so differently is due to the difference between the comic and the tragic environment. Still more it is due to difference in age. Falstaff, with his load of years and flesh, is a static force. Taking his ease at his inn, he uses his caustic materialistic creed and his mastery of moral paradox but as a shield to turn aside the attacks of a more spiritual society. Iago has looked upon the world for only four times seven years. His philosophy is dynamic. It drives him to assume the offensive, to take up arms against what he thinks the stupidity of a too little self-loving world. The flame, which in Falstaff only warms and brightens, sears in Iago; but it is much the same kind of flame, and it attracts the same kind of moths. One may even imagine with a mischievous glee the warping and charring of green wit which would have resulted if Prince Hal and Poins had fluttered about Falstaff when he too was twenty-eight and "not an eagle's talon in the waist" [*1 Henry IV*, II. iv. 330].

Iago is no more a born devil than Falstaff. He too might have gone merrily on drinking and singing, consuming the substance of two generations of Roderigos, till he too waxed fat and inert and unequivocally comic. His diabolism is an accident, thrust upon him early in the play, when in seeking to convince Roderigo of his hate for Othello he convinces himself likewise, and suddenly finds himself over head and ears in the depths of his own egoism, vaguely conscious that he is being used for the devil's purposes, but incapable either of shaping the direction or checking the progress of his drift. There is, indeed, something suggestive of demoniacal possession in the way Iago yields during the first two acts to influences which he recognizes as diabolical, but cannot at all understand. He whispers:

I have 't. It is engender'd. Hell and Night
Must bring this monstrous birth to the world's light;
[I. iii. 403-04]

and again:

. . . 'Tis here, but yet confus'd:
Knavery's plain face is never seen till us'd.
[II. i. 311-12]

What he should say is not "I have 't," but "It has me." Shakespeare is peculiarly careful to exclude the possibility of anything like cold calculation or preconception of purpose.

Iago's ruin results from two by-products of his Falstaffian materialism. In the first place, the materialistic theory of life corrodes the imagination. In Iago's case, as in Falstaff's, it cuts its victim off from his future and ultimately severs his bond of sympathy with his fellows. It leaves him only the sorry garden patch of present personal sensation. There, indeed, the will can fitfully play the gardener, as Iago boasts, "plant nettles, or sow lettuce, set hyssop and weed up thyme, supply it with one gender of herbs, or distract it with many" [I. iii. 321-24]; but it cannot range with large discourse or labor serenely towards a future harvest.

A natural corollary is that the materialist makes large and ever larger demands upon the present. Like the clown in Marlowe's "Faustus," when he buys his shoulder of mutton so dear, he "had need have it well roasted and good sauce to it." Ennui grows constantly more unendurable and more unavoidable. Falstaff's life is a series of desperate escapes from boredom; it is for this that he joins the Gadshill party, that he volunteers for the wars. It is for this that he so carefully husbands Shallow: "I will devise matter enough out of the Shallow to keep Prince Harry in continual laughter the wearing out of six fashions" [*2 Henry IV*, V. i. 78-80]. And Falstaff thinks with rueful envy of the capacity of romantic youth for sensation: "O, it is much that a lie with a slight oath and a jest with a sad brow will do with a fellow that never had the ache in his shoulders!" [*2 Henry IV*, V. i. 81-4].

It is for this that Iago so carefully secures Roderigo and his well-filled purse to spice his life in Cyprus. To avoid tedium is the great purpose of his existence, and truly his efforts are heroic. The brawl scene, with all its sinister potentialities, is for him a triumphant campaign against the blues. When at the close of the second act he looks up into the coming dawn and reviews the doings of the night, he is simply grateful for the anodyne he has ministered to himself. "By the mass," he exclaims, "'tis morning. Pleasure and action make the hours seem short" [II. iii. 378-79]. Be the future what it may, five hours have been saved from dulness!

Of course, Iago clings to a plot which offers such relief. Of course, his narcotized sensibilities prevent him from understanding the exquisite poignancy of others' feelings. Jealousy, we gather, is for him a welcome, though nearly exhausted, source of distraction, offering him the alleviation a man with toothache may get when he bites his finger. How should he know Othello? And so he allows his dread of inactivity, his incorrigible craving for sensation, to drive him on through the temptation scene and all its, to him, fantastic consequences. His plot succeeds so well because he really has no plot. He dances from one mischievous suggestion to another with the agility and unsearchable purposefulness of a sleep-walker.

For Shakespeare, and the Elizabethans, less touchy than we about the particular ideals he shatters, I think Iago was distinctly attractive. Never, probably, was he more delightful to his companions than while his wild scheme spins through his irresponsible brain. Never, doubtless, did he more impress them with his "honesty," his lively, capable, warm-hearted geniality. His spirit is fired with "pleasure and action," and he is almost light-headed. His case is just the converse of Hamlet's. In one play we have the problem of the exhilarated materialist, in the other the problem of the soured idealist.

Shakespeare is a great believer in the school of experience, and his tragedies commonly teach the lessons of that school. Lear is a notable instance; Iago is another. His crusted materialism fails to stand the test of actual practice to which he puts it. Pitted against the idealism of those whom Iago thinks fools, it is first pierced and then broken. When he makes his speech about reputation in the second act, he is no doubt quite honest; the contrary feeling of Cassio awakes his genuine surprise and irritation. But Cassio's is evidently a real feeling and one that challenges consideration. The next morning he paraphrases the idealistic conception:

Good name in man, and woman, dear my lord,
Is the immediate jewel of their souls.
[III. iii. 155-56]

He employs the sentiment, of course, for his own purposes, and perhaps with inward derision, but the day before, he would hardly have believed it could exist in reasonable men. To express the idea at all throws open a window of the soul. Another window is opened when his wife unwittingly presents him with his moral photograph:

I will be hang'd, if some eternal villain,
Some busy and insinuating rogue,
Some cogging, cozening slave, to get some office,
Have not devis'd this slander; I'll be hang'd else.
[IV. ii. 130-33]

Suddenly he sees himself in the new spiritual light which things are taking on, and he recoils incredulous:

> Fie, there is no such man; it is impossible.
>
> [IV. ii. 134]

Last scene of all, we hear Iago in his final soliloquy, hedged about by the desperate perils which his own moral obtuseness has drawn upon him. Only by homicide of the wildest sort can he hope to escape, but he reasons, with a weary detachment, of his chances, and he offers as a chief inducement to the reckless game the new motive of shame:

> . . . If Cassio do remain,
> He hath a daily beauty in his life
> That makes me ugly.
>
> [V. i. 18-20]

Even the "counter-caster," Cassio, whose one admirable trait is his selfless hero-worship of Othello, now seems clothed in a beauty of character which makes the materialist hate himself and drives him to desperate courses. How impossible such an attitude would be to the scornful Iago of the first acts! We have thus a measure of the moral awakening of Iago. His very crimes lead him to a purer sense of the values of life. As elsewhere—in "Lear," "Macbeth," "Hamlet," "Julius Caesar"—the poet's doctrine is that false principles, if left free play, will undo themselves and work their own refutation.

We need a spectroscope for Shakespeare. Our perception of Iago is blurred by the glow of sympathy we feel for Othello and for Desdemona. But in so far as we can eliminate these two luminous figures from our view, we can see the outlines of what I fancy was the poet's original idea, the tragedy of Iago, the tragedy of the honest, charming soldier, who swallowed the devil's bait of self-indulgence, grew blind to ideal beauty, and in his blindness overthrew more than his enemies. (pp. 354-59)

> *Tucker Brooke, "The Romantic Iago," in* The Yale Review, *n.s. Vol. VII, No. 2, January, 1918, pp. 349-59.*

T. S. ELIOT (essay date 1927)

[*Eliot, a celebrated American-born English poet, essayist, and critic, stressed in his criticism the importance of tradition, religion, and morality in literature. His emphasis on imagery, symbolism, and meaning helped to establish the theories of New Criticism. Eliot's concept of the "objective correlative" is considered a major contribution to literary analysis. In his* Selected Essays *(1932), Eliot defines the objective correlative as "a set of objects, a situation, a chain of events which shall be the formula of [a] particular emotion" and which has the ability to evoke that emotion in the reader. In his brief remarks on* Othello, *taken from his essay, "Shakespeare and the Stoicism of Seneca" (1927), Eliot introduces a radically different view of the Moor—one which became extremely influential in later criticism of the play. Using Othello's final speech to illustrate his contention that some Shakespearean heroes adopt a self-dramatizing pose "at moments of tragic intensity," he remarks that in these lines the Moor demonstrates a frailty to which all humans are prone: the wish to view one's actions in the most favorable light possible. Eliot asserts that Othello is here deluding himself about the implications of his actions in an effort to "cheer himself up," and for this reason the critic regards the passage as a "terrible exposure of human weakness—of universal human weakness." In an essay published the same year as Eliot's, Allardyce Nicoll (1927) similarly concluded that the Moor is self-deluded and, in his final speeches, represents himself as something he is not, and most*

recently Jane Adamson (1980) has acknowledged Eliot's insightful assessment of this passage. Eliot's influence can also be noted in the excerpts by F. R. Leavis (1937), G. R. Elliott (1937 and 1953), Derek Traversi (1949), Brents Stirling (1956), Roy W. Battenhouse (1969), and Carol McGinnis Kay (1983), all of whom regard Othello as overly proud and self-centered. However, Jared R. Curtis (1973) and Helen Gardner (see Additional Bibliography) have maintained that Eliot's interpretation of the Moor's concluding speech is in error: Curtis sees no evidence of self-indulgence or self-deception in this passage, and Gardner holds that Othello's references to the services he has done the state are entirely appropriate to the situation, for at the moment when he is about to take his life it is right that "he should be conscious of what has given his life value" and significance. In addition, such other critics as Kenneth O. Myrick (1941), S. L. Bethell (1952), Paul N. Siegel (1953), Irving Ribner (1955 and 1960), G. M. Matthews (1964), and Roy W. Battenhouse (1969) have examined Othello's last speeches and the final moments of the play to determine whether Shakespeare represents the Moor as saved or eternally damned.]

I have always felt that I have never read a more terrible exposure of human weakness—of universal human weakness—than the last great speech of Othello. I am ignorant whether any one else has ever adopted this view, and it may appear subjective and fantastic in the extreme. It is usually taken on its face value, as expressing the greatness in defeat of a noble but erring nature.

> Soft you; a word or two before you go.
> I have done the state some service, and they know't,—
> No more of that.—I pray you, in your letters,
> When you shall these unlucky deeds relate,
> Speak of me as I am; nothing extenuate,
> Nor set down aught in malice: then must you speak
> Of one that loved not wisely but too well;
> Of one not easily jealous, but, being wrought,
> Perplex'd in the extreme; of one whose hand,
> Like the base Indian, threw a pearl away
> Richer than all his tribe; of one whose subdued eyes,
> Albeit unused to the melting mood,
> Drop tears as fast as the Arabian trees
> Their medicinal gum. Set you down this;
> And say, besides,—that in Aleppo once,
> Where a malignant and a turban'd Turk
> Beat a Venetian and traduced the state,
> I took by the throat the circumcised dog,
> And smote him—thus.
>
> [V. ii. 338-56]

What Othello seems to me to be doing in making this speech is *cheering himself up*. He is endeavouring to escape reality, he has ceased to think about Desdemona, and is thinking about himself. Humility is the most difficult of all virtues to achieve; nothing dies harder than the desire to think well of oneself. Othello succeeds in turning himself into a pathetic figure, by adopting an *aesthetic* rather than a moral attitude, dramatising himself against his environment. He takes in the spectator, but the human motive is primarily to take in himself. I do not believe that any writer has ever exposed this *bovarysme* [from Gustave Flaubert's *Madame Bovary*], the human will to see things as they are not, more clearly than Shakespeare. (pp. 110-11)

> *T. S. Eliot, "Shakespeare and the Stoicism of Seneca," in his* Selected Essays, *Harcourt Brace Jovanovich, Inc., 1950, pp. 107-20.*

WYNDHAM LEWIS   (essay date 1927)

[*Lewis wrote in a deliberately provocative style and outside the mainstream of Shakespearean criticism. The majority of his work on Shakespeare is included in his unusual study* The Lion and the Fox *(1927), a title that refers to the struggle between world views which Lewis believed dominated Shakespeare's age. The lion stands for the mystical and feudalistic vision of the age of chivalry; the fox for the rationalism of the coming age of science and industry. Shakespeare himself, according to Lewis, did not take sides in any simple way, but his plays reflect the conflict of these opposing world views. In a section of that work not reproduced here, the critic links Othello with Lear, Antony, Macbeth, Timon, and Coriolanus, describing them as individual representations of the type of colossal or titanic figures originating with Christopher Marlowe's Tamburlaine and characterized by extraordinary majesty, valor, and physical strength. In the following excerpt, Lewis argues that* Othello *depicts "the race of men at war with the race of titans" and that the gods have predetermined that Iago, the petty Everyman, will triumph over the grandeur of Othello. The critic assesses the Moor as the most typical of Shakespeare's colossi "because he is the simplest" and emphasizes his pure, guileless, generous nature and the childlike, defenseless quality of his soul. Lewis considers Iago "no great devil," but instead claims that he represents an ordinary, average, little man; in Lewis's words, he is "the man-in-the-street of any time or place since the emergence of* homo sapiens *on our scene." Other critics who have similarly stressed Iago's human aspects include Richard Grant White (1885), Tucker Brooke (1818), and Robert B. Heilman (1956). Additionally, Lewis disagrees with A. C. Bradley (1904) on two issues. First, whereas Bradley asserts that Iago's statements are not to be believed unless corroborated by other internal evidence, Lewis contends that Iago always speaks the truth in his soliloquies and merits the description of "honest." Second, he disputes Bradley's contention that Iago is unrelated to conventional dramatic Machiavellian figures, asserting that the ensign is closely akin to the stereotypical Machiavellian intriguer of the Elizabethan stage, as distinguished from the political philosopher and writer himself. For additional commentary on the connection between Iago and Machiavellianism, see the excerpts by E. K. Chambers (1908), Allardyce Nicoll (1927), and S. L. Bethell (1952), as well as the essay by Thomas Babington Macaulay cited in the Additional Bibliography.*]

Of all the colossi, Othello is the most characteristic, because he is the simplest, and he is seen in an unequal duel throughout with a perfect specimen of the appointed enemy of the giant—the representative of the race of men at war with the race of titans. The hero comes straight from a world where Machiavelli's black necessities—the obligation, for animal survival, for the lion to couple with the fox—are not known. He is absolutely defenceless: it is as though he were meeting one of his appointed enemies, disguised of course, as a friend, for the first time. He seems possessed of no instinct by which he might scent his antagonist, and so be put on his guard.

So, at the outset, I will present my version of Othello; and anything that I have subsequently to say must be read in the light of this interpretation. For in Othello there is nothing equivocal, I think; and the black figure of this child-man is one of the poles of Shakespeare's sensation.

Who that has read Othello's closing speech can question Shakespeare's intentions here at least? The overwhelming truth and beauty is the clearest expression of the favour of Shakespeare's heart and mind. Nothing that could ever be said would make us misunderstand what its author meant by it. Of all his ideal giants this unhappiest, blackest, most "perplexed" child was the one of Shakespeare's predilection.

The great spectacular "pugnacious" male ideal is represented perfectly by Othello; who was led out to the slaughter on the elizabethan stage just as the bull is thrust into the spanish bull-ring. Iago, the *taurobolus* [bull catcher] of this sacrificial bull, the little David of this Goliath, or the little feat-gilded *espada* [matador], is for Shakespeare nothing but Everyman, the Judas of the world, the representative of the crowds around the crucifix, or of the ferocious crowds at the *corrida* [bull fight], or of the still more abject roman crowds at the mortuary games. Othello is of the race of Christs, or of the race of "bulls"; he is the hero with all the magnificent helplessness of the animal, or all the beauty and ultimate resignation of the god. From the moment he arrives on the scene of his execution, or when his execution is being prepared, he speaks with an unmatched grandeur and beauty. To the troop that is come to look for him, armed and snarling, he says: "Put up your bright swords or the dew will rust them!" [I. ii. 59]. And when at last he has been brought to bay he dies by that significant contrivance of remembering how he had defended the state when it was traduced, and in reviving this distant blow for his own demise. The great words roll on in your ears as the curtain falls:

> And say besides, that in Aleppo once. . . .
>
> [V. ii. 352]

Iago is made to say:

> The Moor, howbeit that I endure him not,
> Is of a constant, loving, noble nature.
>
> [II. i. 288-89]

But we do not need this testimony to feel, in all our dealings with this simplest and grandest of his creations, that we are meant to be in the presence of an absolute purity of human guilelessness, a generosity as grand and unaffected, although quick and, "being wrought, Perplexed in the extreme" [V. ii. 345-46], as deep as that of his divine inventor.

There is no utterance in the whole of Shakespeare's plays that reveals the nobleness of his genius and of its intentions in the same way as the speech with which Othello closes:

> Soft you; a word or two before you go.
> I have done the state some service, and they know it.
> No more of that. I pray you, in your letters,
> When you shall these unlucky deeds relate,
> Speak of me as I am; nothing extenuate,
> Nor set down aught in malice: then, must you speak
> Of one that loved, not wisely, but too well;
> Of one not easily jealous, but, being wrought,
> Perplex'd in the extreme; of one, whose hand,
> Like the base Indian, threw a pearl away,
> Richer than all his tribe; of one, whose subdued
>   eyes, . . .
> Drop tears as fast as the Arabian trees
> Their medicinal gum. Set you down this;
> And say, besides, that in Aleppo once,
> Where a malignant and a turban'd Turk
> Beat a Venetian, and traduced the state,
> I took by the throat the circumcisèd dog,
> And smote him—thus.
>
> [V. ii. 338-48, 350-56]

And it is the speech of a military hero, as simple-hearted as Hotspur [in *Richard II* and *1 Henry IV*]. The tremendous and childlike pathos of this simple creature, broken by intrigue so easily and completely, is one of the most significant things for the comprehension of Shakespeare's true thought. For why should so much havoc ensue from the crude "management" of a very ordinary intriguer? It is no great devil that is pitted against him: and so much faultless affection is destroyed with such a mechanical facility. He is a toy in the hands of a person so much less real than himself; in every sense, human and divine, so immeasurably inferior.

> And say besides, that in Aleppo once.

This unhappy child, caught in the fatal machinery of "shake-spearian tragedy," just as he might have been by an accident in the well-known world, remembers, with a measureless pathos, an event in the past to his credit, recalled as an after-thought, and thrown in at the last moment, a poor counter of "honour," to set against the violence to which he has been driven by the whisperings of things that have never existed.

And it is *we* who are intended to respond to these events, as the Venetian, Lodovico, does, when he apostrophizes Iago, describing him as:

> More fell than anguish, hunger or the sea!
>
> [V. ii. 362]

The eloquence of that apostrophe is the measure of the greatness of the heart that we have seen attacked and overcome. We cannot take that as an eloquent outburst only: it was an expression of the author's conviction of the irreparable nature of the offence, because of the purity of the nature that had suffered. The green light of repugnance and judgment is thrown on to the small mechanical villain at the last.

Professor Bradley in his elaborate analysis of Iago says that many people have seen in Iago one of the traditional Machiavellis of the time; but he repudiates that parentage for him [see excerpt above, 1904]. Yet it hardly seems a thing about which there can be any dispute. There is no question of Shakespeare's finding this *particular* duplicity in the figure of Machiavelli. But it is certain that Iago is a variety of the recognized stage Machiavelli type. Will anyone believe that if a philosophy of duplicity and ruthless mechanical intrigue, directed to the reaching of a definite material end, had never been written by Machiavelli: if Cesare Borgia had not supplied him with a living illustration and hero (as Napoleon was Stendhal's vast living confirmation and original): and if the italian nature had not stood for *intrigue*, of a bold and relentless description, that Iago, the italian "villain" of this italian story, would ever have been created?

In Act I., scene 1, he reveals himself at once, without the least delay or coyness, both to Roderigo and to the audience.

There is nothing that Iago says, in the displays of his mental workings with which we are accommodated, that would be inappropriate in the mouth of any solicitor, stockbroker, politician or man-about-town in England to-day, or in Shakespeare's day. He possesses the same pride in his *cunning*— tells you with a wink that *his* thoughts are not worn on his sleeve but in a deep and secret place, where they cannot easily be found.

There is something at once commonplace and maniacal, "normal" and mad, about the way he speaks of his hiding-place, his mind:

> In following him, I follow but myself;
> Heaven is my judge, not I for love and duty,
> But seeming so, for my peculiar end:
> For when my outward action doth demonstrate

> The native act and figure of my heart
> In compliment extern, 'tis not long after
> But I will wear my heart upon my sleeve
> For daws to peck at: I am not what I am.
>
> [I. i. 58-65]

The last words are the supreme bombast of such people. *I am not what I am.* The small and shoddy, when it meets its kind, knows it at once by this sign—namely, *that it is not what it is.* Both are the votaries of the goddess whose oracle these words convey. Shakespeare's own words—*I am that I am* [*Sonnet* 121]—where in his *Sonnets,* through all the veils of his beautiful rhetoric, he is, as Wordsworth said, "unlocking his heart"—are similarly the supreme defiance of the rarest nature, for ever over against the dark equivocal crowds saturated with falsity. (pp. 190-94)

The secret of Iago, then—if there could be any secret about Iago's nature for an intelligent spectator of the play in which he occurs, for he is as candid as it is possible to be to the audience and to everybody except his victim—is that this particular Everyman is the bluff, commonplace, quite unvillain-like, little "man of the world," mobilized to destroy a great shakespearian hero. [John Webster's] Bossola [in *The Duchess of Malfi*] is a complicated renaissance figure, but Iago is so great a creation because he is not that at all, but just the man-in-the street of any time or place since the emergence of *homo sapiens* on our scene. This plain man is, of course, deeply marked by professional, racial and other stereotyping effects of circumstance; and Iago, for instance, is the *blunt soldier*, and has other characteristics of his calling. But at heart it is one figure, the animal human average.

Most Shakespeare critics, however, when they come to write about Iago, use more or less the language of his wife Emilia on the discovery of his treachery, or of Lodovico, or Gratiano: his "motiveless malignity" [see excerpt above by Samuel Taylor Coleridge, 1808-18] is supposed to be motiveless because it is assumed to be so unusual and so deep. Professor Bradley scouts the idea that his own repeated explanation of his behaviour is to be accepted; and although he will not admit that it is motiveless, with Coleridge, he considers his villainy without parallel in its depth and degradation, and goes off hunting for motives of the most unusual sort (to match the *unusualness* of the crime).

He implores the reader to remember that Iago *under no circumstances* ever tells the truth! Should the reader forget that for a moment, one is almost made to feel he might find himself entrapped by this spartan dog as poor Othello was.

All this appears to me very far from the truth. The most obvious thing about Iago is that he never lies, and is as open (in his villainy) as the day, as we have already said.

He always tells the truth when speaking to the audience or to himself. It is a stroke of genius of Shakespeare to make him always called *honest*—when his actions are so deliberately dishonest, and yet when his nature, rough and direct, does, in another sense, perfectly answer that description. (pp. 194-95)

Iago is a professional soldier, a "man of action," like Othello; and in a sense he is *simple*, like Othello. When he says the Moor is of a constant, loving, noble nature he admires those qualities. He does not sneer as he says it, their psychology has enough in common, just as their way of life has, so that, in spite of his immense respect for the tortuous, he can also admire the open and truthful.

Being in this sense *simple*, like Othello; and believing that Othello has cuckolded him, he reacts to this event in as violent and primitive a way as Othello does. He is, like Othello, very touchy where the faithfulness of his wife is concerned, and likes the idea of being pointed at as a cuckold just as little as Othello does. In other ways, also, Othello has treated him without very much consideration: but the ostensible plot of the play is really the revenge of the sex-vanity of a subordinate on his chief, the revenge taking the form of inspiring his chief with the same feelings of jealousy and wounded vanity that he has experienced himself.

But it is much more than a sex-revenge—*sex* in its way being as deceptive as *money* is in itself a human incentive. It is also, as it were, a *race*-revenge, the vengeance of the small nature upon the great nature. (pp. 196-97)

> Wyndham Lewis, "Othello as the Typical Colossus," in his The Lion and the Fox: The Rôle of the Hero in the Plays of Shakespeare, 1927. Reprint by Methuen & Co. Ltd., 1955, pp. 190-98.

ALLARDYCE NICOLL (essay date 1927)

[An English scholar and educator, Nicoll is the founder of the Shakespeare Institute at Stratford-upon-Avon and served as an editor of the Shakespeare Survey. He is also the author of several studies on English stage history. In the following excerpt from his Studies in Shakespeare (1927), Nicoll proposes that Othello dramatizes delusion and self-delusion interwoven with "the theme of idealism and reality." Tracing these themes throughout the different actions of the three leading characters, he claims that Othello holds an unrealistic, romantic view of life that clashes with his military background and his experiences with such venal women as Emilia and Bianca. According to the critic, these actual experiences of the Moor predispose him to jealousy and prepare the way for his quick descent into suspicion and rage in Act III, Scene iii. Nicoll thus concludes that Othello deludes both his audience and himself in his various protestations of his unsuspicious nature, when in fact jealousy is very much a latent element in his personality. Such other critics as T. S. Eliot (1927), F. R. Leavis (1937), G. R. Elliott (1937 and 1953), Derek Traversi (1949), Brents Stirling (1956), Jane Adamson (1980), and Carol McGinnis Kay (1983) have also commented on Othello's habit of self-deception and self-dramatization, but Jared R. Curtis (1973), Barbara Everett, and Helen Gardner (see Additional Bibliography) have presented differing points of view. Regarding Desdemona, Nicoll argues that she, too, displays a romantic vision of reality—most apparent in her inability to cope with Othello's rage against her—and that she deceives both her father and her husband when she prevaricates out of fear of what the truth might bring. Nicoll discerns in Iago a cynical Machiavellianism that is akin to Othello's and Desdemona's misconceptions of reality, contending that the ancient's amoral self-interest traduces his own superior intelligence, leading him to self-deception and a misunderstanding of the tragic possibilities implicit in his schemes against Othello. For further commentary on Iago's Machiavellianism, see the excerpts by E. K. Chambers (1908), Wyndham Lewis (1927), and S. L. Bethell (1952), as well as the essay by Thomas Babington Macaulay cited in the Additional Bibliography. Other critics who have viewed Iago as self-deceiving or the victim of his own manipulations include William Hazlitt (1817), William Maginn (1839), A. C. Bradley (1904), Tucker Brooke (1918), G. R. Elliott (1937), and Nigel Alexander (see Additional Bibliography). In his conclusion that "the gods are laughing" at Iago as well as the other characters, Nicoll echoes the opinion of such earlier critics as E. K. Chambers (1908), Stopford A. Brooke (1913), and Wyndham Lewis (1927) that Othello depicts a fatalistic, predetermined view of life.]

[In writing *Othello*,] Shakespeare must have realised that a simple dramatisation of Cinthio's story would not make a high tragedy. A mere villain, a mere gullible husband, a mere faithful wife would have made a satisfactory drama of the *Arden of Feversham* type, but they would not have made a tragedy of Shakespearian conception. There is not one of his other tragedies wherein we do not feel the ever-present sense of fate, the sense of divine irony, the mockery of the gods and the weeping of innumerable unseen voices. It would certainly have been peculiar if *Othello* had lacked this spirit, nor is it lacking. Shakespeare, dealing with a theme of more domestic type than he had dealt with in any of his other plays, could not employ the devices utilised by him elsewhere. A ghost in any shape would at once have destroyed the special tone of this tragedy; but use has been made of subtler motives and subtler suggestions. Over the whole drama is cast a note of tragic irony which at once hints to us of forces beyond our ken, and, more important still, there is a common mood which enwraps all the figures in its control, providing a unity of effect and the suggestion of a fatal power over and beyond the actual characters. This common mood is not, as so many have asserted, mere jealousy. Throughout the play run the keynotes of deception and self-deception, the jealousy being only the more obvious result and effect of those forces which move deeply below the whole tragic action.

From a consideration of *Othello* as a play of deception and of self-deception, then, and only as such, does a correct estimation of Shakespeare's purpose seem to me possible. The three main difficulties in Cinthio's plot—the motivating of Iago's actions, the presentation of Othello's acceptance of Iago's machinations as natural, and the providing of Desdemona with such qualities that her failure to pierce Iago's schemes should not be noticed—these are all to be explained by this general mood or theme. It is with Desdemona we may commence.

There is no question here about Shakespeare's prime conception of Desdemona's character. She is presented as a beautiful Venetian maiden, pure and innocent; one who, when married, cannot even conceive of the possibility of loving another man, one who cannot fathom or realise the faintest import of Othello's insinuations. From the point of view of chastity and faithfulness she is a perfect creature. But this is by no means the whole of her story. Those who praise Desdemona and find in her naught but unblemished truth, fail entirely to grasp the purpose of Shakespeare's *Othello*. Desdemona is not a great tragic character, yet Shakespeare has subtly delineated her nature so as to make her a perfect tool for Iago and a perfect foil for Othello. In the first place, she obviously lacks intellect and self-respect. She is no Cordelia [in *King Lear*]; never does she stand forward as a creature of independent spirit and determination. Completely under the domination of her lord, her whole mind is swayed by his. Not only does she show no indignation at his wild insinuations and direct accusations, but she allows herself to be treated by him as a mere slave. In the presence of a Venetian courtier the Moor strikes her, and her only words are:

> I haue not deseru'd this.

> [IV. i. 241]

Othello tirades against her, and she moves away:

> I will not stay to offend you,

> [IV. i. 247]

is the only phrase that rises on her lips. Lodovico wishes her to be called back, and on Othello's cry of "Mistress!" she promptly answers "My lord?" and turns. On his command to depart she obediently moves away. These qualities of lack of intellect and of self-respect detract seriously from our sympathy, but they were rendered necessary by the exigencies of the story. To this Desdemona adds a lack of courage. She can act under the domination of her husband, but she cannot stand out boldly for herself. Had she had courage, intellect, and self-respect, even if she had had any one of these, the tragic issue of Iago's machinations would have been impossible.

These, however, are not the main things in her character; she represents in herself, as do the other main characters, the all-fatal qualities of deception and of self-deception. It is on these Shakespeare has concentrated and it is these which it behoves us most carefully to analyse. It is noticeable that she is shown to us first in the play as deceiving her father. For some considerable time Desdemona must have been encouraging Othello in his love. His account of this we have no reason to disbelieve:

> My Storie being done,
> She gaue me for my paines a world of kisses:
> She swore in faith 'twas strange: 'twas passing strange,
> 'Twas pittifull: 'twas wondrous pittifull.
> She wish'd she had not heard it, yet she wish'd
> That Heauen had made her such a man. She thank'd me,
> And bad me, if I had a Friend that lou'd her,
> I should but teach him how to tell my Story,
> And that would wooe her. Upon this hint I spake.
>
> [I. iii. 158-66]

Yet all this Desdemona had kept carefully concealed from her father, so that he could not conceive but that Othello had used potions to win her affections:

> A Maiden, neuer bold:
> Of Spirit so still, and quiet, that her Motion
> Blush'd at her selfe, and she, in spight of Nature,
> Of Yeares, of Country, Credite, euery thing
> To fall in Loue, with what she fear'd to looke on.
>
> [I. iii. 94-8]

Already Shakespeare has shown to us a flaw in her character, and hints to us, in unmistakable words, that, when the time comes, she will undoubtedly fail. There is nothing of this in the tale of Cinthio. It is Shakespeare's art which has revealed to us with delicate touch wherein lay Desdemona's fatal human weakness. She would never lie for purely evil ends, but, when we add this tendency of her nature to her lack of intellect and courage, we realise that she will probably tell a lie in order to get herself out of any little scrape. The lie will be natural, and its consequences will not come within her limited perception. Indeed, on this Shakespeare lays emphasis, as he was often wont to do. Brabantio's last words to Othello are a warning on this theme:

> Looke to her (Moore) if thou hast eies to see:
> She ha's deceiu'd her Father, and may thee.
>
> [I. iii. 292-93]

Not in Brabantio's sense, but more fatally, was she to deceive her husband.

The way is thus excellently prepared for the climax scene. Desdemona has lost her handkerchief and the Moor questions her concerning it. She has not intellect to see that truth is her only hope of salvation; her courage fails her when she has no one to stand by her side. On Othello's demanding the handkerchief she gives him another. He requests the first. "I haue it not about me," is her answer [III. iv. 53], and her later words tremblingly corroborate her implied lie. "No, indeed, my Lord. . . . Is't possible? . . . Indeed? Is't true? . . . Then would to Heauen, that I had neuer seene't? . . . Why do you speake so startingly and rash? . . . Bless vs! . . . It is not lost: but what and if it were? . . . I say, it is not lost" [III. iv. 54, 68, 75, 77, 79, 81, 83, 84]. Again, her intellect failing her, she tries to turn Othello's mind to Cassio, only succeeding in fanning his preconceived suspicion to a flame of jealousy.

Shakespeare, apparently, felt that even these palpable clues might be overlooked—a not unjustified fear—for this double deception on Desdemona's part is paralleled by a third. She is introduced to us as practising deceit: she ends her life on a lie. Othello has smothered her, and, when help arrives, she can summon only sufficient breath to murmur:

> No body: I my selfe.
>
> [V. ii. 124]

It is a pitiful lie; but all our pity for her should not blind us to the fact that this is entirely characteristic of her—her lack of self-respect, her tendency towards concealing of truth by prevarication. In this way she is responsible for her own doom.

Conscious deception, however, does not wholly explain her position in the drama; like the other characters, she deceives herself. Where is Desdemona if not in a world of romance, of idealism? There she dwells, deceiving herself even when she encounters the fierce torrent of Othello's jealousy. Just as Hamlet wove for himself a sphere of philosophical idealism, so Desdemona created for herself a realm of romance. When reality rudely burst into Hamlet's world of dreams, his intellect turned to abstruse meditation and reflection on the evils of life; but the rough hand of reality leaves Desdemona, because she is unintellectual, bewildered, and at a loss. The first touch of reality comes to her after Othello's outburst of anger in Act IV. In his presence she summons up just sufficient strength to answer his tirades feebly with single phrases. "I hope my Noble Lord esteemes me honest. . . . Alas, what ignorant sin haue I committed? . . . By Heauen, you do me wrong . . . Oh Heauen forgiue vs!" [IV. ii. 65, 70, 81, 89]. Only once does she force herself to give him any sort of reasoned defence:

> No, as I am a Christian.
> If to preserue this vessell for my Lord,
> From any other foule vnlawful touch
> Be not to be a Strumpet, I am none.
>
> [IV. ii. 82-5]

This, however, shows but a momentary flash of spirit. In face of the reality, his anger, she is completely dazed. "Faith, halfe a sleepe" she answers Emilia when the latter asks her how she does [IV. ii. 97]. Her speeches are short and broken: her mind is confused:

> With who? . . .
> Who is thy Lord? . . .
> I haue none: do not talke to me, *Emilia*,
> I cannot weepe: nor answeres haue I none,
> But what should go by water. Prythee to night,
> Lay on my bed my wedding sheetes, remember,
> And call thy husband hither. . . .
> 'Tis meete I should be vs'd so: very meete.
> How haue I bin behau'd, that he might sticke
> The small'st opinion on my least misvse.
>
> [IV. ii. 99, 101, 102-06, 107-09]

Even this does not wholly awaken her, although it arouses her wonder and undoubtedly startles her idealism. In the last act,

"Othello," by H. Hofmann. The Department of Rare Books and Special Collections, The University of Michigan Library.

accordingly, we find her questioning Emilia about sin and still refusing to believe in it. She turns to the world of romance again.

> My Mother had a Maid call'd *Barbarie*,
> She was in loue: and he she lou'd prou'd mad,
> And did forsake her. She had a Song of Willough,
> An old thing 'twas: but it express'd her Fortune,
> And she dy'd singing it: That Song to night,
> Will not go from my mind: I haue much to do,
> But to go hang my head all at one side
> And sing it like poore *Barbarie* . . .
>
>   [IV. iii. 26-33]

Then her mind reverts to reality:

> Dos't thou in conscience thinke (tell me, *Émilia*)
> That there be women do abuse their husbands
> In such grosse kinde? . . .
> Would'st thou do such a deed for all the world? . . .
> Would'st thou do such a deed for all the world? . . .
>   Introth, I thinke thou would'st not. . . .
> Beshrew me, if I would do such a wrong
> For the whole world. . . .
> *I do not thinke there is any such woman.*
>
>   [IV. iii. 61-3, 64, 68, 70, 78-9, 83]

That is Shakespeare's final word on her character. In *Hamlet* he had presented the effects of a shock upon an intellectual nature, in Desdemona he shows the results of a similar shock upon a nature essentially unintellectual. It was as if he were trying the variations of the theme, eternal as the hills, of idealism opposed to reality.

It is evident that this conception of Desdemona's character made possible the success of Iago's evil practice. (pp. 86-93)

In analysing Iago's nature the first thing we note is that, in comparison with the other characters, he is a highly intellectual—or better, intelligent—man. He towers above all the rest with his fertile, acute, and normally far-sighted brain-power. At the same time he is of plebeian descent, and has obviously had no education. His intelligence is native, not cultivated. Partly because of jealous envy, partly because of the consciousness of his own capability, he is inclined to rate his native intelligence over cultured refinement. This man, of plebeian descent and responsible position, is in not too enviable a situation, and it is the consciousness of this which leads towards the development of those more purely evil characteristics which dominate the drama. Iago in his own way is to be considered, not as an individual of overweening villainy, but as a pitiful plaything of circumstance, warped in nature and in his evil bringing others to misery and ruin. (p. 94)

Quite naturally, a man of his upbringing and calibre would have developed a kind of self-help philosophy which logically would develop into a kind of Machiavellianism wherein *virtù*, the individuality, stands for everything, and all moral ideas are rejected as the mere props of weaker spirits.... As for Machiavelli, for Iago there are but two classes of men—the honest fools and the cynical, wise knaves. This does not mean that he follows evil for its own sake. Rather does he find that obsequiousness and the formal semblance of virtue are often more profitable than any amount of knavery. Iago's "honesty" has been practised for long years so that he has become the very spirit of uprightness and Diogenian virtue for them all. So long as this pose is a paying one, Iago is content to persevere in it, but whenever he finds that his "honesty" has carried him as far as it can carry him, he feels it time to cast it off.... His mood, therefore, is not a love of villainy as such, but merely a recognition that, when virtue becomes unprofitable, evil may be called in to aid a sensible man.

As we have seen, Iago's experience had led him to group men into the foolish and the wise. The former, he saw, were by far in the majority, and with something of Hamlet's generalising tendency he was inclined to make them seem even more numerous than they were in reality. Still further, his was an essentially masculine nature, and the women he saw around him he not only despised but ignored. He had probably had experience of frail women. His own wife he suspects of having played him false, and Emilia's words to Desdemona show that he had some justification for his doubt. Quite naturally, then, Iago applies his standard to Desdemona and believes that, no purer than the rest, she might well sin with such a "goodly man" as Cassio. Nor can he conceive that Cassio, given such opportunity, should not aim at this great Venetian beauty:

> That *Cassio* loues her, I do well beleeu't:
> That she loues him, 'tis apt, and of great Credite.
>
> [II. i. 286-87]

His ideas of men and of women are wholly formed on his own experience and on his own theories, which are themselves thoroughly self-interested:

> Oh villanous: I haue look'd vpon the world for foure times seuen yeares, and since I could distinguish betwixt a Benefit, and an Iniurie: I never found man that knew how to loue himselfe. Ere I would say, I would drown my selfe for the loue of a Gynney Hen, I would change my Humanity with a Baboone.... Vertue? A figge, 'tis in our selues that we are thus, or thus.... [Love] is meerly a Lust of the blood, and a permission of the will. Come, be a man: drown thy selfe? Drown Cats, and blind Puppies.
>
> [I. iii. 311-16, 319-20, 334-36]

Iago's philosophy—a picture of true Machiavellianism—is as clearly painted for us as might be; nor is there anything wrong for a man in his position to be a cynic. After all, cynicism is a kind of perverted idealism, and, even as Desdemona's romance might have been cured by a glance at some of the more seamy sides of life, so Iago's cynicism might have been cured by looking more closely at her purity. This may not have been so impossible as it seems, for Shakespeare apparently put a touch of poetry into Iago's being. In the very first scene his words take on a richness and colouring which seems for a moment out of harmony with his villainy, and later, when he conjures up that vision of poppy, mandragora, and all the drowsy syrups of the world, we see a glint of poetry. Here, perhaps, we are given a hint of the might-have-been.

When the play opens Iago's only crime is that of cheating Roderigo of money—but he has serious grievances which he airs to his "fool".... [A] crisis in his career has come. He has followed Othello only for his own ends:

> In following him, I follow but my selfe.
> Heauen is my Iudge, not I for loue and dutie,
> But seeming so, for my peculiar end.
>
> [I. i. 58-60]

His first action has nothing of a deliberate intrigue about it. The calling up of Brabantio is a chance action inspired by a desire to harass Othello as much as lies in his power. Thereafter we lose sight of him till the close of the act, when, in his first soliloquy, he wonders whether he might not be able to emmesh Cassio and Othello in the one net:

> I hate the Moore,
> And it is thought abroad, that 'twixt my sheets
> He ha's done my Office. I know not if't be true,
> But I, for meere suspition in that kinde,
> Will do, as if for Surety. He holds me well,
> The better shall my purpose worke on him:
> *Cassio's* a proper man: Let me see now,
> To get his Place, and to plume vp my will
> In double Knauery. How? how? Let's see.
> After some time, to abuse *Othello's* eares,
> That he is too familiar with his wife:
> He hath a person, and a smooth dispose
> To be suspected: fram'd to make women false.
>
> [I. iii. 386-98]

It is important to note that ... Iago has not the slightest thought of any tragic conclusion. Misjudging men according to his own standards he does not suspect that Othello will burst into such a fury. This is his self-deception, for the gods are laughing at him, too, when he enters upon his intrigue with the lightness of heart of a man too confident in his own cleverness. (pp. 96-100)

Othello, Iago knows, will fly into a passion, but he never imagines he will do more than cast off Desdemona. Still will he love and thank his ancient. So far Iago's main idea is to get Cassio out of office; the other part of his intrigue, spurred by revenge, is "yet confused." ... As we know, he succeeds perfectly. Cassio is degraded; but from this moment Iago is in a trap. In the first place, the lieutenancy is not at once given to him. In the second, Cassio might still be restored to favour. Thirdly, Roderigo needs constant attention. Fourthly, the other part of Iago's plot is unaccomplished. Lastly, and most important of all, his own delight in his superior skill draws him on to further action. Iago, the potential artist, is caught in the toils of his own genius. Pleasure and action, he tells us, make the hours seem short, and this joy in his own workmanship, added to the necessity of dismissing Roderigo and Cassio, sweeps him off his feet. The only method at his command is to abuse the Moor. (pp. 101-02)

The actual poisoning of Othello's mind begins not until the third scene of the third act. In spite of a hesitation which betrays a certain fear in Iago's mind that he has gone too far, the ancient is thoroughly successful in gaining the lieutenancy, but now he cannot stay his hand. He is no longer the centre of the action. He has set Othello's passions aflame, and the conflagration now roars onward beyond his power. The hesitation noted in the third act increases as we advance:

> This is the night
> That either makes me, or foredoes me quight.
>
> [V. i. 129]

From that time on we do not see him until he is brought in guarded, his house of cards fallen in grievous ruin about him. The night had "fordone him quite." Firm-lipped he stands, with exquisite courage, refusing to explain his actions:

> Demand me nothing: what you know, you know:
> From this time forth, I neuer will speake word.
>
> [V. ii. 303-04]

Even Gratiano's tortures, we realise, will not force him to utter a syllable. Iago's end is the best part of his life as we see it presented in the play, and the courage he displays there must have been introduced by Shakespeare for some definite purpose. That purpose, I believe, was to raise an element of sympathy in the audience for this "villain." There is, after all, something pitiful in this man's final doom. He who might have been so great, who had such intelligence and capability, he whose villainy does not seem to have been born with him but to have been the product of circumstance, is caught in the toils of the gods. (pp. 102-03)

He looks upon the world as a rare pageant. He has the idealist's tendency to exalt what he loves and to fix his life wholly upon that. "My life vpon her faith!" [I. iii. 294] he makes answer to Brabantio's warning, and when this faith seems shattered his whole occupation is gone. Even Desdemona's supposed infidelity is viewed by him in an idealistic way. He ceases to look on her as his wife and rises to a generalisation:

> It is the Cause, it is the Cause (my Soule)
> Let me not name it to you, you chaste Starres,
> It is the Cause. Yet Ile not shed her blood,
> Nor scarre that whiter skin of hers, then Snow,
> And smooth as Monumentall Alabaster:
> Yet she must dye, else shee'l betray more men:
> Put out the Light, and then put out the Light.
>
> [V. ii. 1-7]

Opposed to this tendency is his knowledge of a certain part of reality. He is a man who has lived his life in camps. Iago suspects him of adultery with Emilia, and this is not denied throughout the whole of the play: rather is it intensified by Emilia's own words. He shows that he knows the language of the brothel:

> Mistris,
> That have the office opposite to Saint *Peter,*
> And keepes the gate of hell. You, you: I you,
> We have done our course: there's money for your paines:
> I pray you turne the key, and keepe our counsaile.
>
> [IV. ii. 90-4]

The part of life he knows is that part which is associated with women of Emilia's and Bianca's character. Owing to his lack of intellect this portion of life clashes with his romanticism. There is no jealousy in his mind before Iago speaks, but doubt is certainly lying subconscious there. The cardinal scene in the play is the third scene of the third act. On it Shakespeare obviously must have concentrated most. At the opening of this scene Iago first breathes a hint of suspicion. At the close Othello is crying

> Damne her lewde Minx: O damne her, damne her.
> Come go with me a-part, I will withdraw
> To furnish me with some swift meanes of death
> For the faire Diuell.
>
> [III. iii. 476-79]

The duration of the action is not more than a few minutes, yet here is Othello passing from a state of supposedly complete trust in his wife to a passion that knows no bounds. Is this probable of a man "not easily jealous"? [V. ii. 345]. The first part of this scene deserves further attention. Desdemona, Cassio, and Emilia enter; Cassio moves away. "Hah? I like not that," ejaculates Iago, and Othello turns to him with a "What dost thou say?" [III. iii. 35]. From that moment his short sentences show him plunged in thought:

> Was not that *Cassio* parted from my wife? . . .
> I do beleeue 'twas he. . . .
> Who is't you meane? . . .
> Went he hence now? . . .
> Not now (sweet *Desdemon*) some other time.
> No, not to-night. . . .
> I shall not dine at home:
> I meete the Captaines at the Cittadell. . . .
> Prythee no more: Let him come when he will:
> I will deny thee nothing. . . .
> I will deny thee nothing.
> Whereon, I do beseech thee, grant me this,
> To leaue me but a little to my selfe. . . .
> Farewell my *Desdemona,* Ile come to thee strait.
>
> [III. iii. 37, 40, 44, 51, 55, 57, 58-9, 75-6, 83-5, 87]

At the conclusion his thoughts take utterance:

> *Excellent wretch: Perdition catch my Soule*
> *But I do loue thee: and when I love thee not,*
> Chaos is come againe.
>
> [III. iii. 90-2]

"And when I love thee not"—surely here lies one of Shakespeare's clues. To believe that Othello's suspicions were not in embryo before ever Iago spoke is to deny all meaning to Shakespeare's lines. Othello perhaps cheats himself, certainly cheats others, in his affirmation that he is in no wise inclined towards jealousy:

> Why? why is this?
> Think'st thou, I'ld make a Life of Iealousie;
> To follow still the changes of the Moone
> With fresh suspitions. . . .
> 'Tis not to make me Iealious,
> To say my wife is faire, feeds well, loues company,
> Is free of Speech, Sings, Playes, and Dances:
> Where Vertue is, these are more vertuous. . . .
> No *Iago,*
> Ile see before I doubt; when I doubt, proue;
> And on the proofe, there is no more but this,
> Away at once with Loue, or Iealousie.
>
> [III. iii. 176-79, 183-86, 189-92]

Most commentators take these words as a correct analysis of Othello's nature; they overlook the fact that, *without proof,* he is damning his wife and planning her murder. There is no need to dwell on Iago's insinuations; these carry on the play without adding anything new. Othello's die is cast in this one scene.

Deception and self-deception, then, subtly intermingled with the theme of idealism and reality, are the keynotes to Othello. Desdemona deceives her father at the beginning of the tragedy and ends with a lie on her lips. Othello appears in the first act as deceiving himself or his auditors with his declaration that he is "rude of speech"—presenting instead of a "round unvarnish'd tale" [I. iii. 81, 90], one of the most subtle pieces of oratory outside of Antony's similar harangue [in *Julius Caesar*]. He dies with a misconception of his own nature. There is thus a definite unity of effect running through the whole drama. Iago, Desdemona, and Othello, in spite of their difference, all take their parts in the one fatal atmosphere. (pp. 104-09)

> Allardyce Nicoll, "'The Tragedie of Othello, the Moore of Venice'," in his Studies in Shakespeare, Leonard & Virginia Woolf, 1927, pp. 80-109.

G. WILSON KNIGHT   (essay date 1930)

[*Knight was one of the most influential Shakespearean critics of the twentieth century; he helped shape a new interpretive approach to Shakespeare's work and promoted a greater appreciation of many of the plays. In his studies* The Wheel of Fire *(1930) and* The Shakespearian Tempest *(1932), Knight rejected criticism which emphasizes sources, character analysis, psychology, and ethics and outlined his principles of interpretation which, he claimed, would "replace that chaos by drawing attention to the true Shakespearian unity." Knight argued that this unity lay in Shakespeare's poetic use of images and symbols—particularly in the opposition of "tempests" and "music." He also maintained that a play's spatial aspects, or "atmosphere," should be as closely considered as the temporal elements of the plot if one is "to see the whole play in space as well as time." Knight's essay on "The Othello Music," taken from* The Wheel of Fire, *is the first extensive examination of the poetic language of* Othello. *Asserting that Othello's style is the dominant element in determining the dramatic effects of the play, he relates the Moor's poetic expression directly and integrally to what he regards as the central issue—the struggle between the cynicism of Iago and the romanticism of the Moor. In Knight's words, the drama depicts "the cynical intellect pitted against a lovable humanity transfigured by qualities of heroism and grace." Knight characterizes Othello's poetic style as concrete and aloof, its universal images, even when providing a background for human actions, remain essentially isolated, separate, and "decorative." On occasion, the critic declares, the Othello style devolves into "a studied artificiality, nerveless and without force," so that the beauties of the language seem foisted onto Othello's emotion, not integral to them, and his speeches degenerate into exaggerated emotion. The cold or detached quality of Othello's language has also been analyzed by such critics as Derek Traversi (1949), Gayle Greene (1979), and Carol McGinnis Kay (1983). Knight further maintains that the solidity and separateness of Othello's language is also reflected in the concrete, distinct characterization of the three principal figures in the play, adding that "within analysis of these three persons and their interaction lies the meaning of* Othello." *He thus describes Othello as "a symbol of faith in human values of Love, War, [and] Romance"; he judges Desdemona as an intensely human figure as well as a symbolic representation of the divine principle of love worshipped by the Moor; and Iago he calls the opposite of the hero and heroine in his negative persona—the symbol of the "cynical intellect" and the hater of beauty, meaning, and order. Knight locates the transfiguration of Othello and Desdemona into these quintessential, idealized symbols at the moment of their reunion in Cyprus in Act II, Scene i, arguing that Iago's presence, with his dire asides, completes the portrayal of the combat of cynicism and romanticism that is at the heart of the drama; he thus refers to this scene as a "microcosm" of* Othello *itself. Raising another important point, Knight avers that*

Iago's cynicism is his only motivation and his detestation of Othello's and Desdemona's beauty is the sole cause of his malevolence against them. For further commentary on Iago's motives, see the excerpts by Thomas Wilkes (1759), John Potter (1771-72), Richard Hole (1796), Samuel Taylor Coleridge (1808-18), William Hazlitt (1817), William Maginn (1839), Denton J. Snider (1887), A. C. Bradley (1904), Bernard Spivack (1958), G. M. Matthews (1964), and Stanley Edgar Hyman (see Additional Bibliography). Declaring that the degeneration of Othello's poetic style in the temptation scene and thereafter indicates the triumph of Iago's cynicism over love, Knight denies that the success is a lasting one, for he sees in Othello's speeches in Act V, Scene ii a return to the earlier Othello music, signalling the Moor's renewed faith in the human values he had earlier celebrated. For additional commentary on whether Shakespeare depicts Othello as attaining renewed optimism or new understanding at the close of the drama, see the excerpts by G. R. Elliott (1937), F. R. Leavis (1937), E. M. W. Tillyard (1938), Robert B. Heilman (1951 and 1956), G. M. Matthews (1964), and Jared R. Curtis (1973), as well as the essay by Helen Gardner cited in the Additional Bibliography.]

Othello is dominated by its protagonist. Its supremely beautiful effects of style are ever expressions of Othello's personal passion. Thus, in first analysing Othello's poetry, we shall lay the basis for an understanding of the play's symbolism: this matter of style is, indeed, crucial, and I shall now indicate those qualities which clearly distinguish it from other Shakespearian poetry. It holds a rich music all its own, and possesses a unique solidity and precision of picturesque phrase or image, a peculiar chastity and serenity of thought. It is, as a rule, barren of direct metaphysical content. Its thought does not mesh with the reader's: rather it is ever outside us, aloof. This aloofness is the resultant of an inward aloofness of image from image, word from word. The dominant quality is separation, not, as is more usual in Shakespeare, cohesion. Consider these exquisite poetic movements:

> O heavy hour!
> Methinks it should be now a huge eclipse
> Of sun and moon, and that the affrighted globe
> Should yawn at alteration.
>
> [V. ii. 98-101]

Or,

> It is the very error of the moon;
> She comes more nearer earth than she was wont,
> And makes men mad.
>
> [V. ii. 109-11]

These are solid gems of poetry which lose little by divorce from their context: wherein they differ from the finest passages of *Lear* or *Macbeth*, which are as wild flowers not to be uptorn from their rooted soil if they are to live. In these two quotations we should note how the human drama is thrown into sudden contrast and vivid, unexpected relation with the tremendous concrete machinery of the universe, which is thought of in terms of individual heavenly bodies: 'sun' and 'moon'. The same effect is apparent in:

> Nay, had she been true,
> If heaven had made me such another world
> Of one entire and perfect chrysolite,
> I'd not have sold her for it.
>
> [V. ii. 143-46]

Notice the single word 'chrysolite' with its outstanding and remote beauty: this is typical of *Othello*. Now the effect in such passages is primarily one of contrast. The vastness of the night sky, and is moving planets, or the earth itself—here conceived objectively as a solid, round, visualized object—these things, though thrown momentarily into sensible relation with the passions of man, yet remain vast, distant, separate, seen but not apprehended; something against which the dramatic movement may be silhouetted, but with which it cannot be merged. This poetic use of heavenly bodies serves to elevate the theme, to raise issues infinite and unknowable. Those bodies are not, however, implicit symbols of man's spirit, as in *Lear:* they remain distinct, isolated phenomena, sublimely decorative to the play. . . . We meet the same effect in:

> Like to the Pontic sea,
> Whose icy current and conpulsive course
> Ne'er feels retiring ebb, but keeps due on
> To the Propontic and the Hellespont,
> Even so my bloody thoughts, with violent pace,
> Shall ne'er look back, ne'er ebb to humble love,
> Till that a capable and wide revenge
> Swallow them up. Now, by yond marble heaven,
> In the due reverence of a sacred vow
> I here engage my words.
>
> [III. iii. 453-62]

This is, indeed, a typical speech. The long comparison, explicitly made, where in *Lear* or *Macbeth* a series of swiftly evolving metaphors would be more characteristic, is another example of the separateness obtaining throughout *Othello*. There is no fusing of word with word, rather a careful juxtaposition of one word or image with another. And there are again the grand single words, 'Propontic', 'Hellespont', with their sharp, clear, consonant sounds, constituting defind aural solids typical of the Othello music: indeed, fine single words, especially proper names, are a characteristic of this play—Anthropophagi, Ottomites, Arabian trees, 'the base Indian' [V. ii. 347], the Egyptian, Palestine, Mauretania, the Sagittary, Olympus, Mandragora, Othello, Desdemona. This is a rough assortment, not all used by Othello, but it points the Othello quality of rich, often expressly consonantal, outstanding words. Now Othello's prayer, with its 'marble heaven', is most typical and illustrative. One watches the figure of Othello silhouetted against a flat, solid, moveless sky: there is a plastic, static suggestion about the image. (pp. 107-10)

Now this detached style, most excellent in point of clarity and stateliness, tends also to lose something in respect of power. At moments of great tension, the Othello style fails of a supreme effect. Capable of fine things quite unmatched in their particular quality in any other play, it nevertheless sinks sometimes to a studied artificiality, nerveless and without force. For example, Othello thinks of himself as:

> . . . one whose subdued eyes,
> Albeit unused to the melting mood,
> Drop tears as fast as the Arabian trees
> Their medicinal gum.
>
> [V. ii. 348-51]

Beside this we might place Macduff's

> O I could play the woman with mine eyes
> And braggart with my tongue! But, gentle heavens,
> Cut short all intermission . . .
>
> [*Macbeth*, IV. iii. 230-32]

Now Othello's lines here have a certain restrained, melodic beauty, like the 'Pontic sea' passage; both speeches use the typical Othello picturesque image or word; both compare, by simile, the passion of man with some picture delightful in itself, which is developed for its own sake, slightly over-developed—so that the final result makes us forget the emotion in contemplation of the image. Beauty has been imposed on human sorrow, rather than shown to be intrinsic therein. But Macduff's passionate utterance has not time to paint word pictures of 'yon marble heaven', or to search for abstruse geographical images of the Hellespont, or Arabia. There is more force in his first line than all Othello's slightly over-strained phraseology of 'subdued eyes' and 'melting mood'. . . . The Othello style does not compass the overpowering effects of *Macbeth* or *Lear:* nor does it, as a rule, aim at them. At the most agonizing moments of Othello's story, however, there is apparent weakness: we find an exaggerated, false rhetoric. There is a speech in *Othello* that begins in the typical restrained manner, but degenerates finally to what might almost be called bombast. It starts:

> Where should Othello go?
> Now, how dost thou look now? O ill-starr'd wench!
> Pale as thy smock! When we shall meet at compt,
> This look of thine will hurl my soul from heaven,
> And fiends will snatch at it. Cold, cold, my girl!
> Even like thy chastity.
>
> [V. ii. 271-76]

Here we have the perfection of the Othello style. Concrete, visual, detached. Compare it with Lear's, 'Thou art a soul in bliss . . .', where the effect, though perhaps more powerful and immediate, is yet vague, intangible, spiritualized [*King Lear,* IV. vii. 45ff]. Now this speech, started in a style that can in its own way challenge that of *Lear*, rapidly degenerates as Othello's mind is represented as collapsing under the extreme of anguish:

> O cursed slave!
> Whip me, ye devils,
> From the possession of this heavenly sight!
> Blow me about in winds! roast me in sulphur!
> Wash me in steep-down gulfs of liquid fire!
> O Desdemona! Desdemona! dead!
> Oh! Oh! Oh!
>
> [V. ii. 276-82]

There is a sudden reversal of poetic beauty: these lines lack cogency because they exaggerate rather than concentrate the emotion. Place beside these violent eschatological images the passage from *Lear*:

> And my poor fool is hang'd! No, no, no life!
> Why should a dog, a horse, a rat have life,
> And thou no breath at all? Thou'lt come no more,
> Never, never, never, never, never!
> Pray you, undo this button: thank you, Sir.
> Do you see this? Look on her, look, her lips,
> Look there, look there!
>
> [*King Lear,* V. iii. 306-12]

Notice by what rough, homely images the passion is transmitted—which are as truly an integral part of the naturalism of Lear as the mosaic and polished phrase, and the abstruse and picturesque allusion is, in its best passages, a characteristic of Othello's speech. Thus the extreme, slightly exaggerated beauty of Othello's language is not maintained. This is even more true elsewhere. Othello, who usually luxuriates in deliberate and magnificent rhetoric, raves, falls in a trance:

> Lie with her! lie on her! We say lie on her,
> when they belie her. Lie with her! that's ful-
> some—Handkerchief—confessions—handker-

chief! To confess, and be hanged for his labour;
first, to be hanged, and then to confess—I tremble at it. Nature would not invest herself in
such shadowing passion without some instruction. It is not words that shake me thus. Pish!
Noses, ears, and lips.—Is't possible?—Confess—handkerchief!—O devil!

[IV. i. 35-43]

Now, whereas Lear's madness never lacks artistic meaning,
whereas its most extravagant and grotesque effects are presented with imaginative cogency, Othello can voice words like
these. This is the Iago-spirit, the Iago-medicine, at work, like
an acid eating into bright metal. This is the primary fact of
Othello and therefore of the play: something of solid beauty
is undermined, wedged open so that it exposes an extreme
ugliness. When Othello is represented as enduring loss of control he is, as Macbeth and Lear never are, ugly, idiotic; but
when he has full control he attains an architectural stateliness
of quarried speech, a silver rhetoric of a kind unique in Shakespeare:

It is the cause, it is the cause, my soul,—
Let me not name it to you, you chaste stars!—
It is the cause. Yet I'll not shed her blood;
Nor scar that whiter skin of hers than snow,
And smooth as monumental alabaster.
Yet she must die, else she'll betray more men.
Put out the light, and then put out the light:
If I quench thee, thou flaming minister,
I can again thy former light restore,
Should I repent me: but once put out thy light,
Thou cunning'st pattern of excelling nature,
I know not where is that Promethean heat
That can thy light relume. When I have pluck'd the
    rose,
I cannot give it vital growth again,
It needs must wither: I'll smell it on the tree.

[V. ii. 1-15]

This is the noble Othello music: highly-coloured, rich in sound
and phrase, stately. Each word solidifies as it takes its place
in the pattern. This speech well illustrates the Othello style:
the visual or tactile suggestion—'whiter skin of hers than snow',
'smooth as monumental alabaster'; the slightly over-decorative
phrase, 'flaming minister'; the momentary juxtaposition of humanity and the vast spaces of the night, the 'chaste stars'; the
concrete imagery of 'thou cunning'st pattern of excelling nature', and the lengthy comparison of life with light; the presence
of simple forward-flowing clarity of dignified statement and
of simile in place of the superlogical welding of thought with
molten thought as in the more compressed, agile, and concentrated poetry of Macbeth and Lear; and the fine outstanding
single word, 'Promethean'. In these respects Othello's speech
is nearer the style of the aftermath of Elizabethan literature,
the settled lava of that fiery eruption, which gave us the solid
image of Marvell and the 'marmoreal phrase' of Browne: it is
the most Miltonic thing in Shakespeare.

Now this peculiarity of style directs our interpretation in two
ways. First, the tremendous reversal from extreme, almost
over-decorative, beauty, to extreme ugliness—both of a kind
unusual in Shakespeare—will be seen to reflect a primary truth
about the play. That I will demonstrate later in my essay.
Second, the concreteness and separation of image, word, or
phrase, contrasting with the close-knit language elsewhere,
suggests a proper approach to Othello which is not proper to

Macbeth or Lear. Separation is the rule throughout Othello.
Whereas in Macbeth and Lear we have one dominant atmosphere, built of a myriad subtleties of thought and phraseology
entwining throughout, subduing our minds wholly to their respective visions, whereas each has a single quality, expresses
as a whole a single statement, Othello is built rather of outstanding differences. In Othello all is silhouetted, defined,
concrete. Now instead of reading a unique, pervading, atmospheric suggestion—generally our key to interpretation of what
happens within that atmosphere—we must here read the meaning of separate persons. The persons here are truly separate.
Lear, Cordelia, Edmund all grow out of the Lear-universe, all
are levelled by its characteristic atmosphere, all blend with it
and with each other, so that they are less closely and vividly
defined. They lack solidity. Othello, Desdemona, Iago, however, are clearly and vividly separate. All here—but Iago—
are solid, concrete. Contrast is raised to its highest pitch. Othello is statuesque, Desdemona most concretely human and individual, Iago, if not human or in any usual sense 'realistic',
is quite unique. Within analysis of these three persons and their
interaction lies the meaning of Othello. In Macbeth or Lear
we interpret primarily a singleness of vision. Here, confronted
with a significant diversity, we must have regard to the essential
relation existing between the three main personal conceptions.
Interpretation must be based not on unity but differentiation.
Therefore I shall pursue an examination of this triple symbolism, which analysis will finally resolve the difficulty of Othello's speech, wavering as it does between what at first sight
appear an almost artificial beauty and an equally inartistic ugliness.

Othello radiates a world of romantic, heroic, and picturesque
adventure. All about him is highly coloured. He is a Moor; he
is noble and generally respected; he is proud in the riches of
his achievement. Now his prowess as a soldier is emphasized.
His arms have spent 'their dearest action in the tented field'
[I. iii. 85]. . . . But we also meet a curious discrepancy. Othello
tells us:

Rude am I in my speech,
And little bless'd with the soft phrase of peace.

[I. iii. 81-2]

Yet the dominant quality in this play is the exquisitely moulded
language, the noble cadence and chiselled phrase, of Othello's
poetry. Othello's speech, therefore, reflects not a soldier's
language, but the quality of soldiership in all its glamour of
romantic adventure: it holds an imaginative realism. It has a
certain exotic beauty, is a storied and romantic treasure-house
of rich, colourful experiences. He recounts his adventures,
telling of

antres vast and deserts idle,
Rough quarries, rocks, and hills whose heads touch
    heaven,

[I. iii. 140-41]

of Cannibals, and the Anthropophagi, and 'men whose heads
do grow beneath their shoulders' [I. iii. 143-44]. He tells Desdemona of the handkerchief given by 'an Egyptian' to his
mother:

'Tis true: there's magic in the web of it:
A sibyl, that had number'd in the world
The sun to course two hundred compasses,
In her prophetic fury sew'd the work;
The worms were hallow'd that did breed the silk,
And it was dyed in mummy which the skilful
Conserved of maidens' hearts.

[III. iv. 69-75]

Finally there is his noble apostrophe to his lost 'occupation':

Farewell the plumed troop and the big wars,
That make ambition virtue! O, farewell!
Farewell the neighing steed and the shrill trump,
The spirit-stirring drum, the ear-piercing fife,
The royal banner and all quality,
Pride, pomp, and circumstance of glorious war!
And, O you mortal engines, whose rude throats
The immortal Jove's dread clamours counterfeit,
Farewell! Othello's occupation's gone.

[III. iii. 349-57]

Again, we have the addition of phrase to separate phrase, rather than the interdependence, the evolution of thought from thought, the clinging mesh of close-bound suggestions of other plays. Now this noble eulogy of war is intrinsic to the Othello conception. War is in his blood. When Desdemona accepts him, she knows she must not be 'a moth of peace' [I. iii. 256]. Othello is a compound of highly-coloured, romantic adventure—he is himself 'coloured'—and War; together with a great pride and a great faith in those realities. His very life is dependent on a fundamental belief in the validity and nobility of human action—with, perhaps, a strong tendency towards his own achievement in particular. Now War, in Shakespeare, is usually a positive spiritual value, like Love. . . . Soldiership is almost the condition of nobility, and so the Shakespearian hero is usually a soldier. Therefore Othello, with reference to the Shakespearian universe, becomes automatically a symbol of faith in human values of Love, War, of Romance in a wide and sweeping sense. He is, as it were, conscious of all he stands for: from the first to the last he loves his own romantic history. He is, like Troilus, dedicate to these values, has faith and pride in both. Like Troilus he is conceived as extraordinarily direct, simple, 'credulous' [IV. i. 45]. Othello, as he appears in the action of the play, may be considered the high-priest of human endeavour, robed in the vestments of Romance, whom we watch serving in the Temple of War at the Altar of Love's Divinity.

Desdemona is his divinity. She is, at the same time, warmly human. There is a certain domestic femininity about her. She is 'a maiden never bold' [I. iii. 94]. We hear that 'the house affairs' (had Cordelia any?) drew her often from Othello's narrative [I. iii. 147]. But she asks to hear the whole history:

I did consent,
And often did beguile her of her tears,
When I did speak of some distressful stroke
That my youth suffered. My story being done,
She gave me for my pains a world of sighs:
She swore, in faith, 'twas strange, 'twas passing
    strange,
'Twas pitiful, 'twas wondrous pitiful:
She wish'd she had not heard it, yet she wish'd
That heaven had made her such a man.

[I. iii. 155-63]

The same domesticity and gentleness is apparent throughout. She talks of 'to-night at supper' [III. iii. 57] or 'to-morrow dinner' [III. iii. 58]; she is typically feminine in her attempt to help Cassio, and her pity for him. This is how she describes her suit to Othello:

Why, this is not a boon;
'Tis as I should entreat you wear your gloves,

Or feed on nourishing dishes, or keep you warm,
Or sue to you to do a peculiar profit
To your own person . . .

[III. iii. 76-80]

—a speech reflecting a world of sex-contrast. She would bind Othello's head with her handkerchief—that handkerchief which is to become a terrific symbol of Othello's jealousy. The Othello world is eminently domestic, and Desdemona expressly feminine. We hear of her needlework [IV. i. 187-88], her fan, gloves, mask [IV. ii. 9]. In the exquisite 'willow'-song scene, we see her with her maid, Emilia. Emilia gives her 'her nightly wearing' [IV. iii. 16]. Emilia says she has laid on her bed the 'wedding-sheets' [IV. ii. 105] Desdemona asked for. Then there is the Willow-Song, brokenly sung whilst Emilia 'unpins' [IV. iii. 34] Desdemona's dress:

My mother had a maid called Barbara:
She was in love, and he she loved proved mad
And did forsake her . . .

[IV. iii. 26-8]

The extreme beauty and pathos of this scene is largely dependent on the domesticity of it. *Othello* is eminently a domestic tragedy. But this element in the play is yet to be related to another more universal element. Othello is concretely human, so is Desdemona. Othello is very much the typical middle-aged bachelor entering matrimony late in life, but he is also, to transpose a phrase of Iago's, a symbol of human—especially masculine—'purpose, courage, and valour' [IV. ii. 213-14], and, in a final judgement, is seen to represent the idea of human faith and value in a very wide sense. Now Desdemona, also very human, with an individual domestic feminine charm and simplicity, is yet also a symbol of woman in general daring the unknown seas of marriage with the mystery of man. Beyond this, in the far flight of a transcendental interpretation, it is clear that she becomes a symbol of man's ideal, the supreme value of Love. At the limit of the series of wider and wider suggestions which appear from imaginative contemplation of a poetic symbol she is to be equated with the Divine Principle. Now in one scene of *Othello,* and one only, direct poetic symbolism breaks across the vividly human, domestic world of this play. As everything in *Othello* is separated, defined, so the plot itself is in two distinct geographical divisions: Venice and Cyprus. Desdemona leaves the safety and calm of her home for the stormy voyage to Cyprus and the tempest of the following tragedy. Iago's plot begins to work in the second part. The storm-scene, between the two parts, is important.

Storms are continually symbols of tragedy in Shakespeare. Now this scene contains some most vivid imaginative effects, among them passages of fine storm-poetry of the usual kind:

For do but stand upon the foaming shore,
The chidden billow seems to pelt the clouds;
The wind-shaked surge, with high and monstrous mane,
Seems to cast water on the burning bear,
And quench the guards of the ever-fixed pole:
I never did like molestation view,
On the enchafed flood.

[II. i. 11-17]

This storm-poetry is here closely associated with the human element. And in this scene where direct storm-symbolism occurs it is noteworthy that the figures of Desdemona and Othello are both strongly idealized:

Cassio. Tempests themselves, high seas and howling
     winds,
   The gutter'd rocks and congregated sands,—
   Traitors ensteep'd to clog the guiltless keel,—
   As having sense of beauty, do omit
   Their mortal natures, letting go safely by
   The divine Desdemona.
Montano.   What is she?
Cassio. She that I spake of, our great captain's
   captain. . . .

                                          [II. i. 68-74]

Desdemona is thus endued with a certain transcendent quality of beauty and grace. She 'paragons description and wild fame' says Cassio: she is

   One that excels the quirks of blazoning pens,
   And in the essential vesture of creation
   Does tire the ingener.

                                          [II. i. 62-5]

And Othello enters the port of Cyprus as a hero coming to 'bring comfort', to 'give renewed fire' to men. The entry of Desdemona and that of Othello are both heralded by discharge of guns: which both merges finely with the tempest-symbolism and the violent stress and excitement of the scene as a whole, and heightens our sense of the warrior nobility of the protagonist and his wife, subdued as she is 'to the very quality' of her lord [I. iii. 251]. Meeting Desdemona, he speaks:

Othello. O my fair warrior!
Desdemona.   My dear Othello!
Othello. It gives me wonder great as my content
   To see you here before me. O my soul's joy!
   If after every tempest come such calms,
   May the winds blow till they have waken'd death!
   And let the labouring bark climb hills of seas
   Olympus-high and duck again as low
   As hell's from heaven! If it were now to die,
   'Twere now to be most happy; for, I fear,
   My soul hath her content so absolute
   That not another comfort like to this
   Succeeds in unknown fate.

                                          [II. i. 182-93]

This is the harmonious marriage of true and noble minds. Othello, Desdemona, and their love are here apparent, in this scene of storm and reverberating discharge of cannon, as things of noble and conquering strength: they radiate romantic valour. Othello is essential man in all his prowess and protective strength; Desdemona essential woman, gentle, loving, brave in trust of her warrior husband. The war is over. The storm of sea or bruit of cannonade are powerless to hurt them: yet there is another storm brewing in the venomed mind of Iago. Instead of merging with and accompanying tragedy the storm here is thus contrasted with the following tragic events: as usual in *Othello*, contrast and separation take the place of fusion and unity. This scene is thus a microcosm of the play, reflecting its action. Colours which are elsewhere softly toned are here splashed vividly on the play's canvas. Here especially Othello appears a prince of heroes, Desdemona is lit by a divine feminine radiance: both are transfigured. They are shown as coming safe to land, by Heaven's 'grace', triumphant, braving war and tempestuous seas, guns thundering their welcome. The reference of all this, on the plane of high poetic symbolism, to the play as a whole is evident.

Now against these two Iago pits his intellect. In this scene too Iago declares himself with especial clarity:

   O gentle lady, do not put me to't;
   For I am nothing, if not critical.

                                          [II. i. 118-19]

His conversation with Desdemona reveals his philosophy. Presented under the cloak of fun, it exposes nevertheless his attitude to life: that of the cynic. Roderigo is his natural companion: the fool is a convenient implement, and at the same time continual food for his philosophy. Now Othello and Desdemona are radiant, beautiful: Iago opposes them, critical, intellectual. Like cold steel his cynic skill will run through the warm body of their love. Asked to praise Desdemona, he draws a picture of womanly goodness in a vein of mockery. And concludes:

Iago. She was a wight if ever such wight were—
Desdemona. To do what?
Iago. To suckle fools and chronicle small beer.

                                          [II. i. 158-60]

Here is his reason for hating Othello's and Desdemona's love: he hates their beauty, to him a meaningless, stupid thing. That is Iago. Cynicism is his philosophy, his very life, his 'motive' in working Othello's ruin. The play turns on this theme: the cynical intellect pitted against a lovable humanity transfigured by qualities of heroism and grace. As Desdemona and Othello embrace he says:

                  O you are well tuned now!
   But I'll set down the pegs that make this music,
   As honest as I am.

                                          [II. i. 199-201]

'Music' is apt: we remember Othello's rich harmony of words. Against the Othello music Iago concentrates all the forces of cynic villainy. (pp. 111-24)

His plan arises out of the cynical depths of his nature. When, at the end, he says, 'I told him what I thought' [V. ii. 176], he is speaking at least a half-truth. He hates the romance of Othello and the loveliness of Desdemona because he is by nature the enemy of these things. Cassio, he says,

            hath a daily beauty in his life
      That makes mine ugly.

                                          [V. i. 19-20]

This is his 'motive' throughout: other suggestions are surface deep only. He is cynicism loathing beauty, refusing to allow its existence. Hence the venom of his plot: the plot is Iago—both are ultimate, causeless, self-begotten. Iago is cynicism incarnate and projected into action.

Iago is thus utterly devilish: there is no weakness in his casing armour of unrepentant villainy. He is a kind of Mephistopheles, closely equivalent to Goethe's devil, the two possessing the same qualities of mockery and easy cynicism. Thus he is called a 'hellish villain' by Lodovico [V. ii. 368], a 'demi-devil' by Othello [V. ii. 301]. . . . Iago, himself a kind of devil, insidiously eats his way into this world of romance, chivalry, nobility. The word 'devil' occurs frequently in the latter acts: devils are alive here, ugly little demons of black disgrace. They swarm over the mental horizon of the play, occurring frequently. Iago is directly or indirectly their author and originator. 'Devil', 'hell', 'damnation'—these words are recurrent, and continually juxtaposed to thoughts of 'heaven', prayer, angels. We are clearly set amid 'heaven and men and devils'

[V. ii. 221]. Such terms are related here primarily to sexual impurity. In *Othello,* pure love is the supreme good; impurity, damnation. This pervading religious tonal significance relating to infidelity explains lines such as:

> Turn thy complexion there,
> Patience, thou young and rose-lipped cherubin,—
> Ay, there, look grim as hell!
>
> [IV. ii. 62-4]

Othello addresses Emilia:

> You, mistress,
> That have the office opposite to Saint Peter,
> And keep the gate of hell!
>
> [IV. ii. 90-2]

Here faithful love is to be identified with 'the divine', the 'heavenly'; unfaithful love, or the mistrust which imagines it, or the cynic that gives birth to that imagination—all these are to be identified with 'the devil'. The hero is set between the forces of divinity and hell. The forces of hell win and pure love lies slain. Therefore Othello cries to 'devils' to whip him from that 'heavenly' sight [V. ii. 277, 278]. He knows himself to have been entrapped by hell-forces. The Iago-Devil association is of importance.

Now it will be remembered that *Othello* is a play of concrete forms. This world is a world of visual images, colour, and romance. It will also be clear that the mesh of devil-references I have just suggested show a mental horizon black, formless, colourless. They contrast with the solid, chiselled, enamelled Othello-style elsewhere. This devil-world is insubstantial, vague, negative. Now on the plane of personification we see that Othello and Desdemona are concrete, moulded of flesh and blood, warm. Iago contrasts with them metaphysically as well as morally: he is unlimited, formless villainy. He is the spirit of denial, wholly negative. He never has visual reality. He is further blurred by the fact of his being something quite different from what he appears to the others. Is he to look like a bluff soldier, or Mephistopheles? He is a different kind of being from Othello and Desdemona: he belongs to a different world. They, by their very existence, assert the positive beauty of created forms—hence Othello's perfected style of speech, his strong human appeal, his faith in creation's values of Love and War. This world of created forms, this sculptural and yet pulsing beauty, the Iago-spirit undermines, poisons, disintegrates. Iago is a demon of cynicism, colourless, formless, in a world of colours, shapes, and poetry's music. Of all these he would create chaos. Othello's words are apt:

> Excellent wretch! Perdition catch my soul
> But I do love thee! And when I love thee not,
> Chaos is come again.
>
> [III. iii. 90-2]

Chaos indeed. Iago works at the foundations of human values. Cassio is a soldier: he ruins him as a soldier, makes him drunk. So he ruins both Othello's love and warrior-heart. He makes him absurd, ugly. Toward the end of the play there is hideous suggestion. We hear of 'cords, knives, poison' [III. iii. 388, 389], of lovers 'as prime as goats, as hot as monkeys' [III. iii. 403]; we meet Bianca, the whore, told by Cassio to 'throw her vile guesses in the devil's teeth' [III. iv. 184]; there are Othello's incoherent mutterings, 'Pish! Noses, ears and lips!' [IV. i. 42], he will 'chop' Desdemona 'into messes' [IV i. 200]; she reminds him of 'foul toads' [IV. ii. 61]. Watching Cassio, he descends to this:

> O! I see that nose of yours, but not that dog I
> shall throw it to.
>
> [IV. i. 142-43]

Othello strikes Desdemona, behaves like a raging beast. 'Fire and brimstone!' [IV. i. 234] he cries, and again, 'Goats and monkeys!' [IV i. 263]. 'Heaven stops the nose' at Desdemona's impurity [IV. ii. 77]. Othello in truth behaves like "a beggar in his drink" [IV. ii. 120]. In all these phrases I would emphasize not the sense and dramatic relevance alone, but the suggestion—the accumulative effect of ugliness, hellishness, idiocy, negation. It is a formless, colourless essence, insidiously undermining a world of concrete, visual, richly-toned forms. That is the Iago-spirit embattled against the domesticity, the romance, the idealized humanity of the Othello-world. Here, too, we find the reason for the extreme contrast of Othello's two styles: one exotically beautiful, the other blatantly absurd, ugly. There is often no dignity in Othello's rage. There is not meant to be. Iago would make discord of the Othello music. Thus at his first conquest he filches something of Othello's style and uses it himself:

> Not poppy, nor mandragora,
> Nor all the drowsy syrups of the world,
> Shall ever medicine thee to that sweet sleep
> Which thou owed'st yesterday.
>
> [III. iii. 330-33]

To him Othello's pride in his life story and Desdemona's admiration were ever stupid:

> Mark me with what violence she first loved the
> Moor, but for bragging and telling her fantast-
> ical lies: and will she love him still for prating?
>
> [II. i 222-24]

Iago, 'nothing if not critical', speaks some truth of Othello's style—it is 'fantastical'. As I have shown, it is somewhat over-decorative, highly-coloured. The dramatic value of this style now appears. In fact, a proper understanding of Othello's style reveals Iago's 'motive' so often questioned. There is something sentimental in Othello's language, in Othello. Iago is pure cynicism. That Iago should scheme—in this dramatic symbolism forged in terms of interacting persons—to undermine Othello's faith in himself, his wife, and his 'occupation', is inevitable. Logically, the cynic must oppose the sentimentalist: dramatically, he works his ruin by deceit and deception. That Othello often just misses tragic dignity is the price of his slightly strained emotionalism. Othello loves emotion for its own sake, luxuriates in it, like Richard II. As ugly and idiot ravings, disjointed and with no passionate dignity even, succeed Othello's swell and flood of poetry, Iago's triumph seems complete. The honoured warrior, rich in strength and experience, noble in act and repute, lies in a trance, nerveless, paralysed by the Iago-conception:

> Work on, my medicine, work.
>
> [IV. i. 44-5]

But Iago's victory is not absolute. During the last scene, Othello is a nobly tragic figure. His ravings are not final: he rises beyond them. He slays Desdemona finally not so much in rage, as for 'the cause' [V. ii. 1]. He slays her in love. Though Desdemona fails him, his love, homeless, 'perplexed in the extreme' [V. ii. 346], endures. He will kill her and 'love her after' [V. ii. 19]. In that last scene, too, he voices the grandest of his poetry. The Iago-spirit never finally envelops him, masters him, disintegrates his soul. Those gem-like miniatures of poetic movement quoted at the start of my essay are among Othello's last words. His vast love has, it is true, failed in a domestic world. But now symbols of the wide beauty of the universe enrich his thoughts: the 'chaste stars', the 'sun and moon', the 'affrighted globe', the world 'of one entire and perfect chrysolite' that may not but a Desdemona's love. At the end we know that Othello's fault is simplicity alone. He is, indeed, 'a gull, a dolt' [V. ii. 163]; he loves 'not wisely but too well' [V. ii. 344]. His simple faith in himself endures: and at the end, he takes just pride in recalling his honourable service.

In this essay I have attempted to expose the underlying thought of the play. Interpretation here is not easy, nor wholly satisfactory. As all within *Othello*—save the Iago-theme—is separated, differentiated, solidified, so the play itself seems at first to be divorced from wider issues, a lone thing of meaningless beauty in the Shakespearian universe, solitary, separate, unyielding and chaste as the moon. It is unapproachable, yields itself to no easy mating with our minds. Its thought does not readily mesh with our thought. We can visualize it, admire its concrete felicities of phrase and image, the mosaic of its language, the sculptural outline of its effects, the precision and chastity of its form. But one cannot be lost in it, subdued to it, enveloped by it, as one is drenched and refreshed by the elemental cataracts of *Lear;* one cannot be intoxicated by it as by the rich wine of *Antony and Cleopatra*. *Othello* is essentially outside us, beautiful with a lustrous, planetary beauty. Yet the Iago-conception is of a different kind from the rest of the play. This conception alone, if no other reason existed, would force the necessity of an intellectual interpretation. Thus we see the Iago-spirit gnawing at the root of all the Othello-values, the Othello-beauties; he eats into the core and heart of this romantic world, worms his way into its solidity, rotting it, poisoning it. Once this is clear, the whole play begins to have meaning. On the plane of dramatic humanity, we see a story of the cynic intriguing to ruin the soldier and his love. On the plane of poetic conception, in matters of technique, style, personification—there we see a spirit of negation, colourless, and undefined, attempting to make chaos of a world of stately, architectural, and exquisitely coloured forms. The two styles of Othello's speech illustrate this. Thus the different technique of the Othello and Iago conceptions is intrinsic with the plot of the play: in them we have the spirit of negation set against the spirit of creation. That is why Iago is undefined, devisualized, inhuman, in a play of consummate skill in concrete imagery and vivid human delineation. He is a colourless and ugly thing in a world of colour and harmony. His failure lies in this: in the final scene, at the moment of his complete triumph, Emilia dies for her mistress to the words of Desdemona's willow-song, and the Othello music itself sounds with a nobler cadence, a richer flood of harmonies, a more selfless and universalized flight of the imagination than before. The beauties of the Othello-world are not finally disintegrated: they make 'a swan-like end, fading in music' [*The Merchant of Venice*, III. iii. 44-5]. (pp. 125-31)

G. Wilson Knight, ''The Othello Music,'' in his The Wheel of Fire: Essays in Interpretation of Shakespeare's Sombre Tragedies, *Oxford University Press, London, 1930, pp. 107-31.*

MAUD BODKIN (essay date 1934)

[Although not a professional psychoanalyst, Bodkin incorporated into her literary criticism Jungian theories of archetypal patterns in the individual psyche arising from ageless configurations of human experience and providing the ritual origins of art. Whereas the majority of psychoanalytic critics focus upon the pathology of the artist, she sought to discover the manner in which a work of art satisfies the emotions and to identify the relationship of formal structure to the underlying symbolic patterns in the human mind. In the following excerpt from her commentary on Othello, Bodkin offers a view of the kinship between the minds of Othello and Iago that had been prefigured by August Wilhelm Schlegel (1811) and Denton J. Snider (1887) and which was later developed by such critics as G. R. Elliott (1937), F. R. Leavis (1937), and J.I.M. Stewart (1949). Beginning with an endorsement and restatement of G. Wilson Knight's earlier essay on Othello (see excerpt above, 1930), she analyzes the impact on the Moor, during the temptation scene, of Iago's ''half truths'' regarding the possibility of Desdemona's eventual rejection of her husband because of his alien nature and the insubstantial basis of their love. Bodkin asserts that these half-truths actually lie repressed in Othello's own psyche, since his romantic vision of his personal identity cannot accommodate them and remain intact. When Othello denies them conscious acknowledgement, they are projected into the speeches of Iago with ''a terrible power,'' wounding the man who has suppressed them. Bodkin further remarks that Iago is Othello's devil in an archetypal sense, in that he embodies the external and internal forces which imperil the Moor's ''supreme values.'' For additional psychoanalytic interpretations of Othello, see the excerpt by Martin Wangh (1950), as well as the essays by M. D. Faber, Abraham Bronson Feldman, Stanley Edgar Hyman, Stephen Reid, and Gordon Ross Smith cited in the Additional Bibliography.]

I would ask the reader to recall his experience of the play of *Othello,* focusing it at the moment, in Act II, of the meeting of Othello and Desdemona, in presence of Iago. This appears to me one of those moments where the poet's choice of words and shaping of the action leads us to look back and forward, concentrating in its timeless significance the procession of the play's temporal unfolding. Each of the chief figures at this moment appears charged with full symbolic value for feeling. The character of the situation—the fury of the storm braved, Othello's military task accomplished by the elements' aid— prepares for that idealization of the hero and his bride communicated through the words of Cassio:

> Tempests themselves, high seas, and howling winds
> The gutter'd rocks, and congregated sands,
> Traitors ensteep'd to clog the guiltless keel,
> As having sense of beauty, do omit
> Their mortal natures, letting go safely by
> The divine Desdemona. . . .
>
> . . . Great Jove Othello guard,
> And swell his sail with thine own powerful breath,
> That he may bless this bay with his tall ship,
> Make love's quick pants in Desdemona's arms,
> Give renew'd fire to our extincted spirits
> And bring all Cyprus comfort!
>
> [II. i. 68-73, 77-82]

The words of Othello greeting Desdemona communicate the experience of that high rapture which in a tragic world brings fear. We feel a poise of the spirit like that of the sun at its zenith, or of the wheel of fate, before the downward plunge. Consider these words in their place:

> *Othello.* O my fair warrior!
> *Desdemona.*   My dear Othello.
> *Othello.* It gives me wonder great as my content
>   To see you here before me. O my soul's joy!

If after every tempest come such calms
May the winds blow till they have waken'd death!
And let the labouring bark climb hills of seas
Olympus-high, and duck again as low
As hell's from heaven! If it were now to die,
'Twere now to be most happy, for I fear
My soul hath her content so absolute
That not another comfort like to this
Succeeds in unknown fate.

[II. i. 182-93]

The name Othello gives his lady, 'my fair warrior', recalls the events that have led up to this meeting. It reminds us of Othello's story of his wooing—how, moved by his life's tale of warlike adventure,

She swore, in faith, t'was strange, 'twas passing
        strange;
'Twas pitiful, 'twas wondrous pitiful:
She wish'd she had not heard it, yet she wish'd
That heaven had made her such a man; . . .
She lov'd me for the dangers I had pass'd
And I lov'd her that she did pity them.

[I. iii. 160-63, 167-68]

And of Desdemona's confession:

That I did love the Moor to live with him,
My downright violence and storm of fortunes
May trumpet to the world; my heart's subdu'd
Even to the very quality of my lord;
I saw Othello's visage in his mind,
And to his honours and his valiant parts
Did I my soul and fortunes consecrate.
So that, dear lords, if I be left behind,
A moth of peace, and he go to the war,
The rites for which I love him are bereft me.

[I. iii. 248-57]

Desdemona—the 'maiden never bold: Of spirit so still and quiet, that her motion Blush'd at herself' [I. iii. 94-6]—has found, we divine, in Othello the warrior hidden in the depth of her woman's heart. She lives in him as 'essential man in all his prowess and protective strength' [see excerpt above by G. Wilson Knight, 1930], while he finds in her 'essential woman', and lives in her adoring trust and love as in the secret place his own later words describe:

                where I have garner'd up my heart
Where either I must live or bear no life,
The fountain from the which my current runs
Or else dries up. . . .

[IV. ii. 57-60]

In the light that these passages throw upon the relation of the lovers, their high moment appears as, in a manner, a fulfilment of fantasy—the almost inevitable, archetypal fantasy of man and woman in their turning to one another—and this sense of it contributes to the presage of disaster. (pp. 217-19)

To the menace immanent in the form of the ecstatic moment substantial shape is given in the figure of Iago. Already in earlier scenes Iago has become known to us, his hatred of Othello, his pose of the honest clear-sighted friend. Here, as the lovers embrace, the harsh impact of his threatening aside gains intensity from the shadowing fear that lies in excess of happiness:

O! you are well tun'd now,
But I'll set down the pegs that make this music,
As honest as I am.

[II. i. 199-201]

In his essay entitled 'The Othello music', Wilson Knight has enriched our apprehension of the metaphor in these words of Iago by relating it to his view of the main contrast within the play and of the manner in which it is presented [see excerpt above, 1930]. He gives detailed illustration of the way in which Shakespeare has utilized the resources of style in speech to convey the relation between the different worlds, or forces, which the characters represent. The unrealistic beauty of Othello's speech, when he is master of himself, suggests the romantic world of varied colour, form, and sound, to which Othello belongs:

The spirit-stirring drum, the ear-piercing fife,
The royal banner and all quality
Pride, pomp, and circumstance of glorious war!

[III. iii. 352-54]

'Othello's speech reflects not a soldier's language, but the quality of soldiership in all its glamour of romantic adventure' [Knight]. Othello is a symbol of faith in human values of love and war, romantically conceived. Desdemona, as she appears in relation to Othello, is not so much individual woman as the Divinity of love. Iago is cynicism incarnate. He stands for a 'devil-world', unlimited, formless, negative. He is the spirit of denial of all romantic values. His hatred of Othello is something intrinsic to his nature, needing no external motive. Othello's world of colour, shape, and music is undermined by him, poisoned, disintegrated. We are made to feel the disintegration through the direct impact of speech, as Othello's verbal music is transformed by the working of Iago's 'poison' into incoherence—something chaotic, absurd, hideous:

Pish! Noses, ears, and lips. Is it possible?—
Confess!—Handkerchief!—O devil!

[IV. i. 42-3]

Only at the end we feel the partial, hard-won self-maintenance of the world of romantic values in Othello's recovery of his speech-music; as when he gives expression to that longing-recurrent in the Shakespearian tragic hero—for the survival of his memory and his true story among men:

Speak of me as I am; nothing extenuate,
Nor set down aught in malice: then must you speak
Of one that lov'd not wisely but too well;
Of one not easily jealous, but, being wrought,
Perplex'd in the extreme; of one whose hand,
Like the base Indian threw a pearl away
Richer than all his tribe . . .

[V. ii. 342-48]

Upon this characterization of the different worlds or forces that contend within the play, I wish to base a further psychological consideration of the figure of Iago in relation to Othello. Wilson Knight has noted that while Othello and Desdemona have symbolic significance, they are also 'warmly human, concrete'. Iago, on the other hand, is mysterious, inhuman, 'a kind of Mephistopheles'. Iago illustrates, we may say, that different plane of representation noted in relation to Greek and medieval art; and we may raise the question how far it is possible to identify Iago as a projected image of forces present in Othello, in some such fashion as Apatê of the vase-painting represents the blindness of ambition in the Persian king.

We may note first that even when a critic sets out, as A. C. Bradley does, to study Iago's character as if he were an actual living man [see excerpt above, 1904], what seems to emerge most clearly is the dominance of the man by a certain force, or spirit. We can feel, says Bradley, the part of himself that Shakespeare put into Iago—the artist's delight in the development of a plot, a design, which, as it works itself out, masters and possesses him. In regard to this plot it concerns us, as psychological critics, to note that it is built not merely, as Bradley remarks, on falsehoods, but also on partial truths of human nature that the romantic vision ignores. It is such a truth that a woman, 'a super-subtle Venetian' [I. iii. 356], suddenly wedding one in whom she sees the image of her ideal warrior, is liable to experience moments of revulsion from the strange passionate creature she as yet knows so little, movements of nature toward those more nearly akin to her in 'years, manners, and beauties' [II. i. 229-30]. There is an element of apt truth in Iago's thought that a woman's love may be won, but not held, by 'bragging and telling her fantastical lies' [II. i. 223-24]. There is terrible truth in the reflection that if a man is wedded to his fantasy of woman as the steadfast hiding-place of his heart, the fountain whence his current flows, so that he grows frantic and blind with passion at the thought of the actual woman he has married as a creature of natural varying impulse—then he lies at the mercy of life's chances, and of his own secret fears and suspicions.

What is the meaning of that reiteration by Othello of his trust in Iago's honesty? Before Iago has fashioned accident into a trap for Othello, and woven a web of falsehood to ensnare him, at his very first insinuations, Othello shows signs of terror. He fears the monster 'too hideous to be shown' [III. iii. 108] that he discerns lurking in Iago's thought. He begins to harp upon his honesty:

> . . . for I know thou art full of love and honesty,
> And weigh'st thy words before thou giv'st them breath,
> Therefore these stops of thine fright me the more;
>
> [III. iii. 242-43]

As soon as Iago has left him:

> Why did I marry? This honest creature doubtless,
> Sees and knows more, much more, than he unfolds.
>
> [III. iii. 118-20]

And again:

> This fellow's of exceeding honesty,
> And knows all qualities, with a learned spirit
> Of human dealings. . . .
>
> [III. iii. 258-60]

The whole of this dialogue between Othello and Iago, at the very beginning of Iago's plot, shows the uncanny insight of genius, illustrating in anticipation the discoveries of science. Our halting psychological theory has begun to describe for us the manner in which those aspects of social experience that a man's thought ignores leave their secret impress on his mind; how from this impress spring feelings and impulses that work their way toward consciousness, and if refused entrance there project themselves into the words, looks, and gestures of those around, arming these with a terrible power against the willed personality and its ideals. Iago seems to Othello so honest, so wise beyond himself in human dealings, possessed of a terrible power of seeing and speaking truth, because into what he speaks are projected the half truths that Othello's romantic vision ignored, but of which his mind held secret knowledge.

If we attempt to define the devil in psychological terms, regarding him as an archetype, a persistent or recurrent mode of apprehension, we may say that the devil is our tendency to represent in personal form the forces within and without us

that threaten our supreme values. When Othello finds those values, of confident love, of honour, and pride in soldiership, that made up his purposeful life, falling into ruin, his sense of the devil in all around him becomes acute. Desdemona has become 'a fair devil'; he feels 'a young and sweating devil' in her hand [III. iii. 479; III. iv. 42]. The cry 'O devil' breaks out among his incoherent words of raving. When Iago's falsehoods are disclosed, and Othello at last, too late, wrenches himself free from the spell of Iago's power over him, his sense of the devil incarnate in Iago's shape before him becomes overwhelming. If those who tell of the devil have failed to describe Iago, they have lied:

> I look down towards his feet; but that's a fable.
> If that thou be'st a devil, I cannot kill thee.
>
> [V. ii. 286-87]

We also, watching or reading the play, experience the archetype. Intellectually aware, as we reflect, of natural forces, within a man himself as well as in society around, that betray or shatter his ideals, we yet feel these forces aptly symbolized for the imagination by such a figure as Iago—a being though personal yet hardly human, concentrated wholly on the hunting to destruction of its destined prey, the proud figure of the hero. (pp. 220-24)

Maud Bodkin, "The Images of the Devil, of the Hero, and of God," in her Archetypal Patterns in Poetry: Psychological Studies of Imagination, *Oxford University Press, 1934, pp. 217-70.*

G. R. ELLIOTT   (essay date 1937)

[*Elliott was an American educator and literary critic who wrote several works on Shakespeare and other Renaissance writers, including* Scourge and Minister (A Study in "Hamlet") *(1951),* Flaming Minister: A Study of "Othello" as a Tragedy of Love and Hate *(1953), and* Dramatic Providence in "Macbeth" *(1958). In the following excerpt from an essay first published in the* American Review *in 1937, he offers an analysis of* Othello *that diverges sharply from the traditional Romantic interpretation of the play, particularly challenging Samuel Taylor Coleridge's evaluation of the Moor and his love for Desdemona, as well as the earlier critic's assessment of Iago as a "superhuman" villain (see excerpt above, 1813). Elliott acknowledges the intrinsic nobility of the Moor, but asserts that he is also excessively proud and self-centered and that, until the close of the drama, his love for Desdemona is romantic in conception and, relative to the more "penetrating passion" of his wife, comparatively selfish. Like Maud Bodkin (1934), the critic argues that Othello has suppressed his fears that Desdemona may prove false to him and is thus quickly provoked by Iago's initial insinuations in the temptation scene. In fact, Elliott contends, Iago is an actualization of the Moor's "worser self," a point similar to that expressed by such later critics as F. R. Leavis (1937), J. I. M. Stewart (1949), and Kenneth Burke (1951). The most important aspects of the Moor's nature that contribute to his jealous rage, Elliott avers, are the frailties in his love, the forcefulness of his passion, his lack of trust in his wife, and his excessive sense of honor and pride; these, more than the manipulation of Iago, are "the main motive force" in the establishment of Othello's jealousy in Act III, Scene iii. Such other critics as F. R. Leavis (1937), Derek Traversi (1949), Brents Stirling (1956), Roy W. Battenhouse (1969), and Carol McGinnis Kay (1983) have also analyzed the various manifestations of Othello's self-centered nature. With respect to Coleridge's description of Iago as a "superhuman" schemer, Elliott maintains instead that the ensign is a rather inferior villain who badly misjudges the nature of those around him and whose strategies produce results he never intended. The critic contends that Iago does not seek the destruction of Desdemona—a point also put forth by the anonymous critic in the* Bee *(1791), William Maginn (1839), and Richard Grant White (1885)—but, because he fails to calculate the "inward force and danger of Othello's love," he finds that he has to act in concert with the Moor's passion in order to accomplish his goals. Thus, in Elliott's words, from the temptation scene forward Iago becomes "the tool of Othello's passion more than Othello is the tool of his cunning." Other critics who have viewed Iago as the victim of his own schemes include William Hazlitt (1817), William Maginn (1839), A. C. Bradley (1904), Tucker Brooke (1918), Allardyce Nicoll (1927), and Nigel Alexander (see Additional Bibliography). Regarding Desdemona, Elliott asserts that the heroine is portrayed as morally and mentally "limited" through most of the drama, despite the depth of her passion for Othello. But by the end of the play, the critic adds, she achieves what Coleridge called a "holy entireness of love." Elliott focuses on her last, dying speech, claiming that it reflects "a triple truth"—her acknowledgment of her part in the catastrophe, her "self-sacrificing effort to assume the whole guilt," and her "religious vision" of Othello's "potential goodness." Indeed, Elliott concludes, this example of Desdemona's love leads Othello himself to acknowledge the self-centered nature of his feelings for her, and as he judges and condemns himself in his final remarks he passes through a purgatorial process, discarding his pride and recognizing at last the inward, spiritual beauty of Desdemona. For addditional inquiries into whether Othello achieves a new awareness or understanding at the close of the play, see the excerpts by G. Wilson Knight (1930), F. R. Leavis (1937), E. M. W. Tillyard (1938), Robert B. Heilman (1956), G. M. Matthews (1964), and Jared R. Curtis (1973), as well as the essay by Helen Gardner cited in the Additional Bibliography.]*

The following is the gist of the paragraph in which Coleridge summarizes his view of *Othello:*

> Finally, let me repeat that Othello does not kill Desdemona in jealousy, but in a conviction forced upon him by the almost superhuman art of Iago, such a conviction as any man would and must have entertained who had believed Iago's honesty as Othello did. We, the audience, know that Iago is a villian from the beginning; but in considering the essence of the Shakespearean Othello, we must perseveringly place ourselves in his situation, and under his circumstances. Then we shall immediately feel the fundamental difference between the solemn agony of the noble Moor and the wretched fishing jealousies of Leontes and the morbid suspiciousness of Leonatus.... Othello had no life but in Desdemona: the belief that she, his angel, had fallen from the heaven of her native innocence, wrought a civil war in his heart. She is his counterpart; and like him, is almost sanctified in our eyes by her absolute unsuspiciousness, and holy entireness of love. As the curtain drops, which do we pity the most [see excerpt above, 1813]?

This means, first, that Iago is overwhelmingly the cause of the tragedy and, secondly, that Othello's love for Desdemona is on a par with her love for him. (pp. 257-58)

The close of the first third of the present century finds the Coleridgean or Romantic view of *Othello* still predominant. It has been carried on, with modifications of course but without essential change, by one critic after another. It was followed by Professor A. C. Bradley in his authoritative volume on Shakesperean tragedy [see excerpt above, 1904] and by Sir Walter Raleigh in his charming book on Shakespeare's whole

way and work. It literally holds the boards, it dominates the stage; one result being that the modern male star, possessed by the reigning notion that Iago is at least equally important with Othello, wonders in which of the two rôles he may shine at his fullest. Of course I do not mean that this dilemma was originated by Coleridge, but it was firmly established by Romantic criticism. . . . I believe that this conception is ethically wrong, is weakening to morals and religion; but my present point is that it is dramatically untenable.

Read again the long and beautiful speech in which Othello recounts to the Venetian senate the process of his wooing, summing it all up in the lines:

> She loved me for the dangers I had passed,
> And I loved her that she did pity them.
>
> [I. iii. 167-68]

Then proceed immediately to Desdemona's confession:

> That I did love the Moor to live with him,
> My downright violence and storm of fortunes
> May trumpet to the world; my heart's subdued
> Even to the very quality of my lord;
> I saw Othello's visage in his mind,
> And to his honours and his valiant parts
> Did I my soul and fortunes consecrate.
> So that, dear lords, if I be left behind,
> A moth of peace, and he go to the war,
> The rites for which I love him are bereft me,
> And I a heavy interim shall support
> By his dear absence. Let me go with him.
>
> [I. iii. 248-59]

The significant difference between those two speeches is apparent to a reader or spectator alert for a certain dramatic effect at which Shakespeare drives in the early scenes of his chief tragedies and, indeed, in the majority of his plays—namely, the keynote contrast presented by the hero and heroine. And here as in many of his other plays, though far more poignantly, I think, the contrast turns upon two different modes of love. Pity, no doubt, was a ground of Desdemona's love for Othello. But wc cannot imagine her stressing that subordinate emotion in his full and climactic fashion even if she, instead of him, had been asked to explain to the Senate the growth of their affair. Her final statement could not have been that she loved him for the dangers he had passed. Nor on the other hand can we imagine him declaring that his "heart's subdued" to her "very quality", *i.e.*, her inmost nature and character.

Such an interchange of parts cannot be imagined dramatically. But of course if we give way to idealizing fancy instead of being led by dramatic perceptions, we may feel, with Coleridge, that Othello and Desdemona have in common an "entireness of love" which enables each to speak for the heart of the other with complete authority; as a married couple may have a joint bank-account from which each can freely draw with the full concurrence of the other—under ideal conditions. In this case Othello's speech may be regarded as drawing out all the romantic glamour and pathos of their wooing while, with a fine art of reticence, leaving for his wife the very heart of the story, the fact that each loves the inmost nature of the other with equality of knowledge and consecration. But this fiction is not Shakespeare's; and it overrides the whole theatric scheme of the first act.

The act opens and closes with dialogues of Iago and his tool, the foolish Roderigo. In the first scene, the episode of Brabantio serves to bring out dramatically the coarse selfishness of Iago and the thin but, so far, pure devotion of Roderigo for Desdemona. As Roderigo leaves the stage Othello enters; and here we are prepared for what we are made to feel incessantly as the play proceeds, that Roderigo's story is a parody of Othello's, providing relief from it even while illumining it by dramatic suggestion. The suggestion is that Othello's love is touched with the romantic egoism which, so blatant in the case of Roderigo, is potentially so tragic in the case of a great nature like that of Othello. As soon as he enters the scene he stands out above all others. We see his nobility; and we see that his love for Desdemona is potentially noble—potentially, not certainly. For this new relationship presents new difficulties, outward and inward, the like of which he has not previously had to face, and which his self-confidence, fostered hitherto by success, can lead him to underestimate. The outward difficulties are obvious. But Shakespeare also makes clear the inward difficulty, the need of a kind of self-subduing that Othello has not until now been called upon to make. Mainly in connection with his love do we sense that egoism which the words of Iago in the first scene, though obviously biased, had prepared us to find. We sense it without repulsion because, largely accounted for by the circumstances of his life, it has a natural fitness and charm. Nevertheless we see it more and more plainly as the act goes on; we perceive that it has entered into the very quality of his love. Here we discern a tragic danger.

But we discern it wordlessly. It is not put into words by Iago, though his hints come close to it. In the opening lines of the play he speaks of Othello as "loving his own pride and purposes" [I. i. 12]; but these words are inspired by Othello's preference of Cassio over Iago for the lieutenancy. Iago does not connect Othello's pride and Othello's love. Indeed he is incapable of so doing. For in his view, as he informs us in the last episode of the act, the love-sentiment exhibited by Othello, as well as by Roderigo, is merely a superficial and changeable mood. He cannot conceive of love as a lasting and inclusive passion wherein self-pride can be a tragic danger. Othello's vulnerability, from the standpoint of Iago, resides in the fact that

> The Moor is of a free and open nature,
> That thinks men honest that but seem to be so,
> And will as tenderly be led by the nose
> As asses are.
>
> [I. iii. 399-402]

This passage, coming at the close of the act and wearing a summary air, is certainly meant to strike the audience vividly. The first line wins our instant approval because of what we have seen of Othello. But just for that reason, the third line and the three words that follow, sharply set off by the ensuing metrical blank, arouse our instant disagreement. We have seen no reason to suppose that Othello will be asininely submissive to the temptings of a creature like Iago—unless—the thought may still be wordless but certainly it is now pressing—unless his love has in it a kind of frailty, as well as a kind of potency, which Iago has not fathomed.

And so one's mind returns to the words of the lovers themselves. Their confessional speeches are spotlighted, so to put it, at the center of the dramatic pattern of the first act; which comprises an extraordinary range of attitudes towards their love, from the outer darkness of Iago to the inner twilight of the good Duke. With the Duke (and with Coleridge) we see that Othello and Desdemona are indeed counterparts in the sense that each is a complement of the other in a union that

has the beauty of simplicity, purity, and truth. But we also see, with Shakespeare, that their loves are not counterparts (this word is used by Coleridge with seductive ambiguity) in the sense of being facsimiles. Here, as always when he is at his best, Shakespeare displays a difference of inner quality by a sharp difference between the types of poetic style employed by the speakers. Othello's long speech has the simple-elaborate beauty of what may be called "true-love" romance. An example of the same type on a lower level of value is Coleridge's poem "Love", in which the hero wins his lady by telling her a romantic story concerning himself that "disturbed her soul with pity". But Desdemona's brief confession has the higher and more difficult poetry of a strong, plain, utterly self-giving and penetrating passion. Here the physical and spiritual aspects of love are conjoined with a bold delicacy, a superb rightness, of which Othello's romantic style (see the speech which follows hers) is seen to be quite incapable. In other words Desdemona, and she alone, has that "entireness of love" which Coleridge attributes also to Othello. (pp. 258-63)

Continually throughout the play Shakespeare makes a dramatic contrast between Desdemona's unselfish love and the (comparatively, not by any means absolutely) self-centered passion of Othello. And upon that contrast the whole action turns.

In other words this play is a true love-tragedy—not a "true-love" romance with an unhappy ending brought about entirely, or mainly, by "the almost superhuman art of Iago" as Coleridge says. The modern idealization of Iago, as of Milton's Satan, springs from the modern, and often sentimental, cult of unorthodoxy with its admiration of rebels. Iago, according to that cult, is a superb, brainy rebel against our smug rules and gods: he dares to be himself alone! However, this attitude is entirely foreign to Shakespeare. (p. 265)

Iago's "almost superhuman art" may properly be termed sub-human. This fact the spectator, presumably a person of normal humanity, is intended to see more and more, and to enjoy dramatically, in the last three acts of the play. He is supposed not only to condemn the villain morally but to feel superior to him in insight into the human heart. For the audience has been enabled by Shakespeare in the first two acts to perceive that inward force and danger of Othello's love to which Iago has been entirely oblivious. . . . So that the violence of Othello's vengeful outburst in the last phase of the great temptation scene in Act III does not surprise the audience as it does Iago. . . . The fact is that Iago, in spite of his ability in adapting himself to the situation, is astounded and dismayed by the force he has helped to unloose. The murder of Desdemona, which Othello determines upon, had never for an instant been contemplated in the villain's plans. He had intended to

> Make the Moor thank me, love me, and reward me
> For making him egregiously an ass
> And practising upon his peace and quiet
> Even to madness. . . .
>
> [II. i. 308-11]

that is, to such a madness as such "an ass" could have; not the fearful human passion that actually ensues. Iago finds that in order to be thanked, loved, and rewarded, to hear from Othello the coveted words "Now art thou my lieutenant" [III. iii. 479] (in the last line but one of the temptation scene), he must take part in Othello's "black vengeance" with an air of passionate conviction imitated from his master. But he strives to concentre that vengeance on Cassio; whose death—if only it would satisfy the Moor's absurd and bothersome rage—

would clinch the success of his plot. Whereas the killing of Desdemona is quite unnecessary—Iago has adduced no evidence which she could disprove—and may well be embarrassing. His plea, ''But let her live'' [III. iii. 475], means exactly that. And the actor who accompanies these climactic words with a leer of insincerity and intellectual triumph is trying to defeat the legitimate triumph of the audience. We are intended to see, with immense satisfaction, that the villain has overshot his mark. Subdued by his master's violent refusal of his request, he closes the scene with a submissive and dramatic-ironic line, ''I am yours forever'' [III. iii. 480]. For the remainder of the action he is the tool of Othello's passion more than Othello is the tool of his cunning. His self-defeating blindness to the strength of his wife Emilia's love for Desdemona, so brilliantly foreshadowed by the author in the middle of the temptation scene, where the villain appears to be on the crest of fortune's wave, is recognized in the last act as the natural nemesis of one who has failed to fathom the hearts of all the other persons in the play, from Othello down to Roderigo. (pp. 266-68)

Certainly Shakespeare uses Iago superbly in the crucial episode of the play, the first part of the temptation scene. But here the main motive force is not Iago's cunning: it is Othello's deficient love. Coleridge's claim—that Othello's conviction of his wife's unfaithfulness is ''forced upon him'' by Iago and that it is ''such a conviction as any man must and would have entertained who had believed Iago's honesty as Othello did''—confutes itself by the stress it places upon the hero's trustfulness. . . . For surely the ''holy entireness of love'' that Coleridge attributes to Othello must comprise trustfulness: the one person whom he will trust above all others, in the present case, is exactly his wife. The one person, above all others, whose suspicions, in the present case, will not be accepted is exactly Iago. For the more his honesty and loyalty are believed in by his master, the more they account for and explain away his suspicions. Iago is a crude, outside witness. His honesty gives him no access to the inside facts of this case. His view of the matter, as Othello sees and says in a moment of normal vision, is properly to be classed with ''exsufflicate and blown surmises'' [III. iii. 182]. The surmise that *sways* Othello is not Iago's but Othello's.

Iago begins by aspersing Cassio, only Cassio, whose conduct has been doubtful and who of course may be guilty of evil intentions without the slightest complicity on the part of Desdemona. The audience waits in great suspense to hear just what the villain can dare to say of *her*. Finally he ventures the following allusion: ''Good name in man—or *woman*—dear my lord . . .'' [III. iii. 155] (the italics and dashes are of course mine). Ostensibly this clever speech is merely a warning that Cassio may injure Desdemona's reputation and therefore, and above all, filch the good name of Othello. Iago is making a strong appeal to Othello's self-pride, aiming to move him strongly against Cassio; but also hoping, since Cassio's guilt must be incomplete if Desdemona is innocent, to arouse in Othello a suspicion of her virtue. This hope is fulfilled (and here is the very crux of the play) far beyond his expectation, instantly and violently.

Iago for a moment is quite overcome by surprise—such, I think, is the right intent of the stage business; but not so the audience. Like Iago, we have felt all along that Othello's trust in his wife is not impregnable; that it is more assertive than certain, created less by knowledge than by romantic emotion. But, unlike Iago, we have seen what depth of emotion is involved.

Othello's final speech in the first act, expressing immense trust in his wife in the face of Brabantio's warning (''She has deceived her father and may thee'' [I. iii. 293]), is of course packed with dramatic irony. But the irony is intended to be far deeper for the audience than it is for Iago. He can easily sneer at Othello's confidence because he believes, as he presently declares, that love is ''merely a lust of the blood and a permission of the will'' [I. iii. 334-35]. He cannot take seriously Othello's exclamation, ''My life upon her faith!'' [I. iii. 294]. But these ringing words, which linger in our minds and in the end turn out to be literally true, convey to us, when they are first uttered, a tragic premonition. From here on, Shakespeare continually suggests three viewpoints regarding the hero's trust in his wife: that of Othello himself, that of Iago, and that of the audience. If Othello's part is properly acted the audience perceives that he has a suppressed anxiety. ''Repressed emotion'', by the way, is a stock-in-trade device of the Elizabethan stage. Again and again a character is shown to be harboring some good or evil feeling which is less apparent to himself than to the spectators, and which has therefore a strong histrionic effect when it finally breaks forth. Othello's secret fear is fed by a cumulative series of circumstances noted by the audience. And in connection with the drunken brawl supposedly occasioned by Cassio, we are shown the hero's capacity for wrath:

> Now, by heaven,
> My blood begins my safer guides to rule,
> And passion, having my best judgement collied,
> Assays to lead the way. . . .
>
> [II. iii. 204-07]

This, occurring as it does towards the end of Act II, immediately prepares for his outbreak early in Act III in regard to Desdemona. The audience is ready both for the violence of the outbreak and for its direction; while Iago is ready for neither. His animus is against Cassio, not Desdemona. We, however, know that it is natural for Othello's mind to subordinate Cassio, instantly and utterly, to the thought of his wife. I do not mean that the audience is not at all taken by surprise; that would be untrue to theatric actuality. Shakespeare gives us here a *prepared* surprise, a sudden, full revelation of what he has hitherto imparted clandestinely; while also giving us the pleasure of Iago's vivid astonishment.

Othello, seizing the startled villain, cries out, ''By heaven, I'll know thy thoughts'' [III. iii. 162]. And when Iago, recovering himself, refuses to disclose them, his master releases him and turns away, brooding upon his *own* thoughts, which are fully revealed by his single exclamation, ''Ha!'' If the meaning were not unmistakable and if the tone were not one of inner conviction, Iago would not dare in his next speech to translate that monosyllable into the plain terms ''jealousy'' and ''cuckold''. These words, if they were Iago's, merely or even mainly, would bring him a blow on the mouth from his master. That situation must have been perfectly clear to the Elizabethan audience; it is clear to any spectator who watches Othello with a dramatic, instead of a sentimental, sympathy. Here, I believe, is the moment of greatest suspense in the play. A strong repudiating gesture on Othello's part is called for, and the fact that it is not forthcoming means that the word ''cuckold'' is for him merely the verbal echo of the thought that has overcome him. A decisive gesture or word of repudiation would mean that he roots out the evil thing from his mind as soon as he fully faces it. But instead—and only half listening to Iago—he moans to himself, ''O misery.'' The mind that masters him

Act II. Scene i. Othello's arrival at Cyprus. By G. F. Sargent. The Department of Rare Books and Special Collections, The University of Michigan Library.

is not Iago's but his own; though certainly the villain is the dramatic instrument for the unloosing of his black thought, his repressed fear. There is no other means by which that thought and emotion could be unloosed so dramatically. A revealing soliloquy uttered by the hero in solitude would have seemed at this important juncture a very weak device. Instead, Shakespeare gives us soliloquy mingled with dialogue—the self-concealing egoism of the hero put into words by the villain, who is egoism incarnate. Here Iago is a brilliant dramatic version of the evil spirit of allegory, who, as in the case of Marlowe's Faustus, appears at the hero's elbow, typifying his worser self. At the same time he is the culmination of a dramatic series of circumstances serving to bring to the fore the deficiency that there is in Othello's love. (pp. 268-72)

Othello is shown to be mastered by a natural yet sinful and unreasonable doubt of his wife—natural, sinful, unreasonable, in the senses in which those three words would be understood by Shakespeare and (in the year 1605 and perhaps 2005) by the Shakespearean audience. From this first outbreak of jealous passion on the part of the hero, the rest of the play follows. Not that the audience feels here that Othello is surely doomed. There is always the possibility that he will repent before his evil passion leads him to catastrophe. But we see that the chances are against him because of his self-centeredness. Supposing his wife to be really guilty, the hero's rage might well be subdued by sorrow for her and mercy: as in the contemporary

play, Heywood's *A Woman Killed with Kindness*. But Othello's dominant thought is for his own honor and happiness; even in the attempt which he immediately makes to rise above his jealous obsession. His weak spot . . . is at once played upon by Iago:

> I would not have your free and noble nature
> Out of self-bounty be abused; look to 't. . . .
>
> [III. iii. 199-200]

This is indeed diabolical cunning: it voices the self-hidden devil of selfishness at work in Othello's breast.

And that devil is echoed pointedly in the first bit of definite "evidence" against Desdemona which the villain now adduces:

> She did deceive her father, marrying you;
> And when she seemed to shake and fear your looks,
> She loved them most.
>
> [III. iii. 206-08]

Othello accepts this sophistry, but we know that he ought to reject it. It serves, with fine dramatic art of retrospection, to recall to our minds the situation in Act I. She did indeed deceive her father, but because of the bold veracity and urgency of her passion for Othello. And if she appeared to fear his looks while really loving them, the explanation was given in her own words, "I saw Othello's visage in his mind." The sense of this great line, if not the very words, is not and cannot be forgotten by the audience; but it is not remembered by Othello because he has never really grasped it. We recall the inadequacy of his account of her love in Act I; and now we see fully the inadequacy, there suggested, of his love for her compared with hers for him. We know that if she were in his present situation, she would not harbor a doubt of him. Thus—to sum up the matter in well-worn technical terms—the crucial scene of the play is recognized by the audience as entirely developed from the initial situation.

Because of Othello's lack of loving penetration, he can now proceed with Iago's aid to consider his wife less as an individual than as a type. That attitude Desdemona could not possibly assume towards him: she could not think of him mainly as a Moorish mercenary general, an "extravagant and wheeling stranger" [I. i. 136]. But now she becomes such a stranger for him. His mind places her in the category of "Venetian wife" and regards as applicable to her the exposition which Iago gives of the misdemeanors of that class. Here particularly, in the Romantic interpretation of him, the hero is a blind fool; but actually he is a noble person blinded by evil jealousy. In his ensuing soliloquy, designed to sum up the action of the scene so far, his passionate self-concern—"if I do prove her haggard . . . I am abused and my relief must be to loathe her" [III. iii. 260, 267-68]—is displayed as the direct cause of the blindness which permits him in the second half of the speech to break out as follows:

> O curse of marriage!
> That we can call these delicate creatures ours,
> And not their appetites. . . .
>
> [III. iii. 268-70]

These words and those that follow are very terrible words for a gentleman such as Othello to use. (Remember that the Shakespearean audience has always in the back of its mind the idea of "the complete gentleman"). They mean that, while thinking of himself as a finely sensitive person, he reduces Desdemona to a coarse and insensitive type. . . . The speech is the quick utterance of a passion natural and sinful, unreasonable and blinding. Accordingly the histrionic effect is immense when Desdemona herself suddenly enters the scene, even as he is uttering his last black words.

Othello is stunned by the contrast between the actual person, whom he had almost forgotten, and the coarse type alive in his thoughts. He exclaims:

> Look! where she comes.
> If she be false, O! then heaven mocks itself.
> I'll not believe it.
>
> [III. iii. 277-79]

This is a flash of beautiful romantic wonder; it is not a stroke of purifying awe. It is a momentary recrudescence of his former and inadequate kind of confidence in his wife; though this time he does not say, "My life upon her faith!" There is no real insight, no real repenting effort; the whole tone of the lines is otherwise. (This sort of expedient, again, is common in Elizabethan drama, *i.e.*, the contrast between emotion and reality in the speaker, between yearning desire and real insight and effort.) Of course the speech is rich in pathos; accentuated presently by the dramatic irony of the lines that follow upon Desdemona's gentle complaint of his unreadiness for his waiting visitors:

> He: I am to blame.
> She: Why do you speak so faintly?
> Are you not well?
>
> [III. iii. 282-83]

It may be that here he has an inkling of the truth which he is to see at the end of the play: he is to blame, his imagination is diseased. When she comes close to him with loving concern in her eyes (in the beginning he loved her for pitying his troubles) it may be that for a moment and faintly he sees her mind in her visage, as she from the beginning has seen his visage in his mind. But quickly he yields again to self-pain and self-pity; the fleeting chance that *her* pity may renew in him the love that it began is past and gone. He turns aside, and will not look in her eyes again. Thrusting away the hand that tries to relieve his pain by binding his brow with the pitiful handkerchief—it is "too little", he says, as he now feels her pity to be—he exclaims roughly and distantly: "Let it alone. Come, I'll go in with you" [III. iii. 288]. (pp. 274-78)

In the ensuing interval, as the dramatist uses Iago to tell us, the "dangerous conceit" can "burn like the mines of sulphur" [III. iii. 326, 29]; that is, with hidden but increasing power. It is hidden perforce when he is at dinner with his guests; and hence it breaks out with all the more violence when he returns to the stage alone. His exclamation at this point, "Ha! ha! false to me?" [III. iii. 333], certainly refers to Desdemona, not to Iago, whom he does not at first perceive. But the emphasis is on the "me". In this respect his mental farewell here to Desdemona, for such in effect it is, reads like a horrid mocking echo of his greeting to her in the second act. . . . There the thought of himself was at the center of his premonition; here it is the pivot of his black imaginings:

> What sense had *I* of her stolen hours of lust?
> I saw't not, thought it not, it harmed not *me;*
> I slept the next night well, was free and merry;
> I found not Cassio's kisses on her lips. . . .
> I had been happy. . . .
>
> [III. iii. 338-41, 345]

Significantly enough, his ensuing farewell to war is the most rhetorical speech that Shakespeare has so far put in his mouth: the bark climbing hills of seas in Act II [II. i. 185ff.] is out-Heroded here by the "mortal engines whose rude throats the immortal Jove's dread clamours counterfeit" [III. iii. 355-56]. And it is embedded (see the lines which immediately precede and follow it) in the mad, base fancy, far outrunning any suggestion given by the startled Iago, that his wife may have yielded herself to the "general camp", even to the low "pioners" who dig the mud underneath "the pride, pomp, and circumstance of glorious war" [III. iii. 354]. (pp. 278-79)

[The] dramatic contrast between Othello's brutal passion and his spiritual sentiments is followed out relentlessly by Shakespeare. Not that he scorns those sentiments: he portrays them, with sympathy, as potentially noble, but as, in Othello's present state, fatally inadequate and delusive. In Act IV, Scene I, Othello's outcry, "but yet the pity of it, Iago! O! Iago, the pity of it, Iago!" [IV. i. 195-96], is so sincere and moving that, taken by itself, it would seem to express the heart of a man who could not kill the guiltiest of wives. But his next speech is: "I will chop her into messes. Cuckold *me!*" [IV. i. 200]. And in Scene II his pity appears as entirely self-pity in his long speech to Desdemona, "Had it pleased heaven. . . ." [IV. ii. 47ff]. This beautiful passage moves us deeply on Othello's behalf even while we realize that the kind of emotion it expresses is effectually preventing him from discovering the truth of his wife. When he declares, with some effort, that he could even bear the affliction of the loss of honor, the "slow and moving finger" of "the time of scorn" [IV. ii. 56, 55], we feel that he is approaching the patience of unselfish love, the patience that Desdemona has for him. But he is still far from it, and he turns aside from the way thither when he broods upon his own suffering to the exclusion of any touch of mercy for the supposed sinner who has caused that suffering:

> But there, where I have garnered up my heart,
> Where either I must live or bear no life,
> The fountain from the which my current runs
> Or else dries up—To be discarded thence!
> Or keep it as a cistern for foul toads
> To knot and gender in!. . . .
>
> [IV. ii. 57-62]

That thought at once rearouses the grim rage, which, though it had softened for a moment, even to tears, is his controlling mood throughout this episode. The episode means that, having tried to find "a drop of patience" (as he says) in some part of his soul, he finds only the sort of patience that is "grim as hell" [IV. ii. 53, 64]. Presently, after his exit, when Emilia voices her suspicion that some villain has been at work, Desdemona has the simple line: "If any such there be, heaven pardon him!" [IV. ii. 135]. Here is the accent of true mercy, coming from a heart exercised in the patience of love.

Othello's most elaborate effort at patience comes in the catastrophic scene, where he determines to execute his wife in a mood of pure justice and "heavenly sorrow"—and presently murders her in a fit of unjust, hellish rage. Unjust and hellish even if she were guilty. For the acme of the irony that runs through this dreadful episode is the fact that whereas in the beginning Othello, in a tone of mercy, urges Desdemona to pray for heaven's forgiveness—"I would not kill thy soul" [V. ii. 32]—in the end he refuses her plea for time to say "one prayer". So insistent is Shakespeare in exhibiting the weakness of Othello's spiritual sentiments in the face of his selfish passion.

The one who loves Othello best has to die for his cure. Desdemona is a great dramatic creation in that, apart from her deathless love, she is not great at all. Self-secluded as a maid, "tender, fair, and happy" [I. ii. 66], she finds and adores in Othello the virtues that she lacks; and her growing love is able at the close to endue him with the very virtue that he lacks, a virtue above his virtues. He is a great person who becomes obsessed by an evil spirit; she is a small person who becomes possessed of the spirit of redeeming love. Coleridge's question, "As the curtain drops, which do we pity the most?", does not really arise, so entirely is the emotion of pity subjected here to awe, awe in the presence of judging and transforming love. This experience, so familiar in the literature of the seventeenth century, is dulled and confused by the Romantic idealization of Desdemona. Shakespeare certainly intends a very dramatic contrast between what she is and what love does through her. This love is very human and yet it is supernal. Lyrically touched in the sonnets—"eternal love in love's fresh case . . . the star to every wandering bark" [Sonnets 108 and 116]—it touches continually the characters in the plays, but not elsewhere with such invading and cumulative power as in the case of Desdemona. Here illimitable love gradually takes possession of a person who is extremely limited, not just mentally but morally.

Coleridge says that she like Othello is "almost sanctified" by "absolute unsuspiciousness"; but this dictum distorts her no less than it does her husband. (pp. 280-83)

Her "absolute unsuspiciousness", so far from partaking of sanctity, is the fruit of moral naïveté which authentic sanctity excludes. And it is condemned, while pitied, by a dramatic audience, by persons aware that in the exacting drama of life conduct has to be judged by its results as well as by its motives. Dove-like innocence disjoined from the serpent's wisdom may be an absolute value in the world of romance; but in the world of drama it can be tragically wrong. Desdemona's fondness for her husband's friend Cassio is as natural as it is pure. But its obstinate ostentatiousness is not only indelicate, it is morally obtuse; so, and tragically so, is her obstinate refusal to face the plain fact of Othello's jealousy. Act III, Scene IV, where this situation is crucially developed, is equally important with the temptation scene which it follows hard upon. The audience knows very well that Desdemona, and only she, can now check Othello's growing evil passion. Instead, she establishes and intensifies it. Her climactic assertion, "Alas the day! I never gave him cause" [III. iv. 158], is at once judged by the audience: it is an unconscious but tragic equivocation. And its sequel is her ambiguous and fatal outcry regarding Cassio in the final scene, "Alas! he is betrayed and I undone" [V. ii. 76].

She and not Iago is the one who next to Othello, though at a long distance, is the cause of the catastrophe. It is this fact and this alone that gives a real alleviation to our blame of Othello. We see that she is his tragic counterpart, that she like him, though so very differently, loves not wisely but too well; which is just another way of saying that the play is a true love-tragedy. Also it is sublime: love, here, is perfected through suffering. And this occurs in Desdemona—such is the point I would stress—before it occurs or could occur in the case of Othello.

Her "holy entireness of love", in Coleridge's superb phrase, does not exist or at least does not fully exist until the very end. Her love, always entire, is at the first far from holy, in the strict sense of this word. . . . She woos her chosen one, telling him, before he will venture to utter his own feelings, that she wishes "that heaven had made her such a man" [I. iii. 163]. She loves him with a passionate absorption that has at first no touch of the super-earthly. That touch begins to appear in the second half of the play. But Shakespeare keeps it aloof, so to speak, up to the very end; mainly through the exquisite art of the closing episode of the fourth act with its suggestion of Desdemona's pure, full strength of sexual love, a suggestion carried over into the beginning of the final scene. She has no withdrawal from life, no readiness for death; and though she has the patience of love she has no religious meekness in the face of wrongful accusation. The intense personal anger with which she first repudiates Othello's direct charge against her, "By heaven, you do me wrong" [IV. ii. 81]—and which he interprets as the assumed indignation of a "cunning whore"—persists when she is dying. She cries out, "Falsely, falsely murdered. . . . A guiltless death I die" [V. ii. 117, 122].

But then, in the very moment of death, when Emilia demands who has done the deed, she breathes: "Nobody—I myself—commend me to my kind lord" [V. ii. 124-25]. And we see that Shakespeare has from the first designed her to die with her lips murmuring that sublime lie. In the beginning she deceived her father to make sure of her lover; in the middle of the story she tried, vainly and foolishly, to mollify her jealous husband by denying the loss of the handkerchief; in the end, with an inspired wisdom of love far above wisdom, she tells a falsehood to save her murderer, her "kind lord". This dying lie is a triple truth: it is a confession, a sacrifice, and a redeeming vision—a confession of the fact that she herself is not free from blame; a self-sacrificing effort to assume the whole guilt, leaving a wounded name behind; above all, a religious vision of the loved one's potential goodness. At the first she saw Othello's visage in his mind; at the last she sees his black deed in the white light of his "very quality" as love would have it to be.

No wonder that her "kind lord" must now exclaim: "She's like a liar gone to burning hell; 'twas I that killed her" [V. ii. 129-30]. He dare not accept *from* her the heavenly mercy which he has denied *to* her—unless he is to lose himself. Which, of course, is just what happens presently: he loses himself to find himself. He does so with the strong aid of the poor, coarse, and despised Emilia; not mainly because of her information against Iago but because she informs Othello against himself, while giving him the example of her devotion to Desdemona:

> This deed of thine was no more worthy heaven
> Than thou wast worthy her. . . .
> Thou hast not half the power to do me harm
> As I have to be hurt. . . .
>
> [V. ii. 160-61, 162-63]

But mainly Desdemona works upon him from within. . . . He repents; he is converted. The center of himself shifts from himself to her, to the love which her dead face now symbolizes for him:

> when we shall meet at compt,
> This look of thine will hurl my soul from heaven. . . .
>
> [V. ii. 273-74]

"This look", of course, is not a look of condemnation; it is the look of love with which she died, commending herself to him. But it makes him judge himself, calling as he does upon devils to whip him "from the possession of this heavenly sight" [V. ii. 278]. The "compt", the last judgement, is already present to him. We may say that he is saved as by fire; through his self-damnation he finds the way of purgation. Near the close he says that he wishes to be remembered as one who "threw a pearl away richer than all his tribe" [V. ii. 347-48]: her heart, simpler and narrower than his, was richer far in kind. But now his romantic and egoistic passion is purged and lifted towards her "*holy* entireness of love". His new humility appears in his new name for himself. The man "that was Othello" [V. ii. 284] has discarded his own name, of which he was so proud, and will not mention it again. His name is now simply "one whose subdued eyes" [V. ii. 348]. . . . a phrase of great genius, recalling the "my heart's subdued" of Desdemona's confession before the Venetian senate, while her husband watched and listened but did not comprehend. Now, at once criminal and judge, he is on the point of executing himself in the authority of that senate; and his last sight is her face—"this look of thine". At last he has come to see her visage in her mind, her inmost as well as her outward beauty; and his heart's "subdued" to her very quality. (pp. 284-88)

G. R. Elliott, "'Othello' as a Love-Tragedy," in The American Review, *Vol. 8, No. 3, January, 1937, pp. 257-88.*

F. R. LEAVIS (essay date 1937)

[*Leavis was one of the most influential educators and literary critics of the mid-twentieth century. He was a cofounder and editor of* Scrutiny, *a highly regarded literary magazine which had a profound impact on the teaching and interpretation of English literature in Britain and America. Leavis maintained that literary criticism should be based on "intelligent discrimination" and*

"moral seriousness," *contending that close study of texts and attention to a writer's "ethical sensibility" would lead to a discerning evaluation of a work of art. His belief that moral consciousness is the wellspring of poetic creativity led Lionel Trilling to comment that, for Leavis, "literature is what Matthew Arnold said it is, the criticism of life." Leavis often assumed adamant, uncompromising positions in his work, and thus his criticism is frequently contentious and controversial. In the following excerpt on* Othello, *he asserts that the crux of Shakespeare's tragedy lies in the character of the Moor, a noble and heroic man of action whose proclivities for self-dramatization, egotism, and pride suit him for a life of military adventure but make him incapable of coping with the emotional stresses of domestic life. Directly disputing Samuel Taylor Coleridge's and A. C. Bradley's conclusions that the Moor is not easily jealous and that Iago's supremely clever machinations are the sole cause of Othello's rapid decline into murderous suspicion (see excerpts above, 1813, 1822, 1827, and 1904), Leavis maintains that Othello's love for Desdemona is flawed from the very beginning by self-centeredness and a lack of self-understanding that render him easily susceptible to Iago's insinuations. For additional commentary on Othello's pride and self-centeredness, see the excerpts by G. R. Elliott (1937 and 1953), Derek Traversi (1949), Brents Stirling (1956), Roy W. Battenhouse (1969), and Carol McGinnis Kay (1983). Like Maud Bodkin (1934) and G. R. Elliott (1937), Leavis believes that Othello's precipitous fall indicates that the specter raised by Iago is already present in the Moor's mind and that the reason for Iago's quick success is because he voices what has already been engendered in Othello's psyche. Closely analyzing Othello's opening soliloquy in Act V, Scene ii and his final speech leading up to his suicide, the critic further develops the view put forth by T. S. Eliot (1927) and Allardyce Nicoll (1927) that the Moor is excessively preoccupied with self-dramatization and self-delusion. Indeed, Leavis avers, Othello never achieves a clear and accurate perception of himself and dies without attaining "tragic self-discovery," an opinion echoed by Harley Granville-Barker (1945), and Robert B. Heilman (1956). Finally, Leavis disagrees with Elmer Edgar Stoll's interpretation of the play (see excerpt above, 1915), claiming that Othello's jealousy cannot be successfully ascribed to the dramatic conventions of Elizabethan theater without seriously damaging the audience's expectations of "ordinary psychological consistency." Jared R. Curtis (1973), Jane Adamson (1980), and Barbara Everett (see Additional Bibliography) have offered refutations of Leavis's reading of* Othello.]

The generally recognized peculiarity of *Othello* among the tragedies may be indicated by saying that it lends itself as no other of them does to the approach classically associated with Bradley's name: even *Othello* (it will be necessary to insist) is poetic drama, a dramatic poem, and not a psychological novel written in dramatic form and draped in poetry, but relevant discussion of its tragic significance will nevertheless be mainly a matter of character-analysis. It would, that is, have lent itself uniquely well to Bradley's approach if Bradley had made his approach consistently and with moderate intelligence. Actually, however, the section on *Othello* in *Shakespearean Tragedy* is more extravagant in misdirected scrupulosity than any of the others [see excerpt above, 1904]; it is, with a concentration of Bradley's comical solemnity, completely wrongheaded—grossly and palpably false to the evidence it offers to weigh. Grossly and palpably?—yet Bradley's *Othello* is substantially that of common acceptance. And here is the reason for dealing with it, even though not only Bradley but, in its turn, disrespect for Bradley (one gathers) has gone out of fashion (as a matter of fact he is still a very potent and mischievous influence).

According to the version of *Othello* elaborated by Bradley the tragedy is the undoing of the noble Moor by the devilish cunning of Iago. Othello we are to see as a nearly faultless hero whose strength and virtue are turned against him. Othello and

Desdemona, so far as their fate depended on their characters and untampered-with mutual relations, had every ground for expecting the happiness that romantic courtship had promised. It was external evil, the malice of the demi-devil, that turned a happy story of romantic love—of romantic lovers who were qualified to live happily ever after, so to speak—into a tragedy. This—it is the traditional version of *Othello* and has, moreover, the support of Coleridge—is to sentimentalize Shakespeare's tragedy and to displace its centre. (pp. 259-60)

It is all in order, then, that Iago should get one of the two lectures that Bradley gives to the play, Othello sharing the other with Desdemona. And it is all in the tradition: from Coleridge down, Iago—his motivation or his motivelessness—has commonly been, in commentaries on the play, the main focus of attention.

The plain fact that has to be asserted in the face of this sustained and sanctioned perversity is that in Shakespeare's tragedy of *Othello* Othello is the chief personage—the chief personage in such a sense that the tragedy may fairly be said to be Othello's character in action. Iago is subordinate and merely ancillary. He is not much more than a necessary piece of dramatic mechanism—that at any rate is a fit reply to the view of Othello as necessary material and provocation for a display of Iago's fiendish intellectual superiority. Iago, of course, is sufficiently convincing as a person; he could not perform his dramatic function otherwise. But something has gone wrong when we make him interesting in this kind of way:

> His fate—which is himself—has completely mastered him: so that, in the later scenes, where the improbability of the entire success of a design built on so many different falsehoods forces itself on the reader, Iago appears for moments not as a consummate schemer, but as a man absolutely infatuated and delivered over to certain destruction [see excerpt above by Bradley].

> We ought not, in reading those scenes, to be

paying so much attention to the intrinsic personal qualities of Iago as to attribute to him tragic interest of that kind.

This last proposition, though its justice is perhaps not self-evident, must remain for the time being a matter of assertion. Other things come first. Othello has in any case the prior claim on our attention, and it seems tactically best to start with something as easy to deal with as the view—Bradley's and Coleridge's—and of course, Othello's before them—that Othello was 'not easily jealous' [V. ii. 345]. Easy to deal with because there, to point to, is the text, plain and unequivocal. And yet the text was there for Coleridge, and Bradley accompanies his argument with constant particular reference to it. It is as extraordinary a history of triumphant sentimental perversity as literary history can show. Bradley himself saves us the need of insisting on this diagnosis by carrying indulgence of his preconception, his determined sentimental preconception, to such heroic lengths:

> Now I repeat that *any* man situated as Othello was would have been disturbed by Iago's communications, and I add that many men would have been made wildly jealous. But up to this point, where Iago is dismissed [III. iii. 238] Othello, I must maintain, does not show jealousy. His confidence is shaken, he is confused and deeply troubled, he feels even horror; but

he is not yet jealous in the proper sense of that word.

> (pp. 261-62)

It is the vindication of Othello's perfect nobility that Bradley is preoccupied with, and we are to see the immediate surrender to Iago as part of that nobility. But to make absolute trust in Iago—trust at Desdemona's expense—a manifestation of perfect nobility is (even if we ignore what it makes of Desdemona) to make Iago a very remarkable person indeed. And that Bradley, tradition aiding and abetting, proceeds to do.

However, to anyone not wearing these blinkers it is plain that no subtilization and exaltation of the Iago-devil (with consequent subordination of Othello) can save the noble hero of Bradley's devotion. And it is plain that what we should see in Iago's prompt success is not so much Iago's diabolic intellect as Othello's readiness to respond. Iago's power, in fact, in the temptation-scene is that he represents something that is in Othello—in Othello the husband of Desdemona: the essential traitor is within the gates. For if Shakespeare's Othello too is simple-minded, he is nevertheless more complex than Bradley's. Bradley's Othello is, rather, Othello's; it being an essential datum regarding the Shakespearean Othello that he has an ideal conception of himself. (pp. 263-64)

[For Bradley, Othello's] worth is really and solidly there; he is truly impressive, a noble product of the life of action—of

> The big wars
> That make ambition virtue.
>
> [III. iii. 349-50]

'That make ambition virtue'—this phrase of his is a key one: his virtues are, in general, of that kind; they have, characteristically, something of the quality suggested. Othello, in his magnanimous way, is egotistic. He really is, beyond any question, the nobly massive man of action, the captain of men, he sees himself as being, but he does very much see himself:

> Keep up your bright swords, for the dew will rust them.
>
> [I. ii. 59]

In short, a habit of approving self-dramatization is an essential element in Othello's make-up, and remains so at the very end.

It is, at the best, the impressive manifestation of a noble egotism. But, in the new marital situation, this egotism isn't going to be the less dangerous for its nobility. This self-centredness doesn't mean self-knowledge: that is a virtue which Othello, as soldier of fortune, hasn't had much need of. He has been well provided by nature to meet all the trials a life of action has exposed him to. The trials facing him now that he has married this Venetian girl . . . who is so many years younger than himself (his colour, whether or not 'colour-feeling' existed among the Elizabethans, we are certainly to take as emphasizing the disparity of the match)—the trials facing him now are of a different order.

And here we have the significance of the storm, which puts so great a distance between Venice and Cyprus, between the old life and the new, and makes the change seem so complete and so momentous. The storm is rendered in that characteristic heroic mode of the play which Professor Wilson Knight calls the 'Othello music' [see excerpt above, 1930]:

> For do but stand upon the foaming shore,
> The chidden billows seem to chide the clouds;
> The wind-shaked surge, with high and monstrous mane,

Seems to cast water on the burning bear,
And quench the guards of the ever-fixed pole:
I never did like molestation view
On the enchafed flood.

                                        [II. i. 11-17]

This mode (Professor Wilson Knight, in his own way, describes it well) gives the effect of a comparatively simple magnificence; the characteristic verse of *Othello* is firm, regular in outline, buoyant and sonorous. It is in an important sense Othello's own verse, the 'large-mouthed utterance' of the noble man of action. Bradley's way of putting it is that Othello, though he 'has not, indeed, the meditative or speculative imagination of Hamlet,' is 'in the strictest sense of the word' 'more poetic than Hamlet'. . . . We need not ask Bradley what the 'strictest sense of the word' is, or stop to dispute with him whether or not Othello is 'the greatest poet' of all Shakespeare's heroes. If characters in poetic drama speak poetry we ought to be able to notice the fact without concluding that they are poets. In *Othello,* which is poetic drama, Shakespeare works by poetic means: it is through the characteristic noble verse described above that, very largely, we get our sense of the noble Othello. If the impression made by Othello's own utterance is often poetical as well as poetic, that is Shakespeare's way, not of representing him as a poet, but of conveying the romantic glamour that, for Othello himself and others, invests Othello and what he stands for.

For Othello himself—it might be said that to express Othello's sense of himself and make us share it is the essential function of this verse, the 'Othello music.' But, of course, there are distinctions to be noted. The description of the storm quoted above, though it belongs to the general heroic mode of the play, cannot be said to exhibit the element of self-dramatization that is characteristic of Othello's own utterances. On the other hand, the self-dramatizing trick commands subtle modulations and various stops. It is not always as assertive as in

        Behold, I have a weapon,

                                        [V. ii. 259]

or the closing speech. In these speeches, not only is it explicit, it clearly involves, we may note, an attitude *towards* the emotion expressed—an attitude of a kind we are familiar with in the analysis of sentimentality.

The storm, within the idealizing mode, is at the other extreme from sentimentality; it serves to bring out the reality of the heroic Othello and what he represents. For his heroic quality, realized in this verse (here the utterance of others) is a real thing, though it is not, as Othello takes it to be, the whole of the reality. Another way of making the point would be to say that the distinctive style under discussion, the style that lends itself to Othello's self-dramatization and conveys in general the tone and ideal import of this, goes, in its confident and magnificent buoyancy, essentially with the outer storm that both the lovers, in their voyage to Cyprus, triumphantly outride.

With that kind of external stress the noble Othello is well-qualified to deal (if he went down—and we know he won't—he would go down magnificently). But it is not that kind of stress he has to fear in the new life beginning at Cyprus. The stresses of the spiritual climate are concentrated by Iago (with his deflating, unbeglamouring, brutally realistic mode of speech) into something immediately apprehensible in drama and comparable with the storm. In this testing Othello's inner timbers begin to part at once, the stuff of which he is made begins at

once to deteriorate and show itself unfit. There is even a symbolic foundering when, breaking into incoherent ejaculations, he 'falls in a trance' [s.d. IV. i. 43].

As for the justice of this view that Othello yields with extraordinary promptness to suggestion, with such promptness as to make it plain that the mind that undoes him is not Iago's but his own, it does not seem to need arguing. If it has to be argued, the only difficulty is the difficulty, for written criticism, of going in detailed commentary through an extended text. The text is plain enough. Iago's sustained attack begins at about line 90 in Act III, Sc. iii, immediately upon Desdemona's exit and Othello's exclamation:

    Excellent wretch! Perdition catch my soul,
    But I do love thee! and when I love thee not,
    Chaos is come again.

                                        [III. iii. 90-2]

In seventy lines Othello is brought to such a state that Iago can, without getting any reply but

            O misery,

                                        [III. iii. 171]

say

            O, beware, my lord, of jealousy,

                                        [III. iii. 165]

and use the word 'cuckold.' In ninety lines Othello is saying

            Why did I marry?

                                        [III. iii. 242]

The explanation of this quick work is given plainly enough here:

Iago.   I would not have your free and noble nature
            Out of self-bounty be abused; look to't:
            I know our country disposition well;
            In Venice they do let heaven see the pranks
            They dare not show their husbands; their best
                conscience
            Is not to leave't undone, but keep't
                unknown.
Othello.   Dost thou say so?
Iago.   She did deceive her father, marrying you;
            And when she seem'd to shake and fear your
                looks,
            She loved them most.
Othello.   And so she did.

                                        [III. iii. 199-208]

There in the first two lines is, explicitly appealed to by Iago, Othello's ideal conception of himself: it would be a pity if he let it be his undoing (as it actually was—the full irony Iago can hardly be credited with intending). And there, in the last line, we have the noble and magnanimous Othello, romantic hero and married lover, accepting as evidence against his wife the fact that, at the willing sacrifice of everything else, she had made with him a marriage of romantic love. Iago, like Bradley, points out that Othello didn't really know Desdemona, and Othello acquiesces in considering her as a type—a type outside his experience—the Venetian wife. It is plain, then, that his love is composed very largely of ignorance of self as well as ignorance of her: however nobly he may feel about it, it isn't altogether what he, and Bradley with him, thinks it is. It may be love, but it can be only in an oddly qualified sense love of her: it must be much more a matter of self-centred and self-regarding satisfactions—pride, sensual possessiveness, appetite, love of loving—than he suspects. (pp. 265-69)

It is significant that, at the climax of the play, when Othello, having exclaimed

> O blood, blood, blood,
>
> [III. iii. 451]

kneels to take a formal vow of revenge, he does so in the heroic strain of the 'Othello music.' To Iago's

> Patience, I say; your mind perhaps may change,
>
> [III. iii. 452]

he replies:

> Never Iago. Like to the Pontic sea,
> Whose icy current and compulsive course
> Ne'er feels retiring ebb, but keeps due on
> To the Propontic and the Hellespont;
> Even so my bloody thoughts, with violent pace,
> Shall ne'er look back, ne'er ebb to humble love,
> Till that a wide and capable revenge
> Swallow them up. Now, by yond marble heaven,
> In the due reverence of a sacred vow
> I here engage my words.
>
> [III. iii. 453-62]

At this climax of the play, as he sets himself irrevocably in his vindictive resolution, he reassumes formally his heroic self-dramatization—reassumes the Othello of 'the big wars that make ambition virtue.' The part of this conscious nobility, this noble egotism, this self-pride that was justified by experience irrelevant to the present trials and stresses, is thus underlined. Othello's self-idealization, his promptness to jealousy and his blindness are shown in their essential relation. The self-idealization is shown as blindness and the nobility as here no longer something real, but the disguise of an obtuse and brutal egotism. Self-pride becomes stupidity, ferocious stupidity, an insane and self-deceiving passion. The habitual 'nobility' is seen to make self-deception invincible, the egotism it expresses being the drive to catastrophe. Othello's noble lack of self-knowledge is shown as humiliating and disastrous. (pp. 269-70)

With obtuseness to the tragic significance of Shakespeare's play goes insensibility to his poetry—to his supreme art as exhibited locally in the verse (it is still not superfluous to insist that the poetic skill is one with the dramatic). This is Bradley's commentary on Act V, Sc. ii:

> The supposed death of Cassio (V, i) satiates the thirst for vengeance. The Othello who enters the bed-chamber with the words,
>
> > It is the cause, it is the cause, my soul,
> >
> > [V, ii. 1]
>
> is not the man of the Fourth Act. The deed he is bound to do is no murder, but a sacrifice. He is to save Desdemona from herself, not in hate but in honour; in honour, and also in love. . . .

Bradley, in the speech he quotes from, misses all the shifts of tone by which Shakespeare renders the shifting confusion of Othello's mind. For it is a speech one might have chosen with the express view of illustrating that subtle command of tone which marks Shakespeare's mature art, and which makes the poetry of *Othello* so different in kind from that of *Romeo and Juliet,* and the two dramas consequently incomparable.

It opens with the accent of a contained holy revulsion, the containing power appearing as inexorable, impersonal justice:

> It is the cause, it is the cause, my soul!
> Let me not name it to you, you chaste stars!
> It is the cause.
>
> [V. ii. 1-3]

Now comes a shrinking back from the deed:

> Yet I'll not shed her blood,
> Nor scar that whiter skin of hers than snow
> And smooth as monumental alabaster.
>
> [V. ii. 3-5]

Tenderness here quite clearly is that characteristic voluptuousness of Othello's which, since it is unassociated with any real interest in Desdemona as a person, slips so readily into possessive jealousy. Now the accent of impersonal justice is heard again—

> Yet she must die, else she'll betray more men
>
> [V. ii. 6]

—but the accent is so clearly unrelated to any effectual motive in Othello that the concern for justice, the self-bracing to noble sacrifice, appears as self-deception. Next comes misgiving over the finality of the deed:

> Put out the light, and then put out the light:
> If I quench thee, thou flaming minister,
> I can again thy former light restore,
> Should I repent me: but once put out thy light,
> Thou cunning'st pattern of excelling nature,
> I know not where is that Promethean heat
> That can thy light relume. When I have pluck'd the rose
> I cannot give it vital growth again,
> It must needs wither: I'll smell it on the tree.
>
> [V. ii. 7-15]

Tenderness here is less specifically voluptuous sensuality than it was earlier, but we nevertheless remember:

> Get me some poison, Iago; this night, I'll not
> expostulate with her, lest her body and beauty
> unprovide my mind again: this night, Iago.
>
> [IV. i. 204-06]

And there is in Othello a curious and characteristic effect of self-preoccupation, of preoccupation with his emotions rather than with Desdemona in her own right:

> O balmy breath, that almost dost persuade
> Justice to break her sword! One more, one more:
> Be thus when thou art dead, and I will kill thee,
> And love thee after: one more, and this the last:
> So sweet was ne'er so fatal. I must weep,
> But they are cruel tears: this sorrow's heavenly;
> It strikes where it doth love. She wakes.
>
> [V. ii. 16-22]

When she is awake and so is no longer a mere body, but a person, it is not sorrowful love or noble self-bracing to a sacrifice that she becomes aware of in Othello:

> Alas, why gnaw you so your nether lip?
> Some bloody passion shakes your very frame:
> These are portents.
>
> [V. ii. 43-5]

Moreover, though Othello says

I would not kill thy unprepared spirit,

[V. ii. 31]

actually he refuses her the time to say one prayer.

When he discovers his mistake, his reaction is an intolerably intensified form of the common 'I could kick myself':

> Whip me, ye devils
> From the possession of this heavenly sight!
> Blow me about in winds! roast me in sulphur!
> Wash me in steep-down gulfs of liquid fire!
> O Desdemona! Desdemona! dead!
> Oh! Oh! Oh!

[V. ii. 277-82]

But he remains the same Othello; he has discovered his mistake, but there is no tragic self-discovery. The speech closing with the lines just quoted is that beginning

> Behold, I have a weapon,

[V. ii. 259]

one of the finest examples in the play of the self-dramatizing trick. The noble Othello is now seen as tragically pathetic, and he sees himself as pathetic too:

> Man but a rush against Othello's breast,
> And he retires. Where shall Othello go?

[V. ii. 270-71]

He is ruined, but he is the same Othello in whose essential make-up the tragedy lay: the tragedy doesn't involve the idea of the hero's learning through suffering. The fact that Othello tends to sentimentalize should be the reverse of a reason for our sentimentalizing too.

For even, or rather especially, in that magnificent last speech of his Othello does tend to sentimentalize, though to say that and no more would convey a false impression, for the speech conveys something like the full complexity of Othello's simple nature, and in the total effect the simplicity is tragic and grand. The quiet beginning gives us the man of action with his habit of effortless authority:

> Soft you; a word or two before you go.
> I have done the State some service, and they know't.
> No more of that. I pray you in your letters,
> When you shall these unlucky deeds relate,
> Speak of me as I am; nothing extenuate,
> Nor set down aught in malice. . . .

[V. ii. 338-43]

Othello really is, we cannot doubt, the stoic-captain whose few words know their full sufficiency: up to this point we cannot say he dramatizes himself, he simply *is*. But then, in a marvellous way (if we consider Shakespeare's art), the emotion works itself up until in less than half-a-dozen lines the stoic of few words is eloquently weeping. With

> then must you speak
> Of one that loved not wisely but too well,

[V. ii. 343-44]

the epigrammatic terseness of the dispatch, the dictated dispatch, begins to quiver. Then, with a rising emotional swell,

description becomes unmistakably self-dramatization—self-dramatization as un-self-comprehending as before:

> Of one not easily jealous, but being wrought,
> Perplex'd in the extreme; of one whose hand,
> Like the base Indian, threw a pearl away
> Richer than all his tribe; of one whose subdued eyes,
> Albeit unused to the melting mood,
> Drop tears as fast as the Arabian trees
> Their medicinal gum.

[V. ii. 345-51]

—Contemplating the spectacle of himself, Othello is overcome with the pathos of it. But this is not the part to die in: drawing himself proudly up, he speaks his last words as the stern fighting man who has done the state some service:

> Set you down this;
> And say besides, that in Aleppo once,
> Where a malignant and a turban'd Turk
> Beat a Venetian and traduced the state,
> I took by the throat the circumcised dog
> And smote him, thus.   [stabs himself].

[V. ii. 351-56]

It is a superb *coup de théâtre.*

As, with that double force, a *coup de théâtre,* it is a peculiarly right ending to the tragedy of Othello. The theme of the tragedy is concentrated in it—concentrated in the final speech and action as it could not have been had Othello 'learnt through suffering.' That he should die acting his ideal part is all in the part: the part is manifested here in its rightness and solidity, and the actor as inseparably the man of action. The final blow is as real as the blow it re-enacts, and the histrionic intent symbolically affirms the reality: Othello dies belonging to the world of action in which his true part lay. (pp. 271-76)

The title of *Othello,* borne out by the dominating quality of the hero, tells us where we are to focus. As for Iago, we know from the beginning that he is a villain; the business of Roderigo tells us that. In the other scenes we have no difficulty in taking him as we are meant to take him; and we don't (at any rate in the reading, and otherwise it's the actor's problem) ask how it is that appearance and reality can have been so successfully divorced. Considered as a comprehensibly villainous person, he represents a not uncommon kind of grudging, cynical malice (and he's given, at least in suggestion, enough in the way of grievance and motive). But in order to perform his function as dramatic machinery he has to put on such an appearance of invincibly cunning devilry as to provide Coleridge and the rest with some excuse for their awe, and to leave others wondering, in critical reflection, whether he isn't a rather clumsy mechanism. Perhaps the most serious point to be pondered is that, if Othello is to retain our sympathy sufficiently, Iago must, as devil, claim for himself an implicit weight of emotional regard that critical reflection finds him unfit to carry.

'Clumsy,' however, is not the right word for anything in *Othello.* It is a marvellously sure and adroit piece of workmanship; though closely related to that judgment is the further one that, with all its brilliance and poignancy, it comes below Shakespeare's supreme—his very greatest—works.

I refrained, of set purpose, from reading Professor Stoll on *Othello* and its critics till I had written, as Bradley precipitated it, my own account of the play. Professor Stoll is of course known as, in academic Shakespeare criticism, the adversary of the Bradley approach, and now that I have read what he has to say about *Othello* [see excerpt above, 1915] he seems to me to confirm where the critical centre lies by deviating as badly on his side as Bradley does on the other.

Professor Stoll, having first justified with a weight of scholarship my unscholarly assumption that the view of *Othello* represented by Bradley has, since Coleridge's time, been the generally accepted one, exposes unanswerably and at length the absurdity of that view. His own positive account of the play, however, is no less indefensible than Bradley's. He argues that Othello's lapse into jealousy is to be explained in terms, not of Othello's psychology, but of convention. Profiting by the convention of 'the slanderer believed' (for the use of which Professor Stoll gives a long string of instances) Shakespeare simply imposes jealousy on Othello from the outside: that is Professor Stoll's position.

As we contemplate his string of instances we are moved to insist on certain distinctions the importance of which seems to have passed him by. When Shakespeare uses the 'same' convention as Beaumont and Fletcher, Dryden and Voltaire, his use is apt to be such that only by a feat of abstraction can the convention be said to be the same. Who will bother to argue whether jealousy in Beaumont and Fletcher or any of the others is psychologically defensible or not? The unique power by which Shakespeare compels 'faith in the emotions expressed' and beguiles Bradley and company into their absurdities is, of course, recognized by Professor Stoll, though he cannot recognize with any sureness its nature:

> By the sheer potency of art Othello, Iago, Desdemona, and Emilia maintain, through all their incredible vicissitudes, their individual tone. And inconsistent, unpsychological though they be, their passions speak ever true.

To explain this potency, Professor Stoll, urging us to be content with 'mere art,' talks vaguely of 'tact,' 'delicacy' and 'poetry,' makes play with analogies from music, and quotes Shaw's 'it is the score and not the libretto that keeps the work alive and fresh.' Elsewhere he can recognize that 'No one has more imaginative sympathy than Shakespeare; but,' he goes on,

> he employs it by fits and starts, often neglects motivation and analysis, takes a leap as he passes from one "soul-state" to another, and not content with the inconsistencies of life, falls into the contradictions of convention and artifice.

(pp. 278-80)

There are, no doubt, places in Shakespeare of which one may argue that local vividnesses here and there, convincingly living parts, are not related in an inwardly grasped whole, and that Shakespeare has fallen 'into the contradictions of convention and artifice.' That would be an adverse criticism. But before we make it we must make sure what kind of whole Shakespeare is offering us. (p. 280)

By the time [Othello] becomes the jealous husband it has been made plain beyond any possibility of doubt or reversal that we are to take him . . . seriously—at any rate, such a habit of expectation has been set up with regard to him (and he is well established as the main focus of attention) that no development will be acceptable unless the behaviour it imposes on him is reconcilable with our notions of ordinary psychological consistency. Other characters in the play can be 'convincing' on easier terms; we needn't inquire into the consistency of Emilia's

behaviour—we accept her as a datum, and not even about Iago are we—or need we be—so psychologically exacting. His combination of honest seeming with devilish actuality we accept as, at least partly, a matter of tacit convention; convention acceptable because of the convincingly handled tragic theme to which it is ancillary.

And the tragic theme is centred in Othello. Dramatic sleight is not cheating so long as it subserves honesty there. We do not, even when we consider it critically, quarrel with the trick of 'double time,' though it involves impossibilities by the criteria of actual life and yet is at the same time necessary to the plausible conduct of the intrigue; but equivalent tricks or illusions passing off on us mutually incompatible acceptances with regard to Othello's behaviour or make-up *would* be cheating—that is, matter for critical condemnation. To impose by convention sudden jealousy on Leontes in *The Winter's Tale* and Posthumus in *Cymbeline* is one thing: we admit the convention for the sake of an inclusive effect—a dramatic design that does not, we recognize (wherever in the scale of Shakespeare's work we may place these plays), anywhere ask us to endorse dramatic illusion with the feeling of everyday reality. But to impose jealousy by mere convention on Othello is another thing. What end would be served? What profit would accrue?

According to Professor Stoll [in his *Art and Artifice in Shakespeare;* see Additional Bibliography], the profit of 'putting jealousy upon the hero instead of breeding it in him' is an 'enormous emotional effect':

> The end—the enormous emotional effect—justifies the means. . . .

This emotional effect, as Professor Stoll enjoys it, he represents as the product of our being enabled, by Shakespeare's art, to have it both ways: Othello succumbing to jealousy before our eyes acquires an intense dramatic value without incurring in our esteem the disadvantages attendant upon being jealous; there he is, patently jealous, yet he is at the same time still the man who couldn't possibly have become jealous like that.

> The villain, by all this contriving of the poet's, bears in this instance, like the ancient Fate or intruding god, the burden of responsibility; and our sympathy with a hero made of no such baseness is almost wholly without alloy [Stoll].

—Professor Stoll, that is, in spite of the difference of his analysis, sees the play as the triumph of sentimentalization that it has appeared to so many admirers:

> . . . no one in Shakespeare's tragedies more bitterly and wildly reproaches himself . . . Yet not of himself suspicious or sensual, he is now not corrupted or degraded; and amid his misery and remorse he can still hold up his head and declare:
>
> > For nought I did in hate, but all in honour.
> >
> > [V. ii. 295]
>
> > not easily jealous, but, being wrought, Perplex'd in the extreme.
> >
> > [V. ii. 345-46]
>
> He is a more effective tragic figure because he can say that—because, unlike many, he keeps our sympathy and admiration to the end.

—The 'emotional effect' of the tragedy upon Professor Stoll is essentially that celebrated in his own way by Bradley, and Professor Stoll's analysis, in fact, does explain in large measure why such a tragedy should be so widely found in *Othello* and found irresistible.

Fortunately we are not reduced to reversing the critical judgment and censuring Shakespeare. The dilemma that Professor Stoll and Bradley resolve in their different but equally heroic ways—the dilemma represented by a 'not easily jealous' Othello who succumbs at once to Iago's suggestions—needn't be allowed to bother us. Both critics seem to think that, if Othello hasn't exhibited himself in the past as prone to sexual jealousy (and his reputation tells us he hasn't), that establishes him as 'not easily jealous,' so that his plunge into jealousy would, if we had to justify it psychologically (Bradley, of course, prefers not to recognize it), pose us an insoluble problem. Yet surely, as Shakespeare presents him, it is not so very elusive a datum about Othello, or one that ordinary experience of life and men makes it difficult to accept, that his past history hasn't been such as to test his proneness to sexual jealousy—has, in fact, thereby been such as to increase his potentialities in just that respect.

However, he is likely to remain for many admirers the entirely noble hero, object of a sympathy poignant and complete as he succumbs to the machinations of diabolic intellect. (pp. 281-83)

> *F. R. Leavis, "Diabolic Intellect and the Noble Hero: A Note on 'Othello'," in* Scrutiny, *Vol. VI, No. 3, December, 1937, pp. 259-83.*

E. M. W. TILLYARD   (essay date 1938)

[*Tillyard is best known for his influential book,* Shakespeare's History Plays *(1944), considered a leading example of historical criticism. In addition to his historical studies, Tillyard also wrote* Shakespeare's Last Plays *(1938),* Shakespeare's Problem Plays *(1949), and* Shakespeare's Early Comedies *(1965), a book he was working on at the time of his death in 1962. His brief remarks excerpted below, drawn from* Shakespeare's Last Plays, *contain an assertion that* Othello *depicts a regenerative process, embodied in the Moor himself, by which opposing forces are reconciled and "a new order" is born. Tillyard cautions that this rebirth is only hinted at by Shakespeare, but maintains that this subtle intimation is "typical of Shakespearean tragedy." His view that Othello consciously perceives the errors of his conduct and is an altered man at the close of the play is shared by G. Wilson Knight (1930), G. R. Elliott (1937), G. M. Matthews (1964), Jared R. Curtis (1973), and Helen Gardner (see Additional Bibliography) but not by F. R. Leavis (1937), Robert B. Heilman (1956), and John Bayley (1960).*]

In recent talk about tragedy, two conceptions have stood out in strong opposition the one to the other. The first is the stoical. In this view, tragedy is concerned with resistance to circumstance. Through the nature of things, man at his highest can only resist the forces of the universe; he cannot co-operate with them. His courage is the saving virtue in an incurably perverse state of affairs. The other conception, though it can include a measure of stoical resistance, includes some sort of reconciliation in the full tragic pattern. Man is summoned to resist certain things in the universal scheme, and suffering and loss result. But ultimately he is reconciled. There is reconstruction after disintegration. And it is precisely this sense of renewal that accounts for the peculiar tonic effect of the greatest tragedy. Mr. F. L. Lucas represents the stoical view when he writes:

Tragedy is man's answer to the universe which crushes him so pitilessly. Destiny scowls upon him: his answer is to sit down and paint her where she stands.

Such a definition may fit [John] Webster: it does not correspond to what I feel about *Othello*. That play does something more than picture with unflinching courage and accuracy a number of people crushed by the universe. It pictures through the hero not only the destruction of an established way of life, but the birth of a new order. Othello in his final soliloquy is a man of a more capacious mind than the Othello who first meets us. Dover Wilson has the same feeling about Shakespearean tragedy when he says:

> The Lear that dies is not a Lear defiant, but a Lear redeemed. His education is complete, his regeneration accomplished.

True, the new order is cut short in both plays, but its creation is an essential part of the tragic pattern. (pp. 16-17)

Othello is typical of Shakespearean tragedy in merely hinting at a rebirth. (p. 18)

[However] the hints of a regeneration in the mind of Othello count for more than all the dying ecstasies of Antony and Cleopatra or Coriolanus's yielding to his mother. The difference is this. Othello recognises his errors and transmutes them into his new state of mind; Antony, Cleopatra, and Coriolanus abandon their errors without transmuting them. Hence reconciliation is not the word to apply to their states of mind. It is a different thing to pass from A to B, and to fuse A and B into an amalgam C. Antony does the first, Othello the second. When St. Paul was converted he may have freed himself from a kind of devil, but the fierce angel that was born in the conversion incorporated, among other things, that very devil from which he had broken free. That is the true reconciliation. (pp. 21-2)

> *E. M. W. Tillyard, "The Tragic Pattern," in his* Shakespeare's Last Plays, *Chatto and Windus, 1938, pp. 16-58.*

KENNETH O. MYRICK   (essay date 1941)

[*In his "The Theme of Damnation in Shakespearean Tragedy," excerpted below, Myrick became the first commentator to evaluate Othello in relation to specific doctrines of Christian theology. In portions of his essay not reproduced here, he examines evidence of religious beliefs generally held by Elizabethans, demonstrating that Roman Catholics, Anglicans, and Puritans all shared fundamental convictions regarding the fall of man and the importance of repentance. Myrick further explains that Shakespeare's contemporaries believed that Satan was ever present in their daily lives, acknowledged the vulnerability of all humanity to sin and error, and anticipated the existence of their souls throughout eternity, so that "the sight of a heroic but fallible figure assailed by the most treacherous temptations would bring a thrill of tragic pity and fear which no merely human spectacle can easily convey." In the excerpt below, the critic argues that while the idea of damnation is not overtly presented in Othello, it is discernible in the numerous Christian allusions and remains an important element in the "tragic tension of the play." Myrick remarks that, not only do such words as "damned, devil, hell, heaven, and soul" recur more frequently in Othello than in any other Shakespearean drama, but they appear in contexts of intense anxiety, deep emotionalism, or penetrating irony which heighten their significance. He further contends that whereas Shakespeare's original audience would have regarded the Moor with compassionate sympathy, their belief in free will would lead them to view*] *him as guilty of and therefore accountable for the murder of Desdemona—an act for which he must express repentance or face eternal damnation. Indeed, Myrick asserts, in the concluding passages of the play Othello is portrayed as moving through the successive stages of repentance established by Christian doctrine, as he first manifests humble contrition for his crime, openly and frankly confesses his sins, and expiates his treatment of Cassio by apologizing to him. Thus, concludes Myrick, the last impression the audience has of Othello is "not that of a ruined soul, but of a man ennobled by contrition." Other critics who have addressed the issue of Othello's spiritual condition at the close of the drama include Harley Granville-Barker (1945), S. L. Bethell (1952), Paul N. Siegel (1953), Irving Ribner (1955 and 1960), Edward Hubler (1958), G. M. Matthews (1964), and Roy W. Battenhouse (1969). Also, for further discussions of the significance of Shakespeare's allusions to devils and damnation in Othello, see the excerpts by G. Wilson Knight (1930), Edward Hubler (1958), and the essay by Robert H. West cited in the Additional Bibliography.]*

Othello, even more clearly than *Macbeth, Hamlet*, or *Lear*, seems to many students an entirely secular play. Here no supernatural visitor troubles us with "thoughts beyond the reaches of our souls." In the wonderful climax, "the most painful of all tragedies leaves us for the moment free from pain, and exulting in the power of 'love and man's unconquerable mind'" [see excerpt above by A. C. Bradley, 1904]. To many readers, including at one time the writer of this article, it has seemed that considerations of religion would be irrelevant and intrusive in this greatly human play.

But let us consider the text. Emilia has just discovered her dying mistress, and Othello says bitterly,

> She's like a liar gone to burning hell!
> 'Twas I that killed her.
>
> [V. ii. 129-30]

As Emilia herself lies dying, she whispers,

> Moor, she was chaste; she loved thee, cruel Moor.
> So come my soul to bliss as I speak true.
>
> [V. ii. 249-50]

And Othello, when he knows at last what he has done, says to his dead wife,

> O ill-starr'd wench!
> Pale as thy smock! When we shall meet at compt,
> This look of thine will hurl my soul from heaven,
> And fiends will snatch at it. Cold, cold, my girl?
> Even like thy chastity.—O cursed slave!
> Whip me, ye devils,
> From the possession of this heavenly sight!
> Blow me about in winds! roast me in sulphur!
> Wash me in steep-down gulfs of liquid fire!
> O Desdemona, Desdemona! dead!
>
> [V. ii. 272-81]

What are we to think of these plain references to an after-life? In another context they might conceivably be regarded as a conventional manner of speech, no more significant than stereotyped expressions like "'sblood" or "by the mass." But here they occur at the very climax of the tragedy, in lines so charged with intensest emotion that it would be difficult to find their parallel even in Shakespeare.

Their effect is the greater because they do not stand alone. Desdemona's uncle is glad her father is dead, because

> Did he live now,
> This sight would make him do a desperate turn;
> Yea, curse his better angel from his side,
> And fall to reprobance.
>
> [V. ii. 206-09]

And when Iago's villainy is at last discovered, the other persons in the drama leap instinctively to one idea. "Damn'd Iago," Roderigo calls him. "A damned slave" [V. ii. 243], says Montano, and the same epithet is repeated by Lodovico with such variations as "damned villain" and "hellish villain." "Devil" and "demi-devil" are Othello's terms for his destroyer, and Iago's own wife adds her curse:

> If he say so, may his pernicious soul
> Rot half a grain a day.
>
> [V. ii. 155-56]

These phrases are the more emphatic because they are most numerous in the last moments of the drama and because they offer so ironical a contrast to the earlier epithet of "honest Iago." (pp. 235-36)

Now the thought of eternity is not a new idea suddenly intruded into a few passages in the final act. By skilful preparation Shakespeare has given to these passages the further emphasis of dramatic climax. Such key words as *damned, devil, hell, heaven,* and *soul* are repeated again and again from the first scene of the tragedy to the last; occurring more often in *Othello* than in any other of Shakespeare's plays. Evidence of this sort must be used with the greatest caution; but when every allowance has been made for the varying length of the dramas, the evolution of the author's technique, the substitution in the late works of the word *heaven* for the word *God* on account of Puritanical restrictions, the varying connotations of particular words, the incompleteness of evidence based on any five words, and the elements of art which defy analysis, there is still something significant in the frequency with which expressions of Christian coloring are repeated in *Othello*. (pp. 236-37)

But poetic suggestion is not a matter of statistics. Phrases take their imaginative force from their context. And in *Othello* . . . the passages of Christian coloring often occur in the most significant moments of the play, moments of keen suspense, or deep personal emotion, or intense irony. There are Brabantio's vehement words to Othello:

> Damn'd as thou art, thou hast enchanted her!
>
> [I. ii. 63]

Othello's wonderful greeting to Desdemona, on finding her at Cyprus:

> O my soul's joy! . . .
> If it were now to die,
> 'Twere now to be most happy; for I fear
> My soul hath her content so absolute
> That not another comfort like to this
> Succeeds in unknown fate;
>
> [II. i. 184, 189-93]

Iago's exultant invocation:

> Divinity of hell!
> When devils will the blackest sins put on,
> They do suggest at first with heavenly shows,
> As I do now;
>
> [II. iii. 350-53]

Othello's stern words to Cassio and Montano:

> He that stirs next, to carve for his own rage,
> Holds his soul light;
>
> [II. iii. 173-74]

or his cry, after Iago's temptation, when Desdemona appears:

If she be false, O, then heaven mocks itself!

> [III. iii. 278]

or Emilia's

> I durst, my lord, to wager she is honest,
> Lay down my soul at stake.
>
> [IV. ii. 12-13]

There is terrible irony in the words we hear just after Iago, in his first soliloquy, has made clear the real nature of Othello's danger:

> Cassio, though he speak of comfort
> Touching the Turkish loss, yet he looks sadly
> And prays the Moor be safe;
>
> [II. i. 31-3]

in the herald's shout just after the villain's next soliloquy:

> Heaven bless the isle of Cyprus and our noble general
> Othello;
>
> [II. ii. 10-12]

or in the words—at once so funny and so tragic—which Cassio utters in his drunken piety;

> Well, God's above all; and there be souls must
> be saved, and there be souls must not be
> saved. . . . The lieutenant is to be saved before
> the ancient;
>
> [II. iii. 102-04, 109-10]

or in Othello's last happy thoughts of Desdemona:

> Excellent wretch! Perdition catch my soul
> But I do love thee! and when I love thee not,
> Chaos is come again.
>
> [III. iii. 90-2]

Critics have found a premonition in "Chaos has come again," but have ignored the suggestion in "Perdition catch my soul!"

With the Temptation Scene the allusions to perdition take on a new and vehement force. Compare Iago's coolly cynical words to Roderigo at the end of the first act, "If thou wilt needs damn thyself, do it a more delicate way than drowning" [I. iii. 353-54]; with Othello's cry of agony to his tormentor:

> If thou dost slander her and torture me,
> Never pray more; abandon all remorse;
> On horror's head horrors accumulate;
> Do deeds to make heaven weep, all earth amaz'd;
> For nothing canst thou to damnation add
> Greater than that.
>
> [III. iii. 368-73]

In a poetic atmosphere already charged with suggestions of eternity, these terrible words can have only their literal meaning. To take them in any other sense is to reduce intense art to bombast.

Words like these do not so force the idea of damnation upon our attention that we begin to analyze the prospects of Iago or Othello in an after-life. They convey the idea unobtrusively, kindling our imaginations and moving us with wonder and fear. They are part of the tragic tension of the play.

At whom do they chiefly point?

Most obviously, they point at Iago. Othello's words,

> Nothing can'st thou to damnation add,

are echoed instantly in our breasts; and when at last the *dramatis personae* recognize the "honest Iago" for a "demi-devil," the epithets "hellish villain" and "damned slave" only give release to our pent-up feelings of horror. But although the moral certainty that he is damned may help to reconcile us to the spectacle of his villainy, our chief concern is the agony of Othello and Desdemona.

It is part of the overwhelming irony of this play that it is Desdemona whom the Moor first believes to be in danger of perdition. The contrast is only the more fearful between what he believes and what we know. We know her adventurous daring, her modesty, her utter loyalty and singleness of heart. The element of spiritual beauty in her character impresses even the pitiful Roderigo. "She's full of most blessed condition," he tells Iago [II. i. 249-50]. Cassio, when Desdemona first sets foot on Cyprus, to encounter a fate which we partly foresee but of which she has never dreamed, welcomes her in words which have deeper meaning for us than for either of them.

> Hail to thee, lady! and the grace of heaven,
> Before, behind thee, and on every hand,
> Enwheel the round!
>
> [II. i. 85-7]

All the more violent is the shock of Othello's vehement words in his jealousy.

> Damn her, lewd minx. O, damn her!
> Come, go with me apart. I will withdraw
> To furnish me with some swift means of death
> For the fair devil.
>
> [III. iii. 476-79]

> Ay, let her rot, and perish, and be damn'd to-
> night; for she shall not live.
>
> [IV. i. 181-82]

He dwells on the thought that she deserves damnation as well as death.

> Come, swear it, damn thyself;
> Lest, being like one of heaven, the devils themselves
> Should fear to seize thee. Therefore be double-damned—
> Swear thou art honest.
>
> [IV. ii. 35-8]

> Minion, your dear lies dead,
> And your unblest fate hies.
>
> [V. i. 33-4]

But at the last, when thirst for personal revenge has given way to a sense of stern justice, the Moor recoils from the thought that the wife he has loved should find no mercy with heaven.

> If you bethink yourself of any crime
> Unreconcil'd as yet to heaven and grace,
> Solicit for it straight. . . .
> I would not kill thy unprepared spirit.
> No, heaven forfend! I would not kill thy soul.

Des.　Talk you of killing?
Oth.　　　　　　　Ay, I do.
Des.　　　　　　　　　　Then heaven
　　　Have mercy on me.
Oth.　　　　　　　　Amen, with all my heart.

> [V. ii. 26-8, 31-4]

When Desdemona denies her guilt and seems to weep for Cassio, Othello's anger is roused again that on her deathbed she adds perjury to adultery; and when she dies exonerating him of her death, he exclaims with the bitter conviction of one whose generous purpose has been thwarted,

> She's like a liar gone to burning hell!
> 'Twas I that kill'd her!
>
> [V. ii. 129-30]

Emilia's instant cry,

> O, the more angel she,
> And you the blacker devil,
>
> [V. ii. 130-31]

voices the emotion of the audience in one of the great climaxes of the play. All our reverence for Desdemona, intensified by the inconceivably false suspicions of her husband, find expression in her servant's words; and we feel with certitude that for Desdemona—as for Iago—the injustice of this world will be redressed in the judgments of the next.

But what of Othello, who is neither innocent nor a villain? Shakespeare, who knew his audience, must have known how inevitably they would regard the Moor as guilty. Of course, Emilia's tirade against him, by giving release to their indignation, prompts a wave of reaction in his favor, and makes possible a return of their entire sympathy when Othello reproaches himself far more bitterly even than Emilia has done. But can they entirely overlook his guilt when Lodovico asks,

> O thou Othello that wert once so good,
> Fall'n in the practice of a damned slave,
> What shall be said to thee?
>
> [V. ii. 291-93]

No doubt a Calvinist who saw in this tragic figure only an example of man's total depravity would be blind to the whole meaning of the drama. But could the Elizabethan—or for that matter the modern—audience quite exonerate him because he has "fallen into the clutches of some superhuman power"? Nearer to the dramatic truth of the situation, I believe, would be the followers of [Richard] Hooker or St. Thomas [More], who, with their insistence on the freedom of man's will, would hold the Moor accountable for his monstrous act, but would regard him with the deepest compassion. For as Hooker observes [in *Ecclesiastical Polity*],

> Some things we do neither against nor without,
> and yet not simply and merely with our wills,
> but with our wills in such sort moved, that albeit
> there be no impossibility but that we might,
> nevertheless we are not so easily able to do
> otherwise. In this consideration one evil deed
> is made more pardonable than another.

Othello's deed is of this kind, not wholly involuntary, but with his mind "perplexed in the extreme" [V. ii. 346].

How, then, did Shakespeare expect us to feel toward the Moor when thoughts of heaven and hell are suggested to our minds? At times during his jealousy—as when he loses consciousness in the paroxysm of his passion, or strikes his wife before the emissaries of Venice, or calls her an impudent strumpet—part of our tragic terror is lest he . . . sink into entire spiritual ruin. And the dread lest he incur damnation as well as the horrors of jealousy is, I think, not far from our minds. When he furiously curses his wife, bitterly urges her to double-damn herself by swearing innocence, and then begs her on her deathbed to confess and save her soul, the thought must cross our minds that it is Othello who is in danger of perdition. Immediately after the death of Desdemona the thought is brought home to

us with unmistakable emphasis in the words of both Othello and Emilia.

> O, I were damn'd beneath all depth in hell,
> But that I did proceed upon just grounds
> To this extremity.
>
> [V. ii. 137-39]

> This deed of thine is no more worthy heaven
> Than thou wast worthy her.
>
> [V. ii. 160-61]

> When we shall meet at compt,
> This look of thine will hurl my soul from heaven,
> And fiends will snatch at it
>
> [V. ii. 273-75]

But though his life is in ruins, the final impression which the great Moor leaves with us is not that of a ruined soul, but of a man ennobled by contrition. The phrases of conventional piety do not intrude here to reduce a tragic moment to commonplace. But what the theologians would call repentance is here—the utterly humble grief of heart, which is *contrition;* the frank acknowledgment of fault, which is *confession;* the making of amends to the injured party (in this instance the manly apology to Cassio) which is one part of what is called *satisfaction.* "In the majestic dignity and sovereign ascendancy of the close" no doubt the Elizabethan, as the modern, felt the renewed nobility of the hero and rejoiced "in the power of 'love and man's unconquerable mind'" [Bradley]. But mingled with that feeling would be another, which can have as much meaning for us as for our ancestors. For Othello's story is the perfect illustration of man's tragic vulnerability. At his first appearance, his magnificent poise, his modesty, his justice, his genius for command, his elevation of soul all seemed to raise him above the fallibility of the other sons of Adam. His downfall gives the lie to the Stoic boast in the strength of his own virtue, and demonstrates the inability of unaided human nature to govern its own life. In him we see exemplified in the highest degree alike the spiritual greatness and the tragic weakness of men, in both of which the age of Shakespeare had a profound belief. (pp. 237-45)

> *Kenneth O. Myrick, "The Theme of Damnation in Shakespearean Tragedy," in* Studies in Philology, *Vol. XXXVIII, No. 2, April, 1941, pp. 221-45.*

BRENTS STIRLING (essay date 1944)

[*A distinguished literary critic, Stirling has contributed three important books to Shakespearean scholarship:* The Populace in Shakespeare *(1949),* Unity in Shakespearian Tragedy *(1956), and* The Shakespeare Sonnet Order: Poems and Groups *(1968). In the following excerpt from an essay that first appeared in the Shakespeare Association Bulletin in 1944, he offers a refutation of Elmer Edgar Stoll's conclusion that Othello's jealousy is psychologically inconsistent with his noble nature and is explicable only in terms of the dramatic convention of the "calumniator believed" (see excerpt above, 1915). Instead, Stirling asserts, Shakespeare has accurately grounded the Moor's improbable behavior in "psychologically sound processes," which, although not literally drawn from life, are "deliberately rooted in simple psychological truth." To illustrate this proposition, he focuses on three dramatic incidents: Othello's rapid decline into jealousy and rage in Act III, Scene iii; his treatment of Desdemona in Act IV, Scene ii; and his "amazing and disjointed outburst" before falling into a trance in Act IV, Scene i. With respect to the first incident, Stirling argues that Othello's dramatic change from serenity to agitation is convincing because it is shown to arise from his own persistent doubts and demands for proofs of Desdemona's faithlessness. Similarly, when the Moor fails to confront his wife with his suspicions and, instead, levels unspecified charges and innuendoes against her in the brothel scene, he is acting in accordance with another psychological process—"the phenomenon of morbid and malignant secretiveness," in which a person refuses to divulge some knowledge that directly affects another. Finally, Stirling regards Othello's lines preceding his trance as signalling that the recurring assaults on his psyche and the resulting apprehension have caused an "emotional collapse" that is comprehensible to the audience and consistent with our understanding of the operation of the human mind.]*

Mr. Stoll's well-known interpretation denies to *Othello* a psychological motivation of the central character; it asserts, rather, that the play contains what could be called a successful motivation of the audience through stagecraft and skilled poetry, all to such a degree that the audience accepts the psychologically incredible [see excerpt above, 1915]. Although the variations of this argument make simplification objectionable, it may be said that one principle controls throughout Mr. Stoll's view. That principle is that no psychological theory can integrate Othello's experience and his naivete, his swift decision and the crude stimulus for it, his affection for Desdemona and his failure to question her about the slander.

There may be no sound reason for denying this, but there is a reservation which may be made: I suggest that if Mr. Stoll's premises be accepted, the legitimate inference from them is not his conclusion that psychological interpretation of *Othello* be abandoned, but rather that attempts at psychological integration of the character be abandoned. More specifically, I suggest that even if it be true that no psychological theory can make a credible unity of Othello's personality, his improbable acts and beliefs may yet be seen to arise from psychological processes which, apart from their results, are sound and probable. I hope that this will seem less paradoxical as discussion of the play develops.

Our procedure becomes one of examining *Othello* with attention to three well known situations in which the improbable happens, but in each of which a sound psychological process, logically connected with slander and jealousy, is successfully dramatized. There is nothing novel about some of the matters to which attention will be called; certain of them have perhaps become too familiar. There is, however, the usual necessity of surveying old material in order to re-evaluate it.

The first of the psychological processes which have been mentioned as occurring in *Othello* is based upon the principle that effective persuasion of others comes not from frontal assault but from tactics leading the object of persuasion to convince himself of the desired conclusion. It is perhaps well recognized, that Othello is allowed to institute, develop, and confirm suspicion on his own responsibility. I wish to emphasize, however, that I am not calling attention to Iago's often-noted coyness but rather to the phenomenon of Othello's personal initiative and persistence in reaching the conclusion of Desdemona's guilt. In the scene in which his sinister imagination is set in motion, Iago, calling attention to Cassio's departure from Desdemona, remarks cryptically, "Ha! I like not that" [III. iii. 35], and disclaims instantly any significance for the observation. Othello, his curiosity prompted, asks, "Was not that Cassio parted from my wife" [III. iii. 37], and upon Iago's denial discovers for himself, in dialogue with Desdemona, that it was Cassio who had stolen away "so guilty like" [III. iii. 39]. Desdemona asks her boon, Cassio's reinstatement, and as Othello's suspicion dies down Iago broaches the subject: "My

noble lord—*Did* Michael Cassio, when you woo'd my lady, know of your love?" [III. iii. 93, 94]. Iago is tentative to the point of exasperation; Othello, for the next hundred lines, places him under a cogent and dramatic cross-examination, and it is during the course of this that the process of Othello's morbid analysis and self-persuasion starts. Ironically his very disclaimer of jealousy, which caps the passage mentioned, contains his declaration that "to be once in doubt is once to be resolved," and ironically also, his line beginning with "I'll see before I doubt" ends with "when I doubt I'll prove" [III. iii. 179-80, 190]. Iago then alludes to the "pranks" of Venetian wives and to Desdemona's deception of her father; as he leaves, Othello contemplates his course of action: "If I do prove her haggard . . . I'll whistle her off and let her down the wind to prey at fortune" [III. iii. 260, 262-63]. Othello shortly leaves the stage and upon his return later is in great agitation. He tells Iago that he has been set upon the rack and swears that "'tis better to be much abused than but to know't a little" [III. iii. 336-37]. Then in vituperative speech he exhibits what this "little" has become with the accretion of his own thought:

> What sense had I of her stol'n hours of lust?
> I saw it not, thought it not, it harm'd not me. . . .
> I had been happy if the general camp,
> Pioneers and all, had tasted her sweet body,
> So I had nothing known.
>
>   [III. iii. 338-39, 345-47]

Henceforth it is Othello who demands demonstration of Desdemona's guilt. His hysterical requirements of Iago echo with the word "proof"—"ocular proof," "probation" that bears "no hinge or loop" [III. iii. 365]. Othello is only nominally searching for evidence; in actuality he is crying for certainty at any price, and doing so in the office of prosecuting counsel, with Iago in the role of a badgered prurient witness.

It is easy to say, with Mr. Stoll and others, that all this would be melodrama but for the poetic sureness of line which, in Shakspere, often sustains extravaganza where rant or flatulence would destroy it. And it is easy to say that no scene more effectively shows Shakspere to be a master of stagecraft as opposed to consecutive character development. Literally considered, such things are true; abstract out the stagecraft and poetry, then question the causal sequence leading to Othello's paroxysm, and melodrama, perhaps bad melodrama, would remain.

Mr. Stoll and similar interpreters, however, infer from this that the play is devoid of psychological motivation. But is not the scene we have just reviewed grounded upon an assumption that Othello's transition from calm to agitated jealousy is more credible if dramatized as self-developed doubt, self-propelled persuasion? Has not Shakspere dramatized the psychological truism that persuasion and conviction move far more readily by that route? Perhaps these questions may be answered better if we imagine an alternative rendition of the scene; suppose Shakspere had cast Othello in a passive rather than an active role; suppose that not Othello but Iago had forced the issue, that not Othello but Iago had moved step by step to shriller emotion, more abounding rhetoric. Would not the Moor's ultimate belief in Iago have been far less plausible, even with the skillful handling of poetry, tensity, and fast movement? And would not this absence of plausibility have then been attributable simply to a bad psychological mistake made by Shakspere?

Those who share Mr. Stoll's point of view insist, moreover, that the scene just described shows perfectly Shakspere's customary abandonment of psychological development and exploitation of pure situation. Situation it is, but it is "psychological situation" as well as dramatic situation; it is deliberately rooted in simple psychological truth—not literal truth about ordered conduct drawn from life, but a true process regulating the way reluctant belief is most effectively swayed. From this process the improbable (Othello's capitulation) may be said to arise, but the process itself is psychologically sound, and an absence of it would come near cancelling all verisimilitude in the scene. (pp. 135-38)

[There is] a second so-called psychological impossibility in *Othello*, specifically the failure of the Moor to confront Desdemona with interrogation or accusation. This also has come to be viewed in the light of dramatic convention and Shaksperian skill in slurring and blurring. Rightly enough, but Shakspere in using these techniques is not so careless of psychological assumptions as are his interpreters. Gradual, complete, or "real" motivation here also may be impossible, but Shakspere, again in a well-contrived scene, dramatizes a simple and relevant psychological process. It is the phenomenon of morbid and malignant secretiveness—"I have something against you, but you shall not have the satisfaction of knowing what it is." Thus in Act IV, scene 2, Othello does confront Desdemona; he confronts her with innuendo: "Let me see your eyes" [IV. ii. 25]. He orders Emilia to ply her duties as a prostitute's attendant: "Some of your function, mistress" [IV. ii. 27]. He reduces Desdemona to a pulp of anguished mystification, and then shouts that she is as false as hell. In reply to her imploring "To whom, my lord, with whom, how am I false?" he puts her aside in grief with, "O Desdemona away! away! away!" [IV. ii. 39-41].

This scene, like the one first discussed, might never serve to account, in any "real life" sense, for Othello's failure to check elementary facts by consultation with Desdemona. But again, in its forceful dramatization of a psychologically sound principle, in its exploiting of what may be called "psychological situation", it achieves the limit of motivation possible within a factually incredible plot. It shows with maximum effect that the operation of malignant secretiveness is very often a manifestation of morbid suspicion, and it asks us to apply the principle imaginatively to a framework of the non-actual and improbable.

We may consider next the most spectacular of Shakspere's methods of providing, in *Othello*, psychologically sound processes through which the psychologically unlikely transpires. This method is one involving expertly dramatized irrationality in the protagonist. There has been traditionally a tacit avoidance of this emotional crisis of Othello, perhaps because of the feeling that he would lose tragic dignity by ascription to him of something close to madness. Shakspere, however, has emphasized it in a well-known scene in which Othello utterly goes under. After the lie regarding an intimate interview with Cassio and after the setting in motion of the paraphernalia of entrapment, Iago returns to Othello with intelligence. By impetuous questioning Othello drags the news from him: Cassio has blabbed (that is the word) of his lying with Desdemona. Othello, his mind confused and overwhelmed, then breaks the blank verse sequence with his amazing and disjointed outburst:

> Handkerchief—confession—handkerchief!—
> To confess and be hanged for his labor;— First
> to be hanged and then to confess.— I tremble
> at it . . . It is Not words that shake me thus.

Pish! Noses, ears, and lips.—Is't possible?—
confess—handkerchief! O devil!

And in the folio this is followed by the stage direction, "Falls into a trance." [IV. i. 37-9, 41-3]

Mr. Stoll points out that such verbal anarchy is common to Elizabethan stage cuckolds, but the convention does not rob the episode of its quality as a remarkable emotional collapse. An emotional collapse it is by the standards of any place or time, and, significantly here, it has been induced by the process traditionally understood to cause mental and emotional breakdown: a cumulative anxiety aggravated by repetitive irritations. It is scarcely more real insanity than Hamlet's, but it is a profound emotional chaos, and the dramatization of it is in *Othello*. Would a "real" character have undergone such a debacle under the stimulation of Iago? Probably not. But as "psychological situation," Othello's emotional collapse and its causes mentioned above, are in the play with great forthrightness. Such phenomena add immeasurably to the play's motivation, both dramatic and psychological. (pp. 139-41)

> Brents Stirling, "Psychology in 'Othello'," in The Shakespeare Association Bulletin, *Vol. XIX, No. 3, July, 1944, pp. 135-44.*

HARLEY GRANVILLE-BARKER   (essay date 1945)

[Granville-Barker was a noted actor, playwright, director, and critic. His work as a Shakespearean critic is at all times informed by his experience as a director, for he treats Shakespeare's plays not as works of literature better understood divorced from the theater, as did many Romantic critics, but as pieces meant for the stage. As a director, he emphasized simplicity in staging, set design, and costuming. He believed that elaborate scenery obscured the poetry which was of central importance to Shakespeare's plays. Granville-Barker also eschewed the approach of directors who scrupulously reconstructed a production based upon Elizabethan stage techniques; he felt that this, too, detracted from the play's meaning. In the following excerpt on Othello, Granville-Barker examines the dramatic structure of the tragedy and explicates the relation between Shakespeare's manipulation of time and the theme of sexual jealousy. He avers that the passage of time in Act I is realistic and natural, so that the audience is provided with an extended opportunity to become familiar with the central characters. Granville-Barker demonstrates, however, that with the opening of Act II we are introduced to contractions and ambiguities of time that are sustained until Act V, Scene ii, when "'natural' time" is resumed and Shakespeare offers a comprehensive view of the ruined Moor. Remarking that Shakespeare clearly provides references to specific times of day to indicate that from the beginning of Act III, Scene iii until the close of the drama only twenty-four hours of actual time elapses, the critic contends that the precipitous action is both dramatically convincing, as it hurries the audience along, and consistent with the recklessness of Iago and the pathological sexual jealousy that flaws the character of Othello. Granville-Barker also poses the question of why, during this portion of his play, Shakespeare frequently alludes to the passage of a significant span of time, while he also clearly demonstrates that the actual dramatic period is merely a day and a half in duration—in other words, the conflict of long and short time in the play. He concludes that, if Othello were given time to reflect and act sensibly but failed to do so, he would relinquish our esteem and sympathy. Granville-Barker also notes that, with the break in the dramatic action between Acts I and II, Shakespeare has already included one significant lapse of time and that he could not risk destroying the dramatic illusion by introducing another one later in the play. The question of Shakespeare's manipulation of time in Othello *was first raised by Thomas Rymer (1692). For additional commentary on the time*

scheme in the play, see the essays by Ned B. Allen, Horace Howard Furness, Christopher North, M. R. Ridley, and John Dover Wilson cited in the Additional Bibliography. Finally, Granville-Barker contends that although Othello's rapid descent into sexual jealousy and savagery may be shocking or pathetic, it lacks tragic dimension. Unlike the heroes of Shakespeare's other major tragedies, he asserts, the Moor's destruction "comes short of serving for the purgation of our souls, since Othello's own soul stays unpurged." For Granville-Barker, then, Othello remains damned at the close of his life, his only prospect hell, and for this reason he calls Othello "a tragedy without meaning." Other critics who have discussed whether Othello is represented as being saved or eternally damned at the close of the drama include Kenneth O. Myrick (1941), S. L. Bethell (1952), Paul N. Siegel (1953), Irving Ribner (1955 and 1960), Edward Hubler (1958), G. M. Matthews (1964), and Roy W. Battenhouse (1969).]

It has been often enough remarked that in the action of Othello there is, for Shakespeare, an unusually near approach to classic unity. "Had the scene opened in Cyprus", says Johnson, "and the preceding incidents been occasionally related, there had been little wanting to a drama of the most exact and scrupulous regularity" [see excerpt above, 1765]. But this (with due respect to Johnson) makes a misleading approach. There is no aiming at regularity and falling short of it. What unity there is—and it is very defective—is simply the outcome of an economy of treatment peculiar to the needs of the play. Unity of theme, that we have. As to unity of place; this is vaguely and implicitly established for several successive scenes within the bounds of Othello's residence. But Bianca and Roderigo—Bianca particularly—are most unlikely intruders there, where a while before Othello and Desdemona have been domestically disputing over the loss of the handkerchief. And time is given no unity of treatment at all; it is contracted and expanded like a concertina. For the play's opening and closing the time of the action is the time of its acting; and such an extent of "natural" time (so to call it) is unusual. But minutes stand for hours over the sighting, docking and discharging—with a storm raging, too!—of the three ships which have carried the characters to Cyprus; the entire night of Cassio's undoing passes uninterruptedly in the speaking space of four hundred lines: and we have, of course, Othello murdering Desdemona within twenty-four hours of the consummation of their marriage, when, if Shakespeare let us—or let Othello himself—pause to consider, she plainly *cannot* be guilty of adultery.

Freedom with time is, of course, one of the recognised freedoms of Shakespeare's stage; he is expected only to give his exercise of it the slightest dash of plausibility. But in the maturity of his art he learns how to draw positive dramatic profit from it. For this play's beginning he does not, as we have noted, contract time at all. Moreover, he allows seven hundred lines to the three first scenes when he could well have done their business in half the space or less, could even, as Johnson suggests, have left it to be "occasionally related" afterwards. The profit is made evident when later, by contrast, we find him using contraction of time, and the heightening of tension so facilitated, to disguise the incongruities of the action. For he can do this more easily if he has already familiarised us with the play's characters. And he has done that more easily by presenting them to us in the unconstraint of uncontracted time, asking us for no special effort of make-believe. Accepting what they *are*, we the more readily accept what they *do*. It was well, in particular, to make Iago familiarly lifelike. If his victims are to believe in him, so, in another sense, must we. Hence the profuse self-display to Roderigo. That there is as much lying as truth in it is no matter. A man's lying, once we detect it, is as eloquent of him as the truth.

The contraction of time for the arrival in Cyprus has its dramatic purpose too. Shakespeare could have relegated the business to hearsay. But the spectacular excitement, the suspense, the ecstatic happiness of the reuniting of Othello and Desdemona, give the action fresh stimulus and impetus and compensate for the break in it occasioned by the voyage. Yet there must be no dwelling upon this, which is still only prelude to the capital events to come. For the same reason, the entire night of Cassio's undoing passes with the uninterrupted speaking of four hundred lines. It is no more than a sample of Iago's skill, so it must not be lingered upon either. Amid the distracting variety of its comings and goings we do not remark the contraction. As Iago himself has been let suggest to us:

> Pleasure and action make the hours seem short.
>
> [II. iii. 379]

Then, upon the entrance of Cassio with his propitiatory aubade and its suggestion of morning, commences the sustained main stretch of the action. This is set to something more complex than a merely contracted, it goes to a sort of ambiguous scheme of time, not only a profitable, but here—for Shakespeare turning story into play—an almost necessary device. After that we have the long last scene set to "natural" time, the play thus ending as it began. The swift-moving, close-packed action, fit product of Iago's ravening will, is over.

> *Enter Othello, and Desdemona in her bed.*
>
> [s.d. V. ii. 1]

—and, the dreadful deed done, all is done. While the rest come and go about him:

> Here is my journey's end . . .
>
> [V. ii. 267]

he says, as at a standstill, as in a very void of time. And as the "natural" time at the play's beginning let us observe the better the man he was, so relaxation to it now lets us mark more fully the wreck that remains.

The three opening scenes move to a scheme of their own, in narrative and in the presentation of character. The first gives us a view of Iago which, if to be proved superficial, is yet a true one (for Shakespeare will never introduce a character misleadingly), and a sample of his double-dealing. Roderigo at the same time paints us a thick-lipped, lascivious Moor, which we discover in the second scene, with a slight, pleasant shock of surprise at the sight of Othello himself, to have been merely a figment of his own jealous chagrin. There also we find quite another Iago: the modest, devoted, disciplined soldier. . . . The third scene takes us to the Senate House, where Brabantio and his griefs, which have shrilly dominated the action so far, find weightier competition in the question of the war, and the State's need of Othello, whose heroic aspect is heightened by this. (pp. 11-14)

The scenic mobility of Shakespeare's stage permits him up to [I. iii.] to translate his narrative straightforwardly into action. We pass, that is to say, from Brabantio's house, which Desdemona has just quitted, to the Sagittary, where she and Othello are to be found, and from there to the Senate House, to which he and she (later) and Brabantio are summoned. And the movement itself is given dramatic value by its quickening or slackening or abrupt arrest. We have the feverish impetus of Brabantio's torchlight pursuit; Othello's calm talk to Iago set in sequence and contrast; the encounter with the other current of the servants of the Duke upon their errand; the halt, the averted conflict; then the passing on together of the two parties, in sobered but still hostile detachment, towards the Senate House.

Note also that such narrative as is needed of what has passed before the play begins is mainly postponed to the third of these opening scenes. By then we should be interested in the characters, and the more, therefore, in the narrative itself, which is, besides, given a dramatic value of its own by being framed as a cause pleaded before the Senate. Further, even while we listen to the rebutting of Brabantio's accusation of witchcraft by Othello's "round unvarnished tale" [I. iii. 90], we shall be expecting Desdemona's appearance, the one important figure in this part of the story still to be seen. And this expectancy offsets the risk of the slackening of tension which reminiscent narrative must always involve.

Shakespeare now breaks the continuity of the action: and such a clean break as this is with him unusual. He has to transport his characters to Cyprus. The next scene takes place there. An unmeasured interval of time is suggested, and no scene on shipboard or the like has been provided for a link, nor are any of the events of the voyage recounted. The tempest which drowns the Turks, and rids him of his now superfluous war, and has more thrillingly come near besides to drowning the separated Othello and Desdemona—something of this he does

contrive to present to us; and we are plunged into it as we were into the crisis of the play's opening:

> What from the cape can you discern at sea?
>
> Nothing at all. It is a high-wrought flood;
> I cannot, 'twixt the heaven and the main
> Descry a sail.
>
> [II. i. 1-4]

—a second start as strenuous as the first. The excitement offsets the breaking of the continuity. And the compression of the events, of the storm and the triple landing, then the resolution of the fears for Othello's safety into the happiness of the reuniting of the two—the bringing of all this within the space of a few minutes' acting raises tension to a high pitch and holds it there. (pp. 14-16)

The proclamation in [II. ii.] serves several subsidiary purposes. It helps settle the characters in Cyprus. The chances and excitements of the arrival are over. Othello is in command; but the war is over too, and he only needs bid the people rejoice at peace and his happy marriage. It economically sketches us a background for Cassio's ill-fated carouse. It allows a small breathing space before Iago definitely gets to work. It "neutralises" the action for a moment (a herald is an anonymous voice; he has no individuality), suspends its interest without

Act II. Scene i. Othello, Desdemona, Roderigo, Iago, Emilia, Cassio, Montano, Gentlemen, and Attendants. By T. Stothard.

breaking its continuity. Also it brings its present timelessness to an end; events are given a clock to move by, and with that take on a certain urgency. (pp. 22-3)

[In Act III. Scene iii.] the action passes into the ambiguity of time which has troubled so many critics. *Compression* of time, by one means or another, is common form in most drama; we . . . [see] it put to use in the speeding through a single unbroken scene of the whole night of Cassio's betrayal. But now comes—if we are examining the craft of the play—something more complex. When it is acted we notice nothing unusual, and neither story nor characters appear false in retrospect. It is as with the perspective of a picture, painted to be seen from a certain standpoint. Picture and play can be enjoyed and much of their art appreciated with no knowledge of how the effect is gained. But the student needs to know.

We have reached the morrow of the arrival in Cyprus and of the consummation of the marriage. This is plain. It is morning. By the coming midnight or a little later Othello will have murdered Desdemona and killed himself. To that measure of time, plainly demonstrated, the rest of the play's action will move. It comprises no more than seven scenes. From this early hour we pass without interval—the clock no more than customarily speeded—to midday dinner time and past it. Then comes a break in the action (an empty stage; one scene ended, another beginning), which, however, can only allow for a quite inconsiderable interval of time, to judge, early in the following scene, by Desdemona's "Where should I lose that handkerchief, Emilia?" [III. iv. 23]—the handkerchief which we have recently seen Emilia retrieve and pass to Iago. And later in this scene Cassio gives it to Bianca, who begs that she may see him "soon at night" [III. iv. 198]. Then comes another break in the action. But, again, it can involve no long interval of time; since in the scene following Bianca speaks of the handkerchief given her "even now". Later in this scene Lodovico, suddenly come from Venice, is asked by Othello to supper; and between Cassio and Bianca there has been more talk of "tonight" and "supper". Another break in the action; but, again, little or no passing of time can be involved, since midway through the next scene the trumpets sound to supper, and Iago closes it with

> It is now high supper-time and
> the night grows to waste. . . .
>
> [IV. ii. 242-43]

The following scene opens with Othello, Desdemona and Lodovico coming from supper, with Othello's command to Desdemona:

> Get you to bed on the instant. . . .
>
> [IV. iii. 7]

and ends with her good-night to Emilia. The scene after—of the ambush for Cassio—we have been explicitly told is to be made by Iago to "fall out between twelve and one" [IV. ii. 236-37], and it is, we find, pitch dark, and the town is silent. And from here Othello and Emilia patently go straight to play their parts in the last scene of all, he first, she later, as quickly as she can speed.

These, then, are the events of a single day; and Shakespeare is at unusual pains to make this clear, by the devices of the morning music, dinner-time, supper-time and the midnight dark, and their linking together by the action itself and reference after reference in the dialogue. Nor need we have any doubt of his reasons for this. Only by thus precipitating the action can it

be made both effective in the terms of his stage-craft and convincing. If Othello were left time for reflection or the questioning of anyone but Iago, would not the whole flimsy fraud that is practised on him collapse?

But this granted, are they convincing as the events of that particular day, the very morrow of the reunion and of the consummation of the marriage?

Plainly they will not be; and before long Shakespeare has begun to imply that we are weeks or months—or it might be a year or more—away from anything of the sort.

> What sense had I of her stolen hours of lust?
> I saw it not, thought it not; it harmed not me;
> I slept the next night well, was free and merry;
> I found not Cassio's kisses on her lips. . . .
>
> [III. iii. 338-41]

That is evidence enough, but a variety of other implications go to confirm it; Iago's

> I lay with Cassio lately. . . .
>
> [III. iii. 413]

Cassio's reference to his "former suit", Bianca's reproach to him

> What, keep a week away? seven days and nights?
> Eight score eight hours. . . . ?
>
> [III. iv. 173-74]

and more definitively yet, Lodovico's arrival from Venice with the mandate of recall, the war being over—by every assumption of the sort, indeed, Othello and Desdemona and the rest are living the life of Cinthio's episodic story, not at the forced pace of Shakespeare's play. But he wants to make the best of both these calendars; and, in his confident, reckless, dexterous way, he contrives to do so.

Why, however, does he neglect the obvious and simple course of allowing a likely lapse of time between the night of the arrival and of Cassio's disgrace and the priming of Othello to suspect Desdemona and her kindness to him, for which common sense—both our own, and, we might suppose, Iago's—cries out? A sufficient answer is that there has been one such break in the action already, forced on him by the voyage to Cyprus, and he must avoid another.

The bare Elizabethan stage bred a panoramic form of drama; the story straightforwardly unfolded, as many as possible of its more telling incidents presented, narrative supplying the antecedents and filling the gaps. Its only resources of any value are the action itself and the speech; and the whole burden, therefore, of stimulating and sustaining illusion falls on the actor—who, once he has captured his audience, must, like the spellbinding orator he may in method much resemble, be at pains to hold them, or much of his work will continually be to do over again. Our mere acceptance of the fiction, of the story and its peopling, we shall perhaps not withdraw; we came prepared to accept it. Something subtler is involved; the sympathy (in the word's stricter sense) which the art of the actor will have stirred in us. This current interrupted will not be automatically restored. Our emotions, roused and let grow cold, need quick rousing again. And the effects of such forced stoking are apt to stale with repetition.

Hence the help to the Elizabethan actor, with so much dependent on him, of continuity of action. Having once captured his audience, they are the easier to hold. The dramatist finds this too. Shakespeare escapes dealing with minor incidents of the voyage to Cyprus by ignoring them; and he restarts the interrupted action amid the stimulating anxieties of the storm. But such another sustaining device would be hard to find. And were he to allow a likely lapse of time before the attack on Othello's confidence is begun it would but suggest to us when it *is* begun and we watch it proceeding the equal likelihood of an Iago wisely letting enough time pass between assault for the poison's full working. And with that the whole dramatic fabric would begin to crumble. Here would be Cinthio's circumspect Ensign again, and the action left stagnating, the onrush of Othello's passion to be checked and checked again, and he given time to reflect and anyone the opportunity to enlighten him! Give him such respite, and if he then does not, by the single stroke of good sense needed, free himself from the fragile web of lies which is choking him, he will indeed seem to be simply the gull and dolt "as ignorant as dirt" [V. ii. 164] of Emilia's final invective, no tragic hero, certainly.

Shakespeare has to work within the close confines of the dramatic form; and this imposes on him a double economy, a shaping of means to end and end to means, of characters to the action, the action to the characters also. If Othello's ruin is not accomplished without pause or delay, it can hardly be accomplished at all. The circumstances predicate an Iago of swift and reckless decision. These are the very qualities, first, to help him to his barren triumph, then to ensure his downfall. And Othello's precipitate fall from height to depth is tragically appropriate to the man he is—as to the man he is made to be because the fall must be precipitate. Finally, that we may rather feel with Othello in his suffering than despise him for the folly of it, *we* are speeded through time as unwittingly as he is, and left little more chance for reflection.

Most unconscionable treatment of time truly, had time any independent rights! But effect is all. And Shakespeare smooths incongruities away by letting the action follow the shorter, the "hourly" calendar—from dawn and the aubade to midnight and the murder—without more comment than is necessary, while he takes the longer one for granted in a few incidental references. He has only to see that the two do not clash in any overt contradiction.

The change into ambiguity of time is effected in the course of Iago's opening attack upon Othello. This is divided into two, with the summons to dinner and the finding and surrender of the handkerchief for an interlude. In the earlier part—although it is taken for granted—there is no very definite reference to the longer calendar; and Iago, to begin with, deals only in its generalities. Not until the second part do we have the determinate "I lay with Cassio lately . . .", the story of his dream, the matter of the handkerchief, and Othello's own

> I slept the next night well, was free and merry;
> I found not Cassio's kisses on her lips.

with the implication that weeks or months may have passed since the morrow of the landing. But why no tribute to likelihood here of some longer interval than that provided merely by the dinner to "the generous islanders" [III. iii. 280], between the sowing of the poison and its fierce, full fruition? There are two answers. From the standpoint of likelihood a suggested interval of days or weeks would largely defeat its own purpose, since the time given the poison to work would seem time given to good sense to intervene too. From the standpoint simply of the play's action, any interruption hereabouts, actual or suggested, must lower its tension and dissipate

our interest, at the very juncture, too, when its main business, over-long held back, is fairly under way. Shakespeare will certainly not feel called on to make such a sacrifice to mere likelihood. He does loosen the tension of the inmost theme—all else beside, it would soon become intolerable—upon Othello's departure with Desdemona and by the episode of the handkerchief. But with Iago conducting this our interest will be surely held; and, Emilia left behind, the scene continuing, the continuity of action is kept. And when Othello returns, transformed in the interval from the man merely troubled in mind to a creature incapable of reason, "eaten up with passion . . ." [III. iii. 391], his emotion reflected in us will let *us* also lose count of time, obliterate yesterday in today, confound the weeks with the months in the one intolerable moment.

But the over-riding explanation of this show of Shakespeare's stagecraft is that he is not essentially concerned with time and the calendar at all. These, and other outward circumstances, must be given plausibility. But the play's essential action lies in the processes of thought and feeling by which the characters are moved and the story is forwarded. And the deeper the springs of these the less do time, place, and circumstance affect them. His imagination is concerned with fundamental passions, and its swift working demands uncumbered expression. He may falsify the calendar for his convenience; but we shall find neither trickery nor anomaly in the planning of the battle for Othello's soul. And in the light of the truth of this the rest passes unnoticed. (pp. 30-8)

We have seen how, to make the story dramatically viable, the mainspring of the play's action has to be drastically compressed. It follows that the fatal flaw in the hero's character must be one which will develop swiftly and catastrophically too. The story has provided in sexual jealousy about the only one which will.

Of vanity, envy, self-seeking and distrust, which are the seeds of jealousy in general, Othello, it is insisted from the beginning, is notably free, so free that he will not readily remark these qualities in others—in Iago, for instance, in whom they so richly abound. And he has never yet cared enough for a woman to be jealous of her; that also is made clear. It is a nature, then, taught by no earlier minor failings of this kind to resist a gross attack on it, should that come.

But sexual jealousy, once given rein, is a passion like no other. It is pathological, a moral lesion, a monomania. Facts and reason become its playthings. Othello does at first put up a feeble intellectual resistance, in a single soliloquy he struggles a little with himself; but, after this, every defence is swept away, and the poison rages in him unchecked. Here, then, is the sudden and swift descent to catastrophe, which the story, as Shakespeare dramatises it, demands. A bad business, certainly; yet, to this extent, shocking rather than tragic. Indeed, did not Othello suffer so and dispense suffering, the spectacle of his wholly baseless duping and befooling would be more comic than otherwise, the mere upsetting of his confidence and dignity as enjoyable for us as to Iago; and, in a ghastly fashion, it for a few moments becomes so when he is set eavesdropping upon Cassio and Bianca. Shocking, that it is, and pitiful, for all perplexed suffering is pitiful. But there is more to true tragedy than this.

The writing and re-writing of *Hamlet* must surely have shown Shakespeare the limits to the dramatic use that can be made of the purely pathological. Little was to be done in exhibiting the character of a man consistently aping madness who would not reveal himself, but even less was practicable if he were really mad and could not. With Hamlet it is the land near the borderline which proves fruitful, since there we have him acutely conscious of himself, and at his readiest for that work of self-purgation by which the tragic hero finds significance in his fate.

With Othello neither the planning of the play, nor his character, nor the jealous mania which is foreign to every other trait in it, will allow for this. He cannot reason with himself about something which is in its very nature unreasonable, nor can Shakespeare set him searching for the significance of events which exist only in Iago's lies—we, the audience, should resent such futility. He is betrayed and goes ignorantly to his doom. And when, at last, Desdemona dead, he learns the truth, what can he have to say—or we!—but

> O, fool, fool, fool!
>
> [V. ii. 323]

The mere sight of such beauty and nobility and happiness, all wickedly destroyed, must be a harrowing one. Yet the pity and terror of it come short of serving for the purgation of our souls, since Othello's own soul stays unpurged. Hamlet dies spiritually at peace; Lear's madness has been the means to his salvation; by interpreting his life's hell to us even Macbeth stirs us to some compassion. But what alchemy can bring the once noble Moor and the savage murderer into unity again? The "cruel tears" and the kiss and the talk of justice are more intolerable than the savagery itself. Nor can remorse bridge the gulf between the two. Othello wakes as from a nightmare only to kill himself, his prospect hell. And the play's last word is, significantly, not of him, but of tortures for Iago; punishment as barren as the crime. It is a tragedy without meaning, and that is the ultimate horror of it. (pp. 173-75)

Othello's . . . is a story of blindness and folly, of a man run mad. As the play is planned, evil works all but unquestioned in him until it is too late. Of battle between good and evil, his soul the battleground, even of a clarifying consciousness of the evil at work in him, there is nothing. Not until the madman's deed is done, does "he that was Othello" wake to sanity again [V. ii. 284]; his tragedy, then, to have proved that from the seemingly securest heights of his "soul's content" there is no depth of savagery to which man cannot fall.

Shakespeare paints us a merciless picture of the awakened, the broken Othello; of the frenetically repentant creature of Emilia's scornful

> Nay; lay thee down and roar . . .
>
> [V. ii. 198]

of the man with all strength for evil or for good gone out of him, remorse mere mockery as he looks upon the dead Desdemona; of an Othello crying

> Whip me, ye devils,
> From the possession of this heavenly sight!
> Blow me about in winds! roast me in sulphur!
> Wash me in steep down gulfs of liquid fire! . . .
>
> [V. ii. 277-80]

—sheer horror this; the howling of the damned! He speaks his own epitaph before he dies; a last echo of the noble Moor that was. (pp. 183-84)

> Harley Granville-Barker, in his Prefaces to Shakespeare: Othello, fourth series, Sidgwick & Jackson, Ltd., 1945, 223 p.

DEREK TRAVERSI (essay date 1949)

[Traversi, a British scholar, has written a number of books on Shakespeare's plays, including An Approach to Shakespeare (1938), Shakespeare: The Last Phase (1954), Shakespeare: From "Richard II" to "Henry V" (1957), and Shakespeare: The Roman Plays (1963). In the introduction to the first of these studies, Traversi proposed to focus his interpretation of the plays on "the word," stating that the experience which forms the impetus to each of Shakespeare's dramas "will find its most immediate expression in the language and verse." In the following excerpt, taken from an essay on Othello first published in 1949 in a journal entitled The Wind and the Rain, Traversi asserts that the central focus of the play is on "the twin aspects" of physical passion dramatized in the figures of Othello and Iago. Remarking on Shakespeare's use in the Sonnets of the device of the canker within the rose to symbolize the potential destruction contained in sexual love, he argues that Othello is the dramatic portrayal of the devolution of desire into "selfish and destructive 'appetite'"; he adds that although Iago's view of love appears to be in sharp contrast with the Moor's, taken together they represent a complementary vision of the self-destructive tendencies implicit in physical passion. Although he views the Moor as essentially a noble figure, Traversi contends that Othello's poetic expressions of love demonstrate a complacent naiveté and egoism which fatally mar his feelings for Desdemona. He maintains that Othello's passion is rooted in sensuality—although he conceals this from himself—and that Iago's provocations in Act III, Scene iii are designed to ignite the baser, hidden aspects of the Moor's nature. Iago is so successful, Traversi contends, because Othello's "uncritical acceptance of the promptings of passion" is no match for the ancient's "philosophy" of love as sexual appetite or "blood" that, by its very nature, constantly seeks new means by which to sate its desires. Indeed, the critic judges, the "physical intensity" of Iago's cynical disparagements of love demonstrate the forcefulness of that emotion more clearly than does the love poetry of Othello, which the critic describes as frequently cold, aloof, distant, and conventional. However, Traversi discovers in Othello's speeches on his "triumphant soldiership" the force and intensity lacking in his love poetry, noting that before he mourns the loss of Desdemona's love in Act III, Scene iii he first regrets the wound to his pride and "his own integrity as a warrior." For additional discussions of the Moor's poetic language, see the excerpts by G. Wilson Knight (1930), John Bayley (1960), Gayle Green (1979), and Carol McGinnis Kay (1983). Finally, Traversi associates the forcefulness of Othello's speeches on soldiership with his tragic egoism, agreeing with T. S. Eliot (1927) that the Moor has an idealized view of himself which he must constantly strive to uphold and that the "great speeches in which he attains tragic stature by expressing his 'nobility' are, at the same time, merciless exposures of weakness." Other critics who have considered Othello self-centered include G. R. Elliott (1937 and 1953), F. R. Leavis (1937), Brents Stirling (1956), Roy W. Battenhouse (1969), and Carol McGinnis Kay (1983). Also, for further commentary on Shakespeare's presentation of the nature of love in Othello, see the excerpts by Hermann Ulrici (1839), Kenneth Burke (1951), Winifred M. T. Nowottny (1952), Robert B. Heilman (1956), John Bayley (1960), Susan Snyder (1972), Jared R. Curtis (1973), and Jane Adamson (1980).]

Othello is, by common consent, one of Shakespeare's most completely 'objective' plays. The internal conflict of Hamlet, the identification of the hero's tragedy with the effort to achieve self-definition, is now polarized into the more truly dramatic conflict between Othello and Iago. The substitution as vehicles of the tragic emotion of one complex and incoherent character by two simpler, more sharply defined personalities in conflict carries with it an extension of the ability to present the dramatic implications of character. This ability had been partially obscured in the 'problem' plays where the conception of motive is often uncertain and where sentiment is commonly more profound than coherent. Hamlet unites a vast number of impulses and feelings, often contradictory and conflicting, in the utterances of a single man, but it cannot be said that his behaviour is always consistent or his motives fully comprehensible. Othello, on the other hand, is fully and continually a person. His sentiments and actions are throughout perfectly intelligible, perfectly consistent with the character as defined; his emotions, unlike those of Hamlet, are always strictly related to their objective causes as dramatically presented. Othello, indeed, is the first of a series of Shakespearean heroes whose sufferings are explicitly related to their own failings, but who manage in spite of these failings to attain tragic dignity. Like Antony and Coriolanus after him, he dramatizes as 'nobility' his own innate incapacity to cope with life; and, as in their case, the very weakness which is obvious to all around him and by which Iago engineers his downfall, is turned into true tragedy. The dramatic construction of *Othello,* in short, turns upon the close, intricate analysis by which the two contrasted characters of the Moor and his Ancient are at every moment dovetailed, seen for what they are as opposed but strictly related conceptions. Scarcely since the First Part of *Henry IV* had Shakespeare presented character with such assurance; but the objectivity which had there merely illustrated a detached political study is now controlled by the presence of an intense tragic emotion.

To grasp the impulse from which this emotion was derived it is necessary to dwell a little upon certain distinctive poetic qualities of the play. Of all Shakespeare's works *Othello* perhaps dwells with the most exclusive concentration on the theme of physical passion. This concentration, which is even apt to produce in us a certain sense of spiritual claustrophobia, relates the play closely to certain persistent features of Shakespeare's work during the preceding years. The action of *Othello* is dominated at every point by elements already familiar in the Sonnets and 'problem' plays, elements present in the most characteristic utterances of the protagonists and serving to impart an underlying unity to the clear-cut conflict which provides the central dramatic action. The fact is that Othello and Iago are not only distinguished from one another and set in opposition by their contrasted attitude to love. They are also, beneath the obvious division, complementary figures contained in a coherent poetic mood, divergencies within what appears at a deeper level as a common way of feeling; and this mood, this feeling, is concerned with the force of physical passion and with the destructive tendencies that prevent its consummation in perfect union. Even the most positive expressions of emotion in the play suffer from an underlying sensation of failure to achieve fulfilment. The peculiar expression of Othello's passion is in this respect highly significant. His poetry naturally dwells repeatedly upon love, but the feeling expressed in that love is one which, by revealing its own incompleteness, suggests an inability to attain adequate expression. In his meditation, for example, over the sleeping Desdemona before he stifles her (V. ii.) we shall find intensity matched by a remarkable coldness, true sensuous feeling by a curious remoteness from the 'blood'. Beginning with an invocation to 'you *chaste* stars', he goes on to speak of a skin 'whiter than *snow*' and '*smooth* as *monumental alabaster*'; and there is something intense but distant in the apostrophe which follows to 'thy light' and in the almost studied reference to 'Promethean heat' [V. ii. 2, 4, 5, 10, 12]. Collecting together these images, we come to feel that Othello's passion at this critical moment is as cold on the surface as it is intense just below; it combines a certain monumental frigidity in the expression with a tremendous impression of the activity of the senses.

That the senses are present is clearly guaranteed—at this stage in the play—by Othello's own behaviour; and, indeed, the same speech proves that this is so. As he gazes upon his victim, his underlying sensuality is felt above all in the comparison of Desdemona to the 'rose' and in the keenness with which the sense of smell appears in 'balmy breath' and in the phrase 'I'll smell it on the tree' [V. ii. 15]. Even here, however, the sense of incompleteness persists. The impression is one of an overwhelming passion unable to express itself otherwise than in cold and distant imagery: the imagery, never quite freed from the conventional, of the Sonnets. One could not imagine Antony making love to Cleopatra in these terms. Antony's love has at its command a vast, rich, unambiguous range of imagery; Othello's is an intense desire which cannot really surpass the conventional in its expression. Even when he is stressing the full happiness he had hoped to find in perfect love, he chooses to see perfection not in terms of overflowing vitality but in the chill flawlessness of a precious stone:

> Nay, had she been true,
> If heaven would make me such another world
> Of one entire and perfect *chrysolite,*
> I'ld not have sold her for it.
>
> [V. ii. 143-46]

It is not, indeed, in devotion to Desdemona that Othello expresses most powerfully the full possibilities of his nature. The strength of his passionately emotional being finds adequate expression, not in love, but in triumphant soldiership, in his reference to the—

> Pride, pomp, and circumstance of glorious war.
>
> [III. iii. 354]

Here in the poetry of action, untrammelled by reference to objects and needs beyond itself, the egoism essential to the character realizes itself fully and without hindrance. In Othello's love poetry the same intensity fails to express itself completely towards another person; it remains apparently cold on the surface with an intense fire beneath that makes it the more capable of corruption.

This corruption, the central theme of the play, is the work of Iago. The image of the 'rose' already referred to implies, in Shakespeare, that of the 'canker' which destroys it; the simultaneous presence of these twin aspects of passion is here given tragic projection in a clash of opposed attitudes. To understand fully the inadequacy of Othello's passion we have to turn to Iago; for the two characters, as I have said, are contrasted aspects of a single intuition. At first sight the Ancient is all that his general is not, cynical and 'intellectual' where Othello is passionate and trusting to the point of folly. These qualities, however, are not merely opposed but complementary. If Othello's passion expresses itself in a peculiar coldness, Iago's cynicism and belittlement of natural emotion are full of the feeling of 'blood'. 'Blood', or sexual emotion, is the driving force of his intelligence, although it is a force always controlled and criticised by that intelligence. He tells Desdemona on her arrival at Cyprus that he is 'nothing if not critical' [II. i. 119] and he shows Roderigo a passionate (that is the only word for it) contempt for 'blood'; but it is 'blood' which is at the root of the man, criticism and all. Consider the temper of his remarks to Roderigo, when he is advancing the claims of reason and control:

> If the balance of our lives had not one scale of
> reason to poise another of sensuality, the blood
> and baseness of our natures would conduct us

to most preposterous conclusions; but we have
reason to cool our raging motions, our carnal
stings, our unbitted lusts.

[I. iii. 326-31]

How intensely we feel 'blood' at work in the very criticism of
passion! 'Reason' balances—'poises', as Shakespeare so delicately puts it—the scale of sensuality, foreseeing in its unchecked operation the 'most preposterous conclusions'; but the
vigour of the references to 'raging motions', 'carnal stings',
and 'unbitted lusts' demonstrates unmistakeably the source of
Iago's peculiar vitality in action. His is, in fact, the reason of
Hamlet, perverted from its 'god-like' function of harmonizing
the various human faculties in the pursuit of a clearly understood end to a principle of negation and destruction. Although
Iago sees more clearly than Hamlet, his destructive attitude
proceeds from the same inversion of normal human functions,
and his superior clarity only produces a greater consistency in
negation. Where Hamlet's motives for rejecting life are confused, contradictory, those of Iago are consistently cynical and
degrading; but the same negative attitude to the flesh is behind
the judgements of both. Iago's intellect dwells from the first
pungently, insistently upon the bestiality which underlies human passion; but the presence of the despised emotions is
implied by the very intensity with which they are contemplated.
It is impossible not to feel the intense sexuality behind his
feverish activity in the dark at the opening of the play. Revealing itself in the persistent animality with which he incites
Roderigo to disturb 'the fertile climate' [I. i. 70] in which
Desdemona's father dwells and so to 'poison his delight' [I.
i. 68], it dominates both the man and the scene:

> Even now, now, very now, an old black ram
> Is tupping your white ewe. Arise, arise;
> Awake the snorting citizens with the bell,
> Or else the devil will make a grandsire of you.

[I. i. 88-91]

The grotesque tone of the last few lines in itself reflects the
source of the intensity behind Iago's every action. Describing
the relationship between Othello and Desdemona, he speaks
of his general as a 'Barbary horse' and refers to 'coursers' and
'gennets' as the product of their union; he warns Brabantio that
'your daughter and the Moor are now making the beast with
two backs' [I. i. 115-17]. Lastly, in anticipating Desdemona's
faithlessness, his irony expresses itself through a tremendous
sensitivity to the contact of the flesh:

> Lechery, by this hand; an index and obscure
> prologue to the history of lust and foul thoughts.
> They met so near with their lips that their breaths
> embraced together.

[II. i. 257-60]

The 'foul thoughts' are, of course, Iago's own, characteristically transferred by the operation of his own perverted sensuality to the objects of his contemplation. In such passages,
the disgust which underlies *Troilus and Cressida* and *Hamlet*
without there achieving complete definition (except, perhaps,
in the character of Thersites) is gathered up in a tone of Machiavellian cynicism. The 'philosophy' which underlies this
disgust will have to be considered more closely. For the moment it is enough to note that the passionate Othello never
expresses himself in love with such physical intensity as the
sceptical, controlled Iago; in this paradox lies the key to the
whole play.

It is Shakespeare's achievement to have converted into a tragedy this intuition of opposed emotion simultaneously present
in a single situation. To state such an intuition in a single
lyrical moment (as he had done in some of the Sonnets) is one
thing; to bring it into being stage by stage in an action, a closely-
knit development of character and incident within the limits of
a play, is quite another. Othello and Iago, for the three hour
duration of their tragedy, live the conflict active in Shakespeare's imagination. If Iago, to use once more the phrasing
of the Sonnets, represents the 'canker' in the 'rose' of Othello's
love we must watch that canker gaining ground step by step
in the development of the intrigue. The egoistic nature of Othello's love must not only be defined; we must watch it crumble,
through its own blindness, into helplessness and incoherence.
The process must be strictly dramatic. The defects by which
Iago engineers the down-fall of his victim must be those first
stated, or at least implied, in his own utterances. Othello, the
tragic hero in his weakness and nobility, stands at the centre
of the play. In his self-imposed consistency he is the point
upon which the whole action turns; the forces which dissolve
his integrity operate through the hostility of Iago by bringing
to the surface his own deficiencies. The fusion of dramatic
purpose and poetic impulse sought by Shakespeare in the self-
defining complexities of the 'problem' plays is at last achieved
in the full objectivity of his first completely realized and in
some ways most disquieting tragedy.

Shakespeare loses no time in indicating beneath the appearance
of consistency and strength the fundamental weakness of his
hero. One can detect from the first in Othello's every assertion
a note of self-dramatization, as though each action beyond its
intrinsic importance must also be regarded as a contribution to
the rhetorical fiction whose justification is a main purpose of
his life. His real nobility is in acute danger of turning into a
pose because he feels at every moment the need to conform to
a self-portrait of his own creation. His first utterance (I. ii.) is
a round assertion—full, splendid, rhetorical—of his royal lineage and of his services to Venice:

> My service, which I have done the signiory,
> Shall out-tongue his complaint.
>   . . . I fetch my life and being
> From men of royal seige.

[I. ii. 18-19, 21-2]

One need not deny the power of his impulsive rhetoric or
minimize the true stature of the speaker; but one can also sense
in the same incident a touch of irony in the too facile gesture
to his audience which follows: 'When I know that boasting is
an honour' [I. ii. 20]. Othello's rapt declamations are not boasting, because boasting implies a self-consciousness, a conceit
which is far from the essential simplicity of the character; but
they show a certain barbaric complacency which has already
allowed Iago to allude to his speeches as 'bombast circumstance' . . . and will shortly induce him to caricature his description of his love-making as so much 'bragging' and 'fantastical lies'. The complement of this complacency, the defect
of 'a free and open nature' [I. i. 399], is the simplicity which
leads Othello throughout to think 'men honest that but seem
to be so' [I. i. 400], to misread the characters and motives of
those around him in the light of his own naïve self-esteem.

This complacency directly affects his love. Othello, in spite
of himself, submits with a touch of unwillingness to love. He
feels it somehow incongruous with the 'unhoused free condition' [I. ii. 26] in which alone his rhetorical instincts can attain

full expression; and even the first appearance of Desdemona, whose love can so easily become for him a condition of 'circumscription and confine' [I. ii. 27], merely underlines the possibility of tragedy. For Othello is rarely able to get sufficiently far from himself fully to love Desdemona. His happiness in these opening scenes is like everything in his character self-centred, naïve, egoistic; and his account of his wooing (I. iii.) makes this clear. It was, in fact, by his passionate, simple-minded delight in his own magnificent career that he won her; and—we may fairly add—it was mainly because his love-making ministered to his own self-esteem that he valued her:

> She lov'd me for the dangers I had pass'd
> And I lov'd her that *she did pity them*.
> [I. iii. 167-68]

Othello's estimate of his situation is nothing if not simple; but his simplicity is terribly, tragically vulnerable. (pp. 248-53)

If Othello's 'nobility' provides one of the main conceptions upon which the whole closely-knit structure of the play rests, the 'critical' scepticism of Iago is certainly the other. Through his plotting the mysterious poison which had worked, according to Brabantio, upon Othello through Desdemona's 'still and quiet' [I. iii. 95] spirit becomes an active and sinister reality. For Iago *is* that poison, no longer hinted at in ambiguous phrases or obscurely present in minds never fully conscious of it, but turning Brabantio's doubts to destructive activity. His actions, indeed, reflect a 'philosophy', a view of 'nature' in accordance with which Othello's downfall is as inevitable as his love. This conception of 'nature', which plays a prominent part also in *King Lear,* seems to cover the normal conditions of life as they appear to what purports to be the unprejudiced intelligence. It is regarded by those who accept it in the tragedies as favourable to an anarchic conception of life, indulgent to unchecked passion and hostile to any attribution of spiritual value or sense of moral obligation. The chief devotees of 'nature' are Iago, for whom destructive action is a 'pleasure' which makes the hours seem short (II. iii.), and Edmund in *King Lear,* who brings his own father to blindness and follows the impulses of his appetite to destruction. Yet the state of 'nature', though it favours the operations of unchecked individual appetite, is by no means synonymous with irrationality. Possibly a malady of the intellect, it is certainly not a renunciation of the judgement. Both in Edmund and Iago devotion to 'nature' is compatible with keen insight and a critical outlook; but this insight and outlook operate unchecked by considerations that transcend the purely personal. When Iago describes himself to Roderigo as one of those who

> . . . trimmed in forms and visages of duty,
> Keep yet their hearts attending on themselves.
> [I. i. 50-1]

it is worth noting, as evidence of the continuity underlying Shakespeare's thought at this time, that his words are no more than a 'Machiavellian' interpretation of Horatio's reflections on the 'man who is not passion's slave' [*Hamlet,* III. ii. 71-2]. The difference lies in the amoral conception of 'nature' as the background conditioning all human life. 'Nature', as conceived in *Othello* and *Lear,* is completely divorced from 'value' or 'degree', sanctions full independence of action in the pursuit of selfish ends. Edmund, accepting her as his 'goddess' . . . , allows no filial or human consideration to dissuade him from his purpose; and Iago, for whom the following of self-interest is a proof of true manliness ('These fellows have some soul' [I. i. 54]), holds that constancy in love is unnatural, inconsistent

with the conditions of physical desire, and so inconceivable. (pp. 256-57)

Such a 'philosophy' leads Iago, logically enough, to a pessimistic interpretation of love; for satisfaction, in experiences purely physical, leads fatally to satiation and the craving for change. There is nothing in the world of 'nature' to prevent desire from passing easily—and meaninglessly—from one object to another. In the case of Desdemona, Iago's contention is that it must so pass—

> Mark me with what violence she first loved the Moor, but for bragging and telling her fantastical lies; and will she love him still for prating? Let not thy discreet heart think it. Her eye must be fed; and what delight shall she have to look on the devil? When the blood is made dull with the act of sport, there should be again to enflame it and to give satiety a fresh appetite, loveliness in favour, sympathy in years, manners and beauties; all which the Moor is defective in; now, for want of these required conveniences, her delicate tenderness will find itself abused, begin to heave the gorge, disrelish and abhor the Moor; very nature will instruct her in it and compel her to some second choice.
> [II. i. 222-35]

Iago is convinced, in accordance with his own reading of 'nature', that the 'violence' of physical desire is necessarily transient, and that this transience, once the original impulse has been satiated, will *compel* Desdemona to a second choice. Love, being merely a prompting of the senses to which the will gives assent, needs to be continually 'inflamed' if the blood itself is not to be 'made dull with the act of sport' [II. i. 227]. For love, as in *Troilus,* is simply an 'appetite', intense but impermanent like all sensual experiences, and in particular like the impressions of taste. Now 'as luscious as locusts', it will become shortly 'as bitter as coloquintida' [I. iii. 348, 349]; the fact that the keenly palated imagery of the earlier play survives in Iago's statement points once more to the continuity of Shakespeare's interests. In the moment of fulfilment love, Iago tells us, is full of relish, of 'delicate tenderness'; but it must continually be 'fed', lest it turn to abhorrence, 'disrelish' and 'heave the gorge' in nausea at the former object of its choice [II. i. 232, 233]. The original impulse whose satisfaction has led to repletion, equally fatally demands renewal; without this, it turns to indifference and even to loathing. In this way the doubts and reservations that from the first accompany Othello's love in the minds of those who surround him are given clear logical expression. Brabantio had thought that Desdemona's choice of Othello, because prompted by irrational passion, was against the rules of nature; Iago, on the contrary, not only believes that the choice was natural but that 'nature', which had brought her to it, would inevitably drive her to change. It is the conflict between this attitude, at once rational and essentially destructive, and Othello's generous but uncritical acceptance of the promptings of passion that is the subject of the play. (pp. 257-58)

We shall only understand Iago's part in this tragedy if we realize that he plays throughout upon the real weaknesses of his victims. These weaknesses he elevates, following his 'philosophy', into consistent principles, turning what is largely infirmity, susceptibility, or indecision into a positive tendency to evil; but his observations, though they do not account fully for the behaviour of his victims, always pick upon something really vulnerable in them. And that something is invariably connected with desire or 'appetite'. Cassio he describes in this spirit as one who puts on 'the mere form of civil and humane seeming for the better compassing of his salt and most hidden loose affection' [II. i. 239-41]. The description is highly typical. Iago cannot conceive of human weakness as less than fully conscious. Believing in the controlling power of 'corrigible authority' [I. ii. 325-26], and in the will's tendency to follow the impulses which nothing in his conception of 'nature' can prompt it to check, he is led to rationalize Cassio's failing, turning susceptibility into positive cunning; but the short encounter with Bianca ((III. iv.) is there to show that his judgement is not unrelated to fact. Cassio's attitude to Desdemona is thoroughly characteristic of the man. His imagination, stirred by Iago, lingers upon her with intense but passing sensuality. She is 'exquisite', 'a fresh and delicate creature', with an 'inviting' though 'right modest eye' [II. iii. 18, 20-1, 24-5]. He regards her, in short, as a choice morsel to be contemplated, tasted and enjoyed, so that Iago, in speaking of 'provocation' and an 'alarum to love' [II. iii. 26-7], simply gives substance to an innermost thought. For Iago merely brings consistency to unrealized desires, which thereby become in his hands instruments all the more dangerous for being imperfectly understood by his victims. Having observed in Cassio just sufficient 'loose affection' to make his accusations plausible, he uses him to bring out Othello's unconsidered sensuality, to ruin his judgement and destroy his peace.

By inflaming the fuddled Cassio to riot Iago releases the forces of passion on the island. The words in which he describes the origin of the brawl to the roused and angry Othello are notable:

> friends all but now, even now,
> In quarter, and in terms like bride and groom
> Devesting them for bed; and then, but now,
> As if some planet had unwitted men,
> Swords out, and tilting one at other's breast,
> In opposition bloody.
>
> [II. iii. 179-84]

The peace of the island is explicitly related, by the mention of the bridal bed, to the concurrent consummation of Othello's marriage; and his happiness, like the harmony of Cyprus, is broken up by something irrational which 'unwits' him, escapes his understanding. To the sound of the 'dreadful bell' whose sinister clamour, awakening the inhabitants of the isle, frightens them 'from their propriety' [II. iii. 175-76], the prospects of concord between man and man, and between the spiritual and sensual elements in the individual soul, are rapidly, irrecoverably broken. As the drunken revelry, prevailing, takes the mind prisoner, the unchecked forces of 'blood' enter the play in the night of unreason and obscurity. Jealousy, preceded by unreflecting rage, creeps into Othello's mind, as strife enters Cyprus, through Iago's action upon the instability which makes his will—unknown to himself—the slave of passion. (pp. 259-60)

Iago knows that his victim, once confused, is lost; and so his first step is to involve him in uncertainty. For Othello is quite incapable of suspending judgement. Suspense offends his self-confidence, contrasts with the capacity for action upon which above all he prides himself. His nature demands an immediate resolution, which can be in practice nothing but an acceptance of Iago's insinuations:

> to be once in doubt
> Is once to be resolved; exchange me for a goat,
> When I shall turn the business of my soul
> To such exsufflicate and blown surmises
> Matching thy inference.
>
> [III. iii. 179-83]

Few things in the presentation of Othello are more damning than this continual tendency to protest rhetorically against the presence of the very weaknesses that are undoing him. He refers contemptuously to the 'goat', the most notorious symbol of sensuality, just as Iago is poisoning his mind through his blood-inspired imagination; and the reference, strengthened by the sense in 'exsufflicate' of the beast breathing heavily in the external manifestations of passion, is at once grotesque and significant.

Flattering his victim's 'free and open nature' [I. iii. 399], Iago proceeds to clip the wings of his freedom and to convert his frankness into suspicion. He recalls the persistent misgivings that had originally surrounded the marriage—'She did deceive her father, marrying you' [III. iii. 206]; he stressed the inequality of 'clime, complexion, and degree' [III. ii. 230] (note 'degree': Othello, we remember, claimed descent from men 'of royal seige') in a way at once calculated to hurt his pride and to emphasize his ignorance, as a foreigner and a man of alien race, of Desdemona's true motives; above all he insinuates that her apparent purity of purpose may conceal a sensual corruption of the will:

> Foh, one may smell in such a will most rank,
> Foul disproportion, thoughts unnatural.
>
> [III. iii. 232-33]

The last assertion is really the important one. The others do little more than prepare the ground for it. Iago's purpose is, in his own words, 'to act upon the blood' [III. iii. 328], to make the sensual basis of Othello's passion—hitherto concealed from Othello himself—come to the surface in the form of destructive jealousy. The victim's mind must be infected. Iago's conception of love as so much corrupt 'appetite' must take possession of it, demoralize it, destroy it. He must be made to see Desdemona, in short, as Iago's 'philosophy' insists that she really is. She is natural, 'the wine she drinks is made of grapes' [II. ii. 251-52]; therefore, her 'blest condition' must be fatally, inevitably subject to inconstancy. (pp. 261-62)

It is because his 'philosophy' enables him to establish contact with the lower, unconsidered elements of Othello's emotional being that Iago is able to destroy the simplicity of his victim and to reduce him to a mass of contradictions and uncontrolled impulses. Having once deprived him of certainty he plays upon his sensual fancy, describes Cassio's 'dream' with a full insistence upon the grossness of physical contacts, makes him visualize the sin by which Desdemona is offending his self-esteem. Othello responds to these insinuations with an intensity that proceeds from hitherto unsuspected aspects of his nature. He demands instant proof. The completeness of his fall is reflected in the grotesque irony implicit in his demand: 'Villain, be sure thou prove my love a whore' [III. iii. 359]; and Iago leads him on with a sneer that now works like poison on his fantasy:

> . . . how satisfied, my lord?
> Would you, the supervisor, grossly gape on?
> Behold her topp'd?
>
> [III. iii. 394-96]

Here, besides rousing still further the sensual elements in his imagination and giving them added keenness in the barbed sneer of his concluding remark, Iago touches Othello at his most vulnerable point: he offends him in his personal respect. His reaction is a characteristic mixture of pathetic bewilderment and defiant self-esteem. (p. 262)

The increasing insolence—one can call it nothing else—of Iago's comments as he comes to realize that his success is assured is most notable. It is, indeed, an outstanding element in his whole strategy and singularly adapted to the weakness of his victim. Perhaps the irony reaches its climax when the plotter makes his victim stand aside and assist in silence at what he imagines to be Cassio's account of Desdemona's infidelity (IV. i.). Every word is a mortal wound for Othello's pride. Iago sneers, and disclaims the sneer with a phrase that is itself an affirmation of contempt:

> OTHELLO: Dost thou mock me?
> IAGO: I mock you! no, by heaven,
>   Would you would bear your fortune *like a man*!
>
> [IV. i. 60-1]

He roundly taxes the heroic Othello with lack of manliness:

> Whilst you were here o'erwhelmed with your grief—
> *A passion most unsuiting such a man*—
> Cassio came hither . . .
>   . . . Marry, patience;
> Or I shall say you are all in all in spleen,
> *And nothing of a man*.
>
> [IV. i. 76-8, 87-9]

He throws Desdemona's supposed conduct into her duped husband's face, insisting upon the time, the place, the circumstances, and even the future repetition of the betrayal; the bestiality and degradation associated by Iago with the physical act is brought vividly before his eyes by the coarse verb 'cope' with which it is described:

> I will make him tell the tale anew,
> Where, how, how oft, how long ago and when
> He hath and is again to cope your wife.
>
> [IV. i. 84-6]

Nothing could do more than this savage element of caricature in Iago's treatment of Othello to convey the degradation of the victim; no better foil to the Moor's earlier rhetoric—rhetoric which stands in the closest relationship to the subsequent tragedy—could be conceived.

A few phrases from Iago, and Othello has worked himself up into an absolute slavery to passion. Iago himself, in a solitary moment, describes perfectly his own method and achievement:

> The Moor already changes with my poison:
> Dangerous conceits are in their nature poisons:
> Which at the first are scarce found to distaste,
> But with a little act upon the blood
> Even like the mines of sulphur.
>
> [III. iii. 325-29]

The relation of poison to taste, and of both to the action of the 'blood', is by now familiar. It describes the process by which Othello's egoism is reduced to incoherence. He now sees himself, in his imagination, betrayed and it is the knowledge, rather than the betrayal, which affects him:

> I had been happy, if the general camp,
> Pioners and all, had tasted her sweet body,
> *So I had nothing known*.
>
> [III. iii. 345-47]

The form of this confession is highly revealing. The problem of *Othello* is the problem of consciousness, of the relationship of instinctive life to critical detachment. It is precisely because knowledge, reason, is in *Othello* a destructive faculty at war with heroic simplicity that the tragedy takes place. By the end of this crucial scene Othello's new 'knowledge' has had two consequences. It has destroyed the simplicity upon which his real nobility had been based, and it has roused his own sensual impulses to a destructive fury. Sensual passion and prowess in action are, in Othello, mutually exclusive; the entry of the one implies the dissolution of the coherence and self-confidence necessary to the other. The very man who had once declared that 'the young effects' of sensuality were in him defunct now breaks out into the poignancy and physical intensity of the phrase '*tasted* her *sweet* body'. But it is significant that when he becomes aware that his peace is hopelessly undermined he refers to his loss, not first of Desdemona, but of his own integrity as a warrior. On the one hand, the loss of his military prowess in action:

> Farewell the tranquil mind, farewell content!
> Farewell the plumed troop, and the big wars
> That make ambition virtue.
>
> [III. iii. 348-50]

on the other, that sense of Desdemona's supposed promiscuity which grows upon him until Iago can make the ironic comment—'I see, sir, you are eaten up with passion'! [III. iii. 391]. Othello's further history is no more than the aggravation of the condition here defined.

The scene we have been considering forms a kind of pivot upon which the whole subsequent action turns. At the end of it Othello's fate is sealed, and we have only to trace the growth in him of destructive animal feeling and the crumbling into futility of his personal pride. As it closes Othello abjures love and invokes vengeance in a speech which reveals the changing temper of his emotions:

>   Like to the Pontic sea,
> Whose icy current and compulsive course
> Ne'er feels retiring ebb, but keeps due on
> To the Proprontic and the Hellespont;
> Even so my bloody thoughts, with violent pace,
> Shall ne'er look back, ne'er ebb to humble love,
> Till that a capable and wide revenge
> Swallow them up. Now, by yond marble heaven,
> In the due reverence of a sacred vow,
> I here engage my words.
>
> [III. iii. 453-62]

The full rhetoric so typical of the character is still present in the ample opening gesture of the speech; but the power by which Othello is brought to imagine the Pontic sea in its irresistible course is the rising 'violent' power of 'blood', abjuring love—by a vital contradiction—and dedicating itself—but in the fulness of a passion frozen into an '*icy*' current'—to revenge. Iago's preceding comment—'your mind perhaps may change' [III. iii. 452]—is, as usual, perfectly timed to rouse the opposite reaction in Othello. Thwarted in love, his egoism will be consistent in revenge, decisive, irresistible: all the intensity of sensual feeling which was never fully gratified in his relations with Desdemona is now to be exercised in exacting retribution for the ruin of his integrity. The type of passion so notably absent from his declarations of love (or at least so constrained in their expression) reveals itself in a craving for destruction which Iago's activity ceaselessly nourishes.

As the plot advances, and Iago's control over Othello grows, the element of 'blood' which had once been lacking in the expression of his love makes a disturbing appearance—dis-

turbing because it does not come to give warmth and embodiment to his passion, but rather appears as an acute and terrible
repulsion against all contacts of the body. (pp. 263-65)

In the following scenes the action of jealousy, the monster
'begot upon itself' [III. iv. 162], turns openly and apparently
inward to destroy the self. We see and feel its effects upon the
once dominating warrior when he falls into a fit and mumbles
frenziedly, in the presence of the mocking and exultant Iago,
about 'Noses, ears and lips!' [IV. i. 42]. We feel them in those
bestial phrases in which his outraged egoism gropes towards
its revenge: 'I'll tear her all to pieces' [III. iii. 431]; 'I see that
nose of your, but not that dog I shall throw it to' [IV. i. 142-43],
and still more in the combination of affronted self-respect and
rising savagery which prompts the exclamation: 'I will chop
her into messes; cuckold me' [IV. i. 200]. But they appear
most clearly of all, and in clear relation to the love they are
corroding, in that terrible scene (IV. ii.) in which the crazed
Othello turns, with a mixture of intense physical attraction and
open repulsion upon Desdemona. The feeling in that scene—
it is important to note—is very reminiscent of the Sonnets.
Desdemona is a '*rose*-lipp'd cherubin'—such imagery, a compound of poetic convention and deep emotion, is characteristic—and Othello's loathing is expressed in typical sense-im-
agery:

DESDEMONA: I hope my noble lord esteems me
             honest.
OTHELLO: O, ay; as summer flies are in the
             shambles,
             That quicken even with blowing. O,
             thou weed,
             Who art so lovely fair and smell'st so
             sweet
             That the sense aches at thee, would thou
             hadst ne'er been born!
                                        [IV. ii. 65-9]

The mention of 'weed', the reminiscence of convention behind
'lovely fair', and the keen evocation—almost unnaturally sensitive—of the faculty of smell are all suggestive of the Sonnets.
Like 'lilies that fester' [Sonnet 94], their effect depends upon
a sharp opposition of acute sense-impressions. The intensity
of desire implied in 'sense aches at thee' and the feeling for
life behind 'quicken' are set against the loathing which produced 'shambles' and the 'blowing' of the flies. 'Blowing' is
especially subtle in that it speaks of the generation of flies out
of corruption whilst using a word that suggests the opening of
the rosebud into mature beauty. The reminiscence of the Sonnets is not accidental, for the story of *Othello* is precisely a
dramatic representation of the inevitable degeneration, in a
world where 'value' has no foundation, of desire into selfish
and destructive 'appetite'. The whole speech shows the Moor's
passion, still present and insistent even in his denunciation,
turning to corruption in contact with the canker of Iago's cynicism.

This surrender to bestiality involves the collapse of Othello's
integrity as a person. He expresses himself, as I have suggested,
most confidently in the egoistic poetry of war; and it is significant that his acceptance of Iago's insinuations is regarded
by him as tantamount to a renunciation of his prowess as a
soldier. The comments of those who surround him in the last
stage of the play, and particularly of Lodovico (IV. i.), insist

upon the loss of sufficiency, of the mastery over passion which
had always characterized Othello as a warrior:

        Is this the noble Moor, whom our full senate
        Call all in all sufficient? This the nature
        Whom passion could not shake?
                                        [IV. i. 264-66]

Yet, in spite of Iago's reply: 'He is much changed' [IV. i.
268], that sufficiency had itself an egoistic basis which exposure to unfamiliar circumstances has simply brought to the
surface. As his ruin proceeds, the egoism which had always
been a part of the character comes more and more to the fore,
not now in connection with military glory, but rather in his
attitude to his own folly. In the last scene, this folly is completely unmasked. Emilia addresses him as 'dull Moor', and
his own comment is as simple as it is true—'O fool, fool,
fool'! [V. ii. 323]. Yet, in spite of all his folly, his egoism
remains, and with it a considerable degree of tragic dignity.
The weakness and the tragedy stand, in fact, in the closest
relationship. The great speeches in which he attains tragic stature by expressing his 'nobility' are, at the same time, merciless
exposures of weakness. In the first of them, made by Othello
to Desdemona, what emerges above all is the unpreparedness
of the speaker to meet the situation in which he finds himself.
Had life presented to Othello a problem which could have been
met by the active creation of a nobility at once true and flattering to the self-esteem all—we are told—would have been
well:

                    Had it pleased heaven
        To try me with affliction,
                                        [IV. ii. 47-8]

he begins, and in cataloguing the forms which that affliction
might have taken we feel the speaker recovering confidence,
assuring himself that in resistance too there is a kind of heroism,
that the exercise of patience to the limit of endurance is not
incompatible with his conception of his own moral dignity. It
is only in the latter part of the speech that we are shown the
true source of Othello's suffering:

                    ... but, alas, to make me
        A fixed figure for the time of scorn
        To point his slow, unmoving finger at.
                                        [IV. ii. 53-5]

To become an object of ridicule without being able to react,
to assert his own 'nobility'—this is the shame from which
Othello feels that there is no escape, and which accompanies
him to his tragic end.

That end adds little that is new to our knowledge of his character. As T. S. Eliot has noted [see excerpt above, 1927]
Othello's last speech is more than a piece of splendid, self-
centred poetry (though it is most certainly that); it is also the
dupe's attempt at self-justification in an irrelevant pose:

        I have done the state some service and they know't ...
                    ... then must you speak
        Of one that loved not wisely but too well;
        Of one not easily jealous, but, being wrought,
        Perplexed in the extreme.
                                        [V. ii. 339, 343-46]

Who, in point of fact, has ever been more easily jealous than
Othello? It is, we feel, splendid declamation; but it is also
largely beside the point. For the real point lies in the presence,
as Othello speaks, of Desdemona's body, killed by the speaker

himself in his own blindness, and the speech is not only 'poetry' but the revelation of a character. 'Perplexed', betrayed by emotions whose presence and complexity he has never really grasped, Othello's last words are a pathetic return to his original simplicity of nature. Unable to cope effectively with the complicated business of living, he recalls his generous past, and commits the simple act of suicide. But already the critical acid applied by Iago has completely destroyed the structure of his greatness. (pp. 266-68)

Derek Traversi, " 'Othello'," in The Wind and the Rain, *Vol. VI, No. I, Summer, 1949, pp. 248-69.*

J. I. M. STEWART (essay date 1949)

[*A British novelist and short story writer, who frequently writes under the pseudonym of Michael Innes, Stewart has also had a distinguished career as an academician and literary critic, publishing works on writers from the Renaissance to the twentieth century. In the following excerpt from his* Character and Motive in Shakespeare: Some Recent Appraisals Examined *(1949), he reviews several critical approaches to* Othello *and concludes that its central characters, although drawn by Shakespeare with "psychological truth," are presented at critical moments in the play as symbolic abstractions of "violent polarities and ambivalences" in the human psyche. Stewart contends that, particularly in Act III, Othello becomes the symbol of the human soul aspiring to nobility and Iago represents the corrosive inner force seeking to debase it, so that at this stage in the drama their separate identities are conflated into a single "invisible protagonist" caught up in the conflict of spiritual and corporeal impulses. Similarly, he identifies in the love of Othello and Desdemona a contention between emotionalism and rationality, asserting that the Moor symbolizes passion devolving into suspicion while Desdemona becomes a metaphor for trust. For additional discussions of the kinship between Iago and Othello, see the excerpts by August Wilhelm Schlegel (1811), Denton J. Snider (1887), Maud Bodkin (1934), G. R. Elliott (1937), F. R. Leavis (1937), and Kenneth Burke (1951). As mentioned above, Stewart also evaluates the arguments of several seminal critics on the play. For example, he contends that although A. C. Bradley's assessment of Othello as consistently noble and blameless seems closest to the impressions we receive, it fails to address the problem of the hero's sudden and violent transformation by focusing instead on Iago's "superhuman" skills (see excerpt above, 1904). He claims that although Elmer Edgar Stoll's concept of the "calumniator believed" emphasizes the central "element of artifice" at the heart of the drama, it "leads us away from the feeling of the play" and takes no account of the psychological realism operating in conjunction with the fantastic (see excerpt above, 1915). And he maintains that although Maud Bodkin's and F. R. Leavis's respective theories on Othello's repressed fears and doubts would explain the Moor's sudden jealousy, they are not supported "by our experience of the play" (see excerpts above, 1934 and 1937). In Stewart's opinion, a judgment of Othello as stupid, egotistical, and brutal—as Leavis suggests—will not hold up in the face of the Moor's essential nobility and stature.*]

The case against the plausibility of *Othello* begins with Thomas Rymer (see excerpt above, 1692). . . . Rymer says that Shakespeare's object in the play is to surprise us with what is horrible and prodigious. To attain this end he resorts to a fable which is improbable and absurd, and to characters who are unnatural and lacking in all decorum. (p. 97)

And something like Rymer's case is repeated by [Robert] Bridges, who adds that for this audience given over to gross sensation and surprise the complaisant dramatist even took some care to avoid reasonable motives as he went along [see Additional Bibliography]. . . . If the tragedy is intolerably painful this is

not merely because we see Othello being grossly deceived, but because we are ourselves constrained to submit to palpable deception. And particularly Iago is impossible, since a man with a tithe of his wickedness could not pass invisible as he does. Shakespeare aimed merely at sensation, but what was a pleasurable excitement for his obtuse audience is intolerable to us.

Both Rymer and Bridges take exception to *Othello* on what, finally, are moral grounds. But what initially repels both critics is the play's *unnaturalness;* they condemn in it very much what Johnson condemned in *Cymbeline:* "the folly of the fiction, the absurdity of the conduct . . . and the impossibility of the events in any system of life."

Now, most criticism of *Othello*, if it does not ignore these impressions, endeavours to argue them away as incompatible with the evident greatness of the play, which requires that the characters should be humanly plausible and their motives sufficient. Thus for Bradley *Othello* is a profound play of individual character [see excerpt above, 1904]. The hero's very nobility—the fact that his trust, where he trusts, is absolute—makes him unusually open to deception; and, if once wrought to passion, he is likely to act with little reflection, with no delay, and in the most decisive manner conceivable. Iago, again, is a complex but credible figure. Certainly, to pass invisible as he does, his powers of dissimulation and of self-control must have been prodigious, but we may remark that he finds relief in those caustic or cynical speeches which, being misinterpreted, only heightened confidence in his honesty. (pp. 97-8)

All argument like this in favour of the human credibility of *Othello* Stoll turns down as a mere projecting upon Shakespeare's play of modern and historically erroneous ways of thinking [see excerpt above, 1915]. Stoll is thus, in a sense, back with Rymer and Bridges, for whom the characters are unnatural and the motives insufficient or absurd. But, supporting and greatly broadening their indictment, Stoll nevertheless comes to a conclusion altogether different, and one which (he holds) would rehabilitate Shakespeare as a dramatist every whit as great as Bradley claims. Unfavourable criticism of Shakespeare—as also inept laudation—rests upon an insufficient consideration of the canons of dramatic art, and particularly of the admissible and indeed grateful difference between that art and real life. . . . For in . . . Othello's succumbing with incredible facility to Iago's deception we are in the presence, Stoll holds, not of psychology but of literary convention, of a dodge for getting a good story going. The convention of the calumniator believed is as old as the story of Potiphar's wife or of the wicked counsellors of Germanic heroic legend, and here in Shakespeare's tragedy it "summarily, theatrically lifts us over contradiction and paradox as over a rock in the river." (pp. 99-100)

There is one evident weakness in Stoll's argument, here as elsewhere. In considering such immemorial themes as that of the calumniator believed he nowhere presses beyond the conception of their being arbitrary devices for starting a yarn. His general feeling seems to be that the older the story the less correspondence will it hold with any realities of the human situation. . . . [But] just as widespread nativity and crucifixion stories can, at least with an equal colour, be read as adumbrations and intimations of the central fact of history as Christianity views it, and therefore as being so many witnesses to the significance of that fact, just so can the pervasiveness in drama of the "calumniator believed" (as in *Much Ado* or

Cymbeline, Orlando Furioso, Philaster or *The Conquest of Granada*) be read as witnessing to some central human predisposition by which these are prompted and sustained. Nor is this possibility invalidated by the patent absurdity or nullity of many calumniator-fictions, by their evident employment as indeed no more than a storyteller's resource. A convention, like a superstition, may represent a significant perception gone fossilised or inert. And to reanimate a convention, to strip it of sophistication so that its essence is again near the surface and working, is perhaps part of the instinct of the original artist.

And as with the fable so with the agent. Confronted with Iago, Stoll again takes it for granted that what is primitive (in the sense of being directly derived from a rudimentary art) is necessarily crude, superficial and—above all—"unpsychological" or without relevance to the depths. The primitive figure from whom Stoll rightly sees Iago as being, with a rather surprising directness, descended, he views as an arbitrary dummy constructed merely to curdle the blood.

But just so—we might reply to Stoll—may some monstrous idol or totem-pole appear, and yet such a thing is actually the product of a very vivid awareness of actual forces in the human psyche. And thus it may be with Iago. This invisible and indefeasible villain is indeed an immemorial standby in romance, but conceivably he earned his place there not as something stagy, delightfully and horrifically unreal; he earned his place there because he expresses a psychological truth. The error is in supposing that the mature and developed dramatist who dips into fairy-tale thereby dips into something other than human life. When we discard this notion we may see that the "calumniator-believed" theme, the importance of which Stoll accurately distinguishes, can, with all its seeming irrationality, have its place in a picture fully "psychological."

At this point we may conveniently consider the lines upon which modern psychology seems inclined to interpret the particular convention upon which the play is based.

Civilised man is obliged to live far beyond his moral income, and any appearance of stability and solvency which he presents is achieved only through much concealment and subterfuge. His difficulties indeed are such that in order to get along at all he has to ignore them, struggling to confine them within unconscious regions of his mind. Many of the great myths, including those concerning wars in and expulsions from heaven, express this situation. In fact it may be said that every man has his rebel angels, who will not willingly lie long upon the burning marl of a nether world; perpetually they strive by devious routes and guileful policy to gain and carry by assault the empyrean of the conscious mind, of the willed personality and its values. Mysteriously, the conscious man may know little of the battle; may know it only by the exhaustion it brings, or by finding that he bears about with him a secret and inexplicable wound. Part of the force of the assault, indeed, he may be able to exploit like a wrestler, and by this sublimation the dark angels will turn what engines he directs; to the world he will the more appear a tall man of his hands—artist or warrior or saint. But if the struggle becomes desperate the mind brings various emergency measures into play. Thus, and as if to clear itself of the guilt of forbidden impulses forcing a passage from below, it projects these impulses upon the person most injured by them; the mechanism being . . . : "It is not I but you who have this illicit thought or act to answer for." Hence the appearance in the conscious mind of irrational and baseless suspicions. But these suspicions are themselves surrounded by illicit impulses of jealousy, malevolence and destruction, and so the responsibility of instigating and feeding them may also upon the slightest excuse be projected upon some other person. And by thus endowing this other person with impulses working within itself the distraught mind immensely increases the potency for destruction of that person's every word and suggestion. [In a footnote, Stewart acknowledges his indebtedness to Maud Bodkin for this paragraph; see excerpt above, 1934].

These, it is held, are the actual facts of mind underlying the convention of the calumniator believed, and it is clear that, after a fashion not recognized by Stoll, they can be exploited to credibilise the fable of *Othello* at its most perplexing points: namely the flimsiness of the case against Desdemona and the resistlessness of Iago. Iago's villainy draws its potency from Othello's own mind; it is invisible to others because it is, in a sense, *not there;* the devil in the play, like all devils, represents a projection upon some comparatively neutral or insignificant thing; Iago is a device of Othello's by which Othello hears an inner voice that he would fain hear and fain deny. From this complex of ideas much argument can be drawn.

And all this matter is certainly, in my opinion, relevant; there is real light to be gained from it. But can we use it to interpret the play in terms which are, broadly regarded, naturalistic? I do not think that we can. Any attempt to view the play as presenting this picture of things in terms of simple realism— any attempt, that is to say, to rewrite Bradley with a hero drawn from the new psychology—encounters a very real difficulty to which I shall presently come. But first we may notice one or two such Othellos who have, in fact, of late been disengaged from the play.

An early Othello of this sort makes a brief and characteristically discreet appearance in an essay of Mr. T. S. Eliot's:

> What Othello seems to me to be doing in making this [his last] speech is *cheering himself up*. He is endeavouring to escape reality, he has ceased to think about Desdemona, and is thinking about himself. . . . Othello succeeds in turning himself into a pathetic figure, by adopting an *aesthetic* rather than a moral attitude, dramatizing himself against his environment. He takes in the spectator, but the human motive is primarily to take in himself. I do not believe that any writer has ever exposed this *bovarysme*, the human will to see things as they are not, more clearly than Shakespeare [see excerpt above, 1927].

Othello, in fact, is a habitual self-deceiver, and he believes Iago's calumny neither because there is a convention that he must do so in order to start a yarn (which is Stoll) nor because he is too noble to suspect evil (which is Bradley). He believes Iago's calumny because there is something in his nature which leads him to do so.

From this may be developed a variety of arguments endeavouring to rehabilitate a "psychological" Othello in terms of a more realistic (or disillusioned) view of human relationships than Bradley's. And acute observations can be made here. Iago everywhere passes as honest, but of four people to whom he declares or insinuates that Desdemona is unchaste only Othello himself is credulous! Must we not then admit a weakness in Othello, a predisposition to suspicion and jealousy such as Stoll in common with many more orthodox critics is concerned to deny? Is not Othello, in fact, a sombre and searching study in the inner processes of romantic idealism, the portrait of a man who obstinately refuses to face reality? (pp. 100-04)

Argument of this sort is pressed yet further by a writer less concerned, conceivably, with *Othello* in itself than with indicting Bradley as a misleader of undergraduates. Bradley, we are told, failed to approach the play even "with moderate intelligence" and fell indeed into a course of as "triumphant sentimental perversity as literary history can show" [see excerpt above by F. R. Leavis, 1937]. But Bradley's "potent and mischievous influence" may be finally dissipated by showing that Othello, far from being a noble, free and open character fatally practised upon by a diabolically clever antagonist, is from the first a man eaten out by "a habit of approving self-dramatisation." Iago's superhuman arts are moonshine; Othello yields with such promptness as to make it plain that the mind that undoes him is not Iago's but his own; the main datum is not Iago's diabolic intellect but Othello's readiness to respond. And if Bradley is wrong so is Stoll. There is no arbitrary and "unpsychological" stroke effected for the sake of "steep tragic contrast," for the whole tone of the play is such that no development will be acceptable in Othello unless the behaviour it imposes on him is reconcilable with our notions of ordinary psychological consistency. And on the basis of what premiss can that consistency be secured? We must be brought to see that beneath his self-idealising and sentimentalising ways, which are in fact "a disguise," Othello owns only an obtuse and brutal egotism. In his new situation as a married man, which brings problems far different from those of the "big wars," his self-pride quickly becomes stupidity—ferocious stupidity, an insane and self-deceiving passion. It is absurd in Bradley to give a whole lecture to Iago, who is no more than a bit of dramatic mechanism.

Something akin to these readings of *Othello* . . . [is] feasible in *The Winter's Tale,* where Leontes's suppressed impulse to infidelity finds as it were excuse and licence by projecting the infidelity upon another. And a Leontes-Othello, or one deriving from T. S. Eliot's suggestion of a study in *bovarysme,* is less unlikely to have behaved as the play declares him to have behaved than is the noble Othello of Bradley.

And yet I do not think that this will quite do. The line of interpretation we have been following—one arguing for a complete and subtle naturalism—is unsatisfactory for this simple reason: that the play presents no psychological entity answering to Othello as he is here described. Othello's nobility—however related to other facets of the man which older critics may have inadequately acknowledged—is certainly not a "disguise," it is a reality set magnificently before us in both Venice and Cyprus. . . . An *Othello* in which the hero virtually imposes upon Iago Iago's rôle might, I suppose, be written, but it is not given us by our experience of the play. This new Othello is not the Othello who appears before us on the stage; the man we see there (and are, I judge, by the dramatist meant to see) is much nearer to Bradley's Othello.

Moreover in this aspect of the simple impression made by the man, Bradley's Othello and Stoll's are one—the essential difference lying in Bradley's asserting that this Othello *could do it,* and Stoll's asserting that he *could not.* There seems to me to be great force in Stoll's assertion. If we insist, that is to say, on taking the play on the level of straightforward naturalism there is still something like the arbitrary wrenching of the character that Stoll posits, or the character is superior to the situation upon which he is precipitated. On the one hand

Stoll's own interpretation, if we fall back upon it, leads us away from the feeling of the play, or from the weight of it, which intimates something other than a fanciful invention which may please for a while. On the other hand that developed psychological criticism which comes nearer to the roots of the play, and better renders its weight and inwardness, puts forward as Othello a man who does not, in fact, appear before us. How is this somewhat desperate contradiction to be resolved? Perhaps only, as I have hinted, by abandoning *naturalism*—although by no means abandoning *psychological truth.* In poetic drama substantial human truth may be conveyed by means other than those of an entire psychological realism. Shakespeare's plays are basically realistic. But they can artfully and powerfully incorporate elements which, though psychologically highly expressive, are not realistic in themselves. I conclude, therefore, that although the basis of the tragedy is indeed to be found in the inward significance of the "calumniator believed," yet Shakespeare's manner of revealing, or intimating, that significance is different from what I have so far supposed.

In all the argument which we have yet considered there is an element missing; and it is an element for the sharp consciousness of which—though not perhaps for a right understanding of which—we are much indebted to Stoll. I mean the element of artifice, of boldly realistic devices used to significant ends. (pp. 104-06)

[Shakespeare's] instinct is to make of his plays the mirror of life and, broadly speaking, he sets about this by the methods of the naturalistic writer. But he is always ready to follow his intuition behind and beneath life's visible and tangible surfaces and at any time he will shake hands with probability and even possibility when beckoned from some further border of consciousness by an imaginative truth. We must remember the imagination. It is his instrument—and it works, Coleridge tells us, by dissolving and dissipating in order to re-create. We may find an instance of the working of this power in the play's treatment of time.

The chronological contradictions which *Othello* displays when considered realistically go in point of strangeness beyond anything similar in Shakespeare. In Stoll's terms—or Bridge's—it comes to this: that Iago's plot can pass undetected only in the press of rapid action, but other elements in the story are plausible only if there is the contrary impression of a considerable efflux of time; and therefore Shakespeare juggles skilfully with his two clocks. But it strikes me that there is something inward about the oddity of the time-scheme in *Othello.* It is as if Iago only wins out because of something fundamentally treacherous in time, some flux and reflux in it which is inimical to life and love. Mr. Middleton Murry has a fine perception here when he sees that *Iago* and *time* are in some sort of imaginative balance [see Additional Bibliography]. This is one of the things that Iago *is:* an imaginative device for making visible something in the operation of time.

And as with time so it may be with realistic psychology. Liberties are taken with it—but not in the interest of sensation, or of such a fanciful invention as may please for a while. In *Othello* it is conceivable that the psychological integrity of the characters is in places weakened rather as Stoll avers, but by an imaginative power working to ends Stoll does not envisage. In this perhaps lies a solution of the difficulties we face.

That men do project upon others feelings and impulses which they would disavow is a fact obscurely known to us all, and I do not doubt its entering, in some measure, into our experience of *Othello*, with a consequent credibilising of Iago and his power. But we are most of us more aware of the simpler and prior fact of our divided soul, of danger when our blood begins our safer guides to rule, of the conflict of passion and reason—self-division's cause. *Othello* is about this conflict. The core of the play is not this character or that but a love-relationship, and in this relationship passion and reason become suspicion and trust. Desdemona *is* trust and Othello *is* suspicion; we shall etiolate, and not strengthen, Shakespeare's "psychology" if we ignore this element of symbolism in the tragedy. . . . As Desdemona *is* trust and Othello *is* suspicion, so—strangely—Othello *is* the human soul as it strives to be and Iago *is* that which corrodes or subverts it from within. We have evolved a view of the play which renders plausible the mechanism of the "calumniator believed" in terms of modern mental science; and this, I say, is in the tragedy—which in this aspect remains a work of subtle but sufficient naturalism. But this is knit to—I judge is subsidiary to—an aspect in which the play is of imaginative rather than naturalistic articulation. And, in point of the chosen theme, the method is more dramatic, better theatre, and much more apt for a strong and pristine art.

I conjecture, then, that at certain cardinal moments in the play when poetically received Othello and Iago are felt less as individuals each with his own psychological integrity than as abstractions from a single and, as it were, invisible protagonist. There are expressive forms of drama in which we do patently see a man at grips with some externalised facet of himself; in *King Lear* there is perhaps momentarily something of the sort as between Lear himself and the Fool; and this is something familiar to us too in ballet, which is an essence of drama. There is a poetic form—almost a major form—in which much the same thing is rendered in terms of a dialogue between Self and Soul. And something like this I see in the third Act of *Othello:* a realising of the basic mechanisms of the "calumniator believed" not naturalistically but through such an imaginative "splitting" as myth and poetry often employ to express violent polarities and ambivalences in the mind. The true protagonist of the drama (at least at this point) is to be arrived at only, as it were, by conflating two characters; by considering them (rather I should say by intuitively apprehending them) as interlocked forces within a single psyche. It is less a matter of Othello's projecting concealed facets of himself upon an apt Iago (a fundamentally naturalistic handling, such as is offered to us by Miss Maud Bodkin) than of the dramatist's abstracting these facets and embodying them in a figure substantially symbolic. Entailed in this is the view that Othello too is, at times, a figure substantially symbolic.

This hypothesis, I believe, will reconcile much in Stoll (his insistence upon Othello and Iago as not, individually regarded and at a crisis, sufficient and complete personalities) with much in Bradley (both his basic insistence upon the *truth* of the play, its powerful grasp of vehement real life, and upon the essential impression of the nobility of Othello as he appears before us). Again and again one writer whom I have cited jeers at the hopeless naïvety of Bradley in accepting as the *real* Othello what is no more than *Othello*'s Othello. But if we regard the Othello-figure on the stage as being indeed something in the nature of an Othello *persona,* as Othello's ego-ideal or self-exemplar, then Bradley is really right in point of dramatic feeling, since what we have here, in the sort of Soul-and-Body debate which the play essentially is, is indeed the "noble" Othello imaginatively disengaged, though far from immune,

from the lower Othello, the Othello who has been externalised in (rather than merely projected upon) Iago. (pp. 107-09)

     J. I. M. Stewart, "'Steep Tragic Contrast'," in his Character and Motive in Shakespeare: Some Recent Appraisals Examined, *Longmans, Green and Co., 1949, pp. 79-110.*

MARTIN WANGH   (essay date 1950)

[*Employing a psychoanalytical approach to* Othello, *Wangh examines the play for its "hidden content" and concludes that the central motivational force impelling the dramatic action is the repressed homosexual love of Iago for Othello. He asserts that Iago represents a classic example of "delusional jealousy," a term adopted by Sigmund Freud to describe a man's pathological, paranoic denial of love for another man. Noting that the real rival whom Iago must destroy is not Cassio but Desdemona, Wangh points out that this is even more apparent in Cinthio's tale. After remarking on the repeated occasions when Iago interrupts Othello and Desdemona while they are in bed together and his projection onto Desdemona of the sexual attraction he feels toward Othello and Cassio, the critic focuses on Iago's account to Othello—in III. iii. 413-26—of Cassio's alleged dream. Wangh maintains that, in this fabrication, Iago is equating Othello with Cassio and fantasizing that he has made love with the Moor, so that "Iago's dream is a homosexual wish fulfillment." Additionally, he identifies Desdemona's handkerchief as "a fetish, the child's substitution for the breast." Wangh's interpretation of Iago has enjoyed wide currency among both psychoanalytic critics and those who have employed other approaches to* Othello. *For additional examples of psychoanalytic analyses of the play, see the essays by M. D. Faber, Abraham Bronson Feldman, Stanley Edgar Hyman, Stephen Reid, and Gordon Ross Smith cited in the Additional Bibliography.*]

Shakespearean criticism has always held the motivation for Iago's destructive hatred to be too slight. Critics of all lands have spoken of Iago's 'motiveless malignity' [see excerpt above by Samuel Taylor Coleridge, 1808-18]. Some have called him 'monster'; others, the proponent of evil. To none has it seemed that the provocation was sufficient for the pitiless revenge.

One thing, however, has impressed all critics—the repeated shifting of Iago's ground. At first Iago is enraged by the slight he has suffered through Cassio's preferment. Soon the motive shifts to cuckoldry. Iago suspects that Othello and Cassio have slept with Emilia, Iago's wife, and this suspicion grows to a certainty.

Clearly, the two motives do not jibe. There is no direct relation between them; nor does either lead logically to the shocking murder of Desdemona. If the first motivation is the true one, then the play should end in the second act with the displacement of Cassio. If the second motivation is the true one, why is it not presented at once? Why does it not lead to revenge by cuckoldry rather than by murder? How explain Iago's hatred for Desdemona, when it is desire that should animate him? How, also, explain the hold this 'illogical' play has maintained upon the imagination of three and a half centuries of playgoers?

We can conclude only that the apparent motivation is not the basic motivation. The magic of the play lies in its hidden content, which speaks directly to the unconscious of every spectator.

Jealousy grown to the proportion of paranoia is a clinical condition, sufficient to effect the murder of Desdemona. Although it is Othello whom Shakespeare depicts as the person afflicted, I should like to present the view that the prime sufferer is Iago.

It is he who is jealous of Desdemona and hates her. Iago loves Othello. This is never expressed in so many words, but its opposite is repeatedly stressed. From the beginning it is clear that Iago has only disdain for women. He is 'nothing if not critical' [II. i. 119] of the entire sex. As he puts it to Desdemona and Emilia

>   . . . you are pictures out of doors,
> Belles in your parlours, wildcats in your kitchens,
> Saints in your injuries, devils being offended,
> Players in your housewifery, and housewives in your
> beds. . . .
> Nay it is true, or else I am a Turk:
> You rise to play, and go to bed to work.
>   [II. i. 109-12, 114-15]

I should like to consider the tragedy first from the standpoint of the action and its timing, then to follow the emotional conflicts of the character, Iago; for, although the play is called Othello, it is Iago who is the absorbing personality, the evil genius of the play. (pp. 203-04)

[What] are the precipitating factors in Iago's psychopathology? Apparently, before the action of the play Iago has had no conflicts. He has been Othello's trusted aide, very much in the general's confidence, and seemingly deserving of it. Suddenly he is thrown into an explosive frenzy. The first scene finds Iago shouting, 'Thief, thief', under Brabantio's window. Iago thus spectacularly acquaints Desdemona's father with his daughter's elopement with the Moor.

It is night; the town is sleeping when Iago raises his outcry. The disturbance, moreover, occurs immediately after Othello's marriage. Iago has sped to Brabantio's house knowing that Othello and Desdemona have retired to the marriage chamber. We can assume that Iago, being Othello's trusted aide, knew about the plans for the wedding; yet he did not warn Brabantio beforehand. Only when the marriage is about to be consummated does Iago create an uproar.

We should be warranted in reserving judgment were this the only indication of a triangle. But the action is repeated—not once but twice—and each time the uproar has the similar effect of disturbing the marital, sexual relationship. On the night of Othello's arrival in Cyprus, and again later, the couple are roused from bed by the tumult following Rodrigo's attacks on Cassio, both instigated by Iago. The conclusion is inescapable that in disturbing the marital relation Iago has achieved his immediate aim.

So far we can assume only that a triangle exists. On the face of it, Desdemona may be the object of Iago's affection. It may be simply an instance of competitive jealousy based upon the œdipus. Since Othello is a paternal authority, especially for Iago, the Moor's withdrawal to the marriage chamber reawakens the œdipal conflict in Iago. Three times there is a reproduction of the primal scene. (pp. 204-05)

If Iago be motivated by projective jealousy, the object of that jealousy should be his own wife, Emilia; and the manner of revenge should be one of two: Iago should either cuckold Othello or kill him. Since neither of these happens, we are left with delusional jealousy as the final possibility.

Delusional jealousy, Freud says, '. . . represents an acidulated homosexuality and rightly takes its position among the classical forms of paranoia. As an attempt at defense against an unduly strong homosexual impulse it may, in a man, be described in the formula: ''Indeed I do not love him, *she* loves him''' [in

Certain Neurotic Mechanisms in Jealousy, Paranoia and Homosexuality].

In his study of the Schreber case, Freud states that the principal forms of paranoia can all be represented as contradictions of the single proposition: 'I (a man) love him (a man)'. The first contradiction is: 'I do not love him; I hate him'. A second contradiction may be: 'It is not I who love the man; she loves him'. In consonance with these contradictions the sufferer suspects the woman's relation to all the men he himself is tempted to love.

In the very opening lines of the play the first contradiction, 'I do not love him, I hate him', is spoken by Rodrigo, a disappointed suitor for Desdemona's hand. Quoting Iago, he says: 'Thou toldst me thou didst hold him in thy hate' [I. i. 7].

It is noteworthy that in Cinthio's story of the Moor of Venice there is no character Rodrigo. Iago is the unrequited lover, and the drive to murder is ascribed to hurt pride. Shakespeare splits Cinthio's Iago into two characters. Rodrigo represents normal competitive jealousy, expressive of the positive œdipal relationship between Iago and Desdemona; Iago is the pathological counterpart, present under the surface in Cinthio's version as well.

Iago's declaration of his hatred of Othello is stated repeatedly

> Though I do hate him as I do hell-pains,
> Yet, for necessity of present life,
> I must show out a flag and sign of love,
> Which is indeed but sign.
>   [I. i. 154-57]

> I have told thee often, and I retell thee again
> and again, I hate the Moor . . .
>   [I. iii. 364-66]

In an ensuing soliloquy a significant motivation for his hatred is first stated.

>   I hate the Moor;
> And it is thought abroad that 'twixt my sheets
> He hath done my office: I know not if't be true,
> But I, for mere suspicion in that kind
> Will do as if for surety.
>   [I. iii. 386-90]
>   (pp. 205-06)

What evidence is there that Iago denies his love by projecting the part onto a woman? What indication is there that he suspects the woman's relation to all the men he himself is tempted to love?

The evidence for the first is overwhelming. Iago's assertions that Desdemona loves the Moor are too numerous to quote. With respect to the second, it is out of the substitution of Emilia for Desdemona that the thought of Cassio as Desdemona's lover is born. The substitution of Emilia for Desdemona is easy, for their relationship is that of mistress and maid.

Iago reiterates his suspicions of being cuckolded. 'I do suspect', he says, 'the lusty Moor hath leap'd into my seat' [II. i. 295-96]. From this suspicion Iago jumps to another equally unfounded: 'I fear Cassio with my night-cap too' [II. i. 307]. This groundless conjecture is preceded by Iago's suspicion that Cassio loves Desdemona and that she returns his love.

> That Cassio loves her, I do well believe it;
> That she loves him, 'tis apt and of great credit.
>   [II. i. 296-97]

Such rapid shifts are possible for Iago notwithstanding his previous assertion that Desdemona loves the Moor—possible because Iago is so tormented by Othello's love for Desdemona. Iago is driven to separate the pair and, the wish being father to the thought, he accomplishes it by asserting that Desdemona and Othello must tire of each other and that Desdemona must love Cassio. 'She must change for youth', he says, 'she must have change, she must' [I. iii. 350, 351-52]. It is an obsession with him.

This shift from Othello to Cassio certainly resembles a need to suspect the woman in relation to all the men Iago himself is tempted to love. The woman is Emilia who is interchangeable with Desdemona. And so in consonance with the second paranoid contradiction we have a situation in which Iago suspects Desdemona's relation to the two men, Othello and Cassio, whom he is himself tempted to love.

Iago's various projections may be summarized: the Moor has lain with Emilia; therefore Cassio has lain with Emilia; Emilia equals Desdemona; therefore Cassio has lain with Desdemona. All of these serve the function of warding off anxiety and enable Iago to deny by projection his homosexual drive to lie with the Moor.

By the third act the drama has advanced to the point where Othello has been goaded into an intolerable state of jealousy and anxiety. He demands proof that Desdemona is unfaithful, and Iago offers him three. The second of these contains the evidence we need. With mock reluctance Iago pours the following invention into Othello's ready ear.

> I lay with Cassio lately
> And, being troubled with a raging tooth,
> I could not sleep. . . .
> In sleep I heard him say, 'Sweet Desdemona,
> Let us be wary, let us hide our loves!'
> And then, sir, would he gripe and wring my hand,
> Cry, 'O, sweet creature!' and then kiss me hard,
> As if he pluck'd up kisses by the roots
> That grew upon my lips; then laid his leg
> Over my thigh, and sigh'd, and kiss'd; and then
> Cried, 'Cursed fate, that gave thee to the Moor!'
> [III. iii. 413-15, 419-26]

Lies have a psychoanalytic interest similar to fantasies and dreams. A lie told about a dream combines two of these categories. In this instance it is accurate to consider the dream to be a lie and the lie a dream.

Clearly the first and unmistakable purpose of the fabrication is to goad Othello into further jealousy; but behind this there is another, an unconscious motive. Iago's fantasy is an invention to satisfy his own unconscious strivings. We can, then, with confidence assume Iago's fiction to have quite another meaning. The lie can be interpreted as a product of the censorship of the dream, a censorship which contents itself with simple denial.

We feel justified in concluding that Cassio and Othello are equated in function on the accepted evidence that the person to whom a dream is told is himself involved in the dream. In telling the dream to Othello, Iago plainly says: 'I dreamt of you'. It has already been noted that Cassio and the Moor become interchangeable when Iago's jealousy is aroused. At first Iago suspected that the lusty Moor had leaped into his seat, and from this suspicion he immediately jumped to 'I fear Cassio with my night-cap too'. Iago's dream, then, means: 'I lay with

you, Othello, and you made love to me, as you do to Desdemona'. The last line, 'Cursed fate that gave thee [Desdemona] to the Moor' should be reread, 'Cursed fate that gave thee [Desdemona, not me] to the Moor'.

Let us examine the details of Iago's dream and see how far they confirm this interpretation. (pp. 207-09)

The dream begins with an imagined toothache which prevented Iago from sleeping. A tooth is one of the commoner universal symbols of the penis in dreams. 'A raging tooth' would then indicate sexual excitement. Iago's saying that he was 'troubled' with a raging tooth has two meanings: first, of censorship—resistance to his homosexual excitement; second, the wish for and the fear of castration. 'Kisses plucked up by the roots' can be similarly understood as a phrase heavy with castration symbolism, and the whole fantasy is replete with oral erotism. We can conclude that it is in part a fantasy of fellatio. 'He laid his leg over my thigh' is self-explanatory.

These considerations give ample confirmation to the thesis that Iago's dream is a homosexual wish fulfilment, and they are thus strong supporting evidence for the opinion that the basic motivation of the play is Iago's delusional jealousy.

Let us now trace the development of this paranoid condition and review the clinical course of Iago's illness as if the play were a case history.

The sudden onset of his disturbance is most comparable to a state of homosexual panic. In the course of the illness Iago tries to re-establish the countercathexis against the repressed homosexuality. He tries at first to rationalize his excitement. He insists that his jealousy is caused only by his failure to

Act III. Scene iii. Othello and Iago. By S. A. Hart.

attain the post he desired and by its having been conferred on Cassio instead. However, the basic conflict is revealed in Iago's choice of words: 'Preferment goes by letter and affection, and not by the old gradation' [I. i. 36-7]. The words preferment and affection point up the fact that Iago's hurt stems not only from a blow to professional pride, but from a rupture in his love relationship—another has been taken into favor in his stead.

The pathological conflict is hidden behind the verbalization of reasonable ambition. But at the next moment there is a return of the repressed, and Iago next attempts to curb his intolerable torment by denying the need for a love object; he tries to turn his love for Othello into love of himself. 'I never found a man', he says, 'that knew how to love himself. Ere I would say I would drown myself for the love of a guinea-hen, I would change my humanity with a baboon' [I. iii. 313-16]. But this is whistling in the dark. The regression into narcissism fails and Iago is found bolstering resolution by calling on intellect to control emotion. 'Our bodies', he says, 'are our gardens, to the which our wills are gardeners' [I. iii. 320-21].

Now the need to destroy takes possession of Iago. 'Nothing can or shall content my soul till I am even with him wife for wife' [II. i. 298-99]. Cuckolding, however, is not what he wants. Utterly frustrated, at last he makes Desdemona the object of his hate. Much more than Cassio, Desdemona is the rival to be destroyed. Iago will so work upon him that the Moor himself will destroy the hated rival, Desdemona: 'So will I turn her virtue into pitch, and out of her own goodness make the net that shall enmesh them all' [II. iii. 360-62]. His intellectual and emotional awareness apart, he has succeeded in turning over the weight of his intolerable jealousy to Othello, and having projected it thus becomes free to declare his love for Othello. Now he can openly say to the Moor: 'My lord, you know I love you' [III. iii. 117]. From now on he seizes every opportunity to pour out his hate for Desdemona. In a compelling crescendo he vilifies her, triumphs over each occasion when he has brought the Moor to express distaste for his rival. When finally the Moor says, 'Damn her, lewd minx' [III. iii. 475], and in the next breath grants Iago the coveted lieutenancy, Iago lets go completely: 'I am your own forever' [III. iii. 480]. (pp. 209-11)

That Desdemona is the real adversary and that her murder is the objective toward which Iago works is still more clearly represented in the Cinthio version of the story in which Desdemona is murdered by Iago. Othello, to be sure, is an accomplice to the deed, but Iago himself beats her to death with a sand-filled stocking.

In Shakespeare's version the fatal stabbing of Emilia by Iago follows immediately on the murder of Desdemona. It is as though Shakespeare used this means to point up the fact that Iago is the real culprit and that Desdemona and Emilia in his mind are one. (p. 211)

At this point one might well ask: whence comes the driving power of Iago's devouring jealousy? Many writers have given us the key. They have traced jealousy to its outgrowth from oral envy. In addition to the oral imagery of Iago's dream invention in Shakespeare's play, in Cinthio's version of the tale it is not Emilia but Iago who steals the handkerchief from Desdemona and, significantly, he does this while Desdemona is holding his child in her lap. This is the classic situation of the envious older child. The handkerchief, on which the tragedy hinges, has long been identified as a fetish, the child's sub-

stitute for the breast. In this instance, the symbolism is doubly clear. The handkerchief is embroidered with strawberries, easily recognizable symbols of the nipples.

[Iago's] struggle is against his feminine identification with Desdemona, Othello's wife. The power of the repressed homosexuality causes his jealousy, and drives him to contrive the death of Desdemona, his rival. . . . The tragedy occurs for the very reason that Iago must hide the unacceptable truth from himself. Safety for Iago lies only in ignorance and denial; the affliction is too deep to be resolved. His last words are a final closing of the door.

> Demand me nothing: what you know, you know:
> From this time forth I never will speak word.
> [V. ii. 303-04]
(p. 212)

Martin Wangh, " 'Othello': The Tragedy of Iago," in The Psychoanalytic Quarterly, *Vol. XIX, No. 2, April, 1950, pp. 202-12.*

KENNETH BURKE (essay date 1951)

[*Burke is one of the foremost American scholars and controversial literary figures of the twentieth century. Because he advocates a close reading of a literary text, he is frequently associated with such New Critics as I. A. Richards and William Empson, but his approach to literature combines pragmatism with aesthetics and ethical concerns. Burke regards language as symbolic action and perceives the critic's function to be the analysis and interpretation of the symbolic structure embedded in works of art. His pluralism is demonstrated by his use of the multiple perspectives offered by the works of Freud, Marx, and Veblen and by such fields of study as linguistics, sociology, psychology, and theology. Although his remarkable erudition and the complexity of his thought have limited his audience, Burke has had a profound influence on many contemporary literary critics. In the excerpt below, Burke discovers a "ritual design" underlying the dramatic structure of* Othello *that expresses the tension inherent in the perception of monogamous love as a form of property or possession. Endorsing Pierre-Joseph Proudhon's concept of property as "theft" and, hence, always in fear of theft, the critic asserts that Othello's role in the play is that of the possessor—the representation of the spirit of private ownership in the property of "human affections." Burke also claims that the Moor is emblematic of the individual newly enriched by love and marriage to a woman who is his social superior. Thus, he avers, Othello's blackness—a traditional symbol of baseness—is meant to indicate the sense of every lover's inadequacy with respect to the ennobling qualities of the loved one. According to Burke, Iago is the actualized representation of the threat of loss always implicit in the fact of ownership. In this regard, the critic maintains, despite dramatic appearances, the ensign is not an outward force impelling Othello's actions but an inward complement to them; in his words, "villain and hero here are but essentially inseparable parts of the one fascination." Other commentators who have noted the similarities or mutual kinship between Iago and Othello include August Wilhelm Schlegel (1811), Denton J. Snider (1887), Maud Bodkin (1934), G. R. Elliott (1937), F. R. Leavis (1937), and J. I. M. Stewart (1949). Burke further contends that Iago acts as a scapegoat figure by providing the audience with an outlet for the purgation of their antipathy and guilt, since they, too, perceive love in terms of private ownership. Burke argues that Desdemona, as the embodiment of the concept of love's private treasure, forms the third party to this "triune tension" at the heart of* Othello. *He adds that she follows a pattern of conduct that is "Christlike" in her willing forgiveness of her murderer after her death, a point also made by Roy W. Battenhouse (1969). For further commentary on Shakespeare's presentation of love in* Othello, *see the excerpts by Hermann Ulrici (1839), Derek Traversi (1949), Winifred M.*

T. Nowottny (1952), Robert B. Heilman (1956), John Bayley (1960), Susan Snyder (1972), Jared R. Curtis (1973), and Jane Adamson (1980).]

Othello: Act V, Scene ii. Desdemona, fated creature, marked for a tragic end by her very name (Desdemona: "moan-death") lies smothered. Othello . . . has stabbed himself and fallen across her body. (Pattern of Othello's farewell speech: How he spoke of a "base Indian", and we knew by that allusion he meant Othello. When it was told that he "threw a pearl away" [V. ii. 347], for "threw away" we substituted "strangled", and for the pearl, "Desdemona". Hearing one way, we interpreted another. While he was ostensibly telling of a new thing, thus roundabout he induced us to sum up the entire meaning of the story. Who then was the "turban'd Turk" that Othello seized by the throat and smote? By God, it was himself— our retrospective translation thus suddenly blazing into a new present identity, a new act here and now, right before our eyes, as he stabs himself.) Iago, "Spartan dog, / More fell than anguish, hunger, or the sea", is invited by Lodovico to "look on the tragic loading of this bed" [V. ii. 361-63]. *Exeunt omnes* [Exit all], with Iago as prisoner, we being assured that they will see to "the censure of this hellish villain, / The time, the place, the torture" [V. ii. 368-69]. Thus like the tragic bed, himself bending beneath a load, he is universally hated for his ministrations. And in all fairness, as *advocatus diaboli* [devil's advocate] we would speak for him, in considering the cathartic nature of his role.

Reviewing, first, the definition of some Greek words central to the ritual of cure:

Katharma: that which is thrown away in cleansing; the off-scourings, refuse, of a sacrifice; hence, worthless fellow. "It was the custom at Athens," lexicographers inform us, "to reserve certain worthless persons, who in case of plague, famine, or other visitations from heaven, were thrown into the sea," with an appropriate formula, "in the belief that they would cleanse away or wipe off the guilt of the nation." And these were *katharmata.* Of the same root, of course, are our words *cathartic* and *catharsis,* terms originally related to both physical and ritual purgation.

A synonym for *katharma* was *pharmakos:* poisoner, sorcerer, magician; one who is sacrificed or executed as an atonement of purification for others; a scapegoat. It is related to *pharmakon:* drug, remedy, medicine, enchanted potion, philtre, charm, spell, incantation, enchantment, poison.

Hence, with these terms in mind, we note that Iago has done this play some service. Othello's suspicions, we shall aim to show, arise from within, in the sense that they are integral to the motive he stands for; but the playwright cuts through that tangle at one stroke, by making Iago a voice at Othello's ear.

What arises within, if it wells up strongly and presses for long, will seem imposed from without. One into whose mind melodies spontaneously pop, must eventually "hear voices." "Makers" become but "instruments", their acts a sufferance. Hence, "inspiration", "afflatus", "angels", and "the devil". Thus, the very extremity of inwardness in the motives of Iago can make it seem an outwardness. Hence we are readily disposed to accept the dramatist's dissociation. Yet villain and hero here are but essentially inseparable parts of the one fascination.

Add Desdemona to the inseparable integer. That is: add the privacy of Desdemona's treasure, as vicariously owned by Othello in manly miserliness (Iago represents the threat implicit in such cherishing), and you have a tragic trinity of ownership in the profoundest sense of ownership, the property in human affections, as fetishistically localized in the object of possession, while the possessor is himself possessed by his very engrossment (Iago being the result, the apprehension that attains its dramatic culmination in the thought of an agent acting to provoke the apprehension). The single mine-own-ness is thus dramatically split into the three principles of possession, possessor, and estrangement (threat of loss). Hence, trust and distrust, though *living in* each other, can be shown *wrestling with* each other. *La propriété, c'est le vol* [Property is theft, Pierre-Joseph Proudhon]. Property fears theft because it is theft.

Sweet thievery, but thievery nonetheless. Appropriately, the first outcry in this play was of "Thieves, thieves, thieves!" when Iago stirred up Desdemona's father by shouting: "Look to your house, your daughter, and your bags! / Thieves! thieves!" [I. i. 80-1]—first things in a play being as telltale as last things. Next the robbery was spiritualized: "You have lost your soul" [I. i. 87]. And finally it was reduced to imagery both lewd and invidious: "An old black ram is tupping your white ewe" [I. i. 88-9], invidious because of the social discrimination involved in the Moor's blackness. So we have the necessary ingredients, beginning from what Desdemona's father, Brabantio, called "the property of youth and maidenhood" [I. i. 172]. (Nor are the connotations of *pharmakon,* as evil-working drug, absent from the total recipe, since Brabantio keeps circling about this theme, to explain how the lover robbed the father of his property in the daughter. So it is there, in the offing, as imagery, even though rationalistically disclaimed; and at one point, Othello does think of poisoning Desdemona.)

Desdemona's role, as one of the persons in this triune tension (or "psychosis"), might also be illuminated by antithesis. In the article on the Fine Arts (in the eleventh edition of the *Encyclopaedia Britannica*), the elements of pleasure "which are not disinterested" are said to be:

> the elements of personal exultation and self-congratulation, the pride of exclusive possession or acceptance, all these emotions, in short, which are summed up in the lover's triumphant monosyllable, "Mine."

Hence it follows that, for Othello, the beautiful Desdemona was not an aesthetic object. The thought gives us a radical glimpse into the complexity of her relation to the audience (her nature as a rhetorical "topic"). First, we note how, with the increased cultural and economic importance of private property, an aesthetic might arise antithetically to such norms, exemplifying them in reverse, by an idea of artistic enjoyment that would wholly transcend "mine-own-ness". The sharper the stress upon the *meum* [mine] in the practical realm, the greater the invitation to its denial in an aesthetic *nostrum* [ours].

We are here considering the primary paradox of dialectic, stated as a maxim in the formula beloved by dialectician Coleridge: "Extremes meet." Note how, in this instance, such meeting of the extremes adds to our engrossment in the drama. For us, Desdemona *is* an aesthetic object: we never forget that we have no legal rights in her, and we never forget that she is but an "imitation". But *what* is she imitating? She is "imitating" her third of the total tension (the disequilibrium of monogamistic love, considered as a topic). She is imitating a major perturbation of property, as so conceived. In this sense, however aloof from her the audience may be in discounting her nature as a mere playwright's invention, her role can have a full effect upon them only insofar as it draws upon firm beliefs and dark apprehensions that not only move the audience *within* the conditions of the play, but prevail as an unstable and disturbing cluster of motives *outside* the play, or "prior to" it. Here the "aesthetic," even in negating or transcending "mine-own-ness," would draw upon it for purposes of poetic persuasion. We have such appeal in mind when speaking of the "topical" element. You can get the point by asking yourself: "So far as catharsis and wonder are concerned, what is gained by the fact that the play imitates *this particular tension* rather than some other?"

In sum, Desdemona, Othello, and Iago are all partners of a single conspiracy. There were the enclosure acts, whereby the common lands were made private; here is the analogue, in the realm of human affinity, an act of spiritual enclosure. And might the final choking be also the ritually displaced effort to close a thoroughfare, as our hero fears lest this virgin soil that he had opened up become a settlement? Love, universal love, having been made private, must henceforth be shared vicariously, as all weep for Othello's loss, which is, roundabout, their own. And Iago is a function of the following embarrassment: Once such privacy has been made the norm, its denial can be but promiscuity. Hence his ruttish imagery, in which he signalizes one aspect of a total fascination.

So there is a whispering. There is something vaguely feared and hated. In itself it is hard to locate, being woven into the very nature of "consciousness"; but by the artifice of Iago it is made local. The tinge of malice vaguely diffused through the texture of events and relationships can here be condensed into a single principle, a devil, giving the audience as it were flesh to sink their claw-thoughts in. Where there is a gloom hanging over, a destiny, each man would conceive of the obstacle in terms of the instruments he already has for removing obstacles, so that a soldier would shoot the danger, a butcher thinks it could be chopped, and a merchant hopes to get rid of it by trading. But in Iago the menace is generalized. (As were you to see man-made law as destiny, and see destiny as a hag, cackling over a brew, causing you by a spell to wither.)

In sum, we have noted two major cathartic functions in Iago: (1) as regards the tension centering particularly in sexual love as property and ennoblement (monogamistic love), since in reviling Iago the audience can forget that his transgressions are theirs; (2) as regards the need of finding a viable localization for uneasiness (*Angst*) in general, whether shaped by super-human forces or by human forces interpreted as super-human (the scapegoat here being but a highly generalized form of the over-investment that men may make in specialization). Ideally, in childhood, hating and tearing-at are one; in a directness and simplicity of hatred there may be a ritual cure for the bewilderments of complexity; and Iago may thus serve to give a feeling of integrity.

These functions merge into another, purely technical. For had Iago been one bit less rotten and unsleeping in his proddings, how could this play have been kept going, and at such a pitch? Until very near the end, when things can seem to move "of themselves" as the author need but actualize the potentialities already massed, Iago has goaded (tortured) the plot forward step by step, for the audience's villainous entertainment and filthy purgation. (pp. 165-70)

One notable aspect of the tension Shakespeare is exploiting is [Othello's] sense of himself as a parvenu. For ennoblement through love is a new richness (a notable improving of one's status, a destiny that made love a good symbol for secretly containing the political aspirations of the bourgeois as *novus homo* [new man]). Hence, in breaking the proprieties of love into their components, in dramatically carving this idea at the joints, we should encounter also in Othello as lover the theme of the newly rich, the marriage above one's station. And misgivings (which could be dramatized as murderous suspicions) would be proper to this state, insofar as the treasured object stands for many things that no human being could literally be. So, in contrast with the notion of the play as the story of a black (low-born) man cohabiting with (identified with) the high-born (white) Desdemona, we should say rather that the role of Othello as "Moor" draws for its effects upon the sense of the "black man" in every lover. There is a converse ennoblement from Desdemona's point of view, in that Othello is her unquestioned "lord". And could we not further say that such categorical attributing of reverence to the male (in a social context of double sexual standards) necessarily implies again some suspicions of inadequacy. The very sovereignty that the male absolutely arrogates to himself, as an essential aspect of private property in human affection, introduces a secret principle of self-doubt—which would be properly "imitated" in the ascribing of "inferior" origins to Othello, even in the midst of his nobility. And though the reader might not agree with this explanation in detail, it can serve in principle to indicate the *kind* of observation we think the analysis of the dramatis personae requires. (pp. 181-82)

Kenneth Burke, " 'Othello': An Essay to Illustrate a Method," in The Hudson Review, *Vol. IV, No. 2, Summer, 1951, pp. 161-203.*

ROBERT B. HEILMAN   (essay date 1951)

[*An American scholar and educator, Heilman has written* This Great Stage: Image and Structure in "King Lear" *(1948),* Magic in the Web: Action and Language in "Othello" *(1956), and commentary on modern and pre-Shakespearean drama; he has also edited the works of several nineteenth-century novelists. Usually employing a pluralistic approach in his criticism, he is principally concerned with the many dimensions of poetic language and the relation of patterns of imagery to the dramatic action of a play. In the excerpt below, taken from an essay originally published in 1951 in* Essays in Criticism, *Heilman demonstrates the way in which the oppositions of fair and black or light and dark in* Othello *are intensified by recurring images of heaven and hell, order and chaos, purity and foulness, and so on. The critic points out that as Iago transforms Othello's perception of Desdemona, so that in his mind her fairness becomes blackened, he also succeeds in darkening the Moor's "inner brightness," which was affirmed by Desdemona and the Venetian senate in Act I, Scene iii. These transformations, Heilman contends, are "dynamically expressed" by the metaphorical language, which vivifies the twin paradoxes of "fair-as-foul" and "black-as-fair." For additional commentary on the series of contrasts and oppositions in* Othello, *see the excerpts by Victor Hugo (1864), Wyndham Lewis (1927), Allardyce Nicoll (1927), and G. Wilson Knight (1930). Heilman further maintains that Iago's principal function is to confound the truth by blurring distinctions between polarities, pointing out that the ancient is able to convince Othello that light is dark because he himself believes "they are either infinitely convertible, or much the same at bottom." The critic avers, however, that at the close of the drama the Moor recognizes the enormity of his crime and begins once again to be able to distinguish between light and dark; through this insight, Heilman asserts, "he becomes fair again, and the dark recedes." In a later essay on* Othello *(see excerpt below, 1956), Heilman appears to contradict this assessment by contending that Othello never achieves understanding of the significance of Desdemona's love and thus dies ignorant of the true nature of his loss. Such other critics as G. R. Elliott (1937), F. R. Leavis (1937), E. M. W. Tillyard (1938), John Bayley (1960), G. M. Matthews (1964), Jared R. Curtis (1973), and Helen Gardner (see Additional Bibliography) have also considered whether Shakespeare depicts Othello as achieving clarity of vision at the close of the drama. Analyses of the poetic language in* Othello *have also been offered by G. Wilson Knight (1930), Derek Traversi (1949), S. L. Bethell (1952), John Bayley (1960), Gayle Greene (1979), and Carol McGinnis Kay (1983); also, see the essays by Wolfgang Clemen, Madeleine Doran, William Empson, and Caroline F. E. Spurgeon cited in the Additional Bibliography for further commentary on the language and imagery in the play.]*

At the most obvious level of perception *Othello* works in terms of a startling contrast—that, of course, between the 'fair' maid, as she is so often called, and her black lover, Othello of the 'sooty bosom' [I. ii. 70]. Now this opposition of fair and black, of light and dark, is not merely an heirloom which Shakespeare receives passively from literary ancestors and then forgets: on the contrary, the opposition is always, though not obtrusively, being pressed upon our minds, for it has more than one form in the play. Iago, characteristically reducing the relationship of the lovers to the animal level, and intent, of course, upon maddening Brabantio, shouts 'an old black ram / Is tupping your white ewe' [I. i. 88-9]; and he adds even a suggestion, the first of many such, of the darkness of hell: '. . . the devil will make a grandsire of you' [I. i. 91]; Roderigo mildly echoes the contrast when he says that Brabantio's 'fair daughter' is in 'the clasps of a lascivious Moor' [I. i. 126]. The Moor himself is aware of his wife's fairness. He can call her 'fair' [I. iii. 125] as matter-of-factly as others do [IV, ii, 118, 225], but he has much more than a matter-of-fact awareness: when he comes to kill her, he wants not to 'scar that whiter skin of hers than snow' [V. ii. 4]. This final black-white juxtaposition, so clearly set before us in the *white* and *snow* spoken by the dark Othello, is more than pictorial: each character seems to have his own colour symbolically as well as literally. Desdemona, we know, is innocent; and the very language of the play, as we shall see, has had the effect of making Othello, at the end, doubly black.

But Shakespeare does still more than give us a sharp contrast with a symbolic increment: he finds other complications in the black-white issue. To equate black with villainy is easy; but we get beneath surfaces and into the real terrors of experience when black and white become indistinguishable. Note how Iago describes his budding plot:

> Divinity of hell!
> When devils will the blackest sins put on,
> They do suggest at first with heavenly shows,
> As I do now.
>
> [II. iii. 350-53]

Hell and devils find blackest sins congenial; the heavenly, by implication, is white—an identification used throughout the play. The method of Iago's evil is planned confusion; the use of the 'heavenly' to produce 'blackest sins'. Shakespeare uses a brilliant variation of this a few lines later when he has Iago thus describe his scheme for arousing Othello against Desdemona: 'So will I turn her virtue into pitch' [II. iii. 360]. In effect: the fair Desdemona will be made black: good becomes evil, and the world is thrown into utter disorder. How entirely fitting, in this context, is Othello's metaphor for his love of Desdemona:

> and when I love thee not,
> Chaos is come again.
>
> [III. iii. 91-2]

In this doctrine, love—love for the fair Desdemona—is a mode of order; absence of love is chaos—disorder—darkness. In the very next speech after these words of Othello, Iago begins his campaign to restore the anarchy that preceded the creative fiat 'Let there be light'.

The black-white antithesis, then, appears in various extensions: hell-heaven, dark-light, and, as we shall see, foul-pure. Iago's business is to confuse the opposites. Speaking ostensibly of himself, he thus prepares Othello to lose a sense of reality:

> As where's that palace whereinto foul things
> Sometimes intrude not? Who has a breast so pure
> But some uncleanly apprehensions
> Keep leets and law days, and in session sit
> With meditations lawful?
>
> [III. iii. 137-41]

Othello, we have said, is aware of Desdemona's fairness: Shakespeare makes dramatic use of the fairness by having Othello himself tend to symbolize it, to identify it with the virtue that Iago intends to 'turn . . . into pitch'. Iago's success is reflected literally in the words which Othello uses to express his conviction that Desdemona is untrue:

> Her name, that was as fresh
> As Dian's visage, is now begrim'd and black
> As mine own face!
>
> [III. iii. 386-88]

There is a good irony here: Desdemona's name *is* 'begrim'd and black'—not by her own action but by Iago's defiling words. Having brought Othello so far, Iago has recourse to another heavenly show: he kneels as if in prayer and swears devotion 'to wrong'd Othello's service' [III. iii. 467]—and swears how? By 'you ever-burning lights above' [III. iii. 463]—by the *heavenly* and by *lights*. Order is indeed being turned upside down, and light and dark made indistinguishable. In the next-to-the-last line Othello uses words which exactly mark Iago's success: he calls Desdemona 'fair devil' [III. iii. 479]. Later he addresses Desdemona herself: 'O devil, devil!' [IV. i. 244].

Iago continues his 'heavenly shows' by exclaiming to Othello, ' 'tis foul in her' and 'That's fouler' [IV. i. 201, 203]. Talking to Desdemona, Othello wrestles with the contradiction that arises from his identification of fairness and virtue: 'O, thou weed, / Who art so lovely fair, and smell'st so sweet' and 'Was this fair paper, this most goodly book, / Made to write "whore" upon?' [IV. ii. 67-8, 71-2]. After murdering her, Othello must believe he has been just: he cries to Emilia, 'She's like a liar gone to burning hell!' [V. ii. 129], and among Emilia's retorts is the counter-assertion, 'she was heavenly true!' [V. ii. 135]. Up to his enlightenment Othello keeps on protesting: 'honest' Iago, he says, 'hates the slime / That sticks on filthy deeds' and of Desdemona: 'O, she was foul!' [V. ii. 148-49, 200].

The heart of the psychological action is the change of Othello's attitude to Desdemona, a change which for him is really an objective transformation of her. The point here is that this transformation is expressed—anticipated, recorded, commented on—not abstractly, not in chance words, but consistently in images that are related to the basic dramatic facts and that invest those facts with the maximum of suggestiveness. Drama and poetry intimately collaborate. Iago will produce *blackest* sins, turn *fair* Desdemona's virtue into *pitch*, though he swears fidelity to Othello by *lights above*; Desdemona becomes *black* and *foul*; she is called a *devil* and consigned to *hell*. *Chaos* has come sooner than Othello thought.

Now, while blonde Desdemona is being made over into an ironic likeness to Othello, what is happening to Othello himself? Othello's blackness, of course, is always before us as a theatrical fact; yet the fact is not ignored (nor its possible meaningfulness left to chance), but is constantly given special dramatic life by the language. At the beginning we have not only 'sooty bosom' and 'black ram' but the oblique introduction of darkness in the Duke's phrase 'foul proceeding' [I. iii. 65], in Othello's words 'If you do find me foul in her report' [I. iii. 117]—(a fine irony is prepared here: later *she* is found foul in *his* report), and in Brabantio's 'To fall in love with what she fear'd to look on!' [I. iii. 98]. The important thing is that in Act I the black Othello wins, and at the same time the metaphorical darkness is dispelled. Desdemona replies to her father's incredulity: 'I saw Othello's visage in his mind' [I. iii. 252]. His darkness is, in effect, denied; the reality is an inner brightness. How effective, then, is the Duke's summing up, which looks at first like a pair of tag lines, but which actually outlines a major poetic theme:

> If virtue no delighted beauty lack,
> Your son-in-law is far more fair then black.
>
> [I. iii. 289-90]

In punning, the Duke implies the relationship between appearance and moral quality in terms of which, as we have seen, Othello expresses his anguish at what he believes to be the infidelity of the fair Desdemona. But now he is happy: he has been cleared: this official action means a kind of forgiveness for being black. His blackness has been declared skin-deep. Here is the paradox of black-as-fair, which will find its counterpart later in the paradox to be rebelled against and finally accepted by Othello, the paradox of fair-as-foul. (pp. 318-21)

Othello enters the story with the handicap of blackness—a familiar symbol of evil. Then he is declared 'fair'. Then he becomes dark again: his judgment is *collied*, his colour comes into his consciousness, he executes *black* vengeance; he is called a *blacker* devil, a *filthy* bargain, *ignorant* as *dirt*. Iago's victory is that 'black Othello' has earned his blackness—now not an accident of pigmentation but a moral discoloration.

Iago has blackened fair Desdemona for Othello, and, so to speak, reblackened the fair Othello: in two different ways he has turned virtue into pitch. The imagery has not merely decorated the event but has dynamically expressed it, both by utilizing the available fact—in itself dead—of a difference in colour and by defining the general evil implicit in the transformations we have seen. What happens is not the melodramatic irruption of an inimical force which may conventionally be labelled 'dark' or 'black' ('And universal darkness buries all' [Alexander Pope in *The Dunciad*]) but the confusion of dark and light, the taking of light for dark, the darkening of light. This chaos is the really sinister peril, the latent universal which creates the spell of the unique story. Iago, in other words, has not invented an *ad hoc* villainy; rather he has invoked a principle of evil, one to which we are always susceptible. His act has sprung from a credo and a system of values. He is successful against Othello not merely because he is a cool manipulator but because he has faith in the indiscriminate, undifferentiable, lowest-common-denominator universe which he propounds. He can make Othello take light for dark because he believes they are either infinitely convertible, or much the same at bottom. He carries conviction because he is a man of principle. The generality of his position is sketched, with ever so light a touch, in the verses with which he entertains Emilia and Desdemona just before Othello arrives in Cyprus [II. i.

129-60]. He is disparaging women, as a joke of course; but his jokes are of a piece with his most serious operating procedures. What he says is more than a gay verbal echo of issues that have their essential life elsewhere. In Iago's rimes women are characterized as witty and stupid, and as foul or fair or black; but these differences are meaningless, for women become identical through sexuality. What matters foul or fair? A 'black' woman will 'find a white that shall her blackness fit' [II. i. 133]; as for a 'fair and foolish' woman, 'even her folly help'd her to an heir' [II. i. 137]; and in sum,

> There's none so foul, and foolish thereunto,
> But does foul pranks which fair and wise ones do.
>
> [II. i. 141-42]

If the surface manner is comic, the effect is not one of relief; here is a preview—in fact, a full view—of the blurring of distinctions which makes the black-fair pattern a fitting imaginal instrument for the drama. 'Foul and foolish': same as 'fair and wise'. With this sceptical doctrine Iago will corrupt Othello's faith. Iago's credo will become Othello's heresy. Desdemona's comment on Iago after his verse, 'A most profane and liberal counsellor' [II. i. 163-64], is truer than she knows. Iago and Desdemona are opposed in other ways. The scene of Iago's kneeling and swearing fidelity to Othello in the execution of vengeance, 'Witness, you ever-burning lights above' [III. iii. 463], is exactly paralleled by the scene in which Desdemona, calling, ironically enough, upon Iago to help her to regain Othello, swears her fidelity to Othello:

> . . . for, by this light of heaven,
> I know not how I lost him. Here I kneel.
>
> [IV. ii. 150-51]

In his dark purpose, kneeling Iago, the confounder of truth, naturally invokes the light; the oath of kneeling Desdemona strengthens the association of the fair, the light and the pure. Desdemona swears similarly in the next scene when she and Emilia are discussing the infidelity of women—Iago's creed, Othello's induced belief. Would you betray your husband 'for all the world', Desdemona asks Emilia, and quickly replies for herself, 'No, by this heavenly light!' [IV. iii. 64, 65]. Emilia's jocular response—

> Nor I neither by this heavenly light.
> I might do't as well i' th' dark
>
> [IV. iii. 66-7]

introduces twenty lines of witty play on the theme that 'all the world' is 'a great price for a small vice' [IV. iii. 68-9]. Emilia is a foil for Desdemona's girlish earnestness; she can joke in a worldly manner, like Iago; yet she is sharply distinguished from him in that, while his jokes condemn all women, hers only spin a logical fantasy for herself. He always pretends to light; she boldly claims the dark.

We recall all the evil done 'i' th' dark', and, indeed, the prevalence of dark nights in the play. Some important actions take place by day, yet little is made of day as such. . . . *Othello* is predominantly a night-play. All of Act I—with Iago's first move against Othello, the news of enemy advances and Othello's successful defence—takes place at night. Act II is split almost evenly between the happy day-time scene of the safe arrivals at Cyprus, of a victory over storm and the destruction of enemies, and another night scene in which Cassio gets drunk, fights, and thus lays the foundation for the rest of Iago's sinister machinations. When Othello calls Cassio 'night-brawler' and speaks of 'this foul rout' [II. iii. 196, 210], we are reminded that in all the night-scenes there are disturbances and brawling; disorder at night is a good enough symbol of chaos. In Act III, Scene iii, in his first severe attack upon Othello's faith in Desdemona, Iago tells his lie about the night he slept with Cassio and heard him in his sleep make love to Desdemona. Act IV is full of anticipations of the night: Othello plans then to punish Desdemona, Iago tries to whip Roderigo up to decisive action, and Desdemona prepares for bed as Othello has commanded. And all of the action of Act V, like that of Act I, takes place at night—the stabbings on the streets, Othello's murder of Desdemona, and his suicide. On the stage then, at least half of the play is presented in shadow and partial or total darkness—a circumstance which exerts an unmistakable influence on the tone. Here in the external conditions of action—in what we might call the 'theatrical facts'—is a powerful symbol of the darkness of life with which the play is concerned: the conscious evil of Iago and the groping ignorance and misunderstanding of Othello. (pp. 323-26)

The important poetic truth is that in *Othello* night is not just an accident; it is not an idle setting which might just as well be exchanged for something else; nor is it a property of melodrama, an incitement to fear in the easily fearful. Night is not passive but active; its reality is ever pressed upon us; it means not merely physical darkness but spiritual darkness. Everything converges upon the night scenes, and in them there is a confluence of forces—of evil intent or of ignorance—opposed to the true and the fair. If Shakespeare went no further than this in infusing night with meaning, he would have created a very effective symbol. But actually he did not aim only at this and succeed only in this. Night has still other potentialities. Consider some words of Desdemona's . . . :

> Prithee tonight
> Lay on my bed my wedding sheets, remember;
>
> [IV. ii. 104-05]

These lines are a part of the context of darkness; Desdemona is full of foreboding, and her incomprehension of Othello matches his miscomprehension of her. Yet in the words themselves is something which is partly at war with Desdemona's tone; the speech is ambiguous, and night has a second dimension. 'Well, happiness to their sheets!' Iago said earlier [II. iii. 29]. The bed is the marital bed, and even to the end there is some faint possibility that the nocturnal rites may be those of fulfilment rather than sacrifice. From early in the play, indeed, there is a twofold potentiality in night. Night may mean pleasant sleep: even after his indignation at Cassio's 'vile brawl', Othello remarks philosophically: ''Tis the soldier's life / To have their balmy slumbers wak'd with strife' [II. iii. 257-58]. Still earlier Othello, called forth in the first midnight alarum of the play, can cry in the high spirits of the untroubled bridegroom: 'The goodness of the night upon you, friends' [I. ii. 35]. And in this first night-time test, Othello is entirely the victor. The evil that comes at night, then, does not come casually, in place of nothing; it is a reversal, a driving out, of a positive goodness. It falls to Iago to state the issue most specifically—and to state it, with customary indelicacy, but in words that contain less than a full measure of his habitual cynicism:

> Our general cast us thus early for the love of
> his Desdemona; who let us not therefore blame.
> He hath not yet made wanton the night with
> her, and she is sport for Jove.
>
> [II. iii. 14-17]

We have, then, a second kind of night—the night of married love. To this second meaning of night, as is fitting in his design,

Shakespeare gives a comparatively slight development, but yet enough to enrich greatly his total statement. The darkness is sinister because it is not merely an easy external sign but because the evil that happens at night drives out a good. The nocturnal disorders are a brutal interruption of a honeymoon: malice destroys a bridal night. In this ironic juxtaposition of love and hate—of light and dark—*Othello* comes closest to moving us as deeply as the other tragedies. It is as though Shakespeare has kept his human actors balanced upon a delicate border-line of life—a border-line between two realities that are as opposed as night and day and yet may yield to or replace each other in a flash. Love, with its promise of life, suddenly turns into death. In this ironic love-death linkage the play goes furthest beneath the surface and towards the mysteries.

The long night of the play, then, might have been fair as well as dark. With terms transposed, there is the same dual possibility for the villain. Iago says, 'This is the night / That either makes me or fordoes me quite' [V. i. 128-29]. But an earlier speech of Iago's—the closing couplet of Act I—beautifully fits him into the dark-light pattern of the play:

> I have't! It is engend'red! Hell and night
> Must bring this monstrous birth to the world's light.
>
> [I. iii. 403-04]

This couplet does everything: Hell and night, virtually interchangeable throughout the play, are here overtly allied; the rhyming of *night* and *light* sets off the antithetical forces in their symbolic investitures; and the paradoxical inversions of reality essential to the structure are marked in Iago's double-barrelled metaphor—the metaphor of bringing death to life, and darkness to light. The dark underworld and the dark night are fitting midwives for Iago: after his brand of light has been shed on the world . . . , Othello calls Desdemona 'fair devil', and Emilia calls Othello, 'blacker devil'. If we look further, however, we see two counter-processes at work here. While Iago is trying to bring darkness into the happy light of Othello's life, there is an opposing force which tries to bring light into the surrounding darkness. The play, as I have said, actively makes dramatic use of the darkness of night; likewise it makes active use of the lights which must be used at night. Lights could be assumed; necessary properties could be taken for granted. But when what might be only a detail of setting is something of which an author is aware and of which he is carefully transmitting his own awareness to us, we must observe what he is doing. Lights are symbolic as much as darkness is; they may dispel, or try to dispel, or ironically emphasize a failure to dispel, the evil or ignorance or chaos symbolized by the darkness. In Act I, for instance, there is a very remarkable conquest of the dark night—a conquest which, in retrospect, we can see takes place before the powers of darkness have really extended themselves. All the action takes place at night; Iago has admitted his hate and has, through Brabantio, made his initial attack upon Othello, whose blackness he has implied is itself an emblem of wrongdoing. Brabantio, the immediate and incidental victim of Iago's obfuscation, acts quickly, and his first active step lies in this speech:

> Strike on the tinder, ho!
> Give me a taper! Call up all my people! . . .
> Light, I say! light!
>
> [I. i. 140-41, 144]

When he and his servants come down, they come 'with torches' [s.d. I. i. 160], and shortly Brabantio takes up his original cry, 'Get more tapers' [I. i. 166]. In effect, Brabantio seeks the light of knowledge, and he finds the light; if not altogether pleased by what he finds, he nevertheless accepts it. In any case, he does not act in ignorance: in this sense he conquers the Iago night. Other elements in Act I give one a continuous sense of a conquering light. When Othello and his party first appear, they enter 'with torches' [s.d. I. i. 1]; a little later, Cassio and officers enter 'with torches' and Othello asks, 'But look what lights come yond' [I. ii. 28]; then Brabantio, Roderigo, and Officers enter 'with torches' [s.d. I. ii. 55]; and finally the Duke and Senators appear at a table 'with lights' [s.d. I. iii. 1]. At each entry 'with torches' there is also a threat: Brabantio and the others enter 'with torches and weapons' [s.d. I. ii. 55]. But the threats are dispelled, and torches rather than swords are the symbols of the settlement. Brabantio, as we have seen, finds the truth; Othello tells the truth and is corroborated by Desdemona; the Duke is able to see the truth and act in terms of it. Torches, tapers, tinder—they conquer the night. 'Let there be light' is the dominant motif; Iago is defeated in his first effort to make 'chaos . . . come again'. The order of love still holds.

But there are other nights. Now Shakespeare, as is the habit of his imagination, carries this scene over into others, or at least writes others in such a way that they can be read more meaningfully by reference to the management of Act I. Both parts of Act V are dramatically yoked to Act I. Again in Act V it is night; but now Iago's hate, instead of being on the threshold of action, has reached the climax of action. Roderigo has been wounded by Cassio, and Cassio by Iago. Cassio calls, 'O, help, ho! light! a surgeon!' [V. i. 30]. Lodovico says, 'It is a heavy night' [V. i. 42], and, after other calls and excited speeches, somebody comes, as Gratiano says, 'with light and weapons' [V. i. 47]. The newcomer is, of all people, Iago—'with light'! What a fine stroke this is: the very source of darkness as the apparent dispeller of darkness. But like one group of entering characters in Act I [I. ii. 55], Iago carried light *'and weapons':* his equipment defines his pretence and his actuality. In Act I, light conquered the weapons: here, weapons conquer the light. As light bearer (Lucifer in modern dress), Iago is all on the side of chaos, by his plot generally and by his aggravation of the immediate confusion: he pretends ignorance, he pretends helpfulness, he intentionally misidentifies. Wilfully postponing the use of 'light' he uses his weapon to despatch the wounded Roderigo, finding justification in mock-indignant words that exactly define his own role: 'Kill men i' th' dark?' [V. i. 63]. *Then* he calls 'Light, gentlemen' and ostentatiously proffers help to 'brother' Cassio [V. i. 73, 71]. Again he calls, 'Lend me a light. Know we this face or no?' [V. i. 88], now permitting himself a shocked recognition of the Roderigo whom he slew a minute earlier. Later he explains that Cassio was 'set on in the dark' [V. i. 112].

The dark-light pattern is skilfully used here—not only to carry on the good-evil or love-hate oppositions, but to exhibit the sinister counterfeiting of light by dark. At least part of the effect, however, depends on the echoes and reversals of the night-scene in Act I. In that earlier darkness we hear calls for lights and see lights, and real light shines forth; in this later night, we also hear calls for light and see lights—and the darkness increases. The second coming of chaos is almost complete.

It is possible to ignore the symbolic extensions of times of action, properties, and apparently commonplace words. But it is not wise to do so. For to take everything at a flat, literal level is to miss imaginative interconnections which help to set

forth—more, are essential in—the total meaning of the play. To ignore the dark-light symbolism is to miss, above all, the careful preparation for one of the finest speeches in the play, the lines with which Othello opens the final scene. The scene is a bedchamber; Desdemona is asleep; and Othello comes in to kill her. ('This is the night' Iago has said a few lines earlier, closing the scene before.) But his entrance is more than an entrance; he comes in—the last such entrance in the play—'with a light' [s.d. V. ii. 1], the one way best calculated to announce immediately the irony of this scene, by reminding us not only of other like scenes but of the pattern of meaning that orders them all. Here we have a final version, quite different from the others, of the man seeking truth in the midst of darkness. (pp. 328-33)

Othello's light enters directly into the language of the scene—into those affecting lines which help bind together all the parts of the light-dark pattern. First he notices Desdemona's skin 'whiter . . . than snow' [V. ii. 4]. He will not mar it; yet she must die. Then his attention turns to the light:

> Put out the light, and then put out the light.
> If I quench thee, thou flaming minister,
> I can again thy former light restore,
> Should I repent me; but once put out thy light,
> Thou cunning'st pattern of excelling nature,
> I know not where is that Promethean heat
> That can thy light relume.
>
> [V. ii. 7-13]

Othello's words have a primary significance in which the literal and the metaphorical are strikingly juxtaposed—the literal extinction of a lamp, and the metaphorical extinction of life. But in the total play what must impress us still more is a secondary or metaphorical-symbolical significance. For this is the climax of the clash of dark and light which has gone on from the beginning. To put out the light is not only to end a life; it is also to snuff out the good and the true, to end love, to give a victory to what is dark in life. The irony of it is that, in the terms of the story, the dark need not win; the black may become fair, and light can prevail against the power of darkness. But these transformations are not inevitable; man is fallible and may destroy the fair; he may mistake the Iago darkness for light and—put out the true light. Thus he may become an agent of darkness—or, as Emilia called Othello, a 'blacker devil'.

There is an exciting suggestion in the last lines of Othello's light passage: 'I know not where is that Promethean heat / That can thy light relume.' There is a little more here than the literal reference to Prometheus. The Promethean suggests the titanic, immense struggle, agony. These are the terms in which the light may be relumed—not the light of individual life alone, but, in the terms created by the play, the light of truth which sustains the quality of life. In tragedy the light is relumed; in this tragedy, through Othello's agony of recognition and unhesitant penance. Once he sees that what is needed to define the situation is 'a huge eclipse / Of sun and moon' [V. ii. 99-100], he is on the way to distinguishing light and dark. By reaching insight, he becomes fair again; and the dark recedes. (pp. 333-34)

Robert B. Heilman, "More Fair than Black: Light and Dark in 'Othello,'" in Essays in Criticism, *Vol. I, No. 4, October, 1951, pp. 315-35.*

WINIFRED M. T. NOWOTTNY (essay date 1952)

[*Nowottny contends that Shakespeare intended to portray in* Othello *the fundamental incompatibility of love and rational, objective justice, and she postulates that the opposition of these principles, together with the opposition of "belief in 'evidence' and belief in the person one loves," forms the basis of the structural unity of the play. Asserting that Desdemona represents bounteous, generous love, while Othello places a greater value on justice, the critic maintains that throughout the play—especially in Act III, Scene iii—Shakespeare expresses his belief that love is inherently miraculous and, therefore, not subject to the process of rationally evaluating evidence and dispensing justice. Because the Moor is ruled by justice and reason and lacks faith in Desdemona's love for him, Nowottny claims, he is incapable of rejecting Iago's insinuations, which can be countered only by an irrational act of faith. Further, the critic avers that throughout Act IV Othello is shown in search of a "symbolic act" which will resolve the conflicting emotions and principles at war in his soul, and she examines the way in which the murder of Desdemona serves as this symbolic gesture. Closely analyzing Othello's soliloquy at the beginning of Act V, Scene ii, Nowottny discovers in these lines the Moor's contemplation of his seemingly contradictory impulses: to serve the cause of justice by punishing Desdemona, to expiate her alleged guilt, and—because he continues to love the "ideal image" of her—to "possess" her once again. She concludes that this speech is constructed and patterned on the play's central conflict between justice and love. For additional commentary on Shakespeare's representation of the nature of love in* Othello, *see the excerpts by Hermann Ulrici (1839), Derek Traversi (1949), Kenneth Burke (1951), Robert B. Heilman (1956), John Bayley (1960), Susan Snyder (1972), and Jane Adamson (1980). Jared R. Curtis (1973) has disputed Nowottny's claim that the play demonstrates that love and reason are antithetical. For further discussions of whether Othello is motivated to kill Desdemona by justice or honor, see the excerpts by the anonymous critic in the* Bee *(1791), Samuel Taylor Coleridge (1813 and 1822), Hermann Ulrici (1839), G. G. Gervinus (1849-50), Denton J. Snider (1887), A. C. Bradley (1904), Elmer Edgar Stoll (1915), G. M. Matthews (1964), and Carol McGinnis Kay (1983).]*

It is a commonplace of criticism of *Othello* that the Moor, entering in Act V to the murder of Desdemona, sees himself as a minister of Justice. It is apparent that this act is full of references to judgment and of images drawn from it. Yet it is usually assumed that this is but an additional turn of the screw, a means of throwing an even more lurid light on Othello's crime against the innocent Desdemona. It is the purpose of this article to put the case that the insistence on justice in Act V of *Othello* is the culmination to which the drama as a whole is designed to lead, and moreover that a fuller perception of the excellence of the dramatic economy will follow upon the recognition that Shakespeare intends in this play an evaluation of justice in its relation to love.

In *Othello* jealousy is treated as a state in which man experiences the opposition of two kinds of belief—belief in "evidence" and belief in the person one loves—and the opposition of the value of justice (as he conceives it) to the value of love. What is tragic in *Othello* derives from these oppositions. The character of Othello serves but to bring them on; jealousy is the stage on which they stand forth. For in jealousy of this nature and magnitude, justice and love, which in other situations may be conceived of as parallels, meet. It is therefore no accident that *Othello* is full of allusions to justice and of metaphors drawn from it, since, in the jealousy of Othello, the value of justice and the value of love become openly contestant and reveal their essential incompatibility. The trend of the play becomes clear when one considers the difference between two judgments Othello makes, the one on Cassio:

> Cassio, I love thee;
> But never more be officer of mine,
>
> [II. iii. 248-49]

the other on Desdemona: "I kiss'd thee ere I kill'd thee" [V. ii. 358]. The judgment on Cassio can be made, though reluctantly, yet without personal conflict, by subscribing to the idea that justice and love are compatible values; but the judgment on Desdemona is preceded by the personal experience of the conflict of those values, and represents a decision between them.

It is possible to argue that the contention of love and justice begins, in this play, with Brabantio's attempt to bring love under the law, from which attempt it follows that the quality of Othello's and Desdemona's love is declared in a kind of trial scene. Brabantio's accusation and the subsequent inquiry might, it is true, be dismissed as being no more than a means of providing for the necessary exposition of what has gone before. Shakespeare's intentions in this matter are debatable: it could be that the excellence of the device for expository purposes was the whole of his reason for adopting it, or it could be that he saw this device as being "fit not only to advance the action of a special plot and to exhibit certain traits in particular characters, but also to prompt in an audience's mind a special vein of semiconscious comment or a special mood of reverie about certain general ideas" [C. E. Montague, "The Literary Play"]. But whatever we make of Brabantio, we cannot deny significance to Cassio's part in illuminating Othello's attitude to justice and love, since Shakespeare uses him, in III, iv, to point a clear contrast between Othello's attitude to these two values, and Desdemona's. In this scene Cassio asks Desdemona to intercede for the rescinding of Othello's judgment upon him, and weighs his chances of reinstatement in Othello's love:

> If my offence be of such mortal kind
> That nor my service past, nor present sorrows,
> Nor purposed merit in futurity,
> Can ransom me into his love again. . . .
>
> [III. iv. 315-18]

In contrast to this reference to Othello's hierarchy of values, in which justice stands higher than love, there follows Desdemona's reflection on the "unkindness" of Othello and then her immediate penetration of her own absurdity in submitting love to the processes of judgment and thereby constituting herself simultaneously plaintiff, witness, suborner, and judge:

> Beshrew me much, Emilia,
> I was, unhandsome warrior as I am,
> Arraigning his unkindness with my soul;
> But now I find I had suborn'd the witness,
> And he's indicted falsely.
>
> [III. iv. 150-54]

The full development of this theme does not come until Act V, but there Othello and Desdemona play exactly the same roles, he as Justice, she as Love:

> EMIL. O, who hath done this deed?
> DES. Nobody; I myself. Farewell:
> Commend me to my kind lord: O, farewell! . . .
> OTH. She's, like a liar, gone to burning hell:
> 'Twas I that kill'd her.
> EMIL. O, the more angel she,
> And you the blacker devil!
>
> [V. ii. 123-25, 129-31]

This theme, made explicit in Act V, is implicit in all that leads to Act V. In particular, it shapes the treatment of Iago and Othello in Act III. For the very setting of the stage for conflict, the creation of the situation which brings it about (Iago's temptation of Othello) is done in terms of the differing processes pertaining to judgment and love, and emphasizes the difference between the kind of belief relevant to the forming of judgments and the other kind of belief characteristic of love. Shakespeare chooses to make Iago's success depend upon the fatal interaction between two things: the weakness of testimony as such (which is Iago's strength), and the strength of love (which, fitted into the context of Iago, becomes its weakness). The first dialogue of the temptation falls into two parts, separated by Othello's long speech on jealousy [III. iii. 176-92]. In the first part Iago exploits the trickiness of testimony; in the second part he exploits the generosity of love; what is fatal to Othello is the conjunction of the two. It should be stressed that Shakespeare has taken this way of bringing about Othello's mistrust because it allows him to manifest in dramatic terms the pitfalls of reasoning about love and of admitting testimony against it. He shows the process of false testimony succeeding and specifically refers to the reasons why it is impossible to assess it. He posits an Iago entrenched in false opinion; he refers particularly to the impossibility of discriminating between true and false by considering the witness's manner; he shows how the very negatives of testimony can be converted into positives (as Iago, having no proof, makes capital of a feigned reluctance to speak); further, he points to the element of construction inseparable from testimony (when Iago protests that he "imperfectly conceits" the significance of his "scattering and unsure observance" and in so doing is able to divulge exactly what is in his mind). In short, Iago's testimony is strong in proportion as all testimony is weak; his tricks are possible because of the trickiness of testimony itself. Further, in Othello's speech of protest, Shakespeare adverts to the irony at the root of all these ironies: it is useless for Othello to say "I'll see before I doubt; when I doubt, prove" [III. iii. 190], since infidelity does not necessarily produce evidence of itself and fidelity cannot be put to the proof.

Othello's speech over, the dialogue enters its second phase, in which Iago makes capital of the generosity of love. The characteristic irony of this part of the dialogue is prepared for by Iago's words,

> I would not have your free and noble nature,
> Out of self-bounty, be abused; look to 't.
>
> [III. iii. 199-200]

It is precisely this self-bounty of love (both Desdemona's and Othello's) which he now proceeds to abuse. Desdemona's love had been strong enough to be its own conscience, and is therefore open to another verdict in another context:

> IAGO. She did deceive her father, marrying you;
> And when she seem'd to shake and fear your looks,
> She loved them most.
> OTH.   And so she did.
>
> [III. iii. 206-08]

Again, Iago's well-timed "My lord, I see you're moved," makes Othello answer, in loyalty to Desdemona, "I do not think but Desdemona's honest" [III. iii. 224-25]; he cannot, immediately upon that, challenge Iago for proof. Now, significantly, Othello takes the lead, because it is now the finest part of self-bounty (Iago is not fitted to understand it) which plays him wholly into Iago's hands. Desdemona's love had transcended all obstacles in a magnificent departure from ordinary "nature." It had baffled Brabantio by its unreason-

ableness. Othello in turn, in self-deprecation, makes the mistake of bringing it to the bar of reason:

> And yet, how nature erring from itself—
>
> [III. iii. 227]

He does not complete the thought, but its completion is apparent: nature, having left its course, might no doubt lose that fine exaltation and subside to its course again; it would be quite reasonable to suppose that Desdemona had ceased to love. Here for a moment Iago loses track of Othello and takes this to refer to "foul disproportion, thoughts unnatural" [III. iii. 233], but hastily covers up his mistake and achieves an approximation, though a base one, to Othello's thought:

> Her will, recoiling to her better judgement,
> May . . .
>   happily repent.
>
> [III. iii. 236-37, 238]

Othello dismisses him, but the mischief is done, as his soliloquy shows. (pp. 330-33)

[When] Desdemona enters, as Othello comes to the end of his soliloquy, Iago's edifice trembles:

> Desdemona comes:
> If she be false, O, then heaven mocks itself!
> I'll not believe 't.
>
> [III. iii. 277-79]

Immunity from jealousy would lie in the continuance of this simple act of faith. Othello cannot maintain this faith, but if he could, it would still be as non-rational as the jealousy from whose stigma some critics have been anxious to defend him. Shakespeare at this point deliberately forces upon the audience the question, In what strength could Othello reject Iago? The answer would seem to be, By an affirmation of faith which is beyond reason, by the act of choosing to believe in Desdemona. Shakespeare's point is that love is beyond reason. Desdemona's love for Othello has been made "unreasonable" in a way which permits discussion of it in the drama, as when Brabantio tries to bring it to the bar of reason and to punishment by the law, but Othello's race and strangeness (which constitute Brabantio's case) are after all only dramatic heightenings of a simple truism which it is Shakespeare's peculiar excellence to have thought remarkable enough for repeated dramatization: the truism that love, any love, is a miracle. Being a daily miracle, it is not often seen as miraculous; to arrive at that valuation of it costs something, as in *King Lear;* to fail to arrive at it costs more, as in *Othello.* With love, reason and justice have ultimately nothing to do. (pp. 334-35)

Shakespeare has already shown [in III. iii.] . . . that what Othello thinks of as uncertainty of mind is in reality an intolerable emotional tension which demands violent expression:

> I think my wife be honest and think she is not;
> I think that thou art just and think thou art not.
> I'll have some proof. Her name, that was as fresh
> As Dian's visage, is now begrimed and black
> As mine own face. If there be cords, or knives,
> Poison, or fire, or suffocating streams,
> I'll not endure it. Would I were satisfied!
>
> [III. iii. 384-90]

Here we have, first, Othello's attempt to interpret his conflict as uncertainty of mind, and his desire to end it (as he thinks he could) by proof. This counterfeit of the problem is followed immediately by the real problem, the two images of Desdemona: "fresh as Dian's visage"; "begrimed and black." From this tension of incompatibles springs the impulse to violence. With "Would I were satisfied!" he reverts to the illusion that proof will quiet that volcano whose raging we have glimpsed. The very form of this speech, enclosing within two patent rationalizations a reality of experience betrayed directly in imagery, shows that the inner conflict between two modes of belief about Desdemona is the heart of the matter and that Othello, in interpreting it to himself as uncertainty of mind, is simply providing the conflict with a surface rationalization. And it is the urgency of the conflict and of the resultant impulse to end it by violent action that explains Othello's snatching at Iago's lies about Cassio and the handkerchief: by so doing, he can turn the force of his emotions into the current of revenge. It is significant that the image in which he expresses his determination to be revenged (the image of the Pontic sea) contains the promise of release: he promises himself a revenge as "capable and wide" [III. iii. 459] as the Propontic and the Hellespont.

It is one of the finest strokes in the construction of the play that Shakespeare puts the vow of revenge before the test of the handkerchief. By so doing, he makes clear in the action what he has already suggested in the poetry: that the idea of revenge, though it seems to Othello to follow from what he now thinks of Desdemona and offers him the illusion of release from the conflict of his emotions, is not in fact Othello's whole bent. If he could unify himself by revenge, that would be one way out, but he cannot; the test of the handkerchief is a desperate attempt to unify himself in the opposite way—by having Desdemona prove that what Iago has said is false. Othello's description to Desdemona of the mystic nature of the handkerchief—

A sibyl . . .
In her prophetic fury sew'd the work;
The worms were hallow'd that did breed the silk;
And it was dyed in mummy which the skilful
Conserved of maidens' hearts—

[III. iv. 70, 72-5]

is not an irrelevance; he is in reality asking Desdemona to restore to him the sacredness of love. After the failure of this attempt, he is not seen until Act IV, and Act IV concentrates on showing the dreadful interim within Othello when the disjunction of his personality rages for expression and cannot find the means.

It is in Act IV that the nature of the action affords indisputable proof that Shakespeare has in this play a unified design which utterly transcends that concern for immediate theatrical effect which some critics would have us impute to him, for in this act "theatrical effect" is least satisfactory as an explanation of Shakespeare's choice of episodes. Othello falls in a fit; he strikes Desdemona in public; he goes to her as to a prostitute. If these things are chosen only for their immediate effect, the choice is extraordinary, for Act IV is, in itself, hardly to be borne. . . . [It] is wellnigh insupportable. Is not the reason that it is the inescapable outcome of Act III and, more important, the indispensable preparation for Act V, in that the intolerableness of Act IV is the means by which the audience is made to experience, like Othello himself, the necessity for release? The perfection of Shakespeare's art here consists in the economy by which he brings about this participation of the audience in the hero's tragedy: the violence in the action, which creates tension in the audience, is motivated within Othello himself by *his* tension, a tension which is the result of his failure in

Act III to unify himself either by the vow of revenge or by making Desdemona restore to him his undesecrated love. (pp. 337-39)

The episodes of Act IV manifest and communicate this tension by the dreadful spectacle of Othello's attempts to escape from it. The pitch rises as his ways of seeking relief draw, horribly, ever nearer to Desdemona and to the deepest intimacies of love. The falling in a fit is a temporary way of not bearing the tension. That, shocking as it is, affects only himself. The next way is the striking of Desdemona. His striking her in public (for in their private interview there is nothing of this) is a symbolic act: a calling the world's attention to the intolerableness of what he suffers by the intolerableness of what he does. The treating Emilia as a brothel-keeper is an expression of the division in him at its deepest level: to go to his wife as to a prostitute is to try to act out what the situation means to him. Already Othello is driven to symbolize his conflict in act—to seek actions that will express the impossible. But none of these things will serve. Othello is not seen full face again until, in Act V, he finds the perfect symbolic act: to kill, not in hate but in love.

The scene of the murder of Desdemona is a visible demonstration of the laws inherent in the process that led up to it. This is a drama of an error of judgment, the error being in the application of judgment to love. It is not, however, surprising, that the relation of Act V to all that goes before has been imperfectly seen, for the perception about human justice which Shakespeare laid down for himself to work by: as, that justice, however it is conceived of, cannot be executed in love; that love and justice differ in their natures, their processes, and their conclusions; that justice, though ideally conceived of as an expiating sacrifice or as the only cure for a wound in the fitness of things, may be, in its human origin and motivation, indistinguishable from man's need to find redress for what he cannot bear to find in human nature; that, finally, the man who accepts justice as the supreme value in life will, if he be wholly consistent, at last execute himself. I believe all these propositions to be implicit in the play. If their starkness should cause us to deny them or simply not to see that such questions arise, then Act V cannot be seen as the logical outcome of Acts I-IV. The fact that Othello perpetrates injustice in no way weakens the significance of Act V, for the play turns upon the conflict between justice and love, not upon the nature of justice itself. No aspect of Othello's experience of that conflict would have been different if Desdemona had in fact been false (though if she had been false, Othello's experience would have been incommunicable to an audience; the audience's participation in his conflict depends upon its having, as he has, two images of her—his image, and the truth).

In Act V, the significance is so entirely fused with the poetry and the action that it is only by faithful attention to these that we can rightly estimate what Shakespeare was about; this is sufficient reason for pondering every phase of the action, and all the meaning that the poetry carries, even at the risk of being thought to consider too closely or of being accused of attempting to explain poetry and genius.

First, then, let us consider the opening soliloquy of Act V, scene ii: "It is the cause, it is the cause, my soul . . ." [V. ii. 1ff.]. It is to our great loss that we let these words pass as some oracular utterance not susceptible of commentary. We may begin by inquiring what "cause" meant in Elizabethan English. It meant, first, the accusation or charge against someone, as in *King Lear* [IV. vi. 109-11], "What was thy cause? Adultery? . . . die for adultery! No.'' Secondly, in an even more specialized sense, it meant the matter about which a person went to law, or the case of one party in a suit. In a third sense, it meant the end in view or the object for which a deed is done. Or again, in a very pregnant sense, it meant good, proper, and adequate ground for action (as Cassio uses the word in "I never gave you cause" [V. ii. 299]). Which of these meanings does Shakespeare intend? He intends the first, the charge against Desdemona; he also intends the second, Othello's case against her; he intends the fourth, in that Othello thinks himself to have good, proper, and adequate ground for action; and indeed he also intends the third, the end to which the action shall be done. The end to which the murder shall be done is, simply, release from the whole agony. In the phrase itself, as in the action it refers to, Othello's complex attitude is unified: Desdemona is guilty and he has a case against her, but what he is about to do is to him an action just in every way, and what he is about to do has a purpose, the making of an atoning sacrifice which shall make all well. The word unites the personal, the social, and the religious aspects of justice, just as the killing is to answer every need of his nature that he recognizes: the need for punishment, for abstract justice, for the restoration of the ideal image of Desdemona by an atoning sacrifice, and, one might add, a need deeper than all these, the need to possess her again—for murder is now the only act of possession open to him.

Knowing how much "cause" means, we can now grasp the whole phrase, "It is the cause." Said thrice, it evidently has depth under depth of meaning for Othello; two ways, at least, in which the phrase has meaning, are apparent. First, it may be taken as the answer to the unspoken question, "What is it that makes me do this?"—"It is the cause." Secondly, the phrase may be interpreted as an utterance of recognition: "it" (the act of killing) "is" (is the same thing as) "the cause" (the whole state of affairs between us). In other words, Othello has found the act which corresponds to all he feels, though what he feels is a complex of opposites, for the act is symbolic; to describe that act he finds the word which means all that the act means, and the syntax which enables him to describe the act as being the same thing as all those opposites he feels, and therefore their expression, and therefore his release. The killing itself is in this sense symbolic: it is an act which stands for all the warring emotions pent up in Othello. These emotions are now fused in a calm of pure concentration on the symbolic act, an act which is the only possible way for Othello to express at once all that Desdemona means and all that he means. He has the exaltation of having struck a perfect equipoise. But what he is about to do would cease to be an all-embracing symbol if he defined its relevance to any one aspect of the problem: if he were to put the act into defining words, they would break up the symbol, for if the act is vengeance, it cannot be justice or atonement, and if it is any of these, it is not passion; and if it is not all of these, it is not release. Hence Othello's refusal to define:

> Let me not name it to you, you chaste stars!—
> It is the cause.
>
> [V. ii. 2-3]

Because of all that "cause" means to Othello, its real emotional meaning is "solution," and because the solution is simply, and as absolute symbol, the act of killing, there is no transition between those words, "It is the cause" and the next, "Yet I'll not shed her blood" [V. ii. 3]. It is as though he had said, "The solution is to kill, yet I'll not shed her blood." Then,

the moment he looks at Desdemona—at her skin as "smooth as monumental alabaster" [V. ii. 5]—he is forced to give himself a reason why he should destroy her: "Yet she must die, else she'll betray more men" [V. ii. 6]. As soon as *one* reason is given, the symbol begins to dissolve, and to stop the dissolution of his symbol, he must cease to see anything but that—and so, "Put out the light, and then put out the light" [V. ii. 7]. This again is an act of a purely symbolic nature; again he identifies in one action two entities objectively different but emotionally the same: Desdemona, and the light he extinguishes in order not to see her; indeed, it is as though the parallelism of the two acts constituted their logic. The blackness of the act is matched by the blackness in which alone it can be performed. Othello's state is one in which pattern and relationship take the place of reasoning. As in the parallel, "Put out the light, and then put out the light," so in the whole situation: that an act *fits* is the whole reason for its being done. To kill in love; to revenge by justice; to kill the guilty Desdemona for the honour of the innocent Desdemona, or to sacrifice the innocent Desdemona to atone for her guilt; to torture her because she has tortured him and to torture himself in torturing her—in all this it is the pattern that constitutes the logic, for it is the pattern of his feelings. It is moreover only through pattern and symbol (so tranced is his state) that he can consider the finality of his act:

> If I quench thee, thou flaming minister,
> I can again thy former light restore,
> Should I repent me: but once put out thy light. . . .
>
>   When I have pluck'd the rose,
> I cannot give it vital growth again. . . .
>
> [V. ii. 8-10, 13-14]

As if this achievement of expressing emotion through form were not sufficient, Shakespeare has all the while developed, within the tranced patterns of Othello's utterances, the great impersonal pattern of Justice and Love. It is in the growing intensity of Othello's realization of his continuing love, counterpointed by the growing compulsiveness of the sanctions of justice which he must allege to outdo it, that Shakespeare expresses the major conflict of the drama. Faced by the fact that love continues, even in this extremity, Othello is driven to urge higher and higher the claims of that justice which shall destroy it. Justice has already been called in under its aspect of safeguard of society: "Yet she must die, else she'll betray more men." Love persists. Justice is then called in as an abstract ideal. Love, still, can almost persuade her to break her sword, and hints that the threatened act of destruction is at heart the act of possession, of plucking the rose. Justice, in a final terrifying aggrandisement, claims the ultimate possible sanction, the sanction of love: ". . . this sorrow's heavenly; It strikes where it doth love" [V. ii. 21-2]. The process is complete. Justice overrides love by presenting itself as love. In this parallel ascent, where the claims of justice rise with the claims of love, Shakespeare has manifested their tragic contestation, and through the form of the poetry he has shown how the act of killing is related at one level to the tension of opposites in Othello and at a deeper level to the fundamental and eternal opposition of justice and love.

Desdemona wakes. So must Othello. He had thought to strike in heavenly sorrow; he strikes with "Down, strumpet!" From the height of his intention to the depth of the execution the descent is inevitable: at no point in the dialogue could Desdemona's plea for life produce effects other than it does, for the issue of love against justice is settled now; there must inevitably rise up, within Othello's temple of sacrificial justice, the asseverating wrathful self, accusation and self-vindication streaming from its lips:

> O perjured woman! thou dost stone my heart,
> And makest me call what I intend to do
> A murder, which I thought a sacrifice.
>
> [V. ii. 63-5]

It is indeed only the executioner who fully knows the resistance of the sacrificial victim. In human justice as it is commonly ordered the executioner need not question the motive of the judge, nor the judge question his own. With Desdemona, Othello is judge and executioner; he is also plaintiff, and the only possible witness for the defence. In him justice confounds itself by the concentration of all its persons in one, and in being so confounded by unity, throws into relief the indivisible and unconfounded unity of love.

There remains the revelation of the truth. Justice now comes into its own. . . . Othello has killed Desdemona for betraying their love; he kills himself for the same reason. He surveys his life, judges it, passes sentence, and executes it, as long ago he did in Aleppo:

> Where a malignant and a turban'd Turk
> Beat a Venetian and traduced the state,
> I took by the throat the circumcised dog
> And smote him, thus.
>
> [V. ii. 353-56]

Othello's death is perfectly consistent with his life. From first to last, he is the judge. (pp. 339-44)

> *Winifred M. T. Nowottny, "Justice and Love in 'Othello'," in* University of Toronto Quarterly, *Vol. XXI, No. 4, July, 1952, pp. 330-44.*

S. L. BETHELL   (essay date 1952)

[*Bethell contends that the frequent images of diabolism and damnation in* Othello *are used by Shakespeare to underscore the themes of "deceitful appearance" and damnation in the play. He identifies three levels in the drama: the personal one of the tragedy of Desdemona and the Moor; the social, depicting the attempts by Iago—representative of the "atheist-Machiavel"—to destroy the chivalric Othello; and the metaphysical, dramatizing the conflict between the forces of "Good and Evil" in* Othello. *Bethell argues that the metaphorical references to devils and damnation have significance only with respect to the second two levels. Maintaining that all the prominent dramatic characters initially appear to be what they are not, Bethell demonstrates that the action of the play traces the gradual enlightenment of these figures in discerning between appearance and reality until, at the close of the drama, "good and evil are seen for what they are." Robert B. Heilman (1951) has also claimed that the difficulty of distinguishing between appearance and reality is one of the central thematic interests of the play. Bethell further argues that Shakespeare intended to represent Othello as remorseful but unrepentant at the conclusion of the play—guilty not only of the sins of jealousy and murder, but also of suicide. For further commentary on whether Shakespeare represents Othello as purged of his sins or facing eternal damnation, see the excerpts by Kenneth O. Myrick (1941), Harley Granville-Barker (1945), Paul N. Siegel (1953), Irving Ribner (1955 and 1960), Edward Hubler (1958), G. M. Matthews (1964), and Roy W. Battenhouse (1969). Bethell agrees with A. C. Bradley (1904) that Iago is chiefly motivated by the need for self-aggrandizement and is guilty of the sins of "Pride and Envy," and he postulates that, in depicting Iago as atheistic and Machiavellian, Shakespeare sought to demonstrate that this "new man" of the Renaissance would prove to be a destructive force*

in society, unconsciously assisting "the Devil in his constant effort to reduce cosmos to chaos." For further discussions of the connection between Iago and Machiavellianism, see the excerpts by E. K. Chambers (1908), Wyndham Lewis (1927), and Allardyce Nicoll (1927), as well as the essay by Thomas Babington Macaulay cited in the Additional Bibliography.]

[How] are we to understand the great number of diabolic images in *Othello?* They are related closely to Iago, but in what way? I do not think that there is any Elizabethan convention by which the Machiavel or atheist is presented in such terms. . . . In *Othello* those employed by Iago himself are capable of naturalistic explanation up to a point. We might find credible the character of an evil man who, though an unbeliever, likes to dwell on that aspect of religion which fills others with dread and to model himself upon a Devil in whom he does not objectively believe. Alternatively, we could accept Iago as a 'practical atheist', one who lives by an atheistic code without making any deliberate intellectual rejection of religion. There are many such. If this were so, his enjoyment of the devilish might colour his language without implying either belief or disbelief. If naturalistic consistency of character is desired, I suppose that either of these readings might supply it. But Shakespeare leaves us small leisure for such speculation when we are watching *Othello.* What he does, however, is to assail our ears with diabolic imagery throughout, and by no means only in the speeches of Iago. A naturalistic solution is not quite impossible. Accepting either of the naturalistic explanations given above for Iago's use of this sort of imagery, we might argue that the other characters as they come into the circle of his influence take over his forms of expression. But would any Elizabethan, even Shakespeare, entertain such a notion—or even conceive such a character as either of the 'naturalistic' Iagos I have projected? Since . . . Shakespeare's method was fundamentally conventional, there is no need to accept a fantastic naturalistic explanation if a plausible conventional explanation lies to hand.

I shall argue that the diabolic imagery is used to develop poetically an important underlying theme. Of the sixty-four diabolic images in *Othello* not one occurs in Cinthio's *novella.* . . . Shakespeare [added] considerably to the number of religious images in the sources of *Macbeth* and [sharpened] those that were already there, so as to develop poetically a theological theme. Is it not likely that when he introduced a similar type of imagery into *Othello* it was with a similar purpose? There is a steady increase in the use of diabolic imagery from act to act, which looks like thematic development. The figures for each act are, respectively, ten, eleven, thirteen, fourteen, sixteen. I shall outline what I believe to be the general function of this imagery in *Othello* and then consider its operation in detail.

Othello can be interpreted on three levels, the personal, the social and the metaphysical. In *Lear* and *Macbeth* these three levels are so closely interrelated that it is impossible to make sense of the personal or story level without taking the others into consideration. In *Othello* the interrelationship is less complete: the story can be considered alone, with the result that the other elements often remain unnoticed. Unfortunately without them the story itself is liable to misinterpretation. On the personal level we have a straightforward domestic tragedy—Cinthio's *novella,* in fact, with modifications. On the social level we have a study of a contemporary problem, the clash between the 'new man' thrown up by certain aspects of Renaissance culture, the atheist-Machiavel with his principle of pure self-interest, and the chivalric type, representing the traditional values of social order and morality. That Iago is more intelligent than Othello reflects the usual ambivalence of Shakespeare's judgement. On the metaphysical level we see Othello and Iago as exemplifying and participating in the age-long warfare of Good and Evil.

These various planes of meaning coalesce into something like unity. It appears that to Shakespeare Cinthio's ensign suggested *(a)* the contemporary atheist-Machiavel, and *(b)* the Devil himself. It seems to follow that Shakespeare thought of the 'new man', with his contempt for traditional morality and religion, as a disintegrating force seeking to break down the social order that is a part of cosmic order—as, in fact, an instrument (no doubt unconscious) of the Devil in his constant effort to reduce cosmos to chaos. This would be a very natural attitude for a conservative Elizabethan, and to express this attitude is one main function—a general function—of the diabolic imagery in *Othello:* Iago is a "demi-devil" [V. ii. 301], worse than an ordinary devil, a bastard one, and his philosophy is a "divinity of hell" [II. iii. 350].

But Shakespeare's metaphysical interest is not wholly absorbed in the social issue. The problem of good and evil is also presented for itself and in much the same terms as we are familiar with from modern interpretations of *Macbeth*. L. C. Knights has drawn attention to the theme of "the deceitful appearance" in the later play. Good and evil are so readily confused by fallen humanity: "Fair is foul, and foul is fair" [*Macbeth*, I. i. 11]. "There's no art", says Duncan, "To find the mind's construction in the face" [I. iv. 11-12]. This same theme of deceitful appearance runs its course right through the tragedies from *Hamlet* with its smiling villain to the final statement of *Macbeth*. In *Lear* Cornwall suspects Kent of being a sort of Iago:

> These kind of knaves I know, which in this plainness
> Harbour more craft and more corrupter ends
> Than twenty silly ducking observants
> That stretch their duties nicely.
> [*King Lear*, II. ii. 101-04]

I do not think that the ramifications of deceitful appearance in *Othello* have ever received comment. Of course there is Iago—"honest Iago" [II. iii. 177], who is in truth a "hellish villain" [V. ii. 368] but only so revealed at the end of the play. Cinthio's ensign is described as *di bellissima presenza* [of the most beautiful appearance], a fact which actors would do well to note, for Shakespeare surely intended Iago to have this beautiful exterior, since it fits so well with his other arrangements for 'deceit'. His hero, Othello, is a black man, as calculated, in those times, to inspire horror as Iago to inspire confidence. It was well known that the Devil frequently appeared in the form of a black man to his worshippers. "There's no art To find the mind's construction in the face." Contrary to a 'Neoplatonic' doctrine much entertained at the time, Othello and Iago are in appearance the exact opposite of their natures. Ironically enough, they both agree at one point that "men should be what they seem" [III. iii. 126, 128]. Why, again, is Michael Cassio a Florentine? There is nothing in Cinthio to that effect. The Florentines were noted for their fine manners, a quality displayed by Cassio: "'tis my breeding That gives me this bold show of courtesy" [II. i. 98-9]. Florence was also known as the birthplace of Machiavelli and a special degree of subtlety seems to have been ascribed to his fellow-citizens. Cassio is an exception. His exclamation upon Iago, "I never knew A Florentine more kind and honest" [III. i. 40], has several layers of irony and reveals his own simplicity, which is evident also

in the drunken scene. Expectation is again disappointed. Even Desdemona deceives expectation: though a Venetian, she is not a "cunning whore" [IV. ii. 89] as Othello was led frantically to believe. The cunning whores of Venice were well enough known to Elizabethan England: "the name of a Cortezan of Venice is famoused over all Christendome", says [Thomas] Coryate in his *Crudities*. An Elizabethan audience might have expected fickleness in her, not chastity. Yet, though she "deceived her father", a point which is stressed [I. iii. 293; III. iii. 206], and tells a white lie about the handkerchief, she is the most innocent of all deceivers, dying with a noble lie upon her lips: "Nobody; I myself" [V. ii. 124]. Emilia with her materialistic code ought to be a fitting wife for Iago, but her cynical professions conceal a golden heart—which is what Iago pretended about himself. Deceitful appearance thus characterizes all the main figures in *Othello*. Where is the evil one? Who is true and who is false? The play is a solemn game of hunt the devil, with, of course, the audience largely in the know. And it is in this game that the diabolic imagery is bandied about from character to character until the denouement: we know the devil then, but he has summoned another lost soul to his side.

It begins with Iago. In his opening speech he refers to Cassio as "a fellow almost damn'd in a fair wife" [I. i. 21]. We know nothing of the wife and I do not find much significance in the phrase, except as an example of Iago's perversion of values. Perhaps Shakespeare originally intended to introduce Cassio's wife into the plot but omitted her on deciding to use Bianca. "Damn'd" is not important here—I shall try to avoid the image-hunter's fallacy of treating all similar images as equally significant in spite of their context. A more interesting remark occurs shortly afterwards: "I am not what I am" [I. i. 65]. Iago expresses his policy of Machiavellian deceit in a parodied negation of the Scriptural words in which God announces his nature: "I am that I am" (Exodus iii. 14). His own diabolic nature is implied. I do not think that a point such as this is too obscure for an Elizabethan, bred on the Bible and trained in verbal wit, to have apprehended at a first hearing, especially if the actor knew what he was saying. Now comes the calling-up of Brabantio; Othello must be plagued with flies [I. i. 71]. . . . Iago warns Brabantio that "the devil will make a grandsire" of him [I. i. 91]. In the same passage Othello is "an old black ram" [I. i. 88]. Iago thus begins the 'devil-black man' reference which perhaps runs in Brabantio's mind later. The audience, not having listened to Othello yet, might be a little dubious about him. Almost at the same time, however, Iago takes the name of devil to himself: "you are one of those that will not serve God, if the devil bid you" [I. i. 108-09]—it is jocular, and meaningful only in the light of later developments. Its immediate value is that of iteration; the audience is being repeatedly assailed with the idea of the diabolic. A similar value, and no more, attaches to Iago's confidence to Roderigo: he hates Othello as he does hell-pains [I. i. 154]. Brabantio, perhaps inspired by Iago's language earlier accuses Othello: "Damn'd as thou art, thou hast enchanted her" [I. ii. 63]—the black man and black magic naturally falling together. But Othello has an opportunity of showing his true nature, first in preventing bloodshed and afterwards in his speech before the senate. The first endeavour to make a devil of the black man fails to convince the Duke and his senators and leaves the audience persuaded of his high character. No "practices of cunning hell" [I. iii. 102] have been employed. Desdemona "saw Othello's visage in his mind" [I. iii. 252], the sensible converse of popular 'Neoplatonic' theory; her love was unconstrained. So the Duke pronounces Othello "far more fair than black'' [I. iii. 290], putting aside the deceitful appearance. Iago has suffered an initial defeat, but we hear him in good spirits rallying Roderigo: ''If thou wilt needs damn thyself, do it a more delicate way than drowning'' [I. iii. 353-54], hammering again on the theme of damnation. He calls on his ''wits and all the tribe of hell'' [I. iii. 357], and the Venetian scenes close with an ominous couplet:

> I have't. It is engender'd. Hell and night
> Must bring this monstrous birth to the world's light.
>
> [I. iii. 403-04]

On the shore at Cyprus Iago has a chance to vent his cynicism in the guise of entertainment. Women are ''devils being offended'', he says [II. i. iii], but the description would apply more appropriately to himself. There is a moment of high poetry when Othello and Desdemona meet after their safe passage through the storm:

> O my soul's joy!
> If after every tempest come such calms,
> May the winds blow till they have waken'd death!
> And let the labouring bark climb hills of seas
> Olympus-high and duck again as low
> As hell's from heaven! If it were now to die,
> 'Twere now to be most happy.
>
> [II. i. 184-90]

The tragic tempest does indeed drive Othello's bark from heaven to hell; if he had died then in Desdemona's arms he would have been most happy. We move from exalted verse to the flat prose of Iago. What delight shall Desdemona have ''to look on the devil?'' [II. i. 226]. The 'devil-black man' equation is revived for Roderigo's benefit. Cassio, too, is explained to be ''a devilish knave'' [II. i. 244-45]. The limit of Cassio's devilry is reached the same night when he becomes successively possessed by ''the devil drunkenness'' and ''the devil wrath'' [II. iii. 296-97]. Iago must have smarted under Cassio's eschatology: ''there be souls must be saved, and there be souls must not be saved'' [II. iii. 103-04] and ''the lieutenant is to be saved before the ancient'' [II. iii. 109-10]. But he maintains his usual composure, no doubt taking comfort in the thought of the lieutenant's imminent downfall. Cassio, deprived of his rank, exclaims against drunkenness: ''Every inordinate cup is unblessed and the ingredient is a devil'' [II. iii. 307-08]. ''Come, come, good wine is a good familiar creature, if it be well used'' [II. iii. 309-10], says Iago reasonably, having just used it himself for a purpose devilish enough. Iago, it has often been observed, dominates the three night scenes; he is a Prince of Darkness and enjoys them thoroughly. Perhaps Shakespeare took a moment's thought before giving him the one appropriate exclamation as the bell rings out: ''Diablo, ho!'' [II. iii. 161]. The second act ends as he concocts ''divinity of hell'':

> When devils will the blackest sins put on,
> They do suggest at first with heavenly shows,
> As I do now.
>
> [II. iii. 351-53]

Cassio was not a serious candidate for diabolic honours. His penitent self-accusations, the fact that he feels himself to have been possessed because he has been drunk and disorderly, serve merely to demonstrate the daily beauty of his life [V. i. 19]. He has behaved badly, Iago apparently well. But the audience know the truth. Shakespeare has staged a pretty contrast between the apparent sinner and the hypocrite. Iago has not so far shared the stage very much with Othello, but we now pass to the main action, in which the handsome villain and his

hideous but noble dupe stand together in the eye of the audience; fair face and black soul, black face and fair soul in double contrast. Desdemona is to become a devil to Othello, that Othello might become a devil in fact.

> Perdition catch my soul,
> But I do love thee! and when I love thee not,
> Chaos is come again.
>
> [III. iii. 90-2]

This is weighty irony at the turning-point of the play. When he loves her not, chaos does come again, his life is disintegrated, and perdition catches his soul. The Devil's aim, we remember, is to reduce order to its primal chaos once more. There is a microcosm-macrocosm parallel behind the image. Iago now goes to work to arouse Othello's jealousy:

> O, what damned minutes tells he o'er
> Who dotes, yet doubts, suspects, yet strongly loves!
>
> [III. iii. 169-70]

It would be wrong to make anything of the frequent association, in this play, of hell and damnation with sex. Heaven is equally expressed in terms of sexual love. The association is due merely to the particular dramatic medium. The war of good and evil is fought out in this intimate domestic field, just as in *Macbeth* the battleground is a kingdom and the most important relationships are political. Iago is duly warned: ''If thou dost slander her . . . nothing canst thou to damnation add Greater than that'' [III. iii. 368, 372-73]. When he is half convinced of Desdemona's infidelity, Othello exclaims at the thought of it: ''Death and damnation!'' [III. iii. 396]. It is more than an oath. He loses his heaven with his faith in her. Iago takes up the theme: ''damn them then, if ever mortal eyes do see them bolster . . .'' [III. iii. 398-99]. At the end of the scene, Othello, fully persuaded, thinks of Desdemona as a devil while he confers upon Iago the coveted promotion:

> Damn her, lewd minx! O, damn her!
> Come, go with me apart: I will withdraw,
> To furnish me with some swift means of death
> For the fair devil. Now art thou my lieutenant.
>
> [III. iii. 476-79]

''Fair is foul, and foul is fair.'' Bemused by passion, Othello falls into the deep deceit of taking good for evil and evil for good.

At this point we can see how the study of imagery illuminates character problems, even when the imagery is not used for differentiation between characters. Iago is so strongly associated with the diabolic that we are justified in interpreting his character in terms of demonology. All his stated motives may be genuine, but the deepest, as Bradley saw [see excerpt above, 1904], is the desire to plume up his will [I. iii. 393]. He is mastered by the sins which caused the angels to fall, Pride and Envy. He has already acquired, when the play opens, an habitual evil which is expressed in opposition to whatever is good and beautiful. Destruction is the only form of self-assertion left to the proud and envious. The diabolic imagery and the aura it casts about Iago cause the insinuation of jealousy into Othello to take something of the form of a temptation and fall. At bottom Othello's sin is the sin of Adam (as in [John Milton's] *Paradise Lost*): he allows passion to usurp the place of reason. On the night of the brawl he felt passion assaying to lead the way [II. iii. 207]. But Othello was expert in the command of soldiers; he never really lost self-control and so remained in control of the situation. In domestic affairs he was less expert; he had not formed habits of prudence and discretion in a way of life that was new to him. So passion had its way, in the form of jealousy, and like the Pontic sea [III. iii. 453] rushed on blindly to its end. He is to seek swift means of death for Desdemona, whom he sees as a "fair devil". The fair devil, however, is at his side. "I am your own for ever", says Iago [III. iii. 480], but it is Othello who has handed his soul into Iago's keeping. Confused by passion, Othello is on the devil's side without knowing it. Or perhaps he does know in part, for he has already called up "black vengeance from the hollow hell" [III. iii. 447].

With a totally false view of her nature, Othello finds "a young and sweating devil", in Desdemona's palm [III. iv. 42]. The importance of the handkerchief is underlined, for the audience as well as Desdemona:

> To lose't or give't away were such perdition
> As nothing else could match.
>
> [III. iv. 67-8]

"Perdition catch my soul": the handkerchief is central to the plot, and "perdition" to the argument. For a while the devil makes sporadic and rather casual appearances, important only because they keep the word dinning in the audience's ears. Iago compares a cannon to the devil [III. iv. 136]; Cassio bids Bianca throw her vile guesses in the devil's teeth [III. iv. 184]. The fourth act opens with a more serious passage:

> Naked in bed, Iago, and not mean harm!
> It is hypocrisy against the devil:
> They that mean virtuously, and yet do so,
> The devil their virtue tempts, and they tempt heaven.
>
> [IV. i. 5-8]

Ironic because, in spite of his morality, the devil has tempted Othello's virtue and he has fallen—into the sin of jealousy. When Othello drops down in a fit, his last words are "O devil!" [IV. i. 43]. Iago continues to play upon him:

> O, 'tis the spite of hell, the fiend's arch-mock,
> To lip a wanton in a secure couch,
> And to suppose her chaste!
>
> [IV. i. 70-2]

(Bianca keeps up the theme for the audience: "Let the devil and his dam haunt you" [IV. i. 148].) At this stage Othello thinks continuously of Desdemona as a devil or damned soul; this is the measure of his spiritual blindness, his enslavement by Iago: "Ay, let her rot, and perish, and be damned to-night" [IV. i. 181-82]. His exclamations in the presence of Lodovico show how the thought has taken possession of his mind: "Fire and brimstone!" [IV. i. 234]; then, as he strikes her, "Devil!" [IV. i. 240]; and immediately after, "O devil, devil!" [IV. i. 244]. This phase reaches its height in the terrible scene in which he treats Desdemona as a whore and her chamber as a brothel. Emilia, protesting her mistress's innocence, calls down "the serpent's curse" [IV. ii. 16] on the hypothetical beguilder of Othello, but alone with his wife he bids her swear her innocence and damn herself [IV. ii. 35],

> Lest, being like one of heaven, the devils themselves
> Should fear to seize thee: therefore be double damn'd:
> Swear thou art honest.
>
> [IV. ii. 36-8]

He is fully alive to the deceitful appearance; only he ascribes it to the wrong person: "Heaven truly knows that thou art false as hell" [IV. ii. 39]. Even Patience, the "young and rose-lipp'd cherubin" must "look grim as hell" upon her fault [IV. ii. 63-4]. When he summons Emilia again it is as portress of hell [IV. ii. 91]. The connexion with *Macbeth* is not irrelevant. The Devil is at work in Desdemona's chamber, not in the way Othello imagines but as surely as in the castle of Macbeth and with as bloody an outcome.

There is now a lull in the diabolic imagery except for another outburst of Emilia against the unknown villain who has poisoned Othello's mind. When Desdemona prays "If any such there be, heaven pardon him!" she retorts: "A halter pardon him! and hell gnaw his bones!" [IV. ii. 135-36]. The irony of this, spoken in her husband's presence, is strong enough to link up with the denunciations of Iago later. Act IV, scene iii, the 'willow' scene, has no diabolic images, for Shakespeare is a master of decorum. It is more remarkable that Act V, scene i, Iago's last nocturnal scene of devilish activity, should produce only one reference of this kind, when the dying Roderigo recognizes the truth at last: "O damn'd Iago! O inhuman dog!" [V. i. 62]. The murder of Desdemona is carried out, again appropriately enough, without any diabolical imagery: it is a moment for sympathy, not moral judgment. Thus between Othello's departure from Desdemona's chamber after the 'brothel' incident and Desdemona's last words to Emilia from her deathbed there are only two instances of diabolic imagery. In addition to the matter of local propriety this lull prepares very effectively for the continuous torrent of such imagery with which the play closes.

Hitherto the diabolic images have been frequently misapplied—to Othello in his innocence, to Cassio, to Desdemona. Now, immediately after Desdemona's death, the last misapplication is made and corrected. The same sort of images, with all the accumulated force of those that have gone before, will serve to give point and metaphysical depth to the denouement.

> *Oth.*   She's, like a liar, gone to burning hell:
>   'Twas I that kill'd her.
> *Emil.*   O, the more angel she,
>   And you the blacker devil!
> *Oth.*   She turn'd to folly, and she was a whore.
> *Emil.* Thou dost belie her, and thou art a devil.
>
> [V. ii. 129-33]

The formal stichomythia brings out the central importance of the passage. Desdemona quite certainly is angel, not devil, and she has gone to heaven. The imputation has passed from her to Othello, who this time can worthily sustain it. The black man is, after all, a devil: he has earned the title. He himself, however, still believes in the justice of his cause:

> O, I were damn'd beneath all depth in hell,
> But that I did proceed upon just grounds
> To this extremity.
>
> [V. ii. 137-39]

His illusion is soon to be done away. Emilia challenges Iago and, when he maintains Desdemona's guilt, roundly accuses him of telling "an odious, damned lie" [V. ii. 180]. Othello, not yet believing her, attempts to justify himself to Gratiano, whose only reply is to invoke Desdemona's father, now dead:

> did he live now,
> This sight would make him do a desperate turn,
> Yea, curse his better angel from his side,
> And fall to reprobation.
>
> [V. ii. 206-09]

It is to have that effect upon Othello.

Meanwhile the master devil must be identified:

> Let heaven and men and devils, let them all,
> All, all, cry shame against me, yet I'll speak,
>
> [V. ii. 221-22]

says Emilia. When Iago's deceitful appearance has been penetrated at last, there is an end of the game. The devil stands revealed. This is sufficiently emphasized. "O cursed slave!" says Othello [V. ii. 276], and later:

> I look down towards his feet; but that's a fable.
> If that thou be'st a devil, I cannot kill thee.
>
> [V. ii. 286-87]

Iago, wounded, accepts the imputation with what seems like vindictive satisfaction: "I bleed, sir; but not kill'd" [V. ii. 288]. Montano calls him "damned slave" [V. ii. 243], and Lodovico has a variety of epithets of the same type: "damned slave" [V. ii. 292]; "damned villain" [V. ii. 316]; "hellish villain" [V. ii. 368]. But Othello's "demi-devil" [V. ii. 301] is the most appropriate. Prospero explains the term as he applies it to Caliban: "For he's a bastard one" [*Tempest*, V. i. 273]. Iago has not quite the stature of a devil, for the devils *believe* and tremble.

As for Othello, he too has become willy-nilly of the Devil's party:

> when we shall meet at compt,
> This look of thine will hurl my soul from heaven,
> And fiends will snatch at it.
>
> [V. ii. 273-75]

This sounds definite enough, like a statement for the audience. The description of the torments of hell which follows seems to express not only Othello's present state of mind but his future fate:

> Whip me, ye devils,
> From the possession of this heavenly sight!
> Blow me about in winds! roast me in sulphur!
> Wash me in steep-down gulfs of liquid fire!
>
> [V. ii. 277-80]

In this speech he takes an eternal farewell of his heavenly Desdemona. Emilia's words have come home to him:

> This deed of thine is no more worthy heaven
> Than thou wast worthy her.
>
> [V. ii. 160-61]

His suicide, since he is a Christian, seals his fate. . . . We may feel "the pity of it" [IV. i. 196], but the Elizabethans had a harder view of eschatology than is common to-day. After all, to the Middle Ages and to the century after the Reformation it seemed likely that the majority of people would go to hell. And the Elizabethans knew their ascetic theology: Othello shows no sign of penitence, only of remorse, which is another thing. How different is the behaviour of Leontes [in *The Winter's Tale*] when he awakens from his jealous dream. Leontes prepares for a lifetime of penitent devotion, whereas Othello, self-willed to the last, commits the final sin of taking his own life. Shakespeare is no narrow moralist, and Cassio finds the motive for Othello's suicide in his greatness of heart [V. ii. 361]. But Shakespeare was no sentimentalist either: even the great of heart might commit irrevocable sin. There is no contradiction between the feeling of sympathy and a recognition of objective justice in the Elizabethan mind. In *Othello*, as in all Shakespeare's plays, the deceitful appearance is torn away at the end: good and evil are seen for what they are; and, though one soul be lost, good will triumph and order be restored. "Cassio rules in Cyprus" [V. ii. 332] and

> To you, lord governor,
> Remains the censure of this hellish villain.
>
> [V. ii. 367-68]

I would not have it thought that, in proposing three levels of interpretation for Othello and in crediting Shakespeare with a considerable consciousness of what he was about, I intend to countenance any allegorizing of the incidents. The three levels coalesce into one; the deeper meanings, social and metaphysical, are directly applicable to the human story and necessary for a full understanding of its purport. The diabolic images we have considered do not carry us away from the characters into a world of metaphysical speculation in which they have no part. Rather they serve the true purpose of poetic drama, to show the underside, as it were, of ordinary life. It is precisely in such sordid and—to the outsider—trivial domestic quarrels that the Devil is busiest. Shakespeare usually works as a romantic, raising his audience to the cosmic significance of his theme by setting it in remote ages and in the courts of kings. In *Othello* he goes differently to work, showing that the old war of Good and Evil has its centre everywhere, not least in the private household. (pp. 70-9)

S. L. Bethell, "Shakespeare's Imagery: The Diabolic Images in 'Othello'," in Shakespeare Survey: An Annual Survey of Shakespearian Study and Production, Vol. 5, 1952, pp. 62-80.

Act III. Scene iv. Othello and Desdemona. By H. Fradelle. The Department of Rare Books and Special Collections, The University of Michigan Library.

G. R. ELLIOTT (essay date 1953)

[*In* Flaming Minister (1953), *his book-length analysis of* Othello, *Elliott offers a scene-by-scene examination of the play, proposing that the prime mover of the dramatic action is not Iago but the Moor himself and that* "wrong pride as distinguished from right self-esteem" *provides the principal thematic interest. In the following excerpt from the preface to that work, he maintains that Shakespeare's portrayal of the sin of pride forms the basis for the play's dramatic structure, identifying Othello's prideful refusal to reveal to anyone but Iago the reasons for his suspicions as the fundamental cause of the tragic consequences. Arguing that Iago comprehends neither profound love nor profound hatred and is thus unprepared for the violence of Othello's jealousy, Elliott judges his responsibility for the tragedy to be much less than such critics as Samuel Taylor Coleridge (1808-18) and A. C. Bradley (1904) have assigned him; he contends that Cassio's accountability is as great as Iago's, for by importuning Desdemona's assistance in regaining the lieutenancy he unwittingly contributes to Othello's jealousy. Further, the critic asserts that at the beginning of the drama Othello and Desdemona's love for each other is limited, in that each perceives and loves only partial aspects of the other, with Othello enamoured of her outward graces and Desdemona loving an idealized image of his nature. Worse, Elliott adds, each fosters an excessive pride in certain aspects of their respective loves—Desdemona in her belief that she knows her husband completely, Othello in his conviction that their love is perfect, although he admits that he knows little of the real Desdemona. Other commentators who have discussed Othello's pride or egoism include F. R. Leavis (1937), Derek Traversi (1949), Roy W. Battenhouse (1969), and Carol McGinnis Kay (1983). Additionally, Elliott's thesis that* Othello *deals specifically with the distinctions between excessive pride and normal concern with reputation is shared by Brents Stirling (1956), John Arthos (1958), and Madeleine Doran (see Additional Bibliography). Elliott further maintains that at the conclusion of the drama Othello and Desdemona's love has grown to such an understanding that they are truly "wedded in spirit," and he avers that when Othello comprehends at last, after Desdemona's death, her incomparable character and her love for him, the process which began in Act I reaches its culmination; according to the critic, at this point Othello's "wrong pride" is "entirely destroyed" and he attains a "new humility." Other critics who have maintained that Othello gains a deeper awareness of himself and his love for Desdemona by the end of the drama include G. Wilson Knight (1930), E. M. W. Tillyard (1938), G. M. Matthews (1964), Jared R. Curtis (1973), and Helen Gardner (see Additional Bibliography); also, see Elliott's earlier excerpted essay (1937) for further commentary on this point. Finally, Elliott's contention that although* Othello *is, indeed, a domestic tragedy, it is infused with broader religious implications by virtue of its portrayal of the violent conflict between deity and nature may be compared with similar assessments offered by Kenneth O. Myrick (1941), S. L. Bethell (1952), Paul N. Siegel (1953), Irving Ribner (1955 and 1960), and Roy W. Battenhouse (1969). For an opposing view of the play as strictly a domestic romance, see the excerpt by Harry Levin (1964).*]

In old times, pagan and Christian times, pride—wrong pride as distinguished from right self-esteem—was regarded as the worst of all evils and the central source of tragedy in human life and art. The reasons are obvious enough. Pride fixes us where we are, preventing growth of spirit and initiating decay; it is deadly. Traditionally it is the one unforgivable sin, hopelessly affronting God or the gods or supernal law. In other words pride is the essence of all spiritual evil: the insulation of oneself from that which is supremely real in life; the self's refusal of a truer and larger vitality for the self. Pride is therefore not merely *a* sin: it may rightly be regarded as synonymous with sin itself; at any rate it is Sin capitalized. It makes all sins or faults capital by establishing them as unconfessed obstacles to growth. It nullifies our so-called divine dissatisfaction, the human humility essential to human development. Hence it is not merely immoral, in the ordinary or puritan sense of that term, a naughtiness denounced professionally by ancient saints and sages. It is the perennial deadly enemy of humanity, the adversary, the "Satan," opposed to right fulness of human life. (p. xiii)

In the Renaissance the subject of human pride was outstanding. For on the one hand the age-old tradition of the deadliness of pride was fully alive. Conspicuous in the pages of the pagan classic authors, now being freshly studied, it had been immensely reinforced by medieval Christianity: it was a main theme in the Christian humanism that was predominant in art and literature from the thirteenth to the seventeenth century. On the other hand modern pride was rising. Men were inflated by the great discoveries and creations, including the new natural science, though this was still subordinate, that were being achieved by European man. Thus there was a deep-going conflict in the Renaissance spirit. The extraordinary development of man was engendering a pride that was bound finally to undermine, as it has now patently done, that very development. But in the chief creative minds of the time the classic and Judeo-Christian tradition was thoroughly alive: it was not a mere moral convention (as it became in the eighteenth century), but a fresh and vital experience. The greatest thinkers, artists, and poets of the Renaissance *knew* that humility before the Highest was the *sine qua non* of true human growth. And that vital experience of "high humility" in conflict with the new and vivid rise of human pride is a central source of the poetry, and especially the drama, of the Renaissance. (pp. xvi-xvii)

Renaissance tragedy including Shakespearean tragedy is the tragedy of pride. Indeed there is no such thing as *Shakespearean tragedy*, in any deep and inclusive sense, apart from the motif of pride. Consider the extreme contrast between the first and last of the main tragedies: *Hamlet*, so humanely various and charming, and *Coriolanus*, so very univocal and harsh. They might well have been written by two different authors: actually modern criticism has conceived them as written by two very different Shakespeares, i.e. Shakespeare in two utterly diverse states of mind. But in fact the two plays have a central theme in common: right self-esteem turning into wrong pride. And that is the main theme, more or less, of Shakespeare's tragic and semitragic plays from the beginning to the end of his career. . . . Of course Shakespeare's tragic protagonists are highly individualized; each has his own particular values and defects. But the values center in self-esteem and the defects in wrong pride: the defects are rendered *essentially* tragic by, and only by, the pride. The *motives* in Shakespearean tragedy are many, various, and fascinating: its *motif* is pride. (p. xix)

Pride is comical in proportion as it is a minor constituent of vanity, conceit, arrogance, and the like; but wherever it is present in the slightest degree it is potentially disastrous. It is tragic in proportion as it concentrates and erects itself "before high heaven." But since it is always fantastic it is always potentially comic: the Shakespearean smile flickers ever, no matter how remotely, in the background. When pride is utterly catastrophic it could make heavenly (and dramatic) charity laugh if it did not make it "weep." That is the situation preeminently in *Othello*. This story, more than any other of Shakespeare's stories, made very extreme demands upon both his charity and his art. And he met those demands with triumphant success. The general conviction that this play is Shakespeare's greatest achievement in tragidramatic *form*, whatever its deficiencies in other respects, means really that it is his main drama of pride.

Incidentally it is in a broad sense his most Christian drama. Christian believers discern that Shakespeare was a Christian believer; unbelievers believe that he was not. The former are wrong when they find an explicit theology in his work; the latter, when they assert that no theology at all is implicit there. At the least it is certain that the Shakespearean drama is based on the Judeo-Christian conviction, held also by leading pagan thinkers and artists, that *reality* is not monistic but has three distinct (not separate) levels: deity, man, and nature. This conviction underlay Renaissance art and literature as a whole; it was essential to their great dramatic quality. It provided those utmost contrasts which Shakespeare and his fellow playwrights, in England and elsewhere, sought when their art was most intense. The clash in man between the divinely magnanimous and the diabolically brutish was both ultimately real and intensely dramatic. The triform constitution of life and being is in Shakespeare not a dogma: it is, like charity, one with his art. And it is the source of that cogent cosmic atmosphere in his tragedies which modern criticism has tended to regard as merely imagistic, and to eliminate entirely in the case of *Othello*. This play has been regarded as peculiarly domestic and mundane, giving us a sense of "confinement to a comparatively narrow world" [see excerpt above by A. C. Bradley, 1904]— a view incompatible, really, with our belief that Shakespeare's tragic art is in this play supreme. But in fact, . . . the cosmic implications are no less potent in *Othello* than elsewhere because less obtrusive. Indeed God and nature are the more intensively at strife here just because that strife is extraordinarily *domesticated*. (pp. xxiv-xxvi)

The chief cause of Othello's downfall is not his jealousy but the fact that he conceals it from all concerned—except his evil other self, Iago—by reason of his pride. That is the main point of this story; but also the whole pattern of the play turns upon pride. With the exception of Emilia all persons who take any decisive part, even the least, in the main action are in one way or another, and in varying degrees, actuated by pride. Most obvious is the case of Brabantio. In the beginning the old man's violent imperiousness (later to be developed fully in Lear) blasts open, so to speak, the drama's underlying vein of pride. At the opposite pole is the surreptitious arrogance of Iago, displayed to us at the start and at the close of the first act in his dialogues with Roderigo, whose foolish vanity has in it a stiffening touch of pride. In the second act Roderigo and incidentally the complacent Montano help to bring into the foreground a personage who from here to the end—with the aid in Act IV of the humorously proud Bianca—plays a leading part in the tragic action: the chivalrous and charming but proudly, and fatefully, conceited Cassio.

Critics have taken at its face value that young gentleman's complacent remark at the close when he learns of Othello's murderous plot against him: "Dear general, I never gave you cause" [V. ii. 299]. But in fact he had given cause of a very weighty sort. He is possessed of that resonant sense of honor, in certain respects excellent but always questionable and sometimes very wrong, that Shakespeare along with the other dramatists of the time, notably Beaumont and Fletcher, took delight in dramatically criticizing. To spectators normally aware, as the Elizabethan audience was, of the crookedness of pride Cassio's procedure must appear crooked in the extreme. His curious sense of honor prevents him from honorably confessing to his general his luckless fit of drunkenness. Infinitely worse

than that transient insobriety is his fixed intoxication with his honor, his outward repute. This gentleman's improper and very compromising suit to Desdemona is as ungentlemanly, in reality, as it could possibly be. Its sexual purity throws into relief its spiritual impurity, its motive of selfish, blinding pride. Cassio becomes what he unconsciously instigates his best friend, Othello, to be: an excellent gentleman who submerges his better will in a monomaniacal, pride-inspired dream. Romantic tradition to the contrary, Cassio is no less important than Iago as a factor in the tragedy.

But the critics have taken Iago, too, at his word, agreeing with his reiterated claim that the action of the play is mainly the product of his mighty mind. They have missed one of Shakespeare's finest strokes of art, the dramatic contrast, along with likeness of function, between Othello's two friends: Cassio smugly certain, in his refined fashion, that nothing of the catastrophe is due to him; Iago smugly certain, in his coarse way, that all of it is his doing. Moreover, criticism has been visibly embarrassed by the seemingly strange fact that Shakespeare chose to make his major villain also a remarkable buffoon. Explanations of this phenomenon have been many and various. The real point is that Iago's pride is at once very evil and very ludicrous; he is "like an angry ape . . . before high heaven" [*Measure for Measure*, II. ii. 120-21]; and the chief of his "fantastic tricks" is his assumption of intellectual omnipotence. His very acute thinking is, from the standpoint of normal humanity, extremely shallow and often apishly, or asininely, so. That which renders him in the upshot more tragic than absurd is his proud, devilish hate; especially . . . his largely subconscious hatred of Desdemona.

Yet his hate is shallow too in comparison with the "loving hate" [*Romeo and Juliet* I. i. 176] that rises more and more in the breast of Othello, like a billow from the dark cosmic deeps. Iago, devoid of love, is incapable of profoundest hate and has no real understanding of it. Not in the least does it enter into his calculations in the first two acts. And when in the opening of the Temptation scene (III. iii) he incites the Moor's suspicions, with the blind aid of Cassio, he is *just as unconscious as Cassio is* of stirring in their master something far deeper than conventional jealousy: a terrific passion of loving hate or hate-full love. When Iago later in the scene becomes, with surprise and dismay, aware of that passion in Othello he sets himself to foment it. And from then on he believes with increasingly fantastic conceit that he is the creator and absolute controller of it—while the great tide of it sweeps him, along with his master, to his doom. Iago is as simple in his way as Cassio is in his—over against Othello, who, despite the current notion to the contrary, is profoundly complex.

In *Othello* as in Shakespeare's other chief plays the whole design is germinally present in the first act, where, significantly, Iago's active part in the plot is extremely slight. The love of Othello and Desdemona, coming to the fore in the central part of that act, is radiant and harmonious over against the dark background, social and personal, of proud, equivocal, warring intentions. At the same time, however, the dramatist with amazing art makes us feel that the two principals are closely related to the atmosphere surrounding them. Though Othello is not a barbarian and Desdemona far from typical of civic society, they are nevertheless as contrary to each other in their own mode as the Turks and Venetians are in theirs. And the impending warfare that prevents the consummation of their hasty marriage—in modern phrase, a war marriage— adumbrates the fact that the hero and heroine, despite their surface concord, are not wedded in spirit. In basal character, far more than in body and circumstance, they are militantly though tacitly different from each other.

They are opposites in the essential nature of their loves. This veiled but fundamental contrast can be grasped only through a fresh study of Act I. . . . [Neither] of the two, while pure and devoted, sees and loves the other's *whole being*. Othello loves too outwardly, Desdemona too inwardly. He loves all of her except her very self; she thinks she loves all of him in the light of his very self, but her light is too partial. Each loves an image of the other that is true so far as it goes but fearfully inadequate. In general the situation, like that of young Romeo and Juliet, is human and typical: the heroine is the eternal feminine in love, direct and self-giving; the hero, the eternal masculine, romantic and self-involved. But here the situation is extreme and tragic. Desdemona, humble in love, is far from meek in her confidence that she entirely knows Othello; and we feel that if he should turn against her she may (as she does in the second half of the play) become proudly obstinate in refusing to confront the real grounds of the crisis. Still more ominous is the initial bearing of Othello. His pride, entirely justified in his military vocation, goes wrong in his new vocation of love. Considerably aware that his *knowledge* of his wife is deficient, he is *totally* unaware that his *love* for her is far more so, and that this defect is a fateful barrier to an inward knowing of her. In the first act he is serenely (later, dreadfully) confident of the faultlessness of his love for her.

Othello's blind pride-in-love is the central cause of his jealousy and of his wicked concealment of it. In the first half of the play he hides from himself, but reveals to us (*not* to Iago), his growing sense that his wife's devotion *unlike his own*—that is the fatal core of his delusion—is innately infirm. Hence the violence with which his repressed suspicions erupt in the course of the third act. But far more tragic is his violent and yet successful effort, inspired and sustained by pride, to cloak from Desdemona the causes of his fury while trying to make her confess her own supposed sin. Thus he is caught in a hellishly vicious circle. The more he dissembles the more he is sure that she is doing likewise: his refusal to tell the truth prevents him from learning the truth. His diabolic pride far surpasses Iago's: the hero of the play becomes the chief officer and exponent of "hell" [III. iii. 447; IV. ii. 64, 92]. In the fourth act, so much greater and more crucial than the third, Othello's pride is both highly fantastical and deeply tragic. And Desdemona in her great misery learns a new humility: she undergoes a conversion that prepares for the conversion of her husband in the play's final scene. (pp. xxvii-xxxii)

That scene is the dramatic acme . . . of the conversion motif so marked in the literature of the Renaissance, and so foreign to the spirit of humanitarian rationalism. The violent changes of heart evinced by many personages in Elizabethan drama seem very unnatural to the modern reader. In general, however, they exemplify a very human trait: the liability of pride to maintain itself to the last minute and then collapse swiftly, as in Othello. Anticipations and echoes of his case appear in Shakespeare's earlier and later dramas, notably in *Hamlet* and *Measure for Measure, Lear* and *Coriolanus*—Angelo's story reads like a forestudy for the Moor's. But all comparisons serve to throw into relief the spiritual profundity and consummate art of the catastrophe of *Othello*. The "burning hell" [V. ii. 129] of pride, shadowy in the first act, glaring in the fourth, flames out horribly in Othello's repudiation of his dying wife's forgiveness. But soon, at first slowly, then rapidly, that hellish flame subsides—overcome by the heavenly fire, the "flaming minister" [V. ii. 8], of humble love.

Desdemona's love, not completely sacrificial until the end, works upon her husband after her death with the wonderful aid of poor Emilia. Othello goes through a great transformation that appears on the surface precipitous; but actually the process of it began with the beginning of the drama. There Brabantio's treatment of him initiated a series of ever-increasing humiliations. To these the great man reacts with increasing pride— but also, under the surface, with increasing love. Unawares his devotion to the real Desdemona deepens with his hatred of the unreal Desdemona of his imagination, the false image created by his proud and jealous but "great . . . heart" [V. ii. 361]. There is a "soul of goodness" [*Henry V*, IV. i. 4] in his evil hate. He rightly hates, though he does so with dreadful self-righteousness, all the evil he identifies with his wife, while he loves all the more what he wishes she were, and what we know she really is. In the end she surpasses, awfully, the best that he was able to wish and conceive: *that is his crowning humiliation*. So finally he learns with seeming suddenness what "Heaven" [IV. ii. 47] all along has been schooling him in: the utter humility of true and full love. His wrong pride—not his right self-esteem . . .—is as entirely destroyed as the murderer, i.e. himself, whom the justice of love, far more than earthly justice (though this too is a motive), requires him to execute. And his new humility prevents him from seeing what we see: his love, gradually growing and now freed from its egoism, corresponds intimately, in the end, to his wife's love of him. Her love, now so "heavenly" [V. ii. 135, 278], has condemned his sin but has clung to and lifted him. Through death of pride-in-love he and she, strangely and outwardly married in the first act, are at the last wedded in spirit.

Othello is thus a true, and sublime, love tragedy—not a true-love romance with a tragic ending brought about chiefly by a heavy villain. It is *Romeo and Juliet* matured and recomposed. In writing the earlier play Shakespeare was aware, though not deeply aware, that the tragedy of love, when supreme, is also the tragedy of hate. In *Othello* those two passions, comparatively superficial in all his previous stories, are intensified to the uttermost and deeply interwoven. And the atmosphere is at once tense and cosmic. In *Romeo and Juliet* the cosmic touches are pure and bright; in *Antony and Cleopatra*, spacious and picturesque. In *Othello* the air is compressed cosmic fire. Lucent and dusky flames intermingle; foul things stir and move in lurid darkness; bright gleams and flashes, as from great jewels, come and go in chaos: the "black" fire of "hell" [III. iii. 447] tries to smother, but in the end serves to enhance, the striving "heavenly light" [IV. iii. 65 f.]. Universal meanings are not obtruded: they are uniquely implicated here in the common stuff of life. Love, our chief and daily good, working throughout this play in a closely woven pattern of all its main guises—sexual, parental, filial, friendly, duteous, vocational, patriotic, religious—appears as potently ruinous in proportion as it is tainted with our chief evil, the subtly self-disguising demon of pride; which can be conquered only by that same love religiously purged and transfigured. *Othello* is Shakespeare's, and surely the world's, supreme *secular* tragic poem of "human love divine." (pp. xxxii-xxxiv)

G. R. Elliott, "Introduction: On Pride, Renaissance Tragedy, and the Design of 'Othello'," in his Flaming Minister: A Study of "Othello" as Tragedy of Love and Hate, *Duke University Press, 1953, pp. xiii-xxxvi.*

PAUL N. SIEGEL   (essay date 1953)

[*Asserting that* Othello *is not a religious allegory per se, Siegel maintains nevertheless that Christian elements in the play are dramatically important, for they lend "symbolic force" to the action, enhance the significance of the human drama, and would have suggested to Shakespeare's first audience the susceptibility of all "sons of Adam" to ensnarement by Satan. Othello's wrong choice between "Christian love and forgiveness and Satanic hate and vengefulness"—that is, between Desdemona and Iago—in Act III, Scene iii leads him to perdition, the critic contends, and this election is repeated in the final scene of the play. Noting that at the beginning of Act V, Scene ii Othello means to take Desdemona's life not out of revenge but as an act of justice, Siegel contends that her repeated denials of wrongdoing so enrage him that his mood becomes "vengeful" and that, at the moment he denies her the opportunity to pray for her salvation and kills her, "Othello's soul is lost." According to the critic, the Moor's final soliloquy before he slays himself reveals that he knows that he is eternally damned and understands at last the value of his loss. Such other critics as Kenneth O. Myrick (1941), Harley Granville-Barker (1945), S. L. Bethell (1952), Irving Ribner (1955 and 1960), Edward Hubler (1958), G. M. Matthews (1964), and Roy W. Battenhouse (1969) have also discussed whether Shakespeare represents Othello as eternally damned or purged of his sins at the close of the play. Further, like Kenneth Burke (1951), Siegel regards Desdemona as a Christ-like figure, particularly in Act IV, Scene iii, where she rejects Emilia's temptation to sin herself, choosing instead to return "good for evil" by patiently accepting her humiliation. Regarding Iago, Siegel assesses the character as symbolizing the incarnation of evil itself, arising from hell to evoke the destructive force of malevolence in Othello's nature; but he also points out that Iago's "values cannot triumph," for Desdemona remains chaste and faithful to her husband until her tragic end. In 1957, Siegel included a modified version of this essay in his* Shakespearean Tragedy and the Elizabethan Compromise. *In this later work, he compares Othello's "overwhelming sense of guilt without faith in the mercy of God" at the close of Act V and his suicide to the conduct of Judas, who was also guilty of "the heinous sin of despair." This comparison was later developed by Roy W. Battenhouse (1969).*]

Of Shakespeare's four great tragedies the Christian overtones of *Othello* have been least apprehended. Critics have seen in it a noble soul caught in the toils of a diabolically cunning being, who tempts him to doubt the divine goodness of one in whom he has absolute faith, but they have failed to see the symbolic force of the characters and the action. For the Elizabethans, however, the noble soul of Othello, the diabolic cunning of Iago, and the divine goodness of Desdemona would not have had a loosely metaphoric meaning. Desdemona, who in her forgiveness and perfect love, a love requited by death, is reminiscent of Christ, would have represented Christian values; Iago, who in his envious hatred and destructive negativism is reminiscent of Satan, would have represented anti-Christian values. The choice that Othello had to make was between Christian love and forgiveness and Satanic hate and vengefulness. When he exclaimed [III. iii. 447-49], "Arise, black vengeance, from thy hollow cell! / Yield up, O love, thy crown and hearted throne / To tyrannous hate," he was succumbing to the devil, and, like all men who succumb to the devil, his fall was reminiscent of that of Adam.

Elizabethans were habituated to regard human action in terms of such analogy. In the homilies Adam's choice in disobeying God and Christ's choice in sacrificing Himself to redeem mankind were presented again and again as setting a basic pattern for our conduct. Writing for an audience accustomed to think analogically and to regard the history of humanity as a repeated illustration of the truths of the Bible story, Shakespeare implied the great Christian scheme of things in the pattern of events of a specific action, appealing to the poetic imagination rather than outlining it in detail, as the morality plays do. *Othello* is not a retelling of the story of man's fall in allegorical form; it is a drama of human passion which is given deeper significance by the analogies that are suggested in the course of its action. Its characters are lifelike individuals who can be profitably analyzed in the manner of A. C. Bradley [see excerpt above, 1904], but, in following the old pattern of temptation, sin, and retribution, they recall the archetypes of erring humanity, divine goodness, and diabolic evil. (p. 1068)

Like Adam, who was made to question the justice of God's injunction, [Othello] has been made to question Desdemona, who is "heavenly true" [V. ii. 135], and, like Adam, he loses an earthly paradise. After a storm at sea he had come to the island of Cyprus to find Desdemona miraculously waiting for him. The island-citadel of which he was to be governor with Desdemona at his side was his harbor, the blissful end of his life's voyage as the soldier of a maritime state. But there was a serpent in his Eden. There was truly need for the "grace of heaven" [II. i. 85] which Cassio had called upon to encircle Desdemona when she landed upon Cyprus. Even as Othello and Desdemona are voicing the exquisite harmony of their ecstatic love, Iago is expressing with Satanic malice at the sight of the happy pair his intention of destroying that harmony: "O you are well tuned now! / But I'll set down the pegs that make this music, / As honest as I am" [II. i. 199-201].

The loss of his paradise makes Othello, like Adam, the prey of his passion. He had been a commanding personage, grand, self-contained, dignified, "the noble Moor whom our full senate / Call all-in-all sufficient . . . the nature / Whom passion could not shake" [IV. i. 264-66]. His acceptance of Iago's view wrenches him apart and looses the passions which gush forth from within him. . . . Othello contained within himself the utmost potentialities for good and evil. In his greatness and his weakness he showed the possibilities of human nature. That a man of his nobility could fall as he did was a terrifying reminder of the fall of Adam, the noblest of men, and of man's subsequent proneness to soul-destroying sin.

The moment of his kneeling to vow vengeance is the moment of Othello's giving himself over to Iago. "Do not rise yet," commands Iago [III. iii. 462]. He kneels side by side with Othello and vows to be at his service in "what bloody business ever" [III. iii. 469]. The oaths that the two exchange are as horrifying in their solemnity as Faustus' oath: it is a pact with the devil that Othello has made. "I am your own for ever" [III. iii. 480], replies Iago in the last words of the scene. Iago becomes Othello's Mephistopheles, and in making the devil his servant Othello gives himself up into his power.

Like Faustus, however, Othello cannot rest easily in his pact. As he thinks of Desdemona's sweetness, his vengefulness gives way to poignant regret. Each time he voices this regret, however, Iago reminds him of his dedication to revenge—"Nay, you must forget that," "Nay, that's not your way" [IV. i. 180, 186]—and each time Othello is called back to his purpose, only to lapse once more into tender reminiscence. "O! she will sing the savageness out of a bear" [IV. i. 188-89], he exclaims, and for a moment it seems that Desdemona's divine virtues will triumph, that the angelic harmony of her nature will quell the storm within Othello. But Iago overcomes the influence of Desdemona, as the bad angel overcomes the influence of the good angel in the moralities; he rouses Othello's jealousy and sense of outraged honor so that, accepting the drama of Iago's contriving as reality, he goes through with his assigned role of the Italian husband, who was notorious for revenging himself by such means as the hiring of bravoes to kill the gallant and by secret wife-murder. His promise to abide by his vow—"Ay, let her rot, and perish, and be damned tonight; for she shall not live" [IV. i. 181-82]—is a re-affirmation of his pact with the devil which brings him closer to his doom: he himself will be damned that night in the murder of Desdemona.

When Othello comes to kill Desdemona, he does so in the exalted mood of being about to render justice, not to perform revenge. And this justice is to include clemency. Desdemona is to be given the opportunity to pray and ask for heaven's forgiveness [V. ii. 31-2]: "I would not kill thy unpreparèd spirit; / No; heaven forfend! I would not kill thy soul." But the soul that he is about to kill, the divine light that he is about to quench, is his own. In the mood of elevated pity in which he offers Desdemona the opportunity to confess her misdeeds lies Othello's last hope for escaping damnation. "This sorrow's heavenly" indeed [V. ii. 21]. When he says "amen" in reply to Desdemona's "Then Lord have mercy on me," Desdemona cries, "And have you mercy too!" [V. ii. 57-8]. But Othello cannot call up from within him the forgiveness of Christ and, forgetting the Lord's Prayer and Christ's injunction (Matt. vi. 15), "If ye forgive not men their trespasses, neither will your Father forgive your trespass," loses his own claim to God's mercy. When Desdemona denies having been unfaithful to him, his rage is re-kindled: "O perjured woman! thou dost stone my heart, / And makest me call what I intend to do / A murder, which I thought a sacrifice" [V. ii. 63-5]. In his oscillation of feeling he is back to the vengeful spirit in which he had told Iago [IV. i. 182-83], "My heart is turned to stone; / I strike it, and it hurts my hand." No more does he speak of "justice" but of his "great revenge." Desdemona is now not "sweet soul" but "strumpet." When she entreats, "But while I say one prayer" [V. ii. 83], he refuses her what he believes to be the opportunity for salvation which he had previously offered her and stifles her, saying, "It is too late" [IV. ii. 83]. At this moment Emilia pounds on the locked door to tell Othello of the attempted assassination of Cassio, who, escaped from death, can help the truth be revealed, but it is indeed too late: Othello's soul is lost. The noise only makes him hurry the killing of Desdemona. (pp. 1069-71)

The moment he gets his revenge it turns sour. Emilia enters to inform him that Cassio is alive, and Othello exclaims: "Not Cassio kill'd! then murder's out of tune, / And sweet revenge turns harsh" [V. ii. 115-16]. As if to emphasize his words comes Desdemona's cry: "O, falsely, falsely murder'd!" [V. ii. 117]. When she takes upon herself, however, the guilt for her death, Othello, in his bitterness at what he believes to be her final lie, asserts that he killed her and, defending himself against Emilia's charge that Desdemona was "heavenly true" and that he is "a devil," affirms his certitude in words that confirm his damnation: "O, I were damn'd beneath all depth in hell, / But that I did proceed upon just grounds / To this extremity" [V. ii. 137-39]. And when the truth is finally revealed to him, he realizes that he is indeed damned, that in killing Desdemona he had rejected her divine goodness and cast away, as he says in his final speech, a pearl worth more than all the world, losing his soul. Crushed by the sight of Desdemona lying pale on the white marriage sheets, the symbol of her purity, he calls to be transported to hell at once:

> O ill-starr'd wench!
> Pale as thy smock! when we shall meet at compt,
> This look of thine will hurl my soul from heaven,
> And fiends will snatch at it . . .

> Whip me, ye devils,
> From the possession of this heavenly sight!
> Blow me about in winds! roast me in sulphur!
> Wash me in steep-down gulfs of liquid fire!
>   [V. ii. 272-75, 277-80]

His last words, however, are not those of heartbreak or of self-torture. Spoken with the resolution of one who knows his irrevocable fate and with the regret of one who knows the preciousness of what he has lost, they act as a valediction summing up for us the pathos of the ensnarement of this noble nature.

Bradley calls *Othello* . . . "the most painful of all tragedies." If my reading is accepted, it becomes more painful still and indeed may seem to modern readers intolerable. But, although the "tragic waste" of which Bradley speaks . . . becomes greater, the feeling of reconciliation is also heightened. For the victory of Iago is seen to be, like all victories of the devil, a pyrrhic victory. Although he triumphs over Othello, it is at the same time demonstrated that his values cannot triumph. His view of reality is false: Desdemona is pure. She remains heavenly true to Othello, although the cynically worldly Emilia lightheartedly suggests that she revenge herself by cuckolding her husband. "Wouldst thou do such a deed for all the world?" asks Desdemona [IV. iii. 67]. We are reminded of Christ's rejection of the temptation to possess the world. "Marry, I would not do such a thing for a joint-ring," Emilia replies, "nor for measures of lawn, nor for gowns, petticoats, nor caps, nor any petty exhibition; but, for the whole world,—why, who would not make her husband a cuckold to make him a monarch? I should venture purgatory for 't" [IV. iii. 72-7]. Although she is speaking jestingly to divert her mistress, it is clear that Christ's words (Mark viii. 36) "What shall it profit a man to gain the whole world and lose his soul?" have no great significance for her.

This is Desdemona's temptation scene, the counterpart of Othello's temptation scene, as Bradley calls it. Unlike Othello, she does not follow her preceptor's ethic of revenge; she obeys the vow she had made, kneeling in the presence of Iago as Othello had kneeled to vow hatred and revenge, that she would continue in her love and devotion for Othello no matter what he does to her. In doing so she follows the Christian ethic of returning good for evil, accepting ill treatment as a discipline enabling her to grow in virtue: "Good night, good night: heaven me such uses send, / Not to pick bad from bad, but by bad mend!" [IV. iii. 104-05]. Desdemona's suffering, says Bradley . . . , is "the most nearly intolerable spectacle that Shakespeare offers us." It is indeed deeply painful; what makes it tolerable is that as a result of this suffering she is able to reach heights of love and sacrifice that enable her to transcend it. The words in which she accepts her misfortune echo the centuries-long praise of adversity as a teacher of Christian patience and as a means by which we attain the "felicitie or perfytte good which is god" and are guided by "the loue of God," which "kepyth the world in due order and good accorde" and "knytteth together the sacramẽt of wedlocke, with chast loue between man and wyfe" [from *Boethius' Consolation of Philosophy*]. They help to reconcile the audience to her suffering and death, as through her Griselda-like patience and devotion she becomes a saint and a martyr in her love, dying with a divine lie upon her lips, ironically committing the deathbed perjury against which Othello had warned her, but a perjury which makes her, as Emilia says [V. ii. 130], "the more angel."

If Othello loses Desdemona for eternity, the faithful Emilia joins her mistress in death, as did the repentant thief who acknowledged Christ as his Lord as he died by His side and was told by Him (Luke xxiii. 43), "Today shalt thou be with me in paradise." In her easygoing tolerance of her husband, the depths of whose iniquity she does not realize, in her theft of the handkerchief at his behest, Emilia has played a part in her mistress' calamity, but she redeems herself by her trust in Desdemona and her loyalty to her. "I durst, my lord, to wager she is honest," she tells Othello [IV. ii. 12-13], "Lay down my soul at stake." She does indeed stake her soul on the purity of Desdemona. "Moor, she was chaste," she says [V. ii. 249] as she lies dying, "she loved thee, cruel Moor; / So come my soul to bliss, as I speak true" [V. ii. 249-50]. These words, at the supreme moment of death, carry the assurance that in losing her life by heroically defying Iago and revealing the truth she has won her soul.

Desdemona raises and redeems such earthly souls as Emilia. Belief in her, like belief in Christ, is a means of salvation. Cassio, like Othello, is deceived by Iago, but he makes no pact with him, as Othello does, and his worship of Desdemona, expressed in his rapturous welcome of her to Cyprus, is constant. He rejects Iago's insinuating "What an eye she has! methinks it sounds a parley of provocation" with "an inviting eye; and yet methinks right modest" [II. iii. 21-5]. If in Othello Shakespeare's audience had a terrifying reminder of the possibility of even the noblest of men succumbing to the wiles of the devil, in Cassio it had a hopeful reminder of the possibility of the ordinary man—one who like each of them was subject to mortal frailty—achieving salvation through faith and repentance. (pp. 1072-75)

But Cassio's sins are venial, not mortal. Having atoned for his weaknesses with his shame and his blood, he is worthy of the position that Othello, a greater man than he, has lost. "I hold him to be unworthy of his place that does those things," he says [II. iii. 101-02], attempting to regain his dignity when he has got drunk on his watch—unworthy indeed, but repentance wipes out the stains of misdoing. In his realization that he has done wrong he exclaims, albeit with drunken piety, "Forgive us our sin!" [IV. iii. 111-12]. His contrition when he comes to himself is deep. "Confess yourself freely [to Desdemona]," Iago guilefully advises him [II. iii. 318]. "Importune her help to put you in your place again: she is so free, so kind, so apt, so blessed a disposition, she holds it a vice in her goodness not to do more than she is requested" [II. iii. 319-22]. The blessed Desdemona, to whom Cassio dedicates himself as her "true servant" [III. iii. 9] in a feeling of gratitude for her bounteous goodness akin to Mariolatry, does intercede for him after he confesses himself to her. Her intercession brings martyrdom for herself, a martyrdom prefigured in her words "thy solicitor shall rather die / Than give thy cause away" [III. iii. 27-8], which remind us of the steadfastness of Christ in sacrificing Himself for mankind. At the conclusion, however, Cassio gains an even higher place than the one he had lost, as all sons of Adam who repent their sins gain a higher place than they lost when they sinned in Adam. "I hope to be saved" [II. iii. 107], he had said in his drunken religiousness, which, though ludicrous, had serious overtones. He was. (p. 1076)

This element of dramatic justice helps to reconcile us to the damnation of Othello, terrible and pitiful as it is, for it causes us to see it as the sentence of a divine power passing merited judgment upon all. Iago himself, who has put Othello "on the rack" [III. ii. 335], is sentenced to torture. "If thou the next

night following enjoy not Desdemona," he had told Roderigo . . . , knowing this was not to be, "take me from this world with treachery and devise engines for my life" [IV. ii. 214-17]. He is indeed betrayed by the treachery of Emilia, who had been devoted to him, a treachery that is in reality a higher loyalty—as she says [V. ii. 196], "'Tis proper I obey him, but not now"—and has "engines," instruments of torture, ingeniously contrived "cunning cruelty / That can torment him much and hold him long" [V. ii. 333-34], devised for him. These torments are merely the temporal prelude to the eternal torments of hell, to which he returns. "I hate him," he had said of Othello early in the play [I. i. 154], "as I do hell-pains," speaking as if of something with which he is familiar. They are also merely the extreme continuation of the torments he has suffered in life, where his thoughts did, "like a poisonous mineral, gnaw [his] inwards," as hell in Emilia's imprecation upon the unknown villain who is her husband is to "gnaw his bones" [II. i. 297; IV. ii. 136].

And Othello himself, having voiced the pathos of his loss, in killing himself as he had killed "a malignant and a turban'd Turk" who "beat a Venetian and traduced the state" [V. ii. 353-54], visits justice upon himself. The Turk is symbolic in Othello of the evil in human nature destructive of order. "Are we turn'd Turks, and to ourselves do that / Which heaven hath forbid the Ottomites?" exclaims Othello [II. iii. 170-71] at the sight of the fighting which has disturbed Cyprus. "For Christian shame, put by this barbarous brawl" [II. iii. 172]. The threat of the Turks to Cyprus had been dispelled by the destruction of their fleet by a storm, as the Spanish Armada had been destroyed. But this was merely the visible threat from without; the invisible threat from within the island, the evil passions within men that lead to civil strife—and is there not some suggested analogy with Shakespeare's own "scepter'd isle, / This earth of majesty, this seat of Mars, / This other Eden, demi-paradise"? [Richard II, II. i. 40-2]—still remained. Even as Othello is being waited for on the quay after the destruction of the Turkish fleet, Iago, laughingly affirming the validity of his cynical statements about women, says [II. i. 114], "Nay, it is true, or else I am a Turk." It is not true: his statement are the inventions of the Turk inciting to chaos, of Satan seeking to extend the domain of negation. When Othello thrusts his sword into his breast, he is stabbing the Turk, the evil, within himself which Iago, evil incarnate, had aroused. "Good, good: the justice of it pleases: very good," he had said when Iago had suggested, "Do it not with poison, strangle her in her bed, even the bed she hath contaminated" [IV. i. 209-10, 207-08]. He had sought to execute poetic justice in revenging himself and in doing so had laid himself open to such justice at the hands of God. . . . He falls upon the bed upon which he himself has done foul murder. To him, if we take "lust" in the general sense of "passion," apply his words, "Thy bed, lust-stain'd, shall with lust's blood be spotted" [V. i. 36]. His fate is the inevitable consequence of his action. "Perdition catch my soul," he had said . . . , "But I do love thee! and when I love thee not, / Chaos is come again" [III. iii. 90-2]. He has indeed brought chaos to his moral being and perdition to his soul, having traduced divine goodness and violated the law of God. (pp. 1077-78)

Paul N. Siegel, "The Damnation of Othello," in PMLA, *68, Vol. LXVIII, No. 5, December, 1953, pp. 1068-78.*

IRVING RIBNER (essay date 1955)

[*Acknowledging the importance of many other elements in* Othello, *Ribner suggests that the play may be seen as Shakespeare's adaptation of the pattern and philosophy inherent in the medieval morality dramas. He points out that in these traditional plays, humanity is susceptible to evil and to the delusion of mistaking evil for good, but individuals are capable of discovering their errors, rejecting wickedness, and, after serving a term of penance, achieving salvation. Discerning this optimism in* Othello, *Ribner contends that the Moor is a potentially good man who, because of Iago's deceit, elects wickedness, suffers greatly as a result of this choice, but eventually recognizes his mistake and ends his life repentant. The critic directly disputes Paul N. Siegel's assessment that Shakespeare represents the soul of Othello as eternally damned (see excerpt above, 1953), maintaining instead that the hero passes through the progressive stages of repentance—first recognizing his sin and rejecting the devil, then atoning for his transgression with his expiating suicide, and finally becoming reunited with goodness at his death—which clearly demonstrates that he has earned salvation. For additional commentary on whether Shakespeare represents Othello as purged of his sins or eternally damned at the close of the drama, see the excerpts by Kenneth O. Myrick (1941), Harley Granville-Barker (1945), S. L. Bethell (1952), Edward Hubler (1958), G. M. Matthews (1964), and Roy W. Battenhouse (1969), as well as Ribner's subsequently published essay (see excerpt below, 1960). Further, whereas many earlier critics have emphasized the influence of Iago in determining the course of the dramatic action, Ribner argues that the Moor is not Iago's helpless fool, for his wrong choice is the crux of the tragedy. He contends that Iago is "Shakespeare's adaptation of the morality Vice" figure—a vivid recreation of the stock character of medieval drama who was characterized chiefly by his powers of dissimulation, assuming a variety of masks, guises, and demeanors throughout the course of a drama. Bernard Spivack (1958) has provided an extensive analysis of the connection between Iago and the traditional Vice figure, and E. K. Chambers (1908) and Robert G. Hunter (1976) have also considered the relation between Shakespeare's Iago and the villainous characters in medieval and Renaissance drama. In addition, Ribner regards Iago as "a Vice who is a symbol of jealousy," serving to establish early in the play the theme of jealousy which is central to* Othello.]

At the basis of *Othello* is a traditional philosophy of man's relation to the forces of evil in the world. It goes back to the virtual beginnings of Christianity, and in the Middle Ages it had given rise to a distinctive dramatic form: the morality play. It was a basically simple philosophy which held that all men were surrounded by the forces of evil and that any man, no matter how great or noble, could be seduced by evil; man's reason being defective, he was capable of delusion, and the forces of evil could delude man into thinking they were good. Once he had succumbed, however, man was always capable of recognizing his error, recovering from his delusion and casting off evil. If he did so, after a period of penance, he could still triumph over evil and attain salvation. It is in essence an optimistic philosophy of life, and I believe that it is implicit in *Othello*.

With this traditional worldview to express, it was almost inevitable that Shakespeare's dramatic pattern in *Othello* should be the very pattern traditionally used to express that philosophy, that of the morality play. I should like in this essay to show how closely *Othello* conforms to this pattern and to demonstrate that when the play is read with this in mind, the classic question of whether a man like Othello could have succumbed to a man like Iago may be dismissed as a problem irrelevant to Shakespeare's basic design, for Iago was portrayed as a force to whom not only Othello, but any man might succumb. And the problem of Iago's own motivation for evil becomes equally unessential, for the pattern of the play called for an evil force which needed no dramatic motivation. Shakespeare adopted a type which the Elizabethan audience would immediately recognize, for it was an intimate part of their stage tradition, one

whose very nature furnished all of the motivation for evil which was necessary, whose malice could be understood and accepted without question. Iago is, as many critics have pointed out, Shakespeare's adaptation of the morality Vice. It is only with this awareness that we can grasp the essential relation between Othello and his ensign. It is not enough, however, to call Iago a mere primitive survival of the morality drama, as those who have identified him as a Vice have done. That he is a Vice is essential to the framework of the entire play, for Shakespeare did not just incorporate a morality play relic in *Othello*. He cast his entire drama in the morality pattern.

This does not mean that *Othello* is a *mere* morality play any more than it means that Iago is simply a stock stage character. The morality framework is only one of many elements which went into the creation of this rich and varied drama. It has many sides, and it offers many avenues for interpretation. Characters are as richly developed and as adequately motivated as the pattern of the play will allow. Iago, for instance, has an individuality almost unparalleled in the entire field of Elizabethan characterization. Shakespeare brings the Vice to life; he gives it passions, desires, and an intense humanity of which Iago's motive hunting is the supreme example. I do not propose here to deal with the many other elements which went into the creation of *Othello*. I wish merely to define the underlying pattern of the play and to read its philosophical content in the light of it. (pp. 70-2)

It is not surprising that [Shakespeare] should have conceived of *Othello* in morality terms. Not only was the morality pattern a perfect vehicle for the philosophic content of the drama, but the morality tradition had never ceased to be a part of the Elizabethan theater, although it had undergone a continuous development and modification. Shakespeare, in fact, used a popular Medieval survival in order to express a Medieval philosophy of life which was still much a part of the Elizabethan intellectual milieu, but the total drama in which he expressed it is so altered from the morality play "as to be essentially new." (p. 72)

Elizabethan tragedy, moreover, never abandoned the ethical function of the morality play. It never ceased to be concerned with the problem of good and evil, with the great ethical choices which men must make, and it rarely failed to illustrate the results of the choice of evil rather than good. Of this basic moral concern Shakespeare's great tragedies furnish the supreme examples. (p. 73)

The story of *Othello* is that of a man of great potential goodness who chooses evil through deception, suffers the horrible consequences of his choice, and at the end realizes his error and undergoes repentance before death. This is basically the pattern of the morality play.

In *Othello*, Shakespeare is concerned with evil in one of its specific manifestations, jealousy. The Moor, a noble, respected and courageous man, at the height of worldly prosperity and felicity, must come to destruction not through any arbitrary action of fate, but through his deliberate abandonment of the good and his choice of evil in its stead. The ethical choice is never a rational one; it is the product of delusion, but it must be made by Othello himself; he must not be forced to it by circumstances beyond his control, and he must not be a mere pawn in the hands of Iago. If the struggle is not in Othello's own mind and the consequences not the result of his own action, we cease to have a tragedy. Once we attribute Othello's downfall entirely to the machinations of Iago rather than to his own deliberate moral choice, we have merely a story of intrigue, not very skillful and not very convincing at that. It becomes reasonable for a long line of critics, going all the way back to Thomas Rymer's *A Short View of Tragedy* [see excerpt above, 1692], to consider Othello's seduction unbelievable and poorly motivated and the play a dramatic failure, or for such critics as E. E. Stoll to justify it on the basis of so primitive a stage tradition as the "calumniator believed" convention [see excerpt above, 1915]. When, however, we consider Iago as a Vice who is a symbol of jealousy—in fact, a graphic portrait of jealousy itself—such criticism becomes groundless. (pp. 73-4)

It is significant that Iago is the first major character to be introduced and that his first important speech reveals him as jealous of Cassio's position. Shakespeare, thus, even before the introduction of Othello and Desdemona, introduces the theme of jealousy which will run through out. Iago's envy of Cassio shows his jealousy of other men's worldly position and goods; he illustrates sexual jealousy in his groundless suspicions of Emilia, of which Shakespeare reminds his audience throughout the play. He is jealous of Othello's new found joy with Desdemona, and he covets her for himself. Certainly no personification of a deadly sin in the older morality plays ever described himself more clearly to an audience than Iago characterizes himself as the very personification of jealousy.

The Vice of the morality plays developed a definite pattern of action which is easily recognizable. He usually appeared early and made his true nature clear to the audience, just as Iago does. He almost always had a dupe—and often more than one—whom he gulled, and who provided comic interludes between the more serious moments of the play; it is clear that Roderigo performs this function in *Othello*. The Vice's most common trait, however, was that of the masquer or dissimulator. After making clear his true identity, the Vice always pretended to be something which he was not. . . . Often the Vice changed masks with great rapidity, first assuming one pose and then another, and the one pose which he never failed to assume was that of the friend of the hero. This is to be expected when we consider the origins of the morality play in Medieval theology. Man chooses evil because he mistakes it for the good, and thus the task of the devil becomes to pose as good. Certainly the story of the fall of Eve well illustrates this. The devil must disguise himself as the friend of man and thus cause man to forsake the true good and to accept disguised evil in its stead. This essentially is what Iago does for Othello.

To all the world "Honest Iago" is the very epitome of virtue. In the transition from the first scene of Act I, in which Iago reveals his true nature, to the second scene, in which he is shown as the trusted friend of Othello, Shakespeare clearly informs his audience that this is the traditional morality type of evil disguised as good, and that Iago will work his villainy through his disguise. Opposed to Iago are Desdemona and Cassio, who symbolize the true good in two of its most characteristic Renaissance forms, love and friendship. Othello's situation is that of the traditional morality hero; he is faced with a choice between good and evil, and because of his inherent human weakness he finds the disguise of evil so convincing that he rejects the true good and accepts evil in its stead. This is the error which the devil seeks to provoke, and it is the error which leads to Othello's destruction.

Othello has often been called the most structurally perfect of Shakespeare's tragedies. If this is so, it may be because in this play Shakespeare found the formula for a tragedy of moral choice, towards which he had been moving in his earlier plays, and which he partially realized for the first time in *Julius Caesar,* written some four years before. . . . In the first two acts Shakespeare provides a setting for *Othello's* choice. In the great temptation scene in Act III, the crucial scene of the play, Shakespeare shows exactly how Othello comes to choose the false good represented by Iago. The scenes which follow demonstrate the consequences of his choice and complete the morality pattern of repentance and regeneration. (pp. 75-6)

Is Othello, as he calls himself, "one not easily jealous" [V. ii. 345], or is he, as the German critics of the last century liked to think, one in whom the seeds of jealousy are present before Iago begins his work? This is an ancient and much argued question. Within the morality design of Shakespeare's play, however, it is a question of no significance. The morality hero has all human potentialities, and particularly the ability to be ensnared by evil; Othello has it in no greater degree than does any other man. When Shakespeare describes him as "one not easily jealous," he is emphasizing the nobility and freedom from jealousy which Othello enjoys before his temptation, and we must take the dramatist at his word. The hero of a tragedy of moral choice must always be a good man at the play's beginning, but because he is a man and not a god he must have human weakness and susceptibilities. Othello in his tragedy becomes a symbol of mankind, and the manner by which evil ensnares and destroys him, Shakespeare is telling us, is the manner in which evil generally operates in the world. (p. 77)

Shakespeare, in the opening scenes of the play, characterizes Othello as a man of strength, honor, wisdom, justice, and, above all, as one who can master passion with a magnificent and imposing self control. This is evident in his bearing before the council when he is accused by Brabantio and in his:

> Keep up your bright swords, for the dew will rust them.
>
> [I. ii. 59]

But even this example of human excellence is subject to error, and Shakespeare wishes to illustrate to what depths a noble spirit can be brought by jealousy. As soon as Othello becomes united with Iago, he degenerates rapidly, and he begins a course of evil which culminates in his murder of Desdemona. Shakespeare uses all of his art to emphasize the contrast between the two Othellos. All of the hero's virtues abandon him. The man of wisdom becomes a fool who rejects the most obvious testimony of reason and judgment, who is prey to the most shallow artifices imaginable. It is not because of a handkerchief that Othello kills Desdemona, but because he has been reduced by jealousy to a condition in which he cannot see the testimony of the handkerchief in its proper perspective. His calm self control is so reduced that he can strike his wife in the presence of the Venetian ambassador and address her as he would a whore. It must be noted also that Othello convinces himself that it is an act of justice which he is performing and not a murder:

> Yet I'll not shed her blood;
> Nor scar that whiter skin of hers than snow,
> And smooth as monumental alabaster.
> Yet she must die, else she'll betray more men. . . .
>
> [V. ii. 3-7]

It is the ultimate expression of Othello's acceptance of evil under the delusion that it is good.

The early morality drama, because it was concerned essentially with the religious problem of man's salvation, and because the religious doctrine from which it emerged offered the hope of salvation to all, never allowed its hero to be damned; he always recognized his error and attained a new and greater felicity by reunion with the good. But as the morality developed in the early sixteenth century, perhaps under the influence of the Reformation, it came more and more to embody the notion of an inexorable retribution for sin, with the erring mortal suffering final damnation for his evil choice. Out of this ultimately evolved a concept of tragedy as final retribution visited upon man for his sins. . . . (pp. 79-80)

I do not believe, however, that Shakespearean tragedy owes much to this development. His is not a tragedy of damnation, but rather of salvation, as *Hamlet* and *King Lear* supremely illustrate. Paul N. Siegel, who sees strong religious symbolism in *Othello*, with the fall of Othello paralleling that of Adam, and with Desdemona serving as a symbol of Christian salvation which Othello rejects, has argued that Othello's soul is eternally damned [see excerpt above, 1953]. But Siegel pays scant attention to Othello's casting off of evil, his repentance, expiation of his sin, and his symbolic reunion in death with the goodness he has only temporarily rejected. Shakespeare's *Othello*, I believe, is concerned not with the damnation of a soul, but rather with a Christian plan for salvation which had been depicted upon the stage since Medieval times. The design of the play is an expression of Shakespeare's belief that salvation for the sinner who recognized his sin and underwent penance was always possible, a belief equally implicit in the mercy extended to Angelo in *Measure for Measure*, a play almost certainly written in 1604, the very year of *Othello*.

The first step in salvation is the recognition of sin, and this Othello accomplishes. The recognition begins with the entrance of Emilia immediately after the murder, and it is completed with Othello's:

> Are there no stones in heaven
> But what serve for the thunder?—Precious villain!
> [V. ii. 234-35]

He rushes at Iago to kill him, and the union between them is broken. It must be noticed that as soon as Othello casts off Iago he reverts to the man he was at the beginning of the play. His calm self-control and mastery over passion return. This is magnificently illustrated by his bearing towards his captors and in his great speech to Gratiano. His tremendous power of self-understanding is revealed in his final speech before death.

After recognition of sin must come atonement. This Othello accomplishes with his own death, which poetically and dramatically must be viewed as an act of self-punishment in expiation for sin. Othello's suicide is not offered to the audience as evidence of his damnation, as some have supposed; it is the natural culmination of the morality pattern which Shakespeare has presented from the play's beginning. That Othello achieves salvation is further illustrated by his symbolic union in death with Desdemona:

> I kissed thee ere I kill'd thee! no way but this.
> Killing myself to die upon a kiss.
> [V. ii. 358-59]

Othello has forsaken jealousy and, in death, he is reunited with the good. This is the scheme of salvation which Shakespeare carried on from the Medieval moral drama. It is not incorrect to say that Shakespeare's play ends happily. (pp. 80-2)

If we are to understand *Othello* then, we must first recognize the pattern into which the play was cast, a traditional pattern which embodied a traditional concept of the workings of evil in the world. When we have done so, we find that many of the cruxes of modern criticism of the play tend to disappear. We find that Shakespeare was not primarily concerned with presenting credible portraits of life, although that may have been an important secondary consideration, and that action and character which some critics may regard as unrealistic and poorly motivated may often be necessary elements of Shakespeare's basic design and vital to a clear presentation of the philosophical concepts with which the play is concerned. So it certainly is with Iago's apparent lack of motivation and Othello's seemingly excessive gullibility. There is much more in *Othello* than its morality play pattern; this was merely the skeleton with which Shakespeare began, but it is therefore the consideration with which modern criticism must begin. (p. 82)

> *Irving Ribner, '''Othello' and the Pattern of Shakespearean Tragedy,'' in* TSE: Tulane Studies in English, *Vol. V, 1955, pp. 69-82.*

ROBERT B. HEILMAN   (essay date 1956)

[*The following excerpt is from Heilman's seminal study,* Magic in the Web *(1956). In an unexcerpted portion of that work, Heilman offers an in-depth treatment of the imagery in* Othello, *an issue he examined in an earlier essay (see excerpt above, 1951), claiming that the play is based on a series of interrelated contrasts, including hate and love, wit and witchcraft, dark and light, guilt and innocence, chaos and harmony, appearance and reality, blindness and seeing, hell and heaven, and black and white. In the following excerpt, he focuses on the various manifestations of love in* Othello, *stating that Shakespeare's primary intent was to demonstrate the magical, transforming power of love as dramatized in the character of Desdemona. Whereas he regards Othello's affection for his wife as incomplete, egotistical, and self-deceptive—an assessment proposed by such other critics as Allardyce Nicoll (1927), G. R. Elliott (1937 and 1953), F. R. Leavis (1937), Derek Traversi (1949), Roy W. Battenhouse (1969), and Carol McGinnis Kay (1983)—Heilman contends that Desdemona's passion, although naive and somewhat imprudent at first, comes to reflect charity, forgiveness, and spiritual understanding by the close of the play. The critic points to the handkerchief as the physical symbol of this magical love, which, he asserts, Desdemona experiences herself, but which the Moor, caught in his self-obsession, refuses to comprehend. Heilman also emphasizes the importance of Desdemona's three lines before her death to our understanding of her transformation, claiming that they recapitulate the evolution of her love from heedlessness and self-interest to a powerful, redeeming, and sacrificial passion. Like G. R. Elliott (1937), Heilman states that the heroine's final ''lie''— spoken as if from beyond the moral world—demonstrates the fundamental spiritual nature of love, the miracle that human passion finds expression even after death. Othello's ultimate tragedy, he adds, is that he fails to understand the significance of Desdemona's love, relying as he does on Iago's cynical ''wit'' rather than the magic of human passion, and thus he dies ignorant of the true nature of his loss. This assessment may be contrasted with Heilman's earlier evaluation that at the close of the drama the Moor recognizes the enormity of his crime and is able once again to distinguish truth from falsehood (see excerpt above, 1951). Endorsing Winifred M. T. Nowottny's view that in this play Shakespeare presents reason and love as inimicable (see excerpt above, 1952), Heilman argues that Othello's adoption of Iago's mode of rational thought blinds him to reality and leads him to chaos. For opposing views of Othello's awareness at the time of his death, see the excerpts by G. Wilson Knight (1930), G. R. Elliott (1937 and 1953), E. M. W. Tillyard (1938), G. M. Matthews (1964), Jared R. Curtis (1973), and Helen Gardner (see Additional Bibliography); also, see the essay by Curtis for a refutation of Heilman's claim that love and reason are anti-*

thetical in Othello. Other critics who have examined Shakespeare's presentation of love in this play include Hermann Ulrici (1839), Derek Traversi (1949), Kenneth Burke (1951), John Bayley (1960), Susan Snyder (1972), and Jane Adamson (1980).]

Shakespeare presents love in almost innumerable poetic and dramatic forms. In one interpretation that recurs in a number of major dramas, love is a force that binds human beings despite differences that seem prohibitive; it is a means of surmounting great barriers and obstacles, of counterimperatives, even of human limitations. It transcends the family feud of Montagues and Capulets; it rises above the imperial rivalries of Rome and Egypt; and in *Othello* it unites the Venetian and the Moor despite formidable disparities of age, nation, and color. . . . Always, of course, Shakespeare is no less aware of the miracle than of the imperfections of circumstance and character that interfere with it or corrupt it. The very harmony that transcends old oppositions, *Othello* implies, brings into play a new competing divisiveness: synthesis, thesis, antithesis. If we call the impulse to harmony, love, the name for the divisive force is hate: the love of Othello and Desdemona (and the lesser affection of Othello and Cassio) is the occasion for the flowering of Iago's hate. The love which surmounts age and nation and color intimates an absolute reconciliation of contraries; hence it must call forth the most intense hate, the passion to separate (if this were a political myth, we would see in the lovers the possibility of unity in the world and in Iago all the divisiveness). These forces . . . can be understood, in Othello's words, as love and chaos: order and disorder, the bringing together and the tearing apart, the will to create and the will to destroy. Yet Iago is a dramatic vessel, not an allegory, of hate; he has a complex psychological make-up that can be unfolded. If his hate is autonomous, it is still true that that autonomous realm has its own particular structure. Likewise the love of Desdemona and Othello, though it point to the absolute powers of love, is a living experience, not an allegory of love. The transcendent unifying power that works in them is modified by their personalities and hence subject to incompleteness, distortion, and the troubles that flow from foolishness, ignorance, and good intentions.

The spatial form of Act I gives a clue to Shakespeare's way of perceiving the love theme. The act not only begins but also ends with Iago's openly stating his hatred and translating it into schemes against Othello. Twice in the first 150 lines and again twice in the last 50 Iago says unqualifiedly that he "hates" Othello. . . . So Iago has both ends of Act 1; thus his actions symbolically hem in or surround those of Othello and Desdemona, whose love is first dramatized in the middle of the act. (pp. 169-70)

Othello is sure of his love for Desdemona; without it, he tells us in his second speech in the play, he would not his "unhoused free condition / Put into circumscription and confine / For the sea's worth" [I. ii. 26-8]. Thus he shows his awareness of countervalues, in the manner, not indeed of one who regrets, but of one who is recording a transaction. He knows what he has traded in; the bargain is *his;* and it is this sense of himself as negotiator that continues on into his later complaints couched partly in the style of one who has bought defective goods. This incomplete giving, this note of calculation, is one element in his relationship with Desdemona. Then there is the histrionic . . . : Othello has acted out a melodrama of adventure, with special performances for Desdemona: his audience yielded tears and sighs and fell in love with the hero, and the hero, naively pleased with himself rather than yielding to her, "lov'd her that she did pity" [I. iii. 168]. The Duke, charmed by the performance even in summary, and eager to get to state affairs, yields applause: "I think this tale would win my daughter too" [I. iii. 171]. But even his acceptance of the romantic pattern does not obscure the fact that Othello evinces less of devotion than of flattered acceptance of adoration, and we wonder what likelihood there is that, after this glamorous and one-sided beginning, the relationship will achieve depth and durability. He is now so emphatically the man of affairs that his role as lover is almost incidental, as if he were still a careless receiver of benefits rather than a fully reciprocating husband. Even with the Turks threatening, he is rather prompt in declaring his fondness for the hard bed of the warrior, and he goes out of his way to insist that sexual desire is not the reason for taking Desdemona to Cyprus [I. iii. 231-34, 262ff.]. If one did not look carefully enough, this might seem entirely the "noble Othello," a serene conqueror of the lower animal being. But the conqueror's volubility makes one pause. What cloudy irresolutions trouble his awareness of sex? Is he a little unsure of himself here, perhaps mindful of trans-Mediterranean attitudes, fearful of seeming "the lascivious Moor" (a plausible motive in one so generally in need of assurance)? Or is he, by inclination and long practice, the man of public affairs whose private emotional life must tag along as best it may, an appendage rather than an element to be integrated or even an integrating force? Or is there simply a lapse of taste, a partner of his rhetorical tendency, in his vehement relegation of Desdemona to a secondary role that can in no way impinge on "serious and great business"? All these elements have a part in his somewhat protracted statement of his own virtue. Though we know that Othello must seem reliable as leader of the expedition, his heavy emphasis on the establishment of reliability is a giveaway, at least of a deficiency in adult self-awareness. (pp. 171-72)

Further, the disavowal of sensuality is another index of self-deceptiveness. Not, I believe, that there is in Othello a powerful sexuality which he is unconsciously endeavoring to deny or disregard. The general incompleteness of response to Desdemona is the counterpart of a certain physical tepidness; there is a lack of warmth at all levels (it takes jealousy, as ministered to by Iago's aphrodisiac images, to beget intensity of sexual feeling). The lack of urgency, in turn, is symbolically a counterpart of his general deficiency of assurance: together, under pressure, they are convertible into a defensive violence. In denying the "young affects" Othello speaks something close to literal truth; but by implication he denies the power of the whole realm of passion and the irrational. He will order life rationally, as a good general should; no nonsense. The very believer in the magic-webbed handkerchief isn't going to let magic get out of hand; no upsetting passion for him. . . . This is the area of self-deception. His failure to experience a possibly saving irrationality ricochets, we may add, and he is ruined by a destructive irrationality. As in other ways, his experience is representative.

Younger, inexperienced, fascinated by a teller of romantic adventure stories, and now confronted by a sudden nocturnal challenge, Desdemona might well be scared, tremulous, uncertain. But she has the self-possession of one whose new commitment, however romantic in origin, has enough depth to make for strength and security. . . . [She] presses spiritedly for permission to go to Cyprus, an action that is richly characterizing: we see her initiative; her realistic understanding of how her presence at home would affect her father; her romantic love projected from a hearing about into a sharing of adventures, and yet qualified by the facing of military actuality. . . . (pp. 172-73)

In her spontaneous plea to go to Cyprus, Desdemona may not be wise. But at least she is not being self-protective, whereas Othello, though he seconds her request . . . , spends so much time . . . explaining that he has the right reasons and rises to such a hyperbolic conclusion that we cannot fail to sense his self-protectiveness, and even some pompousness in his portrait of himself as the undeflectable commander. . . . In Othello, Shakespeare succeeds in showing something about the love of the hero for the girl who first caught his eye by adoring his exploits, a love in which an over-explicit temperateness reveals some incompleteness of response and in which the man of affairs, not quite consciously nourishing a large image of himself that he has seen in the mirror of affairs, has withheld the self from a transforming devotion. Thus his personal style oddly combines a certain chillness with a florid, flamboyant rhetoric. In his unredeemed egotism lies the force that can ironically convert the temperateness into its opposite—the chilly and florid into the passionate—and endow it with power to ruin. Yet this history is not done simply. For the love that is diluted by a commander's hard pride in duty and by his self-awareness is found in a man of "personality" and courage and straightforwardness—and withal of a subtle self-distrust that is perhaps the inalienable underside of egotism. Strength may coexist with a kind of weakness, and pride joined to such weakness begets instability. (pp. 173-74)

Shakespeare has been careful to show in Othello all the areas of susceptibility to the strains that can be imposed by an earnest dealer in chaos. Iago could not thus work on Desdemona, who, whatever her own simplicity and her mild savoring of wifely influence, is in her love complete and secure.

Iago (the thief, the poisoner, the suborner of fights, the worker in the dark) defines himself when he says "I hate." As an open hater Iago would set up a less difficult problem, but in the actual Iago, destructiveness appears in another key—as friendship, helpfulness, selflessness, devotion to good causes. Hate takes on the guise of love (Iago as protector of property, healer, peacemaker, light-bringer); hence its overwhelming temporary power. In Iago's conduct Shakespeare has found a paradigm of experience affirmed constantly in other observations of life. . . . In Othello it is one of the most ironic variations on the complex theme of love.

Iago can please anybody he wants to, and he "woos" whomever it suits his purposes to seem to love; in the world, evil can charm generally. He uses the word *love* with astonishing frequency. If you drown yourself, he assures Roderigo, "I shall never love thee after" [I. iii. 306], casting even his "morale-building" in the style of that coquetry with which he characteristically helps soften up a victim. He works on Cassio directly: "I think you think I love you," "I protest, in the sincerity of love and honest kindness" [II. iii. 311, 327-29]. Othello, wanting something of Iago, charges him "On thy love" or "If thou dost love me" [II. iii. 178; III. iii. 115]. Othello needs love (his problem of assurance again), and Iago plays to this need; he uses "love" as a weapon, along with "honesty," again with the deep ironic pleasure of simulating what he is destroying.

In 3.3 Iago's style is exactly that of a lover bent on ensnaring a victim and betraying his real attitude to the victim in the obviousness of his devices: "My lord, you know I love you," and Othello, needing to acknowledge this, acknowledges it

twice [III. iii. 117-18]. When Iago is ready to tell a real lie about Desdemona, he attributes it to his "love and duty" [III. iii. 194]. Othello is shocked by what he hears, and Iago promptly covers up with lover's strategy: a careful apology for "too much loving you" and a reassertion that all he says "Comes from my love" [III. iii. 213, 217]. What emerges is a pattern of rival loves: Iago, the lover as operator, works to wean Othello from a counterlove and tie him to his own. It comes out in Othello's threat, "Villain, be sure thou prove my love a whore!" [III. iii. 359]. The other love is on the way down, but the despairing fury of Othello is great enough to make Iago play the seducer's strongest card—the threat to pull out. "I thank you for this profit; and from hence / I'll love no friend, sith love breeds such offence" [III. iii. 379-80]. In effect: "If you don't play my way, I won't love you any more." If we miss the coquetry, we miss the irony of the hater aping the lover to destroy love. (pp. 176-77)

[After] managing the "seduction scene," Iago acts in the assured manner of one who has evoked an infatuation that he can use as he pleases. Aside from having to work to make Othello carry out his many-sided hatred, he can treat his "loved one" with indifference and even contempt. He need not protest or ever mention his love again (just as with Roderigo and Cassio once he has them walking the paths that he has made them think will lead them where they want to go). But Othello, enthralled in the work of hate, takes his seducer's love for granted. He is charmed by Iago's "noble sense of thy friend's wrong" [V. i. 32], for he counts on unearned emotional income as only a self-centered man could. And just before Emilia will tell him the truth, he triumphantly identifies his informer to her: "My friend, thy husband; honest, honest Iago" [V. ii. 154]. "Friend" and "honest" sum up his infatuation.

The amatory style, without which Iago could hardly have managed his great deception of Othello, complicates theme and helps reveal two characters. And it makes possible a second meaning in Emilia's indictment of Iago—"villany hath made mocks with love!" [V. ii. 151]. (pp. 178-79)

If *Othello* may be called the play of love, nevertheless, as I have said, it is not an allegory of love. But in different parts it does enunciate several doctrines of love which help to clarify the symbolic import of the action.

Under Iago's tutelage Othello the lover acquires not only what looks like information but also certain principles of knowledge. Out of passion for a certainty which he might have had by exercising the faith or the charity that love implies he falls into a philosophy that does him little good.

Iago's moral core, we have seen, is hate. Yet he can ape love. We might ask: what would such a man think about love if he theorized about it? What must a man think of that which he does not have but which he can fake and thus use instrumentally? Must he not disparage and minimize it? Here the problem is partly one of distinguishing Iago's beliefs from his strategies. He can encourage Roderigo to count on, and Othello to believe in, Desdemona's infidelity, and Cassio to count on her lovingkindness for strong intercession with Othello; and while hating Othello and plotting against him and Desdemona, he is capable of describing him as "of a constant, loving, noble nature" and her as "fram'd as fruitful / As the free elements" [II. i. 289; II. iii. 341-42]. . . . We remember that Iago regards the world of reality and appearance as fluid, unjelled, subject to manipulation; the only truth is the one that has instrumental value in a given context. At the same time Iago is intellectually capable of recognizing realities—of character and value—that do not shift with context, that exist despite his preferences. . . . By recognition of exceptions to what he believes to be the rule, he knows the good that alone makes evil enjoyable; if sex is the arena, the only victory is that over chastity and devotion. Antipoetic though he is at the core, there is yet something of the ironic poet in him, utilizing contradictory perspectives and even caught in ambivalence of feeling. . . . [Without] a faith in general depravity he could hardly be so consistent in style and so effective in causing others to adopt, for practical purposes, a positivist view of sex. At the heart of his working principle is the reduction of love to sensuality in flux. (pp. 193-95)

Iago has a familiar reductive habit of mind. He is outside the myth of love. He is a kind of scientist of sex. He positivizes it: it consists only of observable physical phenomena. . . . The invisible and the intangible are not real. There is no "idea" of love; we have only the evidence of sensory behavior, which is an absolute. . . . Iago takes away the poetry of love—all the complex interaction of passion and imagination, of self and devotion, of flesh and spirit. He robs men of whatever transcends the physical facts of love—the personality of the thief at work on the philosophic plane; the obscurantist pretending to be the lightbearer; the promoter of what Eric Voegelin calls "spiritual eunuchism." He commits Roderigo, who wants to believe it, to a philosophy of love; he converts Othello to the same philosophy—and Othello does not want to believe. In the end, Iago is engaged in philosophical corruption. He is not merely making statements which are not true, but making statements which might be true if the individual to whom they refer conformed to the general human rule which Iago advances for behavior of this order. His success springs in part from the strength of his belief, in part from his playing upon a human inclination to accept a simplified likeness of truth, even though it promise disaster, rather than to labor with an exacting complex verity. For many human beings it is apparently easier to live with the idea of even a horrifying evil in someone else than to reckon with the complications of good and evil in another and in oneself. (pp. 195-96)

The man of hate conquers by winning others to his theory of love. His own passion is one that, when he can think of it at all, he can think of only as a form of revenge. He wants his "love" to be a tool of hate, and indeed it is shot through with hate. There is high convertibility of elements in the lust-hate compound: hate for the unpossessed, hate for the once-possessed. Lust can be a mode of hate; possess once, without commitment; deny an enduring validity; thus destroy, acting out theory. Iago must fight against the love of Othello and Desdemona: that is the open plot and the metaphysical conflict of the drama. (pp. 207-08)

Although Iago succeeds in dividing husband and wife, he fails in a profounder sense: Desdemona never wavers in the fidelity of which Iago denies the existence. When she protests Othello's harshness or asserts her innocence to him, she has the vigor of incredulity, but she does not fly off into the loud vehemence of offended self-love, just as in defending herself to Iago and Emilia she does not rise above a hurt amazement and a mild earnestness of asseveration. At the height of her happiness, Desdemona assures Othello, "Whate'er you be, I am obedient" [III. iii. 89]; when he strikes her and abuses her, she continues to seek his commands and to do as he says, even when he sneers openly at her obedience [IV. i. 255-56]. Before she knows that anything is wrong, she is solicitous about his

headache; when it first appears that something is wrong, she is solicitous about his tears; after his outright accusations, her only concern is to "win my lord again" [IV. ii. 149]. Instead of looking around for someone to blame, she tries to make a case for Othello's incredible conduct, and she rebukes herself for blaming him. Later, her only theory for what has happened is, "It is my wretched fortune" [IV. ii. 128]—a phrase which recalls the literal meaning of her name: "wretched" or "unhappy." But she does not use wretchedness as a ground for subordinating devotion to self-pity and self-justification; kneeling in the presence of Iago and Emilia, she swears that she "ever will . . . / . . . love him dearly" even though he divorce her [IV. ii. 157-58]. She rejects Emilia's wish that she had never seen Othello and accepts "his stubbornness, his checks, his frowns" [IV. iii. 20]. And the song that "will not go from" her mind has this line: "Let nobody blame him; his scorn I approve" [IV. iii. 31, 52]. Desdemona has matured from the impressionable girl who was romantically charmed by tales of adventure, wondered at the "strange," and sighed for the "pitiful," so that she can without hyperbole define her "sins" paradoxically as the "loves I bear to you" [V. ii. 40]. This is the Desdemona the drama creates for us, not a Desdemona who suffers for the guilt of filial disobedience.

She has an un-Venetian ignorance of the world. She is naive in her astonishment that "women do abuse their husbands / In such gross kind" [IV. iii. 62-3]. She flatters the world by seeing it in her own image (just as Iago, by the same method, traduces it). Perhaps the lack of "sophistication" is a necessary part of her strength of devotion; there is no knowingness to dilute her love. It makes her overintricate to attribute "self-deception" and "deliberate blindness" to her [see the essay by Clifford Leech cited in the Additional Bibliography]. Granted that Iago's cynicism and her naivete give untenably extreme views of human conduct, that her disbelief in the worldly woman described by Emilia [IV. iii. 86] "is as romantically false as Othello's idealism" [see excerpt above by Allardyce Nicoll, 1927]; nevertheless she may act "truly" despite believing "falsely" about the world. Yet the "romantically false" belief comes from the newlywed enthusiasm of a girl who spontaneously generalizes her own incapacity for sexual wandering. It amounts to an intellectual charity that is, after all, a counterpart of the charity of will that she is shortly to achieve. So, confident in her own and of Othello's truth, she inopportunely picks an angry challenge by Othello as the time to resume her plea for Cassio. She simply does not know that the ideal of love may govern Othello's conduct as imperfectly as that of adulterous wives. Perhaps she is willful, perhaps proud, in her way; yet what comes through most directly in the lines is a misestimating of the situation, puzzlement, something like panic, along with a desire not to be overborne, or deflected from her promise to Cassio, by a frightening violence. The very "human" medley of impulses adds up to bad judgment—an avenue to tragedy somewhat like, though less decisive than, Cordelia's refusal to compete with her sisters in the game of love and land. And at the ill-timed moment she resumes her do-good role [III. iv. 50] she has already mishandled the issue of the handkerchief. She knows that it is gone, and she is seriously disturbed [III. iv. 25ff.], but upset by Othello's threatening pressure, she twice tells him it is not lost [III. iv. 83, 85], says she can show it to him "but . . . not now" [III. iv. 86], and jumps to the Cassio theme. Presumably Desdemona, though she "knows" the handkerchief is missing, does not "believe" that it is finally lost but hopes that some miracle will uncover it; "it is not lost" [IV. iii. 83] is a metaphor for this irrational but understandable combination of belief and hope. (pp. 208-10)

Yet it may be virtually impossible for Desdemona, young and inexperienced, to be practically wise about the missing handkerchief after Othello has said ominously, "To lose't or give't away were such perdition / As nothing else could match" [III. iv. 67-8]. For now she learns that the handkerchief is deeply symbolic; and here we look through . . . [an] open window on the inner structure of the drama. The handkerchief, far from being only the trivial object that Rymer saw [see excerpt above, 1692], has a specific symbolic status and, beyond that, the dramatic role of leading us in to the crowning statement in the play of love.

The handkerchief is a talisman: kept by a wife, it guarantees her husband's love; if it is lost or given away, "his spirits should hunt / After new fancies" [IV. iii. 58-63]. Since it is the man who strays, Othello's perturbation as he defines the handkerchief is almost a betrayal of a fear of instability, which would be imaginable in the character as we have read it; too, he may obscurely be justifying, as inevitable, unhusbandlike conduct emotionally seized upon before knowledge of the loss became a live factor in his punitive scheme. (pp. 210-11)

When Othello sums up the myth of the handkerchief, "There's magic in the web of it" [III. iv. 69], he guides us beyond the literal object into the symbolization of love: there is magic in the web of love and in the web of the drama itself. Iago plays with gross facts, all magic out: "beast with two backs" [I. ii. 116-17]. But as soon as Brabantio finds some truth in this "slanted" journalism, he instinctively looks beyond the naturalistic: "Is there not charms / By which the property of youth and maidhood / May be abus'd?" [I. i. 171-73]. This is the essence of his accusation of Othello: "enchanted her!" "chains of magic," "foul charms," "arts inhibited," "spells," "witchcraft." The Duke promises relief, and Othello, picking up Brabantio's literal terms as a metaphor for defense, concludes, "This only is the witchcraft I have us'd" [I. iii. 169]. In Brabantio's usage, witchcraft is an anesthetic; in Othello's, an awakener.

The magic in the web is manifold. The magic of the handkerchief is a seal of the spontaneous human event; it is quasi-sacramental. To Brabantio, magic is a malign working of spells, a compulsion. But at least Brabantio's sense of the magical cause makes it possible for him to understand in his way the magic of love—the harmonizing force that surmounts the barriers of "nature." On the other side is Iago with his minimizing naturalism: all he admits is undifferentiated lubricity. Othello unconsciously edges toward the Iago naturalism: he reduces "charms" to "charm of personality," especially of the histrionic personality. Though his habit of mind is not reductive, he here makes a slight move in a direction that becomes disastrous as he goes further. Yet here again we have a contrast, for "charm of personality" at least saves something. Even this, Iago cannot admit; it is entirely in keeping with his intellectual style to shrink Othello's "charming" story into "bragging and . . . fantastical lies" [II. i. 223-24].

These, then, are the strands of magic in the dramatic web: explicitly, magic as a spell to win unwilling love; magic as the personality that stirs a willing love; magic as the talismanic preserver of love; implicitly, magic as love. We instinctively look for a larger subject, for the dynamics of the personality subject to the magic of love. Iago has put this into words (again the irony of the truth-saying villain) in his sneer at Roderigo: "they say base men being in love have then a nobility in their natures more than is native to them" [II. i. 215-17]. This is a "magic" transformation of the personality. When we turn to

see how Othello and Desdemona, who began in sentiment and romance, are transformed, we come for a necessary final look at the drama of the handkerchief. The handkerchief is stolen when Desdemona, as Emilia says, "let it drop by negligence" [III. iii. 311]. But Desdemona, who has been trying to help Othello cure a headache, has been rebuffed, and in the direct concern of love has forgot the symbol. In rejecting her attention, Othello really rejects the magical powers of love; he *will* not be cured. The handkerchief, he says, "is too little" [III. iii. 287]. Neither the myth nor the family tradition nor the object which so stimulates the eyes and hearts of all who have to do with it can stir him, for the sense of being wronged has become self-enclosure: he will neither love nor let himself be loved. Just before Desdemona's entry he has said he'd "rather be a toad" in a dungeon "Than keep a corner in the thing I love / For others' uses" [III. iii. 270, 272-73]. This "all or nothing" view of love, which is really the essence of self-love, makes it impossible for him to see that he has "all," in any sense that is meaningful; and it defines an ethical nature in which there is a potential addiction to grievance . . . and its consequence, a freezing in the posture of revenge. He closes off the possibility of a magical transformation—of discovering a new "nobility" in his "nature"—and commits himself to a mode of love action which puts the ultimate strain upon the spirit of Desdemona.

We have already spoken of Desdemona's extraordinary, unskeptical constancy, of her progress from the infatuated girl toward the devoted, enduring wife. We have to keep in mind Iago's universal vengefulness, Othello's punitive instinct, Emilia's attributing women's misconduct to men's—the pervasive note of *lex talionis* [law of retaliation]—to appreciate Desdemona's spiritual grace (the "nobility" actualized by the tests of love). She may err in seeking a token submission and in "handling" an angry man. But even after she has been grossly mistreated, her love has not sunk into the self-love of abuse and case-making; her prayer is, "Heaven me such uses send, / Not to pick bad from bad, but by bad mend!" [IV. iii. 104-05]. She is intent on the quality of her behavior. If a villain has slandered her, she prays for him, "heaven pardon him!" [IV. ii. 135]. By putting this line between Iago's "there is no such man" and Emilia's "hell gnaw his bones" [IV. ii. 134, 136], Shakespeare heightens our awareness of the love that can become charity in its rarest form of forgiveness to the deliberate evildoer. Since she can forgive, she can believe in forgiveness; hence she can intercede for Cassio. Her last words on this mission reveal the love of harmony that belongs to love: "I would do much / T'atone them, for the love I bear to Cassio" [IV. i. 232-33]. She fails in life, but Othello and Cassio are indeed "atoned," after her death, an "atonement" which is a reminder of the great mythic act of *caritas* [redeeming love]. The course of her actions after mid-play completes the magic theme, for in her we do see the dynamics of the personality under the magic influence of love; first she felt the static "charm" of Othello's personality and then experienced the full ripening of an outward-turning love which in this context we may call the magical transformation or the miracle of personality.

In *Othello* Shakespeare dramatizes the extremes of hate and love. Without clichés or distortions he gives us devil and saint, for whom, in our more limited horizons, we no longer have an idiom but the sentimental one. . . . There is an almost comparable range in the very portrayal of Desdemona: she fears death and begs for life, in the manner of ordinary humanity; yet she can also achieve the miracle of more than ordinary love. Yet if Shakespeare's interpretation has the authority that comes from an inclusive awareness of human possibilities, he strengthens it with the authority of an extraordinary dramatic action. He knows the utmost extent of "nature" but also knows when to stretch it or go beyond it. There is the bald nature of the death scene: terror and animal destructive lust. Desdemona is dead. Then Emilia enters—the social reality. And then suddenly Desdemona speaks. Acting on the rationalist impulse, we reorder the scene, decide that her death was only apparent, and place the "real" death at the later point. But the fact is that we have felt Desdemona to be dead from the moment when Othello for the second time released her from his grip, and that her speaking comes as a complete shock that takes over the scene. "Still as the grave," Othello has said of her [V. ii. 94]. We must, I think, accept the shock as intended, and must understand a bold and brilliant effort to suggest a voice coming from beyond life—the miracle which completes the pattern of magic in the web. The voice from beyond is anything but tricky theatricalism: the three speeches by Desdemona are a compact dramatic summary of the phases in the "magical transformation" (a reminder of the myth that the dying person recalls his whole life). For Desdemona becomes, rather than simply is, the saint. Her first speech—"O, falsely, falsely murder'd!" [V. ii. 117]—is an accusation with all the emphasis on the evildoer: the most primitive impulse. Here we can remember whatever in her actions was self-regarding—untruths, filial inconsiderateness, love of power, flight from reality, pride, tactlessness (as different critics have it). The second—"A guiltless death I die" [V. ii. 122]—is a self-exculpation: the impulse now freed of accusation and formalized as a legal plea, a simple factual denial of wrongdoing. Then, when Emilia asks, "O, who hath done this deed?" Desdemona speaks for the third and last time: "Nobody—I myself. Farewell. / Commend me to my kind lord. O, farewell!" [V. ii. 124-25]. Here is the last phase: no longer a denial of wrongdoing, but the acting of goodness: the assertion not of one's own innocence or goodness but of that of the evildoer, shielding him but, more than that, forgiving him. And here the verbal drama is very significant, for one of Desdemona's key words—*kind*—is in itself a summation. Once she was "Arraigning his *unkindness* with my soul," and, though she then magnanimously decided that "he's indicted falsely" [III. iv. 152, 154], she could not banish from her mind the idea of unkindness: "his *unkindness* may defeat my life" [IV. ii. 160]. Here, however, she got around the fact by denying its characteristic effect: "But never taint my love" [IV. ii. 161]. Now, with her "Commend me to my *kind* lord," she makes good her prophecy: though life has been defeated, love remains untainted for its ultimate office of denying unkindness. And in *commend*, with its quest for approval, is the humility that reverses whatever pride there was. Here is the perfecting of human nature, which I have called the miracle of personality; its fitting dramatic form is an apparent miracle in the physical world, a "resurrection." Hence one's sense of a surrealistic rightness in Desdemona's return from death, as it were, to say her last words. It is an expressionistic symbol of the metaphysical quality of her love. It is the victory of spirit: the experience of *agape* in a world distraught by *eros*. (pp. 211-16)

Othello's tragedy is crowned by his failure to see what Desdemona's love means. Once he is disabused of his obsession, he recognizes hardly more than that she has been technically true ("Cold . . .? / Even like thy chastity" [V. ii. 275, 276]). He has heard her say, "Nobody—I myself," and has responded only by calling her "liar," which is the first faint symptom of self-doubt or self-disgust. He has also listened to her words, "Commend me to my kind lord," but there is no evidence

that he has "heard" them, much less understood them. . . . [To] complete our estimate of Othello we . . . need to know how much truth there is in the best known lines of his apologia, "lov'd not wisely, but too well" [V. ii. 344]. Not wisely, indeed. But too well? Only if "too well" means too possessively. But the Othello who felt the magic of love that creates a union of the unlike never surrendered to the magic that transforms personality. If we can envision him as striven for, like the protagonist of the morality play, by two versions of love, we realize that he was owned for a while by that version which is a disguise of hate, that he returned to the other where he might have found salvation, but that even in the end he remained largely inaccessible to the spirit of that love. He was never wholly freed from self-love. Othello is not clear what he has done; he knows that he has lost a faithful wife, but he does not know that he has lost the woman who could forgive him and ask him to think well of her. This is his ultimate obtuseness. . . . [Here we have] intimations of the modern variant of tragedy in which the character intended as tragic (or even a whole community) never knows what has happened to him and so exists only as an unripened figure in an object lesson on the stage. The ignorant man is the one most given to self-justification. Othello is only partly ignorant, but still enough so to interlard his self-judgment with justification. "Too well" is less autobiography than a plea of "only partly guilty," but it reminds us how far he fell short of "well."

The world of magic in the web is what Iago cannot help opposing, whether love be the harmonizing force that his divisiveness cannot tolerate, or the perfecter of personality abhorrent to his cynicism. To alter the terms, Desdemona represents the world of spirit which Iago must by philosophical necessity destroy. To her transcendent love he opposes a positivism of sex that takes in both Roderigo and Othello. But it is only after we have become fully aware of Desdemona as the symbolization of spirit that we can grasp all the implications of the lust-hate complex at the center of Iago's feeling for her. . . . As long as Desdemona is faithful to Othello and is alive, she is intolerable to him—a refutation of all his thought (as are, in their own ways, Emilia, whom he kills, and Bianca, whom he tries to destroy). Though he was not present at her death, he would be more likely, through the intuition of absolute enmity, than Othello, who lacked the final intuition of love, to know the spirit of her last words. (pp. 216-18)

[Although Iago] does not take seriously the ennobling power of love, he does not fail to let us know what he does take seriously. When, in his fake oath of loyalty to "wrong'd Othello," he vows "The execution of his wit, hands, heart" [III. iii. 466], Iago's words give a clue to his truth: his heart is his malice, his hands literally wound Cassio and kill Roderigo, and his wit is the genius that creates all the strategy. Wit is reality. How it enters into the dialectic of structure Iago's promises to Roderigo make clear: "If sanctimony and a frail vow betwixt an erring barbarian and a supersubtle Venetian be not too hard for my wits and all the tribe of hell, thou shalt enjoy her" [I. iii. 355-58]. "Tribe of hell" is somewhat rhetorical; the real antagonist is "my wits"—set against the rival power of love, which he cannot tolerate. But even beyond the conscious battle there is a symbolic conflict that is at the heart of the drama. And for this symbolic conflict Iago, again assuaging the pain of Roderigo, inadvertently gives us a name: "Thou know'st we work by wit, and not by witchcraft; / And wit depends on dilatory time" [II. iii. 372-73].

Wit and witchcraft: in this antithesis is the symbolic structure of *Othello*. By *witchcraft*, of course, Iago means conjuring and spells to compel desired actions and states of being. But as a whole the play dramatically develops another meaning of witchcraft which forces itself upon us: *witchcraft* is a metaphor for love. The magic in the web of the handkerchief . . . extends into the fiber of the drama. Love is a magic bringer of harmony and may be the magic transformer of personality; its ultimate power is fittingly marked by a miraculous voice from beyond life. Such events lie outside the realm of "wit"—of the reason, cunning, and wisdom on which Iago rests—and this wit must be hostile to them. Wit must always strive to conquer witchcraft, and there is an obvious sense in which it should conquer; but there is another sense in which, though it try, it should not and cannot succeed: that is what *Othello* is about. Whatever disasters it causes, wit fails in the end: it cuts itself off in a demonic silence before death, while witchcraft—love—speaks after death. (pp. 224-25)

Though Othello seems to be all the naivete of Everyman, and Iago to be all his slyness, Othello gives himself more to wit than to witchcraft because he and Iago, though in different degrees, have much in common—a histrionic bent, an inadequate selfhood that crops up in self-pity and an eye for slights and injuries, an uncriticized instinct to soothe one's own feelings by punishing others (with an air of moral propriety), the need to possess in one's own terms or destroy, an incapacity for love that is the other side of self-love. All this is in another realm from that of witchcraft. When Othello decides to follow Iago and be "wise" and "cunning," he adopts . . . a new code: he will "see" the facts, get the "evidence," "prove" his case, and execute "justice." This is the program of "wit." Now this is not only utterly inappropriate to the occasion on which, under Iago's tutelage, Othello elects to use it, nor is it simply one of a number of possible errors; rather he adopts an attitude or belief or style which is the direct antithesis of another mode of thought and feeling that is open to him. He essays to reason when reason is not relevant: he substitutes a disastrous wit for a saving witchcraft. Shakespeare, as one critic put it, "forces upon the audience the question, In what strength could Othello reject Iago? The answer would seem to be, By an affirmation of faith which is beyond reason, by the act of choosing to believe in Desdemona. Shakespeare's point is that love is beyond reason" [see excerpt above by Winifred M. T. Nowottny, 1952]. Or, in the formulation of C. S. Lewis, "To love involves trusting the beloved beyond the evidence, even against much evidence." Othello, the prime beneficiary of witchcraft, might win all its gifts had he the faith that would open him to its action; but he is short on faith, is seduced by wit (the two actions are simply two faces of the same experience), and ruined. He knew the first miracle of love, but cut himself off from the greater miracle. His final failure is that, though he comes to recognize that he has really been witless, he is never capacious enough in spirit to know how fully he has failed or what he has thrown away. He never sees the full Desdemona witchcraft. (pp. 226-27)

> *Robert B. Heilman, in his* Magic in the Web: Action & Language in "Othello," *University of Kentucky Press, 1956, 298 p.*

BRENTS STIRLING (essay date 1956)

[*Like G. R. Elliott (1953), Stirling regards the issues of pride and reputation as central to* Othello, *asserting that the play presents a dichotomy between the "'normal' regard for esteem and honor" and the "inverted egoistic defensiveness of good name which arises when esteem or honor is threatened." He argues that in*

the early portions of the drama Othello is portrayed as possessing only ordinary concern for this public reputation, but in Act III, Scene iii—because of his excessive pride—he adopts an obsessive, self-centered view of honor and good name; the critic claims that Othello persists in this state of mind until after Desdemona's murder, when he then recovers his previous sense of reputation. Stirling also contends that from the end of Act III, Scene iii until midway through the final scene of the drama, Othello seeks to depersonalize the violent course of conduct he has chosen by converting it into a ceremonial act. Remarking upon the pattern of formal, ritualistic speeches abruptly descending into viciousness and cruelty, the critic asserts that this pattern represents the conflicting attitudes in Othello's psyche and the "moral crisis" in his soul. Stirling discerns the most elaborate expression of Othello's ritualistic attitude in the first part of Act V, Scene ii, in which the Moor simultaneously assumes the roles of "lightbearer," judge, and priest carrying out a sacrifice; however, Stirling adds, the ceremony is a mockery, for Othello's purported sacrifice of Desdemona is shown to be nothing less than murder. For additional commentary on the theme of pride as opposed to a healthy concern with self-esteem or reputation, see the excerpt by John Arthos (1958) and the essay by Madeleine Doran cited in the Additional Bibliography. Such other critics as G. R. Elliott (1937), F. R. Leavis (1937), Derek Traversi (1949), Roy W. Battenhouse (1969), and Carol McGinnis Kay (1983) have also discussed Othello's self-centeredness.]

As a principle which controls character and action in *Othello* the reputation theme has two aspects which are morally opposed but psychologically related. The first of these is an objective, "normal" regard for esteem and honor; the second is an inverted, egoistic defensiveness of good name which arises when esteem or honor is threatened. . . . The distinction I assume between the opposite aspects of reputation, as well as a validity of the distinction in Elizabethan tradition, is made clear in G. R. Elliott's definitive study of the sin of pride as a controlling force in *Othello* [see excerpt above, 1953]. Mr. Elliott differentiates between Othello's "right self-esteem" and "wrong pride," and equates with the most malignant form of pride what I call the egoistic pole of reputation.

Othello's first appearance in the play is a refutation of slander. In I. ii his conduct in facing Brabantio's party ("Keep up your bright swords . . ." [I. ii. 59]) nullifies the "thick lips," the "lascivious Moor," of earlier dialogue and lays a foundation for the council scene in which Othello gains a respect close to veneration. Thus, a deserved reputation, casually sensed by its possessor and pointedly accepted by others, answers the scurrility of Iago and Brabantio. Othello's easy bearing of his good name, his lack of egoistic concern for it, introduces the normal or objective aspect of the reputation theme.

It is Cassio, however, who brings the theme explicitly into the play: "Reputation, reputation, reputation! O, I have lost my reputation! I have lost the immortal part of myself, and what remains is bestial. My reputation, Iago, my reputation!" [II. iii. 262-65]. These lines are given added point by Othello's rebuking of Montano at the time of Cassio's disgrace:

> What's the matter
> That you unlace your reputation thus,
> And spend your rich opinion for the name
> Of a night-brawler?
>
> [II. iii. 193-96]

Both this passage and Cassio's fervent words occur at high points of the scene (II. iii) in which Iago discredits Cassio, so that dramatic force is lent to thematic statement. Reputation becomes the "immortal part" of man, without which he is "bestial," a state well understood to color Shakespeare's portrayal of tragic depths; we may recall Hamlet's phrase, "a beast, nor more" [*Hamlet*, IV. iv. 35], and the chorus of animal imagery which accompanies the tragic descent in *Lear*.

Purely on the face of it, Cassio's lament might imply the egoistic pole of reputation. Only its distraught quality, however, would suggest this, for the passage and its context are free from the cankered defensiveness of Iago and Brabantio. Cassio blames no one but himself and indulges in no recrimination; in all simplicity and modesty he joins Desdemona in her plan to restore his position. Only once in the action leading to III. iii does Cassio show a morbid concern for reputation, and this occurs when he is drunk. In a memorable display of the concern for status shared by tipplers past and present, he says that he wants no more of Iago's singing, and announces (portentous *non sequitur*) that "there be souls must be saved, and there be souls must not be saved" [II. iii. 103-04]. He for one, "no offence to the general, nor any man of quality" [II. iii. 106-07], hopes to be saved.

> *Iago*. And so do I too, Lieutenant.

> *Cassio*. Ay, but, by your leave, not before me; the lieutenant is to be saved before the ancient.
>
> [II. iii. 108-10]

Reputation, reputation! This is Cassio's single and brief "Iago-phase" in which good repute is measured by standards of precedence and "face." When he becomes sober he sets out equably to redeem his lost good name.

Thus, in the first two acts Shakespeare presents his theme in a dramatic triumph by Othello over slander, and in an equally dramatic loss of honor by Cassio which is amplified by strong lyrical expression. In these episodes reputation is asserted within its sound and normal limits. But there is also its inverted aspect; if we return to the beginning of *Othello* we may follow a parallel stressing of good name in the form of self-regard and prideful delusion.

This plane of honor is suggested by Iago's familiar opening speech on the preferment of Cassio, the "counter-caster" who "had th' election" [I. i. 27]:

> He, in good time, must his lieutenant be,
> And I—God bless the mark!—his Moorship's ancient.
>
> [I. i. 32-3]

Brabantio shows a similar quality. A glance at his lines in the street encounter of I. ii will show that his sorrow and anger come not so much from the loss of a daughter as from public humiliation, from loss of reputation. In accusing Othello he protests the "general mock" which Desdemona has incurred by shunning "the wealthy curled darlings" [I. ii. 68] of Venice in her choice of a Moor and an outlander. But it is Iago who fully expresses reputation in its malignant form. Shakespeare has him end two scenes, I. iii and II. i, in parallel soliloquies which clearly express his cast of mind. Brooding upon imagined injury, he cherishes fictions which enhance his degradation and justify retaliation; thence he moves from skeptical pleasure in these fictions to a consuming belief in them.

Iago's passage at the end of I. iii discloses among other things that his hatred of Othello turns upon reputation: "And it is thought abroad that 'twixt my sheets / He has done my office" [I. iii. 387-88]. Iago does not know "if't be true," but led on by self-interest, he dismisses the question of truth: "But I, for mere suspicion in that kind / Will do as if for surety" [I. iii. 388-90]. Here motive is expressed in soliloquy, and it is prob-

ably because of the deliberative air thus given Iago that he is often considered a cynic whose deceit is wholly calculated. In a superficial sense this may be true but it is far from the whole truth when the soliloquy is read as part of a sequence (I. iii-II.i): obsessed with reputation—with what is "thought abroad"—Iago will actually suggest the later Othello as he passes naïvely from surmise to the delusion of certainty. (pp. 111-15)

Since Act III, scene iii of *Othello* is the traditional point of disagreement between psychological interpreters and those who stress the "calumniator believed" convention, an old question may take on new meaning if we examine the scene for its unusual expression of the reputation theme. Concern for good name is made prominent here at two stages. The first is a passage [III. iii. 133ff.] in which Iago crosses the danger line and, half in duplicity, half in real fear, retreats from Othello's questioning. Then, as Othello presses his tempter, Iago dramatically counters with simulated virtue; he cannot utter his "thoughts" because reputation is privileged, and—"Good name in man and woman, dear my lord, / Is the immediate jewel of their souls" [III. iii. 155-56].

The second appearance in III. iii of the reputation theme is equally forceful. It occurs just after Iago's avowal that "not poppy, nor mandragora, / Nor all the drowsy syrups of the world" shall restore Othello's "sweet sleep" [III. iii. 330-32]. Othello resigns himself:

>   O, now, for ever
> Farewell the tranquil mind! farewell content!
> Farewell the plumed troops and the big wars
> That make ambition virtue!
>
> [III. iii. 347-50]

The passage then expands into further symbols of lost career and renown until it ends with "Othello's occupation's gone!" [III. iii. 357] a dramatic echo of Cassio's "Reputation . . . I have lost my reputation!"

It should be clear that neither Iago's invoking of good name nor Othello's withdrawal from public honor is purposive here unless the reputation theme is assumed to be significant. In a run-of-the-mill scene involving temptation to jealousy, Iago's false reluctance would probably take the form of simple concern over drawing Othello into error, and Othello's agony would more aptly appear as a farewell to love instead of to martial glory. Shakespeare, however, turns both situations into lyrical developments of reputation, and so continues a theme which has been present from the beginning. Nor should it be forgotten that the episode is set in motion by Desdemona's move to redeem Cassio's good name. A scene presenting the reputation theme as it affects two characters (Desdemona and Othello) thus arises from efforts to restore the reputation of a third character. (pp. 117-19)

The second phase of III. iii continues the shuttling, both within and between characters, of opposite aspects of the good-name theme. Othello reenters at Iago's line, "Look, where he comes" [III. iii. 330]. The egoistic side of honor then gains full expression as Othello declares he has been set "on the rack," that "'tis better to be much abus'd / Than but to know't a little" [III. iii. 335-37].

> What sense had I of her stol'n hours of lust?
> I saw 't not, thought it not, it harm'd not me.
> I slept the next night well. . . .
>
> [III. iii. 338-40]

Ignorance of slander, a state of being "much abus'd," is now valued above public good name. Concern for the outward world has lapsed:

> I had been happy, if the general camp,
> Pioners and all, had tasted her sweet body,
> So I had nothing known.
>
> [III. iii. 345-47]

Reputation is rejected, but its egoistic counterpart remains. The play of contraries is resumed, however, for directly out of Othello's abandonment of outward honor comes a statement of its priceless quality: "Farewell the plumed troops and the big wars / That make ambition virtue! . . . and all quality / Pride, pomp, and circumstance of glorious war! / . . . Farewell! Othello's occupation's gone!" [III. iii. 349-50, 353-54, 357]. In the logic which controls III.iii, and extends throughout the play, strong affirmation and strong negation imply each other. This, of course, is a logic of the emotions but it represents an actuality of thinking and feeling which is a traditional basis for tragedy.

As with the original "good name" passage and its sequel, egoism now completes the pattern. Just as Othello had previously declared for objective proof ("when I doubt, prove" [III. iii. 190]), so here after the line on occupation his demand runs, ". . . be sure thou prove my love a whore / Be sure of it. Give me the ocular proof / . . . Make me to see 't; or, at the least, so prove it / That the probation bear no hinge nor

Act IV. Scene ii. Othello and Desdemona. By F. Dicksee. The Department of Rare Books and Special Collections, The University of Michigan Library.

loop / To hang a doubt on . . ." [III. iii. 359-60, 364-66]. And as before, objective proof becomes subjective delusion. The proof must be "ocular proof," and it appears as ocular fantasy: "Would you, the supervisor, grossly gape on— / Behold her topp'd?" [III. iii. 395-96]. The "probation" must "bear no hinge or loop / To hang a doubt on," and it consists of Iago's obscene account of Cassio's dream. Finally, again the ocular proof: "Have you not sometimes seen a handkerchief / . . . such a handkerchief— / I am sure it was your wife's—did I today / See Cassio wipe his beard with" [III. iii. 434, 437-39]. Upon introduction of the handkerchief the deception of Othello is complete: "If it be that, —" [III. iii. 439]; and following these ominous words come the lines invoking "black vengeance" and "hollow hell." (pp. 120-21)

Traditionally, the motivation of Othello has been thought to end with his fall in III. iii, and interpreters of the play have seldom assumed that the pyschological growth of his role continues through five acts. Another dramatist might have ended the matter with Cassio's beard wiped by the handkerchief, but Shakespeare chooses to begin at this point a last phase of Othello's commitment to Pride, a phase marked throughout by ritual dedication. Very infrequently have symbolic materials been used with greater meaning or with more regard for the requirements of drama.

As the strawberry-spotted handkerchief ends Othello's doubt, Shakespeare begins the second half of the tragedy in a changed key. From the point of Othello's near-attack upon Iago [III. iii. 368-73] the temptation scene approaches realism in its dialogue of anger and suppressed violence, but some twenty lines from the end Othello subsides ominously into a formal style:

> Like to the Pontic Sea,
> Whose icy current and compulsive course
> Ne'er feels retiring ebb but keeps due on
> To the Propontic and the Hellespont,
> Even so my bloody thoughts with violent pace,
> Shall ne'er look back, ne'er ebb to humble love. . . .
>
> [III. iii. 453-58]

The imagery first expresses hard resolve moving not impulsively but deliberately—"due on"—a tide of Nemesis, depersonalized and immense. Verse rhythms, moreover, carry the same quality. But the Homeric simile then shows a contradiction which suggests Othello's, so that a stock poetic device can be said to reveal character. The initial images with their expression of slow steadiness are suddenly modified by the traditional "so" comparison which completes the figure: "Like to the Pontic sea . . ." it has begun; "Even so," it concludes, "my bloody thoughts with violent pace . . ." Blood, violence, haste thus follow stately tidal motion, but the effect is kept momentary by immediate restatement of the tidal figure; the passage ends: "Shall ne'er look back, ne'er ebb to humble love."

Lest this reading of the Pontic Sea lines be thought conjectural, I may say that my general argument does not depend upon it. I do not wish, however, to minimize it, for it is supported by a passage which follows the one in question. If we can agree that the long simile calls for an actor's break from calm to anger at the "even so" point, we shall find that suggestion of unstable motive by "unstable metaphor" is supplemented by dialogue and action which appear directly afterward. Ceremonialized calm begins again with Othello kneeling:

> Now by yond marble heaven,
> In the due reverence of a sacred vow
> I here engage my words.
>
> [III. iii. 460-62]

Then Iago, quickly taking his cue from Othello's mood:

> Do not rise yet.
> Witness, you ever-burning lights above,
> You elements that clip us round about,
> Witness that here Iago doth give up
> The execution of his wit, hands, heart,
> To wrong'd Othello's service!
>
> [III. iii. 462-67]

This is followed by Othello's almost stilted: "I greet thy love, / Not with vain thanks, but with acceptance bounteous," a deliberative line followed, as before, by an immediate breakthrough to violent haste: "And will upon the instant put thee to 't: / Within these three days let me hear thee say / That Cassio's not alive" [III. iii. 469-70, 471-73]. At this impulsive breach of rite Iago maintains ceremony briefly with his formal "My friend is dead," and provocatively adds, "But let her live" [III. iii. 474-75]. Here the ritual containment ends; what had been a dedication under heaven and the ever-burning stars, a solemn judgment passed upon two offenders, is broken by "Damn her, lewd minx! O, damn her! damn her! / . . . I will withdraw / To furnish me with some swift means of death / For the fair devil" [III. iii. 476-77, 479]. The ritual kneeling and intonation have expressed judicial poise and purified motive just as did the tidal figure in the earlier passage. And as the Pontic Sea image was negated by the "violent pace" comparison which arose from it, so is the kneeling ceremony destroyed by Othello's outcry which comes like a shout in church.

In the remainder of *Othello* we shall find clear development of the character conflict and moral crisis introduced by this episode. It has begun a ceremonial course of action in which Othello, assisted by Iago, invokes the light of heaven as a purifying symbol, and transmutes vengeance into even-handed justice. The dramatist's point of view is ironical: he does not, of course, imply that ritual is evil in itself, but he bases the rest of his tragedy upon subjective delusion fortified by objective ceremony. Personalized violence seeks to become impersonal action. As Shakespeare presents them, Othello's rites not only reinforce error but at the moment of performance contradict their own validity. (pp. 123-26)

We have seen that the ritual tone at the end of III. iii is twice broken by Othello's violence of response. At the next stage of his tragedy another deliberative mood ends in similar contradiction; in IV. i at the great line, "But yet the pity of it, Iago! . . . the pity of it, Iago!" Othello, needled, again destroys the sublimity he has evoked: "I will chop her into messes. Cuckold me!" [IV. i. 194-95, 200]. Once more he moves with violence and pace: "Get me some poison, Iago; this night . . . This night, Iago" [IV. i 204, 206]. Now, however, a return to ceremony, to symbolic action, succeeds the violence. Iago's line, "Do not do it with poison; strangle her in her bed, even the bed she hath contaminated," brings Othello's reply: "Good, good; the justice of it pleases; very good" [IV. i. 207-10].

Symbolic justice has emerged, and the next scene begins appropriately with examination of the criminal. For this purpose Othello invents a strange mock ceremony. Scene: a brothel. Characters: Desdemona, the whore; Emilia, the proprietress; Othello, the patron—the lines which suddenly set the stage are well known. The scene, however, quickly changes as Othello's perverse imagination transforms the cast into a magistrate, a criminal, and a witness. The opening lines suggest the transcript of a court record:

> *Othello.* You have seen nothing then?
> *Emilia.* Nor even heard, nor ever did suspect. . . .
> *Othello.* What, did they never whisper?
> *Emilia.*   Never, my lord.
> *Othello.* Nor send you out o' th' way?
> *Emilia.* Never.
>
> [IV. ii. 1-2, 6-8]

The stylized cross-examination continues with Desdemona's appearance:

> *Othello.*   Pray, chuck, come
>   hither.
> *Desdemona.* What is your pleasure?
> *Othello.*   Let me see your eyes;
>   Look in my face.
>
> [IV. ii. 24-6]

And the tone of official inquiry is sustained:

> *Othello.* Are you not a strumpet?
> *Desdemona.*   No, as I am a
>   Christian. . . .
> *Othello.* What, not a whore?
> *Desdemona.*   No, as I shall be sav'd.
> *Othello.* Is't possible?
> *Desdemona.* O, Heaven forgive us!
> *Othello.*   I cry you mercy, then.
>   I took you for that cunning whore of Venice
>   That married with Othello.
>
> [IV. ii. 82, 86-90]

This "ceremony" differs pointedly, of course, from the ritual oath of III. iii and the coming "sacrifice" of V. ii, but it aptly represents Othello's growing formalism. It also provides an answer to those who question his failure to deal frankly with Desdemona, for his egoistic secretiveness comes forth in an interlude he has composed to express it. In its relation to III. iii and V. ii the "brothel" scene is anti-ritual which presents Othello in a near-parody of his new-found role.

First, then, occurs a rite, designed to sublimate violence, in which violence breaks the spell (III. iii); next, Iago, who had "officiated" on the first occasion, deflects Othello from the violence of poisoning to the path of symbolic justice (IV. i). Appropriately following this, a travesty of judicial ceremony is enacted in an imaginary brothel (IV. ii). These events begin Othello's ritualized course which will end in the sacrificial murder of V. ii.

Act IV, scene ii, however, offers more than a step in this process; it presents the motive, reputation, which by now has become wholly egocentric. Just after his dismissal of Desdemona's plea for understanding, Othello takes the stage in a soliloquy on good name: "Had they rain'd / All kind of sores and shames on my bare head, / . . . I should have found . . . / A drop of patience; but, alas, to make me / The fixed figure for the time of scorn / To point his slow and moving finger at! / Yet could I bear that too, well, very well" [IV. ii. 48-9, 52-6]. Outward disgrace is thus bearable and the insupportable shame is yet to be expressed. It is the violation of self-esteem; concern for reputation takes the final inward turn:

> But there, where I have garner'd up my heart,
> Where either I must live or bear no life;
> The fountain from the which my current runs

Or else dries up; to be discarded thence!
Or keep it as a cistern for foul toads
To knot and gender in!

[IV. ii. 57-62]

Desecration of the inner "fountain" calls for vengeance which, in turn, calls for consecration lest it be unworthy of the inner light. The consecration, the ritual, becomes an enshrinement of self. (pp. 126-29)

Robert Heilman has noted the interesting repetition at this point in *Othello* of a light symbol. With an emphasis and purpose different from his I shall relate this to the subject at hand. In III. iii, Othello kneels, calling upon "yond marble heaven" to witness his dedication, and Iago, quickly kneeling beside him, addresses the "ever-burning lights above." In IV. ii, just after the "anti-ritual" or "brothel" episode, the symbol of celestial light is again invoked, this time by the kneeling Desdemona:

Alas, Iago,
What shall I do to win my lord again?
Good friend, go to him; for, by this light of heaven
I know not how I lost him. Here I kneel.

[IV. ii. 148-51]

And in IV. iii the heavenly light token appears once more, supported by a lively interplay of tragic and comic meaning. Desdemona has asked the wordly Emilia whether "there be women do abuse their husbands / In such gross kind" [IV. iii. 62-3]. This follows:

Emilia. There be some such, no question.
Desdemona. Wouldst thou do such a deed for all the
    world?
Emilia. Why, would not you?
Desdemona. No, by this heavenly light!
Emilia. Nor I neither by this heavenly light;
    I might do't as well i' th' dark.

[IV. iii. 63-7]

Before this there has been little emphasis which would bring the symbol into dramatic relief. It has been latent, appearing first as Othello and Iago kneel in ceremony and then as Desdemona kneels in an impromptu rite which declares her fidelity. But as Emilia responds to Desdemona's second invocation of heavenly light with an engaging quip which repeats it and verbally plays upon it, the device comes into the open; its latent state changes to an active one with emphasis at once retrospective and immediate.

The last and conclusive appearance of the figure occurs where we might expect it, in the murder scene itself. Othello's final obsession is expressed wholly through the ritual theme which, in turn, is controlled by the light symbol. "Enter Othello with a light" [s.d. V. ii. 1]. Little could be made of this stage direction if it were not immediately supported by images of heavenly light which continue the original design, and if the light Othello carries were not made prominent in later lines. The invocation, "Let me not name it to you, you chaste stars!" [V. ii. 2] reintroduces celestial light as symbol of chastity; Desdemona has twice used it in this sense, Emilia has quipped that adultery cannot flourish under it, and now Othello invokes it to express the purity he thinks he is redeeming from violation. With the chaste stars appears also the holy light which is to shine over the act of "sacrifice." In this sense the symbol pointedly recalls III. iii in which the "ever-burning" stars shone upon a consecration of violence.

And now the quenching of the light, a physical prologue to murder which promptly becomes the theme of Othello's soliloquy. With lines abounding in images of light he enters a darkness both dramatically real and metaphorical:

Put out the light, and then put out the light.
If I quench thee, thou flaming minister,
I can again thy former light restore,
Should I repent me; but once put out thy light,
Thou cunning'st pattern of excelling nature,
I know not where is that Promethean heat
That can thy light relume.

[V. ii. 7-13]

Obsession has become ultimate: Othello's ritualized logic is unerring, but his delusion is complete. (pp. 129-32)

Othello's ritual in the murder scene is an elaborate one. In addition to casting himself as light-bearer and minister of Justice, he suggests the role of priest: "Have you pray'd tonight, Desdemon? / . . . Well, do it . . . / I would not kill thy unprepared spirit; / . . . I would not kill thy soul. / . . . Think on thy sins" [V. ii. 25, 30-2, 40]. And after implying the Christian office of absolution he introduces the pagan one of sacrifice:

O perjur'd woman! thou dost stone my heart,
And mak'st me call what I intend to do
A murder, which I thought a sacrifice.

[V. ii. 63-5]

Othello's intended rite has been implicit throughout, but his line, "A murder, which I thought a sacrifice," defeats the intention at the moment of explicit statement. Without real awareness he tells the truth about his ritual act; once more ceremony mocks itself and its contriver. And as liturgy turns into murder, even the symbolic tone of the scene is ended by Emilia, one of Shakespeare's most naturalistic characters. Her cry, "O gull! O dolt! / As ignorant as dirt!" [V. ii. 163-64] brings the denouement.

Here then, under the "heavenly light," the magistrate-priest-sacrificer has performed his last rite of self-delusion. To say this is not to pass final judgment upon Othello, for few of Shakespeare's characters exceed him in ultimate self-knowledge. This knowledge will come, however, only after he advances a last claim to ceremonial honor. Lodovico becomes the accuser:

O thou Othello, that wast once so good,
Fall'n in the practice of a cursed slave,
What shall be said to thee?

[V. ii. 291-93]

And Othello can only reply:

Why anything.
An honourable murder, if you will;
For nought I did in hate, but all in honour.

[V. ii. 293-95]

Pathetically, defensively, now knowing what he has done, he still holds to the rite of hateless sacrifice.

There remain some eighty lines of the play, and within that space Othello gains the self-awareness which Macbeth, Hamlet, and Lear achieve much earlier. In Othello the denouement and the appearance of full tragic stature are almost simultaneous. Othello's reply to Lodovico finds him still holding to honor and its expression in unwrathful rite, so that it would be easy to say that he evolves no further, that even at the end he tries to justify the ceremony of loving bloodshed by dying "upon a kiss" [V. ii. 359]. Honor and rite, however, undergo change, for at his death Othello is free from the egoistic concern for reputation which drove him to the "sacrifice" of V. ii and to the ritual acts which prepared for it. In his last declaration, "Soft you; a word or two before you go" [V. ii. 338], his honor is no longer a formalized defense against the inner knotting and gendering of toads; it is the quality he once showed upon facing Brabantio and the Venetian Council. "I have done the state some service and they know't. / No more of that" [V. ii. 339-40]. "Speak of me as I am; nothing extenuate, / Nor set down aught in malice" [V. ii. 342-43].

> Set you down this;
> And say besides, that in Aleppo once,
> Where a malignant and a turban'd Turk
> Beat a Venetian and traduc'd the state,
> I took by th' throat the circumcised dog,
> And smote him—thus.
>
> [V. ii. 351-56]

With these lines of understatement setting forth a half-forgotten incident, pride is purged as the reputation theme appears for the last time. Killing the nameless dog who "traduc'd" the state was a vindication of Venetian good-name, and Othello's humble irony in speaking of the incident frees him from Iago's inversion of the reputation ideal. (pp. 133-35)

> Brents Stirling, "'Reputation, Reputation, Reputation!'" in his Unity in Shakespearian Tragedy: The Interplay of Theme and Character, 1956. Reprint by Gordian Press, Inc., 1966, pp. 111-38.

JOHN ARTHOS   (essay date 1958)

[*Arthos contends that the opposition of honor and love is the principal thematic interest in* Othello, *arguing that the Moor's integrity and self-definition are originally based on his concept of honor but that throughout the course of the play his love for Desdemona increasingly becomes the essential joy and support of his life. Maintaining that other passions, such as jealousy, are not initially operative in Othello's determination to kill Desdemona, the critic avers that the supposed transgression against his honor impels him to slay her and that he formulates his punishment accordingly, in terms of ceremony and sacrament—an assessment similar to that of Brents Stirling (1956). Citing the commentary of the nineteenth-century French essayist Alfred De Vigny on the "chivalric and sacramental" basis of a soldier's concept of honor, Arthos discerns these elements in Othello's initial reaction to Desdemona's alleged infidelity, but he contends that "the cult of honor" is debased by the Moor himself when he becomes vengeful, hateful, and punitive. Further, this cult does not remain the principal basis of Othello's integrity and joy in life, the critic believes, for by the conclusion of the play it has been superceded by his love for Desdemona. In killing her, Arthos concludes, Othello destroys the source of his happiness and the fundamental meaning of his existence, leaving himself with no alternative but the final sacramental act of suicide. For further discussions of Othello's excessive sense of honor or reputation, see the excerpts by Denton J. Snider (1887), G. R. Elliott (1937 and 1953), F. R. Leavis (1937), Derek Traversi (1949), Roy W. Battenhouse (1969), and Carol McGinnis Kay (1983).*]

In thinking of the downfall of Othello one is drawn to consider certain matters concerning the role of honor in this play, and also to contemplate something that is in a certain sense prior to that, the idea of the integrity of the self. This idea seems to have been constant with Shakespeare, and it was expressed at the very beginning of his work, in Adonis's ultimate ar-

gument: "Before I know myself, seek not to know me" [*Venus and Adonis*]. (p. 95)

The idea of the self as the test of truth and chivalry involves such profound commitments that it is inevitable not only that it should be extended into the complexities of characterization, but that it should also provide an essential qualification for Shakespeare's conception of drama itself. These observations come most naturally, I suppose, when we fix our attention upon the chivalric qualities of such a figure as Othello. Wyndham Lewis' theories [see excerpt above, 1927] were at one place illustrated by a comparison of Othello and Don Quixote, and he spoke of Othello as "the ideal human galleon, twenty storeys high, with his head in the clouds, that the little can vanquish", another Don Quixote who, after some catastrophe or other, could say, "The wound that phantom gave me!" . . . This view of things reinforces Macaulay's way of appealing to common sense, when he suggested how the story itself of Othello might appear to the Italians for whom Machiavelli wrote:

> Othello murders his wife; he gives orders for the murder of his lieutenant; he ends by murdering himself. Yet he never loses the esteem and affection of Northern readers. His intrepid and ardent spirit redeems every thing. . . . Iago, on the contrary, is the object of universal loathing. Many are inclined to suspect that Shakespeare has been seduced into an exaggeration unusual with him, and has drawn a monster who has no archetype in human nature. Now we suspect that an Italian audience in the fifteenth century would have felt very differently. Othello would have inspired nothing but detestation and contempt. The folly with which he trusts the friendly professions of a man whose promotion he had obstructed, the credulity with which he takes unsupported assertions, and trivial circumstances, for unanswerable proofs, the violence with which he silences the exculpation till the exculpation can only aggravate his misery, would have excited the abhorrence and disgust of the spectators. The conduct of Iago they would assuredly have condemned; but they would have condemned it as we condemn that of his victim. Something of interest and respect would have mingled with their disapprobation. The readiness of the traitor's wit, the clearness of his judgment, the skill with which he penetrates the dispositions of others and conceals his own, would have insured to him a certain portion of their esteem [see Additional Bibliography].

But Shakespeare is not mocking chivalry or honor or phantasy. He is himself committed to the idea of the integrity of the self, and whatever we may think is involved in the fall of Othello no cause will ever be given us to question this even when we see honor turn against the self, in violence, and against the truth of the self, in distrusting love. It is true, I think, that the idea of the self and the idea of honor as one sees them in Shakespeare and in chivalry generally are both dependent upon mysticism, but whatever the foundation of these ideas, for Shakespeare the idea of the integrity of the self involves the notion of the adequacy of the self as the judge of truth, even absolute truth. The plays again and again make clear the fatality of delusion, of course, and the cult of honor, in Othello as in Don Quixote, often proposes for adoration delusion instead of truth, but the authority of the touchstone remains.

When Othello asks Iago to be careful of what he says, he speaks of an authority to be observed in an individual's truth that in itself evidently comprehends honor:

> And, for I know thou'rt full of love and honesty,
> And weigh'st thy words before thou giv'st them breath,
> Therefore these stops of thine fright me the more;
> For such things in a false disloyal knave
> Are tricks of custom; but in a man that's just
> They're close dilations, working from the heart
> That passion cannot rule.
>
> [III. iii. 118-24]

The idea that being true to oneself is the basis of honor is part of Othello's demand that Venice requite him in the terms that he deserves:

> If you do find me foul in her report,
> The trust, the office I do hold of you,
> Not only take away, but let your sentence
> Even fall upon my life.
>
> [I. iii. 117-20]

The cult of honor which in its fullest flourishing is the wholeness of his life and his career is dependent on this prior integrity:

> O, now, for ever
> Farewell the tranquil mind! farewell content!
> Farewell the plumed troops and the big wars
> That make ambition virtue! O, farewell!
> Farewell the neighing steed and the shrill trump,
> The spirit-stirring drum, th' ear-piercing fife,
> The royal banner, and all quality,
> Pride, pomp, and circumstance of glorious war!
> And, O you mortal engines, whose rude throats
> Th' immortal Jove's dread clamours counterfeit,
> Farewell! Othello's occupation's gone!
>
> [III. iii. 347-57]

There is egotism here, too, and a selfishness that makes Othello's love less pure than Desdemona's, but allowing Professor G. R. Elliott much in his including many of these matters in the word pride [see excerpt above, 1953], one ought, I think, to give the idea of honor a particular emphasis if only because Shakespeare makes such emphatic use of the term itself. The faults of honor are, of course, the faults of pride in part, and also the faults of "dreaming" or phantasy. It is nonetheless necessary to keep in mind the distinctions between pride and honor and those between honor and truth to oneself since it is the value of honor that is particularly questioned by the failure of Othello's love, and there is no questioning of the idea of the integrity of the self.

Certain remarks of De Vigny [in *Servitude et Grandeur Militaires* (1835)] upon the nature of honor in soldiers help our understanding of the character of Othello. . . . [In] emphasizing the chivalric and sacramental in the traditional military character he incidentally helps explain some of the occasion for the religious language in the play. (pp. 96-8)

What is particularly interesting [in De Vigny's essay], it seems to me, is the special emphasis upon the soldier's sense of dedication to something within himself, and to the solitariness of the cult. Here, as with Othello, there is the alliance or even the identification of the self with truth, the incontestable truth,

which must be enforced by one who, when put to it, would not know how to say what the truth is he enforces. In De Vigny as in Othello the cult of honor supports the sense of the beauty of life, in the most elevated way. But the very structure of such a "religion" is inadequate to the force of life in Othello, and it fails him as it would fail anyone when in defending honor by punishment and vengeance he falls into hate: "I am abus'd; and my relief / Must be to loathe her" [III. iii. 267-68]. Hatred as much as love deprives the cult of honor of its center in the self, and its sufficiency.

Perhaps one can never say what a man hopes to do by killing although it seems that violence is always directed against ideas, and in murder it is directed against the idea of a person. For Othello the need for violence, apart from the activities of war, is most inextinguishably aroused when he is moved to destroy whatever involves the violation of oaths. He must break Cassio on the doubt of his fidelity, and he must break Desdemona. The confusions of jealousy and lust contribute to the cruelty of his treatment of Desdemona, but the impetus is originally soldierly and sacramental.

> Like to the Pontic sea,
> Whose icy current and compulsive course
> Ne'er [feels] retiring ebb, but keeps due on
> To the Propontic and the Hellespont,
> Even so my bloody thoughts, with violent pace,
> Shall ne'er look back, ne'er ebb to humble love,
> Till that a capable and wide revenge
> Swallow them up. Now, by yond marble heaven,
> In the due reverence of a sacred vow
> I here engage my words. . . .
> Damn her, lewd minx! O, damn her! damn her!
>
> [III. iii. 453-62, 476]

The oath, the sacrifice, and, then, worst of all, the curse, brought out by the pain of the betrayal and by the confusion of passion.

It seems that once he had punished Cassio and removed such a cause of weakness and disintegration from the army he could carry on his own dedication unimpaired. The sacrifice to honor in such a case—and the ties that bind Othello and Cassio are not to be lightly broken—is somehow satisfactory. The sacrifice of Desdemona was something else. Having loved her as he did, Othello discovered that she was not to be displaced from his "soul" by whatever efforts towards integrity and purity the cult of honor prescribes.

It is no longer his, he discovers, the wholeness of soul and heart that would allow him to go on as he had, unwed, self-sufficient, glorious. His nature had grown in loving her, had become a more majestical and miraculous self, he had come into quite another life. He is no longer merely the soldier given to his profession and to Venice but he is now also someone inextricably part of Desdemona's life:

> My soul hath her content so absolute
> That not another comfort like to this
> Succeeds in unknown fate.
>
> [II. i. 191-93]

If he loses her he cannot be as he once was:

> But I do love thee! and when I love thee not,
> Chaos is come again.
>
> [III. iii. 91-2]

And if he destroys his ''joy'', even in the cause of honor, he will now be destroying himself.

> The fountain from the which my current runs
> Or else dries up.
>
> [IV. ii. 59-60]

And finally the terrible question will form: ''But why should honour outlive honesty?'' [V. ii. 245]. Why should honor survive when the simplest faithfulness is gone? When joy is gone?

Honor had for Othello the force of absolute authority, and I think we must suppose that the pain of dishonor was felt comparably, an absolute pain, if one might use those words. And the pain of the loss of love was worse. As a kind of pain it quite overcame him, partly in the way of epilepsy and partly in his raging, and so it was that such paroxysms together with *le vertige sensuel* [sensual intoxication] and the stupidity of a man trusting appearances all worked together to sweep him into the final stupidity of logic. And into the usual military error, and the error demanded, I guess, by honor itself when it has an absolute force, to cut off the ''cause'' of the pain.

But the ''cause'' as it happens is not merely another human being, and not merely a dispensable part of a military organization. Desdemona dead, if she can no longer be unfaithful neither can she be faithful any more, and Othello's new life and his joy are lost with her forever. Having admitted and spoiled love, instead of order, hierarchy, obedience, faithfulness, Othello's original equilibrium, there is now only chaos. The new life gone, he and honor are no longer a measure of the truth. Only the meaningless swirl of life is left, the very ''gulfs of liquid fire'' [V. ii. 280], the observance of honor in a world without love and without truth.

It appears that Othello's integrity depended on something other than honor and that he was indeed abused. His fall came with the spoiling of his love, the suspicions that undermined his happiness and sapped his sufficiency, for it was his love that brought the richest fulfillment of his self. When he retreated to the idea of himself as someone who was a stranger to Desdemona, obeying honor and disavowing love, he made still another mistake, taking the word of a liar. This was a foolish fault and it dishonored him, but the other was ruinous beyond that, the spoiling of the capacity of the soul to grow in the love of another. (pp. 99-100)

Othello has been enlarged by love, and then he proved not quite equal to its demands. Honor and the asceticism of the military character, the beauty of the life, the ardency and beauty of its spirit, its purity, all these excellences became the scapegoats of his failure.

Othello never opposes love and honor in the manner developed a few years later on the European stage. The theme is here but the debate is not formulated, and the contrivance of the plot is directed to quite another interest finally, to the presentation of an individual ultimately alone in his mind. In the terms of Kenneth Burke [see excerpt above, 1951], it is conceived in presenting an image of absolute solitude. Commenting on Othello's attitude towards Desdemona, he said:

> In ownership as thus conceived, our play is saying in effect, there is also forever lurking the sinister invitation to an ultimate lie, an illusion carried to the edge of metaphysical madness, as private ownership, thus projected into realms for which there are no unquestionably attested securities, is seen to imply also, pro-

foundly, ultimately, estrangement; hence, we may in glimpses peer over the abyss into the regions of pure abstract loneliness. . . . And, as projected absolutely, all culminated in a last despairing act of total loneliness.

That the revelation of such a state was the conclusion of the play may also be inferred from the way Shakespeare managed the time of the play's action—in a certain respect a duration of days, in another, as if almost no time passed. How important it is that we should hardly feel the passing of time in *Othello,* after the voyage to Cyprus, is made obvious by comparing Cinthio, and in observing what Shakespeare excluded from his original, the aftermath:

> Ere long the Moor, whom Disdemona loved more than her own life, began to feel such sorrow at her loss that he went wandering about as one bereft of reason, searching in every part of the house. And reflecting in his thoughts that the Ensign had been the cause that he had lost, with Disdemona, all joy in life, he conceived so deep a hatred to that wicked man he could not bear to set eyes on him, and had it not been for his fear of the inviolable justice of the Signoria of Venice, he would have slain him openly.

For Shakespeare's Othello there was no such dimension to his life. For one reason, as Granville-Barker said, ''If Othello's ruin is not accomplished without pause or delay, it can hardly be accomplished at all'' [see excerpt above, 1945]. This not only means that Iago's plotting could not succeed indefinitely, but it also means that Othello's view of things might change, and if some other idea should for a moment overcome the sense of dishonor in Othello, the whole meaning of the play would be affected.

The sense of the passing of time would radically alter the play not only from the particular circumstances of the plot but because in dramas where love and honor come into conflict our interest moves past the conflict to the issue. Our interest does not rest with the sight of an individual quite alone with himself in his struggles, but turns towards other persons and his relation to them. What we finally are absorbed in in the best of the plays where love and honor seem irreconcilably opposed are their claims to be reconciled. And our interest in the issue depends upon the play's exploitation of the sense of enough time passing to make the issue seem valid. (pp. 101-02)

Before he met Desdemona Othello had achieved a wonderful equilibrium to the very culmination of his career, but even this balance, this self-sufficiency was enriched by the joy Desdemona brought him. In his union with her Othello felt none of the constriction of one who is owned and on the contrary seemed to know a limitless freedom hitherto unimaginable—''O my soul's joy!'' [II. i. 184]. The quality of this love that can be spoken of as joy, certainly independent of any of the Christian meanings of that word and yet sharing the idea of the absolute absence of care, is emphasized throughout the play by the constant use of the word *soul*. Even Iago, calling Othello uxorious, takes up the word:

> His soul is so enfetter'd to her love,
> That she may make, unmake, do what she list,
> Even as her appetite shall play the god
> With his weak function.
>
> [II. iii. 345-48]

The Senators had given the clue:

> Othello, speak,
> Did you by indirect and forced courses
> Subdue and poison this young maid's affections?
> Or came it by request and such fair question
> As soul to soul affordeth?
>
> [I. iii. 110-14]

The beauty of the love, Othello's "barbaric innocence", and Desdemona's pureness, all presented to us in the language of heaven, saints, souls, and after a while in words about hell and damnation, make it clear that the struggle in Othello's mind was between loyalties each of which claimed absolute power, the love of "souls" (if one takes that not as a passionless thing, but simply as love at its most generous), and honor.

Folly and jealousy and lust corrupt his love as ambition never corrupts his other obligations, but it is not the vices finally that lead him to think of killing Desdemona even though he loathes her, but honor, and even though passion replaces the calculation of Cinthio's Moor—"On leaving the room, the Moor fell to meditating how he should put his wife to death." Lust and jealousy are part of the reality someone more like Don Quixote might never have recognized, but Othello for all his innocence was never that far out of touch with things. He paid one of his debts to reality in striking Desdemona and cursing her, but in killing her he passed beyond jealousy and passion in order to lose sight of her as herself—"It is the *cause*. . ." [V. ii. i]. One might say that the tragic action of *Othello* was the murder in Othello's mind, the substitution of the cause for the person, the displacement of love by the *idea* of the superior sanctity of honor.

But there is no debate and the characters do not take sides.

There were times when Othello thought that the misery that overcame him was the pain of dishonor alone, but when he was preparing to kill himself he made another sacramental gesture something like the ceremonial he developed in killing Desdemona, only this time the religious suggestions were more bitter—

> And say besides, that in Aleppo once,
> Where a malignant and a turban'd Turk
> Beat a Venetian and traduc'd the state,
> I took by th' throat the circumcised dog,
> And smotc him—thus.
>
> [V. ii. 352-56]

Which is to say, for one thing, that this time the vengeance is as empty as a bad joke. It is not the pain of dishonor that has brought him to this imitation of a deed of vengeance and religion but the loss of love, the loss of joy, dying in the kiss of a corpse his distrust had brought to this. (pp. 103-04)

> John Arthos, "The Fall of Othello," in Shakespeare
> Quarterly, *Vol. IX, No. 2, Spring, 1958, pp. 93-104.*

EDWARD HUBLER   (essay date 1958)

[*Declaring that the function of the critic is to consider only what is depicted in the developing dramatic action of the play and avoid raising issues that are not clearly evident in Shakespeare's text, Hubler sharply attacks the contention of S. L. Bethell (1952) and Paul N. Siegel (1953) that the dramatist represents Othello as eternally damned at the close of the drama. His own view of the Moor is that he is a man of great heart, guilty of a grievous*

wrong, but prepared to make atonement for that crime by sacrificing his life. In Hubler's estimation, "Othello's 'eternal destiny,' if he has one, is only of peripheral importance to our experience of the play." Other critics who have examined the condition of Othello's soul at the end of the play include Kenneth O. Myrick (1941), Harley Granville-Barker (1945), Irving Ribner (1955 and 1960), G. M. Matthews (1964), and Roy W. Battenhouse (1969). Siegel's response to Hubler's essay is cited in the Additional Bibliography.]

The Christian approach to [Shakespeare] has produced landmarks in our growing knowledge of him. Yet I am unhappy about some recent studies. They seem to be written by men to whom Christianity has little meaning. It is as though they found it in the library one day, and found it useful. They pillage Christianity, and they pillage it selectively. The result, all too often, is pedantry. My view of pedantry here is that of Shakespeare in *Love's Labour's Lost*—learning unrelated to experience.

This criticism is most often concerned with imagery and symbolism, which are somehow deified, much as some Victorians deified character. They are allowed to take precedence over all the other elements of the play and to suggest things which a more total view of the play would deny. What I miss most in these studies is the view of literature as experience, as something which extends, deepens and elevates the pitifully limited scope of our daily lives. (p. 295)

Since there is nothing to be gained from breaking butterflies, let us begin with an essay of genuine stature from which we can all learn, "The Diabolic Images of *Othello*" by S. L. Bethell [see excerpt above, 1952]. . . . This is an essay which says good things about a number of plays, but the main thing it tells us about *Othello* is that Othello goes to hell and Desdemona to heaven. ". . . the black man, after all, is a devil. . . ." ". . . he has rejected Desdemona, and in so doing he has rejected heaven. Like Judas he fell through loss of faith". . . . And he goes to hell. "His suicide, since he is a Christian, seals his fate. Shakespeare does not leave us in much doubt about the eternal destiny of his tragic heroes". . . . Desdemona, on the other hand, "Quite certainly is angel, not devil, and she has gone to heaven". . . . We learn in passing that Macbeth "presumably goes to hell", that Lear "is fit for heaven", and that "Hamlet is attended to heaven by flights of angels. (It would be quite opposed to Elizabethan dramatic conventions for Horatio to be mistaken at this point about his hero's spiritual state)". . . . There are a number of things to be said about this. (1) There is something of the Victorian deification of character here. A character in a work of fiction has only those attributes his creator endows him with, and unless he is endowed with an "eternal destiny", he doesn't have one. Unless we are told where a character goes when he goes off the stage, he doesn't go anywhere at all. Unless we hold to this principle, we shall get back again to [Mary Cowden Clarke's] *The Girlhood of Shakespeare's Heroines*. (2) We may say, if we will, that Othello is possessed by a devil for a time, but to make him a devil is to make him a villain and negate the tragedy. (3) The view of symbolism here is much too simple; Desdemona, for instance "*is* angel". Without any wish to minimize her angelic qualities, we may assert that a symbol *is* not the thing symbolized and that implications and suggestions should not be solidified into fact, lest we distort the text. (4) I do not know how a Christian audience would know that Horatio is right about Hamlet's spiritual state. (5) Bethell tells us that the Elizabethans knew their ascetic theology. If they knew it better than he does, they would not assume that Othello's suicide ''seals his fate''. To assert that all suicides are damned to hell is to be guilty of blasphemy, for it sets limits on the mercy of God.

The other article is ''The Damnation of Othello'', by Paul N. Siegel [see excerpt above, 1953]. . . . Both Bethell and Siegel decided independently that although at the close of the play Othello is remorseful, he is not truly penitent, and he is therefore damned. Siegel, however, is a more thorough dispenser of justice. He sends both Othello and Roderigo to hell, and both Desdemona and Emilia to heaven. He finds that ''Desdemona is equated to the eternal verities'', and that she ''raises and redeems such earthly souls as Emilia. Belief in her, like belief in Christ, is a means of salvation''. . . . I do not find that this has much relevance to either the text or to Christianity. I find it difficult to recognize the play in this article. There seems to be no awareness of it as a dramatic action. Emergent things are taken as fully developed. The critic views, say, the middle of the play as though the impact of the final scene were fresh in his mind. In my experience of the play Iago is a character who grows in evil and symbolic value until at the end the suggestions of incarnate evil are clinched and he stands revealed as a demi-devil. Surely some of the terror of the close of act three, scene three, is owing to this revelation's not having yet been made. To Siegel this is a scene in which Othello makes a pact with the devil. My point is that we do not view it as such in the theatre. Nor do I recognize Roderigo in the description of him as ''the ordinary weak man led on by his desires to damnation. He at first regards Desdemona as highly as Cassio, speaking of her as 'blessed' [II. ii. 250] in a scene which immediately precedes and contrasts with the one in which Cassio rejects Iago's cynical insinuations''. . . . We may say of this that the scene precedes, but not immediately, the scene with which it contrasts. Roderigo does not call Desdemona ''blessed''. He says that she is ''full of most blessed condition'' [II. ii. 249-50], which is not at all the same thing. He is not the ordinary weak man, nor the ordinary anything else. He is one of Shakespeare's stupidest and most worthless characters. Iago calls him in soliloquy and aside a ''quat'' (that is, a pimple) and a ''snipe'', a bird legendary for its stupidity. At no time does he regard Desdemona as highly as Cassio does. To be sure, he speaks well of her, but he lusts after her and he plans to win his way to her bed through gifts. We are not told that he has gone to hell, nor can I find any suggestion of it. On the contrary we are told that he left some letters disclosing that he was to undertake the death of Cassio and upbraiding Iago for making him brave Cassio upon the watch. Then ''after long seeming dead'', he spoke, saying that ''Iago hurt him, Iago set him on'' [V. ii. 328-29]. It is a little as though he had said with Edmund, ''Some good I mean to do Despite of mine own nature'' [*King Lear*, V. iii. 244-45].

One more instance: ''When she [Desdemona] entreats, 'But while I say one prayer,' he [Othello] refuses her what he believes to be the opportunity for salvation which he had previously offered her and stifles her, saying, 'It is too late' [V. ii. 83]. At this moment Emilia pounds on the door to tell Othello of the attempted assassination of Cassio, who, escaped from death, can help the truth be revealed, but it is indeed too late: Othello's soul is lost''. . . . There are two things to notice here: (1) Emilia does not report the attempted assassination of Cassio; she reports the murder of Roderigo. (2) A Christian audience would have no reason to suppose that at this moment Othello's soul is lost. He is obviously in a state of sin, and just as obviously he is free to repent. As Christian criticism this is not Christian enough. I find it irrelevant to the scene considered

as drama, and it can only be made to seem relevant through the manipulation of ''It is too late.''

The text of the play says that Othello expects to be punished, and he himself asks for punishment:

> Whip me, ye devils,
> From the possession of this heavenly sight!
> Blow me about in winds! roast me in sulphur!
> Wash me in steep down gulfs of liquid fire!
> [V. ii. 277-80]

But this is not to say that Othello was damned. Indeed it could be argued that the sequence of ''Whip me'', ''Blow me about'', ''roast me'', and ''Wash me'' suggests purgation, and it would do no good to argue, as another critic has, that for almost a century the Elizabethans had been taught the non-existence of purgatory. The concept of purgatory served Shakespeare very well in *Hamlet,* and one of his two uses of the word ''purgatory'' occurs at the close of the fourth act of *Othello.* But I shall spare you an elaboration on this because I think that Othello's ''eternal destiny'', if he has one, is only of peripheral importance to our experience of the play. I know very well that to the Catholic morality and eschatology are inseparable. My point here is not theological; it is critical. Othello is not a man; he is a character in a play. When a man writes a play he selects some elements of his subject matter in order that we may concentrate on them. He supresses the others in order that our apprehension of his vision may be the more intense. He gives us a vision of life purified of matters not relevant to his purpose. I take it that what we are being shown in Othello's last speeches is the nature of a man who is ''great of heart'' [V. ii. 361], is greatly wrong, and is now about to make his utmost atonement. The view of tragedy as the dispensation of justice strikes me as childish. (pp. 296-98)

> *Edward Hubler, ''The Damnation of Othello: Some Limitations on the Christian View of the Play,'' in* Shakespeare Quarterly, *Vol. IX, No. 3, Summer, 1958, pp. 295-300.*

BERNARD SPIVACK   (essay date 1958)

[*In his book* Shakespeare and the Allegory of Evil *(1958), Spivack traces the development of Christian allegory from its earliest manifestation in the work of Prudentius, who flourished around 400 A.D. and whose poem* Psychomachia (The Battle for the Soul) *provided the generic name for the most common type of medieval allegory, to the morality plays of the Middle Ages and the ''hybrid drama'' of the sixteenth and seventeenth centuries; these hybrid dramas constituted a transitional form from the allegorical moralities to more naturalistic plays. In the excerpt below from that work, he demonstrates the dramatic lineage of Iago and Shakespeare's debt to the conventional Vice figure in morality drama, whose sole purpose was to bring about, ''through artful dissimulation and intrigue, the spiritual and physical ruin of frail humanity.'' With respect to* Othello, *Spivack contends that the principal theme of the play is love and that the enormity of Iago's evil is, in effect, an ''anti-theme,'' as he proceeds totally to destroy the ideal love of Desdemona and Othello. Further, he finds the source of Iago's hatred of the Moor in his dramatic ancestry, for whereas in the* Psychomachia *Vice and Virtue by nature hate each other and wage war for control of the human soul, in the later moralities and hybrid plays the personified virtues had disappeared and the hero, no longer a ''moral cypher,'' became the possessor of goodness, ''attracting the enmity as well as the aggression of the allegorical foe; thus, Iago as Vice must hate the goodness in Othello, and jealousy and resentment are merely superfluous motivations for him.'' Spivack also compares*

Iago to the Machiavellian figure of the Renaissance in his negation of all Christian or metaphysical values—an attitude, the critic states, best exemplified in his perception of love as mere sexual appetite and physical desire. Other critics who have regarded Iago as a Machiavellian figure include E. K. Chambers (1908), Wyndham Lewis (1927), Allardyce Nicoll (1927), and S. L. Bethell (1952). Also, for further commentary on Iago's role as a Vice figure in Othello, *see the excerpts by Irving Ribner (1955) and Robert G. Hunter (1976).]*

[Iago's] "character," impenetrable to coherent analysis, can be unwoven into two very dissimilar roles governed by two very different motive principles. On the one hand there is the cankered Iago of the thwarted ambition—except that he is never really cankered or ambitious; the passionately moved husband of a wife he believes unfaithful—except that, apart from one flicker of emotion, he is never passionately moved or in any way aware that the adultery he suspects involves his wife; the aspirant who seeks to gain an office by disgracing its incumbent—except that he does not show the slightest interest in the office before or after he achieves it; the hot-blooded Italian whose latent depravity is fired into action by a sense of injury—except that he does not display a sense of injury; the irascible soldier who finds himself deviously and shamefully wronged by Othello and Cassio—except that he proclaims that Othello and Cassio are honest fools, openhearted, generous-minded, noble, ingenuous men, whose artless virtue makes them the easy and natural victims of his duplicity.

On the other hand there appears a figure strange to us, but familiar and fascinating to the Elizabethan playgoer. The Iago who craves revenge for a slight or for dishonor, or seeks advancement to a post held by a rival, dissolves; and in his place appear the features, wrinkled in mocking laughter, of another Iago, concerned with a purpose that has nothing to do with either revenge or ambition. This second Iago is an artist eager to demonstrate his skill by achieving a masterpiece of his craft. He is working upon exactly the right material—ingenuous virtue, or (as in the case of Roderigo) ingenuous folly. His motivation is implicit in his self-proclaimed nature, in the proclaimed nature of his victims, and in the traditional dynamic of his role. His action, he announces, is to be an illustration of his natural talent through a display of virtuosity in aggression against the high spiritual values of love and friendship, and the susceptible naïveté of virtuous, but frail, humanity. (pp. 29-30)

Although Iago is essentially an amoral figure, we fail to grasp the deepest moral *consequence* of his action upon his victims unless we can appreciate the full meaning of his assault upon the "holy cords" [*King Lear*, II. ii. 74] that express Shakespeare's vision of the Good that suffers destruction in all his great tragedies. They are the bonds that knit nature, human society, and the cosmos into hierarchic order and unity and create the divinely ordained harmony of the universe. In the little world of men they are those ties of duty, piety, and humane affection which give a religious meaning to all domestic and social relationships, for in Shakespeare "religion" frequently has this wider sense. . . . Everywhere in his plays, but particularly in his great tragedies, human behavior on every level of life and in every kind of relationship receives its moral definition from its adherence or lack of adherence to the spiritual harmony and order of the universe. It is all religion. Filial piety, matrimonial love, fraternal loyalty, and the immutable social degrees under God's royal regent are spiritual alliances that express man's conformity with the divinely established

order of the cosmos and create the health and happiness—the very possibility in fact—of human society. . . . (p. 48)

The metaphysical range of his moral vision is the main literal and imaginative cargo of the great tragedies, controlling their origin and direction to a degree that still escapes us. The evil in each of them is much broader than simply the violation of private love and natural fealty between person and person. In each a great bond of piety, electric with cosmic meaning, is ruptured; the religious foundations of society are shaken and the universe is racked with disorder. A brother's murder, the unfaithfulness of a wife to the memory of her dead husband, filial ingratitude, the assassination of a king by his subject, the presumed adultery of a wife with her husband's friend—these are acts with infinite repercussion in the poet's ethical imagination. They violate the nature of man, the nature of society, the nature of the universe. It is in this deep sense that they all receive their great condemnation as *unnatural* acts. They are, in fact, all one crime. Their distinguishing details as separate malefactions dissolve and merge into a single large affront to the unity and harmony of the world. The bias of Shakespeare's choice for his great tragic themes and the depth of treatment he brings to them are a double consequence of his vision that evil in its greatest magnitude expresses division and disorder. (p. 49)

This tragic dilation into religious and metaphysical significance of crimes which in our secular modern view have only a personal or social meaning is undoubtedly part of the explanation of Shakespeare's magnitude. His language, subdued to his dramatic purpose, is rarely theological, as Dante's is, and his religious emphasis is upon human society rather than upon eternity. But in the great tragedies Evil receives a treatment that is uniformly metaphysical: it severs the "holy cords" of love and loyalty, cancels and tears to pieces the great bond that holds the universe in order. And in each of them, with one exception, it achieves its cosmic meaning through the language of a moral astronomy and is dyed into high relief by the iterated imagery and visionary atmosphere of the play.

The apparent exception, in spite of the giant evil in it, is *Othello*. From it seems to be absent that quality of transcendental vision that creates in *Hamlet*, in *Lear*, in *Macbeth*, in *Antony and Cleopatra* even, a level of meaning above the merely dramatic level of action, conflict, and passion. Also absent from it is that characteristic thematic imagery which in the other great tragedies elucidates the evil into symbol and metaphor and weaves out of them the imaginative texture of the play. (pp. 50-1)

This is not to say that *Othello* is without its cosmic reference, or devoid of thematic iterations both imagistic and verbal. But these are somehow irrelevant to the enormous evil in the play or lack the clairvoyant power to interpret it into a statement or an atmosphere that could be perspicuous to the imagination of the reader. The cosmic range is there in Othello's words to Desdemona, words reminiscent of Hamlet's to his mother, but they apply in this case to a purely fictitious evil, not to the wicked reality:

> Heaven stops the nose at it, and the moon winks;
> The bawdy wind, that kisses all it meets,
> Is hush'd within the hollow mine of earth
> And will not hear it.
>
> [IV. ii. 77-80]

There is also an abundance of verbal and metaphorical iteration, but it is no less inapplicable. Equally incident in the speech of

Othello and Iago there is the language of the sea, distilling apparently the maritime setting of the play and the salt-water careers of two soldiers in the employ of sea-fostered Venice. And there is, of course, in the word "honest," which adheres to Iago like a constant epithet, the thematic irony that highlights his success in dissimulation and the fatal misapprehension of him entertained by his noble-natured gulls. Furthermore, by himself on several occasions and by others in the last scene, he is equated with the devil; and he wears his satanism with pleasure—first in the vanity of self-comparison:

> When devils will the blackest sins put on,
> They do suggest at first with heavenly shows,
> As I do now.
>
> [II. iii. 351-53]

and later in the polite derision with which he interprets the wound Othello inflicts upon him in wonder-stricken experiment:

> *Oth.* I look down towards his feet—but that's a fable.
> If that thou be'st a devil, I cannot kill thee.
>   [*Wounds Iago*]
> *Iago.* I bleed, sir, but not kill'd.
>
> [V. ii. 286-88]

The importance of such words is not particularly in the diabolism itself, which is an incidental metaphor leading nowhere. For Othello in his passion Desdemona is also a "fair devil," and he applies the epithet to her three times more in the scene in which he strikes her. In the last scene Emilia applies it twice to him. Far back in Iago's ancestry there were devils and the cronies of devils, but his descent is collateral rather than direct, and his association with the diabolic, frequent as it is, is too much a moral cliché to be enlightening. Intrigue, dissimulation, and the seduction of virtue define the enterprise of the Common Enemy throughout the Christian mythos; and the diabolism in the language of this play is a figure for the similar behavior of Iago. But it does not explain him. The Devil is what Iago, considered in human terms, is *like*. What he *is*, is another matter.

But if the diabolism is not in itself enlightening, his joyous self-assertion in respect to it is. The distinction is important, for in Iago's case it makes all the difference between morality and art. The point needs to be examined in the company of another verbal repetition that rings through every scene of the play, reaching in the last one a pitch of clamorous iteration that amounts almost to frenzy. Nothing about Iago's career is more murky than its end. In the last scene he is uncovered and at bay. It is a moment in which the human instinct for self-justification would provoke a declaration of cause out of anyone who had even one of the motives that flourish in Iago's early monologues. The situation fairly pleads for his avowal of his provocations. What has happened to the professional resentment, the jealousy, the hatred? If they all conceal a deeper mystery, here at least in the denouement is the time for revelation; and the express demand for it burns on the lips of the great victim:

> Will you, I pray, demand that demi-devil
> Why he hath thus ensnar'd my soul and body?
>
> [V. ii. 301-02]

But Iago is an alien to the moral conventions of the world of the play, and his real answer would be no more intelligible to Othello than to us. In his reply, therefore, there is no answer:

> Demand me nothing. What you know, you know.
> From this time forth I never will speak word.
>
> [V. ii. 303-04]

These are his last words. Round about him rings a clamor of imprecation. He is called an inhuman dog, a Spartan dog, a viper, a pernicious caitiff, a damned slave, a cursed slave, and a variety of epithets beside—a frantic rhapsody that constricts the imagination, leaving us, in respect to the meaning of the evil, depressed because unenlightened. We look for an explanation that has moral significance either literally or through some liberating symbolism, but find none. And in the words of all the other characters there is none either. Like the reader or playgoer, they belong to the moral world, so they too are unenlightened. They call Iago names.

One name in particular, expressing the sternest kind of moral condemnation, reaches out for Iago in almost every scene of the play. From the exclusively moral viewpoint of the other characters it tells us what Iago appears to them to be in the terms of humanity. In the last scene, where there is almost no end to its iteration, it beats upon him almost beyond, not his endurance, but ours:

> O mistress, villany hath made mocks with love!
>
> I know thou didst not; thou'rt not such a villain.
>
> Villany, villany, villany!
> I think upon't, I think! I smell't! O villany!
>
> Precious villian!
>
> 'Tis a notorious villain.
>
> I'll after that same villain . . .
>
> Bring the villain forth.
>
> O villain!
>
> This damned villain . . .
>
> To you, Lord Governor,
> Remains the censure of this hellish villain.
>
> This wretch hath part confess'd his villany.
>
> O villany, villany!
>
> [V. ii. 151, 174, 190-91, 235, 239, 242, 285, 313, 316, 367-68, 296, 193]

Now perhaps no word in the lexicon of moral condemnation—especially in the theater, where it is a stock epithet—is more common or hackneyed than this one which designates Iago in the frantic rhapsody that ends the tragedy. Sooner or later every malefactor in every play, particularly an Elizabethan play, is a villain, and we are scarcely edified by so universal a stereotype. What is a villain? If that is the extent of what Iago is, how are we helped toward understanding him? No wonder the critics have felt . . . that in *Othello* the liberating symbolism of the other great tragedies does not appear, that in this play of intrigue the imagination of Shakespeare is confined within an uninterpretable evil.

But we need to review these verbal associations and epithets from a different perspective. Although they come off with a moral meaning from the lips of the other characters, they have a further existence in a dimension that is not moral. The endless references by Iago's victims to his honesty is an elaborate piece of tragic irony that is not by itself especially enlightening as to the real meaning of his role. But his own sardonic awareness of the position is most enlightening. He is the very spirit of dishonesty; he is Dishonesty personified, and how joyously and derisively he proclaims it:

Whip me such honest knaves! . . .

[I. i. 49]

The Moor is of a free and open nature
That thinks men honest that but seem to be so . . .

[I. iii. 399-400]

I protest, in the sincerity of love and honest kindness.

[II. iii. 327-28]

O, you are well tun'd now!
But I'll set down the pegs that make this music,
As honest as I am.

[II. i. 199-201]

And although the diabolism, as it is expressed by the others, is a moral metaphor not especially useful, his own happy assumption of the satanic is his absolute definition of his behavior, rendering all moral causation superfluous. And beyond anything else in the play, what is enlightening about his villainy is that he himself proclaims it as his proper name and nature and proceeds thereupon to act accordingly. Villainy is the badge Iago thumbs to announce his dramatic profession. It is an identification card which he himself several times flashes gleefully at the audience, and an Elizabethan audience knew him unmistakably thereby beneath his "motives," for they had seen him many times before in many plays. His role had a stage history that made his villainy self-explanatory in an absolute sense, for villainy such as his defined a stock dramatic figure, and defined, moreover, his purpose on the stage regardless of the plot of the play in which he happened to appear. His essential role, behind the moral façade, exists in a professional and artistic dimension that is perpendicular to the morally conventional plot of the plays in which he survived after the dramatic method that created him disappeared from the English stage.

"Thou art a villain" [I. i. 118], cries out Brabantio upon the dim figure in the darkness below who, with enormous relish, hurls up at the father the gross images that make intolerably vivid to him the elopement of his daughter. And the villain replies in kind, and just as accurately, "You are a senator" [I. i. 118]. Both designations are professionally exact, and the former is the thread that leads us to the fundamental Iago. For he is not essentially a man who is provoked to act villainously, but *Villainy* disguised by late convention to act like a man. The play concerns the oppression of Virtue by Villainy, and if the clamorous iteration of the latter word beats on our brains without enlightening us, that is because we are habituated to look for moral significance in it. But as it is used by Iago to label himself it defines an action that is artistic rather than moral, and it draws its meaning out of an earlier dramatic convention whose characteristic protagonist was at once an abstraction and a professional artist, a laughing *farceur* who had no further purpose than to confound his human victims by a series of intrigues that illustrated the meaning of his abstract name. The First Folio has made a strenuous effort to help us out. There, in the dramatis personae attached to *Othello*, we find professional explanations for most of the roles. Cassio is "an Honourable Lieutenant," Montano "Gouernour of Cyprus," Brabantio "Father to Desdemona," Lodovico and Gratiano "two Noble Venetians," Bianca "a Curtezan." And Iago—what of him?

Iago, a Villaine.

The full stop at the end of the designation proffers a world of meaning. Iago is a villain, and that's all there is to it. He is a

villain in a sense so special it has nothing to do with moral condemnation and is not receptive to the moral symbolism through which evil is interpreted in the other great tragedies. Villainy . . . is Iago's vocation, and it is no sin for a man to labor in his vocation. He is the villain as artist, who, deeply considered, has nothing to do with evil. Into the word "Villain," as it defines his role, is compressed a formula, not moral but profoundly dramaturgic, which determined the nature of the English stage between 1400 and 1570-80, and maintained itself in disguise for several decades thereafter until it was eventually digested by the radically different convention of the *literal* drama that took its place. The formula is that of allegory, and especially that central type of Christian allegory known as the Psychomachia, in which personified forces of good and evil contend for possession of the human soul. Out of medieval allegory came the morality play, which for two centuries provided a type of drama whose purpose and method were homiletic, whose structure was schematic and rigid, whose characters for the most part were personified abstractions with names that expressed the motive and predetermined the nature of their actions.

The morality play not only created allegorical drama out of Christian homiletics but produced also a homilist of amazing popularity. In the early part of Elizabeth's reign he was the *sine qua non* of the stage—so popular and indispensable in fact that his name is the prominent feature of the titles of several plays that have survived in print. In his role as sardonic intriguer in every play in which he appeared he inflicted upon his gullible victims a variety of deceits and seductions—tragedy for them but laughter for him—which illustrated the meaning his abstract name of the moment expressed—Envy, Avarice, Sensual Suggestion, Ill Report, Ambidexter, Iniquity, and numerous designations besides of qualities abstract and pejorative. But all his separate performances, under whatever name, in play after play are merely variations on a single theme—his dexterity in effecting, through artful dissimulation and intrigue, the spiritual and physical ruin of frail humanity; and all his particular names are enveloped within his generic title of *The Vice*. The details of his evolution after 1550 supply the answers to most of the questions that surround Iago. For as the morality play surrendered to the literal drama, its medley of tragic farce giving way to the separate types of comedy and tragedy, the Vice with equal facility moved into both, so entrenched on the popular stage that he outlived by many years the dramatic convention that had created him. His survival in Elizabethan comedy has been to some extent traced and acknowledged. But his significant career in tragedy still goes begging for recognition.

And yet in tragedy he is not so far removed from his origins in homiletic allegory that he does not reveal his breeding through his new title, equally homiletic and almost as abstract, which he proclaims and exemplifies in action. Iniquity has had to be rechristened Iago, but the dominant Vice in him, tenaciously clinging to his old role as artistic intriguer and destroyer, merely acquires a new label—concession to changed surroundings— for his old nature, and an appreciative audience knows him now as the self-proclaimed Villain. And as a further, unavoidable, step in the process of adaptation he acquires something which as an undisguised abstraction in the earlier drama he didn't need—passionate motivation. The energy for his aggressions supplied him previously by allegory is crossbred with the conventional motives of human morality. But since the vital part of him on the stage is still the old Vice, still the laughing, amoral, and self-explanatory artificer of ruin, the motivation is always superfluous, never really fits him, invariably fails to fuse with his archaic nature and function. So criticism writhes. (pp. 51-8)

Cinthio's ensign . . . was a depraved villain of the blackest stripe—lustful, revengeful, deceitful, cunning, and cowardly. But Shakespeare's figure is something else again—a man of principle, with a subtle coherence between what he believes in general and what he believes in particular. He entertains a comprehensive moral attitude toward the world, society, and the individual; and through that attitude appears the "new man," as he has been called, of the Renaissance, his contours sharp and grim against the orthodox values of the poet's age. (p. 423)

Provided we extend the significance of the label beyond Machiavelli, since it embraces concepts of which Tudor England was conscious without the Florentine's instruction, Iago is a Machiavel. Upon the traditional pieties . . . and the system of belief behind them, his derisive assault is fundamental, extending to first principles. When Roderigo whimpers that he is ashamed to be so infatuated but "it is not in my virtue to amend it" [I. iii. 318], the villain's response becomes intelligible only when "virtue" is understood for what it almost certainly does mean: the divine grace flowing into the otherwise helpless nature of man, creating there the power toward good without which salvation is not possible. "Virtue? a fig!" replies Iago, " 'Tis in ourselves that we are thus or thus" [I. iii. 319-20], demolishing in a phrase the theological foundation beneath the whole system of Christian ethics. He is *homo emancipatus a Deo* [man severed from God], seeing the world and human life as self-sufficient on their own terms, obedient only to natural law, uninhibited and uninspired by any participation in divinity. (pp. 423-24)

Labels, however, adhere only to surfaces and mock us with superficiality when we try to apply them to Shakespeare's depths. We detect the type with which he begins but lose it in the unique creation with which he ends. Applied to Iago, the Machiavellian label, while supplying some prefatory enlightenment, is too general to carry us very far into the moral meaning of his role. The high art that wrought him into the dense and exclusive design of his own play does not allow him to remain an undifferentiated specimen of villainous humanity according to the commonplace Elizabethan formula of the Machiavel. He is matched and specialized against a theme, and his evil refined into something rare through the ironic felicity of its polarization and the dramatic felicity of its operation within that theme. His cynical naturalism in respect to human motives and relationships is the first principle from which he moves, through a series of narrowing applications, until it creates his opinion of every other person in the play. It also creates something else: his opinion of his own situation. Unless we follow him closely through the descending gyres of his thought, we lose him and soon begin to wonder what he is talking about. Those of his words, however, which apply to the way we are now concerned with him are invariably consistent with the way he is morally organized, and perspicuous in the terms of that organization. He is wonderfully opposed to the theme of the play as its anti-theme, and is, in fact, the most astonishing product of the Shakespearian technique of contrast.

If the play is about anything it is . . . about love. Its first words concern an elopement and its last the "heavy act" which has brought that elopement's history to its tragic end. Conceivably any sort of villain for any sort of villainous reason might have contrived the intrigue that produces the tragedy, and in Cinthio the motive was frustrated passion. But if one thing more than

another can explain Shakespeare's departures from his sources, especially in matters of character and motive, it is his concern with dramaturgic patterns—in this case the pattern of opposites. Creating in Othello and Desdemona romantic love's most splendid votaries, he also creates in Iago its most derisive atheist. To the kind of love existing between hero and heroine, supplying the bright ideal of the play, the ancient is the dark countertype, the adversary. Although his naturalism is voluble upon a dozen topics, they are all ancillary to its main theme: nothing engrosses him so much as the subject of love or receives from him so mordant a negation. The marriage of true minds, or, for that matter, any level of love above sexual appetite, is exactly what he does not believe in. Nor does he believe that men and women exist in any relationship to each other apart from physical desire. He strikes his proper note in the first scene by the images of animal copulation with which he shocks Brabantio into attention, and descants upon it thereafter through similar images and definitions that are, in fact, consistent deductions from a universal premise: Love, whose imagined mystery bemuses romantic fools like Roderigo, "is merely a lust of the blood and a permission of the will" [I. iii. 334-35]. Before he is through his nimble logic has roped everyone in the play, including himself, into his sexual syllogism. An Othello in love is merely "an erring barbarian" [I. iii. 355-56] momentarily enticed but changeable in his appetites. A Desdemona in love is merely "a supersubtle Venetian" who married the Moor for lust and will leave him for youth "When she is sated with his body" [I. iii. 356, 350]. Cassio is not handsome and young for nothing:

> He hath a person and a smooth dispose
> To be suspected—fram'd to make women false.
> > [I. iii. 397-98]

Emilia, being a woman, is faithful to the promiscuous disposition of her sex:

> *Emil.* Do not you chide; I have a thing for you.
> *Iago.* A thing for me? It is a common thing—
> > [III. iii. 301-02]

He himself, being a man, obeys the disposition of his:

> Now I do love her too;
> Not out of absolute lust (though peradventure
> I stand accountant for as great a sin) . . .
> > [II. i. 291-93]

He thinks like a rigorous geometrician—from his basic proposition straight through to all its corollaries.

Being also a practical man of the world, from corollaries he moves to applications. Since the Moor is what he is and Emilia what she is, it follows that "I do suspect the lusty Moor hath leap'd into my seat" [II. i. 295-96]. On the quay at Cyprus he stands spectator to an exchange of courtesies between Desdemona, who "must change for youth," and Cassio, who is "handsome, young, and hath all those requisites in him that folly and green minds look after" [I. iii. 349-50; II. i. 245-47], and soon imparts to Roderigo what it means: "Desdemona is directly in love with him." Social kissing between the sexes, though never quite free from equivocal suggestion, was permissible in Tudor England (to the astonishment of foreign visitors). Such a kiss between Cassio and Emilia in his presence suggests the interpretation natural to him: "For I fear Cassio with my nightcap too" [II. i. 307]. His formulations are progressive, and parts of his second soliloquy [II. i. 286-312] reach conclusions based on his observations during the reunion of the voyagers at Cyprus a few moments before. He is even obliged, with the air of a man of courage taking a calculated risk, to revise one of his previous estimates (for he has just seen and heard Othello's rapt greeting of Desdemona): "I dare think he'll prove to Desdemona / A most dear husband" [II. i. 290-91]. In the same soliloquy he adverts to his discourse with his gull in order to save us from writing it off as sheer flimflam:

> That Cassio loves her, I do well believe it;
> That she loves him, 'tis apt and of great credit.
>
> [II. i. 286-87]

In other words, "I really do believe what I have just been saying to Roderigo." Something else will save us from the same skepticism—a part of his conversation with Cassio two scenes later:

> *Iago.* Our general cast us thus early for the love of his Desdemona; who let us not therefore blame. He hath not yet made wanton the night with her, and she is sport for Jove.
> *Cas.* She's a most exquisite lady.
> *Iago.* And I'll warrant her full of game.
> *Cas.* Indeed, she's a most fresh and delicate creature.
> *Iago.* What an eye she has! Methinks it sounds a parley to provocation.
> *Cas.* An inviting eye; and yet methinks right modest.
> *Iago.* And when she speaks, is it not an alarum to love?
> *Cas.* She is indeed perfection.
> *Iago.* Well, happiness to their sheets!
>
> [II. iii. 14-29]

He does not get the confirmation for which he probes, but whether he changes his mind about Cassio too we shall never know. His separate suspicions bewilder us less and seem less absurd, at least to our theoretical consideration of him and them, when we see them for what they actually are—related local disturbances moving out from the broad weather front of his sexual doctrine. All of them together, by their mutual reinforcement, exhibit the disposition of his nature, and produce thereby an explanation for the existence of each individually, including the most prominent of them, his personal jealousy regarding his wife and Othello. We need also to reckon with the fact that on his own stage he was supported by a convention of which we are now largely bereft. It would take more than our fingers and toes to count the dramatized husbands round about him who jump to similar jealousies about their wives for no other reason than that they are women and, therefore, in Lear's sufficient phrase, "Down from the waist they are Centaurs" [*King Lear*, IV. vi. 124]; or imagine a rival in every male who is not a certified eunuch.

To the extent that the foregoing interpretation is correct, his suspicions, which otherwise swirl like chaff in the wind, subside into an intelligible pattern. He has only two motives, one of them being his cynical Machiavellianism toward sex, which hovers over everyone in the play and creates his personal provocation when it lights on his wife and "black Othello." The other requires only a word. We have no right to believe that he has a better claim than Cassio's to the lieutenancy, only that he craves it. And his craving is annexed to a credo of service which, at least in our own awareness of his moral qualifications, damns his claim. Besides, by every indication,

he is intended as a coward, just as he was featured by Cinthio: "a very great coward, yet his carriage and conversation were so haughty and full of pretension, that you would have taken him for a Hector or an Achilles." There is no reason to believe that the play changes this estimate. He is fluent with his dagger, but only in special circumstances: Cassio receives it anonymously in the dark, Roderigo already wounded and on his back, his wife when he is cornered ("Fie! your sword upon a woman?" [V. ii. 223-24]); and he likes to stab and run. Finally, we can draw conviction on this point from the fact that to Cassio he is "the bold Iago" and to Lodovico "a very valiant fellow" [II. i. 75; V. i. 52]; for, without exception, every moral attribute applied to him by anyone in the play is an ironic finger pointing to the truth of its opposite. As to his contempt for Cassio's "bookish theoric," it finds its precise equivalent in the feeling that today's master sergeant might entertain for the young second lieutenant just out of West Point. But unless the case is exceptional, we are able to assess the potential superiority of the trained, flexible, theoretical mind against the fossilized know-how of one who has merely slogged through a dozen years of practical experience. Iago's opinion notwithstanding, it tells us something of Cassio's qualifications that Othello should appoint him lieutenant before the beginning of the play and that the Signoria of Venice should appoint him governor of Cyprus before its end. But the question of Iago's justification or lack of it is ultimately meaningless beside the motive fact of his resentment, and his resentment, like his jealousy, belongs to his bad character. We neglect the intention within Shakespeare's irony unless we heed Emilia's inadvertent accuracy in respect to the nature and motives of her husband:

> I will be hang'd if some eternal villain,
> Some busy and insinuating rogue,
> Some cogging, cozening slave, to get some office,
> Have not devis'd this slander. I'll be hang'd else.
>
> The Moor's abus'd by some most villanous knave,
> Some base notorious knave, some scurvy fellow.
>
>   Some such squire he was
> That turn'd your wit the seamy side without
> And made you to suspect me with the Moor.
>
> [IV. ii. 130-33, 139-40, 145-47]

He has every reason for urging her to "Speak within door" [IV. ii. 144], for she has limned him to the life.

Such a portrait, or one reasonably like it, must be accepted because it exists, but it must also be rejected because it does not exist alone. Compromising it by addition and blurring it by invasion is his other life, his other set of features. They derive from nothing discoverable in Cinthio or in any naturalistic intention behind the playwright's revision of Cinthio, but have their source in the spectacular image of evil traditional on the popular stage. We need not expect, however, to find in Iago the massive dislocation visible in Richard [in *Richard III*] ten years before, and even more obvious, because even earlier, in [Christopher Marlowe's] Barabas [in *The Jew of Malta*]. The contrary elements of the conflation, no longer layered in broad distinction, are now relatively merged and granular, with the older image recessive and diminished. For one thing, the bravura image of multiple deceit, though ramifying upon as many victims as before, is no longer tandem and episodic, but deftly organized into a single complex intrigue within a comprehensive dramatic plot. For another, the amoral humor of the moral personification, having ceased to be explosive, has become pervasive—a mood and a tone penetrating Iago's role throughout. In the third place, the homiletic dimension of the role, its didactic voice and naked moral display, is relatively subdued and fragmentary, modified by indirection and mainly limited to sentences and half-sentences that twist in and out of his more relevant phraseology. Finally, while the stark antinomy of the Psychomachia remains, supplying for his aggression an explanation that contradicts his motives, it has suffered attrition, and of the original formula only part survives: ''I hate the Moor'' [I. iii. 386]. (pp. 425-30)

Although all his actions are subdued to the dramatic plot, none of them marked by the pronounced quality of intercalated tour de force so conspicuous in Richard's wooing of Lady Anne, they achieve in their aggregate the same effect. He is not merely being put on display; like his ancestor the Vice he is putting himself on display, and what he displays has villainy for its subject and deceit for its method. Beneath the naturalistic refinements of character and situation lie the deep grooves of the old pattern, and in them he moves, carrying out a purpose that achieves its proper end through repetitive demonstration. (p. 432)

When William Hazlitt described Iago as ''an amateur of tragedy in real life'' [see excerpt above, 1817], when Bradley noted as ''a curious point of technique'' with Shakespeare that Iago's ''soliloquies . . . read almost like explanations offered to the audience'' [see excerpt above, 1904], and when other critics observe the ''histrionic'' or ''artistic'' element in the performance, they all respond to a phenomenon whose real nature, although they do not quite discern it, is by now sufficiently familiar to us. It is once more the homiletic dramaturgy of the moral play, where personified evil demonstrated its destructive operation and preached its own exposure, addressing itself as intimately to its audience as any minister to his congregation or pedagogue to his pupils, with the difference that the dramatized lesson was made trenchant by satire and by action. This method reached its culmination in the Vice and descended from him to the line of villains he fathered. All of them manipulate their victims into comic or tragic confusion in order to exhibit the name and nature of villainy. It is as we have [stated], a declining method, and in Iago it is substantially diminished in its two principal features: the action loses as a demonstration what it gains as an organic plot, and the homily recedes before the enactment of the literal story. But although diminished it remains, exploited by the playwright at the height of his powers. That the action of the villain is still a moral demonstration is made clear by the language of demonstration: ''Thus do I ever make my fool my purse . . .'' [I. iii. 383] and

> Thus credulous fools are caught,
> And many worthy and chaste dames even thus,
> All guiltless, meet reproach.
>
> [IV. i. 45-7]

That the demonstration is addressed unequivocally to the audience is equally clear:

> And what's he then that says I play the villain,
> When this advice is free I give and honest,
> Probal to thinking, and indeed the course
> To win the Moor again?
>
> [II. iii. 336-39]

And it is no less evident that his self-exposure is as absolute as it is inconceivable in any naturalistic estimate of wickedness, no matter how wicked:

> How am I then a villain
> To counsel Cassio to this parallel course,
> Directly to his good? Divinity of hell!

> When devils will the blackest sins put on,
> They do suggest at first with heavenly shows,
> As I do now.
>
> [II. iii. 348-53]

A villain can act this way, but it is only Villainy in a Geneva gown that can talk this way; and the integrity of his sermon includes his victims as well as himself: they are grist for his mill, he says, because one is an ''honest fool,'' another has ''a free and open nature,'' and a third is a ''worthy and chaste'' dame. They qualify as his dupes, he says, because they are too honest to suspect him; but they also qualify in another sense: their virtue provokes him. His meaning on this last point, however, must wait until it is ripe for treatment under the rubric of his ''hate.'' (pp. 436-37)

[Why] does he hate the Moor? The question finds its answer where the whole Elizabethan drama of evil found its first principle: in the moral dualism of the Psychomachia. A quick backward glance helps us forward on this theme. The original allegory pitted personified vice against personified virtue on the field of battle, the most obvious metaphor for the eternal feud between them in the human soul. When the military image disappeared from the moralities, its substitute representation (in plays of the middle period mainly) for the strife between these natural enemies became a debate. . . . Coexistence between vices and virtues being impossible, one side had to drive out the other from the soul of man, whether by original violence, later polemic, or the cunning intrigue of evil which soon became standard. Their enmity gets typical expression in the words of Envy in [the anonymously written] Impatient Poverty:

> I hate conscience, peace loue and reste
> Debate and stryfe that loue I beste
> Accordyng to my properte.

Originally there was nothing for vice to ''hate'' in the generalized figure of mankind: he was a moral vacuum waiting to be filled by good or evil, and it was the job of the vices to capture, persuade, or deceive him while hating their proper adversaries, his guardian virtues. The later evolution of the morality drama brought about, however, a new alignment. All the virtues gradually melt away from the stage, and so do the subsidiary vices, while their leader swells into the portentous figure of the Vice. He, with unique theatrical éclat in the late moralities and in the hybrid plays, carries on the traditional program of moral evil, deceiving his victims into temporary jeopardy or permanent ruin. But in the hybrid plays the Psychomachia, by its adjustment to its new environment, indicates as well its future development in the secular drama. The Vice remains as militant as ever against virtues and values, but these are no longer externalized personifications, and the human hero no longer a moral cypher. Mankind has been replaced by men and women who carry their moral qualities inside them, and to the extent that such persons are good they become the virtuous side of the Psychomachia, attracting the enmity as well as the aggression of the allegorical foe. . . . All the hybrid plays, whether or not their language is explicit on the issue, inherit, along with the Vice, the moral structure of the Psychomachia, and present him arrayed, according to his allegorical ''properte,'' against the virtues incorporated in such heroines as chaste Virginia, godly Susanna, patient and meek Grissill; or against the chivalric and romantic values inherent in the knights and ladies of the dramatized romances in which he appears. The old conflict, along with the enmity proper to it, has not changed, only shifted its ground, now that virtue is no longer distinguishable from its human possessor.

In the secular drama that follows, especially in tragedy, the villain who inherits the mantle of the Vice inherits as well this enmity. In his mouth it becomes the quintessential expression of the Psychomachia—the homiletic revelation of evil's hatred for its opposite. It is properly *allegorical* hatred, having neither psychological explanation nor appropriate emotional content, for it defines the elemental conflict within a moral antinomy, in the sense that Envy, as quoted above, hates Conscience, Peace, Love, and Rest "Accordyng to my properte." In the same sense the villain hates virtues and values, and the persons in whom they are embodied, because, as he says, he is a villain. His avowal to that effect simply repeats, in condensed version, the Vice's obligatory exposition of his name and nature; and it is also, as it was in the moral drama, a comprehensive statement of *allegorical* motivation. (pp. 442-44)

[*Othello*] is very greatly indebted to [the tradition of the Psychomachia], almost as if the playwright, finding in his source a story of villainy highly susceptible to such a dramatization, deliberately undertook to give new brilliance to the old stage image. In Iago the image still retains its integrity as an action, but its verbal structure has crumbled, although all the fragments are still in sight. In his language all parts of the equation are copiously present, but in diffusion and modulated by indirection. In various places he reiterates his villainy, the virtue of his victims, and his hate; and occasionally he even puts two of the ingredients together, as in the following words . . . :

> The Moor (howbeit I endure him not)
> Is of a constant, loving, noble nature . . .

> [II. i. 288-89]

But the linked elements of the original formula, now interpenetrated by naturalism and yielding to the imperative of artistic change, have mainly fallen apart. The role has traveled through too much literal scenery to be able any longer to say, "My name is Iniquity and, according to my property, I hate Virtue"; or even to say less abstractly but with equal coherence, "I hate the Moor because he is a paragon of Christian and romantic virtue and I am a villain." Iago's hatred, in short, having become isolated from its allegorical predication, survives unattached, in spite of what he tells Roderigo about the lieutenancy in the first scene. It simply does not unite with the resentment he expresses then any more than it unites with the jealousy he expresses later, belonging to a realm where such causes have no status. On this point his words to his gull cannot compete in reliability with the testimony of his monologue. There it is starkly

> I hate the Moor;
> And it is thought abroad that 'twixt my sheets
> 'Has done my office.

> [I. iii. 386-88]

What better motive for hatred than his suspicion that Othello has seduced his wife? and how tempting to read "for" instead of "and." But the "and" remains indestructible and wins a place in dramatic history, being the seam between the drama of allegory and the drama of nature, as well as between the kind of motivation proper to each. If he restates his hatred almost as much as he does his villainy, that is because both avowals are heavily stylized realities against his endless pretense of love and honesty:

> Though I do hate him as I do hell pains,
> Yet, for necessity of present life,
> I must show out a flag and sign of love,
> Which is indeed but sign.

> [I. i. 154-57]

His deceit . . . is theatrical bravura according to a traditional design, and designs in Shakespeare, when he is at the top of his powers, are massive as well as subtle, like the imagery and atmosphere in any of the great plays. As for his provocation against Cassio because

> He hath a daily beauty in his life
> That makes me ugly . . .

> [V. i. 19-20]

that is the Psychomachia again, in language that naturalizes it slightly. The sense of the passage is future and its burden self-preservation: "If Cassio do remain" his virtues will, by contrast, show me up as evil and expose me for the villain I am. A certain tenderness about the time to come silts over what is, at bottom, as downright as Lorenzo's hatred of Andrea because "he aimes at honor, / When my purest thoughts work in a pitchy vale . . ." [in the anonymously written *The First Part of Jeronimo* (1603?)]. For it is still the elemental strife between Good and Evil, the metaphor of the moral dualism sustained by the Christian imagination through the dozen centuries between Prudentius and Shakespeare, and it includes Desdemona as well. (pp. 447-49)

Bernard Spivack, "The Family of Iago" and "Iago Revisited," in his Shakespeare and the Allegory of Evil: The History of a Metaphor in Relation to His Major Villains, *Columbia University Press, 1958, pp. 28-59, 415-53.*

JOHN BAYLEY (essay date 1960)

[*In the excerpt below from his* The Characters of Love: A Study in the Literature of Personality *(1960), Bayley considers the principal theme of* Othello *the inherent contradiction in human love. Declaring that "sexual love is at once a prison and a liberation," he contends that the play demonstrates, through Desdemona and Othello, that although love offers a spacious and expansive world to the lovers, it is paradoxically restricted by their romantic egotism and self-contained identities. Bayley notes that while the loves of Othello and Desdemona are both "wildly romantic" and incomplete, her passion is more confident and stable than his, because of her more flexible nature. On the other hand, the critic argues, Othello views Desdemona as a possession that he has acquired—as if by some good fortune or as the result of a military engagement—and his self-image depends heavily on her romantic, idealized perception of him. Thus, Bayley avers, when Othello begins to apprehend, early in Act III, Scene iii, that lovers have different conceptions of love and that love itself is insubstantial, he becomes disturbed and vulnerable to Iago's attack on his vision of Desdemona. The critic also explores the play's concern with identity or self-definition and the various attempts by the characters to "place" themselves in relation to others. Othello's dawning recognition that he and Desdemona do not share identical perceptions of the nature of love, Bayley maintains, signals the disintegration of his identity, because he had defined it exclusively by his perception of her love. Further, the critic examines the language of the play, particularly in Act II, Scene i, where the "power of love" is strongly evoked by the poetry of Othello, Desdemona, and Cassio. Bayley adds that this scene at the quayside in Cyprus also demonstrates the disparities between real and idealized love through contrasting tones of "realistic and operatic" speeches uttered by Iago and the others. Finally, he disagrees with the conclusions of T. S. Eliot (1927) and F. R. Leavis (1937) on the hollowness of Othello's poetry, contending that, because these critics believe the play represents a negative view of love, they were led to make a spurious distinction between heroic and sentimental modes of speech and to view the Moor's romantic flights of language as self-parody. Instead, he concludes, "the 'heroic mode' is the love mode" in this drama, involving the audience in the passions of the dramatic characters and directing us to an appreciation of the vitality and splendor of love. Other critics who have analyzed Shakespeare's portrayal of the nature of love in* Othello *include Hermann Ulrici (1839), Derek Traversi (1949), Kenneth Burke (1951), Winifred M. T. Nowottny (1952), Robert B. Heilman (1956), Susan Snyder (1972), Jared R. Curtis (1973), and Jane Adamson (1980). For further commentary on the poetic language of the play, see the excerpts by G. Wilson Knight (1930), Derek Traversi (1949), Robert B. Heilman (1951), Gayle Greene (1979), and Carol McGinnis Kay (1983).]*

[The] initial fallacy of much *Othello* criticism is the assumption that it is a simple clear-cut affair, and that the task of the critic is to determine what kind of simplicity, so to speak, is involved. For Wilson Knight it is the simplicity of intrigue [see excerpt above, 1930]; for Leavis, that of a special kind of character study [see excerpt above, 1937]; for Bradley (whose approach is less narrowly perspicacious and therefore less inadequate), the more exciting simplicity of a fathomless evil corrupting, though not eclipsing, good [see excerpt above, 1904]. The strong feelings aroused are all directed to one of these particular ends. But if we rather assume, from the nature of the subject and of the response we give to it, that the play is likely to be a highly complex affair, with a Shakespearean variety of perceptions and significances, then we shall cease to be merely pro- or anti-Othello, or under the spell of a *coup de théâtre* [theatrical effect], and instead be more receptive to its totality of effect. (pp. 145-46)

In claiming for the play a far greater degree of complexity than is generally assumed, I am not saying that it closely resembles Shakespeare's other great plays, or that it works in the same way as they do. *Othello* is a tragedy of incomprehension, not at the level of intrigue but at the very deepest level of human dealings. And one would expect that the effect of such a tragedy would be significantly different from those in which a kind of understanding links the actors ever more closely as they suffer or inflict suffering; that it would be, in fact, more like that of a great novel. No one in *Othello* comes to understand himself or anyone else. None of them realize their situation. At the centre, between the poles of the play, Desdemona, Cassio, and Emilia show common sense and humanity, but it is more a matter of good instinct than illumination. Iago maintains to the end the dreadful integrity of his own ignorance, and in spite of—or perhaps because of—the revelation of Desdemona's innocence, Othello retains to the end his agonized incomprehension—the incomprehension which is so moving an aspect of tragedy in sexual love. His love for Desdemona was to him a marvellous revelation of himself rather than a real knowledge of her. And the proof of her innocence is no substitute for such an awareness. This is the final tragic separation, intensified by the conviction that she is going to heaven and he is going to hell. But although the characters never achieve understanding, and although our response to them—as theirs to each other—shifts with the successive and conflicting pulls of emotion and analysis, so that we see Othello through his own eyes and Iago's as well as with our own, yet if we wait for the fullness of what the play has to offer we do reach a state of tragic comprehension; we are left with a greater insight into the passions and the will, and how they operate to cut us off from each other and from ourselves. (pp. 146-47)

[The] whole tendency of *Othello* is to make us partisan, to underline the incommensurability of opposed emotional stances. Just as Desdemona can never see Othello as Iago does, or Iago as does Desdemona, so our own succession of responses follows and reflects the partial and solipsistic attitudes of the protagonists. We are in the bafflingly relative world of social observation, where our own passions and prejudices distort reality as much as those of the people we are watching; and where our discernment of an unconscious motive or a comical lack of awareness—'A's good nature is really selfishness', or, 'Does B ever realize how he bores?'—also reveals our own nature and desires to others who may themselves be noting our unawareness of the fact. In *Othello* love is the agent which precipitates and co-ordinates these responses, keeps them moving, and forces us to reflect in the privacy of our own feelings the stages of an isolated and mysterious struggle.

For love is of all forces in society the most confusing and the most revealing; it stands both for the frightful difficulty of knowing other people and for the possibility of that knowledge; its existence implies the ideal existence of understanding and its absence the total removal of it. The stages of our response to *Othello* compel us to see both with the eye of love and without it, and it is our awareness of what this means that leads us at last to a settled appraisal. The fatal thing is to get stuck at some point, to come to a halt on some premature conviction about the nature of the play, an easy course for the critic whose instinct it is to make up his mind about the nature of the experience he is having. Like all great works of art, *Othello* deprives us of the confident sense of ourselves *vis-à-vis* the rest of the world. (pp. 148-49)

Othello arouses passionate and complex emotions. The 'points of view' in *Othello* have the whole man behind them and not just an argument; an obvious distinction, but worth making in view of the contrasts in the play between poetry and prose. . . . Poetry has a great deal more to do here than in the more organically conceived tragedies, the more so because it is not so native to the world of Othello as to the court of Lear and the castle of Macbeth. *Othello* begins at the moment when the fairy-story ends, and the great 'love-duet' at the beginning of Act II announces what should be the post-marriage *détente:* it is the prelude to domesticity, 'suckling fools and chronicling small beer' [II. i. 160]. The verse must celebrate in heroic terms a domestic situation too realistic even for comedy. But it does not only celebrate it and lift it to a heroic plane, it also analyses it. Although poetry and prose are so sharply differentiated both have the power to dissect and reveal. The antithesis is not, as might be supposed, between simple colourful heroic poetry, and mordant prose, but between the natures of the prose speaker and the poetry speaker. The poetry can be complex and pointed, but it also exalts—as the prose cannot—the bountiful glory and excitement of love. That this excitement has its dangers, even its ugliness and absurdity, both poetry and prose can convey in their separate ways. In using the term 'love-duet' I am suggesting that the unique indicative function of the poetry is indeed comparable with the *aria:* Verdi's *Otello* is the most successful of all operas based on poetic drama, and the greatest performance of Othello was given by Salvini, an actor whose voice and bearing were trained in opera. The magnificence of the poetry embodies the vital splendours of love—Desdemona's as well as Othello's—and is used by those who, like Cassio and the Gentleman at the beginning of Act II, admire and extol such love. It is not used, except as a conscious and horrible parody, by Iago, who . . . produces his own style of verse in deliberate opposition to the love-idiom. . . . Emilia has her own idiom, essentially prose though formally in blank verse, for her important and trenchant speech (Act IV, Scene 3) on the need for give and take between men and women.

Act II, Scene 1 illustrates these points in detail. First Montano and the Gentlemen celebrate in the language of love the storm at sea, that 'storm of fortunes' [I. iii. 249] which the lovers expected and surmounted with such triumphant confidence.... Shakespeare's contrasting storm brings in the powers of love and danger—the latter in both its new and old senses. Cassio now arrives and thanks the previous speakers.

> Thanks, you the valiant of this warlike isle,
> That so approve the Moor! O, let the heavens
> Give him defence against the elements,
> For I have lost him on a dangerous sea.
>
> [II. i. 43-6]

Valiancy and love are connected, their language the same: and with the entry of Cassio the chorus swells to include Desdemona in a paean of praise.

> . . . he hath achieved a maid
> That paragons description and wild fame;
> One that excels the quirks of blazoning pens,
> And in the essential vesture of creation
> Does tire the ingener.
>
> [II. ii. 61-5]

The storm is emphasized once more:

> Tempests themselves, high seas and howling winds,
> The gutter'd rocks and congregated sands—
> Traitors ensteep to enclog the guiltless keel—
> As having sense of beauty, do omit
> Their mortal natures, letting go safely by
> The divine Desdemona.
>
> [II. i. 68-73]

And the power of love is invoked for all its votaries:

> Great Jove, Othello guard,
> And swell his sail with thine own powerful breath,
> That he may bless this bay with his tall ship,
> Make love's quick pants in Desdemona's arms,
> Give renew'd fire to our extinded spirits
> And bring all Cyprus comfort!
>
> [II. i. 77-82]

The paean reaches its climax with the appearance of Desdemona herself,

> O, behold,
> The riches of this ship is come on shore!
> Ye men of Cyprus, let her have your knees.
> Hail to thee, lady, and the grace of heaven
> Before, behind thee, and on every hand,
> Enwheel thee round!
>
> [II. i. 82-7]

It is then abruptly checked and reversed by the presence of Iago. The whole atmosphere of the scene changes at once. Cassio, the noble and enthusiastic leader of the chorus, now appears almost absurd as he administers a gallant peck to the cheek of Emilia, observing

> 'tis my breeding
> That gives me this bold show of courtesy.
>
> [II. i. 98-9]

The little fatuity is endearing enough in its way, but with Iago there Cassio appears in a different light: we see him to some extent through Iago's eyes. We also realize that Cassio has an idea of himself as a well-bred person which can appear fitting and noble or as something a bit vulgar and even—in a comical

way—calculating. Conscious as we are of ideas about personal identity, the *persona* and so forth, we should recognize the swiftness and accuracy with which Shakespeare makes his point about them here and connects it, *via* the realistic and operatic contrasts of the scene, with the enthusiasm and the poetry of love. Love, we might say, brings to a head this problem of identity, and also makes it seem to those in the grip of love a problem to which the answer must instantly be found. Our awareness of Cassio in this scene foreshadows the sense of him that Othello will soon come to have, and furthermore our mixed impression of Cassio as the celebrant of love foreshadows our impressions of Othello himself.

For the next hundred lines or so Iago dominates the gathering. The theme of the passage is 'placing' people in terms of parlour witticisms.

> DESDEMONA: What wouldst thou write of me if thou
>   shouldst praise me?
> IAGO: O gentle lady do not put me to't,
>   For I am nothing if not critical.
>
> [II. i. 117-19]
> (pp. 149-53)

At the end of the Iago passage Cassio again becomes the noble chorus introducing the entrance of Othello. *Lo, where he comes!* [II. i. 181]. The phrase is often met in the tragedies and establishes an entrance with wonderful economy: our obligatory use of the continuous present has deprived us of such naturally ceremonial effects. Iago will use the same phrase when he sees Othello upon the rack.

> Look, where he comes! Not poppy nor mandragora
> Nor all the drowsy syrups of the world
> Shall ever medicine thee to that sweet sleep
> Which thou owedst yesterday.
>
> [III. iii. 330-33]

Iago is deliberately parodying the ceremonial love-idiom of Othello, Cassio, and the others, and the lines reminiscent of Othello's own sonorous style are spoken with mocking glee. The note of parody is emphasized further on in the scene, where Iago produces a horrible simulacrum of Othello's oath of vengeance:

> OTHELLO: . . . Like to the Pontic sea
>   Whose icy currents and compulsive course
>   Ne'er feels retiring ebb, but keeps due on
>   To the Propontic and the Hellespont;
>   Even so my bloody thoughts, with violent
>   pace,
>   Shall ne'er look back, ne'er ebb to
>   humble love
>   Till that a capable and wide revenge
>   Swallow them up. Now, by yond marble
>   heaven,
>   In the due reverence of a sacred vow
>   I here engage my words.
> IAGO: Do not rise yet.
>   Witness, you ever-burning lights above,
>   You elements that clip us round about,
>   Witness that here Iago doth give up
>   The execution of his wit, hands, heart,
>   To wronged Othello's service. Let him
>   command,
>   And to obey shall be in me remorse,
>   What bloody business ever.
>
> [III. iii. 453-69]

The difference between the monumental fervour of Othello's love-hate, and Iago's melodramatic imitation of it, would hardly need commenting on if Eliot [see excerpt above, 1927] and Leavis had not suggested that this liability to parody is the weakness of Othello's poetic idiom, a weakness that reveals the hollowness of the man. Leavis takes Bradley to task for saying that Othello is 'the greatest poet' of all Shakespeare's heroes, and observes very justly that not only do other people in the play speak in the characteristic Othello style, but that 'if characters in poetic drama speak poetry we ought to be able to notice the fact without concluding that they are poets'. Certainly we ought, but where *Othello* is concerned we might also reflect that if certain characters speak poetry it is because it is the idiom of the love theme in the play. This is so obvious that the evasion of it by Eliot and Leavis seems inexplicable, until we remember their essentially negative approach to the play's presentation of love. The poetry of *Othello* is firmly and positively poetic, and so convinced is Leavis of the negative psychological purpose of the play that he is compelled to distinguish between Othello's poetical utterance when it shows 'an attitude *towards* the emotion expressed—an attitude of a kind we are familiar with in the analysis of sentimentality', and the poetry—spoken either by him or by others—which is impersonally 'in the heroic mode', and therefore genuine, its 'firm outline' not concealing an underlying softness. This distinction has no real existence. The 'heroic mode' *is* the love mode, as Dr Leavis must surely have seen if he were not so determined that love in the play is a negative and hollow thing, existing

Act IV. Scene iii. Desdemona and Emilia. By Dante Gabriel Rossetti.

only to be shown up. The power of which the poetry is the expression and symbol is all of a piece, and conveys love in all its aspects—terrible, tender, romantic, domestic, etc. Leavis's contention that 'the heroic mode'—as distinct from the hollow and self-revealing rhetoric of Othello—has only a comparatively simple magnificence, is not borne out by a speech like Desdemona's before the senate.

> That I did love the Moor to live with him
> My downright violence and storm of fortunes
> May trumpet to the world: my heart's subdued
> Even to the very quality of my lord:
> I saw Othello's visage in his mind
> And to his honours and his valiant parts
> Did I my soul and fortunes consecrate . . .
>
> [I. iii. 248-54]

The tone is certainly joyous and magnificent, but it is also as 'revealing' as Leavis claims Othello's rhetoric to be. It reveals Desdemona's mode of being in love, just as Othello's speeches reveal his. As well as being lyrical and romantic, the love-idiom is an expository medium so sensitive that the characters who use it cannot open their mouths without revealing their emotional bias, and their conscious or unconscious conceptions of love. (pp. 154-57)

Moreover we must remind ourselves again of the peculiar operation of the play, its mode of involving us in successive emotions and attitudes comparable to those of the characters themselves, and its sequential rather than simultaneous mode of illumination—a mode entailed on Shakespeare . . . by the intrigue at its roots. The magnificence of the love-choruses may indeed hypnotize us at the outset, and postpone our reception of the vital information they contain, but we shall understand them later as part of the full complexity of the *Othello* world, the world of human love and lovelessness, of the inability of one kind of love to understand another, and of the persistence with which human beings cling to the conception of their love as a part of themselves.

As her speech before the senate shows, Desdemona's way of being in love is as clearly revealed as that of Othello. The love-duet in Act II, Scene 1, adds further touches of significance.

> OTHELLO: O my fair warrior!
> DESDEMONA: My dear Othello!
> OTHELLO: It gives me wonder great as my content
> To see you here before me. O my soul's joy,
> If after every tempest come such calms
> May the winds blow till they have wakened death!
> And let the labouring bark climb hills of seas
> Olympus-high, and duck again as low
> As hell's from heaven! If it were now to die
> 'Twere now to be most happy, for I fear
> My soul hath her content so absolute
> That not another comfort like to this
> Succeeds in unknown fate.
> DESDEMONA: The heavens forbid
> But that our loves and comforts should increase
> Even as our days do grow!

OTHELLO: Amen to that, sweet powers!
             I cannot speak enough of this content,
             It stops me here, it is too much of joy:
             And this, and this, the greatest discords
             be *(kissing her).*
             That e'er our hearts shall make!

                                        [II. i. 182-99]

Two different kinds of love are movingly displayed here. Othello's is the masculine and romantic: his opening hyperbole invokes the romantic commonplace—'Love calls to war'—and also receives Desdemona into his wholly martial personality, just as she had wished in refusing to remain 'a moth of peace' [I. iii. 256]. The glory of the achievement is carried buoyantly on in the image of the ship riding the waves. What battles and dangers wouldn't they undergo for this? But then with the imagined calm a note of brooding appears; the tone changes and deepens; 'If it were now to die . . .' Othello has withdrawn his delighted gaze from Desdemona and is addressing himself and his own vision of love. And in the romantic context that vision has an alarming familiarity. Having achieved his desire, Othello turns naturally to the idea of the *liebestod,* death as the only fit and comparable peer of love. How can the tension otherwise be kept up and the lover remain at the summit of his happiness? Unknowingly Othello is applying this fatal romantic logic, which will not compromise possession with the trivialities of domesticity. And it is of course as a possession, a marvellous and unexpected conquest, that he sees Desdemona. He has won her like a fortune or a battle.

        If heaven had made me such another jewel,
        One whole entire and perfect chrysolite,
        I'd not have changed her for it.

                                        [V. ii. 144-46]

This attitude earns him the disapproval of Eliot and Leavis; but so far from singling out Othello as a type of the ignorant and ungentle lover, Shakespeare portrays him as epitomizing the positive glory of love, which like the glory of war includes and assumes the fact of suffering and injustice. Both love and war are summed up in the image of storm, a manifestation both glorious and terrifying. Yet, as we are finding, there is more in the love-duet than the poetic symbol of the storm and the poetic prolepsis of the lovers' death: there is also the sharp illumination of what men and women in love are like. Othello's sentiments are magnificently commonplace; for he shares with most men the delight of achievement and possession and he feels too the loss of freedom, of the 'unhoused condition', a loss which he has already faced in his large way and put aside. The romantic dangers are there, as with most men, but they do not diagnose his amatory weakness or label him finally. He is not a Tristan or a Lancelot, wholly committed to an intensity in love which is unaware of any freedom outside itself.

Indeed the possibility of development, and the sense of freedom that goes with it, is precisely what the duet most poignantly holds out. Desdemona's love for Othello is also of course wildly romantic—he personifies for her all the romance she has discovered to exist in life—but committing herself to this vision is for her a more matter-of-fact business than it could be for him. Her greeting is as whole-hearted as his, and as characteristic. 'My dear Othello!'—the simple warmth reveals a whole world of feminine actuality behind the male need for hyperbole and symbol. She takes his speech lightly, as the sort of wonderfully gratifying and romantic thing he *would* say—its deeper note doesn't mean much to her except as a stimulus to 'touch wood' and to give her own settled and happy con-

ception of the future. She takes up the word 'comfort' from his speech, the sort of word which in her vision of things presents a concrete and lasting reassurance and satisfaction. The situation has a joyful sense of mutual possibility, the spaciousness which throughout the play is the atmosphere and element of love. Othello's unconsciously romantic sense of an end rather than a beginning is not final: Desdemona's placid confidence touches and lights his own, and he shows the beginnings of a readiness to draw certainty and stability from her, just as she had drawn fire and enthusiasm from him. But this interdependence is not the same as understanding: the singers in the duet are too preoccupied with the vision of their own love really to perceive the nature of their partner's. Desdemona is as much imprisoned in her assumption of love as is Othello in his, and for the same reasons: their kinds of love have produced the relationship in which they find themselves. (pp. 157-61)

Shakespeare's poetry not only indicates with extraordinary compression and subtlety comparable facts about love but also celebrates its infinite potentiality, a freedom based not on error but on the absence of definition. Confined in their separate visions, the lovers do not 'place' each other; their incomprehension is, paradoxically, a form of spaciousness, and it is this which Shakespeare manifests as a positive glory. Nothing is fixed and fated, because of the largeness of love's world, the sheer quality of room it makes available. The magnificence of Othello and his impression of physical size, the sweep of seas and continents that are built up behind him, the heroic Odysseys and adventures of his past—all are there to emphasize the unbounded possibilities of love, and they are brought to an almost Hegelian confrontation with an equally undeniable aspect of love—its confinement in the prison of separate egos.

The fact that both Othello and Desdemona cling at all costs to their own apprehension of love gives its shape and meaning to the last act of the tragedy. Their deaths are the very opposite of the romantic *Liebestod,* but the irony of this is infinitely deeper and truer to human experience, and for that reason strikes us with the greater compassion. Death confirms their separation in love, not their union. In his jealousy Othello accepted Iago's version of Desdemona.

        I know our country disposition well.
        In Venice they do let heaven see the pranks
        They dare not show their husbands.

                                        [III. iii. 199-201]

He has permitted the spaciousness of his own love vision to be enclosed in this horrible 'placing' of the loved object. . . . [Iago's] portrait of Desdemona demoralizes Othello completely well before he begins to manufacture the actual proofs of betrayal. For Othello has apprehended Desdemona as a marvellous mirror through which to see his own experience.

        She loved me for the dangers I had passed;
        And I loved her that she did pity them.

                                        [I. iii. 167-68]

Desdemona gives a meaning to all that has happened to him; the sudden revelation of the importance and splendour of his past is a dazzling thing, which he had taken for granted and never seen in this way before. This revelation is in a sense a loss of innocence: it brings self-consciousness and confers upon him the dramatic part which he can most naturally play. But it is also one of the great positive gifts of love. Desdemona has given it to him and he loves her for it, but ironically the very magnificence of the gift obscures the giver, for the gift—

Othello himself—seems to both of them so much more actual than she. Desdemona's sense of Othello is so much more real to both of them than is the sense of Desdemona to either. (pp. 162-63)

[The first part of Act III, Scene 3] contrasts with the love-duet in its slight but painful suggestion of a discord: their mutuality is no longer perfectly synchronized, for the excellent and commonplace reason that an outside element—neutral and not in itself inimical—prevents the exact intermeshing of the gears.

> DESDEMONA: How now, My Lord!
>   I have been talking with a suitor here,
>   A man that languishes in your
>   displeasure.
> OTHELLO: Who is't you mean?
> DESDEMONA: Why, your lieutenant, Cassio.

Desdemona makes a rhetorical show of mystification, one of those nearly meaningless little demonstrations which none the less convey that the speaker knows she is not being quite straightforward. Perhaps aware of its slight tiresomeness, Othello deliberately ignores her gambit. His query is brusque. It provokes her to a greater formality and a more defensive eloquence. The whole thing, economical as it is, catches exactly the note of connubial exchanges.

>   Why, this is not a boon!
> 'Tis as I should entreat you wear your gloves,
> Or feed on nourishing dishes, or keep you warm,
> Or sue to you to do a peculiar profit
> To your own person.
>
>   [III. iii. 76-80]

Love is no longer talking in the symbolic idiom through which Othello apprehends it. With its touchingly matter-of-fact solicitude, the speech conveys no impression of the Desdemona with whom Othello discovered his own past and personality. On the contrary it is an intrusion comparable to that of the Cassio topic, and it brings Othello's latent irritation to a head.

> I will deny thee nothing:
> Whereon, I do beseech thee, grant me this,
> To leave me but a little to myself.
>
>   [III. iii. 83-5]

Committed as she is, it is natural and agreeable to her to yield the point,

> Shall I deny you? no, farewell, my lord . . .
> Emilia, come. Be as your fancies teach you;
> Whate'er you be, I am obedient.
>
>   [III. iii. 86, 88-9]

Her sweetness produces a warmer reply from him, and the parting is on a friendlier, more understanding note. They are already beginning to learn give and take in such matters. It is the more important to realize this because of a common misunderstanding arising from Othello's next words.

> Excellent wretch! Perdition catch my soul,
> But I do love thee, and when I love thee not
> Chaos is come again.
>
>   [III. iii. 90-2]

Some early critics, and many later ones too, have assumed this to mean that 'the poison of jealousy has already begun to work in Othello'. But in Elizabethan English *wretch* was a word of total and unambiguous endearment. [Jeremy] Collier aptly remarks 'such words are resorted to when those implying love,

admiration, and delight, seem inadequate', and Dr Johnson is equally emphatic. There is the further point that 'when', like the German *wenn*, has here the sense of 'if'. What is significant about the speech is not a display of jealousy by Othello, but his sudden awareness of the nature of his feelings and the insubstantiality of love. What is his love exactly, and where is it to be found? Desdemona's sweetness and domestic solicitude in the glove speech cannot at this moment reassure him, because they are not what he means by love: they so emphatically do not present him with the settled and splendid figure whose reflection he once caught in her eye. He no longer sees his visage in her mind. It disturbs the unthinking and unshakeable confidence which he once had in himself, and which he effortlessly retained at the stormy climax of his fortunes. The armed meeting with Brabantio epitomized this confidence.

> Keep up your bright swords, for the dew will rust them.
> Good signior, you shall more command with years
> Than with your weapons.
>
>   [I. ii. 59-61]

But now the vision and the harmony are in abeyance and are replaced by the uncertainty of two people not yet accustomed to each other. In the process of settling down all lovers become more or less aware of the difference between their conception of their 'love', and what is actually happening to them. Most experience, too, the alarming sensation of the loved person suddenly seeming a total stranger, through the appearance of some unexpected though not necessarily uncongenial aspect of their identity. Any question of identity would be likely to puzzle Othello and throw him off his balance. And there is a difference of identity here which in terms of dramatic poetry is conveyed by the Desdemona of the glove speech, and the Desdemona who proclaimed her love to the senate: it is only the former that Othello knows and loves, but in time he will be able to bridge the gap between the two. Desdemona is unaware of the gap, but her love has a natural resilience which will help to overcome Othello's sense of it. Though she assumes that her lover, to whom she feels so close and with whom she identifies herself completely, will at once see her point about Cassio, she effortlessly modifies this assumption and re-identifies herself with Othello's 'fancies'. She makes the adjustment and goes off quite blithely. But Othello is profoundly shaken. And it is at this moment that Iago, the self-appointed expert in identity, makes his attack. Preoccupied as he is, Othello does not attend for a moment. 'What dost thou say, Iago?' [III. iii. 93]. He is not thinking of Cassio but of Desdemona, groping for his sublime image of her—'one whole, entire, and perfect chrysolite'—and painfully aware of the confusion of the image, as if a stone had scattered a clear reflection. The actor should convey this as a moment of nullity and stasis, a dead spot in love. It is negative, unmeaning, without response or coherence, the 'chaos' which Othello fears. Persons of more emotional experience would know that the mechanism does indeed become inert in this way, for trivial reasons and for short periods, but it is Othello's first taste of such a breakdown. For a man who needs decisiveness so much, the danger of this state is that any suggested cause for it will be eagerly grasped.

This obsession with cause and reason is an ironic aspect of the incomprehension that haunts the play. The word takes on a deep and moving significance at the moment when Othello advances to the act of murder.

> It is the cause, it is the cause, my soul,
> Let me not name it to you, you chaste stars!—
> It is the cause.
>
>   [V. ii. 1-3]

The word seems to hypnotize him, and it is difficult not to feel that he clings to it almost as he once clung to his vision of Desdemona. It gives him a vision of universal connection and necessity, and both visions supply his nature with the grounds for action. 'Yet she must die, else she'll betray more men' [V. ii. 6]. His attitude to the adultery is as visionary and as romantic as his former attitude to Desdemona herself. He needs to be certain of it, as he once needed to be certain of his love-vision of her. 'To be once in doubt is once to be resolved' [III. iii. 179-80]. Doubt is not the lover's state of mind. And it is not the doubting person who is uncomprehending, but the person who must be sure of himself and others: it is no paradox to say that the absence of *doubt* in Othello produces its essential atmosphere of incomprehension and unreality. Othello is torn between his passion for causes and certainties and his natural scope and freedom of impulse, a division that corresponds to the nature of sexual love as at once a prison and a liberation. (pp. 165-69)

As we have seen, Othello . . . suddenly has his confidence in the absolute rightness and solidity of the love-relation (as if love were a force like gravity) effectively shaken. 'When I love thee not, chaos is come again.' He is staggered by the causeless and inexplicable withdrawal of his love vision. Cassio was the seemingly neutral and impersonal occasion of this withdrawal, and it is Cassio's name which is now brought up by Iago and coupled in an unmistakably meaningful way with Othello's love.

> Did Michael Cassio, when you woo'd my lady,
> Know of your love?
>
> [III. iii. 94-5]

Othello takes up the point immediately, for it coincides not with any suspicions he has had but with the inexplicable jar to his own state of love. He seizes eagerly, indeed almost with relief, on the suggestion that Cassio may not be merely the occasion for this but the cause.

> IAGO: I did not think he had been acquainted with
>   her.
> OTHELLO: O yes, and went between us very oft.
>
> [III. iii. 99-100]

The initiative is his once more; his feelings are positive again, on the offensive; he devotes himself to a powerful assault on the now apparently uncomfortable Iago. Like most people in such a situation, Othello is not aware of this deep need to reanimate his own positive feelings. Meanwhile, like a bull-fighter making his cape seem alive, Iago swiftly fashions a Cassio-identity to dangle before Othello's lowered head. He hints that his reasoned analysis of Cassio is very different from the instinctive acceptance of Othello.

> IAGO: Men should be what they seem;
>   Or those that be not, would they might
>   seem none.
> OTHELLO: Certain, men should be what they seem.
> IAGO: Why then I think Cassio's an honest man.
>
> [III. iii. 126-29]

It is Othello's first introduction to the horrible identity game, played laughingly by Iago and Desdemona just before his arrival in Cyprus, but now to be played in earnest. The question of identity must always be absorbing to the lover who reflects on it: it now becomes so for Othello, who fatally has no experience of the problem: 'who is she, and whom does she think I am?' (pp. 174-75)

[It] is part of the skill of [Iago's] approach that he postpones all direct reference to Desdemona. The identity question hangs in the air; Othello is distressed by the momentary disappearance of his image of Desdemona—which has vanished in the actuality of her domestic aplomb and in her introduction of the unfortunate Cassio topic—and it is at this moment that Iago raises the question of what Cassio is *really* like. The world of speculation thus revealed is deeply distasteful to Othello, but it coincides with the disturbance of his vision of Desdemona, a vision which he took for granted with the same sureness and simplicity which he extended to everyone he met. Instead of rejecting this new world out of hand, therefore, Othello listens fascinated to Iago's version of Cassio, the more intently because—as we have seen—conviction of any sort is fatally more acceptable to him than uncertainty. He prefers 'cause' and 'reason' to the withdrawal of emotional initiative and the infliction of mere unease, nullity, emotional slack water. (pp. 194-95)

[Iago's] pretension to omniscience is enough to bewilder and corrupt Othello, and his exhibition of the analytic habit implies that it comes naturally to most people, e.g. to Cassio and Desdemona. Othello is made to feel isolated in an idiom totally different from theirs. Yet he returns a typical and spirited reply to Iago's remarks about jealousy.

> Think'st thou I'd make a life of jealousy
> To follow still the changes of the moon
> With fresh suspicions? No! to be once in doubt
> Is once to be resolved: exchange me for a goat
> When I shall turn the business of my soul
> To such exsufflicate and blown surmises
> Matching thy inference!
>
> [III. iii. 177-83]

He resists passionately the proffered entertainment which is indeed the 'business' of Iago's soul. His whole nature rises to this challenge as it has risen to every other—such a response is almost comfortingly habitual. But he is not to feel this comfort for long. His reply determines Iago to launch his boldest stroke, the climax of his attack: the placing of Desdemona as a typical Venetian girl. It is a risk but it comes off. 'Dost thou say so?' [III. iii. 205]. Fascinated and appalled, Othello struggles to adjust himself to this new way of looking at people, catching now at something he has heard Desdemona's father say, and applying it to his own shaken conviction.

> I do not think but Desdemona's honest . . .
> And yet, how nature erring from itself—
>
> [III. iii. 225, 227]

The hesitating cliché is at once taken up, but to show Othello that he is still congenitally out of things, though he has begun to use the jargon of 'knowing', Iago deliberately misunderstands him and gives *nature* his own meaning.

> —Ay there's the point: as—to be bold with you—
> Not to affect many proposed matches
> Of her own clime, complexion, and degree,
> Whereto we see all things in nature tends—
> Foh! one may smell in such a will most rank,
> Foul disproportion, thoughts unnatural.
> But pardon me, I do not in position
> Distinctly speak of her, though I may fear
> Her will, recoiling to her better judgement,
> May fail to match you with her country forms
> And happily repent.
>
> [III. iii. 228-38]

Othello assumes that it is Desdemona's nature to be honest (i.e. chaste) and that a lapse from this would be unnatural in her; Iago, echoing Brabantio's

> For nature so preposterously to err . . .
> Sans witchcraft could not—
>
> [I. iii. 62, 64]

implies that to the worldly eye the opposite is the case: *nature* determines Desdemona's position as a Venetian girl, with all that that involves. And he gives the concept a further twist by suggesting that Desdemona has shown a viciousness over and above what might be expected of 'our country disposition', by giving way to an unnatural passion for Othello. (pp. 196-98)

After Iago has gone, the corrupted Othello tries to make use of his wisdom and his 'learned spirit' to rationalize his own situation.

> 'tis the plague of great ones.
> Prerogatived are they less than the base;
> 'Tis destiny unshunnable, like death:
> Even then this forked plague is fated to us
> When we do quicken.
>
> [III. iii. 273-77]

There is a subtle piteousness about this which is rare in the drama, rare enough even in the novel, since the novel can hardly command such a merging of the operatic and the realistic. Othello is trying to see his supposed fate as something inevitable for men in his position, and to see it with the worldly calm of an Iago whom nothing puzzles or surprises. Yet he cannot help bringing to the Iago vision a certain ghastly appearance of nobility, just as he later brings to it the instinctive values of his old confident and assertive days. But out of their natural setting these values look incongruous, even hypocritical—

> Yet she must die, else she'll betray more men.

The world's honour, we feel, cannot be preserved so. The muddle which resolves itself into these liturgies is very like the one which underlies Iago's assured pronouncements—it is indeed the same muddle. Iago has compelled Othello to rationalize in the way that he himself does, although with Othello concepts like truth and honour are, with a horrible irony, used in the same way as Iago's negative convictions about love and human nature. And Iago's triumph is the virtual absorption of Othello that comes from getting him wholly *placed*, for how can one place someone better than by compelling him to act strictly inside one's own chosen field of understanding? The fallen Othello is no mystery to Iago: he is behaving as men should behave if they are to lend support to Iago's view of the world. That—'she must die else she'll betray more men'—would have given Iago pure joy if he had heard it, confirming as it does his conviction that all men call their lust, love, and their jealous fury, justice. Iago is driven by the need to make men behave as he thinks they do, and Othello, with his air of massive natural distinction, his absolute singleness of being that cannot be categorized or transfixed with a definition, provides him with a compulsive challenge. He cannot relax until he has Othello safely inside the boundaries of his own perception. Then indeed he can proclaim, reversing their relations with a joyous sarcasm that is lost upon his victim: 'I am your own for ever' [III. iii. 480].

And yet not quite for ever, except in Othello's own estimation. 'That's he that was Othello' [V. ii. 284]. He indeed is convinced that the demi-devil has snared his soul and that he will be eternally damned for what he has done. The fact makes T. S. Eliot's contention that in the final speeches he is 'cheering himself up' seem a trifle uncharitable, to say the least of it. Even Dante would concede that a sinner condemned to everlasting torment is entitled to whatever crumb of comfort he can get by the way. And Othello convinces us that he means what he says, and that he is sure his suicide will cut him off from the last hope of mercy. To ignore this certainty is to ignore the convictions of religion. The past is all that he has, and it is in the past and in the bounty of his remembered self that he escapes from Iago to the freedom of his love for Desdemona, who loved him for the dangers he had passed. It is here that love triumphs—endures rather—for there is nothing unified about it and nothing ideal. As well as in Othello's recollection it has survived and gleamed forth variously and disconnectedly in Desdemona's last moments; in her 'I am very sorry that you are not well' [III. iii. 289]; in the charming heroine-worship of

> Whatever shall become of Michael Cassio
> He's never anything but your true servant;
>
> [III. iii. 8-9]

In the pungent common sense of Emilia's views on sex equality, and her—'Who would not make her husband a cuckold to make him a monarch?' [IV. iii. 75-7]—as well as in her passionate defence of Desdemona. All have a quality and scope that cannot be defined in terms outside themselves; and Iago, the supremely uncharitable impulse, the supreme negation of love, can never wholly succeed in bringing them within the field of his own destructive understanding. (pp. 198-201)

> *John Bayley, "Love and Identity: 'Othello'," in his* The Characters of Love: A Study in the Literature of Personality, *Basic Books, Inc., Publishers, 1960, pp. 125-201.*

IRVING RIBNER (essay date 1960)

[In the excerpt below from his Patterns in Shakespearian Tragedy *(1960), Ribner regards* Othello *as a Christian allegory and judges the paradox of the fortunate fall as "the central intellectual proposition" of the play, shaping and controlling its dramatic action, poetic language, and characterization. As has Paul N. Siegel (1953), he likens the Moor to Adam, encountering evil for the first time in his life and bringing about his own destruction because of his wrong choice; he also compares Othello to the hero of medieval morality drama, the representation of imperfect humanity whose soul is contended for by the forces of good and evil—an idea similarly discussed by Bernard Spivack (1958). The principal sin in* Othello, *Ribner contends, is jealousy, embodied in the figure of Iago, who also represents the "dramatic symbol of evil" in the play. Further, the critic argues that, in rejecting the role of God in determining human affairs and asserting the primacy of human reason, Iago is to be seen as the destroyer of harmony, order, and hierarchy, and thus he also "stands for social disintegration." Arguing that Desdemona's perfect love is a reflection of "the love of Christ for man," Ribner claims that Shakespeare represents her mercy and forgiveness as the agency of Othello's salvation. Indeed, the critic avers, the Moor's suicide should be viewed as expiation for his sins and his final speech at the close of the drama as an explicit rejection of evil, an avowal of his contrition, and a serene acceptance of his fate. Other commentators who have considered whether Shakespeare depicts Othello as repentant or damned at the conclusion of the play include Kenneth O. Myrick (1941), Harley Granville-Barker (1945), S. L. Bethell (1952), Edward Hubler (1958), G. M. Matthews (1964), and Roy W. Battenhouse (1969). Finally, Ribner sees Cassio as representing "ordinary man," temporarily led astray*

by Iago's evil, but never yielding his soul to him; thus, "he can rule in Cyprus at the end of the play, a symbol of rebirth." In an earlier essay (see excerpt above, 1955), Ribner focused more explicitly on Othello's *relation to medieval morality drama.*]

In *Othello* Shakespeare again gave dramatic form to a Christian view of mankind's encounter with evil, the destructive power of that evil, and man's ability to attain salvation in spite of it. He did so with a neatness and precision which reveal that he had matured as an artist in the brief years since the completion of *Hamlet*. Now he evolved a more perfect dramatic form which might in the domestic setting of one man's fall—closer to the immediate world of his audience than that of any other of his tragedies—mirror the fall of all men, just as Judeo-Christian tradition had reflected it in the fall of Adam; and as the paradox of the fortunate fall assured to man the hope of redemption, Shakespeare reflected also this universal hope in *Othello*. (p. 91)

Othello is of great potential virtue, but when he comes upon the scene he is, like the early Hamlet, as yet untried. In spite of his age he has not yet encountered the evil of the world. The play will be his baptism; he will encounter evil as Adam had encountered it, and like Adam he will fall, but in his own destruction he will learn the nature of evil. He will learn to distinguish true virtue from seeming virtue, and from his tragedy he will emerge the kind of man who is capable of salvation. Shakespeare says in the destruction of Othello, as in that of Hamlet, that true virtue and wisdom may come to man only through suffering, struggle and self-mastery. It is the tragedy of human life that this must be so.

In *Hamlet* evil had been passive. Claudius might never have acted against Hamlet, for he was content to let his crime lie buried in the past, but Hamlet had been faced with the task of active struggle against evil. In *Othello* evil is an active force embodied in Iago. He is a dramatic symbol of evil whose function is to cause the downfall of Othello, and although Shakespeare endows him with an illusion of reality so supreme in its artistry that it has escaped analysis as thoroughly as that of Hamlet, in the larger symbolic design of the play he needs no specific motivation. Othello is posing the chief question in the minds of his audience when he asks, 'Will you, I pray, demand that demi-devil / Why he hath thus ensnared my soul and body?' [V. ii. 301-02]; Shakespeare's only answer is to affirm the inscrutability of evil, its self-sufficiency which needs no motive beyond the fact of its existence: 'From this time forth I never will speak word. / Demand me nothing: what you know you know' [V. ii. 303-04]. (pp. 93-4)

Shakespeare achieves directness and precision in this play by symbolizing his force of evil in terms of one specific sin. This is jealousy, in Renaissance terms an aspect of the deadly sin of envy, the antithesis of love which springs from the perversion of love by fear. Iago is the dramatic symbol of jealousy itself, and he mirrors jealousy in all of its possible forms. (p. 94)

Just as Iago stands for jealousy, Desdemona stands for its very opposite, the cardinal virtue of love. It is love in the highest scale of Christian neo-Platonism, love of the mind and understanding:

> I saw Othello's visage in his mind,
> And to his honours and his valiant parts
> Did I my soul and fortunes consecrate.
>
> [I. iii. 252-54]

It is all bounty, all trust and all forgiveness. In the perfection of her love Desdemona reflects the love of Christ for man; she

stands both for self-sacrifice and for redemption. Othello is like the conventional morality play hero between the Satanic Iago and the angelic Desdemona. Both vie for his soul, and in his human imperfection he chooses wrongly. (pp. 94-5)

Like *Hamlet, Othello* begins with evil; it is not the pervasive darkness and gloom which hangs over Elsinore, but a specific agent of evil who wears the outward signs of virtue, life and conviviality. In Iago we see evil as deception and as a direct challenge to the order and harmony of the universe. Iago's superficial brilliance and self-control is the 'reason' of Renaissance scepticism which in Shakespeare's day was challenging the great vision of harmony, order and degree which Christian humanism carried over from the Middle Ages and which was most notably embodied in the writings of Richard Hooker. (p. 96)

Iago stands for social disintegration. In the harmonious world order of which Shakespeare's contemporaries liked to conceive, servants had their just place, their rights and their obligations. They were loyal to their masters out of love, and their masters repaid them with care and protection, all as a part of a social order whose perfection reflected the love of God for man. The true servant of such a system, Iago sees as:

> a duteous and knee-crooking knave,
> That, doting on his own obsequious bondage,
> Wears out his time, much like his master's ass,
> For naught but provender, and when he's old, cashier'd:
> Whip me such honest knaves.
>
> [I. i. 45-9]

Such a servant Iago appears to be, but his semblance of loyalty is but a mask. He is always the self-seeker. He shares none of the 'love and duty' which hold together the social order and link it to God Himself. Iago is all seeming, false appearance:

> In following him, I follow but myself;
> Heaven is my judge, not I for love and duty,
> But seeming so, for my peculiar end:
> For when my outward action doth demonstrate
> The native act and figure of my heart
> In compliment extern, 'tis not long after
> But I will wear my heart upon my sleeve
> For daws to peck at: I am not what I am.
>
> [I. i. 58-65]

The supreme egotism of Iago is a manifestation of the code of 'reason' by which he lives. True human reason in terms of Renaissance Christian humanism was a reflection of the supreme wisdom of God, and it consisted of attuning one's own will to the purposes of God, a recognition that human events are reflections of divine purpose. Iago's 'reason' is the sin of pride, for it denies the supremacy of God and sees man as the sole author of his destiny, able to control himself and others by the power of his mind. . . . Iago would control human passion by an act of will unrelated to the will of God; his action reveals an unbridled passion which gives the lie to his own protestation. In denying the purposes and the power of God, Iago strikes at the root of Christian humanism, for the 'natural law' which it saw as the guiding principle in human affairs was a reflection of the divine law of God, an emanation of God's love for his creation and of the harmonious order by which he ruled the universe. Iago, like the later Edmund [in *King Lear*], stands outside morality. He can see man only as a creature of animal passion, cut off from the grace of God. Love, the guiding principle in God's plan, is only 'a lust of the blood and a permission of the will' [I. iii. 334-35].

Bradley [see excerpt above, 1904] marvelled that the supreme intellect of Iago should finally betray him into such colossal errors as his misjudging both the relationship between Othello and Desdemona and the character of his own wife, Emilia. But it is in the very nature of Iago's intellect that this should be so; for such 'reason', standing outside of moral law, can never recognize the truth of moral law; it can perceive the signs of God's benevolence only as their very opposites. The love of Othello and Desdemona, a love of mind divorced from physical passion, can appear to Iago only as 'a frail vow betwixt an erring barbarian and a super-subtle Venetian' [I. iii. 355-56]. . . . He can perceive only the outward appearance of Othello; he cannot see the qualities for which Desdemona married him, and thus their relationship seems only a product of lust which lust must destroy. Out of Iago's failure of perception will come his own destruction, but this failure is inherent in the very 'reason' by which he lives.

Iago is revealed to the audience as a demi-devil, the incarnation of evil itself, the negation of moral law. This is not, however, how he appears to the other characters in the play: 'Divinity of hell! / When devils will the blackest sins put on, / They do suggest at first with heavenly shows, / As I do now' [II. iii. 350-53]. To the rest of the world, and particularly to Othello, he is always 'honest' Iago, and we must remember that 'honest' has also the implications of chaste. Like the Claudius of *Hamlet*, Iago is evil in its traditional role, disguised as good. (pp. 96-9)

Cassio is deluded like Othello by the seeming virtue of Iago: 'I never knew / A Florentine more kind and honest' [III. i. 40]. This parallel is not his only function in the play. He is used also as a symbol of the true friendship which Othello rejects. His is a genuine honesty contrasted to the seeming honesty of Iago; his conviviality and good fellowship stem, as opposed to Iago's, from a real trust and love of his fellow men. In spite of his deception by Iago, Cassio does not allow himself to be deeply tainted by evil as Othello does. He maintains to the end his faith in Desdemona, symbolically a hope that true love and virtue will restore him to the felicity which his weakness has lost him. Like Banquo in *Macbeth*, Cassio stands for ordinary man, with his mixture of good and evil. He never surrenders his soul to evil, and he emerges triumphant in spite of his encounter with Iago. Thus he can rule in Cyprus at the end of the play, a symbol of rebirth.

Just as in Iago Shakespeare pictures evil in the guise of good, in Othello he pictures true virtue wearing all the outward signs of evil. To do so he developed the suggestion in Cinthio that the marriage was unnatural. Cinthio had not dwelt on the blackness of the Moor, mentioning it only once in his story; but Shakespeare seized upon it as a poetic symbol by which he could emphasize the theme of the unnatural. That Shakespeare intended his audience to think of Othello as a Negro of very dark complexion is clear. We must recognize that a Jacobean audience could not have failed to view the marriage of a white Italian girl to a black African with some horror. Cinthio himself had told the story as an example of a marriage contrary to nature. This is not to attribute racial prejudice to Shakespeare. It is, on the contrary, the most astounding evidence of his freedom from such feeling, for the marriage to which he gives the outward appearance of an evil act contrary to nature, he shows in reality to be the noblest type of spiritual union.

In the Renaissance the colour black was a symbol of lechery—it is commonly so used in the emblem books of the period—and it was also the colour of the devil, whose redness is a

fairly recent innovation. . . . To Shakespeare's audience Othello . . . would have all the outward appearance of the 'blacker devil' [V. ii. 131] which Emilia calls him. His marriage to Desdemona would appear as an aberration in nature. (pp. 100-01)

This motif of unnatural union runs through the first two acts of the play, juxtaposed in thematic counterpoint against the twin motif of Iago's honesty. Othello has the blackness of Satan, Iago the whiteness of truth and virtue. True virtue bears the mark of evil, and evil is marked with the semblance of honesty. Shakespeare assures the audience of the falsity of these outward signs, that Iago is only seeming honest, and that Othello, in spite of his appearance, is a man of true nobility whom Desdemona can love for 'his honours and his valiant parts' [I. iii. 253]. We see his calm bearing and his dignity before the council, and he himself is made to deny the very lechery of which his colour is the outward sign:

> Vouch with me, heaven, I therefore beg it not,
> To please the palate of my appetite,
> Nor to comply with heat—the young affects
> In me defunct—and proper satisfaction,
> But to be free and bounteous to her mind.
>
> [I. iii. 261-65]

Yet so shocking is Shakespeare's deliberate reversal of normal appearances that the audience must be left still incredulous, with an uncertain fear that appearance may still be truth. This fear is supported by Brabantio's warning: 'Look to her, Moor, if thou hast eyes to see: / She has deceived her father, and may thee' [I. iii. 292-93]. Upon this seeming violation of nature, Iago will work in his temptation of Othello. He will cause Othello to see Desdemona as Brabantio has seen her, and thus to cast off as foul and unnatural what appears to be so, but which in reality is the very opposite.

The temptation scene of the third act is cast in the conventional pattern of the morality drama. Othello undergoes a struggle during which he must choose between the two forces which vie for his soul, Iago on the one hand and Desdemona on the other. At the end of the scene Othello rejects Desdemona and embraces Iago in a symbolic ritual union, and from thenceforth he sees the world with the eyes of Iago. The tools with which Iago will work already have been prepared for in the first two acts. He will rely upon his own appearance as honest, which Othello has not yet learned to question, and he will work upon the seeming perversion of nature in Othello's own marriage, appealing to Othello's ignorance of life and to the fears and uncertainties which accompany his human inability to distinguish between appearance and reality. Iago will arouse in Othello a false sense of the demands of honour and reputation, which will reflect the love of mere appearance for which Iago from the first has stood. Othello, in the delusion of his wrong moral choice, will live by the code of Iago. (pp. 102-03)

Desdemona is endowed, like Othello and Iago, with the illusion of reality, but in the total scheme of the play she stands from first to last as an incarnation of self-sacrificing love. She is a reflection of Christ, who must die at the hands of man, but out of whose death may spring man's redemption. We must note that Desdemona undergoes a temptation which parallels that of Othello and which is much like the temptation of Christ in the wilderness. She is offered the bait of evil by Emilia in a scene which parallels that of Othello's seduction by Iago. Emilia justifies sin by the logic of Iago which postulates a world without heavenly control. To sin for the price of the whole world, Emilia argues, would be no sin, for 'Why, the wrong is but a wrong i' the world; and having the world for your labour, 'tis a wrong in your own world, and you might quickly make it right' [IV. ii. 80-2]. This logic Desdemona rejects, and then Emilia suggests that men themselves are to blame for the sins of their wives, and she argues a principle of vengeance:

> But I do think it is their husbands' faults
> If wives do fall: say that they slack their duties,
> And pour our treasures into foreign laps,
> Or else break out in peevish jealousies,
> Throwing restraint upon us; or say they strike us,
> Or scant our former having in despite;
> Why, we have galls, and though we have some grace,
> Yet have we some revenge.
>
> [IV. ii. 86-93]

Emilia lists the very sins against Desdemona of which Othello has been guilty. Desdemona's reply foreshadows her role in the final act, for she is all mercy and all forgiveness, no matter what crimes are done against her:

> Good night, good night: heaven me such uses send,
> Not to pick bad from bad, but by bad mend!
>
> [IV. iii. 104-05]

The evil of her murder she will repay with forgiveness and mercy, out of evil creating good. Her unconquerable love for Othello will be his redemption.

Thus, although Othello dies accepting damnation as his just desert, Shakespeare by his careful delineation of Desdemona as a symbol of mercy has prepared the audience for the salvation of Othello in spite of all. Othello dies truly penitent. He takes the step which Claudius, in spite of his fears of damnation, cannot take. Othello destroys himself in an act of expiation, and his final words are a reminder to the audience of his union in death with the goodness he had tried to destroy:

> I kiss'd thee ere I killed thee: no way but this;
> Killing myself, to die upon a kiss.
>
> [V. ii. 358-59]

The audience knows that in his renunciation of evil, his penance and expiation, Othello has merited salvation.

The calm measured cadence of Othello's death speech recalls his earlier speeches before the Venetian council. It is a renunciation of the values of Iago. Othello denies the dues of reputation, of just reward for his services to Venice. He asks that his deed be considered without bias and in terms of the very justice he had violated in the murder of his wife:

> Soft you; a word or two before you go.
> I have done the state some service, and they know't.
> No more of that. I pray you, in your letters,
> When you shall these unlucky deeds relate,
> Speak of me as I am; nothing extenuate,
> Nor set down aught in malice.
>
> [V. ii. 338-43]

He appeals to the mercy of the onlookers, naming himself an ordinary man, no more vicious than others, but with the very human weaknesses which can lead to error and corruption. He confesses that he has destroyed his greatest good, not willingly, but in the ignorance of delusion, and in his tears he expresses his sincere contrition:

> then must you speak
> Of one that loved not wisely but too well;
> Of one not easily jealous, but being wrought,

> Perplexed in the extreme; of one whose hand,
> Like the base Indian, threw a pearl away
> Richer than all his tribe; of one whose subdued eyes,
> Albeit unused to the melting mood,
> Drop tears as fast as the Arabian trees
> Their medicinal gum.
>
> [V. ii. 343-51]

And with this, as he had once executed justice upon the infidel Turk, he executes it upon himself:

> And say besides, that in Aleppo once,
> Where a malignant and a turban'd Turk
> Beat a Venetian and traduced the state,
> I took by the throat the circumcised dog,
> And smote him, thus.
>
> [V. ii. 352-56]

He destroys the evil within himself, asserting true justice as opposed to the perversion of justice which had led him to kill Desdemona. The speech reveals a new self-knowledge and self-understanding. It is a calm summation of Othello's life-journey. (pp. 112-15)

The tragedy of *Othello*, in its neatness and precision of construction, parallels more closely than any of Shakespeare's other plays what may be called the prototype of tragedy in Christian Europe, that of Adam in the garden of Eden. *Othello* expresses more perfectly than any of the other plays the paradox of the fortunate fall through which the Christian world could postulate a merciful and purposive God in spite of Adam's tragedy. The play is Christian in its symbolism and in the central intellectual proposition which shapes and controls the action, character and poetry of which it is comprised. *Othello* couches its universal propositions in terms of specific action and specific character, which in the speedy movement of the scenes retain an illusion of reality in spite of the logical inconsistencies which the scholar's study may reveal. It creates an emotional equivalent for its central idea and a tension between emotion and intellect which is the essence of tragedy. We participate fully in the horror which falls upon Othello, while rationally we are assured and seconded in our faith in divine order. (p. 115)

Irving Ribner, "The Pattern of Moral Choice: 'Othello'," in his Patterns in Shakespearian Tragedy, *Methuen & Co. Ltd., 1960, pp. 91-115.*

HARRY LEVIN (essay date 1964)

[*Levin contends that it is more appropriate to view* Othello *as a "domestic drama" or romance rather than a tragedy, since it lacks the tragic stature and cosmic significance of such plays as* King Lear, Hamlet, *and* Macbeth. *Because* Othello *does not represent the tragic outcome of the dramatic action as fatally inevitable, he argues, the play is pitiful, not tragic, and therefore should be classed with such other Shakespearean works as* Romeo and Juliet *and* Antony and Cleopatra. *Levin also attributes Thomas Rymer's objections to* Othello *(see excerpt above, 1692) to the strong domestic element in the play, for it disturbed his obsession with "neo-classical decorum" to have the handkerchief and its loss at the heart of the disastrous consequences. Like Robert B. Heilman (1956), Levin views the handkerchief as the embodiment of the "theme of sorcery" in the drama and maintains that its prominence in the tragic outcome demonstrates that human happiness may be determined not by cosmological agents but by such relatively trivial instrumentalities as one man's malice or another's credulity. For additional commentary on the issue of free will versus determinism in* Othello, *see the excerpts by Hermann*

Ulrici (1839), G. G. Gervinus (1849-50), Denton J. Snider (1887), E. K. Chambers (1908), Stopford A. Brooke (1913), Elmer Edgar Stoll (1915), Wyndham Lewis (1927), Allardyce Nicoll (1927), and Robert G. Hunter (1976). Such other critics as John Hughes (1713), Lewis Theobald (1733), Wolstenholme Parr (1795), Nigel Alexander, and John Middleton Murry (see Additional Bibliography) have also analyzed the dramatic function of the handkerchief in the play.]

Mr. Eliot, in one of his portentous *obiter dicta* [casual remarks], avers that he has yet to see a cogent refutation of Thomas Rymer's strictures against *Othello* [see excerpts above, 1927 and 1692]. After that intimidating caveat, any such attempt would seem to be the sheerest bravado. In any case, it is rather too late in the game to try. The fact that no one has risen to Shakespeare's defense—or does Mr. Eliot mean to imply that there have been some ineffectual defenses?—might indicate no more than that Rymer's attack did no substantial damage. . . . [Rymer] was concerned not with the secret springs of behavior but with the outward conformities, with a neoclassical decorum which he construed dogmatically not by a system of ethics but by a code of etiquette. Thus Iago offended him by not behaving as a good soldier correctly should on the stage. Desdemona's conduct was light and unfilial, to say the least; in taking the paternal side against her, it should be added that Rymer has been joined by certain other commentators, and notably by the patriarchal John Quincy Adams [see excerpt above, 1845].

Rymer's anti-Negro sneers at Othello, and at the Venetians for inviting him into their homes and appointing him to a high military post, make the Restoration critic sound to us for all the world like the governor of a southern state. Yet they have the incidental value of attesting that hostile near-contemporaries could recognize and react to the warmth of Shakespeare's compassionate interest in the position of a Negro. Rymer's method of reducing the play to absurdity was to summarize the plot with heavy-handed facetiousness, much as Voltaire would do when he campaigned against *Hamlet*. By dwelling upon its homeliest details, with a zeal for exposing vulgarity which in the long run incriminated himself, Rymer sought to reduce *Othello* to what he termed "a bloody farce." The modern term *domestic drama* would come nearer the mark, and would hint at what was so disturbing to a rigid neoclassicist. That tragedy could hinge upon a commonplace article of domestic utility, so humble an object as a handkerchief, outraged both his personal sense of propriety and all his canons of probability. Jocosely he suggested that *Othello* be retitled *The Tragedy of the Handkerchief*. Archly he proposed a moral: "This may be a warning to all good wives, that they look well to their linen." We should be thankful that Rymer did not compose a commentary on the legend of Saint Veronica.

It should be conceded, for better or worse, that housewivery has a real thematic significance for the play. It is discussed at some length in the banter between Iago and Desdemona, while they are awaiting Othello's arrival at Cyprus. In a sharp series of improvised couplets, with characteristic misogyny, Iago sketches cynical vignettes of woman's role. Desdemona requests a more favorable portrait, and Iago obliges up to a point, building up through a climatic sequence of feminine virtues:

> She was wight, if ever such wight were,—
>
> [II. i. 158]

When Desdemona eagerly asks, "To do what?," he clinches the verses triumphantly:

> To suckle fools and chronicle small beer.
>
> [II. i. 160]

Paragon of the virtues though she be, it will be her anticlimatic lot to have babies and keep household accounts. But alas! such is not to be Desdemona's lot. Not without reason Iago plays upon the polarity of the word *housewife* and its raffish derivative, *hussy*. The courtesan Bianca—and, given the interplay between blacks and whites, her name may have some purport—is introduced as "a housewife that by selling her desires / Buys herself bread and clothes" [IV. i. 94-5]. There is a significant interchange, involving another equivocal key-word, when Emilia calls Bianca a strumpet and the latter flares back:

> I am no strumpet, but of life as honest
> As you that thus abuse me.
>
> [V. i. 122-23]

Desdemona and Bianca, with Emilia midway between them, stand at the polar extremes of womanhood. That the handkerchief should pass from the one to the other, by way of the go-between, is no mere contingency but a sign and a portent—a dumb-show, as it were, of purity bewhored and love confounded with lust.

The original charge against Othello, it will be remembered, was that he has bewitched Desdemona. The truly sinister witchcraft, as it ironically turns out, is the spell cast on Othello by Iago's wit. This theme of sorcery, which is so richly interwoven through the language of the drama, has been traced in rewarding detail by Robert Heilman's *Magic in the Web* [see excerpt above, 1956]. Its concrete embodiment is the handkerchief, which is therefore as meaningful a stage-property as could be imagined. Like Nerissa's ring [in *The Merchant of Venice*], it is a love-token; more than that, it becomes a talisman of life and death. It is hallowed with superstitious awe by Othello's strange tale of the Gypsy charmer and the heirloom from his mysterious past. Shakespeare invests it with romantic mystery as a magic symbol of Othello's passion and a mystic omen of Desdemona's murder, since it will provide the ocular proof that seals Iago's calumny. The stark word *handkerchief* is enunciated no less than twenty-four times, and its vehement iterance by Othello punctuates the most suspenseful dialogue of the play, as who should say upon what trivial hazards our happiness depends. Bianca intends, for Cassio, to *take the work out*, to copy the pattern. But Shakespeare's point is that—though venal loves, like hers for him, can easily be replaced or duplicated—the genuine love of a woman and a man cannot be copied. It is unique and irreplaceable.

When Othello warns Desdemona that the loss of the handkerchief would threaten perdition, the warning reverberates to his earlier avowal:

> Perdition catch my soul,
> But I do love thee! and when I love thee not,
> Chaos is come again.
>
> [III. iii. 90-2]

Chaos does come again; damnation overtakes him; his world is brought down in ruins by the wave of a handkerchief, the neat trick of a wily conjuror abetted by circumstance. Cunning has done its best, and luck its worst. And since the crucial evidence is false, since Desdemona herself is innocent, in the end it is not Iago but Othello who does the motive-hunting:

> It is the cause, it is the cause, my soul.
>
> [V. ii. 1]

But Desdemona has rightly denied it:

> Alas the day! I never gave him cause.
>
> [III. iv. 158]

And Cassio will deny it on his part:

> Dear General, I never gave you cause.
>
> [V. ii. 299]

The catastrophe is needless, then, if not motiveless. The lovers are not star-crossed; the protagonist is neither hounded by fates nor predestinated by oracles; the retrospective design bears the signature, not of necessity, but of chance; we listen in vain for the ring of inevitability. Can *Othello* still be considered a tragedy, in the grander meaning of the form? Should it not be qualified as a domestic drama—if not, to please Bernard Shaw, as "pure melodrama"? [see excerpt above, 1897]. Or, if we prefer more flexible categories, ought we not to consider that Bradley [see excerpt above, 1904] regarded it as the most romantic of Shakespeare's tragedies? Victor Hugo, in a famous manifesto, defined the romantic drama as an admixture of the sublime and the grotesque, and illustrated that definition by the old fairy-tale of Beauty and the Beast [in his preface to *Cromwell*]. A richer illustration would be a picture of Desdemona listening to Othello. It would be highlighted by the recurring imagery of lights and shades. It would harbor the attraction, along with the underlying repulsion, of opposites. There would be implications of bestiality: dogs, goats and monkeys, the beast with two backs. But these would be counterpoised by touches of wonder, which link Desdemona with the heroines of Shakespeare's later romances. Bacon, in his essay "Of Beauty," stressed the element of "strangeness in the proportion." Pater, echoing Bacon, characterized romance as strangeness conjoined with beauty.

Bradley had his hesitations about admitting *Othello* to that canon of major Shakespearean tragedy which, following the lead of Coleridge's lectures, his book did so much to establish. There are good grounds for arguing that the play might more appropriately be flanked by *Romeo and Juliet* on one side and by *Antony and Cleopatra* on the other. Certainly it does not attain the scale of the other three works treated in [Bradley's] *Shakespearean Tragedy*. More particularly, it lacks the terror of *King Lear*, where nature is brought to the verge of her confine, or of *Hamlet* and *Macbeth*, where man is brought face to face with supernatural forces. *Othello* bears the brunt of society rather than nature, and perhaps it compensates with pity for what it misses in terror. Hence Wordsworth deemed it "the most pathetic of human compositions." This did not endear it less to the sympathies of its audiences; Rymer attacked it because it seems to have been, during the seventeenth century, the most popular tragedy on the English stage; and there are many anecdotes of spectators becoming so enthralled in the action that they have sought to intervene between the Moor and his bride. The basis of their mutual understanding, so long as it lasts, is compassion, pathos, pity. When Othello first told Desdemona his tales, she sighed:

> She swore, i' faith 'twas strange, 'twas passing strange,
> 'Twas pitiful, 'twas wondrous pitiful.
>
> [I. iii. 160-61]

And he went on to sum up his case for the Senators:

> She lov'd me for the dangers I had pass'd,
> And I lov'd her that she did pity them.
>
> [I. iii. 167-68]

The conclusion that the tragedy was not inevitable, that the tragic misunderstanding could have been avoided, that so much evil is mere malice and so much folly sheer credulity, and that the essential dignity of man is at the mercy of both malice and credulity—"But yet the pity of it, Iago! O Iago, the pity of it, Iago!" [IV. i. 195-96] (pp. 11-16)

> *Harry Levin, "'Othello' and the Motive-Hunters,"*
> *in* The Centennial Review, *Vol. VIII, No. 1, Winter,*
> *1964, pp. 1-16.*

G. M. MATTHEWS   (essay date 1964)

[*In the following excerpt, Matthews argues that, in making Othello black, Shakespeare was emphasizing the physical and cultural differences that set the Moor apart from the Venetians. He adds that Othello's status as an alien is enhanced by his marriage to Desdemona, which produces a further sense of "isolation and confinement" that grows throughout the play and reaches its fullest expression in Act V, Scene ii. Matthews maintains that although the lovers attempt to "assert 'humane' values" against those of Venice, which he regards as "hierarchical, predatory and therefore not yet fully human," they are unaware that their "humaneness" increases their vulnerability to those around them. The critic also contends that Othello's alien nature is the source of Iago's hatred, and he regards the ensign as a more intense and irrational version of that chauvinistic bias characteristic of Brabantio and other members of the Venetian senate, all of whom tolerate Othello only because of their reliance on his military skill. Such other commentators as G. G. Gervinus (1849-50) and Leslie A. Fiedler (see Additional Bibliography) have also emphasized Othello's alienation from Venetian society. Significantly, Matthews states that Iago's irrationality is best reflected in his use of "systematic unreason" and "magic" to convert the Moor to his debased perception of the world, an assessment at odds with such earlier critics as Robert B. Heilman (1951 and 1956) and Winifred M. T. Nowottny (1952), who claim that Iago works by supplanting reason for passion in Othello's mind. Additionally, whereas such critics as August Wilhelm Schlegel (1811) have emphasized Othello's barbarous origins, Matthews avers that Iago is the barbarian, seeking to transform the civilized Othello into a degenerate creature. However, the critic argues, Iago fails in this attempt, for the Moor slays Desdemona not in passionate hate or revengeful jealousy but in love, perceiving his act as one of justice and duty. At the close, according to Matthews, Othello recovers his dignity and human values, demonstrating in his final speech that he has completely regained "his integrity as a human being." For additional discussions of whether Shakespeare depicts Othello as attaining or regaining clarity of perception at the close of the play, see the excerpts by G. R. Elliott (1937), F. R. Leavis (1937), E. M. W. Tillyard (1938), Robert B. Heilman (1951 and 1956), Jared R. Curtis (1973), and Helen Gardner (see Additional Bibliography). Matthews also believes that although Othello's murder of Desdemona and his suicide would have been viewed by Shakespeare's Jacobean audience as leading to his damnation, it is possible to regard the Moor as saved from this fate—a suggestion he bases on Desdemona's final, forgiving speech, which, the critic states, recalls the Christian doctrine of atonement. Other commentators who have addressed this issue include Kenneth O. Myrick (1941), Harley Granville-Barker (1945), S. L. Bethell (1952), Paul N. Siegel (1953), Irving Ribner (1955 and 1960), Edward Hubler (1958), and Roy W. Battenhouse (1969).*]

Othello presents, in extreme form, the situation of the alien (including the class-alien) in a hierarchical, predatory and therefore not yet fully human society. Othello's colour is thus representative of a much wider human protest than concerns race alone, and Paul Robeson was right in maintaining that

> Shakespeare meant Othello to be a "black moor"
> from Africa.... But the color is essentially

secondary—except as it emphasizes the difference in *culture*. This is the important thing. . . . Shakespeare's Othello has learned to live in a strange society, but he is not *of* it—as an easterner today might pick up western manners and not be western [quoted by Marvin Rosenberg in his *The Masks of Othello* (see Additional Bibliography)].

In another way, however, the colour is of crucial importance in focusing the irrational feelings associated with that difference, as a remarkable footnote by A. C. Bradley [see excerpt above, 1904] illustrates. He is agreeing with Coleridge [see excerpts above, 1808-18 and 1813] that Othello should be 'sunburnt' rather than black on the modern stage:

> Perhaps if we saw Othello coal-black with the bodily eye, *the aversion of our blood, an aversion which comes as near to being merely physical as anything human can, would overpower our imagination* and sink us below not Shakespeare only but the audiences of the seventeenth and eighteenth centuries. (my italics.)

Whatever we make of this, it reminds us that Shakespeare forced his audience to see Othello first with the 'bodily eye' of Iago. This hero is a great human being who, differing *physically* as well as *culturally* from the community he has entered, recognizes (within the limits of his social role) only universal humane values of love and loyalty; but when in his equalitarian innocence he assumes full human rights in a society where other values are dominant, he makes himself and his personal relationships vulnerable to irrational, un-human forces, embodied in Iago, that try to reduce him to a level as irrational as themselves and almost—but not quite—succeed.

Othello's commanding personality and the glamour of his poetic idiom tend to make his actual social position seem much higher than it really is. He is employed by the Venetian republic as a professional soldier, a mercenary, and has become its most reliable and popular general. In his own country he was descended 'From men of royal siege' [I. ii. 22], and he can say without boasting that he merits the position he has reached. Yet in Roderigo's words he is 'an extravagant and wheeling stranger' [I. i. 136] (where *extravagant* means 'straying outside his proper place'), who has lived in Venice, as distinct from the camp, for less than a year [I. iii. 83-5]. The precarious anomaly of Othello's status is vividly dramatized in what are perhaps the most brilliant opening scenes in any Shakespeare play. In the second scene two parties of men are searching for him independently through the streets of Venice: one from the Duke's senate to require his urgent service against the 'enemy Ottoman', the other to imprison him for marrying a senator's daughter. Ironically, one party is at first mistaken for the other in the darkness. Othello himself, not without irony, comments on the paradox; if I obey the prison party, he says, 'How may the duke be therewith satisfied?' [I. ii. 88]. Othello's prestige rests on his indispensability, but being indispensable does not make him socially acceptable in governing circles. Brabantio invited him home and 'loved' him while he recounted his past adventures, but as a future son-in-law he is decidedly *persona non grata,* a 'thing' that no Venetian girl could possibly look at with affection except by some preposterous error of nature. Brabantio never does reconcile himself to the match, the grief of which kills him. There were, of course, 'fortunes' at stake, and the runaway marriage (in contrast to Cinthio's version, which takes place with the reluctant consent of the girl's par-

ents) signifies not rashness but purity of motive. Their secret union, in contempt of the 'many noble matches' [IV. ii. 125] available to Desdemona, is to make it quite clear that no material interests were involved in what was a free love-match. Othello gets nothing from it, while as Desdemona says:

> That I did love the Moor to live with him,
> My downright violence and scorn of fortunes
> May trumpet to the world.
>
> [I. iii. 248-50]

Desdemona affirms her choice in public and with devastating simplicity—devastating because when her father asks her to say where her obedience lies, she answers:

> here's my husband,
> And so much duty as my mother show'd
> To you, preferring you before her father,
> So much I challenge that I may profess
> Due to the Moor, my lord.
>
> [I. iii. 185-89]

She makes no distinction whatever, that is, between her parents' marriage and her own. Brabantio retorts in effect that in that case he is no longer related to her: 'I had rather to adopt a child than get it' [I. iii. 191]. And Desdemona finds, without dismay, that her act has isolated her with Othello, for her father will not admit her into his house, even alone. Desdemona's childlike simplicity, dramatically so effective at the end of the play in heightening the pathos of her helpless isolation, has the effect in this scene of positing the spontaneous, instinctive naturalness of her love for Othello (to Iago her act means the opposite: 'If she had been blest she would never have loved the Moor'). Unlike her father, Desdemona entertains no consideration 'of years, of country, and of credit' [I. iii. 97], only of direct human relationships: parents, lover, husband, friend.

Othello's commitment complements hers. Shakespeare shows that this is the first relationship he has experienced since childhood (Cassio's friendship apart) that was not based on military or political expediency but purely on human feeling. Yet in staking his emotional life on Desdemona he has put his free condition into a 'circumscription and confine' [I. ii. 27] which makes him vulnerable, and that is why the supposed loss of her love exhausts his capacity for suffering. There is nothing egotistical in this attitude; on the contrary. Disease, poverty, slavery, even public disgrace—the loss of all he has valued up to now—he could bear 'well, very well',

> But there, where I have garner'd up my heart,
> Where either I must live or bear no life,
> The fountain from the which my current runs,
> Or else dries up—to be discarded thence!
>
> [IV. ii. 56-60]

Thus both lovers assert 'humane' values against the conventions that debase them; but 'humaneness', so isolated, is itself an abstraction and reliance on it leaves them fatally vulnerable. The emotional innocence of the hero and heroine (like the extreme youth of Romeo and Juliet) reflects both their protest against the social environment and their ultimate helplessness before it.

It is of course between Othello and Iago that the main issue is fought. Here Shakespeare made another significant change in Cinthio's original story. Cinthio's equivalent of Iago did not hate the Moor at all, but deceived him in order to revenge himself on his wife for her refusal to commit adultery. It was only after having her murdered that the Moor, regretting the deed, turned on its instigator and demoted him, and they then began *to hate each other*. In Shakespeare Iago's hatred, which fills the entire play from [I. i. 7] to the end, is one-sided, obsessive, and single-minded. (pp. 126-29)

Why does Iago hate Othello? This has always been the crux of the play. The characters themselves are baffled by hatred of such intensity; the dying Roderigo calls Iago an 'inhuman dog', and to Lodovico he seems 'More fell than anguish, hunger, or the sea' [V. ii. 362]—more implacable than the blind forces of nature. Yet when Othello asks him point-blank why he acted as he did, he shuts up completely. Not that Iago has ever been unwilling to talk, indeed he has just 'part confessed his villainy' [V. ii. 296]: all he refuses to explain is the motive of his hatred. 'What you know you know' [V. ii. 303]. What could he possibly say? 'I was passed over for the lieutenancy'? 'Some people thought Othello had seduced my wife'? The possible rational motives are so ludicrously incommensurate with the effects. But although the quick-witted Iago cannot explain his conduct rationally, Coleridge's verdict of 'motiveless malignity' overlooks the first scene of the play, which shows that his conduct was powerfully motivated. He is no devil from hell, except metaphorically. We learn within twenty lines that he is sensitive to aliens, because one of his first objections to Cassio is that he is a foreigner, 'a Florentine'. And although Iago's avowed policy is to thrive by Othello until he has lined his coat, his first dramatic action is to stir up an unprofitable racial riot against Othello merely in order to 'poison his delight' [I. i. 68] in his marriage, which is described to Brabantio in bestially obscene language:

> *Iago*. Even now, now, very now, an old black ram
> Is tupping your white ewe. . . .
>
> . . . you'll have your daughter cover'd with a Barbary horse; you'll have your nephews [grandchildren] neigh to you; . . . your daughter and the Moor are now making the beast with two backs.
>
> *Brabantio*. Thou art a villain.
> *Iago*.   You are—a Senator.
>   [I. i. 88-9, 111-12, 115-18]

The moment is crucial. The profane wretch and the magnifico suddenly recognize, behind their hostile confrontation, a kind of mutual identity: Brabantio is face to face with his own unconfessed reaction to the news of his daughter's elopement with a black man. Before the Duke that reaction becomes explicit, and Iago afterwards uses it as an invaluable source of quotation in baiting Othello. When Brabantio's 'loved' visitor is also loved by Desdemona he is immediately regarded as a heathen dealer in witchcraft and aphrodisiacs, and the senator's class-prejudice and religious intolerance are revealed in his horrified fear that if such unions are permitted, 'Bond-slaves and pagans shall our statesmen be' [I. ii. 99]. These early scenes demonstrate, therefore, that Iago's view of Othello is not—except in pathological intensity—a unique aberration, but an attitude held by the Venetian ruling class when forced into human relationship with a Moor. The Duke and the rest of his council who are conciliatory and tolerant cannot afford to be otherwise, 'cannot with safety cast him' [I. i. 149]: they need Othello's professional services.

Iago hates Othello because he is a Moor. This irrational but powerful motive, underlying the obsessive intensity of his feeling and the improvised reasons with which he justifies it, continually presses up towards the surface of his language. It breaks through into action at the opening of the play in order to give the audience the key to his character; after this its energies go into the intrigue that will bring the hated object and all its associates to destruction; but it often nearly betrays itself. . . . Iago's mind broods constantly over Othello's colour. After the disembarkation at Cyprus, when Cassio drinks 'To the health of our general' Iago drinks 'to the health of black Othello' [II. iii. 86, 32]. But it is in conversation with Othello himself that the hidden disgust most nearly betrays itself. One exchange is of particular importance. Othello's trust in Desdemona is just beginning to waver:

> *Othello*. And yet, how nature erring from itself—
> *Iago*.   Ay, there's the point: as—to be bold with you—
> Not to affect many proposed matches
> Of her own clime, complexion, and degree,
> Whereto we see in all things nature tends—
> Foh! one may smell in such a will most rank,
> Foul disproportion, thoughts unnatural.
> But pardon me—
>   [III. iii. 227-34]

Othello has been judged stupid for failing to see that this is an open insult, but it is *not* an open insult; Iago is repeating what Brabantio had said in council:

> she—in spite of nature,
> Of years, of country, credit, every thing—
> To fall in love with what she fear'd to look on!
> It is a judgment maim'd and most imperfect
> That will confess perfection so could err
> Against all rules of nature
>   [I. iii. 96-101]

The point lies in two antithetical interpretations of 'nature'. For Othello, as for Desdemona, what was 'natural' was a marriage between two lovers, involving the same duties as their parents had owed each other, and by *nature erring from itself* Othello meant 'a wife forgetting her proper loyalty'. To Brabantio it was against all rules of nature for a Venetian girl to love a Moor, and Iago therefore inverted Othello's phrase *nature erring from itself* to mean 'a woman flouting the laws of colour and class' ('clime, complexion, and degree'). The tragedy is epitomized in this exchange. Human love is what Othello stands by. But for Iago Othello is not a human being at all, he is an animal: a ram, a horse, an ass; his sexual union with Desdemona will produce not children but colts. Since Iago himself admits Othello's qualities ('a constant, loving, noble nature'), he is involved in complete irrationality, forced to argue that it is the very virtues of men that make them beast-like:

> The Moor is of a free and open nature
> . . . And will as tenderly be led by th' nose
> As asses are.
>   [I. iii. 399, 401-02]

This particular beast is loved by his wife and honoured as a brilliant military commander. The real relationship between him and Iago was established . . . when Othello quelled the uproar Iago had raised by saying: 'For Christian shame put by this barbarous brawl' [II. iii. 172]; Othello is the civilized man, Iago the barbarian. Iago's task is to reduce him in actuality to a shape that at first exists only in Iago's fantasy, that of an irrational beast, by

> making him egregiously an *ass*,
> And practising upon his peace and quiet
> Even to *madness*.
>   [II. i. 309-11]

So when Othello exclaims, at the beginning of his ordeal, that Iago would have to 'exchange [him] for a goat' [III. iii. 180] before he would make jealousy the business of his soul, he is describing with unconscious irony exactly what Iago proposes to do. This is not a study of a civilized barbarian reverting to type (for Othello has never been a barbarian, though he has been a slave), but the more subtle one of a white barbarian who tries to make a civilized man into his own image. (pp. 130-33)

The weapon Iago uses is systematic unreason, magic. Brabantio's first assumption on learning that his daughter had fallen in love with a Moor was that she must have been corrupted by sorcery:

> thou hast practis'd on her with foul charms,
> Abus'd her delicate youth with drugs or minerals . . .

> For nature so preposterously to err, . . .
> Sans witchcraft could not.

> [I. ii. 73-4; I. iii. 62, 64]

The Duke's council soon realizes that mutual love was the only 'witchcraft' in the case. Shakespeare is careful to show that the advances came equally from both sides, though at first he plays down the sensual element in Othello's love because men from hot climates were traditionally hot-blooded and this must not be supposed of Othello. The perfect equality of the lovers is symbolized in their playful exchange of roles on arrival in Cyprus, where Othello is Desdemona's 'dear' and Desdemona is Othello's 'fair warrior', while the imagery of Cassio's benediction on them is rich with fertility-feeling:

> Great Jove, Othello guard,
> And swell his sail with thine own powerful breath,
> That he may bless this bay with his tall ship,
> Make love's quick pants in Desdemona's arms,
> Give renew'd fire to our extinct spirits,
> And bring all Cyprus comfort!

> [II. i. 77-82]

It is hard to see how Shakespeare could have made the case clearer. It is not their union but their disunion that is effected by 'drugs or minerals', as the imagery now begins to demonstrate. Iago curbs Roderigo's impatience by reminding him that 'we work by wit and not by witchcraft' [II. iii. 372], meaning 'the job can't be done without planning'; but in this most ironical of Shakespeare's tragedies the statement carries an opposite implication: 'I work by witchcraft, not by reason'. The degrading of Cassio in Act II is a kind of symbolic rehearsal of the method Iago will use with his principal victim. Betrayed into drunkenness and senseless violence Cassio cries in self-disgust: 'To be now a sensible man, by and by a fool, and presently a beast!' [II. iii. 305-06]. The 'medicine' that so 'unwitted' Cassio was alcohol; the drug used on Othello will be more subtle and instead of wine into his mouth Iago will pour pestilence into his ear, but the sequence of results is to be identical. 'The Moor already changes with my poison' [III. iii. 325], Iago says after his first insinuations, and for this the victim has no counter-drug:

> Not poppy, nor mandragora,
> Nor all the drowsy syrups of the world,
> Shall ever medicine thee to that sweet sleep
> Which thou owed'st yesterday.

> [III. iii. 330-33]

This poetry, it has been noticed, is in Othello's own style: Iago is putting on the verbal habits of his victim, as Othello's later

'Goats and monkeys!' [IV. i. 263] will adopt Iago's; but its *content* is quite alien to Othello's thinking, who is not a drug-addict. Othello's characteristic images are of achieved perfection: Desdemona is a pearl, she is as smooth as monumental alabaster, he would not exchange her for a world made of chrysolite; and it is this integrity of love that Iago attacks with the solvents and corrosives of unreason.

The two exceptions are Othello's description of the handkerchief, and his request for poison in order to kill Desdemona. The actual virtue of the handkerchief is simply that both lovers valued it as Othello's first remembrance and to lose it might have been interpreted as a 'symptomatic act' (even Desdemona fears that such a loss might put some men to 'ill thinking'), but Iago's plot loads it with fictitious *mana* as a symbol of infidelity. Naturally Desdemona cannot see it like that, and Othello, mentally unbalanced after his latest interview with Iago, piles more and more on to the supposed properties of the handkerchief in order to scare her into some sense of the enormity of her offence. She feels his urgency but is sceptical of the details ('Sure there's some wonder in this handkerchief' [III. iv. 101] is the furthest she will go), which are evidently new to her; all Othello's previous stories have been factual. Thus it is Iago's magic that went into the web, the absurdity of the hallowed worms and maidens-heart dye corresponding to the irrational significance he has made Othello attach to it. Iago's refusal to agree to the use of poison has been explained as reluctance to implicate himself, but more is implied than mere caution. If Romeo could get poison without signing a register Iago certainly could. Othello surely thinks first of poison because he wants to do the right thing: isn't this the way (his request implies) in which good Italians dispose of unfaithful wives? But Iago cannot allow him to kill Desdemona at a distance, like a civilized Venetian; he must 'strangle her in her bed' [IV. i. 207] with his bare hands, like a savage. Poison is Iago's speciality. 'Work on, my medicine, work!' [IV. i. 44-5]. Just before advising Othello to strangle Desdemona, Iago succeeds in goading him to the point of complete mental breakdown; in the Folio text he 'falls in a trance' [s. d., IV. i. 43], and Iago has the satisfaction of telling Cassio that he sometimes 'breaks out to savage madness' [IV. i. 55] and foams at the mouth. As he recovers his reason, it is with loss of manhood that Iago taunts him. 'A passion most unsuiting such a man'; 'Good sir, be a man'; 'Would you would bear your fortune like a man!' [IV. i. 77, 65, 61]. *Like a man* in this context carries a double irony because the fortune Othello is being advised to bear is that of cuckoldry, so it really means 'like a monster'. From this point on, Othello is absorbed more and more into Iago's mental world. His vicious 'I will chop her into messes' [IV. i. 200] shows him becoming as barbarous as Iago wishes.

How is it that what is rational and human, personified in the hero, is so nearly turned into its opposite by this medicine man? The classic dilemma of *Othello* criticism has been that if the hero is as noble as he seems, a villain of superhuman intelligence would be needed to break him down. There are therefore critics who make Iago superhuman: a symbol or embodiment of Evil. Alternatively, if Iago is as ignoble as he proves, the hero must be a very poor type to be taken in by him. . . . Both views depend ultimately on the Aristotle-Bradley doctrine of the 'tragic flaw'—a doctrine that has obscured the true nature of Shakespearian tragedy far more than any over-emphasis on 'character'. Indeed, it is only when a man's 'character' is pictured as a sort of hard, fixed core somewhere inside him (rather as the essential particles of matter were once pictured as miniature billiard-balls) that looking for 'flaws' in it makes any sense. The idea is that if a dramatic character changes into something different from what he was, he must really have been like that all along; or, at least, he must always have shown some incipient weakness which could lead to that result. In one way this is a truism, for a man obviously cannot develop in any direction unless he is capable of doing so; but the theory is a nuisance because the potentialities of men are infinite, and whatever the greatness of a dramatic hero, any number of potential 'flaws' can be found, or invented, to account for his downfall. Yet in all Shakespeare's tragedies except, perhaps, *Macbeth,* the determining 'flaw' is in society rather than in the hero's supposed distance from perfection. (pp. 135-38)

It is the flaw in society that breaks Othello down and destroys the marriage. In purely human terms his bond with Desdemona is strong, and it is hard to imagine any of the wealthy curled darlings of Venice forging a stronger one, but the phrase 'purely human' is an admission of the price paid in isolation and vulnerability. Othello's pathetic defence in the last Act, sword in hand, of a dead body in an empty bedroom—in fact, the whole claustrophobic movement of the play—reflects this isolation and confinement. *Socially* speaking, the union of what Iago called 'an erring barbarian and a supersubtle Venetian' [I. iii. 355-56] was genuinely frail, and although his words were a parody not a description of the difference between them, he was accurately foreshadowing his line of attack. (p. 139)

Iago's aim has been not Othello's overthrow but his total degradation as a human being: that he should kill what he loved most, in jealous madness, with his bare hands. This aim is almost realized. At least once Othello has broken down into actual madness under Iago's mental drugs; he has solemnly dedicated his heart to hatred and vengeance; and in his insults to Desdemona he has become indistinguishable from the bond-slave Brabantio once compared him to: 'a beggar in his drink Could not have laid such terms upon his callet' [IV. ii. 120-21]. Yet he does not actually commit the murder in jealous revenge but as an act of objective justice, even of civic and religious duty. In a way this makes it worse; but it means that Iago has already partly failed. Othello kills in persisting love, not hate ('O balmy breath, that dost almost persuade Justice to break her sword!' [V. ii. 16-17]), and even against his will: for every two lines of the soliloquy 'It is the cause, it is the cause my soul' [V. ii. 1] there is a word of negation or qualification, *not, nor, yet, but.* Action has restored his self-command and reasserted his public responsibility at the expense of his private inclination. In Desdemona's actual presence, instead of behaving like a mad beast he has to force himself to go through with it. When he says, weeping over the girl he intends not to murder but to sacrifice,

> this sorrow's heavenly;
> It strikes where it doth love.
>
> [V. ii. 1]

he is recognizably trying to administer the same impersonal justice as when he dismissed Cassio:

> Cassio, I love thee;
> But never more be officer of mine.
>
> [V. i. 21-2]

There too, ironically enough, he had been tricked into his act of justice, and here it is a horrible delusion, as Desdemona tries to tell him with her unanswerable 'That death's unnatural that kills for loving' [V. ii. 42]; but from now on Othello is

deluded but responsible, capable of summing himself up with complete self-awareness after his enlightenment as 'an honourable murderer' [V. ii. 294].

This second change in Othello raises one question of importance for an Elizabethan audience at least. Iago has not only destroyed all that Othello valued on earth but has consigned him to eternal punishment by trapping him into murder and suicide. Othello was a Christian convert, and by killing himself he knowingly accepts the fate of being 'damned beneath all depth in hell' [V. ii. 137] for what he has done; to the dead Desdemona he says:

> When we shall meet at compt,
> This look of thine will hurl my soul from heaven,
> And fiends will snatch at it.
>
> [V. ii. 273-75]

If Shakespeare as an orthodox Christian believed the same, what can be the point of emphasizing Othello's recovery of human integrity? Speculation on Shakespeare's religious beliefs is of course unprofitable, but the text does make one broad hint. Some thirty lines after Desdemona has been left for dead, she speaks again, and her last words, in answer to Emilia's question 'O, who hath done this deed?' are: 'Nobody: I myself . . . Commend me to my kind lord: O, farewell!' [V. ii. 123-25]. This attempt to take the blame for her own murder (which provokes Othello into a furious avowal of responsibility: 'She's like a liar gone to burning hell. 'Twas I that killed her' [V. ii. 129-30]) is so piteously absurd that its dramatic point has been queried; but the point is surely obvious. There is a precedent for Desdemona's absurdity in the Christian doctrine of the Atonement. This does not mean that Desdemona is a 'Christ-figure'. In letting her speak as it were from beyond the grave, Shakespeare is suggesting to his audience that whatever might happen 'at compt,' one voice at least—his victim's—was unlikely to be raised against Othello. (pp. 140-42)

Othello's behaviour in the final scene is governed by the way Lodovico discriminates between him and Iago in allotting punishment. Iago has been unmasked, and the Venetian delegation joins with Othello in execrating him. He is sentenced out of hand to be tortured to death—the most savage punishment in Shakespeare, or indeed, anywhere else. Othello is relieved of his post and remanded in custody 'Till that the nature of [his] fault be known To the Venetian state' [V. ii. 336-37]. The customary Elizabethan class-distinction whereby, for example, noble traitors were gracefully beheaded while commoners were hanged, drawn, and quartered may have something to do with this. But the truth is that among the Venetians as in the audience there is strong sympathy for him, and some reluctance to condemn:

> O thou Othello, that was once so good,
> Fall'n in the practice of a damned slave,
> What shall be said to thee?
>
> [V. ii. 291-93]

While Iago is called 'demi-devil', a 'hellish villain', Othello is a 'rash and most unfortunate man' [V. ii. 283]. In Cinthio's story, where the Moor's deed is far less excusable, he escapes with his life. The deferment of judgment, when the facts are so plain, clearly implies that Othello's life may well be spared in view of the circumstances and of his own past merit. So at least Othello understands the position, for as soon as Lodovico's decision is announced he says:

I have done the state some service, and they know't—
[V. ii. 339]

an ironic repetition of his confidence in Act I that his usefulness to the state would outweigh Brabantio's objections to his marriage: 'My services which I have done the signiory Shall outtongue his complaints' [I. ii. 18-19]. He can hardly be 'cheering himself up', as T. S. Eliot oddly interprets [see excerpt above, 1927]; he is recognizing, and rejecting, the possibility of avoiding the death-penalty. He refuses to throw himself on the mercy of the Venetian senators, even though the most powerful of those that might seek vengeance on him, Brabantio, is known to have died. Instead he repudiates the deed—for which his sterile tears flow like the secretions from trees in his native Africa that can restore life to the phoenix—and also dissociates himself from those who would judge him for the deed. They are offered, almost contemptuously, 'a word or two before you go' [V. ii. 338]. Othello is now seeing himself and his social environment with complete objectivity: 'Speak of me as I am; nothing extenuate, Nor set down aught in malice' [V. ii. 342-43], and his own comments are not expressed subjectively but in detached clear-cut images. Whether it is to the 'base Judean' of the Folio or to the 'base Indian' of the Quarto that he compares himself [V. ii. 347], Othello's final image of his relationship with Desdemona is of a white pearl in a black hand. And his self-assessment just before he pronounces sentence on himself broadens the implications of the play in an image that brings its ironies into sharp focus:

> say besides that in Aleppo once,
> Where a malignant and a turban'd Turk
> Beat a Venetian and traduc'd the state,
> I took by th' throat the circumcisèd dog
> And smote him—thus.
>
> [V. ii. 352-56]

Overtly Othello presents himself as a servant of the State, avenging an insult by a foreigner: he is the Turk, the heathen barbarian Iago has tried to make him, who has committed violence on a Venetian citizen and betrayed a public trust, having defiled his human relation with Desdemona and his soldier's honour alike. But the words *malignant, turbaned,* and *circumcisèd dog* are bitterly ironic, because *turbaned* and *circumcisèd* tend to identify the Turk with Othello rather than provide an insulting analogy (for circumcision could be a mark equally of Christian, Moor, Turk and Jew), while *malignant* and *dog* do not fit Othello at all, only Iago. Hence Othello's apparent tit-for-tat in killing the Turk can also be taken in the opposite sense: that he had acted to suppress racial violence in the trading-centre of Aleppo, just as when the play opens we see him suppressing Iago's 'barbarous brawl'. As a final irony, Othello's analogy reminds the Venetians that in dealing with himself as he dealt with the Turk he is in fact depriving them of their main bulwark against Turks. Some of Shakespeare's audience might have remembered that the historical Turkish attack on Cyprus in 1570 had been successful.

Othello's final speech, therefore, though it cannot mitigate what he has done, demonstrates the complete recovery of his integrity as a human being. He will not beg for mercy on the strength of his past greatness, but sums up himself and others with objective self-knowledge, and carries out his own sentence, offering himself by his last gesture as a sacrifice to his victim, since this is the only act of reunion open to him:

> I kiss'd thee ere I kill'd thee. No way but this—
> Killing my self, to die upon a kiss.
>
> [V. ii. 358-59]

Act V. Scene ii. Desdemona and Othello. By John Boydell.

All that Iago's poison has achieved is an object that 'poisons sight': a bed on which a black man and a white girl, although they are dead, are embracing. Human dignity, the play says, is indivisible. (pp. 143-45)

> G. M. Matthews, " 'Othello' and the Dignity of Man," in Shakespeare in a Changing World: Essays, *edited by Arnold Kettle, International Publishers, 1964, pp. 123-45.*

G. R. HIBBARD (essay date 1968)

[*Hibbard discusses the dramatic elements that set* Othello *apart from Shakespeare's other tragedies, focusing particularly on the Moor's final speech and on the structure of the play as a whole. Whereas in such plays as* Hamlet, Macbeth, *and* King Lear *there is a "close interconnexion of the public and the private" levels and the pattern of dramatic action expands to include whole societies in the tragedy of individuals, he argues, the structural design of* Othello *is one of contraction and narrowing focus. Hibbard also contends that although* Othello *has a pattern of destruction that is common to all the tragedies, it is unique in that what is destroyed is not some "great potentiality for good" but "something of transcendent value that has actually been realized and made concrete during the course of the play." Hibbard identifies the perfect love of the Moor and Desdemona as the thing of incomparable worth in* Othello, *and he adds that this passion establishes the hero and heroine as eminently superior to all the other characters in the play. Indeed, the critic contends, with Desdemona dead, there is no one left at the close of the drama— as is generally true in Shakespeare's other tragedies—worthy enough to pronounce a valediction on Othello's life, save the Moor himself; thus, the unusual conclusion of* Othello *demonstrates both the superiority of the heroic Moor and the restrictive focus of the play in general. For additional analyses of the dramatic structure of* Othello, *see the excerpts by Harley Granville-Barker (1945) and Kenneth Burke (1951) and the essays by Terence Hawkes and Barbara Heliodora C. de Mendonça cited in the Additional Bibliography. Also, for further commentary on Shakespeare's presentation of love in the play, see the excerpts by Hermann Ulrici (1839), Derek Traversi (1949), Kenneth Burke (1951), Winifred M. T. Nowottny (1952), Robert B. Heilman (1956), John Bayley (1960), Susan Snyder (1972), Jared R. Curtis (1973), and Jane Adamson (1980).]*

The twelve lines that conclude *Othello* provide an ending that is radically different from the ending of any other of the tragedies. Lodovico's main concern is with Iago and his punishment. There is no formal praise of the hero, the only tribute he receives being Cassio's laconic comment on his suicide: 'For he was great of heart' [V. ii. 361]. His body, and that of Desdemona, are not carried off in state, but hurriedly hidden from view by the drawing of the curtain around the bed on which they lie, because the spectacle they offer is felt as something monstrous and obscene. Nothing is left to be settled and disposed of except the house and fortunes of the Moor, which pass in one brief clipped sentence to Gratiano, Desdemona's next of kin. No interpretation of the events that have led up to the disaster is given, or even promised. Faced with actions which they find shocking and unintelligible, the surviving characters seek, with a haste that is almost indecent, to put them out of sight and out of mind. Their reaction is that of the normal ordinary man, and, as such, serves to underline for the last time the remoteness of Othello from those among whom he has lived and moved. The most immediately and impressively heroic of all the tragic heroes is granted no epic valediction from the mouths of others, no ceremonious rites of funeral; primarily, of course, because he has forfeited all claim to them through his crime in murdering Desdemona, but also, I think, because he is, and always has been, a mystery and a challenge to the unheroic world in which fate and circumstance have placed him. His relationship to that world, and his isolation from it, are both stated in the final couplet. The Venetian state must be acquainted with the death of its greatest soldier and servant; but there is no indication that it will, in any real sense, be seriously affected by that death. Bradley [see excerpt above, 1904] is surely right when he says of Othello:

> his deed and his death have not that influence on the interests of a nation or an empire which serve to idealise, and to remove far from our own sphere, the stories of Hamlet and Macbeth, of Coriolanus and Antony. Indeed he is already superseded at Cyprus when his fate is consummated, and as we leave him no vision rises on us, as in the other tragedies, of peace descending on a distracted land.

The unusual nature of the ending points directly, as Bradley indicates, to the unusual nature of the entire play when seen in the context of Shakespearian tragedy in general. The characteristic pattern of all the other tragedies is an expanding one. Whether the action takes its rise out of a specific act by an individual—Claudius's poisoning of Hamlet's father, and Lear's giving away of his kingdom, for example—or out of the response by a character to some new situation with which he is confronted, as Brutus is by the offering of a crown to Caesar, or Macbeth by his encounter with the witches, it tends to spread and to widen its scope. The initial event that triggers it off is

like a stone thrown into the middle of a pond. A turbulence is set up, which rapidly extends to affect a city, a country, an empire, and, in some cases, even the elements. (p. 39)

The unique quality of Shakespearian tragedy in general, distinguishing it from all other tragedy written at the time, is due in no small measure, it seems to me, to the fact that Shakespeare came to tragedy by way of the history play. It was through the continuous exploration of historical matter that he discovered and penetrated into the intimate connexions between the private decision and its public consequences, between the political action and its repercussions on the individual psyche. It is this unremitting two-way traffic between the private and the public worlds that, more perhaps than anything else, gives his tragedies that density of experience and that closeness to life which sets them apart from the tragedies of his contemporaries. Brutus and Macbeth feel and undergo in themselves, at the moment of temptation, the conflict and the dissension that the decision they are about to take will bring upon their countries.

It is exactly this close interconnexion of the public and the private that is not present in *Othello*—at least not in its usual form—though this fact is by no means evident at the play's opening. In Act I the imminence of a Turkish attack on Cyprus and preparations for the defence of the island demand as much attention from the audience as the marriage of Othello and Desdemona, on which they have a considerable impact, or as Iago's gulling of Roderigo. Indeed, the first spectators to see the play must have thought, up to the beginning of Act II, that they were about to witness an action in which the struggle for the control of the eastern Mediterranean that culminated in the battle of Lepanto would be a leading, if not a central, theme. Shakespeare was touching on more recent history than any he had handled hitherto and on events that had affected the whole of Christendom. (p. 40)

But before Act II begins there have already been indications of the direction in which the action is moving. One of the most striking features of Act I is the frequency with which public affairs of the utmost consequence give way in it to private matters. The third scene opens with the Venetian Senate hurriedly gathered together at night for an extraordinary meeting in order to decide what measures are to be taken to counter the imminent invasion of Cyprus. Yet, despite the extreme urgency of the business, they break off their deliberations to listen, first to Brabantio's complaint against Othello, then to the Moor's defence of himself and his actions, and finally to Desdemona's assertion of her love for him. Only after all this has happened does the Duke invest Othello with the supreme command in Cyprus; and no sooner has Othello accepted this office than the discussion in the Senate turns to the question of whether his wife shall accompany him or not. The incongruous nature of the entire proceedings did not escape the sharp eye and censorious judgement of Thomas Rymer, who expressed his scepticism and disapproval with a vigorous display of that derisive buffoonery which came so easily to him [see excerpt above, 1692]. (pp. 40-1)

Acting in his customary capacity of counsel for the prosecution, Rymer, the lawyer and historian, has made a point that more recent criticism of the play has tended to ignore: by all normal standards of behaviour the actions of the Venetian Senate are highly improbable. Yet they are clearly an essential part of Shakespeare's design, since there is no counterpart to them in the story he was drawing on. The wars between Venice and the Turks have no place in Cinthio's narrative. There Othello merely goes to Cyprus in the regular course of duty as the replacement for a governor whose term of office has expired, not as the man who is best fitted to cope with a great crisis. The setting provided by the momentous affairs of 1571, which meant so much more to an audience in 1604 than they do to an audience today, is something added by Shakespeare to his source for sound dramatic reasons. Improbable though the scene in the Senate may appear when viewed in isolation, it works superbly well within the context of the play, where it has a complex function. It establishes the superior worth and dignity of the hero over those whom he serves; he is the indispensable man in complete control of an ugly situation. It brings out the total devotion of Desdemona to him, since she is prepared to face not only her father's displeasure but also the hazards of war in order to be with the man of her choice. And it leaves the audience with at least a suspicion that, were it not for the military crisis, the attitude of the Duke and the Senate towards the marriage might well be rather different. Rymer is wrong when he says that so far as the Senate is concerned 'the publick may sink or swim'; the point of the scene is that they can see no hope for the state except in Othello.

Once public matters have fulfilled this purpose of helping to define the supreme importance and value of the hero, and of establishing the depth of the love that exists between him and Desdemona, they are dismissed as quickly as possible. They receive their quietus in the brief scene (II, ii) which is given over to Herald's proclamation that the wars are done and that the night is to be devoted to general rejoicing. The last echo of the initial political situation is heard in II, iii, when Othello, faced with the brawl engineered by Iago, speaks of the nameless seaport as 'a town of war, / Yet wild, the people's hearts brimful of fear' [II. iii. 213-14]. But this is the first and the last that we ever hear about the people of Cyprus and their state of mind. They appear only once; they say nothing; they do not matter. The course of the action affects them no more than they affect it. In III, ii Othello sends news to the Venetian Senate, and then goes off to view a fortification. It is his final act as a military commander. From this point onwards public affairs are not mentioned at all again until III, iv, when Desdemona, at a loss to account for Othello's unwonted behaviour to her, invokes them, quite mistakenly, as a possible excuse and explanation, saying to Emilia:

> Something sure of state
> Either from Venice, or some unhatch'd practice
> Made demonstrable here in Cyprus to him,
> Hath puddled his clear spirit. . . .
>
> [III. iv. 140-43]

By this time, however, 'Othello's occupation's gone' [III. iii. 357]; the outer world of military activity and political decision, in which he once moved with such calm assurance and which was his natural sphere, has ceased to exist for him in its own right. When Lodovico arrives in Cyprus towards the end of IV, i, bringing the letters announcing that Cassio is to become governor of the island, Othello receives them with the dignified submission of the great public servant, saying:

> I kiss the instrument of their pleasures.
>
> [IV. i. 218]

But the news itself means nothing to him. His reading of the letters is a mere pretence to cover the avid and unworthy curiosity with which he eavesdrops on the innocent conversation of Desdemona and her kinsman on the subject of Cassio—a conversation that confirms all his worst suspicions and drives him to the outrageous action of striking his wife. Obsessed by

the one consuming passion of jealousy, he can no longer see anything as in itself it really is, otherwise he would realize that if Desdemona were in love with Cassio she would not express joy at hearing news that must mean her separation from him. As it is, however, he draws the words and actions of others into the private nightmare world of confusion and uncertainty in which he now lives, and there they undergo a hideous distortion. Instead of being, like the other tragedies, a play of expansion, *Othello* is a play of contraction. The action does not widen out, it narrows down as public business is increasingly excluded from it until it finds its catastrophe, not on the battle-field, nor in the presence of a court, but in a bedroom at night where two people, united by the closest of ties, speak at cross purposes and misunderstand each other disastrously, with no thought of turning to the independent witness, Emilia, who could reveal the truth and save both of them. Indeed, Othello has taken care to ensure that Emilia shall not be present. The pattern of this tragedy is that of a whirlpool, with its centre in the poisoned mind of the hero which reshapes, distorts, and degrades objective reality. At the heart of *Othello* there is a kind of darkness. Only Iago knows what is true and what is false, and he does his best to confuse the distinction between them in his own mind as well as in the minds of others. Misled and misinformed by him, the rest of the characters misinterpret the events in which they are caught up. Alone of Shakespeare's tragic heroes Othello does not even know who his true antagonist is until the play is within fewer than a hundred and fifty lines of its conclusion.

This radical difference in the tragic pattern is demanded because *Othello*, it seems to me, embodies and defines another sort of tragic experience from that which is to be found in the rest of the tragedies. In them the conflict in which the protagonist is involved and in which he may have been largely responsible for causing, as Brutus, Lear, Coriolanus, and, above all, Macbeth have been, becomes an open one by the end of Act III at the latest. By this stage too it has assumed political dimensions. Even in *Romeo and Juliet* Romeo is banished on the Prince's orders in order to prevent further strife. Having taken on these proportions, the conflict then leads not only to the death of the hero but also to the destruction of some great potential for good—the idealistic hopes of Brutus, the princely promise of Hamlet, the innate nobility of Macbeth. Furthermore, in the course of this conflict, a whole system of values and a way of life are either threatened with destruction or even swept away. At the end of it all, it is true, some positive force, some new kind of order, emerges out of the wreckage; but it is the destructive process that fills the imagination, and that which survives seems an inadequate substitute for that which has been lost. In *Othello*, however, it is not a great potentiality for good that is destroyed but rather something of transcendent value that has actually been realized and made concrete during the course of the play. The love of the Moor and Desdemona is triumphantly rendered through the action and the poetry of the first four scenes. In spite of, or even because of, Iago's denigrations of it, it is this love that dominates the opening which celebrates its achievement. One's awareness of it and admiration for it rise in a crescendo to reach their culmination in the rhapsodic reunion scene, II, i, where Othello voices his sense of its surpassing excellence by saying:

> If it were now to die,
> 'Twere now to be most happy; for I fear
> My soul hath her content so absolute
> That not another comfort like to this
> Succeeds in unknown fate.
>
> [II. i. 189-93]

The happiness is so intense as to be almost unbearable. Yet this happiness is destroyed so completely that at the end of the play one has no sense of any part of it, no matter how small or inadequate, continuing. The ruin is total. Nothing remains of the music of concord that Othello and Desdemona once made together except the poignant memory of its sweetness and its beauty.

Othello is about the wanton destruction of happiness—something so precious and so fragile that its loss is felt as quite irredeemable. This, I think, is the fundamental source of the peculiar sense of pain and anguish that this tragedy, more than any of the others, leaves in the consciousness of a spectator or a reader. But there are two other related features of the play which add to and sharpen the pain. The relationship of the hero and the heroine is—and one of the miracles of *Othello* is the unobtrusive artistry with which Shakespeare produces this effect—a thing of rare and extraordinary beauty. Warm, moving, and vital, it has at the same time some of the qualities of an artifact. The mutual passion of Romeo and Juliet is spontaneous and instinctive; that of Antony and Cleopatra is the fruit of knowledge and experience—there has been an element of deliberate calculation on both sides. But the love of Othello and Desdemona is something that has grown gradually, then been discovered intuitively, then fashioned consciously, and, finally, achieved by them in the face of all the obstacles to it set up by their differences of race and colour, their disparity in years, and the opposition to it of the society to which they belong. Drawn by the fascination of Othello's story of his life into the strange, remote, heroic world which he inhabits, Desdemona has become part of that world, which is itself a work of art created by the hero out of his own experience. Listening to the Moor, as he relates his history to the Senate and re-enacts the drama of his wooing, one is aware of the story as a romantic epic of love and war. There is also a trace of the myth of Pygmalion and Galatea about it all as Othello, first unconsciously, then with a growing awareness of what he is doing, converts the 'maiden never bold, / Of spirit so still and quiet that her motion / Blush'd at herself' into his 'fair warrior', ready to make a 'storm of fortunes', to defy her father and public opinion, and to avow her love in the Senate [I. iii. 94-6; II. i. 182; I. iii. 249]. And just as Othello has, in part at least, created the Desdemona that he loves, actualizing possibilities within her that have hitherto lain dormant, so she, in her love for him, has, as it were, completed him by recognizing in him a beauty invisible to other eyes yet indubitably there. It is Desdemona who gives the finishing touch to the poem that Othello has made of his life when she says:

> I saw Othello's visage in his mind;
> And to his honours and his valiant parts
> Did I my soul and fortunes consecrate.
>
> [I. iii. 252-54]

It is not only the value of what is destroyed in *Othello* that gives pain, but also the sheer loveliness and perfection of what is destroyed. To a far greater extent than in any other of the tragedies the aesthetic sense is directly involved in and affected by the tragic experience that the play provides.

The distinctive feature of the destructive process in *Othello* is its ugliness, for what the hero is subjected to is a deliberate and calculated degradation such as no other of Shakespeare's tragic heroes undergoes. Hamlet is partially corrupted by the corrupt world in which he finds himself, but no one sets out to corrupt him. Macbeth degenerates, but this is a consequence of his own actions. Lear and Gloucester suffer horrible and

degrading cruelty at the hands of their antagonists, but the main end those antagonists have in view is their own material advancement. In *Othello,* however, the urge that impels Iago to his intrigues is no desire for political or military power, not even primarily the desire for gain, but an absolute need to denigrate and undermine all that is true, good, and beautiful. His first reason for seeking Cassio's death is because, as he explains in V, i,

> He hath a daily beauty in his life
> That makes me ugly.
>
> [V. i. 19-20]

The daily life of Othello and Desdemona is infinitely more beautiful than that of Cassio; and the impulse Iago feels to desecrate that beauty is, therefore, correspondingly stronger. It speaks out unequivocally in the opening scene through the coarse and brutal imagery which he employs to describe the union of the lovers. After that first scene there is no need to look for further motives. What D. H. Lawrence calls 'the desire to do dirt on life' is common enough; it is only the intensity with which Iago feels this compulsion that is unusual. As the driving force for a tragic action, however, this hatred of the spiritual and the ideal is without a parallel, so far as I am aware, in the whole range of Elizabethan drama, though the unremitting malice with which the Aragonian brothers ruin their sister's happiness in [John Webster's] *The Duchess of Malfi* looks like a partial imitation of it. If it is, Webster's handling of the matter only serves to point up that which is unique in Shakespeare's. Ferdinand and the Cardinal never succeeded in imposing their warped vision of life on the Duchess as Iago does succeed for a time in imposing his on Othello; and, as a consequence, there is no scene in *The Duchess of Malfi,* despite Webster's fondness for the sensational and the macabre, that is anything like so shocking or painful as that in which Othello strikes Desdemona (IV, i) or that in which he treats her as though she were a whore in a brothel (IV, ii). In both these scenes it is the unmerited suffering of the heroine that causes the immediate distress that Bradley noted, but within the total experience of the play it is the evidence they afford of the degradation Othello has undergone that matters even more, and it is precisely this that Shakespeare draws attention to. Towards the end of IV, i, Lodovico, the dispassionate spectator, expresses his amazement at the change that has taken place in Othello by saying:

> Is this the noble Moor whom our full Senate
> Call all in all sufficient? Is this the nature
> Whom passion could not shake, whose solid virtue
> The shot of accident nor dart of chance
> Could neither graze nor pierce?
>
> [IV. i. 264-68]

The events that follow make Lodovico's questions even more cogent, but the final answer the play gives to them is an emphatic yes, for, terrible and harrowing though the degradation of Othello is, it is not complete. The Moor's speech before he stabs himself is not, as T. S. Eliot suggested [see excerpt above, 1927], an attempt at cheering himself up. It is rather the ultimate defeat of Iago, for it shows that the Ancient has not, after all, ensnared the hero's soul. Enough of the servant of the Venetian republic survives to enable Othello to reaffirm the values by which he once lived and to execute justice on himself. Unlike the other tragic heroes, he speaks his own valediction. He has to, because he is the only character left, now that Desdemona is dead, who is fitted and qualified to do so. The unusual ending of this tragedy is dictated by its unusual nature. (pp. 41-5)

> G. R. Hibbard, " 'Othello' and the Pattern of Shakespearian Tragedy,'' in Shakespeare Survey: An Annual Survey of Shakespearian Study and Production, Vol. 21, 1968, pp. 39-46.

ROY W. BATTENHOUSE (essay date 1969)

[Battenhouse is most noted for his studies on religion and literature and for his theory that Shakespeare's works embody a specifically Christian world view. In the following excerpt, he discusses several parallels between Othello and Judas, first suggested by Paul N. Siegel (1953), and demonstrates how these parallels enhance Shakespeare's portrayal of the Moor as an overly proud figure who is blind to the mercy of God. Noting that Biblical commentators have traditionally judged Judas as guilty of the sin of despair by hanging himself, rather than repenting his betrayal of Christ and trusting to God's forgiveness, Battenhouse maintains that Shakespeare has similarly drawn Othello as "presumptuously playing God" by his self-condemnation and suicide. For additional commentary on Othello's excessive or wrongful pride, see the excerpts by F. R. Leavis (1937), G. R. Elliott (1937 and 1953), Derek Traversi (1949), Brents Stirling (1956), and Carol McGinnis Kay (1983). Whereas such other critics as Kenneth O. Myrick (1941), Irving Ribner (1955 and 1960), and G. M. Matthews (1964) have found signs of repentance in the Moor's concluding speeches in Act V, Scene ii, Battenhouse asserts that Othello is not depicted as either penitent or contrite for the murder of Desdemona, but instead is portrayed as maintaining to the end of his life an obsession with his "quasi-religion of honor." Other commentators who have judged that the Moor is represented as unrepentant and facing eternal damnation at the drama's conclusion include Harley Granville-Barker (1945), S. L. Bethell (1952), and Paul N. Siegel (1953). Additionally, Battenhouse does not equate Desdemona with Christ, but, like Kenneth Burke (1951), he does style her as "Christ-like" in her martyrdom, and he sees Othello's rejection of her proffered grace and mercy as another instance of his sinful errancy.]

Othello in Cyprus has been likened to Adam in a paradise by Paul Siegel [see excerpt above, 1953], who notes also the satanic malice with which Iago sets about untuning the harmony of the newlyweds. This analogy probably occurs to many readers, although in several respects it is an imperfect one. Desdemona is scarcely Eve, or at most distantly so; she chides Iago for his "profane" talk. And Othello, if somewhat like an Adam, nevertheless does not fall by hearkening to his wife in the way Adam did. Obliquely, however, there is an element of analogy. For when Othello says that no contentment of soul could be more "absolute" than his welcome by Desdemona, and then adds that "I dote / In mine own comforts" [II. i. 206-07], he is evidencing a uxoriousness which makes possible the later jealousy into which Iago tempts him. Othello's very concept of bliss has Adam's fault at its basis; then, on top of this, a betrayal of Desdemona develops as a second fault representative of Adamkind's history in some later phase. Since Othello from the start lacks Adam's original innocence, his tragedy has a more complex paradigm than the Genesis one.

The analogy closest to the completed circuit of Othello's career is the one touched on by Siegel when he remarks that this hero's act of self-murder follows the example of Judas. In Scripture the deadliest extent of Adamkind's tragedy is instanced in Judas. And in Othello's own last speeches (although he may be unconscious of this) there are signals of an analogy in his likening himself to "the base Judean" who threw away

a pearl "Richer than all his tribe" [V. ii. 348], and in his final comment:

> I kissed thee ere I killed thee. No way but this,
> Killing myself, to die upon a kiss.
>
> [V. ii. 358-59]

Even if we follow those editors who prefer to read "Indian" (Quarto, 1622) instead of "Iudean" (Folio, 1623), the twin images of priceless pearl and deadly kiss are sufficient to evoke biblical echoes. The Judas who betrayed with a kiss, and whose bargaining away of Christ-the-pearl inverted tragically the parable of the merchant of Matthew 13:45, resembles Othello all too obviously. Othello has become "egregiously an ass," as Iago predicted [II. i. 309], and in this respect is the Jud-as of Elizabethan proverb (see Love's Labor's Lost, [V. ii. 628]). Furthermore, the fact that Judas was Christ's only disciple from his own tribe of Judah, and thus was a traitor to family in betraying Christ, must have made him in Shakespeare's eyes a particularly apt archetype for the domestic tragedy of Othello.

In what more specific ways could the story of Judas be parallel to the tragedy of Othello? Let us recall some aspects of the biblical account. In Matthew 26 (see also John 12), Judas is concerned for the worldly value of a certain "alabaster" cruse, and not for the mystery which this vessel is devoted to celebrating. When the ointment from the alabaster is poured out on the feet of Jesus by Mary of Bethany (in Western tradition usually identified with Mary Magdalene), it signifies her understanding of his mission of sacrifice in the work of atonement. Judas does not understand the mystery of atoning sacrifice. He upbraids Mary's act, by the norm of his own narrower kind of righteousness. He thinks her alabaster vessel should have been committed solely to his treasury, so that he could use it for conventional works of patronizing generosity. Need I expound the analogy of this attitude to that of Othello in his worldly valuing of the "monumental alabaster" [V. ii. 5] of Desdemona's body? Throughout the drama he has supposed that her body should be devoted solely to himself and his own ideals of nobility—and not at all to that "reconciliation" in the name of "grace" for which Desdemona pleads [in III. iii. 46-7] because she wishes to "atone" [IV. i. 233] Othello and Cassio. Judas so resented Mary's act that he decided, then and there, to turn to Christ's enviers to make a covenant for Christ's betrayal. Othello similarly, in his self-righteousness, turns from Desdemona because he is resentful of her Christlike hope for atonement, and makes a covenant with her envious adversary, Iago. At a Last Supper during which Christ speaks of his body as a memorial unto the "forgiveness of sins," Judas arises from the table to go out into the night to keep his bargain of betrayal with a kiss. Likewise Othello, in a final scene of bedroom communion with Desdemona, has no mind for forgiveness but instead, in loyalty to his own blind sense of justice, mocks the reality of communion by celebrating it perversely with a deadly kiss. Judas discovered afterwards, to his shame, that he had betrayed "innocent blood"; and because he was then unable to undo the earthly consequences of his act he hanged himself. Even in his remorse he had not come to understand the meaning of forgiveness. The same is true of Othello, even though he too has seen forgiveness exampled before his very eyes in the spirit of the righteous one he has victimized. Thus Othello's tragedy involves not merely the "mistake" of having conspired against and slain an innocent person but the deeper sin of rejecting grace—by neglecting the "mercy" to which Desdemona was dedicating her alabaster body while also preserving this "vessel" [IV. ii. 83] for Othello.

We need not infer that Shakespeare was equating Desdemona with Christ. In terms of the analogy she is Christlike merely as a faithful follower, like Mary Magdalene. She quite sufficiently identifies herself by her oath ''As I am a Christian'' [IV. ii. 82], and in the bedroom scene by her cry ''Heaven have mercy on me!'' [V. ii. 33-4]. This does not mean that her life has been without fault. Indeed, earlier in the play, out of her pity for human suffering, she has committed a number of indiscretions. One of them is glanced at, I think, by the clown in Act III, scene iv, when he jests: ''I will catechize the world for him; that is, make questions and by them answer'' [III. iv. 16-17]. The clown is here wittily suggesting that Desdemona is better at catechizing than at understanding her pupil—which is certainly the case in her manner of approaching Othello on Cassio's behalf. In this sense, there is some truth in her ultimate testimony, after Othello has strangled her, that ''Nobody, I myself'' [V. ii. 124] is responsible for her death—although it is also true that she dies ''guiltless'' of Othello's specific charge, and yet is forgiving this fault in her ''kind lord.'' These three utterances, spoken almost surrealistically as if from a world beyond death, carry the paradox of a humble confession of fault on the part of a Christian who fulfils charity in her death. Shakespeare is maintaining the real-life complexity of Desdemona's virtue. Yet at the core of the play's meaning is a Christlike martyrdom by Desdemona, fumbling though it be.

This mystery a Judas-like Othello has profaned by backsliding into the noble ''barbarian'' he was before his baptism. His tragedy can be traced to a majestic loyalty to blind ideals. No intentional malice but rather a self-centered mode of virtue has caused him to fall victim to Iago's tempting insinuations, and later, when the facts are set right, to pursue a vain glory one more step into a brutally honorific suicide. Othello thus returns to the action by which in Aleppo once he established his sense of righteousness—when he took by the throat a Turkish traducer of the Venetian state and smote this ''circumcized dog.'' (Shakespeare may be here depicting, by analogy, the temper of those called Judaizers in the New Testament, who took pride in a circumcision of the flesh while neglecting circumcision of the heart.) Othello is displaying at this moment a noble indignation but devoid of all patience and mercy. To vindicate his retaliatory justice he is punishing a culprit, now his own flesh, and prejudging how the state might rule on the matter. This is the story of an aristocratically self-sufficient man—such as we might potentially be, and such as Judas seems to have been. It arouses not our contempt but our pity and fear.

Once we ponder Othello's overall likeness to Judas, it makes fully coherent his underlying psychology. I do not mean that we see him as deliberately cuing his attitude by reference to Judas; indeed, the final allusion in his mouth is probably more of Shakespeare's making than comprehended by its speaker. To us, however, it becomes a clue for understanding this hero as a man whose love of name has made him blind to charity; and thus his jealousy can be seen as something more than a sexual jealousy. We can be aware, in retrospect, of a jealousy for personal honor which both preceded and continues after the episode of disbelief in Desdemona's chastity. And this explains why, in the midst of his sexual jealousy, Othello could exclaim:

> I had been happy if the general camp,
> Pioners and all, had tasted her sweet body,
> So I had nothing known. Oh, now forever
> Farewell the tranquil mind! Farewell content!
>
> [III. iii. 345-48]

His peace of mind is dearer to him than Desdemona. Hence, ironically, he would rather have her defiled and himself ignorant of it, if thereby he might retain an undisturbed confidence in himself. But does not such a narcissistic love of self-image accord with his attitude at the beginning of the play? ''My parts, my title, and my perfect soul / Shall manifest me rightly'' has been his boast [I. ii. 31-2]. He has felt no compassion for Brabantio, or later for Cassio. Having developed none for Desdemona either, he is consistent in denying compassion ultimately to himself, his own flesh and blood.

Othello's stance in his first scene, when Brabantio with officers comes to seize him, is emblematic and constitutes in fact something of a parody of Christ's attitude when arrested at Gethsemane. Othello says chidingly to his accusers: ''Keep up your bright swords, for the dew will rust them'' [I. ii. 59]. Christ had said to Peter: ''Put up your sword into the sheath; the cup which the Father hath given me, shall I not drink it?'' The situations have a strange affinity. But Christ's gentle rebuke was to an over-eager defender, not to his arresters; and it was said out of a willingness to suffer humiliation, not with Othello's intention to ''out-tongue'' complaints against him. In the drama, it is an instance of inverted analogy. And it is possible, perhaps, to see another such upside-down analogy to Christ at a midpoint in the play, when Othello is offered a handkerchief by Desdemona to soothe his anguished head but impatiently brushes aside this napkin. Any playgoer familiar with the Veronica legend (one of the Stations of the Cross in churches) might see here a parody of Christ's suffering brow and a contrast to Christ's acceptance of Veronica's napkin. Whether Shakespeare had in mind these analogies some readers may doubt. But one can say that in the two episodes I have mentioned, both of them at important points in the drama, their artistic shape takes on added meaning if referred to the paradigms I have cited, and we know Shakespeare to have invented both scenes without any hint from Cinthio.

He has invented also a later scene in which Othello, after rejecting Desdemona's testimony that ''Heaven'' knows her honesty, retreats into the self-pity of an ironic Job. Here, in the verbal references to ''affliction,'' ''sores,'' and ''patience,'' all scholars have recognized allusions to Job. But by implication Shakespeare is portraying a grotesque aping of holy Job. Job when tested called on Heaven to resolve his perplexities. Othello is taking his whole vision of life from a Satan-like Iago. And after saluting patience only conditionally, Othello soon calls on the ''cherubin'' Patience to ''look grim as Hell!'' [IV. ii. 64]. Thus he would make the cherubin's office, traditionally that of charity, sanction his own demand for revenge. Ever since his vow by ''yond marble heaven'' [III. iii. 460], his justice has reflected a heart turned to stone. As a would-be priest of this heaven, Othello can weep only over Desdemona's supposed apostasy from his own ideal, and over his own supposed obligation to offer her up in sacrifice to it. He begins Act V, scene ii, by communing self-centeredly with his own soul and its sense of ''cause''; and then, as if aping a celebrant at a service of Tenebrae, he ritualizes his task to ''Put out the light, and then put out the light'' [V. ii. 7]. He is thus like the Judas who gave himself to the ''night'' of a Pharisaic self-righteousness. The accumulative analogies I have touched on are all coherent with the Judas one, which resonates finally in Othello's speech of suicide.

Many of us are familiar with Northrop Frye's useful distinction between two kinds of response to a work of literature [in *Myth and Symbol*]. One kind is a participating sense in time, our absorption in the narrative as it moves in its spontaneous continuity—a precritical response largely. The second kind is a detached response, a consciousness of theme—that is, of what the story is all about when contemplated in its unifying structure. Although these responses somewhat overlap in experience they are distinguishable. The second is our sense of the story's total design, the response by which we see in the words and actions of a character something beyond what they mean to their speaker in the play. We then see the ironies with which the playwright has highlighted the tragic hero's career and we become aware of the analogies by which they are signalized. We discover thus what may be called the "overplot" (Harry Levin's term) and what medieval theorists would have considered the allegorical dimension of the literal fable.

Shakespeare's art in this respect is more subtle than that of, say, Marlowe's *Dr. Faustus,* in which morality play conventions openly interpret each step. Faustus freely confesses his ambition to be a mighty god by outflying Scripture. Quite aware that the god he serves is his own appetite, he deliberately engages in necromancy in order to sell his soul to the devil. Tragedy in this vein is largely exemplum, the illustration of an antisaint's career. As in *psychomachia* drama, the theological aspects are explicitly labelled: "Hell strives with grace for conquest" in the breast of Faustus; good angels and bad angels stalk the stage; the face of a Greekish Helen outweighs the attraction of a vial of "precious grace"; and at the end, the hero's last-minute vision of Christ's saving blood in the firmament is outweighed by a guilty terror of God's wrath. Visible devils carry off this damned man and a chorus moralizes on his "hellish fall." No Shakespearean drama is didactic in this overt and immediate fashion. That is because Shakespeare's focus is on historical verisimilitude—on tragedy as it emerges cumulatively in the arena of temporal events. We may recall, however, that such a focus is also characteristic of the Bible's story of Judas, or Achitophel, or Saul, or Herod. They are not shown debating their eternal destiny or, in the end, carried off to hell. If we infer their fate in eternity we do so on the basis of the moral quality of their behavior before and at death.

Of *Othello,* some readers have sentimentally supposed that the hero ends his life "saved" by punishing himself, or at least that the evidence for his damnation is inconclusive. But is not Shakespeare implying otherwise? The Judas analogy invites us to judge Othello, ultimately, by the light of Christian commentary on Judas. Historically, such commentary begins with Peter's lament, in Acts I, that Judas has "turned aside" from fellowship in the ministry of Christ to go "to his own place"— a place interpreted (by Peter's allusion to Psalm 69) as one of darkened eyes and "punishment upon punishment" from God's anger. Commentary of a more explicit kind was familiar to all readers of Augustine, or Dante, or Calvin. Judas "passed from this life," Augustine said (*City of God* I. 17), "chargeable not only with the death of Christ, but with his own: for though he killed himself on account of his crime, his killing himself was another crime." This act "rather aggravated than expiated" his guilt, since by despairing of God's mercy "he left to himself no place for healing penitence." His so-called "repentance," Calvin explained (*Institutes* III. iii. 4), was no "gospel" repentance, since it apprehended only misery and terror for sin, and not Christ's medicine for sin. Such "repentance" was unlike Hezekiah's or David's, in Calvin's view, but like Cain's or Saul's. Indeed, it was "nothing but a sort of entryway of hell . . . already entered in this life." Dante, understandably, saw Judas as destined for the lowest circle of hell.

With this general tradition of moral analysis Shakespeare was no doubt familiar, either through reading or indirectly through the sensibility of the Christian community in which he lived. He reflects the tradition in his portrait of Othello, who is not shown as achieving a Christian penitence. When made aware of his crime against Desdemona, Othello partly shuffles off responsibility for it onto fate, the stars, and his merely "unlucky" deeds. Instead of being contrite for his vengefulness, he blames only his folly and ignorance. He blames his ignorance of Desdemona's innocence—but not his own ignoring of Christian duty in having sworn a "sacred vow" to serve revenge, nor his now continuing to ignore Christian duty by turning to self-slaughter. On Othello's last speech, Gratiano comments: "All that's spoke is marred" [V. ii. 357]. And Gratiano is a commentator who has earlier told us what a "desperate" turn involves: it involves a "fall to reprobation" [V. ii. 209]. Othello is clearly among the reprobate by Shakespeare's implication.

Othello's own sense of damnation must be shown, however, as somewhat limited and confused. That is, it would be inappropriate to portray him as measuring his own damnation in relation to his neglect of charity. Hence when he speaks of hell, he views it simply as the place of punishment for betrayers of justice. "I were damned beneath all depth in Hell / But that I did proceed on just grounds" [V. ii. 137-38], he says, just before the evidence is supplied him that he has indeed proceeded on unjust grounds. Then, as a deserved retribution for his crime, he calls on devils to whip him and roast him in sulphur. But in thus damning himself he is presumptuously playing God, while overlooking the divine Spirit to which Desdemona's action has testified. Blindly he imagines that when "we meet at compt," her look will "hurl my soul from Heaven" [V. ii. 273-74]; whereas, in fact, only his own pride is doing that. Confusedly he wishes to prove himself "honorable" by killing himself.

Is it true, then, that Othello has loved "not wisely but too well" [V. ii. 344]? Surely not in the sense that he has loved Desdemona too well. Rather, he has loved her not enough, through unwisely loving too well his own honor. A quasireligion of honor guides his final "sacrifice" of himself. We may say of his suicide that it is related to Christian sacrifice by disjunctive analogy—just as Dante's bleeding wood-of-the-suicides is inversely analogous to the holy wood of Calvary. It is we, however, and not Othello, who can understand it thus. His vision must be from within a narrower frame than that which is implied in the play's total design. (pp. 95-102)

Roy W. Battenhouse, "In Search of an Adequate Perspective," in his Shakespearean Tragedy: Its Art and Its Christian Premises, *Indiana University Press, 1969, pp. 45-130.*

SUSAN SNYDER   (essay date 1972)

[*In the following excerpt, Snyder maintains that* Othello *is closely related to Shakespeare's earlier comedies, claiming that in this work the dramatist developed "a tragic view of love" by critically exploring the "romantic assumptions" of human passion which formed the basis of those earlier plays. In an effort to identify these romantic assumptions, the critic examines the presentation of love in* A Midsummer Night's Dream, As You Like It, Twelfth Night, Much Ado about Nothing, *and other comedies, concluding that all these works reflect two underlying assumptions about love: 1) "the value of engagement with a mate and with society at large"; and 2) "the cooperation of forces beyond man, natural and otherwise, in achieving this notion." These romantic comedies also demonstrate the triumph of human passion over rational thought, Snyder adds, and they recognize an instinctive force in nature that propels love and brings it to fruition despite social restrictions. The critic discerns in the first two acts of* Othello *a kind of summation of these assumptions, together with a foreshadowing of the subsequent tragic perspective, which begins to develop in Act III and is controlled by the machinations of Iago. Snyder then emphasizes the transformation of the comic or romantic assumptions about love within this tragic perspective. She points out that while in the comedies passion overcomes reason, in* Othello—*under the influence of Iago's "rational poison"— love becomes vulnerable, weak, and open to defeat; whereas in the comedies nature assists the flowering of love, here it takes on a two-fold enmity against it, for it is both a "personal nature"—namely, the honest, trusting qualities inherent in such characters as Othello, Desdemona and Cassio—and the Hobbesian, reductive concept of nature championed by Iago that the ancient uses to destroy Othello's and Desdemona's love for each other. Snyder also states that whereas in the comedies Shakespeare treated love and marriage as "a new completeness" necessary for the good of both the individual and society, in* Othello *he demonstrates the tragic vulnerability of such an interdependency. The critic suggests that in presenting the union of such contrasting individuals as Othello and Desdemona Shakespeare was emphasizing the impossibility of any ideal marriage. Regarding Iago, Snyder maintains that the ensign is not only "a human being who generates the catastrophe out of his own needs and hatreds," but also "the catalyst who activates destructive forces not of his own creation, forces present in love itself." According to the critic, Iago embodies in his actions the vulnerability of romantic love as presented in the comedies—a point similar to that voiced by Kenneth Burke (1951) in his commentary on the theme of love-as-private property in* Othello. *For further discussions of Shakespeare's presentation of love in this play, see the excerpts by Hermann Ulrici (1839), Derek Traversi (1949), Winifred M. T. Nowottny (1952), Robert B. Heilman (1956), John Bayley (1960), Jared R. Curtis (1973), and Jane Adamson (1980).]*

The motives are sexual love and jealousy; intrigue and deception propel the plot; the outcome is engineered by a clever manipulator; the impact is personal, "domestic," rather than political and cosmic. These features strike us as appropriate to Shakespeare's comedies. Yet they also characterize one of his greatest tragedies. *Othello* is based, not on the chronicles and lives of the great that supply plots for most of the other Shakespearean tragedies, but on a *novella* in Giraldi's *Hecatommithi.* Shakespeare often turned to tales of this sort for the plots and situations of his comedies; in fact, Giraldi's own collection, the certain source of *Othello,* is a probable source for *Measure for Measure* and a possible one for *Twelfth Night.* Yet *Othello* is overwhelmingly tragic in movement and effect. Are the close ties to comedy at all significant, then? I shall argue that they are, that the tragedy is generated and heightened *through* the relation to comedy rather than in spite of it, and that *Othello* develops a tragic view of love by moving from the assumptions of romantic comedy to the darker vision already articulated in some of Shakespeare's lyric poetry.

To see how this is so, we need to look at comedy, and especially at that romantic mode that was dominant in Shakespeare's comic writing in the decade or more preceding *Othello.* What are pertinent here are not the explicit themes of these plays but their common underlying assumptions about love, the values and beliefs that go largely unquestioned and unanalyzed in the dialogue but can be deduced from comic forms and conventions.

Shakespearean comedy invariably presents as all or part of its initial situation individual characters in a single and unsatisfied state and directs them through plot complications toward appropriate pairings-off at the end. Plays like *The Merchant of Venice, As You Like It, Twelfth Night,* even *The Taming of the Shrew,* find their generating tension in barriers between characters, and they stress the uneasiness of isolation even when those barriers are self-imposed. . . . [The] unquestioning drive toward mass marriage suggests that young individuals are to be seen as incomplete identities, the hemispheres of Aristophanes' myth in the *Symposium* which find rest and completion only in union with their opposite halves. The marriage-endings operate as symbols for full participation in life. Marriageable young people who deny or hesitate on the brink are all pushed in. (pp. 123-24)

One basic premise of Shakespeare's comedies, then, is the value of pairing and participation. . . . The naturalness of mating is explicit in some comedies (*Love's Labour's Lost,* for example), implicit in all. Those that promote release and resolution of conflicts by moving the action to an out-of-bounds locale—described for us spatially by Northrop Frye's "green world" and temporally by C. L. Barber's "holiday"—give structural reinforcement to this sense of nature as love's ally. For all of the artificial and magical elements in the forests of *The Two Gentlemen of Verona, A Midsummer Night's Dream,* and *As You Like It,* nature in those places is less trammeled and perverted than in the polite, treacherous court of Milan, Theseus' lawbound Athens, or the dominions where Duke Frederick sets the ethical standard by crimes against his kindred. Turned out or self-exiled from civilization, the lovers are righted and united in the woods.

Love is natural then, as well as right. Comedy answers to our wishes in this respect, not our fears. But comedy also affirms that love is irrational and arbitrary. Here the fear is dealt with not by ignoring but by disarming it. Bottom's comment that reason and love keep little company [in *A Midsummer Night's Dream*] holds true generally in these comedies. (p. 125)

[The] insistence that something as vital as the love-choice is totally beyond rational control might be a disturbing note in comedy, but it is not. Bottom is untroubled by his pronouncement, and by the fairy queen's amazing dotage that provokes it. Lovers generally abandon what reason they have without a struggle, and this course appears to be the approved one: when they attempt to rationalize their new emotions, as Lysander does when the misapplied love-juice compels him to love Helena, the result fools no one.

LYSANDER

Not Hermia but Helena I love:
Who will not change a raven for a dove?
The will of man is by his reason sway'd,
And reason says you are the worthier maid.
Things growing are not ripe until their season;
So I, being young, till now ripe not to reason;
And touching now the point of human skill,
Reason becomes the marshal to my will,
And leads me to your eyes. . . .

HELENA

Wherefore was I to this keen mockery born?
            [*A Midsummer Night's Dream,* II. ii. 113-23]

What provides the security in which we dismiss Lysander's attempts at reason with laughter and adopt instead the spirit of Bottom's "gleek"? In *Midsummer Night's Dream* the most obvious answer is Oberon: love's unreason cannot lead to destruction with this powerful and benevolent figure in charge. The other comedies . . . lack an Oberon, but they share what may be called an Oberon-principle. That is, the people whose extra wit and knowledge put them one up on the others are men and (more usually) women of good will. (p. 126)

The convention of ending comedies with marriage promised (*Love's Labour's Lost, Two Gentlemen, Much Ado About Nothing, Twelfth Night*), or marriage celebrated (*Midsummer Night's Dream, As You Like It*), or marriage ratified emotionally or socially (*Taming of the Shrew, Merchant of Venice, All's Well That Ends Well, Twelfth Night*) has a further corollary. Comedies in this dominant pattern by implication locate the important stresses and decisions of love in the courtship period. Their silence about postmarital shifts of direction suggests that there will be none, that once Jack has Jill nought can go ill— or, if couples like Touchstone and Audrey [in *As You Like It*] seem headed for less than perfect harmony, at least that the "story" is over.

To sum up: Shakespeare's comic forms and conventions assume (1) the value of engagement with a mate and with society at large, and (2) the cooperation of forces beyond man, natural and otherwise, in achieving this mating and forestalling the consequences of human irrationality and malice, as well as plain bad luck. To call these *assumptions* does not, of course, mean that Shakespeare or his audience accepted them without question as universally true. Rather, the playwright's use of the comic formulas and the playgoers' familiarity with them directed which aspects of their diverse perception of experience should be brought forward—wish as well as belief—and which should be held in abeyance. Comedy does not depend for its success on telling the whole truth, any more than tragedy does.

The tragic truth of *Othello* develops out of a closer look at these very assumptions about love, nature, reason. Just as such a scrutiny logically comes *after* the first unquestioning acceptance, so Othello's story is deliberately presented as post-comic. Courtship and ratified marriage, the staple of comic plots, appear in *Othello* as a preliminary to tragedy. The play's action up until the reunion of Othello and Desdemona in Act II, scene i, is a perfect comic structure in miniature. The wooing that Othello and Desdemona describe in the council scene (I. iii) has succeeded in spite of barriers of age, color, and condition of life; the machinations of villain and frustrated rival have come to nothing; the blocking father is overruled by the good Duke; and nature has cooperated in the general movement with a storm that disperses the last external threat, the Turks, while preserving the favored lovers. Othello's reunion speech to Desdemona in Cyprus underlines this sense of a movement accomplished, a still point of happiness like the final scene of a comedy:

> If it were now to die,
> 'Twere now to be most happy; for I fear
> My soul hath her content so absolute
> That not another comfort like to this
> Succeeds in unknown fate.
>
> [II. i. 189-93]

But at the same time that Othello celebrates his peak of joy so markedly, his invocations of death, fear, and unknown fate make us apprehensive about the post-comic future. This impression is reinforced indirectly by Desdemona's mode of agreement ("The heavens forbid / But that our loves and comforts should increase . . ." [II. i. 193-94]) and directly by Iago's threat ("O, you are well tun'd now! / But I'll set down the

pegs that make this music . . ." [II. i. 199-200]). In these few lines Shakespeare has prepared us for tragedy, in part by announcing the end of comedy. The happy ending is completed, but Othello and Desdemona are left to go on from there.

If I am right to see Othello's tragedy as developing from a questioning of comic assumptions, then this initial comic movement ought to contain the seeds of tragedy. And it does, in various ways. Othello's account of their shy, storytelling-and-listening courtship, however moving and beautiful, is in retrospect slightly disturbing. "She lov'd me for the dangers I had pass'd; / And I lov'd her that she did pity them" [I. iii. 167-68]. Is it enough? Some critics upon this hint have proclaimed the Moor totally self-centered, incapable of real love. This is surely too severe. Nevertheless, in his summary their love has a proxy quality. "The dangers I had pass'd" have served as a counter between them, a substitute for direct engagement, or at best a preliminary to something not yet achieved. (pp. 127-29)

Iago is the most obvious potential force for tragedy in the early part of the play. We see him thwarted in his first plot against Othello, but already, at the end of Act I, planning the next. In this speech both overt statement and imagery suggest the thrust beyond the comic, the germination out of the first failure of a deeper evil:

> I ha't—it is engender'd. Hell and night
> Must bring this monstrous birth to the world's light.
>
> [I. iii. 403-04]

To a large extent Iago embodies in himself the play's questioning of comic assumptions. He is the most intelligent character, and reason—or the appearance of reason—is his chief means of controlling others. The *power* of the rational view, so easily dismissed with laughter or overruled by emotion in the comedies, is grimly realized in Iago's accurate estimates of character ("The Moor is of a free and open nature . . . And will as tenderly be led by th' nose . . ." [I. iii. 399, 401]), his telling arguments from experience ("I know our country disposition well: / In Venice they do let God see the pranks / They dare not show their husbands. . . . She did deceive her father, marrying you . . ." [III. iii. 201-03, 206]), his plausible hypotheses ("That Cassio loves her, I do well believe it; / That she loves him, 'tis apt and of great credit . . ." [II. i. 286-87]), his final triumph in converting Othello to the philosophy of "ocular proof." Against him the love of Othello and Desdemona is vulnerable, rooted as it is not in rational evaluation or empirical knowledge, but in instinctive sympathy. The same scene (I. iii) that underlines the indirectness of their courtship indicates the peculiar strength of their love that is also a weakness:

DESDEMONA

I saw Othello's visage in his mind . . .

[I. iii. 252]

OTHELLO

My life upon her faith!

[I. iii. 294]

There is a core of power in this instinctive mutual recognition that survives Iago's rational poison and in a sense defeats it, but this victory comes only in death. In his posing of Iago against Othello / Desdemona, Shakespeare fully explores the conventional dichotomy between reason and love and discovers its deeply tragic implications.

If reason's opposition to love is traditional, nature in *Othello* appears to change sides. Love's ally is now love's enemy, partly because the angle of vision has changed: nature as instinctual rightness gives way to nature as intellectual concept, susceptible like all concepts to distortion and misapplication. Brabantio, Iago, and finally Othello himself see the love between Othello and Desdemona as unnatural—"nature erring from itself" [III. iii. 227]. But there is more to it than this. In key scenes of *Othello* a tension develops between two senses of "nature," the general and the particular. It is to general nature that Brabantio appeals in the council scene, the common experience and prejudice by which like calls to like. Attraction between the young white Venetian girl and the aging black foreigner, since it violates this observed law of nature, could only have been "wrought" by unnatural means:

> She is abus'd, stol'n from me, and corrupted,
> By spells and medicines bought of mountebanks;
> For nature so preposterously to err,
> Being not deficient, blind, or lame of sense,
> Sans witchcraft could not.
>
> [I. iii. 60-4]

The other sense of "nature" is particular and personal. For example, when Iago says in his soliloquy at the end of this scene that the Moor is of "a free and open nature," he uses the term to define individual essence: the inscape of Othello.

Brabantio tries to bring in this nature to support the other. Desdemona is essentially timid, thus by nature (her own) she cannot love the fearsome Moor.

> A maiden never bold,
> Of spirit so still and quiet that her motion
> Blush'd at herself; and she—in spite of nature,
> Of years, of country, credit, every thing—
> To fall in love with what she fear'd to look on!
> It is a judgment maim'd and most imperfect
> That will confess perfection so could err
> Against all rules of nature . . .
>
> [I. iii. 94-101]

But this nature is the very ground of Desdemona's love. In her answer to the Venetian Senate and her father, she relates how, penetrating through the blackness and strangeness, she saw Othello's visage in his mind and subdued her heart to that essence, his "very quality" [I. iii. 251].

For Desdemona, then, nature as individual essence is not the enemy of love. But Iago has the last word in this scene, and his conclusion is ominous: Othello's very generosity and openness will make him take the appearance of honesty for the fact. That is, Othello will act instinctively according to the laws of his own nature, rather than according to reasoned evaluation (which would perceive that most liars pretend to be telling the truth). This internal law of nature, then, implies the same vulnerability we have seen in the instinctive, nonrational quality of Othello's and Desdemona's love.

Brabantio's general nature is implicitly reductive in that it derives rules for individuals from the behavior of the herd. Iago's is explicitly reductive. The view he expounds to Roderigo has no regard for human values and ethical norms. Natural law for Iago, as for Edmund in *Lear*, is Hobbesian—a matter of animal appetites promoted by cleverness, with the strongest and shrewdest winning out. (pp. 129-32)

In Shakespeare's portrayal of Iago we can see a version of the clash I have been describing. In spite of his reductive general

view, he can recognize the essential goodness of Othello ("free and open nature," "constant, loving, noble nature . . ." [II. i. 289]) as well as Desdemona's generosity and Cassio's daily beauty [I. iii. 391; II. i. 245; II. iii. 319-22; V. i. 19-20]. Critics have complained of the inconsistency; and if *Othello* were naturalistic drama they would be right to do so. But Iago is not just an envious spoiler; he is the symbolic enemy of love itself. The play's conception demands that the weapons of both "natures," like those of reason, be put in his hands.

In his great self-summation at the play's end, Othello says he was "wrought" from his true nature, and so he was. His own nature, noble and trusting, gave him an instinctive perception of Desdemona's, a perception which breaks forth at the sight of her even while Iago is poisoning his mind: "If she be false, O, then heaven mocks itself! / I'll not believe it" [III. iii. 278-79]. But Iago is able to undermine this trust with false rationality, the insistence that Desdemona's honor, which is "an essence that's not seen," be made susceptible of ocular proof. He succeeds, where Brabantio failed, in using both conceptions of nature against Othello. The Moor's own generosity of nature, Iago suggests, makes him an easy dupe: "I would not have your free and noble nature / Out of self-bounty be abus'd; look to't" [III. iii. 199-200]. Taught to look instead of trust, Othello soon sees Desdemona's choice of him as an aberration, nature erring from itself, and Iago quickly advances the general nature, the law of "all things," to reinforce the idea:

> Ay, there's the point: as—to be bold with you—
> Not to affect many proposed matches
> Of her own clime, complexion, and degree,
> Whereto we see in all things nature tends—
> Foh! one may smell in such a will most rank,
> Foul disproportion, thoughts unnatural.
>
> [III. iii. 228-33]

And so Othello violates his own peculiar essence and yields to Iago's law of the many. Desdemona soon recognizes uneasily that she is altered ("My lord is not my lord") and, in an ironic reflection of Othello's state, seeks the reason in a generalization: "Men's natures wrangle with inferior things, / Though great ones are their object" [III. iv. 124, 144-45]. Later the Venetian visitors gaze horrified at the change in that nature that passion could not shake, while Othello strikes his wife and then exits mumbling of goats and monkeys. He has internalized Iago's reductive view of man as animal. In the next scene (IV. ii) he will see Desdemona in terms of toads mating and maggots quickening in rotten meat.

In the comedies love was a strength, but in *Othello* it is vulnerable to attacks of reason, arguments from nature. More than that, vulnerability is its very essence. Before falling in love with Desdemona, Othello was self-sufficient, master of himself and the battlefield. After he believes her to be false, his occupation is gone. Why? Love has created a dependency, a yielding of the separate, sufficient self to incorporation with another. What comedy treated as a new completeness becomes in *Othello* the heart of tragedy. Tragic vulnerability is there, even in the play's comic phase. Othello's images for his love-commitment are those of narrowing and confining:

> But that I love the gentle Desdemona,
> I would not my unhoused free condition
> Put into circumscription and confine
> For the seas' worth . . .
>
> [I. ii. 25-8]

To love totally is to give up the freedom of self for the perils of union and the expansive great world for a personal and contingent one. Othello's comparison in the last scene is significant in this connection:

> Nay, had she been true,
> If heaven would make me such another world
> Of one entire and perfect chrysolite,
> I'd not have sold her for it.
>
> [V. ii. 143-46]

"My life upon her faith!" is literally true. Desdemona has become Othello's world.

It is in this light, I think, that we can best understand why Othello responds to Iago's insinuations by renouncing his profession. The great lines on military life notably invoke not chaos and carnage, but *order*. War is individual passion subordinated to a larger plan; martial harmony, formal pageantry, imitation of divine judgment.

> O, now for ever
> Farewell the tranquil mind! farewell content!
> Farewell the plumed troops, and the big wars
> That makes ambition virtue! O, farewell!
> Farewell the neighing steed and the shrill trump,
> The spirit-stirring drum, th' ear-piercing fife,
> The royal banner, and all quality,
> Pride, pomp, and circumstance, of glorious war!
> And O ye mortal engines whose rude throats
> Th' immortal Jove's dread clamours counterfeit,
> Farewell! Othello's occupation's gone.
>
> [III. iii. 347-57]

Stylistically, the formal catalogues and ritual repetitions strengthen this selective picture of war as majestic order. Earlier in this scene, Othello has said that when he stops loving Desdemona chaos will come again, and now it has happened. With his own world dissolving in chaos, his ordering generalship is gone.

Othello's disintegration of self is the dark side of comedy's insistence on interdependence, on completing oneself with another. But Shakespeare goes deeper in his exploration of comic assumptions by showing that the desired merging of self and other is, in any case, impossible. The more or less schematized couplings of the comedies combined necessary opposition (male/female) with a series of sympathies in age, background, temperament. Wit calls to wit in Beatrice and Benedick, Berowne and Rosaline; royalty to royalty in Navarre and the Princess of France; rowdiness to rowdiness in Petruchio and Kate [in *Much Ado About Nothing, Love's Labour's Lost, The Taming of the Shrew,* respectively]. It is enough in comedy to suggest compatibility by outward signs and to look no further than the formal union. But in *Othello* Shakespeare has taken pains in several ways to emphasize the separateness of his lovers.

In the original *novella* Giraldi's Moor is handsome, apparently fairly young, and a long-time Venetian resident. Apart from sex, his only real difference from Desdemona is one of color, and Giraldi does not dwell on it much. But Shakespeare dwells on it a great deal; black-white oppositions continually weave themselves into the verbal fabric of *Othello*. Indeed, the dark skin of Giraldi's hero, which the author capitalizes on so little, may have been one of the story's main attractions for Shakespeare. Certainly he alters other details of the story to reinforce this paradigmatic separation into black and white, to increase Othello's alienness and widen the gulf between his experience

and Desdemona's. Shakespeare's Moor is a stranger to Venice, to civil life in general: his entire life, except for the brief period in which he courted Desdemona, has been spent in camp and battlefield [I. iii. 83-7]. Even Othello's speech constantly and subtly reminds us of his apartness. If not rude, as he claims to the council, it is certainly different. His idiom invokes anthropophagi and Pontic seas, roots itself in the exotic rather than in the details of everyday social life familiar to others but not to him. He knows as little of Venetian ways as Desdemona knows of "antres vast and deserts idle" [I. iii. 140], and he is given no time to learn. While Giraldi's Moor and his bride live for some time in Venice after their marriage, Othello and Desdemona are immediately swept off to Cyprus. When Iago generalizes about his country's habits ("In Venice they do let God see the pranks / They dare not show their husbands . . ."), Othello can only answer helplessly, "Dost thou say so?" [III. iii. 202-03, 205]. Shakespeare has deprived him of any common ground with Desdemona from which he can fight back—not only to facilitate Iago's deception, but to heighten the tragic paradox of human love, individuals dependent on each other but unalterably separate and mysterious to one another in their separateness. To sharpen the contrast, Othello is made middle-aged, thick-lipped—everything Desdemona is not. The image of black man and white girl in conjunction, so repellent to earlier critics that they had to invent a tawny or *café-au-lait* Moor, is basic to the play's conception of disjunction in love, giving visual focus to the other oppositions of war and peace, age and youth, man and woman. This disjunction serves the tragic action: it assists Iago's initial deception, and it provides most of the tension in the period between the deception and the murder, as Desdemona inopportunely pleads for Cassio and Othello can communicate his fears only indirectly, through insults and degradations. But beyond this plot function, it is a tragic vision of love itself.

What I am suggesting is that the action of *Othello* moves us not only as a chain of events involving particular people as initiators and victims, but as an acting out of the tragic implications in any love relationship. Iago is a human being who generates the catastrophe out of his own needs and hatreds, but he is also the catalyst who activates destructive forces not of his own creation, forces present in the love itself. His image of "monstrous birth" quoted above has special significance in this regard: coming at the end of a resolved marriage scene, it suggests that the monster is a product of the marriage. He says, "it is engender'd," not "I have engendered it," because he is not parent but midwife. "Hell and night," embodied in this demidevil who works in the dark, will bring the monster forth, but it is the fruit of love itself. (pp. 132-37)

To call *Othello* a tragic statement about love in general is not to see it as the vehicle of "Shakespeare's philosophy of love." It is one artistic whole, and it expresses one kind of perception, which is demonstrably different not only from that of the romantic comedies but also from those of *Troilus and Cressida, Antony and Cleopatra,* the late romances. No one of these cancels out the others; they are all part of Shakespeare's truth. *Othello* is not an allegory, but a very human drama. Nevertheless, its exploration of romantic love and marriage does give *Othello* a universal dimension, the wider reverberations that many critics have felt to be lacking in the play. We have perhaps spent too much time asking the traditional questions about this play: is Othello culpable in succumbing to Iago's suggestions? and what makes Iago do what he does? These are important questions, but it is also important to see beyond the individual events of *Othello,* beyond the defeat of a more or less noble dupe by an obscurely motivated villain, to the tragic inadequacies and contradictions of all human love. (p. 141)

Susan Snyder, "'Othello' and the Conventions of Romantic Comedy," in Renaissance Drama, n.s. Vol. V, 1972, pp. 123-41.

JARED R. CURTIS   (essay date 1973)

[Disputing the assertions of Winifred M. T. Nowottny (1952) and Robert B. Heilman (1956) that Othello demonstrates the antithetical nature of reason and love or "wit" and "witchcraft," Curtis argues that in this play Shakespeare has presented the way in which the ideal harmony among the faculties of "Reason, Will, and Appetite" is destroyed and then restored. At the beginning of the drama, he contends, both Desdemona and Othello evince the right balance of love and reason, correctly acknowledging that these are not polarities but, instead, exist in equilibrium, "separate but one." Curtis provides an overview of Renaissance psychology to show that Shakespeare's contemporaries believed that imagination and the senses, ordinarily in the service of reason, may distort reality and deceive the mind, placing over one's eyes—in the words of one early seventeenth-century psychological theorist—"green spectacles" which make everything appear green. The critic argues that, because of his superior understanding of human nature, Iago succeeds in distorting Othello's perception by making him see through the "green spectacles" of imagination, obscuring and diminishing his powers of reasoning. Further, Curtis maintains that at the close of the play Othello is shown removing these distorting "spectacles," reestablishing the proper relationship between reason and imagination, and achieving a new understanding of himself. Curtis also takes issue with T. S. Eliot's and F. R. Leavis's claims that Othello's concluding speech reveals "self-indulgence and self-deception" in the Moor (see excerpts above, 1927 and 1937), arguing instead that his final words demonstrate his recognition of "the final harmony, now tragic because lost, between love and reason." For further commentary on Shakespeare's portrayal in Othello of the nature of love, see the excerpts by Hermann Ulrici (1839), Derek Traversi (1949), Kenneth Burke (1951), John Bayley (1960), Susan Snyder (1972), and Jane Adamson (1980). Such other critics as G. R. Elliott (1937), E. M. W. Tillyard (1938), Robert B. Heilman (1956), John Bayley (1960), G. M. Matthews (1964), and Helen Gardner (see Additional Bibliography) have also considered whether Othello's concluding speeches demonstrate a new or renewed awareness and understanding in the character.]

Of the many issues at stake in a discussion of Othello, the central ones are the Moor's nobility and his self-knowledge. But within these issues there lies another: What is the nature of Othello's choice? Any study of the play ordinarily faces this question, and the most obvious but perhaps too simple answer is that his alternatives are "good" on the one hand and "evil" on the other. Recent studies, however, have refined this traditional opposition by describing the play and its tragic hero in terms of a quite different set of polarities, that of love versus judgment or love versus reason or, as Robert Heilman has written, love versus "the whole world of rational demonstration." This view, that love and reason are at odds in the play, has been developed most thoroughly by Heilman in his book, Magic in the Web [see excerpt above, 1956]. . . . [According] to Heilman there are two forces in the play, "witchcraft" or love, and "wit"—the "reason, cunning and wisdom" that destroy love. Under this duality, Iago, because he follows wit, must inevitably strive to overcome witchcraft; Othello, more limited than Desdemona but nevertheless capable of witchcraft, falls, according to Heilman, in electing "a program of 'wit'" when wit is "utterly inappropriate to the occasion." Othello

"essays to reason when reason is not relevant: he substitutes a disastrous wit for a saving witchcraft."

But if reason, even wisdom, must by its very nature destroy love—as the argument goes—then in human intercourse no rational act, which must in some sense depend on "rational demonstration," can be creative, restorative, or even preservative. The question also arises, if love is the "magic bringer of harmony," as Heilman has said, what prevents it from harmonizing with reason? Furthermore, the love-reason dichotomy runs counter to the long tradition of "right" reason from Socrates to Richard Hooker. For "it was the reasonable soul," writes J. V. Cunningham, "that was the central psychological concept of the Renaissance, and a man was praiseworthy, as Horatio was [Hamlet, III. ii. 54-74], in so far as the reasonable soul spoke in him and was hearkened to" [in Tradition and Poetic Structure: Essays in Literary History and Criticism]. Although Shakespeare need not have followed either logic or the humanistic tradition in Othello, I think that within certain limits he wrote from the terms of that tradition. To be sure, in the Renaissance as at other times strong antirational forces influenced intellectual life. From this influence Shakespeare was not immune. But the critics, from T. S. Eliot [see excerpt above, 1927] and F. R. Leavis [see excerpt above, 1937] down to Heilman and others, who see Othello in the last scene as an anti-hero "cheering himself up," do not acknowledge the full view of reason dramatized by the play. (pp. 188-89)

At the turn of the century in England love and reason were not commonly understood as polar opposites, nor was reason thought to prey upon love. It is true that love was regarded as quite beyond reason, especially by poets. In the miraculous union in The Phoenix and the Turtle, "Reason in itself confounded, / Saw division grow together" [ll. 41-2]. But in keeping with the love paradox of "either-neither" in the poem, "reason" is the very metaphor Shakespeare used to express love's ascendance:

> . . . How true a twain
> Seemeth this concordant one!
> Love hath reason, reason none,
> If what parts can so remain.
> [The Phoenix and the Turtle, ll. 45-8]

Love is so refined as to be the image of reason at its best. To regard love as a state beyond reason is not necessarily to see it at war with reason.

Nor does the common Elizabethan theory of mind, based upon classical and medieval thought, support the polarization of the two forces. For nowhere in this scheme of things does the highest "wit" hold a position lower than another faculty, be it Memory, Sensible Reason, Imagination, or Commonsense; and "love," which is apprehended by the Imagination by means of the emotions, functions below the "overseeing and judging power of the highest Understanding, which in turn informs the Will" [William Rossky, "Imagination in the English Renaissance: Psychology and Poetic"]. Moreover, the essence of the system is cooperation or "harmony" of a positive and inclusive sort. Reason, according to one student of the mind and contemporary of Shakespeare, must be kept separate from imagination, not "shuffled up and confounded" with what it must judge, so as to prevent being "thrust out" of its "owne place." Yet at the same time, in judging imagination, reason is prepared to guide the will ("that facultie . . . whereby we desire that which is good, and eschew evil"), for the will "hath no light of itselfe, but is lightned by the minde'' [Pierre de La Primaudaye, in *The French Academie*].

The subtle balance of power is the achievement of a larger harmony than love's victory over reason suggests. Thus the notion of a ''doctrine of sight more profound and veracious'' than ''reason . . . and wisdom,'' is strained, to say the least. And the whole tendency of the system, the course of communication, is in fact to ''transcend the visual evidence'' [Heilman], for the least trustworthy members of the hierarchy are the five primary senses. Only Adam before the fall, according to another psychologist, was blessed with senses which ''perfectly and sincerely delivered the condition of sensible things to the mindes consideration'' [Timothy Bright, in *A Treatise of Melancholie*]. And because the imagination depends wholly upon the senses for its information, and because it has the power to fabricate, in presenting ''images'' to the intellect, it too is suspect. Reason, in fact, is at the mercy of the imagination and the senses and can function truly only when the senses and the imagination neither distort nor are distorted. For when an object is ''not rightly apprehended,'' it is ''delivered otherwise than it standeth in nature,'' and then is ''the hart moved to a disorderly passion.'' Emotions in themselves are not evil, but distorted images of the imagination presented to the heart create distorted, excessive emotions, which in turn bring about evil in thought or action. The body ''affected'' (by passion generated through this process) is to the mind ''as a false stringed lute . . . to the musician'' [Bright].

In several plays Shakespeare revealed his acquaintance with this theory. But most important for our purposes is the frequency and relative accuracy with which he represented the system in *Othello,* represented it to such an extent as to create a kind of dialogue on the relation between reason and love. When Brabantio confronts Othello for having stolen his daughter he charges

> That thou hast practis'd on her with foule Charmes,
> Abus'd her delicate Youth, with Drugs or Minerals,
> That weaken Motion.
>
> [I. ii. 73-5]

Having understood his daughter's love for him only in terms of ''Duty,'' Brabantio is completely surprised by her shift of allegiance in marriage. His only explanation is that Othello has drugged her ''outer'' senses so as to weaken her physically, or more treacherously, has drugged her ''inner'' powers, weakening her ability to tell right from wrong, white from black. However, at Desdemona's appearance before the Senate, she is obviously so much in command of all her faculties that Brabantio's theory collapses [I. iii. 189-98]. Conscious of her ''downe-right violence, and storme of Fortunes'' [I. iii. 249], and of the irrationality, even immorality, with which she may seem to have acted, she explains for her father and the Senate the proper relation between love and reason:

> My heart's subdu'd
> Even to the very quality of my Lord;
> I saw *Othello*'s visage in his mind.
>
> [I. iii. 250-52]

It is a commonplace to speak of these lines as expressing another ''marriage of true minds,'' but her language is less platonic than that of Sonnet 116, more complex than an expression of intuition. The concrete words ''saw'' and ''visage'' balance against the abstract word ''mind,'' making of her definition a striking harmony of parts: sense and mind are separate but one, ''either-neither.''

Othello, taking up this argument on his wife's behalf, applies it to himself, using an elaborate metaphorical language distinctly his own and already familiar to the audience:

> I therefore beg it not
> To please the pallate of my Appetite:
> Nor to comply with heat the yong affects
> In my defunct, and proper satisfaction.
>
> [I. iii. 261-64]

It is not sensual pleasure, rightly his and already tasted, that urges him to defend her joining him in Cyprus. Othello is responding in kind to Desdemona's brilliant defense of her choice. As sense and mind are separate but one in her, so too in him. ''But,'' he goes on, now deliberately echoing Desdemona's earlier statement, he seconds her request in order ''to be free, and bounteous to *her* minde'' [I. iii. 265] (italics mine), just as she was to his. Don't think, he says, that I will ''scant'' ''your serious and great businesse'' [I. iii. 267] because of her presence.

> No, when light wing'd Toyes
> Of feather'd *Cupid,* seele with wanton dulnesse
> My speculative, and offic'd Instrument:
> That my Disports corrupt, and taint my businesse:
> Let House-wives make a Skillet of my Helme,
> And all indigne, and base adversities,
> Make head against my Estimation.
>
> [I. iii. 268-74]

On this speech Othello is made to stand or fall by many critics. Heilman's statement is representative; he finds Othello ''a little unsure of himself here,'' a bit tasteless, and too businesslike on his wedding night. ''The disavowal of sensuality is another index of self deceptiveness,'' Heilman writes; the Moor ''rejects 'light wing'd toys' as Iago does 'the love of a guinea hen.' '' But this is to distort the words to fit a theory externally derived. Othello is no less sure of himself than Desdemona of herself, nor does he ''reject'' anything. He will not allow ''Toyes'' to ''seele'' nor ''Disports'' to ''corrupt''; nor does he slight the ''rites of love'' [I. iii. 257] in either the social or the physical sense. (pp. 189-92)

Othello is not talking about his eyes in the phrase, ''seele . . . my speculative, and offic'd Instrument,'' but of his rational powers, in particular the ''speculative'' wit and the will ''officed'' by the wit, for ''seele'' is but a metaphor for the blinding of the mind. He is echoing familiar Elizabethan concepts: he will not permit the senses, grossly indulged, to fire the imagination, nor will he allow the imagination, to quote another theorist of the mind, to put ''greene spectacles before the eyes of [his] wit to make it see nothing but greene'' [Thomas Wright, in *Passions of the Mind in General*]. His ''disports,'' in themselves not evil but liable to influence evilly, will not impair his rational powers from serving his ''businesse.'' The irony is not that his ''rational'' bent is what destroys him, but rather that his dotage (''I prattle out of fashion, and I doate / In mine owne comforts'' [II. i. 239-40] and Iago's skillful onslaught upon the two lower levels of his ''instrumental'' faculties, the ''outer'' senses and the ''inner'' powers, should taint and corrupt the higher rational powers and thus deprive him of their proper governance.

Of the process of tainting and enervating the rational powers, Iago is master; he is in his way a brilliant practical psychologist. Not only does he preach the doctrine, tongue-in-cheek, to the lust-bitten Roderigo, but he perverts it to serve his destructive cause as well. His sometimes misinterpreted homily on will—

"Vertue? A figge" [I. iii. 320-32]—as J. V. Cunningham has shown, is "a notorious commonplace of the Christian tradition." The doctrine is not diabolically "inverted" but "one of the finest statements, especially in its rhythm, of the traditional and orthodox view of the relation of the reasonable will to the sensitive soul."

Iago is aware that the will must plant and weed the body's garden, that the power and authority for producing industry or idleness "lies in our Wills." But the will is "Corrigeable," capable of being corrected, and its corrector is "The ballance of our lives," with its "scale of Reason." Without this system of checks Iago knows "our Natures would conduct us to most prepostrous Conclusions." He knows the right name of Roderigo's "Love," a "sect, or Seyen," an "unbitted Lust" [I. iii. 332, 331], that with proper husbandry can be controlled as one can shape and improve plants by grafting and cutting. Iago does not undermine the system here but, on the contrary, expresses it clearly and succinctly. Thus when he consciously employs his knowledge of the instrumental faculties in turning Othello from reasoning man into unreasoning animal, his success is more convincing than if, as one critic implies, he were to muddle through error after error to produce evil. I am not arguing that Iago is an intellectual giant, the impression given by Coleridge and A. C. Bradley [see excerpts above, 1808-18 and 1904]. Iago too is subject to fortune, good and bad, and to his own mistakes—he badly miscalculates his wife's strength of character, for example, and he does not dispose of Roderigo and Cassio as neatly as he had planned. But it is important to recognize how unusually skilled he is in putting to use his knowledge of human psychology. (pp. 193-94)

The first stage in the process that thrusts reason out of its own place is signaled by Othello himself, when he is frustrated by Iago's, Cassio's, and Montano's refusal to tell what happened during the first night's watch:

> My blood begins my safer Guides to rule,
> And passion (having my best judgement collied)
> Assaies to leade the way.
>
> [II. iii. 205-07]

The deepest irony, in this play replete with ironies, is Othello's growing conviction that Iago is a "just" man whom "Passion cannot rule" [III. iii. 124]. "Exchange me for a Goat," he says with prophetic irony, "When I shall turne the businesse of my Soule / To such exufflicate, and blow'd Surmises," or when he permits the highest rational power (the soul's business) to be ruled by the swollen and rotted imagination [III. iii. 180-82]. Iago mounts his attack at the very point of Othello's faith in the harmony of mental and physical life. Just as Othello (and Desdemona, too) had affirmed the "balance" of their lives among Reason, Will, and Appetite, so Iago quickly sets the faculties at war with one another. Of Desdemona's choice of the Moor, he says, "One may smell in such, a will most ranke, / Foule disproportions, Thoughts unnaturall" [III. iii. 232-33]. And then, appearing to take back such slander, but cutting deeper still, he says,

> But (pardon me) I do not in position
> Distinctly speake of her, though I may feare
> Her will, recoyling to her better judgement,
> May fal to match you with her country formes
> And happily repent.
>
> [III. iii. 234-38]

"Happily" here means "perhaps" but also carries the sense of "fortunately"; what great good luck for her to be restored

to "balance," as Iago understands it. What follows is not rational demonstration at all but a travesty of reason. Othello searches for a "living reason" in Iago's report of Cassio's dream, which later appears to him "a foregone conclusion" [III. iii. 428], and he finds "Occular proofe" [III. iii. 360] in the infamous handkerchief. The systematic debilitation of Othello's rational faculties, by Iago and by Othello himself once the process is begun, proceeds inexorably to the lowest ebb of these powers, brought on by the thinnest of demonstrations, a trifle "light as ayre" [III. iii. 322], the handkerchief [IV. i. 35-43]. The imagination, no longer "wit's looking glass," the "neere hand-maid to the mind" [John Davies, in *Nosce Teipsum*], but instead its tyrannical ruler, indeed puts "greene spectacles before the eyes of [his] witte to make it see nothing but greene." Significantly, at this juncture Othello's power over speech itself, the mind's most direct instrument of expression, breaks down entirely. (pp. 194-5)

In the last scene the truth is revealed. Emilia in her blunt way calls Othello "foole," for not seeing it sooner, a judgment he concurs in [V. ii. 284, 346]. We need not see in his final speech the "sentimentalist's Othello," nor the absurd reduction to "baboonery" encouraged by the views of T. S. Eliot, F. R. Leavis, and others. Othello's greatness is defined by his removal of the green spectacles and his return to reality and the governance of wit. His final speech re-establishes his rational control and reveals a new inward perceptiveness. (pp. 195-96)

Othello's final words suggest, not self-indulgence and self-deception, but the final harmony, now tragic because lost, between love and reason. Winifred Nowottny's dictum that "with love, reason and justice have ultimately nothing to do" [see excerpt above, 1952] is inappropriate. For wit and witchcraft are not the opposing forces in the play, but wit and the corrupted wit. When the Ghost of Hamlet's father damns "that incestuous, that adulterate beast," Claudius, for the "witchcraft of his wit," he condemns his "wicked" and perverted mind [*Hamlet*, I. v. 42-4]. So too in *Othello* is the perverted mind condemned. Othello's love returns, but so does his reason. To paraphrase *The Phoenix and the Turtle*, love and reason in *Othello* are not combatants but "co-supremes" at the close of the play, "as chorus to their tragic scene" [ll. 51, 52]. (pp. 196-97)

Jared R. Curtis, "The 'Speculative and Offic'd Instrument': Reason and Love in 'Othello'," in Shakespeare Quarterly, *Vol. XXIV, No. 2, Spring, 1973, pp. 188-97.*

ROBERT G. HUNTER (essay date 1976)

[In the following excerpt, Hunter proposes that one way, among others, of viewing Othello *is to see it as "Shakespeare's way of thinking about the possibility that the universe is not providentially ordered." In a dramatic world such as this one, the critic contends, where divine grace is absent and the protagonists' fates are not depicted as predetermined, humanity is free to exercise its will and elect its own destiny. Hunter further assesses the world of* Othello *as based on the precepts of Pelagianism—a doctrine fostered by some fourth- and early fifth-century theologians but condemned as heresy by the Christian Church—which held that human nature is essentially good and the human will is free to determine its own path to salvation; Pelagianism is also optimistic in its denial that human beings are born into sin as a legacy of Adam's original transgression. Hunter maintains that* Othello *tests this optimistic doctrine by asking whether human love can be sustained without divine grace and demonstrating that the "answer, clearly, is 'No.'" Other critics who have analyzed*

Shakespeare's portrayal in Othello *of the issue of free will versus providential control include Hermann Ulrici (1839), G. G. Gervinus (1849-50), Denton J. Snider (1887), E. K. Chambers (1908), Stopford A. Brooke (1913), Elmer Edgar Stoll (1915), Wyndham Lewis (1927), Allardyce Nicoll (1927), and Harry Levin (1964). Contending that the Moor is portrayed as noble and courageous, even superior to most men, Hunter argues that he is also shown to have insufficient strength of reason and will "to keep his hatred in check without the help of love." The critic avers that Othello's struggle to prevent chaos from coming again by sustaining his love for Desdemona bears some resemblance to the structure of the medieval psychomachia, a kind of morality drama in which allegorical figures of vice and virtue contend for the soul or psyche of the protagonist, although it is also reminiscent of the "schiamachia," where the hero must battle with shadows. Hunter asserts that in* Othello, *although the Moor must strive against "the shadows brought into being by Iago's lies," the central contest is between Othello's coexisting capacities for love and hate— between the opposing features of nobility and cruelty inherent not only in his nature but in ours as well. Hunter also notes Iago's resemblance to the vice figure in medieval allegorical drama, but he judges that Iago is supremely both "an 'allegorical' embodiment of the force of hatred" and a vivid, convincing, and painful representation of the "human mind." For additional commentary on the relation of Iago to the medieval vice figure, see the excerpts by Irving Ribner (1955) and Bernard Spivack (1958). By contrast, Hunter argues that Desdemona is not "a human possibility," although she functions effectively in the drama. While Shakespeare has endowed her with incomparable grace and goodness, the critic claims, these are not sufficient in this Pelagian world to forestall the destructive power of hatred. Hunter suggests that had she been more human, with the capacity for hate and sin herself, "she might understand Othello's jealous rage and answer it with a self-preserving fury of her own."]*

At line 90 of scene 3 in act 3 of *Othello,* just before Iago begins his work of destruction, the Moor stands watching Desdemona leave the stage and says:

> Excellent wretch: Perdition catch my Soule
> But I do love thee: and when I love thee not,
> Chaos is come againe.
>
> [III. iii. 90-2]

As prophecy the lines are ironically precise. Othello stops loving his wife, chaos comes again, and it seems likely that when he kills himself at the play's end, perdition catches his soul. But the lines are more than that point of dramatic irony on which the action of the tragedy is poised. They are also the play's clearest direct statement of the action's meaning, and like most such Shakespearean statements they ask more questions than they answer.

According to the lines, the health of a man's mind and soul depends upon his ability to sustain love—an unexceptionable statement whose truth is obviously demonstrated by the tragedy. But the particular language of the lines moves them beyond banality. [The] juxtaposition of love and chaos evokes a conceptual view of the created universe, the view which sees matter as composed of elements that are by nature in contention and whose order is the result of the imposition upon them of divine love. This elemental view is basic to Shakespeare's art, where it coexists with and complements the hierarchical view of order so memorably presented by Ulysses in *Troilus and Cressida.* What the maintaining of degree is to hierarchical order, the maintaining of love is to elemental order. Othello's lines, then, suggest that the particular tragedy of this single man, his psychic and spiritual destruction, is more than personal, or even representatively human. The tragedy is a component of its universe, defining it and defined by it. The laws that destroy and damn Othello govern all men and all created things and express, we must assume, the nature of their creator.

The orthodox optimism of Shakespeare's time accepted, of course, the notion that the creation is an expression of the creator and saw the universal order which exists despite the chaos inherent in it as proof of God's goodness: "How could it be that the elements, so divers and contrary as they be among themselves, should yet agree and abide together in a concord, without destruction one of another to serve our use, if it came not onely of GODS goodnesse so to temper them?" [in *Certaine Sermons or Homilies* (1623)]. Chaos does not come again because God's goodness, his grace and his providence, will not let it. But that statement asks its own question: when chaos comes again, as it does for Othello, does it do so because God lets it? Does our ability to sustain love depend upon God's grace?

Othello, like the other Christian tragedies, asks that question but does not answer it and as usual the refusal (or inability) to answer finds its expression in a series of possible answers. . . . In *Richard III* and *Hamlet* there is a dominant possibility, namely that there is a special providence in the fall of a sparrow, a providence which is equally to be found in the falls of Richard, Claudius, and Hamlet himself. In these plays the paradoxical nature of the concepts of grace and providence is the source for an important part of the power with which these tragedies inspire pity and terror. The destruction of Richard and the triumph of Richmond are evidence for providential control. Even the mutual destruction of Hamlet and Claudius serves to purge Denmark of its rottenness. But the only good that comes of the tragic suffering in *Othello* is the punishment of those who are guilty of inflicting pain upon the innocent. There, the predominance of grace and providence as possible explanations for the action recedes and is replaced by the newly ascendant possibility that the tragedy is the result precisely of that receding. The *Othello* world is one from which God appears to have withdrawn, leaving its disposition to the freed wills of men. (pp. 127-28)

This receding of a sense of grace, providence, and consequently, of predestination as forces operating to determine the action of the play is a part of Shakespeare's larger artistic strategy in *Othello.* In this play he limits himself conceptually just as he narrows his usual range in time, place, and action, and all these efforts of limitation are directed toward the achieving of an emotional intensity that derives from our sense of participating in the mutually destructive interaction of brilliantly imagined human minds. Too strong a suggestion that this conflict is the expression of a divine will rather than the human wills that so thoroughly engage us would distract us from our absorption in the psychological struggle that is this play's great achievement. And so the potentially intrusive concepts are replaced by others that will contribute to the drama's great effect. As always in Shakespeare the conceptual is a means to art and not its end. And yet, among the purposes or inevitable results of Shakespeare's art is the imaginative examination of concepts. *Othello* is, among other things, Shakespeare's way of thinking about the possibility that the universe is not providentially ordered. (pp. 128-29)

I would suggest that what Shakespeare proposes as the clearest possible truth about the *Othello* version of reality is precisely what Homiletic orthodoxy holds to be unthinkable: God has given up his creation to be ruled after our wits and device. In this view of the *Othello* world, man is at liberty. His mind is free of supernatural grace and his will is consequently free to choose its own destiny. This, of course, is precisely Iago's view of the matter:

> 'tis in our selves that we are thus, or thus. Our Bodies are our Gardens, to the which, our Wills are Gardiners. So that if we will plant Nettels, or sowe Lettice: Set Hisope, and weede up Time: Supplie it with one gender of Hearbes, or distract it with many: either to have it sterrill with idlenesse, or manured with Industry, why the power, and Corrigeable authoritie of this lies in our Wills. If the ballance of our lives had not one Scale of Reason, to poize another of Sensualitie, the blood, and basenesse of our Natures would conduct us to most prepostrous Conclusions. But we have Reason to coole our raging Motions, our carnall Stings, our unbitted Lusts: whereof I take this, that you call Love, to be a Sect or Seyen.
>
> [I. iii. 319-32]
> (p. 131)

[The] portrait of the mind given us through Iago's metaphors is Pelagian. Both the garden and the balance are Pelagian images for psychic processes and the poised scales, with the will free to tip the balance, is a precise icon for the Pelagian sense of the will's relationship to the whole mind of which it is a part. It is a view that leaves no room for grace—at least not for grace in any supernatural form. Grace in a Pelagian world may exist in forms exterior to men, but to admit internal, supernatural grace as a working component of the psyche is, to the Pelagian, to deny the freedom of the will. I would suggest that in the creation of the *Othello* world, Shakespeare puts forward this view as the most likely model for the minds of the characters he is creating. In the other Christian tragedies he gives artistic form to the tragic implications of the belief that divine grace is granted to or withheld from the mind of man. In *Othello* he imagines a world in which internal grace may not exist and the mind of man is free to make the choices that will result in the shaping of its own ends. The implications of man's freedom turn out to be at least as tragic as the implications of man's bondage.

But if Iago's Pelagian view of the mind is, in one very basic way, possibly accurate within the context of the play, it is also, in another very basic way, wrong. First of all Iago is very clearly wrong in a parochial sense. What he believes to be true of himself is proved by his actions and fate to be completely untrue. He is, in fact, conducted by the blood and baseness of his nature to the most preposterous of conclusions—death by torture. He does not see that the hatred for Othello which possesses and motivates him totally is as much a sect or scion of what he calls "unbitted lusts" as is Roderigo's love for Desdemona. But this error indicates, I believe, another even more basic than that.

Perhaps the best way of identifying that error is to return to his metaphor and examine the content of the scales. According to Iago, these contain reason and sensuality in equal quantities and the will is therefore free to make a rational choice that will promote its own good. In proper Pelagianism the scales of our life, the components of our nature, consist in equal parts of good and evil, so that the will is enabled by the equilibrium to choose without constraint between sinning and not sinning. In the play, however, these qualities are rather different, though not different in the way Iago would have them. They are pa-

ganized or syncretized into the ultimately pre-Socratic principles of love and strife.

If Iago is right in his basic apprehension of the Pelagian freedom of his mind and universe, then Othello is right in his sense of what preserves mind and universe from destruction. It is neither human reason nor divine grace but human love. The balance of his life consists in a scale of hate poised against one of love and this perilous equilibrium is expressed in the structure of the play with its balancing of antagonist against antiantagonist, Iago against Desdemona. Othello holds and contains the scales and the play questions Pelagian optimism by asking, "Can the unaided force of human love balance the blood and baseness of our natures?" The play's answer, clearly, is "No."

This is an answer that does not flatter our humanity and our natural impulse to evade it leads us to misinterpret the play. Usually such impulses to misinterpretation move us in one of two directions. We may try to alleviate the play's pessimism by overemphasizing its tendency to allegory—a tactic that allows us to see the hatred embodied in Iago as abstract, more diabolical than human, and thus not a dangerously valid comment on the strength of our own ordinary evil. Or we may take an opposite tack and discover, in the realism with which the play characterizes Othello's greatness and his love for Desdemona, evidence for believing that his love and greatness are more than usually flawed and thus not a dangerously valid comment on the weakness of our own ordinary good. Both tendencies are misguided, I think, but both are also in some degree justified by the text and I would like to examine each in turn.

The structural resemblance of *Othello* to allegorized psychomachy is obvious. An heroic everyman, the protagonist is presented with a choice between embodied Vice and Virtue. The text repeatedly draws our attention to the allegorical analogue and Othello sums up this view of the action at the play's end: "Will you, I pray, demand that demy-Divell / Why he hath thus ensnar'd my Soule and Body" [V. ii. 301-02]. But it is wrong to take the diabolical metaphor too literally, and seriously wrong if it allows us to escape the painful implications of Iago's humanity, for Iago is painfully human and his soliloquies, his dialogues with Roderigo and Othello, are brilliantly accurate imitations of real states of mind. Coleridge's famous "motive-hunting of a motiveless malignity" [see excerpt above, 1808-18] is a precise description of Iago's favorite mental activity, but we understand it correctly only so long as we remember that human malignity is by definition motiveless. "Malignity" *is* motive—according to this play (and to Freud) one of the two instinctual drives that move us to our actions. When Iago tells us, repeatedly, that he hates the Moor, it behooves us to believe him. When he tells us why, it behooves us to realize that the emotion precedes the "motives" for it. But to move from that insight to the conclusion that Iago and his hatred are literary conventions instead of profound comments on human reality is to miss—or rather to evade—the point of the characterization. Rational hatred is a possible and common emotion which Iago does not exemplify. Irrational hatred is equally possible and probably more common. For Iago hatred is a necessity. He must have an object for the destructive force that would otherwise destroy its possessor—and does, nonetheless, destroy its possessor. Motives for the choice of Othello as object of the emotion must exist—or rather motives for the particular intensity of the emotion, for hatred in some form is Iago's inevitable response to all human beings. Some of the reasons for the extreme form it takes with regard to Othello are clear. Othello is successful, powerful, noble, and black. That a paranoid should hate him is inevitable and Iago's paranoid tendencies have brought him to the brink of insanity. His soliloquies are a determined effort to convince himself and, thanks to theatrical convention, to convince us that he is sane.

Shakespeare's success in the simultaneous creation of an "allegorical" embodiment of the force of hatred and a convincingly human mind is, in my opinion, total. Iago is an imaginative rethinking back into the human reality from which it emerged of a primary concept, a basic truth about that reality. The result is one of those artifacts whose complexity makes it an apparently inexhaustible source of meaning.

Desdemona's complexity is of another order. Simple in essence, she is, as a result of her simplicity, problematically complex in meaning. Iago's nature partakes of and confirms the complexity of the dramatic world he inhabits. Love, in that world, exists, in Othello himself at least, as the result of the repression of hatred. The Freudian critics of the play have made a (to me) totally convincing case for Iago's hatred as a product of the repression of an inadmissible, unconscious homosexual love. But this ascendant hatred not only represses that love, it simultaneously allows Iago to allow himself to feel love and express it by putting its expression into the admissible mode of deception. Because in his hatred he is deceiving Othello, Iago can kneel in mock-marriage ceremony with him and he can imagine and describe himself in bed with Cassio, being passionately kissed by him. But at the same time that the deception of Othello permits in Iago the expression of a repressed love, it releases in Othello the elemental hatred which has been repressed by his love for Desdemona. Both characters are thus microcosms of an Empedoclean universe in which love and hate coexist in a dynamic and shifting interrelationship.

Desdemona is not such a microcosm. Her simplicity stands in contrast to an otherwise universal doubleness and appears to contradict what would otherwise be a universal human enslavement to the necessity for hatred. There is no hatred in Desdemona's love. Shakespeare has responded to the plot necessity for her technical innocence of adultery by giving her an innocence so complete that it cannot credit the possibility that adultery is ever committed by anyone:

Do'st thou in conscience thinke (tell me *Aemilia*)
That there be women do abuse their husbands
In such grosse kinde? . . .
I do not thinke there is any such woman.
[IV. iii. 61-3, 83]

This is wondrous pitiful, but once we have experienced the pity of it, what are we to make of it? Can we accept it as a human possibility in the way we accept its opposite in Iago? Only, I should say, by accepting it as a temporary possibility, an innocence that must perforce be soon destroyed by experience, Iago or no Iago. But what of the love for Othello that coexists with that innocence? It is not destroyed even by murder:

AEMIL. Oh who hath done this deed?
DES. No body: I my selfe, farewell:
      Commend me to my kinde Lord: oh farewell.
[V. ii. 123-25]

Can we accept Desdemona as a human possibility in the way I, at least, can accept Iago? I cannot. Iago's passions, however basic, are complicated. Desdemona's are impossibly simple,

but this impossible simplicity does not prevent the character from functioning effectively within the work of art. So far as our emotional responses are concerned, her effectiveness is perfectly apparent, but she serves to direct our minds as well.

Shakespeare is testing with his imagination the possible validity of the optimism of a Pelagian world view and in doing so, he appears to have given the Pelagian possibility advantageous odds. He has imagined a heroine who is not only capable of goodness, but incapable of anything else. Desdemona has no need of supernatural grace. She is saved by being what she is—a natural embodiment of grace apparently untainted by original sin. And yet the tragedy occurs despite that grace and innocence. The first meaning of Desdemona's perfection seems to be that the unaided force of human love cannot balance the blood and baseness of our natures, as embodied in Othello, even when the object of that love is perfect. At the same time, this pessimism is qualified (whether to its mitigation or intensification I am not sure) by the sense we have that the tragedy is in part the result of that perfection. Because Desdemona's love is simple, it can answer Othello's hate only with love. So when he strikes her or calls her whore she can only be "obedient, very obedient" [IV. i. 255-56]. If her love were more fully human, if she were innocent of adultery but capable of it, she might understand Othello's jealous rage and answer it with a self-preserving fury of her own. (pp. 132-36)

[In Othello himself] Shakespeare imagines a maker of choices who is a great man, one who is born great and has also achieved greatness, despite his foreignness and blackness, in the power structure of Renaissance Venice. His nobility, courage, and competence are described and demonstrated repeatedly in the course of the first two acts. The envy of Iago and Roderigo and the irrationality of Brabantio emphasize the superiority of the man who inspires their emotions while simultaneously making us begin to fear for a hero whose greatness can arouse so much malignity. The extreme complexity of the results, in terms of our reactions, of Shakespeare's choice of a black hero is well beyond my powers of analysis. Shakespeare is manipulating the racism of his time and that was clearly to some extent different from our own. But several of the more obvious effects of the contrast in pigmentation as opposed to race need to be recognized. The first of these is visibility. Othello's color helps him dominate the stage whenever he is on it. It is to him that our eyes are naturally drawn. The second effect is a function of the first: contrast. Othello is physically apart and this makes the impact of conjunction—particularly sexual conjunction with Desdemona—all the more striking. When Cassio imagines Othello making "love's quick pants in Desdemona's arms" [II. i. 80], we remember Iago's old black ram tupping a white ewe and the symbolic reconciliation of opposites in this act of love becomes the clearer for being black and white.

But perhaps a more important effect of the visible contrast of Othello's blackness is the paradoxical emphasis which it gives to his freedom. Othello, once a black slave, is now supremely at liberty. An extravagant and wheeling stranger, he is socially and racially detached from the world of the play. He can choose to serve or not serve and to love or not love. His decision to marry Desdemona is very carefully presented as an act of free choice. He notices her attraction to him, plays upon it, and finally brings her to a "hint" that is a declaration of love and of willingness to marry. His will rather than hers is presented with the final decision, and it is a decision motivated entirely by love. Despite Iago's claims to the contrary, no worldly advantage comes to Othello from his elopement—only the enmity of Desdemona's powerful father. Othello's subjection to love is deliberate, voluntary, and disinterested:

> But that I love the gentle *Desdemona*,
> I would not my unhoused free condition
> Put into Circumscription, and Confine,
> For the Seas worth.
>
>   [I. ii. 25-8]

In his speech to the senators, in fact, he appears to go so far as to claim that his love for Desdemona is not seriously affected even by sexual passion. When Desdemona asks that she be allowed to accompany him because she wants to live with him, because, in the Quarto version of the line, her heart's subdued "even to the utmost pleasure" of her lord, because if she is left behind "The Rites for why I love him, are bereft me" [I. iii. 251, 257], Othello seconds her but qualifies the physicality of her motives:

>   I therefore beg it not
> To please the pallate of my Appetite:
> Nor to comply with heat the yong affects
> In my defunct, and proper satisfaction.
> But to be free, and bounteous to her minde:
> And Heaven defend your good soules, that you thinke
> I will your serious and great businesse scant
> When she is with me. No, when light wing'd Toyes
> Of feather'd *Cupid*, seele with wanton dulnesse
> My speculative, and offic'd Instrument:
> That my Disports corrupt, and taint my businesse:
> Let House-wives make a Skillet of my Helme,
> And all indigne, and base adversities,
> Make head against my Estimation.
>
>   [I. iii. 261-74]
>   (pp. 141-43)

Othello's overconfidence in his ability to maintain his martial identity against the power of Eros is at least doubly ironic. His social function is to defend Venice from its Moslem enemies, but an Othello in bondage to Eros would not be of much use against the Turk and so Othello protests that he will be able to keep the two scales of his double nature in balance.... Thus apparently obvious good, the control of strife by love, is shown to have potential danger inherent in it. But this irony is complicated by the "providential" destruction of the Turkish fleet, by the consequent evaporation of the need to meet strife with strife, and finally by our suspicion that precisely this loss of function leaves the destructive force in Othello free to destroy the love which should control it.... With Iago's help, of course. Iago ... weaves the net that entraps them all, his magical web constructed from his victim's imagination. (p. 143)

It is tempting to overemphasize the importance of Othello's credulity as a cause of the tragic action. By doing so we can conceal from ourselves the harsher implications about human nature in general that the play contains, taking refuge from them behind an apparently special weakness of the tragic hero. To do so we must, of course, make the assumption, tacit or not, that "we" would not be taken in by Iago, thereby overestimating our own acuity and underestimating Iago's brilliance. That Othello should believe Iago's lies about his wife is a venial sin. That he should kill her is a mortal one. He believes the lies because they are brilliantly told and he kills his wife because he believes the lies. Neither necessary cause is a sufficient one, but the credulity that is the necessary accompaniment to the hero's trust in the villain is far more forgivable than the hatred which converts his mistaken belief into

murderous action. The villain, in other words, is largely responsible for the destruction of Othello's love, but Othello is the source of the fatal hatred which replaces that love. (pp. 143-44)

[In] the Pelagian world of *Othello,* the emergence of good must depend entirely upon man's unaided ability to sustain the good of which he may be momentarily capable. Othello, though a more than ordinarily good man, does not have a rational will sufficiently strong to keep his hatred in check without the help of love. Once he loses faith in the existence of Desdemona's love for him, the scales of his life swing wildly out of balance and hatred becomes the inevitable alternative to lost love: "Shee's gone. I am abus'd, and my releefe / Must be to loath her" [III. iii. 267-68].

As a result chaos comes again within the mind of Othello, and its reign is most vividly dramatized in act 4, scene 1 where the fall of the great man is literalized into an epileptic fit. (pp. 144-45)

The chaos which comes again in *Othello* seems to have no other origin than the human minds of the play's characters and the destructive process which is set in motion by minds in interaction finally can proceed to its catastrophe without the necessity for such interaction, kept going by the force of the hatred released within Othello's mind alone. No supernatural power intervenes to prevent the catastrophe, and we are made aware of no divinity that shapes the ends to which the characters come. We suspect that the psychomachies of Faustus, Richard, Hamlet, and Macbeth are sciamachies because we sense that the outcome of each man's battle may have been predetermined by the will of God. What Coleridge called the civil war in Othello's heart is also a battle of shadows, but of a different kind. (p. 146)

[Shakespeare's] other tragic protagonists ... do battle for and against real things. The crowns that Richard and Macbeth fight for are real and so are the obstacles to their attainment. Hamlet's father really was murdered by Claudius. Our sense of the unreality of their mental struggles comes at the end of their plays, accompanying our suspicion that the outcome has been predetermined by God, that their battles were lost and won before they were fought. In *Othello* the deterministic possibility is quite different and more familiar. What conducts Othello to his preposterous conclusion appears not to be divine will, but the blood and baseness of his own nature. That nature is far less base and bloody than Richard's or Macbeth's, less even, I think, than Hamlet's, but the tragedy is no less horrible as a result. *Richard III, Hamlet,* and *Macbeth* are tragic both in spite of and because of our sense that the events of these plays are providentially directed. *Othello* is tragic in spite of and because of our sense that the events are the result of the working of the free nature of the protagonist. In spite of the nobility of that free nature, the horrors occur; because of the freedom of that nature, human nature, even when noble, is revealed as cruel and unjust, the source of tragic horror. In the providential tragedies we may retain our piety in the face of God's apparent cruelty and injustice, by telling ourselves that the appearance conceals a justice and beneficence which we cannot see by the lights of nature and grace because we do not share in divine omniscience. If we wish to retain an optimistic, Pelagian, Neoplatonic humanism in the face of Othello's apparent cruelty and injustice, we can tell ourselves that the appearance is similarly only appearance. Othello, we can tell ourselves, is not "really" cruel and unjust. He only seems so because he is deceived. But in so excusing Othello, we deceive ourselves.

Act V. Scene ii. Othello and Desdemona. By H. Hofmann. The Department of Rare Books and Special Collections, The University of Michigan Library.

The sciamachy that Othello fights and loses is not just a battle with the shadows brought into being by Iago's lies. It is a struggle between the component parts of Othello's mind and the forces that move him to destruction derive their power from the mind itself, from the "shadowing passion" that emerges out of the unconscious. (pp. 146-47)

> Robert G. Hunter, "'Othello'," in his Shakespeare and the Mystery of God's Judgments, *The University of Georgia Press, 1976, pp. 127-58.*

GAYLE GREENE   (essay date 1979)

[*Greene is the coeditor, with Carol Neely and Carolyn Lenz, of* The Woman's Part: Feminist Criticism of Shakespeare *(1980). In the following excerpt from an essay first published in* Journal of Women's Studies in Literature *in 1979, she argues that Shakespeare's primary purpose in* Othello *is to question the bases or ideals upon which conventional notions of manhood and womanhood are constructed. Maintaining that the drama reveals the playwright's belief that honor and reputation are incomplete foundations of manhood and that chastity is an inadequate basis for a woman's self-definition, Greene identifies the source of the tragedy in Othello and Desdemona's adherence to these traditional conceptions of their genders. She compares the various ways that men in* Othello *misunderstand women, noting that to Iago all* "women are whores," *that Cassio divides women into*

two groups—whores and goddesses—, and that Othello fails to humanize or personalize women, regarding them instead as "types." According to the critic, Othello fails to "see Desdemona as a person" and, although he is clearly "in love with her," he loves the ideal that she represents rather than the woman herself. Further, in an analysis of Othello's language or voice that is reminiscent of Kenneth Burke's essay on the play (see excerpt above, 1951), Greene comments on the Moor's association of Desdemona with words related to exchange, purchase, and possession, and she views these as evidence not only of Othello's conception of his wife as a thing or object, but also of his innate fears that his possession of her cannot be guaranteed or assured. For additional assessments of Othello's poetic voice, see the excerpts by G. Wilson Knight (1930), Derek Traversi (1949), and John Bayley (1960). Further, whereas earlier critics have generally viewed Desdemona as representing ideal femininity, principally because of her submissiveness, selflessness, and solicitude for her husband, Greene regards these very qualities as leading to "her complicity in [the] tragedy." Because she passively accepts the position of compliance and obedience to her husband assigned to her by society, the critic avers, she is unable either to understand the evil that Othello imputes to her or to express any real challenge to his charges. It remains for Emilia, Greene concludes, to express the defiance that the audience waits in vain for Desdemona to utter; and although Shakespeare does not intend us to accept uncritically her view of the world, the critic adds, Iago's wife does indeed provide "an alternative mode of behavior to the destructive passivity of Desdemona." William Hazlitt (1817), Anna Brownell*

Jameson (1833), J. A. Heraud (1865), E. K. Chambers (1908), Allardyce Nicoll (1927), and G. R. Elliott (1937) have also addressed the question of Desdemona's passivity and its effect on the dramatic action of the play.]

For her sweet, silent submission, Desdemona has been praised by generations of critics: "a maiden never bold; / Of spirit . . . still and quiet . . ." [I. iii. 94-5]. Selfless, solicitous of her husband at the expense of herself, obedient to the "fancies" of her "lord": "Be as your fancies teach you / What e'er you be, I am obedient" [III. iii. 88-9], she has struck many as an ideal of femininity. A. C. Bradley [see excerpt above, 1904] praises her "helpless passivity": "She can do nothing whatever. She cannot retaliate even in speech . . . She is helpless because her nature is infinitely sweet and her love absolute." Robert B. Heilman sees in her "the dynamics of the personality under the magic influence of love, the full ripening of outward-turning love which we may call the magical transformation of personality" [see excerpt above, 1956]. What do we do, then, with our outrage, as we suffer through the last half of the play, our attention riveted with horror on Othello's violence, a violence motivated by assumptions that his wife is a "thing" [III. iii. 272] which, "stain'd" or "spotted" [V. i. 36] must be murdered for "Justice[s]" [V. ii. 17] sake? There is no question, of course, that we are meant to condemn him, but it is the basis and extent of our outrage that we must question, testing our "modern" responses against those which can be supported by the play. Shakespeare, we are told, was deeply traditional, a believer in the hierarchical order which was even in his time a thing of the past. Does he see in Desdemona, this woman who goes lyrically to her death, and is, next to Ophelia, the least capable of his women of defending herself, the ideal that so many of his critics have seen?

Just as we look to Othello's character for cause of his vulnerability to Iago, so must we look to Desdemona's character for her vulnerability to Othello. She too is a tragic figure with a flaw analogous to his. Neither is simply a victim; rather, they are manipulable because responsive to and co-operative with their victimizers, a view which, according them some responsibility for their fates, accords them more stature. (pp. 18-19)

Desdemona is [Othello's] counterpart, in love and in tragedy. She is, like him, too noble for the world, and vulnerable because she is virtuous, unable to understand his accusations because incapable of imagining the evil of which she is accused, powerless to challenge him because conditioned to obey, she remains "Truly, an obedient lady" [IV. i. 248]. Her defenselessness is a function of an ideal of womanly behavior that makes her co-operate with him in love and in destruction: as he is "essential man," she is "essential woman" [see excerpt above by G. Wilson Knight, 1930]. They are, as Maud Bodkin calls them, "archetypal fantasy of man and woman" [see excerpt above, 1934], a fantasy that turns to nightmare. Women and relationships are prominent in this play to an unprecedented degree in Shakespeare's tragedies: each of the male characters is shown in relation to a woman, their relationships emphasized by verb forms, "wiv'd" [II. i. 60], "woman'd" [III. iv. 195], "bewhor'd" [IV. ii. 115]. As the play is concerned with a standard of manly behavior, so is it concerned with an ideal of womanly character and conduct, with the question of what women are, what they might be and should be. Such an ideal is suggested by the interplay of the three women characters, and is defined, like the men's, partly in terms of what it is not, partly in terms of language, and related again like the men's, to the capacity for survival. The tragic vulnerability of both male and female protagonists is rooted in ideals and illusions they bring to one another which create their love and destroy it, ideals related to conventional conceptions of man and woman—conceptions which, Shakespeare suggests, are misconceptions. Othello's confusion regarding "honesty", a word that rings through the play with insistent irony, with different meanings for man and for woman, involves more than a personal error: Shakespeare implies a criticism of the ideals themselves, that man's worth is contained in his "honor" and woman's in her "chastity."

Othello is concerned, in action and theme, with men's misunderstanding of women. Throughout the play, we hear men telling us what women are, and what strikes us most about their terms and definitions is their inadequacy. Whether adulating them as goddesses or reviling them as whores, their generalizations tell us more about themselves than about the women they are describing. Iago's slander is simple and all-inclusive, encompassing men as well as women: women are whores, men are knaves. His "alehouse paradoxes," in his exchange with Desdemona as they await Othello's arrival in Cyprus, reduce all to a least common denominator:

> You are pictures out a'doors,
> Bells in your parlors, wild-cats in your kitchens,
> Saints in your injuries, devils being offended . . .
>   [I. ii. 109-11]
>   (pp. 19-20)

Cassio's attitude is slightly more complicated, though equally destructive of the individual, human reality: some women are whores, some are goddesses. His idealization of Desdemona contrasts to Iago's debasement; to him, she is "the riches of the ship" [II. i. 83], to Iago, she is "a land carract" [I. ii. 50], and it is distanced and abstract: "a maid that paragons description," "divine" [II. i. 61-2, 73], "most exquisite," "indeed perfection" [II. iii. 18, 28]. But Cassio reserves his revilement for the "other kind," the woman with whom he is involved: "He, when he hears of her, cannot restrain / From the excess of laughter" [IV. i. 98-9]. Though Bianca shows herself devoted and willing to risk herself for him, it suits him to see her as "caitiff" (and "customer," "monkey," "fitchew" [IV. i. 108, 119, 127, 146]). Cassio, we hear, is "A fellow almost damn'd in a fair wife" [I. i. 21], an enigmatic reference which draws attention to Shakespeare's change in the source: whereas in Cinthio, Cassio was married, Shakespeare shows him in relation to a prostitute, and needing to see her as such.

Cassio divides women into two types, Desdemona and Bianca, but Othello directs his confusions at one woman, his wife. There is no question that Othello is in love with her: "there, where I have garner'd up my heart . . . / The fountain from the which my current runs or else dries up" [IV. ii. 57-60]. But there is a question as to whether he loves her—whether, in human terms, he loves her at all: she is an idea, an ideal, a symbol. Thus even his adulation is curiously egocentric, showing more concern with the feelings she inspires in him— "my soul," "my content"—than with Desdemona. Many of his terms for her are conventional and stereotyped: images like "rose," "balmy breath" [V. ii. 13, 16], and the recurrence of the adjectives "sweet" and "fair" indicate a simplistic and primarily physical response. Shakespeare has elsewhere, in the early Romeo and certain of the sonnets, used such petrarchan terms to indicate immaturity and self-love, a response to one's own projected image rather than to the loved one. Othello's adulation screens out a considerable portion of human reality, and, as Maud Bodkin observes, "If a man is wedded to his fantasy of a woman . . . he grows frantic and blind with passion at the thought of the actual woman . . . as a creature of natural varying impulses.'' Conceiving of Desdemona as one ''type'' it is a short distance to imagining her as the other ''type,'' only a matter of a turn in perspective, which Iago accomplishes, and adulation reverses itself to as extreme a revilement.

Othello's language indicates, as well, certain ambivalences about sexuality. There is suggestion, in images like ''monumental alabaster'' [V. ii. 5] and ''perfect chrysolite'' [V. ii. 145], of what Traversi calls a ''monumental frigidity'' [see excerpt above, 1949]. Othello is never at ease in speaking of sexuality: his terms indicate strain or self-consciousness, a conception of love which is either idealized or reductive, making it more or less than it is—''absolute content,'' or a physical, trifling matter. Certain statements strike a wrong tone: ''The purchase made, the fruits are to ensue / The profit's yet to come 'tween me and you'' [II. iii. 9-10]—and his terms of affection for Desdemona, such as ''honey'' [II. i. 204] and ''sweeting'' [II. iii. 252], are not unlike his derisive term ''chuck'' [IV. ii. 24]. (pp. 21-2)

Implicit in Othello's language is a suspicion of sexuality and the physical being of woman and man, which Iago turns easily to loathing. . . . Iago offers his example of generalized abuse, ''In Venice they do let God see the pranks / They dare not show their husbands'' [III. iii. 202-03]—supplementing his slanders with vivid images of animal copulation: ''Were they as prime as goats, as hot as monkeys . . .'' [III. iii. 403]. Within a few lines, Othello, too, is generalizing

> O curse of marriage!
> That we can call these delicate creatures ours,
> And not their appetites!
>
> [III. iii. 268-70]

and the rank, sexual images have been ''engend'red'' [I. iii. 403] in his language: ''Goats and monkeys!'' [IV. i. 263]. (pp. 22-3)

Othello's response to Iago's insinuations is a righteously vindicated recognition that ''the forked plague'' is ''destiny unshunnable'' [III. iii. 276, 275], a certainty possible only because woman has been suspect from the start. Iago seems so wise to him, ''O, thou art wise, 'tis certain'' [IV. i. 74], because he confirms things Othello has known all along. Othello demands ''satisfaction'', ''Would I were satisfied'' [III. iii. 390], a peculiar word to describe his request for proof, and one which is repeated five times within the next eighteen lines. However, in the confirmation of his deepest fears it is a ''satisfaction'' which takes the place of the consummation which never seems to occur with Desdemona. The language which was frigid in its adoration takes fire from jealousy, and the cold and conventional turns to passionate anguish: ''O ay, as summer flies are in the shambles / That quicken even with blowing'' [IV. ii. 66-7]. Only in the desire to destroy and the assurance of loss does Othello's language attain conviction.

This deep certainty of woman's faithlessness accounts for his obsession with possessing her. Knowing that possession can never be sure, that ''we can call these delicate creatures ours / And not their appetites,'' his passion, in both its loving and destructive aspects, is more involved with Desdemona as possession than as woman, as a ''thing'' to which he has exclusive privileges: ''I had rather be a toad . . . Then keep a corner in the thing I love / For others' uses'' [III. iii. 270, 272-73]. He thus speaks of her in terms of ''exchange'' [I. ii. 25-8], ''purchase'' . . . , something of which he has been ''robb'd'' [III.

iii. 342], which he would ''not have sold'' [V. ii. 146] and though he progresses to an awareness that he ''threw'' [V. ii. 347] her away, a verb indicating more recognition of responsibility, still, he is thinking of her as something that is his to discard. Offended vanity mingles with his motives for murder; he reveals a concern that she has made him appear a ''figure . . . of scorn'' [IV. ii. 54] which follows from his concern with reputation: ''false to me?'' [III. iii. 333], ''Cuckold me!'' ''With mine officer!'' [IV. i. 200, 202].

It is Othello's failure to see Desdemona as a person or to recognize his own uncharted areas that accounts for his easy acceptance of Iago's terms. Men's misconceptions of women are, in Desdemona's words, ''horrible fancies'' [IV. ii. 26], projections of their own worst fears and failings. Man defines woman as ''the other'', in Simone de Beauvoir's term: ''He projects upon her what he desires and what he fears, what he loves and what he hates'' [in *The Second Sex*]. Only once does Othello attempt to ''say what she is'' [IV. i. 187], and though wrenched with ''the pity of it'' [IV. i. 195], he is unable to hold this reality in focus. The final speeches in which he summons the old rhetoric in self-justification and evocation of his heroic past, ''speak of me as I am'' [V. ii. 342], make no mention of the human being he has loved and killed, and are concerned, like so much of what he says, with his tragedy rather than hers. The women, on the other hand, do attempt to adjust their visions of the men and to temper their ideals. Emilia has thought about ''jealous souls'' and their ''cause'' [III. iv. 159, 160], and Desdemona tries to excuse Othello's anger, ''Nay, we must think men are not gods'' [III. iv. 148], and to understand the human being with concerns besides herself:

> Something sure of state . . .
> Hath puddled his clear spirit; and in such cases
> Men's natures wrangle with inferior things
> Though great ones are their object.
>
> [III. iv. 140, 143-45]

But none of the men succeeds; Othello himself only once even tries to adjust his ideas and ''images'' of women to the human reality.

The characters of the three women illuminate aspects of one another, Emilia and Bianca providing potentials of character and behavior available to Desdemona. In this system of contrasts and parallels, an association between Desdemona and Bianca is established by the juxtaposition of the eavesdropping and ''brothel'' scenes, analogous in the cruelty with which men impose ''fancies'' on women. Bianca enters the scene, which Iago has devised, in the midst of the laughter characteristic of Cassio's habitual response to her; in a feeble attempt at self-assertion, she returns the handkerchief she believes to be from another woman, but ends by begging him to accompany her home, an incident which constitutes ''proof'' for Othello of his own wife's adultery. Though the scene is comic in tone, it provides comment on the next scene which is not. As Cassio has called Bianca ''caitiff'' and ''customer'' [IV. i. 108, 119], Othello imposes the same ''fancy'' on Desdemona, reducing the reality of a woman who loves him to ''strumpet'' and ''whore'' [IV. ii. 81, 82, 85, 89], a role and relationship that justifies his abuse. Though least alike in terms of innocence and experience, Bianca and Desdemona are analogous in that to which they are subject and in an ability to return devotion for revilement which is simultaneously virtue and folly.

We watch Desdemona progress, in the course of the play, through a variety of roles traditionally assigned to woman: she is defined and disowned as daughter, then adulated as lover and wife, reviled as whore, and finally deprived of all designations. Her first words define her carefully within the social order, as daughter and wife; in her description of herself as "divided" in "duty" between father and husband she provides an emblem of her situation. The words she uses to describe these relationships, "bound," "duty," "due" [III. i. 181, 182, 184, 186, 189], indicate circumscription, a deeply-engrained obedience for which she is finally literally strangled. (Othello's first plan is to poison her, but he eagerly accepts Iago's suggestion that he strangle her: "The justice of it pleases" [IV. i. 209]). Only in relation to her love for Othello does her language assume the more active qualities of "storm," "violence" [I. iii. 249] and "challenge" [I. iii. 188], but her elopement, though a challenge to the social order, is still a circumscribed form of rebellion which follows the prescribed path from father to husband, a husband whom she nearly always addresses as "my lord," true to the filial relationship determined by their difference in years. And though her love for Othello is touching, bold, wonderful, hers is still that romantic illusion of the merging of identity, "My heart's subdu'd / Even to the quality of my lord" [I. iii. 250-51], and the verb "subdued" is accurate, since, as de Beauvoir notes, it is an ideal that must result in the obliteration of self: if, as Catherine says, "I am Heathcliffe" [in Emily Brontë's *Wuthering Heights*], that leaves only one of them.

Defined by men and in relation to men, woman's identity is precarious, and we see how precarious within this scene when Brabantio dissolves his ties to Desdemona, casting her off as daughter, "Dead . . . to me" [I. iii. 59], "I give thee that . . ." [I. iii. 193]. Having betrayed him, she is no longer his daughter, nor even a person, but a "that." (So, for that matter, is Othello called a "thing" [I. ii. 71], and the de-humanizing terms suggest a similarity between racial and sexual stereotyping which we have come to recognize). Brabantio's warning, "Look to her, Moor, if thou hast eyes to see; / She has deceiv'd her father and may thee" [I. iii. 292-93], suggests similarities between Desdemona's relations with both husband and father, though not those which Brabantio imagines. Othello, too, will dissolve his ties to her, and redefine her, no longer as his wife, but as "that cunning whore of Venice / That married with Othello" [IV. ii. 89-90], a re-definition that strips her of identity and finally of life "My wife? . . . I have no wife" [V. ii. 97].

Though Desdemona's "divided duty" may represent orthodox Elizabethan doctrine, it is her acceptance of these terms and assumptions that leaves her powerless to understand her situation, let alone deal with it. We watch the course of her love for Othello, from simple adoration, to confusion ("What shall I do to win my lord again?" [IV. ii. 149]), through attempts to justify him ("something sure of state . . ."), to justify herself: "You do me wrong" [IV. ii. 81]; "I have not deserv'd this" [IV. i. 241]. We watch her struggle with her sense of outraged worth, subduing her rebellion, remaining solicitous of him at the expense of herself ("Am I the motive for these tears, my lord?" [IV. ii. 43]), siding, finally, with him against herself: "My love doth so approve him, / That even his stubborness, his checks, his frowns . . . have grace and favor in them" [IV. iii. 19-21]; "Let nobody blame him, his scorn I approve" [IV. iii. 52]; and ending, finally, resolutely faithful in her acceptance of blame: "Nobody; I myself . . . / Commend me to my kind lord" [V. ii. 124, 125]. Her defenselessness

is partly a patter of naivety, and partly linguistic: she cannot pronounce the word "whore", "I cannot say 'whore'. / It does abhor me now I speak the word" [IV. ii. 161-62]. As Othello "throws despite and heavy terms upon her" [IV. ii. 116], she can barely understand them, "What doth your speech import?", let alone defend herself against them: "I understand a fury in your words, / But not the words" [IV. ii. 31-3]. For this she has been praised by a critic as astute as Heilman:

> She does not fly off into the loud vehemence of offended self-love [or] rise above a hurt amazement and a mild earnestness of assertion . . . Instead of looking around for someone to blame, she tries to make a case for Othello's incredible conduct, and she rebukes herself for blaming him . . . But she does not . . . subordinate devotion to self-pity and self-justification.

But though this mildness may have appeal in the abstract, to approve it is contrary to our experience of these last scenes, to the tension and frustration created as Desdemona is brought together with her raving husband and is unable to rise above "hurt amazement." What began as the "archetypal fantasy of man and woman" turns to another "complementary mythic fantasy," what [Leslie] Fiedler calls "the male nightmare of unmerited betrayal and the female dream of patient suffering rewarded" [see Additional Bibliography]. Precisely what is required of Desdemona is "self-love" and "self-justification," defiance of the role in which Othello has cast her; we long to hear her ask, inquire, answer, challenge, shout, to find a voice by which she can express her innocence and defend herself, but it is her acceptance of his terms, not "whore," but the premises and assumptions that make her "inferior thing", that renders her helpless and inarticulate. What has been lost in her "divided duty" is duty to herself, and Othello's irony strikes a terrible truth: "And she's obedient, as you say, obedient; / Very obedient" [IV. i. 255-56]. Though, to his question, "What art thou," she can reply, "Your wife, my lord; your true / And loyal wife" [IV. ii. 33-4], she is not able to find a language strong or clear enough to counteract his "fancy," and in fact, manages consistently to say just the wrong thing, pursuing Cassio's suit at the moment when it does her most harm, struggling for life when the desire to live convicts her of guilt: "Kill me tomorrow, let me live tonight!" [V. ii. 80]. We cringe as she finds just the words to infuriate him: "He [Cassio] will not say so" [V. ii. 71]; "Alas, he is betray'd and I undone!" [V. ii. 76]. "Bewhor'd," she is bewildered, "half asleep" [IV. ii. 97], and overcome.

Is this her "wretched fortune" [IV. ii. 128], as she calls it, and as her name implies? In a sense, it is her fate as a woman, quintessential woman, the "jewell" [I. iii. 195] of her father, "pearl" [V. ii. 347] of her husband, treasure, but possession, and her acceptance of her position that renders her incapable of self-defense. That defiance is what is required in her situation, and is an Elizabethan as well as a modern possibility, is indicated by Shakespeare's structuring of the murder scene in such a way that expression is given the rebellion we have longed to hear, and an alternative mode of behavior is provided. Bursting in on the scene, demanding "a word" [V. ii. 90], it is Emilia who finds the voice of protest that makes itself heard: "You told a lie, an odious, damned lie! / Upon my soul, a lie! a wicked lie" [V. ii. 180-81], a voice which is contrast and antidote to the muffled silence of her mistress. From the beginning, Emilia has had this ability to name things clearly, precisely, if at times a bit crassly. Speaking on her own behalf, she gives expression to the human reality which we have heard stereotyped:

> But I do think it is their husbands' faults
> If wives do fall . . .
> Why, we have galls; and though we have some grace,
> Yet have we some revenge. Let husbands know
> Their wives have sense like them: they see, and smell,
> And have their palates both for sweet and sour,
> As husbands have . . . And have we not affections,
> Desires for sport, and frailty, as men have?
> Then let them use us well; else let them know
> The ills we do, their ills instruct us so.
>
> [IV. iii. 86-7, 92-6, 100-03]

A simple truth, yet beyond any of the men in the play: that woman is neither goddess nor whore, but a being with "frailty," desire, and point of view, combined of both "grace" and "gall." Not that Emilia's is a perspective to which we wholly ascribe, entrenched as it is in a material reality, but her vision complements Desdemona's, and represents some of the body and toughness that Desdemona lacks: "The world's a huge thing . . . and the wrong is but a wrong i' th' world; and having the world for your labor, 'tis a wrong in your own world, and you might quickly make it right" [IV. iii. 69, 80-2]. Such relativism has its strengths: an acknowledgement, like irony, of other points of view, and it is irony of which Desdemona and Othello are tragically incapable; but that relativism plays no part in Emilia's actions is seen in her unhesitating sacrifice of her life. If we try to account for her character, we may speculate that this clarity is partly a matter of social class: never adulated, no one's "jewel," she has remained clear-eyed and without illusions, although she is, like Desdemona, too tolerant of her husband's "fantasy" [III. iii. 299]. Thus it is she who finds the voice Desdemona cannot, which despells the nightmarish unreality: "I am bound to speak" [V. ii. 184], "Let me have leave to speak" [V. ii. 195], "Let heaven and men and devils let them all / All cry shame against me, yet I'll speak" [V. ii. 221-22]. And her simple refusal expresses the defiance we have long wished to hear: "'Tis proper I obey him; but not now. / Perchance, Iago, I will ne'er go home" [V. ii. 196-97]. (pp. 23-8)

Bianca provides a reflection of what Desdemona is, Emilia a potential of what she might be: an autonomous being capable of speaking from her own center of self and finding a language which is strong and clear because it does come from that center. Desdemona needs more of the one, less of the other. As Desdemona's defenselessness is explicable in terms of a "feminine" docility, so too are Othello's limitations traceable to the "manly" ideal of character and conduct involved in his "occupation." As with Lear, Hamlet, and Antony, the experience of betrayal makes the tragic protagonist doubt his very identity, but unlike the others, Othello assumes that selfhood can be recovered by an act of physical violence and destruction of the loved one. Though we are tempted to cry with Emilia, "What should such a fool / Do with so good a wife?" [V. ii. 233-34], and though his years and her youth make him the more reprehensible, we must realize that Othello and Desdemona co-operate in their destruction: cut off in tragic incomprehension from one another, they speak two different languages, and she is no more capable of entering into his experience than he is into hers. But, by not defying him, Desdemona destroys both of them. She may have an inkling of her complicity in their tragedy, when, about to die, she confesses her sins as "loves I bear you" [V. ii. 40].

Othello's investment of his "manhood" in his "honesty," in an ideal of honor as reputation that requires Desdemona's death, and in his confusion of her character with her "chastity," points to an error, not only of fact, but one involved in the conceptions themselves, not only of Othello, but of society as a whole. Though to the end, Othello is still thinking in such terms, justifying himself as "an honorable murderer" who "did all in honor" [V. ii. 294, 295], "But why should honor out-live honesty?" [V. ii. 245], Shakespeare is suggesting that woman's virtue need be defined as a more active and positive quality than chastity, the "preservation of this vessel for my lord" [IV. ii. 83], and that the "honor" for which Othello so readily kills be made of sterner stuff than "the bubble reputation" [As You Like It, II. vii. 152]. The ideal of manly and womanly behavior that the play finally affirms is something closer to a combination of masculine and feminine than that recognized or represented by Desdemona or Othello: it is the ideal, familiar elsewhere in Shakespeare, that the best of women has something of man in her, and the best of men something of woman.

This is not to imply that the complexities of this tragedy are reducible to a tract on the subject of woman. The sense we are left with is one of woe and wonder, the paradox that we kill what we most love, and that what is grand about these characters, their faith and absolute commitment, is also their doom. But while recognizing and responding to what is splendid in their love, we can question what fatal quality condemns it to death, and whether it need be a *liebestod* [love-death], allied so inevitably to destruction. Perhaps we must finally accept this connection of love and death as an inexorable condition of our lives, man's revulsion from woman accountable . . . in Freudian terms of man's earliest desire for his mother. But so much of what Freud considered "inexorable" has been traced, in the past fifty years, to social conditions, and "essentially" male and female characteristics may not be "essential," but socially determined. It is equally possible to see man's ambivalence toward woman in terms of his suspicion that he has wronged her: binding her to a double standard in which she has not been consulted, to which she has not consented, he expects her revenge to take the form of sexual betrayal. The social dimension in this play is prominent by virtue of Othello's blackness and the carefully delineated backgrounds, classes, and "occupations" of each of the characters. This man of action, who has never looked within, and his obedient lady are fatally interlocked in the ancient rite of love and death. Though Desdemona comes closer than he does to recognizing the human being and adjusting her ideal accordingly, theirs is not a marriage of true minds, not based on a recognition of persons, and though touching and wondrous, is fatally flawed; what Heilman calls "the magical transformation of love" destroys them both. Shakespeare is suggesting, in his radical critique of some of society's most cherished notions, that accepted ideals of manly and womanly behavior are distortive and destructive of the human reality, and that relations be based on saner and more certain ground than "this that you call love" [I. iii. 331-32]. (pp. 29-30)

> *Gayle Greene, "'This That You Call Love': Sexual and Social Tragedy in 'Othello'," in* Journal of Women's Studies in Literature, *Vol. 1, No. 1, Winter, 1979, pp. 16-32.*

JANE ADAMSON   (essay date 1980)

[*In an unexcerpted portion of her* "Othello" *as Tragedy: Some Problems of Judgment and Feeling (1980), Adamson declares that the focus of her book is "the relationship between . . . the characters' treacherous habits of thought and feeling and judgment, and . . . our own in response to them," and she contends that the significance of* Othello *is its power to make us recognize the similarity between the characters' propensities and fallibilities and our own. In the excerpt below, she argues that T. S. Eliot's description of Othello's final speech as evasive and self-dramatizing is insightful (see excerpt above, 1927), but she denies that the Moor is an egotist or a moral coward. Adamson also claims that A. C. Bradley's emphasis on Othello's nobility fails to acknowledge his culpability and even extenuates his murder of Desdemona (see excerpt above, 1904) and that F. R. Leavis's insistence on Othello's guilt leads him to ignore the Moor's obvious "pain and suffering" and to judge him too harshly (see excerpt above, 1937). The critic maintains instead that Shakespeare has not intended the audience to censure or blame Othello, but to regard his tendency to make quick judgments and to seek simplistic solutions as an all-too-human susceptibility shared by each of us. She argues that Othello's self-dramatizing represents an attempt to avoid reality, noting that his "mastery of speech" in the early portion of the play enables him to restructure external impressions by "projecting images of himself" that are received by the other characters as portraits of the essential Moor. But, Adamson contends, from Act III, Scene iii onwards, reality progressively masters him and his powers of speech deteriorate until, by the end of the play, all he has to defend himself against the truth is his "instinctive weapon of self-dramatization," which has by now become withered and impotent. She avers that Othello's concluding speech must be read, not just for its evident elements of self-pity and denials of reality, but also as a harrowing acknowledgment that his attempt to avoid a clear and accurate perception of himself and his conduct has failed inexorably. What he comes to apprehend and accept, the critic asserts, is the play's consistent portrayal of love's tragic dilemma: that "to love absolutely" is to "risk total, irreparable loss" and that the possibility of being wounded by one's lover is "a necessary condition of loving." For additional commentary on the self-dramatizing or self-deluding aspects of Othello's nature, see the excerpts by Allardyce Nicoll (1927), G. R. Elliott (1937), Brents Stirling (1956), and Carol McGinnis Kay (1983), as well as the essays by Barbara Everett and Helen Gardner cited in the Additional Bibliography. Shakespeare's portrayal of the nature of love in* Othello *has also been discussed by Hermann Ulrici (1839), Derek Traversi (1949), Kenneth Burke (1951), Winifred M. T. Nowottny (1952), Robert B. Heilman (1956), John Bayley (1960), Susan Snyder (1972), and Jared R. Curtis (1973).]*

The crucial test of any view of *Othello* is its last scene, the culmination and climax of the whole drama. We have had to watch the hero vilify and strike his wife; we now have to watch while he kills her for a 'sin' we know she never committed, and then watch while he kills himself as well. At this point, the central critical questions become acute. What does the play eventually bring us to think and feel about Othello? How far, here and all through, are we brought to consider him as the victim, and how far the agent, of his fate? What bearing does our sense of these issues have on our estimate of the nature, scope and quality of the play as a whole? In relation to Shakespeare's other tragedies is *Othello* really a 'comparatively simple', 'rather limited' play, as we have so often been told?

On the first of these questions—what we are to make of Othello's behaviour, especially during the second half of the play—most people seem to have very fixed views. Generally speaking, they tend to take one of two positions about the play: to some, Shakespeare's main impulse is evidently to present the case *for* his hero; to others, it is evidently to present the case against him. On the one side, it is Othello's vulnerability that seems most important. Arguing on much the same lines as Coleridge and Bradley [see excerpts above, 1813 and 1904],

for example, many critics see Othello's conduct as the natural, and therefore condonable reaction of such a man to extreme pressure; more than anything else, they claim, the play evokes our pity for him as the noble, 'not easily jealous' victim of Iago's hellish cunning. On the other side, it is Othello's culpability that seems most important. Arguing on much the same lines as Leavis [see excerpt above, 1937], for example, many see Othello as 'noble' in certain limited ways; but more than anything else, they claim, the play judges him (and evokes our judgment of him) as an egotist made brutal by a jealousy that is largely self-generated, a man guilty not only of maltreating and killing his innocent wife, but of not even having the grace, courage or humility to accept his guilt. (pp. 11-12)

The strength of the first view—what we might call the Bradleyan or, better, the 'pro-Othello', view—is fairly obvious; so too is its weakness, at least since Leavis's celebrated (some would say notorious) attack on the sentimentality of Bradley's account of the play. If we can dispense with Leavis's scathing vehemence, we may notice that Bradley does at least insist on the play's power to make us feel *for* Othello in some way. On the other hand, his particular account of those feelings does seem soggy and crude, and is certainly distorted and undermined by his flat refusal, or incapacity, to acknowledge Othello's guilt. After extolling the hero at some length, Bradley arrives at the awkward fact that Othello's record blackens somewhat half-way through III, iii. In response to this, however, Bradley calmly remarks, 'but the play is a tragedy, and from this point we may abandon the ungrateful and undramatic task of awarding praise and blame'. It is a neat tactical policy-revision, which has the consoling effect of allowing him to extenuate Othello's abominable behaviour by blaming it all on the villainous Iago, whose skill he covertly praises as well. Like all of Othello's partisans Bradley cannot bring himself to recognize that, psychologically and physically, Othello—and Othello alone—kills Desdemona. As Leavis acidly pointed out, Bradley clings so blindly to the notion that his hero is merely a victim, that his account of the play's final scene actually argues that Othello is now his old noble self again (now that 'chaos has come and gone') and that 'there is almost nothing here to diminish the admiration and love which heighten pity'. Like all such extenuations of Othello—and they are legion—this is open to the crushing objection that it quite overlooks (or reduces to 'almost nothing') our feelings for *Desdemona* at this point. In what sense can the play be called a 'great tragedy' if it urges us simply to admire and pity a man as he disposes of his innocent wife? Indeed, what is true here is true of all such 'noble Othello' views of the play, that they are inadequate precisely to the extent that they overlook or understate the shocking fact that Othello commits murder.

The problem with the second main view of the play—what we might call the Leavisian or 'anti-Othello' one—is roughly the reverse. Its strength lies in the obvious reasons the play gives us to judge Othello as culpable. Its weakness, however, is that it indulges in judgment and blame of Othello at the cost of any sympathetic feeling for him at all. In this, Leavis's account of the play, which is the classic statement of the anti-Othello view, demonstrates the point most clearly. So determined is Leavis to reject Bradley's sentimentality and to insist that Othello himself, not Iago, is the primary agent of his fate, that he fails even to consider how far Othello, like any human being, is open to pain and suffering. Like all anti-Othello critics, he either ignores such vulnerability or treats it simply as moral weakness based on egotism, to be merely despised. Yet in what sense is the play a tragedy if it leaves us so detached from its hero as scarcely to care when he kills himself—or, rather, scarcely to recognize that he does actually kill himself? (pp. 12-14)

Is the play a tragedy, or not? Is Othello a tragic hero or isn't he? The contradiction between the two statements points directly to the chief critical problem with the play; is it possible fully to acknowledge Othello's culpability and his habit of evading it in self-dramatizing rhetoric, and yet at the same time to feel intensely for and with him, without sentimentalizing? To put the issue quite simply, I think we can call the play a tragedy in the fullest sense only if—and only to the extent that—it makes us face squarely the implications of Othello's habitually self-bolstering mode of speech, while simultaneously making us assent to such acute feelings about the ending as, for example, Dr Johnson experienced:

> I am glad that I have ended my revisal of this dreadful scene. It is not to be endured [see excerpt above, 1765].
>
> (pp. 17-18)

[But we] do 'endure' the play's ending, terrible though we may feel it to be. Just *how* we can endure it without evading the play's impact (and the same is equally true of Desdemona's death) largely depends on how far—if at all—we have been brought to recognize their deaths as both truly terrible and yet truly inevitable within the play's created world, rather than just a Shakespearean whim to make the end pathetic. But our sense of that of course depends on how we have responded to everything else in the play that bears on, conditions or effects the tragedy of love that is the fate of its central figures.

Like some kind of statutory trade-mark on all anti-sentimentalist accounts of *Othello*, T. S. Eliot's remarks about the play's ending [see excerpt above, 1927] have been repeated so often that it is hard now to view them with a fresh eye. This is a pity, because what he said can help us understand why judgments and feelings collide so terribly in the final scene. (pp. 24-5)

Eliot's very ability to diagnose Othello's state [before his suicide] is itself the most significant difference between him as 'spectator' and the 'spectators' left on stage—Lodovico, Cassio and the others. Unlike them (and unlike Bradley) Eliot is not 'taken in' by Othello's rhetoric: he remains sufficiently detached to see that rhetoric as an attempt on Othello's part, not to countenance painful truths, but to shield himself from them.

However, to agree with Eliot (as . . . I think we must) about the evasive impulse of Othello's speech at this point is not necessarily to agree with Leavis and others that Eliot's perception 'gives us the cue' for an anti-Othello case. It is rather surprising that Eliot's account gives scarcely any sense of the sheer terribleness of the play's ending, and that his remarks about Othello's state sound so coolly analytic. For it was Eliot who in an earlier essay ["Tradition and the Individual Talent" (1917)], speaking about poetic impersonality, was moved to add that 'only those who have personality and emotions know what it means to want to escape from these things'. Had he only followed his own hint here Eliot might have seen that, for Othello in the final scene, that 'want' has become a sheer necessity. In so far as his remarks about Othello's valediction prompt us to see this they are illuminating; but in so far as his commentary implicitly gives us a cue merely to censure Othello, it is to that extent misleading. Shakespeare does not reveal Othello's evasiveness to us in order to condemn it as egotism or moral cowardice. The ending makes far deeper demands on

our imaginative and moral understanding than that. For at the very same time as we realize that Othello is indeed, as Eliot claimed, trying to cheer himself up, 'endeavouring to escape reality', we realize too the terrible futility of the endeavour. If he succeeds at all, the success is inevitably partial and evanescent. His attempt is to tidy things up, to salvage some dignity from the wreckage of his life; but at the end of the speech, far from having achieved any real self-comfort, he remains so desperate that he kills himself. So we are pushed towards a more basic question, which has been there for us to ponder ever since the third act: why, exactly does Othello so urgently *need* to try to cheer himself up? And the most basic kind of answer the play gives us is (to put it in Eliot's own words in 'Burnt Norton') that

> human kind
> Cannot bear very much reality.
> Time past and time future
> What might have been and what has been
> Point to one end, which is always present.

In short, the last scene makes us face squarely the question of what 'reality' it is that Othello now can bear so little that he kills himself rather than have to face or endure it a moment more. For us, to respond fully to the drama is to treat as 'real' both Othello's rhetoric *and* the act of suicide to which it finally brings him and which it fails to forestall. We have to acknowledge not only that his urgent 'primary motive' is 'to take in himself' but also that he fails. The attempt and the failure are equally crucial and equally significant; and they surely forbid us the simple comforts of extolling his 'nobility' or denouncing his 'escapism' and of assuming that such praise or censure is the upshot of the play's judgment too. (pp. 25-8)

In the early acts . . . , Othello's mastery of speech was the manifest sign, and sometimes the very means, of his mastery in and over his world. It not only sounded authoritative and conscious of its power, but was actually forceful enough to disarm Brabantio and others:

> Keep up your bright swords, for the dew will rust them.
> Good signor, you shall more command with years
> Than with your weapons.
>
> [I. ii. 59-61]

The commanding eloquence of that was no mere trick of language, but sprang from and bespoke the real authority of Othello's self. As so often in the first half of the play, his speech realized his earned warrant to think of himself as a man whose proven 'worth' and 'valour' had won him the right, reflected and assumed in his language, to be respected, admired and obeyed. More than that, however, . . . his gift of speech had also constantly empowered him—either in fact or in his own 'fancy'—to master reality, including that of his inner experience, by restructuring it, re-creating it, by projecting images of it (or of himself) which were figured, and therefore disposable, in accordance with obscure pressures and needs in himself. Early on—as in his reported wooing-speeches—he deployed language to represent and so to confirm the reality both of himself and his world by touching up, but not fundamentally altering, the truth of both. But ever since III, iii, his power to 'master' and control experience in this way has become ever more distorting and ever more urgently necessary to him as reality has threatened increasingly to master *him*. By V, ii, after the deaths of Desdemona and Emilia, he is—and seems half-aware that he is—almost 'naked', almost helpless now to hold it at bay. Having been 'disarmed' in various ways by Montano's action, by Emilia's words, and worst of all by Desdemona's love and charity, he can use only the most tried and trusted weapon, the blade of speech, the 'ice-brook's temper' [V. ii. 253], to temper and disarm reality now.

Yet for that instinctive weapon of self-dramatization to work at all, he needs an audience, consolation, not isolation. Clearly he dreads to be alone, dreads the moment when solitude should deliver him to the tyranny of self-reflection.

OTHELLO	I have another weapon in this chamber....
	[*To Gratiano*] Uncle, I must come forth.
GRATIANO	[*within*] If thou attempt it, it will cost thee dear;
	Thou hast no weapon, and perforce must suffer.
OTHELLO	Look in upon me then, and speak with me,
	Or naked as I am I will assault thee.

> [V. ii. 252, 254-58]

Gratiano's words are far truer and far more ironic than he can possibly know. Despite Othello's secret 'weapon', he is in fact psychically almost stripped bare, and whatever he attempts must necessarily cost him dear; whatever verbally self-protective trappings he tries to wear, he 'perforce must suffer', just because in the end he 'must come forth', naked to his own gaze as well as to that of the world. The heated urgency of his voice makes his command and his threat sound more like a desperate plea—'Uncle, I must come forth'—and it is this pleading note which most sharply makes us realize the distance he has travelled from the cool composure of his remark in Act I: 'I must be found. / My parts, my title, and my perfect soul / Shall manifest me rightly'' [I. ii. 30-2]. Here in the final scene, his need to 'come forth' and 'be found' has to overcome his equally urgent need to be weaponed, to fortify himself with eloquent self-images which, if only for a time, can 'manifest' him falsely—*prevent* his real self from being 'found'. (pp. 284-86)

[Othello's] sole remaining 'weapon' is his instinct for 'how to tell my story'—his capacity to project a tolerable image of his self with such eloquence as might seduce his hearers, including himself, into believing it. But if this power to gloss over his real state should be denied him by denying him an audience, or if it should break down, it will leave him with nothing with which he could go on living. Dramatically, therefore, it is both unsurprising and perfectly right that his next speech, the famous one beginning 'Behold, I have a weapon' [V. ii. 259], should be at once so eloquent and so desperately flailing in its rhetoric, its abrupt breaks and about-turns. With terrible clarity, it demonstrates the unwitting truth of the Duke's remark to Brabantio upon *his* crisis and imminent collapse in the play's first act:

> ... take up this mangled matter at the best:
> Men do their broken weapons rather use
> Than their bare hands.

> [I. iii. 173-75]

As if to shore himself up against the ruin of his last fragments of consolation, Othello in this speech runs the whole gamut of his characteristic stratagems to fend off reality. One by one he attempts every defensive posture or habit we have witnessed in the play, as if the sheer multiplicity of such guises might somehow compensate for the increasingly evident threadbareness of each. This speech, 'Behold I have a weapon . . .',

certainly exhibits what Leavis called Othello's 'rhetorical trick of self-boosting'.

Nevertheless, we cannot simply label and dismiss it any more than we [can] do so with everyone else's 'self-boostings'. Once we notice how transparent Othello's self-dramatizations are, we also recognize how crucially necessary they are to him: without them, he could not survive. Hence, they prompt us to a much more complex and disturbing judgment than Leavis's frowningly superior comment that Othello exhibits 'an attitude *towards* the emotion expressed—an attitude of a kind we are familiar with in the analysis of sentimentality'. The 'sentimentality' is Othello's own, not Shakespeare's, and what Shakespeare imaginatively grasps and dramatizes and makes us respond to are the vital reasons for, and the vital reality of, this man visibly straining *not* to recognize how idealizing and sentimental—indeed, how false—his extenuating self-images are. What we are dramatically shown is more than Othello's exhibition of 'an attitude towards the emotion expressed'. We are shown a desperate action: specifically, Othello's effort to dull his emotions, even to replace them with 'attitudes', since he can neither express nor bear nor transform them in any other way. As in Acts III and IV, his mind projects and focuses on an 'attitude towards feelings' *instead* of those feelings which would prove insupportable. If this is a form of 'bovarysme', as Eliot claimed, it is a form so acute and so desperate that attaching moralistic labels seems only to betray a blindness or evasiveness in our own feelings about the tragedy.

The same seems to me true of the terms Eliot applied to the end of the play: 'Humility is the most difficult of all virtues to achieve; nothing dies harder than the desire to think well of oneself.' Phrases like 'sentimentality', 'humility', 'virtue', 'desire to think well of oneself' and so on, seem both inadequate and misleading; for what the ending reveals is rather that nothing dies harder than the need not to think so ill of oneself that the self actually disintegrates, being unable any longer to delude itself that it has not been totally and irredeemably a 'fool, fool, fool' [V. ii. 323]. (pp. 287-89)

The opening of [Othello's] famous valedictory speech is clipped, direct, controlled—at least on the surface:

> Soft you; a word or two before you go.
> I have done the state some service and they know't:
> No more of that.

> [V. ii. 338-40]

The tone of quiet and courteous authority may recall that of his speeches in the opening acts, but now it barely holds his self together. He is straining to reconstruct—and momentarily perhaps forgive—the self he is bound to obliterate. Almost inevitably, therefore, his speech becomes more rhetorical, as he seeks from others the exculpation his own heart denies. Small self-extentuations—'these unlucky deeds' [V. ii. 341]—give way to larger more pitiably self-pitying ones. For a last time, 'fancy' and 'conscience' (to use Johnson's phrases) come to 'act interchangeably' upon him, and they so often 'shift their places' that 'the illusions of one are not distinguished from the dictates of the other'. The speech reveals as sharply as any so far how compulsively Othello's fancy takes wing against reality whenever he is faced with the pressure and dread of his guilt. Thus, the humbly polite request—'I pray you in your letters . . . / Speak of me as I am: nothing extenuate, / Nor set down aught in malice' [V. ii. 340, 342-43]—rapidly transforms itself into fully fledged, overt command. Othello attempts to *dictate* the story about himself that 'must' be published abroad:

'Then you must speak / Of one that loved not wisely, but too well' [V. ii. 343-44]. The size of that understatement—'not wisely'—is matched only by the size of his need to speak it and believe it. Fancy is driven to supply the self-image, 'one that loved . . . too well', by a conscience dictating the as yet unutterable truth, 'too much, too desperately, and too little'. As Coleridge so well put it, 'Othello wishes to excuse himself on the score of ignorance, and yet not to excuse himself—to excuse himself by accusing.' The great struggle of feeling in him is audible in the resonance of this public rhetoric stretched tight over the aching, unmed'cinable 'hollow hell' within. He creates, for the last time, a 'shadow' of himself—a vividly projected semblance of what he wishes he had been, is, and will be thought to have been. (pp. 293-94)

Throughout Acts IV and V he has struggled to kill in himself the very capacity to feel; he has sought to 'whistle off' Desdemona, to sever his very 'heart-strings' and turn his heart into unliving, invulnerable stone. From the first moment that some need, some lack of faith in himself, turned to lack of faith in Desdemona's faith to him, and dread created the object it needed—'she's gone, I am abused' [III. iii. 267]—he has sought 'remedy' to kill his suffering; yet *we* have never been able to doubt that the search has been doomed to fail, and to bring him ultimately face to face with the mortal guilt he has incurred in the course of it. For us, his act of stabbing himself is the inevitable completion of the psychic self-murder he had attempted in murdering Desdemona. Killing her could not stifle or still the insufferable motions of his own heart. Except by literally stabbing his heart, there is literally 'no way but this' [V. ii. 358] to endure the pressure of his feelings, to break free of what has bound him to Iago, and to acknowledge his inseverable bond with Desdemona which—in his demented attempts to sever it—has driven him to murder and brought him to the point of suicide.

At the end, with the extraordinary tact and integrity that are the signs of his greatest art, Shakespeare realizes and leaves open several ways for us to comprehend Othello's act of suicide. We can see it as an outward action that demonstrates 'in complement extern' the 'native act and figure' [I. i. 63, 62] of Othello's heart—his heart kills itself. We can see his act, that is, as representing a self-indictment so total that it actually *is* the act of self-annihilation. Alternatively, yet no less dreadfully, it can be seen as his last desperate effort *not* to have to face a guilt so total that his mind would shatter in the recognition of it. Indeed, the play has pressed us to enter into Othello's inner experience so far that we can see his final action as both these at once. But we can see too that, beyond these, his ultimate act is also paradoxically a recognition of his own ineradicable humanity, an acknowledgment that he can never finally gainsay the 'dictates' of his heart. His self-murder implies his final acknowledgment of what he has sometimes fleetingly recognized as the absolute ground of his emotional and moral life, but which another current of his being has always striven to master and deny: his absolute need of Desdemona's unalterable love—the need, always impossible of fulfilment in the flux of human life, to rest forever secure in her total love of him and her entire acceptance of his love. It is as if, at last, in this single act, he at once *acknowledges, accepts* and *cancels* that need and that impossibility forever. As her love for him gave him the power to hurt her past all surgery, so his love for her—with all her consequent power to reject and deny it—has all along empowered her to make him feel his capacity to *be* hurt past all surgery: and that necessary condition of loving is simultaneously confirmed and annulled by his suicide. This

is why, in anticipation of the act, his very last words, which arise from and attest his dependence, are for the first time free of fear and all self-protective rhetoric. At last he can speak to her as 'thee', in a voice that is utterly simple, direct, and naked in its love:

> I kissed thee, ere I killed thee: no way but this,
> Killing myself, to die upon a kiss.
>
> [V. ii. 358-59]

Just because they circumscribe, no articulated words could adequately sum up everything the end of the play brings us to think and feel. For all its inevitable bathos, Gratiano's ejaculation when Othello stabs himself is strictly true:

> All that's spoke is marred . . .
>
> [V. ii. 357]

But the closing lines of the play, after Othello's death, bring us partially to realize something further as well:

> LODOVICO   O, Spartan dog,
> More fell than anguish, hunger, or the sea,
> Look on the tragic loading of this bed:
> This is thy work. The object poisons sight:
> Let it be hid.
>
> [V. ii. 361-65]

Because we share a common bond of humanity with men like Cassio and Lodovico we too find it impossible to contemplate steadily 'the tragic loading' of the play's end. Our natural impulse, too, is to shield ourselves from its full recognition, to hide it from our sight. No doubt this would be so even if we knew only what the characters know about the disaster; but of course the play has brought us to know and realize far more than any of them can. And in the face of what we find hardest to contemplate steadily and whole, we too—more than any of the people left alive in the play—inevitably seek precisely the sort of 'relief' from our feelings that Othello had so disastrously sought for his: we instinctively try to divert our attention from 'what's past help' [*The Winter's Tale*, III. ii. 222], by imagining punitive reprisals. Trying to compensate where no real compensation is possible, we embrace the comforting idea of blaming Iago, 'enforcing torture' on him, needing to let our feelings erupt in 'the censure of this hellish villain' [V. ii. 368].

The urge to take control of the situation, to punish, to justify oneself and to mete out 'justice' on others, is partly what caused the tragedy of course; equally, the fear of negation, real loss and utter chaos was what aggravated that need in both Iago and Othello—the need not to have to suffer and be patient, not to have to 'be circumstanced', the need to find some or any 'cure' for what otherwise seemed insupportable. In Othello himself, ever since Act III, these needs have been all-consuming, insatiable. He has lurched from all to nothing, from a sense of Desdemona as an angel to the conviction that she must be a devil. The poles of his mind, like Hamlet's, were always heaven and hell; and amidst the violent storm of his feelings his capacity even to 'distinguish' them was 'quench'd', in the very moment when his only chance of 'bearing it out' lay in recognizing and accepting the possibility of some 'midway 'twixt these extremes' [*Antony and Cleopatra*, III. iv. 19-20].

Because we have been shown and brought to feel the force of the whole story, the whole process by which Othello founders on the 'guttered rocks and congregated sands' [II. i. 69] of his own latent fears, moral panic and self-mistrust, we cannot at the end of the play find it sufficient to our fullest response to say what Lodovico (who knows only half the story) says to Iago: 'this is thy work'. For one thing, we have been shown that, as always in real tragedies (in literature as in life), the sources of this tragedy also lay in Othello and Desdemona's extraordinary positive capacities, their capacities to love absolutely and so risk total, irreparable loss, as much as they lay in their ordinary human shortcomings and susceptibilities. For another thing, we have seen that, despite our wish to think otherwise, it was not Iago who brought Othello to commit murder and suicide: it was Othello's own need for moral and emotional finality, moral and emotional certainty. So little could he stand any doubt, any moral query, that he presumed every 'if' meant 'must' and snatched at it before it could be given any 'overt test' at all. The working of that insecurity in him aborted every attempt to deny or leave in abeyance for a single moment his need to know for sure where he stood and who he was in relation to the woman who was his very source of life. For us, it is impossible not to realize what the play has shown in such dreadful detail: the pain and misery that can attend on trying to keep one's heart open to love and so open to being negated. . . . (pp. 296-99)

Because we have seen the whole story from outside as well as from within, we understand how and why Othello's frantic lust for assurance has proved not less but infinitely more devastating than his self-wrung struggles to live in suspense, to try to distinguish what really is from what he darkly fears. Thus, at the heart of the play, and centred in its full realization of both Desdemona's and Othello's anguish, is Shakespeare's insight into the dire necessity for, and the often impossible difficulty of sustaining, a life open to doubt and uncertainty and therefore always at risk.

As usual, what applies to the play's characters applies equally to us. Much of the power of *Othello* as a tragedy, I believe, is to make us acutely aware of our *own* needs for emotional and moral certainty, simplicity and finality—our own impulse . . . to categorize people as fair or foul in accordance with our own hot feelings about them. In revealing the web of self-strung delusions in which its characters trap themselves, the play forbids us (unless we delude ourselves) to judge its characters absolutely in terms of moral 'debit and credit', as angels or devils, virtuous victims or hellish villains. But another part of its power is to make us none the less urgently— in spite of *and* because of all that it has shown us—continue to seek some way of sheltering ourselves from the full reality of its ending. As with the characters, so with us: to recognize that (as Iago put it) 'there's no remedy' [I. i. 35] is not to overcome our need for one. Even, indeed especially, at the end of the play, our rational awareness of the situation and our feelings about it pull in different directions. Inevitably, *we* seek to cheer ourselves up, 'endeavour to escape reality': by thinking, for example, that Othello's suicide somehow morally balances out the murder of Desdemona; or by trying to persuade ourselves that perhaps they are somehow better off dead than alive in a world that contained a Iago; or supposing that 'really' the catastrophe was entirely Iago's work; or by reminding ourselves a little too quickly that what we have witnessed is after all 'only a play'. Of course it is only a play—we are never in any doubt of it. Indeed, the comfort of being always in some sense aware that it is a fiction, together with the strange exhilaration which comes from contemplating the energy of Shakespeare's fully mature art, is exactly what enables us to stand what we see. But while we can bear the dramatic illusion, the full brunt of the tragedy, our urgent 'primary motive', willynilly, is to reach for some moral simplicity to lessen it. And

it seems to me that our very need to try to lessen it is perhaps the clearest 'proof' of Shakespeare's insight here into the problems of reconciling honest judgment with honest feeling. In thinking about Shakespeare's art in *Othello* it is vital not to get trapped into too-ready feelings or too-ready judgments about its 'greatness' or its 'limitations'. Much more to the point is Lodovico's sober advice—'As you shall prove us, praise us' [V. i. 66]: the need and the difficulty of doing that are the subject and the substance of the tragedy. Like all the very greatest tragic works, *Othello* makes us realize with especial force that the fate of loving is precisely the conjunction of that difficulty and that need. (pp. 300-01)

> *Jane Adamson, in her "Othello" as Tragedy: Some Problems of Judgment and Feeling, Cambridge University Press, 1980, 301 p.*

CAROL McGINNIS KAY (essay date 1983)

[*Disputing F. R. Leavis's assessment of Othello as supremely confident (see excerpt above, 1937) and arguing that the Moor possesses only a negligible sense of himself, in that he requires others' perceptions of him to create his self-image, Kay likens Othello to a psychological type known as an "immature ego"— that is, one whose self-concept has been arrested in its development. The critic maintains that Othello is clearly deficient in self-confidence, relying on Desdemona's "grand romantic" view of him and Iago's suggestion that he is, indeed, a rational, "wise judge" as the means of formulating his identity. Further, Othello has no concept of Desdemona's individuality, aside from the selfimage he has projected onto her, Kay argues, and this is evident both in the "cold and inhuman" nature of the objects he associates her with and in his conviction that, if she has been false to him, he has lost his identity as a heroic warrior. G. Wilson Knight (1930), Derek Traversi (1949), Kenneth Burke (1951), and Gayle Greene (1979) have also commented on the frigid or lifeless allusions Othello uses in connection with Desdemona. Whereas T. S. Eliot (1927) has seen Othello's last speech as an attempt to "cheer himself up" after discovering that his sacrifice of Desdemona was actually murder, Kay holds that the Moor's speeches throughout the play reveal this same, childlike need to reassure himself, or be reassured by others, of his nobility and worth. She compares that final speech with the earlier one in which his intended suicide is aborted by the arrival of the gentlemen and Iago (V. ii. 259 ff.), noting that in both he begins by attempting to "gather an audience," proceeds to remind his auditors of his military accomplishments, blames his actions on fate or other people, and focuses attention on himself rather than on Desdemona or his guilt. Finally, Kay remarks that, unlike Shakespeare's other tragic heroes, Othello has only one soliloquy, and she attributes this to the fact that the Moor has merely a "scant private 'self' for him to deal with"; thus, his attempts at self-justification for his actions must be played out before an audience. For an opposing assessment of the significance of Othello's final speeches, see the excerpt by Jane Adamson (1980).*]

Othello is remarkable among Shakespeare's tragic heroes in having two deathbed speeches, one interrupted before he can kill himself and the other concluded by his successful suicide. Curiously, both speeches are carefully orchestrated to onstage persons—*curiously* because Othello goes out of his way in both instances to have an audience for which there is no apparent need. Othello clearly wants witnesses to what is usually an intensely private act. We may well ask, why? What kind of person stages his own suicide as a public event? Answering these questions should inform our understanding of Othello's character and action.

The first deathbed speech occurs just after Montano, Lodovico, and the other Venetians have rushed out in pursuit of Iago, leaving Othello disarmed and locked in his bedchamber with Emilia, who has received a fatal wound from Iago. Before she dies, Emilia reminds Othello that Desdemona had loved him. Instead of responding to her words or her death, Othello is preoccupied with his own business:

> I have another weapon in this chamber,
> It is a sword of Spain, the ice-brook's temper;
> O, here it is. . . .
>
> [V. ii. 252-54]

He calls out to Gratiano, posted outside his door, "uncle, I must come forth" [V. ii. 254].

When Gratiano tells Othello not to try to come out, Othello demands, *"Look in upon me* then, and speak to me, / Or, naked as I am, I will assault thee" ([V. ii. 257-58]; italics added). Gratiano enters, asking, "What is the matter?" [V. ii. 259]. Othello responds with what he assumes will be his final words (his sword is held against his own chest, not that of Gratiano):

> Be not afraid, though you do see me weapon'd:
> Here is my journey's end, here is my butt,
> And very sea-mark of my utmost sail.
>
> [V. ii. 266-68]

His plan, however, is thwarted by the return of the other men, with Iago as prisoner. Othello turns his sword instead against Iago. Disarmed a second time, Othello uncovers yet a third weapon and some sixty lines later delivers what proves to be his actual deathbed speech.

Both the aborted and the genuine deathbed speeches are alike in context, structure, and tone. Each begins with Othello exerting considerable effort to gather an audience. In the first instance he has to threaten Gratiano to get him to come into the room, and in the second he stops the departing crowd with "Soft you, a word or two" [V. ii. 338]. Othello then reminds both audiences of his past military services. In the first speech he says, "I have seen the day, / That with this little arm, and this good sword, / I have made my way through more impediments / Than twenty time your stop" [V. ii. 261-64]. In the second this is condensed into the simple declaration, "I have done the state some service, and they know't" [V. ii. 339]. Further, in both cases Othello blames his current plight on external forces. In the first instance he says, "Who can control his *fate*?" [V. ii. 265]. Later he says, "When you shall these *unlucky* deeds relate, / Speak of them as they are" ([V. ii. 341-42]; italics added). He devotes the remainder of both passages, by far the largest portion, to drawing the witnesses' attention to himself—not to the innocent Desdemona whom he has just killed, nor to his culpability in that murder, but to his own present and future suffering. When, in the first speech, he looks at the body of Desdemona, he sees her only in terms of what her murder does to him:

> . . . when we shall meet at count,
> This look of thine will hurl my soul from heaven,
> And fiends will snatch at it. . . .
>
> [V. ii. 273-75]

Desdemona reflects his future torment as a citizen of Hell, being washed "in steep-down gulfs of liquid fire!" [V. ii. 280]. Similarly, in the second speech Othello asks his onstage audience who will, so he assumes, focus on him in their letters home, to speak of him as a weeping lover who "took by the throat the circumcised dog, / And smote him . . ." [V. ii. 355-56]. After his two major attempts to maneuver others into seeing him as he would like to be seen, Othello finally kills himself while a circle of horrified witnesses stands by. They react with precisely the combination of astonishment and regret that Othello has hoped to elicit from them.

The childlike "Look at me" quality of Othello's two deathbed speeches is characteristic of his language throughout the play. His first speech in the play, an answer to Iago's warning about Brabantio, is a defense of his own virtues: "Let him [Brabantio] do his spite; / My services, which I have done the signiory, / Shall out-tongue his complaints . . ." [I. ii. 17-19]. The peremptory quality of these initial words establishes Othello's "voice" for the duration of the action. Almost every subsequent speech by him rings with "I," "me," and "my." Othello seems to take personally everything said to him, and he constantly calls attention to his own worth, or position, or action. His urging that the senators comply with Desdemona's suit to accompany him to Cyprus is couched more in terms of a denial of his own uxoriousness than in terms of support for her request. The need for approval and reassurance from others that we find embedded in Othello's words does much to undercut the critical view that Othello is proud or vain. My argument is that Othello is anything but F. R. Leavis' heroic man of "great consciousness of worth and confidence of respect" [see excerpt above, 1937]. Othello may be considered ego*centric* in that he directs much of his energy and that of others into defining and bolstering a sense of his own identity, but this is because his sense of self is so weak and so ill-defined as to require constant reinforcement. Beneath his apparent self-confidence is a void of genuine confidence. In fact, Othello exhibits what psychologists call an "immature ego." (pp. 261-63)

Othello is typical of an adult whose psychological birth into separateness and selfhood was somehow aborted and who now tries to know himself, almost to create himself, through others' perceptions of him.

The kind of selfhood that is sought through others' reflections should not be confused with the kind of selfhood attained through what Stephen Greenblatt has called "self-fashioning," a completely artful process of shaping one's own adult identity through deliberate and manipulative efforts. . . . The kind of search for identity that we see in Othello lies far below and antecedent to this conscious level of act and thought; indeed, he himself manifests no awareness of the search itself or of the modes of behavior he slips into in the process of the search. He seems genuinely unaware of the true nature of his relationships with his two primary psychological "mirrors": Desdemona and Iago, the two persons closest to him, and the persons who serve as the "beacons of orientation" he had apparently not received in his fictional infancy.

Othello's use of Desdemona as a psychic mirror is first made evident in his account of their courtship, a story that is also the nearest thing we have to a biography of Othello. (p. 264)

Othello describes his courtship of Desdemona in Act I, scene iii, when he stands publicly accused by Brabantio of having used magic to woo her. Othello tells the Venetian senators the story of his life as he had earlier told it to Brabantio, with Desdemona listening whenever she had the chance. These exotic adventures had appealed to her, he says, and she had hinted that such a narrative could win her love: ". . . Upon this hint

I spake: / *She* love'd *me* for the dangers *I* had pass'd, / And *I* lov'd *her* that she did pity them'' ([I. iii. 166-68]; italics added). The basis for their love, then, is the grand romantic picture of Othello that they both admire and pity, the image of Othello that Desdemona reflects to him. He does not have a reciprocal concept of her as a human being. Instead, he projects onto Desdemona the image of himself he wants to see reflected there: Othello calls her "my fair warrior" [II. i. 182] and through identification with her he too becomes a fair warrior in his own consciousness. Significantly, Othello's love for Desdemona is expressed best when she is absent, as in his account of their courtship before the Venetian council, or when she is silent, as in the final scene when he admires her beauty as she sleeps. He thinks of her in terms of objects, often cold and inhuman ones: she has skin "whiter . . . than snow, / And smooth, as monumental alabaster" [V. ii. 4-5]; she is a "cunning pattern of excelling nature" [V. ii. 11]; and she is "false as water" [V. ii. 134]. If she had been honest, Othello says, he would not have sold her for "one entire and perfect chrysolite" [V. ii. 145]; she is "a pearl . . . / Richer than all his tribe" [V. ii. 347-48]. As long as she fulfills his need for a reflecting statue, Othello loves her. But when Desdemona's own humanity intrudes, whenever she begins to speak, Othello's affections and confidence falter. We see this degenerative process in such instances as Desdemona's silent entrance in the middle of Act III, scene iii, when she arrives to invite Othello in to dinner. Othello takes one *look* at her and sweeps aside all of Iago's insinuations: "If she be false, O, then heaven mocks itself, / I'll not believe it" [III. iii. 278-79]. But as soon as Desdemona *speaks*, Othello begins to insinuate that she is making him a cuckold. And when he returns from their dinner together he has become utterly convinced—without Iago's presence—that Desdemona has been unfaithful to him.

And what is his first action after this mistaken conclusion? In a seemingly incongruent gesture, he bids farewell to his position as a general:

> O now for ever
> Farewell the tranquil mind, farewell content:
> Farewell the plumed troop, and the big wars,
> That makes ambition virtue: O farewell,
> Farewell the neighing steed, and the shrill trump,
> The spirit-stirring drum, the ear-piercing fife;
> The royal banner, and all quality,
> Pride, pomp, and circumstance of glorious war!
>
>   [III. iii. 347-54]

Many commentators have tried to explain why a man whose wife is presumed to be unfaithful would give up his job. Certainly it is true that a military leader needs the respect of his men, and that a cuckold, a figure of derision, might find it difficult to maintain his men's respect. But if this were the reason for Othello's farewell to his occupation, then we might expect to find some hint of it in or near the farewell speech. There is none. Instead, the speech is a moving dismissal of all the glories of war incorporated into Desdemona's initial grandiose reflection of Othello as romantic hero. If Othello's mirror—that is, Desdemona—is proven false, then the image reflected in that mirror is proven just as false. If the oneness Othello attempted to achieve with Desdemona has failed, then the separate identity he has so tentatively established through her has also failed. If "She's gone" [III. iii. 367], then "Farewell, Othello's occupation's gone!" [III. iii. 357].

Othello's other primary mirror is Iago. This is a reflector he had used long before he met Desdemona, and it is one whose reflected image he has come to trust and need. The self-portrait he sees when he turns to Iago is not *the romantic warrior* reflected by Desdemona. Rather, through Iago he sees the other major side of the human psyche, that is, the rational. Through Iago he defines himself as *the wise judge*, a thoughtful man of reason and decisiveness, who considers all the arguments and acts objectively and persistently. This is the fictive Othello who listens to Iago's hints early in Act III, scene iii, assuring Iago that he would never become such a miserable, jealous creature as Iago has described:

> Think'st thou I'ld make a life of jealousy?
> To follow still the changes of the moon
> With fresh suspicions? No, to be once in doubt,
> Is once to be resolv'd. . . .
>
>   [III. iii. 177-80]

He claims to be confident that he could never be made jealous either by praise of his wife or by dispraise of himself. He is, above all, objective:

> . . . 'tis not to make me jealous,
> To say my wife is fair, feeds well, loves company,
> Is free of speech, sings, plays, and dances well;
> Where virtue is, these are more virtuous:
> Nor from mine own weak merits will I draw
> The smallest fear, or doubt of her revolt,
> For she had eyes, and chose me. . . .
>
>   [III. iii. 183-89]

And if ever faced with a reason to suspect his wife, Othello says, he would act with the same rational decisiveness exercised earlier by the Venetian council: "I'll see before I doubt, when I doubt, prove, / And on the proof, there is no more than this: / Away at once with love or jealousy!" [III. iii. 190-92].

After setting up this paradigm of reasoned deliberation for himself, Othello needs Iago to notice how well he follows it, for in showing Iago he is showing himself. When the scene concludes with Othello's complete acceptance of his wife's alleged infidelity—"Now do I see 'tis true" [III. iii. 444]—he does not dismiss Iago and engage in a soliloquy as Hamlet or Macbeth might do in a moment of such intense personal anguish. Instead, Othello turns to Iago and says "*look here, Iago,* / All my fond love thus do I blow to heaven, . . . / 'Tis gone" ([III. iii. 444-46]; italics added). Approval for doing precisely what he had said he would do in such a situation appears to be as important to Othello as the act itself, for the approval validates the act and confirms the actor.

Then, still mindful of his audience, Othello kneels and swears vengeance, a theatrical gesture intended for Iago's reaction. Iago responds to Othello's desperate self-consciousness with a psychologically perfect gesture: he kneels before the kneeling Othello and swears a corresponding vow of vengeance. The mirror image of the two kneeling revengers facing each other literalizes the symbiotic nature of the psychological bond established between them.

That the wise judge of unswerving determination displayed in Act III, scene iii is largely a fiction of Iago's—and therefore Othello's—creation is demonstrated in Othello's brief soliloquy. In the middle of the temptation scene Iago leaves briefly, and Othello speaks completely alone for the only time in the play. Less than fifty lines after he had assured Iago that no one could make him jealous either by praising Desdemona or by dispraising him, in private he submits to the opposite conclusion: "Haply, for I am black, / And have not those soft parts of conversation / That chamberers have, or for I am declin'd / Into the vale of years,—yet that's not much— / She's gone, I am abus'd, and my relief / Must be to loathe her . . ." [III. iii. 263-68]. An insecure sense of self is apparent in Othello's focus on his own presumed frailty, and in his immediate assumption that he has lost Desdemona. To Iago he had spoken of a step-by-step process of ratiocination, but to himself he leaps from a speculation that he may "prove her haggard" [III. iii. 260] to an unproven conclusion that she is an adulteress.

In addition to his use of Desdemona and Iago as sustaining mirrors, Othello's vulnerability to external concepts of self takes many other forms. Othello has only the one brief soliloquy, referred to above, and very few asides. Because there is scant private "self" for him to deal with, most of his words are directed to other people, and, as we have seen, most of them are self-dramatizing and self-congratulatory. The play therefore lacks the introspection and personal revelations of a *Hamlet* or a *Macbeth*. By the same token, Othello shows little awareness of anything beyond the superficial in words directed to him by others, and he frequently seems naive, simplistic, or obtuse. (pp. 265-68)

In the murder scene, Othello's concern, typically, is for his own justification. His own fate matters far more to him than does any concern for Desdemona as murder victim. He tells Emilia,

> O, I were damn'd beneath all depth in hell,
> But that I did proceed, upon just grounds,
> To this extremity. . . .
>
> [V. ii. 137-39]

He then spends the major portion of the scene trying in vain to convince everyone that he has done precisely that: proceeded "upon just grounds." He clings to the Iago-reflected image of himself as the wise judge, and he tries to prove that he was justified in what he did. The play's final scene, therefore, becomes an analogue to the trial scene in Act I, scene iii, where Othello had been accused of using witchcraft to win Desdemona. Once again Venetians, functioning as embodiments of reasoned order, serve as jurors to determine Othello's guilt or innocence. Othello himself frequently acknowledges their presence: when Emilia calls everyone's attention to Desdemona's body on the bed, Othello turns to the Venetians and says, "Nay, stare not, masters, it is true indeed" [V. ii. 188]. He later rises from the bed where he had fallen "roar[ing]" [V. ii. 198], according to Emilia, to say to Gratiano in incongruously conversational tones, "I scarce did know you, uncle, there lies your niece, / Whose breath indeed these hands have newly stopp'd; / I know this act shows terrible and grim" [V. ii. 201-03].

When Emilia establishes that Iago has framed Desdemona, Othello does not blame himself—indeed, nowhere in the scene does he suggest an overt recognition of his own responsibility in the murder scene except perhaps in the problematic line "Fool, fool, fool!" [V. ii. 323]—but instead shifts the blame to another. As soon as he realizes that Iago has manipulated him, he tries to stab Iago. When prevented by Montano, who takes his sword away, Othello's reaction is self-revelatory: he sees the incident primarily as a personal affront. "I am not

valiant neither, / But every puny whipster gets my sword" [V. ii. 243-44].

I realize that much of what I am saying draws near to T. S. Eliot's observation that Othello in the final scene is trying to "cheer himself up" [see excerpt above, 1927]. But Eliot's description is a limited one in that it refers to Othello's behavior in only one scene, and it does not place that action in the context of the whole play or account for it in terms of Othello's total personality. What interests me far more than the fact that Othello bolsters his self-esteem at the moment he realizes that he is murderer is the fact that this moment is but another manifestation of the psychological profile that helps us see why Othello's ego needs that bolstering. A healthy person would respond to such a realization with some variation of self-directed fury. The superego—the voice of conscience, the "inner mother" developed by the healthy individual—would tell that person that he had erred on a gigantic scale. Instead of this mature self-judgment, Othello insists on Desdemona's guilt long past the point at which the truth is obvious to everyone else. He shifts the blame to Iago, to fate, and to bad luck. He asks pardon only of Cassio for mistrusting him. And he stages two very calculated suicide speeches, both filled with self-praise. As he delivers his final "Look at me" speech, he concludes with the precise description he wants the Venetians to use in their reports of him:

> When you shall these unlucky deeds relate,
> Speak of them as they are; nothing extenuate,
> Nor set down aught in malice; then must you speak
> Of one that lov'd not wisely, but too well.
>
> [V. ii. 341-44]

Then, calling attention to his own brave action, he stabs himself. As he falls upon the bed, he calls his audience's attention to his final dramatic gesture. "I kiss'd thee ere I kill'd thee, no way but this, / Killing myself, to die upon a kiss" [V. ii. 358-59]. The self-consciousness of Othello's words and actions, his need for reassurance from an audience, and his insistent defensiveness are *not* the random efforts of a newly unhappy man trying to cheer himself up. Nor are the analogous self-dramatizations earlier in the play the manifestations of a healthy self-confidence. They are the characteristic—even pathological—actions of a psyche trapped in an arrested state of development.

The immature ego is exemplified by many of the qualities that audiences and readers of *Othello* have historically found so infuriating or inexplicable about Othello: his seeming obtuseness, his apparently hasty actions and reactions, his lack of critical self-awareness, his simplicity, his touchiness, his naiveté about other people, and his apparent vanity. This is not to deny Othello's admirable and heroic qualities, his abilities as a general, his bravery, his eloquence, and so forth. Rather, it is to assert that Othello's words and behavior may be understood as a coherent pattern of action that typifies a single recognized personality type, the immature ego. That such an individual is psychologically incapable of achieving Hamlet's sophisticated introspection, or Macbeth's honest self-awareness, or Lear's moving anagnorisis may do much to explain why *Othello* as a play keeps slipping into the genre of melodrama, in spite of our frequent critical efforts to maintain its position in the small circle of high tragedies. (pp. 268-70)

Carol McGinnis Kay, "Othello's Need for Mirrors," in Shakespeare Quarterly, *Vol. 34, No. 3, Autumn, 1983, pp. 261-70.*

ADDITIONAL BIBLIOGRAPHY

Abernethy, Julian Willis. "Honest Iago." *The Sewanee Review* XXX, No. 3 (July 1920): 336-44.

Considers *Othello* supremely effective "as an acting play," but not of the same poetic stature as *Hamlet, King Lear,* and *Macbeth.* Abernethy claims that this play is "un-Aristotelian" in that it "neither elevates nor consoles"; he also remarks that the conventional figure of the cuckolded husband belongs more properly to comedy than tragedy and charges that Shakespeare's characterizations of Othello and Iago are inferior, because the Moor does not grow or develop during the course of the dramatic action and Iago explains himself directly to the audience, instead of being "explained by the action." Abernethy also examines Iago's "grim, sardonic" humor and suggests that Shakespeare's original intention was to represent him as a comic character.

Adamson, W. D. "Unpinned or Undone? Desdemona's Critics and the Problem of Sexual Innocence." *Shakespeare Studies* XIII (1980): 169-86.

Asserts that Shakespeare has drawn Desdemona as "legally innocent of adultery, morally innocent of idly considering it, and psychologically innocent of even being capable of it." Adamson rejects the conclusions of those critics who have either idealized Desdemona into a saintly figure or regarded her innocence as neurotic and self-destroying. The critic compares these assessments to Othello's inability to acknowledge Desdemona's vibrant sexuality and Iago's nihilistic view of female chastity.

Alexander, Nigel. "Thomas Rymer and 'Othello'." *Shakespeare Survey* 21 (1968): 67-77.

Argues that in his interpretation of *Othello* Thomas Rymer misconstrued the function of the dramatist, revealed his own racial bias, and mistakenly assumed that he held all the answers to the puzzles raised by the play. By accusing Shakespeare of violating poetic justice in depicting the murder of Desdemona, Alexander maintains, Rymer erroneously defined the role of the playwright as apologist or explicator, rather than portrayer, of the "differences which divide mankind" and "the problem of evil." He further contends that Rymer's bigotry is akin to that of several characters in the drama, because, like Iago, Brabantio, and Roderigo, Rymer views Desdemona's love for Othello as unnatural and thus fails to grasp that the tragic action necessarily ensues because men like Rymer himself can only see the lovers' union as "monstrous."

Allen, Ned B. "The Two Parts of 'Othello'." *Shakespeare Survey* 21 (1968): 13-29.

Explains the discrepancies between Long Time and Short Time in *Othello* by arguing that Shakespeare wrote Acts III through V first and composed Acts I and II at some later date. Noting that the dramatist followed Cinthio's tale much more closely in the final three acts than in the first two, Allen contends that the contradictions in the time scheme of the play result from the fact that when Shakespeare composed Acts III through V he treated the characters "not as having arrived in Cyprus on the previous day, but as having long been there—as in Cinthio," but when he came to write Acts I and II he shifted to a different pace, with the result that Othello murders Desdemona one day after the consummation of their marriage.

Auden, W. H. "The Joker in the Pack." In his *The Dyer's Hand and Other Essays,* pp. 246-72. New York: Random House, 1948.

Compares Iago to a practical joker who himself has no personal feelings or values, but contemptuously uses the very real desires of other people to gull and manipulate them. Auden also examines the institutionalized racism of Venice and contends that Othello prizes his marriage to Desdemona not because of any great love he holds for her, but because this signals to him, mistakenly, that he is "loved and accepted as a person, a brother in the Venetian community." Arguing that Cassio is much happier in the company of women than men—"because he is unsure of his masculinity"

and feels threatened by the aggressive virility of his fellow soldiers—the critic asserts that the Florentine is incapable of real passion and can only indulge his sexual impulses with a prostitute whom he regards with "insufferable" contempt.

Berry, Ralph. "Pattern in *Othello*." In his *Shakespearean Structures,* pp. 64-86. Totowa, N. J.: Barnes & Noble Books, 1981.

Disputes the notion that jealousy is the central theme of the play and maintains, instead, that both Iago and Othello are shown to be inherently distrustful of women, doubting their wives' fidelity because they fail to consider all the evidence or possible proofs of their chastity. Arguing that "the unresolvable appearance-reality dualism" is the basis of the structural design of *Othello,* Berry contends that the Moor is "not a pure innocent subverted by Iago," but rather a man whose destruction stems from his lack of reliance on Desdemona's innocence and from his inability to distinguish between what is true and what is only apparent.

Bowman, Thomas D. "In Defense of Emilia." *The Shakespeare Association Bulletin* XXII, No. 3 (July 1947): 99-104.

Assesses Emilia as consistently loyal to Desdemona, warm-hearted and well intentioned, and "the unconscious victim of tragic error." Claiming that she misunderstands the significance of the handkerchief, Bowman points out that it is snatched from her hands by Iago and that she can hardly contradict her mistress when Desdemona denies that it is lost, and he praises her conduct throughout the final act. The critic also regards Emilia's last speech in Act IV, Scene iii as an eloquent plea for sexual equality and the derogation of the double standard of morality for men and women.

Bridges, Robert. "The Influence of the Audience on Shakespeare's Drama." In his *Collected Essays Papers &c. of Robert Bridges,* Vol. 1. London: Oxford University Press, 1927, 29 p.

Remarks on the various improbabilities in *Othello,* particularly the apparent inconsistencies of time in Acts II through V, Emilia's failure to disclose the whereabouts of the handkerchief, and the failure of everyone to discern the wickedness of Iago. Noting that Shakespeare could easily have provided a lapse of time for the purported affair of Cassio and Desdemona by delaying Othello's ship on its passage to Cyprus, Bridges concludes that the dramatist deliberately intended to generate in his audience feelings of anxiety and excitement "to the limit of their endurance."

Bullough, Geoffrey. Introduction to *Othello,* by William Shakespeare. In *Narrative and Dramatic Sources of Shakespeare,* Vol. VII, edited by Geoffrey Bullough, pp. 193-238. London: Routledge and Kegan Paul, 1978.

Extended discussion of Shakespeare's adaptation of Cinthio's novella. Bullough remarks that in Acts III and IV of *Othello,* Shakespeare followed his source more closely and departed from it more strikingly in Acts I, II, and V, and he contends the dramatist was most drawn to the story by "the clever way in which Cinthio's Ensign played on the Moor's simplicity and perverted him from a noble officer and loving husband into a brutal murderer." He asserts that Shakespeare's introduction of the Turkish conflict and his elevation of the military and social stations of Othello and Desdemona add dignity and significance to the theme of domestic love and jealousy. Bullough also describes several probable and possible sources in fifteenth- and sixteenth-century translations of Matteo Bandello, Leo Africanus, and Pliny and in Elizabethan and Jacobean historical accounts of the wars between Venice and Turkey. In addition to discerning both long and short time in the duration in the drama, as had Christopher North (see entry below), the critic postulates a third, psychological time, apparent in Othello's confused sense of "past and present."

Campbell, Lily B. "*Othello*: A Tragedy of Jealousy." In her *Shakespeare's Tragic Heroes: Slaves of Passion,* pp. 148-74. 1930. Reprint. New York: Barnes & Noble, 1960.

Asserts that jealousy is the central theme of *Othello* and that Shakespeare intended to demonstrate the impact of this emotion on men of different races. Noting the Elizabethan belief that Africans are naturally disposed to jealousy, Campbell argues that Othello's suspicions of Desdemona's innocence arise from his high regard for reputation and good name, a concern the critic regards as not unexpected in a black man who must accommodate himself to a society that views him as an alien.

Champion, Larry S. "The Tragic Perspective of *Othello*." *English Studies* 54, No. 5 (October 1973): 447-60.

Examines the way in which Othello's increasing emotional isolation from Act III, Scene iii to the conclusion of the play is enhanced by Shakespeare's shifting of dramatic perspective from Iago to the Moor in the temptation scene itself. Just as Iago's evident irrational hatred of Othello generates our sympathy for the Moor in the first part of the drama, Champion contends, Shakespeare enables us to experience the full "emotional impact of [Othello's] destruction" by forcing us to perceive the tragic action in the second half from his point of view.

Charlton, H. B. "Shakespeare's *Othello*." *Bulletin of the John Rylands Library* 31, No. 1 (January 1948): 28-53.

Extended comparison of Cinthio's tale and Shakespeare's *Othello* which contends that although the source presents the ancient as the principal cause of the tragedy, in Shakespeare's play Iago is merely an agent of the calamity and not "an indispensable cause" of it. Charlton emphasizes Othello's alienation from Venetian society, "his native nobility" of soul which is not equalled by superior powers of intellect and reasoning, and the Moor's acquired habits of self-control over his passionate emotions, and he argues that, although by themselves these do not suit him as a tragic protagonist, Othello is elevated to heroic stature by virtue of the incomparable love he shares with Desdemona.

Clemen, Wolfgang. "*Othello*." In his *The Development of Shakespeare's Imagery*, pp. 119-32. London: Methuen and Co., 1977.

Discusses Shakespeare's use of metaphorical language in *Othello* to characterize Iago and the Moor and to heighten the contrasts between these two figures. Remarking that Iago's imagery is artificial and deliberate, static, "cold and cynical," and consciously contrived to influence and persuade the person he is addressing, Clemen argues that, by comparison, Othello's metaphors are "spontaneous and unconscious," dynamic, emotive, and uttered "from the heart." From Act III, Scene iii to the play's conclusion, however, the critic notes that Othello's speech increasingly contains foul and repulsive images which had before been the sole prerogative of his ensign, denoting the progressive poisoning of the Moor's mind by the base insinuations of Iago.

Cohen, Eileen Z. "Mirror of Virtue: The Role of Cassio in *Othello*." *English Studies* 57, No. 2 (April 1976): 115-27.

Views Cassio as a reflection of Othello's noble and virtuous aspects and argues that the lieutenant's ascendancy at the close of the play underscores the Moor's final reconciliation with Desdemona and his ultimate triumph over evil represented by Iago. Maintaining that Cassio's drunken behavior in Act II, Scene iii foreshadows Othello's similar intoxication by Iago later in the drama, Cohen notes that from the close of that scene until Iago's villainy is revealed in Act V, Scene ii, Othello has no "direct contact" with Cassio, and she remarks that during this period he increasingly loses touch with his own nobility and virtue, which are restored to him only when he comprehends that justice must be served by his suicide.

Cook, Ann Jennalie. "The Design of Desdemona: Doubt Raised and Resolved." *Shakespeare Studies* XIII (1980): 187-96.

Compares Shakespeare's ambiguous portrayal of Desdemona through the first half of *Othello* by means of doling out "information or innuendo," manipulating the audience's expectations, and offering situations "that seem to enlighten but may in fact mislead" to Iago's parallel manipulation of the Moor. Remarking that a Renaissance audience would have initially judged Desdemona's marrying without her father's approval and authority as scandalous, Cook argues that it is not until Act III—just at the point where Othello begins to be unsure of Desdemona—that the

dramatist provides us with total assurance of her constancy and virtuousness, and thus the design of the play has provided us with an experience which "precisely parallels Othello's."

Dash, Irene. "A Woman Tamed: *Othello*." In her *Wooing, Wedding, and Power: Women in Shakespeare's Plays*, pp. 103-30. New York: Columbia University Press, 1981.

Contends that *Othello* demonstrates "the cost to husband and wife . . . of attempting to conform to stereotyped ideals of marriage." Noting that throughout Acts I and II Desdemona is portrayed as independent, self-confident, and courageous, Dash argues that when the "mutual respect" she and Othello held for each other during their courtship is supplanted by Othello's more conventional view of marriage. Desdemona fails to recognize that by subordinating her life to his she denigrates her own identity. Because of her inability to discard her self-confident approach to Othello, the critic adds, Desdemona cannot adjust to these "new patterns of behavior," and her tragedy is complete and demonstrable in her public and private humiliation in Act IV.

Doran, Madeleine. "Good Name in *Othello*." *Studies in English Literature: 1500-1900* VII, No. 2 (Spring 1967): 195-217.

Examines Othello's concern for his reputation in terms of Renaissance concepts of good name as "most precious, yet most precarious," and maintains that in the sixteenth century it was widely held that for a man "to lose his name is to lose himself." Arguing that Shakespeare apprehended the important difference between acts committed out of "rash passion" and those conceived in "deliberate malice," Doran avers that Othello's final speech represents his entreaty that the audience recognize the distinction between his inherent goodness and his conduct, which was the result of reckless passion and Iago's malicious envy. She also interprets Cassio's last words as the restitution of the Moor's integrity and "the act of grace which clears Othello's name."

————. "Iago's 'if': An Essay on the Syntax of *Othello*." In *The Drama of the Renaissance: Essays for Leicester Bradner*, edited by Elmer M. Blistein, pp. 69-99. Providence, R.I.: Brown University Press, 1970.

An exhaustive analysis of syntactical patterns in *Othello* which demonstrates Shakespeare's strategic use of conditional sentences to emphasize Othello's inability to countenance doubt and to mark off the turns in the catastrophic action of the play. Noting Iago's method of employing conditional sentences that express "a condition assumed to be possible," Doran contends that Othello's sentences are normally declarative, "in the indicative mood," and rarely reveal "unthought-of possibilities" without the instigation of Iago. She concludes that the Moor's final speech should be read straight-forwardly as a plea for impartial judgment and as an affirmation "of his love, his jealousy, his folly, and his remorse."

Draper, John W. *The "Othello" of Shakespeare's Audience*. Paris: Marcel Didier, 1952, 246 p.

Views *Othello* from the perspective of Elizabethan psychology, rhetoric, and attitudes toward citizens of foreign nations. Asserting that "historical criticism can explain most of the difficulties in the play," Draper offers a detailed examination of the various backgrounds—military, family, political, marriage conventions, and infidelity—from which, he argues, the play must be explored, and he applies these to his assessments of the various dramatic elements, including characters, setting, plot, and theme.

Empson, William. "Honest in Othello." In his *The Structure of Complex Words*, pp. 218-49. London: Chatto & Windus, 1951.

Extended analysis of the many possible connotations an Elizabethan audience would perceive in the words "honest" and "honesty" in *Othello*, especially as they are used by or applied to Iago. These include: generous and "loving towards friends," chaste, "exposer of false pretensions," honorable, and "frankness to yourself about your own desires." Contending that Shakespeare's characterization of Iago offers an almost full range of these possible meanings, so that the intended effect is sometimes ambiguous and sometimes ironic, Empson concludes that the audience's confused reaction to Iago is symbolized "by the confusion of the word" honesty itself.

Evans, K. W. "The Racial Factor in Othello." *Shakespeare Studies* V (1969): 124-40.
    Contends that by portraying Othello's "self-development" from a romantic idealist, who has only a superficial understanding of passion, to a man who ultimately understands love's true mysteries, Shakespeare persuaded his Elizabethan audience to transcend their conventional ideas of Moors, recognize that Othello shares a common humanity with them, and experience within themselves his painful tragedy. Othello's credulity and belief in magic were traits commonly associated with Moors, Evans argues, but Shakespeare manipulated "Elizabethan psychology" by depicting his protagonist as finally rejecting Iago's view of human passion and affirming, through the manner in which he murders Desdemona, his "belief in the magic of love."

Everett, Barbara. "Reflections on the Sentimentalist's Othello." *Critical Quarterly* 3, No. 2 (Summer 1961): 127-38.
    Argues that F. R. Leavis's essay on *Othello* (see excerpt above, 1937) raises valuable questions but errs in presenting the Moor as egotistical and self-centered. Noting that self-dramatization is a quality shared by all protagonists of Renaissance drama, Everett contends that Shakespeare consistently portrays Othello as a heroic individual whose idealism becomes "horrifying as it becomes more attached to Iago's principles and practice" and as a character with the capacity to turn away from such conduct and return to goodness, thus recognizing his responsibility for the tragic events. Whereas Leavis views Othello's behavior in the second half of the drama as essentially corrupt, Everett maintains that Shakespeare has drawn him, and the other central characters as well, not only with the potential for good and evil, but also with the freedom to choose a course of action. She claims that "the first and essential destructive action, the will to pervert and corrupt, comes from Iago."

Faber, M. D. "*Othello:* The Justice of It Pleases." *American Imago* 28, No. 3 (Fall 1971): 228-46.
    Focuses on the psychoanalytic significance of Iago's proposal that Desdemona be strangled in her bed and Othello's "enthusiastic reception of this idea." Like Stephen Reid (see entry below), Faber contends that Othello is maternally fixated and exhibits clinical symptoms of delusional jealousy, and he regards the Moor's response to Iago's plan of murder as evincing a pathological orality, concluding that Othello's frustrated oral desires lead him to a murderous form of "oral retaliation" against his mother.

Feldman, Abraham Bronson. "Othello's Obsessions." *American Imago* 9, No. 2 (June 1952): 147-63.
    A psychoanalytic discussion of Othello's jealousy which discerns a repressed homosexual love of Cassio as its source. Arguing that Othello's conduct in Act III, Scene iii reveals that his love for Desdemona is merely superficial, and that there are many indications in the play that the Moor is plagued by doubts about his own virility, Feldman concludes that he is driven mad by the thought of Cassio betraying their close relationship and, further, that "the essence of Othello is effeminate."

Fiedler, Leslie A. "The Moor as Stranger; or, 'Almost damned in a fair wife . . .'." In his *The Stranger in Shakespeare*, pp. 139-96. New York: Stein and Day, 1972.
    Maintains that Othello's blackness is "primarily symbolic," denoting his extreme cultural alienation from Desdemona and heightening Shakespeare's depiction of him as "forever homeless" and never entirely integrated into European and Christian cultures. Remarking on the comic elements in *Othello*, Fiedler also contends that the play may be seen as a burlesque on the conventional male view that, since the marriage system treats men and women unequally, women—who are by nature inherently lustful—will seek revenge by committing adultery.

Flatter, Richard. *The Moor of Venice.* London: William Heinemann, 1950, 225 p.
    Extended analyses of minor as well as major characters in *Othello*. Flatter disputes the view that Othello and Iago are "complementary sections of one personality split in two," arguing instead that they are independent of each other and depicted naturalistically rather than ideally. The critic similarly denies that Shakespeare has represented Desdemona as saintly throughout the drama, contending that in Act I, Scene iii she exhibits such human weaknesses as selfishness, deception, and immodesty, but that when she speaks at her death in Act V, Scene ii she clearly demonstrates the unshakeable and "boundless confidence in her husband's love"— an act that raises her to saintliness, according to Flatter.

Fortin, René. "Allegory and Genre in *Othello.*" *Genre* IV, No. 2 (June 1971): 153-72.
    Contends that Shakespeare intentionally represented in *Othello* a confusion of generic elements from religious and social allegory, Italian *commedia dell'arte,* traditional and domestic tragedy, medieval morality patterns, and naturalistic drama to demonstrate that the ultimate mystery of evil may have multiple levels of significance, thus resisting simplistic interpretations.

French, Marilyn. "The Late Tragedies: *Othello.*" In her *Shakespeare's Division of Experience,* pp. 204-19. New York: Summit Books, 1981.
    Analyzes the portrayal of "the political situation of women and their personal identities apart from men" in *Othello.* Arguing that for both aristocratic and lower-class Venice the principal values are control, power, and possession, French traces the evidence in the play that Othello and Iago—representatives of the former and latter group, respectively—embody this value structure. Both men, she asserts, are "profoundly misogynistic" in their denigration of the feminine principles of loyalty, obedience, and emotion, and they attempt to control sexuality either by idealizing love and denying its erotic element or by denying "the loving element in eros." French views Emilia as not only the "spokeswoman for the females of the play," but also as the only dramatic character who regards women as human individuals, implicitly rejecting the limitations of the idealized women/whore dichotomy.

Furness, Horace Howard, ed. *Othello,* by William Shakespeare. A New Variorum Edition. Philadelphia: J. B. Lippincott, 1886, 471 p.
    Includes excerpted essays by principal nineteenth-century scholars on the date, text, and sources of *Othello,* together with commentary on such issues as the characterization in the play and whether Shakespeare intended to present Othello as a black man. Furness endorses Christopher North's assessment of Double Time in the play (see entries below) and reprints extended passages from North's essays and several critical appraisals of North's analyses.

Gardner, Helen. "The Noble Moor." *Proceedings of the British Academy* XLI (1955): 189-205.
    A spirited defense of the thematic significance of *Othello* and the essential heroic nobility of the Moor himself. Arguing that the play dramatizes the belief that lapses and "recoveries of faith" are natural to the "rhythm" of the human heart, Gardner asserts that Othello's lapse of faith should be attributed not to some "psychological weakness," but instead to his stature as a noble, tragic hero who acts without any thought of the consequences to himself. Shakespeare portrayed the Moor as driven by an inner compulsion to act out his fate and to murder the woman he mistakenly regards as a sinner, Gardner maintains, and she declares that "tragic responsibility is not the same as moral guilt."

———. "'Othello': A Retrospect, 1900-67." *Shakespeare Survey* 21 (1968): 1-12.
    Comprehensive discussion of the contributions to *Othello* criticism from the beginning of the twentieth century to 1967, with particular focus on the influence of A. C. Bradley (see excerpt above, 1904). Gardner contends that Bradley's assessment that the tragedy stems from Othello's unsuspecting nature and his judgment that the play lacks the universal or symbolic significance of *Hamlet, King Lear,* and *Macbeth* have formed the basis of most sub-

sequent commentary on the drama, even for critics who maintain that they are anti-Bradleyian, for they, too, are frequently concerned with the effect of the Moor's imperfect nature on the tragic outcome of the drama. Citing several critics who share her view, Gardner maintains that the center of interest lies, not in the figure of Othello, but in Shakespeare's dramatization of the tragic defeat of "human needs and aspirations."

Grudin, Robert. "Contrariety as Structure: The Later Tragedies." In his *Mighty Opposites: Shakespeare and Renaissance Contrariety*, pp. 119-79. Berkeley and Los Angeles: University of California Press, 1979.

Avers that Desdemona's "type of lamblike femininity" is compelling to Othello but not to Shakespeare and thus the dramatist demonstrates that her passive helplessness is implicitly ironic, for it "sharpens the impulse to aggression in others." The ambiguities of her virtue are comparable, Grudin maintains, to the complexities of Iago's wickedness.

Hallett, W. Hughes, "Honest, Honest Iago." *Fortnightly Review* LXXIII n.s., No. CCCCXXXIV (1 February 1903): 275-86.

An analysis of the character of Iago which emphasizes his commonplace or prosaic qualities and his inferior social status. Contending that Iago is neither superhumanly wicked nor motiveless, Hallett asserts that behind his schemes is a "low, narrow-minded" cunning. The critic adds that Iago's loss of the military promotion is a "legitimate cause for grievance."

Hallstead, R. N. "Idolatrous Love: A New Approach to *Othello*." *Shakespeare Quarterly* XIX, No. 2 (Spring 1968): 107-24.

Argues that after the consummation of Othello and Desdemona's marriage in Cyprus, the Moor's love for his wife becomes so excessive that it is theologically idolatrous. Asserting that *Othello* is "a morality play in a completely realistic framework," Hallstead contends that the Moor is shown renouncing Christianity when he swears a pagan vow with Iago at the close of Act III, Scene iii, but the critic also discovers in the final scene of the drama a clear pattern of Christian penance, concluding that Shakespeare has manifestly portrayed "the return of Othello's Christianity."

Hapgood, Robert. "The Trials of Othello." In *Pacific Coast Studies in Shakespeare*, edited by Waldo F. McNeir and Thelma N. Greenfield, pp. 134-47. Eugene: University of Oregon Books, 1966.

Contends that the self-righteousness of Othello serves as a warning to the audience to be wary of making judgments on the dramatic characters in the play and to acknowledge the connection between the Moor's presumptive judgments and our own "human injudiciousness." Hapgood maintains that the justice theme in *Othello* is underscored by the Moor's "excessive assurance of his innate rectitude—both in judging himself and others" and that it is this trait which keeps him from openly confronting Desdemona and Cassio with his suspicions.

Hawkes, Terence. "Iago's Use of Reason." *Studies in Philology* LVII (January 1961): 160-69.

Analyzes Shakespeare's portrayal in *Othello* of the clash between rational and intuitive modes of thinking and compares this struggle to the tension in the Elizabethan age between science and religion. Hawkes argues that the play's dramatic structure is grounded in Othello's choice between Iago's rationality and the exalted world of Desdemona and her love, which are beyond rational explication. He maintains that Iago's successful use of the tools of ratiocination, such as observation, analysis, explanation, definition, "logical necessity, and rational certitude," leads the Moor to substitute his ancient's version of reality for the truth and implicates Iago "to the hilt in the age-old sin of the intellect."

Heilman, Robert B. "Dr. Iago and His Potions." *Virginia Quarterly Review* 28, No. 4 (Autumn 1952): 568-84.

Assesses the significance of the frequent association of Iago with metaphors of illness and health, poison and medicine, destructive practitioner and healing physician, and concludes that this pattern serves to intensify Shakespeare's portrayal of wickedness and treachery in the play. Emphasizing that at the beginning of the drama Iago is depicted merely as an "aggrieved human being," Heilman traces the ancient's descent into inhumanity in the subsequent action of the drama.

Holloway, John. "*Othello*." In his *The Story of the Night: Studies in Shakespeare's Major Tragedies*, pp. 37-56. London: Routledge & Kegan Paul, 1961.

Argues that *Othello* must be interpreted in light of Renaissance concepts of right conduct in public and private affairs and literary conventions of Elizabethan tragedy. Holloway contends that Shakespeare has depicted the Moor as a great and noble figure, acting with dignity and courtesy in both his public and private roles until his reason is overcome by jealousy and his nature becomes monstrously transformed, but recovering his lost reason and fully understanding the extent of his aberrant behavior at the close of the drama. He further avers that in Elizabethan tragedy the final speech of the protagonist "is no piece of private musing," but rather a summation of and commentary upon his role in the dramatic action, and thus Othello's concluding words "are an authoritative and exact account of what has happened in the play."

Homan, Sidney R. "Iago's Aesthetics: Othello and Shakespeare's Portrait of an Artist." *Shakespeare Studies* V (1969): 141-48.

Suggests that in *Othello* Shakespeare may have been assessing the validity of "negative or pejorative views of the artist and his work in the Renaissance." Noting that Iago's artistry and creativity allow him to distort the reality of Cassio's friendship and Desdemona's faithfulness for the benefit of his single auditor, Homan offers a detailed analysis of the ways in which Iago as artist embodies "all the negative qualities that critics in the Renaissance found in poets and playwrights."

Hunter, G. K. "Othello and Colour Prejudice." *Proceedings of the British Academy* LIII (1967): 139-63.

A noteworthy discussion of the dramatic significance of Othello's blackness and Shakespeare's manipulation of the expectations which the Moor's race engendered in the play's first audiences. Hunter offers an extensive review of the Renaissance attitude toward black-skinned people derived from Graeco-Roman literature and Christian eschatology, concluding that the "widespread and ancient tradition associating black-faced men with wickedness" survived to the time of *Othello*'s composition and would likely have shaped or informed the prejudicial and xenophobic assumptions of a Jacobean audience. Arguing that the dramatist leads us to discard these assumptions by identifying them with Iago, the critic contends that Shakespeare achieved this effect in one manner by presenting in the play a contrasting pattern of thought, which held that the fairness of one's soul was more important than the color of one's skin, and that, indeed, "all men are within the scope of the Christian ministry." Further maintaining that the theme of appearance and reality is central to *Othello*, Hunter contends that the audience becomes guiltily aware that the strangeness of foreigners disappears when we become familiar with them and that a "prejudicial foreign appearance may conceal a vision of truth." Hunter notes that Renaissance commentators had begun to question the discrepancies between "the capacities and ideals claimed by Christendom" and the conduct of sixteenth-century explorers who cruelly mistreated indigenous populations, and he asserts that *Othello* presses its audience to consider—through its portrayal of "prejudice and vision, appearance and reality"—the pietism of European civilization.

Hyman, Stanley Edgar. *Iago: Some Approaches to the Illusion of His Motivation*. New York: Atheneum, 1970, 180 p.

Assesses Iago's motives for destroying Othello and Desdemona from five different critical perspectives, alternately questioning whether the ensign should be viewed as "a stage villain, or Satan, or an artist, or a latent homosexual, or a Machiavel." A pluralistic approach to this critical issue, Hyman argues, demonstrates the "tension, paradox, and irony" in Shakespeare's portrayal of Iago, whereas a single line of inquiry can only produce one perspective that is "inevitably reductive and partial."

Jones, Eldred. *Othello's Countrymen: The African in English Renaissance Drama*. London: Oxford University Press, 1965, 158 p.

Analyzes the manner in which Moors were represented in English masques, pageants, and eleven plays from this period, concluding that Moors were usually portrayed as either black-skinned villains or tawny colored oriental rulers, equally capable of cruel or noble conduct. In *Othello*, Jones contends, Shakespeare transcended both types, portraying a noble hero endowed with universal human frailties and overwhelmed by circumstances, while achieving the "complete humanization of a type character who for most of his contemporaries [had] only decorative or a crude moral significance."

Jorgenson, Paul A. "*Honesty* in *Othello*." *Studies in Philology* XLVII, No. 3 (July 1950): 557-67.

Analyzes the recurring treatment in Elizabethan dramatic and non-dramatic literature, including *Othello*, of one of the dominant questions of the period: "How may one know the honest man from the knave?" Demonstrating that the figure of Honesty in morality plays was typically portrayed as a professional distinguisher of honest and villainous men, employed by royalty and nobility to assess the sincerity of their other retainers, Jorgenson maintains that Iago's protestations of his honesty, his reputation for acuity and forthrightness, his apparent distrust of Cassio's glibness, and his frequent expressions of "moral indignation" are all characteristics of the Honesty figure, and he concludes that Shakespeare has drawn him, not as a variation on the allegorical Vice in morality drama, but as "a knave posing as Honesty, a hunter of knaves."

Kirschbaum, Leo. "The Modern Othello." *ELH* 11, No. 4 (December 1944): 283-96.

Develops the opinion of T. S. Eliot (see excerpt above, 1927) that Othello is self-deluded and charges that Elmer Edgar Stoll (see excerpt above, 1915) has overemphasized dramatic conventions in his study of the play, neglecting the psychological consistency of Shakespeare's portrayal of the Moor. Kirschbaum argues that Othello is shown to be responsible for his fate, frequently assuming "the god pose" that reflects his romantic idealization of himself, and similarly regarding Desdemona as an idealized symbol rather than an individual woman. Stoll's response to this essay was published in *ELH* in 1946 (see entry below).

Kittredge, George Lyman. *Shakspere: An Address*. Cambridge: Harvard University Press, 1916, 54 p.

Asserts that Iago is not a superhuman fiend but an individual drawn to human proportions, motivated by sexual jealousy and anger over losing the lieutenancy. Arguing that Iago does not start out with the intention of destroying Othello and Desdemona, Kittredge also emphasizes "his highly intellectual cynicism" and contends that his conduct demonstrates what may ensue when will and reason suppress "the cultivation of the moral faculties."

Kott, Jan. "The Two Paradoxes of Othello." In his *Shakespeare Our Contemporary*, translated by Boleslaw Taborski, pp. 99-125. New York: W. W. Norton & Co., 1964.

Maintains that the struggle between Othello and Iago is a dramatic representation of a "dispute on the nature of the world" and an enquiry into the purpose of human existence. Kott focuses specifically on two paradoxical events in the play: Iago's own victimization by the evil he himself sets in motion and Desdemona's delight in the erotic aspects of love which leads Othello to believe her capable of betraying him.

Lerner, Laurence. "The Machiavel and the Moor." *Essays in Criticism* IX, No. 4 (October 1959): 339-60.

Argues that *Othello* produces a melodramatic rather than a tragic effect, largely because of Shakespeare's portrayals of Iago and the Moor. Lerner contends that although Shakespeare provides no smooth transitions when he switches abruptly from symbolic to naturalistic methods of characterizing Iago, we are willing to suspend belief because we recognize that the play is a melodrama. Lerner also maintains that Shakespeare depicted Othello with a dual personality and represented his fall in Act III, Scene iii as a reversion to his essential nature—namely, that of a jealous, barbarous savage who renounces his acquired role as a noble Christian soldier.

Long, Michael. "The Moor of Venice." In his *The Unnatural Scene: A Study in Shakespearean Tragedy*, pp. 37-58. London: Methuen & Co., 1976.

Focuses on the "Courtesy-world" of Venice and its inhabitants. Long avers that Shakespeare portrayed the Venetians as prone to collapse because of their inherent vulnerability and incapacity to accommodate manifestations of the ambiguities between their ideal world and the actual, physical one. What critics have described as a "hollowness" in Othello, Long asserts, is a reflection of the central focus of the play: the hollowness, instability, and lack of vitality of Venetian culture and its elite members.

Macaulay, Thomas Babington. "Oeuvres Complètes de Machiavel, traduites par J. V. Perier." *Edinburgh Review* XLV, No. XC (March 1827): 259-95.

The earliest association of Iago with Machiavellianism. Macaulay contends that because of the political precepts held by Renaissance Italians, they would likely have admired Iago for his quick-wittedness, his discerning judgment of human nature, and his dissimulation. Conversely, the critic adds, Renaissance Italians would have found Othello contemptible and despised his gullibility, his credulousness, and his violent behavior.

Mason, H. A. "*Othello*." In his *Shakespeare's Tragedies of Love: An Examination of the Possibility of Common Readings of "Romeo and Juliet," "Othello," "King Lear" & "Antony and Cleopatra,"* pp. 59-161. London: Chatto & Windus, 1970.

Contends that *Othello* is disturbing and excruciatingly painful "rather than profoundly moving" because it lacks a central point "embodying wisdom about life." Maintaining that the absence of a deep center is "the central defect of the play," Mason also finds additional evidence of flawed composition and craftsmanship, and he hypothesizes that Shakespeare began writing the drama "without knowing how it was going to develop," inexplicably failing to reread and revise his completed manuscript.

McDonald, Russ. "Othello, Thorello, and the Problem of the Foolish Hero." *Shakespeare Quarterly* 30, No. 1 (Winter 1979): 51-67.

An overview of the treatment of the subject of adultery in comic and tragic dramas written at the turn of the seventeenth century, focusing on plays which depict a foolish husband who, by virtue of his vanity and an overactive imagination, believes that his wife has betrayed him. McDonald argues that Shakespeare "devised a collision between the [original] audience's normally scornful reaction to the 'imaginary cuckold' and the response dictated by the tragic nature of Othello's story" in order to heighten "the power of the action." He asserts that Othello's kinship with the comic figure of the gull should not blind us to his essential nobility, imaginative faculties, and greatness of heart.

Mendonça, Barbara Heliodora C. de. "'Othello': A Tragedy Built on a Comic Structure." *Shakespeare Survey* 21 (1968): 31-8.

An examination of Shakespeare's manipulation of elements from Italian *commedia dell'arte* and how they enhance his criticism in the play of Venetian society. Mendonça contends that the conflict between Othello and Venice arises from the hero's "moral convictions which are more impassioned and exacting than those of the super-subtle Venetians," whose moral attitude had become devoid of significance. She further notes that Iago—like the *commedia dell'arte* figures of Zanni-Arlecchino-Brighella—fails to understand his master and the possible implications of his intrigue, ending up the victim of his own self-interest.

Mercer, Peter. "*Othello* and the Form of Heroic Tragedy." *Critical Quarterly* 11, No. 1 (Spring 1969): 45-61.

An analysis of Othello's rhetorical diction in light of the dramatic convention governing the language of tragic heroes. Mercer contends that the play "turns upon the suggested discrepancy between the linguistic and the existential worlds," noting that language is in effect an interpretation of reality or recorded events. He maintains that Othello's heroic idealism cannot admit doubts, ambiguities, or uncertainties and that his mind is unhinged by "the impossibility of knowledge and the torments of jealousy," but he concludes that Othello's final speech is consonant with the tradition of the tragic hero's ultimate assertion of remorse and his reaffirmation of his heroic dignity.

Money, John. "Othello's 'It is the cause . . .': An Analysis." *Shakespeare Survey* 6 (1953): 94-105.

A detailed examination of Othello's opening speech in Act V, Scene ii which focuses on such linguistic elements as the repetitions and alliterations, the changes in tempo, ambiguous words and phrases, and the contrived or artificial tone. Money maintains that this speech exposes just as evidently as does the Moor's final one at the play's conclusion Othello's proclivity for self-deception.

Muir, Kenneth. "The Jealousy of Iago." In *English Miscellany: A Symposium of History, Literature and the Arts 2*, edited by Mario Praz, pp. 65-83. Rome: Edizioni di Storia e Letteratura, 1951.

A rejection of the judgment—first espoused by Coleridge (see excerpt above, 1808-18) and endorsed by many later critics—of Iago's soliloquies as "motive-hunting." Muir contends that Shakespeare has provided Iago with several reasons for his actions and that these are revealed through his soliloquies. Of these, Muir identifies envy and "a pathological jealousy of his wife" as the bases for Iago's conduct, postulating that the ancient is less concerned with Emilia's unfaithfulness than he is with the idea that, as a cuckold, he is a despicable and pitiable figure, an assessment that "is intolerable to his self-esteem."

———. "The Text of *Othello*." *Shakespeare Studies* I (1965): 227-39. Discusses the textual problems that confront modern editors of *Othello*. Contending that the First Folio text is "generally more accurate" and reliable than that of the 1622 Quarto, Muir asserts that, on occasion, an editor should accept the quarto reading instead and, from time to time, should even reject both possibilities. Muir offers analyses of thirty-five passages in the play which differ from quarto to Folio, theorizing in each instance whether the variants are the result of copyist's or compositor's errors, changes made by Shakespeare on the manuscript used by the printer, or deliberate alterations attributable to the editors of the Folio.

———. "*Othello*." In his *Shakespeare's Tragic Sequence*, pp. 93-116. New York: Barnes & Noble Books, 1979.

Dissents from the critical assumption that Othello is not a jealous man and avers that, although he is clearly drawn as noble, he is also shown to become "desperately jealous" because of his credulousness and the deceitfulness of Iago. Muir also diverges from the viewpoint of such critics as T. S. Eliot and F. R. Leavis (see excerpts above, 1927 and 1937), maintaining that Othello is neither egotistical nor prone to self-dramatization and that the Moor's final speech reveals his grief and repentance—"the natural expression of proper pride"—and the conviction that in making Desdemona the sole meaning of his life he indeed loved her too well.

Murry, John Middleton. "Desdemona's Handkerchief." In his *Shakespeare*, pp. 311-21. London: Jonathan Cape, 1936.

Argues that Desdemona's loss of the handkerchief symbolizes the perfection of her love for Othello, for she became heedless of it only "when Othello was sick and her concern for the man she loved drove out all concern for the token of their love." Murry contends that at the heart of the tragedy is Shakespeare's recognition and portrayal of the impossibility of attaining the complete merging of two separate identities that is love's ideal and that, in this straining after the unattainable, human love "has within it the seed of its own death."

Neely, Carol Thomas. "Women and Men in *Othello*: 'what should such a fool / Do with so good a woman?'" *Shakespeare Studies* X (1977): 133-58.

An analysis of the kinship between the women in *Othello* and the heroines in Shakespeare's earlier comedies which emphasizes their similar capacities to initiate courtship, to tolerate men's fancies, and to balance romantic idealism with a realistic view of sexuality, but which also contrasts the failure of the women in this play to "transform or be reconciled with the men" with the resolution of conflict that is the conventional conclusion of the comedies. Arguing that the foolish vanity of male figures in the comedies degenerates into a murderous obsession with reputation and manliness in *Othello*, Neely maintains that reconciliation between the sexes is not attained in this play because the men misunderstand the women and "the women overestimate the men." She judges that Desdemona's loss of the handkerchief represents her loss of "women's civilizing power" and that when she lies to Othello about its disappearance she loses both "her maiden's power" to sustain their relationship and her ability to repel the destructive attacks against it posed by Iago and Othello. Neely concludes that, in its representation of the destruction of the development of romantic love, "the play's ending is less like tragedy than cankered comedy."

North, Christopher [pseudonym of John Wilson]. "Christopher under Canvas." *Blackwood's Edinburgh Magazine* LXVI, No. CCCCXIV (April 1850): 481-512.

The earliest examination of the double time scheme in *Othello*. North demonstrates that the events in Cyprus are alternately presented as occurring within the space of thirty-six hours and over a period of many weeks. Comparing the multiple allusions in Acts III through V to specific hours and events of a single day, and contending that Act III begins on the morning following the reunion in Cyprus and Cassio's disgrace, North concludes that less than two full days elapse between their arrival on the island and Othello's murder of Desdemona. The critic argues that an extended period of time "seemed necessary" to convince the audience that the noble Moor of Acts I and II believes he has cause to slay his wife; hence Shakespeare provided many indications that the characters had been on Cyprus for at least two months in order to suggest the lapse of a certain period of time in which the supposedly adulterous relationship could have developed.

———. "Christopher under Canvas." *Blackwood's Edinburgh Magazine* LXVI, No. CCCCXV (May 1850): 622-39.

A continuation of the critic's earlier essay (see entry above), in which he hypothesizes that the compressed or short time conveys the "tragical vehemency" and "impetuous energy" of Othello's passion, while the protracted or long time imparts verisimilitude to the dramatic action. Particularly noting the way in which Othello's four entrances onto the stage at different intervals in Act III, Scene iii "have a strangely deluding effect" and serve to dislocate the audience's sense of the passage of time during this scene, North contends that long time serves a variety of dramatic necessities, most of all, "the necessity of our not knowing that Iago begins the Temptation, and that Othello extinguishes the Light of his Life all in one day."

Reid, Stephen. "Othello's Jealousy." *American Imago* 25, No. 3 (Fall 1968): 274-93.

A psychoanalytic appraisal of Othello's delusional jealousy as based not on "an unconscious homosexual impulse," as has been argued by Abraham Bronson Feldman (see entry above), but on the Moor's suddenly released oedipal anxieties and his subconscious fear of castration. Reid contends that Desdemona's seeming inaccessibility and her belief in and acceptance of the Moor's "heroic fancies" "reproduces all too perfectly the situation Othello had longed to experience with his mother," and thus, subsequent to the consummation of their marriage, Othello behaves as if he had acted out his repressed childhood desires toward his mother, projecting his own guilty feelings onto Desdemona for betraying him "into a dangerous situation."

Rice, Julian C. "Desdemona Unpinned: Universal Guilt in *Othello*." *Shakespeare Studies* VII (1974): 209-26.

Argues that although Desdemona is apparently the most virtuous of women, she shares with Othello and all the other characters in the drama the frailties, imperfections, and moral vulnerability that are inherent in human nature. Rice maintains that Desdemona is partially responsible for her own murder through her "overconfidence in the power of virtue to triumph."

Richmond, Hugh. "Love and Justice: *Othello*'s Shakespearean Context." In *Pacific Coast Studies in Shakespeare*, edited by Waldo F. McNeir and Thelma N. Greenfield, pp. 148-72. Eugene: University of Oregon Books, 1966.

Assesses *Othello* as a subtle and complex exploration of idealistic love. The Moor's absolutism leads him to value that type of love which is most inaccessible, Richmond contends, and the pursuit of this ideal must inevitably direct him towards the final and complete distancing of lover and beloved found only in death. The critic further argues that the very characteristics that have drawn Othello and Desdemona to each other—her "unusual toughness and integrity" and his "resoluteness" and "promptness of response"—are also the ones that destroy their relationship, for it is Desdemona's persistence in pleading Cassio's cause that alienates her husband and Othello's intolerance of uncertainties and confusion of his superior intelligence with omniscience that leads him to judge himself and others with "fatal harshness."

Ridley, M. R. Introduction to *Othello*, by William Shakespeare, edited by M. R. Ridley, pp. xv-lxx. The New Arden Edition of the Works of William Shakespeare, edited by Una Ellis-Fermor and Harold F. Brooks. London: Methuen & Co., 1958.

An overview of several aspects of *Othello*, including its date, sources, time scheme, and characterization, as well as the textual issues associated with the play. Ridley doubts whether there is "any real chance of establishing an 'authoritative' text for *Othello*," but he offers conjectural reasons for his greater reliance on the 1622 Quarto than on the First Folio of 1623, postulating that the former represents a more direct transmission from Shakespeare to the compositor than does the latter and rejecting the claim of Alice Walker (see entry below) that the Folio text is generally regarded as more accurate and reliable. He also disputes Samuel Taylor Coleridge's contentions that Shakespeare did not intend Othello to be a black man and that Iago's malignity is motiveless (see excerpts above, 1808-18 and 1813).

Rogers, Stephen. "*Othello:* Comedy in Reverse." *Shakespeare Quarterly* XXIV, No. 2 (Spring 1973): 210-20.

Traces the process by which Shakespeare adapted, rearranged, and inverted in *Othello* dramatic techniques and materials usually associated with comedies of manners in order to enhance the impact of the Moor's metamorphosis from hero into fool. Rogers focuses on Iago's employment of devices used by comic schemers to manipulate the perceptions and identities of other characters, noting particularly that his method for causing Othello to misinterpret the meeting between Cassio and Bianco in Act IV, Scene i echoes the familiar comic device of the "concealed witness," with one exception: whereas such scenes in comic drama generally lead to revelation of truth and the removal of "obstacles to love," this simulated disclosure convinces Othello that Desdemona has been false to him.

Rosenberg, Marvin. *The Masks of Othello: The Search for the Identity of Othello, Iago, and Desdemona by Three Centuries of Actors and Critics.* Berkeley: University of California Press, 1961, 313 p.

An overview of the interpretations of Othello, Desdemona, and Iago by actors and actresses from the Restoration to the mid-twentieth century. Seeking to synthesize the commentary of literary critics with the interpretations offered by leading performers, Rosenberg emphasizes the essential humanity of the play's three central dramatic figures, rejecting as limited both symbolist criticism that focuses narrowly on the poetic language and scholarly readings of the play which view it solely in terms of Elizabethan

dramatic conventions. Rosenberg maintains that both viewpoints fail to take into account the impact of the play when it is performed in the theater—"its proper medium."

Ross, Lawrence J. "World and Chrysolite in *Othello*." *Modern Language Notes* LXXVI, No. 8 (December 1961): 683-92.

A detailed analysis of Othello's "chrysolite" speech (V. II. 143-46) and a review of the moral and emblematic significance of the chrysolite jewel as expressed in writing of the late sixteenth and early seventeenth centuries. Maintaining that for Shakespeare's contemporaries the chrysolite signified a Christ-like truth and purity, Ross argues that the dramatist uses the image here to indicate that Othello, through his own compulsive possessiveness and his unfaithfulness to his wife, has lost not only Desdemona, but also the spiritual value "which she incarnated and which the chrysolite symbolizes."

Rossiter, A. P. "*Othello:* A Moral Essay." In his *Angel with Horns and Other Shakespeare Lectures*, edited by Graham Storey, pp. 189-208. New York: Theatre Arts Books, 1961.

Disputes the view held by Samuel Taylor Coleridge (see excerpts above, 1813, 1822, and 1827) and A. C. Bradley (see excerpt above, 1904) that Othello is not inherently jealous and would not have acted as he did except for the extraordinary cleverness and wickedness of Iago. Noting that the term jealousy may connote either mere suspicion or "extreme sexual jealousy," and that the emotion is generally regarded as both wicked and as an indication of the intensity of one's love for another, Rossiter discovers the same ambivalence in Othello's use of the word in his concluding speech and relates this to the drama's ambiguous and insubstantial depiction of love itself.

Sedgewick, G. G. "Irony as Dramatic Preparation: *Othello*." In his *Of Irony: Especially in Drama*, pp. 87-114. Toronto: University of Toronto Press, 1935.

Analyzes the dramatic action in *Othello* from the beginning of the play to Act III, Scene iii and demonstrates that, through the use of "irony as dramatic preparation," the audience is led to expect that a catastrophe is "not only probable but inevitable" and to feel "impatient for its coming." Contending that throughout the first part of the drama the marriage of Desdemona and Othello evokes uneasiness in the Venetian senators, outrage in Brabantio, and vilification in Iago and Roderigo, Sedgewick asserts that we begin to sense that the continued stability of the union is unlikely, even while it is apparently triumphant at the close of the council scene and exalted at the couple's reunion in Cyprus. Thus, the critic argues, when the Moor succumbs to Iago in the temptation scene, the speed of his decline does not surprise us, for it is "positively demanded by the action of the play" and by our carefully developed expectations.

Sewell, Arthur. "Tragedy and 'The Kingdom of Ends'." In his *Character and Society in Shakespeare*, pp. 91-121. Oxford: At the Clarendon Press, 1951.

Contends that in *Othello* the essential conflict is between the functionalism, expediency, prestige, and conduct of the temporal world of Venice and the value, integrity, principles, and "moral being" of the spiritual world represented by the Moor himself. Sewell also regards Othello's downfall as a reenactment of "the Fall of Man," and he finds in the play "no hint of regeneration or redemption."

Siegel, Paul N. Letter to the editor of *Shakespeare Quarterly* IX, No. 3 (Summer 1958): 433-35.

A response to Edward Hubler's attack on Siegel's interpretation of *Othello* (see excerpts above, 1958 and 1953). Asserting that Hubler offers no detailed evidence from the text itself to demonstrate "where I had wrenched or disregarded it," Siegel charges that the critic's attempted refutation is principally "devoted to generalities" about Elizabethan religious views. With regard to Hubler's claim that Shakespeare has not "told" us what happens to the characters after they leave the stage and, therefore, it is specious to claim that the Moor has incurred eternal damnation,

Siegel argues that a dramatist addresses his audience only indirectly, "through the implications of the words and actions of his characters and of the consequences of these words and actions" and that it is the function of the critic to attend to these implications and overtones.

Smith, Gordon Ross. "Iago the Paranoiac." *American Imago* 16, No. 2 (Summer 1959): 155-67.

Generally endorses Martin Wangh's interpretation of Iago as a victim of delusional jealousy stemming from repressed homosexual impulses (see excerpt above, 1950). Noting Iago's repeated expressions of ambivalence toward both Othello and Cassio, the evidence of an extreme inner conflict in the definitions he offers of himself, and his "incessant allusions to sexual matters" that strongly suggest he lacks satisfactory sexual outlets, Smith contends that, in his portrayal of the ancient, Shakespeare demonstrated an understanding of the personality configuration known to psychoanalysts as paranoia and of its characteristic "suspicion, its destructiveness, and its relation to homosexuality."

Spencer, Theodore. "*Othello* and *King Lear*." In his *Shakespeare and the Nature of Man*, pp. 122-52. New York: The Macmillan Co., 1942.

Contends that Othello's innate nobility and self-mastery of his sensuality and passion are clearly evident in the first part of the drama and that Shakespeare subsequently portrays the Moor as tragically misusing his superb powers. Spencer also assesses Iago as dispassionate and cynical, the embodiment of the evil that ensues when man overvalues his own individualism and negates the significance of any connection to other persons or principles, becoming, in effect, "an emotional eunuch."

Spurgeon, Caroline F. E. *Shakespeare's Imagery and What It Tells Us*, 1935. Reprint. Cambridge: At the University Press, 1971, 408 p.

Identifies, in several discussions of *Othello* dispersed throughout the book, two central patterns of imagery in the play: the first consisting of allusions to predatory or socially irresponsible animals and the second reflected in the frequent use of metaphors associated with the sea. Spurgeon also discovers a subsidiary metaphoric pattern of olfactory sensations, particularly to denote "the evil smell of evil deeds."

Stempel, Daniel. "The Silence of Iago." *PMLA* 84, No. 2 (March 1969): 252-63.

Traces the elements which constituted the Elizabethan caricature of the Jesuitical Machiavel and demonstrates that Iago embodies the evils which Shakespeare's contemporaries assigned to members of the Society of Jesus, especially with regard to the ancient's assertion of the autonomy of the human will. Through an examination of late sixteenth- and early seventeenth-century ecclesiastical writings, Stempel shows that strict Thomist Catholics, Anglicans, and Puritans generally viewed Jesuits as casuistic, morally expedient, untrustworthy—because they cloaked their destructive intents under "the garment of amity and friendship"—and theologically guilty of extenuating the grace of God by their claim that free will and divine grace operate equally in determining human conduct. The critic concludes that, in depicting Iago as the exemplification of these characteristics, Shakespeare sought to dramatize and confute the Jesuitical doctrine of "the autonomous will."

Stoll, Elmer Edgar. "*Othello*." In his *Art and Artifice in Shakespeare: A Study in Dramatic Contrast and Illusion*, pp. 6-55. Cambridge: At the University Press, 1933.

Charges that critics of *Othello* who have sought psychological realism in Iago's successful temptation of the Moor have failed to distinguish between life and art. Stoll contends that by ascribing the downfall of Othello entirely to Iago's manipulations and by providing a mechanical stage convention as an explanation for the rapid development of the Moor's jealousy—namely, that of "the blameless hero" and "the calumniator believed"—Shakespeare permitted us to retain a compassionate attitude toward Othello, while simultaneously accepting the fact that he does indeed become jealous. The critic's assessment of the play offered in this essay is similar to his earlier interpretation (see excerpt above, 1915).

———. "An Othello All Too Modern." *ELH* 13, No. 1 (March 1946): 46-58.

Charges that Leo Kirschbaum's assessment of the character of Othello (see entry above) is erroneous and unsupported by textual evidence from the play. Stoll argues that the passages which Kirschbaum maintains reveal Othello to be indulging in god-like posturing are actually examples of Shakespeare's use of "self-descriptive techniques" common to Renaissance tragic drama, frequently employed by Shakespeare and others to designate the speaker as a figure of lofty stature and to emphasize his inherent nobility.

Tannenbaum, Samuel A. "The Wronged Iago." *Shakespeare Association Bulletin* XII, No. 1 (January 1937): 57-62.

Contends that Shakespeare provides clear evidence in *Othello* that the Moor is guilty of adultery with Emilia and that Iago does believe he has been cuckolded. Maintaining that the play has a "moralistic purpose," as do all Elizabethan dramas, Tannenbaum holds that Othello's death represents the sure and ultimate punishment of his "sin and error."

Walker, Alice. "The 1622 Quarto and the First Folio Texts of *Othello*." *Shakespeare Survey* 5 (1952): 16-24.

Advances the theory that the First Folio of 1623 was printed from an emended copy of the 1622 Quarto and that the inferiority of the Quarto is traceable to the fact that it is "the work of a bookkeeper who relied on his knowledge of the play as acted and on his invention where memory failed." Noting the many errors common to both texts, Walker hypothesizes that inaccuracies in the Quarto were overlooked during the process of improving and correcting it for the printer of the Folio.

West, Robert H. "The Christianness of *Othello*." *Shakespeare Quarterly* XV, No. 3 (Summer 1964): 333-43.

Contends that *Othello* does not provide "decisive evidence" regarding the damnation of the Moor and that Paul N. Siegel (see excerpt above, 1953) has imposed a Christian design on the play. Arguing that the resemblances between Othello and Adam are not "detailed, explicit, and consistent enough to be really indispensable to our understanding of the play," West rejects the notion that these similarities imply that the Moor faces the same condemnation as Adam. He views the biblical references and echoes of Christian theology as devices to intensify the emotional effect of the dramatic action rather than to promulgate religious doctrine, concluding that Act V, Scene ii is "theologically unexplicit" and provides no evidence to confirm either Othello's salvation or his consignment to perdition.

Whitaker, Virgil K. "The Way to Dusty Death: *Othello* and *Macbeth*." In his *The Mirror up to Nature: The Technique of Shakespeare's Tragedies*, pp. 241-75. San Marino, Calif.: The Huntington Library, 1965.

Locates Othello's principal error in his doting uxoriousness that leads him to place his love for Desdemona "above his duty to God." Whitaker maintains that the Moor's excessive self-confidence renders him particularly vulnerable to self-deception and that in the temptation scene he makes the wrong moral choice because, inflamed by passion, he is unable to evaluate rationally the evidence Iago presents to him. Whitaker contends that Othello's ensuing conduct leads him to damnation, although he asserts that Shakespeare did not sufficiently prepare us to believe Othello "when he tells us explicitly that he is damned." The critic also sees other shortcomings in this play, and he argues that, because of the overly lengthy dramatic exposition, Shakespeare had to compress the development of Othello's jealousy into one scene, leaving us insufficient time to experience for ourselves the Moor's "horror and distress"; because of this, we fail to empathize fully with his tragic decline.

Wilson, John Dover. Introduction to *Othello,* by William Shakespeare, edited by Alice Walker and John Dover Wilson, pp. ix-lvi. Cambridge: At the University Press, 1957.

    A comprehensive overview of *Othello,* including discussions of such topics as composition date, Shakespeare's adaptation of Cinthio's tale, image patterns, and the issue of double time in the play's dramatic action. Dover Wilson asserts that the character and motivation of Iago are essentially enigmatic and will continue to resist all attempts to explicate them. He also maintains that the dramatist intended the audience to regard Othello as noble throughout the play, and he assesses the Moor's death as self-execution rather than suicide, arguing that Othello's final tears are joyous because he understands at last that Desdemona has remained faithful to him and that ''her soul is in bliss.''

Yoder, R. A. ''The Two Worlds of *Othello.*'' *South Atlantic Quarterly* 72, No. 2 (Spring 1973): 213-25.

    Contends that the representation of society as purified and renewed ''through the expulsion or death of a scapegoat hero''—a pattern Shakespeare used in his other tragedies—is absent from *Othello.* Yoder maintains that Venice is portrayed in this play as a society based upon moral expediency and that the removal of the dramatic action to Cyprus leads, not to reconciliation, but to the imposition on the Moor of Venetian perceptions of life, so that at the close of the drama the values espoused by Othello and Desdemona are obliterated and Venice dominates ''in fact as well as fancy.''

Titus Andronicus

DATE: External evidence indicates that *The Most Lamentable Romaine Tragedie of Titus Andronicus* was written and performed sometime between 1589 and 1594. An entry in the STATIONERS' REGISTER of February 6, 1594, lists "a booke intituled a Noble Roman Historye of Tytus Andronicus" and "the ballad thereof," although many critics believe that this allusion refers not to Shakespeare's play, but to a prose history that served as his source. The earlier date of 1589 was established by Ben Jonson, who in the Induction to his *Bartholomew Fair,* published in 1614, listed *Titus* along with Thomas Kyd's *The Spanish Tragedy* as works composed "five and twenty, or thirtie yeeres" hence; the later date is supported by Philip Henslowe, a theater owner and contemporary of Shakespeare, who in his diary entry of January 24, 1594, noted the performance of a new play entitled "Titus and Ondronicus." However, many scholars have questioned the validity of both Jonson's and Henslowe's accounts and have turned to the play's internal evidence in attempts to establish a more accurate date. Linguistic similarities to *1 Henry VI* and significant stylistic and thematic parallels between *Titus, Venus and Adonis,* and *The Rape of Lucrece* have led numerous critics to conjecture that *Titus Andronicus* was composed in 1592-93, the years Shakespeare is known to have written these other works. Yet, despite the wealth of information on the question, no consensus has been reached concerning the date of *Titus*'s composition or its first performance.

TEXT: There are four known texts for *Titus Andronicus,* and commentators generally agree on their authority and relationship. The First Quarto (Q1) was published in 1594 and is considered the most authoritative text. Many scholars believe that Q1 is based on a transcription of Shakespeare's FOUL PAPERS—uncorrected manuscript written in the author's own hand—because of such telling characteristics as irregular speech prefixes and cryptic stage directions. The Second Quarto (Q2) was printed in 1600; it contains minor corrections to the text of Q1 but includes as well a number of superficial COMPOSITOR errors, such as misspelled words and incorrect speech headings. The Third Quarto (Q3) was issued in 1611 and includes fewer corrections and more corruptions than Q2. The final version of the play is the FIRST FOLIO text (F1), published in 1623. Based on a copy of Q3, F1 adds several stage directions and an entirely new scene—the so-called "fly-killing incident" of Act III, Scene ii—that do not appear in any of the QUARTOS. Many critics theorize that this scene was copied from Shakespeare's original manuscript which is now lost. This in turn would refute the hypothesis that Q1 was based on a transcription of this manuscript, since the scene does not appear in that text; others simply claim that Shakespeare added the scene to the copy of Q3 used by the compositors of the FOLIO text. Regardless of the answer, relatively few difficulties have been attributed to TEXTUAL CORRUPTION in F1 or the presence of the extra scene. Apart from textual considerations, what controversy does exist in *Titus* criticism—and has existed since the seventeenth century—surrounds the question of Shakespeare's authorship of the play. Commentators have variously argued that Shakespeare either wrote the drama in its entirety, revised the work of another playwright, or had nothing to do with its composition. Basing their conclusions on the depiction of Aaron in the play, a number of critics in the latter half of the nineteenth century

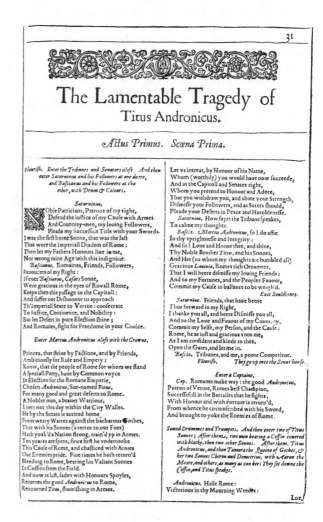

claimed that Christopher Marlowe wrote *Titus.* Such twentieth-century scholars as John Dover Wilson, W. Arthur Turner, and T. W. Baldwin discovered apparent stylistic anomalies within the play and advanced the theory that Shakespeare either collaborated with or revised the work of George Peele. Most recent critics, however, generally regard *Titus Andronicus* as Shakespeare's first tragedy, avoiding the question of authorship for a lack of conclusive information.

SOURCES: According to many modern scholars, the text entered in the Stationers' Register on February 6, 1594, may be Shakespeare's main source for *Titus Andronicus* rather than the play itself. The discrepancy between the title page of Q1 and the book described in the entry, as well as the inclusion in the latter of a "ballad," have often been cited to support this theory. In addition, many recent commentators have concluded that an eighteenth-century chapbook, or pamphlet, entitled *The History of Titus Andronicus, the Renowned Roman General,* which contains a prose narrative and a ballad derived from that story, is more likely a reprint of this source work, or at least a version of the narrative which Shakespeare used as the major source for his play. The similarities between the narrative and Shakespeare's *Titus Andronicus* tend to confirm this hypothesis, although Shakespeare's version is considerably elaborated. For example, both works include essentially the same characters, although Shakespeare's portraits of Aaron, Tamora, and Titus are more detailed than they are in the narrative. Both works present an invasion of Rome by the Goths; but whereas the prose version offers a simple account of this event, Shakespeare includes a factional dispute within the Roman society that complicates and confuses the broader struggle for power. Finally, the narrative contains many of the same classical allusions to SENECA's *Thyestes* and OVID's *Metamorphoses* that are found in *Titus Andronicus,* although Shakespeare emphasizes and extends the references to Ovid as an integral part of his plot.

Thomas Kyd's *The Spanish Tragedy* and Christopher Marlowe's portrait of Barabas in his *The Jew of Malta* have also been suggested as probable influences. Some critics have conjectured that Shakespeare ensured the success of *Titus* by deliberately imitating the style of these playwrights, whose works exemplify the revenge tragedy genre that was well received by Elizabethan audiences.

CRITICAL HISTORY: Despite strong evidence that reinforces Shakespeare's authorship of *Titus Andronicus,* such as FRANCIS MERES's listing of the play in his *Palladis Tamia* in 1598 and its inclusion by the editors John Heminge and Henry Condell in the First Folio, critics in the eighteenth and nineteenth centuries were unwilling to recognize *Titus* as primarily Shakespeare's work. Often disturbed or repelled by the play's violence, these commentators focused predominantly on the question of authorship, claiming for Shakespeare a secondary role. Although twentieth-century scholars have continued this controversy, most have generally accepted Shakespeare as the sole author of *Titus Andronicus.* Modern critics have concentrated on the play itself, examining its structure, themes, characterization, imagery, and language in order to understand its meaning and establish its importance to Shakespeare's canon.

The seventeenth-century dramatist Edward Ravenscroft, who characterized *Titus Andronicus* as ''a heap of Rubbish'' and claimed that Shakespeare provided only ''some Master-touches'' to the work of an unknown playwright, was the first commentator to suggest that the play was not totally Shakespeare's. Such eighteenth-century scholars as Charles Gildon, Lewis Theobald, and Edmond Malone in effect concurred with Ravenscroft by stating that Shakespeare merely added superficial revisions to an existing work. In support of his conclusion, Gildon asserted that events and characterization in *Titus* were ''contrary to Nature and Art,'' and for this reason he could not imagine that Shakespeare wrote any part of it. Theobald, basing his conclusion on Jonson's rather vague reference to the play's date of composition, argued that the original *Titus* was composed before Shakespeare settled in London and began writing drama. He maintained that Shakespeare only reintroduced the work some years later with ''his own masterly Touches.'' And though Malone did not cite his evidence, he contended that information in the Dulwich College Papers— documents which include the memoirs and correspondences of Philip Henslowe and the actor Edward Alleyn, two of Shakespeare's contemporaries—prove that Shakespeare revised an existing version of the play.

In addition to those commentators who theorized that Shakespeare collaborated to some degree on *Titus Andronicus,* several Neoclassical critics rejected the possibility that the dramatist was responsible for any part of the play. John Upton accepted Theobald's hypothesis concerning Shakespeare's

whereabouts at the time of *Titus*'s original composition as proof that Shakespeare could not have written or even revised the play, and he further remarked that it should never have been included among Shakespeare's genuine works. Samuel Johnson, on the other hand, rejected Theobald's argument, declaring that Shakespeare's touch is nowhere discernible in the drama. George Steevens, like Johnson, also maintained that the play does not conform to Shakespeare's recognized style.

A number of eighteenth-century commentators, however, did argue in favor of Shakespeare's authorship of *Titus Andronicus,* claiming that his style is apparent throughout the play. Benjamin Heath rejected the theory presented by both Theobald and Upton and regarded *Titus* instead as an example of Shakespeare's apprentice work, a drama ''written and acted before his poetical genius had had time to unfold and form itself.'' Edward Capell, the first critic to note a close connection between *Titus* and the popular Elizabethan revenge tragedy, theorized that Shakespeare imitated this genre in order to ensure the financial success of his own drama. The theories advanced by Heath and Capell received additional support and consideration in the nineteenth century by such prominent critics as August Wilhelm Schlegel, Hermann Ulrici, and Charles Knight.

The controversy over the authorship of *Titus Andronicus* continued throughout the nineteenth century, with critical opinion divided into the three categories established in the 1700s. The German scholar Schlegel expanded the arguments of Heath and Capell and contended that it is more realistic to view *Titus* as a work of Shakespeare's apprenticeship than to attribute it to an inferior playwright. In turn, Schlegel's commentary initiated a series of responses from such critics as William Hazlitt, Hermann Ulrici, Charles Knight, G. G. Gervinus, and Edward Dowden. Both Hazlitt and Dowden rejected the remarks of Schlegel and other German scholars and denied Shakespeare's authorship of *Titus Andronicus.* Hazlitt specifically argued against Schlegel's conclusion, claiming that the play's violence is totally unlike Shakespeare and that the entire work shows nothing of an immature effort, but instead demonstrates a ''confirmed habit'' and a ''full grown'' style. In a similar vein, Dowden asserted that *Titus* lacks the ''bright and tender play of fancy and feeling'' apparent in Shakespeare's other early works. Ulrici and Knight supported Schlegel's theory by agreeing that *Titus* is undoubtedly one of Shakespeare's early endeavors, written before he fully realized the depth and power of his genius. Knight also supported the theory that the violence and barbarity of *Titus* is a result of Shakespeare's personal experience—a biographical reading of the play strongly opposed by Gerald Massey and Dowden. Gervinus recognized *Titus* as one of Shakespeare's earliest works, but, like many of the eighteenth-century commentators, he contended that the play's unnatural characterization and improbable action indicate that Shakespeare did not write the drama, but simply revised the work of another playwright.

Although the efforts of most nineteenth-century critics were devoted to the question of *Titus*'s authorship, some commentators briefly examined other aspects of the play. Ulrici noted, as did Gerald Massey, that the work's major defect is not the abundance of horrors which seem to overwhelm its tragic design, but the absence of that conciliatory message or element of pity necessary to all serious tragedy. Knight declared that the actions and speeches of Tamora and Aaron display Shakespeare's ability—unique among Elizabethan dramatists—to maintain the ''entire conception of, and power over, the design of a drama.'' And Frederick S. Boas commented on *Titus*'s "clear and compact plot," as well as its relation to some of Shakespeare's later plays, such as *King Lear, Othello,* and *Richard III.* Unlike Ulrici, Boas also claimed that *Titus* does not lack a conciliatory message or end in "unmitigated gloom," but projects the optimism of "a new social order." However, the question of authorship continued to dominate critics' interests, as seen in the essays by L. M. Griffiths and Arthur Symons, both of whom followed the so-called "Ravenscroft tradition" and interpreted *Titus* as Shakespeare's revision of an unknown playwright's work.

In the twentieth century, critics have continued to address the question of Shakespeare's part in *Titus Andronicus,* with such scholars as John Dover Wilson, W. Arthur Turner, and T. W. Baldwin advancing the theory that Shakespeare either collaborated with or revised the work of George Peele. But a shift in critical emphasis to detailed analyses of the play itself, suggests solely that most modern commentators are willing to accept *Titus* as Shakespeare's work, and one of his first dramatic endeavors. The concentration on the different facets of the play's construction has led to a reassessment of previous critical assumptions, as well as a reexamination of *Titus*'s relationship to the other plays in Shakespeare's canon; it has also brought about an increasing interest in such fundamental issues as Shakespeare's tragic design, his synthesis of language and dramatic action, and his mixture of various sources and influences, including Seneca, Ovid, the revenge tragedy, and medieval morality drama.

At the turn of the century, H. Bellyse Baildon compared the characterization of *Titus* to that of other Shakespearean tragedies and maintained that the earlier play served as the archetype of those later works. Expanding the list of parallels noted by L. M. Griffiths in the nineteenth century, Baildon claimed that Tamora was Shakespeare's model for Lady Macbeth and Cleopatra and that Titus provided a rough pattern for the characters of Lear, Coriolanus, and Hamlet. He also considered Aaron a crude version of Iago, and in the tragic figure of Lavinia he perceived elements of Cordelia's character. Although Baildon's conclusions have been widely accepted, the dramatic complexity of such characters as Aaron and Titus was more fully examined by such later commentators as Fredson Thayer Bowers, Muriel C. Bradbrook, Bernard Spivack, and Irving Ribner. Bowers studied Shakespeare's handling of the revenge tragedy tradition by comparing the plot structures of *Titus* and Kyd's *The Spanish Tragedy.* Despite their obvious similarities, he noted that Shakespeare's play differs from Kyd's in several ways, including a fuller treatment of the protagonist and the inclusion of Aaron, "an important villainous character who is only loosely connected with the main plot." Bowers concluded that, by introducing the Moor as the central villain from Act II onward, Shakespeare diverts attention away from Tamora—the original instigator of the villains' revenge—and thus destroys the structural unity of his drama. Consequently, Bowers characterized *Titus* as an experimental play in which Shakespeare tried, unsuccessfully, to combine two different types of revenge tragedy: one Marlovian, the other Kydian. Bradbrook commented on the emblematic quality of the characters in *Titus Andronicus* and illustrated Shakespeare's indebtedness to medieval sources for his structure and characterization. She considered the medieval influence so pervasive in *Titus* that she labelled it "more like a pageant than a play," and she argued that the critics who focused primarily on the revenge pattern misunderstood Shakespeare's intent. Concentrating on the symbolic quality of Aaron's role, Spivack identified Aaron as the Vice figure of medieval allegorical drama—

in his words, "an entrenched theatrical image originating in metaphor." Ribner located the tragic theme of *Titus Andronicus* within the damnation of the play's protagonist. According to him, Titus emulates the classic tragic hero whose virtues, when exaggerated, become faults and whose destruction is guaranteed by his failure to alter his behavior and accept salvation. Ribner also suggested the manner in which Shakespeare's first audiences would have viewed Titus's behavior by noting the play's Elizabethan and Christian concept of mercy as a greater ideal than human justice, and by demonstrating how Titus forsakes this doctrine for a lesser good. The influence of Elizabethan concepts of justice or retribution on *Titus Andronicus* was also discussed later in the twentieth century by Ronald Broude.

Despite many essays in the last fifty years which attest to the complexity of the characterization in *Titus,* a number of critics deprecated Shakespeare's handling of his personae as well as his material in general. H. B. Charlton regarded the play as nothing more than a melodrama in which the plot, characterization, and moral foundation are all based on a mechanical manipulation of events for theatrical effect, rather than on a serious concern for the laws of tragedy. Wolfgang H. Clemen, although primarily concerned with the conflict between image and action in the play, also criticized the characterization and events as vague and unjustified. Larry S. Champion argued that Titus lacks "philosophic depth" and fails in his role as a tragic protagonist. According to Champion, Titus's failure results from Shakespeare's choice of an external narrative approach to develop Titus's character, through which such supporting figures as Marcus and Lucius define his personality rather than through the effective use of soliloquies and asides, the technique Shakespeare adopted in his later plays. It is for this reason, Champion concluded, that Titus's emergence as a sophisticated avenger in the play's dénouement remains unconvincing.

Twentieth-century criticism of *Titus Andronicus* has demonstrated that the problems with characterization, language, and action in the play are closely related to the question of Shakespeare's tragic design. In fact, this question has occupied the interest of commentators since Bowers identified a combination of Elizabethan revenge tragedy elements within the play and E.M.W. Tillyard compared it to the later histories, specifically with respect to Shakespeare's theme of rightful succession. One of the most unconventional interpretations of Shakespeare's design in *Titus Andronicus* is that presented by John Dover Wilson, who argued that the portions written by Shakespeare demonstrate a deliberate attempt at parody rather than serious tragedy. According to Dover Wilson, Shakespeare compensated for his unpleasant experience in revising the play by "mocking" its fundamental style of language and characterization—a theory he substantiated by comparing such passages as Marcus's discovery of the mutilated Lavinia and those of Titus's lamentations to similar scenes in such contemporary works as *The Rape of Lucrece* and *Love's Labour's Lost.* Other critics noted a disparity between the play's poetry and action. Clemen also pointed to Marcus's lyrical outburst at the sight of the mutilated Lavinia to underscore his displeasure with Shakespeare's dramatic structure, which he concluded is based on an "absurd contrast between occasion and image."

One of the most important essays on the conflict between language and action in *Titus Andronicus,* as well as the nature of Shakespeare's tragic structure, was written by Eugene M. Waith. Waith disputed the interpretations proposed by both Dover

Wilson and Clemen and contended instead that Shakespeare was well aware of the incongruity inherent in his play. Waith maintained that Shakespeare was attempting to develop "a special tragic mode" in which he dramatized certain concepts from Ovid's *Metamorphoses* within the structure of an Elizabethan political and moral tragedy. He acknowledged that Shakespeare's experiment could not "be fully realized by the techniques of drama" because the primary concept he borrowed from Ovid—the transformation of individuals through passion and suffering—cannot be successfully conveyed onstage. Waith's essay is significant because it is one of the first comprehensive investigations of Ovid's influence on the language and structure of *Titus* and because it identifies the conflict between image and action in the play as an essential part of Shakespeare's design.

Following Waith's study, critics returned repeatedly to the question of Shakespeare's tragic structure in *Titus Andronicus*. Alan Sommers regarded the play's central theme as the struggle between "ideal civilization" and "the barbarism of primitive, original nature," and he declared that Shakespeare's tragic vision of the moral and political dissolution and regeneration of an entire society parallels Friedrich Nietzsche's metaphysic in *The Birth of Tragedy*. Sommers also stressed the importance in *Titus* of the conflict between Rome's principle of justice and what he characterized as the primal energy of the "forest-symbol," a point discussed more fully by D. J. Palmer and Albert H. Tricomi. Other critics who examined the tragic structure of Shakespeare's play as well as the dramatist's handling of his Ovidian and Senecan sources include A. C. Hamilton, James L. Calderwood, and Palmer. Hamilton called *Titus* the "archetype" of Shakespeare's later tragedies and claimed that it is more than an early, immature work or an imitation of Kyd's *The Spanish Tragedy*; instead, he regarded it as a "very ambitious" play in which Shakespeare combined elements from Senecan and medieval morality drama with the "major literary tradition in Ovid." Unlike Waith, who found the mixture of Ovid's "cultured style" and the violent content in *Titus* dramatically unsuccessful, Hamilton advocated that this synthesis is essential to the play's dramatic reality and tragic form. In an examination of the "metadramatic theme" of *Titus Andronicus*, Calderwood interpreted the play as Shakespeare's attempt to unite poetry and action, word and deed, Ovid and Seneca within the structure of a popular art form. To Calderwood, *Titus* reveals Shakespeare's frustration as a beginning dramatist forced to adapt his poetic language to satisfy dramatic convention. On the symbolic level, he thus defined Lavinia as poetic expression and her violation by the barbarous Goths as essentially the rape and mutilation of language when it is made to embody dramatic action. Shakespeare's purpose was to reestablish the importance of lyrical expression in his Senecan world of horror, according to Calderwood; but, he concluded, Shakespeare was unable at this point in his career to resolve the opposition of language and action which *Titus* presents, achieving instead, through his reliance on the banquet scene from Seneca's *Thyestes*, a conclusion that projects the drama even further into "pure physical action." As such, Calderwood echoes Waith's final assessment of *Titus*, namely, that Shakespeare failed to dramatically combine his Ovidian and Senecan, or lyrical and representational, materials. Palmer agreed with Hamilton that *Titus Andronicus* is "a highly-ordered and elaborately-designed work." Also like Hamilton, he disagreed with Waith's opinion that Shakespeare's dramatization of Ovid's language of metamorphosis inhibits the reality of the play's action. He claimed instead that Shakespeare actually sought, through the use of ritualized expression, to express the unutterable and to stabilize reality for both his characters and his audience. Palmer also identified the cyclic repetition of revenge as the work's primary dramatic pattern, and he concluded by describing the play as Shakespeare's "thesis in tragedy, anticipating many of the formal techniques and devices used in later tragedies."

Two other important essays include the imagery study of Albert H. Tricomi and the psychoanalytical interpretation of *Titus* presented by David Willbern. Tricomi challenged Clemen's assertion that the imagery in the play does not proceed organically from the dramatic action and contended instead that the poetic language, especially the imagery of animals and vegetation, reveals the tragedy's thematic structure, which he defined as the image of a pastoral garden—represented by Lavinia, the Andronici family, and Rome itself—assaulted by the "predatory principle of malevolence" personified in the characters of Tamora and Aaron. Tricomi concluded that this image of the "mutilated garden" also suggests a larger religious issue informing the tragic events: the question of divine justice. He asserted that the existence of divine justice is affirmed in the play, although Shakespeare also implies that this providential order does not necessarily prohibit human suffering. Willbern also focused on the imagery and symbolism in *Titus Andronicus*, identifying certain sexual implications based on the play's ambivalent presentation of "attack and defense, rape and rescue, and a further enactment of [a] murderous hostility toward women." He perceived in the figure of Tamora an image of humanity's worst fear, that is, the "dreaded devouring mother," and he compared her with the image of the forest pit or mouth, both of which unconsciously suggest dismemberment and destruction. Willbern concluded that Titus's final revenge—his Thyestean banquet—is on its deepest level an "oral vengeance" in which the fear of Tamora's latent tendencies are returned to their source, both symbolically and dramatically.

Titus Andronicus has never been considered one of Shakespeare's more successful efforts. Despite the studies that have established the play's intended structural and thematic unity, scholars have generally recognized a disparity between the tragedy's poetic conception and dramatic realization, and the conflict between the play's words and actions remains unresolved. However, the play remains important as an archetype of Shakespeare's later tragedies. In the words of Larry S. Champion, *Titus* provides "a base from which to measure and evaluate the nature of Shakespeare's growth as a tragic playwright."

BEN JONSON (essay date 1614)

[*Jonson, one of the most prominent Elizabethan playwrights, is thought to have been a strong rival of Shakespeare's as a writer of comedies. Yet Jonson was also a close friend of Shakespeare's, and, in the preface he composed for the First Folio of Shakespeare's plays, he praised Shakespeare's genius, saying, "He was not of an age, but for all time!" Elsewhere, Jonson wrote of Shakespeare, "I lov'd the man, and doe honour his memory (on this side Idolatry) as much as any." Their friendship, however, did not prevent Jonson from making critical comments on Shakespeare's plays or pointing out that the "Sweet Swan of Avon" had "small Latine, and lesse Greeke." Jonson's reference to* Titus Andronicus *in the Induction to his* Bartholomew Fair *(1614), excerpted below, has been cited by many critics in their attempts to establish the date of composition for Shakespeare's play. Jonson's allusion indicates a date no later than 1589.]*

Hee that will sweare *Ieronimo* [Thomas Kyd's *The Spanish Tragedy*] or *Andronicus* are the best playes, yet shall passe unexcepted at, heere, as a man whose Iudgement shewes it is constant, and hath stood still, these five and twentie, or thirtie yeeres.

> *Ben Jonson, in an extract from* The Shakspere Al-lusion-Book: A Collection of Allusions to Shakspere *from 1591-1700, Vol. I, edited by John Munro, revised edition, 1932. Reprint by Books for Libraries Press, 1970; distributed by Arno Press, Inc., p. 247.*

EDWARD RAVENSCROFT (essay date 1686)

[*Ravenscroft was a seventeenth-century English dramatist whose adaptation of* Titus Andronicus *was first performed in 1678. The following excerpt is taken from the preface to the quarto edition of his* Titus Andronicus, or the Rape of Lavinia, *written in 1686. He is the first critic to suggest that Shakespeare merely provided "some Master-touches" to the work of an unknown playwright—an opinion supported by many scholars in the eighteenth and nineteenth centuries. This theory is now referred to as "the Ravenscroft tradition."*]

I think it a greater theft to Rob the dead of their Praise, then the Living of their Money. That I may not appear Guilty of such a Crime, 'tis necessary I should acquaint you, that there is a Play in Mr. *Shakespears* Volume under the name of *Titus Andronicus,* from whence I drew part of this. I have been told by some anciently conversant with the Stage, that it was not Originally his, but brought by a private Author to be Acted, and he only gave some Master-touches to one or two of the Principal Parts or Characters; this I am apt to believe, because 'tis the most incorrect and indigested piece in all his Works, It seems rather a heap of Rubbish then a Structure.

> *Edward Ravenscroft, in an extract from* The Shakspere Allusion-Book: A Collection of Allusions to Shakspere *from 1591-1700, Vol, II, edited by John Munro, revised edition, 1932. Reprint by Books for Libraries Press, 1970; distributed by Arno Press, Inc., p. 319.*

CHARLES GILDON (essay date 1710)

[*Gildon was the first critic to write an extended commentary on Shakespeare's plays. Like many other Neoclassicists, he regarded Shakespeare as an imaginative playwright who nevertheless lacked knowledge of the dramatic "rules" necessary for correct writing. In the excerpt below, Gildon echoes Edward Ravenscroft (1686) by stating that Shakespeare only added "some few Touches" to* Titus Andronicus; *he further contends that the play's characterization is "contrary to Nature and Art."*]

As [*Titus Andronicus*] is not founded in any one Particular, on the *Roman* History tho' palm'd upon *Rome,* so the whole is so very shocking, that if there be any Beauties in the Diction I cou'd not find them, or at least they are very faint and very few. I can easily believe what has been said, that this is none of *Shakespear's* Play that he only introduc'd it and gave it some few Touches. Such Devils incarnate are not fit for the *Drama* the Moor describes himself a Degree more abandon'd than the Devil himself, and *Tamora* when *Lavinia* is seiz'd, and *Bassianus* kill'd shows her self not much better. This is so contrary to Nature and Art, that all the Crimes are monstrously beyond the very Name of Scandalous. (pp. 367-68)

> *Charles Gildon, "Remarks on the Plays of Shake-spear," in* The Works of Mr. William Shakespear, *Vol. 7, by William Shakespeare, 1710. Reprint by AMS Press, Inc., 1967, pp. 257-444.*

LEWIS THEOBALD (essay date 1733)

[*Theobald, a dramatist and classical scholar, was also one of the most important editors of Shakespeare's plays in the first half of the eighteenth century. Although his reputation as a Shakespearean editor declined after his death and opinion of the value of his work remains divided today, he nonetheless contributed significant emendations which have been adopted by modern editors. However, his adaptations of Shakespeare's plays, revised to adhere to Neoclassical dramatic rules, have been less well received. In the following excerpt, Theobald cites Ben Jonson's reference to* Titus Andronicus *(see excerpt above, 1614) and regards his dating of the play as accurate. Theobald argues that the play was written before Shakespeare arrived in London and that he only reintroduced the work with "his own masterly Touches" some years later. Other critics who accept* Titus Andronicus *as Shakespeare's revision of an earlier work include Edward Ravenscroft (1686), Edmond Malone (1790), Samuel Taylor Coleridge (1811), G. G. Gervinus (1849-50), L. M. Griffiths (1884), Arthur Symons (1885), and Joseph S. G. Bolton (1933).*]

[*Titus Andronicus*] is one of those Plays, which I have always thought, with the better Judges, ought not to be acknowledg'd in the List of *Shakespeare's* genuine Pieces. And, perhaps, I may give a Proof to strengthen this Opinion, that may put the Matter out of Question. *Ben Jonson* in the Induction to his *Bartlemew*-Fair, (which made its first Appearance in the Year 1614) couples *Jeronymo* and *Andronicus* together in Reputation, and speaks of them as Plays then of 25 or 30 Years standing. Consequently, *Andronicus* must have been on the Stage, before *Shakespeare* left *Warwickshire* to come and reside in *London:* and I never heard it so much as intimated, that he had turn'd his Genius to Stage-Writing, before he associated with the Players, and became one of their Body. However, that he afterwards introduc'd it a-new on the Scene, with the Addition of his own masterly Touches, is incontestable: and thence, I presume, grew his Title to it. The Diction in general, where he has not taken the Pains to raise it, is even beneath that of the Three Parts of *Henry* VI. (pp. 307-08)

> *Lewis Theobald, in a note on "Titus Andronicus," in* The Works of Shakespeare, *Vol. 5 by William Shakespeare, edited by Lewis Theobald, 1733. Reprint by AMS Press, 1968, pp. 307-08.*

JOHN UPTON (essay date 1748)

[*In the following excerpt from his* Critical Observations on Shakespeare *(1748), Upton, an eighteenth-century clergyman and Spenserean scholar, agrees with Lewis Theobald (1733) that* Titus Andronicus *must have been written before Shakespeare arrived in London. Upton, however, denies the possibility that Shakespeare wrote or revised any part of the play. Other critics who deny any presence of Shakespeare's hand in* Titus Andronicus *include Samuel Johnson (1765), George Steevens (1778), William Hazlitt (1817), Gerald Massey (1866), Edward Dowden (1881), and A. H. Bullen (1885).*]

[The] whole play intitled *Titus Andronicus* should be flung out the list of Shakespeare's works. What tho' a purple patch might here and there appear, is that sufficient reason to make our poet's name father this or other anonymous productions of the stage? But Mr Theobald has put the matter out of all question;

for he informs us 'that Ben Jonson in the induction to his *Bartlemew-Fair* . . . couples *Jeronimo* and *Andronicus* together in reputation, and speaks of them as plays then of 25 or 30 years standing. Consequently *Andronicus* must have been on the stage, before Shakespeare left Warwickshire to come and reside in London' [see excerpt above, 1733]. So that we have all the evidence, both internal and external, to vindicate our poet from this bastard issue; nor should his editors have printed it among his genuine works. (p. 307)

> *John Upton, in an extract from* Shakespeare, the Critical Heritage: 1733-1752, Vol. 3, *edited by Brian Vickers, Routledge & Kegan Paul, 1975, pp. 306-07.*

BENJAMIN HEATH   (essay date 1765)

[*In the following excerpt from his* A Revisal of Shakespeare's Text, wherein the Alterations Introduced into It by the More Modern Editors and Critics Are Particularly Considered *(1765), Heath, a student of classical literature, rejects as unfounded the hypotheses of both Lewis Theobald (1733) and John Upton (1748) that* Titus Andronicus *was not originally Shakespeare's play because it was written before he moved to London. To Heath, the internal evidence in* Titus Andronicus *argues against Shakespeare's authorship, yet he still finds enough of Shakespeare's style in the play to conjecture that it is his "most juvenile performance," written "before his poetical genius had had time to unfold and form itself." For additional commentary on* Titus Andronicus *as one of Shakespeare's earliest works, see the excerpts by Edward Capell (1768), August Wilhelm Schlegel (1808), Hermann Ulrici (1839), Charles Knight (1849).*]

[Mr Upton] gives us a calculation of Mr Theobald's, founded on a passage in Ben Jonson's Induction to his *Bartholomew Fair* [see excerpts above, 1748, 1733, and 1614], by which it appears that [*Titus Andronicus*] made its first appearance on the stage not later at least than the year 1589, and this he affirms (upon what grounds I know not) was before Shakespeare left Warwickshire to come and reside at London. From these premises Mr Upton concludes that this play is spurious, and could not possibly be Shakespeare's. But his conclusion is a little too hasty. That year was the twenty-fifth of Shakespeare's age, and it is scarce conceivable that so strong a propensity of genius towards the drama could have lain so long dormant without exerting itself in some production. This production might have been sent to town and brought on the stage before he himself quitted Warwickshire, and might have been the very circumstance that introduced him to his acquaintance with the players upon his first arrival. The internal evidence against the play is much stronger. The fable is at the same time shocking and puerile, without the least appearance of art or conduct. The characters are unnatural and undistinguishable, or rather absolutely none, whereas those of Shakespeare are always strongly marked beyond those of any other poet that ever lived. The sentiments are poor and trivial, the stile flat and uniform, utterly destitute of that strength and variety of expression which, with a certain obscurity sometimes attending it, are the distinguishing characters of Shakespeare. There are, however, scattered here and there, many strokes something resembling his peculiar manner, though not his best manner, which, as they could not be imitated from him would incline one to believe this might possibly be his most juvenile performance, written and acted before his poetical genius had had time to unfold and form itself. (p. 560)

> *Benjamin Heath, in an extract from* Shakespeare, the Critical Heritage: 1753-1765, Vol. 4, *edited by Brian*

Vickers, Routledge & Kegan Paul, 1976, pp. 550-64.

SAMUEL JOHNSON   (essay date 1765)

[*Johnson has long held an important place in the history of Shakespearean criticism. He is considered the foremost representative of moderate English Neoclassicism and is credited by some literary historians with freeing Shakespeare from the precepts of the three unities valued by strict Neoclassicists: that dramas should have a single setting, take place in less than twenty-four hours, and have a causally connected plot. More recent scholars portray him as a critic who was able to synthesize existing critical theory rather than as an innovative theoretician. Johnson was a master of Augustan prose style and a personality who dominated the literary world of his epoch. In his essay on* Titus Andronicus, *taken from his 1765 edition of* The Plays of William Shakespeare, *Johnson agrees with Lewis Theobald (1733) and earlier critics that* Titus *is a "spurious" work. But he does not believe that Shakespeare reintroduced the play with his own revisions. In fact, Johnson finds no evidence of Shakespeare's hand apparent anywhere in the play, an opinion adopted by such later critics as George Steevens (1778), William Hazlitt (1817), Gerald Massey (1866), Edward Dowden (1881), and A. H. Bullen (1885).*]

All the editors and cricticks agree with Mr. Theobald in supposing [*Titus Andronicus*] spurious. I see no reason for differing from them; for the colour of the stile is wholly different from that of the other plays, and there is an attempt at regular versification, and artificial closes, not always inelegant, yet seldom pleasing. The barbarity of the spectacles, and the general massacre which are here exhibited, can scarcely be conceived tolerable to any audience; yet we are told by Jonson, that they were not only borne but praised. That Shakespeare wrote any part, though Theobald declares it "incontestable," I see no reason for believing. (p. 750)

The chronology of this play does not prove it not to be Shakespeare's. If it had been written twenty-five years, in 1614, it might have been written when Shakespeare was twenty-five years old. When he left Warwickshire I know not, but at the age of twenty-five it was rather too late to fly for deer-stealing.

Ravenscroft, who, in the reign of Charles II. revised this play, and restored it to the stage, tells us in his preface, from a theatrical tradition I suppose, which in his time might be of sufficient authority, that this play was touched in different parts by Shakespeare, but written by some other poet [see excerpt above, 1686]. I do not find Shakespeare's touches very discernible. (p. 751)

> *Samuel Johnson, "Notes on Shakespeare's Plays: 'Titus Andronicus'," in his* The Yale Edition of the Works of Samuel Johnson: Johnson on Shakespeare, *Vol. VIII, edited by Arthur Sherbo, Yale University Press, 1968, pp. 746-51.*

EDWARD CAPELL   (essay date 1768)

[*Capell was the first Shakespearean editor to practice using good quarto texts as the basis for his editions of the plays, which he published between 1768 and 1783. In the following excerpt, taken from the first volume of that collection, Capell regards Shakespeare as the sole author of* Titus Andronicus, *attributing its anomalous style and structure to the idea that Shakespeare was writing mainly for profit and, therefore, naturally imitated the style of such successful playwrights as Thomas Kyd and Christopher Marlowe. This theory is further elaborated in the essays* by August Wilhelm Schlegel (1808), Hermann Ulrici (1839), and Charles Knight (1849).]

Commentators, editors, every one (in short) who has had to do with Shakespeare, unite all in condemning [*Titus Andronicus*], as a very bundle of horrors, totally unfit for the stage, and unlike the Poet's manner and even the style of his other pieces. All which allegations are extreamly true, and we readily admit of them, but can not admit the conclusion that therefore it is not his. . . . (p. 319)

The books of that time afford strange examples of the barbarism of the publick taste both upon the stage and elsewhere. A conceited one of *John* Lyly's set a nation a madding; and for a while every pretender to politeness 'parl'd Euphuism,' as it was phras'd, and no writings would go down with them but such as were pen'd in that fantastical manner. . . . [Some] other writers who rose exactly at that time succeeded better in certain tragical performances, though as outragious to the full in their way, and as remote from nature as these comick ones of Lyly's. For, falling in with that innate love of blood which has been often objected to *British* audiences, and choosing fables of horror which they made horrider still by their manner of handling them, they produc'd a set of monsters that are not to be parallel'd in all the annals of play-writing. Yet they were receiv'd with applause, and were the favourites of the publick for almost ten years together ending at 1595. . . . Now Shakespeare, whatever motives he might have in some other parts of it, at this period of his life wrote certainly for profit; and seeing it was to be had in this way (and in this way only, perhaps) he fell in with the current, and gave his sorry auditors a piece to their tooth in this contested play of *Titus Andronicus;* which as it came out at the same time with [such plays as *The Wars of Cyrus, Tamburlaine, The Spanish Tragedy, Soliman and Perseda,* and *Selimus*] is most exactly like them in almost every particular. Their very numbers, consisting all of ten syllables with hardly any redundant, are copy'd by this *Proteus,* who could put on any shape that either serv'd his interest or suited his inclination. And this, we hope, is a fair and unforc'd way of accounting for *Andronicus;* and may convince the most prejudic'd that Shakespeare might be the writer of it. . . . (pp. 319-20)

> Edward Capell, in an extract from Shakespeare, the Critical Heritage: 1765-1774, Vol. 5, *edited by Brian Vickers, Routledge & Kegan Paul, 1979, pp. 303-27.*

FRANCIS GENTLEMAN　(essay date 1774)

[*In the following excerpt from* Bell's Edition of Shakespeare's Plays *(1774), Gentleman, in a typically Neoclassical response on the function of art, states that if a literary work is not of use to society, it is not worth evaluation. As such, he claims that* Titus Andronicus *is worthless and wonders how Shakespeare could have written it; yet, Gentleman seems willing to regard the play as at least primarily Shakespeare's—an assessment reached by such earlier critics as Benjamin Heath (1765) and Edward Capell (1768).*]

Without some evident use to society in general no literary production, however fanciful or plausible, can claim estimation. Upon this principle, though in different parts *Titus Andronicus* bears strong, nay evident, marks of *Shakespeare's* pen yet he has fixed upon such characters and incidents as are totally offensive. Human nature is shewn in a most partial and deplorable state; depraved as we sometimes find it, it is scarce to be imagined that such an infernal groupe as is huddled

together in this piece could meet in so small a compass. Hence this play must be horrid in representation, and is disgustful in perusal. Indeed it is matter of great wonder how *Shakespeare's* humane heart could endure the contemplation of such inhuman actions and events, through the course of five acts.

> Francis Gentleman, in an extract from Shakespeare, the Critical Heritage: 1774-1801, Vol. 6, *edited by Brian Vickers, Routledge & Kegan Paul, 1981, p. 104.*

MRS. [ELIZABETH] GRIFFITH　(essay date 1775)

[*Griffith's criticism exemplifies the seventeenth- and eighteenth-century preoccupation with searching through Shakespeare's plays for set speeches and passages that could be read out of dramatic context for their own sake. Griffith, however, avoided the more usual practice of collecting and commenting on poetic "beauties" and concentrated instead on the "moral" subjects treated in the text. In the excerpt below, Griffith presents an unconventional argument for Shakespeare's authorship of* Titus Andronicus: *the play is so thoroughly barbarous that it could not have been anyone else's work. She also presents a passage which she considers characteristic of Shakespeare's style and criticizes Samuel Johnson (1765) for not recognizing the existence of such passages throughout the play.*]

It has been much disputed among the Commentators, whether [*Titus Andronicus*] be originally Shakespeare's, or only the work of some elder Author, revised and improved for representation by him: though, if I might be allowed to venture a criticism upon this subject, I should suppose the intire Piece to be his, and for a very singular reason; Because the whole of the fable, as well as the conduct of it, is so very *barbarous*, in every sense of the word, that I think, however he might have been tempted to make use of the legend, in some hurry or other, for his own purpose, he could hardly have adopted it from any other person's composition. We are quick-sighted to the faults of others, though purblind to our own. Besides, he would never have strewed such sweet flowers upon a *caput mortuum* ["worthless remnant"], if some child of his had not lain entombed underneath. (p. 403)

I should imagine, from the many shocking spectacles exhibited in this Play, that it could never have been represented on any theatre. . . . And yet Ben Jonson assures us that it was performed, in his time, *with great applause* [see excerpt above, 1614]; and we are also told that it was revived again, in the reign of Charles the Second, *with the same success* [see excerpt above by Edward Ravenscroft, 1686]. The different humours and tastes of times! It would be not only hissed, but driven off the stage at present. (pp. 403-04)

> *Titus.*　If there were reason for these miseries,
> 　　Then into limits could I bind my woes.
> 　　When Heaven doth weep, doth not the earth o'er-flow?
> 　　If the winds rage, doth not the sea wax mad,
> 　　Threat'ning the welkin with his big-swoln face?
> 　　And wilt thou have a reason for this coil? . . . .
> 　　*Then give me leave, for losers will have leave*
> 　　*To ease their stomachs with their bitter tongues.*
> 　　　　　　　　　　　　　　　　　[III. i. 219-33]
> 　　　　　　　　　　　　　　　　　　　(p. 405)

In the two last lines above, Shakespeare has given an elevation to the common expression of *losers have leave to speak*. . . . This is one of his characteristics; and, indeed, I think that his stile and manner are so strongly marked, throughout this Play, (take the above speech, for one instance) that I own it surprizes me Doctor Johnson should say, ''he did not think Shakespeare's 'touches discernible in it''' [see excerpt above, 1765]. (p. 406)

> Mrs. [Elizabeth] Griffith, '''Titus Andronicus','' in her The Morality of Shakespeare's Drama Illustrated, 1775. Reprint by Frank Cass & Co. Ltd., 1971, pp. 403-06.

GEORGE STEEVENS   (essay date 1778)

[*Steevens was an English scholar who collaborated with Samuel Johnson on a ten-volume edition of Shakespeare's works in 1773. The subsequent revision of this collection, along with Steevens's own edition of 1793, formed the textual basis for the first two Variorum editions of Shakespeare's plays. In the following excerpt, taken from the 1778 edition of Shakespeare's plays on which he collaborated with Edmond Malone, Steevens lists the ways in which* Titus Andronicus *does not fit Shakespeare's recognized style, and he comments that the play contains more classical allusions than the rest of Shakespeare's dramas combined. Other critics who reject Shakespeare's authorship of* Titus Andronicus *include Samuel Johnson (1765), William Hazlitt (1817), Gerald Massey (1866), Edward Dowden (1881), and A. H. Bullen (1885).*]

Whatever were the motives of Heminge and Condell for admitting [*Titus Andronicus* among the tragedies] of Shakespeare, all it has gained by their favour is to be delivered down to posterity with repeated remarks of contempt;—a Thersites babbling among heroes, and introduced only to be derided. (p. 196)

[It is] deficient in such internal marks as distinguish the tragedies of Shakespeare from those of other writers; I mean, that it presents no struggles to introduce the vein of humour so constantly interwoven with the business of his serious dramas. It can neither boast of his striking excellencies nor his acknowledged defects; for it offers not a single interesting situation, a natural character, or a string of quibbles, from the first scene to the last. That Shakespeare should have written without commanding our attention, moving our passions, or sporting with words, appears to me as improbable as that he should have studiously avoided dissyllable and trissyllable terminations in this play and in no other. . . .

Could the use of particular terms employed in no other of his pieces be admitted as an argument that he was not its author, more than one of these might be found; among which is *palliament* for *robe*, a Latinism which I have not met with elsewhere in any English writer, whether ancient or modern; though it must have originated from the mint of a scholar. I may add that *Titus Andronicus* will be found on examination to contain a greater number of classical allusions &c. than are scattered over all the rest of the performances on which the seal of Shakespeare is undubitably fixed.—Not to write any more *about and about* this suspected *thing*, let me observe that the glitter of a few passages in it has perhaps misled the judgment of those who ought to have known that both sentiment and description are more easily produced than the interesting fabrick of a tragedy. Without these advantages many plays have succeeded; and many have failed, in which they have been dealt about with the most lavish profusion. It does not follow that he who can carve a frieze with minuteness, elegance, and ease has a conception equal to the extent, propriety, and grandeur of a temple. (pp. 196-97)

> George Steevens, in an extract from Shakespeare, the Critical Heritage: 1774-1801, Vol. 6, edited by

> Brian Vickers, Routledge & Kegan Paul, 1979, pp. 196-97.

EDMOND MALONE   (essay date 1790)

[*An eighteenth-century Irish literary scholar and editor, Malone was the first critic to establish a chronology of Shakespeare's plays. He was also the first scholar to prepare a critical edition of Shakespeare's Sonnets and to write a comprehensive history of the English stage based on extensive research into original sources. As the major Shakespearean editor of the eighteenth century, Malone collaborated with George Steevens on Steevens's second and third editions of Shakespeare's plays and issued his own edition in 1790. His importance resides not so much in textual emendation as in his unrivaled knowledge of primary sources. In the excerpt below, Malone reiterates the theory first suggested by Edward Ravenscroft (1686) that Shakespeare did not write, but merely revised* Titus Andronicus; *he bases his argument on evidence contained in the Dulwich College Papers, although he fails to state exactly what this evidence is. These documents include the memoirs and correspondence of theater owner Philip Henslowe and actor Edward Alleyn, two of Shakespeare's contemporaries, and have since become valuable resources for the study of the Elizabethan-Jacobean stage. For a similar interpretation of Shakespeare's part in the composition of* Titus Andronicus, *see the excerpts by Lewis Theobald (1733), Samuel Taylor Coleridge (1811), G. G. Gervinus (1849-50), L. M. Griffiths (1884), Arthur Symons (1885), and Joseph S. G. Bolton (1933). Also, for a refutation of Malone's methodology, see the excerpt by Charles Knight (1849).*]

It has long been thought that *Titus Andronicus* was not written originally by Shakspeare; about seventy years after his death, Ravenscroft having mentioned that he had been ''told by some anciently conversant with the stage, that our poet only gave some master-touches to one or two of the principal parts or characters'' [see excerpt above, 1686]. The very curious papers lately discovered in Dulwich College, from which large extracts are given at the end of the History of the Stage, prove, what I long since suspected, that this play, and *the First Part of K. Henry VI*. were in possession of the scene when Shakspeare began to write for the stage; and the same manuscripts shew, that it was then very common for a dramatick poet to alter and amend the work of a preceding writer. The question therefore is now decisively settled; and undoubtedly some additions were made to both [*Pericles* and *Titus Andronicus*] by Shakspeare. (p. lix)

> Edmond Malone, in a preface to The Plays and Poems of William Shakspeare, Vol. 1 by William Shakespeare, edited by Edmond Malone, 1790. Reprint by AMS Press, 1968, pp. i-lxxix.

AUGUST WILHELM SCHLEGEL   (lecture date 1808)

[*A prominent German Romantic critic, Schlegel holds a key place in the evolution of Shakespeare's reputation in European criticism. His translations of thirteen of the plays are still considered the best German editions of Shakespeare. Schlegel was also a leading spokesman for the Romantic movement, which permanently overthrew the Neoclassical contention that Shakespeare was a child of nature whose plays lacked artistic form. The following excerpt was originally part of a lecture delivered by Schlegel in 1808 and subsequently published in his Über dramatische Kunst und Literatur in 1811. Like Benjamin Heath (1765) and Edward Capell (1768), Schlegel regards* Titus Andronicus *as a ''feeble and immature work'' of Shakespeare's apprenticeship, a time when the poet had few models on which to fashion his art and had not yet developed his own style. Because art ''must be* acquired by practice and experience,'' Schlegel asserts, Shakespeare must have produced some failures, and Titus is one. Schlegel's theory is supported by such later critics as Hermann Ulrici (1839) and Charles Knight (1849). For an opposing assessment of Shakespeare's part in the composition of Titus Andronicus, see the excerpts by John Upton (1748), William Hazlitt (1817), Gerald Massey (1866), Edward Dowden (1881), and A. H. Bullen (1885).]

[Titus Andronicus] is framed according to a false idea of the tragic, which by an accumulation of cruelties and enormities, degenerates into the horrible, and yet leaves no deep impression behind: the story of Tereus and Philomela is heightened and overcharged under other names, and mixed up with the repast of Atreus and Thyestes, and many other incidents. In detail there is no want of beautiful lines, bold images, nay, even features which betray the peculiar conception of Shakespeare. Among these we may reckon the joy of the treacherous Moor at the blackness and ugliness of his adulterous offspring; and in the compassion of Titus Andronicus, grown childish through grief, for a fly which had been struck dead, while his rage afterwards, when he imagines he discovers in it his black enemy, we recognize the future poet of Lear. Are the critics afraid that Shakspeare's fame would be injured, were it established that in his early youth he ushered into the world a feeble and immature work? Was Rome the less the conqueror of the world, because Remus could leap over its first walls? Let any one place himself in Shakspeare's situation at the commencement of his career. He found only a few indifferent models, and yet these met with the most favourable reception, because in the novelty of an art, men are never difficult to please, before their taste has been made fastidious by choice and abundance. Must not this situation have had its influence on him before he learned to make higher demands on himself, and by digging deeper in his own mind, discovered the rich veins of noble metal that ran there? It is even highly probable that he must have made several failures before he succeeded in getting into the right path. Genius is in a certain sense infallible, and has nothing to learn; but art is to be learned, and must be acquired by practice and experience. In Shakspeare's acknowledged works we find hardly any traces of his apprenticeship, and yet apprenticeship he certainly had. This every artist must have, and especially in a period where he has not before him the examples of a school already formed. I consider it as extremely probable that Shakspeare began to write for the theatre at a much earlier period than the one which is generally stated, namely, after the year 1590. It appears that, as early as the year 1584, when only twenty years of age, he had left his paternal home and repaired to London. Can we imagine that such an active head would remain idle for six whole years without making any attempt to emerge by his talents from an uncongenial situation? That in the dedication of the poem of Venus and Adonis he calls it ''the first heir of his invention,'' proves nothing against the supposition. It was the first which he printed; he might have composed it at an earlier period; perhaps, also, in this term, ''heirs of his invention,'' he did not indulge theatrical labours, especially as they then conferred but little to his literary dignity. The earlier Shakspeare began to compose for the theatre, the less are we enabled to consider the immaturity and imperfection of a work a proof of its spuriousness in opposition to historical evidence, if only we can discern in it prominent features of his mind. (pp. 442-44)

> *August Wilhelm Schlegel, ''Criticisms on Shakspeare's Historical Dramas,'' in his* A Course of Lectures on Dramatic Art and Literature, *edited by Rev. A.J.W. Morrison, translated by John Black,*

revised edition, 1846. Reprint by AMS Press, Inc., 1965, pp. 414-46.*

SAMUEL TAYLOR COLERIDGE　(essay date 1811?)

[Coleridge's lectures and writings on Shakespeare form a major chapter in the history of English Shakespearean criticism. As the channel for the critical ideas of the German Romantics and as an original interpreter of Shakespeare in the new spirit of Romanticism, Coleridge played a strategic role in overthrowing the last remains of the Neoclassical approach to Shakespeare and in establishing the modern view of the dramatist as a conscious artist and masterful portrayer of human character. Coleridge's remarks on Shakespeare come down to posterity largely as fragmentary notes, marginalia, and reports by auditors on the lectures, rather than in polished essays. The excerpt below is taken from Coleridge's marginalia believed to have been written in 1811. In it, he dismisses the conjecture of Lewis Theobald (1733) that Titus Andronicus was written before Shakespeare arrived in London, and therefore by another dramatist, and argues instead that portions of both Titus and Thomas Kyd's The Spanish Tragedy contain examples of Shakespeare's earliest work.]

That Shakespeare never 'turned his genius to stage-writing' (as Theobald Theobaldicè phrases it) [until he became an actor in London] is an assertion of about as much authority as the precious story that he left Stratford for deer-stealing, and lived by holding gentlemen's horses at the doors of the theatres, and other trash of that arch-gossip, old Aubrey. The metre [in Titus Andronicus] is an argument against its being Shakespeare's worth a score such chronological surmises. Yet I incline to think that both in this and in Jeronymo [Thomas Kyd's The Spanish Tragedy] Shakespeare wrote some passages, and that they are the earliest of his compositions. (p. 3)

> *Samuel Taylor Coleridge, ''Notes on the Tragedies of Shakespeare: 'Titus Andronicus','' in his* Shakespearean Criticism, Vol. 1, *edited by Thomas Middleton Raysor, second edition, Dutton, 1960, pp. 3-4.*

WILLIAM HAZLITT　(essay date 1817)

[Hazlitt is considered a leading Shakespearean critic of the English Romantic movement. A prolific essayist and critic on a wide range of subjects, Hazlitt remarked in the preface to his Characters of Shakespear's Plays, first published in 1817, that he was inspired by the German critic August Wilhelm Schlegel and was determined to supplant what he considered the pernicious influence of Samuel Johnson's Shakespearean criticism. Hazlitt's approach is typically Romantic in its emphasis on character studies. Unlike his fellow Romantic critic Samuel Taylor Coleridge, Hazlitt was a dramatic critic whose experience of Shakespeare in the theater influenced his interpretations. In the following excerpt, Hazlitt posits that Shakespeare did not write Titus Andronicus and rejects the hypothesis that it is an example of Shakespeare's dramatic apprenticeship, an idea most recently suggested by Schlegel (1808). To Hazlitt, Titus is not an imperfect first attempt at drama, but rather demonstrates a ''confirmed habit,'' a systematic preference for violence that is totally un-Shakespearean. He also notes that the play's ''grammatical construction'' is not Shakespeare's. Other critics who deny Shakespeare's authorship of Titus Andronicus include John Upton (1748), Samuel Johnson (1765), George Steevens (1778), Gerald Massey (1866), Edward Dowden (1881), and A. H. Bullen (1885).]

Titus Andronicus is certainly as unlike Shakespear's usual style as it is possible. It is an accumulation of vulgar physical horrors, in which the power exercised by the poet bears no proportion to the repugnance excited by the subject. The character of Aaron the Moor is the only thing which shews any originality of conception; and the scene in which he expresses his joy "at the blackness and ugliness of his child begot in adultery" [see excerpt above by August Wilhelm Schlegel, 1808], the only one worthy of Shakespear. Even this is worthy of him only in the display of power, for it gives no pleasure. Shakespear managed these things differently. Nor do we think it a sufficient answer to say that this was an embryo or crude production of the author. In its kind it is full grown, and its features decided and overcharged. It is not like a first imperfect essay, but shews a confirmed habit, a systematic preference of violent effect to every thing else. There are occasional detached images of great beauty and delicacy, but these were not beyond the powers of other writers then living. The circumstance which inclines us to reject the external evidence in favour of this play being Shakespear's is, that the grammatical construction is constantly false and mixed up with vulgar abbreviations, a fault that never occurs in any of his genuine plays. (pp. 210-11)

> William Hazlitt, "Characters of Shakespear's Plays:
> Doubtful Plays of Shakespear," in his Characters of
> Shakespear's Plays & Lectures on the English Poets,
> Macmillan and Co. Limited, 1903, pp. 204-11.*

HERMANN ULRICI   (essay date 1839)

[*A German scholar, Ulrici was a professor of philosophy and the author of works on Greek poetry and Shakespeare. The following excerpt is from an English translation of his* Über Shakspeares dramatische Kunst, und sein Verhältniss zu Calderon und Göthe, *a work first published in 1839. This study exemplifies the "philosophical criticism" developed in Germany during the nineteenth century. The immediate sources for Ulrici's critical approach appear to be August Wilhelm Schlegel's conception of the play as an organic, interconnected whole and Georg Wilhelm Friedrich Hegel's view of drama as an embodiment of the conflict of historical forces and ideas. Unlike his fellow German Shakespearean critic G. G. Gervinus, Ulrici sought to develop a specifically Christian aesthetics, but one which, as he carefully points out in the introduction to the work mentioned above, in no way intrudes on "that unity of idea, which preeminently constitutes a work of art a living creation in the world of beauty." Like Edward Capell (1768) and August Wilhelm Schlegel (1808), Ulrici contends that because* Titus Andronicus *was Shakespeare's first dramatic endeavor, he most likely imitated the successful style of established, popular dramatists such as Christopher Marlowe. Although Ulrici notes a number of the play's defects, he challenges the assumption that "Shakespeare has here confounded the tragical with the horrible," stating that the latter is a necessary element of* Titus *and that the former is reinforced by the "thwarting of human greatness and nobility" and the achievement of "poetic justice" at the close of the action. He also asserts that* Titus *surpasses the works of Thomas Kyd and Marlowe because it depicts the tragedy of human nobility falling "of its own frailty." To Ulrici, the play's theme, or "organic ideal focus," illustrates a decaying society where, in the conflict between good and evil, evil destroys both itself and good. For additional commentary on the principal conflict in* Titus Andronicus, *see the excerpts by Eugene M. Waith (1955) and Alan Sommers (1960). Ulrici remarks that the play's major defect is the absence of the conciliatory element in tragedy, for both Titus and Lavinia die without realizing the extent of their guilt and thus cannot be purified by the tragic experience. This aspect of the play's structure is further discussed by Irving Ribner (1960) and Albert H. Tricomi (1976).*]

[The] peculiarities of the language and versification [in "Titus Andronicus"], which it is pretended could not possibly be Shakspeare's, . . . become not only easy to be accounted for,

but what we should naturally look for, when we consider that the young Shakspeare, like the young Raphael, must unquestionably have directed his first essays by the models of older and more famous masters; in the present case, those of Marlowe, in whom all these peculiarities are found in abundance. On the contrary, it would have been as singular if he had not done so, as it would be wonderful if his first essays had been at once complete masterpieces. Such the "Titus Andronicus" is not by any means: on the contrary, its great defects are obvious. The incidents and revolutions of fortune are horrible in the highest degree, and in this respect it as much surpasses Marlowe's well-known pieces of violence and rage as it is superior to them in tragic energy and moral earnestness. The most fearful crimes are rapidly accumulated with steadily advancing enormity. When we think we have reached the summit of these most unnatural cruelties and vice, the next scene suddenly opens to our view a still higher ascent. The characters are sketches done with the coarsest touches and darkest colouring; one personage, Aaron the Moor, is, *perhaps,* (I fear, however, *only perhaps*), perfectly untrue to nature; he appears to be a very devil, and no man. It is, alas! too true, that the nature of human wickedness is most difficult to understand, and but too easy to depict. Again, the action is hurried on certainly with precipitate haste, and without adequate motives, if not absolutely without consideration.

These certainly are no trifling defects. But if we call to mind the wild tragedies of Marlowe, so popular in Shakspeare's day, and the other favourite pieces of the English public, such as the "Spanish Tragedy," &c. it will appear but natural—we might venture to say, inevitable—that Shakspeare's rich and exuberant poetical genius should in the luxuriance of youth have fallen into such aberrations. His only school of art was his own artistic experience. It was necessary for him to pass through the existant position of dramatic art, which he was afterwards to leave so far behind him; and that he should in Tragedy have felt himself more attracted to Marlowe than to Greene, admits of being explained by the same reason as disposed Pindar to follow Stesichorus rather than Simonides. How far he surpassed his models even in their own style, those acquainted with the old English theatre will easily discern, provided they seek to discover the merits as well as the defects of "Titus Andronicus." It cannot with truth be said, that Shakspeare has here confounded the tragical with the horrible; at most he has but given to the former the incomplete and consequently inappropriate form of the latter. The horrible is no doubt in and by itself not tragical, but still it *can* become so, even because its essence lies simply in the outward form of human action and suffering. It is not horrible to kill a man with the thrust of a dagger, but it is so to rack him to death by torture. "Titus Andronicus" retains a just claim to the title of tragical, in so far as it exhibits the thwarting of human greatness and nobility, by its own frailty and besetting sinfulness. For the tragic fate which overwhelms the hero of the piece is not undeserved. He has fully merited his doom by the cold-blooded indifference with which he devotes Tamora's eldest son to be sacrificed as a peace-offering to the manes—an act of cruelty which his sons perpetrate—as well as by the passionate heat with which he slays his child for a pardonable opposition to his will, and lastly, the fearful and inhuman revenge which he wreaks upon the doubtless equally inhuman queen. Moreover, the common ruin which ultimately overtakes all the guilty, is but the satisfaction due to poetic justice. Lastly, it must not be forgotten, that the historical basis on which the whole rests is the later times of the Roman Empire, which were so abundant in dark deeds, and every kind of horror, that the sober history outstrips the boldest fancy. The *historical* character of these times forms so decidedly the background of the whole dramatic picture, that the piece approximates closely to the character of an historical play, and therefore requires to be considered and examined by no other than the spirit of the age. When this is done, it will we think be found, that in this piece the tragic element hardly admitted of being presented otherwise than it actually is, and we may ask why, if the horror does really exist in history, the tragic may not for once assume this form? Tragedy, in its full historical significance, was not made for tender weak-nerved spirits. It requires strong shoulders to support the whole burthen of the tragical, which the life of humanity contains. (pp. 234-36)

The fault of the piece consists principally in this, that what by its nature is merely an isolated, special exceptional reality, is *inconsiderately* made the *universal* and *sole* form of the tragical. The fundamental idea of the piece is in short nothing else than the fact of this corruption of the tragic into the horrible, which is found inevitably amidst the universal decay of a great people and polity, and leads good and noble minds, like Titus, to break through the most necessary and strongest ties of nature, disregarding even the voice of parental affection. Such is the first crime out of which the whole tissue of the successive scenes of horror are spun out; this has awakened the fiendish nature of Tamora, and excited the brutish rage of Aaron. When evil has once been challenged to the lists by good itself, it destroys not only itself but the good also, which indeed has by this act ceased to be truly good. It is from such a view of life that the entire drama is conceived: this is the organic ideal focus towards which all the separate rays converge. But the horrors thus accumulated, and represented as the ordinary and natural elements of life, required some more *special* grounding. It was not sufficient to suppose a general state of corruption, since even in such a state of things the horrible is not the *universal* form of the tragic. But even this fault might be tolerated and pardonable, at least it is not wholly without excuse. What is properly the leading defect, is the total absence of the *soothing* elements of Tragedy. Titus Andronicus perishes without a sense or suspicion of his own guilt, or of the duty of humble submission to the will of the gods—in short, without a thought of his need of mercy. So, too, his younger sons: even Lavinia, whose character was intended for one of noble womanhood, could hold unmoved the basin to catch the blood of two human victims, and it is while attending at this frightful sacrifice that she perishes by the dagger of her own father. Aaron, Tamora, Saturnin, die as they had lived; and Lucius marks his elevation to the dignity of Governor with a command for the inhuman and revolting execution of the Moor. Thus fearfully does the conclusion jar upon our feelings; we have still the cheerless prospect that even behind the fallen curtain things will go on as they had begun; and we turn with horror from such a view of human nature, and are almost impiously led to demand why such a race was ever called into being.

That, nevertheless, this drama is rich in isolated beauties, profound thoughts, and striking peculiarities, Shakspearean imagery, which like lightning flashes over and illumines the whole piece, and that single scenes are even deeply affecting and highly poetical, is generally admitted, and requires no proof. It will be sufficient to call attention to the scenes of the shooting the arrows, and of the interview between Titus and Tamora, who announces herself to the old man, whom she believes to be mad, as the Goddess of Vengeance. Moreover, the wonderful self-possession of the latter, that *chiaro-oscuro* between madness and forecast deliberation, between playful thought-

lessness and energetic presence of mind, is painted with the most wonderful profundity and verisimilitude. Even in default of any historical evidence, such passages would be sufficient to prove that the work must have been the youthful essay of the greatest poet of all times. (pp. 236-37)

> *Hermann Ulrici, "Criticisms of Shakspeare's Dramas: 'Titus Andronicus', and 'Timon of Athens'," in his* Shakspeare's Dramatic Art: And His Relation to Calderon and Goethe, *translated by Rev. A.J.W. Morrison, Chapman, Brothers, 1846, pp. 233-45.**

CHARLES KNIGHT   (essay date 1849)

[*Knight, an English author and publisher, dedicated his career to providing education and knowledge to the Victorian working class. In the following excerpt, he supports the conclusions of August Wilhelm Schlegel (1808) and Hermann Ulrici (1839), both of whom regarded* Titus Andronicus *as one of Shakespeare's earliest works. He argues that Shakespeare wrote the play before he realized the depth and power of his genius and that he was attempting to reconcile a popular dramatic form with his own concepts of truth and human nature. To support his explanation of the play's inferiority, Knight includes a translated extract from Franz Horn's* Shakspeare's Schanspiele (1823-31), *in which the German critic claims that Shakespeare's inexperience and the "unfavourable circumstances" of his early years in London hampered his poetic talent and consequently affected the composition of* Titus. *Knight also asserts, however, that Shakespeare was the only Elizabethan playwright who could maintain the "entire conception of, and power over, the design of a drama" and that* Titus *displays this ability. He cites Tamora's speeches, Aaron's affection for his child, and Lucius's mourning for Titus as the work of an author who conceived and controlled the play's entire dramatic movement; with these examples, Knight refutes the methodology of Edmond Malone, who, through an analysis of these scenes and speeches, determined that Shakespeare revised another dramatist's efforts. For further discussion of the dramatic unity in* Titus Andronicus, *see the excerpts by Frederick S. Boas (1896), Irving Ribner (1960), A. C. Hamilton (1967), D. J. Palmer (1972), and Albert H. Tricomi (1976).*]

We can scarcely subscribe to Mr. [Henry] Hallam's strong opinion, given with reference to [the] question of the authorship of 'Titus Andronicus,' that, "in criticism of all kinds, we must acquire a dogged habit of resisting testimony, when *res ipsa per se vociferatur* ['the thing itself speaks'] to the contrary." The *res ipsa* may be looked upon through very different media by different minds: *testimony*, when it is clear, and free from the suspicion of an interested bias, although it appear to militate against conclusions that, however strong, are not infallible, because they depend upon very nice analysis and comparison, *must* be received, more or less, and *cannot* be doggedly resisted. Mr. Hallam says, " 'Titus Andronicus' is now, by common consent, denied to be, in *any* sense, a production of Shakspeare." Who are the interpreters of the "common consent?" Theobald, Johnson, Farmer, Steevens, Malone, M. Mason. These critics are wholly of one school; and we admit that they represent the "common consent" of their own school of English literature upon this point—till within a few years the only school. But there is another school of criticism, which maintains that 'Titus Andronicus' is in *every* sense a production of Shakspere. The German critics, from W. Schlegel to Ulrici, agree to reject the "common consent" of the English critics. The subject, therefore, cannot be hastily dismissed; the external testimony cannot be doggedly resisted. But, in entering upon the examination of this question with the best care we can bestow, we consider that it possesses an importance much higher than belongs to the proof, or disproof, from the internal evidence, that this painful tragedy was written by Shakspere. The question is not an isolated one. It requires to be treated with a constant reference to the state of the early English drama,— the probable tendencies of the poet's own mind at the period of his first dramatic productions,—the circumstances amidst which he was placed with reference to his audiences,—the struggle which he must have undergone to reconcile the contending principles of the practical and the ideal, the popular and the true,—the tentative process by which he must have advanced to his immeasurable superiority over every contemporary. It is easy to place 'Titus Andronicus' by the side of 'Hamlet,' and to say,—the one is a low work of art, the other a work of the highest art. It is easy to say that the versification of 'Titus Andronicus' is not the versification of 'A Midsummer Night's Dream.' It is easy to say that Titus raves and denounces without moving terror or pity; but that Lear tears up the whole heart, and lays bare all the hidden springs of thought and passion that elevate madness into sublimity. But this, we venture to think, is not just criticism. . . . No one who has deeply contemplated the progress of the great intellects of the world, and has traced the doubts, and fears, and throes, and desperate plunges of genius, can hesitate to believe that excellence in art is to be attained by the same process through which we may hope to reach excellence in morals—by contest, and purification,—until habitual confidence and repose succeed to convulsive exertions and distracting aims. He that would rank amongst the heroes must have fought the good fight. *Energy* of all kinds has to work out its own subjection to principles, without which it can never become *power*. In the course of this struggle what it produces may be essentially unlike to the fruits of its after-peacefulness:—for the good has to be reached through the evil—the true through the false—the universal through the partial. The passage we subjoin is from Franz Horn; and we think that it demands a respectful consideration:—

> A mediocre, poor, and tame nature *finds itself* easily. It soon arrives, when it endeavours earnestly, at a knowledge of what it can accomplish, and what it cannot. Its poetical tones are single and gentle spring-breathings; with which we are well pleased, but which pass over us almost trackless. A very different combat has the higher and richer nature to maintain with itself; and the more splendid the peace, and the brighter the clearness, which it reaches through this combat, the more monstrous the fight which must have been incessantly maintained.

> Let us consider the richest and most powerful poetic nature that the world has ever yet seen; let us consider Shakspere, *as boy and youth,* in his circumscribed external situation,—without one discriminating friend, without a patron, without a teacher,—without the possession of ancient or modern languages,—in his loneliness at Stratford, following an uncongenial employment; and then, in the strange whirl of the so-called great world of London, contending for long years with unfavourable circumstances,—in wearisome intercourse with this great world, which is, however, often found to be little;—but also with nature, with himself, and with God:—What materials for the deepest contemplation! This rich nature, thus circumstanced, desires to explain the enigma of the

human being and the surrounding world. But it is not yet disclosed to himself. Ought he to wait for this ripe time before he ventures to dramatise? Let us not demand anything superhuman: for, through the expression of error in song, will he find what accelerates the truth; and well for him that he has no other sins to answer for than poetical ones, which later in life he has atoned for by the most glorious excellences!

The elegiac tone of his juvenile poems allows us to imagine very deep passions in the youthful Shakspere. But this single tone was not long sufficient for him. He soon desired, from that stage 'which signifies the world' (an expression that Schiller might properly have invented for Shakspere), to speak aloud what the world seemed to him,—to him, the youth who was not yet able thoroughly to penetrate this seeming. Can there be here a want of colossal errors? Not merely single errors. No: we should have a whole drama which is diseased at its very root,—which rests upon one single monstrous error. Such a drama is this 'Titus.' The poet had here nothing less in his mind than to give

Title page of the First Quarto of Titus Andronicus *(1594). By permission of the Folger Shakespeare Library.*

us a grand Doomsday-drama. But what, as a man, was possible to him in 'Lear,' the youth could not accomplish. He gives us a torn-to-pieces world, about which Fate wanders like a bloodthirsty lion, or as a more refined or more cruel tiger, tearing mankind, good and evil alike, and blindly treading down every flower of joy. Nevertheless a better feeling reminds him that some repose must be given; but he is not sufficiently confident of this, and what he does in this regard is of little power. The personages of the piece are not merely heathens, but most of them embittered and blind in their heathenism; and only some single aspirations of something better can arise from a few of the best among them;—aspirations which are breathed so gently as scarcely to be heard amidst the cries of desperation from the bloody waves that roar almost deafeningly. (pp. 42-3)

It is scarcely necessary to point out that this argument of the German critic is founded upon the simple and intelligible belief that Shakspere is, in *every* sense of the word, the author of 'Titus Andronicus.' . . . The drama belongs to the province of the very highest poetical art; because a play which fully realizes the objects of a scenic exhibition requires a nicer combination of excellences, and involves higher difficulties, than belong to any other species of poetry. Taking the qualities of invention, power of language, versification, to be equal in two men, one devoting himself to dramatic poetry, and the other to narrative poetry, the dramatic poet has chances of failure which the narrative poet may entirely avoid. The dialogue, and especially the imagery, of the dramatic poet are secondary to the invention of the plot, the management of the action, and the conception of the characters. Language is but the drapery of the beings that the dramatic poet's imagination has created. They must be placed by the poet's power of combination in the various relations which they must maintain through a long and sometimes complicated action: he must see the whole of that action vividly, with reference to its capacity of manifesting itself distinctly to an audience, so that even the deaf should partially comprehend: the pantomime must be acted over and over again in his mind, before the wand of the magician gives the agents voice. When all this is done, all contradictions reconciled, all obscurities made clear, the interest prolonged and heightened, and the catastrophe naturally evolved and matured, the poet, to use the terms of a sister-art, has completed that design which colour and expression are to make manifest to others with something like the distinctness with which he himself has seen it. We have no hesitation in believing that one of the main causes of Shakspere's immeasurable superiority to other dramatists is that all-penetrating power of combination by which the action of his dramas is constantly sustained; whilst in the best pieces of his contemporaries, with rare exceptions, it flags or breaks down into description,—or is carried off by imagery,—or the force of conception in one character overpowers the management of the other instruments—cases equally evidencing that the poet has not attained the most difficult art of controlling his own conceptions. And thus it is that we so often hear Christopher Marlowe, or Philip Massinger,—to name the very best of them,—speaking themselves out of the mouths of their puppets, whilst the characterization is lost, and the action is forgotten. But when do we ever hear the individual voice of the man William Shakspere? When does he come forward to bow to the audience, as it were, between the scenes? Never is there any pause with him, that we may see the com-

placent author whispering to his auditory—''This is not exactly what I meant; my inspiration carried me away; but is it not fine?'' The great dramatic poet sits out of mortal ken. He rolls away the clouds and exhibits his world. There is calm and storm, and light and darkness; and the material scene becomes alive; and we see a higher life than that of our ordinary nature: and the whole soul is elevated; and man and his actions are presented under aspects more real than reality, and our control over tears or laughter is taken away from us; and, if the poet be a philosopher,—and without philosophy he cannot be a poet,—deep truths, before dimly seen, enter into our minds and abide there. Why do we state all this? Utterly to reject the belief that Shakspere was a line-maker: that, like Gray, for example, he was a manufacturer of mosaic poetry;—that he made verses to order:—and that his verses could be produced by some other process than an entire conception of, and power over, the *design* of a drama. (pp. 44-5)

From the first, Shakspere, with that consummate judgment which gave a fitness to everything that he did, or proposed to do, held his genius in subjection to the apprehension of the people, till he felt secure of their capability to appreciate the highest excellence. In his case, as in that of every great artist, perfection could only be attained by repeated efforts. He had no models to work upon; and in the very days in which he lived the English drama began to be created. . . . He took the thing as he found it. The dramatic power was in him so supreme that, compared with the feeble personifications of other men, it looks like instinct. He seized upon the vague abstractions which he found in the histories and comedies of the Blackfriars and the Bel Savage, and the scene was henceforth filled with living beings. But not as yet were these individualities surrounded with the glowing atmosphere of burning poetry. The philosophy which invests their sayings with an universal wisdom that enters the mind and becomes its loadstar was scarcely yet evoked out of that profound contemplation of human actions and of the higher things dimly revealed in human nature, which belonged to the maturity of his wondrous mind. The wit was there in some degree from the first, for it was irrepressible; but it was then as the polished metal, which dazzlingly gives back the brightness of the sunbeams; in after times it was as the diamond, which reflects everything, and yet appears to be self-irradiated in its lustrous depths. If these qualities, and if the humour which seems more especially the ripened growth of the mental faculty, could have been produced in the onset of Shakspere's career, it is probable that the career would not have been a successful one. He had to make his audience. (pp. 45-6)

We hold, then, that Malone's principle of marking with inverted commas those passages in which he supposed the hand of Shakspere might be traced in this play of 'Titus Andronicus' is based upon a vital error. It is not with us a question whether the passages which Malone has marked exhibit, or not, the critic's poetical taste: we say that the passages could not have been written except by the man, whoever he be, who conceived the action and the characterization. Take the single example of the character of Tamora. She is the presiding genius of the piece; and in her we see, as we believe, the outbreak of that wonderful conception of the union of powerful intellect and moral depravity which Shakspere was afterwards to make manifest with such consummate wisdom. Strong passions, ready wit, perfect self-possession, and a sort of oriental imagination, take Tamora out of the class of ordinary women. It is in her mouth that we find, for the most part, what readers of Malone's school would call the poetical language of the play. . . .

> The birds chant melody on every bush;
> The snake lies rolled in the cheerful sun;
> The green leaves quiver with the cooling wind,
> And make a chequer'd shadow on the ground:
> Under their sweet shade, Aaron, let us sit,
> And—whilst the babbling echo mocks the hounds,
> Replying shrilly to the well-tuned horns,
> As if a double hunt were heard at once—
> Let us sit down. . . .
>
>   [II. iii. 12-20]

> A barren detested vale, you see, it is:
> The trees, though summer, yet forlorn and lean,
> O'ercome with moss and baleful misseltoe.
> Here never shines the sun; here nothing breeds,
> Unless the nightly owl, or fatal raven. . . .
>
>   [II. iii. 93-7]

> King, be thy thoughts imperious, like thy name.
> Is the sun dimm'd, that gnats do fly in it?
> The eagle suffers little birds to sing,
>   And is not careful what they mean thereby;
> Knowing that, with the shadow of his wing,
>   He can at pleasure stint their melody. . . .
>
>   [IV. iv. 81-6]

> Know thou, sad man, I am not Tamora;
> She is thy enemy, and I thy friend:
> I am Revenge; sent from the infernal kingdom,
> To ease the gnawing vulture of thy mind,
> By working wreakful vengeance on thy foes.
> Come down, and welcome me to this world's light.
>
>   [V. ii. 28-33]

The first two of these passages are marked by Malone as the additions of Shakspere to the work of an inferior poet. If we had adopted Malone's theory, we should have marked the two other passages; and have gone even further in our selection of the poetical lines spoken by Tamora. But we hold that the lines could not have been produced, according to Malone's theory, even by Shakspere. Poetry, and especially dramatic poetry, is not to be regarded as a bit of joiner's work—or, if you please, as an affair of jewelling and enamelling. The lines which we have quoted may not be amongst Shakspere's highest things; but they could not have been produced except under the excitement of the full swing of his dramatic power—bright touches dashed in at the very hour when the whole design was growing into shape upon the canvass, and the form of Tamora was becoming alive with colour and expression. To imagine that the great passages of a drama are produced like "a copy of verses," under any other influence than the large and general inspiration which creates the whole drama, is, we believe, utterly to mistake the essential nature of dramatic poetry. It would be equally just to say that the nice but well-defined traits of character, which stand out from the physical horrors of this play, when it is carefully studied, were superadded by Shakspere to the coarser delineations of some other man. Aaron, the Moor, in his general conception is an unmitigated villain—something alien from humanity—a fiend, and therefore only to be detested. But Shakspere, by that insight which, however imperfectly developed, must have distinguished his earliest efforts, brings Aaron into the circle of humanity; and then he

is a thing which moves us, and his punishment is poetical justice. One touch does this—his affection for his child:

> Come on, you thick-lipp'd slave, I'll bear you hence;
> For it is you that puts us to our shifts:
> I'll make you feed on berries, and on roots,
> And feed on curds and whey, and suck the goat,
> And cabin in a cave; and bring you up
> To be a warrior, and command a camp.
>
>   [IV. ii. 175-80]

Did Shakspere put in these lines, and the previous ones which evolve the same feeling, under the system of a cool editorial mending of a second man's work? The system may do for an article; but a play is another thing. Did Shakspere put these lines into the mouth of Lucius, when he calls to his son to weep over the body of Titus?—

> Come hither, boy; come, come, and learn of us
> To melt in showers: Thy grandsire lov'd thee well:
> Many a time he danced thee on his knee,
> Sung thee asleep, his loving breast thy pillow;
> Many a matter hath he told to thee,
> Meet and agreeing with thine infancy;
> In that respect then, like a loving child,
> Shed yet some small drops from thy tender spring,
> Because kind nature doth require it so.
>
>   [V. iii. 160-68]

Malone has not marked these; they are too simple to be included in his poetical gems. But are they not full to overflowing of those deep thoughts of human love which the great poet of the affections has sent into so many welcoming hearts? Malone marks with his commas the address to the tribunes at the beginning of the third act. The lines are lofty and rhetorical; and a poet who had undertaken to make set speeches to another man's characters might perhaps have added these. Dryden and Tate did this service for Shakspere himself. But Malone does not mark *one* line which has no rhetoric in it, and does not *look* like poetry. The old man has given his hand to the treacherous Aaron, that he may save the lives of his sons; but the messenger brings him the heads of those sons. It is for Marcus and Lucius to burst into passion. The father, for some space, speaks not; and then he speaks but one line:—

> *When will this fearful slumber have an end?*
>
>   [III. i. 252]

Did Shakspere make this line to order? The poet who wrote the line conceived the whole situation, and he could not have conceived the situation unless the whole dramatic movement had equally been his conception. Such things must be wrought out of the redheat of the whole material—not filled up out of cold fragments. (pp. 46-7)

It is easy to understand how Shakspere, at the period when he first entered upon those labours which were to build up a glorious fabric out of materials that had been previously used for the basest purposes,—without models,—at first, perhaps, not voluntarily choosing his task, but taking the business that lay before him so as to command popular success,—ignorant, to a great degree, of the height and depth of his own intellectual resources,—not seeing, or dimly seeing, how poetry and philosophy were to elevate and purify the common staple of the coarse drama about him,—it is easy to conceive how a story of fearful bloodshed should force itself upon him as a thing that he could work into something better than the dumb show and fiery words of his predecessors and contemporaries. It was in after-years that he had to create the tragedy of passion. (p. 50)

Charles Knight, " 'Titus Andronicus'," in his Studies of Shakspere, 1849. Reprint by George Routledge and Sons, 1868, pp. 41-52.

G. G. GERVINUS   (essay date 1849-50)

[*One of the most widely read Shakespearean critics of the latter half of the nineteenth century, the German critic Gervinus was praised by such contemporaries as Edward Dowden, F. J. Furnivall, and James Russell Lowell; however, he is little known in the English-speaking world today. Like his predecessor Hermann Ulrici, Gervinus wrote in the tradition of the "philosophical criticism" developed in Germany in the mid-nineteenth century. Under the influence of August Wilhelm Schlegel's literary theory and Georg Wilhelm Friedrich Hegel's philosophy, German critics like Gervinus focused their analyses around a search for the literary work's organic unity and ethical import. Gervinus believed that Shakespeare's work contained a rational, ethical system independent of any religion—in contrast to Ulrici, for whom Shakespeare's morality was basically Christian. In his discussion of* Titus Andronicus, *first published in his* Shakespeare *in 1849-50, Gervinus initially follows the tradition promulgated by Edward Capell (1768), August Wilhelm Schlegel (1808), Hermann Ulrici (1839), and Charles Knight (1849), categorizing the play as one of Shakespeare's earliest works. After reviewing the evidence that either supports or challenges Shakespeare's authorship of the play, however, he contests that the "coarseness of the characterisation," the improbability of events, and the lack of sufficient motives all point to an author other than Shakespeare. To support his argument, Gervinus claims that it is "scarcely possible" that Shakespeare was able to create natural characters in such early works as* Venus and Adonis, *but in* Titus *was satisfied with such a "harsh and distorted touch." Thus, he acquiesces to what he terms the "Ravenscroft tradition" and concludes that Shakespeare revised an earlier work to please his first audiences. Other critics who regard* Titus Andronicus *as Shakespeare's revision of another playwright's work include Edward Ravenscroft (1686), Lewis Theobald (1733), Edmond Malone (1790), Samuel Taylor Coleridge (1811), L. M. Griffiths (1884), Arthur Symons (1885), and Joseph S. G. Bolton (1933).*]

It is indisputable that 'Titus Andronicus,' if a work of Shakespeare's at all, is one of his earliest writings. Ben Jonson . . . said, in the year 1614, that the 'Andronicus'—by which he could hardly allude to any other play—had been acted for twenty-five or thirty years [see excerpt above]; it would, therefore, in any case have been produced during the first years of Shakespeare's life in London. There are few, however, among the readers who value Shakespeare who would not wish to have it proved that this piece did not proceed from the poet's pen. This wish is met by the remark of a man named Ravenscroft, who, in 1687, remodelled this tragedy, and who had heard from an old judge of stage matters that the piece came from another author, and that Shakespeare had only added 'some master-touches to one or two of the principal characters' [see excerpt above, 1686]. (p. 102)

That which we wish we willingly believe. But in this case great and important reasons in evidence of Shakespeare's authorship stand opposed to the wish and the ready belief. The express testimony of Meres, a learned contemporary, who in the year 1598 mentions a list of Shakespeare's plays, places 'Titus' positively among them. The friends of Shakespeare received it in the edition of his works. Neither of these facts certainly contradicts the tradition of Ravenscroft, but at all events they

prevent the piece from being expunged as supposititious without examination.

In accordance with these contradictory external testimonies, internal evidence and the arguments deduced from it appear also to lead rather to doubt than to certainty. It is true that 'Titus Andronicus' belongs in matter as well as in style entirely to the older school which was set aside by Shakespeare. Reading it in the midst of his works, we do not feel at home in it: but if the piece is perused in turn with those of Kyd and Marlowe, the reader finds himself upon the same ground. If, agitated by Shakespeare's most terrible tragedies, we enter into the accumulated horrors of this drama, we perceive without effort the difference that exists between the liberal art which sympathises with the terribleness of the evil it depicts and quickly passes over it—and which, for that reason, suffers no evil to overtake men that cannot be laid to their own guilt and nature—and the rudeness of a style which unfeelingly takes pleasure in suffering innocence, in paraded sorrow, in tongues cut out and hands hewn off, and which depicts such scenes with the most complacent diffuseness of description. He who compares the most wicked of all the characters which Shakespeare depicted with this Aaron, who cursed 'the day in which he did not some notorious ill' [V. i. 127], will feel that in the one some remnant of humanity is ever preserved, while in the other a 'ravenous tiger' commits unnatural deeds and speaks unnatural language. But if the whole impression which we receive from this barbarous subject and its treatment speaks with almost overwhelming conviction against the Shakesperian origin of the piece, it is well also to remember all the circumstances of the poet and his time which can counterbalance this conviction. The refinement of feeling which the poet acquired in his maturity was not of necessity equally the attribute of his youth. If the play, such as it is, were the work of his youthful pen, we must conclude that a mighty, indeed almost violent revolution, early transformed his moral and aesthetic nature, and as it were with one blow. Such a change, however, took place even in the far less powerful poetic natures of our own Goethe and Schiller; it has in some more or less conspicuous degree *at any rate* taken place in Shakespeare. The question might be asked, whether, in the first impetuosity of youth, which so readily is driven to misanthropical moods, this violent expression of hatred, of revenge, and of bloodthirstiness, conspicuous throughout the piece, denotes more in such a man and at such a time, than Schiller's 'Robbers' or Gerstenberg's 'Ugolino' did, which were written in Germany, in the eighteenth century, for a far more civilised generation. When a poet of such self-reliance as Shakespeare ventured his first essay, he might have been tempted to compete with the most victorious of his contemporaries; this was Marlowe. To strike him with his own weapons would be the surest path to ready conquest. And how should an embryo poet disdain this path? At that period scenes of blood and horror were not so rare on the great stage of real life as with us; upon the stage of art they commended a piece to hearers to whom the stronger the stimulant the more it was agreeable. . . . Besides this approval of the people, the author of 'Titus' could claim yet higher approbation. Whoever he might be, he was imbued just as much as the poet of 'Venus' and 'Lucrece' with the fresh remembrance of the classical school; Latin quotations, a predilection for Ovid and Virgil, for the tales of Troy and the Trojan party, and constant references to old mythology and history, prevail throughout the play. An allusion to Sophocles' 'Ajax,' and similarity to passages of Seneca, have been discovered in it. All the tragic legends of Rome and Greece were certainly present to the poet, and we know how full they are of terrible matter. The learned poet gathered them together, in order to compose his drama and its action, from the most approved poetical material of the ancients. When Titus disguises his revenge before Tamora, he plays the part of Brutus; when he stabs his daughter, that of Virginius; the dreadful fate of Lavinia is the fable of Tereus and Progne; the revenge of Titus on the sons of Tamora, that of Atreus and Thyestes; other traits remind of Aeneas and Dido, of Lucretia and Coriolanus. Forming his one fable from these shreds of many fables, and uniting the materials of many old tragedies into one, the poet might believe himself most surely to have surpassed Seneca.

The inference drawn from the subject and contents of the play concerns its form also. With Coleridge the metre and style alone decided against its authenticity [see excerpt above, 1811]. Shakespeare has nowhere else written in this regular blank verse. The diction, for the most part devoid of imagery, and without the thoughtful tendency to rare expressions, to unusual allusions, and to reflective sayings and sentences, is not like Shakespeare. The grand typhon-like bombast in the mouth of the Moor, and the exaggerated mimic play of rage, is in truth that out-heroding Herod which we find the poet so abhorring in 'Hamlet.' Yet even here the objection may be raised, that it was natural for a beginner like Shakespeare to allow himself to be carried away by the false taste of the age, and that it was easy for a talent like his to imitate this heterogeneous style. If we had no testimony as to the genuineness of Shakespeare's narrative poems, scarcely anyone would have considered even them as his writing. Just as with a master's hand he could imitate the conceits of the pastorals, the lyric of the Italians, and the tone of the popular Saxon song, just as well and indeed with far more ease could he affect the noisy style of a Kyd and a Marlowe. At the same time we must confess that at least here and there the diction is not quite alien to Shakespeare. The second act possesses much of that Ovid luxuriance, of that descriptive power, and of those conceits, which we find also in 'Venus' and 'Lucrece,' of which indeed single passages and expressions remind us. It was in these passages that even Coleridge perceived the hand of Shakespeare, and he had in these matters the keenest perception.

Amid these conflicting doubts, these opposing considerations, we more readily acquiesce in Ravenscroft's tradition, that Shakespeare only elaborated in 'Titus' an older play. The whole, indeed, sounds less like the early work of a great genius than the production of a mediocre mind, which in a certain self-satisfied security felt itself already at its apex. But that which, in our opinion, decides against its Shakespeare authorship is the coarseness of the characterisation, the lack of the most ordinary probability in the actions, and the unnatural motives assigned to them. The *style* of a young writer may be perverted, and his *taste* almost necessarily at first goes astray; but that which lies deeper than all this exterior and ornament of art—namely, the estimate of man, the deduction of motives of action, and the general contemplation of human nature—this is the power of an innate talent, which, under the guidance of sound instinct, is usually developed at an early stage of life. Whatever piece of Shakespeare's we regard as his first, everywhere, even in his narratives, the characters are delineated with a firm hand; the lines may be weak and faint, but nowhere are they drawn, as here, with a harsh and distorted touch. And besides, Shakespeare ever knew how to devise the most natural motives for the strangest actions in the traditions which he undertook to dramatise, and this even in his earliest plays; but nowhere has he grounded, as in this piece, the story of his play upon the most apparent improbability. . . . Whoever compares [the] rough psychological art [in 'Titus'] with the fine touches with which in the poet's first production, 'Venus and Adonis,' even amid the perversion of an over-refined descriptive style, those two figures are so agreeably and truly delineated that the painter might without trouble copy them from the hand of the poet, will consider it scarcely possible that the same poet, even in his greatest errors, could have so completely deadened that finer nature which he nowhere else discards.

If it be asked, how it were possible that Shakespeare with this finer nature could ever have chosen such a play even for the sake alone of appropriating it to his stage, we must not forget that the young poet must always in his taste do homage to the multitude, and that in the beginning of his career he would be stimulated by speculation upon their applause, rather than by the commands and laws of an art ideal. (pp. 102-06)

> *G. G. Gervinus, "'Titus Andronicus' and 'Pericles',"* in his Shakespeare Commentaries, *translated by F. E. Bunnètt, revised edition, 1877. Reprint by AMS Press Inc., 1971, pp. 102-12.*

GERALD MASSEY   (essay date 1866)

[*Massey was a nineteenth-century English poet, journalist, and political activist. In the excerpt below, he compares the linguistic style of* Titus Andronicus *with that of Shakespeare's early poems, and because he finds none of the condensed thought, "gusto of language," or nearness to nature evident in Shakespeare's other early works, concludes that Shakespeare had nothing to do with the play. In addition, Massey questions Charles Knight's biographical interpretation of the play (see excerpt above, 1849) by declaring that Shakespeare never experienced a period of "storm and stress" and that his entire career demonstrates "the poise of a rich genius flowering in joy." Massey thus finds no justification for Shakespeare's authorship of* Titus, *and he concludes by attributing it instead to the pens of Christopher Marlowe and Thomas Nashe. For additional commentary on* Titus Andronicus *as the work of Marlowe, see the excerpt by A. H. Bullen (1885).*]

['Titus Andronicus'] has none of the Shakspearian condensation of thought which, in his earliest work, is loosed in the most utter sweetnesses and felicities of expression. None of the Shakespearian gusto of language which makes many of his cordial words as it were the audible kiss of sound and sense. . . . In the whole play, there is no single touch that his closest acquaintances instantly and for ever recognise as the master's; not one of those nearnesses to nature that we know as Shakspearian; and yet he could not write thirty lines without emitting an authentic flash of such revelation.

In short, those who accept 'Titus Andronicus' as Shakspeare's work cannot only not have followed out his nearness to nature in the more delicate touches and opalescent graces of his poetry, but they totally misapprehend the quality of his coarseness; the signs of his immaturity. 'Pericles' is an early play. Dryden calls it the earliest, and I see no cause for doubting the tradition, but many reasons for accepting it. And this play contains the unmistakeable Shakspearian touch of life, of prompt and pregnant thought, of phrase that glows like the serene fire in a gem. But it is impossible to find any proof of Shakspeare's presence from beginning to end of the 'Titus Adronicus.'

Shakspeare's is the tragedy of Terror; this is the tragedy of Horror. His tragedy is never bloodily sensual; his genius has ever a spiritualising influence. Blood may flow, but he is dealing with more than blood. This play is a perfect slaughter-house, and the blood makes appeal to all the senses. The murder is committed in the very gateways of the sense. It reeks blood, it smells of blood, we almost feel that we have handled blood; it is so gross. The mental stain is not whitened by Shakspeare's sweet springs of pity; the horror is not hallowed by that appalling sublimity with which he invested his chosen ministers of death. It is tragedy only in the coarsest material relationships; the tragedy of Horror.

Mr. Knight whose views on the subject of our poet's earliest work, compel his arguments to straddle over impossible spaces past all power of standing, endeavours to show that this play was written by Shakspeare in some period of 'storm and stress' when he was in the throes and agonies of labouring might too big for birth, and had not yet attained to his repose of power.

Yet, directly after, he remarks that from the first, Shakspeare, 'with that consummate judgment which gave fitness to everything he did or proposed to do, held his genius in subjection to the apprehension of the people till he felt secure of their capability to appreciate the highest excellence' [see excerpt above, 1849]. But this equally implies his power to stand over his work and hold his genius in such subjection as should effectually prevent its breaking out in the wild way it must have done supposing him to be the author of 'Titus Andronicus.' It is demonstrable however that Shakspeare did not pass through any such period of agitation or mental green-sickness. His work is healthy from the first. He makes no absurd endeavours to embrace immensity; had no assumptions of strength that collapse in spasm. No tearing of things to pieces tooth and nail. No blind haste or threatening rant. But everywhere the ease, the depth, the fulness, the poise of a rich genius flowering in joy, whose power was from the visible beginning supreme in its range and according to its theme.

We shall best apprehend the superb and happy health of the man by entering into the *humour* of his 'Venus and Adonis.' His merry motive all through is to tantalize the passion with which he plays so provokingly. And this he does with the large ease, the sure touch, the ripe humour of human nature's great master. The man who could so early take such an attitude of assured sovereignty could not have afterwards become the fretting fuming slave of 'Storm and Stress.' Besides which we may learn from the Marlowe group of Sonnets that as early as 1592 or 1593 Shakspeare was fully conscious of the gross faults and defects, the surfeiting comparisons, the Brobdignagian bombast that Marlowe and others revelled in. . . . (pp. 580-82)

One of the greatest differences betwixt Shakspeare and Marlowe was that the latter poet had not sufficient humour to hinder his taking the step from the sublime to the ridiculous, whereas Shakspeare had a most active and ticklish sense of the absurd. This must have been one of his quickest, keenest, most self-preserving instincts!—the liveliest part of his self-consciousness. This alone would have prevented his following in the track of Marlowe save for the purpose of sketching on the back of the other poet as it were, a portrait in caricature of his more prominent features—making a face for the fun of the thing, such as setting Pistol to parody Tamburlane, and devoting some of his earliest merriest satire to mock those who talked unlike men of God's making. And yet Shakspeare is supposed to have written or re-written a drama which contains many of Marlowe's worst characteristics, the unnatural spirit of which is far worse than anything in the expression. (p. 583)

My conviction is that ['Titus Andronicus'] was mapped out and partly written by Marlowe who was the great poet at Henslowe's Theatre. His 'Jew of Malta,' and the 'Titus Andronicus'

were running there alternately and to judge by Henslowe's receipts the latter play was a success. Marlowe's death in June 1593 would prevent his finishing the play and be the chief cause why his name slipped out of sight. It was entered in the Stationers' Registers 1593 but not completed for performance till early in the next year. And whose was the hand that finished the play? Whose should it be but Nash's? he who was united with Marlowe in the production of 'Queen Dido.' It appears to me that no great amount of insight is necessary to discover the same workmanship in both plays. The drama may have been removed to Shakspeare's Theatre on account of Nash's part in it and because both Nash and Marlowe were under the patronage of Shakspeare's friend, Southampton, in whose interest the play may have been completed and at whose request it may have been adopted by the Blackfriars Company. It was published without a name in 1594. And if our Poet made a copy in his own hand-writing that may have misled the Editors of the first folio. As for Meres, it is far easier to believe that he made one mistake in his list of an unpublished literature than it is to accept 'Titus Adronicus' as Shakspeare's work in any sense. (pp. 584-85)

> Gerald Massey, "Appendix D: 'Titus Andronicus'," in his Shakspeare's Sonnets Never Before Interpreted, *Longmans, Green, and Co., 1866, pp. 580-85.*

EDWARD DOWDEN   (essay date 1881)

[*Dowden was an Irish critic and biographer whose* Shakspere: A Critical Study of His Mind and Art *(rev. ed. 1881) is the leading example of the biographical criticism popular in the English-speaking world near the end of the nineteenth century. Biographical critics sought in the plays and poems a record of Shakespeare's personal development. As that approach gave way in the twentieth century to aesthetic theories with greater emphasis on the constructed, artificial nature of literary works, Dowden and other biographical critics came to be considered limited. In the following excerpt, Dowden disputes the interpretation of* Titus Andronicus *as a play reflecting the "Sturm und Drang"—the storm and stress—of Shakespeare's early career, an assessment he attributes to German critics. He argues that Shakespeare never experienced any such turbulent phase during his youth and that his early work consistently demonstrates a "bright and tender play of fancy and of feeling." Like Gerald Massey (1866), Dowden rejects Shakespeare's authorship of the play and thus opposes the commentary of such critics as Edward Capell (1768), August Wilhelm Schlegel (1808), Hermann Ulrici (1839), and Charles Knight (1849).*]

[*Titus Andronicus*] belongs to the pre-Shaksperian school of bloody dramas. If any portions of it be from Shakspere's hand, it has at least this interest—it shows that there was a period of Shakspere's authorship when the poet had not yet discovered himself, a period when he yielded to the popular influences of the day and hour; this much interest, and no more. That Shakspere himself entered with passion or energy into the literary movement which the "Spanish Tragedy" of Kyd may be taken to represent, his other early writings forbid us to believe. The supposed *Sturm und Drang* period of Shakspere's artistic career exists only in the imagination of his German critics. The early years of Shakspere's authorship were years of bright and tender play of fancy and of feeling. If an epoch of storm and stress at any time arrived, it was when Shakspere's genius had reached its full maturity, and *Lear* was the product of that epoch. But *then,* if the storm and stress were prolonged and urgent, Shakspere possessed sufficient power of endurance, and had obtained sufficient grasp of the strong sure roots of life, to save him from being borne away into the chaos or in any direction across the borders of the ordered realm of art. Upon the whole, *Titus Andronicus* may be disregarded. Even if it were a work of Shakspere, we should still call it un-Shaksperian. (p. 48)

> Edward Dowden, "*The Growth of Shakspere's Mind and Art*," in his Shakspere: A Critical Study of His Mind and Art, *third edition, Harper & Brothers Publishers, 1881, pp. 37-83.*

L. M. GRIFFITHS   (essay date 1884)

[*Griffiths argues that in writing* Titus Andronicus *Shakespeare considerably altered the work of another dramatist, whom he does not name; he supports this theory by drawing parallels between* Titus *and a number of Shakespeare's plays of undisputed authorship. For further commentary on the similarities between* Titus *and Shakespeare's other plays, see the excerpt by H. Bellyse Baildon (1904). Also, Joseph S. G. Bolton (1933) presents an analysis of* Titus Andronicus *as Shakespeare's revision of a work written by another dramatist.*]

In common no doubt with many other persons, I was before reading [*Titus Andronicus*] quite convinced that Shakespeare had nothing or very little to do with it. But having read the play a few times, I have come to quite a different conclusion, and so far from thinking that Shakespeare had only slightly touched an old play. I now believe that he adapted the older play as his own and made in it very considerable alterations and such as no other writer could have done. . . . Many of the criticisms upon the play as a whole, seem to me undeservedly harsh. Gerald Massey says, "this play is a perfect slaughter-house and the blood makes appeal to all the senses. It reeks blood, it smells of blood, we almost feel that we have handled blood—it is so gross" [see excerpt above, 1866].

I appeal to all those who have carefully studied the play, to say with me that this is a far-fetched and highly coloured description. I will spend just a few words to show that it goes far beyond just criticism. The sacrifice of Marbus and the killing of Mutius in the first scene are both carried out without any prominence being given to details. The same may be said of the murder of Bassianus and of the nurse. The description of the slaughter of Chiron and Demetrius I would willingly believe to be unaltered from the old play. The mutilation of Lavinia is dwelt upon with very little detail—most of it being by Marcus, who is so good a fellow generally, that nothing can be urged against him on the score of impropriety. This and the amputation of Titus's hand are of course main and essential incidents of the story and Shakespeare having made the play his own, has dealt with these details in that considerate way which so characterizes him when he has perforce to mention incidents of revolting outrages. There is then the general slaughter at the end of the tragedy, where Lavinia, Tamora, Titus and Saturninus all meet with violent deaths. But I must remind you that just such a slaughter occurs at the end of *Hamlet,* where within the space of fifty lines the Queen, the King, Laertes and Hamlet all die. (pp. 201-02)

In the last scene of *Lear,* also, there is by no means an inconsiderable number of dead bodies. The passage in which Macbeth falsely attempts to justify the slaughter of the murdered King's attendants will run any passage in *Titus* very closely for first honors in detail of horror. . . .

And Thersites [in *Troilus and Cressida*] and Apemantus [in *Timon of Athens*], although they do not deal in deeds of blood, yet give utterance to sentiments just as shocking to modern ears unused to the like as the recital of details of slaughter. (p. 202)

When first I conceived the notion of writing this desultory paper, I intended to call it "An Apology for *Titus Andronicus,*" but on looking more and more into the play I decided to give it the more ambitious title of "A Vindication of *Titus Andronicus.*" To justify this title I now propose to look at this play somewhat more in detail, and in doing so to adopt the plan of comparing the characterization of this, with that of the undoubted plays and citing from those plays passages parallel to some in *Titus Andronicus.* . . . Titus himself is powerfully drawn. He acts almost throughout in a dignified and consistent manner. He compares favourably with Coriolanus, who presents many points of similarity to him.

When as the successful warrior returning to his home he is offered the government of the people, he treats the offer in a far more dignified way than Coriolanus, whose behaviour to the people largely partakes of affectation. Titus asks for the suffrages of the people only, that he may bestow them upon their legitimate possessor. When newly possessed with power which he owes to the generosity of Titus, Saturninus begins to make his plans entirely ignoring him to whose generalship the safety of the country is owing, the proud spirit of Titus finds expression in those pathetic words which realize the deep felt grief which possessed him.

> I am not bid to wait upon the bride.
> Titus, when wert thou wont to walk alone,
> Dishonoured thus?
>
> [I.i.338-40]

But his is no mutinous spirit and he is ready to give obedience to the new Ruler of Rome, and in the trusting innocence of his heart finds new life in the specious words of Tamora, who already makes Saturninus the tool of her revenge upon her captor.

> I thank your Majesty and her my lord.
> These words, these looks infuse new life in me.
>
> [I.i.460-61]

What more natural than this episode as illustrating the greatness of the mind of a true lover of his country. When his wrongs are past explanation or gloss, and they are so brought home to him as for a time to cloud his reason, there is, notwithstanding a few strained metaphors and bombastic talking, from which Shakespeare is not quite free, even in later plays, a nobleness pervading his actions which shows that the character is drawn by no common hand. I am anxious to know if there is any character in contemporary literature dealt with so finely as this of Titus? Cast in an entirely different mould his brother Marcus presents to us another finely-drawn picture. Marcus seems to me—I know not if there is any reason for it—a much older man than Titus, and one whose every action is dictated by a wish to benefit the common weal. (pp. 202-03).

He reminds me now of Nestor [in *Troilus and Cressida*], now of Prospero, and now of Antonio [in *The Tempest*]. His character is strongly marked with the Shakespearian freshness and strength, and it would be difficult to find in all the plays a more gentle, lovable, self-denying old man. There is no need to go with detail into the character of Tamora, but there are in it many points of resemblance to that of Cleopatra. The details of the characters of Aaron and Richard of Gloster [*Richard III*] bear evidence of a common author.

Let us look very briefly at the Clown. Consider carefully his appearance in IV, 3, and although I do not lay special stress on this as a proof of authorship, I think it must be admitted that there we have an unmistakable Shakespearian clown, given with only a few touches, but those of so life-like a nature that they furnish some small portion of evidence as to the authorship. I will now quote a few passages which seem to me to bear decided evidence of Shakespeare's style, and such that may not merely be apologised for as productions of his prentice-hand, but that will bear favorable comparison with many of his acknowledged later compositions. . . .

> And if thy sons were ever dear to thee,
> O think my son to be as dear to me.
> Sufficeth not that we are brought to Rome
> To beautify thy triumphs and return
> Captive to thee and to thy Roman yoke,
> But must my sons be slaughtered in the streets
> For valiant doings in their country's cause?
> O, if to fight for King and common weal
> Were piety in thine, it is in these,
> Andronicus, stain not thy tomb with blood,
> Wilt thou draw near the nature of the gods?
> Draw near them, then, in being merciful.
>
> [I.i.107-18]

The speech would have been worthy Constance in her calmer moments [*King John*, III. iv. 25-35]. If Constance's apostrophe to death had been found in *Titus Andronicus*, we should, I doubt not, have had a chorus of critics adducing it as further evidence of the pre-Shakespearian bombast. The likeness of part of this speech of Tamora's to a passage in Portia's speech on Mercy [in *The Merchant of Venice* can be seen], and also parallel passages in [*I Henry VI*, V. iii. 78-9] and [*Richard III*, I. ii. 227-28] to *Titus Andronicus*, [II. i. 82-3]. Only a few lines further on we have a passage which for dignity and concentration of thought is rarely surpassed in any of the later plays:

> In peace and honour rest you here my sons,
> Rome's readiest champions, repose you here in rest
> Secure from worldly chances and mishaps.
> Here lurks no treason, here no envy swells.
> Here grow no damned grudges, here are no storms,
> No noise, but silence and eternal sleep.
> In peace and honour rest you here, my sons.
>
> [I. i. 150-56]

The dirge of Guiderius and Arvirages over the supposed corpse of Imogen [in *Cymbeline*], which may be cited as a somewhat parallel passage, is to my ear a far feebler one than this. (pp. 203-04)

The outburst of Titus' grief at the treatment he had received at the hands of the Tribunes is given with such vigour, that, making allowance for the hyperbole, which not unnaturally would characterize the passionate outpouring of a much-wronged soul, I think it would be difficult to find in the whole of Shakespeare's contemporaries, writing at their best, any passage at all comparable with this. . . .

If I am met with the objection that in *Titus* there is so much inferior work that the play cannot be looked upon as Shakespeare's, I reply that I admit that there is much that is obviously non-Shakespearian, . . . but the existence of these parts is accounted for by the theory of Shakespeare retouching an old play and leaving much of it as he found it, and also by the fact that in the best of Shakespeare's plays there is many a

passage which, if taken by itself, we should think could not have been written by the master-hand of the unparalleled dramatist. (p. 204)

> *L. M. Griffiths, "A Vindication of 'Titus Andronicus'," in* Shakespeariana, *Vol. I, No. 8, June, 1884, pp. 201-04.*

JOHN ADDINGTON SYMONDS　(essay date 1884)

[*Symonds was a nineteenth-century English art historian, critic, and poet who, in his* Shakspere's Predecessors in the English Drama *(1884), introduced and defined the term "Tragedy of Blood" to characterize the type of play produced by such Elizabethan dramatists as Thomas Kyd, Christopher Marlowe, and John Marston. Symonds considers* Titus Andronicus *interesting for its blending and heightening of all the elements typically found in the Tragedy of Blood. For additional comparisons of* Titus *and the works of Kyd and Marlowe, see the excerpts by Arthur Symons (1885) and Fredson Thayer Bowers (1940).*]

The sympathies of the London audience on which our playwrights worked might be compared to the chords of a warrior's harp, strung with twisted iron and bulls' sinews, vibrating mightily, but needing a stout stroke to make them thrill. This serves to explain that conception of Tragedy which no poet of the epoch expressed more passionately than Marston in his prologue to 'Antonio's Revenge,' and which early took possession of the stage. The reserve of the Greek Drama, the postponement of physical to spiritual anguish, the tuning of moral discord to dignified and solemn moods of sustained suffering, was unknown in England. Playwrights used every conceivable means to stir the passion and excite the feeling of their audience. They glutted them with horrors; cudgelled their horny fibres into sensitiveness. Hence arose a special kind of play, which may be styled the Tragedy of Blood, existing, as it seems to do, solely in and for bloodshed. The action of these tragedies was a prolonged tempest. Blows fell like hailstones; swords flashed like lightning; threats roared like thunder; poison was poured out like rain. As a relief to such crude elements of terror, the poet strove to play on finer sympathies by means of pathetic interludes and 'lyrical interbreathings'—by the exhibition of a mother's agony or a child's trust in his murderer, by dialogues in which friend pleads with friend for priority in death or danger, by images leading the mind away from actual horrors to ideal sources of despair, by the soliloquies of a crazed spirit, by dirges and songs of 'old, unhappy, far-off things,' by crescendos of accumulated passion, by the solemn beauty of religious resignation. This variety of effect characterises the Tragedies of Blood. These lyrical and imaginative elements idealise their sanguinary melodrama. (pp. 485-86)

Marlowe, finding [this species of drama] already popular, raised it to higher rank by the transfiguring magic of his genius. 'The Jew of Malta' marks a decided step in advance upon the plays which I have noticed. Two dramas of superior merit, clearly emanating from the school of Marlowe, may also be reckoned among the Tragedies of Blood in this second period of elaboration. These are 'Titus Andronicus,' which, on the faith of an old anecdote, we may perhaps infer to have been the work of an amateur, dressed for the theatre by Shakspere; and 'Lust's Dominion; or, The Lascivious Queen,' a play ascribed to Marlowe, but now believed to have been written by Dekker, Haughton, and Day. Both in 'Titus Andronicus' and in 'Lust's Dominion,' Marlowe's sanguinary Jew is imitated. Barabas, Aaron, and Eleazar are of the same kindred. (p. 490)

[Symonds adds in a footnote:] Aaron seems to me as inferior to Barabas in poetic and dramatic pith, as he exceeds him in brutality. But the play of *Titus Andronicus* is interesting, independently of this villain's character, for its systematic blending, and in some sense heightening, of all the elements which constitute a Tragedy of Blood. We have a human sacrifice and the murder of a son by his father in the first act; in the second, a murder and the rape and mutilation of a woman; in the third, two executions and the mutilation of the hero; in the fourth, a murder; in the fifth, six murders, a judicial death by torture, and a banquet set before a queen of her two dead sons' flesh. The hyperbolical pathos of Lavinia's part, the magnificent lunacy of Titus (so like to that of Hieronymo in quality), and the romantic lyrism which relieves and stimulates imagination, belong to the very essence of the species. So also does the lust of Tamora and the frantic devilishness of her paramour.

(p. 491)

John Addington Symonds, "Tragedy of Blood," in his Shakspere's Predecessors in the English Drama, *Smith, Elder, & Co., 1884, pp. 485-98.**

ARTHUR SYMONS (essay date 1885)

[*Symons was an English critic, essayist, and poet. His analysis of* Titus Andronicus *was originally published in 1885 as the introduction to a facsimile of the play's first quarto edition. In the following excerpt, Symons examines the play's relationship to the Tragedy of Blood tradition first discussed by John Addington Symonds (1884), stressing the similarities between Aaron, Barabas, from Marlowe's* The Jew of Malta, *and Eleazar, from Decker's* Lust's Dominion. *He also notes inconsistencies in the characterization of Titus and Lavinia that, to him, suggest that* Titus *is the work of more than one author. In conclusion, Symons argues that the play was originally written by an unknown minor author who imitated the Tragedy of Blood structure, and that Shakespeare revised or added certain portions. For additional commentary on the characterization in* Titus Andronicus, *see the excerpts by H. Bellyse Baildon (1904), Joseph S. G. Bolton (1933), Eugene M. Waith (1955), Bernard Spivack (1958), and Irving Ribner (1960).*]

It is on the internal evidence, and the internal evidence alone, that the burden of proof [concerning Shakespeare's authorship of *Titus Andronicus*] really rests; all that we can require of a hypothesis intelligibly constructed from the evidence of the play itself, is that it shall not be at variance with the few external facts, on a rational interpretation of them.

We know, almost to a certainty, that Shakespeare's earliest dramatic work consisted in adapting to the stage old plays in the stock of his players' company, and very probably in revising new works by unknown and unskilful playwrights. The second and third parts of *King Henry VI* are examples to our hand of the former manner of work: *Titus Andronicus* may with some probability be conjectured to be an instance of the latter. I shall try to show that such a supposition is the least violent and fanciful that we can well make; accepting Ravenscroft's tradition [see excerpt above, 1686], not from any particular reliance on its probable authenticity, but because, in the absence of any definite information to the contrary, it supplies me with a theory which most nearly agrees with my impressions after a careful examination of the text itself.

Titus Andronicus is a crude and violent, yet in certain respects superior, study in that pre-Shakespearian school which Symonds distinguishes as "The Tragedy of Blood" [see excerpt above, 1884]. This Tragedy of Blood, loud, coarse, violent, extravangantly hyperbolical, extravagantly realistic, was the first outcome of a significant type of Elizabethan character, a hardy boisterousness of nature, a strength of nerve and roughness of taste, to which no exhibition of horror or cruelty could give anything but a pleasurable shock. A popular audience required strong food, and got it.

In the early days of the drama, when playwrights were as yet new to their trade, and without much sense of its dignity as an art, this popular style of tragedy, in the hands of its popular manufacturers, was merely horrible. There were blood and vengeance, strong passions and unrestrained wantonness, but as yet there was no conception of the difference between the horrible and the terrible. Later on, in the hands of Shakespeare and Webster, the old rank Tragedy of Blood, the favourite of the people, became transformed. The horrible became the terrible, a developed art guided the playwright's hand in covering with a certain magnificence the bare and grim outlines of malevolence and murder. It was the same thing, and yet new. (pp. 63-5)

A careful examination of the plays left to us of the period at which *Titus Andronicus* must have been written will show us the exact nature of this species of bloody tragedy, its frequency, and its importance and influence. There may be traced a foreshadowing of it in the copious but solemn blood-shedding of the very first English dramas, the pseudo-classical *Gorboduc* and *The Misfortunes of Arthur*. . . . [In these plays] there is no attempt to move by thrilling; a would-be classical decorum is preserved in the midst of carnage, and the sanguinary persons of the drama comment on their actions with singular gravity. But while the barbarous violence of action is reported as having happened, with a steady suppression of sights and details of blood, it is already potentially present in the background, in readiness for more powerful use by more powerful playwrights.

In *Jeronymo* (or *Hieronymo*) and *The Spanish Tragedy*, in reality a single play of colossal proportions, we have perhaps the first, and at once the foremost, representative of the genuine Tragedy of Blood. The stilted and formal phraseology is still employed, in a much modified and improved form, but there is a real attempt to move the hardy susceptibilities of an audience; the murders occur on the stage, and are executed with much fierceness, and the language of overblown rant is at least intended (and was probably found) to be very stirring. The action of both plays is slow, dull, wearisome, without vivacity or naturalness; the language alternates from the ridiculously trivial to the ridiculously inflated; while in the way of character there are the very slightest indications of here and there a mood or a quality. But the play is important by reason of its position at the head of a long line of tragedies, containing more than one of the dramas of Marlowe, and scarcely coming to an end in the masterpiece of Webster. (pp. 65-7)

Contemporaneous with *The Spanish Tragedy* but less representative of the movement, are several other melodramas; the anonymous *Soliman and Perseda,* and Peele's *Battle of Alcazar,* for instance. Becoming, not more human, but more artistic, the Tragedy of Blood found a willing exponent in the great, daring, but unballasted genius Marlowe, and in the authors of *Lust's Dominion.*

It is to this period that *Titus Andronicus* belongs; a period of more mature art, more careful construction, more power of characterization, but of almost identical purpose. These plays are distinguished from *The Spanish Tragedy* on the one hand, but they are after all still more sharply distinguished from *Lear, The Duches of Malfi,* or even *The Revenger's Tragedy,* and the harsh, powerful dramas of Marston, on the other.

Marlowe's *Jew of Malta* is the most generally known of the Tragedies of Blood, and it is indeed not an ill specimen of the developed style. . . . [It] belongs distinctly to the school of Kyd, but it is raised above its precursors, not only by reason of the frequent splendour of its poetry, but still more by the presence of a finely-imagined character, an idealizing of the passion of greed. The play is Barabas; with his entrance and exit the good in it comes in and goes out. The captains, brutes, and bullies, the shadowy Abigail, all the minor characters, are hasty sketches, rank if not bodiless, mere foils to the malevolent miser. Barabas himself, as it has been so often pointed out, is a creation only in the first two acts, where he foreshadows Shylock; in all the later portion of the play he is only that "monster with a large painted nose" of whom Lamb has spoken. Marlowe and Shakespeare, it is sad to recollect, alike degraded their art, Marlowe more than once, Shakespeare at least once, to please the ears of the groundlings. The intentional debasement of Barabas, in the latter half of *The Jew of Malta,* from a creation into a caricature, is only equalled, but it is equalled, by that similar debasement of Falstaff in *The Merry Wives of Windsor,* from the prophet and philosopher of this world's cakes and ales into an imbecile buffoon, helpless, witless, and ridiculous.

Lust's Dominion, a play issued under the name of Marlowe, but assigned by Mr. Collier, with great probability, to Dekker, Haughton, and Day, is a play of the same class as *The Jew of Malta,* overloaded to an inconceivable extent with the most fiendish crimes, but in several scenes really beautiful and fanciful, and containing, like *The Jew of Malta,* a single predominant character, the villain Eleazar, drawn with abundant strength and some precision. This play is the very quintessence of the Tragedy of Blood; crammed from end to end with the most ingeniously atrocious villanies, but redeemed from utter vulgarity by a certain force and even delicacy of expression, and a barbaric splendour of horror not untinged with ferocious irony. It is a work of art, if of a gross and immature kind, in a sense in which *The Spanish Tragedy* is not. The old outlines remain, but they are filled in with bold but glaring colouring, with coarsely-painted human figures, and are set in a distinct, though loud, key of colour. The thing is revolting, but it is no longer contemptible.

Between these two plays, but rather in company with the former than the latter, I would place *Titus Andronicus.* Like *The Jew of Malta* and *Lust's Dominion,* it contains the full-length portrait of a villain; like *The Spanish Tragedy,* its most powerful scenes are devoted to the revengeful madness of a wronged old man.

In construction *Titus Andronicus* belongs distinctively to the Tragedy of Blood: it is full of horrors and of bloodthirsty characters. . . . [There] is in Titus a fine note of tragic pathos, in Aaron a certain vigour and completeness of wickedness, in Tamora a faint touch of power, but in Lavinia, in Bassianus, in Saturninus, in the sons of Titus and Tamora, scarcely the semblance of an attribute. The powerful sketch of Aaron is a good deal indebted to the Barabas of Marlowe. There is much the same comprehensive malevolence, feeding on itself rather than on any external provocation; a malevolence even deeper in dye, if less artistic in expression. Both have a delight in

evil, apart from the pleasure anticipated from an end gained: they revel in it, like a virtuous egoist in the consciousness of virtue. Eleazar, in *Lust's Dominion,* is a slightly different type of the complete villain. His is a cold, calculating wickedness, not raving nor furious, but set on a certain end. He enjoys his villany, but in a somewhat sad and sober fashion. He is supremely ambitious, to that ambition all other qualities of evil bow, his lust, his cruelty, his spite, his pride; everything. . . . The three villains, Barabas, Aaron, and Eleazar, are three of the earliest, three primary types, of that long series in which the Elizabethan dramatists attempted to read the problem of Renaissance Italy: of wickedness without moral sense, without natural conscience, wickedness cultivated almost as an aesthetic quality, and attaining a strenuous perfection.

The character of Titus is on a higher plane than that of Aaron; it has more humanity, and a pathos that is the most artistic quality of the play. Titus is the one character, absolutely the only one, who moves us to any sympathy of emotion. The delineation is unequal, there are passages and scenes of mere incoherency and flatness, speeches put into his mouth of the most furious feebleness, but at its best, in the later scenes of half real and half pretended madness, the character of Titus is not so very much below the Hieronymo of the "additions." At its worst it sinks to almost the level of the original Hieronymo. Such curious inequality is not observable in any other person of the play. Aaron and Tamora are the Aaron and Tamora of a single conception, worked out with more or less skill on a level line. The dummies of the play are consistent dummies. Lavinia is a single and unmixed blunder. But Titus, by his situation the most interesting character of the play, is at one time fine, at another foolish, in a way for which it is difficult to account if a single author wrote the whole play.

Lavinia, I have said, is a single and unmixed blunder. There is no other word for it. I can never read the third scene of the second act without amazement at the folly of the writer, who, requiring in the nature of things to win our sympathy for his afflicted heroine, fills her mouth with the grossest and vilest insults against Tamora, so gross, so vile, so unwomanly, that her punishment becomes something of a retribution instead of being wholly a brutality. There is every dramatic reason why the victim should not share the villain's soul, every dramatic reason why her situation should be one of pure pathos. Nothing but the coarseness of nature of the man who first wrote it can explain the absurdity. And this is Shakespeare's first heroine, the first of the series which ends with Imogen, in the opinion of those critics who assign the whole of *Titus Andronicus* to the young Shakespeare! The character of Lavinia is alone enough to disprove this opinion; and the character of Lavinia only belongs to the general conception of the play, which is not at all better than might be expected of a clever follower of approved models, a disciple of Marlowe in his popular melodrama. But when we have said this, we have not said everything. The beauty and force of certain passages, and the impressiveness of certain scenes, are so marked, and so markedly above the level of the surrounding work, that we may well hesitate to deny to Shakespeare all part or lot in it.

Two positions I think we are justified in assuming. First, that *Titus Andronicus* is so absolutely unlike all Shakespeare's other early work, that it is, to say the least, improbable that the whole play can be his; and second, that the assumption of a revision by him of another man's work is, on the face of it, quite probable and likely. . . . *Titus Andronicus* is full of gross horror, sickening with the scent of blood, materially moving.

It seems nothing less than impossible that the same hand should have written, first this play, in which the playwright revels coarsely in blood and horror; then *Romeo and Juliet,* in which a tragic story is treated with only a lyrical rendering of the tragedy; then *King Lear,* burdened with an almost intolerable weight of terror, but kept sweet, and pure, and fair by the twin quality of pity. Unless Shakespeare wrote *Titus Andronicus* he never touched tragedy without making it either lyrically pathetic or piteously terrible. And it is only natural to suppose that he never did, and never could have done so.

On the other hand, taking into consideration the differences of workmanship traceable in the play, and the comparative force and beauty of certain parts, it is not impossible that Shakespeare had, if not a hand, at least some finger in it. . . . Suppose a new play, by a "private author," written, somewhat clumsily, in a popular style, to be offered to the theatre: what would be more likely than that the thing should be handed over to the dramatic journeyman, young Shakespeare, for brief revision and rectification? Young Shakespeare, little as he may care for the style, of course must hold himself subservient to the ideals of the original playwright; but he heightens, where he can, the art of the delineations, inserts some passages of far more impressive significance, perhaps almost some scenes, and touches the dead level of the language into something of grace and freshness. Thus we have a stupid plot, a medley of horrible incidents, an undercurrent of feeble language; and, in addition, some powerful dramatic writing, together with bright passages here and there, in which a fresh and living image is expressed finely.

Coleridge's fancy or theory as to Shakespeare's way of dealing with a play in revising it; beginning indifferently, adding only a line here and there, but getting more interested as he went on, applies very well to *Titus Andronicus.* All the first act is feeble and ineffectual; here and there a line, a couplet, a short passage, such as the touch on mercy, or the speech of Titus [I. i. 187-200] puts a colour on the pale outline, and permits us for a moment to think of Shakespeare. But the "purple patches" are woefully far apart. (pp. 68-79)

With the second act there is a decided improvement. Aaron, the notable villain of the piece makes his first appearance; Tamora blossoms out into the full flower of wickedness; and in the mouths of these anything but idyllic personages we have some of those fine idyllic passages which seem not unlike the early style of Shakespeare. (pp. 79-80)

The last three acts are far superior to the first two. They are mainly concerned with the wrongs and madness of Titus, which I suspect to have been entered into by Shakespeare with more sympathy than the other parts of the play, and almost throughout dignified and humanized by him. I do not mean to say that Shakespeare wrote all, or most, of the speeches assigned to Titus throughout the play, or even in the last three acts. The touches by which a great poet can raise the work of a small poet from puerility to fineness may be slight and delicate; and are, indeed, far too delicate to be distinguished and emphasized by the critic. Nor is the service, which I suspect Shakespeare to have rendered his predecessor, complete. Not a few empty and rhetorical passages put into the mouth of the suffering hero seem like untouched fragments of the former stuff. . . . All the ending of the play, the grotesquely horrible dish of human flesh, the tortures, is, of course, entirely due to the original author. Nothing is more clearly and more closely connected with the model Tragedy of Blood; and nothing certainly could be more unlike Shakespeare.

Act V. Scene ii. Titus, Demetrius, Caius, Lavinia, Publius, Valentine, and Chiron. Frontispiece to the Rowe edition (1709). By permission of the Folger Shakespeare Library.

Thus we see, on glancing through the play, that *Titus Andronicus,* in its plot, general conception, and most of its characters, belongs distinctly to the Tragedy of Blood, and, being in these respects inferior to the best of it, may be considered the work of a disciple of the school, not of an acknowledged master; while in certain parts it seems to be lifted above itself, vivified and dignified: a combination which naturally suggests the revision of an inferior work by a superior master. The closer we examine it, the more natural does this view become, and the more probable does it seem that in *Titus Andronicus* we have the work of an unknown writer revised by the young Shakespeare. To consider it the work of an amateur, a disciple of the School of Blood, but not a great writer, raised to its present interesting and imperfect state by Shakespeare's early revision (which is substantially the Ravenscroft tradition) seems to explain the otherwise inexplicable mixture in this singular play of good and bad, twaddle and impressiveness; and seems to explain, on the one hand, why it is so good as it is, on the other, why it is no better. I do not think it is very sensible to try to assign the play, as originally written, to some well-known author of the time, such as Greene or Marlowe, rather than to the "private author." Such resemblances of these writers as occur might naturally be imitations; but to father on Marlowe, in especial, the meaner parts of the play, is a quite gratuitous insult to his memory. (pp. 83-7)

Arthur Symons, "'Titus Andronicus' and the Tragedy of Blood," in his Studies in the Elizabethan Drama,
E. P. Dutton & Company, 1919, pp. 61-87.*

A. H. BULLEN (essay date 1885)

[An English scholar best known for his studies of Christopher
Marlowe, Bullen regards Titus Andronicus as one of Marlowe's
earliest works. Like John Addington Symonds (1884) and Arthur
Symons (1885), Bullen points to parallels between Aaron and the
character of Barabas in Marlowe's The Jew of Malta; but whereas
both Symonds and Symons attribute a certain share of the play
to Shakespeare, Bullen finds nothing to support this assessment.
Gerald Massey (1866) also considered Marlowe the author of
Titus Andronicus, although he stated that the dramatist began the
composition late in his career and that it was completed by Thomas
Nashe.]

As I re-read [Titus Andronicus] after coming straight from the
study of Marlowe, I find again and again passages that, as it
seems to me, no hand but his could have written. It is not easy
in a question of this kind to set down in detail reasons for our
belief. Marlowe's influence permeated so thoroughly the dramatic literature of his day, that it is hard sometimes to distinguish between master and pupil. When the master is writing
at his best there is no difficulty, but when his work is hasty
and ill-digested, or has been left incomplete and has received
additions from other hands, then our perplexity is great. In our
disgust at the brutal horrors that crowd the pages of Titus
Andronicus, we must beware of blinding ourselves to the imaginative power that marks much of the writing. In Aaron's soliloquy at the opening of act ii., it is hard to believe that we
are not listening to the young Marlowe. There is the ring of
Tamburlaine in such lines as these:—

> As when the golden sun salutes the morn,
> And, having gilt the ocean with his beams,
> Gallops the zodiac in his glistering coach,
> And overlooks the highest-peering hills.
>
> [II. i. 5-8]

Both rhythm and diction in the following lines remind us of
Marlowe's earliest style:—

> Madam, though Venus govern your desires,
> Saturn is dominator over mine:
> What signifies my deadly-standing eye,
> My silence and my cloudy melancholy,
> My fleece of woolly hair that now uncurls
> Even as an adder when she doth unroll
> To do some fatal execution?
> No, madam, these are no venereal signs:
> Vengeance is in my heart, death in my hand,
> Blood and revenge are hammering in my head.
>
> [II. iii. 30-9]

Aaron's confession of his villainies (in V. i) will recall to every
reader the conversation between Barabas and Ithamore in the
third scene of the second act of the Jew of Malta. The character
of Aaron was either drawn by Marlowe or in close imitation
of him; and it seems to me more reasonable to suppose that
Titus Andronicus is in the main a crude early work of Marlowe's
than that any imitator could have written with such marked
power. But the great difficulty lies in determining to whom
we should assign the frantic ravings of old Andronicus. They
appear to be by another hand than Marlowe's; and they cannot,
with any degree of plausibility, be assigned to Shakespeare. . . . What share Shakespeare had in the play I must

confess myself at a loss to divine. I have sometimes thought
that there are traces of his hand in the very first scene,—and
not beyond it; that he began to revise the play, and gave up
the task in disgust. It is of Shakespeare rather than of Marlowe
that we are reminded in such lines as—

> Wilt thou draw near the nature of the gods?
> Draw near them then in being merciful:
> Sweet mercy is nobility's true badge.
>
> [I. i. 117-19]

But however closely we may look for them, we shall find very
few Shakespearean passages. Of Marlowe's earliest style we
are constantly and inevitably reminded. (pp. lxxvi-lxxviii)

A. H. Bullen, in an introduction to The Works of
Christopher Marlowe, Vol. I, edited by A. H. Bullen,
Houghton, Mifflin and Company, 1885, pp. ix-lxxxiv.*

FREDERICK S. BOAS (essay date 1896)

[Boas was a nineteenth- and early twentieth-century scholar specializing in Elizabethan and Tudor drama. In his Shakespearean
criticism, he focused on both the biographical elements and the
historical influence apparent in Shakespeare's works. For this
reason, many scholars today regard him as occupying a transitional position in the history of Shakespearean criticism between
the biographical methods of Edward Dowden and Frank Harris
and the historical approach of E. E. Stoll, Hardin Craig, and
E. M. W. Tillyard. Boas asserts in the following excerpt that the
signs of Shakespeare's handiwork are evident throughout Titus
Andronicus. He claims that the play's "clear and compact" plot,
consistent versification, animal and nature imagery, and characterization all display Shakespeare's "master-hand." Boas also
describes the play's conclusion as typically Shakespearean in its
projection "beyond the darkness" to "the dawn of a new social
order"—a conciliatory element that such earlier critics as Hermann Ulrici (1839) and Gerald Massey (1866) find lacking
throughout the play. For further discussion of the tragic structure
of Titus Andronicus, see the excerpts by E. M. W. Tillyard (1944),
Alan Sommers (1960), Irving Ribner (1960), D. J. Palmer (1972),
and Albert H. Tricomi (1976).]

[The plot of Titus Andronicus is] a tissue of horrors, and they
are accentuated unsparingly throughout. It is this repulsive
realism that has led English critics to deny that the play is a
genuine specimen of Shaksperean tragedy, which wellnigh uniformly shuns all that is barbarous or gross. In Titus Andronicus
the worst excesses of Kyd's Spanish Tragedy are reproduced,
combined with the most unnatural horrors of classic fable. The
ghastly legends of Atreus and Thyestes, of Tereus and Philomela directly suggest incidents in the play, while other episodes
are borrowed from the stories of the Tarquins, of Virginius,
and Coriolanus. The running fire of classical allusion throughout every act, united to occasional quotations from Latin authors in the original, has been urged as an additional proof that
the play was not written by Shakspere. But it is far from
impossible that the Stratford poet may have poured out, in this
early work, his stock of grammar-school reminiscences, and
have drawn upon them for the materials of a blood-curdling
tragedy of the approved type. In any case neither this peculiarity
of style, nor the loathsome nature of so many incidents in the
play, justifies the attitude which English criticism has adopted.
External evidence ascribes the play to Shakspere, and the conjecture that he merely added revising touches to it finds no
support in the character of the work. For, whatever its demerits
are, it has an unmistakable stamp of unity. The plot is clear
and compact, and the versification is singularly homogeneous
throughout. Moreover, a close examination reveals certain

characteristics of style and spirit, which temper the horrors, and which anticipate the later methods of the Stratford dramatist. A breeze from the Warwickshire glades blows fresh at times through the reeking atmosphere, and amidst the festering corruptions of a decadent society we have glimpses of nature that make us less forlorn. The constant allusions, however, to animals and birds in *Titus Andronicus*, as in other of the early plays and poems, are due not only to Shakspere's familiarity with the country, but to the influence of Euphuism, one of whose most notable features is the persistent use of illustrations from the natural world. Other passages anticipate speeches or situations in the dramatist's later works, and afford strong confirmation of the Shaksperean authorship of the play. But yet weightier evidence is to be found in the character-drawing where, amidst much that is intolerably crude, there are already signs of the master-hand. Titus forfeits our sympathies in the first act by his tyrannical attempt to separate his daughter from her betrothed, and by his hot-headed murder of the son who stands forth in her defence. But as the action proceeds he becomes a man more sinned against than sinning, and he atones for his misdeeds in the scene where he sacrifices his hand in the vain hope of saving Quintus and Martius from their doom. Thus, like Lear, he expiates his crimes by suffering, though his horrible revenge upon his enemies at the close proves that his moral purgation has been but superficial, and Nemesis justly claims him as a victim. More noteworthy, however, than Titus is Aaron the Moor, the arch-villain of the drama. In the cynical effrontery of his wickedness, he resembles some of Marlowe's creations, especially Barabas. But he further displays, though in rudimentary form, two leading characteristics of Shakspere's criminals: he has an acid humour, and he has the faculty of adroitly turning to his own purposes the vicious desires of his fellow-men. A redeeming touch, that keeps him within the pale of humanity, is his affection for his bastard child; but otherwise he is an incarnation of motiveless malignity, thus prefiguring, strangely enough, Iago, who ruins a very different type of the Moorish race. Among the crowd of repellent figures the boy Lucius forms an attractive picture, with his combined nervousness and high spirit, his precocious intelligence, and his tender memories of the loving mother who left him his Ovid's *Metamorphoses*. He is of the same kin as the two young princes in *Richard III*, and one hand must have created them all. But the most distinctively Shaksperean feature of the play is its close. It is a uniform law in the dramatist's tragedies that, however terrible be the catastrophe in which they culminate, they never end in unmitigated gloom. Individuals may perish, the victims of their own or others' misdeeds, but their fate has in it something of sacrificial efficacy, and beyond the darkness we foresee the dawn of a new social order. So here the choice of the valiant soldier Lucius, the sole surviving son of Titus, to be emperor is of good omen for the future, and gives hope of a sounder era when Rome shall no longer 'herself be bane unto herself' [V. iii. 73]. (pp. 138-41)

> Frederick S. Boas, "Shakspere's Dramatic Appren-
> ticeship," in his Shakspere and His Predecessors,
> Charles Scribner's Sons, 1896, pp. 130-57.

H. BELLYSE BAILDON (essay date 1904)

[*In his introduction to the original Arden edition of* Titus Andronicus, *excerpted below, Baildon examines information on the date and sources of the play and discusses the controversy surrounding its authorship. In an unexcerpted portion of this introduction, he refutes those critics who have "discarded the direct evidence" of Shakespeare's hand in the drama, and he attributes* the critical rejection of Titus *as a Shakespearean play to prejudice rather than fact or scholarly judgment. In the following excerpt, Baildon focuses on the main characters in the play and compares them to figures from other Shakespearean tragedies. For example, he identifies Tamora as the precursor of Lady Macbeth and Cleopatra, the former in her ambition and hypocrisy, the latter in her overriding sexual desires. He considers Titus "a first study" from which the characters of Lear, Coriolanus, and Hamlet were later developed. And he maintains that Aaron is a partially successful attempt to humanize the typically Marlovian stage villain as well as a crude forerunner of Iago. Baildon's comparative approach echoes that of Frederick S. Boas (1896), and his conclusion that* Titus *is primarily Shakespeare's play agrees with the theories of Edward Capell (1768), August Wilhelm Schlegel (1808), Hermann Ulrici (1839), and Charles Knight (1849).*]

Whenever we ask ourselves what is the first essential to the making of a great and perennially interesting author of fiction in its widest sense, whether the form be narrative or dramatic, prose or verse, we are always driven back on the one answer, that it is what we are pleased to call "creative power" and in particular the power of creating characters. Gradually, as time goes on, these *creators, poets, makers,* emerge from the multitude of lesser writers, however accomplished, and take their stations at an altitude that the others can never attain. (p. xxix)

Of this life-giving power, not to use any disputable instance, we have certainly three great exemplars in our literature—Chaucer, especially in his Prologue, Shakespeare, and Scott. Five centuries have not weakened the pulse of life in one of the Canterbury Pilgrims, and the grave Knight and the gay Squire, the genteel Prioress and the vulgar Wife of Bath are living as when their palfreys raised the dust on Kentish roads. While there are some classes of Scott's characters whose original *anoemia* has proved fatal to them, there are others whose cheeks are still fresh and ruddy as winter apples. But high above these, almost in a world of their own, survive in imperishable beauty and vitality the creations of Shakespeare. Here and there, but only here and there, do we find a character looking a little sick and ghostly among the rest, and this almost entirely in his earlier plays. In *Love's Labour's Lost* we have little more than graceful pen-and-ink sketches and first studies for what were to be his great creations later on; and, in like manner, in *Titus Andronicus* we find a series of powerful, and even exaggerated, studies for the great characters that peopled his later tragedies. Already in this play the author shows a marvellous power, one of those absolutely essential in the creation of character in fiction, that of discriminating between two characters apparently extremely alike. This power has been pointed out as characteristic of Shakespeare; but I do not remember that anyone has noticed that the two sons of Tamora are a marvellous example of this. At first sight nothing would seem more difficult than to discriminate between these two utter ruffians. But Shakespeare has done it, and he has done it in a peculiarly bold way. The distinction is this, that he makes Chiron, the younger, at once the more sentimental and the more ruthless. At first it comes on us with a kind of shock when we find the sentimentalist, who was going to sacrifice everything to win Lavinia, suddenly accepting with gusto the horrible proposition of Aaron and his brother. But we have observed human nature but ill if we do not recognise the profound truth of Shakespeare's psychology here, in that sentiment is often but a thin mask worn by the sentimentalist to disguise from himself and others a pitiless lust. How many other dramatists, if any, would have ventured on such a stroke and torn the disguise aside so ruthlessly? It is certainly a psychologic subtlety, far beyond the reach of Kyd, and probably even of Greene or Marlowe.

It is a natural transition from these two [rogues] to their worthy mother, to whose ''codding spirit,'' as Aaron, who ought to know, says, their lustful natures were due.

My own feeling is that up to the scene when she tries to personate Revenge, Tamora's character is magnificently handled. Lustful and ferocious as she is, she has a quality of greatness, such as perhaps only Shakespeare can impart to his wicked women. Her first appearance and her appeal to Titus is as queenly and noble as anything in the range of dramatic art. And here Shakespeare is careful, and this also is characteristic, to give her an excuse for, if not a justification of, her subsequent actions. The barbarous treatment of her eldest born son, Alarbus, was enough to rouse in her strong and passionate nature a thirst for an adequate and terrible revenge. . . . Tamora, like all Shakespeare's heroines, good or bad, largely dominates the play; for even Aaron is often merely her emissary and agent, carrying out her terrific programme with malicious pleasure no doubt, but with no other advantage to himself. Tamora, doubtless, is the slave of her passion for Aaron, or rather, like the Semiramis to whom she was compared in the play, or Catherine of Russia, the slave of her own insatiable desires. This passion and those desires brought about her downfall. On her character the author lavishes all his powers, as, with the exception of Aaron's soliloquy at the opening of the second Act, all the finest pieces of poetic rhetoric are assigned to her. Nor does Tamora, with all her wickedness and cruelty and lust, ever cease to be the woman. (pp. xxx-xxxii)

But, further, we have in Tamora an early study for at least two of Shakespeare's great women characters—Lady Macbeth and Cleopatra. Tamora's relation to Saturninus and her hypocrisy to Titus are extremely like Lady Macbeth's instigation of her husband and her hypocrisy to Duncan. In Cleopatra, again, we have, in a less gross form perhaps, a woman in whom sexual desire is the ruling passion. And in Lady Macbeth we have the same view of the ability of the sexes, for, ready as Lady Macbeth is in planning the single murder of Duncan, she falls into the background as soon as Macbeth embarks in the more comprehensive scheme of crime which the first murder involved; and so one of the great elements of pathos in Lady Macbeth's position is that she is no longer any use to her husband, and only a source of danger to him, through her sleepwalking, and it is characteristic of Shakespeare's maturer treatment that he does not let us see Lady Macbeth defeated and humiliated, as we see Tamora, at the end of our play. (p. xxxiii)

It seems nearly incredible that most of Shakespeare's critics and commentators have missed the seemingly obvious fact that in the character of Titus we have strong suggestions of no less than three of the great male characters in his acknowledged masterpieces, namely, Lear, Coriolanus, and Hamlet. The resemblance to Lear is perhaps the most complete and significant. The faults of Titus' character and that of his family, from which, as in *Lear,* the whole tragic situation arises, are identical. Just as Lear fancied he had a true and disinterested love for his children, so did Titus; and yet in the very opening of both plays their mistake is at once demonstrated. . . . But the resemblance does not end here. Titus has the Empire of Rome within his grasp, and, like Lear, feeling some of the languor of age coming over him, he declines, as Lear wishes to resign, the burden of power. But they both deceive themselves; they do not wish *really* to resign their *power itself,* but merely its burdens and toils. Lear pictures himself loved, honoured and revered, and still consulted and obeyed by his children. Titus,

thinking he had earned the deathless gratitude of Saturninus, seems really to have expected to retain much of his honour and influence, and to be regarded as sort of guardian or grand vizier to the Emperor of his own creation. He, like Lear, is bitterly disappointed; for he finds himself suddenly neglected and of no account. He thus, like Lear, by his own acts, by his cruelty towards Alarbus, his injustice to Lavinia and Bassianus, and his murder of his son, furnishes all the elements in the ensuing tragedy; and as Lear and Cordelia are intimately associated in the final and terrible results, so, in cruder fashion, are Titus and Lavinia.

The resemblance to Coriolanus is yet more simple and obvious. We have the same military and warlike qualities, the same immense pride, the same inordinate claim on the gratitude of his countrymen, the same almost traitorous readiness to turn against them when they offend him.

In regard to his real or feigned madness, Titus has points of resemblance to both Lear and Hamlet. That his madness, like Hamlet's, was mainly assumed, I think there can be no doubt; for whenever he chooses he is not only sane, but capable. But I think also that his troubles are meant to bring him to *the border of real madness,* and just as a man partially drunk can play complete drunkenness more easily than a perfectly sober man, so a man on the verge of madness will probably feign insanity more naturally than one who is perfectly sane. Lear's madness is, of course, not feigned, but that of Edgar in the same play is.

Shakespeare, indeed, is very fond of repeating himself up to a certain point, and it is just beyond that point when his extraordinary power of variation on like themes comes in. There are, indeed, few characters in Shakespeare which could not, at least, be duplicated from his works, and yet no two are the same, any more than two sisters or two brothers are the same person. It seems as if here also he revels in his unequalled power of discrimination. (pp. xxxiii-xxxv)

But let no one run away with the idea that I am holding up Titus himself as being equal in either conception or execution to the other masterpieces of characterisation with which I have compared him: he is only a first study out of which the others were developed. With the general conception of the character there is no fault to find, but with the execution there is a good deal, for either Shakespeare had not got over the influence of a false style which piled up and elaborated images and classical allusions, which embarrassed rather than assisted the effective expression of the emotions and thought, or he has carried forward a good deal of defective matter from some older version of the piece. Perhaps, indeed, we are safer to say that we have both these causes in operation to render the play inferior to Shakespeare's maturer work. (p. xxxvi)

But I think we always get our best test of Shakespeare in his final and total effects rather than in detail, and the final effect of Titus upon us approximates to that of Lear in being superhuman, titanic, something out of the ordinary scale of humanity; and the same is true, even more so, of Tamora: who, as always seems to me, ought to be on the scale of Keats' heathen goddess, one ''who would have ta'en Achilles by the hair and bent his neck.''

Let us now turn to the only other character of absolutely first importance in the drama, Aaron the Moor.

Now, in the character of Aaron, Shakespeare seems to have made a great, if only partially successful, attempt to humanise the ordinary stage villain or monster, as then rendered, even by so great a man as Marlowe. And Marlowe, be it noted, makes no attempt to redeem his villains. He loves them to be monsters; and monsters they remain in his hands. But Shakespeare aimed obviously, not at whitewashing his villains, as a modern author might do . . . , but at humanising them, which is unfortunately quite another thing. And this is the object of the whole of the business of Aaron and his black baby, than which nothing in Shakespeare or out is more admirably managed; and could he have left the character then, it might have been set, as an artistic creation, on a level at least with Richard III., if not Iago. Unfortunately he lapses towards the end of the play into the crudely monstrous and devilish. At the same time, this is not altogether out of nature, certainly not out of Shakespeare's conception of it; for more subtly as Iago is undoubtedly managed, he is in reality very nearly of the same purely malicious and fiendish character as Aaron. . . . [We] need not be surprised that a so faithful, and even sternly faithful, delineator of character as Shakespeare should frequently delineate characters which seem hopelessly bad and incapable of repentance, as Regan and Goneril, Claudius, Richard III., and Iago. These wilfully wicked characters are indeed curiously abundant in Renaissance times, and we have only to recall the Borgia and the Medici families in order to convince ourselves of the fact. The Renaissance indeed, while inaugurating a great artistic and intellectual revival, seems to have had the effect of almost annihilating conscience. The encountering tides of mediaeval Christianity and revived Pagan naturalism seem to have, and that in the greatest men and women of that time, obliterated all moral distinctions,—a phenomenon exemplified in *The Prince* of Machiavelli, which itself became a sort of Devil's Bible which taught one to unlearn all that was honourable and noble in the one ethical system, and all that was kind and merciful in the other. Hence Marlowe, who himself in his life too well exemplifies this, introduces Machiavelli as the presiding evil genius in *The Jew of Malta*. . . . Therefore one is not much at a loss to guess where Shakespeare and even Marlowe got models for their "perfect fiends." So that, crude as Aaron seems to us, who live in times when such crimes are the exception and not the rule, we cannot reasonably maintain that it is out of nature; and, indeed, in our own criminal annals, do we not find monsters of cruelty and iniquity not unworthy of comparison even with Aaron? (pp. xxxix-xli)

[Aaron is] by no means as unnatural as his own rhodomontade towards the end of the play would make us believe. His pure malignity, and avowed love of evil for its own sake, is at least mitigated by self-interest, by zeal for the party he belonged to and for a mistress he admired, if he did not love. On the other hand, his tenderness to his child must not be rated too highly. It is in the first place intensely selfish; it is as a *bit of himself,* a second self, that he cherishes it. And this very tenderness to his child brings out his want of love and consideration for Tamora, whom he at first proposes to leave to her fate. Of any really noble and unselfish feeling Aaron, like Iago, Regan, Goneril, and Richard III., is represented as incapable, and so, according to Shakespeare's ethical or spiritual system, he is a lost soul. From the *Sonnets* onward to *Lear,* Shakespeare's doctrine of redemption, through the love which is a power and faculty in the soul of the lover and not dependent on the attractions or the natural relationship of the object of the love, is continually proclaimed. In Titus, as in Lear, instinctive parental love is shown up in its inability to stand the test of any, even moderate, trial. Both these men think they love their children, but they only love them selfishly, as their own offspring, with an instinctive, almost animal, love, and not with

a personal love, which in Shakespeare's view is the only love worth the name. (p. xliii)

Shakespeare's view seems to have been, not that natural and even sexual love were evils, as Bacon seems to hold, but that in them lay the germs of true love, and that only through them could the higher forms of love be reached. He did not fail to observe—what, indeed, did he fail to observe in human nature?—that this purer form of love springs yet more readily from what we may call the more disinterested forms of "kindly" or natural love, as in this very play he makes the love of brother and uncle, of Lucius and Marcus, a purer affection than Titus' had been, until Lavinia's sufferings develop in him a more personal love, what Tennyson, that great disciple of Shakespeare in such matters, calls "The love of a soul for a soul."

In Aaron we have this "kindly" and instinctive love at its lowest, and yet we feel that there, if anywhere, lies the hope of redemption for so dark a soul as that of the Moor; and we can quite imagine, had it suited Shakespeare's *dramatic* purpose, that he could have portrayed for us such a redemption. (pp. xliv-xlv)

Another coincidence in the treatment of Aaron and Iago . . . is that Shakespeare, regarding mere death as an inadequate punishment for such villains, reserves them both for horrible tortures later on. Tamora and the others are regarded as adequately or appropriately punished, the one by death and the horrible meal she had to make, and [her two sons] by being coolly slaughtered and bled, like the beasts they were. Poor Desdemona suffers more than enough for her indiscretion and disobedience, and Othello for his distrust of her. But Aaron and Iago are reserved for a more terrible fate; and yet we feel assured that these monsters of malice and wickedness will, like many a modern criminal and Richard III. himself, "die game"; for there is in both a strength of spirit, in the pursuit of evil though it be, that wrings from us a genuine, if reluctant, admiration, such as we feel for the sublime malignity and unconquerable endurance of Milton's Satan.

There is one remaining character of first importance in the play, and one who seems to have been almost as cruelly mishandled by the critics of this play, as she was by the two ruffians in the drama itself. I mean, of course, the unfortunate and cruelly-used Lavinia. (pp. xlvi-xlvii)

[Lavinia's speeches are, all through *Titus Andronicus*], simply *maladroit,* and intentionally *maladroit.* For, be it observed, the difficulty with the dramatist is not to secure our sympathy with Lavinia, to whom it naturally flows, but to mitigate our pity for her by making her provocative. No one can fail to sympathise with Lavinia, and the object of the dramatist is rather to divide our sympathies than concentrate them. So in *Lear,* Cordelia's speech to her father is also very *maladroit,* and partly alienates our sympathies. Both Lavinia and Cordelia have a share of the family failings, and both exemplify, whether intentionally or no, the saying, that there is nearly always about virtue an element of harshness. And it seems to me that the reader who allows his sympathy to be diverted so easily from poor Lavinia, has just incontinently fallen into the pit the subtle dramatist has dug for the unwary. The Andronici, like the Lear family, were too uncompromising, for good or evil; and even Lucius, who is made to be chastened and softened, as the play goes on, by pity and affection, is at first harsh and cruel; and the Alarbus incident, which is apparently the pure invention of the author of this version of the play, is at once the test of the Andronicus character, and the key to the stern justice of the piece. And the justice is terribly stern, especially so in the case of Lavinia, as in *Lear* in that of Cordelia. But, perhaps, it would be fairer to Shakespeare to say that what he aims at showing is not exactly the justice so much as the inexorable logic or causality of events. For while Lear and Titus have largely deserved their sufferings, this cannot be justly said of either Lavinia or Cordelia. They are involved in a fatal coil, and, though they do not deserve, yet their faults, slight as they seem, *contribute to* their own misfortunes and the general catastrophe. So far, then, from being "an unmixed blunder" [see excerpt above by Arthur Symons, 1885], and, therefore, we are told, not Shakespeare's work (as if such an essential character in the plot could possibly be wholly the work of a different hand to the rest), Lavinia is not only no blunder, but particularly subtly managed and specially characteristic of Shakespeare. For not only has she her successor in Cordelia, but she has her predecessor or contemporary in Lucrece, as Tamora has her successors in Lady Macbeth and Cleopatra, and her predecessors or contemporaries in Venus and Queen Margaret. (pp. xlix-l)

Titus Andronicus is, I verily believe, Shakespeare's first essay in Tragedy, and it has all the characteristics of a first essay. It is the work of a man learning his business, copying too closely his predecessors, unsure of himself, and still unconscious of his superior powers; afraid of making trenchant alterations in his plot, unskilled in entwining it, as he so well could do later, with a second plot, timid and half-hearted in his attempt to give comic relief to the strain of the tragic interest, afraid of mulcting his audience of the sensationalism they loved. Yet he has the root of the matter in him: his power of distinctive characterisation; his working to a certain moral balance, development and resultant; his gift of humanising grotesque types of wickedness; his interest in psychologic and moral problems, which he afterwards returned to and triumphantly illustrated. He has already command of a noble poetic rhetoric, and the beginnings at least of fine versification. For both of which he may, and probably was, deeply indebted to Marlowe; but he was to put them to yet greater and nobler dramatic use. (pp. lxvii-lxviii)

> *H. Bellyse Baildon, in an introduction to* The Works of Shakespeare: The Lamentable Tragedy of Titus Andronicus *by William Shakespeare, edited by H. Bellyse Baildon, Methuen and Co., 1904, pp. ix-lxxxiv.*

JOSEPH S. G. BOLTON (essay date 1933)

[*Bolton concentrates on the structure, characterization, and poetic style of* Titus Andronicus *in order to prove that Shakespeare revised the work of another dramatist. He contends that the shift in emphasis from Tamora in Act I, to Aaron in the middle acts, and back to Tamora in Act V indicates an extensive, though incomplete revision rather than crudity or inexperience on the part of the playwright. He states that many of the supporting characters, depicted as "brief-spoken vigorous men of action" in the first act, are transformed into loquacious men of sentiment and sensitivity in the middle portions of the play. To Bolton, however, the presence of two authors is most obvious in the portrait of Titus, who is "visited with two kinds of mental derangement": the hallucinations of Thomas Kyd's Hieronymo and the melancholia and emotional imbalance of Richard II. Bolton also notes that the poetic style of Shakespeare's early works—rich in simile, sentiment, and description—is evident in the revised portions of* Titus, *particularly in the characterization of acts II to IV. For additional discussion of* Titus Andronicus *as Shakespeare's revision of another playwright's work, see the excerpts by Edward Ravenscroft (1686), Lewis Theobald (1733), Edmond*

Malone (1790), Samuel Taylor Coleridge (1811), G. G. Gervinus (1849-50), L. M. Griffiths (1884), and Arthur Symons (1885).]

In its central portion [*Titus Andronicus*] seems to me to show that type of distortion which is associated with extensive, although not complete, revision. The formula for Elizabethan tragedies of revenge is simple and effective. Wickedness schemes, virtue suffers; virtue retaliates, and wickedness falls,—as does virtue along with it. But in *Titus Andronicus* the wickedness of the first and last acts is not the same as that of the central three. In Act I the savage Queen of the Goths promises herself the pleasure of torturing the entire Andronicus family, upon which *gens* do come, in terrifying succession, woes of sufficient variety and scope to satisfy a sadist, until, at the conclusion, the survivors of the family succeed in their turn in engulfing the lady and her faction in a punishment as spectacular as it is revolting. But the sufferings that have been theirs through Acts II, III, and IV, are by no means the work of the malignant queen. They have been devised and, for the most part, executed by a character scarcely noticeable at the beginning of the play, and so little a part of Act V as to be given no place in the elaborately constructed scene of retribution. A picturesque, but relatively unimportant, attendant upon the queen, this unlovely individual is raised to leadership with a suddenness that suggests the hand of a second author, and is then allowed to sink back to his former position.

Act I had indeed promised a meteoric career for the captive queen. She had been forced to see her oldest son slain in an expiatory sacrifice to the souls of the dead Andronici. Notwithstanding her plea that "mercy is nobility's true badge" [I. i. 119], the boy's limbs were lopped and hewn and his entrails fed to the sacrificing fire. Little wonder if she burst forth in a passionate threat to massacre them all—

> And make them know what 'tis to let a queen
> Kneel in the streets and beg for grace in vain.
> [I. i. 454-55]

Little wonder, too, if the reader looks to her, now that she has become Empress of Rome, for a spectacular fulfillment of her promise. And only the celerity with which the subsequent atrocities follow one another prevents him from realizing that she is in truth not their author.

Similarly indicative of the original playwright's purpose is the surprisingly innocuous conduct, at the beginning of the play, of the black-faced scoundrel who for three acts displaces Tamora as protagonist of evil. Oddly enough, this character is given no speech at all in Act I, although present half the time. He is but appended, somewhat as an after-thought, to a thrice-repeated stage-direction: *Enter Tamora and her two sons, with Aaron the Moor.* It is only when his racial superiors have withdrawn and left the stage to him that he speaks aloud, and tells, in his 25-line soliloquy, of his illicit love for his royal mistress. (pp. 211-12)

The corresponding rise in importance of the Mephistophelean Moor—now that the reviser seems to have begun his work—may be guessed from his second soliloquy. Thoughts of love have given way, for no observable reason, to high schemes of villainy, and, when his royal mistress tempts him to idle dalliance, he rebukes her masterfully. Venus may govern *her* desires; Saturn dominates his. In his heart is vengeance; in his hand, death, while blood and revenge are hammering in his head. There is no question as to his leadership. (p. 213)

Although at this point in the story the queen shows herself to be little more than an emotional onlooker, definite suggestions of her earlier importance survive, if I am correct in my deductions, in the speeches of the suffering Andronici. These pitiable wretches continue to fear her as the she-bear fighting for her whelps, and fail correspondingly to appreciate the true position of the Moor. He is to them but her black paramour—the mark of her single evil-mindedness. And save for their utterances in the subsequently added second scene of Act III, the words that they speak betray not so much bitterness toward him as contempt. (pp. 213-14)

As Act IV draws to its conclusion, however—and the revision becomes more superficial—the lady comes again into actual prominence.

> Why, thus it shall become
> High-witted Tamora to gloze with all!
>
> [IV. iv. 34-5]

she exclaims—she who has so far glozed with no one—and in Act V she bestirs herself to match wits with Titus and protect her docile husband. But although she regains her ascendancy over the imperial party, she fails of winning success. The time has come for retribution; the characters proceed to die in order; and the queen's primacy appears only in her capacity to suffer. (p. 214)

It is only after the uproar has subsided that [Aaron] is sent to his undramatic, though sufficiently unpleasant, death off-stage, in a manner strongly suggesting interpolation; and the play closes with the new emperor giving orders for the disposal of the dead bodies that crowd him on the stage. (pp. 214-15)

Although pre-Shakespearean plays were at best inconsistent in motivation and confused in plot-structure, a double shift of emphasis such as this can hardly be ascribed to mere crudity and dramatic inexperience. A certain logic inheres of necessity in the first conception of a piece, and its absence here would suggest some sort of revision. In its original form, I imagine, the tragedy exhibited the malevolent lady as prime mover in the incriminating of Titus' sons in the murder of Bassianus, as well as originator of the scheme to rob the venerable hero of his hand. The amorous Moor would have appeared little more than an unnatural lover for her Gothic Majesty and a ready messenger to fetch Titus's hand and bring him back and his two sons' heads. He would thus have ranked in importance slightly below her own sons. It is probable that he lived to see a negroid child born to his royal mistress, but, in all likelihood, he dropped out of the play—at the end of a rope—immediately after his capture by Lucius's soldiery, as was his fate in the German version of the tragedy of the year 1620. For the queen alone was reserved the chief horror of the ghastly banquet-scene.

From this irregularity in the structure of *Titus Andronicus* one may deduce a general rewriting of the middle portion of the piece, designed possibly to adapt to a repertory company now possessing two masculine leads a tragedy that had centered around a wicked queen and an aged warrior. To arrive at a more exact conception of the limits of the reviser's work—as well as to substantiate the oft-questioned pronouncement of Meres regarding its authorship—one need consider points of characterization and poetic style. Significant in this respect are the changes that come over individual characters as they pass from the first act to the second. Throughout Act I, for instance, the younger sons of Titus are brief-spoken, vigorous men of action, conventional enough to be known simply as "2nd Son"

and "3rd Son." In the succeeding act they appear sentimental, loquacious, effeminate. They have become the colorful Quintus and Martius, who tremble at the sight of blood, who faint on the edge of a pit, and who speak fluently of rude-growing briars and morning dew and tapers shining in a monument. Less convincing as Roman warriors, they have yet gained in vitality, in vividness, and in sensitivity. Similarly the tribune Marcus Andronicus drops the reticence and restraint that had marked his initial conduct as he watched his nephew killed and refused burial by his brother, and his brother insulted and threatened by the emperor, and on entering the second act discovers a vein of sentiment worthy of an adolescent Keats. (pp. 215-16)

Although, as a rule, the minor characters appear too rarely to show similar changes, there is a significant contrast between those who are restricted to the beginning of the play and those who find themselves still alive in the central portion. Two of the former—Titus' son Mutius, who lived young, and his son-in-law Bassianus, who did not survive his honeymoon—differ markedly in their matter-of-fact brevity and directness from the two minor characters of the middle portion of the play—the honest clown, who "never drank with Jupiter in his life" [IV. iii. 85-6], and the bewildered child. This last little personage, in fact, is entirely qualified to enter that group of sentimental, self-conscious, but on the whole likable, little boys who appear in the plays from *Richard III* to *The Winter's Tale*. Young Lucius sees the other characters in the drama as real people; he gives evidence of having lived a life beyond the covers of the book; and he has had a mother!

It is, however, in the title rôle of the piece that a second hand is most clearly evident. To the long-suffering Titus the probable revision would seem to have brought one added woe. The venerable hero is now visited by two kinds of mental derangement. At times he sees such hallucinations of abstract qualities, of Justice and Revenge personified, as make him blood-brother to Kyd's Hieronimo. He shoots messages at the planets and even hits a constellation. And appropriately an attempt is made by the queen to befuddle him with visions of Rape and Murder and Revenge—all highly suggestive of the 1580's. At other times, his mental sufferings take the form of intense melancholia and emotional unbalance, shadowing forth, with occasional eloquence, the picturesque lamentations of that second Richard who dreamed away a kingdom and then wept for it in the dust. (p. 217)

[The] matter of Shakespeare's earliest poetic manner is yet, it is true, in a highly debatable state. Some critics assume it to have been a pale reflection of the style of his maturity, and look in vain for his hand in *Titus Andronicus*. Others deem it scarcely distinguishable from that of Peele or Greene or Kyd or Lodge, and give up as hopeless the task of identifying the great man's part in the early plays of multiple authorship. With neither can I agree. Banish from your ears the rhythms of *Hamlet* and of *Lear,* and read in succession the earliest pieces generally agreed upon as the work of Shakespeare alone—free even from later revision by himself—and you will find constantly present a style that is highly individualized and yet strikingly unlike the cadences of 1600. *Venus and Adonis* and *The Rape of Lucrece, The Two Gentlemen of Verona,* and *The Comedy of Errors, King John* and *Richard II*—all written, it now seems probable, within two or three years of the first recorded production of *Titus Andronicus*—offer you a style rich in similes, sentiment, and description, a style that is more turgid than Marlowe's, more vivid than Peele's, more emotional than Greene's. And such is the style that my ear distinguishes throughout the greater part of *Titus Andronicus*.

In fact, there are but three scenes in which I do not find it present and predominant: the very long first scene, wherein Tamora loses a son, wins a husband, and plans the utter humiliation of the Andronicus family; the very short third scene (II, ii), in which the hunt is inaugurated with winded horns and marriage quips; and the first 76 lines of Act IV, scene iii, where Titus shoots his celestial arrows. The rest of the play is, I believe, substantially Shakespeare's. In it are to be found the more sensitively drawn characterizations, the more striking similes, and the closest parallels to the poet's undisputed work. (pp. 219-20)

If one may look, with some assurance, upon certain scenes and episodes in this play as being the distinctive work of Shakespeare, whether as originator or as sympathetic reviser, these scenes will assume new importance in the eyes of critics as possible guides to the interests and the ability of the youthful dramatist. In a task, however, as precarious as this of attempting to deduce Shakespeare's personality from his plays, one must proceed cautiously and tentatively, and only so far as may be substantiated by evidence from his other early work. A consideration of the play suggests that the dramatist at thirty was alive to the possibilities of the Marlowesque villain, the sentimental child, and the anguished father,—that he was already experimenting with his Iagos, his Arthurs, and his Lears. (p. 221)

In particular, his ability appears in the delineation of Aaron the Moor. This character exhibits, to an appreciable extent, that vivid living quality which marks such divergent individuals as Faulconbridge and Juliet and Shylock, and makes them so unlike earlier figures in English drama. Despite his regrettable anti-social tendencies, the scoundrel has vitality. Perhaps it is his air of sophistication and his very evident intellectual superiority, which suggests a similar intellectual power in his creator. Perhaps it is his ironic humor, that lights up with weird color the deep-dyed villainy of his soul. Perhaps it is his rude affection for his little son, so in keeping with his barbaric nature. But, whatever his secret, this figure is outstanding in the drama of 1594. (pp. 221-22)

Joseph S. G. Bolton, "'Titus Andronicus': Shakespeare at Thirty," in Studies in Philology, *Vol. XXX, No. 2, April, 1933, pp. 208-24.*

FREDSON THAYER BOWERS　(essay date 1940)

[An American scholar and educator, Bowers is known for both his meticulous textual criticism of Shakespeare's plays and his studies of the revenge tragedy popular during the Elizabethan era. In the excerpt below, he examines Shakespeare's handling of the revenge tradition by comparing the plot of Titus Andronicus *to that of Thomas Kyd's* The Spanish Tragedy. *He notes, for example, that Shakespeare conforms to an important element of this tradition by making his protagonist delay his revenge until he discovers the identity of his foes. Bowers also emphasizes Shakespeare's innovations, paying particular attention to his treatment of Aaron. According to Bowers, Shakespeare blurs Tamora's motive for revenge and weakens the dénouement by making Aaron an important character when he is "only loosely connected with the main plot." Bowers thus concludes that* Titus Andronicus *is an imperfect experimental play, a Kydian revenge tragedy in which Shakespeare attempted to incorporate a Marlovian villain, combining two dissimilar approaches to tragedy. For further commentary on Aaron's function in* Titus Andronicus, *see the excerpts*

by Bernard Spivack (1958), Alan Sommers (1960), D. J. Palmer (1972), Albert H. Tricomi (1976), and David Willbern (1978).]

Titus Andronicus is very similar in construction to *The Spanish Tragedy*. . . . As in the older play it is the revenge of the villains that calls forth in answer the blood-revenge of the protagonist. Although Shakespeare motivates Tamora's revenge by the murder of her son Alarbus and thus gives her better grounds than Lorenzo and Balthazar possessed, the earlier version of the play (if the [Dutch and German] versions be accepted as indications of an early state) followed *The Spanish Tragedy* in the weakness of the villains' original motives.

A second important change comes in the early disclosure of the faultiness of Titus's character. In the German version he is wholly good until the catastrophe; in the Dutch, Titus's cruel demand that Aran be slain is an incomplete omen of what is to come. Shakespeare avoided the sudden change in character that befell Hieronimo by emphasizing so strongly Titus's faults at the very beginning that the audience would not be too shocked at the conclusion. His consciousness of power makes Titus overbearingly proud and haughty. Although his demand that Alarbus be slain is justified by his religious beliefs, it is, as Tamora exclaims, a "cruel, irreligious piety" [I. i. 130]. His murder of his son Mutius, though admirable according to the Roman patriarchal and stoic standards, is a misguided piece of callous, proud cruelty, calculated to remove from him the audience's personal sympathy and to leave him only the abstract admiration due his undoubted honesty. He is so egoistic, so sure the justice of his actions cannot be questioned, that, despite his share in the death of Alarbus, he expects Tamora's gratitude. Such a conception is infinitely more rounded than Hieronimo's, and, in combination with Titus's far more frightful sufferings, and the equally fiendish retaliations they provoke, undoubtedly prepares the audience for the final justice of his death.

In Shakespeare the revenge of the villains starts almost immediately when Tamora vows requital for the death of Alarbus. It is strengthened by the winning over of Saturninus, and reaches an early fruition in the second act rape of Lavinia. This deed is not originally accomplished by any set plan of Tamora's, but it is linked to her revenge when, reminded of Alarbus, she refuses Lavinia's pleas for pity. Whereas the villains of *The Spanish Tragedy* achieved their single revenge and stopped, the rape of Lavinia is merely incidental to the larger plans to strike at Titus through his sons. It must be noted that Aaron, not Tamora, contrives the plans although her help is indispensable.

The revenge has been almost completed by the end of the second act and Titus made practically helpless. The revengers have one more scheme, however, and in the third act Titus is tricked into the loss of his hand. For an act and a half he has received blow after blow. His son-in-law Bassianus has been killed, his sons are accused and condemned for the murder, his daughter has been ravished and mutilated, his pleas have been unheard, his son Lucius banished, and finally he has lost his hand in a vain attempt to save the lives of two more sons. Such a chain of incidents was missing from *The Spanish Tragedy* where the revenger is never personally injured and has only the death of his son to revenge. But they are a necessary part of the plot of *Titus Andronicus* to fill the action . . . until the protagonist starts his vengeance. In *Titus* the turning-point comes at the end of the third act when the final indignity affects Titus's mind, and his sudden laugh foreshadows his madness. For the moment incipient insanity sharpens his wits. He solemnly swears revenge and plans the invasion of the Goths under Lucius as the first step.

The succeeding scenes face the same problem as in *Hamlet* and *The Spanish Tragedy:* the revenger must discover the identity of his foes but must be prevented from instant vengeance. Kyd had solved the problem differently in both his plays. In the *Ur-Hamlet* the counter-action had gone steadily forward against the revenger and, barring the prayer scene, no occasion had presented itself until finally the counter-action designed to kill Hamlet had backfired and in the midst of disaster presented Hamlet with his long-awaited opportunity to revenge. In *The Spanish Tragedy* the revenger was delayed by lack of knowledge as to the identity of his opponents, and when that ignorance was resolved had made a thwarted attempt to secure revenge. Foiled in that, and hampered by the weakening of his will in fits of madness, he was forced to bide his time. Opportunity finally came, he conceived a plan to ensnare his foes, and carried it to a successful completion.

The plotting of both plays is drawn upon to prepare for the catastrophe of *Titus Andronicus*. Titus is yet ignorant of the assailants of Lavinia, although he knows his other foes. The revelation of this information follows without the delay of Kyd's plays so that Titus by the first scene of the fourth act, immediately after his vow of revenge, has all the information he needs. One avenue for delay is closed, and others must be sought. Therefore the opposing action, having rested satisfied as in *The Spanish Tragedy,* is once more set in motion, as in *Hamlet,* by the new knowledge of danger from the revenger. This information is given the villains, however, by incidents arising from the revenger's delay through his madness, as in *The Spanish Tragedy*. Titus for a time does nothing personally to revenge his wrongs. In fits of madness he relieves his feelings by sending ominous tokens to the sons of Tamora and to Saturninus. One of these tokens seems about to start the counteraction, when the enraged recipient, Saturninus, orders Titus to be dragged before his court, but actually the news of Lucius's rebellion is the eventual cause of Tamora's final trickery.

In the old play, if we may judge from the German version, Tamora's scheme involved the assassination of Titus and Lucius, a plan which owes much to *Hamlet,* while in the Dutch, Tamora merely tries to turn Titus's mind against Lucius and to dispose in that way of the menace of the invasion. Shakespeare's Tamora, trusting to her wiles to reconcile all parties and save Rome, desires only to know what plans are afoot. The plotting of *The Spanish Tragedy* now comes to the fore. Titus has no plan until Tamora's move presents him with an opportunity which he seizes as the means for revenge. Just as Hieronimo's complaisance tricks Lorenzo into taking part in the play, so Titus by his feigning of harmless madness lures the villains to his house and secures possession of Tamora's sons. (pp. 111-14)

The dénouement of *Titus Andronicus* follows *Hamlet* only so far as the chance to revenge is offered by the opponents' final counter-plot, which was set in motion to dispose of a new danger after they had thought their previous plots successful. The two differ, however, since the new plot against Titus is not aimed directly at his life. Madness is given a new and unique dramatic importance, for the villains' final device is based on the assumption that the revenger is mad. Such a situation had already been partially suggested in the Hamlet-Ofelia scene, but in *Titus Andronicus* the trick is given a far greater importance by its position in leading to the catastrophe. That Titus, although unbalanced, is not absolutely insane and

so can detect the motives of the villains, spells their downfall. The feigning of madness which was absent in *The Spanish Tragedy* and never quite legitimately motivated in *Hamlet,* is here an essential part of the plot to bring on the dénouement and is therefore more closely and ironically bound to the revenge.

For this reason the catastrophe of *Titus Andronicus* differs from the essential plan of Kyd's two plays. Hamlet is unaware of the plot behind the fencing-match, while Titus sees through the device of the banquet and is able to plan his revenge beforehand. Hieronimo's revenge is perhaps more premeditated than Titus's, since his plans, although dependent on the request for entertainment, are not forced upon him, as in *Titus,* in order to wreck the villains' plot to nullify his revenge. In *Titus* it is the weakness of Tamora's overconfident device which brings about her downfall. Since her plot was not laid against his life, Titus is killed by Saturninus in just such an unpremeditated fashion as Hamlet stabbed the king. The deaths in the catastrophe lack, thus, the premeditation of *The Spanish Tragedy* or even the ironic miscarrying of *Hamlet*. (p. 115)

The chief variations in *Titus* from Kyd's plays are (1) the adequate but undeveloped motivation of blood-revenge as a cause for the villains' machinations; (2) the increased importance and complexity of the villains' actions before the start of the protagonist's revenge; (3) the number of faults in the revenger's character, which, though balanced by obvious virtues, make necessary a tragic ending for his bloodstained life; (4) the more logical and ironic use of the revenger's madness; (5) the change in the manner of bringing about the catastrophe, although the plotting here suffers from haste; (6) the inclusion of an important villainous character who is only loosely connected with the main plot.

This character, Aaron, illustrates clearly the influence of Marlowe's Barabas in his delight in villainy for its own sake. He is thus placed before the audience as a creature of "motiveless malignity" [see essay by Clarence Valentine Boyer in the Additional Bibliography], a conception heightened by his place in Shakespeare's plot. Aaron himself is never personally injured, and whatever grudge he holds against the Andronici can result only from his original defeat and capture, a motive not touched upon. After the rape of Lavinia, which first inspired his villainous aid, his plans seem governed simply by the desire to preserve their new positions in Rome against the inevitable revenger for the deed; but it soon becomes obvious that the plot he envisages will fall in with Tamora's revenge and may even lead to further advancement at court. His natural love of villainy is thus turned to the uses of his mistress. (pp. 116-17)

If Aaron had been merely a clever, villainous accomplice, his part in the play would have been more closely connected with the main plot and its important dénouement. But as it is, he plays his rôle, drops out, and has nothing to do with the direction of the ending. Indeed, the clear-cut outlines of the play are blurred because it is really he who has devised the methods of revenge, and is abetted instead of commanded by Tamora, the chief person injured. The blurring is carried still further when the villain's part is so absorbed by Aaron that blood-revenge for Alarbus, the prime motivation of Tamora's revenge, disappears from her thoughts shortly after the start and is never mentioned by her sons. The incidents arise not from the originally announced clear-cut motive, the thirst of Tamora for revenge for blood, but rather from Aaron's natural villainy finding in Titus a fit subject on which to spend itself. The

Act IV. Scene ii. Chiron, Demetrius, Nurse (holding Aaron's child), and Aaron. Frontispiece to the Hanmer edition by F. Hayman (1744). By permission of the Folger Shakespeare Library.

conflict is drawn between Titus and Aaron, and the catastrophe loses force when Aaron is not included in its workings.

The imitation of the Marlovian protagonist villain Barabas (himself sprung from Lorenzo, the villain of the counter-plot) as a quasi-accomplice in a Kydian revenge tragedy, meant first the deepening of Aaron's villainy and second his inevitable extension beyond the limits of an accomplice's part. By this extension the balance of forces was disordered, the natural villain Tamora was forced into the background and the normal conflict between injurer and revenger was so modified that the justness and symmetry of the plot was disturbed. Shakespeare's *Titus Andronicus,* then, must be considered as an experimental play, uniting in an imperfect form two wholly dissimilar methods of plotting and theories of tragedy. (pp. 117-18)

Fredson Thayer Bowers, "The School of Kyd," in his Elizabethan Revenge Tragedy, 1587-1642, *1940. Reprint by Peter Smith, 1959, pp. 101-53.**

E. M. W. TILLYARD (essay date 1944)

[*Tillyard's* Shakespeare's History Plays *(1944), one of the most influential twentieth-century works in Shakespearean studies, is considered a leading example of historical criticism. Tillyard's thesis, which is shared, with variations, by other historical critics,* discerns a systematic world view in Shakespeare's plays—and one common to educated Elizabethans—in which reality is understood to be structured in a hierarchal Great Chain of Being. On a social level such a philosophy valued order, hierarchy, and civil peace as the chief political goals. Further, Tillyard notes a basic acceptance in Shakespeare's histories of "the Tudor myth," the critic's term for an interpretation of English history from Richard II to Henry VIII. According to this concept, Henry IV was a usurper, and his seizure of the throne set into motion the disastrous chain of events which culminated in the War of the Roses (1455 to 1485). In the excerpt below, Tillyard compares Titus Andronicus with The Comedy of Errors, *describing both as "academic, ambitious, and masterfully plotted" works. He even characterizes the atrocities in* Titus *as "exquisitely proportioned" and "necessary," including the scene in which Tamora is tricked into eating her own sons' flesh. But Tillyard's primary concern is with the political theme of rightful succession, which he finds dominant throughout the play. He maintains that Shakespeare, although young, demonstrates in* Titus *a serious interest in this issue—an issue on which he sided with Elizabeth's court, favoring the law of primogeniture. The political themes in* Titus *are also examined in the essays by Eugene M. Waith (1955) and Alan Sommers (1960).]*

That so profound a student of the artificial mode of the detective story as T. S. Eliot should have gone completely wrong over *Titus Andronicus* is surprising. He calls it "one of the stupidest and most uninspired plays ever written, a play in which it is incredible that Shakespeare had any hand at all." Actually this play has exactly the same large qualities as the *Comedy of Errors:* it is academic, ambitious, and masterfully plotted. . . . Classical tags litter the pages thickly. . . . Shakespeare in his youthful ambition must needs outdo Seneca. So he brings in Ovid and much else besides. Although there is a little confusion at the beginning with the rapid courtship of Tamora by Saturninus, Bassianus's abduction of Lavinia and the quarrels among the Andronici, the plotting of the whole is masterly. The author holds everything in his head, and event follows event with measured precision. The very violences are exquisitely proportioned. The culminating horror of Tamora eating her own son is made necessary, for nothing less violent would have had any emphasis after the many violences already transacted.

Apart from these general qualities . . . , there are many things added. *Titus Andronicus* is indeed an abounding play which, though academic, breaks out on many sides beyond its prescribed classical limits. There are beautiful lyrical passages, fresh descriptions of nature, while Aaron is a magnificent comic villain. Aaron is also related to other Shakespearean characters. He is bluff and hearty, as well as villainous. He looks forward to the hearty effrontery of Richard III and is the evil counterpart of the plain good characters such as Humphrey of Gloucester and the Bastard Falconbridge. The scene where he defends his blackamoor baby from Chiron and Demetrius is brilliant. . . . It is an astonishing speech, because it is so rich, so bursting with promise. In another sense it is the very reverse of astonishing, because it is precisely the kind of writing that common sense would expect from the young Shakespeare.

But for my present purpose the most interesting incidental quality is the strong political trend of parts of the play. . . . Questions of title and succession were crucial in Elizabethan thought, and their importance had been tragically set forth in the acts of the Wars of the Roses. *Titus Andronicus* begins with a dispute about the succession: Saturninus, the elder son of the late king, claiming the throne by primogeniture; Bassianus, the younger, on the plea of merit, to be backed by a free election. Marcus Andronicus, the tribune, tells the two princes that the Roman people have already elected his brother,

Titus Andronicus, king. The princes consent to disband their followers and await the return of Titus and the verdict of the people. Titus returns with Gothic captives and followed by the populace. His brother offers him the crown, but he refuses as too old to sustain it. But the tribunes and the people will accept anyone he chooses. Titus, with Elizabethan correctness, chooses Saturninus, the late king's elder son. Poetically the scene is stiff, the work of a young man being solemn beyond the capacity of his years, but of a young man *interested* in his theme, and minding about his politics, not dragging them in to satisfy convention. Titus, now the servant of the new emperor, proceeds to behave with the correctness of a loyal subordinate and lays all his martial trophies at his master's feet. Saturninus promises never to forget his fealty. Later, before the main melodrama of the play begins (II. 3) Titus tells his sons "to attend," as he will, "the emperor's person carefully" [II. ii. 8].

The high political theme, that of the wounds of civil war and their cure, recurs at the end of the play. Rome has been in an uproar; Lucius Andronicus, Titus's son, having fled for safety to the Goths, returns with an army (not unlike the Earl of Richmond from Brittany) and survives, the sole possible successor to the throne. These are the words Marcus Andronicus addresses to the people to introduce to them his nephew, Lucius, the future king.

> You sad-fac'd men, people and sons of Rome,
> By uproar sever'd like a flight of fowl
> Scatter'd by winds and high tempestuous gusts,
> O, let me teach you how to knit again
> This scatter'd corn into one mutual sheaf,
> These broken limbs again into one body;
> Lest Rome herself be bane unto herself,
> And she whom mighty kingdoms court'sy to,
> Like a forlorn and desperate castaway,
> Do shameful execution on herself.
>
> [V. iii. 67-76]

And Lucius, chosen emperor, says,

> May I govern so,
> To heal Rome's harms and wipe away her woe.
>
> [V. iii. 147-48]

Marcus's speech is in the high political vein. . . . The tempests of the air duplicate the commotions of the commonwealth, and the commonwealth is figured in the anatomy of a man. Rome must cease to be a bane to herself, as England is later to be told it will never fear a foreign foe, if it "to itself do rest but true" [*King John*, V. vii. 118].

From the political theme of *Titus* it is a natural step to my next concern: the likenesses between that play and *I Henry VI*. First, let me revert to the place [I. i. 244] where Titus does homage to the newly created emperor. This scene is followed, ironically, by the complicated brawl after Bassianus's seizure of Lavinia. The pattern recurs at the end of Act 3 of *I Henry VI*. Here Talbot does homage to Henry VI, just crowned in Paris, and lays his conquest at his king's feet in precisely the same manner; and this scene is followed by a brawl between partisans of York and Lancaster. Titus and Talbot are indeed the same character, the disinterested and utterly brave warrior, unswerving servant of his royal master, though Titus is pictured the elder by many years. In his madness, of course, Titus comes close to Kyd's Hieronymo, but none the less in his sanity he is an elderly Talbot. Again it is a woman who, by fascinating the king or prince, defeats the good designs of the warrior-

hero in each play. Tamora is indeed not at all the same character as Joan, but she is a bad woman, a foreigner, and she is the prime enemy of Titus. Joan, too, is Talbot's evil genius. Tamora works evil by seducing Saturninus, yet being unfaithful to him. Joan fascinates Charles the Dauphin but confesses to adultery before her execution. I think the two plays must have been written about the same time.

The *Comedy of Errors* and *Titus Andronicus* revealed their author as ambitious. If he wrote *I Henry VI* about the same time, the extent of his ambitions is enlarged. Here we have a young man trying his hand in three great literary modes, classical comedy, Senecan tragedy, and, in keeping with the political proclivities of his age, a highly serious historical play. We find, not the brilliant apprentice and tinker of others' matter, but an original poet, educated, confident of himself, already dedicated to poetry; a man passing through the states common to any very great artist, akin to Dante and Milton not only through mature achievement but in the manner in which he began his life-work. (pp. 139-41)

> *E. M. W. Tillyard, "The Early Shakespeare," in his* Shakespeare's History Plays, *Chatto & Windus, 1944, pp. 129-46.*

H. B. CHARLTON   (lecture date 1946-47)

[*An English scholar, Charlton is best known for his* Shakespearian Tragedy *(1948) and* Shakespearian Comedy *(1938)—two important studies in which he argues that the proponents of New Criticism, particularly T. S. Eliot and I. A. Richards, were reducing Shakespeare's drama to its poetic elements and in the process losing sight of his characters. In his introduction to* Shakespearian Tragedy, *Charlton describes himself as a "devout" follower of A. C. Bradley, and like his mentor he adopted a psychological, character-oriented approach to Shakespeare's work. Charlton's commentary on* Titus Andronicus *was originally part of a series of lectures delivered in 1946-47. To him, the play is nothing more than a melodrama that lacks the essential inner design of tragedy. He claims that the actions of the characters are motivated by neither passion nor reason, and that the play's implied moral system of "virtue," "nobility," and "honor" is ambiguously presented and fails to justify the events presented. Charlton concludes that there is no "inner world" to* Titus, *since the characters are "mechanized puppets" who seldom react humanely. For additional discussions of the tragic design of* Titus Andronicus, *see the excerpts by Alan Sommers (1960), Irving Ribner (1960), A. C. Hamilton (1967), and D. J. Palmer (1972).*]

Titus Andronicus is melodrama, the crudest of Shakespeare's tragedies, magnificent only in this, that its language is always adequate to its own dramatic and theatrical demands, crude or low, spectacular or sentimental, as on varying occasion they may be. But as drama it can never disguise its own quality. It is a rudimentary type of tragedy. It appeals only to the eye and to the other senses. Response to it is confined to the nervous system. Its thrills and throbs are not transmissible to the mind in forms more intellectual than mere sensation. They induce a nightmare of horrors. As sensations of horror, if they are felt as such at all and not laughed off by man's sense of the ludicrous, they strike so heavily and so frequently that the mind is incapacitated from attempting to translate them into its own discursive idiom. So great is the weight of horror that the response of the senses themselves is finally stunned to stupor, and the disabled sensibility is deprived of the power to prompt mind and imagination to cope with such tremendous issues as are the essence of tragedy, the ultimate mysteries of human destiny. (pp. 18-19)

As a piece of serious drama, *Titus Andronicus* has little of worth except its theatrically stirring situations. Even these occur in isolation. A momentary spectacle can be given as much conviction as is needed for the achievement of its stage effect by craftsmanship of no higher order in the art of poetry than is the stage-carpenter's in the art of drama. But a sustained representation of human action in a continuous dramatic plot makes greater demands. As Aristotle put it, what happens must happen according to the law of the probable and the necessary. As human action, it must be intelligible. The men and women in the play must act as human beings do act. When their action seems to be spontaneously prompted by passion or by instinct rather than by considered choice, those passions and instincts must be shown to be of that sort which in our experience of life seems likely to break out in that way. When the doers of such deeds plead also the sanction of deliberate choice, the systems of conduct to which they appeal must appear to have impetus vital enough to make their compulsion inevitable. However, a qualification must here be made. Sanctions, like the systems of law and morality which give them their warrant, are but rarely eternal and are often flagrantly ephemeral. . . . But in drama, sanctions which are pleaded as constraints to a decisive course of action must have something more than a merely historic warrant to give them effective dramatic force. The compulsion must be felt by the audience as a power which might well compel human beings to such deeds. (pp. 19-20)

With a mind conscious of these considerations, turn to *Titus Andronicus*, and enquire how far its action is autonomously and organically propelled. Very soon, its nominal hero, Titus, is a comparative pawn in the theatrical game, and the real protagonists are the villains, Aaron and Tamora. The incidents of the play, and especially the more theatrical of them, proceed in the main as the deliberate purposes of the villain's evil designs. These purposes are those of sinners whose prevalent passion is lust, that which no passion is more deeply seated in the human animal, none more primary nor more insatiable. The dramatist can therefore permit to them the extremest of enormities; the law of human probability can be pleaded for suspending for them its own normal requirements. . . . Moreover, with such human devils as these for the outstanding figures, other characters and episodes in the play can be stretched to extravagant limits. Titus in his turn can execute his own son. In these ways, the dramatist is easily provided with a string of melodramatic incidents in unbroken sequence. But it is merely the sequence of succession, each item owing its occurrence not to what has gone immediately before, but as the accidental next in the cumulative outcome of the bestial passions of the main contrivers.

There is, however, some attempt to give to this succession a specious appearance of causal sequence. Action is sometimes expressed, not as the spontaneous consequence of passion, but as the recognisable manifestation of some sort of world-order.

The first scene sets up the façade of the universe in which its action is to occur. The 'righteous heavens', 'the gods of Rome' preside over it; priests minister at their solemn services, sometimes with 'holy water', sometimes with 'sacrificial rites'; its men lift up their 'vows to heaven', and 'sumptuously' maintain the sacred 'monuments' in which their dead are solemnly interred. But it is a mere façade. The moral system which would give such a universe a credible substance manifests itself as an incoherent chaos. There is talk of 'virtue' and 'nobility', yet they appear to comprise nothing but a primitive valour in martial enterprise. 'Piety' is named; but it gives nothing beyond

a moment's historic authenticity to a Roman father's right to kill his son, and such historic authentication may even be an obstacle to dramatic plausibility. . . . In *Titus Andronicus* the standard of moral currency most in use is 'honour'. The word occurs a score of times in the scene in which Titus kills his son; it is made more prominent by another half-score instances of its opposite, 'dishonour'. But it is utterly impossible to define the content of the moral concept implied, and quite impossible therefore to assess its potency as a moral agent in motivating action. Titus is 'dishonoured' because his sons do not immediately obey his edict, and no less 'dishonoured' because Bassianus, with what appear to be highly honourable intentions, marries Titus' daughter. Saturninus is 'dishonoured' because someone has revealed the flagrant truth that he is a scoundrel, and even more 'dishonoured' because others have helped him to secure the throne instead of recognising his right to it without help. The audience, with more justice than Falstaff, may well enquire 'what is this honour?' [*I Henry IV*, V. i. 135]. The play gives no answer, for nothing consistently recognisable as 'honour' animates its action. Hence its incidents sink to melodrama. There are crucial examples in this first scene.

Take one which relies on an alleged ancient practice: the noblest prisoner taken must be sacrificed to appease 'the groaning shadows of the slain' [I. i. 127]. Tamora's son is the victim chosen by Titus' sons, and they will 'hew his limbs and on a pile *Ad manes fratrum* sacrifice his flesh' [I. i. 97-8]. Tamora appeals, with far less ancient terms and with more intelligible instinct, for the exercise of the 'sweet mercy which is nobility's true badge' [I. i. 119]. But Titus is placidly unmoved: for 'their brethren slain' his sons 'religiously ask a sacrifice' [I. i. 122, 125]; they have marked her son for this, and 'die he must'. He is haled away by Titus' sons with fervent zeal, and in a twinkling they return to tell that his 'limbs are lopped',

> And entrails feed the sacrificing fire
> Whose smoke, like incense, doth perfume the sky.
>
> [I. i. 143-45]

As a mere record in human archaeology, such a scene can doubtless be freely paralleled; but its persons have not here inspired the psychological resuscitation which would give them dramatic personality. Their motives, therefore, implicit and explicit, are dramatically inert; the 'must' of 'die he must' is merely arbitrary and void of all power to excite in the audience a willing concurrence in its compulsiveness. Or take the incident in which Titus, exercising the Roman *jus patrium* ["the right of the father"], slays his son Mutius for a single act of sudden disobedience. Mutius' action is completely intelligible in common sense and in the simplest psychology; moreover, it commands enough moral sympathy to make it instantly credible to the audience. So, in despite of assurances from historical record, it is impossible for the audience to slip into a requisite and subconscious understanding of Titus. For them he is a lay-figure, humanly, and therefore dramatically, unreal.

As in its first scene, so throughout the whole play. There is no inner world to it. Hence its plot is factitious; its people are mechanised puppets wearing masks of human faces, but seldom reacting even with a faint semblance of humanity except when their deeds are crimes which are prompted by a primitive human passion, crimes such as are still occasionally committed by the more bestial members of the human race. It is sheer melodrama and not tragedy; for, as *The New British Theatre* even as long ago as 1814 distinguished them, 'in tragedy and comedy, the final event is the effect of the moral operations of the different characters, but in melodrama the catastrophe is the physical result of mechanical stratagem'. And melodrama, lacking an inner world, can have none of the philosophic significance which is the peculiar function of tragedy; it can throw no light on the great mysteries of human fate. (pp. 21-4)

H. B. Charlton, "Apprentice Pieces: 'Titus Andronicus', 'Richard III' and 'Richard II'," in his Shakespearian Tragedy, *Cambridge at the University Press, 1948, pp. 18-48.*

JOHN DOVER WILSON   (essay date 1947)

[*Dover Wilson was a highly regarded Shakespearean scholar involved in several aspects of Shakespeare studies. As an editor of the* New Cambridge Shakespeare, *he made numerous contributions to twentieth-century textual criticism of Shakespeare, making use of the scientific bibliography developed by W. W. Greg and Charlton Hinman. As a critic, Dover Wilson combines several contemporary approaches and does not fit easily into any one critical "school." He is concerned with character analysis in the tradition of A. C. Bradley; he delves into Elizabethan culture like the historical critics, but without their usual emphasis on hierarchy and the Great Chain of Being; and his interest in visualizing possible dramatic performances of the plays links him with his contemporary, Harley Granville-Barker. The following excerpt is taken from Dover Wilson's introduction to the Cambridge edition of* Titus Andronicus, *written in 1947. Most of the introduction deals with such issues as the date, text, sources, and authorship of the play. It is with respect to this final question that Dover Wilson devotes the greater part of his attention, arguing that George Peele originally wrote the play in 1593 and that Shakespeare only revised certain portions of the work later that year. In the excerpt below, Dover Wilson claims that Shakespeare undertook the task of revising* Titus *strictly for money and that the material was somewhat foreign to him. But he suggests that the dramatist "took out compensation for himself in kind" for the unpleasantness of the task by "mocking" Peele's hyperbolic style. In support of this assertion, Dover Wilson points to the scene where Marcus discovers Lavinia after her rape and to passages during Titus's lamentations, claiming that it is obvious, especially when compared to similar passages in* Lucrece *and* Love's Labour's Lost, *that Shakespeare is caricaturing or mocking a certain style of language. Dover Wilson's essay signaled a shift in the criticism of* Titus Andronicus *from the early perception of the play as strictly a revenge tragedy to the later assessment of it as a more complex work. For Dover Wilson,* Titus—*at least Shakespeare's portion of the drama—reflects a deliberate attempt at parody; for such later critics as Muriel C. Bradbrook (1951), Eugene M. Waith (1955), Alan Sommers (1960), Irving Ribner (1960), A. C. Hamilton (1967), James L. Calderwood (1971), D. J. Palmer (1972), and Albert H. Tricomi (1976), Shakespeare's design is more serious. Many of these commentators, in fact, regard the play as a highly elaborate investigation of language and form, word and action, and art and reality, as well as Shakespeare's attempt to combine numerous influences, such as Seneca, Ovid, and elements from the morality plays.*]

No one, I think, who has followed [an] examination of Peele's style in [his work] will suppose for a moment that Shakespeare felt anything but conempt for it. When he set to work upon [*Titus Andronicus*] he was nearing the end of his thirtieth year and had attained, not of course his full stature, but surely a mood of self-confidence, together with a pleasing sense of mastery in his art. Two years had passed since a spokesman of the old school, addressing his fellows, had confessed the 'upstart's' triumph and his own defeat in bitter terms from his death-bed; and since then the upstart had published *Venus and Adonis*, the most popularly successful poem of the age, had secured the patronage of a member of the inner ring at Eliz-

abeth's court, and had probably been recently entertaining 'divers of worship' with *Love's Labour's Lost* and *Richard III*, which, wherever you place them in the rank of his plays, were written by a man at once very sure of his powers and delighting in their exercise. It is therefore exceedingly unlikely that he would cherish deferential feelings for this particularly poor specimen of the old school, which he was called upon to patch up.

What then? The play, for all its faults, partly because of its faults, had money in it, big money. The plague, moreover, had been raging in London for over two years and the whole acting profession was wellnigh ruined. Shakespeare put the job through to relieve a very pressing necessity, and in the doing of it produced one of the most popular, and therefore most profitable, of Elizabethan plays. But having undertaken it against the grain he took out compensation for himself in kind. Once catch the trick of it, you can see him laughing behind his hand through most of the scenes he rehandled. Look for example at that long speech of Marcus in 2. 4, which 'presents' Lavinia to the audience upon her first appearance after Tamora's sons have 'trimmed' her, and expatiates upon almost every detail of her deflowered and mutilated person, in forty-seven lines of inordinately figured verse. . . . [Either] Shakespeare wrote this 'tawdry rant' or 'bleating pathos', as Symons [see excerpt above, 1885] and Robertson justly call it, because he could no other, or he wrote it deliberately, knowing it for what it was. In pondering this problem I would ask the reader to savour its successive phrases upon his palate. Let him mark, for instance, the inept curiosity and bland surprise of

> Speak gentle niece, what stern ungentle hands
> Hath lopped and hewed and made thy body bare
> Of her two branches?
>
> [II. iv. 16-18]

—a woodman, discovering an injury to one of his trees, would have shown more indignation; or the studied triviality of

> Fair Philomel, why she but lost her tongue,
> And in a tedious sampler sewed her mind;
>
> [II. iv. 38-9]

or the sublime image of Lavinia as a public conduit from which the blood gushes in 'three issuing spouts'! [II. iv. 30]. And having marked these things, let him ask himself whether he can conceive Shakespeare writing such stuff in earnest at any period of his poetic development.

It is true that this descanting upon physical suffering and wounds and effusion of blood, together with the lamentation which occupies so large a portion of the verse in Act 3, belong to a vogue of the age; there is plenty of both, for example, in Sidney's *Arcadia*. It is true also that they are a marked feature of Shakespeare's first phase. As for the analogy between wind and rain and the storms of human passion and grief, that runs all through Shakespeare and the pastoral romances alike. But . . . what is in question in *Titus* is not the material handled but the manner and spirit of the handling. In others of his early plays, in *2 and 3 Henry VI* and *Richard III*, for instance, which were almost certainly composed or revised by him before 1594, or in *The Comedy of Errors, The Taming of the Shrew, The Two Gentlemen of Verona*, and *Romeo and Juliet*, some of which may be a little before, others a little after *Titus*, nothing remotely resembling the tone of this scene is to be found, and certainly nothing that can be styled 'bleating pathos' or 'tawdry rant'. But we can best put the matter to the test by comparing a particularly egregious, or offensive, portion of Marcus' speech with something [in *Lucrece*] which resembles it closely in matter and diction. . . . The scene afer Lucrece has stabbed herself is thus described [II. 1730-43]:

Stone-still, astonished with this deadly deed,
Stood Colatine, and all his lordly crew;
Till Lucrece' father, that beholds her bleed,
Himself on her self-slaughtered body threw;
And from the purple fountain Brutus drew
    The murderous knife, and, as it left the place,
    Her blood, in poor revenge, held it in chase;

And bubbling from her breast, it doth divide
In two slow rivers, that the crimson blood
Circles her body in on every side,
Who like a late-sacked island, vastly stood,
Bare and unpeopled in this fearful flood.
    Some of her blood still pure and red remained,
    And some looked black, and that false Tarquin stained.

And this is how Marcus speaks of Lavinia's mouth from which the tongue had been torn [II. iv. 22-5]:

Alas, a crimson river of warm blood,
Like to a bubbling fountain stirred with wind,
Doth rise and fall between thy roséd lips,
Coming and going with thy honey breath.

The two passages furnish an excellent example of identity of theme, coupled with verbal parallelism, and verbal parallelism of high quality, seeing that the blood is crimson, bubbling, a river, and a fountain in both. Yet, what a world of difference in tone or spirit! The first, a period piece with an elaborated conceit that may repel the modern reader, is nevertheless the unquestionable product of a serious artistic impulse, executed with restraint and considerable skill, and striking no false note. The second is a bundle of ill-matched conceits held together by sticky sentimentalism. Or, to select one detail, consider the controlled metaphor in

And from the purple fountain Brutus drew
    The murderous knife,

                              [*Lucrece*, II. 1734-35]

and compare it with the flaccid and turgid simile uscd a little later by Marcus:

And notwithstanding all this loss of blood,
As from a conduit with three issuing spouts. . . .

                              [II. iv. 29-30]

Is it not clear that the whole speech is caricature, or rather that Shakespeare is drawing upon imagery already put to serious use in *Lucrece* in order to disport himself with the ridiculous *Titus*?

And in the next scene Titus out-bleats his brother Marcus. Take this for an introduction:

When I did name her brothers, then fresh tears
Stood on her cheeks, as doth the honey-dew
Upon a gathered lily almost withered.

                              [III. i. 111-13]

It comes from the same corner of Shakespeare's brain as the King's 'sonnet' in *Love's Labour's Lost* [IV. iii. 25-8] which begins

So sweet a kiss the golden sun gives not
    To those fresh morning drops upon the rose,
As thy eye-beams, when their fresh rays have smote
    The night of dew that on my cheeks down flows.

Both passages are in mocking vein; but whereas the latter mocks at love in a rather absurd conceit consistently developed, the former mocks at the conceit itself by reducing it to sheer bathos. And if we should chance to overlook the strange phenomenon of the dews of heaven falling upon cut flowers in a vase, the cautious word 'almost' shows us the author pulling our leg. But the scene consists in the main of the lamentations of Titus; and it is these which provide most of the fun. Having just lost his right hand, the old man lifts the left to heaven, and kneels to pray for pity, only to find the handless, tongueless Lavinia kneeling beside him; a heart-rending tableau, upon which he comments as follows:

What, wouldst thou kneel with me?
Do then, dear heart, for heaven shall hear our prayers,
Or with our sighs we'll breathe the welkin dim,
And stain the sun with fog, as sometime clouds
When they do hug him in their melting bosoms.

                              [III. i. 209-13]

It is just the kind of three-piled hyperbole, which the prentice boys and citizens' wives could never have enough of. But the voice of common sense (and Shakespeare) is heard in a querulous interjection from Marcus—of all people!

O brother, *speak with possibility*,
And do not break into these deep extremes.

                              [III. i. 214-15]

The rising tide of hysteria is not thus to be checked, however; and when Titus replies, Bottom-like,

Is not my sorrow deep, having no bottom?
Then be my passions bottomless with them,

                              [III. i. 216-17]

and Marcus objects once more,

But yet let reason govern thy lament,

                              [III. i. 218]

Titus finally silences him in a speech which, outsoaring the earlier fog of sighs that stains the sun, identifies Lavinia with the weeping welkin and himself with the sea, or the earth (he is not certain which), and then suddenly crashes to the ground with these ineffable lines:

Then must my earth with her continual tears
Become a deluge, overflowed and drowned:
For why? my bowels cannot hide her woes,
But like a drunkard must I vomit them.
Then give me leave, for losers will have leave
To ease their stomachs with their bitter tongues.

                              [III. i. 228-33]

And he continues to ease his stomach for the rest of the act. 'The ugly figure of vomiting woes like a drunkard may be matched', Parrott notes [see Additional Bibliography], 'with a line from *Lucrece* [1. 703],

Drunken Desire must vomit his receipt.

But what is in question in *Lucrece* is the foul lust of Tarquin, to which 'the ugly figure' is as appropriate as it is outrageous when Titus applies it to his sorrows. Similarly, the close parallel Parrott points out in *Romeo and Juliet*, [III. v. 132 *Seq.*] to 'the elaborate comparison' which Titus draws 'between mortal grief and the windswept sea' has this much in common with it, that what Capulet utters in comic raillery, Titus is supposed to be howling in tragic despair. Many more instances of the same kind of thing might be given, but there the text lies; and

I would not spoil the reader's enjoyment of Shakespeare's by doling out the fun piecemeal. And if there be anyone who still thinks these turgid lamentations were written, or should be read, with a straight face, he will I presume also accept as tragic earnest Lavinia's puppy-dog exit with the hand of Titus between her teeth, or—to take a minor absurdity of another kind—Saturninus' exit on the grandiloquent, but philologically impossible, flourish,

> Then go successantly, and plead with him.
>
> [IV. iv. 113]

Yet *Titus* is not all burlesque and melodramatic travesty; not only a huge joke which, we may guess, Shakespeare enjoyed twice over, once in the penning of it, and again in performance, while he watched his dear groundlings, and most of those in the more expensive parts of the theatre also, gaping ever wider to swallow more as he tossed them bigger and bigger gobbets of sob-stuff and raw beef-steak. For he had one weakness, which, though the secret of his strength, often thwarted his first intentions and sometimes went near to ruining a whole drama: he could not help falling in love with his characters. Even old man Titus succeeds in winning him over before the end. Absurd as their occasion and action may be, the scenes in which he kills the black fly and in which the witless-witty Tamora visits him disguised as Revenge and leaves her sons behind in his power, give an impression of real dignity and pathos, while the second of them is also steeped in tragic irony, so that those who find here adumbrations, unmistakable if faint, of *King Lear* are not putting the thing too high. (pp. l-lvii)

> *John Dover Wilson, in an introduction to* Titus Andronicus *by William Shakespeare, edited by John Dover Wilson, Cambridge at the University Press, 1948, pp. vii-lxv.*

WOLFGANG H. CLEMEN (essay date 1951)

[A German Shakespearean scholar, Clemen was among the first critics to consider Shakespeare's imagery an integral part of the development of his dramatic art. J. Dover Wilson described Clemen's method as focusing on "the form and significance of particular images or groups of images in their context of the passages, speech, or play in which they occur." This approach is quite different from that of the other leading image-pattern analyst, Caroline F. E. Spurgeon, whose work is more statistical in method and partly biographical in purpose. In the following excerpt from his The Development of Shakespeare's Imagery, *originally published in German in 1936, and revised and published in English in 1951, Clemen, like H. B. Charlton (1946-47), criticizes the action and characterization in* Titus Andronicus *as poorly developed, unjustified, and, at times, as obstacles to the progression of the plot. But unlike Charlton, Clemen also applies this criticism to the play's imagery; he states that, like the action and characterization, it does not proceed organically and exists merely as an "addition" to the thought being conveyed. For Clemen, the play's imagery is disruptive in other ways: its quality is one of number, or multiplicity, rather than of function, which is based on clarity. According to Clemen, this often results in a situation where image and object stand in "absurd contrast" to one another, such as the scene in which Marcus describes Lavinia's mutilation in pastoral language. Ultimately, Clemen attributes all of the shortcomings he perceives in* Titus *to Shakespeare's immature desire to demonstrate his knowledge and to outdo such contemporaries as Thomas Kyd and Christopher Marlowe in "grand effects and frightful deeds." For additional discussion of the imagery in* Titus Andronicus, *see the excerpts by Muriel C. Bradbrook (1951), A. C. Hamilton (1967), Albert H. Tricomi (1976), and David Willbern (1978).]*

When we have read *Titus* or have seen it on the stage we are under the impression that we have witnessed prodigious events and prodigious speeches without having any clear notion of their necessity or their logical motivation. The frightful deeds of horror, the terrific outbursts of passion take us by surprise with their suddenness, but they fail to convince us. This happens not only because real motivation is lacking, but also because the nature and character of the persons from whom these gigantic effects derive do not yet appear to us as truly great. We apprehend in *Titus* only the great effects, the consequences of the nature of the characters, but not their source and essential foundation in the personalities. This means, if transferred to the words and the style of *Titus*, that many expressions and speeches remain for us little more than an empty gesture. The words are not yet necessarily individual to the character by whom they are uttered. Some other could as well have spoken them. And there are many passages in *Titus* which neither serve the characterization nor further the course of events, the action of the play. The pleasure derived from impassioned forms of expression, from bombastic and high-flown speech and lurid effects leads again and again to a deviation from the inner organic structure of the drama.

Hence it is characteristic of *Titus* that the desire for effective expression is greater than what is to be expressed; the dramatist's own conception of those colossal deeds and people was not plastic and realistic enough to mould the means of expression. If we are to credit Shakespeare with *Titus* at all, it was not his own experience and conviction but rather the desire to surpass Kyd and Marlowe by grand effects and frightful deeds which is at the root of the play.

In the nature and use of the imagery this inner disproportion becomes apparent through the predominance of the unrestrained desire for expression over any real necessity for it. The images "run wild", they are not yet organically related to the framework of the play, just as all the other means of expression are but little disciplined in *Titus*. The failure in organic connection between the images and their context can be recognized by a stylistic feature. In *Titus* the comparison *added on* by means of "like" or "as" prevails. The particles "as" and "like" not only make the image stand out from the text and isolate it in a certain way; they also show that the object to be compared and the comparison are felt as being something different and separate, that image and object are not yet viewed as an identity, but that the act of comparing intervenes. It would be false to exaggerate the importance of such a fact, because in Shakespeare's late plays we also find many comparisons introduced with "like" or "as". Nevertheless the frequency of such comparisons with "as" and "like" in *Titus Andronicus* is noteworthy, and this loose form of connection corresponds entirely to the real nature of these images. If we take, for example, passages such as these:

> . . . then fresh tears
> Stood on her cheeks, as doth the honey-dew
> Upon a gather'd lily almost wither'd. [III. i. 111-13]

> . . . that kiss is comfortless
> As frozen water to a starved snake.   [III. i. 250-51]

we see that these images are simply added on to the main sentence afterwards, dove-tailed into the context, appended to what has already been said as flourish and decoration. They occurred to Shakespeare as an afterthought, as "illustration", as "example", but they were not there from the very beginning as simultaneous poetic conception of object and image. One could leave out these images without the text's losing any of its comprehensibility and clarity. (pp. 21-3)

Here we might speak of a tendency to make the images independent. Shakespeare writes a sentence suggesting an image to him. He then proceeds to enlarge upon this image and to elaborate it for its own sake—and in the meantime also forgets the starting-point. The comparison in this case is an independent enclosure. It belongs to the order of the epic-descriptive similes such as often appear in Spenser's *Faerie Queene,* for example. Hence, Shakespeare may be said to employ here a type of image which does not generically belong to the drama and in consequence appears here as an extraneous addition. Although it is a characteristic of the epic style to expand upon every detail and to interrupt the action time and again by broad descriptions and elaborated digressions, the drama cannot afford such a lingering manner and such an easy, calm, delineation of the circumstances. (p. 23)

This lack of internal and external connection between the images and the framework of the text or the train of thought is itself only one aspect of the principle of addition which characterizes the whole style of *Titus.* If we take any one of the longer speeches and investigate whether the image concerned has been prepared for by other stylistic means, whether it grows organically out of what has gone before or is the climax of a passage, we must answer all these questions in the negative: one line is tacked on to the other and the images are added on just as much without preparation as the thoughts. This principle of addition finds its metrical counterpart in the general absence of *enjambement* resulting in a pause after every line, and the necessity for every new line to start off afresh:

> The birds chant melody on every bush,
> The snake lies rolled in the cheerful sun,
> The green leaves quiver with the cooling wind
>
> [II. iii. 12-14]

Moreover, this manner of adding on, of letting the separate motifs stand side by side in isolation from each other, may also be observed in the structure of the thought of the speeches. In every speech we can neatly divide the separate thoughts and themes. In each case a subject is brought up, carried through to its end, and with no transition the new theme commences. The art of transition, of inner connection, is lacking in the structure of the whole drama just as much as in the style and in the imagery. Suddenly the characters make their most important decisions, their attitude changes from one extreme to the other in a twinkling (cf. Titus' behaviour in I. ii.; III. i., etc.). Shakespeare is not yet quite aware of the fact that great deeds must bud and ripen in the "womb of time", that conflict and collision develop gradually and in a manifold, complicated dependency upon all the other happenings. Instead of preparing us for *one* great event, for *one* climax and leading us through all the stages of development up to this peak, Shakespeare overwhelms us from the first act on with "climaxes", with a multiplicity of fearful events and high-sounding words.

What thus holds true of the action on a larger scale can now be observed on a smaller scale in the style of the whole drama. The language adds and accumulates and would seek to replace clarity and definiteness by multiplicity. The heaping up of images is a token of the fact that the pleasure taken in building up comparisons is greater than the need for unequivocal met-

aphorical characterization. As an example of such piling up of imagery we quote a passage from the second act:

MART. Upon his bloody finger he doth wear
A precious ring, that lightens all the hole,
Which, like a taper in some monument,
Doth shine upon the dead man's earthy cheeks,
And shows the ragged entrails of the pit:
So pale did shine the moon on Pyramus
When he by night lay bathed in maiden blood.
O brother, help me with thy fainting hand—
[II. iii. 226-33]

The learned comparison with Pyramus is a second image for Bassianus' ring, which has already been compared with the taper. It is a learned addition, quite uncalled for, which could just as well have been omitted. (pp. 24-5)

The passage just quoted leads to another question. For what is the occasion for this image? Martius has just fallen into a deep pit, upon the corpse of Bassianus concealed therein. In this gruesome situation, almost ready to faint, as he himself admits, Martius produces these learned and circumstantial comparisons for Bassianus' ring.

The best example of such absurd contrast between occasion and image is offered by the speech of forty-seven lines which Marcus makes upon finding the cruelly mutilated Lavinia in the wood [II. iv. 11-57]. It is not only the idea that a human being at sight of such atrocities can burst forth into a long speech full of images and comparisons which appears so unsuitable and inorganic; but it is rather the unconcerned nature of these images, as it were, their almost wanton playfulness which reveals the incongruity. The stream of blood gushing from the mouth of the unfortunate Lavinia is compared by Marcus "to a bubbling fountain stirr'd with wind", her cheeks "look red as Titan's face", and of her lily hands he says in retrospect that they "tremble, like aspen-leaves upon a lute, and make the silken strings delight to kiss them". The speech is, moreover, adorned with a number of studied mythological references (Tereus and Philomela, Cerberus).

In this connection the use of mythology in *Titus* is very instructive. In the later plays Shakespeare employs mythology in order to lend an event or a person a particular and individual colour (the parallel mythological situation often being vividly represented to us). In *Titus,* on the other hand, the use of mythological comparisons is still wholly due to the desire of displaying *knowledge.* When it is said of Saturnine's virtues that they "reflect on Rome as Titan's rays on earth" [I. i. 226] or of Tamora that she outshines the Roman women "like the stately Phoebe 'mongst her nymphs" [I. i. 316], these are stereotyped images, at best—in the case of more abstruse mythological comparisons—learned quotations with which Shakespeare seeks to prove that he is as much a master of mythology as Greene.

It is this ambition to display his own command of the fashionable stylistic devices of the time which leads Shakespeare so often to the involved conceits we already meet in *Titus.* Today the conceit may appear to us as a form in which the spontaneous image has become frozen into a mathematical figure. In the early Shakespeare we often find passages in which the simple image is expanded into an elaborate conceit. Whereas the simple image, the metaphor, can lend a greater passionateness to the speech, the effect of the conceit which is developed out of it is often quite the contrary. The rational, circumstantial manner in which the conceit splits up a whole situation is apt to rob the speech of its passionate movement, making it appear as cold and artificial. When Titus cries out:

> Let my tears stanch the earth's dry appetite;
>
> [III. i. 14]

this still seems natural. In the lines following, however, a long conceit is spun out of that line. In this way the spontaneity of this outburst of feeling is subsequently lamed by the artificial working out of the image. . . . To be sure, these are judgements according to modern standards of taste, for the Elizabethans themselves took pleasure in the skilful invention and clever intricacy of their conceits. Shakespeare, nevertheless, with his sense of proportion in all things, turned away more and more from the unnatural character of the conceits; and although he still uses conceits in the tragedies he no longer employs them in that artificial manner. (pp. 25-7)

We may add one further observation. In no play of Shakespeare's are there so many rhetorical questions as in *Titus*. The frequency of this stylistic device throws light upon the attitude of the characters to one another. For the rhetorical question is a question which expects no answer and awaits no answer, a question which is put for its own sake. The dialogue in *Titus* often only pretends to be dialogue; in reality the characters are not yet talking with *each other,* but are delivering pompous orations to the audience. The revelling in rhetorical questions to be observed in *Titus* is a token of the padding of the language with mere rhetorical decoration, with empty gesture and pomp. . . . However, rhetorical style is not restricted to the early works of Shakespeare; it frequently reappears even in the late tragedies, but there it has become the adequate form of expression of the character and is in harmony with the inner and outer situation. (p. 29)

> *Wolfgang H. Clemen, " 'Titus Andronicus',"in his*
> *The Development of Shakespeare's Imagery, second*
> *edition, Methuen and Co. Ltd., 1977, pp. 21-9.*

M[URIEL] C. BRADBROOK (essay date 1951)

[*Bradbrook is an English scholar specializing in the development of Elizabethan drama and poetry. In her Shakespearean criticism, she combines both biographical and historical research, focusing especially on stage conventions popular during Shakespeare's lifetime. Her* Shakespeare and Elizabethan Poetry (1951) *is a comprehensive work in which she examines the evolution of Shakespeare's verse as well as its relation to the poetry of George Chapman, Christopher Marlowe, Edmund Spenser, and Philip Sidney. One of the first critics to stress the relationship between* Titus Andronicus *and medieval literature, Bradbrook interprets the structure of the play as a combination of "accepted designs," such as the medieval Complaint—a nondramatic monologue or lyric in which the speaker laments personal misfortunes—the morality play, and the Elizabethan revenge drama written in the manner of Thomas Kyd's* The Spanish Tragedy. *In support of her interpretation, Bradbrook focuses on the "emblematic or heraldic quality" of all the characters in* Titus *as the primary element Shakespeare adopted from medieval literature, and she further illustrates how this "moral heraldry" continues throughout the play, even beyond the point where the revenge pattern supercedes. For Bradbrook, this emblematic quality is enhanced by the dramatic imagery and the formal texture of Shakespeare's writing. She concludes by describing* Titus *as "more like a pageant than a play"; she also claims that many commentators, focusing strictly on the revenge pattern present in the drama, have misunderstood Shakespeare's intentions, and that the poet himself was possibly unsure of his design, which took shape years later in his depiction of pain and madness in* King Lear. *This emphasis on the play's importance to Shakespeare's later design in* King Lear *can also*

be found in the essays by Frederick S. Boas (1896), H. Bellyse Baildon (1904), and Joseph S. G. Bolton (1933). For further commentary on the language and imagery in Titus Andronicus, *see the excerpts by Wolfgang H. Clemen (1951), A. C. Hamilton (1967), D. J. Palmer (1972), Albert H. Tricomi (1976), and David Willbern (1978).*]

[In *Titus Andronicus* and *The Rape of Lucrece*], where Shakespeare was trying his hand in the high style, he models from accepted designs. Early Elizabethan tragedy was closely connected with the nondramatic Complaint: *Lucrece* is comparable with Daniel's *Rosamund's Complaint,* and *Titus* is largely a dramatic lament. The Complaint was a late medieval form: in *The Mirror for Magistrates,* the medieval tradition was transmitted to the Elizabethans. The Vergilian journey to the underworld, the allegorical figures and wailing ghosts, the imagery of hell and judgment and the demonstration of the turn of Fortune's wheel as Chaucer described it . . . are all transferred to the stage in the early revenge play, the other parent-stock from which *Titus Andronicus* derives. Kyd's *Spanish Tragedy* provided the dramatic model: Ovid's *Metamorphoses,* part of the story, which is based on the Rape of Philomel. Shakespeare was drawing on as many good authorities as he could. . . . (pp. 104-05)

There is an emblematic or heraldic quality about all the characters of *Titus Andronicus.* Formal grouping appears with the first great scene of lament where, after the procession of Titus's condemned sons, Lucius, his banished heir, stands with sword drawn, whilst Titus kneels and pleads with the stones under his feet.

> A stone is silent and offendeth not,
> And tribunes with their tongues doom men to death.
>
> [III. i. 46-7]

he says, working out the emblematic contrast of the stony-hearted men at great length. Next, the ravished Lavinia is brought to her father; he invites the whole family to sit on the earth together and wipe one another's eyes in a kind of ballet of lamentation. Titus sees himself as a figure in a tapestry or a picture, something to move the sorrows of spectators. . . . His ravished daughter would be woeful enough if she were only a pictured figure, he says: but she is alive. Nevertheless the effect is that of a living picture rather than of life itself. Titus points out all his woeful family in turn and comments on them: when he has mutilated himself in a vain attempt to save his sons' lives, and receives as reward their two decapitated heads, his brother takes up the role of commentator, and points out the tragic spectacle, including himself

> Even like a stony image, cold and numme
>
> [III. i. 258]

He invites Titus to rage and lament, instead of trying to restrain him. Instead, Titus bursts into a terrific laugh. It is the turning-point of the play: Titus has dropped the role of Lamenter to take up that of Revenger. (pp. 105-06)

Moral heraldry is devised in the other scene of lament, the mourning feast at Titus's house, where he moralizes formally on his daughter—'this map of woe' [III. ii. 12] he calls her. In this scene also he has a speech of madness in which he rebukes his brother for killing a fly, until told that it was a black fly, emblematic of the wicked Aaron. (p. 106)

The moral heraldry of *Titus Andronicus* is not confined to grouping and imagery. The figure of Aaron is the only one which beside Titus has any life in it. He is portentous and diabolic: his blackness an outward symbol of his diabolic nature, recognized by all. . . . Aaron is clearly related to both Ithamore and Barabas of *The Jew of Malta*. In the long speech in which he confesses before his death, he echoes the Jew:

> Even now I curse the day and yet I thinke
> Few come within the compass of my curse,
> Wherein I did not some notorious ill. . . .
>
> [V. i. 125-27]

Murder, rape, perjury, the kind of crime against 'poor men's cattle' [V. i. 132] and their barns and haystacks which the common witch was accused of are all jumbled together, and neatly linked with Titus's lament by the final simile:

> Tut, I have done a thousand dreadfull things,
> As willingly as one would kill a flie. . . .
>
> [V. i. 141-42]

Aaron is half-symbol, half stage-formula. The medieval devil, witty and exuberant, has contributed to his character, and so has the conscienceless Machiavel, with his delight in plots, his manipulation of the poor victims to engineer their own undoing, and his rapid action by violence when 'policy' will not serve. He is an atheist of course, and regards an oath as 'popish' [V. i. 76].

His wit throws the laments of the tragic characters into high relief—whether he is crying 'weke, weke' as he stabs the nurse ('so cries a pigge prepared to the spit' [IV. ii. 146], 'almost splitting his sides with extreme laughter' [V. i. 113] as Titus mutilates himself, or dandling the coal-black baby which Tamora bears him, and defying her sons:

> Yee white limde walles, yee alehouse painted signes. . . .
>
> [IV. ii. 98]

But when the Revenge action is on foot, Titus becomes witty and ironic in turn, sends his ominous presents to the young princes, shoots his arrows at the gods, and outplays Aaron at his own game of countermining.

Murder and Rape are finally personified upon the stage and the Empress Tamora herself appears as Revenge, the spirit which had prompted her first acts, and which now prompts Titus. Throughout the play the murders, rapes, mutilations and other atrocities remain mere moral heraldry, with no more sense of physical embodiment than if all the characters had been given such names.

This is ensured by the formal quality of the writing, which is learned, rhetorical, full of conceits. The imagery of 'black night', 'hollow caves' and the gloomy journey to hell in search of revenge belong to the tragic tradition of Kyd. Yet sometimes a decorus pastoral landscape appears, which jars most violently against the subject with which it is related, as in the description of the ravished Lavinia, when villains had

> lopt and hewde and made thy body bare,
> Of her two branches, those sweet Ornaments,
> Whose circling Shadowes, Kings have sought to
> sleepe in . . .
> Alas, a crimson River of warme blood,
> Like to a bubling Fountaine stirde with winde,
> Doth rise and fall between thy Rosed lips,
> Comming and going with thy honie breath . . .
> One houres storme will drowne the fragrant
> meades . . .
>
> [II. iv. 17-54]

This imagery is meant to work by contrast, like some of the imagery in the narrative poems. The writer is saying by means of the images, 'Look here upon this picture, and on this'. The contrast of remembering happiness in misery is the very material of the lament. (pp. 107-09)

Titus Andronicus is then more like a pageant than a play. But unlike such pageants as those at the end of the third book of the *Faerie Queene*, it is not provided with an interpretation, and no doubt it was enjoyed by the groundlings as an atrocity play. They would take what it had in common with *Lust's Dominion* and ignore what was different. This learned and decorous work may have achieved popular success only through misunderstanding of the young author's intentions.

It is quite possible that Shakespeare himself did not know exactly what he meant by this play. But in the laments of Titus, which are the core of the piece, can be felt some faint foreshadowing of the pain and madness that were ultimately to issue in *King Lear*. The play seems a first crude attempt to portray some experience that Shakespeare was only to recognize, understand and embody in a 'lively image' at a much later stage. Because that later image exists, we may guess at the unfulfilled intention of the earlier writing, where the meaning is given in terms of doctrine, not of experience: stated, not realized: shadowed, not portrayed. (p. 110)

> M[uriel] C. Bradbrook, "Moral Heraldry: 'Titus Andronicus', 'Rape of Lucrece', 'Romeo and Juliet'," in her Shakespeare and Elizabethan Poetry: A Study of His Earlier Work in Relation to the Poetry of the Time, *Chatto and Windus, 1951, pp. 104-22.*

EUGENE M. WAITH (lecture date 1955)

[*Waith discusses* Titus Andronicus *in relation to Ovid's* Metamorphoses. *In an unexcerpted portion of his essay, he outlines the physical and mental changes that Ovid's characters undergo, stressing that Ovid "was more interested in the transforming power of intense emotion than in pointing a moral." He also states that Ovid combined emotional excitement with objective distance in his work to create an impersonal aura and to emphasize the phenomenon of transformation itself rather than the characters who are changed. In the following excerpt, Waith concentrates on the manner in which Ovid's themes and method of characterization inform* Titus Andronicus. *He maintains that the theme of Shakespeare's play—the conflict beween moral and political disorder and the integrating forces of friendship, brotherly love, justice, and wise government—parallels that of the* Metamorphoses. *Waith also responds to those critics, most notably John Dover Wilson (1947) and Wolfgang H. Clemen (1951), who have questioned the combination of horrifying violence and fanciful description in* Titus. *Unlike Dover Wilson, who regarded this contrast of style and action as Shakespeare's attempt at parody, and unlike Clemen, who regarded it as the work of an immature playwright, Waith argues that Shakespeare was well aware of the incongruity inherent in his play. He suggests that the poet was striving to achieve "a special tragic mode," in which he incorporated Ovid's concept of transformation into an Elizabethan political and moral tragedy. The failure of this experiment, Waith concludes, can be attributed to Shakespeare's Ovidian material, which requires narration rather than dramatic action to convey individual metamorphosis. For additional discussion of the Ovidian influence in* Titus Andronicus, *see the excerpts by A. C. Hamilton (1967) and D. J. Palmer (1972). Waith's essay was originally delivered as a lecture at the International Shakespeare Conference in 1955.*]

The theme of *Titus Andronicus* is too commonplace to attribute to any one source. It is, I take it, the opposition of moral and political disorder to the unifying force of friendship and wise government, a theme in which Shakespeare was interested all his life. Tillyard noted several years ago the relation of this tragedy to the history plays [see exceprt above, 1944], and it extends to the Roman plays, to *King Lear, Macbeth* and much else that Shakespeare wrote. Marcus states the theme at the end of the play:

> You sad-faced men, people and sons of Rome,
> By uproar severed, as a flight of fowl
> Scattered by winds and high tempestuous gusts,
> O, let me teach you how to knit again
> This scattered corn into one mutual sheaf,
> These broken limbs again into one body.
>
> [V. iii. 67-72]

The rape and mutilation of Lavinia is the central symbol of disorder, both moral and political, resembling in this respect the rape of Lucrece as Shakespeare portrays it. The connexion between the two sorts of disorder is made explicit in the play's two references to Tarquin, once as ravisher [IV. i. 63-4] and once as the evil, exiled king [III. i. 299]. The association is still present in Shakespeare's mind many years later, when he has Macbeth speak of "wither'd murder" moving "with Tarquin's ravishing strides" [*Macbeth*, II. i. 55].

The integrating force, which through most of the play is too weak to impose itself upon chaos, appears in the guise of friendship, brotherly love, justice, and gratitude. Marcus addresses Titus at the beginning of the play as the "friend in justice" to the people of Rome [I. i. 180], and at the end calls Lucius "Rome's dear friend" [V. iii. 80]. Brotherly love is demonstrated in the bizarre episodes of Quintus losing himself in the effort to help his brother Martius out of the pit, and of Marcus offering his hand for that of Titus. The absence of brotherly love appears in the first scene in the quarrel of Saturninus and Bassianus, and injustice and gratitude are the subjects of complaint throughout the play.

The theme of *Titus Andronicus* is at least consonant with what many interpreters supposed Ovid to be saying [in his *Metamorphoses*]. Friendship is one of the ordering forces; Golding [the Elizabethan translator of Ovid] uses this word in translating Ovid's account of how the strife between the elements was ended. . . . Titus laments the departure of justice by quoting "Terras Astraea reliquit" [IV. iii. 4] from Ovid's description of the iron age, just before the time of the giants and the flood. Disorder is represented by the acts of wanton violence and one of the most powerful metaphors in the play, "Rome is but a wilderness of tigers" [III. i. 54], seems to echo Golding's lines about disorder in the state.

We may ask then whether any of the characterization is in an Ovidian mode. "Tiger" is one of several animal and bird epithets applied to the passionate Tamora, whose story would fit easily into the scheme of the *Metamorphoses*. When we first see her, she is a captive "distressèd queen", pleading for mercy to her son. We must sympathize, though we are given very little time to do so, with her protest against Titus's inflexibility: "O cruel, irreligious piety!" [I. i. 130]. Demetrius then compares her to Hecuba, who was given the opportunity to revenge the loss of her son on Polymestor. The allusion reminds one of the guile and the ferocity of Hecuba in carrying out her vengeance and of her final transformation into a dog. The end of Tamora's career is quite consistent with this introduction. Her disguise as Revenge, though part of her plot to deceive Titus, obviously labels for us the passion which dom-

inates her character. She dies a victim of an outrage prompted by the outrage in which she had assisted, and the last words of the play leave no doubt of her complete assimilation into the animal kingdom:

> As for that ravenous tiger, Tamora,
> No funeral rite, nor man in mourning weed,
> No mournful bell shall ring her burial;
> But throw her forth to beasts and birds of prey.
> Her life was beastly and devoid of pity,
> And being dead, let birds on her take pity.
>
> [V. iii. 195-200]
> (pp. 44-5)

The character of Tamora is so intimately related to the character of Titus, for which it is a foil, that the two must be discussed together. Once more we have a story which could easily be put with the *Metamorphoses*. We see Titus at the beginning a man of absolute integrity but cursed, somewhat like Coriolanus, with an unbending and blind fixity of character. If his piety, ignoring all pleas for mercy, warrants Tamora's adjective, "cruel", his slaying of Mutius and his refusal to have him entombed deserve the charges of injustice, impiety, and barbarity brought by his brother and sons. His choice of a principle rather than a man, when he throws the election to Saturninus, is palpable folly. Thus his closely related virtues and faults are well established in the first act. In the succeeding acts the cruelties of his enemies are heaped upon him in a steady succession. After he has cut off his hand, the unbearable horror of his situation causes him to exclaim,

> Is not my sorrow deep, having no bottom?
> Then be my passions bottomless, . . .
> If there were reason for these miseries,
> Then into limits could I bind my woes.
>
> [III. i. 216-17, 219-20]

If this speech suggests some of the attitudes . . . in Ovid, so do the comments of Marcus after the messenger has brought Titus the heads of his sons:

> These miseries are more than may be borne! . . .
> Ah! now no more will I control thy griefs: . . .
> Now is a time to storm, why art thou still?
>
> [III. i. 243, 259, 263]

From this point the character of Titus is markedly altered by grief. Although Marcus says that Titus is "so just that he will not revenge" [IV. i. 128], it gradually becomes clear that revenge is his obsession. At first he takes refuge in fantasy, but when he finally has Chiron and Demetrius in his power his words reveal clearly his true state of mind and do so in a series of Ovidian allusions. After a grisly account of his plans for the banquet, he says:

> This is the feast that I have bid her to,
> And this the banquet she shall surfeit on;
> For worse than Philomel you used my daughter,
> And worse than Progne I will be revenged. . . .
> Come, come, be every one officious
> To make this banquet, which I wish may prove
> More stern and bloody than the Centaurs' feast.
>
> [V. iii. 192-95, 201-03]

Here surely is a psychic metamorphosis which provides one of the truly powerful moments in the depiction of the hero. His cruelty is monstrous yet, thanks to the indications of the first act, not incredible.

Act IV. Scene ii. Chiron (seated), Demetrius, and Aaron. By G. F. Sargent. The Department of Rare Books and Special Collections, The University of Michigan Library.

Because of this consistent development Titus is a more successful character than Tamora, who is not always depicted as the woman obsessed by revenge. In the second act we find her more lustful than revengeful, while Aaron, described in terms of the same birds and beasts to which Tamora is compared, becomes in a sense the projection of her revenge. But unfortunately for the unity of design, Aaron, though a brilliant dramatic creation, belongs to the un-Ovidian tradition of Barabas and Eleazar. His villainy invites a less complicated response than does the obsessive behaviour of Tamora and Titus.

Although the references to Procne and to the battle of the Lapiths and the centaurs show the horrifying effect of the fixation on revenge. Titus, unlike Tamora, is not finally shown as bestial or degenerate. His slaying of Lavinia, also somewhat prepared for by the first act, has overtones of nobility, though Saturninus' comment "unnatural and unkind" [V. iii. 498], is uncomfortably close to the truth. The final comments on his character are all praise and pity, sharply contrasted with the abuse heaped on Aaron and Tamora. Marcus gives the core of the defence:

> Now judge what cause had Titus to revenge
> These wrongs, unspeakable, past patience,
> Or more than any living man could bear.
>   [V. iii. 125-27]

So at the end it is Titus rather than Tamora who produces an effect like that of Ovid's Hecuba, for whom even the gods felt pity when revenge had dreadfully transformed her. Or we might describe the difference by saying that the depiction of Tamora is in the mode of the moralized Ovid, while the depiciton of Titus more closely resembles Roman Ovid.

The underlying theme of *Titus Andronicus,* to which I have referred, is not so important an organizing principle as Shakespeare's themes are in his later tragedies. I think that, like Ovid, he was more interested here in portraying the extraordinary pitch of emotion to which a person may be raised by the most violent outrage. The passions of Titus transcend the limits of character to become in their own right, so to speak, phenomena of nature: his grief, like the Nile, "disdaineth bounds" [III. i. 71]. The grotesqueries of his mad scenes contribute to this effect, and the end is pure frenzy. If the violence of the play serves the theme as an emblem of disorder, it also serves as both agent and emblem of a metamorphosis of character which takes place before our eyes. Character in the usual sense of the word disintegrates completely. What we see is a personified emotion.

We come finally to Lavinia, the third character who may profitably be seen against this Ovidian background. She has been one of the chief stumbling-blocks to the appreciation of the play: to many critics she has seemed smug in her contemptuous speeches to Tamora [II. iii. 66ff], and intolerably pathetic or ludicrous thereafter. Dover Wilson gave the most unkindest cut of all when he likened her to "a little puppy-dog", trotting after Titus with his severed hand in her teeth [see excerpt above, 1947]. Yet as an inhabitant of the Ovidian world she is neither absurd nor difficult to understand. Her proud self-confidence with Tamora clearly points up the shocking suddenness of her change to a weeping suppliant—an initial metamorphosis somewhat comparable to Niobe's.

Lavinia's second metamorphosis is accomplished in a description which has proved to be the most unpalatable passage in the play. It is also the most Ovidian. This is the passage in which Marcus compares Lavinia to a tree whose branches have been cut, her blood to a river, a bubbling fountain, her lips to roses, her cheeks to the sun, her lost hands, once more, to the leaves of a tree [II. iv. 16-57]. In a somewhat different category is the comment on her loss of blood "As from a conduit with three issuing spouts", a comparison reminiscent of Ovid's description of the death of Pyramus. . . . Like Ovid's comparisons, these of Shakespeare's are unexpected, fanciful, and yet exact. Miss Bradbrook has pointed to Shakespeare's use of opposites in description in *Venus and Adonis* and here in *Titus Andronicus*. The imagery of the description of Lavinia is meant, she believes, to "work by contrast. . . . The writer is saying by means of the images, 'Look here upon this picture, and on this'" [see exceprt above, 1951]. It is the "contrast of remembering happiness in misery" to which she refers, and agreeing that the observation is just, I should like to add some other ways in which contrast works here. These pleasant and familiar images of trees, fountains, and conduits bring the horror that has been committed within the range of comprehension. They oblige us to see clearly a suffering body, yet as they do so they temporarily remove its individuality, even its humanity, by abstracting and generalizing. Though not in themselves horrible, they point up the horror; though familiar, they point up the strangeness. The suffering becomes an object of contemplation.

This technique of description is not inappropriate to this sort of situation. The trouble is that it is a narrative rather than a dramatic device. Though many writers have used it in plays, its function is to present to the mind's eye something which is not on the stage for the physical eye to see. When Duncan is described, "His silver skin lac'd with his golden blood" [*Macbeth*, II. ii. 112], there is also an incongruity between mortal wounds and decorative language, but Duncan himself is not there to compete with the description. The imagination of the spectator is free to contemplate a spectacle simultaneously horrible and kingly. The narrative intrusion is brief and clearly separated from dramatic action. For the Ovidian description of Lavinia to work as it might work in the *Metamorphoses* an even greater freedom is required. A physical impersonation of the mutilated Lavinia should not block our vision.

Though this objection sounds like Lamb's criticism of *King Lear,* I believe it is more valid because of the different way in which metamorphosis is related to the meaning of *Titus Andronicus*. In *King Lear* the transformation brought about by extraordinary suffering is not a loss of humanity but a step toward greater understanding. Dramatic action reinforces at every point what the poetry suggests. In Ovid's *Metamorphoses* the unendurable emotional state robs the character of his humanity and the story ends, so to speak, with a point of exclamation. It is easy to see that the melodramatic tale of Titus, Tamora, and Lavinia, partly inspired by Ovid, is susceptible of the full Ovidian treatment. It ends logically with what Joyce might have called an "epiphany" of the state of mind at which

each of the principal characters has arrived. This would be shown by a physical metamorphosis or by a passage of description or by both together. In *Titus Andronicus* we have the many speeches insisting upon what is extraordinary in the situation of the hero—what makes it beyond human endurance—but the final transformation which would complete the suggestion cannot take place. We have the description which almost transforms Lavinia, but in the presence of live actors the poetry cannot perform the necessary magic. The action frustrates, rather than re-enforces, the operation of the poetry.

A simple formulation of the source of critical dissatisfaction with the play might seem to follow logically here: the style is inappropriate. Shakespeare, like some Elizabethan builders, has reached out for a bit of classical design and has come up with some decoration which does not fit his basic structure. But this pronouncement rests on an oversimplification, for the Ovidian borrowing in *Titus Andronicus* has more significance than the mere application of decorative detail.

In taking over certain Ovidian forms Shakespeare takes over part of an Ovidian conception which cannot be fully realized by the techniques of drama. This is the conception of the protagonist as a man so worked upon that by sheer intensity of passion he ultimately transcends the normal limits of humanity. I believe that there is a reason why such a treatment of character might appeal to an Elizabethan writer of tragedy, and hence why he might attempt what seems to us a patently impossible task.

In describing the proper effect of tragedy many Renaissance critics emphasized what they called "admiration". In the sixteenth century the word was sometimes used with approximately its modern meaning, but usually retained its basic meaning of "wonder" or "astonishment". . . . There is no doubt that such ideas about tragedy were in the air at the end of the sixteenth century and hence that playwrights, whether or not they had read the theorists, might look for material and language suitable to arouse admiration. Seneca was obviously a rich mine, but often it was the Latin writers of verse narrative who furnished models; astonishing passages were freely borrowed or imitated from Virgil, Lucan, Statius. Marlowe and Chapman each developed what might be called a rhetoric of admiration. . . . This genre of tragedy is most uncongenial to our times. We are inclined to deny that it is tragedy at all and to dismiss it as mere posturing and rant. (pp. 45-8)

Titus Andronicus is Shakespeare's contribution to a special tragic mode. Its final spectacle is both horrible and pathetic, but above all extraordinary. Ovid more than Seneca or the epic poets was the model for both characterization and style, with the result that Shakespeare's rhetoric of admiration, as seen in such lines as Marcus' description of Lavinia, is more elegantly florid than that of his contemporaries. The hero, in this respect like Tamburlaine or Bussy D'Ambois, is almost beyond praise or blame, an object of admiration. (p. 48)

> *Eugene M. Waith, "The Metamorphosis of Violence in 'Titus Andronicus',"in* Shakespeare Survey: An Annual Survey of Shakespearian Study and Production, *Vol. 10, 1957, pp. 39-49.*

BERNARD SPIVACK   (essay date 1958)

[*In his* Shakespeare and the Allegory of Evil *(1958), Spivack relates the traditions of late medieval drama to the characterizations of Shakespeare's major villains. He also discusses those dramatic techniques of the Elizabethan stage that reflect its tran-*

sition from the conventions of medieval allegory to the naturalism of modern drama, suggesting that such knowledge might help to explain some of the major problems critics encounter in Shakespeare's works. Spivack demonstrates in the excerpt below that, despite Shakespeare's effort to inform Aaron with an individual identity based on such Machiavellian motives as revenge or ambition, he is in reality little more than the traditional Vice figure of medieval allegorical drama. Spivack concentrates on aspects of Aaron's character, such as his disruptive influence on political harmony and the lack of specific motives for his actions, as qualities typical of the traditional Vice figure. Shakespeare's reliance on medieval dramatic traditions for the characterization of Titus Andronicus *is also discussed by Muriel C. Bradbrook (1951).*]

Titus is an Elizabethan tragedy of violent revenge in the popular style, in imitation of Seneca and with borrowings from Ovid. It is not the only violent play that Shakespeare wrote, but it is the earliest of them, and it troubles us more than the others because its violence is so stark, because it lacks the rich moral organization and poetic subtlety by which the later Shakespeare of *Hamlet* and *Macbeth* sublimed melodrama and murder. The action in *Titus* lurches like a brazen engine in a field of blood. Most of its sounds—there are lovely exceptions—belong to the rhetoric of passion or oratory, and most of its gestures are sword thrusts. We should remember that here Shakespeare handles a Roman story for the first time, and, like all Elizabethans, he was very conscious of the special quality of the Roman *virtus*. He is aiming for the kind of character that fits the *Imperium* and the Forum—the high fashion of the antique Roman—and if his Romans in this play succeed chiefly in being *high,* they do much better in others which come later.

More pleasing perhaps than anything the Romans say and do is Aaron's affection for his child, and Aaron, although a Moor, is the one important figure unmistakably in [England's] native dramatic tradition—both halves of him. . . . If "Aaron is Shakespeare's master-stroke in Titus," as Dover Wilson says, the compliment finds its proper object in the effective combination between the young playwright's powers and the theatrical image which descended to him from the allegorical stage.

Aaron is not always the Vice, of course, for he is a hybrid. The other part of him is properly Aaron the Moor—in his first soliloquy, his vicious counsel to Chiron and Demetrius, his relations with Tamora and with his child, in much of the play in fact. But the older stage image weaves in and out of him, and we can see it best by placing him alongside his partner in evil, the villainous Tamora. Her deeds are no better than his, but she, although not profoundly drawn, is perfectly credible. She is a bad character whom revenge sets in motion; and she does not need to protest her villainy, she acts it. Her actions, moreover, are organic to the plot, not a stylized performance based on premises outside it. As Queen of the Goths she is the natural enemy of Rome who "will charm Rome's Saturnine / And see his shipwrack and his commonweal's" [II. i. 23-4]. As a captive led in triumph she is the natural enemy of her captors, the Andronici. Her sharper cause against them, a consistent theme throughout, is their sacrifice of her son Alarbus; and when she turns Lavinia over to her remaining sons her words agree with her sentiments everywhere in the play:

Remember, boys, I pour'd forth tears in vain
To save your brother from the sacrifice;
But fierce Andronicus would not relent.
Therefore away with her, and use her as you will;
The worse to her, the better lov'd of me.
[II. iii. 163-67]

Her wickedness stays in clear moral focus because it belongs *exclusively* to her character and her motives, and she is not a dramatic problem. The only time she threatens to become one, it is none of her doing, but when Aaron, with his homiletic voice, describes her as

our Empress, with her sacred wit
To villany and vengeance consecrate . . .
[II. i. 120-21]

But these words, of which the paired nouns in the second line expose the hyphenated role, tell us about Aaron, and the dimension in which he is intermittently cast, not about Tamora.

In Aaron the homiletic projection and bravura demonstration of the old morality role, still relatively unsubdued by the crescent naturalism to which it is united, create once more the familiar hybrid. The old metaphor is gone, of course, but its traditional stage features remain and combine with the historical or legendary Moor who, along with the rest of the plot, may have come to Shakespeare out of some story now lost—combine with him to theatricalize him according to the established dramatic formula that still counted for more with the popular audience than the human validity of which it deprived him. When Titus, by a benevolent deception . . . , manages that his own hand, rather than that of Marcus or Lucius, is cut off to redeem his condemned sons, Aaron has his text for a sneering commentary that distills the essence of the role whose history we follow—the bravura deceit that was once a moral metaphor for the insinuation of evil into the human heart, but is now superficially grafted to a new rationale in revenge and ambition:

[Aside] If that be call'd deceit, I will be honest
And never whilst I live deceive men so.
But I'll deceive you in another sort,
And that you'll say ere half an hour pass.
He cuts off Titus' hand.
[III. i. 188-91]

A moment later his words shape themselves into a late version of the Vice's verbal trick, breathe the Vice's laughter upon the grief of his victims, and engage the audience with a directness to which the editorialized direction does scant justice:

I go, Andronicus, and for thy hand
Look by-and-by to have thy sons with thee.
[Aside] Their heads, I mean. O, how this villany
Doth fat me with the very thoughts of it!
Let fools do good, and fair men call for grace,
Aaron will have his soul black like his face.
[III. i. 200-05]

We need not doubt his laughter in this scene, even though it is not explicit in the text, for later he refers to it expressly when he boasts to Lucius of his versatile iniquity . . . :

I play'd the cheater for thy father's hand,
And when I had it, drew myself apart
And almost broke my heart with extreme laughter.
I pried me through the crevice of a wall
When for his hand he had his two sons' heads,
Beheld his tears, and laugh'd so heartily
That both my eyes were rainy like to his.
[V. i. 111-17]

This is exactly the mood of the inherited role, just as the deed itself remains for Aaron exactly what it has always been for the Vice—sport:

> And when I told the Empress of this sport,
> She sounded almost at my pleasing tale
> And for my tidings gave me twenty kisses.
>
> [V. i. 118-20]

The moral effect of his actions, no less than their style and mood, bears the impress of the same inheritance. In addition to mischief of every kind through which his deceit and cunning can illustrate themselves, enmity and internecine strife are his special object and the special mark of his achievement. The play has a large political theme, the unity of Rome, which is emphatic in the opening scene with its turmoil of rivalry between Saturninus and Bassianus for the vacant throne—rivalry which carries to the edge of civil war before it is put to rest by the patriotic efforts of Marcus and Titus. When the bloody events at the end vacate the throne once more and throw the populace into confusion and terror, Marcus invokes them in language expounding the most urgent of Elizabethan political tenets, the need for internal order and unity:

> You sad-fac'd men, people and sons of Rome,
> By uproar sever'd, as a flight of fowl
> Scatt'red by winds and high tempestuous gusts,
> O, let me teach you how to knit again
> This scattered corn into one mutual sheaf,
> These broken limbs again into one body;
> Lest Rome herself be bane unto herself,
> And she whom mighty kingdoms cur'sy to,
> Like a forlorn and desperate castaway,
> Do shameful execution on herself.
>
> [V. iii. 67-76]

Creating and sustaining this unity, for the time it lasts, is the reconciliation in the first scene between the houses of Andronicus and Saturninus, sincere on the one side even if only pretended on the other. Having become the wife of Saturninus, Tamora announces that "this day all quarrels die" [I. i. 465], and her husband, the new emperor, follows suit by proclaiming "a love-day." The royal pair invite the Andronici to a double marriage celebration and become, in turn, their guests for the hunt of the day following.

Aaron's "excellent piece of villany" [II. iii. 7] has its social meaning as an assault upon this harmony. He lays his snare for the sake of "their unrest / That have their alms out of the Empress' chest" [II. iii. 8-9], and we shall see that one part of his vocational agenda consists in setting "deadly enmity between two friends" [V. i. 131]. His contrivance incriminates the innocent sons of Titus in the murder of the Emperor's brother and is at the heart of a train of events inciting the Emperor to tyranny and the Andronici to rebellion and regicide. The deception by which he persuades Andronicus to cut off his own right hand is the straw that breaks the patience of Lucius and makes him leader of the Goths against Rome. In effect he pours the sweet milk of concord into hell, his achievement this way being standard for the role of the Vice in any morality with political or social implications. . . . (pp. 379-83)

In nothing, however, does his heritage reveal itself more clearly than in its liquidation of the conventional motives that naturalize him to the play as Aaron the Moor, follower and lover of evil Tamora as well as a criminal in his own right. Except for the moment he utters them they are everywhere annulled

in his performance by its homiletic dimension and traditional impetus. The conventional ambition that appears in his adjuration to himself "To mount aloft with thy imperial mistress" [II. i. 13] and the conventional vengeance in his vague rhetoric to her about "Blood and revenge . . . hammering in my head" [II. iii. 39] not only have neither coherence with his behavior nor even verbal endurance in his utterance, they are sunk fathoms deep by the mood and method of villainy for the sake of homiletic display. In the archaic stratum of his performance his wickedness is neither acquisitive nor retaliatory; it is demonstrative—a serial exhibition perpetuating the veteran stage image of almost two centuries. His behavior has its absolute meaning in his self-proclaimed villainy—that composite homiletic label which replaces, of necessity, the exposition of his name and nature by the Vice of the moralities. Shaped by the same homiletic perspective, his stratagems exist, not as instruments of practical purpose, but as illustrations of a talent in villainous deceit that, by his traditional intimacy with them, he invites the audience to acknowledge. . . . (pp. 383-84)

Even more destructive of his moral status as a person with passions and motives is his *moral pedigree* as he recites it in the fifth act. It is overwhelming testimony to his lineage, being one more version of the stylized rhetoric of exposure by which the Vice explains his aggressive business in the play as just another example of his characteristic activity always and everywhere. Barabas and Edricus . . . translate into literal villainies the precise method of this homiletic rhetoric, and in Aaron we have it once more—the long speech of evil explication which universalizes and immortalizes the Vice. No longer in naked intimacy with the audience, he declaims it in response to the question of Lucius, his captor: "Art thou not sorry for these heinous deeds?" [V. i. 123] after Aaron has gleefully itemized his villainies throughout the play. But Aaron is sorry only for his lack of industry:

> Ay, that I had not done a thousand more.
> Even now I curse the day (and yet I think
> Few come within the compass of my curse)
> Wherein I did not some notorious ill:
> As kill a man, or else devise his death;
> Ravish a maid, or plot the way to do it;
> Accuse some innocent, and forswear myself;
> Set deadly enmity between two friends;
> Make poor men's cattle break their necks;
> Set fire on barns and haystacks in the night
> And bid the owners quench them with their tears.
> Oft have I digg'd up dead men from their graves
> And set them upright at their dear friends' door
> Even when their sorrow almost was forgot,
> And on their skins, as on the bark of trees,
> Have with my knife carved in Roman letters
> 'Let not your sorrow die, though I am dead.
> Tut, I have done a thousand dreadful things
> As willingly as one would kill a fly;
> And nothing grieves me heartily indeed
> But that I cannot do ten thousand more.
>
> [V. i. 124-44]

In all these words we hear a personification speaking according to the formula of self-exposure once requisite for such a speaker on the abstract and didactic stage. The fifth, sixth, and seventh lines, let us notice, exactly document his activity in the play— against Bassianus, against Lavinia, and against the two sons of Titus; and the eighth describes his divisive enterprise as we have already reviewed it. They also tell us all we need to know about the meaning of this activity and the source of its energy: it springs from what he everlastingly is and always does. The whole speech saturates his behavior with its allegorical explanation, and into this plenum motives such as revenge or ambition have no entry. They exist, of course, just as they exist for other figures we have examined, being part of the literal vesture without which the old role is no longer viable. But they have no real affinity with his mood and impetus, which imitate, not human life, but an entrenched theatrical image originating in metaphor.

Also, like the other members of his race who survive in the literal and serious drama, Aaron is homiletically fond of diabolic bravado: "If there were devils, would I were a devil" [V. i. 147]. No less a sign of the unnaturalistic convention in his role is the bravery of his end. He confronts the ingenious torment awaiting him with a defiance that justifies nothing, extenuates nothing, repents nothing, but flaunts instead the archaic allegiance of a performance whose meaning lies a world away from revenge or ambition. His last words transform, without concealing, the Vice's allegorical *property and kind*. In Aaron they become the Villain's unswerving addiction to villainy and his regret for nothing except the cessation of his enterprise on earth:

> I am no baby, I, that with base prayers
> I should repent the evils I have done.
> Ten thousand worse than ever yet I did
> Would I perform if I might have my will.
> If one good deed in all my life I did,
> I do repent it from my very soul.
>
> [V. iii. 185-90]
> (pp. 384-86)

Bernard Spivack, "The Hybrid Image in Shakespeare," in his Shakespeare and the Allegory of Evil: The History of a Metaphor in Relation to His Major Villains, *Columbia University Press, 1958, pp. 379-414.*

ALAN SOMMERS   (essay date 1960)

[*In a structural analysis of* Titus Andronicus, *Sommers examines Shakespeare's development of the play's fundamental conflict and central theme, which he describes as the struggle between "ideal civilization" and "the barbarism of primitive, original nature." Although this conflict was noted by earlier critics, Sommers identifies "a more intricate series of contrasts" in the play which he feels increases our understanding of the primary conflict and "forms the core of the poet's conception." He identifies these contrasts as the juxtaposition of Saturninus and Bassianus—the self-willed versus the ideal ruler—and the juxtaposition of Rome's principle of justice and what he calls the primal energy of the "forest-symbol," best personified in the figures of Tamora and Aaron. Sommers then shifts his perspective and evaluates* Titus *strictly as a tragedy. He declares that the play's "tragic vision" of the moral and political dissolution and regeneration of a civilization follows Friedrich Nietzsche's metaphysic in* The Birth of Tragedy. *In that influential nineteenth-century work, Nietzsche developed his theory on the birth of Hellenic tragedy out of the conflict between Apollonian and Dionysian forces, the former representing the tendency towards restraint, harmony, and measure best expressed in Greek sculpture and architecture, the latter reflecting the savage yet creative power of the universe displayed in the drunken orgies of the Dionysian festivals. By extension, Nietzsche applied his theory to other forms of civilization, and even to the destruction and rebirth of civilizations themselves. Sommers also maintains that the tragic structure of* Titus *is quite different from Shakespeare's later plays, especially in its depen-*

dence on emotional release, which he maintains dissolves pain and "the knowledge of error," but which simultaneously compromises the tragic heightening and emotional complexity necessary for "high" tragedy. Yet, Sommers concludes, the tragic conception of the play's central conflict remains intact, despite Shakespeare's emphasis on such nontragic elements as symbolic characterization and horrifying events. Sommers's essay reflects a growing concern among twentieth-century critics with the nature of the tragic structure in Titus Andronicus, *also demonstrated in the essays by H. B. Charlton (1946-47), Eugene M. Waith (1955), Irving Ribner (1960), A. C. Hamilton (1967), James L. Calderwood (1971), and D. J. Palmer (1972).*]

The essential conflict in *Titus Andronicus* is the struggle between Rome, and all that this signifies in the European tradition to which we, and Shakespeare, belong, and the barbarism of primitive, original nature. It is this opposition which realises itself in the play's striking events and startling atmospheric contrasts. Both the opposing principles are indigenous to Shakespeare's world: a nature-bound vitality almost characterises the poet's early work, while the Roman idea, pervasive in the historical plays and elsewhere, is fairly central, finally entwining itself with the thought of England's destiny in *Cymbeline*. A poetic conception, composite both of traditional and of genuinely classical values, as Roman 'virtue', 'justice', 'piety'—the words all recur significantly in *Titus Andronicus*—is in this earlier vision threatened by forces of unregenerate barbarism, comprising natural gifts and some natural instinct, but constituting a specific reaction from civilisation, religion and humanity. . . . The opposition is stark, and the drama leaves it unresolved. Nevertheless, a most interesting pattern of values becomes evident.

In the opening scene there is strong and vivid ethical feeling. It may, perhaps, seem strange to use such terms; 'ethic' and 'value' would be remote abstractions and the play a mere melodrama but for the way in which the dramatist insists upon such reference. It is in these terms that one *must* speak of the cruelty of Titus in countenancing the ritual murder of the eldest son of the captive queen. This error releases the whole conflict; it is the source of the tragedy. The evil character of the decision is underlined. There is Tamora's plea for mercy:

> Wilt thou draw near the nature of the gods?
> Draw near them then in being merciful;
> Sweet mercy is nobility's true badge.
>
> [I. i. 117-19]

which, if not 'in character', suffices at least to stamp the episode as Shakespearian and to condemn the act, by reference to Christian values, similarly invoked in other plays. . . . It seems to derive none the less from an authentic Roman virtue, 'piety'. The Andronici are distinguished by family piety, and in this value, an aspect of the Virgilian *pietas*, lies their real strength. But a virtue such as this is not, alone, sufficient. Others may possess it equally, as Tamora says [I. i. 114-15]. Her subsequent complaint is no less just:

> O cruel, irreligious piety!
>
> [I. i. 130]

What is lacking is not only the 'mercy' pleaded for but also, more precisely, pity. . . . The word is to be reiterated as we see that the quality is more completely lacking in the non-Roman party. Tamora, splendid animal but barbaric, is pitiless. At the end Lucius is to declare that

> Her life was beast-like, and devoid of pity;
> And, being so, shall have like want of pity.
>
> [V. iii. 199-200]

The initial crime of the protagonist is not glossed over, and it is not excused. But while it is logical that Rome's want of pity should be avenged on the Andronici by a subsequent transference of power to pitiless barbarism, and though our inevitable sympathy with Rome is strained to the utmost by this very impressive opening, there is no doubt as to which side must ultimately maintain its right. The Andronici, strong in 'piety', are, like the hero of the *Oresteia,* finally justified. Lucius becomes Emperor.

The structure of the tragedy has one important characteristic: the whole action develops from, depends upon, and in a sense returns to, the opening situation. The opposition already defined, of ideal civilisation and barbarism, coincides obviously with the separation of the dramatic persons into two parties, 'good' and 'evil', which is one of many points of resemblance between this play and *King Lear.* There is, however, a more intricate series of contrasts: the juxtaposition and interaction of persons, incidents and impressions serve to develop, and add to the significance of, the main conflict, which forms the core of the poet's conception.

A fine symbolic juxtaposition opens the play. The speeches of the two contestants of the Empire are of interest here:

> *Saturninus.* Noble patricians, patrons of *my right,*
> Defend the justice of *my cause* with arms;
> And, countrymen, *my loving followers,*
> Plead *my successive title* with your
> swords . . .
>
> *Bassianus.* Romans, friends, followers, favourers of
> my right,
> If ever Bassianus . . .
> Were *gracious* in the eyes of *royal* Rome
> suffer not dishonour to approach
> The *imperial* seat, to *virtue consecrate,*
> To *justice, continence,* and *nobility;*
> and let *desert* in *pure* election *shine,*
> And, Romans, fight for *freedom* in your
> choice.
>
> [I. i. 1-17]

The speech of Bassianus demands attention. Its penetrative colouring of imaginative positives in contrast to evil suggests the later Shakespeare, of Banquo's speeches, and Malcolm's catalogue of the 'king-becoming graces', in *Macbeth.* As frequently with Shakespeare, the Roman Empire is seen, through mediaeval tradition, in conjunction with the principle of Christian royalty. Yet classical republican ideals, opposed to the imperial spirit in *Julius Caesar,* are here specifically included. Bassianus's subsequent speeches in the scene show a similar colouring, and he himself typifies that Roman character which persistently excites the poet's instinctive admiration. The speech of Saturninus differs, particularly, in tone, its halting movement conveying his uneasiness as he falls back upon personal dignity and primogeniture. He is a 'degenerate' type. But the conflict is, in fact, yet more dramatic. Bassianus, conscious of inferior claims as an individual [I. i. 63], stands for the ideal, perhaps mainly to create a 'pure election', but this ideal is immediately relevant, 'dishonour' referring not to a threat of armed force, which both sides offer, but to Saturninus, the betrayer of Rome, who is judged throughout by the standard which Bassianus invokes, and represents. Apparently it is intended here to point to some previous degradation. . . . At least, the subsequent revelation of the contrasting natures of the two men enforces such a view: Bassianus is to be seen as

potentially the ideal ruler, by 'Roman' principles, while Saturninus, distinguished by a shifty self-will, ingratitude, vain prejudice, and rash injustice, is surely the obverse of Roman nobility.

At first, these two figures dominate. The split in Rome forms a prelude to the greater conflict, its opposing forces merging into the main antagonism. The Andronici, except for the protagonist, align themselves with Bassianus, while Saturninus falls a ready prey to Tamora. Thus the initial juxtaposition links the main conflict with the problem of Roman integrity, and points vividly the national and political background of Titus's actions.

The crown of the play's idealism (the unsatisfying term is used with a provisional apology) is its conception of *justice.* This word, an abstraction radiating poetic authority, recurs persistently after Bassianus's first speech. In the opening scene it connotes the ruling values, communal and imperial, before the start of the tragic disintegration. It defines each error of the protagonist, subsequent to the killing of Alarbus, which errors condition and motive the later tragedy, a living chaos which subsists in the absence of a resolving and determining spiritual authority, 'justice'. (pp. 276-80)

Like Lear, [Titus] is to become the unforeseeing arbiter of his own fate, but he [initially] bears a spiritual, almost priest-like, responsibility for the perpetuation of the values of Roman civilisation; he is 'Rome's best champion' and 'patron of virtue' [I. i. 65]. His first offence has already been noticed. To the people of Rome he has hitherto been—the phrasing is significant—'friend in justice' [I. i. 180]. He now seeks in Saturninus 'virtues' which will:

> Reflect on Rome as Titan's rays on earth,
> And ripen *justice* in this commonweal.
>
> [I. i. 226-27]

Here is Shakespeare's royal sun-symbol self-interpreted, though as for Saturninus, Lucius sees more clearly now [I. i. 208-09], as later:

> What boots it thee, to call thyself a sun?
>
> [V. iii. 18]

Bassianus, by contrast already pointed, is the human embodiment of ideal justice. Titus's fundamental error is thus manifest: he loses sight of the supreme Roman values, electing to throw the people's suffrages upon the worthless elder brother. . . . [Tragedy] begins at this point because, although the hero's choice is correct by the standard of normal rule and precedent, a higher order of value, made clear through word and symbol in the drama, impinges upon the immediate event: that which would elevate, and preserve, is denied access.

The events which follow are necessary consequence. In Bassianus, symbolism unites the personal and impersonal; not only his words, but his actions too are comprised; notice how, in the very significant ordering of the events of this scene, his interference with Titus's course is withheld until Lavinia, his rightful bride handed over by her father to Saturninus, is insulted by the latter. Bassianus in seizing her acts 'justly' [I. i. 285]. Marcus comments:

> *Suum cuique* is our Roman justice:
> This prince in justice seizes but his own.
>
> [I. i. 280-81]

The repetition is emphatic. It is, precisely, justice which Titus ignores, wrongs, flouts and finally, in his youngest son, slays.

The irony of this is increased by the Roman ethic according to which a son might thus die *for* justice: the words of Lucius 'My lord, you are unjust' [I. i. 292] point the standing accusation.

Two errors, offences to justice and to Bassianus, are thus added to the account beginning with the hero's initial crime. His error of judgement compromises justice in the abstract; he is next forced into unjust action: a sort of analogue, it might be observed, to the fall of Man. The pattern of the scene is indeed worked through the most intricate detail. Titus's misdeeds all spring from a perverse *piety;* it is in piety towards Saturninus that he wrongs the family in piety to which he had offended Tamora. After investing power in the new Emperor he presents him with the latter as a captive; the gradation of authority is at once reversed, and Titus has in effect cast himself upon the mercy of those whom he has mortally offended, and to whom he has refused mercy. Despite his essential nobility, the consistency of his actions is superficial; their effect, in terms of value, is chaos. (pp. 280-82)

The perversion of communal justice produces a veritable convulsion not merely in the commonwealth, but, quite literally, on the cosmic level. The meaning of this in moral-philosophical terms is aptly expressed by the statement, through the now familiar Elizabethan cosmography, of Ulysses's speech on 'degree' [*Troilus and Cressida* I. iii. 75-137]. But in the tragic action of *Titus Andronicus,* the justice of heaven, taken inevitably for granted in such doctrinal passages, is *challenged.* A striking scene consists of Titus's directions, during his madness, to his kinsmen, who are to search for 'justice' by land and sea:

> Then, when you come to Pluto's region,
> I pray you, deliver him this petition;
> Tell him, it is for justice and for aid,
> And that it comes from old Andronicus,
> Shaken with sorrows in ungrateful Rome.
>
>   [IV. iii. 13-17]

Justice has been 'shipp'd' from Rome by Saturninus [IV. iii. 23], who has indeed given his authority into foreign hands. This bold and profoundly suggestive fantasy provides a necessary key to the play's structure: the nightmare of its central acts is the state of the complete absence of 'justice' from Rome, human actions, the external world, and from the internal world of human passions; from, one might say, earth and hell. Therefore, says Titus:

> sith there's no justice in earth nor hell,
> We will solicit heaven and move the gods
> To send down Justice for to wreak our wrongs.
>
>   [IV. iii. 50-2]

They proceed to supplicate the gods with arrows, which fall within the court of Saturninus, and partly occasion further injustice. But the prayer is answered; the evil world is swiftly destroyed and with the death of 'this wicked emperor' and his associates, justice is restored to Rome.

It is not Saturninus, however, who dominates these fearful scenes. Their 'presiding genius' is Aaron the Moor, the precursor of Iago. The terrible sufferings of humanity witnessed take on a metaphysical horror precisely because in this world— and who shall deny a certain relevance to the present century at this point?—power has been completely divorced from justice. An essential authority, denied to Bassianus and invested, by the protagonist, in Saturninus, passes to Tamora and thence

to Aaron, who thus becomes the contriver and the symbol of nightmare disintegration and revolting barbarism. (pp. 282-83)

Titus's revenge brings about the restoration of the Roman order ('justice') not, indeed, directly, but through the sacrificial tragedy and the death-ritual of the feast. Such a ritualised catastrophe is surely a right and inevitable end to the orgiastic chaos of the middle scenes. Titus does indeed pull justice out of Acheron as he threatened [IV. iii. 45]. But the rhythm of life cannot begin again automatically; hence the long speeches of the conclusion, in which the tragedy, now at a distance, is recounted and in part re-enacted before the people of Rome. By this dramatic projection of the Andronici, the commonwealth is again given due prominence, and the play closes with the promise of the new emperor to:

>   order well the state,
> That like events may ne'er it ruinate.
>
>   [V. iii. 203-04]

The original errors, which had given birth to the 'events' of the play, are thus recognised, atoned for, and corrected. (p. 283)

The terrible scenes of the second Act are set in a forest, and this forest, though the place of the 'Roman hunting' [II. ii. 20], is a wild, uncivilised part, blending finely with the natures of the persons to whom authority at the centre of civilisation has passed. . . . [Here] the forest-symbol on the barbarian side balances the Roman 'justice'—concrete and abstract are juxtaposed—as the expression of Dionysiac powers of nature opposed to 'ambitious Rome' [I. i. 132]. This dramatic symbol does not, like much poetic symbolism, merely suggest a reality apprehended but otherwise indefinable: the forest is itself a power, or is the home of powers, active within the play, and it *actively* defines the threat to civilisation. Tamora is also such a threat, and her power is one with that of the element which she here inhabits. Cruel, barbarous, 'insatiate' [V. i. 87], a 'heinous tiger' [V. iii. 195], she all but personifies riotous nature, becoming the spirit or demiurge of the place where her vengeance is effected. The peculiar dramaturgic power of her speeches is justified aesthetically by its correspondence to her power *within* the drama. She is compared to Diana [II. iii. 57, 61], in point of power. While she remains in the forest her vengeance is irresistible. Bassianus and Lavinia are trapped, and their struggle is brief and futile; Quintus and Martius are overpowered by the very nature of the place to which they are brought [II. iii. 191-245]. The situation is contrived, deliberately, by Aaron, 'chief architect and plotter' of the tragic events, who possesses autonomous authority over Tamora, and over her sons, who represent a certain type of unregenerate human nature, well fitted for such tuition [V. i. 98]. But Aaron, too, is a creature of wild nature, so conceived in many descriptive similes, and particularly in his words to his child:

> I'll make you feed on berries and on roots,
> And feed on curds and whey, and suck the goat,
> And cabin in a cave . . .
>
>   [IV. ii. 177-79]

His final fate, suggesting that of the Erinyes at Athens, is to be fixed alive in the earth. (pp. 284-85)

The evil so potent in this drama springs partly from the spiritual conflict with Rome, initiated by Titus's grave offence to Tamora, and partly from an obscure, dark source, defined by Titus's lines about the 'ruthless, vast, and gloomy woods' [IV. i. 53], and symbolised by Aaron. The dual vision is true to life. The subtle impressionism of the forest scene, idyllic and sombre, its Diana and Actaeon, the real hidden gold, the

> rude-growing briers,
> Upon whose leaves are drops of new-shed blood
> As fresh as morning's dew distill'd on flowers.
>   [II. iii. 199-201]

all serve to provide a microcosm of the total nature-vision in the drama. Nature itself is seen by the strange light of a humanity not quite human, divested of both goodness and spirituality. (pp. 285-86)

The significance of the conflict thus elucidated, it remains to be decided what valuation can be placed upon *Titus Andronicus* as a tragedy. The foregoing conceptions at least seem to possess some correspondence to the metaphysic of Nietzsche's *The Birth of Tragedy*. The definition of the forest-symbol, and description of the barbarian party in their naturalistic aspect, characterise these as specifically *Dionysian,* in the primary sense of their association with a powerful inspiration from the heart of nature which actuates the poet. . . . The Dionysian phenomenon is originally an incursion of barbarism; Rome here, threatened by such an incursion, is in apt contrast an *Apollonian* conception. The acceptance of these terms would at least remove such inconvenient words as 'idealism' from the description.

Furthermore, the destruction and regeneration of Rome already noticed in the play constitute a tragic vision according to Nietzsche's description of this. Now this process takes place in later tragedies, but with a difference: in *King Lear* and *Othello* it is in the soul of the protagonist that destruction and rebirth take place; in *Titus Andronicus* the tragic conception is less humanised and in a sense the city is the real protagonist of the drama. A vision of that which, in the words of Shelley's *Hellas,* 'builds itself' again 'impregnably' from apparent 'wreck', recreates its identity through 'tragic' disintegration, by the creative power in its own essence, is precisely the idea of Dionysus preached by the author of *The Birth of Tragedy*. Shakespeare's Rome is a 'tragic civilisation'. (pp. 286-87)

[The tragedy of *Titus Andronicus*] is created through, or melts into, a strangely liquid emotionalism—the pervasive water-images should be noted—a rich phantasmagoria of the passional element, luxuriating, dissolving and sublimating pain and the knowledge of error. There is effective emotional release and a simultaneous failure to attain the artistic level of high tragedy, which makes somewhat different use of the emotions of 'pity' and 'terror'. This will become clear by imagining a phrase such as Lear's 'No, I'll not weep' transferred to Titus's lament (III. i). The lack of tragic heightening at this point (lack of 'emotional complexity') is perhaps the main justification for sensing an inherent weakness of development later.

Tragedy is essentially a representation of man's encounter with impersonal, vast, often explicitly cosmic powers, interlocking their sway with his purposes, and of the catastrophes resulting from such conflicts, thus revealed in a wider significance. Though in *Titus Andronicus* interest is in reality centred in the opposition of different impersonal forces the persons of the play, though not highly individualised, are not unimpressive. Many, it has been observed, have primarily a symbolic function; others, like the protagonist, are scarcely symbolic in any sense. It might be noted further that the 'symbolic' persons tend to disappear from the action around the crisis in Act II: this is partly explained by a certain dramatic reduction, and partly by the suggested necessity of the failure of the 'ideal'

in a tragic world. In the scenes following, there are moving pictures of the remnant of a tragic family, concluding with Titus's pose as a cook [V. iii. 26]. The reduction of interests to the domestic and cosmic elements is paralleled in *King Lear*. But the imperial and communal reference is not lost: the presence of the tribune, Marcus—this is perhaps his main function—is an effective reminder of it, and there are other allusions. Titus Andronicus himself, the agent and principal victim of the dissolution, is exquisitely conceived, in the mould of later Shakespearian tragic heroes. An old man, yet a Titan in his sorrows, he has dignity and piety at his worst. . . . He does not, indeed, personally attain to a full and perfect regeneration, but he cannot be denied tragic status.

Nor will it be possible, in the future, to deny tragic meaning to the play. The revelation of the central scenes is abysmal: a vision of suffering and evil the content of which may be allowed to be more appalling than that of any other tragedy, yet poetical coherence and truth are not thus denied. As in other tragedies the power of evil is swiftly brought to nothing. The exceptional quality of the play has indeed been somewhat exaggerated. The 'horrors', to which objection is taken, strictly speaking number only three events, or at most four, two of which are of subsidiary importance. They are, however, atmospherically enforced, suffered to play upon the imagination, that is, though not—let producers note—upon the nerves, which is an essentially modern refinement of consciousness. As a result of this they become isolated emotional crises, whereas the horrors of *Othello* and *King Lear* serve mainly for contrast as parts of a complex pattern. As effects, they belong to the thaumaturgic traditions of popular drama; they are clumsy symbolisms in an outdated mode, scarcely essential to a mature tragic conception. . . . But it is unwise to rely unduly on contemporary attitudes to life: the play's relation of horror and disintegration to the now familiar tendency to evade the responsibility of a course of imaginative action is a palpable hit in return. Tragedy will not be understood in terms of modern thought until it is written in terms of modern experience. In the meantime, it will be wiser to allow for the range and depth of a nobler conception of life in Shakespeare's work. (pp. 287-89)

> *Alan Sommers, "'Wilderness of Tigers': Structure and Symbolism in 'Titus Andronicus'," in* Essays in Criticism, *Vol. X, No. 3, July, 1960, pp. 275-89.*

IRVING RIBNER   (essay date 1960)

[*Ribner examines the factors in* Titus Andronicus *that contribute to the tragic downfall of the play's protagonist. According to Ribner, Titus represents Shakespeare's "prototype of erring humanity," a tragic hero whose virtues are eventually warped through self-deception and pride and whose behavior guarantees his own destruction. Ribner discusses in detail Titus's three tragic errors: the sacrifice of Alarbus, the violation of Lavinia's betrothal to Bassianus, and the slaying of his son Mutius. He also maintains that Shakespeare's Christian audiences would have condemned Titus's acts of justice as contradicting the greater ideal of Christian mercy. For additional commentary on the tragic design in* Titus Andronicus, *see the excerpts by H. B. Charlton (1946-47), Eugene M. Waith (1955), Alan Sommers (1960), A. C. Hamilton (1967), James L. Calderwood (1971), and D. J. Palmer (1972). Also, for an examination of the play's underlying concept of Elizabethan justice and Christian retribution, see the excerpt by Ronald Broude (1979).*]

In terms of dramatic craftsmanship alone, *Titus Andronicus* is superior to *The Spanish Tragedy*. It does not have the divided action of Kyd's play, with the ghost of Andrea at the beginning calling for revenge and then quite forgotten while the action shifts to Hieronimo and his scarcely related affairs. In spite of its obvious shortcomings, *Titus Andronicus* in poetry and in characterization is superior to any play written before it. This usually has been recognized, but *Titus Andronicus* has been called a failure because 'it lacks a sense of morality, seriousness and consistency'. But it is the very sense of morality and the serious purpose with which Shakespeare approached his crude unpalatable material which, above all else, make *Titus Andronicus* so much greater than *The Spanish Tragedy*.

Shakespeare shaped what he found in his source to fit the general pattern of the Kydian revenge play, but he made significant changes from his source, and these tend to make *Titus Andronicus* somewhat different from *The Spanish Tragedy*. Shakespeare's play is profoundly influenced, moreover, by his reading of Ovid, not only by the story of Philomela which he borrowed, but by the entire *Metamorphoses,* with its emphasis upon the transformation of man into beast through excess of passion. This transformation of Titus is set within a specific moral system which the play in its totality affirms. (pp. 16-17)

[Shakespeare's] most important innovation is in his conception of the principal characters and their relations to one another. Titus Andronicus is a commanding figure. He is a great and initially virtuous man, the first of Shakespeare's heroic figures whose very virtues are the source of their sins. In many ways he is a forerunner of Coriolanus. Titus embodies all the ancient Roman virtues: 'A nobler man, a braver warrior, / Lives not this day within the city walls' [I. i. 25-6]. He has given his life and his sons unselfishly in the cause of his country. He might now be emperor, but he respects hereditary right and chooses Saturninus instead. He is stern and he is proud, the master of his family, the last of the ancient Romans.

Titus is a superman, but being human he must, like all men, face the forces of evil in the world. In his encounter with evil Titus fails. He rejects the way of redemption which is offered him in the choral commentary of his brother, Marcus, and he moves towards inevitable damnation. By the life journey of his hero, Shakespeare explores in imaginative terms the universal way of damnation, for Titus becomes a prototype of erring humanity. In this early tragedy Shakespeare already is trying to shape his tragic hero as a symbol of mankind, and in the description of his fall to pose not so much the problem of an individual as that of humanity at large. (p. 17)

Although Shakespeare makes his audience acutely aware of the hero's blindness, he causes them also to hope to the very end that he will learn the way of redemption before it is too late. So as not entirely to alienate his audience from Titus, while he depicts the moral degeneration which will lead to the final crime against nature, Shakespeare uses the pathos of Lavinia and the *naïveté* of Titus' grandchild. In the source Titus kills the emperor, but Shakespeare spares his hero the additional taint of regicide. The kissing of the dead body of Titus is another such attempt to win sympathy for him, crude as it may be, for the audience is invited to participate emotionally in the sorrow of his death.

Shakespeare tries also to place the fall of Titus within a larger framework in which evil too is destroyed, so that the audience, while lamenting the damnation of one soul, may have a renewed awareness of the perfection of God's order and of the operation of justice in the world. Marcus points out the path which Titus might have taken, and Lucius brings about a reconciliation when the forces both of good and evil lie dead upon the stage and the world is ready for rebirth. In the portrait of the degeneration and damnation of a noble figure because of weaknesses which spring from those very traits in him which the audience admires, and in the reconciliation which comes from the destruction of evil in spite of his fall, we have a formula for tragedy which postulates the reality of evil, man's free moral choice in spite of it, and divine justice in a harmonious moral order.

In *Titus Andronicus* the forces of good and evil are neatly arranged against one another. Of all the evil characters, Aaron is not only the most fully developed but also the manipulator of the evil action, the specific author of Titus' misfortunes. He may be regarded as a symbol of evil itself. He is black, the traditional colour of the devil (and more specifically of lechery), and like the devil he can never know remorse or penance. He remains defiant to the very end. . . . Shakespeare's contemporaries commonly believed that the devil had power to infuse himself into the bodies of men and govern their actions. The devil may be tortured as Aaron is, but he can never be penitent, a suggestion Shakespeare was further to develop in Iago. As a dramatic embodiment of a specific vice, the lechery which governs Tamora, Aaron affords the first clear example of the symbolic use of character which is to be so marked a feature of the great plays of Shakespeare's maturity. Evil in *Titus Andronicus* is already envisaged as a motiveless force which operates through deception, and Shakespeare has learned to express its mode of operation in the appearance and action of a dramatic character.

Evil is always present in the world, but Titus brings it upon himself. To make this clear Shakespeare created the incidents of the first act, in which Titus gives himself to evil by three specific deeds: the sacrifice of Alarbus, the violation of Lavinia's betrothal to Bassianus, and the slaying of Mutius. Each of these acts proceeds out of a virtue corrupted into vice.

The ancient Roman code demanded that a captive enemy be sacrificed to appease the souls of those who have died in battle. There is a stern virtue in Titus' respect for this decree, a reverence for a primitive type of justice. There is no rancour in his reply to Tamora:

> Patient yourself, madam, and pardon me.
> These are their brethren, whom you Goths beheld
> Alive and dead, and for their brethren slain
> Religiously they ask a sacrifice:
> To this your son is mark'd, and die he must,
> To appease their groaning shadows that are gone.
> [I. i. 121-26]

Allegiance to the ancient ideal of justice, however, blinds Titus to the greater good of mercy. Shakespeare's audience saw the play not in terms of a Roman morality but in terms of an Elizabethan one which upheld mercy as a greater ideal than justice, and which would have agreed entirely with Tamora's argument:

> But must my sons be slaughter'd in the streets,
> For valiant doings in their country's cause?
> O, if to fight for king and commonweal
> Were piety in thine, it is in these. . . .
> Wilt thou draw near the nature of the gods?
> Draw near them then in being merciful:
> Sweet mercy is nobility's true badge.
> [I. i. 112-19]

Shakespeare poses the problem which is to occupy him in *The Merchant of Venice* and *Measure for Measure:* the relation of mercy to justice. Titus, like a later Shylock or Angelo, makes a wrong moral choice; his sin is in adherence to a Roman code of justice to the dead, in spite of the pleas of a Christian ideal of mercy and of the Renaissance creed that those who fight bravely for their country must be honoured even in defeat.

Elizabethans generally would have approved of Titus' refusal of the throne and of his choice of Saturninus over Bassianus, for he is the elder brother who claims the throne by just and lawful succession. There is virtue also in the intense family pride of Titus and in his loyalty to his emperor. It is only fitting that his daughter be a queen, and when Saturninus claims Lavinia as his bride, Titus readily agrees to the union as proper. Further, his emperor wills it, and the loyal subject must obey. This loyalty, this famly pride, this respect for his own position and merits, and the sense of the honour which his emperor is offering him cause him to forget that Lavinia has already been betrothed to another. A betrothal in Elizabethan England was a binding contract with all of the force of law; to break it was to violate a woman's honour. Shakespeare's audience would have sided fully with the sons of Titus in their opposition to his decree. Similarly, an Elizabethan audience would have respected the position of Titus as master of his household; to his sons his word must be law, and for them to oppose him unthinkable. What Mutius stands for, however, is his sister's honour, and when Titus murders his son for his opposition, he is carrying the authority of the father to an excess in defiance of justice, honour and reason.

All of Titus' crimes proceed from perversions of virtuous instincts; in each instance Titus makes a wrong moral choice in which he sacrifices the greater good for the lesser one. This is a conventional definition of evil, which in Christian terms involved a blinding by pride which might cause a man to accept a lesser finite good rather than the greater infinite good of God's will. By his attempt to be a God, Titus violates the law of God.

Titus sins in the first act. In acts two and three we see Titus made to suffer by the evil forces which his own sins have unleashed upon him. By the second scene of the third act, Titus has begun to plot his revenge, and the rest of the play is concerned with its execution. This revenge is a rejection of the Christian way of redemption which called for a submission to the will of God in faith that God would protect man from evil, reward the virtuous and punish the guilty. The madness of Titus symbolizes the defect of reason which makes it impossible for him to see the Christian way out of his difficulties. Marcus counsels him, 'But yet let reason govern thy lament' [III. i. 218]. Reason here would mean an attuning of human will to divine will, with faith in the perfection of God's harmonious order. Titus, however, shoots arrows in defiance of the Gods. His damnation is inevitable.

In spite of the damnation of Titus, the audience is left not with a feeling of despair, but with a renewed acceptance of divine order and purpose. This feeling of reconciliation is supported by the destruction of evil, which in spite of Titus' damnation vindicates divine justice. The audience participates emotionally in the relief from suffering which comes to Lavinia and Titus, and in the promise of a new day for Rome with the coming of Lucius and his crowning as emperor:

> Thanks, gentle Romans: may I govern so,
> To heal Rome's harms, and wipe away her woe!
> [V. iii. 147-48]

The Department of Rare Books and Special Collections, The University of Michigan Library.

In spite of the crudity of style and the Senecan horrors which alienate modern readers, there is a controlling idea of tragedy behind *Titus Andronicus,* a conception of how evil operates in the world and may cause the destruction of a virtuous man by his own moral choice. This wrong moral choice is shown as the product of self-deception and pride, an adherence to an ideal of virtue which is not virtue at all. That evil operated through deception, disguised as good, is a basic Christian notion, going back to the story of Eve's seduction in the garden of Eden. It was at the heart of the medieval morality play, and Shakespeare was to use it again and again, most notably in *Othello.*

Shakespeare in *Titus Andronicus* already conceived of tragedy as an examination of man's relation to the forces of evil in the world, and he altered both his prose source and the dramatic tradition of the Kydian revenge play so that he might express some such relation in a meaningful complex of events. Shakespeare was not yet a great dramatist when he wrote *Titus Andronicus,* but he had a greater awareness of the potentialities of tragedy than usually has been allowed him. (pp. 18-22)

Irving Ribner, ''Senecan Beginnings: 'Titus Andronicus', 'Richard III', 'Romeo and Juliet','' in his Pat-

terns in Shakespearian Tragedy, *Methuen & Co. Ltd.,*
*1960, pp. 14-35.**

A. C. HAMILTON   (essay date 1967)

[*Hamilton considers* Titus Andronicus *the "archetype" of Shake-*
speare's later tragedies, and he maintains that the play is more
than an early, immature work or an imitation of Thomas Kyd's
The Spanish Tragedy; *instead, he characterizes it as a "very*
ambitious tragedy" in which Shakespeare combined elements from
Senecan and medieval morality dramas with the "major literary
tradition in Ovid." Like Eugene M. Waith (1955), Hamilton ex-
amines the manner in which Shakespeare incorporated elements
from Ovid's Metamorphoses, *specifically the myth of the world's*
fall from the golden to the iron age signified by the flight of
Astraea, the goddess of justice, from earth. But Hamilton dis-
agrees with Waith's assessment that the "cultured style" and
violent content of Ovid's work fail when transformed into the
dramatic structure of Titus; *instead, he argues that Shakespeare*
gave dramatic reality and tragic form to Ovid's myth. Hamilton
then discusses the methods Shakespeare adopted to intensify the
significance of the characters in Titus *and to heighten the play's*
tragic effect. For a similar interpretation of Shakespeare's use of
Ovid, see the excerpt by D. J. Palmer (1972).]

A critical effort to understand Shakespeare's first experiment
in tragedy, and its place among his early plays, may not ignore
dissatisfaction with the play. *Titus Andronicus* has always provoked strong response. Critics have accepted it grudgingly, if
at all, into the canon of Shakespeare's plays. (p. 63)

The play's apparent failure as a Shakespearean tragedy—that
is, our failure to accept it as such—calls for excuse and explanation. One excuse maintains that Shakespeare was too young
to do better. . . . At the same time, we may infer as easily
that his first tragedy would be deliberately conceived and executed. Its *excess,* characteristic of all of Shakespeare's early
work, may be a sign of strength, not of weakness. An explanation for the play's failure has been found in the age itself:
when we cannot accommodate ourselves to a work, we are
tempted to accommodate it to some contemporary setting. The
excessive violence of its plot has been blamed on the cult of
Seneca or on the native tradition of the Tragedy of Blood seen
in Kyd's *Spanish Tragedy.* Far from being a simple Senecan
exercise, however, the play goes far beyond Seneca in its
violence. (p. 65)

The excessive artifice of its style has been blamed on the
Elizabethan cult of Ovid. Eugene M. Waith believes that the
cool, detached, and florid rhetoric suitable in the *Metamor-*
phoses remains intractable in drama: "We have the description
which almost transforms Lavinia, but in the presence of live
actors the poetry cannot perform the necessary magic. The
action frustrates, rather than re-enforces, the operation of the
poetry" [see excerpt above, 1955]. This explanation is tempting. Yet Shakespeare challenges Ovid deliberately. . . . Both
in the cultured style and in the violence rendered through the
style Shakespeare seeks to overgo Ovid. In imitating him, he
would not be unaware of the dramatic problems involved, though
the nature and degree of his success must be analyzed.

Titus Andronicus is a very ambitious tragedy. Even on the
technical level, it displays a mastery of stage resources. It is
comprehensive in combining earlier traditions of tragedy—both
the native morality plays and Seneca—with the major literary
tradition in Ovid. . . . Consequently, it shows an accomplishment that is distinctively Shakespearean, being both popular
and literary, a stage play and a work of literature. While its

accomplishment may be demonstrated, its conception is even
more significant: the play reveals Shakespeare's architectonic
skill. . . . It foreshadows the later tragedies because it is their
archetype. Instead of being dismissed as an immature tragedy
written for its age, it deserves to be approached as a central
and seminal play in the canon of Shakespeare's works.

The Elizabethans did not share our need to offer excuse and
explanation for the play. In the *Induction* to *Bartholomew Fair*
[see excerpt above, 1614], Jonson records their regard for it,
with *The Spanish Tragedy,* as "the best playes." We cannot
dismiss their judgment simply as a taste for violence that could
be glutted indifferently by its excessive horrors or by a public
execution. Surely it is no historical accident that Shakespeare's
most popular play imitates *Thyestes,* Seneca's most popular
play, which in turn imitates the most popular theme of Greek
tragedy, the boiling and eating of Pelops. Shakespeare, too,
tells the story of a father who devours his own sons. Titus
sacrifices twenty-two of them for the sake of honor, and, by
slaying Tamora's son, he brings her revenge upon those remaining. In defense of his honor he slays one son himself and
rejects the rest. He plans the hunt that brings Lavinia's rape
and finds the note that condemns two of his sons to death.
Lucius alone escapes to join his father's enemy, the Goths—
a dramatically awkward point, as critics have noted, but thematically correct, since he stands opposed to his father from
the beginning.

Nothing more than sure dramatic instinct may have led Shakespeare to the story of Pelops. Yet his choice of Saturninus as
the name of the emperor whose state the play projects suggests
some awareness of the myth. In Ovid the story of Philomel,
which Shakespeare uses, follows that of Tantalus' serving his
son Pelops to the gods. That story in turn would lead him to
the story of Saturn in Ovid's first book. Renaissance iconog-
raphy shows Saturn devouring his child. His wife is Rhea, the
earth, and in the play Saturninus' wife eats her children, "Like
to the earth, swallow[ing] her own increase" [V. ii. 191]. Since
the myth of Saturn was interpreted in the Renaissance as an
allegory of the Fall, perhaps its choice is inevitable for Shakespeare's first tragedy. (pp. 66-8)

Shakespeare's reason for turning to Ovid becomes clear when
Titus reads "the tragic tale of Philomel / [That] treats of Tereus' treason and his rape" [IV. i. 47-8]. "See, see!" he cries,
as he reads the Sixth Book of the *Metamorphoses:*

Ay, such a place there is where we did hunt—
O, had we never, never hunted there!—
Pattern'd by that the poet here describes,
By nature made for murders and for rapes.

[IV. i. 55-8]

To Ovid's pattern Shakespeare gives dramatic reality. That
reality is almost greater than Titus can bear. When he confronts
his mutilated daughter, he says:

Had I but seen thy picture in this plight,
It would have madded me; what shall I do
Now I behold thy lively body so?

[III. i. 103-05]

Ovid distances Philomel from us as a picture, shielding her
reality through the sophistication of his art. Shakespeare shows
Lavinia in her indescribable reality: "Now I behold thy lively
body *so.*" The play provides no release from reality through
metamorphosis. When Lucius falls prostrate on seeing Lavinia,
Titus tells him (and us): "Faint-hearted boy, arise, and *look*

upon her'' [III. i. 65]. That reality may be greater than we can bear. . . . The play becomes a test of how much reality the tragic genre can contain.

The story of Lavinia shows Shakespeare's use of Ovid in giving tragic form to the tale of Philomel. The rape of Lavinia, which is carried out near a pit, suggests the ancient ritual in which Pluto, the son of Saturn, ravishes Persephone and takes her to the underworld. The similarity is the more striking since Demetrius, a ''son'' of Saturninus, asserts that he is in hell through lust for Lavinia: ''Per Styga, per manes vehor'' [II. i. 135]. Later he and his brother are named ''a pair of cursed hellhounds'' [V. ii. 144]. Lavinia is central to the play, not merely as the instrument through which Tamora seeks revenge against Titus, but as a tragic symbol. Hailed at the beginning as ''Gracious Lavinia, Rome's rich ornament'' [I. i. 52], she is chosen by the emperor as ''Rome's royal mistress'' [I. i. 241]. By mutilating her, Tamora's sons offend against Nature herself, as Pluto does by raping Persephone. . . . Her ''martyred'' and ''mangled'' body symbolizes that fallen Nature which the tragedy projects. His opening words to her as ''the cordial of mine age'' and his prayer that she ''outlive thy father's days, / And fame's eternal date, for virtue's praise!'' [I. i. 166-68] point with heavy irony to the tragic action through which her shame becomes his sorrow. At the end he must slay her as a scapegoat for his sorrow. Her ''descent into hell'' is the vehicle for the tragic action.

More specifically, Ovid provides Shakespeare with the pattern for his tragedy. The first book of the *Metamorphoses* tells how the overthrow of Saturn brings the fall from the golden to the iron age. When Astraea, the goddess of Justice and last of the immortals, leaves the earth, the giants challenge the gods. Lycaon serves Jove a banquet of human flesh; in his anger Jove overwhelms the land with the sea. In the tragic world of Shakespeare's play, Saturninus, as his name suggests, inverts the golden age of Saturn when the goddess Astraea leaves the earth. Titus laments: ''Terras Astraea reliquit'' [IV. iii. 4]. Yet he himself banishes her when he refuses to weigh Bassianus' merit against Saturninus' right and, ironically, chooses the latter in the hope that he will ''ripen justice'' [I. i. 227]. Upon being denied justice, Bassianus ''rapes'' his ''true betrothed love'' [I. i. 406] according to the narrow rule that

> Suum cuique is our Roman justice:
> This prince in justice seizeth but his own.
>
> [I. i. 280-81]

The final downward step comes when Chiron and Demetrius vow to rape Lavinia ''sit fas aut nefas'' [II. i. 133].

Since Justice has left the earth, desire for revenge governs the action: Tamora seeks revenge against all the Andronici; Titus against her; Saturninus against him and Marcus; and Lucius against the Romans. Further, the desire for revenge is often added to motivate actions doubly: in the forest Tamora arouses her sons to revenge, even though their plot to murder Bassianus has already been laid. . . . Though Lucius has already agreed to come to his father's house, for her revenge Tamora persuades Titus to invite him. The cycle permits no escape, and the play ends, as it began, with plans for revenge. In this world without Justice, the action culminates in cannibalism, which, in Ovid, brings Jove's curse upon the earth. Yet, unlike the giants who challenge the gods, Titus cannot bear the wrongs he suffers:

> Marcus, we are but shrubs, no cedars we,
> No big-bon'd men fram'd of the Cyclops' size;
> But metal, Marcus, steel to the very back,
> Yet wrung with wrongs more than our backs can bear.
>
> [IV. iii. 45-8]

He describes himself as the earth flooded with Lavinia's tears . . . :

> I am the sea; hark how her sighs do blow.
> She is the weeping welkin, I the earth;
> Then must my sea be moved with her sighs;
> Then must my earth with her continual tears
> Become a deluge, overflow'd and drown'd.
>
> [III. i. 225-29]

In him we see the last stage of the Fall in Ovid, the earth overwhelmed by the sea. (pp. 70-2)

The scope of the play's action as a tragedy is outlined in the first act. As the play opens, Titus is hailed as

> Patron of virtue, Rome's best champion,
> Successful in the battles that he fights,
> With honour and with fortune . . . return'd.
>
> [I. i. 65-7]

From this pinnacle he first overreaches himself by agreeing to his sons' demands that Tamora's son be sacrificed. . . . Her reproof, ''O cruel, irreligious piety!'' [I. i. 130], marks his descent from one who was ''surnamed Pius'' [I. i. 23]. He further offends justice when the people choose him as their candidate in the contest for the throne, ''For many good and great deserts to Rome'' [I. i. 24]. Bassianus also claims the throne on grounds of desert: ''. . . let desert in pure election shine; / And, Romans, fight for freedom in your choice'' [I. i. 16-17]. Saturninus, on the other hand, claiming the throne in terms of birthright, calls repeatedly for force to support his cause. When Titus elects Saturninus, he rejects justice and cancels the honor due him through desert. Finally, in killing his own son in defense of his honor, he commits an act of injustice, as Lucius charges. . . . Consequently, in refusing his slain son proper burial, he becomes guilty of impiety. . . . His first act brings Tamora's curse upon himself and his family; the second unwittingly brings the emperor's curse; and the last directly offends the gods. He destroys the bonds of family by slaying his own son, the laws of society by denying Lavinia's lawful betrothal to Bassianus, the order of the state by denying the Romans ''pure election . . . And . . . freedom in . . . choice,'' . . . and divine laws, like Creon, by refusing burial to the dead. At the beginning, crowned with the highest honors, he sees Tamora kneeling before him; near the end of the first act, she enters ''aloft'' . . . with the emperor, and he walks alone, brooding upon his fall. . . . By the end of the first act, Shakespeare has, like Chaucer, told the story

> Of hym that stood in greet prosperitee,
> And is yfallen out of heigh degree
> Into myserie, and endeth wrecchedly.
>
> [*Prologue* to *The Monk's Tale*, ll. 1975-77]
>
> (pp. 75-6)

In the next four acts Shakespeare is on his own, with little in earlier or contemporary practice to guide him. His method intensifies the significance of the hero's fall through rhetorical elaboration and expands it through metaphor. . . . To keep his violence sweet, Shakespeare formalizes both his language and the action of his play. The tragic ''affects'' are focused upon one central question that becomes the ''cause'' of the tragedy.

> O, why should nature build so foul a den,
> Unless the gods delight in tragedies?
>
> [IV. i. 59-60]

Not only do language and action become a metaphor of the play, the play itself—or rather, the world that it reveals—becomes a metaphor of that "cause." (p. 77)

In the beginning, though Titus has sacrificed nearly all his sons for the sake of honor and slays another without remorse, "For two and twenty sons" he "never wept" [III. i. 10]. After his fall, when two more of his sons are condemned to death, he weeps "that never wept before" [III. i. 25]. The sight of his mutilated daughter inflicts his next sorrow. . . . When his grief breaks out, it is registered in one word—a simple change from present to past tense:

It *was* my dear, and he that wounded her
Hath hurt me more than had he kill'd me dead.

[II. i. 91-2]

Now he sees himself standing

as one upon a rock,
Environ'd with a wilderness of sea,
Who marks the waxing tide grow wave by wave,
Expecting ever when some envious surge
Will in his brinish bowels swallow him.

[III. i. 93-7]

It would not seem possible to develop further the image of a man's grief.

Yet Shakespeare intensifies that image in two great dramatic moments. As Titus catalogs the griefs that overwhelm him, he turns suddenly from himself to Lavinia:

Look, Marcus! Ah, son Lucius, look on her!
When I did name her brothers, then fresh tears
Stood on her cheeks, as doth the honey dew
Upon a gath'red lily almost withered.

[III. i. 110-13]

At this turning point in the play, her tears teach him that his sons are innocent: ". . . they would not do so foul a deed; / Witness the sorrow that their sister makes" [III. i. 118-19]. She teaches Titus and the others again to weep, and Titus gathers them all in "a sympathy of woe" [III. i. 148]. The further shock of losing his hand now overwhelms him:

I am the sea; hark how her sighs do blow.
She is the weeping welkin, I the earth;
Then must my sea be moved with her sighs;
Then must my earth with her continual tears
Become a deluge, overflow'd and drown'd.

[III. i. 225-29]

Here Titus and nature are identified. The inner chaos of his nature, signified by "a wilderness of sea" [III. i. 94] overwhelming the land, expresses the chaos of the outer world. . . . By using the allegorical equation of the sea with the perturbations of the soul, Shakespeare shows man absorbed by nature.

The second great dramatic moment comes after the shock of his condemned sons' deaths, when Titus is urged by Marcus to storm. Instead he remains silent, collapses into mad laughter, and then says quietly:

I have not another tear to shed;
Besides, this sorrow is an enemy,
And would usurp upon my wat'ry eyes
And make them blind with tributary tears.

[III. i. 266-69]

Now in a state beyond grief, he awaits revenge. At the end, with revenge assured, he slays Lavinia, "for whom my tears have made me blind" [V. iii. 49].

Through such control over language, Shakespeare controls the horror that the play arouses. . . . In the most shocking scene in Shakespeare's play, Act V, Scene ii, we watch Titus cut the throats of Tamora's sons while Lavinia holds the vessel to receive their blood. Out of context it may appear the crude work of an inexperienced dramatist catering to a debased public taste for the merely horrific. In the dramatic context, however, it is not murder that we witness, not even personal revenge, but a solemn sacrifice. Tamora's sons have offended not alone against the Andronici but also, as we are told, against Nature herself. . . . [Titus's] references to Lavinia as Philomel and to himself as Progne and to the banquet as "More stern and bloody than the Centaurs' feast" [V. ii. 203] further thrust the event into an enveloping framework of myth. His victims are no longer Tamora's sons; their disguise reveals them for what they are: Revenge's sons, Murder and Rape. . . . Such control does not mitigate the horror; it intensifies it.

The horror is turned inward to point to the agony framed in the question:

O, why should nature build so foul a den,
Unless the gods delight in tragedies?

[IV. i. 59-60]

Chaucer may have suggested to Shakespeare this link between the rape of Philomel and the problem of evil in the opening lines of his *Legend of Philomela*. The dark forest with the pit at the center becomes the dramatic symbol upon which the whole play turns and through which Shakespeare raises the second tragic "affect" of admiration or wonder.

In the opening scene of the play, a gaping tomb dominates the action, addressed by Titus as

O sacred receptacle of my joys,
Sweet cell of virtue and nobility.

[I. i. 92-3]

Its place is taken in the second act, after Titus' downfall, by the forest, which is described by Aaron, in Spenserian terms, as a place "Fitted by kind for rape and villainy" [II. i. 116], "ruthless, dreadful, deaf, and dull" [II. i. 128], "shadowed from heaven's eye" [II. i. 130], where Tamora's sons may rape Lavinia. . . . The forest with the pit as its center stands for a vision of a destroyed and destroying Nature that only tragedy dare face. (pp. 78-82)

Within this Nature, the progress of human life becomes a descent into hell. The tragic world becomes a diabolical mirror that reflects our world in inverted pastoral terms. For this reason the play parodies Virgil's fourth eclogue: in place of the age of gold that heralds a new birth of peace, with the earth pouring out her fruits and all beasts living in concord, it shows the age of Saturninus, where Tamora uses gold for revenge against the Andronici, and Rome becomes "a wilderness of tigers" [III. i. 54]. . . . In this infernal world, the air is the sighs of the suffering, water is their tears, and the earth is a blood-drinking pit. (pp. 82-3)

Yet not all is evil. The Messenger who brings Titus his hand and his sons' heads pities him "More than remembrance of my father's death" [III. i. 240]. Again, Titus' rise partly balances Tamora's descent into evil. At the beginning, as the loving mother, she pleads for her son's life. Later she plays the lustful Semiramis [II. i. 22] with Aaron. When she rouses her sons to slay Bassianus, she becomes herself. Lavinia cries: "Ay, come, Semiramis—nay, barbarous Tamora" [II. iii. 118]. When Tamora denies Lavinia's plea to be killed, she forgoes all humanity: "No grace? no womanhood? Ah, beastly creature" [II. iii. 182]. Finally she becomes an abstraction, Revenge itself.

Titus, on the other hand, appears most inhuman at the beginning, when he sacrifices his children for the sake of honor. Later, he sacrifices his hand for his sons' lives. Further, in his frenzy of grief he confesses his fault:

> Ah, Rome! Well, well, I made thee miserable
> What time I threw the people's suffrages
> On him that thus doth tyrannize o'er me.
>
> [IV. iii. 18-20]

Marcus calls upon the heavens to revenge Titus, who is "so just that he will not revenge" [IV. i. 128]. At Publius' offer of Revenge, Titus seeks Justice instead [IV. iii. 37-51]; in the same scene, he shoots his arrows to the gods while Marcus shoots his into the court. While others seek revenge, he seeks justice, until Revenge comes to him. Finally, he appears as the loving grandfather to the young Lucius [V. iii. 160-75]. Further, at the end, unlike Titus at the beginning, Marcus and Lucius submit themselves to the will of the Romans. Frances Yates suggests that "The apotheosis of Lucius at the end of the play . . . represents the Return of the Virgin—the return of the just empire and the golden age" [see Additional Bibliography]. Her claim may seem excessive, and yet the choice of Lucius, who was "the first king of the Britains that received the faith of Jesus Christ," according to Holinshed, would seem deliberate. Marcus and Lucius promise "to knit . . . / These broken limbs again into one body" [V. iii. 70-2], as the gods restored the body of Pelops. (pp. 84-5)

> A. C. Hamilton, "The Early Tragedy: 'Titus Andronicus'," in his The Early Shakespeare, The Huntington Library, 1967, pp. 63-89.

LARRY S. CHAMPION   (essay date 1971)

[Champion argues that the tragic perspective of Titus Andronicus—what he describes as the "touchstone to the artistry of the dramatist's later work"—is created primarily through the development of the protagonist Titus and Shakespeare's manipulation of the audience's attitude toward that character, which in turn establishes "an anticipation for the pattern of the action." Yet, Champion maintains that Shakespeare ultimately confounds his audience's expectations by failing to grant Titus the knowledge necessary to a tragic hero and, more importantly, necessary to the structure of his play. Champion lists several ways in which Shakespeare could have ended Titus's struggles, all of which he claims would have worked within the play's structure. For Champion, the conclusion Shakespeare did provide is the very one the play will not support: Titus's emergence as a sophisticated revenger ready to outwit his adversaries. Champion identifies the problem in Titus's lack of "philosophic depth," which he attributes to Shakespeare's choice of an external narrative approach to developing his character, allowing such figures as Marcus and Lucius to define Titus's personality rather than suggesting important psychological traits through the effective use of soliloquies and asides. Both H. B. Charlton (1946-47) and Wolfgang H. Clemen (1951) also criticized Shakespeare's portrait of Titus, as well as the play's characterization in general. For other commentary on the protagonist's character, see the excerpts by H. Bellyse Baildon (1904), Eugene M. Waith (1955), Alan Sommers (1960), and Irving Ribner (1960).]

Analysis of Titus Andronicus would be largely an exercise in futility did it not provide a base from which to measure and evaluate the nature of Shakespeare's growth as a tragic playwright. (p. 14)

For, whether Shakespeare is responsible for all, part, or none of this play, the tragic perspective—the nature of the protagonist and his development and the structural devices by which to control the spectator's attitude toward him and by which to establish an anticipation for the pattern of the action—is a touchstone to the artistry of the dramatist's later work.

Most significant is the establishment in the initial scene of a potentially powerful tragic protagonist. Specifically, the juxtaposition in Act I of Titus' magnitude and heroism (as visualized in the words of others and in his posture as conquering hero) with his precipitous actions and bestial fury quite logically establishes the thematic anticipation of a great man, flawed to the core, whose implacable pride has provoked disastrous error and who, in the subsequent scenes, must be expected to endure a spiritual wheel of fire. This concept of character, along with the structural devices which control the spectators' attitude, need not be explained away as unworthy of a fledgling Shakespeare. To be sure, the design is executed only in part, the full potential of the protagonist never realized. But as D. A. Stauffer has remarked, the play is a "storehouse of themes and episodes and attitudes and images and situations which Shakespeare later was to develop" [see Additional Bibliography]. (pp. 14-15)

Certainly Shakespeare consciously underscores Titus' merits at the outset. Marcus, the Captain, Lavinia, the Tribunes—all are direct pointers to guide and control the spectators' initial response. . . . That Marcus and "the people of Rome" have selected Titus to stand as a candidate for "the empery" is attestation to their regard. When he modestly refuses the honor and factionalism bursts forth again between Saturninus and Bassianus, that the citizens would readily accept Titus' word for selecting the next ruler ("To gratify . . . / And gratulate his safe return to Rome" [I. i. 221-22] suggests virtual idolatry.

Yet, directly in the face of what others have said about him, Titus' actions in the first act reflect a man who is furiously proud and stubborn beyond measure. The spectator can only be disturbed by the hero's implacable determination to sacrifice Alarbus. . . . Indeed, Shakespeare is at some pain to focus the worst light of this situation on Titus. For one thing, the human sacrifice is never justified; the occasional comments that this is a "sacrifice of expiation" . . . simply fail to provide the rationale so distinctly needed when the action has been openly challenged; no god's name is invoked, no spiritual efficacy described. For another thing, Titus agrees to the sacrifice in the face of a description which flashes its most gruesome and inhuman aspects. Lucius requests his father to "Give [him] the proudest prisoner" so that he "may hew his limbs, and on a pile . . . sacrifice his flesh" [I. i. 96-8]. . . . Even more emphatically, Titus' determination to proceed with the ritual death assumes cruelty when juxtaposed with Tamora's impassioned pleas that her son be spared:

> [R]ue the tears I shed,
> A mother's tears in passion for her son; . . .
> Wilt thou draw near the nature of the gods?
> Draw near them in being merciful.
>
> [I. i. 105-06, 117-18]

In effect, it is she who, invoking the names both of mother and gods, momentarily captures the spectator's emotional fancy.

If Titus' pride is implicit in his treatment of Alarbus, certainly it is explicit in his brutal slaying of his son. When Mutius attempts to prevent his father's pursuing Bassianus and Lavinia, Titus strikes him down with a monstrous arrogance: "Bar'st me my way in Rome?" [I. i. 291]. And to Lucius' charge that Titus is "unjust" and has slain "in wrongful quarrel" [I. i. 293], the father retorts that anyone who dishonors him is no real son. So too, in his white-hot wrath, he for a time denies Mutius burial in the family tomb, spurning the charge of impiety and branding sons and brother "traitors." . . . Stained thus by passion, he is easily duped by Tamora into believing that she, who a few moments earlier was coldly repudiated in pleading for the life of her son, is now a merciful intercessor on behalf of the murderer. Just as earlier he could use his own punctured ego as justification for the most blatant atrocities, so now he is unable to see beyond the glitter of his reconciliation and the apparent restitution of his wonted dignity and adulation.

The structure of Act I, in brief, establishes a fundamental thrust for the plot; the juxtaposition of numerous choric characters parroting Titus' heroics with a flurry of actions precipitated by the sudden and uncontrolled fury of his pride creates for the spectator a pattern of anticipation in which the focus is on the central character and the consequences he must suffer as a result of his tragic foolishness and, if the cycle is to be complete, the insights which he may ultimately achieve. Indeed for a time the experiences of Titus in moving from wrath to self-pity to madness—and the interpretation of them as the spectator is directed by the choric characters—support this assumption. (pp. 15-16)

Quite pointedly, his wrath is converted to self-pity in Act III. Lying on the ground before the Judges, Senators, and Tribunes, he pleads for his sons "For pity of mine age," "For all my blood," and "for these bitter tears" [III. i. 2, 4, 6]; his entreaties spurned, he moans that he will "tell [his] sorrows to the stones" because at least they "Receive [his] tears, and seem to weep with [him]" [III. i. 37, 42]. (pp. 16-17)

Throughout the act the comments of the surrounding characters maintain the focus on Titus and his reactions to his sufferings. Lucius, for example, stands by as Titus pleads before the judges, informing him that he "lament[s] in vain. . . . [Y]ou recount your sorrows to a stone" [III. i. 27, 29]; his choric function is similar later in the scene when, the ravished Lavinia standing before her father, he implores Titus to "cease [his] tears" [III. i. 136] because of the effect that they are having upon her. Marcus most extensively provides such comments. . . . Even his grandson on one occasion begs Titus to "leave these bitter deep laments" [III. ii. 46].

In Act IV, his sanity is the victim of his extreme pride stretched on the rack of ignominy and suffering. Indeed, his actions suggest a mounting degree of insanity—his macabre laughter when the mutilated Lavinia kisses her grieving father, his assertion that he is "mad with misery" [III. ii. 9], "no man should be mad but I" [III. ii. 24], his berating Marcus for killing a fly, his suggestion of inscribing words on a leaf of brass to be blown by the angry northern wind, his presents to the empress' sons, his assertion that justice has abandoned the earth. . . . (p. 17)

As the surrounding characters reinforce Titus' statements of sufferings and self-pity in Act III, so their remarks—coupled with his actions and the absence of any comment from him to suggest that such action is but an antic posture—convince the spectators that he is indeed mad. Even at the height of Titus' passion in Act I, Martius preplots with the observation that Andronicus "is not with himself" [I. i. 368]. In similar fashion, young Lucius later glosses Lavinia's actions: "I have heard my grandsire say full oft / Extremity of griefs would make men mad" [IV. i. 18-19]. Marcus, again, is the most significant tragic pointer. Of his brother's actions in the fly scene, he notes, "Alas, poor man! grief has so wrought on him, / He takes false shadows for true substances" [III. ii. 79-80]. So, later, after Lavinia has revealed the identity of her attackers, Marcus' attempt to initiate some form of revenge indicates his assumption that Titus—plagued by the "mutiny" in his "thoughts"—is unable to mount such an effort. . . . (p. 18)

Demonstrably, Shakespeare has focused the first four and one half acts primarily on the character of Titus. Largely through the consistent pattern of comments from the surrounding characters, the spectators' attention has been directed to a powerful Roman soldier who, once past the awesomely furious and active moments of his pride in Act I, is by degrees broken through pain and madness. He has, in effect, become relatively passive and impotent—on occasions speaking of vengeance but apparently incapable of a concerted effort. Certainly, then, the thrust of the play is toward some final and climactic development in the character of Titus—whether it be some form of stoic resignation by which spiritually to rise above the conditions that destroy him, or some recognition of the destructive nature of uncontrolled passion, or some form of poetic redress by which a chastened Titus could regain something of his former status without his former abilities, or some scheme of vengeance directed by Marcus through which Titus either in life or death could enact some measure of retributive justice. At least the structure of the play could accommodate such a conclusion.

What Shakespeare provides is the very conclusion the structure will not support, the sudden and, from the perspective of the audience, absolutely unanticipated emergence of Titus as a rather sophisticated revenger outwitting his adversaries at their own game. One is shocked to hear Titus, in an aside well into Act V (indeed 264 lines from the end), suddenly affirm his sanity:

> I knew them all, though they suppos'd me mad,
> And will o'er-reach them in their own devices,
> A pair of cursed hell-hounds and their dam.
>
> [V. ii. 142-44]

Even here, of course, the spectators have no assurance of a degree of sanity sufficient for his devising a scheme; nor for that matter is the audience made aware of what Titus' macabre designs are until he explains them to Chiron and Demetrius even at the point of cutting their throats. In no way arising from the pattern of the plot and in no way consistent with the character of Titus, the events of the final moments occur so rapidly and so amazingly as to command interest as an end in themselves, and—the perspective for the spectator totally destroyed—the emphasis is narrational rather than dramatic. (pp. 18-19)

The central problem of the play, then, is the protagonist—the direction in which he is developed in the first twelve scenes and the anomalous point at which he has suddenly arrived in the last two scenes. Certainly it is patently inaccurate to assert that Titus is totally flat, a character without development. The development from wrath to self-pity to madness, which Shakespeare is to reiterate in Lear, is profoundly human and, even amidst the bombastic rhetoric and the diversionary horrors of Aaron the Moor, not totally ineffective. On the other hand, to develop a character and to provide him with philosophic depth are two different matters. In this play the playwright, to indicate the progressive degeneration in Titus, depends almost exclusively upon the external structural device of the pointer characters—Marcus primarily, but, on occasion, other figures such as the sons, young Lucius, Publius, the Captain, Aaron, Tamora, and Saturninus. Totally absent are significant soliloquies and asides, devices which permit the spectator to see within the character, to perceive . . . where the struggle occurs which gives universal meaning to external actions. (pp. 19-20)

Shakespeare himself may well have realized something of the weakness arising from the total lack of philosophic dimension. References to the gods and the heavens are quite frequent in the last half of the play (seventeen to the gods, fifteen to the heavens). The effect, however, is entirely peripheral; no relationship is at any time suggested between Titus and the heavens or his concept of the will of the gods. (p. 20)

Whatever the nature of Titus' development, the spectator remains entirely outside of him because of the playwrights' total reliance on external pointers. This structural device is further demonstrated in the final act. A successful revenger who, in the process, shocks us further by sacrificing his daughter without warning, Titus experiences no form of regeneration which in itself would strengthen the emotional rapport between spectator and protagonist; again the playwright attempts to create through the comments of the surrounding characters an impression of sympathy and nobility. (p. 21)

By pointers and character contrast, then, the playwright attempts to elevate Titus to a final tragic stature even though there is no significant internal regeneration. This effort is undermined, however, by the unpleasant ambiguities concerning the leader under whom the ultimate restoration of peace and order is achieved. To be sure it is almost commonplace for the Elizabethan tragic conclusion to accommodate a restoration of national harmony—whether the issue be of primary significance as with Richmond in *Richard III* and Malcom of *Macbeth* or of secondary significance as with Albany in *Lear*. . . . Unless the intent is to produce a conscious ambivalence as with Bolingbroke in *Richard II,* the dramatist is careful to protect the image of this person in order that the final view of the stage-world will be a positive one. Thus, it is not unusual to have Lucius, Titus' son, proclaimed emperor following the elimination of Saturninus and Bassianus. The disturbing factor is the rather vicious and cruel streak which Lucius on occasion displays. . . . [The] cruelty of Lucius is not fundamentally different in kind from that of Titus which instigated the whole vicious cycle. With no visible difference in Titus—and none in Lucius, one is left wondering just what has been purged, what wisdom gained as a result of the whole experience. (pp. 21-2)

Certainly, by the standard of Shakespeare's later work, the structure of *Titus Andronicus* is disjointed and the results disconcerting. The tragic perspective is blurred by the inconsistencies of the protagonist coupled with an absence of effective philosophic depth; the structural devices—by which externally, through pointer characters and character parallels to focus and direct the spectators' attention and internally, through soliloquy and aside to probe the depths of character motivation and internal struggle—are in large measure ineffectively utilized. Nevertheless, the raw material for an effective tragic perspective is present. (p. 24)

In brief, *Titus Andronicus* as an Elizabethan tragedy is embryonic. But its unrealized potential does indeed provide a guideline to the various aspects of dramatic form with which Shakespeare is to experiment in his subsequent early tragedies and through which he is to achieve the firm tragic perspective of his major work. (p. 25)

> *Larry S. Champion, "'Titus Andronicus' and Shakespeare's Tragic Perspective," in* Ball State University Forum, *Vol. XII, No. 2, Spring, 1971, pp. 14-25.*

JAMES L. CALDERWOOD (essay date 1971)

[*Calderwood has examined what he calls Shakespeare's "metadrama" in two studies,* Shakespearean Metadrama *(1971) and* Metadrama in Shakespeare's Henriad *(1979). In the introduction to his earlier book, Calderwood claims that "Shakespeare's plays are not only about . . . various moral, social, political, and other thematic issues," but also about dramatic art itself—"its materials, its media of language and theater, its generic forms and conventions, its relationship to truth and the social order." It is this synthesis of aesthetic concerns which Calderwood terms "metadrama." In the following excerpt, Calderwood examines the "metadramatic theme" of* Titus Andronicus, *and in the process finds a biographical basis for its emergence. The metadramatic concern of the play he interprets as Shakespeare's attempt to unite poetry and action, word and deed, Ovid and Seneca within the structure of a popular art form that resists meaningful expression; the biographical basis for this concern he identifies as Shakespeare's feeling during his apprenticeship that his language as a poet was being violated when put to the task of dramatic construction. Calderwood interprets* Titus Andronicus *within this framework, characterizing Lavinia as a symbol of poetic expression, and her rape and mutilation by the barbarous Goths as the rape and violation of language when forced to embody dramatic action. Lavinia's rape also suggests that Rome itself has become barbaric, its inhabitants unable to communicate in terms other than the "nonlanguage of barbarism," or physical action. For Calderwood, the dramatic structure threatens to collapse into chaos unless Shakespeare manages to find "a merger of language and action"; but Lavinia has lost the ability to speak and Titus, until the final movement of the play, has lost the motivation to act—a situation Calderwood finds grotesquely symbolized in the scene where "the useless hand of action" is carried away "in the tongueless mouth of Lavinia." Ultimately, Calderwood asserts, Shakespeare was unable at this point in his career to solve the opposition of language and action inherent in* Titus Andronicus. *Instead, he maintains, Shakespeare relies upon the authority of Seneca to resolve his conflict, just as he had relied on Ovid for the story of Lavinia's rape that precipitated the tragedy; but the banquet scene, taken from Seneca's* Thyestes, *rather than unifying word and deed in one dramatic stroke, actually projects the play further into "pure physical action ungraced by language." Calderwood's assertion that Shakespeare failed in his synthesis of Ovid and Seneca is reminiscent of the remarks of Eugene M. Waith (1955); a similar emphasis on the language and structure of* Titus *can be found in the essays by Wolfgang H. Clemen (1951), A. C. Hamilton (1967), D. J. Palmer (1972), and Albert H. Tricomi (1976).*]

Had Shakespeare wanted to suggest the poet's sacrifice of verbal autonomy when writing for the theater he could hardly have found a better myth to dramatize than that of Philomela, with which he was of course familiar in Arthur Golding's translation of Ovid's *Metamorphoses*. In his prefatory "Epistle" to the translation Golding betrays considerable anxiety to underscore Ovid's "dark Philosophie" and high moral purpose, which if not immediately apparent in tales of nubile nymphs and light-hoofed satyrs becomes visible under close allegorical scrutiny.

Wearing Golding's tropological spectacles, Shakespeare would have discovered that the story of Philomela illustrates the fact that "distresse doth drive a man to looke about / And seeke all corners of his wits, what way to wind him out." However, since Philomela's problem is linguistic and is solved by "art"— her weaving into the "warp of white upon a frame of Thracia" the purple lettering that indicts Tereus—we might expect Shakespeare to have seen in the tale not so much Golding's platitude about necessity mothering invention as the more specific literary problem of embodying thought in language and language in expressive forms, the problem that becomes particularly aggravating to the poet turned playwright and forced to deal in forms that must, initially at any rate, impede rather than enhance expression. If it is the artistic aspects of Philomela's plight that interest Shakespeare, then we might expect these to be reflected in the plight of Lavinia, the Philomela-substitute in the play.

Philomela's métier may have been weaving, but Shakespeare repeatedly associates Lavinia with poetry. . . . Not only do poets speak through her, but her own tongue is given to melodic, lyric speech—or once was, Marcus reflects:

> O, that delightful engine of her thoughts,
> That blabbed them with such pleasing eloquence,
> Is torn from forth that pretty hollow cage,
> Where, like a sweet melodious bird, it sung
> Sweet varied notes, enchanting every ear!
>
> [III. i. 82-6]

Marcus is equally impressed by the musical expressiveness of Lavinia's hands:

> O, had the monster seen those lily hands
> Tremble, like aspen-leaves, upon a lute
> And make the silken strings delight to kiss them,
> He would not then have touched them for his life!
>
> [II. iv. 44-7]

In the lines immediately following these, Shakespeare combines the eloquence of the hands trembling on a lute and that of the tongue whose varied notes enchant every ear into the figure of that first and greatest of all lyric poets, the Thracian Orpheus:

> Or, had he heard the heavenly harmony
> Which that sweet tongue hath made,
> He would have dropped his knife, and fell asleep
> As Cerberus at the Thracian poet's feet.
>
> [II. iv. 48-51]

This is a curious equation—Lavinia, demure and lovely, a most domestic lyricist compared to the wide-wandering Orpheus, tamer of beasts, free spirit whose art is his passport even to Hades and back. Yet there is a point at which their experiences coincide, a moment for each of them when the harmonics of tongue and harp lose their enchantment. In this metaphoric frame, the rape and mutilation of Lavinia become analogous to the death of Orpheus, so vividly described in the opening lines of the eleventh book of Golding's Ovid:

> With blowing shalmes, and beating drummes, and
>   bedlem howling out,
> And clapping hands on every syde by Bacchus drunken
>   rout,
> Did drowne the sownd of Orphyes harp. . . .

We might hesitate to read the Orpheus myth at this point as a euhemeristic account of the progressive cultural killing off (by *sparagmos,* or ritual dismemberment) of early Greek lyric poetry by Dionysiac ritual drama; but it seems unlikely that Shakespeare could have read such a passage without reflecting on the fate of the poet in the theater, where the melodies of his harp must submit to being "clapper-clawed with the palmes of the vulgar" (preface to *Troilus and Cressida*). From the expressive freedom of wandering Orpheus to the squalid confines of the Theatre in Shoreditch: what a verbal lopping off was there!

What I am suggesting is that *Titus Andronicus* metadramatically presents us with a rape of language, with the mutilation that the poet's "tongue" suffers when forced to submit to the rude demands of the theater. The major image of this barbarizing of language by the theater is of course the rape and mutilation of Lavinia by the Goth brothers. "Barbarizing" is an apt term here because in the Renaissance "Goth" and "barbarity" are virtually synonyms—and the word "barbarous" appears more often in *Titus* than in any other of Shakespeare's plays ("barbarous Tamora," "barbarous Moor," "barbarous, beastly villains," etc.). Moreover, the word "barbarian"—as Shakespeare suggests when he has Marcus admonish the ireful Titus "Thou art a Roman, be not barbarous" [I. i. 378]—once meant anyone who did not speak Greek or (later on) Latin and whose speech therefore sounded like "bar-bar-bar" according to Herodotus. So it is appropriate that Lavinia of the melodic speech be assaulted by the Goths, who have been advised by the equally barbarous Aaron to "strike her home by force, if not by words" [II. i. 118].

Lavinia's rape follows naturally from the fact that Rome has itself become barbaric. As Tamora says after her marriage to Saturninus, "Titus, I am incorporate in Rome" [I. i. 462]. With the nonlanguage of barbarism in the ascendant, the play abounds in images of linguistic distress, corruption, and mutilation. (pp. 27-30)

In Lavinia's rape and mutilation is figured the deflowering of the chaste poetic word, the private possession of the lyric-narrative poet, when it encounters the "barbarities" of the public theater and suffers the mauling of a raucous audience anxious for just such horrors as Lavinia's experience provides. Linguistic authority then passes into the possession of the Goths, and Titus's solicitations for his sons [before the senate] cannot elicit a merciful word. Titus's vow to revenge—the verbal promise that is to be redeemed by the vengeful act—implies Shakespeare's own sense of the necessity of finding a merger of language and action without the lyric Lavinia. But neither he nor Titus has found how to effect that merger, and the immediate emblem of this frustration is the useless hand of action being carried in the tongueless mouth of Lavinia [at the end of Act III, Scene i]. We arrive here at a grotesque parody of the proper union of word and deed in drama.

Drama becomes truly expressive through the marriage of the right language to the right actions. In the theatrical world of *Titus Andronicus* Lavinia cannot survive, but with the loss of her melodious tongue the play threatens to dissolve into meaninglessness. Drama that tries to prevail by violent action alone delivers itself up to pure brutality without point or purpose. With the mutilation of Lavinia Rome degenerates into "a wilderness of tigers" whose medium of communication is not words but mangled bodies [III. i. 54]. Whatever meaning is to be found must be found in Lavinia if the play is to regain any sense of dramatic direction. . . . Even action, which thus far has barbarized the play, could constitute a kind of language or expressive form if one only had the wit to find it out. In any event Lavinia's secrets must be discovered before any meaningful action can occur. The manner of their discovery—her turning the pages of Ovid's *Metamorphoses* to the tale of Philomela—is curiously relevant since the Philomela myth is not merely analogous to but a model for her own experience. In fact Ovid is a model for nature as well: the forest that so silently collaborated in Lavinia's violation was, as Titus says, "Patterned by that the poet here describes, / By nature made for murders and for rapes" [IV. i. 57-8].

The stress on literary models is entirely fitting. Lavinia's turning the pages of the *Metamorphoses* is an almost literal representation of Shakespeare's own technique of writing *Titus Andronicus*. Not only did he find Lavinia herself (as Philomela) in those pages, as she is doing within the play, but like her he found a mode of expression—a tongue, language, verbal style—which he has incorporated into *Titus Andronicus*, though not with eminent success. For the verbal style has had to encounter, in theatrical action, a kind of opposition which Ovidian poetry was spared, and the conjunction of the two has produced a rape instead of a marriage.

The marriage is lacking from the play because, presumably, it is lacking in its author at this time. Unable to create an interplay of language and action—to write poetry from which acts freely issue and to envisage stage situations in which poetry is implicit, to write a dynamic language of words and to create a visual language of movements, gestures, and deeds—Shakespeare presents us with verbal design on one side and physical violence on the other. The verbal design is primarily Ovidian, lush in imagery and conceit, full of expansive figuration but fatally indifferent to dramatic context. The obvious example is Marcus's forty-seven lines of detached mythological and metaphorical doodling when he comes upon the deflowered, blood-spurting Lavinia. . . . In *Titus* Shakespeare fails to mold his verbal style to the contours of shifting dramatic occasions; and as a result word and deed become dislocated and often grotesque in their mutual isolation or come together with a disfiguring clash.

The Ovidian poet then can function neither freely nor effectively in the dramatic mode. Lavinia has found in Ovid a means of expressing herself, but it is a less than ideal substitute for living speech. Pointing out her Ovidian forerunner, Philomela tells roughly what happened to her, but Ovid cannot help her say who has played the role of Tereus. Identifying the barbarous brothers requires a most barbaric mode of expression: writing in the sand with a stick held between her teeth. The analogy to the trials of the poet-turned-playwright may seem fetched in from afar, but it remains consistent with the metadramatic theme sustained throughout the play. Such writing is not only rather tricky but highly frustrating since the medium of the stage performance is as ephemeral, compared to the permanence of the printed pages of Ovid just consulted, as the sand in which Lavinia writes. (pp. 32-5)

If all this suggests the frustrations of the theatrical trade, still Lavinia's identifying the villains promises something by way of a solution to the word-deed dilemma. The teeth that hold the "pen" are after all the same teeth that held Titus's hand earlier in a dumb show of linguistic and actional disfigurement. Rendered useless in the absence of Lavinia's tongue, the hand of revenge is now empowered to act meaningfully. Unfortunately, the agent of action, Titus, has been drifting away from meaning for some time, his mind slipping into madness. Precisely when it appears that all the prerequisites to revenge have been fulfilled and a sense of direction restored to the plot, Titus

spends the remainder of Act 4 futilely petitioning the authorities, including the gods, for justice. Thus the play returns to its earlier phase of arrested motion. This curious stress on clearing away all obstacles to dramatic advancement, only to have the play continue to mark time, raises some structural issues that merit looking into. There are after all precedents for such undeveloping developments.

In the middle of *Titus Andronicus,* through most of the third and fourth acts, the mad hero is baffled by the problem of securing justice. In a similar case T. S. Eliot has argued that Hamlet's indecision is "a prolongation of the bafflement of his creator in the face of his artistic problem." However it may be with Hamlet, Titus's bafflement can be seen to reflect not merely Shakespeare's artistic problem, but also his means of solving it. The artistic problem, I have been urging, is how to bring about the marriage of word and deed in drama, how to suit the action to the word and the word to the action, presumably without trampling on, let alone merely o'erstepping, the modesty of nature.

Confronted by an artistic problem a literary novice in the Renaissance would consider nothing more customary and logical than to seek guidance from classical authorities. And as modern texts like *Shakespeare's Plutarch, Shakespeare's Ovid,* and the ever-expanding *Narrative and Dramatic Sources of Shakespeare* indicate, Shakespeare especially finds it natural to turn to literary models—Plautus, Seneca, Ovid, Plutarch but also Lyly, Kyd, Greene, Marlowe, and perhaps Beaumont and Fletcher later on. (pp. 36-7)

If we back off and consider the play structurally it divides into two major actions: the rape and mutilation of Lavinia in Act 2 and the Thyestean banquet in Act 5. The former action derives from Ovidian poetry, the latter from Senecan drama; the former presents us with an image of linguistic mutilation, the latter with a macabre act which revenges that mutilation. Separating the two is a period of poetic and dramatic frustration in which Lavinia cannot speak and, when she can, Titus cannot act. The principal emblem of this frustration has been the grotesque conjunction of Titus's mutilated hand and Lavinia's mutilated mouth. (p. 37)

The hiatus between the two major events of the play—the period during the third and fourth acts in which Titus seeks justice from various authorities—results from Shakespeare's own reliance on authority, specifically the form of Senecan revenge tragedy. For the most arbitrary yet inevitable feature of that form is the "delay," that is, an essentially static phase following the commission of the offense and preceding the scene of retribution which provides a natural climax to the play. Unlike other Senecan practitioners, Shakespeare seems to have realized that the delay constitutes a conventional caesura between the revenger's usually ritualized "vow" to revenge and his final "act" of revenge. With this built-in separation of word and act the Senecan form structurally puts asunder those two cardinal elements of drama whose marriage the playwright seeks to negotiate, and so appears to defeat him in his principal task. However, it can also be said to assist him in performing that task since it guides him to the eventual fulfillment of the word by the act after a period of structurally authorized frustration. A consciousness of this paradox seems reflected in Shakespeare's having made the division between word and act—a division already implicit in the form—unusually prominent by having the offense be against Lavinia's "tongue" and by repeatedly symbolizing the word-act dilemma

Act IV. Scene ii. Demetrius, Chiron, Aaron, Nurse, and Aaron's child. By T. Kirk (n.d.).

as the play gradually maneuvers toward the Senecan action that avenges her.

This reliance on the authority of a dramatic form becomes increasingly apparent as the final revenge approaches. When Titus next appears he is in his study preparing a script for revenge:

> what I mean to do
> See here in bloody lines I have set down,
> And what is written shall be executed.
>
> [V. ii. 13-15]

His opportunity to enact his revenge drama arises when the Goths unexpectedly show up at his house to perform a play of their own. Not so mad as he seems, Titus easily perceives the identities of the actors within their roles of Revenge, Rape, and Murder and out of the failure of their drama weaves the success of his own, being inspired as he says to "o'erreach them in their own devices" [V. ii. 143].

To overreach the Goths in their own devices, however, is to outbarbarize the barbarians, which is precisely what Shakespeare implies as Titus prepares for the banquet scene. Guided by the principle expressed by Atreus in Seneca's *Thyestes,* "A wrong is not revenged but by a worse wrong," Titus tells the Goth brothers "For worse than Philomel you used my daughter, / And worse than Progne I will be revenged" [V. ii. 194-95], and in the same vein he later hopes his banquet will "prove / More stern and bloody than the Centaurs' feast" [V. iii. 202-03]. This emphasis on outdoing classical authority—Ovid, Se-

neca, Greek mythology—is especially apt because Titus is the one character in the play whose conduct is dominated by a sense of authority and tradition. (pp. 38-9)

So it is in keeping with Titus's character that the first murder in the banquet scene should be sanctioned by classical authority; he carefully establishes beforehand that Virginius's murder of his daughter (referred to by Seneca in *Octavia*) will serve as

> A reason mighty, strong, and effectual;
> A pattern, precedent, and lively warrant
> For me, most wretched, to perform the like.
> Die, die, Lavinia, and thy shame with thee.
>
> [V. iii. 43-6]

It is also to the metadramatic point that when Tamora asks "Why hast thou slain thine only daughter thus?" Titus disclaims responsibility:

> Not I—'Twas Chiron and Demetrius.
> They ravished her, and cut away her tongue;
> And they, 'twas they, that did her all this wrong.
>
> [V. iii. 56-8]

Only metaphorically can the Goths be said to have murdered Lavinia; but the effect of forcing the metaphor here is to equate Titus and the Goths and thus to underscore the barbarity of his action. "Thou art a Roman," he was admonished in Act I, "be not barbarous" [I. i. 378]. Such an easy distinction between Roman and barbarian is no longer available since the noble Roman has indeed "o'erreached them in their own devices."

Would this not suggest Shakespeare's awareness of artistic failure in *Titus Andronicus* and his recognition of the reason for it? Relying as he so rigorously has upon the "pattern, precedent, and lively warrant" [V. iii. 44] of Senecan revenge drama has led him to traffic in a kind of theatrical sensationalism as barbarous in its way as the Goths in theirs. . . . Amid [the] climactic flurry of stage action—it is instructive how many stage directions must be interpolated to make texts of the play intelligible to a reader at this point—the words "do," "did," "done," and "deed" (not to mention the more violent actional terms) sound eight times in the space of nineteen lines. The dramatic medium, in short, is now very nearly pure physical action ungraced by language. And that should remind us that during all the elaborate preparations for the banquet the mute Lavinia has been moving dutifully about the stage carrying out Titus's bloody instructions, playing her silent part in an action as calculatedly sadistic as that by which she lost her tongue. So employed she provides us even before she is killed with a visual representation of the barbarizing of language in the theater. In turning to Senecan authorities for theatrical instruction Shakespeare no doubt hoped to find how to render art dramatically expressive, how in the broadest sense to coalesce word and act. What he seems conscious of having brought about, however, is a mutilation of words, ultimately a ruthless silencing of graceful speech, by sensational actions. The result, as Sonnet 66 has it, "art made tongue-tied by authority."

In the final, post-banquet part of *Titus Andronicus* still another authority comes into incriminating focus. Before going on to that, however, I need to return to [V. i.] and consider the role of Aaron in the metadramatic theme. (pp. 40-1)

Aaron is the indispensable character on whose plots Shakespeare's own plot hinges. Of course one could say that about any important character in a play. However, Aaron is pointedly associated with the kind of plotting that produces not only revenges but revenge dramas. . . . Aaron is not merely a plot-wright of timeless tragedies but a veritable Johannes factotum of the theater—actor, director, messenger, prop gatherer, prompter—the man who tutors the Goth brothers, plants the gold, writes the "fatal-plotted scroll," coaches Tamora how to perform, fetches Titus's sons and directs them to the guileful hole, skips off and back again with Saturninus, reveals the bag of gold, etc. And so he goes throughout the play. Yet despite his manifold manipulations and scurryings about, his real identity as controlling intelligence is effectively concealed from nearly everyone else. Late in the play then when he encounters Lucius, Aaron the master-plotter contains the secret of Shakespeare's play—a secret that is in danger of disappearing forever: "And this shall all be buried in my death / Unless thou swear to me my child shall live" [V. i. 67-8].

From this standpoint what seems especially noteworthy about the Aaron-Lucius transaction is that the "drama" Aaron is privy to can be rescued from oblivion only if the merciful word can be found and sworn to. It is much too late for Shakespeare's play to be redeemed by the language of mercy, but that mercy is what it lacks seems abundantly evident. Thus the drama Aaron reveals to Lucius is a drama of blood and he himself the "bloody mind" behind it, the matrix and guiding principle of revenge tragedy. (pp. 44-5)

[Aaron] is identified as the foul, murderous core of the play, as to be sure he must be if his meeting with Lucius is to serve as a point of dramatic and moral transformation in the play: Aaron the black plotter actuated by vengeance giving way to the fair Lucius, who will convert revenge tragedy into a political morality play in which Rome's recovery is framed by justice and mercy. Essential to such a transformation is the purging of the state, which means that as much evil as possible must be funneled into Aaron so that Rome can be cleansed by his death. Shakespeare gets that task done by inflating Aaron into a symbol of motiveless malignity analogous to the allegorizing of Tamora and sons as Fury, Rapine, and Murder in the following scene [V. ii.].

But Aaron as we have seen is also associated with Titus. And it is significant that Shakespeare chooses this point—that is, before the Thyestean banquet—to introduce so arrestingly the concept of mercy. The effect is to cast doubt on the ethical propriety of revenge, or at least to bring before the audience a moral perspective that cannot help influencing its assessment of Titus's climactic revenges later in the act. Thus the play moves toward the elimination of evil (Tamora, sons, Saturninus) but also toward an exposure of the evil involved in that process itself.

The Aaron-as-dramatist metaphor may suggest that in looking back over *Titus Andronicus* Shakespeare has himself come to feel a bit monstrous and Aaron-like. At any rate since the play moves on to the banquet scene in which Aaron is out-monstered by Titus it is not surprising that the post-banquet portion of that scene is the most stiffly self-conscious piece of casemaking in Shakespeare. (pp. 45-6)

[The] exoneration of the Andronici, so formally staged with risings aloft and speakings down, is a species of internal epilogue that in typical epilogue fashion makes a bid for the sympathy and forgiveness of the audience. The most immediate audience is the gathering of "sad-faced men, people and sons of Rome" [V. iii. 67], but beyond this audience are the equally sad-faced men, people and sons of London gathered in the Theatre at Shoreditch, not to mention generations of sad-faced

critics. . . . The lives of the Andronici and the theatrical life of Shakespeare's play are equally dependent on the judgment of their respective audiences, noble Romans and penny knaves. (pp. 47-8)

My suggesting that Shakespeare here submits the life of his play to the judgment of his audience in the Theatre seems to contradict my earlier claim that it is precisely the theatrical milieu, including the audience, that debases the poet turned playwright. However, just as the Thyestean banquet scene revealed how the poet could become inarticulate by relying on classical authority, this address to the audience now suggests, perhaps a bit cynically, how the poet may become equally inarticulate through the theatrical necessity of securing the approval of the "common voice," which is no less corruptive than Seneca. That is, the play is based on one authority and directed to another. (p. 48)

Consider for instance the irony in the appeal to the audience and in what happens afterward. Lucius, forgiven by *his* audience and indeed so thoroughly endorsed by it that he is elevated to emperor, thus becoming official spokesman of the common voice, pauses for a final elegiac moment over the body of Titus, and then with considerable executive efficiency sentences Aaron to a breast-deep burial alive and orders the body of Tamora to be cast forth to scavenging birds and animals. . . . With the popular voice behind him, Lucius is as unrelenting as Aaron. The voice of the lyric is nowhere heard in this desert; the Orphic artist must of necessity be sacrificed to the vulgar. In fact if Shakespeare's audience bestows grace on this play, as we know it repeatedly did in his time, that is because its desire for sensational and sadistic brutality has been catered to by a playwright who must bid for mercy by being cruel.

At the end Aaron and Lucius hold the stage, the latter capable only of the language of repellent justice—the "sentence" that kills by torture—and the former suppressing words that sue for grace in favor of his own brand of speech: "Ah, why should wrath be mute and fury dumb?" [V. iii. 184]. Neither has been; only the voice of Lavinia has been permanently stilled. "If one good deed in all my life I did, / I do repent it from my very soul" [V. iii. 189-90]. There seems no need for Aaron or the play to repent on that score, since in both of them "bad" words and "bad" deeds have abounded. In that perverted form the play has suited the action to the word, the word to the action, after all. But at the same time it has created a coherent metadramatic theme, a mode of autistic meaning in which Shakespeare has played, for the most part ironically, on the goals and frustrations and the sense of loss of the poet exploring the complexities of drama. (p. 49)

> *James L. Calderwood, " 'Titus Andronicus': Word, Act, Authority," in his* Shakespearean Metadrama: The Argument of the Play in "Titus Andronicus," "Love's Labour's Lost," "Romeo and Juliet," "A Midsummer Night's Dream" and "Richard II," *University of Minnesota Press, 1971, pp. 23-51.*

D. J. PALMER (essay date 1972)

> [*Like A. C. Hamilton (1967), Palmer argues that* Titus Andronicus *is a "highly-ordered and elaborately-designed work." Also like Hamilton, Palmer disagrees with Eugene M. Waith's assessment that Shakespeare's dramatization of Ovid's concept of metamorphosis inhibits the reality of the play's action; in Waith's words, Shakespeare transformed states of violent emotion into speeches of "interested but somewhat detached contemplation"*

(see excerpt above, 1955). According to Palmer, Shakespeare actually sought, through the use of ritualized language, to express the unutterable and to stabilize reality for both his characters and his audiences. For example, he considers Marcus's formal lament at the sight of Lavinia's mutilation—the speech which Wolfgang H. Clemen (1951) regarded as an "absurd contrast" between image and occasion—an effort to understand an action that defies comprehension. Palmer also analyzes the structure of Titus Andronicus, *identifying the play's cyclic repetition of revenge as its primary dramatic pattern. He discusses the substitution of different characters within this pattern, noting the drama's movement from Roman ceremony to barbarian blood-letting (and the assimilation of both thereafter), and interprets the characters'— particularly Titus's—enactment of ritual, game, and even farce as their means of attempting to comprehend reality. Palmer concludes that* Titus *could well be called Shakespeare's "thesis in tragedy, anticipating many of the formal techniques and devices used in the later tragedies." He also echoes Waith's final comment on Shakespeare's reason for attempting such an undramatic experiment, stating that the action "moves to admiration" rather than to compassion and sympathy; admiration, to both Palmer and Waith, is that aesthetic principle valued by Elizabethans as the ultimate effect of tragedy.]*

The extremities of horror and suffering in *Titus Andronicus* seem to stretch the capacities of art to give them adequate embodiment and expression. Perhaps it was this sense of testing the limits of his poetic and dramatic resources that attracted Shakespeare to the subject at the beginning of his career, for his early work in general is characterised by its tendency to display rhetorical and technical virtuosity, as well as by a desire to emulate and outdo his models. The early Shakespeare is more prone to excessive ingenuity than to a lack of skill or inventiveness. But the question at issue in *Titus Andronicus* has for a long time been whether the nature of the material over-extended Shakespeare's abilities. (p. 320)

The charge that the form and style are at odds with the situations they are supposed to express finds a point of focus in the episode where Lavinia, 'her hands cut off, and her tongue cut out, and ravish'd' [S.D., II, iv], is encountered by her uncle Marcus. Marcus addresses her gruesome figure in a speech of formal lamentation, dwelling on the details of her mutilation and shame with such elaborate and fanciful conceits, mixing sweetness with the grotesque, that many have thought the effect of lines like these to be an insensitive mockery of the physical and emotional reality of the situation:

> Alas, a crimson river of warm blood,
> Like to a bubbling fountain stirr'd with wind,
> Doth rise and fall between thy rosed lips,
> Coming and going with thy honey breath . . .
> And not withstanding all this loss of blood—
> As from a conduit with three issuing spouts—
> Yet do thy cheeks look red as Titan's face
> Blushing to be encount'red with a cloud.
>
> [II. iv. 22-32]

The effect is certainly bizarre, and intrinsic to it is the mute presence on stage of Lavinia herself. Indeed for that reason I find it difficult to accept the defence of this kind of rhetoric in the play made by E. M. Waith, who argues that it derives from the style of Ovidian metamorphosis [see excerpt above, 1955]. . . . Waith finds that the effect of such curious conceits is to transform states of violent emotion, at their point of extremity, into 'interested but somewhat detached contemplation', but he acknowledges that the device belongs essentially to narrative and descriptive poetry, and 'cannot be fully realized by the techniques of drama'. Detached contemplation, how-

ever, is hardly appropriate to the formal lament that Marcus is uttering, and it seems more in keeping with the techniques of drama to take these lines as an expression of Marcus' own feelings, moved by the sight of such affliction, rather than as directly descriptive of Lavinia. . . . Marcus' lament is the expression of an effort to realise a sight that taxes to the utmost the powers of understanding and utterance. The vivid conceits in which he pictures his hapless niece do not transform or depersonalise her: she is already transformed and depersonalised, as she stands before him the victim of a strange and cruel metamorphosis. The opening words of his speech are 'Who is this?' [II. iv. 11] and his first response is to doubt the reality of what he sees:

> If I do dream, would all my wealth would wake me!
> If I do wake, some planet strike me down,
> That I may slumber an eternal sleep!
>
> [II. iv. 13-15]

Far from being a retreat from the awful reality into some aesthetic distance, then, Marcus' conceits dwell upon this figure that is to him both familiar and strange, fair and hideous, living body and object: this is, and is not, Lavinia.

Lavinia's silence is as moving, and as appalling, as the sight of her bleeding wounds, and following his envisagement of her, Marcus gives dramatic embodiment to another function of rhetoric in this episode as in the play as a whole:

> Shall I speak for thee? Shall I say 'tis so?
> O, that I knew thy heart, and knew the beast,
> That I might rail at him to ease my mind!
> Sorrow concealed, like an oven stopp'd,
> Doth burn the heart to cinders where it is.
>
> [II. iv. 33-7]

Lavinia's plight is literally unutterable: Ovid's Philomela, as Marcus says, at least had her hands to tell her story in a woven sampler, but in thus surpassing Ovid Shakespeare also makes fully dramatic the testing of his own expressive resources. By realising Lavinia's tragedy, Marcus' formal lament articulates unspeakable woes.

The formality and stylisation of this speech, therefore, instead of being incongruously related to the horror of the situation, arise reality. Here and throughout the play, the response to the intolerable is ritualised, in language and action, because ritual is the ultimate means by which man seeks to order and control his precarious and unstable world. (pp. 320-22)

The progression of the play's first two Acts represents the metamorphosis of Roman civilisation into Gothic barbarism through a transition from solemn ceremony to wild and brutal sport. So clearly structured is the sequence of action in this opening phase of the play, leading to the violation of Lavinia, that its significance can be followed almost entirely in terms of the strongly-defined patterns of stage-spectacle and movement. We attend as much to Shakespeare's choreography as to the dialogue, while the shifting tableaux of groups of figures, their physical movements and gestures, create a series of expressive parallels and contrasts in rhythm, emotional pitch and tone. The tragic issues are here presented in the language of theatrical form. (pp. 326-27)

The action begins with a brief tableau in which the two brothers Saturninus and Bassianus enter with drums and trumpets from opposite sides, confronting each other with their followers as rivals for their father's crown, as Marcus, the people's representative, appears above them holding the crown: the pyramidal grouping expresses both the rule of law, the formal majesty of the state, and the tensions that threaten to tear it apart. At the news of Titus' approach, this pageant disperses to make way for another. The triumphal entry of Titus is obviously a splendid and elaborate spectacle, carefully ordered by the stage-direction. . . . At this point however the victory march turns into a funeral procession: the triumph of Titus culminates in the burial of his sons, and the conjunction of these two cere-monies creates an ambiguity, reflected in Titus' speech, as though his glory is the sacrifice of his sons. Such an incon-gruous mingling of triumph and mourning has the effect of questioning the values underlying this Roman piety and sac-rifice, as the tomb of the Andronici is opened to gape like the jaws of some god appeased by devouring its offspring: the stage-image is powerful in suggestion. Moreover, this effect is intensified by our knowledge that Titus is re-enacting a rite he has performed five times before: repetition of an act itself establishes a ritualistic pattern.

The ensuing sacrifice of Alarbus to appease the sons of Titus who have themselves been sacrificed confirms our sense of inhuman cruelty in this ritual sequence. Tamora comes forward to plead for her son in a spontaneous movement that breaks the ceremonial ordering of the scene, yet also creates a new tableau in the pleading that ironically parallels Titus' prayer for his sons to the gods. . . . The mounting tension of the scene erupts into open violence as Alarbus is unceremoniously dragged off to be dismembered for interment; Tamora's cry, 'O cruel irreligious piety!' [I. i. 130] underlines the strong contradiction between formal ritual and such a brutal show of physical force. The dramatic situation has now been trans-formed, or rather it has developed according to an inner logic and momentum which now accelerates.

The contradictions of Titus' behaviour become increasingly apparent as he refuses to wear the ceremonial 'palliament' of the 'candidatus', but instead nominates Saturninus in his place, and as he offers Lavinia to Saturninus (much as he has sacrificed his sons to the state), provoking the open rebellion of Bassianus and the ensuing family brawl in which Titus kills his son Mu-tius. This slaughter takes place on-stage, but since Titus acts to uphold the same piety for which his other sons have died, the deed is akin to their sacrifices. This is the climactic point of the scene, and as if to reinforce our sense of a complete reversal of the opening situation, at this moment Saturninus enters 'aloft' as the new Emperor, with his former enemy but now his bride-to-be Tamora, her two sons and the still-silent Aaron: in the separation between lower and upper stage we see the divisions that are to dismember Rome itself. (pp. 327-28)

Aaron, a mute spectator of events in the opening Act, begins the following scene with a soliloquy. As so often in Shake-speare, the scene of crowded public activity is succeeded by a more intimate interlude that comments on the previous action from a new point of view. The transposition of style and tone is equally marked, as Aaron's Marlovian rhetoric of aspiration gives way to low comedy with the entry of Tamora's two clownish sons, Chiron and Demetrius. Instead of brooding upon vengeance for Alarbus, as we might have expected, they are engaged in a quarrel over Lavinia, adopting the comically inappropriate postures of rival lovers. This exhibition of a brotherly brawl itself parodies the action of the previous scene, and Aaron is once again the amused bystander until he inter-venes to prevent them from killing each other. Like the old Vice of the morality plays, Aaron acts with avuncular humour and superior intelligence to chide them and effect their rec-

onciliation by means of a scheme that promises further mis-chief. In the remainder of the scene he devises the plot that will satisfy the desires of each in the forest where the hunt is to take place.

The shift of location from court to forest, thus prepared for, suggest emblematically a reversion from civilised values to what we now call 'the law of the jungle'. Yet from what we have seen of Roman ceremonials, and of the breakdown of order that has already taken place, court and forest, like Roman and barbarian, have been assimilated to each other. As the 'solemn hunting' proposed by Titus is another form of ritualised bloodletting, so the dreadful fates that await Lavinia, her hus-band and two of her brothers are not only the consequences of events in Act One, but re-enactments of the cruel rites per-formed before. The gloomy pit which will consume its victims parallels the open tomb of the first scene. . . . It is the focal image of desecration, of the vile plot hatched by Aaron and acted out under his direction; moreover, 'this unhallow'd and blood-stained hole', as Martius calls it, 'the swallowing womb of this deep pit' [II. iii. 210, 239-40], as it is described by Quintus, are images that not only make it a fit place to avenge Alarbus' sacrificial death, but that relate both tomb and pit at the beginning of the play to the final banquet at which Tamora will 'Like to the earth, swallow her own increase' [V. ii. 191].

So the logic and the ritual of revenge involve a hideous pattern of re-enactment in the play. This pattern calls for the substi-tution of different figures in cyclic repetition, and the idea of displacement is one of the unifying elements in the play. (pp. 328-29)

Ritual and game, the solemn and the farcical, are also gro-tesquely mingled in Titus' enactment of his suffering, as though it is only in these forms of play that he can realise extremities of horror and cruelty that defy normal comprehension. The horrific of its very nature is that from which the mind shrinks, that which repels the senses, feelings and understanding, but for Titus there is no such evasion. Titus' passion is a continued struggle, not merely to endure the unendurable, but to express the inexpressible; he *performs* his woes out of the need to grasp what is all too real but virtually inconceivable in its enormity. The impulse to play, in other words, arises in Titus not as a retreat from the hideous reality that confronts him, but as a means of registering its full significance. His more bizarre fantasies, in which his mind seems to have collapsed under the unbearable suffering, are certainly symptoms of a precarious sanity, yet far from losing his grip on reality, through these obsessive pantomimes Titus' mind becomes fixed on its object. (p. 330)

The style of Titus' lamentation . . . is not mere formless rant: on the contrary, its imagery and ordering express the struggle to maintain an equilibrium in bringing the eyes to focus on such appalling and as yet totally inexplicable atrocity. Titus' 'consuming sorrow' is related to the imagery of devouring that is basic to the play:

> For now I stand as one upon a rock,
> Environ'd with a wilderness of sea,
> Who marks the waxing tide grow wave by wave,
> Expecting ever when some envious surge
> Will in his brinish bowels swallow him.
>
> [III. i. 93-7]

But as the waxing tide of calamity around him, and of his passions within, threatens to overwhelm him, there is a rock of identity that rises from this 'wilderness of sea': the very urge to clarification through a dramatised sense of self is enacted in these lines. And in the sequence of the following lines there is both a gathering momentum of mounting woes and a stabilising effect deriving from the balanced litany of enumeration:

> This way to death my wretched sons are gone;
> Here stands my other son, a banish'd man,
> And here my brother, weeping at my woes.
> But that which gives my soul the greatest spurn
> Is dear Lavinia, dearer than my soul.
> Had I but seen thy picture in this plight,
> It would have madded me; what shall I do
> Now I behold thy lively body so?
> Thou hast no hands to wipe away thy tears,
> Nor tongue to tell me who hath martyr'd thee;
> Thy husband he is dead, and for his death
> Thy brothers are condemn'd, and dead by this.
> Look, Marcus! Ah, son Lucius, look on her!
>
> [III. i. 98-110]

The dramatic power of these lines also arises from the way in which the patriarchal figure of Titus embraces all their afflictions, includes them within his own agony, and celebrates their union in suffering like a high priest of Sorrow. There is as yet no protest, no execration, no demand for justice; only 'a sympathy of woes' [III. i. 148], in which pity, so totally repressed in the opening scenes, now reasserts itself as the supremely humanising quality. Pity is enacted as the compelling need to identify with its object, to take its part and become one with what it beholds. . . . As an expression of pity, Titus' identification with Lavinia's suffering and his assimilation of his family's plight into his own ritualised performance gives another meaning to the motif of substitution in the play, and one that inverts the pattern of pitiless expiation in the earlier scenes. Pity moves Titus to a sustained act of imagination which alone can realise and express the magnitude of the suffering in which he participates.

Titus does not have long to wait before his compulsion to identify with Lavinia and to stand in place of his sorrowing kin is satisfied, by Aaron's entry with the offer of a reprieve for the condemned sons in exchange for a severed hand from one of the Andronici. Since this is Aaron's sadistic jest, it is fitting that it should reduce Titus, Marcus and Lucius to a ludicrous rivalry in their frantic efforts to volunteer the required article, but any laughter surely stops abruptly when Titus, outwitting his brother and son, is actually dismembered on-stage. Aaron alone continues to see the funny side of this spectacle, confiding to the audience that it is only the heads of his two sons that Titus will be given in return. Anticipating the outcome of this grisly practical joke, we now hear Titus break out into the most passionate of his laments, despite Marcus' attempts to restrain him. . . . [While the images of this speech] express a sense of boundless uncontrollable anguish, linked in their physical immediacy to the horrific spectacle we have just witnessed, there is a modulation through the imagery from the idea of limitless and therefore ungovernable woe to that of relief and purgation through utterance itself. . . . Once more, a tension is set up in the style of the dramatic verse between violent anarchic energies and a ritualistic impulse towards the formal devices of their enactment, and it is the turbulent energies themselves that are felt to seek such a formalised means of expression.

The Messenger who now enters, bearing the heads of Titus' sons and the severed hand, echoes by a characteristically Shakespearian touch the scene's major concern with 'a sympathy of woes', as he reports Aaron's cruel deception and proffers his own compassion for Titus. . . . This is the turning-point of the whole scene: as Marcus and Lucius bear the burden of inveighing against Aaron's malicious trick, Titus, now wrought to breaking-point, finds his only possible response in the terrible mirthless laugh that parodies the mockery of Aaron himself. He vows to seek 'Revenge's cave' (another metamorphosis of the devouring mouth), and makes a prophecy that will eventually be fulfilled to the very letter:

> I shall never come to bliss
> Till all these mischiefs be return'd again
> Even in their throats that have committed them.
>
> [III. i. 272-74]

The grisly pageant in which Titus . . . leaves the stage, carrying the head of one son while Marcus carries that of the other, and Lavinia brings up the rear with her Father's severed hand between her teeth, may be regarded as horror toppling over into farce through sheer excess. But this kind of laughter, as Titus has just shown, may also be a very effective release of hysterical tension: the emotional pitch, wrought steadily higher by the progression of the scene, is suddenly snapped by Titus' laugh, and his vows of revenge are calculating and deliberate, not distraught or frantic. So as he leaves the stage in this grotesque procession, the urge to laughter which the spectacle provokes in us secures and intensifies for the moment our complicity with his mood. It is a culminating effect which, in terms of the scene's internal dynamics, resolves the mounting pressure on our responses, and allows the scene to end in an abrupt shift of emotional perspective before the concluding sobriety of Lucius' soliloquy. (pp. 330-34)

Language is assimilated to ritual and game throughout the play, not only through the formal style of speeches of lamentation and prayer, through the witty wordplay of Aaron and the obsessive puns of Titus, but through the use of literary allusions and analogues. The power of utterance, like the impulse to perform tableaux that solemnise or parody reality, involves both the idea of repetition or re-enactment and that of substitution. 'Shall I speak for thee?' asks Marcus [II. iv. 33], moved to his lament by the spectacle of his mutilated niece, and his words reiterate her tragic plight by speaking on her behalf. So do the words of Ovid, in the scene where Lavinia opens the book of *Metamorphoses* at the tale of Tereus and Philomela [IV. i.]: her story is a reiteration of the poet's fiction, a substitution of one set of characters for another enacting the same pattern of events. Shakespeare's use of the Ovidian fable here, like that of the tapestry depicting the Fall of Troy in *The Rape of Lucrece,* is akin to the device of the play-within-the-play, in which art holds the mirror up to nature. But in *Titus Andronicus,* with its reiterative imagery of the devouring mouth, the revenge action itself is also a ritualised sequence of repetition through substitution.

The capacity of words to speak for woes brings relief through clarification. . . . Consequently the action of the play as a whole seems to turn upon the dual nature of the mouth that utters and devours: Lavinia's deprivation of speech is finally avenged by a banquet of uneatable flesh. Yet while extremities of horror and suffering seek comfort in utterance, of their very nature they are too dreadful to be named. Pleading in vain to Tamora before the outrage is committed upon her, Lavinia cannot bring herself to speak of rape except as 'one thing more, / That womanhood denies my tongue to tell' [II. iii. 173-74]; and when at last she reveals that crime by writing in the sand, the word she uses is Latin, 'Stuprum' [IV. i. 79]. In a sense, since this is a Roman play, that word does not conceal the horrid deed in the decent obscurity of a dead language, but rather, like Caesar's 'Et tu Brute', it gives a sudden actuality to the dramatic moment. When Chiron and Demetrius fall prey to Titus, they are seized with a thrice-repeated command:

> And stop their mouths if they begin to cry . . .
> Stop close their mouths, let them not speak a word . . .
> Sir, stop their mouths, let them not speak to me;
> But let them hear what fearful words I utter.
>
> [V. ii. 161-68]

The cutting of their throats on-stage is not therefore simply a gratuitous piece of butchery before they are dispatched to the kitchen: by a precise and macabre irony, the knife is again used to silence the voice. (pp. 334-36)

At the end of the play, after unspeakable woes have been reiterated in word and action, and the pattern of repetition which is the logic of revenge has gone its full circle, Marcus bids Lucius recount the tragic events to the people of Rome (it is we, the audience, who are to be addressed). . . . So Lucius speaks for Marcus, and for Titus and the others who have now themselves receded into the frame of a sad story, 'chanced in the time of old'. As the Andronici take their last farewell of the dead in ritual obsequy, Lucius reminds his young son of Titus:

> Many a story hath he told to thee,
> And bid thee bear his pretty tales in mind
> And talk of them when he was dead and gone.
>
> [V. iii. 164-66]

The tragedy that has been performed before us hardly makes a pretty tale, but it has shown us that through the reiterative processes of fiction and drama we confront, name and expiate the worst that is in us, and that in speaking for us tragedy enables us to become whole again.

My claim for *Titus Andronicus* is not only that it is a highly-ordered and elaborately-designed work, but that it is also one in which Shakespeare takes some extremely bold yet calculated risks with the resources of his art. Its faults are those of an excessively conscious theatrical and poetic ingenuity rather than those of crude sensationalism. It moves to admiration, in the Elizabethan sense of wonder and amazement, more often than to compassion or sympathy; even the laughter it provokes (although it is to the dread of modern theatre-directors) can be trusted as determined and controlled by Shakespeare's skilful management of tone and emotional pitch, disconcerting though it often is. The play is rich in dramatic and stylistic invention, and so full of analogues to its own art that it might be described as Shakespeare's thesis in tragedy, anticipating many of the formal techniques and devices used in the later tragedies. But it is for all that and above all an exciting piece for performance, and one which should stand in little need of apology in an age when our contemporary drama also seems to be exploring the basis of its own existence. (pp. 337-39)

> *D. J. Palmer, "The Unspeakable in Pursuit of the Uneatable: Language and Action in 'Titus Andronicus'," in* Critical Quarterly, *Vol. 14, No. 4, Winter, 1972, pp. 320-39.*

ALBERT H. TRICOMI (essay date 1976)

[Tricomi counters Wolfgang H. Clemen's assertion that the imagery in Titus Andronicus *does not proceed organically from the dramatic action (see excerpt above, 1951); instead, he stresses that the play's poetic language, especially its encompassing imagery of animals and vegetation, reveals the tragedy's "thematic integrity and imaginative power," which he finds rooted in "a dialectical contrast between the play's predatory animal images and its cardinal emblem of the enduring but mutilated garden." According to Tricomi, the play's imagery progresses from the early figure of the pastoral forest, established in the scene of Tamora's illicit union with Aaron, to the repeated violation of this idyllic garden, reflected primarily in the rape of Lavinia, with whom the pastoral imagery is continually identified. Tricomi states that Lavinia's mutilation also symbolizes the destruction of the Andronici family, with whom Tricomi also associates the play's image of "vegetative . . . civilized life," and by further extension, the destruction of Rome itself, which the Andronici represent by their political attachments. This mutilation, Tricomi remarks, is the result of the evil machinations of Tamora and Aaron—the two characters most closely associated with the play's beast or animal imagery. Tricomi concludes that the symbolism of the pastoral garden violated by the "predatory principle of malevolence" suggests the larger religious issue of divine justice. Ultimately, he asserts,* Titus *demonstrates that the gods are just, but that this justice does not necessarily preclude human tragedy. Although Titus and his family become the instrument of the gods' vindication, their acts of retribution permanently negate their previous creative and humane existence; however, their sacrifice also prepares the way for a revitalized Roman garden. Tricomi's interest in the function of Shakespeare's poetry and language in* Titus Andronicus *exemplifies an emerging critical trend in twentieth-century commentary on the play, which can also be found in the essays by Wolfgang H. Clemen (1951), Muriel C. Bradbrook (1951), Eugene M. Waith (1955), A. C. Hamilton (1967), James L. Calderwood (1971), and D. J. Palmer (1972).]*

Customary though it has been to highlight the ornamentality and decorativeness of the poetry in *Titus Andronicus*, its images create a thematic matrix that is impressive considering the early date of the tragedy. This thematic matrix, which governs the imagistic structure of the play, culminates in a dialectic contrast between the play's predatory animal images and its cardinal emblem of the enduring but mutilated garden. Through these central image patterns, the play reveals the tragic efforts of the Andronici to preserve a world of civilized virtues from the onslaught of a demonic barbarism. Oddly enough then, the very qualities of language in *Titus Andronicus* that once excited critical contumely hold the potential for revealing the play's thematic integrity and imaginative power.

Wolfgang Clemen observes of *Titus Andronicus* that the images lack "internal and external connection" with the structure of the tragedy; they appear to be "tacked on" [see excerpt above, 1951]. The focal point of his strictures, as well as those of Miss Bradbrook [see excerpt above, 1951] and a host of other reputable critics, is the prettified Ovidian monologue in Act II, scene iv, in which Marcus Andronicus discovers that his niece, Lavinia, has been raped and mutilated. Clemen's excoriation of the passage . . . is characteristic of many; however, it goes too far, for when on a broader level of generalization Clemen declares, "The images 'run wild,' they are not yet organically related to the framework of the play . . . ," his devastating judgment blinds us to the imagistic achievements of the play. The thematic integrity of the play's pastoral images, although couched in a context of Senecan horror, is not so very ludicrous at all. In fact, the same monologue that has become a cynosure of derision establishes the principal images of the garden setting that are basic to the thematic structure of the tragedy.

In this passage Marcus responds to the sight of Lavinia's mutilation by likening her to a denuded shade tree. . . . Having made this elaborate arboreal comparison, Marcus soon compares Lavinia's bleeding body, in a notorious simile, to a bubbling fountain. . . . In perusing this speech, we must notice that its central images of the denuded shade tree and the bubbling fountain are integrally related to one another, both being drawn from a pastoral setting, and are by no means ornamental. They also bear considerable symbolic weight in supporting the imagistic framework of the play. (pp. 89-91)

Lavinia and the forest in *Titus Andronicus* are imagined as one or nearly one throughout the play. Through this association, which becomes manifest by degrees, Shakespeare both defines and magnifies the significance of Lavinia's violation.

Before the forest is ever explicitly identified with Lavinia, that is before Marcus' speech at II. iv. 11, it begins to assume increasingly symbolic importance. As the title of Sommers' article, "Wilderness of Tigers," suggests, the forest in *Titus Andronicus* eventually becomes synonymous with barbarism and chaos [see excerpt above, 1960], but in the early acts, we must remember, it is often depicted as lovely and attractive. For Titus and for Saturninus the forest is initially an appealing, fit place to celebrate an Emperor's marriage with a recreational hunt. (pp. 91-2)

Through most of the second act Shakespeare delineates the forest as a pastoral haven so that even Tamora's illicit tryst with Aaron in the secluded bower bears the earmarks of an idyllic retreat or demi-paradise. In this wooded retreat "The birds chant melody on every bush" [II. iii. 12] and the green leaves "quiver with the cooling wind" while offering a pleasing shade [II. iii. 14-15]. Here, Tamora observes, lovers may enjoy "a golden slumber" while the "sweet melodious birds" act as "a nurse's song / Of lullaby to bring her babe asleep" [II. iii. 27-9]. We do well to savor the luxurious details of Tamora's pastoral description, for in the scenes immediately following, these very pastoral images reappear in Marcus' delineations of his niece Lavinia. However inappropriate his poeticizing otherwise appears, Marcus establishes the visual and aural correspondences between Lavinia and this idyllic retreat. In phrases that cannot help but recall Tamora's pastoral narration, Marcus describes Lavinia as "a sweet melodious bird" [III. i. 85], as a tree under "Whose circling shadows kings have sought to sleep in" [II. iv. 19], as a deer "straying in the park" [III. i. 88], and as one whose hands are "like aspenleaves" [II. iv. 45]—all of which suggests not only that Lavinia is associated with this pastoral demi-paradise but that her person appears to embody it.

Were this idyllic view of the forest unqualified throughout the play, we could indeed conclude that the images associated with it are part of a largely ornamental, albeit integrated, display. But there is dramatic tension in our perception of the forest from the outset. Aaron alone amongst the principal characters believes the forest to be "ruthless, dreadful, deaf, and dull" [II. i. 128], "Fitted by kind for rape and villainy" [II. i. 116]. Tamora's oafish sons, who are the henchmen of Aaron's thoughts, enter the forest in eager expectation of a rape; "Chiron, we hunt not, we, with horse nor hound, / But hope to pluck a dainty doe to ground" [II. ii. 25-6]. If we attend as well to the pastoral landscape that presides over Tamora's adulterous liaison with her black paramour, we will find in it a cause for eerie fascination and alarm, for in the midst of this paradisic haven we find that the coiled snake lies motionless in the cheerful sun [II. iii. 13].

As the symbol of the forest unfolds, then, we see in it a pastoral haven ominously threatened by an impending act of doom, the rape of Lavinia. That the forest and Lavinia are intimately associated with one another and that they share the same fate is made clear by Tamora's elaborate dissimulation that Lavinia's husband Bassianus intends to rape her. In creating this false witness, Tamora paints a new picture of the forest that inadvertently prophesies what it actually becomes:

> A barren detested vale you see it is;
> The trees, though summer, yet forlorn and lean,
> Overcome with moss and baleful mistletoe:
> Here never shines the sun: here nothing breeds,
> Unless the nightly owl or fatal raven:
> And when they show'd me this abhorred pit,
> They told me, here, at dead time of the night,
> A thousand fiends, a thousand hissing snakes,
> Ten thousand swelling toads, as many urchins,
> Would make such fearful and confused cries,
> As any mortal body hearing it
> Should straight fall mad, or else die suddenly.
> [II. iii. 93-104]

As if in ghoulish anticipation of the rape scene that is immediately to follow, Tamora's dissembling narration presents us with a metamorphosis of the pastoral garden she had previously portrayed. . . . Thus, in striking contradiction to Tamora's earlier account, the pastoral haven now reveals itself to be the pit of hell; the sleeping snake in the first account now hisses and is in its diabolism multiplied a thousandfold as the idyllic setting, now transfigured, is about to preside over Lavinia's own disfiguration. The metamorphosis of the pastoral forest *is* the metamorphosis of Lavinia writ large; the dual transfiguration is part of the same symbolic event.

At the center of these images that identify Lavinia with this pastoral setting and with the violation of its gardenlike condition stands the symbol of the bubbling fountain. As the most vividly developed metaphor in Marcus' ode to Lavinia's lost beauty, the image only appears to suffer from ornamentality and to disassociate itself from the pastoral imagery that otherwise dominates the speech. Not only is the fountain a proverbial fixture in the Renaissance pastoral, but it is also conventionally associated with the female sexual organs. . . . Given this cultural context, Marcus' comparison of Lavinia to a bubbling fountain and his earlier identification of Lavinia with the pastoral image of the shade tree reveals itself to be anything but decorative. The delineation of Lavinia as a bubbling fountain—that is, as an opened fountain whose seals have been broken—is an appropriate, tasteful, and almost conventional image of lost virginity and consequent shame.

In the mutilated form of her body as well, with tongue and hands cut out, Lavinia becomes just what Marcus says of her, "a conduit with three issuing spouts" [II. iv. 30]. In the seemingly endless streams of blood that spurt from her body, Lavinia becomes an emblem of ceaseless suffering and loss. She *is,* indeed, the fountain of sorrowful life; her maimed body has been sculpted in its image.

In all the important details of its imagined construction, in fact, the fountain image in *Titus Andronicus* reflects the tragedy that has befallen the Andronici. Not long after her mutilation, Marcus brings Lavinia to her father Titus who, although unaware of Marcus' earlier speech, employs a second figure of the fountain. This time the image functions explicitly as an emblem of irremediable sorrow:

> And thou [Lavinia], and I, sit round about some
>   fountain,

Looking all downwards to behold our cheeks
How they are stain'd, like meadows yet not dry,
With miry slime left on them by a flood?
And in the fountain shall we gaze so long
Till the fresh taste be taken from that clearness.
And made a brine-pit with our bitter tears?

[III. i. 123-29]

If the bubbling fountain waters as Marcus imagines them symbolize Lavinia's violated chastity and the mutilated condition of her limbs as well, the fountain basin as Titus imagines it is transfigured into "a brine-pit." This pit of brine evokes a memory of the pit into which Aaron craftily lures two of Lavinia's brothers so that they are later executed for the murder of Bassianus. At the same time, the waters in the fountain basin reflect the disconsolate faces of Titus and Lavinia. In this way the image of the fountain, which originates in the specific symbolism of Lavinia's violation, soon embraces as emblem all the suffering Andronici.

Because the fountain image iterates the metamorphosis of Lavinia and of the Andronici fortunes in general, it becomes a locus for the metaphysical anxiety that underlies the tragedy. As Titus gazes tearfully into the fountain basin, he finds not only the disfigured reflection of Lavinia but the sullied remains of a once verdant world. In Titus' imagination the salt drops from his eyes transform the clear waters of the fountain into a briny sea. This briny sea, fed by a flood of grief, overwhelms the earthen world and mires with slime its meadows. Through this image we discover once more the metamorphosis of the green landscape, but, even more importantly, we find the transfiguration of Titus' inner world. The same grief that mires with slime the weeping cheeks of Titus and Lavinia so mires their spirits with thirst for vengeance that they can never again regain the humanity they lose. In this inward transformation of Titus and Lavinia, the fountain water, now imagined as brinish with tears, reveals itself to be a symbol of the broken-bodied, broken-spirited, Andronici. Far from functioning as ornamental brocade, the image of the fountain, as Marcus employs it and as Titus later develops it, is fully integrated into the pastoral imagery in the play. Moreover, as Marcus delineates it, the spurting fountain embodies by the very details of its construction the most pervasive features of the tragedy, the maimed and bleeding human body. In this latter regard, the fountain with seals unstopped richly symbolizes Lavinia's violation, the violation of the pastoral garden, and the emergence of that power of blackness whose malignity the forest had always latently contained.

The hyperbolic events of plotting—the rape and disfigurement of Lavinia, the emperor's scornful rejection of the "gift" of Titus' right hand, and the heartless executions of Quintus and Martius—flamboyantly raise in theatrical terms the ontological issue of whether civilized men can withstand the enormity of evil that the world contains and still retain their humanity. The issue is visualized concretely in the literal opposition between Aaron's blackness of person and character and Lavinia's assailed whiteness of body and spirit. Through these emblematic characterizations, which beget a rich web of associative images, Shakespeare endeavors to explore the power of blackness in its eternal antagonism to its opposite. (pp. 92-6)

On the day of the fateful forest hunt, we hear that Titus and the court have prepared to hunt the panther and the deer. The hunted deer, we ironically discover, is to be Lavinia herself; but even more ironically, the panther, whom we never really see, begins to hunt his hunters and soon reveals itself to be identified with Aaron. (p. 96)

The "abhorred pit" that Tamora had imagined earlier in the fecundity of her malediction is in this scene with Aaron objectified and given life, which is to say that the unseen power of malevolence that Tamora first delineates is now rendered visible and real. At the same time we also recognize that while no real panther lies at the bottom of the pit, only the imagined pretence of one, Aaron's fraudulence is a genuine manifestation of his own fiendish imagination—and that power of blackness Martius and Quintus do discover at the bottom of the pit. Aaron is indeed the black panther of the tragedy, and it is the reality of that diabolism that Martius and Quintus discover when they find the decapitated body of their brother Bassianus and are subsequently charged with perpetrating the bloody deed. (p. 97)

Stated imagistically, the dialectic clash between dark and light, black and white, barbarism and civilization is subsumed in the play's two great imagistic clusters—its animal imagery and its mutilated plant imagery. Through these two great clusters of images, the play's poetic dialectic takes on dramatic life. According to the terms of this tragedy, Lavinia and the Andronici, depicted as mutilated trees and flora, are piece by piece literally torn apart by the savage animal principals of the play and cannot ever flourish until the latter are themselves destroyed.

The animal symbolism that identifies Aaron and Tamora and their scions is exuberant and unsurprising—Aaron is characteristically identified with the dark creatures of the earth. . . . Tamora and her brood are depicted as savage carnivores preying upon the Andronici, who are the flesh and blood of civilized Rome.

At the same time that the Andronici are depicted as the anguished human victims of an animal barbarism, they are also depicted emblematically as plants cut down or stunted in their growth. That is to say, when Marcus discovers Lavinia wandering in the woods and likens her to a shade tree hewed and lopped of its branches, he establishes the central emblem of the tragedy and the second of its irreducible imagistic terms. From this perspective, the opposition between the animal and the plant imagery ought not, strictly speaking, to be viewed in terms of the predator's relation to its victim since by definition the carnivore is not herbivorous and the metaphor is mixed in any case; rather, the relationship between the two great emblems of the tragedy functions as an affective device that underscores the helplessness of the Andronici and the initially unlike natures of the two opposing principals. More particularly, these antithetic emblems delineate the antagonism between a powerful, predatory principle of malevolence embodied in Tamora and Aaron and a vegetative principal of creative, civilized life, originally embodied in Lavinia and the other Andronici.

The meaning of this tragic conflict between the animal and the plant principles returns inevitably to the destruction of the pastoral world in Act II, scene iv, for once the panther and the tigress with her whelps overrun the forest and rape Lavinia, the park then loses its pastoral identity and becomes indeed in Titus' famous phrase, "a wilderness of tigers" [III. i. 54]. And the onslaught against the Andronici, both literal and imagistic, is relentless. (pp. 99-100)

Because of [the] relentless "trimming" of the Andronici, their hands, formerly victorious and able, are, like Lavinia's, rendered useless one by one. In the first act, Lavinia's request that Titus bless her "with thy victorious hand" [I. i. 163] proves, in view of her unhappy fate, utterly futile, as does Quintus' brotherly offer of a helping hand to Martius in the second act and as does Titus' unavailing gift of his hand to ransom the lives of his two sons from Saturninus in the third act. . . . In the mutilation of the Andronici, we witness the visual image of Rome's own mutilation, for in this tragedy the fortunes of the patriotic Andronici become synonymous with the destiny of the Roman state and civilization in general.

Tied to the political tragedy and expressed by the same imagery of mutilation is a large religious issue concerning the nature of life. Behind Titus' allusions to the uselessness of hands there stands the haunting emblem of the trimmed tree of Lavinia's body and the fundamental question of God's ultimate providence in reconstituting the garden of life. The hands of the Andronici, we are told explicitly, once possessed the creative power of feeding life, but now they have been rendered useless. Even their outstretched hands calling for the aid of Providence have gone unheeded.

Marcus' question to Titus, "Oh, why should nature build so foul a den, / Unless the gods delight in tragedies?" [IV. i. 59-60], explicitly voices this ontological concern. The answer in terms of *The Tragedy of Titus Andronicus* is that the gods are just but the justice they mete out does not preclude human tragedy. Lavinia and Titus, who at first helplessly endure the barbarian onslaught, begin to enact a retributive justice of their own. . . . No longer the mere object of Aaron's animal cunning, no longer a mere withered herb, Titus becomes in vengeance another carnivore in the wilderness of tigers. Thus, he dismembers the bodies of Lavinia's assailants and serves them to their mother Tamora in a baked pie. And because the revenge is accomplished in dumb show—Tamora, Chiron, and Demetrius are disguised respectively as Revenge, Rapine, and Murder—the allegorical significance of the event is played out fully before us. (pp. 100-02)

The gods are just, but they are not kind. Transformed by the horrors they have undergone, Titus and Lavinia cannot restore the processes of creative life, nor can they ever emerge humanely whole again. Titus' slaying of his own dishonored daughter out of pity before he is himself slain is tacit recognition that this world which has made a mangled ruin of their bodies has also transformed them utterly in spirit. With their thirst for revenge sated, there is nothing left for either Lavinia or the maddened Titus but the surcease of sorrow in death.

Yet, whatever the cost in body and spirit, Titus' retribution successfully extirpates the Gothic tigress and whelps from Rome. This accomplished, the state can be knit together again by others and the mutilated garden can once more grow healthily. This image of the fractured and dismembered state being knit together again is the play's resolving metaphor. (p. 102)

Such a sustained dialectic of imagistic ideas demonstrates Shakespeare's ability, even at this early stage of his career, to thrust seemingly ornamental images into a coherent poetic matrix. There is, of course, no point in denying that the play often suffers from a manifest discontinuity between its poetic conception and its dramatic realization. For this reason alone *Titus Andronicus* will surely remain one of Shakespeare's minor tragedies, but even so we need not be ashamed of it. Through its synthesizing emblem of the mutilated garden and all the images attendant upon its transformation, *Titus Andronicus* reveals the integrity of its imagistic structure and the authenticity of its tragic idea. (p. 103)

Albert H. Tricomi, "The Mutilated Garden in 'Titus Andronicus'," in Shakespeare Studies: An Annual Gathering of Research, Criticism, and Reviews, *Vol. IX, 1976, pp. 89-105.*

DAVID WILLBERN (essay date 1978)

[*Willbern undertakes a psychoanalytic interpretation of* Titus Andronicus, *focusing on the "manifest sexual, symbolic, and sadistic elements of the play." These latent sexual elements he identifies within the characters, imagery, and the structure of the play, which he considers based on the "ambivalent action of attack and defense, rape and rescue." For example, Willbern characterizes both Lavinia and Tamora as two opposing "symbolic personifications of female Rome"; the former is pure and virtuous, vulnerable to attack or invasion, and, like Rome itself, fought over by two brothers. Her rape by Tamora's sons in Act II, Scene iii is both a revenge and a rescue—the rescue of Tamora from the supposed attack on herself which she fabricates in order to incriminate Lavinia and Bassianus, and a revenge by Chiron and Demetrius against the threat to their mother's honor. On the other hand, Tamora is dangerous, seductive, and, also like the city under her leadership, malevolent, even cannibalistic. She ultimately represents, according to Willbern, "the catastrophic enactment of maternal malevolence: the dreaded devouring mother." Thus because her sexuality is completely oral, Willbern compares her role with that of the forest pit, both unconsciously suggesting the presence of a tomb, a womb, and, most importantly, a mouth—the last with all its potentialities for dismemberment and destruction. Since their threat is primarily oral, as Willbern states, the "revenge in Shakespeare's play is at its deepest level an oral vengeance." Willbern concludes that Titus's final revenge—his Thyestean banquet—returns to Tamora the vengeance she represents throughout* Titus Andronicus, *namely, all of humanity's unconscious fantasies of the devouring mother. The final image of retribution, as Willbern asserts, is essentially Shakespeare's hyperbolic dramatization of that threat. Willbern's treatment is the most comprehensive psychoanalytic interpretation of* Titus Andronicus *so far, yet many elements in his analysis—such as the emphasis on the forest pit as a controlling image in the drama and the interpretation of Lavinia and Tamora as personifications of Rome—can be found in the essays by Alan Sommers (1960), A. C. Hamilton (1967), and D. J. Palmer (1972).*]

[*Titus Andronicus*] opens with a choreographed confrontation of opposites, which provides a highly formal structure to contain potential violence: *"Enter the Tribunes and Senators aloft; and then enter Saturninus and his followers at one door, and Bassianus and his followers at the other, with drums and trumpets"* [I. i. S.D.]. This balanced entrance of opposing forces establishes a careful visual patterning which dramatizes the conflict between the two Roman brothers. Their opening speeches maintain this tension, and reveal the two basic impulses which energize the play: attack and defense. (p. 160)

These two speeches emerge from very different motivations. Saturninus makes his plea to Rome's fathers (*patres*, patricians) on the basis of his own reflection of his "father's honours." He urges his followers to use their swords in the confirmation of patrilineal primogeniture. The "love" he solicits involves a violent attack against other Roman citizens. Bassianus, on the other hand, appeals to his own favored position "in the eyes of royal Rome" [I. i. 11] in asking his followers to defend "this passage" from the "dishonour" which Saturninus' attack would mean.

Beyond indicating the different character traits of the two brothers, these opening speeches establish a balance of attack and defense on which the action of *Titus Andronicus* is structured. More precisely, attack in this play means sexual attack (rape),

Act II. Scene iii. Tamora, Demetrius, Lavinia, Chiron, and the body of Bassanius. By Samuel Woodforde (n.d.).

and these speeches glance at this central event. Bassianus' wish to defend the Mother of Cities from assault and "dishonour" is primarily a wish to protect her from rape, to defend her "passage" and preserve her "virtue" and her "continence." For Rome in this play is clearly feminine. Bassianus' personification of the city ("in the eyes of royal Rome") suggests the significance of Rome herself as a character in the play, over whose possession the two "suitors" quarrel [I. i. 44]. Saturninus implies a similar personification when he agrees to dismiss his suit in favor of Titus' judgment: "Rome, be as just and gracious unto me / As I am confident and kind to thee. / Open the gates and let me in" [I. i. 60-2]. . . . Saturninus implicitly voices a desire for maternal affection and acceptance. As we shall see, the wished-for opening of the gates is latently sexual and highly ambivalent: entry into the mother's body, in both genital and oral terms, is unconsciously as terrifying as it may be pleasurable. (p. 161)

Titus, too, associates Rome with a mother's womb: especially the center of his Rome, the ancestral tomb of the Andronici:

> O sacred receptacle of my joys,
> Sweet cell of virtue and nobility,
> How many sons hast thou of mine in store,
> That thou wilt never render to me more!
>
> [I. i. 92-5]

In burying his sons, Titus returns them to their origin (notice that his language echoes Bassianus' description of the Capitol, "the imperial seat, to virtue consecrate, / . . . and nobility";

later he refers to the sacred sepulchre as "virtue's nest" [I. i. 376]). The equation of womb and tomb is central to the unconscious action of *Titus Andronicus.*

In giving Rome to Saturninus by choosing him emperor, Titus in effect gives him a maternal woman. In fact, he immediately gives him Lavinia, who is "Rome's rich ornament," "Rome's royal mistress" [I. i. 52, 241]. Lavinia, the symbol of female Rome, is moreover almost a magical restorative to Titus: "the cordial of mine age," as he calls her [I. i. 166]. Fought over by imperial claimants, attacked by barbarian Goths, and finally avenged by the Andronici, she repeats by her personal fate the larger fate of Rome herself. (pp. 162-63)

Tamora is in an important respect a substitute for Lavinia, and is herself highly symbolic. Saturninus accepts her in place of Lavinia as the new empress of Rome. Her own maternal status is evident: as she describes her relationship to Saturninus, she "will a handmaid be to his desires, / A loving nurse, a mother to his youth" [I. i. 331-32].

Both Lavinia and Tamora may be seen as symbolic personifications of female Rome. They enact contrasting aspects: the pure and virtuous mother, threatened with attack and invasion, who needs protection and rescue; and the dangerous, seductive, threatening mother, *from* whom one needs protection. Revenge against the latter will lead magically to restoration of the former. The defeat of evil Rome, under Saturninus and Tamora, and the re-establishment of virtuous Rome, under a new emperor, are the basic political and psychological goals of the play.

Saturninus concludes Act I by proclaiming "a love day," since it is the wedding-day of both himself and his brother (Tamora has urged a treacherous reconciliation). Titus then suggests a hunt for the next day, to "give [his] grace bonjour" [I. i. 491-94]. Hunting thus becomes implicitly a version of what happens after marriage, as the ensuing events in the woods will reveal, and as Saturninus discloses with his coy allusion to the wedding-night:

> *Titus.* I promised your grace a hunter's peal.
> *Saturninus.* And you have rung it lustily, my lords;
> Somewhat too early for new-married ladies.
>
> [II. ii. 13-15]

Hunting and sexuality are traditionally connected in myth and literature, as well as by the common word "venery." These sexual undertones are intensified by the fiendish plans of Tamora's sons, whose hunt is not for the usual game: "Chiron," Demetrius tells his brother, "we hunt not, we, with horse nor hound, / But hope to pluck a dainty doe to ground" [II. ii. 25-6]. These two vicious Goths begin Act II by quarreling over Lavinia. Their dispute is another version of the quarrel which opened the play: two brothers arguing over the possession of a woman. (pp. 164-65)

Aaron urges the brothers to stop quarreling and take their pleasures by force, and they depart to join the hunt. The Moor's own amusements are more subtle, and he now begins to instigate his vicious villainy by burying gold under a tree. "This gold," he tells us,

> . . . must coin a stratagem,
> Which, cunningly effected, will beget
> A very excellent piece of villainy:
> And so repose, sweet gold, for their unrest
> That have their alms out of the empress' chest.
>
> [II. iii. 5-9]

Aaron's imagination plays with very sexual metaphors ("coin," "beget," "piece"). His villainy will figuratively be born out of his implanted stratagem. The final line is puzzling. It seems to echo Aaron's previous advice to Chiron and Demetrius, to "revel in Lavinia's treasury" [II. iii. 131], with a similar sexual meaning (reinforced by the sexual metaphor which precedes it). In this sense, it alludes to the dangers of the sexually seductive Tamora. There is, however, another non- (or rather pre-) genital meaning of the word "chest": it means "breast," and Shakespeare uses it in this way in *The Rape of Lucrece* [l. 761]. Since "alms" refers to charitable sustenance—free nurturance, one might say—the phrase also suggests the Empress in her malignant and frustrating maternal role. . . . Any connection with Tamora becomes dangerous. In psychoanalytic terms, and in the ultimate dramatic terms of the play, Tamora— "this queen, / This goddess, this Semiramis, this nymph, / This siren" [II. i. 22-3]—is the catastrophic enactment of maternal malevolence: the dreaded devouring mother.

Tamora's entrance at this precise moment coincides exactly with Aaron's ambiguous allusion to her, and her proposal of amorous "conflict" actualizes the metaphor of Aaron's speech. Describing the grove they are in as "green" and "cooling" and "sweet," she suggests love-making, and then, later, she tells Aaron,

> We may, each wreathed in the other's arms,
> Our pastimes done, possess a golden slumber,
> Whiles hounds and horns and sweet melodious birds
> Be unto us as is a nurse's song
> Of lullaby to bring her babe asleep.
>
> [II. iii. 25-9]

Her proposal characterizes sexuality in regressive oral terms, culminating in the obvious maternal image of the nurse and her babe. (pp. 165-66)

Faced with the underlying danger of Tamora's seductive sexuality, Aaron rejects her proposition while simultaneously affirming his own threatened phallic potency. Symbolic images of arousal ("my deadly-standing eye," "my fleece of woolly hair that now uncurls" [II. iii. 32, 34]) represent an active apotropaic defense against Tamora's wiles. Denying the sexual temptation, Aaron asserts that "these are no venereal signs" [II. iii. 37], but marks of potent revenge. Sexuality is displaced onto vengeance, which becomes its symbolic substitute. Revenge is both a substitute for sexuality and a defense against it: it is both threat and rescue. (p. 166)

In psychoanalytic terms, Aaron's latent character is "phallic" but not "genital." He plays no direct part in the rape of Lavinia, although an audience might plausibly expect him to, and the black baby which results from his secret union with Tamora immediately becomes the object of her hatred and his defense:

> *Chiron.*   It shall not live.
> *Aaron.*   It shall not die.
> *Nurse.*   Aaron, it must; the mother wills it so.
>
> [IV. ii. 80-2]

This bald expression of maternal malevolence rouses Aaron to a heroic speech [IV. ii. 88-105] in which he challenges the Titans, Heracles, and Ares to try to take his child away. He will raise his son alone, in the wilderness, without a mother, "to be a warrior" [IV. ii. 178-81]. In this heroic male fantasy, the threatened child is rescued and preserved, independent of and invulnerable to the female. (p. 167)

[Tamora] makes one last attempt to embrace [Aaron] just as Bassianus and Lavinia discover them [II. iii. 50-2]. Aaron then leaves Tamora to face her accusers. "Who have we here?" asks Bassianus, and he sarcastically compares her with Diana. Tamora replies by showing him the fate of Actaeon, another luckless hunter who saw what he should not have seen:

> Had I the pow'r that some say Dian had,
> Thy temples should be planted presently
> With horns, as was Actaeon's; and the hounds
> Should drive upon thy new-transformed limbs,
> Unmannerly intruder as thou art.
>
> [II. iii. 61-5]

This mythological allusion—to spying, interruption, dismemberment, and death (by being devoured)—portrays a miniature enactment of the ensuing fatal events. Unmannerliness results in unmanning. For their untimely interruption, Bassianus will be killed and Lavinia raped and mutilated. The moment dramatizes the fearsome aspect of "the stately Phoebe 'mongst her nymphs," as Tamora was once described [I. i. 316]. (pp. 167-68)

At this point Chiron and Demetrius appear, already tutored in their sadistic duties by Aaron. They are given superfluous motives for their villainy, however, by the strange fantasy which their mother produces to accuse Bassianus and Lavinia:

> These two have 'ticed me hither to this place:
> A barren detested vale you see it is;
> The trees, though summer, yet forlorn and lean,
> Overcome with moss and baleful mistletoe:
> Here never shines the sun: here nothing breeds,
> Unless the nightly owl or fatal raven:
> And when they show'd me this abhorred pit,
> They told me, here, at dead time of the night,
> A thousand fiends, a thousand hissing snakes,
> Ten thousand swelling toads, as many urchins,
> Would make such fearful and confused cries,
> As any mortal body hearing it
> Should straight fall mad, or else die suddenly.
> No sooner had they told this hellish tale,
> But straight they told me they would bind me here
> Unto the body of a dismal yew,
> And leave me to this miserable death.
> And then they called me foul adulteress,
> Lascivious Goth, and all the bitterest terms
> That ever ear did hear to such effect;
> And had you not by wondrous fortune come,
> This vengeance on me had they executed.
> Revenge it, as you love your mother's life,
> Or be ye not henceforth call'd my children.
>
> [II. iii. 92-115]

Here is Freud's plenty. The passage expresses highly sadistic fantasies of sexual attack and matricide, from which the mother must then be rescued by an act of filial revenge. Sexual symbols abound in this frightening vision of a classic *locus horrendus*. "The abhorred pit" will soon assume its central and over-determined symbolic significance as vagina, womb, tomb, and mouth, and all those "snakes" and "urchins" (hedgehogs or goblins) and "swelling toads" may plausibly be imagined as grotesquely distorted phallic threats. The context of the entire scene has been sexual, and Tamora implicitly admits that sexuality is a basis for her fantasy when she calls herself "foul adulteress, / Lascivious Goth." She demands revenge, but she also terms the fantasized attack on herself "this vengeance":

revenge is hence a complex of sexual attack, punishment for sexual activity, and rescue from sexual threat. After being subjected, in fantasy or in reality, to sadistic rape, the woman is rescued by revenge. Tamora's nightmarish vision traces the unconscious genesis of revenge in *Titus Andronicus:* the threat of rape or dishonor or invasion to the maternal figure (Lavinia, Tamora, Rome) requires dutiful vengeance. The first act of revenge will be to kill the man while rescuing the woman. Bassianus suffers in Act II what Mutius (Titus' son) suffered in Act I, and what Saturninus will suffer in Act V. Chiron and Demetrius kill Bassianus in the "rescue" of Tamora, just as Titus killed his son "in the rescue of Lavinia" [I. i. 417], and as Lucius will kill Saturninus in the rescue of maternal Rome. (pp. 168-69)

These [matricidal and incestuous] impulses are central to the attack on Lavinia, who is taken away to her horrible fate while her murdered husband is carried off to the pit. Aaron now enters, leading two of Titus' sons, Quintus and Martius, to "the loathsome pit" where he says he "espied a panther fast asleep" [II. iii. 194]. The symbol of this pit lies at the absolute core of the play. As A. C. Hamilton states, "the dark forest with the pit at the center becomes a major dramatic symbol upon which the play turns" [see excerpt above, 1967]. Martius falls into the "subtle hole," and his brother's description is revealing:

> What, art thou fallen? What subtle hole is this,
> Whose mouth is covered with rude-growing briers,
> Upon whose leaves are drops of new-shed blood
> As fresh as morning dew distill'd on flowers?
> A very fatal place it seems to me.
>
> [II. iii. 198-202]

The description—considered symbolically—is almost anatomical. It represents a detailed natural image of a violated vagina (the "flowers" in line 201 recall the word "deflower" used ten lines before to refer to Lavinia). This onstage symbolic event occurs simultaneously with the offstage rape of Lavinia by the other set of brothers. Any unconscious expectation of Lavinia's ravishment, frustrated to an extent by its apparent enactment offstage, is satisfied by its symbolic substitute. (p. 170)

At one level these strange adventures are a repetition, or symbolic reenactment, of the rape of Lavinia, and thereby suggest the latent identity of these two sets of brothers (and the Andronici are punished for what their Gothic counterparts do). But the symbol of the pit is not confined to genital significance. It is both womb and tomb, and vagina, but it is also and most importantly a *mouth,* as its description clearly reveals. This connection of the facts of birth and copulation and death with fantasies of being devoured is crucial to *Titus Andronicus,* as it is to psychoanalytic theory. For the unconscious fear of women—more precisely, of female genitals—may originate from a more primary source than castration anxiety. It can emerge from a fear of the catastrophically perceived preoedipal mother, who threatens total dismemberment and destruction (the devouring mother). This threat is seen as primarily oral and, consequently, revenge in Shakespeare's play is at its deepest level an oral vengeance. What else, after all, could a cannibalistic feast be? The "detested, dark, blood-drinking pit" [II. iii. 224] will again practice its proper action of devouring in the grisly climax of the bloody banquet. (p. 171)

Of course, the "pit" in *Titus Andronicus* is also Hell. The theatrical trapdoor "Hell-mouth" which serves as the actual

pit in performance makes the allusion visibly possible. But this parallel significance by no means alters the basic bodily source, since for Shakespeare "Hell" ("there's hell, there's darkness, / There's the sulphurous pit" [*King Lear*, IV. vi. 126-27]) can also symbolize female genitals.

> And whether that my angel be turned fiend,
> Suspect I may, yet not distinctly tell,
> But being both from me both to each friend,
> I guess one angel in another's Hell.
>   Yet that shall I ne'er know, but live in doubt,
>   Till my bad angel fire my good one out.
>
> [Sonnet 144]

The bawdy word-play on intercourse ("in . . . Hell") and venereal disease ("fire") is typical of other sonnets, and present in Lear's tirade as well. But the burning and consumption which terrify Lear represent more than merely a fear of infection. The "pit" locates those primal fears of total destruction which haunt both *King Lear* and *Titus Andronicus.* Shakespeare's later tragedy is obsessed with the same fantasy which informs his earliest one. Gloucester's ravaged face, with its "bleeding rings, / Their precious stones new lost" [*Lear*, V. iii. 190-91], is a mirror of Lavinia's.

When we finally see the mutilated bride, *"her hands cut off, and her tongue cut out, and ravished"* [II. iv. S.D.], she has accumulated a great deal of symbolic significance. Her lamentable condition is a stark visual reminder of the unconscious proximities of sexuality, rape, death, and dismemberment on which the play builds. The shock of her sudden appearance is accompanied by Marcus' epilogue-like speech which concludes Act II. Her uncle's first reference to her missing hands includes the statement that "kings have sought to sleep in" her arms [II. iv. 18-19]. An echo of the events of Act I, when Bassianus and Saturninus were temporary rivals for her love (and committed her initial "rape"), the phrase reminds us of the central force behind Lavinia's fate: sexual desire. Before Marcus specifically discovers her rape, he is alluding to its gentler counterpart. "Come, let us go, and make thy father blind, / For such a sight will blind a father's eye" [II. iv. 52-3], says Marcus as he leads his niece offstage, "a fearful sight of blood and death" [II. iii. 216] like the pit of which she is now a living symbol. The imagined blindess is both a defense against having to look at such a horrible symbolic image, and also a punishment *for* seeing it. Lavinia has become a kind of Medusa: when Lucius sees her he exclaims, "Ay me, this object kills me" [III. i. 64], and young Lucius is understandably frightened by her [see IV. i. 1-7]. She presents a grim image of the dangers of sexuality, and a constant visual reminder of the bloody pit at the deepest core of this play.

After the explosive release of violence and sadism in Act II, Act III provides a balance of grief and punishment. It is the accumulation of horrors in this act which drives Titus to the verge of madness and beyond to the diabolical calculation of suitable revenge. (pp. 172-73)

To avoid being swallowed up by either grief or future villainy, Titus . . . must turn villainy back against the villains. Pushed finally by the pressure of intolerable outrage into a position beyond sorrow and grief-stricken self-posturing, [he] begins the crafty and deliberate plotting of revenge. His goal is to see that "all these mischiefs be return'd again / Even in their throats that hath committed them" [III. i. 273-74]. His ultimate vengeance will literalize the cliché, by meeting the oral threat with its mirror, oral revenge. "Come," he directs the remnants of his family: "let me see what task I have to do" [III. i. 275]. The task is to "plot some device of further misery, / To make us wonder'd at in time to come" [III. i. 134-35]. This choice of active plotting involves the rejection of passive, pageant-like suffering: "Or shall we bite our tongues, and in dumb shows / Pass the remainder of our hateful days?" [III. i. 131-32]. Titus' image is most precise: oral sadism, in submission turned inward ("bite our tongues"), in revenge turns outward. (p. 174)

Having learned of the fact of Lavinia's rape through a literary reference to the tale of Philomela [IV. i. 41 ff.], Titus imagines himself the appropriate literary avenger: "For worse than Philomel you used my daughter," he tells Chiron and Demetrius, "And worse than Progne I will be reveng'd" [V. ii. 194-95]. "I'll play the cook," he exults, with true theatrical zeal. His actions repeat an artistic pattern. He appeals to another such pattern when he stabs his daughter during the climactic banquet: the example of Virginius, who killed his own daughter to prevent her defilement, provides "a reason mighty, strong, and effectual; / A pattern, president, and lively warrant" for Titus [V. iii. 43-45]. This confused (and in terms of the literary example, inaccurate) gesture of mad vengeance and paternal love, in which a father kills his daughter in order belatedly to save her, presents another instance of the ambivalent action of attack and defense, rape and rescue, and a further enactment of the murderous hostility toward women which informs the play. (p. 175)

Tamora assumes that her tantalizing wiles will entrap Titus. . . . The strategy of her temptation is to disguise herself as "Revenge, sent from th' infernal kingdom" [V. ii. 30], and to call on Titus as he sits in his study "ruminat[ing]"—i.e., chewing—"strange plots of dire revenge" [V. ii. 6]. The staging of this "Senecan playlet" is especially interesting. "Revenge" is traditionally an infernal figure (as, for example, in *The Spanish Tragedy*), and Tamora pretends to have been "sent from below," "from th' infernal kingdom" [V. ii. 3, 30]. . . . Her invitations to Titus to "Come down" [V. ii. 33, 43] would then be enticements into Hell itself. That Hell is of course the theatrical "Hellmouth," and in *Titus Andronicus* its fearful characteristics have been defined by its use in the "pit" episodes. Tamora, the devouring mother, stands within the symbol of her dreadful power: the true panther in the pit, beckoning Titus to enter (to his death). This staging makes a strong visual connection between the Empress and the blood-drinking pit— a connection which will be reinforced in the actual blood-drinking of the final scene.

Titus, of course, only pretends to swallow the bait Tamora offers him. He takes it only to seize his opportunity to reciprocate Gothic villainy with gruesome gusto. The vainly disguised Chiron and Demetrius hear him exclaim,

> Hark, villains, I will grind your bones to dust,
> And with your blood and it I'll make a paste,
> And of the paste a coffin I will rear,
> And make two pasties of your shameful heads,
> And bid that strumpet, your unhallowed dam,
> Like to the earth swallow her own increase.
> [V. ii. 186-91]

Titus' recitation of his vengeful plans, which plays with the familiar nursery rhyme, is stylized like a diabolic incantation. The ritualistic rhetoric manages the most horrible fantasy. One critic contends that "in context, it is not murder that we witness, nor even personal revenge, but a solemn sacrifice" (like

the sacrifice of Alarbus in Act I) [see excerpt above by A. C. Hamilton, 1967]. Titus' retaliation is fiendishly ingenious; he will return the villains to the womb which engendered them, re-incorporating them into the dark and dangerous place from which they came. For the womb is also a tomb, like the pit which is a kind of coffin (like the coffin carried onstage at the opening of the play [I. i. 69 S.D.]) as well as a devouring mouth: it contains a corpse. Titus will create a "coffin" (pastry) to be devoured as the perfect mirror-vengeance for the coffin that devours. The "devouring receptacle," "the swallowing womb," "the blood-drinking pit" [II. iii. 224], is once again dramatically symbolized as Tamora sits "eating the flesh that she herself hath bred" [V. iii. 62]. All of the unconscious fantasies which accompany the primal fear of being devoured find expression in this banquet, an action as over-determined as the bloody pit which prefigured it. Being eaten by the mother symbolizes incestuous intercourse (entry into the mother's body) as well as death by dismemberment and dissolution. It is simultaneously a rape and the retaliatory punishment such rape requires. It enacts the threat of maternal malevolence at its most hyperbolic, but directed against the monster's own flesh. Revenge returns, even in her throat.

With the bloody banquet, Titus' revenge is perfected, and the killings which now follow in rapid-fire order and within an almost ludicrous rhymed interlude are anti-climactic. The chaotic violence which finally erupts from the formal confines of the ritualistic revenge ultimately exhausts itself by slaughtering aggressors and victims alike—and they *are* alike at this final moment, indistinguishable in the furious vengeance that engulfs them. (pp. 177-80)

Marcus and Lucius share the task of "tell[ing] the tale" [V. iii. 94] of Rome and the Andronici, of providing a formal close to the sad events. Half of this final scene is devoted to the rehearsal in words of everything that has occurred by deeds. This repetition of the past is essential to the process of developing psychological control over the ferocities just passed. Remembrance becomes re-membering. The strategy functions for the audience as well as for the dramatic characters.

Lucius, once banished by ungrateful Rome, is now welcomed by the grateful city which he has rescued, and is made emperor. Notice the focus of the attack against Rome, which he has both enacted and repulsed:

> I am the turn'd forth, be it known to you,
> That have preserv'd her welfare in my blood
> And *from her bosom* took the enemy's point,
> Sheathing the steel in my advent'rous body.
> [V. iii. 109-12; critic's italics]

Titus' son becomes the eventual hero, now in complete control of both Romans and Goths, able to restore the shattered city under his purely masculine rule. He has invaded Rome and killed the Emperor, at the head of a barbarian army, but as filial rescuer and not as traitorous aggressor. His revenge is a literal enactment of those fears of invasion implicit in Act I, but it is a just retaliation and not an unjust attack. The rescue repeats the threat, but from a different attitude (in psychoanalytic terms, a superego attitude). By means of an identification with the aggressor, Lucius has become the ruler and judge of the world of the play.

Titus Andronicus, like *The Spanish Tragedy* and other revenge plays, ends with the decree of appropriate punishments to the major villains: Aaron, the "breeder of these dire events," and "that ravenous tiger, Tamora" [V. iii. 178, 195]. Aaron's fate is especially revealing. Fulfilling his previous vow that the Moor should ''receive no sustenance'' after he is captured [V. iii. 6], Lucius commands

> Set him breast-deep in the earth, and famish him;
> There let him stand and rave and cry for food.
> If anyone relieves or pities him,
> For the offence he dies. This is our doom.
> Some stay to see him fast'ned in the earth.
> *Aaron.* Ah, why should wrath be mute, and fury dumb?
> I am no baby, I, that with base prayers
> I should repent the evils I have done. . . .
>
>   [V. iii. 179-86]

Aaron's denial discloses an unconscious fantasy. He is indeed like a baby, half-born and half-buried and half-devoured by the earth, crying for food. Anyone who would dare serve as a mother to him will be killed. Matricide pursues even those who would only act the part. Aaron's torment is moreover an image of that of the mythical Tantalus, whose fate represents the *locus classicus* of oral revenge.

Enforced starvation is not the only kind of oral revenge. Tamora's corpse is to be thrown ''to beasts and birds to prey'' [V. iii. 198]. The threatening devourer will herself be devoured. Revenge comes full circle, finally repeating as punishment what once was feared. As the revenger identifies with the aggressor, so revenge identifies with the offense. In the primitive logic of the unconscious, and in the primary strategies of the revenge play, *lex talionis* is the inexorable rule. (pp. 180-82)

> David Willbern, ''Rape and Revenge in 'Titus Andronicus','' in English Literary Renaissance, *Vol. 8, No. 2, Spring, 1978, pp. 159-82.*

RONALD BROUDE   (essay date 1979)

[*Broude claims that the ''guiding force'' in* Titus Andronicus *''is something very much like the Christian Providence of Shakespeare's histories.'' He contends that within the framework of his general ''theme of revenge as an instrument of political regeneration,'' Shakespeare depicts four types of retribution found in Elizabethan society and which figured predominantly in the so-called ''Tudor myth'' of the dramatist's lifetime; these include human sacrifice, the blood vendetta, state justice, and providential retribution. Broude characterizes the sacrifice of Alarbus and Tamora's ''blood revenge'' as examples of pagan vengeance—methods of retribution that, as events in* Titus *demonstrate, provoke a ''potentially endless chain of aggression and retaliation.'' Broude asserts that Shakespeare combined the latter two forms of revenge—state justice and providential retribution—in the figure of Titus, a ''divine avenger'' whose punitive exercises in the last act restore order and justice to Rome. For additional commentary on the role of divine justice in* Titus Andronicus, *see the excerpt by Irving Ribner (1960).*]

In *Titus Andronicus,* Shakespeare depicts four forms of vengeance, each based upon its own definition of right and wrong, each prescribing its own means of effecting retribution, and each functioning within the context of its own religious or social system. We encounter the human sacrifice by which the ghosts of the slain are placated with the blood of their slayers; the vendetta, in which families ruthlessly avenge past injuries in order to discourage future ones; the state justice which maintains civil order by punishing those who transgress its laws; and the divine vengeance which upholds cosmic order, and, directed by Providence, turns crime and punishment alike to the uses of an inscrutable Purpose.

The pagan setting of *Titus Andronicus* enables Shakespeare to underline the differences between ''non-Christian'' and ''Christian'' forms of vengeance. The former—human sacrifice and certain kinds of vendetta—are presented as fundamentally futile, motivated by superstition and misguided family loyalty. Unlike Christian retribution, Shakespeare's pagan vengeance presupposes a more or less continuous state of bloody strife, a state which renders superfluous all inquiry into the circumstances surrounding any particular outrage. Every deed of violence, whether justified or not, is understood to require a response, and so there is forged a potentially endless chain of vengeance in which each act of revenge is both the answer to a previous act and the provocation to a new one.

On the other hand, state justice and divine vengeance, which Shakespeare represents along the lines of approved Tudor models, assume as the norm of human existence a condition of order which crime may temporarily disrupt but which is re-established by the retribution that inevitably follows. Such a norm is presupposed in *Titus,* for—notwithstanding the paganism of the characters—the guiding force in the play is something very much like the Christian Providence of Shakespeare's histories. For this force, retribution is not simply the exaction of blood for blood but is rather an instrument of regeneration: the string of revenges which culminates in the Thyestean banquet of Act V is so directed that it not only balances accounts of blood but also makes possible the amalgamation of the Goth and Roman peoples. The sacrifice of Alarbus is presented by Shakespeare as a characteristic example of pagan vengeance, an instance of the way in which superstition and obligations of blood may combine to shake the foundations of a mighty commonweal. (pp. 495-96)

Such sacrifices represent the darker side of Greco-Roman religion: they are examples of the rites called ''ceremonies of avoidance.'' It is not the gods above but rather the spirits of the dead below—the *manes*—who demand such offerings. Kinsmen who fail to satisfy the *manes'* desire for their enemies' blood may well become themselves the object of the hatred of these potentially dangerous spirits. Fear thus plays an important part in these grim ceremonies: the ill will of the *manes* must be avoided at all costs, and the living are often little-disposed to be chary about the means employed to satisfy the dead.

Shakespeare handles Alarbus' sacrifice with full appreciation of its archaeological significance. . . . The sinister tone of superstitious dread is effectively conveyed by Lucius' reference to ''prodigies'' and by his use of ''unappeas'd.'' This note is echoed by Titus, who shortly afterward insists that Alarbus must die ''T'appease their groaning shadows that are gone'' [I. i. 126].

We are expected to condemn Alarbus' sacrifice on religious, humanitarian, and political grounds. Tamora, in an oxymoron that would have had added meaning for a Christian audience, unwittingly puts her finger on the paradoxical aspect of Titus' zeal when she assails her son's sacrifice as ''irreligious piety'' [I. i. 130]. There is certainly piety in Titus' determination that the sacrifice go on: the sincerity of his motives is never in question. But the rite is ''irreligious'' because the supernatural beings in whose name it is carried out are false gods. As Tamora also reminds us [I. i. 112-20], Alarbus' sacrifice is both cruel and unjust. The criteria which doom Alarbus are too few to admit the claims of anyone but the *manes*. Neither the circumstances under which the slain Andronici died nor the part (if any) Alarbus may have played in their deaths is considered relevant. Thus, in their haste to placate the vindictive shadows, the Andronici condemn Alarbus for having displayed the same courage and patriotism for which they honor their own slain kinsmen. That such vengeance may have grave consequences, with both personal and social repercussions, is demonstrated almost immediately, as Tamora and her remaining sons set about to respond in kind.

The vengeance taken for the death of Alarbus is an example of blood revenge—in particular of the form which we today call the unrestricted vendetta. Blood revenge functions in the interests of families, clans, and similar social units, the security of which it helps to ensure. Ordinarily, blood revenge operates in the absence of state machinery able to guarantee the safety of life and property. (pp. 496-98)

All blood revenge is predicated upon the principle of collective responsibility, although different species of blood revenge define this principle in different ways. In the unrestricted vendetta, collective responsibility is understood to obligate all members of the blood group to revenge offenses against a kinsman, and to hold the entire group liable to retaliation by other groups for offenses committed against them by any one of its members. No restraint is set upon the kind or degree of the vengeance which may be taken. The restricted vendetta, on the other hand, ordinarily limits the privilege of revenge to the offended party or his nearest kinsmen, and fixes the penalty to which the offender and his kinsmen may be liable. (p. 498)

It is the antisocial aspects of blood revenge that Shakespeare stresses in depicting the revenge taken for Alarbus. Tamora and her sons show not the slightest hesitation in satisfying the claims of blood at the expense of the Roman commonweal. The murder of Bassianus and the rape of Lavinia defy the laws of both Rome and the heavens. The device by which Martius and Quintus are ''framed'' subverts the machinery of Rome's government to private ends. And, as this interfamily struggle takes on political dimensions, Rome is threatened first by factionalism and then by civil war.

As forms of vengeance, both human sacrifice and the unrestricted vendetta are fraught with potential danger. This danger is substantial even when the revenger is, like Titus, just and honorable, intent only upon fulfilling his obligations to the dead. It is, however, immeasurably increased when the revenger's motives are not pure but mixed. Such is the case with Tamora and her party: for them revenge proves to be not simply the payment of the debt due Alarbus but also the excuse for the satisfaction of Chiron and Demetrius' lust, Tamora's craving for power, and Aaron's sheer love of deviltry. Revenge thus becomes the narrow end of the wedge which opens Rome to the most terrible of social and political evils. Moreover, whereas Titus, confident of the propriety of his actions, had sacrificed Alarbus in a public ceremony, Alarbus' revengers, knowing that they must conceal their deeds, proceed by ''secret crime,'' thereby laying upon Rome a burden of guilt which can be lifted only by the exposure and punishment of the criminals.

The rape of Lavinia and the murders of Bassianus, Martius, and Quintus are wrongs which offend not only the Andronici but also Rome and the heavens, whose laws they violate. Responsibility for responding to transgressions of human and divine law rests, according to Tudor theory, with the king and magistrates, whose offices are ordained by God for the maintenance of civic and cosmic order. (pp. 499-500)

Titus's Rome, faced with the tasks of assimilating the newly conquered Goths and erasing the memories of the recently

concluded hostilities, finds itself strained beyond its capacities and unable to meet its responsibilities in even the most basic matters of justice. The failure of Roman justice is symbolized by the treatment accorded Titus, who, although his services to Rome entitle him to honor and security, is nevertheless subjected to public humiliation and left to the mercy of powerful enemies. Saturninus, who, as Emperor, should enforce the laws impartially, takes part in the factionalism which threatens to destroy Rome. Although he does not seem to have been a party to either the violation of Lavinia or the framing of Martius and Quintus, his hatred of the Andronici predisposes him to believe Titus' sons guilty and so to forgo the inquiry which might uncover the real culprits. The breakdown of Roman justice is clearly related to the growing influence which Tamora—and through her, Aaron—exercises over the weak Emperor: the corruption of the Roman empery is symbolized by the black-amoor child which Aaron fathers upon Saturninus' wife. When, according to Tudor theory, state justice proves unable to do its part in maintaining civil and cosmic order, the heavens can be expected to intervene—to punish the criminal and to chastize the magistrate whose negligence has allowed the criminal to escape retribution. (p. 500)

To fill the place of the state justice rendered all but inoperative by the negligence of Saturninus, the heavens call upon the Andronici. In selecting the Andronici to be the agents of their vengeance—and the instruments of Rome's regeneration—the heavens acknowledge both the privileges of blood and the unique position which the Andronici hold as pillars of the Roman

Act IV. Scene i. Marcus, Titus, Young Lucius, and Lavinia. By T. Kirk (n.d.).

commonweal. The identity of the criminals is revealed to the revengers in IV. i, and the revelation is interpreted as a divine mandate to proceed. (p. 501)

The appalling form which Titus' vengeance takes is an integral part of its meaning. Titus' revenge is a horrifying response to a horrifying series of events. On the personal level, it is the act of an overwrought man "wrung with wrongs more than our backs can bear" [IV. iii. 49]. On the social level, it is the sort of violence which is bred by the state's failure to suppress violence. In the opinion of some, the most proper course for Titus would be not to take action himself: Marcus expresses this view when he speaks of Titus as "so just that he will not revenge" [IV. i. 128]. But the circumstances which have driven Titus to act make it difficult to condemn him out of hand. Thus, when Marcus, having catalogued the crimes of Tamora and her party, invites the populace to "judge what cause had Titus to revenge" [V. iii. 125], the Romans render their verdict by acclaiming Lucius Emperor.

Like Hieronimo [in Kyd's The Spanish Tragedy] and Hamlet, Titus is a figure with a strong sense of justice and duty selected by the heavens to act as the agent of their vengeance in a society where human justice has ceased to function. As Christians, however, both the Spanish knight marshal and the Danish prince have access to the doctrine which enables them eventually to understand and accept the role for which they have been chosen. The pagan Titus, on the other hand, is unable to penetrate the mystery of the Justice whose agent he is. Although he sees his revenge as a duty prescribed by the gods, Titus does not envision it as an act which can serve any interests beyond those of his family. Like Tamora, he views revenge within the context of the vendetta tradition. Significantly, the vengeance which Tamora seeks to personify for Titus' benefit is the vengeance of the vendetta. The rape and murder which she and her sons pretend they will revenge are seen not as violations of human and divine laws but rather as offenses against the Andronici. . . . Ironically, while Tamora presents herself as the vengeance of the vendetta, it is the heavens' vengeance which her masquerade unwittingly serves.

Although Tamora and Titus are both conducting vendettas, the vengeance of the Andronici differs from that of their enemies in two important ways. First, the Andronici act in as scrupulous a manner as the circumstances allow. Their motives are unmixed: they seek only to respond to wrongs perpetrated secretly against their kinsmen; they harm none but those who are actually guilty; and they make their actions public as soon as they have accomplished their ends. Second, the vengeance of the Andronici serves the justice which, by distributing reward and punishment in accordance with men's deserts, helps to maintain order in commonweal and cosmos. It is this justice which Saturninus, by accepting the empery, undertakes to uphold, and which, by employing his power in the interests of factionalism, he shamelessly betrays. It is this justice whose loss Titus laments when he sends his kinsmen to seek Astraea in the depths of the ocean and at the center of the earth [IV. iii. 4ff]. And it is this justice that the final act of this vendetta—the sentencing and execution of Aaron—re-establishes in Rome. With the punishment of Aaron, the offenses against the Andronici, Rome, and the heavens are wiped out, and the burden of guilt under which Rome has lain is lifted. (pp. 502-04)

Titus Andronicus reflects the Elizabethan awareness of revenge's immense potential both for good and for ill. Sensitive to this paradoxical aspect of his theme, Shakespeare portrays revenge on the one hand as the violence which destroys civil order and on the other as the violence which restores it. In dealing with the socially beneficial qualities of revenge, however, Shakespeare presents revenge as something more than simply a dangerous medicine with which to counter a dangerous illness. In Titus, revenge is an essential part of the regenerative process by which Rome will be cleansed of blood guilt and Romans and Goths will be reconciled and united in a harmonious and prosperous commonweal. In employing the theme of revenge as an instrument of political regeneration, Shakespeare makes use of a concept which had played an important part of sixteenth-century English thought. It had figured in the "Tudor myth," which explained the vengeance visited upon Richard III as a necessary precondition for England's renewal under Henry VII, and it had been adduced in the arguments of Protestant thinkers who represented the Reformation as the process by which the Church would be purged of corruption and returned to its primitive purity. (p. 505)

The regeneration of Titus' Rome entails not simply the founding of a new dynasty but also the establishment of a new justice. The movement in Titus Andronicus is away from the self-government whose tenets underlie the human sacrifice and blood revenge of the first four and a half acts to the principles of the state justice which Lucius affirms upon his accession in the play's final moments. The fact that both Goths and Romans acknowledge Lucius as their Emperor means that neither need think that resorting to force is the only means to right their wrongs. Thus the potentially endless chain of aggression and retaliation is closed off by the creation of a viable government able and willing to administer impartially the laws of Rome and of the gods. (p. 507)

Ronald Broude, "Four Forms of Vengeance in 'Titus Andronicus'," in The Journal of English and Germanic Philology, *Vol. LXXVIII, No. 4, October, 1979, pp. 494-507.*

ADDITIONAL BIBLIOGRAPHY

Baker, Howard. "The Spanish Tragedy, Titus Andronicus, and Senecanism" and "Transformations of Medieval Structure: Titus Andronicus and the Shakespearean Practice." In his Induction to Tragedy: A Study in the Development of Form in "Gorbudoc," "The Spanish Tragedy," and "Titus Andronicus," pp. 106-53, pp. 154-79. 1939. Reprint. New York: Russell & Russell, 1965.
    Traces the influence of Senecan and medieval tragic forms on the structure of Elizabethan revenge tragedies. Baker was one of the first critics to maintain that for Titus Andronicus Shakespeare relied more heavily on Ovid than on Seneca. He also notes that Shakespeare's expansion of Ovid's tale of Philomel resembles the medieval English poet John Gower's treatment of the same myth in his Confessio Amantis. Baker concludes that Titus displays "traits of classical-medieval narrative art."

Baldwin, T. W. On the Literary Genetics of Shakespeare's Plays: 1592-1594. Urbana: The University of Illinois Press, 1959, 562 p.
    Contends that Shakespeare and George Peele collaborated in 1593-94 to revise the original dramatic version of Titus Andronicus, which was written, according to Baldwin, in 1589-90 by an unknown author and based on the prose narrative The History of Titus Andronicus, the Renowned Roman General. Baldwin examines Peele's works as well as the relationship between the narrative source and the Shakespearean, German, and Dutch versions of the play in order to support his theory.

Boyer, Clarence Valentine. "The Revengeful Villain-Hero." In his *The Villain As Hero in Elizabethan Tragedy*, pp. 99-132. 1914. Reprint. New York: Russell & Russell, 1964.

Defines Aaron as a Machiavellian character who is similar in many respects to Marlowe's Barabas in *The Jew of Malta*. Boyer also asserts that Aaron is motivated by revenge rather than by lust, a motive that he finds unjustified by the action in *Titus Andronicus*.

Brooke, Nicholas. "The Tragic Spectacle in *Titus Andronicus* and *Romeo and Juliet*." In *Shakespeare: The Tragedies: A Collection of Critical Essays*, edited by Clifford Leech, pp. 243-56. Chicago: The University of Chicago Press, 1965.

Regards *Titus Andronicus* and *Romeo and Juliet* as "conscious experiments in poetic drama." According to Brooke, the stylistic differences between these two tragedies are based on their relationships to Shakespeare's poems: *Titus* parallels the Ovidian themes in *Venus and Adonis* and *The Rape of Lucrece*, while *Romeo and Juliet* echoes Shakespeare's romantic sonnets.

Brower, Reuben A. "Most Lamentable Romaine Tragedie." In his *Hero and Saint: Shakespeare and the Graeco-Roman Heroic Tradition*, pp. 173-203. New York: Oxford University Press, 1971.

Maintains that *Titus Andronicus* is a transitional work in Shakespeare's canon because of the deliberate imitation of classical, medieval, and contemporary theatrical modes throughout the drama. Brower also examines the play for early indications of Shakespeare's mature tragic and moral perspective.

Brown, Huntington. "Enter the Shakespearean Tragic Hero." *Essays in Criticism* III, No. 3 (July 1953): 285-302.

Contends that Shakespeare's "unsympathetic heroes"—Titus, Timon, and Coriolanus—"betray no hint of any inner division of mind or heart," nor do they display their "inner man."

Brucher, Richard T. " 'Tragedy, Laugh On': Comic Violence in *Titus Andronicus*." *Renaissance Drama* 10 (1979): 71-91.

Outlines the development of comic violence in Elizabethan drama and highlights its purpose and probable effect on contemporary audiences. Brucher argues that the laughter provoked by the grisly humor in *Titus Andronicus* reflects an effort "to put the bizarre action in perspective" and to reconcile the tragic situation with the characters' ludicrous behavior. He further claims that the play's violence raises questions concerning our "cherished notions about human values and conduct."

Chambers, E. K. "*Titus Andronicus* (1906)." In his *Shakespeare: A Survey*, pp. 31-9. 1926. Reprint. New York: Hill & Wang, 1958.

Calls for an objective critical approach to *Titus Andronicus* that is not based on emotional reactions to the play.

Cutts, John P. "The Early Tragedies: *Titus Andronicus*." In his *The Shattered Glass: A Dramatic Pattern in Shakespeare's Early Plays*, pp. 59-75. Detroit: Wayne State University Press, 1968.

Studies the portrait of Titus in relation to Shakespeare's technique of depicting a character's progress toward self-awareness. Cutts stresses that Titus blinds himself to his own weaknesses by viewing his lust for power and public recognition as "the pursuit of noble honor and high ideals." Cutts concludes that Titus never realizes his own faults and destroys himself rather than face life without the trappings of power and glory.

Fawcett, Mary L. "Arms/Words/Tears: Language and the Body in *Titus Andronicus*." *ELH* 50, No. 2 (Summer 1983): 261-78.

Suggests that *Titus* should be examined as a "meditation" on the relationship between the body, language, and writing. To Fawcett, Lavinia symbolizes Shakespeare's conception of the body as the physical expression of conscious thought.

Fuller, Harold DeWolf. "The Sources of *Titus Andronicus*." *Publications of the Modern Language Association of America* n.s. IX, No. 1 (1901): 1-65.

Explores the relationship between Shakespeare's *Titus Andronicus* and the seventeenth-century German and Dutch editions of the play. Fuller concludes that all three versions were based on the same sources.

Granger, Frank. "Correspondence: Shakespeare and the Legend of Andronicus." *The Times Literary Supplement*, No. 950 (1 April 1920): 213.

Contends that Shakespeare's depiction of Titus was influenced by the historical accounts of the Byzantine emperor, Andronicus Comnenus.

Harrison, Thomas P. "*Titus Andronicus* and *King Lear*: A Study in Continuity." In *Shakespearean Essays*, edited by Alwin Thaler and Norman Sanders, pp. 121-30. Knoxville: The University of Tennessee Press, 1964.

Defends Shakespeare's authorship of *Titus* by identifying its "marked similarities" to *King Lear*.

Hill, R. F. "Shakespeare's Early Tragic Mode." *Shakespeare Quarterly* 9, No. 4 (Autumn 1958): 455-69.

Describes the rhetorical style in Shakespeare's first tragedies as "ultimately Senecan in origin."

Hulse, S. Clark. "Wresting the Alphabet: Oratory and Action in *Titus Andronicus*." *Criticism: A Quarterly for Literature and the Arts* XXI, No. 2 (Spring 1979): 106-18.

Characterizes *Titus* as Shakespeare's "first experiment with the shifting levels of dramatic action and their capacity to portray the depravity of human action." Hulse asserts that the movement from the interior significance of speech to the external effect of action makes *Titus* a "worthy predecessor" to *Hamlet*.

Hunter, G. K. "Shakespeare's Earliest Tragedies: *Titus Andronicus* and *Romeo and Juliet*." *Shakespeare Survey* 27 (1974): 1-9.

Compares and contrasts the plot structures of *Titus* and *Romeo and Juliet* and contends that the two plays represent the "extreme polarities" of Shakespeare's tragic range: the examination of man's bestiality in the former and the tragic dramatization of material suited for comedy in the latter.

Kermode, Frank. Introduction to *Titus Andronicus*. In *The Riverside Shakespeare*, by William Shakespeare, edited by G. Blakemore Evans, pp. 1019-22. Boston: Houghton Mifflin Co., 1974.

States that Shakespeare broadened the scope of *Titus* from the typical blood feud of the Elizabethan revenge tragedies to include material on Roman politics and civilization. Kermode also comments that the play introduces the "fantastic range of possibilities" that Shakespeare explored in his later works.

Kramer, Joseph E. "*Titus Andronicus*: The 'Fly-Killing' Incident." *Shakespeare Studies* V (1969): 9-19.

Examines the function and purpose of the "fly-killing" scene and rejects it as unnecessary and remote from the content of the play. Kramer concludes that the episode is definitely not a part of Shakespeare's original dramatic conception.

Law, Robert Adger. "The Roman Background of *Titus Andronicus*." *Studies in Philology* XL, No. 2 (April 1943): 145-53.

Adds Plutarch and Virgil to the list of classical sources Shakespeare used for *Titus*.

Maxwell, J. C. Introduction to *Titus Andronicus*, by William Shakespeare, edited by J. C. Maxwell, pp. xi-xlv. The Arden Edition of the Works of William Shakespeare, edited by Harold F. Brooks and Harold Jenkins. London: Methuen & Co., 1961.

A comprehensive overview of the date, publication history, texts, editorial problems, and sources of *Titus*.

Parrott, Thomas Marc. "Shakespeare's Revision of *Titus Andronicus*." *The Modern Language Review* XIV, No. 1 (January 1919): 16-37.

Uses metrical analysis to speculate that Shakespeare merely revised certain scenes from an existing dramatic version of *Titus*.

Price, Hereward T. "The Authorship of *Titus Andronicus*." *The Journal of English and Germanic Philology* XLII, No. 1 (January 1943): 55-81.

Investigates external and internal evidence, compares Shakespeare's style with that of his predecessors, and concludes that Shakespeare wrote *Titus*.

————. "The First Quarto of *Titus Andronicus*." *The English Institute Essays, 1947* (1948): 137-68.

> Presents evidence that indicates Q1 was copied from a manuscript written in Shakespeare's hand.

Sargent, Ralph M. "The Source of *Titus Andronicus*." *Studies in Philology* XLVI, No. 2 (April 1949): 167-83.

> The first detailed study of the eighteenth-century chapbook entitled *The History of Titus Andronicus, the Renowned Roman General,* which contains the prose narrative regarded by most modern scholars as a version of the main source Shakespeare used to write *Titus*.

Spencer, Hazelton. "Trial Flights in Tragedy: The Tragedy of *Titus Andronicus*." In his *The Art and Life of William Shakespeare*, pp. 207-13. New York: Harcourt, Brace and Co., 1940.

> Declares that *Titus* fails as a tragedy because it lacks a hero who enlists our full sympathy. Spencer further maintains that the play, because of the abundant use of the revenge motif, is "a welter of vendettas instead of a clean-cut story of a hero's dedication to a sacred duty."

Stamm, R. "The Alphabet of Speechless Complaint: A Study of the Mutilated Daughter in *Titus Andronicus*." *English Studies* 55, No. 4 (August 1974): 325-39.

> Focuses on Lavinia's function in *Titus* as both a "purely visual" theatrical tool and an example of Shakespeare's experimentation with methods of coordinating speech, gesture, poetical patterns, and stage situations.

Stauffer, Donald A. "The Country Mouse: *Titus Andronicus*." In his *Shakespeare's World of Images: The Development of His Moral Ideas*, pp. 113-19. New York: W. W. Norton & Co., 1949.

> Considers *Titus Andronicus* a poorly constructed amalgam of classical Latin stories and themes. Stauffer finds, however, that the play provided the foundation for many of Shakespeare's later themes, attitudes, and situations. He also notes that the dramatist's love of nature is evident even in this "bloody play."

Stimpson, Catharine R. "Shakespeare and the Soil of Rape." In *The Woman's Part: Feminist Criticism of Shakespeare*, edited by Carolyn Ruth Swift Lenz, Gayle Green, and Carol Thomas Neely, pp. 56-64. Urbana: University of Illinois Press, 1980.

> Explores the structure and metaphoric significance of Shakespeare's rape sequences in *Titus Andronicus* and *The Rape of Lucrece*. Stimpson finds that Shakespeare presents the act of rape as a moral and physical test of the violator and as a traumatic injustice to the woman. She concludes that Shakespeare's attitude toward the violated woman is more sympathetic than "that of many of our contemporaries."

Teller, Stephen J. "Lucius and the Babe: Structure in *Titus Andronicus*." *The Midwest Quarterly* XIX, No. 4 (Summer 1978): 343-54.

> Outlines the relationship between Shakespeare's play and the prose narrative regarded as his main source. Teller also discusses Lucius's "suitability as the restorer of the moral order" in the play.

Thompson, Ann. "Philomel in *Titus Andronicus* and *Cymbeline*." *Shakespeare Survey* 31 (1978): 23-32.

> Discusses Shakespeare's handling of Ovid's tale of Philomel in both *Titus* and *Cymbeline*. Thompson argues that Lavinia's rape is used, in a latent form, as a political and moral symbol, while the same sequence in *Cymbeline* establishes a variety of interrelated analogies. To Thompson, the contextual function of these two scenes demonstrates the development of Shakespeare's dramatic skills.

Toole, William B., III. "The Collision of Action and Character Patterns in *Titus Andronicus*: A Failure in Dramatic Structure." *Renaissance Papers 1971* (1972): 25-39.

> Identifies a structural conflict between *Titus Andronicus*'s pattern of imagery and action and Shakespeare's depiction of Titus. Toole claims that "the atmosphere of mounting horror interferes with the atmosphere of mounting sympathy" the reader feels toward Titus and, as such, creates a sense of "emotional dislocation" at the conclusion of the play.

Tricomi, Albert H. "The Aesthetics of Mutilation in *Titus Andronicus*." *Shakespeare Survey* 27 (1974): 11-19.

> Considers Shakespeare's symbolism in *Titus* a significant dramatic experiment in which metaphoric language is used to describe "the literal reality of the play's events" rather than to translate the action beyond the boundaries of the stage. Tricomi regards this experiment as Shakespeare's attempt "to integrate the power of the poetic language with the immeasurable potential of dramatic action itself."

Van Doren, Mark. "*Titus Andronicus*." In his *Shakespeare*, pp. 38-43. New York: Henry Holt & Co., 1939.

> Considers *Titus* an extreme parody of the Tragedy of Blood genre as well as the only "unfeeling" drama in Shakespeare's canon.

West, Grace Starry. "Going by the Book: Classical Allusions in Shakespeare's *Titus Andronicus*." *Studies in Philology* LXXIX, No. 1 (Winter 1982): 62-77.

> Contends that the juxtaposition of classical allusions and violent action in *Titus* indicates that Shakespeare was "exploring the relationship between Roman education—the source of all the bookish allusions—and the disintegration" of Roman civilization. According to West, the characters' education taught them to be evil rather than good.

Yates, Frances A. "Queen Elizabeth As Astraea." *Journal of the Warburg and Courtauld Institutes* X (1947): 27-82.

> Studies the development of dramatic symbolism that equated Queen Elizabeth with Astraea, the virgin goddess of justice in classical mythology. In her brief remarks on *Titus Andronicus*, Yates mentions that John Foxe's *Book of Martyrs* begins with Lucius, the first Christian King of England, and ends with Elizabeth. She suggests that, since it was Lucius's arrow that struck Virgo (Astraea) in the play's arrow-shooting scene—and "presumably brought her down to earth"—his apotheosis represents "the return of the just empire and the golden age" of Queen Elizabeth.

Appendix

The following is a listing of all sources used in Volume 4 of *Shakespearean Criticism*. Included in this list are all reprint rights and acknowledgments for those essays for which permission was obtained. Every effort has been made to trace copyright, but if omissions have been made, please let us know.

THE EXCERPTS IN SC, VOLUME 4, WERE REPRINTED FROM THE FOLLOWING PERIODICALS:

The American Review, v. 8, January, 1937.

Ball State University Forum, v. XII, Spring, 1971 for " 'Titus Andronicus' and Shakespeare's Tragic Perspective" by Larry S. Champion. © 1971 Ball State University. Reprinted by permission of the author.

The Bee; or, Literary Weekly Intelligencer, v. I, January 12, January 19, January 29, and February 2, 1791.

Bentley's Miscellany, v. V, 1839.

The Bristol Gazette, November 11, 1813.

The British Journal of Medical Psychology, v. XIV, 1934.

The Censor, n. 36, January 12, 1717.

The Centennial Review, v. VIII, Winter, 1964 for " 'Othello' and the Motive-Hunters" by Harry Levin. © 1964 by The Centennial Review. Reprinted by permission of the publisher and the author.

Critical Quarterly, v. 14, Winter, 1972. © Manchester University Press 1972. Reprinted by permission of Manchester University Press.

ELH, v. XXIX, September, 1962. Reprinted by permission.

English Literary Renaissance, v. 8, Spring, 1978. Copyright © 1978 by *English Literary Renaissance*. Reprinted by permission.

Essays and Studies, n.s. v. 3, 1950.

Essays in Criticism, v. I, October, 1951./ v. X, April, 1960 for " 'The Merchant of Venice': A Reconstruction" by Graham Midgley; v. X, July, 1960. Both reprinted by permission of the Editors of *Essays in Criticism* and the author.

THE EXCERPTS IN SC, VOLUME 4, WERE REPRINTED FROM THE FOLLOWING BOOKS:

Adams, John Quincy. From ''Misconceptions of Shakespeare, upon the Stage,'' in *Notes and Comments upon Certain Plays and Actors of Shakespeare*. By James Henry Hackett. Carleton, Publisher, 1863.

Adamson, Jane. From *''Othello'' as Tragedy: Some Problems of Judgment and Feeling*. Cambridge University Press, 1980. © Cambridge University Press 1980. Reprinted by permission of the publisher.

Baildon, H. Bellyse. From *The Works of Shakespeare: The Lamentable Tragedy of Titus Andronicus*. By William Shakespeare, edited by H. Bellyse Baildon. Methuen & Co. Ltd., 1904.

Barber, C. L. From *Shakespeare's Festive Comedy: A Study of Dramatic Form and Its Relation to Social Custom*. Princeton University Press, 1959. Copyright © 1959 by Princeton University Press. All rights reserved. Excerpts reprinted with permission of the publisher.

Baskervill, Charles Read. From *The Manly Anniversary Studies in Language and Literature*. The University of Chicago Press, 1923.

Battenhouse, Roy W. From *Shakespearean Tragedy: Its Art and Its Christian Premises*. Indiana University Press, 1969. Copyright © 1969 by Indiana University Press. All rights reserved. Reprinted by permission of the author.

Bayley, John. From *The Characters of Love: A Study in the Literature of Personality*. Basic Books, 1960. Copyright © 1960 by John Bayley. Reprinted by permission of Basic Books, Inc., Publishers.

Boas, Frederick S. From *Shakespeare and His Predecessors*. Charles Scribner's Sons, 1896.

Bodenstedt, Friederich. From an extract translated by William Henry Furness, in *A New Variorum Edition of Shakespeare: Othello, Vol. VI*. Edited by Horace Howard Furness. J. B. Lippincott Company, 1886.

Bodkin, Maud. From *Archetypal Patterns in Poetry: Psychological Studies of Imagination*. Oxford University Press, Inc., 1934.

Bowers, Fredson Thayer. From *Elizabethan Revenge Tragedy, 1587-1642*. Princeton University Press, 1940. Copyright © 1940 by Princeton University Press. Renewed 1967 by Fredson T. Bowers. Excerpts reprinted by permission of the publisher.

Bradbrook, M. C. From *Shakespeare and Elizabethan Poetry: A Study of His Earlier Work in Relation to the Poetry of the Time*. Chatto and Windus, 1951.

Bradley, A. C. From *Shakespearean Tragedy: Lectures on ''Hamlet,'' ''Othello,'' ''King Lear,'' ''Macbeth.''* Macmillan and Co., Limited, 1904.

Brooke, Stopford A. From *Ten More Plays of Shakespeare*. Constable and Company Ltd., 1913.

Brown, John Russell. From *Shakespeare and His Comedies*. Methuen & Co. Ltd., 1957.

Bryant, J. A., Jr. From *Hippolyta's View: Some Christian Aspects of Shakespeare's Plays*. University of Kentucky Press, 1961. Copyright © 1961 by The University Press of Kentucky. Reprinted by permission of the publisher.

Bullen, A. H. From *The Works of Christopher Marlowe, Vol. I*. Edited by A. H. Bullen. Houghton Mifflin and Company, 1885.

Calderwood, James L. From *Shakespearean Metadrama: The Argument of the Play in ''Titus Andronicus,'' ''Love's Labour's Lost,'' ''Romeo and Juliet,'' ''A Midsummer Night's Dream'' and ''Richard II.''* University of Minnesota Press, 1971. © copyright 1971 by the University of Minnesota. All rights reserved. Reprinted by permission of the publisher.

Capell, Edward. From *Mr. William Shakespeare: His Comedies, Histories, and Tragedies, Vol. I*. By William Shakespeare, edited by Edward Capell. J. & R. Tonson, 1768.

Chambers, E. K. From *Shakespeare: A Survey*. Sidgwick & Jackson, 1925.

Charlton, H. B. From *Shakespearian Tragedy*. Cambridge at the University Press, 1948.

Clemen, Wolfgang. From *The Development of Shakespeare's Imagery*. Second edition. Methuen, 1977. Copyright 1951 and 1977 Wolfgang Clemen. Reprinted by permission of Methuen & Co. Ltd.

Coleridge, Samuel Taylor. From *The Literary Remains of Samuel Taylor Coleridge, Vol. II*. Edited by Henry Nelson Coleridge. William Pickering, 1836.

Coleridge, Samuel Taylor. From *Shakespearean Criticism, Vol. I*. Edited by Thomas Middleton Raysor. Cambridge, Mass: Harvard University Press, 1930.

Coleridge, Samuel Taylor. From *Specimens of the Table Talk of the Late Samuel Taylor Coleridge, Vol. I*. Edited by H. N. Coleridge. John Murray, 1835.

Colie, Rosalie L. From *Shakespeare's Living Art*. Princeton University Press, 1974. Copyright © 1974 by Princeton University Press. All rights reserved. Excerpts reprinted with permission of the publisher.

Colman, George. From "Critical Reflections on the Old English Dramatick Writers," in *The Dramatic Works of Philip Massinger*. By Philip Massinger, edited by Thomas Coxeter, N.p., 1761.

Danson, Lawrence. From *The Harmonies of "The Merchant of Venice"*. Yale University Press, 1978. Copyright © 1978 by Yale University. All rights reserved. Reprinted by permission of the publisher.

Dowden, Edward. From *Shakspere: A Critical Study of His Mind and Art*. Third edition. Harper & Brothers Publishers, 1881.

Eliot, T. S. From *Selected Essays*. Harcourt Brace Jovanovich, 1950. Copyright 1950 by Harcourt Brace Jovanovich, Inc. Renewed 1978 by Esme Valerie Eliot. Reprinted by permission of Harcourt Brace Jovanovich, Inc. In Canada by Faber & Faber Ltd.

Elliott, G. R. From *Flaming Minister: A Study of "Othello" as Tragedy of Love and Hate*. Duke University Press, 1953.

Elze, Karl. From *Essays on Shakespeare*. Translated by L. Dora Schmitz. Macmillan and Co., 1874.

Evans, B. Ifor. From *The Language of Shakespeare's Plays*. Methuen & Co. Ltd., 1952.

Foakes, R. A. From *Shakespeare, the Dark Comedies to the Last Plays: From Satire to Celebration*. University Press of Virginia, 1971. Copyright © R. A. Foakes 1971. Reprinted by permission.

Forman, Simon. From "Contemporary Notices of the Plays and Poems: Dr. Simon Forman," in *The Riverside Shakespeare*. Edited by G. Blakemore Evans. Houghton Mifflin, 1974. Copyright © 1974 by Houghton Mifflin Company. All rights reserved. Reprinted by permission of Houghton Mifflin Company.

Frye, Northrop. From *A Natural Perspective: The Development of Shakespearean Comedy and Romance*. Columbia University Press, 1965. Copyright © 1965 Columbia University Press. All rights reserved. Reprinted by permission of the publisher.

Furness, Horace Howard. From *A New Variorum Edition of Shakespeare: The Tragedie of Cymbeline*. By William Shakespeare, edited by Horace Howard Furness. J. B. Lippincott Company, 1913. Copyright, 1913, by H. H. Furness, Jr. Renewed 1941 by Fairman R. Furness. Reprinted by permission of the Literary Estate of Horace Howard Furness.

Gentleman, Francis. From a note to "Titus Andronicus," in *Bell's Edition of Shakespeare's Plays, Vol. VIII*. By William Shakespeare. J. Bell, 1774.

Gervinus, G. G. From *Shakespeare Commentaries*. Translated by F. E. Bunnett. Revised edition. Smith, Elder, & Co., 1877.

Gildon, Charles. From *Miscellaneous Letters and Essays*. B. Bragg, 1694.

Gildon, Charles. From "Remarks on the Plays of Shakespear," in *The Works of Mr. William Shakespear, Vol. 7*. By William Shakespeare. E. Curll and E. Sanger, 1710.

Girard, René. From "'To Entrap the Wisest': A Reading of 'The Merchant of Venice'," in *Literature and Society: Selected Papers from the English Institute, 1978*. Edited by Edward W. Said. The Johns Hopkins University Press, 1980. Copyright © 1980 by the English Institute. All rights reserved. Reprinted by permission of the publisher.

Goddard, Harold C. From *The Meaning of Shakespeare*. University of Chicago Press, 1951. Copyright 1951 by The University of Chicago. Renewed 1979 by Margaret G. Holt and Eleanor G. Worthen. All rights reserved. Reprinted by permission of the publisher.

Gollancz, Sir Israel. From *Allegory and Mysticism in Shakespeare: A Medievalist on "The Merchant of Venice"*. Edited by Alfred W. Pollard. George W. Jones, 1931.

Granville-Barker, Harley. From *Prefaces to Shakespeare, second series*. Sidgwick & Jackson, Ltd., 1930.

Granville-Barker, Harley. From *Prefaces to Shakespeare: Othello, fourth series*. Sidgwick & Jackson, Ltd., 1945.

Griffith, Elizabeth. From *The Morality of Shakespeare's Drama Illustrated*. T. Cadell, 1775.

Hamilton, A. C. From *The Early Shakespeare*. Huntington Library, 1967. Copyright 1967 The Henry E. Huntington Library and Art Gallery. Reprinted by permission.

Hawkins, William. From *Cymbeline: A Tragedy Altered from Shakespeare*. J. Rivington & J. Fletcher, 1759.

Hazlitt, William. From *Characters of Shakespear's Plays*. R. Hunter, 1817, C. H. Reynell, 1817.

Heath, Benjamin. From *A Revisal of Shakespear's Text, Wherein the Alterations Introduced into It by the More Modern Editors and Critics Are Particularly Considered*. W. Johnston, 1765.

Heilman, Robert B. From *Magic in the Web: Action & Language in "Othello"*. University of Kentucky Press, 1956. Copyright © 1956 by the University Press of Kentucky. Renewed 1984 by Robert B. Heilman. Reprinted by permission of the publisher.

Heine, Heinrich. From *Heine on Shakespeare: A Translation of His Notes on Shakespeare Heroines*. Translated by Ida Benecke. Archibald Constable and Co., 1895.

Heraud, J. A. From *Shakspere, His Inner Life as Intimated in His Works*. J. Maxwell and Company, 1865.

Hole, Richard. From *Essays, by a Society of Gentlemen at Exeter*. N.p., 1796.

Hugo, Victor. From *William Shakespeare*. Translated by Melville B. Anderson. A. C. McClurg and Company, 1887.

Hunter, Robert G. From *Shakespeare and the Mystery of God's Judgments*. University of Georgia Press, 1976. Copyright © 1976 by the University of Georgia Press. All rights reserved. Reprinted by permission of the publisher.

Hunter, Robert Grams. From *Shakespeare and the Comedy of Forgiveness*. Columbia University Press, 1965. Copyright © 1965 Columbia University Press. Reprinted by permission of the publisher.

Ihering, Rudolf von. From an extract translated by Horace Howard Furness, in *A New Variorum Edition of Shakespeare: The Merchant of Venice, Vol. VII*. By William Shakespeare, edited by Horace Howard Furness. J. B. Lippincott Company, 1888.

Jameson, Anna Brownell. From *Characteristics of Women: Moral, Poetical, and Historical*. Second edition. N.p., 1833.

Johnson, Samuel. From notes in *The Plays of William Shakespeare, Vol. II*. By William Shakespeare, edited by Samuel Johnson. J. & R. Tonson, 1765.

Johnson, Samuel. From *The Plays of William Shakespeare, Vol. VI*. By William Shakespeare, edited by Samuel Johnson. J. & R. Tonson, 1765.

Johnson, Samuel. From *The Plays of William Shakespeare, Vols. VII & VIII*. By William Shakespeare, edited by Samuel Johnson. J. & R. Tonson, 1765.

Jonson, Ben. From *The Workes of Benjamin Jonson, Vol. 2*. Richard Meighen, 1640.

Kenny, Thomas. From *The Life and Genius of Shakespeare*. Longman, Green, Longman, Roberts, and Green, 1864.

Kirsch, Arthur C. From *Jacobean Dramatic Perspectives*. The University Press of Virginia, 1972. Copyright © 1972 by the Rector and Visitors of the University of Virginia. Reprinted by permission of the publisher.

Knight, Charles. From *Studies of Shakspere*. Charles Knight, 1849.

Knight, G. Wilson. From *The Crown of Life: Essays in Interpretation of Shakespeare's Final Plays*. Oxford University Press, 1947.

Knight, G. Wilson. From *The Wheel of Fire: Essays in Interpretation of Shakespeare's Sombre Tragedies*. Oxford University Press, London, 1930.

Kreyssig, Friedrich. From an extract, translated by Horace Howard Furness, in *A New Variorum Edition of Shakespeare: The Merchant of Venice, Vol. VII*. By William Shakespeare, edited by Horace Howard Furness. J. B. Lippincott Company, 1888.

Langbaine, Gerard. From *An Account of the English Dramatick Poets*. G. West and H. Clements, 1691.

Leavis, F. R. From *The Common Pursuit*. Chatto & Windus, 1952, Hogarth Press, 1984. Copyright 1952 by F. R. Leavis. Reprinted by permission of Chatto & Windus: The Hogarth Press.

Lennox, Charlotte. From *Shakespear Illustrated; or, The Novels and Histories, on Which the Plays of Shakespear Are Founded, Vol. I*. A. Millar, 1753.

Lewis, Wyndham. From *The Lion and the Fox: The Rôle of the Hero in the Plays of Shakespeare*. Grant Richards Ltd., 1927. Copyright 1927 Wyndham Lewis and the Estate of Mrs. G. A. Wyndham Lewis. Reprinted by permission of The Wyndham Lewis Memorial Trust, a registered charity.

Malone, Edmond. From *The Plays and Poems of William Shakspeare, Vol. 1*. By William Shakespeare, edited by Edmond Malone. J. Rivington and Sons, 1790.

Martin, Helena Faucit, Lady. From *On Some of Shakespeare's Female Characters: Ophelia, Portia, Desdemona, Juliet, Imogen, Rosalind, Beatrice*. Scribner and Welford, 1887.

Massey, Gerald. From *Shakspeare's Sonnets Never Before Interpreted*. Longmans, Green, and Co., 1866.

Matthews, Brander. From *Shakspere as a Playwright*. Charles Scribner's Sons, 1913. Copyright, 1913, by Charles Scribner's Sons. Renewed 1941 by Nelson Macy, Jr. Reprinted with the permission of Charles Scribner's Sons.

Matthews, G. M. From "'Othello' and the Dignity of Man," in *Shakespeare in a Changing World: Essays*. Edited by Arnold Kettle. International Publishers, 1964. © International Publishers Co., Inc., 1964. Reprinted by permission.

Moody, A. D. From *Shakespeare: "The Merchant of Venice"*. Edward Arnold (Publishers) Ltd., 1964. © A. D. Moody 1964. Reprinted by permission.

Murry, John Middleton. From *Shakespeare*. Jonathan Cape, 1936. Copyright 1936 by Harcourt Brace & Co., Inc. Renewed 1963 by Mary Middleton Murry. Reprinted by permission of The Society of Authors as the literary representative of the Estate of John Middleton Murry.

Nicoll, Allardyce. From *Studies in Shakespeare*. Leonard & Virginia Woolf, 1927. Copyright 1928 by Leonard & Virginia Woolf. Renewed 1955 by Allardyce Nicoll. Reprinted by permission of the author and the Hogarth Press.

Parr, Wolstenholme. From *The Story of the Moor of Venice*. By Giovanni Battista Giraldi, translated by Wolstenholme Parr. N.p., 1795.

Peterson, Douglas L. From *Time, Tide and Tempest: A Study of Shakespeare's Romances*. Huntington Library, 1973. Copyright © 1973 Huntington Library Publications, San Marino, CA. Reprinted by permission.

Phialas, Peter G. From *Shakespeare's Romantic Comedies: The Development of Their Form and Meaning*. University of North Carolina Press, 1966. Copyright © 1966 by The University of North Carolina Press. Reprinted by permission of the publisher and the author.

Pietscher, A. From an extract, translated by Horace Howard Furness, in *A New Variorum Edition of Shakespeare: The Merchant of Venice, Vol. VII*. By William Shakespeare, edited by Horace Howard Furness. J. B. Lippincott Company, 1888.

Pope, Alexander. From *The Works of Shakespear, Vol. 6*. By William Shakespeare, edited by Alexander Pope. Jacob Tonson, 1723.

Potter, John. From *The Theatrical Review; or, New Companion to the Play-House, Vol. I*. S. Crowder, 1772.

Quiller-Couch, Arthur. From an introduction to *The Merchant of Venice*. By William Shakespeare. Cambridge at the University Press, 1926.

Rabkin, Norman. From *Shakespeare and the Problem of Meaning*. University of Chicago Press, 1981. © 1981 by The University of Chicago. All rights reserved. Reprinted by permission of the publisher.

Raleigh, Walter. From *Shakespeare*. Macmillan and Co., Limited, 1907.

Ravenscroft, Edward. From *Titus Andronicus; or, The Rape of Lavinia*. J. Hindmarsh, 1687.

Reik, Theodor. From *The Search Within: The Inner Experiences of a Psychoanalyst*. Farrar, Straus and Cudahy, 1956. Copyright © 1956 by Theodor Reik. Copyright renewed © 1984 by Arthur Reik. Reprinted by permission of Farrar, Straus and Giroux, Inc.

Ribner, Irving. From *Patterns in Shakespearian Tragedy*. Methuen, 1960. © 1960 Irving Ribner. Reprinted by permission of Methuen & Co. Ltd.

Rowe, Nicholas. From *The Works of Mr. William Shakespeare, Vol. I.* By William Shakespeare, edited by Nicholas Rowe. Jacob Tonson, 1709.

Rymer, Thomas. From *A Short View of Tragedy*. Richard Baldwin, 1692.

Schlegel, Augustus William. From *A Course of Lectures on Dramatic Art and Literature*. Edited by Rev. A. J. W. Morrison, translated by John Black. Revised edition. Henry G. Bohn, 1846.

Shaw, Bernard. From *Short Stories, Scraps and Shavings*. Dodd, Mead, 1934. Copyright 1933, 1934 by George Bernard Shaw. All rights reserved. Reprinted by permission of Dodd, Mead & Company, Inc.

Shebbeare, John. From *Letters on the English Nation*. N.p., 1755.

Snider, Denton J. From *The Shakespearian Drama, a Commentary: The Tragedies*. Sigma Publishing Co., 1887.

Snider, Denton J. From *The Shakespearian Drama, a Commentary: The Comedies*. Sigma Publishing Co., 1890?

Spivack, Bernard. From *Shakespeare and the Allegory of Evil: The History of a Metaphor in Relation to His Major Villains*. Columbia University Press, 1958. © 1958, Columbia University Press. Reprinted by permission of the publisher.

Spurgeon, Caroline F. E. From *Shakespeare's Imagery and What It Tells Us*. The Macmillan Company, 1935, Cambridge at the University Press, 1935.

Stauffer, Donald A. From *Shakespeare's World of Images: The Development of His Moral Ideas*. Norton, 1949. Copyright 1949 by W. W. Norton & Company, Inc. Renewed 1977 by Ruth M. Stauffer. Reprinted by permission of W. W. Norton & Company, Inc.

Steevens, George. From notes on ''Titus Andronicus,'' in *The Plays of William Shakspeare, Vol. VIII.* By William Shakespeare, edited by George Steevens and Samuel Johnson. Revised edition. C. Bathurst, 1778.

Steevens, George. From *The Plays of William Shakspeare, Vol. XIII.* By William Shakespeare, edited by Samuel Johnson and George Steevens. Revised edition. T. Longman, 1793.

Stewart, J. I. M. From *Character and Motive in Shakespeare: Some Recent Appraisals Examined*. Longmans, Green and Co., 1949.

Stirling, Brents. From *Unity in Shakespearian Tragedy: The Interplay of Theme and Character*. Columbia University Press, 1956. © 1956, Columbia University Press. Renewed 1984 by Brents Stirling. Reprinted by permission of the author.

Stoll, Elmer Edgar. From *''Othello'': An Historical and Comparative Study*. The University of Minnesota, 1915.

Stoll, Elmer Edgar. From *Shakespeare Studies: Historical and Comparative in Method*. The Macmillan Company, 1927.

Swander, Homer D. From '' 'Cymbeline': Religious Idea and Dramatic Design,'' in *Pacific Coast Studies in Shakespeare*. Edited by Waldo F. McNeir and Thelma N. Greenfield. University of Oregon, 1966. Copyright © 1966 University of Oregon. Reprinted by permission of the publisher.

Swinburne, Algernon Charles. From *A Study of Shakespeare*. R. Worthington, 1880.

Symonds, John Addington. From *Shakspere's Predecessors in the English Drama*. Smith, Elder, & Co., 1884.

Symons, Arthur. From *Studies in the Elizabethan Drama*. Dutton, 1919. Copyright 1919 by E. P. Dutton, renewed 1946 by Nona Hill. All rights reserved. Reprinted by permission of the publisher, E. P. Dutton, a division of New American Library. In Canada by the Literary Estate of Arthur Symons.

Theobald, Lewis. From *The Works of Shakespeare, Vol. 5*. By William Shakespeare, edited by Lewis Theobald. A. Bettesworth and C. Hitch, 1733.

Theobald, Lewis. From *The Works of Shakespeare, Vol. 7*. By William Shakespeare, edited by Lewis Theobald. A Bettesworth and C. Hitch, 1733.

Tillyard, E. M. W. From *Shakespeare's History Plays*. Chatto & Windus, 1944. © 1944 by Chatto & Windus. Copyright renewed © 1971 by Stephen Tillyard, Mrs. V. Sankaran and Mrs. A. Ahlers. Reprinted by permission of the author's Literary Estate and Chatto & Windus.

Tillyard, E. M. W. From *Shakespeare's Last Plays*. Chatto and Windus, 1938.

Tovey, Barbara. From ''The Golden Casket: An Interpretation of 'The Merchant of Venice','' in *Shakespeare as Political Thinker*. Edited by John Alvis and Thomas G. West. Carolina Academic Press, 1981. © 1981 John Alvis and Thomas G. West. All rights reserved. Reprinted by permission.

Traversi, D. A. From *An Approach to Shakespeare*. Revised edition. Doubleday, 1969. Copyright © 1956 by Doubleday & Company, Inc. Copyright © 1960, 1969 by Derek A. Traversi. All rights reserved. Reprinted by permission of the publisher.

Traversi, Derek. From *Shakespeare: The Last Phase*. Hollis & Carter, 1954.

Ulrici, Hermann. From *Shakspeare's Dramatic Art: And His Relation to Calderon and Goethe*. Translated by A. J. W. Morrison. Chapman, Brothers, 1846.

Upton, John. From *Critical Observations on Shakespeare*. Second edition. G. Hawkins, 1748.

Van Doren, Mark. From *Shakespeare*. Henry Holt and Company, 1939.

Walley, Harold R. From ''Shakespeare's Portrayal of Shylock,'' in *Essays in Dramatic Literature: The Parrott Presentation Volume*. Edited by Hardin Craig. Princeton University Press, 1935.

Walwyn, B. From *An Essay on Comedy*. N.p., 1782.

Warburton, William. From *The Works of Shakespear, Vol. VIII*. By William Shakespeare, edited by William Warburton. J. and P. Knapton, 1747.

Wendell, Barrett. From *William Shakspere: A Study in Elizabethan Literature*. Charles Scribner's Sons, 1894.

White, Richard Grant. From *Studies in Shakespeare*. Houghton, Mifflin and Company, 1886.

Wilkes, Thomas. From *A General View of the Stage*. J. Coote, 1759.

Wilson, John Dover. From *Titus Andronicus*. By William Shakespeare, edited by John Dover Wilson. Cambridge at the University Press, 1948.

Wright, Abraham. From an extract in *Historical Papers, Part I*. Edited by Philip Bliss and Bulkeley Bandinel. W. Nicol, Shakspeare Press, 1846.

Glossary

APOCRYPHA: A term applied to those plays which have, at one time or another, been ascribed to Shakespeare, but which are outside the canon of the thirty-seven dramas generally accepted as authentic. The second issue of the THIRD FOLIO included seven plays not among the other thirty-six of the FIRST FOLIO: *Pericles, The London Prodigal, Thomas Lord Cromwell, Sir John Oldcastle, The Puritan, A Yorkshire Tragedy,* and *Locrine.* These seven were also included in the FOURTH FOLIO, but of them only *Pericles* is judged to be the work of Shakespeare. Four other plays that were entered in the STATIONERS' REGISTER in the seventeenth century listed Shakespeare as either an author or coauthor: *The Two Noble Kinsmen* (1634), *Cardenio* (1653), *Henry I* and *Henry II* (1653), and *The Birth of Merlin* (1662); only *The Two Noble Kinsmen* is thought to be, at least in part, written by Shakespeare, although *Cardenio*—whose text is lost—may also have been by him. Scholars have judged that there is strong internal evidence indicating Shakespeare's hand in two other works, *Sir Thomas More* and *Edward III.* Among other titles that have been ascribed to Shakespeare but are generally regarded as spurious are: *The Troublesome Reign of King John, Arden of Feversham, Fair Em, The Merry Devil of Edmonton, Mucedorus, The Second Maiden's Tragedy,* and *Edmund Ironside.*

ASSEMBLED TEXTS: The theory of assembled texts, first proposed by Edmond Malone in the eighteenth century and later popularized by John Dover Wilson, maintains that some of the plays in the FIRST FOLIO were reconstructed for the COMPOSITOR by integrating each actor's part with the plot or abstract of the play. According to Dover Wilson, this reconstruction was done only for those plays which had not been previously published in QUARTO editions and which had no company PROMPT-BOOKS in existence, a list he limits to three of Shakespeare's works: *The Two Gentlemen of Verona, The Merry Wives of Windsor,* and *The Winter's Tale.*

BAD QUARTOS: A name attributed to a group of early editions of Shakespeare's plays which, because of irregularities, omissions, misspellings, and interpolations not found in later QUARTO or FOLIO versions of the same plays, are considered unauthorized publications of Shakespeare's work. The term was first used by the twentieth-century bibliographical scholar A. W. Pollard and has been applied to as many as ten plays: The First Quartos of *Romeo and Juliet, Hamlet, Henry V,* and *The Merry Wives of Windsor; The First Part of the Contention betwixt the two famous Houses of Yorke and Lancaster* and *The True Tragedy of Richard Duke of Yorke,* originally thought to have been sources for Shakespeare's *2* and *3 Henry VI,* but now generally regarded as bad quartos of those plays; the so-called ''Pied Bull'' quarto of *King Lear;* the 1609 edition of *Pericles; The Troublesome Reign of King John,* believed to be a bad quarto of *King John,* and *The Taming of a Shrew,* which some critics contend is a bad quarto of Shakespeare's Shrew drama. The primary distinction of the bad quartos is the high degree of TEXTUAL CORRUPTION apparent in the texts, a fact scholars have attributed to either one of two theories: some have argued that each quarto was composed from a stenographer's report, in which an agent for the printer was employed to surreptitiously transcribe the play during a performance; others have held the more popular explanation that the questionable texts were based on MEMORIAL RECONSTRUCTIONS by one or more actors who had performed in the plays.

BANDELLO, MATTEO: (b. 1480? - d. 1561) Italian novelist and poet who was also a churchman, diplomat, and soldier. His literary reputation is principally based on the *Novelle,* a collection of 214 tragic, romantic, and historical tales derived from a variety of material from antiquity to the Renaissance. Many of the stories in the *Novelle* are coarse and lewd in their presentation of love, reflecting Bandello's secular interests rather than his clerical role. Together with the dedications to friends and patrons that accompany the individual stories, the *Novelle* conveys a vivid sense of historical events and personalities of the Renaissance. Several translations and adaptations appeared in the third quarter of the sixteenth century, most notably in French by Francois Belleforest and Pierre Boaistuau and in English by William Painter and Geoffrey Fenton.

BLACKFRIARS THEATRE: The Blackfriars Theatre, so named because it was located in the London precinct of Blackfriars, was originally part of a large monastary leased to Richard Farrant, Master of the Children of Windsor, in 1576 for the purpose of staging children's plays. It was acquired in 1596 by James Burbage, who tried to convert the property into a professional theater, but was thwarted in his attempt by surrounding residents. After Burbage died, the Blackfriars was taken over by his son, Richard, who circumvented the objections of his neighbors and, emulating the tactics of Farrant's children's company, staged both children's and adult plays under the guise of a private house, rather than a public theater. This arrangement lasted for five years until, in 1605, the adult company was suspended by King James I for its performance of the satire *Eastward Ho!* Shortly thereafter, the children's company was also suppressed for performing George Chapman's *Conspiracy and Tragedy of Charles Duke of Byron.* In 1608, Burbage organized a new group of directors consisting of his brother Cuthbert and several leading players of the KING'S MEN, including Shakespeare, John Heminge, Henry Condell, and William Sly. These ''housekeepers,'' as they were called, for they shared no profits accruing to the actors, arranged to have the Blackfriars used by the King's Men alternately with the GLOBE THEATRE, an arrangement that lasted from the autumn of 1609 to 1642. Because it was a private house, and therefore smaller than the public theaters of London at that time, the Blackfriars set a higher price for tickets and, as such, attracted a sophisticated and aristocratic audience. Also, through its years of operation as a children's theater, the Blackfriars developed a certain taste in its patrons—one which appreciated music, dance, and masque in a dramatic piece, as well as elements of suspense, reconciliation, and rebirth. Many critics attribute the nature of Shakespeare's final romances to the possibility that he wrote the plays with this new audience foremost in mind.

BOOKKEEPER: Also considered the bookholder or prompter, the bookkeeper was a member of an Elizabethan acting company who maintained custody of the PROMPT-BOOKS, or texts of the plays. Many scholars believe that the bookkeeper also acted as the prompter during any performances, much as a stage manager would do today; however, other literary historians claim that another official satisfied this function. In addition to the above duties, the bookkeeper obtained a license for each play, deleted from the dramatist's manuscript anything offensive before it was submitted to the government censor, assembled copies of the players' individual parts from the company prompt-book, and drew up the "plot" of each work, that is, an abstract of the action of the play emphasizing stage directions.

COMPOSITOR: The name given to the typesetter in a printing shop. Since the growth of textual criticism in modern Shakespearean scholarship, the habits and idiosyncrasies of the individual compositors of Shakespeare's plays have attracted extensive study, particularly with respect to those works that demonstrate substantial evidence of TEXTUAL CORRUPTION. Elizabethan compositors set their type by hand, one letter at a time, a practice that made it difficult to sustain a sense of the text and which often resulted in a number of meaningless passages in books. Also, the lack of uniform spelling rules prior to the eighteenth century meant that each compositor was free to spell a given word according to his personal predilection. Because of this, scholars have been able to identify an individual compositor's share of a printed text by isolating his spelling habits and idiosyncrasies.

EMENDATION: A term often used in textual criticism, emendation is a conjectural correction of a word or phrase in a Shakespearean text proposed by an editor in an effort to restore a line's original meaning. Because many of Shakespeare's plays were carelessly printed, there exist a large number of errors in the early editions which textual scholars through the centuries have tried to correct. Some of the errors—those based on obvious misprints—have been easily emended, but other more formidable TEXTUAL CORRUPTIONS remain open to dispute and have solicited a variety of corrections. Perhaps the two most famous of these are the lines in *Henry V* (II. iii. 16-17) and *Hamlet* (I. ii. 129).

FAIR COPY A term often applied by Elizabethan writers and theater professionals to describe the corrected copy of an author's manuscript submitted to an acting company. According to available evidence, a dramatist would presumably produce a rough copy of a play, also known as the author's FOUL PAPERS, which would be corrected and revised either by himself or by a professional scribe at a later date. Eventually, the fair copy of a play would be modified by a BOOKKEEPER or prompter to include notes for properties, stage directions, and so on, and then be transcribed into the company's PROMPT-BOOK.

FIRST FOLIO: The earliest collected edition of Shakespeare's plays, edited by his fellow-actors John Heminge and Henry Condell and published near the end of 1623. The First Folio contains thirty-six plays, exactly half of which had never been previously published. Although this edition is considered authoritative for a number of Shakespeare's plays, recent textual scholarship tends to undermine this authority in calling for a broader consideration of all previous versions of a Shakespearean drama in conjunction with the Folio text.

FOLIO: The name given to a book made up of sheets folded once to form two leaves of equal size, or four pages, typically 11 to 16 inches in height and 8 to 11 inches in width.

FOURTH FOLIO: The fourth collected edition of Shakespeare's plays, published in 1685. This, the last of the FOLIO editions of Shakespeare's dramas, included a notable amount of TEXTUAL CORRUPTION and modernization—751 editorial changes in all, most designed to make the text easier to read.

FOUL PAPERS: The term given to an author's original, uncorrected manuscript, containing the primary text of a play with the author's insertions and deletions. Presumably, the foul papers would be transcribed onto clean sheets for the use of the acting company which had purchased the play; this transcribed and corrected manuscript was called a FAIR COPY. Available evidence indicates that some of Shakespeare's early QUARTOS were printed directly from his foul papers, a circumstance which would, if true, explain the frequent errors and inconsistencies in these texts. Among the quartos alleged to be derived from Shakespeare's foul papers are the First Quartos of *Much Ado about Nothing, A Midsummer Night's Dream, Love's Labour's Lost, Richard II,* and *1* and *2 Henry IV;* among the FIRST FOLIO editions are *The Comedy of Errors, The Taming of the Shrew,* and *Coriolanus.*

GLOBE THEATRE: Constructed in 1599 on Bankside across the Thames from the City of London, the Globe was destroyed by fire in 1613, rebuilt the following year, and finally razed in 1644. Accounts of the fire indicate that it was built of timber with a thatched roof, and sixteenth-century maps of Bankside show it was a polygonal building, but no other evidence exists describing its structure and design. From what is known of similar public theaters of the day, such as the Fortune and the Swan, it is conjectured that the Globe contained a three-tiered gallery along its interior perimeter, that a roof extended over a portion of the three-storied stage and galleries, and that the lowest level of the stage was in the form of an apron extending out among the audience in the yard. Further, there is speculation that the Globe probably included a tiring room or backstage space, that the first two stories contained inner stages that were curtained and recessed, that the third story sometimes served as a musicians' gallery, and that beneath the flat roof, which was also known as "the heavens," machinery was stored for raising and lowering theatrical apparatus. It is generally believed that the interior of the Globe was circular and that it could accommodate an audience of approximately two thousand people, both in its three galleries and the yard. The theater was used solely by the LORD CHAMBERLAIN'S MEN, later known as the KING'S MEN, who performed there throughout the year until 1609, when the company alternated performances at the fully-enclosed BLACKFRIARS THEATRE in months of inclement weather.

HALL (or HALLE), EDWARD: (b. 1498? - d. 1547) English historian whose *The Union of the Noble and Illustre Famelies of Lancastre and York* (1542; enlarged in 1548 and 1550) chronicles the period from the death of Richard II through the reign of Henry VIII. Morally didactic in his approach, Hall shaped his material to demonstrate the disasters that ensue from civil wars and insurrection against monarchs. He traced through the dynastic conflicts during the reigns of Henry VI and Richard III a pattern of cause and effect in which a long chain of crimes and divine retribution was ended by the accession of Henry VII to the English throne. Hall's eye-witness account of the pageantry and festivities of the court of Henry VIII is remarkable for its vivacity and embellished language. His heavy bias on the side of Protestantism and defense of Henry VIII's actions against the Roman Church led to the prohibition of his work by Queen Mary in 1555, but his interpretation of the War of the Roses was adopted by all subsequent Tudor historians. Hall's influence on Shakespeare is most evident in the English history plays.

HOLINSHED, RAPHAEL: (d. 1580?) English writer and editor whose *Chronicles of England, Scotlande, and Irelande* (1577; enlarged in 1587) traced the legends and history of Britain from Noah and the flood to the mid-sixteenth century. The *Chronicles* reveal a Protestant bias and depict the history of the British monarchy in terms of the "Tudor myth," which claimed that Henry VI's usurpation of the crown from Richard II set off a chain of disasters and civil strife which culminated in the reign of Henry VI and continued until the accession to the throne of Henry VII, who, through his marriage to Elizabeth of York, united the two feuding houses of Lancaster and York and brought harmony and peace to England. Holinshed was the principal author of the *Chronicles,* being responsible for the "Historie of England," but he collaborated with William Harrison—who wrote the "Description of England," a vivid account of six-teenth-century customs and daily life—and Richard Stanyhurst and Edward Campion, who together wrote the "Description of Ireland." "The History and Description of Scotland" and the "History of Ireland" were translations or adaptations of the work of earlier historians and writers. The *Chronicles* were immediately successful, in part because of the easily accessible style in which they were composed and because their patriotic celebration of British history was compatible with the rise of nationalistic fervor in Elizabethan England. As in the case of EDWARD HALL, Holinshed's influence on Shakespeare is most evident in the English history plays.

INNS OF COURT: Four colleges of law located in the City of London—Gray's Inn, the Middle Temple, the Inner Temple, and Lincoln's Inn. In the sixteenth and seventeenth centuries, the Inns were not only academic institutions, but were also regarded as finishing schools for gentlemen, providing their students with instruction in music, dance, and other social accomplishments. Interest in the drama ran high in these communities; in addition to producing their own plays, masques, and revels, members would occasionally employ professional acting companies, such as the LORD CHAMBERLAIN'S MEN and the KING'S MEN, for private performances at the Inns. Existing evidence indicates that at least two of Shakespeare's plays were first performed at the Inns: *The Comedy of Errors* and *Twelfth Night.*

KING'S MEN: An acting company formerly known as the LORD CHAMBERLAIN'S MEN. On May 19, 1603, shortly after his accession to the English throne, James I granted the company a royal patent, and its name was altered to reflect the King's direct patronage. At that date, members who shared in the profits of the company included Shakespeare, Richard Burbage, John Heminge, Henry Condell, Augustine Phillips, William Sly, and Robert Armin. Records of the Court indicate that this was the most favored acting company in the Jacobean era, averaging a dozen performances there each year during that period. In addition to public performances at the GLOBE THEATRE in the spring and autumn, the King's Men played at the private BLACKFRIARS THEATRE in winter and for evening performances. Because of the recurring plague in London from 1603 onward, theatrical companies like the King's Men spent the summer months touring and giving performances in the provinces. Besides the work of Shakespeare, the King's Men's repertoire included plays by Ben Jonson, Francis Beaumont and John Fletcher, Thomas Dekker, and Cyril Tourneur. The company continued to flourish until 1642, when by Act of Parliament all dramatic performances were suppressed.

LORD ADMIRAL'S MEN: An acting company formed in 1576-77 under the patronage of Charles Howard, Earl of Nottingham. From its inception to 1585 the company was known as the Lord Howard's Men, from 1585 to 1603 as the Lord Admiral's Men, from 1604 to 1612 as Prince Henry's Men, and from 1613 to 1625 as the Palsgrave's Men. They were the principal rivals of the LORD CHAMBERLAIN'S MEN; occasionally, from 1594 to 1612, these two troupes were the only companies authorized to perform in London. The company's chief player was Edward Alleyn, an actor of comparable distinction with Richard Burbage of the Lord Chamberlain's Men. From 1591 the company performed at the ROSE THEATRE, moving to the Fortune Theatre in 1600. The detailed financial records of Philip Henslowe, who acted as the company's landlord and financier from 1594 until his death in 1616, indicate that an extensive list of dramatists wrote for the troupe throughout its existence, including Christopher Marlowe, Ben Jonson, George Chapman, Anthony Munday, Henry Chettle, Michael Drayton, Thomas Dekker, and William Rowley.

LORD CHAMBERLAIN'S MEN: An acting company formed in 1594 under the patronage of Henry Carey, Lord Hunsdon, who was the Queen's Chamberlain from 1585 until his death in 1596. From

1596 to 1597, the company's benefactor was Lord Hunsdon's son, George Carey, and they were known as Hunsdon's Men until the younger Carey was appointed to his late father's office, when the troupe once again became officially the Lord Chamberlain's Men. The members of the company included Shakespeare, Will Kempe—the famous 'clown' and the most popular actor of his time—, Richard Burbage—the renowned tragedian—, and John Heminge, who served as business manager for the company. In 1594 they began performing at the Theatre and the Cross Key's Inn, moving to the Swan on Bankside in 1596 when the City Corporation banned the public presentation of plays within the limits of the City of London. In 1599 some members of the company financed the building of the GLOBE THEATRE and thus the majority became "sharers," not only in the actors' portion of the profits, but in the theatre owners' allotment as well. This economic independence was an important element in the unusual stability of their association. They became the foremost London company, performing at Court on thirty-two occasions between 1594 and 1603, whereas their chief rivals, the LORD ADMIRAL'S MEN, made twenty appearances at Court during that period. No detailed records exist of the plays that were in their repertoire. Ben Jonson wrote several of his dramas for the Lord Chamberlain's Men, but the company's success is largely attributable to the fact that, after joining them in 1594, Shakespeare wrote for no other company.

MEMORIAL RECONSTRUCTION: One hypothesis used to explain the texts of the so-called BAD-QUARTOS. Scholars have theorized that one or more actors who had appeared in a Shakespearean play attempted to reconstruct from personal memory the text of that drama. Inevitably, there would be lapses of recall with resultant errors and deviations from the original play. Characteristics of these corrupt "reported texts" include the transposition of phrases or entire speeches, the substitution of new language, omission of dramatically significant material, and abridgements of extended passages. It has been speculated that memorial reconstructions were produced by companies touring the provinces whose PROMPT-BOOKS remained in London, or by actors who sold the pirated versions to printers. W. W. Greg, in his examination of the bad quarto of *The Merry Wives of Windsor,* was the first scholar to employ the term.

MERES, FRANCIS: (b. 1565 - d. 1647) English cleric and schoolmaster whose *Palladis Tamia, Wit's Treasury* (1598) has played a valuable role in determining the dates of several of Shakespeare's plays and poems. The work is a collection of observations and commentary on a wide range of subjects, including religion, moral philosophy, and the arts. In a section entitled "A Comparative discourse on our English Poets with the Greeke, Latine, and Italian Poets," Meres compared Shakespeare's work favorably with that of OVID, PLAUTUS, and SENECA and listed the titles of six of his tragedies, six comedies, and two poems, thus establishing that these works were composed no later than 1598. Meres also praised Shakespeare as "the most excellent" of contemporary writers for the stage and remarked that, in addition to his published poetry, he had written some "sugred sonnets" which were circulated among a group of his "private friends."

MIRROR FOR MAGISTRATES, A: A collection of dramatic monologues in which the ghosts of eminent historical figures lament the sins or fatal flaws that led to their downfalls. Individually and collectively, the stories depict the evils of rebellion against divinely constituted authority, the obligation of rulers to God and their subjects, and the inconstancy of Fortune's favor. William Baldwin edited the first edition (1559) and wrote many of the tales, with the collaboration of George Ferrers and six other authors. Subsequently, six editions appeared by 1610, in which a score of contributors presented the first-person narrative complaints of some one hundred heroic personages, from King Albanact of Scotland to Cardinal Wolsey and Queen Elizabeth. The first edition to include Thomas Sackville's *Induction* (1563) is the most notable; Sackville's description of the poet's descent into hell and his encounters with allegorical figures, such as Remorse, Revenge, Famine, and War, is generally considered the most poetically meritorious work in the collection. With respect to Shakespeare, scholars claim that elements from *A Mirror for Magistrates* are most apparent in the history plays on the two Richards and on Henry IV and Henry VI.

OCTAVO: The term applied to a book made up of sheets of paper folded three times to form eight leaves of equal size, or sixteen pages. The dimensions of a folded octavo page may range from 6 to 11 inches in height and 4 to 7½ inches in width.

OVID [PUBLIUS OVIDIUS NASO]: (b. 43 B.C. - d. 18 A.D.) Roman poet who was extremely popular during his lifetime and who greatly affected the subsequent development of Latin poetry; he also deeply influenced European art and literature. Ovid's erotic poetry is molded in elegaic couplets, a highly artificial form which he reshaped by means of a graceful and fluent style. These erotic poems—*Amores, Heroides, Ars amatoria,* and *Remedia amoris*—are concerned with love and amorous intrigue, depicting these themes in an amoral fashion that some critics have considered licentious. Ovid's *Metamorphoses,* written in rapidly flowing hexameters, presents some 250 stories from Greek and Roman legends that depict various kinds of transformations, from the tale of primeval chaos to the apotheosis of Julius Caesar into a celestial body. *Metamorphoses* is a superbly unified work, demonstrating Ovid's supreme skills in narration and description and his ingenuity in linking a wide variety of sources into a masterly presentation of classical myth. His brilliance of invention, fluency of style, and vivid descriptions were highly praised in the Renaissance, and familiarity with his work was considered an essential part of a formal education. Ovid has been cited as a source for many of Shakespeare's plays, including *The Merry Wives of Windsor, A Midsummer Night's Dream, The Tempest, Titus Andronicus, Troilus and Cressida,* and *The Winter's Tale.*

PLAUTUS, TITUS MACCIUS: (b. 254? - d. 184 B.C.) The most prominent Roman dramatist of the Republic and early Empire. The esteem and unrivaled popularity he earned from his contemporaries have been ratified by scholars and dramatists of the past five hundred years. Many playwrights from the sixteenth to the twentieth century have chosen his works, particularly *Amphitruo, Aulularia, Captivi, Menaechmi, Miles Gloriosus, Mostellaria,* and *Trinummus,* as models for their own. Plautus adapted characters, plots, and settings from Greek drama, combined these with elements from Roman farce and satire, and introduced into his plays incongruous contemporary allusions, plays upon words, and colloquial and newly coined language. His dramatic style is further characterized by extensive use of song and music, alliteration and assonance, and variations in metrical language to emphasize differences in character and mood. His employment of stock character types, the intrigues and confusions of his plots, and the exuberance and vigor of his comic spirit were especially celebrated by his English Renaissance audience. The plays of Shakespeare that are most indebted to Plautus include *The Comedy of Errors, The Taming of the Shrew, The Merry Wives of Windsor, The Two Gentlemen of Verona, Romeo and Juliet,* and *All's Well That Ends Well.* His influence can also be noted in such Shakespearean characters as Don Armado (*Love's Labour's Lost*), Parolles (*All's Well That Ends Well*), and Falstaff (*Henry IV* and *The Merry Wives of Windsor*).

PLUTARCH: (b. 46? - d. 120? A.D.) Greek biographer and essayist whose work constitutes a faithful record of the historical tradition, moral views, and ethical judgments of second century A.C. Graeco-Roman culture. His *Parallel Lives*—translated into English by Sir Thomas North and published in 1579 as *The Lives of the Noble Grecianes and Romans compared together*—was one of the most widely read works of antiquity from the sixteenth to the nineteenth century. In this work, Plutarch was principally concerned with portraying the personal character and individual actions of the statesmen, soldiers, legislators, and orators who were his subjects, and through his warm and lively style with instructing as well as entertaining his readers. His portrayal of these classical figures as exemplars of virtue or vice and his emphasis on the successive turns of Fortune's wheel in the lives of great men were in close harmony with the Elizabethan worldview. His miscellaneous writings on religion, ethics, literature, science, and politics, collected under the general title of *Moralia,* were important models for sixteenth- and seventeenth-century essayists. Plutarch is considered a major source for Shakespeare's *Julius Caesar, Antony and Cleopatra,* and *Coriolanus,* and a minor source for *A Midsummer Night's Dream* and *Timon of Athens.*

PRINTER'S COPY: The manuscript or printed text of a work which the compositor uses to set type pages. The nature of the copy available to the early printers of Shakespeare's plays is important in assessing how closely these editions adhere to the original writings. Bibliographical scholars have identified a number of forms available to printers in Shakespeare's time: the author's FOUL PAPERS; a FAIR COPY prepared either by the author or a scribe; partially annotated foul papers or a fair copy that included prompt notes; private copies, prepared by a scribe for an individual outside the acting company; the company's PROMPT-BOOK; scribal transcripts of a prompt-book; a stenographer's report made by someone who had attended an actual performance; earlier printed editions of the work, with or without additional insertions provided by the author, a scribe, or the preparer of a prompt-book; a transcript of a MEMORIAL RECONSTRUCTION of the work; and an ASSEMBLED TEXT.

PROMPT-BOOK: Acting version of a play, usually transcribed from the playwright's FOUL PAPERS by a scribe or the dramatist himself. This copy, or ''book,'' was then presented to the Master of the Revels, the official censor and authorizer of plays. Upon approving its contents, he would license the play for performance and endorse the text as the ''allowed book'' of the play. A prompt-book represents an alteration or modification of the dramatist's original manuscript. It generally contains detailed stage directions, including cues for music, off-stage noises, and the entries and exits of principal characters, indications of stage properties to be used, and other annotations to assist the prompter during an actual performance. The prompt-book version was frequently shorter than the original manuscript, for cuts would be made in terms of minor characters or dramatic incidents to suit the resources of the acting company. Printed editions of plays were sometimes based on prompt-books.

QUARTO: The term applies to a book made up of sheets of paper folded twice to form four leaves of equal size, or eight pages. A quarto page may range in size from 8½ inches to 12½ inches in height and 6¾ to 10 inches in width.

ROSE THEATRE: Built in 1587 by Philip Henslowe, the Rose was constructed of timber on a brick foundation, with exterior walls of lath and plaster and a roof of thatch. Its location on Bankside—across the Thames River from the City of London—established this area as a new site for public theaters. Its circular design included a yard, galleries, a tiring house, and ''heavens.'' A half-dozen acting companies played there, the most important being the LORD ADMIRAL'S MEN, the chief rival to the LORD CHAMBERLAIN'S MEN, who performed at the Rose from 1594 to 1600, when they moved to the new Fortune Theatre constructed by Henslowe in Finsbury, north of the City of London. Among the dramatists employed by Henslowe at the Rose were Thomas Kyd, Christopher Marlowe, Shakespeare, Robert Greene, Ben Jonson, Michael Drayton, George Chapman, Thomas Dekker, and John Webster. The building was razed in 1606.

SECOND FOLIO: The second collected edition of Shakespeare's plays, published in 1632. While it is essentially a reprint of the FIRST FOLIO, more than fifteen hundred changes were made to modernize spelling and to correct stage directions and proper names.

SENECA, LUCIUS ANNAEUS: (b. 4? B.C. - d. 65 A.D.) Roman philosopher, statesman, dramatist, and orator who was one of the major writers of the first century A.D. and who had a profound influence on Latin and European literature. His philosophical essays castigating vice and teaching Stoic resignation were esteemed by the medieval Latin Church, whose members regarded him as a great moral teacher. His nine tragedies—*Hercules Furens, Thyestes, Phoen-issae, Phaedra, Oedipus, Troades, Medea, Agamemnon,* and *Hercules Oetaeus*—were trans-lated into English in 1581 and exerted a strong influence over sixteenth-century English dramatists. Seneca's plays were composed for reading or reciting rather than for performing on the stage, and they evince little attention to character or motive. Written in a declamatory rhetorical style, their function was to instruct on the disastrous consequences of uncontrolled passion and political tyranny. Distinctive features of Senecan tragedy include sensationalism and intense emotionalism, the depiction of wicked acts and retribution, adultery and unnatural sexuality, murder and revenge, and the representation of supernatural beings. Shakespeare's use of Seneca can be discerned most readily in such plays as *King John,* the histories from *Henry VI* to *Richard III, Antony and Cleopatra, Titus Andronicus, Julius Caesar, Hamlet,* and *Macbeth.*

STATIONERS' REGISTER: A ledger book in which were entered the titles of works to be printed and published. The Register was maintained by the Stationers' Company, an association of those who manufactured and those who sold books. In Tudor England, the Company had a virtual monopoly—aside from the university presses—on printing works written throughout the coun-try. Having obtained a license authorizing the printing of a work, a member of the Company would pay a fee to enter the book in the Register, thereby securing the sole right to print or sell that book. Many registered texts were acquired by questionable means and many plays were published whose titles were not entered in the records of the Company. However, the Stationers' Register is one of the most important documents for scholars investigating the literature of that period.

TEXTUAL CORRUPTION: A phrase signifying the alterations that may occur as an author's original text is transmitted through the subsequent stages of preparation for performance and printing. In cases where the PRINTER'S COPY was not an author's FAIR COPY, the text may contain unin-telligible language, mislineations, omissions, repetitious lines, transposed verse and prose speeches, inaccurate speech headings, and defective rhymes. Through their investigation of the nature of the copy from which a COMPOSITOR set his type, textual scholars attempt to restore the text and construct a version that is closest to the author's original manuscript.

THIRD FOLIO: The third collected edition of Shakespeare's plays, published in 1663. Essentially a reprint of the SECOND FOLIO, it contains some corrections to that text and some errors not found in earlier editions. The Third Folio was reprinted in 1664 and included ''seven Playes, never before Printed in Folio.'' One of these seven—*Pericles*—has been accepted as Shakespeare's work, but the other six are considered apocryphal (see APOCRYPHA).

VARIORUM: An edition of a literary work which includes notes and commentary by previous editors and scholars. The First Variorum of Shakespeare's works was published in 1803. Edited by Isaac Reed, it was based on George Steevens's four eighteenth-century editions and includes

Glossary

extensive material from Samuel Johnson's edition of 1765, together with essays by Edmund Malone, George Chalmers, and Richard Farmer. The Second Variorum is a reprint of the First, and it was published in 1813. The Third Variorum is frequently referred to as the Boswell-Malone edition. Containing prefaces from most of the eighteenth-century editions of Shakespeare's work, as well as the poems and sonnets, which Steevens and Reed omitted, the Third Variorum was published in 1821. Edited by James Boswell the younger and based on the scholarship of Malone, it includes such a wealth of material that it is generally regarded as the most important complete edition of the works of Shakespeare. The Fourth Variorum, known as the ''New Variorum,'' was begun by Horace Howard Furness in 1871. Upon his death, his son, Horace Howard Furness, Jr., assumed the editorship, and subsequently—in 1936—a committee of the Modern Language Association of America took on the editorship. The Fourth Variorum is a vast work, containing annotations, textual notes, and excerpts from eminent commentators throughout the history of Shakespearean criticism.

ISBN 0-8103-6128-0

90000

REFERENCE